A STATISTICAL ABSTRACT SUPPLEMENT

HISTORICAL STATISTICS

of the United States

Colonial Times to 1957

Prepared by the Bureau of the
Census with the Cooperation of the
Social Science Research Council

U.S. DEPARTMENT OF COMMERCE, Frederick H. Mueller, *Secretary*
BUREAU OF THE CENSUS, Robert W. Burgess, *Director*

Bureau of the Census

ROBERT W. BURGESS, *Director*
A. Ross Eckler, *Deputy Director*
Howard C. Grieves, *Assistant Director*
Conrad Taeuber, *Assistant Director*
Morris H. Hansen, *Assistant Director for Statistical Standards*
Lowell T. Galt, *Assistant Director for Operations*
Walter L. Kehres, *Assistant Director for Administration*
Calvert L. Dedrick, *Chief, International Statistical Programs Office*
A. W. von Struve, *Acting Public Information Officer*

HERMAN P. MILLER, *Historical Statistics Project Director*

This volume stems from a joint interest by the Bureau of the Census and the Social Science Research Council. It was planned, assembled, edited, and published by the Bureau, with the advice and assistance of the Committee on Historical Statistics appointed by the Council. Many other individuals and agencies cooperated and made significant contributions to this project. General acknowledgments for each chapter are presented on p. VII; other acknowledgments frequently appear in the text discussions of the various chapters.

The volume was prepared in the Bureau of the Census under the general direction of Edwin D. Goldfield, Chief, Statistical Reports Division. Herman P. Miller served as the Project Director and was primarily responsible for the planning, organizing, and supervising of all aspects of the compilation of the data. Dr. Miller also served as executive secretary of the Committee on Historical Statistics, handled liaison matters for the Committee, and participated in its selection of experts to serve as consultants. O. Halbert Goolsby acted as staff assistant.

Morris B. Ullman, who supervised the preparation of the previous volume, *Historical Statistics of the United States, 1789-1945*, was responsible for planning during the early stages of the project.

William Lerner, Assistant Chief, Statistical Reports Division, was primarily responsible for the planning and supervising of the publication aspects of the volume and for the review and editing of the text and tables. Dorothy M. Belzer was responsible for the tabular presentation of the data and preparation of the material for the printer. The Census Library Branch, Louise H. Clickner, Chief, also lent valuable assistance.

Social Science Research Council

The Committee on Historical Statistics appointed by the Social Science Research Council participated actively in the preparation of this volume, in the extension of the subjects to be added, and in planning the general procedures for securing expert assistance on each subject. As the project was developed the Committee, especially the Chairman, was primarily responsible for consideration of problems of data selection and format, for general appraisal of the quality of the series suggested for inclusion, and for the selection of consultant-specialists for the various subjects. The Committee as a whole, or through specially qualified members, reviewed the plans for inclusion of specific series and discussed areas of study which presented unusual problems.

Committee on Historical Statistics of the Social Science Research Council
(Advisory to the Bureau of the Census)

G. Heberton Evans, Jr., *Chairman*
Chairman of Department of Political Economy
The Johns Hopkins University

Herman P. Miller, *Executive Secretary*
Bureau of the Census

Otis Dudley Duncan
Associate Director of Population
Research and Training Center
The University of Chicago

Solomon Fabricant
Director of Research
National Bureau of Economic
Research, Inc.

Maurice I. Gershenson
Department of Industrial Relations
State of California

Richard M. Scammon
Director of Elections Research
Governmental Affairs Institute

Willard L. Thorp
Director of Merrill Center for
Economics
Amherst College

Harold F. Williamson
Professor of Economics
Northwestern University

Paul Webbink, Vice President, Social Science Research Council, attended Committee meetings and acted as the Council's representative. Stanley Lebergott, Office of Statistical Standards, Bureau of the Budget, also participated in the meetings.

Second Printing, 1961

Suggested brief citation: U.S. Bureau of the Census, *Historical Statistics of the United States, Colonial Times to 1957*, Washington, D.C., 1960

Library of Congress Card No. A 60–9150

For sale by the Superintendent of Documents, U.S. Government Printing Office, Washington 25, D.C.   Price $6.00

Contents

[The numbers following subjects are series numbers]

CONTENTS

CONTENTS

CONTENTS

> Corrections of errors discovered after
> the first printing appear on p. xii.

Acknowledgments for Chapter Contributions

[See Introduction for description of consultants' responsibilities]

Chapter A. Population

Principal consultant—Population Division, Bureau of the Census
Review consultant—Irene B. Taeuber, Princeton University
Other contributor—Donald S. Akers, Bureau of the Census

Chapter B. Vital Statistics and Health and Medical Care

VITAL STATISTICS

Principal consultant—Robert D. Grove, National Office of Vital Statistics
Review consultant—Irene B. Taeuber, Princeton University
Other contributors—Joseph Schachter and Mildred L. McKinnon, National Office of Vital Statistics; Wilson H. Grabill, Bureau of the Census

HEALTH AND MEDICAL CARE

Principal consultant—Maryland Y. Pennell, Public Health Service
Review consultant—Antonio Ciocco, University of Pittsburgh

Chapter C. Migration

INTERNAL MIGRATION

Principal consultants—Everett S. Lee and Dorothy S. Thomas, University of Pennsylvania
Review consultant—Irene B. Taeuber, Princeton University
Other contributor—Anne S. Lee, University of Pennsylvania

INTERNATIONAL MIGRATION AND NATURALIZATION

Principal consultant—Edward P. Hutchinson, University of Pennsylvania
Review consultant—Niles Carpenter, The University of Buffalo
Other contributors—Helen F. Eckerson and Gertrude D. Krichefsky, Immigration and Naturalization Service

Chapter D. Labor

LABOR FORCE

Principal consultant—Seymour L. Wolfbein, Bureau of Labor Statistics
Review consultant—Clarence D. Long, The Johns Hopkins University

HOURS, WAGES, AND WORKING CONDITIONS

Principal consultants—H. Gregg Lewis and Albert Rees, The University of Chicago
Review consultant—Harry M. Douty, Bureau of Labor Statistics

Chapter E. Prices and Price Indexes

Principal consultant—Ethel D. Hoover, Bureau of Labor Statistics
Review consultants—Arthur H. Cole, Harvard University; Geoffrey H. Moore, National Bureau of Economic Research, Inc.

Chapter F. National Income and Wealth

Principal consultant—Richard A. Easterlin, University of Pennsylvania
Review consultant—Simon Kuznets, The Johns Hopkins University
Other contributor—Raymond W. Goldsmith, National Bureau of Economic Research, Inc.

Chapter G. Consumer Income and Expenditures

FAMILY AND INDIVIDUAL INCOME

Principal consultant—Selma F. Goldsmith, Office of Business Economics
Review consultant—Dorothy S. Brady, University of Pennsylvania

CONSUMER EXPENDITURE PATTERNS

Principal consultant—Faith M. Williams, Bureau of Labor Statistics
Review consultant—Rose D. Friedman, Chicago, Illinois
Other contributors—Joseph A. Clorety, Anna-Stina L. Ericson, Helen H. Lamale, Bureau of Labor Statistics; Marguerite C. Burk, Agricultural Marketing Service, and Jean L. Pennock, Agricultural Research Service

Chapter H. Social Statistics

SOCIAL SECURITY AND WELFARE

Principal consultant—Ida C. Merriam, Social Security Administration
Review consultant—Eveline M. Burns, Columbia University
Other contributor—George Rohrlich, Bureau of Employment Security

EDUCATION

Principal consultant—Emery M. Foster, Office of Education
Review consultants—Helen M. Walker, Columbia University; John Walton, The Johns Hopkins University
Other contributors—Henry G. Badger, W. Vance Grant, and Rose Marie Smith, Office of Education; Charles B. Nam, Bureau of the Census

CRIME AND CORRECTION

Principal consultant—Ronald H. Beattie, California Department of Justice, State of California
Review consultant—Thorsten Sellin, University of Pennsylvania
Other contributors—Benjamin Frank, Henry C. Lanpher, James A. McCafferty, Bureau of Prisons

RECREATION

Principal consultant—Marion Clawson, Resources for the Future, Inc.
Review consultant—Thomas C. Fichandler, The Twentieth Century Fund
Other contributor—George D. Butler, National Recreation Association

RELIGIOUS AFFILIATION

Principal consultant—Benson Y. Landis, National Council of the Churches of Christ in the United States of America
Review consultant—Edmund deS. Brunner, Columbia University

Chapter J. Land, Water, and Climate

LAND AND WATER UTILIZATION

Principal consultants—Ernst H. Wiecking and Hugh H. Wooten, Agricultural Research Service; Walter L. Picton, Business and Defense Services Administration
Review consultant—Marion Clawson, Resources for the Future, Inc.

CLIMATE

Principal consultants—Helmut E. Landsberg and J. Murray Mitchell, Jr., Weather Bureau
Review consultant—George S. Benton, The Johns Hopkins University
Other contributor—Milton L. Blanc, Weather Bureau

Chapter K. Agriculture

Principal consultant—Department of Agriculture (Earl E. Houseman, Coordinator)
Review consultant—Theodore W. Schultz, The University of Chicago

Chapter L. Forestry and Fisheries

FORESTS AND FOREST PRODUCTS

Principal consultant—Dwight Hair, Forest Service
Review consultant—William A. Duerr, Syracuse University

FISHERIES

Principal consultant—Harvey L. Moore, Fish and Wildlife Service
Review consultant—F. Heward Bell, International Pacific Halibut Commission
Other contributor—Edward A. Power, Fish and Wildlife Service

Chapter M. Minerals

Principal consultants—Sam H. Schurr and Elizabeth K. Vogely, Resources for the Future, Inc.
Review consultant—Vivian E. Spencer, Bureau of the Census
Other contributor—Robert E. Herman, Bureau of Mines

Chapter N. Construction and Housing

Principal consultant—Leo Grebler, University of California, Los Angeles
Review consultant—Raymond W. Goldsmith, National Bureau of Economic Research, Inc.

Chapter P. Manufactures

Principal consultant—Daniel Creamer, National Industrial Conference Board, Inc.
Review consultant—John W. Kendrick, George Washington University
Other contributor—John A. Waring, Washington, D.C.

Chapter Q. Transportation

Principal consultant—Thor Hultgren, National Bureau of Economic Research, Inc.
Review consultant—George R. Taylor, Amherst College
Other contributor—Bureau of Public Roads

Chapter R. Communications

Principal consultants—Hyman H. Goldin and Robert E. Stromberg, Federal Communications Commission
Review consultant—Melville J. Ulmer, American University

Chapter S. Power

Principal consultant—Lawrence D. Jennings, Federal Power Commission
Review consultant—Herbert B. Dorau, New York University

Chapter T. Distribution and Services

Principal consultants—Reavis Cox and Charles S. Goodman, University of Pennsylvania
Review consultant—Harold Barger, Columbia University

Chapter U. Foreign Trade and Other International Transactions

FOREIGN TRADE

Principal consultant—Herbert B. Woolley, New York University
Review consultant—Douglass C. North, University of Washington

BALANCE OF INTERNATIONAL PAYMENTS AND INVESTMENT POSITION

Principal consultant—Nancy F. Culbertson, Office of Business Economics
Review consultant—Walter S. Salant, The Brookings Institution
Other contributors—Douglass C. North, University of Washington; Matthew Simon, Pace College

Chapter V. Business Enterprise

BUSINESS POPULATION

Principal consultant—Morris A. Adelman, Massachusetts Institute of Technology
Review consultant—Irwin Friend, University of Pennsylvania

CORPORATE ASSETS, LIABILITIES, AND INCOME

Principal consultant—Sergei P. Dobrovolsky, Rensselaer Polytechnic Institute
Review consultant—Irwin Friend, University of Pennsylvania

Chapter W. Productivity and Technological Development

PRODUCTIVITY INDEXES

Principal consultant—Leon Greenberg, Bureau of Labor Statistics
Review consultant—John W. Kendrick, George Washington University
Other contributors—Robert T. Adams and Julian Frechtman, Bureau of Labor Statistics

COPYRIGHTS, PATENTS, AND TRADEMARKS

Principal consultant—Jacob Schmookler, University of Minnesota
Review consultant—Fritz Machlup, The Johns Hopkins University
Other contributor—P. J. Federico, Patent Office

RESEARCH AND DEVELOPMENT

Principal consultant—Kathryn S. Arnow, National Science Foundation
Review consultant—Irving H. Siegel, Council of Economic Advisers

Chapter X. Banking and Finance

BANKING, MONEY SUPPLY, MONEY RATES, AND CREDIT

Principal consultants—Susan S. Burr and Caroline H. Cagle, Board of Governors of the Federal Reserve System
Review consultant—Milton Friedman, The University of Chicago
Other contributor—Clark Warburton, Federal Deposit Insurance Corporation

PRIVATE INSURANCE

Principal consultant—Albert I. Hermalin, Institute of Life Insurance
Review consultant—James J. O'Leary, Life Insurance Association of America

Chapter Y. Government

ELECTIONS AND POLITICS

Principal consultant—Richard M. Scammon, Governmental Affairs Institute
Review consultant—V. O. Key, Harvard University

GOVERNMENT EMPLOYMENT AND FINANCE

Principal consultants—Jacob M. Jaffe, Bureau of the Census; James M. Jarrett, Internal Revenue Service; I. M. Labovitz, Library of Congress; and Flora M. Nicholson, Civil Service Commission
Review consultant—I. M. Labovitz, Library of Congress
Other contributors—Paul B. Trescott, Kenyon College; Paul P. Van Riper, Cornell University

ARMED FORCES AND VETERANS

Principal consultants—Milton C. Forster, Veterans Administration; Michael S. March, Bureau of the Budget
Review consultant—Irving H. Siegel, Council of Economic Advisers
Other contributor—Sydney M. Ratcliffe, Department of the Army

Chapter Z. Colonial Statistics

Principal consultant—Lawrence A. Harper, University of California
Review consultant—Richard B. Morris, Columbia University
Other contributors—Robert E. Gallman, Ohio State University; Jacob M. Price, University of Michigan; Stella H. Sutherland, Oakland City College, Indiana

Introduction

This volume is the second in the *Historical Statistics* series issued by the Bureau of the Census as a supplement to the annual *Statistical Abstract of the United States*. The first volume, *Historical Statistics of the United States, 1789-1945*, was published in 1949. It provided, in a single volume, a wide range of series quantifying various aspects of the economic and social development of the Nation. A *Continuation to 1952* was issued in 1954 to provide data for 1946 to 1952 for the series shown in the first volume.

Limited resources confined the scope of the first volume to those data most readily available, usually from governmental sources. Nevertheless, some 3,000 statistical time series were presented. Because of the huge and intricate task of inspection, evaluation, and selection of time series, the compilers recognized from the outset that the first volume would have to serve as a working document to break the ground and set a pattern for a subsequent more comprehensive and definitive volume. The present publication is intended to achieve the purpose foreshadowed in the original volume.

The *Historical Statistics* volumes are designed to bring together historical series of wide general interest and to inform the user where additional data can be found. All of the broad subject areas covered in the first volume have been included and expanded in this volume, and a number of new subjects have been added. The new subjects include consumer expenditure patterns, social security, education, crime and correction, recreation, religious affiliation, climate, communications, distribution and services, business population, corporate assets, research and development, private insurance, Armed Forces and veterans, and colonial statistics.

This volume also presents the results of a complete review of the subject matter shown in the earlier volume. In a number of cases, series in the latter have been replaced or supplemented. Finally, an attempt was made to reduce the unevenness in scope and quality which characterized the text materials in the earlier work. Critical notes have been added along with further bibliographic material, cross references to other statistical compendia, and previously unpublished data (in some instances).

Origin of *Historical Statistics of the United States*

The volume, *Historical Statistics of the United States, 1789-1945*, was formally initiated by a recommendation in 1945 by the Social Science Research Council that the Secretary of Commerce consider compilation and publication by the Bureau of the Census of a source book of economic statistics.

Earlier the same year, J. Frederic Dewhurst urged the development of a historical source book in a proposal to the American Statistical Association and the American Economic Association. A joint committee to explore the practical problems of preparing such a volume was named by these associations, joined by the Economic History Association. Dr. Dewhurst's proposal coincided closely with Bureau of the Census plans, then under consideration, to prepare a historical supplement to the *Statistical Abstract of the United States*. The formal decision in 1945 by the Bureau of the Census to compile and publish such a volume led to the reconstitution of the joint committee, which then became the Social Science Research Council Committee on the Source Book of Historical Statistics, Advisory to the Bureau of the Census.

After the first volume was issued in June 1949, the Economic History Association, in response to a request from the Bureau of the Census, appointed an advisory committee in September 1950 to evaluate the volume and to make specific recommendations affecting the question of its revision. This committee, formally designated as the Committee

of the Economic History Association on the Revision of *Historical Statistics of the United States, 1789-1945*, was under the chairmanship of G. Heberton Evans, Jr., The Johns Hopkins University, and included the following as members: Arthur H. Cole, Harvard University; Shepard Clough, Columbia University; T. C. Cochran, University of Pennsylvania; and Solomon Fabricant, National Bureau of Economic Research, Inc. In April 1952 the committee submitted a report to the Bureau of the Census entitled "On the Revision of *Historical Statistics of the United States, 1789-1945*." The conclusions and comments presented in this report were subsequently influential in getting underway the project for a revised volume.

Both *Historical Statistics* volumes have been prepared by the Bureau of the Census with the cooperation of the Social Science Research Council. A description of the relationship established for the first volume between the Bureau and the Social Science Research Council appears in the introduction to that volume. For the present volume, the Bureau designated a project director who served also as secretary of the Committee on Historical Statistics appointed by the Social Science Research Council to guide the Bureau in the program. The Bureau again assumed the responsibility for publishing the volume as a part of its *Statistical Abstract* program. The Social Science Research Council, in turn, obtained a grant from the Ford Foundation which provided funds for the procurement of services of experts in each field. More than 125 such specialists were engaged (although not all were paid) to serve as consultants. To make further use of the information assembled for this project, the Council also made arrangements with some of the consultants for the preparation of bibliographic essays on statistics in selected fields. Several of these essays have been published in the *Journal of the American Statistical Association*.

The Problem of Historical Statistics

Statistics are an indispensable adjunct to historical analysis. Few fields exist in which qualitative historical records cannot be clarified and enriched by quantitative data. For some time, however, it has been evident that users of historical data are faced with the paradox of overabundance and scarcity. On the one hand, a burdensome multiplicity of sources has frequently to be consulted in order to reconstruct one quantitative aspect of a particular subject. On the other hand, users are confronted just as often by a discouraging barrenness of data, discoverable only after much costly work and delay.

The scattered sources of historical statistics of the United States include the annual reports of the executive heads of the agencies of the Federal Government, reports of special Federal commissions, the volumes of the censuses of the United States, printed debates of the Congress, published reports of committees of the Congress and transcripts of hearings on important legislative measures, published reports and documents of the State governments, statistical publications of private research foundations and organizations and of the universities and colleges of the Nation, together with the great mass of statistical volumes printed by other private organizations and individuals.

It has been noted that on occasion compilers, desiring to save the time and effort required to obtain data directly from the original sources, make use of successive issues of the annual *Statistical Abstract of the United States* to construct long-term time series. The results of such a procedure are not always sound, since the space available in the *Statistical Abstract* for describing major revisions in time series may not permit adequate clarification. Of the many revised figures appearing in each issue, most revisions apply to the immediate preceding years, but revisions of much earlier years are not uncommon. Moreover, the revisions shown have followed no systematic pattern and may be scattered irregularly over many issues.

Impediments to the use of historical statistics, then, include the initial difficulty of determining whether the data in fact exist, of identifying the public or private document in which the data may be found, of constructing time series where the data may not be arranged in suitable form, and of identifying and interpreting changes in concept and coverage. Definitions employed in published historical tables, moreover, may have to be sought in separate publications if, indeed, they have been published at all.

The objective of the *Historical Statistics* volumes is to provide a convenient reference source which has two functions, *collecting* and *referring*. The *collecting* function consists of assembling, selecting, and arranging data from hundreds of sources and making them available within a single source. The *referring* function consists of text annotations to the data which act as a guide to sources of greater detail. The annotations also define terms used in the tables and include essential qualifying statements.

Planning and Compilation

As a first step in the actual preparation of this volume, the Bureau of the Census, with the advice and cooperation of the Committee on Historical Statistics, prepared a working outline and statement of basic premises to guide the selection of material. After an agreement on a basic framework, responsibility for the duties of "principal" or "review" consultant for specific subjects was assigned either to a Government agency or to an individual specialist.

As stated previously, a number of subjects are included in this volume which were not included in the first. Principal consultants responsible for these subjects had to prepare their material from inception, advise on the series to be used, and prepare descriptive, analytical, and bibliographic notes to accompany the tabular data. All other principal consultants were required to examine the presentation of data in their fields in the first volume and to make detailed recommendations for additions, deletions, and other changes. The relative importance of the data in the first volume had to be judged in light of historical series made available from more recent studies. These studies often contained an abundance of data from which consultants had to select specific series for inclusion here. The accompanying text also had to be prepared. Principal consultants were also called upon to resolve problems that arose during the processing and editing of the material. Review consultants were responsible for critical review of the data and text to be included during each phase of their preparation.

Coordination, final processing, and editing of the materials were carried out by the Bureau of the Census. A multitude of source publications was assembled. Data were excerpted, reviewed, and arranged in appropriate form and sequence. Source citations, text, titles, headnotes, and footnotes were brought into a consistent style and reviewed for clarity. Problems that emerged during preparation and review of the material were resolved in consultation with consultants.

Technical Notes and Explanations

Arrangement of the data. Data are arranged by subject in lettered chapters and numbered series. Subject-listing under chapter titles in the table of contents, together with the index, will facilitate reference, chapter titles being necessarily somewhat arbitrary. Each series or tabular column is assigned a number, the first series in each chapter beginning with 1. Each series is further identified in the table titles and cross references by prefixing the chapter letter. Thus, the 44th series in the chapter on agriculture is designated K 44 to distinguish it from the 44th series in the chapter on transportation designated Q 44. Because of possible confusion with numerals, the capital letters I and O have been omitted in identifying chapters.

All series begin with the most recent year for which data have been obtained and run backward in time. This arrangement was selected because it lent itself to more compact, less space-consuming presentation than the alternative of beginning with the earliest year. Insofar as possible, there are uniformly placed spaces above every year ending in 0 or 5. No data are shown for years subsequent to 1957, because most of the 1958 figures were still unavailable or preliminary at the time this volume was in preparation. Figures for 1958 and later years for most of the current series are presented in the *Statistical Abstract of the United States* beginning with the 1960 edition.

Basic guidelines. Before work was begun on the volume, certain guidelines were established to aid the Census Bureau staff and the consultants in the selection and presentation aspects of the operation. These guidelines, however, were not always rigidly adhered to. The problems encountered because of the scope and the variety of the subject matter and the attempt to achieve a relatively balanced presentation between subject fields made it necessary to modify the rules in a number of places. The guidelines applied and the elements subject to application are discussed below.

Area coverage. Unless otherwise specified, data are for continental United States as of 1958 (i.e., excluding Alaska and Hawaii). In some instances, the sources used for data failed to specify the area covered. Where practicable, the data were examined and the appropriate qualifications were added.

Because of limitations of space, data are not generally shown for regions, States, or localities. Some exceptions were permitted, however, in the following instances: Where regional statistics are essential for correct interpretation of data, such as presentation of merchant marine statistics separately for each coast and for inland waters; where data in the subject field cannot (by definition) be summarized effectively for continental United States, such as internal migration data; where summary data for a given subarea or market are indicative of general trend or level, such as prices on the New York Stock Exchange or cattle prices at Chicago; where data for a given area effectively represent the national picture because of concentration of production, etc., as Pennsylvania anthracite; where data are available for only a given area as in the case of many series concerned with early American history which are limited to the Atlantic seaboard.

Time coverage. In general, only annual or census-period data which cover at least 20 years are presented. Exceptions were permitted primarily in the case of newly developed series of basic importance.

The general requirements as to time coverage were specifically designed to permit inclusion of "lapsed" series, particularly those falling within the nineteenth century. The lapsed series, which begin and terminate in the past, represent major fields of interest during various phases of American historical development; frequently they must be sought in out-of-print documents which are available in few libraries.

The identification of time-periods was complicated by failure of some sources to state whether the data were prepared on a calendar-year or on a fiscal-year basis; by shifts in time coverage from calendar to fiscal year during the period of the series, and, in some instances, by the lack of identification of the beginning or ending date of the fiscal year where this basis was used. In all such cases, particularly where time shifts seemed likely to have occurred, an effort was made to identify the correct basis.

Frequency of data. Annual data are given preference but certain series are presented only for census years (years in which a national census was conducted) and, in some instances (for example, telephone and telegraph rates), only for the few dates for which the data are available. Where both annual figures and decennial or quinquennial benchmark or census data exist, both series are sometimes shown.

Series linkage. No formal attempt was made to extend a single series back through time by linking it to another series which terminated at or near the date on which the first began. In a number of instances, however, such series are presented in adjoining columns, with an overlap for a period of years when available.

Unpublished figures. In general, only published materials or unpublished estimates from the files of a Government agency or from a responsible private organization like the National Bureau of Economic Research were used. Unpublished estimates of private scholars, with rare exceptions, are not included in the volume.

Subject detail. Because of space limitations, series selected are confined to those regarded as of major importance in each field. The criteria of selection varied broadly, depending upon the subject. Within each subfield, the amount of subject detail was held to a minimum. Generally, only summary measures are shown and detailed cross classifications and information of a highly specialized character have been avoided. Presentation of data in excessive detail, such as for specific commodities, was discouraged. Exceptions were allowed, however, where it was considered more meaningful to present long series for selected specific commodities than to present an aggregate which is difficult to interpret.

Presentation of absolute rather than derived data. Primary emphasis was placed on the presentation of absolute figures rather than on derived data since the absolute figures offer somewhat greater flexibility to the user. The major exception was the presentation of index numbers. In general, percentage distributions of absolute data already shown are not presented. Other percentage data, and averages, medians, ratios, and rates were used only where they resulted in a significant economy in space or where they facilitated interpretation. No attempt was made, in view of the technical problems involved, to convert various series of index numbers to a common base year or period.

Omissions of data, "blank" cells. The significance of dashes in tabular cells varies from series to series. In general, the presence of cell "leaders" or "dashes" indicates merely that no information was provided for this volume. Dash entries may mean that no information exists for the given year; that the entry, if shown, would be zero; the information was not available; or the information is believed to exist in published form but it was not practicable to do the research necessary to locate the appropriate source. The user will have to judge from the context which meaning is appropriate in each particular instance.

The practices of the various sources of information differ as to the meaning of dashes in cells, the extent to which they label material as "not available," the meaning of the term "not available," the use of the zero entry, etc. In general, the policy adopted in preparing this volume was to retain "not available" notations where they appeared for intermediate years in the series; to change them to dashes where they appeared at the beginning or end of the series. Where cells were left blank in the sources, they were filled with dashes in this volume.

Since series of varying length taken from different sources are frequently found in adjoining columns in a table, the stub listings for years necessarily encompass the earliest and latest date for which any of the series in the table are shown. In itself, this tends to create many additional blank cells since missing entries have been replaced by dashes in order to make it easier for the user's eye to trace the entries for a given year across the entire table.

Text. For every series used, the text presents the precise source of the data. Where possible, the text also includes the definition of the concepts used, and sufficient methodological and historical information to permit intelligent use of the data. For many series the text includes a reference to where more detail can be found. Unusual values in a series are explained and major changes which affect comparability are noted. Where adjusted or derived figures are used, the methods used are described, often with a reference to a more complete description.

Responsibility

Because of the multitude of sources and the varied subject matter covered, the Bureau of the Census cannot accept responsibility for the accuracy or limitations of data other than those which it collects Every attempt has been made, within the limits of time and available personnel, to verify and correctly identify the material. Final responsibility for selection of the material, and for its accurate and proper presentation, rests with the Bureau of the Census, even though carried out with the cooperation of many individuals and agencies who devoted much time and energy in providing data and descriptions of series for this publication.

The information presented in this volume supersedes all similar information presented in *Historical Statistics of the United States, 1789-1945*, and in *Continuation to 1952 of Historical Statistics of the United States, 1789-1945*.

FOR ADDITIONAL INFORMATION ON DATA PRESENTED

write to the agency indicated in the source note in the descriptive text for the given statistical series.

SUGGESTIONS AND COMMENTS
should be sent to:

The Director
Bureau of the Census
Washington 25, D.C.

CORRECTIONS

Listed below are errors which have been discovered since the first printing of this volume.

Page 178 (table), series G 191. Insert a footnote against the column head which should read as follows: "Includes expenditures for 'other housing' not shown separately. 'Other housing' includes expenditures for transient hotels, tourist cabins, clubs, schools, and institutions."

Page 329 (table), series L 196-202, footnote 1. Should read, "Included in series L 196-197," not ". . . L 197-198."

Page 349 (table), series M 1-12, footnote 11. Should read, "Less than $500,000," not ". . . $5000,000."

Page 405 (text), series P 196. Last sentence should read, "For 1954-1957, . . .," not "For 1953-1957, ..."

Page 491 (table), series R 95-98. Figures are rounded to thousands. Should have unit indicators of "1,000."

Page 557 (text), series U 168-192. Right-hand column, lines 27-30, should read as follows: ". . . world. Since 1919, resi-

dents of the United States comprise residents of continental United States, Alaska, Hawaii, Puerto Rico, American Samoa, and Virgin Islands. Beginning 1940, residents of the Panama Canal Zone are also included."

Page 566 (table), series U 207, 1817-1819. Footnote symbol should be 1, not 5.

Page 566 (table), series U 208-213. The figures for 1956 and 1957 are transposed for the category of "Transportation, communication, and public utilities." The same also applies for the category of "Other."

Page 730 (table), series Y 672, 1902-1950. Footnote symbol should be 2, not 1.

Page 754 (text), series Z 337-356, right-hand column, the order of lines 19 and 20 should be reversed.

Page No.	Series No.	Year	Now reads--	Should read--	Page No.	Series No.	Year	Now reads--	Should read--
118	E 52	1946	78.7	...	364	M 188	1955	1,067	1,007
118	E 53	1946	...	78.7	429	Q 48	1957	386,996	386,978
168	G 171	1955	5,382	5,384	564	U 192	1918	1,817	+1,817
168	G 173	1955	5,584	5,582	684	Y 46	1952	10R	10D
208	H 247	1950	5,437,004	5,437,044	684	Y 50	1856	14R	13R
356	M 98	1955	7,756	7,856					

Population

A 1–263. General note.

The principal source of population data is the Decennial Census of Population, a house-to-house enumeration made by the Bureau of the Census. In accordance with a Constitutional provision for a decennial canvass of the population, the first census enumeration was made in 1790. The primary reason for the Census of Population, as set forth in the Constitution, is to provide a basis for the apportionment of Members of the House of Representatives among the several States. Until 1902, the census organization was temporary. In 1902, the Bureau of the Census was established as a permanent agency of the Government charged with responsibility for the decennial census and for compiling statistics on other subjects as needed. Currently, this Bureau supplies intercensal data based on surveys and estimates in addition to making the comprehensive decennial census enumeration.

In accordance with Census practice dating back to 1790, each person is counted as an inhabitant of his usual place of residence or usual place of abode, that is, the place where he lives and sleeps most of the time. This place is not necessarily the same as his legal residence, voting residence, or domicile, although, in the vast majority of cases, the use of these different bases of classification would produce identical results. Indians living in Indian Territory or on reservations were not included in the population count until 1890 and in earlier censuses large tracts of unorganized and sparsely settled territory were not covered by enumerators.

Most of the population data presented are based on complete counts. However, some of the 1950 data were obtained from representative samples of 20 percent or 3⅓ percent of the population. A few series also include 1940 data obtained on a sample basis.

Several series present statistics based on the Current Population Survey, conducted monthly by the Bureau of the Census. Until May 1956, the Survey covered a sample of approximately 21,000 interviewed households spread over a sample of areas throughout the United States. Since then, the sample has been expanded to approximately 35,000 interviewed households in a larger number of areas.

Exact agreement is not to be expected among the various samples, nor between them and the complete census count, but the sample data may be used with confidence where large numbers are involved, and may be assumed to indicate patterns and relationships where small numbers are involved. Detailed statements regarding the sampling errors are given in the original sources.

Many errors appear in the Censuses of 1790–1840. The data for these censuses were adjusted by county and color, and the revised estimates were published in the 1870 Census. Later, the data by sex and age in the 1790–1840 Censuses were adjusted to agree with the estimates published in 1870.

The Bureau of the Census has always been concerned about the degree of completeness of enumeration in the decennial censuses. Prior to 1950, the population counts were evaluated by indirect methods only since no method had been devised to give an over-all direct measure of the completeness of enumeration for the total population. For the most part, dis-

cussion in Census reports was confined to qualitative statements. In the 1950 Census, the population was reenumerated on a sample basis in a carefully conducted postenumeration survey, thereby providing a direct check on a case-by-case basis. The results of this survey indicate a net underenumeration in the census count of the total population of the United States of about 2,100,000, or 1.4 percent. It is also estimated that the net underenumeration was about 1.6 percent in 1940 and about 0.7 percent in 1930.

One of the indirect methods of evaluating the completeness of enumeration for censuses prior to 1950 is a comparison of rates of change with respect to consistency and reasonableness. On this basis, it is believed that the figures for the South show unreasonably low rates of increase for the decade 1860–1870 and abnormally high rates of increase for 1870–1880. The differences are so great that it appears evident that the enumeration of 1870 in these areas was seriously incomplete, undoubtedly as a result of the unsettled conditions of the reconstruction period. For the portion of the United States outside the South, the rate of increase for 1860–1870 was almost exactly the same as for 1870–1880. Therefore, the number initially enumerated in 1870 for the South was revised on the assumption that the rate of increase for these two decades was the same.

Comparisons of census data with independent counts of corresponding segments of the population are sometimes possible in the case of certain age-sex groups. For example, there have been several studies for both World Wars I and II relating figures for males of military age from the census to registration figures. Interpretation of the differences is complicated by the fact that there are no adequate measures of the Selective Service figures. Nonetheless, these studies do suggest an appreciable underenumeration of males in appropriate age groups, particularly among Negroes, in the Censuses of 1920 and 1940.

A 1–3. Estimated population of the United States, 1790–1957.

Source: 1790–1899, Bureau of the Census estimates based on linear interpolation between decennial census years; 1900–1957, Bureau of the Census, *Current Population Reports*, Series P–25, Nos. 71, 114, 173, and unpublished Census Bureau records.

Estimates for 1900–1909 are sums of State estimates prepared from local data indicative of population change. Estimates for 1910–1957 are based on decennial censuses and statistics of births, deaths, immigration, emigration, and Armed Forces. These estimates are as of July 1 and therefore may differ from other estimates in this section which are as of the date of the census.

A 4–16. Population of continental United States and outlying areas, 1880–1950.

Source: With the exceptions noted below for series A 6 and A 8, *U. S. Census of Population: 1950*, vol. I, pp. 1–3, 51–4, 52–5, 53–6, 54–3, 54–5, 54–7, 54–9. **Series A 6**, population abroad, 1900, Twelfth Census Reports, *Population*, vol. I, part 1, p. xxiii; 1910–1920, Fourteenth Census Reports, *Population*, vol. I, p. 13. Series A 8, Philippine Islands, 1900–1940, *Historical Statistics of the United States, 1789–1945*, p. 25.

A 17–21. Area and population of continental United States, 1790–1950.

Source: Reports of Fourteenth, Fifteenth, Sixteenth, and Seventeenth Censuses, *Population*, vol. I, and other reports and records. See also Sixteenth Census Report, *Areas of the United States, 1940*.

Area figures for each census year represent all continental area under the jurisdiction of the United States on the indicated date, including in some cases considerable areas not then organized or settled, and not covered by the census. Area figures for prior years have been adjusted to bring them into agreement with remeasurements made in 1940. For a further discussion of areas covered by the censuses, see *U. S. Census of Population: 1950*, vol. I, p. xi.

A 22–33. Estimated population, by sex, color, and age, 1900–1957.

Source: Bureau of the Census, *Current Population Reports*, Series P–25, Nos. 98, 114, 146, and 170.

These estimates are as of July 1 and therefore may differ from other estimates in this section, which are as of the date of the census.

The age estimates for 1900–1919 were prepared by mathematical interpolation for identical age groups within color-sex groups from five successive censuses. For the 1900–1909 decade, the 1880–1920 Censuses were used; annual estimates for 1910–1919 were based on the 1890–1930 Censuses. The estimates since 1920 are based on censuses and vital statistics; estimates of net migration and mortality rates were computed from life tables.

The classification of the population by color is not ordinarily based on replies to census questions asked by the enumerators, but rather is obtained by observation. This concept does not, therefore, reflect a clear-cut definition of biological stock. The nonwhite population consists of Negroes, American Indians, Japanese, Chinese, Filipinos, and some other groups. Persons of mixed parentage are placed in the color classification of the nonwhite parent. Persons of Mexican birth or ancestry who are not definitely Indian or of other nonwhite stock have been classified as white in all censuses except that of 1930. The data for 1930 used in these series have been revised to include Mexicans as white. For a more detailed discussion of the definition of color, see *U. S. Census of Population: 1950*, vol. II, part 1, Introduction.

A 34–50. Population, by sex, residence, and color, 1790–1950.

Source: See detailed listing below.

See also text for series A 22–33 for definition of color.

The Bureau of the Census has employed several definitions of urban population. According to the definition adopted for the 1950 Census, the urban population comprises all persons living in (1) places of 2,500 inhabitants or more incorporated as cities, boroughs, and villages, (2) incorporated towns of 2,500 inhabitants or more except in New England, New York, and Wisconsin, where the term "town" is used to designate minor civil divisions of counties, (3) the densely settled urban fringe, including both incorporated and unincorporated areas, around cities of 50,000 inhabitants or more, and (4) unincorporated places of 2,500 inhabitants or more outside any urban fringe. The remaining population is classified as rural. According to the definition used in 1940, the urban population was limited to all persons living in incorporated places of 2,500 inhabitants or more and in other areas classified as urban under special rules relating to population size and density. For a discussion of these different definitions of the urban population, see *U. S. Census of Population: 1950*, vol. I, pp. xv and xviii. The population is shown classified in accordance with the urban definition used in the 1940 Census for 1790–1950. Classification in accordance with the definition used in the 1950 Census is given only for 1950.

The first official publication of figures formally presenting the urban population was made following the Census of 1870 in the *Statistical Atlas of the United States*. The population of cities and towns of 8,000 inhabitants or more was presented as the "urban population." In the reports of the 1880, 1890, and 1900 Censuses, the urban population was variously defined as the population living in places of 4,000 inhabitants or more, or 8,000 inhabitants or more. The first publication in which the population of places having 2,500 inhabitants or more was officially designated as urban was the *Supplementary Analysis of the Twelfth Census (1900)*. This definition, with minor modifications, was used in later censuses up to and including 1940. For purposes of comparison, the data for 1950 were also tabulated in accordance with this urban definition.

In the *Statistical Atlas* for 1870, the rural population was defined as the population residing outside the cities or towns of 8,000 inhabitants or more, but the data were used simply to calculate the density of counties. A new definition of the rural population was presented in the reports of the Census of 1890. In that year, the rural population was obtained by subtracting from the total population, county by county, the population of "all cities or other compact bodies of population which number 1,000 or more." In the report of the Census of 1900, the rural population was presented as the population living outside incorporated places. For 1910–1940, the rural population was defined as all of the population not classified as urban.

For a discussion of the development of the urban-rural classification, see Bureau of the Census, *Current Population Reports*, "The Development of the Urban-Rural Classification in the United States: 1874 to 1949," Series P–23, No. 1.

The farm population for 1950 included all persons living on farms, as determined by the question in the 1950 Census of Population, "Is this house on a farm (or ranch)?" Persons on "farms" who were paying cash rent for their home and yard only were classified as nonfarm, as were persons in institutions, summer camps, motels, and tourist camps. The definition of farm population prior to 1950 differed somewhat, but remained a residence rather than an occupational classification and depended primarily upon the respondent's conception of what was meant by the word "farm." Consequently it reflected local usage rather than the uniform application of an objective definition.

A 34–35. Total population, by sex, 1820–1950.

Source: 1820–1840, reports of Fourth, Fifth, and Sixth Censuses, and unpublished Census Bureau records; 1850–1950, *U. S. Census of Population: 1950*, vol. II, part 1, p. 1-88.

A 36–38. Total population, by residence, 1790–1950.

Source: 1790–1950, urban and total rural population, *U. S. Census of Population: 1950*, vol. I, p. 1-5; 1920, rural-farm and rural-nonfarm population, Sixteenth Census Reports, *Population*, vol. II, part 1, p. 18; 1930–1950, *U. S. Census of Population: 1950*, vol. II, part 1, p. 1-87.

A 39–44. Population, by residence, by sex, 1900–1950.

Source: 1900, Fourteenth Census Reports, *Population*, vol. III, p. 15; 1910 and 1920, Sixteenth Census Reports, *Population*, vol. II, part 1, p. 20; 1930–1950, *U. S. Census of Population: 1950*, vol. II, part 1, p. 1-87.

A 45–50. Population, by color, by sex, 1790–1950.

Source: 1790–1840, first six population censuses and unpublished Census Bureau records; 1850–1950, *U. S. Census of Population: 1950*, vol. II, part 1, p. 1–88.

See text for series A 22–33 for definition of color.

A 51–58. White population, by sex and nativity, 1850–1950.

Source: See detailed listing below.

See also text for series A 22–33 for definition of color.

A native is defined as a person born in continental United States, Puerto Rico, or the Territories or possessions, or born abroad to American parents. Persons for whom place of birth was not reported are included with the natives. The 1890 Census was the first to make the distinction between native and foreign parentage. Data on aliens are not shown for 1890, 1900, and 1910, because the information collected in those censuses was restricted to males 21 years of age and over.

A 51, 55. Total native white, by sex, 1850–1950.

Source: *U. S. Census of Population: 1950*, vol. II, part 1, p. 1–88.

A 52, 56. Native white of foreign or mixed parentage, by sex, 1890–1950.

Source: *U. S. Census of Population: 1950*, vol. IV, Special Reports, *Nativity and Parentage*, p. 3A–11.

A 53, 57. Total foreign born, by sex, 1850–1950.

Source: *U. S. Census of Population: 1950*, vol. II, part 1, p. 1–88.

A 54, 58. Foreign-born aliens, by sex, 1920–1950.

Source: 1920, Fifteenth Census Reports, *Population*, vol. II, p. 405; 1930 and 1940, Sixteenth Census Reports, *Population*, vol. II, part 1, p. 30; 1950, *U. S. Census of Population: 1950*, vol. II, part 1, p. 1–178.

A 59–70. Nonwhite population, by sex and race, 1820–1950.

Source: With the exception of series A 60 and A 66 (slaves, by sex), data are from following sources: 1820–1840, Fourth, Fifth, and Sixth Censuses, and unpublished Census Bureau records; 1850–1950, *U. S. Census of Population: 1950*, vol. II, part 1, p. 1–88. **Series A 60 and A 66** are from the following sources: 1820–1850, *The Seventh Census of the United States: 1850*, p. xxxvi and revisions on record; 1860, *The Eighth Census of the United States: 1860*, "Population Recapitulation," p. 595.

Data on the population classified by race (but not by sex) for 1790–1840 and estimates for 1870 appear in Fifteenth Census Reports, *Population, General Report: Statistics by Subject*, p. 32. Data for slaves (not by sex) for 1790–1860 appear in *Negro Population in the United States: 1790–1915*, chap. V, p. 53.

The classification of the population by race is not ordinarily based on replies to census questions asked by the enumerators, but rather is obtained by observation. This concept does not, therefore, reflect a clear-cut definition of biological stock. "All other races" include Filipinos, Koreans, Asian Indians, Indonesians, Polynesians, and other Asians. The Asian groups are identified largely in terms of country or area of origin. Persons of mixed nonwhite parentage are classified according to the race of the father, except that mixtures of Negro and Indian are classified as Negro unless the Indian stock is clearly predominant or unless the individual is accepted in the community in which he resides as an Indian.

The category Indian includes unmixed American Indians together with persons who are of mixed white and Indian ancestry if they are enrolled on an Indian reservation or agency roll. Persons who are part Indian are included as Indian if they are one-fourth or more Indian, or if they are regarded as Indians in the community in which they reside.

The Census of 1860 was the first in which Indians were distinguished from other classes in the population. Prior to 1890, enumeration of Indians was limited to Indians living in the general population of the various States; Indians in Indian Territory and on Indian reservations were excluded. In 1910, a special effort was made to secure a complete enumeration of persons with any perceptible amount of Indian ancestry. This probably resulted in the enumeration as Indian of a considerable number of persons who would have been reported as white in earlier censuses. There were no special efforts in 1920, and the returns showed a much smaller number of Indians than in 1910. Again in 1930 emphasis was placed on securing a complete count of Indians, with the results that the returns probably overstated the decennial increase in the number of Indians.

A 71–85. Population, by age, sex, race, and nativity, 1790–1950.

Source: Total population: 1850–1870, Ninth Census Reports, *Vital Statistics*, vol. II, pp. 552–558; 1880–1950, *U. S. Census of Population: 1950*, vol. II, part 1, p. 1–93. Male and white population: 1790–1840, reports of the first six censuses and unpublished Census Bureau records; 1850–1950, same as source for total population. Foreign-born white: 1870, Ninth Census Reports, *Vital Statistics*, vol. II, pp. 552–558; 1880, Fifteenth Census Reports, *Population*, vol. II, p. 580; 1890–1950, *U. S. Census of Population: 1950*, vol. IV, Special Reports, *Nativity and Parentage*, p. 3A–3. Negro: 1820–1840, reports of the Fourth, Fifth, and Sixth Censuses, and unpublished Census Bureau records; 1850–1870, Ninth Census Reports, *Vital Statistics*, vol. II, pp. 552–558; 1880, Thirteenth Census Reports, *Population*, vol. X, p. 323; 1890–1920, Fifteenth Census Reports, *Population*, vol. II, p. 580; 1930–1940, Sixteenth Census Reports, *Population*, vol. II, part 1, p. 22; 1950, *U. S. Census of Population: 1950*, vol. IV, Special Reports, *Nonwhite Population by Race*, p. 3B–16.

See text for series A 51–58 and A 59–70 for definitions of race and nativity.

A 86–94. Median age of population, by color and sex, 1790–1950.

Source: 1790–1940, Sixteenth Census Reports, *Population*, vol. IV, part 1, p. 3; 1950, *U. S. Census of Population: 1950*, vol. II, part 1, p. 1–92.

See text for series A 22–33 for definition of color.

The median age is that age which divides the population into two equal groups, one-half being older and one-half younger than the median. The median age is ordinarily 1 or 2 years younger than the average or mean age of the population. Medians have been computed on the basis of 5-year age intervals, except those for censuses earlier than 1840, where broader age groups were used.

A 95–122. Population, by race and nativity, for regions, 1790–1950.

Source: See detailed listing below.

See also text for series A 22–33 and A 59–70 for definition of color and race and A 51–58 for definition of nativity.

Figures for 1810 include in the North Central Region the population of that part of the Louisiana Territory which subsequently became the State of Arkansas (a southern State).

The divisional and State composition of Census regions is as follows:

Northeast Region:	South Region—Con.
New England Division:	South Atlantic Division—Con.
Maine	Virginia
New Hampshire	West Virginia
Vermont	North Carolina
Massachusetts	South Carolina
Rhode Island	Georgia
Connecticut	Florida
Middle Atlantic Division:	East South Central Division:
New York	Kentucky
New Jersey	Tennessee
Pennsylvania	Alabama
North Central Region:	Mississippi
East North Central Division:	West South Central Division:
Ohio	Arkansas
Indiana	Louisiana
Illinois	Oklahoma
Michigan	Texas
Wisconsin	West Region:
West North Central Division:	Mountain Division:
Minnesota	Montana
Iowa	Idaho
Missouri	Wyoming
North Dakota	Colorado
South Dakota	New Mexico
Nebraska	Arizona
Kansas	Utah
South Region:	Nevada
South Atlantic Division:	Pacific Division:
Delaware	Washington
Maryland	Oregon
District of Columbia	California

A 95, 102, 109, and 116. Population, for regions, 1790–1950.

Source: *U. S. Census of Population: 1950*, vol. I, pp. 1-8 and 1-9.

A 96, 103, 110, and 117. White population, for regions, 1790–1950.

Source: 1790–1910, *Negro Population in the United States: 1790–1915*, chap. 3, pp. 43–45; 1920, Fourteenth Census Reports, *Population*, vol. II, chap. 1, p. 31; 1930, Fifteenth Census Reports, *Population*, vol. II, p. 35; 1940, Sixteenth Census Reports, *Population*, vol. II, part 1, p. 52; 1950, *U. S. Census of Population: 1950*, vol. II, part 1, p. 1-106.

A 97, 104, 111, and 118. Native white population, for regions, 1850–1950.

Source: 1850–1890, Fifteenth Census Reports, *Population*, vol. II, p. 53; 1900–1930, *U. S. Census of Population: 1950*, vol. IV, Special Reports, *Nativity and Parentage*, p. 3A-12; 1940, Sixteenth Census Reports, *Population*, vol. II, part 1, p. 52; 1950, *U. S. Census of Population: 1950*, vol. II, part 1, p. 1-106.

A 98, 105, 112, and 119. Foreign-born white, for regions, 1850–1950.

Source: See source for series A 97, 104, 111, and 118.

A 99, 106, 113, and 120. Negro population, for regions, 1790–1950.

Source: See source for series A 96, 103, 110, and 117.

A 100, 107, 114, and 121. Negro slaves, for regions, 1790–1860.

Source: Ninth Census Reports, *Population and Social Statistics*, vol. I, p. 7.

A 101, 108, 115, and 122. Other races, for regions, 1860–1950.

Source: 1860–1890, Fifteenth Census Reports, *Population*, vol. II, p. 53; 1900–1950, see source for series A 96, 103, 110, and 117.

A 123–180. Population, for States, 1790–1950.

Source: For the population enumerated in continental United States and in the several States, *U. S. Census of Population: 1950*, vol. I, pp. 1-8 and 1-9; for the boundaries of the States and Territories for 1790–1900, Twelfth Census Reports, *A Century of Population Growth, 1790–1900*, pp. 52 and 53.

A 181–194. Number of places in urban and rural territory, by size of place, 1790–1950.

Source: *U. S. Census of Population: 1950*, vol. I, pp. 1-6 and 1-7.

The number of places shown for 1790–1940 and for 1950, according to the urban definition used in the 1940 and prior Censuses (see text for series A 34–50), represents the number of incorporated places (cities, boroughs, villages, and, in certain States, towns) and the number of places urban under special rules. The number of places shown for 1950, according to the urban definition used in the 1950 Census, represents the number of incorporated places and those unincorporated places delineated by the Bureau of the Census for the 1950 Census which had 1,000 inhabitants or more.

A 195–209. Population in urban and rural territory, by size of place, 1790–1950.

Source: *U. S. Census of Population: 1950*, vol. I, pp. 1-6 and 1-7.

See text for series A 34–50.

A 210–227. Marital status of persons 14 years old and over, by sex, 1890–1957.

Source: 1890–1940, *U. S. Census of Population: 1950*, vol. II, part 1, p. 1-179; 1947–1957, Bureau of the Census, *Current Population Reports*, Series P–20, Nos. 10, 23, 26, 38, 44, 50, 56, 62, 72, and 81.

Marital status (single, married, widowed, and divorced) represents the status of persons at the time of the enumeration. Persons classified as "married" include those who have been married only once, remarried after having been widowed or divorced, separated, and living in common-law marriages. Persons reported as never married or with annulled marriages are classified as single. Since it is probable that some divorced persons are reported as single, married, or widowed, the census figures may understate somewhat the actual number of divorced persons who have not remarried.

Percentages shown are standardized for age to offset the effect of changes in the age distribution of the population. Using the civilian population in March 1950 as a standard, the age-standardized proportions of each sex in each of the marital status categories were computed for the age groups 14–17 years, 18 and 19 years, 20–24 years, 25–34 years, 35–44 years, 45–54 years, 55–64 years, and 65 years and over. The age-specific proportions of persons in each marital status category during a given year were then each multiplied by the proportion of persons in that age group in the 1950 civilian population. The sum of the products is the standardized proportion of persons in the given marital status category.

A 228–229. Median age at first marriage, by sex, 1890–1957.

Source: 1890–1954, Bureau of the Census, *Current Population Reports*, Series P–20, No. 72; 1955–1957, Bureau of the Census and Department of Defense, records.

The median age at first marriage, as shown here, is an approximation derived indirectly from tabulations of marital status and age. (See source for detailed explanation of computation procedures.) These estimates differ from those based on annual marriage records or census questions on age at first marriage. Data on age at first marriage are available only for certain States and from census questions only for selected dates. Moreover, median age at first marriage based on records is affected by changes in the age distribution of the population, whereas the median age at first marriage shown here can be interpreted as applying to the cohort born "n" years earlier, where "n" is the median age at first marriage.

A 230–241. Households, by sex and age of head, 1890–1957.

Source: 1890 and 1950, *U. S. Census of Population: 1950*, vol. IV, Special Reports, *General Characteristics of Families*, p. 2A–10; 1930, Fifteenth Census Reports, *Population*, vol. VI, *Families*, p. 27, and Sixteenth Census Reports, *Population*, *Families—Size of Family and Age of Head*, p. 123, and unpublished Census Bureau records; 1940, Sixteenth Census Reports, *Population*, vol. IV, p. 28; 1956 and 1957, Bureau of the Census, *Current Population Reports*, Series P–20, Nos. 72 and 81.

According to the current Census Bureau definition, a household includes all the persons who occupy a house, an apartment, or other group of rooms, or a room that constitutes a dwelling unit. In general, a group of rooms occupied as separate living quarters is a dwelling unit if it has separate cooking equipment or if it constitutes the only living quarters in the structure. A household includes the related family members (the head of the household and others in the dwelling unit related to the head) and also the unrelated persons, if any, such as lodgers (if fewer than 5), foster children, wards, or employees who share the dwelling unit. A person living alone in a dwelling unit, or a group of unrelated persons sharing a dwelling unit as partners, is also counted as a household.

All persons not living in households are considered to live in quasi-households. A quasi-household is a group of persons living in quarters not classified as a dwelling unit, for example, in a house with at least 5 lodgers, or in a hotel, dormitory, institution, labor camp, or military barracks.

The figures for number of households are not strictly comparable from year to year. In general, the definitions of household for 1790, 1900, 1930, 1940, 1950, and 1957 are similar. Very minor differences result from the fact that in 1950 and 1957 dwelling units with 5 or more lodgers were excluded from the count of households, whereas in 1940 and 1930 dwelling units with 11 lodgers or more were excluded, and in 1790 and in 1900 no precise definition of the maximum allowable number of lodgers was made. The definition of household for 1850–1890, 1910, and 1920 differs slightly from that given above. For these years, no distinction was made between households and quasi-households, and thus the numbers include both households and quasi-households.

In 1950 and 1957 the number of households has been equal, by definition, to the number of occupied dwelling units enumerated for housing statistics. In 1940, the definition of household was not completely the same as that of occupied dwelling units. In that year there were 95,000 more households than occupied dwelling units.

A 242–244. Households, by residence, 1900–1957.

Source: 1900–1946, Bureau of the Census, *Current Population Reports*, Series P–20, No. 92; 1947–1957, *Current Population Reports*, Series P–20, Nos. 59 and 76.

See text for series A 230–241 for definition of household, and A 34–50 for definition of residence.

Data for 1900–1946 represent estimates of the number of married women with their spouse in their own household, and the number of household heads in the remaining population. These estimates were based on available census and survey data and on additional information on construction activity, vacancy rates, marriage rates, divorce rates, economic indexes, etc. Although the figures are shown as of a given date, they should be regarded as an approximation of the annual average number of households.

The estimates by residence were made by subdividing the total into farm and nonfarm components, using estimates of the average size of farm households in conjunction with annual estimates of the farm population (see joint report of Bureau of the Census and Bureau of Agricultural Economics, *Estimates of the Farm Population: 1910 to 1950*, Series Census–BAE, No. 16A). Since the annual changes in the number of households which are implied in these series may be in substantial error, caution should be used in the interpretation of small changes.

The farm household series for 1910–1946 relates to the total farm population, whereas that for 1947–1957 relates to the rural-farm population. There were 88,000 urban-farm households in 1940 and 96,000 in 1950.

A 245–247. Married couples with or without own household, 1910–1957.

Source: Bureau of the Census, *Current Population Reports*, Series P–20, Nos. 17, 59, and 76.

A married couple, as defined for census purposes, is a husband and his wife enumerated as members of the same household or quasi-household. The married couple may or may not have children living with them.

A 248–254. Population, by household relationship, 1910–1957.

Source: 1910, Thirteenth Census Reports, *Population*, vol. I, p. 1285, and unpublished Census Bureau records; 1930, Fifteenth Census Reports, *Population*, vol. VI, p. 10, *Current Population Reports*, Series P–20, No. 53, and unpublished Census Bureau records; 1940, Sixteenth Census Reports, *Population*, vol. IV, p. 26; 1947, Bureau of the Census, *Current Population Reports*, Series P–20, Nos. 10, 17, and 55; 1950, *Current Population Reports*, Series P–20, No. 55, and unpublished Census Bureau records; 1954 and 1957, *Current Population Reports*, Series P–20, Nos. 56 and 81.

See text for series A 230–241 for definition of household.

Prior to 1947, persons living in houses with 5 to 10 lodgers were classified as living in households rather than quasi-households. Thus, the figures for 1910, 1930, and 1940 include such persons in the total number living in households, whereas the figures for 1947, 1950, 1954, and 1957 include them as living in quasi-households.

A 255–263. Selected characteristics of households, 1790–1950.

Source: See detailed listing below.

See also text for series A 230–241 for definition of household and A 59–70 for definition of race.

A 255. Number of households, 1790–1957.

Source: 1790, Twelfth Census Special Reports, *A Century of Population Growth, 1790–1900*, p. 96; 1850–1880, Eleventh Census Reports, *Population*, part 1, p. 914; 1890–1950, *U. S. Census of Population: 1950*, vol. IV, Special Reports, *General Characteristics of Families*, p. 2A–8; 1957, Bureau of the Census, *Current Population Reports*, Series P–20, No. 81.

A 256. Median size of households, 1790–1940.

Source: Figures for 1790–1900 computed from following sources: 1790, Twelfth Census Special Reports, *A Century of Population Growth, 1790–1900*, p. 98; 1890, Eleventh Census Reports, *Population*, part 1, p. 951; 1900, Twelfth Census Reports, *Population*, vol. II, part 2, p. 611; 1930, Sixteenth Census Special Reports, *Families—Size of Family and Age of Head*, p. 3; 1940, Sixteenth Census Reports, *Housing*, vol. II, part 1, p. 32; 1950, computed from *U. S. Census of Housing: 1950*, vol. I, part 1, p. 1-8; 1957, computed from Bureau of the Census, *Current Population Reports*, Series P–20, No. 83.

A 257. Population per household, 1790–1957.

Source: 1790–1880, computed from Twelfth Census Special Reports, *A Century of Population Growth, 1790–1900*, p. 80;

1890–1950, *U. S. Census of Population: 1950*, vol. IV, Special Reports, *General Characteristics of Families*, p. 2A-8. Population figures used in computing population per household for 1957 are from Bureau of the Census, *Current Population Reports*, Series P–25, No. 169.

These figures were computed by dividing the total population (the total free population for 1790, 1850, and 1860) by the number of household heads. As explained previously, the number of household heads for 1850–1890, 1910, and 1920 also include the heads of quasi-households. Since these are such a small fraction of the total number of household heads, the population per household is only slightly affected by the change in definition for these years.

A 258–260. Race of head, 1890–1957.

Source: 1890–1930, Sixteenth Census, Special Reports, *Families—General Characteristics*, p. 4; 1940, Sixteenth Census Reports, *Population*, vol. IV, part 1, p. 26, and Sixteenth Census Special Reports, *Population—Characteristics of the Nonwhite Population by Race*, p. 30; 1950, *U. S. Census of Population: 1950*, vol. IV, Special Reports, *General Characteristics of*

Families, p. 2A-8; 1957, Bureau of the Census, *Current Population Reports*, Series P–20, No. 83.

A 261–262. Sex of head, 1890–1957.

Source: 1890, Eleventh Census Reports, *Farms and Homes: Proprietorship and Indebtedness*, p. 172; 1900, Twelfth Census Reports, *Population*, vol. II, part 2, p. ccviii; 1930, Sixteenth Census Special Reports, *Families—General Characteristics*, p. 32; 1940, Sixteenth Census Reports, *Population*, vol. IV, part 1, p. 26; 1950, *U. S. Census of Population: 1950*, vol. IV, Special Reports, *General Characteristics of Families*, p. 2A-10; 1957, Bureau of the Census, *Current Population Reports*, Series P–20, No. 81.

A 263. Median age of head, 1890–1957.

Source: 1890 and 1930–1940, Sixteenth Census Special Reports, *Families—Size of Family and Age of Head*, pp. 3 and 123; 1900, Twelfth Census Reports, *Population*, vol. II, part 2, p. ccx; 1950, *U. S. Census of Population: 1950*, vol. IV, Special Reports, *General Characteristics of Families*, p. 2A-10; 1957, Bureau of the Census, *Current Population Reports*, Series P–20, No. 81.

Series A 1–3. Estimated Population of the United States: 1790 to 1957

[In thousands. As of July 1]

Year	Total population including Armed Forces overseas (1)	Total population residing in the United States (2)	Civilian population (3)
1957	171,229	170,333	168,406
1956	168,174	167,259	165,339
1955	165,270	164,303	162,307
1954	162,417	161,191	159,086
1953	159,636	158,313	156,046
1952	157,028	155,761	153,366
1951	154,360	153,384	151,082
1950	151,683	151,234	150,202
1949	149,188	148,665	147,578
1948	146,631	146,093	145,168
1947	144,126	143,446	142,566
1946	141,389	140,054	138,385
1945	139,928	132,481	127,573
1944	138,397	132,885	126,708
1943	136,739	134,245	127,499
1942	134,860	133,920	130,942
1941	133,402	133,121	131,595
1940	132,122	131,954	131,658
1939	131,028	130,880	130,683
1938	129,969	129,825	129,635
1937	128,961	128,825	128,639
1936	128,181	128,053	127,879
1935	127,362	127,250	127,099
1934	126,485	126,374	126,228
1933	125,690	125,579	125,436
1932	124,949	124,840	124,694
1931	124,149	124,040	123,886
1930	123,188	123,077	122,923
1929	---------	121,770	---------
1928	---------	120,501	---------
1927	---------	119,038	---------
1926	---------	117,399	---------
1925	---------	115,832	---------

Year	Total population residing in the United States (2)
1924	114,113
1923	111,950
1922	110,055
1921	108,541
1920	106,466
1919 [1]	104,512
1918 [1]	103,203
1917 [1]	103,266
1916	101,966
1915	100,549
1914	99,118
1913	97,227
1912	95,331
1911	93,868
1910	92,407
1909	90,492
1908	88,709
1907	87,000
1906	85,437
1905	83,820
1904	82,165
1903	80,632
1902	79,160
1901	77,585
1900	76,094
1899	74,799
1898	73,494
1897	72,189
1896	70,885
1895	69,580
1894	68,275
1893	66,970
1892	65,666
1891	64,361

Year	Total population residing in the United States (2)
1890	63,056
1889	61,775
1888	60,496
1887	59,217
1886	57,938
1885	56,658
1884	55,379
1883	54,100
1882	52,821
1881	51,542
1880	50,262
1879	49,208
1878	48,174
1877	47,141
1876	46,107
1875	45,073
1874	44,040
1873	43,006
1872	41,972
1871	40,938
1870	39,905
1869	39,051
1868	38,213
1867	37,376
1866	36,538
1865	35,701
1864	34,863
1863	34,026
1862	33,188
1861	32,351
1860	31,513
1859	30,687
1858	29,862
1857	29,037

Year	Total population residing in the United States (2)
1856	28,212
1855	27,386
1854	26,561
1853	25,736
1852	24,911
1851	24,086
1850	23,261
1849	22,631
1848	22,018
1847	21,406
1846	20,794
1845	20,182
1844	19,569
1843	18,957
1842	18,345
1841	17,733
1840	17,120
1839	16,684
1838	16,264
1837	15,843
1836	15,423
1835	15,003
1834	14,582
1833	14,162
1832	13,742
1831	13,321
1830	12,901
1829	12,565
1828	12,237
1827	11,909
1826	11,580
1825	11,252
1824	10,924
1823	10,596

Year	Total population residing in the United States (2)
1822	10,268
1821	9,939
1820	9,618
1819	9,379
1818	9,139
1817	8,899
1816	8,659
1815	8,419
1814	8,179
1813	7,939
1812	7,700
1811	7,460
1810	7,224
1809	7,031
1808	6,838
1807	6,644
1806	6,451
1805	6,258
1804	6,065
1803	5,872
1802	5,679
1801	5,486
1800	5,297
1799	5,159
1798	5,021
1797	4,883
1796	4,745
1795	4,607
1794	4,469
1793	4,332
1792	4,194
1791	4,056
1790	3,929

[1] Total population including Armed Forces overseas (in thousands), 1917: 103,414; 1918: 104,550; 1919: 105,063; civilian population (in thousands), 1917: 102,796; 1918: 101,488; 1919: 104,158.

Series A 4–16. Population of Continental United States and Outlying Areas: 1880 to 1950

Year	Total (4)	Continental United States (5)	Population abroad [1] (6)	Outlying areas Total (7)	Philippine Islands [2] (8)	Puerto Rico (9)	Hawaii (10)	Alaska (11)	Guam (12)	Canal Zone (13)	Virgin Islands (14)	American Samoa (15)	All other (16)
1950	154,233,234	150,697,361	[3]481,545	3,054,328	----------	2,210,703	499,794	128,643	59,498	52,822	26,665	18,937	[4]57,266
1940	150,622,754	131,669,275	118,933	18,834,546	16,356,000	1,869,255	422,770	[5]72,524	22,290	51,827	24,889	12,908	[6]2,083
1930	138,439,069	122,775,046	89,453	15,574,570	13,513,000	1,543,913	368,300	[5]59,278	18,509	39,467	22,012	10,055	[7]36
1920	118,107,855	105,710,620	117,238	12,279,997	10,599,000	1,299,809	255,881	55,036	13,275	22,858	[8]26,051	8,056	[7]31
1910	102,370,018	91,972,266	55,608	10,342,144	8,886,000	1,118,012	191,874	64,356	11,806	[9]62,810	----------	[9]7,251	[7]35
1900	84,371,985	75,994,575	91,219	8,286,191	7,100,000	[10]953,243	154,001	63,592	[11]9,676	----------	----------	5,679	
1890	62,979,766	62,947,714	----------	32,052	----------	----------	----------	32,052	----------	----------	----------	----------	
1880	50,189,209	50,155,783	----------	33,426	----------	----------	----------	33,426	----------	----------	----------	----------	

[1] Excludes U. S. citizens temporarily abroad on private business, travel, etc.
[2] Estimates derived by extrapolation and interpolation of the censuses of 1903, 1918, and 1939. No figure shown for 1950 since Philippine Islands were granted independence in 1946.
[3] Estimate based on 20-percent sample of reports received.
[4] Includes population of Canton (272), Corn (1,304), Johnston (46), Midway (416), Swan (36), and Wake (349) Islands, and Trust Territory of the Pacific Islands (54,843).
[5] Census taken as of October 1 of the preceding year.
[6] Includes population of Baker, Howland, and Jarvis (10), Canton and Enderbury (44), Corn (1,523), Johnston (69), and Midway (437) Islands.
[7] Population for Midway Island.
[8] Population as of 1917 Census.
[9] Population as of 1912 Census.
[10] Population as of 1899 Census.
[11] Population as of 1901 Census.

Series A 17–21. Area and Population of Continental United States: 1790 to 1950

Year	Area (square miles)			Population		Year	Area (square miles)			Population	
	Gross area	Land	Water	Number	Per square mile of land area		Gross area	Land	Water	Number	Per square mile of land area
	17	18	19	20	21		17	18	19	20	21
1950 (Apr. 1)	3,022,387	2,974,726	47,661	150,697,361	50.7	1860 (June 1)	3,022,387	2,969,640	52,747	31,443,321	10.6
1940 (Apr. 1)	3,022,387	2,977,128	45,259	131,669,275	44.2	1850 (June 1)	2,992,747	2,940,042	52,705	23,191,876	7.9
1930 (Apr. 1)	3,022,387	2,977,128	45,259	122,775,046	41.2						
1920 (Jan. 1)	3,022,387	2,969,451	52,936	105,710,620	35.6	1840 (June 1)	1,788,006	1,749,462	38,544	17,069,453	9.8
1910 (Apr. 15)	3,022,387	2,969,565	52,822	91,972,266	31.0	1830 (June 1)	1,788,006	1,749,462	38,544	12,866,020	7.4
						1820 (Aug. 7)	1,788,006	1,749,462	38,544	9,638,453	5.6
1900 (June 1)	3,022,387	2,969,834	52,553	75,994,575	25.6	1810 (Aug. 6)	1,716,003	1,681,828	34,175	7,239,881	4.3
1890 (June 1)	3,022,387	2,969,640	52,747	62,947,714	21.2	1800 (Aug. 4)	888,811	864,746	24,065	5,308,483	6.1
1880 (June 1)	3,022,387	2,969,640	52,747	50,155,783	16.9						
1870 (June 1)	3,022,387	2,969,640	52,747	¹39,818,449	¹13.4	1790 (Aug. 2)	888,811	864,746	24,065	3,929,214	4.5

¹ Revised to include adjustments for underenumeration in Southern States.

Series A 22–33. Estimated Population, by Sex, Color, and Age: 1900 to 1957

[In thousands. As of July 1, 1940–1957; includes Armed Forces outside continental United States]

Year	Total	Sex		Color		Age (in years)						
		Male	Female	White	Nonwhite	Under 14	14 to 24	25 to 34	35 to 44	45 to 54	55 to 64	65 and over
	22	23	24	25	26	27	28	29	30	31	32	33
1957	171,229	84,858	86,371	152,464	18,766	49,206	25,502	23,767	23,341	19,711	14,954	14,749
1956	168,174	83,399	84,775	149,877	18,297	47,915	24,711	24,014	23,080	19,296	14,753	14,407
1955	165,270	82,016	83,255	147,423	17,848	46,406	24,358	24,152	22,825	18,911	14,548	14,069
1954	162,417	80,656	81,761	144,995	17,423	44,788	24,215	24,235	22,585	18,562	14,333	13,698
1953	159,636	79,337	80,299	142,633	17,003	43,148	24,204	24,241	22,360	18,242	14,107	13,333
1952	157,028	78,104	78,923	140,412	16,616	41,617	24,230	24,199	22,145	17,960	13,883	12,995
1951	154,360	76,825	77,536	138,120	16,241	40,110	24,286	24,083	21,894	17,691	13,655	12,644
1950	151,683	75,530	76,153	135,818	15,865	38,605	24,458	23,926	21,569	17,413	13,424	12,287
1949	149,188	74,335	74,853	133,598	15,590	37,238	24,709	23,729	21,187	17,260	13,145	11,921
1948	146,631	73,130	73,502	131,308	15,323	35,865	25,008	23,494	20,794	17,107	12,824	11,538
1947	144,126	71,946	72,180	129,059	15,067	34,499	25,286	23,236	20,421	16,970	12,528	11,185
1946	141,389	70,631	70,757	126,565	14,824	32,906	25,565	22,954	20,073	16,820	12,244	10,828
1945	139,928	70,035	69,893	125,266	14,662	32,360	25,922	22,734	19,787	16,642	11,988	10,494
1944	138,397	69,378	69,020	124,009	14,388	31,827	26,269	22,511	19,505	16,419	11,719	10,147
1943	136,739	68,546	68,194	122,605	14,134	31,389	26,390	22,194	19,226	16,199	11,472	9,867
1942	134,860	67,597	67,263	120,992	13,868	30,765	26,454	21,911	18,950	15,976	11,220	9,584
1941	133,402	66,920	66,482	119,731	13,671	30,545	26,468	21,691	18,692	15,759	10,959	9,288
1940	132,122	66,352	65,770	118,629	13,494	30,521	26,454	21,446	18,422	15,555	10,694	9,031
1939	130,880	65,713	65,166	117,524	13,355	30,671	26,267	21,176	18,178	15,336	10,487	8,764
1938	129,825	65,235	64,590	116,592	13,233	30,844	26,133	20,953	18,001	15,077	10,310	8,508
1937	128,825	64,790	64,035	115,706	13,118	31,091	25,969	20,723	17,866	14,785	10,132	8,258
1936	128,053	64,459	63,594	115,022	13,031	31,478	25,817	20,505	17,783	14,495	9,949	8,027
1935	127,250	64,110	63,140	114,309	12,941	31,900	25,612	20,275	17,712	14,208	9,739	7,803
1934	126,374	63,726	62,648	113,527	12,847	32,294	25,401	20,022	17,640	13,933	9,502	7,583
1933	125,579	63,384	62,195	112,815	12,764	32,742	25,221	19,750	17,569	13,684	9,249	7,362
1932	124,840	63,070	61,770	112,154	12,686	33,141	25,092	19,484	17,504	13,481	8,992	7,146
1931	124,040	62,726	61,314	111,433	12,606	33,442	24,984	19,242	17,412	13,296	8,735	6,929
1930	123,077	62,297	60,780	110,559	12,518	33,638	24,852	19,039	17,270	13,096	8,477	6,706
1929	121,770	61,684	60,086	109,385	12,385	33,863	24,498	18,942	16,917	12,761	8,315	6,475
1928	120,501	61,100	59,401	108,245	12,256	33,966	24,138	18,952	16,538	12,431	8,176	6,298
1927	119,038	60,402	58,636	106,939	12,099	33,960	23,733	18,949	16,173	12,093	7,999	6,131
1926	117,399	59,590	57,809	105,469	11,930	33,822	23,315	18,866	15,845	11,786	7,804	5,961
1925	115,832	58,820	57,012	104,065	11,767	33,677	22,939	18,724	15,578	11,523	7,604	5,788
1924	114,113	57,987	56,126	102,513	11,601	33,406	22,537	18,557	15,339	11,276	7,389	5,609
1923	111,950	56,864	55,086	100,511	11,438	33,032	21,974	18,230	15,070	11,068	7,161	5,415
1922	110,055	55,891	54,164	98,768	11,287	32,691	21,537	17,924	14,824	10,898	6,952	5,229
1921	108,541	55,292	53,250	97,417	11,124	32,308	21,230	17,748	14,666	10,721	6,793	5,077
1920	106,466	54,295	52,171	95,511	10,955	31,756	20,858	17,417	14,383	10,503	6,620	4,929
1919	¹104,512	²53,107	51,405	93,681	10,831	31,384	20,468	16,911	14,007	10,402	6,457	4,883
1918	¹103,203	²51,968	51,234	92,354	10,849	31,360	20,047	16,445	13,880	10,290	6,358	4,823
1917	¹103,266	²52,786	50,481	92,437	10,829	30,911	20,822	16,914	13,647	10,069	6,191	4,712
1916	101,966	52,238	49,728	91,202	10,764	30,488	20,837	16,776	13,390	9,845	6,026	4,604
1915	100,549	51,572	48,977	89,850	10,699	30,063	20,789	16,578	13,131	9,620	5,867	4,501
1914	99,118	50,889	48,229	88,483	10,635	29,643	20,718	16,370	12,876	9,398	5,712	4,401
1913	97,227	49,961	47,266	86,705	10,522	29,095	20,538	16,074	12,564	9,134	5,539	4,283
1912	95,331	49,020	46,311	84,924	10,407	28,560	20,334	15,769	12,254	8,875	5,371	4,168
1911	93,868	48,292	45,576	83,529	10,339	28,174	20,190	15,528	12,005	8,661	5,234	4,076
1910	92,407	47,554	44,853	82,137	10,270	27,806	20,024	15,276	11,761	8,454	5,101	3,985
1909	90,492	46,546	43,945	80,338	10,153	27,394	19,656	14,924	11,472	8,204	4,965	3,877
1908	88,709	45,595	43,114	78,659	10,050	27,049	19,281	14,585	11,203	7,974	4,841	3,776
1907	87,000	44,679	42,321	77,051	9,950	26,729	18,911	14,256	10,945	7,755	4,724	3,680
1906	85,437	43,836	41,600	75,575	9,861	26,452	18,564	13,950	10,706	7,553	4,620	3,592
1905	83,820	42,968	40,852	74,059	9,760	26,153	18,203	13,635	10,460	7,351	4,514	3,504
1904	82,165	42,082	40,083	72,516	9,649	25,832	17,833	13,315	10,211	7,149	4,409	3,416
1903	80,632	41,263	39,369	71,088	9,544	25,538	17,491	13,019	9,975	6,963	4,311	3,334
1902	79,160	40,480	38,680	69,721	9,440	25,249	17,167	12,736	9,747	6,787	4,218	3,256
1901	77,585	39,649	37,936	68,270	9,315	24,910	16,827	12,440	9,504	6,608	4,121	3,176
1900	76,094	38,869	37,226	66,901	9,193	24,581	16,514	12,162	9,271	6,439	4,027	3,100

¹ Estimates including Armed Forces overseas (in thousands), 1917: 103,414; 1918: 104,550; 1919: 105,063.

² Estimates including Armed Forces overseas (in thousands), 1917: 52,934; 1918: 53,316; 1919: 53,658.

Series A 34–50. Population, by Sex, Residence, and Color: 1790 to 1950

[In thousands. For total population, see series A 20]

Year	Total by sex		Residence[1] by sex									Color by sex					
	Male	Female	Both sexes			Male			Female			Both sexes		Male		Female	
			Urban	Rural non-farm	Rural farm	Urban	Rural non-farm	Rural farm	Urban	Rural non-farm	Rural farm	White	Non-white	White	Non-white	White	Non-white
	34	35	36	37	38	39	40	41	42	43	44	45	46	47	48	49	50
1950 (1950 urban def.)[2]	74,833	75,864	96,468	31,181	23,048	46,892	15,863	12,079	49,576	15,318	10,970	134,942	15,755	67,129	7,704	67,813	8,051
1950 (1940 urban def.)[2]			88,927	38,693	23,077	43,117	19,622	12,094	45,810	19,071	10,983						
1940	66,062	65,608	74,424	27,029	30,216	36,364	13,758	15,940	38,060	13,272	14,276	118,215	13,454	59,449	6,613	58,766	6,841
1930[3]	62,137	60,638	68,955	23,663	30,158	34,155	12,118	15,864	34,800	11,545	14,293	110,287	12,488	55,923	6,215	54,364	6,274
1920	53,900	51,810	54,158	20,159	31,393	27,203	10,337	16,360	27,101	9,710	14,999	94,821	10,890	48,431	5,470	46,390	5,420
1910	47,332	44,640	41,999	49,973		21,496	25,836		21,127	23,513		81,732	10,240	42,178	5,154	39,554	5,086
1900	38,816	37,178	30,160	45,835		15,087	23,730		15,294	21,885		66,809	9,185	34,202	4,615	32,607	4,571
1890	32,237	30,711	22,106	40,841								55,101	7,846	28,270	3,967	26,831	3,880
1880	25,519	24,637	14,130	36,026								43,403	6,753	22,131	3,388	21,272	3,365
1870	19,494	19,065	9,902	28,656								[4]33,589	[4]4,969	17,029	2,464	16,560	2,505
1860	16,085	15,358	6,217	25,227								26,923	4,521	13,811	2,274	13,111	2,247
1850	11,838	11,354	3,544	19,648								19,553	3,639	10,026	1,811	9,527	1,828
1840	8,689	8,381	1,845	15,224								14,196	2,874	7,256	1,433	6,940	1,441
1830	6,530	6,336	1,127	11,739								10,537	2,329	5,363	1,166	5,174	1,162
1820	4,897	4,742	693	8,945								7,867	1,772	3,998	899	3,869	873
1810			525	6,714								5,862	1,378	2,988		2,874	
1800			322	4,986								4,306	1,002	2,195		2,111	
1790			202	3,728								3,172	757	1,615		1,557	

[1] Residence for both sexes tabulated according to the old urban (or 1940) definition (series A 36–38) from 1790 to 1940, and for male and for female separately for 1930 and 1940. Tabulations of residence for male and for female from 1900 to 1920 are according to the definitions current at those censuses.

[2] See text for series A 34–50 for explanation of definitions.

[3] Figures for color by sex in 1930 revised to include Mexicans as white. Mexicans were classified as nonwhite in the 1930 reports.

[4] Adjustment for underenumeration in the South (see series A 20 above) shows a population of 39,818,000 of whom 34,337,000 were white and 5,481,000 were nonwhite.

Series A 51–58. White Population, by Sex and Nativity: 1850 to 1950

[Prior to 1920, citizenship figures restricted to males 21 and over]

Year	Male				Female				Year	Male			Female		
	Native		Foreign born		Native		Foreign born			Native		Foreign born	Native		Foreign born
	Total	Foreign or mixed parentage	Total	Alien[1]	Total	Foreign or mixed parentage	Total	Alien[1]		Total	Foreign or mixed parentage		Total	Foreign or mixed parentage	
	51	52	53	54	55	56	57	58		51	52	53	55	56	57
1950	61,952,802	[2]11,426,110	5,176,390	[2]804,395	62,828,058	[2]12,152,265	4,984,778	[2]1,130,400	1890	23,318,521	5,781,571	4,951,858	22,660,870	5,722,104	4,170,009
1940	53,437,533	[2]11,558,280	6,011,015	1,502,023	53,358,199	[2]11,599,300	5,408,123	1,841,791	1880	18,609,265	(3)	3,521,635	18,234,026	(3)	3,038,044
1930	48,420,037	12,824,751	7,502,491	2,912,960	47,883,298	13,077,632	6,480,914	2,684,461	1870	14,086,509	(3)	2,942,579	14,009,156	(3)	2,551,133
1920	40,902,333	11,265,552	7,528,322	3,696,544	40,205,828	11,420,652	6,184,432	2,746,128	1860	11,619,157	----------	2,192,230	11,206,627	----------	1,904,523
1910	34,654,457	9,425,239	7,523,788	----------	33,731,955	9,472,598	5,821,757	----------	1850	8,786,968	----------	1,239,434	8,525,565	----------	1,001,101
1900	28,686,450	7,836,603	5,515,285	----------	27,908,929	7,809,414	4,698,532	----------							

[1] Includes those with first papers; excludes those with citizenship unknown, of which, for both sexes, there were 698,695 in 1950; 825,072 in 1940; 491,263 in 1930; and 790,823 in 1920.

[2] Based on 20-percent sample in 1950 and 5-percent in 1940. Comparable sample totals differ slightly from figures based on a complete count.

[3] Native white of foreign or mixed parentage, for both sexes, amounted to 8,274,867 in 1880 and 5,324,268 in 1870. (See Fifteenth Census of the United States: 1930, vol. II, p. 33.)

Series A 59–70. Nonwhite Population, by Sex and Race: 1820 to 1950

Year	Male						Female					
	Negro[1]		Indian	Japanese	Chinese	All other	Negro[1]		Indian	Japanese	Chinese	All other
	Total	Slave					Total	Slave				
	59	60	61	62	63	64	65	66	67	68	69	70
1950	7,298,722	----------	178,824	76,649	77,008	[2]72,844	7,743,564	----------	164,586	65,119	40,621	[2]37,396
1940	6,269,038	----------	171,427	71,967	57,389	43,223	6,596,480	----------	162,542	54,980	20,115	7,244
1930	5,855,669	----------	170,350	81,771	59,802	46,960	6,035,474	----------	162,047	57,063	15,152	4,018
1920	5,209,436	----------	125,068	72,707	53,891	8,674	5,253,695	----------	119,369	38,303	7,748	814
1910	4,885,881	----------	135,133	63,070	66,856	3,092	4,941,882	----------	130,550	9,087	4,675	83
1900	4,386,547	----------	119,484	23,341	85,341	----------	4,447,447	----------	117,712	985	4,522	----------
1890	3,735,603	----------	125,719	1,780	103,620	----------	3,753,073	----------	122,534	259	3,868	----------
1880	3,253,115	----------	[3]33,985	134	100,686	----------	3,327,678	----------	[3]32,422	14	4,779	----------
1870	[4]2,393,263	----------	[3]12,534	47	58,633	----------	[4]2,486,746	----------	[3]13,197	8	4,566	----------
1860	2,216,744	1,982,625	[3]23,924	----------	33,149	----------	2,225,086	1,971,135	[3]20,097	----------	1,784	----------
1850	1,811,258	1,602,535					1,827,550	1,601,778				
1840	1,432,988	1,246,467					1,440,660	1,240,888				
1830	1,166,276	1,012,823					1,162,366	996,220				
1820	898,892	786,022					872,764	752,000				

[1] Sex not reported before 1820. Total for both sexes from 1790 to 1810 is as follows: For 1810, total 1,377,808, slaves 1,191,362; 1800, total 1,002,037, slaves 893,602; and 1790, total 757,208, slaves 697,681.

[2] Includes persons of mixed white, Negro, and Indian ancestry in certain communities in eastern United States.

[3] Excludes Indians in Indian Territory and on Indian reservations.

[4] Adjustment for underenumeration in Southern States shows 5,392,172 Negroes for both sexes combined.

Series A 71-85. Population, by Age, Sex, Race, and Nativity: 1790 to 1950

[Age at last birthday, except for 1890 which is age at nearest birthday. For total population, see series A 20]

Year	Under 5 years	5 to 9 years	10 to 14 years	15 to 19 years	20 to 24 years	25 to 29 years	30 to 34 years	35 to 39 years	40 to 44 years	45 to 49 years	50 to 54 years	55 to 59 years	60 to 64 years	65 and over	Age unknown
	71	72	73	74	75	76	77	78	79	80	81	82	83	84	85
TOTAL															
1950	16,163,571	13,199,685	11,119,268	10,616,598	11,481,828	12,242,260	11,517,007	11,246,386	10,203,973	9,070,465	8,272,188	7,235,120	6,059,475	12,269,537	----------
1940	10,541,524	10,684,622	11,745,935	12,333,523	11,587,835	11,096,638	10,242,388	9,545,377	8,787,843	8,255,225	7,256,846	5,843,865	4,728,340	9,019,314	----------
1930	11,444,390	12,607,609	12,004,877	11,552,115	10,870,378	9,833,608	9,120,421	9,208,645	7,990,195	7,042,279	5,975,804	4,645,677	3,751,221	6,633,805	94,022
1920	11,573,230	11,398,075	10,641,137	9,430,556	9,277,021	9,086,491	8,071,193	7,775,281	6,345,557	5,763,620	4,734,873	3,549,124	2,982,548	4,933,215	148,699
1910	10,631,364	9,760,632	9,107,140	9,063,603	9,056,984	8,180,003	6,972,185	6,396,100	5,261,587	4,469,197	3,900,791	2,786,951	2,267,150	3,949,524	169,055
1900	9,170,628	8,874,123	8,080,234	7,556,089	7,335,016	6,529,441	5,556,039	4,964,781	4,247,166	3,454,612	2,942,829	2,211,172	1,791,363	3,080,498	200,584
1890 [1]	7,634,693	7,573,998	7,033,509	6,557,563	6,196,676	5,227,777	4,578,630	3,866,161	3,185,518	2,731,640	2,326,262	1,672,336	1,458,034	2,417,288	162,165
1880	6,914,516	6,479,660	5,715,186	5,011,415	5,087,772	4,080,621	3,368,943	3,000,419	2,468,811	2,089,445	1,839,883	1,271,434	1,104,219	1,723,459	----------
1870	5,514,713	4,814,713	4,786,189	4,040,588	3,748,299	3,075,118	2,562,829	2,314,976	1,939,712	1,578,932	1,367,969	876,552	778,971	1,153,649	5,161
1860	4,842,496	4,171,200	3,720,780	3,361,495	5,726,400		4,021,248		2,614,330		1,585,879		1,347,982		51,511
1850	3,497,773	3,241,268	2,890,629	2,529,792	4,277,318		2,825,819		1,846,660		1,109,540		958,792		14,285
MALE															
1950	8,236,164	6,714,555	5,660,399	5,311,342	5,606,293	5,972,078	5,624,723	5,517,544	5,070,269	4,526,366	4,128,648	3,630,046	3,037,838	5,796,974	----------
1940	5,354,808	5,418,823	5,952,329	6,180,153	5,692,392	5,450,662	5,070,312	4,745,659	4,419,135	4,209,269	3,752,750	3,011,364	2,397,816	4,406,120	----------
1930	5,806,174	6,381,108	6,068,777	5,757,825	5,336,815	4,860,180	4,561,786	4,679,860	4,136,459	3,671,924	3,131,645	2,425,992	1,941,508	3,325,211	51,816
1920	5,857,461	5,753,001	5,369,306	4,673,792	4,527,045	4,538,233	4,130,783	4,074,361	3,285,543	3,117,550	2,535,545	1,880,065	1,581,800	2,483,071	92,875
1910	5,380,596	4,924,123	4,601,753	4,527,282	4,580,290	4,244,348	3,656,768	3,367,016	2,786,350	2,378,916	2,110,013	1,488,437	1,185,966	1,985,976	114,443
1900	4,633,612	4,479,396	4,083,041	3,750,451	3,624,580	3,323,543	2,901,321	2,616,865	2,255,916	1,837,836	1,564,622	1,145,257	917,167	1,555,418	127,423
1890 [1]	3,884,869	3,830,352	3,574,787	3,248,711	3,104,893	2,698,311	2,425,664	2,051,044	1,654,604	1,418,102	1,208,922	871,663	758,710	1,233,719	103,529
1880	3,507,709	3,275,131	2,907,481	2,476,088	2,554,684	2,109,741	1,744,308	1,527,159	1,243,773	1,078,695	966,702	674,927	584,858	867,564	----------
1870	2,797,257	2,437,442	2,435,585	1,989,695	1,835,946	1,515,671	1,273,633	1,179,366	990,021	839,578	740,360	469,495	407,491	578,230	3,795
1860	2,449,547	2,109,545	1,900,868	1,650,012	2,911,558		2,129,017		1,392,223		835,350		679,194		27,890
1850	1,769,460	1,640,407	1,473,116	1,237,680	2,194,469		1,490,135		967,573		575,685		479,962		9,173
1840 [2]	1,270,743	1,024,050	879,530	756,106	1,322,453		866,452		536,606		314,538		278,966		6,100
1830 [2]	972,980	782,075	669,734	573,196	956,487		592,535		367,840		229,284		211,002		8,275
1820 [2]	1,345,220		[3] 612,535	[4] 776,150			[5] 766,283					495,066			2,459
1810 [2]	1,035,258		[3] 468,183	[4] 547,597			[5] 572,347					364,736			----------
1800 [2, 6]	763,461		[3] 343,150	[4] 392,846			[5] 432,428					262,654			766
1790 [2, 6]		[7] 800,492							[8] 814,942						----------
WHITE															
1950	14,184,504	11,596,572	9,694,529	9,330,520	10,179,187	10,924,804	10,356,331	10,058,473	9,190,290	8,169,354	7,535,439	6,695,732	5,652,606	11,373,687	----------
1940	9,229,505	9,328,951	10,352,695	10,964,047	10,340,149	9,904,270	9,206,478	8,516,660	7,936,083	7,532,756	6,680,307	5,426,845	4,416,693	8,379,431	----------
1930 [9]	10,142,169	11,161,663	10,694,424	10,248,779	9,612,669	8,708,998	8,210,912	8,278,268	7,266,892	6,381,570	5,445,743	4,319,301	3,496,777	6,239,973	78,602
1920	10,373,921	10,087,245	9,369,322	8,314,155	8,185,341	8,141,690	7,338,790	6,965,805	5,755,547	5,188,040	4,317,266	3,305,671	2,771,433	4,583,026	123,663
1910	9,322,914	8,475,173	7,918,408	7,968,391	7,986,411	7,257,136	6,267,276	5,731,845	4,780,272	4,061,062	3,555,313	2,564,206	2,069,323	3,640,003	134,224
1900	7,919,952	7,638,326	6,959,238	6,543,189	6,335,044	5,762,980	5,004,444	4,460,575	3,852,143	3,105,678	2,633,981	2,021,217	1,620,658	2,806,719	145,052
1890 [1]	6,579,648	6,473,168	5,991,972	5,675,347	5,448,467	4,646,687	4,144,832	3,439,930	2,865,648	2,449,220	2,090,949	1,531,659	1,323,110	2,202,112	121,141
1880	5,800,151	5,442,419	4,880,531	4,351,650	4,402,472	3,541,701	2,979,254	2,648,492	2,190,735	1,861,892	1,627,892	1,154,915	977,308	1,543,558	----------
1870	4,719,792	4,151,715	4,136,461	3,511,036	3,235,028	2,681,552	2,265,065	2,047,320	1,715,255	1,406,615	1,204,243	794,771	686,679	1,030,782	3,063
1860	4,117,445	3,528,098	3,113,753	2,852,581	4,917,349		3,503,591		2,282,332		1,399,675		1,182,555		25,158
1850	2,896,458	2,704,128	2,402,129	2,128,716	3,627,561		2,416,939		1,588,788		958,171		819,871		10,307
1840	2,474,062	2,010,990	1,716,160	1,548,329	2,576,043		1,645,572		1,038,789		619,390		560,370		6,100
1830	1,894,914	1,532,816	1,308,590	1,169,450	1,874,898		1,148,066		723,886		452,788		420,840		11,130
1820	2,625,770		[3] 1,217,921	[4] 1,557,521			[5] 1,502,883					957,854			848
1810	2,016,684		[3] 916,507	[4] 1,109,265			[5] 1,116,503					703,114			----------
1800 [6]	1,489,081		[3] 666,939	[4] 794,453			[5] 844,449					501,758			766
FOREIGN-BORN WHITE															
1950 [10]	63,550	62,035	63,260	92,245	207,555	352,645	322,255	527,035	787,020	1,057,480	1,225,405	1,325,015	1,314,805	2,695,110	----------
1940	8,321	21,584	53,751	164,785	209,509	424,276	709,091	1,048,395	1,263,070	1,503,905	1,565,568	1,318,750	1,068,875	2,059,258	----------
1930 [9]	34,009	142,373	178,534	377,106	747,188	1,114,932	1,320,810	1,702,431	1,745,900	1,610,052	1,345,130	1,048,476	925,893	1,679,855	10,716
1920	44,984	169,884	331,362	527,942	926,844	1,454,363	1,651,475	1,737,805	1,428,099	1,299,675	1,167,377	908,722	715,731	1,328,227	20,264
1910	102,507	298,509	358,330	673,761	1,430,381	1,662,696	1,505,715	1,408,093	1,303,475	1,146,360	925,055	693,520	627,583	1,183,349	26,211
1900	52,369	147,192	311,565	561,746	919,482	1,097,229	1,173,683	1,177,566	966,112	840,220	803,392	643,003	545,031	950,347	24,880
1890 [1]	86,629	248,351	396,379	521,295	917,374	1,072,239	942,320	870,592	859,954	787,815	709,220	525,131	477,647	682,304	24,617
1880	62,371	122,697	238,439	378,812	528,255	671,116	762,631	789,265	712,890	630,941	577,087	373,114	310,463	401,598	----------
1870	83,912	174,233	205,538	325,426	609,068	708,526	689,595	667,992	600,749	452,826	369,778	203,516	180,931	220,029	1,593
NEGRO															
1950 [11]	1,884,219	1,530,885	1,356,764	1,226,930	1,235,035	1,253,520	1,111,950	1,142,520	973,127	862,950	704,789	516,197	386,444	859,268	----------
1940	1,249,080	1,294,546	1,330,660	1,304,606	1,195,227	1,145,284	992,879	985,833	815,096	692,807	550,435	397,219	295,904	615,942	----------
1930	1,230,206	1,368,381	1,251,542	1,250,528	1,203,191	1,071,787	864,514	890,900	687,423	630,065	504,590	309,397	242,169	372,719	13,731
1920	1,143,699	1,266,207	1,236,914	1,083,215	1,054,847	909,739	697,865	773,931	559,701	551,589	399,110	229,980	200,118	332,713	23,503
1910	1,263,288	1,246,553	1,155,266	1,060,416	1,030,795	881,227	668,089	633,449	455,413	385,909	326,070	209,622	186,502	294,124	31,040
1900	1,215,655	1,202,758	1,091,990	982,022	969,172	737,479	524,607	474,687	367,216	326,384	290,987	179,176	161,687	261,363	48,811
1890 [1]	[12] 1,047,574	[12] 1,093,494	[12] 1,033,701	871,118	731,548	559,551	409,977	707,581		499,679		268,320		211,684	35,813
1880 [13]	1,114,365	1,037,241	834,655	659,765	685,300	538,920	389,689	351,927	278,076	227,553	211,991	116,519	126,911	179,901	----------

[1] Exclusive of Indian Territory and Indian reservations with a population of 325,464 not distributed by age, of whom 169,221 were male, 117,368 were white, and 18,636 were Negro. These areas were not enumerated prior to 1890.
[2] White males only. [3] 10 to 15 years old. [4] 16 to 25 years old. [5] 26 to 44 years old.
[6] Age detail partly estimated. [7] Under 16 years old. [8] 16 years old and over.
[9] Revised to include Mexicans classified as nonwhite in the 1930 reports.
[10] Based on 20-percent sample; figures for total white population in series A 71-85 based on complete count.
[11] Due to processing errors, the sum of the various ages of Negroes in 1950 (series A 71-85) will differ slightly from the number of Negroes shown elsewhere.
[12] Estimates based on total Negroes under 15 and age distribution of nonwhites.
[13] Nonwhite population. Age not tabulated for Negroes separate from other nonwhite races.

Series A 71–85. Population, by Age, Sex, Race, and Nativity: 1790 to 1950—Con.

Year	Under 5 years	5 to 9 years	10 to 14 years	15 to 19 years	20 to 24 years	25 to 29 years	30 to 34 years	35 to 39 years	40 to 44 years	45 to 49 years	50 to 54 years	55 to 59 years	60 to 64 years	65 and over	Age unknown
	71	72	73	74	75	76	77	78	79	80	81	82	83	84	85
NEGRO—Con.															
1870	791,421	659,831	645,311	520,550	498,854	379,048	284,749	258,838	216,820	168,968	161,362	80,857	91,314	122,058	28
1860	719,084	637,806	601,647	501,593	783,603		500,598		324,519		183,693		163,029		26,258
Free colored	65,918	61,857	60,399	52,747	85,562		61,732		44,726		27,991		26,966		172
Slave	653,166	575,949	541,248	448,846	698,041		438,866		279,793		155,702		136,063		26,086
1850	601,315	537,140	488,500	401,076	649,757		408,880		257,872		151,369		138,921		3,978
Free colored	60,821	58,052	52,308	43,794	77,547		55,225		37,940		24,353		24,169		286
Slave	540,494	479,088	436,192	357,282	572,210		353,655		219,932		127,016		114,752		3,692
1840	955,395		[14]890,720		[15]552,114				[16]343,099				132,320		
Free colored	111,346		[14]109,397		[15]77,003				[16]58,635				24,912		
Slave	844,049		[14]781,323		[15]475,111				[16]284,464				102,408		
1830	797,167		[14]712,554		[15]431,562				[16]277,365				109,994		
Free colored	96,004		[14]91,217		[15]60,191				[16]46,598				25,589		
Slave	701,163		[14]621,337		[15]371,371				[16]230,767				84,405		
1820		[17]763,747		[18]456,372			[5]367,156					184,381			
Free colored		[17]93,551		[18]52,848			[5]50,741					36,494			
Slave		[17]670,196		[18]403,524			[5]316,415					147,887			

[5] 26 to 44 years old.   [14] 10 to 23 years old.   [15] 24 to 35 years old.   [16] 36 to 54 years old.   [17] Under 14 years old.   [18] 14 to 25 years old.

Series A 86–94. Median Age of Population, by Color and Sex: 1790 to 1950

[In years. Because of change in computation procedure, medians for 1850 to 1930 differ slightly from those published in the population census reports for 1930 and previous years]

Year	All classes			White			Nonwhite			Year	All classes			White			Nonwhite		
	Total	Male	Female	Total	Male	Female	Total	Male	Female		Total	Male	Female	Total	Male	Female	Total	Male	Female
	86	87	88	89	90	91	92	93	94		86	87	88	89	90	91	92	93	94
1950	30.2	29.9	30.5	30.8	30.4	31.1	26.1	25.9	26.2	1860	19.4	19.8	19.1	19.7	20.2	19.3	17.5	17.5	17.5
1940	29.0	29.1	29.0	29.5	29.5	29.5	25.2	25.4	25.1	1850	18.9	19.2	18.6	19.2	19.5	18.8	17.4	17.3	17.4
1930	26.5	26.7	26.2	26.9	27.1	26.6	23.5	23.9	23.1	1840	17.8	17.8	17.7	17.9	17.9	17.8	17.3	17.0	17.5
1920	25.3	25.8	24.7	25.6	26.1	25.1	22.4	23.1	21.9	1830	17.2	17.1	17.3	17.2	17.2	17.3	16.9	16.7	17.1
1910	24.1	24.6	23.5	24.5	24.9	23.9	21.1	21.5	20.6	1820	16.7	16.6	16.7	16.5	16.5	16.6	17.2	16.9	17.1
1900	22.9	23.3	22.4	23.4	23.8	22.9	19.7	20.0	19.5	1810				16.0	15.9	16.1			
1890	22.0	22.3	21.6	22.5	22.9	22.1	18.4	18.5	18.3	1800				16.0	15.7	16.3			
1880	20.9	21.2	20.7	21.4	21.6	21.1	18.0	17.9	18.0	1790				15.9					
1870	20.2	20.2	20.1	20.4	20.6	20.3	18.5	18.2	18.9										

Series A 95–122. Population, by Race and Nativity, for Regions: 1790 to 1950

[For total population, see series A 20]

Year	Northeast Total	White Total	White Native	White Foreign born	Negro Total	Negro Slave	Other races	North Central Total	White Total	White Native	White Foreign born	Negro Total	Negro Slave	Other races
	95	96	97	98	99	100	101	102	103	104	105	106	107	108
1950	39,477,986	37,398,684	32,204,834	5,193,850	2,018,182	———	61,120	44,460,762	42,119,384	39,407,638	2,711,746	2,227,876	———	113,502
1940	35,976,777	34,566,768	28,545,927	6,020,841	1,369,875	———	40,134	40,143,332	38,639,970	35,291,033	3,348,937	1,420,318	———	83,044
1930	34,427,091	33,244,081	26,135,432	7,108,649	1,146,985	———	36,025	38,594,100	37,249,272	32,902,458	4,346,814	1,262,234	———	82,594
1920	29,662,053	28,957,919	22,174,690	6,783,229	679,234	———	24,900	34,019,792	33,164,249	28,569,009	4,595,240	793,075	———	62,468
1910	25,868,573	25,360,966	18,720,401	6,640,565	484,176	———	23,431	29,888,542	29,279,243	24,598,792	4,680,451	543,498	———	65,801
1900	21,046,695	20,637,888	15,898,900	4,738,988	385,020	———	23,787	26,333,004	25,775,870	21,624,468	4,151,402	495,751	———	61,383
1890	17,406,969	17,121,985	13,247,119	3,874,866	269,906	———	15,078	22,410,417	21,913,813	17,860,356	4,053,457	431,112	———	65,492
1880	14,507,407	14,273,844	11,465,448	2,808,396	229,417	———	4,146	17,364,111	16,961,423	14,049,225	2,912,198	385,621	———	17,067
1870	12,298,730	12,117,269	9,599,990	2,517,279	179,738	———	1,723	12,981,111	12,698,503	10,367,625	2,330,878	273,080	———	9,528
1860	10,594,268	10,438,028	8,419,243	2,018,785	156,001	18	239	9,096,716	8,899,969	7,357,376	1,542,593	184,239	114,948	12,508
1850	8,626,851	8,477,089	7,153,512	1,323,577	149,762	236	———	5,403,595	5,267,988	4,617,913	650,075	135,607	87,422	———
1840 [1]	6,761,082	6,618,758	———	———	142,324	765	———	3,351,542	3,262,195	———	———	89,347	58,604	———
1830 [1]	5,542,381	5,417,167	———	———	125,214	2,780	———	1,610,473	1,568,930	———	———	41,543	25,879	———
1820	4,359,916	4,249,192	———	———	110,724	18,001	———	859,305	841,045	———	———	18,260	11,329	———
1810	3,486,675	3,384,438	———	———	102,237	27,081	———	292,107	285,173	———	———	6,934	3,304	———
1800	2,635,576	2,552,510	———	———	83,066	36,370	———	51,006	50,371	———	———	635	135	———
1790	1,968,040	1,900,616	———	———	67,424	40,354	———	———	———	———	———	———	———	———

[1] Excludes persons (6,100 in 1840 and 5,318 in 1830) on public ships in the service of the United States, not credited to any region.

Series A 95–122.   Population, by Race and Nativity, for Regions: 1790 to 1950—Con.

	South							West						
Year	Total	White			Negro		Other races	Total	White			Negro		Other races
		Total	Native	Foreign born	Total	Slave			Total	Native	Foreign born	Total	Slave	
	109	110	111	112	113	114	115	116	117	118	119	120	121	122
1950	47,197,088	36,849,529	36,092,010	757,519	10,225,407	--------	122,152	19,561,525	18,574,431	17,076,378	1,498,053	570,821	--------	416,273
1940	41,665,901	31,658,578	31,032,902	625,676	9,904,619	--------	102,704	13,883,265	13,349,554	11,925,870	1,423,684	170,706	--------	363,005
1930	37,857,633	28,371,969	27,571,198	800,771	9,361,577	--------	124,087	11,896,222	11,421,418	9,694,247	1,727,171	120,347	--------	354,457
1920	33,125,803	24,132,214	23,285,022	847,192	8,912,231	--------	81,358	8,902,972	8,566,533	7,079,440	1,487,093	78,591	--------	257,848
1910	29,389,330	20,547,420	19,821,249	726,171	8,749,427	--------	92,483	6,825,821	6,544,328	5,245,970	1,298,358	50,662	--------	230,831
1900	24,523,527	16,521,970	15,959,395	562,575	7,922,969	--------	78,588	4,091,349	3,873,468	3,112,616	760,852	30,254	--------	187,627
1890	20,028,059	13,193,453	12,672,558	520,895	6,760,577	--------	74,029	3,102,269	2,872,007	2,199,358	672,649	27,081	--------	203,181
1880	16,516,568	10,555,427	10,113,361	442,066	5,953,903	--------	7,238	1,767,697	1,612,276	1,215,257	397,019	11,852	--------	143,569
1870	[2] 12,288,020	[2] 7,863,209	7,467,542	395,667	[2] 4,420,811	--------	4,000	990,510	910,396	660,508	249,888	6,380	--------	73,734
1860	11,133,361	7,033,973	6,642,201	391,772	4,097,111	3,838,765	2,277	618,976	550,567	406,964	143,603	4,479	29	63,930
1850	8,982,612	5,630,414	5,390,314	240,100	3,352,198	3,116,629	--------	178,818	177,577	150,794	26,783	1,241	26	--------
1840 [1]	6,950,729	4,308,752	--------	--------	2,641,977	2,427,986	--------							
1830 [1]	5,707,848	3,545,963	--------	--------	2,161,885	1,980,384	--------							
1820	4,419,232	2,776,560	--------	--------	1,642,672	1,508,692	--------							
1810	3,461,099	2,192,462	--------	--------	1,268,637	1,160,977	--------							
1800	2,621,901	1,703,565	--------	--------	918,336	857,097	--------							
1790	1,961,174	1,271,390	--------	--------	689,784	657,327	--------							

[1] Excludes persons (6,100 in 1840 and 5,318 in 1830) on public ships in the service of the United States, not credited to any region.

[2] Adjustment for underenumeration shows a total for the South of 13,548,098, of whom 8,611,124 were white and 4,932,974 were Negro.

Series A 123–180.   Population, for States: 1790 to 1950

[Insofar as possible, population shown is that of present area of State. For U. S. total population, see series A 20. However, in 1830, series A 20 includes 5,318 persons on public ships in the service of the United States not credited to any State; the corresponding figure for 1840 is 6,100]

Series No.	State	1950	1940	1930	1920	1910	1900	1890	1880
123	**New England**	9,314,453	8,437,290	8,166,341	7,400,909	6,552,681	5,592,017	4,700,749	4,010,529
124	Maine	913,774	847,226	797,423	768,014	742,371	694,466	661,086	648,936
125	New Hampshire	533,242	491,524	465,293	443,083	430,572	411,588	376,530	346,991
126	Vermont	377,747	359,231	359,611	352,428	355,956	343,641	332,422	332,286
127	Massachusetts	4,690,514	4,316,721	4,249,614	3,852,356	3,366,416	2,805,346	2,238,947	1,783,085
128	Rhode Island	791,896	713,346	687,497	604,397	542,610	428,556	345,506	276,531
129	Connecticut	2,007,280	1,709,242	1,606,903	1,380,631	1,114,756	908,420	746,258	622,700
130	**Middle Atlantic**	30,163,533	27,539,487	26,260,750	22,261,144	19,315,892	15,454,678	12,706,220	10,496,878
131	New York	14,830,192	13,479,142	12,588,066	10,385,227	9,113,614	7,268,894	6,003,174	5,082,871
132	New Jersey	4,835,329	4,160,165	4,041,334	3,155,900	2,537,167	1,883,669	1,444,933	1,131,116
133	Pennsylvania	10,498,012	9,900,180	9,631,350	8,720,017	7,665,111	6,302,115	5,258,113	4,282,891
134	**East North Central**	30,399,368	26,626,342	25,297,185	21,475,543	18,250,621	15,985,581	13,478,305	11,206,668
135	Ohio	7,946,627	6,907,612	6,646,697	5,759,394	4,767,121	4,157,545	3,672,329	3,198,062
136	Indiana	3,934,224	3,427,796	3,238,503	2,930,390	2,700,876	2,516,462	2,192,404	1,978,301
137	Illinois	8,712,176	7,897,241	7,630,654	6,485,280	5,638,591	4,821,550	3,826,352	3,077,871
138	Michigan	6,371,766	5,256,106	4,842,325	3,668,412	2,810,173	2,420,982	2,093,890	1,636,937
139	Wisconsin	3,434,575	3,137,587	2,939,006	2,632,067	2,333,860	2,069,042	1,693,330	1,315,497
140	**West North Central**	14,061,394	13,516,990	13,296,915	12,544,249	11,637,921	10,347,423	8,932,112	6,157,443
141	Minnesota	2,982,483	2,792,300	2,563,953	2,387,125	2,075,708	1,751,394	1,310,283	780,773
142	Iowa	2,621,073	2,538,268	2,470,939	2,404,021	2,224,771	2,231,853	1,912,297	1,624,615
143	Missouri	3,954,653	3,784,664	3,629,367	3,404,055	3,293,335	3,106,665	2,679,185	2,168,380
144	North Dakota	619,636	641,935	680,845	646,872	577,056	319,146	190,983	36,909
145	South Dakota	652,740	642,961	692,849	636,547	583,888	401,570	348,600	98,268
146	Nebraska	1,325,510	1,315,834	1,377,963	1,296,372	1,192,214	1,066,300	1,062,656	452,402
147	Kansas	1,905,299	1,801,028	1,880,999	1,769,257	1,690,949	1,470,495	1,428,108	996,096
148	**South Atlantic**	21,182,335	17,823,151	15,793,589	13,990,272	12,194,895	10,443,480	8,857,922	7,597,197
149	Delaware	318,085	266,505	238,380	223,003	202,322	184,735	168,493	146,608
150	Maryland	2,343,001	1,821,244	1,631,526	1,449,661	1,295,346	1,188,044	1,042,390	934,943
151	Dist. of Columbia	802,178	663,091	486,869	437,571	331,069	278,718	230,392	177,624
152	Virginia	3,318,680	2,677,773	2,421,851	2,309,187	2,061,612	1,854,184	1,655,980	1,512,565
153	West Virginia	2,005,552	1,901,974	1,729,205	1,463,701	1,221,119	958,800	762,794	618,457
154	North Carolina	4,061,929	3,571,623	3,170,276	2,559,123	2,206,287	1,893,810	1,617,949	1,399,750
155	South Carolina	2,117,027	1,899,804	1,738,765	1,683,724	1,515,400	1,340,316	1,151,149	995,577
156	Georgia	3,444,578	3,123,723	2,908,506	2,895,832	2,609,121	2,216,331	1,837,353	1,542,180
157	Florida	2,771,305	1,897,414	1,468,211	968,470	752,619	528,542	391,422	269,493
158	**East South Central**	11,477,181	10,778,225	9,887,214	8,893,307	8,409,901	7,547,757	6,429,154	5,585,151
159	Kentucky	2,944,806	2,845,627	2,614,589	2,416,630	2,289,905	2,147,174	1,858,635	1,648,690
160	Tennessee	3,291,718	2,915,841	2,616,556	2,337,885	2,184,789	2,020,616	1,767,518	1,542,359
161	Alabama	3,061,743	2,832,961	2,646,248	2,348,174	2,138,093	1,828,697	1,513,401	1,262,505
162	Mississippi	2,178,914	2,183,796	2,009,821	1,790,618	1,797,114	1,551,270	1,289,600	1,131,597
163	**West South Central**	14,537,572	13,064,525	12,176,830	10,242,224	8,784,534	6,532,290	4,740,983	3,334,220
164	Arkansas	1,909,511	1,949,387	1,854,482	1,752,204	1,574,449	1,311,564	1,128,211	802,525
165	Louisiana	2,683,516	2,363,880	2,101,593	1,798,509	1,656,388	1,381,625	1,118,588	939,946
166	Oklahoma	2,233,351	2,336,434	2,396,040	2,028,283	1,657,155	790,391	258,657	--------
167	Texas	7,711,194	6,414,824	5,824,715	4,663,228	3,896,542	3,048,710	2,235,527	1,591,749
168	**Mountain**	5,074,998	4,150,003	3,701,789	3,336,101	2,633,517	1,674,657	1,213,935	653,119
169	Montana	591,024	559,456	537,606	548,889	376,053	243,329	142,924	39,159
170	Idaho	588,637	524,873	445,032	431,866	325,594	161,772	88,548	32,610
171	Wyoming	290,529	250,742	225,565	194,402	145,965	92,531	62,555	20,789
172	Colorado	1,325,089	1,123,296	1,035,791	939,629	799,024	539,700	413,249	194,327
173	New Mexico	681,187	531,818	423,317	360,350	327,301	195,310	160,282	119,565
174	Arizona	749,587	499,261	435,573	334,162	204,354	122,931	88,243	40,440
175	Utah	688,862	550,310	507,847	449,396	373,351	276,749	210,779	143,963
176	Nevada	160,083	110,247	91,058	77,407	81,875	42,335	47,355	62,266
177	**Pacific**	14,486,527	9,733,262	8,194,433	5,566,871	4,192,304	2,416,692	1,888,334	1,114,578
178	Washington	2,378,963	1,736,191	1,563,396	1,356,621	1,141,990	518,103	357,232	75,116
179	Oregon	1,521,341	1,089,684	953,786	783,389	672,765	413,536	317,704	174,768
180	California	10,586,223	6,907,387	5,677,251	3,426,861	2,377,549	1,485,053	1,213,398	864,694

Series A 123–180. Population, for States: 1790 to 1950—Con.

Series No.	State	1870	1860	1850	1840	1830	1820	1810	1800	1790
123	**New England**	3,487,924	3,135,283	2,728,116	2,234,822	1,954,717	1,660,071	1,471,973	1,233,011	1,009,408
124	Maine	626,915	628,279	583,169	501,793	399,455	298,335	228,705	151,719	96,540
125	New Hampshire	318,300	326,073	317,976	284,574	269,328	244,161	214,460	183,858	141,885
126	Vermont	330,551	315,098	314,120	291,948	280,652	235,981	217,895	154,465	85,425
127	Massachusetts	1,457,351	1,231,066	994,514	737,699	610,408	523,287	472,040	422,845	378,787
128	Rhode Island	217,353	174,620	147,545	108,830	97,199	83,059	76,931	69,122	68,825
129	Connecticut	537,454	460,147	370,792	309,978	297,675	275,248	261,942	251,002	237,946
130	**Middle Atlantic**	8,810,806	7,458,985	5,898,735	4,526,260	3,587,664	2,699,845	2,014,702	1,402,565	958,632
131	New York	4,382,759	3,880,735	3,097,394	2,428,921	1,918,608	1,372,812	959,049	589,051	340,120
132	New Jersey	906,096	672,035	489,555	373,306	320,823	277,575	245,562	211,149	184,139
133	Pennsylvania	3,521,951	2,906,215	2,311,786	1,724,033	1,348,233	1,049,458	810,091	602,365	434,373
134	**East North Central**	9,124,517	6,926,884	4,523,260	2,924,728	1,470,018	792,719	272,324	51,006	----------
135	Ohio	2,665,260	2,339,511	1,980,329	1,519,467	937,903	581,434	230,760	[1] 45,365	----------
136	Indiana	1,680,637	1,350,428	988,416	685,866	343,031	147,178	[2] 24,520	[2] 5,641	----------
137	Illinois	2,539,891	1,711,951	851,470	476,183	157,445	55,211	[3] 12,282	----------	----------
138	Michigan	1,184,059	749,113	397,654	212,267	[4] 31,639	[4] 8,896	[4] 4,762	----------	----------
139	Wisconsin	1,054,670	775,881	305,391	[5] 30,945	----------	----------	----------	----------	----------
140	**West North Central**	3,856,594	2,169,832	880,335	426,814	140,455	66,586	19,783		
141	Minnesota	439,706	172,023	6,077	----------					
142	Iowa	1,194,020	674,913	192,214	[6] 43,112					
143	Missouri	1,721,295	1,182,012	682,044	383,702	140,455	66,586	19,783		
144	North Dakota	2,405	[7] 4,837	----------						
145	South Dakota	11,776	----------							
146	Nebraska	122,993	28,841	----------						
147	Kansas	364,399	107,206	----------						
148	**South Atlantic**	5,853,610	5,364,703	4,679,090	3,925,299	3,645,752	3,061,063	2,674,891	2,286,494	1,851,806
149	Delaware	125,015	112,216	91,532	78,085	76,748	72,749	72,674	64,273	59,096
150	Maryland	780,894	687,049	583,034	470,019	447,040	407,350	380,546	341,548	319,728
151	Dist. of Columbia	131,700	75,080	51,687	33,745	30,261	23,336	15,471	8,144	----------
152	Virginia	1,225,163	1,219,630	1,119,348	1,025,227	1,044,054	938,261	877,683	807,557	691,737
153	West Virginia	442,014	376,688	302,313	224,537	176,924	136,808	105,469	78,592	55,873
154	North Carolina	1,071,361	992,622	869,039	753,419	737,987	638,829	555,500	478,103	393,751
155	South Carolina	705,606	703,708	668,507	594,398	581,185	502,741	415,115	345,591	249,073
156	Georgia	1,184,109	1,057,286	906,185	691,392	516,823	340,989	252,433	162,686	82,548
157	Florida	187,748	140,424	87,445	54,477	34,730	----------	----------	----------	----------
158	**East South Central**	4,404,445	4,020,991	3,363,271	2,575,445	1,815,969	1,190,489	708,590	335,407	109,368
159	Kentucky	1,321,011	1,155,684	982,405	779,828	687,917	564,317	406,511	220,955	73,677
160	Tennessee	1,258,520	1,109,801	1,002,717	829,210	681,904	422,823	261,727	105,602	35,691
161	Alabama	996,992	964,201	771,623	590,756	309,527	127,901	[8] 9,046	[8] 1,250	----------
162	Mississippi	827,922	791,305	606,526	375,651	136,621	75,448	[9] 31,306	[9] 7,600	----------
163	**West South Central**	2,029,965	1,747,667	940,251	449,985	246,127	167,680	77,618	----------	----------
164	Arkansas	484,471	435,450	209,897	97,574	30,388	14,273	1,062	----------	----------
165	Louisiana	726,915	708,002	517,762	352,411	215,739	153,407	76,556	----------	----------
166	Oklahoma	----------	----------	----------	----------	----------	----------	----------	----------	----------
167	Texas	818,579	604,215	212,592	----------	----------	----------	----------	----------	----------
168	**Mountain**	315,385	174,923	72,927	----------	----------	----------	----------	----------	----------
169	Montana	20,595	----------	----------						
170	Idaho	14,999	----------	----------						
171	Wyoming	9,118	----------	----------						
172	Colorado	39,864	34,277	----------						
173	New Mexico	91,874	[10] 93,516	61,547	----------					
174	Arizona	9,658	----------	----------						
175	Utah	86,786	[11] 40,273	11,380	----------					
176	Nevada	42,491	[12] 6,857	----------						
177	**Pacific**	675,125	444,053	105,891	----------	----------	----------	----------	----------	----------
178	Washington	23,955	[13] 11,594	[14] 1,201	----------					
179	Oregon	90,923	52,465	12,093	----------					
180	California	560,247	379,994	92,597	----------					

[1] Territory northwest of the Ohio River.
[2] 1810 includes population of area separated in 1816; 1800 includes 3,124 persons in those portions of Indiana Territory which were taken to form Michigan and Illinois Territories in 1805 and 1809, respectively, and that portion which was separated in 1816.
[3] Illinois Territory.
[4] Michigan Territory as then constituted; boundaries changed in 1816, 1818, 1834, and 1836.
[5] Includes that part of Minnesota northeast of Mississippi River.
[6] Includes that part of Minnesota lying west of Mississippi River and a line drawn from its source northwards to Canadian boundary.

[7] Dakota Territory.
[8] Those parts of Mississippi Territory now in present State.
[9] Those parts of present State included in Mississippi Territory as then constituted.
[10] Includes area taken to form part of Arizona Territory in 1863.
[11] Utah Territory exclusive of that part of present State of Colorado taken to form Colorado Territory in 1861.
[12] Nevada Territory as organized in 1861.
[13] Includes population of Idaho and parts of Montana and Wyoming.
[14] Parts of Oregon Territory taken to form part of Washington Territory in 1853 and 1859.

Series A 181–194. Number of Places in Urban and Rural Territory, by Size of Place: 1790 to 1950

[In 1930 each pair of the following was counted as a single place: Bluefield, Va., and Bluefield, W. Va.; Bristol, Tenn., and Bristol, Va.; Delmar, Del., and Delmar, Md.; Harrison, Ohio, and West Harrison, Ind.; Junction City, Ark., and Junction City, La.; Texarkana, Ark., and Texarkana, Tex. Texhoma, Okla., and Texhoma, Tex.; and Union City, Ind., and Union City, Ohio. In all other years they were counted as separate incorporated places. For description of urban definition, see text]

Series No.	Class and population size	1950		1940	1930	1920	1910	1900	1890	1880
		1950 urban definition	1940 urban definition							
181	Urban territory	4,741	4,023	3,464	3,165	2,722	2,262	1,737	1,348	939
182	Places of 1,000,000 or more	5	5	5	5	3	3	3	3	1
183	Places of 500,000 to 1,000,000	13	13	9	8	9	5	3	1	3
184	Places of 250,000 to 500,000	23	23	23	24	13	11	9	7	4
185	Places of 100,000 to 250,000	65	66	55	56	43	31	23	17	12
186	Places of 50,000 to 100,000	126	128	107	98	76	59	40	30	15
187	Places of 25,000 to 50,000	252	271	213	185	143	119	82	66	42
188	Places of 10,000 to 25,000	778	814	665	606	465	369	280	230	146
189	Places of 5,000 to 10,000	1,176	1,133	965	851	715	605	465	340	249
190	Places of 2,500 to 5,000	1,846	1,570	1,422	1,332	1,255	1,060	832	654	467
191	Places under 2,500	457	---	---	---	---	---	---	---	(1)
192	Rural territory	13,807	13,235	13,288	13,433	12,855	11,830	8,931	6,490	(1)
193	Places of 1,000 to 2,500	4,158	3,408	3,205	3,087	3,030	2,717	2,128	1,603	(1)
194	Places under 1,000	9,649	9,827	10,083	10,346	9,825	9,113	6,803	4,887	(1)

Series No.	Class and population size	1870	1860	1850	1840	1830	1820	1810	1800	1790
181	Urban territory	663	392	236	131	90	61	46	33	24
182	Places of 1,000,000 or more									
183	Places of 500,000 to 1,000,000	2	2	1	---	---	---	---	---	---
184	Places of 250,000 to 500,000	5	1	---	1	---	---	---	---	---
185	Places of 100,000 to 250,000	7	6	5	2	1	1	---	---	---
186	Places of 50,000 to 100,000	11	7	4	2	3	2	2	1	---
187	Places of 25,000 to 50,000	27	19	16	7	3	2	2	2	2
188	Places of 10,000 to 25,000	116	58	36	25	16	8	7	3	3
189	Places of 5,000 to 10,000	186	136	85	48	33	22	17	15	7
190	Places of 2,500 to 5,000	309	163	89	46	34	26	18	12	12

1 Not available.

Series A 195–209. Population in Urban and Rural Territory, by Size of Place: 1790 to 1950

[For U. S. total population, see series A 20]

Series No.	Class and population size	1950		1940	1930	1920	1910	1900	1890	1880
		1950 urban definition	1940 urban definition							
195	Urban territory	[1]96,467,686	88,927,464	74,423,702	68,954,823	54,157,973	41,998,932	30,159,921	22,106,265	14,129,735
196	Places of 1,000,000 or more	17,404,450	17,404,450	15,910,866	15,064,555	10,145,532	8,501,174	6,429,474	3,662,115	1,206,299
197	Places of 500,000 to 1,000,000	9,186,945	9,186,945	6,456,959	5,763,987	6,223,769	3,010,667	1,645,087	806,343	1,917,018
198	Places of 250,000 to 500,000	8,241,560	8,241,560	7,827,514	7,956,228	4,540,838	3,949,839	2,861,296	2,447,608	1,300,809
199	Places of 100,000 to 250,000	9,478,662	9,614,111	7,792,650	7,540,966	6,519,187	4,840,458	3,272,490	2,781,894	1,786,783
200	Places of 50,000 to 100,000	8,930,823	9,073·363	7,343,917	6,491,448	5,265,408	4,178,915	2,709,338	2,027,569	947,918
201	Places of 25,000 to 50,000	8,807,721	9,495,862	7,417,093	6,425,693	5,075,041	4,023,397	2,800,627	2,268,786	1,446,366
202	Places of 10,000 to 25,000	11,866,505	12,467,229	9,966,898	9,097,200	7,034,668	5,548,868	4,338,250	3,451,258	2,189,447
203	Places of 5,000 to 10,000	8,138,596	7,878,675	6,681,894	5,897,156	4,967,625	4,217,420	3,204,195	2,383,685	1,717,146
204	Places of 2,500 to 5,000	6,490,406	5,565,269	5,025,911	4,717,590	4,385,905	3,728,194	2,899,164	2,277,007	1,617,949
205	Places under 2,500	577,992	---	---	---	---	---	---	---	(2)
206	Rural territory	54,229,675	61,769,897	57,245,573	53,820,223	51,552,647	49,973,334	45,834,654	40,841,449	36,026,048
207	Places of 1,000 to 2,500	6,473,315	5,382,637	5,026,834	4,820,707	4,712,007	4,234,406	3,298,054	2,508,642	(2)
208	Places under 1,000	4,031,148	4,129,049	4,315,843	4,362,746	4,254,968	3,930,222	3,003,479	2,249,332	(2)
209	Other rural territory	43,725,212	52,258,211	47,902,896	44,636,770	42,585,672	41,808,706	39,533,121	36,083,475	(2)

Series No.	Class and population size	1870	1860	1850	1840	1830	1820	1810	1800	1790
195	Urban territory	9,902,361	6,216,518	3,543,716	1,845,055	1,127,247	693,255	525,459	322,371	201,655
196	Places of 1,000,000 or more									
197	Places of 500,000 to 1,000,000	1,616,314	1,379,198	515,547	---	---	---	---	---	---
198	Places of 250,000 to 500,000	1,523,820	266,661	---	312,710	---	---	---	---	---
199	Places of 100,000 to 250,000	989,855	992,922	659,121	204,506	202,589	123,706	---	---	---
200	Places of 50,000 to 100,000	768,238	452,060	284,355	187,048	222,474	126,540	150,095	60,515	---
201	Places of 25,000 to 50,000	930,119	670,293	611,328	235,424	105,243	70,474	80,342	67,734	61,653
202	Places of 10,000 to 25,000	1,709,541	884,433	560,783	404,822	240,371	121,613	108,980	54,479	48,182
203	Places of 5,000 to 10,000	1,278,145	976,436	596,086	328,744	230,859	155,035	116,271	94,394	47,569
204	Places of 2,500 to 5,000	1,086,329	594,515	316,496	171,801	125,711	95,887	69,771	45,249	44,251
206	Rural territory	28,656,010	25,226,803	19,648,160	15,224,398	11,738,773	8,945,198	6,714,422	4,986,112	3,727,559

1 Includes population of unincorporated parts of urbanized areas (7,344,026).   2 Not available.

Series A 210–227. Marital Status, by Sex: 1890 to 1957

[In thousands. Total population, 1890 to 1940, and civilian population, 1947 to 1956. 1947 to 1957 based on sample figures from Current Population Survey. Civilian population includes members of the Armed Forces living off post or with their families on post. For total population, see series A 1]

	Male, 14 years old and over									Female, 14 years old and over								
						Percent, standardized for age									Percent, standardized for age			
Date	Total	Single	Married	Widowed	Divorced	Single	Married	Widowed	Divorced	Total	Single	Married	Widowed	Divorced	Single	Married	Widowed	Divorced
	210	211	212	213	214	215	216	217	218	219	220	221	222	223	224	225	226	227
March 1957	57,470	13,754	40,490	2,186	1,040	24.5	70.3	3.5	1.8	61,863	11,487	41,204	7,778	1,394	18.6	67.7	11.5	2.3
March 1956	56,744	13,516	39,967	2,335	926	24.7	70.0	3.8	1.6	60,975	11,126	40,650	7,707	1,492	18.5	67.4	11.6	2.5
April 1955 [1]	55,994	13,522	39,125	2,357	990	25.1	69.3	3.9	1.7	60,250	10,962	40,327	7,595	1,366	18.6	67.4	11.8	2.3
April 1954 [1]	55,297	13,004	39,042	2,171	1,080	24.7	69.8	3.7	1.9	59,542	11,043	39,869	7,256	1,374	19.0	67.2	11.5	2.3
April 1953 [1]	54,784	13,000	38,612	2,228	944	24.8	69.7	3.8	1.7	58,940	10,774	39,426	7,404	1,336	18.6	67.1	12.0	2.3
April 1952	53,564	12,868	37,830	2,102	764	24.6	70.2	3.8	1.4	58,034	11,068	38,670	6,972	1,324	19.3	66.6	11.8	2.3
April 1951	53,420	12,984	37,354	2,216	866	24.6	69.6	4.1	1.6	57,354	10,946	38,124	7,084	1,200	19.2	66.4	12.3	2.1
March 1950 [1]	54,762	14,322	37,227	2,296	917	26.2	68.0	4.2	1.7	56,970	11,139	37,633	6,967	1,231	19.6	66.1	12.2	2.2
April 1949	53,448	13,952	36,474	2,181	842	25.7	68.5	4.2	1.6	56,001	11,174	37,012	6,582	1,233	19.7	66.0	12.1	2.2
April 1948	53,227	14,734	35,411	2,055	1,027	26.9	67.1	4.0	1.9	55,364	11,623	35,783	6,725	1,233	20.5	64.6	12.7	2.2
April 1947	52,350	14,760	34,638	2,134	818	27.2	66.9	4.3	1.6	54,806	12,078	35,212	6,376	1,140	21.1	64.5	12.3	2.1
April 1940	50,554	17,593	30,192	2,144	624	31.1	62.8	4.8	1.3	50,549	13,936	30,090	5,700	823	24.3	61.0	12.9	1.7
April 1930	[2]45,088	16,159	26,328	2,025	489	30.9	62.1	5.6	1.2	[2]44,013	12,478	26,175	4,734	573	23.7	61.2	13.7	1.3
January 1920	[2]37,954	13,998	21,852	1,758	235	31.8	61.3	6.1	0.7	[2]36,190	10,624	21,324	3,918	273	24.1	60.4	14.6	0.8
April 1910	[2]33,362	13,485	18,093	1,471	156	32.5	60.4	6.2	0.5	[2]30,959	9,842	17,688	3,176	185	24.5	60.1	14.7	0.6
June 1900	[2]26,414	11,090	13,956	1,178	84	33.1	59.9	6.4	0.4	[2]25,024	8,337	13,814	2,718	115	25.0	58.7	15.7	0.5
June 1890	[2]21,501	9,379	11,205	815	49	32.8	61.2	5.6	0.3	[2]20,298	6,928	11,126	2,155	72	24.3	59.4	15.9	0.4

[1] Not strictly comparable with figures for 1951 and 1952. See text of Series P-20, Nos. 50 and 81. [2] Includes marital status not reported.

Series A 228–229. Median Age at First Marriage, by Sex: 1890 to 1957

[In years. 1947 to 1957 based on sample figures from Current Population Survey]

Year	Male	Female	Year	Male	Female	Year	Male	Female	Year	Male	Female	Year	Male	Female	Year	Male	Female
	228	229		228	229		228	229		228	229		228	229		228	229
1957	22.5	20.3	1954	23.0	20.3	1951	22.9	20.4	1948	23.3	20.4	1940	24.3	21.5	1910	25.1	21.6
1956	22.3	20.1	1953	22.8	20.2	1950	22.8	20.3	1947	23.7	20.5	1930	24.3	21.3	1900	25.9	21.9
1955	22.5	20.2	1952	23.0	20.2	1949	22.7	20.3				1920	24.6	21.2	1890	26.1	22.0

Series A 230–241. Households, by Sex and Age of Head: 1890 to 1957

[In thousands. 1956 and 1957 based on sample figures from Current Population Survey]

	Male head						Female head					
Year	Total	Under 25 years	25 to 34 years	35 to 44 years	45 to 54 years	55 years and over	Total	Under 25 years	25 to 34 years	35 to 44 years	45 to 54 years	55 years and over
	230	231	232	233	234	235	236	237	238	239	240	241
1957	40,903	1,993	8,814	9,830	8,516	11,750	8,640	340	738	1,133	1,631	4,798
1956	40,420	2,003	8,735	9,652	8,292	11,738	8,365	274	763	1,206	1,506	4,616
1950 [1]	35,863	1,850	8,139	8,676	7,274	9,925	6,380	164	541	935	1,264	3,486
1940	29,680	1,260	6,539	7,286	6,716	7,879	5,269	113	470	879	1,144	2,663
1930	[2]26,112	1,266	5,879	7,082	5,743	6,123	[2]3,793	[3]120	[3]371	[3]685	[3]862	[3]1,749
1890	10,857	572	2,962	2,883	2,184	2,256	1,833	59	230	387	466	691

[1] Based on 20-percent sample of 1950 Census returns. [2] Total for males includes 18,345 persons of unknown age and total for females, 6,567 of unknown age. [3] Number of female heads in each age group estimated from data on white and Negro heads with marital status and age reported.

Series A 242–244. Households, by Residence: 1900 to 1957

[In thousands. 1900 to 1946 as of July; 1947 to 1949 and 1951 to 1955 as of April; and 1950, 1956, and 1957 as of March]

Year	Total	Nonfarm	Farm	Year	Total	Nonfarm	Farm	Year	Total	Nonfarm	Farm	Year	Total	Nonfarm	Farm
	242	243	244		242	243	244		242	243	244		242	243	244
1957	49,543	44,325	5,218	1942	36,445	29,433	7,012	1927	28,632	21,941	6,691	1913	21,606	15,187	6,419
1956	48,785	43,136	5,649	1941	35,929	28,786	7,143	1926	28,101	21,325	6,776	1912	21,075	14,727	6,348
												1911	20,620	14,358	6,262
1955	47,788	42,243	5,545	1940	35,153	28,001	7,152	1925	27,540	20,745	6,795				
1954	46,893	41,399	5,493	1939	34,409	27,249	7,160	1924	26,941	20,182	6,759	1910	20,183	13,989	6,194
1953	46,334	40,503	5,831	1938	33,683	26,518	7,165	1923	26,298	19,492	6,806	1909	19,734		
1952	45,504	39,554	5,950	1937	33,088	25,917	7,171	1922	25,687	18,780	6,907	1908	19,294		
1951	44,656	38,587	6,069	1936	32,454	25,253	7,201	1921	25,119	18,255	6,864	1907	18,863		
												1906	18,394		
1950	43,554	37,279	6,275	1935	31,892	24,665	7,227	1920	24,467	17,668	6,799				
1949	42,182	35,687	6,495	1934	31,306	24,118	7,188	1919	23,873	17,307	6,566	1905	17,989		
1948	40,532	34,116	6,416	1933	30,802	23,653	7,149	1918	23,519	16,846	6,673	1904	17,521		
1947	39,107	32,673	6,434	1932	30,439	23,541	6,898	1917	23,323	16,643	6,680	1903	17,108		
1946	38,370	31,944	6,426	1931	30,272	23,476	6,796	1916	22,926	16,291	6,635	1902	16,716		
												1901	16,345		
1945	37,503	31,158	6,345	1930	29,997	23,268	6,729	1915	22,501	15,949	6,552	1900	15,992		
1944	37,115	30,722	6,393	1929	29,582	22,851	6,731	1914	22,110	15,630	6,480				
1943	36,833	30,206	6,627	1928	29,124	22,416	6,708								

Series A 245–247. Married Couples With or Without Own Household: 1910 to 1957

[In thousands. All years as of April, except 1945 as of September, 1946 as of June, and 1950, 1956, and 1957 as of March. 1945 to 1957 based on sample figures from Current Population Survey]

Year	Total	With own household	Without own household	Year	Total	With own household	Without own household	Year	Total	With own household	Without own household
	245	246	247		245	246	247		245	246	247
1957	38,940	37,711	1,229	1951	36,136	34,378	1,758	1946 [1]	31,550	28,850	2,700
1956	38,306	37,043	1,263					1945 [1]	28,200	26,835	1,365
				1950	36,091	34,075	2,016				
1955	37,570	36,266	1,304	1949	35,425	33,257	2,168	1940	28,517	26,571	1,946
1954	37,346	35,875	1,471	1948	34,364	31,900	2,464	1930	25,174	23,649	1,525
1953	37,106	35,560	1,546	1947	33,543	30,612	2,931	1910	17,175	16,250	925
1952	36,696	35,138	1,558								

[1] Not strictly comparable with 1947 to 1957. Latter are estimates taking into account 1950 Census totals, whereas 1945 and 1946 were estimated as projections from 1940 Census totals.

Series A 248–254. Population, by Household Relationship: 1910 to 1957

[In thousands. 1947, 1950, 1954, and 1957 based on sample figures from Current Population Survey. Total population, 1910 to 1940, and civilian population, 1947 to 1957. Civilian population includes members of the Armed Forces living off post or with their families on post]

Date	Total population	Living in households					Living in quasi-households
		Total	Head of household	Wife of head	Other relative of head	Non-relative of head	
	248	249	250	251	252	253	254
March 1957	168,122	165,558	49,543	37,711	75,335	2,969	2,564
April 1954	159,223	156,443	46,893	35,875	70,412	3,263	2,780
March 1950	149,838	146,835	43,554	34,075	65,064	4,142	3,003
April 1947	142,061	139,114	39,107	30,612	64,774	4,621	2,947
April 1940	131,669	128,427	34,949	26,571	61,411	5,496	3,242
April 1930	122,775	119,812	29,905	23,649	60,721	5,537	2,963
April 1910	91,972	90,528	20,256	16,250	49,517	4,505	1,444

Series A 255–263. Selected Characteristics of Households: 1790 to 1957

Year	All households			Race of head			Sex of head		Median age of head
	Number	Median size [1]	Population per household	White	Negro	Other	Male	Female	
	255	256	257	258	259	260	261	262	263
1957 [2]	49,543,000	3.02	3.42	44,886,000	[3]	[3]	40,903,000	8,640,000	46.9
1950	42,857,335	3.05	3.52	[4] 38,429,035	[3]	[3]	[4] 35,862,900	[4] 6,388,515	[4] 45.9
1940	34,948,666	3.28	3.77	31,679,766	3,141,883	127,017	29,679,718	5,268,948	46.06
1930 [5]	29,904,663	3.40	4.11	26,982,994	2,803,756	117,913	26,111,761	3,792,902	[6] 44.45
1920	24,351,676	--------	4.34	21,825,654	2,430,828	95,194	--------	--------	--------
1910	20,255,555	--------	4.54	[3]	2,173,018	[3]	--------	--------	--------
1900	15,963,965	4.23	4.76	14,063,791	1,833,759	66,415	14,022,546	1,941,419	42.99
1890	12,690,152	4.48	4.93	11,255,169	1,410,769	24,214	10,857,249	1,832,903	42.55
1880	9,945,916	--------	5.04	--------	--------	--------	--------	--------	--------
1870	7,579,363	--------	5.09	--------	--------	--------	--------	--------	--------
1860 [7]	5,210,934	--------	5.28	--------	--------	--------	--------	--------	--------
1850 [7]	3,598,240	--------	5.55	--------	--------	--------	--------	--------	--------
1790	557,889	5.43	5.79	--------	--------	--------	--------	--------	--------

[1] 1790 and 1940–1957 relate to households only but include lodgers and other non-relatives in addition to the head and his relatives; 1890 and 1900 include all persons whether related to the head or not, in both households and quasi-households; 1930 includes the household head and his relatives only.
[2] Based on sample figures from Current Population Survey.
[3] Not available.

[4] Based on 20-percent sample of census returns.
[5] Figures for race of head revised to include Mexicans as white. Mexicans were classified as nonwhite in the 1930 reports.
[6] Based on white and Negro households for which marital status of head was reported.
[7] Free population only.

Vital Statistics and Health and Medical Care

VITAL STATISTICS (Series B 1–179)

B 1–179. General note.

Vital statistics, including statistics of births, deaths, marriages, and divorces, are compiled for the country as a whole by the National Office of Vital Statistics. Originally, the collection of these data was the responsibility of the Bureau of the Census. In July 1946, this function was transferred to the Federal Security Agency, which in 1953, was reconstituted as the Department of Health, Education, and Welfare. The National Office of Vital Statistics is a part of the Public Health Service in that Department.

The live-birth, death, and fetal-death statistics prepared by the National Office of Vital Statistics are based principally on copies of vital records received from registration offices of all States, of certain cities, and of the District of Columbia, Alaska, Hawaii, Puerto Rico, and the Virgin Islands. The marriage and divorce statistics are based on reports from State registration offices that maintain central registers of marriage or divorce, from local officials, and from the District of Columbia, Alaska, Hawaii, Puerto Rico, and the Virgin Islands. Figures shown here, however, are limited to events occurring within continental United States; Alaska, Hawaii, Puerto Rico, and the Virgin Islands are excluded, as are births, deaths, marriages, and divorces of American nationals in other parts of the world. For States or areas for which numbers of marriages are not available, numbers of marriage licenses are used as the nearest approximations.

The annual report, *Vital Statistics of the United States,* presents final figures for continental United States, Alaska, Hawaii, Puerto Rico, and the Virgin Islands. A series of national summaries, *Vital Statistics—Special Reports,* is also issued each year, containing data on particular subjects. Information regarding unpublished data is contained in each annual report under "Guide to Tabulations," which is a complete index to all tabulated statistics on live births, deaths, and fetal deaths for the year.

Although every State has adopted a law requiring the registration of births, deaths, and fetal deaths, these laws are not uniformly observed. One condition for admission to the national registration areas was a demonstrated registration completeness of at least 90 percent. On the basis of this criterion, all of the States were admitted to both the birth- and death-registration areas by 1933. It is recognized, however, that the methods then used in testing completeness were subject to considerable error.

Accurate measures of birth-registration completeness on a nationwide basis were obtained for the first time in 1940, when studies were made in connection with the population census of that year. They showed that, for the United States as a whole, birth registration was 92.5 percent complete. A corresponding study 10 years later indicated that registration had improved considerably, with 97.9 percent of the births in 1950 being recorded. Only in a few States was underregistration shown to be still a problem. The results of this study have been published in considerable detail and provide a basis for adjusting registered birth data for underreporting and for making estimates of registration completeness in post-

censal years. Birth registration has continued to improve since 1930, and in 1956, 98.7 percent of the live births were registered. (See National Office of Vital Statistics, "Birth-Registration Completeness in the United States and Geographic Areas, 1950," parts I, II, and III, *Vital Statistics—Special Reports,* vol. 39, Nos. 2 and 4, and vol. 45, No. 9.)

Death registration is believed to be at least as complete as birth registration. However, quantitative information on the completeness with which deaths are reported is limited to that obtained years ago in applying the "90-percent" standard for entry into the death registration area and to information obtained from occasional local area studies. While under-registration for the country as a whole is negligible, local studies furnish evidence that in certain isolated places under-reporting of deaths may still be a problem. Registration of fetal deaths is probably significantly incomplete in all areas.

In 1956 and 1957, pilot tests of the registration completeness of marriages and of divorces and annulments were undertaken, and in two States, Tennessee and Michigan, Statewide tests of marriage-registration completeness were undertaken. The final results of these tests have not been published but preliminary results indicate that marriage-registration completeness in both States is well above 95 percent.

Population statistics published or made available by the Bureau of the Census have been used in computing the vital rates shown here. Rates for 1940 and 1950 are in all cases based on the population enumerated in the censuses of those years which were taken as of April 1. With the exception of series B 10–18 and B 24–30, which are based on estimated population as of April 1 for 1941–1949, rates for all other years are based on the latest midyear (July 1) estimates of population made by the Bureau of the Census.

Except for 1941–1946, vital rates are based on the population residing in continental United States. In those years, the transfer overseas of several million men precluded the computation of birth and divorce rates strictly comparable with such rates for prewar years. For 1941–1946, the birth and divorce rates are based on the population including the Armed Forces overseas. (For a discussion of the interpretation of rates during wartime, see "Summary of Natality and Mortality Statistics, United States, 1943," *Vital Statistics—Special Reports,* vol. 21, No. 1, and "Marriage and Divorce in the United States, 1937 to 1945," *Vital Statistics—Special Reports,* vol. 23, No. 9.)

Vital statistics showing color and race are compiled from entries which appear on certificates filed with vital registration offices. The classification white includes persons reported as Mexican and Puerto Rican. The Negro group includes persons of mixed Negro and other ancestry. Other mixed parentage is classified according to the race of the nonwhite parent and mixtures of nonwhite races according to the race of the father.

B 1–5. Growth of birth- and death-registration area, 1900–1933.

Source: National Office of Vital Statistics, *Vital Statistics of the United States, 1955,* vol. I, p. xviii. For a description of the historical development of the vital statistics system in the United States, see *Vital Statistics of the United States, 1950*, vol. I, chap. 1.

The first death statistics published by the Federal Government were for 1850 and covered the entire United States. These figures were based on the decennial census of that year. As an approximation of births in 1850, data on the population under one year old as reported in the 1850 Census were used. Although these reports were incomplete, similar data were collected in each census up to and including the Census of 1900.

In 1880, the Bureau of the Census established a national "registration area" for deaths. The original area consisted of only two States (Massachusetts and New Jersey), the District of Columbia, and several large cities having efficient systems for the registration of deaths. By 1900, eight other States had been admitted. For 1880, 1890, and 1900, mortality data were received from the States and cities included in this expanding area, but for other parts of the country death figures were still compiled from the census. Since relatively reliable mortality statistics are available for Massachusetts over a longer period than for the Nation, several annual series for that State are included here (see series B 76–91, B 113, and B 155–175).

The annual collection and publication of mortality statistics for the registration area began in 1900. In 1902, the Bureau of the Census was authorized to obtain, annually, copies of records filed in the vital statistics offices of those States and cities having adequate death-registration systems. The death-registration area for 1900 consisted of 10 States, the District of Columbia, and a number of cities located in nonregistration States. This original registration area included 40.5 percent of the population of continental United States (26.2 percent, excluding the reporting cities in nonregistration States), but it was predominantly urban and it had a high proportion of white persons. Between 1900 and 1933, the death-registration area was steadily expanded until, by 1933, all 48 States and the District of Columbia were included.

As it was more difficult to obtain accurate and complete registration of births than of deaths, the national birth-registration area was not established until 1915, and no birth statistics were published by the Bureau of the Census for 1900–1914. The original birth-registration area of 1915 consisted of 10 States and the District of Columbia. Beginning with 1933, the birth-registration area has included the 48 States and the District of Columbia.

B 6. Live births, 1909–1956.

Source: 1909–1934, National Office of Vital Statistics, *Vital Statistics—Special Reports*, vol. 33, No. 8; 1935–1956, *Vital Statistics of the United States, 1956*, vol. I, p. lxxvi.

B 7. Deaths, 1933–1956.

Source: 1933–1956, National Office of Vital Statistics, *Vital Statistics of the United States, 1956*, vol. I, p. xcvi.

B 8–9. Marriages and divorces, 1920–1956.

Source: 1920–1956, National Office of Vital Statistics, *Vital Statistics of the United States, 1956*, vol. I, pp. xxii, lxxi.

B 10–18. Birth rate, by live-birth order, for native white women, 1920–1956.

Source: 1920–1956, National Office of Vital Statistics, *Vital Statistics of the United States, 1956*, vol. I, p. lxxx.

For estimates for 1920–1939, as prepared by P. K. Whelpton, see *Vital Statistics—Special Reports*, vol. 33, No. 8.

Figures contain estimates for cases not reporting order of birth, including those in Massachusetts where birth-order reporting is not required. By limiting these rates to the native

white group, it is possible to exclude the effect of the varying fertility patterns of foreign-born and nonwhite women.

B 19–21. Birth rate, by color, 1800–1956.

Source: Series B 19, 1820–1900, Henry D. Sheldon, *The Older Population of the United States*, John Wiley and Sons, New York, 1958, p. 145. Series B 20, 1800–1900, Warren S. Thompson and P. K. Whelpton, *Population Trends in the United States*, McGraw-Hill, New York, 1933, p. 263. Series B 19–21, 1910, National Office of Vital Statistics, *Vital Statistics—Special Reports*, vol. 33, No. 8, p. 141; 1920–1956, *Vital Statistics of the United States, 1956*, vol. I, p. lxxvi.

B 22–24. Birth rate, women 15 to 44 years old, by color, 1800–1956.

Source: Series B 22–23, 1800–1910, Warren S. Thompson and P. K. Whelpton, *Population Trends in the United States*, McGraw-Hill, New York, 1933, p. 263; 1910–1939, unpublished estimates prepared by National Office of Vital Statistics; 1940–1956, National Office of Vital Statistics, *Vital Statistics of the United States, 1956*, vol. I, p. lxxvii. Series B 24, 1920–1956, *Vital Statistics of the United States, 1956*, vol. I, p. lxxx.

Rates are computed by relating total births, regardless of the age of mother, to the female population 15 to 44 years old.

B 25–30. Birth rate, native white women, by age of mother, 1920–1955.

Source: 1920–1939, National Office of Vital Statistics, *Vital Statistics—Special Reports*, vol. 33, No. 8, p. 143; 1940–1955, unpublished estimates prepared by the National Office of Vital Statistics.

The age-specific rates shown here express the number of live births to native white women in a specified age group per 1,000 native white women in that age group.

B 31–36. Gross and net reproduction rates, by color, 1905–10 to 1956.

Source: 1905–10 to 1935–40, Bureau of the Census, Sixteenth Census Reports, *Differential Fertility, 1940 and 1910—Standardized Fertility Rates and Reproduction Rates;* 1935, National Office of Vital Statistics, *Vital Statistics of the United States, 1950*, vol. I, p. 87; 1940–1956, *Vital Statistics of the United States, 1956*, vol. I, p. lxxix.

The gross reproduction rate represents the number of daughters a hypothetical cohort of 1,000 women entering the childbearing period would have during their lives, if they were subject to the age-specific birth rates observed in a given time period, and if none of the cohort were to die before the childbearing period was completed. This rate is the sum of the age-specific birth rates of female infants per 1,000 women. It shows the maximum possible replacement of women that might be expected from the given set of age-specific birth rates. If no migration took place and if the gross reproduction rate remained below 1,000, no improvement in mortality alone could prevent the population from declining when a stable age distribution had been reached.

The net reproduction rate is based on the specific fertility and mortality conditions existing in a given time period. If the age-specific birth and death rates of a certain year (or years) were to continue until the population became stable, a net reproduction rate of 1,000 would mean that a cohort of 1,000 newly born girls would bear just enough daughters to replace themselves.

Reproduction rates are useful in the analyses of fertility and mortality conditions of a given period, but they are not indicators of future population growth. They do not take into account such factors as nuptiality, marital duration, and size of family, and they assume the continuation of the age-specific rates in a given year throughout the lifetime of a cohort of women. Since the United States has experienced major changes in marriage and fertility rates over short periods of time, variations in reproduction rates should not be taken as indications of long-run movements in family formation and rates of fertility and mortality.

B 37–68. Number of children under 5 years old per 1,000 women 20 to 44 years old, by race and residence, by geographic divisions, 1800–1950.

Source: **Series B 37–38**, Bureau of the Census, *Forecasts of the Population of the United States, 1945–1975*, p. 16. **Series B 39–68**, 1800–1840 and 1910–1950, Wilson H. Grabill, Clyde V. Kiser, and Pascal K. Whelpton, *The Fertility of American Women*, John Wiley and Sons, New York, 1958; 1850–1900, Bureau of the Census, unpublished estimates.

Figures for series B 37–38 were adjusted for underreporting on the basis of factors obtained for 1925–1930. They have also been standardized for age (except for white women for 1800–1820) using the 1930 age distribution of women to offset the effect of changes in the age distribution of the female population. Therefore, the figures represent the fertility rates of women having the same age distribution as those in 1930. Rates for 1800–1860 are partly estimated.

For definition of geographic divisions, see text for series A 95–122.

The urban-rural classification is the one used by the Bureau of the Census in 1940. The urban population includes all persons living in incorporated places of 2,500 inhabitants or more and in other areas classified as urban under special rules relating to population size and density. The remaining area of the country is classified as rural. See also text for series A 34–50.

B 69–75. Percent distribution of ever-married women (survivors of birth cohorts of 1835–39 to 1900–04), by number of children ever born, 1910, 1940, and 1950.

Source: Conrad and Irene B. Taeuber, *The Changing Population of the United States, 1790–1955*, John Wiley and Sons, New York, 1957, pp. 255–256.

These data are based on an analysis of the 1910, 1940, and 1950 Censuses. In each of these censuses, women who had ever married were asked about the number of children they had ever borne. When these women are classified according to age, it is possible to suggest the trend of fertility among women who had completed their childbearing at each census. On p. 255, the source presents the following caution regarding the use of these data:

There are many difficulties in the analysis and interpretation of data on numbers of children ever born to married women. The cumulative reproductive performance of the women can be related directly to age, marital status, urban or rural residence, migrant history, ethnic affiliation, and social and economic characteristics. However, the characteristics of the women are those of the time of the census rather than of the time when marriage occurred or children were born. There may be selective factors in memory as age advances, or there may be pride in achievement that leads to exaggeration. Marital status is correlated with social and economic status and with ethnic affiliation, so relations between marital status and fertility may be derivative. Illegitimate births are underreported and erroneously reported in unknown proportions. The possibility of selective associations between fertility, mortality, and migration become increasingly great as age advances.

B 76–91. Expectation of life at specified ages, by sex, 1850–1956.

Source: See detailed listing below.

The expectation of life at a specified age is the average number of years that members of a hypothetical cohort would continue to live if they were subject throughout the remainder of their lives to the mortality rates for specified age groups observed in a given time period.

B 76–83. Expectation of life at specified ages, white population (death-registration area), 1900–1956.

Source: 1900–02 to 1929–31, Bureau of the Census, *United States Life Tables, 1900–1931*, pp. 4–7, 20–23, 28–31, and 40–51; 1939–41 to 1956, National Office of Vital Statistics, *Vital Statistics of the United States, 1956*, vol. I, p. xciii.

See also text for series B 92–100.

B 84–91. Expectation of life in Massachusetts, 1850 to 1949–51.

Source: 1850, 1878–82, 1893–97, Metropolitan Life Insurance Company, *Statistical Bulletin*, vol. 9, No. 3, March 1928, pp. 7–8; 1855, Edgar Sydenstricker, *Health and Environment*, McGraw-Hill, New York, 1933, p. 164; 1890, 1900–02, 1909–11, Bureau of the Census, *United States Life Tables, 1890, 1901, 1910, and 1901–1910*; 1919–20, Sydenstricker, *op. cit.*, and Bureau of the Census, *United States Abridged Life Tables, 1919–1920*, pp. 24–27; 1929–31, National Resources Committee, *Population Statistics 2, State Data*, p. 38; 1939–41 to 1949–51, Bureau of the Census and National Office of Vital Statistics, annual report, *Vital Statistics of the United States*, vol. I.

B 92–100. Expectation of life at birth, by color and sex (death-registration area), 1900–1956.

Source: 1900–1956, National Office of Vital Statistics, *Vital Statistics—Special Reports*, vol. 48, No. 6, p. 154.

Derivation of estimates is described in "Estimated Average Length of Life in the Death-Registration States," *Vital Statistics—Special Reports*, vol. 33, No. 9.

The expectation of life at birth is the average number of years that members of a hypothetical cohort would live if they were subject throughout their lives to the age-specific mortality rates observed at the time of their birth. This is the most usual measure of the comparative longevity of different populations. There is some objection to the use of the average duration of life as a standard of comparison because the method of calculating it gives great weight to the relatively large number of deaths occurring in the first year of life. This influence may be entirely eliminated by considering instead the average lifetime remaining to those members of the cohort surviving to age 1, or, in other words, the expectation of life at age 1. However, this objection is growing less valid as infant mortality decreases.

B 101–103. Fetal death ratio, by color, 1922–1956.

Source: 1922–1956, National Office of Vital Statistics, *Vital Statistics of the United States, 1956*, vol. I, p. lxxxviii.

Lack of uniformity in requirements for registration and variation in completeness of registration influence the comparability of the data over the years, especially in the series based on all reported fetal deaths. Considering the probable total effect of these factors, as well as that of incompleteness of the registration area until 1933, it appears likely that the ratios understate any decline in fetal mortality. Changes in the regulations have more often been in the direction of broadening the base of fetal death reporting, than in the other direction. With respect to completeness of reporting, the situation has probably improved because of the increases in the number of women receiving hospital and medical care at childbirth and also because of the general strengthening of the vital registration system.

B 104–106.   Neonatal mortality rate, by color, 1915–1956.

Source: 1915–1929, National Office of Vital Statistics, *Vital Statistics of the United States, 1950*, vol. I, pp. 258–259; 1930–1950, *Vital Statistics—Special Reports*, vol. 45, No. 1, pp. 8–10; 1951–1956, *Vital Statistics of the United States, 1956*, vol. I, p. cxiv.

The neonatal mortality rate represents the number of deaths of infants under 28 days (exclusive of fetal deaths) per 1,000 live births.

B 107–109.   Infant mortality rate, by color, 1915–1956.

Source: 1915–1950, National Office of Vital Statistics, *Vital Statistics—Special Reports*, vol. 45, No. 1, p. 7; 1951–1956, *Vital Statistics of the United States, 1956*, vol. I, p. cxiv.

The infant mortality rate represents the number of deaths under 1 year (exclusive of fetal deaths) per 1,000 live births. The rates have been computed by the conventional method in which the infant deaths occurring in a specified period are related to the number of live births occurring during the same period. Rates computed in this way are influenced by changes in the number of births and will not be comparable if the birth rate is fluctuating widely. Deaths under 1 year of age occurring during any calendar year are deaths not only of infants born during that year but also of infants born during parts of the previous year. An approximate correction of this error can be made by relating infant deaths during a specified year to the year in which those infants were born. See Bureau of the Census, "Effect of Changing Birth Rates Upon Infant Mortality Rates," *Vital Statistics—Special Reports*, vol. 19, No. 21.

B 110–112.   Maternal mortality rate, by color, 1915–1956.

Source: 1915–1955, National Office of Vital Statistics, *Vital Statistics—Special Reports*, vol. 46, No. 17, p. 438; 1956, *Vital Statistics—Special Reports*, vol. 48, No. 15, p. 412. Rates prior to 1940, see also Bureau of the Census, *Vital Statistics Rates in the United States, 1900–1940*, pp. 574–575, 622, and 656–662.

The maternal mortality rate represents the number of deaths from deliveries and complications of pregnancy, childbirth, and the puerperium per 10,000 live births.

B 113.   Infant mortality rate, for Massachusetts, 1851–1956.

Source: 1851–1900, *77th Annual Report of Vital Statistics of Massachusetts*, p. 132; 1900–1956, Bureau of the Census and National Office of Vital Statistics, annual report, *Vital Statistics of the United States*, vol. I.

B 114–128.   Death rate, for selected causes (death-registration area), 1900–1956.

Source: All data except series B 116, 1900–1950, National Office of Vital Statistics, *Vital Statistics of the United States, 1950*, vol. I, p. 218; 1951–1956, *Vital Statistics of the United States, 1956*, vol. I, p. c. Series B 116, 1900–1920, *Vital Statistics of the United States, 1950*, vol. I, p. 218; 1921–1940, *Vital Statistics Rates in the United States, 1900–1940*, p. 266; 1941–1956, National Office of Vital Statistics, unpublished data.

Mortality data are classified according to the numbers and titles of the detailed International List of Causes of Death. A large proportion of the death certificates filed annually in the United States report two or more diseases or conditions as joint causes of death. General statistical practice requires that cases involving more than one cause of death be changed to a single cause.

In the French edition of the International List (1900), certain principles for determining the single cause to be selected from the joint causes given were incorporated as a part of the general classification scheme. As an outgrowth of practices in this country after 1902, definite relationships among the various conditions represented by items in the International List were put in concrete form in the *Manual of Joint Causes of Death*, first published in 1914, and revised to conform with successive revisions of the International List. This manual, which was developed for use in the United States, was followed until 1949, when an international procedure for joint-cause selection was adopted. The new international rules place the responsibility on the medical practitioner to indicate the underlying cause of death. This change, in conjunction with the Sixth Revision of the International List in 1948 and the Seventh Revision in 1955, has introduced rather serious breaks in statistical continuity.

Time-trend studies of causes of death would be facilitated if the International List were maintained without change over a long period of years. However, if the list were rigidly fixed it would be inconsistent with current medical knowledge and terminology. To obtain the advantages of frequent revision, and yet to retain a fixed list for a number of years, revisions are made at an international conference every 10 years. In the process of revision, discontinuities are introduced into the time trends of death rates for certain specific causes of death (see National Office of Vital Statistics, "The Effect of the Sixth Revision of the International List of Diseases and Causes of Death Upon Comparability of Mortality Trends," *Vital Statistics—Special Reports*, vol. 36, No. 10).

Improvement in diagnostic procedures and development of medical knowledge and facilities are other important factors in the study of changes in death rates for certain causes.

B 129–135.   Death rate, by color and sex (death-registration area), 1900–1956.

Source: 1900–1956, National Office of Vital Statistics, *Vital Statistics of the United States, 1956*, vol. I, p. xcvi.

B 136–142.   Age-adjusted death rate, by color and sex (death-registration area), 1900–1956.

Source: 1900–1956, National Office of Vital Statistics, *Vital Statistics of the United States, 1956*, vol. I, p. xcvii. See also *Vital Statistics Rates in the United States, 1900–1940*, p. 127, and Bureau of the Census, *Vital Statistics—Special Reports*, vol. 23, No. 1, p. 17.

The age-adjusted death rate is a convenient summary index that "corrects" for differences in age composition. These rates were computed by taking the age-distribution of the population in 1940 as the "standard" without regard to sex, color, or other characteristics. The age-specific death rates actually observed in a given year were applied to the age distribution of this standard population and a total death rate was computed. For a detailed description of the direct method by which these rates were computed, see *Vital Statistics Rates in the United States, 1900–1940*, pp. 66–69.

B 143–154.   Death rate, by age and sex (death-registration area), 1900–1956.

Source: 1900–1939, National Office of Vital Statistics, *Vital Statistics—Special Reports*, vol. 43, No. 1, pp. 10–12; 1940–1954, Bureau of the Census and National Office of Vital Statistics, *Vital Statistics of the United States, 1954*, vol. I, p. xlix; 1955–1956, *Vital Statistics of the United States, 1956*, vol. I, p. xcviii.

B 155–162. Death rate, by sex and by selected cause, for Massachusetts, 1860–1956.

Source: 1860–1899, computed from *48th Annual Registration Report for Massachusetts* and *77th Annual Report on the Vital Statistics of Massachusetts*; 1900–1956, Bureau of the Census and National Office of Vital Statistics, annual reports, *Vital Statistics of the United States.*

B 163–175. Death rate, by age, for Massachusetts, 1865–1900.

Source: *48th Annual Registration Report for Massachusetts*, p. 321, and *77th Annual Report on the Vital Statistics of Massachusetts*, p. 126.

B 176–179. Marriage and divorce rates, 1920–1956.

Source: 1920–1956, National Office of Vital Statistics, *Vital Statistics—Special Reports*, vol. 48, No. 3, pp. 53, 58.

For series B 176 and B 178, see also *Vital Statistics of the United States, 1956*, vol. I, p. lxxi.

See also Commissioner of Labor, *A Report on Marriage and Divorce in the United States, 1867 to 1886;* Bureau of the Census, *Marriage and Divorce, 1867–1906; Marriage and Divorce, 1916;* and *Marriage and Divorce*, annual reports, 1922–1932; S. A. Stauffer and L. M. Spencer, "Recent Increases in Marriage and Divorce," *American Journal of Sociology*, vol. 44, No. 4 (for 1933–1936); Bureau of the Census, "A Review of Marriage and Divorce Statistics: United States, 1887–1937," *Vital Statistics—Special Reports*, vol. 9, No. 60; Bureau of the Census, "Estimated Number of Marriages by State: United States, 1937–1940," *Vital Statistics—Special Reports*, vol. 15, No. 13; Bureau of the Census, "Estimated Number of Divorces by State: United States, 1937–1940," *Vital Statistics—Special Reports*, vol. 15, No. 18. For exact population base figures, see *Vital Statistics—Special Reports*, vol. 46, No. 12, p. 330.

Marriage and divorce records are filed only at the county level in some States, but gradually the various States are requiring by law that such events be recorded at the State level. The completeness of reporting to the State offices varies, but there has been no nationwide test. A marriage-registration area covering 30 States and 5 independent areas, established by the National Office of Vital Statistics, became effective in January 1957. A major criterion for admission of a State to the registration areas was agreement with the National Office of Vital Statistics to conduct a test of marriage registration completeness. A divorce- and annulment-registration area with 14 States and 3 independent areas was inaugurated in January 1958.

The marriage and divorce rates shown in series B 177 and B 179 are based on those segments of the female population that may be considered as subject to possible marriage and divorce.

Series B 1–5. Growth of Birth- and Death-Registration Area: 1900 to 1933

Year	Continental United States, midyear population	Birth-registration area [1]			Death-registration area [1]			Year	Continental United States, midyear population	Birth-registration area [1]			Death-registration area [1]		
		Midyear population		Number of States	Midyear population		Number of States			Midyear population		Number of States	Midyear population		Number of States
		Number	Percent of total		Number	Percent of total				Number	Percent of total		Number	Percent of total	
	1	2	3	------	4	5	------		1	2	3	------	4	5	------
	1,000	*1,000*			*1,000*				*1,000*	*1,000*			*1,000*		
1933	125,579	125,579	100.0	48	125,579	100.0	48	1916	101,966	32,944	32.3	11	66,971	65.7	26
1932	124,840	118,904	95.2	47	118,904	95.2	47	1915	100,549	31,097	30.9	10	61,895	61.6	24
1931	124,040	117,455	94.7	46	118,149	95.3	47	1914	99,118	--------	----		60,963	61.5	24
1930	123,077	116,545	94.7	46	117,238	95.3	47	1913	97,227				58,157	59.8	23
1929	121,770	115,317	94.7	46	115,317	94.7	46	1912	95,331				54,848	57.5	22
1928	120,501	113,636	94.3	44	113,636	94.3	44	1911	93,868				53,930	57.5	22
1927	119,038	104,321	87.6	40	107,085	90.0	42								
1926	117,399	90,401	77.0	35	103,823	88.4	41	1910	92,407				47,470	51.4	20
								1909	90,492				44,224	48.9	18
1925	115,832	88,295	76.2	33	102,032	88.1	40	1908	88,709				38,635	43.6	17
1924	114,113	87,000	76.2	33	99,318	87.0	39	1907	87,000				34,553	39.7	15
1923	111,950	81,072	72.4	30	96,788	86.5	38	1906	85,437				33,782	39.5	15
1922	110,055	79,561	72.3	30	92,703	84.2	37								
1921	108,541	70,807	65.2	27	87,814	80.9	34	1905	83,820				21,768	26.0	10
								1904	82,165				21,332	26.0	10
1920	106,466	63,597	59.7	23	86,079	80.9	34	1903	80,632				20,943	26.0	10
1919	104,512	61,212	58.6	22	83,158	79.6	33	1902	79,160				20,583	26.0	10
1918	103,203	55,154	53.4	20	79,008	76.6	30	1901	77,585				20,237	26.1	10
1917	103,266	55,198	53.5	20	70,235	68.0	27	1900	76,094				19,965	26.2	10

[1] District of Columbia excluded from count of number of States but included in the population figures in series B 1–5.

Series B 6–9. Live Births, Deaths, Marriages, and Divorces: 1909 to 1956

[In thousands. Birth, marriage, and divorce figures represent estimates of all such events; death figures, the number of registered events]

Year	Live births	Deaths [1]	Marriages	Divorces [2]	Year	Live births	Deaths [1]	Marriages	Divorces [2]	Year	Live births	Marriages	Divorces [2]
	6	7	8	9		6	7	8	9		6	8	9
1956	[3] 4,218	1,564	1,585	382	1940	2,559	1,417	1,596	264	1924	2,979	1,185	171
1955	4,104	1,529	1,531	377	1939	2,466	1,388	1,404	251	1923	2,910	1,230	165
1954	[3] 4,078	1,481	1,490	379	1938	2,496	1,381	1,331	244	1922	2,882	1,134	149
1953	[3] 3,965	1,518	1,546	390	1937	2,413	1,450	1,451	249	1921	3,055	1,164	160
1952	[3] 3,913	1,497	1,539	392	1936	2,355	1,479	1,369	236				
1951	[3] 3,823	1,482	1,595	381						1920	2,950	1,274	171
					1935	2,377	1,393	1,327	218	1919	2,740	----	----
1950	3,632	1,452	1,667	385	1934	2,396	1,397	1,302	204	1918	2,948	----	----
1949	3,649	1,444	1,580	397	1933	2,307	1,342	1,098	165	1917	2,944	----	----
1948	3,637	1,444	1,811	408	1932	2,440	--------	982	164	1916	2,964	----	----
1947	3,817	1,445	1,992	483	1931	2,506	--------	1,061	188				
1946	3,411	1,396	2,291	610						1915	2,965	----	----
					1930	2,618	--------	1,127	196	1914	2,966	----	----
1945	2,858	1,402	1,613	485	1929	2,582	--------	1,233	206	1913	2,869	----	----
1944	2,939	1,411	1,452	400	1928	2,674	--------	1,182	200	1912	2,840	----	----
1943	3,104	1,460	1,577	359	1927	2,802	--------	1,201	196	1911	2,809	----	----
1942	2,989	1,385	1,772	321	1926	2,839	--------	1,203	185	1910	2,777	----	----
1941	2,703	1,398	1,696	293	1925	2,909	--------	1,188	175	1909	2,718	----	----

[1] Excludes fetal deaths.   [2] Includes reported annulments.   [3] Based on 50-percent sample.

Series B 10–18. Birth Rate, by Live-Birth Order, for Native White Women: 1920 to 1956

[Based on estimated total live births per 1,000 native white female population 15 to 44 years old]

Year	Total	Live-birth order								Year	Total	Live-birth order							
		1st	2d	3d	4th	5th	6th	7th	8th and over			1st	2d	3d	4th	5th	6th	7th	8th and over
	10	11	12	13	14	15	16	17	18		10	11	12	13	14	15	16	17	18
1956 [1]	116	33	32	23	13	7	3	2	3	1937	75	29	18	10	6	4	3	2	4
1955	114	33	32	23	13	6	3	2	2	1936	74	28	18	10	6	4	3	2	4
1954 [1]	114	33	33	23	12	6	3	2	2										
1953 [1]	111	33	33	22	11	5	3	2	2	1935	75	28	17	10	7	4	3	2	4
1952 [1]	110	34	33	21	10	5	3	1	2	1934	76	26	18	11	7	5	3	2	4
1951 [1]	108	35	33	20	9	5	2	1	2	1933	74	24	17	11	7	5	3	2	4
										1932	79	26	18	11	7	5	4	2	5
1950	103	34	32	18	8	4	2	1	2	1931	82	27	19	12	8	5	4	3	5
1949	105	37	33	17	8	4	2	1	3										
1948	106	41	31	16	8	4	2	1	3	1930	86	29	20	12	8	6	4	3	5
1947	114	49	31	16	8	4	2	1	3	1929	86	28	20	13	8	6	4	3	5
1946	103	41	29	15	7	4	2	2	3	1928	90	29	20	13	9	6	4	3	6
										1927	95	30	21	14	9	6	5	3	6
1945	85	30	24	13	7	4	2	2	3	1926	96	30	22	14	10	6	5	3	6
1944	89	32	25	14	7	4	3	2	3										
1943	95	37	27	14	7	4	2	2	3	1925	100	31	22	15	10	7	5	3	7
1942	92	40	24	12	6	4	2	2	3	1924	104	32	23	16	10	7	5	4	7
1941	83	34	21	11	6	4	2	2	3	1923	103	31	24	15	10	7	5	4	7
										1922	104	32	24	15	10	7	5	4	7
1940	78	30	20	11	6	4	2	2	3	1921	112	36	23	16	11	8	6	4	8
1939	76	30	19	10	6	4	2	2	3	1920	109	35	23	16	11	7	6	4	7
1938	78	31	19	10	6	4	3	2	4										

[1] Based on 50-percent sample.

Series B 19–30. Birth Rate, by Color, and by Age of Mother: 1800 to 1956

[Based on estimated total live births per 1,000 population for specified group]

Year	Rate by color			Women 15 to 44 years			Rate by age of mother, native white					
	Total	White	Nonwhite	Total	White	Native white	15 to 19 years	20 to 24 years	25 to 29 years	30 to 34 years	35 to 39 years	40 to 44 years [1]
	19	20	21	22	23	24	25	26	27	28	29	30
1956 [2]	25.2	24.0	35.4	120.8	115.6	116						
1955	25.0	23.8	34.7	118.0	113.2	114	79	235	188	112	57	15
1954 [2]	25.3	24.1	34.9	117.6	113.1	114	79	231	186	113	57	15
1953 [2]	25.0	24.0	34.1	114.7	110.6	111	77	220	181	110	56	15
1952 [2]	25.1	24.1	33.6	113.5	109.8	110	74	213	178	111	54	15
1951 [2]	24.9	23.9	33.8	111.3	107.4	108	76	207	172	106	52	15
1950	24.1	23.0	33.3	106.2	102.3	103	70	190	164	102	52	15
1949	24.5	23.6	33.0	107.1	103.6	105	72	195	165	102	52	15
1948	24.9	24.0	32.4	107.3	104.3	106	71	198	164	104	53	15
1947	26.6	26.1	31.2	113.3	111.8	114	70	211	180	114	58	16
1946	24.1	23.6	28.4	101.9	100.4	103	51	184	165	111	58	16
1945	20.4	19.7	26.5	85.9	83.4	85	43	138	135	101	56	16
1944	21.2	20.5	27.4	88.8	86.3	89	46	152	140	99	54	16
1943	22.7	22.1	28.3	94.3	92.3	95	53	164	153	100	52	15
1942	22.2	21.5	27.7	91.5	89.5	92	53	165	147	92	47	14
1941	20.3	19.5	27.3	83.4	80.7	83	48	143	131	85	45	15
1940	19.4	18.6	26.7	79.9	77.1	78	45	131	123	83	46	15
1939	18.8	18.0	26.1	77.6	74.8	76	45	125	118	80	46	15
1938	19.2	18.4	26.3	79.1	76.5	78	47	128	119	81	47	16
1937	18.7	17.9	26.0	77.1	74.4	75	45	124	115	80	47	16
1936	18.4	17.6	25.1	75.8	73.3	74	44	121	114	79	49	18
1935	18.7	17.9	25.8	77.2	74.5	75	44	121	115	81	51	19
1934	19.0	18.1	26.3	78.5	75.8	76	43	122	117	85	52	20
1933	18.4	17.6	25.5	76.3	73.7	74	41	118	114	82	53	21
1932	19.5	18.7	26.9	81.7	79.0	79	44	126	120	86	57	22
1931	20.2	19.5	26.6	84.6	82.4	82	46	131	125	89	59	23
1930	21.3	20.6	27.5	89.2	87.1	86	50	139	130	93	62	24
1920	27.7	26.9	35.0	117.9	115.4	109	55	167	160	122	86	35
1910	30.1	29.2		126.8	117	117						
1900	32.3	30.1				130						
1890		31.5				137						
1880	39.8	35.2				155						
1870		38.3				167						
1860	44.3	41.4				184						
1850		43.3				194						
1840	51.8	48.3				222						
1830		51.4				240						
1820	55.2	52.8				260						
1810		54.3				274						
1800		55.0				278						

[1] Computed by relating births to native white women 40 years old and over to the native white population 40 to 44 years old.   [2] Based on 50-percent sample of births.

Series B 31–36. Gross and Net Reproduction Rates, by Color: 1905–10 to 1956

[Based on estimated total live births]

Year	Gross reproduction rate			Net reproduction rate			Year or period	Gross reproduction rate			Net reproduction rate		
	Total	White	Non-white	Total	White	Non-white		Total	White	Non-white	Total	White	Non-white
	31	32	33	34	35	36		31	32	33	34	35	36
1956 [1]	1,793	1,719	2,333	1,724	1,660	2,178	1945	1,212	1,175	1,493	1,132	1,106	1,323
1955	1,741	1,671	2,251	1,673	1,613	2,097	1944	1,249	1,214	1,520	1,163	1,139	1,334
1954 [1]	1,723	1,657	2,212	1,654	1,598	2,058	1943	1,323	1,294	1,548	1,228	1,211	1,348
1953 [1]	1,665	1,603	2,114	1,594	1,543	1,955	1942	1,277	1,250	1,487	1,185	1,171	1,293
1952 [1]	1,635	1,577	2,059	1,561	1,514	1,894	1941	1,168	1,131	1,458	1,075	1,052	1,242
1951 [1]	1,591	1,532	2,025	1,519	1,471	1,864	1940	1,121	1,082	1,422	1,027	1,002	1,209
1950	1,505	1,446	1,940	1,435	1,387	1,780	1935	1,091	1,059	1,350	975	958	1,108
1949	1,515	1,461	1,906	1,439	1,396	1,741	1935–40	1,101	1,063	1,413	978	957	1,137
1948	1,514	1,468	1,846	1,435	1,401	1,680	1930–35	1,108	1,080	1,336	984	972	1,074
1947	1,593	1,568	1,766	1,505	1,492	1,594	1905–10	1,793	1,740	2,240	1,336	1,339	1,329
1946	1,430	1,406	1,600	1,344	1,331	1,435							

[1] Based on 50-percent sample of births.

VITAL STATISTICS AND HEALTH AND MEDICAL CARE

Series B 37–68. Number of Children Under 5 Years Old Per 1,000 Women 20 to 44 Years Old, by Race and Residence, by Geographic Divisions: 1800 to 1950

[Adjusted data standardized for age of women, and allowance made for undercount of children in Censuses; see text. Definition of urban and rural based on 1940 Census of Population]

Series No.	Area	1950	1940	1930	1920	1910	1900	1890	1880	1870	1860	1850	1840	1830	1820	1810	1800
	Adjusted number of children per 1,000 women:																
37	White	587	419	506	604	631	666	685	780	814	905	892	1,085	1,145	1,295	1,358	1,342
38	Negro	706	513	554	608	736	845	930	1,090	997	1,072	1,087	------	------	------	------	------
	Unadjusted number of children per 1,000 white women:																
39	United States	551	400	485	581	609	644	667	754	792	886	877	1,070	1,134	1,236	1,290	1,281
40	Urban	479	311	388	471	469							701	708	831	900	845
41	Rural	673	551	658	744	782							1,134	1,189	1,276	1,329	1,319
42	New England	516	347	441	518	482	478	440	498	544	622	621	752	812	930	1,052	1,098
43	Urban	486	321	417	500	468							592	614	764	845	827
44	Rural	612	443	541	602	566							800	851	952	1,079	1,126
45	Middle Atlantic	471	320	424	539	533	549	547	624	679	767	763	940	1,036	1,183	1,289	1,279
46	Urban	432	286	386	501	495							711	722	842	924	852
47	Rural	596	457	590	680	650							1,006	1,100	1,235	1,344	1,339
48	East North Central	552	388	458	548	555	599	653	757	869	999	1,022	1,270	1,467	1,608	1,702	1,840
49	Urban	491	326	400	485	470							841	910	1,059	1,256	
50	Rural	679	533	605	668	672							1,291	1,484	1,616	1,706	1,840
51	West North Central	600	431	495	584	630	710	781	905	990	1,105	1,114	1,445	1,678	1,685	1,810	
52	Urban	514	324	365	416	426							705	1,181			
53	Rural	702	538	614	711	760							1,481	1,703	1,685	1,810	
54	South Atlantic	572	464	593	694	760	779	777	851	811	918	937	1,140	1,174	1,280	1,325	1,345
55	Urban	450	305	401	458	485							770	767	881	936	861
56	Rural	677	596	744	851	894							1,185	1,209	1,310	1,347	1,365
57	East South Central	631	539	655	734	817	834	850	926	903	1,039	1,099	1,408	1,519	1,631	1,700	1,799
58	Urban	494	333	414	441	469							859	863	1,089	1,348	
59	Rural	720	648	781	846	922							1,424	1,529	1,635	1,701	1,799
60	West South Central	607	474	584	686	845	925	968	1,043	935	1,084	1,046	1,297	1,359	1,418	1,383	
61	Urban	542	342	410	445	504							846	877	866	727	
62	Rural	703	591	723	823	977							1,495	1,463	1,522	1,557	
63	Mountain	663	526	582	664	661	720	757	872	967	1,051	886	------	------	------	------	------
64	Urban	584	404	428	470	466							------	------	------	------	------
65	Rural	754	643	712	807	810							------	------	------	------	------
66	Pacific	539	339	360	425	460	512	587	775	888	1,026	901	------	------	------	------	------
67	Urban	478	283	306	344	360							------	------	------	------	------
68	Rural	652	466	507	603	640							------	------	------	------	------

Series B 69–75. Percent Distribution of Ever-Married Women (Survivors of Birth Cohorts of 1835–39 to 1900–04), by Number of Children Ever Born: 1910, 1940, and 1950

Year of birth of women	Census year	Age of women (years)	Percent of women, by number of births						Children per 1,000 women	Year of birth of women	Census year	Age of women (years)	Percent of women, by number of births						Children per 1,000 women
			None	1 and 2	3 and 4	5 and 6	7 to 9	10 or more					None	1 and 2	3 and 4	5 and 6	7 to 9	10 or more	
			69	70	71	72	73	74	75				69	70	71	72	73	74	75
1900–04	1950	45–49	20.4	41.5	22.4	8.4	5.0	2.2	2,492	1865–69	1940	70–74	12.3	26.6	26.1	16.0	12.5	6.4	3,901
1895–99	1950	50–54	18.6	39.0	23.9	10.0	5.8	2.6	2,706	1860–64	1910	45–49	9.5	22.4	22.0	17.3	17.6	11.2	4,744
1890–94	1940	45–49	16.8	35.3	25.0	12.2	7.7	3.1	2,998	1855–59	1910	50–54	8.9	20.6	21.3	17.9	19.0	12.3	4,972
1885–89	1940	50–54	16.6	33.1	25.1	13.1	8.6	3.6	3,146	1850–54	1910	55–59	8.3	18.8	20.8	17.8	20.4	13.9	5,218
1880–84	1940	55–59	16.7	30.7	24.7	14.1	9.6	4.2	3,301	1845–49	1910	60–64	8.2	18.5	20.3	18.3	20.8	14.0	5,266
1875–79	1940	60–64	15.0	30.5	25.2	14.4	10.3	4.7	3,462	1840–44	1910	65–69	7.9	17.9	20.1	18.1	21.6	14.3	5,364
1870–74	1940	65–69	13.9	28.4	25.1	15.2	11.6	5.8	3,700	1835–39	1910	70–74	7.7	17.3	20.0	18.7	21.6	14.7	5,395

Series B 76–91. Expectation of Life at Specified Ages, by Sex: 1850 to 1956

[In years]

Year or period	Death-registration area [1] (white population)								Massachusetts [2]							
	At birth		Age 20		Age 40		Age 60		At birth		Age 20		Age 40		Age 60	
	Male	Female	Male	Female	Male	Femal	Male	Female	Male	Female	Male	Female	Male	Female	Male	Female
	76	77	78	79	80	81	82	83	84	85	86	87	88	89	90	91
1956	67.3	73.7	50.1	55.9	31.6	36.7	15.9	19.3								
1955	67.3	73.6	50.1	55.8	31.7	36.7	16.0	19.3								
1949–51	66.31	72.03	49.52	54.56	31.17	35.64	15.76	18.64	66.71	72.09	49.33	54.19	30.67	35.15	15.35	18.28
1939–41	62.81	67.29	47.76	51.38	30.03	33.25	15.05	17.00	63.25	67.62	47.41	50.95	29.30	32.55	14.45	16.42
1929–31	59.12	62.67	46.02	48.52	29.22	31.52	14.72	16.05	59.29	62.63	46.14	48.50	28.96	31.23	14.34	15.79
1919–21	56.34	58.53	45.60	46.46	29.86	30.94	15.25	15.93								
1919–20									54.07	56.56	44.6	45.5	28.8	30.0	14.4	15.4
1909–11	50.23	53.62	42.71	44.88	27.43	29.26	13.98	14.92	49.33	53.06	42.48	44.85	26.97	29.04	13.42	14.79
1901–10	49.32	52.54	42.39	44.39	27.55	29.28	14.17	15.09	46.07	49.42	41.82	43.71	27.17	29.00	13.90	15.06
1900–02	48.23	51.08	42.19	43.77	27.74	29.17	14.35	15.23								
1893–97									44.09	46.61	41.20	42.79	27.41	29.00	14.38	15.74
1890									42.50	44.46	40.66	42.03	27.37	28.76	14.73	15.70
1878–82									41.74	43.50	42.17	42.78	28.86	30.29	15.60	16.91
1855									38.7	40.9	39.8	39.9	27.0	28.8	14.4	15.6
1850									38.3	40.5	40.1	40.2	27.9	29.8	15.6	17.0

[1] Data for 1929–31 to 1956 are for continental United States; those for 1919–21, for death-registration States of 1920; those for earlier years, for death-registration States of 1900.

[2] Data for 1919–20 and 1929–31 are for white population only.

Series B 92–100. Expectation of Life at Birth, by Color and Sex: 1900 to 1956

[Prior to 1933 for death-registration area only. See series B 4 and B 5]

Year	Total Both sexes	Total Male	Total Female	White Both sexes	White Male	White Female	Nonwhite Both sexes	Nonwhite Male	Nonwhite Female	Year	Total Both sexes	Total Male	Total Female	White Both sexes	White Male	White Female	Nonwhite Both sexes	Nonwhite Male	Nonwhite Female
	92	93	94	95	96	97	98	99	100		92	93	94	95	96	97	98	99	100
1956	69.6	66.7	73.0	70.2	67.3	73.7	63.2	61.1	65.9	1927	60.4	59.0	62.1	62.0	60.5	63.9	48.2	47.6	48.9
1955	69.5	66.7	72.9	70.2	67.3	73.6	63.2	61.2	65.9	1926	56.7	55.5	58.0	58.2	57.0	59.6	44.6	43.7	45.6
1954	69.6	66.8	72.9	70.3	67.4	73.6	63.1	61.0	65.8	1925	59.0	57.6	60.6	60.7	59.3	62.4	45.7	44.9	46.7
1953	68.8	66.1	72.1	69.6	66.8	72.9	61.7	59.7	64.4	1924	59.7	58.1	61.5	61.4	59.8	63.4	46.6	45.5	47.8
1952	68.6	65.9	71.8	69.4	66.6	72.7	61.1	59.1	63.7	1923	57.2	56.1	58.5	58.3	57.1	59.6	48.3	47.7	48.9
1951	68.4	65.8	71.5	69.2	66.5	72.4	61.0	59.1	63.3	1922	59.6	58.4	61.0	60.4	59.1	61.9	52.4	51.8	53.0
1950	68.2	65.7	71.3	69.1	66.5	72.2	60.8	59.1	62.9	1921	60.8	60.0	61.8	61.8	60.8	62.9	51.5	51.6	51.3
1949	68.0	65.4	71.0	68.8	66.2	71.9	60.6	58.9	62.7										
1948	67.2	64.7	70.2	68.0	65.5	71.0	60.0	58.1	62.5	1920	54.1	53.6	54.6	54.9	54.4	55.6	45.3	45.5	45.2
1947	66.8	64.4	69.7	67.6	65.2	70.5	59.7	57.9	61.9	1919	54.7	53.5	56.0	55.8	54.5	57.4	44.5	44.5	44.4
1946	66.7	64.4	69.4	67.5	65.1	70.3	59.1	57.5	61.0	1918	39.1	36.6	42.2	39.8	37.1	43.2	31.1	29.9	32.5
										1917	50.9	48.4	54.0	52.0	49.3	55.3	33.8	37.0	40.8
1945	65.9	63.6	67.9	66.8	64.4	69.5	57.7	56.1	59.6	1916	51.7	49.6	54.3	52.5	50.2	55.2	41.3	39.6	43.1
1944	65.2	63.6	66.8	66.2	64.5	68.4	56.6	55.8	57.7										
1943	63.3	62.4	64.4	64.2	63.2	65.7	55.6	55.4	56.1	1915	54.5	52.5	56.8	55.1	53.1	57.5	38.9	37.5	40.5
1942	66.2	64.7	67.9	67.3	65.9	69.4	56.6	55.4	58.2	1914	54.2	52.0	56.8	54.9	52.7	57.5	38.9	37.1	40.8
1941	64.8	63.1	66.8	66.2	64.4	68.5	53.8	52.5	55.3	1913	52.5	50.3	55.0	53.0	50.8	55.7	38.4	36.7	40.3
										1912	53.5	51.5	55.9	53.9	51.9	56.2	37.9	35.9	40.0
1940	62.9	60.8	65.2	64.2	62.1	66.6	53.1	51.5	54.9	1911	52.6	50.9	54.4	53.0	51.3	54.9	36.4	34.6	38.2
1939	63.7	62.1	65.4	64.9	63.3	66.6	54.5	53.2	56.0										
1938	63.5	61.9	65.3	65.0	63.2	66.8	52.9	51.7	54.3	1910	50.0	48.4	51.8	50.3	48.6	52.0	35.6	33.8	37.5
1937	60.0	58.0	62.4	61.4	59.3	63.8	50.3	48.3	52.5	1909	52.1	50.5	53.8	52.5	50.9	54.2	35.7	34.2	37.3
1936	58.5	56.6	60.6	59.8	58.0	61.9	49.0	47.0	51.4	1908	51.1	49.5	52.8	51.5	49.9	53.3	34.9	33.8	36.0
										1907	47.6	45.6	49.9	48.1	46.0	50.4	32.5	31.1	34.0
1935	61.7	59.9	63.9	62.9	61.0	65.0	53.1	51.3	55.2	1906	48.7	46.9	50.8	49.3	47.3	51.4	32.9	31.8	33.9
1934	61.1	59.3	63.3	62.4	60.5	64.6	51.8	50.2	53.7										
1933	63.3	61.7	65.1	64.3	62.7	66.3	54.7	53.5	56.0	1905	48.7	47.3	50.2	49.1	47.6	50.6	31.3	29.6	33.1
1932	62.1	61.0	63.5	63.2	62.0	64.5	53.7	52.8	54.6	1904	47.6	46.2	49.1	48.0	46.6	49.5	30.8	29.1	32.7
1931	61.1	59.4	63.1	62.6	60.8	64.7	50.4	49.5	51.5	1903	50.5	49.1	52.0	50.9	49.5	52.5	33.1	31.7	34.6
										1902	51.5	49.8	53.4	51.9	50.2	53.8	34.6	32.9	36.4
1930	59.7	58.1	61.6	61.4	59.7	63.5	48.1	47.3	49.2	1901	49.1	47.6	50.6	49.4	48.0	51.0	33.7	32.2	35.3
1929	57.1	55.8	58.7	58.6	57.2	60.3	46.7	45.7	47.8	1900	47.3	46.3	48.3	47.6	46.6	48.7	33.0	32.5	33.5
1928	56.8	55.6	58.3	58.4	57.0	60.0	46.3	45.6	47.0										

Series B 101–112. Fetal Death Ratio; Neonatal, Infant, and Maternal Mortality Rates, by Color: 1915 to 1956

[Prior to 1933 for registration area only. See series B 2–5]

Year	Fetal death ratio per 1,000 live births [1] Total	White	Nonwhite	Neonatal mortality rate per 1,000 live births Total	White	Nonwhite	Infant mortality rate per 1,000 live births Total	White	Nonwhite	Maternal mortality rate per 10,000 live births Total	White	Nonwhite
	101	102	103	104	105	106	107	108	109	110	111	112
1956	16.5	14.6	27.2	18.9	17.5	27.0	26.0	23.2	42.1	4.1	2.9	11.1
1955	17.1	15.2	28.4	19.1	17.7	27.2	26.4	23.6	42.8	4.7	3.3	13.0
1954	17.5	15.5	28.9	19.1	17.8	27.0	26.6	23.9	42.9	5.2	3.7	14.4
1953	17.8	15.9	29.6	19.6	18.3	27.4	27.8	25.0	44.7	6.1	4.4	16.6
1952	18.3	16.1	32.2	19.8	18.5	28.0	28.4	25.5	47.0	6.8	4.9	18.8
1951	18.8	16.7	32.1	20.0	18.9	27.3	28.4	25.8	44.8	7.5	5.5	20.1
1950	19.2	17.1	32.5	20.5	19.4	27.5	29.2	26.8	44.5	8.3	6.1	22.2
1949	19.8	17.5	34.6	21.4	20.3	28.6	31.3	28.9	47.3	9.0	6.8	23.5
1948	20.6	18.3	36.5	22.2	21.2	29.1	32.0	29.9	46.5	11.7	8.9	30.1
1947	21.1	18.7	39.6	22.8	21.7	31.0	32.2	30.1	48.5	13.5	10.9	33.5
1946	22.8	20.4	40.9	24.0	23.1	31.5	33.8	31.8	49.5	15.7	13.1	35.9
1945	23.9	21.4	42.0	24.3	23.3	32.0	38.3	35.6	57.0	20.7	17.2	45.5
1944	27.0	24.5	45.4	24.7	23.6	32.5	39.8	36.9	60.3	22.8	18.9	50.6
1943	26.7	24.2	46.2	24.7	23.7	32.9	40.4	37.5	62.5	24.5	21.1	51.0
1942	28.2	25.5	49.3	25.7	24.5	34.6	40.4	37.3	64.6	25.9	22.2	54.4
1941	29.9	26.5	54.0	27.7	26.1	39.0	45.3	41.2	74.8	31.7	26.6	67.8
1940	31.3	27.7	56.7	28.8	27.2	39.7	47.0	43.2	73.8	37.6	32.0	77.3
1939	32.0	28.2	59.0	29.3	27.8	39.6	48.0	44.3	74.2	40.4	35.3	76.2
1938	32.1	28.1	61.1	29.6	28.3	39.1	51.0	47.1	79.1	43.5	37.7	84.9
1937	33.4	29.2	63.2	31.3	29.7	42.1	54.4	50.3	83.2	48.9	43.6	85.8
1936	34.4	29.8	66.9	32.6	31.0	43.9	57.1	52.9	87.6	56.8	51.2	97.2
1935	35.8	31.1	68.7	32.4	31.0	42.7	55.7	51.9	83.2	58.2	53.1	94.6
1934	36.2	31.4	70.1	34.1	[2]32.3	[2]45.3	60.1	[2]54.5	[2]94.4	59.3	[2]54.4	[2]89.7
1933	37.0	32.2	71.1	34.0	[2]32.1	[2]45.8	58.1	[2]52.8	[2]91.3	61.9	[2]56.4	[2]96.7
1932	37.8	32.7	74.4	33.5	[2]32.0	[2]43.7	57.6	[2]53.3	[2]86.2	63.3	[2]58.1	[2]97.6
1931	38.2	33.4	74.1	34.6	33.2	45.2	61.6	57.4	93.1	66.1	60.1	111.4
1930	39.2	34.0	79.9	35.7	34.2	47.4	64.6	60.1	99.9	67.3	60.9	117.4
1929	39.5	34.4	79.7	36.9	35.6	47.3	67.6	63.2	102.2	69.5	63.1	119.9
1928	40.2	35.0	81.5	37.2	35.7	48.8	68.7	64.0	106.2	69.2	62.7	121.0
1927	38.8	34.8	74.8	36.1	35.0	46.1	64.6	60.6	100.1	64.7	59.4	113.3
1926	38.1	35.1	73.0	37.9	37.1	48.0	73.3	70.0	111.8	65.6	61.9	107.1
1925	38.1	35.1	73.1	37.8	36.8	49.5	71.7	68.3	110.8	64.7	60.3	116.2
1924	39.3	35.8	76.2	38.6	37.4	51.2	70.8	66.8	112.9	65.6	60.7	117.9
1923	38.9	35.9	71.8	39.5	38.6	49.9	77.1	73.5	117.4	66.5	62.6	109.5
1922	39.4	36.4	73.4	39.7	38.8	49.9	76.2	73.2	110.0	66.4	62.8	106.8
1921	---	---	---	39.7	38.7	50.3	75.6	72.5	108.5	68.2	64.4	107.7
1920	---	---	---	41.5	40.4	55.0	85.8	82.1	131.7	79.9	76.0	128.1
1919	---	---	---	41.5	40.3	55.2	86.6	83.0	130.5	73.7	69.6	124.4
1918	---	---	---	44.2	43.3	60.5	100.9	97.4	161.2	91.6	88.9	139.3
1917	---	---	---	43.4	42.6	58.0	93.8	90.5	150.7	66.2	63.2	117.7
1916	---	---	---	44.1	43.5	68.9	101.0	99.0	184.9	62.2	60.8	117.9
1915	---	---	---	44.4	---	---	99.9	98.6	181.2	60.8	60.1	105.6

[1] For 1945–1956 includes only deaths for which the period of gestation was given as 20 weeks or more or not stated. For earlier years, includes all fetal deaths, regardless of gestation. In 1945 ratios based on all fetal deaths, regardless of gestation, were: Total, 26.6; white, 24.1; nonwhite, 44.6.
[2] Mexicans included with "nonwhite."

VITAL STATISTICS AND HEALTH AND MEDICAL CARE

Series B 113. Infant Mortality Rate, for Massachusetts: 1851 to 1956

[Deaths under 1 year per 1,000 live births. Excludes fetal deaths. Data for 1940 to 1956 are by place of residence; for earlier years, by place of occurrence]

Year or period	Rate 113	Period	Rate 113	Period	Rate 113	Period	Rate 113
1956	22.4	1930–34	53.9	1900–04	141.4	1870–74	170.3
1955	21.9	1925–29	67.6	1895–99	153.2	1865–69	146.3
1950–54	22.8	1920–24	78.7	1890–94	163.2	1860–64	142.5
1945–49	28.4	1915–19	100.2	1885–89	158.5	1855–59	122.9
1940–44	34.3	1910–14	116.7	1880–84	161.3	1851–54	131.1
1935–39	43.2	1905–09	134.3	1875–79	156.3		

Series B 114–128. Death Rate, for Selected Causes: 1900 to 1956

[Number of deaths, excluding fetal deaths, per 100,000 population. Prior to 1933 for death-registration area only. See series B 4 and B 5]

Year	Tuberculosis, all forms	Syphilis and its sequelea [1]	Typhoid and paratyphoid fever	Diphtheria	Whooping cough	Measles	Malignant neoplasms [2]	Diabetes mellitus	Major cardiovascular-renal diseases	Influenza and pneumonia [3]	Gastritis, duodenitis, enteritis, and colitis [4]	Cirrhosis of liver	Motor vehicle accidents [5]	All other accidents [6]	Suicide
	114	115	116	117	118	119	120	121	122	123	124	125	126	127	128
1956	8.4	2.3	0.0	0.1	0.2	0.3	147.9	15.7	510.7	28.2	4.5	10.7	23.7	33.0	10.0
1955	9.1	2.3	0.0	0.1	0.3	0.2	146.5	15.5	506.0	27.1	4.7	10.2	23.4	33.5	10.2
1954	10.2	3.0	0.0	0.1	0.2	0.3	145.6	15.6	495.1	25.4	4.9	10.1	22.1	33.8	10.1
1953	12.3	3.3	0.0	0.1	0.2	0.3	144.7	16.3	514.6	33.0	5.4	10.4	24.0	36.1	10.1
1952	15.8	3.7	0.1	0.1	0.3	0.4	143.3	16.4	511.6	29.7	5.6	10.2	24.3	37.5	10.0
1951	20.1	4.1	0.1	0.2	0.6	0.4	140.5	16.3	513.0	31.4	5.2	9.8	24.1	38.4	10.4
1950	22.5	5.0	0.1	0.3	0.7	0.3	139.8	16.2	510.8	31.3	5.1	9.2	23.1	37.5	11.4
1949	26.3	5.8	0.1	0.4	0.5	0.6	138.8	16.9	502.1	30.0	6.7	9.2	21.3	39.3	11.4
1948	30.0	8.0	0.2	0.4	0.8	0.6	134.9	26.4	488.0	38.7	6.0	11.3	22.1	44.8	11.2
1947	33.5	8.8	0.2	0.6	1.4	0.3	132.3	26.2	491.0	43.1	5.6	10.4	22.8	46.4	11.5
1946	36.4	9.3	0.3	0.9	0.9	0.9	130.0	24.8	476.8	44.5	5.8	9.6	23.9	45.9	11.5
1945	39.9	10.6	0.4	1.2	1.3	0.2	134.0	26.5	508.2	51.6	8.7	9.5	21.2	50.9	11.2
1944	41.2	11.2	0.4	0.9	1.4	1.4	128.8	26.3	500.5	61.6	9.9	8.6	18.3	53.0	10.0
1943	42.5	12.1	0.5	0.9	2.5	1.0	124.3	27.1	510.8	67.1	9.6	9.3	17.7	55.7	10.2
1942	43.1	12.2	0.6	1.0	1.9	1.0	122.0	25.4	479.5	55.7	8.8	9.4	21.1	50.1	12.0
1941	44.5	13.3	0.8	1.0	2.8	1.7	120.1	25.4	475.3	63.8	10.5	8.9	30.0	45.9	12.8
1940	45.9	14.4	1.1	1.1	2.2	0.5	120.3	26.6	485.7	70.3	10.3	8.6	26.2	47.0	14.4
1939	47.1	15.0	1.5	1.5	2.3	0.9	117.5	25.5	466.3	75.7	11.6	8.3	24.7	45.6	14.1
1938	49.1	15.9	1.9	2.0	3.7	2.5	114.9	23.9	456.8	80.4	14.3	8.3	25.1	46.7	15.3
1937	53.8	16.1	2.1	2.0	3.9	1.2	112.4	23.7	454.6	114.9	14.7	8.5	30.8	50.4	15.0
1936	55.9	16.2	2.5	2.4	2.1	1.0	111.4	23.7	461.1	119.6	16.4	8.3	29.7	55.7	14.3
1935	55.1	15.4	2.8	3.1	3.7	3.1	108.2	22.3	431.2	104.2	14.1	7.9	28.6	49.3	14.3
1934	56.7	15.9	3.4	3.3	5.9	5.5	106.4	22.2	430.0	96.9	18.4	7.7	28.6	50.8	14.9
1933	59.6	15.1	3.6	3.9	3.6	2.2	102.3	21.4	413.6	95.7	17.3	7.4	25.0	46.9	15.9
1932	62.5	15.4	3.7	4.4	4.5	1.6	102.3	22.0	418.2	107.3	16.1	7.2	23.6	47.2	17.4
1931	67.8	15.4	4.5	4.8	3.9	3.0	99.0	20.4	407.1	107.5	20.5	7.4	27.1	50.7	16.8
1930	71.1	15.7	4.8	4.9	4.8	3.2	97.4	19.1	414.4	102.5	26.0	7.2	26.7	53.1	15.6
1929	75.3	15.6	4.2	6.5	6.2	2.5	95.8	18.8	418.9	146.5	23.3	7.2	25.5	54.2	13.9
1928	78.3	16.4	4.9	7.2	5.4	5.2	95.7	19.0	419.1	142.5	26.4	7.5	23.2	54.9	13.5
1927	79.6	16.4	5.3	7.7	6.8	4.1	95.2	17.4	398.3	102.2	27.1	7.4	21.6	55.5	13.2
1926	85.5	17.1	6.4	7.4	8.8	8.3	94.6	17.9	410.6	141.7	32.9	7.2	19.9	57.3	12.6
1925	84.8	17.3	7.8	7.8	6.7	2.3	92.0	16.8	391.5	121.7	38.6	7.2	16.8	59.7	12.0
1924	87.9	17.8	6.6	9.3	8.1	8.2	90.4	16.4	383.4	115.2	33.7	7.3	15.3	58.5	11.9
1923	91.7	17.9	6.7	12.0	9.6	10.7	88.4	17.7	380.8	151.7	39.1	7.1	14.6	59.7	11.5
1922	95.3	18.0	7.4	14.6	5.5	4.3	86.2	18.3	366.6	132.3	38.9	7.4	12.4	55.9	11.7
1921	97.6	17.5	8.8	17.7	9.1	4.2	85.5	16.7	351.2	98.7	50.7	7.3	11.3	55.5	12.4
1920	113.1	16.5	7.6	15.3	12.5	8.8	83.4	16.1	364.9	207.3	53.7	7.1	10.3	59.7	10.2
1919	125.6	16.2	9.2	14.9	5.6	3.9	81.0	15.0	348.6	223.0	55.2	7.9	9.3	61.8	11.5
1918	149.8	18.7	12.3	14.0	17.0	10.8	80.8	16.1	387.0	588.5	72.2	9.6	9.3	72.2	12.3
1917	143.5	19.1	13.3	15.6	10.5	14.1	80.8	16.9	396.4	164.5	75.2	10.9	8.6	77.4	13.0
1916	138.4	18.6	13.2	13.9	10.5	11.4	81.0	16.9	389.4	163.3	75.5	11.8	7.1	74.5	13.7
1915	140.1	17.7	11.8	15.2	8.2	5.2	80.7	17.6	383.5	145.9	67.5	12.1	5.8	67.7	16.2
1914	141.7	16.7	14.7	17.2	10.2	6.8	78.7	16.2	374.5	132.4	75.1	12.5	4.2	72.5	16.1
1913	143.5	16.2	17.5	18.1	10.1	12.8	78.5	15.4	370.6	140.8	86.7	12.9	3.8	79.9	15.4
1912	145.4	15.1	16.1	17.6	9.2	7.2	77.0	15.1	375.7	138.4	79.6	13.1	2.8	78.0	15.6
1911	155.1	15.3	20.1	18.4	11.0	9.9	74.2	15.1	366.5	145.4	86.8	13.6	2.1	81.5	16.0
1910	153.8	13.5	22.5	21.1	11.6	12.4	76.2	15.3	371.9	155.9	115.4	13.3	1.8	82.4	15.3
1909	156.3	12.9	20.2	19.9	10.0	10.0	74.0	14.1	362.0	148.1	101.8	13.4	1.2	77.5	16.0
1908	162.1	12.4	23.4	21.9	10.7	10.6	71.5	13.8	356.7	150.9	112.5	13.5	0.8	82.1	16.8
1907	174.2	12.4	28.2	24.2	11.3	9.6	71.4	14.2	389.8	180.0	115.0	14.8	0.7	94.1	14.5
1906	175.8	14.1	30.9	26.3	16.1	12.9	69.3	13.4	364.3	156.3	123.6	14.1	0.4	94.0	12.8
1905	179.9	13.8	22.4	23.5	8.9	7.4	73.4	14.1	384.0	169.3	118.4	14.0	———	81.3	13.5
1904	188.1	13.9	23.9	29.3	5.8	11.3	71.5	14.2	388.8	192.1	111.5	13.9	———	85.4	12.2
1903	177.2	13.2	24.6	31.1	14.3	8.8	70.0	12.7	364.4	169.3	100.3	13.5	———	81.4	11.3
1902	174.2	12.9	26.4	29.8	12.4	9.3	66.3	11.7	349.8	161.3	104.9	13.0	———	72.5	10.3
1901	189.9	12.5	27.6	33.5	8.7	7.4	66.4	11.6	347.7	197.2	118.5	13.1	———	83.8	10.4
1900	194.4	12.0	31.3	40.3	12.2	13.3	64.0	11.0	345.2	202.2	142.7	12.5	———	72.3	10.2

[1] Excludes aneurysm of the aorta for 1900–1920.
[2] Includes neoplasms of lymphatic and hematopoietic tissues.
[3] Excludes pneumonia of newborn for all years, and capillary bronchitis for 1900–1920.
[4] Excludes diarrhea of newborn for all years; includes ulcer of duodenum for 1900–1920.
[5] Excludes automobile collisions with trains and streetcars, and motorcycle accidents for 1906–1925.
[6] Includes legal executions for 1900–1921, food poisoning for 1900–1908, and motor vehicle accidents for 1900–1905.

Series B 129–142. Death Rate, by Color and Sex: 1900 to 1956

[Number of deaths, excluding fetal deaths, per 1,000 population. Prior to 1933 for death-registration area only. See series B 4 and B 5]

Year	Death rate							Age-adjusted death rate						
	Total	White			Nonwhite			Total	White			Nonwhite		
		Both sexes	Male	Female	Both sexes	Male	Female		Both sexes	Male	Female	Both sexes	Male	Female
	129	130	131	132	133	134	135	136	137	138	139	140	141	142
1956	9.4	9.3	10.8	7.8	10.1	11.4	8.8	7.7	7.4	9.2	5.8	10.9	12.4	9.5
1955	9.3	9.2	10.7	7.8	10.0	11.3	8.8	7.7	7.4	9.2	5.8	10.8	12.3	9.4
1954	9.2	9.1	10.6	7.6	10.1	11.4	8.8	7.7	7.4	9.1	5.8	10.9	12.3	9.5
1953	9.6	9.4	11.0	7.9	10.8	12.3	9.4	8.1	7.7	9.5	6.1	11.7	13.3	10.2
1952	9.6	9.4	11.0	8.0	11.0	12.5	9.6	8.2	7.8	9.5	6.2	11.9	13.4	10.5
1951	9.7	9.5	11.0	8.0	11.1	12.5	9.8	8.3	7.9	9.6	6.3	12.1	13.4	10.7
1950	9.6	9.5	10.9	8.0	11.2	12.5	9.9	8.4	8.0	9.6	6.5	12.3	13.6	10.9
1949	9.7	9.5	11.0	8.1	11.2	12.5	10.0	8.5	8.1	9.7	6.6	12.3	13.5	11.1
1948	9.9	9.7	11.2	8.3	11.4	12.7	10.1	8.8	8.3	10.0	6.8	12.5	13.8	11.2
1947	10.1	9.9	11.4	8.5	11.4	12.5	10.3	9.0	8.6	10.1	7.1	12.5	13.6	11.4
1946	10.0	9.8	11.2	8.5	11.1	12.2	10.0	9.1	8.8	10.2	7.3	12.4	13.5	11.3
1945	10.6	10.4	12.5	8.6	11.9	13.5	10.5	9.5	9.1	10.7	7.5	13.1	14.5	11.9
1944	10.6	10.4	12.2	8.8	12.4	13.8	11.1	9.7	9.3	10.8	7.8	13.8	14.9	12.6
1943	10.9	10.7	12.2	9.2	12.8	14.0	11.6	10.2	9.7	11.2	8.2	14.5	15.7	13.4
1942	10.3	10.1	11.4	8.7	12.7	14.0	11.4	9.9	9.4	10.9	8.0	14.5	15.8	13.3
1941	10.5	10.2	11.4	8.9	13.5	14.8	12.2	10.3	9.7	11.2	8.3	15.6	16.9	14.3
1940	10.8	10.4	11.6	9.2	13.8	15.1	12.6	10.8	10.2	11.6	8.8	16.3	17.6	15.0
1939	10.6	10.3	11.3	9.2	13.5	14.7	12.4	10.7	10.2	11.4	8.9	16.0	17.1	14.9
1938	10.6	10.3	11.3	9.2	14.0	15.2	12.9	10.9	10.3	11.5	9.1	16.6	17.7	15.5
1937	11.3	10.8	12.0	9.6	14.9	16.4	13.4	11.7	11.1	12.4	9.7	17.8	19.2	16.3
1936	11.6	11.1	12.3	9.9	15.4	16.9	13.9	12.2	11.5	12.8	10.1	18.5	20.1	17.0
1935	10.9	10.6	11.6	9.5	14.3	15.6	13.0	11.6	11.1	12.3	9.8	17.3	18.5	16.1
1934	11.1	10.6	11.7	9.6	14.8	16.0	13.5	11.9	11.3	12.5	10.0	17.9	19.0	16.7
1933	10.7	10.3	11.2	9.3	14.1	15.1	13.1	11.6	11.0	12.2	9.9	17.2	18.1	16.4
1932	10.9	10.5	11.3	9.6	14.5	15.4	13.5	11.9	11.3	12.3	10.2	17.8	18.6	17.0
1931	11.1	10.6	11.5	9.6	15.5	16.5	14.5	12.1	11.4	12.5	10.3	19.0	19.9	18.1
1930	11.3	10.8	11.7	9.8	16.3	17.4	15.3	12.5	11.7	12.8	10.6	20.1	21.0	19.2
1929	11.9	11.3	12.2	10.4	16.9	18.0	15.8	13.2	12.4	13.5	11.4	21.0	21.9	20.0
1928	12.0	11.4	12.3	10.5	17.1	18.0	16.2	13.4	12.6	13.6	11.5	20.9	21.7	20.2
1927	11.3	10.8	11.6	10.0	16.4	17.2	15.6	12.6	11.9	12.8	10.9	19.8	20.4	19.3
1926	12.1	11.6	12.3	10.8	17.8	18.7	16.9	13.5	12.7	13.6	11.8	21.4	22.1	20.8
1925	11.7	11.1	11.8	10.4	17.4	18.2	16.6	13.0	12.3	13.2	11.4	20.9	21.4	20.4
1924	11.6	11.0	11.8	10.3	17.1	17.9	16.3	12.9	12.2	13.1	11.3	20.5	21.1	20.0
1923	12.1	11.7	12.3	11.0	16.5	17.0	16.0	13.5	12.9	13.7	12.1	19.8	20.0	19.7
1922	11.7	11.3	11.9	10.7	15.2	15.7	14.8	13.0	12.6	13.3	11.8	18.3	18.4	18.4
1921	11.5	11.1	11.6	10.6	15.5	15.7	15.4	12.7	12.2	12.7	11.6	18.2	18.0	18.6
1920	13.0	12.6	13.0	12.1	17.7	17.8	17.5	14.2	13.7	14.2	13.1	20.6	20.4	21.0
1919	12.9	12.4	13.0	11.8	17.9	18.1	17.8	14.0	13.4	14.1	12.8	20.5	20.3	20.8
1918	18.1	17.5	19.3	15.8	25.6	26.7	24.4	19.0	18.4	20.2	16.6	28.0	28.9	27.1
1917	14.0	13.5	14.6	12.4	20.4	21.4	19.4	15.3	14.7	16.0	13.4	23.4	24.1	22.7
1916	13.8	13.4	14.4	12.4	19.1	19.9	18.4	15.1	14.7	15.8	13.4	22.2	22.6	21.6
1915	13.2	12.9	13.7	12.0	20.2	20.8	19.5	14.4	14.1	15.1	13.0	23.1	23.5	22.6
1914	13.3	13.0	13.9	12.1	20.2	20.9	19.4	14.5	14.1	15.2	13.0	22.6	23.3	21.9
1913	13.8	13.5	14.5	12.5	20.3	21.0	19.6	15.0	14.6	15.8	13.4	22.7	23.3	22.0
1912	13.6	13.4	14.3	12.4	20.6	21.3	19.7	14.8	14.6	15.7	13.4	23.1	24.0	22.2
1911	13.9	13.7	14.5	12.8	21.3	21.9	20.6	15.2	14.9	15.9	13.8	23.7	24.4	22.9
1910	14.7	14.5	15.4	13.6	21.7	22.3	21.0	15.8	15.6	16.7	14.4	24.1	24.8	23.2
1909	14.2	14.0	14.9	13.2	21.8	22.3	21.2	15.3	15.0	16.1	14.0	24.1	24.8	23.3
1908	14.7	14.5	15.3	13.6	22.4	22.8	22.0	15.8	15.5	16.6	14.4	24.7	25.3	24.1
1907	15.9	15.7	16.8	14.5	24.3	25.0	23.5	17.1	16.8	18.2	15.4	26.6	27.5	25.7
1906	15.7	15.5	16.5	14.4	24.2	24.7	23.6	16.7	16.4	17.6	15.1	26.2	27.0	25.5
1905	15.9	15.7	16.5	14.8	25.5	26.8	24.3	16.7	16.5	17.6	15.4	28.3	29.7	26.9
1904	16.4	16.2	17.1	15.3	26.1	27.6	24.7	17.3	17.1	18.1	16.0	29.1	30.7	27.4
1903	15.6	15.4	16.2	14.6	24.5	25.5	23.4	16.5	16.2	17.2	15.3	27.2	28.5	25.9
1902	15.5	15.3	16.2	14.4	23.6	24.8	22.3	16.2	16.0	17.0	14.9	25.9	27.5	24.5
1901	16.4	16.2	17.1	15.4	24.3	25.6	23.1	17.2	17.0	18.0	16.0	26.9	28.4	25.5
1900	17.2	17.0	17.7	16.3	25.0	25.7	24.4	17.8	17.6	18.4	16.8	27.8	28.7	27.1

VITAL STATISTICS AND HEALTH AND MEDICAL CARE

Series B 143–154.   Death Rate, by Age and Sex: 1900 to 1956

[Number of deaths, excluding fetal deaths, per 1,000 population for specified group.   Prior to 1933 for death-registration area only.   See series B 4 and B 5]

Year	Total [1]	Under 1 year	1 to 4 years	5 to 14 years	15 to 24 years	25 to 34 years	35 to 44 years	45 to 54 years	55 to 64 years	65 to 74 years	75 to 84 years	85 years and over
	143	144	145	146	147	148	149	150	151	152	153	154
BOTH SEXES												
1956	9.4	29.6	1.1	0.5	1.1	1.5	3.0	7.4	17.5	39.9	89.0	189.7
1955	9.3	29.6	1.1	0.5	1.1	1.5	3.1	7.5	17.3	39.6	89.4	186.2
1954	9.2	30.3	1.2	0.5	1.1	1.5	3.1	7.7	17.4	39.0	87.6	174.6
1953	9.6	31.4	1.3	0.5	1.2	1.6	3.3	8.1	18.4	40.2	92.5	186.7
1952	9.6	32.7	1.4	0.6	1.3	1.7	3.4	8.3	18.6	40.0	92.1	186.3
1951	9.7	32.6	1.4	0.6	1.3	1.8	3.5	8.4	18.8	40.5	93.3	194.4
1950	9.6	33.0	1.4	0.6	1.3	1.8	3.6	8.5	[2] 19.0	[2] 41.0	93.3	202.0
1949	9.7	35.2	1.5	0.7	1.3	1.8	3.7	8.7	19.3	40.8	93.0	203.2
1948	9.9	35.7	1.6	0.7	1.4	2.0	3.9	9.0	19.7	41.4	95.1	213.2
1947	10.1	34.5	1.6	0.7	1.5	2.1	4.1	9.2	20.1	42.1	97.0	216.9
1946	10.0	46.3	1.8	0.8	1.7	2.3	4.2	9.2	19.8	41.2	95.1	210.6
1945	10.6	42.5	2.0	0.9	1.9	2.7	4.6	9.6	20.5	42.6	98.4	209.6
1944	10.6	44.2	2.3	0.9	2.0	2.7	4.6	9.7	20.8	43.9	101.7	215.3
1943	10.9	44.0	2.6	1.0	2.1	2.7	4.8	10.2	21.5	46.2	107.5	230.3
1942	10.3	48.8	2.4	0.9	1.9	2.8	4.8	10.1	21.0	44.9	101.6	211.1
1941	10.5	52.6	2.8	1.0	2.0	2.9	5.0	10.3	21.3	46.2	105.8	218.7
1940	10.8	54.9	2.9	1.0	2.0	3.1	5.2	10.6	[2] 22.2	[2] 48.4	112.0	235.7
1939	10.6	53.7	3.2	1.1	2.1	3.2	5.3	10.7	22.1	47.2	112.5	223.3
1938	10.6	58.0	3.8	1.2	2.3	3.4	5.6	10.9	22.1	47.1	110.9	212.6
1937	11.3	61.3	4.2	1.4	2.6	3.9	6.2	11.8	23.5	49.0	117.0	227.2
1936	11.6	62.9	4.4	1.5	2.8	4.1	6.5	12.1	24.1	50.8	121.7	242.7
1935	10.9	60.9	4.4	1.5	2.7	4.0	6.2	11.6	23.2	48.7	113.1	224.6
1934	11.1	66.8	5.1	1.5	2.8	4.1	6.2	11.8	23.5	49.4	114.1	224.8
1933	10.7	61.3	4.7	1.5	2.7	4.1	6.2	11.4	23.2	49.0	111.3	222.3
1932	10.9	61.3	4.6	1.5	2.9	4.2	6.3	11.6	23.4	50.0	114.3	233.3
1931	11.1	64.4	5.3	1.7	3.2	4.5	6.7	12.0	23.6	49.9	110.5	222.8
1930	11.3	69.0	5.6	1.7	3.3	4.7	6.8	12.2	24.0	51.4	112.7	228.0
1929	11.9	71.6	6.3	1.9	3.6	5.0	7.3	12.7	24.5	54.0	122.2	254.3
1928	12.0	73.1	6.5	1.9	3.7	5.0	7.5	12.8	24.2	54.3	125.2	268.3
1927	11.3	68.8	5.9	1.9	3.5	4.7	7.1	12.0	22.9	51.2	115.9	250.1
1926	12.1	77.9	7.2	1.9	3.7	4.9	7.4	12.7	24.1	53.8	125.4	279.7
1925	11.7	75.4	6.4	2.0	3.8	4.8	7.2	12.2	23.3	51.7	119.3	272.3
1924	11.6	76.8	6.8	2.0	3.8	4.8	7.1	12.1	23.0	51.0	117.2	261.8
1923	12.1	81.1	8.1	2.1	3.9	5.0	7.3	12.2	23.9	53.3	123.5	279.7
1922	11.7	77.6	7.4	2.1	3.8	5.0	7.1	11.8	23.2	52.2	117.5	258.1
1921	11.5	80.6	8.0	2.5	3.9	4.9	6.8	11.2	22.1	49.0	111.2	239.1
1920	13.0	92.3	9.9	2.6	4.9	6.8	8.1	12.2	23.6	52.5	118.9	248.3
1919	12.9	91.0	9.3	2.7	5.3	7.5	8.6	12.3	23.1	50.0	107.8	222.2
1918	18.1	111.7	15.7	4.1	10.7	16.4	13.4	15.2	26.5	55.1	113.0	222.1
1917	14.0	104.6	10.7	2.6	4.7	6.5	9.0	13.9	26.8	57.3	123.9	245.9
1916	13.8	105.7	11.1	2.5	4.4	6.2	8.8	13.6	26.5	57.2	123.9	250.4
1915	13.2	102.4	9.2	2.3	4.1	5.8	8.3	13.1	25.5	55.6	120.1	240.3
1914	13.3	107.2	10.2	2.5	4.2	6.0	8.5	13.1	25.1	54.1	115.6	231.5
1913	13.8	114.8	11.9	2.7	4.4	6.2	8.7	13.5	25.5	54.1	117.9	235.9
1912	13.6	111.1	10.9	2.5	4.3	6.1	8.6	13.4	25.8	54.5	120.2	242.2
1911	13.9	114.0	11.8	2.7	4.5	6.4	8.9	13.5	25.8	55.0	120.1	246.4
1910	14.7	131.8	14.0	2.9	4.5	6.5	9.0	13.7	26.2	55.6	122.2	250.3
1909	14.2	126.7	13.5	2.8	4.4	6.3	8.7	13.3	25.6	53.9	118.4	244.9
1908	14.7	133.2	14.0	3.0	4.8	6.7	9.0	13.8	26.2	53.8	119.5	248.6
1907	15.9	138.6	14.7	3.2	5.3	7.5	10.2	15.1	28.6	58.8	128.7	269.1
1906	15.7	144.8	15.8	3.3	5.3	7.5	9.8	14.5	27.1	55.0	120.4	255.1
1905	15.9	141.2	15.0	3.4	5.2	7.4	9.8	14.7	27.7	56.2	122.4	261.5
1904	16.4	139.2	15.9	3.7	5.5	7.8	10.2	15.1	28.5	58.2	126.1	270.0
1903	15.6	132.6	15.4	3.4	5.2	7.5	9.8	14.3	27.2	55.0	120.8	253.7
1902	15.5	138.9	16.6	3.3	5.1	7.5	9.6	14.0	25.9	52.9	114.1	235.6
1901	16.4	141.4	17.0	3.5	5.5	8.0	10.3	15.0	27.8	56.2	124.6	260.8
1900	17.2	162.4	19.8	3.9	5.9	8.2	10.2	15.0	27.2	56.4	123.3	260.9
MALE												
1956	10.8	33.6	1.2	0.6	1.6	1.9	3.7	9.6	23.1	49.8	102.3	193.9
1955	10.8	33.4	1.2	0.6	1.6	1.9	3.8	9.7	22.7	49.2	101.9	191.1
1954	10.7	34.1	1.3	0.6	1.6	2.0	3.8	9.9	22.7	48.0	99.3	181.4
1953	11.1	35.5	1.4	0.7	1.7	2.1	4.1	10.4	23.9	49.1	104.3	195.8
1952	11.1	36.8	1.5	0.7	1.8	2.2	4.2	10.5	24.0	48.5	103.3	193.9
1951	11.1	37.0	1.5	0.7	1.7	2.2	4.3	10.6	23.9	49.1	104.3	207.4
1950	11.1	37.3	1.5	0.7	1.7	2.2	4.3	10.7	[2] 24.0	[2] 49.3	104.3	216.4
1949	11.1	39.6	1.6	0.8	1.7	2.2	4.4	10.8	24.2	48.4	103.8	215.0
1948	11.3	40.2	1.7	0.8	1.8	2.3	4.7	11.2	24.6	48.8	105.1	226.4
1947	11.5	38.8	1.8	0.8	1.9	2.4	4.8	11.3	25.0	49.2	106.6	229.3
1946	11.3	52.1	2.0	1.0	2.1	2.6	4.9	11.2	24.3	47.5	104.1	221.1
1945	12.6	47.6	2.2	1.1	2.7	3.5	5.5	11.6	25.0	49.1	107.7	220.7
1944	12.4	49.1	2.5	1.1	2.8	3.2	5.4	11.7	25.0	50.2	110.7	225.5
1943	12.4	49.3	2.8	1.1	2.6	3.2	5.5	12.2	25.7	52.6	117.2	242.6
1942	11.7	54.4	2.6	1.1	2.3	3.2	5.6	12.1	25.1	51.3	111.0	222.1
1941	11.8	58.6	3.0	1.1	2.3	3.3	5.7	12.2	25.3	52.6	115.2	231.9
1940	12.0	61.9	3.1	1.2	2.3	3.4	5.9	12.5	[2] 26.1	[2] 54.6	121.3	246.4
1939	11.7	60.3	3.4	1.3	2.4	3.4	6.0	12.5	25.5	52.7	120.7	232.6
1938	11.7	65.2	4.1	1.4	2.5	3.6	6.2	12.6	25.3	52.5	118.8	222.2
1937	12.5	68.7	4.5	1.5	2.9	4.2	7.0	13.8	27.2	54.5	126.4	238.0
1936	12.7	70.7	4.7	1.7	3.0	4.4	7.4	14.1	27.7	56.1	130.6	252.7
1935	12.0	68.9	4.7	1.7	2.9	4.3	7.0	13.3	26.3	53.7	121.7	234.7
1934	12.1	74.8	5.4	1.7	3.0	4.3	7.0	13.5	26.6	54.3	122.2	235.1
1933	11.6	68.3	5.0	1.7	2.9	4.3	6.8	12.9	26.0	53.6	118.3	232.7
1932	11.7	68.5	4.9	1.7	3.0	4.3	6.9	12.9	26.1	54.1	121.1	242.3
1931	12.0	72.2	5.6	1.8	3.4	4.7	7.4	13.4	26.2	54.4	117.5	234.1
1930	12.3	77.0	6.0	1.9	3.5	4.9	7.5	13.6	26.6	55.8	119.1	236.7
1929	12.8	80.0	6.6	2.1	3.7	5.2	8.0	14.1	26.9	58.4	128.9	259.8
1928	12.8	82.3	6.8	2.1	3.8	5.1	8.0	14.1	26.5	58.5	132.3	271.5
1927	12.1	77.5	6.2	2.1	3.5	4.8	7.6	13.2	25.0	55.2	122.6	254.2
1926	12.9	87.1	7.6	2.1	3.7	5.0	7.9	13.9	26.0	57.6	131.8	281.3

See footnotes at end of table.

Series B 143–154. Death Rate, by Age and Sex: 1900 to 1956—Con.

Year	Total [1]	Under 1 year	1 to 4 years	5 to 14 years	15 to 24 years	25 to 34 years	35 to 44 years	45 to 54 years	55 to 64 years	65 to 74 years	75 to 84 years	85 years and over
	143	144	145	146	147	148	149	150	151	152	153	154
MALE—Con.												
1925	12.4	84.6	6.7	2.2	3.8	4.9	7.6	13.3	25.1	55.4	125.3	273.5
1924	12.3	86.2	7.2	2.2	3.8	4.8	7.6	13.1	24.9	54.7	122.8	263.8
1923	12.7	90.2	8.5	2.3	3.9	5.1	7.7	13.1	25.6	56.2	127.4	279.4
1922	12.3	87.0	7.9	2.3	3.8	5.0	7.4	12.5	24.7	55.1	121.8	257.8
1921	11.9	90.1	8.4	2.7	3.8	4.8	6.9	11.6	23.3	51.1	114.4	241.2
1920	13.4	103.6	10.3	2.8	4.8	6.4	8.2	12.6	24.6	54.5	122.1	253.0
1919	13.5	101.9	9.7	2.8	5.3	7.4	9.1	12.9	24.4	51.9	111.0	229.6
1918	19.8	124.5	16.0	4.2	12.2	19.0	15.3	16.7	28.7	58.5	118.1	227.6
1917	15.0	117.4	11.2	2.7	5.0	7.1	10.1	15.5	29.3	61.1	129.0	251.1
1916	14.8	118.2	11.7	2.6	4.5	6.6	9.7	15.1	29.0	60.6	128.7	255.5
1915	14.0	114.5	9.7	2.4	4.2	6.2	9.1	14.4	27.7	58.8	124.6	246.7
1914	14.2	118.9	10.7	2.6	4.4	6.4	9.4	14.5	27.4	57.8	120.5	236.9
1913	14.8	127.6	12.5	2.8	4.7	6.7	9.7	15.0	27.9	57.7	122.8	241.4
1912	14.5	123.3	11.5	2.6	4.5	6.5	9.5	14.9	28.2	57.9	125.2	248.6
1911	14.7	125.9	12.2	2.8	4.7	6.7	9.8	14.9	28.0	58.1	125.1	249.3
1910	15.6	145.5	14.6	3.0	4.8	6.9	10.0	15.2	28.7	58.7	127.4	255.8
1909	15.1	139.9	14.1	2.9	4.6	6.6	9.5	14.8	27.7	57.0	123.9	251.4
1908	15.5	147.0	14.6	3.1	5.0	7.0	9.8	15.2	28.4	56.4	125.9	251.5
1907	17.0	152.9	15.3	3.3	5.8	8.1	11.4	16.8	31.1	62.7	134.0	275.0
1906	16.7	160.2	16.4	3.4	5.7	7.9	10.9	16.0	29.4	58.2	126.5	261.6
1905	16.7	156.6	15.8	3.4	5.3	7.6	10.6	16.0	29.8	59.0	128.8	270.5
1904	17.3	153.9	16.6	3.7	5.5	8.0	11.1	16.4	31.1	61.7	132.6	280.7
1903	16.4	146.6	15.9	3.5	5.3	7.7	10.4	15.5	29.0	58.5	126.8	262.7
1902	16.4	153.4	17.1	3.4	5.2	7.7	10.3	15.1	28.0	56.5	120.5	248.6
1901	17.3	156.4	17.7	3.7	5.7	8.3	11.0	16.1	29.5	59.2	129.7	268.1
1900	17.9	179.1	20.5	3.8	5.9	8.2	10.7	15.7	28.7	59.3	128.3	268.8
FEMALE												
1956	7.9	25.5	1.0	0.4	0.7	1.1	2.3	5.3	12.2	31.0	78.4	186.2
1955	7.9	25.7	1.0	0.4	0.7	1.1	2.4	5.4	12.2	31.0	79.2	182.7
1954	7.8	26.2	1.1	0.4	0.7	1.1	2.4	5.7	12.3	30.7	78.0	170.2
1953	8.1	27.2	1.2	0.4	0.7	1.2	2.6	6.0	13.1	32.1	82.8	180.4
1952	8.1	28.4	1.3	0.5	0.8	1.3	2.7	6.1	13.4	32.1	82.6	180.9
1951	8.2	28.1	1.3	0.5	0.9	1.4	2.8	6.3	13.8	32.5	84.1	185.4
1950	8.2	28.5	1.3	0.5	0.9	1.4	2.9	6.4	[2] 14.0	[2] 33.3	84.0	191.9
1949	8.3	30.6	1.4	0.5	0.9	1.5	3.0	6.6	14.3	33.6	83.8	194.4
1948	8.5	31.0	1.5	0.6	1.1	1.6	3.2	6.8	14.8	34.3	86.4	203.1
1947	8.7	30.0	1.5	0.6	1.2	1.8	3.3	7.1	15.2	35.3	88.5	207.2
1946	8.6	40.1	1.7	0.7	1.3	1.9	3.5	7.1	15.3	35.1	87.3	203.0
1945	8.8	37.2	1.9	0.7	1.4	2.1	3.8	7.5	15.9	36.3	90.2	201.3
1944	9.0	39.0	2.2	0.8	1.4	2.2	3.9	7.6	16.4	37.8	93.7	207.8
1943	9.4	38.5	2.4	0.8	1.5	2.4	4.1	8.1	17.2	39.9	99.0	221.2
1942	9.0	42.9	2.3	0.7	1.6	2.4	4.1	8.0	16.7	38.7	93.4	202.9
1941	9.2	46.3	2.6	0.8	1.7	2.6	4.3	8.3	17.1	39.8	97.3	208.8
1940	9.5	47.7	2.7	0.9	1.8	2.7	4.5	8.6	[2] 18.0	[2] 42.0	103.7	227.6
1939	9.5	46.8	2.9	0.9	1.9	2.9	4.6	8.9	18.6	41.7	105.1	216.3
1938	9.6	50.7	3.6	1.1	2.1	3.1	4.9	9.1	18.6	41.8	103.7	205.4
1937	10.0	53.6	3.9	1.2	2.3	3.5	5.4	9.7	19.6	43.4	108.4	219.0
1936	10.4	54.9	4.1	1.3	2.5	3.8	5.6	10.0	20.3	45.4	113.5	235.3
1935	9.9	52.8	4.1	1.4	2.5	3.8	5.4	9.8	19.8	43.7	105.1	217.0
1934	10.0	58.5	4.7	1.4	2.5	3.8	5.5	9.9	20.2	44.4	106.5	217.1
1933	9.7	54.0	4.4	1.3	2.6	3.9	5.5	9.8	20.1	44.3	104.7	214.4
1932	10.0	53.9	4.4	1.4	2.7	4.0	5.7	10.1	20.6	45.8	108.0	226.6
1931	10.1	56.5	4.9	1.5	3.0	4.3	6.0	10.4	20.7	45.4	104.0	214.3
1930	10.4	60.7	5.2	1.5	3.2	4.4	6.1	10.6	21.2	46.8	106.6	221.4
1929	11.0	62.9	5.9	1.7	3.5	4.8	6.6	11.1	21.8	49.4	116.0	250.2
1928	11.1	63.6	6.1	1.7	3.6	4.8	6.9	11.3	21.8	49.9	118.6	265.9
1927	10.5	60.0	5.6	1.7	3.4	4.6	6.5	10.8	20.6	47.0	109.6	247.0
1926	11.3	68.4	6.8	1.7	3.7	4.8	6.8	11.4	22.0	49.9	119.5	278.4
1925	10.9	66.0	6.1	1.8	3.8	4.8	6.7	11.0	21.2	47.9	113.8	271.3
1924	10.9	67.0	6.4	1.8	3.8	4.7	6.6	11.1	21.0	47.1	112.0	260.3
1923	11.5	71.6	7.7	2.0	3.9	5.0	6.9	11.2	22.0	50.4	119.8	279.9
1922	11.1	67.9	7.0	2.0	3.8	5.1	6.8	11.0	21.5	49.2	113.7	258.4
1921	11.0	70.8	7.6	2.3	3.9	5.0	6.6	10.7	20.8	46.8	108.3	237.6
1920	12.6	80.7	9.5	2.5	5.0	7.1	8.0	11.7	22.4	50.5	115.9	244.7
1919	12.3	79.7	8.8	2.6	5.3	7.6	8.1	11.5	21.6	48.0	105.0	216.8
1918	16.4	98.5	15.5	4.1	9.4	14.0	11.3	13.6	24.0	51.5	108.3	218.1
1917	12.9	91.5	10.1	2.4	4.4	5.9	7.9	12.0	24.0	53.4	119.2	242.1
1916	12.8	92.8	10.5	2.3	4.2	5.7	7.7	11.9	23.9	53.6	119.5	246.6
1915	12.3	90.0	8.8	2.2	3.9	5.4	7.4	11.6	23.2	52.5	116.0	235.3
1914	12.4	95.1	9.7	2.4	4.0	5.6	7.5	11.6	22.7	50.4	111.0	227.3
1913	12.8	101.7	11.4	2.5	4.1	5.7	7.7	11.8	22.9	50.5	113.4	231.7
1912	12.7	98.5	10.4	2.3	4.0	5.7	7.6	11.6	23.3	51.1	115.5	237.1
1911	13.0	101.8	11.3	2.6	4.3	6.0	7.9	11.9	23.4	51.9	115.5	244.2
1910	13.7	117.6	13.4	2.9	4.2	6.1	7.9	12.1	23.7	52.4	117.4	246.0
1909	13.4	113.2	12.9	2.7	4.2	6.0	7.8	11.7	23.4	50.8	113.3	239.9
1908	13.8	119.1	13.4	2.9	4.5	6.3	8.0	12.2	23.9	51.1	113.7	246.4
1907	14.8	123.9	14.1	3.0	4.8	6.9	8.8	13.1	25.9	54.9	124.0	264.7
1906	14.7	129.2	15.2	3.2	4.9	7.0	8.5	12.9	24.6	51.8	114.8	250.3
1905	15.0	125.5	14.2	3.3	5.1	7.2	8.9	13.3	25.6	53.5	116.7	254.9
1904	15.5	124.2	15.2	3.6	5.5	7.6	9.2	13.7	26.0	54.9	120.3	262.1
1903	14.8	118.3	14.9	3.4	5.0	7.3	9.0	13.0	25.4	51.8	115.4	247.1
1902	14.6	124.1	16.0	3.2	5.1	7.3	8.8	12.8	23.9	49.5	108.3	226.1
1901	15.6	126.1	16.2	3.4	5.4	7.8	9.6	13.9	26.0	53.4	120.0	255.6
1900	16.5	145.4	19.1	3.9	5.8	8.2	9.8	14.2	25.8	53.6	118.8	255.2

[1] Age not reported included in "Total," but not distributed among specified age groups.

[2] Based on enumerated population adjusted for age bias in the nonwhite population 55 to 69 years old.

VITAL STATISTICS AND HEALTH AND MEDICAL CARE

Series B 155–162. Death Rate, by Sex and by Selected Cause, for Massachusetts: 1860 to 1956

[Includes only deaths, excluding fetal deaths, occurring within Massachusetts except for 1940-1956. For these years data are for deaths occurring to residents of Massachusetts

Year	Total	Male	Female	Tuberculosis of respiratory system	Diphtheria	Typhoid and paratyphoid fever	Measles	Smallpox
	155	156	157	158	159	160	161	162
1956	11.0			8.6	0.1	0.0	0.0	0.0
1955	11.2			9.3	0.0	0.0	0.4	0.0
1950	10.5	11.6	9.5	20.2	0.2	0.0	0.0	0.0
1945	12.2			36.9	0.3	0.1	0.2	0.0
1940	11.9	12.6	11.1	34.6	0.2	0.2	0.3	0.0
1935	11.5	12.2	10.8	42.9	0.7	0.3	0.8	0.0
1930	11.6	12.2	11.1	57.2	4.3	0.9	3.3	0.0
1925	12.5	13.0	11.9	70.1	8.0	1.8	8.4	0.0
1920	13.8	13.9	13.6	96.8	15.1	2.4	9.1	0.1
1915	14.3	15.0	13.7	116.8	19.8	6.7	7.3	0.3
1910	16.1	17.0	15.3	138.3	21.0	12.5	11.6	0.0
1905	16.7	17.6	15.8	163.5	22.1	17.9	8.4	0.1
1900	18.4	19.2	17.6	190.3	52.8	22.1	11.7	0.1
1899	17.4			190.4	38.2	22.3	8.8	0.5
1898	17.5			197.4	26.4	24.7	3.1	0.0
1897	18.1			207.4	54.5	23.2	6.0	0.2
1896	19.3			216.4	65.5	28.3	5.4	0.0
1895	19.0	19.9	18.2	223.4	71.4	27.2	4.7	0.0
1894	19.1			223.4	73.6	30.6	4.0	1.3
1893	20.5			231.0	58.3	31.4	11.5	0.4
1892	20.9			244.8	62.2	35.3	3.8	0.1
1891	19.7			239.6	53.2	35.9	10.3	0.1
1890	19.4	20.0	18.9	258.6	72.6	37.3	5.1	0.0
1889	19.2			256.5	101.7	40.9	7.9	0.3
1888	19.9			270.8	86.6	44.6	10.4	0.4
1887	19.8			285.6	79.2	44.8	22.1	0.1
1886	18.6			295.1	78.0	40.0	6.5	0.0
1885	19.6	20.2	19.0	306.6	78.4	39.5	16.1	1.0
1884	19.0			303.6	86.2	45.8	3.9	0.2
1883	20.1			316.0	86.4	45.8	17.1	0.3
1882	19.9			317.9	96.0	58.5	3.7	2.4
1881	20.1			324.5	131.4	59.1	12.7	2.6
1880	19.8	20.3	19.3	308.1	134.3	49.5	13.2	2.1
1879	18.1			297.4	130.6	36.3	1.1	0.4
1878	18.1			308.4	145.5	39.3	17.6	0.1
1877	18.4			320.4	186.6	47.8	7.9	1.4
1876	19.8			317.6	196.4	52.5	2.8	1.8
1875	21.7	21.8	20.5	347.4	113.8	64.1	14.1	2.1
1874	18.6			328.0	56.7	71.2	10.0	1.6
1873	21.6			353.6	47.4	89.5	11.5	42.5
1872	22.9			362.6	49.1	111.1	27.9	67.2
1871	18.7			339.3	50.0	74.7	8.8	19.7
1870	18.8	19.5	18.6	343.3	46.4	91.5	18.5	9.0
1869	18.4			328.8	54.3	85.0	15.7	4.2
1868	18.6			322.0	56.7	65.0	20.8	1.5
1867	17.0			325.5	45.3	72.0	14.5	14.6
1866	18.2			353.0	63.7	83.7	8.4	10.8
1865	20.6	21.7	19.6	367.9	92.8	133.7	10.7	17.4
1864	22.8			375.7	158.7	106.7	25.4	19.2
1863	22.2			372.6	182.4	115.1	11.3	3.4
1862	18.5			342.8	92.1	91.1	29.6	3.2
1861	19.5			365.2	89.2	79.9	16.9	2.7
1860	18.7	19.3	18.4		68.0	76.1	18.2	27.1

Series B 163–175. Death Rate, by Age, for Massachusetts: 1865 to 1900

[Includes only deaths, excluding fetal deaths, occurring within Massachusetts. Rate per 1,000 population for specified group]

Year	Total	Under 1 year	1 to 4 years	5 to 9 years	10 to 14 years	15 to 19 years	20 to 29 years	30 to 39 years	40 to 49 years	50 to 59 years	60 to 69 years	70 to 79 years	80 years and over
	163	164	165	166	167	168	169	170	171	172	173	174	175
1900	18.2	190.1	57.8	5.3	2.9	4.8	7.0	8.8	12.0	21.3	41.0	85.8	197.8
1895	19.0	215.9	64.5	6.2	3.2	5.3	7.1	9.7	12.7	20.5	39.4	82.4	184.7
1890	19.4	223.6	68.1	6.6	3.6	6.3	8.4	10.4	13.4	20.4	37.5	76.0	174.2
1885	19.6	212.5	67.0	7.5	3.8	6.4	9.1	10.6	13.0	19.7	36.2	76.2	182.3
1880	19.8	191.3	68.1	8.5	3.8	6.6	9.5	10.3	11.7	17.9	33.9	73.1	184.0
1875	21.2	226.6	74.0	9.8	4.7	7.7	10.5	11.3	13.0	18.3	34.8	71.1	176.4
1870	18.8	188.1	62.9	5.9	3.7	7.2	10.5	10.6	12.0	17.0	30.1	68.9	170.0
1865	20.6	205.3	68.6	9.6	5.1	9.6	12.6	11.7	11.9	17.5	32.9	70.5	168.2

Series B 176–177. Marriage Rate: 1920 to 1956

Year	Per 1,000 population	Per 1,000 unmarried females [1]
	176	177
1956	9.5	82.3
1955	9.3	80.9
1954	9.2	79.9
1953	9.8	83.7
1952	9.9	83.2
1951	10.4	86.6
1950	11.1	90.2
1949	10.6	85.5
1948	12.4	98.0
1947	13.9	106.8
1946	16.4	120.7
1945	12.2	84.5
1944	10.9	76.8
1943	11.7	83.8
1942	13.2	93.6
1941	12.7	88.8
1940	12.1	82.7
1939	10.7	73.9
1938	10.3	70.8
1937	11.3	78.0
1936	10.7	74.0
1935	10.4	72.5
1934	10.3	71.8
1933	8.7	61.3
1932	7.9	56.0
1931	8.6	61.9
1930	9.2	67.6
1929	10.1	
1928	9.8	
1927	10.1	
1926	10.2	
1925	10.3	
1924	10.4	
1923	11.0	
1922	10.3	
1921	10.7	
1920	12.0	92.0

[1] 15 years old and over.

Series B 178–179. Divorce Rate: 1920 to 1956

[Includes reported annulments]

Year	Per 1,000 population	Per 1,000 married females [1]
	178	179
1956	2.3	9.4
1955	2.3	9.3
1954	2.4	9.5
1953	2.5	9.9
1952	2.5	10.1
1951	2.5	9.9
1950	2.6	10.3
1949	2.7	10.8
1948	2.8	11.3
1947	3.4	13.7
1946	4.3	17.8
1945	3.5	14.5
1944	2.9	12.1
1943	2.6	11.0
1942	2.4	10.1
1941	2.2	9.4
1940	2.0	8.8
1939	1.9	8.5
1938	1.9	8.4
1937	1.9	8.7
1936	1.8	8.3
1935	1.7	7.8
1934	1.6	7.5
1933	1.3	6.1
1932	1.3	6.1
1931	1.5	7.1
1930	1.6	7.5
1929	1.7	
1928	1.7	
1927	1.6	
1926	1.6	
1925	1.5	
1924	1.5	
1923	1.5	
1922	1.4	
1921	1.5	
1920	1.6	8.0

[1] 15 years old and over.

chapter B

HEALTH AND MEDICAL CARE (Series B 180–281)

B 180–181. Physicians, 1850–1957.

Source: 1850, Superintendent of the U. S. Census, *Statistical View of the United States . . . a Compendium of the Seventh Census;* 1860, Superintendent of the U. S. Census, *Population of the United States in 1860;* 1870–1930 (decennial years), Bureau of the Census, Sixteenth Census Reports, *Comparative Occupation Statistics for the United States, 1870 to 1940,* p. 111; 1940 and 1950, *U. S. Census of Population, 1950,* vol. II, part 1, pp. 1-266 to 1-269; 1870–1934, R. G. Leland, *Distribution of Physicians in the United States,* American Medical Association, Chicago, 1936, pp. 7, 79; 1936–1957, the *American Medical Directory,* vols. 14–20 (a summary for 1906–1957 is shown in table 2 of the 1958 edition); 1950–1954, estimates prepared by Public Health Service.

The census data for 1940 and 1950 are for employed civilian physicians; figures for prior years are largely for gainful workers and may include physicians not in active medical practice. See text for series D 36–45 for explanation of difference between employed persons and gainful workers. The 1910 figure includes osteopaths; earlier figures include osteopaths, chiropractors, and healers (not elsewhere classified).

The *American Medical Directory* figures pertain to the total number of physicians, including those retired or not in practice for other reasons and those in the Federal service. They exclude graduates of the years concerned.

Population figures used to compute physician-population rate for census years, 1850–1930, include Armed Forces overseas; only the civilian population is used for 1940 and 1950. Rates for other years are based on the Census Bureau population estimates as of July 1, including Armed Forces overseas.

B 182–183. Dentists, 1810–1957.

Source: 1810 and 1840, John T. O'Rourke and Leroy M. S. Miner, *Dental Education in the United States,* W. B. Saunders Co., Philadelphia, 1941, p. 298; 1820 and 1830, Harris' *Principles and Practice of Dental Surgery,* Lindsay and Blakiston, Philadelphia, 1848, pp. 36–37; 1850–1950 (decennial years), same sources as series B 180–181; 1893–1928, *Polk's Dental Register and Directory of the United States and Dominion of Canada,* R. L. Polk and Co., Chicago, 1928, pp. 9, 22, and prior editions; 1947–1957, *Distribution of Dentists in the United States by State, Region, District and County,* American Dental Association, Chicago, 1958, and prior editions.

The census data for 1940 and 1950 are for employed civilian dentists; figures for prior years are largely for gainful workers and may include dental students and dentists not in active dental practice. See text for series D 36–45 for explanation of difference between employed persons and gainful workers.

The 14 editions of *Polk's Dental Register and Directory of the United States and Dominion of Canada* list by State all dentists for 1893–1928. The *American Dental Directory,* first published in 1947, lists by State all dentists, including those retired or not in practice for other reasons and those in the Federal dental service. The figures for all dates include graduates of the years concerned.

The population figures used to compute the dentist-population rate are the same as those used for the physician-population rate. See text for series B 180–181.

B 184–185. Graduate nurses, 1910–1955.

Source: 1910–1950, Public Health Service, *Health Manpower Source Book 2, Nursing Personnel,* pp. 14–15; 1953 and 1955, American Nurses Association, *Facts About Nursing,* New York, 1956–57 edition, p. 8.

The estimates for 1910–1950 were obtained by subtracting student nurses from the number of nurses reported in the decennial censuses.

Census data for 1910–1930 are for gainful workers; for 1940 they include employed nurses and those seeking work; and for 1950 they include employed civilian nurses. See text for series D 36–45 for explanation of difference between employed persons and gainful workers.

The estimates for 1953 and 1955, were prepared jointly by the American Nurses Association, the National League for Nursing, and the Public Health Service. They are based partly on information supplied by hospitals, schools of nursing, public health agencies, boards of education, and nursing homes. Estimates of nurses in private duty, doctors' offices, industry, and other nursing fields were based on the American Nurses Association Inventory of 1951 adjusted according to trends observed in more recent State surveys of nursing needs and resources.

Population figures used to compute nurse-population rate for 1910–1940 include Armed Forces overseas. The 1950 rate is based on the civilian population. Rates for 1953 and 1955 are based on the Census Bureau population estimates as of January 1, 1954 and 1956, respectively, including Armed Forces overseas.

B 186–188. Medical schools, students, and graduates, 1810–1957.

Source: 1810–1840, *1956 American Medical Directory;* later years, annual reports of the Council on Medical Education and Hospitals of the American Medical Association as follows: 1850–1919, *Journal of the American Medical Association,* vol. 79, No. 8, pp. 629–633, August 1922; 1920–1930, *Journal of the American Medical Association,* vol. 105, No. 9, p. 686, August 1935; 1931–1957, Edward L. Turner, *et al., Journal of the American Medical Association,* vol. 165, No. 11, p. 1420, November 1957.

Data on the number of medical schools, students, and graduates prior to 1900 are fragmentary and of dubious accuracy. The first medical school in the United States was founded in 1765. In 1800 three schools graduated students, with the number of schools increasing steadily from 52 in 1850 to a maximum of 162 in 1906. From 1906 to 1929 the number of schools declined sharply, largely because of the inspection and classification system begun in 1904 by the American Medical Association Council on Medical Education. By 1929 only one unapproved school remained.

B 189. Dental schools, 1840–1957.

Source: 1840–1945, Harlan Hoyt Horner, *Dental Education Today,* copyrighted 1947 by University of Chicago, p. 30; 1946–1957, American Dental Association Council on Dental Education, *Dental Students' Register,* Chicago, annual publications.

Horner's data are compiled from Dorothy Fahs Beck, *The Development of the Dental Profession in the United States,* dissertation of the University of Chicago, 1932, and from records of the Council on Dental Education of the American Dental Association. Additional data may be obtained from the following sources cited by Beck: W. J. Gies, *Dental Education in the United States and Canada*, Carnegie Foundation for the Advancement of Teaching, Bulletin No. 19, 1926, p. 42; *Polk's Dental Register and Directory of the United States and Canada*, R. L. Polk and Co., Chicago, 1925, p. 35; W. J. Gies, "Additional Remarks on a Reference to the Carnegie Foundation's Study of Dental Education," *Journal of Dental Research*, vol. 10, p. 32, February 1930; W. J. Greenleaf, *Dentistry*, Career Series, Leaflet No. 7, Office of Education, pp. 7-10. The Beck tabulation also appears in Frederick B. Noyes, "Dental Education, 1911-36," *Oral Hygiene*, vol. 26, p. 24, January 1936.

The first dental school in the United States was organized in 1840. Before that, all physicians practiced some dentistry, a few limiting their practice to this specialty. The dental practitioners who were not physicians learned their trade as apprentices or were self-taught. From 1840 to 1880 apprentice training was the chief source of supply, but by 1880 most States had enacted laws requiring graduation from a dental school.

B 190. Dental students, 1921-1957.

Source: 1921-1934, Frederick B. Noyes, *Oral Hygiene*, vol. 26, p. 28, January 1936; 1935-1957, American Dental Association Council on Dental Education, *Dental Students' Register*, annual publications. Sources cited by Noyes are: W. J. Gies, *Journal of the American Dental Association*, vol. 18, p. 593, April 1931; and Dental Educational Council of America, statistical reports.

B 191. Dental graduates, 1850-1957.

Source: See source for series B 189.

Annual figures for graduates for 1841-1924, are also presented in *Polk's Dental Register*, 1925, p. 34; but the figures for the early years far exceed those shown elsewhere in histories of dentistry as well as those shown here.

B 192-194. Nursing schools, students, and graduates, 1880-1957.

Source: 1880-1927 and 1931, Office of Education, *Biennial Survey of Education in the United States: 1934-36*, vol. II, chap. IV, p. 294; 1929 and 1932, The Committee on the Grading of Nursing Schools, *The Second Grading of Nursing Schools*, New York, 1932, p. 9; 1935-1939, The Nursing Information Bureau of the American Nurses' Association, *Facts About Nursing, 1946*, New York, 1946, pp. 32, 34; 1940-1956, *Facts About Nursing, 1957*, pp. 67, 71; 1957, *Facts About Nursing, 1958*, pp. 70, 74.

Nursing education began in this country in 1873 with the opening of three schools. These schools offered students an opportunity to learn by doing, under the tutorship for 1 year of a superintendent who had been trained in one of the European schools . . . By 1893 about 70 schools were in operation . . . . As State licensing bodies came into existence, counts of State approved schools and of their students began to be available. Since only graduates of State approved schools could stand for licensure examinations, nonapproved schools tended to close as the effect of licensure became felt. Not until 1923 was machinery for approving schools in operation in every State. (Public Health Service, *Health Manpower Source Book 2, Nursing Personnel*, p. 33.)

B 195-208. Hospitals and beds, by type of service and ownership (AHA), 1946-1957.

Source: 1946-1954, Administrators Guide issue of *Hospitals, Journal of the American Hospital Association*, vol. 29, No. 8, August 1955, part II, pp. 7, 12; 1955-1956, Guide issue of *Hospitals*, vol. 31, No. 15, August 1957, part 2, pp. 348, 355; 1957, Guide issue of *Hospitals*, vol. 32, No. 15, August 1958, part 2, pp. 364, 366.

These figures may not be entirely comparable with those shown in series B 209-220 because the standards required for "listing" or "recognition" of hospitals by the American Hospital Association differ from those required by the American Medical Association. The American Hospital Association collects data annually from all hospitals which it accepts for listing, a basic recognition extended to hospitals and related institutions in accordance with official requirements adopted by its House of Delegates. The Guide issue of *Hospitals* also presents data on admissions, average daily census, births, assets, total expense, payroll expense, and total personnel.

Short-term hospitals have an average patient stay of 30 days or less; long-term, an average stay of longer duration. General hospitals accept patients for a variety of acute medical and surgical conditions, and, for the most part, do not admit cases of contagious disease, tuberculosis, and nervous and mental disease. Special hospitals are those devoted to the treatment of some particular disease or group of diseases or some particular group in the population. Among the former are orthopedic, contagious disease, chronic and convalescent, and eye, ear, nose, and throat hospitals; the latter include maternity, children's, and industrial hospitals. Psychiatric hospitals include those providing temporary or prolonged care for the mentally ill and institutions for the mentally deficient and epileptic. Tuberculosis hospitals include sanatoria or hospitals specifically for the care of tubercular patients.

Number of beds includes beds, cribs, and pediatric bassinets normally available for inpatients. It excludes newborn infant bassinets.

An additional source of information on civilian hospital beds since 1948 is the inventory contained in the comprehensive State plans for hospital and medical facility construction (see *Public Health Reports*, vol. 70, No. 5, May 1955, p. 488).

B 209-220. Hospitals and beds, by type of service (AMA), 1909-1953.

Source: 1909, 1914, 1918, and 1921, *American Medical Directory*, American Medical Association, Chicago, 1921 and prior editions; 1920 and 1923-1953, the following issues of the *Journal of the American Medical Association*, Hospital Number: 1920, April 1921 issue, pp. 1083-1103; 1923, 1927-1933, March 1934 issue, pp. 1008-1009; 1924, March 1925 issue, pp. 961-970; 1925, April 1926 issue, pp. 1009-1055; 1926, March 1927 issue, pp. 789-839; 1934-1953, May 1954 issue, pp. 9-10.

Until 1953, when it discontinued registration of hospitals, the American Medical Association collected data annually from all hospitals registered by it, and published them in the Hospital Number of the *Journal of the American Medical Association*. Registration was a basic recognition extended to hospitals and related institutions in accordance with requirements officially adopted by its House of Delegates. Although its annual census was begun in 1920, complete data on the number of hospital beds classified by type of service are available only from 1925. In addition to information on number of hospitals and beds, the Hospital Number of the AMA Journal presented statistics on admissions, average daily census, and births. For definition of type of service, see text for series B 195-208.

B 221-234. Hospitals and beds, by ownership or control (AHA), 1946-1957.

Source: 1946-1947, American Hospital Association, *American Hospital Directory*, 1947 and 1948 issues; 1948-1955, Administrators Guide issues for 1949-1956 of *Hospitals, Journal of the American Hospital Association;* 1956, Guide issue of *Hospitals*, vol. 31, No. 15, August 1957, part 2, p. 364; 1957, Guide issue of *Hospitals*, vol. 32, No. 15, August 1958, part 2, pp. 366-369.

Governmental hospitals include those operated by Federal, State, and local governments, the latter including county, city, city-county, and hospital district. Nonprofit hospitals are those operated not for profit by churches and by associations of citizens or fraternal organizations. Proprietary hospitals are operated for profit by individuals, partnerships, or corporations.

B 235-248. Hospitals and beds, by ownership or control (AMA), 1909-1953.

Source: The following issues of the *Journal of the American Medical Association*, Hospital Number: 1909, 1914, 1918, and 1934-1953, May 1954 issue, pp. 4, 7-8; 1923 and 1927-1933, March 1934 issue, pp. 1006-1007; 1924, March 1925 issue, pp. 961-970; 1925, April 1926 issue, pp. 1009-1055; 1926, March 1927 issue, pp. 789-839.

For definition of ownership or control, see text for series B 221-234.

B 249-260. Average daily census and admissions to hospitals, by type of service and ownership (AHA), 1946-1957.

Source: American Hospital Association publications, as follows: 1947, 1949, and 1951, Administrators Guide issue of *Hospitals*, vol. 29, No. 8, August 1955, part II, p. 7; 1946, 1948, 1950, 1952-1956, Guide issue of *Hospitals*, vol. 31, No. 15, August 1957, part 2, p. 355; 1957, Guide issue of *Hospitals*, vol. 32, No. 15, August 1958, part 2, p. 372.

Admissions refer to patients who enter a hospital during the course of a year, either as first admissions or readmissions. For definitions of type of service and ownership, see text for series B 195-208.

B 261-270. Average daily census and admissions to hospitals, by type of service (AMA), 1923-1953.

Source: The following issues of the *Journal of the American Medical Association*, Hospital Number: 1925, April 1926 issue, p. 1009; 1923, 1927, and 1929-1933, March 1934 issue, pp. 1008-1009; 1934-1953, May 1954 issue, pp. 9-10.

Admissions refer to patients who enter a hospital during a year, either as first admissions or readmissions. For definitions of type of service, see text for series B 195-208.

B 271-274. Admissions of patients to hospitals for mental disease, 1831-1956.

Source: 1831-1880, report of the Tenth Census, vol. xxi, *Report on the Defective, Dependent, and Delinquent Classes . . .*, pp. 166-171; 1890-1904, Census Office Special Report, *Insane and Feeble-Minded in Hospitals and Institutions, 1904*; 1910, Bureau of the Census, *Insane and Feeble-Minded in Institutions, 1910*; 1922-1946, same agency annual reports (varying titles), *Patients in Mental Institutions*; 1947-1956, Public Health Service annual reports, *Patients in Mental Hospitals*.

For 1923-1932, the annual enumerations of patients in mental institutions, conducted by the Bureau of the Census, were confined to State hospitals for mental disease and State institutions for mental defectives and epileptics. Since 1933, the annual censuses (conducted by the Bureau of the Census until 1946 and subsequently by the Public Health Service) have covered all types of hospitals and institutions caring for the mentally ill, mental defectives, and epileptics. For a discussion of these developments, see the *1947* issue, pp. 1-4, of the source cited above for 1947-1956. See the latter also for additional information on admissions, patients, personnel, and expenditures of institutions for mental defectives and epileptics, as well as for hospitals for mental disease, see the annual reports of the Public Health Service, *Patients in Mental Hospitals*.

The figures for admissions represent patients who enter hospitals (admissions or readmissions) which provide care solely for the mentally ill, as distinguished from the physically

ill and from the mentally deficient and epileptic. These hospitals may provide care over an unlimited period of time or temporary care as in psychopathic hospitals. Hospitals included are those under control of State and local governments, nonprofit and proprietary organizations, the Veterans Administration, and the Federal Government in the District of Columbia (included here under State hospitals).

The rates are computed in relation to the total population of continental United States, as of July 1 of each year prior to 1940; in relation to the civilian population since then.

B 275-281. Specified reportable diseases, 1912-1956.

Source: 1912-1919, Public Health Service, *Public Health Reports*, various issues; 1920-1950, National Office of Vital Statistics, *Vital Statistics—Special Reports*, vol. 37, No. 9; 1951-1956, National Office of Vital Statistics, annual reports, *Vital Statistics of the United States*, vol. I.

The rates refer to the number of notifiable diseases occurring within continental United States per 100,000 population. Each State makes its own laws and regulations prescribing the diseases to be reported, the agencies and persons required to report, and penalties for failure to report. All States have entered voluntarily into a cooperative agreement to report to the Federal Government.

The notification of disease in the United States began in the Colonial period on a local basis, particularly in port cities. It was usually limited to periods when epidemics of pestilential disease threatened or were in progress. Statewide notification was not required until 1883, when Michigan passed a law requiring physicians and householders to report certain diseases to health officers or boards of health. During the next three decades all States made similar requirements.

In response to the need for nationwide statistical information on epidemic diseases, a law was passed in 1878 providing for the collection of such statistics. By 1912, data were supplied regularly by 19 States and the District of Columbia on diphtheria, measles, poliomyelitis, scarlet fever, tuberculosis, typhoid fever, and smallpox. State health authorities now report weekly on 25 diseases and annually on about 40. Most States require the reporting of additional diseases.

The Public Health Service has changed its form of reporting several times and some of the rates shown here do not appear in the published reports. Since the data were originally shown only for the individual States, a rate for the country was obtained for each disease by combining the information only for those States reporting it.

For trends of sickness and accident among groups of male and female industrial workers (1917-1950, for cases disabling for 1 day or longer, and 1921-1952, for cases disabling for 8 days or longer), see W. M. Gafafer, "Industrial Sickness Absenteeism Among Males and Females During 1950," *Public Health Reports*, vol. 66, No. 47, pp. 1550-1552, November 1951. See also "Rates for Specific Causes in 1952 for the Year and Last Two Quarters—Industrial Sickness Absenteeism," *Public Health Report*, vol. 68, No. 11, pp. 1052-1055, November 1953; and S. D. Collins, "Long-Time Trends in Illness and Medical Care," *Public Health Monograph*, No. 48, p. 32.

Civilian illness rates for the United States are not available for a long period. However, records of illness (admission to sick report) among the active-duty personnel of the Army are available back to 1819, and those for the Navy back to 1865. See U. S. Army, *Annual Reports of the Surgeon General on Medical Statistics*, and U. S. Navy, *Annual Reports of the Surgeon General on Medical Statistics*. For annual days sick per person, computed from Army and Navy data, see S. D. Collins, "Long-Time Trends in Illness and Medical Care," *Public Health Monograph*, No. 48, p. 37.

Series B 180–194. Physicians, Dentists, and Nurses; and Medical, Dental, and Nursing Schools: 1810 to 1957

[Census figures in italics. Figures for schools and students are for academic session ending in the specified year]

Year	Physicians Number	Physicians Rate per 100,000 population	Dentists Number	Dentists Rate per 100,000 population	Active professional graduate nurses Number	Active professional graduate nurses Rate per 100,000 population	Medical schools Number [1]	Medical schools Students	Medical schools Graduates	Dental schools Number [2]	Dental schools Students	Dental schools Graduates	Professional nursing schools Number	Professional nursing schools Students	Professional nursing schools Graduates
	180	181	182	183	184	185	186	187	188	189	190	191	192	193	194
1957	226,625	132	100,534	59			[3] 82	[3] 28,852	[3] 6,796	45	13,004	3,050	[4] 1,115	[4] 114,674	
1956			99,227	59			[3] 82	[3] 28,639	[3] 6,845	43	12,730	3,038	[4] 1,125	[4] 114,423	[4] 29,591
1955	218,061	132	97,529	59	[5] 430,000	258	[3] 81	[3] 28,583	[3] 6,977	43	12,601	3,081	[4] 1,139	[4] 107,572	[4] 28,729
1954	214,200	132	95,883	59			[3] 80	[3] 28,227	[3] 6,861	43	12,516	3,084	[4] 1,141	[4] 103,019	[4] 28,539
1953	210,900	132	93,726	59	[5] 401,600	249	79	27,688	6,668	42	12,370	2,945	[4] 1,148	[4] 102,019	[4] 29,308
1952	207,900	132	91,638	58			79	27,076	6,080	42	12,169	2,975	[4] 1,167	[4] 102,550	[4] 29,016
1951	205,500	133					79	26,186	6,135	42	11,891	2,830	[4] 1,183	[4] 103,433	28,794
1950	203,400	134	89,441	59	[5] 375,000	251	79	25,103	5,553	41	11,460	2,565	[4] 1,203	[4] 98,712	25,790
1950	*191,947*	*128*	*74,855*	*50*											
1949	201,277	135					78	23,670	5,094	41	10,132	1,574	1,215	88,817	21,379
1948							77	22,739	5,543	40	8,996	1,755	1,245	91,643	34,268
1947			82,990	58			77	23,900	6,389	40	8,287	2,225	1,253	106,900	40,744
1946							77	23,216	5,826	39	7,274	2,666	1,271	128,828	36,195
1945							77	24,028	5,136	39	[6] 8,590	3,212	1,295	126,576	31,721
1944							77	[6] 48,195	[6] 10,303	39	[6] 9,014	2,470	1,307	112,249	28,276
1943							76	22,631	5,223	39	[6] 8,847	1,926	1,297	100,486	26,816
1942	180,496	134					77	22,031	5,163	39	[6] 8,355	1,784	1,299	91,457	25,613
1941							77	21,379	5,275	39	7,720	1,568	1,303	87,588	24,899
1940	175,163	133			[5] 284,200	216	77	21,271	5,097	39	7,407	1,757	1,311	85,156	23,600
1940	*165,989*	*126*	*69,921*	*53*											
1939							77	21,302	5,089	39	7,331	1,794	1,328	82,095	22,485
1938	169,628	131					77	21,587	5,194	39	7,184	1,704	1,349	74,305	20,655
1937							77	22,095	5,377	39	7,397	1,739	1,389	73,286	20,400
1936	165,163	129					77	22,564	5,183	39	7,306	1,736	1,417	69,589	18,600
1935							77	22,888	5,101	39	7,175	1,840	1,472	67,533	19,600
1934	161,359	128					77	22,799	5,035	39	7,160	1,864			
1933							77	22,466	4,895	39	7,508	1,986			
1932							76	22,135	4,936	38	8,031	1,840	1,781	84,290	25,312
1931	156,406	126					76	21,982	4,735	38	8,129	1,842	1,844	100,419	25,971
1930					[5] 214,300	174	76	21,597	4,565	38	7,813	1,561			
1930	*153,803*	*125*	*71,055*	*58*											
1929	152,503	125					76	20,878	4,446	40	8,200	2,442	1,885	78,771	23,810
1928			67,334	56			80	20,545	4,262	40		2,563			
1927	149,521	126					80	19,662	4,035	40	10,333	2,642	1,797	77,768	18,623
1926							79	18,840	3,962	44		2,610			
1925	147,010	127	64,481	56			80	18,200	3,974	43	11,863	2,590			
1924							79	17,728	3,562	43		3,422			
1923	145,966	130					80	16,960	3,120	45	13,099	3,271			
1922							81	15,635	2,520	45		1,765			
1921	145,404	134					83	14,466	3,186	45	11,745	1,795			
1920					[5] 103,900	98	85	13,798	3,047	46		906	1,755	54,953	14,980
1920	*144,977*	*137*	*56,152*	*53*											
1919							85	13,052	2,656	46		3,587			
1918	147,812	141					90	13,630	2,670	46		3,345			
1917			45,988	44			96	13,764	3,379	46		3,010			
1916	145,241	142					95	14,012	3,518	49		2,835			
1915							96	14,891	3,536	49		2,388	1,509	46,141	11,118
1914	142,332	144	42,606	43			102	16,502	3,594	48		2,254			
1913							107	17,015	3,981	51		2,022			
1912	137,199	144	38,866	41			118	18,412	4,483	52		1,940			
1911							122	19,786	4,273	54		1,742			
1910	135,000	146	37,684	41	[5] 50,500	55	131	21,526	4,440	54		1,646	1,129	32,636	8,140
1910	*151,132*	*164*	*39,997*	*43*											
1909	134,402	149					140	22,145	4,515	56		1,761			
1908			36,670	41			151	22,602	4,741	55		2,005			
1907							159	24,276	4,980	55		1,724			
1906	134,688	158	35,238	41			162	25,204	5,364	55		1,519			
1905							158	26,147	5,600	55		2,621	862	19,824	5,795
1904	128,950	157	32,204	39			160	28,142	5,747	56		2,168			
1903							160	27,615	5,698	55		2,198			
1902	123,196	156	28,109	36			160	27,501	5,009	56		2,294			
1901							160	26,417	5,444	57		2,304			
1900	119,749	157	25,189	33			160	25,171	5,214	57		2,091	432	11,164	3,456
1900	*132,002*	*173*	*29,665*	*39*											
1898	115,524	157	23,911	33						54		1,894			
1896	104,554	147	20,063	28						48		1,432			
1893	103,090	154								37					
1890	100,180	159					133	15,404	4,454	31		960	35	1,552	471
1890	*104,805*	*166*	*17,498*	*28*											
1886	87,521	151								23		473			
1880	82,000	163					100	11,826	3,241	14		315	15	323	157
1880	*85,671*	*171*	*12,314*	*25*											
1870	60,000	150					75			10		147			
1870	*64,414*	*162*	*7,988*	*20*											
1860	*55,055*	*175*	*5,606*	*18*			65			3		64			
1850	*40,755*	*176*	*2,923*	*13*			52			2		17			
1840			1,000	6			35			1					
1830			300	2			20								
1820			100	1			10								
1810			50	1			5								

[1] Approved medical and basic science schools.
[2] For 1840 and 1926–1931, schools offering courses in dentistry; for 1850–1925, schools conferring degrees; for other years, schools in operation.
[3] Includes Puerto Rico.
[4] Includes Hawaii and Puerto Rico.
[5] Census estimate adjusted to exclude student nurses enumerated as graduates.
[6] Reflects enrollment of more than 1 class in some schools under accelerated program in operation during World War II.

Series B 195–208. Hospitals and Beds, by Type of Service and Ownership (AHA): 1946 to 1957

Year	Total		Non-Federal								Federal, all types		Beds per 1,000 population	
			Short-term general and special		Long-term general and special		Psychiatric		Tuberculosis					
	Hospitals	Beds	Hospitals	Beds	Hospitals	Beds	Hospitals	Beds	Hospitals	Beds	Hospitals	Beds	Total	Short-term [1]
	195	196	197	198	199	200	201	202	203	204	205	206	207	208
1957	6,818	1,558,691	5,309	594,529	340	77,608	452	641,455	280	62,097	437	183,002	9.2	3.5
1956	6,966	1,607,692	5,299	586,498	395	75,646	525	695,331	315	66,096	432	184,121	9.6	3.5
1955	6,956	1,604,408	5,237	567,612	402	76,278	542	707,162	347	70,194	428	183,162	9.8	3.5
1954	6,970	1,577,961	5,212	553,068	406	70,926	554	691,176	368	73,558	430	189,233	9.8	3.4
1953	6,978	1,580,654	5,212	545,903	406	68,039	541	691,855	384	72,253	435	202,604	10.0	3.5
1952	6,903	1,561,809	5,122	530,669	405	69,731	546	675,749	391	72,642	439	213,018	10.0	3.4
1951	6,832	1,521,959	5,066	516,020	394	62,768	551	655,932	399	72,642	422	214,597	9.9	3.4
1950	6,788	1,455,825	5,031	504,504	412	70,136	533	619,530	398	72,178	414	189,477	9.6	3.3
1949	6,277	1,435,288	4,585	476,584	395	79,145	507	614,465	414	78,330	376	186,764	9.7	3.2
1948	6,160	1,411,450	4,499	471,555	362	77,040	504	601,103	409	75,906	386	185,846	9.7	3.2
1947	6,173	1,400,318	4,475	465,209	385	84,758	499	580,273	411	70,307	403	199,771	9.8	3.2
1946	6,125	1,435,778	4,444	473,059	389	83,415	476	568,473	412	74,867	404	235,964	10.3	3.4

[1] Non-Federal short-term general and special hospitals.

Series B 209–220. Hospitals and Beds, by Type of Service (AMA): 1909 to 1953

Year	Total		General		Mental		Tuberculosis		All other		Beds per 1,000 population	
	Hospitals	Beds	Hospitals	Beds	Hospitals	Beds	Hospitals	Beds	Hospitals	Beds	Total	General
	209	210	211	212	213	214	215	216	217	218	219	220
1953	6,840	1,573,014	5,087	653,752	593	749,393	420	88,406	740	81,463	9.9	4.1
1952	6,665	1,541,615	4,924	640,923	585	732,929	428	89,571	728	78,192	9.9	4.1
1951	6,637	1,529,988	4,890	640,207	596	728,187	430	88,379	721	73,215	10.0	4.2
1950	6,430	1,456,912	4,713	587,917	579	711,921	431	85,746	707	71,328	9.6	3.9
1949	6,572	1,439,030	4,761	574,683	606	705,423	444	83,470	761	75,454	9.7	3.9
1948	6,335	1,423,520	4,589	576,459	586	691,499	438	81,993	722	73,569	9.7	3.9
1947	6,276	1,425,222	4,539	592,453	585	680,913	441	81,328	711	70,528	9.9	4.1
1946	6,280	1,468,714	4,523	641,331	575	674,930	450	83,187	732	69,266	10.5	4.6
1945	6,511	1,738,944	4,744	922,549	563	657,393	449	78,774	755	80,228	13.1	7.0
1944	6,611	1,729,945	4,833	925,818	566	648,745	453	79,848	759	75,534	13.0	7.0
1943	6,655	1,649,254	4,885	850,576	575	650,993	455	79,860	740	67,825	12.3	6.3
1942	6,345	1,383,827	4,557	594,260	586	646,118	468	82,372	734	61,077	10.3	4.4
1941	6,358	1,324,381	4,518	533,498	596	638,144	477	82,365	767	70,374	9.9	4.0
1940	6,291	1,226,245	4,432	462,360	602	621,284	479	78,246	778	64,355	9.3	3.5
1939	6,226	1,195,026	4,356	444,947	600	606,284	480	75,972	790	67,823	9.1	3.4
1938	6,166	1,161,380	4,286	425,324	592	591,822	493	76,022	795	68,212	8.9	3.3
1937	6,128	1,124,548	4,245	412,091	579	570,616	508	76,751	796	65,090	8.7	3.2
1936	6,189	1,096,721	4,207	402,605	584	548,952	506	73,692	892	71,472	8.6	3.1
1935	6,246	1,075,139	4,257	406,174	592	529,311	496	70,373	901	69,281	8.4	3.2
1934	6,334	1,048,101	4,198	393,425	614	513,845	495	70,063	1,027	70,768	8.3	3.1
1933	6,437	1,027,046	4,237	386,713	621	498,955	497	70,682	1,082	70,696	8.2	3.1
1932	6,562	1,014,354	4,305	395,543	624	479,548	512	69,676	1,121	69,587	8.1	3.2
1931	6,613	974,115	4,309	384,333	587	451,245	509	65,923	1,208	72,614	7.9	3.1
1930	6,719	955,869	4,302	371,609	561	437,919	515	65,940	1,341	80,401	7.8	3.0
1929	6,665	907,133	4,268	357,034	572	414,386	502	61,310	1,323	74,403	7.4	2.9
1928	6,852	892,934	4,361	363,337	553	394,268	508	62,113	1,430	73,216	7.4	3.0
1927	6,807	853,318	4,322	345,364	563	373,364	508	63,170	1,414	71,420	7.2	2.9
1926	6,946	859,445	--------	--------	--------	--------	--------	--------	--------	--------	7.3	--------
1925	6,896	802,065	4,041	293,301	589	341,480	466	49,131	1,800	118,153	6.9	2.5
1924	7,370	813,926	--------	--------	--------	--------	--------	--------	--------	--------	7.1	--------
1923	6,830	755,722	3,793	--------	593	--------	476	--------	1,968	--------	6.8	--------
1921	[1]6,236	--------	--------	--------	--------	--------	--------	--------	--------	--------	--------	--------
1920	6,152	817,020	4,013	311,159	521	295,382	52	10,150	1,566	200,329	7.7	2.9
1918	5,323	612,251	--------	--------	--------	--------	--------	--------	--------	--------	5.9	--------
1914	5,047	532,481	--------	--------	--------	--------	--------	--------	--------	--------	5.4	--------
1909	4,359	421,065	--------	--------	--------	--------	--------	--------	--------	--------	4.7	--------

[1] Excludes hospitals with less than 10 beds.

Series B 221-234. Hospitals and Beds, by Ownership or Control (AHA): 1946 to 1957

Year	Total		Governmental						Nonprofit				Proprietary	
			Federal		State		Local		Church		Other			
	Hospitals	Beds	Hospitals	Beds	Hospitals	Beds	Hospitals	Beds	Hospitals	Beds	Hospitals	Beds	Hospitals	Beds
	221	222	223	224	225	226	227	228	229	230	231	232	233	234
1957	6,818	1,558,691	437	183,002	543	686,255	1,238	194,740	1,220	180,291	2,291	267,555	1,089	46,848
1956	6,966	1,607,692	432	184,121	553	728,151	1,263	202,368	1,206	176,972	2,304	265,633	1,208	50,447
1955	6,956	1,604,408	428	183,162	552	739,153	1,253	203,179	1,101	162,283	2,339	264,761	1,283	51,870
1954	6,970	1,577,961	430	189,233	552	717,558	1,248	202,312	1,196	169,685	2,225	247,658	1,319	51,515
1953	6,978	1,580,654	435	202,604	556	710,802	1,239	203,836	1,110	157,597	2,259	251,712	1,379	54,103
1952	6,903	1,561,809	439	213,018	(1)	(1)	1,747[1]	896,596[1]	(2)	(2)	3,348[2]	398,530[2]	1,369	53,665
1951	6,832	1,521,959	422	214,597	(1)	(1)	1,701[1]	870,517[1]	(2)	(2)	3,297[2]	383,102[2]	1,412	53,743
1950	6,788	1,455,825	414	189,477	(1)	(1)	1,654[1]	843,672[1]	(2)	(2)	3,250[2]	368,137[2]	1,470	54,539
1949	6,277	1,435,288	376	186,764	(1)	(1)	1,511[1]	842,089[1]	(2)	(2)	3,044[2]	355,331[2]	1,346	51,104
1948	6,160	1,411,450	386	185,846	(1)	(1)	1,474[1]	826,377[1]	(2)	(2)	3,022[2]	349,310[2]	1,278	49,917
1947	6,173	1,400,318	403	199,771	(1)	(1)	1,490[1]	807,602[1]	(2)	(2)	2,981[2]	342,120[2]	1,299	50,825
1946	6,125	1,435,778	404	235,964	(1)	(1)	1,504[1]	811,702[1]	(2)	(2)	2,921[2]	334,867[2]	1,296	53,245

[1] State hospitals included with "Local."   [2] Church-operated and affiliated hospitals included with "Other."

Series B 235-248. Hospitals and Beds, by Ownership or Control (AMA): 1909 to 1953

Year	Total		Governmental						Nonprofit				Proprietary	
			Federal		State		Local		Church		Other			
	Hospitals	Beds	Hospitals	Beds	Hospitals	Beds	Hospitals	Beds	Hospitals	Beds	Hospitals	Beds	Hospitals	Beds
	235	236	237	238	239	240	241	242	243	244	245	246	247	248
1953	6,840	1,573,014	392	200,535	550	711,824	1,194	200,645	1,169	164,053	2,206	243,653	1,329	52,304
1952	6,665	1,541,615	386	211,510	549	691,408	1,143	196,705	1,136	158,389	2,146	232,598	1,305	51,005
1951	6,637	1,529,988	388	216,939	554	683,376	1,090	197,405	1,116	154,053	2,121	225,903	1,368	52,312
1950	6,430	1,456,912	355	186,793	552	665,019	1,005	185,229	1,097	150,078	2,072	218,788	1,349	51,005
1949	6,572	1,439,030	361	182,254	573	656,611	1,003	186,290	1,090	146,315	2,067	213,576	1,478	53,984
1948	6,335	1,423,520	372	185,098	567	648,386	961	186,283	1,068	144,036	2,016	208,936	1,351	50,781
1947	6,276	1,425,222	401	213,204	563	626,648	953	190,353	1,051	141,920	1,965	202,661	1,343	50,436
1946	6,280	1,468,714	464	264,486	557	628,363	941	189,885	1,050	138,096	1,942	198,885	1,326	48,999
1945	6,511	1,738,944	705	546,384	549	619,642	929	190,692	1,036	135,481	1,954	195,805	1,338	50,940
1944	6,611	1,729,945	798	551,135	539	609,025	925	192,118	1,020	133,090	1,961	195,624	1,368	48,953
1943	6,655	1,649,254	827	476,673	531	610,115	926	189,351	1,004	130,488	1,952	192,219	1,415	50,408
1942	6,345	1,383,827	474	220,938	530	606,437	920	188,406	977	126,141	1,949	190,150	1,495	51,755
1941	6,358	1,324,381	428	179,202	530	600,320	906	185,989	993	123,331	1,917	182,140	1,584	53,399
1940	6,291	1,226,245	336	108,928	521	572,079	910	192,682	998	120,809	1,903	177,681	1,623	54,066
1939	6,226	1,195,026	329	96,338	523	560,575	888	188,233	1,001	120,740	1,839	172,765	1,646	56,375
1938	6,166	1,161,380	330	92,248	523	541,279	875	181,609	981	119,521	1,776	169,980	1,681	56,743
1937	6,128	1,124,548	329	97,951	522	508,913	871	181,885	975	115,283	1,718	162,474	1,713	58,042
1936	6,189	1,096,721	323	84,234	524	503,306	877	176,300	969	113,288	1,742	162,586	1,754	57,007
1935	6,246	1,075,139	316	83,353	526	483,994	882	174,365	970	113,268	1,670	155,300	1,882	64,859
1934	6,334	1,048,101	313	77,865	544	473,035	892	166,988	970	113,263	1,676	154,449	1,939	62,501
1933	6,437	1,027,046	295	75,635	557	459,646	924	159,192	984	115,840	3,677[1]	216,733[1]	(1)	(1)
1932	6,562	1,014,354	301	74,151	568	442,601	935	162,615	1,001	117,555	3,757[1]	217,432[1]	(1)	(1)
1931	6,613	974,115	291	69,170	576	419,282	949	153,072	1,011	116,935	3,786[1]	215,656[1]	(1)	(1)
1930	6,719	955,869	288	63,581	581	405,309	943	150,836	1,017	116,846	3,890[1]	219,297[1]	(1)	(1)
1929	6,665	907,133	292	59,901	578	385,706	925	136,930	1,024	113,555	3,846[1]	211,041[1]	(1)	(1)
1928	6,852	892,934	294	61,765	595	369,759	924	135,910	1,056	114,613	3,983[1]	210,887[1]	(1)	(1)
1927	6,807	853,318	301	60,444	592	354,786	916	129,939	1,060	108,582	3,938[1]	199,567[1]	(1)	(1)
1926	6,946	859,445	----	63,553	----	334,984	----	----	----	----	----	----	----
1925	6,896	802,065	299	57,091	351	317,264	----	----	----	----	----	----	----
1924	7,370	813,926	310	62,352	632	321,399	1,050	125,302	1,233	110,760	1,748	131,439	2,397	62,674
1923	6,830	755,722	220	53,869	601	302,208	915	115,871	893	77,941	2,439	160,114	1,762	45,719
1918	5,323	612,251	110	18,815	303	262,254	----	----	----	----	----	----	----	----
1914	5,047	532,481	93	12,602	294	232,834	----	----	----	----	----	----	----	----
1909	4,359	421,065	71	8,827	232	189,049	----	----	----	----	----	----	----	----

[1] Proprietary hospitals and beds included with "Other nonprofit."

Series **B 249–260.** Average Daily Census and Admissions to Hospitals, by Type of Service and Ownership (AHA): 1946 to 1957

[In thousands]

Year	Total		Non-Federal								Federal, all types	
			Short-term general and special		Long-term general and special		Psychiatric		Tuberculosis			
	Average daily census	Admissions during year	Average daily census	Admissions during year	Average daily census	Admissions during year	Average daily census	Admissions during year	Average daily census	Admissions during year	Average daily census	Admissions during year
	249	250	251	252	253	254	255	256	257	258	259	260
1957	1,320	22,993	438	21,002	67	198	609	303	49	71	157	1,419
1956	1,356	22,090	425	20,107	63	175	659	343	53	76	156	1,388
1955	1,363	21,073	407	19,100	65	158	677	312	56	87	157	1,415
1954	1,343	20,345	393	18,392	61	155	668	289	61	89	160	1,421
1953	1,342	20,184	394	18,098	56	160	663	291	62	77	168	1,558
1952	1,336	19,624	385	17,413	58	156	651	392	62	76	180	1,586
1951	1,298	18,783	378	16,677	51	163	636	275	62	83	171	1,586
1950	1,253	18,483	372	16,663	60	164	607	293	62	79	152	1,284
1949	1,240	17,224	352	15,428	68	132	597	269	66	128	157	1,268
1948	1,241	16,821	361	15,072	70	128	595	267	66	112	149	1,241
1947	1,190	17,689	354	15,908	73	149	558	266	55	94	150	1,271
1946	1,142	15,675	341	13,655	63	139	517	202	55	85	166	1,593

Series **B 261–270.** Average Daily Census and Admissions to Hospitals, by Type of Service (AMA): 1923 to 1953

[In thousands]

Year	Total		General		Mental		Tuberculosis		All other	
	Average daily census	Admissions during year	Average daily census	Admissions during year	Average daily census	Admissions during year	Average daily census	Admissions during year	Average daily census	Admissions during year
	261	262	263	264	265	266	267	268	269	270
1953	1,333	19,869	477	18,693	719	328	75	108	61	739
1952	1,309	18,915	475	17,760	704	312	75	110	55	733
1951	1,294	18,237	471	17,066	698	307	74	107	52	757
1950	1,243	17,024	433	15,830	688	307	72	113	49	773
1949	1,225	16,660	429	15,450	675	308	69	113	51	789
1948	1,217	16,423	438	15,160	664	305	66	106	49	852
1947	1,217	15,830	457	14,665	652	292	63	99	46	773
1946	1,239	15,153	496	14,052	636	271	62	100	45	731
1945	1,405	16,257	665	15,228	624	249	60	86	56	694
1944	1,299	16,037	570	15,060	619	226	63	88	47	662
1943	1,257	15,375	529	14,455	619	209	65	92	43	620
1942	1,126	12,546	405	11,634	610	214	70	102	41	596
1941	1,087	11,596	364	10,647	603	209	71	101	50	639
1940	1,026	10,088	325	9,219	591	190	67	91	43	587
1939	996	9,879	308	9,018	577	190	65	91	46	580
1938	966	9,421	293	8,546	562	199	66	101	44	576
1937	944	9,222	288	8,350	547	196	65	102	44	574
1936	909	8,647	272	7,756	525	185	63	99	49	607
1935	876	7,717	261	6,875	507	173	61	86	46	583
1934	830	7,147	237	6,292	488	172	60	82	45	601
1933	810	7,038	232	6,072	475	171	60	84	43	711
1932	808	7,228	250	6,304	455	170	60	93	43	662
1931	775	7,156	248	6,322	427	----------	56	81	45	----------
1930	763	----------	240	----------	415	----------	56	----------	52	----------
1929	727	----------	234	----------	395	----------	51	----------	47	----------
1927	672	----------	228	----------	350	----------	51	----------	43	----------
1925	629	----------	194	----------	322	----------	40	----------	74	----------
1923	553	----------	----------	----------	----------	----------	----------	----------	----------	----------

Series B 271–274. Admissions of Patients to Hospitals for Mental Disease: 1831 to 1956

Year	Admissions — All hospitals (271)	Admissions — State hospitals (272)	Rate per 100,000 population — All hospitals (273)	Rate per 100,000 population — State hospitals (274)
1956	296,359	176,245	179.2	106.7
1955	302,543	169,512	186.4	104.4
1954	276,025	163,071	173.5	102.5
1953	274,968	159,002	176.2	101.9
1952	270,087	152,479	176.1	99.4
1951	255,605	141,588	169.2	93.7
1950	255,748	141,493	170.3	94.2
1949	251,978	139,103	170.7	94.3
1948	252,341	133,514	173.8	92.0
1947	240,503	123,392	168.7	86.6
1946	218,545	116,807	157.9	84.4
1945	189,648	110,914	148.7	86.9
1944	171,967	107,907	135.7	85.2
1943	160,998	106,698	126.3	83.7
1942	157,284	109,059	120.1	83.3
1941	162,724	107,914	123.7	82.0
1940	158,253	105,420	120.2	80.1
1939	156,526	103,844	119.6	79.3
1938	154,491	100,493	119.0	77.4
1937	154,118	98,646	119.6	76.6
1936	147,297	94,897	115.0	74.1
1935	134,077	89,964	105.4	70.7
1934	135,339	87,647	107.1	69.4
1933	125,384	86,407	99.8	68.8
1932	[1]	83,460	--------	66.9
1931	115,679	82,334	93.3	66.4
1930	[1]	78,452	--------	63.7
1929	[1]	75,601	--------	62.1
1928	[1]	73,388	--------	60.9
1927	[1]	69,318	--------	58.2
1926	[1]	65,348	--------	55.7
1922	89,455	61,182	81.3	55.6
1910	60,769	45,873	65.8	49.6
1904	49,622	41,391	60.4	50.4
1903	[1]	38,931	--------	48.3
1902	[1]	37,766	--------	47.7
1901	[1]	37,689	--------	48.6
1900	[1]	41,165	--------	54.1
1899	[1]	33,304	--------	44.5
1898	[1]	34,045	--------	46.3
1897	[1]	31,612	--------	43.8
1896	[1]	30,531	--------	43.1
1895	[1]	30,977	--------	44.5
1894	[1]	28,771	--------	42.1
1893	[1]	28,446	--------	42.5
1892	[1]	27,164	--------	41.4
1891	[1]	26,580	--------	41.3
1890	[1]	24,651	--------	39.1

Year	Admissions, all hospitals (271)	Rate per 100,000 population, all hospitals (273)	Year	Admissions, all hospitals (271)	Rate per 100,000 population, all hospitals (273)
1880	12,235	24.3	1855	4,501	16.4
1879	13,051	26.5	1854	4,347	16.4
1878	13,647	28.3	1853	4,106	16.0
1877	13,392	28.4	1852	3,658	14.7
1876	13,145	28.5	1851	3,286	13.6
1875	12,181	27.0	1850	2,979	12.8
1874	12,447	28.3	1849	2,982	13.2
1873	11,223	26.1	1848	3,117	14.2
1872	11,554	27.5	1847	2,685	12.5
1871	11,173	27.3	1846	2,266	10.9
1870	10,010	25.1	1845	2,182	10.8
1869	9,319	23.9	1844	1,810	9.2
1868	8,740	22.9	1843	1,618	8.5
1867	7,702	20.6	1842	1,202	6.6
1866	7,376	20.2	1841	1,344	7.6
1865	7,019	19.7	1840	1,082	6.3
1864	6,311	18.1	1839	1,142	6.8
1863	5,998	17.6	1838	932	5.7
1862	5,724	17.2	1837	873	5.5
1861	5,874	18.2	1836	789	5.1
1860	5,846	18.6	1835	820	5.5
1859	5,636	18.4	1834	611	4.2
1858	5,047	16.9	1833	558	3.9
1857	4,764	16.4	1832	358	2.6
1856	4,380	15.5	1831	394	3.0

[1] Not available.

Series B 275–281. Specified Reportable Diseases: 1912 to 1956

[Rate per 100,000 population enumerated as of April 1 for 1940 and 1950, and estimated as of July 1 for all other years]

Year	Typhoid and paratyphoid fever [1] (275)	Scarlet fever and streptococcal sore throat [2] (276)	Diphtheria (277)	Whooping cough (278)	Meningococcal infections (279)	Acute poliomyelitis (280)	Smallpox (281)
1956	5.0	105.5	0.9	19.0	1.6	9.1	0.0
1955	4.4	89.8	1.2	38.2	2.1	17.6	0.0
1954	4.7	91.7	1.3	37.8	2.8	23.9	0.0
1953	3.9	84.0	1.5	23.5	3.2	22.5	0.0
1952	3.2	73.0	1.9	28.9	3.1	37.2	0.0
1951	2.5	54.9	2.6	44.8	2.7	18.5	0.0
1950	2.5	42.8	3.8	80.1	2.5	22.1	0.0
1949	2.7	58.7	5.4	46.7	2.4	28.3	0.0
1948	2.5	62.5	6.5	51.1	2.3	19.0	0.0
1947	2.8	65.2	8.5	109.1	2.4	7.5	0.1
1946	2.8	89.6	11.7	78.4	4.1	18.3	0.2
1945	3.7	140.1	14.1	101.0	6.2	10.3	0.3
1944	4.2	150.9	10.6	82.7	12.3	14.3	0.3
1943	4.1	112.0	11.0	142.9	13.6	9.3	0.6
1942	5.0	101.4	12.1	142.9	2.9	3.1	0.6
1941	6.5	104.7	13.5	166.9	1.5	6.8	1.0
1940	7.4	125.9	11.8	139.6	1.3	7.4	2.1
1939	10.0	132.3	18.4	140.0	1.5	5.6	7.5
1938	11.5	152.8	23.5	175.1	2.2	1.3	11.5
1937	12.4	183.5	22.2	166.6	4.4	7.4	9.1
1936	12.4	195.6	23.4	115.0	5.9	3.5	6.1
1935	14.4	211.0	30.8	141.9	4.7	8.5	6.3
1934	17.6	180.0	34.1	209.9	2.0	5.9	4.3
1933	18.6	174.4	40.2	142.6	2.4	4.0	5.2
1932	21.4	172.7	48.0	172.5	2.6	3.1	9.0
1931	21.4	166.3	57.1	139.1	4.7	13.3	24.4
1930	22.1	144.5	54.1	135.6	7.0	7.7	39.7
1929	19.1	152.9	70.1	162.1	8.7	2.4	34.7
1928	22.6	148.9	75.9	134.3	5.0	4.3	32.7
1927	29.2	179.8	89.8	152.4	2.9	8.8	31.6
1926	35.5	166.7	80.7	172.2	2.2	2.4	28.7
1925	40.6	164.4	83.3	133.2	1.9	5.4	34.7
1924	31.8	164.2	105.6	145.0	1.8	4.8	49.6
1923	31.0	158.8	131.4	154.2	2.1	3.3	27.6
1922	33.0	148.1	156.9	107.7	2.0	2.3	30.5
1921	46.0	188.9	201.5	--------	2.5	6.5	100.3
1920	37.5	168.3	154.3	--------	3.2	2.5	107.0
1919	42.9	118.3	144.7	--------	3.1	2.3	63.8
1918	50.0	94.5	101.5	--------	7.2	2.8	83.1
1917	63.0	139.2	133.0	--------	6.2	4.9	52.7
1916	82.3	114.5	129.2	--------	2.7	41.1	23.4
1915	74.0	108.6	132.7	--------	2.9	3.1	50.2
1914	82.4	133.0	152.5	--------	3.4	2.4	66.4
1913	84.2	143.1	142.1	--------	3.4	4.0	55.7
1912	81.8	138.2	139.0	--------		5.5	30.8

[1] Excludes paratyphoid fever for 1912 to 1919 and includes other salmonella infections for 1950 to 1955.   [2] Excludes streptococcal sore throat for 1912 to 1919.

Migration

INTERNAL MIGRATION (Series C 1–87)

C 1–73. General note.

Data concerning internal migration of the native population are based on information concerning State of birth and State of residence collected during the decennial censuses of population. Caution is required in the interpretation of these data because the migration measured by each census is the net movement from the time of birth to the census date. Migrants as defined here include only those persons who have moved from one State to another and are, on the census date, living in States other than those in which they were born. Persons who moved from their State of birth and then returned to it by the time of the census are classified as nonmigrants.

These statistics for migrants do not represent the total number of persons who have moved from the State or geographic division in which they were born to other States or divisions during any given period of time. Some of those who moved from one State to another died before the following census date. Some moved from and returned, between censuses, to their State of birth. Others moved to places outside continental United States.

A native is defined as a person born in continental United States, Puerto Rico, or the Territories or possessions, or born abroad to American parents. Persons for whom place of birth was not reported are included with the natives.

The classification of the population by color is not ordinarily based on replies to census questions asked by the enumerators, but rather is obtained by observation. This concept does not, therefore, reflect a clear-cut definition of biological stock. The nonwhite population consists of Negroes, American Indians, Japanese, Chinese, Filipinos, and some other groups. Persons of mixed parentage are placed in the color classification of the nonwhite parent. Persons of Mexican birth or ancestry who are not definitely Indian or of other nonwhite stock have been classified as white in all censuses except that of 1930. The lack of comparability introduced by this factor is substantial in the West South Central, Mountain, and Pacific Divisions. For revised 1930 figures for regions showing Mexicans classified as white, see series B 215–230 in *Historical Statistics of the United States, 1789–1945.*

C 1–14. Native population, by residence within or outside State, division, and region of birth, by color, 1850–1950.

Source: Special compilations made by the University of Pennsylvania Studies of Population Redistribution and Economic Growth from the following: 1850, *The Seventh Census of the United States: 1850*, pp. xxxvi–xxxviii; 1860, *Eighth Census of the United States: 1860*, table 5 for each State, pp. 10–589, various pages, and pp. 616–619; 1870, Ninth Census Reports, vol. I, pp. 327–335; 1880, Tenth Census Reports, *Population*, pp. 484–491; 1890, Eleventh Census Reports, *Population*, part 1, pp. 564–567 and 576–579; 1900, Twelfth Census Reports, *Population*, vol. I, part 1, pp. 686–693 and 702–705; 1910, Thirteenth Census Reports, *Population*, vol. I, pp. 730–744; 1920, Fourteenth Census Reports, *Population*, vol. II, pp. 626–

640; 1930, Fifteenth Census Reports, *Population*, vol. II, pp. 153–167; 1940, Sixteenth Census Reports, *State of Birth of the Native Population*, pp. 20–39; 1950, *U. S. Census of Population: 1950*, vol. IV, Special Reports, *State of Birth*, pp. 4A-24 to 4A-43.

In 1860, persons who were born in territories and who were then residing in territories were assumed to be residing in the territory of their birth.

See general note for definition of color and nativity; see also text for series A 95–122 for definitions of division and region.

C 15–24. Native population born in each division, by division of residence, by color, 1850–1950.

Source: See source for series C 1–14.

See also general note for definition of color and nativity.

C 25–73. Estimated net intercensal migration of total, native white, foreign-born white, and Negro population surviving from the preceding census date, by States, 1870–1950.

Source: Everett S. Lee, Ann Ratner Miller, Carol P. Brainerd, and Richard A. Easterlin, *Population Redistribution and Economic Growth: United States, 1870–1950*, vol. I, Philadelphia, the American Philosophical Society, 1957, pp. 107–231.

See general note for definition of color and nativity.

The estimates of net migration were obtained by a residual method, using survival ratios derived from census data. The loss through mortality during an intercensal period was estimated on the basis of the ratios of appropriate age groups as enumerated in successive decennial censuses. The difference between the enumerated population at the end of the decennial period and the estimated survivors from the beginning to the end of the period was assumed to be net migration. Computations were by age groups for each sex, the figures presented in series C 25–73 being summations for ages 10 years and over at the end of each intercensal period. For the native population, the figures show the estimated amount of net internal migration. For the foreign born, the figures represent the estimated net change attributable to direct movement into the State from abroad and the net gain or loss in the exchange of foreign-born residents with other States.

C 74–79. Estimated annual movement of the farm population, 1920–1957.

Source: 1920–1954, Agricultural Marketing Service, *Farm Population, Migration to and From Farms, 1920–1954*, AMS-10, 1954; 1955–1957, *Farm Population, Estimated for (specific years)*, AMS-80, 1955, 1956, and 1957.

Estimates of the total farm population and of the annual changes in its components utilize data from the censuses of population and agriculture and the Current Population Survey conducted by the Bureau of the Census in addition to data from a questionnaire mailed by the Department of Agriculture to lists of crop reporters. Estimates of the components of change are derived from information supplied by the crop reporters and adjusted for internal consistency with available birth and death figures and data on movements in and out of the Armed Forces. For a history of the procedures used and the successive revisions of the series, see Department of Agriculture, *Major Statistical Series of the U. S. Department of Agriculture,* vol. 7, Agricultural Handbook No. 118, 1957.

Farm population figures relate to the civilian population living on farms, regardless of occupation or source of income. The determination of whether a household is located on a farm has been made largely by the residents themselves. If the respondent in reply to the inquiry, "Is this house on a farm (or ranch)?" answers affirmatively, it is, in most cases, classified as a farm dwelling unit and the occupants as part of the farm population. Excluded are the following: Persons living on farmland who rent for cash a home and yard only; persons in summer camps, motels, and tourist camps; and persons in institutions on farmland.

C 80–87. Mobility status and type of mobility of the civilian population one year old and over, 1947–1957.

Source: Bureau of the Census, *Current Population Reports,* Series P–20, No. 82.

The civilian population was classified by mobility status on the basis of a comparison between the place of residence of each individual on the survey date and the place of residence one year earlier. Persons classified as movers include all those whose place of residence in the United States was different at the end of the period and at the beginning of the period.

For similar information for earlier years, see Donald J. Bogue, Henry S. Shryock, Jr., and Siegried A. Hoermann, "Subregional Migration in the United States, 1935–40," vol. 1, *Streams of Migration Between Subregions,* Miami, Ohio, Scripps Foundation Studies in Population Distribution, No. 5, 1957.

Series C 1–14. Native Population, by Residence Within or Outside State, Division, and Region of Birth, by Color: 1850 to 1950

Color [1] and year	Native population	Born in State of residence		Born in other States				Born in outlying areas	Born abroad or at sea	State of birth not reported	Born in division of residence		Born in region of residence	
				Contiguous to State of residence		Noncontiguous to State of residence								
		Number	Percent	Number	Percent	Number	Percent				Number	Percent	Number	Percent
	1	2	3	4	5	6	7	8	9	10	11	12	13	14
TOTAL														
1950 [2]	139,868,715	102,788,385	73.5	14,589,035	10.4	20,695,185	14.8	329,970	96,355	1,369,785	113,477,915	81.1	119,490,510	85.4
1940	120,074,379	92,609,754	77.1	12,588,482	10.5	14,322,504	11.9	156,956	122,169	279,514	101,694,396	84.7	106,734,907	88.9
1930	108,570,897	82,677,619	76.2	12,200,290	11.2	13,187,810	12.1	136,032	130,677	238,469	91,382,402	84.2	96,447,180	88.8
1920	91,789,928	71,071,013	77.4	9,741,781	10.6	10,532,669	11.5	38,020	92,863	313,582	77,906,515	84.9	82,308,490	89.7
1910	78,456,380	61,185,305	78.0	7,959,860	10.1	7,959,860	11.4	7,365	67,911	285,685	66,746,379	85.1	70,864,304	90.3
1900	65,653,299	51,901,722	79.0	6,308,975	9.6	7,192,070	11.0	2,923	67,151	180,458	56,248,496	85.7	60,025,002	91.4
1890 [3]	53,372,703	41,872,656	78.5	4,628,768	8.7	6,464,295	12.1	322	10,010	396,652	45,022,600	84.4	48,398,175	90.7
1880	43,475,840	33,882,734	77.9	4,083,004	9.4	5,509,760	12.7	51	291	---------	36,582,390	84.1	39,530,266	90.9
1870	32,991,142	25,321,340	76.8	3,182,563	9.6	4,474,757	13.6	51	169	12,262	27,363,803	82.9	29,634,393	89.8
WHITE														
1950 [2]	124,382,950	91,984,035	74.0	13,195,215	10.6	17,629,445	14.2	289,435	88,065	1,196,755	101,491,050	81.6	107,061,705	86.1
1940	106,795,732	82,533,805	77.3	11,298,723	10.6	12,492,817	11.7	99,170	117,933	253,284	90,586,586	84.8	95,225,370	89.2
1930 [1]	95,497,800	72,821,481	76.2	10,824,966	11.3	11,452,788	12.0	71,582	125,060	201,923	80,492,581	84.3	85,075,201	89.1
1920	81,108,161	62,524,789	77.1	8,675,416	10.7	9,521,420	11.7	26,476	88,838	271,222	68,601,740	84.6	72,563,235	89.5
1910	68,386,412	52,806,091	77.2	7,018,331	10.3	8,245,872	12.0	6,413	64,356	245,349	57,703,559	84.4	61,361,087	89.7
1900	56,595,379	44,278,021	78.2	5,534,957	9.8	6,562,833	11.6	2,563	63,366	153,639	48,102,508	85.0	51,407,811	90.8
1890 [3]	45,862,023	35,524,287	77.5	4,064,121	8.9	5,926,722	12.9	279	9,543	337,071	38,315,138	83.5	41,227,682	89.9
1880	36,843,291	28,310,081	76.8	3,576,340	9.7	4,956,596	13.5	50	224	---------	30,681,197	83.3	33,126,949	89.9
1870	28,095,665	21,355,242	76.0	2,779,526	9.9	3,951,487	14.1	38	160	9,212	23,130,521	82.3	24,914,093	88.7
1860 [4]	23,353,385	17,527,069	75.1	2,529,494	10.8	3,242,190	13.9	---------	2,618	52,014	18,969,880	81.2	20,481,089	87.7
1850 [4]	17,772,270	13,624,902	76.7	2,105,724	11.9	2,006,033	11.3	---------		35,611	14,707,719	82.8	15,765,010	88.7
NONWHITE														
1950 [2]	15,485,765	10,804,350	69.8	1,393,820	9.0	3,065,740	19.8	40,535	8,290	173,030	11,986,865	77.4	12,428,805	80.3
1940	13,278,647	10,075,949	75.9	1,284,759	9.7	1,829,687	13.8	57,786	4,236	26,230	11,107,810	83.7	11,509,537	86.7
1930 [1]	13,073,097	9,856,138	75.4	1,375,324	10.5	1,735,022	13.3	64,450	5,617	36,546	10,889,821	83.3	11,371,979	87.0
1920	10,681,767	8,546,224	80.0	1,066,365	10.0	1,011,249	9.5	11,544	4,025	42,360	9,304,775	87.1	9,745,255	91.2
1910	10,069,968	8,379,214	83.2	941,529	9.3	704,382	7.0	952	3,555	40,336	9,042,820	89.8	9,503,217	94.4
1900	9,057,920	7,623,701	84.2	774,018	8.5	629,237	6.9	360	3,785	26,819	8,145,988	89.9	8,617,191	95.1
1890 [3]	7,510,680	6,348,369	84.5	564,647	7.5	537,573	7.2	43	467	59,581	6,707,462	89.3	7,170,493	95.5
1880	6,632,549	5,572,653	84.0	506,664	7.6	553,164	8.3	1	67	---------	5,901,193	89.0	6,403,317	96.5
1870	4,895,477	3,966,098	81.0	403,037	8.2	523,270	10.7	13	9	3,050	4,233,282	86.5	4,720,300	96.4

[1] Mexicans classified as nonwhite in 1930, as white in other censuses.
[2] Based on 20-percent sample of persons enumerated.
[3] Excludes population of Indian Territory and Indian reservations, specially enumer-ated in 1890, with a native population of 117,368 white, and 208,083 nonwhite, not distributed by State of birth.
[4] Free colored included with white.

Series C 15–24. Native Population Born in Each Division, by Division of Residence, by Color: 1850 to 1950

[Excludes persons born outside continental U. S. and persons for whom State of birth was not reported]

Color, [1] census year, and division of birth	Total	Division of residence								
		New England	Middle Atlantic	East North Central	West North Central	South Atlantic	East South Central	West South Central	Mountain	Pacific
	15	16	17	18	19	20	21	22	23	24
WHITE										
1950 [2]	122,808,695	7,765,220	23,667,205	26,038,680	12,848,660	15,490,860	8,652,720	11,564,885	4,543,490	12,236,975
New England	8,123,805	7,040,420	445,570	130,600	31,000	185,885	16,245	35,245	30,575	208,265
Middle Atlantic	25,133,815	456,510	21,967,895	883,575	119,430	800,850	61,425	124,225	113,220	606,685
East North Central	26,253,590	90,555	434,780	22,344,070	801,785	498,185	208,910	292,995	314,300	1,268,010
West North Central	15,804,720	40,080	142,145	925,255	11,186,855	180,270	66,485	532,565	697,650	2,033,415
South Atlantic	14,808,615	66,925	434,560	461,355	70,370	12,976,715	326,755	174,420	63,965	233,550
East South Central	10,389,290	19,555	82,350	908,915	132,160	613,630	7,795,585	523,035	75,205	238,855
West South Central	12,022,265	18,830	69,435	223,550	314,375	141,435	150,350	9,699,470	357,420	1,047,400
Mountain	3,945,625	11,210	34,890	79,265	109,840	36,690	10,845	98,400	2,721,865	842,620
Pacific	6,326,970	21,135	55,580	82,095	82,845	57,200	16,120	84,530	169,290	5,758,175
1940	106,325,345	6,788,754	21,562,277	22,892,971	12,296,354	12,766,703	7,936,741	10,255,758	3,698,071	8,127,716
New England	7,091,608	6,292,313	410,907	101,637	25,600	91,015	6,952	12,776	16,803	133,605
Middle Atlantic	22,321,593	340,901	20,113,804	765,363	123,075	440,461	30,373	64,963	66,229	376,424
East North Central	23,255,752	62,294	393,318	20,031,073	896,605	301,011	155,711	238,290	242,314	935,136
West North Central	14,401,132	25,609	120,901	818,929	10,705,594	102,722	45,398	516,685	633,440	1,431,854
South Atlantic	12,601,815	35,011	360,021	314,513	54,368	11,290,451	246,371	135,018	39,439	126,623
East South Central	9,333,222	9,258	59,151	616,381	133,904	432,330	7,336,524	531,150	59,299	155,225
West South Central	10,085,283	7,189	43,268	142,119	237,853	69,671	105,050	8,669,708	270,484	539,941
Mountain	3,089,040	6,431	26,562	59,659	85,530	18,445	5,519	61,359	2,271,873	553,662
Pacific	4,145,900	9,748	34,345	43,297	33,825	20,597	4,843	25,809	98,190	3,875,246

[1] Mexicans classified as nonwhite in 1930, as white in other censuses.
[2] Based on 20-percent sample of persons enumerated.

Series C 15–24. Native Population Born in Each Division, by Division of Residence, by Color: 1850 to 1950—Con.

Color,[1] census year, and division of birth	Total	Division of residence								
		New England	Middle Atlantic	East North Central	West North Central	South Atlantic	East South Central	West South Central	Mountain	Pacific
	15	16	17	18	19	20	21	22	23	24
WHITE—Con.										
1930	95,099,235	6,204,011	19,780,421	20,990,462	11,778,688	11,025,521	7,158,480	8,906,478	2,999,731	6,255,443
New England	6,535,693	5,752,888	392,102	114,311	36,849	65,025	6,084	12,825	19,829	135,780
Middle Atlantic	20,610,693	321,693	18,427,461	834,310	179,234	314,394	27,532	69,246	78,751	358,072
East North Central	21,523,034	53,302	362,359	18,167,867	1,102,154	229,645	151,942	278,633	275,415	901,717
West North Central	13,113,754	21,386	106,542	760,889	9,918,618	68,103	39,461	558,788	562,360	1,077,607
South Atlantic	11,319,720	29,326	353,731	322,548	72,008	9,955,907	271,607	166,797	42,096	105,700
East South Central	8,531,783	7,315	52,209	596,959	153,991	326,357	6,563,867	635,683	61,895	133,507
West South Central	8,039,544	5,401	34,716	101,431	202,164	44,638	90,120	7,117,591	179,510	263,973
Mountain	2,317,079	5,090	22,734	53,880	82,608	10,884	4,219	47,331	1,699,814	390,519
Pacific	3,107,935	7,610	28,567	38,267	31,062	10,568	3,648	19,584	80,061	2,888,568
1920	80,721,625	5,420,554	16,651,261	17,641,695	10,798,750	9,311,926	6,286,445	7,615,242	2,730,830	4,264,922
New England	5,613,387	5,003,487	251,361	103,025	53,349	49,436	5,803	13,680	25,804	107,442
Middle Atlantic	17,754,221	305,384	15,714,467	746,504	252,354	264,186	27,434	74,672	99,028	270,192
East North Central	18,836,603	48,079	273,633	15,606,106	1,292,533	179,169	136,431	306,576	319,171	674,905
West North Central	11,077,968	17,259	72,434	462,835	8,699,489	50,549	32,428	534,721	529,090	679,163
South Atlantic	9,605,593	24,111	246,672	232,580	90,706	8,487,281	222,844	180,365	45,179	75,855
East South Central	7,445,580	5,815	36,076	377,338	179,126	234,259	5,791,383	663,654	63,268	94,661
West South Central	6,358,200	4,562	21,272	53,305	141,216	30,900	64,080	5,791,839	133,956	117,070
Mountain	1,785,103	4,997	15,165	32,948	62,656	7,714	3,300	34,621	1,442,878	180,824
Pacific	2,244,970	6,860	20,181	27,054	27,321	8,432	2,742	15,114	72,456	2,064,810
1910	68,070,294	4,641,157	14,003,037	14,791,593	9,682,750	7,765,765	5,657,676	6,344,580	2,063,208	3,120,528
New England	4,867,376	4,305,759	215,838	97,016	73,131	28,394	5,221	11,024	30,999	99,994
Middle Atlantic	15,123,715	247,999	13,264,960	652,982	337,132	191,251	26,602	60,485	110,309	231,995
East North Central	16,287,667	37,814	211,088	13,239,961	1,411,304	111,408	129,227	309,955	291,913	544,997
West North Central	9,210,184	13,453	48,916	323,844	7,410,156	22,494	26,257	484,944	378,359	501,761
South Atlantic	8,273,219	19,347	201,618	167,764	109,371	7,244,553	220,304	204,527	42,174	63,561
East South Central	6,631,841	4,461	24,205	250,933	196,661	145,352	5,198,232	686,321	52,956	72,720
West South Central	4,909,800	3,879	13,329	27,218	91,459	15,183	48,275	4,563,489	84,119	62,849
Mountain	1,206,525	3,876	11,416	17,638	36,206	3,417	2,055	15,963	1,024,876	91,078
Pacific	1,559,967	4,569	11,667	14,237	17,330	3,713	1,503	7,872	47,503	1,451,573
1900	56,375,811	4,063,335	11,764,269	13,037,883	8,501,171	6,487,097	4,947,654	4,494,019	1,281,152	1,799,231
New England	4,304,088	3,782,347	175,529	117,475	95,473	21,464	4,972	7,981	27,658	71,189
Middle Atlantic	12,994,778	213,818	11,203,366	725,710	410,130	152,668	24,477	39,005	88,623	136,981
East North Central	13,990,407	31,065	162,945	11,539,206	1,424,563	83,300	119,482	192,025	180,312	257,557
West North Central	7,211,362	11,316	33,376	267,723	6,142,945	15,230	22,391	305,129	190,402	222,850
South Atlantic	7,028,299	14,206	152,680	154,152	125,802	6,105,309	221,912	197,884	24,638	31,716
East South Central	5,696,181	3,111	16,105	195,986	209,595	95,892	4,515,686	597,479	26,407	35,920
West South Central	3,330,565	1,888	7,950	18,745	58,754	9,877	36,961	3,143,786	28,208	24,396
Mountain	765,078	1,716	4,543	9,280	21,396	1,446	823	6,401	685,356	34,117
Pacific	1,055,053	3,868	7,775	9,604	12,513	1,911	1,000	4,329	29,548	984,505
1890[3]	45,515,130	3,498,667	9,620,523	10,679,859	7,053,073	5,376,140	4,186,475	2,937,889	856,949	1,305,555
New England	3,869,022	3,308,754	157,962	141,909	126,561	21,469	5,802	7,058	28,966	70,541
Middle Atlantic	11,026,901	149,620	9,222,526	769,746	507,162	115,883	24,664	29,588	84,419	123,293
East North Central	11,459,737	18,588	95,477	9,280,356	1,464,505	57,949	94,521	112,084	138,062	198,195
West North Central	5,083,535	5,555	16,549	137,664	4,511,678	8,284	14,461	121,395	113,722	154,227
South Atlantic	5,988,960	9,927	107,554	159,824	151,969	5,101,959	232,107	177,366	20,095	28,159
East South Central	4,794,666	2,026	9,597	171,757	238,208	62,460	3,790,050	466,533	20,572	33,463
West South Central	2,138,369	1,275	5,167	11,125	36,260	6,446	23,981	2,019,570	15,988	18,607
Mountain	452,657	756	1,664	3,155	10,025	523	341	2,074	417,647	16,472
Pacific	701,283	2,166	4,027	4,323	6,705	1,167	598	2,221	17,478	662,598
1880	36,843,017	3,177,460	8,287,904	9,098,915	4,950,250	4,483,127	3,563,017	2,067,174	468,678	746,492
New England	3,614,346	3,031,308	176,366	178,124	123,105	17,545	4,886	6,645	21,169	55,198
Middle Atlantic	9,693,744	116,499	7,921,093	899,051	479,473	103,764	21,758	23,520	51,848	76,738
East North Central	9,062,808	12,806	73,777	7,521,118	1,126,361	42,533	67,865	69,347	62,709	86,292
West North Central	3,117,714	3,176	11,055	101,161	2,801,794	4,361	11,515	78,285	43,790	62,577
South Atlantic	5,169,015	8,618	90,530	192,311	149,700	4,256,663	272,498	168,103	12,170	18,422
East South Central	4,077,215	1,725	7,269	192,398	232,785	52,704	3,164,256	390,416	12,557	23,105
West South Central	1,410,432	1,016	4,219	9,494	28,023	4,633	19,693	1,328,521	5,920	8,913
Mountain	265,689	711	1,096	1,941	4,925	339	177	1,083	248,307	7,110
Pacific	432,054	1,601	2,499	3,317	4,084	585	369	1,254	10,208	408,137
1870	28,086,255	2,807,945	6,788,821	7,325,414	3,038,215	3,469,244	2,835,457	1,161,542	224,834	434,783
New England	3,270,626	2,704,882	180,779	212,928	97,087	14,708	5,552	4,418	9,181	41,091
Middle Atlantic	8,065,869	83,537	6,479,733	967,899	339,388	84,225	23,259	13,223	20,533	54,072
East North Central	6,550,805	8,463	48,589	5,625,542	704,106	19,407	48,469	24,898	20,631	50,705
West North Central	1,684,544	1,621	5,031	62,386	1,524,350	2,051	8,851	33,449	11,644	35,161
South Atlantic	4,206,178	6,497	65,515	230,689	138,450	3,308,462	313,905	123,369	5,032	14,259
East South Central	3,165,831	1,206	4,920	214,814	210,645	37,442	2,420,279	253,883	4,766	17,876
West South Central	765,053	730	2,651	7,885	20,005	2,591	14,865	707,821	1,487	7,018
Mountain	153,772	66	138	432	2,169	52	65	159	147,771	2,920
Pacific	223,577	943	1,465	2,839	2,015	306	212	327	3,789	211,681
1860[4]	23,298,753	2,663,062	5,898,979	5,715,955	1,702,245	3,358,465	2,538,909	984,856	150,116	286,166
New England	3,144,598	2,584,262	212,218	224,230	57,324	12,213	7,269	5,930	6,006	35,146
Middle Atlantic	6,944,042	64,518	5,582,854	946,080	184,972	68,452	24,020	15,661	10,348	47,137
East North Central	4,562,911	5,057	29,662	4,044,329	358,725	10,445	32,248	24,038	17,053	41,354
West North Central	848,692	652	1,965	27,496	756,018	915	5,842	23,459	7,188	25,157
South Atlantic	4,264,749	6,777	66,971	265,569	125,982	3,236,171	411,919	133,672	3,046	14,642
East South Central	2,781,432	797	3,061	202,798	210,990	28,932	2,048,662	263,132	4,306	18,754
West South Central	550,043	522	1,648	4,322	7,759	1,230	8,887	518,799	950	5,926
Mountain	100,739	(5)	(5)	(5)	(5)	(5)	(5)	(5)	100,739	(5)
Pacific	101,547	477	600	1,131	475	107	62	165	480	98,050

[1] Mexicans classified as nonwhite in 1930, as white in other censuses.
[3] Excludes population of Indian Territory and Indian reservations, specially enumerated in 1890, with a native population of 117,368 white and 208,083 nonwhite, not distributed by State of birth.
[4] Includes free colored.
[5] Not available.

Series C 15-24. Native Population Born in Each Division, by Division of Residence, by Color: 1850 to 1950—Con.

Color,[1] census year, and division of birth	Total	Division of residence								
		New England	Middle Atlantic	East North Central	West North Central	South Atlantic	East South Central	West South Central	Mountain	Pacific
	15	16	17	18	19	20	21	22	23	24
WHITE—Con.										
1850 [4]	17,736,659	2,423,178	4,884,300	3,965,269	695,231	2,907,947	2,207,677	503,295	68,484	81,278
New England	2,821,823	2,367,932	237,367	171,172	9,404	11,074	5,922	5,522	1,131	12,299
Middle Atlantic	5,483,951	46,635	4,566,495	725,056	39,123	55,210	19,778	12,656	2,286	16,712
East North Central	2,757,356	2,410	16,349	2,582,600	96,708	7,048	21,821	14,616	2,511	13,293
West North Central	373,500	181	568	12,794	334,662	495	2,951	11,619	1,341	8,889
South Atlantic	3,764,808	5,100	60,734	286,195	80,838	2,811,305	446,391	65,489	482	8,274
East South Central	2,179,505	507	1,840	184,634	131,053	21,951	1,705,017	123,282	823	10,398
West South Central	286,016	378	934	2,812	3,435	858	5,796	270,104	88	1,611
Mountain	59,802	(5)	(5)	(5)	(5)	(5)	(5)	(5)	59,802	(5)
Pacific	9,898	35	13	6	8	6	1	7	20	9,802
NONWHITE										
1950 [2]	15,263,910	136,825	1,771,205	1,799,890	469,245	5,068,460	2,687,045	2,473,610	214,980	642,650
New England	95,105	74,260	11,345	2,245	350	3,780	410	515	270	1,930
Middle Atlantic	884,085	6,990	798,465	20,225	1,675	41,660	3,180	3,280	1,175	7,435
East North Central	754,760	1,605	19,745	675,230	11,170	13,040	11,310	5,920	1,915	14,825
West North Central	362,865	790	6,165	45,560	268,130	3,660	3,420	7,830	5,980	21,330
South Atlantic	6,125,050	43,895	810,945	269,290	8,740	4,882,210	60,780	18,125	2,960	28,105
East South Central	3,634,040	5,730	91,980	604,445	89,670	104,760	2,569,950	108,770	6,020	52,715
West South Central	2,954,750	2,575	25,165	169,690	85,170	15,965	36,775	2,323,380	32,520	263,510
Mountain	183,680	145	1,425	2,520	2,150	1,015	355	1,800	158,355	15,915
Pacific	269,575	835	5,970	10,685	2,190	2,370	865	3,990	5,785	236,885
1940	13,190,395	95,035	1,208,567	1,084,123	401,916	4,706,493	2,779,679	2,489,075	163,606	261,901
New England	72,448	58,883	9,094	1,190	142	2,143	228	150	58	560
Middle Atlantic	571,445	4,352	526,569	12,397	945	22,910	1,084	779	324	2,085
East North Central	469,788	762	13,421	420,714	9,676	8,114	7,444	3,391	1,111	5,155
West North Central	304,282	275	3,971	31,247	240,766	1,918	2,635	8,471	4,933	10,066
South Atlantic	5,484,716	27,275	585,734	188,711	8,733	4,579,081	62,448	19,370	1,753	11,611
East South Central	3,359,873	2,016	50,942	340,816	74,444	82,512	2,664,877	125,376	4,036	14,854
West South Central	2,615,711	735	13,731	85,882	64,924	8,126	40,421	2,329,478	17,136	55,278
Mountain	144,576	69	793	1,357	1,610	596	240	1,151	131,955	6,805
Pacific	167,556	668	4,312	1,809	676	1,093	302	909	2,300	155,487
1930	12,966,484	85,473	980,056	957,610	394,534	4,421,188	2,655,398	2,797,906	298,651	375,668
New England	60,784	47,909	8,543	1,308	191	1,964	152	166	83	468
Middle Atlantic	405,404	4,380	365,212	12,886	1,046	17,792	1,109	917	405	1,657
East North Central	355,312	617	11,840	307,789	10,799	6,950	7,522	4,144	1,366	4,285
West North Central	295,827	243	3,229	33,085	229,087	1,531	2,675	11,592	5,841	8,544
South Atlantic	5,215,766	29,024	531,014	197,586	11,337	4,316,289	85,900	31,498	2,444	10,674
East South Central	3,197,521	1,779	45,220	321,450	74,933	68,994	2,515,818	153,257	4,486	11,584
West South Central	2,855,954	574	11,050	79,125	62,438	6,528	41,697	2,588,627	20,299	45,616
Mountain	303,676	73	783	2,162	3,782	368	219	5,937	258,301	32,051
Pacific	276,240	874	3,165	2,219	921	772	306	1,768	5,426	260,789
1920	10,623,838	68,704	562,963	522,270	311,204	4,315,975	2,516,980	2,110,266	105,563	109,913
New England	46,726	36,756	5,356	1,023	292	2,051	343	453	152	300
Middle Atlantic	265,307	4,315	235,108	8,594	1,178	13,020	733	705	689	965
East North Central	225,537	501	6,458	190,121	10,630	4,709	5,336	3,390	1,686	2,706
West North Central	242,757	220	2,089	20,419	194,448	2,093	2,721	10,710	5,407	4,650
South Atlantic	4,771,502	24,251	280,607	86,850	12,137	4,231,573	76,086	47,528	5,097	7,373
East South Central	2,923,262	1,423	25,506	190,571	58,241	56,648	2,399,065	178,676	6,134	6,998
West South Central	1,981,385	371	5,096	22,118	31,599	4,588	32,076	1,867,040	6,868	11,629
Mountain	85,376	85	593	840	2,020	472	331	951	77,728	2,356
Pacific	81,986	782	2,150	1,734	659	821	289	813	1,802	72,936
1910	10,025,125	60,931	407,348	311,737	278,717	4,103,893	2,646,426	2,048,401	95,408	72,264
New England	39,839	32,693	3,944	598	265	1,414	185	344	133	263
Middle Atlantic	219,137	4,018	196,486	5,117	1,178	9,186	966	989	415	782
East North Central	192,088	405	4,471	162,724	9,180	3,160	5,131	3,718	1,397	1,902
West North Central	238,996	211	1,294	13,386	198,839	1,138	3,076	12,660	5,225	3,167
South Atlantic	4,497,605	21,394	191,612	35,299	12,656	4,048,161	108,763	71,118	2,700	5,902
East South Central	2,849,182	967	5,787	88,363	40,006	37,547	2,494,110	173,531	4,361	4,510
West South Central	1,848,608	285	1,448	5,011	14,034	2,203	33,650	1,783,963	3,363	4,651
Mountain	82,771	64	581	281	2,145	462	320	1,415	76,130	1,373
Pacific	56,899	894	1,725	958	414	622	225	663	1,684	49,714
1900	9,026,956	56,174	325,698	267,124	276,104	3,723,920	2,496,880	1,750,800	80,317	49,939
New England	34,186	28,948	2,803	625	206	1,002	136	186	120	160
Middle Atlantic	183,339	3,999	166,691	4,070	947	5,640	520	676	332	464
East North Central	170,049	346	3,494	148,199	7,232	2,002	4,267	2,805	978	726
West North Central	237,297	122	752	10,828	203,858	507	3,032	12,603	4,182	1,413
South Atlantic	4,133,276	21,417	145,557	30,787	14,038	3,684,080	134,831	96,632	2,772	3,162
East South Central	2,628,985	633	4,066	68,777	38,282	28,514	2,327,272	156,214	3,327	1,900
West South Central	1,524,820	241	1,052	3,405	8,624	1,790	26,633	1,480,511	1,317	1,247
Mountain	70,780	27	335	152	2,741	77	70	868	66,036	474
Pacific	44,224	441	948	281	176	308	119	305	1,253	40,393
1890 [3]	7,450,589	42,248	219,834	210,343	225,426	3,249,541	2,105,538	1,342,049	26,286	29,324
New England	28,981	24,677	2,201	468	216	736	142	242	102	197
Middle Atlantic	150,505	3,438	136,516	3,555	1,051	3,738	605	665	389	548
East North Central	136,704	142	1,483	121,167	6,422	1,292	2,752	2,027	915	504
West North Central	178,589	56	569	6,448	157,506	372	2,765	7,100	2,741	1,032
South Atlantic	3,627,912	13,252	76,277	27,938	15,723	3,223,865	148,595	116,874	2,700	2,688
East South Central	2,183,937	322	1,639	48,570	37,189	18,188	1,932,764	141,602	2,365	1,359
West South Central	1,103,866	274	663	2,059	7,086	1,100	17,493	1,073,379	790	1,022
Mountain	17,177	11	284	47	225	29	364	85	15,873	259
Pacific	22,918	76	202	91	69	221	58	75	411	21,715

[1] Mexicans classified as nonwhite in 1930, as white in other censuses.
[2] Based on 20-percent sample of persons enumerated.
[3] Excludes the population of Indian Territory and Indian reservations, specially enumerated in 1890, with a native population of 117,368 white and 208,083 nonwhite, not distributed by State of birth.
[4] Includes free colored.
[5] Not available.

Series C 15–24. Native Population Born in Each Division, by Division of Residence, by Color: 1850 to 1950—Con.

Color,[1] census year, and division of birth	Total	Division of residence								
		New England	Middle Atlantic	East North Central	West North Central	South Atlantic	East South Central	West South Central	Mountain	Pacific
	15	16	17	18	19	20	21	22	23	24
NONWHITE—Con.										
1880	6,632,481	39,430	188,000	191,082	206,963	2,939,779	1,926,935	1,087,916	23,548	28,828
New England	29,078	25,077	1,843	466	210	648	235	399	41	159
Middle Atlantic	149,988	3,309	136,808	3,445	900	3,061	995	895	155	420
East North Central	116,353	150	739	105,676	3,728	1,236	2,753	1,641	233	197
West North Central	159,284	29	147	6,194	141,665	180	2,981	6,742	1,005	341
South Atlantic	3,340,699	10,369	46,950	30,110	16,439	2,917,316	197,100	120,570	729	1,116
East South Central	1,942,781	288	963	43,205	35,325	16,183	1,708,900	136,846	657	414
West South Central	847,230	167	419	1,902	8,583	1,073	13,918	820,685	220	263
Mountain	19,932	24	80	52	78	37	19	100	19,345	197
Pacific	27,136	17	51	32	35	45	34	38	1,163	25,721
1870	4,892,405	30,847	146,581	134,896	145,086	2,216,892	1,463,794	738,385	3,456	12,468
New England	22,477	19,514	1,426	405	135	345	155	236	43	218
Middle Atlantic	120,810	2,904	110,845	2,941	664	1,786	444	611	113	502
East North Central	67,523	100	430	62,667	2,220	375	857	718	69	87
West North Central	117,168	31	78	4,817	101,335	159	3,096	7,011	296	345
South Atlantic	2,622,615	7,873	32,620	27,869	15,027	2,201,827	210,996	124,766	384	1,253
East South Central	1,426,109	244	828	34,648	21,324	11,437	1,238,885	118,026	295	422
West South Central	504,139	167	328	1,512	4,306	940	9,345	486,997	352	192
Mountain	1,952	2	3	9	59	4	3	9	1,813	50
Pacific	9,612	12	23	28	16	19	13	11	91	9,399

[1] Mexicans classified as nonwhite in 1930, as white in other censuses.

Series C 25–73. Estimated Net Intercensal Migration of Total, Native White, Foreign-Born White, and Negro Population Surviving From the Preceding Census Date, by States: 1870 to 1950

[In thousands]

Series No.	State	1940 to 1950	1930 to 1940	1920 to 1930	1910 to 1920	1900 to 1910	1890 to 1900	1880 to 1890	1870 to 1880
	TOTAL POPULATION [1]								
	New England:								
25	Maine	−35.8	−1.2	−39.3	−8.3	10.6	4.1	−15.9	−33.3
26	New Hampshire	−9.1	9.1	−10.2	−3.6	3.2	20.4	20.7	10.1
27	Vermont	−23.8	−18.7	−20.6	−17.6	−3.7	−2.4	−13.3	−26.2
28	Massachusetts	−29.5	−69.5	22.1	192.2	307.3	334.9	295.7	140.2
29	Rhode Island	2.7	−2.3	11.4	12.8	66.1	45.9	42.5	27.9
30	Connecticut	89.5	39.2	64.1	122.1	112.7	90.8	72.9	22.4
	Middle Atlantic:								
31	New York	83.8	396.3	1,062.1	467.4	1,061.0	604.8	395.4	61.7
32	New Jersey	200.7	−28.2	442.3	278.2	376.1	218.3	151.3	48.4
33	Pennsylvania	−447.2	−301.0	−252.9	51.9	444.6	262.0	285.1	19.1
	East North Central:								
34	Ohio	151.6	−56.6	214.7	499.4	207.7	77.7	41.9	−12.9
35	Indiana	56.7	10.6	−0.9	16.0	−54.4	33.4	−86.7	−70.2
36	Illinois	−22.1	−60.8	414.0	255.6	223.0	340.0	170.3	−59.0
37	Michigan	251.4	17.1	549.6	465.2	117.2	62.0	172.3	161.4
38	Wisconsin	−95.1	−10.9	−17.9	37.6	9.2	84.3	100.8	9.0
	West South Central:								
39	Minnesota	−160.9	36.0	−106.2	59.1	72.6	148.4	264.1	156.2
40	Iowa	−178.8	−73.4	−167.2	−18.3	−207.5	21.7	−5.6	85.1
41	Missouri	−168.6	−20.8	−98.7	−134.7	−163.8	−17.2	56.4	−30.4
42	North Dakota	−109.4	−105.8	−76.3	−46.0	137.3	63.8	⎫ 243.4	86.8
43	South Dakota	−71.2	−101.4	−45.0	−31.2	86.9	0.3	⎭	
44	Nebraska	−123.0	−139.5	−78.1	−34.5	−28.8	−153.9	362.5	204.4
45	Kansas	−86.8	−163.8	−83.1	−74.5	20.0	−149.8	159.7	366.8
	South Atlantic:								
46	Delaware	14.5	16.0	−3.5	5.1	2.7	−1.2	4.3	−2.3
47	Maryland	213.3	87.0	10.2	43.1	−8.3	8.2	−10.7	−11.2
48	District of Columbia	78.5	157.8	27.3	97.0	41.0	34.3	36.1	18.1
49	Virginia	152.0	0.2	−231.6	−27.7	−73.7	−91.5	−80.9	−51.1
50	West Virginia	−210.8	−73.6	−53.8	−1.7	46.1	17.2	−4.8	24.0
51	North Carolina	−202.8	−85.4	−7.9	−74.3	−80.4	−88.8	−57.7	−14.4
52	South Carolina	−172.4	−102.5	−256.9	−80.9	−80.6	−75.5	−35.9	25.7
53	Georgia	−224.3	−134.1	−414.9	−98.1	−41.7	−56.1	−19.5	−40.0
54	Florida	510.9	280.3	297.6	101.6	103.5	36.9	51.1	12.1
	East South Central:								
55	Kentucky	−319.2	−93.5	−206.1	−167.1	−177.8	−65.1	−96.8	−47.2
56	Tennessee	−102.8	−14.9	−113.8	−131.2	−156.9	−95.4	−77.7	−91.8
57	Alabama	−271.0	−165.3	−149.2	−113.9	−47.8	−40.4	−11.5	−60.7
58	Mississippi	−349.9	−90.3	−101.6	−199.3	−46.4	−44.5	−60.6	−5.6

[1] For 1870–1890, only white population for the 11 Western States; no estimates made for Negroes.

Series C 25–73. Estimated Net Intercensal Migration of Total, Native White, Foreign-Born White, and Negro Population Surviving From the Preceding Census Date, by States: 1870 to 1950—Con.

[In thousands]

Series No.	State	1940 to 1950	1930 to 1940	1920 to 1930	1910 to 1920	1900 to 1910	1890 to 1900	1880 to 1890	1870 to 1880
	TOTAL POPULATION [1]—Con.								
	West South Central:								
59	Arkansas	−320.4	−128.8	−191.3	−74.7	−27.2	−82.8	75.1	84.0
60	Louisiana	−112.1	5.7	−23.2	−64.7	10.6	1.4	−3.0	−12.0
61	Oklahoma	−356.1	−269.4	−51.8	62.4	491.5	501.3	44.5	(²)
62	Texas	132.9	−72.8	243.5	114.3	131.1	147.7	151.2	308.5
	Mountain:								
63	Montana	−42.2	−19.3	−72.9	90.1	86.5	63.5	70.6	12.1
64	Idaho	−29.6	20.5	−50.6	37.3	104.1	39.8	34.2	11.7
65	Wyoming	−4.6	−0.1	−1.2	20.7	33.3	15.6	28.7	7.2
66	Colorado	32.4	1.0	−16.6	39.8	159.8	51.9	146.8	119.1
67	New Mexico	9.8	18.6	−22.9	−20.2	63.1	1.2	6.4	−3.3
68	Arizona	117.4	−3.5	23.5	75.4	50.7	21.4	10.9	19.8
69	Utah	6.4	−30.5	−30.8	−0.2	24.9	8.9	17.9	16.7
70	Nevada	28.8	12.5	6.9	−6.4	32.9	−5.1	−15.6	6.6
	Pacific:								
71	Washington	351.3	109.2	81.6	97.5	464.7	80.4	205.4	28.7
72	Oregon	244.0	94.1	96.5	56.0	189.9	43.0	85.9	39.0
73	California	2,399.1	974.6	1,695.2	804.1	694.1	172.7	214.2	129.6
	NATIVE WHITE POPULATION								
	New England:								
25	Maine	−41.6	−2.2	−46.6	−22.7	−18.4	−20.6	−40.8	−46.5
26	New Hampshire	−12.6	8.3	−14.4	−12.8	−15.7	−2.5	−7.1	−7.1
27	Vermont	−25.8	−14.6	−25.2	−19.7	−17.2	−10.9	−21.9	−24.7
28	Massachusetts	−73.8	−45.6	−101.7	−6.0	−23.3	46.9	31.9	13.5
29	Rhode Island	−0.2	0.8	−8.7	−10.5	5.1	3.3	2.4	4.1
30	Connecticut	49.0	30.2	6.4	18.7	−10.9	5.4	2.8	−6.5
	Middle Atlantic:								
31	New York	−270.8	140.3	138.1	−76.5	−74.9	−18.6	−146.4	−167.4
32	New Jersey	88.6	−18.8	179.3	72.0	71.4	46.3	9.4	−8.9
33	Pennsylvania	−531.3	−260.9	−380.2	−199.4	−178.1	−60.2	−70.0	−105.2
	East North Central:								
34	Ohio	28.5	−58.6	58.2	233.4	−40.4	−29.6	−96.7	−92.8
35	Indiana	15.0	7.1	−43.3	−33.1	−111.9	−7.6	−120.4	−101.2
36	Illinois	−202.9	−58.7	80.3	−36.2	−198.9	44.0	−170.7	−192.5
37	Michigan	51.7	18.1	239.9	181.5	−35.9	−26.8	−19.7	25.8
38	Wisconsin	−110.3	−10.0	−53.2	−37.3	−103.3	−25.7	−75.6	−78.8
	West North Central:								
39	Minnesota	−163.1	27.1	−113.6	−1.2	−61.4	25.9	37.2	38.2
40	Iowa	−180.9	−70.5	−164.0	−45.9	−249.1	−29.9	−108.2	2.7
41	Missouri	−197.4	−36.8	−141.4	−173.7	−228.1	−50.0	2.4	−43.2
42	North Dakota	−103.6	−99.1	−72.8	−46.3	81.8	20.4	} 126.0	43.5
43	South Dakota	−71.3	−96.8	−46.1	−33.7	59.6	−26.5		
44	Nebraska	−125.9	−135.5	−81.1	−53.2	−62.4	−159.2	244.3	139.2
45	Kansas	−90.1	−156.2	−84.6	−86.9	−18.2	−156.6	106.3	290.1
	South Atlantic:								
46	Delaware	11.2	12.8	−3.8	0.3	−3.0	−3.7	−1.1	−2.6
47	Maryland	167.6	72.2	−4.5	16.8	−26.9	−5.8	−29.4	−16.1
48	District of Columbia	6.7	101.2	5.5	69.3	22.2	20.1	18.1	8.6
49	Virginia	169.1	33.7	−111.7	−9.5	−35.6	−25.8	−33.6	−16.5
50	West Virginia	−193.0	−66.7	−62.7	−29.3	−6.2	3.5	−12.3	18.1
51	North Carolina	−81.6	−27.1	5.2	−47.7	−54.4	−41.7	−19.8	−7.6
52	South Carolina	−15.7	−8.7	−52.4	−8.0	−10.5	−10.8	−17.5	9.1
53	Georgia	−38.2	−44.2	−155.1	−27.4	−30.8	−31.4	−35.1	−20.8
54	Florida	438.7	208.4	221.1	84.5	46.6	10.1	24.8	7.3
	East South Central:								
55	Kentucky	−299.1	−83.8	−188.4	−153.1	−159.9	−58.9	−85.6	−39.6
56	Tennessee	−68.6	−24.4	−100.6	−103.2	−127.3	−76.7	−64.9	−67.0
57	Alabama	−108.6	−101.0	−69.7	−45.3	−32.8	−41.1	−12.1	−25.9
58	Mississippi	−94.3	−32.0	−33.8	−70.3	−19.0	−35.8	−47.7	−22.7
	West South Central:								
59	Arkansas	−207.1	−95.5	−144.4	−74.4	−55.2	−77.6	25.3	53.0
60	Louisiana	−4.7	15.3	2.9	−17.8	15.8	9.2	−12.2	−11.8
61	Oklahoma	−319.5	−253.4	−51.2	54.5	414.2	404.3	39.6	(²)
62	Texas	134.4	−1.7	197.5	−28.4	60.5	95.5	90.9	233.9
	Mountain:								
63	Montana	−41.9	−14.8	−66.9	75.4	51.0	37.1	39.8	8.2
64	Idaho	−30.7	20.8	−49.5	31.5	81.9	31.0	24.6	8.5
65	Wyoming	−5.6	2.2	−1.8	19.9	19.8	11.7	19.1	5.5
66	Colorado	21.1	7.4	−17.6	29.2	108.8	33.1	101.1	86.7
67	New Mexico	3.8	22.5	−17.2	−32.0	52.7	−2.3	2.7	−5.9
68	Arizona	97.6	12.4	31.8	39.9	25.7	15.1	7.2	11.7
69	Utah	1.0	−27.5	−31.5	−7.6	2.8	−2.5	2.7	0.6
70	Nevada	24.2	13.8	5.1	−6.1	21.5	−3.9	−10.0	0.8
	Pacific:								
71	Washington	303.9	100.3	49.2	51.9	311.4	54.0	133.2	20.8
72	Oregon	222.9	90.4	74.3	38.2	132.0	29.2	57.4	25.7
73	California	1,874.7	899.5	1,244.5	537.7	425.2	96.3	109.6	56.0
	FOREIGN-BORN WHITE POPULATION								
	New England:								
25	Maine	5.9	0.8	7.5	14.3	28.9	24.4	25.0	13.4
26	New Hampshire	3.3	1.0	4.0	9.2	18.9	22.7	27.9	17.1
27	Vermont	2.0	−4.0	4.7	3.0	12.7	8.6	8.6	−1.4
28	Massachusetts	33.6	−26.6	120.9	191.3	324.8	278.0	259.3	123.7
29	Rhode Island	1.7	−3.6	21.0	22.7	60.3	41.1	38.9	22.9
30	Connecticut	27.5	6.8	52.5	98.1	123.2	82.9	69.0	28.1

[1] For 1870–1890, only white population in the 11 Western States; no estimates made for Negroes.   [2] Not available.

Series C 25–73. Estimated Net Intercensal Migration of Total, Native White, Foreign-Born White, and Negro Population Surviving From the Preceding Census Date, by States: 1870 to 1950—Con.

[In thousands]

Series No.	State	1940 to 1950	1930 to 1940	1920 to 1930	1910 to 1920	1900 to 1910	1890 to 1900	1880 to 1890	1870 to 1880
	FOREIGN-BORN WHITE POPULATION—Con.								
	Middle Atlantic:								
31	New York	111.0	120.1	751.3	480.9	1,100.2	589.7	532.0	221.5
32	New Jersey	58.5	−18.9	196.0	181.6	286.2	154.2	133.5	54.4
33	Pennsylvania	−5.5	−60.4	25.6	168.7	589.8	282.9	334.3	115.6
	East North Central:								
34	Ohio	16.5	−18.8	65.8	196.5	232.5	102.1	133.4	77.3
35	Indiana	9.5	−5.0	19.3	28.8	53.4	32.9	29.9	24.3
36	Illinois	1.0	−51.5	214.4	222.0	398.3	273.4	332.6	124.8
37	Michigan	36.4	−29.0	223.6	245.1	151.1	88.3	193.2	134.0
38	Wisconsin	3.4	−1.9	30.9	72.7	112.0	107.0	176.3	86.5
	West North Central:								
39	Minnesota	−0.5	7.8	6.9	58.1	131.7	116.5	225.4	116.5
40	Iowa	1.1	−2.6	−1.3	23.7	39.4	50.1	102.1	80.2
41	Missouri	3.0	−3.3	6.7	11.8	63.3	32.8	58.1	17.2
42	North Dakota	−5.8	−6.6	−3.4	0.3	55.2	38.6	} 117.4	43.0
43	South Dakota	−0.2	−4.4	1.2	2.5	27.0	12.7		
44	Nebraska	−0.2	−4.6	8.0	13.4	32.0	7.7	110.9	64.1
45	Kansas	1.1	−7.5	−4.4	7.0	35.6	7.4	50.7	62.0
	South Atlantic:								
46	Delaware	0.8	0.8	−0.3	5.3	6.0	3.1	5.1	1.7
47	Maryland	15.7	4.1	9.7	19.4	30.0	20.6	26.2	12.4
48	District of Columbia	10.7	9.1	5.8	9.3	9.1	5.5	4.7	3.3
49	Virginia	13.4	3.4	−2.7	9.0	11.3	5.1	6.2	2.9
50	West Virginia	−1.1	−2.8	−3.9	12.1	37.0	8.0	4.0	3.8
51	North Carolina	6.1	1.6	2.7	2.2	2.3	1.5	0.6	1.1
52	South Carolina	2.3	0.6	−0.2	1.6	2.0	0.7	0.3	0.9
53	Georgia	5.1	0.5	0.2	4.0	5.4	2.5	3.3	1.1
54	Florida	65.0	22.0	22.4	13.9	16.2	3.4	10.5	3.4
	East South Central:								
55	Kentucky	2.7	−0.7	−1.0	2.7	4.4	6.0	11.2	5.5
56	Tennessee	4.0	1.0	0.7	1.3	4.7	0.4	5.9	−0.2
57	Alabama	3.0	−0.5	1.1	2.2	7.0	2.4	6.3	1.3
58	Mississippi	2.5	−0.2	1.1	0.7	3.4	1.7	0.3	−0.6
	West South Central:								
59	Arkansas	2.8	(³)	−0.6	0.8	5.5	2.6	5.1	5.6
60	Louisiana	6.4	−1.1	−0.6	4.3	10.9	13.8	5.8	1.2
61	Oklahoma	2.3	−2.9	−2.4	7.1	22.6	17.8	2.7	(²)
62	Texas	65.8	−76.1	36.4	137.5	80.8	45.0	47.6	53.6
	Mountain:								
63	Montana	−0.5	−4.4	−5.9	14.8	35.2	26.4	30.9	4.0
64	Idaho	0.7	−0.3	−0.9	5.6	21.9	8.9	9.5	3.3
65	Wyoming	−0.3	−2.1	0.6	1.4	12.3	4.0	9.6	1.7
66	Colorado	5.1	−7.3	0.3	9.9	47.9	18.7	45.6	32.4
67	New Mexico	3.7	−5.4	−2.7	7.8	10.4	3.5	3.6	2.6
68	Arizona	13.0	−19.4	−10.2	29.8	24.8	6.4	3.8	8.2
69	Utah	4.2	−3.2	1.0	7.1	21.6	11.4	15.2	16.1
70	Nevada	1.7	−1.5	1.6	−0.2	11.1	−1.1	−5.7	5.8
	Pacific:								
71	Washington	29.6	7.7	32.3	44.4	149.8	26.4	72.2	8.0
72	Oregon	14.3	3.3	22.1	17.2	57.5	13.8	28.5	13.4
73	California	265.4	33.8	414.2	250.3	259.1	76.4	104.7	73.6
	NEGRO POPULATION								
	New England:								
25	Maine	−0.1	0.2	−0.2	0.1	0.2	0.3	−0.1	−0.2
26	New Hampshire	0.2	−0.3	0.2	(³)	(³)	0.1	(³)	0.1
27	Vermont	0.1	−0.2	(³)	−0.9	0.8	−0.1	(³)	(³)
28	Massachusetts	10.6	2.7	2.9	6.9	5.9	9.9	4.4	3.0
29	Rhode Island	1.2	0.6	−0.7	0.6	0.6	1.5	1.2	0.8
30	Connecticut	12.9	2.2	5.2	5.3	0.5	2.5	1.1	0.8
	Middle Atlantic:								
31	New York	243.6	135.9	172.8	63.1	35.8	33.8	9.9	7.6
32	New Jersey	53.6	9.5	67.0	24.5	18.5	17.7	8.4	2.9
33	Pennsylvania	89.6	20.3	101.7	82.5	32.9	39.2	20.8	8.7
	East North Central:								
34	Ohio	106.7	20.7	90.7	69.4	15.6	5.2	5.2	2.6
35	Indiana	32.1	8.6	23.2	20.3	4.1	8.1	3.9	6.6
36	Illinois	179.8	49.4	119.3	69.8	23.5	22.7	8.4	8.7
37	Michigan	163.3	28.0	86.1	38.7	1.9	0.4	−1.2	1.6
38	Wisconsin	11.9	1.0	4.4	2.2	0.5	3.0	0.1	1.3
	West North Central:								
39	Minnesota	2.7	1.0	0.6	2.1	2.3	5.9	1.5	1.5
40	Iowa	1.0	−0.4	−1.9	3.9	2.1	1.6	0.4	2.3
41	Missouri	25.7	19.2	35.9	27.2	1.0	(³)	−4.0	−4.3
42	North Dakota	0.1	−0.1	−0.1	−0.1	0.3	4.9	} (³)	0.3
43	South Dakota	0.2	−0.1	−0.2	(³)	0.3	14.0		
44	Nebraska	3.0	0.6	(³)	5.2	1.6	−2.3	7.3	1.2
45	Kansas	2.3	−0.1	6.0	5.4	2.6	−0.6	2.7	14.7
	South Atlantic:								
46	Delaware	2.4	2.4	0.5	−0.6	−0.4	−0.7	0.3	−1.4
47	Maryland	29.9	10.7	5.0	7.0	−11.4	−6.5	−7.5	−7.5
48	District of Columbia	61.2	47.5	16.0	18.3	9.8	8.7	13.4	6.2
49	Virginia	−30.6	−36.9	−117.2	−27.2	−49.3	−70.8	−53.4	−37.6
50	West Virginia	−16.7	−4.1	12.8	15.5	15.3	5.8	3.6	2.1
51	North Carolina	−127.3	−60.0	−15.7	−28.9	−28.4	−48.7	−38.4	−7.9
52	South Carolina	−159.0	−94.4	−204.3	−74.5	−72.0	−65.5	−18.6	15.7
53	Georgia	−191.2	−90.3	−260.0	−74.7	−16.2	−27.3	12.3	−20.3
54	Florida	7.2	49.9	54.2	3.2	40.7	23.4	15.8	1.4

² Not available.   ³ Less than 50.

Series C 25–73. Estimated Net Intercensal Migration of Total, Native White, Foreign-Born White, and Negro Population Surviving From the Preceding Census Date, by States: 1870 to 1950—Con.

[In thousands]

Series No.	State	1940 to 1950	1930 to 1940	1920 to 1930	1910 to 1920	1900 to 1910	1890 to 1900	1880 to 1890	1870 to 1880
	NEGRO POPULATION—Con.								
	East South Central:								
55	Kentucky	−22.8	−9.1	−16.6	−16.6	−22.3	−12.2	−22.4	−13.1
56	Tennessee	−38.2	8.6	−14.0	−29.3	−34.3	−19.0	−18.7	−24.6
57	Alabama	−165.4	−63.8	−80.7	−70.8	−22.1	−1.7	−5.8	−36.1
58	Mississippi	−258.2	−58.2	−68.8	−129.6	−30.9	−10.4	−13.2	17.6
	West South Central:								
59	Arkansas	−116.1	−33.3	−46.3	−1.0	22.5	−7.9	44.7	25.4
60	Louisiana	−113.8	−8.4	−25.5	−51.2	−16.1	−21.6	3.3	−1.3
61	Oklahoma	−38.9	−13.0	1.9	0.8	54.8	79.3	2.3	(²)
62	Texas	−67.2	4.9	9.7	5.2	−10.2	7.1	12.6	21.0
	Mountain:								
63	Montana	0.1	(³)	−0.2	−0.1	0.3			
64	Idaho	0.3	(³)	−0.1	0.3	0.3			
65	Wyoming	1.3	−0.2	−0.1	−0.6	1.2			
66	Colorado	6.1	0.9	0.8	0.7	3.1			
67	New Mexico	2.3	1.5	−2.9	4.1	(³)			
68	Arizona	6.7	3.5	1.9	5.8	0.2			
69	Utah	1.1	0.2	−0.3	0.4	0.5			
70	Nevada	2.8	0.2	0.2	−0.1	0.4			
	Pacific:								
71	Washington	17.8	1.2	0.2	1.1	3.4			
72	Oregon	6.9	0.5	0.2	0.7	0.5			
73	California	258.9	41.2	36.4	16.1	9.8			

² Not available.   ³ Less than 50.

Series C 74–79. Estimated Annual Movement of the Farm Population: 1920 to 1957

[In thousands]

Year	Farm population, April 1	Net change: Births and deaths	Migration[1] Net	Migration[1] To farms	Migration[1] From farms	Change through change in classification of residence[2]	Year	Farm population, April 1	Net change: Births and deaths	Migration[1] Net	Migration[1] To farms	Migration[1] From farms	Change through change in classification of residence[2]
	74	75	76	77	78	79		74	75	76	77	78	79
1957	20,396	375	−2,236	459	2,695		1939	30,840	405	−420	823	1,243	−125
1956	22,257	355	−256	497	753		1938	30,980	375	−529	872	1,401	−132
							1937	31,266	363	−690	719	1,409	−144
1955	22,158	359	−91	544	635		1936	31,737	375	−642	825	1,467	−157
1954	21,890	382	−1,171	675	1,846								
1953	22,679	392	−1,996	528	2,524		1935	32,161	383	−415	783	1,198	−112
1952	24,283	394	−271	643	914		1934	32,305	375	−482	951	1,433	19
1951	24,160	404	−1,302	597	1,899		1933	32,393	398	325	1,544	1,219	282
							1932	31,388	387	−79	1,683	1,762	235
1950	25,058	418	−1,314	995	2,309		1931	30,845	377	−306	1,740	2,046	245
1949	25,954	422	−371	1,171	1,542								
1948	25,903	465	−1,686	1,016	2,702		1930	30,529	426	−477	1,604	2,081	
1947	27,124	490	151	1,768	1,617		1929	30,580	454	−422	1,698	2,120	
1946	26,483	324	864	2,585	1,721		1928	30,548	475	−457	1,705	2,162	
							1927	30,530	458	−907	1,427	2,334	
1945	25,295	364	−564	916	1,480		1926	30,979	491	−702	1,336	2,038	
1944	25,495	377	−1,563	1,095	2,658								
1943	26,681	422	−2,975	824	3,799		1925	31,190	500	−487	1,581	2,068	
1942	29,234	385	−1,424	822	2,246		1924	31,177	494	−807	1,355	2,162	
1941	30,273	359	−633	696	1,329		1923	31,490	518	−1,137	1,115	2,252	
							1922	32,109	550	−564	759	1,323	
1940	30,547	410	−583	819	1,402	−120	1921	32,123	485	−336	560	896	
							1920	31,974					

[1] Beginning 1940, includes persons going into or returning from Armed Forces, and includes changes through migration and in classification of residence. From 1930 to 1939, excludes entrance into or withdrawal from the farm population without migration. Comparability of figures for 1930–1939 with those for subsequent years may be obtained by adding net migration figures (series C 76) to figures showing change in classification of residence (series C 79).
[2] Changes resulting from cessation of or beginning of farm operations on places from which residents did not move.

Series C 80–87. Mobility Status and Type of Mobility of the Civilian Population One Year Old and Over: 1947 to 1957

[In thousands]

Period	Total civilian population[1]	Same house (nonmovers)	Different house in the United States (movers) Total	Different house in the United States (movers) Same county	Different county (migrants) Total	Different county (migrants) Within a State	Different county (migrants) Between States	Abroad at beginning of period
	80	81	82	83	84	85	86	87
April 1956 to April 1957	164,371	131,648	31,834	21,566	10,268	5,192	5,076	889
March 1955 to March 1956	161,497	127,457	33,098	22,186	10,912	5,859	5,053	942
April 1954 to April 1955	158,609	126,190	31,492	21,086	10,406	5,511	4,895	927
April 1953 to April 1954	155,679	125,654	29,027	19,046	9,981	4,947	5,034	998
April 1952 to April 1953	153,038	121,512	30,786	20,638	10,148	4,626	5,522	740
April 1951 to April 1952	150,494	120,016	29,840	19,874	9,966	4,854	5,112	638
April 1950 to April 1951	148,400	116,936	31,158	20,694	10,464	5,276	5,188	306
March 1949 to March 1950	146,864	118,849	27,526	19,276	8,250	4,360	3,889	491
April 1948 to April 1949	144,101	116,498	27,127	18,792	8,335	3,992	4,344	476
April 1947 to April 1948	141,698	113,026	28,210	19,202	9,008	4,638	4,370	462

[1] Population 1 year old and over at end of survey interval.

INTERNATIONAL MIGRATION AND NATURALIZATION (Series C 88–283)

C 88–151. General note.

The continuous record of immigration to the United States began in 1819, under the Act of 1819, which required the captain or master of a vessel arriving from abroad to deliver to the local collector of customs a list or manifest of all passengers taken on board. This list was to designate the age, sex, and occupation of each passenger, "the country to which they severally belonged," and the number that had died on the voyage. Copies of these manifests were to be transmitted to the Secretary of State, who reported the information periodically to Congress. Subsequently, the Act of 1855 prescribed quarterly reports to the Secretary of State and annual reports to Congress. Later acts have continued to require the collection of such information.

Although the reporting of alien arrivals was required by the Act of 1798, which expired two years later, the number arriving before 1819 is not known. William J. Bromwell, in his *History of Immigration to the United States*, 1856 (pp. 18–19), estimated the number of passengers of foreign birth arriving here from the close of the Revolutionary War to 1819, at 250,000. This estimate was used by the Bureau of Statistics which later compiled the official statistics of immigration.

Immigration statistics were compiled by the Department of State for 1820–1870; by the Treasury Department, Bureau of Statistics, for 1867–1895; and since 1892, by a separate Office or Bureau of Immigration, now a part of the Immigration and Naturalization Service. For 1892–1932, the Bureau of Immigration issued annual reports. For 1933–1940, the data were summarized in the *Annual Report of the Secretary of Labor;* for 1941, they were issued in the *Annual Report of the Attorney General;* for 1942, no report was published; and for subsequent years, the statistics appeared in the *Annual Report of the Immigration and Naturalization Service.*

Since 1820 the official immigration data have undergone many changes in the reporting area covered. During the first decades only arrivals by vessel at Atlantic and Gulf ports were reported. Arrivals at Pacific ports were first included in 1850. During the Civil War the only Southern ports that reported were those controlled by the Federal Government. Later the reporting area was expanded to include arrivals at outlying possessions. Arrivals in Alaska were first reported in 1871, but only irregularly thereafter until 1904, after which Alaska was regularly included among the places of entry. Arrivals in Hawaii were first included in 1901, Puerto Rico in 1902, and the Virgin Islands in 1942.

Counting arrivals at the land borders was not required by the early immigration acts, and the counting of such arrivals did not approach completeness until after 1904. For 1820–1823, a few arrivals by land borders were included. Complete reporting was attempted in 1855 with only partial success, was interrupted for several years by the Civil War, and was discontinued in 1885. Beginning in 1894, European immigrants who arrived at Canadian ports with the declared intention of proceeding to the United States were included in the immigration statistics. Some immigration was reported at land border stations established in 1904. More stations were opened in the following years, but reporting of land border arrivals was not fully established until 1908.

The statistical treatment of Canadian and Mexican immigrants at times has differed from that of other immigrants. When reporting of arrivals by land borders was discontinued in 1885, regular reporting of Canadian and Mexican arrivals by vessel was also discontinued; however, a few Canadian and Mexican immigrants were reported in most of the following years. Arrivals of Canadians and Mexicans by land borders began to be reported in 1906, and reporting was fully established in 1908 under authority of the Act of 1907, which provided for the inspection of Canadians and Mexicans at the land borders.

Not all aliens entering via the Canadian and Mexican borders are counted for inclusion in the immigration statistics. Before 1930, no count was made of residents of a year or longer of Canada, Newfoundland, or Mexico who planned to remain in the United States less than 6 months. For 1930–1945 the following classes of aliens entering via the land borders were counted and included in the statistics of immigration:

(1) Those who have not been in the United States within 6 months, who come to stay more than 6 months; (2) those for whom straight head tax is a prerequisite to admission, or for whom head tax is specially deposited and subsequently converted to straight head tax account; (3) those required by law or regulation to present an immigration visa or reentry permit, and those who surrender either, regardless of whether they are required by law or regulation to do so; (4) those announcing an intention to depart via a seaport of the United States for Hawaii or insular possessions of the United States, or for foreign countries, except arrivals from Canada intending to return thereto by water; and (5) those announcing an intention to depart across the other land boundary.

These classes were revised in 1945 so that the statistics of arriving aliens at land border ports of entry for 1945–1952 included (1) arriving aliens who came into the United States for 30 days or more; and (2) returning alien residents who had been out of the United States more than 6 months. Arriving aliens who came into the United States for 29 days or less were not counted except those certified by public health officials, aliens held for a board of special inquiry, aliens excluded and deported, and aliens in transit who announced an intention to depart across another land boundary, or by sea.

Since 1953, all arriving aliens at land border ports of entry are counted and included except: (1) Canadian citizens and British subjects resident in Canada who were admitted for 6 months or less; (2) Mexican citizens who were admitted for 72 hours or less in the United States; and (3) returning residents who had been out of the United States for more than 6 months. Beginning with February 1956, residents returning from stays in Western Hemisphere countries of less than 6 months have not been counted. Because of changes in regulations in 1957, returning residents without reentry permits or visas who have been abroad for 1 year or less are not counted.

Persons who cross the land borders for brief periods (border crossers) are not included in the immigration and emigration statistics, but the Immigration and Naturalization Service publishes statistics on alien and citizen border crossers in the *Annual Report.*

Arrivals in and departures from the Philippine Islands were recorded in the port tables for 1910–1924, but were not included in the total immigration data. For 1925–1931, such arrivals and departures were obtained annually from the Bureau of Insular Affairs, War Department, and published in separate tables. The Immigration Service has no records since 1932 of arrivals in, or departures from, the Philippine Islands to foreign countries.

Data on aliens admitted to continental United States from insular possessions have been compiled since 1908 but are not included in the immigration totals. Aliens admitted from Hawaii and Puerto Rico have been reported continuously since 1908. Aliens admitted from the Philippine Islands were reported from 1908–1934, but since then all arrivals from and departures to the Philippine Islands have been included with data from other foreign countries. Aliens admitted from the Virgin Islands have been recorded since 1917. The departure of aliens from the mainland to Hawaii and Puerto Rico was first recorded in 1918. Records are available since 1918 of aliens passing between insular possessions. Data on aliens from Guam are available since 1929; Samoa, since 1932. Records of United States citizens' arrival in continental United States from insular possessions, and in insular possessions from continental United States and other insular possessions, are available since 1920.

Definition of terms. For 1820–1867, immigration totals (compiled by the Department of State) were shown as alien passenger arrivals, but may have included alien passengers who died before arrival, and did include, for 1856–1867, temporary visitors among arriving alien passengers. For the 12-year period, the temporary visitors constituted about 1½ percent of the alien passenger arrivals.

For 1868–1891, the Bureau of Statistics immigrant arrival figures (excluding temporary visitors), were reported. Since 1892, official immigration data have been compiled by the Office of Immigration (and its successors) and for 1892–1895 its totals were 7 to 8 percent lower than those for the Bureau of Statistics for that period. The difference is largely attributable to the limitation of the Office of Immigration figures to alien steerage passengers; cabin class passengers were not again included as immigrants until 1904. A further difference was that the Bureau of Statistics figures were for arrivals and those of the Office of Immigration were for admissions.

For 1895–1897, the Office of Immigration readopted arrivals and the figures include the 2,419 aliens debarred in 1895, the 2,799 in 1896, and 1,880 in 1897. In later years, the immigration data were further refined to exclude aliens in transit through the United States (1904), and resident aliens returning from a visit abroad (1906).

In 1906 arriving aliens were divided into two classes: Immigrants, or those who intended to settle in the United States, and nonimmigrants, or admitted aliens who declared an intention not to settle in the United States, and all aliens returning to resume domiciles formerly acquired in the United States.

The official record of emigration began in 1907. It was made possible by the Immigration Act of 1907, which required all steamship companies carrying departing aliens to furnish manifests similar to those required for arriving aliens.

For 1908–1932, aliens arriving in or departing from the United States were classified as follows: Arriving aliens with permanent domicile outside the United States who intended to reside permanently in the United States were classed as immigrants; departing aliens with permanent residence in the United States who intended to reside permanently abroad were classed as emigrants; all alien residents making a temporary trip

abroad and all aliens residing abroad making a temporary trip to the United States were classed as nonimmigrants on the inward journey and nonemigrants on the outward. Permanent residence was defined as a residence of 1 year or longer. (*Annual Report of the Commissioner General of Immigration, 1908,* p. 6.)

Since 1933, aliens arriving in or departing from the United States have been classified as follows: Immigrants are non-resident aliens admitted to the United States for permanent residence; they are further classified as quota immigrants, or those admitted under established quotas from European countries, Asia, Africa, and the Pacific, and colonies, dependencies, and protectorates of European countries; and nonquota immigrants, i.e., natives from the independent countries of the Western Hemisphere, their wives and unmarried children under 18 years of age; wives, husbands, and unmarried children of citizens of the United States; ministers and professors who enter to carry on their professions, and their wives and children; and others. Since 1952 (Immigration and Nationality Act), professors have been removed from the nonquota classes. Husbands as well as wives of ministers and of natives of independent countries in the Western Hemisphere may be admitted as nonquota.

Nonimmigrants are alien residents of the United States returning from a temporary visit abroad, or nonresident aliens admitted to the United States for a temporary period. Included in this group are visitors, transients, treaty traders (treaty investors since December 1952), students, foreign government officials, officials to international organizations, wives and unmarried children of these groups, and agricultural laborers from the West Indies (and from Japan since 1957). Excluded are travelers between the United States and insular possessions, commuters and others who frequently cross the international land boundaries, and agricultural laborers from Mexico and Canada.

Emigrants are aliens who have resided in the United States for a year or longer and who are leaving the United States for a permanent residence abroad. Nonemigrants are resident aliens of the United States who are leaving the United States for a temporary period abroad, or nonresident aliens of the United States who have been in the United States for less than a year and who are returning to permanent residence abroad.

Except for returning alien residents, the definition of immigrants used in the statistical tables resembles the legal definition given above. Under the law, returning alien residents are classed as nonquota immigrants, whereas in the statistics they are defined as nonimmigrants.

The definitions of immigrant and emigrant, nonimmigrant and nonemigrant, have to some extent impaired the reliability of net immigration figures. While an immigrant is admitted for permanent residence, he may change his mind and depart prior to residence of 1 year, in which case he is counted as an immigrant on arrival and a nonemigrant on departure. An alien who comes for a temporary visit and fails to depart within a year is classed as a nonimmigrant on arrival and an emigrant on departure.

C 88–114. Immigrants, by country, 1820–1957.

Source: 1820–1932, Immigration and Naturalization Service, unpublished records, and Bureau of Immigration, *Annual Reports of the Commissioner General of Immigration* as follows: 1820–1926, *Report* for 1926, pp. 170–178; 1927–1931, *Report* for 1931, pp. 222–223; 1932, *Report* for 1932, pp. 120–125; and 1933–1957, Immigration and Naturalization Service, records.

Data prior to 1906 cover countries from which the aliens came; data for years following, countries of last permanent residence. Owing to changes in the list of countries separately reported and to changes in boundaries, data for certain countries are not comparable throughout. Under the provisions of the Immigration and Nationality Act, subquotas of 100 each were established for colonies or dependencies, to be charged against the quota of the mother country. Because of these provisions, since January 1953, statistics have been compiled for each colony or dependency having a subquota.

The principal changes in reporting immigrants by country since 1820 are shown in the detailed listing below.

See also general note for series C 88–151.

C 89–100. Immigration from Europe, 1820–1957.

Source: See source for series C 88–114.

Since 1820, territorial transfers in Europe have to a certain extent impaired the comparability of immigration statistics from that continent. Data for Austria-Hungary were not reported until 1861. Austria and Hungary have been reported separately since 1905. For 1938–1945, Austria is included with Germany. Bulgaria, Serbia, and Montenegro were first reported in 1899. In 1920 Bulgaria was reported separately, as was the Kingdom of Serbs, Croats, and Slovenes (identified as Yugoslavia since 1922). Prior to 1925 Northern Ireland was included with Ireland (Eire). The figures for Norway and Sweden were combined from 1820–1868, but since 1869 each country has been reported separately. Poland was recorded as a separate country for 1820–1898 and since 1920. During 1899–1919 Poland was included with Austria-Hungary, Germany, and Russia. There is no record of immigration from Rumania prior to 1880.

International transfers in territory following World War I resulted in the establishment of several countries. In 1920, Czechoslovakia, Finland, Poland, and the Kingdom of Serbs, Croats, and Slovenes (designated as Yugoslavia in 1925) were added to the immigration lists; in 1924, Albania, Estonia, Latvia, and Lithuania were added; in 1925, the Free City of Danzig and Luxembourg were added.

The Immigration Act of 1924, which established quotas for all independent countries in Europe, Asia, Africa, and the Pacific has effected a further change in the immigration lists of countries. This change, however, was not fully felt until 1931. In that year Andorra, Iceland, Liechtenstein, Monaco, and San Marino were added to the European countries, and the Russian Empire was classified into European Russia (designated as U.S.S.R. in Europe since 1947) and Siberia, or Asiatic Russia. The principal effect of the 1924 Act, however, was in the extension of the lists of Asian, African, and Western Hemisphere countries.

In 1950, Bessarabia and the northern portion of Bukovina were included in the U.S.S.R. instead of in Rumania. The Dodecanese Islands were included in Greece instead of Italy. The Free Territory of Trieste, formerly a part of Italy and Yugoslavia, was established as an independent country.

C 101–105. Immigration from Asia, 1820–1957.

Source: See source for series C 88–114.

China and India are the only countries in Asia for which the records of immigration to the United States date back to 1820. A few immigrants from Japan were recorded in 1861, 1866, and 1867, but complete records for Japan begin in 1869. Figures for Turkey in Asia are available since 1869. Data on some immigration from Arabia are recorded for 1876–1895; from Armenia for 1874–1895; and from Persia for 1871–1895. For 1896–1923, immigration from Asia included only China, India, Japan, Turkey in Asia, and "other Asia." In 1924, Syria was added, and in 1925 Armenia, Palestine, and Persia

(Iran) were added to the lists of Asian countries. Since 1934 Armenia has been included in Russia. In 1931 Siberia, or Asiatic Russia, was separated from European Russia, and Iraq and Siam (Thailand) were added to the lists.

In 1945, the classification of country in the country-of-birth statistics (on which the Quota Law is based) was adopted for the immigration statistics. This change resulted in the addition to the immigration lists of Afghanistan, Arabian Peninsula, Bhutan, Muscat, Nepal, Saudi Arabia, and Asiatic colonies, dependencies, and protectorates of European countries. Since 1948, the following countries have been added to the immigration lists: (1948) Burma, Ceylon, Jordan, Korea, and Pakistan; (1949) Israel (formerly included with Palestine), Lebanon (formerly included with Syria), and Yemen; (1950) Indonesia; (1952) Bonin Volcano Islands, Ryukyu Islands, Cambodia, and Laos; (1957) Formosa.

C 106–109. Immigration from America, 1820–1957.

Source: See source for series C 88–114.

Prior to 1920 Canada and Newfoundland were recorded under country of last permanent residence as British North America. Combined figures are available for Canada and Newfoundland for 1920–1924; for 1925–1948 each was reported separately. Since 1950, Newfoundland has been included in Canada.

Statistics of European immigrants arriving in Canada en route to the United States have been available since 1894. For 1894–1906, the data refer principally to European aliens arriving at Canadian Atlantic and Pacific ports en route to the United States. Inspection of Canadians and Mexicans was first authorized by the Act of 1907, and 1908 is, therefore, the first complete year for which all immigration via the land borders was recorded.

Immigration from Mexico has been recorded for 1820–1885 and for 1894 to the present. Immigration statistics for the West Indies have been available since 1820. For 1820–1860 there was no classification of the West Indies, by country. For 1860–1898, some immigration was recorded from Antigua (1873–1895), Bahamas (1871–1895), Barbados (1869–1895), Bermuda (1861–1895), Cuba (1869–1898), Curacao (1873–1895), Haiti (1869–1895), Jamaica (1869–1895), Puerto Rico (1869–1895), Saint Croix (1871–1895), Saint Thomas (1872–1895), and Trinidad (1874–1895). For 1899–1924, there again was no classification by country of immigration from the West Indies. Immigration from Cuba has been separately recorded since 1925; from the British West Indies, Dominican Republic, Dutch West Indies, French West Indies, and Haiti since 1931; and from Bermuda since 1945. For detailed data, see *Annual Report of Commissioner General of Immigration* for each year, 1892–1932. Since January 1953, all countries in the West Indies have been reported.

Immigration from Central America has been recorded since 1820, but not by country during most of that period. Separate statistics are available for 1895–1898 for Guatemala, Honduras, Nicaragua, and Salvador; and for 1895–1897 for Costa Rica. British Honduras was also enumerated separately for 1874–1910. With the above exceptions, only figures for total immigration were available for Central America until 1925. Immigration has been reported separately from British Honduras since 1925, and from the Canal Zone, Costa Rica, Guatemala, Honduras, Nicaragua, Panama, and Salvador since 1931.

Immigration from South America has also been reported in total since 1820 but, with the following exceptions, not by country until 1925. For 1869–1895, separate enumerations were made for Brazil, Chile, Colombia, Ecuador, Guiana, Peru, and Venezuela; and for 1871–1895 for the Argentine Republic. Separate figures for Brazil have been again available since 1925;

and since 1931 for Argentina, Bolivia, British Guiana, Dutch Guiana, French Guiana, Chile, Colombia, Ecuador, Paraguay, Peru, Uruguay, and Venezuela.

C 110.   Immigration from Africa, 1820–1957.

Source: See source for series C 88–114.

Immigration from Africa has been recorded since 1820, but, with few exceptions, was not classified by country until 1931. There is record of some immigration from Liberia in 1829, 1839, 1844, and for 1857–1893; Algeria, 1872–1894; Egypt, 1869–1895; and South Africa, 1869–1895. For 1890–1924, only immigration for continental Africa was reported. Immigration from Egypt was again recorded in 1925. Immigration from Ethiopia (Abyssinia), Liberia, Morocco, and Union of South Africa, has been recorded since 1931. In 1945 "other Africa" was classified into Cameroons (British Mandate), Cameroons (French Mandate), Ruanda and Urundi (trust territory, Belgium), South-West Africa (Mandate of the Union of South Africa), Tanganyika (trust territory, United Kingdom), Togoland (British Mandate), Togoland (trust territory, France), and colonies, dependencies, or protectorates of Belgium, France, Great Britain, Italy, Portugal, and Spain.

Since 1945, the following countries have been added: 1953: Libya and Somaliland (Italian administration), and Southern Rhodesia. Eritrea, which was federated with Ethiopia, was included with Ethiopia. 1957: Ghana (composed of British territories, Gold Coast and British Togoland), Sudan, and Tunisia.

C 111–113.   Immigration from Australasia, 1870–1957.

Source: See source for series C 88–114.

Immigration from Australia was recorded separately in 1822, 1839–1840, and for most of the years 1854–1898. For 1899–1924, a combined total was recorded for Australia, Tasmania, and New Zealand, and since 1925 Australia has been again reported separately. Separate figures for New Zealand are available for 1870–1890. For 1891–1893, New Zealand was included in "all other countries"; for 1894–1898 in "Pacific Islands, not specified," and for 1899–1924 with Australia and Tasmania. Separate figures for New Zealand have again been available since 1925.

The following countries were added to the immigration lists of the Pacific in 1945: Nauru (British Mandate); Territory of New Guinea including appertaining islands (Australian Mandate); Western Samoa (New Zealand Mandate); Yap and other Pacific Islands under Japanese Mandate; and colonies, dependencies, or protectorates of France, Great Britain, Japan, Netherlands, and Portugal. In 1952, the Pacific Islands (trust territory, U. S. administration) were added.

C 115–132.   Immigrants, by major occupation group, 1820–1957.

Source: 1820–1890, Treasury Department, Bureau of Statistics, *Arrivals of Alien Passengers and Immigrants in the United States, 1820–1890*, pp. 42–49; 1891, Treasury Department, Bureau of Statistics, *Immigration into the United States Showing Number, Nationality, Sex, Age, Occupation, Destination, ... from 1820–1903*; 1892–1898, Bureau of Immigration, *Annual Reports of Commissioner General of Immigration*; 1899–1944, Immigration and Naturalization Service, unpublished records; 1945–1957, *Annual Reports of the Immigration and Naturalization Service*.

The major occupation groups for 1820–1898 include the following categories: Professional—occupations which involve a liberal education or its equivalent and mental rather than manual skills; commercial—agents, bankers, hotelkeepers, manufacturers, and merchants and dealers; skilled—occupations requiring special training of a manual rather than mental nature.

A "farmer" is one who operates a farm, either for himself or for others; a "farm laborer" is one who works on a farm for the man who operates it. The "no occupation" group includes dependent women and children, other aliens without occupation, and aliens whose occupations were not stated.

Although the data are shown in broad occupation groups, the instructions for compiling statistics specified that the occupation should be described as precisely as possible. For example, civil engineer, stationary engineer, mining engineer, brass polisher, steel polisher, iron molder, wood turner, etc., should be so described, and not entered simply as engineer, polisher, molder, turner, or other indefinite designation.

In 1945 the Immigration and Naturalization Service adopted the major occupation groups as shown in the *Sixteenth Census of the United States, Alphabetical Index of Occupations and Industries*. It also grouped occupations of immigrants for 1899–1944 (compiled in unpublished records) as closely as possible into the new groups. Since 1951, occupations have been coded and grouped in accordance with the definitions in *U. S. Census of Population: 1950, Alphabetical Index of Occupations and Industries*.

The occupation figures include all immigrants, those with and without work experience. The "no occupation" group includes housewives, unemployed, retired persons, students, children under 14 years of age, aliens with no occupation, and occupation unknown or not reported.

See also general note for series C 88–151.

C 133, 135–138.   Immigrants, by age, 1820–1957.

Source: 1820–1897, Treasury Department, Bureau of Statistics, *Monthly Summary of Commerce and Finance of the U. S.*, No. 12, series 1902–1903, pp. 4358 and 4362; 1898–1932, *Annual Reports of the Commissioner General of Immigration*; 1933–1957, data are from Immigration and Naturalization Service, records.

Some of the published estimates have been revised because of apparent printing errors in the source.

The age groups used to classify immigrants have changed a number of times since 1820, thereby impairing to a certain extent their comparability. For 1820–1898, the classification was: Under 15 years, 15 to 40, and over 40 years. In addition, the age of nearly 250,000 immigrants, or 4 percent of the total, for 1820–1866 was not reported.

For 1899–1917 the age classification was: Under 14 years, 14 to 44, and 45 years and over; for 1918–1924 it was under 16 years, 16 to 44, and 45 years and over.

Although only three age groups were generally used before 1925, a more detailed classification was used for 1910–1924 for single females: 15 to 19 years, 20 to 24, 25 to 29, and 30 to 34 in 1910; 14 to 21 years, 22 to 29, 30 to 37, and 38 to 44 for 1911–1917; 16 to 21 years, 22 to 29, 30 to 37, and 38 to 44 for 1918–1924.

In 1925 the age classification was enlarged from 3 to 6 groups: Under 16 years, 16 to 21, 22 to 29, 30 to 37, 38 to 44, and 45 years and over. In 1940, it was enlarged to 12 groups, with a lower limit of under 11 years, 5-year age groups until 60, and an upper limit of over 60 years. In 1945, it was further enlarged into 5-year groups, with a lower age limit of under 5 years and an upper open-end limit of 100 years and over.

See also general note for series C 88–151.

C 134.   Percent male immigrants, 1820–1957.

Source: 1820–1910, Senate Doc. No. 756, 61st Congress, *Reports of the Immigration Commission*, vol. 3, pp. 6 and 7; 1911–1931, Bureau of Immigration, *Annual Report of the*

Commissioner General of Immigration, 1931, p. 238; 1932, *Annual Report of the Commissioner General of Immigration,* 1932, p. 58; 1933–1957, Immigration and Naturalization Service, records.

Although the Act of 1819 required that arriving immigrants be recorded by sex, these data were not satisfactorily compiled before 1869. (See Senate Doc. No. 756 cited above, p. 5.) The earlier reports of the Secretary of State to Congress contain partial data on this subject, and in 1911 the Immigration Commission compiled these data to show the approximate sex distribution for 1820–1867. Therefore the percentages given in series C 134 cannot be reduced to numbers. Moreover, the data are not complete, as in most years sex was not reported for a considerable number of immigrants; but on the whole the percentages may be accepted as fairly representative of the sex distribution in the years considered.

C 139–151. Annual quota and aliens admitted, by classes, 1925–1957.

Source: *Annual Reports of Immigration and Naturalization Service* and Presidential Proclamations on quotas.

For 1925–1929, the annual quota (series C 139) of 164,667 was based on 2 percent of the foreign-born residents in the United States as determined by the 1890 Census. The present "national origin" formula for determining quotas, which has not changed since 1929, provides that the annual quota equal one-sixth of one percent of the number of white inhabitants in continental United States in 1920, less Western Hemisphere immigrants and their descendants. The annual quota for any nationality for each fiscal year is the number which bears the same ratio to 150,000 as the number of inhabitants in continental United States in 1920 having that national origin bears to the number of inhabitants in continental United States in 1920, but the minimum quota for any nationality is 100.

Changes in quotas since 1929 have been due chiefly to changes in territorial boundaries of quota areas and to the establishment of new quotas for countries that have become independent.

The classes presented in these series are legal classes of admission, as defined in the Act of 1924, and the Immigration and Nationality Act of 1952. Returning resident aliens, who have been counted before as immigrants, are included with nonimmigrants.

In general, statistics on aliens admitted have been derived from manifests or entry documents. Changes in regulations extending documentary waivers for nonimmigrants entering via the Canadian or Mexican border, or from adjacent islands, have impaired comparability of the nonimmigrant statistics. For example, the figure on nonimmigrant admissions dropped in 1953 because beginning with 1953, the nonimmigrant figures have excluded, with certain exceptions, Canadian citizens and British subjects resident in Canada who were admitted for 6 months or less. In prior years the nonimmigrant figures excluded entries over the Canadian border for 29 days or less. The reduction in the number of returning residents in 1956 and 1957 may be attributed to changes in regulations extending documentary waivers to resident aliens returning from stays in Western Hemisphere countries of less than 6 months. The waiver has recently been extended further to returning residents who have been abroad less than 1 year.

See also general note for series C 88–151.

C 152–155. Aliens deported, voluntarily departing, and excluded, 1892–1957.

Source: *Annual Report of Immigration and Naturalization Service,* 1957, pp. 46, 50.

C 153, aliens deported. Undesirable aliens who have violated certain immigration laws may be expelled or deported under formal deportation proceedings. Deportation of alien contract laborers within one year after entry was authorized by the Act of 1888. Deportation statistics, however, have been compiled only since 1892, shortly after enactment of the Act of 1891, which provided for the deportation of all aliens who entered unlawfully. The classes of deportable aliens were extended by subsequent acts and are now defined in the Immigration and Nationality Act of 1952. The principal deportable classes are criminals (including violators of narcotic laws), immoral classes, mental or physical defectives, public charges, subversives, and those who entered illegally or failed to maintain or comply with the conditions of admission.

C 154, aliens voluntarily departing. An alien may concede deportability and be permitted to depart voluntarily at his own expense. Statistics on aliens voluntarily departing have been recorded only since 1927.

C 155, aliens excluded. Prior to 1882, various State laws were enacted excluding from admission to the United States undesirable aliens such as paupers, felons, and diseased aliens. The first Chinese exclusion law was passed in 1882. Lunatics, idiots, and persons likely to become public charges were first excluded by the Act of 1882.

Statistics on aliens excluded were first compiled in 1892, shortly after passage of the Act of 1891, which extended the classes of excludable aliens. Subsequent acts, principally the Immigration Act of 1917, and the Immigration and Nationality Act of 1952, extended these classes further. At present, the principal classes excluded are attempted illegal entries, criminals (including violators of narcotic laws), immoral persons, subversive or anarchistic persons, and mental or physical defectives.

C 156–157. Aliens departing, 1908–1957.

Source: 1908–1910, Bureau of Immigration, *Annual Report of the Commissioner General of Immigration,* 1931, pp. 213 and 239; 1911–1956, *Annual Report of the Immigration and Naturalization Service,* 1956, p. 48; 1957, *Ibid,* 1957 reports, p. 31.

For definition of terms, see general note for series C 88–151.

C 158–170. General note.

Prior to 1906, individual courts kept records of naturalizations, but no national data were compiled. The Act of 1906 required all courts conducting naturalization proceedings to file with a central Federal agency a copy of each declaration of intention and petition of naturalization filed and of each certificate of naturalization issued.

For 1907–1912 naturalization statistics were compiled by the Bureau of Immigration and Naturalization. For 1913–1932 they were compiled by the Bureau of Naturalization. For 1933–1940, they were given in the *Annual Reports of the Secretary of Labor* and for 1941 in the *Annual Report of the Attorney General.* No report was published in 1942. For subsequent years, the statistics appeared in *Annual Reports of the Immigration and Naturalization Service.*

C 158. Declarations filed, 1907–1957.

Source: 1907–1910, *Annual Report of the Secretary of Labor,* 1940, p. 115; 1911–1957, *Annual Report of Immigration and Naturalization Service,* 1957, p. 67.

See also general note for series C 158–170.

Section 331 of the Nationality Act of 1940 provided that an applicant for naturalization after reaching the age of 18 years must make under oath, not less than 2 nor more than 7 years prior to his petition for naturalization, a signed declaration of intention to become a citizen. This section contained substantially the requirements of the Basic Naturalization Act of 1906 concerning the declaration of intention. The Immigration and Nationality Act of 1952, which repealed the Nationality Act of 1940, provides that a declaration of intention may be filed, but it is not a prerequisite to naturalization. In a number of States, in order to obtain employment, a license, etc., an alien applicant must prove that he intends to become a citizen. The law permits the filing of a declaration to show such intent.

Prior to 1930 the number of declarations of intention was far in excess of the number of aliens naturalized. This was due mainly to the failure of many aliens to file a petition for naturalization within the prescribed time limit, as well as the denial of a number of petitions for naturalization. In most of the years since 1930 the number of aliens naturalized has exceeded the declarations filed, because of the increasing number of persons who were exempted from the general requirements for a declaration of intention.

Since 1907, a number of laws have been passed exempting special classes of persons from the general requirement of a declaration of intention. Most of these laws were codified into the Nationality Act of 1940. Included among such exempted classes were noncitizen spouses of United States citizens; certain former citizens; noncitizens who, because of misinformation, erroneously exercised the rights of citizenship; noncitizens who, at the time of entering the United States, were under 16 years of age; certain noncitizens who served honorably in the United States Armed Forces or on certain vessels; and certain noncitizen children.

C 159. Aliens naturalized, 1907–1957.

Source: See source for series C 158.

"Aliens naturalized" are aliens upon whom naturalization was conferred in the United States by a naturalization court or outside of the United States by a representative of the Immigration and Naturalization Service. The total number of aliens naturalized includes both civilian and military naturalizations.

The statistics of aliens naturalized do not include the following groups: Repatriations under section 323 of the Nationality Act of 1940 of former citizens of the United States who lost citizenship by entering the armed forces of allied countries during World War I, and former citizens who lost citizenship of the United States by voting in a political election in a foreign state (other than a state at war with the United States during World War II); repatriations of women who were citizens at birth but who lost or were believed to have lost citizenship through marriage to an alien and whose marriages were terminated; repatriations under the Act of 1936, as amended, of native-born women who lost citizenship by marriage; and repatriations of persons who lost citizenship by voting in a political election or plebiscite in Italy (Act of 1951) and in occupied Japan (Act of 1954).

Separate statistics on these repatriations are compiled by the Immigration and Naturalization Service which also compiles statistics on certificates of derivative citizenship granted and denied, expatriations and certificates of naturalization revoked, and petitions for naturalization denied.

C 160–161. Aliens naturalized, by sex, 1923–1957.

Source: 1923–1932, Bureau of Naturalization, *Annual Report of the Commissioner of Naturalization, 1923–1932;* 1933–1940, *Annual Report of the Secretary of Labor, 1933–1940;* 1941–1957, *Annual Report of the Immigration and Naturalization Service* for 1949 and 1957.

See also general note for series C 158–170 and text for series C 159.

C 162–169. Aliens naturalized, by place of former allegiance, 1923–1957.

Source: 1923–1932, *Annual Report of the Commissioner of Naturalization;* 1933–1935, Immigration and Naturalization Service, records; 1936–1957, *Annual Report of the Immigration and Naturalization Service.*

See also general note for series C 158–170.

"Country of former allegiance or nationality" is the country of which the alien at the time was a citizen or subject. Data on the number of aliens naturalized, by country or region of former allegiance, have been compiled only from 1922. Owing to changes in the list of countries separately reported and to changes in boundaries, data for certain countries are not comparable throughout. The principal changes in reporting since 1923 are shown for individual series below.

C 162, Northwestern Europe. Includes the British Empire, Norway, Sweden, Denmark, Netherlands, Belgium, Luxembourg, Switzerland, France, and, beginning with 1948, Iceland. For 1924–1932, the figures for the British Empire were classified by country. Canada is shown separately for 1923–1932, and since 1948; for 1933–1947, Canada is included in the British Empire. Beginning with 1948, Ireland has been reported separately. Australia has been reported separately from 1951, and included in "all other" (series C 169). See text for series C 166, C 168, and C 169 for former British territories.

C 163, Central Europe. Includes Germany, Poland, Czechoslovakia, Austria, Hungary, Yugoslavia, and Montenegro. For 1938–1947, Austria was included with Germany. For 1923–1932, Yugoslavia was recorded as the Kingdom of Serbs, Croats, and Slovenes.

C 164, Eastern Europe. Includes the Union of Soviet Socialist Republics, Latvia, Estonia, Lithuania, Finland, Rumania, Bulgaria, and Turkey. For 1923–1928, Latvia and Estonia were included with Russia. For 1923–1927, Lithuania comprised portions of Russia and Germany. European and Asiatic Turkey are included in Eastern Europe.

C 165, Southern Europe. Includes Greece, Italy, Spain, Portugal, and, for 1929–1957, "other Europe," which comprises Albania, the Free City of Danzig, Liechtenstein, San Marino, Monaco, Andorra, and, since 1950, Trieste. For 1923–1928, "other Europe" was recorded under the "miscellaneous" group of countries and is included with "all other" (C 169).

C 166, Asia. For 1923–1927, Asia was included under "all other" (C 169). The Asian countries reported separately and the beginning dates are shown below:

Afghanistan (1929); Arabian Peninsula (1943); Bhutan (1945); Burma (1949); Ceylon (1948); China (1932); India (1948, British Empire formerly); Indonesia (1950); Iran (1929); Iraq (1929); Israel (1950, Palestine formerly); Japan (1932); Jordan (1948, formerly called Trans-Jordan and included with Palestine prior to 1948); Korea (1948, Japan formerly); Lebanon (1950, included in Syria formerly); Muscat and Oman (1945); Nepal (1945); Pakistan (1948, included in British Empire formerly); Palestine (reported separately 1929–1944 and since 1948; included in British Empire 1945–1947); Philippines (1929); Saudi Arabia (1945); Syria (reported separately 1928–1944 and since 1948; included in France, 1944–1947); Thailand (Siam, 1944); Vietnam (1952); Yemen (1950); and Formosa (1957).

Until 1953 racial restrictions upon naturalization limited the naturalization of aliens who were citizens or subjects of countries located in Asia. (See text for series C 170.)

C 167, Canada. For 1923–1932, and since 1948, Canada is shown separately; it is included in the British Empire for 1933–1947.

620722 O–62–5

C 168, Other America. Includes Mexico, the West Indies, Central and South America. Figures for "other America" countries were not compiled separately in 1923. Figures for Mexico date from 1924; for the West Indies (Cuba, Dominican Republic, and Haiti separately) from 1929. For 1924–1928, the figures for Central and South America were combined. Separate figures have been compiled for independent countries in Central and South America beginning with 1929, except in 1933.

C 169, All other. Includes "miscellaneous" countries 1923–1928; repatriated Americans, 1924–1934; "stateless" nationals from 1945; Ethiopia from 1929; Liberia from 1929; and countries which were former territories. Former territories and the beginning dates of separate report are shown below:

Formerly French territory: Libya (1953); Tunisia (1957); Sudan (1957). Formerly British territory: Egypt, reported separately 1929–1944 and since 1948, included in British Empire, 1945–1947; South West Africa (1952); Southern Rhodesia (1953); Union of South Africa (1948); Australia (1951); Nauru (1952); New Guinea (1952); New Zealand (1952); and Western Samoa (1952). Formerly Italian administration: Somaliland (1953). Formerly international administration: Tangier (1953). Separate figures are available for the following United States possessions: American Samoa, Canal Zone, Puerto Rico, Virgin Islands, and Wake and Midway Islands (1945–1951 and since 1955); Hawaii (since 1955); Guam (1944–1951, and since 1955).

C 170. Petitions denied, 1907–1957.

Source: 1907–1921, *Reports of Commissioner of Naturalization* as follows: 1907–1917, *Report* for 1917, p. 5; 1918–1919, *Report* for 1919, p. 4; 1920, *Report* for 1920, pp. 5–6; 1921–1957, see *Annual Report of Immigration and Naturalization Service*, 1957, p. 72.

See also general note for series C 158–170.

Statistics on petitions denied have been compiled since 1907. The Basic Naturalization Act of 1906 and subsequent naturalization laws specified the eligibility requirements for naturalization. Petitions for naturalization of aliens who fail to meet the prerequisites for naturalization may be denied by the courts at the final naturalization hearing. Included among the reasons for denial are lack of knowledge and understanding of history, principles, and form of government of the United States, failure to establish good moral character, lack of attachment to the Constitution of the United States, inability to speak (read, write) the English language, failure to establish lawful admission to the United States or to meet residence requirements, etc.

In the early laws the right to become naturalized was limited to white persons, and petitions of persons of ineligible races were denied. Gradually such restrictions were removed with respect to Negroes, Filipinos, races indigenous to North and South America and adjacent islands, Chinese, and Guamanians. In 1952, the Immigration and Nationality Act removed all racial restrictions to naturalization. Japanese aliens in the United States were the largest class of aliens that benefited by this law.

C 171–184. Citizenship status of the population, 1890–1950.

Source: 1890–1940, total, native, and total foreign-born population, and 1930–1940, citizenship status of foreign born and persons 21 years old and over, Sixteenth Census Reports, *Population*, vol. II, part 1, pp. 19, 30–33; 1890–1920, data on persons 21 years old and over, and 1920, citizenship status of foreign born, Fifteenth Census Reports, *Population*, vol. II, p. 405; 1950, *U. S. Census of Population: 1950*, vol. II, part 1, pp. 1–178.

The classification of citizenship by the Bureau of the Census embraces the two major categories, citizen and alien. Citizens are subdivided into native and naturalized. Aliens are subdivided into those having first papers (that is, having made formal declaration of intention to become citizens of the United States) and those not having first papers. In addition to the citizen and alien categories, there is a third group made up of foreign-born persons for whom no report on citizenship was obtained, designated as "citizenship not reported" or "unknown citizenship." Since it is likely that most of these persons are aliens, they are often included in summary figures for total aliens. The population 21 years old and over is also given separately by citizenship, in order to show the number of potential voters.

These statistics relate to the citizenship status of the population at the date of the specified decennial census.

C 185–217. Native white population of foreign or mixed parentage, by country of origin of parents, 1900–1950.

Source: 1900–1940, Sixteenth Census Reports, *Population, Country of Origin of Foreign Stock*, p. 10; 1950, *U. S. Census of Population: 1950*, vol. IV, Special Reports, *Nativity and Parentage*, p. 3A-75.

A native is defined as a person born in continental United States, Puerto Rico, or the Territories or possessions, or born abroad to American parents. Persons for whom place of birth was not reported are included as native. The nativity of parents was defined in the same way as it was for the individual.

Persons of foreign parentage are allocated to the country of birth of the foreign parent. The classification by country of birth of parents is, of course, subject to the same limitations and may be presumed to be less accurate than the classification of the foreign born by country of birth.

The definition of country of birth of parents is similar to that used in series C 218–283, below, with several important exceptions. The classification by country of birth of parents for 1930 and later years is made on the basis of boundaries existing at the date of the specified decennial census. The 1920 data on country of birth of parents, however, are based on pre-World War I boundaries because of the difficulty of obtaining correct replies on the basis of postwar boundaries for parents of persons enumerated. The procedure differs from that used for series C 218–283 where the boundaries used for 1920 and for all other years were those in existence at the time of the census.

For definition of color, see text for series A 22–33.

C 218–283. Foreign-born population, by country of birth, 1850–1950.

Source: 1850–1930, total foreign born, Fifteenth Census Reports, *Population*, vol. II, p. 233; 1910–1940, foreign-born white, Sixteenth Census Reports, *Population*, vol. II, part 1, p. 43; 1950, foreign-born white, *U. S. Census of Population: 1950*, vol. IV, Special Reports, *Nativity and Parentage*, p. 3A-71.

The foreign-born population comprises all persons born outside the United States or any of the outlying possessions, except certain persons whose parents at the time of their birth were American citizens. Persons born in any of the outlying Territories or possessions, and American citizens born abroad or at sea, are regarded as native.

The statistics on country of birth are generally based on the political boundaries of foreign nations existing at the date of the specified decennial census. Because of boundary changes following World War I and World War II, accurate comparisons over the entire period, 1850–1950, can be made for relatively few countries. These countries include England, Scotland, Wales, Norway, Sweden, Netherlands, Switzerland, Spain, Portugal, Canada (total of Canada-French, other, and Newfoundland), and Mexico. For several other countries, as for example, Italy, France, and Belgium, the figures are slightly affected by boundary changes; but these changes have not been so great as to destroy entirely the value of comparative figures. The boundaries of other countries, as for example, U.S.S.R., Austria, Hungary, Rumania, and Greece, have been so changed that comparisons over time are subject to a large margin of error.

Statistics on country of birth of the foreign born have generally been restricted to those countries which had at the time of the census a separate political entity. For 1860–1900, however, an exception was made in the case of Poland. Although Poland was not restored to its original status as an independent country until the end of World War I, its historical position was such that Polish immigrants generally reported Poland as their country of birth regardless of the political sovereignty over their birthplace. For 1860–1890, persons reported as born in Poland were so tabulated without qualification. In the Census of 1900 an attempt was made to distinguish Austrian, German, and Russian Poland, and separate statistics for each were presented. In the Census of 1910, persons reported as born in Poland were assigned either to Russia, Germany, or Austria. The figures for 1910, however,

have been adjusted on the basis of mother tongue data, to conform as nearly as possible to the conditions in 1930.

Since World War I, the greatest difficulties encountered in the tabulation of country-of-birth statistics has been the classification of persons born in the former Austro-Hungarian Empire. Many persons born within the prewar boundaries of this Empire could not or did not give to the enumerator the information needed for the determination of their country of birth on the basis of postwar geography. It is therefore quite possible that some persons were assigned to Austria who were really born within the present areas of either Czechoslovakia or Yugoslavia, and that persons were assigned to Hungary who were born within the present areas of Rumania or Yugoslavia. Similarly, it is possible that some persons born in Latvia, Estonia, or Lithuania were assigned to Russia. Persons for whom Austria-Hungary was reported in the 1950 Census were allocated on the basis of surname to the various countries created out of the territory of the old empire after World War I. Even with this procedure, however, there appears to be some indication that Austria and Hungary are overreported at the expense of Yugoslavia and Czechoslovakia. In 1950 the situation was further complicated by the fact that, although there were extensive de facto boundary changes as a result of World War II, only a small number of these changes were officially recognized by the United States at that time.

For definition of color, see text for series A 22–33.

Series C 88–114.   Immigrants, by Country: 1820 to 1957

[For continuation of list of countries, see series C 101–114.   For years ending June 30, except: 1820–1831 and 1844–1849, years ending Sept. 30; and 1833–1842 and 1851–1867, years ending Dec. 31; 1832 covers 15 months ending Dec. 31; 1843, 9 months ending Sept. 30; 1850, 15 months ending Dec. 31; 1868, 6 months ending June 30]

		Europe											
			Northwestern Europe				Central Europe			Eastern Europe		Southern Europe	
Year	All countries [1]	Total	Great Britain	Ireland [2]	Scandinavia [3]	Other Northwestern [4]	Germany [5]	Poland [6]	Other Central [7]	U. S. S. R. and Baltic States [8]	Other Eastern [9]	Italy	Other Southern [10]
	88	89	90	91	92	93	94	95	96	97	98	99	100
1957	326,867	169,625	24,020	8,227	6,189	25,109	60,353	571	15,498	663	558	19,624	8,813
1956	321,625	156,866	19,008	5,607	5,681	15,254	44,409	263	10,284	643	394	40,430	14,893
1955	237,790	110,591	15,761	5,222	5,159	10,707	29,596	129	4,133	523	134	30,272	8,955
1954	208,177	92,121	16,672	4,655	5,459	11,853	33,098	67	2,873	475	104	13,145	3,720
1953	170,434	82,352	16,639	4,304	5,537	11,145	27,329	136	2,885	609	86	8,432	5,250
1952	265,520	193,626	22,177	3,526	5,416	12,476	104,236	235	23,529	548	137	11,342	10,004
1951	205,717	149,545	14,898	3,144	5,502	10,973	87,755	98	10,365	555	223	8,958	7,074
1950	249,187	199,115	12,755	5,842	5,661	10,857	128,592	696	17,792	526	277	12,454	3,663
1949	188,317	129,592	21,149	8,678	6,665	12,288	55,284	1,673	7,411	694	246	11,695	3,809
1948	170,570	103,544	26,403	7,534	6,127	13,721	19,368	2,447	6,006	897	485	16,075	4,481
1947	147,292	83,535	23,788	2,574	4,918	14,562	13,900	745	4,622	761	249	13,866	3,550
1946	108,721	52,852	33,552	1,816	1,278	8,651	2,598	335	511	153	98	2,636	1,224
1945	38,119	5,943	3,029	427	224	365	172	195	206	98	97	213	917
1944	28,551	4,509	1,321	112	281	619	238	292	316	157	109	120	944
1943	23,725	4,920	974	165	239	1,531	248	394	206	159	54	49	901
1942	28,781	11,153	907	83	371	5,622	2,150	343	396	197	117	103	864
1941	51,776	26,541	7,714	272	1,137	9,009	4,028	451	786	665	299	450	1,730
1940	70,756	50,454	6,158	839	1,260	7,743	21,520	702	3,628	898	491	5,302	1,913
1939	82,998	63,138	3,058	1,189	1,178	5,214	33,515	3,072	5,334	1,021	620	6,570	2,367
1938	67,895	44,495	2,262	1,085	1,393	3,352	17,199	2,403	5,195	960	542	7,712	2,392
1937	50,244	31,863	1,726	531	971	2,512	10,895	1,212	3,763	629	533	7,192	1,899
1936	36,329	23,480	1,310	444	646	1,745	6,346	869	2,723	378	424	6,774	1,821
1935	34,956	22,778	1,413	454	688	1,808	5,201	1,504	2,357	418	453	6,566	1,916
1934	29,470	17,210	1,305	443	557	1,270	4,392	1,032	1,422	607	347	4,374	1,461
1933	23,068	12,383	979	338	511	1,045	1,919	1,332	981	458	352	3,477	991
1932	35,576	20,579	2,057	539	938	1,558	2,670	1,296	1,749	636	592	6,662	1,882
1931	97,139	61,909	9,110	7,305	3,144	4,420	10,401	3,604	4,500	1,396	1,192	13,399	3,438
1930	241,700	147,438	31,015	23,445	6,919	9,170	26,569	9,231	9,184	2,772	2,159	22,327	4,647
1929	279,678	158,598	21,327	19,921	17,379	9,091	46,751	9,002	8,081	2,450	2,153	18,008	4,435
1928	307,255	158,513	19,958	25,268	16,184	9,079	45,778	8,755	7,091	2,652	1,776	17,728	4,244
1927	335,175	168,368	23,669	28,545	16,860	9,134	48,513	9,211	6,559	2,933	1,708	17,297	3,939
1926	304,488	155,562	25,528	24,897	16,818	8,773	50,421	7,126	6,020	3,323	1,596	8,253	2,807
1925	294,314	148,366	27,172	26,650	16,810	8,548	46,068	5,341	4,701	3,121	1,566	6,203	2,186
1924	706,896	364,339	59,490	17,111	35,577	16,077	75,091	28,806	32,700	20,918	13,173	56,246	9,150
1923	522,919	307,920	45,759	15,740	34,184	12,469	48,277	26,538	34,038	21,151	16,082	46,674	7,008
1922	309,556	216,385	25,153	10,579	14,625	11,149	17,931	28,635	29,363	19,910	12,244	40,319	6,477
1921	805,228	652,364	51,142	28,435	22,854	29,317	6,803	95,089	77,069	10,193	32,793	222,260	76,409
1920	430,001	246,295	38,471	9,591	13,444	24,491	1,001	4,813	5,666	1,751	3,913	95,145	48,009
1919	141,132	24,627	6,797	474	5,590	5,126	52	---------	53	1,403	51	1,884	3,197
1918	110,618	31,063	2,516	331	6,506	3,146	447	---------	61	4,242	93	5,250	8,471
1917	295,403	133,083	10,735	5,406	13,771	6,731	1,857	---------	1,258	12,716	369	34,596	45,644
1916	298,826	145,699	16,063	8,689	14,761	8,715	2,877	---------	5,191	7,842	1,167	33,665	46,779
1915	326,700	197,919	27,237	14,185	17,883	12,096	7,799		18,511	26,187	2,892	49,688	21,441
1914	1,218,480	1,058,391	48,729	24,688	29,391	25,591	35,734		278,152	255,660	21,420	283,738	55,288
1913	1,197,892	1,055,855	60,328	27,876	32,267	28,086	34,329		254,825	291,040	18,036	265,542	43,526
1912	838,172	718,875	57,148	25,879	27,554	22,921	27,788		178,882	162,395	20,925	157,134	38,249
1911	878,587	764,757	73,384	29,112	42,285	25,549	32,061		159,057	158,721	21,655	182,882	40,051
1910	1,041,570	926,291	68,941	29,855	48,267	23,852	31,283		258,737	186,792	25,287	215,537	37,740
1909	751,786	654,875	46,793	25,033	32,496	17,756	25,540		170,191	120,460	11,659	183,218	21,729
1908	782,870	691,901	62,824	30,556	30,175	22,177	32,309		168,509	156,711	27,345	128,503	32,792
1907	1,285,349	1,199,566	79,037	34,530	49,966	26,512	37,807		338,452	258,943	36,510	285,731	52,079
1906	1,100,735	1,018,365	67,198	34,995	52,781	23,277	37,564		265,138	215,665	18,652	273,120	29,975
1905	1,026,499	974,273	84,189	52,945	60,625	24,693	40,574		275,693	184,897	11,022	221,479	18,156
1904	812,870	767,933	51,448	36,142	60,096	23,321	46,380		177,156	145,141	12,756	193,296	22,197
1903	857,046	814,507	33,637	35,310	77,647	17,009	40,086		206,011	136,093	12,600	230,622	25,492
1902	648,743	619,068	16,898	29,138	54,038	10,322	28,304		171,989	107,347	8,234	178,375	14,423
1901	487,918	469,237	14,985	30,561	39,234	9,279	21,651		113,390	85,257	8,199	135,996	10,685
1900	448,572	424,700	12,509	35,730	31,151	5,822	18,507		114,847	90,787	6,852	100,135	8,360
1899	311,715	297,349	13,456	31,673	22,192	5,150	17,476		62,491	60,982	1,738	77,419	4,772
1898	229,299	217,786	12,894	25,128	19,282	4,698	17,111	4,726	39,797	29,828	1,076	58,613	4,633
1897	230,832	216,397	12,752	28,421	21,089	5,323	22,533	4,165	33,031	25,816	943	59,431	2,893
1896	343,267	329,067	24,565	40,262	33,199	7,611	31,885	691	65,103	51,445	954	68,060	5,292
1895	258,536	250,342	28,833	46,304	26,852	7,313	32,173	790	33,401	35,907	768	35,427	2,574
1894	285,631	277,052	22,520	30,231	32,400	9,514	53,989	1,941	38,638	39,278	1,027	42,977	4,537
1893	439,730	429,324	35,189	43,578	58,945	17,888	78,756	16,374	57,420	42,310	625	72,145	6,094
1892	579,663	570,876	42,215	51,383	66,295	21,731	119,168	40,536	76,937	81,511	1,331	61,631	8,138
1891	560,319	546,085	66,605	55,706	60,107	21,824	113,554	27,497	71,042	47,426	1,222	76,055	5,047
1890	455,302	445,680	69,730	53,024	50,368	20,575	92,427	11,073	56,199	35,598	723	52,003	3,960
1889	444,427	434,790	87,992	65,557	57,504	22,010	99,538	4,922	34,174	33,916	1,145	25,307	2,725
1888	546,889	538,131	108,692	73,513	81,924	23,251	109,717	5,826	45,811	33,487	1,393	51,558	2,959
1887	490,109	482,829	93,378	68,370	67,629	17,307	106,865	6,128	40,265	30,766	2,251	47,622	2,248
1886	334,203	329,529	62,929	49,619	46,735	11,737	84,403	3,939	28,680	17,800	670	21,315	1,702

[1] For 1820–1867 excludes returning citizens; therefore for those years, does not agree with series C 115 and C 133.
[2] Comprises Eire and Northern Ireland.
[3] Comprises Norway, Sweden, Denmark, and Iceland.
[4] Comprises Netherlands, Belgium, Luxembourg, Switzerland, and France.
[5] Includes Austria, 1938 to 1945.
[6] Between 1899 and 1919, included with Austria-Hungary, Germany, and Russia.
[7] Comprises Czechoslovakia (since 1920), Yugoslavia (since 1920), Hungary (since 1861), and Austria (since 1861, except for the years 1938–1945, when Austria was included with Germany).
[8] Comprises U. S. S. R. in Europe, Latvia, Estonia, Lithuania, and Finland.
[9] Comprises Rumania, Bulgaria, and Turkey in Europe.
[10] Comprises Spain, Portugal, Greece, and other Europe, not elsewhere classified.

Series C 88–114. Immigrants, by Country: 1820 to 1957—Con.

Year	All countries [1]	Total	Europe										
			Northwestern Europe				Central Europe			Eastern Europe		Southern Europe	
			Great Britain	Ireland [2]	Scandinavia [3]	Other Northwestern [4]	Germany [5]	Poland [6]	Other Central [7]	U.S.S.R. and Baltic States [8]	Other Eastern [9]	Italy	Other Southern [10]
	88	89	90	91	92	93	94	95	96	97	98	99	100
1885	395,346	353,083	57,713	51,795	40,704	13,732	124,443	3,085	27,309	17,158	941	13,642	2,561
1884	518,592	453,686	65,950	63,344	52,728	18,768	179,676	4,536	36,571	12,689	388	16,510	2,526
1883	603,322	522,587	76,606	81,486	71,994	24,271	194,786	2,011	27,625	9,909	163	31,792	1,944
1882	788,992	648,186	102,991	76,432	105,326	27,796	250,630	4,672	29,150	16,918	134	32,159	1,978
1881	669,431	528,545	81,376	72,342	81,582	26,883	210,485	5,614	27,935	5,041	102	15,401	1,784
1880	457,257	348,691	73,273	71,603	65,657	15,042	84,638	2,177	17,267	5,014	35	12,354	1,631
1879	177,826	134,259	29,955	20,013	21,820	9,081	34,602	489	5,963	4,453	29	5,791	2,063
1878	138,469	101,612	22,150	15,932	12,254	6,929	29,313	547	5,150	3,048	29	4,344	1,916
1877	141,857	106,195	23,581	14,569	11,274	8,621	29,298	533	5,396	6,599	32	3,195	3,097
1876	169,986	120,920	29,291	19,575	12,323	10,923	31,937	925	6,276	4,775	38	3,015	1,842
1875	227,498	182,961	47,905	37,957	14,322	11,987	47,769	984	7,658	7,997	27	3,631	2,724
1874	313,339	262,783	62,021	53,707	19,178	15,998	87,291	1,795	8,850	4,073	62	7,666	2,142
1873	459,803	397,541	89,500	77,344	35,481	22,892	149,671	3,338	7,112	1,634	53	8,757	1,759
1872	404,806	352,155	84,912	68,732	28,575	15,614	141,109	1,647	4,410	1,018	20	4,190	1,928
1871	321,350	265,145	85,455	57,439	22,132	7,174	82,554	535	4,887	673	23	2,816	1,457
1870	387,203	328,626	103,677	56,996	30,742	9,152	118,225	223	4,425	907	6	2,891	1,382
1869	352,768	315,963	84,438	40,786	43,941	10,585	131,042	184	1,499	343	18	1,489	1,638
1868	138,840	130,090	24,127	32,068	11,985	4,293	55,831	--------	192	141	4	891	558
1867	315,722	283,751	52,641	72,879	8,491	12,417	133,426	310	692	205	26	1,624	1,040
1866	318,568	278,916	94,924	36,690	14,495	13,648	115,892	412	93	287	18	1,382	1,075
1865	248,120	214,048	82,465	29,772	7,258	7,992	83,424	528	422	183	14	924	1,066
1864	193,418	185,233	53,428	63,523	2,961	5,621	57,276	165	230	256	11	600	1,162
1863	176,282	163,733	66,882	55,916	3,119	3,245	33,162	94	85	77	16	547	590
1862	91,985	83,710	24,639	23,351	2,550	4,386	27,529	63	111	79	11	566	425
1861	91,918	81,200	19,675	23,797	850	3,769	31,661	48	51	34	5	811	499
1860	153,640	141,209	29,737	48,637	840	5,278	54,491	82	--------	65	4	1,019	1,056
1859	121,282	110,949	26,163	35,216	1,590	3,727	41,784	106	--------	91	10	932	1,330
1858	123,126	111,354	28,956	26,873	2,662	4,580	45,310	9	--------	246	17	1,240	1,461
1857	251,306	216,224	58,479	54,361	2,747	6,879	91,781	124	--------	25	11	1,007	810
1856	200,436	186,083	44,658	54,349	1,330	12,403	71,028	20	--------	9	5	1,365	916
1855	200,877	187,729	47,572	49,627	1,349	14,571	71,918	462	--------	13	9	1,052	1,156
1854	427,833	405,542	58,647	101,606	4,222	23,070	215,009	208	--------	2	7	1,263	1,508
1853	368,645	361,576	37,576	162,649	3,396	14,205	141,946	33	--------	3	15	555	1,198
1852	371,603	362,484	40,699	159,548	4,106	11,278	145,918	110	--------	2	3	351	469
1851	379,466	369,510	51,487	221,253	2,438	20,905	72,482	10	--------	1	2	447	485
1850	369,980	308,323	51,085	164,004	1,589	11,470	78,896	5	--------	31	15	431	797
1849	297,024	286,501	55,132	159,398	3,481	7,634	60,235	4	--------	44	9	209	355
1848	226,527	218,025	35,159	112,934	1,113	9,877	58,465	--------	--------	1	3	241	232
1847	234,968	229,117	23,302	105,536	1,320	24,336	74,281	8	--------	5	2	164	163
1846	154,416	146,315	22,180	51,752	2,030	12,303	57,561	4	--------	248	4	151	82
1845	114,371	109,301	19,210	44,821	982	9,466	34,355	6	--------	1	3	137	320
1844	78,615	74,745	14,353	33,490	1,336	4,343	20,731	36	--------	13	10	141	292
1843	52,496	49,013	8,430	19,670	1,777	4,364	14,441	17	--------	6	5	117	186
1842	104,565	99,945	22,005	51,342	588	5,361	20,370	10	--------	28	2	100	139
1841	80,289	76,216	16,188	37,772	226	6,077	15,291	15	--------	174	6	179	288
1840	84,066	80,126	2,613	39,430	207	7,978	29,704	5	--------	--------	1	37	151
1839	68,069	64,148	10,271	23,963	380	7,891	21,028	46	--------	7	1	84	477
1838	38,914	34,070	5,420	12,645	112	3,839	11,683	41	--------	13	--------	86	231
1837	79,340	71,039	12,218	28,508	399	5,769	23,740	81	--------	19	--------	36	269
1836	76,242	70,465	13,106	30,578	473	5,189	20,707	53	--------	2	3	115	239
1835	45,374	41,987	8,970	26,927	68	3,369	8,311	54	--------	9	--------	60	219
1834	65,365	57,510	10,490	24,474	66	4,468	17,686	54	--------	15	1	105	151
1833	58,640	29,111	4,916	8,648	189	5,355	6,988	1	--------	159	1	1,699	1,155
1832	60,482	34,193	5,331	12,436	334	5,695	10,194	34	--------	52	--------	3	114
1831	22,633	13,039	2,475	5,772	36	2,277	2,413	--------	--------	1	--------	28	37
1830	23,322	7,217	1,153	2,721	19	1,305	1,976	2	--------	3	2	9	27
1829	22,520	12,523	3,179	7,415	30	1,065	597	--------	--------	1	1	23	212
1828	27,382	24,729	5,352	12,488	60	4,700	1,851	1	--------	7	6	34	230
1827	18,875	16,719	4,186	9,766	28	1,829	432	1	--------	19	1	35	422
1826	10,837	9,751	2,319	5,408	26	968	511	--------	--------	4	2	57	456
1825	10,199	8,543	2,095	4,888	18	719	450	1	--------	10	--------	75	287
1824	7,912	4,965	1,264	2,345	20	671	230	4	--------	7	2	45	377
1823	6,354	4,016	1,100	1,908	7	528	183	3	--------	7	2	33	245
1822	6,911	4,418	1,221	2,267	28	522	148	3	--------	10	4	35	180
1821	9,127	5,936	3,210	1,518	24	521	383	1	--------	7	--------	63	209
1820	8,385	7,691	2,410	3,614	23	452	968	5	--------	14	1	30	174

[1] For 1820–1867 excludes returning citizens; therefore for those years, does not agree with series C 115 and C 133.
[2] Comprises Eire and Northern Ireland.
[3] Comprises Norway, Sweden, Denmark, and Iceland.
[4] Comprises Netherlands, Belgium, Luxembourg, Switzerland, and France.
[5] Includes Austria, 1938 to 1945.
[6] Between 1899 and 1919, included with Austria-Hungary, Germany, and Russia.
[7] Comprises Czechoslovakia (since 1920), Yugoslavia (since 1920), Hungary (since 1861), and Austria (since 1861, except for the years 1938–1945, when Austria was included with Germany).
[8] Comprises U. S. S. R. in Europe, Latvia, Estonia, Lithuania, and Finland.
[9] Comprises Rumania, Bulgaria, and Turkey in Europe.
[10] Comprises Spain, Portugal, Greece, and other Europe, not elsewhere classified.

Series C 88–114.　Immigrants, by Country: 1820 to 1957—Con.

Year	Asia					America				Africa, total	Australasia			All other countries [3]
	Total	Turkey in Asia [1]	China	Japan [2]	Other Asia [3]	Total	Canada and Newfoundland [4]	Mexico	Other America		Total	Australia and New Zealand	Other Pacific Islands [3]	
	101	102	103	104	105	106	107	108	109	110	111	112	113	114
1957	20,008	77	2,098	6,829	11,004	134,160	46,354	49,321	38,485	1,600	1,458	1,228	230	16
1956	17,327	48	1,386	5,967	9,926	144,713	42,363	61,320	41,030	1,351	1,346	1,171	175	22
1955	10,935	54	568	4,150	6,163	110,436	32,435	43,702	34,299	1,203	1,028	932	96	3,597
1954	9,970	33	254	3,846	5,837	95,587	34,873	30,645	30,069	1,248	910	845	65	8,341
1953	8,231	13	528	2,579	5,111	77,650	36,283	17,183	24,184	989	782	742	40	430
1952	9,328	12	263	3,814	5,239	61,049	33,354	9,079	18,616	931	578	545	33	8
1951	3,921	3	335	271	3,312	47,631	25,880	6,153	15,598	845	527	490	37	3,248
1950	3,779	13	1,280	100	2,386	44,191	21,885	6,744	15,562	849	517	460	57	736
1949	6,438	40	3,415	529	2,454	49,334	25,156	8,083	16,095	995	776	661	115	1,182
1948	10,739	16	7,203	423	3,097	52,746	25,485	8,384	18,877	1,027	1,336	1,218	118	1,178
1947	5,823	22	3,191	131	2,479	52,753	24,342	7,558	20,853	1,284	2,960	2,821	139	937
1946	1,633	16	252	14	1,351	46,066	21,344	7,146	17,576	1,516	6,106	6,009	97	548
1945	442	13	71	1	357	29,646	11,530	6,702	11,414	406	1,663	1,625	38	19
1944	227	15	50	4	158	23,084	10,143	6,598	6,343	112	615	577	38	4
1943	334	36	65	20	213	18,162	9,761	4,172	4,229	141	160	120	40	8
1942	564	31	179	44	310	16,377	10,599	2,378	3,400	473	163	120	43	51
1941	1,801	16	1,003	289	493	22,445	11,473	2,824	8,148	564	255	194	61	170
1940	1,913	7	643	102	1,161	17,822	11,078	2,313	4,431	202	228	207	21	137
1939	2,162	15	642	102	1,403	17,139	10,813	2,640	3,686	218	222	213	9	119
1938	2,376	11	613	93	1,659	20,486	14,404	2,502	3,580	174	248	228	20	116
1937	1,065	13	293	132	627	16,903	12,011	2,347	2,545	155	174	145	29	84
1936	721	20	273	91	337	11,786	8,121	1,716	1,949	105	165	147	18	72
1935	682	31	229	88	334	11,174	7,782	1,560	1,832	118	141	132	9	63
1934	597	22	187	86	302	11,409	7,945	1,801	1,663	104	147	130	17	3
1933	552	27	148	75	302	9,925	6,187	1,936	1,802	71	137	122	15	--------
1932	1,931	43	750	526	612	12,577	8,003	2,171	2,403	186	303	291	12	--------
1931	3,345	139	1,150	653	1,403	30,816	22,183	3,333	5,300	417	652	616	36	--------
1930	4,535	118	1,589	837	1,991	88,104	65,254	12,703	10,147	572	1,051	1,026	25	--------
1929	3,758	70	1,446	771	1,471	116,177	66,451	40,154	9,572	509	636	619	17	--------
1928	3,380	80	1,320	550	1,430	144,281	75,281	59,016	9,984	475	606	578	28	--------
1927	3,669	73	1,471	723	1,402	161,872	84,580	67,721	9,571	520	746	712	34	--------
1926	3,413	37	1,751	654	971	144,393	93,368	43,316	7,709	529	591	556	35	--------
1925	3,578	51	1,937	723	867	141,496	102,753	32,964	5,779	412	462	416	46	--------
1924	22,065	2,820	6,992	8,801	3,452	318,855	200,690	89,336	28,829	900	679	635	44	58
1923	13,705	2,183	4,986	5,809	727	199,972	117,011	63,768	19,193	548	759	711	48	15
1922	14,263	1,998	4,406	6,716	1,143	77,448	46,810	19,551	11,087	520	915	855	60	25
1921	25,034	11,735	4,009	7,878	1,412	124,118	72,317	30,758	21,043	1,301	2,281	2,191	90	130
1920	17,505	5,033	2,330	9,432	710	162,666	90,025	52,361	20,280	648	2,185	2,066	119	702
1919	12,674	19	1,964	10,064	627	102,286	57,782	29,818	14,686	189	1,310	1,234	76	46
1918	12,701	43	1,795	10,213	650	65,418	32,452	18,524	14,442	299	1,090	925	165	47
1917	12,756	393	2,237	8,991	1,135	147,779	105,399	17,869	24,511	566	1,142	1,014	128	77
1916	13,204	1,670	2,460	8,680	394	137,424	101,551	18,425	17,448	894	1,574	1,484	90	31
1915	15,211	3,543	2,660	8,613	395	111,206	82,215	12,340	16,651	934	1,399	1,282	117	31
1914	34,273	21,716	2,502	8,929	1,126	122,695	86,139	14,614	21,942	1,539	1,446	1,336	110	136
1913	35,358	23,955	2,105	8,281	1,017	103,907	73,802	11,926	18,179	1,409	1,340	1,229	111	23
1912	21,449	12,788	1,765	6,114	782	95,926	55,990	23,238	16,698	1,009	898	794	104	15
1911	17,428	10,229	1,460	4,520	1,219	94,364	56,830	19,889	17,645	956	1,043	984	59	39
1910	23,533	15,212	1,968	2,720	3,633	89,534	56,555	18,691	14,288	1,072	1,097	998	99	43
1909	12,904	7,506	1,943	3,111	344	82,208	51,941	16,251	14,016	858	892	839	53	49
1908	28,365	9,753	1,397	15,803	1,412	59,997	38,510	6,067	15,420	1,411	1,179	1,098	81	17
1907	40,524	8,053	961	30,226	1,284	41,762	19,918	1,406	20,438	1,486	1,989	1,947	42	22
1906	22,300	6,354	1,544	13,835	567	24,613	5,063	1,997	17,553	712	1,733	1,682	51	[5] 33,012
1905	23,925	6,157	2,166	10,331	5,271	25,217	2,168	2,637	20,412	757	2,166	2,091	75	161
1904	26,186	5,235	4,309	14,264	2,378	16,420	2,837	1,009	12,574	686	1,555	1,461	94	90
1903	29,966	7,118	2,209	19,968	671	11,023	1,058	528	9,437	176	1,349	1,150	199	25
1902	22,271	6,223	1,649	14,270	129	6,698	636	709	5,353	37	566	384	182	103
1901	13,593	5,782	2,459	5,269	83	4,416	540	347	3,529	173	498	325	173	1
1900	17,946	3,962	1,247	12,635	102	5,455	396	237	4,822	30	428	214	214	13
1899	8,972	4,436	1,660	2,844	32	4,316	1,322	161	2,833	51	810	456	354	217
1898	8,637	4,275	2,071	2,230	61	2,627	352	107	2,168	48	201	153	48	--------
1897	9,662	4,732	3,363	1,526	41	4,537	291	91	4,155	37	199	139	60	--------
1896	6,764	4,139	1,441	1,110	74	7,303	278	150	6,875	21	112	87	25	--------
1895	4,495	2,767	539	1,150	39	3,508	244	116	3,148	36	155	155	--------	--------
1894	4,690	--------	1,170	1,931	1,589	3,551	194	109	3,248	24	244	244	--------	70
1893	2,392	--------	472	1,380	540	2,593	(6)	(7)	2,593	(6)	248	248	(6)	5,173
1892	--------					(6)	(6)	(7)	(6)	(6)	267	267	(6)	8,520
1891	7,678	2,488	2,836	1,136	1,218	5,082	234	(7)	4,848	103	1,301	777	524	70
1890	4,448	1,126	1,716	691	915	3,833	183	(7)	3,650	112	1,167	699	468	62
1889	1,725	593	118	640	374	5,459	28	(7)	5,431	187	2,196	1,000	1,196	70
1888	843	273	26	404	140	5,402	15	(7)	5,387	65	2,387	697	1,690	61
1887	615	208	10	229	168	5,270	9	(7)	5,261	40	1,282	528	754	73
1886	317	15	40	194	68	3,026	17	(7)	3,009	122	1,136	522	614	73

[1] No record of immigration from Turkey in Asia until 1869.
[2] No record of immigration from Japan until 1861.
[3] Philippine Islands are included in "Other Asia" in 1952 (1,179), 1953 (1,074), 1954 (1,234), 1955 (1,598), 1956 (1,792), and 1957 (1,874). From 1934 to 1951, inclusive, they are included in "All other countries."
[4] Prior to 1920 Canada and Newfoundland were recorded as British North America. From 1820 to 1898 the figures include all British North American possessions.
[5] Includes 32,897 persons returning to their homes in the United States.
[6] Included in "All other countries."
[7] No record of immigration from Mexico for 1886 to 1893.

Series C 88–114. Immigrants, by Country: 1820 to 1957—Con.

Year	Asia					America				Africa, total	Australasia			All other countries [3]
	Total	Turkey in Asia [1]	China	Japan [2]	Other Asia [3]	Total	Canada and Newfoundland [4]	Mexico	Other America		Total	Australia and New Zealand	Other Pacific Islands [3]	
	101	102	103	104	105	106	107	108	109	110	111	112	113	114
1885	198	----	22	49	127	41,203	38,336	323	2,544	112	679	449	230	71
1884	510	----	279	20	211	63,339	60,626	430	2,283	59	900	502	398	98
1883	8,113	----	8,031	27	55	71,729	70,274	469	986	67	747	554	193	79
1882	39,629	----	39,579	5	45	100,129	98,366	366	1,397	60	889	878	11	99
1881	11,982	5	11,890	11	76	127,577	125,450	325	1,802	33	1,191	1,188	3	103
1880	5,839	4	5,802	4	29	101,692	99,744	492	1,456	18	954	953	1	63
1879	9,660	31	9,604	4	21	33,043	31,286	556	1,201	12	816	813	3	36
1878	9,014	7	8,992	2	13	27,204	25,592	465	1,147	18	606	606	----	15
1877	10,640	3	10,594	7	36	24,065	22,137	445	1,483	16	914	912	2	27
1876	22,943	8	22,781	4	150	24,686	22,505	631	1,550	89	1,312	1,205	107	36
1875	16,499	1	16,437	3	58	26,640	24,097	610	1,933	54	1,268	1,104	164	76
1874	13,838	6	13,776	21	35	35,339	33,020	386	1,933	58	1,193	960	233	128
1873	20,325	3	20,292	9	21	40,335	37,891	606	1,838	28	1,414	1,135	279	160
1872	7,825	----	7,788	17	20	42,205	40,204	569	1,432	41	2,416	2,180	236	164
1871	7,240	4	7,135	78	23	48,835	47,164	402	1,269	24	21	18	3	85
1870	15,825	----	15,740	48	37	42,658	40,414	463	1,781	31	36	36	----	27
1869	12,949	2	12,874	63	10	23,767	21,120	320	2,327	72	----	----	----	17
1868	5,171	----	5,157	----	14	3,415	2,785	129	501	3	----	----	----	161
1867	3,961	----	3,863	67	31	24,715	23,379	292	1,044	25	----	----	----	3,270
1866	2,411	----	2,385	7	19	33,582	32,150	239	1,193	33	----	----	----	3,626
1865	2,947	----	2,942	----	5	22,778	21,586	193	999	49	----	----	----	8,298
1864	2,982	----	2,975	----	7	4,607	3,636	99	872	37	----	----	----	559
1863	7,216	----	7,214	----	2	4,147	3,464	96	587	3	----	----	----	1,183
1862	3,640	----	3,633	----	7	4,175	3,275	142	758	12	----	----	----	448
1861	7,528	----	7,518	1	9	2,763	2,069	218	476	47	----	----	----	380
1860	5,476	----	5,467	----	9	6,343	4,514	229	1,600	126	----	----	----	486
1859	3,461	----	3,457	----	4	5,466	4,163	265	1,038	11	----	----	----	1,395
1858	5,133	----	5,128	----	5	5,821	4,603	429	789	17	----	----	----	801
1857	5,945	----	5,944	----	1	6,811	5,670	133	1,008	25	----	----	----	22,301
1856	4,747	----	4,733	----	14	9,058	6,493	741	1,824	6	----	----	----	542
1855	3,540	----	3,526	----	14	9,260	7,761	420	1,079	14	----	----	----	334
1854	13,100	----	13,100	----	----	8,533	6,891	446	1,196	----	----	----	----	658
1853	47	----	42	----	5	6,030	5,424	162	444	8	----	----	----	984
1852	4	----	----	----	4	7,695	6,352	72	1,271	----	----	----	----	1,420
1851	2	----	----	----	2	9,703	7,438	181	2,084	3	----	----	----	248
1850	7	----	3	----	4	15,768	9,376	597	5,795	----	----	----	----	45,882
1849	11	----	3	----	8	8,904	6,890	518	1,496	3	----	----	----	1,605
1848	8	----	----	----	8	7,989	6,473	24	1,492	10	----	----	----	495
1847	12	----	4	----	8	5,231	3,827	62	1,342	----	----	----	----	608
1846	11	----	7	----	4	5,525	3,855	222	1,448	1	----	----	----	2,564
1845	6	----	6	----	----	5,035	3,195	498	1,342	4	----	----	----	25
1844	6	----	3	----	3	3,740	2,711	197	832	14	----	----	----	110
1843	11	----	3	----	8	2,854	1,502	398	954	6	----	----	----	612
1842	7	----	4	----	3	3,994	2,078	403	1,513	3	----	----	----	616
1841	3	----	2	----	1	3,429	1,816	352	1,261	14	----	----	----	627
1840	1	----	----	----	1	3,815	1,938	395	1,482	6	----	----	----	118
1839	----	----	----	----	----	3,617	1,926	353	1,338	10	----	----	----	294
1838	1	----	----	----	1	2,990	1,476	211	1,303	10	----	----	----	1,843
1837	11	----	----	----	11	3,628	1,279	627	1,722	2	----	----	----	4,660
1836	4	----	----	----	4	4,936	2,814	798	1,324	6	----	----	----	831
1835	17	----	8	----	9	3,312	1,193	1,032	1,087	14	----	----	----	44
1834	6	----	----	----	6	2,779	1,020	885	874	1	----	----	----	5,069
1833	3	----	----	----	3	3,282	1,194	779	1,309	1	----	----	----	26,243
1832	4	----	----	----	4	2,871	608	827	1,436	2	----	----	----	23,412
1831	1	----	----	----	1	2,194	176	692	1,326	2	----	----	----	7,397
1830	----	----	----	----	----	2,296	189	983	1,124	2	----	----	----	13,807
1829	2	----	1	----	1	3,299	409	2,290	600	1	----	----	----	6,695
1828	3	----	----	----	3	2,090	267	1,089	734	6	----	----	----	554
1827	1	----	----	----	1	580	165	127	288	4	----	----	----	1,571
1826	1	----	----	----	1	831	223	106	502	----	----	----	----	254
1825	1	----	1	----	----	846	314	68	464	1	----	----	----	808
1824	1	----	----	----	1	559	155	110	294	----	----	----	----	2,387
1823	----	----	----	----	----	382	167	35	180	----	----	----	----	1,956
1822	1	----	----	----	1	378	204	5	169	----	----	----	----	2,114
1821	----	----	----	----	----	303	184	4	115	2	----	----	----	2,886
1820	5	----	1	----	4	387	209	1	177	1	----	----	----	301

[1] No record of immigration from Turkey in Asia until 1869.
[2] No record of immigration from Japan until 1861.
[3] Philippine Islands are included in "Other Asia" in 1952 (1,179), 1953 (1,074), 1954 (1,234), 1955 (1,598), 1956 (1,792), and 1957 (1,874). From 1934 to 1951, inclusive, they are included in "All other countries."
[4] Prior to 1920 Canada and Newfoundland were recorded as British North America. From 1820 to 1898 the figures include all British North American possessions.

Series C 115–132. Immigrants, by Major Occupation Group: 1820 to 1957

[For years ending June 30, except: 1820–1831 and 1844–1850, years ending Sept. 30; and 1833–1842 and 1850–1866, years ending Dec. 31; 1832 covers 15 months ending Dec. 31; 1843, 9 months ending Sept. 30; 1851, 15 months ending Dec. 31]

Year	Total	Professional, technical, and kindred workers	Farmers and farm managers	Managers, officials, and proprietors, exc. farm	Clerical, sales, and kindred workers	Craftsmen, foremen, operatives, and kindred workers	Private household workers	Service workers, exc. private household	Farm laborers and foremen	Laborers, exc. farm and mine	No occupation
	115	116	117	118	119	120	121	122	123	124	125
1957	326,867	24,489	3,506	6,127	25,897	46,338	11,457	8,761	4,585	21,826	173,881
1956	321,625	18,995	5,727	5,814	23,413	44,950	15,347	7,922	9,050	27,807	162,600
1955	237,790	14,109	4,446	5,114	18,060	34,218	11,824	6,512	5,486	17,518	120,503
1954	208,177	13,817	3,846	5,296	16,018	32,151	8,096	5,203	1,622	10,061	112,067
1953	170,434	12,783	3,393	5,025	15,171	26,975	6,852	4,390	1,538	5,369	88,938
1952	265,520	16,496	10,566	5,968	16,724	42,315	9,653	6,418	6,289	8,969	142,122
1951	205,717	15,269	10,214	5,493	14,098	34,041	7,243	5,292	4,972	5,481	103,614
1950	249,187	20,502	17,642	6,396	16,796	41,450	8,900	4,970	3,976	5,693	122,862
1949	188,317	13,884	8,937	6,014	14,797	27,964	6,990	3,937	933	6,192	98,669
1948	170,570	12,619	4,884	6,207	15,298	23,816	6,389	4,350	946	4,826	91,235
1947	147,292	10,891	3,462	5,886	13,961	19,306	4,922	3,882	442	2,831	81,709
1946	108,721	6,198	947	3,616	8,378	8,826	2,464	2,153	189	1,473	74,477
1945	38,119	2,852	497	1,457	3,715	4,511	1,495	1,047	225	886	21,434
1944	28,551	2,616	349	894	2,368	3,533	1,125	811	203	1,030	15,622
1943	23,725	2,695	235	988	1,840	2,587	770	707	164	681	13,058
1942	28,781	3,518	254	2,305	1,638	2,061	872	740	92	493	16,808
1941	51,776	6,232	356	5,640	2,837	3,513	1,503	829	129	732	30,005
1940	70,756	6,802	847	7,415	4,361	5,710	2,891	949	252	2,120	39,409
1939	82,998	7,199	1,186	8,929	4,794	6,532	5,420	1,979	415	2,070	44,474
1938	67,895	5,418	1,508	5,408	3,119	5,697	5,919	1,794	609	2,411	36,012
1937	50,244	4,130	852	3,422	2,126	3,996	3,213	1,426	378	1,904	28,797
1936	36,329	2,564	535	1,782	1,449	2,490	1,944	1,056	324	1,195	22,990
1935	34,956	2,244	593	1,347	1,024	2,689	1,418	1,390	408	1,355	22,488
1934	29,470	2,101	425	1,207	933	2,267	805	1,216	233	1,154	19,129
1933	23,068	1,615	292	690	600	1,821	550	933	134	887	15,546
1932	35,576	2,100	403	1,331	919	2,053	1,232	1,063	254	1,157	25,064
1931	97,139	4,120	2,743	2,384	4,229	9,555	9,740	3,128	3,422	4,806	53,012
1930	241,700	8,585	8,375	4,620	14,414	32,474	29,073	6,749	13,736	18,080	105,594
1929	279,678	8,792	8,309	4,709	15,354	36,437	31,841	6,820	19,849	27,873	119,694
1928	307,255	9,332	8,773	5,287	16,344	42,765	28,751	8,846	24,161	37,904	125,092
1927	335,175	9,883	10,324	5,772	20,140	42,394	31,344	10,070	23,698	55,989	125,561
1926	304,488	9,203	9,720	5,374	19,086	38,682	30,587	14,340	17,390	45,199	114,907
1925	294,314	8,942	13,875	5,508	15,363	36,927	26,924	15,399	16,022	36,610	118,744
1924	706,896	20,926	20,320	15,668	27,373	123,923	51,680	29,261	27,492	112,344	277,909
1923	522,919	13,926	12,503	12,086	17,931	87,899	52,223	22,244	25,905	86,617	191,585
1922	309,556	9,696	7,676	9,573	10,055	40,309	44,531	12,340	10,529	33,797	131,050
1921	805,228	12,852	22,282	18,286	18,922	109,710	102,478	24,298	32,400	162,859	301,141
1920	430,001	10,540	12,192	9,654	14,054	55,991	37,197	18,487	15,257	83,496	173,133
1919	141,132	5,261	3,933	4,247	6,524	21,671	6,277	11,571	4,412	18,922	58,314
1918	110,618	3,529	2,583	3,940	4,239	17,501	7,816	6,367	4,538	15,142	44,963
1917	295,403	7,499	7,764	8,329	10,554	38,660	31,885	11,784	22,328	52,182	104,418
1916	298,826	9,024	6,840	8,725	9,907	36,086	29,258	10,989	26,250	56,981	104,766
1915	326,700	11,453	6,518	10,728	9,377	45,591	39,774	11,976	24,723	49,620	116,940
1914	1,218,480	13,454	14,442	21,903	17,933	149,515	144,409	19,621	288,053	228,935	320,215
1913	1,197,892	12,552	13,180	19,094	15,173	139,091	140,218	17,609	320,105	223,682	297,188
1912	838,172	10,913	7,664	14,715	13,782	107,893	116,529	13,580	184,154	137,872	231,070
1911	878,587	11,275	9,709	15,416	14,723	128,717	107,153	11,051	176,003	158,518	246,022
1910	1,041,570	9,689	11,793	14,731	12,219	121,847	96,658	8,977	288,745	216,909	260,002
1909	751,786	7,603	8,914	11,562	8,467	75,730	64,568	5,849	171,310	176,490	221,293
1908	782,870	10,504	7,720	16,410	11,523	106,943	89,942	10,367	138,844	147,940	242,677
1907	1,285,349	12,016	13,476	20,132	12,735	169,394	121,587	13,578	323,854	293,868	304,709
1906	1,100,735	13,015	15,288	23,515	12,226	156,902	115,984	10,439	239,125	228,781	285,460
1905	1,026,499	12,582	18,474	27,706	12,759	159,442	125,473	5,849	142,187	290,009	232,018
1904	812,870	12,195	4,507	26,914	11,055	133,748	104,937	6,400	85,850	212,572	214,692
1903	857,046	6,999	13,363	15,603	7,226	110,644	92,686	11,482	77,518	321,824	199,701
1902	648,743	2,937	8,168	9,340	3,836	71,131	69,913	6,298	80,562	243,399	153,159
1901	487,918	2,665	3,035	8,294	3,197	57,346	42,027	5,352	54,753	162,563	148,686
1900	448,572	2,392	5,433	7,216	2,870	54,793	40,311	4,406	31,949	164,261	134,941
1899	311,715	1,972	3,973	6,815	2,473	38,608	34,120	4,580	17,343	92,452	109,379

Series C 115-132. Immigrants, by Major Occupation Group: 1820 to 1957—Con.

Year	Total[1]	No occupation	Professional	Commercial	Skilled	Farmers	Servants	Laborers	Miscellaneous
	115	125	126	127	128	129	130	131	132
1898	229,299	90,569	1,347	5,959	33,145	16,243	23,656	52,531	5,849
1897	230,832	91,624	1,732	7,159	33,161	22,560	23,739	46,198	4,659
1896	343,267	123,196	2,324	6,174	46,807	29,251	38,926	91,262	5,327
1895	258,536	92,193	2,029	5,314	43,844	13,055	35,960	61,430	4,711
1894	285,631	113,247	1,791	6,033	49,736	21,762	29,653	56,732	6,677
1893	439,730	209,767	2,362	837	51,145	34,070	(2)	114,295	[2]27,254
1892	579,663	255,832	2,932	2,683	63,128	51,630	(2)	171,483	[2]31,975
1891	560,319	248,635	3,431	11,340	54,951	36,398	32,596	167,290	5,678
1890	455,302	195,770	3,236	7,802	44,540	29,296	28,625	139,365	6,668
1889	444,427	208,761	2,815	7,359	50,457	28,962	30,220	111,809	4,044
1888	546,889	243,900	3,360	7,597	59,985	29,335	27,310	170,273	5,129
1887	490,109	224,073	2,882	8,032	52,403	30,932	27,510	140,938	3,339
1886	334,203	157,952	2,078	6,237	36,522	20,600	20,198	86,853	3,763
1885	395,346	211,730	2,097	6,707	39,817	27,585	20,213	83,068	4,129
1884	518,592	277,052	2,284	7,691	55,061	42,050	24,249	106,478	3,727
1883	603,322	322,318	2,450	8,280	62,505	39,048	27,988	136,071	4,662
1882	788,992	402,835	2,992	10,102	72,664	61,888	23,010	209,605	5,896
1881	669,431	355,670	2,812	9,371	66,457	58,028	19,342	147,816	9,935
1880	457,257	217,446	1,773	7,916	49,929	47,204	18,580	105,012	9,397
1879	177,826	81,772	1,639	5,202	21,362	19,907	6,804	36,897	4,243
1878	138,469	62,622	1,510	4,475	16,531	14,843	6,157	26,656	5,675
1877	141,857	63,316	1,885	4,667	21,006	13,188	5,158	25,482	7,155
1876	169,986	71,111	2,400	4,963	24,200	14,536	6,493	38,847	7,436
1875	227,498	106,723	2,426	5,029	33,803	16,447	10,579	46,877	5,614
1874	313,339	155,122	2,476	5,641	38,700	28,775	12,427	65,895	4,303
1873	459,803	239,307	2,980	7,593	48,792	36,983	16,259	104,423	3,466
1872	404,806	213,959	1,905	7,156	44,967	38,159	11,108	85,934	1,618
1871	321,350	172,215	2,247	5,553	33,577	27,042	13,814	65,936	966
1870	387,203	207,174	1,831	7,139	35,698	35,656	14,261	84,577	867
1869	352,768	181,453	1,700	8,837	33,345	28,102	10,265	88,649	417
1868	282,189	150,983	1,398	8,556	32,197	23,046	6,561	59,151	297
1867	342,162	182,794	2,288	14,706	44,097	32,626	7,715	57,419	517
1866	359,957	202,456	2,242	15,827	41,091	30,302	8,883	58,629	527
1865	287,399	161,580	1,743	12,700	36,522	20,012	9,231	45,247	364
1864	221,535	106,656	1,120	9,473	26,542	13,837	15,623	48,041	243
1863	199,811	99,039	1,173	7,590	24,155	12,348	9,103	46,198	205
1862	114,463	62,860	788	7,774	11,986	9,265	3,683	17,752	355
1861	112,702	60,760	668	7,683	11,601	11,668	739	19,413	170
1860	179,691	93,925	792	11,207	19,342	21,742	1,415	31,268	----------
1859	155,509	78,228	858	12,495	24,628	16,323	1,281	21,696	----------
1858	144,906	71,320	662	10,217	18,742	20,506	1,142	22,317	----------
1857	271,982	153,963	570	12,114	26,062	34,702	1,322	43,249	----------
1856	224,496	130,647	462	11,101	18,797	24,722	1,748	37,019	----------
1855	230,476	117,603	780	14,759	17,463	34,693	2,598	42,580	----------
1854	460,474	235,216	699	15,173	36,468	87,188	3,357	82,373	----------
1853	400,982	223,390	722	12,782	20,806	56,322	3,938	83,022	----------
1852	397,343	223,861	572	11,502	27,176	58,023	942	75,267	----------
1851	474,398	257,376	938	14,983	36,297	59,095	3,733	101,976	----------
1850	315,334	188,931	918	6,400	26,369	42,873	3,203	46,640	----------
1849	299,683	157,657	972	3,508	32,021	39,675	3,671	62,179	----------
1848	229,483	118,528	517	3,407	24,705	31,670	4,433	46,223	----------
1847	239,482	126,005	703	4,218	25,895	43,594	3,198	35,869	----------
1846	158,649	91,132	592	4,189	13,250	27,944	3,349	18,193	----------
1845	119,896	65,055	542	5,049	10,857	19,349	2,492	16,552	----------
1844	84,764	49,843	755	3,960	9,476	9,831	1,174	9,725	----------
1843	56,529	32,842	578	3,226	6,093	8,031	413	5,346	----------
1842	110,980	60,526	744	4,976	14,553	12,966	1,264	15,951	----------
1841	87,805	46,197	541	5,267	11,111	12,343	923	11,423	----------
1840	92,207	47,305	481	5,311	10,811	18,476	183	9,640	----------
1839	74,666	37,985	584	5,692	10,026	12,410	99	7,870	----------
1838	45,159	24,627	459	4,005	5,675	6,667	42	3,684	----------
1837	84,959	52,011	522	3,893	8,483	10,835	120	9,095	----------
1836	80,972	50,684	472	3,379	8,879	8,770	39	8,749	----------
1835	48,716	28,736	487	3,875	6,005	6,117	599	2,897	----------
1834	67,948	45,906	561	3,021	7,190	7,160	1,236	2,874	----------
1833	59,925	30,944	459	4,913	12,800	6,618	82	4,109	----------
1832	61,654	33,840	176	5,424	10,333	8,502	56	3,323	----------
1831	23,880	15,218	183	2,368	2,383	2,685	115	928	----------
1830	24,837	19,363	136	1,427	1,745	1,424	22	720	----------
1829	24,513	15,535	252	2,661	2,579	1,264	337	1,885	----------
1828	30,184	18,066	331	2,328	3,868	2,542	421	2,628	----------
1827	21,777	12,415	262	2,076	3,056	2,071	136	1,761	----------
1826	13,908	7,478	190	1,943	2,129	1,382	70	716	----------
1825	12,858	7,031	204	1,841	1,416	1,647	69	650	----------
1824	9,627	4,965	187	1,926	1,237	918	13	381	----------
1823	8,265	4,247	179	1,427	1,268	800	6	338	----------
1822	8,549	4,302	151	1,431	1,397	834	20	414	----------
1821	11,644	6,670	204	1,441	1,533	1,249	94	453	----------
1820	10,311	6,836	105	933	1,090	874	139	334	----------

[1] For 1820-1867 includes returning citizens.

[2] Servants included with "miscellaneous" (series C 132).

Series C 133–138. Immigrants, by Age: 1820 to 1957

[For years ending as follows: 1820–1832, ending Sept. 30; 1833–1842, ending Dec. 31; 1844–1850, ending Sept. 30; 1851–1865, ending Dec. 31; 1867–1957, ending June 30. For intermediate periods, see footnotes]

Left section

Year	Total Number [1] (133)	Percent male (134)	Under 16 years (135)	16 to 44 years (136)	45 and over (137)
1957	326,867	47.5	80,140	207,664	39,063
1956	321,625	48.6	74,429	206,770	40,426
1955	237,790	47.1	51,829	156,001	29,960
1954	208,177	45.9	45,105	135,731	27,341
1953	170,434	42.9	37,016	110,860	22,558
1952	265,520	46.6	64,513	159,788	41,219
1951	205,717	48.3	44,023	121,823	39,871
1950	249,187	47.8	50,468	152,358	46,361
1949	188,317	42.7	32,728	123,340	32,249
1948	170,570	39.5	24,095	112,453	34,022
1947	147,292	36.5	18,881	101,459	27,002
1946	108,721	25.1	11,092	85,797	11,832
1945	38,119	35.1	5,645	25,482	6,992
1944	28,551	40.0	4,092	[2]18,511	[2]5,948
1943	23,725	41.4	3,179	[2]15,282	[2]5,264
1942	28,781	41.7	3,710	[2]17,529	[2]7,542
1941	51,776	45.4	7,982	[2]30,747	[2]13,047
1940	70,756	47.3	9,602	[2]45,026	[2]16,128
1939	82,998	47.5	12,204	54,235	16,559
1938	67,895	44.1	10,181	47,068	10,646
1937	50,244	43.1	8,326	33,907	8,011
1936	36,329	40.7	6,925	23,391	6,013
1935	34,956	40.1	6,893	22,557	5,506
1934	29,470	41.1	5,389	18,987	5,094
1933	23,068	40.0	4,131	15,033	3,904
1932	35,576	39.1	6,781	22,905	5,890
1931	97,139	41.8	17,320	67,100	12,719
1930	241,700	48.4	40,777	177,059	23,864
1929	279,678	50.8	47,935	207,990	23,753
1928	307,255	54.0	49,680	230,832	26,743
1927	335,175	57.9	51,689	254,574	28,912
1926	304,488	56.0	47,347	228,527	28,614
1925	294,314	55.5	50,722	213,980	29,612
1924	706,896	59.9	132,264	513,788	60,844
1923	522,919	58.8	91,816	383,960	47,143
1922	309,556	48.4	63,710	210,164	35,682
1921	805,228	55.8	146,613	587,965	70,650
1920	430,001	57.6	81,890	307,589	40,522
1919	141,132	59.0	26,373	97,341	17,418
1918	110,618	55.9	21,349	76,098	13,171

Year	Total Number [1] (133)	Percent male (134)	Under 14 years (135)	14 to 44 years (136)	45 and over (137)
1917	295,403	59.1	47,467	214,616	33,320
1916	298,826	61.0	47,070	220,821	30,935
1915	326,700	57.2	52,982	244,472	29,246
1914	1,218,480	65.6	158,621	981,692	78,167
1913	1,197,892	67.5	147,158	986,355	64,379
1912	838,172	63.2	113,700	678,480	45,992
1911	878,587	64.9	117,837	714,709	46,041
1910	1,041,570	70.7	120,509	868,310	52,751
1909	751,786	69.2	88,393	624,876	38,517
1908	782,870	64.8	112,148	630,671	40,051
1907	1,285,349	72.4	138,344	1,100,771	46,234
1906	1,100,735	69.5	136,273	913,955	50,507
1905	1,026,499	70.6	114,668	855,419	56,412
1904	812,870	67.6	109,150	657,155	46,565
1903	857,046	71.5	102,431	714,053	40,562
1902	648,743	71.9	74,063	539,254	35,426
1901	487,918	67.9	62,562	396,516	28,840
1900	448,572	67.8	54,624	370,382	23,566
1899	311,715	62.6	43,983	248,187	19,545

Year	Total Number [1] (133)	Percent male (134)	Under 15 years (135)	15 to 40 years (136)	Over 40 (137)
1898	229,299	59.2	38,267	164,905	26,127
1897	230,832	58.5	38,627	165,181	27,024
1896	343,267	61.9	52,741	254,519	36,007
1895	279,948	57.6	33,289	233,543	13,116
1894	314,467	59.3	41,755	258,162	14,550
1893	502,917	63.8	57,392	419,701	25,824
1892	623,084	62.4	89,167	491,839	42,078
1891	560,319	63.2	95,879	405,843	58,597

Right section

Year	Total Number [1] (133)	Percent male (134)	Under 15 years (135)	15 to 40 years (136)	Over 40 (137)	Age not reported (138)
1890	455,302	61.9	86,404	315,054	53,844	
1889	444,427	59.2	92,534	303,885	48,058	
1888	546,889	63.2	97,287	396,990	52,612	
1887	490,109	62.6	94,278	345,575	50,256	
1886	334,203	60.1	66,188	232,118	35,897	
1885	395,346	57.3	92,880	257,551	44,915	
1884	518,592	59.5	123,562	335,572	59,458	
1883	603,322	60.3	143,865	390,406	69,051	
1882	788,992	63.2	171,021	540,677	77,294	
1881	669,431	61.4	153,480	454,495	61,456	
1880	457,257	62.9	87,154	327,662	42,441	
1879	177,826	62.9	34,554	122,731	20,541	
1878	138,469	62.3	24,285	95,938	18,246	
1877	141,857	64.9	23,754	100,366	17,737	
1876	169,986	65.8	27,875	121,734	20,377	
1875	227,498	61.5	44,254	154,621	28,623	
1874	313,339	60.4	63,578	199,840	49,921	
1873	459,803	60.0	104,672	288,272	66,859	
1872	404,806	59.3	90,510	263,213	51,083	
1871	321,350	59.3	71,148	210,366	39,836	
1870	387,203	60.8	89,129	250,965	47,109	
1869	352,768	60.9	79,803	232,397	40,568	
1868	282,189	([3])	57,637	188,359	36,193	
1867	342,162	62.0	65,335	236,017	40,810	
1866 [4]	185,892	62.7	27,011	112,692	18,034	28,155
1865	287,399	59.9	46,524	175,501	32,190	33,184
1864	221,535	59.4	41,912	151,711	27,778	134
1863	199,811	60.1	37,433	142,009	20,108	261
1862	114,463	58.4	20,641	80,725	12,888	209
1861	112,702	57.1	18,878	81,515	11,221	1,088
1860	179,691	58.6	28,620	133,919	16,795	357
1859	155,509	58.2	24,670	114,110	16,115	614
1858	144,906	57.8	25,914	102,921	15,545	526
1857	271,982	53.9	50,548	177,093	22,808	21,533
1856	224,496	57.8	42,732	141,986	19,905	19,873
1855	230,476	58.8	53,045	151,440	25,155	836
1854	460,474	57.6	100,013	312,301	47,377	783
1853	400,982	56.7	87,331	267,876	44,558	1,217
1852	397,343	58.8	90,274	246,076	43,394	17,599
1851	408,828	57.7	89,241	274,359	44,072	1,156
1850 [5]	65,570	62.2	13,825	43,699	7,621	425
1850	315,334	---------	62,543	181,468	26,085	45,238
1849	299,683	60.0	67,331	200,899	30,679	774
1848	229,483	58.9	53,213	151,148	23,066	2,056
1847	239,482	57.9	57,161	156,627	20,800	4,894
1846	158,649	57.5	36,878	103,263	17,160	1,348
1845	119,896	57.7	26,182	79,448	12,059	2,207
1844	84,764	56.0	19,913	54,745	8,655	1,451
1843 [6]	56,529	57.4	14,930	34,606	5,197	1,796
1842	110,980	61.0	25,516	74,499	9,709	1,256
1841	87,805	61.5	19,732	58,864	8,590	619
1840	92,207	64.2	21,727	62,461	7,556	463
1839	74,666	64.0	15,167	51,063	7,201	1,235
1838	45,159	63.3	8,822	28,713	5,748	1,876
1837	84,959	63.4	16,014	54,312	8,421	6,212
1836	80,972	63.8	16,665	54,738	8,141	1,428
1835	48,716	62.0	10,635	32,412	5,431	238
1834	67,948	67.8	15,383	42,811	6,818	2,936
1833	59,925	67.5	17,425	35,002	4,855	2,643
1832 [5]	7,303	65.6	1,946	3,774	425	1,158
1832	54,351	---------	16,485	31,069	4,273	2,524
1831	23,880	64.4	7,040	13,598	1,863	1,379
1830	24,837	72.5	2,878	6,347	1,173	14,439
1829	24,513	65.2	3,686	11,603	1,764	7,460
1828	30,184	65.4	8,117	18,397	3,036	634
1827	21,777	71.7	3,905	14,089	2,148	1,635
1826	18,908	70.9	2,261	10,025	1,281	341
1825	12,858	74.2	1,825	9,392	1,151	490
1824	9,627	80.1	94	6,550	1,106	1,877
1823	8,265	79.0	17	5,314	984	1,950
1822	8,549	77.5	51	5,430	956	2,112
1821	11,644	74.2	170	7,047	1,396	3,031
1820	10,311	69.8	1,313	6,064	1,518	1,416

[1] For 1820–1867 includes returning citizens.
[2] For years 1940–1944, figures in series C 136 include, and those in series C 137 exclude, immigrants 45 years old.
[3] Not reported.
[4] 6 months ending June 30.
[5] 3 months ending December 31.
[6] 9 months ending September 30.

Series C 139–151. Annual Quota and Aliens Admitted, by Classes: 1925 to 1957

[For years ending June 30]

Year	Annual quota	Immigrants					Nonimmigrants						
		Total	Quota¹	Nonquota: Spouses and children of U. S. citizens	Nonquota: Natives of Western Hemisphere countries²	Nonquota: Other³	Total	Temporary visitors	Transit aliens	Students	Foreign government and international officials	Returning resident aliens	Other⁴
	139	140	141	142	143	144	145	146	147	148	149	150	151
1957	154,857	326,867	97,178	32,359	113,488	83,842	758,858	537,760	107,399	30,760	34,904	⁵10,617	37,418
1956	154,657	321,625	89,310	31,742	124,032	76,541	686,259	471,969	65,214	28,013	32,299	52,136	36,628
1955	154,657	237,790	82,232	30,882	94,274	30,402	620,946	401,090	71,301	27,192	32,291	61,442	27,630
1954	154,657	208,177	94,098	30,689	80,526	2,864	566,613	353,754	78,526	25,425	28,696	55,887	24,325
1953	154,657	170,434	84,175	22,543	61,099	2,617	485,714	306,715	67,684	13,533	30,614	50,397	16,771
1952	154,277	265,520	194,247	19,315	48,408	3,550	516,082	356,351	77,899	8,613	27,404	44,980	835
1951	154,277	205,717	156,547	11,462	35,274	2,484	465,106	314,205	72,027	7,355	26,407	44,212	900
1950	154,206	249,187	197,460	16,275	33,238	2,214	426,837	287,794	68,640	9,744	18,985	40,903	771
1949	153,929	188,317	113,046	35,854	36,394	3,023	447,272	299,083	81,615	10,481	18,445	36,984	664
1948	153,929	170,570	92,526	36,830	37,968	3,246	476,006	284,983	124,780	11,914	20,881	32,464	984
1947	153,929	147,292	70,701	38,739	35,640	2,212	366,305	214,558	96,825	11,003	20,320	22,818	781
1946	153,879	108,721	29,095	49,267	29,502	857	203,469	134,826	31,124	5,855	17,689	13,306	669
1945	153,879	38,119	11,623	3,078	22,828	590	164,247	107,729	28,174	2,866	18,054	6,896	528
1944	153,774	28,551	9,394	1,302	17,614	241	113,641	48,689	34,856	1,643	23,630	4,745	78
1943	153,774	23,725	9,045	875	13,522	283	81,117	27,700	31,906	1,021	16,328	4,102	60
1942	153,774	28,781	14,597	1,262	12,596	326	82,457	25,135	28,305	1,368	12,038	15,462	149
1941	153,774	51,776	36,220	2,122	12,586	848	100,008	34,660	18,749	1,766	9,269	35,246	318
1940	153,774	70,756	51,997	5,474	11,985	1,300	138,032	65,325	36,304	2,044	7,448	26,105	806
1939	153,774	82,998	62,402	7,043	12,223	1,330	185,333	88,309	44,115	2,182	7,777	42,196	754
1938	153,774	67,895	42,494	10,262	14,379	760	184,802	79,840	45,146	2,451	6,221	50,266	878
1937	153,774	50,244	27,762	9,536	12,152	794	181,640	89,455	31,822	1,828	6,493	51,223	819
1936	153,774	36,329	18,675	8,824	8,066	764	154,570	73,313	26,571	1,515	5,312	47,166	693
1935	153,774	34,956	17,207	9,228	7,747	774	144,765	61,633	24,931	1,377	5,194	50,885	745
1934	153,774	29,470	12,483	7,891	8,237	859	134,434	49,833	23,687	1,048	4,363	54,928	575
1933	153,831	23,068	8,220	6,658	7,549	641	127,660	36,899	22,693	877	4,053	62,460	678
1932	153,831	35,576	12,983	9,490	9,461	3,642	139,295	40,465	28,678	147	2,966	66,879	160
1931	153,714	97,139	54,118	17,264	21,287	4,470	183,540	55,636	32,169	272	3,951	91,201	311
1930	153,714	241,700	141,497	32,105	63,147	4,951	204,514	70,823	27,991	552	5,326	99,056	766
1929	164,667	279,678	146,918	30,245	97,548	⁶4,967	199,649	64,310	27,776	561	5,273	100,879	850
1928	164,667	307,255	153,231	25,678	123,534	⁶4,812	193,376	64,581	27,257	517	5,340	94,368	1,313
1927	164,667	335,175	158,070	18,361	147,399	⁶11,345	202,826	60,508	28,312	524	4,769	95,502	13,211
1926	164,667	304,488	157,432	11,061	134,305	1,690	191,618	56,614	25,574	1,878	5,638	83,744	18,170
1925	164,667	294,314	145,971	7,159	139,389	1,795	164,121	35,326	22,697	1,397	1,930	64,617	38,154

¹ Includes persons admitted under the Displaced Persons Act of 1948, as amended, of whom there were 39,899 in 1949, 132,577 in 1950, 97,960 in 1951, 119,982 in 1952, 5,123 in 1953, 5,235 in 1954, and 1,093 in 1955. In addition, between 1949 and 1953, inclusive, 4,157 displaced persons were admitted as nonquota immigrants.
² Includes spouses and children.
³ Includes persons admitted under the Refugee Relief Act of 1953, of whom there were 821 in 1954, 29,002 in 1955, 75,473 in 1956, and 82,444 in 1957.
⁴ From 1953 on includes, among others, exchange aliens, of whom there were 12,584 in 1953, 15,260 in 1954, 16,077 in 1955, 17,204 in 1956, and 17,849 in 1957; and temporary workers and industrial trainees of whom there were 3,021 in 1953, 7,479 in 1954, 9,750 in 1955, 17,077 in 1956, and 16,856 in 1957.
⁵ Figures are incomplete because of documentary waivers.
⁶ Does not agree with source; adjusted to conform to definitions used in later years.

Series C 152–155. Aliens Deported, Voluntarily Departing, and Excluded: 1892 to 1957

[For years ending June 30]

Year	Aliens expelled: Total (152)	Aliens expelled: Deported (153)	Aliens expelled: Voluntarily departing¹ (154)	Aliens excluded (155)	Year	Aliens expelled: Total (152)	Aliens expelled: Deported (153)	Aliens expelled: Voluntarily departing¹ (154)	Aliens excluded (155)	Year	Aliens deported (153)	Aliens excluded (155)
1957	68,461	5,082	63,379	907	1935	16,297	8,319	7,978	5,558	1913	3,461	19,938
1956	88,188	7,297	80,891	1,709	1934	16,889	8,879	8,010	5,384	1912	2,456	16,057
1955	247,797	15,028	232,769	2,667	1933	30,212	19,865	10,347	5,527	1911	2,788	22,349
1954	1,101,228	26,951	1,074,277	3,313	1932	30,201	19,426	10,775	7,064			
1953	905,236	19,845	885,391	5,647	1931	29,861	18,142	11,719	9,744	1910	2,695	24,270
1952	723,959	20,181	703,778	5,050						1909	2,124	10,411
1951	686,713	13,544	673,169	5,647	1930	28,018	16,631	11,387	8,233	1908	2,069	10,902
					1929	38,796	12,908	25,888	18,127	1907	995	13,064
1950	579,105	6,628	572,477	5,256	1928	31,571	11,625	19,946	18,839	1906	676	12,432
1949	296,337	20,040	276,297	5,541	1927	26,674	11,662	15,012	19,755			
1948	217,555	20,371	197,184	7,113	1926	10,904	10,904	----------	20,550	1905	845	11,879
1947	214,543	18,663	195,880	7,435						1904	779	7,994
1946	116,320	14,375	101,945	2,942	1925	9,495	9,495	----------	25,390	1903	547	8,769
					1924	6,409	6,409	----------	30,284	1902	465	4,974
1945	80,760	11,270	69,490	2,341	1923	3,661	3,661	----------	20,619	1901	363	3,516
1944	39,449	7,179	32,270	1,642	1922	4,345	4,345	----------	13,731			
1943	16,154	4,207	11,947	1,495	1921	4,517	4,517	----------	13,779	1900	356	4,246
1942	10,613	3,709	6,904	1,833	1920	2,762	2,762	----------	11,795	1899	263	3,798
1941	10,938	4,407	6,531	2,929	1919	3,068	3,068	----------	8,626	1898	199	3,030
					1918	1,569	1,569	----------	7,297	1897	263	1,617
1940	15,548	6,954	8,594	5,300	1917	1,853	1,853	----------	16,028	1896	238	2,799
1939	17,792	8,202	9,590	6,498	1916	2,781	2,781	----------	18,867			
1938	18,553	9,275	9,278	8,066						1895	177	2,419
1937	17,617	8,829	8,788	8,076	1915	2,564	2,564	----------	24,111	1894	417	1,389
1936	17,446	9,195	8,251	7,000	1914	4,610	4,610	----------	33,041	1893	577	1,053
										1892	637	2,164

¹ First recorded in 1927.

Series C 156–157. Aliens Departing: 1908 to 1957

[For years ending June 30]

Year	Emigrant 156	Non-emigrant 157	Year	Emigrant 156	Non-emigrant 157	Year	Emigrant 156	Non-emigrant 157	Year	Emigrant 156	Non-emigrant 157
1957	23,933	(1)	1945	7,442	85,920	1932	103,295	184,362	1920	288,315	139,747
1956	22,824	692,376	1944	5,669	78,740	1931	61,882	229,034	1919	123,522	92,709
			1943	5,107	53,615				1918	94,585	98,683
1955	31,245	634,555	1942	7,363	67,189	1930	50,661	221,764	1917	66,277	80,102
1954	30,665	568,496	1941	17,115	71,362	1929	69,203	183,295	1916	129,765	111,042
1953	24,256	520,246				1928	77,457	196,899			
1952	21,880	487,617	1940	21,461	144,703	1927	73,366	180,142	1915	204,074	180,100
1951	26,174	446,727	1939	26,651	174,758	1926	76,992	150,763	1914	303,338	330,467
			1938	25,210	197,404				1913	308,190	303,734
1950	27,598	429,091	1937	26,736	197,846	1925	92,728	132,762	1912	333,262	282,030
1949	24,586	405,503	1936	35,817	157,467	1924	76,789	139,956	1911	295,666	222,549
1948	20,875	427,343				1923	81,450	119,136			
1947	22,501	300,921	1935	38,834	150,216	1922	198,712	146,672	1910	202,436	177,982
1946	18,143	186,210	1934	39,771	137,401	1921	247,718	178,313	1909	225,802	174,590
			1933	80,081	163,721				1908	395,073	319,755

1 Series discontinued.

Series C 158–170. Aliens Naturalized, by Sex and Place of Former Allegiance: 1907 to 1957

[For years ending June 30, except as noted]

Year	Declarations filed 158	Total naturalized 159	Male 160	Female 161	Northwestern Europe 162	Central Europe 163	Eastern Europe 164	Southern Europe 165	Asia 166	Canada 167	Other America 168	All other 169	Petitions denied 170
1957	15,911	138,043	60,289	77,754	25,878	47,656	18,062	15,762	7,548	10,891	8,977	3,269	2,948
1956	12,870	2 145,885	64,962	80,923	28,183	47,186	21,017	14,200	10,412	11,539	10,795	2,553	3,935
1955	10,855	2 209,526	95,850	113,676	46,253	62,557	22,795	23,955	16,000	18,151	15,321	4,494	4,571
1954	9,100	2 117,831	54,477	63,354	31,085	28,341	7,848	16,024	12,170	13,062	7,210	2,091	2,084
1953	23,558	92,051	34,657	57,394	23,238	26,676	5,440	13,507	4,966	10,303	5,181	2,740	2,300
1952	111,461	88,655	28,597	60,058	23,688	25,933	5,392	13,360	3,749	10,004	4,548	1,981	2,163
1951	91,497	54,716	18,711	36,005	17,069	11,864	3,485	8,503	2,886	5,872	3,827	1,210	2,395
1950	93,527	66,346	25,745	40,601	20,260	13,946	4,300	12,200	4,802	5,882	4,133	823	2,276
1949	64,866	66,594	27,865	38,729	20,782	14,471	5,244	11,716	4,993	5,347	3,607	434	2,271
1948	60,187	70,150	33,147	37,003	18,834	17,495	6,150	13,059	7,201	3,860	3,188	368	2,887
1947	37,771	2 93,904	52,998	40,906	27,017	24,220	7,281	15,661	11,741	(3)	4,676	3,308	3,953
1946	28,787	2 150,062	76,296	73,766	41,772	46,802	14,481	30,336	3,450	(3)	7,144	6,077	6,575
1945	31,195	2 231,402	4 116,691	4 114,711	57,997	82,195	23,948	51,629	2,545	(3)	8,590	4,498	9,782
1944	42,368	2 441,979	4 202,698	4 239,281	114,801	139,304	48,382	122,638	5,592	(3)	11,099	163	7,297
1943	115,664	2 318,933	4 157,663	4 161,270	122,708	86,365	42,012	51,758	6,133	(3)	9,866	91	13,656
1942	221,796	270,364	112,040	158,324	117,607	71,762	41,586	31,047	2,075	(3)	6,247	40	8,348
1941	224,123	277,294	136,348	140,946	96,375	86,122	35,844	51,819	1,844	(3)	5,249	41	7,769
1940	203,536	235,260	132,406	102,854	78,357	75,024	29,146	47,236	1,523	(3)	3,930	44	6,549
1939	155,691	188,813	113,934	74,879	62,430	59,636	22,209	40,452	1,331	(3)	2,709	46	5,680
1938	150,673	162,078	92,041	70,037	55,359	51,359	19,809	32,235	1,311	(3)	1,976	29	4,854
1937	176,195	164,976	97,696	67,280	58,002	55,789	18,970	29,169	1,290	(3)	1,710	46	4,042
1936	148,118	141,265	86,777	54,488	54,852	47,289	14,781	22,194	901	(3)	1,220	28	3,124
1935	136,524	118,945	82,182	36,763	44,605	39,554	11,825	21,171	760	(3)	987	43	2,765
1934	108,079	113,669	82,465	31,204	39,481	38,859	11,476	20,349	703	(3)	896	1,905	1,133
1933	83,046	113,363	78,293	35,070	40,795	37,068	12,544	19,498	706	(3)	780	1,972	4,703
1932	101,345	136,600	95,901	40,699	39,123	43,334	14,884	24,851	676	10,144	721	5 2,867	5,478
1931	106,272	143,495	106,715	36,780	38,465	48,041	17,428	27,793	822	7,173	989	5 2,784	7,514
1930	62,138	169,377	120,572	48,805	38,915	56,540	24,046	37,481	993	7,566	651	5 3,185	9,068
1929	280,645	224,728	167,665	57,063	50,554	72,267	33,652	53,234	1,445	8,223	664	5 4,689	11,848
1928	254,588	233,155	181,875	51,280	46,059	72,111	34,962	63,989	1,334	7,712	506	5 6,482	12,479
1927	258,295	199,804	165,833	33,971	37,293	65,592	27,399	55,924	(6)	5,237	455	7,904	11,946
1926	277,539	146,331	121,561	24,770	28,317	49,696	23,158	33,750	(6)	5,078	283	6,049	13,274
1925	277,218	152,457	133,881	18,576	29,006	55,262	23,154	31,671	(6)	7,013	290	6,061	15,613
1924	424,540	150,510	135,739	14,771	28,780	55,915	23,348	32,232	(6)	5,765	270	4,200	18,324
1923	296,636	145,084	139,073	6,011	29,107	56,112	22,897	28,392	(6)	6,546	(6)	2,030	24,884
1922	273,511	170,447											29,076
1921	303,904	181,292											18,981
1920	299,076	177,683											15,586
1919	391,156	217,358											13,119
1918	342,283	151,449											12,182
1917	440,651	88,104											9,544
1916	209,204	87,831											11,927
1915	247,958	91,848											13,691
1914	214,104	104,145											13,133
1913	182,095	83,561											10,891
1912	171,133	70,310											9,635
1911	189,249	56,683											9,017
1910	169,348	39,448											7,781
1909	145,745	38,374											6,341
1908	137,571	25,975											3,330
1907 7	73,658	7,941											250

1 See text for list of countries.
2 Includes 1,425 in 1943, 6,496 in 1944, 5,666 in 1945, 2,054 in 1946, 5,370 in 1947, 2,981 in 1954, 2,539 in 1955, and 2,236 in 1956, in various theaters of war or areas occupied by American Forces. No provision for naturalization in these areas for 1948-1953.
3 Included in Northwestern Europe as part of British Empire.
4 Data are from records of the Immigration and Naturalization Service and do not agree with source quoted. Source excludes Armed Forces overseas whereas the data shown here include Armed Forces overseas.
5 Includes 469 in 1928, 501 in 1929, 342 in 1930, 318 in 1931, and 489 in 1932 naturalized in outlying possessions, country of former allegiance not specified.
6 Included in "All other."
7 September 27, 1906, to June 30, 1907.

Series C 171–184. Citizenship Status of the Population: 1890 to 1950

[Prior to 1920, the citizenship inquiry of the Population Census was restricted to males 21 years old and over. 1950 figures based on 20-percent sample; therefore differ from similar series based on complete count]

	All ages							21 years old and over						
			Foreign-born population							Foreign-born population				
Year	Total population	Native population	Total	Natural-ized	Having first papers	No papers	Unknown citi-zenship	Total population	Native population	Total	Natural-ized	Having first papers	No papers	Unknown citi-zenship
	171	172	173	174	175	176	177	178	179	180	181	182	183	184
BOTH SEXES														
1950	150,216,110	139,868,715	10,347,395	7,562,970	(1)	(1)	2,784,425	96,732,900	86,712,450	10,020,450	7,466,445	(1)	(1)	2,554,005
1940	131,669,275	120,074,379	11,594,896	7,280,265	924,524	2,555,128	834,979	83,996,629	72,703,808	11,292,821	7,159,643	910,416	2,424,976	797,786
1930	122,775,046	108,570,897	14,204,149	7,919,536	1,266,419	4,518,341	499,853	72,943,624	59,607,271	13,336,353	7,681,681	1,237,255	3,946,176	471,241
1920	105,710,620	91,789,928	13,920,692	6,489,883	1,222,553	5,406,780	801,476	60,886,520	48,200,127	12,686,393	6,218,801	1,197,698	4,529,756	740,138
MALE														
1950	74,200,085	68,941,830	5,258,255	4,033,070	(1)	(1)	1,225,185	47,137,460	42,045,230	5,092,230	3,981,895	(1)	(1)	1,110,335
1940	66,061,592	59,939,945	6,121,647	4,137,027	581,713	1,008,071	394,836	42,004,816	36,035,228	5,969,588	4,076,207	574,296	942,855	376,230
1930	62,137,080	54,489,990	7,647,090	4,365,403	955,942	2,081,710	244,035	37,056,757	29,837,780	7,218,977	4,247,704	939,875	1,800,295	231,103
1920	53,900,431	46,224,996	7,675,435	3,449,547	1,137,021	2,695,042	393,825	31,403,370	24,339,776	7,063,594	3,320,226	1,119,982	2,259,310	364,076
1910	47,332,277	39,664,529	7,667,748	--------	--------	--------	--------	26,999,151	20,218,937	6,780,214	3,038,303	571,521	2,390,426	779,964
1900	38,816,448	33,186,258	5,630,190	--------	--------	--------	--------	21,134,299	16,124,013	5,010,286	2,848,807	412,271	1,014,219	734,989
1890	32,237,101	--------						16,940,311	12,591,852	4,348,459	2,545,753	236,061	1,189,452	377,193
FEMALE														
1950	76,016,025	70,926,885	5,089,140	3,529,900	(1)	(1)	1,559,240	49,595,440	44,667,220	4,928,220	3,484,550	(1)	(1)	1,443,670
1940	65,607,683	60,134,434	5,473,249	3,143,238	342,811	1,547,057	440,143	41,991,813	36,668,580	5,323,233	3,083,436	336,120	1,482,121	421,556
1930	60,637,966	54,080,907	6,557,059	3,554,133	310,477	2,436,631	255,818	35,886,867	29,769,491	6,117,376	3,433,977	297,380	2,145,881	240,138
1920	51,810,189	45,564,932	6,245,257	3,040,336	85,532	2,711,738	407,651	29,483,150	23,860,351	5,622,799	2,898,575	77,716	2,270,446	376,062

[1] Not available.

Series C 185–217. Native White Population of Foreign or Mixed Parentage, by Country of Origin of Parents: 1900 to 1950

[1940 figures based on 5-percent sample; 1950 on 20-percent sample]

Series No.	Country of origin of parents	1950	1940	1930	1920	1910	1900
185	Total	23,589,485	23,157,580	25,902,383	22,686,204	18,897,837	15,646,017
186	England and Wales	1,443,230	1,466,900	1,890,051	1,864,345	1,822,264	1,695,558
187	Scotland	463,325	446,540	545,268	514,436	484,699	447,524
188	Northern Ireland	29,890	270,820	517,167	} 3,122,013	3,304,015	3,375,546
189	Ireland (Eire)	1,891,495	1,838,920	2,341,712			
190	Norway	652,380	662,600	752,246	701,096	609,068	478,531
191	Sweden	864,695	856,320	967,453	888,497	752,695	542,032
192	Denmark [1]	318,710	305,640	349,668	320,410	256,175	187,844
193	Netherlands	272,535	261,320	280,833	249,339	188,015	(2)
194	Belgium	85,500	76,400	82,897	68,961	46,222	(2)
195	Switzerland	215,660	205,680	260,993	257,341	217,459	178,691
196	France	253,665	246,120	336,373	288,350	226,059	214,592
197	Germany	3,742,615	3,998,840	5,264,289	5,346,004	5,670,611	5,340,147
198	Poland	1,925,015	1,912,380	2,073,615	1,303,351	725,924	326,764
199	Czechoslovakia	705,890	664,620	890,441	(3)	(3)	(3)
200	Austria	816,465	781,340	583,734	[4]1,235,097	716,753	391,636
201	Hungary	437,080	371,840	316,318	[4]538,518	215,295	81,897
202	Yugoslavia	239,920	222,300	257,979	(3)	(3)	(3)
203	U. S. S. R.	1,647,420	1,569,360	1,516,214	} 1,508,604	775,654	} 288,098
204	Lithuania	249,525	229,040	245,589			
205	Finland	172,370	167,080	178,058	152,161	85,672	
206	Rumania	130,100	131,760	147,060	64,776	26,934	(2)
207	Greece	195,235	163,420	129,225	52,083	9,985	(2)
208	Italy	3,143,405	2,971,200	2,756,453	1,751,091	771,645	254,550
209	Spain	69,490	61,700	52,305	} 137,284	74,548	(2)
210	Portugal	117,675	114,060	97,917			(2)
211	Other Europe	128,030	75,660	101,652			(2)
212	Asia	239,525	183,260	152,347	(2)	(2)	(2)
213	Canada-French	519,495	635,020	735,307	562,360	562,709	456,030
214	Canada-Other	1,468,325	1,231,020	1,323,617	1,279,245	1,088,112	933,440
215	Mexico	891,980	699,220	583,422	253,176	162,959	(2)
216	Other America	101,240	91,980	75,220	51,259	30,169	(2)
217	All other and not reported	157,300	245,220	96,960	176,407	74,196	453,137

[1] Includes Iceland prior to 1930.
[2] Included with "All other and not reported."
[3] Included with Austria and Hungary.
[4] Areas as defined in 1910.

Series C 218–283. Foreign-Born Population, by Country of Birth: 1850 to 1950

[1950 figures based on 20-percent sample. Data are given for each country for all census years since 1850 for which figures are available]

Series No.	Country of birth	Foreign-born white						Total foreign born								
		1950	1940	1930	1920	1910	1930	1920	1910	1900	1890	1880	1870	1860	1850
218	All countries	10,158,854	11,419,138	13,983,405	13,712,754	13,345,545	14,204,149	13,920,692	13,515,886	10,341,276	9,249,560	6,679,943	5,567,229	4,138,697	2,244,602
219	Northwestern Europe	2,326,887	2,825,671	3,726,844	3,828,876	4,237,373	3,728,050	3,880,094	4,239,067	4,202,683	4,880,752	3,494,484	3,124,638	2,472,211	1,437,475
220	England	554,525	621,975	808,684	812,828	876,455	809,563	813,853	877,719	840,513	909,092	664,160	555,046	433,494	278,675
221	Scotland	244,200	279,321	354,323	254,567	261,034	354,570	254,570	261,076	233,524	242,231	170,136	140,835	108,518	70,550
222	Wales	30,060	35,360	60,205	67,066	82,479	60,205	67,066	82,488	93,586	100,079	83,302	74,533	45,763	29,868
223	Northern Ireland	15,398	106,416	178,832	{1,037,233}	{1,352,155}	178,832								
224	Ireland (Eire)	504,961	572,031	744,810			744,810	1,037,234	1,352,251	1,615,459	1,871,509	1,854,571	1,855,827	1,611,304	961,719
225	Norway	202,294	262,088	347,852	363,862	403,858	347,852	363,863	403,877	336,388	322,665	181,729	114,246	43,995	12,678
226	Sweden	324,944	445,070	595,250	625,580	665,183	595,250	625,585	665,207	582,014	478,041	194,337	97,332	18,625	3,559
227	Denmark	107,897	138,175	179,474	189,154	181,621	179,474	189,154	181,649	153,690	132,543	64,196	30,107	9,962	1,838
228	Iceland	2,455	2,104	2,764			2,764	2,049							
229	Netherlands[1]	102,133	111,064	133,183	131,766	120,053	133,183	131,766	120,063	94,931	81,828	58,090	46,802	28,281	9,848
230	Belgium	52,891	53,958	64,194	62,686	49,400	64,194	62,687	49,400	29,757	22,639	15,535	12,553	9,072	1,313
231	Luxembourg	5,590	6,886	9,048	12,585	3,071	9,048	12,585	3,071	3,031	2,882	12,836	5,802		
232	Switzerland	71,515	88,293	113,010	118,659	124,834	113,010	118,659	124,848	115,593	104,069	88,621	75,153	53,327	13,358
233	France	107,924	102,930	135,265	152,390	117,236	135,592	153,072	117,418	104,197	113,174	106,971	116,402	109,870	54,069
234	Central and Eastern Europe	4,218,908	4,958,368	5,897,795	6,134,825	6,013,720	5,897,799	6,134,845	6,014,028	4,136,646	3,420,629	2,187,776	1,784,449	1,311,722	586,240
235	Germany	984,331	1,237,772	1,608,814	1,686,102	[2]2,311,237	1,608,814	1,686,108	[2]2,311,237	2,663,418	2,784,894	1,966,742	1,690,533	1,276,075	583,774
236	Poland[2]	861,184	993,479	1,268,583	1,139,978	[2]987,884	1,268,583	1,139,979	[2]987,884	383,407	147,440	48,557			
237	Czechoslovakia	278,268	319,971	491,638	362,436	845,506	491,638	362,438	845,555	432,798	241,377	124,024	70,797	25,061	946
238	Austria	408,785	479,906	370,914	575,625	495,600	370,914	575,627	495,609	145,714	62,435	11,526	3,737		
239	Hungary	268,022	290,228	274,450	397,282	495,600	274,450	397,283	495,600						
240	Yugoslavia[5]	143,956	161,093	211,416	169,437		211,416	169,439							
241	U. S. S. R.	894,844	1,040,884	1,153,624	1,400,489	[2]1,184,382	1,153,628	1,400,495	[2]1,184,412	423,726	182,644	35,722	4,644	3,160	1,414
242	Latvia	31,590	18,636	20,673			20,673								
243	Estonia	10,085	4,178	3,550			3,550								
244	Lithuania	147,765	165,771	193,606	135,068		193,606	135,068							
245	Finland	95,506	117,210	142,478	149,824	129,669	142,478	149,824	129,680	62,641	149,824				
246	Rumania	84,952	115,940	146,393	102,823	65,920	146,393	102,823	65,923	15,032	102,823				
247	Bulgaria	9,615	8,888	9,399	10,477	11,453	9,399	10,477	11,498	[3]9,910	[3]1,889	[3]1,205	[3]302	[3]128	[3]106
248	Turkey in Europe	[3]	4,412	2,257	5,284	[4]432,221	2,257	5,284	[4]432,230						
249	Southern Europe	1,706,640	1,896,886	2,093,976	1,902,781	1,523,934	2,106,295	1,911,213	1,525,875	530,200	206,648	58,265	25,853	20,365	8,152
250	Greece	169,083	163,252	174,526	175,972	101,264	174,526	175,976	101,282	8,515	1,887	776	390	328	86
251	Albania[4]	10,510		8,814			8,814	5,608	[4]						
252	Italy	1,427,145	1,623,580	1,790,424	1,610,109	1,343,125	1,790,429	1,610,113	1,343,125	484,027	182,580	44,230	17,157	11,677	3,679
253	Spain	45,565	47,707	47,707	49,247	21,977	59,362	49,535	21,977	7,050	6,185	5,121	3,764	4,116	3,113
254	Portugal	54,387	62,347	69,993	67,453	57,623	73,164	69,981	59,360	30,608	15,996	8,138	4,542	4,116	1,274
255	Other Europe	15,670	19,819	[4]25,065	11,509	[5]12,851	16,255	5,901	12,871	2,251	12,579	3,786	1,678	1,403	1,135
256	Danzig						1,483	2,049							
257	Europe, not specified						14,772	3,882	[5]12,571	2,251	12,579	3,786	1,678	1,403	1,135
258	Asia	[3]179,900	149,909	157,580	110,450	64,814	275,665	237,950	191,484	120,248	113,396	107,630	64,565	36,796	1,135
259	Armenia	[6]540	[6]	[6]			32,166	36,628							
260	Palestine		7,047	6,135	3,202		6,137	6,187							
261	Syria	35,325	50,859	57,227	51,900	59,702	57,227	51,901	59,729						
262	Turkey in Asia	[3]71,780	52,479	46,651	11,014	59,729	46,654	11,019							
263	China	11,985	9,484	46,129	43,560	56,756	46,129	43,560	56,756	81,534	106,701	104,468	63,042	35,565	758
264	Japan	4,650	9,484	70,993	81,502	67,744	70,998	81,502	67,744	24,788	2,292	401	73		
265	India	5,370	7,638	5,017	4,074	4,664	10,514	4,912	4,664	3,897	2,143	1,707	586		377
266	Other Asia	50,300	28,770	30,333	16,855	7,562	33,623	18,551	8,228	4,733	5,006	1,054	864	1,231	377
267	America	1,564,189	1,509,855	2,011,224	1,656,801	1,453,186	2,122,209	1,727,017	1,489,231	1,317,380	1,088,245	807,230	551,335	288,285	168,484
268	Canada—French	[7]238,409	273,366	370,852	370,786	385,083	[7]370,852	307,786	385,083	[7]395,126	[7]302,496	717,157	493,464	249,970	147,711
269	Canada—Other	[7]756,183	770,758	907,660	810,092	810,987	915,587	817,189	819,554	[7]784,796	[7]678,442				
270	Newfoundland		21,361	23,971	13,242	5,076	13,249	13,249	15,080						
271	Cuba	29,295	15,277	16,089	13,842	12,869	18,493	14,872	15,133	11,081	23,256	6,917	5,319	7,353	5,772
272	Other West Indies	22,735	15,257	15,511	13,526	12,869	18,498	14,872	15,183	14,354	9,484	104,468	6,251	27,466	13,817
273	Mexico	450,562	377,433	639,017	478,383	219,802	641,462	486,418	221,915	103,393	77,853	68,399	42,435	233	141
274	Central America	23,475	7,638	7,791	4,074	1,507	10,514	4,912	1,736	1,192	707	1,707	301	233	141
275	South America	43,510	28,770	30,333	16,855	7,562	33,623	18,551	8,228	4,733	5,006	4,566	3,263	3,263	1,543
276	All other	146,715	58,630	70,921	67,512	40,167	77,876	73,672	43,330	31,868	27,811	20,772	14,711	7,915	48,116
277	Africa	13,260	10,998	12,720	10,801	8,938	8,859	5,781	3,992	2,588	2,204	2,207	2,657	1,526	551
278	Australia	19,900	10,914	12,816	10,914		12,816	10,914	9,085	6,807	5,984	4,906	3,118	1,419	
279	Azores	26,025	25,751	35,432	33,788	15,795	35,611	33,995	18,274	9,768	9,739	7,641	4,434	1,361	
280	Other Atlantic Islands	4,695	3,232	4,053	5,196		9,467	10,345		2,013	3,369	1,953	910	721	588
281	Pacific Islands	[5]5,760	17,638	13,753	12,425	8,549	4,527	3,712	2,415		479		954	1,366	
282	Country not specified	77,175	1,011	4,968	5,302	6,885	1,588	3,589	2,687	2,546		4,068	2,638	2,522	41,977
283	Born at sea						5,008	5,836	6,927	8,196	5,533				

[1] Listed as Holland prior to 1910.
[2] Persons reported in 1910 as of Polish mother tongue and combined as Poland. Persons born in Austria, Germany, and U. S. S. R. have been deducted from their respective countries and combined as Poland.
[3] For 1950, Turkey in Europe included with Turkey in Asia; for 1850–1900, Turkey in Europe included with Turkey in Asia.
[4] Albania included with Turkey in Europe for 1910; for 1930 and 1940, included with "Other Europe."
[5] Includes persons born in Serbia and in Montenegro, which became part of Yugoslavia in 1918.
[6] Armenia included with "Other Asia."
[7] Newfoundland included with Canada prior to 1910 and for 1950.
[8] Excluding possessions of the United States.

Labor

LABOR FORCE (Series D 1-572)

D 1-35. General note.

The conceptual structure and techniques for measurement of current labor force data were developed during the late 1930's by the Work Projects Administration (see John N. Webb, "Concepts Used in Unemployment Surveys," *Journal of the American Statistical Association*, March 1939). However, prior to 1940, especially during the 1930's, the economically active sector was differentiated on the basis of its ability and willingness to work. Thus, most surveys during the 1930's counted as unemployed those persons not working but "willing and able to work." Willingness and ability, however, turned out to be extremely subjective in practice, and since these concepts were dependent on the attitudes of the persons involved, it was difficult to compile data on a comparable basis from place to place and from time to time.

The 1929–1939 estimates shown here have been prepared on as comparable a basis as possible with the concepts used since 1940. For the techniques used in preparing these data, see their source (as stated in the text for series D 1–12). On the other hand, the decennial census data shown here are not directly comparable with annual data because of differences in collection techniques, time reference, and other factors.

For another set of labor force estimates, 1890–1950, see Clarence D. Long, *The Labor Force Under Changing Income and Employment*, National Bureau of Economic Research, New York, 1958, appendix tables A-4, A-6, and A-20.

The concepts and procedures used since 1940 are based principally upon an individual's actual activity, that is, whether he was working, looking for work, or doing something else during the time reference of the survey. (At present, the Census Bureau's *Monthly Report on the Labor Force* collects its information for the week containing the 12th of each month.) Instead of questions about a person's attitudes with respect to his labor market status (e.g., "Are you able to work?" or "Are you willing to work?" or "Do you want work?"), the present concept makes labor market participation depend on the more overt test of working or actively seeking work. Thus, in the surveys and censuses conducted by the Bureau of the Census since 1940, persons are classified with regard to employment status into the following categories.

Employed. Includes all persons who, during the week of reference (1) did any work for pay or for profit, on or off a farm, or worked at least 15 hours as an unpaid family worker in a business or on a farm operated by a member of the family; and (2) those who neither were at work or actively sought work, but who did have jobs from which they were temporarily absent because of such reasons as illness, bad weather, vacation, labor management dispute, etc. Volunteer work for religious or charitable institutions, as well as work around the house, is excluded.

Unemployed. Includes all persons (1) not at work during the survey week but actively seeking work within the preceding 60 days (efforts to find employment include registration at an employment office, writing letters of application, applying at the factory gate, running a situations-wanted ad in the newspaper, etc.); and (2) not at work but waiting to be called back to a job from which they had been laid off, or waiting to report to a new wage or salary job to start in the next 30 days (and not in school during the survey week), or who would have been actively looking for work except that they were temporarily ill or believed there was no work in their line available in their community.

Labor force. The civilian labor force is the sum of the employed and the unemployed. It is confined to persons 14 years of age and over, since labor market participation by persons under that age is relatively small. Information on the size of the Armed Forces is obtained from official sources and added to the civilian labor force to provide the total labor force figures.

Not in the labor force. Includes all persons 14 years of age and over not classified as employed, unemployed, or in the Armed Forces.

Current labor force data are produced by the Current Population Survey of the Bureau of the Census on the basis of a scientifically designed sample of households in 330 areas, with coverage in every State and the District of Columbia. The present size and composition of the sample dates from May 1956. From January 1954 through April 1956 the sample covered 230 areas, all of which were continued in the new and expanded sample. Prior to 1954, the interviewed households were concentrated in 68 sample areas. Household interviews totaled about 21,000 until the currently expanded sample beginning in May 1956 raised the total to about 35,000.

The household interview method (population approach) involves direct enumeration and interrogation of individuals to obtain information on employment activity from workers or members of workers' households. Each employed worker is counted only once, even though he may have held two or more jobs during a given period. This approach encompasses direct enumeration of all employed and unemployed persons including the self-employed, unpaid family workers, domestic servants, and others who do not ordinarily appear on the payrolls of any establishment. For a more detailed description of the concepts, techniques, estimation procedures, and adequacy and reliability of these data, see Bureau of the Census, *Current Population Reports*, Series P-23, No. 5.

D 1-12. Labor force status of the population, 1890–1957.

Source: Annual data, 1929–1939, population, Bureau of the Census, *Current Population Reports*, Series P-25, No. 114 (figures adjusted to include Armed Forces overseas); labor force, "Labor Force, Employment and Unemployment, 1929–39: Estimating Methods," *Monthly Labor Review*, July 1948, p. 50.

Annual data, 1940–1957, population and labor force, Bureau of the Census, *Current Population Reports*, Series P-50, Nos. 2, 13, 19, 31, 40, 45, 59, 67, 72, and 85. The population estimates are adjusted to include the institutional population; both population and labor force data for 1940–1952 are also adjusted to include about 150,000 members of the Armed Forces stationed outside continental United States in 1940 and not enumerated in the 1940 Census and therefore excluded from the original 1940–1952 estimates.

Decennial data, population, 1890–1950, and labor force, 1950, *U. S. Census of Population: 1950*, vol. II, part 1, pp. 1-100, 1-102, and 1-179; labor force, 1890–1940, John D. Durand, *The Labor Force in the United States, 1890–1960*, Social Science Research Council, New York, 1948, p. 208.

D 13–25. Labor force, by age and sex, 1890–1957.

Source: Annual data, see source for series D 1–12, annual data, 1940–1957. Decennial data, 1890–1940, John D. Durand (see source for series D 1–12); 1950, *U. S. Census of Population: 1950*, vol. IV, Special Reports, *Employment and Personal Characteristics*, p. 1A-62.

D 26–35. Civilian labor force, by color and sex, and marital status of women, 1890–1957.

Source: Annual data, labor force totals and percents, 1940–1946, *Current Population Reports*, Series P–50, No. 2; totals, and percents by color and sex, 1947–1953, Series P–50, Nos. 13, 19, 31, 40, 45, and 67; labor force by color and sex, and percents, 1954–1957, *Current Population Reports*, Series P–57, Nos. 142, 154, 166, and 178; marital status, 1940, 1944, and 1947–1957, *Current Population Reports*, Series P–50, Nos. 22, 29, 39, 44, 62, 73, and 76.

Decennial data, numbers, 1890–1940, and percents, 1890 and 1940, John D. Durand (see source for series D 1–12), pp. 208, 216; numbers and percents, 1950, *U. S. Census of Population: 1950*, vol. IV, Special Reports, *Employment and Personal Characteristics*, p. 1A-100; percents, 1920–1940 based on labor force data from Durand and population data from Bureau of the Census, Sixteenth Census Reports, *Population*, vol. III, part 1, p. 25, and *U. S. Census of Population: 1950*, vol. II, part 1, p. 1-179.

D 36–45. Gainful workers, by age, sex, and farm-nonfarm occupations, 1820–1930.

Source: Sixteenth Census Reports, *Comparative Occupation Statistics for the United States, 1870–1940*, pp. 93, 100, and 142.

The gainful worker concept differs radically from current labor force concepts as described in the general note for series D 1–35. The primary purpose of the gainful worker statistics was a count of occupations. The data were based on a question relating to occupational status and not to employment status as currently defined. Thus, census enumerators were instructed to find and enter the occupation of each person 10 years of age and over who followed an occupation in which he earned money or its equivalent, or in which he assisted in the production of marketable goods. In sum, gainful workers were people for whom a gainful occupation was entered in response to this question.

The question as posed by the enumerator made no reference to time. The response thus varied substantially with the individual. Many persons who were retired or permanently disabled and who had not worked for some time reported their former line of work and were counted as gainful workers. On the other hand, many employed persons did not enter themselves as gainful workers, because they considered themselves as students or housewives and their current employment as only temporary.

These and other factors made for incomparabilities among different age and occupational groups from one decennial census to the next. The gainful worker statistics, however, are considered as a generally reliable measure of long-term trends during the time period covered.

For a more detailed discussion of the gainful worker concept and the data themselves, see John D. Durand (see source for series D 1–12), p. 191 *et seq.*; John D. Durand, "Development of the Labor Force Concept, 1930–40," *Labor Force Definition and Measurement*, appendix A, Social Science Research Council, Bulletin 56, 1947; and Sixteenth Census Reports, *Population*, "Estimates of Labor Force, Employment, and Unemployment in the U. S.: 1940 and 1930."

D 46–47. Unemployment, annual averages, 1900–1957.

Source: 1900–1928, Stanley Lebergott, "Annual Estimates of Unemployment in the United States, 1900–1954," *The Measurement and Behavior of Unemployment*, National Bureau of Economic Research, New York, 1956, pp. 213–241; 1929–1957, see source for annual data on labor force for series D 1–12.

Prior to 1940, these figures represent estimates of unemployment on as comparable a basis to current labor force concepts as is presently possible. There have been many estimates of unemployment for these years prepared by such agencies as the National Industrial Conference Board and by authors such as Paul Douglas in *Real Wages in the United States, 1890–1926* (these are discussed and compared in the sources of pre-1940 figures cited above). In all of these, including the series presented here, unemployment is calculated as a residual. That is, estimates are first made of the civilian labor force, then of employment; the difference between the two provides the estimates of unemployment. The figures for decennial census years are used as benchmarks, with interpolations made for intercensal years from a variety of available sources.

D 48–56. Employees in nonagricultural establishments, by major industry division, 1919–1957.

Source: Bureau of Labor Statistics, *Employment and Earnings*, vol. 5, No. 8, p. 1.

These data are compiled from monthly reports made by employers, i.e., businesses or industrial establishments, to the Bureau of Labor Statistics. The "establishment approach" permits data on wages, hours worked, labor turnover, and industrial affiliation to be more accurately obtained from employers' records than from inquiries directed to a worker or a member of his household (the "population approach"). Workers appearing on more than one payroll for the same time period are counted more than once in establishment statistics. For a discussion of labor force data obtained by the "population approach," see general note for series D 1–35.

The data summarized in these series are available in considerable industrial detail (estimates are provided for about 400 different industries each month). For a discussion of available historical data, see Bureau of Labor Statistics, *Guide to Employment Statistics of BLS*, 1954; for an analysis of historical trends, see Seymour L. Wolfbein, "Changing Patterns of Industrial Employment," *Monthly Labor Review*, March 1956.

D 57–71. Industrial distribution of gainful workers, 1820–1940.

Source: Solomon Fabricant, "The Changing Industrial Distribution of Gainful Workers: Some Comments on the American Decennial Statistics for 1820–1940," *Studies in Income and Wealth*, vol. 11, National Bureau of Economic Research, New York, 1949, p. 42.

The data are based almost entirely on estimates in the following monographs which were prepared mainly from data collected in the decennial censuses of population: P. K. Whelpton, "Occupational Groups in the United States, 1820–1920," *Journal of the American Statistical Association*, September 1926; Sixteenth Census Reports, *Comparative Occupation Statistics for the United States, 1870 to 1940;* and Daniel Carson, "Industrial Composition of Manpower in the United States, 1870–1940," *Studies in Income and Wealth,* vol. 11.

D 72–122. Major occupation group of the economically active population, by sex, 1900–1950.

Source: David L. Kaplan and M. Claire Casey, *Occupational Trends in the United States, 1900–1950,* Bureau of the Census, Working Paper No. 5, 1958.

These data constitute primarily an updating by Kaplan and Casey of the material in Sixteenth Census Reports, *Comparative Occupation Statistics in the United States, 1870–1940.* Separate series developed by Alba M. Edwards in the above report were brought together and a number of new estimates were prepared to fill gaps. The appropriate figures were then adjusted to conform to the definitions used in the 1950 occupational classification system. Except where there was firm evidence to support a change, Edwards' basic assumptions and estimates were utilized throughout.

The source cautions that the data, particularly those for 1900, are approximations only. The estimates for 1900 "were included mainly for the purpose of rounding out a half-century of information, despite some obvious deficiencies. Particularly prior to 1910, there is little information available on the exact definitions used for the several occupational categories. And, even for fairly recent years, there is often only meager statistical intelligence on which to base adjustments for comparability with the 1950 definitions."

The universe covered in the series is described as the "economically active population." Prior to 1940, this refers to civilian gainful workers 10 years old and over; for 1940 and 1950, it refers to persons 14 years old and over in the experienced civilian labor force (all employed and unemployed workers with previous work experience). Two incomparabilities should be noted. First, there are important differences between the gainful worker and labor force concepts (see general note for series D 1–35, and text for series D 36–45). Second, there is the difference in age limitation. The inclusion of the 10-to-13 group prior to 1940, and their exclusion in 1940 and 1950, follows the census practice in those years.

D 123–572. Detailed occupation of the economically active population, 1900–1950.

Source: David L. Kaplan and M. Claire Casey, *Occupational Trends in the United States, 1900–1950,* Bureau of the Census, Working Paper No. 5, 1958.

See text for series D 72–122.

Series D 1–12. Labor Force Status of the Population: 1890 to 1957

[In thousands of persons 14 years old and over. Annual estimates are averages of monthly figures except as noted. Beginning January 1953, labor force and employment figures not exactly comparable with previous years as a result of introduction of material from 1950 Census into estimating procedure; for effects of this change, see *Current Population Reports*, Series P–50, No. 59]

Year	Population [1]	Total labor force		Civilian labor force					Not in the labor force			
		Number [2]	Percent of population	Total	Employed			Unemployed	Total	Keeping house	In school	Other
					Total	Agriculture	Nonagricultural					
	1	2	3	4	5	6	7	8	9	10	11	12
CURRENT POPULATION REPORTS [3]												
1957 [4]	121,889	70,746	58.0	67,946	65,011	6,222	58,789	2,936	51,143	33,891	7,048	10,204
1956	120,178	70,387	58.6	67,530	64,979	6,585	58,394	2,551	49,792	33,399	6,593	9,800
1955	118,832	68,896	58.0	65,847	63,193	6,730	56,463	2,654	49,936	33,722	6,569	9,645
1954	117,663	67,818	57.6	64,468	61,238	6,504	54,734	3,230	49,845	33,893	6,310	9,642
1953	116,538	67,362	57.8	63,815	62,213	6,562	55,651	1,602	49,176	....	6,040	8,616
1952	114,551	66,560	58.1	62,966	61,293	6,805	54,488	1,673	47,991	33,334	6,040	8,616
1951	113,355	65,982	58.2	62,884	61,005	7,054	53,951	1,879	47,373	33,105	5,829	8,440
1950	112,210	64,749	57.7	63,099	59,957	7,507	52,450	3,142	47,462	33,058	6,197	8,207
1949	111,054	63,721	57.4	62,105	58,710	8,026	50,684	3,395	47,332	33,068	6,093	8,173
1948	109,809	62,898	57.3	61,442	59,378	7,973	51,405	2,064	46,910	32,850	6,178	7,883
1947	108,785	61,758	56.8	60,168	58,027	8,266	49,761	2,142	47,027	32,441	6,446	8,139
1946	107,700	60,970	56.6	57,520	55,250	8,320	46,930	2,270	46,730	31,020	6,360	9,350
1945	106,700	65,290	61.2	53,860	52,820	8,580	44,240	1,040	41,410	27,760	4,830	8,820
1944	105,810	66,040	62.4	54,630	53,960	8,950	45,010	670	39,770	27,350	4,540	7,880
1943	104,840	64,560	61.6	55,540	54,470	9,080	45,390	1,070	40,280	27,320	5,100	7,860
1942	103,790	60,380	58.2	56,410	53,750	9,250	44,500	2,660	43,410	28,690	6,370	8,350
1941	102,700	57,530	56.0	55,910	50,350	9,100	41,250	5,560	45,170	....	....	....
1940	101,560	56,180	55.3	55,640	47,520	9,540	37,980	8,120	45,380	....	....	....
COMPARABLE WITH CURRENT POPULATION REPORTS [3]												
1939	100,360	55,600	55.4	55,230	45,750	9,610	36,140	9,480	44,760	....	....	....
1938	99,120	54,950	55.4	54,610	44,220	9,690	34,530	10,390	44,170	....	....	....
1937	97,870	54,320	55.5	54,000	46,300	9,820	36,480	7,700	43,550	....	....	....
1936	96,700	53,740	55.6	53,440	44,410	10,000	34,410	9,030	42,960	....	....	....
1935	95,460	53,140	55.7	52,870	42,260	10,110	32,150	10,610	42,320	....	....	....
1934	94,190	52,490	55.7	52,230	40,890	9,900	30,990	11,340	41,700	....	....	....
1933	92,950	51,840	55.8	51,590	38,760	10,090	28,670	12,830	41,110	....	....	....
1932	91,810	51,250	55.8	51,000	38,940	10,170	28,770	12,060	40,560	....	....	....
1931	90,710	50,680	55.9	50,420	42,400	10,290	32,110	8,020	40,030	....	....	....
1930	89,550	50,080	55.9	49,820	45,480	10,340	35,140	4,340	39,470	....	....	....
1929	88,010	49,440	56.2	49,180	47,630	10,450	37,180	1,550	38,570	....	....	....
DECENNIAL CENSUS												
1950 (April)	112,354	[5] 60,054	53.5	59,072	56,239	6,885	49,354	2,832	52,300	32,180		
1940 (April)	101,103	53,299	52.7	....	....	....	....	....	47,804	....		
1930 (April)	89,101	47,404	53.2	....	....	....	....	....	41,697	....		
1920 (Jan.)	74,144	40,282	54.3	....	....	....	....	....	33,862	....		
1900 (June)	51,438	27,640	53.7	....	....	....	....	....	23,798	....		
1890 (June)	41,799	21,833	52.2	....	....	....	....	....	19,966	....		

[1] 1929–1939 figures as of July 1.
[2] 1940–1952 figures revised to include Armed Forces overseas; see text.
[3] For 1940–1957, figures from Bureau of the Census, *Current Population Reports*; for 1929–1939, Bureau of Labor Statistics estimates; see text.
[4] Beginning 1957, certain limited changes have been made in definitions of employment and unemployment with the result that each month about 200,000 to 300,000

workers, formerly classified as employed, were counted as unemployed. On the basis of old definitions, unemployment in 1957 averaged 2,693,000. See *Current Population Reports*, Series P–57, No. 176.
[5] Based on full count and therefore differs from that shown in series D 13 and D 26 which are based on 3⅓-percent sample.

Series D 13–25. Labor Force, by Age and Sex: 1890 to 1957

[In thousands of persons 14 years old and over. Annual estimates are averages of monthly figures. 1940–1952 figures revised to include Armed Forces overseas; see text. Beginning 1953, data not exactly comparable with previous years; see headnote, series D 1–12]

Year	Total labor force	Male						Female					
		Total	14 to 19 years	20 to 24 years	25 to 44 years	45 to 64 years	65 and over	Total	14 to 19 years	20 to 24 years	25 to 44 years	45 to 64 years	65 and over
	13	14	15	16	17	18	19	20	21	22	23	24	25
NUMBER													
Current population reports:													
1957 [1]	70,746	48,649	3,669	4,781	22,293	15,428	2,477	22,097	2,198	2,453	9,384	7,249	813
1956	70,387	48,579	3,610	4,814	22,286	15,266	2,603	21,808	2,183	2,467	9,322	7,019	822
1955	68,896	48,054	3,378	4,851	22,297	15,002	2,525	20,842	1,987	2,458	9,069	6,546	780
1954	67,818	47,847	3,298	4,959	22,215	14,850	2,525	19,972	1,941	2,441	8,939	5,988	666
1953	67,362	47,692	3,338	5,085	22,138	14,591	2,544	19,668	1,952	2,447	8,842	5,729	693
1952	66,560	47,001	3,396	5,223	21,636	14,331	2,416	19,559	2,002	2,519	8,779	5,669	590
1951	65,982	46,674	3,476	5,268	21,325	14,137	2,469	19,308	2,018	2,670	8,612	5,459	551
1950	64,749	46,069	3,444	5,224	20,996	13,952	2,453	18,680	1,982	2,681	8,267	5,167	584
1949	63,721	45,674	3,480	5,198	20,747	13,797	2,454	18,048	2,054	2,662	7,999	4,778	556
1948	62,898	45,300	3,580	5,114	20,478	13,742	2,384	17,599	2,083	2,722	7,744	4,538	514
1947	61,758	44,843	3,641	5,093	20,199	13,534	2,376	16,915	2,067	2,725	7,426	4,252	445
1946	60,970	44,130	3,700	4,930	19,740	13,410	2,350	16,840	2,160	2,810	7,410	4,030	440
1945	65,290	46,020	4,530	5,760	19,900	13,370	2,460	19,270	2,720	3,300	8,350	4,420	490
1944	66,040	46,670	4,950	5,940	20,050	13,300	2,430	19,370	2,900	3,340	8,320	4,320	490
1943	64,560	45,750	4,700	5,710	19,810	13,200	2,320	18,810	2,930	3,170	8,240	3,970	490
1942	60,380	44,260	--------	--------	--------	--------	--------	16,120	--------	--------	--------	--------	--------
1941	57,530	42,890	--------	--------	--------	--------	--------	14,640	--------	--------	--------	--------	--------
1940	56,180	42,020	3,270	5,490	19,150	12,170	1,950	14,160	1,700	2,900	6,440	2,780	330
Decennial census:													
1950 (April) [2]	59,671	43,118	2,543	4,537	20,389	13,275	2,373	16,553	1,441	2,521	7,666	4,416	509
1940 (April)	53,299	40,284	2,619	5,035	18,817	11,954	1,859	13,015	1,395	2,688	6,107	2,550	275
1930 (April)	47,404	37,008	2,795	4,747	17,498	10,173	1,795	10,396	1,591	2,316	4,404	1,842	243
1920 (Jan.)	40,282	32,053	2,947	4,080	15,353	8,290	1,383	8,229	1,640	1,785	3,314	1,310	180
1900 (June)	27,640	22,641	2,834	3,302	10,560	4,958	987	4,999	1,230	1,179	1,791	672	127
1890 (June)	21,833	18,129	1,997	2,836	8,513	3,937	846	3,704	984	938	1,216	476	90
LABOR FORCE PARTICIPATION RATE													
Current population reports:													
1957 [1]	58.0	81.6	49.0	88.6	96.2	91.1	36.6	35.5	30.3	45.8	39.2	40.9	10.2
1956	58.6	82.4	50.9	89.5	96.4	91.5	39.1	35.6	31.7	46.2	38.9	40.4	10.6
1955	58.0	82.4	49.0	89.8	96.7	91.3	38.5	34.5	29.7	45.8	38.0	38.5	10.3
1954	57.6	82.7	48.6	90.4	96.5	91.6	39.5	33.4	29.5	45.1	37.5	35.9	9.1
1953	57.8	83.0	50.2	91.0	96.6	91.3	40.4	33.3	30.2	44.4	37.3	35.1	9.7
1952	58.1	83.4	51.4	90.9	96.4	91.0	41.6	33.6	31.3	44.6	37.6	34.8	9.0
1951	58.2	83.6	53.3	89.9	96.0	90.7	43.8	33.6	31.8	46.4	37.3	34.1	8.7
1950	57.7	83.2	52.7	88.0	95.5	90.4	44.7	32.8	31.3	45.9	36.2	32.9	9.5
1949	57.4	83.2	53.1	86.6	95.4	90.6	45.9	32.1	32.2	44.9	35.4	31.0	9.4
1948	57.3	83.3	54.1	84.6	95.5	91.5	45.7	31.7	32.4	45.2	34.7	30.1	9.0
1947	56.8	83.3	53.7	83.8	95.5	91.6	46.8	30.8	31.4	44.7	33.8	28.8	8.0
1946	56.6	82.5	53.5	81.0	94.3	92.0	47.4	31.1	32.1	46.2	34.3	27.9	8.3
1945	61.2	86.7	.64.2	94.3	96.2	93.0	50.8	35.9	39.7	53.9	39.1	31.3	9.3
1944	62.4	88.4	69.2	97.1	97.6	93.5	50.9	36.5	41.7	54.7	39.5	31.2	9.6
1943	61.6	87.3	64.8	94.3	97.4	94.0	49.5	35.8	41.4	52.3	39.6	29.2	9.8
1942	58.2	85.3	--------	--------	--------	--------	--------	31.0	--------	--------	--------	--------	--------
1941	56.0	83.5	--------	--------	--------	--------	--------	28.5	--------	--------	--------	--------	--------
1940	55.3	82.6	44.0	95.2	96.7	90.4	44.2	27.9	23.1	49.1	32.1	21.7	7.2
Decennial census:													
1950 (April) [2]	53.4	79.0	39.5	81.9	93.3	88.2	41.4	29.0	22.6	42.9	33.3	28.8	7.8
1940 (April)	52.7	79.7	35.4	88.4	95.6	89.4	42.2	25.7	19.0	45.6	30.6	20.0	6.0
1930 (April)	53.2	82.1	40.1	88.8	95.8	91.0	54.0	23.6	22.8	41.8	24.6	18.0	7.3
1920 (Jan.)	54.3	84.6	51.5	89.9	95.6	90.7	55.6	22.7	28.4	37.5	21.7	16.5	7.3
1900 (June)	53.7	85.7	62.0	90.6	94.7	90.3	63.1	20.0	26.8	31.7	17.5	13.6	8.3
1890 (June)	52.2	84.3	50.0	90.9	96.0	92.0	68.3	18.2	24.5	30.2	15.1	12.1	7.6

[1] See footnote 4, series D 1–12.

[2] See footnote 5, series D 2.

Series D 26–35.   Civilian Labor Force, by Color and Sex, and Marital Status of Women: 1890 to 1957

[In thousands of persons 14 years old and over.   Beginning 1953, data not exactly comparable with previous years; see headnote, series D 1-12]

Year	Labor force, by color and sex							Marital status of women in the labor force		
	Both sexes			Male		Female				
	Total	White	Nonwhite	White	Nonwhite	White	Nonwhite	Single	Married, husband present	Other
	26	27	28	29	30	31	32	33	34	35
NUMBER										
Current population reports: [1]										
1957	66,951	59,771	7,180	40,981	4,448	18,791	2,732	5,378	11,529	4,617
1956	66,555	59,540	7,015	40,966	4,395	18,573	2,620	5,167	11,126	4,549
1955	64,647	57,925	6,723	40,266	4,228	17,659	2,495	5,087	10,423	4,643
1954	64,063	57,326	6,737	40,127	4,210	17,199	2,527	5,412	9,923	4,391
1953	63,155							5,223	9,763	4,319
1952	61,744							5,532	9,222	4,058
1951	61,789							5,430	9,086	4,086
1950	62,183							5,621	8,550	3,624
1949	60,835							5,682	7,959	3,526
1948	60,524							5,943	7,553	3,659
1947	59,120							6,181	6,676	3,466
1946	56,450									
1945	54,180									
1944	54,220							7,542	6,226	4,681
1943	54,860									
1942	55,880									
1941	54,980									
1940	54,870							6,710	4,200	2,930
Decennial census: [2]										
1950 (April) [3]	59,671	53,502	6,168	39,059	4,058	14,443	2,110	5,274	7,697	3,581
1940 (April)	53,299	47,670	5,626	36,499	3,783	11,171	1,843	6,429	4,623	1,963
1930 (April)	47,404	41,911	5,493	33,286	3,722	8,625	1,771			
1920 (Jan.)	40,282	35,554	4,728	28,807	3,246	6,747	1,482			
1900 (June)	27,640	23,871	3,769	20,057	2,584	3,814	1,185			
1890 (June)	21,833	18,932	2,901	16,094	2,035	2,838	866	2,565	500	638
PERCENT OF CIVILIAN NONINSTITUTIONAL POPULATION										
Current population reports:										
1957	57.1	56.7	61.2	81.4	81.0	34.1	43.7	46.8	29.6	40.4
1956	57.6	57.3	60.8	82.5	81.3	34.2	42.7	46.4	29.0	39.4
1955	56.7	56.4	59.2	82.2	79.7	32.9	41.2	46.4	27.7	39.6
1954	56.9	56.5	60.5	82.9	81.0	32.4	42.5	49.0	26.6	39.4
1953	56.7	56.4	59.8	83.0	82.9	32.3	39.6	48.5	26.3	39.1
1952	56.5	56.1	59.8	82.9	83.6	31.9	39.7	50.0	25.3	38.8
1951	56.8	56.4	60.4	83.1	82.4	31.8	41.5	49.6	25.2	39.3
1950	56.9	56.5	61.2	83.3	83.5	31.1	42.1	50.5	23.8	37.8
1949	56.4	56.0	60.2	83.5	83.3	29.9	40.1	50.9	22.5	37.1
1948	56.6	56.2	60.1	83.4	83.4	30.3	39.9	51.1	22.0	38.7
1947	55.9	55.2	61.9	83.2	85.3	28.7	41.0	51.2	20.0	37.4
1946	55.2									
1945	58.2									
1944	58.1							58.6	21.7	41.7
1943	57.8									
1942	56.2									
1941	55.1									
1940	55.0							48.1	14.7	36.2
Decennial census: [2]										
1950 [3] (April)	53.4	53.1	56.1	79.2	76.6	28.1	37.1	46.3	21.6	35.5
1940 (April)	52.7	52.1	58.1	79.7	80.0	24.5	37.3	46.1	15.4	30.1
1930 (April)	53.2	52.1	63.2	81.7	86.1	21.8	40.5			
1920 (Jan.)	54.3	53.2	64.2	84.1	87.5	20.7	40.6			
1900 (June)	53.7	52.4	65.0	85.4	88.5	17.3	41.2			
1890 (June)	52.2	51.0	62.4	84.0	86.6	15.8	37.7	36.9	4.5	28.6

[1] As of April, except marital status for 1950, 1956, and 1957 as of March.
[2] Relates to total labor force and total population.
[3] See footnote 5, series D 2.

Series D 36–45.   Gainful Workers, by Age, Sex, and Farm-Nonfarm Occupations: 1820 to 1930

[In thousands of persons 10 years old and over]

Year	Total workers	Occupation		Sex		Age (in years)					Year	Total workers	Occupation	
		Farm	Non-farm	Male	Female	10 to 15	16 to 44	45 to 64	65 and over	Un-known			Farm	Non-farm
	36	37	38	39	40	41	42	43	44	45		36	37	38
1930	48,830	10,472	38,358	38,078	10,752	667	33,492	12,422	2,205	44	1860	10,533	6,208	4,325
1920	42,434	11,449	30,985	33,797	8,637	1,417	29,339	9,914	1,691	73	1850	7,697	4,902	2,795
1910	37,371	11,592	25,779	29,926	7,445	1,622	26,620	7,606	1,440	83	1840	5,420	3,720	1,700
1900	29,073	10,912	18,161	23,754	5,319	1,750	20,223	5,804	1,202	94	1830	3,932	2,772	1,160
1890	23,318	9,938	13,380	19,313	4,006	1,504	16,162	4,547	1,009	97	1820	2,881	2,069	812
1880	17,392	8,585	8,807	14,745	2,647	1,118	16,274							
1870	12,925	6,850	6,075	11,008	1,917	765	12,160							

Series D 46–47. Unemployment: 1900 to 1957

[In thousands of persons 14 years old and over. Annual averages]

Year	Un-employed	Percent of civilian labor force	Year	Un-employed	Percent of civilian labor force	Year	Un-employed	Percent of civilian labor force	Year	Un-employed	Percent of civilian labor force	Year	Un-employed	Percent of civilian labor force
	46	47		46	47		46	47		46	47		46	47
1957 [1]	2,936	4.3	1945	1,040	1.9	1933	12,830	24.9	1922	3,220	7.6	1911	2,290	6.2
1956	2,551	3.8	1944	670	1.2	1932	12,060	23.6	1921	5,010	11.9	1910	2,150	5.9
1955	2,654	4.0	1943	1,070	1.9	1931	8,020	15.9	1920	1,670	4.0	1909	1,870	5.2
1954	3,230	5.0	1942	2,660	4.7	1930	4,340	8.7	1919	950	2.3	1908	2,960	8.5
1953	1,602	2.5	1941	5,560	9.9	1929	1,550	3.2	1918	560	1.4	1907	600	1.8
1952	1,673	2.7	1940	8,120	14.6	1928	2,080	4.4	1917	1,920	4.8	1906	280	0.8
1951	1,879	3.0	1939	9,480	17.2	1927	1,890	4.1	1916	1,920	4.8	1905	1,000	3.1
1950	3,142	5.0	1938	10,390	19.0	1926	880	1.9	1915	3,840	9.7	1904	1,490	4.8
1949	3,395	5.5	1937	7,700	14.3	1925	1,800	4.0	1914	3,110	8.0	1903	800	2.6
1948	2,064	3.4	1936	9,030	16.9	1924	2,440	5.5	1913	1,680	4.4	1902	800	2.7
1947	2,142	3.6	1935	10,610	20.1	1923	1,380	3.2	1912	1,960	5.2	1901	710	2.4
1946	2,270	3.9	1934	11,340	21.7							1900	1,420	5.0

[1] See footnote 4, series D 1–12.

Series D 48–56. Employees in Nonagricultural Establishments, by Major Industry Division: 1919 to 1957

[In thousands. Annual averages. Includes all full- and part-time employees who worked during, or received pay for, any part of the pay period reported. Excludes proprietors self-employed persons, farm workers, unpaid family workers, domestic servants, and personnel of Armed Forces. Data for the latest year are adjusted to 1st quarter 1957 benchmark levels indicated by data from Government social insurance programs, and are comparable with the series for earlier years]

Year	Total	Mining	Contract construction	Manufacturing	Transportation and public utilities	Wholesale and retail trade	Finance, insurance, and real estate	Service and miscellaneous	Government
	48	49	50	51	52	53	54	55	56
1957	52,162	809	2,808	16,782	4,151	11,302	2,348	6,336	7,626
1956	51,766	807	2,929	16,903	4,161	11,221	2,308	6,160	7,277
1955	50,056	777	2,759	16,563	4,062	10,846	2,219	5,916	6,914
1954	48,431	777	2,593	15,995	4,009	10,520	2,122	5,664	6,751
1953	49,681	852	2,622	17,238	4,221	10,527	2,038	5,538	6,645
1952	48,303	885	2,634	16,334	4,185	10,281	1,967	5,411	6,609
1951	47,347	916	2,603	16,104	4,166	10,012	1,892	5,264	6,389
1950	44,738	889	2,333	14,967	3,977	9,645	1,824	5,077	6,026
1949	43,315	918	2,165	14,178	3,949	9,513	1,765	4,972	5,856
1948	44,448	982	2,169	15,321	4,141	9,519	1,741	4,925	5,650
1947	43,462	943	1,982	15,290	4,122	9,196	1,672	4,783	5,474
1946	41,287	852	1,661	14,461	4,023	8,602	1,619	4,474	5,595
1945	40,037	826	1,132	15,302	3,872	7,522	1,428	4,011	5,944
1944	41,534	883	1,094	17,111	3,798	7,260	1,409	3,934	6,043
1943	42,106	917	1,567	17,381	3,619	7,189	1,435	3,919	6,080
1942	39,779	983	2,170	15,051	3,433	7,333	1,469	3,857	5,483
1941	36,220	947	1,790	12,974	3,248	7,416	1,480	3,705	4,660
1940	32,058	916	1,294	10,780	3,013	6,940	1,436	3,477	4,202
1939	30,311	845	1,150	10,078	2,912	6,612	1,399	3,321	3,995
1938	28,902	882	1,055	9,253	2,840	6,453	1,347	3,196	3,876
1937	30,718	1,006	1,112	10,606	3,114	6,543	1,355	3,233	3,749
1936	28,802	937	1,145	9,653	2,956	6,076	1,313	3,060	3,662
1935	26,792	888	912	8,907	2,771	5,692	1,262	2,883	3,477
1934	25,699	874	862	8,346	2,736	5,552	1,247	2,784	3,298
1933	23,466	735	809	7,258	2,659	4,999	1,225	2,614	3,167
1932	23,377	722	970	6,797	2,804	4,907	1,270	2,682	3,225
1931	26,383	864	1,214	8,021	3,243	5,531	1,333	2,913	3,264
1930	29,143	1,000	1,372	9,401	3,675	6,064	1,398	3,084	3,149
1929	31,041	1,078	1,497	10,534	3,907	6,401	1,431	3,127	3,066
1928	29,710	1,041	1,606	9,786	3,822	6,137	1,360	2,962	2,996
1927	29,691	1,105	1,608	9,839	3,891	6,165	1,295	2,871	2,917
1926	29,539	1,176	1,555	9,997	3,940	6,033	1,235	2,755	2,848
1925	28,505	1,080	1,446	9,786	3,824	5,810	1,166	2,591	2,802
1924	27,770	1,092	1,321	9,523	3,806	5,626	1,163	2,516	2,723
1923	28,128	1,203	1,229	10,155	3,882	5,494	1,123	2,431	2,611
1922	25,569	920	1,185	8,986	3,505	5,084	1,079	2,268	2,542
1921	24,125	953	1,012	8,132	3,459	4,754	1,097	2,187	2,531
1920	27,088	1,230	848	10,534	3,998	4,623	1,110	2,142	2,603
1919	26,829	1,124	1,021	10,534	3,711	4,664	1,050	2,054	2,671

Series D 57–71. Industrial Distribution of Gainful Workers: 1820 to 1940

[In thousands]

Year	Total	Agriculture	Forestry and fisheries	Mining	Manufacturing and hand trades	Construction	Transportation and other public utilities	Trade	Finance and real estate	Educational service	Other professional service	Domestic service	Personal service	Government not elsewhere classified	Not allocated
	57	58	59	60	61	62	63	64	65	66	67	68	69	70	71
1940	53,300	9,000	140	1,110	11,940	3,510	4,150	7,180	1,550	1,680	2,320	2,610	3,100	1,690	3,330
1930 [1]	47,400	10,180	120	1,160	10,770	3,030	4,810	6,190	1,470	1,630	1,720	2,550	2,500	1,130	[2]145
1930 [3]	48,830	10,480	270	1,150	10,990	3,030	4,850	6,030	1,420	1,650	1,760	2,330	2,490	1,050	1,340
1920	41,610	11,120	280	1,230	10,880	2,170	4,190	4,060	800	1,170	1,080	1,700	1,630	920	380
1910	36,730	11,340	250	1,050	8,230	2,300	3,190	3,370	520	900	770	2,150	1,520	540	600
1900	29,070	10,710	210	760	6,340	1,660	2,100	2,760		650	500	1,740	970	300	370
1890	23,740	9,990	180	480	4,750	1,440	1,530	1,990		510	350	1,520	640	190	170
1880	17,390	8,610	95	310	3,170	830	860	1,220		330	190	1,080	360	140	195
1870 [4]	12,920	6,430	60	200	2,250	750	640	830		190	140	940	250	100	140
1870 [3]	12,920	6,850	60	180	2,750			1,350				[5]1,700			30
1860	10,530	6,210	50	170	1,930			780				1,310			80
1850	7,700	4,900	25	90	1,260			420				940			65
1840	5,420	3,720	(6)	15	790			(6)				(6)			895
1830	3,930	2,770	(6)	(6)	(6)			(6)				(6)			1,160
1820	2,880	2,070	(6)	(6)	350			(6)				(6)			460

[1] Comparable with 1940.
[2] Difference between number of persons not reporting industrial affiliation (1,335,000), and excess of the "gainful worker" total over the "labor force" total (1,190,000).
[3] Comparable with data for earlier years.
[4] Comparable with data for later years.
[5] Figure corrected for apparent error in source; components now add to total, series D 57.
[6] Not available.

Series D 72–122. Major Occupation Group of the Economically Active Population, by Sex: 1900 to 1950

[In thousands]

Series No.	Major occupation group and sex	1950	1940	1930	1920	1910	1900
	BOTH SEXES						
72	Total	58,999	51,742	48,686	42,206	37,291	29,030
73	White-collar workers	21,601	16,082	14,320	10,529	7,962	5,115
74	Professional, technical, and kindred workers	5,081	3,879	3,311	2,283	1,758	1,234
75	Managers, officials, and proprietors, except farm	5,155	3,770	3,614	2,803	2,462	1,697
76	Clerical and kindred workers	7,232	4,982	4,336	3,385	1,987	877
77	Sales workers	4,133	3,450	3,059	2,058	1,755	1,307
78	Manual and service workers	30,445	26,666	24,044	20,287	17,797	13,027
79	Manual workers	24,266	20,597	19,272	16,974	14,234	10,401
80	Craftsmen, foremen, and kindred workers	8,350	6,203	6,246	5,482	4,315	3,062
81	Operative and kindred workers	12,030	9,518	7,691	6,587	5,441	3,720
82	Laborers, except farm and mine	3,885	4,875	5,335	4,905	4,478	3,620
83	Service workers	6,180	6,069	4,772	3,313	3,562	2,626
84	Private household workers	1,539	2,412	1,998	1,411	1,851	1,579
85	Service workers, except private household	4,641	3,657	2,774	1,901	1,711	1,047
86	Farmworkers	6,953	8,995	10,321	11,390	11,533	10,888
87	Farmers and farm managers	4,375	5,362	6,032	6,442	6,163	5,763
88	Farm laborers and foremen	2,578	3,632	4,290	4,948	5,370	5,125
	MALE						
89	Total	42,554	39,168	37,933	33,569	29,847	23,711
90	White-collar workers	12,974	10,434	9,564	7,176	6,019	4,166
91	Professional, technical, and kindred workers	3,074	2,271	1,829	1,275	1,032	800
92	Managers, officials, and proprietors, except farm	4,456	3,356	3,321	2,612	2,312	1,623
93	Clerical and kindred workers	2,730	2,282	2,090	1,771	1,300	665
94	Sales workers	2,715	2,525	2,323	1,518	1,376	1,079
95	Manual and service workers	23,228	20,247	18,956	16,172	13,469	9,664
96	Manual workers	20,581	17,877	17,138	14,923	12,320	8,924
97	Craftsmen, foremen, and kindred workers	8,098	6,069	6,140	5,377	4,209	2,985
	MALE—Con.						
	Manual and service workers—Con.						
	Manual workers—Con.						
98	Operative and kindred workers	8,743	7,067	5,822	4,839	3,739	2,456
99	Laborers, except farm and mine	3,740	4,742	5,177	4,707	4,372	3,482
100	Service workers	2,647	2,370	1,818	1,250	1,149	740
101	Private household workers	80	135	89	51	67	53
102	Service workers, except private household	2,568	2,235	1,729	1,199	1,082	687
103	Farmworkers	6,352	8,487	9,414	10,221	10,359	9,880
104	Farmers and farm managers	4,255	5,205	5,769	6,165	5,884	5,451
105	Farm laborers and foremen	2,097	3,282	3,645	4,056	4,475	4,429
	FEMALE						
106	Total	16,445	12,574	10,752	8,637	7,445	5,319
107	White-collar workers	8,627	5,648	4,756	3,353	1,943	949
108	Professional, technical, and kindred workers	2,007	1,608	1,482	1,008	726	434
109	Managers, officials, and proprietors, except farm	700	414	292	191	150	74
110	Clerical and kindred workers	4,502	2,700	2,246	1,614	688	212
111	Sales workers	1,418	925	736	541	379	228
112	Manual and service workers	7,217	6,419	5,088	4,327	3,363	
113	Manual workers	3,685	2,720	2,134	2,052	1,914	1,477
114	Craftsmen, foremen, and kindred workers	253	135	106	105	106	76
115	Operative and kindred workers	3,287	2,452	1,870	1,748	1,702	1,264
116	Laborers, except farm and mine	145	133	158	199	106	137
117	Service workers	3,532	3,699	2,954	2,063	2,413	1,886
118	Private household workers	1,459	2,277	1,909	1,360	1,784	1,526
119	Service workers, except private household	2,073	1,422	1,045	703	629	359
120	Farmworkers	601	508	908	1,169	1,175	1,008
121	Farmers and farm managers	120	157	263	277	279	311
122	Farm laborers and foremen	481	351	645	892	895	697

Series D 123–572. Detailed Occupation of the Economically Active Population: 1900 to 1950

[In thousands. "N. e. c." means not elsewhere classified]

Professional, technical, and kindred workers; Farmers; Managers (Series 123–190)

Series No.	Occupation	1950	1940	1930	1920	1910	1900
123	Total	58,999	51,742	48,686	42,206	37,291	29,030
124	Professional, technical, and kindred workers	5,081	3,879	3,311	2,283	1,758	1,234
125	Accountants and auditors	390	238	192	118	39	23
126	Actors and actresses	20	21	76	48	48	31
127	Athletes	13	9				
128	Dancers and dancing teachers	18	14				
129	Entertainers (n. e. c.)	17	12				
130	Sports instructors and officials	47	25				
131	Airplane pilots and navigators	14	5	6	1		
132	Architects	25	22	23	17	16	11
133	Artists and art teachers	83	66	57	35	34	25
134	Authors	17	14	12	7	4	
135	Chemists	77	57	45	28	16	9
136	Clergymen	171	141	149	127	118	114
137	Religious workers	42	42	71	46	19	7
138	Recreation and group workers	95	77				
139	Social and welfare workers, except group	127	77	62	33	16	30
140	College presidents, prof'rs, & instructors (n. e. c.)	127	71	71	56	40	45
141	Dentists	76	32	98	67	45	32
142	Designers	41	82	39	39	36	
143	Draftsmen	127	66	61			
144	Editors and reporters	93	66				
145	Engineers, technical	543	297	217	134	77	38
146	Engineers, civil	128	97	88	56	40	20
147	Engineers, chemical	23	13	14	11	7	3
148	Engineers, metallurgical and metallurgists		12				
149	Engineers, mining						
150	Engineers, electrical	110	65	58	27	15	14
151	Engineers, industrial	42	13				
152	Engineers, aeronautical	13					
153	Engineers, mechanical	207	97	58	39	15	
154	Engineers (n. e. c.)	41	40	34	24	21	16
155	Farm and home management advisors	13	12	4	3	1	
156	Funeral directors and embalmers	41					
157	Lawyers and judges	184	182	161	123	115	108
158	Librarians	57	39	30	15	7	3
159	Musicians and music teachers	166	167	165	130	139	92
160	Nurses, professional	491	377	294	149	82	12
161	Nurses, student professional	15	10	5	7		
162	Optometrists						
163	Pharmacists	90	83	84	64	54	46
164	Photographers	56	38	33	29	30	25
165	Physicians and surgeons	195	168	157	146	152	131
166	Osteopaths	5	6	6	5		
167	Chiropractors	13	11	12			
168	Therapists and healers (n. e. c.)	25	18	14	12	5	
169	Radio operators	17	17	15	5	4	
170	Surveyors	27			5		6
171	Teachers (n. e. c.)	1,149	1,086	1,044	752	595	436
172	Technicians, medical and dental	158	73	73			
173	Technicians, testing			20	4		
174	Technicians (n. e. c.)	28	11	12	13	12	8
175	Veterinarians	14					
176	Dietitians and nutritionists						
177	Foresters and conservationists						
178	Natural scientists (n. e. c.)	302	153	73	32	20	12
179	Personnel and labor relations workers						
180	Social scientists						
181	Professional, technical, and kindred workers (n. e. c.)	14	11				
182	Farmers and farm managers	4,375	5,362	6,032	6,442	6,163	5,763
183	Farmers (owners and tenants)	4,839	5,324	5,992	6,884	6,132	5,752
184	Farm managers	36	38	40	58	31	10
185	Managers, officials, and proprietors, exc. farm	5,155	3,770	3,614	2,803	2,462	1,697
186	Buyers and department heads, store	147	74	35	20	15	12
187	Buyers and shippers, farm products	29	43	42	48	51	43
188	Conductors, railroad	57	48	73	75	66	75
189	Credit men	34	30	22	14	31	2
190	Floormen and floor managers, store	11	7	6	4	4	2

Managers, officials, & propr's, exc. farm—Con.; Clerical; Sales workers (Series 191–255)

Series No.	Occupation	1950	1940	1930	1920	1910	1900
191	Inspectors (n. e. c.), public administration	58	43				
192	Officials (n. e. c.), public administration	158	122	124	100	72	58
193	Inspectors (n. e. c.), Federal public administration and postal service	28	20				
194	Officials and administrators (n. e. c.), Federal public administration and postal service	51	40	40	42	20	18
195	Inspectors (n. e. c.), State public administration	10	11				
196	Officials & admins. (n. e. c.), State public administration	24	21	15	9	7	4
197	Inspectors (n. e. c.), local public administration	20	12				
198	Officials & admins. (n. e. c.), local public admin	83	61	70	49	44	35
199	Managers and superintendents, building	68	72	71	43	32	(¹)
200	Officers, pilots, pursers, and engineers, ship	43	35	49	49	45	43
201	Officials, lodge, society, union, etc.	28	26	15	12	8	(¹)
202	Postmasters	39	40	34	29	25	19
203	Purchasing agents and buyers (n. e. c.)	65	34	29	18	8	7
204	Managers, officials, and proprietors (n. e. c.)	4,419	3,197	3,113	2,390	2,135	1,511
205	Construction	296	175	199	107	183	58
206	Manufacturing	665	432	447	406	350	174
207	Transportation	151	90	184	162	167	66
208	Telecommunications, & utilities & sanitary services	68	54	96	97	85	6
209	Wholesale trade	343	225	39	62	5	78
210	Retail trade	1,977	1,620	1,592	1,220	1,119	930
211	Eating and drinking places	570	270	165	106	129	110
212	Food & dairy products stores, & milk retailing	512	469	540	444	395	
213	General merchandise and five and ten cent stores	128	111	184	162	167	
214	Apparel and accessories stores	130	99	96	97	85	
215	Motor vehicles and accessories retailing	119			62	5	
216	Gasoline service stations	186	183	89	15	2	
217	Furniture, home furnishings, and equipment stores	98	57				
218	Hardware, farm implement, & bldg. material retail	131	95	456	368	336	820
219	Other retail trade	305	271				
220	Banking and other finance	143	126	174	122	75	76
221	Insurance and real estate	117	65	66	38	29	14
222	Automobile repair services and garages	86	66	93	8	5	
223	Miscellaneous repair services	35	14		6	7	(¹)
224	Personal services	216	129	105	76	88	72
225	Business services	63	33	140	107	74	36
226	All other industries (incl. not reported)	259	169				
227	**Clerical and kindred workers**	7,232	4,982	4,336	3,385	1,987	877
228	Agents (n. e. c.)	128	73	102	64	28	59
229	Collectors, bill and account	24	45	43	31	36	
230	Attendants and assistants, library	13	24	28	14	3	1
231	Attendants, physician's and dentist's office	43	35	9	6	6	
232	Baggagemen, transportation	35	6	8	12	12	19
233	Bookkeepers	994	721	738	616	447	232
234	Cashiers						
235	Express messengers and railway mail clerks	19	23	26	22	22	28
236	Mail carriers	171	124	121	91	81	
237	Stenographers, typists, and secretaries	1,661	1,223	1,097	786	387	134
238	Messengers and office boys	60	64	80	110	103	66
239	Telegraph messengers	8	17	16	9	9	
240	Telegraph operators	36	42	68	75	66	56
241	Telephone operators	375	214	249	190	98	19
242	Ticket, station, and express agents	61	47	38	37	35	27
243	Office machine operators	150	66	38			
244	Shipping and receiving clerks	304	233				
245	Bank tellers						
246	Dispatchers and starters, vehicle						
247	Clerical and kindred workers (n. e. c.)	3,178	2,026	1,681	1,323	654	235
248	**Sales workers**	4,133	3,450	3,059	2,058	1,755	1,307
249	Advertising agents and salesmen	35	41	40	25	11	12
250	Auctioneers	6	4	8	5	4	3
251	Demonstrators	14	10				
252	Hucksters and peddlers	24	55	57	50	80	77
253	Insurance agents and brokers	312	253	257	120	88	78
254	Newsboys	101	58	39	28	30	34
255	Real estate agents and brokers	145	119	150	89	78	

¹ Not available.

Series D 123–572. Detailed Occupation of the Economically Active Population: 1900 to 1950—Con.

[In thousands]

Panel 1

Series No.	Occupation	1900	1910	1920	1930	1940	1950
	Sales workers—Con.						
256	Stock and bond salesmen	4	6	11	22	18	11
257	Salesmen and sales clerks (n. e. c.):						
258	Wholesale trade					2,893	3,485
259	Retail trade	1,089	1,454	1,724	2,482		
260	Other industries (incl. not reported)						
261	**Craftsmen, foremen, and kindred workers**	3,062	4,315	5,482	6,246	6,203	8,350
262	Bakers	70	90	98	141	139	128
263	Boilermakers	31	45	74	50	33	40
264	Bookbinders	26	17	19	19	18	33
265	Brickmasons, stonemasons, and tile setters	149	160	135	171	141	181
266	Cabinetmakers	36	43	50	63	60	78
267	Carpenters	596	815	885	917	776	1,016
268	Cement and concrete finishers	3	4	8	8	32	34
269	Electrotypers and stereotypers	3	5	5	8	9	12
270	Engravers, except photoengravers	22	4			9	10
271	Photoengravers and lithographers	22	23	23	28	23	29
272	Compositors and typesetters	136	128	140	184	181	182
273	Pressmen and plate printers, printing	20	20	19	31	36	51
274	Decorators and window dressers	3	5	9	20	30	46
275	Electricians	51	108	192	253	221	332
276	Cranemen, derrickmen, and hoistmen					112	218
277	Excavating, grading, and road machinery operators					53	223
278	Stationary engineers	134	219	258	294	201	222
279	Blacksmiths	220	238	209	136	99	60
280	Forgemen and hammermen						
281	Foremen (n. e. c.)	318	485	551	585	867
282	Construction	15	14	43	79	62
283	Manufacturing	164	296	293	310	525
284	Metal industries					218
285	Machinery, including electrical				112	72
286	Transportation equipment	164	296	293	53	235
287	Textiles, textile products, and apparel					
288	Other durable goods				144	
289	Other nondurable goods (incl. not specified mfg.)					
290	Railroads and railway express service	69	81	83	51	55
291	Transportation, except railroad	24	31	44	15	20
292	Telecommunications, & utilities & sanitary services	45	63	88	27	41
293	Other industries (incl. not reported)	164	296	293	104	164
294	Furriers	7	8	9	12	16	14
295	Painters, construction and maintenance	221	288	265	446	451	447
296	Glaziers		3	6	7	11	11
297	Heat treaters, annealers, and temperers	2	2	7	7	17	18
298	Inspectors, scalers, and graders, log and lumber	22	53	77	78	8	19
299	Inspectors (n. e. c.)	1	28	3	9	82	99
300	Construction		28	3	7	30	37
301	Railroads and railway express service	20	43	39	39	14	13
302	Transp. exc. railroad, commun., & other pub. util.	1	10	10	17	30	40
303	Other industries (incl. not reported)		14	21	17		49
304	Jewelers, watchmakers, goldsmiths, and silversmiths	23	33	39	39	36	49
305	Linemen & servicemen, telegraph, telephone, & power	18	35	106	104	116	219
306	Locomotive engineers	107	99	113	104	67	74
307	Locomotive firemen	76	91	67	67	50	57
308	Loom fixers	13	16	19	19	25	32
309	Job setters, metal					16	75
310	Machinists	304	520	1,168	1,387	535	571
311	Mechanics and repairmen, airplane					28	
312	Mechanics and repairmen, automobile					448	693
313	Mechanics and repairmen, railroad and car shop					46	49
314	Mechanics and repairmen, office machine						
315	Mechanics and repairmen, radio and television					436	987
316	Mechanics and repairmen (n. e. c.)						
317	Toolmakers, and die makers and setters					100	160
318	Millers, grain, flour, feed, etc.	25	23	23	16	16	10
319	Millwrights	17	17	38	42	44	61
320	Molders, metal	97	121	124	105	86	65
321	Motion picture projectionists		10	13	24	27	27
322	Opticians, and lens grinders and polishers	6	9	11	13	20	20

Panel 2

Series No.	Occupation	1900	1910	1920	1930	1940	1950
	Craftsmen, foremen, and kindred workers—Con.						
323	Paperhangers	22	26	19	28	31	23
324	Pattern and model makers, except paper	15	24	28	30	31	38
325	Piano and organ tuners and repairmen	4	7	7	7	5	8
326	Plasterers	35	48	38	70	53	66
327	Plumbers and pipe fitters	92	148	207	238	211	304
328	Rollers and roll hands, metal	6	18	25	31	33	32
329	Roofers and slaters	9	12	12	24	33	50
330	Shoemakers and repairers, except factory	102	70	79	68	68	60
331	Stone cutters and stone carvers	37	36	23	15	15	9
332	Structural metal workers		18	31	33	47	57
333	Tailors and tailoresses	134	205	192	169	120	88
334	Tinsmiths, coppersmiths, and sheet metal workers	49	60	75	83	91	133
335	Upholsterers	26	20	24	42	43	65
336	Craftsmen and kindred workers (n. e. c.)	60	73	66	43	47	76
337	Members of the Armed Forces[2]					3	38
338	**Operatives and kindred workers**	3,720	5,441	6,587	7,691	9,518	12,030
339	Apprentice carpenters	2	6	5	4	6	11
340	Apprentice electricians		3	10	5	8	9
341	Apprentice plumbers and pipefitters	3		7	6	5	13
342	Apprentice printing trades	4	12	12	6	10	16
343	Apprentice machinists and toolmakers			39	14	20	16
344	Apprentice auto mechanics						
345	Apprentice bricklayers and masons						
346	Apprentice mechanics, except auto	57	86	66	49	33	42
347	Apprentices, building trade (n. e. c.)						
348	Apprentices, metalworking trades (n. e. c.)						
349	Apprentices, other specified trades						
350	Apprentices, trade not specified					12	15
351	Asbestos and insulation workers			1	3	6	17
352	Attendants, auto service and parking		2	18	144	245	253
353	Blasters and powdermen			7	7	7	12
354	Boatmen, canalmen, and lock keepers	1	2	6	6	6	9
355	Brakemen, railroad	13	5	13	77	82	82
356	Switchmen, railroad	107	160	208	173	50	63
357	Chainmen, rodmen, and axmen, surveying				4	11	8
358	Conductors, bus and street railway	24	57	64	37	18	12
359	Deliverymen and routemen	167	230	170	187	294	253
360	Dressmakers and seamstresses, except factory	413	467	259	198	172	147
361	Dyers	5	14	15	18	28	26
362	Filers, grinders, and polishers, metal	17	50	60	79	117	160
363	Fruit, nut, & veget. graders & packers, exc. factory	13	13	24	33	25	37
364	Furnacemen, smeltermen, and pourers	5	26	16	15	20	59
365	Heaters, metal	13	10	10	15	10	10
366	Laundry and dry cleaning operatives	91	132	142	265	314	462
367	Meat cutters, except slaughter and packing house	33	41	61	120	160	180
368	Milliners	75	100	50	25	15	13
369	Mine operatives and laborers (n. e. c.):						
370	Coal mining	660	907	995	892	845	620
371	Crude petroleum and natural gas extraction		3	12	17	20	25
372	Mining and quarrying, except fuel	37	56	63	58	39	27
373	Motormen, mine, factory, logging camp, etc.		14	25	31	40	63
374	Motormen, street, subway, and elevated railway	55	111	144	83	104	130
375	Oilers and greasers, except auto	14	49	61	83	104	126
376	Painters, except construction and maintenance	55	55	61	71	104	126
377	Photographic process workers	2	2	3	8	15	30
378	Power station operators		12	21	29	22	22
379	Sailors and deckhands	40	47	55	65	47	55
380	Sawyers	18	43	34	36	50	100
381	Spinners, textile	56	74	83	81	113	88
382	Stationary firemen	73	111	144	127	128	130
383	Bus drivers						
384	Taxicab drivers and chauffeurs					1,515	1,808
385	Truck and tractor drivers		46	285	972		
386	Weavers, textile	155	202	219	225	109	105
387	Welders and flame-cutters		3	54	37	137	288
388	Operatives and kindred workers (n. e. c.)	1,592	2,451	3,284	3,634	4,654	6,627
	Manufacturing	1,443	2,318	3,076	3,189	4,225	5,847

[1] Consists solely of civilians seeking work whose last job was as a member of the Armed Forces.

[2] ... member of the Armed Forces.

Series D 123–572. Detailed Occupation of the Economically Active Population: 1900 to 1950—Con.

[In thousands]

Private household workers and Service workers, except private household (Series D 457–523)

Series No.	Occupation	1900	1910	1920	1930	1940	1950
457	**Private household workers**	1,579	1,851	1,411	1,998	2,412	1,539
458	Laundresses, private household—living in	280	513	375	344	203	76
459	Laundresses, private household—living out						
460	Housekeepers, private household—living in					410	150
461	Housekeepers, private household—living out						
462	Private household workers (n. e. c.)—living in	1,299	1,338	1,036	1,654	1,799	1,313
463	Private household workers (n. e. c.)—living out						
464	**Service workers, except private household**	1,047	1,711	1,901	2,774	3,657	4,641
465	Attendants, hospital and other institution	109	133	157	198	102	216
466	Midwives					115	151
467	Practical nurses		133	157	198		133
468	Attendants, professional & personal service (n. e. c.)		2	3	4	42	52
469	Attendants, recreation and amusement	6	9	13	29	64	66
470	Ushers, recreation and amusement		6	22		22	26
471	Barbers, beauticians, and manicurists	133	193	214	371	449	396
472	Bartenders	89	101	26		131	214
473	Boarding and lodging housekeepers	71	165	133	144	74	30
474	Bootblacks	8	14	15	19	16	15
475	Charwomen and cleaners	29	29	31	52	72	128
476	Cooks, except private household	117	174	200	292	349	478
477	Elevator operators	13	25	41	68	87	97
478	Firemen, fire protection	15	36	51	73	82	112
479	Guards, watchmen, and doorkeepers	116	78	116	148	216	255
480	Policemen and detectives, government	34	68	94	145	135	176
481	Policemen and detectives, private	57	9	7	9	21	21
482	Marshals and constables	42	45	52	61	9	7
483	Housekeepers and stewards, except private household	5	113	179	310	90	112
484	Janitors and sextons	107	96	102	151	377	482
485	Porters	9	7	11	15	182	179
486	Sheriffs and bailiffs		200	242	415	16	19
487	Counter and fountain workers		10	13	13	636	836
488	Waiters and waitresses		203	203	259	10	12
489	Watchmen (crossing) and bridge tenders	2				360	561
490	Service workers, except private household (n. e. c.)						
491	**Farm laborers and foremen**	5,125	5,370	4,948	4,290	3,632	2,578
492	Farm foremen	7	19	35	28	17	17
493	Farm laborers, wageworkers	5,115	2,832	2,271	2,597	2,405	1,617
494	Farm laborers, unpaid family workers		2,514	1,660	1,660	1,208	934
495	Farm service laborers, self-employed	4	6	10		3	10
496	**Laborers, except farm and mine**	3,620	4,478	4,905	5,335	4,875	3,885
497	Fishermen and oystermen	69	68	53	73	64	75
498	Garage laborers and car washers and greasers		4	33	77	63	72
499	Gardeners, except farm, and groundskeepers	24	65	71	168	163	159
500	Longshoremen and stevedores	29	63	86	74	74	73
501	Lumbermen, raftsmen, and woodchoppers	117	139	180	147	169	196
502	Teamsters	374	441	412	120	31	23
503	Laborers (n. e. c.)	3,007	3,696	4,070	4,675	4,312	3,288
	Manufacturing	723	1,487	2,169	1,960	1,598	1,209
504	Sawmills, planing mills, and millwork	139	289	280	292	230	152
505	Furniture and fixtures	7	24	35	40	27	18
506	Miscellaneous wood products	15	25	30	28	35	21
507	Glass and glass products	13	36	30	39	26	16
508	Cement & concrete, gypsum, & plaster products	42	78	49	60	39	24
509	Structural clay products	6	6	12	11	11	29
510	Pottery and related products	7	7	5	8	7	7
511	Miscellaneous nonmetallic mineral & stone prod					14	9
512	Motor vehicles and motor vehicle equipment	16	16	83	124	71	51
513	Ship and boat building and repairing	12	12	69	17	23	16
514	Blast furnaces, steelworks, and rolling mills					201	145
515	Other primary iron and steel industries					128	111
516	Fabricated steel products		419	544	492	46	43
517	Office and store machines and devices					6	1
518	Miscellaneous machinery					11	14
519	Not specified metal industries					4	4
520	Agricultural machinery and tractors					8	6
521	Aircraft and parts						
522	Railroad & miscellaneous transportation equipment	145	419	544	492		

Operatives and kindred workers—Con. (Series D 389–456)

Series No.	Occupation	1900	1910	1920	1930	1940	1950
	Operatives and kindred workers (n. e. c.)—Con.						
	Manufacturing—Con.						
389	Sawmills, planing mills, and millwork	75	105	92	91	63	151
390	Miscellaneous wood products		44	52	72	36	46
391	Furniture and fixtures	19	42	45	72	82	132
392	Glass and glass products	25	13	10	41	54	76
393	Cement & concrete, gypsum, & plaster products	9	13	16	11	13	30
394	Structural clay products	13	16	17	13	16	23
395	Pottery and related products	16	9	6	23	25	35
396	Miscellaneous nonmetallic mineral & stone prod	9			18	18	28
397	Motor vehicles and motor vehicle equipment	121	21	125	170	208	371
398	Ship and boat building and repairing		6	53	11	19	15
399	Blast furnaces, steelworks, and rolling mills				105	105	133
400	Other primary iron and steel industries		286	370	397	209	324
401	Fabricated steel products					24	40
402	Office and store machines and devices			192	172	123	273
403	Miscellaneous machinery	102	133			12	4
404	Not specified metal industries					21	52
405	Agricultural machinery and tractors					27	67
406	Aircraft and parts					11	19
407	Railroad & miscellaneous transportation equipment			21	30	29	258
408	Primary nonferrous industries	11	27	32	34	48	98
409	Fabricated nonferrous metal products	18	25	65	117	150	356
410	Electrical machinery, equipment, and supplies					29	60
411	Professional equipment and supplies	102	133	192	172	172	258
412	Photographic equipment and supplies						
413	Watches, clocks, and clockwork-operated devices						
414	Miscellaneous manufacturing industries						
415	Meat products	11	26	50	53	91	132
416	Canning & preserving fruits, veget., & seafood	13	8	18	26	52	95
417	Dairy products		12	19	26	36	62
418	Grain-mill products	4	4	8	7	17	33
419	Bakery products	9	9	20	28	45	68
420	Confectionery and related products	27	31	52	44	49	51
421	Beverage industries	13	20	10	7	36	57
422	Food preparations & kindred products	2	16	21	30	29	51
423	Not specified food industries						
424	Tobacco manufactures	116	152	145	104	86	70
425	Knitting mills	13	16	104	129	192	154
426	Dyeing and finishing textiles, except knit goods	10	15	18	20	24	26
427	Carpets, rugs, and other floor covering	1	4	14	17	21	26
428	Yarn, thread, and fabric mills	202	269	323	324	426	477
429	Miscellaneous textile mill products	31	48	46	35	35	32
430	Apparel and accessories	225	336	365	422	734	824
431	Miscellaneous fabricated textile products	21	18	21	15	53	58
432	Pulp, paper, and paperboard mills	21	36	55	64	87	106
433	Miscellaneous paper and pulp products		10	14	17	28	61
434	Paperboard containers and boxes	19	18	20	14	41	64
435	Printing, publishing, and allied industries	16	42	48	51	59	80
436	Synthetic fibers				21	31	27
437	Paints, varnishes, and related products	3	4	6	8	12	18
438	Drugs and medicines	9	33	51	53	72	149
439	Miscellaneous chemicals and allied products	4	4	14	27	30	48
440	Petroleum refining	1	2	2	2	5	7
441	Miscellaneous petroleum and coal products						
442	Rubber products	15	32	86	81	85	127
443	Leather: tanned, curried, and finished	26	34	32	29	35	32
444	Footwear, except rubber	98	181	206	210	228	226
445	Leather products, except footwear	31	29	33	26	44	50
446	Not specified manufacturing industries	67	93	207	139	74	43
447	Nonmanufacturing industries (incl. not reported)	149	132	208	445	429	780
448	Construction	7	182	111	145	40	71
449	Railroads and railway express service		61		98	73	96
450	Transportation, except railroad					24	37
451	Telecommunications, & utilities & sanitary serv.	137	19	30	57	24	52
452	Wholesale and retail trade		27	40	74	145	311
453	Business and repair services		6	8	30	38	54
454	Public administration		3	4	6	11	54
455	Personal services		9	12	165	75	105
456	All other industries (incl. not reported)	5					

Series D 123-572. Detailed Occupation of the Economically Active Population: 1900 to 1950—Con.

[In thousands]

Series No.	Occupation	1950	1940	1930	1920	1910	1900
	Laborers, except farm and mine—Con.						
	Laborers (n.e.c.)—Con.						
	Manufacturing—Con.						
524	Primary nonferrous industries	38	43	39	43	33	15
525	Fabricated nonferrous metal products	33	30	37	27	11	8
526	Electrical machinery, equipment, and supplies	4	4				
527	Professional equipment and supplies						
528	Photographic equipment and supplies						
529	Watches, clocks, and clockwork-operated devices	18	27	74	101	43	30
530	Miscellaneous manufacturing industries						
531	Meat products	37	47	43	60	34	12
532	Canning & preserving fruits, veget., & seafood	27	34	26	19	10	10
533	Dairy products	15	17	17	15	5	5
534	Grain-mill products	20	21	16	18	9	10
535	Bakery products	10	8	12	12	5	5
536	Confectionery and related products	4	8	6	7	3	3
537	Beverage industries	25	22	9	11	19	3
538	Miscellaneous food preparations & kindred prod	24	29	26	32	17	12
539	Not specified food industries						
540	Tobacco manufactures	10	17	21	35	16	14
541	Knitting mills	3	5	9	12	8	8
542	Dyeing and finishing textiles, except knit goods	6	7	8	11	10	10
543	Carpets, rugs, and other floor coverings	5	5	5	4	4	4
544	Yarn, thread, and fabric mills	50	71	94	120	59	44
545	Miscellaneous textile mill products	4	7	5	8	8	8
546	Apparel and accessories	9	10	14	12	8	5
547	Miscellaneous fabricated textile products	3	3	1	1	31	1
548	Pulp, paper, and paperboard mills	29	44	52	52	2	14
549	Miscellaneous paper and pulp products	9	6	4	3		

Series No.	Occupation	1900	1910	1920	1930	1940	1950
	Laborers, except farm and mine—Con.						
	Laborers (n.e.c.)—Con.						
	Manufacturing—Con.						
550	Paperboard containers and boxes	1	1	3	3	10	12
551	Printing, publishing, and allied industries	4	5	8	11	10	12
552	Synthetic fibers				5	5	3
553	Paints, varnishes, and related products	2	3	5	6	6	5
554	Drugs and medicines	15	45	79	80	77	61
555	Miscellaneous chemical and allied products	11	11	32	41	28	25
556	Petroleum, refining	5	11	9	5	8	6
557	Miscellaneous petroleum and coal products	6	14	51	29	20	17
558	Rubber products	16	21	27	18	11	8
559	Leather: tanned, curried, and finished	5	10	19	17	12	6
560	Footwear, except rubber	3	4	8	18	3	2
561	Leather products, except footwear						
562	Not specified manufacturing industries	79	109	191	114	44	11
563	Nonmanufacturing industries (incl. not reported)	2,284	2,210	1,901	2,715	2,714	2,079
564	Construction	284	531	391	710	1,340	788
565	Railroads and railway express service	86	599	543	490	278	293
566	Transportation, except railroad	68	195	199	249	98	119
567	Telecommunications, & utilities & sanitary serv		152	182	253	103	135
568	Wholesale and retail trade					250	345
569	Business and repair services	1	2	2	7	52	107
570	Public administration		56	93	134	64	83
571	Personal services		675	490	864	520	194
572	All other industries (incl. not reported)	1,825					

HOURS, WAGES, AND WORKING CONDITIONS (Series D 573–792)

D 573–577. Daily hours and indexes of daily wages in all industries and in building trades, January 1860–1891.

Source: U. S. Congress, "Aldrich Report," Senate Report No. 1394, 52d Congress, 2d Session, part I, pp. 173–180.

The Aldrich Report is the leading source of data on average wages and hours for 1840–1891. The only other large body of data relating to this period covers 1860–1880 (Joseph D. Weeks, *Report on the Statistics of Wages in Manufacturing Industries*, Tenth Census, vol. 20).

The basic wage data of the Aldrich Report were collected in 1891 and 1892 from the records of wages by occupation in 88 establishments in the Northeast, including Maryland. Those occupational wage series going back to 1860 were combined into industry indexes. Series starting after 1860 were not used in the indexes.

D 573–575 cover 21 industries including railroads, building trades, groceries, dry goods, city public works, illuminating gas, sidewalks, and 14 manufacturing industries. The source also contains data for the same period on wages in the coal, iron, glass, and pottery industries, and on teachers' salaries in certain areas.

In computing the weighted averages for series D 573 and D 574, shifting employment weights based on occupational data from the censuses of population were used.

Data for 1840–1859 for series D 573–577 are shown in the source, but the coverage is so inadequate that they are of little value.

The Aldrich Report indexes have been severely criticized by A. L. Bowley, Wesley C. Mitchell, and others, on several grounds including the failure to use the wage data for July of each year, the use of simple averages to combine occupations, and the overweighting of industries for which data were scanty. Mitchell's alternative processing of the wage data is shown in series D 578–588; however, it extends only to 1880. For 1880–1891, the Aldrich Report indexes are the only published summary of these wage data that covers all years. For certain industries and years, alternative indexes are presented in A. L. Bowley, "Comparison of the Rates of Increase of Wages in the United States and in Great Britain," *Economic Journal*, vol. V, 1895, pp. 368–383.

D 578–588. Indexes of average daily wages in all industries, in selected industries, and by degree of skill, January and July, 1860–1880.

Source: Wesley C. Mitchell, *Gold, Prices, and Wages Under the Greenback Standard*, University of California Press, Berkeley, 1908, pp. 120, 145–152.

The data underlying these indexes are from the Aldrich Report (see text for series D 573–577). The source also presents indexes of the medians and deciles of wages for most of the industries in series D 578–586, some indexes of means by

sex, indexes of medians and deciles by occupation, and indexes of means, medians, and deciles by initial wage level. In addition, the source contains a similar processing of the wage data of the Weeks Report (see text for series D 573–577).

D 578–586 are weighted arithmetic means of wage indexes by occupation for all industries covered in the Aldrich Report and for establishments in each industry. The weights are the number of workers included in each series at each date.

D 587 is an index of the median of wage indexes by occupation for unskilled men in all industries, excluding one establishment (Establishment 35, City Public Works, New York) that included about half the total number of unskilled men covered in the Aldrich Report.

D 588 is an index of the median of wage indexes by occupation for skilled men, excluding foremen and overseers and helpers of craftsmen.

D 589–602. Hours and earnings in manufacturing, in selected nonmanufacturing industries, and for "lower-skilled" labor, 1890–1926.

Source: Paul H. Douglas, *Real Wages in the United States, 1890–1926*, Houghton Mifflin Company, New York, 1930.

D 589–590 are weighted averages of series D 591 and D 593 and series D 592 and D 594, respectively. The union scales of wages are substantially higher and less flexible than the wages of all workers in the "union" industries. Since the weight of the "union" industries in the all-manufacturing average is based on the total number of skilled and semiskilled workers in the industries, the total manufacturing average is too high (see Leo Wolman, "American Wages," *Quarterly Journal of Economics*, XLVI, 1932, pp. 398–406).

D 591–592, beginning in 1907, are weighted averages of trade union scales for occupations. The weights are union membership by crafts. The series are extrapolated back to 1890 by use of payroll data from the sources of series D 593 and D 594.

D 593–594, average hours and earnings for "payroll" manufacturing industries, are averages weighted by employment data from employer payrolls (see text for series D 618–625), given in various Bureau of Labor Statistics (BLS) bulletins and in the *Nineteenth Annual Report of the Commissioner of Labor*. Until 1913, the original data are for selected occupations only, and exclude most laborers and some other unskilled workers. Therefore, for 1890–1913 the series are extrapolations backward from the 1914 level.

Differences between series D 591–592 and D 593–594 are not necessarily reliable indicators of differences in wages and hours between workers in union and nonunion industries. Because the biases in series D 591–592 are probably much greater than those in series D 593–594, it may sometimes be desirable to use only the latter to represent all manufacturing.

D 595, average hours in bituminous coal mining, is estimated from union contracts and their coverage for 1890–1903; after 1903, it is based on data from the U. S. Geological Survey.

D 596, average hourly earnings, was obtained by dividing series D 612, average annual earnings, by average days

Note. The series on wages and earnings in this section are in "current" (or money) dollars rather than dollars of fixed purchasing power. Although the current dollar is the proper unit for measuring wages and earnings for many purposes, it often tends to be a misleading indicator of purchasing power. If information is desired on the changes in purchasing power of earnings, money wages or earnings should be converted to real terms by dividing them by an appropriate index of consumer prices. Several such indexes are given in chapter E.

worked, as reported by the U. S. Geological Survey; the resulting series was divided by daily hours worked.

D 597, average full-time earnings on railroads, is based on average daily wages by occupations, 1895–1914; for 1914–1926, it is based on average hourly wages as reported by the Interstate Commerce Commission and estimated daily hours.

D 598–599, average hours and earnings in the building trades, were obtained in the same way as series D 591–592.

D 600, average hours for postal employees, is based on nominal hours as set by law, adjusted (after 1920) for sick leave.

D 601, average hourly earnings, is estimated by dividing series D 615 by 52 to obtain weekly earnings and then by dividing again by series D 600 to obtain hourly earnings.

D 602, average full-time weekly earnings for "lower-skilled" labor, is reproduced in the source from Whitney Coombs, *The Wages of Unskilled Labor in Manufacturing Industries in the United States, 1890–1924*, Columbia University Press, New York, 1926, p. 99. It is based on the wages of the least skilled or lowest paid occupations reported for each industry in BLS bulletins and in the *Nineteenth Annual Report of the Commissioner of Labor*, except that the figure for 1920 is based on the data of the National Industrial Conference Board. Since these sources exclude most laborers before 1914, the series is labelled here as "lower skilled," though it is called "unskilled" by Coombs and by Douglas.

D 603–617. Average annual earnings in all industries and in selected industries and occupations, 1890–1926.

Source: See source for series D 589–602.

D 603–604, all industries averages, are weighted averages of series D 605–617 and an additional series beginning in 1902 for anthracite coal. The weights change annually and are based on decennial census employment estimates. Interpolations of weights for intercensal years are based on State employment data when available; elsewhere they are linear.

The weights for decennial census years and 1926 are shown in the source, p. 390.

D 605, wage earners in manufacturing, is based on data from the census of manufacturers for census years (total wages paid and wage earners). Figures for intercensal years are interpolated using similar data from the labor bureaus of a number of States. Census data for 1890 are adjusted to eliminate the hand trades.

D 606, wage earners of steam railroads, is based on Interstate Commerce Commission data since 1905, and extrapolated back to 1890 using data from several State railroad commissions.

D 607, street railways, is based on the Eleventh Census (1890) and the censuses of electrical industries. Figures for intercensal years are interpolations based on data from several State railroad and public utility commissions and State labor bureaus.

D 608–609, telephone and telegraph industries, are based on censuses of electrical industries. Figures for intercensal years are interpolations based on data published by the Pennsylvania Department of Internal Affairs.

D 610, gas and electricity, is based on the censuses of electrical industries (electricity) and on the censuses of manufactures (gas). Figures for intercensal years are interpolations based on data for New York City, Wisconsin, Illinois, and Pennsylvania, from State sources.

D 611, clerical workers in manufacturing and steam railroads, is based on: Average earnings of salaried workers in manufacturing computed from the censuses of manufactures

for census years, with data from 3 States used to interpolate for other years; and beginning in 1895, earnings of salaried workers in railroads from the Interstate Commerce Commission, with data from 2 State railway commissions and 1 railroad used to extrapolate back to 1890.

D 612, bituminous coal mining, is based on aggregate wage payments from the censuses of mines and quarries of 1889, 1902, 1909, and 1919 as revised in the Fourteenth Census (1920), divided by employment figures reported by the U. S. Geological Survey. Figures for intercensal years are interpolations based on data from the State labor bureaus or departments of mines of 5 major coal-producing States.

D 613, farm labor, is based on the Department of Agriculture series of daily wages of farm labor without board and of monthly wages of farm labor without board. Data for 1900–1909 are linear interpolations covering from 1 to 3 years each.

D 614, Federal employees, covers employees of Federal executive departments in Washington, D. C., only. The data are from the *Official Register*, adjusted to include bonuses paid during 1917–1924.

D 615, postal employees, covers letter carriers and, beginning in 1906, postal clerks in first and second class post offices. The data are from the *Annual Reports of the Postmaster General*, adjusted to calendar years.

D 616, public school teachers, covers teachers, principals, and supervisors in public elementary and secondary schools. The data are from the *Annual Reports of the U. S. Commissioner of Education*, adjusted to a calendar-year basis. Data for some years after 1915 are interpolations based on studies of the National Education Association.

D 617, ministers, covers salaries of Methodist and Congregational ministers as reported in the *Methodist Year Book* and the *Annual Congregational Gray Book*.

D 618–625. Indexes of wages, hours, and earnings in manufacturing and in the building trades, 1890–1907.

Source: Department of Commerce and Labor, *Bulletin of the Bureau of Labor, No. 77*, 1908, p. 7; Leo Wolman, "Hours of Work in American Industry," *Bulletin 71*, National Bureau of Economic Research, 1938, p. 2.

Beginning in 1900, the Bureau of Labor of the Department of Commerce and Labor undertook, in somewhat modified form, a continuation of the Aldrich Report (see text for series D 573–577). The *Nineteenth Annual Report of the Commissioner of Labor*, 1904, contains the results of the studies for 1890–1903. Somewhat similar surveys were made for 1904–1907 and the information for the entire period was summarized in *Bulletin No. 77*, cited above. The *Nineteenth Annual Report* and the subsequent *Bulletins* (Nos. 59, 65, 71, and 77) show the basic wage, hour, and employment averages for each of the individual occupations and industries and for selected occupations by States and for large cities.

The Bureau of Labor figures (series D 618–620) include the building and other hand and neighborhood trades. Wolman's figures (series D 621) exclude the building and hand trades.

The data in the *Nineteenth Annual Report* are based on information obtained from 3,475 establishments in 67 industries, covering 519 occupations. Agents of the Bureau of Labor collected wages, hours, and employment data separately by occupation and sex from the records of each establishment. Such data were taken only for what were judged principal occupations in each industry and only for the period within each year that was judged "normal" for the establishment. By and large, the basic data for each occupation (separately by sex) were for establishments whose records were complete enough to supply the data for each year 1890–1903.

For 1890–1903, average hourly wages and average full-time weekly hours, weighted by employment, were computed for each occupation, separately by sex. Each of the occupational series was converted to an index number with the average for 1890–1899 as the base. Within each industry, simple arithmetic means of the individual occupational indexes were then computed. Series D 622 and D 624 are unweighted means of the occupational indexes in the building trades. The "all manufacturing" index numbers (series D 618 and D 620), however, are weighted means of the indexes of the 67 separate industries included, each industry weighted by the payroll of that industry as estimated from the 1900 Census. Series D 619 is the product of series D 618 and D 620. Similarly, series D 623 is the product of series D 622 and D 624.

For 1904–1907, the procedures used by the Bureau of Labor were similar to those used for 1890–1903, with the following exceptions: (1) Some small industries covered in 1890–1903 were dropped although the number of establishments covered was increased; and (2) the indexes were chain-linked to those for 1890–1903.

Series D 621 and D 625, for average full-time weekly hours, are based on Wolman's reworking of the basic data for series D 620 and D 624. Series D 621 shows the index numbers computed from the weighted average of the hours figures in the *Nineteenth Annual Report* for 456 occupations in 48 manufacturing industries and excludes the building trades and other hand and neighborhood trades covered in the report. The weight for each occupation in each year is the number of employees covered in the survey of that occupation in the year. Series D 625 is the index number calculated from the similarly weighted average computed by Wolman for the 19 building trades occupations. For the building trades, Wolman expressed the opinion that the hours data in the *Nineteenth Annual Report* were those established by unions.

Wolman's report is a basic source of information of hours of work in American industry. It contains 15 summary tables of historical data on hours of work in manufacturing, building construction, steam railroads, and coal mining for various dates, 1890–1937.

D 626–634. Hours and earnings for production workers in manufacturing, 1909–1957.

Source: 1909–1946, Bureau of Labor Statistics, *Handbook of Labor Statistics*, 1950 edition; 1947–1957, *Monthly Labor Review*, various issues.

The figures for 1909–1931 represent estimates based largely on periodic wage and hour surveys conducted by the Bureau of Labor Statistics during that period for a narrow list of manufacturing industries. These figures are an extension of, and are adjusted for comparability with, the figures for 1932–1957. For a discussion of the methods and data used to derive the figures for 1909–1931, see the *Monthly Labor Review*, July 1955, pp. 801–806.

The estimates of average weekly earnings for 1909–1931, based primarily on census data, tend to be more accurate than those for average hourly earnings, and average weekly hours. It is likely that the hourly earnings figures are overstated and the weekly hours understated because the BLS surveys of wages tended to sample large firms more heavily than small firms.

For 1932–1957, the underlying employment, payroll, and man-hour figures are obtained by means of a mail questionnaire sent monthly to cooperating establishments. Each establishment reports the following information: (1) The number of production workers or nonsupervisory employees who worked or received pay for any part of the payroll period ending nearest the 15th of the month; (2) the total gross payrolls for these employees before such deductions as Social Security taxes, withholding taxes, union dues, etc. (the payroll figures include pay for overtime, shift premiums, sick leave, holidays, vacations, and production bonuses, but exclude payments in kind, retroactive pay, nonproduction bonuses, employer contributions to private welfare funds, insurance and pension plans, and similar fringe payments); and (3) total man-hours paid for these employees including hours paid for vacations, holidays, sick leave, travel time, lunch time, etc.

Within each detailed industry the payroll, employment, and man-hours figures for reporting establishments are aggregated, and average hourly earnings, average weekly hours, and average weekly earnings are computed. The average hourly earnings and average weekly hours for a group of industries are weighted arithmetic means of the corresponding averages for the industries within the group. The weights used for earnings are estimates of aggregate production-worker man-hours and those used for hours are estimates of aggregate production-worker employment. Average weekly earnings for the group is the product of the average hourly earnings and the average weekly hours for the group.

Average weekly hours worked or paid for differ from average full-time or standard hours (before payment at overtime premium rates) and from average hours worked per week. During periods of substantial unemployment, average weekly hours paid for often may be considerably below the full-time level of hours or the level at which premium payments for overtime begin. On the other hand, during periods of relatively full employment, overtime hours tend to raise the average weekly hours above the full-time level.

Until the 1940's, the distinction in most industries between hours paid for and hours worked was relatively unimportant. The widespread adoption of paid vacations of increasing length and of an increasing number of paid holidays (and in some industries paid travel time, lunch time, etc.), however, has raised average weekly hours (which are hours paid for) above average hours worked by increasing amounts. By 1957, the difference may have grown to as much as 5 percent in manufacturing industries on the average; in some industries, such as bituminous coal mining, the difference was substantially larger. Since the middle 1940's, figures for weekly hours tend to understate the downward movement of hours worked per week.

Average hourly earnings figures exclude such fringe payments as employer contributions to private health, welfare, and insurance funds and include premium payments for overtime and for night work.

D 635–637. Hours and earnings for bituminous coal mines, 1909–1957.

Source: Bureau of Labor Statistics, *Employment and Earnings*, and *Hours and Earnings* (multilithed releases).

For 1909–1931, estimates are based on a variety of sources including special studies by the BLS and data collected by the Bureau of the Census, the Bureau of Mines, and reports of various State coal commissions. For 1932–1957, figures are strictly comparable in concept and method of estimation with those for manufacturing in series D 626–634. See text also for same series regarding hours paid for in contrast to hours worked and the exclusion from average hourly earnings of fringe payments which are particularly applicable to coal mining.

Before 1945, lunch time was not paid for in the mines. Beginning April 1945, mine operators paid for 15 minutes of lunch time per day; in July 1947, the lunch time paid for was increased to one-half hour. Similarly, before November 1943, working time was computed on a "face-to-face" basis. From November 1943 to April 1945, inside mine workers were paid for 45 minutes of travel time per day at two-thirds of the regular rate. Since April 1945, inside workers have been paid for all travel time at the applicable hourly rate.

Data published by the Bureau of Mines (*Minerals Yearbook*, 1946, p. 81) show that in 1944 travel time amounted, on the average, to 10–15 percent of total time paid for. Therefore, average weekly hours figures since 1945 may have a serious upward bias if used to measure hours actually worked, and the average hourly earnings figures may have a correspondingly serious downward bias if used to measure average earnings per hour actually worked.

Average hourly earnings figures exclude contributions of coal mine employers to the miners' health and welfare fund. These contributions have increased from 5 cents per ton in 1946 to 40 cents per ton in 1952 and later years. In 1953 wage supplements in bituminous coal mining, chiefly employer contributions to the health and welfare fund in the industry, amounted to 16 percent of total wages and salaries in the industry.

D 638–641. Hours and earnings for Class I steam railroads, 1921–1957.

Source: Bureau of Labor Statistics, *Employment and Earnings*, and *Hours and Earnings* (multilithed releases); BLS, *Handbook of Labor Statistics*, 1947 and 1950 editions; and Interstate Commerce Commission, *Wage Statistics of Class I Railroads in the United States*, various issues.

Figures for Class I railroads are based on their monthly reports to the Interstate Commerce Commission. Until 1951, the figures covered all hourly rated employees of Class I railroads excluding (except in 1921–1927) Class I switching and terminal companies. Since 1951, the figures cover all employees (excluding switching and terminal companies) except executives, officials, and staff assistants. Although the figures since 1951 are not strictly comparable with those for earlier years, the difference is not large.

Average hourly earnings are computed by dividing the total compensation of covered employees by total man-hours paid for. Average weekly earnings are derived by multiplying average weekly hours by average hourly earnings. Average weekly hours equal total man-hours paid for (during a month) reduced to a weekly basis, divided by the full-month count of employees on the payroll. The full-month count generally tends to be somewhat larger than a count for the payroll period ending nearest the 15th of the month, which is used for other industries. For this reason both the weekly earnings and the weekly hours figures tend to be slightly lower than they would be if computed on the latter basis.

For 1921–1927, straight-time average hourly earnings (series D 641) are computed by dividing compensation for straight time actually worked by hours of straight time actually worked. For 1928–1950, figures are ratios of compensation for straight time paid for to hours of straight time paid for. Since 1951, the figures have been computed from the ICC's *Wage Statistics*, which provides monthly and annual data on employment, man-hours, and compensation by detailed occupation as well as by major occupational groups.

D 642–653. Indexes of union hourly wage rates and weekly hours, for building and printing trades, 1907–1956.

Source: Bureau of Labor Statistics, *Union Wages and Hours: Building Trades*, July 1957, pp. 5 and 14; and *Union Wages and Hours: Printing Industry*, July 1956, pp. 6 and 15.

Studies by the Bureau of Labor Statistics of union scales of wages and hours prior to 1936 included at various times building and printing trades, barbers, linemen, longshoremen, and workers employed in breweries, laundries, metal trades, millwork, restaurants, soft drink production, theaters, baking, trucking, and local transit. Since 1936, the studies have been confined to the printing and building trades, trucking, local transit, and baking. The baking study was discontinued in 1953.

For each trade, the local union is asked to submit data on the minimum union wage rate, the weekly hours (before overtime becomes effective), and the number of active union members working or available for work on a single specified date (recently July 1) each year.

The earliest studies covered 13 journeymen and 7 helper and labor classifications in building construction, and 7 book and job and 4 newspaper classifications in the printing trades in 39 cities. The most recent study covered 24 journeymen and 9 helper and labor classifications in the building trades in 52 cities of over 100,000 population, and 12 book and job and 8 newspaper classifications in the printing trades in 53 such cities.

Indexes for all years were computed by the chain-link relative method, except 1921–1929, which were based on weighted arithmetic means for each year. The figures reflect minimum union contract scales and exclude premium pay for overtime. During periods of unemployment, the contract rates may be higher than the actual wage rates paid. Wage rates above contract scales may be paid during periods of high employment or rapid inflation. Thus, the union figures tend to have smaller cyclical fluctuations than actual wage rates paid to union employees. Furthermore, since overtime pay is excluded, union wage rates fluctuate less cyclically than average hourly earnings.

The hours figures also reflect union contract straight-time hours. They do not measure hours actually worked, which vary for the building trades with climatic conditions and the amount of construction work available.

D 654–668. Hours and earnings, for production workers in 25 manufacturing industries, by sex and degree of skill, 1914–1948.

Source: National Industrial Conference Board, *The Economic Almanac for 1950*, New York, 1950, pp. 336–344.

The underlying data were collected by the National Industrial Conference Board (NICB) from a sample of companies representing 25 industries (durable and nondurable goods) by means of a monthly mail questionnaire. The number of firms included in the sample, as well as the distribution of these firms by size and geographical location, varied somewhat from time to time. In 1936, the sample included 1,886 firms employing about one-third of all wage earners in the 25 industries covered and about one-fifth of all wage earners in all manufacturing industries. The average firm in the sample (in most of the 25 industries) was substantially larger (in terms of employment) than the average firm in the population from which the sample was taken. Although some tendency toward an upward bias in the level of earnings of the sample firms may exist, it is not clear that this bias also had a trend or varied with the business cycle.

Within each industry, average hourly earnings was obtained by dividing the aggregate payroll for reporting companies by the aggregate man-hours. Average weekly hours and average weekly earnings were obtained in a similar manner. The averages for all industries taken together were weighted means of the separate industry averages with fixed employment weights estimated for each industry with the help of the 1923 Census of Manufactures.

The distinction in classification between unskilled males and other male workers was not precisely stated by NICB and the classification was made by the reporting firms.

D 669–684. Hours and earnings, for production workers in selected nonmanufacturing industries, 1932–1957.

Source: Bureau of Labor Statistics, *Employment and Earnings*, and *Hours and Earnings* (multilithed releases); and *Handbook of Labor Statistics*, 1947 edition, pp. 80–86.

See text for series D 626–634.

D 685–695. Average annual compensation per full-time employee, by major industry, 1919–1929.

Source: Computed from Simon Kuznets, *National Income and its Composition, 1919–1938*, National Bureau of Economic Research, New York, 1941, pp. 314–315.

These data were obtained by dividing Kuznets' estimates of aggregate employee compensation for each major industry division by the corresponding estimates of number of full-time equivalent employees. The source also presents similar compensation and employment data for 1930–1938, and for industry groups within the major industry divisions.

Employee compensation figures include wages and salaries, and government relief payments. In addition, bonuses, commissions, gratuities, payments in kind, pensions, and compensation for injuries were included for industries in which they were a significant proportion of total compensation and could be estimated from available data.

Kuznets' employment estimates include both wage earners and salaried employees and are stated in full-time equivalent units (the number of persons that would have been employed if each had worked full-time for a full year), or, in effect, the number of full-time positions filled. In practice, Kuznets used estimates of employment similar to those used by BLS; namely, annual averages of monthly figures, based on a payroll count for a single payroll period in each month, except in a few industries in which part-time work was important and for which he derived full-time equivalent employment by dividing aggregate wage payments by estimates of annual earnings for full-time workers.

D 696–707. Average annual earnings per full-time employee, by major industry, 1929–1957.

Source: 1929–1945, Office of Business Economics, *National Income: 1954 Edition*, pp. 200–201; 1946–1957, *U. S. Income and Output, 1958*, table VI-15.

These estimates are ratios of aggregate wage and salary payments, by industry, to the aggregate number of full-time equivalent employees, by industry (the sources also present estimates for industry groups within major industries). Wages and salaries include executives' compensation, bonuses, tips, and payments in kind, and exclude those sources of labor income appearing in series D 708–727 as "supplements to wages and salaries."

Full-time equivalent employment measures man-years of full-time employment of wage and salary earners and its equivalent in work performed by part-time workers. For a discussion of the concept of full-time equivalent employment and the methods of estimation involved in converting part-time work to its full-time equivalent, see the *Survey of Current Business*, June 1945, pp. 17–18.

The difference between the Kuznets' figures for average annual earnings (series D 685–695) and these Office of Business Economics figures is slight prior to World War II. Kuznets' compensation figures include both wages and salaries and some "supplements to wages and salaries." For 1919–1938, however, supplements were a small fraction of wages and salaries in most industries. The concept of full-time equivalent employment used by Kuznets also was essentially the same as that used by the Office of Business Economics.

The employment and payrolls estimates were derived by combining separate estimates for those industries covered by Social Security programs and those not covered by such programs. For 1929–1938, for those industries covered (as of 1957) by Social Security programs, the employment and payrolls figures are extrapolations backward from 1939, based on sources and methods similar to those for series D 685–695.

Since 1939, for those industries (virtually all industrial and commercial employment) covered by Social Security programs, estimates of aggregate wages and salaries were obtained as follows (employment estimates came from essentially the same sources). Figures for payrolls covered by Old-Age and Survivors Insurance (OASI) or the Railroad Retirement Act came from the records of the State Unemployment Insurance programs and from the Interstate Commerce Commission's *Statistics of Railways*, and provide employer-reported data by industry for about 95 percent of total payrolls covered by Social Security. Payrolls of firms covered by OASI but not by State Unemployment Insurance were estimated from periodic special tabulations of OASI data for these firms. Similarly payrolls covered by the Railroad Retirement Act but not reported to the Interstate Commerce Commission were estimated from Railroad Retirement Board data.

This general method was followed except for categories for which more reliable data were available from other sources or where the proportion of firms not covered by Social Security programs was large: Agricultural services, forestry, and fisheries; banking (before 1943); water transportation (before 1947); medical and other health services; and legal services. Data for these were obtained from various population and industry censuses, the Maritime Commission, governmental banking regulatory bodies, and special surveys made by the Department of Commerce.

Estimates of employment and payrolls not covered by Social Security programs, accounting for roughly one-fifth of total wages and salaries, are based on a variety of sources, chief among which are: (1) For the Federal Government, reports of the Civil Service Commission, records of the armed services, and (for 1933–1943) records of the Federal work relief projects; (2) for State and local governments, reports of the Bureau of the Census, the Office of Education, etc.; (3) for farms, the Census of Agriculture and estimates of the Department of Agriculture; (4) for private households, the Census of Population. For further details, see *National Income: 1954 Edition*, pp. 70–72.

D 708–719. Average annual supplements to wages and salaries per full-time employee, by major industry, 1929–1957.

Source: Computed from the following: 1929–1945, Office of Business Economics, *National Income: 1954 Edition*, pp. 183 and 196–197; 1946–1957, *U. S. Income and Output, 1958*, tables VI-3 and VI-13.

These figures have been computed by dividing estimates by industry of aggregate supplements to wages and salaries by the corresponding estimates of the aggregate number of full-time equivalent employees. For discussion of estimates of full-time equivalent employees, see text for series D 696–707; for discussion of supplements to wages and salaries, see text for series D 720–727.

D 720–727. Average annual supplements to wages and salaries per full-time equivalent employee, by type of supplement, 1929–1957.

Source: Computed from the following: 1929–1945, Office of Business Economics, *National Income: 1954 Edition*, pp. 196–197 and 210–211; 1946–1957, *U. S. Income and Output, 1958*, tables I-8, III-6, and VI-13.

These figures have been computed by dividing estimates by type of aggregate supplements to wages and salaries by estimates of full-time equivalent employees in all industries. For discussion of estimates of full-time equivalent employees, see text for series D 696–707. The source presents figures for a more detailed classification of supplements.

The averages shown for the different types of supplements may tend to be somewhat lower than they should be because the employment figures used to obtain the averages include employees for whom no contributions or payments were made and who would not therefore be recipients of supplemental compensation.

Data for items under "employer contributions for social insurance" (series D 721–724) have a high degree of reliability since they are obtained almost exclusively from the accounting records of the agencies administering the programs. Estimates for items under "other labor income" are less reliable.

Data on supplements to wages and salaries are obtained from a variety of sources. Reports filed by employers with the administrative agencies or with the United States Treasury are the sources of figures for employer contributions under old-age and survivors insurance, State unemployment insurance and cash sickness compensation, railroad retirement and unemployment insurance, and the Federal unemployment tax. Payments made by the Federal Government to its civilian employee retirement systems are obtained from Treasury Department records and the records of the administrative agencies. Estimates of Federal Government contributions made to Government life insurance programs are based on monthly reports of the Veterans Administration.

Contributions to State and local retirement systems are based on data supplied, since 1936, by the Department of Health, Education, and Welfare. Estimates for 1929–1935 are extrapolations from the 1936 figure based on a sample survey of State and local government units.

Estimates of compensation for injuries are based on data in the annual *Insurance Yearbook* (Spectator Company) and on reports of State insurance funds, and on information furnished by State accident compensation commissions.

Employer contributions to private pension plans are estimated for 1945–1956 chiefly from tabulations prepared by the Internal Revenue Service. Contributions to health and welfare funds are estimated from data obtained from the Amalgamated Clothing Workers of America, the International Ladies' Garment Workers' Union, the United Mine Workers of America, and the American Telephone and Telegraph Company, and from data appearing chiefly in Bureau of Labor Statistics publications.

Employer contributions for group insurance (series D 726) are based upon studies made by the Department of Health, Education, and Welfare and the National Industrial Conference Board and upon reports from life insurance companies, Blue Cross and Blue Shield, and other sources.

Data on the pay of military reservists have been obtained from the armed services or from the annual *Budget of the United States Government* and data on Federal payments to enemy prisoners of war were obtained from the Department of Defense. Other items in "other labor income" have always been small in amount.

D 728. Annual salary of public school teachers, 1930–1954.

Source: Office of Education, *Biennial Survey of Education in the United States*, various years.

Estimates are based on biennial reports made to the Office of Education by the departments of education in the 48 States and the District of Columbia. Average annual salary is the ratio of salary expenditures for principals, supervisors, and teachers to the number of such staff members. It is not possible to determine precisely from the *Biennial Surveys*, particularly in the earlier years, the extent to which number of teachers is number of teaching positions rather than number of teachers on the payroll. In recent years the concept used presumably is number of teaching positions. To the extent that the surveys have shifted from a payroll to a position count, average salaries in recent years tend to be overstated relative to those of earlier years. For additional information and longer series, see Chapter H, general note for series H 1–89, and series H 12, H 13, and H 14–16.

D 729. Annual salary of college teachers, 1929–1952.

Source: George J. Stigler, *Trends in Employment in the Service Industries*, Princeton University Press, Princeton, 1956, p. 134.

These figures refer to college teachers in large public institutions. The average annual salary is the weighted arithmetic mean of median salaries estimated separately for the four categories: Instructors, assistant professors, associate professors, and professors.

For 1929–1932, the median salaries by rank are based on Viva Boothe's *Salaries and the Cost of Living in Twenty-seven State Universities and Colleges, 1913–1932*, Ohio State University Press, 1932.

For 1935–1942, 1950, and 1952, Stigler estimated median salaries by rank from data in various reports of the Office of Education. The weights used in calculating the weighted mean of the median salaries by rank were the relative numbers in each of the ranks in public universities, colleges, and professional schools in New York State as shown in annual reports of the University of the State of New York.

For 1943–1949, the figures were interpolated by Stigler on the basis of expenditures on resident instruction per teacher.

Figures for 1908–1928 approximately comparable to those shown here and for median salaries for each of the four college teaching ranks for 1908–1942 appear in George J. Stigler, *Employment and Compensation in Education*, National Bureau of Economic Research, New York, 1950.

D 730. Annual net income of nonsalaried lawyers, 1929–1954.

Source: 1929–1946, William Weinfeld, "Income of Lawyers, 1929–1948," *Survey of Current Business*, August 1949, p. 18; 1947–1954, Maurice Liebenberg, "Income of Lawyers in the Postwar Period," *Survey of Current Business*, December 1956, p. 27.

Nonsalaried lawyers are those who engage in private practice as entrepreneurs. The average shown is the arithmetic mean. For some of the years, the sources also give median net income. Net income is excess of gross receipts from legal practice over the total of the payroll, rent, and other costs of legal practices. Part-year incomes have been converted to full-year equivalents.

The estimates are based on a series of sample mail surveys of the legal profession made by the Department of Commerce. The results of the various surveys are reported in the *Surveys of Current Business* for April 1938, August 1943, May 1944, August 1949, July 1952, and December 1956. These reports, particularly those of August 1949 and December 1956, contain for selected years mean and median net income figures and detailed frequency distributions by size of income not only for nonsalaried lawyers but also for salaried and part-salaried lawyers. Tabulations by various other characteristics are also shown in the sources.

D 731. Annual net income of nonsalaried physicians, 1929–1951.

Source: 1929–1949, William Weinfeld, "Income of Physicians, 1929–49," *Survey of Current Business*, July 1951, p. 11; 1950–1951, "Incomes of Physicians, Dentists, and Lawyers, 1949–51," *Survey of Current Business*, July 1952, p. 6.

A nonsalaried physician is one whose sole source of medical income is from independent practice. The average shown is the arithmetic mean. For some of the years, the sources also give estimates of median net income. Net income is the gross receipts from medical practice less the total of payroll, rent, supplies, equipment depreciation, and other expenses of medical practice. Part-year incomes have not been converted to full-time equivalents.

The estimates of mean net income are based chiefly on a series of sample mail surveys of the medical profession made by the Department of Commerce. The results of the various surveys are reported in the *Surveys of Current Business* for April 1938, October 1943, July 1951, and July 1952. These reports, particularly July 1951, show for selected years mean and median net and gross incomes and income distributions by size of income not only for nonsalaried physicians but also for salaried and part-salaried physicians. Tabulations by various other characteristics are also shown in the sources.

D 732. Annual net income of nonsalaried dentists, 1929–1951.

Source: 1929–1948, William Weinfeld, "Income of Dentists, 1929–48," *Survey of Current Business*, January 1950, p. 9; 1949–1951, "Incomes of Physicians, Dentists, and Lawyers, 1949–51," *Survey of Current Business*, July 1952, p. 6.

Nonsalaried dentists are those who engage in private practice as entrepreneurs. The average shown is the arithmetic mean. Medians are given in the source for some but not all of the years. Net income is gross receipts from dental practice less the total of the payroll, rent, and other costs of dental practice. Part-year incomes have not been converted to full-year equivalent incomes.

The estimates of average annual net income are based on a series of sample mail surveys made by the Department of Commerce. The 1938 survey of dental incomes is reported in Herman Lasken, *Economic Conditions in the Dental Profession, 1929–37*, Department of Commerce, September 1939; the 1942 survey in the *Survey of Current Business*, April 1944, and the 1949 survey in the *Survey of Current Business*, January 1950.

These reports contain, for selected years, mean and median net and gross incomes and detailed income distributions by size of income not only for nonsalaried dentists but also for salaried and part-salaried dentists. Tabulations by various other characteristics are also shown in the sources.

D 733. Median base monthly salary rate, engineers, 1929–1953.

Source: David M. Blank and George J. Stigler, *The Demand and Supply of Scientific Personnel*, National Bureau of Economic Research, New York, 1957, pp. 114 and 116.

The estimates for 1929, 1932, and 1934 were based on data obtained by the Bureau of Labor Statistics from a 1935 survey of all professional engineers in the United States who could be located. The survey placed heavy reliance on membership lists of engineering societies for its mailing list. Approximately 173,000 questionnaires were mailed and about one-third were returned with usable data.

The estimates for 1939, 1943, and 1946 are for all engineers, both graduate and nongraduate, who were members of the 6 engineering societies of the Engineers Joint Council in May 1946. The Council obtained income data from a mail questionnaire sent to 87,000 member engineers. Approximately 47,000 questionnaires were returned. The basic tabulations made by the Council were based on returns from engineers who had maintained residence as civilians in the United States continuously during 1939–1946.

The estimate for 1953 is for graduate engineers only and is the monthly equivalent of the annual rate given in the source used by Blank and Stigler. It is based on data obtained by the Engineers Joint Council from a sample survey of graduate engineers employed in industry and government.

Blank and Stigler give not only median monthly salary rates, but also first and third quartile monthly salary rates. In addition, other tables, particularly in appendix A, provide average income data for selected years (in some cases as far back as 1890) for engineers classified by years of experience and engineering specialization.

D 734. Annual pay and allowances, U. S. Regular Army commissioned officers, 1929–1952.

Source: George J. Stigler, *Trends in Employment in the Service Industries*, Princeton University Press, Princeton, 1956, pp. 134–135.

The figures are weighted averages of average annual earnings, computed according to specified years of cumulative service for each rank. The weights used throughout were fixed weights derived from the distribution of Army officers by rank in 1941. Stigler's basic sources were: *Official Army Register*, Adjutant General's Office, 1930, 1933, 1947, and 1950 and the *Annual Report of the Secretary of the Army*, Department of the Army, 1941.

D 735–740. Labor union membership, by affiliation, 1897–1934.

Source: Bureau of Labor Statistics, records, and Leo Wolman, *Ebb and Flow in Trade Unionism*, National Bureau of Economic Research, New York, 1936.

The data are based on reports and statements made by unions in their official journals, reports, and convention proceedings; on correspondence of the compilers of the series with union officials; and on per capita dues payments of national and international unions to over-all federations. Different unions define membership differently. Some include and others exclude unemployed members, retired members, apprentices, members involved in work stoppages, and members in the Armed Forces. Because of such variations, different series estimating the membership of the same groups of unions can differ substantially.

The figures include Canadian members of unions with headquarters in the United States, and some other members outside continental United States. Wolman estimates the number of Canadian members at 255,000 in 1920, and 203,000 in 1930.

D 735–736. Total union membership, 1897–1934.

Source: See source for series D 737–740.

Series D 735 is the sum of series D 738 and D 740; series D 736 is the sum of series D 739 and D 740.

D 737–740. Unions and membership of American Federation of Labor, and membership in independent or unaffiliated, 1897–1934.

Source: *Proceedings*, 65th Convention of the American Federation of Labor, 1946, p. 43; Lewis L. Lorwin, *The American Federation of Labor*, Brookings Institution, Washington, 1933, p. 488; *Proceedings* of the A. F. of L. Conventions of 1897, 1898, and 1933–34; and Leo Wolman, *Ebb and Flow in Trade Unionism*, National Bureau of Economic Research, New York, 1936.

D 738 represents "total paid membership of the affiliated national and international organizations and directly chartered trade and federal labor unions" based on "the actual per capita tax" remitted by affiliated unions. Such per capita tax payments can and frequently do cover either fewer or more members than the affiliated union reports in its own statements.

Total membership in series D 739 differs from that in series D 738 because series D 739 uses the direct reports of affiliated unions where available in preference to the membership indicated by per capita tax payments.

D 740, membership of independent and unaffiliated unions, covers national and international unions not affiliated with the A. F. of L. It excludes independent unions that are purely local in character or whose jurisdiction is confined to the employees of a single employer. In most years about half the workers covered by this series were members of the four brotherhoods of workers in the railroad train and engine service. This series is from Wolman, cited above, pp. 138–139, adjusted in 1929–1934 to include the membership of the Trade Union Unity League. For 1932 and 1934, the membership of the Trade Union Unity League has been interpolated from figures for adjacent years.

For Wolman's estimates of union membership by industry, see series D 746–763. Annual estimates of the membership of individual national and international unions for 1897–1934 may be found in Wolman's book cited above and in his *The Growth of American Trade Unions, 1880–1923*, National Bureau of Economic Research, 1924.

D 741–745. Labor union membership and membership as percent of nonagricultural employment, 1930–1956.

Source: Bureau of Labor Statistics, "Union Membership as a Proportion of Labor Force, 1930–1956," January 1958 (mimeographed release).

See also text for series D 735–740.

D 741, total union membership, is a continuation of series D 735. For 1935–1947, the membership of A. F. of L. unions included is based on per capita taxes; the membership of independent unions included was estimated by BLS from fragmentary data. For 1948, 1949, and 1950, the figure shown is the midpoint of an estimated range of 14,000,000 to 16,000,000. For 1951 and 1952 the figure shown is the midpoint of an estimated range of 16,500,000 to 17,000,000. These ranges are based on membership data from surveys of national and international unions made by BLS. The level of the series may be more accurate during 1948–1952 than during 1939–1947. Prior to 1947, the series seems to include substantially inflated membership claims of some unions (see the alternative figures

for 1939 below). The year-to-year movement of this series from 1947–1953, and in particular the drop in membership from 1947–1948, should not be considered as reliable.

Starting in 1953, the estimates are based on biennial surveys of national and international unions. See *Directory of National and International Labor Unions in the United States, 1957*, BLS Bulletin No. 1222, and the 1955 *Directory*, Bulletin No. 1185. The figures also include the members of directly chartered local labor unions affiliated with the major national federations and members of local unaffiliated unions.

Estimates of union membership by affiliation (A. F. of L., CIO, and independent) for 1934–1950 appear in BLS, *Handbook of Labor Statistics*, 1950 edition, p. 139. For 1954 and 1956 such estimates are given in the directories cited above (the 1956 estimates are for the merged AFL-CIO and for independent unions). The directories also give the membership of individual national and international unions, membership by sex, and detailed data on membership reporting practices. The 1957 directory gives data on membership by industry and distributions of unions by percentage of white-collar workers.

D 742, Canadian membership of U. S. unions, is from the Department of Labour of Canada, except for 1954 and 1956 which are from the BLS directories cited above.

D 743, union membership excluding Canada, is obtained by subtracting series D 742 from D 741. The year-to-year movement for 1947–1953 is unreliable for the reasons given above. A better estimate might be obtained for these years by holding the percentage in series D 745 constant at 34.0 and by applying this figure to series D 744.

D 745, union membership (excluding Canada) as a percent of employees in nonagricultural establishments, is computed from series D 743 and D 744. Wolman has also estimated for three decennial census years the number of trade union members exclusive of Canada as a percentage of the total number of nonagricultural employees. These percentages are 9.9 in 1910, 19.4 in 1920, and 10.2 in 1930. The percentage shown for 1930 in series D 745 is larger than the corresponding percentage given by Wolman because Wolman's estimated union membership figure exclusive of Canada (3,190,000) is smaller than that shown in series D 743, and also because Wolman's nonagricultural employment estimate (30,247,000), based on census data, is larger than the number of employees in nonagricultural establishments shown in series D 744. Wolman's figure excludes many salaried professional and managerial workers included in series D 744, and includes domestic servants, excluded from series D 744.

Independent estimates of union membership for 1939 and 1953, both including and excluding Canadian membership, are available in Leo Troy, *Distribution of Union Membership Among the States, 1939 and 1953*, National Bureau of Economic Research, New York, 1957, pp. 3–5. Troy's estimates of total union membership, including Canadian members, are 6,730,000 for 1939 and 17,147,000 for 1953. The corresponding estimates, excluding Canadian members, are 6,518,000 for 1939 and 16,217,000 for 1953.

Troy's estimates are based mainly on financial reports and other records supplied by approximately 200 national unions. Although his coverage of unaffiliated unions was admittedly incomplete, the discrepancies between his estimates and those of BLS for 1939 are too large to be accounted for by such incompleteness of coverage. The work by Troy includes estimates of union membership by major industry, by State and region, and by affiliation (A. F. of L., CIO, unaffiliated).

D 746–763. Labor union membership, by industry, 1897–1934.

Source: Leo Wolman, *Ebb and Flow in Trade Unionism*, National Bureau of Economic Research, New York, 1936, pp. 172–193.

These figures were obtained by classifying national and international unions into industrial categories and totalling the membership of the unions in each category in each year.

In the latter part of the period, series D 763, "Miscellaneous," consists largely of two unions, the Firemen and Oilers and the Operating Engineers. The Industrial Workers of the World is included from 1905–1914, and is the largest union in the series for some years. The Horseshoers are important in the early years, declining rapidly in the 1920's. Unions affiliated with the Trade Union Unity League in 1929–1934 are excluded.

Some errors of classification arise when a union has membership in more than one category. For example, the Meat Cutters and Butcher Workmen, classified in food, liquor, and tobacco had many members in retail meat stores; the Operating Engineers, classified as miscellaneous, had many members in building construction. These problems are less important in 1897–1934 than they would be in recent years.

The source gives annual estimates of the percentage distribution of union membership by industrial categories. For 1910, 1920, and 1930, it gives estimates of the percentage of employees organized in each of the industrial categories shown here, and in more detailed categories.

D 764–778. Work stoppages, workers involved, man-days idle, major issues, and average duration, 1881–1957.

Source: Bureau of Labor Statistics, various bulletins, especially *Analysis of Work Stoppages, 1957*, Bulletin No. 1234, and *Strikes in the United States, 1880–1936*, Bulletin No. 651.

Work stoppages include strikes and lockouts. A strike is defined as a temporary stoppage of work by a group of employees in order to express a grievance or to enforce a demand. A lockout is defined as a temporary withholding of work from a group of employees by an employer (or a group of employers) in order to enforce acceptance of the employer's terms. Most work stoppages are strikes rather than lockouts.

The individual strike or lockout is the unit counted regardless of the number of unions or employers jointly involved in the controversy. Excluded, however, are strikes involving fewer than 6 workers or lasting less than a full shift, strikes of American seamen in foreign ports, and strikes of foreign crews on foreign ships in American ports.

Figures for workers involved include all workers made idle in the establishment where the stoppage occurs, even though they may not all be participants in the controversy. The figures exclude indirect or secondary idleness in other establishments which suspend or curtail operations because of shortages of materials or services resulting from a stoppage. The number of workers involved is the number on the day of maximum idleness; however, the figures for man-days idle (series D 767) take into account variations in the number idle during the strike and include all days on which work was scheduled.

The duration of stoppages (series D 774) is counted in calendar days rather than working days. Strikes that are never formally settled are considered ended when a majority of vacant jobs are filled, whether by former strikers or by others, or when the establishment affected is permanently closed.

The classification of causes of strikes (series D 771–773 and D 776–778) necessarily lacks precision, since many strikes involve more than one issue. In particular, strikes for union organization often involve demands concerning wages or hours.

Beginning in 1951, the number of employed workers used as a base for the percentages in series D 766 is the BLS series on employment in nonagricultural establishments. Before 1951, the base is "all workers except those in occupations and professions in which strikes rarely occur." The excluded groups were the self-employed, domestic workers, employees on farms with fewer than 6 employees, most managerial and professional workers, employees of Federal and State governments, and elected and appointed officials of local governments. The change in base affects the series by less than one-tenth of a percentage point in most years. The estimated working time used as a base for the percentages in series D 768 is the base for series D 766 times the number of days worked by most employees, excluding Saturdays when customarily not worked, Sundays, and established holidays.

Unions are involved in the great majority of work stoppages. Thus in 1956 only 42 of 3,825 work stoppages, accounting for 3,280 of the 1,900,000 workers involved, did not involve any union. For some purposes, therefore, workers involved in strikes as a percent of union membership is a more useful statistic than workers involved as a percent of all workers.

Data for 1881–1886 were first published in the *Third Annual Report of the Commissioner of Labor, 1887*. This report also gives fragmentary data for earlier years. Data for 1887–1894 are given in the *Tenth Annual Report, 1894*; for 1895–1900 in the *Sixteenth Annual Report, 1901*; and for 1900–1905 in the *Twenty-first Annual Report, 1906*. References to strikes and lockouts during 1881–1905 were located by the Bureau of Labor by examination of the daily and trade press. Agents of the Bureau then collected data from the parties involved.

No government agency collected data on work stoppages for 1906–1913. For 1914–1915 BLS collected data on the number of stoppages and major issues. For 1916–1926 the count of stoppages was made from press notices, and questionnaires were sent to determine the number of workers involved. This number was reported for only about two-thirds of the known stoppages.

Methods of compiling the series have been fairly uniform since 1927. Information on the existence of a stoppage is obtained from press clippings from a large number of newspapers throughout the country and from reports from unions, employers, and a number of Federal and State agencies. Improvement in the sources of these "leads," especially through State employment security agencies, increased the number of strikes reported over previous years by about 5 percent in 1950 and by about 10 percent in 1951 and 1952. The increase from this source in the reported number of workers involved and man-days idle was about 2 percent in 1950 and 3 percent in 1951 and 1952. When the existence of a strike is known, a questionnaire is mailed to the parties reported as involved to obtain data on the number of workers involved, duration, issues, etc. In some instances, field representatives of the BLS call on the parties.

D 779–784. Average monthly labor turnover rates in manufacturing, by class of turnover, 1919–1957.

Source: Bureau of Labor Statistics, *Monthly Labor Review*, July 1929, pp. 64–65; BLS, *Employment and Earnings*, June 1957, p. 95; and Office of Business Economics, *Business Statistics*, 1957 biennial edition, p. 69.

The figures for 1919–1929 are those of the Metropolitan Life Insurance Company which pioneered in collecting labor turnover data on a regular basis, beginning in January 1926. Subsequently, the Company secured data that enabled it to estimate turnover rates monthly back to January 1919.

The Company obtained its turnover data by means of a mail questionnaire sent monthly to reporting firms. (The sample of reporting firms, 160 in November 1926, had grown to 350 by mid-1929.) Each firm was asked to report each month: (1) The daily average number of employees on the payroll, and the total number of (2) accessions, (3) voluntary quits, (4) discharges, and (5) layoffs during the month. The accession rate for each company was computed by dividing the total number of accessions during the month by the daily average number on the payroll during the month. The composite or average accession rate for all reporting firms was the unweighted median of the accession rates computed for individual firms. The annual average was the arithmetic mean of the 12 monthly median accession rates. Discharges, quits, and layoffs were handled in a similar fashion. (The total separation rate, however, was computed as the sum of the median discharge rate, the median quit rate, and the median layoff rate.)

The figures for 1919–1929 are stated as equivalent annual rates rather than monthly rates. They have been converted in series D 779–783 to monthly rates by dividing by 12.

In July 1929, BLS took over the work of the Metropolitan Life Insurance Company. At that time there were approximately 350 large manufacturers employing 700,000 workers in the sample of reporting firms. Over the years the list of cooperating firms has grown greatly, the amount of industry detail has expanded, and methods of computation have been somewhat changed.

BLS turnover rate estimates are based on reports made monthly on a mail questionnaire by a sample of cooperating firms. In 1957, the sample covered approximately 10,000 establishments in manufacturing employing nearly 6,000,000 employees, 120 metal minining establishments with 57,000 workers, 220 coal mining establishments with 77,000 workers, and telephone and telegraph establishments employing about 690,000 workers. The reporting firms are considerably larger on the average than all firms within the population sampled. This large-firm bias may cause underestimation of turnover rates. Furthermore, the BLS sample of manufacturing firms and its estimates of turnover for manufacturing exclude printing, publishing, and allied industries (since April 1943); canning and preserving fruits, vegetables, and seafoods; women's and misses' outerwear; and fertilizers. The last three industries tend to have exceptionally high turnover rates seasonally. Plants experiencing work stoppages are excluded.

Each cooperating firm is asked to report each month: (1) Total accessions, (2) total separations, (3) total quits, (4) total discharges, (5) total layoffs, (6) total military separations, (7) total miscellaneous separations, and (8) the total number of employees who worked or received pay for any part of the payroll period ending nearest the 15th of the month. Prior to 1940 "miscellaneous" separations were included with "quits." Since January 1943 the labor turnover rates pertain to all employees; before that date the rates were for production workers only. Furthermore, before October 1945 the employment base was the average of the number of employees on the payroll the last day of the preceding month and the last day of the current month. The effect of changing the employment base to the number on the midmonth payroll was negligible.

Discharges are terminations of employment by management for cause (incompetence, laziness, etc.). Layoffs are terminations of employment for more than a week, initiated by management, without prejudice to the worker. Quits are terminations of employment initiated by employees; they include unauthorized absences of more than a week. Miscellaneous separations are terminations of employment for military duty of over 30 days and other separations than those itemized (deaths, retirements, etc.). For January 1942–June 1944, the military separation rate was published separately.

D 785. Work-injury frequency rates in manufacturing, 1926–1956.

Source: Bureau of Labor Statistics, *Handbook of Labor Statistics*, 1950 edition, p. 179; and *Monthly Labor Review*, various issues.

The Bureau of Labor Statistics' first continuing compilation of injury-rate statistics began in 1910 for the iron and steel industry. In 1925, the injury-rate compilations were expanded to cover 24 industries. By 1952, the compilations covered over 200 manufacturing and nonmanufacturing industry classifications.

Efforts to standardize the compilation of work-injury statistics were initiated by BLS in 1911 and resulted in 1920 in the first standardized procedures. In 1926 the American Engineering Standards Committee, later the American Standards Association, undertook a revision of these procedures. Their work led to the publication in 1937 of the first American Standard Method of Compiling Industrial Injury Rates. This standard was again revised in 1954.

The standard injury-frequency rate is the average number of disabling injuries per million man-hours worked. A disabling injury is an injury incurred in the course of and arising out of employment, which results in death or permanent physical impairment, or renders the injured person unable to perform any regularly established job, open and available to him, during the entire time interval corresponding to the hours of his regular shift on one or more days after the injury.

The BLS annual injury-rate estimates are based on a sample mail survey conducted once a year. Cooperating firms are asked to report for all employees (1) average employment, (2) aggregate man-hours worked by all employees, (3) aggregate number of disabling work injuries by extent of disability, and (4) time lost because of disabilities. The manufacturing sample covers approximately 50,000 establishments. The injury-rate series for manufacturing excludes petroleum refining, smelting and refining of nonferrous metals, cement and lime manufacturing, and coke production, which are covered in similar surveys conducted by the Bureau of Mines (see text for series D 786–790).

Prior to 1936 the data in series D 785 are based on surveys covering only wage earners in 30 manufacturing industries. Since 1936 the data refer to all employees in all manufacturing industries. Separate injury-frequency rates have been computed since 1936 for component industries by dividing aggregate injuries by aggregate man-hours in reporting establishments. In computing the average rate for all manufacturing the separate averages for the component industries are weighted by estimated total employment in these industries. Before 1936 the weights implicitly were aggregate man-hours in the reporting firms in each industry.

D 786–790. Work-injury frequency rates in mining, 1924–1956.

Source: Bureau of Mines, *Minerals Yearbook*, 1956 and earlier annual issues.

Except for coal mining since 1941, the Bureau of Mines estimates of work-injury frequency rates in "mining" industries are based on reports made voluntarily by mining establishments. Coal mining firms since 1941 have been obliged by Federal law to report work-injury and related data to the Bureau of Mines.

D 791-792. Work-injury frequency rates on Class I railroads, 1922-1956.

Source: Interstate Commerce Commission, *Accident Bulletin*, various issues.

Both series exclude work injuries suffered by employees of Class I switching and terminal companies after 1932. They are based on monthly accident reports that the Class I railroads are required by Federal law to make to the Interstate Commerce Commission. The two series thus result from essentially complete censuses of man-hours worked and of reportable work injuries.

Before 1936 a reportable work-injury was either a fatality or a nonfatal injury to an employee "sufficient to incapacitate him from performing his ordinary duties for more than 3 days in the aggregate in the 10 days immediately following the accident." Series D 792 includes only such work-injuries. Beginning in 1936 the railroads have been required to report work-injuries incapacitating employees for 1-3 days immedi-ately following an accident as well as more serious injuries. Series D 791 is series D 792 plus the average work-injury frequency rate for "1-3 day" injuries.

The concept of "disabling injury" underlying series D 785-790 is essentially the same as that underlying series D 791. Series D 792, which excludes "1-3 day" injuries, is not comparable to series D 785-790 in level, and series D 791 also tends to have a downward bias in trend relative to series D 785-790. It has been included to indicate at least crudely the trend in the average injury-frequency rates on Class I railroads before 1936.

Both series cover all employees of Class I railroads. The man-hour base of both series is the aggregate number of straight-time hours actually worked and overtime hours paid for in millions of man-hours. Days worked by daily-rated employees have been converted to man-hours worked by multiplying days worked by 8. The average injury-frequency rate is the ratio of the aggregate number of work-injuries to the man-hour base.

Series D 573–577. Daily Hours and Indexes of Average Daily Wages in all Industries and in Building Trades: January 1860 to 1891

Year	All industries Weighted average daily hours [1]	Indexes of average daily wages (Jan. 1860=100) Weighted	Indexes of average daily wages (Jan. 1860=100) Unweighted [1]	Building trades Average daily hours	Building trades Index of average daily wages (Jan. 1860=100)	Year	All industries Weighted average daily hours [1]	Indexes of average daily wages (Jan. 1860=100) Weighted	Indexes of average daily wages (Jan. 1860=100) Unweighted [1]	Building trades Average daily hours	Building trades Index of average daily wages (Jan. 1860=100)
	573	574	575	576	577		573	574	575	576	577
1891	10.0	168.6	160.7	9.4	172.5	1875	10.3	158.0	158.4	9.9	169.2
1890	10.0	168.2	158.9	9.6	172.7	1874	10.5	162.5	161.5	9.9	178.1
1889	10.0	162.9	156.7	9.6	170.1	1873	10.5	166.1	167.1	9.9	179.4
1888	10.0	157.9	155.4	9.7	170.9	1872	10.5	167.1	166.0	9.9	183.3
1887	10.0	156.6	153.7	9.7	170.1	1871	10.5	166.4	163.6	10.0	182.7
1886	10.2	155.8	150.9	9.8	170.3						
						1870	10.5	167.1	162.2	10.0	185.5
1885	10.3	155.9	150.7	9.9	169.9	1869	10.6	167.4	162.0	10.0	189.2
1884	10.3	155.1	152.7	9.9	168.5	1868	10.6	164.9	159.2	10.0	185.5
1883	10.3	159.2	152.7	9.9	166.0	1867	10.8	164.0	157.6	10.0	185.1
1882	10.3	152.9	149.9	9.9	165.1	1866	10.8	155.6	152.4	10.0	170.0
1881	10.3	150.7	146.5	9.9	160.1						
						1865	10.7	148.6	143.1	10.0	161.1
1880	10.3	143.0	141.5	9.9	142.7	1864	10.8	134.0	125.6	10.1	143.7
1879	10.3	139.4	139.9	9.9	137.9	1863	10.8	118.8	110.5	10.1	119.7
1878	10.3	140.9	142.5	9.9	140.7	1862	10.8	103.7	102.9	10.1	106.3
1877	10.3	143.8	144.9	9.9	146.3	1861	10.9	100.7	100.8	10.1	100.4
1876	10.3	151.4	152.5	9.9	158.6	1860	11.0	100.0	100.0	10.1	100.0

[1] Restricted coverage, especially for earlier years; see text.

Series D 578–588. Indexes of Average Daily Wages in all Industries, in Selected Industries, and by Degree of Skill: January and July, 1860 to 1880

[January 1860=100]

Year and month	All industries	Cotton textiles and ginghams	Woolen textiles	Metals and metallic goods	Building trades	Stone	Railroads	Illuminating gas	City public works	Degree of skill Unskilled men	Degree of skill Skilled men
	578	579	580	581	582	583	584	585	586	587	588
1880: July	144	154	144	135	146	133	153	159	135	127	140
January	142	152	143	130	138	124	153	158	133	122	136
1879: July	139	149	143	128	139	125	147	157	123	122	135
January	142	149	142	127	139	125	146	162	135	122	138
1878: July	143	153	147	131	137	130	138	156	134	123	137
January	145	153	144	132	141	133	139	169	143	127	141
1877: July	143	150	144	133	140	130	142	165	140	125	140
January	147	149	139	135	143	140	147	184	150	134	144
1876: July	153	154	144	141	160	141	151	173	166	139	150
January	162	160	148	146	160	169	150	193	190	148	150
1875: July	163	163	152	148	170	161	158	182	181	150	160
January	167	162	150	151	168	167	161	200	193	160	160
1874: July	175	177	149	159	182	180	160	200	193	173	169
January	176	175	145	158	178	182	160	212	199	181	169
1873: July	183	189	150	163	186	198	162	204	195	187	175
January	180	185	149	161	180	182	158	221	196	182	171
1872: July	185	189	148	161	190	203	171	205	201	201	175
January	179	190	148	158	185	186	167	196	198	175	172
1871: July	184	184	149	159	187	198	170	195	204	195	179
January	183	182	148	158	178	188	171	199	213	198	175
1870: July	179	172	147	159	188	201	158	189	202	203	172
January	181	169	147	161	192	200	165	192	210	208	170
1869: July	179	173	146	160	199	205	162	189	191	205	171
January	176	168	149	160	195	196	156	195	192	191	170
1868: July	170	167	145	159	195	175	161	186	190	165	173
January	167	166	141	159	180	178	156	185	186	175	165
1867: July	168	169	148	159	186	162	160	185	188	159	166
January	168	168	149	158	174	168	155	183	186	182	166
1866: July	164	166	153	157	171	158	148	181	182	158	164
January	161	159	149	155	162	172	138	183	181	174	153
1865: July	155	146	142	150	158	151	146	175	178	155	150
January	152	135	142	149	145	155	144	176	175	152	150
1864: July	142	124	128	139	143	135	112	162	169	135	137
January	131	116	122	126	128	143	114	157	144	140	120
1863: July	119	108	114	120	118	113	109	142	123	114	112
January	116	108	120	114	118	100	106	125	122	111	105
1862: July	104	103	111	108	107	90	103	103	99	97	102
January	102	101	108	105	103	96	105	100	99	99	100
1861: July	99	102	107	103	102	91	105	99	91	98	100
January	102	100	106	102	101	128	105	100	100	100	100
1860: July	100	100	103	101	102	100	103	99	100	100	100
January	100	100	100	100	100	100	100	100	100	100	100

Series D 589–602. Hours and Earnings in Manufacturing, in Selected Nonmanufacturing Industries, and for "Lower-Skilled" Labor: 1890 to 1926

Year	Manufacturing industries						Bituminous coal mining		Rail-roads, average full-time weekly earnings	Building trades		Postal employees		"Lower-skilled" labor, average full-time weekly earnings
	Total		Union		Payroll									
	Average weekly hours	Average hourly earnings	Average weekly hours	Average hourly earnings	Average weekly hours	Average hourly earnings	Average weekly hours (standard)	Average hourly earnings		Average weekly hours (union)	Average hourly earnings (union)	Average weekly hours	Average hourly earnings	
	589	590	591	592	593	594	595	596	597	598	599	600	601	602
1926	50.3	$0.647	45.9	$1.007	52.2	$0.488	48.4	$0.719	$32.16	43.8	$1.313	47.2	$0.867	--------
1925	50.3	.645	45.9	.989	52.2	.493	48.5	.724	31.80	43.9	1.229	47.2	.836	--------
1924	50.4	.636	46.1	.970	52.1	.502	48.5	.811	30.66	43.8	1.188	47.2	.788	--------
1923	51.0	.620	46.3	.913	53.0	.491	48.4	.864	30.24	43.9	1.107	47.2	.762	--------
1922	51.2	.574	46.2	.873	53.4	.443	48.4	.834	30.30	43.8	1.006	47.4	.748	--------
1921	50.7	.607	46.1	.921	52.7	.467	48.2	.846	31.14	43.8	1.076	47.4	.759	--------
1920	51.0	.663	45.7	.884	53.5	.561	48.2	.784	34.14	43.8	1.052	48.0	.739	$25.98
1919	52.3	.529	46.2	.706	55.1	.448	48.4	.699	27.66	44.0	.780	48.0	.648	23.83
1918	53.6	.448	47.2	.602	56.6	.374	48.7	.599	26.40	44.1	.684	48.0	.536	21.69
1917	54.6	.364	47.6	.499	57.9	.299	49.8	.484	18.84	44.4	.624	48.0	.484	17.18
1916	54.9	.320	48.0	.464	58.2	.250	51.6	.379	16.62	44.5	.587	48.0	.471	13.78
1915	55.0	.287	48.6	.439	58.2	.212	51.6	.337	15.78	44.8	.569	48.0	.466	10.65
1914	55.2	.287	48.8	.438	58.3	.213	51.6	.323	15.36	44.7	.567	48.0	.464	10.78
1913	55.5	.285	49.2	.430	58.8	.211	51.6	.316	15.12	44.9	.557	48.0	.450	10.84
1912	56.0	.274	49.5	.416	59.3	.200	51.6	.320	14.79	45.0	.544	48.0	.437	10.32
1911	56.4	.263	49.8	.411	59.6	.191	51.6	.305	14.49	45.0	.531	48.0	.429	10.13
1910	56.6	.260	50.1	.403	59.8	.188	51.6	.299	14.07	45.2	.520	48.0	.420	10.65
1909	56.8	.252	50.3	.392	60.2	.179	51.6	.292	13.59	45.6	.510	48.0	.409	10.37
1908	56.8	.250	50.4	.388	60.3	.175	51.6	.293	13.47	45.6	.505	48.0	.395	10.22
1907	57.3	.257	50.8	.396	60.6	.186	51.6	.288	13.35	45.7	.498	48.0	.378	10.76
1906	57.3	.248	51.0	.385	60.7	.176	51.6	.293	12.84	45.9	.481	48.0	.369	10.34
1905	57.7	.239	51.1	.378	61.1	.168	51.6	.276	12.45	46.1	.454	48.0	.375	9.91
1904	57.7	.236	51.1	.374	61.1	.164	51.6	.271	12.36	46.1	.443	48.0	.373	9.84
1903	57.9	.236	51.4	.372	61.2	.167	52.2	.267	12.12	46.3	.436	48.0	.372	9.64
1902	58.3	.227	51.8	.362	61.5	.162	52.3	.244	11.73	46.7	.413	48.0	.374	9.25
1901	58.7	.219	52.4	.350	61.9	.153	52.4	.231	11.49	47.5	.391	48.0	.375	9.05
1900	59.0	.216	53.0	.341	62.1	.152	52.6	.204	11.43	48.3	.374	48.0	.371	8.83
1899	59.1	.209	53.0	.338	62.1	.146	52.7	.185	11.37	48.9	.361	48.0	.370	8.70
1898	59.3	.204	53.4	.331	62.2	.143	52.8	.170	11.31	49.5	.348	48.0	.376	8.53
1897	59.1	.203	53.4	.330	61.9	.141	60.0	.138	11.25	49.8	.346	48.0	.381	8.40
1896	59.2	.205	53.5	.330	62.1	.143	60.0	.147	11.22	50.1	.343	48.0	.378	8.46
1895	59.5	.200	53.5	.327	62.3	.141	60.0	.158	11.22	50.3	.341	48.0	.375	7.45
1894	59.1	.200	53.6	.326	61.7	.140	60.0	.171	11.25	50.5	.339	48.0	.368	8.34
1893	59.7	.205	53.9	.331	62.2	.151	60.0	.188	11.37	50.4	.347	48.0	.361	8.73
1892	59.8	.203	54.0	.333	62.3	.147	60.0	.179	11.46	50.6	.348	48.0	.360	8.75
1891	59.7	.202	54.0	.328	62.1	.148	60.0	.169	11.27	51.0	.341	48.0	.358	9.74
1890	60.0	.199	54.4	.324	62.2	.149	60.0	.180	11.38	51.3	.341	48.0	.352	8.71

Series D 603–617. Average Annual Earnings in all Industries and in Selected Industries and Occupations: 1890 to 1926

| Year | All industries | | Wage earners, manu-facturing | Wage earners, steam railroads | Street railways | Tele-phones | Tele-graphs | Gas and electricity | Clerical workers, mfg. and steam railroads | Bitumi-nous coal mining | Farm labor | Federal em-ployees [1] | Postal em-ployees | Public school teachers | Ministers |
| | Including farm labor | Excluding farm labor | | | | | | | | | | | | | |
	603	604	605	606	607	608	609	610	611	612	613	614	615	616	617
1926	$1,376	$1,473	$1,309	$1,613	$1,566	$1,117	$1,215	$1,477	$2,310	$1,247	$593	$1,809	$2,128	$1,277	$1,826
1925	1,336	1,434	1,280	1,597	1,565	1,108	1,161	1,448	2,239	1,141	587	1,776	2,051	1,263	1,769
1924	1,303	1,402	1,240	1,570	1,544	1,104	1,150	1,436	2,196	1,120	574	1,708	1,934	1,247	1,678
1923	1,299	1,393	1,254	1,585	1,493	1,069	1,133	1,355	2,126	1,246	572	1,658	1,870	1,224	1,620
1922	1,201	1,305	1,149	1,591	1,436	1,064	1,110	1,343	2,067	954	508	1,625	1,844	1,188	1,622
1921	1,233	1,349	1,180	1,632	1,539	1,038	1,159	1,364	2,134	1,013	522	1,593	1,870	1,082	1,556
1920	1,407	1,489	1,358	1,817	1,608	980	1,145	1,432	2,160	1,386	810	1,648	1,844	936	1,428
1919	1,201	1,272	1,158	1,509	1,387	844	967	1,291	1,914	1,097	706	1,520	1,618	810	1,238
1918	1,047	1,115	980	1,424	1,111	690	831	1,092	1,697	1,211	604	1,380	1,339	689	1,186
1917	830	887	774	989	872	616	769	853	1,477	976	481	1,295	1,207	648	1,069
1916	708	765	651	867	798	567	806	679	1,359	750	388	1,211	1,175	605	1,017
1915	633	687	568	815	748	529	792	644	1,267	589	355	1,152	1,162	578	984
1914	627	682	580	795	737	476	742	651	1,257	543	351	1,140	1,157	564	938
1913	621	675	578	760	704	438	717	661	1,236	631	360	1,136	1,124	547	899
1912	592	646	550	721	674	438	669	641	1,209	614	348	1,128	1,091	529	879
1911	575	629	537	705	685	419	670	648	1,213	553	338	1,116	1,071	509	856
1910	574	630	558	677	681	417	649	622	1,156	558	336	1,108	1,049	492	802
1909	543	594	518	644	671	430	622	618	1,136	524	328	1,106	1,021	476	831
1908	516	563	475	667	650	420	639	595	1,111	487	324	1,102	987	455	833
1907	542	595	522	661	658	412	635	623	1,091	580	319	1,094	944	431	831
1906	520	569	506	607	662	412	592	581	1,074	537	315	1,084	921	409	773
1905	503	554	494	589	646	401	581	543	1,076	500	302	1,072	935	392	759
1904	490	540	477	600	610	392	601	556	1,056	470	290	1,066	931	377	759
1903	489	543	486	593	582	397	573	--------	1,037	522	277	1,067	928	358	761
1902	467	519	473	562	576	408	544	--------	1,025	490	264	1,061	934	346	737
1901	454	508	456	549	601	--------	--------	615	1,009	465	255	1,047	936	337	730
1900	438	490	435	548	604	--------	--------	620	1,011	438	247	1,033	925	328	731
1899	428	480	426	543	591	--------	--------	612	1,004	379	239	1,017	924	318	722
1898	417	468	412	542	558	--------	--------	698	1,010	316	228	1,025	939	306	739
1897	411	462	408	543	552	--------	--------	703	970	270	224	1,057	950	298	750
1896	411	462	406	544	531	--------	--------	665	954	282	220	1,084	944	294	764

[1] Executive departments.

Series D 603–617. Average Annual Earnings in all Industries and in Selected Industries and Occupations: 1890 to 1926—Con.

Year	All industries Including farm labor	All industries Excluding farm labor	Wage earners, manu- facturing	Wage earners, steam railroads	Street railways	Tele- phones	Tele- graphs	Gas and electricity	Clerical workers, mfg. and steam railroads	Bitumi- nous coal mining	Farm labor	Federal em- ployees [1]	Postal em- ployees	Public school teachers	Ministers
	603	604	605	606	607	608	609	610	611	612	613	614	615	616	617
1895	$415	$468	$416	$546	$509	--------	--------	$640	$941	$307	$216	$1,104	$935	$289	$787
1894	400	448	386	546	508			670	928	292	214	1,110	919	283	824
1893	430	480	420	563	526			627	923	383	232	1,101	902	276	809
1892	445	495	446	563	535			625	885	393	238	1,096	899	270	809
1891	438	487	442	554	529			587	882	377	236	--------	894	264	786
1890	438	486	439	560	557			687	848	406	233	--------	878	256	794

[1] Executive departments.

Series D 618–625. Indexes of Wages, Hours, and Earnings in Manufacturing and in the Building Trades: 1890 to 1907
[1890–1899 = 100]

Year	All manufacturing Average hourly wages [1]	Average full-time weekly earnings [1]	Average full-time weekly hours Bureau of Labor [1]	Wolman	Building trades Average hourly wages	Average full-time weekly earnings	Average full-time weekly hours Bureau of Labor	Wolman
	618	619	620	621	622	623	624	625
1907	128.8	122.4	95.0	--------	144.6	131.0	90.6	87.8
1906	124.2	118.5	95.4	--------	140.2	127.4	90.9	--------
1905	118.9	114.0	95.9	--------	132.2	120.6	91.2	--------
1904	117.0	112.2	95.9	--------	129.7	118.4	91.3	--------
1903	116.3	112.3	96.6	97.3	126.8	116.4	91.8	93.1
1902	112.2	109.2	97.3	98.1	121.1	112.1	92.6	92.9
1901	108.0	105.9	98.1	98.6	114.5	108.1	94.4	94.4
1900	105.5	104.1	98.7	99.1	109.9	105.0	95.5	96.3
1899	102.0	101.2	99.2	99.6	105.3	102.7	97.5	97.4

Year	All manufacturing Average hourly wages [1]	Average full-time weekly earnings [1]	Average full-time weekly hours Bureau of Labor [1]	Wolman	Building trades Average hourly wages	Average full-time weekly earnings	Average full-time weekly hours Bureau of Labor	Wolman
	618	619	620	621	622	623	624	625
1898	100.2	99.9	99.7	100.0	102.8	100.8	98.1	98.7
1897	99.6	99.2	99.6	99.6	101.3	99.9	98.6	99.2
1896	99.7	99.5	99.8	99.8	99.9	99.1	99.2	99.6
1895	98.3	98.4	100.1	100.0	98.4	98.7	100.3	100.0
1894	97.9	97.7	99.8	99.5	97.6	98.3	100.7	100.5
1893	100.9	101.2	100.3	100.1	100.0	100.5	100.5	100.4
1892	100.8	101.3	100.5	100.6	99.9	100.6	100.7	100.5
1891	100.3	100.8	100.5	100.3	97.9	99.7	101.8	101.5
1890	100.3	101.0	100.7	100.5	97.0	99.4	102.5	102.2

[1] Includes the building trades and other hand and neighborhood trades.

Series D 626–634. Hours and Earnings for Production Workers in Manufacturing: 1909 to 1957

Year	All manufacturing Average hourly earnings	Average weekly hours	Average weekly earnings	Durable goods Average hourly earnings	Average weekly hours	Average weekly earnings	Nondurable goods Average hourly earnings	Average weekly hours	Average weekly earnings
	626	627	628	629	630	631	632	633	634
1957	$2.07	39.8	$82.39	$2.20	40.3	$88.66	$1.88	39.1	$73.51
1956	1.98	40.4	79.99	2.10	41.1	86.31	1.80	39.5	71.10
1955	1.88	40.7	76.52	2.01	41.4	83.21	1.71	39.8	68.06
1954	1.81	39.7	71.86	1.92	40.2	77.18	1.66	39.0	64.74
1953	1.77	40.5	71.69	1.87	41.3	77.23	1.61	39.5	63.60
1952	1.67	40.7	67.97	1.77	41.5	73.46	1.54	39.6	60.98
1951	1.59	40.7	64.71	1.67	41.6	69.47	1.48	39.5	58.46
1950	1.465	40.5	59.33	1.537	41.2	63.32	1.378	39.7	54.71
1949	1.401	39.2	54.92	1.469	39.5	58.03	1.325	38.8	51.41
1948	1.350	40.1	54.14	1.410	40.5	57.11	1.278	39.6	50.61
1947	1.237	40.4	49.97	1.292	40.6	52.46	1.171	40.1	46.96
1946	1.086	40.4	43.82	1.156	40.2	46.49	1.015	40.5	41.14
1945	1.023	43.4	44.39	1.111	44.1	49.05	.904	42.3	38.29
1944	1.019	45.2	46.08	1.117	46.6	52.07	.861	43.1	37.12
1943	.961	44.9	43.14	1.059	46.6	49.30	.803	42.5	34.12
1942	.853	42.9	36.65	.947	45.1	42.73	.723	40.3	29.13
1941	.729	40.6	29.58	.808	42.1	34.04	.640	38.9	24.92
1940	.661	38.1	25.20	.724	39.3	28.44	.602	37.0	22.27
1939	.633	37.7	23.86	.698	38.0	26.50	.582	37.4	21.78
1938	.627	35.6	22.30	.686	35.0	24.01	.584	36.1	21.05
1937	.624	38.6	24.05	.674	40.0	26.91	.577	37.4	21.53
1936	.556	39.2	21.78	.586	41.0	24.04	.529	37.7	19.94
1935	.550	36.6	20.13	.577	37.3	21.52	.530	36.1	19.11
1934	.532	34.6	18.40	.556	33.9	18.87	.515	35.1	18.05
1933	.442	38.1	16.73	.472	34.8	16.43	.427	40.0	16.89
1932	.446	38.3	17.05	.497	32.6	16.21	.420	41.9	17.57
1931	.515	40.5	20.87	--------	--------	21.28	--------	--------	20.50
1930	.552	42.1	23.25	--------	--------	24.77	--------	--------	21.84
1929	.566	44.2	25.03	--------	--------	27.22	--------	--------	22.93
1928	.562	44.4	24.97	--------	--------	27.24	--------	--------	22.88
1927	.550	45.0	24.74	--------	--------	26.66	--------	--------	23.01
1926	.548	45.0	24.65	--------	--------	26.61	--------	--------	22.75
1925	.547	44.5	24.37	--------	--------	26.39	--------	--------	22.44
1924	.547	43.7	23.93	--------	--------	25.84	--------	--------	22.07
1923	.522	45.6	23.82	--------	--------	25.78	--------	--------	21.94
1922	.487	44.2	21.51	--------	--------	--------	--------	--------	--------
1921	.515	43.1	22.18	--------	--------	--------	--------	--------	--------
1920	.555	47.4	26.30	--------	--------	--------	--------	--------	--------
1919	.477	46.3	22.08	--------	--------	--------	--------	--------	--------
1914	.223	49.4	11.01	--------	--------	--------	--------	--------	--------
1909	.193	51.0	9.84	--------	--------	--------	--------	--------	--------

Series D 635–641. Hours and Earnings for Bituminous Coal Mines and Class I Steam Railroads: 1909 to 1957

Year	Bituminous coal mines — Average weekly earnings (635)	Average weekly hours (636)	Average hourly earnings (637)	Class I steam railroads [1] — Average weekly earnings (638)	Average weekly hours (639)	Average hourly earnings — Total (640)	Straight time (641)
1957	$110.53	36.6	$3.02	$94.47	41.8	$2.26	$2.25
1956	106.22	37.8	2.81	88.40	41.7	2.12	2.09
1955	96.26	37.6	2.56	82.12	41.9	1.96	1.93
1954	80.85	32.6	2.48	78.74	40.8	1.93	1.91
1953	85.31	34.4	2.48	76.33	40.6	1.88	1.86
1952	78.09	34.1	2.29	74.30	40.6	1.83	1.81
1951	77.79	35.2	2.21	70.93	41.0	1.73	1.71
1950	70.35	35.0	2.010	63.20	40.8	1.549	1.516
1949	63.28	32.6	1.941	61.73	43.5	1.419	1.390
1948	72.12	38.0	1.898	60.34	46.1	1.309	1.272
1947	66.59	40.7	1.636	54.17	46.3	1.170	1.135
1946	58.03	41.6	1.401	51.22	45.9	1.116	1.080
1945	52.25	42.3	1.240	45.69	48.5	.942	.899
1944	51.27	43.4	1.186	46.06	49.1	.938	.898
1943	41.58	36.6	1.139	43.68	48.7	.897	.862
1942	35.02	32.9	1.059	38.65	46.9	.824	.804
1941	30.86	31.1	.993	34.25	45.6	.751	.736
1940	24.71	28.1	.883	31.55	44.0	.717	.706
1939	23.88	27.1	.886	30.99	43.4	.714	.714
1938	20.80	23.5	.878	30.26	42.5	.712	.703
1937	23.84	27.9	.856	29.20	43.2	.676	.666
1936	22.71	28.8	.794	28.01	42.5	.659	.648
1935	19.58	26.4	.745	26.76	41.1	.651	.643
1934	18.10	27.0	.673	24.32	40.4	.602	.594
1933	14.47	29.5	.501	23.09	38.8	.595	.587
1932	13.91	27.2	.520	23.34	38.9	.600	.593
1931	17.69	28.3	.647	26.76	41.1	.651	.643
1930	22.21	33.5	.684	27.76	43.1	.644	.635
1929	25.72	38.4	.681	28.49	44.8	.636	.625
1928	24.66	35.6	.716	27.71	44.4	.624	.613
1927	24.33	33.5	.751	27.43	44.6	.615	.598
1926	28.63	37.7	.786	27.12	44.9	.604	.587
1925	26.47	34.2	.800	26.91	44.4	.606	.584
1924	23.59	30.0	.813	26.37	44.1	.598	.577
1923	25.60	31.3	.845	26.65	45.4	.587	.565
1922	---------	---------	---------	26.70	45.4	.588	.560
1921	---------	---------	---------	25.87	43.4	.596	.580
1919	25.69	35.5	.759	---------	---------	---------	---------
1914	12.24	35.2	.359	---------	---------	---------	---------
1909	11.82	37.8	.323	---------	---------	---------	---------

[1] Beginning 1951, covers all employees except "executives, officials, and staff assistants"; for prior years, covers all hourly-rated employees. For 1921–1927, includes switching and terminal companies.

Series D 642–653. Indexes of Union Hourly Wage Rates and Weekly Hours, for Building and Printing Trades: 1907 to 1956

Year	Building trades (1947–49 = 100) — All trades Hourly wage rate (642)	Weekly hours (643)	Journeymen Hourly wage rate (644)	Weekly hours (645)	Helpers and laborers Hourly wage rate (646)	Weekly hours (647)	Printing trades (Jan. 2, 1948–July 1, 1949 = 100) — All printing Hourly wage rate (648)	Weekly hours (649)	Book and job Hourly wage rate (650)	Weekly hours (651)	Newspaper Hourly wage rate (652)	Weekly hours (653)
1956	147.7	100.1	146.2	100.1	157.4	100.1	134.1	99.1	134.9	98.7	132.1	99.0
1955	141.2	100.1	140.0	100.1	148.5	100.1	130.7	99.2	131.4	98.9	128.9	99.1
1954	136.4	100.1	135.4	100.1	142.4	100.1	127.1	99.4	127.6	99.1	125.9	99.2
1953	131.6	100.1	130.7	100.1	136.5	100.1	123.5	99.5	124.0	99.2	122.3	99.3
1952	125.1	100.1	124.6	100.1	127.7	100.1	118.8	99.5	119.3	99.2	117.6	99.3
1951	117.8	100.1	117.4	100.1	119.9	99.9	112.4	99.7	112.1	99.5	112.7	99.4
1950	110.7	100.2	110.5	100.2	112.2	100.0	107.9	99.8	108.2	99.8	107.4	99.5
1949	106.1	100.1	106.0	100.1	106.4	100.0	105.7	99.9	105.7	99.9	105.7	99.7
1948	101.8	100.0	101.7	100.0	102.3	100.0	94.3	100.1	94.3	100.1	94.3	100.3
1947	92.1	100.0	92.3	99.9	91.1	100.1	(1)	(1)	(1)	(1)	(1)	(1)
1946	80.5	100.1	80.9	100.1	77.9	100.1	74.3	102.0	74.2	102.4	74.5	101.3
1945	72.2	101.1	73.0	101.2	67.0	100.8	63.5	104.6	63.1	106.1	64.1	101.7
1944	70.8	101.1	71.7	101.2	64.0	100.8	62.6	104.6	62.3	106.1	63.3	101.7
1943	70.2	100.9	71.2	101.0	63.3	100.8	61.1	104.6	60.7	106.1	61.9	101.7
1942	69.7	101.0	70.8	100.8	62.5	101.5	59.3	104.3	59.1	105.8	59.4	101.7
1941	65.6	100.2	67.0	99.5	56.9	102.4	56.8	104.6	56.6	105.8	56.9	101.8
1940	63.3	99.8	64.7	99.0	54.3	102.1	56.2	104.6	56.0	105.8	56.2	102.2
1939	62.3	99.9	63.8	99.0	53.2	102.7	55.4	104.8	55.5	106.0	55.0	102.5
1938	61.8	100.1	63.4	99.1	52.8	102.9	54.9	105.1	55.1	106.3	54.3	103.0
1937	56.8	101.8	58.3	100.9	48.0	104.6	53.2	105.7	53.3	106.8	52.9	103.5
1936	53.1	101.4	54.6	100.5	44.1	104.2	51.5	106.2	51.6	107.0	51.0	104.5
1935	51.3	101.4	52.8	100.5	41.7	104.0	50.3	106.6	50.2	106.9	50.3	105.8
1934	50.7	102.2	52.2	101.3	41.5	104.7	48.5	108.4	49.1	108.5	47.4	107.6
1933	50.3	106.1	51.9	105.1	40.3	108.1	47.5	114.3	47.8	112.5	46.8	116.9
1932	51.8	106.4	53.4	105.5	42.2	108.6	50.5	115.2	50.6	113.6	50.0	117.5
1931	60.6	108.4	62.4	107.4	49.4	111.1	50.8	119.2	51.1	118.2	50.1	120.6
1930	60.4	109.7	62.2	108.9	49.7	112.0	50.6	119.3	50.8	118.2	50.0	120.6
1929	58.0	112.9	59.7	112.2	47.3	114.6	49.8	119.4	49.9	118.3	49.5	120.8
1928	57.2	113.9	59.0	112.9	46.5	116.9	49.1	119.5	49.2	118.4	48.6	121.0
1927	56.9	114.6	58.5	113.7	46.0	117.0	48.2	119.5	48.6	118.4	47.4	121.3
1926	55.0	114.8	56.6	114.0	45.2	117.0	46.8	119.6	47.4	118.4	46.1	121.6
1925	51.6	115.0	53.0	114.2	41.5	117.3	45.8	119.7	46.4	118.6	45.1	121.4
1924	49.7	115.0	51.1	114.2	40.1	117.5	45.1	119.7	45.9	118.5	44.3	121.7
1923	46.0	115.0	47.4	114.2	37.1	117.5	43.0	120.2	44.1	118.5	41.8	123.4
1922	41.7	114.9	42.9	114.1	35.0	117.3	41.8	120.8	42.4	119.2	41.3	123.6
1921	44.4	114.9	45.6	114.0	38.4	117.6	41.3	121.2	42.2	120.7	40.9	121.3
1920	43.6	115.0	44.7	114.1	38.1	117.6	37.7	129.0	38.4	131.2	37.6	121.6
1919	32.3	115.5	33.4	114.6	26.2	118.4	29.4	132.9	29.4	136.3	30.8	121.7
1918	28.2	116.1	29.3	115.0	22.7	119.5	24.0	132.9	23.9	136.4	25.5	121.5
1917	25.4	116.7	26.5	115.7	19.6	119.9	22.1	132.9	21.5	136.4	24.3	121.5
1916	23.9	117.0	25.1	115.9	17.8	120.4	21.4	132.9	20.8	136.4	23.7	121.5
1915	23.2	117.4	24.3	116.4	17.2	120.7	21.2	132.9	20.5	136.4	23.6	121.6
1914	23.0	117.5	24.1	116.5	17.1	120.8	21.0	132.9	20.4	136.4	23.5	121.7
1913	22.5	118.0	23.5	116.8	16.9	121.5	20.7	133.0	20.0	136.4	23.2	122.0
1912	22.0	118.2	23.0	117.1	16.4	121.5	20.3	133.1	19.6	136.4	22.8	122.1
1911	21.5	118.6	22.5	117.5	16.3	121.9	19.9	133.2	19.3	136.5	22.4	122.3
1910	21.2	119.0	22.1	117.9	16.2	122.1	(1)	(1)	18.8	136.5	22.0	122.3
1909	20.4	120.5	21.2	119.3	15.7	124.3	(1)	(1)	17.8	136.9	21.3	122.6
1908	19.4	122.2	20.2	120.8	15.2	126.9	(1)	(1)	16.6	138.1	20.4	122.9
1907	18.2	124.1	19.0	122.6	14.5	129.6	(1)	(1)	15.0	144.8	19.4	123.5

[1] Not available.

Series D 654–668. Hours and Earnings, for Production Workers in 25 Manufacturing Industries, by Sex and Degree of Skill: 1914 to 1948

Year	All production workers			Male			Female			Unskilled, male			Skilled and semiskilled, male		
	Average hourly earnings	Average weekly hours	Average weekly earnings	Average hourly earnings	Average weekly hours	Average weekly earnings	Average hourly earnings	Average weekly hours	Average weekly earnings	Average hourly earnings	Average weekly hours	Average weekly earnings	Average hourly earnings	Average weekly hours	Average weekly earnings
	654	655	656	657	658	659	660	661	662	663	664	665	666	667	668
1948 [1]	$1.431	40.3	$57.22	$1.503	40.7	$60.98	$1.090	38.4	$41.86	$1.227	40.7	$49.88	$1.567	40.6	$63.52
1947	1.342	40.4	54.27	1.414	40.9	57.77	1.007	38.7	38.99	1.147	40.9	46.80	1.478	40.9	60.35
1946	1.190	40.1	47.55	1.260	40.4	50.72	.876	39.0	34.14	1.015	40.4	40.86	1.320	40.3	53.10
1945	1.097	44.2	48.46	1.185	45.2	53.47	.787	40.8	32.18	.917	44.8	41.03	1.248	45.2	56.39
1944	1.067	45.6	48.83	1.164	46.9	54.65	.752	41.3	31.21	.892	46.0	41.07	1.227	47.1	57.85
1943	1.014	45.0	45.88	1.103	46.2	51.05	.699	41.1	28.83	.854	45.4	38.86	1.164	46.4	54.10
1942	.924	43.0	40.03	.987	43.9	43.46	.609	39.2	23.95	.773	43.1	33.49	1.043	44.3	46.31
1941	.814	41.2	33.62	.867	41.8	36.18	.533	38.0	20.29	.682	41.4	28.19	.914	42.0	38.32
1940	.739	38.6	28.54	.784	39.2	30.64	.491	35.5	17.43	.611	39.3	23.91	.827	39.2	32.41
1939	.720	37.6	27.05	.765	38.0	28.96	.475	35.8	17.02	.594	38.6	22.82	.808	37.9	30.53
1938	.716	34.3	24.43	.758	34.6	26.07	.482	32.6	15.69	.586	35.5	20.67	.802	34.4	27.49
1937	.695	38.7	26.80	.735	39.3	28.72	.473	36.1	17.02	.570	39.6	22.41	.777	39.3	30.39
1936	.619	39.5	24.39	.651	40.1	26.02	.434	36.2	15.74	.501	40.0	20.00	.689	40.1	27.58
1935	.599	37.2	22.23	.628	37.5	23.49	.437	35.2	15.37	.495	37.0	18.32	.665	37.7	24.98
1934	.580	34.7	20.06	.607	34.8	21.07	.427	34.0	14.50	.479	34.4	16.46	.643	35.0	22.45
1933	.491	36.4	17.71	.518	36.3	18.69	.340	36.6	12.35	.401	37.4	14.91	.550	37.1	20.27
1932	.498	34.8	17.05	.526	34.4	17.96	.325	36.3	11.73	.400	36.4	14.48	.559	35.1	19.48
1931	.564	40.4	22.62	.597	40.4	24.00	.371	39.8	14.69	.460	41.8	19.18	.634	39.7	25.05
1930	.589	43.9	25.84	.622	44.5	27.66	.395	40.5	15.98	.478	45.9	21.90	.663	44.0	29.17
1929	.590	48.3	28.55	.625	49.1	30.64	.398	44.2	17.61	.486	50.2	24.40	.668	48.8	32.60
1928	.579	47.9	27.80	.614	48.8	29.95	.396	43.4	17.15	.474	50.4	23.89	.659	48.5	31.94
1927	.576	47.7	27.53	.610	48.5	29.59	.398	43.7	17.37	.471	49.9	23.54	.656	48.1	31.51
1926	.568	48.1	27.42	.601	49.1	29.51	.398	43.5	17.27	.461	50.2	23.21	.652	48.5	31.61
1925	.561	48.2	27.08	.592	49.0	29.00	.389	44.1	17.17	.455	50.3	22.93	.644	48.6	31.29
1924	.562	46.9	26.43	.592	47.8	28.27	.393	42.6	16.75	.458	48.9	22.41	.644	47.5	30.55
1923	.541	49.2	26.61	.570	50.0	28.39	.383	45.0	17.24	.443	50.3	22.28	.619	49.9	30.81
1922 [2]	.494	49.2	24.29	.520	50.0	25.90	.352	45.0	15.84	.402	50.5	20.30	.566	49.8	28.11
1921	.524	45.6	23.77	.554	46.0	25.35	.362	43.2	15.63	.437	46.5	20.28	.599	45.9	27.36
1920 [3]	.606	48.2	29.39	.642	49.2	31.69	.414	43.0	17.71	.529	49.2	26.06	.687	49.4	34.10
1914 [4]	.247	51.5	12.68	.262	52.2	13.65	.155	50.1	7.75	.203	52.9	10.71	.291	51.7	14.99

[1] Average of 7 months, January-July.
[2] Average of 6 months, July-December.
[3] Average of 7 months, June-December.
[4] July.

Series D 669–684. Hours and Earnings, for Production Workers in Selected Nonmanufacturing Industries: 1932 to 1957

Year	Building construction [1]			Wholesale trade [2]			Retail trade [3]			Electric light and power [4]			Laundries			Insurance carriers, [5] average weekly earnings
	Average hourly earnings	Average weekly hours	Average weekly earnings	Average hourly earnings	Average weekly hours	Average weekly earnings	Average hourly earnings	Average weekly hours	Average weekly earnings	Average hourly earnings	Average weekly hours	Average weekly earnings	Average hourly earnings	Average weekly hours	Average weekly earnings	
	669	670	671	672	673	674	675	676	677	678	679	680	681	682	683	684
1957	$2.97	36.1	$107.22	$2.10	40.2	$84.42	$1.65	38.1	$62.87	$2.30	41.3	$97.06	$1.09	39.8	$43.38	$80.69
1956	2.80	36.4	101.92	2.01	40.4	81.20	1.57	38.6	60.60	2.25	41.5	93.38	1.05	40.3	42.32	77.50
1955	2.66	36.2	96.29	1.90	40.6	77.14	1.50	39.0	58.50	2.13	41.2	87.76	1.01	40.3	40.70	73.29
1954	2.60	36.2	94.12	1.83	40.4	73.93	1.45	39.1	56.70	2.05	41.3	84.67	1.00	40.1	40.10	70.08
1953	2.48	37.0	91.76	1.77	40.5	71.69	1.40	39.2	54.88	1.97	41.4	81.56	.98	40.5	39.69	67.29
1952	2.31	38.1	88.01	1.67	40.6	67.80	1.32	39.9	52.67	1.84	41.4	76.18	.94	41.1	38.63	63.38
1951	2.19	37.2	81.47	1.58	40.7	64.31	1.26	40.2	50.65	1.74	41.9	72.91	.92	41.1	37.81	61.31
1950	2.031	36.3	73.73	1.483	40.7	60.36	1.176	40.5	47.63	1.630	41.6	67.81	.861	41.2	35.47	58.49
1949	1.935	36.7	70.95	1.414	40.7	57.55	1.137	40.4	45.93	1.564	41.5	64.91	.843	41.5	34.98	56.47
1948	1.848	37.3	68.85	1.359	40.9	55.58	1.088	40.3	43.85	1.469	42.0	61.70	.817	41.9	34.23	54.93
1947	1.681	37.6	63.30	1.268	41.0	51.99	1.009	40.3	40.66	1.371	41.9	57.44	.767	42.6	32.71	52.58
1946	1.478	38.1	56.24	1.150	41.5	47.73	.893	40.7	36.35	1.256	41.6	52.04	.704	42.9	30.20	50.94
1945	1.379	39.0	53.73	1.029	42.7	43.94	.783	40.3	31.55	1.141	43.5	50.05	.648	42.8	27.73	47.13
1944	1.319	39.6	52.18	.985	42.9	42.26	.731	40.4	29.53	1.107	43.1	48.04	.605	42.9	25.95	44.87
1943	1.252	38.4	48.13	.933	42.2	39.37	.679	40.3	27.36	1.053	41.6	44.16	.538	42.9	23.08	41.87
1942	1.148	36.4	41.80	.860	41.3	35.52	.626	41.1	25.73	.983	40.1	39.60	.482	42.2	20.34	38.37
1941	1.010	34.8	35.14	.793	41.0	32.51	.580	42.1	24.42	.920	39.8	36.54	.444	42.1	18.69	37.54
1940	.958	33.1	31.70	.739	41.2	30.45	.553	42.5	23.50	.884	39.7	35.10	.429	41.8	17.93	36.55
1939	.932	32.6	30.39	.715	41.7	29.82	.542	42.7	23.14	.869	39.6	34.38	.422	41.8	17.64	36.32
1938	.908	32.1	29.19	.700	42.2	29.54	.543	42.6	[6] 23.13	.858	39.9	34.15	.414	41.6	17.22	36.30
1937	.903	33.4	30.14	.698	42.8	29.87	.551	43.3	[6] 23.86	.853	40.3	34.22	.395	42.6	16.83	39.29
1936	.824	32.8	27.01	.667	42.6	28.41	.522	43.5	[6] 22.71	.803	40.1	32.22	.378	42.7	16.14	37.99
1935	.815	30.1	24.51	.648	41.3	26.76	.521	41.8	[6] 21.78	.790	39.3	31.07	.376	41.0	15.42	36.22
1934	.795	28.9	22.97	(⁷)	(⁷)	26.37	.528	41.5	[6] 21.91	.775	38.8	29.98	.378	39.4	14.89	35.02
1933	(⁷)	(⁷)	(⁷)	(⁷)	(⁷)	26.11	(⁷)	(⁷)	[8] 21.16	.693	42.0	29.23	(⁷)	(⁷)	(⁷)	34.29
1932	(⁷)	(⁷)	(⁷)	(⁷)	(⁷)	27.72	(⁷)	(⁷)	[8] 22.85	.696	44.0	30.78	(⁷)	(⁷)	(⁷)	36.99

[1] Figures for 1947 and earlier refer only to on-site workers on privately financed construction; figures for 1948 and later cover both on-site and off-site workers on both private and public projects.
[2] Data for 1937 and earlier years not strictly comparable with those for later years. Data for later years, but not those for 1937 and earlier, exclude supervisory employees.
[3] Data for 1938 and earlier years not strictly comparable with those for later years.
[4] Figures for 1947 and later years include only companies engaged exclusively in producing and distributing electricity; figures for 1946 and earlier years also include combined gas and electric utilities whose income results primarily from sale of electricity.
[5] Data for 1947 and later years are for "insurance carriers"; figures for 1946 and earlier years for "insurance."
[6] Average hourly earnings times average weekly hours.
[7] Not available.
[8] These figures bear the same ratios to the 1934 figures as the corresponding figures for 1932 and 1933 as shown in the *Handbook of Labor Statistics* (1947 edition) bear to the 1934 *Handbook* figures.

Series D 685–695. Average Annual Compensation Per Full-Time Employee, by Major Industry: 1919 to 1929

Year	Total	Agriculture	Mining	Manufacturing	Construction	Transportation and other public utilities	Trade	Finance	Service	Government	Miscellaneous
	685	686	687	688	689	690	691	6 2	693	694	695
1929	$1,489	$651	$1,481	$1,508	$1,883	$1,679	$1,546	$1,904	$1,245	$1,703	$1,431
1928	1,478	646	1,514	1,500	1,934	1,656	1,526	1,886	1,229	1,673	1,428
1927	1,459	648	1,573	1,467	1,921	1,629	1,494	1,864	1,234	1,642	1,416
1926	1,450	651	1,598	1,442	1,872	1,619	1,570	1,854	1,191	1,593	1,428
1925	1,421	642	1,563	1,417	1,862	1,595	1,522	1,844	1,176	1,545	1,398
1924	1,394	629	1,681	1,394	1,822	1,572	1,447	1,795	1,161	1,515	1,359
1923	1,382	614	1,774	1,372	1,815	1,546	1,462	1,751	1,132	1,510	1,352
1922	1,294	551	1,601	1,255	1,459	1,531	1,410	1,782	1,109	1,473	1,266
1921	1,311	567	1,751	1,306	1,552	1,599	1,354	1,717	1,103	1,429	1,248
1920	1,424	830	1,700	1,497	1,924	1,721	1,418	1,623	1,081	1,375	1,315
1919	1,220	725	1,372	1,264	1,560	1,412	1,399	1,467	897	1,151	1,177

Series D 696–707. Average Annual Earnings Per Full-Time Employee, by Major Industry: 1929 to 1957

Year	All industries [1]	Private industries										Government and government enterprises
		Total	Agriculture, forestry, and fisheries	Mining	Contract construction	Manufacturing	Wholesale and retail trade	Finance, insurance, and real estate	Transportation	Communications and public utilities	Services	
	696	697	698	699	700	701	702	703	704	705	706	707
1957	$4,211	$4,248	$1,690	$5,218	$4,922	$4,781	$4,019	$4,304	$5,246	$4,813	$3,146	$4,040
1956	4,042	4,074	1,639	5,015	4,674	4,584	3,860	4,141	4,972	4,612	3,008	3,888
1955	3,847	3,876	1,554	4,701	4,414	4,351	3,702	3,968	4,697	4,426	2,867	3,710
1954	3,670	3,707	1,515	4,377	4,324	4,116	3,558	3,828	4,503	4,229	2,786	3,501
1953	3,587	3,632	1,540	4,353	4,225	4,049	3,446	3,663	4,398	4,039	2,677	3,388
1952	3,414	3,444	1,544	4,057	3,991	3,828	3,284	3,503	4,205	3,799	2,545	3,282
1951	3,231	3,255	1,481	3,879	3,711	3,606	3,171	3,356	3,994	3,547	2,367	3,114
1950	3,008	3,006	1,349	3,448	3,339	3,300	3,034	3,217	3,696	3,318	2,220	3,015
1949	2,851	2,849	1,330	3,207	3,211	3,092	2,899	3,034	3,556	3,153	2,172	2,863
1948	2,795	2,801	1,353	3,387	3,126	3,040	2,832	2,954	3,456	3,002	2,114	2,758
1947	2,589	2,591	1,288	3,113	2,829	2,793	2,632	2,740	3,145	2,792	2,005	2,574
1946	2,356	2,359	1,207	2,719	2,537	2,517	2,378	2,570	2,948	2,567	1,872	2,341
1945	2,189	2,253	1,127	2,621	2,600	2,517	2,114	2,347	2,734	2,425	1,688	2,052
1944	2,108	2,190	1,027	2,499	2,602	2,517	1,946	2,191	2,679	2,248	1,538	1,924
1943	1,951	2,018	867	2,162	2,503	2,349	1,781	2,041	2,493	2,075	1,347	1,777
1942	1,709	1,731	673	1,796	2,191	2,023	1,608	1,885	2,183	1,883	1,132	1,623
1941	1,443	1,454	498	1,579	1,635	1,653	1,478	1,777	1,885	1,766	1,020	1,388
1940	1,300	1,291	408	1,388	1,330	1,432	1,382	1,725	1,756	1,718	953	1,344
1939	1,264	1,250	385	1,367	1,268	1,363	1,360	1,729	1,723	1,692	952	1,337
1938	1,230	1,207	369	1,282	1,193	1,296	1,352	1,731	1,676	1,674	942	1,336
1937	1,258	1,240	360	1,366	1,278	1,376	1,352	1,788	1,644	1,601	938	1,355
1936	1,184	1,164	307	1,263	1,178	1,287	1,295	1,713	1,582	1,522	898	1,279
1935	1,137	1,109	286	1,154	1,027	1,216	1,279	1,632	1,492	1,486	873	1,292
1934	1,091	1,056	251	1,108	942	1,153	1,228	1,601	1,393	1,426	857	1,284
1933	1,048	1,002	230	990	869	1,086	1,183	1,555	1,334	1,351	854	1,328
1932	1,120	1,070	247	1,016	907	1,150	1,315	1,652	1,373	1,438	918	1,477
1931	1,275	1,241	312	1,221	1,233	1,369	1,495	1,858	1,549	1,514	1,008	1,547
1930	1,368	1,348	388	1,424	1,526	1,488	1,569	1,973	1,610	1,497	1,066	1,553
1929	1,405	1,390	397	1,526	1,674	1,543	1,594	2,062	1,643	1,474	1,079	1,551

[1] Includes residual classification, "rest of the world," not shown separately here.

Series D 708–719. Average Annual Supplements to Wages and Salaries Per Full-Time Employee, by Major Industry: 1929 to 1957

Year	All industries	Private industries										Government and government enterprises
		Total	Agriculture, forestry, and fisheries	Mining	Contract construction	Manufacturing	Wholesale and retail trade	Finance, insurance, and real estate	Transportation	Communications and public utilities	Services	
	708	709	710	711	712	713	714	715	716	717	718	719
1957	$292	$295	$33	$549	$277	$418	$179	$390	$394	$489	$117	$279
1956	258	264	29	515	250	368	160	347	360	443	104	229
1955	236	247	28	488	232	345	149	331	324	427	96	187
1954	212	226	19	429	222	312	137	293	297	411	92	151
1953	195	207	17	403	203	286	121	254	279	379	78	142
1952	188	196	15	358	191	269	121	246	269	366	73	152
1951	180	187	14	352	189	256	120	213	255	353	70	149
1950	160	159	9	308	167	210	112	196	233	319	55	168
1949	138	127	7	214	147	160	91	175	218	266	47	200
1948	119	116	6	206	139	140	85	155	200	244	44	136
1947	124	113	6	160	133	134	86	134	224	235	42	192
1946	123	99	6	117	120	117	77	132	176	221	41	229
1945	104	102	5	106	137	129	72	120	164	221	37	109
1944	81	97	4	100	134	120	68	130	157	194	34	44
1943	69	85	3	97	128	102	59	128	151	152	30	28
1942	66	73	3	87	120	87	55	105	139	132	26	36
1941	63	67	2	83	98	81	55	105	117	131	25	43
1940	60	61	3	79	87	75	54	103	110	127	23	55
1939	60	61	2	81	85	74	56	104	108	123	24	53
1938	58	60	2	80	84	72	56	102	106	123	25	49
1937	50	50	2	66	74	58	44	88	99	97	20	51
1936	28	26	1	32	45	27	19	59	59	61	10	40
1935	20	16	1	19	36	15	10	42	40	47	5	45
1934	19	15	1	19	36	12	8	35	55	39	5	41
1933	20	15	1	20	40	13	9	35	45	40	5	48
1932	21	16	2	22	44	16	10	42	41	31	6	55
1931	20	17	2	22	43	16	10	45	40	31	5	50
1930	19	16	2	24	42	15	10	47	36	28	5	49
1929	18	15	1	24	38	14	9	50	33	28	4	49

Series D 720–727. Average Annual Supplements to Wages and Salaries Per Full-Time Equivalent Employee, by Type of Supplement: 1929 to 1957

Year	Total supplements	Employer contributions for social insurance				Other labor income		
		Total	Public retirement systems [1]	Unemployment insurance [2]	Other [3]	Total	Employer contributions to private pension and welfare funds	Compensation for injuries and other [4]
	720	721	722	723	724	725	726	727
1957	$292	$134	$99	$34	(5)	$158	$123	$35
1956	258	117	83	33	(5)	140	108	33
1955	236	106	76	28	$2	130	101	29
1954	212	96	69	26	1	116	89	28
1953	195	87	56	29	1	109	83	25
1952	188	90	57	30	3	98	74	24
1951	180	90	54	33	3	90	68	23
1950	160	82	50	30	2	78	56	22
1949	138	74	38	27	10	64	43	21
1948	119	63	36	25	2	56	37	19
1947	124	75	33	29	13	49	33	16
1946	123	84	28	26	30	40	26	14
1945	104	71	23	24	24	33	21	13
1944	81	53	22	27	5	28	17	10
1943	69	49	20	29	(5)	20	11	9
1942	66	48	19	28	1	18	8	10
1941	63	46	18	28	(5)	17	7	9
1940	60	42	17	26	(5)	18	7	10
1939	60	42	16	26	(5)	17	7	10
1938	58	41	15	25	(5)	17	7	10
1937	50	34	15	18	(5)	16	6	10
1936	28	12	5	7	(5)	16	7	9
1935	20	5	5	(5)	(5)	15	6	9
1934	19	5	5	(5)	(5)	14	5	9
1933	20	5	5	----------	(5)	15	5	10
1932	21	5	4	----------	(5)	17	5	12
1931	20	4	3	----------	(5)	17	5	11
1930	19	3	3	----------	(5)	16	5	11
1929	18	3	3	----------	(5)	16	5	11

[1] Old-age, survivors insurance; railroad retirement insurance; Federal civilian employee retirement systems; State and local employee retirement systems.
[2] State unemployment insurance; Federal unemployment tax; railroad unemployment insurance.
[3] Cash sickness compensation funds; government life insurance.
[4] Includes pay of military reservists.
[5] Less than $0.50.

Series D 728–734. Earnings in Selected Professional Occupations: 1929 to 1954

| Year | Average annual salary | | Average annual net income | | | Median base monthly salary rate, engineers [2] | Average annual pay and allowances, U. S. Regular Army commissioned officers |
| | Public school teachers [1] | College teachers | Nonsalaried lawyers | Nonsalaried physicians | Nonsalaried dentists | | |
	728	729	730	731	732	733	734
1954	$3,825		$10,258				
1953			9,392			$518	
1952	3,450	$5,106	9,021				$6,552
1951			8,855	$13,432	$7,820		6,552
1950	3,010	4,354	8,349	12,324	7,436		6,552
1949		4,234	7,971	11,744	7,146		6,552
1948	2,639	4,123	8,003	11,327	7,089		5,528
1947		3,736	7,437	10,726	6,610		5,528
1946	1,995	3,465	6,951	10,202	6,381	409	5,528
1945		3,277	6,861	10,975	6,922		5,096
1944	1,728	3,331	6,504	9,802	6,649		5,096
1943		3,039	5,945	8,370	5,715	334	5,096
1942	1,507	2,914	5,527	6,735	4,625		5,096
1941			4,794	5,047	3,782		4,800
1940	1,441	2,906	4,507	4,441	3,314		4,800
1939			4,391	4,229	3,096	277	4,800
1938	1,374	2,861	4,273	4,093	2,870		4,800
1937		2,843	4,483	4,285	2,883		4,800
1936	1,283	2,732	4,394	4,204	2,726		4,800
1935		2,666	4,272	3,695	2,485		4,800
1934	1,227		4,218	3,382	2,391	210	4,800
1933			3,868	2,948	2,188		4,800
1932	1,417	3,111	4,156	3,178	2,479	235	4,800
1931		3,134	5,090	4,178	3,422		4,800
1930	1,420	3,065	5,194	4,870	4,020		4,800
1929		3,056	5,534	5,224	4,267	289	4,800

[1] Public elementary and secondary school teachers, supervisors, and principals. Figures are for "school" years ending in the year indicated; for example, the figure shown for 1954 is for the school years 1953–1954.

[2] For 1953, graduate engineers only. All other figures are for graduates and nongraduates. The corresponding figure for graduate engineers for 1946 is $405.

Series D 735–740. Labor Union Membership, by Affiliation: 1897 to 1934

[Includes Canadian members of labor unions with headquarters in U. S.]

Year	Total union membership (1,000)		American Federation of Labor			Independent or un-affiliated unions, total membership (1,000), Wolman
			Number of affiliated unions, BLS	Total membership (1,000)		
	BLS	Wolman		BLS	Wolman	
	735	736	737	738	739	740
1934	3,249	3,671	109	2,608	3,030	641
1933	2,857	3,048	108	2,127	2,318	730
1932	3,226	3,191	106	2,532	2,497	694
1931	3,526	3,379	105	2,890	2,743	636
1930	3,632	3,416	104	2,961	2,745	671
1929	3,625	3,461	105	2,934	2,770	691
1928	3,567	3,480	107	2,896	2,809	671
1927	3,600	3,546	106	2,813	2,759	787
1926	3,592	3,502	107	2,804	2,715	788
1925	3,566	3,519	107	2,877	2,831	689
1924	3,549	3,536	107	2,866	2,853	683
1923	3,629	3,622	108	2,926	2,919	703
1922	3,950	4,027	112	3,196	3,273	754
1921	4,722	4,781	110	3,907	3,967	815
1920	5,034	5,048	110	4,079	4,093	955
1919	4,046	4,125	111	3,260	3,339	786
1918	3,368	3,467	111	2,726	2,825	642
1917	2,976	3,061	111	2,371	2,457	605
1916	2,722	2,773	111	2,073	2,124	649
1915	2,560	2,583	110	1,946	1,968	614
1914	2,647	2,687	110	2,021	2,061	626
1913	2,661	2,716	111	1,996	2,051	665
1912	2,405	2,452	112	1,770	1,818	635
1911	2,318	2,343	115	1,762	1,787	556
1910	2,116	2,140	120	1,562	1,587	554
1909	1,965	2,006	119	1,483	1,524	482
1908	2,092	2,131	116	1,587	1,625	505
1907	2,077	2,080	117	1,539	1,542	538
1906	1,892	1,907	119	1,454	1,469	438
1905	1,918	2,022	118	1,494	1,598	424
1904	2,067	2,073	120	1,676	1,682	391
1903	1,824	1,914	113	1,466	1,556	358
1902	1,335	1,376	97	1,024	1,065	311
1901	1,058	1,125	87	788	854	270
1900	791	868	82	548	625	243
1899	550	611	73	349	410	201
1898	467	501	67	278	312	189
1897	440	447	58	265	272	175

Series D 741–745.　Labor Union Membership and Membership as Percent of Nonagricultural Employment: 1930 to 1956

[In thousands]

Year	Union membership			Nonagricultural employment		Year	Union membership			Nonagricultural employment	
	Total	Canadian members of U. S. unions	Excluding Canadian members	Total	Membership [1] as percent of total		Total	Canadian members of U. S. unions	Excluding Canadian members	Total	Membership [1] as percent of total
	741	742	743	744	745		741	742	743	744	745
1956	18,477	987	17,490	51,878	33.7	1942	10,762	382	10,380	39,779	26.1
1955	17,749	947	16,802	50,056	33.6	1941	10,489	288	10,201	36,220	28.2
1954	17,955	933	17,022	48,431	35.1						
1953	17,860	912	16,948	49,681	34.1	1940	8,944	227	8,717	32,058	27.2
1952	16,750	858	[2] 15,900	48,303	32.9	1939	8,980	217	8,763	30,311	28.9
1951	16,750	804	[2] 15,900	47,347	33.7	1938	8,265	231	8,034	28,902	27.8
						1937	7,218	217	7,001	30,718	22.8
1950	15,000	733	[2] 14,300	44,738	31.9	1936	4,164	175	3,989	28,802	13.8
1949	15,000	718	[2] 14,300	43,315	33.0						
1948	15,000	681	[2] 14,300	44,448	32.2	1935	3,728	144	3,584	26,792	13.4
1947	15,414	627	14,787	43,462	34.0	1934	3,249	161	3,088	25,699	12.0
1946	14,974	579	14,395	41,287	34.9	1933	2,857	168	2,689	23,466	11.5
						1932	3,226	176	3,050	23,377	13.0
1945	14,796	474	14,322	40,037	35.8	1931	3,526	216	3,310	26,383	12.5
1944	14,621	475	14,146	41,534	34.1	1930	3,632	231	3,401	29,143	11.7
1943	13,642	429	13,213	42,106	31.4						

[1] Excludes Canadian members.　　　　　　　　　　　　　　　　　[2] Rounded to nearest hundred.

Series D 746–763.　Labor Union Membership, by Industry: 1897 to 1934

[In thousands]

Year	Total	Mining, quarrying, and oil	Building construction	Metals, machinery, shipbuilding	Textiles	Leather and shoes	Clothing	Lumber and woodworking	Paper, printing, and bookbinding	Chemicals, clay, glass, stone	Food, liquor, tobacco	Transportation and communication	Public service	Theaters and music	Trade	Hotel and restaurant services	Domestic and personal service	Miscellaneous
	746	747	748	749	750	751	752	753	754	755	756	757	758	759	760	761	762	763
1934	[1] 3,609	579	605	222	40	117	405	10	162	47	82	645	299	127	6	53	64	137
1933	2,973	355	583	180	16	76	336	8	153	27	58	609	296	127	5	32	55	57
1932	3,144	357	806	173	29	29	211	8	160	29	56	699	300	128	9	31	63	57
1931	3,358	309	890	191	34	38	224	12	166	33	60	816	276	132	10	38	70	60
1930	3,393	230	904	203	35	44	230	13	165	35	62	882	264	134	10	44	73	64
1929	3,443	271	919	211	35	47	218	13	162	38	65	892	247	135	10	45	67	67
1928	3,480	333	905	205	35	45	239	13	162	39	66	890	224	132	10	46	66	69
1927	3,546	397	903	204	35	49	267	13	162	41	70	889	212	113	10	47	66	68
1926	3,502	386	867	202	36	55	292	11	158	42	75	884	204	112	10	46	63	61
1925	3,519	439	837	205	36	54	292	10	156	42	75	893	193	110	10	46	60	60
1924	3,536	493	814	218	38	47	282	11	154	45	76	893	185	108	10	46	57	61
1923	3,622	530	790	257	37	56	295	11	151	50	76	907	180	104	10	45	56	67
1922	4,027	387	826	506	37	90	310	12	160	50	99	1,039	171	107	17	60	61	95
1921	4,781	470	869	728	88	96	323	20	182	53	146	1,240	172	106	21	69	55	143
1920	5,048	439	888	859	149	113	374	24	164	52	181	1,256	161	99	21	60	51	157
1919	4,125	419	802	618	60	104	324	16	148	48	168	959	137	88	15	61	42	119
1918	3,467	433	701	396	49	75	258	14	144	51	137	777	105	87	15	65	44	114
1917	3,061	373	606	310	41	73	222	18	137	52	120	695	102	82	15	65	44	105
1916	2,773	338	553	267	29	61	210	18	126	52	117	623	96	87	15	59	40	82
1915	2,583	332	533	224	22	53	174	21	116	53	119	576	90	87	15	61	38	69
1914	2,687	380	542	226	30	58	158	25	111	58	145	562	91	92	15	72	37	86
1913	2,716	432	553	219	29	55	164	25	107	56	141	557	86	82	15	69	34	92
1912	2,452	343	509	204	23	56	131	26	102	60	137	530	67	77	15	48	32	94
1911	2,343	311	479	210	21	50	145	29	97	59	128	513	66	69	15	43	31	76
1910	2,140	275	459	196	21	47	98	28	90	60	123	480	58	60	15	37	29	64
1909	2,006	307	426	178	14	40	80	19	83	57	119	438	44	52	15	37	29	66
1908	2,131	290	445	200	17	40	73	20	87	55	112	470	39	47	50	39	30	118
1907	2,080	312	433	212	16	40	65	27	86	55	110	460	31	45	50	36	27	73
1906	1,907	265	389	187	14	40	54	36	88	55	103	422	26	43	50	34	29	72
1905	2,022	297	373	166	14	41	63	42	91	51	104	446	24	38	50	39	27	158
1904	2,073	279	392	213	15	43	78	52	92	49	136	444	23	28	50	49	30	100
1903	1,914	280	369	205	19	42	77	48	88	46	122	339	22	20	50	39	29	119
1902	1,376	197	263	137	15	24	59	34	70	39	93	258	19	15	30	19	20	84
1901	1,125	218	192	104	7	15	38	32	55	33	77	216	18	13	25	10	14	59
1900	868	131	153	81	8	10	25	26	48	30	69	189	15	9	20	5	7	42
1899	611	75	97	59	7	8	15	16	43	27	51	158	11	9	8	2	4	22
1898	501	44	74	46	8	12	15	12	39	25	46	130	11	8	6	2	3	18
1897	447	21	67	50	8	15	15	6	38	23	46	116	11	7	4	2	2	17

[1] Includes 11,000 union members in the professional service industry, not shown separately.

Series D 764–778. Work Stoppages, Workers Involved, Man-Days Idle, Major Issues, and Average Duration: 1881 to 1957

Year	Work stoppages and man-days idle						Major issues and average duration								
	Stoppage beginning in year			Man-days idle			Stoppages[3]				Average duration of stoppages (days)	Workers involved (1,000)			
	Total	Workers involved		Number (1,000)	Percent of estimated working time[2]	Per worker involved	Total	Major issues				Total	Major issues		
		Number (1,000)	Percent of employed wage earners[1]					Wages and hours	Union organization	Other and not reported			Wages and hours	Union organization[4]	Other and not reported
	764	765	766	767	768	769	770	771	772	773	774	775	776	777	778
1957	3,673	1,390	3.1	16,500	0.14	11.4	3,673	1,730	751	1,192	19.2	1,390	752	72	563
1956	3,825	1,900	4.3	33,100	0.29	17.4	3,825	1,821	774	1,230	18.9	1,900	1,270	183	447
1955	4,320	2,650	6.2	28,200	0.26	10.7	4,320	2,154	844	1,322	18.5	2,650	1,780	244	625
1954	3,468	1,530	3.7	22,600	0.21	14.7	3,468	1,726	588	1,154	22.5	1,530	886	54	591
1953	5,091	2,400	5.6	28,300	0.26	11.8	5,091	2,825	745	1,521	20.3	2,400	1,460	162	781
1952	5,117	3,540	8.8	59,100	0.57	16.7	5,117	2,447	839	1,831	19.6	3,540	1,450	841	1,244
1951	4,737	2,220	5.5	22,900	0.23	10.3	4,737	2,102	888	1,747	17.4	2,220	1,180	136	904
1950	4,843	2,410	6.9	38,800	0.44	16.1	4,843	2,559	919	1,365	19.2	2,410	1,460	130	819
1949	3,606	3,030	9.0	50,500	0.59	16.7	3,606	1,682	781	1,143	22.5	3,030	1,540	82	1,410
1948	3,419	1,960	5.5	34,100	0.37	17.4	3,419	1,737	780	902	21.8	1,960	1,210	228	518
1947	3,693	2,170	6.5	34,600	0.41	15.9	3,693	1,707	1,102	884	25.6	2,170	805	931	431
1946	4,985	4,600	14.5	116,000	1.43	25.2	4,990	2,238	1,617	1,135	24.2	4,940	3,710	568	663
1945	4,750	3,470	12.2	38,000	0.47	11.0	4,616	1,956	946	1,714	9.9	3,070	1,340	671	1,060
1944	4,956	2,120	7.0	8,720	0.09	4.1	4,958	2,146	808	2,004	5.6	2,130	810	395	922
1943	3,752	1,980	6.9	13,500	0.15	6.8	3,734	1,906	585	1,243	5.0	1,970	1,220	226	523
1942	2,968	840	2.8	4,180	0.05	5.0	3,036	1,423	943	670	11.7	852	429	191	232
1941	4,288	2,360	8.4	23,000	0.32	9.8	4,314	1,535	2,138	641	18.3	2,360	1,110	744	512
1940	2,508	577	2.3	6,700	0.10	11.6	2,493	753	1,243	497	20.9	573	235	190	148
1939	2,613	1,170	4.7	17,800	0.28	15.2	2,639	699	1,411	529	23.4	1,180	352	641	185
1938	2,772	688	2.8	9,150	0.15	13.3	2,772	776	1,385	611	23.6	688	252	224	211
1937	4,740	1,860	7.2	28,400	0.43	15.3	4,720	1,410	2,728	582	20.3	1,950	436	1,160	347
1936	2,172	789	3.1	13,900	0.21	17.6	2,156	756	1,083	317	23.3	710	251	365	94
1935	2,014	1,120	5.2	15,500	0.29	13.8	2,003	760	945	298	23.8	1,102	663	288	151
1934	1,856	1,470	7.2	19,600	0.38	13.4	1,817	717	835	265	19.5	1,480	346	762	372
1933	1,695	1,170	6.3	16,900	0.36	14.4	1,672	926	533	213	16.9	1,144	544	465	135
1932	841	324	1.8	10,500	0.23	32.4	852	560	162	130	19.6	325	234	73	18
1931	810	342	1.6	6,890	0.11	20.2	796	447	221	128	18.8	346	155	116	74
1930	637	183	0.8	3,320	0.05	18.1	651	284	207	160	22.3	182	73	76	33
1929	921	289	1.2	5,350	0.07	18.5	924	373	382	169	22.6	286	104	102	80
1928	604	314	1.3	12,600	0.17	40.2	620	222	226	172	27.6	323	140	95	88
1927	707	330	1.4	26,200	0.37	79.5	666	273	240	153	26.5	319	232	45	43

Year	Stoppages[3]				Workers involved (1,000)				Year	Stoppages[3]				Workers involved (1,000)			
	Total	Major issues			Total	Major issues				Total	Major issues			Total	Major issues		
		Wages and hours	Union organization	Other and not reported		Wages and hours	Union organization[4]	Other and not reported			Wages and hours	Union organization	Other and not reported		Wages and hours	Union organization[4]	Other and not reported
	770	771	772	773	775	776	777	778		770	771	772	773	775	776	777	778
1926	1,035	478	206	351	----	----	----	----	1899	1,838	1,014	471	353	432	288	66	79
1925	1,301	537	219	545	----	----	----	----	1898	1,098	645	236	217	263	184	30	49
1924	1,249	537	244	468	----	----	----	----	1897	1,110	680	193	237	416	335	36	45
1923	1,553	721	308	524	----	----	----	----	1896	1,066	547	297	222	249	160	53	36
1922	1,112	583	208	321	----	----	----	----	1895	1,255	810	217	228	407	305	51	51
1921	2,385	1,501	373	511	----	----	----	----	1894	1,404	865	206	333	690	469	25	196
1920	3,411	2,038	622	751	----	----	----	----	1893	1,375	783	257	335	288	162	59	66
1919	3,630	2,036	869	725	----	----	----	----	1892	1,359	693	261	405	239	122	59	57
1918	3,353	1,869	584	900	----	----	----	----	1891	1,786	867	334	585	330	221	55	54
1917	4,450	2,268	799	1,383	----	----	----	----	1890	1,897	1,039	318	540	373	276	32	66
1916	3,789	2,036	721	1,032	----	----	----	----	1889	1,111	662	173	276	260	207	29	24
1915	1,593	770	312	511	----	----	----	----	1888	946	540	163	243	163	100	23	41
1914	1,204	403	253	548	----	----	----	----	1887	1,503	836	299	368	439	249	91	99
1906–13	----	----	----	----	----	----	----	----	1886	1,572	1,073	210	289	610	445	79	87
1905	2,186	942	800	444	302	191	57	54	1885	695	486	67	142	258	214	14	30
1904	2,419	944	964	511	574	272	210	92	1884	485	341	50	94	165	145	4	16
1903	3,648	1,778	1,200	670	788	396	235	156	1883	506	372	55	79	170	131	28	12
1902	3,240	1,604	1,051	585	692	279	279	134	1882	476	353	38	85	159	133	12	14
1901	3,012	1,413	1,016	583	564	288	161	115	1881	477	382	32	63	130	118	5	7
1900	1,839	931	414	494	568	210	282	76									

[1] "Employed wage earners" include all workers except those in occupations and professions in which strikes rarely if ever occur.

[2] Estimated working time computed by multiplying the average number of "employed wage earners" each year by the days worked by most employees during the year.

[3] Figures are for stoppages beginning in calendar years 1881–1927 and 1947–1957. For 1928–1946, figures are for those ending in calendar years.

[4] Wages and hours were important issues in many of these stoppages also.

LABOR

Series D 779–784. Average Monthly Labor Turnover Rates in Manufacturing, by Class of Turnover: 1919 to 1957

[Monthly rate per 100 employees. Beginning July 1929, averages are arithmetic means; prior to that, unweighted medians. See text for further discussion]

Year	Accessions	Separations				
		Total	Discharge	Layoff	Quit	Miscellaneous
	779	780	781	782	783	784
1957	2.9	3.6	0.2	1.7	1.4	0.2
1956	3.4	3.5	0.3	1.5	1.6	0.2
1955	3.7	3.3	0.3	1.2	1.6	0.2
1954	3.0	3.5	0.2	1.9	1.1	0.2
1953	3.9	4.3	0.4	1.3	2.3	0.3
1952	4.4	4.1	0.3	1.1	2.3	0.3
1951	4.4	4.4	0.3	1.2	2.4	0.5
1950	4.4	3.5	0.3	1.1	1.9	0.2
1949	3.5	4.3	0.2	2.4	1.5	0.1
1948	4.4	4.6	0.4	1.3	2.8	0.1
1947	5.1	4.8	0.4	1.0	3.4	0.1
1946	6.7	6.1	0.4	1.2	4.3	0.2
1945	6.3	8.3	0.6	2.3	5.1	0.3
1944	6.1	6.8	0.6	0.6	5.1	0.5
1943	7.5	7.3	0.6	0.6	5.2	0.9
1942	7.6	6.5	0.4	1.1	3.8	1.3
1941	5.4	3.9	0.2	1.3	2.0	0.4
1940	4.4	3.4	0.2	2.2	0.9	0.1
1939	4.1	3.1	0.1	2.2	0.8	
1938	3.8	4.1	0.1	3.4	0.6	
1937	3.5	4.4	0.2	3.0	1.3	
1936	4.4	3.4	0.2	2.0	1.1	
1935	4.2	3.4	0.2	2.5	0.9	
1934	4.7	4.1	0.2	3.0	0.9	
1933	5.4	3.8	0.2	2.7	0.9	
1932	3.3	4.4	0.2	3.5	0.7	
1931	3.1	4.0	0.2	2.9	0.9	
1930	3.1	5.0	0.4	3.0	1.6	
1929 [1]	5.7	6.3	0.8	2.1	3.4	
1929 [2]	5.1	3.9	0.5	0.4	3.0	
1928	3.7	3.1	0.4	0.5	2.2	
1927	3.3	3.3	0.5	0.7	2.1	
1926	4.5	3.9	0.6	0.5	2.9	
1925	5.2	4.0	0.5	0.4	3.1	
1924	3.3	3.8	0.5	0.6	2.7	
1923	9.0	7.5	1.0	0.3	6.2	
1922	8.0	5.3	0.7	0.4	4.2	
1921	2.8	4.4	0.4	1.8	2.2	
1920	10.1	10.3	1.1	0.8	8.4	
1919	10.1	7.5	1.1	0.6	5.8	

[1] July to December average.

[2] January to May average.

Series D 785–792. Work-Injury Frequency Rates in Manufacturing, Mining, and Class I Railroads: 1922 to 1956

[Rate is average number of disabling injuries per million man-hours worked]

Year	Manufacturing[1]	Mining					Class I railroads[7]	
		Total[2]	Bituminous coal[3]	Metals[4]	Non-metals[5]	Stone quarries[6]	All injuries[8]	Excluding 1-3 day injuries[9]
	785	786	787	788	789	790	791	792
1956	12.0	32.8	44.0	37.5	31.0	21.3	14.7	7.7
1955	12.1	34.4	43.7	43.2	37.8	22.0	13.9	7.2
1954	11.9	33.9	44.7	38.9	32.6	22.0	12.6	6.5
1953	13.4	36.7	46.2	40.0	47.3	23.7	13.6	6.7
1952	14.3	40.3	48.5	42.9	40.9	24.5	13.7	7.0
1951	15.5	41.8	48.7	43.4	45.4	26.2	14.7	7.5
1950	14.7	42.9	48.6	45.3	44.2	25.4	14.2	7.3
1949	14.5	44.7	52.6	48.6	42.1	26.8	13.7	7.0
1948	17.2	48.5	57.4	47.9	42.9	28.3	16.2	8.5
1947	18.8	52.4	58.6	53.6	45.8	32.4	18.2	9.7
1946	19.9	54.6	59.9	57.0	51.9	32.8	19.0	10.5
1945	18.6	52.0	57.6	49.7	47.2	32.8	20.5	11.9
1944	18.4	52.5	57.2	55.4	50.5	34.9	20.6	11.8
1943	20.0	54.1	59.2	56.9	53.4	34.0	20.3	11.9
1942	19.9	56.6	61.6	56.6	55.5	35.7	17.6	10.2
1941	18.1	58.1	60.3	64.2	51.6	40.1	14.6	8.3
1940	15.3	59.6	63.0	66.8	44.2	35.7	11.5	6.7
1939	14.9	59.6	61.9	69.4	42.2	36.5	11.1	6.7
1938	15.1	62.3	65.0	71.3	41.1	38.2	11.1	6.8
1937	17.8	64.9	69.6	78.9	48.7	40.6	13.6	8.2
1936	16.6	64.7	67.0	76.3	48.6	39.5	13.7	8.3
1935	17.9	67.1	72.9	65.8	50.7	38.2	---	6.7
1934	20.2	69.0	70.8	71.4	52.4	41.8	---	7.0
1933	19.3	67.5	70.2	65.8	53.3	42.0	---	6.9
1932	19.6	70.0	74.4	57.2	45.2	38.5	---	7.4
1931	18.9	74.3	81.6	58.0	47.5	41.0	---	7.5
1930	23.1	---	85.6	---	---	40.3	---	9.4
1929	24.0	---	---	---	---	46.9	---	13.8
1928	22.5	---	---	---	---	47.5	---	16.2
1927	22.6	---	---	---	---	59.2	---	19.4
1926	24.2	---	---	---	---	58.0	---	23.9
1925	---	---	---	---	---	61.4	---	26.1
1924	---	---	---	---	---	62.9	---	27.3
1923	---	---	---	---	---	---	---	30.9
1922	---	---	---	---	---	---	---	27.1

[1] Excludes petroleum refining, smelting and refining of nonferrous metals, cement and lime manufacturing, and coke production.
[2] Includes anthracite coal mining, coke production, and metallurgical plants, not shown separately.
[3] Includes lignite.
[4] Copper, gold-placer, gold-silver, iron, lead-zinc, and miscellaneous.
[5] Barite, feldspar, fluorspar, gypsum, magnesite, mica, phosphate rock, rock salt, sulphur, and miscellaneous. Excludes stone quarries.
[6] Granite, limestone, marble, sandstone, slate and traprock quarrying, and cement and lime manufacturing.
[7] For 1922–1932, includes switching and terminal companies; excluded thereafter.
[8] Includes fatalities and nonfatal injuries incapacitating employees for at least 1 day in 10 days immediately following date of injury.
[9] Includes fatalities and nonfatal injuries incapacitating employees for more than 3 days in 10 days immediately following date of injury.

Prices and Price Indexes

E 1–186. General note.

An early interest in the statistics of prices is evident at the beginning of the 19th century, with the appearance in 1806 of Samuel Blodgett, Jr.'s *Economica: A Statistical Manual for the United States of America*, which included a collection of prices for 16 important commodities in 5 markets for 1785–1805. Many other contemporary accounts contained references to prices, but the first serious attempt to summarize comprehensive price data for the United States in the form of index numbers was made by Horatio C. Burchard, Director of the Mint. His report to the Secretary of the Treasury in 1881 contained wholesale prices for many individual articles and an index number (which contains some serious inadequacies). In 1886, a special report containing retail prices of about 60 "necessaries of life" was included in volume 20 of the Tenth Census, *Report on the Statistics of Wages in Manufacturing Industries*, by Joseph D. Weeks (usually called the *Weeks Report*). No summary figures were included in this volume.

In 1891, a Senate Resolution led to the collection of a voluminous body of data which covered wholesale prices for 1840–1891 and retail prices for a 28-month period ending September 1891, for more than 200 commodities. The information assembled was summarized by Roland P. Falkner, whose indexes have been widely used as evidence of price changes for 1840–1891. These indexes were prepared as estimates of changes in wage earners' cost of living, but, in actuality, they were indexes of wholesale prices for one month of each year. Their technical adequacy was the subject of considerable controversy at the time, but the deficiencies in the indexes do not detract from the historical value of the basic price data collected for the Senate Committee and published in the "Aldrich Reports," including *Wholesale Prices, Wages, and Transportation* (4 parts), Senate Report No. 1394, 1893, and *Retail Prices and Wages* (3 parts), Senate Report No. 986, 1892.

In 1900, Roland Falkner extended his indexes to 1899 with quotations for 142 articles collected by the Department of Labor, with some adjustments in his methods. The results are published in Department of Labor Bulletin No. 27, *Wholesale Prices: 1890 to 1899*, pp. 237–313. In 1902, the Department of Labor began publication of its index of wholesale prices, which has continued since without interruption.

Interest in price measurements following the upturn in prices after 1897 led to the preparation of a number of wholesale price indexes for the United States, in addition to the official Department of Labor index series. John R. Commons published an index of wholesale prices of 66 commodities for 1878–1900 in the *Quarterly Bulletin of the Bureau of Economic Research* for July and October 1900. Bradstreet's indexes of wholesale prices of about 96 commodities were established in 1897 and carried back to 1890. Dun's index numbers of wholesale prices for about 350 commodities were published in *Dun's Review* on a continuous basis beginning in 1901 and gradually extended back to 1860. These last 2 series were expressed as sums of actual prices rather than in the conventional index number form. Several other relatively short-lived series were also compiled during the next 10 to 20 years.

After 1902, when the Department of Labor's wholesale price index was continuously available, additions to wholesale price index numbers were mainly to obtain a better historical perspective. In 1932, the series of wholesale price indexes for 1720–1932 were completed by G. F. Warren and F. A. Pearson (see series E 1–12). Part of this work was done under the auspices of the International Scientific Committee on Price History referred to below.

Walter B. Smith and Arthur H. Cole computed wholesale commodity price indexes covering 1792–1862 for *Fluctuations in American Business, 1790–1860*, Harvard Economic Studies, Harvard University Press, Cambridge, 1935. The series include wholesale commodity price indexes for Boston, 1792–1820; for Boston, New York, and Philadelphia, 1815–1845; and New York (primarily), 1843–1862.

Wholesale prices in Cincinnati were assembled from newspapers for 1844–1914 and an index for this market was published by Henry E. White in *Wholesale Prices at Cincinnati and New York*, Cornell University Agricultural Experiment Station, *Memoir 182*, Ithaca, 1935.

The most extensive historical price investigations, however, were undertaken under the auspices of the International Scientific Committee on Price History. The results of these research projects for 6 important marketing centers were summarized by Arthur H. Cole in *Wholesale Commodity Prices in the United States, 1700–1861*, Harvard University Press, Cambridge, 1938. The historical indexes are given in series E 68–100.

Wholesale price indexes were compiled by Frederick C. Mills for commodities grouped according to economically significant factors. Mill's studies of price relationships and price movements contain a number of special indexes which he derived by recombining price relatives for commodities in the BLS indexes. These indexes include some special commodity groupings not used by BLS, e.g., crops, as well as classifications by stage of processing and by durability. Some series were first published for 1890–1931 in *Economic Tendencies in the United States*, National Bureau of Economic Research, No. 21, New York, 1932, pp. 584–588. Additional indexes for 1913–1935 appeared in *Prices in Recession and Recovery*, NBER, No. 31, New York, 1936, pp. 491–547. Indexes through June 1943 were included in an appendix to *Prices in a War Economy*, NBER, Occasional Paper No. 12, October 1943, and through March 1948 in *The Structure of Postwar Prices*, NBER, Occasional Paper No. 27, July 1948.

The volume of information available for wholesale prices is not matched at the retail level, especially for the early years. The official Consumer Price Index of the BLS was initiated in 1904 with a food index. The *Eighteenth Annual Report of the Commissioner of Labor, 1903: Cost of Living and Retail Prices of Food* contained an index of retail prices of food for 1890–1903 weighted by family consumption in 1901. This food index was continued until the end of World War I, when it became one component group of a comprehensive "cost-of-living" index, originated as part of a study of cost of living in shipbuilding cities in 1918 and 1919. Supplementary price information had been collected by the BLS over the years, and a comprehensive index was compiled back to 1913. Since

World War I, the index has undergone a number of changes in coverage and methodology, most of them in the direction of improvement in the quantity and quality of data. At present, the index is issued monthly under the official title Consumer Price Index, in mimeographed releases and in the *Monthly Labor Review* (see text for series E 113-147).

The National Industrial Conference Board also compiled a Consumer Price Index from 1918 to 1958. This index was similar to the BLS Consumer Price Index but the collection of data was primarily by mail instead of by personal visit. A description of the NICB index as it was compiled before discontinuance is included in the August 1954 issue of *Management Record*.

The index numbers of prices received and paid by farmers compiled by the Department of Agriculture were also initiated after World War I; see chapter K, series K 122-138.

Prior to 1913, except for the data in the *Weeks Report* and the *Aldrich Reports*, readily available retail price data are extremely spotty and inadequate. As a result, many of the indexes widely used to approximate changes in retail prices, rest entirely or partially on changes in wholesale prices. A serious limitation in these indexes is that allowance was not made for the slow-moving rents and services nor was account always taken of the difference in movement between wholesale and retail prices of commodities. Falkner's indexes referred to above, for example, were calculated entirely from wholesale price information. Adjustments to wholesale price movements combined with available BLS retail prices formed the basis for Douglas' index of the cost of living (series E 159). The only "cost-of-living" indexes now available for any years before 1913, computed from retail price data, are Wesley C. Mitchell's *Relative Cost of Living for 1860 to 1880*, the *Consumer Price Index for 1851 to 1880* compiled by Ethel Hoover (series E 148-156), and Rees' cost-of-living index, 1890-1914 (series E 160). The cost-of-living index computed by Wesley C. Mitchell for *Gold, Prices, and Wages Under the Greenback Standard*, University of California Publications in Economics, vol. 1, Berkeley, March 1908, p. 91, utilized a portion of the retail data in the *Weeks Report* for 1860-1880. The Mitchell series was included as one of the links in the cost-of-living index estimate of the Federal Reserve Bank of New York (series E 157). The Hoover Consumer Price Index for 1851-1880 was based largely on a summarization of all of the usable retail price information from the *Weeks Report*, with some additions from other sources. The Rees' cost-of-living index utilized some components of the Douglas' index, but most of the data were compiled from mail-order catalogs, newspapers, and other sources.

Over the years there has been considerable improvement in the quality of the price reporting, in the scope of the data, and in the construction of index numbers. The lists of commodities that are now included in the price collection program cover a wider range of goods in the market, and services are represented in the "cost-of-living" indexes. Commodities and services are now defined fairly precisely and the current collection methods give the opportunity of securing supplementary data on discounts, terms of delivery, and other necessary information to measure price change. Data for weighting systems for index numbers can now be taken from the greatly improved expenditure studies, censuses, and other official statistics.

As the indexes and price reports were extended to earlier years, many of these advantages making for better price measures were not present. The range of commodities and services for which information could be obtained from sur-

viving records was very limited. At the wholesale level, the commodity coverage was limited primarily to raw materials and goods in the early stages of processing. The limited coverage of finished goods, especially after the Civil War, is an important factor in the interpretation of price changes. At retail, the available price data were relatively scant and the emphasis was on food and dry goods prices, with little information for other less important commodities and for rents and services. The perennial problem of changes in qualities, which is still present to some extent in the current indexes, becomes accentuated as price comparisons are made over longer periods of time.

The newspapers and other sources from which prices were assembled for the early years give only brief or vague descriptions for the commodities quoted and the compiler could not always be assured that quotations over time were for the same quality. Incomplete files, nominal prices, and nonpublication in some issues were among the many other problems encountered. Data obtained from records of surviving firms raise the further question of how well these surviving firms represented the movement of prices for all firms for the period under consideration.

E 1-100. General note.

Wholesale price indexes are compiled from prices in primary markets; that is, prices pertaining to the first major commercial transaction for each commodity. The quotations are usually selling prices of manufacturers or producers, or prices quoted on organized exchanges or markets. They are not prices received by wholesalers, distributors, or jobbers.

In addition to the indexes presented here, brief descriptions of the coverage and calculation techniques for other indexes may be found in G. F. Warren and F. A. Pearson, *Wholesale Prices for 213 Years, 1720-1932*, Cornell University Agricultural Experiment Station, Memoir 142, Ithaca, 1932, pp. 167-196; and in BLS Bulletin No. 284, *Index Numbers of Wholesale Prices in the United States and Foreign Countries*, 1921, pp. 115-175. This bulletin also contains Wesley C. Mitchell's "The Making and Using of Index Numbers."

See also general note for series E 1-186.

E 1-12. Wholesale price indexes (Warren and Pearson), by major product groups, 1749-1890.

Source: George F. Warren and Frank A. Pearson, *Prices*, John Wiley and Sons, New York, 1933, pp. 11-13, 25-27.

The indexes are also presented in *Wholesale Prices for 213 Years, 1720-1932* (see general note, series E 1-100), part 1, pp. 7-10 and 84-111. The "all-commodities" index for 1749-1889, converted to the base of 1926, is included in BLS Bulletin No. 572, *Wholesale Prices, 1931, 1933*, appendix, pp. 111-114.

The primary aim of Warren and Pearson was to present monthly comprehensive index numbers for the 19th century corresponding to those of BLS for 1890 and later years. The full series constitutes the longest index now available for 1720-1932. For 1890-1932, Warren and Pearson used the BLS indexes (series E 13-24) converted to the base 1910-14. Their work covered the period 1797-1890, and the index was extended back to 1720 by Herman M. Stoker.

The bulk of the prices on which the index is based relate to New York City and were obtained from newspapers, supplemented with prices published in the *Report of the Secretary of the Treasury on the State of the Finances* (usually referred to as the *U. S. Finance Report*) for 1863. The number of products included in the all-items index numbers for 1797-1890 varied from a low of 113 in 1830 to 146 in 1880. For the extension back to 1720, Stoker encountered some serious gaps in the available source materials, especially for years prior to 1749. For 1720–1748, the price data were scarce and irregular, and an index could be computed only for certain months in each year. For 1749–1782, the number of commodities included generally varied from 11 to 19; and for 1783–1796, 71 series were available for most years.

The index numbers for 1797–1890 are weighted arithmetic averages of relatives, computed first on the 1876–91 base then converted to the 1910–14 base using the relationship with BLS index numbers for 1890–1893. When one commodity was substituted for another, a linking procedure was employed. Two all-commodity indexes were prepared, one with fixed group weights throughout the whole period, and one with varying group weights. The latter is presented here as series E 1.

Separate subindexes (series E 2–12) were computed by Warren and Pearson for the 10 groups of commodities formerly used by BLS with a supplemental index for spirits. Within each group, weights representing the importance of the priced commodities in the total trade of the United States were varied over the years to represent, insofar as possible, changes in importance. (Specific mention should be made of the reduction in the importance of cotton during the Civil War period. Cotton was scarce and prices very high so weights were based on the amount available for consumption for 1861–1866 and on production for 1867–1871.) Censuses, imports, exports, and similar official figures were used as weighting factors. However, data were meager for the early years and some arbitrary weight assignments were necessary.

For 1787–1800, Stoker constructed a "71-commodity index" with the same commodity group classification and methods of calculation as those employed by Warren and Pearson. These all-commodity and group indexes were linked to the Warren-Pearson indexes. His "15-commodity index" for 1720–1787 based on the 11–19 items (practically all farm products and foods) was in turn linked to the 71-commodity index.

There are discrepancies between *Prices* and *Memoir 142* for farm products (series E 2) for 1807, 1808, and 1827. The figures shown in series E 2 are averages of monthly data in *Memoir 142*.

E 13–24. Wholesale price indexes (BLS), by major product groups, 1890–1951.

Source: 1890–1950, BLS, *Handbook of Labor Statistics*, 1950 edition, p. 118; 1951, 1951 supplement to the *Handbook*, p. 42.

Since 1902, when BLS began regular publication of wholesale price indexes, there have been a number of changes in lists of items, weighting factors, base periods, and methods of computing the indexes. Detailed descriptions of the early unweighted index numbers, and later the weighted indexes, are included in various annual bulletins on wholesale prices beginning with Bulletin No. 39, issued in March 1902. The figures shown in series E 13–24 are weighted index numbers of the fixed base weighted aggregative type.

In 1914, BLS recalculated its series back to 1890 using as weights the quantity of each priced item marketed in 1909 but retained the base 1890–99. The system of classification for group indexes was generally according to origin rather than end use and each commodity was included in only one group index. For 1914–1921, the index series were continued with little change except for expanding the list of priced items and rebasing the indexes several times. In 1920, the year 1913 was adopted as the base period in order to provide a prewar standard for measuring price changes.

In 1921, a revision of the indexes extended the commodity coverage to include about 400 items as compared with 250 to 325 in previous years. The weighting factors were changed to represent the quantity of each priced item marketed in 1919. At this time an important change was made in the method of grouping commodities. Articles properly classified in more than one major group were included in the appropriate groups with their total weights but, in the all-commodities index, the weights for such articles were counted only once. In addition, a rearrangement of commodities within groups was made to provide separate indexes for 37 subgroups.

When the 1926 base period was adopted in 1927, the indexes were recalculated back to 1913 with new sets of weights (see BLS Bulletin No. 473, *Wholesale Prices, 1913 to 1927*, pp. 2–5). The figures for 1890–1912 were converted, not recalculated in detail.

In subsequent years, the weighting factors were brought up to date from time to time. Major additions to the lists of priced items in 1931 and again in 1940 provided better coverage of manufactured articles than in earlier indexes. By 1951, when these indexes were discontinued, the number of subgroups for which separate series were available had been enlarged to 49.

Because of changes in the list of commodities and in the weighting factors, the indexes were calculated by the chain relative method. In this way, comparisons between any two periods were based on the same commodities with the same weights. Throughout the whole period, the weight used for each priced commodity was the quantity marketed for that class of commodity. Classes of commodities not represented by an item in the list priced were not represented in the weighting factors.

Table I contains a summary of the number of commodities and the weights used for the indexes in series E 13.

Table I. Number of Price Series and Weighting Factors Used in BLS Wholesale Price Index (All Commodities, Series E 13): 1890 to 1951

Year	Number of series	Weights used
1949–1951	900–947	Quantities marketed 1929 and 1931
1940–1948	881–890	
1938–1939	813	
1934–1937	784	
1932–1933	784	Quantities marketed 1927 and 1929
1931	784	Quantities marketed 1925 and 1927
1930	550	
1926–1929	404–550	Quantities marketed 1923 and 1925
1924–1925	526–528	
1922–1923	450–478	Quantities marketed 1921 and 1923
1920–1921	390–450	Quantities marketed 1919 and 1921
1914–1919	296–371	Quantities marketed 1914 and 1919
1913	252	Quantities marketed 1909 and 1914
1890–1912	251–261	Quantities marketed 1909

The price quotations on which the indexes were based were obtained by mail from leading manufacturers or selling agents or from such other sources as standard trade publications, reports of boards of trade, and produce exchanges. Before 1913, most of the data referred to the New York market but after 1913, quotations were obtained in several major markets for a number of important commodities.

For articles subject to frequent fluctuations in price, monthly averages were made up of quotations for one day in each week and for a portion of the period from daily quotations. For other articles, monthly, quarterly, or semiannual quotations were secured.

Considerable attention was devoted to obtaining descriptive details so that price comparisons were based on the same or comparable commodities. By 1931, BLS had developed a specification for each commodity in the index. These specifications defined quality as precisely as possible, including the principal price-determining characteristics, terms of sale, and other details. These specifications were refined and improved over the years.

The prices used in the index were usually net cash prices, f.o.b., for the article described by the specification. Delivered prices were included only when it was customary for an industry to quote on the delivered basis.

See also general note for series E 1–100.

E 25–41. Wholesale price indexes (BLS), by major product groups, 1913–1957.

Source: BLS Bulletin No. 1235, *Wholesale Prices and Price Indexes, 1957*, p. 26.

The current (1958) BLS wholesale price indexes on the 1947–49 base period were begun in 1952 but calculated to 1947, using new samples of items and new weights. However, the 1947–49 base period index is the official index beginning with January 1952, and does not replace the 1926 base series as the official index for 1947–1951. The new series of indexes was spliced to the former series (converted) by linking as of January 1947. Indexes shown for 1913–1946 are conversions of series E 13–24. The former group indexes were spliced with the new ones when the value aggregate of commodities in the former group represented 50 percent or more of the value of shipments in 1947 for all commodities (priced and unpriced) in the group.

With the revision in 1952, the conceptual definition of the index was not altered, but major changes in coverage and methods were adopted. The list of priced commodities was expanded from 947 to approximately 1,800, embracing nearly 5,000 separate series. The weighting factors for each commodity represented the value of shipments for the specific commodity priced and for all others in the same group which were known (or assumed) to have price movements similar to those for the commodity priced. By this method of weighting, values for all commodities in a group are accounted for and the group automatically has its proper representation in the all-commodities index. The weight universe includes the net selling value of all commodities included in the producing and processing sector of the economy *including* sales for exports and imports for consumption but *excluding* interplant transfers, military goods, construction, real estate, transportation, securities, printing and publishing, and transactions for services.

The indexes are calculated as averages of relatives weighted by values of shipments. This is algebraically equivalent to quantity weighted aggregative indexes but allows for more flexibility in processing. As in all the official indexes, the linking process is used when there are changes in lists of commodities, changes in weighting factors, or other changes making for noncomparability. In the case of quality changes, adjustments are made to obtain month-to-month relatives for the same quality insofar as possible. If the change in description is minor, direct comparisons are made between the price of the old and the new items. For major quality changes, efforts are made to secure from the producer an estimate of the proportion of the gross price change due to quality differences and to a price change. When such information cannot be obtained, the new quality is linked into the index, thus assuming that the full price change is due to quality change.

Since the revised index was initiated, there have been two changes in the weighting factors. Value of shipments in 1952 and 1953 were introduced in 1955 and only relatively minor changes were made in the list of items priced. Another revision in the weighting factors to represent value of shipments in 1954 was introduced beginning January 1958.

Most of the prices in the index are collected by mail directly from the manufacturer or other producer. A few are reported by trade associations or organized exchanges and some are obtained from authoritative trade publications or from other government agencies that collect price data for their regular work.

Before 1952, prices used were monthly averages of 1-day-a-week prices. Thereafter, prices have been for the most part those of the Tuesday of the week which includes the 15th of the month. However, for some commodities another day may be used as a more representative day.

Whenever possible, prices are obtained at the production point or at the central marketing point. Delivered prices are used only when it is the practice of the industry to quote prices on this basis. Prices obtained from manufacturers or other producers are subject to the applicable trade and quantity discounts. Cash discounts are deducted from the price when it is determined that most buyers avail themselves of the reduced prices. Excise taxes are excluded from the price. Closeout sales prices are usually not used. Free deals or allowances are used when possible in arriving at the net price to be used for index calculation. Nominal prices are used when they are indicative of the market situation and no other price is available.

For a complete description of techniques used in the Wholesale Price Index, see BLS Bulletin No. 1168, *Techniques of Preparing Major BLS Statistical Series*, 1954, chap. 10.

See also general note for series E 1–100.

E 42–55. Wholesale price indexes (BLS), for economic sectors, by stage of processing, 1913–1957.

Source: 1913–1946, **series E 42, 43, 47, and 53**, BLS Bulletin No. 1235, *Wholesale Prices and Price Indexes, 1957*, p. 26; (these series on a 1926 base appear in the following publications: 1913–1941, BLS, *Handbook of Labor Statistics*, 1941 edition, p. 733; 1942–1946, BLS Bulletin No. 947, *Wholesale Prices, 1947*, p. 6); 1947–1957, BLS Bulletin No. 1235, *op. cit.*, p. 27.

Although the basic weights, the price data, and the calculation methods for these indexes were the same as those used for the regular indexes, the series shown comprise two parts, one for 1913–1946 and the second for 1947–1957. Prior to the revision of the regular Wholesale Price Index (WPI) in 1952 (which was carried back to 1947), each commodity in the WPI was classified in one of three groups: Raw, semimanufactured, or manufactured. The prices were weighted using quantities as specified for series E 13–24. The list of commodities included in each classification is shown in BLS Bulletin No. 473, p. 62.

The more refined economic sector classification used for 1947–1957 required adjustments to these procedures. Many commodities were considered to fall appropriately in more than one category. The base weight for each such article was, therefore, distributed among the economic sectors on the basis of percentage distributions by end use, derived from the BLS interindustry studies for 1947. The same price series was used in several sectors when a commodity was classified in more than one sector. It was recognized that this procedure had some disadvantages, but it was believed to have little effect on the measurement of price trend.

In splicing the two parts, the index for "raw materials" was considered as most nearly comparable with the new "crude materials for further processing"; "semimanufactured" with "intermediate materials, supplies, and components"; and "manufactured" with "finished goods."

E 56–64. Wholesale price indexes (BLS), by durability of product, 1947–1957.

Source: BLS Bulletin No. 1235, *Wholesale Prices and Price Indexes, 1957*, pp. 32 and 33.

These indexes were constructed by recombining commodity segments of the regular BLS Wholesale Price Index according to durability. The basic weights, the price data, and the calculation methods were the same as for the regular indexes (see text for series E 25–41). The commodity groups included in each of these special indexes are listed in the source, pp. 12–14.

Manufactured commodities were generally classified on the same basis as that used by the Federal Reserve Board for its Index of Industrial Production. The classification of the "raw or slightly processed goods" was based for the most part on that used by Frederick C. Mills in *Prices in Recession and Recovery*, National Bureau of Economic Research, New York, 1936, pp. 472–474.

E 65–67. Wholesale price indexes (BLS), by 2 levels of processing, for identical commodities, 1890–1926.

Source: BLS Bulletin No. 440, *Wholesale Prices, 1890 to 1926*, pp. 28–29.

These series were calculated for the first time in 1915, were extended back to 1890, and continued through 1926. The items in each of the indexes were selected from those included in the BLS regular wholesale price index (see series E 13). The indexes are fixed weight aggregative indexes, derived by weighting the price series with the estimated quantity of each article marketed in 1919. Similar figures for 1890–1914 on the 1914 base, using 1909 quantity weights may be found in BLS Bulletin No. 181, *Wholesale Prices, 1890–1914*, pp. 28–29.

E 68–100. General note.

The inadequacy of the available statistics on commodity-price and wage movements over long periods of time led to the formation of the International Scientific Committee on Price History in 1929. In the United States, the attention of this Committee was directed to providing long series of prices for important commodities for pre-Civil War years. Price history research was initiated or expanded for 6 important markets—Philadelphia, Charleston, S.C., Cincinnati, New Orleans, New York City, and Boston. Information is presented here only for the first 4 of these markets.

The results of the investigations in all 6 areas were summarized in the form of wholesale price index numbers by the individual research directors and presented by Arthur H. Cole in *Wholesale Commodity Prices in the United States, 1700 to 1861*, Harvard University Press, Cambridge, 1938. A statistical supplement to Cole's report contains the actual monthly quotations for approximately 45 commodities for the years covered in each market.

The source materials for the price data included newspapers, merchants price lists, account books, and similar records that could be located. Differences in the availability of price and weighting data from area to area contributed to differences in the indexes derived, particularly with respect to the appropriate base periods, the length of the series, and the classifications of commodities for subindexes.

E 68–81. Wholesale price indexes (Bezanson), for Philadelphia, unweighted geometric average, 1784–1861.

Source: Anne Bezanson, Robert D. Gray, and Miriam Hussey, *Wholesale Prices in Philadelphia, 1784–1861*, part I, University of Pennsylvania Industrial Research Study No. 29, Philadelphia, 1936, p. 392.

See also general note for series E 68–100.

Records of prices for Philadelphia provided continuous price reports for 186 series covering 140 different commodities for 1784–1861 and 205 series for 157 commodities for 1819–1861. Monthly relative prices for the individual commodities and changes in the description of the commodities quoted are included in part II of the source, published as Industrial Research Study No. 30. Bezanson and her associates have also computed indexes for 1852–1896, corresponding to those for the earlier part of the century, which are available in a BLS pamphlet, *Wholesale Price Indexes for Philadelphia, 1852–96: Annual Group Totals*.

Indexes for all commodities and for subindexes using different modes of classification were computed as unweighted geometric averages of price relatives. Two all-commodities indexes were prepared, one based on 140 commodities (series E 68) and one for a more limited period for 157 commodities.

In addition to the subindexes selected for inclusion here, other subindexes for commodity groupings generally comparable to those of the BLS were also calculated. All indexes are available on a monthly basis.

E 82. Wholesale price indexes (Bezanson), for Philadelphia, unweighted arithmetic average, 1720–1861.

Source: See source for series E 68–81.

For the colonial period, Bezanson and her associates obtained some price data for 82 series. Because of the gaps in the data, however, indexes for the early years were based on prices for many fewer commodities.

Indexes for 1720–1861 were computed as unweighted arithmetic averages of relatives of prices for the same 12 commodities for the full period. The source also includes an unweighted geometric index of 20 commodities for 1731–1861.

E 83–89. Wholesale price indexes (Taylor), for Charleston, S. C., 1732–1861.

Source: Arthur H. Cole, *Wholesale Commodity Prices in the United States, 1700–1861*, Harvard University Press, Cambridge, 1938, pp. 153, 155–157, and 159–167.

See also articles by George Rogers Taylor, "Wholesale Commodity Prices at Charleston, S. C., 1732–1791," *Journal of Economic History*, February 1932, pp. 356–377, and "Wholesale Commodity Prices at Charleston, S. C., 1796–1861," August 1932 supplement to the *Journal*, pp. 848–868.

See also general note for series E 68–100.

Taylor's research in commodity prices was summarized in separate index numbers for 8 different periods. The choice of time periods was made partly to reflect business conditions in Charleston and partly to take account of availability of data. Newspapers and original manuscript materials produced price series for a maximum of 32 items for 1818–1842 and a minimum of 6 for 1732–1747. Gaps were relatively frequent and no quotations at all appeared for 1792–1795.

Indexes for each period were weighted arithmetic averages of price relatives, with weights representing the approximate importance of each commodity in South Carolina commerce. The weights were unchanged for all years within each time period but were changed from period to period. An all-commodities series was made up of prices for 6 articles for

1732–1747, 10 articles for 1748–1761, and 16 articles for 1762–1775. In each period, rice represented 50 to 64 percent of the total weight. For the 5 later time intervals, weighted sub-indexes were combined with group weights based on the following total number of price series: 1780–1791, 20; 1796–1812, 18; 1813–1822, 13; 1818–1842, 32; 1843–1861, 20. During these years, the importance of rice declined from about 37 percent of the total weight to 5 to 7 percent, while the importance of cotton increased from zero in 1791 to almost 35 percent in 1843–1861.

The all-commodity series (E 83) was obtained by splicing the indexes for the separate periods.

E 90–92. Wholesale price indexes (Berry), for Cincinnati, 1816–1861.

Source: **Series E 90**, 1816–1860, Arthur H. Cole, *Wholesale Commodity Prices in the United States, 1700–1861*, Harvard University Press, Cambridge, 1938, p. 185 (averages of the monthly data were computed from the source); 1861, estimated by Ethel Hoover from series E 91 and E 92 with weights shown in Cole (cited above), p. 81. **Series E 91–92**, Thomas S. Berry, *Western Prices Before 1861*, Harvard University Press, Cambridge, 1943, p. 564.

See also general note for series E 68–100.

These indexes were weighted arithmetic averages of price relatives, computed for 3 separate time periods which were spliced to obtain the continuous series. For 1816–1825, prices for 21 commodities were assembled, 13 "identified with northern agriculture" and 8 "not identified with northern agriculture." For 1824–1846, the total was 37 with 20 in the first category and 17 in the second. For 1846–1861, the total was 50, with 29 for northern agriculture, and 21 for other. The weighting factors for the first period were estimated from New Orleans receipts in 1825, while those for the 2 later periods were based on receipts at Cincinnati for 1845–1848 and 1852–1856. Berry's analysis is accompanied by many tabulations of supplementary data, including actual prices for individual articles.

E 93–95. Wholesale price indexes (Berry), for Ohio River Valley, 1788–1817.

Source: Thomas S. Berry, *Western Prices Before 1861*, Harvard University Press, Cambridge, 1943, pp. 563–564.

See also general note for E 68–100.

In his study of Cincinnati prices, Berry encountered considerable difficulty in obtaining price information for years before 1816. He enlarged his geographical coverage for the market to include Lexington and Louisville, Ky., and Pittsburgh, Pa., and was successful in constructing 14 commodity price series for 1788–1816 from data in "account books of backwoods merchants" and from local journals.

The indexes were computed as unweighted averages of price relatives. The annual prices used to obtain the relatives were medians of all Ohio Valley quotations for each item each year.

E 96–100. Wholesale price indexes (Taylor), for New Orleans, 1800–1861.

Source: Arthur H. Cole, *Wholesale Commodity Prices in the United States, 1700–1861*, Harvard University Press, Cambridge, 1938, pp. 170–179.

See also general note for series E 68–100.

A considerable difference was found in the volume of information available for New Orleans from decade to decade. Therefore, New Orleans indexes were prepared for 4 separate time periods. Data for 8 commodities, primarily agricultural, were combined into an index for "Louisiana" products for 1800–1812 (July). For a part of this period, 1804–1812 (April), 2 series were constructed, 1 for 29 domestic products and the other for 15 imported goods. For 2 later periods, the volume of data was sufficient to set up 3 sub-indexes, classifying the commodities by origin. The number of articles included was: For 1815–1842, 5 Louisiana products, 34 other domestic products, and 11 foreign imports; for 1840–1861, the corresponding numbers of articles were 4, 37, and 8.

All of the index numbers were calculated using the method of weighted averages of relatives. The weights in the several time periods represented the importance of the various commodities in the trade of New Orleans.

The all-commodities index (series E 96) was obtained by splicing the "all-commodities" indexes for the different periods.

E 101–112. General note.

From among the several hundred commodities for which wholesale prices have been published in various reports, 12 were selected for publication in the form of actual prices. Generally, consideration was given to representation of commodities in different product groups, importance in U. S. trade, and the length of the series available.

The descriptions for each commodity insofar as they could be determined and the sources from which the prices were compiled are shown below in the detailed notes for each series. When annual averages were not available in the original source, they were computed for this publication. If 12 monthly figures were presented, a simple average was calculated, but if only quarterly figures were given, straight line interpolation was used to estimate missing months.

It was not possible to obtain one continuously comparable series for the full period. The data were assembled from several sources for each commodity and there were, frequently, changes in the basis of quotation even in the same source. Two prices are shown for each year in which a change in the series occurred, if it was possible to obtain the information. In some instances, mostly prior to 1890, changes in the basis of quotation occurred and no overlapping prices were available. Such changes are noted in the text.

Prices for earlier years for some commodities are available in the same sources as those indicated for 1800, and in other publications. Because of limitations of time and space, however, figures prior to 1800 were not included in this chapter. For example, prices of wheat back to 1700 may be found in the publication by Cole cited as the source for wheat prices for 1800–1825. Wheat prices in the New England colonies at 10-year intervals for 1630–1750 are included with prices for several other commodities in BLS Bulletin No. 604, *History of Wages in the United States From Colonial Times to 1928*, p. 19.

The *Annual Report of the Director of the Mint*, cited as the source for practically all series for some part of the period for 1825–1880, was used despite the lack of commodity descriptions. The prices included in this report were summaries of the New York prices included in the *U. S. Finance Reports* of 1863, 1873, and 1874 which had been compiled from the newspaper, *The New York Shipping and Commercial List*. Prices for 1875–1880 were also compiled from this source. Such descriptions as appear in the notes for each series when prices were taken from *U. S. Finance Reports* were obtained from the report for 1863.

An alternate source for many of the price series included in the *Aldrich Reports* (cited for data prior to 1890) is *Monthly Summary of Commerce and Finance in the United States*, 57th Congress, 2d Session, House Doc. No. 15, part 1, 1902, pp. 59–100. This summary covers not only the years included in the *Aldrich Reports*, but also extends the data through July 1902.

E 101. Wheat, 1800–1957.

Source: A.—1800–1825, Arthur H. Cole, *Wholesale Commodity Prices in the United States, 1700–1861*, Statistical Supplement, Harvard University Press, Cambridge, 1938; B.—1825–1880, *Annual Report of the Director of the Mint to the Secretary of the Treasury for the Fiscal Year Ended June 30, 1881*, p. 50; C.—1880–1890, *Wholesale Prices, Wages, and Transportation*, Senate Report No. 1394, 52d Congress, 2d Session, part 2, 1893, p. 61 (one of the reports usually referred to as the *Aldrich Reports*); D.—1890–1957, compiled from Bureau of Labor Statistics records.

For 1800–1825, prices are for Philadelphia (commodity description not available). For 1825–1880, prices are for New York, "Northern" wheat; the *1863 U. S. Finance Report* (from which these prices were partially compiled) shows prices for "genesee" for most years, 1825–1863, but for a few years prices refer to "North River," "prime white," "western," "western red," or "mixed and red." For 1880–1890, prices are for "wheat No. 2, Winter, Chicago." For 1890–1913, prices are for Chicago "Range No. 1 Northern Spring and No. 2 Red Winter" in carlots. For 1913–1948, prices are for Kansas City, "No. 2, hard (ordinary)" in carlots. For 1949–1957, prices are for Kansas City, "No. 2, hard winter, closing spot market price, carlots, f.o.b. track."

See also general note for series E 101–112.

E 102. Wheat flour, 1800–1957.

Source: See sources cited for series E 101; 1800–1825, source A; 1825–1870, source B; 1870–1890, source C, p. 79; 1890–1957, source D.

For 1800–1825, prices are for Philadelphia, "Superfine" flour, per barrel of 196 pounds. For 1825–1870, prices are for New York, "Superfine" flour, per barrel. For 1870–1890, prices were provided by a New York firm (commodity description not available). For 1890–1913, prices are for "winter straights, f.o.b., New York," per barrel. For 1913–1943, prices are for "Straights, hard winter, white, in carlots, f.o.b., Kansas City," per barrel. During 1943, the basis of quotation was changed from per barrel to flour in sacks, per 100 pounds. For 1950–1957, prices are for "hard winter, bakery, short patents, plain or enriched, in 100-pound sacks, carlots, f.o.b. mill, Kansas City," per 100 pounds. During 1918 and a part of 1946, prices were quoted on the standard provided under government regulation.

See also general note for series E 101–112.

E 103. Sugar, 1800–1957.

Source: See sources for series E 101; 1800–1825, source A; 1825–1860, source B; 1860–1890, source C, p. 114; 1890–1957, source D.

For 1800–1825, prices are for the Philadelphia market. Prices for 1800 refer to "Muscovado, brown"; 1801–1802 (October), "Muscovado"; 1802 (November)–1813 (October), "Muscovado, first quality"; 1813 (November)–1815 (April), "Muscovado, unspecified"; 1815 (May)–1825, "Muscovado, prime." For 1825–1860, prices are for New York, "Cuba" sugar; the *1863 U. S. Finance Report* (from which the data were compiled) quoted "Muscovado" for 1825–1829 and 1845–1860, "Cuba Muscovado" for 1830–1836 and "Cuba" for 1837–1844. For 1860–1890, prices are for "Refined, granulated" sugar (no market specified). For 1890–1946, prices are for New York, "Granulated" sugar. Prices were quoted for sugar in barrels until 1955 when the basis of quotation was changed to 100-pound paper bags. For 1947–1957, the description was amplified to "granulated, domestic, cane, refined, New York,"

per pound. Prices for 1934–1957 include the excise tax of 53½ cents per 100 pounds, effective in May 1934.

See also general note for series E 101–112.

E 104. Cotton, raw, 1800–1957.

Source: 1800–1890, Mathew B. Hammond, *The Cotton Industry, an Essay in American Economic History*, American Economic Association, New Series No. I, Macmillan, New York, 1897, p. 358; 1890–1957, see source D for series E 101.

For 1800–1890, prices refer to "Middling uplands" cotton for the New York market and are available back to 1790. For 1800–1820, prices are estimates made by merchants or government officials. For 1821–1890, prices were taken from James L. Watkin, *Production and Price of Cotton for One Hundred Years*, published by the Department of Agriculture, 1895. For 1890–1941, prices are for New York, "Upland, Middling" cotton, spot. In 1936, "7/8 inch" was added to the description. For 1941–1954 (July), prices are for "Middling, 15/16 inch," 10 spot market average. For 1954 (July)–1956 (August), the number of markets included in the average was increased from 10 to 14. The July 1954 average for 10 markets was $0.342 per pound and for 14 markets, $0.341 per pound. For 1956 (August)–1957, prices are for "Middling, 1-inch," 14 spot market average. In August 1956, the average for 15/16-inch staple was $0.348 per pound and for 1-inch staple $0.357 per pound.

See also general note for series E 101–112.

E 105. Wool, 1813–1957.

Source: See sources cited for series E 101; 1813–1825, source A; 1825–1850, source B, p. 60; 1850–1890, source C, p. 387; 1890–1957, source D.

For 1813–1825, prices are for Philadelphia, "Merino clean" wool except for 1819 and 1820 when description was "Merino" wool. For 1825–1850, prices are for New York, "Merino" wool. For 1850–1890, prices are for Boston, "Ohio, fine fleece, scoured." For 1890–1913, prices are for, "Domestic, Ohio, fine fleece (x and xx grades), scoured"; for 1913–1945, for Boston, "Domestic, Territory, staple, fine and fine medium, scoured"; for 1946–1949 for Boston, "Domestic, Territory, staple, fine combing, graded, scoured." For 1950–1957, the description was changed with no difference in price level to "Domestic, fine, good French combing and staple, clean basis."

See also general note for series E 101–112.

E 106. Cotton sheeting, 1800–1957.

Source: See sources cited for series E 101; 1800–1847, source A; 1847–1890, source C, p. 155; 1890–1957, source D.

Prices are for Philadelphia, "Russian, unspecified" for 1800–1804, "Russian, brown" for 1805–1814 and 1824–1847, and "Russian, half bleached" for 1815–1823. Prices were shown "per piece" (approximately 100 yards). For 1847–1890, prices are for "sheeting, brown, 4-4, Atlantic A," per yard (no market specified). For 1890–1912, prices are for "brown, Indian head, 4-4, 2.85 yards to pound, factory." For 1913–1941, description same except that the width designation was changed in 1913 to "36-inch" instead of "4/4," and "48x48, carded yarn" was added in 1923. For 1941–1943 (May), prices are for "Unbleached, 36-inch, 48x48, 2.85 yards per pound, Class A, nonfeeler, f.o.b. mill." For 1943 (May)–1947, description same except for change from "48x48" to "48x44." For 1948–1957, prices are for "Unbleached (series 1), 40-inch, 48x48, 2.85 yards per pound, Class A, nonfeeler, f.o.b. mill." The January 1948 price for the former description (36-inch, 48x44) was $0.279 and of the new description (40-inch, 48x48) was $0.289 per pound.

See also general note for series E 101–112.

E 107.   Coal, anthracite, 1800–1957.

Source: See sources cited for series E 101; 1800–1825, source A; 1825–1833, source B; 1890–1957, source D. For 1833–1890, American Iron and Steel Association, *Statistics of the American and Foreign Iron Trades for 1896*, Philadelphia, 1897, p. 91.

Prices are for Philadelphia, "Virginia" coal for 1800–1811 and 1814–1825, and "Domestic" for 1812 and 1813. There was no description for 1826–1833. For 1825–1833, prices are for New York, "anthracite coal (Schuylkill)." For 1833–1890, prices are for "Schuylkill white ash lump" coal, by the cargo, at Philadelphia, per gross ton. For 1890–1957, prices are for "Pennsylvania anthracite, chestnut," but the basis of quotation was changed several times. For 1890–1928, the basis was "New York Tidewater," per gross ton; for 1928–1931, "destination on tracks," per gross ton; for 1931–1947, per net ton (2000 pounds); and 1947–1957, "f.o.b. cars at mine" per net ton.

See also general note for series E 101–112.

E 108.   Steel rails, 1847–1957.

Source: 1847–1890, American Metal Market and Daily Iron and Steel Report, *Metal Statistics*, 1921, p. 91. For 1891–1957, see source D for series E 101.

For 1847–1867, prices are for "Iron rails, Eastern Pennsylvania mill" (production of steel rails did not exceed production of iron rails until 1877). The source also shows prices of iron rails of this description for 1868–1882. For 1867–1870, prices are for New York "Steel rails, Bessemer," per gross ton. For 1871–1890, prices are for "Steel rails, Pennsylvania mill." For 1891–1913, prices are for "Bessemer, Standard, f.o.b. mill, Pittsburgh," per long ton; for 1913–1946, for "Open hearth, standard, f.o.b. mill"; for 1947–1953 (April), for "Standard, heavier than 60 pounds, No. 1 open hearth, f.o.b. mill" (refinement of previous specification and quoted per 100 pounds— no break in series); and for 1953 (May)–1957, for "Standard, carbon steel, No. 1 open hearth, 115 pounds per linear yard, control cooled, base quantity, f.o.b. mill."

See also general note for series E 101–112.

E 109.   Nails, 1800–1957.

Source: See sources cited for series E 101; 1800–1828, source A; 1828–1834, source B, p. 54; 1890–1957, source D. For 1835–1890, see source for series E 107, 1833–1890, p. 87. (For 1835–1849, prices were compiled from the *Report of the Secretary of the Treasury*, 1849; for 1850–1859, by the American Iron and Steel Association from the books of the Duncannon Iron Company; and for 1860–1890, by an official of the Duncannon Iron Company.)

For 1800–1828, prices are for the Philadelphia market. For 1814–1827, prices are for "Cut nails, all sizes"; for other years, "assorted sizes." For 1828–1834, prices are for New York, "Nails, cut." For 1835–1890, prices are for "Cut nails." For 1890–1953, prices refer to "wire, 8 penny, fence and common, 100-pound keg, f.o.b. Pittsburgh." "Base price" was added to the description in 1926 and fence nails were not included after 1947. For 1953–1957, prices refer to "wire, carbon steel, 8 d, common, carload lots, f.o.b. mill." The April 1953 price for former specification was $7.41, and for the new specification was $7.33 per 100 pounds. "Packed in fiberboard boxes" was added to description in 1955.

See also general note for series E 101–112.

E 110.   Copper, 1800–1957.

Source: See sources cited for series E 101; 1800–1825, source A; 1825–1860, source B, p. 52; 1890–1957, source D. For 1860–1889, see source for series E 108, 1847–1867, p. 299.

For 1800–1825, prices are for the Philadelphia market. Prices are for "Copper in sheets," 1800–1801 (April) and 1805 (June)–1809 (June); "Sheathing unspecified," 1801 (May)–1802 (December), 1809 (July)–1818 (April), and 1824 (September)–1825; "Sheathing, cold rolled," 1803–1805 (May); and "Sheeting unspecified," 1818 (May)–1824 (August). For 1825–1860, prices are for New York, "Sheathing." For 1860–1889, prices are for New York, "Lake Copper." Price shown for 1890 is the same as that in *Metal Statistics, 1921*. For 1890–1907, prices are for New York, "Lake Copper"; for 1907–1927, for "Copper ingot, electrolytic, early delivery, refinery in New York"; for 1927–1953, for "Copper, electrolytic, delivered, Connecticut Valley"; and for 1954–1957, for "Copper ingot, electrolytic, producers' prices, delivered, f.o.b. cars, U. S. destination."

See also general note for series E 101–112.

E 111.   Turpentine, 1800–1957.

Source: See sources cited for series E 101; 1800–1825, source A; 1825–1840, source B, p. 56; 1840–1890, source C, p. 240; 1890–1957, source D.

For 1800–1825, prices are for the Philadelphia market per barrel (31½ gallons per barrel). No description was available, but a comparison of prices indicates that they may be for "soft" turpentine. For 1825–1840, prices are for the New York market (no description is available). For 1840–1890, prices are for New York, "Spirits of turpentine." For 1890–1942, prices are for "Southern, barrels, at New York." The description was amplified in 1936 by the addition of "carlots, ex dock, gum spirits." For 1942–1951, prices refer to "Gum spirits, bulk, f.o.b. Savannah, Ga." For 1952–1956 (October), quotations are for "Spirits of turpentine, tank cars, at New York." The January 1952 price for the former specification (Savannah) was $0.80 per gallon and for the new (New York), $0.76 per gallon. For 1956 (November)–1957, prices are for "gum, tank cars" at New York. The October 1956 price for the former specification (spirits) was $0.640 per gallon and for the new (gum), $0.635 per gallon.

See also general note for series E 101–112.

E 112.   Brick, 1849–1957.

Source: See sources cited for series E 101; 1849–1890, source C, p. 222; 1890–1957, source D.

For 1849–1890, prices are for "common domestic building" (market not indicated). For 1890–1933, prices are for "Common, Red, Domestic, at New York"; 1933–1947, for "Common building, f.o.b. plant" (composite of approximately 50 firms); for 1947–1957, for "Building brick, f.o.b. plant or New York dock" (composite of approximately 25 firms). Changes in list of firms from time to time did not result in any significant differences in the annual average prices.

See also general note for series E 101–112.

E 113–160.   General note.

An appropriate name for indexes of retail price changes has been the subject of considerable discussion. Most indexes that have at some time been called "cost-of-living" indexes measure changes in retail prices for the goods and services families buy. Insofar as possible, the retail prices are for the same list of items in the same localities, the same qualities, and the same quantities from one period to the next. The indexes, therefore, measure changes in costs for living in the same way and in the same place.

Generally, people tend to think of the amount of money they spend for commodities and services as their cost of living. Changes in total expenditures reflect changes in costs resulting from differences in the place or manner of living, such as shifts in the kinds of goods and services bought, and may represent a better or a worse standard than at some earlier date.

The term "Consumer Price Index" was adopted by the Bureau of Labor Statistics and the National Industrial Conference Board after much controversy during World War II regarding the BLS *Cost of Living Index*. For a discussion of differences in concept and measurement of the cost of living, see the *Report of the President's Committee on Cost of Living*, Office of Economic Stabilization, 1945.

E 113–139. Consumer price indexes (BLS), by major groups and subgroups, 1890–1957.

Source: BLS, *U. S. Consumer Price Indexes (1947–49 =100)*; *Historical Series A–1 to I–1*.

See also general note for series E 113–160.

The BLS Consumer Price Index measures changes in retail prices of the goods and services bought by city wage earners and clerical workers. It was originated on a comprehensive basis at the end of World War I when data were in demand for wage negotiations in shipbuilding cities. A Department of Labor study of the cost of living in 92 shipbuilding and other industrial centers was made in 1918–1919, as reported in BLS Bulletin No. 357, *Cost of Living in the United States*. The first publication of changes in the "cost of living" was in the *Monthly Labor Review* for October 1919 and regular publication has continued since February 1921. The frequency of publication was increased from semiannually to quarterly in 1935. Since September 1940, the index has been computed and published monthly in mimeograph releases and in the *Monthly Labor Review*.

The present index (1958) is based on prices of about 300 individual items. The list of goods and services priced for the index are those important in family expenditures and were chosen to represent price trends for all goods and services bought by families of wage earners and clerical workers. The selection was made on the basis of a detailed study of expenditures of 8,000 families in 1950 and studies of price trends for many individual items to determine items with similar price fluctuations. The average size of the families covered by the index was estimated to be about 3.3 persons and their average family income after taxes was estimated at about $4,160 in 1952.

The sample of 46 cities on which the index is based was chosen to represent all urban places with population of 2,500 or more in 1950. Characteristics of different city types which affect the way families spent their money were taken into account, including size, climate, density of population, level of income, and distance to market center (for small cities). Prices for foods and fuels and some services are obtained monthly in all cities. Prices for most other goods and services are obtained monthly in the 5 largest cities and quarterly on a rotating cycle in 41 cities. Separate indexes are computed for 20 large cities.

All retail price data are collected with the use of specifications to ensure comparisons from period to period of prices for the same or similar qualities insofar as possible. These specifications include the quality factors associated with price differences and other physical characteristics needed for identification from store to store and from one pricing period to the next. A discussion of the use of specifications is contained in BLS Bulletin No. 1182, *Average Retail Prices: Collection and Calculation Techniques and Problems*. Every effort is made to obtain the prices paid by the customer, not list prices from which discounts are normally given. Sales taxes are reflected wherever applicable.

Food prices are obtained from about 2,000 food stores, including all important types of food retailers in each city. Rent figures are collected from tenants for approximately 30,000 rental units selected from block listings of the total rental housing market in each city. Prices for other goods and services are obtained from about 4,000 retail and service establishments patronized by wage earner and clerical families and including department stores, specialty shops, etc., with a minimum of 4 quotations per item per city in most cases. For most cities, the samples of reporters are located in the city limits, but for rents, data are obtained from the "urbanized areas" as defined by the Census Bureau.

Price collection for the majority of goods and services is made by personal visit of BLS full-time field representatives. Food prices are collected by local part-time agents while for some items mail collection is supplemented by occasional personal visits.

The indexes are calculated using a variation of the base quantity weighted index formula. In practice, the aggregates are obtained by applying price relatives to "value weights" representing the cost of 1951–1952 quantities as determined from the 1950 family expenditure study. The importance of each item in the index represents the expenditure for the item and in addition the expenditure for all items it represents. City indexes are computed using the expenditure weights for each city. National indexes are calculated by combining city data with weights representing their 1950 population.

For a more complete description of the current index see *Techniques of Preparing Major BLS Statistical Series*, BLS Bulletin No. 1168, chap. 9.

A number of changes in coverage, methodology, classification, and base periods have been made since these indexes were first issued in 1919 with index numbers back to 1913. Until 1935, the "cost-of-living" indexes were calculated using quantity weights derived from the BLS family expenditure study in 1917–1919. The weights related to the individual items priced and to geographic areas rather than to individual cities. Group indexes were combined with percentages representing the importance of the group in total expenditures. The goods and services included were described in general terms only. The measurement of price change for comparable articles was accomplished by careful attention on the part of the field representative in obtaining price quotations for the same quality from one period to the next from the same respondents.

A major improvement in the index calculation method was introduced in 1935 and is described in Faith M. Williams, Margaret H. Hogg, and Ewan Clague, "Revision of Index of Cost of Goods Purchased by Wage Earners and Lower-Salaried Workers," *Monthly Labor Review*, September 1935, pp. 819–837. In the 1935 revision, consumption weights for individual cities were derived from the 1917–1919 expenditure study, and population weights (average population in 1920 and 1930) were used to combine city data. At this time, indexes back to 1913 were recalculated based on the prices collected for the former indexes. "Specification pricing" was also introduced in 1935; see John H. Cover, *Retail Price Behavior*, University of Chicago Press, 1935.

Another revision was completed in 1940 to take into account the results of a study of family expenditures in 1934–1936. At this time, indexes back to 1935 were recalculated with weights derived from this study. Indexes for earlier years were not recalculated completely, but the former group indexes were recombined with revised weights. Other improvements introduced are described in *The Bureau of Labor*

Statistics' New Index of Cost of Living, Serial No. R. 1156, reprinted from the August 1940 issue of the *Monthly Labor Review.*

Table II. Number of Cities Included in BLS Consumer Price Index for All Items (E 113) and for Foods (E 114-115), and Weights Used: 1913 to 1957

Period	Number of cities		Weights used	
	All items	Food	Family expenditures in—	Population in—
1913-1917	19	40-45	1917-19	none
1918-1924	32	45-51	1917-19	1920 and 1930
1925-1930	32	51	1917-19, [1] 1934-36	1920 and 1930
1930-1934	33	51	[1] 1934-36	1930
1935-1942	33-34	56-64	1934-36	1930
1943-1949	34	56	1934-36	May 1942
1950-1952	34	56	[2] 1947-49	1950
1953-1957	46	46	[3] 1950	1950

[1] Individual item weights for 1913-1935 were derived from the 1917-19 study. Group weights as shown.
[2] Family expenditures in 7 cities.
[3] Adjusted to 1952 for price change.

During World War II, shortages and rationing imposed many measurement problems. The adjustments made by BLS in weights and in pricing are described in Faith M. Williams, "Bureau of Labor Statistics Cost of Living Index in Wartime," *Monthly Labor Review*, July 1943.

Prior to the comprehensive revision in 1953, when present index procedures and coverage were introduced, an "interim adjustment" was made in 1951. This adjustment included a correction for "new unit bias" in the rent index (resulting from wartime rent controls) for 1940-1950 and the introduction of revised commodity weights based on expenditure surveys in 7 cities during 1947-1949. The revised commodity weights were used to recalculate indexes back to January 1950 but not earlier years. A description of the adjustment is in BLS Bulletin No. 1039, *Interim Adjustment of Consumer Price Index.* The "interim adjustment" resulted in the publication of two index series for 1940-1952—the "old series" and the "adjusted series." When the comprehensive revision was completed in 1953, the revised indexes were linked to the "adjusted series."

In the 1953 revision, the city sample was changed to include small and medium-sized cities and the expenditure concept was broadened to include the purchase price of a house. (See February and April 1956 issues of *Monthly Labor Review* for a discussion of housing costs in the CPI.) Pricing of restaurant meals and home repair and maintenance items was begun and several other items were added. Items were regrouped into 8 major groups.

The BLS Consumer Price Index has been the subject of extensive analysis and investigation. A comprehensive review made by a committee of the American Statistical Association in 1933 led to the 1935 revision. During World War II, the effect of such factors as quality deterioration, "black market" prices, disappearance of special sales prices and low-end merchandise, and similar wartime developments was estimated by the President's Committee on the Cost of Living to have produced an understatement of the rise in retail prices from January 1941 to September 1944 by a maximum of 3 to 4 index points. The Committee also estimated that if small cities were included in the national average, an additional half point would be added. The various reports submitted to and by the President's Committee are included in its report cited in the general note for series E 113-160. The continuation of

wartime conditions was taken into account in December 1945 when the Office of War Mobilization and Reconversion estimated that for the full period January 1941 to September 1945, the understatement amounted to a total of 5 index points for large and small cities combined.

In 1949, the Joint Committee on the Economic Report reviewed BLS methods in the compilation, composition, and presentation of the Consumer Price Index; see *The Consumers Price Index: Report of the Joint Committee on the Economic Report*, Joint Committee Print, 80th Congress, 2d Session, 1949.

In 1951, a Special Subcommittee of the House of Representatives held extensive hearings and concluded that the Consumer Price Index was generally adequate for the purpose for which it was intended. See *Consumers Price Index—Report of a Special Subcommittee of the Committee on Education and Labor*, House of Representatives, 82d Congress, 1st Session, Subcommittee Report No. 2, 1951.

E 140-147. Consumer price indexes (BLS), for special groups, 1935-1957.

Source: 1935-1946, BLS, *Consumer Price Index: Price Indexes for Selected Items and Groups*, July 1956, p. 2, March 1957, p. 9, and mimeographed historical tables; 1947-1957, *Monthly Labor Review*, April 1958, p. 468.

These indexes are based on a reclassification of the items priced for the Consumer Price Indexes (series E 113-139). The goods and services included in each series are listed in footnotes in the April 1958 issue of the *Monthly Labor Review.* The basic weights, price data, and calculation methods were the same as those used for the regular CPI.

E 148-156. Consumer price index (Hoover), 1851-1880.

Source: Ethel D. Hoover, "Prices in the 19th Century," *Studies in Income and Wealth*, vol. 24, Princeton University Press (forthcoming).

See also general note for series E 113-160.

The basic price data for these series are from Joseph D. Weeks, "The Average Retail Prices of Necessaries of Life," *Report on Statistics of Wages in Manufacturing Industries*, Tenth Census, vol. 20, 1886. Averages of retail prices for 58 commodities were calculated by making simple averages of the prices reported for each item by one or two storekeepers in approximately 40 cities. The consistency of price movement and price level between prices identified as of "June 1" and those as "year" averages led to the inclusion of all prices to calculate an all-city average for each year. In calculating the relative prices for each commodity, a comparability procedure was used; that is, for each year two average prices were calculated—one comparable with the preceding year and the other comparable with the following year. Data for these 58 commodities were supplemented with estimates of price change for services (shoe repairs and medical care) as well as some additional items important in family spending estimated from other sources. The number of price series included in each of the index groups was food, 40; clothing, 12; rents, 2; fuel and light, 5; and other, 7.

Relative prices for the individual commodities were combined with value weights derived from the study of family expenditures in Massachusetts in 1875, supplemented by detailed expenditures of 232 families as given in the *Aldrich Reports* (*Wholesale Prices*, part 1, pp. 62-63). The formula for calculation of the index was the algebraic equivalent of the Laspeyre index.

E 157. Cost-of-living indexes (Federal Reserve Bank of N.Y.), 1820–1913.

Source: Federal Reserve Bank of New York, *Index of Estimated Cost of Living in the United States* (1938 revision mimeographed).

Indexes for 1820–1952 converted to the 1947–49 base and figures showing purchasing power of the dollar "in terms of retail prices" for the same period are available in a mimeographed release with same title dated March 17, 1953.

See also general note for series E 113–160.

This index was obtained by splicing together parts of indexes already available to approximate a continuous series. No adjustments were made to the original series other than those necessary to convert to a common base period. Indexes for 1820–1839 were taken from Alvin H. Hansen's cost-of-living indexes which were based on wholesale prices for these years. For 1840–1859, the indexes used were also obtained from Hansen's index which had in turn utilized the weighted index of wholesale prices (assuming all unpriced items moved with all priced items) computed by Roland P. Falkner for the Senate Committee on Finance. The Falkner indexes for 1840–1891 may be found in Senate Report No. 1394 (*Aldrich Report*), *Wholesale Prices, Wages, and Transportation*, U. S. Senate Committee on Finance, 1893, p. 93. For 1860–1879, the Federal Reserve Bank used the relative cost-of-living series prepared by Wesley C. Mitchell, who calculated his index from retail price data for 60 of the "necessaries of life" included in the *Weeks Report*. The original series may be found in Mitchell's *Gold, Prices, and Wages Under the Greenback Standard*, University of California Publications in Economics, vol. 1, Berkeley, March 1908, p. 91. For 1880–1889, the indexes were those of W. Randolph Burgess in *Trends of School Costs* (see series E 158). For 1890–1909, Paul Douglas' "Most Probable Index of the Total Cost of Living for Workingmen" (see series E 159) as published in *American Economic Review*, March 1926 supplement, p. 22, was used. Indexes for 1910–1912 were derived from the cost-of-living index for Massachusetts appearing in the Department of Labor and Industries of the Commonwealth of Massachusetts, *Report of the Commission on the Necessaries of Life*, February 1920, p. 118.

E 158. Cost-of-living index (Burgess), 1841–1920.

Source: *The Review of Economic Statistics*, February 1934, vol. XVI, No. 2, p. 26.

Original data in dollars are shown in W. Randolph Burgess, *Trends of School Costs*, Russell Sage Foundation, New York City, 1920, p. 54.

See also general note for series E 113–160.

To determine changes in the purchasing power of teacher's salaries for his study of *Trends in School Costs*, Burgess compiled the series, "Cost of Living Per Week for a Small Family Using the Same Amount of the Same Commodities Over the Entire Period." This series is based on prices for 10 foods important in wage earners' spending. Quantity weights, derived from BLS 1901–1902 consumer expenditure studies, were used to combine prices of the 10 foods. On the assumption that other less important items fluctuated with food prices, the total food cost was adjusted upward to approximate the total weekly cost for all items for a typical wage earners' family of man, wife, and two children. The factor used for adjustment was based on the ratio of food costs to total costs in 1901. The source of the price data is indicated by general reference to BLS, the Massachusetts Bureau of Statistics of Labor, the *Aldrich Reports*, records of

purchases by the Army and Navy, and miscellaneous publications.

E 159. Cost-of-living index (Douglas), 1890–1926.

Source: Paul H. Douglas, *Real Wages in the United States, 1890–1926*, Houghton Mifflin Company, Boston and New York, 1930, p. 60.

See also general note for series E 113–160.

This index was called the "Most Probable Index of the Movement of the Total Cost of Living for Workingmen" by Douglas, who constructed the series for his study of real wages during this period. The all-item indexes are available for two base periods, 1890–1899 and 1914.

For 1890–1914, the sources of the price data were BLS wholesale and retail reports. The available retail prices for foods were supplemented with wholesale prices for additional foods. These wholesale data were adjusted for the variation in movement between retail and wholesale prices for identical foods. Wholesale prices were also adjusted to approximate retail prices for clothing, fuel and light, furniture, tobacco, and spirits. The combined index for all items is a weighted arithmetic average of price relatives, using weights derived from the BLS consumer expenditure study of 1901–1902. No estimates were made for rent movements because of lack of data. For 1913–1926, the individual city indexes in the BLS "Cost-of-Living Index" were combined with city population weights.

E 160. Cost-of-living index (Rees), 1890–1914.

Source: National Bureau of Economic Research, *Thirty-eighth Annual Report*, New York, May 1958, pp. 59–60.

Rees' cost-of-living index was based largely on retail prices. Douglas' estimates were adopted for food at retail, and tobacco and spirits at wholesale prices (see text for series E 159), but retail data were assembled to compute new components for fuel, rent, clothing, and housefurnishings. Prices for gas obtained from utility companies, and retail prices of kerosene as used for the New Jersey State cost-of-living index, were included in fuels. Wholesale prices of coal were included before 1907 and for kerosene before 1898. Rents for six cities were compiled from newspaper advertisements. Prices for clothing and housefurnishings were compiled from mail-order catalogs.

The index is a weighted average of price relatives, using weights derived largely from the BLS consumer expenditure study of 1901–1902.

E 161–176. Retail prices of selected food in U. S. cities (BLS), 1890–1957.

Source: 1890–1922, BLS Bulletin No. 396, *Retail Prices, 1890 to 1924*, pp. 8–10; 1923–1934, BLS Bulletin No. 635, *Retail Prices of Food, 1923–36*, pp. 77–89; 1935–1939, Serial No. R. 1172 (August 1940), *Retail Prices*, pp. 28–35; 1940–1957, annual or biennial bulletins, *Retail Prices of Food* (including Serial No. R. 1264, and Bulletin Nos. 707, 799, 899, 938, 965, 1032, 1055, 1141, 1183, and 1217).

While there were scattered statistics of prices of many individual commodities in various publications, it was not until 1901, when BLS began the collection of food prices on a regular basis, that a regular price collection program was initiated by the Federal Government. At that time, information was secured from dealers' books for 1890–1901. Since then, retail prices of food have been obtained by BLS, first at annual intervals, then monthly or semimonthly.

As the pricing program was expanded to other commodities and services purchased by families for daily living, the available resources and review of data requirements for the over-all

Consumer Price Index resulted in sampling and methodology changes for foods. The growth in importance of some foods and declines for others, changes in kinds and sizes of packages, different methods of preparation of foods for retail stores, and similar developments were taken into consideration in the adjustments made to the list of foods priced. Of the many foods included for most of the period since 1890, only 16 were selected for publication here.

The list of cities in which food prices were collected changed over the years. In the main, the cities covered were industrial localities in 30 to 40 States up to 1952. Beginning in 1953, the collection of food prices was restricted to the 46 cities included in the CPI.

The number of stores in each city reporting food prices, after the initial collections through 1904, generally ranged from 25 in the larger cities to 15 in the smaller cities until 1932. Average prices for the United States were obtained by making simple averages of quotations from the total number of firms reporting for each food for 1915–1932. Average relative prices for each commodity were applied to prices in 1915 to estimate national averages for 1890–1914. Some chain stores were added to the samples as their sales volumes became significant in each city.

During 1932–1934 the store samples were expanded, particularly in the larger cities, and the method of averaging prices was adjusted to reflect food sales by chain and independent stores in each city. National averages were obtained by combining weighted city averages with the use of consumption and population weights. Refinements to the sampling and the weighting system have been introduced from time to time (see "Store Samples for Retail Food Prices," *Monthly Labor Review*, January 1947).

During the revision of the CPI in the late 1930's, comparable revised national averages were calculated back to 1923. The national averages shown here are those estimated by price relatives for 1890–1915, simple averages of quotations from all cities for 1916–1922, and weighted city averages beginning with 1923.

Food price data were collected by use of mail schedules and occasional personal visits until 1934. Since that year, all prices have been collected by personal visit of BLS representatives. Changes in descriptions for the foods priced, the cities covered, sizes and designs of samples of stores, and methods of processing introduce some noncomparabilities into the series. However, the only change, which is significant on a national basis, is the change in the description of the commodity.

The BLS publications have regularly included actual prices for individual nonfoods only for fuels, gas, and electricity. For review of retail prices available for articles other than foods and fuels, see BLS Bulletin No. 1182, *Average Retail Prices: Collection and Calculation Techniques and Problems*, pp. 90–105.

E 161, flour. Prices are for general all-purpose white wheat flour. The size of package on which quotations were secured were: 1890–1928, 1/8 or 1/4 of a barrel although some smaller units were also included; 1929–1938, 12 or 24 lb. sack; 1939–1942, 5–12 lb. sack; 1943–1957, 5 lb. sack.

E 162, bread. Prices are for white bread, pan style excluding all specialty type bread. For 1913–1936, prices were obtained from bakeries for 16 or 18 ounces in the dough and converted to 16 ounces baked weight. Both wrapped and unwrapped breads were included. Beginning in 1937, prices have been obtained primarily from grocery stores for the volume-selling size loaf of wrapped bread. The baked weight

as given on the wrapper or reported by the store was converted to 16 ounces.

National averages have not been computed for 1890–1913. Prices for individual firms are available in the early retail price bulletins.

E 163, round steak. For 1890–1939, the averages include quotations for the best cut of the best grade handled in each store for whole round or top round, mostly bone-in. For 1940–1957, prices were for top round, bone-in, U. S. choice grade (comparable to U. S. good grade prior to the changes in grades by the Department of Agriculture in 1950).

E 164, chuck roast. For 1913–1939, quotations were reported for the best cut of the best grade handled in each store and include both bone-in and boneless. Since then, all quotations have been for "bone-in" roasts. The grade priced for 1940–1957 was the same as for round steak. Beginning in 1951, the more precise description of the cut was "blade pot-roast cut from upper part of shoulder before rib roast and behind neck, U. S. choice, bone-in."

National averages have not been computed for 1890–1913. Prices for individual firms are available in the early retail price bulletins.

E 165, pork chops. For 1890–1935, quotations were for loin chops of the best grade handled. Rib chops and chops from the thick end of the loin were excluded. Beginning in 1935, prices were obtained for center cut loin chops of U. S. No. 1 grade.

E 166, bacon. Most of the quotations included in the average were for sliced bacon for all years. In the early years (probably before 1930) bacon was sliced when sold and prices for slab bacon may be included. Sliced and packaged bacon has been priced since about 1930 in 1 pound or two ½ pound packages of cellophane or similar material. Grade descriptions were: 1890–1942, best but not fancy grade; 1943–1945, first quality or fancy grade; 1946–1957, standard Grade A.

E 167, butter. All prices refer to creamery butter, 92 to 93 score or better for 1890–1942 and 92 score for 1943–1957. Tub or print butter was priced up to 1940, roll or print in 1941 and 1942, package of 4 sticks or quarters for 1943–1946, and package print or roll, including quarters for 1947–1957.

E 168, eggs. Averages are for fresh eggs for all years. For 1890–1942, prices are for the highest grade sold in volume in each store; for 1943–1944, U. S. extras or Grade A; for 1945–1952, the highest grade and size sold in volume in each store; since 1953, large Grade A eggs in most cities, although some ungraded eggs included in some small cities.

E 169, milk, delivered. Until 1935, prices are for fresh fluid milk, raw or pasteurized, no grade designation, in quart bottle or in bulk, delivered to homes; for 1935–1946, raw or pasteurized milk of the dominant grade in each city in quart bottles or cartons; for 1947–1949, same grades, but sizes included 1-quart, 2-quart, and 4-quart containers in many cities; for 1950–1956, pasteurized milk, homogenized or nonhomogenized, without Vitamin D, of the volume-selling grade in each city in quart or half-gallon cartons or bottles; for 1957, pasteurized, homogenized milk with Vitamin D added, 3.25 percent or over butterfat content in quart or half-gallon cartons or bottles.

E 170, oranges. California and Florida oranges of the variety and size constituting the bulk of sales each month were quoted from 1919 to about 1935. After that time, the size range was narrowed to include only size 176–222 in standard box of U. S. No. 1 grade (good quality).

E 171, potatoes. White or Irish potatoes, excluding large baking types, have been priced consistently for all years in the quantities in which sales have customarily been made. The designation of U. S. No. 1 grade was added in 1935.

E 172, tomatoes, canned. The volume selling brands of canned tomatoes, standard grade, in No. 2 can were priced for 1919–1954. For 1955–1957, the description was expanded to specify "small and large pieces, with a maximum of 50 percent liquid, standard grade (C)" and the can size was changed to No. 303. Prices for 1919–1954 have been converted to No. 303 can.

E 173, navy beans. Dried beans, white, navy, or pea beans, No. 1 choice, hand picked, packaged or bulk were priced for 1915–1957. For 1949–1952, California small white beans were also included and for 1953–1957, Great Northern beans.

E 174, coffee. For 1913–1956, whole bean or ground roasted coffee was priced. Bulk or packaged coffee was quoted up to 1938. For 1939–1955, coffee in cans, glass, cardboard, or paper containers were averaged. For 1956 and 1957, prices are for ground roasted coffee in airtight cans only.

E 175, margarine. Prices are for uncolored oleomargarine, animal and vegetable, in 1-pound cartons for 1919–1948. For 1949 and 1950, uncolored vegetable margarine in 1-pound carton was quoted. For 1951–1957, averages are for colored vegetable margarine in 1-pound cartons.

E 176, sugar. Prices are for white granulated cane or beet sugar but the size package has varied over the years. For 1890–1916, prices for the volume-selling quantity were quoted; for 1917–1928, 1 pound; for 1929–1942, 10 pounds; and for 1943–1957, 5 pounds. For a short period during World War II, the 2-pound unit was the only one available.

E 177–185. General note.

The collection of retail prices for fuel and light was initiated in 1911 with coal and gas data for 1907–1911. After that time, the program was expanded to include gas, electricity, and the heating fuels used in important quantities in the cities covered. Prices were collected semiannually up to 1920, and at quarterly or monthly intervals from 1920 on.

The number of cities for which prices for this group have been compiled has varied widely. Before 1947, the city coverage had gradually been extended until prices for fuels and utility rates were obtained in 51 cities. In 1947, this program was cut back to the 34 cities in the CPI. The revision of the CPI in 1952 resulted in changing the city sample and enlarging the number to 46 cities.

The changing importance of particular kinds of fuel in particular localities, coupled with the over-all change in the city sample over the years, produced many changes in the volume of data for the indexes. The amount of supplementary information for deriving weights has also varied. In order to produce continuous index numbers, all changes in samples and methods of averaging were handled by the linking process.

All prices have been collected by mail from retailers and utility companies in each city, except that reports for electricity have been secured through the Federal Power Commission since 1937.

The terms of sale for the quotations were net cash payment basis, delivered to the residential consumer in specified quantities. Charges for special services were excluded but all applicable sales taxes were included. Annual averages were computed using standard BLS procedures.

The following bulletins contain the history of the collection and publication of prices for this group: BLS Bulletin No. 664, *Changes in Retail Prices of Electricity, 1923–38*, pp. 17–19; BLS Bulletin No. 628, *Changes in Retail Prices of Gas, 1923–36*, pp. 48–52; BLS Bulletin No. 950, *Residential Heating*

Fuels: Retail Prices, 1941–48, pp. 1–4. These reports contain references to earlier bulletins and include other index and price series.

E 177. Indexes of retail prices of electricity for household use, composite, 1913–1957.

Source: BLS, *Retail Price Indexes of Fuels and Electricity, January 1935–December 1957* (issued September 1958).

See also general note for series E 177–185.

This composite is an extension backward of a current BLS series. For 1913–1934, the index is based on the average price per kilowatt-hour for the average amount of electricity used by families in each of the 32 cities included in the CPI. Average prices for the 32 cities were combined as simple averages.

In 1938, a new method of computation for the revised CPI was inaugurated, and data were extended back to 1935. Net monthly bills for typical residential services were calculated from rate schedules for each city. The number of cities in the composite included 34 cities for 1935–1952, and 46 cities for 1953–1957. Some changes were also made in the typical services. For 1935–1952, bills were based on 25, 40, 100, and 250 kilowatt-hours. Since December 1952, 3 services have been priced, 40, 100, and 200 kilowatt-hours.

The net monthly bills for the typical services above were first combined into an index for each city by using weights approximating the importance of each of the services in that city. The city indexes were then combined with the consumption and population weights of the CPI.

E 178. Indexes of retail prices of electricity for household use, 100 kilowatt-hours, 1923–1957.

Source: See source for series E 177.

See also general note for series E 177–185.

This index is based on net monthly bills for one of the typical services included in the composite, series E 177. When the new method of calculation was inaugurated in 1938, net monthly bills were obtained from rate schedules supplied by the companies or in BLS files. The indexes were originally calculated on the 1923–25 base and converted to later base periods when the CPI was revised.

For 1923–June 1947, the cities in the series totaled 51 (including the 34 CPI cities). Thereafter, only CPI cities were included. The weights used for 1923–June 1947 represented the number of residential customers as of December 31, 1935. Since July 1947, the weights were the CPI consumption and population factors.

E 179. Indexes of retail prices of gas for household space heating, 1935–1957.

Source: See source for series E 177.

See also general note for series E 177–185.

The use of gas for home heating grew in importance as additional pipelines made natural gas available to more and more cities. Although gas for space heating was not included in the CPI before 1953, a special study in 1943 provided information on the volume of sales for space heating as of 1940 and rate schedule data back to 1935 for cities in which gas was an important heating fuel. The number of cities included varied from 27 of the 51 cities for 1935–1946 to 16 of the 34 CPI cities for 1947–1952, and 28 of the 46 CPI cities for 1953–1957.

The price for each city was calculated as an average of the rates per therm in all of the heating rate blocks of the rate schedule, weighted by the total number of therms sold by the gas company in that rate block for residential heating. For 1935–1952, the average rates per therm for the various cities were then combined, using total thermal sales for residential heating in each city as weights. After 1952, they were combined with consumption and population weights in the CPI.

E 180. Indexes of retail prices of gas for household uses other than space heating, all types, 1935–1957.

Source: See source for series E 177.

See also general note for series E 177–185.

In 1935, BLS adopted the method of computing net monthly bills based upon a definite number of heat units (therms of 100,000 BTU each) for each of 4 selected services—10.6, 19.6, 30.6, and 40.6 therms. These 4 typical services were continued through 1952. For 1953–1957, net monthly bills for 10 and 25 therms were used. This method of calculating prices has provided a better measure of price changes since differences in heating values over time could be taken into account.

Indexes based on 10.6 and 30.6 therms back to 1923 and a description of the methods adopted in 1935 are included in BLS Bulletin No. 628, *Changes in Retail Prices of Gas.*

For the number of cities included and methods of combining monthly bills used, see text for series E 177.

E 181. Indexes of retail prices of manufactured gas for household uses, 10 therms, 1907–1956.

Source: 1907–1913, unpublished data compiled by BLS; 1935–1957, see source for series E 177.

See also general note for series E 177–185.

When price collection for gas was begun by the BLS in 1911, the majority of cities were served with manufactured gas. As a result of the increasing trend to the use of straight natural gas, the number of cities for which BLS obtained prices for manufactured gas declined from 35 out of 39 cities in 1911 and 42 of 51 cities in 1923, to none of the 46 cities in the CPI in 1957.

For 1907–1922, the index was based on simple averages of net prices per 1,000 cubic feet (approximately 5.3 therms) based on consumption of 3,000 cubic feet. For 1923–June 1947, the net monthly bill for 10.6 therms was computed for each city, and cities were combined using the number of residential customers as of December 1934. For July 1947–1956, prices were obtained for 10 therms and city averages were combined with the consumption and population weights of the CPI.

Annual averages were estimated from April figures for 1907–1920 and from quarterly figures for 1921–1951. Prices were collected monthly beginning in 1952.

E 182. Indexes of retail prices of natural gas for household uses, 10 therms, 1913–1957.

Source: See source for series E 177.

See also general note for series E 177–185.

The increase in distribution of natural gas is reflected in the number of cities for which BLS obtained prices over the years. In 1913, 8 or 9 of 50 cities were using natural gas, 18 of the 50 were reporting natural gas prices by 1935, and by 1957, 33 of 46 cities then covered were being served with natural gas.

For 1913–1923, the index was computed from simple averages of net prices per 1,000 cubic feet (approximately 10 therms) based on consumption of 5,000 cubic feet. Net monthly bills for 10.6 therms were used for 1923–1952 and for 10 therms for 1953–1957. For the frequency of collection and the methods employed to combine city data, see text for series E 181.

E 183. Indexes of retail prices of Pennsylvania anthracite, stove size, 1913–1957.

Source: See source for series E 177.

See also general note for series E 177–185.

Data for the early years by type of coal for each firm reporting were published in BLS Bulletin No. 105, *Retail Prices, 1890–1911.* Similar data for 1912–1917 are included in later issues of *Retail Prices.* Since the first collection, BLS has continuously obtained retail prices for all locally important fuels.

This index is based on average prices per net ton delivered at the curb or in the bin if there was no extra charge. Prices from dealers in each city have always been combined as a simple average for each city. For 1913–1928, city averages were also combined on an unweighted basis. Through a revision of method in 1936, city average prices for 1929–1952 were weighted by fixed weights based on anthracite shipments to each city by rail during the year ending July 1936. Beginning 1953, the city averages were combined with consumption and population weights of the CPI.

Cities for which anthracite prices were obtained varied partly because of change in consumer demand and partly due to CPI revisions. Generally the number of cities has declined until, at the end of 1957, only 8 of the 46 cities in the CPI were reporting prices for anthracite. (For complete listing through 1948, see BLS Bulletin No. 950, *Residential Heating Fuels*, p. 2.)

E 184. Indexes of retail prices of bituminous coal, all domestic sizes, 1913–1957.

Source: See source for series E 177 and E 183.

See also general note for series E 177–185.

For methods of collection and averaging of prices, see text for series E 183. Generally, the index was based on unweighted averages of all prices for all sizes and types of bituminous coal for 1913–June 1947, and on city averages weighted with CPI weighting factors for July 1947–1957.

E 185. Indexes of retail prices of No. 2 fuel oil for household use, 1935–1957.

Source: See source for series E 177.

See also general note for series E 177–185.

Retail prices of petroleum fuels were first collected in 24 cities beginning in 1937 and data were obtained back to 1935. Thereafter the number of cities was increased as fuel oil for heating became more important. Beginning in 1947, the city coverage was restricted to those included in the CPI and since that time has usually covered about 20 cities.

The prices from which the index was computed refer to prices per 100 gallons delivered in "the amount usually delivered at one time." No. 2 fuel oil has been priced continuously and for 1939–1947, No. 3 oil was also priced and included. Average prices for each city were simple averages of quotations from a sample of dealers. For 1935–1938, city averages were combined with CPI consumption and population weights. For 1939–1946, weighting factors to combine city averages were obtained from 1941 shipments to each city as measured by OPA rationing authorities. CPI weights were again employed after 1946 to obtain the U. S. averages.

E 186. Rent indexes (Warren and Pearson) for dwelling units in 5 large cities, 1860–1880.

Source: George F. Warren and Frank A. Pearson, *Prices,* John Wiley and Sons, New York, 1933, p. 267.

See also G. F. Warren and F. A. Pearson, *Wholesale Prices for 213 Years, 1720–1932,* Cornell University Agricultural Experiment Station, *Memoir 142,* Ithaca, New York, 1932, p. 27.

The method of calculating this index was not indicated. The rental data were obtained from the special report by J. D. Weeks, "Report on the Average Retail Prices of Necessaries of Life in the United States" in volume 20 of the Tenth Census of the United States, pp. 104–107.

Series E 1–12. Wholesale Price Indexes (Warren and Pearson), by Major Product Groups: 1749 to 1890

[1910–14 = 100]

Year	All commodities	Farm products	Foods	Hides and leather products	Textile products	Fuel and lighting	Metals and metal products	Building materials	Chemicals and drugs	House-furnishing goods	Spirits	Miscellaneous
	1	2	3	4	5	6	7	8	9	10	11	12
1890	82	71	86	74	103	72	123	84	90	91	----	89
1889	81	67	79	80	99	71	116	81	101	94	74	80
1888	86	75	86	86	98	72	121	80	103	94	80	73
1887	85	71	86	92	98	70	119	81	97	92	77	75
1886	82	68	78	101	100	70	110	82	99	94	79	74
1885	85	72	84	105	105	72	109	81	100	99	79	78
1884	93	82	93	111	109	77	124	84	105	105	81	78
1883	101	87	103	107	116	89	144	85	110	110	83	93
1882	108	99	114	108	119	92	157	88	114	109	80	93
1881	103	89	106	109	119	91	150	83	120	109	81	90
1880	100	80	96	113	128	92	166	81	120	117	83	91
1879	90	72	90	100	114	80	134	74	120	105	82	90
1878	91	72	93	95	115	93	126	72	127	109	82	88
1877	106	89	115	109	125	108	141	80	136	118	86	95
1876	110	89	113	104	138	127	157	84	140	123	86	98
1875	118	99	120	123	141	128	175	90	149	134	88	98
1874	126	102	126	128	151	135	194	101	176	149	78	111
1873	133	103	122	132	175	148	243	106	181	160	75	115
1872	136	108	121	130	177	153	257	107	175	159	73	125
1871	130	102	130	126	170	152	203	102	177	154	74	120
1870	135	112	139	128	179	134	200	101	199	164	78	128
1869	151	128	154	134	194	166	227	110	227	178	86	136
1868	158	138	171	126	197	149	225	116	204	178	117	153
1867	162	133	167	132	220	144	248	120	229	196	146	162
1866	174	140	173	146	245	160	278	128	283	220	154	170
1865	185	148	180	152	266	214	306	118	300	214	150	175
1864	193	162	189	164	264	197	354	114	297	222	106	189
1863	133	113	123	133	206	125	236	88	234	165	45	146
1862	104	86	107	108	147	87	180	69	206	124	28	122
1861	89	75	89	90	120	80	152	63	174	110	21	98
1860	93	77	96	102	119	98	149	65	175	117	23	98
1859	95	82	99	115	120	93	150	64	168	118	24	98
1858	93	76	97	110	123	90	154	67	168	121	23	102
1857	111	95	123	139	138	97	173	73	171	130	27	107
1856	105	84	116	121	129	97	174	73	176	128	30	114
1855	110	98	126	104	125	102	176	71	178	129	31	103
1854	108	93	117	100	124	121	191	70	174	129	27	103
1853	97	83	98	84	119	102	186	67	169	128	22	96
1852	88	77	95	70	113	93	144	64	156	118	19	89
1851	83	71	84	65	115	87	141	61	153	117	20	86
1850	84	71	84	67	116	95	147	61	154	114	21	88
1849	82	62	88	64	111	93	155	58	152	110	21	92
1848	82	59	87	56	113	93	170	61	153	111	22	99
1847	90	72	96	66	117	90	186	61	156	117	24	99
1846	83	58	84	57	122	88	191	64	164	110	20	86
1845	83	58	84	63	125	96	189	64	178	107	21	85
1844	77	52	72	66	125	90	179	59	187	108	20	96
1843	75	48	77	69	114	87	172	58	188	99	19	109
1842	82	53	80	72	132	94	183	62	203	113	17	111
1841	92	64	90	86	140	111	204	67	220	121	19	113
1840	95	65	102	80	146	105	204	65	238	128	21	108
1839	112	86	126	90	159	122	220	70	250	----	25	122
1838	110	82	128	80	157	121	219	70	257	----	25	120
1837	115	84	132	80	167	130	243	70	264	----	25	119
1836	114	89	128	78	177	130	241	53	251	----	25	130
1835	100	75	107	74	170	111	206	52	225	----	23	126
1834	90	64	93	70	161	101	201	52	212	----	19	109
1833	95	69	100	76	162	111	205	51	220	----	22	105
1832	95	63	99	85	161	137	212	49	226	----	22	110
1831	94	61	98	91	179	112	209	49	211	----	23	111
1830	91	58	94	85	181	116	209	47	207	----	19	111
1829	96	59	100	85	182	133	227	49	222	----	19	117
1828	97	58	99	90	190	138	234	51	251	----	19	113
1827	98	59	100	87	186	137	243	51	287	----	21	112
1826	99	62	98	91	188	138	269	52	298	----	21	110
1825	103	67	100	99	198	131	279	50	313	----	22	114
1824	98	61	99	97	191	133	242	48	304	----	19	119
1823	103	64	108	97	209	131	247	49	320	----	20	119
1822	106	70	109	93	218	138	257	50	342	----	21	118
1821	102	64	102	89	215	142	261	50	306	----	21	129
1820	106	68	109	83	211	157	270	53	300	----	22	124
1819	125	87	140	101	233	162	285	55	306	----	24	144
1818	147	117	172	113	275	149	279	56	318	----	29	149
1817	151	126	184	95	268	141	277	60	327	----	31	156
1816	151	119	172	86	274	190	310	68	376	----	34	177
1815	170	117	187	85	300	318	399	76	538	----	41	202
1814	182	112	181	96	300	525	464	69	814	----	48	246
1813	162	104	172	77	291	334	419	63	848	----	37	251
1812	131	81	141	72	257	185	356	58	735	----	34	234
1811	126	82	140	73	243	166	325	57	570	----	31	204

Series E 1–12. Wholesale Price Indexes (Warren and Pearson), by Major Product Groups: 1749 to 1890—Con.

[1910–14 = 100]

Year	All commodities	Farm products	Foods	Hides and leather products	Textile products	Fuel and lighting	Metals and metal products	Building materials	Chemicals and drugs	Spirits	Miscellaneous	Year	All commodities
	1	2	3	4	5	6	7	8	9	11	12		1
1810	131	90	139	75	278	167	332	59	483	29	208	1778	140
1809	130	83	129	73	323	147	350	60	538	27	197	1777	123
1808	115	71	113	79	279	148	336	57	455	23	164	1776	86
1807	130	92	142	82	274	161	327	59	440	22	173		
1806	134	95	150	85	280	153	328	58	519	23	179	1775	75
												1774	76
1805	141	106	162	85	270	196	309	58	511	24	165	1773	84
1804	126	89	142	84	252	182	300	56	493	23	149	1772	89
1803	118	83	135	83	232	152	290	53	431	25	138	1771	79
1802	117	84	132	80	230	153	301	55	377	24	145		
1801	142	113	177	71	236	167	348	55	445	27	173	1770	77
												1769	77
1800	129	99	157	62	225	159	322	51	427	25	194	1768	74
1799	126	98	147	62	227	150	310	51	523	24	206	1767	77
1798	122	93	145	65	226	131	304	51	442	26	177	1766	73
1797	131	98	163			144	299	54		26	177		
1796	146	116	186			150	284	58		31	204	1765	72
												1764	74
1795	131	102	163			155	259	56		25	220	1763	79
1794	108	76	135			125	258	40		23	158	1762	87
1793	102	75	125			122	240	39		22	163	1761	77
1791	85	57	99			100	240	34		19	148		
												1760	79
1790	90	68	104			95	247	35		17	141	1759	79
1789	86	68	94			99	250	35		16	152	1758	70
1787	90	78	103			127	236	36		15	148	1757	65
1786	90	75										1756	66
1785	92											1755	66
1784												1754	65
1783												1753	65
1782												1752	66
1781	216											1751	65
1780	225											1750	60
1779	226											1749	68

Series E 13–24. Wholesale Price Indexes (BLS), by Major Product Groups: 1890 to 1951

[1926 = 100]

Year	All commodities	All commodities other than farm products and foods	Farm products	Foods	Hides and leather products	Textile products	Fuel and lighting	Metals and metal products	Building materials	Chemicals and allied products	House-furnishing goods	Miscellaneous
	13	14	15	16	17	18	19	20	21	22	23	24
1951	180.4	169.4	196.1	186.9	221.4	172.2	138.2	189.2	225.5	143.3	176.0	141.0
1950	161.5	153.2	170.4	166.2	191.9	148.0	133.2	173.6	206.0	122.7	153.2	120.9
1949	155.0	147.3	165.5	161.4	180.4	140.4	131.7	170.2	193.4	118.6	145.3	112.3
1948	165.1	151.0	188.3	179.1	188.8	149.8	134.2	163.6	199.1	135.7	144.5	120.5
1947	152.1	135.2	181.2	168.7	182.4	141.7	108.7	145.0	179.7	127.3	131.1	115.5
1946	121.1	109.5	148.9	130.7	137.2	116.3	90.1	115.5	132.6	101.4	111.6	100.3
1945	105.8	99.7	128.2	106.2	118.1	100.1	84.0	104.7	117.8	95.2	104.5	94.7
1944	104.0	98.5	123.3	104.9	116.7	98.4	83.0	103.8	115.5	95.2	104.3	93.6
1943	103.1	96.9	122.6	106.6	117.5	97.4	80.8	103.8	111.4	94.9	102.7	92.2
1942	98.8	95.5	105.9	99.6	117.7	96.9	78.5	103.8	110.2	95.5	102.4	89.7
1941	87.3	89.0	82.4	82.7	108.3	84.8	76.2	99.4	103.2	84.4	94.3	82.0
1940	78.6	83.0	67.7	71.3	100.8	73.8	71.7	95.8	94.8	77.0	88.5	77.3
1939	77.1	81.3	65.3	70.4	95.6	69.7	73.1	94.4	90.5	76.0	86.3	74.8
1938	78.6	81.7	68.5	73.6	92.8	66.7	76.5	95.7	90.3	77.0	86.8	73.3
1937	86.3	85.3	86.4	85.5	104.6	76.3	77.6	95.7	95.2	82.6	89.7	77.8
1936	80.8	79.6	80.9	82.1	95.4	71.5	76.2	87.0	86.7	78.7	81.7	70.5
1935	80.0	77.9	78.8	83.7	89.6	70.9	73.5	86.4	85.3	79.0	80.6	68.3
1934	74.9	78.4	65.3	70.5	86.6	72.9	73.3	86.4	86.2	75.3	81.5	69.7
1933	65.9	71.2	51.4	60.5	80.9	64.8	66.3	79.8	77.0	72.1	75.8	62.5
1932	64.8	70.2	48.2	61.0	72.9	54.9	70.3	80.2	71.4	73.9	75.1	64.4
1931	73.0	75.0	64.8	74.6	86.1	66.3	67.5	84.5	79.2	79.3	84.9	69.8
1930	86.4	85.2	88.3	90.5	100.0	80.3	78.5	92.1	89.9	88.7	92.7	77.7
1929	95.3	91.6	104.9	99.9	109.1	90.4	83.0	100.5	95.4	94.0	94.3	82.6
1928	96.7	92.9	105.9	101.0	121.4	95.5	84.3	97.0	94.1	95.0	95.1	85.4
1927	95.4	94.0	99.4	96.7	107.7	95.6	88.3	96.3	94.7	96.1	97.5	91.0
1926	100.0	100.0	100.0	100.0	100.0	100.0	100.0	100.0	100.0	100.0	100.0	100.0
1925	103.5	102.6	109.8	100.2	105.3	108.3	96.5	103.2	101.7	101.8	103.1	109.0
1924	98.1	99.7	100.0	91.0	101.5	106.7	92.0	106.3	102.3	98.9	104.9	93.6
1923	100.6	104.3	98.6	92.7	104.2	111.3	97.3	109.3	108.7	101.1	108.9	99.7
1922	96.7	102.4	93.8	87.6	104.6	100.2	107.3	102.9	97.3	100.3	103.5	92.8
1921	97.6	104.9	88.4	90.6	109.2	94.5	96.8	117.5	97.4	115.0	113.0	109.2
1920	154.4	161.3	150.7	137.4	171.3	164.8	163.7	149.4	150.1	164.7	141.8	167.5
1919	138.6	128.8	157.6	129.5	174.1	135.3	104.3	130.9	115.6	157.0	105.9	139.1
1918	131.3	124.6	148.0	119.1	125.7	137.2	109.2	136.5	98.6	182.3	93.3	134.4
1917	117.5	114.2	129.0	104.5	123.8	98.7	105.4	150.6	88.2	165.0	74.2	122.1
1916	85.5	88.3	84.4	75.7	93.4	70.4	74.3	116.5	67.6	160.7	61.4	100.6
1915	69.5	68.0	71.5	65.4	75.5	54.1	51.8	86.3	53.5	112.0	56.0	86.9
1914	68.1	66.4	71.2	64.7	70.9	54.6	56.6	80.2	52.7	81.4	56.5	89.9
1913	69.8	70.0	71.5	64.2	68.1	57.3	61.3	90.8	56.7	80.2	56.1	93.1
1912	69.1		72.6	66.8	64.5	55.7	51.4	89.5	55.9	80.7	53.0	106.4
1911	64.9		66.8	62.0	58.8	55.5	46.7	80.8	55.3	81.6	52.7	108.6

Series E 13–24. Wholesale Price Indexes (BLS), by Major Product Groups: 1890 to 1951—Con.

[1926 = 100]

Year	All commodities	All commodities other than farm products and foods	Farm products	Foods	Hides and leather products	Textile products	Fuel and lighting	Metals and metal products	Building materials	Chemicals and allied products	House-furnishing goods	Miscellaneous
	13	14	15	16	17	18	19	20	21	22	23	24
1910	70.4	--------	74.3	64.9	60.2	58.4	47.6	85.2	55.3	82.0	54.0	152.7
1909	67.6	--------	69.6	62.6	61.5	56.5	51.6	84.5	53.7	79.9	51.7	129.6
1908	62.9	--------	62.2	58.7	55.6	54.8	53.7	86.3	52.0	79.6	51.6	97.8
1907	65.2	--------	62.2	57.0	58.0	63.5	54.4	109.8	56.8	78.5	55.0	108.2
1906	61.8	--------	57.3	53.4	57.7	58.7	52.0	102.4	54.0	76.8	51.3	115.3
1905	60.1	--------	56.4	55.1	53.9	54.1	49.6	89.1	48.1	82.3	49.7	117.4
1904	59.7	--------	58.5	54.0	49.7	52.9	53.3	79.9	45.0	84.1	50.3	109.5
1903	59.6	--------	55.6	52.0	49.9	52.8	60.3	90.2	46.7	84.1	50.9	98.9
1902	58.9	--------	58.4	53.3	50.8	49.4	51.8	91.0	45.3	86.5	49.2	88.1
1901	55.3	--------	52.8	50.5	48.9	48.1	44.6	93.1	44.3	84.2	48.9	93.4
1900	56.1	--------	50.5	50.8	49.4	53.3	46.3	98.0	46.2	82.1	48.9	102.0
1899	52.2	--------	45.8	47.7	49.4	47.7	41.2	100.0	43.6	81.1	45.0	97.4
1898	48.5	--------	44.9	47.8	48.3	44.9	34.5	65.3	39.6	77.4	44.0	93.4
1897	46.6	--------	42.5	45.5	45.9	42.9	33.9	65.0	37.4	70.9	42.5	92.5
1896	46.5	--------	39.6	44.1	45.2	43.1	39.5	71.2	38.9	65.0	43.4	90.2
1895	48.8	--------	43.9	47.3	49.4	44.3	40.3	70.4	38.8	64.7	43.5	88.9
1894	47.9	--------	44.6	48.2	43.0	46.1	34.3	65.7	39.8	65.5	45.3	86.4
1893	53.4	--------	51.3	54.7	45.1	54.1	35.3	76.8	41.6	72.7	48.1	89.0
1892	52.2	--------	49.5	51.0	47.2	55.2	34.8	84.0	41.7	74.6	48.1	86.6
1891	55.8	--------	54.2	54.8	47.9	54.6	37.0	92.2	44.2	74.0	50.4	94.3
1890	56.2	--------	50.4	55.5	47.5	57.8	38.1	105.3	46.5	73.2	49.9	97.9

Series E 25–41. Wholesale Price Indexes (BLS), by Major Product Groups: 1913 to 1957

[1947–49 = 100]

Year	All commodities	All commodities other than farm products and foods	Farm products	Processed foods	Textile products and apparel	Hides, skins, leather, and leather products	Fuel, power, and lighting materials	Chemicals and allied products	Rubber and rubber products	Lumber and wood products	Pulp, paper, and allied products	Metals and metal products	Machinery and motive products	Furniture and other household durables	Non-metallic minerals, structural	Tobacco manufactures and bottled beverages	Miscellaneous products
	25	26	27	28	29	30	31	32	33	34	35	36	37	38	39	40	41
1957	117.6	125.6	90.9	105.6	95.4	99.4	117.2	109.5	145.2	119.0	129.6	151.2	146.1	122.2	134.6	126.1	89.6
1956	114.3	122.2	88.4	101.7	95.3	99.3	111.2	107.2	145.8	125.4	127.2	148.4	137.8	119.1	129.6	122.3	91.0
1955	110.7	117.0	89.6	101.7	95.3	93.8	107.9	106.6	148.8	123.6	119.3	136.6	128.4	115.9	124.2	121.6	92.0
1954	110.3	114.5	95.6	105.3	95.2	94.2	108.1	107.0	126.9	118.0	116.3	128.0	124.6	115.4	120.9	120.6	102.5
1953	110.1	114.0	97.0	104.6	97.3	98.5	109.5	105.7	125.0	120.2	116.1	126.9	123.0	114.2	118.2	115.7	97.8
1952	111.6	113.2	107.0	108.8	99.8	97.2	106.6	104.5	134.0	120.3	116.5	123.0	121.5	112.0	113.6	111.8	108.3
1951	114.8	115.9	113.4	111.4	110.6	120.3	106.7	110.0	148.0	123.9	119.6	122.8	119.0	114.1	113.6	109.4	104.9
1950	103.1	105.0	97.5	99.8	99.2	104.6	103.0	96.3	120.5	113.9	100.9	110.3	108.6	105.3	106.9	103.5	96.6
1949	99.2	101.3	92.8	95.7	95.5	96.9	101.9	94.8	98.9	99.2	98.5	104.8	106.6	103.1	104.4	102.3	96.1
1948	104.4	103.4	107.3	106.1	104.4	102.1	107.1	103.8	102.1	107.2	102.9	103.9	100.9	101.4	101.7	100.5	103.1
1947	96.4	95.3	100.0	98.2	100.1	101.0	90.9	101.4	99.0	93.7	98.6	91.3	92.5	95.6	93.9	97.2	100.8
1946	78.7	78.3	83.2	77.6	82.6	74.6	76.2	76.3	99.4	60.3	--------	73.9	80.3	83.0	84.2	89.7	--------
1945	68.8	71.3	71.6	60.8	71.1	64.2	71.1	70.6	98.9	52.5	--------	65.9	71.6	78.6	79.1	85.8	--------
1944	67.6	70.4	68.9	60.4	69.9	63.4	70.3	70.2	102.0	51.9	--------	64.8	71.0	78.4	75.9	83.4	--------
1943	67.0	69.3	68.5	61.6	69.2	63.9	68.4	69.5	103.3	48.0	--------	64.8	71.0	76.4	74.5	83.0	--------
1942	64.2	68.3	59.2	59.1	68.9	64.0	66.4	69.3	100.6	45.4	--------	64.9	71.2	76.8	74.1	79.1	--------
1941	56.8	63.7	46.0	50.5	60.3	58.9	64.5	61.6	86.5	41.8	--------	64.0	68.6	71.2	71.3	78.1	--------
1940	51.1	59.4	37.8	43.6	52.4	54.8	60.7	56.6	80.2	35.2	--------	62.8	66.2	66.8	69.7	77.3	--------
1939	50.1	58.1	36.5	43.3	49.5	52.0	61.8	55.8	86.3	31.6	--------	62.6	65.3	65.4	69.5	76.4	--------
1938	51.1	58.4	38.3	45.6	47.4	50.5	64.7	55.9	82.7	30.8	--------	63.1	--------	65.6	71.1	76.4	--------
1937	56.1	61.0	48.3	52.4	54.2	56.9	65.7	59.0	84.4	33.7	--------	65.6	--------	67.2	73.4	76.5	--------
1936	52.5	56.9	45.2	50.1	50.8	51.9	64.5	56.4	71.7	28.7	--------	57.3	--------	60.6	71.7	75.8	--------
1935	52.0	55.7	44.0	52.1	50.4	48.7	62.2	56.0	66.4	27.4	--------	56.2	--------	59.8	71.6	75.9	--------
1934	48.7	56.0	36.5	42.6	51.8	47.1	62.0	53.7	65.8	28.5	--------	56.2	--------	60.2	71.6	76.0	--------
1933	42.8	50.9	28.7	36.3	46.0	44.0	56.1	51.2	56.8	24.2	--------	50.9	--------	55.5	66.9	72.8	--------
1932	42.1	50.2	26.9	36.5	39.0	39.7	59.5	--------	53.8	20.3	--------	49.9	--------	55.4	63.4	81.4	--------
1931	47.4	53.6	36.2	44.8	47.1	46.8	57.2	--------	62.0	23.8	--------	54.1	--------	62.8	67.6	84.6	--------
1930	56.1	60.9	49.3	53.3	57.1	54.4	66.5	--------	73.0	29.4	--------	60.3	--------	68.2	72.4	87.1	--------
1929	61.9	65.5	58.6	58.5	64.2	59.3	70.2	--------	83.5	31.9	--------	67.0	--------	69.3	72.6	86.6	--------
1928	62.9	66.4	59.2	59.4	66.0	58.5	71.4	--------	96.0	30.8	--------	64.5	--------	69.9	73.8	86.9	--------
1927	62.0	67.2	55.5	56.7	67.9	58.5	74.7	--------	121.0	31.6	--------	64.6	--------	71.7	71.4	88.0	--------
1926	65.0	71.5	55.9	58.2	71.1	54.4	84.6	--------	159.3	33.7	--------	68.9	--------	73.5	74.5	88.0	--------
1925	67.3	73.4	61.3	57.8	77.0	57.3	81.7	--------	--------	--------	--------	70.7	--------	75.4	--------	--------	--------
1924	63.8	71.3	55.9	53.3	75.8	55.2	77.9	--------	--------	--------	--------	70.1	--------	76.3	--------	--------	--------
1923	65.4	74.6	55.1	55.1	79.1	56.7	82.4	--------	--------	--------	--------	74.2	--------	80.3	--------	--------	--------
1922	62.8	73.2	52.4	51.0	71.2	56.9	90.8	--------	--------	--------	--------	62.7	--------	76.0	--------	--------	--------
1921	63.4	75.0	49.4	54.0	67.1	59.4	81.9	--------	--------	--------	--------	67.1	--------	85.2	--------	--------	--------
1920	100.3	115.3	84.2	81.9	117.1	93.1	138.5	--------	--------	--------	--------	97.7	--------	101.5	--------	--------	--------
1919	90.1	92.1	88.0	78.2	96.1	94.7	88.3	--------	--------	--------	--------	85.3	--------	75.2	--------	--------	--------
1918	85.3	89.1	82.7	73.1	97.5	68.3	92.4	--------	--------	--------	--------	98.4	--------	63.6	--------	--------	--------
1917	76.4	81.7	72.1	63.6	70.1	67.3	89.2	--------	--------	--------	--------	116.7	--------	53.4	--------	--------	--------
1916	55.6	63.1	47.1	45.8	50.0	50.8	62.9	--------	--------	--------	--------	84.5	--------	46.6	--------	--------	--------
1915	45.2	48.6	39.9	39.9	38.4	41.1	43.8	--------	--------	--------	--------	52.7	--------	43.9	--------	--------	--------
1914	44.3	47.5	39.8	39.2	38.8	38.5	47.9	--------	--------	--------	--------	44.3	--------	43.4	--------	--------	--------
1913	45.4	50.0	39.9	38.2	40.7	37.0	51.9	--------	--------	--------	--------	51.4	--------	43.4	--------	--------	--------

Series E 42–55.　Wholesale Price Indexes (BLS), for Economic Sectors, by Stage of Processing: 1913 to 1957
[1947–49 =100]

Year	All commodities	Crude materials for further processing				Intermediate materials, supplies, and components						Finished goods [1]		
		Total	Food-stuffs and feed-stuffs	Nonfood materials, except fuel	Fuel	Total	Materials and components for—		Processed fuels and lubricants	Containers, non-returnable	Supplies	Total	Con-sumer	Pro-ducer
							Manufac-turing	Construc-tion						
	42	43	44	45	46	47	48	49	50	51	52	53	54	55
1957	117.6	97.2	87.7	112.5	119.7	125.1	126.9	132.9	113.0	134.3	112.5	118.1	111.1	146.7
1956	114.3	95.0	84.0	114.2	113.3	122.1	123.7	132.0	106.7	128.5	111.3	114.0	108.0	138.1
1955	110.7	94.5	85.7	110.1	105.8	117.0	118.2	125.6	103.5	119.8	108.5	110.9	106.4	128.5
1954	110.3	98.3	94.7	104.2	106.0	114.8	115.4	120.9	103.5	118.2	110.2	110.7	107.1	124.7
1953	110.1	99.2	94.6	106.2	111.0	114.1	115.2	120.2	103.6	116.2	107.8	110.4	107.1	123.1
1952	111.6	107.4	105.7	110.9	107.2	113.5	113.4	118.3	102.8	116.0	113.5	111.5	109.0	121.3
1951	114.8	116.9	112.3	128.1	106.5	116.9	118.4	119.1	104.2	122.7	113.5	112.1	110.3	119.3
1950	103.1	101.8	97.0	111.0	104.6	104.3	104.5	108.9	99.7	104.4	100.8	102.4	100.9	108.7
1949	99.2	93.4	90.5	97.2	105.0	99.9	99.6	103.5	97.8	101.7	97.5	100.6	99.2	106.1
1948	104.4	108.0	108.8	106.8	105.6	104.0	104.0	103.2	107.4	101.3	103.5	103.5	104.1	101.1
1947	96.4	98.6	100.7	96.0	89.4	96.2	96.4	93.3	94.8	97.0	99.0	95.9	96.8	92.8
1946	78.7	80.0	-----	-----	-----	72.6	-----	-----	-----	-----	78.7	-----	-----	-----

Year	All commodities	Crude materials for further processing	Inter-mediate materials, supplies, and com-ponents	Finished goods [1]	Year	All commodities	Crude materials for further processing	Inter-mediate materials, supplies, and com-ponents	Finished goods [1]	Year	All commodities	Crude materials for further processing	Inter-mediate materials, supplies, and com-ponents	Finished goods [1]
	42	43	47	53		42	43	47	53		42	43	47	53
1945	68.8	69.4	62.8	69.0	1934	48.7	40.8	47.7	53.0	1923	65.4	58.5	77.7	67.3
1944	67.6	67.3	61.6	68.4	1933	42.8	33.6	42.8	47.8	1922	62.8	57.0	64.8	65.4
1943	67.0	66.6	60.8	67.9	1932	42.1	32.7	38.8	47.7	1921	63.4	52.5	62.9	70.0
1942	64.2	59.8	60.6	66.9	1931	47.4	39.0	45.2	52.2					
1941	56.8	49.6	56.9	60.4						1920	100.3	90.2	129.8	101.6
					1930	56.1	50.1	53.6	59.7	1919	90.1	86.7	103.3	88.6
1940	51.1	42.7	51.8	55.3	1929	61.9	57.9	61.5	64.1	1918	85.3	80.7	100.7	84.6
1939	50.1	41.7	50.4	54.5	1928	62.9	58.9	61.9	65.0	1917	76.4	72.9	98.5	74.0
1938	51.1	42.8	49.4	55.7	1927	62.0	57.3	61.8	64.4	1916	55.6	49.1	77.5	55.8
1937	56.1	50.4	55.9	59.1	1926	65.0	59.4	65.5	67.8					
1936	52.5	47.5	49.7	55.6						1915	45.2	39.9	53.2	46.7
1935	52.0	45.8	48.2	55.7	1925	67.3	63.4	69.0	68.2	1914	44.3	40.2	45.8	46.0
					1924	63.8	58.0	71.2	65.3	1913	45.4	40.9	49.0	47.1

[1] Goods to users, including raw foods and fuel.

Series E 56–64.　Wholesale Price Indexes (BLS), by Durability of Product: 1947 to 1957
[1947–49 =100]

Year	All commodities			Manufactures			Raw or slightly processed goods		
	Total	Durable	Nondurable	Total	Durable	Nondurable	Total	Durable	Nondurable
	56	57	58	59	60	61	62	63	64
1957	117.6	141.4	104.7	123.2	142.0	108.4	98.9	122.3	97.7
1956	114.3	136.7	102.1	119.5	136.8	105.8	97.0	136.3	94.9
1955	110.7	128.2	101.2	115.0	128.5	104.3	96.6	121.6	95.3
1954	110.3	123.3	103.4	113.7	124.1	105.5	99.3	100.9	99.2
1953	110.1	122.2	103.6	112.8	122.6	105.2	101.1	110.6	100.6
1952	111.6	119.8	107.2	112.9	120.0	107.4	107.3	116.0	106.8
1951	114.8	119.3	112.4	115.5	119.3	112.5	112.5	119.6	112.1
1950	103.1	108.8	100.1	104.1	108.9	100.3	99.9	105.9	99.6
1949	99.2	104.7	96.2	100.3	105.1	96.5	95.5	91.1	95.8
1948	104.4	102.5	105.4	103.8	102.1	105.1	106.4	113.3	106.0
1947	96.4	92.8	98.4	95.9	92.7	98.5	98.1	95.6	98.2

Series E 65–67.　Wholesale Price Indexes (BLS), by 2 Levels of Processing, for Identical Commodities: 1890 to 1926
[1913 =100]

Year	All commod-ities (97 series)	Raw commod-ities (27 series)	Manu-factured commod-ities (70 series)	Year	All commod-ities (97 series)	Raw commod-ities (27 series)	Manu-factured commod-ities (70 series)	Year	All commod-ities (97 series)	Raw commod-ities (27 series)	Manu-factured commod-ities (70 series)
	65	66	67		65	66	67		65	66	67
1926	145.3	139.4	154.6	1914	99.6	98.7	101.0	1901	75.8	72.2	81.5
				1913	100.0	100.0	100.0				
1925	154.1	150.7	159.6	1912	96.9	95.1	99.7	1900	76.8	72.8	83.0
1924	142.6	139.1	148.2	1911	88.9	86.3	92.9	1899	71.7	67.4	78.5
1923	142.0	138.2	148.1					1898	66.1	61.2	73.6
1922	133.5	130.0	139.1	1910	97.8	95.4	101.4	1897	62.7	57.2	71.2
1921	131.6	121.2	147.7	1909	93.7	91.1	97.8	1896	61.7	56.2	70.1
				1908	87.3	83.7	92.8				
1920	225.3	220.3	233.2	1907	89.6	86.6	94.2	1895	65.2	60.5	72.5
1919	215.4	216.0	214.6	1906	83.7	81.3	87.5	1894	63.0	56.8	72.4
1918	205.9	208.0	202.6					1893	71.7	64.2	83.2
1917	183.3	184.0	182.1	1905	82.3	78.2	88.5	1892	69.7	62.0	81.5
1916	127.6	125.4	131.0	1904	81.9	79.1	86.2	1891	75.1	68.3	85.6
				1903	80.2	76.5	85.9				
1915	102.9	101.0	105.9	1902	81.0	77.1	86.9	1890	76.1	69.3	86.6

Series E 68–82. Wholesale Price Indexes (Bezanson), for Philadelphia: 1720 to 1861

Year	All commod- ities	Source		Type		Major groups									Un- weighted arith- metic average (1741–45 =100)
		Do- mestic	Im- ported	Agri- cul- tural	Indus- trial	Farm		Im- ported foods	Lumber products and naval stores	Industrial		Fish	Furs	Wine	
						Crops	Deriva- tives			Raw	Con- sump- tion				
	68	69	70	71	72	73	74	75	76	77	78	79	80	81	82
1861	88.2	94.7	85.3	111.6	79.9	117.9	106.4	67.3	125.0	82.5	76.2	118.5	50.6	125.0	167.5
1860	88.8	95.7	84.9	118.0	83.2	113.8	121.7	64.7	100.0	87.0	77.8	150.8	47.6	122.2	164.3
1859	89.4	98.7	83.0	123.3	84.0	124.3	122.4	63.1	103.3	87.1	79.6	152.4	49.9	108.5	176.5
1858	89.7	94.8	88.0	115.4	85.3	115.6	115.2	66.0	97.2	86.9	82.9	136.5	49.4	127.2	165.3
1857	100.9	106.1	99.9	134.8	92.5	136.8	133.1	86.5	99.9	93.8	90.5	161.9	54.3	130.8	198.4
1856	99.1	103.7	99.2	128.8	93.9	129.9	127.9	83.0	92.5	94.3	93.4	156.8	51.4	126.4	194.6
1855	99.3	107.6	96.5	142.5	93.1	147.7	138.2	75.1	100.2	92.7	93.6	153.4	44.4	125.6	234.9
1854	95.8	105.6	91.5	131.8	90.7	135.5	128.7	75.1	111.0	92.1	88.8	156.7	45.4	90.4	211.6
1853	87.7	96.8	82.3	117.4	82.8	116.4	118.3	71.8	101.2	86.8	77.2	146.5	54.5	74.2	171.9
1852	80.4	89.5	74.8	107.7	75.1	107.6	107.7	65.4	92.9	78.2	70.7	135.7	57.1	70.3	152.8
1851	80.3	86.4	76.7	102.2	75.9	110.0	95.9	71.3	87.9	78.9	71.6	118.7	56.0	70.3	144.8
1850	79.9	85.2	76.7	98.6	77.1	109.2	90.3	71.5	79.1	80.1	72.8	126.1	56.0	70.6	147.3
1849	76.5	81.6	72.9	94.0	76.1	100.1	89.1	64.3	73.2	78.1	73.1	104.0	56.0	68.7	146.8
1848	78.5	84.2	74.9	97.4	78.7	103.7	92.4	64.8	72.6	80.6	75.9	118.4	56.0	69.9	149.3
1847	83.5	90.7	78.4	112.8	80.6	123.1	104.6	72.2	75.3	82.6	77.7	123.1	57.3	71.9	177.5
1846	80.1	83.4	78.3	93.2	78.9	101.7	86.4	71.7	78.4	80.9	76.1	119.6	64.5	71.1	144.1
1845	79.7	82.3	78.4	90.1	78.6	94.2	86.6	73.1	75.5	81.4	74.7	128.3	65.5	73.4	142.5
1844	76.9	77.4	77.3	81.1	79.0	87.7	75.9	68.6	70.2	82.4	74.2	126.5	56.6	73.6	129.3
1843	75.4	77.2	74.6	81.1	78.7	88.0	75.5	64.3	75.7	81.7	74.3	107.7	45.4	66.5	131.4
1842	79.1	85.1	74.1	89.0	83.2	97.1	82.6	60.8	83.0	87.2	77.5	109.3	61.1	64.7	135.7
1841	85.2	93.6	77.5	102.2	87.1	111.8	94.6	65.0	88.6	90.9	81.8	131.8	70.2	68.0	152.3
1840	87.4	96.8	78.2	107.6	89.8	109.5	106.0	63.7	90.1	93.1	85.2	139.7	74.3	68.7	165.4
1839	95.9	110.8	82.0	136.6	95.6	146.7	128.5	67.2	95.0	99.3	90.5	177.5	72.0	70.6	203.8
1838	91.9	103.2	80.2	123.3	92.6	123.9	122.9	67.4	94.0	94.7	89.6	130.7	66.1	71.2	211.4
1837	95.3	109.7	80.5	131.0	93.3	132.0	130.3	68.5	97.6	92.6	92.6	120.3	88.8	72.4	233.8
1836	97.6	113.0	82.4	135.7	93.8	142.8	129.8	75.0	105.2	97.4	88.6	124.9	92.2	77.3	217.7
1835	90.7	99.9	81.4	115.4	87.3	126.6	106.5	74.8	99.0	89.9	83.6	111.5	83.2	80.2	181.9
1834	85.8	91.6	79.1	97.6	86.4	101.3	94.6	68.0	94.1	90.1	81.3	91.8	88.4	81.6	163.0
1833	88.1	93.8	81.6	101.9	88.3	102.2	101.7	71.7	91.6	90.1	85.7	92.8	85.4	85.9	171.2
1832	89.3	91.8	86.6	99.7	88.2	99.6	99.8	84.4	87.4	88.7	87.5	86.3	84.9	84.8	166.7
1831	87.7	89.7	87.1	97.0	87.1	94.3	99.4	81.2	84.7	88.6	84.9	97.1	86.8	83.3	165.2
1830	84.0	84.7	85.4	87.3	84.2	84.3	89.9	80.7	80.9	85.3	82.7	88.0	85.2	82.5	150.2
1829	88.8	90.2	88.6	90.9	88.7	91.1	90.7	84.9	89.8	89.9	87.0	91.4	97.6	87.6	172.4
1828	91.0	90.7	91.6	89.5	90.2	86.5	92.2	90.1	96.2	91.8	87.9	96.4	101.4	90.9	165.4
1827	93.0	93.2	92.3	95.0	92.2	96.8	93.4	91.9	95.5	94.4	89.0	95.4	93.1	92.2	161.5
1826	95.9	96.3	94.7	100.3	94.0	106.7	95.1	96.1	98.0	97.2	89.4	84.1	101.0	96.4	160.4
1825	98.5	97.4	99.9	97.0	97.0	100.5	94.1	102.4	102.8	101.0	91.4	89.3	111.8	99.1	163.6
1824	94.3	94.4	93.8	92.6	94.9	91.4	93.7	92.3	97.8	95.5	93.9	99.4	99.0	92.1	163.0
1823	98.6	99.7	97.3	101.5	98.2	101.8	101.3	95.3	100.1	97.6	99.1	105.0	101.0	95.4	179.3
1822	104.2	105.4	102.9	107.9	103.3	107.7	108.1	103.6	102.5	102.2	104.9	106.8	103.8	103.4	183.4
1821	102.0	100.5	103.8	97.5	104.7	95.3	99.4	103.5	95.6	101.8	109.3	99.2	82.6	109.3	160.2
1820	106.6	108.6	104.7	109.2	105.7	112.9	106.2	107.7	109.1	101.8	111.8	108.5	73.4	114.0	180.7
1819	119.4	123.8	116.4	132.9	113.5	136.7	129.6	126.1	121.5	109.6	119.4	137.9	75.0	122.8	223.2
1818	130.6	138.8	125.0	160.3	121.8	162.5	158.4	136.6	126.9	118.3	127.0	164.4	80.3	123.0	276.2
1817	132.6	145.1	122.9	178.0	121.8	183.5	173.5	133.0	123.4	117.2	128.8	155.1	93.7	122.7	307.6
1816	151.9	159.5	146.6	177.8	143.2	185.0	171.8	157.8	146.3	141.8	145.1	196.8	107.0	147.9	298.3
1815	173.1	160.8	186.4	161.1	175.1	154.1	167.3	194.8	165.8	175.1	175.0	220.5	111.5	167.1	337.1
1814	189.7	159.0	223.4	151.5	205.6	147.5	154.9	217.7	176.6	209.5	199.9	227.8	89.6	192.0	371.3
1813	161.0	135.5	187.8	133.4	175.9	133.2	133.7	182.4	132.9	177.0	174.2	174.7	90.7	164.5	286.3
1812	142.3	125.6	158.6	126.3	153.7	120.5	131.6	143.8	120.7	158.3	147.0	165.0	93.5	151.9	257.3
1811	135.3	134.2	139.4	129.4	141.8	122.2	135.9	127.0	132.5	146.1	135.7	157.7	97.6	137.0	260.2
1810	138.7	131.6	147.3	133.4	146.2	130.3	136.1	134.2	138.6	151.3	138.9	140.2	90.7	128.9	249.6
1809	135.6	121.9	151.1	119.3	145.9	115.7	122.5	146.8	131.3	148.1	142.6	136.9	83.8	113.0	224.0
1808	123.1	112.4	133.6	109.4	132.6	108.7	110.0	135.7	113.9	136.3	127.4	128.1	78.5	97.7	192.6
1807	123.7	121.9	123.7	126.0	128.4	125.9	126.0	128.8	114.3	133.9	120.7	167.6	82.7	89.1	217.9
1806	128.1	125.8	128.8	135.5	131.7	132.3	138.2	138.3	114.8	135.3	126.4	171.7	75.0	89.4	233.1
1805	131.5	131.6	130.8	142.0	131.3	145.5	139.0	142.8	124.7	131.9	133.3	163.0	81.7	96.7	262.9
1804	128.1	123.9	132.6	126.9	129.5	130.9	123.4	142.2	126.6	131.6	126.5	147.9	85.3	103.5	241.0
1803	120.2	115.9	124.9	114.7	123.1	120.6	109.9	130.8	125.0	126.1	118.9	138.2	72.9	98.7	212.1
1802	122.5	118.1	129.5	120.5	124.0	121.7	119.4	137.3	115.2	125.7	121.4	167.1	72.4	103.6	211.2
1801	131.9	129.5	137.4	143.8	131.6	142.7	144.8	144.2	120.5	132.1	130.9	169.4	77.6	101.7	274.4
1800	128.3	121.1	138.0	129.6	130.5	129.0	130.1	155.3	116.2	131.5	129.1	124.6	74.4	93.9	------
1799	127.3	115.6	142.2	123.3	133.4	127.4	120.0	158.7	104.8	132.9	134.2	146.2	60.5	89.9	------
1798	127.1	123.4	131.9	128.8	129.0	136.6	122.4	152.3	122.7	125.4	134.6	189.5	58.1	81.5	
1797	133.5	134.4	135.8	135.9	130.0	142.8	130.2	169.3	133.9	125.4	137.1	226.3	75.1	85.7	266.7
1796	139.1	140.7	142.6	144.6	136.0	147.8	141.8	178.3	130.7	126.1	152.0	211.0	85.7	87.1	295.8
1795	130.7	125.3	141.3	129.6	130.0	124.1	134.6	173.3	114.2	124.9	138.9	200.3	70.1	86.5	257.8
1794	109.6	101.6	120.7	108.7	110.7	104.6	112.3	143.7	86.6	104.2	121.0	141.9	59.3	83.3	
1793	96.3	91.2	103.0	97.8	92.8	98.8	96.9	133.3	79.1	91.7	94.4	113.8	61.9	78.6	174.9
1792	91.5	85.5	99.3	88.0	89.4	88.4	87.7	132.5	72.4	88.7	90.6	116.5	62.2	71.3	156.5
1791	89.7	84.7	96.5	88.4	87.0	88.3	88.4	128.7	74.2	87.3	86.5	117.1	57.7	67.1	149.2
1790	86.5	83.4	89.9	93.5	85.4	96.6	90.8	109.3	67.0	89.9	79.2	105.5	58.9	64.0	160.3
1789	82.4	76.5	88.8	80.7	85.2	84.6	77.4	102.7	60.5	91.1	77.1	103.5	55.8	62.7	128.6
1788	83.3	78.1	89.7	84.5	85.4	89.3	80.6	107.5	56.5	91.7	76.8	103.5	52.8	65.2	120.5
1787	88.4	85.4	92.7	97.5	88.3	104.2	92.1	110.9	59.9	93.7	80.8	116.2	55.3	69.1	135.8
1786	91.0	90.0	93.8	101.6	88.6	106.1	97.9	113.0	69.6	95.9	78.7	117.8	65.4	69.1	145.0
1785	94.1	97.0	93.5	101.8	90.9	105.9	98.4	110.7	92.4	100.6	78.3	121.9	72.4	66.0	158.0
1784	100.1	104.8	97.7	107.0	96.9	101.7	111.8	122.0	104.3	103.9	87.4	127.9	76.9	59.1	172.6

Series E 68–82. Wholesale Price Indexes (Bezanson), for Philadelphia: 1720 to 1861—Con.

Year	Un-weighted arithmetic average (1741–45 =100) 82	Year	Un-weighted arithmetic average (1741–45 =100) 82	Year	Un-weighted arithmetic average (1741–45 =100) 82	Year	Un-weighted arithmetic average (1741–45 =100) 82	Year	Un-weighted arithmetic average (1741–45 =100) 82	Year	Un-weighted arithmetic average (1741–45 =100) 82
1774	127.5	1763	136.4	1752	111.9	1741	112.6			1730	98.0
1773	133.7	1762	133.4	1751	112.8					1729	92.5
1772	141.0	1761	121.2			1740	87.3			1728	92.8
1771	126.7			1750	113.0	1739	82.2			1727	97.6
		1760	125.7	1749	121.5	1738	91.1			1726	101.0
1770	121.6	1759	125.0	1748	124.7	1737	91.1				
1769	115.9	1758	109.6	1747	110.6	1736	83.6	1725	96.6		
1768	119.7	1757	107.1	1746	99.7			1724	88.9		
1767	123.7	1756	109.6			1735	87.8	1723	84.3		
1766	124.7			1745	92.7	1734	87.2	1722	81.6		
		1755	107.3	1744	90.9	1733	90.0	1721	78.6		
1765	118.4	1754	109.1	1743	95.6	1732	83.6				
1764	119.4	1753	109.9	1742	108.3	1731	87.1	1720	86.2		

Series E 83–89. Wholesale Price Indexes (Taylor), for Charleston, S. C.: 1732 to 1861

Year	All commodities (1818–42 =100) 83	All commodities 84	S. C. export staples 85	U. S. products, other than S. C. export staples [1] 86	Foreign imports [1] 87
	1843–61 =100				
1861	113	133	105	144	166
1860	94	111	116	113	96
1859	94	111	120	112	92
1858	90	106	120	99	94
1857	106	125	135	123	109
1856	97	114	116	116	109
1855	98	115	108	132	95
1854	88	103	100	111	93
1853	84	99	108	96	89
1852	77	91	96	91	79
1851	78	92	97	90	84
1850	87	102	123	88	91
1849	73	86	85	85	90
1848	67	79	66	86	92
1847	90	105	110	100	107
1846	75	88	83	85	105
1845	70	82	72	82	102
1844	68	80	73	74	106
1843	66	77	66	74	106
	1818–42 =100				
1842	74	74	67	80	75
1841	85	85	81	88	86
1840	83	83	75	90	83
1839	107	107	108	114	90
1838	103	103	88	123	92
1837	108	108	92	133	90
1836	121	121	129	124	100
1835	108	108	123	100	91
1834	93	93	97	91	91
1833	93	93	94	93	89
1832	86	86	78	91	89
1831	81	81	70	88	86
1830	82	82	78	80	93
1829	82	82	72	85	97
1828	85	85	80	81	103
1827	87	87	77	87	104
1826	92	92	83	96	104
1825	109	109	133	84	110
1824	93	93	99	82	102
1823	98	98	94	94	111
1822	108	108	100	108	122
1821	101	101	103	92	113
1820	110	110	121	97	114
1819	133	133	131	138	128
1818	179	179	220	160	135

Year	All commodities (1818–42 =100) 83	All commodities 84	S. C. export staples 85	Other than S. C. export staples [1] 86, 87
	1813–22 =100			
1822	108	77	75	79
1821	101	71	74	67
1820	110	78	86	71
1819	133	98	96	99
1818	179	135	160	110
1817	189	138	145	131
1816	172	125	134	116
1815	149	109	102	115
1814	123	90	70	110
1813	109	79	57	101
	1796–1812 =100			
1812	95	84	63	106
1811	96	85	70	100
1810	96	85	80	91
1809	90	79	74	85
1808	87	76	70	83
1807	107	94	100	88
1806	109	97	101	92
1805	126	111	116	105
1804	114	101	100	102
1803	112	98	106	90
1802	106	93	96	91
1801	136	120	122	118
1800	123	108	114	103
1799	133	117	125	110
1798	129	114	123	106
1797	122	108	108	108
1796	145	128	134	122

Year	All commodities (1818–42 =100) 83	S. C. products (1762–74 =100) 88	Imported [2] (1781, 1784–91 =100) 89
1791	92	110	106
1790	97	119	106
1789	88	113	86
1788	97	128	87
1787	108	142	97
1786	108	142	98
1785	100	135	84
1784	110	150	86
1783			
1782	[3]192	[3]250	[3]178
1781	138	170	150
1780	[3]118	[3]137	[3]146

[1] Combination for 1796 to 1822 designated as "Other than South Carolina export staples."   [3] Based on part of year only.
[2] Includes goods imported from abroad and from other parts of the United States.

Series E 83–89. Wholesale Price Indexes (Taylor), for Charleston, S. C.: 1732 to 1861—Con.

Year	All commodities (1818–42 =100) 83	S. C. products (1762–74 =100) 88	Year	All commodities (1818–42 =100) 83	S. C. products (1762–74 =100) 88	Year	All commodities (1818–42 =100) 83	S. C. products (1762–74 =100) 88	Year	All commodities (1818–42 =100) 83	S. C. products (1762–74 =100) 88
1775	³80	³102	1764	67	86	1753	88	112	1742	66	85
1774	81	104	1763	72	92	1752	76	97	1741	76	97
1773	91	116	1762	60	77	1751	65	83			
1772	107	137	1761	62	80				1740	60	77
1771	84	108				1750	78	100	1739	65	84
			1760	72	92	1749	75	96	1738	³98	³125
1770	72	93	1759	87	112	1748	68	88	1737	92	117
1769	81	104	1758	67	86	1747	54	69	1736	75	96
1768	80	102	1757	61	78	1746	35	45			
1767	74	94	1756	60	77				1735	82	105
1766	78	100				1745	36	46	1734	84	108
			1755	67	86	1744	50	64	1733	62	80
1765	68	87	1754	67	86	1743	54	70	1732	62	79

³ Based on part of year only.

Series E 90–95. Wholesale Price Indexes (Berry), for Cincinnati, 1816 to 1861, and Ohio River Valley, 1788 to 1817

Year	Cincinnati, weighted (1824–46 =100) All commodities 90	Identified with northern agriculture 91	Not identified with northern agriculture 92	Year	Ohio River Valley, unweighted (1788–1817 =100) All commodities 93	Identified with northern agriculture 94	Not identified with northern agriculture 95
1861	103	123	76	1817	125	145	75
1860	110	133	80	1816	116	131	75
1859	114	140	79				
1858	102	120	77	1815	108	117	86
1857	128	154	94	1814	122	134	90
1856	121	141	93	1813	106	114	86
				1812	77	84	60
1855	123	153	81	1811	79	78	82
1854	110	128	85				
1853	104	118	84	1810	87	88	85
1852	93	112	68	1809	90	87	97
1851	90	107	68	1808	95	89	110
				1807	95	92	104
1850	86	98	72	1806	95	95	96
1849	77	87	65				
1848	75	83	65	1805	86	86	89
1847	90	102	76	1804	87	85	90
1846	76	81	69	1803	84	82	88
				1802	88	84	99
1845	87	97	68	1801	90	89	94
1844	77	81	71				
1843	72	73	70	1800	93	88	106
1842	72	70	76	1799	97	89	117
1841	89	91	87	1798	109	108	113
				1797	133	134	129
1840	104	111	91	1796	127	125	132
1839	138	150	116				
1838	129	137	115	1795	111	110	114
1837	131	142	112	1794	96	95	100
1836	145	159	121	1793	106	110	96
				1792	98	101	92
1835	117	125	102	1791	92	88	104
1834	95	93	97				
1833	102	101	102	1790	98	90	118
1832	101	103	98	1789	102	87	139
1831	99	100	98	1788	104	93	130
1830	93	86	106				
1829	98	91	112				
1828	92	81	113				
1827	91	79	114				
1826	93	81	115				
1825	100	85	127				
1824	98	85	122				
1823	101	87	129				
1822	98	78	166				
1821	86	68	160				
1820	140	112	237				
1819	193	164	265				
1818	190	160	264				
1817	205	175	272				
1816	196	164	289				

Series E 96–100. Wholesale Price Indexes (Taylor), for New Orleans: 1800 to 1861

Year	All commodities (1824–42 =100) 96	All commodities 97	La. products 98	U. S. products, other than La. 99	Foreign imports 100
1843–61 = 100					
1861	117	125	102	138	206
1860	105	112	113	110	110
1859	107	114	118	110	106
1858	104	111	118	104	106
1857	136	144	156	136	115
1856	114	121	121	124	107
1855	103	110	96	129	107
1854	90	96	82	114	101
1853	91	97	94	101	96
1852	85	90	91	91	84
1851	89	95	98	93	86
1850	103	110	123	95	95
1849	80	85	85	85	81
1848	68	73	66	81	80
1847	93	99	108	90	82
1846	78	83	88	77	83
1845	74	79	77	80	85
1844	75	80	84	74	84
1843	70	74	75	70	89
1842	75	78	76	79	93
1841	93	100	102	97	104
1840	91	97	88	106	105
1824–42 = 100					
1842	75	75	73	78	75
1841	93	93	89	100	85
1840	91	91	78	110	82
1839	116	116	105	136	93
1838	107	107	98	123	96
1837	108	108	103	118	98
1836	132	132	140	129	103
1835	123	123	133	114	95
1834	96	96	99	95	87
1833	99	99	103	95	95
1832	88	88	84	92	102
1831	80	80	74	86	97
1830	86	86	85	82	103
1829	90	90	84	94	108
1828	91	91	92	86	110

Year	All commodities (1824–42 =100) 96	All commodities 97	La. products 98	U. S. products, other than La. 99	Foreign imports 100
1824–42 = 100—Con.					
1827	90	90	88	87	112
1826	95	95	97	88	116
1825	130	130	155	96	123
1824	110	110	122	90	123
1823	105	105	112	90	132
1822	124	124	140	94	152
1821	115	115	130	83	160
1820	119	119	126	98	190
1819	151	151	160	127	200
1818	200	200	224	146	220
1817	197	197	218	150	151
1816	214	214	227	184	182
1815	170	170	178	142	-----
1805–11 = 100 [1]					
1811	110	87	87		89
1810	119	95	91		108
1809	120	95	91		112
1808	112	89	90		83
1807	133	106	109		92
1806	142	113	114		106
1805	147	117	118		111
1804	126	100	100		101
1805–11 = 100					
1811	110		83		
1810	119		87		
1809	120		88		
1808	112		89		
1807	133		112		
1806	142		118		
1805	147		124		
1804	126		99		
1803	115		95		
1802	130		106		
1801	146		120		
1800	[2]138		[2]114		

[1] Combination of series E 98 and E 99 designated as "Domestic products."   [2] Based on part of year only.

Series E 101–112. Wholesale Prices of Selected Commodities: 1800 to 1957

In dollars per unit. Where 2 prices are shown for a single year, those in italic are comparable to preceding years, and those in regular type comparable with following years; see text for detailed explanation]

Year	Wheat	Wheat flour	Sugar	Cotton, raw	Wool	Cotton sheeting	Coal, anthracite	Steel rails	Nails	Copper	Turpentine	Brick
	101	102	103	104	105	106	107	108	109	110	111	112
	Bu.	100 lb.[1]	Lb.	Lb.	Lb.	Yd.[2]	Ton[3]	100 lb.[4]	100 lb.	Lb.	Gallon[5]	1,000
1957	2.201	5.680	0.090	0.338	1.608	0.205	14.67	5.442	9.596	0.303	0.662	30.86
1956	2.219	5.676	.086	[6].335 / *[7].351*	1.373	.229	13.53	4.946	8.917	.418	.645	30.61
1955	2.256	5.935	.084	.336	1.423	.213	12.93	4.663	8.180	.373	.640	29.15
1954	2.307	6.133	.086	.341	1.705	.210	14.01	4.463	7.651	.300	.653	28.22
1953	2.238	5.649	.086	.329	1.729	.222	15.45	[8]4.086 / *[9]3.775*	7.440	.290	.594	27.85
1952	2.387	5.477	.084	.387	1.665	.226	14.30	3.672	7.123	.245	.632	27.35
1951	2.403	5.750	.082	.416	2.702	.275	14.19	3.600	6.930	.245	.812	27.33
1950	2.225	5.429 / *5.215*	.078	.362	1.991	.259	12.58	3.415	6.339	.216	.528	25.67
1949	2.149	5.036	.078	.316	1.662	.212	12.04	3.208	6.136	.195	.387	24.73
1948	2.409	5.445	.076	.338	1.646	.243	11.57	2.938	5.823	.223	.481	23.65
1947	2.602	6.200	.081	.345	1.242	.264	10.33 / *14.11*	2.606	4.467 / *3.971*	.213	.751	20.98 / *20.50*
1946	1.895	4.487	.064	.305	1.025	.201	13.06	47.90 (per gross ton)	3.477	.141	.953	18.13
1945	1.664	3.181	.054	.226	1.192	.153	11.89	42.94	2.850	.120	.794	15.89
1944	1.604	3.184	.055	.212	1.188	.145	11.47	40.00	2.550	.120	.776	14.29
1943	1.440	3.170	.055	.206	1.183	.142	10.89	40.00	2.550	.120	.668	13.43
1942	1.189	5.448	.055	.193	1.195	.141	10.31	40.00	2.550	.120	.619 / *7.06*	13.21
1941	.992	4.752	.049	.139 / *.146*	1.091	.115 / *.121*	10.01	40.00	2.550	.120	.617	12.59

See footnotes at end of table.

Series E 101–112. Wholesale Prices of Selected Commodities: 1800 to 1957—Con.

[In dollars per unit. Where 2 prices are shown for a single year, those in italic are comparable to preceding years, and those in regular type comparable with following years; see text for detailed explanation]

Year	Wheat 101	Wheat flour 102	Sugar 103	Cotton, raw 104	Wool 105	Cotton sheeting 106	Coal, anthracite 107	Steel rails 108	Nails 109	Copper 110	Turpentine 111	Brick 112
	Bu.	100 lb.¹	Lb.	Lb.	Lb.	Yd.²	Ton³	100 lb.⁴	100 lb.	Lb.	Gallon⁵	1,000
1940	0.871	4.307	0.044	0.104	0.966	0.085	9.55	40.00	2.550	0.115	0.371	12.13
1939	.755	3.872	.046	.095	.823	.079	9.14	40.00	2.461	.112	.314	12.05
1938	.777	4.364	.045	.087	.691	.076	9.44	41.79	2.575	.102	.294	12.00
1937	1.201	5.606	.047	.114	.971	.107	9.37	41.89	2.773	.131	.387	12.05
1936	1.123	5.441	.048	.121	.881	.097	9.74	36.63	2.229	.097	.438	11.74
1935	1.040	6.197	.049	.119	.723	.110	9.59	36.38	2.628	.089	.500	11.77
1934	.932	5.755	.044	.123	.817	.109	9.64	36.38	2.623	.087	.529	12.00
1933	.724	4.633	.043	.087	.663	.088	10.06	39.33	2.089	.073	.463	{ 10.53 / *9.19* }
1932	.494	3.104	.040	.064	.459	.062	10.88	42.38	2.050	.058	.431	9.54
1931	.606	3.570	.044	.085	.621	.072	{ 11.40 / *12.77* }	43.00	1.978	.084	.447	10.02
1930	.900	4.865	.047	.135	.763	.105	12.72	43.00	2.191	.132	.473	10.10
1929	1.180	5.794	.051	.191	.987	.125	12.89	43.00	2.667	.184	.550	10.73
1928	1.324	6.406	.056	.200	1.159	.135	{ 13.00 / *10.93* }	43.00	2.676	.148	.565	13.00
1927	1.372	6.686	.058	.176	1.107	.120	10.95	43.00	2.638	{ .132 / *.130* }	.621	13.88
1926	1.496	7.252	.055	.175	1.152	.123	11.48	43.00	2.750	.138	.930	16.46
1925	1.670	7.678	.055	.235	1.392	.147	11.19	43.00	2.820	.141	1.013	14.70
1924	1.232	5.980	.074	.287	1.407	.161	11.37	43.00	2.989	.131	.912	17.04
1923	1.112	5.353	.084	.293	1.379	.163	10.88	43.00	3.035	.145	1.171	19.81
1922	1.213	6.130	.059	.212	1.238	.129	10.60	40.69	2.610	.134	1.150	17.34
1921	1.326	7.034	.062	.151	.828	.131	10.53	45.65	3.056	.126	.681	15.21
1920	2.455	11.580	.127	.339	1.604	.288	9.50	53.83	4.187	.180	1.734	21.85
1919	2.418	10.695	.089	.325	1.775	.232	8.27	49.26	3.518	.191	1.210	15.96
1918	2.159	10.302	.078	.318	1.815	.235	6.86	56.00	3.600	.247	.594	11.93
1917	2.296	10.551	.077	.235	1.568	.145	5.94	40.00	3.633	.294	.488	8.89
1916	1.329	6.091	.069	.145	.845	.088	5.57	33.33	2.596	.275	.491	8.04
1915	1.290	5.612	.056	.102	.707	.068	5.33	30.00	1.746	.173	.459	6.05
1914	.939	4.125	.047	.121	.593	.080	5.32	30.00	1.679	.134	.473	5.53
1913	{ .877 / *.953* }	{ 3.847 / *4.308* }	.043	.128	{ .562 / *.589* }	.084	5.31	{ 30.00 / *28.00* }	1.819	.157	.428	6.56
1912	1.049	4.686	.051	.115	.647	.081	5.28	28.00	1.740	.164	.470	6.76
1911	.984	3.984	.053	.130	.647	.088	5.00	28.00	1.804	.125	.679	5.89
1910	1.097	4.691	.050	.151	.686	.084	4.81	28.00	1.888	.129	.683	5.72
1909	1.200	5.451	.048	.121	.738	.075	4.82	28.00	1.917	.131	.491	6.39
1908	.990	4.291	.049	.105	.716	.078	4.82	28.00	2.100	.133	.453	5.10
1907	.907	3.988	.047	.119	.718	.084	4.82	28.00	2.117	{ .208 / *.213* }	.634	6.16
1906	.793	3.615	.045	.110	.718	.080	4.86	28.00	1.958	.196	.665	8.55
1905	1.010	4.543	.053	.096	.759	.076	4.82	28.00	1.896	.158	.628	8.10
1904	1.039	4.826	.048	.121	.686	.080	4.83	28.00	1.906	.131	.576	7.49
1903	.790	3.592	.046	.112	.655	.068	4.83	28.00	2.075	.137	.572	5.91
1902	.741	3.489	.045	.089	.577	.063	4.46	28.00	2.104	.120	.474	5.39
1901	.719	3.309	.051	.086	.545	.063	4.33	27.33	2.365	.169	.373	5.77
1900	.704	3.349	.053	.096	.659	.062	3.92	32.29	2.633	.166	.477	5.25
1899	.711	3.382	.049	.066	.623	.054	3.65	28.13	2.388	.177	.458	5.69
1898	.885	4.145	.050	.060	.615	.054	3.55	17.63	1.438	.119	.322	5.75
1897	.795	4.361	.045	.072	.496	.059	3.74	18.75	1.485	.113	.292	4.94
1896	.641	3.620	.045	.079	.394	.062	3.56	28.00	2.925	.110	.274	5.06
1895	.600	3.231	.042	.073	.377	.059	2.98	24.33	2.118	.108	.292	5.31
1894	.559	2.750	.041	.070	.445	.060	3.54	24.00	1.652	.095	.293	5.00
1893	.677	3.283	.048	.083	.564	.068	4.17	28.13	1.992	.109	.300	5.83
1892	.788	4.122	.044	.077	.612	.065	3.94	30.00	2.190	.115	.323	5.77
1891	.962	4.905	.047	.086	.686	.073	3.46	29.92	2.467	.131	.380	5.71
1890	{ .893 / *.865* }	{ 4.652 / *6.039* }	{ .062 / *.063* }	{ .111 / *.115* }	{ .716 / *.733* }	{ .073 / *.067* }	{ 3.35 / *3.92* }	31.78	{ 2.965 / *2.00* }	.158	{ .408 / *.414* }	6.56
1889	.895	6.540	.080	.107	.735	.067	4.04	29.25	2.00	.138	.461	7.00
1888	.886	6.120	.071	.103	.680	.069	4.21	29.83	2.03	.168	.398	6.52
1887	.769	5.817	.059	.103	.733	.068	4.05	37.08	2.30	.113	.358	7.40
1886	.797	6.119	.062	.094	.740	.064	4.00	34.52	2.27	.110	.395	7.58
1885	.864	6.275	.064	.105	.713	.067	4.10	28.52	2.33	.111	.351	6.36
1884	.913	7.043	.068	.106	.805	.069	4.42	30.75	2.39	.138	.328	6.52
1883	1.038	7.735	.087	.106	.860	.075	4.54	37.75	3.06	.159	.432	8.14
1882	1.198	9.020	.095	.122	.905	.079	4.61	48.50	3.47	.185	.518	10 7.58
1881	1.154	8.895	.097	.113	.955	.080	4.53	61.08	3.09	.183	.476	11 7.50
1880	{ 1.057 / *1.253* }	8.895	.099	.120	1.028	.081	4.53	67.52	3.68	.215	.383	6.94
1879	1.223	8.632	.086	.104	.718	.076	2.70	48.21	2.69	.186	.315	5.26
1878	1.252	9.101	.092	.113	.748	.074	3.22	42.21	2.31	.166	.298	4.89
1877	1.685	10.806	.111	.117	.910	.080	2.59	45.58	2.57	.190	.362	4.94
1876	1.320	9.898	.106	.130	.870	.084	3.87	59.25	2.98	.210	.371	5.71
1875	1.403	10.218	.107	.150	1.045	.099	4.39	68.75	3.42	.227	.345	7.00
1874	1.517	10.728	.106	.170	1.153	.109	4.55	94.28	3.99	.220	.396	7.44
1873	1.787	11.498	.112	.182	1.198	.128	4.27	120.58	4.90	.280	.497	8.02
1872	1.780	12.141	.124	.205	1.568	.135	3.74	111.94	5.46	.356	.618	9.96
1871	1.581	10.245	.131	.170	1.068	.125	4.46	102.52	4.52	.241	.549	9.31
1870	1.373	{ 9.281 / *5.029* }	.135	.240	.898	.140	4.39	106.79	4.40	.212	.427	8.40
1869	1.651	5.725	.162	.290	.905	.153	5.31	132.25	4.87	.243	.458	11.33
1868	2.541	7.912	.163	.249	.888	.160	3.86	158.50	5.17	.230	.510	12.08
1867	2.844	9.164	.159	.316	1.133	.174	4.37	{ 166.00 / *83.12* }	5.92	.254	.639	10.85
1866	2.945	7.920	.166	.432	1.313	.236	5.80	86.75	6.97	.343	.810	11.44

See footnotes at end of table.

Series E 101–112. Wholesale Prices of Selected Commodities: 1800 to 1957—Con.

[In dollars per unit. Where 2 prices are shown for a single year, those in italic are comparable to preceding years, and those in regular type comparable with following years; see text for detailed explanation]

Year	Wheat 101 Bu.	Wheat flour 102 100 lb.[1]	Sugar 103 Lb.	Cotton, raw 104 Lb.	Wool 105 Lb.	Cotton sheeting 106 Yd.[2]	Coal, anthracite 107 Ton[3]	Steel rails 108 100 lb.[4]	Nails 109 100 lb.	Copper 110 Lb.	Turpentine 111 Gallon[5]	Brick 112 1,000
1865	2.160	7.706	0.207	0.834	1.660	0.370	7.86	98.62	7.08	0.393	1.525	9.67
1864	1.942	8.062	.235	1.015	1.770	.513	8.39	126.00	7.85	.470	2.978	8.27
1863	1.640	5.690	.146	.672	1.515	.342	6.06	76.87	5.13	.339	2.924	6.41
1862	1.390	5.165	.113	.313	.938	.176	4.14	41.75	3.47	.219	1.574	4.16
1861	1.425	4.965	.090	.130	.828	.093	3.39	42.37	2.75	.223	.833	3.88
1860	1.495	5.190	.096 / *.085*	.110	1.025	.082	3.40	48.00	3.13	.229 / *.262*	.423	4.49
1859	1.435	5.110	.088	.121	1.093	.080	3.25	49.37	3.86	.261	.481	5.00
1858	1.325	4.295	.087	.122	.825	.078	3.43	50.00	3.53	.260	.460	3.96
1857	1.675	5.785	.118	.135	1.020	.085	3.87	64.25	3.72	.301	.453	4.21
1856	1.755	6.420	.098	.103	1.048	.072	4.11	64.37	3.92	.312	.401	4.29
1855	2.435	8.760	.072	.104	.858	.072	4.49	62.87	4.10	.297	.427	4.31
1854	2.210	8.945	.067	.110	.913	.075	5.19	80.12	4.76	.302	.556	4.89
1853	1.390	5.780	.072	.110	1.070	.074	3.70	77.25	4.85	.291	.593	5.42
1852	1.105	5.005	.070	.095	.818	.066	3.46	48.37	3.13	.235	.452	4.63
1851	1.075	4.520	.075	.121	.855	.066	3.34	45.62	3.28	.205	.353	4.69
1850	1.275	5.550	.074	.123	.833 / *.400*	.073	3.64	47.87	3.71	.215	.334	4.85
1849	1.240	4.510	.069	.076	.361	.064	3.62	53.87	4.00	.215	.333	3.85
1848	1.175	5.960	.067	.080	.343	.066	3.50	62.25	4.25	.215	.370	----------
1847	1.365	6.685	.077	.112	.352	.078 / *8.50*	3.80	69.34	4.50	.232	.402	----------
1846	1.085	5.060	.085	.079	.323	8.45	3.90	----------	4.50	.235	.450	----------
1845	1.040	4.935	.059	.056	.351	8.10	3.46	----------	4.75	.227	.405	----------
1844	.975	4.670	.062	.077	.400	7.67	3.20	----------	4.50	.215	.335	----------
1843	.981	4.855	.057	.073	.305	7.92	3.27	----------	4.25	.212	.338	----------
1842	1.140	5.570	.046	.079	.320	8.57	4.18	----------	4.75	.227	.338	----------
1841	1.185	5.585	.060	.095	.442	8.92	5.79	----------	5.25	.250	.319	----------
1840	1.055	5.295	.058	.089	.391	9.26	4.91	----------	5.50	.245	.266 / *.276*	----------
1839	1.245	7.300	.068	.134	.512	9.22	5.00	----------	6.12	.245	.335	----------
1838	1.920	7.956	.069	.101	.381	9.60	5.27	----------	6.00	.255	.320	----------
1837	1.775	9.140	.070	.133	.424	10.56	6.72	----------	6.00	.270	.390	----------
1836	1.780	7.495	.090	.165	.586	10.50	6.64	----------	6.00	.270	.550	----------
1835	1.220	5.855	.078	.175	.539	8.62	4.84	----------	6.00	.235	.548	----------
1834	1.058	4.980	.071	.129	.488	8.53	4.84	----------	5.50	.235	.471	----------
1833	1.193	5.565	.072	.123	.490	8.74	5.23 / *6.82*	----------	5.00	.230	.415	----------
1832	1.260	5.770	.065	.094	.475	9.28	10.21	----------	5.80	.225	.365	----------
1831	1.185	5.710	.058	.097	.535	10.00	7.08	----------	5.60	.222	.292	----------
1830	1.070	4.985	.070	.100	.390	10.24	9.05	----------	5.50	.220	.292	----------
1829	1.245	6.452	.076	.099	.345	9.44	10.72	----------	7.10	.235	.360	----------
1828	1.218	5.580	.086	.103	.370	8.99	10.92	----------	7.50 / *7.08*	.247	.376	----------
1827	.992	5.140	.085	.093	.390	9.17	11.34	----------	6.76	.262	.365	----------
1826	.940	4.810	.082	.122	.495	9.94	10.92	----------	7.21	.297	.302	----------
1825	.920 / *.998*	5.130 / *5.11*	.093 / *.115*	.186	.585 / *.530*	10.52	9.16 / *.250*	----------	7.33	.304 / *.303*	.405 / *[10] 2.619*	----------
1824	1.103	5.61	.118	.148	.550	9.80	.300	----------	8.87	.252	2.556	----------
1823	1.354	6.84	.120	.114	.717	14.50	.325	----------	9.80	.260	2.692	----------
1822	1.248	6.58	.122	.143	.750	15.00	.325	----------	9.80	.282	2.543	----------
1821	.880	4.78	.114	.143	.750	16.00	.325	----------	9.80	.300	2.219	----------
1820	.928	4.71	.123	.170	.750	16.00	.317	----------	9.80	.290	2.368	----------
1819	1.344	6.89	.153	.240	.825	16.50	.338	----------	9.67	.302	2.877	----------
1818	1.981	9.97	.148	.240	.892	16.99	.327	----------	9.60	.293	3.542	----------
1817	2.406	11.72	.158	.265	.750	17.96	.322	----------	10.90	.273	2.902	----------
1816	1.942	9.80	.184	.295	.975	19.47	.360	----------	12.83	.364	3.688	----------
1815	1.565	8.57	.215	.210	1.333	20.00	.597	----------	12.50	.449	4.478	----------
1814	1.482	8.11	.220	.150	3.312	22.68	1.134	----------	11.25	.600	6.665	----------
1813	1.622	8.94	.205	.125	[12]2.750	21.60	.919	----------	8.50	.504	3.083	----------
1812	1.774	9.34	.142	.105	----------	19.04	.412	----------	8.50	.463	2.425	----------
1811	1.846	10.06	.129	.155	----------	19.04	.370	----------	9.33	.356	3.228	----------
1810	1.796	9.65	.125	.160	----------	21.58	.369	----------	9.50	.428	3.937	----------
1809	1.248	6.86	.127	.160	----------	25.17	.295	----------	9.50	.449	3.835	----------
1808	1.000	5.53	.120	.190	----------	22.50	.276	----------	9.50	.456	3.052	----------
1807	1.308	7.12	.120	.215	----------	20.69	.297	----------	9.50	.508	2.548	----------
1806	1.379	7.27	.125	.220	----------	21.83	.323	----------	9.50	.520	2.979	----------
1805	1.953	10.07	.140	.230	----------	21.27	.399	----------	10.50	.505	3.610	----------
1804	1.357	8.21	.138	.200	----------	19.21	.293	----------	10.50	.480	3.500	----------
1803	1.133	6.85	.122	.190	----------	16.00	.290	----------	10.52	.430	3.625	----------
1802	1.193	6.90	.114	.190	----------	16.00	.290	----------	11.65	.409	2.981	----------
1801	1.835	10.40	.118	.440	----------	17.35	.303	----------	10.67	.500	2.667	----------
1800	[13]1.819	10.03	.134	.240	----------	17.38	.309	----------	10.67	.526	[13]2.500	----------

[1] Beginning 1943, per 100 pounds; for prior years, per 196-lb. barrel.
[2] Beginning 1847 (in regular type), per yard; for prior years, "per piece"; see text.
[3] Beginning 1825 (in regular type), per ton; for prior years, per 80-lb. bushel.
[4] Beginning 1947, per 100 pounds; for prior years, per gross ton.
[5] Beginning 1825 (in regular type), per gallon; for prior years, per 31½-gal. barrel.
[6] July through December.
[7] January through July.
[8] May through December.
[9] January through April.
[10] July price.
[11] January price.
[12] December price.
[13] June through December.

Series E 113–139. Consumer Price Indexes (BLS), by Major Groups and Subgroups: 1890 to 1957

[1947–49 = 100]

Year	All items	Food							Housing						House furnish-ings	House-hold operation
		All foods [1]	Food at home						Total [2]	Rent	Fuel, electricity, and refrigeration					
			Total	Cereals and bakery products	Meats, poultry, and fish	Dairy products	Fruits and vegetables	Other food at home			Total	Gas and electricity	Solid fuels and fuel oil			
	113	114	115	116	117	118	119	120	121	122	123	124	125		126	127
1957	120.2	115.4	113.8	130.5	105.2	111.8	118.6	112.9	125.6	135.2	(3)	113.0	137.4		104.6	127.5
1956	116.2	111.7	110.2	125.6	97.1	108.7	119.0	112.8	121.7	132.7	(3)	111.8	130.7		103.0	122.9
1955	114.5	110.9	109.7	123.9	101.6	105.9	113.5	111.5	120.0	130.3	(3)	110.7	125.2		104.1	119.1
1954	114.8	112.6	111.9	121.9	108.0	106.1	111.9	114.8	119.1	128.5	(3)	107.9	123.5		106.1	117.4
1953	114.4	112.8	112.5	119.1	109.9	109.6	113.5	112.2	117.7	124.1	(3)	106.6	123.9		107.9	115.3
1952	113.5	114.6	114.6	116.8	116.2	111.5	117.2	109.3	114.6	117.9	113.5	104.5	118.7		108.5	111.8
1951	111.0	112.6	112.6	114.0	117.2	107.0	106.7	114.6	112.4	113.1	111.6	103.1	116.4		111.2	109.0
1950	102.8	101.2	101.2	104.5	104.9	95.9	97.6	101.2	106.1	108.8	107.9	102.7	110.5		100.3	101.2
1949	101.8	100.0	100.0	102.7	100.5	96.9	101.9	97.5	103.3	105.0	105.1	102.5	106.8		99.6	100.1
1948	102.8	104.1	104.1	103.4	106.1	106.3	100.5	102.5	101.7	100.7	102.4	100.0	104.4		103.2	102.6
1947	95.5	95.9	95.9	94.0	93.5	96.7	97.6	100.1	95.0	94.4	92.6	97.6	88.8		97.2	97.2
1946	83.4	79.0	79.0	75.6	69.4	85.7	89.3	--------	88.3	91.4	85.9	97.9	77.9		83.9	85.8
1945	76.9	68.9	68.9	65.9	56.5	69.5	86.7	--------	86.1	90.9	84.3	100.7	73.0		76.9	82.5
1944	75.2	67.4	67.4	65.6	55.9	69.4	82.4	--------	84.7	90.6	83.9	101.6	71.7		71.9	80.9
1943	74.0	68.3	68.3	65.1	57.6	69.9	82.7	--------	82.8	90.3	82.3	101.9	68.7		66.2	77.9
1942	69.7	61.3	61.3	63.6	54.2	65.1	64.1	--------	81.8	90.4	80.6	102.5	65.5		64.4	74.4
1941	62.9	52.2	52.2	59.2	46.3	58.2	50.5	--------	78.3	88.4	78.1	103.0	61.6		56.6	69.9
1940	59.9	47.8	47.8	58.6	41.2	52.6	47.3	--------	76.4	86.9	76.2	103.9	58.0		53.0	68.5
1939	59.4	47.1	47.1	57.2	41.6	49.8	46.3	--------	76.1	86.6	75.7	104.9	56.4		53.4	68.4
1938	60.3	48.4	48.4	60.4	42.6	51.7	45.6	--------	76.6	86.5	76.4	105.0	57.5		54.5	69.0
1937	61.4	52.1	52.1	62.5	45.5	54.7	52.8	--------	75.4	83.8	76.6	105.1	57.9		55.0	69.0
1936	59.3	50.1	50.1	60.9	42.6	52.8	51.3	--------	72.8	80.1	76.6	106.9	56.8		50.8	68.7
1935	58.7	49.7	49.7	61.6	43.0	50.6	48.8	--------	71.8	78.2	77.0	109.0	56.0		50.0	69.1
1934	57.2	46.4	46.4	--------	--------	--------	--------	--------	--------	78.4	77.5	--------	--------		48.9	--------
1933	55.3	41.6	41.6	--------	--------	--------	--------	--------	--------	83.6	76.5	--------	--------		44.4	--------
1932	58.4	42.8	42.8	--------	--------	--------	--------	--------	--------	97.1	79.1	--------	--------		45.0	--------
1931	65.0	51.4	51.4	--------	--------	--------	--------	--------	--------	108.2	83.3	--------	--------		51.7	--------

Year	Apparel					Transportation			Medical care	Personal care	Reading and recrea-tion	Other goods and services
	Total	Men's and boys'	Women's and girls'	Foot-wear	Other apparel [4]	Total	Private	Public				
	128	129	130	131	132	133	134	135	136	137	138	139
1957	106.9	109.0	99.2	127.9	92.1	136.0	125.8	178.8	138.0	124.4	112.2	125.5
1956	105.5	107.4	98.7	123.9	91.4	128.7	118.8	172.2	132.6	120.0	108.1	122.0
1955	103.7	105.7	98.0	117.7	90.6	126.4	117.1	165.7	128.0	115.3	106.6	120.2
1954	104.3	106.8	98.9	116.4	90.7	128.0	119.2	161.1	125.2	113.4	107.0	120.1
1953	104.8	107.4	99.7	115.2	92.1	129.7	122.2	150.9	121.3	112.8	108.0	118.2
1952	105.8	108.2	100.9	115.3	92.1	126.2	119.9	141.5	117.2	111.8	107.0	115.4
1951	106.9	107.7	102.2	117.7	101.6	118.4	112.4	132.8	111.1	110.5	106.5	109.7
1950	98	99.5	94.8	104.0	92.0	111.3	107.6	120.3	106.0	101.1	103.4	105.2
1949	9ა.4	100.0	98.1	102.4	93.2	108.5	107.4	111.2	104.1	101.1	104.1	103.4
1948	103.5	102.7	103.8	103.2	108.6	100.9	101.2	100.2	100.9	101.3	100.4	100.5
1947	97.1	97.3	98.0	94.5	98.1	90.6	91.4	88.6	94.9	97.6	95.5	96.1
1946	83.7	82.2	84.6	75.6	72.0	82.1	80.5	84.8	87.7	87.4	89.7	88.6
1945	76.3	72.4	78.8	67.3	65.4	78.1	76.1	82.3	83.1	81.5	86.8	85.7
1944	72.6	69.5	74.8	65.7	62.1	78.2	76.2	82.3	81.2	79.0	83.4	82.4
1943	67.8	66.3	69.4	63.1	60.2	78.2	76.3	82.2	78.7	73.8	75.3	80.2
1942	64.9	63.3	66.4	59.9	59.0	78.5	77.6	82.0	75.1	66.9	69.5	76.3
1941	55.6	54.3	57.5	53.0	46.9	72.2	68.2	81.4	73.1	61.0	66.4	74.2
1940	53.2	51.6	55.0	51.1	42.5	69.8	64.8	81.3	72.7	59.5	64.1	72.8
1939	52.5	50.8	54.5	50.3	40.6	70.2	65.5	81.3	72.6	59.6	63.0	70.6
1938	53.4	51.7	55.3	51.0	41.6	71.9	68.0	81.0	72.5	59.8	62.9	69.4
1937	53.7	52.0	55.7	50.9	44.5	71.3	67.5	80.1	72.3	58.5	60.8	68.8
1936	51.0	49.3	53.0	48.4	42.7	70.2	65.5	80.9	71.6	55.3	59.1	67.0
1935	50.6	48.7	52.6	47.7	42.7	69.6	64.3	81.7	71.4	54.6	58.1	67.2
1934	50.2	--------	--------	--------	--------	--------	--------	--------	70.9	--------	--------	--------
1933	45.9	--------	--------	--------	--------	--------	--------	--------	71.0	--------	--------	--------
1932	47.5	--------	--------	--------	--------	--------	--------	--------	72.7	--------	--------	--------
1931	53.6	--------	--------	--------	--------	--------	--------	--------	74.1	--------	--------	--------

[1] Beginning 1953, includes "food away from home" (restaurant meals and other food bought and eaten away from home), not shown separately.

[2] Beginning 1953, includes "other shelter" (home purchase and other homeowner costs), not shown separately.

[3] Not available.

[4] Includes diapers, yard goods, and miscellaneous apparel.

Series E 113–139. Consumer Price Indexes (BLS), by Major Groups and Subgroups: 1890 to 1957—Con.

[1947–49 = 100]

Year	All items	Food at home, total	Housing			Apparel, total	Medical care	Year	Food at home, total
			Rent	Fuel, electricity, and refrigeration	House-furnishings				
	113	115	122	123	126	128	136		115
1930	71.4	62.4	114.2	85.2	57.4	58.9	74.2	1910	36.8
1929	73.3	65.6	117.4	86.0	58.9	60.3	73.5	1909	35.1
1928	73.3	64.8	120.3	86.7	59.6	60.9	72.7	1908	33.4
1927	74.2	65.5	123.2	88.2	61.1	61.8	72.2	1907	32.5
1926	75.6	68.0	125.2	89.6	62.6	63.0	[5] 72.1	1906	31.2
1925	75.0	65.8	126.4	88.2	64.0	64.0	----------	1905	30.3
1924	73.1	60.8	125.9	86.9	65.4	65.3	----------	1904	30.1
1923	72.9	61.4	121.6	88.1	66.5	65.8	----------	1903	29.7
1922	71.6	59.4	118.5	86.5	61.9	65.7	----------	1902	29.9
1921	76.4	63.5	115.1	87.2	73.0	80.9	----------	1901	28.3
1920	85.7	83.6	100.2	81.7	86.8	105.1	----------	1900	27.2
1919	74.0	74.2	85.3	69.6	70.7	88.2	----------	1899	26.8
1918	64.3	66.5	78.8	64.4	56.1	66.6	----------	1898	26.6
1917	54.8	57.9	77.4	55.4	43.6	49.2	----------	1897	25.9
1916	46.6	45.0	78.1	49.7	37.4	40.9	----------	1896	25.7
1915	43.4	40.0	77.2	47.8	33.5	37.3	----------	1895	26.3
1914	42.9	40.5	76.6	47.6	32.0	36.5	----------	1894	26.8
1913	42.3	39.6	76.6	47.3	31.2	36.2	----------	1893	28.1
1912	----------	38.6	----------	----------	----------	----------	----------	1892	27.4
1911	----------	36.4	----------	----------	----------	----------	----------	1891	28.0
								1890	27.6

[5] December data.

Series E 140–147. Consumer Price Indexes (BLS), for Special Groups: 1935 to 1957

[1947–49 = 100]

Year	All items, excluding food	All items, excluding rent	Commodities				Services	
			Total	Excluding food			Including rent	Excluding rent
				Total	Durable	Non-durable		
	140	141	142	143	144	145	146	147
1957	122.8	117.8	113.6	112.3	108.8	116.1	137.7	138.6
1956	118.8	114.0	110.1	108.9	105.1	113.0	132.6	133.0
1955	116.7	112.4	109.0	107.5	105.1	110.6	129.8	130.1
1954	116.4	113.0	110.2	108.6	108.3	110.6	127.5	127.7
1953	115.7	113.1	111.3	110.0	112.6	110.1	124.2	124.6
1952	113.5	112.7	111.7	109.8	113.8	109.1	119.3	120.1
1951	110.8	110.5	110.3	108.9	112.4	108.5	114.1	114.6
1950	104.2	102.0	101.2	101.3	104.4	100.9	108.5	108.1
1949	103.0	101.3	100.6	101.5	103.3	101.1	105.1	105.2
1948	101.9	103.1	103.2	102.9	101.8	103.1	100.4	100.1
1947	95.1	95.6	96.3	95.7	94.9	95.7	94.5	94.7
1946	87.0	82.3	80.1	84.7	87.5	83.3	90.8	90.2
1945	83.4	74.8	72.3	79.7	83.7	77.6	89.0	87.0
1944	81.5	72.9	70.2	76.7	77.8	74.9	87.9	85.2
1943	78.5	71.6	69.4	72.7	71.2	71.3	85.8	81.3
1942	76.4	66.6	63.8	69.8	68.9	68.4	84.2	77.8
1941	71.4	59.1	55.7	62.7	60.7	61.8	81.6	74.5
1940	69.4	55.8	51.1	59.8	56.8	59.3	80.6	73.6
1939	69.1	55.4	51.6	59.4	57.3	58.7	80.4	73.5
1938	69.6	56.4	52.7	60.4	58.5	59.6	80.3	73.5
1937	68.9	58.0	54.7	60.4	57.5	59.9	78.7	72.9
1936	66.5	56.2	52.7	57.9	54.1	57.6	76.4	72.2
1935	65.8	55.5	52.0	57.3	53.3	57.1	75.6	72.6

Series E 148–156. Consumer Price Index (Hoover): 1851 to 1880

[1860 = 100]

Year	All items				Food	Cloth-ing	Rent	Fuel and light	Other
	Total	Less food	Less rent	Less food and rent					
	148	149	150	151	152	153	154	155	156
1880	110	108	106	96	111	94	127	95	133
1879	108	105	105	95	110	94	122	92	134
1878	111	107	108	96	113	95	124	93	135
1877	118	109	117	101	125	99	123	98	138
1876	119	113	118	106	124	104	123	106	138
1875	123	116	122	108	129	105	129	110	140
1874	129	122	128	116	134	115	133	114	141
1873	133	128	131	122	136	122	139	120	142
1872	135	132	133	125	136	126	144	122	141
1871	135	133	134	127	137	128	144	125	142
1870	141	137	141	135	143	141	142	126	143
1869	147	141	148	141	151	148	141	132	145
1868	154	141	157	143	164	148	138	133	144
1867	157	149	161	157	163	166	135	140	144
1866	167	163	172	178	169	194	138	152	146
1865	175	181	183	209	170	238	134	159	147
1864	176	187	185	222	167	261	130	155	141
1863	139	151	144	173	129	197	113	136	115
1862	113	120	115	131	107	143	101	112	105
1861	101	103	102	107	99	110	95	103	102
1860	100	100	100	100	100	100	100	100	100
1859	100	99	101	98	102	98	100	98	99
1858	99	100	99	100	99	99	100	103	98
1857	105	102	106	102	108	100	100	109	98
1856	102	102	102	101	102	100	103	106	96
1855	104	102	104	102	105	99	103	109	97
1854	101	103	101	103	100	100	102	113	96
1853	93	100	92	100	88	100	100	102	95
1852	93	100	91	100	87	101	100	99	95
1851	92	99	90	99	86	100	100	99	95

Series E 157–160. Cost-of-Living Indexes, (Federal Reserve Bank of N. Y., Burgess, Douglas, Rees): 1820 to 1926

Year	Federal Reserve Bank of N. Y. (1913=100)	Burgess (1913=100)	Douglas [1] (1890–99=100)	Rees [2] (1914=100)
	157	158	159	160
1926			241	
1925			240	
1924			234	
1923			234	
1922			229	
1921			246	
1920		203.7	286	
1919		188.7	247	
1918		171.1	218	
1917		147.8	179	
1916		113.4	149	
1915		101.1	136	
1914		102.5	139	100
1913	100	100.0	137	99
1912	102	92.8	133	97
1911	96	91.5	132	95
1910	96	93.1	128	95
1909	91	88.6	121	91
1908	91	84.4	121	92
1907	95	82.0	126	94
1906	90	78.2	119	90
1905	87	76.0	115	89
1904	87	76.1	115	89
1903	88	74.8	116	88
1902	84	74.8	111	86
1901	82	70.6	108	85
1900	80	67.7	106	84
1899	77	66.1	102	83
1898	75	65.9	100	83
1897	75	63.9	100	83
1896	74	62.9	99	84
1895	73	64.2	97	84
1894	73	65.3	97	86
1893	75	69.1	100	90
1892	77	67.5	102	91
1891	76	68.8	101	92

Year	Federal Reserve Bank of N. Y. (1913=100)	Burgess (1913=100)	Rees [2] (1914=100)
	157	158	160
1890	78	67.8	91
1889	78	67.8	
1888	78	67.5	
1887	76	65.4	
1886	76	65.3	
1885	75	64.6	
1884	77	66.4	
1883	81	71.7	
1882	86	76.1	
1881	83	73.8	
1880	80	71.3	
1879	79	68.8	
1878	80	69.6	
1877	80	77.2	
1876	81	78.0	
1875	86	81.2	
1874	88	83.1	
1873	88	84.7	
1872	90	86.3	
1871	89	86.9	
1870	91	92.5	
1869	95	97.8	
1868	98	104.2	
1867	102	103.5	
1866	103	107.4	
1865	102	108.1	
1864	95	104.6	
1863	78	80.0	
1862	69	66.0	
1861	63	61.2	
1860	61	63.0	
1859	63	63.7	
1858	69	61.2	
1857	70	67.3	
1856	68	63.9	

Year	Federal Reserve Bank of N. Y. (1913=100)	Burgess (1913=100)
	157	158
1855	67	64.1
1854	64	60.9
1853	64	53.9
1852	60	53.7
1851	60	53.0
1850	54	58.4
1849	51	61.1
1848	54	63.1
1847	58	63.4
1846	58	59.0
1845	54	56.3
1844	52	54.9
1843	51	53.6
1842	55	53.5
1841	60	55.9
1840	60	---
1839	71	
1838	71	
1837	72	
1836	68	
1835	60	
1834	51	
1833	58	
1832	57	
1831	56	
1830	54	
1829	58	
1828	57	
1827	57	
1826	55	
1825	58	
1824	57	
1823	61	
1822	64	
1821	62	
1820	65	

[1] Douglas' index for 1890 is 104.

[2] Preliminary figures. Final figures and full description to be published at a later date.

PRICES AND PRICE INDEXES

Series E 161–176. Retail Prices of Selected Foods in U. S. Cities (BLS): 1890 to 1957

[In cents per unit indicated]

Year	Flour	Bread	Meats				Dairy products and eggs			Fruits and vegetables				Other		
			Round steak	Chuck roast	Pork chops	Bacon	Butter	Eggs	Milk, delivered	Oranges	Potatoes	Tomatoes, canned	Navy beans	Coffee	Marga-rine	Sugar
	161	162	163	164	165	166	167	168	169	170	171	172	173	174	175	176
	5 lb.	Lb.	Lb.	Lb.	Lb.	Lb.	Lb.	Doz.	Qt.	Doz.	10 lb.	303 can	Lb.	Lb.	Lb.	5 lb.
1957	54.6	18.8	93.6	52.5	86.6	73.8	74.3	57.3	25.0	57.9	57.1	15.0	16.1	101.7	29.9	55.2
1956	53.3	17.9	88.2	48.4	78.2	57.3	72.1	60.2	24.2	58.3	67.7	15.2	16.3	103.4	28.9	52.8
1955	53.8	17.7	90.3	50.1	79.3	65.9	70.9	60.6	23.1	52.8	56.4	15.1	(¹)	93.0	28.9	52.1
1954	53.6	17.2	90.7	51.4	86.3	81.7	72.4	58.5	23.0	55.4	52.6	²14.6	17.6	110.8	29.9	52.6
1953	52.3	16.4	91.5	52.9	82.7	78.5	79.0	69.8	23.4	49.0	53.8	14.8	17.0	89.2	29.4	52.8
1952	52.3	16.0	111.2	73.5	80.3	64.9	85.5	67.3	24.2	50.6	76.0	14.8	16.1	86.8	29.4	51.5
1951	51.9	15.7	109.3	74.1	79.4	67.2	81.9	73.7	23.1	48.7	50.8	15.8	16.7	86.8	34.7	50.6
1950	49.1	14.3	93.6	61.6	75.4	63.7	72.9	60.4	20.6	49.3	46.1	12.4	15.3	79.4	30.8	48.7
1949	47.9	14.0	85.3	55.5	74.3	66.5	72.5	69.6	21.1	51.8	54.6	12.8	16.4	55.4	30.8	47.6
1948	49.0	13.9	90.5	64.4	77.2	76.9	86.7	72.3	21.8	44.7	55.9	13.9	22.0	51.4	41.4	47.0
1947	48.2	12.5	75.6	51.5	72.1	77.7	80.5	69.6	19.6	43.4	50.3	16.3	21.3	46.9	40.8	48.6
1946	35.4	10.4	52.1	36.6	48.5	53.3	71.0	58.6	17.6	49.9	46.8	12.6	14.0	34.4	28.3	38.4
1945	32.1	8.8	40.6	28.1	37.1	41.1	50.7	58.1	15.6	48.5	49.3	10.3	11.4	30.5	24.1	33.4
1944	32.4	8.8	41.4	28.8	37.3	41.1	50.0	54.5	15.6	46.0	46.5	10.1	10.7	30.1	24.1	33.6
1943	30.6	8.9	43.9	30.2	40.3	43.1	52.7	57.2	15.5	44.3	45.6	10.6	10.1	30.0	23.6	34.2
1942	26.4	8.7	43.5	29.3	41.4	39.4	47.3	48.4	15.0	35.7	34.2	9.9	9.0	28.3	22.1	34.1
1941	22.6	8.1	39.1	25.5	34.3	34.3	41.1	39.7	13.6	31.0	23.5	7.7	7.4	23.6	17.1	28.6
1940	21.5	8.0	36.4	23.5	27.9	27.3	36.0	33.1	12.8	29.1	23.9	7.2	6.6	21.2	15.9	26.0
1939	19.0	7.9	36.0	23.4	30.4	31.9	32.5	32.1	12.2	28.9	24.7	7.2	6.2	22.4	16.7	27.2
1938	19.8	8.6	34.9	22.8	32.9	36.7	34.7	35.5	12.5	26.7	21.3	7.5	6.3	23.2	17.5	26.6
1937	24.0	8.6	39.1	25.7	36.7	41.3	40.7	36.2	12.5	38.9	27.9	7.9	9.6	25.5	19.2	28.2
1936	23.8	8.2	34.1	22.3	34.1	40.7	39.5	37.1	12.0	33.6	31.9	8.0	6.7	24.3	18.5	27.9
1935	25.3	8.3	36.0	24.0	36.1	41.3	36.0	37.6	11.7	32.0	19.1	8.6	6.2	25.7	18.8	28.2
1934	24.5	8.3	28.1	17.5	25.5	29.1	31.5	32.5	11.2	34.1	23.0	8.8	6.1	26.9	13.5	27.5
1933	19.5	7.1	25.7	16.0	19.8	22.6	27.8	28.8	10.4	27.3	23.0	7.7	5.3	26.4	13.2	26.5
1932	16.0	7.0	29.7	18.5	21.5	24.2	27.8	30.2	10.7	30.2	17.0	7.8	5.2	29.4	15.4	25.0
1931	18.0	7.7	35.4	22.7	29.6	36.6	35.8	35.0	12.6	35.0	24.0	8.5	8.1	32.8	19.9	28.0
1930	23.0	8.6	42.6	28.6	36.2	42.5	46.4	44.5	14.1	57.1	36.0	10.2	11.7	39.5	25.0	30.5
1929	25.5	8.8	46.0	31.4	37.5	43.9	55.5	52.7	14.4	44.7	32.0	10.8	14.1	47.9	27.0	32.0
1928	26.5	8.9	43.7	29.6	35.2	44.4	56.9	50.3	14.2	58.6	27.0	9.9	11.8	48.2	27.3	34.5
1927	27.5	9.2	38.7	25.2	37.2	47.8	56.3	48.7	14.1	52.0	38.0	10.0	9.4	47.4	28.3	36.0
1926	30.0	9.3	37.1	23.7	39.9	50.8	53.6	51.9	14.0	51.6	49.0	9.9	9.4	50.2	30.1	34.0
1925	30.5	9.3	36.2	22.8	37.0	47.1	55.2	55.4	13.9	57.1	36.0	11.1	10.3	50.4	30.2	35.0
1924	24.5	8.9	34.8	21.6	31.0	38.4	52.2	51.0	13.4	44.8	28.0	10.8	9.9	42.6	29.3	45.0
1923	23.5	8.8	34.3	20.8	30.3	39.7	55.8	49.9	13.9	49.7	30.0	10.5	10.9	36.9	28.1	49.5
1922	25.5	8.7	32.3	19.7	33.0	39.8	47.9	44.4	13.1	57.4	28.0	11.3	9.9	36.1	28.0	36.5
1921	29.0	9.9	34.4	21.2	34.9	42.7	51.7	50.9	14.6	49.6	31.0	10.2	8.2	36.3	31.6	40.0
1920	40.5	11.5	39.5	26.2	42.3	52.3	70.1	68.1	16.7	63.2	63.0	12.5	11.4	47.0	42.3	97.0
1919	36.0	10.0	38.9	27.0	42.3	55.4	67.8	62.8	15.5	53.2	38.0	13.6	12.6	43.3	41.3	56.5
1918	33.5	9.8	36.9	26.6	39.0	52.9	57.7	59.0	13.9	--------	32.0	--------	17.3	30.5	--------	48.5
1917	35.0	9.2	29.0	20.9	31.9	41.0	48.7	48.1	11.2	--------	43.0	--------	17.9	30.2	--------	46.5
1916	22.0	7.3	24.5	17.1	22.7	28.7	39.4	37.5	9.1	--------	27.0	--------	11.0	29.9	--------	40.0
1915	21.0	7.0	23.0	16.1	20.3	26.9	35.8	34.1	8.8	--------	15.0	--------	7.8	30.0	--------	33.0
1914	17.0	6.3	23.6	16.7	22.0	27.5	36.2	35.3	8.9	--------	18.0	--------	--------	29.7	--------	29.5
1913	16.5	5.6	22.3	16.0	21.0	27.0	38.3	34.5	8.9	--------	17.0	--------	--------	29.8	--------	27.5
1912	17.5	--------	19.9	--------	19.2	24.4	37.4	34.1	8.7	--------	22.0	--------	--------	--------	--------	31.5
1911	17.0	--------	17.5	--------	17.9	24.7	33.7	32.3	8.5	--------	22.0	--------	--------	--------	--------	30.5
1910	18.0	--------	17.4	--------	19.2	25.5	35.9	33.7	8.4	--------	17.0	--------	--------	--------	--------	30.0
1909	18.0	--------	16.4	--------	17.4	22.4	34.5	31.9	8.1	--------	19.0	--------	--------	--------	--------	29.5
1908	16.5	--------	15.9	--------	16.0	20.7	32.8	29.7	8.0	--------	19.0	--------	--------	--------	--------	29.5
1907	15.5	--------	15.2	--------	15.6	20.1	32.7	27.8	7.8	--------	18.0	--------	--------	--------	--------	29.0
1906	14.5	--------	14.5	--------	15.2	19.6	30.4	27.8	7.4	--------	17.0	--------	--------	--------	--------	28.5
1905	16.0	--------	14.0	--------	13.9	18.1	29.0	27.2	7.2	--------	17.0	--------	--------	--------	--------	30.0
1904	16.0	--------	14.1	--------	13.7	18.0	28.0	27.1	7.2	--------	18.0	--------	--------	--------	--------	29.5
1903	13.5	--------	14.0	--------	14.0	18.2	28.7	25.9	7.2	--------	17.0	--------	--------	--------	--------	28.0
1902	12.5	--------	14.7	--------	14.1	17.7	28.7	24.7	7.0	--------	18.0	--------	--------	--------	--------	28.0
1901	12.5	--------	13.8	--------	13.0	15.8	26.5	21.9	6.8	--------	18.0	--------	--------	--------	--------	30.0
1900	12.5	--------	13.2	--------	11.9	14.3	26.1	20.7	6.8	--------	14.0	--------	--------	--------	--------	30.5
1899	12.5	--------	12.9	--------	11.2	13.4	25.1	20.9	6.7	--------	15.0	--------	--------	--------	--------	29.5
1898	14.0	--------	12.7	--------	10.9	13.1	24.4	19.9	6.7	--------	16.0	--------	--------	--------	--------	29.5
1897	14.0	--------	12.5	--------	10.8	12.7	23.9	18.9	6.7	--------	14.0	--------	--------	--------	--------	28.0
1896	12.5	--------	12.4	--------	10.7	12.6	23.8	19.2	6.8	--------	12.0	--------	--------	--------	--------	28.0
1895	12.0	--------	12.3	--------	11.0	13.0	24.9	20.6	6.8	--------	14.0	--------	--------	--------	--------	26.5
1894	11.5	--------	12.2	--------	11.2	13.5	26.1	19.9	6.8	--------	15.0	--------	--------	--------	--------	27.5
1893	12.5	--------	12.4	--------	11.8	14.2	28.3	22.4	6.8	--------	17.0	--------	--------	--------	--------	29.5
1892	14.0	--------	12.4	--------	11.1	12.9	27.5	22.1	6.8	--------	14.0	--------	--------	--------	--------	28.0
1891	15.0	--------	12.4	--------	10.9	12.6	27.4	22.1	6.8	--------	18.0	--------	--------	--------	--------	30.0
1890	14.5	--------	12.3	--------	10.7	12.5	25.5	20.8	6.8	--------	16.0	--------	--------	--------	--------	34.5

¹ Not available.　　　　　Average of January–September inclusive.

Series E 177–185. Retail Price Indexes (BLS), of Electricity, Gas, and Fuel for Household Use: 1907 to 1957

[1947–49 = 100]

Year	Electricity		Gas				Coal		Fuel oil, No. 2 [4]
	Composite [1]	100 kw. hrs.	For space heating, all types	For other household uses			Pennsylvania anthracite, stove size	Bituminous, all domestic sizes	
				All types [2]	Manu-factured 10 therms [3]	Natural 10 therms [3]			
	177	178	179	180	181	182	183	184	185
1957	106.9	104.3	122.8	117.4	‑‑‑‑‑	107.1	146.2	129.8	137.2
1956	106.5	103.8	121.5	115.1	112.8	105.5	136.6	124.8	130.5
1955	106.1	103.4	120.6	112.6	109.1	102.6	128.1	120.4	124.4
1954	104.7	102.2	114.6	109.1	108.0	100.0	129.0	119.1	120.4
1953	104.3	101.2	111.5	107.5	107.6	99.0	134.6	119.2	119.6
1952	103.0	100.3	105.8	105.4	107.2	96.2	127.0	116.8	113.7
1951	102.0	100.1	102.6	103.8	106.6	94.4	125.2	114.6	111.1
1950	101.2	99.4	101.6	104.0	106.5	97.5	113.0	112.1	105.1
1949	100.9	99.4	101.2	103.9	109.8	99.5	107.5	108.1	104.0
1948	100.0	100.9	99.9	99.7	99.1	99.5	101.7	104.3	109.7
1947	99.1	99.6	99.0	96.3	91.2	100.9	90.8	87.6	86.2
1946	100.3	100.4	98.0	95.5	87.0	102.1	83.7	74.1	72.3
1945	104.4	102.4	99.0	97.1	86.7	107.1	75.4	70.4	71.7
1944	104.9	102.5	99.8	98.3	86.6	109.6	72.8	68.9	75.1
1943	105.2	103.2	100.3	98.8	86.5	111.4	68.9	66.5	75.0
1942	105.3	103.2	100.6	99.8	86.1	113.6	65.0	63.7	69.0
1941	105.9	103.7	102.5	100.1	86.2	114.9	62.5	60.6	60.2
1940	106.7	105.1	104.3	101.2	86.5	117.2	59.4	57.1	58.6
1939	107.8	106.4	105.3	101.9	85.8	117.4	56.6	56.6	55.9
1938	109.5	107.8	105.6	100.8	85.5	113.8	57.5	57.0	61.4
1937	111.2	109.3	109.2	99.5	85.1	114.2	57.9	56.6	64.5
1936	113.7	111.7	118.5	100.5	85.1	114.6	61.6	55.4	55.6
1935	117.4	116.6	121.4	101.2	85.2	115.9	59.9	54.3	53.4
1934	123.6	120.0	‑‑‑‑‑	‑‑‑‑‑	84.6	119.5	63.9	54.0	‑‑‑‑‑
1933	133.6	123.5	‑‑‑‑‑	‑‑‑‑‑	84.4	120.5	63.6	50.1	‑‑‑‑‑
1932	135.0	124.5	‑‑‑‑‑	‑‑‑‑‑	84.9	120.7	65.8	50.4	‑‑‑‑‑
1931	136.5	129.2	‑‑‑‑‑	‑‑‑‑‑	85.2	120.7	71.7	54.4	‑‑‑‑‑
1930	138.6	133.8	‑‑‑‑‑	‑‑‑‑‑	85.4	120.7	73.5	57.8	‑‑‑‑‑
1929	141.2	138.0	‑‑‑‑‑	‑‑‑‑‑	84.8	120.8	74.2	57.9	‑‑‑‑‑
1928	146.4	143.8	‑‑‑‑‑	‑‑‑‑‑	84.6	112.3	74.6	58.7	‑‑‑‑‑
1927	149.1	149.2	‑‑‑‑‑	‑‑‑‑‑	84.9	110.4	75.4	60.7	‑‑‑‑‑
1926	151.2	154.0	‑‑‑‑‑	‑‑‑‑‑	84.9	108.4	76.9	61.1	‑‑‑‑‑
1925	153.3	157.2	‑‑‑‑‑	‑‑‑‑‑	85.2	104.7	75.9	59.3	‑‑‑‑‑
1924	155.0	161.2	‑‑‑‑‑	‑‑‑‑‑	85.1	100.1	75.7	60.1	‑‑‑‑‑
1923	156.2	165.1	‑‑‑‑‑	‑‑‑‑‑	85.4	98.2	75.7	67.6	‑‑‑‑‑
1922	159.5	‑‑‑‑‑	‑‑‑‑‑	‑‑‑‑‑	87.5	93.4	74.2	66.4	‑‑‑‑‑
1921	161.3	‑‑‑‑‑	‑‑‑‑‑	‑‑‑‑‑	89.5	86.0	74.6	69.9	‑‑‑‑‑
1920	158.3	‑‑‑‑‑	‑‑‑‑‑	‑‑‑‑‑	78.4	77.2	70.9	69.8	‑‑‑‑‑
1919	158.5	‑‑‑‑‑	‑‑‑‑‑	‑‑‑‑‑	72.2	75.0	59.3	53.6	‑‑‑‑‑
1918	153.2	‑‑‑‑‑	‑‑‑‑‑	‑‑‑‑‑	66.7	68.9	50.5	51.3	‑‑‑‑‑
1917	152.7	‑‑‑‑‑	‑‑‑‑‑	‑‑‑‑‑	63.3	62.6	45.8	47.3	‑‑‑‑‑
1916	156.9	‑‑‑‑‑	‑‑‑‑‑	‑‑‑‑‑	63.2	60.1	40.9	38.4	‑‑‑‑‑
1915	161.0	‑‑‑‑‑	‑‑‑‑‑	‑‑‑‑‑	63.9	59.7	37.9	36.5	‑‑‑‑‑
1914	166.2	‑‑‑‑‑	‑‑‑‑‑	‑‑‑‑‑	64.5	59.7	37.9	37.1	‑‑‑‑‑
1913	[5] 169.6	‑‑‑‑‑	‑‑‑‑‑	‑‑‑‑‑	65.1	[6] 59.7	37.8	36.2	‑‑‑‑‑
1912	‑‑‑‑‑	‑‑‑‑‑	‑‑‑‑‑	‑‑‑‑‑	64.3	‑‑‑‑‑	‑‑‑‑‑	‑‑‑‑‑	‑‑‑‑‑
1911	‑‑‑‑‑	‑‑‑‑‑	‑‑‑‑‑	‑‑‑‑‑	64.5	‑‑‑‑‑	‑‑‑‑‑	‑‑‑‑‑	‑‑‑‑‑
1910	‑‑‑‑‑	‑‑‑‑‑	‑‑‑‑‑	‑‑‑‑‑	65.7	‑‑‑‑‑	‑‑‑‑‑	‑‑‑‑‑	‑‑‑‑‑
1909	‑‑‑‑‑	‑‑‑‑‑	‑‑‑‑‑	‑‑‑‑‑	66.6	‑‑‑‑‑	‑‑‑‑‑	‑‑‑‑‑	‑‑‑‑‑
1908	‑‑‑‑‑	‑‑‑‑‑	‑‑‑‑‑	‑‑‑‑‑	67.3	‑‑‑‑‑	‑‑‑‑‑	‑‑‑‑‑	‑‑‑‑‑
1907	‑‑‑‑‑	‑‑‑‑‑	‑‑‑‑‑	‑‑‑‑‑	[6] 68.0	‑‑‑‑‑	‑‑‑‑‑	‑‑‑‑‑	‑‑‑‑‑

[1] Combination of 40, 100, and 200 kw.-hrs. from 1953 to 1957, and 25, 40, 100, and 250 kw.-hrs. from 1935 to 1952, and the "average consumption" in each component city prior to 1935.

[2] Combination of 10 and 25 therms from 1953 to 1957, and 10.6, 19.6, 30.6, and 40.6 therms prior to 1953.

[3] 10 therms, 1953–1957; 10.6 therms, 1923–1952; prior to 1923, price per 1,000 cu. ft. based on consumption of 3,000 cu. ft. for mnaufactured gas and 5,000 cu. ft. for natural gas.

[4] Includes fuel oils No. 2 and 3 from 1939 through 1947.

[5] December only.

[6] April only.

Series E 186. Rent Indexes (Warren and Pearson) for Dwelling Units in 5 Large Cities: 1860 to 1880

[1860 = 100. Covers Boston, Philadelphia, Cincinnati, Louisville, and St. Louis]

Year	Index 186	Year	Index 186	Year	Index 186	Year	Index 186	Year	Index 186
1880	151	1875	162	1870	180	1865	175		
1879	148	1874	166	1869	187	1864	168		
1878	152	1873	173	1868	179	1863	123		
1877	148	1872	173	1867	167	1862	101		
1876	147	1871	173	1866	187	1861	101		
						1860	100		

National Income and Wealth

NATIONAL PRODUCT AND INCOME (Series F 1-157)

F 1-157.   General note.

In broad terms, national product or its equivalent, national income, is a comprehensive measure of the Nation's total annual production of commodities and services. Only the end products of a year's economic activity are included. For example, since the output of bread is included, the output of wheat used in producing the bread is excluded. At any given time, national product may be measured as the sum of the value added in various forms of economic activity (agriculture, mining, manufacturing, etc.) ; as the total of the incomes accruing to persons supplying different productive factors (wages and salaries, profits, including undistributed corporate profits, etc.) ; or as the aggregate value of the final products of the economy (food, clothing, shelter, etc.).   While each of these approaches yields the same total (given a consistent scheme of valuation), the component detail illuminates different facets of the process of production, distribution, and consumption of the Nation's output, and, hence, serves different uses. These three approaches, of course, do not exhaust the possibilities.

Changes in national product may be measured either in current prices or in prices of a given year. In the latter case, the change ideally reflects only the change in the real volume of commodities and services. Each of these two forms of valuation has its particular uses. For example, in a study of financial developments or market trends, the current price series is often preferable, while for analysis of consumer levels of living or national productivity, the constant price series is more appropriate.

It may be useful to indicate briefly some of the more general conceptual limitations of national product estimates. First, national product is primarily a measure of the output of the market economy. Only a few items of "income in kind" are included. The most important are the value of food and fuel produced and consumed by farm families and the rental value of owner-occupied dwellings. No account is taken of items such as the value of the housewife's services or of home repairs, home dressmaking, or noncommercial recreation. Since economic growth generally involves a progressive commercialization of such activities, the increase of national product reflects to some extent a transfer of production from the nonmarket to the market sector rather than a real growth in the total volume of production.

Second, there is no complete agreement on all of the goods that may properly be considered end products of the economy. National product, as ordinarily constituted, includes, among other things, all items of consumer expenditure. This leads to the inclusion of such things as expenditures on transportation to work and payments to labor unions, which the consumer may not consider end products in themselves, but rather a necessary means under modern industrial organization to secure the money income needed to obtain goods that do constitute the goal of economic activity, such as food, clothing, and recreation. Also, since national product typically includes all government expenditure for commodities and services, criticism has been voiced regarding the inclusion of war and defense goods and government services to business, such as police and fire protection for factories and warehouses. If

this argument is accepted, national product measures would be viewed as overstating the growth of the final product of the economy over time, since these items tend on balance to increase in relative importance as the economy develops.

Third, because of the techniques used in adjusting for price changes, national product in constant prices fails to reflect fully changes in the quality of goods during economic growth. In contrast to the foregoing limitation, this one would tend to understate the growth of national product, since on the average, quality of products probably tends to improve over time.

Finally, national product may fail to measure accurately changes in the material level of living provided by economic activity, even when placed on a per capita basis, since the aggregate figures do not reflect changes in the distribution of income between rich and poor, in consumption needs arising from changes in the age composition of the population, or in man-hours spent in economic activity.

Despite these shortcomings of national product measures for historical analysis, there are wide areas of agreement on the proper means of constructing and interpreting such measures. Their usefulness in providing insights into the nature and growth of the economy is attested to by the wide acceptance of the figures.

Most of the series presented here are based on recent work. The principal works of comprehensive nature used are: Office of Business Economics, *U. S. Income and Output*, 1958, *National Income: 1954 Edition, A Supplement to the Survey of Current Business*, and *Survey of Current Business*, July 1957; Simon Kuznets, *Capital in the American Economy: Its Formation and Financing*, National Bureau of Economic Research, New York (forthcoming), and "Long-Term Changes in the National Income of the United States of America Since 1870," in International Association for Research in Income and Wealth, *Income and Wealth of the United States: Trends and Structure*, Income and Wealth Series II, Bowes and Bowes, Cambridge, 1952; John W. Kendrick, *Productivity Trends in America*, National Bureau of Economic Research, New York (forthcoming); and Raymond W. Goldsmith, Dorothy S. Brady, and Horst Mendershausen, *A Study of Saving in the United States*, vol. III, Princeton University Press, Princeton, 1956.   Earlier works of historical nature are: Robert F. Martin, *National Income in the United States, 1799–1938*, National Industrial Conference Board, New York, 1939; Simon Kuznets, *National Income and Its Composition, 1919–1938*, National Bureau of Economic Research, New York, 1941, and *National Product Since 1869*, National Bureau of Economic Research, New York, 1946; *Enterprise and Social Progress*, National Industrial Conference Board, New York, 1939; Willford I. King, *The Wealth and Income of the People of the United States*, Macmillan, New York, 1915. A basic source for discussion of conceptual issues in the field is Conference on Research in Income and Wealth, *Studies in Income and Wealth*, vols. 1-24, National Bureau of Economic Research, New York.

The extent of detail presented was limited by space requirements; greater detail is frequently available in the original source.   No attempt was made to utilize estimates of contemporaries available for the 19th century, since these figures have not yet been subjected to critical review in the light of modern concepts and techniques. (See George Tucker, *Progress of the United States in Population and Wealth in Fifty Years*, Press of Hunt's Merchants' Magazine, New York, 1843; Ezra C. Seaman, *Essays on the Progress of Nations*, Charles Scribner, New York, 1868; *Annual Report of the Commissioner of Patents for the Year 1848*; David A. Wells, *Our Burden and Our Strength*, Loyal Publication Society, New York, 1864; Edward Atkinson, *The Distribution of Products*, New York, 1885; and Michael G. Mulhall, *Industries and Wealth of Nations*, Longmans, Green, London, 1896.)

F 1–5. Gross national product, total and per capita, in current and 1929 prices, 1869–1957.

Source: Series F 1 and F 2, 1869–1873 to 1928, John W. Kendrick, *Productivity Trends in the United States*, National Bureau of Economic Research, New York (forthcoming); 1929–1945, Office of Business Economics, *Survey of Current Business*, July 1957, pp. 8–9; 1946–1957, Office of Business Economics, *U. S. Income and Output*, 1958. Series F 3, 1869–1945, John W. Kendrick (cited above); 1946–1955, computed by applying Kendrick's implicit price index for 1946–1955 to the revised gross national product figures in *U. S. Income and Output*, 1958. Series F 4, computed by dividing gross national product by population estimates in series A 1–2. Series F 5, computed by dividing Kendrick's current price series of gross national product by the constant price series.

Gross national product, as defined by the Department of Commerce, is the market value of the output of goods and services produced by the Nation's economy, before deduction of depreciation charges and other allowances for business and institutional consumption of durable capital goods. Other business products used up by business in the accounting period are excluded. The Nation's economy in this context refers to the labor and property supplied by residents of the Nation. Gross national product comprises the purchase of goods and services by consumers and government, gross private domestic investment (including the change in business inventories), and net foreign investment.

The current dollar estimates for 1929–1957 are the official estimates prepared by the Department of Commerce. For the years prior to 1929, the underlying estimates are those of Simon Kuznets, but they have been adjusted for 1889–1928 by John W. Kendrick to the same conceptual basis as the Commerce figures. The estimates for years before 1889 are in terms of the somewhat different Kuznets concept of gross national product. As is clear from the overlap values for 1889–1893, however, the quantitative difference between the two series is less than 5 percent for these early years. The specific nature of the conceptual differences is indicated below in connection with the discussion of series F 104–130. The constant dollar estimates at all dates are basically those of Simon Kuznets (see text for series F 131–157), but have been adjusted to the Department of Commerce concept for 1889–1955 by Kendrick, who prepared constant dollar estimates for the reconciliation items between the two series.

With regard to statistical reliability, the Commerce estimates are considered to be "subject to only a small percentage of error." The same is very likely true of the estimates for 1919–1928, but for the years prior to 1919 the margin of error widens noticeably. For further discussion of the margin of error in the early estimates, see text for series F 104–130.

F 6–9. Net national product, national income, personal income, and disposable income, in current prices, 1897–1957.

Source: 1897–1928, computed by adjusting the gross national product totals in series F 1 by the estimated values of the items accounting for the difference between gross national product and the given aggregate. (See the reconciliation among the aggregates in table I below.) The values of the reconciliation items are given in Raymond W. Goldsmith, Dorothy S. Brady, and Horst Mendershausen, *A Study of Saving in the United States*, vol. III, Princeton University Press, Princeton, 1956, pp. 435 and 441; 1929–1945, Office of Business Economics, *Survey of Current Business*, July 1957, pp. 10 and 11; 1946–1957, Office of Business Economics, *U. S. Income and Output*, 1958.

The following are definitions used by the Department of Commerce:

Net national product is the market value of the net output of goods and services produced by the Nation's economy. All business products used up by business in the accounting period are excluded. Net national product comprises the purchases of goods and services by consumers and government, net private domestic investment (including the change in business inventories), and net foreign investment.

National income (sometimes called national income at factor cost) represents the aggregate earnings of labor and property which arise from the current production of goods and services by the Nation's economy. Thus, it measures the total factor costs of the goods and services produced by the economy. Earnings are recorded in the forms in which they accrue to residents of the Nation, inclusive of taxes on those earnings. As such, they consist of the compensation of employees, the profits of corporate and unincorporated enterprises, net interest, and the rental income flowing to persons.

Personal income represents the current income received by persons from all sources, inclusive of transfers from government and business but exclusive of transfers among persons. Not only individuals (including owners of unincorporated enterprises), but also nonprofit institutions, private trust funds, and private pension, health, and welfare funds are classified as "persons." Personal income is measured on a before-tax basis, as the sum of wage and salary disbursements, other labor income, proprietors' and rental income, interest and dividends, and transfer payments, minus personal contributions for social insurance.

Disposable income is the income remaining to persons after the deduction from personal income of personal tax and nontax payments to general government.

The precise relations among the various national accounts aggregates for 1957 are presented below in table I.

Table I. Relation of Gross National Product, Net National Product, National Income, Personal Income, and Disposable Income: 1957

[In billions of dollars]

Item	1957
Gross national product	440.3
Less: Capital consumption allowances	37.7
Equals: Net national product	402.6
Plus: Subsidies minus current surplus of government enterprises	1.3
Less:	
Indirect business tax and nontax liability	37.6
Business transfer payments	1.6
Statistical discrepancy	.7
Equals: National income	364.0
Less:	
Undistributed corporate profits	9.4
Corporate profits tax liability	21.6
Corporate inventory valuation adjustment	−1.5
Contributions for social insurance	14.2
Excess of wage accruals over disbursements	
Plus:	
Net interest paid by government	6.2
Government transfer payments	19.9
Business transfer payments	1.6
Equals: Personal income	347.9
Less: Personal tax and nontax payments	42.7
Equals: Disposable personal income	305.1

Theoretically, net national product and national income are superior to gross national product as measures of the final output of the economy, since some duplication is involved by the inclusion in the latter of the production of fixed capital which serves merely for replacement purposes. However, the depreciation charges, taken as an approximation of the value of capital currently consumed in deriving net national product and national income, are largely in terms of original cost, and hence are on a basis of valuation not comparable to that of the gross production of fixed capital (see *National Income: 1954 Edition*, p. 43). In practice, therefore, the measures of the net product of the economy which are obtained are not fully satisfactory.[1]

While net national product and national income are both measures of current national production (ideally, free from the duplication involved in gross national product), they differ in the manner in which this production is valued. Conceptually, in net national product, current production is valued at market prices, while in national income, it is valued at factor costs, that is, at the cost of the capital and labor used in producing it. In practice, as table I shows, the principal difference between these two forms of valuation is indirect business taxes.

Personal income, which measures the actual current income receipts of persons from all sources, differs from the national income in that it excludes certain types of income which accrue in production but are not received by persons (for instance, the undistributed part of corporate profits) and, on the other hand, includes certain types of income which do not arise in current productive activity but constitute personal receipts (such as relief and unemployment benefits). Hence personal income, unlike the national product and national income aggregates, is not a measure of national production. Personal income net of taxes (i.e., disposable income) is the closest over-all statistical approximation to consumer purchasing power derived from current incomes.

The Department of Commerce figures (1929–1957) are believed to be subject to only a small percentage error. Personal income figures are more reliable than those for national income because the major items included in personal income (but not in national income) are reliable, and the exclusions either do not affect reliability or actually increase it.

Since the estimates for the period prior to 1929 were derived by adjusting the gross national product estimates in series F 1, the remarks concerning the reliability of the gross national product figures for this period apply to the present series also. The estimates for the items needed to move from gross national product to the other aggregates were made in a manner and from sources as closely comparable as possible with the Department of Commerce current figures. However, the estimates for these adjusting items "are probably affected by a larger margin of error for the period before 1929 than the Department of Commerce figures for the same items. . . . In addition, two adjustments were ignored altogether for the period before 1929 because no reasonable estimates could be made for them, viz, subsidies less current surplus of government enterprises and business transfer payments" (*A Study of Saving . . .* , vol. III, p. 424). However, these items are quite small at the present time, and were probably relatively less important prior to 1929.

---

[1] Unofficial estimates of depreciation valued on a basis comparable to that of the gross production of fixed capital are available for most years shown in these series. Cf. Raymond W. Goldsmith, Dorothy S. Brady, and Horst Mendershausen, *A Study of Saving in the United States*, vol. III, p. 437.

F 10–21. Value added by selected industries, and value of output of fixed capital, in current and 1879 prices, 1839–1899.

Source: Robert E. Gallman, "Commodity Output in the United States, 1839–1899," Conference on Research in Income and Wealth, *Studies in Income and Wealth*, vol. 24, National Bureau of Economic Research, New York (forthcoming).

Value added in agriculture, mining, manufacturing, and construction, though narrower in scope than national product, is the most reliable output series of fairly comprehensive coverage for the period prior to 1870. "Value added" is the value of output, at producers' prices, less the value of commodities consumed in production, at delivered prices. Viewed from the income side, it comprises for any given sector the sum of payments to factors of production (net income originating), payments made to noncommodity producing firms (including government, but excluding transportation), and depreciation. Generally speaking, the coverage of the total for the four sectors combined is fairly close to that for finished commodity output plus construction materials (see also text for series P 250–306). It differs from gross national product primarily in that it excludes the value of transportation and distributive services and of services to ultimate consumers, such as medical and educational services, and refers to the product produced within a given area rather than that accruing to the residents of the area.

The series for agriculture includes the value of food, fuel, and manufactures produced and consumed on the farm; that for mining excludes the output of precious metals mining; and that for manufacturing excludes home manufactures and the products of the independent hand trades. Forestry and fisheries are not covered in any of the series.

Estimates in constant prices were obtained for each sector as the difference between the constant price value of the output of the sector and the constant price value of the sector's purchases of materials.

The series on value of output of fixed capital covers the value of construction, manufactured producers' durables, and farm improvements. The value of repairs and maintenance is included only in the estimates for construction. Fixed capital produced by the independent hand trades—chiefly artisans' tools and agricultural implements—is not included. As noted in connection with the earlier series, the figures relate to output, not domestic use. Constant price estimates were obtained for construction by deflating the current price series by an index of the cost of labor and construction materials. For producers' durables, an index of selling prices was chiefly used, and for farm improvements, use was made of a series on acres of land improved.

In general, the principal sources were the Federal and State censuses of the period, but a wide range of additional materials was used either directly for the estimates or to test the results. Compared with the national product estimates for the late 19th century, the present series might be considered less reliable, because of the greater scarcity of materials at the earlier dates and the lower reliability of the census returns. On the other hand, restriction of scope to the commodity sectors would tend to improve reliability relative to the national product estimates, since the basic sources for the service estimates included in the latter are much less satisfactory than those for commodity output. The estimates for the different commodity producing sectors are believed about equally reliable, except that for construction which is substantially inferior to the others. Also, because of the greater relative importance of construction in the fixed capital series, it is less reliable than the value-added series for all sectors combined.

F 22–48. General note.

These series present distributions of total income or product by industrial origin. In obtaining such a distribution, the income originating in an industry is generally measured by summing employee compensation, income of unincorporated enterprises and corporate profits (both including adjustment for inventory valuation), and net interest. Because of statistical difficulties, rental income of persons is assigned wholly to the real estate industry, rather than to the industry of origin.

One of the most important uses of a distribution by industrial origin is to indicate the changing importance of various productive activities in the economy. For example, such a distribution shows whether agriculture is growing or declining, and how it is changing relative to other sectors. However, certain qualifications must be attached to such an interpretation of the sector totals. In the distribution of employee compensation by industry, establishments are classified wholly in the industry that accounts for the principal part of their activity, even though they may perform other functions that should properly be classified in another industry. Thus, the distributive functions carried on by a manufacturing establishment are generally classified under manufacturing rather than under trade. Hence, shifts in the relative weights of different industrial sectors may reflect in part a transfer of activities from one sector to another rather than a change in the relative magnitude of the functions performed. An even greater departure from an activity classification occurs when corporate profits and net interest are distributed by industry. In this case, the distribution is based, because of statistical necessity, on the principal industrial attachment of the company, though the company may include establishments engaged in several industrial lines. Thus, the industrial distributions only approximate a true distribution by type of activity.

Aside from this, changes in the relative importance of the income totals for different industrial sectors may reflect not only changes in the relative magnitude of different productive activities, but also differential movements in the prices received for products or the prices paid for material and service inputs. However, in series F 44–48, which present a constant dollar distribution by industrial origin, the influence of differential price movements has been removed, though unfortunately this adjustment is presently possible for only a few sectors. For an analysis of the difference between the current and constant dollar distributions, by industrial origin, see Simon Kuznets, "Long-Term Changes in the National Income . . . Since 1870" . . . , pp. 92–106 (for complete citation, see source for series F 34–43).

A distribution by industrial origin may also be viewed as an approximation to the incomes of groups in the population attached to particular industries. For this purpose the current dollar figures are more appropriate than the constant dollar figures, though adjustment of the current dollar figures for cost-of-living differences among the various groups would be still more satisfactory. On the other hand, there are important limitations that should be kept in mind in attempting to identify the income of a group in the population with the income originating in an industry. For example, while farmers draw most of their income from agriculture, they may also receive income from part-time employment or investments outside agriculture. Conversely, some income originating in agriculture, such as interest paid on mortgages held by nonfarm landlords, may be paid to persons not engaged in farming. Indeed, for property income in general (profits, interest, and rent), identification of the income originating in an industry with a particular social group is difficult, because those persons to whom property income is important are likely to receive income from diverse industrial sources and are not likely to depend on a single industry. Finally, the income shares of the various industries are shown before deduction for personal and, for 1929–1957, corporate income taxes. These taxes have a differential effect on the various sector totals.

F 22–33. National income, by industrial origin, in current prices, 1929–1957.

Source: 1929–1945, Office of Business Economics, *National Income: 1954 Edition, A Supplement to the Survey of Current Business*, pp. 176–177; 1946–1957, *U. S. Income and Output*, 1958.

The income total used in this distribution is that of national income (see text for series F 7). The industrial classification follows closely that of the Standard Industrial Classification Manual published by the Office of Statistical Standards of the Bureau of the Budget. For a comparison of the classification used in the national income accounts and the Standard Industrial Classification, see *National Income: 1954 Edition*, pp. 66–68.

In the discussion of series F 49–54 below, it is noted that there are differences in the reliability of the estimates for various *types* of income, and, in particular, that the estimates for proprietors' income and for rental income are of a much lower order of accuracy. This information may be used to draw some inferences concerning the relative accuracy of the industry estimates, since, generally speaking, the estimates for those sectors in which the least reliable types of income bulk large will be lowest in statistical accuracy. Accordingly, the estimates for the construction, trade, and service sectors should be considered least reliable, since in each of these, proprietors' income accounts for a disproportionately large share. The estimate for the sector labeled "finance, insurance, and real estate" should also be included in this category, because rental income is of preponderant importance. The most reliable estimates are those for mining, manufacturing, transportation, communications and public utilities, and government, while those for agriculture would probably rank somewhat below these, but noticeably above the least reliable group.

F 34–43. Percent distribution of national income or aggregate payments, by industry, in current prices, 1869–1948.

Source: Simon Kuznets, "Long-Term Changes in the National Income of the United States of America Since 1870," in International Association for Research in Income and Wealth, *Income and Wealth of the United States: Trends and Structure*, Income and Wealth Series II, Bowes and Bowes, Cambridge, 1952, p. 89.

The basic estimates used in deriving this series are those of Robert F. Martin, *National Income in the United States, 1799–1938*, National Industrial Conference Board, New York, 1939; and Simon Kuznets, *National Income and Its Composition, 1919–1938*, National Bureau of Economic Research, New York, 1941. The Kuznets series was extended through 1948 on the basis of appropriately adjusted Department of Commerce figures.

This measure of income originating in an industry differs somewhat from that employed in the Department of Commerce estimates, series F 22–33, corporate taxes having been excluded and interest on government debt included. Also, in the Martin series on "aggregate payments," undistributed corporate profits are not included. Hence, aside from variations in statistical technique and sources, the income totals differ somewhat for the years where the three sets of estimates overlap.

Also, there is some variation in industrial classification. The finance and miscellaneous category in the National Bureau of Economic Research estimates includes items such as income originating in fisheries and in bus, truck, and air transportation, and dividend and interest flows from the rest of the world. In the Martin estimates this category also includes income from fisheries and the net international flow of interest and dividends, as well as income from miscellaneous professional occupations, such as the clergy, and from the hand trades. (In the other two sets of estimates these last two categories are classified in the service sector.) Also, in the Martin estimates shown in the last three lines of series F 34–43, rents are distributed among the various industries, whereas, in the estimates for all other years they are classified under the "finance" sector.

The comments made above in connection with series F 22–33 regarding variations in the statistical reliability of the estimates for the different sectors are relevant here. (See also *National Income and Its Composition, 1919–1938*, pp. 509–523.) Also, the Martin estimates, particularly for the dates prior to 1899, should be considered of a definitely lower order of reliability.

F 44–48. Gross domestic product originating in private farm and nonfarm sectors and government, in 1929 prices, 1869–1955.

Source: John W. Kendrick, *Productivity Trends in the United States*, National Bureau of Economic Research, New York (forthcoming).

Gross domestic product in series F 44 differs from gross national product in series F 3 in that the former excludes net factor income from abroad. Thus the return on capital located abroad but owned by United States residents is excluded, while the income from capital owned abroad but located in this country is included. However, the quantitative difference between the two series is not great.

Kendrick derived these estimates as follows: Gross national product in constant prices, as given in series F 3, was adjusted by a constant price estimate of net factor income from abroad to obtain gross domestic product. A constant dollar estimate of gross farm product was derived as the difference between constant dollar estimates of the total value of farm output and of the value of intermediate products consumed. This procedure is preferable to the more common one of taking the physical outputs of an industry and weighting them by unit values in the base year. The latter procedure yields a measure that includes purchases from other industries, and the figures for a number of industries cannot be summed without duplication. For example, assume that the output of artificial fertilizers was to increase and to cause higher yields in agriculture; the effect on the combined output of agriculture and manufacturing (which would include the manufacture of artificial fertilizers) would be exaggerated if the individual sector estimates were derived without allowance for changes in the constant dollar value of purchases from other sectors.

"Farm" as used in series F 46 differs slightly from "agriculture" in series F 23 in that F 46 excludes agricultural services, forestry, and fisheries.

Gross government product, in accordance with present Department of Commerce concepts, consists of a deflated series on compensation of general government employees. The deflation procedure used does not allow for changes in the productivity of these employees.

Gross private product was obtained as the difference between gross domestic product and gross government product. Gross nonfarm product is the difference between gross private and gross farm product.

The reliability of gross domestic product is essentially the same as that of gross national product, from which it was derived (see text for series F 1–5). While the estimates for farm and government product, the two directly estimated components, are probably less accurate, they are nevertheless based on fairly satisfactory sources, even for the earlier dates.

F 49–66. General note.

These series present distributions of total income by type of income (employee compensation, entrepreneurial income, interest, etc.). Perhaps the chief interest attaching to a distribution of this kind lies in the indication it may provide of the changing manner in which total income in the economy is divided between returns from labor and returns from property. However, the figures as given suffer from certain limitations for this purpose, one of the most important being that entrepreneurial income (including rental income) includes a return both on invested capital and on personal services. Also the income shares are before deduction for personal (and, in the case of series F 53 and F 59, corporate) taxes. Since these taxes have a differential impact on the several shares, it would sometimes be desirable to eliminate them.

Three other recent studies, drawing largely on the same sources as those used here, which present historical data on the distribution of income by type should be noted: Daniel Creamer, *Personal Income During Business Cycles*, Princeton University Press, Princeton, 1956, appendix A; George J. Schuller, "The Secular Trend in Income Distribution by Type, 1869–1948: A Preliminary Estimate," *The Review of Economics and Statistics*, vol. xxxv, No. 4, November 1953, pp. 302–324; and Edward C. Budd, "United States Factor Shares, 1850–1910," Conference on Research in Income and Wealth, *Studies in Income and Wealth*, vol. 24, National Bureau of Economic Research, New York (forthcoming).

F 49–54. National income, by type of income, in current prices, 1929–1957.

Source: 1929–1945, Office of Business Economics, *Survey of Current Business*, July 1957, pp. 8–9; 1946–1957, *U. S. Income and Output*, 1958.

The following are definitions used by the Department of Commerce:

For the definition of national income, see text for series F 7. Compensation of employees represents the income accruing to persons in an employee status as remuneration for their work. From the employer's standpoint, it is the direct cost of employing labor. It includes wages and salaries, i.e., the monetary remuneration of employees commonly regarded as wages and salaries, inclusive of executives' compensation, commissions, tips, and bonuses, and payments in kind which represent income to the recipients. It also includes supplements to wages and salaries such as employer contributions for social insurance; employer contributions to private pension, health, and welfare funds; compensation for injuries; directors' fees; pay of the military reserve; and a few other minor items of labor income.

Income of unincorporated enterprises represents the monetary earnings and income in kind of sole proprietorships, partnerships, and producers' cooperatives from their current business operations other than the supplementary income of individuals derived from renting property. Capital gains and losses are excluded and no deduction is made for depletion. An inventory valuation adjustment is included, which measures the excess of the value of the change in the volume of inventories, valued at average prices during the period, over the change in the book value of inventories. The adjustment is required because income of unincorporated enterprises is taken inclusive of inventory profit or loss, as is customary in business accounting, whereas only the value of the real change in inventories is counted as current output in the national product.

Rental income of persons represents the monetary earnings of persons from the rental of real property, except those of persons primarily engaged in the real estate business; the imputed net rental returns to owner-occupants of nonfarm dwellings; and the royalties received by persons from patents, copyrights, and rights to natural resources.

Corporate profits before taxes represent the earnings of corporations organized for profit which accrue to residents of the Nation, measured before Federal and State profit taxes, without deduction of depletion charges and exclusive of capital gains and losses. In most major respects, the definition of profits is in accordance with Federal income tax regulations. As in the case of income of unincorporated enterprises, an inventory valuation adjustment has been made in order to eliminate inventory profits.

Net interest represents total interest (monetary and imputed, private and government) accruing to United States persons and governments, minus total interest paid by United States governments. The imputed interest component of net interest is measured in general as the excess of property income received by financial intermediaries from funds entrusted to them by persons over property income actually returned in monetary form by these intermediaries to persons.

The figures are official Department of Commerce estimates. The relative accuracy of the various series as evaluated by the Department is, in terms of decreasing reliability: Employee compensation, corporate profits before taxes, net interest, income of unincorporated enterprises, and rental income. In particular, "the entrepreneurial income estimates [including rental income] are subject to significant shortcomings when compared with the other income shares."

F 55–60. Percent distribution of national income, by type of income, in current prices, 1900–1952.

Source: D. Gale Johnson, "The Functional Distribution of Income in the United States, 1850–1952," *Review of Economics and Statistics*, vol. xxxvi, No. 2, May 1954, p. 178.

The definitions for series F 55–60 are the same as those for series F 50–54, except that prior to 1929 corporate profits before taxes (series F 59) does not include an inventory valuation adjustment, and income of unincorporated enterprises (series F 57) includes one only for farm income. Also, imputed interest is not included in the series used to extrapolate the Department of Commerce estimates of net interest prior to 1929.

The underlying figures were prepared by D. Gale Johnson, who carried the Department of Commerce estimates (series F 49–54) back to 1900 on the basis of Kuznets' estimates for 1919–28; King's for 1909–1918; Martin's for 1899–1908; and certain other sources. (Simon Kuznets, *National Income and Its Composition, 1919–1938*, National Bureau of Economic Research, New York, 1941; Willford I. King, *The National Income and Its Purchasing Power*, National Bureau of Economic Research, New York, 1930; and Robert F. Martin, *National Income in the United States, 1799–1938*, National Industrial Conference Board, New York, 1939.)

The procedures followed are summarized by Johnson as follows:

For the period 1910–28 the Bureau of Agricultural Economics' estimates of farm operators' income is used. The estimate of corporate profits is taken from a series of net profits after taxes published by the National Industrial Conference Board, to which is added the amount of corporate taxes paid. Kuznets' series for wages and salaries, nonfarm entrepreneurial income, and rent were accepted as published for 1919–28. His interest series is substantially below that of the Department of Commerce after interest paid by governments is eliminated. It was linked with the Department of Commerce series in terms of average relationship for the period 1929–33. The estimates of King for 1909–18 and Martin for 1899–1908 were adjusted in a similar fashion.

The evaluation of the relative accuracy of series F 50–54 applies also to the present series, though for the years prior

to 1929, and particularly before 1919, the general level of reliability of all series is less than for the later period. For 1929–1952, there may be minor discrepancies between the percentage distribution shown in series F 55–60 and those derived from series F 49–54, since the latter series incorporate some recent revisions.

F 61–66. Percent distribution of aggregate payments, by type of income, in current prices, 1870–1948.

Source: See source for series F 34–43, p. 136.

These series provide a somewhat longer historical perspective on the trend in the distribution of income by type, chiefly by drawing on an earlier study by Willford I. King, *The Wealth and Income of the People of the United States*, Macmillan, New York, 1919. However, the reliability of these earlier figures is uncertain, as is clear from the following statement accompanying presentation of the table in the source:

[The following table] assembles the information available on [the] distribution of aggregate payments by type for the period under consideration. W. I. King's figures are of somewhat doubtful usefulness in this connection, since the treatment of corporate and government savings is not clear from his analysis, and the statistical basis for the estimates is quite thin. Although Martin's figures are on a somewhat more secure basis, the differences in level between [the overlap values for 1909–1918] indicate lack of comparability with the more acceptable estimates for recent decades. One must, therefore, pick one's way with caution in any attempt to infer long-term changes in the distribution of income payments by type.

These series are based on a somewhat different aggregate than those in series F 49–54 and F 55–60, the most important difference being that the "aggregate payments" concept includes only corporate dividends rather than corporate profits before taxes. Hence, corporate profits tax liability, undistributed corporate profits, and the corporate inventory valuation adjustment are all excluded from the total underlying series F 61. In addition, the interest series includes government interest and excludes imputed interest (though in bringing the National Bureau of Economic Research series up to date by means of the Department of Commerce data, the first three entries in series F 65, a series including imputed interest was used). With regard to the remaining three series (employee compensation, entrepreneurial income, and rent), the underlying concepts correspond closely to their counterparts in series F 50, F 51, and F 52, though the statistical procedures followed differ somewhat.

F 67–157. General note.

These series provide a summary view of the end products of the economy. From these data one can determine, among other things, to what extent the annual flow of production took the form of consumers' goods, on the one hand, and capital goods, on the other. In addition, one can examine the composition of the flow of goods to consumers (in terms of broad categories such as services, nondurable goods, and durable goods), and of capital formation, classified according to types such as construction, producers' durable equipment, etc.

F 67–86. Gross national product, by major type of product, in current prices, 1929–1957.

Source: 1929–1945, Office of Business Economics, *Survey of Current Business*, July 1957, pp. 8–9; 1946–1957, *U. S. Income and Output*, 1958.

The following are definitions used by the Department of Commerce:

For the definition of gross national product, see text for series F 1–5. Personal consumption expenditures (series F 68) represent the market value of purchases of goods and services by individuals and nonprofit institutions and the value of food, clothing, housing, and financial services received by them as income in kind. It includes the rental value of owner-occupied houses but does not include purchases of dwellings, which are classified as capital goods. Consumer durable commodities are generally defined as those having an average life of 3 years or longer. Gross private domestic investment (series F 72) consists of acquisitions of newly produced capital goods by private business and nonprofit institutions and of the value of the change in the volume of inventories held by business. It covers all private new dwellings, including those acquired by owner occupants. Producers' durable equipment is defined in terms of items having an average life of one or more years. Net foreign investment (series F 80) is the net change in international assets and liabilities, including the monetary gold stock, arising out of the current international flow of goods and services, factor incomes, and cash gifts and contributions. Government purchases of goods and services (series F 81) measures purchases of goods and services by government bodies, exclusive of acquisitions of land and used depreciable assets and of current outlays of government enterprises. It consists of general government expenditures for compensation of employees, purchases from business (net of sales by government of consumption goods and materials), net government purchases from abroad and international contributions, and the gross investment of government enterprises. Transfer payments, government interest, subsidies, and loans are excluded. Federal national security expenditures include, in addition to national defense outlays, expenditures for international security and foreign relations (other than military assistance) and promotion of the merchant marine.

The figures are official Department of Commerce estimates. With regard to the relative accuracy of the different product series, the Department states that government purchases of goods and services, particularly Federal Government purchases, is highest on the scale of reliability, while the change in business inventories (which includes an inventory valuation adjustment) is lowest. Lying between these extremes are, in order of decreasing accuracy: Producers' purchases of durable equipment and personal consumption expenditures for durables and nondurables; personal consumption expenditures for services; and new construction. While the estimate of net foreign investment is based on a good deal of statistical information, it is nevertheless liable to substantial percentage error because it is derived as the difference between much larger numerical values.

F 87–103. Gross national product, by major type of product, in 1954 prices, 1929–1957.

Source: Office of Business Economics, *U. S. Income and Output*, 1958.

These series present estimates in 1954 prices for most of the current price series presented in series F 67–86. The general procedure followed by the Department of Commerce was to divide the current price figures (organized in a product breakdown much finer than that shown in series F 67–86) by appropriate price indexes based on 1954 = 100. The price indexes used in deriving the 1954 price estimates do not generally allow for quality change. Therefore, the constant price figures do not reflect part of the secular quality improvement in the economy. Also, the present series overstate somewhat short-run fluctuations in output, because available price information understates effective short-run fluctuations in prices. The choice of a recent year price base rather than an earlier year base (for example, 1929) to derive the constant price estimates tends to reduce somewhat the magnitude of the long-term growth in gross national product.

F 104–130. Gross and net national product, by major type of product, in current prices, 1869–1931.

Source: Simon Kuznets, *Capital in the American Economy: Its Formation and Financing*, National Bureau of Economic Research, New York (forthcoming).

The difference between the gross national product series presented in series F 104 and the Department of Commerce series in series F 1 and F 67 is primarily conceptual, and relates almost wholly to the treatment of government in the estimation of national product. In series F 104, government purchases of goods and services is omitted as a component of gross national product. However, an estimate of government services to consumers is added to personal consumption expenditures to obtain an estimate of "flow of goods to consumers" and government capital formation (consisting of both war and nonwar public construction, purchases of durable equipment including durable munitions, and the change in the stock of monetary metals) is added to private capital formation. In addition, series F 104 excludes from flow of goods to consumers and from gross national product the imputed value of unpaid services of financial intermediaries.

The effect of these adjustments is to yield a lower aggregate for gross national product, chiefly because government expenditures which are considered not to take the form of services to consumers or capital formation are omitted from the total. In effect, these omitted expenditures are treated as yielding intermediate services that facilitate the flow of goods to consumers or capital formation, but do not in themselves constitute final products; just as the production of wheat contributes to the production of bread but is not counted as a final product in addition to bread. For the earlier years, the quantitative difference between the two series (F 1 and F 104) arising from this conceptual difference is fairly small, but for the most recent decades it would be quite large, because of the great relative expansion in Government expenditures for military and defense purposes, which in the Kuznets concept are largely excluded from the total.

Net national product differs from gross national product in that an allowance for capital consumed during the year in the process of production has been deducted from the gross national product total. In the present case, capital consumption, both private and public, is valued at reproduction cost. Thus, a piece of equipment used up during the current year is valued at the current cost of replacement, irrespective of the original cost of the equipment. In addition, the capital consumption estimate includes an allowance for depletion of natural resources.

The differences between the present series and the Department of Commerce series with regard to the major components (that is, between personal consumption expenditures and flow of goods to consumers, and between gross private domestic investment and private and public capital formation) have been indicated above in the discussion of the differences in the gross national product concepts. Consumer perishables, semidurables, and durables are commodities that, without marked change and retaining their essential physical identity are ordinarily employed, respectively, less than 6 months, from 6 months to 3 years, and more than 3 years. Because of differences, usually minor, in the scope or method of derivation of the figures, the estimates presented here differ somewhat from those for apparently comparable categories (such as consumers' durables) in series F 67–86.

With regard to the statistical reliability of the estimates, the following quotation, relating to decade rather than the quinquennial averages presented here, is relevant:

For the comprehensive totals of national product and their major components, such as flow of goods to consumers, gross value of producer durables, gross construction, the maximum error in the estimates for the decades before 1919 can be said to be 15 percent; for the later three decades [1919–28, 1924–33, 1929–38] less than 10 percent. The maximum errors may be somewhat larger for the various categories of the flow of goods to consumers; and, on a percentage basis, much larger for the net totals—net producer durables, net construction, changes in inventories, changes in claims against foreign countries, particularly the last two.

Owing to possible shortages in the underlying data or errors inherent in some of the assumptions, the comprehensive totals for the 1869–78 decade may be understated by as much as 10 percent; for the 1874–83 decade by as much as 5 percent; for the subsequent decades through 1899–1908 by as much as 2 to 3 percent. (Simon Kuznets, *National Product Since 1869*, National Bureau of Economic Research, New York, 1946, pp. 85–86.)

This statement, though made with respect to an earlier set of estimates, is also applicable to the revised figures presented here, but since the present estimates refer to quinquennial periods, the allowance for maximum error should be increased.

F 131–157. Gross and net national product, by major type of product, in 1929 prices, 1869–1931.

Source: See source for series F 104–130.

See also text for same series.

These series are exact counterparts of series F 104–130, except that the estimates are expressed in 1929 prices instead of current prices.

The estimates were derived as follows: For commodity production, the current dollar estimates used in deriving series F 104–130, but in the narrowest categories that production statistics permitted, and at producers' prices, were deflated by price indexes for corresponding product groups. The resulting estimates of commodity output in 1929 prices were then adjusted upward by a constant ratio to allow for transportation and distributive margins, thus yielding commodity output at final cost to consumers. The current dollar estimates of services included in series F 104–130 were deflated by the implicit average price index for all consumer commodities, except in the case of rent, which was deflated by a specific rent index.

The discussion of margins of error with regard to series F 104–130 applies here also, except that the deflation procedure increases the possible error somewhat. In particular, since the price indexes used for deflation do not adequately allow for quality change or new goods, an element of downward bias is introduced that is not present in the current dollar estimates.

Series F 1–5. Gross National Product, Total and Per Capita, in Current and 1929 Prices: 1869 to 1957

[5-year periods are annual averages]

Year	Current prices Total	Current prices Per capita	1929 prices Total	1929 prices Per capita	Implicit price index (1929 = 100)	Year or period	Current prices Total	Current prices Per capita	1929 prices Total	1929 prices Per capita	Implicit price index (1929 = 100)
	1	2	3	4	5		1	2	3	4	5
	Bil. dol.	Dollars	Bil. dol.	Dollars			Bil. dol.	Dollars	Bil. dol.	Dollars	
Dept. of Commerce concept:						Dept. of Commerce concept—Con.					
1957	440.3	2,572	(1)	(1)	(1)	1930	91.1	740	95.1	772	96
1956	419.2	2,493	(1)	(1)	(1)	1929	104.4	857	104.4	857	100
						1928	98.2	815	98.5	817	100
1955	397.5	2,405	230.8	1,396	172	1927	96.3	809	97.3	817	99
1954	363.1	2,236	212.6	1,309	171	1926	97.7	832	96.4	821	101
1953	365.4	2,289	215.3	1,349	170						
1952	347.0	2,210	206.7	1,317	168	1925	91.3	788	90.5	781	101
1951	329.0	2,131	199.9	1,295	165	1924	87.6	768	88.4	775	99
						1923	86.1	769	85.8	766	100
1950	284.6	1,876	187.1	1,233	152	1922	74.0	672	75.8	689	98
1949	258.1	1,730	171.1	1,147	151	1921	74.0	682	71.6	660	103
1948	259.4	1,769	174.4	1,189	149						
1947	234.3	1,626	165.6	1,149	141	1920	88.9	835	73.3	688	121
1946	210.7	1,490	166.8	1,179	126	1919	78.9	755	74.2	710	106
1945	213.6	1,526	180.9	1,293	118	1917–1921	75.6	719	71.9	683	105
1944	211.4	1,527	183.6	1,327	115	1912–1916	40.3	408	62.5	632	64
1943	192.5	1,408	170.2	1,245	113	1907–1911	31.6	349	55.0	608	57
1942	159.1	1,180	154.7	1,147	103	1902–1906	24.2	294	46.8	569	52
1941	125.8	943	138.7	1,040	91	1897–1901	17.3	231	37.1	496	47
						1892–1896	13.6	199	29.6	434	46
1940	100.6	761	121.0	916	83	1889–1893	13.5	210	27.3	424	49
1939	91.1	695	111.0	847	82						
1938	85.2	656	103.2	794	83	Kuznets concept:					
1937	90.8	704	109.1	846	83	1889–1893	13.1	204	26.1	405	50
1936	82.7	645	100.9	787	82	1887–1891	12.3	199	24.0	388	51
						1882–1886	11.3	204	20.7	374	55
1935	72.5	569	91.4	718	79	1877–1881	9.18	186	16.1	327	57
1934	65.0	514	80.8	639	80	1872–1876	7.53	171	11.2	254	67
1933	56.0	446	74.2	590	75	1869–1873	6.71	165	9.11	223	74
1932	58.5	468	76.4	611	77						
1931	76.3	615	89.5	721	85						

¹ Not available.

Series F 6–9. Net National Product, National Income, Personal Income, and Disposable Income, in Current Prices: 1897 to 1957

[In billions of dollars. 5-year periods are annual averages]

Year	Net national product	National income	Personal income	Disposable income	Year	Net national product	National income	Personal income	Disposable income	Year or period	Net national product	National income	Personal income	Disposable income
	6	7	8	9		6	7	8	9		6	7	8	9
1957	402.6	364.0	347.9	305.1	1942	149.0	137.7	123.5	117.5	1927	88.2	81.7	79.6	77.4
1956	384.5	349.4	330.5	290.5	1941	116.8	104.7	96.3	93.0	1926	89.9	83.7	79.5	77.4
1955	365.5	330.2	310.2	274.4	1940	92.5	81.6	78.7	76.1	1925	84.0	78.2	75.0	73.0
1954	334.3	301.8	289.8	256.9	1939	83.3	72.8	72.9	70.4	1924	80.7	75.2	73.2	71.4
1953	338.9	305.6	288.3	252.5	1938	77.4	67.6	68.6	65.7	1923	79.5	74.3	71.5	69.7
1952	323.0	292.2	273.1	238.7	1937	83.0	73.6	73.9	71.0	1922	67.9	63.1	62.0	60.3
1951	307.0	279.3	256.7	227.5	1936	75.2	64.9	68.5	66.2	1921	68.1	64.0	62.1	60.2
1950	265.5	241.9	228.5	207.7	1935	65.3	57.1	60.2	58.3	1920	83.0	79.1	73.4	71.5
1949	240.8	217.7	208.3	189.7	1934	57.9	49.0	53.6	52.0	1919	73.8	70.2	65.0	63.3
1948	244.0	223.5	210.4	189.3	1933	48.8	40.2	47.2	45.7					
1947	221.3	198.2	191.6	170.1	1932	50.9	42.5	50.1	48.7	1917–1921	70.3	66.9	62.5	61.0
1946	200.0	180.9	179.3	160.6	1931	68.1	59.7	65.7	63.8	1912–1916	36.9	34.8	33.7	33.3
										1907–1911	28.9	27.2	26.7	26.4
1945	201.0	181.2	171.2	150.4	1930	82.6	75.7	76.9	74.4	1902–1906	22.1	20.7	20.2	20.0
1944	199.4	182.6	165.7	146.8	1929	95.8	87.8	85.8	83.1	1897–1901	15.8	14.6	14.3	14.1
1943	181.6	170.3	151.4	133.5	1928	89.7	82.8	79.8	77.5					

Series F 10–21. Value Added by Selected Industries, and Value of Output of Fixed Capital, in Current and 1879 Prices: 1839 to 1899

[In billions of dollars]

Year	Current prices Total	Current prices Agriculture	Current prices Mining	Current prices Manufacturing	Current prices Construction	Current prices Value of output of fixed capital	1879 prices Total	1879 prices Agriculture	1879 prices Mining	1879 prices Manufacturing	1879 prices Construction	1879 prices Value of output of fixed capital
	10	11	12	13	14	15	16	17	18	19	20	21
1899	*10.20	3.40	0.47	5.04	1.29	3.47	11.75	3.92	0.55	6.26	1.02	3.35
1894	7.83	2.64	.29	3.60	1.30	--------	10.26	3.27	.39	5.48	1.12	--------
1889	7.87	2.77	.28	3.73	1.10	2.82	8.66	3.24	.35	4.16	.92	--------
1884	7.09	2.84	.20	3.05	1.01	--------	7.30	3.00	.23	3.22	.86	2.72
1879	5.30	2.60	.15	1.96	.59	1.64	5.30	2.60	.15	1.96	.59	1.64
1874	5.40	2.53	.15	2.07	.65	--------	4.30	1.98	.11	1.69	.52	--------
1869	4.83	2.54	.13	1.63	.54	1.51	3.27	1.72	.07	1.08	.40	1.09
1859	2.57	1.50	.03	.82	.23	.62	2.69	1.49	.03	.86	.30	.73
1854	2.39	1.46	.03	.66	.23	--------	2.32	1.32	.03	.68	.30	--------
1849	1.40	.83	.02	.45	.11	.31	1.66	.99	.02	.49	.16	.39
1844	1.09	.69	.01	.31	.08	--------	1.37	.94	.01	.29	.13	--------
1839	1.04	.71	.01	.24	.08	.20	1.09	.79	.01	.19	.11	.25

Series F 22–33. National Income, by Industrial Origin, in Current Prices: 1929 to 1957

[In billions of dollars]

Year	Total	Agriculture, forestry, and fisheries	Mining	Contract construction	Manufacturing	Wholesale and retail trade	Finance, insurance, and real estate	Transportation	Communications and public utilities	Services	Government and government enterprises	Rest of the world
	22	23	24	25	26	27	28	29	30	31	32	33
1957	364.0	16.2	6.2	19.6	112.5	59.6	34.6	17.3	13.3	39.4	42.9	2.2
1956	349.4	16.1	6.3	19.1	109.9	57.3	32.1	16.8	12.5	37.0	40.3	2.0
1955	330.2	16.1	5.6	17.4	104.5	55.0	30.9	15.8	11.7	33.7	37.8	1.8
1954	301.8	16.9	4.9	16.0	91.1	50.6	29.3	14.4	10.8	30.2	35.9	1.6
1953	305.6	17.5	5.2	15.9	98.0	49.8	27.6	15.8	10.1	29.2	35.3	1.3
1952	292.2	19.5	5.2	15.4	90.2	49.0	25.6	15.4	9.2	26.9	34.5	1.3
1951	279.3	20.5	5.5	14.2	88.5	47.2	23.6	14.9	8.3	25.1	30.2	1.4
1950	241.9	17.9	5.0	11.8	74.4	42.7	21.8	13.3	7.2	23.1	23.5	1.2
1949	217.7	16.9	4.3	10.5	62.7	40.6	20.0	11.9	6.6	21.3	21.9	1.0
1948	223.5	21.9	5.2	10.6	66.8	41.5	17.6	12.7	5.9	20.7	19.7	1.0
1947	198.2	19.3	4.2	8.4	58.7	37.3	15.3	11.5	5.1	18.9	18.6	.8
1946	180.9	18.7	3.0	6.5	48.5	34.4	14.5	10.2	4.8	17.2	22.6	.6
1945	181.2	14.9	2.7	4.3	52.0	28.0	12.8	10.5	4.2	14.6	36.8	.4
1944	182.6	14.5	2.9	4.1	60.1	25.7	12.2	11.2	4.1	13.6	33.7	.4
1943	170.3	14.1	2.7	5.5	58.1	23.8	11.6	10.8	3.9	12.3	27.0	.4
1942	137.7	12.4	2.6	6.5	45.3	20.3	10.6	8.6	3.7	11.0	16.3	.4
1941	104.7	8.5	2.3	4.2	33.0	17.3	9.2	6.3	3.3	9.8	10.5	.4
1940	81.6	6.2	1.9	2.6	22.3	14.3	8.2	5.0	3.1	8.9	8.8	.4
1939	72.8	5.9	1.6	2.3	17.9	12.5	7.9	4.6	2.9	8.3	8.5	.3
1938	67.6	5.9	1.5	2.0	15.0	11.9	7.7	4.1	2.7	7.9	8.5	.4
1937	73.6	7.2	1.9	2.1	19.3	12.2	7.2	4.6	2.7	8.2	7.8	.3
1936	64.9	5.4	1.5	2.0	16.2	10.6	6.6	4.3	2.5	7.5	8.1	.3
1935	57.1	6.4	1.2	1.3	13.3	9.2	5.9	3.7	2.3	6.7	6.7	.4
1934	49.0	3.7	1.2	1.1	10.9	8.1	5.6	3.4	2.2	6.2	6.3	.3
1933	40.2	3.7	.6	.8	7.6	5.5	5.7	3.0	2.0	5.6	5.3	.4
1932	42.5	3.3	.7	1.1	7.2	6.4	6.8	3.2	2.3	6.1	5.2	.4
1931	59.7	4.9	1.0	2.2	12.4	9.7	8.6	4.4	2.6	7.9	5.4	.5
1930	75.7	6.2	1.6	3.2	18.2	12.2	10.6	5.6	2.8	9.2	5.3	.7
1929	87.8	8.3	2.0	3.8	21.9	13.4	12.7	6.6	2.9	10.3	5.1	.8

Series F 34–43. Percent Distribution of National Income or Aggregate Payments, by Industry, in Current Prices: 1869 to 1948

[Percents based on annual averages of periods shown]

Period	Total	Agriculture	Mining	Manufacturing	Contract construction	Transportation and other public utilities	Trade	Service	Government	Finance and miscellaneous
	34	35	36	37	38	39	40	41	42	43
Based on NBER estimates of national income:										
1939 to 1948	100.0	9.4	1.6	27.1	3.4	7.3	13.3	10.5	17.2	10.2
1934 to 1943	100.0	9.2	1.7	24.2	2.9	8.5	13.2	12.1	15.4	12.7
1929 to 1938	100.0	8.5	1.7	19.4	2.9	10.0	13.6	13.9	14.4	15.6
1924 to 1933	100.0	8.7	1.9	19.6	4.2	10.4	13.3	13.4	11.8	16.7
1919 to 1928	100.0	10.5	2.5	21.9	4.4	9.8	13.6	11.6	9.6	16.1
Based on Martin's estimates of aggregate payments:										
1919 to 1928	100.0	12.2	3.1	22.2	3.9	11.3	13.7	9.4	8.6	15.7
1914 to 1923	100.0	15.2	3.3	22.2	3.0	11.0	14.0	8.3	7.9	15.0
1909 to 1918	100.0	17.7	3.3	20.8	3.2	10.7	14.5	8.2	6.3	15.4
1904 to 1913	100.0	17.0	3.3	18.9	4.3	11.0	15.0	8.9	5.4	16.2
1899 to 1908	100.0	16.7	3.1	18.4	4.5	10.7	15.3	9.6	5.6	16.0
1889 and 1899	100.0	17.1	2.5	18.2	4.9	10.7	16.8	11.8	6.0	12.0
1879 and 1889	100.0	16.1	2.1	16.6	5.5	11.9	16.6	13.6	4.9	12.6
1869 and 1879	100.0	20.5	1.8	13.9	5.3	11.9	15.7	14.7	4.4	11.7

Series F 44–48. Gross Domestic Product Originating in Private Farm and Nonfarm Sectors and Government, in 1929 Prices: 1869 to 1955

[In billions of dollars]

Year	Gross domestic product	Gross private product			Government product	Year	Gross domestic product	Gross private product			Government product
		Total	Farm	Nonfarm				Total	Farm	Nonfarm	
	44	45	46	47	48		44	45	46	47	48
1955	226.2	212.9	14.1	198.8	13.3	1940	120.6	112.7	11.4	101.3	7.9
1954	210.5	197.0	13.5	183.5	13.5	1939	110.6	103.0	11.5	91.5	7.6
1953	213.1	199.3	13.1	186.2	13.8	1938	102.8	95.2	11.4	83.8	7.6
1952	204.9	191.1	12.2	178.9	13.9	1937	108.8	101.8	10.9	90.9	7.0
1951	198.5	185.5	12.1	173.4	13.0	1936	100.5	93.0	9.8	83.2	7.5
1950	186.6	176.2	12.9	163.3	10.4	1935	91.0	84.7	10.4	74.3	6.3
1949	169.9	159.8	12.7	147.1	10.1	1934	80.4	74.5	9.5	65.0	5.9
1948	172.3	162.7	12.8	149.9	9.6	1933	73.8	68.8	11.0	57.8	5.0
1947	163.5	153.9	11.9	142.0	9.6	1932	75.9	71.4	10.7	60.7	4.5
1946	165.2	152.7	12.4	140.3	12.5	1931	88.8	84.2	11.2	73.0	4.6
1945	180.6	157.2	12.2	145.0	23.4	1930	94.4	89.8	10.0	79.8	4.6
1944	183.2	159.2	12.7	146.5	24.0	1929	103.6	99.3	10.7	88.6	4.3
1943	169.9	148.9	12.6	136.3	21.0	1928	97.7	93.5	10.4	83.1	4.2
1942	154.3	140.6	13.2	127.4	13.7	1927	96.6	92.5	10.6	81.9	4.1
1941	138.3	128.7	12.3	116.4	9.6	1926	95.7	91.7	10.3	81.4	4.0

Series F 44–48. Gross Domestic Product Originating in Private Farm and Nonfarm Sectors and Government, in 1929 Prices: 1869 to 1955—Con.

[In billions of dollars. Annual averages for periods shown]

Year or period	Gross domestic product	Gross private product			Govern-ment product	Period	Gross domestic product	Gross private product			Govern-ment product
		Total	Farm	Nonfarm				Total	Farm	Nonfarm	
	44	45	46	47	48		44	45	46	47	48
1925	89.8	85.9	10.4	75.5	3.9	1912–1916	62.5	59.9	10.1	49.8	2.6
1924	87.7	84.0	9.7	74.3	3.7	1907–1911	55.1	52.9	9.2	43.7	2.2
1923	85.1	81.5	10.2	71.3	3.6	1902–1906	46.9	45.2	8.9	36.3	1.8
1922	75.2	71.7	9.6	62.1	3.5	1897–1901	37.3	35.8	8.4	27.4	1.5
1921	71.3	67.7	9.0	58.7	3.6	1892–1896	29.8	28.5	6.8	21.7	1.3
1920	72.9	69.3	9.5	59.8	3.7	1889–1893	27.5	26.3	6.6	19.7	1.2
1919	73.6	68.7	9.7	59.0	5.0	1879–1888	21.2	20.2	5.8	14.4	1.0
1917–1921	71.6	67.0	9.7	57.3	4.6	1869–1878	11.6	10.9	4.1	6.8	.7

Series F 49–54. National Income, by Type of Income, in Current Prices: 1929 to 1957

[In billions of dollars]

Year	Total	Compensa-tion of employees	Income of unincorpo-rated enterprises	Rental income of persons	Corporate profits before tax	Net interest	Year	Total	Compensa-tion of employees	Income of unincorpo-rated enterprises	Rental income of persons	Corporate profits before tax	Net interest
	49	50	51	52	53	54		49	50	51	52	53	54
1957	364.0	254.6	43.0	11.8	41.9	12.6	1942	137.7	85.3	23.9	4.5	19.7	4.3
1956	349.4	241.8	42.4	10.9	42.9	11.3	1941	104.7	64.8	17.4	3.5	14.5	4.5
1955	330.2	223.9	42.1	10.7	43.1	10.4	1940	81.6	52.1	13.0	2.9	9.1	4.5
1954	301.8	207.6	40.4	10.9	33.7	9.1	1939	72.8	48.1	11.6	2.7	5.7	4.6
1953	305.6	208.8	40.7	10.5	37.3	8.2	1938	67.6	45.0	11.1	2.6	4.3	4.6
1952	292.2	195.0	42.2	10.2	37.7	7.1	1937	73.6	47.9	12.7	2.1	6.2	4.7
1951	279.3	180.3	42.3	9.4	41.0	6.3	1936	64.9	42.9	10.5	1.8	5.0	4.7
1950	241.9	154.2	37.5	9.0	35.7	5.5	1935	57.1	37.3	10.4	1.7	2.9	4.8
1949	217.7	140.8	35.6	8.3	28.2	4.8	1934	49.0	34.3	7.0	1.7	1.1	4.9
1948	223.5	141.0	40.2	7.3	30.8	4.2	1933	40.2	29.5	5.6	2.0	−2.0	5.0
1947	198.2	128.8	35.5	6.5	23.6	3.8	1932	42.5	31.1	5.3	2.7	−2.0	5.4
1946	180.9	117.7	36.6	6.2	17.3	3.1	1931	59.7	39.7	8.7	3.8	1.6	5.8
1945	181.2	123.2	30.8	5.6	18.4	3.2	1930	75.7	46.8	11.5	4.8	6.6	6.0
1944	182.6	121.3	29.6	5.4	23.0	3.3	1929	87.8	51.1	14.8	5.4	10.1	6.4
1943	170.3	109.6	28.2	5.1	23.8	3.7							

Series F 55–60. Percent Distribution of National Income, by Type of Income, in Current Prices: 1900 to 1952

[Percents based on annual averages for periods shown]

Period	Total	Compen-sation of employees	Income of unincor-porated enterprises	Rental income of persons	Corporate profits before tax	Net interest	Period	Total	Compen-sation of employees	Income of unincor-porated enterprises	Rental income of persons	Corporate profits before tax	Net interest
	55	56	57	58	59	60		55	56	57	58	59	60
1947–1952	100.0	64.5	15.7	3.4	14.1	2.2	1920–1929	100.0	60.5	17.6	7.6	8.2	6.2
1940–1949	100.0	64.3	16.9	3.6	12.9	2.2	1915–1924	100.0	57.2	21.0	7.6	8.9	5.3
1935–1944	100.0	64.4	16.1	4.0	11.5	4.0	1910–1919	100.0	53.2	24.2	7.7	9.7	5.2
1930–1939	100.0	66.8	15.0	5.0	4.9	8.2	1905–1914	100.0	55.2	22.9	9.1	6.9	5.8
1925–1934	100.0	63.0	15.8	6.6	6.4	8.1	1900–1909	100.0	55.0	23.6	9.1	6.8	5.5

Series F 61–66. Percent Distribution of Aggregate Payments, by Type of Income, in Current Prices: 1870 to 1948

[Percents based on annual averages for periods shown]

Period	Total	Employee compen-sation	Entrepre-neurial income	Divi-dends	Interest	Rent	Period	Total	Employee compen-sation	Entrepre-neurial income	Divi-dends	Interest	Rent
	61	62	63	64	65	66		61	62	63	64	65	66
Based on Dept. of Commerce estimates:							Based on Martin's estimates of aggregate payments:[1]						
1939–1948	100.0	69.6	18.4	3.5	4.5	4.0	1909–1918	100.0	59.7	23.3	6.5	4.9	5.7
1934–1943	100.0	67.6	16.7	4.7	6.6	4.4	1904–1913	100.0	59.6	23.3	5.7	5.1	6.3
1929–1938	100.0	64.1	14.7	6.1	10.0	5.1	1899–1908	100.0	59.5	23.8	5.3	5.1	6.4
Based on NBER estimates of aggregate payments:							Based on King's estimates of value of product:						
1929–1938	100.0	64.9	15.9	6.6	8.4	4.3							
1924–1933	100.0	63.1	16.6	6.5	7.8	5.9	1900 and 1910	100.0	47.1	28.8	15.9		8.3
1919–1928	100.0	61.7	19.5	5.6	6.1	7.1	1890 and 1900	100.0	50.4	27.3	14.7		7.7
1914–1923	100.0	59.2	22.5	5.6	5.6	7.2	1880 and 1890	100.0	52.5	23.0	16.5		8.2
1909–1918	100.0	56.2	24.6	6.1	5.4	7.6	1870 and 1880	100.0	50.0	26.4	15.8		7.8

[1] Excluding entrepreneurial savings.

Series F 67–86. Gross National Product, by Major Type of Product, in Current Prices: 1929 to 1957

[In billions of dollars]

Year	Gross national product	Personal consumption expenditures				Gross private domestic investment				
		Total	Durable goods	Nondurable goods	Services	Total	New construction			Producers' durable equipment
							Total	Residential nonfarm	Other	
	67	68	69	70	71	72	73	74	75	76
1957	440.3	284.4	39.9	138.0	106.5	65.3	36.5	17.0	19.5	27.9
1956	419.2	269.4	38.4	131.4	99.6	68.2	35.7	17.7	18.1	27.0
1955	397.5	256.9	39.6	124.8	92.5	63.8	34.9	18.7	16.2	23.1
1954	363.1	238.0	32.4	119.3	86.3	48.9	29.7	15.4	14.3	20.8
1953	365.4	232.6	32.9	118.0	81.8	50.3	27.6	13.8	13.8	22.3
1952	347.0	219.8	29.1	115.1	75.6	49.9	25.5	12.8	12.7	21.3
1951	329.0	209.8	29.5	110.1	70.2	56.3	24.8	12.5	12.3	21.3
1950	284.6	195.0	30.4	99.8	64.9	50.0	24.2	14.1	10.1	18.9
1949	258.1	181.2	24.6	96.6	60.0	33.0	18.8	9.6	9.2	17.2
1948	259.4	178.3	22.7	98.7	56.9	43.1	19.5	10.1	9.3	18.9
1947	234.3	165.4	20.6	93.4	51.4	31.5	15.3	7.5	7.7	16.7
1946	210.7	147.1	15.9	84.8	46.4	28.1	11.0	4.8	6.3	10.7
1945	213.6	121.7	8.1	73.2	40.4	10.4	3.8	1.1	2.7	7.7
1944	211.4	109.8	6.8	65.4	37.7	7.1	2.7	.8	1.9	5.4
1943	192.5	100.5	6.6	59.3	34.7	5.6	2.3	.9	1.4	4.0
1942	159.1	89.7	7.0	51.3	31.5	9.9	3.7	1.7	2.0	4.3
1941	125.8	81.9	9.7	43.2	29.0	18.1	6.6	3.5	3.1	6.9
1940	100.6	71.9	7.8	37.2	26.9	13.2	5.5	3.0	2.5	5.5
1939	91.1	67.6	6.7	35.1	25.8	9.3	4.8	2.7	2.1	4.2
1938	85.2	64.6	5.7	34.0	25.0	6.7	4.0	2.0	2.0	3.6
1937	90.8	67.3	6.9	35.2	25.1	11.7	4.4	1.9	2.5	5.1
1936	82.7	62.6	6.3	32.8	23.5	8.4	3.3	1.6	1.7	4.2
1935	72.5	56.3	5.1	29.3	21.9	6.3	2.3	1.0	1.3	3.1
1934	65.0	51.9	4.2	26.7	21.0	2.9	1.7	.6	1.1	2.3
1933	56.0	46.4	3.5	22.3	20.7	1.4	1.4	.5	1.0	1.6
1932	58.5	49.3	3.6	22.8	22.9	.9	1.9	.6	1.2	1.6
1931	76.3	61.3	5.5	28.9	26.9	5.5	4.0	1.6	2.4	2.8
1930	91.1	71.0	7.2	34.0	29.8	10.3	6.2	2.1	4.1	4.5
1929	104.4	79.0	9.2	37.7	32.1	16.2	8.7	3.6	5.1	5.9

Year	Gross private domestic investment—Con.			Net foreign investment	Government purchases of goods and services					
	Change in business inventories				Total	Federal				State and local
	Total	Nonfarm	Farm			Total	National security	Other	Less: Government sales	
	77	78	79	80	81	82	83	84	85	86
1957	1.0	0.2	0.8	4.9	85.7	49.4	44.3	5.5	0.4	36.3
1956	5.4	5.9	−.5	2.8	78.8	45.7	40.3	5.7	.3	33.1
1955	5.8	5.5	.3	1.1	75.6	45.3	39.1	6.6	.4	30.3
1954	−1.6	−2.1	.5	1.0	75.3	47.5	41.2	6.7	.3	27.7
1953	.4	1.1	−.6	−.4	82.8	58.0	49.3	9.0	.3	24.9
1952	3.1	2.1	.9	1.3	76.0	52.9	46.4	6.7	.3	23.2
1951	10.2	9.1	1.2	2.4	60.5	38.8	33.9	5.2	.3	21.7
1950	6.8	6.0	.8	.6	39.0	19.3	14.3	5.2	.1	19.7
1949	−3.1	−2.2	−.9	3.8	40.2	22.2	13.6	8.9	.2	17.9
1948	4.7	3.0	1.7	3.5	34.5	19.3	11.6	8.2	.5	15.2
1947	−.5	1.3	−1.8	9.0	28.4	15.7	11.4	5.4	1.1	12.7
1946	6.4	6.4	----------	4.9	30.5	20.6	18.8	4.5	2.7	9.9
1945	−1.1	−.6	−.5	−1.4	82.9	74.8	75.9	1.0	2.2	8.1
1944	−1.0	−.6	−.4	−2.1	96.5	89.0	88.6	1.6	1.2	7.5
1943	−.8	−.6	−.2	−2.2	88.6	81.2	80.4	1.5	.6	7.4
1942	1.8	.7	1.2	−.2	59.7	52.0	49.6	2.7	.2	7.7
1941	4.5	4.0	.5	1.1	24.8	16.9	13.8	3.2	(1)	7.8
1940	2.2	1.9	.3	1.5	14.1	6.2	2.2	4.0	(1)	7.9
1939	.4	.3	.1	.9	13.3	5.2	1.3	3.9	(1)	8.2
1938	−.9	−1.0	.1	1.1	12.8	5.3	5.3		(1)	7.5
1937	2.2	1.7	.5	.1	11.7	4.6	4.6		(1)	7.2
1936	1.0	2.1	−1.1	−.1	11.8	4.8	4.8		(1)	7.0
1935	.9	.4	.5	−.1	10.0	2.9	2.9		(1)	7.1
1934	−1.1	.2	−1.3	.4	9.8	3.0	3.0		(1)	6.8
1933	−1.6	−1.4	−.3	.2	8.0	2.0	2.0		(1)	6.0
1932	−2.6	−2.6	(1)	.2	8.1	1.5	1.5		(1)	6.6
1931	−1.3	−1.6	.3	.2	9.2	1.5	1.5		(1)	7.7
1930	−.4	−.1	−.3	.7	9.2	1.4	1.4		(1)	7.8
1929	1.7	1.8	−.2	.8	8.5	1.3	1.3		(1)	7.2

¹ Less than $50,000,000.

142

Series F 87–103. Gross National Product, by Major Type of Product, in 1954 Prices: 1929 to 1957

[In billions of dollars]

Year	Gross national product	Personal consumption expenditures				Gross private domestic investment									Net foreign invest-ment	Government purchases of goods and services		
		Total	Durable goods	Non-durable goods	Services	Total	New construction			Pro-ducers' durable equip-ment	Change in business inventories					Total	Federal	State and local
							Total	Resi-dential non-farm	Other		Total	Non-farm	Farm					
	87	88	89	90	91	92	93	94	95	96	97	98	99	100	101	102	103	
1957	407.0	270.3	38.1	132.7	99.4	57.8	32.3	15.5	16.9	24.1	1.4	0.1	1.4	3.9	75.0	42.7	32.3	
1956	402.2	263.7	37.9	130.2	95.6	63.1	32.8	16.4	16.4	24.8	5.6	5.5	.0	2.4	72.9	42.0	30.9	
1955	392.7	256.0	39.6	125.4	91.0	62.5	33.9	18.2	15.7	22.5	6.1	5.4	.7	.9	73.2	43.5	29.7	
1954	363.1	238.0	32.4	119.3	86.3	48.9	29.7	15.4	14.3	20.8	−1.6	−2.1	.5	1.0	75.3	47.5	27.7	
1953	369.0	235.1	33.1	118.3	83.7	50.6	27.6	13.6	14.0	22.5	.5	1.1	−.7	−.9	84.3	58.8	25.5	
1952	353.5	224.2	28.5	115.0	80.8	50.4	26.0	12.8	13.2	21.8	2.6	2.2	.4	1.2	77.7	53.3	24.5	
1951	341.8	218.5	29.2	111.2	78.2	57.7	26.0	12.9	13.2	22.0	9.7	9.0	.7	2.2	63.3	39.3	24.1	
1950	318.1	216.8	32.1	109.2	75.5	55.9	27.4	15.5	11.9	21.3	7.2	6.5	.7	.2	45.1	21.6	23.5	
1949	292.7	204.3	26.3	106.3	71.7	38.5	22.3	11.2	11.1	19.8	−3.6	−2.6	−1.0	2.6	47.2	25.3	21.9	
1948	293.1	199.3	24.6	105.1	69.6	49.8	22.7	11.4	11.2	22.8	4.4	3.0	1.4	2.0	42.1	22.9	19.2	
1947	282.3	195.6	23.3	105.3	67.0	41.5	19.9	9.6	10.3	21.7	−.1	1.4	−1.6	8.0	37.2	19.4	17.8	
1946	282.5	192.3	19.4	107.6	65.3	42.4	17.3	7.3	10.0	16.1	9.0	9.1	−.1	3.8	43.9	28.2	15.8	
1945	314.0	171.4	9.8	101.4	60.2	17.0	6.6	1.8	4.8	12.7	−2.4	−1.6	−.8	−5.6	131.2	117.1	14.0	
1944	317.9	160.2	8.6	94.0	57.6	12.3	4.8	1.4	3.4	9.2	−1.7	−1.1	−.6	−6.7	152.2	138.4	13.8	
1943	296.7	154.6	9.4	90.0	55.2	10.7	4.4	1.7	2.7	6.9	−.6	−.5	.0	−6.6	137.9	123.9	14.0	
1942	266.9	150.8	10.9	87.3	52.6	18.8	7.8	3.6	4.2	7.4	3.6	1.6	2.0	−2.9	100.1	84.7	15.4	
1941	238.1	154.3	17.6	85.6	51.1	36.7	15.3	7.9	7.4	12.9	8.6	7.6	1.0	−.6	47.7	30.7	16.9	
1940	205.8	144.6	15.3	80.2	49.1	29.0	13.6	7.3	6.3	10.9	4.5	3.8	.6	1.1	31.1	13.1	18.0	
1939	189.3	137.3	13.3	76.7	47.3	21.6	12.2	6.8	5.4	8.5	1.0	.6	.4	.3	30.1	11.0	19.1	
1938	175.1	129.9	11.2	72.8	45.9	15.5	10.1	5.1	5.0	7.3	−1.8	−2.3	.4	.8	28.8	11.4	17.4	
1937	183.5	132.1	13.8	71.6	46.8	27.0	11.3	5.0	6.3	10.5	5.2	3.4	1.8	−1.6	26.0	9.6	16.4	
1936	173.3	127.7	13.1	69.2	45.3	21.0	9.4	4.6	4.9	9.2	2.4	4.3	−2.0	−2.2	26.9	10.3	16.6	
1935	152.9	115.8	10.7	62.1	42.9	16.1	6.7	3.1	3.6	6.7	2.6	.9	1.7	−1.9	23.0	6.7	16.3	
1934	138.5	108.9	8.6	58.8	41.5	7.4	5.1	1.9	3.2	5.0	−2.8	.3	−3.1	−.6	22.8	6.9	15.8	
1933	126.6	103.5	7.5	55.2	40.8	4.0	4.6	1.6	3.0	3.7	−4.2	−3.5	−.7	−.8	19.9	5.3	14.6	
1932	130.1	106.0	7.8	56.9	41.4	3.9	6.0	2.1	3.9	3.5	−5.6	−6.3	.7	−.3	20.5	3.9	16.6	
1931	153.0	116.6	10.3	61.8	44.6	15.0	10.9	4.2	6.6	5.9	−1.8	−3.5	1.7	−.3	21.6	3.7	17.9	
1930	164.5	120.3	11.8	62.1	46.4	23.6	15.4	5.1	10.4	8.8	−.7	−.3	−.4	.2	20.5	3.4	17.1	
1929	181.8	128.1	14.9	65.3	48.0	35.0	20.9	8.7	12.2	11.1	3.0	3.2	−.3	.2	18.5	2.9	15.6	

Series F 104–130. Gross and Net National Product, by Major Type of Product, in Current Prices: 1869 to 1931

[In billions of dollars. 5-year periods are annual averages]

Period	Gross national product	Net national product	Flow of goods to consumers					Private and public capital formation						
			Total	Commodities			Services	Total		Gross construction				
				Perish-able	Semi-durable	Durable		Gross	Net	Total	Private		Public	
											Nonfarm resi-dential	Other	Nonwar	War
	104	105	106	107	108	109	110	111	112	113	114	115	116	117
1927–1931	89.9	79.4	73.0	25.1	9.46	7.76	30.7	16.8	6.35	10.3	3.22	4.46	2.56	0.02
1922–1926	84.8	75.1	66.8	23.3	9.31	7.56	26.7	18.0	8.30	10.6	4.50	4.21	1.88	.01
1917–1921	71.6	62.6	54.9	22.9	8.33	5.15	18.5	16.7	7.68	5.85	1.19	2.98	.99	.69
1912–1916	38.9	34.6	30.8	12.5	3.93	2.72	11.7	8.05	3.80	4.17	1.26	2.27	.64	.01
1907–1911	30.4	27.2	24.1	10.0	3.20	1.97	8.90	6.35	3.15	4.25	1.19	2.56	.50	-------
1902–1906	23.5	21.2	18.2	7.68	2.49	1.52	6.53	5.29	2.96	3.29	.93	2.05	.31	-------
1897–1901	16.8	15.0	12.9	5.60	1.79	1.03	4.44	3.89	2.13	2.26	.65	1.43	.18	-------
1892–1896	13.1	11.8	10.1	4.44	1.48	.84	3.38	3.01	1.63	2.21	.72	1.35	.14	-------
1887–1891	12.3	11.0	9.58	4.09	1.54	.87	3.08	2.69	1.44	1.91	.81	.98	.12	-------
1882–1886	11.3	10.3	9.10	4.09	1.41	.74	2.85	2.21	1.23	1.40	.57	.74	.10	-------
1877–1881	9.18	8.48	7.33	3.24	1.20	.56	2.33	1.86	1.16	.91	.31	.52	.07	-------
1872–1876	7.53	6.92	5.94	2.58	1.05	.53	1.78	1.59	.97	.90	.25	.59	.07	-------
1869–1873	6.71	6.20	5.38	2.29	1.01	.50	1.59	1.34	.82	.77	.22	.50	.06	-------

Series F 104–130. Gross and Net National Product, by Major Type of Product, in Current Prices: 1869 to 1931—Con.

[In billions of dollars. 5-year periods are annual averages]

Period	Gross producers' durables			Net construction					Net producers' durables			Net change in—	
					Private		Public						Claims against foreign countries
	Total	Nonwar	War	Total	Nonfarm residential	Other	Nonwar	War	Total	Nonwar	War	Inventories	
	118	119	120	121	122	123	124	125	126	127	128	129	130
1927–1931	5.85	5.68	0.17	3.69	1.59	0.72	1.56	−0.17	1.94	1.96	−0.02	0.04	0.68
1922–1926	5.54	5.44	.10	4.95	3.16	.90	1.08	−.19	1.49	1.99	−.50	1.21	.65
1917–1921	5.57	4.53	1.04	.88	.09	−.14	.38	.55	1.50	.93	.57	2.54	2.75
1912–1916	2.28			1.71	.64	.69	.37	.01	.49			.67	.93
1907–1911	1.62			2.28	.66	1.31	.32		.39			.46	.02
1902–1906	1.36			1.81	.56	1.07	.18		.50			.47	.17
1897–1901	.84			1.14	.36	.69	.10		.20			.47	.31
1892–1896	.60			1.31	.50	.74	.07		.13			.22	−.03
1887–1891	.64			1.10	.63	.40	.06		.20			.24	−.10
1882–1886	.53			.78	.45	.28	.05		.18			.33	−.06
1877–1881	.45			.46	.23	.20	.03		.19			.44	.06
1872–1876	.41			.54	.18	.33	.03		.16			.39	−.11
1869–1873	.39			.46	.16	.28	.02		.18			.35	−.18

Series F 131–157. Gross and Net National Product, by Major Type of Product, in 1929 Prices: 1869 to 1931

[In billions of dollars. 5-year periods are annual averages]

Period	Gross national product	Net national product	Flow of goods to consumers						Private and public capital formation						
			Total	Commodities				Services	Total		Gross construction				
												Private		Public	
				Perishable	Semi-durable	Durable			Gross	Net	Total	Nonfarm residential	Other	Nonwar	War
	131	132	133	134	135	136	137		138	139	140	141	142	143	144
1927–1931	93.4	82.6	76.0	26.6	9.77	8.18	31.5		17.4	6.58	10.6	3.34	4.57	2.66	0.02
1922–1926	84.4	74.6	66.4	24.1	8.40	7.55	26.3		18.0	8.19	10.8	4.70	4.34	1.75	.01
1917–1921	67.7	59.0	52.4	20.0	6.44	4.85	21.1		15.2	6.58	6.0	1.31	2.99	.92	.74
1912–1916	59.7	52.6	46.6	18.5	6.72	4.33	17.0		13.1	6.05	7.4	2.34	3.92	1.12	.02
1907–1911	52.5	46.6	40.9	16.5	5.79	3.74	14.9		11.7	5.71	8.0	2.30	4.73	.95	
1902–1906	45.0	40.2	34.3	14.1	5.02	3.27	11.8		10.8	5.94	7.0	2.10	4.21	.65	
1897–1901	35.4	31.4	26.7	11.4	3.96	2.62	8.7		8.7	4.73	5.5	1.72	3.30	.43	
1892–1896	28.3	24.9	20.9	9.0	3.21	2 11	6.6		7.4	3.98	5.5	2.02	3.14	.34	
1887–1891	24.0	21.3	18.1	7.5	2.92	1.95	5.7		5.9	3.24	4.4	2.09	2.01	.27	
1882–1886	20.7	18.7	16.2	7.1	2.49	1.50	5.1		4.5	2.52	3.1	1.41	1.47	.21	
1877–1881	16.1	14.6	12.4	5.4	1.96	1.07	4.0		3.7	2.23	2.1	.82	1.14	.16	
1872–1876	11.2	10.1	8.5	3.5	1.37	.77	2.9		2.6	1.62	1.8	.55	1.13	.13	
1869–1873	9.1	8.3	7.0	2.8	1.22	.64	2.4		2.1	1.30	1.5	.47	.92	.11	

Period	Gross producers' durables			Net construction					Net producers' durables			Net change in—	
					Private		Public						Claims against foreign countries
	Total	Nonwar	War	Total	Nonfarm residential	Other	Nonwar	War	Total	Nonwar	War	Inventories	
	145	146	147	148	149	150	151	152	153	154	155	156	157
1927–1931	6.05	5.87	0.18	3.80	1.64	0.71	1.62	−0.17	1.98	2.00	−0.02	0.11	0.69
1922–1926	5.58	5.48	.10	5.06	3.31	.93	1.00	−.18	1.50	2.01	−.51	1.00	.64
1917–1921	5.09	4.09	1.00	.95	.09	−.10	.34	.61	1.44	.86	.58	1.60	2.60
1912–1916	3.57			3.11	1.19	1.24	.66	.02	.76			.85	1.33
1907–1911	2.98			4.31	1.29	2.41	.61		.72			.65	.03
1902–1906	2.72			3.85	1.24	2.22	.40		1.01			.75	.32
1897–1901	1.75			2.80	.96	1.60	.23		.41			.87	.66
1892–1896	1.47			3.29	1.40	1.70	.19		.32			.42	−.05
1887–1891	1.82			2.61	1.63	.84	.14		.42			.41	−.20
1882–1886	1.00			1.79	1.11	.57	.11		.32			.51	−.10
1877–1881	.77			1.13	.60	.45	.08		.33			.66	.10
1872–1876	.51			1.11	.40	.65	.07		.19			.46	−.16
1869–1873	.46			.93	.34	.54	.05		.22			.39	−.24

chapter F

NATIONAL WEALTH AND SAVING (Series F 158–345)

F 158–251. General note.

The national balance sheet is derived by summing similar balance sheets for groups of transactors in the economy—nonfarm households, agriculture, unincorporated business, corporations, etc. The balance sheet of each group is in turn derived by summing the balance sheets of the constituent units, based as far as possible on a comparable valuation of assets and liabilities. In deriving the balance sheet, no creditor-debtor or owner-issuer relationships among units are eliminated; for example, the debts of households to corporations appear on one side as assets of corporations and on the other as liabilities of households. When all relationships among constituent units are canceled, whether these units be in the same or different groups, the balance sheet reduces to a national wealth statement. This statement shows only tangible assets plus the net balance of United States claims against foreign countries, in effect, consolidated net national worth. (In the series shown, the estimate for total tangible assets in the national balance sheet differs very slightly from that in the national wealth statement because of a minor disparity in the treatment of monetary metals.)   Thus, the national balance sheet adds to the national wealth statement a comprehensive summary of the various types of financial obligations outstanding at a particular date, and provides perspective on the magnitude of financing activities in the Nation's economy.

The national balance sheet falls somewhat short of the goal of a comprehensive summary of the assets, liabilities, and net worth of all transactors in the economy, since, for lack of data, obligations among households are not included, and in the case of corporations with subsidiaries, the balance sheet of the parent company is used, thus eliminating relationships among the subsidiary units. In addition, intangibles such as goodwill and patent rights are excluded from the balance sheet. Finally, and this limits the comprehensiveness of the national wealth statement as well, inventories of nondurable goods in the hands of consumers, expenditures on soil improvement, subsoil assets, and military and naval equipment held by the government are omitted. Needless to say, no account is taken of the economic value of the stock of the Nation's human resources.

The value for "equity" in the national balance sheet exceeds total national wealth, that is, consolidated net national worth. This is primarily because in the balance sheet the net worth of the various constituent units are added together. For example, the net worth of a corporation is added to the net worth of the stockholders. In the national wealth statement, however, they are consolidated. That is, the outstanding stock of the corporation is canceled against the holdings of the owners, leaving only the net worth of the stockholders and the undistributed earnings of the corporations. Stated differently, the "equity" entry in the balance sheet includes the equity of intermediaries as well as of ultimate owners.

F 158–196. National balance sheet, in current prices, 1900–1955.

Source: 1900–1949, Raymond W. Goldsmith, et al., *A Study of Saving in the United States*, vol. III, Princeton University Press, Princeton, 1956, pp. 60–61; 1955, National Bureau of Economic Research, *Thirty-Seventh Annual Report*, p. 36.

The figures for 1955, which were prepared by Raymond W. Goldsmith and Morris Mendelson, represent preliminary estimates and in some cases are not fully comparable with those for earlier dates.

The national balance sheet is derived by summing similar balance sheets for various transactor groups in the economy—nonfarm households, agriculture, unincorporated business, etc. (see general note for series F 158–251). For most of these groups, however, balance sheets of the constituent units are nonexistent, so that in practice the group balance sheet is compiled from separate estimates of the various categories of assets and liabilities, net worth being derived as a residual. Only in the case of corporations and the Federal Government does a substantial proportion of the items come from their own financial statements.

The estimates presented are in current prices rather than original cost. Essentially this means that reproducible tangible assets are valued at reproduction cost, and nonreproducible tangible assets and intangibles at market value, though some intangibles, particularly short-term claims, are valued at par or face value.

In deriving the estimates, a problem sometimes arose because of a difference between two groups in the value at which the same item is carried on the balance sheet, a difference not attributable to bad debt reserves alone. Where this was the case, no attempt was made to force consistency. Both valuations were carried over into the national balance sheet on the appropriate sides. This, together with the treatment of net holdings of foreign assets and liabilities, principally accounts for differences between the asset and liability totals for certain intangible items; differences which are generally small compared with the balance sheet totals.

The following statement from the source bears on the reliability of the estimates:

There is unfortunately no way of estimating the margin of error in the individual items of assets and liabilities and net worth, or in the balance sheet totals. This is due partly to conceptual difficulties, i.e., the difficulty of agreeing [as to] what should be regarded as the true figure for a given asset or liability of a given group at a given date, even if the basic principle of valuation at current prices is accepted. It also reflects the absence, in almost all cases, of benchmark or alternative estimates. The margin of error obviously is considerably lower for assets like cash, inventories, bonds, and farm and residential mortgages, and for the corresponding liabilities, than for items like structures and equipment, land, accounts receivable and payable, common stock, and interest in unincorporated business. The estimates of net worth, being derived as residuals, are of course particularly subject to error, and the more so, the smaller the proportion of net worth to total assets and liabilities. Similarly, the figures are as a rule more reliable—for the same class of assets or liabilities—for groups like corporations and agriculture, for which comprehensive balance sheets of some type have been available, than for nonfarm individuals, unincorporated business, personal trust departments, and governments, for which they have had to be developed practically from the ground up. Finally, the margin of error is undoubtedly smaller—again for the same group and type of asset or liability—for the last three benchmark dates [1939, 1945, and 1949] than for earlier dates. This statement, however, must be qualified by the fact that over-all national wealth statements, which provide valuable checks, exist for the first three benchmark dates, but are entirely absent for later ones.

The source provides considerable additional detail, in particular, balance sheets for separate transactor groups, such as nonfarm households, agriculture, etc., and makes it possible to trace the patterns of claims and counterclaims among the various groups.

F 197–221. National wealth, by type of asset, in current prices, 1850–1956.

Source: 1850–1900, Raymond W. Goldsmith, "The Growth of Reproducible Wealth of the United States of America From 1805 to 1950," International Association for Research in Income and Wealth, *Income and Wealth of the United States: Trends and Structure*, Income and Wealth Series II, Bowes and Bowes, Cambridge, 1952, p. 306 (estimates for 1805 presented in this publication have not been reproduced here because of questionable reliability); 1900–1945, see source for series F 158–196, pp. 14–15; 1949, 1956, preliminary estimates by Raymond W. Goldsmith, following the methods of *A Study of Saving in the United States*, vol. III; final estimates to be published by National Bureau of Economic Research.

The estimates for 1900 to the present were constructed by Goldsmith by means of the "perpetual inventory method." In this method, the stock of an asset in existence at a given point in time is estimated from annual output totals extending back over a period equal to the average life of the asset, the output total for every year being depreciated to the end of the period, and the results summed. The underlying estimates for 1850 appear in the Census Office, *Preliminary Report of the Eighth Census*, 1862, p. 195; and those for 1880, 1890, and 1900 in Simon Kuznets, *National Product Since 1869*, National Bureau of Economic Research, New York, 1946, pp. 202–215. In every case, the original estimates were adjusted by Goldsmith, that for 1880 substantially, to improve comparability with the estimates for 1900–1956. The basic sources for these earlier estimates were returns on stocks of various assets in the industrial censuses and censuses of wealth. Hence, there is a sharp break in the method of derivation between the earlier and later estimates. However, the figures for the overlap year, 1900, agree reasonably well. The figures for 1850 exclude the value of slaves.

The estimates for 1900–1956 are in "current prices," that is, each asset is valued at its replacement cost in the given year. This is preferable to valuation at original cost, whether depreciated or undepreciated. Assets appearing in the wealth statement for any given date were produced in different years, and since prices change from year to year, summation of original cost values would often result in an arithmetic aggregate without economic meaning. (However, totals in original cost are also given in *A Study of Saving in the United States*. . . .) For the estimates for 1850 to 1900, which are primarily from the Federal censuses, the basis of valuation is not always certain, and is not uniform among types of assets and among industries. It is possible that the figures may approximate either current market values or original cost, depreciated or undepreciated, or some combination of the two. Some assurance as to the comparability of the earlier and later sets of figures on this score is provided, however, by the overlapping values for 1900, though this comparison applies only to a single year.

As to the reliability of the estimates, the source (*Income and Wealth of the United States: Trends and Structure*, p. 264) states "that the margin of error in the estimates is substantial, amounting to hardly less than 10 to 20 percent at any date; that this relative margin increases as we go back in time; but that it is not at all certain that comparability is impaired by as much as the size of the margin may imply because the error probably tends in the same direction for most if not all benchmarks although it is likely that the understatement is more pronounced in the early part of the period than in the latter." With regard to the estimates for 1900–1956, derived by the perpetual inventory method, it is noted that "the most important source of error . . . resides in the estimates of

expenditures on construction . . . ." (same source, p. 259). For some of the components of total wealth, the reliability is strengthened because of the possibility of checks against alternative estimates. "This is the case primarily for residential real estate, farm structures, inventories and international assets . . . . Checks are less satisfactory for nonfarm business structures and equipment . . . but the information provided in corporate balance sheets submitted to the Bureau of Internal Revenue assures us that the Perpetual Inventory estimates are not too far off the mark for the last 20 years. The only sectors of reproducible tangible wealth in which the Perpetual Inventory estimates can be subject to no checks, or to only very unsatisfactory ones, are consumers' durables and government fixed assets . . . ." (same source, pp. 260–261).

The same source also presents considerably greater detail (for example, annual estimates for 1896–1949). Estimates of national wealth by contemporaries are also available for various dates during the 19th century. See, for example, Samuel Blodget, Jr., *Economica; A Statistical Manual for the United States*, 1806 edition, and *Annual Report of the Director of the Mint, 1881*.

F 222–246. National wealth, by type of asset, in 1929 and 1947–49 prices, 1850–1956.

Source: 1850–1900, see source for series F 197–221, p. 307; 1900–1945, see source for series F 158–196, pp. 20–21; 1945–1956, see source for series F 197–221.

These estimates were derived by adjusting the current dollar figures for a given class of assets in series F 197–221 for the change in price or cost of construction of that type of asset between each year and the base year. Thus, conceptually, changes over time in the constant price value of a category of assets reflect changes in the physical stock of that asset and not in its value. For 1945–1956, a different base year was necessary because estimates in 1929 prices for the most recent years are not available. This shift in base years introduces some element of incomparability, since the relative weights of individual assets in the price index differ between the two years.

For 1900–1956, an attempt was made to adjust for price changes by fairly narrow classes of assets, using construction cost or price indexes referring specifically to the assets in each class. For 1880, 1890, and 1900, a more summary adjustment was used. Only three separate deflators were employed for construction (residential, other private, and farm), and a single deflator was used for all types of equipment. For 1850, the same price index (Snyder's index of the general price level) was applied to all types of structures and equipment, although for the adjustment of inventories the wholesale price index was used.

Goldsmith states that the conceptual significance of a constant price estimate for land is open to question. If land is carried for all dates at its absolute value in the base year, the relation to the constant price value of reproducible assets tends to become unrealistic, particularly at dates fairly far removed from the base year. In the present estimate, an alternative procedure is followed, a constant price value of land being derived, generally speaking, as a fixed proportion of the constant price value of structures. This permits derivation of a constant price series for aggregate national wealth, but it should be recognized that the deflated estimates of land values included in the totals cannot be conceived as reflecting changes in physical units alone.

The adjustment for price changes introduces errors in the estimates in addition to those discussed in connection with series F 197–221. On balance, any error is likely to lead towards an overstatement of the price rise over the period and hence an understatement of growth rates because the techniques used in adjusting for price change fail to make adequate allowance for improvement in the quality of the assets, and there is no evidence that the error is larger for one part of the period than for another, although the possibilities of error are certainly greater in the 19th century than the 20th. In addition, it is likely that the failure to allow for quality improvement has a differential effect on the different components of wealth. In particular, it leads to a more serious understatement in the growth of components such as producer and consumer durables and livestock than for structures and inventories.

F 247–251. Value of stock of structures and equipment in specified sectors, in 1929 prices, 1880–1948.

Source: Simon Kuznets, *Capital in the American Economy: Its Formation and Financing*, National Bureau of Economic Research, New York (forthcoming).

These estimates fall somewhat short of the value of all reproducible wealth in each sector, since the value of inventories is omitted, and considerably short of total wealth, since land is excluded. Also, data are not available for other business sectors; for example, trade and the service industries are omitted. However, it is estimated that the four sectors included here accounted for about 80 percent of the stock of structures and equipment in 1880.

The underlying sources of the estimates are three monographs prepared in connection with the National Bureau of Economic Research Study of Capital Formation and Financing: Alvin S. Tostlebe, *Capital in Agriculture: Its Formation and Financing Since 1870*, Princeton University Press, Princeton, 1957; Daniel Creamer, Israel Borenstein, and Sergei P. Dobrovolsky, *Capital Formation and Financing in Manufacturing and Mining* (forthcoming); and Melville J. Ulmer, *Capital in Transportation, Communication, and Public Utilities: Its Formation and Financing* (forthcoming). With the exception of the last monograph, the approach followed in deriving the estimates of capital stock differed rather noticeably from that chiefly employed in obtaining the figures presented in series F 197–246, since the basic data, such as census returns on capital or balance sheet items in *Statistics of Income*, related to stocks rather than output flows. Further detail on capital investment by type and/or minor industrial sector is given in these monographs.

F 252–345. General note.

Statistics of saving provide the link between the statements of national income or product, on the one hand, and the national wealth statement and balance sheet, on the other. Generally speaking, for the Nation as a whole, aggregate saving, which equals national income less national consumption, is identical with net national investment, and the latter, in turn, is equal to the change in real national wealth. For the individual economic unit, however, saving is equal not to the change in holdings of real assets, but to the difference between the change in total assets (both tangible and intangible) and total liabilities. The national balance sheet registers the effect of saving on the stock of intangibles as well as tangibles.

The link provided by the saving statistics is imperfect for both conceptual and statistical reasons. To note only some of the principal conceptual differences, there are, first, variations in the treatment of government. In the Department of Commerce estimates of income and saving, government investment and government saving are excluded, while in the Kuznets income estimates, and the Goldsmith saving and wealth estimates, Government saving and investment are included, though

the Goldsmith estimates exclude military assets. Another important difference is in the treatment of consumer durables, which in both the Department of Commerce and Kuznets income estimates is not considered investment, but in the Goldsmith estimates of saving and wealth is so considered. Finally, there are important differences in the scope and valuation of capital consumption allowances. Beyond the conceptual differences, there are variations in the sources and techniques employed by the different estimators. The broad outlines of the relationships among the different social accounts can, nevertheless, be distinguished. In addition, the saving statistics throw important light on the nature of the different groups of savers in the economy and the forms that saving takes.

F 252–260. Gross private saving, in current prices, 1929–1957.

Source: 1929–1945, Office of Business Economics, *National Income: 1954 Edition, A Supplement to the Survey of Current Business*, pp. 164–165; 1946–1957, *U. S. Income and Output*, 1958.

The following are definitions used by the Department of Commerce:

Gross private saving represents the sum of series F 253–256 and F 260. Generally speaking, it is the total of household and business saving. Saving through government, including government insurance funds, is excluded. Household expenditures for consumer durables, except on residential construction, are not treated as saving. Series F 252 is "gross" in that it includes business capital consumption allowances and depreciation on residences.

Personal saving represents the excess of personal income over the sum of personal consumption expenditures and personal tax and nontax payments. It includes the current saving of individuals (including owners of unincorporated business), nonprofit institutions, and private pension, health, welfare, and trust funds. Personal saving may be in such forms as changes in cash and deposits, security holdings, indebtedness, and reserves of life insurance companies and mutual savings institutions, the net investment of unincorporated enterprises, and the acquisition of real property net of depreciation. Inventory profits and other capital gains are excluded.

Undistributed corporate profits represent the difference between corporate profits after tax and dividends. Corporate profits after tax are the earnings of corporations organized for profit which accrue to the residents of the Nation, measured after Federal and State profit taxes, without deduction of depletion charges and exclusive of capital gains and losses. Dividends measure cash dividend disbursements by corporations organized for profit to stockholders who are residents of the United States.

Corporate inventory valuation adjustment is the excess of the value of the change in the volume of nonfarm corporate business inventories, valued at average prices during the period, over the change in the book value of nonfarm corporate inventories.

Capital consumption allowances represent the sum of business depreciation charges, accidental damage to fixed business capital, and capital outlays charged to current expense.

Business depreciation charges are charges made by private business against receipts for the current consumption of durable capital goods and comparable allowances for nonprofit institutions. They include depreciation charges against owner-occupied houses. Depreciation reported by business is not adjusted for changes in the replacement value of capital goods, except for farm enterprises.

Accidental damage to fixed business capital represents the value of the physical losses by fire, natural events, and other

147

accidents to fixed capital of private business not covered by depreciation charges.

Capital outlays charged to current expense represent new construction and purchases of new durable capital goods included in gross private domestic investment (series F 72) that are charged as current expense by business rather than entered on capital account.

Excess of wage accruals over disbursements represents wages earned during the current period but not disbursed.

With respect to reliability of these estimates, the Department of Commerce notes that the margin of error in the estimates of gross private saving and its components tends generally to be high. Because personal saving is derived as the difference between two much larger totals, it is subject to large percentage error in both level and movement. Undistributed corporate profits is more accurate, but the corporate inventory valuation adjustment is liable to considerable error, so that the reliability of the two items combined is not high. Furthermore, while approximately half of the estimate for capital consumption allowances is based on fairly solid data, the remainder is estimated on the basis of a variety of sources and methods, and some of these are subject to a wide margin of error.

F 261–303. Individuals' saving, by components, in current prices, 1929–1957.

Source: 1929–1932, Irwin Friend and Vito Natrella, *Individuals' Saving*, John Wiley & Sons, New York, 1954, pp. 85 and 91 (except series F 293 for 1929–1932, Raymond W. Goldsmith, *A Study of Saving in the United States*); 1933–1957, Securities and Exchange Commission, records.

Conceptually, individual saving in series F 261 is identical with that in series F 253. However, the total is derived in an entirely different way. In the procedure followed in obtaining series F 261, referred to as the direct or balance sheet method of estimating saving, the total is derived by summing the changes in the various assets and liabilities of the economic units included in the personal sector. Since the reliability of the underlying components varies widely, it is not possible to state unequivocally that the total in series F 261 is subject to a smaller margin of error than that in series F 253. Rather the two series should be viewed as providing a reciprocal check, with the present series also presenting detail on the various types of saving. While the difference between the two series is substantial for a few dates, they are generally in fair agreement with regard to absolute amount.

The estimates for saving in the form of currency and deposits (including deposits in savings and loan associations) have a relatively small margin of error, while those for saving in the form of corporate and State and local securities probably have a greater margin of error. Generally speaking, the estimates for the earlier years, particularly 1929–1932, are subject to greater error than those for the later years. For a discussion of the limitations of the estimates for a number of the components, see the source (Friend and Natrella).

F 304–315. National saving, by major saver groups, in current prices, 1897–1945.

Source: Raymond W. Goldsmith, *A Study of Saving in the United States*, vol. I, Princeton University Press, Princeton, 1955, p. 345 (saving, excluding consumer durables, computed by subtraction of estimates of saving in consumer durables for nonagricultural individuals, p. 359, and for agriculture, p. 756).

In contrast to series F 252–260, these series provide an estimate of saving by government (thus permitting the derivation of aggregate national saving), and estimates of personal

saving subdivided among three major groups—nonagricultural individuals (including private nonprofit institutions and personal trust funds), agriculture, and unincorporated business. There are also some differences in the scope of the saving concept. While these estimates include all forms of saving covered in series F 252–260, they also cover saving in the form of consumer durables, and of brokers' and dealers' commissions and profits on change of hands of existing assets. In addition, in deriving these estimates of net saving, capital consumption allowances have been valued at replacement cost. Neither set of figures, however, includes saving in the form of soil improvement or additions to military assets. An important difference also exists between the two sets of estimates in the technique of derivation. The estimates in series F 252–260 were derived by the income approach; these figures, with the exception of those for corporate saving, were obtained by the balance sheet method. In this respect, they are similar to the estimates of personal saving presented in series F 261–303, though differences in techniques and in concept cause the actual estimates for personal saving to differ between the two tables, e.g. because of inclusion in series F 337 (but not in series F 289) of stock issues of small corporations not distributed by security dealers.

The following statement from the source (pp. 40–41) provides an indication of the reliability of the estimates:

Evaluation of the possible errors in the individual series from which the estimates of group and national saving have been constructed indicates that the margin of error is hardly under 10 percent for any given year or for the average annual figure in any series, that it is probably in the order of magnitude of 20 to 30 percent in many of them, that it may run even higher in not a few cases, but that the relative margin of error in most cases is reduced for sequences of several years and generally the smaller the longer the period. . . .

Most of the components utilized in building the estimates of saving of any of the major saver groups are statistically independent; and the estimates for the major saver groups are very largely independent of each other except for those of nonfarm households and unincorporated business enterprises. Accordingly since the number of components of saving is large for each of the groups, running to several dozen even if only those of substantial quantitative importance are taken into account, there is reason to assume that errors in one direction, i.e. overstatements or underestimates of saving, made in any one year in some of the component series will be offset by errors in the opposite direction in other series. As a result, the relative error in the estimates of saving by the major groups, and still more the estimates of broad aggregates such as national or personal saving, may be expected to be considerably lower than the average of the relative errors in the component series. Indeed, it is quite possible that, if we take account of the number of independent component series and their relative size, and even take a pessimistic view of errors in constituent series, the relative error of national or personal saving in any one year does not on the average exceed something like 10 percent.

The quality of most of the individual series used in the measurement of saving has undoubtedly improved. It would seem to be substantially poorer for the period before the thirties than for the last two decades, and within the earlier period, in turn, to be particularly poor for the years before approximately 1905. Nevertheless, there is no statistical evidence, such as might be provided by the difference between estimates of saving and investment, that the estimates of aggregate saving have larger relative errors in the earlier part of the period than in the later part. Indeed, from that point of view, the relative error in the estimates would have to be regarded as substantially the same through the thirties, and as considerably lower only for the last decade. There is, however, evidence . . . that the error is . . . in the direction of an overstatement of saving in the first three decades and an understatement during the thirties.

F 316–345. Personal saving, by major components, in current prices, 1897–1956.

Source: 1897–1945, see source for series F 304–315, pp. 353–355; 1946–1956, preliminary estimates by Raymond W. Goldsmith and Morris Mendelson, following the methods of *A Study of Saving in the United States;* final estimates to be published by the National Bureau of Economic Research.

See text for series F 304–315 regarding concept and reliability of personal saving estimates.

The estimates for 1946–1956 are not fully comparable with those for earlier years. The savings and loan association liability called loans in process and the surplus of mutual financial intermediaries are imputed to personal saving in the new estimates, though not in the earlier figures. Furthermore, in the estimates for the earlier years brokers and dealers were not distinguished from other unincorporated businesses, and the estimates for the components of saving included the changes in the assets and liabilities of these brokers and dealers. In the new estimates, brokers and dealers are treated as financial organizations and personal saving through brokers and dealers is assumed to take the form of changes in equity in these organizations. Changes in loans in process, surplus of mutual financial organizations, and equity in brokers and dealers are all included in total personal saving (series F 316 and F 317), but not included in any of the components shown in series F 316–345. The data for these three forms of personal saving are given in the tabulation below.

There are also other differences between the new and old estimates which reduce comparability. The estimates of accrued tax liabilities were not carried forward and as a result the estimates of personal saving are somewhat higher in most and lower in a few years than they would otherwise be. Finally, in several instances, changes in the sources of data used influences comparability. The most important of them is the substitution of flow-of-funds for Securities and Exchange

Commission data, particularly in the case of net trade debt of nonfarm, noncorporate business (included in series F 344). This change was made primarily to achieve consistency with other bodies of data utilized in the National Bureau's postwar Capital Market Study where flow-of-funds data are used extensively. The result is that the present estimates of personal saving diverge more from the SEC estimates than do those of earlier years.

Year	Loans in process of saving and loan association	Other savings in mutual financial institutions	Equity in brokers and dealers
	Bil. dol.	Bil. dol.	Bil. dol.
1956	−.02	.61	.12
1955	.12	.54	−.17
1954	.24	.63	.27
1953	.06	.47	.09
1952	.08	.37	−.06
1951	.02	.41	−.03
1950	.14	.40	.04
1949	.04	.42	.01
1948	−.04	.35	.06
1947	.06	.30	−.09
1946	.10	.25	−.14

Series F 158–196.   National Balance Sheet, in Current Prices: 1900 to 1955

[In billions of dollars. As of end of year]

Year	Total assets (F 181 plus F 196)	Tangible assets	Intangible assets									
			Total	Currency	Deposits in—		Life insurance reserves	Pension and retirement funds		Receivables from—		Loans on securities
					Commercial banks	Other financial institutions		Private	Government	Business	Households	
	158	159	160	161	162	163	164	165	166	167	168	169
1955	3,074.0	1,329.0	1,745.0	54.0	145.0	112.0	80.0	15.0	58.0	123.0	44.0	9.0
1949	2,016.0	881.3	1,134.7	49.0	131.1	53.4	58.8	6.8	38.8	64.0	26.8	3.6
1945	1,557.5	570.3	987.2	45.0	137.9	44.0	44.3	2.9	25.5	41.0	11.7	8.1
1939	877.2	395.0	482.2	22.4	54.1	28.8	29.2	1.0	6.2	26.3	14.6	2.7
1933	733.1	322.4	410.7	8.1	36.2	18.8	20.9	.7	3.0	30.2	11.9	5.2
1929	981.8	426.9	554.8	6.5	44.8	17.9	17.5	.5	1.5	46.7	15.3	16.3
1922	653.0	326.2	326.8	6.9	34.2	10.5	8.7	.1	.3	32.7	11.1	6.7
1912	308.6	167.6	141.0	2.5	15.8	4.5	4.1	--------	--------	17.2	5.6	2.3
1900	159.0	90.2	68.8	1.4	6.7	2.6	1.6	--------	--------	10.9	1.9	1.3

Year	Intangible assets—Con.										
	Mortgages		Securities				Equity in—			Accruals	Other
	Nonfarm	Farm	U.S. government	State and local governments	Corporate bonds	Preferred and common stock	Unincorporated business	Financial nonprofit institutions	Government corporations		
	170	171	172	173	174	175	176	177	178	179	180
1955	121.0	9.0	272.0	46.0	69.0	437.0	83.0	9.0	(1)	60.0	
1949	60.8	5.4	253.3	21.9	39.5	158.8	68.8	5.0	26.5	23.4	39.1
1945	33.1	4.7	274.4	15.9	25.9	150.8	51.7	3.3	17.2	19.0	30.7
1939	32.0	6.6	47.0	19.8	32.5	100.1	26.1	2.3	4.5	7.8	18.0
1933	33.5	7.7	23.9	19.1	37.7	101.7	17.6	2.3	3.1	5.4	24.0
1929	37.3	9.6	16.2	16.9	38.1	186.7	27.5	2.1	.4	7.6	45.3
1922	16.3	10.8	23.0	10.4	23.7	76.1	22.2	1.2	.7	4.7	26.6
1912	7.5	4.3	1.2	4.4	14.5	38.0	8.9	.6	--------	1.1	8.2
1900	4.4	2.3	1.2	2.0	5.2	13.9	6.3	.3	--------	.7	6.0

Year	Liabilities															Equity
	Total	Currency	Deposits in—		Life insurance reserves	Pension and retirement funds		Payables to—			Borrowing on securities	Mortgages	Bonds and notes	Accruals	Other	
			Commercial banks	Other financial institutions		Private	Government	Financial intermediaries	Other business	Households						
	181	182	183	184	185	186	187	188	189	190	191	192	193	194	195	196
1955	1,265.0	54.0	165.0	112.0	82.0	15.0	58.0	63.0	77.0	--------	9.0	130.0	397.0	104.0		1,809.0
1949	874.0	49.2	131.1	53.9	58.8	6.8	38.8	34.8	51.1	.9	3.6	66.2	316.1	23.4	39.3	1,142.0
1945	772.5	44.8	137.9	43.5	44.3	2.9	25.5	18.6	31.7	.8	8.1	37.8	320.3	19.0	37.3	784.9
1939	356.5	22.2	54.1	29.0	29.2	1.0	6.2	17.4	24.6	.4	2.7	38.6	107.3	7.8	15.9	520.6
1933	281.4	7.7	36.2	18.9	20.9	.7	3.0	18.3	19.4	.3	5.2	41.1	83.8	5.4	20.6	451.7
1929	324.3	6.4	44.8	17.9	17.5	.5	1.5	25.4	28.6	1.2	16.3	46.9	76.1	7.6	33.5	657.4
1922	222.4	6.8	34.2	10.5	8.7	.1	.3	20.4	23.0	.5	6.7	27.1	59.5	4.7	19.9	430.6
1912	94.1	2.5	15.8	4.5	4.1	--------	--------	10.1	10.8	.2	2.3	11.8	23.9	1.1	6.8	214.5
1900	47.2	1.2	6.7	2.6	1.6	--------	--------	4.3	7.6	.1	1.3	6.7	10.4	.7	4.0	111.9

[1] Consolidated into Federal Government.

Series F 197–221. National Wealth, by Type of Asset, in Current Prices: 1850 to 1956

In billions of dollars. As of end of year except as noted. Figures in italics for 1900 are comparable with earlier years; those in regular type are comparable with later years]

Year [1]	Total national wealth	Reproducible tangible assets										
		Total	Structures							Equipment		
			Total	Nonfarm		Mining (underground)	Farm	Institutional	Government	Total	Producer durables	Consumer durables
				Residential	Nonresidential							
	197	198	199	200	201	202	203	204	205	206	207	208
1956	1,448.2	1,199.6	721.7	350.1	151.7	26.1	34.3	22.2	137.3	331.2	177.6	153.6
1949	900.2	728.7	432.9	216.0	91.6	13.6	24.8	12.4	74.6	188.1	98.0	90.1
1945	561.2	446.1	275.7	143.2	56.0	7.8	16.3	7.0	45.4	94.5	48.3	46.2
1939	395.6	305.3	188.5	86.3	49.4	4.7	9.0	5.4	33.8	66.7	34.2	32.5
1933	330.2	241.0	159.4	69.6	46.7	3.4	8.7	4.8	26.2	54.9	29.2	25.7
1929	439.1	313.2	189.8	89.5	55.0	4.1	12.2	5.6	23.4	80.6	38.4	42.2
1922	334.2	233.2	134.5	56.6	42.6	3.3	12.4	4.1	15.5	61.7	30.8	30.9
1912	165.2	109.1	62.5	25.4	22.6	.9	5.6	2.0	5.9	27.3	13.8	13.6
1900	87.7	59.1	35.0	15.7	12.5	.4	3.3	1.1	2.0	12.6	6.5	6.0
1900 [1]	----------	*63.8*	*35.0*	*15.0*	*14.3*		*3.6*	*2.1*		*15.3*	*9.3*	*6.0*
1890 [1]	----------	*46.1*	*25.0*	*10.8*	*10.3*		*2.7*	*1.2*		*10.3*	*5.8*	*4.5*
1880 [1]	----------	*25.8*	*13.3*	*4.9*	*5.8*		*2.0*	*.6*		*5.4*	*3.0*	*2.4*
1850 [1]		*4.5*	----------		*.8*	[2]*1.1*	*.7*	*.1*		----------	[2]*.2*	*.3*

Year	Reproducible tangible assets—Con.						Land						Net foreign assets
	Inventories					Monetary gold and silver	Total	Private				Public	
	Total	Private			Public			Agricultural	Nonfarm		Forests		
		Livestock	Crops	Nonfarm					Residential	Nonresidential			
	209	210	211	212	213	214	215	216	217	218	219	220	221
1956	120.2	11.2	7.1	95.0	7.0	26.5	230.8	74.0	54.4	51.1	12.2	39.1	17.8
1949	79.2	12.9	6.0	56.9	3.4	28.4	157.7	50.7	33.9	34.3	7.5	31.3	13.8
1945	52.0	9.7	6.0	33.6	2.7	23.9	117.4	43.5	22.6	23.3	3.8	24.2	-2.3
1939	30.4	5.1	2.2	22.1	1.0	19.6	88.6	23.2	22.9	22.2	2.9	17.4	1.7
1933	21.9	3.2	1.8	16.9	.1	4.7	81.1	22.8	18.7	22.1	2.2	15.4	8.1
1929	38.0	6.5	3.0	28.4	.1	4.8	113.5	34.9	24.1	36.1	3.1	15.3	12.4
1922	32.6	5.4	3.1	24.0	.1	4.4	92.8	41.5	15.4	19.8	3.5	12.6	8.2
1912	16.7	5.6	2.6	8.4	----------	2.5	58.2	31.6	7.0	10.2	2.0	7.5	-2.1
1900	10.0	3.1	1.4	5.4	----------	1.6	30.9	14.5	4.4	6.5	1.5	4.0	-2.3
1900 [1]	*11.8*	*3.3*	----------	*8.5*	----------	*1.7*	(3)	(3)	(3)	(3)	(3)	(3)	*-1.1*
1890 [1]	*9.6*	*2.6*	----------	*7.0*	----------	*1.2*	(3)	(3)	(3)	(3)	(3)	(3)	*-1.6*
1880 [1]	*6.6*	*2.0*	----------	*4.6*	----------	*.6*	(3)	(3)	(3)	(3)	(3)	(3)	*-.5*
1850 [1]	*1.1*	*.5*	*.2*	*.5*	----------	*.2*	(3)	(3)	(3)	(3)	(3)	(3)	*-.2*

[1] As of June 1.
[2] Producer durables in the hands of nonagricultural business included with nonfarm nonresidential construction.
[3] Not available.

Series F 222–246. National Wealth, by Type of Asset, in 1929 and 1947–49 Prices: 1850 to 1956

[In billions of dollars. As of end of year except as noted. Figures in italics for 1900 are comparable with earlier years; those in regular type comparable with later years]

Year	Total national wealth	Total	Reproducible tangible assets — Structures							Equipment		
			Total	Nonfarm Residential	Nonfarm Nonresidential	Mining (underground)	Farm	Institutional	Government	Total	Producer durables	Consumer durables
	222	223	224	225	226	227	228	229	230	231	232	233
1947–49 PRICES												
1956	1,118.9	940.6	541.0	266.7	107.7	19.8	27.8	16.1	102.9	268.5	128.0	140.5
1949	885.4	719.2	430.0	212.8	88.0	13.4	24.3	12.1	79.4	181.2	91.9	89.3
1945	774.3	617.1	403.0	198.5	81.6	11.3	22.2	11.6	77.9	119.1	61.5	57.5
1929 PRICES												
1945	435.6	331.5	185.3	84.0	44.5	5.2	10.1	4.4	37.2	89.4	42.6	46.9
1939	424.8	317.8	191.7	86.3	49.8	4.5	10.4	5.1	35.5	78.8	34.7	44.1
1933	421.5	301.5	194.1	87.4	55.5	4.1	11.3	5.7	30.1	72.0	33.9	38.1
1929	445.8	318.7	193.5	90.6	56.8	4.2	12.5	5.6	23.8	83.0	39.1	43.8
1922	336.6	238.0	140.4	60.8	44.8	3.3	12.0	4.3	15.1	60.7	31.8	28.9
1912	265.3	186.3	113.2	48.2	39.0	1.7	9.4	3.8	11.2	49.6	24.6	25.0
1900	179.5	122.6	73.0	33.1	24.9	.8	6.8	2.3	5.1	30.0	13.5	16.6
1900[1]		*139.0*	*81.5*	*35.4*	*32.9*		*8.5*		*4.7*	*36.5*	*19.9*	*16.6*
1890[1]		*99.7*	*58.4*	*26.0*	*23.2*		*6.5*		*2.7*	*24.3*	*11.7*	*12.6*
1880[1]		*53.7*	*31.1*	*11.6*	*13.2*		*4.9*		*1.4*	*11.2*	*4.7*	*6.5*
1850[1]		*10.8*	---------	*2.1*	*[2]3.0*		*1.7*		*.3*	---------	*[2].4*	*.8*

Year	Reproducible tangible assets—Con.					Monetary gold and silver	Land						Net foreign assets
	Inventories						Private						
	Total	Private Livestock	Crops	Nonfarm	Public		Total	Agricultural	Nonfarm Residential	Nonfarm Nonresidential	Forests	Public	
	234	235	236	237	238	239	240	241	242	243	244	245	246
1947–49 PRICES													
1956	107.2	14.7	8.2	76.5	7.8	23.9	164.3	50.9	41.3	33.3	5.3	33.5	14.0
1949	81.7	13.6	7.5	56.9	3.8	26.2	153.4	49.4	33.4	33.0	5.7	32.0	12.9
1945	73.3	14.9	7.9	46.9	3.7	21.7	160.0	53.8	31.3	34.2	5.9	34.8	-2.7
1929 PRICES						*							
1945	44.0	7.2	3.9	30.8	2.1	12.7	103.3	35.9	20.9	22.5	3.1	20.8	.8
1939	36.4	6.6	3.2	24.9	1.6	10.9	105.0	31.8	22.9	26.4	3.4	20.4	2.1
1933	31.2	7.1	3.0	21.1	.1	4.2	109.2	34.5	23.4	28.5	2.9	20.0	10.8
1929	38.0	6.5	3.0	28.4	.1	4.3	114.7	34.9	24.4	37.0	3.1	15.3	12.4
1922	32.9	7.2	3.2	22.4	.1	4.0	90.4	35.5	16.6	22.7	3.2	12.4	8.2
1912	21.3	6.5	3.6	11.2	---------	2.1	82.2	36.3	13.3	20.2	2.6	9.9	-3.2
1900	18.2	6.4	2.6	9.2	---------	1.3	61.6	28.0	9.2	15.2	2.5	6.7	-4.7
1900[1]	*19.3*	*6.4*	*2.6*	*10.3*	---------	*1.7*	(3)	(3)	(3)	(3)	(3)	(3)	*-5.1*
1890[1]	*15.6*	*6.2*	*2.3*	*7.1*	---------	*1.2*	(3)	(3)	(3)	(3)	(3)	(3)	*-3.6*
1880[1]	*10.8*	*4.5*	*2.0*	*4.3*	---------	*.6*	(3)	(3)	(3)	(3)	(3)	(3)	*-1.0*
1850[1]	*2.2*	*1.1*	*.3*	*.8*	---------	*.3*	(3)	(3)	(3)	(3)	(3)	(3)	*-.3*

[1] As of June 1.
[2] Producer durables in the hands of nonagricultural business included with nonfarm nonresidential construction.
[3] Not available.

Series F 247–251. Value of Stock of Structures and Equipment in Specified Sectors, in 1929 Prices: 1880 to 1948

[In billions of dollars. Figures in italics for 1900 are comparable with earlier years; those in regular type are comparable with later years]

Year	Total, specified sectors	Agriculture[1]	Mining	Manufacturing	Transportation and other public utilities	Year	Total, specified sectors	Agriculture[1]	Mining	Manufacturing	Transportation and other public utilities
	247	248	249	250	251		247	248	249	250	251
1948, Dec. 31	103.9	18.5	5.3	34.8	45.3	1912, Dec. 31	65.1	13.4	3.4	15.3	33.0
1940, April 1	85.2	13.5	4.7	25.3	41.6	1900, June 1	38.5 / *39.0*	8.8	1.6	7.2 / *7.6*	21.0
1930, April 1	92.9	15.5	6.2	27.0	44.2	1890, June 1	29.1	7.3	0.8	4.5	16.5
1922, Dec. 31	78.0	15.3	5.3	22.0	35.4	1880, June 1	20.6	6.6	0.4	1.9	11.8

[1] Includes value of farm residences.

Series F 252–260. Gross Private Saving, in Current Prices: 1929 to 1957

[In billions of dollars]

Year	Gross private saving	Personal saving	Undistributed corporate profits	Corporate inventory valuation adjustment	Capital consumption allowances				Excess of wage accruals over disbursements
					Total	Business depreciation charges	Accidental damage to fixed business capital	Capital outlays charged to current expense	
	252	253	254	255	256	257	258	259	260
1957	66.32	20.71	9.42	−1.55	37.74	33.70	0.90	3.14	----------
1956	64.21	21.05	11.03	−2.56	34.69	30.76	.73	3.20	----------
1955	59.58	17.51	11.82	−1.74	31.99	27.94	1.06	2.99	----------
1954	54.35	18.86	7.00	−.32	28.81	25.20	.92	2.69	−0.08
1953	54.14	19.83	8.86	−1.00	26.53	23.07	.81	2.65	−.02
1952	52.18	18.94	8.28	.98	24.00	20.87	.68	2.45	−.02
1951	49.20	17.68	10.68	−1.20	21.97	18.75	.91	2.31	.07
1950	40.32	12.64	13.56	−4.97	19.07	16.50	.62	1.95	.02
1949	36.10	8.50	8.52	1.86	17.28	15.09	.52	1.67	−.05
1948	37.62	10.99	13.27	−2.15	15.47	13.10	.57	1.80	.04
1947	23.57	4.70	11.72	−5.90	13.03	11.06	.57	1.40	.02
1946	26.52	13.46	7.66	−5.26	10.70	9.04	.41	1.25	−.03
1945	44.25	28.66	3.60	−.56	12.55	11.25	.38	.92	.01
1944	54.15	36.93	5.70	−.29	12.01	10.79	.36	.85	−.19
1943	49.30	33.01	6.00	−.77	10.87	9.85	.40	.61	.21
1942	41.90	27.77	5.18	−1.20	10.16	9.16	.48	.51	----------
1941	22.59	11.11	4.91	−2.47	9.04	8.08	.27	.69	----------
1940	14.59	4.20	2.44	−.20	8.15	7.32	.25	.59	----------
1939	11.16	2.87	1.17	−.71	7.84	7.12	.22	.50	----------
1938	8.88	1.05	−.92	.96	7.78	6.94	.39	.46	----------
1937	11.50	8.74	.05	−.03	7.75	6.91	.30	.53	----------
1936	10.15	3.61	−.22	−.74	7.50	6.70	.38	.42	----------
1935	8.37	2.03	−.67	−.23	7.24	6.67	.24	.33	----------
1934	4.96	.09	−1.62	−.63	7.12	6.60	.24	.28	----------
1933	1.94	−.65	−2.43	−2.14	7.16	6.66	.28	.23	----------
1932	2.05	−.65	−5.97	1.05	7.62	7.04	.33	.25	----------
1931	7.72	2.51	−5.37	2.41	8.17	7.55	.35	.26	----------
1930	12.20	3.41	−3.01	3.26	8.54	7.74	.39	.42	----------
1929	15.70	4.17	2.45	.47	8.62	7.70	.41	.51	----------

Series F 261–303. Individuals' Saving, by Components, in Current Prices: 1929 to 1957

[In billions of dollars]

Year	Individuals' saving (F 276 + F 279 minus F 294)	Investment in tangible assets													
		Gross investment									Depreciation [2]				
		Total	Non-farm homes	Other construction and producers' durable equipment				Inventories of noncorporate and farm enterprises			Total	Non-farm homes	Noncorporate nonfarm enterprises	Farm enterprises	Non-profit institutions
				Total	Noncorporate nonfarm enterprises	Farm enterprises [1]	Nonprofit institutions	Total	Nonfarm	Farm					
	261	262	263	264	265	266	267	268	269	270	271	272	273	274	275
1957	22.30	30.58	15.17	14.60	8.10	4.07	2.44	0.80	0.04	0.76	14.33	4.64	5.24	3.92	0.52
1956	19.50	30.67	16.22	14.80	8.86	3.83	2.12	−.36	.12	−.48	13.36	4.26	4.85	3.75	.49
1955	18.15	32.99	17.34	14.80	8.60	4.19	2.01	.86	.56	.30	12.81	3.92	4.68	3.74	.48
1954	16.64	27.61	14.24	13.09	7.02	4.19	1.87	.29	−.20	.49	12.14	3.61	4.46	3.63	.45
1953	21.09	25.53	12.75	13.14	6.91	4.70	1.53	−.36	.26	−.62	11.58	3.32	4.31	3.53	.43
1952	19.16	25.24	11.96	12.44	6.32	4.71	1.41	.84	−.08	.92	10.89	3.02	4.07	3.42	.39
1951	19.93	26.29	11.61	12.99	6.48	4.99	1.53	1.68	.50	1.18	10.26	2.83	3.85	3.24	.33
1950	10.01	27.73	12.70	13.04	6.96	4.65	1.44	1.99	1.18	.82	9.01	2.53	3.45	2.74	.29
1949	8.09	18.36	8.23	11.49	5.76	4.52	1.21	−1.35	−.49	−.86	8.21	2.29	3.22	2.44	.26
1948	11.19	22.41	9.00	10.76	5.53	4.28	.95	2.66	.92	1.73	7.15	2.12	2.72	2.07	.24
1947	7.05	14.97	6.76	9.91	6.01	3.33	.57	−1.70	.06	−1.76	6.15	1.94	2.37	1.62	.23
1946	12.13	11.49	4.42	6.66	4.34	1.86	.45	.41	.38	.03	5.04	1.84	1.76	1.23	.22
1945	29.52	4.31	1.09	3.25	2.05	1.08	.12	−.03	.43	−.46	5.57	1.81	1.51	2.04	.20
1944	35.14	3.18	.98	2.15	.96	1.13	.06	.05	.50	−.44	5.38	1.80	1.47	1.91	.20
1943	33.73	2.68	1.14	1.84	.78	1.02	.03	−.30	−.12	−.18	5.14	1.79	1.45	1.71	.20
1942	29.99	5.62	1.90	2.38	1.16	1.11	.11	1.34	.18	1.16	4.84	1.76	1.37	1.51	.20
1941	11.12	8.96	3.67	4.10	2.55	1.31	.24	1.18	.73	.45	4.33	1.68	1.16	1.29	.19
1940	5.13	6.92	3.15	3.18	2.04	.93	.21	.59	.32	.27	3.94	1.62	1.02	1.13	.18
1939	4.03	5.54	2.79	2.63	1.68	.73	.22	.12	.06	.06	3.81	1.56	.95	1.12	.17
1938	.41	4.08	1.83	2.28	1.36	.69	.22	−.02	−.13	.10	3.84	1.58	.96	1.12	.18
1937	4.06	5.45	1.63	3.09	2.03	.87	.19	.73	.21	.52	3.77	1.54	.97	1.09	.17
1936	3.96	3.05	1.27	2.42	1.68	.60	.14	−.64	.48	−1.11	3.65	1.53	.95	1.00	.17
1935	1.64	3.02	.54	1.78	1.26	.44	.09	−.70	.16	.54	3.45	1.47	.90	.91	.16
1934	.42	.07	.19	1.19	.94	.17	.08	−1.31	.01	−1.32	3.37	1.47	.87	.87	.16
1933	−3.17	.10	.09	.78	.70	(³)	.08	−.76	−.50	−.26	3.32	1.48	.83	.84	.16
1932	1.57	.62	.35	1.01	.69	.12	.20	−.75	−.78	.04	3.26	1.42	.79	.89	.16
1931	5.64	3.23	1.25	2.19	1.25	.54	.40	−.21	−.52	.31	3.48	1.46	.82	1.05	.16
1930	5.19	4.73	1.52	3.68	2.02	1.14	.53	−.47	−.22	−.25	3.66	1.46	.82	1.23	.16
1929	5.82	7.78	3.20	4.57	2.43	1.58	.56	(³)	.26	−.25	3.68	1.44	.81	1.27	.16

¹ Includes farm dwellings.
² Includes accidental damage to fixed property.
³ Less than $5 million.

Series F 261–303. Individuals' Saving, by Components, in Current Prices: 1929 to 1957—Con.

[In billions of dollars]

Year	Investments in tangible assets—Con. / Net investment in tangible assets — Total (F 262 minus F 271)	Nonfarm homes	Other	Increase in financial assets [4] — Total	Currency and bank deposits — Total	Currency	Demand deposits	Time and savings deposits [5]	Savings and loan association shares	Securities — Total	U.S. savings bonds [6]	Other U.S. Government	State and local government	Corporate and other
	276	277	278	279	280	281	282	283	284	285	286	287	288	289
1957	16.24	10.53	5.71	24.29	5.65	−0.03	−0.92	6.60	4.80	6.02	−1.91	1.95	1.98	3.99
1956	17.31	11.96	5.35	22.90	4.87	.03	.57	4.27	4.83	5.16	−.09	1.54	1.44	2.27
1955	20.18	13.42	6.76	22.46	3.81	.37	−.06	3.50	4.79	6.29	.26	1.62	1.68	2.73
1954	15.47	10.63	4.84	17.40	5.41	−.36	1.08	4.68	4.45	.23	.60	−1.60	.66	.57
1953	13.94	9.44	4.50	18.85	4.93	.58	−.21	4.56	3.64	3.41	.20	.06	1.83	1.32
1952	14.34	8.94	5.40	20.06	7.14	1.11	1.52	4.51	3.05	3.48	.09	.35	.96	2.07
1951	16.03	8.78	7.25	14.06	6.00	.77	3.08	2.14	2.07	.58	−.47	−1.00	.38	1.67
1950	18.72	10.17	8.55	11.09	3.74	−.06	3.20	.59	1.54	.99	.25	−.46	.49	.71
1949	10.15	5.94	4.21	6.94	−1.38	−.79	−1.56	.97	1.51	2.51	1.46	−.10	.41	.73
1948	15.26	6.88	8.38	6.98	−1.78	−.46	−2.23	.91	1.19	3.42	1.60	−.28	.98	1.12
1947	8.82	4.83	3.99	9.47	2.07	−.43	.22	2.28	1.20	2.26	2.08	−.85	.33	.69
1946	6.45	2.58	3.86	13.48	10.61	.12	5.12	5.37	1.18	−2.03	1.22	−3.10	−.15	(3)
1945	−1.26	−.72	−.54	34.38	19.01	2.96	7.19	8.86	1.06	9.93	6.85	4.44	−.20	−1.16
1944	−2.20	−.81	−1.38	37.90	17.57	4.55	5.87	7.15	.81	15.71	11.80	4.64	−.05	−.68
1943	−2.46	−.65	−1.81	33.94	16.20	4.72	7.12	4.36	.55	14.14	11.14	3.37	−.12	−.26
1942	.79	.14	.64	24.14	10.95	4.12	6.05	.78	.25	10.33	7.98	2.56	−.22	.01
1941	4.63	1.98	2.64	10.04	4.84	2.18	2.54	.11	.36	2.64	2.75	.66	−.28	−.50
1940	2.97	1.53	1.44	4.60	2.93	.77	1.45	.71	.20	−.43	.86	−.39	−.46	−.44
1939	1.73	1.22	.51	4.02	3.04	.45	1.90	.69	.04	−.83	.66	−.64	−.23	−.62
1938	.24	.24	(3)	1.60	.42	.04	.36	.02	(3)	−.42	.41	−.61	−.23	.02
1937	1.68	.09	1.59	2.74	.46	.20	−.49	.74	−.11	.57	.42	.71	−.05	−.51
1936	−.60	−.27	−.33	5.01	3.66	.52	2.04	1.09	−.06	−.34	.28	.58	−.47	−.73
1935	−.43	−.93	.50	2.12	2.47	.23	1.02	1.22	−.20	−1.76	.13	−.56	−.12	−1.20
1934	−3.29	−1.27	−2.02	2.80	1.81	−.10	.24	1.67	−.29	−.09	---------	1.09	−.79	−.39
1933	−3.21	−1.39	−1.82	−1.47	−1.28	.16	1.21	−2.65	−.58	−.23	---------	.60	−.67	−.16
1932	−2.64	−1.06	−1.59	−1.39	−1.70	.28	−.54	−1.44	−.59	.61	---------	.70	−.29	.20
1931	−.25	−.20	−.05	.45	−1.58	1.01	−.31	−2.27	−.38	1.54	---------	.84	.58	.12
1930	1.07	.07	1.00	1.03	−1.46	.03	−2.18	.69	.06	1.28	---------	−.49	.78	.98
1929	4.10	1.76	2.34	2.37	−3.57	−.12	−2.54	−.92	.48	4.25	---------	−1.27	.88	4.64

Year	Increase in financial assets—Con. / Private insurance and pension reserves — Total	Insurance reserves	Insured pension reserves	Noninsured pension funds	Increase in debt to corporations and financial intermediaries — Total	Consumer debt	Securities loans	Mortgage debt — Total	On nonfarm homes	On noncorporate nonfarm enterprises	On farms	Net trade debt of noncorporate nonfarm enterprises	Nonreal-estate farm debt	Bank debt, not elsewhere classified
	290	291	292	293	294	295	296	297	298	299	300	301	302	303
1957	7.81	3.56	1.58	2.68	18.23	2.58	−0.07	10.15	8.25	1.53	0.38	3.52	0.64	1.41
1956	8.05	4.44	1.20	2.41	20.71	3.14	−.75	12.41	10.38	1.53	.50	3.96	.23	1.72
1955	7.57	4.19	1.30	2.08	24.49	6.09	.60	13.98	11.93	1.48	.57	−.18	.54	3.46
1954	7.31	4.21	1.18	1.93	16.24	.96	.86	10.54	9.01	1.20	.34	1.57	.34	1.97
1953	6.88	3.94	1.10	1.84	11.70	3.65	.40	8.58	7.30	1.00	.29	−.47	−.37	−.09
1952	6.39	3.76	1.12	1.51	15.25	4.36	.60	7.89	6.52	1.02	.35	2.17	.30	−.08
1951	5.41	3.09	.98	1.35	10.16	.99	−.30	8.36	6.59	1.48	.30	.35	.96	−.21
1950	4.82	3.92		.90	19.81	3.64	.22	8.86	7.29	1.30	.27	2.42	.81	3.85
1949	4.31	3.71		.60	9.00	2.64	.32	5.34	4.12	1.03	.19	−.96	.41	1.25
1948	4.15	3.75		.40	11.05	2.41	.43	5.87	4.72	1.07	.08	1.84	.70	−.20
1947	3.94	3.64		.30	11.24	2.81	−.76	5.54	4.62	.81	.11	1.25	.60	1.80
1946	3.72	3.42		.30	7.79	2.32	−2.34	4.37	3.60	.79	−.02	1.11	.45	1.87
1945	4.38	3.46		.93	3.61	.48	1.48	.14	.22	.16	−.25	.86	.03	.61
1944	3.81	3.21		.60	.57	.14	1.38	−.54	−.05	−.13	−.36	−.32	−.10	.01
1943	3.05	2.85		.20	−2.26	−1.03	.58	−1.05	−.38	−.20	−.48	−.64	.04	−.15
1942	2.61	2.49		.12	−5.07	−2.96	.27	−.37	.10	−.15	−.31	−2.01	−.01	.01
1941	2.22	2.14		.08	3.55	.69	−.11	.93	.82	.16	−.06	1.28	.29	.47
1940	1.90	1.85		.05	2.44	1.01	−.20	.86	.85	.04	−.03	.53	.21	.03
1939	1.77	1.72		.05	1.72	.81	−.23	.48	.50	.11	−.13	.33	.26	.07
1938	1.60	1.54		.06	1.43	−.62	−.12	.16	.17	.08	−.09	1.77	.20	.04
1937	1.82	1.76		.06	.36	.58	−.49	.07	.01	.15	−.08	.43	.10	−.34
1936	1.75	1.67		.08	.45	1.29	.06	−.44	−.09	−.28	−.07	−.43	−.04	.01
1935	1.60	1.55		.05	.04	.83	−.04	−.32	−.13	−.24	.06	−.55	.19	−.06
1934	1.38	1.33		.05	−.91	.40	−.47	.98	.55	−.04	.47	−1.38	−.30	−.14
1933	.62	.57		.05	−1.50	−.10	−.25	−.22	−.62	.66	−.26	−.31	−.26	−.35
1932	.29	.24		.05	−5.60	−1.13	−1.06	−1.44	−.89	−.24	−.31	−.98	−.41	−.58
1931	.87	.82		.05	−5.45	−1.22	−2.10	−.64	−.34	−.17	−.13	−.32	−.46	−.71
1930	1.15	1.10		.05	−3.09	−.57	−2.20	.40	.11	.41	−.12	−.16	−.22	−.34
1929	1.21	1.05		.16	.64	.84	−1.66	1.11	.86	.37	−.12	.06	−.10	.38

3 Less than $5 million.
4 Includes changes in assets of noncorporate enterprises of the types specified. Excludes changes in government insurance and pension reserves, and small amounts of Armed Forces leave bonds.
5 Includes shares and deposits in credit unions and the Postal Saving System.
6 Includes increases in redemption value of outstanding bonds.

Series F 304–315.　National Saving, by Major Saver Groups, in Current Prices: 1897 to 1945

[In billions of dollars]

Year	National saving		Personal saving							Unincorporated business	Corporate saving	Government saving	
			Total		Nonagricultural individuals		Agriculture					State and local	Federal
	Including consumer durables	Excluding consumer durables	Including consumer durables	Excluding consumer durables	Including consumer durables	Excluding consumer durables	Including consumer durables	Excluding consumer durables				
	304	305	306	307	308	309	310	311	312	313	314	315
1945	−7.31	−6.56	36.41	37.15	29.31	29.92	3.61	3.75	3.48	2.51	2.59	−48.81
1944	−7.28	−5.61	39.30	40.96	30.78	32.21	4.22	4.44	4.31	4.79	3.17	−54.53
1943	−3.64	−2.14	36.17	37.67	27.85	29.37	4.40	4.38	3.92	4.23	2.72	−46.76
1942	4.50	5.81	33.24	34.55	23.80	25.15	5.04	5.01	4.39	2.86	1.82	−33.42
1941	14.31	11.23	13.97	10.89	10.54	7.71	2.74	2.49	.69	1.70	1.72	−3.08
1940	10.98	8.76	8.54	6.31	6.54	4.39	.95	.86	1.06	1.62	1.85	−1.02
1939	4.84	3.47	6.85	5.49	6.08	4.86	.83	.69	−.06	−.09	.80	−2.73
1938	2.00	1.87	3.72	3.58	3.95	3.78	.39	.43	−.63	−.57	1.50	−2.64
1937	7.29	5.32	7.32	5.35	6.32	4.50	1.29	1.14	−.29	−.55	1.31	−.79
1936	1.56	−.21	5.28	3.51	4.26	2.67	−.02	−.20	1.04	−1.41	1.23	−3.54
1935	.24	−.33	2.35	1.79	.62	.18	1.25	1.13	.48	−1.29	.75	−1.58
1934	−4.42	−3.76	−.95	−.29	−1.45	−.80	−1.13	−1.12	1.63	−2.72	1.41	−2.16
1933	−8.85	−7.34	−3.81	−2.30	−3.38	−2.06	.02	.20	−.44	−4.69	.77	−1.12
1932	−10.49	−8.39	−3.27	−1.17	−.72	1.08	.19	.50	−2.75	−5.03	−.95	−1.23
1931	−3.31	−2.21	2.47	3.56	6.01	6.85	.01	.26	−3.55	−3.36	−.48	−1.93
1930	5.82	5.89	5.62	5.67	7.99	7.92	−.18	−.05	−2.20	−.51	.90	−.19
1929	15.97	14.02	11.49	9.53	10.98	9.16	.13	−.01	.38	2.14	1.25	1.10
1928	10.91	9.25	6.01	4.35	6.28	4.72	.11	.01	−.38	2.11	1.75	1.04
1927	13.69	12.02	10.07	8.40	10.17	8.44	−.11	−.06	.02	1.37	1.11	1.14
1926	15.89	13.18	10.10	7.40	9.30	6.69	−.04	−.14	.85	3.39	1.22	1.17
1925	15.45	12.82	10.74	8.11	10.52	8.09	.07	−.14	.16	2.37	1.32	1.02
1924	12.13	10.29	8.62	6.77	7.74	5.88	.58	.59	.30	1.46	1.27	.80
1923	13.61	11.42	9.88	7.70	9.81	7.67	.33	.29	−.26	2.35	.41	.96
1922	7.95	7.05	6.30	5.40	5.96	4.89	−.20	−.03	.54	.95	.50	.20
1921	2.26	2.57	1.29	1.59	3.01	2.76	−1.84	−1.29	.12	1.34	.09	−.45
1920	9.97	9.46	6.57	6.06	6.50	5.77	−1.63	−1.42	1.71	3.44	−.19	.15
1919	6.57	6.10	9.76	9.30	10.33	10.08	−1.76	−1.97	1.19	2.48	.13	−5.81
1918	1.61	1.91	12.69	12.99	10.92	11.29	1.50	1.43	.27	.42	.06	−11.56
1917	9.93	9.26	10.07	9.40	8.65	8.30	1.22	.90	.20	2.53	.16	−2.83
1916	9.58	8.74	5.56	4.72	5.85	5.14	−1.10	−1.23	.81	3.19	.22	.61
1915	6.27	6.07	4.68	4.47	4.47	4.34	.21	.12	.01	1.25	.20	.15
1914	3.51	3.35	2.55	2.38	2.07	1.95	.40	.36	.07	.74	.20	.03
1913	4.14	3.69	2.67	2.22	2.85	2.44	−.66	−.70	.48	.92	.45	.10
1912	5.23	4.76	4.24	3.76	3.88	3.48	.27	.19	.09	.57	.30	.13
1911	2.93	2.58	2.09	1.74	2.78	2.50	−.65	−.72	−.04	.58	.20	.06
1910	4.60	4.11	3.24	2.76	2.79	2.41	−.01	−.11	.46	1.10	.16	.09
1909	3.69	3.24	3.00	2.55	3.08	2.72	.10	.00	−.17	.42	.22	.05
1908	2.45	2.35	2.00	1.90	2.30	2.24	.03	−.01	−.33	.41	.08	−.04
1907	3.13	2.70	2.10	1.67	2.25	1.87	−.27	−.32	.12	.77	.16	.10
1906	4.21	3.70	3.24	2.73	2.90	2.44	.10	.04	.25	.73	.12	.12
1905	4.31	3.94	3.46	3.08	2.87	2.53	.10	.06	.49	.68	.14	.04
1904	2.04	1.82	1.42	1.19	1.56	1.36	.08	.05	−.22	.40	.23	−.00
1903	2.77	2.49	1.50	1.22	1.61	1.35	−.14	−.16	.03	1.07	.14	.06
1902	3.95	3.67	2.94	2.67	2.21	1.97	.48	.45	.25	.72	.22	.06
1901	2.20	1.98	1.36	1.14	1.78	1.58	−.35	−.37	−.07	.65	.12	.09
1900	2.10	1.92	1.27	1.10	1.07	.91	−.03	−.05	.24	.67	.12	.03
1899	2.82	2.59	2.19	1.96	1.72	1.52	.11	.08	.36	.55	.07	.01
1898	1.62	1.49	1.29	1.16	.82	.72	.23	.21	.23	.37	.07	−.11
1897	.93	.79	.55	.41	.66	.54	.04	.02	−.15	.29	.07	.02

NATIONAL INCOME AND WEALTH

Series F 316–345. Personal Saving, by Major Components, in Current Prices: 1897 to 1956

[In billions of dollars]

Year	Total[1]		Nonfarm construction		Farm construction	Consumer durables	Producer durables	Inventories	Currency	Commercial bank deposits	Savings bank deposits	Credit unions and cooperatives	Savings and loan associations	Mortgage holdings	Life insurance reserves
	Including consumer durables	Excluding consumer durables	Residential	Non-residential											
	316	317	318	319	320	321	322	323	324	325	326	327	328	329	330
1956	35.60	28.96	10.71	1.98	0.25	6.65	0.81	−1.02		3.87		0.66	4.85	1.75	4.97
1955	33.33	22.20	12.02	1.80	.40	11.13	.91	.97		3.80		.60	4.77	1.31	5.41
1954	27.59	21.78	8.34	1.38	.47	5.81	.62	.55		6.29		.54	4.41	1.19	5.32
1953	28.61	21.60	7.90	.97	.57	7.02	1.54	−.56		4.28		.53	3.60	1.04	4.92
1952	27.27	22.59	6.93	.66	.77	4.68	1.79	1.00		6.96		.47	2.99	.81	4.81
1951	28.67	22.09	7.10	.91	.75	6.58	2.44	2.41		4.68		.39	2.07	.82	4.12
1950	25.30	13.44	7.29	.72	.64	11.86	2.62	2.73		3.54		.35	1.49	.55	3.84
1949	16.58	8.48	4.07	.40	.55	8.09	2.51	−1.57		−1.42		.30	1.48	.66	3.75
1948	22.22	14.16	5.00	.29	.65	8.06	2.95	2.44		−1.43		.29	1.21	1.13	3.63
1947	19.12	10.57	2.46	−.07	.48	8.55	2.46	−1.68		2.48		.28	1.20	1.28	3.51
1946	21.33	15.34	1.01	.18	.36	5.99	1.11	.32		9.48		.16	1.18	1.46	3.36
1945	36.41	37.16	−1.33	−.30	−.17	−.75	.67	.05	2.87	13.26	2.75	.21	1.11	.65	3.38
1944	39.30	40.97	−1.44	−.44	−.11	−1.67	.46	.35	4.58	10.59	2.32	.17	.83	.02	3.19
1943	36.17	37.68	−1.19	−.50	−.05	−1.51	−.18	−.17	4.67	9.98	1.57	.11	.61	−.24	2.87
1942	33.24	34.55	−.26	−.39	−.04	−1.31	.15	1.64	4.21	6.26	.28	.11	.30	−.23	2.50
1941	13.97	10.89	1.78	−.10	.09	3.08	.83	.79	2.13	2.54	.03	.15	.40	.08	2.20
1940	8.54	6.31	1.29	−.16	.02	2.23	.49	.56	.89	2.00	.25	.11	.29	−.28	1.84
1939	6.85	5.50	.95	−.19	−.02	1.35	.20	.13	.45	2.44	.36	.08	.17	−.29	1.72
1938	3.72	3.58	.14	−.21	−.09	.14	.09	−.02	−.01	.34	.19	.07	−.00	−.20	1.61
1937[2]	7.32	5.36	−.06	−.17	−.04	1.96	.52	.90	.20	.35	.23	.07	−.09	−.09	1.62
1936	5.28	3.51	−.31	−.25	−.10	1.77	.33	−.67	.53	2.77	.35	.06	−.18	.10	1.69
1935	2.35	1.79	−.99	−.44	−.14	.56	.00	.80	.18	2.48	.21	.06	−.30	.13	1.51
1934	−.95	−.29	−1.50	−.44	−.26	−.66	−.35	−1.31	−.01	2.14	.34	.05	−.24	−.53	1.13
1933	−3.81	−2.31	−1.60	−.41	−.26	−1.50	−.59	−.82	.19	−1.83	−.02	−.02	−.36	−.90	.54
1932	−3.27	−1.17	−1.45	−.24	−.29	−2.10	−.70	−.54	.31	−1.98	.31	−.00	−.42	−.23	.27
1931	2.47	3.57	−.51	.04	−.23	−1.10	−.44	−.23	.75	−3.66	1.03	−.00	−.23	−.18	.77
1930	5.62	5.69	−.07	.45	−.13	−.07	−.07	.03	−.00	−.90	.76	−.00	.20	.78	1.01
1929	11.49	9.54	1.45	.65	.05	1.95	.36	.20	.00	−.80	.16	.03	.53	1.89	1.12
1928	6.01	4.34	2.73	.69	.10	1.67	.18	−.26	−.06	−1.75	.59	.03	.69	1.65	1.29
1927	10.07	8.39	3.17	.81	.15	1.68	.20	−.23	−.05	2.64	.66	.03	.74	1.32	1.25
1926	10.10	7.40	3.79	.85	.06	2.70	.31	.03	−.04	−.36	.54	.03	.63	.68	1.14
1925	10.74	8.11	4.00	.72	.08	2.63	.23	.10	−.10	1.58	.47	.03	.60	.43	1.02
1924	8.62	6.78	3.75	.51	.06	1.84	.07	−.92	−.03	2.08	.51	.03	.60	−.46	.82
1923	9.88	7.70	3.16	.47	.09	2.18	.18	.47	.09	1.25	.44	.03	.45	.18	.79
1922	6.30	5.40	2.19	.40	.04	.90	−.12	.11	.13	2.47	.40	.03	.35	−.18	.66
1921	1.29	1.59	.90	.27	−.04	−.30	−.37	−.80	−.91	−1.36	.28	.03	.28	.28	.53
1920	6.57	6.06	.54	.24	.39	.51	.36	1.97	.37	−1.02	.51	.03	.28	2.24	.52
1919	9.76	9.30	.75	.07	.64	.46	.23	.56	−.02	4.06	.44	.03	.17	1.14	.53
1918	12.69	12.99	−.06	−.01	.41	−.30	.25	−.17	.96	1.46	.18	.03	.11	.51	.37
1917	10.07	9.40	.38	.13	.44	.67	.28	1.19	.61	2.85	.15	.03	.13	1.11	.37
1916	5.56	4.72	.69	.17	.29	.84	.13	−.82	.33	2.92	.35	.02	.09	.55	.35
1915	4.68	4.47	.61	.06	.17	.21	−.00	.41	.30	1.73	.17	.02	.10	.27	.27
1914	2.55	2.38	.60	.09	.17	.17	.06	.50	−.14	.21	.13	.02	.08	.47	.20
1913	2.67	2.23	.73	.20	.17	.44	.16	−.21	.05	.50	.19	.02	.08	.62	.23
1912	4.24	3.76	.72	.15	.18	.48	.15	.51	.09	.76	.20	.01	.09	.26	.23
1911	2.09	1.74	.65	.10	.16	.35	.07	−.45	−.07	.79	.16	.01	.08	.25	.25
1910	3.24	2.75	.73	.13	.18	.49	.11	.47	.04	.46	.15	.01	.06	.22	.21
1909	3.00	2.55	.78	.14	.16	.45	.10	−.06	.06	.67	.17	.01	.06	.06	.21
1908	2.00	1.90	.55	.14	.13	.10	.05	−.03	−.28	−.10	.06	.01	.04	.08	.18
1907	2.10	1.67	.68	.24	.12	.43	.18	−.24	.12	−.28	.07	.01	.04	.07	.17
1906	3.24	2.72	.61	.18	.12	.52	.17	.25	.06	.47	.17	.01	.03	.04	.21
1905	3.46	3.09	.55	.13	.12	.37	.10	.27	.22	1.12	.18	.01	.02	.07	.19
1904	1.42	1.18	.36	.11	.12	.24	.07	−.13	−.07	.14	.13	.01	.02	.07	.17
1903	1.50	1.22	.40	.15	.12	.28	.09	−.04	.06	.22	.12	.01	.01	.07	.15
1902	2.94	2.67	.27	.23	.12	.27	.14	.54	.06	.45	.15	.01	.01	.06	.15
1901	1.36	1.14	.14	.19	.11	.22	.06	−.57	.04	.63	.13	.01	−.01	.05	.14
1900	1.27	1.09	.00	.20	.10	.18	.03	.19	.06	.29	.19	.01	−.01	.05	.11
1899	2.19	1.96	.07	.12	.08	.23	.02	.21	.12	.59	.12	.01	−.02	.06	.10
1898	1.29	1.17	.04	.13	.09	.12	−.01	.27	.04	.33	.12	.01	.00	.06	.10
1897	.55	.40	.07	.15	.07	.15	−.04	−.10	.03	.18	.09	.00	−.02	.06	.08

[1] Components do not add to total for years 1946–1956; see text for explanation.   [2] Components do not add to total; source offers no explanation.

Series F 316–345. Personal Saving, by Major Components, in Current Prices: 1897 to 1956—Con.

[In billions of dollars]

Year	Pension and retirement funds			Securities				Share in saving of foreign corporations other than U.S. subsidiaries	Less change in liabilities — Nonfarm mortgage debt on—		Farm mortgage debt	Debt to banks and other institutions	Borrowing on securities	Consumer and other debt	Tax liabilities
	U.S. Government	State and local	Private	U.S. Government	State and local	Corporate and foreign bonds	Stocks		Residential structures	Nonresidential structures					
	331	332	333	334	335	336	337	338	339	340	341	342	343	344	345
1956	2.05	1.41	2.50	0.95	1.67	1.67	3.50	0.05	10.90	0.97	0.84	0.45	-0.02	1.25	------
1955	1.90	1.30	2.16	2.63	1.87	2.03	3.21	.05	12.58	.81	.78	3.01	.95	7.31	------
1954	1.48	1.22	2.00	-1.34	1.10	-.68	2.13	.04	9.44	.71	.52	1.74	.70	1.29	------
1953	2.31	1.04	1.79	.20	1.84	.25	1.90	.03	7.80	.46	.51	-.32	.50	4.22	------
1952	3.37	.96	1.69	.15	1.13	-.17	2.42	.03	7.01	.42	.59	.17	.41	5.98	------
1951	3.22	.84	1.48	-1.47	.26	-.64	2.56	.03	6.92	.44	.61	-.27	-.10	2.68	------
1950	.52	.74	1.02	-.39	.59	-.23	2.14	.03	7.29	.37	.49	4.09	.33	2.77	------
1949	1.98	.62	.73	-.85	.72	-.47	1.50	.02	4.42	.37	.29	.42	.19	2.97	------
1948	2.94	.53	.68	-.18	1.11	-.17	1.71	.03	5.21	.48	.22	-.37	-.03	3.48	------
1947	3.34	.39	.66	2.08	.50	-.47	1.76	.03	4.98	.53	.17	1.87	-.03	2.87	------
1946	3.33	.34	.54	-.34	-.22	-1.17	-1.70	.03	4.28	.51	.14	2.28	-1.50	2.00	------
1945	4.80	.25	.80	11.84	-.31	-1.58	1.25	.05	.39	.04	-.25	.48	1.38	1.46	-.41
1944	4.41	.26	.60	17.80	-.08	-1.14	.52	.04	-.11	-.09	-.46	.05	1.57	.31	.70
1943	3.71	.24	.20	14.67	-.15	-.65	.47	.04	-.55	-.19	-.56	-.04	.56	-1.51	.61
1942	2.42	.22	.13	10.57	-.18	.06	.19	.04	-.23	-.14	-.42	-.55	.06	-4.20	-1.09
1941	1.68	.20	.08	3.40	-.15	-.96	.63	.04	.96	-.06	-.11	.82	-.09	.98	2.44
1940	1.14	.19	.05	.29	-.13	-.42	.49	.04	.78	-.08	-.09	.49	-.28	1.30	.49
1939	1.11	.18	.05	-.08	-.12	-.67	.57	.03	.57	-.11	-.18	.28	-.15	1.10	.08
1938	.96	.16	.06	.00	-.05	-.05	.23	.03	.20	-.06	-.16	-.10	-.10	.42	-.54
1937	1.25	.16	.06	1.03	.10	-1.06	.83	.03	.11	-.06	-.15	.28	-.52	1.22	-.22
1936	.45	.13	.08	.98	-.36	-.92	.19	.03	-.20	.02	-.19	.15	-.03	1.10	.55
1935	.14	.12	.05	-.90	-.01	-.94	-.07	.03	-.23	-.10	-.09	.17	-.11	.23	.26
1934	.05	.11	.05	-.23	-.86	.04	.42	.03	.01	-.09	-.03	-.23	-.28	-.85	.39
1933	.03	.09	.05	1.11	-.91	-.10	.44	.03	-1.26	-.08	-.71	-.95	-.04	-.46	.48
1932	-.04	.07	.05	.69	.13	-.40	.23	.03	-1.15	-.14	-.60	-.88	-1.03	.44	.33
1931	-.40	.07	.05	.72	1.78	.56	.60	.03	-.56	.07	-.28	-1.22	-2.01	1.14	-.19
1930	.13	.07	.05	-.23	.59	.67	1.28	.03	.57	.21	-.22	-.99	-2.05	1.28	-.51
1929	.16	.07	.16	-.47	.51	.66	4.79	.04	1.95	.39	-.12	.05	-1.33	1.09	-.03
1928	.13	.07	.08	-.98	.38	1.63	3.41	.04	2.50	.55	.01	.19	1.65	.98	.40
1927	.13	.06	.07	-2.26	.45	2.02	2.08	.03	2.39	.54	.11	-.23	1.33	.35	.38
1926	.16	.05	.04	-.64	.15	1.90	1.76	.03	2.60	.54	-.05	-.04	-.00	.45	.19
1925	.16	.04	.03	-.30	.23	1.94	2.09	.03	2.18	.80	-.19	.21	1.48	.64	.15
1924	.09	.04	.02	-1.52	.20	1.44	1.25	.02	1.74	.55	-.74	-.83	.84	.15	.08
1923	.04	.04	.01	-.28	.62	1.57	1.23	.02	1.70	.55	-.11	.64	-.10	.30	.18
1922	.04	.03	.03	-2.69	.75	1.26	1.35	.01	1.00	.30	.09	-.21	.66	.13	-.10
1921	.03	.03	.01	-.61	.70	1.40	.96	.01	.81	.20	.49	-1.48	-.08	-.15	.25
1920	.02	.02	------	-.67	.68	1.67	1.82	.01	1.17	.35	1.77	.92	-.67	.57	-.19
1919	.01	.01	------	3.15	.03	.52	2.00	.01	.36	.15	1.31	1.78	.79	.65	-.02
1918	.01	.01	------	8.67	.50	1.01	.96	.01	.27	.10	.60	.41	.37	.15	.30
1917	------	.01	------	3.40	.21	.69	.96	.01	.62	.19	.71	1.04	.14	.26	.61
1916	------	.01	------	-.12	.22	1.09	1.38	.01	.33	.12	.57	.63	.28	.32	.68
1915	------	.01	------	-.00	.30	1.46	.69	.01	.25	.10	.27	.64	.40	.19	.24
1914	------	.00	------	-.00	.23	.47	.46	.00	.36	.13	.28	.01	.11	.10	.18
1913	------	.00	------	-.00	.01	.20	.54	.00	.41	.14	.36	.11	-.02	.14	.14
1912	------	.00	------	.00	.14	.67	.93	.00	.22	.08	.42	.32	.10	.16	.04
1911	------	.00	------	.02	.11	.41	.25	.00	.20	.08	.41	.14	.05	.14	.02
1910	------	.00	------	.01	.14	-.03	.80	.00	.24	.09	.31	.16	.01	.12	.02
1909	------	.00	------	-.03	.01	.53	.75	.00	.23	.08	.12	.30	.11	.17	.02
1908	------	.00	------	.00	.21	.61	.66	.00	.13	.06	.11	.03	.04	.01	.02
1907	------	.00	------	-.08	.12	.08	.69	.00	.14	.06	.11	-.03	-.05	.09	.02
1906	------	.00	------	.01	.07	.42	.81	.00	.19	.07	.10	.34	.04	.13	.02
1905	------	.00	------	-.01	05	.66	.35	.00	.17	.07	.10	.33	.14	.11	.02
1904	------	.00	------	-.02	.02	.30	.36	.00	.13	.06	.10	.04	.03	.06	.02
1903	------	.00	------	-.02	.02	.08	.48	.00	.11	.05	.09	.28	.07	.07	.02
1902	------	.00	------	-.02	.00	.47	.72	.00	.10	.05	.09	.27	.08	.08	.02
1901	------	.00	------	-.03	.03	.39	.56	.00	.06	.04	.09	.30	.15	.07	.02
1900	------	.00	------	-.05	.02	.24	.26	.00	.06	.04	.08	.23	.11	.06	.02
1899	------	.00	------	.13	.06	.29	.54	.00	.03	.03	.08	.22	.11	.06	.02
1898	------	.00	------	.09	.03	.12	.10	.00	.02	.03	.08	.07	.07	.05	.02
1897	------	.00	------	-.02	.03	.06	.11	.00	-.00	.02	.07	.14	.07	.03	.02

Consumer Income and Expenditures

FAMILY AND INDIVIDUAL INCOME (Series G 1–190)

G 1–190. General note.

The development of reasonably reliable nationwide estimates of income distribution for families and individuals was dependent on the availability of comprehensive basic source material from Federal individual income tax returns and from representative sample field surveys of family incomes. Annual tabulations of tax-return data originated during World War I, but until the 1940's, when the minimum income requirement for filing returns was substantially lowered, these tabulations provided information for only a small fraction of the upper-income population. Sample field surveys of family incomes that were designed to cover all income and occupation groups in the Nation were not introduced until the 1930's.

Reflecting the lack of adequate source data, the early estimators of income distribution had to piece together various sets of sample income statistics that were available for selected occupation groups or local areas, and combine these figures with income data from State or Federal income tax returns or with income distribution series derived by applying yield rates to estimated size-class distributions of wealth. Among the early estimators were Charles B. Spahr who constructed a family income distribution in 1896, Willford I. King who developed income distribution estimates by size-class for families for 1910, and for individuals for 1921 and 1928, Frederick R. Macaulay who constructed income distributions for individuals for 1918, and Maurice Leven who did the same for families and individuals for 1929.

The following publications relate to these early efforts:

C. L. Merwin, "American Studies of the Distribution of Wealth and Income by Size," *Studies in Income and Wealth*, vol. 3, Conference on Research in Income and Wealth, National Bureau of Economic Research, New York, 1939.

Charles B. Spahr, *The Present Distribution of Wealth in the United States*, New York, 1896.

Willford I. King, *Wealth and Income of the People of the United States*, New York, 1915; also unpublished manuscript at the National Bureau of Economic Research, New York.

W. C. Mitchell, W. I. King, F. R. Macaulay, and O. W. Knauth, *Income in the United States*, National Bureau of Economic Research, New York, 1921 and 1922.

Maurice Leven, H. G. Moulton, and Clark Warburton, *America's Capacity to Consume*, The Brookings Institution, Washington, D. C., 1934.

The Consumer Purchases Study of 1935–36 was the first sample field survey in the United States in which income data were collected from all types of families without restriction as to occupation or earnings group. Based largely on the 300,000 family income schedules collected in that study and on tax returns for upper incomes, the National Resources Committee constructed estimates of family income, by income size-class, for a 12-month period during 1935 and 1936. Aside from their firmer statistical basis, the figures developed by Dr. Hildegarde Kneeland and her staff represented a marked improvement over earlier estimates by providing separate income distributions for numerous subgroups, e.g., for families classified by major occupation of the head, type and size of community, region, color, and family size. (See National Resources Committee, *Consumer Incomes in the United States: Their Distribution in 1935–36*, Washington, D. C., 1938.)

The Survey of Spending and Saving in Wartime provided the only other pre-World War II statistics on the distribution of families, by total income brackets, on a nationwide basis. This survey for 1941, though much smaller in size than the 1935–36 study, represented a further advance in that the sample of families selected for interview was designed specifically for the purpose of "inflating" the results to produce nationwide estimates of family income distribution. (See Bureau of Labor Statistics, *Family Spending and Saving in Wartime*, BLS Bulletin 822, 1945; also Bureau of Human Nutrition and Home Economics, *Rural Family Spending and Saving in Wartime*, U. S. Department of Agriculture Misc. Publication No. 520, 1943.)

Detailed distributions of families, and of persons 14 years old and over, by size-class of their money wage and salary income in 1939, were provided by the 1940 Census of Population, the first decennial census to include income questions. For items of income other than wages or salaries, the census obtained only a "yes" or "no" response as to the receipt of $50 or more, so that over-all size-class distributions on a total income basis are not available. A 5-percent sample of these returns was tabulated with extensive cross-classifications. For many types of analysis, e.g., for studying occupational differentials in wage-salary earnings distribution, these tabulations for 1939 comprise the best available data for comparisons between the prewar and postwar periods. (See Bureau of the Census, *Population—The Labor Force (Sample Statistics): Wage or Salary Income in 1939*; and *Population—Families: Family Wage or Salary Income in 1939*. For other decennial census reports that include income data, and for list of available tabulations, see Edwin D. Goldfield, "Decennial Census and Current Population Survey Data on Income," *Studies in Income and Wealth*, vol. 23, Conference on Research in Income and Wealth, National Bureau of Economic Research, Princeton, 1958.)

For postwar years, annual nationwide sample survey data are available from two sources: The annual Current Population Surveys of the Census Bureau which present distributions by total money income brackets for families and for persons 14 years old and over for 1944–1957; and the annual Surveys of Consumer Finances conducted by the Survey Research Center of the University of Michigan for the Board of Governors of the Federal Reserve System, which furnish distributions by total money income brackets for families and for "spending units" for 1945–1957. Income size-class distributions from both these sets of sample survey data are available for numerous subgroups of the population. (See Bureau of the Census, *Current Population Reports: Consumer Income*, Series P–60, Nos. 1–29, and Series P–S, Nos. 22 and 22–S; and Board of Governors of the Federal Reserve System, "1958 Survey of Consumer Finances: The Financial Position of Consumers," *Federal Reserve Bulletin*, September 1958, and corresponding articles for earlier years.)

In the 1950 Census of Population the income questions covered all items of money income, not just wages and salaries. The tabulations based on this census show separate money income distributions for families for local areas, and for persons 14 years old and over, classified by demographic and socioeconomic characteristics. (See Bureau of the Census, *1950 Census of Population*, vol. II; see also article by Goldfield, cited above.) Comparative distributions for 1939 and 1949 of persons classified by money wage or salary brackets and cross-classified by sex and detailed occupation and industry groups have been compiled from the census material by H. P. Miller. (See Herman P. Miller, *Income of the American People*, John Wiley and Sons, New York, 1955; and "Changes in the Industrial Distribution of Wages in the United States, 1939–1949," *Studies in Income and Wealth*, vol. 23, Conference on Research in Income and Wealth, National Bureau of Economic Research, Princeton, 1958.)

In addition to these nationwide surveys and censuses, other postwar surveys providing income data for selected population groups are the income-expenditure surveys conducted by the Bureau of Labor Statistics, which show urban family income distributions for 1944 and 1950, several studies of farm family incomes by the Department of Agriculture, and a number of surveys in individual localities conducted by the Bureau of the Census. (See Bureau of Labor Statistics, "Expenditures and Savings of City Families in 1944," *Monthly Labor Review*, January 1946; "City Family Composition in Relation to Income, 1941 and 1944," *Monthly Labor Review*, February 1946; and *Study of Consumer Expenditures, Incomes and Savings, Statistical Tables, Urban U.S.—1950*, vol. XI, *Details of Family Accounts for Incomes, Savings, Insurance and Gifts and Contributions*, tabulated by the Bureau of Labor Statistics for the Wharton School of Finance and Commerce, University of Pennsylvania, 1957; Department of Agriculture and Department of Commerce, *Farms and Farm People, A Special Cooperative Report*, 1953; and *Farmers' Expenditures, A Special Cooperative Survey*, 1956.)

Since 1937, income distributions are also available for workers covered under the Old-Age and Survivors Insurance Program. These figures show workers classified by size brackets of "covered" wages and salaries (and, since 1951, "covered" self-employment income). The group of workers covered by these series was substantially expanded in the postwar period, but the usefulness of the series is limited by the upper limit of $4,200 for "covered" earnings for 1955–1957 ($3,000 prior to 1951; $3,600 for 1951–54). (See Social Security Administration, *Handbook of Old-Age and Survivors Insurance Statistics: Employment, Wages, and Insurance Status of Workers in Covered Employment, 1953–54*, 1957, and earlier issues.)

Distributions of Federal individual income tax returns by income bracket are available annually since 1913. Until World War II, the minimum filing requirements were relatively high so that the tabulations covered only a small fraction of the population. Successive lowering of the filing limit coupled with the rise in incomes after the depression of the 1930's led to a very marked expansion in coverage so that all but a very few groups of the population are included in the postwar tabulations. (See Internal Revenue Service, *Statistics of Income, Individual Income Tax Returns*, annual.)

Tax-return data have been used in several studies to measure changes in relative income distribution over time. Rufus Tucker applied measures of dispersion to tax-return distributions for 1863–1935. He included in his series some less reliable tax data for the Civil War period. (See Rufus S. Tucker, "The Distribution of Income Among Income Taxpayers in the United States, 1863–1935," *Quarterly Journal of Economics*, vol. L II, 1938, pp. 547–587.) The most detailed

study of the tax-return statistics is that by Simon Kuznets (see text for series G 131–146).

A number of the family income distribution estimates for the pre-World War II period were developed by integrating tax-return and survey data. Among them are the estimates of The Brookings Institution for 1929 and the National Resources Committee for 1935–36, both cited earlier, and the Survey of Spending and Saving in Wartime distribution for 1941 as subsequently adjusted in the light of tax-return data by Joseph Pechman. (See Joseph Pechman, "Distribution of Income Before and After Federal Income Tax, 1941 and 1947," *Studies in Income and Wealth*, vol. 13, Conference on Research in Income and Wealth, National Bureau of Economic Research, New York, 1951.) In developing these prewar distributions, data from Federal individual income tax returns could be used only to construct estimates for the top ranges of the family income scale, which were then linked directly to field survey data for the low and middle income brackets.

The much broader coverage of Federal individual income tax returns introduced in World War II, coupled with the availability of annual postwar sample survey data, made possible the construction of family income distributions for the postwar period that are more firmly based statistically than the earlier estimates. As part of its national income work, the Office of Business Economics has developed distributions of families and family income by brackets of family personal income for 1944, 1946, 1947, and for each year, 1950–1957, by combining the two sets of source data and adjusting the results so that they accord statistically and definitionally with the personal income series prepared in that office. (See Office of Business Economics, *Income Distribution in the United States by Size, 1944–1950*, 1953; revised and brought up to date in articles on income distribution in the *Survey of Current Business*, March 1955, June 1956, April 1958 and 1959.)

In order to derive meaningful comparisons over time, the family distributions for the prewar period required adjustment to make them consistent with postwar series. Adjusted family income distributions reasonably comparable with the postwar series of the Office of Business Economics were developed for 1935–36 and 1941 by Selma Goldsmith, et al (see source cited for series G 1–28 for 1935–36 and 1941). Mrs. Goldsmith also adjusted the figures in The Brookings Institution study for 1929 to remove the major elements of incomparability. (See Selma F. Goldsmith, "The Relation of Census Income Distribution Statistics to Other Income Data," *Studies in Income and Wealth*, vol. 23, Conference on Research in Income and Wealth, National Bureau of Economic Research, Princeton, 1958.)

Direct comparability among income distribution series is frequently precluded by variations in definition or coverage which are due in many instances to the different purposes for which the data were collected. Definitional differences may apply to the basic unit of classification, to the definition of the income measure, or to the time period to which the income data or the definition of the family unit refers. (See Simon Kuznets, "The Why and How of Distributions of Income by Size," *Studies in Income and Wealth*, vol. 5, Conference on Research in Income and Wealth, National Bureau of Economic Research, New York, 1943, and "Economic Growth and Income Inequality," *American Economic Review*, March 1955, vol. XLV, No. 1; Dorothy S. Brady, "Research on the Size Distribution of Income," *Studies in Income and Wealth*, vol. 13, Conference on Research in Income and Wealth, National Bureau of Economic Research, New York, 1951; and *Income Distribution in the United States . . .*, cited above.) For measures of the effect of alternative income definitions on changes observed over time in relative income shares of top income groups, see Selma F. Goldsmith, "Changes in the Size Distribution of Income," *American Economic Review*, May 1957, vol. XLVII, No. 2.

Aside from definitional variations, the several sets of income distribution statistics differ with respect to the extent to which adjustments have been made to allow for incomplete reporting of family incomes. Tabulations of the postwar sample data on family incomes from the Current Population Surveys and the Surveys of Consumer Finances, for example, represent "inflated" income data obtained directly through interviews with sampled families. These tabulations understate family money income as estimated from business and governmental data sources. Income distributions from these field surveys are therefore not directly comparable with the Office of Business Economics income distribution series which account for larger money income aggregates for most major types of income. The inclusion of selected nonmoney income items in the OBE income measures, and their exclusion from the postwar sample surveys, is a further reason for differences between the series, particularly in the lower ranges of the family income scale.

For the prewar period, also, direct comparison is not warranted between certain sets of income distribution statistics. For example, for 1941, the income classification in series G 508–522 is in terms of family money income brackets, and in series G 1–28, it is in terms of family personal income brackets. For 1929 and 1935–36, the income for series G 523–543 and for series G 1–28 are not directly comparable because of adjustments incorporated in the latter as noted above.

G 1–28. Families and unattached individuals and family personal income, by income level, 1935–36 to 1957.

Source: 1935–36 and 1941, Selma F. Goldsmith, George Jaszi, Hyman Kaitz, and Maurice Liebenberg, "Size Distribution of Income Since the Mid-Thirties," *Review of Economics and Statistics*, February 1954, p. 4; 1944–1957, Office of Business Economics, *Survey of Current Business*, April 1959, p. 14.

The definitions of families and unattached individuals in these series conform with those used by the Census Bureau. Families are units of two or more persons related by blood, marriage, or adoption, and residing together; unattached individuals are persons other than institutional inmates who are not living with any relatives. The total number of families and unattached individuals is estimated as of the end of the calendar year to which the income data pertain (for 1935–36, the estimate refers to July 1, 1936). It is derived, for most years, by interpolating between Census Bureau figures after adjustment to exclude certain minor groups of individuals.

Family personal income represents the current income received by families and unattached individuals from all sources, including wage and salary receipts (net of social insurance contributions), other labor income, proprietors' and rental income, dividends, personal interest income, and transfer payments. In addition to monetary income flows, family income includes certain nonmoney items such as wages in kind, the value of food and fuel produced and consumed on farms, the net imputed rental value of owner-occupied homes, and imputed interest. Total family personal income is a somewhat smaller amount in each year than the personal income aggregate from which it is derived, because it excludes the income received by institutional residents (including military personnel not living with their families), or retained by nonprofit institutions, private trust, pension, and welfare funds.

For discussion of these definitions, see Office of Business Economics, *Income Distribution in the United States by Size, 1944–1950*, 1953, pp. 17–25. For limitations of the prewar

distributions with respect to their comparability with the postwar series, see source for prewar figures.

G 29–56. Families and family personal income, by income level, 1935–36 to 1957.

Source: 1935–36 and 1941, compiled from unpublished tabulations underlying estimates shown in source for series G 1–28; 1944–1954, Office of Business Economics, *Survey of Current Business*, April 1958, p. 15; 1955–1957, *Survey of Current Business*, April 1959, p. 14.

For definitions of terms, see text for series G 1–28.

G 57–74. Families and unattached individuals and family personal income, by income level in 1950 dollars, 1929–1957.

Source: 1929, Selma F. Goldsmith, "The Relation of Census Income Distribution Statistics to Other Income Data," *Studies in Income and Wealth*, vol. 23, Conference on Research in Income and Wealth, National Bureau of Economic Research, Princeton, 1958, p. 93; 1935–36 to 1944, see source for series G 1–28 (1935–36 and 1941); 1950, *Survey of Current Business*, April 1959, p. 14; 1957, Office of Business Economics, records.

1957 data were computed by applying the OBE price index used for deflating personal consumption expenditures (of the national income accounts) to the income distribution expressed in current dollars for that year; the latter appears in the *Survey of Current Business*, April 1959, p. 11. For definitions of terms, see text for series G 1–28.

The price-deflated income size distributions such as are shown here represent only approximate measures of real income distribution because separate price indexes applicable to the various income brackets are not available. It is therefore necessary to use the same index throughout the income range even though all brackets may not have been affected by the price rise in the same way. Moreover, available price indexes which refer to consumer expenditures for goods and services must be applied to income totals that include income taxes and saving as well as outlays for consumption. For interpolation procedures used in deflating income size distributions, see Office of Business Economics, *Income Distribution in the United States by Size, 1944–1950*, p. 38.

Because of inadequacies in the basic source data, the estimates for 1929 are less reliable than for other years in the series. For limitations of the prewar data, see the sources.

G 75–98. Families and unattached individuals and family personal income after Federal individual income tax liability, by after-tax income level, 1941–1957.

Source: 1941, compiled from unpublished tabulations underlying estimates shown for 1941, series G 1–28; 1950–1954, Office of Business Economics, *Survey of Current Business*, April 1958, p. 18; 1955–1957, *Survey of Current Business*, April 1959, p. 16.

Federal individual income tax liability which has been deducted from family personal income in these series includes liability reported on Federal individual income tax returns, plus an estimate for amounts uncovered by subsequent audit, minus liability of military personnel not living with their families, minus liability on net capital gain. See also definitions in text for series G 1–28.

G 99–117. Family personal income received by each fifth and top 5 percent of families and unattached individuals, 1929–1957.

Source: 1929 (series G 99–105), see source for 1929, series G 57–74, p. 92; 1929 (series G 106–117), unpublished tabulations underlying estimates shown in source for 1929, series G 57–74; 1935–36 and 1941, see source for same years, series

G 1–28, p. 9; 1944–1947, Office of Business Economics, *Income Distribution in the United States by Size, 1944–50*, 1953, p. 81; 1950–1954, *Survey of Current Business*, April 1958, p. 17; 1955–1957, *Survey of Current Business*, April 1959, p. 16.

For definitions of terms, see text for series G 1–28.

G 118–130. Number and average size of families and unattached individuals, and average family personal income before and after Federal individual income tax liability, 1929–1957.

Source: 1929-1941, unpublished tabulations underlying estimates shown in source for 1935-36, series G 1–28; 1944-1954, Office of Business Economics, *Survey of Current Business*, April 1958, pp. 11 and 16-19 (except series G 127, G 129, and G 130, for the following years: 1944-1947, *Income Distribution in the United States by Size, 1944-1950*, 1953, pp. 82-84; 1950-1951, *Survey of Current Business*, March 1955, pp. 25-26; 1952, *Survey of Current Business*, June 1956, p. 13. Series G 121 and G 123, 1944-1954, and series G 122, 1944-1946, Office of Business Economics, records); 1955-1957, *Survey of Current Business*, April 1959, pp. 10 and 15-16, and Office of Business Economics, records.

For definitions of terms, see text for series G 1–28 and G 75–98.

Farm-operator families cover all families operating farms as defined in the Census of Agriculture; the total number is estimated annually by the Agricultural Marketing Service. Nonfarm families include all multiperson units other than farm-operator families.

G 131–146. Percent shares of total income received by top 1 percent and 5 percent of total population, 1913–1948.

Source: Simon Kuznets, *Shares of Upper Income Groups in Income and Savings*, National Bureau of Economic Research, New York, 1953, pp. 582, 585, 635, 637, 646, and 649.

The top percentiles in these series represent the 1 or 5 percent of men, women, and children covered on those individual income tax returns reporting the largest per capita

incomes in each year. The basic variant is the total of employee compensation, entrepreneurial income, rent, interest, and dividends; the economic variant represents the basic variant adjusted to allow for such factors as the nonreporting of State and local government salaries prior to 1938, the omission of imputed rent on owner-occupied houses, and, most important, the effects of classifying the tax data by an inappropriate base and unit; the disposable income variant is derived by deducting from the economic income variant Federal income taxes paid, and adding the net balance of realized gains and losses from sales of assets.

G 147–168. Median money wage or salary income of primary families and individuals with wage or salary income, by selected characteristics, 1939–1957.

Source: All years (except 1953–1954 for all series, and 1953-1957 for series G 147), Bureau of the Census, *Current Population Reports*, Series P–60, Nos. 5, 7, 9, 12, 24, 27, and 30; for the exceptions, Bureau of the Census, records.

The term "primary family" refers to the head of a household and all other persons in the household related to the head by blood, marriage, or adoption. If no one in the household is related to the head, then the head himself constitutes a "primary individual."

Money wages or salaries are defined as total money earnings received for work performed as an employee during the calendar year, including wages, salary, commissions, tips, piece-rate payments, and cash bonuses earned, before deductions were made for taxes, bonds, pensions, union dues, etc.

G 169–190. Median money wage or salary income of all workers with wage or salary income, and of year-round full-time workers, by sex, color, and major occupation group, 1939–1957.

Source: Bureau of the Census, *Current Population Reports*, Series P–60, Nos. 9, 11, 14, 16, 19, 23, 27, and 30.

See text for series G 147–168.

Series G 1-28. Families and Unattached Individuals and Family Personal Income, by Income Level: 1935-36 to 1957

Series No.	Income level (before income taxes)	1957	1956	1955	1954	1953	1952	1951	1950	1947	1946	1944	1941	1935-36
	FAMILIES AND UNATTACHED INDIVIDUALS (1,000)													
1	Total	53,510	52,850	52,170	51,150	50,510	50,210	49,480	48,890	44,740	43,330	40,880	41,370	38,410
2	Under $1,000	7,512	7,776	8,241	3,071	2,956	3,282	3,227	3,861	3,748	3,826	4,352	12,003	16,718
3	$1,000 to $1,999				5,889	5,554	5,687	6,022	7,464	7,370	7,606	8,108	12,381	13,121
4	$2,000 to $2,999	5,352	5,561	5,917	6,509	6,364	6,541	7,164	8,091	8,459	8,628	8,791	9,193	5,050
5	$3,000 to $3,999	6,672	7,105	7,339	7,291	7,061	7,636	8,192	8,586	8,628	8,590	8,762	4,089	1,702
6	$4,000 to $4,999	7,006	7,222	7,328	7,118	7,117	7,631	7,455	7,054	5,725	5,364	4,585	1,627	642
7	$5,000 to $5,999	6,396	6,217	6,321	6,032	6,152	6,072	5,580	4,694	3,474	3,065	2,515	1,170	604
8	$6,000 to $7,499	7,320	7,038	6,925	6,284	6,379	5,801	5,323	3,836	3,151	2,547	2,259		
9	$7,500 to $9,999	6,626	6,045	5,203	4,734	4,768	4,121	3,390	2,758	2,170	1,751	1,385	372	231
10	$10,000 to $14,999	4,206	3,742	3,068	2,661	2,636	2,041	1,899	1,536	1,199	1,070	707		
11	$15,000 to $19,999		1,081	883	745	734	598	523	414	386	332	246		
12	$20,000 to $24,999	2,420	425	378	313	308	316	274	218	167	143	108	535	342
13	$25,000 to $49,999		504	452	397	383	384	336	294	208	191	140		
14	$50,000 and over		134	115	106	98	100	95	84	55	54	40		
1	**Percent**	100.0	100.0	100.0	100.0	100.0	100.0	100.0	100.0	100.0	100.0	100.0	100.0	100.0
2	Under $1,000	14.0	14.7	15.8	6.0	5.9	6.5	6.5	7.9	8.4	8.8	10.7	29.0	43.5
3	$1,000 to $1,999				11.5	11.0	11.3	12.2	15.3	16.5	17.6	19.8	29.9	34.2
4	$2,000 to $2,999	10.0	10.5	11.3	12.7	12.6	13.0	14.5	16.6	18.9	20.3	21.4	22.3	13.1
5	$3,000 to $3,999	12.5	13.4	14.1	14.3	14.0	15.2	16.5	17.6	19.3	19.8	18.9	9.8	4.4
6	$4,000 to $4,999	13.1	13.7	14.0	13.9	14.1	15.2	15.1	14.4	12.8	12.4	11.1	4.0	1.7
7	$5,000 to $5,999	11.9	11.8	12.1	11.8	12.2	12.1	11.3	9.6	7.8	7.1	6.2	2.8	1.6
8	$6,000 to $7,499	13.7	13.3	13.3	12.3	12.6	11.6	10.7	7.9	7.0	5.9	5.5		
9	$7,500 to $9,999	12.4	11.4	10.0	9.2	9.4	8.2	6.8	5.6	4.8	4.0	3.4	0.9	0.6
10	$10,000 to $14,999	7.9	7.1	5.9	5.2	5.2	4.1	3.8	3.1	2.7	2.5	1.7		
11	$15,000 to $19,999		2.1	1.7	1.5	1.4	1.2	1.1	0.8	0.8	0.8	0.6		
12	$20,000 to $24,999	4.5	0.8	0.7	0.6	0.6	0.6	0.6	0.4	0.4	0.3	0.3	1.3	0.9
13	$25,000 to $49,999		1.0	0.9	0.8	0.8	0.8	0.7	0.6	0.5	0.4	0.3		
14	$50,000 and over		0.2	0.2	0.2	0.2	0.2	0.2	0.2	0.1	0.1	0.1		
	AGGREGATE FAMILY PERSONAL INCOME ($1,000,000)													
15	Total	331,771	314,669	294,239	273,956	272,186	257,162	242,652	217,262	184,598	170,705	147,721	91,406	62,654
16	Under $1,000	8,440	8,765	9,326	1,571	1,518	1,688	1,680	1,943	1,973	2,017	2,390	6,964	9,654
17	$1,000 to $1,999				8,951	8,438	8,627	9,084	11,333	11,231	11,570	12,338	18,529	18,781
18	$2,000 to $2,999	13,437	13,970	14,871	16,345	15,998	16,411	17,945	20,273	21,176	22,007	21,988	22,693	12,222
19	$3,000 to $3,999	23,471	24,966	25,815	25,615	24,817	26,792	28,696	29,983	30,045	29,906	26,960	13,982	5,787
20	$4,000 to $4,999	31,516	32,511	33,021	32,055	32,057	34,305	33,552	31,533	25,583	23,956	20,261	7,237	2,830
21	$5,000 to $5,999	35,044	34,073	34,648	33,033	33,702	33,200	30,502	25,603	18,957	16,725	13,739	6,938	3,612
22	$6,000 to $7,499	49,014	47,023	46,311	41,947	42,611	38,759	35,596	25,578	20,812	16,833	14,942		
23	$7,500 to $9,999	56,930	51,886	44,468	40,333	40,707	34,660	28,531	23,364	18,454	14,905	11,802	3,201	1,982
24	$10,000 to $14,999	50,566	45,038	36,915	31,856	31,561	24,212	22,617	18,310	14,300	12,784	8,483		
25	$15,000 to $19,999		18,546	15,129	12,749	12,557	10,214	8,933	7,083	6,586	5,692	4,215		
26	$20,000 to $24,999	63,353	9,447	8,382	6,931	6,821	6,986	6,063	4,826	3,700	3,165	2,395	11,862	7,786
27	$25,000 to $49,999		16,950	15,140	13,294	12,793	12,633	11,097	9,743	6,879	6,308	4,651		
28	$50,000 and over		11,494	10,213	9,276	8,606	8,675	8,356	7,690	4,902	4,837	3,607		
15	**Percent**	100.0	100.0	100.0	100.0	100.0	100.0	100.0	100.0	100.0	100.0	100.0	100.0	100.0
16	Under $1,000	2.5	2.8	3.2	0.6	0.6	0.7	0.7	0.9	1.1	1.2	1.6	7.6	15.4
17	$1,000 to $1,999				3.3	3.1	3.3	3.7	5.2	6.1	6.8	8.4	20.3	30.0
18	$2,000 to $2,999	4.0	4.4	5.1	6.0	5.9	6.4	7.4	9.3	11.5	12.9	14.9	24.8	19.5
19	$3,000 to $3,999	7.1	7.9	8.8	9.4	9.1	10.4	11.8	13.8	16.3	17.5	18.3	15.3	9.2
20	$4,000 to $4,999	9.5	10.3	11.2	11.7	11.8	13.3	13.8	14.5	13.8	14.0	13.7	7.9	4.5
21	$5,000 to $5,999	10.6	10.8	11.8	12.1	12.4	12.9	12.6	11.8	10.2	9.8	9.3	7.6	5.8
22	$6,000 to $7,499	14.8	15.0	15.8	15.3	15.6	15.1	14.7	11.8	11.3	9.9	10.1		
23	$7,500 to $9,999	17.2	16.5	15.1	14.7	14.9	13.5	11.8	10.8	10.0	8.7	8.0	3.5	3.2
24	$10,000 to $14,999	15.2	14.3	12.5	11.6	11.6	9.4	9.3	8.4	7.7	7.5	5.7		
25	$15,000 to $19,999		5.9	5.1	4.6	4.6	4.0	3.7	3.3	3.6	3.3	2.9		
26	$20,000 to $24,999	19.1	3.0	2.8	2.5	2.5	2.7	2.5	2.2	2.0	1.9	1.6	13.0	12.4
27	$25,000 to $49,999		5.4	5.1	4.8	4.7	4.9	4.6	4.5	3.7	3.7	3.1		
28	$50,000 and over		3.7	3.5	3.4	3.2	3.4	3.4	3.5	2.7	2.8	2.4		

Series G 29–56. Families and Family Personal Income, by Income Level: 1935–36 to 1957

Series No.	Income level (before income taxes)	1957	1956	1955	1954	1953	1952	1951	1950	1947	1946	1944	1941	1935–36
	FAMILIES (1,000)													
29	Total	43,670	43,350	42,670	41,750	41,110	40,770	40,420	39,790	37,025	35,860	33,300	32,920	30,430
30	Under $1,000	} 3,472	3,700	3,948	{ 1,039	937	1,179	1,084	1,462	1,503	1,499	1,859	7,886	11,653
31	$1,000 to $1,999				3,436	3,100	3,161	3,495	4,730	4,897	5,139	5,453	9,601	10,910
32	$2,000 to $2,999	3,275	3,511	3,808	4,367	4,235	4,389	5,079	6,001	6,740	7,210	7,304	8,049	4,579
33	$3,000 to $3,999	5,074	5,586	5,862	5,910	5,676	6,294	6,989	7,546	7,889	7,939	7,151	3,884	1,598
34	$4,000 to $4,999	6,054	6,369	6,561	6,429	6,421	6,968	6,894	6,628	5,467	5,156	4,348	1,528	599
35	$5,000 to $5,999	5,874	5,772	5,943	5,731	5,843	5,794	5,358	4,531	3,367	2,974	2,435	} 1,111	551
36	$6,000 to $7,499	7,010	6,774	6,704	6,104	6,195	5,635	5,178	3,721	3,071	2,484	2,201		
37	$7,500 to $9,999	6,439	5,887	5,065	4,616	4,649	4,009	3,300	2,693	2,126	1,714	1,351	354	217
38	$10,000 to $14,999	4,115	3,664	3,002	2,604	2,578	1,987	1,854	1,501	1,175	1,048	687	} 507	323
39	$15,000 to $19,999	} 2,357	1,059	864	728	717	581	508	401	376	323	236		
40	$20,000 to $24,999		414	367	303	298	307	266	211	161	138	102		
41	$25,000 to $49,999		486	436	382	368	370	324	284	201	184	134		
42	$50,000 and over		128	110	101	93	96	91	81	52	52	39		
29	Percent	100.0	100.0	100.0	100.0	100.0	100.0	100.0	100.0	100.0	100.0	100.0	100.0	100.0
30	Under $1,000	} 8.0	8.5	9.3	{ 2.5	2.3	2.9	2.7	3.7	4.1	4.2	5.6	24.0	38.3
31	$1,000 to $1,999				8.2	7.6	7.8	8.6	11.9	13.2	14.3	16.4	29.2	35.8
32	$2,000 to $2,999	7.5	8.1	8.9	10.5	10.3	10.8	12.5	15.1	18.2	20.1	21.9	24.4	15.1
33	$3,000 to $3,999	11.6	12.9	13.7	14.2	13.8	15.4	17.3	19.0	21.3	22.1	21.5	11.8	5.2
34	$4,000 to $4,999	13.9	14.7	15.4	15.4	15.6	17.1	17.0	16.6	14.8	14.4	13.0	4.6	2.0
35	$5,000 to $5,999	13.4	13.3	13.9	13.7	14.2	14.2	13.3	11.3	9.1	8.3	7.3	} 3.4	1.8
36	$6,000 to $7,499	16.0	15.6	15.7	14.6	15.1	13.8	12.8	9.4	8.3	6.9	6.6		
37	$7,500 to $9,999	14.8	13.6	11.9	11.1	11.3	9.8	8.2	6.8	5.8	4.8	4.1	1.1	0.7
38	$10,000 to $14,999	9.4	8.5	7.0	6.3	6.3	4.9	4.6	3.8	3.2	2.9	2.1	} 1.5	1.1
39	$15,000 to $19,999		2.4	2.0	1.7	1.7	1.4	1.3	1.0	1.0	0.9	0.7		
40	$20,000 to $24,999		1.0	0.9	0.7	0.7	0.8	0.7	0.5	0.4	0.4	0.3		
41	$25,000 to $49,999	} 5.4	1.1	1.0	0.9	0.9	0.9	0.8	0.7	0.5	0.5	0.4		
42	$50,000 and over		0.3	0.3	0.2	0.2	0.2	0.2	0.2	0.1	0.2	0.1		
	AGGREGATE FAMILY PERSONAL INCOME ($1,000,000)													
43	Total	303,087	288,069	268,939	250,255	248,350	233,896	221,379	197,724	169,340	156,670	134,102	80,238	54,275
44	Under $1,000	} 4,264	4,547	4,890	{ 606	561	679	636	748	837	852	1,108	4,901	6,798
45	$1,000 to $1,999				5,285	4,767	4,847	5,316	7,261	7,551	7,895	8,376	14,494	15,735
46	$2,000 to $2,999	8,267	8,867	9,636	11,052	10,723	11,083	12,795	15,135	16,967	18,130	18,377	19,924	11,103
47	$3,000 to $3,999	17,929	19,701	20,703	20,858	20,044	22,174	24,565	26,415	27,503	27,682	25,009	13,292	5,433
48	$4,000 to $4,999	27,292	28,722	29,609	28,987	28,957	31,361	31,072	29,655	24,444	23,044	19,436	6,797	2,636
49	$5,000 to $5,999	32,197	31,659	32,599	31,395	32,021	31,692	29,301	24,718	18,375	16,232	18,304	} 6,599	3,298
50	$6,000 to $7,499	46,958	45,279	44,843	40,753	41,394	37,658	34,632	24,811	20,288	16,420	14,560		
51	$7,500 to $9,999	55,340	50,534	43,292	39,335	39,694	33,716	27,768	22,807	18,085	14,595	11,517	3,053	1,862
52	$10,000 to $14,999	49,485	44,116	36,136	31,187	30,880	23,571	22,078	17,887	14,009	12,525	8,247	} 11,178	7,410
53	$15,000 to $19,999	} 61,355	18,168	14,805	12,457	12,264	9,932	8,681	6,858	6,411	5,533	4,057		
54	$20,000 to $24,999		9,205	8,140	6,723	6,608	6,791	5,885	4,662	3,568	3,043	2,278		
55	$25,000 to $49,999		16,364	14,596	12,789	12,285	12,139	10,692	9,408	6,636	6,089	4,437		
56	$50,000 and over		10,907	9,690	8,828	8,152	8,253	7,958	7,359	4,666	4,630	3,396		
43	Percent	100.0	100.0	100.0	100.0	100.0	100.0	100.0	100.0	100.0	100.0	100.0	100.0	100.0
44	Under $1,000	} 1.4	1.6	1.8	{ 0.2	0.2	0.3	0.3	0.4	0.5	0.6	0.8	6.1	12.5
45	$1,000 to $1,999				2.1	1.9	2.1	2.4	3.7	4.5	5.0	6.2	18.1	29.0
46	$2,000 to $2,999	2.7	3.1	3.6	4.4	4.3	4.7	5.8	7.6	10.0	11.6	13.7	24.8	20.5
47	$3,000 to $3,999	5.9	6.8	7.7	8.3	8.1	9.5	11.1	13.4	16.2	17.7	18.7	16.6	10.0
48	$4,000 to $4,999	9.0	10.0	11.0	11.6	11.6	13.4	14.0	15.0	14.4	14.7	14.5	8.5	4.8
49	$5,000 to $5,999	10.6	11.0	12.1	12.6	12.9	13.6	13.3	12.5	10.8	10.3	9.9	} 8.2	6.1
50	$6,000 to $7,499	15.5	15.7	16.7	16.3	16.7	16.1	15.6	12.5	12.0	10.5	10.9		
51	$7,500 to $9,999	18.3	17.5	16.1	15.7	16.0	14.4	12.5	11.5	10.7	9.3	8.6	3.8	3.4
52	$10,000 to $14,999	16.3	15.3	13.5	12.5	12.4	10.1	10.0	9.0	8.3	8.0	6.2	} 13.9	13.7
53	$15,000 to $19,999	} 20.3	6.3	5.5	5.0	4.9	4.2	3.9	3.5	3.8	3.5	3.0		
54	$20,000 to $24,999		3.2	3.0	2.7	2.7	2.9	2.7	2.4	2.1	1.9	1.7		
55	$25,000 to $49,999		5.7	5.4	5.1	5.0	5.2	4.8	4.8	3.9	3.9	3.3		
56	$50,000 and over		3.8	3.6	3.5	3.3	3.5	3.6	3.7	2.8	3.0	2.5		

Series G 57–74. Families and Unattached Individuals and Family Personal Income, by Income Level in 1950 Dollars: 1929 to 1957

Series No.	Income level in 1950 dollars (before income taxes)	Families and unattached individuals (1,000)						Series No.	Family personal income in 1950 dollars ($1,000,000)					
		1957	1950	1944	1941	1935–36	1929		1957	1950	1944	1941	1935–36	1929
57	Total_____	53,510	48,890	40,880	41,370	38,410	36,100	66	283,808	217,262	190,093	151,586	112,809	121,387
58	Under $1,000_____	} 9,246	{ 3,861	2,996	6,232	7,478	5,754	67	} 10,438	{ 1,943	1,522	4,082	4,487	2,365
59	$1,000 to $1,999_____		7,464	5,588	8,236	11,231	9,239	68		11,333	8,548	12,412	16,846	13,845
60	$2,000 to $2,999_____	6,827	8,091	6,326	7,643	7,959	9,275	69	17,220	20,273	15,714	19,039	19,619	23,043
61	$3,000 to $3,999_____	8,192	8,586	7,189	6,488	4,709	4,395	70	28,679	29,983	24,850	22,604	16,293	15,206
62	$4,000 to $4,999_____	7,778	7,054	6,004	5,069	2,806	2,590	71	34,862	31,533	26,973	22,657	12,502	11,551
63	$5,000 to $7,499_____	12,201	8,530	7,540	4,983	2,582	2,655	72	74,052	51,181	45,348	29,655	15,359	15,935
64	$7,500 to $9,999_____	4,609	2,758	2,853	1,304	686	1,130	73	39,303	23,364	24,281	10,998	5,877	9,750
65	$10,000 and over_____	4,657	2,546	2,384	1,415	959	1,062	74	79,254	47,652	42,857	30,139	21,826	29,692
57	Percent_____	100.0	100.0	100.0	100.0	100.0	100.0	66	100.0	100.0	100.0	100.0	100.0	100.0
58	Under $1,000_____	} 17.3	{ 7.9	7.3	15.1	19.5	15.9	67	} 3.7	{ 0.9	0.8	2.7	4.0	2.0
59	$1,000 to $1,999_____		15.3	13.7	19.9	29.2	25.6	68		5.2	4.5	8.2	14.9	11.4
60	$2,000 to $2,999_____	12.8	16.6	15.5	18.5	20.7	25.7	69	6.1	9.3	8.3	12.6	17.4	19.0
61	$3,000 to $3,999_____	15.3	17.6	17.6	15.7	12.3	12.2	70	10.1	13.8	13.1	14.9	14.4	12.5
62	$4,000 to $4,999_____	14.5	14.4	14.7	12.3	7.3	7.2	71	12.3	14.5	14.2	14.9	11.1	9.5
63	$5,000 to $7,499_____	22.8	17.5	18.4	12.0	6.7	7.4	72	26.1	23.6	23.8	19.6	13.6	13.1
64	$7,500 to $9,999_____	8.6	5.6	7.0	3.1	1.8	3.1	73	13.8	10.8	12.8	7.2	5.2	8.0
65	$10,000 and over_____	8.7	5.1	5.8	3.4	2.5	2.9	74	27.9	21.9	22.5	19.9	19.4	24.5

Series G 75–98. Families and Unattached Individuals and Family Personal Income After Federal Individual Income Tax Liability, by After-Tax Income Level: 1941 to 1957

Series No.	Income level after Federal individual income tax liability	1957	1956	1955	1954	1953	1952	1951	1950	1941	Percent								
											1957	1956	1955	1954	1953	1952	1951	1950	1941
	FAMILIES AND UNATTACHED INDIVIDUALS (1,000)																		
75	Total_____	53,510	52,850	52,170	51,150	50,510	50,210	49,480	48,890	41,370	100.0	100.0	100.0	100.0	100.0	100.0	100.0	100.0	100.0
76	Under $1,000_____	} 7,989	8,288	8,758	{ 3,074	2,963	3,393	3,350	3,978	12,022	} 14.9	15.7	16.8	{ 6.0	5.9	6.8	6.8	8.1	29.1
77	$1,000 to $1,999_____		6,466	6,196	6,237	6,541	7,940	12,536		12.6	12.3	12.4	13.2	16.3	30.3
78	$2,000 to $2,999_____	5,911	6,172	6,510	7,079	6,988	7,247	7,849	8,664	9,405	11.0	11.7	12.5	13.8	13.8	14.4	15.9	17.7	22.7
79	$3,000 to $3,999_____	7,437	7,842	7,992	7,881	7,762	8,408	8,763	9,109	3,976	13.9	14.9	15.3	15.4	15.3	16.7	17.7	18.6	9.6
80	$4,000 to $4,999_____	7,908	8,041	8,197	7,917	8,193	8,622	8,142	7,226	1,522	14.8	15.2	15.7	15.5	16.2	17.2	16.5	14.8	3.7
81	$5,000 to $5,999_____	6,733	6,720	6,694	6,370	6,383	5,909	5,559	4,487		12.6	12.7	12.8	12.5	12.6	11.8	11.2	9.2
82	$6,000 to $7,499_____	6,733	6,200	6,050	5,323	5,251	5,082	4,459	3,297		12.6	11.7	11.6	10.4	10.4	10.0	9.0	6.7
83	$7,500 to $9,999_____	5,468	4,866	4,082	3,688	3,591	2,751	2,397	2,131		10.2	9.2	7.7	7.2	7.1	5.5	4.8	4.4
84	$10,000 to $14,999_____	3,578	3,160	2,590	2,212	2,142	1,614	1,525	1,278	1,909	6.7	6.0	5.0	4.3	4.2	3.2	3.1	2.6	4.6
85	$15,000 to $19,999_____	} 1,753	{ 863	729	597	562	518	453	375	} 3.3	{ 1.6	1.4	1.2	1.1	1.0	0.9	0.8
86	$20,000 and over_____		698	618	543	484	479	442	405		1.3	1.2	1.1	1.0	1.0	0.9	0.8
	AFTER-TAX FAMILY PERSONAL INCOME ($1,000,000)																		
87	Total_____	298,471	282,769	265,539	247,656	242,886	229,462	218,552	198,942	87,206	100.0	100.0	100.0	100.0	100.0	100.0	100.0	100.0	100.0
88	Under $1,000_____	} 9,170	9,552	10,119	{ 1,574	1,524	1,797	1,800	2,058	6,982	} 3.1	3.4	3.8	{ 0.6	0.6	0.8	0.8	1.0	8.0
89	$1,000 to $1,999_____		9,852	9,437	9,528	9,961	12,122	18,728		4.0	3.9	4.2	4.6	6.1	21.5
90	$2,000 to $2,999_____	14,877	15,560	16,401	17,808	17,564	18,224	19,714	21,762	23,170	5.0	5.5	6.2	7.2	7.2	7.9	9.0	11.0	26.6
91	$3,000 to $3,999_____	26,147	27,522	28,039	27,647	27,249	29,476	30,632	31,809	13,600	8.8	9.7	10.5	11.2	11.2	12.8	14.0	16.0	15.5
92	$4,000 to $4,999_____	35,611	36,146	36,826	35,581	36,846	38,701	36,502	32,285	6,752	11.9	12.8	13.9	14.4	15.2	16.9	16.7	16.2	7.8
93	$5,000 to $5,999_____	36,918	36,868	36,665	34,844	34,940	32,299	30,316	24,445		12.4	13.1	13.8	14.1	14.4	14.1	13.8	12.3
94	$6,000 to $7,499_____	44,941	41,421	40,275	35,442	34,958	33,557	29,709	21,921		15.0	14.6	15.2	14.3	14.4	14.6	13.6	11.0
95	$7,500 to $9,999_____	46,611	41,393	34,303	31,284	30,457	23,239	20,289	18,034	17,974	15.6	14.6	12.9	12.6	12.5	10.1	9.3	9.1	20.6
96	$10,000 to $14,999_____	42,635	37,573	30,836	26,246	25,401	19,110	18,047	15,118		14.3	13.3	11.6	10.6	10.5	8.3	8.3	7.6
97	$15,000 to $19,999_____	} 41,561	{ 14,671	12,437	10,179	9,604	8,913	7,800	6,409	} 13.9	{ 5.2	4.7	4.1	4.0	3.9	3.6	3.2
98	$20,000 and over_____		22,063	19,638	17,199	14,906	14,618	13,782	12,984		7.8	7.4	6.9	6.1	6.4	6.3	6.5

CONSUMER INCOME AND EXPENDITURES

Series G 99–117. Family Personal Income Received by Each Fifth and Top 5 Percent of Families and Unattached Individuals: 1929 to 1957

Series No.	Fifths ranked by family personal income	1957	1956	1955	1954	1953	1952	1951	1950	1947	1946	1944	1941	1935–36	1929
	PERCENT DISTRIBUTION OF AGGREGATE FAMILY PERSONAL INCOME														
99	Total	100.0	100.0	100.0	100.0	100.0	100.0	100.0	100.0	100.0	100.0	100.0	100.0	100.0	100.0
100	Lowest fifth	4.8	4.8	4.8	4.8	4.9	4.9	5.0	4.8	5.0	5.0	4.9	4.1	4.1	} 12.5
101	Second fifth	11.3	11.3	11.3	11.1	11.3	11.4	11.3	10.9	11.0	11.1	10.9	9.5	9.2	
102	Third fifth	16.3	16.3	16.4	16.4	16.6	16.6	16.5	16.1	16.0	16.0	16.2	15.3	14.1	13.8
103	Fourth fifth	22.3	22.3	22.3	22.5	22.5	22.4	22.3	22.1	22.0	21.8	22.2	22.3	20.9	19.3
104	Highest fifth	45.3	45.3	45.2	45.2	44.7	44.7	44.9	46.1	46.0	46.1	45.8	48.8	51.7	54.4
105	Top 5 percent	20.2	20.2	20.3	20.3	19.9	20.5	20.7	21.4	20.9	21.3	20.7	24.0	26.5	30.0
	AVERAGE (MEAN) FAMILY PERSONAL INCOME (CURRENT DOLLARS)														
106	Total	6,200	5,954	5,640	5,356	5,389	5,122	4,904	4,444	4,126	3,940	3,614	2,209	1,631	2,335
107	Lowest fifth	1,477	1,427	1,355	1,289	1,322	1,249	1,221	1,056	1,023	982	882	450	337	} 725
108	Second fifth	3,482	3,353	3,200	2,975	3,038	2,918	2,775	2,418	2,275	2,178	1,979	1,044	749	
109	Third fifth	5,037	4,889	4,634	4,401	4,471	4,255	4,034	3,579	3,308	3,156	2,920	1,694	1,146	1,606
110	Fourth fifth	6,913	6,634	6,290	6,019	6,072	5,782	5,473	4,911	4,542	4,290	4,014	2,463	1,708	2,252
111	Highest fifth	14,091	13,516	12,722	12,096	12,041	11,455	11,016	10,254	9,483	9,091	8,272	5,396	4,216	6,327
112	Top 5 percent	25,079	24,062	22,893	21,761	21,481	21,028	20,287	19,066	17,226	16,796	14,963	10,617	8,654	13,960
	LOWER INCOME LIMIT [1] (CURRENT DOLLARS)														
113	Second fifth	2,610	2,520	2,390	2,200	2,260	2,170	2,090	1,810	1,730	1,660	1,510	740	560	(2)
114	Third fifth	4,260	4,100	3,920	3,700	3,770	3,610	3,420	3,020	2,800	2,680	2,450	1,370	930	1,340
115	Fourth fifth	5,860	5,620	5,370	5,120	5,180	4,910	4,680	4,160	3,830	3,650	3,410	2,040	1,380	1,860
116	Highest fifth	8,260	7,920	7,410	7,100	7,160	6,760	6,450	5,850	5,470	5,130	4,800	2,940	2,120	2,810
117	Top 5 percent	14,400	13,860	13,070	12,350	12,320	11,480	11,110	10,200	9,560	9,180	8,240	5,010	3,910	5,690

[1] Rounded to nearest $10. [2] Not available.

Series G 118–130. Number and Average Size of Families and Unattached Individuals, and Average Family Personal Income Before and After Federal Individual Income Tax Liability: 1929 to 1957

Series No.	Item	1957	1956	1955	1954	1953	1952	1951	1950	1947	1946	1944	1941	1935–36	1929
	All families and unattached individuals (consumer units):														
118	Number of consumer units_____mil	53.5	52.8	52.2	51.2	50.5	50.2	49.5	48.9	44.7	43.3	40.9	41.4	38.4	36.1
119	Average (mean) number of persons per consumer unit	3.16	3.14	3.12	3.12	3.10	3.06	3.06	3.05	3.19	3.22	3.07	3.15	3.28	3.34
	Average (mean) family personal income per consumer unit: Before tax:														
120	In current dollars_____dol	6,200	5,954	5,640	5,356	5,389	5,122	4,904	4,444	4,126	3,940	3,614	2,209	1,631	2,335
121	In constant (1950) dollars_____do	5,304	5,246	5,054	4,833	4,902	4,719	4,593	4,444	4,379	4,592	4,650	3,664	2,937	3,363
	After tax:														
122	In current dollars_____do	5,578	5,350	5,090	4,842	4,809	4,570	4,417	4,069	3,719	3,575	3,212	2,108	1,608	2,318
123	In constant (1950) dollars_____do	4,772	4,714	4,561	4,369	4,375	4,211	4,137	4,069	3,947	4,167	4,133	3,496	2,895	3,339
	All families:														
124	Number of families_____mil	43.7	43.4	42.7	41.8	41.1	40.8	40.4	39.8	37.0	35.9	33.3	32.9	30.4	27.9
125	Average (mean) number of persons per family	3.64	3.60	3.59	3.60	3.58	3.54	3.52	3.52	3.64	3.68	3.54	3.70	3.88	4.03
126	Average (mean) family personal income per family, in current dollars_____dol	6,940	6,645	6,303	5,994	6,041	5,737	5,477	4,969	4,574	4,369	4,027	2,437	1,784	------
	Farm-operator families:														
127	Number of families_____mil	4.9	5.0	5.1	5.2	5.3	5.4	5.6	5.7	5.9	5.9	5.9	6.1	6.7	------
128	Average (mean) family personal income per family, in current dollars_____dol	4,024	4,015	3,917	3,881	3,905	4,147	4,114	3,498	3,583	3,385	2,860	1,552	951	------
	Nonfarm families:														
129	Number of families_____mil	38.8	38.4	37.6	36.5	35.8	35.4	34.8	34.1	31.1	30.0	27.4	26.8	23.7	------
130	Average (mean) family personal income per family, in current dollars_____dol	7,305	6,986	6,626	6,295	6,358	6,013	5,721	5,232	4,775	4,573	4,267	2,638	2,020	------

Series G 131–146. Percent Shares of Total Income Received by Top 1 Percent and 5 Percent of Total Population: 1913 to 1948

Year	Shares of total income						Shares of different types of income (basic variant)									
	Basic income variant		Economic income variant		Disposable income variant		Employee compensation		Entrepreneurial income		Dividends		Interest		Rent	
	Top 1 percent	Top 5 percent	Top 1 percent	Top 5 percent	Top 1 percent	Top 5 percent	Top 1 percent	Top 5 percent	Top 1 percent	Top 5 percent	Top 1 percent	Top 5 percent	Top 1 percent	Top 5 percent	Top 1 percent	Top 5 percent
	131	132	133	134	135	136	137	138	139	140	141	142	143	144	145	146
1948	8.38	17.63	-------	-------	-------	-------	3.78	10.87	15.16	30.72	53.56	69.84	15.76	26.47	12.77	22.60
1947	8.49	17.41	-------	-------	-------	-------	3.90	10.61	15.16	30.04	50.23	65.43	17.20	27.95	10.98	20.39
1946	8.98	18.20	9.58	19.96	7.71	17.66	3.76	10.37	18.28	34.39	50.90	67.94	19.17	31.94	10.15	19.20
1945	8.81	17.39	9.37	19.27	7.27	16.65	3.33	9.73	23.00	38.94	(¹)	(¹)	(¹)	(¹)	9.11	16.82
1944	8.58	16.62	8.98	18.68	6.61	15.75	3.33	9.92	22.00	34.83	(¹)	(¹)	(¹)	(¹)	8.94	15.79
1943	9.38	17.75	9.95	20.86	6.44	16.66	3.75	10.86	23.35	35.68	52.30	65.54	22.70	33.03	9.76	17.47
1942	10.06	18.94	10.70	22.47	7.81	19.03	4.89	13.07	18.84	29.27	52.72	65.26	25.98	37.04	9.96	18.24
1941	11.39	21.89	12.32	25.67	9.89	22.98	6.00	15.60	16.88	28.52	57.81	72.85	25.30	38.35	11.35	22.85
1940	11.89	22.71	12.87	26.83	11.39	25.44	6.41	16.86	14.81	26.02	63.23	75.99	23.65	36.44	13.01	23.35
1939	11.80	23.45	13.12	27.77	12.14	26.81	6.36	17.80	14.21	25.92	62.02	75.21	24.27	36.22	12.78	24.51
1938	11.45	22.80	12.75	27.62	12.01	26.85	6.57	17.75	13.17	24.32	61.33	75.69	22.61	33.16	13.26	24.99
1937	12.84	23.80	13.96	28.20	12.81	27.06	6.55	17.46	12.69	23.01	67.55	80.29	25.37	35.87	13.00	24.29
1936	13.14	24.35	14.46	28.82	13.52	27.92	6.43	17.08	15.27	27.73	65.41	77.40	25.17	36.93	12.68	26.09
1935	12.05	23.73	13.58	28.77	12.74	27.89	6.77	18.86	11.70	21.80	68.00	80.04	23.92	34.23	12.54	26.38
1934	12.48	24.88	14.08	30.26	12.84	28.95	6.19	19.00	15.26	29.98	66.59	78.14	22.63	32.49	12.84	28.10
1933	12.48	25.34	14.76	31.73	13.01	30.21	7.23	20.06	15.30	29.62	66.25	78.55	19.66	29.83	13.94	32.06
1932	13.25	26.71	15.65	32.99	12.62	30.40	7.45	20.55	14.82	31.24	67.32	79.17	21.01	33.76	15.83	34.50
1931	13.31	26.27	15.57	32.03	14.56	31.23	6.82	18.40	14.03	31.12	65.44	79.34	22.32	36.63	15.54	37.65
1930	14.12	26.19	15.88	31.34	15.38	30.95	6.64	17.25	14.23	31.15	67.05	78.61	26.11	40.72	14.58	30.81
1929 ²	14.65	26.36	17.31	32.19	19.08	33.81	6.26	16.37	17.12	32.47	71.26	83.37	28.41	43.26	13.42	29.21
1929 ³	14.50	26.09	17.15	31.88	18.92	33.49	6.17	16.13	16.16	30.65	66.02	77.24	31.13	47.40	17.17	37.39
1928	14.94	26.78	17.18	32.06	19.12	34.06	6.41	16.67	17.16	32.10	71.35	81.80	32.02	49.39	16.08	33.95
1927	14.39	25.96	16.46	31.19	17.22	31.92	6.23	15.71	15.79	31.03	72.86	85.18	31.70	49.08	16.75	36.56
1926	13.93	25.25	15.77	30.21	16.26	30.78	6.08	14.85	15.11	30.80	73.26	85.66	30.77	48.18	17.86	40.18
1925	13.73	25.20	15.74	30.24	16.54	31.09	6.24	15.24	15.60	31.49	67.89	78.91	28.73	45.08	17.22	38.73
1924	12.91	24.29	14.69	29.06	14.28	28.73	6.05	14.28	14.47	31.71	68.83	81.08	27.83	45.64	14.84	36.15
1923	12.28	22.89	14.02	28.08	13.08	27.05	5.81	13.38	13.04	29.70	64.60	77.49	28.97	45.74	14.62	32.41
1922	13.38	24.79	15.58	30.39	14.39	29.04	6.33	16.56	14.80	27.89	71.66	85.26	30.66	45.09	15.43	29.77
1921	13.50	25.47	16.15	31.70	14.20	29.32	6.82	17.29	15.73	28.94	65.33	82.00	29.90	45.66	16.12	34.30
1920	12.34	22.07	13.64	25.76	11.80	23.96	5.82	14.40	13.78	24.93	72.40	84.47	32.55	45.69	14.86	28.54
1919 ²	12.84	22.91	14.04	26.10	12.21	24.27	6.14	14.92	12.68	23.76	74.09	86.23	37.34	51.09	14.23	29.48
1919 ³	12.96	23.13	-------	-------	-------	-------	6.58	16.01	11.47	21.48	66.55	77.45	42.35	57.96	14.23	29.48
1918	12.69	22.69	-------	-------	-------	-------	5.96	15.10	10.63	20.45	61.74	70.25	47.01	66.69	14.90	30.73
1917	14.16	24.60	-------	-------	-------	-------	6.64	16.90	9.15	19.29	72.39	78.77	44.59	53.01	14.89	33.21
1916	15.58	-------	-------	-------	-------	-------										
1915	14.32	-------	-------	-------	-------	-------										
1914	13.07	-------	-------	-------	-------	-------										
1913	14.98	-------	-------	-------	-------	-------										

¹ Data on dividends and interest are not separately available for 1944 and 1945. The combined data for 1944 and 1945 are, respectively: Top 1 percent, 38.88 and 37.80; for the top 5 percent, 52.30 and 52.24.

² Comparable with later years.
³ Comparable with earlier years.

Series G 147–168. Median Money Wage or Salary Income of Primary Families and Unrelated Individuals With Wage or Salary Income, by Selected Characteristics: 1939 to 1957

Series No.	Selected characteristics	1957	1956	1955	1954	1953	1951	1950	1949	1947	1945	1944	1939
147	Total	$4,594	$4,453	$4,137	$3,960	$4,011	$3,515	$3,216	$2,959	$2,854	$2,390	$2,378	$1,231
	COLOR												
148	White families and individuals	4,831	4,685	4,331	4,150	4,201	3,673	3,390	3,138	2,999	(¹)	(¹)	1,325
149	Nonwhite families and individuals	2,536	2,429	2,418	2,333	2,357	1,943	1,671	1,533	1,448	(¹)	(¹)	489
	SEX, MARITAL STATUS, AND AGE OF HEAD												
150	Families with male head, married, wife present	5,033	4,858	4,467	4,286	4,324	3,773	3,486	3,194	3,042	(¹)	(¹)	1,319
	Age of head:												
151	Under 35 years	4,890	4,700	4,279	4,118	4,189	3,665	3,305	2,998	2,733	(¹)	(¹)	1,171
152	35 to 44 years	5,500	5,312	4,872	4,719	4,640	4,111	3,805	3,418	3,398	(¹)	(¹)	1,449
153	45 to 54 years	5,489	5,308	4,944	4,633	4,660	3,957	3,752	3,564	3,514	(¹)	(¹)	1,481
154	55 years and over	4,045	3,985	3,757	3,570	3,722	3,303	3,031	2,848	2,788	(¹)	(¹)	1,243
155	Other families with male head	4,244	4,321	3,857	3,636	4,009	3,412	3,092	2,972	2,909	(¹)	(¹)	1,159
156	Families with female head	2,902	2,780	2,651	2,546	2,750	2,407	2,122	2,185	2,195	(¹)	(¹)	909
	SIZE OF FAMILY												
157	2 persons	4,296	4,148	3,835	3,709	3,788	3,365	3,002	2,777	2,587	(¹)	(¹)	1,219
158	3 persons	4,868	4,754	4,417	4,172	4,320	3,694	3,394	3,116	2,897	(¹)	(¹)	1,297
159	4 persons	5,234	5,045	4,646	4,468	4,419	3,891	3,619	3,361	3,232	(¹)	(¹)	1,374
160	5 persons	5,208	5,043	4,506	4,535	4,565	3,952	3,632	3,376	3,403	(¹)	(¹)	1,322
161	6 persons or more	4,664	4,500	4,146	3,894	4,024	3,556	3,182	3,100	3,284	(¹)	(¹)	1,134

¹ Not available.

Series G 147–168. Median Money Wage or Salary Income of Primary Families and Unrelated Individuals With Wage or Salary Income, by Selected Characteristics: 1939 to 1957—Con.

Series No.	Selected characteristics	1957	1956	1955	1954	1953	1951	1950	1949	1947	1939
	FAMILIES, BY NUMBER OF CHILDREN UNDER 18 YEARS OF AGE										
162	None	$4,697	$4,558	$4,227	$4,006	$4,163	$3,662	$3,349	$3,113	$2,942	$1,368
163	1	4,855	4,644	4,343	4,188	4,285	3,662	3,421	3,120	2,964	1,315
164	2	5,047	4,911	4,518	4,450	4,386	3,761	3,493	3,261	3,122	1,288
165	3 or more	4,783	4,605	4,157	3,933	4,009	3,544	3,082	2,858	2,812	956
	NONFARM FAMILIES, BY NUMBER OF WAGE OR SALARY EARNERS										
166	1	(1)	(1)	(1)	(1)	(1)	3,332	(1)	(1)	2,653	1,195
167	2	(1)	(1)	(1)	(1)	(1)	4,547	(1)	(1)	3,671	1,680
168	3 or more	(1)	(1)	(1)	(1)	(1)	6,139	(1)	(1)	(2)	2,415

[1] Not available.   [2] More than $5,000.

Series G 169–190. Median Money Wage or Salary Income of All Workers With Wage or Salary Income, and of Year-Round Full-Time Workers, by Sex, Color, and Major Occupation Group: 1939 to 1957

Series No.	Sex, color, and major occupation group in survey week	All workers									Year-round full-time workers			
		1957	1956	1955	1954	1953	1952	1951	1950	1939	1957	1956	1955	1939
	MALE													
	Color [1]													
169	White	$4,396	$4,260	$3,986	$3,754	$3,760	$3,507	$3,345	$2,982	$1,112	$4,950	$4,710	$4,458	$1,419
170	Nonwhite	2,436	2,396	2,342	2,131	2,233	2,038	2,060	1,828	460	3,137	2,912	2,831	639
	Major occupation group [2]													
171	Professional, technical, and kindred workers	5,601	5,465	5,055	4,905	4,816	4,691	4,071	3,874	1,809	5,990	5,847	5,382	2,100
172	Farmers and farm managers	469	455	461	577	493	479	482	711	373	454	479	414	430
173	Managers, officials, and proprietors, except farm	5,872	5,589	5,290	5,234	5,071	4,696	4,134	4,171	2,136	6,110	5,967	5,584	2,254
174	Clerical and kindred workers	4,252	4,150	3,870	3,735	3,766	3,421	3,366	3,002	1,421	4,564	4,388	4,162	1,564
175	Salesworkers	4,379	4,275	4,315	3,823	3,716	3,576	3,539	3,148	1,277	5,143	5,005	4,937	1,451
176	Craftsmen, foremen, and kindred workers	4,777	4,619	4,356	4,246	4,156	3,756	3,601	3,405	1,309	5,216	4,981	4,712	1,562
177	Operatives and kindred workers	3,984	3,824	3,586	3,349	3,415	3,216	3,064	2,736	1,007	4,397	4,235	4,046	1,268
178	Service workers, except private household	2,894	2,946	2,778	2,818	2,806	2,374	2,426	2,299	833	3,605	3,521	3,565	1,019
179	Farm laborers and foremen	940	892	971	923	817	847	982	986	309	1,518	1,526	(3)	365
180	Laborers, except farm and mine	2,763	2,635	2,387	2,358	2,406	2,244	2,170	1,850	673	3,710	3,410	3,105	991
	FEMALE													
	Color [1]													
181	White	2,240	2,179	2,065	2,046	2,049	1,976	1,855	1,698	676	3,107	2,958	2,870	863
182	Nonwhite	1,019	970	894	914	994	814	781	626	246	1,866	1,637	1,637	327
	Major occupation group [2]													
183	Professional, technical, and kindred workers	3,344	3,114	2,963	3,008	2,929	2,695	2,495	2,264	1,023	3,810	3,650	3,500	1,277
184	Managers, officials, and proprietors, except farm	3,118	2,976	3,158	(3)	2,548	2,705	2,679	2,089	1,107	3,890	3,525	(3)	1,218
185	Clerical and kindred workers	2,802	2,699	2,597	2,468	2,420	2,270	2,147	2,064	966	3,287	3,145	3,065	1,072
186	Salesworkers	1,342	1,204	1,182	1,348	1,158	1,075	1,176	1,148	636	2,289	2,090	(3)	745
187	Craftsmen, foremen, and kindred workers	(3)	(3)	(3)	(3)	(3)	2,075	(3)	(3)	827	(3)	(3)	2,489	995
188	Operatives and kindred workers	2,130	2,130	2,048	1,852	1,901	1,908	1,739	1,616	582	2,611	2,632	2,489	742
189	Private household workers	459	486	502	495	554	433	447	448	296	980	879	(3)	339
190	Service workers, except private household	1,249	1,151	1,135	1,154	1,223	1,128	996	895	493	1,995	1,950	1,759	607

[1] For wage or salary workers at time of survey.
[2] For experienced civilian labor force. 1939 excludes public emergency workers and persons having less than $100 of wage or salary income, but includes members of the Armed Forces; 1950 excludes persons having less than $100 of wage or salary income.

[3] Fewer than 100 cases in the sample reporting with $1 or more of wage or salary income.

chapter G

CONSUMER EXPENDITURE PATTERNS (Series G 191–584)

G 191–218. Personal consumption expenditures, by type of product, 1929–1957.

Source: 1929–1945, Office of Business Economics, *National Income: A Supplement to the Survey of Current Business, 1954 Edition*, pp. 206–208; 1946–1957, *U. S. Income and Output, 1958*.

Detailed estimates by the Department of Commerce of consumer expenditures for commodities and services since 1929 were first published in the *Survey of Current Business*, June 1944. The figures on personal consumption expenditures for commodities were calculated by the "commodity flow methods" developed by Simon Kuznets, *Commodity Flow and Capital Formation*, National Bureau of Economic Research, New York, 1938. Estimates of personal consumption expenditures for services are based on a variety of source materials which cannot be summarized briefly. For further detail, see *National Income: 1954 Edition*.

As defined by the Department of Commerce, personal consumption expenditures represent the market value of purchases of goods and services by individuals and nonprofit institutions and the value of food, clothing, housing, and financial services received by them as income in kind. Rental value of owner-occupied houses is included; purchases of dwellings, which are classified as capital goods, are excluded.

G 219–243. Personal consumption expenditures, by type of product, 1909–1929.

Source: J. Frederic Dewhurst and Associates, *America's Needs and Resources, A New Survey*, The Twentieth Century Fund, New York, 1955, pp. 965–980.

The first detailed estimates of aggregate consumer expenditures for goods and services in the United States over a period of time appeared in William H. Lough (with the assistance of Martin Gainsbrugh), *High-Level Consumption*, McGraw-Hill, New York, 1935. These pioneer estimates covered the years 1909, 1914, 1919, 1921, 1923, 1925, 1927, 1929, and 1931. The data for the later years were revised and extended by Harold Barger, *Outlay and Income in the United States, 1921–1938*, National Bureau of Economic Research, New York, 1942. In the 1940's, J. Frederic Dewhurst and Associates (*America's Needs and Resources*, 1947) revised these various estimates and expanded those on recreational expense to take account of estimates by Julius Weinberger, "The Economic Aspects of Recreation," *Harvard Business Review*, Summer issue, 1937.

G 244–543. General note.

Collection of data on consumer expenditures, and, especially wage earners' expenditures, began in the United States in the 1870's. It was undertaken on a small scale by a number of different State agencies using a great variety of methods. The most substantial of these studies was that made for Massachusetts by Carroll D. Wright, Bureau of Statistics of Labor of Massachusetts. He undertook a carefully planned survey of the earnings and expenditures of 397 families of skilled and unskilled workers in 1875. The usefulness of the data gathered in this study led the Congress to request further studies of this type on a broader base by the newly formed U.S. Bureau of Labor of which Wright had become Commissioner.

Some of the results of the large-scale studies made by the Bureau of Labor for 1888–91 and 1901 are given in series G 303–321. The data on food expenditures obtained in the 1901 survey were used to provide the design for an index of prices of food purchased by workingmen. This index was used generally as a deflator for workers' incomes and expenditures for all kinds of goods until World War I.

During that period, the need for a more inclusive index of retail prices became clearer because food prices rose so much faster than those of many other commodities and of rents. A nationwide study of the expenditures of wage earners and clerical workers was undertaken in 1918 to provide a list of items to be priced for such an index and also to provide data on the relative importance of each item. Because of the number of wage disputes in the shipbuilding centers, the survey was first undertaken in seacoast cities. It was later expanded into what was regarded as a representative sample of industrial centers in the United States.

The first study made in this country of the over-all consumer expenditures of a group of farm families was made in Livingston County, N.Y., in 1909. In the early 1920's, the Department of Agriculture initiated a cooperative project on the subject with the State Agricultural Experiment Stations under the direction of E. L. Kirkpatrick. In 1925, it was decided, for lack of any other data on farm family expenditures extending across State lines, to average the data that had been collected in 11 States covering one year in the period 1923–1925. The resulting averages given in series G 488–507 have been widely used, but other State studies made in the next few years indicated that the averages for the 2,886 families were too high to be representative of the expenditures of farm-operator families throughout the country at that time.

Dramatic increases in productivity in industry and agriculture during the 1920's and the economic collapse which began in 1929 led a number of economists to study the factors affecting consumer expenditures and to estimate changes in consumption patterns over time. The pioneer investigation in this field was made by Simon Kuznets, *Commodity Flow and Capital Formation*, National Bureau of Economic Research, New York, 1938. This study shows national aggregates for four types of consumer goods and services. The Brookings Institution published, in 1934, estimates of expenditure patterns at different income levels of farm and nonfarm families and single individuals in 1929 (see M. Leven, H. G. Moulton, and C. Warburton, *America's Capacity to Consume*, The Brookings Institution, Washington, D. C., 1934). The figures were prepared by Clark Warburton on the basis of scattered sample studies made during the 1920's and early 1930's and correlated with national income estimates made by Maurice Leven (see text for series G 482–487 and G 538–543). In 1935, estimates of aggregate consumer expenditures in detail for 1909 and 1929 and selected years between were prepared by Martin Gainsbrugh and published in William H. Lough, *High-Level Consumption* (see text for series G 219–243). This book included a comparison with The Brookings Institution's aggregates for 1929, showing that the two estimates were very close for food expense, and reasonably close for attire and home maintenance; but the estimates by Lough and Gainsbrugh of expenditures for all other items were much higher than the Brookings' figures.

In the middle 1930's, two national cross-section studies of consumer expenditure patterns were undertaken. The first, conducted by the Bureau of Labor Statistics, covered employed city wage and clerical workers and was initiated to provide a new list of items and weights for the Consumer Price Index of the Bureau of Labor Statistics. The second, the Study of Consumer Purchases, conducted jointly by the BLS and the Bureau of Home Economics in the Department of Agriculture, related to families (with native-born heads) who were not on public relief rolls during the survey year, and was initiated to provide data relating the effect on expenditure patterns of income, occupation of the head, race, family composition, and type of community. The results of the second study were used by the National Resources Planning Board as the basis for a national estimate of consumer expenditures (see text for series G 409–426, G 464–481, and G 523–537). The data from this study were supplemented by information from the Bureau of Internal Revenue on income distribution and receipts from excise taxes, and from a few studies of the expenditures of families on public relief rolls and of those with foreign-born heads.

A small nationwide survey covering 1941 conducted by the Bureau of Labor Statistics and the Bureau of Home Economics (see text for series G 391–408 and G 445–463) provides the most recent detailed data on the expenditure patterns of rural and urban families in the same year. BLS also conducted a sample national study of urban family expenditures in 1944 (see text for series G 373–390). Another BLS urban study covering 1950, intended primarily to serve as a basis for revision of the Consumer Price Index, subsequently provided detailed tabulations of consumer expenditures, income, and savings (see text for series G 244–263). The Department of Agriculture, in cooperation with the Bureau of the Census, conducted a survey of farm family expenditures in 1955 (see text for series G 427–444) to obtain data to revise the Parity Index and improve the basis for estimating farm operators' production expenses, which provides detailed data on farm family expenditures.

In recent years, there have been a number of nationwide surveys of consumer expenditures by income level for specified types of goods. See, for example, individual reports in the series published by Department of Agriculture, *Household Food Consumption Survey*, 1955. The reports of this survey provide detailed data for farm and nonfarm households on quantities and values of food consumed and on dietary levels by money income after taxes in the United States as a whole and in four major regions.

The annual Surveys of Consumer Finances, conducted for the Board of Governors of the Federal Reserve System by the Survey Research Center of the University of Michigan, yield data on consumer purchases of selected durable goods by income level of all "spending units" in the United States. Reports of these surveys appear in the *Federal Reserve Bulletin*.

Other recent national sample surveys conducted for use in marketing research have covered a very large proportion, but not all types, of consumer goods and services. The most comprehensive of these is the study of consumer expenditures conducted for Life Magazine by Alfred Politz Research, Inc., which is based on a sample designed to represent all individuals, 20 years of age and over, in continental United States. The study provides an unusual amount of detailed material on expenditures for commodities along with data on buying habits of households of different types.

The lack of continuity in the tables shown here which present data by income level is, at least in part, due to the fact that the coverage and definitions used in obtaining the data differ so greatly from study to study. The chief differences in population coverage and in the classification and definition of goods and services purchased are briefly specified in the tables and in the text which follows. Differences in definition primarily affect the figures on income, expenditures for housing, and for "sundries" or "miscellaneous goods and services."

The figures on income represent annual income before deduction of direct personal taxes, i.e., income, poll, and personal property, except the following, which represent annual income after deduction of taxes: Urban families in 1917–19 (series G 283–302), 1944 (series G 373–390), and 1950 (series G 244–263 and G 353–372); and farm-operator families in 1955 (series G 427–444).

Direct personal taxes, as well as indirect taxes, were generally tabulated as an item of current expenditure in the consumer expenditure surveys made before the 1930's. Since the Consumer Purchases Study of 1935–36, such taxes have been presented separately and have not been included in consumer expenditures. For the series presented here, direct personal taxes were deducted from expenditure figures in the earlier surveys, wherever possible, to insure greater comparability with the most recent surveys.

Social Security taxes paid by the worker (first collected in 1937) were treated as savings in the 1941 and 1944 surveys, and handled with personal insurance as a separate class of disbursements in the 1950 urban and the 1955 farm surveys.

In the early studies of wage earners' incomes and expenditures, no attempt was made to evaluate the products received by a family from its garden, poultry, hogs, or cows. Most studies of the incomes and expenditures of farm-operator families include data on the value of food and fuel produced by the family for its own use, sometimes valued at prices which would have been paid for them had they been purchased through nearby trade channels, and sometimes at prices which would have been received if the products had been sold.

The treatment of imputed income resulting from expenditures for owned homes varies considerably from one series to another. Series G 191–243 include rental value of owned homes, but not capital expenditures for housing. In the early studies of wage earners' expenditures, the statistical difficulties of handling homeowners' housing expenditures were avoided by excluding homeowners from the "normal" family group and including only renters. In studies made in the middle 1930's and early 1940's information was obtained not only on homeowners' current year expenditures for housing and for investments in their homes, but also on the net rental value of their homes. These figures are not presented here, but are available in the original sources.

Conceptually, premiums paid on life insurance policies may be classified wholly as current expenditures or partly as savings and partly current expenditures, depending on the type of policy; but in sample surveys it is difficult to obtain from respondents information on the type of policies on which premiums are paid.

Series G 191–243 include as consumer expenditures the part of insurance premiums paid which covers the expense of handling life insurance, but not the part which will eventually be returned to the consumer buyer or his beneficiaries. In sample surveys of consumer expenditures made before the 1930's, the difficulty of obtaining information on the types of policies held resulted in classifying payments on such premiums in the sundries or miscellaneous group as current expenditures. In expenditure surveys made since 1930, it has been the practice to exclude insurance premiums from current expenditure data, handling them either as savings or as a separate class of disbursements.

In addition to the sources of the individual series, students of the history of the subject are referred to the following:

Dorothy S. Brady and Faith M. Williams, "Advances in the Techniques of Measuring and Estimating Consumer Expenditures," *Journal of Farm Economics*, May 1945, vol. 27, No. 2.

"Consumer Survey Statistics, Report of Consultant Committee on Consumer Survey Statistics, organized by the Board of Governors of the Federal Reserve System at the request of the Subcommittee on Economic Statistics of the Joint Committee on the Economic Report, July 1955," *Hearings Before the Subcommittee on Economic Statistics*, 84th Congress, July 19 and 26, October 4 and 5, 1955, pp. 251–372.

Solomon Fabricant, "Measuring National Consumption," *Studies in Income and Wealth*, vol. 8, National Bureau of Economic Research, New York, 1946.

Helen Humes Lamale, *Methodology of the Survey of Consumer Expenditures in 1950*, Wharton School of Finance and Commerce, University of Pennsylvania, 1959.

William H. Shaw, "Consumption Expenditures, 1929–1943," *Survey of Current Business*, June 1944.

Bureau of Home Economics, *Study of Consumer Purchases, Urban, Village, and Farm Series*, 1935–1936 (22 volumes).

Agricultural Research Service, *Farm Family Spending and Saving in Illinois*, Agricultural Information Bulletin, No. 101.

Agricultural Research Service, *Condensed vs. Detailed Schedule for Collection of Family Expenditure Data*, FE-51, March 1954.

Bureau of Labor Statistics, *Money Disbursements of Wage Earners and Clerical Workers, 1934–1936*, Bulletin Nos. 636–641, inclusive. (No. 638 is the summary volume.)

Bureau of Labor Statistics, *Study of Consumer Purchases, Urban Series, 1935–1936*, Bulletin Nos. 642–649, inclusive.

Clark Warburton, "Three Estimates of the Value of the Nation's Output of Commodities and Services," *Studies in Income and Wealth*, vol. 3, National Bureau of Economic Research, New York, 1939.

Faith M. Williams, "International Comparisons of Patterns of Family Consumption," in *Consumer Behavior: Research on Consumer Reactions*, Harper and Brothers, 1958.

Faith M. Williams and Carle C. Zimmerman, *Family Living Studies in the United States and Other Countries*, Department of Agriculture, Miscellaneous Publication No. 223.

Chase Going Woodhouse and Faith M. Williams, *Comparison of Schedule and Account Methods of Collecting Data on Family Living*, Department of Agriculture, Technical Bulletin 386.

G 244–330.　General note.

Data on the consumption expenditures of families of city wage and clerical workers of two or more persons were collected at irregular intervals and for a variety of purposes. Only the 1950 BLS Study of Consumer Expenditures was based on a sample representing families of all types in these occupational groups in cities of all sizes throughout the entire country. Insofar as the original publications make it possible, the figures from the earlier studies have been adjusted as to definition and classification of consumer expenditures so as to conform to those used in 1950.

See also general note for series G 244–543.

G 244–263.　Consumption expenditures, in current prices, of families of city wage and clerical workers of 2 or more persons, by income class, 1950.

Source: Department of Labor, *How American Buying Habits Change*, 1959.

These series are based on a *Study of Consumer Expenditures, Incomes and Savings; Statistical Tables: Urban U.S.—1950*, a joint study by the Bureau of Labor Statistics and the Wharton School of Finance and Commerce, University of Pennsylvania, 1956, vols. I, II, III, IX, and X.

The survey of consumer expenditures in 1950 was conducted by BLS to provide the basis for revising its Consumer Price Index. The survey was undertaken during the first half of 1951 in 91 urban areas throughout the United States ranging in size from places of 2,500 inhabitants to the greater New York area with a population of 9 million. Complete and usable reports were obtained from 12,489 consumer units. Since the study was directed toward the determination of expenditure weights for the BLS revised CPI, the data for family expenditures for individual consumption goods and services purchased by the 7,007 wage-earner and clerical-worker families of 2 or more persons were tabulated and averaged for each of the 91 cities surveyed.

Subsequently, the same data were tabulated in considerable detail and published as part of the study of consumer expenditures, income, and savings, which was made by the Wharton School of Finance and Commerce in cooperation with BLS under a grant from the Ford Foundation.

To obtain data for wage-earner and clerical-worker families of 2 or more, the following groups were excluded: Single consumers; self-employed; salaried professionals; officials, etc.; and persons not gainfully employed. Within the 9 classes of cities averaged for the Wharton School publications (large cities, suburbs, and small cities in the North, South, and West), averages were based on the sample families as weights; in combining the resulting averages, universe (total consumer units, i.e., families and single consumers) weights were used.

G 264–282.　Consumption expenditures, in current prices, of families of employed city wage and clerical workers of 2 or more persons, by income class, 1934–36.

Source: Bureau of Labor Statistics, records.

These series are based on Faith M. Williams and Alice C. Hanson, *Money Disbursements of Wage Earners and Clerical Workers*, Bureau of Labor Statistics, Bulletin No. 638, summary volume, 1941.

The data in this 1934–36 study were gathered to provide the basis for revising the BLS Consumer Price Index. The survey (conducted in a period of mass unemployment) was restricted to families of two or more in large cities, who had an income of at least $500 and who had not been on public relief rolls during the survey year. These limits precluded from the pattern on which the CPI was to be based the irregular spending of workers on "relief" and those employed so irregularly that their purchases could not have been typical of long-range consumption patterns. The survey covered 12,903 white families and 1,566 Negro families in 42 cities with population 50,000 or more.

These series derived from Bulletin No. 638 have been adjusted for comparability with definitions and classifications of the 1950 *Study of Consumer Expenditures* . . . (see text for series G 244–263), as follows: "Vocation" outlays shown in table 1 were deducted from both "average annual current expenditures" in table 1 and from "average annual amount" of total net family income in table 7. "Community welfare" and "gifts and contributions to persons outside the economic family" were deducted from "average annual current consumption expenditures" in table 7.

G 283–302.　Consumption expenditures, in current prices, of families of city wage and clerical workers with at least 1 child, by income class, 1917–19.

Source: Bureau of Labor Statistics, Bulletin No. 357, *Cost of Living in the United States, 1917–19*.

These data were collected from white city worker families having husband and wife and at least 1 child, who was not a boarder or lodger. The families could have no boarders and not over 3 lodgers; at least 75 percent of family income had to come from the principal breadwinner or others who contributed all earnings to the family fund; slum or charity families or non-English speaking families who had been in the United States less than 5 years were excluded.

This survey was first undertaken in shipbuilding centers for the purpose of providing market baskets which could be used in computing consumer price indexes for cities most affected by the inflation which occurred during and just after World War I. It was later broadened to cover 92 cities and localities throughout the entire country.

The income and expenditure figures presented in Bulletin No. 357 were adjusted for comparability with definitions and classifications used in the 1950 *Study of Consumer Expenditures* . . . (see text for series G 244–263). Thus, average money income after taxes (see series G 285) was derived by deducting dues to labor organizations, personal property and poll taxes, and expenditures for tools (Bulletin No. 357, pp. 448 and 454) from total average income per family (Bulletin No. 357, p. 4). Average expenditures for current consumption (see series G 286) were derived by deducting from total average yearly expenses per family (Bulletin No. 357, p. 5) the same items deducted from income and, in addition, life insurance premiums; contributions to church, charity, and patriotic purposes; and gifts (Bulletin No. 357, pp. 447 and 448). Each consumption group was adjusted for maximum comparability with the corresponding groups as classified in the 1950 *Study* (when they differed from the original published table).

G 303–312. **Consumption expenditures, in current prices, of normal families of city wage and clerical workers of 2 or more persons, by income class, 1901.**

Source: Department of Labor, *How American Buying Habits Change*, 1959.

These series are based on 18th Annual Report of the Commissioner of Labor, Document No. 23, Bureau of Labor, 1903, *Cost of Living and Retail Prices of Food*, pp. 581, 592, and 593.

Earnings and expenditure data from this report covered families with wage and salary incomes not exceeding $1,200 a year, and were collected through personal interviews by experienced special agents of the Bureau of Labor. About 15 percent of these families had incomes from boarders and lodgers and other sources. The latter income raised a few families total income above $1,200. Therefore their expenditures could be, and were, above $1,200. Altogether, data were collected from 25,440 families of all types but only those from the 11,156 families defined as "normal" were summarized by income levels. These "normal" families had a husband at work, a wife, not more than 5 children and none over 14 years of age; no dependents, boarders, lodgers, or servants; and provided data on expenditures for rent, fuel, lighting, food, clothing, and sundries.

The 1901 study had a wide city and industry coverage in 32 States and the District of Columbia, and appears to have provided a very good picture of "normal" families in wage and salaried occupations. The selection of the number of persons interviewed in each geographical area was roughly apportioned in accordance with the number of persons employed in the manufacturing industries of the States.

G 313–321. **Consumption expenditures, in current prices, of normal families of city wage and clerical workers of 2 or more persons in 9 basic industries, by income class, 1888–91.**

Source: Department of Labor, *How American Buying Habits Change*, 1959.

These series are based on Sixth Annual Report of the Commissioner of Labor, 1890, *Cost of Production*, part III; and Seventh Annual Report of the Commissioner of Labor, 1891,

Cost of Production, vol. II, part III. Only data for so-called "normal" families in all industries (identified by budget numbers, Seventh Annual Report, pp. 1826-1839, 1887-1898) were used for comparative purposes. Family size, income, and expenditures were tabulated from the Sixth Annual Report (pp. 790–801, 914–925, 984–989, 1076–1085, 1128–1131, 1160–1162), and the Seventh Annual Report (pp. 1170–1206, 1374–1390, and 1552–1569). Those data provided the basis for calculation of average family size, income, and total expenditures for all "normal" families by income class. The percentage distributions of total expenditures for "normal" families, in the Seventh Annual Report (pp. 2012 and 2013), were applied to the appropriate averages to estimate the dollar expenditure by income class.

Earnings and expenditure data in the study covered 2,562 "normal" families. "Normal" families had both a husband and wife, not more than 5 children, no one of whom was over 14 years of age; no dependents or boarders; did not own its own dwelling place; and had expenditures for rent, fuel, lighting, clothing, and food. The study covered workers in the following industries: Pig iron, bar iron, steel, bituminous coal, coke, iron ore, cotton, woolen, and glass.

G 322–330. **Consumption expenditures, in current prices, of Massachusetts, families of city wage and clerical workers of 2 or more persons, by income class, 1874–75.**

Source: Department of Labor, *How American Buying Habits Change*, 1959.

These data are based on Massachusetts Bureau of Statistics of Labor, Sixth Annual Report, March 1875, Public Document No. 31, pp. 221-354, 372, 373, and 441. The data were collected from families of wage earners in 15 cities and 21 towns by trained agents of the Bureau of Statistics of Labor who approached 1,000 families before they were able to find 397 who had enough information about their affairs to answer the questions put to them and who were also willing to "having their private life inquired into." The families included about equal numbers of skilled and unskilled workers, and were those who, with comparatively few exceptions, had children dependent on them for support.

Series G 322–330 were computed from data in the Massachusetts report which show, by income class, the number of families from whom figures were received, their aggregate earnings and expenses in each class, and percentages of expenditure as regards income, by income class, for five major categories of expense. The resulting weighted averages for all families' earnings and expenses were found to check with all family averages shown elsewhere in the report. Average figures on money earnings, expenses for all goods and services and for fuel also checked with such averages in the report. The figures on expenses for food, rent, and sundries checked within a few dollars (differences probably caused by rounding of the percentages).

In this report, the items of expenditure not specifically for subsistence, clothing, rent, and fuel were listed as sundries. The report states that sundry items of expense are those which "although . . . not absolutely necessary for the life of the body, are, in their way, imperative necessity in a man's social life." Some specified sundries include furniture, carpets, books and papers, societies, religion, charity, sickness, care of parents, care of house, recreation, housegirl, travel to work, and life insurance.

G 331–352. **Consumption expenditures, in 1950 prices, of families of city wage and clerical workers of 2 or more persons, 1888–91 to 1950.**

Source: Department of Labor, *How American Buying Habits Change*, 1959.

Figures on average money receipts and outlays of wage and clerical workers' families of two or more persons in large cities have been converted into dollars of 1950 purchasing power for each of the survey years since 1888–91. The BLS Consumer Price Index was used to convert current expenditures and average income into dollars of 1950 purchasing power for the surveys of 1917–19 and 1934–36. The cost-of-living index developed by Paul Douglas (see *American Economic Review*, Supplement, March 1926, p. 22) was used to convert income and total consumption expenditures for the 1888-91 and 1901 studies; the BLS Retail Food Index was used to convert the expenditures for food and drink. Other categories of expenditures were not converted into 1950 dollars because no indexes are available for these categories prior to 1913.

Series G 331–352 for 1950, 1934–36, and 1917–19 relate to expenditures of wage and clerical workers' families in large cities, i.e., with populations of 30,500 and over in 1950; 50,000 and over in 1934–36 and 1917–19. Populations of the large industrial centers surveyed in the two earliest surveys were not specified.

G 353–426. General note.

For discussion of the surveys from which these series were taken, see general note for series G 244–543 and the text for series separately grouped by survey which follows.

G 353–372. Consumption expenditures, in current prices, of all families of 2 or more persons in cities of 2,500 and over, by income class, 1950.

Source: *Study of Consumer Expenditures, Incomes and Savings; Statistical Tables: Urban U. S.—1950*, cited above, vol. XVIII, pp. 14-23.

For a description of this survey, see text for series G 244–263. To obtain the data for all families of two or more persons, only single consumers were excluded; all occupational groups were included. Within the nine classes of cities averaged for the Wharton School publications (large cities, suburbs, and small cities in the North, South, and West), averages were based on the sample families as weights. In combining the resulting averages, universe (total consumer units) weights were used.

G 373–390. Consumption expenditures, in current prices, of all families of 2 or more persons in cities of 2,500 and over, by income class, 1944.

Source: Bureau of Labor Statistics, *Monthly Labor Review*, January 1946, p. 4; and Bulletin No. 838, *Wartime Food Purchases*, pp. 1-4, and appendix.

A study of expenditures and savings in 1944 of city families was undertaken by BLS for the primary purpose of comparing prices reported by city consumers with prices indicated by urban store reports. The survey was made in two parts. The first part, made in the fall of 1944, provided detailed information on food purchases during 1 week, purchases of clothing and household textiles during the first 8 months of the year, tenure and rental in August 1944, and sufficient information on family composition, living arrangements, and income to provide a basis for classification. The second part provided data on purchases of food during 1 week early in 1945, of clothing and other textiles during the last 4 months of 1944, and of other goods and services throughout 1944.

The sample used in this survey was very similar to that used in the 1941 survey (see text for series G 391–408) and related to the civilian noninstitutional population in cities of 2,500 or more scattered throughout the country. The sample included approximately 1,700 families and single persons in 28 metropolitan districts and 20 cities with a population under 50,000 outside of metropolitan districts. These places were selected to represent, with respect to region, State, and city size, all cities in the United States with a population of 2,500 or more.

Family income represents the sum of all types of income received by family members during 1944; included are wage and salary earnings after payroll deductions of income taxes, entrepreneurial net income or withdrawals, and nonearned income from all sources except inheritances, large gifts, and lump-sum insurance settlements.

Although the figures were originally published as preliminary and subject to slight revisions, no revisions were subsequently issued.

G 391–408. Consumption expenditures, in current prices, of all families of 2 or more persons in cities of 2,500 and over, by income class, 1941.

Source: Bureau of Labor Statistics, Bulletin No. 822, *Family Spending and Saving in Wartime*, pp. 68, 70, 71, 76, 102, and 109.

The survey of family spending and saving in wartime is the only survey which was conducted for the primary purpose of providing national estimates of expenditures and savings by income class.

The method of drawing the sample used for this survey differed in several important respects from that followed in earlier surveys of family incomes and expenditures. A description of these changes appears in part I, "Scope and Method," of the source. The coverage of population was more complete than in any previous survey and included such segments of the population as families on public relief rolls, foreign-born and broken families, single consumers, occupational groups, and city-size classes; but it excluded inmates of institutions, residents of military camps, and persons in labor camps.

The sample was smaller than in any previous survey on which national estimates have been based. The sample for urban areas covered about 1,300 families and single persons in 62 cities of 2,500 or more scattered throughout the country. The cities were so selected as to give proper representation to (1) each city-size group; (2) proximity to a metropolis (for cities under 50,000); (3) each region and State; (4) low, medium, and high rent cities; and (5) cities of differing racial composition.

Information was obtained on both money and nonmoney income, although only money income figures are shown here. Expenditures for family living were reported in detail under 14 categories of expense. All purchases of durable goods made during the year, except payments on homes and improvements on homes, were considered current expenditures. Financing charges, interest on installment and other credit purchases, and shipping and delivery charges were considered as part of the expenditure. Discounts and trade-in allowances were deducted from the gross price. Sales and excise taxes were included in the expenditure for each article except in the case of the details for food expenditure.

Sample data for the $5,000 to $10,000 and the $10,000 and over classes are included, although the averages for these classes are based on a small number of cases and are therefore quite irregular and subject to a wide margin of error. They should be considered as statements of sample results only, and not as estimates of actual expenditures by the entire group of families in those income groups.

G 409–426. Consumption expenditures, in current prices, of all families of 2 or more persons in cities of 2,500 and over, by income class, 1935–36.

Source: National Resources Planning Board, *Family Expenditures in the United States, Statistical Tables and Appendixes*, 1941, pp. 61, 120, and 157.

The study of family expenditures is part of the *Study of Consumer Purchases*, conducted by the Bureau of Labor Statistics and the Bureau of Home Economics, in cooperation with the National Resources Committee, the Central Statistical Board, and the Works Progress Administration. The Bureau of Home Economics conducted the survey in rural-farm and rural-nonfarm areas and in the majority of the small cities covered, and the Bureau of Labor Statistics conducted the surveys in the other small cities and all of the larger urban communities.

The study of consumer purchases was the most detailed analysis of family expenditures in the United States made up to that time. Data were published on over 90 categories of outlays. They are classified to permit study of differences between the farm, rural-nonfarm, and urban population, of regional variations, of differences with respect to size of family and between white and Negro families, as well as of differences between income levels.

Detailed information on expenditures and savings during a 12-month period between January 1935 and December 1936 was secured from a sample of about 60,000 families living in cities of different sizes, in villages, and on farms in 30 States, of which 54,000 were used in preparing the family expenditure data. The urban sample covered 51 cities and approximately 30,000 expenditure schedules. Both the sample expenditure data and the population weights used in preparing the estimates (shown in these series) of family expenditures by income class exclude families receiving any direct or work-relief assistance (however little) at any time during the year.

Income was defined to include total net money income received during the year by all members of the economic family, plus the value of certain items of nonmoney income such as net value of owner-occupied homes and rent received as pay. Consumption data were collected only from native white families in most sample communities and from native Negro families in the Southeast, in New York City, and Columbus, Ohio.

G 427–507. General note.

For discussion of the surveys from which these series were obtained, see general note for series G 244–543 and the text for series separately grouped by survey which follows.

G 427–444. Consumption expenditures, in current prices, of farm-operator families of 2 or more persons, by income class, 1955.

Source: Derived from Department of Agriculture, Statistical Bulletin No. 224, *Farmers' Expenditures in 1955 by Regions*, 1958, and from unpublished records of the Agricultural Research Service.

These data are based on a weighted sample of approximately 4,000 schedules, selected on the basis of the 1954 Census of Agriculture distribution of farms by economic class of farm (value of all products sold). The number of families included a small number not reporting income. Federal and State personal taxes have been deducted from money income. Expenditures for dwelling upkeep included for owned homes an assigned share of real estate taxes and special assessments, insurance premiums, mortgage interest charges, legal and settlement charges; and for both owned and rented homes expense for repairs, replacements, alterations and improvements, and cash rent for off-farm rented dwellings. Expense for lodging away from home and for vacation homes was also included. Expenditures for automobile and truck transportation include family share of purchase and upkeep. Expenditures for other goods and services include expense for funerals for family members, legal fees, bank charges for service and deposit box, rental of post office box, money lost or stolen, interest paid on

borrowing for family use, occupational expense, union dues, poll taxes, and personal property taxes.

G 445–463. Consumption expenditures, in current prices, of farm-operator families of 2 or more persons, by income class, 1941.

Source: Department of Agriculture, Miscellaneous Bulletin No. 520, *Rural Family Spending and Saving in Wartime*, June 1943, pp. 156 and 159.

These data were obtained from a study conducted in 1942 by the Bureau of Home Economics in areas representing the entire rural population of the country. The survey was paralleled by a study of the income and expenditures of urban families and single consumers conducted by the Bureau of Labor Statistics (see text for series G 391–408). The study was based on a sample of 1,000 rural-nonfarm families and single consumers and 760 farm families and single consumers in 45 counties, stratified to give representation to all regions and to economic groups in the rural population.

The data collected included nonmoney as well as money income; the former was limited to that received in the form of food, housing, fuel, ice, clothing, or household furnishings. However, classification in these series is by money income only. Expenditures for family living were reported in detail under 15 categories of expense. All purchases of durable goods made during the year, except payments on homes and improvements on homes, were considered as current expenditures. Financing charges and interest on installment and other credit purchases, shipping and delivery charges were considered as part of the expenditure. Discounts and trade-in allowances were deducted from the gross price. Sales and excise taxes were included in the expenditures for each article except in the case of the details for food expenditure. Although the survey included expenditures of families and single consumers, these series cover farm families only.

G 464–481. Consumption expenditures, in current prices, of farm-operator families, by income class, 1935–36.

Source: National Resources Planning Board, *Family Expenditures in the United States, Statistical Tables and Appendixes*, June 1941, pp. 51, 120, and 157.

These data are based on information obtained as part of the Works Progress Administration study (see text for series G 409–426) and summarized for the United States by the National Resources Planning Board. The definition of income used in this study includes, in addition to money income, the nonmoney income items of net rental value of owner-occupied homes and housing received as pay and the net imputed value of food produced at home for the family's own use. For farm families, it also includes the net imputed value of certain other farm-produced goods used by the family, i.e., fuel, ice, tobacco, and wool, plus or minus the value of any increase or decrease in the amount of livestock owned or of crops stored for sale.

Estimates for approximately 15,000 native farm families (excluding those on public relief rolls) living in rural areas are presented in these series. For the main categories of disbursement, 140 villages and 66 farm countries in 30 States were surveyed. The farm sample represents the more important types of farming. Farm families operating part-time farms were excluded from the consumption sample (except in Oregon).

G 482–487. Consumption expenditures, in current prices, of farm-operator families, by income class, 1929.

Source: Computed from M. Leven, H. G. Moulton, and C. Warburton, *America's Capacity to Consume*, The Brookings Institution, Washington, D. C., 1934, p. 260.

Aggregates presented in the original source were divided by the number of families in each income class to derive average expenditures per family.

The number of families is based on the distribution of families by income estimated by Maurice Leven. The estimates of consumer expenditures were made by Clark Warburton on the basis of 6 sample studies of the value of consumer goods and services used by farm families in one year between 1924 and 1930.

The income figures shown here represent both annual money and nonmoney income. Included in nonmoney income are imputed value of home-produced food and fuel, and of owned homes. The expenditure for "other" items includes direct taxes and contributions.

G 488–507. Consumption expenditures of farm-operator families, by income class, 1922–1924.

Source: Computed from E. L. Kirkpatrick, *The Farmer's Standard of Living: A Socio-Economic Study of 2,886 White Farm Families of Selected Localities in 11 States*, Department of Agriculture, Bulletin 1466, pp. 29 and 34.

These data were derived from a number of special studies made by the Department of Agriculture in cooperation with 12 colleges or universities. The studies were planned to show the following items among others: Tenure, acres per farm, and value of land per acre; quantities and value of food, fuel, and other materials furnished during the year; quantities and costs of food, fuel, furniture and furnishings, household supplies, and household labor purchased during the year; and expenditures for other items such as clothing, health, education, recreation, personal care, etc.

The economic level of farm business resources and of farm family living was the chief consideration in the selection of the localities represented in this study. The localities were situated in 11 States (New Hampshire, Vermont, Massachusetts, Connecticut, Kentucky, South Carolina, Alabama, Missouri, Kansas, Iowa, and Ohio). Of the 2,886 families represented in the study, 1,950 were owners, 867 were cash and share tenants including croppers, and 69 were hired men or managers. The study was limited to families who had an adult man operating the farm and an adult woman as homemaker; generally the operator and homemaker were man and wife.

Total expenditures for current consumption and expenditures for each consumption category were derived from figures in the source showing percentage distribution of the value of all goods. Expenditures for life and health insurance were deducted from the total. Consumer goods and services purchased include food, fuel, and housing furnished by the farm. Food and fuel provided by the farm were valued at prices halfway between what they would have brought and what they would have cost in the open market; housing provided was valued at 10 percent of the estimated value of the house occupied.

The class intervals shown in series G 488-507 as value of goods purchased and goods furnished in kind are ambiguously referred to in the original as "total value or income" groups. A comparison with other studies by the author indicates that the classes are not representative of income. Series G 488-507 therefore differs in this respect from the other series in this chapter.

G 508–543. General note.

For discussion of the surveys from which these series were obtained, see general note for series G 244–543 and the text for series separately grouped by survey which follows.

G 508–522. Consumption expenditures, in current prices, of families and single consumers combined, by income class, 1941.

Source: See source for series G 391–408, p. 75.

For a description of this study, see text for series G 391–408 and G 445–463.

The expenditure data in these series represent expenditures of all families and single consumers including families with negative incomes and incomes of $5,000 and over not shown separately, for the country as a whole. Nonmoney income is not included. The expenditure patterns are based on a sample of 3,100 families and single consumers in 62 cities and 45 rural counties.

G 523–537. Consumption expenditures, in current prices, of all families and single consumers combined, by income class, 1935–36.

Source: National Resources Committee, *Consumer Expenditures in the United States, Estimates for 1935–36*, pp. 77 and 84.

The study from which these series were derived was part of the Works Progress Administration study already described in the text for series G 409–426 and G 464–481, supplemented by data from other sources on expenditures of families with foreign-born heads, and of families having received public relief assistance. The expenditure data were secured from a sample of more than 60,000 families living in cities of different size, in villages, and on farms in 30 States. Similar patterns for single men and women were built up from less extensive sample data available from the Study of Consumer Purchases and from various supplementary sources. Average consumption patterns for broad groups of the population and for the Nation as a whole were obtained by weighting the patterns for the component groups of families and single individuals according to their relative importance at each income level. The population weights for this purpose and for estimating the aggregate consumption of the Nation in 1935-36 were derived from the study of consumer incomes (see National Resources Committee, *Consumer Incomes in the United States, Their Distribution in 1935–36*).

G 538–543. Consumption expenditures, in current prices, of all families and single consumers combined, by income class, 1929.

Source: Computed from M. Leven, H. G. Moulton, and C. Warburton, *America's Capacity to Consume*, The Brookings Institution, Washington, D. C., 1934, pp. 260, 261, and 265.

For the purpose of presenting these series in a form roughly comparable with those from other sources for earlier years, average consumption expenditures of all families and single consumers were derived by combining aggregate consumption expenditures (in millions of dollars), by income class, of farm and urban families and single consumers, as given in the report, and dividing these by the total number of consumers (in thousands) in each income class.

The estimates of consumer expenditures presented in *America's Capacity to Consume* were made by Clark Warburton who based his figures on sample surveys of expenditures of nonfarm families for 1918–1930, of farm families for 1924–1930 (see text for series G 482–487), and of single persons for 1918–1933 from a variety of sources. In addition, he used the results of a questionnaire concerning incomes, expenditures, and savings in 1929 circulated by The Brookings Institution to families of business and professional men.

G 544. Index of volume of food marketings and home consumption, 1910–1957.

Source: Agricultural Marketing Service, *National Food Situation*, July 1958; and the 1956 supplement to *Consumption of Food in the United States, 1909–52*, Agriculture Handbook No. 62.

This index was derived for 1940–1957 by weighting the quantities of the major farm-produced foodstuffs sold or used in farm households by average farm prices in 1947–1949. For 1910–1939, average prices for 1935–1939 were used and the series was "spliced" to the levels indicated by the newer weights on the basis of overlapped calculations for 1940. This index, as well as others including nonfood commodities, is described in *Major Statistical Series of the U. S. Department of Agriculture*, Agriculture Handbook No. 118, vol. 2, pp. 38–49. For a comparison of this index with the production subindex (series K 104) of the index of supply-utilization of farm food commodities, see *Measuring the Supply and Utilization of Farm Commodities*, Agriculture Handbook No. 91, 1955, pp. 37–39.

G 545. Index of food consumption per capita, 1909–1957.

Source: See source for series G 544.

This index was derived by weighting per capita consumption of food, retail weight equivalents, by average retail prices in 1947–1949. Details of the construction of this index are described in *Consumption of Food in the United States, 1909–52*. Revised retail weight data were published in the Supplement for 1956 to that bulletin. The retail weight data are derived from such series as those on per capita food consumption (series G 552–584), by means of average conversion factors for nonprocessed and partially processed items which allow for wastes and losses in distribution between the particular primary distribution level at which each series is measured and the retail store level.

This index measures changes in quantity, primarily, although it also reflects certain changes in quality of foods consumed, such as the shift from lower-priced to higher-priced foods. It does not reflect price changes as such, because base-period prices are used throughout. Subindexes and a comparison with other measures of food consumption are given in *Major Statistical Series of the U.S. Department of Agriculture*, Agriculture Handbook No. 118, vol. 5, pp. 65–68.

G 546–551. Nutrients available, per capita per day, 1909–1957.

Source: See source for series G 544.

These figures are averages for the total population, 1909–1940, and for the civilian population only, 1941–1957. Data are computed on the basis of estimates of apparent civilian consumption (retail basis) including estimates of consumption from urban home gardens. No deductions have been made in the nutrient estimates for the loss or waste of food in the home or for the destruction or loss of nutrients during the preparation of food. Deductions have been made for inedible refuse.

The computations were made by multiplying the estimated per capita quantity of each food consumed by appropriate food composition figures. The composition values are those published in Department of Agriculture, *Composition of Foods . . . Raw, Processed, Prepared*, Agriculture Handbook No. 8, supplemented by a few unpublished values.

Since the early 1940's, there has been enrichment or fortification of several types of foods with minerals and vitamins. Composition figures used include these added minerals and vitamins. Foods that are commonly enriched or fortified are white flour and bread, breakfast cereals, and margarine.

The consumption of vitamins and mineral preparations, other than those used in the enrichment or in the fortification of foods mentioned, is not included here. Quantities of calcium or other minerals added to flour to make it self-rising or phosphated are not included nor is the nutritive content of baking powder, yeast, or dough conditioner.

G 552–584. Apparent civilian per capita consumption of food, 1849–1957.

Source: See source for series G 544.

Department of Agriculture estimates of the consumption of major foods are based on a great variety of information pertaining to supplies moving through trade channels for use by the civilian population. All estimates for foods other than cane and beet sugar are derived from data obtained primarily for other purposes. This accounts (1) for the lesser degree of reliability which should be placed on data in many of the series for earlier years, particularly before 1924 and (2) for the several levels in distribution at which the official estimates of consumption of individual foods are measured.

From the annual supply of each food (production plus beginning stocks, plus imports) are deducted feed, seed, industrial, and other nonfood use, exports and shipments, government purchases, and ending stocks. The residual is taken as a measure of the quantities moving into domestic civilian consumption during a given calendar year. Data used are from the following sources:

Item	Source of data
Stocks	Agricultural Marketing Service; Department of Commerce; trade reports.
Production	Agricultural Marketing Service; Fish and Wildlife Service.
Foreign trade	Department of Commerce; shipment data of Agricultural Marketing Service.
Nonfood use	Agricultural Marketing Service.
Military procurement	Special reports submitted to Department of Agriculture.

Data on military takings during World War I were so incomplete that they could not be used. Accordingly, data on total domestic food "disappearance" for 1909–1940 were divided by the total population. For 1941–1957, the total food supplies available for civilian consumption were divided by the number of people eating from civilian supplies. For 1941–1945, adjustments were made for members of the Armed Forces who were on leave or were, for other reasons, eating in homes or restaurants in this country.

The basic disappearance data are in varied terms, such as the carcass weight of meats at the slaughter level and the farm weight of fresh fruits and vegetables. However, such variation does not impede comparisons for a given food through time. Although disappearance data are not the same as consumption data, since they measure the quantities of food going into the distribution system instead of the quantities bought or consumed by consumers, they are the only available estimates of consumption. The possibility of error is present throughout, but the data are internally consistent. All disappearance data are on a national basis and no regional or State estimates can be made without the collection of much additional statistical information.

Some scattered data that are basic to estimates of apparent consumption have been gathered from decennial censuses prior to 1900. The food production data from the Census of Agriculture for 1910 were more complete, and are the first important benchmark for most food consumption estimates. The completeness and accuracy of the data have been greatly improved as the crop reporting system has developed. Data on consumption of major foods since about 1924 are viewed as much more reliable and comparable.

Extensive descriptions of methodology, sources, and inherent limitations for all series are given in *Consumption of Food . . .* (cited above) and are summarized in *Major Statistical Series of the U.S. Department of Agriculture*, Agriculture Handbook No. 118, vol. 5, chap. 3.

G 552–555, meat. Consumption is measured at the wholesale level in terms of weights of dressed carcass, excluding offal. Carcass weight of pork includes head meat, but excludes cuts rendered into lard. Quantities slaughtered under the Emergency Government Relief Purchase Program in 1934 and 1935 are included.

G 556, total fats and oils. Data are measurements at wholesale level and include fat content of butter, margarine, lard, shortening, and "other edible fats and oils." Other edible fats and oils are those used in cooking and salad oils and for minor uses such as fish canning, etc.

G 560, fresh fruit. Consumption is measured at the farm level. Includes apples (from commercial areas only, 1934–1957), apricots, avocados, bananas, cherries, cranberries, figs, grapes, nectarines, peaches, pears, pineapples, plums and prunes, strawberries, and citrus fruits. Excludes supplies used in processing.

G 561, citrus fruits. Includes oranges, tangerines, lemons, limes, and grapefruit.

G 562, canned fruit. Includes apples and applesauce, apricots, berries, cherries, cranberries, figs, fruit salad and cocktail, peaches (including spiced), pears, pineapple, plums and prunes, olives, and citrus segments. Data in terms of net weight reflect disappearance from the wholesale level of distribution.

G 563, canned fruit juice. Consumption is measured at wholesale level. It includes grapefruit, orange, blended citrus and lemon juices (single strength juices, 1930–1957; concentrated juices converted to single strength basis, 1941–1957), and apple, berry, fruit nectars, grape, pineapple, prune, and tangerine juices. Prior to 1928 only grape juice was covered.

G 564, dried fruit. Includes apples, apricots, dates (pits-in basis), figs, peaches, pears, prunes (excludes quantities used for juice), and raisins and currants. Disappearance or consumption since 1941 has been measured at the wholesale level.

G 565, frozen fruits and fruit juices. Includes blackberries, raspberries, strawberries, other berries, apples, apricots, cherries, grapes and pulp, peaches, citrus juices (product weight), and miscellaneous frozen fruits. Disappearance is measured at the wholesale level.

G 566, potatoes. Consumption is measured at the farm level. It excludes quantities supplied by nonfarm home gardens and quantities frozen or canned because they are counted in processed form, but includes quantities used for other purposes, such as for potato chips.

G 567, sweetpotatoes. Consumption is measured at the farm level. It excludes quantities canned and supplies from nonfarm home gardens.

G 568, fresh vegetables. Consumption is measured in terms of farm weights at the farm level, and includes tomatoes, artichokes, asparagus, lima beans, snap beans, broccoli, Brussels sprouts, cabbage, carrots, kale, lettuce and escarole, green peas, peppers, spinach, beets, cauliflower, celery, corn, cucumbers, eggplant, garlic, onions and shallots, and minor vegetables. It excludes quantities produced in home gardens and all supplies going into commercial processing.

G 569, canned vegetables. Excludes soups, baby food, and baked beans; but includes asparagus, lima beans, snap beans, carrots, peas, pumpkin and squash, spinach, tomatoes, tomato catsup and chili sauce, paste and sauce, and pulp and puree, tomato and other vegetable juices, beets, corn, pickles, sauerkraut, potatoes, sweetpotatoes, miscellaneous greens, pimientos, and mixed vegetables. Information on January 1 stocks was not available before 1943. Disappearance measured at wholesale level.

G 570, frozen vegetables. Includes asparagus, snap beans, lima beans, carrots, peas, peas and carrots, pumpkin and squash, broccoli, Brussels sprouts, spinach, cauliflower, corn (cut basis), succotash, rhubarb, potato products, and miscellaneous frozen vegetables. Disappearance measured at wholesale level.

G 571, melons. Consumption is measured at the farm level and includes watermelons, cantaloups, and honey dew and honey ball melons. Excludes quantities produced in home gardens.

G 572, dry beans. Disappearance is measured at the farm level, includes quantities used for canned baked beans and soups, and excludes supplies produced in home gardens.

G 573, total milk for human consumption. The total is measured in terms of whole milk equivalent, on fat solids basis, of all dairy products.

G 574, fluid milk and cream. Includes fluid cream on a whole milk equivalent basis (about 4 percent butterfat) and covers fresh use only; excludes fluid skim and buttermilk.

G 575, condensed and evaporated milk. Evaporated milk is unskimmed, unsweetened, case goods; the condensed milk is unsweetened (plain condensed), unskimmed bulk goods; and sweetened condensed milk, unskimmed, case and bulk goods. Data are measured at the processing level.

G 576, cheese. Includes all whole and part whole milk cheeses; excludes cottage, pot, and bakers' cheese and full-skimmed American.

G 577, ice cream. Data measured at the processing level in terms of product weight. Figures exclude frozen dairy product desserts such as sherbet, frozen custard and malted, and ice milk and mellorine (which is made from skim milk products and vegetable fats).

G 578, eggs. Consumption is measured at approximately the wholesale level of distribution and includes all eggs used in processed foods. Eggs were assumed to weigh approximately 1.5 pounds per dozen through 1946. To adjust for the increasing size of eggs, this factor was increased, beginning in 1947 by 0.01 pound each year through 1952, continued at 1.56 for 1953–1956, and raised to 1.57 for 1957.

G 579, chickens and turkeys. Consumption is measured at the wholesale level. Although most poultry was sold in dressed form until recent years, more is now sold ready-to-cook. The entire series was put on this basis to achieve comparability. Ready-to-cook includes the weight of giblets. Prior to 1947, the factor used to derive ready-to-cook weight from dressed weight for chicken was 0.75; for turkey, 0.824; beginning in 1947, data were computed using differing factors for the various items of supply and distribution.

G 580, sugar, cane and beet. Represents sugar used for all purposes, including quantities in processed fruit and vegetable items and ice cream. Data for 1875–1908 were obtained from Henry Schultz, *Theory and Measurement of Demand* (based on data in *Concerning Sugar*, a looseleaf service by United States Sugar Manufacturers Association, which had been derived from Willett and Gray, *Weekly Statistical Sugar Trade Journal*).

G 581, wheat flour. Includes white, whole wheat, and semolina flour (which is used primarily for macaroni and spaghetti); excludes use in breakfast cereals, but includes use in all other processed foods.

G 582, corn flour and meal. Estimates are based on census data. In recent years approximately 50 percent of cornmeal has been degermed.

G 583, peanuts. Excludes quantities crushed for oil; includes commercially cleaned and shelled peanuts plus quantities used on farms and farm sales for food use.

G 584, coffee. Consumption is measured in terms of green-bean equivalent of all types of coffee, reflecting disappearance from the wholesale roasting level.

Series G 191–218. Personal Consumption Expenditures, by Type of Product: 1929 to 1957

[In millions of dollars]

Year	Total consumption expenditures	Food and beverages [1] Total	Purchased meals and beverages	Tobacco products	Clothing and related products	Jewelry and watches	Laundering and cleaning, etc., in establishments	Personal care	Rental value of — Owner-occupied [2]	Tenant-occupied [2]	Farm-houses	Household furniture, equipment, and supplies Durable	Non-durable	Gas
	191	192	193	194	195	196	197	198	199	200	201	202	203	204
1957	284,442	75,567	15,589	6,074	25,339	1,894	2,752	3,963	22,064	10,395	1,794	14,344	3,512	2,343
1956	269,400	71,237	15,062	5,638	25,107	1,920	2,692	3,726	19,854	10,146	1,744	14,554	3,474	2,210
1955	256,940	67,942	14,371	5,350	23,976	1,835	2,619	3,399	18,033	10,018	1,741	13,781	3,337	1,984
1954	238,025	66,213	13,766	5,218	22,532	1,682	2,535	3,151	16,720	9,803	1,711	12,026	3,088	1,762
1953	232,649	65,241	13,722	5,365	22,527	1,611	2,530	2,973	15,520	9,373	1,765	12,101	3,224	1,560
1952	219,774	64,369	13,419	5,153	22,416	1,577	2,456	2,786	14,266	8,611	1,736	11,752	3,231	1,445
1951	209,805	61,507	12,936	4,743	21,690	1,465	2,384	2,626	13,134	7,800	1,608	11,964	3,388	1,324
1950	195,013	55,238	11,749	4,432	20,125	1,370	2,300	2,452	12,117	6,978	1,464	11,531	3,162	1,171
1949	181,158	54,112	11,686	4,272	19,824	1,353	2,274	2,324	10,915	6,370	1,408	9,835	2,828	1,028
1948	178,313	56,061	11,996	4,155	20,654	1,436	2,266	2,311	9,755	5,723	1,505	10,416	2,823	956
1947	165,409	54,405	11,939	3,869	19,344	1,463	2,145	2,253	8,471	5,113	1,447	9,532	2,575	862
1946	147,109	49,018	11,709	3,478	18,796	1,506	1,913	2,086	7,343	4,750	1,303	7,516	2,465	754
1945	121,699	41,601	10,063	2,972	16,927	1,243	1,536	1,982	6,492	4,596	980	4,240	1,955	705
1944	109,833	37,416	8,472	2,717	15,092	1,050	1,370	1,834	6,060	4,729	791	3,526	1,834	667
1943	100,541	33,676	7,392	2,677	13,819	968	1,239	1,616	5,588	4,737	727	3,514	1,617	648
1942	89,748	28,787	5,865	2,381	11,302	743	1,037	1,354	5,192	4,692	684	4,018	1,349	623
1941	81,875	23,633	4,738	2,108	9,070	562	889	1,162	4,706	4,438	646	4,315	1,104	575
1940	71,881	20,340	3,974	1,883	7,680	414	768	1,036	4,310	4,154	625	3,442	911	573
1939	67,578	19,164	3,633	1,767	7,342	355	709	1,004	4,179	3,994	620	3,106	830	538
1938	64,641	18,888	3,392	1,697	6,969	323	699	951	4,104	3,870	622	2,810	697	523
1937	67,259	19,879	3,528	1,673	7,053	333	706	961	3,950	3,639	636	3,168	770	528
1936	62,616	18,420	2,985	1,535	6,753	265	643	864	3,759	3,365	620	2,864	703	516
1935	56,289	16,187	2,610	1,434	6,203	233	574	802	3,646	3,199	621	2,304	579	503
1934	51,894	14,182	2,248	1,367	5,837	198	527	760	3,643	3,158	615	2,009	536	494
1933	46,392	11,524	1,816	1,233	4,784	172	482	660	3,844	3,296	587	1,706	460	495
1932	49,306	11,382	2,102	1,322	5,228	252	562	817	4,416	3,753	655	1,821	445	537
1931	61,333	14,731	2,541	1,489	7,145	328	744	979	5,101	4,200	754	2,573	600	556
1930	70,968	17,964	2,788	1,450	8,322	513	878	1,039	5,552	4,397	830	2,987	703	560
1929	78,952	19,535	2,911	1,695	9,685	560	948	1,116	5,868	4,500	829	3,745	860	542

Year	Electricity	Water, other fuel, and ice	Telephone, etc. [3]	Domestic and other household service [4]	Medical care and death expenses [5]	Personal business [6]	User-operated transportation New cars and net purchases of used cars	Gasoline and oil	Other	Other transportation	Recreation	Private education and research	Religious and welfare activities	Foreign travel and remittance (net)
	205	206	207	208	209	210	211	212	213	214	215	216	217	218
1957	3,899	4,577	3,539	7,770	16,399	15,736	14,575	10,220	8,259	3,291	15,908	3,047	3,607	2,460
1956	3,606	4,447	3,239	7,345	15,293	14,520	13,260	9,558	7,741	3,217	15,161	2,848	3,441	2,399
1955	3,300	4,340	2,966	6,814	14,014	12,993	15,800	8,770	7,609	3,162	14,220	2,597	3,106	2,288
1954	3,017	4,091	2,693	6,061	13,049	11,663	11,347	8,007	6,823	3,151	13,256	2,389	2,988	2,175
1953	2,730	3,995	2,616	6,049	12,200	10,783	11,822	7,547	6,962	3,288	12,892	2,244	2,778	2,126
1952	2,453	3,976	2,386	5,704	11,252	9,586	8,872	6,705	6,329	3,259	12,257	2,109	2,696	1,623
1951	2,210	3,990	2,160	5,749	10,485	8,927	9,444	6,040	5,869	3,173	11,704	1,951	2,483	1,282
1950	1,964	3,855	1,942	5,378	9,711	8,005	10,729	5,375	5,547	3,003	11,278	1,801	2,364	1,082
1949	1,748	3,523	1,737	4,952	9,003	7,015	8,077	5,003	4,697	3,087	10,122	1,683	2,235	1,131
1948	1,561	3,911	1,579	4,986	8,674	6,560	5,724	4,435	4,442	3,193	9,808	1,553	2,227	994
1947	1,406	3,414	1,383	4,777	7,658	5,707	4,587	3,630	4,099	3,074	9,352	1,411	2,032	837
1946	1,270	2,917	1,312	3,858	6,893	4,993	2,436	3,034	3,534	3,062	8,621	1,162	1,915	770
1945	1,194	2,608	1,189	3,639	5,756	4,431	357	1,809	1,826	2,853	6,139	974	1,735	1,621
1944	1,125	2,450	1,077	3,353	5,383	4,141	322	1,384	1,339	2,803	5,422	972	1,667	1,004
1943	1,045	2,386	973	2,927	4,832	3,881	410	1,339	1,110	2,680	4,961	957	1,428	555
1942	1,017	2,235	825	2,660	4,312	3,743	415	2,090	1,076	1,948	4,677	813	1,207	316
1941	965	2,042	695	2,255	3,852	3,894	2,706	2,649	1,676	1,407	4,239	702	1,060	629
1940	910	1,908	615	2,120	3,533	3,646	2,217	2,273	1,382	1,271	3,761	641	1,012	223
1939	849	1,741	576	1,984	3,347	3,548	1,679	2,181	1,268	1,237	3,452	628	938	317
1938	810	1,638	542	1,845	3,172	3,472	1,228	2,145	1,080	1,180	3,241	619	923	376
1937	766	1,748	542	2,003	3,180	3,663	1,988	2,143	1,157	1,229	3,381	600	900	452
1936	726	1,737	511	1,764	2,978	3,391	1,921	1,945	1,090	1,175	3,020	546	899	412
1935	697	1,592	472	1,590	2,728	3,119	1,508	1,743	966	1,064	2,630	507	862	352
1934	671	1,564	443	1,492	2,581	2,927	1,024	1,640	920	1,012	2,441	483	870	339
1933	645	1,421	436	1,303	2,370	2,912	779	1,466	790	952	2,202	481	872	367
1932	662	1,416	482	1,416	2,542	2,986	635	1,476	824	1,046	2,442	571	973	467
1931	674	1,614	554	1,854	3,029	3,497	1,144	1,540	1,063	1,256	3,302	665	1,125	601
1930	660	1,838	577	2,260	3,382	4,035	1,642	1,748	1,271	1,485	3,990	683	1,209	756
1929	616	1,886	569	2,517	3,544	5,086	2,588	1,814	1,558	1,652	4,331	664	1,196	799

[1] Includes value of food produced and consumed on farms and alcoholic beverages.
[2] Nonfarm dwellings.
[3] Telephone, telegraph, cable, and wireless.
[4] Includes cleaning and polishing preparations, and miscellaneous household supplies and paper products.
[5] Includes drug preparations and sundries, ophthalmic products, and orthopedic appliances, physicians, dentists, other professional services, privately controlled hospitals and sanitariums, and medical care and hospitalization insurance.
[6] Includes brokerage charges and interest, bank service charges, value of financial services, legal services, interest on personal debt, and other.

Series G 219–243. Personal Consumption Expenditures, by Type of Product: 1909 to 1929

[In millions of dollars]

Year	Total consumption expenditures	Food and non-alcoholic beverages	Alcoholic beverages	Tobacco products [1]	Clothing and related products Purchases	Cleaning, repair, and maintenance	Personal care	Rent and imputed rent [2]	Household equipment and operation Furniture and furnishings	Mechanical appliances	Fuel, ice, and lighting supplies	Electricity, gas, and water	Domestic services [3]
	219	220	221	222	223	224	225	226	227	228	229	230	231
1929	80,761	19,674	2,000	1,700	9,832	965	1,116	11,421	3,698	768	1,694	1,397	1,501
1927	74,569	18,318	1,800	1,617	9,894	851	1,042	11,319	3,630	667	1,882	1,230	1,429
1925	71,750	17,919	1,700	1,521	9,422	734	903	11,454	3,668	548	1,646	1,137	1,327
1923	66,594	16,138	1,500	1,476	9,575	672	873	10,613	3,589	511	2,160	1,004	1,191
1921	55,766	13,908	1,400	1,481	8,162	572	602	9,682	2,474	294	1,817	828	1,005
1919	60,573	18,554	2,000	1,429	8,413	539	615	8,045	2,841	400	1,492	707	967
1914	33,395	8,954	2,000	732	4,059	344	305	6,222	1,333	167	1,190	460	697
1909	28,814	7,369	1,800	627	3,735	281	261	5,563	1,229	145	985	362	712

Year	Household operation—Con. Communication	Cleaning, repair, and maintenance	Financial, legal, and insurance [4]	Medical care	Insurance [5]	Transportation New cars and net purchases of used cars (private)	Other private transportation [6]	Public carrier	Recreation [7]	Education (private)	Religion and welfare activities	Occupational and miscellaneous expenses
	232	233	234	235	236	237	238	239	240	241	242	243
1929	860	805	5,645	2,915	108	2,588	3,216	2,203	3,836	1,170	1,469	180
1927	721	754	3,770	2,599	91	1,995	3,114	2,081	3,141	1,007	1,447	170
1925	641	681	3,166	2,411	80	2,411	3,214	1,953	2,840	894	1,310	170
1923	557	656	2,482	2,130	65	2,289	2,406	1,819	2,624	813	1,291	160
1921	466	535	1,948	1,483	53	1,157	1,972	1,679	2,068	746	1,364	70
1919	427	625	2,073	2,019	41	1,300	2,172	1,411	2,157	751	1,455	140
1914	214	307	977	881	24	417	673	1,042	997	493	837	70
1909	174	259	870	782	17	167	493	829	859	416	819	60

[1] Includes smoking supplies.
[2] Includes rent of transient accommodations.
[3] Excludes practical nurses.
[4] Includes death expenses.
[5] Accident, health, and prepayment. 1909–1927, estimated at 11 percent of life insurance expenditures.
[6] Includes expenditures for automobile parts, repair, and maintenance, gasoline and oil, luggage, and 1909–1927 for horse-drawn vehicles and equipment, and blacksmith's services.
[7] Figures differ from comparable estimates shown in series H 500. See text for series H 500–515 for explanation.

Series G 244–330. Consumption Expenditures, in Current Prices, of Families of City Wage and Clerical Workers of 2 or More Persons, by Income Class: 1874–75 to 1950

Series No.	Item	All income classes	Income class (after taxes) Under $1,000	$1,000 to $2,000	$2,000 to $3,000	$3,000 to $4,000	$4,000 to $5,000	$5,000 to $6,000	$6,000 to $7,500	$7,500 to $10,000	$10,000 and over
	1950: FAMILIES IN CITIES OF 2,500 AND OVER										
244	Number of families in sample	7,007	64	498	1,423	2,180	1,453	749	427	164	49
245	Average family size_____persons	3.4	2.3	2.9	3.1	3.4	3.5	3.7	3.9	4.2	4.5
246	Average income after taxes	$3,923	$651	$1,629	$2,564	$3,487	$4,454	$5,434	$6,606	$8,394	$13,292
247	**Average expenditures for current consumption**	3,925	1,683	1,924	2,795	3,573	4,408	5,262	6,187	7,161	10,342
248	Food	1,205	540	690	946	1,139	1,324	1,514	1,691	1,992	2,656
249	Alcoholic beverages	70	8	25	41	58	82	102	134	158	289
250	Tobacco	79	29	50	66	73	88	96	107	130	126
251	Housing	415	283	249	336	390	454	511	590	606	976
252	Fuel, light, and refrigeration	163	122	111	140	158	174	194	208	228	287
253	Household operation	155	77	71	108	135	169	213	245	304	814
254	Furnishings and equipment	278	86	117	193	242	331	388	462	435	805
255	Clothing	453	131	197	286	385	508	648	822	1,026	1,588
	Transportation:										
256	Automobile	472	107	131	248	421	561	737	887	1,052	1,002
257	Other	69	25	37	53	56	73	98	113	158	202
258	Medical care	200	112	102	150	194	221	246	294	333	411
259	Personal care	91	35	51	69	84	99	118	132	161	212
260	Recreation	177	33	46	93	155	219	256	324	397	605
261	Reading	34	14	17	26	33	38	44	50	55	80
262	Education	17	1	6	7	14	20	29	39	43	84
263	Miscellaneous	47	81	25	34	37	49	70	89	84	206

Series G 244–330. Consumption Expenditures, in Current Prices, of Families of City Wage and Clerical Workers of 2 or More Persons, by Income Class: 1874–75 to 1950—Con.

Series No.	Item	All income classes	Income class (before taxes)									
			$500 to $600	$600 to $900	$900 to $1,200	$1,200 to $1,500	$1,500 to $1,800	$1,800 to $2,100	$2,100 to $2,400	$2,400 to $2,700	$2,700 to $3,000	$3,000 and over
	1934–36: FAMILIES OF EMPLOYED WORKERS IN CITIES (50,000 INHABITANTS OR MORE)											
264	Number of families in sample	14,469	116	1,215	2,952	3,444	2,937	2,185	810	391	188	231
265	Average family size __persons	3.6	3.1	3.2	3.4	3.5	3.6	3.8	4.0	4.3	4.4	4.8
266	Average income	$1,518	$550	$775	$1,062	$1,348	$1,634	$1,928	$2,241	$2,507	$2,867	$3,450
267	**Average expenditures for current consumption**	1,463	637	832	1,081	1,332	1,576	1,804	2,075	2,305	2,550	3,093
268	Food and alcoholic beverages	508	250	315	398	472	540	597	683	756	837	1,021
269	Tobacco	29	11	15	20	26	31	36	44	51	58	75
270	Housing	259	132	169	215	246	281	300	324	346	370	411
271	Fuel, light, and refrigeration	108	64	76	94	106	114	123	136	131	131	148
272	Household operation	58	20	30	38	49	63	77	92	102	119	142
273	Furnishings and equipment	60	13	28	39	55	70	77	90	96	83	112
274	Clothing	160	49	74	102	136	173	211	258	309	388	471
	Transportation:											
275	Automobile	87	9	20	40	73	99	137	162	161	197	212
276	Other	38	17	25	29	33	40	43	52	65	78	115
277	Medical care	59	22	33	42	53	64	78	81	97	109	115
278	Personal care	30	13	17	22	27	32	37	43	51	59	71
279	Recreation	38	11	15	23	32	40	49	62	73	88	116
280	Reading	15	6	8	11	14	16	19	23	28	31	41
281	Education	7	2	2	4	5	7	11	14	19	17	22
282	Miscellaneous	7	18	5	4	5	6	9	11	20	25	21

Series No.	Item	All income classes	Income class (after taxes)						
			Under $900	$900 to $1,200	$1,200 to $1,500	$1,500 to $1,800	$1,800 to $2,100	$2,100 to $2,500	$2,500 and over
	1917–19: FAMILIES WITH AT LEAST 1 CHILD								
283	Number of families in survey	12,096	332	2,423	3,959	2,730	1,594	705	353
284	Average family size __persons	4.9	4.3	4.7	5.0	5.1	5.7	6.4	
285	Average income after taxes	$1,505	$810	$1,070	$1,336	$1,622	$1,914	$2,261	$2,777
286	**Average expenditures for current consumption**	1,352	804	1,016	1,234	1,452	1,656	1,937	2,331
287	Food	549	372	456	516	572	627	712	860
288	Alcoholic beverages	7	4	7	7	7	7	9	16
289	Tobacco	17	12	14	15	17	20	21	28
290	Housing [1]	187	122	150	180	207	232	248	260
291	Household operation	37	18	14	32	41	51	61	63
292	Fuel, light, and refrigeration	74	57	64	73	79	87	93	102
293	Furnishings and equipment	62	28	43	54	71	79	93	105
294	Clothing	238	112	156	206	257	307	384	503
	Transportation:								
295	Automobile	16	1	4	9	18	31	50	58
296	Other	26	11	18	23	29	32	43	54
297	Medical care	64	36	46	58	71	78	87	102
298	Personal care	14	9	11	13	15	17	19	24
299	Recreation	33	8	15	25	38	52	69	97
300	Reading	11	6	8	10	11	13	15	16
301	Education	7	4	3	5	8	11	16	22
302	Miscellaneous	10	4	7	8	11	12	17	21

Series No.	Item	All income classes	Income class (before taxes)											
			Under $200	$200 to $300	$300 to $400	$400 to $500	$500 to $600	$600 to $700	$700 to $800	$800 to $900	$900 to $1,000	$1,000 to $1,100	$1,100 to $1,200	$1,200 and over
	1901: NORMAL FAMILIES													
303	Number of families	11,156	32	115	545	1,676	2,264	2,336	2,094	806	684	340	96	168
304	Average family size persons	4.0	3.2	3.4	3.8	3.8	3.9	3.9	4.0	4.2	4.1	4.3	4.0	3.8
305	Average income	$651	(2)	(2)	(2)	(2)	(2)	(2)	(2)	(2)	(2)	(2)	(2)	(2)
306	**Average expenditures for current consumption**	618	$196	$312	$389	$466	$540	$612	$693	$771	$816	$900	$973	$1,052
307	Food	266	100	148	187	218	249	266	287	319	326	349	367	384
308	Rent	112	33	56	73	87	100	113	126	132	144	158	161	183
309	Fuel	28	13	19	23	26	27	28	29	30	31	34	35	41
310	Light	7	2	4	4	5	6	7	8	8	9	10	11	12
311	Clothing	80	17	27	39	53	65	79	94	105	117	136	145	165
312	Sundries	124	31	59	63	77	93	119	150	177	189	213	254	267

[1] Excludes 301 families whose rent included the cost of either heat or light or both.   [2] Not available.

Series G 244–330. Consumption Expenditures, in Current Prices, of Families of City Wage and Clerical Workers of 2 or More Persons, by Income Class: 1874–75 to 1950—Con.

Series No.	Item	All income classes	Income class (before taxes)						
			Under $200	$200 to $400	$400 to $600	$600 to $800	$800 to $1,000	$1,000 to $1,200	$1,200 and over
	1888–91: NORMAL FAMILIES OF WORKERS IN 9 BASIC INDUSTRIES								
313	Number of families in sample	2,562	24	500	1,168	492	206	86	86
314	Average family size_____persons	3.9	3.4	3.7	3.9	3.9	4.1	4.2	4.3
315	Average money income	$573	$156	$335	$486	$674	$883	$1,064	$1,450
316	**Average expenditures for current consumption**	534	233	363	476	608	746	878	1,128
317	Food	219	116	165	212	245	271	295	323
318	Housing	80	36	54	73	95	116	126	142
319	Fuel and light	32	18	26	31	34	37	38	34
320	Clothing	82	30	51	70	97	119	151	177
321	Sundries	121	33	67	90	137	203	268	452

Series No.	Item	All income classes	Income class (before taxes)				
			$300 to $450	$450 to $600	$600 to $750	$750 to $1,200	$1,200 and over
	1874–75: MASSACHUSETTS—FAMILIES OF WAGE EARNERS IN 15 CITIES AND 21 TOWNS						
322	Number of families in sample	397	6	52	143	188	8
323	Average family size_____persons	5.1	5.0	5.2	4.8	5.3	6.9
324	Average money income	$763	$395	$549	$679	$871	$1,383
325	Average expenditures for goods and services	738	410	555	668	832	1,212
326	Subsistence [1]	427	262	350	401	466	618
327	Clothing	106	29	58	94	125	230
328	Rent	117	82	86	94	141	182
329	Fuel	44	25	33	40	50	60
330	Sundry expenses	44	12	28	40	50	121

[1] Includes kerosene.

Series G 331–352. Consumption Expenditures, in 1950 Prices, of Families of City Wage and Clerical Workers of 2 or More Persons: 1888–91 to 1950

Series No.	Item	1950 [1]	1934–36 [1]	1917–19 [2]	1901 [3]	1888–91 [4]	Series No.	Item	1950 [1]	1934–36 [1]	1917–19 [2]
331	Number of families covered	5,994	14,469	12,096	11,156	2,562		**AVERAGE OUTLAYS—Con.**			
332	Average family size_____persons	3.3	3.6	[5] 4.9	[6] 4.0	[6] 3.9		**Current outlays for goods and services—Con.**			
							341	Fuel, light, refrigeration, and water	153	158	126
	AVERAGE MONEY RECEIPTS						342	Housefurnishings and equipment	281	119	109
333	Money income before personal taxes	$4,299	$2,661				343	Household operation	167	80	
334	Total receipts, after taxes	4,038	2,663				344	Automobile purchase and operation	457	150	
335	Money income	4,005	2,659	$2,408	$1,914	$1,793	345	Other transportation	81	57	
336	Other receipts	33	4				346	Medical care	213	88	
	AVERAGE OUTLAYS						347	Personal care	93	55	
											479
337	**Current outlays for goods and services**	4,076	2,564	2,163	1,817	1,671	348	Recreation	191	67	
338	Food and drink	1,335	1,030	854	952	797	349	Reading	36	27	
339	Clothing	473	309	343			350	Education	19	11	
340	Shelter (current expense)	448	356	252			351	Tobacco	80	46	
							352	Miscellaneous goods and services	49	11	

[1] Derived from Faith M. Williams, "Standards and Levels of Living of City-Worker Families," *Monthly Labor Review*, Sept. 1956. Figures do not correspond to those given in series G 244–263 because these relate to wage and clerical workers' families in large cities only; those in G 244–263 relate, in addition, to such families in suburbs and small cities.
[2] Derived from Bureau of Labor Statistics, *Cost of Living in the United States*, Bulletin No. 357.
[3] Derived from Departments of Commerce and Labor, Eighteenth Annual Report of the Commissioner of Labor, *Cost of Living and Retail Prices of Food*.
[4] Derived from the Sixth Annual Report of the Commissioner of Labor, 1890, *Cost of Production*, part III, "Cost of Living"; and Seventh Annual Report of the Commissioner of Labor, 1891, *Cost of Production*, vol. II, part III, "Cost of Living."
[5] Families of 3 or more persons.
[6] Refers to "normal" families; see text, series G 303–321.

Series G 353-426. Consumption Expenditures, in Current Prices, of All Families of 2 or More Persons in Cities of 2,500 and Over, by Income Class: 1935-36 to 1950

Series No.	Item	All income classes	Income class (after taxes)								
			Under $1,000	$1,000 to $2,000	$2,000 to $3,000	$3,000 to $4,000	$4,000 to $5,000	$5,000 to $6,000	$6,000 to $7,500	$7,500 to $10,000	$10,000 and over
	1950: FAMILIES										
353	Number of families in sample	10,791	284	982	1,962	2,807	2,058	1,191	793	425	289
354	Average family size persons	3.3	2.4	2.7	3.1	3.3	3.5	3.7	3.7	4.0	3.7
355	Average income after taxes	$4,224	$622	$1,556	$2,549	$3,492	$4,464	$5,449	$6,638	$8,432	$15,932
356	**Average expenditures for current consumption**	4,119	1,863	1,892	2,809	3,613	4,469	5,277	6,062	7,160	10,808
357	Food	1,221	605	679	944	1,135	1,313	1,498	1,648	1,925	2,423
358	Alcoholic beverages	67	15	20	37	55	74	96	112	140	223
359	Tobacco	74	25	41	60	71	85	88	95	103	112
360	Housing	455	278	262	343	408	485	536	620	704	1,146
361	Fuel, light, and refrigeration	172	137	126	146	161	179	196	211	242	306
362	Household operation	191	89	79	114	144	184	235	281	389	968
363	Furnishings and equipment	290	105	103	190	242	334	383	438	456	906
364	Clothing	476	131	168	282	388	511	649	776	971	1,535
	Transportation:										
365	Automobile	490	133	120	252	422	572	728	841	973	1,172
366	Other	69	22	35	51	57	70	89	103	140	199
367	Medical care	215	142	111	154	202	227	256	302	378	453
368	Personal care	92	37	46	68	84	99	116	129	150	203
369	Recreation	185	40	45	92	155	217	251	317	365	598
370	Reading	37	19	18	27	34	40	45	52	59	83
371	Education	26	9	4	9	15	26	35	48	70	166
372	Miscellaneous	60	76	34	41	39	53	76	88	95	316

Series No.	Item	All income classes	Income class (after taxes)								
			Under $500	$500 to $1,000	$1,000 to $1,500	$1,500 to $2,000	$2,000 to $2,500	$2,500 to $3,000	$3,000 to $4,000	$4,000 to $5,000	$5,000 and over
	1944: FAMILIES										
373	Percent of families in each class	100.0	1.5	5.2	5.3	10.7	14.0	14.7	23.0	11.2	14.4
374	Average number of persons [1]	3.42	2.45	2.45	2.78	3.03	3.10	3.13	3.69	4.01	4.13
375	Average income after taxes	$3,411	$313	$776	$1,243	$1,779	$2,259	$2,757	$3,480	$4,408	$7,595
376	**Average expenditures for current consumption**	2,633	887	1,053	1,407	1,788	2,051	2,410	2,838	3,439	4,305
377	Food and beverages [2]	947	374	434	555	701	797	913	1,043	1,150	1,386
378	Tobacco	52	16	15	21	41	41	48	59	71	76
379	Clothing	430	42	80	163	234	283	364	462	623	848
380	Housing, fuel, light, and refrigeration [3]	450	257	251	298	341	394	430	488	547	616
381	Household operation	138	56	47	66	83	93	110	140	166	295
382	Furnishings and equipment	89	5	25	39	49	60	88	95	132	157
	Transportation:										
383	Automobile	104	16	19	29	42	69	105	119	177	171
384	Other	61	7	20	26	44	50	51	63	84	109
385	Medical care	148	62	88	94	105	104	123	149	190	265
386	Personal care	63	21	19	33	41	48	56	65	84	110
387	Recreation	75	3	15	28	46	55	63	82	105	137
388	Reading	28	14	13	14	18	22	27	31	37	43
389	Education, formal	17	1	2	2	11	9	15	13	29	42
390	Other	32	13	25	39	32	26	17	29	44	50

Series No.	Item	All income classes	Income class (before taxes)								
			Under $500	$500 to $1,000	$1,000 to $1,500	$1,500 to $2,000	$2,000 to $2,500	$2,500 to $3,000	$3,000 to $5,000	$5,000 to $10,000	$10,000 and over
	1941: FAMILIES										
391	Estimated number of families 1,000	20,419	750	2,237	2,703	3,735	3,472	2,816	3,384	524	798
392	Average family size [1] persons	3.44	2.64	3.17	3.05	3.39	3.30	3.70	3.71	4.43	4.62
393	Average money income	$2,672	$323	$736	$1,257	$1,756	$2,240	$2,745	$3,726	$6,208	$14,196
394	**Average expenditures for current consumption**	2,290	457	781	1,288	1,662	2,137	2,572	3,234	4,717	8,731
395	Food and beverages [2]	706	183	324	468	575	666	839	949	1,330	1,943
396	Tobacco	48	9	15	34	40	49	52	71	108	97
397	Housing, fuel, light, and refrigeration	423	123	185	290	354	418	458	526	696	1,433
398	Household operation	120	20	31	44	70	84	104	162	262	890
399	Furnishings and equipment	122	9	30	67	80	116	163	210	202	329
400	Clothing	278	26	69	139	191	233	310	432	663	1,146
	Transportation:										
401	Automobile	223	23	39	78	112	239	264	353	495	996
402	Other	53	5	12	27	31	36	62	62	138	356
403	Personal care	50	8	17	27	36	45	55	74	106	188
404	Medical care	107	33	29	58	85	113	90	154	244	399
405	Recreation	101	9	14	32	51	78	105	155	297	633
406	Reading	23	6	7	13	19	21	26	32	51	82
407	Education	18	1	5	2	6	16	18	34	89	174
408	Other	18	2	4	9	12	23	26	20	36	65

[1] Family size is based on equivalent persons, with 52 weeks of family membership considered equivalent to 1 person; 26 weeks equivalent to 0.5 person, etc.   [2] Includes alcoholic beverages.

[3] Includes rent for tenant-occupied dwellings and for lodging away from home, and current operation expenses of homeowners. Excludes principal payment on mortgages on owned homes.

Series G 353–426. Consumption Expenditures, in Current Prices, of All Families of 2 or More Persons in Cities of 2,500 and Over, by Income Class: 1935–36 to 1950—Con.

Series No.	Item	Income class (money plus nonmoney, before taxes)											
		Under $500	$500 to $750	$750 to $1,000	$1,000 to $1,250	$1,250 to $1,500	$1,500 to $1,750	$1,750 to $2,000	$2,000 to $2,500	$2,500 to $3,000	$3,000 to $4,000	$4,000 to $5,000	$5,000 to $10,000
	1935–36: FAMILIES												
409	Number of families	780	1,448	2,284	3,009	3,310	3,168	3,270	5,299	2,617	2,635	1,036	878
410	Average family size_____persons	3.1	3.4	3.5	3.5	3.6	3.6	3.7	3.7	3.9	4.0	4.2	4.1
411	Average family income	$329	$649	$886	$1,134	$1,374	$1,626	$1,875	$2,235	$2,733	$3,454	$4,438	$6,912
412	**Average expenditures for current consumption**	593	739	934	1,152	1,350	1,567	1,769	2,043	2,411	2,882	3,523	5,050
413	Food and beverages	232	290	354	414	472	519	568	627	706	793	899	1,143
414	Tobacco	11	15	21	26	30	34	37	42	46	51	56	68
415	Housing	147	167	198	236	268	308	342	385	447	538	643	963
416	Housing operation	77	96	116	138	155	174	198	225	272	346	439	676
417	Furnishings	10	16	30	41	51	59	72	79	91	99	115	176
418	Clothing	39	54	73	100	122	152	174	215	266	342	430	601
	Transportation:												
419	Automobile	11	18	35	62	80	112	143	187	235	281	371	543
420	Other	7	9	13	15	19	22	23	26	31	36	46	67
421	Medical care	26	30	39	47	61	74	81	98	115	142	186	284
422	Personal care	13	17	21	26	30	35	39	45	53	63	72	98
423	Recreation	8	12	18	26	35	44	54	67	87	113	151	245
424	Education	2	3	3	5	7	10	12	17	27	36	59	104
425	Reading	6	8	10	12	15	17	19	21	25	29	36	45
426	Other items	4	4	3	4	5	7	7	9	10	13	20	37

Series G 427–507. Consumption Expenditures, in Current Prices, of Farm-Operator Families, by Income Class: 1922–1924 to 1955

Series No.	Item	All income classes	Income class (after taxes)									
			Under $1,000				$1,000 to $1,499	$1,500 to $1,999	$2,000 to $2,999	$3,000 to $3,999	$4,000 to $7,499	$7,500 and over
			Total	Under $250	$250 to $499	$500 to $999						
	1955: FAMILIES OF 2 OR MORE PERSONS											
427	Number of families represented by sample 1,000	4,534	1,111	399	193	519	480	469	822	594	663	173
428	Average family size_____persons	4.0	3.5	3.6	3.6	3.4	3.7	3.9	4.2	4.3	4.4	4.4
429	**Average expenditures for current consumption**	$2,984	$1,887	$2,238	$1,716	$1,680	$2,077	$2,513	$2,952	$3,395	$4,459	$6,560
430	Food and beverages	868	612	690	598	558	653	781	857	982	1,204	1,592
431	Tobacco	51	38	43	38	34	44	50	52	57	66	70
432	Dwelling upkeep	195	119	160	91	98	124	143	173	204	324	552
433	Housefurnishings and equipment	213	122	126	105	125	145	183	219	244	330	505
434	Fuel, light, refrigeration, water	193	136	169	114	118	148	179	201	222	256	321
435	Other household operation	114	69	83	70	58	79	92	111	123	172	312
436	Clothing	419	249	290	232	224	281	369	430	459	630	973
	Transportation:											
437	Automobile and truck	370	175	204	159	157	207	258	352	466	669	976
438	Other	17	6	6	5	6	9	12	18	21	24	78
439	Medical care	248	196	262	162	157	196	213	252	274	322	437
440	Personal care	71	44	50	42	41	52	63	71	76	107	158
441	Recreation	126	64	77	59	57	77	96	126	158	202	323
442	Reading	19	11	14	9	10	14	17	19	22	28	46
443	Education	25	11	15	5	9	15	22	24	29	42	80
444	Other goods and services	52	36	51	25	28	35	34	47	59	83	137

Series No.	Item	All income classes[1]	Income class (before taxes)							
			0 to $250	$250 to $499	$500 to $749	$750 to $999	$1,000 to $1,499	$1,500 to $1,999	$2,000 to $2,999	$3,000 to $4,999
	1941: FAMILIES OF 2 OR MORE PERSONS									
445	Number of farm-operator families	733	104	135	102	85	110	79	64	28
446	Average family size_____persons	4.15	3.93	3.95	4.11	4.16	4.74	4.39	3.56	4.54
447	Average money income	$1,163	$139	$378	$628	$866	$1,226	$1,701	$2,441	$3,776
448	**Average expenditures for current consumption**	841	313	451	617	806	921	1,207	1,562	1,836
449	Food and beverages	254	114	152	193	258	295	340	444	467
450	Tobacco	17	9	14	13	17	17	22	27	24
451	Housing	22	4	12	19	22	25	26	45	44
452	Fuel, light, and refrigeration	53	16	26	40	55	60	77	97	109
453	Other household operation	35	12	15	22	33	37	47	72	94
454	Furnishings and equipment	67	15	30	44	62	74	117	138	144
455	Clothing	139	58	83	112	128	152	180	234	308
	Transportation:									
456	Automobile	104	16	42	74	98	103	187	220	307
457	Other	7	5	4	8	3	7	9	12	4
458	Medical care	62	30	35	41	60	65	96	116	126
459	Personal care	20	7	11	15	19	21	29	37	50
460	Recreation	27	8	12	16	19	32	40	48	109
461	Reading	8	3	4	5	8	8	11	15	16
462	Formal education	9	2	5	6	7	9	11	10	20
463	Miscellaneous	17	14	6	9	17	16	15	47	14

[1] Includes a small number of families with negative incomes and incomes of $5,000 or more, not shown separately.

Series G 427–507. Consumption Expenditures, in Current Prices, of Farm-Operator Families, by Income Class: 1922–1924 to 1955—Con.

Series No.	Item	Income class (money plus nonmoney, before taxes)											
		Under $500	$500 to $750	$750 to $1,000	$1,000 to $1,250	$1,250 to $1,500	$1,500 to $1,750	$1,750 to $2,000	$2,000 to $2,500	$2,500 to $3,000	$3,000 to $4,000	$4,000 to $5,000	$5,000 to $10,000
	1935–36: FAMILIES												
464	Number of farm-operator families	2,548	2,616	2,390	1,821	1,510	1,111	761	1,011	538	466	143	108
465	Average family size_____persons	4.0	4.4	4.4	4.5	4.6	4.5	4.5	4.6	4.6	4.6	4.7	4.8
466	Average income per family	$339	$633	$878	$1,127	$1,374	$1,620	$1,864	$2,218	$2,716	$3,390	$4,396	$6,587
467	**Average expenditures for current consumption**	537	720	919	1,113	1,266	1,404	1,528	1,704	1,881	2,149	2,395	2,946
468	Food and beverages	288	393	474	537	585	610	635	681	729	788	850	868
469	Tobacco	10	13	14	16	16	17	17	20	22	20	24	33
470	Housing	51	67	96	128	152	188	212	244	256	319	376	488
471	Household operation	54	65	79	97	111	123	135	146	163	182	205	302
472	Furnishings	12	16	21	29	38	43	51	58	73	86	90	117
473	Clothing	47	64	83	104	125	137	148	174	191	221	280	348
	Transportation:												
474	Automobile	31	40	65	88	106	132	158	181	217	253	254	395
475	Other	1	2	2	2	3	3	4	5	6	6	11	14
476	Medical care	22	29	40	50	55	64	77	83	90	111	106	152
477	Personal care	7	9	13	17	20	22	23	27	30	35	42	48
478	Recreation	6	9	14	21	26	32	33	43	51	60	78	87
479	Education	2	4	8	11	12	15	16	23	30	37	46	57
480	Reading	3	4	5	7	8	9	9	11	12	13	16	20
481	Other items	3	5	5	6	9	9	10	8	11	18	17	17

Series No.	Item	All income classes	Income class (money plus nonmoney, before taxes)						
			Under $1,000	$1,000 to $1,500	$1,500 to $2,000	$2,000 to $3,000	$3,000 to $4,000	$4,000 to $5,000	$5,000 to $7,000	$7,000 to $10,000
	1929: FAMILIES									
482	Estimated number of families____1,000	5,796	3,164	1,005	607	614	230	102	59	15
483	**Average expenditures for current consumption**	$990	$602	$1,130	$1,359	$1,634	$1,983	$2,216	$2,407	$2,800
484	Food	439	336	491	550	611	665	706	729	800
485	Home	234	119	260	339	435	570	637	678	733
486	Attire	146	75	180	209	261	322	363	373	467
487	Other	171	73	200	260	327	426	510	627	800

Series No.	Item	All families	Value of goods purchased and goods furnished in kind								
			Under $600	$600 to $899	$900 to $1,199	$1,200 to $1,499	$1,500 to $1,799	$1,800 to $2,099	$2,100 to $2,399	$2,400 to $2,699	$2,700 to $2,999	$3,000 and over
	1922–1924: VALUE OF CURRENT CONSUMPTION OF FARM-OPERATOR FAMILIES IN 11 STATES											
488	Number of farm-operator families	2,886	58	280	579	614	492	332	196	116	83	136
489	Average family size_____persons	4.4	3.0	3.4	3.7	4.1	4.8	4.8	5.3	5.4	5.7	6.2
490	Average size of household____do	4.8	3.3	3.6	4.0	4.5	5.1	5.3	5.9	6.0	6.5	7.0
491	Average value, all goods____dollars	1,598	486	779	1,055	1,339	1,639	1,932	2,240	2,529	2,854	3,779
492	**Average expenditures for current consumption____do**	1,556	484	769	1,038	1,315	1,597	1,884	2,171	2,446	2,771	3,609
493	Food____do	658	264	406	502	606	705	769	833	916	959	1,160
494	Clothing____do	235	56	93	133	185	248	298	354	392	457	620
495	Rent____do	200	61	90	137	170	200	261	282	311	374	412
496	Furniture and furnishings____do	40	7	12	22	31	48	48	63	71	80	110
497	Operation goods____do	212	64	110	150	182	211	257	302	344	354	472
498	Maintenance____do	61	10	20	32	47	56	75	103	96	191	181
499	Advancement____do	105	9	21	38	59	90	122	168	248	277	506
500	Personal____do	42	11	16	24	32	38	48	58	63	77	144
501	Unclassified____do	3	--------	1	--------	3	2	6	7	5	3	4
	Proportion of living:											
502	Furnished by farm____percent	42.8	55.6	52.9	48.9	46.3	44.0	42.1	39.5	38.2	38.1	31.7
503	Purchased____do	57.2	44.4	47.1	51.1	53.7	56.0	57.9	60.5	61.8	61.9	68.3
	Proportion of food:											
504	Furnished by farm____do	66.9	69.0	70.6	67.9	67.5	67.5	66.0	65.5	64.7	67.8	63.2
505	Purchased____do	33.1	31.0	29.4	32.1	32.5	32.5	34.0	34.5	35.3	32.2	36.8
	Number of rooms:											
506	Per household	6.8	4.4	5.4	6.2	6.6	7.0	7.5	7.9	8.2	8.2	8.6
507	Per person	1.4	1.3	1.5	1.5	1.5	1.4	1.4	1.3	1.4	1.3	1.2

Series G 508–543. Consumption Expenditures, in Current Prices, of Families and Single Consumers Combined, by Income Class: 1929 to 1941

Series No.	Item	All income classes [1]	Income class (before taxes)					
			Under $500	$500 to $1,000	$1,000 to $1,500	$1,500 to $2,000	$2,000 to $3,000	$3,000 to $5,000
	1941							
508	**Average expenditures for current consumption**	$1,666	$374	$740	$1,173	$1,566	$2,214	$3,088
509	Food and beverages	516	144	272	402	521	693	894
510	Tobacco	35	9	18	27	37	47	65
511	Housing, fuel, light, and refrigeration	290	63	135	221	295	394	494
512	Household operation	85	16	30	46	67	92	158
513	Furnishings and equipment	93	14	37	68	87	135	201
514	Clothing	205	45	85	137	184	262	410

[1] Includes a small number of families with negative incomes and incomes of $5,000 or more, not shown separately.

Series G 508–543. Consumption Expenditures, in Current Prices, of Families and Single Consumers Combined, by Income Class: 1929 to 1941–Con.

Series No.	Item	All income classes [1]	Income class (before taxes)					
			Under $500	$500 to $1,000	$1,000 to $1,500	$1,500 to $2,000	$2,000 to $3,000	$3,000 to $5,000
	1941—Con.							
	Average expenditures for current consumption—Con.							
	Transportation:							
515	Automobile	$171	$21	$56	$100	$141	$248	$359
516	Other	34	5	12	20	27	43	55
517	Medical care	84	27	40	63	86	102	152
518	Personal care	36	8	16	26	34	47	70
519	Recreation	69	12	19	33	50	85	144
520	Reading	16	3	7	12	17	22	29
521	Education	15	2	5	4	7	18	33
522	Other	17	5	8	14	13	26	24

Series No.	Item	All income classes	Income class (money plus nonmoney, before taxes)												
			Under $500	$500 to $750	$750 to $1,000	$1,000 to $1,250	$1,250 to $1,500	$1,500 to $1,750	$1,750 to $2,000	$2,000 to $2,500	$2,500 to $3,000	$3,000 to $4,000	$4,000 to $5,000	$5,000 to $10,000	$10,000 to $15,000	$15,000 and over
	1935–36															
523	**Average expenditures for current consumption**	$1,273	$420	$673	$886	$1,099	$1,285	$1,480	$1,652	$1,925	$2,269	$2,681	$3,219	$4,369	$6,060	$12,563
524	Food and beverages	428	187	285	357	415	466	510	543	601	677	753	831	1,010	1,195	2,044
525	Tobacco	24	7	13	19	24	29	31	34	39	42	49	53	63	78	118
526	Housing	241	94	135	170	208	237	272	306	352	406	489	584	807	1,258	2,437
527	Household operation	134	40	66	89	114	131	150	170	195	246	296	368	531	697	1,612
528	Furnishings	36	6	11	20	30	37	47	57	64	76	90	98	139	201	342
529	Clothing	133	32	62	84	105	129	150	169	208	254	314	406	551	821	1,775
	Transportation:															
530	Automobile	96	9	20	37	63	84	113	142	186	232	277	363	502	675	1,460
531	Other	22	9	14	17	19	22	24	26	30	30	38	46	63	131	421
532	Medical care	56	16	24	33	43	53	67	75	88	107	131	159	248	255	724
533	Personal care	26	9	15	19	23	27	31	34	41	48	53	64	85	108	197
534	Recreation	42	4	13	20	29	38	48	55	69	87	112	142	215	350	781
535	Reading	14	5	8	11	13	15	16	18	21	23	28	32	42	56	101
536	Education	13	1	3	5	7	9	11	14	18	28	34	51	72	198	444
537	Other items	8	1	4	5	6	8	10	9	13	13	17	22	41	37	107

Series No.	Item	All income classes	Income class (money plus nonmoney, before taxes)							
			Under $1,000	$1,000 to $1,500	$1,500 to $2,000	$2,000 to $3,000	$3,000 to $4,000	$4,000 to $5,000	$5,000 to $7,000	$7,000 to $10,000	$10,000 and over
	1929										
538	Estimated number of families....1,000..	36,462	10,020	7,782	5,993	6,059	2,695	1,350	1,190	626	747
539	**Average expenditures for current consumption**	$2,062	$767	$1,218	$1,596	$2,124	$2,885	$3,624	$4,583	$6,054	$18,284
540	Food	544	298	448	552	671	788	859	901	974	1,359
541	Home	590	198	334	448	600	847	1,120	1,493	1,998	5,051
542	Attire	304	118	201	265	329	422	515	639	850	2,194
543	Other	624	152	235	331	524	828	1,130	1,550	2,232	9,680

[1] Includes a small number of families with negative incomes and incomes of $5,000 or more, not shown separately.

Series G 544–551. Food Production and Consumption Indexes and Nutrients Available: 1909 to 1957

Year	Index (1947–49 = 100)		Nutrients available, per capita per day						Year	Index (1947–49 = 100)		Nutrients available, per capita per day					
	Food marketings and home consumption	Food consumption per capita	Food energy	Calcium	Vitamin A value	Thiamine	Ascorbic acid	Protein		Food marketings and home consumption	Food consumption per capita	Food energy	Calcium	Vitamin A value	Thiamine	Ascorbic acid	Protein
	544	545	546	547	548	549	550	551		544	545	546	547	548	549	550	551
			Calories	Grams	Int. units	Mgs.	Mgs.	Grams				Calories	Grams	Int. units	Mgs.	Mgs.	Grams
1957 (prel.)	113	102	3,180	1.03	7,200	1.80	108	96	1933	74	88	3,340	0.91	8,000	1.53	113	91
1956	116	104	3,220	1.03	7,400	1.84	106	97	1932	73	88	3,380	0.91	8,300	1.56	115	91
									1931	74	90	3,440	0.91	8,000	1.59	117	92
1955	110	102	3,220	1.03	7,400	1.85	108	96	1930	73	91	3,500	0.91	7,900	1.57	110	93
1954	108	101	3,200	1.03	7,400	1.83	108	96	1929	74	91	3,520	0.92	8,100	1.61	119	94
1953	106	101	3,210	1.01	7,500	1.83	110	96	1928	74	91	3,540	0.90	7,700	1.60	111	94
1952	104	100	3,240	1.03	7,500	1.89	107	95	1927	73	91	3,510	0.90	8,000	1.58	112	95
1951	101	98	3,200	1.01	7,500	1.88	110	94	1926	72	92	3,510	0.90	7,800	1.55	111	95
1950	100	100	3,300	1.02	8,000	1.88	108	95	1925	70	91	3,500	0.89	7,300	1.56	112	95
1949	100	99	3,240	1.03	8,000	1.91	112	94	1924	73	92	3,510	0.89	7,300	1.63	114	96
1948	98	99	3,250	1.03	8,100	1.90	116	94	1923	71	91	3,490	0.88	7,700	1.64	115	96
1947	102	102	3,320	1.06	8,400	1.96	125	97	1922	68	89	3,480	0.89	7,900	1.56	110	94
1946	102	104	3,360	1.12	9,000	2.18	127	103	1921	65	85	3,240	0.88	7,500	1.53	108	91
1945	103	101	3,340	1.10	9,500	2.08	131	103	1920	64	87	3,330	0.89	7,500	1.55	108	94
1944	103	100	3,400	1.05	9,100	2.11	130	100	1919	67	88	3,480	0.88	7,500	1.57	104	97
1943	98	97	3,410	1.04	9,000	2.08	122	100	1918	67	87	3,420	0.90	7,200	1.62	104	97
1942	93	96	3,380	1.02	8,600	1.86	123	97	1917	62	85	3,370	0.85	7,200	1.57	101	96
1941	85	97	3,440	0.97	8,300	1.68	119	94	1916	63	86	3,430	0.83	6,900	1.59	99	96
1940	82	95	3,380	0.96	8,100	1.56	119	93	1915	62	86	3,480	0.84	7,100	1.62	107	97
1939	79	94	3,400	0.96	8,300	1.53	121	92	1914	60	87	3,490	0.85	6,800	1.60	103	98
1938	77	91	3,300	0.95	8,200	1.48	118	91	1913	59	87	3,510	0.87	6,800	1.64	104	100
1937	73	90	3,290	0.94	8,300	1.45	117	90	1912	60	89	3,510	0.89	7,000	1.67	106	102
1936	73	91	3,340	0.94	8,000	1.46	117	92	1911	59	88	3,530	0.82	6,900	1.64	101	101
1935	69	87	3,240	0.92	8,300	1.42	120	88	1910	57	88	3,500	0.85	7,100	1.65	108	102
1934	75	89	3,300	0.91	8,200	1.51	116	91	1909		89	3,580	0.87	7,100	1.70	107	104

CONSUMER INCOME AND EXPENDITURES

Series G 552–584.   Apparent Civilian Per Capita Consumption of Foods: 1849 to 1957

[In pounds, except eggs. Calendar years, except as noted]

Year	Meats (carcass weight)				Edible fats and oils				Fruits						Potatoes (farm weight)	Sweet-potatoes (farm weight)
	Total	Beef and veal	Pork, excluding lard	Lamb and mutton	Total [1] (fat content)	Lard [2]	Marga-rine [3] (actual weight)	Butter, farm and factory (actual weight)	Fresh (farm weight)		Processed					
									Total [4]	Citrus [5]	Canned fruit [6]	Canned fruit juice [7]	Dried fruit [8]	Frozen fruits and juices (product weight)		
	552	553	554	555	556	557	558	559	560	561	562	563	564	565	566	567
1957	159.1	93.4	61.5	4.2	44.4	9.5	8.6	8.4	98.3	37.0	22.4	12.2	3.6	9.0	105	7.2
1956	166.7	94.9	67.4	4.4	45.3	9.8	8.2	8.7	100.4	39.0	21.8	13.1	3.6	8.8	100	7.6
1955	162.8	91.4	66.8	4.6	45.9	10.1	8.2	9.0	101.6	41.7	22.6	12.9	3.6	8.7	106	8.2
1954	154.7	90.1	60.0	4.6	45.4	10.2	8.5	8.9	106.1	41.2	21.1	13.2	3.9	7.4	106	8.0
1953	155.3	87.1	63.5	4.7	44.1	11.4	8.1	8.5	111.3	43.4	21.3	13.6	3.7	7.1	106	8.0
1952	146.0	69.4	72.4	4.2	44.1	11.8	7.9	8.6	112.5	44.4	21.0	13.8	3.8	6.6	101	7.3
1951	138.0	62.7	71.9	3.4	42.1	12.3	6.6	9.6	115.5	45.1	19.5	14.8	3.8	4.8	113	8.1
1950	144.6	71.4	69.2	4.0	45.9	12.6	6.1	10.7	107.4	41.2	22.0	13.4	4.1	4.3	106	12.1
1949	144.6	72.8	67.7	4.1	42.6	11.8	5.8	10.5	123.3	47.8	19.7	15.1	4.1	3.5	110	11.7
1948	145.5	72.6	67.8	5.1	42.6	12.7	6.1	10.0	131.1	54.4	18.8	17.1	3.9	3.0	105	11.5
1947	155.3	80.4	69.6	5.3	42.0	12.6	5.0	11.2	142.3	62.2	18.2	15.6	3.7	3.2	127	14.5
1946	154.1	71.6	75.8	6.7	40.0	11.9	3.9	10.5	136.5	59.1	22.3	17.8	4.5	3.1	123	17.2
1945	145.2	71.3	66.6	7.3	39.1	11.7	4.1	10.9	142.0	66.6	14.4	10.9	6.0	2.3	122	18.3
1944	154.2	68.0	79.5	6.7	40.9	12.3	3.9	11.9	141.7	68.2	9.3	10.3	6.1	2.0	136	19.7
1943	146.8	61.5	78.9	6.4	42.0	13.0	3.9	11.8	119.7	60.3	12.6	7.4	5.9	1.1	125	21.4
1942	140.3	69.4	63.7	7.2	44.9	12.8	2.8	15.9	131.4	57.7	17.3	8.5	4.2	1.4	127	20.4
1941	143.7	68.5	68.4	6.8	47.6	13.8	2.8	16.1	148.9	57.7	17.8	8.5	4.3	1.3	128	18.4
1940	142.4	62.3	73.5	6.6	46.4	14.4	2.4	17.0	142.1	56.7	19.1	7.2	6.0	1.3	123	16.2
1939	133.6	62.3	64.7	6.6	46.4	12.7	2.3	17.4	151.5	61.4	16.1	5.9	6.4	1.1	122	19.7
1938	127.1	62.0	58.2	6.9	45.3	11.1	3.0	16.6	135.3	49.1	15.4	4.6	5.5	1.0	129	21.3
1937	126.2	63.8	55.8	6.6	45.5	10.5	3.1	16.8	142.5	44.5	13.5	4.5	5.8	0.5	126	21.5
1936	130.6	68.9	55.1	6.6	45.7	11.3	3.1	16.8	129.1	46.2	16.7	2.4	5.4	0.7	130	19.8
1935	117.4	61.7	48.4	7.3	44.1	9.6	3.0	17.6	136.5	44.6	13.4	2.0	5.9	0.5	142	25.6
1934	143.9	73.2	64.4	6.3	44.5	13.0	2.1	18.6	119.1	39.8	12.5	0.5	5.1	0.5	135	24.4
1933	136.1	58.6	70.7	6.8	43.0	14.0	1.9	18.2	127.2	39.4	11.8	0.5	5.2	0.5	132	24.0
1932	131.1	53.3	70.7	7.1	42.9	14.4	1.6	18.5	128.9	36.7	10.2	0.4	5.4	0.6	134	27.7
1931	130.7	55.2	68.4	7.1	44.4	13.6	1.9	18.3	163.6	42.3	10.9	0.4	4.7	0.4	136	20.6
1930	129.0	55.3	67.0	6.7	--------	12.7	2.6	17.6	133.6	31.2	12.8	0.3	5.4	0.5	132	18.3
1929	131.2	56.0	69.6	5.6	--------	12.7	2.9	17.6	143.1	39.8	12.3	0.3	5.3	0.6	159	22.4
1928	131.6	55.2	70.9	5.5	--------	13.2	2.6	17.6	150.1	29.5	12.6	0.1	6.2	0.5	147	20.7
1927	134.9	61.9	67.7	5.3	--------	12.7	2.3	18.3	129.7	32.2	12.6	0.3	6.3	0.3	141	25.0
1926	138.0	68.5	64.1	5.4	--------	12.2	2.0	18.3	164.3	31.4	12.0	0.2	6.1	0.1	128	21.1
1925	140.1	68.1	66.8	5.2	--------	12.3	2.0	18.1	135.8	28.9	11.1	0.2	6.3	0.2	157	17.7
1924	147.3	68.1	74.0	5.2	--------	14.2	2.0	17.8	151.1	33.9	8.9	0.1	6.4	--------	154	17.6
1923	147.3	67.8	74.2	5.3	--------	14.3	2.0	17.8	147.5	32.5	9.0	0.3	5.5	--------	174	24.8
1922	137.7	66.9	65.7	5.1	--------	13.3	1.7	17.1	147.9	24.6	7.5	0.2	6.6	--------	143	28.9
1921	134.0	63.1	64.8	6.1	--------	10.8	2.0	16.3	115.9	30.5	8.2	0.3	5.5	--------	156	27.2
1920	136.0	67.1	63.5	5.4	--------	12.0	3.4	14.9	145.4	26.0	9.4	0.6	6.7	--------	140	29.1
1919	138.9	69.3	63.9	5.7	--------	10.7	3.4	15.2	125.0	23.5	9.7	0.3	6.9	--------	152	29.3
1918	141.6	75.8	61.0	4.8	--------	11.8	3.3	14.1	122.0	16.5	7.5	0.4	4.4	--------	174	26.7
1917	135.3	71.9	58.9	4.5	--------	10.0	2.7	15.7	132.2	22.0	7.7	0.3	6.3	--------	146	27.9
1916	140.1	65.3	69.0	5.8	--------	11.6	1.8	17.3	136.2	22.0	7.1	0.4	5.1	--------	143	24.5
1915	134.9	62.3	66.5	6.1	--------	11.5	1.4	17.2	157.3	23.1	5.6	0.6	5.0	--------	185	25.3
1914	140.0	67.8	65.1	7.1	--------	10.6	1.4	17.0	163.8	24.1	5.7	0.1	4.1	--------	157	22.1
1913	143.7	69.6	66.9	7.2	--------	10.7	1.5	16.5	133.6	16.6	4.2	0.3	3.7	--------	189	23.6
1912	145.9	71.5	66.7	7.7	--------	11.2	1.5	16.6	159.7	18.5	4.2	0.5	4.5	--------	179	24.0
1911	151.9	75.6	69.0	7.3	--------	12.1	1.1	18.6	156.1	19.8	3.9	0.2	4.3	--------	157	24.0
1910	146.4	77.6	62.3	6.5	--------	12.5	1.6	18.3	137.9	17.8	3.6	0.5	3.5	--------	198	26.2
1909	155.2	81.5	67.0	6.7	--------	12.5	1.2	17.8	138.2	16.2	3.0	--------	4.2	--------	187	26.2
1908	163.3	79.3	77.7	6.3	--------	14.4	1.0	19.7	--------	--------	--------	--------	--------	--------	--------	--------
1907	158.2	77.8	74.1	6.3	--------	13.2	0.9	17.6	--------	--------	--------	--------	--------	--------	--------	--------
1906	155.6	78.3	71.0	6.3	--------	11.7	0.8	17.8	--------	--------	--------	--------	--------	--------	--------	--------
1905	155.2	77.9	71.0	6.3	--------	11.8	0.6	19.9	--------	--------	--------	--------	--------	--------	--------	--------
1904	152.7	75.6	70.6	6.5	--------	12.5	0.6	18.5	--------	--------	--------	--------	--------	--------	--------	--------
1903	152.1	77.0	68.2	6.9	--------	11.8	0.6	18.3	--------	--------	--------	--------	--------	--------	--------	--------
1902	144.8	71.0	66.7	7.1	--------	12.1	0.9	17.6	--------	--------	--------	--------	--------	--------	--------	--------
1901	151.1	73.3	70.8	7.0	--------	12.8	1.6	20.0	--------	--------	--------	--------	--------	--------	--------	--------
1900	150.7	72.3	71.9	6.5	--------	13.2	1.3	20.1	--------	--------	--------	--------	--------	--------	--------	--------
1899	150.7	72.4	71.8	6.5	--------	12.8	1.4	19.6	--------	--------	--------	--------	--------	--------	--------	--------

[1] Computed from unrounded numbers.
[2] Includes small quantity of lard used in other fats and oils products 1899–1908; beginning 1909 excludes quantities so used.
[3] Prior to 1909, data are for year beginning July.
[4] Beginning 1934 excludes apples from noncommercial areas. Citrus fruits on crop year 1941 to date.
[5] From 1941 to date, year begins October or November prior to year indicated.
[6] Data on pack-year basis 1909–1942, beginning early June of year indicated.
[7] Citrus juice on pack-year basis beginning November prior to year indicated and year for grape juice in 1909–1933 and 1948 to date begins November prior to year indicated.
[8] Pack-year data, beginning middle of year indicated.

Series G 552–584. Apparent Civilian Per Capita Consumption of Foods: 1849 to 1957—Con.

[In pounds, except eggs]

Year	Vegetables: Fresh (farm weight)	Canned [9]	Frozen	Melons (farm weight)	Dry beans [10]	Dairy products: Total milk for human consumption	Fluid milk and cream [11]	Condensed and evaporated milk	Cheese	Ice cream (product weight)	Eggs (number)	Chicken and turkey [12] (ready-to-cook)	Sugar, cane and beet (refined)	Wheat flour	Corn flour and meal	Peanuts (shelled) [13]	Coffee (green-bean basis)
	568	569	570	571	572	573	574	575	576	577	578	579	580	581	582	583	584
1957	104.6	43.9	7.5	25.7	7.5	691	350	15.5	7.7	17.9	358	31.4	97.1	119	8.4	4.5	15.8
1956	106.9	43.9	7.3	27.8	8.0	706	354	15.9	8.0	18.0	368	29.8	98.4	121	8.6	4.4	15.5
1955	104.6	43.5	6.6	29.2	7.3	707	352	16.2	7.9	18.0	371	26.4	97.5	123	8.8	4.1	15.3
1954	107.3	42.0	5.9	28.9	8.2	701	348	16.8	7.9	17.4	376	28.1	96.3	126	9.3	4.2	14.8
1953	108.3	43.3	5.4	28.2	7.6	692	347	17.4	7.5	18.0	379	26.7	97.9	128	9.8	4.4	16.9
1952	111.0	42.0	5.3	25.7	8.1	700	352	17.6	7.6	17.9	390	26.8	98.2	131	10.4	4.4	16.9
1951	111.6	42.2	4.3	26.1	8.1	715	352	18.3	7.2	17.4	392	26.1	93.8	133	10.8	4.6	16.5
1950	114.6	42.1	3.4	24.9	8.6	741	349	20.1	7.7	17.2	389	24.7	100.8	135	11.8	4.5	16.2
1949	115.8	39.1	3.0	26.8	6.9	734	352	19.7	7.3	17.6	383	22.9	95.8	136	12.7	4.1	18.7
1948	123.0	37.9	3.0	27.3	6.8	724	355	20.2	6.9	18.5	389	21.4	94.0	137	12.8	4.6	18.4
1947	122.4	40.5	2.6	28.0	6.5	769	369	20.4	6.9	20.1	383	21.7	95.5	139	13.1	4.5	17.4
1946	129.9	46.8	2.0	30.6	8.7	786	389	18.6	6.7	23.1	379	23.1	75.1	156	15.2	5.3	20.1
1945	133.8	43.2	1.9	29.7	7.8	788	399	18.3	6.7	15.7	402	25.1	73.9	161	17.6	6.6	16.4
1944	123.4	34.4	1.6	28.0	8.1	763	381	15.7	4.9	14.3	354	23.1	89.5	149	19.2	6.0	15.8
1943	116.4	37.0	0.7	21.7	8.9	750	371	18.8	4.9	13.1	347	25.7	80.7	163	20.5	5.7	12.9
1942	118.3	39.7	1.1	22.5	11.1	833	354	18.4	6.4	15.8	318	20.7	81.8	157	19.8	6.2	13.6
1941	113.5	36.9	0.7	24.5	8.8	803	334	18.5	5.9	13.6	311	18.3	104.3	156	20.6	4.8	15.9
1940	116.9	34.4	0.6	26.5	8.4	819	331	19.3	6.0	11.4	319	17.0	95.7	155	21.8	5.0	15.5
1939	116.6	31.8	0.5	25.4	9.3	825	332	17.8	5.9	11.0	313	16.6	100.8	158	21.7	4.4	14.9
1938	114.5	31.1	0.4	27.2	9.6	796	329	17.2	5.9	10.4	310	15.0	95.2	160	22.1	4.3	14.9
1937	111.0	29.4	0.4	28.8	7.8	798	331	16.7	5.6	10.6	308	15.9	96.4	159	23.8	4.4	13.3
1936	112.5	27.7	--------	26.4	9.0	792	330	15.9	5.4	9.5	289	15.9	97.3	163	24.2	4.6	13.7
1935	111.2	26.2	--------	27.2	8.4	801	326	16.2	5.3	8.1	280	14.8	97.1	158	24.7	4.0	13.4
1934	115.2	23.3	--------	25.6	9.1	814	322	15.0	4.9	7.1	289	15.3	93.7	157	25.3	3.3	12.3
1933	104.5	22.0	--------	25.3	7.1	814	337	13.8	4.5	6.1	296	16.7	93.7	162	25.7	3.6	12.8
1932	108.8	22.1	--------	27.1	7.4	832	339	14.0	4.4	6.3	313	16.1	94.7	170	26.5	4.1	12.4
1931	108.3	25.3	--------	32.8	8.8	838	335	13.4	4.5	8.6	333	15.5	100.5	169	26.6	4.4	13.0
1930	111.9	28.4	--------	33.0	9.5	819	337	13.6	4.7	9.8	331	17.2	109.6	171	28.3	3.2	12.5
1929	112.6	25.9	--------	32.1	7.8	811	340	13.6	4.7	10.7	334	15.7	96.9	177	30.5	4.1	12.2
1928	104.2	23.0	--------	30.6	8.6	804	337	12.3	4.4	9.9	338	14.6	103.7	179	29.9	3.8	11.9
1927	106.0	22.3	--------	30.8	8.7	813	336	11.7	4.6	9.9	342	15.2	102.4	181	28.8	3.9	12.2
1926	100.6	25.9	--------	36.4	7.6	818	338	11.8	4.6	9.5	339	14.2	104.5	182	28.9	3.4	12.4
1925	101.3	25.7	--------	34.4	7.3	802	337	11.7	4.7	9.7	318	14.3	104.3	180	29.4	3.6	10.6
1924	100.9	23.0	--------	35.7	7.8	796	336	11.9	4.6	8.8	324	13.7	99.5	180	32.4	3.5	12.6
1923	90.1	21.5	--------	29.1	5.9	787	328	11.4	4.5	9.0	326	14.6	90.5	180	35.8	3.2	12.6
1922	92.8	17.1	--------	37.3	5.1	783	342	10.9	4.3	8.2	316	14.2	104.4	180	36.4	2.7	11.8
1921	82.2	16.9	--------	34.9	4.8	768	346	9.9	4.2	7.6	300	13.4	87.3	167	34.4	2.7	12.0
1920	95.0	18.5	--------	31.8	5.7	736	348	8.6	4.0	7.6	299	13.7	85.5	179	35.2	3.0	11.7
1919	76.6	21.3	--------	24.8	5.4	733	335	9.8	4.2	6.8	303	14.2	86.6	192	35.4	4.6	11.8
1918	--------	22.3	--------	--------	7.4	725	361	10.3	3.9	6.4	284	13.3	74.6	179	49.7	2.8	10.0
1917	--------	18.9	--------	--------	7.5	729	328	9.4	3.7	4.8	281	13.3	78.0	191	46.5	4.2	12.1
1916	--------	16.1	--------	--------	5.1	747	315	9.6	3.8	4.3	299	13.8	76.8	204	45.1	2.8	11.5
1915	--------	18.0	--------	--------	5.8	751	318	9.5	4.1	3.9	313	14.4	77.6	205	44.3	2.8	10.6
1914	--------	19.2	--------	--------	6.4	747	321	8.9	4.2	3.4	295	14.5	81.0	207	45.0	2.5	9.2
1913	--------	19.8	--------	--------	6.1	754	342	7.9	4.2	3.0	303	14.5	81.3	209	45.9	2.5	9.0
1912	--------	18.7	--------	--------	6.8	763	355	7.1	3.9	2.7	312	14.9	75.9	211	47.8	2.3	10.8
1911	--------	15.6	--------	--------	6.3	749	301	6.4	4.0	2.3	329	15.6	77.4	213	49.6	2.3	8.3
1910	--------	14.5	--------	--------	6.5	759	315	5.8	4.3	1.9	306	15.5	75.4	214	51.1	2.5	9.2
1909	--------	15.3	--------	--------	6.8	770	343	5.5	3.8	1.6	293	14.7	73.7	217	53.0	2.4	--------
1908	--------	--------	--------	--------	--------	--------	--------	5.1	3.8	--------	--------	--------	81.2	--------	--------	--------	--------
1907	--------	--------	--------	--------	--------	--------	--------	4.7	3.5	--------	--------	--------	77.5	--------	--------	--------	--------
1906	--------	--------	--------	--------	--------	--------	--------	4.4	3.5	--------	--------	--------	76.1	--------	--------	--------	--------
1905	--------	--------	--------	--------	--------	--------	--------	4.1	4.1	--------	--------	--------	70.5	--------	--------	--------	--------
1904	--------	--------	--------	--------	--------	--------	--------	3.8	4.1	--------	--------	--------	75.3	--------	--------	--------	--------
1903	--------	--------	--------	--------	--------	--------	--------	3.5	4.0	--------	--------	--------	70.9	--------	--------	--------	--------
1902	--------	--------	--------	--------	--------	--------	--------	3.2	4.0	--------	--------	--------	72.8	--------	--------	--------	--------
1901	--------	--------	--------	--------	--------	--------	--------	3.0	4.5	--------	--------	--------	68.7	--------	--------	--------	--------
1900	--------	--------	--------	--------	--------	--------	--------	2.7	3.7	--------	--------	--------	65.2	--------	--------	--------	--------
1899	--------	--------	--------	--------	--------	--------	--------	2.5	3.7	--------	--------	--------	62.6	--------	--------	--------	--------

Year	Butter (actual weight) 559	Cheese 576	Sugar, cane and beet (refined) 580	Year	Butter (actual weight) 559	Cheese 576	Sugar, cane and beet (refined) 580	Year	Butter (actual weight) 559	Cheese 576	Sugar, cane and beet (refined) 580
1898	19.8	3.4	61.5	1887	16.3	3.2	52.7	1876	14.5	2.6	38.5
1897	20.8	3.6	64.8	1886	16.8	2.8	56.9	1875	12.4	3.1	40.3
1896	22.2	2.9	62.5	1885	16.1	3.0	51.8	1874	13.4	2.6	--------
1895	18.4	2.9	63.4	1884	15.3	3.1	53.4	1873	13.4	2.9	--------
1894	15.4	2.9	66.7	1883	15.2	3.3	51.1	1872	10.6	3.0	--------
1893	15.5	2.9	64.4	1882	13.9	3.1	48.4	1871	11.7	2.4	--------
1892	15.9	3.7	63.8	1881	15.2	3.2	44.2	1870	10.7	3.2	--------
1891	16.7	3.5	66.3	1880	15.5	2.7	42.7	1869	13.6	3.0	--------
1890	18.2	3.8	52.8	1879	15.6	2.2	38.1	1859	14.8	2.9	--------
1889	20.5	3.5	51.8	1878	14.6	3.5	38.6	1849	13.7	4.1	--------
1888	16.0	3.5	56.7	1877	14.4	2.7	46.1				

[9] For 1909–1942, calendar-year data were derived from pack-year data by combining proportional parts of each pack-year involved.
[10] Cleaned basis.
[11] Cream included on whole-milk equivalent basis.
[12] Chicken only 1909–1928, but turkey consumption very small during that time.
[13] On September-August year through 1939; August-July year thereafter.

Social Statistics

SOCIAL SECURITY AND WELFARE (Series H 1–222)

H 1–222. General note.

The concept of social welfare used in these series, and more particularly in series H 1–45, includes all governmental programs directed specifically toward promoting the well-being of individuals and families. Except for the veterans program, social welfare activities in the United States remained largely a local responsibility throughout most of the 19th century. State governments began to establish separate State institutions for the mentally ill and other dependent groups in the late 1850's and State boards of health were in operation in a number of States by 1900. State laws authorizing pensions for the blind, for orphans and their mothers, and for the aged were adopted in a number of States during the period 1900–1930. Workmen's compensation spread rapidly between 1911 and 1920. Special retirement systems for State and local government employees, principally teachers, policemen, and firemen, were in existence in a few localities before 1900. The civil service retirement system for Federal employees was established in 1920.

It was not until the Social Security Act of 1935, however, that the Federal Government participated in any major way in permanent welfare programs for the general population. The Social Security Act established a national system of old-age insurance (now old-age, survivors, and disability insurance) and a Federal-State system of unemployment insurance, and provided Federal grants-in-aid to the States for public assistance, child health and welfare services, general public health services, and vocational rehabilitation services.

Since 1936, a substantial volume of statistical data relating to old-age, survivors, and disability insurance, unemployment insurance, and public assistance is available from the operating records of the administering agencies. Statistics based on operating data can also be obtained for the railroad retirement program, the civil service retirement program, and the four State temporary disability insurance programs. Estimates of expenditures under State workmen's compensation programs and State and local employee retirement systems since 1934 have been made by the Social Security Administration.

The principal source of statistics of social insurance and welfare programs is the Social Security Administration, which presents annual figures in the *Annual Statistical Supplement* to the monthly *Social Security Bulletin* (for the years 1939–1948 in the *Social Security Yearbook;* for 1949–1954, in the September 1950–1955 issues of the *Bulletin;* since 1956, issued separately), and in annual articles in the October issues of the *Social Security Bulletin* (since 1955).

Figures shown for recent years are subject to revision. All figures represent the latest estimates available and may differ from those shown in the sources cited. In all such cases, the revised figures were obtained from the Social Security Administration records or estimates.

H 1–29. Social welfare expenditures under civilian public programs, 1890–1956.

Source: 1935, 1940, 1945, and 1950–1956, Social Security Administration, *Social Security Bulletin*, October issues; all other years, Social Security Administration, records.

Estimates presented for 1890, 1913, and 1929 were primarily based on the following: R. A. Musgrave and J. M. Culbertson, "The Growth of Public Expenditures in the U. S., 1890–1948," *National Tax Journal*, June 1953; and J. Frederic Dewhurst and Associates, *America's Needs and Resources*, Twentieth Century Fund, New York, 1955; and reports of official agencies.

Scattered data relating to social welfare programs in particular localities or States may be found in other sources. The definitions used in these sources, however, are highly variable and the original source of the data is frequently not indicated. Further historical study might yield some additional quantitative information, but no data comparable to those shown for later years are readily available.

The data for education, workmen's compensation, and State and local retirement programs relate to continental United States. For the other programs, some payments and expenditures outside continental United States are included, primarily payments in Territories covered by the programs and payments to beneficiaries living in other countries.

Estimates of expenditures for public assistance and for other public aid in the 1930's differ in various sources because different accounting concepts were used. There are differences in methods of allocating work program expenditures by years and in treatment of funds from the Federal Emergency Relief Administration. In some sources, FERA funds are treated as general relief payments (and therefore as State and local expenditures for public assistance); in others, they are treated as other public aid from Federal funds. The estimates for the 1930's shown here (series H 13–15) correspond to those in the National Resources Planning Board report, *Security, Work, and Relief Policies*, 1942, appendix 19, except for the substitution of more recent estimates of the value of surplus commodities and minor revisions of some figures on public assistance payments. See also text for series H 186–198 and H 199–206.

The estimates for health and medical services (series H 16) are derived from the Census of Governments and the Federal Budget. They include net public expenditures for hospital and medical care (after deduction of fee payments), hospital construction, community and related public health services, maternal and child health services, the operation of sanitation services (but not sewer construction or water supply), food and drug inspection, and medical research. They exclude expenditures for domiciliary care (other than in mental and tuberculosis institutions) which are included under institutional care (series H 19). They also exclude expenditures for health and medical services provided in connection with veterans programs, public education, public assistance, workmen's compensation, State temporary disability insurance, and vocational rehabilitation; these are included in the total expenditures shown for those programs. Also excluded are international health activities, medical activities of the Department of Defense and the Atomic Energy Commission, and medical activities subordinate to the performance of other functions, such as those of the Civil Aeronautics Authority. (For detailed discussion, see *Social Security Bulletin*, October 1956 and 1957.)

The estimates for veterans programs (series H 23–28) were obtained from the *Annual Report of the Veterans Administration*, supplemented by unpublished data. The figures exclude expenditures for bonus payments (regarded as deferred pay, rather than as social insurance benefits), appropriations to the Government life insurance trust fund (impossible to allocate by years on an incurred cost basis), and accounts of several small revolving funds (which are in the nature of business activities). The appropriate administrative costs are included in each of the five categories of expenditure shown, thereby facilitating the addition of veterans health expenditures to other health and medical expenditures, veterans education expenditures with other education programs, etc.

See also general note for series H 1–222.

H 30–45. Social welfare expenditures under civilian public programs, by source of funds, 1890–1956.

Source: See source for series H 1–29.

Federal grants-in-aid are classified as expenditures from Federal funds (contrary to the practice in the national income accounts which includes them as expenditures from State and local funds). Benefit payments under the State unemployment insurance programs are classified as expenditures from State funds (in the national income accounts they are classified as Federal expenditures, based on the fact that the State unemployment insurance trust funds are held and invested by the Secretary of the Treasury). Federal grants to the States for the administration of unemployment insurance and the employment service are classified as expenditures from Federal funds.

See also general note for series H 1–222 and text for series H 1–29.

H 46–48. Civilian labor force, 1934–1957.

Source: 1934 and 1939, **series H 46**, Bureau of Labor Statistics, *Monthly Labor Review*, July 1948, p. 50; **series H 47–48**, Social Security Administration, records; 1944–1957, Bureau of the Census, *Current Population Reports*, Series P–50, Nos. 2, 19, 59, 67, 72, and 85.

H 49–54. Workers covered under social insurance programs, 1934–1957.

Source: 1934–1954, Social Security Administration, records; 1954 (Dec.)–1957, *Social Security Bulletin, Annual Statistical Supplement*, various issues.

See general notes for series H 1–222 and series H 115–161, and text for series H 55–67.

H 55–67. Estimated payrolls in employment covered by selected social insurance programs, 1937–1957.

Source: 1937–1948, Social Security Administration, records; 1949–1957, *Social Security Bulletin, Annual Statistical Supplement*, various issues.

The Office of Business Economics is the original source for total earnings and wage and salary disbursements (series H 55–57). The Social Security Administration is the original source for payrolls covered by State and local government retirement systems and by workmen's compensation (series H 62 and H 67). See also text for series H 175–185. Figures for series H 58–61 and H 63–66 are based on reports of the agencies administering the programs specified.

Annual estimates of the number of workers and the amount of payrolls covered by workmen's compensation laws are based on data compiled by the Social Security Administration for certain benchmark years—1940, 1946, and 1953. For the intervening years, coverage estimates have been projected on the basis of the percentage change under the unemployment insurance laws, with adjustments, where necessary, for changes in coverage under the two programs. Coverage estimates for the benchmark years are based primarily on payroll data provided by the National Council on Compensation Insurance, the major rate-making organization in the country. The number covered is the average of the number of workers in covered employment in the pay period ending nearest the 15th of each month. All the estimates are submitted to the respective State workmen's compensation administrative agencies for review and comment at least every 2 or 3 years.

H 68–114. Monthly benefits and beneficiaries under social insurance and related programs, by risk and program, 1940–1957.

Source: Social Security Administration, *Social Security Bulletin, Annual Statistical Supplement*, various issues.

Lump-sum payments are excluded. Data for workmen's compensation and State and local retirement systems are for continental United States only; data for other programs include benefits paid and beneficiaries in Territories or in other countries.

Most of the data are derived from operating statistics of the administering agencies. For the basis of estimates of workmen's compensation payments, see text for series H 175–185.

Estimates of the operations of State and local government retirement systems (series H 73 and H 97) are based primarily on Bureau of the Census reports on city and State government finances. Fiscal-year data in these reports show, both for State-administered and city-administered systems, the contributions by the government and by employees and the total payments (with benefits and withdrawals separately identified when available). These figures must be adjusted to derive estimates of benefits for several reasons. Systems administered by counties, for example, are not included. On the other hand, comparison with reports of the systems themselves (specifically for the New York systems) indicates that contributions borrowed by members may be included as benefit payments. Moreover, benefit payments may include withdrawals made as refunds to members leaving the system and lump-sum death payments. The 1957 Census of Governments survey of employee retirement systems will make possible considerable refinement of this series.

H 115–161. General note.

The national system of old-age, survivors, and disability insurance originally covered employees in industry and commerce. Beginning in 1951 (as a result of the 1950 amendments of the Social Security Act) coverage was extended to regularly employed agricultural and domestic workers, to most urban self-employed persons, and on a group-voluntary basis to employees of nonprofit organizations and to employees of State and local governments not covered by separate retirement programs. In January 1955, coverage was further extended to self-employed farmers and additional farm workers, to most professional self-employed persons, on a group-voluntary basis to most State and local government employees covered by their own retirement system, and on an individual-voluntary basis to ministers. Effective with taxable years ending after 1955, additional self-employed professional groups and certain farm owners and operators were covered. As of January 1957, military personnel were covered on a compulsory basis. Free wage credits for military service from September 1940 through December 1956 are reflected in benefits paid in the years covered by the series (primarily in benefits to young survivors) but do not enter into the count of covered workers or taxable earnings. The additional cost of benefits paid in any year as a result of these credits is met by a transfer to the trust funds from general revenues.

An individual in covered employment may not be covered for the full amount of his earnings. Contributions were payable only on earnings up to $3,000 a year during the period 1937–1950, up to $3,600 a year for 1951–1954, and up to $4,200 a year for 1955–1957. Taxable earnings represented about 93 percent of total earnings in covered employment in 1938, about 80 percent in 1950, about 85 percent in 1951, about 80 percent in 1954, about 84 percent in 1955, and about 82 percent in 1956.

Contributions were payable on taxable earnings at the following rates: 1937–1949, employers and employees 1 percent each; 1950–1953, employers and employees 1½ percent each, self-employed 2¼ percent; 1954–1956, employers and employees 2 percent each, self-employed 3 percent; 1957, employers and employees 2¼ percent each, self-employed 3⅜ percent or 1½ times this amount.

Lump-sum death payments became payable in 1937, monthly benefits in 1940. The original Social Security Act provided for monthly old-age benefits only. Amendments adopted in 1939 added benefits for dependents (wives 65 years old and over, and children under 18) and for survivors (widows 65 years old and over, children under 18 and their widowed mothers, and dependent parents 65 years old and over when there was no surviving widow or child). Beginning in September 1950, aged husbands or widowers who had been dependent on their wife's earnings became eligible for benefits. As a result of amendments adopted in 1956, the age at which women became eligible for benefits was lowered to 62, effective November 1956, and monthly disability benefits became payable in January 1957 to dependent disabled children 18 years old and over who were totally disabled before attaining age 18 and in July 1957 to permanently and totally disabled insured individuals 50–64 years old.

Insured workers who retire from any substantially gainful work may receive benefits beginning at age 65 (since November 1956 at age 62 for women who elect to receive an actuarially reduced benefit). The test of substantially gainful work was taxable earnings of $15 a month or more during 1940–1950; $50 a month in 1951–1952; $75 a month for wage workers in 1953–1954 and $600 and $900 a year, respectively, for self-employed workers during the same period, with no restrictions for workers aged 75 or over; $1,200 per year beginning 1955, with no restrictions for workers aged 72 or over.

H 115–125. Old-age, survivors, and disability insurance—coverage and benefits, 1937–1957.

Source: Social Security Administration, *Social Security Bulletin, Annual Statistical Supplement*, various issues.

See general note for series H 115–161.

H 126–136. Old-age, survivors, and disability insurance—monthly beneficiaries, by type of benefit, 1940–1957.

Source: See source for series H 115–125, except for series H 122 which is from Social Security Administration, records.

H 137–148. Old-age, survivors, and disability insurance—families in receipt of monthly benefits and average monthly benefit, for selected family groups, 1940–1956.

Source: See source for series H 115–125.

See general note for series H 115–161.

H 149–161. Old-age, survivors, and disability insurance—workers retiring, and retired workers receiving benefits, by sex, 1940–1957.

Source: See source for series H 115–125.

See general note for series H 115–161.

H 162–174. Unemployment insurance—coverage, benefits, and financing under State programs, 1941–1957.

Source: Bureau of Employment Security, *The Labor Market and Employment Security* and the monthly *Statistical Supplement*.

Most of these series also appear in the *Social Security Bulletin, Annual Statistical Supplement*. Data relate only to State programs under Title IX of the Social Security Act. Note that data in series H 1–114 include, in addition, the railroad unemployment insurance system, unemployment allowances for veterans, reconversion unemployment benefits for seamen, and unemployment benefits for Federal employees paid by the States as agents of the Federal Government.

In all States, covered employment represents employment in industrial and commercial establishments of 8 or more for 1941–1955, and 4 or more for 1956–1957 (coverage required under the Federal statute); in some States, covered employment also represents employment in smaller establishments and employment for additional groups of workers, such as State and local employees or seamen. Taxable wages represent wages up to $3,000 a year in all States except Delaware, Nevada, Oregon, and Rhode Island, where the limit has been $3,600 since January 1956; in Alaska, wages up to $3,600 were taxable in calendar 1956 and up to $4,200 since January 1957. Contributions payable by employers to the Federal Government (0.3 percent of taxable wages), and used primarily for Federal grants to the States for the cost of administering unemployment insurance and employment services, are not included in these series. Employer contributions to States for unemployment insurance vary in rate depending on the individual employer's experience (in earlier years not all States permitted variable rates), ranging generally from 0.5 percent or less to 2.7 percent or more of taxable payrolls. In 1941, 5 States also collected contributions for this program from employees; by 1958, only Alabama, New Jersey, and Alaska did so.

In most States, a waiting period of 1 week must be served before payments begin. Benefits are payable for a maximum number of weeks, ranging from 16 to 30 weeks among the States; maximum weekly benefits without dependents' allowances range from $25 to $45 under the several State laws. In 11 States, maximum allowances for dependents ranging from $3 to $25 raise the range of maximum augmented benefits to $30 to $70.

H 175–185. Workmen's compensation—payments, by type of benefit and type of insurance, 1939–1957.

Source: 1939–1952, Social Security Administration, *Social Security Bulletin*, March 1954; 1953–1957, *Social Security Bulletin*, December issues, and Social Security Administration, records.

The figures include estimated payments under State workmen's compensation laws (46 States in 1939; 48 States, 1948–1957) and under Federal workmen's compensation laws covering employees of the Federal Government, private employees in the District of Columbia, and longshoremen and harbor workers. Most of the State workmen's compensation laws exempt employment in agriculture, domestic service, and casual labor; the majority exempt employers who have fewer than a specified number of employees. Occupational diseases, or at least specified diseases, are compensable under nearly all laws.

To make certain that benefit payments will be made when due, the covered employer is required by law to obtain insurance from a private insurance carrier, from a State insurance fund, or to give proof of his qualifications to carry his own risk, which is known as self-insurance.

Estimates of workmen's compensation payments depend on a variety of sources of published information, supplemented by correspondence with State agencies. Data on payments by private insurance companies and some of the competitive State funds are obtained from annual issues of *Spectator: Insurance by States of Fire, Marine, Casualty, Surety and Miscellaneous Lines.* Data on payments made by the remaining State funds are obtained from annual or biennial reports issued by State Workmen's Compensation Bureaus or Divisions, or State Insurance Departments, and from the annual publication of the Bureau of the Census, *Compendium of State Government Finances.* Data on payments by self-insurers in some States are obtained directly from State reports. For most States, however, estimates are calculated using one of several ratios (e.g., reported accidents, claims filed, taxes paid, etc.) that exist between firms which are insured with private carriers, or State funds, and firms which self-insure.

See also text for series H 55–67.

H 186–198. Public assistance—recipients and average monthly payments, by program, 1936–1957.

Source: Social Security Administration, *Social Security Bulletin, Annual Statistical Supplement, 1957,* p. 74.

Assistance programs financed in part by Federal grants-in-aid were in effect on a State-wide basis in 1936 in 42 States for old-age assistance, 27 States for aid to dependent children, and 25 States for aid to the blind. Programs have been in effect in all 48 States and the District of Columbia beginning 1938 for old-age assistance, 1955 for aid to dependent children,

and 1953 for aid to the blind. Approval of the first plans for aid to the permanently and totally disabled was effective October 1950, and in 1957, 44 States and the District of Columbia were participating. General assistance, provided from State or local funds or both, is available to certain other categories of needy persons in all States. In 1956, about one-third of the States did not provide general assistance to employable persons and in 16 States, general assistance was provided entirely from local funds.

H 199–206. Emergency public assistance and Federal work programs—recipients and assistance, 1933–1943.

Source: See source for series H 186–198, various issues.

The estimates shown here for 1933–1939 are very similar to those in the National Resources Planning Board report on *Security, Work, and Relief Policies,* 1942, appendixes 9 and 10.

See also text for series H 1–29 and H 30–45.

H 207–212. Old-age assistance recipients and insurance beneficiaries per 1,000 population 65 years old and over; and children receiving aid, and child insurance beneficiaries per 1,000 population under age 18, 1936–1957.

Source: See source for series H 186–198, various issues and records.

A special study of concurrent receipt of public assistance and old-age, survivors, and disability insurance has been conducted each year since 1950 by the Bureau of Public Assistance and the findings are generally published in the October or November issues of the *Social Security Bulletin.*

H 213–222. Services under child health and welfare service programs, 1937–1957.

Source: Children's Bureau, *Statistical Series* and Social Security Administration, records.

Series H 1-29. Social Welfare Expenditures Under Civilian Public Programs: 1890 to 1956

[In millions of dollars. Represents expenditures from public funds (general and special) and trust accounts, and other expenditures under public law; excludes transfers to such accounts and loans; includes capital outlay for hospitals, public elementary and secondary schools, and publicly controlled higher education; includes administrative expenditures except as noted. Years ending June 30 for Federal Government, most States, and some localities; for other States and localities covers various 12-month periods ending in specified year. (State temporary disability insurance programs operate in 4 States only.)]

Year	Total expenditures			Social insurance									Public aid		
	Total	Percent of gross national product	Percent of all government expenditures [1]	Total	Old-age, survivors, and disability insurance	Railroad retirement	Public employee retirement [2]	Unemployment insurance and employment services [3]	Railroad unemployment insurance	Railroad temporary disability insurance	State temporary disability insurance	Workmen's compensation [4]	Total	Public assistance [5]	Other [6]
	1	2	3	4	5	6	7	8	9	10	11	12	13	14	15
1956	34,748	8.4	33.0	10,645	5,485	603	1,560	1,621	60	53	233	1,030	3,113	3,022	91
1955	32,210	8.2	32.1	9,865	4,436	576	1,365	2,114	159	54	219	943	3,002	2,940	62
1954	29,142	8.1	28.5	8,245	3,364	490	1,251	1,880	100	46	211	903	2,787	2,775	12
1953	26,542	7.4	25.6	6,600	2,717	465	1,114	1,144	58	45	198	859	2,726	2,726	---------
1952	25,075	7.4	26.9	5,665	2,067	391	999	1,187	26	28	178	790	2,583	2,583	1
1951	24,006	7.7	35.1	4,759	1,569	321	921	1,051	28	29	140	702	2,591	2,584	7
1950	24,100	9.2	37.8	4,765	784	304	743	2,082	120	31	72	628	2,495	2,489	6
1949	21,623	8.3	36.4	3,687	661	283	646	1,382	51	32	51	582	2,088	2,087	1
1948	18,922	7.7	36.2	2,862	559	227	563	901	36	29	34	513	1,701	1,700	---------
1947	16,658	7.5	33.5	2,653	466	178	493	986	51	---------	15	464	1,441	1,441	---------
1946	11,868	5.9	16.0	2,576	358	154	409	1,202	24	---------	5	424	1,150	1,148	2
1945	7,992	3.7	7.4	1,364	267	145	383	162	4	---------	5	398	1,030	1,028	2
1944	7,098	3.5	6.7	1,237	217	137	352	152	4	---------	5	372	1,032	1,014	18
1943	7,338	4.1	8.1	1,206	177	133	296	253	4	---------	1	342	1,496	1,011	485
1942	8,569	6.1	19.5	1,314	137	129	280	445	11	---------	---------	311	2,730	1,061	1,669
1941	9,112	8.2	39.8	1,267	91	124	265	504	21	---------	---------	263	3,465	1,107	2,357
1940	9,101	9.5	49.4	1,215	28	117	255	552	19	---------	---------	245	3,597	1,123	2,474
1939	9,578	10.9	52.6	1,113	14	109	243	512	2	---------	---------	234	4,230	1,102	3,129
1938	8,172	9.3	52.7	791	5	83	234	230	---------	---------	---------	240	3,233	991	2,242
1937	7,761	8.9	51.0	473	(7)	2	226	16	---------	---------	---------	230	3,436	779	2,657
1936	7,140	9.2	49.7	425	---------	---------	218	15	---------	---------	---------	193	3,080	656	2,424
1935	6,811	9.9	51.7	384	---------	---------	210	(7)	---------	---------	---------	174	2,998	624	2,374
1929	4,310	4.1	42.0	340	---------	---------	(7)	---------	---------	---------	---------	(7)	(8)	(7)	(7)
1913	1,000	2.8	34.0	15	---------	---------	(7)	---------	---------	---------	---------	(7)	(8)	(7)	(7)
1890	318	2.4	38.0	---------	---------	---------	(7)	---------	---------	---------	---------	---------	(8)	(7)	(7)

Year	Health and medical programs [9]	Other welfare services					Education	Veterans programs						Public housing [14]
		Total	Vocational rehabilitation	Institutional care [10]	School lunch [10]	Child welfare		Total [11]	Pensions and compensation [12]	Readjustment allowances	Health and medical care	Education	Welfare and other [13]	
	16	17	18	19	20	21	22	23	24	25	26	27	28	29
1956	3,250	683	55	189	293	146	12,334	4,612	2,826	(15)	751	804	232	111
1955	3,074	566	42	150	238	135	11,251	4,363	2,712	(15)	755	700	196	89
1954	2,979	868	36	466	239	126	10,084	4,115	2,534	(15)	740	590	148	65
1953	2,896	761	35	410	195	121	9,291	4,221	2,468	(15)	737	705	197	47
1952	2,823	676	33	376	153	113	8,574	4,720	2,195	1	765	1,382	235	34
1951	2,674	661	31	356	165	109	7,783	5,506	2,121	11	691	2,021	328	32
1950	2,388	616	30	323	159	105	7,289	6,535	2,093	148	742	2,689	391	12
1949	1,923	555	27	297	130	102	6,355	7,009	1,983	541	711	2,818	435	6
1948	1,505	484	25	245	116	99	5,485	6,880	1,911	715	560	2,620	458	6
1947	1,191	385	20	185	101	79	4,290	6,689	1,831	1,512	572	2,251	365	10
1946	1,103	305	14	164	57	70	3,711	3,014	1,266	1,037	245	363	57	9
1945	996	285	10	156	47	72	3,393	914	756	24	115	10	10	11
1944	898	255	7	144	34	70	3,041	623	521	---------	101	---------	2	13
1943	805	220	6	134	23	57	3,041	556	468	---------	88	---------	1	14
1942	791	213	5	143	23	42	2,970	538	453	---------	84	---------	1	14
1941	755	209	5	149	14	42	2,873	535	453	---------	81	---------	1	9
1940	799	171	4	126	(7)	41	2,780	535	448	---------	86	---------	1	4
1939	807	170	4	121	---------	45	2,741	513	434	---------	78	---------	1	3
1938	751	164	4	111	---------	49	2,738	494	419	---------	74	---------	1	2
1937	724	115	3	111	---------	1	2,527	485	413	---------	71	---------	1	---------
1936	665	114	3	111	---------	---------	2,375	480	415	---------	64	---------	1	---------
1935	642	113	2	111	---------	---------	2,225	450	390	---------	59	---------	1	---------
1929	470	8 500	---------	(7)	---------	(7)	2,450	550	(7)	---------	(7)	---------	(7)	---------
1913	150	8 114	---------	(7)	---------	(7)	525	196	(7)	---------	(7)	---------	(7)	---------
1890	18	8 41	---------	(7)	---------	(7)	146	113	(7)	---------	(7)	---------	(7)	---------

[1] Government expenditures are from general revenues and social insurance trust funds; excludes workmen's compensation and temporary disability insurance payments made through private carriers. Although these are included as social welfare expenditures, series H 1 (under statutory provisions).

[2] Excludes refunds of employee contributions to those leaving service. Federal expenditures include retirement pay of military personnel.

[3] Includes unemployment compensation for Korean veterans (beginning 1953) and for Federal employees (beginning 1955).

[4] Payments by private insurance carriers, State funds, and self-insurers of benefits payable under State law and estimated State costs of administering State funds and of supervising private operations and payments and administration cost under Federal employees compensation programs. Administrative costs of private insurance carriers and self-insurers not available. Prior to 1949 excludes all administrative costs for workmen's compensation.

[5] Old-age assistance, aid to dependent children, aid to the blind, aid to the permanently and totally disabled (beginning 1951), and from State and local funds, general assistance.

[6] Work program earnings, other emergency aid programs, and value of surplus food distributed to needy persons. (From 1936 to 1940, includes unknown amount of surplus food distributed to institutions.)

[7] Not available.

[8] Some public aid expenditures included under "Other welfare services."

[9] Excludes expenditures included under other programs.

[10] Includes value of surplus foods for school lunches or nonprofit institutions. (See footnote 6.)

[11] Beginning 1946, total exceeds sum of items because of inclusion of State payments to veterans.

[12] Includes burial awards.

[13] Vocational rehabilitation, specially adapted homes and automobiles for disabled veterans, counseling, beneficiaries' travel, loan guarantees, and, beginning 1950, domiciliary care; for earlier years, domiciliary care included with health and medical services.

[14] Federal and State subsidies (and administrative costs) for low-cost housing.

[15] Net refunds.

Series H 30–45. Social Welfare Expenditures Under Civilian Public Programs, by Source of Funds: 1890 to 1956

[In millions of dollars]

Year	From Federal funds								From State and local funds [1]							
	Total	Social insurance	Public aid	Health and medical programs	Other welfare services	Education	Veterans programs	Public housing	Total	Social insurance [2]	Public aid	Health and medical programs	Other welfare services	Education	Veterans programs	Public housing
	30	31	32	33	34	35	36	37	38	39	40	41	42	43	44	45
1956	14,676	7,528	1,554	349	322	309	4,523	91	20,050	3,095	1,559	2,901	361	12,025	89	20
1955	13,186	6,429	1,503	299	245	334	4,302	74	19,024	3,436	1,499	2,775	320	10,917	62	15
1954	11,407	5,074	1,418	312	265	275	4,012	51	17,734	3,171	1,369	2,667	602	9,808	103	14
1953	10,542	4,214	1,359	342	195	291	4,107	34	16,001	2,386	1,367	2,554	566	9,000	114	13
1952	9,806	3,330	1,210	350	143	174	4,577	22	15,269	2,335	1,373	2,473	533	8,400	143	12
1951	9,664	2,710	1,195	319	167	83	5,171	19	14,342	2,049	1,397	2,355	493	7,700	335	13
1950	9,585	1,911	1,102	257	167	73	6,063	12	14,515	2,853	1,393	2,132	450	7,216	471	--------
1949	9,414	1,595	940	183	134	67	6,489	6	12,208	2,091	1,148	1,740	421	6,288	520	--------
1948	8,639	1,313	723	149	125	60	6,264	6	10,283	1,549	978	1,356	359	5,425	616	--------
1947	8,579	1,115	616	153	102	54	6,530	10	8,079	1,538	825	1,039	283	4,236	159	--------
1946	4,540	851	448	129	79	57	2,967	9	7,328	1,725	702	974	226	3,654	47	--------
1945	2,376	705	419	127	87	113	914	11	5,617	659	610	869	198	3,280	--------	--------
1944	1,995	624	428	107	74	127	623	13	5,103	613	604	791	181	2,914	--------	--------
1943	2,165	524	765	73	53	181	556	14	5,172	682	731	732	168	2,860	--------	--------
1942	2,943	481	1,652	61	35	162	538	14	5,626	833	1,078	730	178	2,808	--------	--------
1941	3,296	431	2,129	55	36	103	535	9	5,816	837	1,336	700	174	2,770	--------	--------
1940	3,236	350	2,244	51	10	42	535	4	5,865	865	1,353	748	161	2,739	--------	--------
1939	3,784	302	2,871	44	10	41	513	3	5,794	811	1,359	763	161	2,700	--------	--------
1938	2,897	243	2,075	39	4	40	494	2	5,275	548	1,158	712	160	2,698	--------	--------
1937	3,172	122	2,494	40	4	27	485	--------	4,589	351	942	684	112	2,500	--------	--------
1936	2,955	115	2,310	21	2	25	480	--------	4,185	310	770	644	111	2,350	--------	--------
1935	2,966	99	2,374	17	2	25	450	--------	3,845	285	624	625	111	2,200	--------	--------
1929	625	--------	--------	--------	--------	--------	--------	--------	3,685	--------	--------	--------	--------	--------	--------	--------
1913	196	--------	--------	--------	--------	--------	--------	--------	804	--------	--------	--------	--------	--------	--------	--------
1890	115	--------	--------	--------	--------	--------	--------	--------	203	--------	--------	--------	--------	--------	--------	--------

[1] Includes expenditures from State accounts in unemployment trust fund; excludes Federal grants-in-aid.

[2] Includes payments by private insurance carriers and self-insurers of benefits payable under State workmen's compensation and temporary disability insurance laws.

Series H 46–54. Civilian Labor Force And Workers Covered Under Social Insurance Programs: 1934 to 1957

[In millions. Monthly average except as noted]

Year	Civilian labor force			Retirement systems			Workmen's compensation	Unemployment insurance [4]	Temporary disability insurance [5]
	Total [1]	Paid employees	Self employed	Old-age, survivors, and disability insurance [2]	Railroad retirement	Public employee [3]			
	46	47	48	49	50	51	52	53	54
1957 (Dec.)	67.8	53.9	9.2	53.1	1.1	4.1	42.0	43.2	11.3
1956 (Dec.)	67.0	54.1	9.1	52.8	1.2	4.8	42.0	43.4	11.6
1955 (Dec.)	66.6	53.4	9.4	51.7	1.3	4.7	40.0	41.5	11.1
1954 (Dec.)	63.5	50.0	9.5	45.2	1.2	4.7	39.0	37.0	10.8
1954	64.5	49.9	9.7	45.0	1.2	4.7	38.5	36.2	10.6
1949	62.1	45.9	10.8	34.3	1.4	4.4	34.5	33.0	5.3
1944	54.6	41.9	9.3	31.5	1.7	4.7	33.0	31.6	.2
1939	55.2	33.2	10.4	24.0	1.2		22.0	22.6	
1934	52.2	28.9	10.0			1.4	17.0		

[1] Bureau of the Census total of persons 14 years old and over in the civilian labor force; includes unpaid family members and the unemployed, not shown separately.

[2] Beginning in 1954, includes persons covered under both a government retirement system and old-age, survivors, and disability insurance (about 1,000,000 in December 1956, 600,000 in December 1955, and 300,000 in December 1954); excludes persons who were eligible for coverage but not actually covered (about 3.5 million in December 1956); also excludes railroad employees jointly covered by OASDI and their own retirement program.

[3] Includes persons covered under both a government retirement system and old-age, survivors, and disability insurance; see footnote 2.

[4] State, railroad, and Federal employee programs.

[5] State and railroad programs. Excludes government employees covered by sick-leave provisions.

Series H 55–67. Estimated Payrolls in Employment Covered by Selected Social Insurance Programs: 1937 to 1957

[In millions of dollars. Continental United States, except as noted. Earnings and payroll data are gross, before deduction of social insurance contributions]

Year	Total earnings [1]	Wages and salaries [2]		Payrolls covered by retirement programs						Net earnings of self-employed covered by old-age, survivors, and disability insurance [6]	Payrolls covered by unemployment insurance programs			Payrolls covered by workmen's compensation program [8]
		Total	Civilian	Total [3]	Old-age, survivors, and disability insurance [4]	Railroad retirement [4][5]	Federal civil service retirement	State and local government retirement			Total [7]	State unemployment insurance [4]	Railroad unemployment insurance [4][5]	
	55	56	57	58	59	60	61	62	63		64	65	66	67
1957	281,121	238,120	228,486	229,204	203,000	6,178	10,116	15,240	30,000		190,539	173,139	6,178	186,500
1956	269,739	227,304	217,636	210,303	184,000	6,203	9,560	13,840	29,000		180,998	163,959	6,203	177,000
1955	253,051	210,902	201,124	193,951	169,000	5,801	8,290	12,540	25,000		164,240	148,144	5,801	165,000
1954	236,701	196,259	186,308	177,460	154,000	5,630	6,980	11,650	26,700		142,224	136,594	5,630	153,000
1953	238,829	198,106	187,769	178,447	155,000	6,147	6,950	10,670	16,900		144,804	138,657	6,147	153,500
1952	227,090	184,857	174,385	165,934	143,000	6,185	6,929	9,820	16,300		133,505	127,320	6,185	141,500
1951	211,585	170,776	162,136	152,376	131,000	6,101	6,395	8,880	16,200		124,344	118,243	6,101	129,700
1950	182,666	146,391	141,392	128,834	109,439	5,327	6,068	8,000	---------		108,162	102,835	5,327	113,500
1949	168,528	134,379	130,131	117,825	99,645	5,133	5,707	7,340	---------		98,653	93,520	5,133	100,500
1948	173,531	135,142	131,172	118,450	101,892	5,589	4,469	6,550	---------		101,270	95,731	5,539	101,500
1947	157,276	122,843	118,775	107,450	92,088	5,113	4,809	5,440	---------		91,347	86,234	5,113	91,500
1946	147,131	111,866	104,048	93,621	79,003	4,883	5,195	4,540	---------		78,028	73,145	4,883	79,500
1945	148,398	117,577	95,758	85,455	71,317	4,530	5,840	3,768	---------		70,941	66,411	4,530	74,000
1944	146,581	117,016	96,983	86,403	73,060	4,523	5,600	3,220	---------		73,409	68,886	4,523	--------
1943	133,806	105,619	91,486	81,619	69,379	4,100	5,100	3,040	---------		69,971	65,871	4,100	--------
1942	106,016	82,109	75,941	67,664	57,950	3,394	3,600	2,720	---------		57,942	54,548	3,394	--------
1941	79,487	62,086	60,220	52,485	45,286	2,697	1,912	2,590	---------		44,682	41,985	2,697	--------
1940	62,828	49,818	49,255	41,620	35,560	2,280	1,430	2,350	---------		34,632	32,352	2,280	--------
1939	57,551	45,941	45,553	36,892	31,488	2,149	1,221	2,034	---------		31,218	29,069	2,149	--------
1938	54,104	42,976	42,611	33,755	28,635	2,010	1,139	1,971	---------		28,210	26,200	2,010	--------
1937	58,798	46,107	45,753	37,705	32,532	2,265	1,050	1,858	---------		(9)	(9)	2,265	--------

[1] Includes earnings of self-employed.
[2] Wage and salary disbursements paid in cash and in kind in continental United States and pay of Federal personnel in all areas.
[3] Beginning 1953, adjusted for duplication of payrolls covered by both old-age, survivors, and disability insurance and State and local retirement systems.
[4] Taxable plus estimated nontaxable wages and salaries in employment covered by programs.
[5] Includes a small amount of taxable wages for Alaska and Hawaii.
[6] Preliminary.
[7] Beginning 1955, includes payrolls of Federal civilian employees in all areas.
[8] Payrolls of employers insuring with private carriers, State funds, or self-insured, and Federal programs; excludes railroads (covered by Employers' Liability Act).
[9] Not available.

Series H 68–114. Monthly Benefits and Beneficiaries Under Social Insurance and Related Programs, by Risk and Program: 1940 to 1957

[Partly estimated. Refunds of employee contributions excluded, for State and local government, Federal civil service, and other contributory retirement plans]

Series No.	Risk and program	1957	1956	1955	1954	1953	1952	1951	1950	1949
	AMOUNT OF BENEFITS ($1,000,000)									
68	Total	[1]15,550	13,002	11,901	10,962	8,771	7,603	6,718	6,215	6,472
69	Old-age retirement	7,452	5,913	5,127	3,954	3,300	2,574	2,189	1,403	1,227
70	Old-age, survivors, and disability insurance [2]	5,688	4,361	3,748	2,698	2,175	1,539	1,321	651	437
71	Railroad retirement	420	380	336	325	282	267	187	177	169
72	Federal Government retirement [3]	730	631	541	467	414	370	346	287	356
73	State and local government retirement [4]	550	470	427	385	343	310	273	230	203
74	Veterans programs [5]	64	71	75	79	86	87	62	58	62
75	Survivorship—Monthly benefits only	2,606	2,244	2,067	1,741	1,570	1,354	1,179	902	795
76	Old-age, survivors, and disability insurance	1,521	1,244	1,108	880	744	592	507	277	197
77	Railroad retirement	144	133	122	93	83	74	50	44	39
78	Federal Government retirement [3]	61	52	41	34	27	20	14	8	4
79	State and local government retirement [4]	45	40	38	35	32	30	29	26	25
80	Veterans programs	755	699	688	629	613	573	519	492	477
81	Workmen's compensation [6]	80	75	70	70	70	65	60	55	52
82	Disability	[1]3,579	3,333	3,175	2,976	2,851	2,632	2,487	2,443	2,180
83	Workmen's compensation [6]	620	578	520	498	491	460	416	360	331
84	Veterans programs [5]	2,109	2,081	1,982	1,842	1,754	1,635	1,586	1,675	1,630
85	Railroad retirement	118	111	103	104	92	94	82	77	72
86	Federal Government [3]	311	299	281	256	248	211	202	189	35
87	State and local government retirement [4]	55	50	45	40	35	30	28	24	22
88	State temporary disability insurance [7]	258	216	193	186	185	168	148	89	59
89	Railroad temporary disability insurance	51	50	52	49	45	35	26	28	30
90	Unemployment	1,913	1,512	1,531	2,292	1,051	1,044	863	1,466	2,271
91	State unemployment insurance [8]	1,766	1,381	1,350	2,027	962	998	840	1,373	1,737
92	Railroad unemployment insurance	94	70	93	157	47	42	20	60	104
93	Veterans allowances [9]	53	61	88	108	42	4	2	35	430
	NUMBER OF BENEFICIARIES (1,000) [10]									
	Old-age retirement:									
94	Old-age, survivors, and disability insurance [2]	7,623.3	6,190.9	5,443.2	4,589.6	3,888.7	3,187.3	2,756.8	1,918.1	1,574.6
95	Railroad retirement	363.6	347.3	329.2	307.7	288.5	268.6	182.0	174.8	164.3
96	Federal Government retirement [3]	331.6	295.7	270.8	248.9	231.6	218.2	209.5	184.3	209.1
97	State and local government retirement [4]	395.0	345.0	315.0	292.0	270.0	250.0	230.0	213.0	200.0
98	Veterans programs [5]	50.2	55.9	59.6	65.7	71.8	78.4	57.3	53.5	57.4
	Survivorship—Monthly benefits only:									
99	Old-age, survivors, and disability insurance	2,633.0	2,282.3	2,096.6	1,891.9	1,687.5	1,484.6	1,286.8	1,093.9	983.9
100	Railroad retirement	220.7	210.6	196.5	167.2	157.7	149.9	146.8	136.3	121.8
101	Federal Government retirement [3]	93.8	82.1	72.0	61.5	50.4	40.0	30.2	18.3	9.4
102	State and local government retirement [4]	50.0	50.0	50.0	48.0	46.0	44.0	42.0	40.0	38.0
103	Veterans programs	1,176.9	1,173.9	1,152.9	1,122.2	1,086.0	1,044.2	1,011.2	991.7	971.2
104	Workmen's compensation	(11)	(11)	(11)	(11)	(11)	(11)	(11)	(11)	(11)

See footnotes at end of table.

Series H 68–114. Monthly Benefits and Beneficiaries Under Social Insurance and Related Programs, by Risk and Program: 1940 to 1957—Con.

Series No.	Risk and program	1957	1956	1955	1954	1953	1952	1951	1950	1949
	NUMBER OF BENEFICIARIES—Con. (1,000) [10]									
	Disability: [1]									
105	Workmen's compensation	(11)	(11)	(11)	(11)	(11)	(11)	(11)	(11)	(11)
106	Veterans programs [5]	2,745.1	2,682.4	2,610.8	2,527.7	2,437.0	2,343.9	2,319.1	2,301.8	2,260.0
107	Railroad retirement	91.2	89.8	87.1	84.9	81.9	80.3	79.1	76.0	70.0
108	Federal Government [3]	156.6	153.3	146.6	139.2	130.2	116.5	106.9	99.0	39.7
109	State and local government retirement [4]	55.5	50.0	50.0	45.0	42.0	38.0	35.0	32.0	29.0
110	State temporary disability retirement [7]	91.4	86.5	80.9	81.7	83.4	75.0	71.3	54.1	28.0
111	Railroad temporary disability insurance [12]	30.7	30.3	31.9	31.5	33.2	31.5	28.9	31.2	33.6
	Unemployment:									
112	State unemployment insurance [13]	1,250.2	1,037.0	1,099.5	1,614.9	812.1	873.6	796.9	1,305.0	1,666.1
113	Railroad unemployment insurance [12]	59.6	47.6	63.1	110.4	40.2	42.6	29.0	76.8	120.4
114	Veterans allowances [9]	44.6	50.7	72.4	89.3	33.5	15.2	3.8	33.6	427.9

Series No.	Risk and program	1948	1947	1946	1945	1944	1943	1942	1941	1940
	AMOUNT OF BENEFITS ($1,000,000)									
68	**Total**	**5,195**	**5,313**	**5,684**	**2,556**	**1,573**	**1,339**	**1,519**	**1,431**	**1,504**
69	Old-age retirement	1,034	888	741	602	523	459	420	379	326
70	Old-age, survivors, and disability insurance [2]	352	288	222	157	119	97	80	55	17
71	Railroad retirement	150	139	118	106	99	95	92	88	83
72	Federal Government retirement [3]	278	232	185	141	122	110	104	104	103
73	State and local government retirement [4]	190	175	158	143	135	125	115	107	103
74	Veterans programs [5]	64	54	57	55	49	33	29	24	20
75	Survivorship—Monthly benefits only	696	619	529	422	282	232	208	192	162
76	Old-age, survivors, and disability insurance	172	149	128	104	77	58	42	25	6
77	Railroad retirement	36	19	2	2	2	2	2	2	1
78	Federal Government retirement [3]	1	(14)	(14)	(14)	(14)	(14)	(14)	(14)	----
79	State and local government retirement [4]	23	22	21	20	19	18	18	17	16
80	Veterans programs	414	383	334	254	144	116	111	112	106
81	Workmen's compensation [6]	50	46	44	42	40	38	36	37	32
82	Disability	2,132	2,020	1,536	956	701	567	540	501	481
83	Workmen's compensation [6]	309	280	250	244	227	206	186	149	129
84	Veterans programs [5]	1,647	1,622	1,212	643	407	299	296	296	298
85	Railroad retirement	58	39	31	31	31	31	31	31	31
86	Federal Government [3]	31	25	22	19	17	16	15	14	13
87	State and local government retirement [7]	20	18	16	15	14	12	11	11	10
88	State temporary disability insurance [7]	36	26	5	5	5	3	----	----	----
89	Railroad temporary disability insurance	31	11	----	----	----	----	----	----	----
90	Unemployment	1,332	1,786	2,878	575	67	81	350	359	535
91	State unemployment insurance [8]	793	776	1,095	446	62	80	344	344	519
92	Railroad unemployment insurance	29	39	40	2	1	1	6	15	16
93	Veterans allowances [9]	510	971	1,744	127	4	----	----	----	----
	NUMBER OF BENEFICIARIES (1,000) [10]									
	Old-age retirement:									
94	Old-age, survivors, and disability insurance [2]	1,294.9	1,068.1	842.7	591.8	463.4	386.1	322.8	271.5	77.2
95	Railroad retirement	156.0	147.1	139.7	129.1	121.5	117.0	114.1	112.6	102.0
96	Federal Government retirement [3]	168.4	148.4	123.9	101.1	90.1	86.3	86.6	84.0	80.8
97	State and local government retirement [4]	190.0	180.0	167.0	155.0	146.0	136.0	126.7	117.2	113.0
98	Veterans programs [5]	59.8	61.6	62.5	59.1	52.4	46.8	42.0	39.1	29.2
	Survivorship—Monthly benefits only:									
99	Old-age, survivors, and disability insurance	872.4	767.4	661.0	533.5	402.8	304.3	217.4	168.5	35.7
100	Railroad retirement	101.6	40.5	4.5	4.4	4.2	4.0	3.7	3.6	3.0
101	Federal Government retirement [3]	2.0	.4	.4	.3	.2	.1	.1	(14)	----
102	State and local government retirement [4]	36.0	35.0	34.0	32.0	30.0	29.0	28.2	26.0	25.0
103	Veterans programs	950.0	901.5	790.5	542.1	342.0	314.9	316.4	318.5	323.2
104	Workmen's compensation	(11)	(11)	(11)	(11)	(11)	(11)	(11)	(11)	(11)
	Disability:									
105	Workmen's compensation	(11)	(11)	(11)	(11)	(11)	(11)	(11)	(11)	(11)
106	Veterans programs [5]	2,252.0	2,283.7	2,010.1	1,148.1	763.6	581.1	581.1	583.6	580.9
107	Railroad retirement	63.0	51.2	39.3	39.0	39.1	39.6	39.7	40.3	39.3
108	Federal Government [3]	35.8	31.6	27.3	23.7	21.2	19.8	(15) 18.4	17.6	15.5
109	State and local government retirement [4]	27.0	25.0	23.0	21.0	19.5	17.6	16.3	15.0	14.3
110	State temporary disability retirement [7]	24.2	23.0	5.6	5.4	5.9	4.6	----	----	----
111	Railroad temporary disability insurance [12]	33.2	23.6	----	----	----	----	----	----	----
	Unemployment:									
112	State unemployment insurance [13]	821.1	852.4	1,152.2	465.0	79.3	115.5	541.5	523.0	982.4
113	Railroad unemployment insurance [12]	38.2	52.6	52.7	3.3	.8	1.5	12.4	22.4	41.5
114	Veterans allowances [9]	513.5	941.9	1,588.7	101.0	10.9	----	----	----	----

[1] Includes $56,676,000 and 123.7 thousand beneficiaries under old-age, survivors, and disability insurance for 1957, not shown separately.

[2] Includes benefits paid to aged wives, to dependent husbands (first payable Sept. 1950), and to children of retired-worker beneficiaries.

[3] Includes Federal civil service and other contributory systems and Federal noncontributory systems. For contributory systems, prior to 1954, includes small but unknown amount and number of disability and survivor benefits and beneficiaries (included with old-age retirement). For noncontributory systems, for 1940, significant amount and number of disability payments included with old-age retirement. Before 1954, small but unknown amount and number of survivor payments included with old-age retirement.

[4] For fiscal year, usually ending June 30. Data for 1957 preliminary. Under survivorship, number represents families.

[5] Under Veterans Administration. Old-age retirement data are for veterans of the Spanish-American War, the Boxer Rebellion, and the Philippine Insurrection; beginning Oct. 1951, include all service pensions. Disability data include pensions and compensation, and subsistence payments to disabled veterans undergoing training.

[6] Small but unknown amount of lump-sum death payments included with monthly survivor payments. Disability benefits exclude payments for medical care.

[7] Benefits first payable in Rhode Island, Apr. 1943; in California, Dec. 1946; in New Jersey, Jan. 1949; and in New York, July 1950. Includes maternity data for Rhode Island. Excludes hospital benefits in California and hospital, surgical, and medical care benefits paid under approved plans in New York. Number represents average weekly number of beneficiaries; excludes private-plan beneficiaries in California and New Jersey.

[8] Beginning 1955, includes payments to unemployed Federal employees made by the States as agents of the Federal Government.

[9] For unemployment allowances (under the Servicemen's Readjustment Act beginning Sept. 1944 and under the Veterans' Readjustment Assistance Act beginning Oct. 1952), average weekly number. For self-employment allowances under the Servicemen's Readjustment Act beginning Nov. 1944, average monthly number. For 1953 to 1957, a small number and amount of self-employment allowances included with unemployment benefits; not shown separately.

[10] Average monthly number, except as noted.

[11] Not available.

[12] Average number of beneficiaries during a 14-day registration period.

[13] Average weekly number.

[14] Less than $500,000, or 500 beneficiaries.

[15] Revised unpublished estimate.

Series H 115–125. Old-Age, Survivors, and Disability Insurance—Coverage and Benefits: 1937 to 1957

Year	Living covered workers [1] beginning of following year		New entrants [2] to covered employment	Workers with taxable earnings during year [3]	Taxable earnings [4]		Employers reporting taxable wages [5]	Contributions of employees, employers, and self-employed persons [6]	Total benefits paid	Trust fund assets at end of year [7]	Average old-age benefit in current payment status at end of year
	Insured	Uninsured			Total	Average per worker					
	115	116	117	118	119	120	121	122	123	124	125
	1,000	1,000	1,000	1,000	Mil. dol.	Dol.	1,000	Mil. dol.	Mil. dol.	Mil. dol.	Dol.
1957	(8)	(8)	[9]3,500	[9]74,000	[9]182,000	[9]2,460	[9]5,200	6,825	7,404	23,042	64.58
1956	[9]72,500	[9]30,400	[9]4,500	[9]69,000	[9]175,000	[9]2,540	[9]5,100	6,172	5,715	22,519	63.09
1955	[9]70,900	[9]28,400	[9]5,000	[9]66,000	[9]158,100	[9]2,400	[9]5,000	5,713	4,968	21,663	61.90
1954	[9]70,700	[9]24,600	[9]2,500	[9]59,700	[9]133,800	[9]2,240	[9]4,350	5,163	3,670	20,576	59.14
1953	[9]71,000	[9]22,500	[9]3,400	[9]61,000	[9]136,100	[9]2,230	[9]4,350	3,945	3,006	18,707	51.10
1952	[9]68,200	[9]22,700	[9]3,800	[9]59,600	[9]128,800	[9]2,160	4,450	3,819	2,194	17,442	49.25
1951	62,800	25,100	6,170	58,100	121,000	2,083	4,440	3,367	1,885	15,540	42.14
1950	59,800	22,600	2,520	48,283	87,498	1,812	3,345	2,671	961	13,721	43.86
1949	45,700	34,900	1,958	46,796	81,808	1,748	3,316	1,670	667	11,816	26.00
1948	44,800	34,400	2,635	49,018	84,122	1,716	3,298	1,688	556	10,722	25.35
1947	43,400	33,700	2,685	48,908	78,372	1,602	3,246	1,558	466	9,360	24.90
1946	41,800	33,200	3,078	48,845	69,088	1,414	3,017	1,295	378	8,150	24.55
1945	40,300	32,100	3,477	46,392	62,945	1,357	2,614	1,285	274	7,121	24.19
1944	38,600	30,900	4,691	46,296	64,426	1,392	2,469	1,316	209	6,005	23.73
1943	34,900	30,500	7,337	47,656	62,423	1,310	2,394	1,239	166	4,820	23.42
1942	31,200	27,300	7,965	46,363	52,939	1,142	2,655	1,012	131	3,688	23.02
1941	27,500	23,500	6,436	40,976	41,848	1,021	2,646	789	88	2,762	22.70
1940	24,900	20,000	4,430	35,393	32,974	932	2,500	325	35	2,031	22.60
1939	22,900	17,800	4,450	33,751	29,745	881	2,366	580	14	1,724	----------
1938	----------	----------	3,930	31,822	26,502	833	2,239	360	10	1,132	----------
1937	----------	----------	32,904	32,904	29,615	900	2,421	765	1	766	----------

[1] Estimates; not adjusted to reflect effect of provisions that coordinate old-age and survivors insurance and railroad retirement programs, and wage credits for military service. Only partially adjusted to eliminate duplicate count of persons with taxable earnings reported on more than 1 account number; effect of such duplication is substantially less significant for insured workers than for uninsured.
[2] Workers with first taxable earnings under program in specified year.
[3] Partly adjusted for workers having more than 1 account.
[4] Not adjusted for earnings excluded in benefit computations, i.e., amounts above taxable base earned by workers with more than one employer or source of earnings and on which employee contributions were subsequently refunded. Annual wages in excess of $3,000 before 1951, $3,600 during 1951–1954, and $4,200 beginning 1955, paid to workers by any 1 employer, were not taxable. Beginning with 1951, self-

employment earnings were taxable; amount taxable may not exceed amounts specified above from a combination of wages and self-employment earnings.
[5] Represents number of different employers filing tax reports. A report may relate to more than 1 establishment if employer operates separate establishments.
[6] Includes insurance contributions, adjusted for refunds, and transfers during calendar years 1947–1951 from general funds equivalent to additional payments arising from extension of survivors insurance protection to certain veterans of World War II (Social Security Act Amendments of 1946).
[7] Before 1940, represents operations of old-age reserve account.
[8] Not available.
[9] Preliminary estimate.

Series H 126–136. Old-Age, Survivors, and Disability Insurance—Monthly Beneficiaries, by Type of Benefit: 1940 to 1957

[In thousands. Number in current payment status at end of year]

Year	Total beneficiaries			Old-age			Wife's or husband's	Widow's or widower's	Parent's	Child's	Mother's
	Total	Payable to beneficiaries		Total	Male	Female					
		65 or over	Under 65 years								
	126	127	128	129	130	131	132	133	134	135	136
1957	[1]11,129	8,390	2,129	6,198	4,198	2,000	1,827	1,095	29	1,502	328
1956	9,128	7,089	2,039	5,112	3,572	1,540	1,434	913	27	1,341	301
1955	7,961	6,335	1,625	4,474	3,252	1,222	1,192	701	25	1,276	292
1954	6,886	5,405	1,482	3,775	2,803	972	1,016	638	25	1,161	272
1953	5,981	4,633	1,348	3,222	2,438	784	888	541	24	1,053	254
1952	5,026	3,824	1,202	2,644	2,052	592	738	455	21	939	229
1951	4,379	3,300	1,079	2,278	1,819	459	647	384	19	846	204
1950	3,477	2,599	878	1,771	1,469	302	508	314	15	700	169
1949	2,743	1,951	792	1,286	1,100	186	391	261	13	639	152
1948	2,315	1,591	723	1,048	900	148	321	210	12	581	142
1947	1,978	1,318	660	875	756	119	269	164	10	525	135
1946	1,642	1,051	590	702	610	92	216	127	7	462	128
1945	1,288	777	511	518	447	71	159	94	6	390	121
1944	955	567	388	378	323	55	116	68	5	298	90
1943	748	448	299	306	261	45	92	46	4	229	70
1942	598	368	230	260	224	36	77	29	3	173	57
1941	434	274	160	200	175	25	57	15	2	117	42
1940	222	147	75	112	99	13	30	4	1	55	20

[1] Includes 150,000 monthly beneficiaries 50 to 64 years old.

Series H 137–148.   Old-Age, Survivors, and Disability Insurance—Families in Receipt of Monthly Benefits and Average Monthly Benefit, for Selected Family Groups: 1940 to 1956

[Number in current payment status at end of year]

	Retired-worker families					Survivors' families						
	Worker only			Worker and aged wife [2]	Worker, young wife, [3] and 1 child	Aged widows	Widowed mother and children			Children only		1 aged dependent parent
Year [1]	Total	Male	Female				1 child	2 children	3 or more children	1 child	2 children	
	137	138	139	140	141	142	143	144	145	146	147	148
FAMILIES (1,000)												
1956	3,662	2,133	1,528	1,359	38	912	128	88	83	225	90	24
1955	3,266	2,054	1,212	1,123	36	700	126	86	80	210	86	22
1954	2,744	1,780	964	958	31	637	117	82	72	189	76	22
1953	2,321	1,543	778	839	26	540	113	74	64	168	70	20
1952	1,893	1,306	588	699	21	454	103	67	56	151	61	18
1951	1,618	1,162	456	614	19	384	92	61	49	141	54	17
1950	1,240	939	301	498	5	314	82	53	33	115	47	13
1949	872	687	186	390	---	261	78	44	26	106	49	11
1948	708	560	148	321	---	210	73	41	24	96	43	10
1947	590	471	119	269	---	164	69	39	23	83	37	9
1946	473	380	92	216	---	127	66	37	21	68	30	6
1945	349	278	71	159	---	94	62	35	19	51	23	5
1944	256	200	55	116	---	68	46	25	15	40	19	4
1943	206	161	45	92	---	46	34	20	11	28	14	3
1942	176	146	30	77	---	29	29	17	7	19	9	2
1941	136	114	22	57	---	15	20	13	4	11	6	2
1940	78	65	12	30	---	4	10	6	3	3	2	1
AVG. MONTHLY BENEFITS												
1956	$59.90	$66.10	$51.10	$105.90	$127.80	$50.10	$109.90	$141.00	$138.70	$49.20	$84.70	$51.00
1955	59.10	64.60	49.80	103.50	122.80	48.70	106.80	135.40	133.20	48.20	82.70	50.10
1954	56.50	61.60	47.00	99.10	114.60	46.30	103.90	130.50	126.80	47.40	80.80	47.60
1953	48.80	52.90	40.60	85.00	97.60	40.90	90.10	111.90	109.00	41.80	71.50	42.20
1952	47.10	50.70	39.10	81.60	89.60	40.70	87.50	106.00	101.30	41.00	69.90	41.50
1951	40.30	43.20	33.00	70.20	60.40	36.00	77.30	93.80	92.00	35.80	60.80	36.80
1950	42.20	44.60	34.80	71.70	68.40	36.50	76.90	93.90	92.40	35.20	60.00	36.80
1949	25.30	26.50	20.60	41.40	---	20.80	36.50	50.40	54.00	13.50	26.60	13.80
1948	24.60	25.80	20.10	40.40	---	20.60	36.00	49.80	53.00	13.40	26.20	13.70
1947	24.20	25.30	19.90	39.60	---	20.40	35.40	48.80	52.20	13.20	25.60	13.60
1946	23.90	24.90	19.60	39.00	---	20.20	34.60	48.20	51.40	13.00	25.10	13.20
1945	23.50	24.50	19.50	38.50	---	20.20	34.10	47.70	50.40	12.90	24.70	13.20
1944	23.00	24.10	19.30	37.90	---	20.20	34.40	47.30	50.10	12.90	24.90	13.20
1943	22.90	23.80	19.10	37.50	---	20.20	34.20	46.60	50.40	12.80	24.70	13.20
1942	22.50	23.30	18.70	36.80	---	20.20	33.90	46.50	50.70	12.80	24.70	13.20
1941	22.20	22.90	18.50	36.30	---	20.20	33.70	46.60	51.00	12.90	24.90	13.10
1940	22.10	22.80	18.40	36.40	---	20.30	33.90	47.10	51.30	13.00	25.10	13.20

[1] Estimated for 1940–1943; thereafter, based on sample tabulations.   [2] Wife aged 65 or over; beginning 1956, includes wife aged 62 to 64 with no entitled child in her care.   [3] Wife under age 65 with 1 or more entitled children in her care.

Series H 149–161.   Old-Age, Survivors, and Disability Insurance—Workers Retiring, and Retired Workers Receiving Benefits, by Sex: 1940 to 1957

	Workers retiring during year [1]							Retired workers receiving benefits at end of year [2]					
			Percent of retired workers							Percent of old-age beneficiaries			
Year	Total (1,000)	Average age	Total	65 years	66 to 69 years	70 to 74 years	75 and over	Total (1,000)	Average age	Total	65 to 69 years	70 to 74 years	75 and over
	149	150	151	152	153	154	155	156	157	158	159	160	161
MALE													
1957	---	---	---	---	---	---	---	4,198	72.9	100.0	34.9	34.2	30.9
1956	772	69.0	100.0	32.5	30.8	24.1	12.6	3,572	72.9	100.0	34.2	35.2	30.6
1955	604	68.2	100.0	38.2	30.3	25.5	6.1	3,252	72.7	100.0	35.7	34.8	29.5
1954	592	67.9	100.0	38.4	35.8	17.9	7.9	2,803	72.6	100.0	37.2	32.8	30.0
1953	521	67.9	100.0	39.2	34.9	17.3	8.6	2,438	72.6	100.0	37.3	32.5	30.2
1952	475	68.8	100.0	32.8	33.9	17.9	15.4	2,052	72.6	100.0	36.9	32.9	30.2
1951	352	68.0	100.0	40.2	32.8	17.4	9.6	1,819	72.3	100.0	38.8	32.4	28.8
1950	644	69.0	100.0	22.8	43.1	21.2	12.9	1,469	72.2	100.0	39.1	33.7	27.3
1949	284	68.4	100.0	30.4	39.6	20.8	9.1	1,100	72.3	100.0	36.3	37.0	26.6
1948	228	68.6	100.0	28.9	39.0	22.0	10.1	900	72.3	100.0	35.6	39.1	25.3
1947	252	68.9	100.0	25.4	39.7	24.0	10.9	756	72.1	100.0	36.5	40.4	23.2
1946	252	69.4	100.0	17.3	42.3	28.1	12.3	610	71.9	100.0	38.0	41.1	20.9
1945	180	69.4	100.0	17.0	42.7	27.9	12.4	447	71.7	100.0	39.9	40.2	19.8
1944	100	69.4	100.0	18.5	41.4	27.3	12.8	323	71.5	100.0	42.7	38.6	18.8
1943	76	69.1	100.0	22.2	40.1	25.8	12.0	261	71.1	100.0	49.2	34.1	16.7
1942	86	69.1	100.0	24.1	38.0	26.0	11.9	224	70.5	100.0	57.3	28.6	14.2
1941	97	69.1	100.0	23.7	37.8	26.7	11.8	175	69.8	100.0	65.6	23.0	11.5
1940	127	68.2	100.0	17.9	57.8	16.6	7.6	99	68.8	100.0	74.4	17.4	8.2
FEMALE													
1957	---	---	---	---	---	---	---	1,999	70.5	[4] 100.0	[4] 39.7	28.2	18.9
1956	569	65.5	[3] 100.0	[3] 27.1	14.3	7.7	3.6	1,540	70.9	[4] 100.0	[4] 42.5	30.7	19.5
1955	280	67.4	100.0	47.6	30.1	17.6	4.7	1,222	71.3	100.0	47.8	32.3	19.8
1954	258	67.5	100.0	46.0	31.9	15.2	6.9	972	71.2	100.0	49.0	31.2	19.8
1953	213	67.5	100.0	46.7	31.3	15.1	6.9	784	71.1	100.0	49.8	30.9	19.4
1952	195	68.4	100.0	37.8	32.4	17.7	12.1	592	71.0	100.0	50.2	30.9	18.8
1951	119	67.2	100.0	49.3	31.7	14.0	5.1	459	70.8	100.0	51.5	30.6	17.9
1950	204	68.1	100.0	24.0	50.4	19.8	5.8	302	71.1	100.0	48.4	32.9	18.7
1949	47	68.1	100.0	32.3	40.4	20.5	6.8	186	71.7	100.0	39.8	39.0	21.2
1948	39	68.2	100.0	30.6	40.6	21.6	7.1	148	71.6	100.0	39.9	41.3	18.7
1947	39	68.4	100.0	27.6	41.9	23.4	7.0	119	71.4	100.0	41.2	42.6	16.3
1946	32	68.6	100.0	23.1	43.8	25.3	7.8	92	71.1	100.0	43.3	42.5	14.2
1945	21	68.4	100.0	25.4	43.7	23.6	7.3	71	70.8	100.0	47.1	40.0	12.8
1944	14	68.1	100.0	27.9	44.6	20.7	6.8	55	70.5	100.0	52.6	36.1	11.4
1943	12	68.0	100.0	30.3	43.6	19.6	6.6	45	70.0	100.0	60.4	29.8	9.7
1942	13	68.1	100.0	31.1	41.4	20.8	6.7	36	69.5	100.0	68.4	23.5	8.1
1941	14	68.2	100.0	30.2	41.6	21.2	7.0	25	68.9	100.0	75.2	18.2	6.6
1940	16	67.5	100.0	21.9	61.1	12.7	4.4	13	68.1	100.0	82.6	12.8	4.5

[1] Age on birthday in year of entitlement.   [2] Age at birthday in stated year.   [3] In 1956, 47.2 percent of the retiring women were 62 to 64 years old.
[4] In 1956, 7.3 percent of the retired women were 62 to 64 years old; in 1957, the percentage was 13.3.

Series H 162–174. Unemployment Insurance—Coverage, Benefits, and Financing Under State Programs: 1941 to 1957

[Includes Alaska and Hawaii, except as noted]

Year	Average covered employment [1]	Average weekly insured unemployment	First payments	Average weekly initial claims [2]	Average weekly benefit [3] Amount	Average weekly benefit [3] Percent of average weekly wage	Average actual duration of benefit payments	Claimants exhausting benefits [4]	Duration of benefits for exhaustees[5]	Total benefits paid [6]	Contributions collected [7]	Taxable wages [8]	Reserves [9] (end of year)
	162	163	164	165	166	167	168	169	170	171	172	173	174
	1,000	*1,000*	*1,000*	*1,000*	*Dollars*		*Wks.*	*1,000*	*Wks.*	*Mil. dol.*	*Mil. dol.*	*Mil. dol.*	*Mil. dol.*
1957	39,670	1,474	5,071	278	28.21	34.8	11.6	1,191	20.5	1,734	1,544	112,826	8,662
1956	38,929	1,212	4,729	235	27.02	33.3	11.4	1,020	20.0	1,381	1,463	109,879	8,574
1955	36,590	1,254	4,508	235	25.04	32.1	12.4	1,272	20.3	1,350	1,209	101,575	8,264
1954	35,372	1,865	6,590	315	24.93	33.5	12.8	1,769	20.0	2,027	1,136	96,539	8,219
1953	36,667	995	4,228	225	23.58	32.3	10.1	764	19.2	962	1,348	99,630	8,913
1952	35,577	1,024	4,384	222	22.79	33.0	10.4	931	19.3	998	1,368	94,670	8,328
1951	34,858	969	4,127	218	21.09	32.2	10.1	811	17.9	840	1,493	90,252	7,782
1950	32,887	1,503	5,212	252	20.76	34.4	13.0	1,853	19.3	1,373	1,191	81,545	6,972
1949	31,695	1,976	7,364	340	20.48	36.0	11.8	1,935	18.7	1,736	987	76,268	7,010
1948	33,088	1,002	4,008	210	19.03	34.1	10.7	1,028	[10] 18.0	790	1,000	78,536	7,603
1947	32,278	1,009	3,984	187	17.83	34.6	11.1	1,272	17.8	775	1,096	72,981	7,303
1946	30,234	---------	4,461	189	18.50	39.6	13.4	1,986	18.5	1,095	912	63,690	6,860
1945	28,407	---------	[5] 2,823	116	18.77	41.6	8.5	[11] 254	14.5	446	1,162	58,545	6,914
1944	30,044	---------	533	29	15.90	35.9	7.7	[11] 102	13.8	62	1,317	60,637	6,072
1943	30,828	---------	664	36	13.84	33.6	9.0	[11] 194	14.3	80	1,325	59,049	4,716
1942	29,349	---------	2,815	122	12.66	35.3	10.0	[11] 1,078	12.6	344	1,139	49,721	3,388
1941	26,814	---------	3,439	164	11.06	36.6	9.4	[11] 1,544	12.1	344	1,006	38,677	2,524

[1] Before 1945, average of workers in last pay period of each type (weekly, semi-monthly, etc.) ending within the month; thereafter, ending nearest 15th of each month. Excludes Alaska and Hawaii.
[2] Includes initial transitional claims.
[3] For total unemployment; includes dependents' allowance.
[4] Based on date final payments were issued.
[5] Excludes Wisconsin for all years; in addition excludes data as follows: 1941, for 5 states; 1942–1943, 3 States; 1944, 7 States; 1945, 11 States; 1948–1949, 1 State.
[6] Excludes small amounts of reconversion unemployment benefits for seamen in 1947–1950.
[7] Includes contributions, penalties, and interest from employers; employee contributions in States which tax workers; and $40.6 million deposited by Federal Government in 1938 to trust funds of 15 States, representing payroll taxes collected by the former in 1936.

[8] Wages subject to State unemployment insurance taxes.
[9] Funds available for benefits. Excludes transfers as follows; To railroad unemployment insurance program, $8 million in 1941; to States' temporary disability funds, $200,000 in 1946, $15 million in 1947, and $64 million in 1948. Includes in 1955, $3 million advance to Alaska from Federal account in Unemployment Insurance Trust Fund, which advance was repaid in December 1956. Includes $33.4 million allocation to the States in July 1956, based on 1955 taxable wages in accord with Employment Security Administrative Financing Act of 1954.
[10] Excludes January-March 1948 data for all States.
[11] Excludes Indiana, Wisconsin, and Wyoming from 1940–1943; Wisconsin and Wyoming in 1944; and Wisconsin in January-November 1945.

Series H 175–185. Workmen's Compensation—Payments, by Type of Benefit and Type of Insurance: 1939 to 1957

[In millions of dollars]

Year	Total payments	Medical and hospitalization payments	Type of benefits — Compensation payments Total	Disability	Survivor	Insurance losses paid by private insurance carriers [1] Amount	Insurance losses paid by private insurance carriers [1] Percent of total	State fund disbursements [2] Amount	State fund disbursements [2] Percent of total	Self-insurance payments [3] Amount	Self-insurance payments [3] Percent of total
	175	176	177	178	179	180	181	182	183	184	185
1957	1,064	365	699	619	80	660	62.0	272	25.6	132	12.4
1956	1,003	350	653	578	75	618	61.7	259	25.8	125	12.5
1955	915	325	590	520	70	563	61.4	238	26.1	114	12.5
1954	876	308	568	498	70	541	61.7	225	25.7	110	12.6
1953	841	280	561	491	70	524	62.3	210	25.0	107	12.7
1952	785	260	525	460	65	491	62.5	193	24.6	101	12.9
1951	709	233	476	416	60	444	62.7	170	24.0	94	13.3
1950	615	200	415	360	55	381	62.0	149	24.2	85	13.8
1949	566	185	381	329	52	353	62.3	132	23.3	81	14.4
1948	534	175	359	309	50	335	62.7	121	22.7	78	14.6
1947	486	160	326	280	46	302	62.1	110	22.7	74	15.2
1946	434	140	294	250	44	270	62.1	96	22.1	68	15.8
1945	408	125	283	241	42	253	61.9	91	22.3	65	15.8
1944	385	120	265	225	40	237	61.4	86	22.3	63	16.3
1943	353	112	241	203	38	213	60.4	81	22.8	59	16.8
1942	329	108	221	185	36	190	57.9	81	24.7	57	17.4
1941	291	100	191	157	34	160	55.0	77	26.6	54	18.4
1940	256	95	161	129	32	135	52.7	73	28.4	48	18.9
1939	235	85	150	120	30	122	52.0	68	29.2	44	18.8

[1] Net cash and medical benefits paid during calendar year by private insurance carriers under standard workmen's compensation policies.
[2] Net cash and medical benefits paid by State funds, and Federal system for Government employees. Data for fiscal years for some funds.
[3] Cash and medical benefits paid by self-insurers, plus value of medical benefits paid by employers carrying workmen's compensation policies that exclude standard medical coverage. Estimated from available State data.

Series H 186–198.   Public Assistance—Recipients and Average Monthly Payments, by Program: 1936 to 1957

[As of December.   Through 1942, continental United States only; thereafter data include Alaska and Hawaii and, beginning October 1950, Puerto Rico and the Virgin Islands]

	Number of recipients (1,000)							Average monthly payment					
Year	Old-age assistance	Aid to dependent children			Aid to the blind	Aid to the permanently and totally disabled [2]	General assistance (cases) [3]	Old-age assistance	Aid to dependent children		Aid to the blind	Aid to the permanently and totally disabled [2]	General assistance (per case) [3]
		Families	Total recipients [1]	Children					Per family	Per recipient [1]			
	186	187	188	189	190	191	192	193	194	195	196	197	198
1957	2,487	667	2,498	1,913	108	291	344	60.68	100.72	26.90	66.35	60.02	59.74
1956	2,514	616	2,271	1,732	107	269	305	57.99	95.05	25.79	63.15	58.83	56.14
1955	2,553	603	2,193	1,661	105	244	314	53.93	88.61	24.35	58.08	56.18	55.04
1954	2,565	604	2,174	1,640	102	224	351	51.90	86.21	23.96	56.37	54.93	57.29
1953	2,591	548	1,942	1,464	100	195	270	51.50	84.22	23.77	55.67	53.44	50.53
1952	2,646	570	1,992	1,495	99	164	280	50.90	83.83	23.98	54.91	53.50	49.82
1951	2,708	593	2,044	1,524	97	127	323	46.00	77.08	22.36	49.05	49.46	47.09
1950	2,789	652	2,234	1,662	98	69	413	43.95	72.42	21.13	46.56	45.41	46.65
1949	2,736	599	--------	1,521	93	--------	562	44.76	74.19		46.11		50.47
1948	2,498	475	--------	1,214	86	--------	398	42.02	71.88		43.54		47.39
1947	2,332	416	--------	1,060	81	--------	356	37.42	63.01		39.58		42.79
1946	2,196	346	--------	885	77	--------	315	35.31	62.23		36.67		39.47
1945	2,056	274	--------	701	71	--------	257	30.88	52.05		33.52		32.72
1944	2,066	254	--------	639	72	--------	258	28.43	45.58		29.31		28.77
1943	2,149	272	--------	676	76	--------	292	26.66	41.57		27.95		27.76
1942	2,227	348	--------	849	79	--------	460	23.37	36.25		26.54		25.23
1941	2,234	390	--------	941	77	--------	798	21.27	33.62		25.82		24.40
1940	2,066	370	--------	891	73	--------	1,239	20.26	32.38		25.38		24.28
1939	1,909	315	--------	760	70	--------	1,558	19.30	31.77		25.44		24.89
1938	1,776	280	--------	648	67	--------	1,631	19.56	31.96		25.22		25.06
1937	1,577	228	--------	565	56	--------	1,626	19.46	31.46		27.20		25.36
1936	1,106	162	--------	404	45	--------	1,510	18.79	29.82		26.11		24.13

[1] Includes as recipients, the children and 1 parent or other adult relative in families in which the requirements of at least 1 such adult were considered in determining the amount of assistance. Beginning October 1950, Federal funds were available for payments to these adults under the 1950 Social Security Act amendments.

[2] Program initiated October 1950 under the 1950 Social Security Act amendments.
[3] Excludes Idaho for 1957 and Nebraska for 1952 and 1953.

Series H 199–206.   Emergency Public Assistance and Federal Work Programs—Recipients and Assistance: 1933 to 1943

[In thousands.   Data through 1942 refer to continental United States only; 1943 public assistance data include Alaska and Hawaii]

Year	Federal Emergency Relief Administration	Farm Security Administration	Civilian Conservation Corps	National Youth Administration		Work Projects Administration	Civilian Works Administration	Other Federal projects
				Student program	Out-of-school program			
	199	200	201	202	203	204	205	206
RECIPIENTS (OR PERSONS EMPLOYED), DECEMBER								
1943								
1942				86		300		
1941		26	126	333	283	1,023		2
1940		45	246	449	326	1,826		22
1939		96	266	434	296	2,109		141
1938		115	275	372	240	3,156		167
1937		109	284	304	136	1,594		235
1936	11	135	328	411	178	2,243		506
1935	96	130	459	283		2,667		408
1934	459		330					331
1933	101		290				3,597	264
ASSISTANCE (OR EARNINGS) DURING YEAR								
1943				[1] $3,794		[1] $46,737		
1942		$6,271	$34,030	11,328	$32,009	503,055		$730
1941		12,281	155,604	25,118	94,032	937,366		12,904
1940		18,282	215,846	26,864	65,211	1,269,617		92,604
1939		19,055	230,513	22,707	51,538	1,565,515		247,285
1938		22,579	230,318	19,598	41,560	1,751,053		186,505
1937	$467	35,894	245,756	24,287	32,664	1,186,266		324,639
1936	3,873	20,365	292,397	26,329	28,883	1,592,039		498,415
1935	114,996	2,541	332,851	6,364		238,018		289,897
1934	61,069		260,957				$503,060	275,161
1933	5,753		140,736				214,956	30,718

[1] Program discontinued before end of 1943.

Series H 207–212. Old-Age Assistance Recipients and Insurance Beneficiaries Per 1,000 Population 65 Years Old and Over; and Children Receiving Aid, and Child Insurance Beneficiaries Per 1,000 Population Under Age 18: 1936 to 1957

[June of each year. For 1936–1950, 51 jurisdictions, States, and Territories; 1951–1957, 53 jurisdictions, States, and Territories. OAA denotes old-age assistance; OASDI, old-age survivors and disability insurance; and ADC, aid to dependent children]

Year	Number per 1,000 population 65 years old and over receiving—				Number per 1,000 child population under 18 years old receiving—[1]		Year	Number per 1,000 population 65 years old and over receiving—				Number per 1,000 child population under 18 years old receiving—[1]	
	OAA, OASDI, or both	OAA	OASDI	Both OAA and OASDI	ADC	OASDI		OAA, OASDI, or both	OAA	OASDI	Both OAA and OASDI	ADC	OASDI
	207	208	209	210	211	212		207	208	209	210	211	212
1957	657	168	527	38	30	23	1946	274	194	87	7	19	10
1956	570	173	454	36	29	22							
							1945	251	194	62	5	15	8
1955	559	179	415	36	29	21	1944	251	205	50	4	16	6
1954	511	187	358	34	28	20	1943	257	219	41	3	18	5
1953	474	194	314	33	28	19	1942	266	234	34	3	23	4
1952	432	203	260	31	29	17	1941	254	233	23	2	23	2
1951	421	215	235	28	32	16							
1950	375	226	170	21	35	14	1940	224	217	7	1	20	1
1949	351	218	149	17	29	13	1939	----	210	----	----	18	----
1948	318	205	126	13	25	12	1938	----	194	----	----	15	----
1947	299	202	106	10	23	11	1937	----	156	----	----	11	----
							1936	----	81	----	----	9	----

[1] A small number of children were in families receiving both OASDI and ADC.

Series H 213–222. Services Under Child Health and Welfare Service Programs: 1937 to 1957

Year	Crippled children's program [1]		Maternal and child health program [2]						Child welfare program	
			Maternity medical clinic		Child health clinic service					
					Infants		Other children			
	Children served	Rate per 10,000 children	Mothers served [3]	Rate per 1,000 live births	Number served	Rate per 1,000 infants	Number served	Rate per 1,000 children 1 to 4 years old	Children served	Rate per 10,000 children under 21
	213	214	215	216	217	218	219	220	221	222
1957	313,000	47	240,630	(4)	557,801	144	768,476	(5)	330,000	49
1956	296,000	46	225,624	(4)	517,243	139	769,102	(5)	305,000	47
1955	278,000	45	188,988	46	448,058	121	576,896	39	296,000	47
1954	271,000	45	190,667	47	446,772	123	576,966	39	289,000	48
1953	252,000	43	177,580	44	411,907	117	591,959	41	282,000	48
1952	238,000	42	180,265	45	433,911	126	576,260	41	279,000	49
1951	229,000	41	188,541	48	402,279	120	580,344	41	277,000	50
1950	211,000	39	175,270	47	302,892	94	420,334	31	270,000	49
1949	207,000	39	168,234	45	294,998	91	398,582	31	265,000	50
1948	195,000	37	152,691	41	263,819	81	379,472	31	260,000	50
1947	175,000	34	151,117	38	245,514	69	320,263	28	255,000	50
1946	155,000	32	130,909	37	187,045	75	275,969	25	250,000	51
1945	130,000	27	116,961	31	169,965	67	256,815	24	241,000	51
1944	125,000	27	129,596	43	169,799	66	266,774	26		
1943	115,000	24	147,599	46	185,729	67	264,817	28		
1942	133,000	27	161,367	52	185,562	78	307,344	33		
1941	147,000	30	167,002	61	185,139	85	314,238	36		
1940	127,000	26	146,440	55	175,357	84	299,174	34		
1939	127,000	26	125,667	51	138,280	69	277,703	33		
1938	114,000	24	119,623	48	156,749	80	266,466	32		
1937	110,000	24	75,193	31	127,365	66	200,022	25		

[1] General coverage of State reports: 1937–1947, services administered or financed in whole or in part by official State agencies under the Social Security Act; 1948–1949, services provided or purchased by official State agencies exclusive of prediagnostic services; 1950–1956, "physician's services" consisting of clinic service, hospital care, convalescent home care, and other services by physicians. Data for 1937 are for 45 States, the District of Columbia, Alaska, Hawaii (Georgia, Louisiana, Oregon not participating); for 1938, Georgia and Oregon also included and for 1939, Louisiana as well (except for first quarter). Puerto Rico excluded beginning with the last half of 1940, and Virgin Islands beginning the last half of 1947; prior to these dates they were included. Arizona, which did not participate 1950–1956, excluded for these years.

Rates for each year are based on the population of States participating in those years.
[2] Includes services administered or supervised by official State health agencies. Reports were received each year except 1941 from 48 States, the District of Columbia, Alaska, Hawaii. Missouri was not participating in 1941. Puerto Rico is included beginning with 1940, and the Virgin Islands beginning with the last half of 1947.
[3] Prior to 1956 antepartum service only.
[4] Rates no longer computed because mothers may receive maternity medical clinic service in more than one calendar year and in years different from year of giving birth.
[5] Rates no longer computed as older children are included.

chapter H

EDUCATION (Series H 223–411)

H 223–411. General note.

Nationwide statistics on education have been collected and published primarily by the Office of Education and the Bureau of the Census. Data on education have also been collected and published by other Federal and State and local governmental agencies, and by independent research organizations.

The Office of Education generally obtains data from reports of State and local school systems and institutions of higher learning. These data relate to school enrollment and attendance, graduates, instructional staff, curricula, school district organization, receipts, and expenditures for elementary and secondary schools, and enrollment, faculty, degrees conferred, income, expenditures, property, and plant fund operations for institutions of higher education.

Data from the Bureau of the Census are obtained through household interviews in decennial censuses and current sample surveys, and relate essentially to school enrollment, literacy, and educational attainment of the general population.

H 223–315. General note.

The Office of Education has issued statistical reports on elementary and secondary education since 1870. For 1870–1917, statistics were included as part of the *Annual Report of the United States Commissioner of Education*. Since 1918, a report has been issued for each even-numbered school year under the title, *Biennial Survey of Education in the United States*. Chapter 1 of the *Biennial Survey*, "Statistical Summary of Education," and chapter 2, "Statistics of State School Systems," are primary sources for some derived measures relating to education. Beginning with 1941 and ending with 1951, chapter 2 was supplemented by an abridged report issued as a circular for each odd-numbered school year. Data from the odd-year biennial circulars have not been included in the present compilation. Biennial survey data are based on report forms completed by State departments of education (a copy of the report form appears in the *Biennial Survey* of 1952–1954). Beginning with the *Biennial Survey* of 1952–1954, these forms have been completed by education officials in accordance with detailed instructions contained in the Office of Education, *Handbook I, the Common Core of State Educational Information*. Prior to that date, the forms were completed in accordance with various circulars of information distributed by the Office of Education.

One of the major factors in presenting accurate statistical data on a national basis is the uniformity with which all recording units use standard terms, definitions, and procedures. Prior to 1909, this was controlled only by definitions on the questionnaires requesting information. Since 1909, the Office of Education in cooperation with other national and State organizations has improved uniform recording and reporting through the means of national committees, publications, and national and regional conferences.

A major problem in the collection and processing of comprehensive nationwide school statistics is that of getting all the schools to respond within reasonable time limits. The school authorities are not compelled to report to the Office of Education. There is some evidence that the proportion of schools reporting has increased through the years. This increase is most evident in the data for secondary schools. Prior to 1930,

a complete list of public secondary day schools had not been compiled, and consequently there is no way to measure the degree of response in the earlier years. In 1930, there were 23,930 public secondary day schools on file, and reports were received from 22,237. In 1938, the number of schools on file increased to 25,308, and the number reporting was 25,091. In 1952, there were 23,757 schools, and replies were received from all but 12 schools. The data for the missing schools were estimated, and the published totals for 1952 cover all public secondary day schools.

Since 1870, there have been both major and minor changes in the collection patterns with changes in the administration of the program. Some patterns lasted for many years. With voluntary response and no field service (until 1924), response rates varied in their completeness for both reporting in general and for specific items. The completeness of the coverage is not always made evident in the publication. Field service supplemented returns by mail for the 1923–1924 biennial chapters. Visits were made to State departments of education and colleges and universities to complete the coverage from basic or secondary records that were available in the State departments of education or at individual schools and institutions. The introduction of sampling in recent years has also insured adequate coverage.

The data in these historical tables will not always agree with similar data in the publications cited as sources for a specific year because tabulations were "kept open" for many years and as data came in they were added and reflected in future historical tables.

H 223–233. Elementary and secondary schools, enrollment and attendance, and high school graduates, 1870–1956.

Source: 1870–1916, Office of Education, *Annual Report of the United States Commissioner of Education*, various issues (except for 1890 for series H 228, see source for 1918–1956); 1918–1956, *Biennial Survey of Education in the United States*, chapter 2, various issues (except for series H 228 for 1918 and 1928–1934, and for series H 232–233, see Chapter 1, "Statistical Summary of Education").

Enrollment data are also collected and issued by the Bureau of the Census; see series H 374–382 and H 383–394.

A public school is defined as one operated by publicly elected or appointed school officials in which the program and activities are under the control of these officials and which is supported by public funds. School enrollment and other figures are for public elementary and secondary day schools in continental United States. Excluded are public schools in the Territories and outlying parts of the United States, public schools operated directly by the Federal Government on military reservations and schools for Indians and Alaskan natives, public residential schools for exceptional children, and subcollegiate departments of institutions of higher education. Only regular day school pupils are included; pupils enrolled in night schools and summer schools are excluded.

A nonpublic school is defined as one established by an agency other than the State or its subdivisions, primarily supported by other than public funds, and the operation of whose program rests with other than publicly elected or appointed officials. Nonpublic schools include both denominational and nonsectarian schools, but not private schools for exceptional children or private vocational or trade schools. Enrollment figures include only regular day school pupils; they exclude summer school pupils.

Nonpublic school figures (series H 228) for 1920–1956, which appear in the separate issues of "Statistics of State School Systems" for those years, are not strictly comparable. For example, for 1928–1934, enrollment in kindergarten was not included, and in some of the earlier years, the figures include enrollment of secondary pupils in subcollegiate departments of institutions of higher education, normal schools, etc. For data substituted from other sources, see the exceptions cited in the source note above.

Figures for average daily attendance in public schools were computed by dividing the total number of days attended by all pupils enrolled by the number of days school was actually in session. Only days on which the pupils were under the guidance and direction of teachers are considered as days in session.

Figures for high school graduates include graduates from public and nonpublic schools and exclude persons granted equivalency certificates.

Population estimates used in computing series H 225 and H 233 were provided by the Bureau of the Census.

See also general note for series H 223–315.

H 234–245. Public elementary and secondary day schools' instructional staff, school districts, and schools, 1870–1956.

Source: 1870–1916, Office of Education, *Annual Report of the United States Commissioner of Education*, various issues; 1918–1956, *Biennial Survey of Education in the United States*, various issues, and Pamphlet No. 92, *Are the One-Teacher Schools Passing?*

A principal is defined as the administrative head of a school to whom has been delegated the major responsibility for the coordination and supervision of the activities of the school. Supervisors of instruction or consultants are school personnel who have the responsibility of assisting teachers in improving the learning situation and instructional methods.

School districts (series H 241) are administrative units at the local level which exist primarily to operate schools or to contract for school services. Normally, taxes can be levied against citizens or property or both within the units for school purposes. These units may or may not be coterminous with county, city, or town boundaries.

A school (series H 242–244) is defined as a division of the school system consisting of a group of pupils composed of one or more grade groups, organized as one unit with one or more teachers to give instruction of a defined type, and housed in a school plant of one or more buildings. More than one school may be housed in one school plant, as is the case when the elementary and secondary programs are housed in the same school plant.

One-teacher public schools (series H 245) are schools in which one teacher is employed to teach all grades authorized in the school, regardless of the number of rooms in the building.

See also general note for series H 223–315 and text for series H 223–233.

H 246–251. Public elementary and secondary schools' receipts, by source, 1890–1956.

Source: 1890–1916, Office of Education, *Annual Report of the United States Commissioner of Education*, various issues; 1918–1956, *Biennial Survey of Education in the United States*, various issues.

Revenue receipts represent additions to assets (cash) from taxes, appropriations, and other funds which do not incur an obligation that must be met at some future date and do not represent exchanges of property for money. Receipts from county and other intermediate sources are included with local receipts. Other sources of revenue (series H 251) include gifts and tuition, and transportation fees from patrons.

Nonrevenue receipts represent amounts which either incur an obligation that must be met at some future date or change the form of an asset from property to cash and therefore decrease the amount and the value of school property. Money received from loans, sale of bonds, sale of property purchased from capital funds, and proceeds from insurance adjustments constitute most of the nonrevenue receipts.

See also general note for series H 223–315 and text for series H 223–233.

H 252–261. Public elementary and secondary schools' expenditures, by purpose, 1870–1956.

Source: 1870–1916, Office of Education, *Annual Report of the United States Commissioner of Education*, various issues; 1918–1956, *Biennial Survey of Education in the United States*, various issues.

Expenditures for administration (series H 255) include those for the central office staff for administrative functions and all general control which is systemwide and not confined to one school, subject, or narrow phase of school services. Instruction expenditures (series H 256) include salaries of instructional staff and clerical assistants, and expenditures for free textbooks, school library books, and supplies and other expenditures for instruction. Plant operation and maintenance expenditures (series H 257) include salaries of custodians, engineers, carpenters, painters, etc.; fuel, light, water, and power; and supplies, expenses, and contractual service. Other current expenditures (series H 258) include expenditures for fixed charges and for attendance, health, transportation, food, and miscellaneous school services.

Capital outlay (series H 259) includes expenditures for the acquisition of fixed assets or additions to fixed assets (such as land or existing buildings, improvement of grounds, construction of buildings, additions to buildings, remodeling of buildings, and initial or additional equipment). Interest (series H 260) includes interest payments on short-term and current loans from current funds, and on bonds from current and sinking funds. Other expenditures (series H 261) include expenditures, when separately reported, for summer schools, community colleges, and adult education.

See also general note for series H 223–315 and text for series H 223–233.

H 262–315. Public secondary day school pupils enrolled in specified subjects, 1890–1949.

Source: Office of Education, *Biennial Survey of Education in the United States, 1948–1950.*

For 1910–1934, the percentages are based on the number of pupils enrolled in the last 4 years of all schools that returned usable questionnaires. For 1890, 1900, and 1949, the figures are based on the total number of pupils enrolled in the last 4 years of all schools. The source states that "when necessary, the subjects reported in previous surveys were analyzed, and appropriate components were either recombined, separately listed, or eliminated (with corresponding changes in the number and percentage enrolled) in a manner to yield as close comparability as possible with the data in the current (1948–49) survey."

H 316–373. General note.

The Office of Education has issued statistical reports on higher education on a periodic basis since 1870. Until 1916, these statistics appeared in the *Annual Report of the United States Commissioner of Education*. There was no report for 1917. Since 1918, statistical reports have been issued biennially, as chapters of the *Biennial Survey of Education in the United States*. In addition, an annual report on conferral of earned degrees has been issued since 1948 and one on early fall enrollments since 1946. An annual report on current income and expenditures and other finance items was also issued from 1933 to 1940, first under the title, *The Economic Outlook in Higher Education* and later under the title, *College Income and Expenditures*.

Among the major problems involved in the collecting and processing of nationwide statistics of higher education have been those of uniformity and promptness of reporting, and completeness of coverage of the field. The problem of uniformity of reporting was attacked in 1930 with the formation of the National Committee on Standard Reports for Institutions of Higher Education; this committee was disbanded in 1935. Its successor, the Financial Advisory Service of the American Council on Education, carried on the work until 1940, when it, too, was discontinued. These two organizations, voluntary in character and operating with no official status, did much to conventionalize finance accounting and reporting procedures in universities and colleges.

The problems of promptness of reporting and completeness of coverage stem from the fact that only the land-grant institutions (fewer than 4 percent of all the institutions in the Nation) are under legal obligation to submit financial or statistical reports to the Office of Education. The percent of institutions supplying usable reports within a reasonable time, however, has increased materially in the last two or three decades, in spite of the fact that inquiries emanating from the Office of Education have increased in number and scope.

Another problem in the compilation of historical statistics of higher education is the double counting of data for some institutions. Until 1916, the tabulations of the Office of Education were built largely around the various professional curricula, with the result that in many instances the data of a professional school within a university were included both in the over-all tabulations of universities and colleges and in those of the profession involved. With the inception of the *Biennial Survey of Education* in 1918, the emphasis in tabulation was shifted to the administrative organization and the data relating to certain professional schools were so tabulated that any possible duplication was identifiable without too much difficulty. Since 1932, the Office of Education has maintained a master list of all institutions in the Nation; thus, the problem of duplicate tabulation is no longer an important one.

H 316–324. Institutions of higher education—number, faculty, and enrollment, 1870–1956.

Source: 1870–1916, Office of Education, *Annual Report of the United States Commissioner of Education*, various issues; 1918–1956, *Biennial Survey of Education in the United States*, various issues.

Institutions reporting include universities, colleges, professional schools, junior colleges, teachers colleges, and normal schools, both privately and publicly controlled, regular session. The figures for institutions represent administrative organizations rather than individual campuses, i.e., a university operating one or more branches away from the main campus is counted as one institution. There is probably some (undeterminable) underreporting in some of the earlier years. Since 1946, this underreporting has been corrected by the use of estimated reports prepared from secondary sources for nonrespondent institutions.

Faculty figures include full-time and part-time faculty members. Except in 1932, no attempt is made to evaluate these services on a full-time equivalent basis. Faculty figures also include the entire administrative, instructional, research, and other professional personnel. Resident instructional staff, however, excludes administrative and other professional personnel not engaged in instructional activities.

Enrollment data are cumulative and cover the entire academic year concerned, except for 1954 and 1956, where data are for November 1953 and 1955, respectively.

A special student is a resident student taking courses on a college level but not working for a degree.

See also general note for series H 316–373.

H 325–326. Junior colleges, 1918–1954.

Source: See source for series H 316–324.

A junior college is defined as one that offers at least one but less than four years of work and does not grant the bachelor's degree.

H 327–338. Institutions of higher education—degrees conferred, by sex, 1870–1957.

Source: Office of Education, records.

The basic sources of data for earned degrees for 1870–1916 are the various issues of the *Annual Report of the United States Commissioner of Education;* for 1918–1946, various issues of the *Biennial Survey of Education;* and for 1948–1957, *Earned Degrees Conferred by Higher Educational Institutions.*

The figures presented here were estimated from summaries and compilations from the original source material previously published by the Office of Education in *Education for Victory*, August 21, 1944; and *Higher Education*, vol. XII, No. 7, March 1956; and in Walter C. Eells, *American Universities and Colleges*, Seventh Edition, 1956, or directly from the basic sources for recent years.

The first-level degree (designated as "bachelor's or first professional") is defined as the first degree granted upon completion of a course of study in a given field. The degree must be based on at least 4 years of college work or the equivalent thereof. The same classification (namely, "first level") is given to a degree, e.g., LL. B., regardless of whether the degree is based on 7 years' preparation, 6 years' preparation, or less; and regardless of whether the student had previously earned a degree in another field. The first-level degree is ordinarily a bachelor's degree, but important exceptions occur in certain of the professional fields. The second-level degree is a degree beyond the first level but below the doctorate; ordinarily, a master's degree. The doctorate (the highest level of earned degrees) includes such advanced degrees as Ph.D., Ed.D., D.Eng., and Dr. P.H.; it includes only earned degrees, not honorary.

H 339–350. Institutions of higher education—current income, 1890–1954.

Source: 1890–1910, Office of Education, *Annual Report of the United States Commissioner of Education*, various issues; 1920–1954, *Biennial Survey of Education in the United States*, various issues.

Total current income represents funds accruing to, or received by, higher educational institutions, usable for their recurring day-to-day activities. It does not include additions to plant funds nor those to endowment and other nonexpendable funds (included in series H 362–369). Educational and general income is perhaps best understood as income available for educational and general expenditures. Income from auxiliary enterprises and activities includes income of dormitories, dining halls, cafeterias, union buildings, college bookstores, university presses, student hospitals, faculty housing, intercollegiate athletic programs, concerts, industrial plants operated on a student self-help basis, and other enterprises conducted primarily for students and staff and intended to be self-supporting without competing with the industries of the community in which the institution is located. Other current income includes moneys becoming available for student aid (scholarships, fellowships, prizes). Until the last few years, it also included earnings of funds subject to annuity or living trust agreements, as well as some few funds so minor in amount or so infrequent in recurrence as to make special classification inadvisable.

See also general note for series H 316–373.

H 351–361. Institutions of higher education—current expenditures, 1930–1954.

Source: Office of Education, *Biennial Survey of Education in the United States*, various issues.

Expenditure data were not tabulated for all institutions of higher education until 1930. Prior to that time they were collected from land-grant institutions and teacher-education institutions only. Other professional schools and non-land-grant institutions were omitted from the surveys.

H 362–369. Institutions of higher education—plant fund operations, 1930–1954.

Source: Office of Education, *Biennial Survey of Education in the United States*, various issues.

Data represent moneys received and spent by higher educational institutions for expanding their physical holdings (land, buildings, equipment of various sorts) held or utilized primarily for instructional, recreational, or student residence purposes. Real estate held and operated for investment purposes is not included.

H 370–373. Property of institutions of higher education, 1890–1954.

Source: See source for series H 339–350.

Data represent value of all permanent or quasi-permanent assets which include lands, buildings, and equipment; funds held for investment purposes only (the income from such funds being available for current use); funds subject to annuity or living trust agreements; and funds the principal of which may be lent to students to help defray their living expenses or tuition bills. The term "fund" is used in its accounting sense of cash or other valuable assets (real estate, bonds, stock certificates, and other evidences of ownership or equity).

H 374–382. School enrollment rates, by color and sex, 1850–1957.

Source: 1850–1930, Bureau of the Census, Fifteenth Census Reports, *Population*, vol. II, pp. 1094 and 1095; 1940–1950, *U. S. Census of Population: 1950*, vol. II, part 1, p. 1-206; 1954–1957, *Current Population Reports*, Series P–20, Nos. 54, 66, 74, and 80.

The statistics for decennial years refer to the total population within the specified age group; figures for 1954–1957 refer to the civilian noninstitutional population. Persons not covered for the later years (Armed Forces and institutional population) are known to have low enrollment rates.

In the Census of Population for 1940 and 1950, and in the Current Population Survey (1954–1957), enrollment was defined as enrollment in "regular" schools only—that is, those schools where enrollment may lead to an elementary or high school diploma, or to a college, university, or professional school degree. Such schools are public, private, or parochial schools; colleges, universities, or professional schools, either day or night. Enrollment was either full time or part time.

If a person was receiving regular instruction at home from a tutor and if the instruction was considered comparable to that of a regular school or college, the person was counted as enrolled. Enrollment in a correspondence course was counted only if the course was given by a regular school, such as a university, and the person received credit thereby in the regular school system.

Children enrolled in kindergarten were not included in the "regular" school enrollment figures in the 1950 Census of Population; however, they have been included here to make the data comparable with earlier years and with current practice. In censuses prior to 1950, no attempt was made to exclude children in kindergarten so that the statistics for those years include varying proportions attending kindergarten. Also, in censuses prior to 1940, the data were not restricted as to type of school or college the person was attending.

In addition to differences in definitions of school enrollment and in population coverage, the enrollment data for different years may differ because of variations in the dates when the questions were asked and time periods to which enrollment referred. Data from the current surveys were obtained in October and refer to enrollment in the current school term. In 1940 and 1950, the censuses were taken as of April 1, but enrollment related to any time after March 1 in 1940 and any time after February 1 in 1950. The corresponding question in the censuses from 1850 to 1930 applied to a somewhat longer period: In 1910, 1920, and 1930, to the period between the preceding September 1 and the census date (April 15 in 1910, January 1 in 1920, and April 1 in 1930); and in 1850 to 1900, to the 12 months preceding the census date.

Information on school enrollment is also collected and published by the Office of Education (see series H 223–228 and H 321–324). These data are obtained from reports of school systems and institutions of higher learning, and from other surveys and censuses. They are, however, only roughly comparable with data collected by the Bureau of the Census by household interviews, because of differences in definitions, time references, population coverage, and enumeration methods.

See also general note for series H 223–411.

H 383–394. School enrollment, by age, 1910–1957.

Source: 1910–1950 (decennial data), Bureau of the Census, *U. S. Census of Population: 1950*, vol. II, part 1, p. 1-95; 1945–1957 (annual data), *Current Population Reports*, Series P–20, Nos. 30, 52, 54, 66, 74, and 80.

See text for series H 374–382 for definitions and qualifications of data.

The decennial data and the annual data differ as to the enrollment rates for each age group in part because of differences in the time of year at which the questions were asked and the period to which they referred, and because of differences in the age of persons at the time of the inquiry. For example, some persons 18 or 19 years old may not yet have completed their schooling by April 1, but may have finished before October of that year. Also, some of the differences may have been caused by variations in the accuracy of reporting. Although the same definitions of enrollment were used in the 1950 Census and in the Current Population Survey, there is evidence that some persons, particularly at post-compulsory school ages, were counted as enrolled in the census who should not have been included under the definition. For the current survey, as compared to the census, more detailed questions are asked and the enumerators are generally more experienced and have better training and supervision.

See also general note for series H 223–411.

H 395–406. Median years of school completed, by age, sex, and color, 1940 and 1950.

Source: Bureau of the Census, *U. S. Census of Population: 1950*, vol. II, part 1, pp. 1-236 to 1-239.

In general, the data refer to education ever received in "regular" schools. For the definition of "regular" schools and enrollment in these schools, see text for series H 374–382.

The median year of school completed is defined as the value which divides the population group into two equal parts—one-half having completed more schooling and one-half having completed less schooling than the median. The medians are expressed in terms of a continuous series of numbers representing years of school completed. For example, the fourth year of high school is indicated by 12 and the first year of college by 13. The procedure used both in 1940 and 1950 for calculating the median year of school completed made allowance for the fact that many persons reported as having completed a given full school year had also completed a part of the next higher grade. Thus, it is assumed that persons who reported 12 full years of school completed had actually completed 12.5 years, on the average.

Differences in the quality of education data for the two censuses may have resulted in part from changes in the way the information was requested. In 1940, a single question was asked on highest grade of school completed. In 1950, data on years of school completed were obtained from a combination of responses to two questions, one asking for the highest grade of school attended and another whether that grade was finished. Analysis of data from the 1940 Census returns and from surveys conducted by the Bureau of the Census, using the same question wording used in 1940, indicated that respondents frequently reported the year or grade they had last attended, instead of the one completed. There is evidence that, as a result of the change in the questions in 1950, there was relatively less exaggeration in reporting educational attainment than in 1940. Hence, the indicated increases in attainment between 1940 and 1950 tend slightly to understate the true increase.

Although the statistics on median years of school completed have been available only since 1940, the data by age give further indication of time trends.

See also general note for series H 223–411.

H 407–411. Percent illiterate in the population, by color and nativity, 1870–1952.

Source: 1870–1930, Bureau of the Census, Fifteenth Census Reports, *Population*, vol. II, p. 1223; 1940 and 1947, *Current Population Reports*, Series P–20, No. 20, pp. 4, 7; 1950 and 1952, *Current Population Reports*, Series P–20, No. 45, pp. 7, 22.

Persons were regarded as illiterate who could not read and write, either in English or some other language. Information on illiteracy of the population was obtained from direct questions in the censuses of 1870–1930. The data for 1947 and 1952 were obtained from sample surveys, and the statistics for the census years 1940 and 1950 were derived by estimating

procedures. In 1947, the literacy question was asked only of persons who completed less than 5 years of school; in 1952, the same general procedure was used but the question was asked of those who completed less than 6 years of school.

Some variation has existed over the years in the way the question on illiteracy was asked. Since 1930, reference has been made as to whether or not the person was able to read and write. In censuses of 1870–1930, two questions were asked, one on whether the person was able to read and one on whether he could write. Illiteracy was defined as inability to write "regardless of ability to read." Since the data showed that nearly all persons who were able to write could also read, the earlier statistics should be generally comparable with data obtained through the consolidated question used in later years.

Ability to read and write cannot be defined so precisely in a census as to cover all cases with certainty. No specific test of ability to read and write was used, but enumerators were instructed not to classify a person as literate simply because he was able to write his name. Analysts of earlier census data assumed that the illiterate population comprised only those persons who had no education whatever. Information on the educational attainment of illiterates obtained in recent sample surveys indicates, however, that some persons cannot read and write even though they have had some formal schooling. For example, data from the Current Population Survey of October 1952 show that among persons 14 years old and over the proportion reported as illiterate ranged from 77.8 percent of those who had not completed a year of school to 1.3 percent of those who had completed 5 years.

Data on illiteracy were also collected in the censuses of 1840, 1850, and 1860, but are not included here because they are not comparable with statistics for subsequent years, and because of limitations in the quality of data for those early years. In 1840, the head of the family was asked for the total number of illiterates in each family, a method which undoubtedly led to some understatement. Beginning with 1850, the individual entry system was used, the question being asked regarding each member of the family. By 1870, another change in census methods was introduced, separate questions being asked on ability to read and ability to write. In addition to changes in the form of the inquiry, the statistics on illiteracy for 1840, 1850, and 1860 related to the population 20 years old and over, whereas in the 1870 and later censuses they referred to the population 10 years old and over.

The percentages of illiterates in the total population 20 years old and over, as recorded in those earlier censuses, were as follows: 1840, 22.0 percent; 1850, 22.6 percent; and 1860, 19.7 percent. The comparable percentages for the white population 20 years old and over in those years were: 9.0, 10.7, and 8.9 percent, respectively. The apparent increases in illiteracy of white persons in 1850 and 1870 may be due, in part, to the large influx of immigrants during those periods, many of whom could not read and write in any language. It is more likely, however, that the apparent increases resulted from improvements in the way the information was obtained at those census dates.

See also general note for series H 223–411.

Series H 223-233. Elementary and Secondary Schools, Enrollment and Attendance, and High School Graduates: 1870 to 1956

School year ending—	Total[1]	School enrollment					Public school attendance			High school graduates[3]	
		Public day schools				Nonpublic schools[2]	Average daily attendance (all grades)	Average length of school term (days)	Average number of days attended per enrolled pupil	Number	Percent of population 17 years old
		Total		Kindergarten and grades 1 to 8	Grades 9 to 12 and post-graduates						
		Number	Percent of population 5 to 17 years old								
	223	224	225	226	227	228	229	230	231	232	233
1956	35,872,203	31,162,843	83.6	24,290,257	6,872,586	4,709,360	27,740,149	178.0	158.5	1,414,800	62.3
1954	33,175,215	28,836,052	83.5	22,545,807	6,290,245	4,339,163	25,643,871	178.6	158.9	1,276,100	60.0
1952	30,372,028	26,562,664	84.7	20,680,867	5,881,797	3,809,364	23,256,523	178.2	156.0	1,196,500	58.6
1950	28,491,566	25,111,427	81.6	19,386,806	5,724,621	3,380,139	22,284,000	177.9	157.9	1,199,700	59.0
1948	26,998,446	23,944,532	79.4	18,291,227	5,653,305	3,053,914	20,910,000	177.6	155.1	1,189,909	54.0
1946	26,124,441	23,299,941	80.5	17,677,744	5,622,197	2,824,500	19,848,507	176.8	150.6	1,080,033	47.9
1944	25,757,907	23,266,616	80.4	17,713,096	5,553,520	2,491,291	19,602,772	175.5	147.9	1,019,233	42.3
1942	27,179,002	24,562,473	84.2	18,174,668	6,387,805	2,616,529	21,031,322	174.7	149.6	1,242,375	51.2
1940	28,044,589	25,433,542	85.3	18,832,098	6,601,444	2,611,047	22,042,151	175.0	151.7	1,221,475	50.8
1938	28,662,591	25,975,108	84.4	19,748,174	6,226,934	2,687,483	22,298,200	173.9	149.3	1,120,079	45.6
1936	29,005,873	26,367,098	83.4	20,392,561	5,974,537	2,638,775	22,298,767	173.0	146.3	1,015,345	----------
1934	29,162,732	26,434,193	81.6	20,765,037	5,669,156	2,728,539	22,458,190	171.6	145.8	914,853	----------
1932	29,061,403	26,275,441	82.0	21,135,420	5,140,021	2,785,962	22,245,344	171.2	144.9	826,991	----------
1930	28,329,059	25,678,015	81.3	21,278,593	4,399,422	2,651,044	21,264,886	172.7	143.0	666,904	29.0
1928	27,810,309	25,179,696	81.5	21,268,417	3,911,279	2,630,613	20,608,353	171.5	140.4	596,655	----------
1926	27,180,193	24,741,468	82.3	20,984,002	3,757,466	2,438,725	19,855,881	169.3	135.9	561,469	----------
1924	26,016,072	24,288,808	82.8	20,898,930	3,389,878	1,727,264	19,132,451	168.3	132.5	494,006	----------
1922	24,820,100	23,239,227	81.2	20,366,218	2,873,009	1,580,873	18,432,213	164.0	130.6	357,000	----------
1920	23,277,797	21,578,316	77.8	19,377,927	2,200,389	1,699,481	16,150,035	161.9	121.2	311,266	16.8
1918	22,515,917	20,853,516	75.3	18,919,695	1,933,821	1,662,401	15,548,914	160.7	119.8	285,047	----------
1916	22,171,897	20,351,687	75.8	18,895,626	1,456,061	1,820,210	15,358,927	160.3	120.9	259,396	----------
1915	21,474,344	19,704,209	74.6	18,375,225	1,328,984	1,770,135	14,985,900	159.4	121.2	239,728	----------
1914	20,934,953	19,153,786	73.7	17,934,982	1,218,804	1,781,167	14,216,459	158.7	117.8	218,784	----------
1913	20,347,796	18,609,040	72.7	17,474,269	1,134,771	1,738,756	13,613,656	158.1	115.6	199,783	----------
1912	19,830,041	18,182,937	72.2	17,077,577	1,105,360	1,647,104	13,302,303	158.0	115.6	180,574	----------
1911	19,636,348	18,035,118	72.5	17,050,441	984,677	1,601,230	12,871,980	156.8	111.8	167,918	----------
1910	19,372,289	17,813,852	73.5	16,898,791	915,061	1,558,437	12,827,307	157.5	113.0	156,429	8.8
1909	18,994,876	17,506,175	72.2	16,664,902	841,273	1,488,701	12,684,837	155.3	112.6	141,574	----------
1908	18,609,023	17,061,962	69.3	16,291,506	770,456	1,547,061	12,154,172	154.1	109.8	128,654	----------
1907	18,200,182	16,890,818	69.6	16,139,737	751,081	1,309,364	11,925,672	151.8	107.3	127,194	----------
1906	18,055,625	16,641,970	70.4	15,919,278	722,692	1,413,655	11,712,300	150.6	106.0	125,860	----------
1905	17,806,168	16,468,300	70.3	15,788,598	679,702	1,337,868	11,481,531	150.9	105.2	119,329	----------
1904	17,560,258	16,256,038	70.6	15,620,230	635,808	1,304,220	11,318,256	146.7	102.1	111,736	----------
1903	17,205,084	16,009,361	70.7	15,417,148	592,213	1,195,723	11,054,502	147.2	101.7	105,231	----------
1902	17,125,976	15,917,385	71.5	15,366,774	550,611	1,208,591	11,064,164	144.7	100.6	99,277	----------
1901	17,072,410	15,702,517	71.7	15,160,787	541,730	1,369,893	10,716,094	143.7	98.0	97,221	----------
1900	16,854,832	15,503,110	72.4	14,983,859	519,251	1,351,722	10,632,772	144.3	99.0	94,883	6.4
1899	16,473,939	15,176,219	72.0	14,699,992	476,227	1,297,720	10,389,407	143.0	97.9	89,528	----------
1898	16,458,764	15,103,874	72.7	14,654,274	449,600	1,354,890	10,356,458	143.0	98.0	84,173	----------
1897	16,140,059	14,823,059	72.4	14,413,626	409,433	1,317,000	10,052,554	142.0	96.3	79,758	----------
1896	15,833,756	14,498,956	71.8	14,118,463	380,493	1,334,800	9,781,475	140.5	94.8	75,813	----------
1895	15,454,985	14,243,765	71.5	13,893,666	350,099	1,211,220	9,548,722	139.5	93.5	72,019	----------
1894	15,314,157	13,995,357	71.3	13,706,083	289,274	1,318,800	9,187,505	139.5	91.6	65,320	----------
1893	14,826,168	13,483,340	69.7	13,229,317	254,023	1,342,828	8,855,717	136.3	89.6	59,178	----------
1892	14,555,521	13,255,921	69.5	13,016,365	239,556	1,299,600	8,560,603	136.9	88.4	53,039	----------
1891	14,540,732	13,050,132	69.4	12,838,536	211,596	1,490,600	8,329,234	135.7	86.6	48,380	----------
1890	14,479,409	12,722,581	68.6	12,519,618	202,963	1,756,828	8,153,635	134.7	86.3	43,731	3.5
1889	13,660,821	12,392,260	68.2	----------	----------	1,268,561	8,005,969	133.7	86.4	38,516	----------
1888	----------	12,182,600	68.3	----------	----------	----------	7,906,986	132.3	85.9	33,301	----------
1887	----------	11,884,944	68.0	----------	----------	----------	7,681,806	131.3	84.9	32,146	----------
1886	----------	11,664,460	68.1	----------	----------	----------	7,526,351	130.4	84.1	32,997	----------
1885	----------	11,398,024	68.0	----------	----------	----------	7,297,529	130.7	83.6	32,468	----------
1884	----------	10,982,364	67.0	----------	----------	----------	7,055,696	129.1	82.9	30,962	----------
1883	----------	10,651,828	66.4	----------	----------	----------	6,652,392	129.8	81.1	28,348	----------
1882	----------	10,211,578	65.0	----------	----------	----------	6,331,242	131.2	81.3	27,151	----------
1881	----------	10,000,896	65.0	----------	----------	----------	6,145,932	130.1	80.0	24,954	----------
1880	----------	9,867,505	65.5	9,757,228	110,277	----------	6,144,143	130.3	81.1	23,634	2.5
1879	----------	9,504,458	64.6	----------	----------	----------	5,876,077	130.2	80.5	23,128	----------
1878	----------	9,438,883	65.7	----------	----------	----------	5,783,065	132.0	80.9	21,939	----------
1877	----------	8,965,006	63.9	----------	----------	----------	5,426,595	132.1	80.0	20,693	----------
1876	----------	8,869,115	64.7	----------	----------	----------	5,291,376	133.1	79.4	20,448	----------
1875	----------	8,785,678	65.5	----------	----------	----------	5,248,114	130.4	77.9	19,707	----------
1874	----------	8,444,251	64.4	----------	----------	----------	5,050,840	128.8	77.0	18,966	----------
1873	----------	8,003,614	62.4	----------	----------	----------	4,745,459	129.1	76.5	18,225	----------
1872	----------	7,815,306	62.2	----------	----------	----------	4,658,844	133.4	79.5	17,483	----------
1871	----------	7,561,582	61.5	7,481,355	80,227	----------	4,545,317	132.1	79.4	16,741	----------
1870	----------	6,871,522	57.0	----------	----------	----------	4,077,347	132.2	78.4	16,000	2.0

[1] Partially estimated. Includes enrollment in regular public and nonpublic day schools. Excludes pupils enrolled in residential schools for exceptional children, subcollegiate departments of institutions of higher education, and Federal schools.

[2] Partially estimated.

[3] Includes graduates from public and nonpublic schools. Nonpublic graduates are partially estimated.

Series H 234–245.　Public Elementary and Secondary Day Schools' Instructional Staff, School Districts, and Schools: 1870 to 1956

School year ending—	Instructional staff								Schools			One-teacher public schools
	Total	Average annual salary [1]	Classroom teachers and other nonsupervisory staff [2]			Principals	Other supervisors or consultants	School districts	Total	Public	Private	
			Total	Male	Female							
	234	235	236	237	238	239	240	241	242	243	244	245
1956	1,213,459	4,156	1,149,223	[3]294,170	[3]838,923	50,973	13,263	54,773	146,732	130,473	16,259	34,964
1954	1,098,320	3,825	1,042,313	[3]253,518	[3]778,620	45,729	10,278	62,969	152,164	136,512	15,652	42,825
1952	1,012,384	3,450	962,864	234,942	727,922	39,695	9,825	70,993	161,497	147,509	13,988	50,742
1950	962,174	3,010	913,671	194,968	718,703	39,314	9,189	83,614	166,473	152,767	13,706	59,652
1948	907,013	2,639	860,678	161,913	698,765	37,144	9,191	94,817	185,607	172,244	13,363	75,096
1946	867,248	1,995	831,026	138,209	692,817	29,416	6,806	[4]101,273	197,698	184,541	13,157	86,563
1944	865,038	1,728	827,990	126,672	701,318	31,569	5,479	111,274	212,174	198,878	13,296	96,302
1942	898,001	1,507	858,888	183,194	675,694	33,057	6,056	115,384	221,531	208,235	13,296	107,692
1940	911,835	1,441	875,477	194,725	680,752	31,521	4,837	116,999	238,169	223,295	14,874	113,600
1938	918,715	1,374	877,266	185,103	692,163	36,484	4,965	118,892	260,446	247,127	13,319	121,178
1936	906,376	1,283	870,963	179,073	691,890	29,570	5,843	----------	271,145	257,826	13,319	131,101
1934	880,226	1,227	847,120	161,949	685,171	28,068	5,038	----------	274,269	260,950	13,319	139,166
1932	901,204	1,417	871,607	153,861	717,746	23,910	5,687	127,422	272,182	259,159	13,023	143,391
1930	892,027	1,420	854,263	141,771	712,492	30,876	6,888	----------	274,769	262,236	12,533	149,282
1928	868,422	1,364	831,934	138,193	693,741	28,829	7,659	----------				156,066
1926	849,502	1,277	814,169	138,810	675,359	26,933	8,400	----------				162,756
1924	787,113	1,227	761,308	128,731	632,577	17,881	7,924	----------				169,718
1922	755,698	1,166	722,976	118,085	604,891	18,616	14,106	----------				180,762
1920	699,754	871	[5]679,533	95,654	583,648	13,638	6,583	----------				190,655
1918	----------	635	650,709	105,194	545,515	----------	----------	----------				196,037
1916	----------	553	622,371	123,038	499,333	----------	----------	----------				[6]200,094

School year ending—	Instructional staff				School year ending—	Instructional staff				School year ending—	Instructional staff			
	Average annual salary [1]	Classroom teachers and other nonsupervisory staff [2]				Average annual salary [1]	Classroom teachers and other nonsupervisory staff [2]				Average annual salary [1]	Classroom teachers and other nonsupervisory staff [2]		
		Total	Male	Female			Total	Male	Female			Total	Male	Female
	235	236	237	238		235	236	237	238		235	236	237	238
1915	543	604,301	118,449	485,852	1900	325	423,062	126,588	296,474	1885	224	325,916	121,762	204,154
1914	525	580,058	114,662	465,396	1899	----------	414,272	131,207	283,065	1884	----------	314,015	118,905	195,110
1913	512	565,483	113,213	452,270	1898	----------	410,813	132,257	278,556	1883	----------	304,389	116,388	188,001
1912	492	547,289	114,559	432,730	1897	----------	404,958	131,221	273,737	1882	----------	299,079	118,892	180,187
1911	466	533,606	110,328	423,278	1896	----------	400,296	130,373	269,923	1881	----------	293,860	122,511	171,349
1910	485	523,210	110,481	412,729	1895	286	398,042	129,706	268,336	1880	195	286,593	122,795	163,798
1909	----------	506,453	108,300	398,153	1894	----------	388,949	125,402	263,547	1879	----------	280,330	121,490	158,840
1908	----------	495,463	104,495	390,968	1893	----------	383,010	122,056	260,954	1878	----------	277,147	119,404	157,743
1907	----------	481,316	104,414	376,902	1892	----------	374,226	121,573	252,653	1877	----------	267,050	114,312	152,738
1906	----------	466,063	109,179	356,884	1891	----------	368,388	123,360	245,028	1876	----------	259,618	109,780	149,838
1905	386	460,269	110,532	349,737	1890	252	363,922	125,525	238,397	1875	----------	257,865	108,791	149,074
1904	----------	455,242	113,744	341,498	1889	----------	356,577	124,467	232,110	1874	----------	248,447	103,465	144,982
1903	----------	449,287	117,035	332,252	1888	----------	347,134	126,240	220,894	1873	----------	237,513	97,790	139,723
1902	----------	441,819	120,883	320,936	1887	----------	339,460	127,093	212,367	1872	----------	229,921	94,992	134,929
1901	----------	431,918	125,838	306,080	1886	----------	331,393	123,792	207,601	1871	----------	220,225	90,293	129,932
										1870	189	200,515	77,529	122,986

[1] Computed for teaching positions only, prior to 1920; beginning 1920, also includes supervisors and principals.
[2] Prior to 1938, number of different persons employed rather than number of positions. Includes librarians and guidance and psychological personnel.
[3] Classroom teachers only. Excludes other nonsupervisory instructional staff.
[4] Excludes 1,840 districts in Texas "in legal existence" which do not operate schools.
[5] Includes 231 part-time teachers not classified by sex.
[6] Partially estimated.

Series H 246–251.　Public Elementary and Secondary Schools' Receipts, by Source: 1890 to 1956
[In thousands of dollars]

School year ending—	Total (revenue and non-revenue)	Sources of revenue receipts					School year ending—	Sources of revenue receipts		
		Total [1]	Federal	State [2]	Local [3]	Other		Total [1]	State [2]	Local [3]
	246	247	248	249	250	251		247	249	250
1956	12,042,866	9,686,677	441,442	3,828,886	5,394,059	22,291	1912	469,111	75,814	346,898
1954	9,690,856	7,866,852	355,237	2,944,103	4,547,254	20,258	1911	451,151	69,071	333,832
1952	7,636,884	6,423,816	227,711	2,478,596	3,716,421	1,086	1910	433,064	64,605	312,222
1950	6,401,022	5,437,004	155,849	2,165,689	3,115,386	121	1909	403,647	63,547	288,643
1948	4,869,431	4,311,534	120,270	1,676,362	2,514,572	330	1908	381,920	58,097	259,341
1946	3,318,173	3,059,845	41,378	1,062,057	1,956,156	254	1907	355,016	44,706	231,738
1944	2,699,076	2,604,322	35,886	859,183	1,708,980	274	1906	322,106	47,943	223,491
1942	2,593,959	2,416,580	34,305	759,993	1,622,035	246	1905	301,819	44,349	210,168
1940	2,521,470	2,260,527	39,810	684,354	1,536,069	294	1904	279,134	42,553	193,216
1938	2,492,598	2,222,885	26,535	655,996	1,540,053	300	1903	251,637	40,456	173,731
1936	[4]2,178,106	[4]1,971,402	[4]9,850	578,369	1,382,389	294	1902	245,498	39,216	173,151
1934	1,940,251	1,810,652	21,548	423,178	1,365,554	372	1901	235,339	36,281	168,897
1932	2,229,423	2,068,029	8,262	410,550	1,648,687	530	1900	219,766	37,887	149,487
1930	2,469,311	2,038,557	7,334	353,670	1,726,709	844	1899	203,337	35,341	144,898
1928	2,324,708	2,025,750	6,174	333,279	1,685,330	967	1898	199,833	35,122	135,516
1926	2,171,845	1,830,017	5,552	284,569	1,539,896	----------	1897	191,959	33,942	130,318
1924	1,958,529	1,618,438	3,986	261,997	1,290,239	----------	1896	182,480	35,032	124,880
1922	1,743,192	1,444,242	2,891	230,517	1,184,530	----------	1895	176,565	34,638	118,915
1920	1,155,507	970,120	2,475	160,085	807,561	----------	1894	170,404	32,750	112,785
1918	802,613	736,876	1,669	122,256	612,951	----------	1893	165,023	33,695	108,425
1916	----------	633,901	----------	95,278	488,120	----------	1892	157,175	29,908	105,630
1915	----------	589,652	----------	91,104	456,956	----------	1891	147,915	27,632	100,359
1914	----------	561,743	----------	87,895	425,457	----------	1890	143,195	26,345	97,222
1913	----------	507,227	----------	78,376	375,582	----------				

[1] For 1922, 1924, and years prior to 1918, includes receipts undistributed by source.
[2] Prior to 1918, excludes receipts from sources other than State taxes and appropriations.
[3] Includes county and other intermediate sources of income. Prior to 1918, excludes receipts from sources other than local taxes and appropriations.
[4] Includes only Federal aid for vocational education.

Series H 252–261. Public Elementary and Secondary Schools' Expenditures by Purpose: 1870 to 1956

[In thousands of dollars, except as noted]

School year ending—	Total expenditures for all schools	Current expenditures for day schools — Total[1] Amount	Current expenditures for day schools — Total[1] Per pupil in average daily attendance[2]	Administration	Instruction[3]	Plant operation and maintenance	Other[4]	Capital outlay	Interest	Other expenditures[5]
	252	253	254	255	256	257	258	259	260	261
1956	10,955,047	8,251,420	294.22	372,956	5,501,921	1,072,299	1,304,244	2,387,187	215,699	100,743
1954	9,092,449	6,790,923	264.76	310,995	4,552,349	907,542	1,020,037	2,055,178	153,884	92,464
1952	7,344,237	5,722,162	244.24	265,636	3,781,837	757,249	917,440	1,477,332	114,310	30,432
1950	5,837,643	4,687,274	208.83	220,050	3,112,340	641,751	713,132	1,014,176	100,578	35,614
1948	4,311,176	3,794,702	179.43	169,999	2,571,539	526,164	526,999	412,467	76,331	27,676
1946	2,906,886	2,707,441	136.41	132,899	1,853,911	371,535	349,097	111,046	76,923	11,477
1944	2,452,581	2,293,337	116.99	110,631	1,590,634	316,098	275,975	53,856	96,805	8,583
1942	2,322,698	2,067,660	98.31	101,463	1,457,877	288,651	219,670	137,552	108,781	8,704
1940	2,344,049	1,941,799	88.09	91,571	1,403,285	267,687	179,257	257,974	130,909	13,367
1938	2,233,110	1,870,090	83.87	86,441	1,359,704	260,168	163,777	238,853	114,102	10,065
1936	1,968,898	1,656,799	74.30	67,436	1,214,363	233,264	141,736	171,322	132,983	7,794
1934	1,720,105	1,515,530	67.48	64,093	1,120,874	203,477	127,086	59,277	137,037	8,262
1932	2,174,651	1,809,939	81.36	74,910	1,333,332	257,424	144,273	210,996	140,235	13,480
1930	2,316,790	1,843,552	86.70	78,680	1,317,727	294,882	152,263	370,878	92,536	9,825
1928	2,184,337	1,705,538	82.76	77,266	1,219,820	278,367	130,085	382,996	92,025	3,778
1926	2,026,308	1,537,874	77.45	68,426	1,127,009	243,510	98,929	411,038	71,901	5,495
1924	1,820,744	1,368,584	71.53	54,753	1,001,356	220,951	91,523	388,469	58,963	4,729
1922	1,580,671	1,234,669	66.98	51,327	903,474	202,785	69,266	305,941	35,788	4,273
1920	1,036,151	861,120	53.52	36,752	632,555	146,139	45,673	153,543	18,212	3,277
1918	763,678	629,441	40.48	25,179	444,138	132,958	27,165	119,083	15,155	----------
1916	640,717	537,210	34.98	15,483	377,841	----------	143,886	103,507	----------	----------
1915	605,461	502,704	33.55	13,499	358,210	----------	130,995	102,756	----------	----------
1914	555,077	463,471	32.60	12,428	335,489	----------	115,554	91,606	----------	----------
1913	521,546	437,941	32.17	9,948	315,909	----------	112,083	91,606	----------	----------
1912	482,887	404,868	30.44	8,577	294,857	----------	101,434	78,019	----------	----------
1911	446,727	371,171	28.84	6,266	273,483	----------	91,422	75,556	----------	----------
1910	426,250	356,272	27.85	6,827	260,179	----------	89,265	69,978	----------	----------
1909	401,398	319,519	25.19	----------	237,014	----------	82,505	81,879	----------	----------
1908	371,344	297,704	24.49	----------	219,780	----------	77,924	73,640	----------	----------
1907	336,898	271,565	22.77	----------	202,048	----------	69,517	65,333	----------	----------
1906	307,766	247,158	21.10	----------	186,483	----------	60,674	60,608	----------	----------
1905	291,617	235,201	20.49	----------	177,463	----------	57,738	56,416	----------	----------
1904	273,216	223,763	19.77	----------	167,825	----------	55,938	49,453	----------	----------
1903	251,458	205,169	18.56	----------	157,110	----------	48,058	46,289	----------	----------
1902	238,262	198,299	17.92	----------	151,444	----------	46,856	39,963	----------	----------
1901	227,523	187,651	17.51	----------	143,379	----------	44,272	39,872	----------	----------
1900	214,965	179,514	16.67	----------	137,688	----------	41,826	35,451	----------	----------
1899	200,155	168,926	16.26	----------	129,346	----------	39,579	31,229	----------	----------
1898	194,293	162,878	15.73	----------	124,192	----------	38,685	31,415	----------	----------
1897	187,682	155,306	15.45	----------	119,311	----------	35,995	32,376	----------	----------
1896	183,499	150,909	15.43	----------	117,140	----------	33,769	32,590	----------	----------
1895	175,809	146,372	15.33	----------	113,872	----------	32,500	29,437	----------	----------
1894	172,503	142,495	15.51	----------	109,202	----------	33,293	30,008	----------	----------
1893	164,171	133,877	15.12	----------	104,560	----------	29,317	30,294	----------	----------
1892	155,817	126,472	14.77	----------	100,298	----------	26,174	29,345	----------	----------
1891	147,495	121,047	14.53	----------	96,303	----------	24,744	26,448	----------	----------
1890	140,507	114,300	13.99	----------	91,836	----------	22,463	26,207	----------	----------
1889	132,540	109,144	13.63	----------	87,568	----------	21,576	23,396	----------	----------
1888	124,245	----------	----------	----------	83,023	----------	----------	----------	----------	----------
1887	115,784	----------	----------	----------	78,640	----------	----------	----------	----------	----------
1886	113,323	----------	----------	----------	76,270	----------	----------	----------	----------	----------
1885	110,328	----------	----------	----------	72,879	----------	----------	----------	----------	----------
1884	103,213	----------	----------	----------	68,384	----------	----------	----------	----------	----------
1883	96,750	----------	----------	----------	64,799	----------	----------	----------	----------	----------
1882	88,990	----------	----------	----------	60,595	----------	----------	----------	----------	----------
1881	83,643	----------	----------	----------	58,012	----------	----------	----------	----------	----------
1880	78,095	----------	----------	----------	55,943	----------	----------	----------	----------	----------
1879	76,192	----------	----------	----------	54,640	----------	----------	----------	----------	----------
1878	79,083	----------	----------	----------	56,155	----------	----------	----------	----------	----------
1877	79,440	----------	----------	----------	54,974	----------	----------	----------	----------	----------
1876	83,083	----------	----------	----------	55,358	----------	----------	----------	----------	----------
1875	83,504	----------	----------	----------	54,722	----------	----------	----------	----------	----------
1874	80,054	----------	----------	----------	50,786	----------	----------	----------	----------	----------
1873	76,238	----------	----------	----------	47,932	----------	----------	----------	----------	----------
1872	74,234	----------	----------	----------	45,936	----------	----------	----------	----------	----------
1871	69,108	----------	----------	----------	42,581	----------	----------	----------	----------	----------
1870	63,397	----------	----------	----------	37,833	----------	----------	----------	----------	----------

[1] Prior to 1918, includes expenditures for interest.
[2] In dollars. For 1948–1956, excludes expenditures not allocated to pupil costs.
[3] Prior to 1910, includes only expenditures for salaries of teachers and superintendents.
[4] Prior to 1918, includes plant operation and maintenance; prior to 1910, includes all current expenditures except salaries of teachers and superintendents.
[5] Beginning 1954, includes expenditures for community services, previously included in "current expenditures for day schools."
[6] Includes $7,816,000 in undistributed expenses.

Series H 262–315.   Public Secondary Day School Pupils Enrolled in Specified Subjects: 1890 to 1949

[In percents.   Figures cover enrollment in last 4 years of school.   For school years ending in year indicated]

Series No.	Specified subject	1949	1934	1928	1922	1915	1910	1900	1890
262	Total enrollment	5,399,452	4,496,514	2,896,630	2,155,460	1,165,495	739,143	519,251	202,963
263	English	92.9	90.5	93.1	76.7	58.4	57.1	38.5	
264	Journalism	1.9	0.7	0.2	0.1				
265	Radio speaking and broadcasting	0.1							
266	United States history	22.8	17.3	17.9	15.3	} [2]50.5	[2]55.0	[2]38.2	[2]27.3
267	English history	(1)	0.5	0.9	2.9				
268	World history	16.2	11.9	6.1					
269	Civil government	8.0	6.0	6.6	} 19.3	15.7	15.6	21.7	
270	Community government	(3)	10.4	13.4					
271	Geography	5.6	2.1	0.3					
272	Problems of democracy	5.2	3.5	1.0					
273	Economics	4.7	4.9	5.1	4.8				
274	Sociology	3.4	2.5	2.7	2.4				
275	Psychology	0.9	0.3	1.0	0.9	1.2	1.0	2.4	
276	Consumer education	0.7							
277	General science	20.8	17.8	17.5	18.3				
278	Biology	18.4	14.6	13.6	8.8	6.9	1.1		
279	Botany	0.1	0.9	1.6	3.8	9.1	15.8		
280	Physiology	1.0	1.8	2.7	5.1	9.5	15.3	27.4	
281	Zoology	0.1	0.6	0.8	1.5	3.2	6.9		
282	Earth science	0.4	1.7	2.8	4.5	15.3	21.0	29.8	
283	Chemistry	7.6	7.6	7.1	7.4	7.4	6.9	7.7	10.1
284	Physics	5.4	6.3	6.8	8.9	14.2	14.6	19.0	22.8
285	Algebra	26.8	30.4	35.2	40.2	48.8	56.9	56.3	45.4
286	General mathematics	13.1	7.4	7.9	12.4				
287	Geometry	12.8	17.1	19.8	22.7	26.5	30.9	27.4	21.3
288	Trigonometry	2.0	1.3	1.3	1.5	1.5	1.9	1.9	
289	Spanish	8.2	6.2	9.4	11.3	2.7	0.7		
290	Latin	7.8	16.0	22.0	27.5	37.3	49.0	50.6	34.7
291	French	4.7	10.9	14.0	15.5	8.8	9.9	7.8	5.8
292	German	0.8	2.4	1.8	0.6	24.4	23.7	14.3	10.5
293	Italian	0.3	0.2	0.1	(1)				
294	Portuguese	(1)							
295	Russian	(1)							
296	Industrial subjects	26.6	21.0	13.5	13.7	11.2			
297	General business training	5.2	6.2	3.0					
298	Business arithmetic	4.6	4.9	6.9	1.5				
299	Bookkeeping	8.7	9.9	10.7	12.6	3.4			
300	Typewriting	22.5	16.7	15.2	13.1				
301	Shorthand	7.8	9.0	8.7	8.9				
302	Business law	2.4	3.2	2.6	0.9				
303	Business English	1.0	0.9	0.5					
304	Economic geography	1.7	4.0	4.8	1.7				
305	Office practice	2.0	1.8	1.5	0.4				
306	Retailing	0.5							
307	Salesmanship and advertising	1.0	0.7	0.4	0.3				
308	Cooperative office training	0.4							
309	Cooperative store training	0.3							
310	Home economics	24.2	16.7	16.5	14.3	12.9	3.8		
311	Agriculture	6.7	3.6	3.7	5.1	7.2	4.7		
312	Physical education	69.4	50.7	15.0	5.7				
313	Music	30.1	25.5	26.0	25.3	31.5			
314	Art	9.0	8.7	11.7	14.7	22.9			
315	Teacher training	(1)	0.1	1.8	1.0				

[1] Less than 0.05 percent, or fewer than 1 pupil in 2,000.   [2] Includes ancient history and medieval and modern history.   [3] Comparable data for 1949 not available.

Series H 316–326.   Institutions of Higher Education—Number, Faculty, and Enrollment: 1870 to 1956

School year ending—	Number of institutions	All institutions								Junior colleges	
		Faculty				Enrollment (1,000)				Number	Enrollment (1,000)
		Total			Resident instructional staff	Total		Under-graduate [1]	Graduate [1]		
		Both sexes	Male	Female		Number [1]	Percent of population 18 to 21 years old [2]				
	316	317	318	319	320	321	322	323	324	325	326
1956 [3]	1,850	298,910	230,342	68,568	228,188	2,637		2,387	250		
1954 [3]	1,863	265,911	204,871	61,040	207,365	2,200	29.90	1,977	223	[4]495	[4]325
1952	1,832	244,488	187,136	57,352	183,758	2,302	26.78	2,069	233	[5]480	[5]230
1950	1,851	246,722	186,189	60,533	190,353	2,659	29.88	2,422	237	483	243
1948	1,788	223,660	164,616	59,044	174,204	2,616	28.87	2,442	174	472	240
1946	1,768	165,324	116,134	49,190	125,811	1,677	20.84	1,556	121	464	156
1944	1,650	150,980	106,254	44,726	105,841	[6]1,155	12.73	[7]1,100	[7]59	413	89
1942	1,720	151,066	109,309	41,757	114,693	1,404	14.68	[7]1,319	[7]85	461	141
1940	1,708	146,929	106,328	40,601	110,885	1,494	15.68	1,388	106	456	150
1938	1,690	135,989	97,362	38,627	102,895	1,351	13.96	1,270	91	453	122
1936	1,628	121,036	86,567	34,469	92,580	1,208	12.50	1,129	79	415	102
1934	1,418	108,873	78,369	30,504	86,914	1,055	11.20	964	71	322	78
1932	1,460	[8]100,789	[8]71,680	[8]29,109	88,172	1,154	12.62	[9]1,028	78	342	85
1930	1,409	82,386	60,017	22,369	82,386	1,101	12.42	1,054	47	277	56
1928	1,415				76,080	1,054	12.13			248	45
1926	1,377				70,674	941	11.27			153	27
1924					63,999	[10]823	10.27			132	21
1922					56,486	681	8.87			80	12

See footnotes at end of table.

Series H 316–326. Institutions of Higher Education—Number, Faculty, and Enrollment: 1870 to 1956—Con.

School year ending—	Number of institutions	All institutions									Junior colleges	
		Faculty				Enrollment (1,000)					
		Total			Resident instructional staff	Total		Under-graduate [1]	Graduate [1]	Number	Enrollment (1,000)
		Both sexes	Male	Female		Number [1]	Percent of population 18 to 21 years old [2]				
	316	317	318	319	320	321	322	323	324	325	326
1920	1,041	48,615	35,807	12,808	(11)	598	8.09	582	16	52	8
1918						441	6.00			46	5
1916						441					
1915						404					
1914						379					
1913						361					
1912						356					
1911						354					
1910	951	36,480	29,132	7,348		355	5.12	346	9		
1905						264					
1900	977	23,868	19,151	4,717		238	4.01	232	6		
1890	998	[7]15,809	[7]12,704	[7]3,105		157	3.04	154	2		
1880	811	[7]11,552	[7]7,328	[7]4,194		116	2.72				
1870	563	[7]5,553	[7]4,887	[7]666		52	1.68				

[1] Special students tabulated by level (undergraduate and graduate) in November 1953; all special students tabulated with undergraduates in 1952 and earlier years. In some instances, a student may be enrolled simultaneously as both a graduate and an undergraduate, with the result that the total in series H 321 (different individuals) is less than the sum of series H 323 and H 324.

[2] Percentages for 1910, 1920, 1930, and 1940–1954 are based on population, 18 to 21 years old, as of July 1 prior to the opening of school; for all other years based on July 1 population after the closing of school in June. Beginning in 1946, percentages are based on all enrolled students rather than merely nonveteran students. The percentages, biennially, of nonveteran students to the population for 1946–1954 are, respectively: 15.10, 15.01, 19.44, 21.84, and 25.93.

[3] 1956 data as of November 1955; 1954 as of November 1953. Cumulative figures for academic year 1954 are total, 2,535,000; undergraduate, 2,257,000; and graduate, 278,000.

[4] Excludes 23 public junior colleges (normal schools) having a combined enrollment of 1,108.

[5] Excludes 26 public junior colleges (normal schools) having a combined enrollment of 1,184.

[6] Includes military students.

[7] Distributions estimated.

[8] Full-time equivalent; total number of different persons not tabulated.

[9] Estimated.

[10] Data for 1924 and previous years taken from *Education for Victory*, vol. 3, No. 6, 1944.

[11] Estimates for 1920 not shown because available figures exclude "instructors in normal courses" in teachers colleges and normal schools.

Series H 327–338. Institutions of Higher Education—Degrees Conferred, by Sex: 1870 to 1957

School year ending—	All degrees			Bachelor's or first professional			Master's or second professional			Doctor's or equivalent		
	Total	Male	Female	Total	Male	Female	Total	Male	Female	Total	Male	Female
	327	328	329	330	331	332	333	334	335	336	337	338
1957	408,324	270,352	137,972	337,663	221,231	116,432	61,909	41,308	20,601	8,752	7,813	939
1956	376,973	245,627	131,346	308,812	198,233	110,579	59,258	39,376	19,882	8,903	8,018	885
1955	352,140	229,186	122,954	285,138	182,463	102,675	58,165	38,712	19,453	8,837	8,011	826
1954	356,608	232,830	123,778	290,825	186,528	104,297	56,788	38,122	18,666	8,995	8,180	815
1953	372,315	248,254	124,061	303,049	199,793	103,256	60,959	40,946	20,013	8,307	7,515	792
1952	401,203	276,507	124,696	329,986	225,981	104,005	63,534	43,557	19,977	7,683	6,969	714
1951	454,960	331,099	123,861	382,546	278,240	104,306	65,077	46,196	18,881	7,337	6,663	674
1950	496,874	376,051	120,823	432,058	328,841	103,217	58,183	41,220	16,963	6,633	5,990	643
1949	421,282	303,347	117,935	365,492	263,608	101,884	50,741	35,212	15,529	5,049	4,527	522
1948	317,607	208,042	109,565	271,186	175,615	95,571	42,432	28,931	13,501	3,989	3,496	493
1946	157,349	69,728	87,621	136,174	58,664	77,510	19,209	9,484	9,725	1,966	1,580	386
1944	141,582	63,456	78,126	125,863	55,865	69,998	13,414	5,711	7,703	2,305	1,880	425
1942	213,491	121,104	92,387	185,346	103,889	81,457	24,648	14,179	10,469	3,497	3,036	461
1940	216,521	128,915	87,606	186,500	109,546	76,954	26,731	16,508	10,223	3,290	2,861	429
1938	189,503	113,580	75,923	164,943	97,678	67,265	21,628	13,400	8,228	2,932	2,502	430
1936	164,197	99,940	64,257	143,125	86,067	57,058	18,302	11,503	6,799	2,770	2,370	400
1934	157,279	96,313	60,966	136,156	82,341	53,815	18,293	11,516	6,777	2,830	2,456	374
1932	160,084	97,728	62,356	138,063	83,271	54,792	19,367	12,210	7,157	2,654	2,247	407
1930	139,752	84,486	55,266	122,484	73,615	48,869	14,969	8,925	6,044	2,299	1,946	353
1928	124,995	76,635	48,360	111,161	67,659	43,502	12,387	7,727	4,660	1,447	1,249	198
1926	108,407	69,636	38,771	97,263	62,218	35,045	9,735	6,202	3,533	1,409	1,216	193
1924	92,097	61,362	30,735	82,783	54,908	27,875	8,216	5,515	2,701	1,098	939	159
1922	68,488	46,318	22,170	61,668	41,306	20,362	5,984	4,304	1,680	836	708	128

Series H 327–338. Institutions of Higher Education—Degrees Conferred, by Sex: 1870 to 1957—Con.

School year ending—	All degrees			Bachelor's or first professional			Master's or second professional			Doctor's or equivalent		
	Total	Male	Female	Total	Male	Female	Total	Male	Female	Total	Male	Female
	327	328	329	330	331	332	333	334	335	336	337	338
1920	53,516	35,487	18,029	48,622	31,980	16,642	4,279	2,985	1,294	615	522	93
1918	42,041	28,566	13,475	38,585	26,269	12,316	2,900	1,806	1,094	556	491	65
1916	49,823	35,372	14,451	45,250	31,852	13,398	3,906	2,934	972	667	586	81
1915	48,100	34,604	13,496	43,912	31,417	12,495	3,577	2,638	939	611	549	62
1914	48,097	34,925	13,172	44,268	32,183	12,085	3,270	2,256	1,014	559	486	73
1913	45,959	33,814	12,145	42,396	31,312	11,084	3,025	2,021	1,004	538	481	57
1912	42,943	32,211	10,732	39,408	29,560	9,848	3,035	2,215	820	500	436	64
1911	40,434	30,817	9,617	37,481	28,547	8,934	2,456	1,821	635	497	449	48
1910	39,755	30,716	9,039	37,199	28,762	8,437	2,113	1,555	558	443	399	44
1909	40,531	31,543	8,988	37,892	29,433	8,459	2,188	1,713	475	451	397	54
1908	36,162	28,226	7,936	33,800	26,376	7,424	1,971	1,511	460	391	339	52
1907	34,202	26,804	7,398	32,234	25,269	6,965	1,619	1,215	404	349	320	29
1906	34,189	26,939	7,250	32,019	25,215	6,804	1,787	1,366	421	383	358	25
1905	33,813	26,813	7,000	31,519	24,934	6,585	1,925	1,538	387	369	341	28
1904	32,514	25,879	6,635	30,501	24,237	6,264	1,679	1,340	339	334	302	32
1903	31,962	25,559	6,403	29,907	23,872	6,035	1,718	1,385	333	337	302	35
1902	31,117	24,953	6,164	28,966	23,225	5,741	1,858	1,464	394	293	264	29
1901	30,790	24,838	5,952	28,681	23,099	5,582	1,744	1,405	339	365	334	31
1900	29,375	23,812	5,563	27,410	22,173	5,237	1,583	1,280	303	382	359	23
1899	27,867	22,666	5,201	25,980	21,064	4,916	1,542	1,275	267	345	327	18
1898	26,816	21,831	4,985	25,052	20,358	4,694	1,440	1,188	252	324	285	39
1897	26,963	22,012	4,951	25,231	20,550	4,681	1,413	1,163	250	319	299	20
1896	26,342	21,525	4,817	24,593	20,076	4,517	1,478	1,213	265	271	236	35
1895	25,712	21,094	4,618	24,106	19,723	4,383	1,334	1,124	210	272	247	25
1894	23,352	19,191	4,161	21,850	17,917	3,933	1,223	1,013	210	279	261	18
1893	19,989	--------	--------	18,667	15,342	3,325	1,104	--------	--------	218	--------	--------
1892	17,722	--------	--------	16,802	13,840	2,962	730	--------	--------	190	--------	--------
1891	17,803	--------	--------	16,840	13,902	2,938	776	--------	--------	187	--------	--------
1890	16,703			15,539	12,857	2,682	1,015	--------	--------	149	147	2
1889	16,305			15,020	12,397	2,623	1,161	--------	--------	124		
1888	16,383			15,256	12,562	2,694	987	--------	--------	140		
1887	14,402			13,402	11,008	2,394	923	--------	--------	77		
1886	14,040			13,097	10,731	2,366	859	--------	--------	84		
1885	15,882			14,734	12,043	2,691	1,071	--------	--------	77		
1884	13,732			12,765	10,408	2,357	901	--------	--------	66		
1883	16,029			15,116	12,294	2,822	863	--------	--------	50		
1882	15,928			14,998	12,168	2,830	884	--------	--------	46		
1881	15,830			14,871	12,035	2,836	922	--------	--------	37		
1880	13,829			12,896	10,411	2,485	879	--------	--------	54	51	3
1879	13,036			12,081	9,808	2,273	919	--------	--------	36		
1878	12,381			11,533	9,416	2,117	816	--------	--------	32		
1877	10,915			10,145	8,329	1,816	731	--------	--------	39		
1876	12,871			12,005	9,911	2,094	835	--------	--------	31		
1875	12,616			11,932	9,905	2,027	661	--------	--------	23		
1874	12,366			11,493	9,593	1,900	860	--------	--------	13		
1873	11,723			10,807	9,070	1,737	890	--------	--------	26		
1872	8,660			7,852	6,626	1,226	794	--------	--------	14		
1871	12,370			12,357	10,484	1,873	--------	--------	--------	13		
1870	9,372	--------	--------	9,371	7,993	1,378	--------	--------	--------	1	1	--------

Series H 339–350. Institutions of Higher Education—Current Income: 1890 to 1954

[In thousands of dollars]

School year ending—	Total income	Educational and general income									Auxiliary enterprises and activities	Other current income
		Total	Student fees	Endowment earnings	Government			Private gifts and grants	Organized activities related to instructional departments	Other sources		
					Federal	State	Local					
	339	340	341	342	343	344	345	346	347	348	349	350
1954	2,945,550	2,338,569	551,424	127,475	417,097	740,043	88,198	190,899	164,880	58,553	574,769	32,212
1952	2,562,451	2,020,878	446,591	112,859	451,011	611,302	72,013	149,826	136,442	40,834	509,546	32,027
1950	2,374,645	1,833,845	394,610	96,341	524,319	491,958	61,378	118,627	111,987	34,625	511,265	29,535
1948	2,027,051	1,538,076	304,601	86,680	526,476	352,281	47,521	91,468	92,725	36,324	465,154	23,821
1946	1,169,394	924,958	214,345	89,763	197,250	225,161	31,005	77,572	67,084	22,779	244,436	(1)
1944	1,047,298	863,654	154,485	75,196	308,162	175,169	26,449	50,449	53,577	20,167	183,644	(1)
1942	783,720	626,296	201,365	74,075	58,232	166,532	27,057	45,916	40,308	12,811	157,424	(1)
1940	715,211	571,288	200,897	71,304	38,860	151,222	24,392	40,453	32,777	11,383	143,923	(1)
1938	652,631	522,108	178,996	70,654	29,345	140,959	22,091	36,908	27,947	15,208	130,523	(1)
1936	597,585	491,106	158,134	60,090	43,234	119,585	21,050	37,115	24,943	26,955	106,479	(1)
1934	486,362	388,725	138,257	55,533	19,827	[2] 117,551	(3)	27,468	17,759	12,330	87,983	9,653
1932	566,264	451,997	150,649	60,903	(3)	[2] 174,663	(3)	29,948	21,008	14,826	103,269	10,998
1930	554,511	483,065	144,126	68,605	20,658	[2] 150,847	(3)	26,172	(1)	72,657	60,419	11,027
1920	199,922	172,929	42,254	26,482	[5] 12,783	[6] 61,690	(3)	7,584	(1)	22,135	26,993	(1)
1910		76,053	--------	--------	--------	--------	--------	--------	(1)	--------	--------	--------
1900		35,084	--------	--------	--------	--------	--------	--------	--------	--------	--------	--------
1890		21,464	--------	--------	--------	--------	--------	--------	--------	--------	--------	--------

[1] Data not collected. [2] Includes local government.
[3] Included with State government.
[4] Includes Federal and local governments.

[5] Universities, colleges, and professional schools only; teachers colleges and normal schools omitted.
[6] May also include Federal funds for teachers colleges and normal schools.

Series H 351–361. Institutions Of Higher Education—Current Expenditures: 1930 to 1954
[In thousands of dollars]

School year ending—	Total expenditures	Educational and general expenditures								Auxiliary enterprises and activities	Other expenditures
		Total	Administration and general expense	Resident instruction	Organized research	Libraries	Plant operation and maintenance	Organized activities related to instructional departments	Extension		
	351	352	353	354	355	356	357	358	359	360	361
1954	2,882,864	2,271,296	288,147	960,556	372,643	72,944	277,874	186,905	112,227	537,533	74,035
1952	2,471,008	1,921,209	233,844	823,117	317,928	60,612	240,446	147,854	97,408	477,672	72,127
1950	2,245,661	1,706,444	213,070	780,994	225,341	56,147	225,110	119,108	86,674	476,401	62,816
1948	1,883,269	1,391,594	171,829	657,945	159,090	44,208	201,996	85,346	71,180	438,988	52,687
1946	1,088,422	820,326	104,808	375,122	86,812	26,560	110,947	60,604	55,473	242,028	26,068
1944	974,118	656,802	69,668	334,189	58,456	20,452	81,201	48,415	44,421	199,344	[1]117,972
1942	738,168	572,465	66,968	298,558	34,287	19,762	72,594	37,771	42,525	137,328	28,375
1940	674,688	521,990	62,827	280,248	27,266	19,487	69,612	27,225	35,325	124,184	28,514
1938	614,385	473,171	56,406	253,006	25,213	17,588	62,738	24,031	34,189	115,620	[2]25,594
1936	541,391	417,303	48,069	225,144	22,091	15,531	56,802	20,241	29,427	95,332	[2]28,755
1934	469,329	362,159	43,155	203,332	17,064	13,387	51,046	14,155	20,020	78,730	[2]28,440
1932	536,523	415,394	47,232	232,645	21,978	11,379	56,797	21,297	24,066	90,897	[2]30,232
1930	507,142	377,903	42,929	221,302	18,007	9,622	61,061	[3]	24,982	3,127	126,112

[1] Includes $97,043,886 expended for Federal contract courses.
[2] Includes unitemized educational and general expenditures amounting to $2,020,311 (1937–38); $2,579,553 (1935–36); $7,502,347 (1933–34); $5,238,649 (1931–32).
[3] Not tabulated separately; probably included in series H 361, "Other expenditures."

Series H 362–373. Institutions of Higher Education—Plant Fund Operations and Property: 1890 to 1954
[In thousands of dollars]

School year ending—	Plant fund operations									Property (at end of year)			
	Receipts by source								Expenditures	Physical plant [1]	Nonexpendable funds		
	Total	Government			Private gifts and grants	Loans	Other sources				Endowment [2]	Annuities	Student loans
		Federal	State	Local									
	362	363	364	365	366	367	368		369	370	371	372	373
1954	468,667	8,380	132,113	13,956	103,776	132,837	77,605		530,804	8,032,700	3,193,889	67,253	49,085
1952	355,614	12,657	144,187	16,075	71,606	47,907	63,182		403,317	6,755,915	2,868,530	74,640	46,784
1950	528,747	12,358	283,920	19,373	72,620	[3]	140,476		416,831	5,272,590	[4]2,601,223	[5]	43,100
1948	364,902	[3]	[3]	[3]	[3]	[3]	[3]		306,370	3,996,000	2,384,487	69,050	44,190
1946	121,837	3,548	71,492	1,818	44,979	[6]	[6]		71,403	[6]	[6]	[6]	[6]
1944	22,587	[3]	[3]	[3]	[3]	[3]	[3]		27,427	[7]	[7]	[7]	[7]
1942	30,096	1,563	12,450	1,119	14,964	[6]	[6]		50,202	2,759,261	[8]1,766,664	[5]	[5]
1940	66,209	22,987	18,404	2,154	22,663	[6]	[6]		83,765	2,753,780	1,686,283	49,537	28,784
1938	58,264	[3]	[3]	[3]	20,665	[3]	[9]37,599		70,466	2,556,075	1,652,620	43,782	25,439
1936	[3]	[3]	[3]	[3]	[3]	[3]	[3]		47,369	2,359,418	1,553,610	42,029	27,466
1934	41,803	[3]	[3]	[3]	10,171	[3]	[9]31,632		29,503	2,252,877	1,472,946	43,757	23,024
1932	56,257	[3]	[3]	[3]	[3]	[3]	[3]		98,290	2,207,295	1,372,349	[7]	91,058
1930	82,078	[3]	[10]30,621	[11]	51,457	[3]	[3]		125,106	2,065,050	1,372,068	[6]	[6]
1920										741,333			
1910										460,532			
1900										253,599			
1890										95,426			

[1] Includes unexpended plant funds. [2] Includes funds functioning as endowment. [7] Data not tabulated. [8] Includes annuity and student loan funds.
[3] Not tabulated separately. [4] Includes annuity funds. [9] Includes items not tabulated separately.
[5] Included with endowment funds. [6] Data not collected. [10] Includes local government. [11] Included with State government.

Series H 374–382. School Enrollment Rates, by Color and Sex: 1850 to 1957
[Statistics for 1954–1957 are estimates based on Current Population Survey sample; 1950 based on 20-percent sample. Rate per 100 population. Figures for 1890 and 1940–1957, refer to population 5 to 19 years old; 1850–1880, enrollment refers to all ages and population base to those 5 to 19 years old; 1900–1930 figures refer to population 5 to 20 years old]

Year	Both sexes			Male			Female		
	Total	White	Nonwhite	Total	White	Nonwhite	Total	White	Nonwhite
	374	375	376	377	378	379	380	381	382
CURRENT POPULATION SURVEY									
1957	87.8	88.2	85.3	89.4	90.0	85.6	86.2	86.4	85.0
1956	87.2	87.8	83.6	88.6	89.4	83.6	85.8	86.1	83.5
1955	86.5	87.0	82.9	88.4	88.9	84.6	84.5	85.0	81.2
1954	86.2	87.0	80.8	87.5	88.4	80.9	84.8	85.4	80.7
DECENNIAL CENSUS									
1950	78.7	79.3	74.8	79.1	79.7	74.7	78.4	78.9	74.9
1940	74.8	75.6	68.4	74.9	75.9	67.5	74.7	75.4	69.2
1930 [1]	69.9	71.2	60.3	70.2	71.4	59.7	69.7	70.9	60.8
1920	64.3	65.7	53.5	64.1	65.6	52.5	64.5	65.8	54.5
1910	59.2	61.3	44.8	59.1	61.4	43.1	59.4	61.3	46.6
1900	50.5	53.6	31.1	50.1	53.4	29.4	50.9	53.9	32.8
1890	54.3	57.9	32.9	54.7	58.5	31.8	53.8	57.2	33.9
1880	57.8	62.0	33.8	59.2	63.5	34.1	56.5	60.5	33.5
1870	48.4	54.4	9.9	49.8	56.0	9.6	46.9	52.7	10.0
1860	50.6	59.6	1.9	52.6	62.0	1.9	48.5	57.2	1.8
1850	47.2	56.2	1.8	49.6	59.0	2.0	44.8	53.3	1.8

[1] Revised to include Mexicans as white persons.

Series H 383–394. School Enrollment, by Age: 1910 to 1957

[Number in thousands. Figures for 1945–1957 are estimates based on Current Population Survey sample, except for 1950 Census data which are based on 20-percent sample]

Year	Total, 5 to 19 years			5 to 13 years			14 to 17 years			18 and 19 years		
	Population	Enrolled		Population	Enrolled		Population	Enrolled		Population	Enrolled	
		Number	Percent		Number	Percent		Number	Percent		Number	Percent
	383	384	385	386	387	388	389	390	391	392	393	394
CURRENT POPULATION SURVEY												
1957	44,407	39,010	87.8	30,231	28,534	94.4	10,134	9,067	89.5	4,042	1,409	34.9
1956	42,832	37,363	87.2	29,314	27,543	94.0	9,540	8,413	88.2	3,978	1,407	35.4
1955	41,342	35,750	86.5	28,268	26,548	93.9	9,169	7,970	86.9	3,905	1,232	31.5
1954	39,972	34,448	86.2	27,118	25,396	93.6	8,936	7,784	87.1	3,918	1,268	32.4
1953	38,445	32,934	85.7	25,885	24,216	93.6	8,775	7,538	85.9	3,785	1,180	31.2
1952	36,972	31,158	84.3	24,643	22,756	92.3	8,631	7,341	85.1	3,698	1,061	28.7
1951	35,398	29,705	83.9	23,171	21,513	92.8	8,458	7,201	85.1	3,769	991	26.3
1950	34,722	28,859	83.1	22,330	20,716	92.8	8,351	6,953	83.3	4,041	1,190	29.4
1949	34,850	28,659	82.2	22,486	20,853	92.7	8,302	6,778	81.6	4,062	1,028	25.3
1948	34,320	27,969	81.5	21,769	20,011	91.9	8,342	6,824	81.8	4,209	1,134	26.9
1947	33,446	26,950	80.6	20,817	19,206	92.3	8,492	6,737	79.3	4,137	1,007	24.3
1946	32,705	25,780	78.8	20,117	17,996	89.5	8,666	6,900	79.6	3,922	884	22.5
1945	31,835	25,204	79.2	19,725	17,580	89.1	8,878	6,956	78.4	3,232	668	20.7
DECENNIAL CENSUS												
1950	35,092	27,605	78.7	22,305	19,136	85.8	8,443	7,068	83.7	4,344	1,401	32.3
1940	34,764	25,998	74.8	20,025	16,840	84.1	9,720	7,709	79.3	5,019	1,449	28.9
1930	36,165	26,558	73.4	22,230	18,567	83.5	9,341	6,826	73.1	4,593	1,165	25.4
1920	31,470	21,226	67.4	19,993	15,791	79.0	7,736	4,768	61.6	3,741	666	17.8
1910	27,931	17,491	62.6	17,020	12,552	73.7	7,220	4,250	58.9	3,691	689	18.7

Series H 395–406. Median Years of School Completed, by Age, Sex, and Color: 1940 and 1950

[Statistics for 1950 are estimates based on 20-percent sample; 1940 from a complete count]

Series No.	Age	Total		Male						Female					
				All classes		White		Nonwhite		All classes		White		Nonwhite	
		1950	1940	1950	1940	1950	1940	1950	1940	1950	1940	1950	1940	1950	1940
395	Total, 25 and over	9.3	8.6	9.0	8.6	9.3	8.7	6.4	5.4	9.6	8.7	10.0	8.8	7.2	6.1
396	25 to 29 years	12.1	10.3	12.0	10.1	12.4	10.5	8.4	6.5	12.1	10.5	12.2	10.9	8.9	7.5
397	30 to 34 years	11.6	9.5	11.4	9.2	11.9	9.7	7.8	6.2	11.8	9.9	12.1	10.3	8.4	7.0
398	35 to 39 years	10.7	8.8	10.3	8.7	10.7	8.8	7.1	5.8	10.7	8.9	11.2	9.1	7.8	6.5
399	40 to 44 years	9.8	8.6	9.4	8.6	9.9	8.7	6.5	5.5	10.1	8.7	10.5	8.8	7.2	6.1
400	45 to 49 years	8.9	8.5	8.9	8.4	8.9	8.5	6.0	5.2	9.0	8.5	9.5	8.6	6.7	5.7
401	50 to 54 years	8.7	8.4	8.6	8.3	8.7	8.4	5.6	4.8	8.8	8.4	8.9	8.5	6.1	5.2
402	55 to 59 years	8.5	8.3	8.4	8.2	8.5	8.3	5.1	4.6	8.6	8.4	8.7	8.5	5.8	4.9
403	60 to 64 years	8.4	8.3	8.3	8.2	8.3	8.3	4.7	4.3	8.4	8.3	8.5	8.4	5.3	4.5
404	65 to 69 years	8.2	8.2	8.1	8.1	8.2	8.2	4.0	3.7	8.3	8.2	8.4	8.3	4.5	3.8
405	70 to 74 years	8.2	8.1	8.0	8.0	8.1	8.1	3.9	2.9	8.3	8.2	8.4	8.3	4.2	2.8
406	75 years and over	8.1	8.0	7.9	7.7	8.1	8.0	3.1	1.5	8.2	8.1	8.3	8.2	3.4	1.0

Series H 407–411. Percent Illiterate in the Population, by Color and Nativity: 1870 to 1952

[Data for 1870 to 1940 are for population 10 years old and over; data for 1947, 1950, and 1952 are for population 14 years old and over]

Year	Total	White			Non-white	Year	Total	White			Non-white
		Total	Native	Foreign born				Total	Native	Foreign born	
	407	408	409	410	411		407	408	409	410	411
1952	2.5	1.8	(1)	(1)	10.2	1910	7.7	5.0	3.0	12.7	30.5
1950	²3.2	(1)	(1)	(1)	(1)	1900	10.7	6.2	4.6	12.9	44.5
1947	2.7	1.8	(1)	(1)	11.0						
						1890	13.3	7.7	6.2	13.1	56.8
1940	2.9	2.0	1.1	9.0	11.5	1880	17.0	9.4	8.7	12.0	70.0
1930	4.3	3.0	1.6	10.8	16.4						
1920	6.0	4.0	2.0	13.1	23.0	1870	20.0	11.5	(1)	(1)	79.9

¹ Not available.
² See source, pp. 6 and 7, for an explanation of the estimating procedure used to obtain this figure and a possible explanation as to why it is somewhat higher than others in recent years.

CRIME AND CORRECTION (Series H 412–454)

H 412–454. General note.

In the United States there are many difficulties to be faced in drawing together national statistics on crime and correction. There is no one body of criminal law or procedure that relates to the United States as a whole. Under the United States constitution, the police powers are reserved to the States. Thus, there are 48 sovereign jurisdictions of crime control in the 48 States in this country and a 49th in the District of Columbia which has a penal code and a criminal enforcement system provided by Act of Congress.

Federal criminal jurisdiction is something quite apart from State jurisdiction. Federal crimes are defined by Acts of Congress in connection with enforcing laws relating primarily to customs, taxation, and interstate matters. Therefore, except for offenses committed within the limited geographical area of a Federal reservation, crimes such as murder, robbery, burglary, larceny, rape, arson, etc., are juridically State crimes rather than Federal.

Within each State, the enforcement of the criminal law is predominantly the responsibility of local agencies. Police departments, prosecutors, and courts are in most instances either municipal or county agencies. To a large extent, even the correctional processes such as probation and misdemeanant imprisonment are functions administered by local authorities. Direct State responsibility is largely confined to providing penal institutions for those offenders convicted and committed to long-term imprisonment.

The inherent difficulties of collecting only the basic information about crime from hundreds of independent police departments, prosecutors, courts, and correctional agencies within a single State, not to mention the difficulties encountered in attempting to synthesize such information for the 48 States and the District of Columbia, have limited the development of adequate national compilations of criminal statistics.

There have been three different collections of nationwide criminal statistics undertaken in recent years: One summarized data on offenders committed to prison; the second, data on crimes known to the police and arrests; and the third, statistics on criminal defendants prosecuted in the trial courts. The first two of these are still being carried on.

Statistics on prisoners were collected by the Bureau of the Census in connection with each decennial Census of Population from 1850 to 1890. Independent enumerations of prisoners were made in 1904, 1910, 1923, and 1933. The first nationwide collection of criminal data on an annual basis was made in 1926 by the Bureau of the Census (a compilation of prisoners received and released from State and Federal prisons and reformatories). This agency published an annual summary and an analysis of these data from 1926 to 1946, and a very brief summary in 1947. Subsequently, the Federal Bureau of Prisons assumed this responsibility.

These annual reports have, from the beginning, covered most of the States, never less than 44 of the 49 jurisdictions plus reports from the Federal prison system, and have been consistent and complete enough to offer historical data that have some acceptable comparability (see series H 412–431).

The second annual nationwide collection began in 1930. Summary reports on serious offenses known to the police and arrests made by them were collected from a large number of police departments by the Federal Bureau of Investigation. Annual and semiannual statistics have been regularly issued ever since in *Uniform Crime Reports.* Because the sources of data for this series are cooperating individual police departments in all of the States, there have never been data available which represented complete reporting from all police departments in any one State. Further, the variability in procedure and practice in the reporting of crimes known to the police and the lack of uniformity in the definition of offenses are serious obstacles in compiling valid historical series on crimes and arrests in the United States as a whole.

A third collection of data on a national basis was made under the auspices of the Bureau of the Census in 1932 when reports were obtained from a number of States accounting for defendants prosecuted and convicted and sentenced in courts of general trial jurisdiction. The usual pattern throughout the country is that there is one such court in each county and there are over 3,000 counties in the 48 States. This series was continued for 15 years, and reports summarizing these data were issued annually by the Bureau of the Census under the title, *Judicial Criminal Statistics.* However, at no time were there more than 32 States involved in this reporting system. Partly because of its limited existence and incomplete coverage, its inclusion here is not justified. In addition, the variations from State to State and even within States from county to county that occurred in the reporting of the data created many unresolved questions of comparability and completeness.

H 412–420. Prisoners present in Federal and State institutions, prisoners received from courts, and conditional-release violators returned, 1926–1957.

Source: 1926–1939, Bureau of the Census, *Prisoners in State and Federal Prisons and Reformatories;* series H 412–417, 1940–1957, Federal Bureau of Prisons, *National Prisoner Statistics,* Bulletin No. 19, July 1958; series H 418–420, 1940–1957, Federal Bureau of Prisons, *National Prisoner Statistics,* annual issues.

These data, as well as those shown in series H 421–431, are based on information reported for State prisons and reformatories and for Federal prisons with the following exceptions: No data were reported for Delaware or the District of Columbia prior to 1931. The New Castle County Workhouse was the only reporting institution for Delaware for 1931-1956 except for 1933 when no data were reported; in 1957, all State prisoners in Delaware were included. No data were reported in 1926 for Alabama, Florida, Idaho; in 1927 for Alabama; in 1928 for Mississippi, Idaho; in 1929 for Alabama, Georgia, Mississippi; in 1930 for Alabama, Georgia, Idaho. For 1931–1937, inclusive, no data were reported for Alabama, Georgia, or Mississippi. South Carolina was omitted in 1932. The Milwaukee House of Correction in Wisconsin is excluded in series H 414 and H 417 for 1937-1939; it is also excluded in series H 420 for 1937-1946. In 1938 and 1939, all States except Alabama and Georgia were included. Rhode Island data include both misdemeanant and felony prisoners for all years except 1957 when only felony prisoners were included. Although there have been years since 1940 when 2 or 3 States did not report, the published data have been adjusted to include estimates for these missing States. Therefore, the data presented for 1940-1957 represent prisons and reformatories in all States and the District of Columbia. However, a significant change was introduced in the series in 1940 by the addition of reports for 9 Federal correctional institutions and 2 detention headquarters to the Federal totals. Also for 1940-1957, series H 414 and H 417 include felony prisoners present at the end of the year and received from court for North Carolina Road Camps; series H 420 excludes such prisoners except for 1957.

Institutions for adult offenders may include a sizable number of juveniles for certain States.

H 421–431. Prisoners released from Federal and State institutions, by type of release, 1926–1957.

Source: 1926–1946, Bureau of the Census, *Prisoners in State and Federal Prisons and Reformatories;* 1947 and 1948, Bureau of Prisons, records; 1949-1957, Bureau of Prisons, *National Prisoner Statistics,* and records.

Data are for live releases. Between 1926 and 1957 only 2,177 prisoners died in Federal institutions; 32 of these were executions carried out between 1927 and 1957. In State institutions, there were 30,528 deaths between 1926 and 1957. Of these, 4,003 were executions. Most of these executions were carried out by State authorities, however, some were carried out by local authorities. The data on executions by State and local authorities are incomplete for 1926-1929.

All the limitations on completeness of coverage of series H 412-420 are also applicable for these series.

Series H 421-431 exclude escapees, temporary releases, etc.

H 432–444. Prisoners executed under civil authority, by race and offense, 1930–1957.

Source: Federal Bureau of Prisons, *National Prisoner Statistics,* Bulletin No. 20, February 1959.

Figures represent all executions occurring within the States whether they were carried out in a State institution or by local agencies. Executions by military authorities are excluded. The Army (including Air Force) carried out 157 executions (148 between 1942 and 1950, and 3 each in 1954, 1955 and 1957); 104 of the 157 were executed for murder (including 21 involving rape), 52 for rape, and 1 for desertion. The Navy carried out no executions during the period.

H 445–451. Urban crime, by type of major offense, 1937–1957.

Source: Federal Bureau of Investigation, *Uniform Crime Reports,* Annual Bulletin, 1957, vol. XXVIII, No. 2, p. 85. (The source also shows estimates for rape and larceny.)

Figures are from the same 353 cities for each year. Their total population was 36.5 million in 1940 and 42.7 million in 1950. If a police department is known to have made major

changes in its records procedures during the period covered, its reports have been excluded.

The fact that the basic source of these data is 353 individual reporting areas scattered over the 48 States, that there are differences among the States in the definition of some of these offenses, and that there has been improvement in reporting procedures on the part of some police agencies over this period of years makes the matter of interpreting these figures as reflecting a relatively exact measure of crime somewhat doubtful. It is likely that the reliability of reports on murder and robbery is higher than those for other offenses as these 2 offenses are more clearly and consistently defined throughout the various States than are the other types of offenses shown.

H 452–454. Persons lynched, by race, 1882–1956.

Source: 1882–1951, *1952 Negro Year Book,* William H. Wise and Co., p. 278; 1952–1956, Tuskegee Institute, Department of Records and Research, unpublished estimates.

Additional information and more detailed figures can be found in Arthur F. Raper, *The Tragedy of Lynching,* University of North Carolina Press, Chapel Hill, 1933, pp. 480–484, and James E. Cutler, *Lynch Law: An Investigation Into the History of Lynching in the United States,* Longmans-Green, New York, 1905, pp. 160–161. Raper presents statistics of lynchings for whites and Negroes for 1889–1932, based on the *Negro Year Book,* 1931–1932, and on material obtained from the Department of Records and Research, Tuskegee Institute. For 1916–1932, Raper's estimates agree with those shown here; but for all earlier years there are differences which are due to subsequent revisions made in the series by Tuskegee Institute. Cutler's estimates are based on the annual record kept by the Chicago Tribune (daily newspaper). Estimates shown here are for whites and Negroes only. During the period 1882–1903, Cutler found that 45 Indians, 12 Chinese, 1 Japanese, and 20 persons of Mexican ancestry had been lynched.

The *1952 Negro Year Book* presents a detailed discussion concerning the difficulty of defining the term "lynching." According to this source, ". . . agencies concerned about the lynching problem have not been able to come to a conclusive agreement even when using the same criteria in classifying cases of lynching." The same source refers to a conference held on December 11, 1940, at Tuskegee Institute which established the following criteria to cover persons considered as victims of lynching:

1. There must be legal evidence that a person was killed;
2. The person must have met death illegally;
3. A group must have participated in the killing;
4. The group must have acted under pretext of service to justice, race, or tradition.

Series H 412–420. Prisoners Present in Federal and State Institutions, Prisoners Received From Courts, and Conditional-Release Violators Returned: 1926 to 1957

[Prisoners in institutions for adult offenders only. Figures for 1926–1939 exclude institutions in certain States for which data are not available; 1940–1957 cover all States]

Year	Prisoners present (at end of year)			Prisoners received from courts (during year)			Conditional-release violators returned to prison (during year)		
	Total	Federal institutions	State institutions	Total	Federal institutions	State institutions	Total	Federal institutions	State institutions
	412	413	414	415	416	417	418	419	420
1957	195,414	20,420	174,994	80,409	13,305	67,104	12,096	1,092	11,004
1956	189,565	20,134	169,431	77,869	13,454	64,415	11,720	1,032	10,688
1955	185,915	20,088	165,827	78,349	15,286	63,063	11,002	980	10,022
1954	182,901	20,003	162,898	80,796	16,685	64,111	10,355	902	9,453
1953	173,579	19,363	154,216	74,149	16,375	57,773	10,036	956	9,080
1952	168,233	18,014	150,219	70,845	15,305	55,540	9,465	995	8,470
1951	165,680	17,395	148,285	67,164	14,120	53,044	9,124	1,226	7,898
1950	166,165	17,134	149,031	69,515	14,237	55,278	8,692	1,371	7,321
1949	163,749	16,868	146,881	68,836	13,130	55,706	9,079	1,529	7,550
1948	155,977	16,328	139,649	63,696	12,430	51,266	8,226	1,099	7,127
1947	151,304	17,146	134,158	64,735	12,948	51,787	8,263	946	7,317
1946	140,079	17,622	122,457	61,302	14,950	46,352	7,324	688	6,636
1945	133,649	18,638	115,011	53,212	14,171	39,041	6,792	632	6,160
1944	132,356	18,139	114,217	50,162	14,047	36,115	7,087	599	6,488
1943	137,220	16,113	121,107	50,082	12,203	37,879	6,728	708	6,020
1942	150,384	16,623	133,761	58,858	13,725	45,133	7,007	742	6,265
1941	165,439	18,465	146,974	68,700	15,350	53,350	7,252	898	6,354
1940	173,706	19,260	154,446	73,104	15,109	57,995	6,655	834	5,821
1939	161,075	16,967	144,108	64,816	12,027	52,789	5,899	645	5,254
1938	159,382	17,083	142,299	66,890	12,538	54,352	5,964	558	5,406
1937	149,357	15,309	134,048	62,069	11,171	50,898	5,928	437	5,491
1936	143,573	15,373	128,200	60,925	11,459	49,466	4,575	348	4,227
1935	144,665	14,777	129,888	65,723	11,837	53,886	4,795	292	4,503
1934	138,220	12,080	126,140	62,251	9,275	52,976	4,154	161	3,993
1933	136,947	10,851	126,096	62,801	8,333	54,468	4,073	177	3,896
1932	137,183	12,282	124,901	67,477	9,652	57,825	4,257	172	4,085
1931	137,082	12,964	124,118	71,520	10,615	60,905	3,658	120	3,538
1930	127,495	12,181	115,314	66,013	9,800	56,213	3,158	79	3,079
1929	120,496	12,964	107,532	58,906	9,734	49,172	2,820	42	2,778
1928	116,626	8,204	108,422	55,746	5,570	50,176	2,750	63	2,687
1927	106,517	7,722	98,795	51,936	5,021	46,915	2,393	36	2,357
1926	96,125	6,803	89,322	48,108	5,010	43,098	2,228	26	2,202

Series H 421–431. Prisoners Released From Federal and State Institutions, by Type of Release: 1926 to 1957

[Prisoners in institutions for adult offenders only. Figures for 1926–1939 exclude institutions in certain States for which data are not available; 1940–1957 cover all States]

Year	Total, Federal and State institutions	Released from Federal institutions					Released from State institutions				
		Total	Conditional		Unconditional		Total	Conditional		Unconditional	
			Parole	Other	Expiration of sentence	Other		Parole	Other	Expiration of sentence	Other
	421	422	423	424	425	426	427	428	429	430	431
1957	85,356	14,029	3,822	3,258	6,941	8	71,327	39,535	2,147	26,467	3,178
1956	83,099	14,285	3,975	3,087	7,209	14	68,814	38,288	1,888	25,489	3,149
1955	82,924	15,776	3,823	2,617	9,328	8	67,148	37,631	1,842	24,678	2,997
1954	78,184	16,743	4,410	2,507	9,825	1	61,441	33,551	1,779	23,276	2,835
1953	75,125	15,813	3,793	2,361	9,659	---------	59,312	32,525	1,508	22,693	2,586
1952	74,268	15,524	3,642	2,121	9,761	---------	58,744	32,712	1,387	22,037	2,608
1951	73,937	14,974	3,495	4,049	7,422	8	58,963	32,936	1,466	22,064	2,497
1950	72,179	15,187	3,294	6,172	5,710	11	56,992	31,428	1,342	22,147	2,075
1949	69,051	13,999	3,051	5,596	5,317	35	55,052	28,267	2,590	22,368	1,827
1948	65,978	14,243	3,822	5,124	5,146	151	51,735	27,062	3,206	19,798	1,669
1947	60,080	14,246	4,020	4,893	5,317	16	45,834	25,107	2,766	17,107	854
1946	59,289	15,544	5,362	5,191	4,869	122	43,745	24,571	3,641	14,959	574
1945	57,500	13,598	3,101	5,242	5,229	26	43,902	24,255	4,145	14,935	567
1944	59,860	12,457	3,272	4,784	4,263	138	47,403	26,029	4,574	16,520	280
1943	69,723	13,190	3,101	5,853	4,223	13	56,533	30,526	5,331	20,426	250
1942	81,630	16,032	3,079	7,162	5,776	15	65,598	30,980	7,849	26,143	626
1941	86,887	16,998	2,723	7,583	6,669	23	69,889	32,246	6,372	30,500	771
1940	88,640	16,280	2,572	7,988	5,702	18	72,360	30,360	8,081	32,092	1,827
1939	66,303	11,794	2,315	6,932	2,538	9	54,509	25,568	5,554	22,898	489
1938	62,771	11,102	2,416	6,795	1,876	15	51,669	25,220	4,300	21,754	395
1937	60,462	11,477	2,944	6,566	1,950	17	48,985	24,331	3,521	20,766	367
1936	62,750	10,965	2,445	6,256	2,263	1	51,785	28,686	407	21,778	914
1935	60,475	9,010	2,369	4,294	2,345	2	51,465	28,039	391	20,990	2,045
1934	60,732	8,310	2,709	2,887	2,709	5	52,422	29,747	184	20,761	1,730
1933	63,640	10,206	4,242	1,203	4,756	5	53,434	30,597	---------	21,194	1,643
1932	66,863	10,394	5,050	---------	5,314	30	56,469	32,087	---------	20,530	3,852
1931	60,930	9,749	4,643	---------	5,105	1	51,181	30,339	---------	20,321	521
1930	54,925	8,926	4,157	---------	4,764	5	45,999	25,352	---------	20,112	535
1929	45,986	5,610	1,347	---------	4,261	2	40,376	22,791	---------	16,931	654
1928	45,124	4,983	1,082	---------	3,900	1	40,141	22,887	---------	16,575	679
1927	41,356	4,179	688	---------	3,491	---------	37,177	20,964	---------	14,964	1,249
1926	39,044	4,248	834	---------	3,413	1	34,796	19,088	---------	14,418	1,295

Series H 432–444. Prisoners Executed Under Civil Authority, by Race and Offense: 1930 to 1957

Year	All offenses				Murder [2]			Rape			Other offenses		
	Total	White	Negro	Other [1]	Total [3]	White	Negro	Total	White	Negro	Total [4]	White [5]	Negro
	432	433	434	435	436	437	438	439	440	441	442	443	444
1957	65	34	31		54	32	22	10	2	8	1		1
1956	65	21	43	1	52	20	31	12		12	1	1	
1955	76	44	32		65	41	24	7	1	6	4	2	2
1954	81	38	42	1	71	37	33	9	1	8	1		1
1953	62	30	31	1	51	25	25	7	1	6	4	4	
1952	83	36	47		71	35	36	12	1	11			
1951	105	57	47	1	87	55	31	17	2	15	1		1
1950	82	40	42		68	36	32	13	4	9	1		1
1949	119	50	67	2	107	49	56	10		10	2	1	1
1948	119	35	82	2	95	32	61	22	1	21	2	2	
1947	153	42	111		129	40	89	23	2	21	1		1
1946	131	46	84	1	107	45	61	22		22	2	1	1
1945	117	41	75	1	90	37	52	26	4	22	1		1
1944	120	47	70	3	96	45	48	24	2	22			
1943	131	54	74	3	118	54	63	[3] 13		11			
1942	147	67	80		116	57	59	24	4	20	7	6	1
1941	123	59	63	1	102	55	46	20	4	16	1		1
1940	124	49	75		105	44	61	15		13	4	3	1
1939	159	80	77	2	144	79	63	12		12	3	1	2
1938	190	96	92	2	155	90	63	25	1	24	10	5	5
1937	147	69	74	4	133	67	62	13	2	11	1		1
1936	195	92	101	2	181	86	93	10	2	8	4	4	
1935	199	119	77	3	184	115	66	13	2	11	2	2	
1934	168	65	102	1	154	64	89	14	1	13			
1933	160	77	81	2	151	75	74	7	1	6	2	1	1
1932	140	62	75	3	128	62	63	10		10	2		2
1931	153	77	72	4	137	76	57	15	1	14	1		1
1930	155	90	65		147	90	57	6		6	2		2

[1] All were for murder except 2 for rape in 1943.
[2] Includes 29 females; 18 white, 11 nonwhite.
[3] Total includes other nonwhite, not shown separately.
[4] 21 armed robbery, 16 kidnaping, 11 burglary, 8 espionage (6 in 1942 and 2 in 1953), 4 aggravated assault.
[5] Includes 2 females.

Series H 445–451. Urban Crime, by Type of Major Offense: 1937 to 1957

[Offenses known to police in 353 cities with 25,000 inhabitants or more, and having a total 1950 population of 42,719,693, based on 1950 Census of Population]

Year	Total	Criminal homicide		Robbery [3]	Aggravated assault [4]	Burglary—breaking or entering [5]	Auto theft [6]
		Murder, non-negligent manslaughter [1]	Manslaughter by negligence [2]				
	445	446	447	448	449	450	451
1957	457,370	2,533	1,722	34,641	39,833	247,845	130,796
1956	410,170	2,502	1,766	31,471	39,439	218,248	116,744
1955	373,761	2,410	1,643	30,675	38,785	202,660	97,588
1954	373,735	2,352	1,573	34,139	37,976	206,426	91,269
1953	362,988	2,439	1,599	31,813	38,064	191,339	97,734
1952	343,044	2,471	1,688	28,644	36,136	181,216	92,889
1951	316,175	2,302	1,557	26,086	31,884	169,209	85,137
1950	306,402	2,370	1,544	25,909	32,350	170,708	73,521
1949	307,205	2,332	1,308	29,693	32,144	173,312	68,416
1948	296,880	2,533	1,450	27,850	31,014	163,965	70,068
1947	305,948	2,535	1,481	29,395	31,004	164,709	76,824
1946	334,228	2,629	1,724	31,028	30,228	171,029	97,590
1945	322,190	2,361	1,723	27,671	28,026	156,835	105,574
1944	271,273	2,141	1,424	22,301	25,698	132,768	86,941
1943	257,868	2,030	1,428	22,636	22,126	127,368	82,280
1942	242,598	2,278	1,698	22,903	22,914	123,642	69,163
1941	264,004	2,295	1,852	24,212	20,736	138,043	76,866
1940	266,969	2,208	1,469	25,269	20,312	146,361	71,350
1939	264,837	2,223	1,229	26,347	19,063	145,208	70,767
1938	263,917	2,133	1,428	27,836	18,765	138,939	74,816
1937	276,426	2,479	1,978	26,696	19,841	137,757	87,675

[1] Includes all willful felonious homicides; excludes suicides and justifiable homicides.
[2] Includes deaths primarily attributable to gross negligence on the part of some individual other than the victim.
[3] Includes the stealing or taking of anything of value by force or violence or by threat of force or violence; includes attempted robbery.
[4] Includes assault with intent to kill. Excludes simple assault, assault and battery, fighting, etc.
[5] Includes any unlawful entry to commit a felony or a theft. Includes attempted burglary and burglary followed by larceny.
[6] Includes all cases where motor vehicles are driven away and abandoned. Excludes those taken for temporary use when actually returned by the taker.

Series H 452–454. Persons Lynched, by Race: 1882 to 1956

Year	Total	White	Negro	Year	Total	White	Negro	Year	Total	White	Negro	Year	Total	White	Negro	Year	Total	White	Negro
	452	453	454		452	453	454		452	453	454		452	453	454		452	453	454
1956				1940	5	1	4	1925	17		17	1910	76	9	67	1895	179	66	113
1955	3		3	1939	3	1	2	1924	16		16	1909	82	13	69	1894	192	58	134
1954				1938	6		6	1923	33	4	29	1908	97	8	89	1893	152	34	118
1953				1937	8		8	1922	57	6	51	1907	60	2	58	1892	230	69	161
1952				1936	8		8	1921	64	5	59	1906	65	3	62	1891	184	71	113
1951	1		1																
1950	2	1	1	1935	20	2	18	1920	61	8	53	1905	62	5	57	1890	96	11	85
1949	3		3	1934	15		15	1919	83	7	76	1904	83	7	76	1889	170	76	94
1948	2	1	1	1933	28	4	24	1918	64	4	60	1903	99	15	84	1888	137	68	69
1947	1		1	1932	8	2	6	1917	38	2	36	1902	92	7	85	1887	120	50	70
1946	6		6	1931	13	1	12	1916	54	4	50	1901	130	25	105	1886	138	64	74
1945	1		1	1930	21	1	20	1915	69	13	56	1900	115	9	106	1885	184	110	74
1944	2		2	1929	10	3	7	1914	55	4	51	1899	106	21	85	1884	211	160	51
1943	3		3	1928	11	1	10	1913	52	1	51	1898	120	19	101	1883	130	77	53
1942	6		6	1927	16		16	1912	63	2	61	1897	158	35	123	1882	113	64	49
1941	4		4	1926	30	7	23	1911	67	7	60	1896	123	45	78				

RECREATION (Series H 455–525)

H 455–525. General note.

Statistics on recreation have not been generally compiled and published in a systematic way. One major difficulty is that recreation, as a field of human activity and of social science research, has not been clearly defined in a manner accepted by all students. This general problem, and some of the consequent statistical problems, have been explored in the study by Marion Clawson, "Statistical Data Available for Economic Research on Certain Types of Recreation," *Journal of the American Statistical Association,* March 1959.

In general, many more data are available in the files of public agencies or private groups than have been published; and much of the publication is in forms not physically permanent nor likely to be preserved in libraries and other reference sources. Much of the data are inaccessible and therefore essentially unavailable. The series presented here represent only the more readily available data.

All series except H 500–522 were obtained from the report by Marion Clawson, *Statistics on Outdoor Recreation,* Resources for the Future, Inc., Washington, D. C., 1958. The original sources of these data are discussed below in the text for the various series. *Statistics on Outdoor Recreation* includes much more detail than it has been possible to include here; in particular, it includes much data for individual States and other geographic regions.

H 455–470. National parks, monuments, and allied areas—number, area, and visits, 1850–1956.

Source: Marion Clawson, *Statistics on Outdoor Recreation,* Resources for the Future, Inc., Washington, D. C., 1958.

Data on number and area of units were compiled by the National Park Service. Data on visits appear in the annual reports of the National Park Service or of the Secretary of the Interior. Figures on recreation in these areas are contained in the annual reports of the Director of the National Park Service, in annual reports on *Areas Administered by the National Park Service,* and in periodic reports on attendance at the various units. The records of the National Park Service also contain data on area and visits to each of the units of the national park system, at least for recent years and, in some cases, for years before 1910.

The estimates cover all areas now administered by the National Park Service, although some have in the past been administered by the Department of Agriculture or by the War Department. These areas were established by law or by Executive Order. Areas are tabulated according to their legal designation at the time of tabulation. When designations were changed, numbers of areas and acreages in each series were shifted accordingly. Data do not include areas which are named national historic sites administered by States.

Series H 469–470, national recreation areas, include national seashore recreational areas, but exclude recreation demonstration areas which existed from about 1933 until 1952. In 1932, there were 46 such areas with a total acreage of 395,844. By 1952, all had been disposed of to States or absorbed into the national park system.

Gross acres are reported for 1850–1934; federally owned acreage for 1935–1956. (Series F 17 and F 18 in *Historical Statistics of the United States, 1789–1945,* dealt with area within the national park system and total visits to it, respectively. Those data related only to continental United States, whereas series H 456–457 presented here include the Territories as well.) Data on acreage are compiled from both official and unofficial reports, internal records, and memoranda, among which are many unresolved inconsistencies, particularly for the early years. Acreage data, therefore, should not be considered either final or official.

In many areas, visitors are required to pay an entrance fee, and an actual count of visitors or of cars is obtained. In other areas, visits must be estimated. Each person is counted each time he enters any area of the system. Hence, the number of visits is substantially in excess of the number of different individuals. No data are available on the latter. Data do not include visits to parts of the system when they were not under National Park Service administration. After 1936, all areas which were a part of the system were also administered by the National Park Service. In general, the use of these areas prior to 1936 was not large.

H 471–474. Recreational use of national forest lands, 1924–1956.

Source: See source for series H 455–470.

The basic data are published in annual reports of the Forest Service and in *Agricultural Statistics;* however, a great deal of detailed information is made available in annual processed releases or is in the files of the Forest Service. This is particularly true of data for individual areas. More data, by Forest Service regions, by purpose of visit, and by month are to be found in *Statistics on Outdoor Recreation.*

The national forests are open to several kinds of recreation. In some areas, actual counts of visits are obtained; in most, however, estimates are necessary. A recreational use includes a stop of at least 15 minutes; data do not include a count of persons who drove over highways through national forests but made no other use of the areas. Use of a national forest area for recreation for a period of ¼ to 3 hours is counted as ¼ day; of 3–5 hours, as ½ day; of 5–7 hours as ¾ day; and of 7–24 hours as a full-day use. As with the national park data, a visitor is counted each time he visits an area. Therefore, the number of different persons involved is substantially fewer than numbers of visits.

H 475–487. State parks—acreage, expenditures, funds, revenue, employees, and attendance, 1939–1956.

Source: See source for series H 455–470.

Many different kinds of areas and names are used to describe State-owned areas open for public recreation. Data on such areas are collected by the National Park Service and published in two series. *State Park Statistics* is published annually in mimeographed form and contains data for one year on expenditures, sources of funds, attendance, areas and acreages, personnel, and anticipated expenditures for the next year. *State Parks—Areas, Acreages, and Accommodations* is published quinquennially. Each series is based upon voluntary reports by State agencies to the National Park Service. The latter report for 1955 lists some 55 different kinds of State park areas, or, at least, 55 different names are applied to such areas.

In making its 1956 annual survey, the National Park Service sent questionnaires to some 94 different State agencies. Returns were received from 89 agencies in 47 States. The areas included in these studies vary in size from less than 50 acres each (35 percent of the number of areas) to over 50,000 acres each (0.4 percent). The larger areas, however, contain 64 percent of the total area of the entire system.

The areas as defined in these studies exclude State forests and wildlife areas, some of which have important recreational facilities, and also exclude wayside areas if administered by State highway departments. The extent of the reporting has been variable; however, the more important States and agencies have usually reported. Considerably more data, particularly by individual States, is found in *Statistics on Outdoor Recreation.*

Acreage data are based upon reports from most but not all States, the extent of the coverage increasing in recent years. Land acquired includes purchases, gifts, transfers from other State or Federal agencies, and other means. Of the total, only 38 percent has been by purchase.

Funds available for expenditure include not only current appropriations, but also carryovers from previous appropriations, revenues from operations of concessions and other sources when these are available for expenditure, and "other." Revenue from operations include revenues from publicly operated facilities, from leased concessions, from entrance and parking fees, and from "other."

Attendance data at recreational areas are often estimated, sometimes on various bases. Comparability of figures in these series (H 485–487) is somewhat marred by the transfer in California of numerous very popular beaches from State to county control. This accounts for the apparent drop in total attendance for 1947–1948, when, in fact, attendance was rising rather rapidly.

H 488–499. Municipal recreation—parks, leadership, and facilities, for cities of 100,000 inhabitants or more in 1950, 1880–1955.

Source: See source for series H 455–470.

Statistics on municipal parks and recreation have been collected for many years by the National Recreation Association of New York, a private organization. Questionnaires are sent to all cities of 2,500 and over, to many smaller communities, and to all counties which are believed to have county park systems; and within each, to all agencies known or believed to have administration over parks or recreational programs. Provision of information is voluntary, and in spite of the best efforts of the Association, there is apparently a large degree of underreporting. Between 50 and 60 percent of all cities reported; however, the reporting was complete for the largest cities, fair for middle-size ones, and low for small ones. Many of the latter had no parks, but it is not possible to differentiate between those with no parks and those making no report. Perhaps as many as 90 percent or more of all parks are reported. Data from these surveys have been published in Bureau of Labor Statistics, *Park Recreation Areas in the United States,* Misc. Series Bulletin No. 462, 1928, and No. 565, 1932; George D. Butler, *Municipal and County Parks in the United States, 1935,* National Park Service and National Recreation Association; and the following National Recreation Association publications: *Municipal and County Parks in the United States, 1940; Recreation and Park Yearbook—Midcentury Edition—*

A Review of Local and County Recreation and Park Developments, 1900–1950; 1956 Recreation and Park Yearbook; and other *Yearbooks* published annually for 1910–1940 and biennially for 1942–1950. In the published reports, no effort was made to correct for underreporting, but the number of cities reporting is shown.

However, the estimates shown here have been adjusted for nonresponse. These estimates are based on special tabulations prepared by the National Recreation Association. The extent and basis of estimating is described in *Statistics on Outdoor Recreation.* In general, the amount of estimating was small and it is believed the totals here reported are approximately correct. In *Statistics on Outdoor Recreation* these data are shown for individual cities; there are also shown selected totals for all cities reporting at each period.

H 500–515. Personal consumption expenditures for recreation, 1909–1957.

Source: 1909–1927, Twentieth Century Fund, unpublished estimates (prepared for *Survey of Time, Work, and Leisure*); 1929–1945, Office of Business Economics, *National Income: A Supplement to the Survey of Current Business,* 1954 edition, p. 206; 1946–1957, *U. S. Income and Output,* 1958.

The data for 1909–1927 are based on J. Frederic Dewhurst and Associates, *America's Needs and Resources: A New Survey,* Twentieth Century Fund, New York, 1955. Dewhurst in turn drew his data on recreation from William H. Lough, *High-Level Consumption,* McGraw-Hill, New York, 1935; and Julius Weinberger, "Economic Aspects of Recreation," *Harvard Business Review,* Summer 1937.

For more detailed definitions of the specific series, see the Department of Commerce publications defining these series. Payments are those made by consumers at point of use; expenditures for clothing, transportation, food and drink, shelter, and other items, even though primarily for the purpose of recreation, are excluded here. However, expenditures for most of these items are included in Chapter G, Consumer Expenditure Patterns. For expenditures in constant dollars, see Dewhurst, *America's Needs and Resources.*

H 516–525. General note.

The items included here were selected because they are of some importance, and data are available for them. Other items of perhaps equal importance have been omitted for lack of data or have been included in other chapters. For data on radio and television, for example, see series R 90–98.

H 516–517. Bowling, 1896–1957.

Source: 1896–1946, American Bowling Congress, *Bowling Magazine,* September 1956, Milwaukee, Wis., p. 117; 1947–1957, series H 516, American Bowling Congress records, and series H 517, *Bowling Magazine,* September 1958, p. 118.

While some bowling is not covered by these data, it is believed that they give a fair picture of the growth of this activity. Additional data are available in the publications of the Congress.

H 518. Horse racing attendance, 1940–1957.

Source: 1940–1952, *New Encyclopedia of Sports, 1947,* and *Encyclopedia of Sports, 1953,* A. S. Barnes and Co., New York; 1953–1957, The National Association of State Racing Commissioners, *Statistical Reports on Horse Racing in the United States,* Lexington, Ky., various issues.

Statistics exclude attendance at quarter-horse and harness racing and races at fairs. Sources also contain data on number of racing days, number of races run, number of horses run, and money distributed as purses; in some cases as far back as 1908.

H 519–520.   Major league baseball attendance, 1916–1956.

Source: New York World-Telegram, *World Almanac,* annual issues, and *New Encyclopedia of Sports, 1947.*

H 521.   Boxing, gross receipts, 1944–1956.

Source: *The Ring,* Nat S. Fleischer (publisher), New York.

The basic data are compiled from reports of State boxing commissions.

H 522.   Movies, average weekly attendance, 1922–1955.

Source: *1956 Yearbook of Motion Pictures,* Film Daily, New York.

H 523–524.   Paid hunting and fishing license holders, 1923–1956.

Source: See source for series H 455–470.

Additional data on number of nonresident licenses, and amounts paid for licenses, all by States, are shown in the source. The original data are from reports made by the various State game commissions or departments of the Fish and Wildlife Service, and released annually in mimeographed statements.

H 525.   Outboard motors sold, 1919–1956.

Source: Outboard Boating Club of America, Chicago.

These and other data on outboard motors, boats, and trailers, including some data by States for recent years, are summarized in *Statistics on Outdoor Recreation.*

Series H 455-470. National Parks, Monuments, and Allied Areas—Number, Area, and Visits: 1850 to 1956

[For years ending September 30 prior to 1941; thereafter, years ending December 31. Embraces all areas now administered by the National Park Service. Includes areas in Alaska, Hawaii, Virgin Islands, and Puerto Rico. However, excludes National Capital Parks (Washington, D. C. area) which are similar to other municipal parks and hence not comparable with national parks and monuments]

Year	Total, enumerated areas [1]			National parks			National monuments			National historical and military areas [3]			National parkways		National recreation areas	
	Number	Area	Visits [2]	Number	Area	Visits	Number	Area	Visits	Number	Area	Visits	Number	Area	Number	Area
	455	456	457	458	459	460	461	462	463	464	465	466	467	468	469	470
		1,000 acres	1,000		1,000 acres	1,000		1,000 acres	1,000		1,000 acres	1,000		1,000 acres		1,000 acres
1956	180	24,359	54,923	29	13,131	20,055	83	8,957	8,769	60	137	9,243	3	85	5	2,050
1955	180	23,889	50,008	28	12,670	18,830	84	8,976	7,953	58	116	8,561	5	82	5	2,045
1954	178	23,873	47,834	28	12,641	17,969	83	8,999	7,805	58	113	8,465	4	78	5	2,042
1953	179	23,863	46,225	28	12,640	17,372	85	9,000	7,540	57	112	8,382	4	76	5	2,035
1952	176	23,801	42,300	28	12,589	17,143	85	9,010	6,807	55	106	7,683	4	76	4	2,020
1951	177	23,702	37,106	28	12,557	15,079	85	8,964	6,187	57	103	6,508	4	69	3	2,010
1950	178	23,836	33,253	28	12,222	13,919	86	9,439	5,310	57	102	5,354	4	64	3	2,010
1949	176	22,976	31,736	28	11,420	12,968	86	9,383	4,923	56	102	5,195	3	61	3	2,010
1948	178	22,955	29,859	28	11,347	11,293	86	9,279	4,438	56	102	4,526	3	59	5	2,167
1947	175	22,824	25,534	28	11,347	10,674	85	9,279	4,027	54	66	4,258	3	55	5	2,077
1946	172	22,424	21,752	27	11,062	8,991	86	9,284	3,603	52	44	3,667	3	55	4	1,979
1945	168	22,126	11,714	27	11,061	4,538	84	9,286	2,512	53	44	1,653	3	55	1	1,680
1944	169	22,107	8,340	27	11,055	2,646	84	9,274	1,851	54	44	1,270	3	55	1	1,680
1943	167	21,061	6,828	26	10,303	2,054	84	9,186	1,578	53	44	1,067	3	49	1	1,478
1942	165	20,827	9,371	26	10,300	3,815	83	9,015	1,831	52	44	1,704	3	49	1	1,418
1941	163	20,817	21,237	26	10,285	8,459	82	9,008	3,745	51	38	4,024	3	46	1	1,440
1940	160	20,762	16,755	26	10,258	7,358	82	8,994	2,817	48	33	3,007	3	36	1	1,440
1939	153	19,942	15,531	27	9,459	6,854	78	8,984	2,592	44	31	2,897	3	29	1	1,440
1938	143	18,637	16,331	27	9,409	6,619	73	7,498	2,364	41	30	3,982	1	1	1	1,700
1937	135	16,537	15,133	27	8,750	6,705	72	7,756	1,966	35	29	2,867	1	1	--------	--------
1936	132	15,333	11,990	26	8,692	5,791	67	6,614	1,681	38	26	1,905	1	1	--------	--------
1935	129	15,115	7,676	24	8,486	4,056	68	6,609	1,332	37	20	2,287	--------	--------	--------	--------
1934	114	15,244	6,337	22	8,532	3,517	67	6,687	1,386	25	24	1,435	--------	--------	--------	--------
1933	113	15,140	3,482	22	8,485	2,867	66	6,681	523	25	24	91	--------	--------	--------	--------
1932	108	12,968	3,755	22	8,417	2,949	61	4,527	406	25	24	400	--------	--------	--------	--------
1931	105	12,523	3,545	22	8,027	3,153	60	4,473	392	23	23	--------	--------	--------	--------	--------
1930	99	10,581	3,247	22	7,797	2,775	59	2,766	472	18	17	--------	--------	--------	--------	--------
1929	96	10,538	3,248	21	7,755	2,757	57	2,766	491	18	17	--------	--------	--------	--------	--------
1928	92	10,359	3,025	20	7,581	2,569	57	2,761	456	15	17	--------	--------	--------	--------	--------
1927	89	10,320	2,798	20	7,570	2,381	57	2,733	417	12	17	--------	--------	--------	--------	--------
1926	86	10,249	2,315	20	7,501	1,942	57	2,733	373	9	14	--------	--------	--------	--------	--------
1925	82	9,987	2,054	20	7,286	1,762	55	2,687	292	7	14	--------	--------	--------	--------	--------
1924	73	8,813	1,671	19	7,278	1,424	47	1,520	247	7	14	--------	--------	--------	--------	--------
1923	71	8,790	1,494	19	7,278	1,281	45	1,497	213	7	14	--------	--------	--------	--------	--------
1922	64	8,781	1,216	19	7,278	1,045	38	1,489	172	7	14	--------	--------	--------	--------	--------
1921	63	8,452	1,172	19	6,950	1,007	37	1,488	164	7	14	--------	--------	--------	--------	--------
1920	63	8,452	1,059	19	6,950	920	37	1,488	139	7	14	--------	--------	--------	--------	--------
1919	60	8,372	811	18	6,873	757	35	1,485	54	7	14	--------	--------	--------	--------	--------
1918	59	7,554	455	16	6,255	452	36	1,285	3	7	14	--------	--------	--------	--------	--------
1917	60	7,491	490	17	6,254	488	36	1,223	2	7	14	--------	--------	--------	--------	--------
1916	54	5,984	358	15	4,742	356	34	1,229	2	5	14	--------	--------	--------	--------	--------
1915	49	5,880	335	14	4,666	335	30	1,200	--------	5	14	--------	--------	--------	--------	--------
1914	48	5,986	240	13	4,437	240	30	1,535	--------	5	14	--------	--------	--------	--------	--------
1913	46	5,984	252	13	4,437	252	28	1,533	--------	5	14	--------	--------	--------	--------	--------
1912	46	5,977	229	13	4,431	229	28	1,533	--------	5	14	--------	--------	--------	--------	--------
1911	46	5,978	224	13	4,431	224	28	1,533	--------	5	14	--------	--------	--------	--------	--------
1910	44	5,998	199	13	4,431	199	26	1,553	--------	5	14	--------	--------	--------	--------	--------
1909	38	5,013	86	12	3,449	86	21	1,550	--------	5	14	--------	--------	--------	--------	--------
1908	32	4,363	69	12	3,449	69	15	900	--------	5	14	--------	--------	--------	--------	--------
1907	24	3,547	61	12	3,444	61	7	89	--------	5	14	--------	--------	--------	--------	--------
1906	17	3,265	31	12	3,251	31	--------	--------	--------	5	14	--------	--------	--------	--------	--------
1905	15	3,471	141	10	3,457	141	--------	--------	--------	5	14	--------	--------	--------	--------	--------
1904	15	3,471	121	10	3,457	121	--------	--------	--------	5	14	--------	--------	--------	--------	--------
1903	14	3,470	--------	9	3,456	--------	--------	--------	--------	5	14	--------	--------	--------	--------	--------
1902	13	3,459	--------	8	3,445	--------	--------	--------	--------	5	14	--------	--------	--------	--------	--------
1901	12	3,300	--------	7	3,286	--------	--------	--------	--------	5	14	--------	--------	--------	--------	--------
1900	12	3,300	--------	7	3,286	--------	--------	--------	--------	5	14	--------	--------	--------	--------	--------
1899	12	3,300	--------	7	3,286	--------	--------	--------	--------	5	14	--------	--------	--------	--------	--------
1898	10	3,287	--------	6	3,274	--------	--------	--------	--------	4	13	--------	--------	--------	--------	--------
1897	10	3,287	--------	6	3,274	--------	--------	--------	--------	4	13	--------	--------	--------	--------	--------
1896	10	3,287	--------	6	3,274	--------	--------	--------	--------	4	13	--------	--------	--------	--------	--------
1895	10	3,287	--------	6	3,274	--------	--------	--------	--------	4	13	--------	--------	--------	--------	--------
1894	8	3,058	--------	6	3,052	--------	--------	--------	--------	2	7	--------	--------	--------	--------	--------
1893	8	3,058	--------	6	3,052	--------	--------	--------	--------	2	7	--------	--------	--------	--------	--------
1892	8	3,058	--------	6	3,052	--------	--------	--------	--------	2	7	--------	--------	--------	--------	--------
1891	7	3,058	--------	5	3,051	--------	--------	--------	--------	2	7	--------	--------	--------	--------	--------
1890	3	2,889	--------	3	2,889	--------	--------	--------	--------	--------	--------	--------	--------	--------	--------	--------
1872–1889 [4]	2	1,921	--------	2	1,921	--------	--------	--------	--------	--------	--------	--------	--------	--------	--------	--------
1850–1871 [5]	1	1	--------	1	1	--------	--------	--------	--------	--------	--------	--------	--------	--------	--------	--------

[1] Not the same as the "national park system." Definition of the latter has changed from time to time; for instance, National Recreation Areas were included prior to 1943, and after that excluded. Series H 455-457 are merely totals of the other items listed.

[2] Total for some years includes visits not shown separately.

[3] Includes national historical parks, national military parks, national battlefield parks, national battlefield sites, national cemeteries, national historic sites, and one national memorial park. Does not include historical areas established under the Antiquities Act of 1906 and designated national monuments.

[4] Yellowstone National Park, the first national park, established 1872.

[5] Hot Springs Reservation set aside by the Federal Government in 1832 and established as a national park in 1921. Initial Federal acreage was much greater than indicated, but over a period of years was subdivided into tracts and sold, some 900-odd acres being permanently reserved to the Federal Government. These series begin with 1850, the first year following the establishment of the Department of the Interior.

Series H 471–474. Recreational Use of National Forest Lands: 1924 to 1956

[Calendar-year data, except 1933–1938 which are on fiscal-year basis. Includes continental United States and Territories]

Year	Total use of recreational resources		Visits to areas improved by Federal funds	Visits to all other areas [1]	Year	Total use of recreational resources		Visits to areas improved by Federal funds	Visits to all other areas [1]
	Man-days	Visits				Man-days	Visits		
	471	472	473	474		471	472	473	474
	1,000	*1,000*	*1,000*	*1,000*		*1,000*	*1,000*	*1,000*	*1,000*
1956	69,714	52,556	25,053	27,503	1939	39,480	14,332	11,466	2,866
1955	62,103	45,713	22,317	23,396	1938		14,496	10,810	3,686
1954	54,847	40,304	19,747	20,557	1937		11,831	8,810	3,021
1953	48,750	35,403	17,199	18,204	1936		10,781	8,233	2,548
1952	45,861	33,007	15,929	17,078					
1951	43,789	29,950	14,857	15,093	1935		9,719	7,722	1,996
					1934		8,581	6,953	1,628
1950	38,932	27,368	13,061	14,307	1933		8,166	6,576	1,590
1949	37,538	26,080	13,277	12,803	1932		7,896	6,227	1,669
1948	35,190	24,011	12,391	11,620	1931		8,074	5,959	2,115
1947	34,576	21,331	10,506	10,825					
1946	33,561	18,241	8,763	9,478	1930		6,911	5,253	1,658
					1929		7,132	4,959	2,173
1945	24,480	10,074	5,072	5,002	1928		6,550	4,783	1,767
1944	16,364	7,152	3,585	3,567	1927		6,136	4,469	1,667
1943	11,322	6,274	3,412	2,862	1926		6,044	4,460	1,584
1942	17,036	10,407	6,066	4,341					
1941	26,077	18,005	10,688	7,317	1925		5,623	4,217	1,406
					1924		4,660	3,460	1,200
1940	42,421	16,163	13,062	3,101					

[1] Unimproved public areas, e.g., wilderness areas, and a few public areas improved by non-Federal means.

Series H 475–487. State Parks—Acreage, Expenditures, Funds, Revenue, Employees, and Attendance: 1939 to 1956

Year	Acreage			Expenditures [1]			Funds available for expenditure	Revenue from operations	Employees		Attendance [1]		
	Total	Land acquired	Land disposed of	Total	Operation and maintenance	Capital expenditures [2]			Total, year round	Total seasonal	Total	Day visitors	Overnight use
	475	476	477	478	479	480	481	482	483	484	485	486	487
	1,000 acres	*Acres*	*Acres*	*1,000 dol.*	*1,000 dol.*	*1,000 dol.*	*1,000 dol.*	*1,000 dol.*			*1,000*	*1,000*	*1,000*
1956	5,165	61,535	3,967	65,844	38,047	27,797	88,255	14,928	6,048	8,884	200,705	185,325	12,642
1955	5,085	70,148	2,996	55,093	34,028	21,065	69,075	13,816	5,657	7,980	183,187	169,123	11,056
1954	5,005	92,215	983	49,134	31,646	17,488	64,059	13,099	5,105	7,299	166,427	155,817	9,472
1953	4,876	20,991	8,670	49,565	30,158	19,407	68,791	10,776	5,080	7,906	159,116	148,189	8,347
1952	4,928	53,994	4,049	40,469	26,139	14,329	60,886	9,349	4,753	7,363	149,255	139,578	7,812
1951	4,877	48,491	12,729	38,545	22,841	15,704	62,859	6,652	4,376	6,937	120,722	114,024	6,698
1950		62,042		36,399	21,384	15,015	52,283	6,646	4,191	6,435	114,291	108,212	6,079
1949		68,176		31,921	19,122	12,780	44,176	6,089	4,004	6,245	106,792	100,105	6,687
1948		73,303		32,059	17,279	14,781	42,497	5,794	3,987	6,238	105,248	100,222	5,026
1947		100,812		25,991	13,844	12,147	36,813	4,731	3,489	5,900	109,995	105,624	4,231
1946		121,590		15,445	9,937	5,508	20,711	4,118	2,771	3,879	92,507	88,923	3,139
1945		87,837		10,564	7,115	3,449	11,973	2,595	2,433	4,800	57,649	51,619	2,622
1944		154,260		6,466	5,755	710	9,788	1,979	2,233	2,754	39,668	33,991	2,069
1943		105,224		6,570	5,406	1,164	7,684	1,910	2,186	2,547	38,306	35,190	2,312
1942		39,863		9,373	6,774	2,599	9,993	2,488	1,518	2,107	70,359	50,496	2,188
1941				10,022	6,944	3,009	10,372	3,177	2,025	605			
1940				9,443	6,226	3,195	9,078						
1939				7,429	4,524	2,635	8,169						

[1] Detail does not add to total because some States do not report detail.   [2] In recent years, roughly three-quarters spent for improvements; the rest for land acquisition.

Series H 488–499. Municipal Recreation—Parks, Leadership, and Facilities, for Cities of 100,000 Inhabitants or More in 1950: 1880 to 1955

Year	Parks		Recreational leadership			Facilities						
	Number	Acreage	Leaders		Playgrounds under leadership	Ball diamonds	Bathing beaches	Golf courses	Outdoor swimming pools	Tennis courts	Recreation buildings	Indoor recreation centers
			Total	Full-time year-round								
	488	489	490	491	492	493	494	495	496	497	498	499
1955	9,558	323,049	31,649	5,454	7,113	8,919	158	225	695	6,039	1,718	3,758
1950	8,671	301,492	27,712	4,571	6,426	7,967	158	222	549	6,328	1,419	2,617
1948			23,319	4,069	5,956	7,425	153	199	518	6,187	1,395	2,237
1946			20,130	3,561	5,288	2,075	175	190	550	6,390	969	1,737
1944			18,872	3,364	4,986	------	119	204	488	------		
1942			15,810	2,793	4,858	1,992	164	197	459	6,645	1,038	1,478
1941			15,480	2,838	5,120	2,100	182	197	455	6,908	1,021	1,766
1940	8,339	267,753	14,768	2,703	5,165	2,023	164	201	449	7,003	961	2,080
1939			15,550	2,555	5,010	2,089	156	193	466	6,485	969	2,134
1938			15,033	2,461	4,984	2,041	171	189	430	6,184	868	2,109
1937			14,419	2,379	5,020	2,025	158	195	432	6,102	779	1,881
1936			13,348	2,156	4,855	1,915	157	194	414	5,772	764	2,001
1935	6,989	228,093	12,604	2,111	4,386	2,027	143	197	402	5,534	707	2,048
1934			11,926	1,760	3,820	2,073	133	190	371	5,346	551	2,052
1933			13,870	1,865	3,897	2,248	141	189	402	5,876	501	2,520
1932			15,201	1,766	3,874	2,149	120	181	405	5,259	450	1,312
1931			16,659	2,159	4,282	2,295	134	168	414	5,361	418	1,434

Series H 488–499. Municipal Recreation—Parks, Leadership, and Facilities, for Cities of 100,000 Inhabitants or More in 1950: 1880 to 1955—Con.

Year	Parks Number (488)	Parks Acreage (489)	Leaders Total (490)	Leaders Full-time year-round (491)	Playgrounds under leadership (492)	Ball diamonds (493)	Bathing beaches (494)	Golf courses (495)	Outdoor swimming pools (496)	Tennis courts (497)	Recreation buildings (498)	Indoor recreation centers (499)
1930	6,368	201,067	16,249	2,028	4,236	2,139	135	168	387	5,120	426	1,422
1929			15,004	2,090	4,273	2,024	130	155	380	4,890	415	1,618
1928			13,817		3,955	1,814	114	158	346	4,673	251	1,693
1927			13,134		3,579	1,660	120	139		4,509	196	1,487
1926	4,778	152,203	11,469		3,204							
1925			10,329		2,817							
1924			11,091		2,624							
1923			8,453		3,015							
1922			8,044									
1921			8,547									
1920			7,546									
1919			5,642									
1918			6,150									
1917			6,302									
1916	2,816	93,240	5,768									
1915 [1]			5,664									
1913			4,953									
1912			4,502									
1911			3,651									
1910			2,760									
1905		61,616										
1890	1,054	32,880										
1880	508	18,355										

[1] No survey taken in 1914.

Series H 500–515. Personal Consumption Expenditures for Recreation: 1909 to 1957

[In millions of dollars]

Year	Total (500)	Nondurable toys and sport supplies (501)	Wheel goods, durable toys, sport equipment, boats, and pleasure aircraft (502)	Radio and television receivers, records, and musical instruments (503)	Radio and television repair (504)	Admission to specified spectator amusement Total (505)	Motion picture theaters (506)	Theater entertainment (plays, operas, etc.) of nonprofit institutions, except athletics (507)	Spectator sports (508)	Clubs and fraternal organizations, except insurance (509)	Commercial participant amusements (510)	Pari-mutuel, net receipts (511)	Books and maps (512)	Magazines, newspapers, and sheet music (513)	Flowers, seeds, and potted plants (514)	Other (515)
1957	15,908	2,048	1,698	2,988	652	1,658	1,116	296	246	671	725	431	1,026	2,170	824	1,017
1956	15,161	2,008	1,575	2,872	585	1,741	1,225	276	240	627	668	408	1,006	1,954	770	947
1955	14,220	1,842	1,397	2,792	522	1,700	1,217	251	232	582	615	375	888	1,917	721	869
1954	13,256	1,624	1,174	2,741	475	1,660	1,210	225	225	549	565	362	806	1,825	687	788
1953	12,892	1,694	1,093	2,608	428	1,594	1,172	200	222	525	545	367	831	1,776	675	756
1952	12,257	1,709	994	2,373	389	1,646	1,233	192	221	506	510	323	790	1,689	634	694
1951	11,704	1,663	904	2,264	350	1,708	1,299	188	221	483	490	253	778	1,573	582	656
1950	11,278	1,396	878	2,457	281	1,775	1,367	185	223	467	463	237	677	1,495	524	628
1949	10,122	1,172	847	1,704	201	1,868	1,445	183	240	458	440	246	630	1,454	504	598
1948	9,808	1,079	980	1,479	174	1,918	1,503	182	233	438	436	256	588	1,374	483	603
1947	9,352	910	972	1,429	140	2,004	1,594	188	222	399	415	255	536	1,243	475	574
1946	8,621	843	809	1,143	115	2,066	1,692	174	200	359	379	241	594	1,099	447	526
1945	6,139	553	400	344	88	1,714	1,450	148	116	281	284	153	520	965	378	459
1944	5,422	459	323	311	72	1,563	1,341	142	80	236	241	131	450	880	327	429
1943	4,961	393	271	403	60	1,455	1,275	118	62	217	215	79	366	838	274	390
1942	4,677	404	306	634	46	1,204	1,022	92	90	205	213	69	291	703	241	361
1941	4,239	362	314	607	36	995	809	79	107	203	210	65	255	636	229	327
1940	3,761	306	254	494	32	904	735	71	98	203	197	55	234	589	201	292
1939	3,452	285	228	420	28	821	659	64	98	199	183	41	226	554	191	276
1938	3,241	268	210	339	25	816	663	58	95	200	164	44	221	514	176	264
1937	3,381	269	210	385	23	818	676	53	89	203	194	38	243	518	186	294
1936	3,020	242	171	333	21	759	626	50	83	198	165	29	208	490	159	245
1935	2,630	216	136	248	21	672	556	44	72	197	141	26	183	456	130	204
1934	2,441	200	118	229	17	625	518	42	65	199	135	19	165	441	116	177
1933	2,202	181	93	195	14	573	482	41	50	208	121	6	152	419	90	150
1932	2,442	207	110	268	19	631	527	57	47	242	132	4	153	428	89	159
1931	3,302	266	159	478	24	854	719	78	57	277	175	6	253	479	134	197
1930	3,990	281	172	921	27	892	732	95	65	294	203	7	264	512	190	227
1929	4,331	336	219	1,012	26	913	720	127	66	302	207	8	309	538	221	240
1927	3,120 [1]	470		713		769	526	195	48	283	159		(1)	(1)	183	(2)
1925	2,835 [1]	411		739		588	367	174	47	275	145		(1)	(1)	182	(2)
1923	2,620 [1]	455		637		528	336	146	46	242	148		(1)	(1)	176	(2)
1921	2,055 [1]	338		439		412	301	81	30	242	128		(1)	(1)	128	(2)
1919	2,180 [1]	377		667		(2)	336		(2)	242	55		(1)	(1)	135	(2)
1914	1,000 [1]	186		193		(2)	191		(2)	140	25		(1)	(1)	56	(2)
1909	860 [1]	143		166		(2)	167		(2)	121	22		(1)	(1)	70	(2)

[1] Totals include only 42 percent of the national estimated expenditures for books and maps and magazines, newspapers, and sheet music. The remaining 58 percent were classified as educational rather than recreational outlay. Expenditures for these items classified as "recreation" expenditures (42 percent of the total) are (in millions of dollars): 1927—349; 1925—318; 1923—270; 1921—239; 1919—204; 1914—131; 1909—104.

[2] Not available.

Series H 516–525. Participation in Selected Recreational Activities: 1896 to 1957

Year	Bowling Number of teams	Bowling Number of alley beds	Horse-racing attendance	Major league baseball attendance Regular season	World series	Boxing, gross receipts	Movies, average weekly attendance	Paid hunting and fishing license holders Hunting	Fishing	Outboard motors sold
	516	517	518	519	520	521	522	523	524	525
			1,000	*1,000*	*1,000*	*$1,000*	*Millions*	*1,000*	*1,000*	*1,000*
1957	492,249	65,127	28,851	----	----	----	----	----	----	----
1956	425,089	60,654	28,342	16,519	346	4,448	----	14,462	18,702	647
1955	386,912	58,203	27,774	16,617	362	6,335	46	14,192	18,855	515
1954	368,231	56,861	28,021	15,936	252	4,285	49	14,073	18,581	[1] 479
1953	351,506	55,739	27,969	14,384	307	4,183	46	14,803	17,652	463
1952	333,300	55,272	26,435	14,633	341	3,988	51	13,902	17,128	337
1951	322,277	54,943	23,808	16,127	342	5,100	54	12,661	16,027	[2] 284
1950	320,878	52,488	22,526	17,463	196	3,800	60	12,638	15,338	367
1949	310,299	49,555	23,234	20,216	237	5,001	70	12,759	15,479	329
1948	284,777	45,296	24,340	20,921	358	11,240	90	11,392	14,078	499
1947	250,117	44,028	25,866	19,953	390	13,500	90	12,067	12,620	584
1946	184,000	40,146	26,834	18,613	250	14,000	90	9,854	11,069	398
1945	172,000	38,023	18,900	11,375	333	13,000	85	8,191	8,280	----
1944	151,000	37,104	18,000	8,977	207	10,840	85	7,491	7,830	----
1943	150,000	38,582	14,000	7,699	277	----	85	8,081	8,029	----
1942	190,000	39,812	11,500	9,410	277	----	85	8,521	8,423	----
1941	163,000	34,195	13,500	10,252	236	----	85	7,913	8,004	170
1940	132,000	26,382	8,500	10,182	282	----	80	7,646	7,931	130
1939	103,000	22,866	----	9,349	184	----	85	7,511	7,858	120
1938	93,000	18,238	----	----	201	----	85	6,903	7,436	100
1937	64,000	16,285	----	9,448	238	----	88	6,860	6,902	100
1936	52,000	11,655	----	8,585	303	----	88	6,658	5,832	50
1935	41,000	11,473	----	----	287	----	80	5,988	5,121	41
1934	32,000	9,760	----	----	282	----	70	5,918	4,856	23
1933	29,000	9,473	----	----	163	----	60	5,742	4,858	15
1932	39,000	9,277	----	----	192	----	60	5,777	----	12
1931	44,000	8,897	----	----	232	----	75	6,368	----	14
1930	43,000	10,796	----	----	213	----	90	6,901	----	44
1929	27,000	9,366	----	----	190	----	80	6,429	----	59
1928	22,000	8,426	----	----	199	----	65	6,463	----	54
1927	18,000	7,419	----	----	202	----	57	5,998	----	42
1926	15,000	6,818	----	----	328	----	50	5,332	----	33
1925	12,000	6,299	----	----	283	----	46	4,905	----	27
1924	10,000	5,776	----	----	284	----	46	4,395	----	21
1923	11,000	----	----	----	301	----	43	4,341	----	21
1922	7,500	----	----	----	186	----	40	----	----	16
1921	4,800	----	----	----	270	----	----	----	----	12
1920	5,100	----	----	----	174	----	----	----	----	17
1919	2,700	----	----	----	237	----	----	----	----	12
1918	3,100	----	----	----	186	----	----	----	----	----
1917	3,300	----	----	----	129	----	----	----	----	----
1916	3,200	----	----	----	163	----	----	----	----	----

Year	Bowling, number of teams 516	Year	Bowling, number of teams 516	Year	Bowling, number of teams 516	Year	Bowling, number of teams 516
1915	2,100	1910	1,400	1905	630	1900	150
1914	1,500	1909	1,300	1904	470	1899	120
1913	1,700	1908	1,320	1903	400	1898	100
1912	1,700	1907	1,266	1902	220	1897	75
1911	1,200	1906	970	1901	200	1896	60

[1] Production disrupted due to labor arbitration.

[2] Production disrupted due to material allocation under the Controlled Materia Plan.

chapter H

RELIGIOUS AFFILIATION (Series H 526–543)

H 526–543. General note.

National statistics for all religious bodies, on an interdenominational basis, have been compiled at intervals since 1850 and until 1936 by the Bureau of the Census, and during the past few decades by the *Christian Herald*, a periodical published in New York, and by the National Council of Churches in the *Yearbook of American Churches*, which contains statistical data furnished by all faiths.

Practically all national religious bodies compile reports or estimates from time to time based on records kept by local churches (congregations or parishes), or from estimates furnished by the local churches. Probably about half the national bodies receive reports from their local churches annually and then issue the figures to their constituencies or to the public. The bodies which report annually the figures systematically received from their local churches are mainly the larger denominations. The other national bodies report their statistics at irregular intervals.

For those denominations which have standard forms, the records are kept locally as determined by the national body. For other denominations, the records are kept in accordance with the wishes of the local churches. The statistics are gathered by the denominations for their own, often different, purposes, thus leading to variety in the forms used and in the nature of the information gathered. In addition, local church records are usually kept by persons untrained in the keeping of statistical records, or persons with only the most elementary instruction or experience.

All denominations make their own definitions of membership or affiliation, and accordingly there are also variations in the basis of compilation. However, the bodies reporting have made no major changes in their definitions since the Census of Religious Bodies, 1926. The definitions used since that date for the larger bodies are as follows:

The Eastern Churches report estimates of the total number of persons within the cultural or nationality group served.

The Jewish Congregations report on the number of Jews in communities having congregations.

The Roman Catholic Church, the Lutheran bodies, and the Protestant Episcopal Church report as members the total number of baptized persons, including infants.

Most Protestant bodies report as members those persons who have attained full membership, usually at about age 13.

Variations in definitions for years prior to 1926 are noted below in the text for specific series.

One relatively large body, the Church of Christ, Scientist, with headquarters in Boston, Mass., now forbids the enumeration of its members and the publication of statistics of affiliation. The local churches of this body reported a total membership of 268,915 in the Census of Religious Bodies for 1936, but have made no public report since then. A few relatively small bodies also do not report membership figures to compilers of national data. However, it is believed that the figures presented here cover all but a fraction of one percent of total religious affiliation.

H 526–530. Church denominations, members, and edifices, 1850–1936.

Source: 1850–1890 and 1916, Bureau of the Census, *Religious Bodies, 1916*, part I; 1906–1936, *Religious Bodies*, 1906, 1926, and 1936 volumes.

Data presented are not directly comparable from census period to census period. Special note must be taken in the case of the data for 1936 in relation to other years. The compilation for that year was less complete than those of other years for reasons noted below.

Limited information on religious bodies (number of congregations and buildings, and value of edifices) was first published in the census report for 1850 and similar information was included in the reports for 1860 and 1870. In 1880, the figures gathered by the Census Office were not published. In 1890, the Census Office collected figures from religious organizations concerning membership, number and value of edifices, number of ministers, etc.

The 1906 Census of Religious Bodies (2 parts) was the first to be compiled by means of a questionnaire mailed to the pastors or clerks of the local churches. The Jewish Congregations reported heads of families only (101,457, principally male, persons). It is indicated that, in most denominations, 99 percent of the local churches to which forms were mailed made returns.

The 1916 Census reported 41,926,854 members, a figure adjusted in the 1926 report to read 43,311,648 persons, for reasons there given. The Jewish Congregations reported only heads of families (357,135 persons). The methods used in the 1916 and 1926 Censuses were essentially the same as those used in the 1936 Census (see below).

Students of church statistics regard the compilation of 1926 as probably the most adequate one ever made. In this census, every local organization was classed as a church whether it was commonly known as a church, a congregation, a meeting, a society, a mission, a station, a chapel, or by some other term. "A local church may have had officers and an enrolled membership, or it may have been little more than an association or fellowship, but to be included in this enumeration it must have had a religious purpose and a distinctive membership."

For all denominations except the Jewish Congregations, the 1926 Census reported 50,495,104 members, compared with a corrected total figure, partly estimated, of 42,954,512 persons in 1916. The Jewish Congregations reported "all Jews in communities where there is a congregation," whereas in 1916 they reported only "heads of families, seat holders, and other contributors." The figures for Jews were admittedly incomplete. With this census also, the Lutheran bodies, the Protestant Episcopal Church, and the Christian Reformed Church began to report on a more inclusive basis than in previous censuses.

The data for the 1936 Census were obtained by means of a schedule for local church organizations mailed to the clergyman or the lay clerk of the local parish or congregation. The data collected were for the year 1936, "or to the church record year most nearly conforming to the end of that year." The

Census Bureau established contact with persons in authority in the various religious bodies in order to secure lists of pastors or clerks of the local religious organizations. Special agents were employed for the purpose of securing data from "some loosely organized denominations, or those averse to publishing the statistics of their organizations." The census received only halfhearted support from a few denominations and undoubtedly the total membership figures would have been much larger if all churches had furnished statistics. The incompleteness of returns is also reflected by the fact that total value of church edifices (series H 530) is lower in 1936 than in 1926. A private compilation for 1936, published in the *Christian Herald*, New York, July 1937, based on official reports of the religious bodies, listed 244,147 local churches. It seems probable that about 20 percent of the officers of active local churches in 1936 did not report to the Bureau of the Census. The *Christian Herald* stated, for example, that the *Southern Baptist Handbook* for 1937 reported 4,482,315 members for 1936, while the Bureau of the Census reported only 2,700,155 members.

Differences among the religious bodies in defining the term "member" were noted. The Jewish Congregations, continuing a basis begun in 1926, reported "all persons of the Jewish faith living in communities in which local congregations are situated. . . . Among the Roman Catholic and Eastern churches, all persons, even infants, are considered members, provided they have been baptized according to the rites of the church . . . The Protestant Episcopal Church, and the Lutheran bodies, because they also count as members all baptized persons in the congregation, tend toward the more inclusive definition of the term." In the large majority of Protestant bodies, the term "member" is applied only to "communicants," or to persons who have attained to full membership, usually at age 13.

H 531–537. Membership of religious bodies, 1890–1957, and by major groups, 1951–1957.

Source: 1890–1926 and 1936, Bureau of the Census, *Religious Bodies*, various issues; 1931–1935, 1937, and 1945–1949, The Christian Herald Association, *Christian Herald*, New York, various issues; 1938–1944 and 1950–1957, National Council of the Churches of Christ, *Yearbook of American Churches*, various issues.

The Bureau of the Census usually secured information for the year indicated, but it also accepted a figure for the church year nearest to that for which data were sought. In the compilations of private agencies the "latest information" is published for each denomination; in a number of instances, the actual figures of a denomination are for a previous period. For 1956, e.g., most bodies reported figures for that year, but many others had available only the data compiled for previous years. The lag is usually only of several years duration, but in a few instances (for small bodies) the actual figures are from the 1936 Census of Religious Bodies. Data for certain years, which do not appear in these series, appear in the *Christian Herald*; these data are not comparable as they include only the "communicant" or adult membership.

For definition of membership used by the larger groups (Eastern Orthodox, Jewish Congregations, Roman Catholic,

and Protestant bodies), see general note for series H 526–543. See also text for series H 526–530.

H 538. Roman Catholic members, 1891–1957.

Source: Records of P. J. Kenedy & Sons (publishers of the *Official Catholic Directory*), New York.

Certain of the typographical errors appearing in the annual published reports issued by this firm have been corrected in this series. Figures are compiled from reports by dioceses and parishes. For definition of membership, see general note for series H 526–543.

H 539. Presbyterian members, 1826–1956.

Source: 1826–1926, Presbyterian Church in the U. S. A., *Presbyterian Statistics Through One Hundred Years, 1826 to 1926*, Philadelphia; 1927–1957, Presbyterian Church in the U. S. A., records.

Figures include persons who have attained full membership, usually at age 13; exclude foreign members.

H 540. Protestant Episcopal members, 1927–1957.

Source: *The Episcopal Church Annual*, Morehouse-Goreham Co., New York, 1957.

Data include an unpublished number of members living outside the United States. The source gives the number of "communicants" residing abroad, but not the total number of members. The foreign residents among the communicants have numbered less than one-half of one percent of the total communicants during the period for which the figures are given. For definition of membership, see general note for series H 526–543.

H 541. Methodist members, 1790–1956.

Source: 1790–1948, Statistical Office of the Methodist Church, *Methodist History as Revealed in Statistical Form* (loose insert in *The Methodist Fact Book*), Chicago, 1949; 1949–1956, *The Methodist Fact Book*, 1957.

The Methodist Church was formed in 1939 by a merger of the Methodist Episcopal Church; the Methodist Episcopal Church, South; and the Methodist Protestant Church. Figures include all three bodies prior to 1939. Members are persons who have attained full membership, usually at age 13.

H 542. Seventh-day Adventist members, 1907–1957.

Source: Records of the Statistical Secretary of the Seventh-day Adventist Church, Tacoma Park, Washington, D. C.

The members of this body are mainly 13 years old and over. The latest year for which age grouping was reported was 1936, when the local churches of the body reported that only about 3 percent of their members were less than 13 years of age.

H 543. Southern Baptist members, 1845–1957.

Source: Southern Baptist Convention, *Southern Baptist Handbook, 1958*, Convention Press, Nashville.

Membership in the Southern Baptist churches consists only of individuals who present themselves to the church, request membership, and are baptized. Infant baptism is not practiced.

Series H 526–530. Church Denominations, Members, and Edifices: 1850 to 1936

Year	Denominations reporting 526	Local organizations 527	Members [1] 528	Church edifices Number 529	Value [2] 530	Year	Denominations reporting 526	Local organizations 527	Members [1] 528	Number 529	Value [2] 530
			1,000		$1,000				1,000		$1,000
1936	256	199,302	55,807	179,742	3,411,875	1890	145	165,151	21,699	142,487	679,426
1926	212	232,154	54,576	210,924	3,839,501	1870	----------	72,459	----------	63,082	354,484
1916	200	227,487	41,927	203,432	1,676,601	1860	----------	54,009	----------	----------	171,398
1906	186	212,230	35,068	192,795	1,257,576	1850	----------	38,061	----------	----------	87,329

[1] Represents members as defined by each denomination. Figures do not furnish an adequate basis for computing membership growth, not only because of organic denominational changes, but also because of basic changes in the definition of "member" by certain denominations.
[2] For churches reporting.

Series H 531–537. Membership of Religious Bodies, 1890 to 1957, and by Major Groups: 1951 to 1957

[In thousands]

Year	Total membership 531	Buddhist 532	Old Catholic and Polish National Catholic 533	Eastern Orthodox 534	Jewish 535	Roman Catholic 536	Protestant 537	Year	Total membership 531	Year	Total membership 531	Year	Total membership 531
1957	104,190	10	469	2,540	5,500	35,847	59,824	1949	81,862	1940	64,502	1933	60,813
1956	103,225	63	351	2,598	5,500	34,564	60,149	1948	79,436	1938	64,157	1932	60,157
								1947	77,386	1937	63,848	1931	59,798
1955	100,163	63	368	2,387	5,500	33,397	58,449	1946 [1]	73,673			1926	54,576
1954	97,483	63	368	2,024	5,500	32,403	57,124			1936	[2] 55,807		
1953	94,843	63	366	2,100	5,000	31,476	55,837	1945 [1]	71,700	1935	62,678	1916	41,927
1952	92,277	73	367	2,354	5,000	30,253	54,230	1944	72,493	1934	62,007	1906	35,068
1951	88,673	73	337	1,859	5,000	29,242	52,162	1942	68,501			1890	21,699
1950	86,830												

[1] Includes only bodies with memberships over 50,000.

[2] The *Christian Herald* reported 1936 membership as 63,222,000.

Series H 538–543. Membership of Selected Religious Bodies: 1790 to 1957

[In thousands]

Year	Roman Catholic [1] 538	Presbyterian 539	Protestant Episcopal 540	Methodist 541	Seventh-day Adventist 542	Southern Baptist [2] 543	Year	Roman Catholic [1] 538	Presbyterian 539	Methodist 541	Seventh-day Adventist 542	Southern Baptist [2] 543
1957	34,564	----------	3,163	----------	292	8,966	1925	18,654	1,829	7,066	103	3,649
1956	33,574	2,722	3,111	9,445	283	8,709	1924	18,560	1,787	6,604	102	3,575
							1923	18,261	1,760	6,522	98	3,494
1955	32,576	2,650	3,014	9,313	277	8,475	1922	18,105	1,718	6,444	96	3,366
1954	31,648	2,572	2,907	9,223	270	8,169	1921	17,886	1,686	6,289	94	3,220
1953	30,425	2,497	2,791	9,152	261	7,886						
1952	29,408	2,442	2,716	9,180	254	7,634	1920	17,736	1,603	6,140	91	3,149
1951	28,635	2,399	2,643	9,066	246	7,373	1919	17,549	1,571	5,937	91	2,961
							1918	17,416	1,604	6,006	88	2,887
1950	27,766	2,364	2,541	8,936	237	7,080	1917	17,023	1,579	5,970	83	2,844
1949	26,718	2,319	2,512	8,793	230	6,761	1916	16,584	1,541	5,829	76	2,744
1948	26,076	2,266	2,437	8,651	223	6,489						
1947	25,268	2,208	2,350	8,568	216	6,271	1915	16,309	1,493	5,698	74	2,686
1946	24,402	2,115	2,301	8,430	208	6,079	1914	16,068	1,428	5,394	69	2,589
							1913	15,154	1,388	5,402	69	2,523
1945	23,964	2,104	2,270	8,084	201	5,866	1912	15,016	1,353	5,261	66	2,446
1944	23,420	2,040	2,228	8,046	196	5,668	1911	14,619	1,331	5,168	65	2,421
1943	22,945	1,996	2,189	7,979	190	5,493						
1942	22,556	1,986	2,168	7,838	186	5,367	1910	14,347	1,315	5,073	64	2,332
1941	22,293	1,961	2,162	7,683	181	5,238	1909	14,235	1,299	4,977	65	2,219
							1908	13,877	1,276	4,851	65	2,139
1940	21,403	1,971	2,172	7,360	175	5,104	1907	13,089	1,305	4,735	65	2,015
1939	21,407	1,930	2,157	7,590	167	4,949	1906	12,652	1,127	4,612	----------	1,947
1938	21,167	1,906	2,110	7,507	162	4,770						
1937	20,959	1,928	2,095	7,387	155	4,596	1905	12,463	1,090	4,518	----------	1,899
1936	20,735	1,915	2,068	7,346	152	4,482	1904	11,887	1,068	4,477	----------	1,833
							1903	11,290	1,044	4,389	----------	1,806
1935	20,523	1,921	2,038	7,320	149	4,389	1902	10,977	1,024	4,354	----------	1,737
1934	20,323	1,934	2,040	7,254	143	4,277	1901	10,775	1,000	4,302	----------	1,683
1933	20,268	1,917	2,015	7,153	136	4,174						
1932	20,236	1,958	1,986	7,301	128	4,066	1900	10,130	983	4,226	----------	1,658
1931	20,215	1,950	1,957	7,247	121	3,945	1899	9,907	961	4,186	----------	1,608
							1898	9,857	955	4,230	----------	1,587
1930	20,204	1,937	1,939	7,319	114	3,850	1897	9,596	939	4,134	----------	1,569
1929	20,113	1,959	1,876	7,245	112	3,771	1896	9,411	924	4,086	----------	1,529
1928	19,689	1,919	1,878	7,248	108	3,706						
1927	19,483	1,886	1,789	7,171	107	3,674	1895	9,078	903	3,990	----------	1,469
1926	18,879	1,868	----------	6,830	105	3,617	1894	8,902	877	3,841	----------	1,431

[1] Beginning 1923, includes membership in Alaska, and beginning 1927, includes membership in Hawaii.

[2] Beginning 1951, includes membership in Alaska, and beginning 1954, includes membership in Hawaii. Excludes membership of Baptist Missionary Association beginning 1925; included prior to that time.

Series H 538-543. Membership of Selected Religious Bodies: 1790 to 1957—Con.

[In thousands]

Year	Roman Catholic [1]	Presby-terian	Methodist	Southern Baptist [2]	Year	Presby-terian	Methodist	Southern Baptist [2]	Year	Presby-terian	Methodist	Year	Methodist
	538	539	541	543		539	541	543		539	541		541
1893	8,806	837	3,705	1,363	1867	245	1,565	----------	1841	134	917	1815	212
1892	8,618	812	3,619	1,322	1866	238	1,428	----------	1840	127	856	1814	212
1891	8,277	790	3,511	1,282								1813	215
					1865	232	1,381	----------	1839	128	798	1812	196
1890	----------	761	3,442	1,236	1864	231	1,438	----------	1838	178	744	1811	185
1889	----------	739	3,290	1,195	1863	227	1,581	----------	1837	221	700		
1888	----------	706	3,168	1,166	1862	303	1,549	----------	1836	219	651	1810	175
1887	----------	681	3,104	1,126	1861	300	1,617	----------				1809	164
1886	----------	648	3,059	1,072					1835		655	1808	153
					1860	292	1,661	650	1834	248	641	1807	145
1885	----------	627	2,974	1,013	1859	279	1,561	639	1833	234	602	1806	131
1884	----------	607	2,907	975	1858	259	1,510	618	1832	217	551		
1883	----------	593	2,794	935	1857	244	1,372	580	1831	182	515	1805	120
1882	----------	585	2,727	915	1856	233	1,348	569				1804	114
1881	----------	575	2,665	961					1830	173	478	1803	104
					1855	231	1,326	542	1829	163	450	1802	87
1880	----------	573	2,694	1,673	1854	225	1,187	519	1828	146	423	1801	73
1879	----------	568	2,638	1,516	1853	219	1,121	496	1827	135	384		
1878	----------	563	2,412	1,484	1852	210	1,254	467	1826	127	362	1800	65
1877	----------	553	2,346	1,418	1851	210	1,223	424				1799	62
1876	----------	531	2,224	1,342					1825		342	1798	60
					1850	207	1,186	--------	1824		330	1797	59
1875	----------	503	2,185	1,249	1849	201	1,158	405	1823		314	1796	57
1874	----------	493	2,118	1,200	1848	192	1,196	386	1822		299		
1873	----------	470	2,026	1,099	1847	179	1,102	377	1821		282	1795	61
1872	----------	466	1,987	956	1846	175	1,168	367				1794	67
1871	----------	454	1,915	----------					1820		258	1793	68
					1845	172	995	352	1819		242	1792	66
1870	----------	445	1,822	----------	1844	166	1,143	--------	1818		230		
1869	----------	258	1,748	----------	1843	159	1,175	----------	1817		226	1791	76
1868	----------	251	1,667	----------	1842	140	1,072	----------	1816		215	1790	58

[1] Beginning 1923, includes membership in Alaska, and beginning 1927, includes membership in Hawaii.

[2] Beginning 1951, includes membership in Alaska, and beginning 1954, includes membership in Hawaii. Excludes membership of Baptist Missionary Association beginning 1925; included prior to that time.

Land, Water, and Climate

LAND AND WATER UTILIZATION (Series J 1–108)

J 1–2. Territorial expansion of the United States, 1790–1947.

Source: Bureau of the Census, reports and records.

Boundaries of territories listed under continental United States were indefinite, at least in part, at time of acquisition. Area figures shown here represent precise determinations of specific territories which have been marked upon maps, based upon interpretations of the several treaties of cession, which are necessarily debatable. These determinations were made by a committee consisting of representatives of various governmental agencies in 1912. Subsequently these figures were adjusted to bring them into agreement with remeasurements made in 1940.

"All other" (38 square miles) includes the following islands with gross areas as indicated: Midway (2), Wake (3), Canton and Enderbury (combined area, 27), Swan (1), Navassa (2), Baker, Howland, and Jarvis (combined area, 3), Johnston and Sand (combined area, less than 0.5), Kingman Reef, Quita Sueno Bank, Roncador Cay, and Serrana Bank (each less than 0.5). Other possessions include the following islands for which area figures are not available: Caroline, Christmas, Danger (Pukapuka), Flint, Funafuti, Malden, Manahiki, Nukufetau, Nukulailai, Nurakita, Penrhyn, Rakahanga, Starbuck, Vostok, Phoenix Group (except Canton and Enderbury), and Union (Tokelau) Group, not enumerated in decennial censuses.

J 3–5. Acquisition of the territory of the United States, 1783–1853.

Source: Department of the Interior, *Areas of Acquisitions to the Territory of the United States*, 1922.

All areas are given as computed in 1912 by a Federal Government committee representing the General Land Office, the Geological Survey, Bureau of Statistics, and the Bureau of the Census. Figures for 1957 have been adjusted for the new area measurements for the United States which were made for the 1940 Decennial Census. For the revised figures in square miles, see series J 1–2.

Recognition of its sovereignty over its present continental land area of 2,977,128 square miles, or about 1,905 million acres (as recomputed for the 1940 Decennial Census), was acquired by the Federal Government through a series of international agreements and treaties. The United States, however, did not gain title to all of these lands by such agreements. At the time of acquisition of sovereignty over the areas involved, title to about 463 million acres rested in individual States and their political subdivisions or in private owners, which title was not relinquished to the United States. Title to the remaining 1,442 million acres passed to the Federal Government during the period from 1781 to 1853.

J 6–8. Acquisition of the original public domain, 1781–1853.

Source: See source for series J 3–5.

For area by States, see Bureau of Land Management, *Annual Report of the Director*, Statistical Appendix, 1957.

By acts of cession, during the period 1781–1802, 7 of the original 13 States relinquished to the Federal Government for the common good their claims to the "western lands," roughly the area north of the Ohio River and east of the Mississippi River and the area embraced by the present States of Alabama and Mississippi. The State of Maryland ceded the present area of the District of Columbia in 1788. In 1850, the State of Texas sold its land outside its present boundaries to the United States. Title to the remaining area west of the Mississippi River (except the State of Texas) and to Florida passed to the Federal Government as sovereign at the time of their addition to the Nation during the period 1803–1853. For detailed information, see E. M. Douglas, *Boundaries, Areas, Geographic Centers and Altitudes of the United States and the Several States . . .*, Geological Survey Bulletin No. 817, 1939 edition, and B. H. Hibbard, *History of the Public Land Policies*, Macmillan Co., New York, 1924.

With the exception of land in the District of Columbia, the total of 1,442 million acres of land area (see series J 7), title to which became vested in the Government, is known as the *original public domain*. Any of such lands which the Government has not disposed of under the public-land laws are generally referred to as *public-domain lands*.

In addition to the public domain, the Federal Government has from time to time acquired by purchase, condemnation, and gift, tracts of land needed for various public purposes, such as sites for public buildings, defense installations, and natural-resource conservation activities. Such lands are often referred to as *acquired lands*, to distinguish them from public-domain lands. Complete statistics are not available as to the extent of such acquisitions.

J 9. Estimated area of the public domain, 1802–1957.

Source: 1802–1956, Bureau of Land Management; 1957, General Services Administration, *Inventory Report*, 1957.

For definition of public domain, see text for series J 6–8.

J 10–18. General note.

For definition of public-domain lands and acquired lands, see text for series J 6–8. The laws which govern the management, use, and sale or other disposal of public-domain lands are known as the *public-land laws*. The policy of the Federal Government in the early years was to pass the public lands into private ownership as rapidly as possible. Congress passed thousands of laws providing for the disposal of the original public domain to States and their subdivisions and to private owners. Initially this was done to raise revenue and later to hasten the settlement and development of the country. Under these laws, approximately 285 million acres have been patented to homesteaders, 225 million acres have been granted to States for various public purposes, 90 million acres have been granted to railroad corporations to aid in financing the construction of railroads, and about 430 million acres have been sold or otherwise disposed of. Disposals have reduced the original public domain to its present area of about 410 million acres (see series J 9). Special laws provide for the disposal of surplus *acquired lands*, as, for example, the Surplus Property Act of 1944.

J 10. Vacant public lands, 1904–1957.

Source: Bureau of Land Management (formerly the General Land Office), *Annual Report of the Director*, various issues, and records.

Data are estimates as of June 30 of each year; they do not include public lands in Alaska.

The vacant public lands of the United States are public-domain lands (see text for series J 6–8) which are not reserved for any purpose other than for reclassification and which are not covered by any non-Federal right or claim other than permits, leases, right-of-way, or unreported mining claims. They are subject to acquisition by applicants under appropriate laws, such as the laws governing homesteads or grants to States. It is upon these laws for the most part that entries and selections (see text for series J 13–15) are made. The Bureau of Land Management administers the public-land laws relating to such entries and selections, a function transferred to it from the General Land Office as a part of Reorganization Plan No. 3 of 1946 (U. S. Congress).

J 11. Cash receipts of the Bureau of Land Management, 1881–1957.

Source: Bureau of Land Management, *Annual Report of the Commissioner of the General Land Office*, 1946, Statistical Appendix, pp. 120–121, and thereafter, annual reports of the Bureau of Land Management.

Figures are for fiscal years and include receipts from such sources as: Sales of public and ceded Indian lands; fees and commissions; mineral rentals, royalties, and bonuses; sales of timber; grazing fees and rentals; and land rentals. These data represent the total receipts of the General Land Office and Bureau of Land Management covered into the Treasury for 1881–1957 and include the relatively small receipts from land and resources in Alaska. They do not include the receipts which other Government agencies realized from their operations on Federal lands, although they do include some receipts from lands under the administration of such agencies. For example, mineral leases for public-domain lands within areas administered by the National Forest Service were issued by the General Land Office, which also collected the mineral rentals, royalties, and bonuses from such lands. Also for 1935 through part of 1940, the General Land Office collected grazing fees for lands within grazing districts; and, for 1908 through the first half of 1913, it collected water-right charges in connection with the Bureau of Reclamation irrigation projects. Other examples of multiple jurisdiction exist.

For receipts from sales of public lands as reported by the Treasury Department, see series Y 263. The data representing receipts from sales of public lands which are included here, however, are not identical to those shown for series Y 263, since the General Land Office reports of receipts from sales did not cover the same period as the Treasury reports.

J 12. Land granted by the United States to the several States, 1802–1938.

Source: Bureau of Land Management, *Annual Report of the Commissioner of the General Land Office*, 1946, Statistical Appendix, pp. 108–119.

See also *General Land Office Information Bulletin No. 1, 1939 series.*

The data on land grants to the States for various public purposes are presented according to the calendar year in which the granting legislation was passed by the Congress. Some variation in the series is possible since the language of some of the statutes, including that of amendatory legislation, offers alternatives in the selection of the year to which individual

grants could be assigned. As with the land grants for the construction of canals and other transportation improvements (series J 44–48), many of these grants were satisfied through delivery of evidence of legal title throughout the years.

J 13–15. Original entries and selections, final entries, and patents and certifications, 1869–1957.

Source: 1869–1919, Department of Commerce, *Statistical Abstract of the United States*, various issues, 1879–1919 (data for 1903–1908 are revised as shown in the *Statistical Abstract*, 1909); 1920–1957, Bureau of Land Management, *Annual Report of the Director*, various issues.

The data on entries, selections, patents, and certifications refer to transactions which involve the disposal, under the public-land laws (including the homestead laws), of Federal public-domain lands to non-Federal owners. In general terms, *original entries* and *selections* are applications to secure title to public-domain lands which have been accepted as properly filed. Some types of applications, however, are not reported until the final certificate is issued and are, therefore, not included in series J 13.

Applications become *final entries* upon issuance of a *final certificate* which is given to the applicant after he has complied fully with the requirements of the laws relating to his application. These requirements may include, in particular cases, settlement upon and improvement of the lands entered, or payment of statutory fees or purchase money. A *final certificate* passes equitable title to the land to the applicant. With respect to certain State selections, no final certificate is issued. Such selections are, therefore, not included in series J 14 (final entries). *Patents* are instruments which pass legal title to the lands to the applicant. *Certifications* are issued in lieu of patents in connection with certain State selections.

The data do not include the area of certain lands which have been granted to the States to aid in the support of common schools. Title to such lands usually passes to the States upon survey of the lands by the Federal Government. Owing to legal complexities, detailed statistical records were not kept of these lands. Figures published here have been subjected to minor adjustments to improve comparability. They have not been checked, however, for internal accuracy or for strict comparability which would require analysis of supporting records. Data include disposals of lands in Alaska.

J 16–18. Homestead entries, except on ceded Indian lands, 1863–1957.

Source: Series J 16, 1863–1883, Thomas Donaldson, *The Public Domain*, Government Printing Office, 1884, pp. 351–355; 1884–1957, Bureau of Land Management, *Annual Report of the Director*, various issues. Series J 17, Department of Commerce, *Statistical Abstract of the United States*, 1889–1957, various issues. Series J 18, 1868–1928, *Statistical Abstract*, 1929, p. 130; 1929–1957, *Statistical Abstract*, various issues.

For definitions of the terms *original entries* and *final entries*, see text for series J 13–15.

Figures for original homestead entries exclude applications which were accepted for lands ceded by the Indians to the United States with the provision that proceeds from their disposal would be covered into the Treasury to the credit of the Indians. Detailed statistics on such homestead entries were not published in the reports of the Commissioner of the General Land Office prior to 1924. Such reports contain general information as to the disposal of ceded Indian lands. The records upon which the reports were based are for the most part on file in the National Archives.

Acreage figures of final entries (series J 18) do not include commuted homesteads. A *commuted homestead entry* is a homestead entry not exceeding 160 acres in connection with which the entryman pays the minimum statutory price for the land in consideration for reduction in residence and other requirements. Only certain classes of homestead entries can be commuted.

J 19–24. Revenues from public-domain, revested, and acquired land, 1785–1956.

Source: Marion Clawson and Burnell Held, *The Federal Lands: Their Use and Management*, The Johns Hopkins Press, Baltimore, 1957, text table 8 and appendix tables 25 and 27.

The original data for 1785–1880 are from J. R. Mahoney, *Natural Resources Activity of the Federal Government*, Public Affairs Bulletin No. 76, Library of Congress, 1950. Data for 1881–1956 are from annual reports of the Bureau of Land Management.

These are gross cash revenues, from which certain payments were made to States.

O & C lands are those areas granted to the Oregon and California Railroad Company in 1866. Later the Federal Government repossessed this land because the terms of the grant were not carried out.

J 25–31. Receipts from timber sales and grazing fees and use from public-domain lands, 1935–1956.

Source: See source for series J 19–24, appendix tables 12 and 14.

Data were compiled from annual reports of the Bureau of Land Management (formerly General Land Office and Grazing Service). Value of timber sold (series J 25) is the sum of amounts involved in timber sale contracts concluded during the fiscal year; actual cash receipts and volume of timber cut on each contract are spread over several months, often for 2 years or more, after the contract is signed. Data are for fiscal years; grazing receipts are credited to the year received even though part of the period covered extends into the following year.

An animal-unit-month represents the forage required to maintain 5 sheep or goats or ½ horse or 1 cow for a month. Data on grazing exclude grazing on reclamation land, land utilization projects where not part of a grazing district, O & C lands (see text for series J 19–24 for definition of O & C lands), and Alaskan grazing; include lands rented and sublet under the Pierce Act (43 USC 315M). Amount of grazing in districts (series J 29–31) includes free-use, crossing, and trailing permits in addition to regular paid use.

J 32–40. Oil and gas leases of public-domain lands—acreage, receipts, and output, 1920–1957.

Source: 1920–1955, see source for series J 19–24, appendix table 15; 1956 and 1957, records of Bureau of Land Management and the Geological Survey.

Original data for 1920–1955 are from annual reports of the Bureau of Land Management (formerly General Land Office) and the Geological Survey.

J 41–42. Livestock permitted to graze in National forests, 1905–1956.

Source: See source for series J 19–24.

Original data were obtained from Forest Service, annual reports and records.

Data are for the number of animals under paid permit, not necessarily the actual number grazed.

J 43. Public land sales, 1800–1860.

Source: Walter B. Smith and Arthur H. Cole, *Fluctuations in American Business, 1790–1860*, Harvard University Press, Cambridge, 1935.

Data were derived from Hibbard, *A History of the Public Land Policies*, 1924, pp. 100, 103, 106, and from *Annual Report of the Commissioner of the General Land Office*, various issues. The data differ from those presented by Hibbard (p. 106) for the years after 1850. After 1850, Hibbard's data shifts from calendar years to fiscal years ending June 30.

J 44–48. Public land grants by United States to aid in construction of railroads, wagon roads, canals, etc., 1823–1871.

Source: Bureau of Land Management, *Annual Report of the Commissioner of the General Land Office*, 1946, Statistical Appendix, pp. 100–107.

Figures include only the area of lands for which title passed to the grantee States and corporations. The exact extent of practically all of these grants was, owing to their terms, indeterminate at the time the granting acts were passed by the Congress. The procedures for the satisfaction of the grants generally required the grantees to submit lists of lands to which they requested evidence of legal title on the basis of the provisions of the authorizing legislation. This process of issuance of instruments of title has not been fully completed by the Department of the Interior; a relatively small area remains to be adjudicated.

For the series presented, the areas shown in the instruments of title which were issued for each grant over the years were totaled and shown as of the fiscal year in which the grant was *originally enacted*, even though in certain instances grants were revived at a later date after the expiration of statutory time limits while others were enlarged by subsequent legislation. Because the tabulation is based on instruments of title, the data do not reflect the area of those portions of grants which could not be satisfied under the law for various reasons or of those grants or portions of grants which were forfeited.

J 49–79. General note.

Area measurements in the United States began with measurements for the country as a whole; and, as mapping progressed, included measurements for the States and later for counties and minor civil divisions. For total figures (gross, land, and water) in square miles, 1790–1950, see series A 17–19. In 1940, a remeasurement of the United States was made for the Sixteenth Census of the United States. The last previous measurement was that for the Census of 1880. Differences between the two measurements are due primarily to the more accurate determination of the outer limits of the United States, the improvement in mapping, and omission of certain bodies of water included in the previous measurements. See Bureau of the Census, *Areas of the United States, 1940*, Sixteenth Census of the United States, 1942, pp. 1–5.

Collection of land utilization statistics began with the Census of 1850, when farmland was enumerated as "improved land" or "unimproved land." In 1890 and later census years, these inquiries were expanded and revised. After the turn of the century, collection of various land utilization statistics was begun by branches of the Department of Agriculture, while other contributions to the literature on this subject were made by numerous agencies, State universities, and individuals.

The Census of Agriculture is the primary source of data concerning land in farms in census years. Statistics concerning land not in farms are less complete, except for forest land, and have been collected by various interested agencies for individual items (e.g., acreage of forest land by the Forest Service, public-domain lands by the Department of the Interior) and for local areas by Federal, State, and private agencies and individuals. During the 1930's, studies by the National Resources Planning Board and assisting agencies contributed greatly to the available statistics on total land utilization. Since 1920, the former Bureau of Agricultural Economics and the Agricultural Research Service have prepared periodic inventories of land use.

Data on the utilization of farmland for 1850–1925 are chiefly estimates made by the former Bureau of Agricultural Economics based on the Census of Agriculture conducted by the Bureau of the Census. The estimates for 1930–1954 are from the Census of Agriculture, except for an adjustment made by the Agricultural Research Service in cropland harvested and other land in farms for 1950 and 1954. This adjustment was made to compensate for some of the underenumeration of cropland indicated by the postenumeration surveys conducted by the Bureau of the Census and to obtain greater conformity with the total acreage of crops harvested as reported by the Agricultural Marketing Service.

Acreages of nonfarm uses of land were estimated by the former Bureau of Agricultural Economics and the Agricultural Research Service from records and reports of State and Federal agencies concerned with management of public land, conservation of land, public services, and assessment of land for taxation.

Changes in total farmland for 1850–1954 represent in part increased agricultural activity and in part more complete census enumeration and changes in census definition of *land in farms*. Uses not reported by the Bureau of the Census and additions to census data for 1925–1954 are based largely on agricultural statistics assembled by the Department of Agriculture. Forest-land inventories and grazing-land studies during this period are believed to have improved the reliability of the estimates of these items for this period as contrasted with earlier years. Estimates for 1925 and prior census years for land not in farms are based on more limited evidence, such as available charts, maps, records, and reports on land areas and uses.

J 49. Total land area, 1850–1954.

Source: Department of Agriculture, *Major Uses of Land in the United States: Summary for 1954*, Agriculture Information Bulletin No. 168, 1957, pp. 36 and 37.

See also *1940 Census of Agriculture*, vol. III, p. 33, for additional detail for 1850–1940. For total land area for 1950 and 1954, see *U.S. Census of Agriculture: 1950*, vol. II, p. 64, and *U.S. Census of Agriculture: 1954*, vol. II, p. 60.

Total land area, as defined by the Census for the 1940 remeasurement includes "dry land and land temporarily or partially covered by water, such as marshland, swamps and river flood plains . . . (except tidal flats) . . . streams, sloughs, estuaries, and canals less than 1/8 of a statute mile in width; and lakes, reservoirs, and ponds having less than 40 acres of area." The total land area reported by the Bureau of the Census for 1950 and 1954 is less than that reported for 1940 mainly because of the completion of additional reservoirs.

J 50–64. Land utilization, by type, 1850–1954.

Source: Department of Agriculture, *Major Uses of Land in the United States: Summary for 1954*, Agriculture Information Bulletin No. 168, 1957, pp. 36 and 37. (Data for series J 56–57 and J 61–62 for 1900 from records of Agricultural Research Service.)

These data are based on estimates from the following sources: Bureau of the Census, *U.S. Census of Agriculture: 1954*, vol. II, pp. 8 and 9; Department of Agriculture publications, as follows: *Pasture Land on Farms in the United States*, Bulletin No. 626, 1918; *Agriculture Yearbook, 1923*, 1924, pp. 415–506; *Inventory of Major Land Uses, United States, 1945*, Miscellaneous Publication 663, 1948; *Major Uses of Land in the United States*, Technical Bulletin No. 1082, and Supplement, *Basic Land Use Statistics, 1950*; and National Resources Board, *A Report on National Planning and Public Works. . .*, 1934, pp. 108–113.

Cropland used for crops includes cropland harvested, crop failure, and cultivated summer fallow. *Cropland idle or in cover crops* includes idle land left unplanted for a year or two only, as well as some poorer cropland abandoned for crop purposes and soil-improvement crops not harvested and not pastured. *Grassland pasture* includes cropland used only for pasture and all other nonforested pasture in farms. *Farm woodland* includes grazed or ungrazed farm wood lots or timber tracts, natural or planted, and cutover land with young growth, which has or will have value as wood or timber. Chaparral and woody shrubs are omitted. *Other land in farms* includes farmsteads, roads, lanes, wasteland, and so on.

Nonfarm grazing land comprises the open grassland and shrub grazing lands and the woodland and forest area grazed. *Nonfarm forest land not used for grazing* excludes forested areas in parks, wildlife refuges, military areas, recreation sites, and arid woodland, brushland, and forest land used for grazing. *Other nonfarm land* includes urban, industrial, and residential areas outside farms; parks and wildlife refuges; military lands; roads; railroads; ungrazed desert, rock, swamp, and other unused wasteland.

J 65–79. Private and public land ownership, by major uses, 1920–1954.

Source: 1920, Bureau of Agricultural Economics and Agricultural Research Service, records; 1930–1954, see source for series J 50–64, pp. 90–92.

See also Department of Agriculture, *Federal and State Rural Lands, 1950, with Special Reference to Grazing*, Circular No. 909, 1952. For definitions and for longer series on total land area, see text for series J 49 and J 50–64.

The figures were compiled from a number of Federal and State reports and records and varying degrees of reliability attach to them. The figures used are applicable for different dates. All of them were assembled for some other purpose than that for which they are used here. The areas of all unsurveyed lands are estimated, and the areas of many lands based on surveys are subject to correction. Some of the data are not complete and are used merely for comparison. Therefore, although they are the best available, the figures given here are not strictly accurate, often not complete, and are not comparable among themselves. Nevertheless, they give some idea of the major features of land use and control for the country as a whole.

Private land is land held or owned by private individuals, groups, and corporations, and is generally used for private purposes. Indian lands held in trust and administered by the Federal Government for the benefit and use of groups or tribes of the Indian people are included in private land, as three-fourths of this land is used directly for farming and grazing by Indian farmers and stockmen. Much of the rest is leased for farming and grazing to other farmers and ranchers and the proceeds are received by the Indian owners. These lands are subject to eventual private individual ownership by the Indians.

Public land as used here is land owned or administered by Federal, State, county, municipal, or other governments for common or public purposes (e.g., highways, airports, national defense, flood control, water supply, forests, and parks). Public land frequently is used for farming and grazing by private parties under a system of permits or leases. However, most of it is dry, rough, rocky, swampy, or otherwise unsuited for farming. When used by individuals, public land is sometimes included in reporting statistics on acreages in farms. More often, when public land is used in common by several persons, it is not reported as in farms.

J 80–90. Land drainage and irrigation, 1890–1954.

Source: Series J 80, Bureau of the Census, *Drainage of Agricultural Lands*, 1950, p. 2; series J 81–83, *Drainage of Agricultural Lands*, 1940, p. 1; series J 84–86, 1890–1950, *Irrigation of Agricultural Lands*, 1950, vol. III, pp. 34–37, 1954, Bureau of the Census, records; series J 87–90, *Irrigation of Agricultural Lands*, 1940 and 1950, and *U.S. Census of Agriculture: 1954*, vol. II, p. 9.

The date of each drainage census was January 1 of the census year. The data on condition and use of the land refer to the year preceding the date of the census. The number of States covered has varied from census to census. The New England States and West Virginia have never been included. The 1920 Census also excluded the Middle Atlantic States, Alabama, Delaware, Maryland, and Virginia. This was also true for 1930 except that Virginia was included. In addition, New Jersey, New York, and Pennsylvania were omitted in 1940 and Pennsylvania in 1950.

The Bureau of the Census has collected irrigation statistics by means of two censuses: (1) The Censuses of Agriculture, which have provided irrigation statistics since 1890 and represent a direct enumeration of farmers; and (2) the Special Censuses of Irrigation Enterprises, taken decennially since 1910, which collect information from irrigation enterprises and cover only the States where irrigation is very extensive. In addition, a special census of irrigation was taken in 1902 and the statistics were published in 1904 in *Bulletin 16* of the Census Bureau.

For reasons of comparability with the acreage series on cropland and pasture shown here, the irrigation data presented here are from the Censuses of Agriculture.

The States included for series J 86–88 are: Arizona, California, Colorado, Idaho, Kansas, Montana, Nebraska, Nevada, New Mexico, North Dakota, Oklahoma, Oregon, South Dakota, Texas, Utah, Washington, and Wyoming.

For series J 89–90, the States included are: Alabama, Arkansas, Connecticut, Delaware, Florida, Georgia, Illinois, Indiana, Iowa, Kentucky, Louisiana, Maine, Maryland, Massachusetts, Michigan, Minnesota, Mississippi, Missouri, New Hampshire, New Jersey, New York, North Carolina, Ohio, Pennsylvania, Rhode Island, South Carolina, Tennessee, Vermont, Virginia, West Virginia, and Wisconsin.

Although both types of reclamation are important, drainage development overshadows irrigation in acreage of land already converted to farming and in land that still may be developed. Drainage developments are concentrated mainly in the humid areas of the Eastern and Central States, whereas irrigation developments are located predominantly in the arid and semiarid areas of the West. However, in irrigated areas, drainage

also must be provided to carry away any water not required by crops.

J 91–102. Water use, 1900–1955.

Source: Business and Defense Services Administration, *Water Use in the United States, 1900–1975*, July 1959. (The source also contains a detailed bibliography on water utilization.)

The figures are based on nationwide estimates of water uses as developed by various agencies whose primary interest lies within this field. The estimates shown here are considered conservative and are subject to revision as new information permits readjustment in the several categories of water use.

Public water supplies (series J 95 and J 96) include those basic systems furnishing water for domestic, commercial, and industrial purposes within their area of distribution. Self-supplied use applies to all water uses which are individually provided, and without assistance from a publicly owned supply. Domestic use (series J 97 and J 98) includes all water used primarily for household purposes, the watering of livestock, the irrigation of gardens, lawns, shrubbery, etc., surrounding a house or domicile. Industrial and miscellaneous use (series J 99 and J 100) includes manufacturing industries, mineral industries, air conditioning, resorts, motels, rural, commercial, military, and other miscellaneous uses not elsewhere included, all self-supplied. Steam electric power use (series J 101 and J 102) applies to all water used in the production of steam for the generation of electric energy. The increase in industrial production, accompanied by increasing mechanization and automation, has rapidly increased consumption of electric power, the major portion of which is produced by steam generation.

J 103–108. Water wells in use, 1900–1955.

Source: Business and Defense Services Administration, records. (Estimates are shown in chart form in Walter L. Picton, "The Water Picture Today," *Water Well Journal*, April 1956.)

In the formulation of these estimates, due consideration has been given to growth in population, the population served by public water supplies, the rural-farm and nonfarm self-served population, and the relative essential water facility requirements to serve them. In addition to population growth, the increase in per capita domestic water use, irrigation requirements, and industrial demands have been considered.

Although the trend appears to be upward in all segments of the water well industry, the extent of increase cannot be firmly measured on a region-to-region basis. In the absence of measurable data, the level of activity in the field has been gauged by the process of deduction, utilizing the populations of rural and other areas not serviced by public water supplies.

Series J 1–2. Territorial Expansion of the United States: 1790 to 1947

Accession	Date	Gross area (land and water)	Accession	Date	Gross area (land and water)
	1	2		1	2
		Sq. mi.			*Sq. mi.*
Total		**3,628,130**	Alaska	1867	586,400
			Hawaii	1898	6,423
Continental United States		3,022,387	Puerto Rico	1899	3,435
Territory in 1790 [1]		888,811			
Louisiana Purchase	1803	827,192	Other areas:		
By treaty with Spain:			The Philippines	1898	[2] 115,600
Florida	1819	58,560	Guam	1899	206
Other areas	1819	13,443	American Samoa	1900	76
			Canal Zone [3]	1904	553
Texas	1845	390,144	Corn Islands [4]	1914	4
Oregon	1846	285,580	Virgin Islands of the U. S.	1917	133
Mexican Cession	1848	529,017	Trust Territory of the Pacific Islands [5]	1947	8,475
Gadsden Purchase	1853	29,640	All other		38

[1] Includes that part of drainage basin of Red River of the North, south of 49th parallel, sometimes considered part of Louisiana Purchase.
[2] Not included in total. Ceded by Spain in 1898, the Philippines constituted a territorial possession of the United States until 1946. Granted independence July 4, 1946.
[3] Under jurisdiction of United States in accordance with treaty of Nov. 18, 1903, with Republic of Panama.

[4] Leased (1914) from Republic of Nicaragua for 99 years.
[5] Under trusteeship with the United States as administering authority. See *Trusteeship Agreement for the Former Japanese Mandated Islands (Documentary Supplement No. 1)* of the Security Council of the United Nations which became effective on July 18, 1947.

Series J 3–9. Acquisition and Extent of Territory and Public Domain, Continental United States: 1781 to 1957

[Areas are as computed in 1912, hence do not agree with total figures (in square miles) shown in series J 2, or with figures (in acres) shown for 1940 and 1945 in series J 49 and J 65]

Year and how acquired	Acquisition of the territory of the United States			Acquisition of the original public domain			Estimated area of the public domain [1] (selected years)
	Total area	Land area	Water area	Total area	Land area	Water area	
	3	4	5	6	7	8	9
	Acres	*Acres*	*Acres*	*Acres*	*Acres*	*Acres*	*Acres*
Aggregate	1,934,327,680	1,903,824,640	30,503,040	1,462,466,560	1,442,200,320	20,266,240	
1957, estimate of public domain							[2] 410,000,000
1956, estimate of public domain							[2] 411,000,000
1950, estimate of public domain							[2] 412,000,000
1946, estimate of public domain							[2] 413,000,000
1912, estimate of public domain							600,000,000
1880, estimate of public domain							900,000,000
1853, Gadsden Purchase	18,988,800	18,961,920	26,880	18,988,800	18,961,920	26,880	
1850, estimate of public domain							1,200,000,000
1850, Purchase from Texas				78,926,720	78,842,880	83,840	
1848, Mexican Cession [3]	338,680,960	334,479,360	4,201,600	338,680,960	334,479,360	4,201,600	
1846, Oregon Compromise	183,386,240	180,644,480	2,741,760	183,386,240	180,644,480	2,741,760	
1845, Annexation of Texas [3]	249,066,240	246,777,600	2,288,640				
1819, Cession from Spain	46,144,640	43,342,720	2,801,920	46,144,640	43,342,720	[4] 2,801,920	
Red River Basin [5]	29,601,920	29,066,880	535,040	29,601,920	29,066,880	535,040	
1803, Louisiana Purchase [3]	529,911,680	523,446,400	6,465,280	529,911,680	523,446,400	6,465,280	
1802, estimate of public domain							200,000,000
1783, Treaty with Great Britain	541,364,480	526,570,240	14,794,240				
1781–1802 (State Cessions)				236,825,600	233,415,680	3,409,920	

[1] Estimated from imperfect data available for indicated years.
[2] Includes Indian Trust properties.
[3] Data for Louisiana Purchase exclude area eliminated by the Treaty of 1819 with Spain. Such areas are included in figures for annexation of Texas and the Mexican Cession.

[4] Includes 33,920 acres subsequently recognized as part of the State of Texas which is not a public-domain State.
[5] Represents drainage basin of the Red River of the North, south of the 49th parallel. Authorities differ as to the method and exact date of its acquisition. Some hold it as a part of the Louisiana Purchase, others maintain it was acquired from Great Britain.

Series J 10–18. Vacant Lands, and Disposal of Public Lands: 1802 to 1957

[For Treasury receipts from sale of public land, see series Y 263]

Year	Vacant public lands	Cash receipts of Bureau of Land Management	Land granted to States, as of June 30, 1946 [1]	All entries, selections, patents, etc. [2]			Homestead entries, except on ceded Indian lands		
				All original entries and selections [3]	All final entries	Patents and certifications	Original entries		Final entries [4]
							Number	Acreage	
	10	11	12	13	14	15	16	17	18
	Million acres	*1,000 dollars*	*1,000 acres*	*1,000 acres*	*1,000 acres*	*1,000 acres*	*Number*	*1,000 acres*	*1,000 acres*
1957	169	112,059		180	279	561	662	79	64
1956	170	212,217		151	267	629	455	57	40
1955	170	239,549		251	250	539	482	60	37
1954	171	77,487		306	239	416	474	60	43
1953	171	66,846		310	177	364	482	61	39
1952	172	64,518		113	165	374	458	59	38
1951	174	49,082		121	198	388	363	49	63
1950	170	36,177		142	150	492	523	73	46
1949	170	37,149		134	116	390	681	82	37
1948	171	33,286		117	56	287	635	78	18
1947	170	21,012		76	53	403	474	55	26
1946	170	13,840		27	61	154	143	18	29
1945	170	14,147		40	61	217	182	22	35
1944	168	15,169		91	85	402	157	20	51
1943	169	10,543		63	168	637	211	29	102
1942	174	9,914		135	252	1,055	283	37	188
1941	172	8,655		76	491	1,039	400	51	390

See footnotes at end of table.

Series J 10–18. Vacant Lands, and Disposal of Public Lands: 1802 to 1957—Con.

Year	Vacant public lands	Cash receipts of Bureau of Land Management	Land granted to States, as of June 30, 1946 [1]	All entries, selections, patents, etc. [2]			Homestead entries, except on ceded Indian lands		
				All original entries and selections [3]	All final entries	Patents and certifications	Original entries		Final entries [4]
							Number	Acreage	
	10	**11**	**12**	**13**	**14**	**15**	**16**	**17**	**18**
	Million acres	*1,000 dollars*	*1,000 acres*	*1,000 acres*	*1,000 acres*	*1,000 acres*	*Number*	*1,000 acres*	*1,000 acres*
1940	(5)	7,520	----	54	756	1,904	349	46	652
1939	(5)	7,804	----	302	1,198	1,982	378	66	1,089
1938	(5)	8,430	2	131	1,478	1,944	447	78	1,362
1937	(5)	7,375	1	125	2,026	2,184	561	111	1,915
1936	(5)	5,194	200	426	1,938	1,359	1,209	357	1,765
1935	(5)	4,800	(6)	1,759	1,772	1,610	3,297	1,166	1,640
1934	166	4,035	3	3,585	1,225	1,362	7,507	2,787	1,124
1933	172	3,859	193	3,118	980	1,866	7,527	2,642	907
1932	173	4,129	77	4,552	1,333	2,013	10,639	3,914	1,210
1931	177	4,836	2	5,219	1,537	2,126	12,640	4,757	1,353
1930	179	6,801	1	5,435	1,577	2,253	12,708	4,723	1,371
1929	190	6,194	100	4,613	2,030	2,648	11,598	4,178	1,701
1928	194	6,710	252	3,726	2,168	2,519	10,429	3,367	1,816
1927	194	9,202	55	3,595	3,011	4,586	10,500	3,237	2,584
1926	7 196	11,414	----	3,243	3,962	4,600	10,354	2,875	3,451
1925	185	10,766	1	3,641	4,489	5,627	11,010	3,041	4,049
1924	187	16,373	(6)	4,564	5,229	9,082	13,886	3,873	4,791
1923	186	10,700	----	6,415	6,201	10,352	18,942	5,524	5,594
1922	183	11,785	----	10,367	8,074	13,761	29,263	8,980	7,307
1921	190	14,508	(6)	15,632	8,772	10,930	43,813	13,662	7,727
1920	200	6,132	----	16,437	9,778	13,327	48,532	13,511	8,373
1919	213	4,304	----	11,871	----	----	39,341	10,204	6,525
1918	222	5,432	----	10,147	----	----	35,875	7,420	8,236
1917	231	6,150	(6)	16,202	----	----	58,896	12,021	8,497
1916	255	5,445	4	18,708	----	----	65,282	13,628	7,278
1915	280	5,395	2	16,861	----	----	62,360	12,440	7,181
1914	291	6,148	----	16,523	----	----	62,229	12,117	9,291
1913	298	6,956	----	15,867	----	----	57,800	11,222	10,009
1912	315	9,973	(8)	14,575	----	----	52,991	13,624	4,306
1911	327	11,090	----	19,211	----	----	70,720	17,639	4,620
1910	344	11,464	17,150	26,391	----	----	98,598	18,329	3,796
1909	363	12,216	(6)	19,893	----	----	75,445	12,302	3,699
1908	387	12,716	16	19,090	----	----	87,057	13,586	4,243
1907	406	11,553	(6)	20,998	----	----	93,957	14,755	3,741
1906	424	7,586	3,114	19,431	----	----	89,600	13,975	3,527
1905	449	7,018	(6)	17,057	----	----	70,344	12,896	3,419
1904	474	9,283	20	16,332	----	----	69,175	10,171	3,233
1903	----	11,025	----	22,824	----	----	80,188	11,193	3,577
1902	----	6,262	(6)	19,372	----	----	98,829	14,033	4,343
1901	----	4,972	----	15,453	----	----	68,648	9,497	5,241
1900	----	4,380	8	13,391	----	----	61,270	8,478	3,478
1899	----	3,070	50	9,091	----	----	45,776	6,178	3,134
1898	----	2,278	5,600	8,422	----	----	44,980	6,207	3,095
1897	----	2,088	(6)	7,754	----	----	33,250	4,452	2,778
1896	----	2,106	----	13,174	----	----	36,548	4,831	2,790
1895	----	2,033	69	8,364	----	----	37,336	5,009	2,981
1894	----	2,768	8,470	10,377	----	----	56,632	8,047	2,930
1893	----	4,480	----	11,802	----	----	48,436	6,809	3,477
1892	----	4,860	8	13,567	----	----	55,113	7,716	3,260
1891	----	5,429	(6)	10,357	----	----	37,602	5,040	3,955
1890	----	7,781	7,678	12,666	----	----	40,244	5,532	4,061
1889	----	9,686	15,367	17,026	----	----	42,183	6,029	3,682
1888	----	13,547	(6)	24,161	----	----	46,236	6,677	3,175
1887	----	12,289	----	25,111	----	----	52,028	7,594	2,749
1886	----	9,031	----	20,992	----	----	61,638	9,145	2,664
1885	----	8,628	----	20,114	----	----	60,877	7,416	3,033
1884	----	12,789	46	26,834	----	----	54,982	7,832	2,946
1883	----	11,714	----	19,031	----	----	56,565	8,172	2,504
1882	----	8,395	----	13,999	----	----	45,331	6,348	2,219
1881	----	5,409	276	10,763	----	----	36,999	5,028	1,928
1880	----	----	(6)	9,152	----	----	47,293	----	1,938
1879	----	----	----	8,724	----	----	41,005	----	2,071
1878	----	----	----	7,210	----	----	35,630	----	2,663
1877	----	----	----	3,495	----	----	18,675	----	2,408
1876	----	----	----	4,292	----	----	25,104	----	2,591
1875	----	----	3,842	3,792	----	----	20,668	----	2,069
1874	----	----	----	4,784	----	----	29,126	----	1,586
1873	----	----	----	6,386	----	----	31,561	----	1,225
1872	----	----	----	7,248	----	----	38,742	----	707
1871	----	----	----	7,119	----	----	39,768	----	629
1870	----	----	----	6,663	----	----	33,972	----	520
1869	----	----	----	6,678	----	----	25,628	----	504
1868	----	----	----	----	----	----	23,746	----	355

Year	Land granted to States, as of June 30, 1946 [1]	Homestead entries except on ceded Indian lands
	12	**16**
	1,000 acres	*Number*
1867	4	16,957
1866	226	15,355
1865	----	8,924
1864	4,955	9,405
1863	----	8,223
1862	9,420	----
1861	3,052	----
1859	3,498	----
1857	2,974	----
1855	46	----
1853	5,587	----
1850	55,401	----
1849	9,491	----
1846	1,081	----
1845	2,076	----
1841	7,807	----
1836	2,146	----
1832	24	----
1831	6	----
1827	46	----
1826	25	----
1823	92	----
1820	1,317	----
1819	986	----
1818	1,186	----
1817	824	----
1816	740	----
1812	807	----
1803	793	----
1802	24	----

[1] Includes grants for such public purposes as the following: Educational, penal, and other public institutions and buildings; bridges, reservoirs, and other internal improvements; reclamation of swamp and arid lands; experiment stations; recreational areas; wildlife and forestry areas; military camps; and payment of bonds issued by local governments. Does not include grants tabulated in series J 44–48. Does not include acreage of swamplands lost to the States, for which the States received indemnity in cash. [2] Includes homesteads.
[3] Previous to 1911 the data included, in addition to original entries and selections, some classes of final entries and patents.

[4] Exclusive of commuted homesteads.
[5] Not reported.
[6] Less than 1,000 acres.
[7] The increase in area over 1925 was reported as the result of a "special check" of field office records which was "used as a basis for a complete revision of the vacant land statistics."
[8] Grants of unsurveyed lands to Wisconsin for forestry purposes; area not determined.

Series J 19–24.   Revenues From Public-Domain, Revested, and Acquired Land: 1785 to 1956

[In millions of dollars]

Period	Total	Sales of public domain	Grazing fees and rentals [1]	Timber sales [1] (O & C, and public domain)	Mineral Leasing Act receipts— public-domain and acquired land [1]	Miscellaneous [2]
	19	20	21	22	23	24
Total	[3]1,573.1	414.2	27.2	123.0	615.4	139.7
1951–1956	[3]709.2	8.8	12.5	94.4	335.0	4.9
1941–1950	199.4	2.4	11.5	24.9	158.0	2.6
1931–1940	58.0	1.4	3.2	3.7	46.0	3.7
1921–1930	104.5	6.7			76.4	21.4
1911–1920	67.0	27.9				39.1
1901–1910	94.1	64.8				29.3
1891–1900	33.5	21.3				12.2
1881–1890	99.3	76.9				22.4
1785–1880	208.1	204.0				4.1

[1] Revenues of earlier years included under "Miscellaneous." (See text for definition of O & C lands.)
[2] Includes fees and commissions, sales of Indian lands, various rentals and permits, and a varied assortment of minor items. For the period roughly 1910–1920 contains relatively minor amounts from mineral leases of various kinds. For the period roughly 1910–1945, contains minor amounts from sale of dead, down, or damaged timber, including trespass damages for timber cutting; and for the period roughly 1910–1934, includes minor amounts for grazing, including grazing trespass damages. From 1916 through 1932, also includes receipts from sale of O & C timber.
[3] Includes $253.6 million of mineral leasing submerged areas of outer Continental Shelf not shown separately.

Series J 25–31.   Receipts From Timber Sales and Grazing Fees and Use From Public-Domain Lands: 1935 to 1956

[In thousands]

Year	Value of timber sold	Grazing [1]						Year	Grazing [1]			
		Receipts			Animal-unit-months of use				Receipts			Total, animal-unit-months of use
		Total [2]	In grazing districts	Outside grazing districts	Total	Cattle and horses	Sheep and goats		Total [2]	In grazing districts	Outside grazing districts	
	25	26	27	28	29	30	31		26	27	28	29
1956	$2,331	$2,386	$2,050	$335	15,301	10,223	5,078	1945	$996	$765	$231	15,572
1955	1,489	2,219	1,879	339	15,367	10,186	5,181	1944	1,015	813	202	15,745
1954	1,055	2,039	1,678	359	15,686	10,371	5,315	1943	979	785	194	15,061
1953	1,100	2,095	1,764	328	15,780	10,483	5,297	1942	1,095	900	195	15,271
1952	1,183	1,985	1,658	322	15,403	10,157	5,246	1941	1,113	922	191	15,369
1951	1,348	1,694	1,382	306	14,331	9,211	5,120					
1950	396	1,534	1,146	383	14,461	9,205	5,256	1940	747	595	152	13,832
1949	585	1,239	1,060	173	14,522	9,117	5,405	1939	1,038	886	152	13,789
1948	166	1,415	1,165	244	14,726	9,078	5,648	1938	850	800	49	13,376
1947	78	1,046	819	221	14,993	9,195	5,798	1937	488	415	73	14,383
1946	47	964	736	228	15,254			1936	48	48		11,106
								1935	1	1		6,507

[1] Includes free-use, crossing, and trailing permits in addition to regular paid use.   [2] Includes minor receipts from grazing on privately owned lands within grazing districts (Pierce Act lands) which were administered by Bureau of Land Management

Series J 32–40.   Oil and Gas Leases of Public-Domain Lands—Acreage, Receipts, and Output: 1920 to 1957

[Excludes acquired lands, military and naval oil reserves, and submerged lands.   Data are for fiscal years, except as noted]

Year or period	Number in effect	Average under lease	Receipts			Volume of output			
			Total	Rentals [1]	Royalties	Total petroleum equivalent [2]	Petroleum	Natural gas	Gasoline and butane
	32	33	34	35	36	37	38	39	40
	1,000	Mil. acres	Mil. dol.	Mil. dol.	Mil. dol.	Mil. bbl.	Mil. bbl.	Bil. cu. ft.	Mil. gal.
1957	108.0	80.3	73.4	20.0	[3]53.4	187.8	130	317	207
1956	100.9	75.4	62.8	16.4	[3]46.4	168.1	118	272	203
1955	96.4	73.3	59.9	19.6	40.3	159.5	111	261	211
1954	87.7	66.0	53.6	15.5	38.1	146.9	105	223	197
1953	78.8	59.9	43.8	12.8	30.9	127.2	94	173	184
1952	63.2	48.6	46.8	19.2	27.5	121.6	92	152	179
1951	42.5	32.9	34.3	7.9	26.4	105.9	82	123	141
1950	28.9	23.6	26.7	4.3	22.4	100.5	76	126	145
1949	21.3	19.0	28.4	4.9	23.5	100.5	76	124	158
1948	13.4	10.7	24.1	2.9	21.2	98.3	74	124	152
1947	12.5	8.1	14.5	2.2	12.3	83.3	64	98	126
1946	8.8	6.0	9.3	1.0	8.3	78.9	60	96	121
1945	7.0	4.6	9.4	2.0	7.4	78.0	56	96	250
1944	5.3	3.1	10.3	3.4	6.9	69.2	54	80	78
1943	4.5	2.8	6.6	.5	6.1	66.6	50	87	90
1942	4.3	3.3	6.3	.7	5.7	61.4	45	88	71
1941	5.3	5.5	5.3	.4	4.9	57.9	43	82	52
1931–1940						43.7	462.4	328	698	759
1920–1930						59.4	302.3	260	198	390

[1] Includes bonuses. Rentals are estimates derived by deducting royalties from total receipts.   [2] Includes gasoline and butane on an equal basis with petroleum (42 gallons per barrel), and 6,000 cubic feet of natural gas equal to 1 barrel of petroleum.   [3] Estimated from Geological Survey, calendar year data.

Series J 41–42. Livestock Permitted to Graze in National Forests: 1905 to 1956

[In thousands. Excludes animals under 6 months of age. Data are for fiscal years prior to 1921, calendar years thereafter]

Year	Cattle, horses, and swine	Sheep and goats	Year	Cattle, horses, and swine	Sheep and goats	Year	Cattle, horses, and swine	Sheep and goats	Year	Cattle, horses, and swine	Sheep and goats	Year	Cattle, horses, and swine	Sheep and goats
	41	42		41	42		41	42		41	42		41	42
1956	1,095	2,730	1945	1,206	3,889	1935	1,345	5,691	1925	1,621	6,432	1915	1,727	7,284
1955	1,106	2,822	1944	1,225	4,280	1934	1,419	6,161	1924	1,753	6,597	1914	1,620	7,619
1954	1,008	2,910	1943	1,212	4,539	1933	1,399	6,162	1923	1,864	6,712	1913	1,557	7,868
1953	1,108	2,964	1942	1,191	4,758	1932	1,397	6,321	1922	1,987	6,892	1912	1,503	7,552
1952	1,096	3,000	1941	1,176	4,787	1931	1,376	6,608	1921	2,080	6,980	1911	1,448	7,449
1951	1,088	3,013				1930	1,358	6,714	1920	2,217	7,881	1910	1,498	7,649
1950	1,092	3,006	1940	1,177	4,949	1929	1,399	6,964	1919	2,234	7,996	1909	1,586	7,820
1949	1,126	3,092	1939	1,209	5,132	1928	1,415	6,784	1918	2,243	8,512	1908	1,382	7,087
1948	1,226	3,322	1938	1,250	5,307	1927	1,486	6,704	1917	2,054	7,636	1907	1,200	6,657
1947	1,247	3,403	1937	1,284	5,485	1926	1,559	6,503	1916	1,861	7,886	1906	1,015	5,762
1946	1,203	3,713	1936	1,311	5,645							1905	692	1,710

Series J 43. Public Land Sales: 1800 to 1860

[In thousands]

Year	Acres 43	Year	Acres 43	Year	Acres 43	Year	Acres 43	Year	Acres 43
1860	2,543.4	1847	2,521.3	1835	12,564.5	1822	710.0	1810	285.8
1859	4,011.7	1846	2,263.7	1834	4,658.2	1821	782.5	1809	275.0
1858	3,663.6			1833	3,856.2			1808	209.2
1857	4,220.1	1845	1,843.5	1832	2,462.3	1820	814.0	1807	320.9
1856	5,247.0	1844	1,754.8	1831	2,777.9	1819	2,968.4	1806	506.0
		1843	1,605.3			1818	3,491.0		
1855	11,959.8	1842	1,129.2	1830	1,929.7	1817	1,886.2	1805	582.0
1854	12,823.0	1841	1,164.8	1829	1,244.9	1816	1,742.5	1804	398.2
1853	3,787.1			1828	965.6			1803	174.2
1852	894.8	1840	2,236.9	1827	926.7	1815	1,306.4	1802	271.1
1851	2,055.9	1839	4,976.4	1826	848.1	1814	1,176.1	1801	497.9
		1838	3,414.9			1813	505.6		
1850	1,405.8	1837	5,601.1	1825	999.0	1812	386.1	1800	67.8
1849	1,329.9	1836	20,074.9	1824	737.0	1811	575.1		
1848	1,887.6			1823	652.1				

Series J 44–48. Public Land Grants by United States to Aid in Construction of Railroads, Wagon Roads, Canals, etc.: 1823 to 1871

[In thousands of acres]

Year	Total grants	Railroads	Wagon roads	Canals	River improvements	Year	Total grants	Railroads	Wagon roads	Canals	River improvements
	44	45	46	47	48		44	45	46	47	48
1871	3,253	3,253				1853	3,379	2,629		750	
1870	129	129				1852	1,773	1,773			
1869	105		105			1851	3,752	3,752			
1867	25,173	23,535	1,538	100							
1866	200			200		1847	1,845	840			1,005
1865	42,794	41,452	941	401		1838	139			139	
1864	2,349	2,349									
1863	31,401	30,877	524			1828	1,338			938	400
1857	6,689	6,689				1827	2,273		202	2,071	
1856	14,085	14,085				1823	49			49	

Series J 49–64. Land Utilization, by Type: 1850 to 1954

[In millions of acres]

Year	Total land area	Land in farms — Total	Cropland — Total	Cropland — Used for crops	Cropland — Idle or in cover crops	Grassland pasture	Farm woodland — Total	Farm woodland — Pastured	Farm woodland — Not pastured	Special uses	Other	Land not in farms — Total	Grazing land	Forest land not used for grazing	Special uses	Other
	49	50	51	52	53	54	55	56	57	58	59	60	61	62	63	64
1954	1,904	1,158	399	380	19	526	197	121	76	23	13	746	353	238	87	68
1950	1,904	1,159	409	387	22	485	220	135	85	24	21	745	400	201	81	63
1945	1,905	1,142	403	379	24	529	166	95	71	24	20	763	428	186	76	73
1940	1,905	1,061	399	363	36	461	157	100	57	44		844	504	203	137	
1935	1,903	1,055	416	375	41	410	185	108	77	44		848	533	184	131	
1930	1,903	987	413	379	34	379	150	85	65	21	24	916	578	208	53	77
1925	1,903	924	391	365	26	331	144	77	67	58		979	646	203	130	
1920	1,903	956	402	374	28	328	168	77	91	58		947	661	160	126	
1910	1,903	879	347	324	23	284	191	98	93	57		1,024	739	162	123	
1900	1,903	889	319	(1)	(1)	276	191	87	103	54		1,064	768	175	121	
1890	1,903	623	248	(1)	(1)	144	190	(1)	(1)	41		1,280	818	344	118	
1880	1,903	536	188	(1)	(1)	122	190	(1)	(1)	36		1,367	883	368	116	
1870	1,903	408	189	(1)	(1)	-------	219	(1)	(1)	(1)		1,495	(1)	(1)	(1)	
1860	1,903	407	163	(1)	(1)	-------	244	(1)	(1)	(1)		1,496	(1)	(1)	(1)	
1850	1,884	294	113	(1)	(1)	-------	181	(1)	(1)	(1)		1,590	(1)	(1)	(1)	

¹ Not available.

Series J 65–79. Private and Public Land Ownership, by Major Uses: 1920 to 1954

[In millions of acres]

Year	Total land area					Private land					Public land				
	All land	Crop-land	Pasture and grazing land	Forest and wood-land not grazed	Other land	Total	Crop-land	Pasture and grazing land	Forest and wood-land not grazed	Other land	Total	Crop-land	Pasture and grazing land	Forest and wood-land not grazed	Other land
	65	66	67	68	69	70	71	72	73	74	75	76	77	78	79
1954	1,904	399	1,000	314	191	1,399	396	704	211	88	505	3	296	103	103
1950	1,904	409	1,020	286	189	1,399	405	724	184	86	505	4	296	102	103
1945	1,905	403	1,052	265	185	1,396	401	748	156	91	509	2	304	109	94
1940	1,905	399	1,065	260	181	1,404	398	766	150	90	501	1	299	110	91
1930	1,903	413	1,042	273	175	1,409	411	745	168	85	494	2	297	105	90
1920	1,903	402	1,066	251	184	1,404	401	766	145	92	499	1	300	106	92

Series J 80–90. Land Drainage and Irrigation: 1890 to 1954

[In thousands of acres, except number of farms]

Year	Drainage, United States, acreage in drainage enterprises				Irrigation, United States		Irrigation, 17 Western States [2]			Irrigation, 31 Eastern States [2]	
	Total	Improved land	Unimproved land	Cropland planted	Total acreage irrigated [1]	Number of farms with irrigated land	Land in irrigated farms	Total acreage irrigated [1]	Number of farms with irrigated land	Total acreage irrigated [1]	Number of farms with irrigated land
	80	81	82	83	84	85	86	87	88	89	90
1954					29,552	320,236	188,898	26,971	279,896	2,581	40,340
1950	[3] 102,688	[4] 82,138	[4] 20,550		25,787	305,061	166,074	24,271	281,476	1,516	23,585
1945					20,539	288,195		19,431	270,629	1,108	17,566
1940	86,967	67,389	19,578	49,614	17,983	299,604	110,942	17,243	283,089	740	16,515
1935								12,441	281,910		
1930	84,408	63,514	20,894	54,428	14,689		77,083	14,086	258,463	[5] 603	
1920	65,495	44,288	21,207		14,482			[6] 13,883	215,152	[5] 599	
1910					11,667			[6] 11,259	159,801	[5] 408	
1900					7,789			7,543	109,298	246	
1890					3,717			3,632	54,136	85	

[1] Acreage irrigated as reported by the agricultural census for the year preceding the date of the census.
[2] Excludes data for 17 States prior to 1920 as some States had not yet been admitted to the Union.
[3] Includes 4,110,000 acres reported drained by irrigation enterprises.
[4] Estimate based on increase in acreage of improved land, 1930 to 1940, and increase in acreage of land in drainage enterprises, 1940 to 1950.
[5] Arkansas and Louisiana. Data for the other 29 Eastern States not available.
[6] Data for 1910 and 1920 for the 17 Western States are interpolated from censuses of irrigation for these years.

Series J 91–102. Water Use: 1900 to 1955

[In billions of gallons, daily average]

Year	Total water use		Irrigation [1]		Public water supplies		Self-supplied use					
							Domestic [2]		Industrial and miscellaneous [3]		Steam electric power	
	Total	Ground	Total	Ground	Total	Ground	Total	Ground	Total	Ground	Total	Ground
	91	92	93	94	95	96	97	98	99	100	101	102
1955	263.80	47.79	116.30	29.08	16.30	4.27	5.40	4.91	49.20	9.45	76.60	0.08
1950	202.70	35.19	100.00	19.80	14.10	3.78	4.60	4.09	38.10	7.47	45.90	0.05
1946	165.74	27.88	86.44	15.04	12.00	3.25	3.50	3.06	33.00	6.50	30.80	0.03
1945	170.46	28.33	83.06	14.12	12.00	3.28	3.20	2.78	41.00	8.12	31.20	0.03
1944	178.43	29.19	80.65	13.55	12.00	3.30	3.18	2.76	48.00	9.55	34.60	0.03
1940	136.43	22.56	71.03	11.22	10.10	2.82	3.10	2.64	29.00	5.86	23.20	0.02
1930	110.50	18.18	60.20	9.09	8.00	2.30	2.90	2.40	21.00	4.37	18.40	0.02
1920	91.54	15.78	55.94	8.17	6.00	1.79	2.40	1.94	18.00	3.87	9.20	0.01
1910	66.44	11.68	39.04	5.27	4.70	1.49	2.20	1.76	14.00	3.15	6.50	0.01
1900	40.19	7.28	20.19	2.22	3.00	1.05	2.00	1.60	10.00	2.40	5.00	0.01

[1] For agricultural purposes only. Includes delivery losses but not reservoir evaporation.
[2] Nonfarm domestic and farm domestic and farm stock wells.
[3] Manufacturing industry, mineral industry, commercial, air conditioning, resorts, motels, military, and miscellaneous.

Series J 103–108. Water Wells in Use: 1900 to 1955

[In thousands]

Year	Total	Domestic wells		Public water supplies	Industrial and miscellaneous	Irrigation	Year	Total	Domestic wells		Public water supplies	Industrial and miscellaneous	Irrigation
		Farm	Nonfarm						Farm	Nonfarm			
	103	104	105	106	107	108		103	104	105	106	107	108
1955	13,730	5,248	8,035	28	278	142	1925	9,265	5,139	3,952	13	105	55
1950	12,766	5,620	6,800	23	216	107	1920	8,844	5,080	3,600	12	100	53
1945	11,273	6,063	4,943	22	170	75	1915	8,104	4,712	3,244	10	92	45
1940	10,362	5,935	4,200	18	144	65	1910	7,336	4,305	2,900	9	84	38
1935	9,843	5,457	4,195	16	115	60	1905	7,046	4,038	2,898	9	75	26
1930	9,601	5,220	4,200	15	110	56	1900	6,866	3,975	2,800	7	67	17

CLIMATE (Series J 109–265)

J 109–265. General note.

Climate may be defined as the statistical summary of the state of the atmosphere at a given place for a given period of time. However, each element of this definition deserves comment.

The "state" of the atmosphere properly includes many weather elements in addition to the most influential ones like temperature, precipitation, and wind; not all of these are given much attention, nor have they been adequately measured throughout the United States. Virtually every human pursuit finds itself sensitive to one or more factors of its climatic environment, particularly when and where they range beyond critical limits as, for example, the freezing temperature of water.

In view of the significance of ranges of climatic elements, mere arithmetic averages are usually unsatisfactory in specifying the state of the atmosphere, although the description of climate in much of the Nation has had to be so limited. Fully as significant, if less convenient to summarize, are the probability distribution and extreme values of individual weather elements, the joint frequency distributions of two or more elements, and certain specialized indices involving many elements.

Climate often differs significantly in a surprisingly short distance through the air or along the ground and a rather careful definition of the "place" to which an observed climate refers is required. The collection of climatological statistics is, therefore, essentially a sampling process, and in many respects existing statistics should be taken as indicative rather than definitive.

Climate is known to be changing irregularly. The numerical description of climate thus depends somewhat on the period of history over which weather statistics are compiled. A standard climatological period has been defined by the World Meteorological Organization to consist of the 30 years ending with the most recent decade year. At present, the standard period includes 1921 to 1950. Averages over this period are defined as *normals*; averages over other periods should properly be called by other names.

The longest climatological series in the United States are not homogeneous, and no exact statistical methods exist for making them so. (A homogeneous series is one which refers to the same "place" or to equivalent places throughout the period of record, and whose sampling bias is randomly distributed in time around its average bias which, in turn, need not equal zero.) These long series, widely published in the past without qualifying notes, must therefore be used with discrimination.

The representativeness and hence utility of all climatological series is more or less constrained by a variety of sampling and data-processing uncertainties. (See Charles F. Brooks, *The Climatic Record: Its Content, Limitations, and Geographic Value*, Annals of the Association of American Geographers, vol. XXXVIII, No. 3, 1948, pp. 153-168.) Observed climate at a point is valuable merely as a sample of the climate of other points in the surrounding region. Typically, this region is nonuniform in geographical character, and the sample is complexly biased. Even today, with the best

coverage by climatological stations in the history of the United States, the average temperature station must represent over 500 square miles of land surface. (Precipitation stations now average one in about 300 square miles; "first-order" Weather Bureau stations with observations of most other elements average one in about 10,000 square miles.) This sampling density is insufficient to interpolate the climate of every hamlet and bean patch; it is, however, more than sufficient to indicate relative *variations* of temperature, precipitation, and certain other elements from one year (or decade) to another because simultaneous departures of these from their normals are closely parallel over large areas. For this reason, homogeneous series for one station may reflect satisfactorily the historical variations of climate over 10,000 or even 100,000 square miles, while surely not the climate itself.

Many factors operate to compromise the homogeneity of typical climatic series. These chiefly derive from observational practice which, being flexibly geared to ever-changing requirements, has never been well adapted to the special application of historical comparison of climate. The longest series to which so much attention has traditionally been given have exclusively come from stations within slowly expanding cities. This fact has introduced warming trends in temperature and complex changes in precipitation which are not representative of their rural surroundings. Also, the occasional need to move stations to new locations with their slightly different climates has blemished their combined record with discontinuities.

Changes in daily observation time and in exposure of instruments have caused further discontinuities; this problem is especially acute in records prior to the establishment of standardized Weather Bureau practices in these respects in the 1880's. Other sources of inhomogeneity derive from neglect of occasionally missing daily records in forming monthly averages, and from familiar human errors in instrument reading, observation copying, editing, computing, and printing. These have been reduced since 1948 by better universal quality control methods but cannot be eliminated entirely.

Virtually all "first-order" Weather Bureau stations had been located (and relocated) in cities until recent years when (at various times since the 1930's) many were transferred to nearby airports. Resulting discontinuities in their records can rarely be corrected for; in some published versions of the records wherein corrections were attempted, insufficient details of the methods are given by which to judge their merits.

Only 2 or 3 percent of the city stations have remained in one location for their full history. (See station histories in Weather Bureau, *Local Climatological Data*, published annually for each station.) Many cooperative stations staffed by uncompensated cooperative Weather Bureau observers, on the other hand, are beyond range of major city influences on climate; some can be found which have not been significantly moved since their inception. Moreover, the *per se* climatological basis of their program has ensured against its repeated disruption for the convenience of other programs.

"Climatological benchmark network." Since less than one percent of the total reporting network, suitably distributed, would be sufficient for sampling historical variations of climate in the Nation, it is potentially possible to select a network

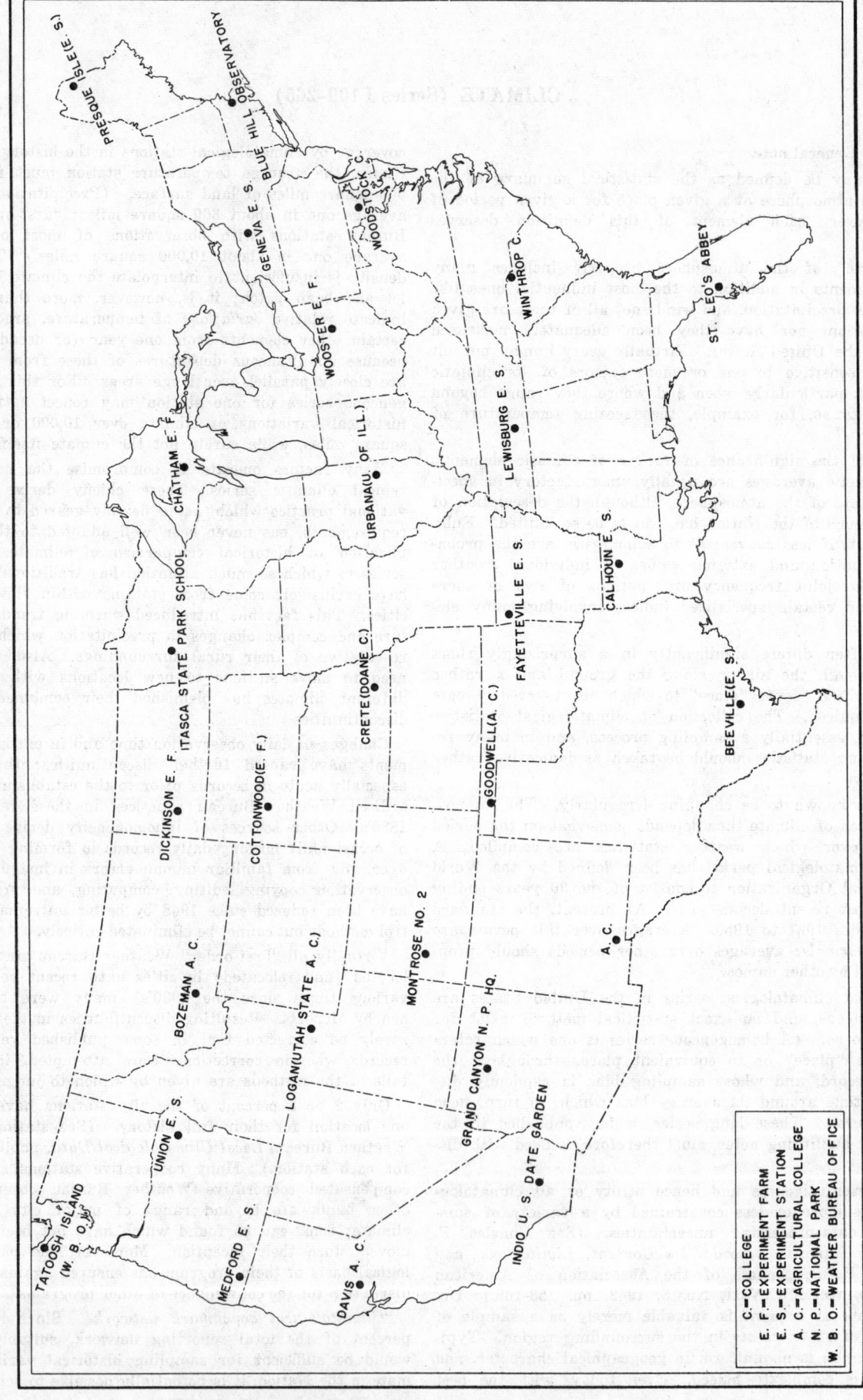

Fig. I. Climatological Benchmark Station Network

C = COLLEGE
E. F. = EXPERIMENT FARM
E. S. = EXPERIMENT STATION
A. C. = AGRICULTURAL COLLEGE
N. P. = NATIONAL PARK
W. B. O. = WEATHER BUREAU OFFICE

in which each station not only (1) possesses fairly long and unbroken records, but also (2) has suffered few if any relocations of instruments, (3) has a good ground exposure little influenced by environmental changes such as city growth or sheltering trees, and (4) is preferably operated by a public or private agency which, by reason of its own interest in the data, will ensure future perpetuation of the station.

A network which comes as nearly as possible to meeting these requirements is the "Climatological benchmark network." Twenty-eight continental stations in the network presented here have thus far been chosen on a tentative basis; others will be added in the future. The best qualified are among those maintained by Federal or State agencies (parks, forests, experiment stations, reclamation projects, etc.), colleges and universities, religious organizations, and public utility companies. Most of them are at agricultural colleges and agricultural experiment stations.

The program now in progress of checking benchmark station records should, in the future, minimize the drawback of relatively low quality control. While the drawback of limited variety of measured elements at cooperative stations generally remains, it is pertinent to add that the records of the larger variety of elements at first-order stations are irretrievably blemished by the effects of many station moves, changes in observational routine, and local city growth. Historical series based on such records must always be suspect.

The latitude, longitude, and altitude of the benchmark stations are given in table 1. The choice of stations to use in a particular data application may be facilitated by figure I.

Table I. Climatological Benchmark Stations

[Abbreviations: A. C.—Agricultural College; E. F.—Experiment Farm; E. S.—Experiment Station; N. P.—National Park; WBO—Weather Bureau Office; and Obs.—Observatory]

Station	Latitude	Longitude	Altitude
Northeast:			
Blue Hill Obs., Mass	42° 13′	71° 07′	640
Geneva E. S., N. Y	42° 53′	77° 00′	615
Presque Isle E. S., Maine	46° 39′	68° 00′	606
North Central:			
Chatham E. F., Mich	46° 21′	86° 56′	875
Cottonwood E. F., S. Dak	43° 58′	101° 52′	2,414
Crete (Doane College), Nebr	40° 37′	96° 57′	1,368
Dickinson E. F., N. Dak	46° 53′	102° 48′	2,460
Itasca State Park School, Minn	47° 13′	95° 13′	1,500
Urbana (U. of Ill.), Ill	40° 06′	88° 14′	743
Wooster E. F., Ohio	40° 47′	81° 56′	1,030
The South:			
Beeville E. S., Tex	28° 27′	97° 42′	225
Calhoun E. S., La	32° 31′	92° 20′	180
Fayetteville E. S., Ark	36° 06′	94° 10′	1,270
Goodwell A. C., Okla	36° 36′	101° 39′	3,300
Lewisburg E. S., Tenn	35° 27′	86° 48′	787
St. Leo's Abbey, Fla	28° 20′	82° 15′	178
Winthrop College, S. C	34° 57′	81° 03′	690
Woodstock College, Md	39° 20′	76° 52′	415
The West:			
Agricultural College, N. Mex	32° 17′	106° 45′	3,909
Bozeman A. C., Mont	45° 40′	111° 00′	4,856
Davis A. C., Calif	38° 32′	121° 45′	51
Grand Canyon N. P. Hdq., Ariz	36° 03′	112° 08′	6,890
Indio U. S. Date Garden, Calif	33° 43′	116° 15′	11
Logan (Utah State A. C.), Utah	41° 44′	111° 49′	4,775
Medford E. S., Oreg	42° 18′	122° 52′	1,457
Montrose No. 2, Colo	38° 29′	107° 53′	5,830
Tatoosh Island (W.B.O.), Wash	48° 23′	124° 44′	101
Union E. S., Oreg	45° 13′	117° 53′	2,765

It is anticipated that application of these data will be attempted in both correlation studies and trend analyses. The first kind of application, in which temporary deviations of climate are related to those of other statistical series, is a sound one to be encouraged where appropriate. The second application, to the extent that trends of general climate are derived with high quantitative precision and related to trends in other statistics, is not recommended, however.

Long-period trends in homogeneous climatic series are usually small and irregular. Because there are many opportunities for observational inhomogeneities to introduce trends and discontinuities into climatic series, which are not characteristic of the climate at large, real trends in the latter are easily distorted or obscured. Not even the "climatological benchmark" data are above all reproach in this respect.

Concerning climatic trends, it is important to realize that in many instances they could readily be duplicated fortuitously in random number series of equal variance. While this obviously means that statistically observed climatic trends cannot be extrapolated into past or future time reliably, they are nonetheless capable of inducing important trends in concurrent climate-dependent series.

Monthly and annual values of average temperature and total precipitation can most conveniently be found in the following official Weather Bureau publications:

Local Climatological Data, annual summary. This is issued annually for each of approximately 280 stations. With few exceptions, these are first-order Weather Bureau city and/or airport stations. The contents partially include normal values of temperature and precipitation, and comparative data for each month and year back to 1900 or the beginning of record, whichever is later. They also include a station history giving the various station locations and elevations of instruments.

Climatological Data, annual summary. This bulletin is issued annually by climatological sections. In most instances, a section is a State. Nearly all cooperative climatological stations as well as first-order Weather Bureau stations are included. This publication was founded in the 1880's, but was included as part of the Weather Bureau *Monthly Weather Review* from 1911 to 1913, inclusive.

Climatic Summary of the United States (Bulletin "W"). Monthly and annual series of total precipitation at all stations and mean temperature at selected (first-order) stations are also contained in this publication. Values from the beginning of record up through 1930 are given by geographical sections in the earlier Bulletin, published in the early 1930's. Values for later years are given in *Climatic Summary of the United States—Supplement for 1931 Through 1952*, by States, published variously since 1954.

Length-of-record series of monthly and annual temperature, pressure, and precipitation up to 1940 may also be found in H. H. Clayton (ed.), *World Weather Records*, Smithsonian Miscellaneous Collections, vol. 79 (1944), vol. 90 (1944), and vol. 105 (1947). A new volume by the Weather Bureau will bring the series up through 1950. Some station history information is included, and records are listed for nearly 50 Weather Bureau stations in the United States. Temperature data are corrected for differences in daily observation time, and, being reduced to 24-hour means, differ somewhat in value from the same data appearing in Weather Bureau publications.

For daily data on extreme values, or on elements other than temperature and precipitation, see monthly editions of *Climatological Data* and, since 1948, *Local Climatological Data*.

J 109–135. Climatological benchmark stations—normal monthly, seasonal, and annual temperature.

Source: **Series J 109–131, J 133–135,** Weather Bureau, unpublished records (figures computed from monthly temperature data in *Climatological Data*). **Series J 132,** *Local Climatological Data*, annual editions. (Data for series J 110 appear in *Local Climatological Data*, but the temperatures there have been adjusted to values based on 24 daily observations and so are incompatible with other temperature data for that station given here.)

Nearly all weather stations have been moved several times in their history (see general note, above). Consequently, the Weather Bureau has adopted the practice of using "normal" values of temperature and precipitation for comparative purposes rather than long-term means which are derived from records taken at the several different locations the stations may have had over the years.

Normal values of temperature and precipitation are based on records for the 30-year period 1921 to 1950, inclusive. Where a station had a record for the entire 30 years from the same instrument site, monthly precipitation normals are the mean of the monthly values for the 30 years. For such stations, the temperature normals were obtained in a similar manner, using normal maximum and normal minimum values to obtain monthly normals. The annual normal temperature is obtained by dividing the sum of the annual normal maximum value and the annual normal minimum value for temperature by 2.

For stations that did not have continuous records from the same instrument site for the entire 30 years, 1921 to 1950, the means have been adjusted to the record at the present site. In these adjustments, a "difference factor" was used for temperature and a "ratio factor" for precipitation. These factors were determined by parallel comparison, either between records at the actual station sites or through a second station that had a continuous record to compare against both sites for obtaining the resultant adjusting factors. Normals were thereafter obtained as outlined above.

This system of normals has three characteristics: (1) The 30-year period (1921 to 1950) adopted for the computations is consistent with the term of years accepted by the World Meteorological Organization for climatic normals; (2) where the station and exposure for records in a given locality have been changed, the whole record has been carefully studied and adjusted to the latest source of records and reports; (3) the normals for maximum and minimum temperatures are separately tabulated and made available for the first time.

See also general note for series J 109–265.

J 136–162. Climatological benchmark stations—normal monthly, seasonal, and annual precipitation.

Source: See source for series J 109–135.

See also text for series J 109–135.

J 163–245. Climatological benchmark stations—temperature, precipitation, and description of year, 1884–1957.

Source: Weather Bureau, *Climatological Data*, annual summary.

The description of the year is given by three digits; the first digit applies to the year as a whole, the second applies to the summer season (June, July, and August), and the third applies to the winter season (December *of the previous year,* January, and February). The following code defines the meaning of each digit:

Code	Temperature	Precipitation
1	In warmest quartile	In wettest quartile
2	Near normal	In wettest quartile
3	In coldest quartile	In wettest quartile
4	In warmest quartile	Near normal
5	Near normal	Near normal
6	In coldest quartile	Near normal
7	In warmest quartile	In driest quartile
8	Near normal	In driest quartile
9	In coldest quartile	In driest quartile

For example, a code 5–1–9 indicates that, for a particular year and station, the annual mean temperature and annual total precipitation were both near normal (i.e., not within either extreme quartile of their distributions in the normal 1921–1950 period); but that the summer season was unusually warm and wet, while the winter season was unusually cold and dry.

Smoothed ogives of the distribution of average values in the 30-year normal period were used to obtain the upper and lower quartile limits of temperature and precipitation for each season and for the year as a whole. Any given quartile therefore separates approximately one-quarter of the number of years in the normal period, but probably more or less than one-quarter of the total years in any full length-of-record series owing to the presence of climatic trends or variations.

J 246–265. Long-record city stations—annual mean temperature and annual total precipitation, 1780–1957.

Source: Series J 246, J 247, J 250–255, J 257–265, 1780–1940, H. H. Clayton (ed.), *World Weather Records*, Smithsonian Miscellaneous Collections, vol. 79 (1944), vol. 90 (1944), vol. 105 (1947); 1941–1950, Weather Bureau, *World Weather Records*, 1941–1950 (forthcoming); 1951–1957, Weather Bureau, *Local Climatological Data* (corrected to 24-hour means), annual editions. Series J 248, J 249, and J 256, *Local Climatological Data* and *Climatic Summary of the United States*, annual editions.

The series for city stations selected for presentation here are among the longest existing climatological series for the United States. They were selected with the realization that they are not homogeneous, but have comparative value in the earlier years and have been less frequently affected by changes of station location. The series, however, are not adjusted for known station changes, and coming as they do from growing cities, they contain climatic trends which in part are typical only of major metropolitan centers.

Each long-record station has suffered several changes of location and exposure of instruments. The following station history notes are extracted from the annual editions of *Local Climatological Data*, and indicate all known changes likely to have affected the temperature and/or precipitation records. The history of each station prior to the date of establishment by the Federal weather service is essentially unknown; occasional exposure changes in earlier years undoubtedly occurred whose effects, although significant, may never be discovered.

Records for 2 of the 10 stations shown refer in recent years to airport locations; the observation program in New Haven city terminated in 1943, and that in St. Paul-Minneapolis terminated in 1937. With one exception, all other records are continuously available from city locations although the major part of Weather Bureau activities in each case has been transferred to airport stations. The exception is Santa Fe, where interpolations have been required to complete the city record in recent years.

In the following notes, "temperature means" indicate the combination of hourly temperature readings each day which were averaged together to form means. For example, 1/3 (7, 15, 21) indicates an average of readings at 7 a.m., 3 p.m., and 9 p.m. local standard time. The formula 1/3 (7:35, 16:35, 23) was in general use for 1870–1879 (Nov.), and the formula 1/3 (7, 15, 23) for 1879–1888, the times referring to the 75th meridian (Washington). Since about 1888, however, daily maximum and minimum temperatures, observed with special registering thermometers, have been averaged to obtain means.

Numbers in parentheses refer to elevations of the thermometers and rain gauge, respectively; the example (51/70) indicates the thermometers were 51 feet above ground, and the rain gauge funnel was 70 feet above ground (roof exposures). Asterisks indicate that heights are estimated from circumstantial information; a question mark indicates unknown.

Albany, N.Y. Temperature means: 1795–1796, unknown; 1813–1814, 1/3 (7, 15, 21); 1820–1870, 1/3 (7, 14, 21). Station established by Army Signal Service in Dudley Heights December 1873 (11/ ?); instruments moved July 1874 (17/1). Station moved 1.3 miles W March 1880 (51/70), 400 feet E

October 1884 (80/100). Exposure changed July 1888 (84/99), October 1901 (102/100), October 1928 (107/100). Station moved 100 feet N April 1935 (97/88).

Baltimore, Md. Temperature means: 1817–1870, unknown. Station established December 1870 (34/69); thermometers relocated October 1885 (76/69). Station moved 0.1 mile January 1889 (86/78), 0.8 mile June 1891 (87/80), 0.7 mile September 1895 (120/116), 0.6 mile August 1896 (69/73), 0.8 mile January 1908 (100/91). Recording instruments only after July 1949 (100/90).

Charleston, S. C. 1738–1861, discontinuous records by various doctors. Temperature means: 1823–1872, unknown. Station established January 1871 (40/57); thermometers moved January 1886 (60/55). Station moved 0.2 mile N February 1897 (11/76); rain gauge moved July 1932 (11/3); thermometers moved August 1949 (6/3).

New Haven, Conn. Temperature means: 1780–1865, unknown but corrected to 24 hours; 1866–1872, unknown, monthly temperatures available to whole degrees only. Station established December 1872 (85/109); instruments moved February 1881 (118/110). Station moved 600 feet E March 1919 (74/68). City station closed and observations taken over by airport station 4 miles SE July 1943 (4/3).

New York, N. Y. (Central Park). 1822–1864, records from Jamaica, N.Y.; 1865–1868, records from 86th St. Reservoir, N. Y. Temperature means: 1822–1842, 1/3 (7, 14, 21); 1843–1870, 1/4 (Sunrise, 9, 15, 21). Station established December 1868 (61/64); moved 1 mile N January 1920 (6/22).

Philadelphia, Pa. Temperature means: 1825–1870, unknown. Station established December 1870 (?/?); moved 0.3 mile E September 1871 (100*/91), 0.7 mile W February 1882 (54*/106*), 0.1 mile E April 1884 (169/167). Instruments moved February 1904 (117/114); thermometers moved January 1914 (124/114). Station moved 0.6 mile E December 1934 (175/166).

San Francisco, Calif. Temperature means: 1851–1853, 1/4 (Sunrise, 9,15,21); 1854, 1/3 (9,12,21); 1857–1859, 1/3 (7,14, 21); 1861–1868, 1/4 (7,14,21 weighted twice). Station estab-

lished February 1871 (48/75); moved 0.5 mile SW September 1890 (109/101), 0.3 mile NE November 1892 (161/154), 3.1 miles W May 1906 (29/40), 3.0 miles E October 1906 (200/191). Instruments moved October 1914 (209/200). Station moved 1.0 mile SW May 1936 (112/104). Temperature probably affected at times by nearby ventilators April 1919–May 1936.

Santa Fe, N. Mex. Temperature means: 1849–1854, 1/4 (Sunrise, 9,15,21); 1855–1872, 1/3 (7,14,21). Station established November 1871 (30*/27*); moved March 1878 (5*/2*), March 1882 (50*/50*), November 1884 (35*/32*), January 1892 (53*/50*), March 1893 (42*/39*), July 1907 (5*/2*), April 1912 (52*/49*), March 1922 (34*/31*). Continued as cooperative station 0.5 mile NE September 1941 (39*/36*). Instruments moved May 1942 (5*/2*), October 1942 (23*/20*). Station moved about 1 mile SE May 1944, few hundred feet NW July 1947, 1 mile SE October 1950, about 0.3 mile NW October 1951, few hundred feet March 1954, and 1.5 miles SE May 1955. Ground exposures, approximately (5/2), at last six locations.

St. Louis, Mo. Temperature means: 1836–1870, unknown but corrected to 24 hours. Station established October 1870 (70/93). Several suspected changes of thermometer exposure; station then moved 0.2 mile WNW March 1873 (105/100), 250 feet E August 1903 (208/199), 300 feet E September 1913 (264/258), 0.4 mile SW November 1935 (179/172).

St. Paul, Minn. Records from Fort Snelling 1820–1855, from Minneapolis 1856–1858. Temperature means: 1820–1858, unknown; 1859–1870, 1/4 (7,14,21 weighted twice). Station established November 1870 (30/36); moved 0.2 mile WSW December 1871 (34/44), 0.2 mile ENE April 1878 (33/58), 0.2 mile NE April 1883 (45/61), 0.2 mile NNW July 1885 (103/92), 0.1 mile SE July 1904 (171/162). Instruments moved January 1911 (201/195), July 1918 (237/227). Station moved 0.3 mile W April 1931 (114/106). Record July 1933–April 1937 8.8 miles WNW at Minneapolis City (102/91); April 1937–December 1955 7.5 miles SSE at Minneapolis–St. Paul International Airport (43/40).

Series J 109–135. Climatological Benchmark Stations—Normal Monthly, Seasonal, and Annual Temperatures

[In Fahrenheit degrees. Figures are "normal" values based on records for the 30-year period 1921–1950; see text. Record for Medford Experiment Station, Oreg., too short to obtain normals]

Series No.	Station	January	February	March	April	May	June	July	August	September	October	November	December	Summer	Winter	Annual
	NORTHEAST															
109	Blue Hill Observatory, Mass	26.4	26.4	35.1	45.1	56.3	65.2	70.5	69.1	62.5	52.3	41.4	29.6	68.2	27.5	48.3
110	Geneva Experiment Station, N. Y.	26.5	26.2	34.9	46.1	57.7	67.6	72.3	70.3	63.8	52.2	40.9	29.5	70.1	27.4	49.0
111	Presque Isle Experiment Station, Maine	11.5	12.5	23.1	35.2	50.8	60.4	66.0	63.6	55.2	43.1	30.4	17.0	63.3	13.6	39.1
	NORTH CENTRAL															
112	Chatham Experiment Farm, Mich	16.6	16.8	24.8	37.4	47.8	59.8	65.4	63.6	54.3	44.2	32.4	21.3	62.9	18.2	40.4
113	Cottonwood Experiment Farm, S. Dak	18.8	23.0	33.1	46.6	56.8	66.7	75.1	73.2	62.5	49.9	34.3	23.3	71.7	21.7	46.9
114	Crete (Doane College), Nebr	24.8	29.6	39.9	52.8	62.4	72.5	78.7	76.9	68.2	56.3	39.8	28.7	76.0	27.7	52.6
115	Dickinson Experiment Farm, N. Dak	10.4	13.5	25.7	41.3	52.6	61.5	69.4	66.5	55.9	44.1	27.9	15.7	65.8	13.2	40.4
116	Itasca State Park School, Minn	5.8	9.5	21.9	38.9	51.7	61.2	67.1	64.3	53.4	43.7	26.0	11.6	64.2	9.0	37.9
117	Urbana (U. of Ill.), Ill	27.9	31.1	40.3	51.5	61.9	71.6	76.1	73.8	67.1	56.0	41.5	30.7	73.8	29.9	52.4
118	Wooster Experiment Farm, Ohio	28.2	29.3	37.7	48.1	58.6	68.4	72.3	70.4	64.4	52.9	40.7	30.5	70.3	29.3	50.1
	THE SOUTH															
119	Beeville Experiment Station, Tex	55.1	58.9	64.5	71.3	77.0	81.7	83.8	84.3	80.3	73.4	63.5	57.3	83.3	57.1	70.9
120	Calhoun Experiment Station, La	48.4	51.8	57.6	65.4	72.2	79.8	82.3	82.5	77.4	66.7	56.2	49.9	81.5	50.0	65.8
121	Fayetteville Experiment Station, Ark	38.2	42.0	49.2	59.4	66.0	74.9	79.0	78.8	71.7	61.3	48.8	40.8	77.6	40.3	59.2
122	Goodwell Agricultural College, Okla	34.5	39.1	42.2	55.4	64.3	74.6	79.2	78.2	68.1	56.9	43.3	36.6	77.3	36.7	56.0
123	Lewisburg Experiment Station, Tenn	40.3	42.7	49.8	59.0	67.0	75.7	78.7	77.7	72.4	60.5	48.6	41.7	77.4	41.6	59.5
124	St. Leo's Abbey, Fla	61.2	62.8	66.2	71.2	76.1	80.0	80.9	81.4	79.8	73.7	66.0	62.0	80.8	62.0	71.8
125	Winthrop College, S. C	44.4	46.5	53.0	61.5	69.8	77.6	79.4	77.9	73.7	63.3	52.4	44.8	78.3	45.2	62.0
126	Woodstock College, Md	33.4	34.2	43.0	52.2	62.5	71.0	74.8	73.0	66.9	55.3	44.9	34.9	72.9	34.2	53.8
	THE WEST															
127	Agricultural College, N. Mex	40.3	45.7	51.1	58.9	67.1	76.0	79.1	77.2	71.3	60.8	47.7	41.6	77.4	42.5	59.7
128	Bozeman Agricultural College, Mont	19.4	23.5	30.7	42.2	51.0	57.5	66.1	64.6	54.8	45.1	31.8	23.4	62.7	22.1	42.5
129	Davis Agricultural College, Calif	44.4	49.2	53.4	58.1	64.4	70.8	75.0	73.1	70.1	62.4	52.8	45.6	73.0	46.4	59.9
130	Grand Canyon National Park Headquarters, Ariz	29.5	32.8	38.6	46.8	55.6	64.7	70.2	67.7	62.2	51.0	39.7	32.5	67.5	31.6	49.3
131	Indio U. S. Date Garden, Calif	54.1	58.8	64.8	71.9	79.2	86.3	92.0	90.6	85.3	74.7	63.0	55.6	89.6	56.2	73.0
132	Logan (Utah State Agricultural College), Utah	22.8	28.8	37.2	47.9	56.7	64.4	73.7	72.0	62.4	51.1	36.7	27.5	70.0	26.4	48.4
133	Montrose No. 2, Colo	24.8	31.5	39.1	48.7	57.8	66.9	72.7	70.3	62.5	51.0	37.0	28.0	70.0	28.1	49.2
134	Tatoosh Island (Weather Bureau Office), Wash	42.0	43.2	44.7	47.5	50.9	54.0	55.5	55.7	54.5	51.9	47.4	44.1	55.0	43.1	49.3
135	Union Experiment Station, Oreg	28.5	33.9	40.4	47.3	53.9	59.3	66.6	64.9	56.9	48.8	39.2	32.5	63.6	31.6	47.7

Series J 136–162. Climatological Benchmark Stations—Normal Monthly, Seasonal, and Annual Precipitation

[In inches. Figures are "normal" values based on records for the 30-year period 1921–1950; see text. Record for Medford Experiment Station, Oreg., too short to obtain normals]

Series No.	Station	January	February	March	April	May	June	July	August	September	October	November	December	Summer	Winter	Annual
	NORTHEAST															
136	Blue Hill Observatory, Mass	4.09	3.58	3.86	3.99	3.49	4.17	3.71	4.05	3.77	3.44	4.20	3.92	11.93	11.54	46.22
137	Geneva Experiment Station, N. Y	2.37	2.30	2.69	2.89	3.10	3.51	3.18	2.76	2.80	2.75	2.89	2.36	9.45	7.03	33.60
138	Presque Isle Experiment Station, Maine	1.91	1.41	1.97	2.19	2.83	3.66	3.65	3.29	3.31	3.35	2.81	2.11	10.60	5.43	32.49
	NORTH CENTRAL															
139	Chatham Experiment Farm, Mich	2.28	1.65	1.71	1.90	2.89	3.61	3.23	2.98	3.98	2.94	3.05	2.09	9.82	6.02	32.31
140	Cottonwood Experiment Farm, S. Dak	0.43	0.24	0.77	1.72	2.48	2.92	1.91	1.49	0.92	0.96	0.45	0.32	6.32	0.99	14.61
141	Crete (Doane College), Nebr	0.69	0.86	1.41	2.30	3.72	4.38	3.09	3.32	2.97	1.64	1.35	0.74	10.79	2.29	26.47
142	Dickinson Experiment Farm, N. Dak	0.51	0.41	0.72	1.32	2.08	3.93	2.06	1.39	1.30	0.94	0.62	0.47	7.38	1.39	15.75
143	Itasca State Park School, Minn	0.70	0.71	1.10	2.24	3.19	3.94	3.14	3.22	2.21	1.64	1.21	0.78	10.30	2.19	24.08
144	Urbana (U. of Ill.), Ill	2.23	1.90	3.55	3.91	4.15	4.35	3.12	3.55	3.75	3.10	2.73	2.32	11.02	6.45	38.66
145	Wooster Experiment Farm, Ohio	2.84	2.20	3.23	3.07	3.82	4.13	3.68	3.40	2.98	2.17	2.52	2.42	11.21	7.46	36.46
	THE SOUTH															
146	Beeville Experiment Station, Tex	2.13	1.60	2.44	2.19	3.35	3.13	3.29	2.00	3.59	2.24	1.94	2.73	8.42	6.46	30.63
147	Calhoun Experiment Station, La	5.75	4.69	5.19	5.04	4.86	3.34	4.28	2.83	2.48	3.33	4.36	6.12	10.45	16.56	52.27
148	Fayetteville Experiment Station, Ark	2.84	2.74	3.30	5.09	5.54	5.25	3.22	3.54	4.46	3.78	3.28	2.85	12.01	8.43	45.89
149	Goodwell Agricultural College, Okla	0.39	0.60	0.82	1.31	2.63	2.57	2.86	2.31	1.72	1.54	0.74	0.45	7.74	1.44	17.94
150	Lewisburg Experiment Station, Tenn	5.21	5.49	5.81	4.30	4.15	4.12	4.18	3.63	2.69	2.90	4.19	4.75	11.93	15.45	51.42
151	St. Leo's Abbey, Fla	2.24	2.57	3.86	2.94	4.33	9.01	9.08	7.74	7.57	3.79	1.39	2.17	25.83	6.98	56.69
152	Winthrop College, S. C	4.17	3.95	4.39	3.61	3.44	3.43	5.25	4.60	3.73	3.06	2.98	4.11	13.28	12.23	46.72
153	Woodstock College, Md	3.44	2.78	3.30	3.44	3.93	3.65	4.07	3.78	3.64	3.21	2.98	2.74	11.50	8.96	40.96
	THE WEST															
154	Agricultural College, N. Mex	0.41	0.41	0.31	0.19	0.42	0.50	1.47	1.71	1.37	0.74	0.43	0.56	3.68	1.38	8.52
155	Bozeman Agricultural College, Mont	0.93	0.77	1.40	1.62	2.30	2.86	1.33	1.20	1.69	1.42	1.18	0.94	5.39	2.64	17.64
156	Davis Agricultural College, Calif	2.89	3.21	2.14	1.36	0.50	0.15	0.00	0.00	0.06	0.88	1.61	3.17	0.15	9.27	15.97
157	Grand Canyon National Park Headquarters, Ariz	1.23	1.71	1.38	0.94	0.62	0.41	1.66	2.24	1.74	1.06	0.76	1.60	4.31	4.54	15.35
158	Indio U. S. Date Garden, Calif	0.42	0.48	0.25	0.15	0.04	0.02	0.11	0.31	0.45	0.30	0.21	0.88	0.44	1.78	3.62
159	Logan (Utah State Agricultural College), Utah	1.40	1.36	1.88	2.14	1.84	1.23	0.53	0.72	1.15	1.65	1.35	1.54	2.48	4.30	16.79
160	Montrose No. 2, Colo	0.52	0.51	0.82	0.92	0.91	0.55	0.84	1.29	1.08	0.92	0.53	0.60	2.68	1.63	9.49
161	Tatoosh Island (Weather Bureau Office), Wash	10.19	8.70	7.82	5.23	3.31	2.58	1.99	2.01	3.64	8.72	9.52	12.04	6.58	30.93	75.75
162	Union Experiment Station, Oreg	0.96	1.00	1.21	1.40	1.37	1.74	0.38	0.49	0.85	1.17	1.21	1.09	2.61	3.05	12.87

Series J 163–245. Climatological Benchmark Stations—Temperature, Precipitation, and Description of Year: 1884 to 1957

[Italicized figures are based on interpolated monthly values. Standard error of interpolated figures: For temperature, less than 1° F.; for precipitation, less than 0.5 inch]

	Northeast									North Central					
	Blue Hill Observatory, Mass.			Geneva Experiment Station, N. Y.			Presque Isle Experiment Station, Maine			Chatham Experiment Farm, Mich.			Cottonwood Experiment Farm, S. Dak.		
Year	Annual mean temperature	Annual total precipitation	Description¹ of year	Annual mean temperature	Annual total precipitation	Description¹ of year	Annual mean temperature	Annual total precipitation	Description¹ of year	Annual mean temperature	Annual total precipitation	Description¹ of year	Annual mean temperature	Annual total precipitation	Description¹ of year
	163	164	165	166	167	168	169	170	171	172	173	174	175	176	177
	°F.	Inches		°F.	Inches		°F.	Inches		°F.	Inches		°F.	Inches	
1957	50	35.5	7-7-5	48	26.1	8-8-8	40	31.3	5-9-5	41	30.2	8-8-8	47	22.5	2-2-5
1956	48	59.2	2-8-2	47	34.2	6-6-6	39	30.8	5-6-4	41	*25.2*	8-5-7	48	14.6	5-4-2
1955	49	64.4	1-1-5	49	42.4	2-4-6	40	34.2	5-4-1	43	26.5	7-7-8	48	12.9	4-7-5
1954	49	57.4	2-6-4	48	29.2	8-8-7	40	52.4	2-3-1	42	32.2	5-8-4	49	13.0	4-8-4
1953	51	59.6	1-7-1	50	26.3	7-5-4	42	35.4	4-8-4	44	36.0	1-4-1	49	18.6	1-5-1
1952	50	39.8	7-7-1	49	31.6	5-8-4	41	36.4	4-4-1	43	31.7	4-1-7	47	16.7	5-5-3
1951	50	50.9	1-5-4	48	31.3	6-6-5	*41*	40.2	*2-2-1*	40	39.8	2-3-5	43	20.9	3-3-2
1950	49	42.0	8-8-4	47	36.9	6-6-1	41	37.4	2-2-4	38	33.3	6-6-5	44	11.9	6-9-6
1949	51	33.7	7-7-7	50	22.8	7-4-7	42	*33.5*	4-4-4	43	*37.7*	1-1-4	46	14.8	5-7-3
1948	48	47.8	5-5-3	49	32.9	5-5-9	40	31.0	5-8-9	40	27.3	8-8-9	46	17.0	5-3-8
1947	49	44.9	5-5-7	49	35.7	5-2-5	*41*	34.1	*4-4-1*	41	*34.5*	5-5-5	47	13.0	5-5-5
1946	50	42.0	7-3-3	50	29.6	7-6-8	41	31.2	4-8-5	42	29.0	8-6-5	49	17.8	1-5-7
1945	49	54.4	1-5-6	49	40.4	2-8-6	41	37.1	1-4-5	40	32.4	6-9-6	47	11.4	5-5-8
1944	49	45.6	4-4-8	50	32.1	5-4-8	41	30.4	7-7-8	42	33.1	5-5-7	*45*	12.9	*6-6-5*
1943	48	34.9	8-7-5	48	37.1	6-4-3	39	33.8	5-2-5	40	33.6	6-1-5	46	11.0	8-5-8
1942	48	46.3	5-6-5	50	38.9	2-8-5	41	28.0	7-5-4	42	32.8	4-8-7	47	19.3	2-6-8
1941	49	32.6	8-5-8	50	30.2	7-5-5	40	33.0	5-5-2	44	40.9	1-4-1	49	18.6	1-2-4
1940	46	45.0	6-9-6	47	36.9	6-5-3	39	36.9	3-2-5	41	38.4	2-5-1	47	9.8	8-5-2
1939	*48*	*37.8*	8-7-5	50	28.9	8-8-2	39	36.6	6-1-5	41	36.5	2-5-2	50	8.4	7-7-5
1938	49	58.5	1-1-5	50	35.2	4-1-5	*38*	33.4	6-2-9	42	34.1	4-5-2	48	14.9	4-8-5
1937	49	46.1	5-7-1	49	38.2	2-4-1	41	31.8	4-4-4	41	32.7	5-4-5	46	14.6	5-1-6
1936	47	59.1	3-6-3	49	30.1	8-8-6	39	44.0	2-6-2	40	25.5	9-8-3	47	7.1	8-7-3
1935	47	43.7	6-5-3	48	35.5	6-2-6	39	28.4	6-4-6	40	31.8	6-5-5	48	15.7	5-5-4
1934	47	41.2	9-9-6	48	23.4	9-8-6	38	36.4	6-3-3	*39*	32.6	6-9-6	51	12.0	4-4-4
1933	48	52.8	2-6-7	50	26.9	7-4-7	39	*32.5*	5-8-7	40	29.8	8-7-2	49	14.5	4-7-5
1932	49	48.9	4-5-4	50	40.5	1-5-1	40	34.0	5-5-7	41	40.9	2-2-4	46	17.3	5-5-2
1931	50	49.3	4-2-5	52	31.7	4-7-5	42	37.1	1-5-8	45	32.0	4-4-7	50	9.6	7-7-7
1930	49	41.3	7-4-5	50	26.8	8-5-5	41	*29.1*	8-1-5	*41*	26.9	*8-5-6*	48	23.0	2-2-2
1929	48	47.0	9-8-5	48	35.5	5-9-8	39	29.7	8-6-7	39	32.7	6-6-6	44	18.2	3-5-6
1928	48	46.8	5-2-5	49	33.5	5-2-2	*39*	36.7	*2-6-2*	40	36.1	2-6-5	*47*	14.0	5-3-5
1927	49	51.6	1-3-5	49	42.8	6-3-5	*39*	36.8	*2-6-3*	40	31.0	8-9-8	44	21.0	3-3-8
1926	46	48.9	6-6-5	46	36.2	6-3-5	37	*35.4*	6-9-2	38	37.8	3-6-5	47	13.5	5-5-1
1925	49	50.4	1-4-8	48	36.8	6-5-5	*38*	*43.6*	7-8-6	40	21.7	8-8-9	47	10.4	8-5-2
1924	47	42.8	9-5-2	46	32.2	6-6-8	38	24.6	9-9-5	*42*	*35.6*	*1-3-2*	44	11.2	9-6-5
1923	47	44.9	6-9-3	47	31.2	6-6-3	*37*	29.5	9-9-6	40	30.8	9-2-9	46	22.3	3-3-6
1922	48	54.0	2-1-9	49	39.8	2-2-5	39	33.7	5-2-5	*42*	*34.7*	*4-5-2*	44	22.4	3-2-3
1921	49	51.8	2-2-5	52	29.4	7-7-4	40	31.1	5-5-2	*43*	*32.0*	*4-4-8*	49	10.9	7-4-7
1920	46	63.8	3-3-3	48	37.2	6-2-5	39	43.6	2-2-6	*39*	*32.6*	6-5-9	46	19.4	3-5-5
1919	47	56.2	3-3-5	49	35.4	5-5-7	*38*	29.2	9-9-5	40	27.8	9-8-4	45	16.0	6-5-5
1918	47	44.9	6-6-6	48	34.4	6-6-6	*37*	*35.9*	6-3-3	39	*36.4*	3-6-9	46	15.0	5-5-6
1917	45	48.8	6-5-5	45	35.4	6-2-6	36	41.3	3-1-_	34	*30.3*	9-6-9	44	13.2	6-8-3
1916	46	45.5	6-3-5	48	*42.0*	5-5-2	--------	--------	--------	*38*	*41.9*	3-5-3	44	12.3	6-5-6
1915	48	44.0	5-3-2	48	*29.0*	5-6-5	--------	--------	--------	40	42.2	3-3-2	44	27.6	3-3-3
1914	46	40.3	9-6-5	48	*33.4*	5-5-9	--------	--------	--------	38	33.0	3-6-5	48	15.0	5-8-2
1913	49	45.1	4-8-4	*51*	*33.5*	4-8-4	--------	--------	--------	*39*	26.7	9-9-9	48	10.5	8-7-8
1912	47	40.4	9-9-9	--------	--------	--------	--------	--------	--------	36	27.0	9-9-6	*46*	14.1	6-5-2
1911	48	44.6	5-2-9	--------	--------	--------	--------	--------	--------	40	37.2	3-2-5	49	12.3	4-8-5
1910	48	34.3	8-8-5	--------	--------	--------	--------	--------	--------	40	27.9	9-8-3	*48*	*10.0*	8-8-3
1909	48	43.6	6-9-5	--------	--------	--------	--------	--------	--------	39	30.2	9-2-5	*47*	*6.6*	8-1-_
1908	49	37.7	8-4-2	--------	--------	--------	--------	--------	--------	41	27.6	8-8-5	--------	--------	--------
1907	46	47.6	6-9-6	--------	--------	--------	--------	--------	--------	37	29.3	9-9-3	--------	--------	--------
1906	48	45.5	5-6-4	--------	--------	--------	--------	--------	--------	40	30.7	9-5-2	--------	--------	--------
1905	46	39.4	9-6-6	--------	--------	--------	--------	--------	--------	38	33.4	6-6-3	--------	--------	--------
1904	45	46.2	6-9-6	--------	--------	--------	--------	--------	--------	37	32.5	6-6-6	--------	--------	--------
1903	47	46.8	6-6-2	--------	--------	--------	--------	--------	--------	40	39.1	2-6-2	--------	--------	--------
1902	48	42.7	6-9-2	--------	--------	--------	--------	--------	--------	40	34.8	5-6-2	--------	--------	--------
1901	47	54.0	3-4-9	--------	--------	--------	--------	--------	--------	41	42.0	2-5-8	--------	--------	--------
1900	49	48.1	5-7-5	--------	--------	--------	--------	--------	--------	*41*	*33.4*	5-_-_	--------	--------	--------
1899	48	40.6	8-8-5	--------	--------	--------	--------	--------	--------	--------	--------	--------	--------	--------	--------
1898	48	58.7	2-2-5	--------	--------	--------	--------	--------	--------	--------	--------	--------	--------	--------	--------
1897	47	45.4	6-6-8	--------	--------	--------	--------	--------	--------	--------	--------	--------	--------	--------	--------
1896	47	47.4	6-6-5	--------	--------	--------	--------	--------	--------	--------	--------	--------	--------	--------	--------
1895	47	46.2	6-9-9	--------	--------	--------	--------	--------	--------	--------	--------	--------	--------	--------	--------
1894	*48*	*35.8*	8-8-5	--------	--------	--------	--------	--------	--------	--------	--------	--------	--------	--------	--------
1893	46	45.1	6-6-8	--------	--------	--------	--------	--------	--------	--------	--------	--------	--------	--------	--------
1892	47	39.7	9-5-4		36.7	--------	--------	--------	--------	--------	--------	--------	--------	--------	--------
1891	48	50.3	5-6-3		33.8		--------	--------	--------	--------	--------	--------	--------	--------	--------
1890	47	50.8	3-9-7		44.3		--------	--------	--------	--------	--------	--------	--------	--------	--------
1889	48	54.6	2-3-2		40.0		--------	--------	--------	--------	--------	--------	--------	--------	--------
1888	45	55.8	3-6-6	--------	--------	--------	--------	--------	--------	--------	--------	--------	--------	--------	--------
1887	46	43.7	6-6-3	--------	--------	--------	--------	--------	--------	--------	--------	--------	--------	--------	--------
1886	47	47.0	6-9-_	--------	--------	--------	--------	--------	--------	--------	--------	--------	--------	--------	--------

¹ For definition of codes, see text.

Series **J 163–245.** Climatological Benchmark Stations—Temperature, Precipitation, and Description of Year: 1884 to 1957—Con.

[Italicized figures are based on interpolated monthly values. Standard error of interpolated figures: For temperature, less than 1° F.; for precipitation, less than 0.5 inch]

North Central—Con.

Year	Crete (Doane College), Nebr. Annual mean temperature	Annual total precipitation	Description of year	Dickinson Experiment Farm, N. Dak. Annual mean temperature	Annual total precipitation	Description of year	Itasca State Park School, Minn. Annual mean temperature	Annual total precipitation	Description of year	Urbana (U. of Ill.), Ill. Annual mean temperature	Annual total precipitation	Description of year	Wooster Experiment Farm, Ohio Annual mean temperature	Annual total precipitation	Description of year
	178	179	180	181	182	183	184	185	186	187	188	189	190	191	192
	°F.	Inches		°F.	Inches		°F.	Inches		°F.	Inches		°F.	Inches	
1957	51	33.0	3-2-8	41	22.2	2-2-8	39	33.9	2-2-5	52	41.6	5-5-5	50	44.6	2-3-5
1956	53	24.4	5-5-9	42	12.7	7-4-8	39	20.7	8-5-5	53	27.3	8-5-8	49	43.4	3-3-5
1955	53	15.9	8-8-5	42	14.6	4-4-5	40	20.4	7-7-4	54	38.5	4-5-5	50	38.2	5-5-6
1954	54	33.7	1-1-1	42	16.3	4-2-4	40	25.4	4-5-1	55	29.7	7-4-4	50	32.0	5-9-4
1953	54	21.5	7-7-4	44	19.4	1-5-7	41	31.7	1-2-7	55	26.1	7-7-4	51	25.9	8-8-4
1952	51	35.1	3-3-2	42	12.0	7-5-2	40	21.8	4-2-2	54	33.9	8-4-4	50	32.0	5-7-1
1951	49	44.4	3-3-2	37	16.7	6-6-5	36	30.9	3-6-5	51	38.4	6-6-3	49	41.0	6-8-3
1950	50	30.7	3-6-5	36	15.1	6-9-6	35	29.9	3-6-3	51	43.0	3-6-1	48	49.1	2-3-1
1949	51	38.8	3-3-3	40	10.8	8-7-3	39	35.5	2-1-2	54	45.5	1-4-1	52	32.8	4-1-4
1948	52	28.6	5-5-3	40	16.1	5-5-5	38	23.5	5-5-5	53	41.4	5-2-6	50	35.1	5-5-9
1947	53	27.6	5-2-8	40	17.2	5-3-5	38	24.2	5-2-5	52	36.9	5-2-8	50	45.4	2-2-5
1946	55	27.8	4-5-4	42	14.5	4-5-8	39	27.7	2-5-5	54	35.5	4-5-6	51	34.6	4-6-9
1945	51	25.4	6-6-5	40	12.2	9-9-8	37	22.3	5-6-5	51	48.0	3-5-8	50	39.1	5-5-9
1944	52	38.5	2-3-4	40	20.6	2-3-7	40	32.6	1-2-7	53	40.7	5-4-5	49	30.2	9-8-8
1943	52	24.2	5-1-5	39	15.0	6-5-6	38	23.5	5-4-6	52	35.5	5-7-9	48	30.2	9-5-6
1942	52	29.5	2-5-2	40	19.8	2-3-4	40	29.5	1-2-3	52	42.4	5-5-5	49	29.8	9-9-5
1941	52	30.9	2-8-5	42	31.2	1-2-7	41	27.4	1-4-3	54	42.9	1-5-8	51	29.9	8-1-8
1940	50	21.2	9-8-6	41	17.1	5-5-8	38	21.9	5-8-3	51	30.6	8-5-9	47	39.7	6-2-6
1939	54	18.3	7-5-5	42	15.8	4-5-5	40	20.7	3-5-2	54	38.0	4-2-1	51	30.7	8-5-5
1938	54	28.3	4-5-5	42	16.6	4-5-2	40	25.4	4-4-5	54	42.8	1-2-5	51	36.7	4-5-5
1937	51	21.7	9-4-6	39	16.3	6-2-6	36	24.6	6-4-3	51	37.6	6-5-2	50	42.2	2-5-1
1936	53	12.4	8-7-6	40	6.7	8-7-6	36	17.6	9-7-6	52	35.1	8-7-6	50	36.9	5-1-6
1935	53	26.8	5-7-7	40	15.0	5-5-7	38	28.7	2-2-5	52	37.2	5-5-5	50	46.3	2-2-8
1934	56	17.2	7-7-1	44	7.9	7-5-7	39	18.6	8-6-5	53	35.2	8-4-8	50	29.9	8-4-8
1933	55	26.8	4-4-8	42	11.5	7-7-5	38	22.6	5-7-5	54	34.5	7-7-4	52	33.5	4-7-4
1932	51	27.3	6-2-2	40	17.2	5-4-5	38	20.8	8-8-7	53	30.5	8-5-4	51	34.6	4-8-1
1931	55	36.3	1-4-7	44	16.2	4-4-4	43	20.4	7-5-7	55	36.5	4-4-7	53	35.7	4-4-7
1930	54	22.5	7-4-5	41	13.8	8-4-2	39	21.4	5-8-2	53	25.1	8-8-2	51	28.8	7-8-1
1929	50	24.4	6-9-6	37	17.2	6-8-3	36	13.9	9-8-6	50	44.1	3-3-6	49	44.4	2-5-2
1928	52	28.2	5-6-8	41	15.3	5-3-3	38	27.0	2-3-2	51	33.0	6-6-2	49	33.5	6-2-2
1927	52	26.4	5-6-5	38	19.6	3-6-5	36	21.4	6-6-5	52	55.6	2-3-8	51	43.3	2-6-5
1926	52	26.4	5-8-4	41	13.1	8-8-4	38	21.0	8-9-4	50	43.5	3-5-5	48	39.4	6-5-6
1925	52	26.3	5-2-3	41	12.2	8-5-6	38	28.8	2-3-6	52	29.4	8-3-3	50	30.4	5-8-5
1924	50	22.5	9-6-8	37	15.1	8-6-6	36	22.2	6-9-5	49	40.4	6-3-2	48	38.9	6-3-2
1923	52	31.2	2-3-7	41	19.7	5-2-5	38	19.7	8-5-3	52	40.4	5-5-5	50	36.3	5-8-2
1922	53	23.0	8-5-6	39	18.2	2-5-3	39	24.9	5-5-2	53	36.7	5-8-5	51	34.4	4-5-5
1921	54	20.3	4-2-7	42	15.8	1-4-7	41	24.3	4-4-4	55	41.7	4-7-4	53	41.9	1-7-4
1920	51	23.0	9-6-9	41	15.8	2-2-5	38	23.6	5-2-6	51	29.3	9-9-9	49	39.7	6-3-9
1919	51	33.4	3-5-4	41	8.4	8-7-4	37	27.5	2-1-1	52	35.2	5-5-4	51	43.1	1-1-4
1918	53	26.2	5-7-6	41	12.4	8-5-6	39	18.9	8-8-9	51	43.2	3-5-9	50	33.8	5-8-6
1917	49	24.8	6-6-8	38	9.2	6-5-7	35	16.3	9-8-6	48	32.2	9-5-9	46	31.9	9-5-6
1916	50	23.9	6-6-3	38	18.4	3-5-5	35	26.5	6-2-3	51	29.7	9-8-3	49	34.9	6-5-2
1915	50	36.0	3-3-3	40	20.0	2-3-8	38	23.6	5-3-5	51	34.2	9-3-6	49	42.1	3-3-6
1914	52	29.6	2-5-2	42	22.7	1-2-7	38	28.0	2-2-8	52	24.7	8-7-5	49	37.4	6-2-5
1913	47	27.0	6-7-6	42	14.9	4-5-8	39	22.4	5-5-9	53	38.2	5-8-5	51	51.2	2-5-2
1912	50	23.8	6-9-3	39	19.1	3-6-4	38	17.8	8-8-9	50	31.5	9-9-5	48	46.6	3-3-6
1911	53	25.4	5-7-6	40	15.6	5-5-5	--------	24.2	-1-	53	32.3	8-8-5	51	47.2	2-5-5
1910	52	25.3	5-6-3	42	13.3	7-5-3	--------	--------	--------	51	28.0	9-9-6	49	35.4	6-9-3
1909	51	33.6	3-8-5	40	21.3	2-2-5	--------	--------	--------	50	47.0	3-3-2	50	44.2	2-2-1
1908	52	38.1	2-3-4	42	19.5	1-5-4	--------	--------	--------	52	33.3	8-9-2	51	33.9	5-5-2
1907	51	29.6	3-3-5	39	13.7	9-6-3	--------	--------	--------	50	40.2	6-3-2	48	40.0	6-6-2
1906	52	29.7	2-6-7	41	20.5	2-5-4	--------	--------	--------	52	34.2	8-5-5	51	42.8	2-1-7
1905	50	33.0	3-6-6	42	16.6	4-5-5	--------	--------	--------	50	29.6	9-5-6	49	42.9	3-2-6
1904	50	30.2	3-6-6	40	15.2	5-5-2	--------	--------	--------	49	29.8	9-9-6	47	41.3	3-9-3
1903	50	33.5	3-6-3	42	16.9	4-5-6	--------	--------	--------	50	32.5	9-6-6	49	40.4	3-3-3
1902	50	42.9	3-3-6	44	16.1	4-9-2	--------	--------	--------	--------	--------	--------	50	33.0	5-3-9
1901	52	24.0	5-4-5	44	12.9	7-4-7	--------	--------	--------	--------	--------	--------	49	35.9	6-4-9
1900	53	34.0	2-3-6	45	11.8	7-4-4	--------	--------	--------	--------	--------	--------	51	36.6	5-1-5
1899	50	30.3	3-3-6	38	17.2	6-5-6	--------	--------	--------	--------	--------	--------	50	32.9	5-8-6
1898	51	22.8	9-6-5	38	11.9	8-8-7	--------	--------	--------	--------	--------	--------	50	47.8	2-1-5
1897	51	30.3	3-6-4	40	13.5	8-8-2	--------	--------	--------	--------	--------	--------	49	36.8	5-6-5
1896	52	41.0	2-3-7	38	18.5	3-8-2	--------	--------	--------	--------	--------	--------	50	39.1	5-3-5
1895	51	20.7	9-9-4	38	11.8	9-6-8	--------	--------	--------	--------	--------	--------	48	30.9	9-8-6
1894	52	22.4	8-6-6	40	15.5	5-7-5	--------	--------	--------	--------	--------	--------	51	30.6	8-8-5
1893	--------	22.1	--------	38	11.6	9-7--	--------	--------	--------	--------	--------	--------	48	40.6	3-8-3

[1] For definition of codes, see text.

Series J 163–245. Climatological Benchmark Stations—Temperature, Precipitation, and Description of Year: 1884 to 1957—Con.

[Italicized figures are based on interpolated monthly values. Standard error of interpolated figures: For temperature, less than 1° F.; for precipitation, less than 0.5 inch]

The South

Year	Beeville Experiment Station, Tex.			Calhoun Experiment Station, La.			Fayetteville Experiment Station, Ark.			Goodwell Agricultural College, Okla.			Lewisburg Experiment Station, Tenn.			St. Leo's Abbey, Fla.		
	Annual mean temperature	Annual total precipitation	Description of year	Annual mean temperature	Annual total precipitation	Description of year	Annual mean temperature	Annual total precipitation	Description of year	Annual mean temperature	Annual total precipitation	Description of year	Annual mean temperature	Annual total precipitation	Description of year	Annual mean temperature	Annual total precipitation	Description of year
	193	194	195	196	197	198	199	200	201	202	203	204	205	206	207	208	209	210
	°F.	Inches		°F.	Inches		°F.	Inches		°F.	Inches		°F.	Inches		°F.	Inches	
1957	70	40.1	3-8-4	66	69.1	2-6-4	57	62.5	3-6-4	56	15.4	5-5-8	60	65.3	2-8-1	73	58.8	4-5-4
1956	71	19.3	8-7-8	66	43.3	8-8-5	59	38.7	8-5-9	59	10.3	7-4-8	60	52.3	5-5-5	72	45.4	8-8-5
1955	72	19.4	7-5-8	66	50.1	5-6-8	59	42.6	5-6-2	57	14.5	5-8-8	59	59.8	2-9-6	72	43.1	8-8-6
1954	72	15.4	7-7-8	68	30.9	7-7-7	60	35.3	7-5-6	60	10.1	7-4-4	60	47.3	4-7-5	72	45.0	8-4-5
1953	72	19.3	7-7-8	67	54.6	4-7-5	60	35.6	8-7-8	60	12.2	7-4-7	60	48.1	5-5-5	73	81.1	1-4-5
1952	71	32.2	5-7-4	64	34.0	9-7-1	59	34.8	8-4-7	58	9.2	7-7-7	60	48.9	5-4-8	72	42.6	8-7-1
1951	73	25.5	7-7-8	66	48.4	5-4-5	57	48.1	6-5-6	56	16.2	5-5-5	59	52.9	5-8-6	72	50.1	8-7-6
1950	73	13.9	7-5-4	67	67.2	1-3-1	57	50.7	6-3-2	57	26.9	2-2-7	58	66.6	3-6-1	72	57.4	4-4-7
1949	72	35.5	4-2-4	68	53.0	4-5-1	58	47.0	6-6-2	56	22.2	5-2-2	60	49.8	5-5-4	74	50.8	7-8-4
1948	71	19.9	8-7-6	66	39.2	8-7-6	58	48.3	5-5-6	56	24.0	2-2-3	59	63.7	3-8-6	74	51.3	7-4-5
1947	70	19.3	8-8-9	68	57.1	4-4-6	58	40.0	9-5-9	56	23.0	2-2-7	58	41.4	9-6-5	72	68.5	2-3-5
1946	72	37.1	5-5-5	68	71.5	1-2-2	60	52.6	2-5-5	58	26.0	1-5-5	60	54.7	5-9-3	74	51.8	4-5-2
1945	72	25.7	7-5-8	68	61.9	1-3-3	58	64.7	3-3-2	57	15.5	5-6-2	59	62.5	3-9-3	72	81.9	1-2-5
1944	71	27.4	5-4-5	66	56.6	5-5-5	59	48.0	5-5-2	56	21.6	6-5-3	60	58.1	5-7-5	72	54.3	5-4-5
1943	71	33.6	5-5-7	66	32.2	8-4-8	59	40.7	5-7-5	57	15.0	5-4-4	59	42.1	8-4-8	72	63.3	2-1-5
1942	70	40.0	2-2-5	65	44.5	5-4-5	59	56.9	2-2-6	57	27.0	2-2-4	59	44.8	6-2-6	72	60.1	5-1-3
1941	70	47.5	2-3-2	66	54.6	5-5-5	60	50.5	5-5-2	56	26.2	2-3-5	60	38.6	8-2-8	72	60.0	5-4-2
1940	70	33.0	5-2-8	64	62.2	3-3-6	57	40.5	5-6-9	56	16.2	5-8-5	57	43.8	6-6-8	70	43.9	9-5-6
1939	73	16.7	7-4-5	67	45.0	7-4-5	61	36.4	7-7-4	58	13.6	7-5-2	59	59.4	2-2-2	73	50.1	7-2-7
1938	73	21.1	7-7-1	67	47.1	4-5-7	61	48.3	4-5-1	59	14.9	4-7-7	61	46.8	4-5-5	72	49.2	8-8-8
1937	71	23.3	8-7-8	65	62.1	2-5-2	58	42.4	5-4-5	57	11.3	8-7-5	59	64.4	3-2-1	72	60.7	5-5-1
1936	68	34.9	6-3-6	65	32.9	8-8-9	60	29.3	7-7-9	57	9.7	5-7-6	59	51.1	5-4-9	72	55.8	5-8-3
1935	70	33.2	6-6-5	66	48.4	5-8-5	59	58.5	5-2-7	58	11.7	7-7-7	59	46.8	5-5-5	70	57.6	6-3-9
1934	71	32.1	5-8-1	67	54.8	4-4-4	61	40.0	7-7-7	60	14.3	4-7-1	60	41.3	8-4-5	71	69.8	3-3-5
1933	72	29.7	4-3-5	68	62.8	1-2-2	61	54.2	2-4-2	58	12.6	7-4-6	61	49.6	4-5-5	72	65.0	2-3-4
1932	70	42.7	3-5-1	66	51.8	5-7-1	60	45.1	5-5-1	55	14.7	6-8-2	60	61.8	1-4-1	73	40.5	7-7-7
1931	70	37.8	3-3-2	66	58.6	5-6-6	60	41.9	4-5-5	57	16.2	5-8-5	61	41.3	7-8-8	70	45.2	9-8-3
1930	70	26.9	6-8-3	66	44.9	8-8-8	59	40.2	5-8-5	52	18.5	6-5-9	60	41.7	8-7-4	69	51.9	6-9-6
1929	70	38.4	3-6-3	65	43.1	9-5-6	58	52.8	3-5-3	50	18.4	6-3-6	59	58.0	5-5-6	72	52.3	5-6-4
1928	70	36.8	5-4-5	65	49.8	6-5-9	59	52.9	2-6-5	55	24.3	3-6-5	59	43.0	9-2-8	70	64.8	3-2-6
1927	73	20.6	7-4-4	67	49.8	4-9-1	60	66.6	2-3-4	57	16.3	5-3-5	61	54.5	4-6-4	71	48.5	8-5-8
1926	69	31.6	6-6-6	64	49.8	6-2-8	58	42.5	5-6-8	56	17.3	5-5-8	59	63.5	2-2-8	71	55.4	6-5-3
1925	70	31.2	5-5-5	67	54.6	4-4-5	60	27.0	8-7-5	57	15.9	5-5-6	61	42.4	7-7-5	73	53.8	4-4-4
1924	70	21.8	9-8-3	64	29.5	9-7-5	57	38.8	8-5-8	55	12.1	9-8-5	57	45.8	6-8-5	72	62.2	2-7-5
1923	71	46.4	2-5-1	65	72.8	3-6-4	60	46.3	5-7-4	56	24.1	2-5-7	59	59.2	3-8-2	71	53.9	6-6-8
1922	71	37.7	2-2-8	65	60.8	3-6-2	60	35.6	7-5-4	58	14.8	4-5-5	61	55.8	4-8-5	71	61.8	2-6-5
1921	72	27.5	4-7-8	66	49.5	5-3-5	62	39.3	7-5-4	59	16.9	4-6-1	62	50.1	4-4-5	71	58.1	5-9-5
1920	70	22.3	9-5-6	63	71.1	3-3-9	58	44.0	5-5-9	56	14.8	5-9-5	59	57.3	6-6-5	69	50.3	9-6-6
1919	69	47.4	3-3-3	64	59.6	6-6-9	59	45.5	5-2-4	54	14.9	6-9-3	60	55.1	5-5-5	71	63.3	3-3-3
1918	70	29.6	6-8-9	64	44.0	9-2-9	60	39.5	8-7-8	56	20.1	5-4-9	60	49.1	5-5-6	71	54.4	6-6-6
1917	70	12.1	8-7-8	63	39.0	8-6-8	57	40.0	8-6-5	55	16.6	6-6-5	57	52.8	6-5-5	70	54.0	6-3-2
1916	72	23.4	7-1-7	65	36.4	9-6-8	60	43.0	4-7-2	58	11.7	4-5-8	59	57.6	5-3-4	71	50.6	8-6-8
1915	72	13.1	8-7-9	64	48.8	6-6-6	59	58.2	2-3-6	50	26.8	3-2-5	59	57.4	6-3-6	70	53.5	6-8-3
1914	70	46.6	3-1-8	65	48.2	6-2-9	60	38.8	8-4-2	58	22.5	1-2-2	59	46.8	5-1-8	71	51.9	6-8-2
1913	69	32.8	6-6-9	64	62.7	3-6-2	59	47.3	5-4-5	51	19.0	6-5-6	60	53.1	4-4-2	72	50.6	8-6-4
1912	70	30.0	6-8-3	64	50.6	6-6-3	57	40.4	6-5-6	47	17.5	6-5-3	58	61.0	3-3-6	72	64.1	2-9-3
1911	73	23.5	7-7-7	67	54.4	4-5-7	61	38.9	7-5-7	59	15.5	4-4-4	62	60.3	1-2-5	73	54.9	4-2-9
1910	71	29.8	5-5-6	65	41.7	8-6-6	59	33.4	8-6-6	59	11.4	7-4-2	59	46.7	6-6-6	70	53.8	6-3-6
1909	72	30.8	4-2-7	66	44.7	8-5-4	61	34.0	7-7-7				60	50.5	5-5-4	72	53.3	5-2-8
1908	72	35.7	4-1-8	65	64.0	2-3-5	60	50.5	5-3-5				60	50.4	4-5-6	72	41.7	8-3-3
1907	72	19.1	7-7-7	65	47.5	6-3-7	60	40.7	4-5-4				60	51.5	5-2-4	72	46.6	8-8-8
1906	70	31.2	5-5-6	64	57.8	6-3-9	58	51.6	6-3-6				60	57.1	5-2-5	71	60.0	5-2-3
1905	69	39.6	3-5-6	63	65.3	2-3-3	56	54.7	3-6-9				60	62.8	2-2-6	71	62.3	2-2-5
1904				65	49.1	6-3-9	58	43.5	6-3-6				60	37.4	8-8-9	71	50.7	6-3-2
1903				63	50.3	6-3-6	56	45.3	6-6-3				59	51.1	6-6-5	70	54.9	6-9-2
1902				64	52.1	6-5-9	58	48.2	5-5-6				60	52.3	5-4-6	72	45.5	8-7-6
1901				62	36.7	9-5-9	58	28.9	8-7-8				58	45.0	6-1-8			
1900				64	57.7	6-3-6	59	37.7	8-5-6				60	53.6	6-3-6			
1899				64	30.7	9-8-9	59	40.2	5-5-9				59	47.4	5-7-6			
1898				67	53.6	4-3-5	58	66.1	2-3-5					49.8	--5--			
1897				65	45.5	8-5-9	59	37.2	8-5-5									
1896				66	37.3	8-7-9	61	38.5	7-7-5									
1895				62	48.4	6-3-9	57	41.6	5-2-9									
1894				64	55.2	6-6-6	59	47.1	5-5-5									
1893				64	43.5	9-6-6	58	58.5	3-3-9									
1892					65.5		57	51.3	6-6-6									--5--
1891					52.5		56	34.6	9-6-8									
1890													60	53.0	5-6--			
1889													58	48.6	6-3--			
1888														53.3				
1887																		
1886																		
1884								51.9										

[1] For definition of codes, see text.

Series J 163–245. Climatological Benchmark Stations—Temperature, Precipitation, and Description of Year: 1884 to 1957—Con.

[Italicized figures are based on interpolated monthly values. Standard error of interpolated figures: For temperature, less than 1° F.; for precipitation, less than 0.5 inch]

	The South—Con.						The West											
	Winthrop College, S. C.			Woodstock College,[2] Md.			Agricultural College, N. Mex.			Bozeman Agricultural College, Mont.			Davis Agricultural College, Calif.			Grand Canyon National Park Headquarters, Ariz.		
Year	Annual mean temperature	Annual total precipitation	Description[1] of year	Annual mean temperature	Annual total precipitation	Description[1] of year	Annual mean temperature	Annual total precipitation	Description[1] of year	Annual mean temperature	Annual total precipitation	Description[1] of year	Annual mean temperature	Annual total precipitation	Description[1] of year	Annual mean temperature	Annual total precipitation	Description[1] of year
	211	212	213	214	215	216	217	218	219	220	221	222	223	224	225	226	227	228
	°F.	Inches		°F.	Inches		°F.	Inches		°F.	Inches		°F.	Inches		°F.	Inches	
1957	*63*	50.0	5-8-4	54	41.1	5-8-4	61	9.3	4-4-1	43	*16.5*	5-1-8	61	15.3	4-7-8	48	*20.9*	*3-3-4*
1956	63	36.7	8-8-8	54	44.1	5-2-8	60	4.8	7-4-4	43	11.3	7-7-5	60	13.0	5-8-1	50	7.6	7-8-7
1955	63	43.9	5-5-5	54	46.8	2-1-8	61	7.3	4-6-9	41	17.2	5-8-5	60	13.6	5-5-6	48	11.9	9-2-6
1954	63	35.7	4-7-2	54	30.5	8-8-7	62	5.8	7-8-8	44	12.7	5-5-4	60	18.3	5-5-4	51	12.5	4-5-7
1953	61	42.1	5-5-5	55	47.2	1-9-1	60	3.8	7-7-5	46	16.4	5-4-4	61	10.0	7-2-1	50	10.9	8-2-8
1952	62	49.5	5-2-5	*54*	60.8	*2-1-1*	60	6.2	5-4-4	43	19.6	5-5-2	60	21.5	2-5-2	48	17.8	3-5-3
1951	62	37.2	5-5-9	54	41.4	5-5-5	61	5.0	7-7-8	40	20.2	5-6-5	60	12.9	5-5-4	49	17.2	5-5-7
1950	62	44.5	5-3-7	53	48.8	2-3-4	62	5.3	7-5-4	42	18.2	5-3-5	61	20.0	1-8-6	50	10.3	7-6-5
1949	*62*	58.9	*2-3-4*	56	39.0	4-4-1	61	9.0	4-7-3	43	17.1	5-4-3	59	10.6	9-5-6	47	17.9	3-6-3
1948	62	49.8	5-8-9	54	53.5	2-5-3	58	5.2	9-7-3	42	*19.5*	5-2-5	58	16.0	6-2-8	49	13.5	6-2-5
1947	61	51.1	6-6-5	54	36.5	8-5-8	59	6.1	6-5-5	44	23.6	1-2-4	60	11.3	8-2-9	49	11.8	8-6-7
1946	63	41.3	4-9-6	54	38.5	4-3-5	60	7.1	4-7-6	43	18.6	4-8-2	59	10.8	9-5-6	49	18.7	2-2-5
1945	63	45.2	5-5-5	54	53.9	2-3-3	59	5.8	9-5-8	42	19.5	5-3-8	60	19.9	2-4-5	49	12.6	5-5-7
1944	62	47.0	5-8-2	53	41.1	5-4-8	58	9.8	3-3-2	42	20.9	2-3-8	60	19.5	2-6-5	48	10.9	9-8-5
1943	62	39.9	8-4-5	54	35.4	8-7-5	61	7.6	4-4-4	42	17.2	6-6-8	61	15.6	4-6-1	51	12.3	4-5-4
1942	62	53.1	2-2-6	54	47.2	2-2-5	60	9.8	2-2-5	41	17.2	6-9-3	60	18.4	5-7-1	50	9.7	7-4-5
1941	62	45.2	5-2-9	54	29.9	8-5-5	60	19.6	2-3-1	43	22.9	2-5-4	61	28.8	1-5-1	48	24.6	2-5-1
1940	60	41.1	6-5-6	51	41.4	6-9-9	60	9.2	5-6-5	44	18.6	4-4-2	62	29.4	1-8-1	50	22.7	1-4-4
1939	63	46.9	4-1-1	54	38.8	5-5-2	59	5.8	8-8-6	44	14.0	7-5-8	60	5.9	8-5-8	50	17.7	2-7-6
1938	63	40.1	7-5-4	54	33.2	7-7-8	59	9.3	6-3-4	43	20.4	1-8-4	59	20.6	3-5-2	49	17.2	5-5-2
1937	62	55.3	2-4-1	53	48.7	2-4-1	60	7.0	5-8-5	41	18.0	6-5-3	60	21.6	2-5-3	49	19.3	2-8-3
1936	61	63.3	3-5-3	53	39.1	6-5-3	60	9.5	4-5-2	43	12.8	5-7-6	61	18.2	4-2-1	50	15.8	5-5-5
1935	61	39.3	9-8-8	52	39.5	6-8-3	60	12.7	2-1-7	42	15.5	8-8-4	59	16.6	5-5-5	49	14.1	5-1-5
1934	61	45.1	6-7-8	53	46.2	3-7-6	61	4.6	7-7-8	47	10.5	4-7-4	62	11.2	7-2-4	52	10.5	7-5-7
1933	63	32.6	7-5-4	55	50.1	1-1-4	59	4.7	9-5-6	44	15.9	4-4-6	60	12.5	5-4-9	51	10.6	7-4-6
1932	63	51.4	4-4-1	55	45.6	4-5-4	59	8.8	6-5-3	42	17.3	6-2-5	60	8.4	8-5-5	50	12.7	5 7-3
1931	63	50.0	5-2-9	56	35.6	7-1-8	60	13.3	2-2-2	44	15.3	7-7-5	61	16.1	4-1-7	49	15.0	5-4-8
1930	62	36.2	8-8-8	55	20.1	7-7-7	60	6.9	5-5-8	42	14.2	8-4-8	59	12.1	6-6-4	48	14.7	6-2-7
1929	61	60.8	3-6-5	54	40.3	5-9-5	59	9.2	6-6-8	41	15.8	6-4-6	59	8.6	8-3-9	49	10.8	8-2-6
1928	61	48.8	6-2-5	*53*	*41.0*	*6-8-5*	60	9.4	5-6-5	42	16.2	5-6-6	60	13.9	5-8-8	50	13.1	4-4-5
1927	63	43.8	4-6-4	54	38.1	5-9-5	60	9.5	5-3-4	41	21.8	3-6-2	59	18.1	6-2-5	50	22.9	2-3-2
1926	62	38.4	8-4-5	52	43.2	6-6-5	59	14.4	3-9-6	43	19.8	2-5-1	61	23.0	1-4-5	50	17.4	5-5-8
1925	63	32.6	7-7-2	54	35.0	8-5-5	60	7.8	5-2-8	44	19.4	4-5-8	60	15.4	5-4-5	49	17.6	3-3-6
1924	60	58.4	3-8-5	52	52.4	3-6-1	59	4.8	9-4-5	40	20.9	3-9-2	59	13.8	6-8-8	49	15.6	5-8-5
1923	62	48.0	5-5-5	54	39.1	5-5-5	60	10.4	2-5-1	42	15.3	8-5-8	60	7.8	8-5-5	*48*	18.6	*3-3-4*
1922	*62*	52.9	*2-5-2*	55	38.9	4-2-5	60	5.6	7-7-7	40	17.7	6-2-6	59	22.6	2-7-3	48	16.4	6-5-3
1921	*63*	40.1	7-4-5	56	38.3	4-5-4	62	7.6	4-5-8	42	15.2	8-4-4	60	13.4	5-7-5	48	15.8	6-8-9
1920	61	51.6	5-2-3	53	49.9	3-2-6	60	8.2	5-2-4	40	19.2	3-6-5	60	15.4	5-4-8	*47*	*12.6*	6-9-1
1919	63	54.2	2-2-2	55	42.3	4-5-1	60	8.0	5-8-6	42	11.0	9-7-8	59	14.6	5-5-3	48	*18.4*	*3-5-6*
1918	62	47.8	5-5-9	54	40.9	5-5-6	60	7.2	5-4-8	42	18.9	6-5-2	60	16.7	5-7-7	48	19.9	3-3-8
1917	58	40.6	9-6-8	52	38.2	6-2-6	60	5.6	8-5-8	41	15.7	6-8-3	61	9.5	7-7-2	47	10.7	9-8-6
1916	*61*	*43.8*	*6-3-8*	54	39.9	5-2-5	61	7.8	4-8-7	38	21.2	3-6-6	60	20.1	2-5-1	46	14.5	6-6-2
1915	62	48.0	5-5-2	54	47.6	2-3-2	59	7.4	6-8-2	42	25.0	2-3-8	60	21.0	2-7-2	46	13.9	6-9-6
1914	61	45.8	6-1-5	54	36.1	8-4-2	61	11.8	1-2-5	43	16.5	5-6-8	59	22.2	6-3-2	48	*13.0*	*6-6-2*
1913	62	52.4	2-5-4	56	39.0	4-4-4	58	11.7	3-2-6	40	18.7	6-6-6	59	17.9	5-5-9	47	15.8	6-6-3
1912	61	47.4	6-3-6	*53*	40.8	*6-5-6*	58	9.2	6-2-9	40	21.6	3-6-5	58	11.0	9-3-8	43	9.6	9-9-9
1911	63	40.0	7-4-8	55	*44.7*	*4-2-9*	60	5.8	7-8-4	40	18.1	6-6-5	57	22.4	3-6-2	*46*	*21.7*	*3-3-1*
1910	61	42.5	6-3-5	*53*	29.6	8-9-6	63	4.0	7-4-8	43	18.7	5-8-6	-------	7.0	-------	48	12.0	*6-3-3*
1909	62	40.9	8-2-7	*53*	*33.7*	7-7-7	61	4.9	7-7-7	40	22.3	3-5-8	-------	25.8	-------	*45*	*26.1*	*3-5-2*
1908	62	55.0	2-2-3	*54*	*35.7*	*5-2-3*	60	6.0	7-5-4	41	25.3	3-6-5	-------		-------	*45*	22.5	*3-3-5*
1907	61	49.3	6-3-7	52	47.5	6-3-6	63	6.4	4-4-4	41	17.2	6-3-5	-------		-------	*49*	36.7	*2-3-1*
1906	62	55.6	2-2-3	54	*53.1*	*2-1-8*	61	8.8	4-8-2	*41*	*16.9*	6-6-5	-------		-------	*48*	*22.3*	*3-3-6*
1905	*61*	*45.5*	*6-2-6*	52	*42.9*	*6-4-6*	60	17.1	1-5-1	*41*	*14.7*	*9-6-5*	-------		-------	*48*	*29.6*	*3-3-2*
1904	60	35.4	9-3-9	*50*	*34.4*	*9-6-9*	60	10.1	1-5-8	42	16.2	5-9-2	-------		-------	*50*	17.6	*5-2-3*
1903	61	43.6	6-5-3	*53*	*41.6*	*6-3-3*	59	10.3	3-2-2	41	17.6	6-6-5	-------		-------	-------	-------	-------
1902	61	48.8	6-5-3	*53*	51.6	*3-6-3*	60	10.9	1-2-7	42	15.5	8-6-5	-------		-------	-------	-------	-------
1901	59	64.1	3-3-6	*52*	39.7	*6-4-9*	61	12.0	1-1-4	*44*	15.5	7-8-5	-------		-------	-------	-------	-------
1900	62	44.9	5-4-6	*53*	32.5	*8-4-8*	61	8.4	4-7-4	*44*	*14.2*	*7-8--*	-------		-------	-------	-------	-------
1899	-------	-------	-------	*51*	40.8	*6-5-3*	57	9.7	3-3-6	-------		-------	-------		-------	-------	-------	-------
1898	-------	-------	-------	*53*	36.8	*9-4-6*	53	14.4	3-3-9	-------		-------	-------		-------	-------	-------	-------
1897	-------	-------	-------	*51*	*49.3*	*3-3-6*	58	9.0	6-6-8	-------		-------	-------		-------	-------	-------	-------
1896	-------	-------	-------	*51*	*33.3*	*9-6-3*	59	-------	*-6-*	-------		-------	-------		-------	-------	-------	-------
1895	-------	-------	-------	*50*	28.0	*9-9-9*	-------	-------	-------	-------		-------	-------		-------	-------	-------	-------
1894	-------	-------	-------	*52*	35.4	*9-9-9*	-------	-------	-------	-------		-------	-------		-------	-------	-------	-------
1893	-------	-------	-------	*50*	39.0	*6-9-6*	-------	-------	-------	-------		-------	-------		-------	-------	-------	-------

[1] For definition of codes, see text.

[2] Figures corrected for station move about Jan. 1914.

Series J 163–245. Climatological Benchmark Stations—Temperature, Precipitation, and Description of Year: 1884 to 1957—Con.

[Italicized figures are based on interpolated monthly values. Standard error of interpolated figures: For temperature, less than 1° F.; for precipitation, less than 0.5 inch. Record for Medford Experiment Station, Oreg., too short to obtain normals; therefore description of year omitted]

The West—Con.

Year	Indio U.S. Date Garden, Calif.			Logan (Utah State Agricultural College), Utah			Medford Experiment Station, Oreg.		Montrose No. 2, Colo.			Tatoosh Island (Weather Bureau Office), Wash.			Union Experiment Station, Oreg.		
	Annual mean temperature	Annual total precipitation	Description of year	Annual mean temperature	Annual total precipitation	Description of year	Annual mean temperature	Annual total precipitation	Annual mean temperature	Annual total precipitation	Description of year	Annual mean temperature	Annual total precipitation	Description of year	Annual mean temperature	Annual total precipitation	Description of year
	229	230	231	232	233	234	235	236	237	238	239	240	241	242	243	244	245
	°F.	Inches		°F.	Inches		°F.	Inches	°F.	Inches		°F.	Inches		°F.	Inches	
1957	74	3.0	4-4-5	48	17.8	5-5-5	52	23.2	50	15.4	2-2-2	50	71.6	5-1-6	47	15.6	2-8-6
1956	73	0.4	8-5-8	48	11.7	8-8-2	52	26.7	50	6.7	7-4-4	48	79.4	6-2-6	48	15.8	2-2-2
1955	72	1.7	6-6-6	46	17.0	5-5-6	52	15.8	48	7.8	6-5-6	47	80.8	6-3-8	46	11.8	6-8-8
1954	74	2.7	4-6-7	50	12.5	7-5-4	52	18.1	52	8.6	4-5-7	49	86.2	2-3-2	48	12.5	4-3-4
1953	73	0.8	8-5-5	50	14.0	7-5-7	52	28.7	50	10.8	2-4-5	50	92.2	1-8-1	49	18.3	1-6-1
1952	73	6.5	2-8-3	48	12.8	8-5-3	52	20.7	49	9.7	5-4-2	48	68.7	6-6-6	48	11.7	5-2-6
1951	72	3.2	6-2-8	47	18.9	6-6-4	53	20.9	49	5.8	8-8-4	48	80.0	6-9-2	48	13.9	5-5-4
1950	74	0.7	8-6-8	48	19.9	2-6-2	52	28.4	50	6.8	7-9-2	47	101.6	3-6-9	48	13.0	5-5-8
1949	72	2.3	6-8-6	47	19.8	2-5-3	51	11.5	49	8.4	5-6-2	48	73.6	6-5-6	47	10.0	8-8-6
1948	72	2.0	6-6-5	47	17.3	5-5-8	49	25.7	48	10.8	6-3-2	48	89.3	3-4-5	46	16.9	3-3-5
1947	73	1.0	8-5-4	48	18.8	5-2-4	52	16.2	50	12.5	2-3-7	50	77.3	4-4-5	48	14.6	4-3-4
1946	72	1.8	6-8-5	49	20.5	2-5-8	51	17.1	50	9.1	4-4-8	49	82.2	5-3-5	48	15.4	2-5-5
1945	72	5.0	6-3-8	47	24.6	2-3-5	52	23.0	49	8.2	5-5-5	49	83.7	2-6-4	48	14.4	5-6-4
1944	71	3.0	6-8-3	47	18.9	3-8-8	51	17.5	50	10.4	2-5-6	50	72.7	4-9-4	48	10.6	5-3-8
1943	73	8.1	2-2-5	50	18.1	4-2-5	52	19.3	51	9.7	4-2-5	49	58.6	8-5-5	47	12.4	5-3-2
1942	73	3.2	5-1-5	47	18.0	6-5-3	52	23.8	50	7.8	5-8-5	50	58.9	7-1-4	48	17.2	2-2-2
1941	72	8.3	3-3-2	48	19.6	2-2-4	53	24.7	49	16.9	2-2-2	52	64.7	7-4-7	50	21.3	1-2-4
1940	74	4.9	4-7-4	52	17.0	4-7-4	54	22.0	50	10.1	4-7-5	52	78.1	4-4-7	50	18.8	1-7-1
1939	73	10.8	2-8-2	50	12.4	7-5-5	53	17.9	50	6.4	8-4-6	50	75.0	5-5-3	49	6.1	8-8-8
1938	73	4.1	6-5-4	50	17.8	4-5-4	53	19.3	48	13.3	2-8-2	49	60.9	8-9-2	49	11.8	5-4-1
1937	74	1.3	4-7-6	48	20.4	2-5-3	53	26.6	47	7.0	8-9-6	49	75.8	5-2-6	47	12.8	5-5-6
1936	74	6.8	1-2-5	50	18.3	4-4-2	--------	--------	50	7.6	7-4-5	50	63.4	8-1-8	48	9.8	8-4-6
1935	73	3.5	6-4-2	49	13.5	8-7-5	--------	--------	50	7.2	7-4-4	49	80.4	5-5-8	47	8.0	8-5-7
1934	76	0.5	7-5-7	53	11.8	7-4-4	--------	--------	53	7.9	4-7-4	51	82.1	4-5-4	51	10.8	4-5-4
1933	73	0.8	9-7-6	49	11.9	8-7-6	--------	--------	49	7.5	8-7-6	48	88.4	3-6-3	46	12.7	6-5-6
1932	72	3.5	6-5-6	46	16.4	6-2-3	--------	--------	48	8.9	6-5-6	49	93.2	2-2-5	46	11.3	6-9-6
1931	73	4.6	5-5-5	48	12.3	8-7-9	--------	--------	49	7.6	8-4-8	50	89.5	2-2-4	48	9.9	8-7-8
1930	73	3.3	5-5-4	47	20.3	3-2-5	--------	--------	47	9.1	6-2-6	49	69.3	5-2-3	47	13.5	6-5-2
1929	73	1.5	5-4-8	48	16.0	5-5-6	--------	--------	46	10.4	6-5-9	48	49.6	9-5-6	46	11.0	6-1-9
1928	73	0.7	8-8-2	48	10.8	8-6-8	--------	--------	49	11.3	2-5-8	50	73.1	5-8-5	48	9.4	8-8-9
1927	72	7.9	3-3-2	49	18.4	5-5-5	--------	--------	49	12.7	2-2-2	49	82.7	2-5-6	46	16.5	3-5-2
1926	74	6.2	1-5-7	50	16.0	4-5-4	--------	--------	49	10.8	2-8-8	51	71.8	4-7-4	48	15.9	2-4-4
1925	73	3.6	5-5-8	50	16.3	4-3-5	--------	--------	49	10.0	5-2-3	49	71.4	5-5-5	49	11.6	4-4-5
1924	74	0.7	7-7-7	47	12.4	9-8-8	--------	--------	47	9.1	6-5-3	48	79.1	2-9-5	46	9.4	9-6-5
1923	73	0.5	8-5-7	46	16.9	6-6-2	--------	--------	48	9.0	6-5-4	49	71.1	5-7-3	48	17.5	2-2-2
1922	73	1.7	5-4-3	47	15.2	6-4-3	--------	--------	49	7.6	8-4-8	48	60.3	9-9-3	46	8.3	9-7-9
1921	74	6.6	2-2-9	49	18.3	5-8-5	--------	--------	51	10.6	1-2-5	48	100.4	3-3-5	48	14.8	5-7-2
1920	72	6.8	3-2-5	47	19.2	3-6-8	--------	--------	48	10.1	6-5-8	48	89.8	3-3-8	46	14.8	6-5-9
1919	73	3.1	5-1-9	48	15.7	5-7-7	--------	--------	48	9.9	6-8-3	48	73.9	6-9-2	46	9.5	9-4-5
1918	73	2.0	5-4-8	49	16.9	5-4-1	--------	--------	48	11.0	3-5-2	49	82.6	2-6-5	48	12.4	5-4-1
1917	73	2.1	5-4-6	46	18.1	6-8-3	--------	--------	47	7.8	6-5-6	48	82.4	6-4-6	46	15.0	6-5-3
1916	72	5.1	6-5-2	47	18.8	5-8-2	--------	--------	49	13.1	2-5-1	47	77.8	6-5-3	45	13.3	6-6-6
1915	72	5.2	6-5-3	50	15.2	4-9-8	--------	--------	48	9.0	6-5-3	50	72.2	4-7-5	48	16.9	1-5-8
1914	74	2.7	4-5-5	48	19.6	2-2-2	--------	--------	49	13.2	2-2-3	49	83.4	2-9-5	49	11.6	4-5-4
1913	72	2.0	6-6-6	47	17.8	5-3-8	--------	--------	47	8.1	6-9-6	48	78.3	6-1-9	46	17.3	3-3-9
1912	72	4.5	6-5-8	46	18.9	6-3-8	--------	--------	48	10.9	3-2-8	49	72.8	5-2-5	46	17.7	3-3-2
1911	72	2.5	6-5-5	46	19.1	3-9-2	--------	--------	49	11.8	2-5-1	47	52.6	9-9-6	--------	--------	--------
1910	75	1.0	7-4-6	50	11.7	7-8-3	--------	--------	47	4.7	9-9-6	48	67.1	9-9-6	--------	--------	--------
1909	72	4.1	6-2-5	48	22.3	2-4-2	--------	--------	45	11.2	3-3-2	47	74.9	6-6-9	--------	--------	--------
1908	73	3.6	6-5-5	46	18.8	6-3-8	--------	--------	46	9.9	6-3-8	48	72.4	6-9-8	--------	--------	--------
1907	73	3.9	5-8-2	48	22.0	2-3-1	--------	--------	48	11.5	3-3-7	48	61.1	9-9-6	--------	--------	--------
1906	73	7.1	2-2-5	48	26.4	2-3-6	--------	--------	48	13.4	3-6-5	49	69.2	5-5-5	--------	--------	--------
1905	73	5.4	3-7-1	49	12.5	8-5-8	--------	--------	45	11.2	3-6-2	50	63.7	8-8-5	--------	--------	--------
1904	--------	--------	--------	49	13.5	8-5-5	--------	--------	45	7.5	9-6-3	49	78.7	5-6-8	--------	--------	--------
1903	--------	--------	--------	46	14.0	9-8-6	--------	--------		8.1	--------	49	68.9	5-5-5	--------	--------	--------
1902	--------	--------	--------	48	13.3	8-6-7	--------	--------		6.5	--------	48	91.6	3-6-5	--------	--------	--------
1901	--------	--------	--------	50	14.5	7-5-7	--------	--------		6.2	--------	49	101.3	2-6-5	--------	--------	--------
1900				50	15.1	4-8-8	--------	--------		5.9	--------	50	101.4	1-1-2	--------	--------	--------
1899				47	12.6	9-6-9	--------	--------		9.2	--------	50	114.0	2-9-3	--------	--------	--------
1898				46	13.2	9-8-9	--------	--------		7.8	--------	49	86.4	2-4-2	--------	--------	--------
1897				47	17.4	6-6-5	--------	--------		15.6	-6-2	48	95.2	3-2-2	--------	--------	--------
1896				48	16.2	5-2-8	--------	--------		6.5	-7-2	48	100.8	3-4-2	--------	--------	--------
1895				45	13.5	9-9-6	--------	--------		12.3		48	93.0	3-5-5	--------	--------	--------
1894				46	14.4	9-6-5	--------	--------				47	114.3	3-5-3	--------	--------	--------
1893				46	14.5	9-9-6	--------	--------	48	9.5	6-5-2	47	104.2	3-2-6	--------	--------	--------
1892				--------	--------	--------			48	9.0	6-9-3	--------	--------	--------			
1891				--------	--------	--------				11.4	-6-	--------	--------	--------			
1890				--------	--------	--------				9.1	--------	--------	--------	--------			
1889				--------	--------	--------				7.2	-_-6	--------	--------	--------			
1888				--------	--------	--------			48	8.5	6-6-_	--------	--------	--------			
1887				--------	--------	--------				9.6	--------	--------	--------	--------			
1886				--------	--------	--------				9.9	--------	--------	--------	--------			
1885				--------	--------	--------				10.9	--------	--------	--------	--------			

[1] For definition of codes, see text.

Series J 246–265. Long-Record City Stations—Annual Mean Temperature and Annual Total Precipitation: 1780 to 1957

[Italicized figures are based on interpolated monthly values]

Year	Albany, N.Y. Annual mean temperature (246)	Albany, N.Y. Annual total precipitation (247)	Baltimore, Md. Annual mean temperature (248)	Baltimore, Md. Annual total precipitation (249)	Charleston, S.C. Annual mean temperature (250)	Charleston, S.C. Annual total precipitation (251)	New Haven, Conn. Annual mean temperature (252)	New Haven, Conn. Annual total precipitation (253)	New York, N.Y. Annual mean temperature (254)	New York, N.Y. Annual total precipitation (255)	Philadelphia, Pa. Annual mean temperature (256)	Philadelphia, Pa. Annual total precipitation (257)	San Francisco, Calif. Annual mean temperature (258)	San Francisco, Calif. Annual total precipitation (259)	Santa Fe, N. Mex. Annual mean temperature (260)	Santa Fe, N. Mex. Annual total precipitation (261)	St. Louis, Mo. Annual mean temperature (262)	St. Louis, Mo. Annual total precipitation (263)	St. Paul, Minn. Annual mean temperature (264)	St. Paul, Minn. Annual total precipitation (265)
	°F.	Inches	°F.	Inches	°F.	Inches	°F.	Inches	°F.	Inches	°F.	Inches	°F.	Inches	°F.	Inches	°F.	Inches	°F.	Inches
1957	51	29.1	59	37.7	66	51.8	[1]53	[1]41.1	56	36.5	[2]56	[2]35.0	56	22.8	49	17.6	57	52.7	46	27.8
1956	49	32.6	58	37.8	66	35.1	[1]51	[1]48.4	54	36.2	55	44.8	56	15.1	50	6.7	58	33.7	45	26.8
1955	50	41.5	57	47.9	66	40.5	[1]52	[1]51.3	55	39.9	56	33.7	54	21.0	49	10.8	58	33.0	46	21.1
1954	50	41.0	59	30.5	66	31.0	[1]52	48.5	55	35.6	56	36.9	55	19.8	52	14.1	59	30.0	46	23.7
1953	52	41.0	59	49.3	67	44.0	[1]54	56.7	57	45.2	58	50.5	56	12.6	50	12.8	60	23.0	47	27.9
1952	51	39.2	58	55.9	66	39.2	[1]53	49.7	55	41.5	57	51.1	54	31.5	49	11.4	58	26.7	46	23.7
1951	50	43.6	57	46.9	66	38.2	[1]53	50.5	55	44.4	56	42.0	54	22.9	50	9.3	55	38.6	42	34.6
1950	49	37.8	57	44.0	66	43.4	51	42.5	54	36.9	55	45.4	55	26.3	51	10.4	55	43.2	42	21.6
1949	52	28.5	59	37.7	67	46.0	54	39.9	57	36.2	58	43.3	54	16.2	49	17.7	57	46.5	46	25.1
1948	49	39.9	57	54.7	66	61.3	51	50.7	54	46.9	55	49.5	55	16.5	49	16.9	57	34.5	46	17.0
1947	49	37.6	57	46.2	65	67.4	51	47.6	54	40.8	55	52.1	56	14.4	49	11.0	56	37.1	45	21.1
1946	50	33.0	58	37.6	67	49.0	52	40.6	55	38.4	57	40.9	55	12.3	50	13.5	59	57.1	46	29.0
1945	49	47.3	57	46.6	66	74.9	[1]52	[1]50.4	54	45.0	56	47.0	56	25.0	49	11.5	55	49.8	44	27.2
1944	48	39.6	57	45.5	66	51.2	[1]52	49.1	55	45.7	56	39.5	55	25.6	48	14.6	57	33.5	47	29.1
1943	48	36.1	58	36.8	65	36.2	[1]51	37.2	54	36.7	55	36.8	56	17.7	50	9.6	56	34.8	44	22.7
1942	50	44.2	58	46.0	66	41.4	51	57.7	54	38.9	56	41.2	56	24.9	49	13.0	57	45.1	46	30.6
1941	50	28.0	58	34.7	66	62.6	52	36.7	55	39.0	56	32.2	58	35.2	49	17.7	58	32.1	48	27.0
1940	45	35.9	55	44.3	64	45.5	49	48.7	52	45.1	53	44.8	57	34.8	50	16.4	56	25.0	44	28.5
1939	47	31.2	58	40.9	67	49.0	51	46.4	55	38.6	56	45.4	56	11.2	49	13.4	58	40.2	46	24.5
1938	49	40.2	56	34.8	67	31.1	52	57.8	54	48.5	56	48.5	56	22.2	50	15.6	59	41.2	47	29.6
1937	50	38.5	57	50.8	66	48.8	52	53.2	54	53.0	55	37.4	56	25.8	50	15.7	55	35.5	46	22.6
1936	49	40.0	56	44.6	66	40.2	50	59.6	53	49.8	55	38.7	57	22.4	50	14.4	57	26.1	44	18.5
1935	48	33.7	56	51.5	66	54.1	50	37.0	53	33.8	54	46.4	56	20.6	49	12.9	56	39.4	45	27.5
1934	47	36.5	56	50.9	66	38.8	50	49.0	54	49.8	55	38.4	58	15.0	52	13.3	58	29.2	47	22.7
1933	50	38.2	58	53.0	68	52.8	51	45.4	54	53.8	56	51.4	55	17.0	49	13.1	59	34.8	47	23.5
1932	49	34.2	57	49.6	67	44.8	52	45.6	55	43.9	56	43.9	56	12.0	48	15.4	57	38.0	45	23.6
1931	51	33.2	59	39.6	66	28.8	53	44.2	56	36.1	58	36.1	57	22.9	49	15.9	60	37.4	51	22.6
1930	50	25.5	58	21.6	65	32.4	52	34.7	54	39.9	57	34.0	57	16.7	48	13.2	58	23.2	46	20.0
1929	49	31.7	57	42.5	66	45.0	51	43.1	54	40.4	56	41.6	56	10.0	48	21.5	55	38.6	42	24.4
1928	49	33.6	56	43.4	65	42.8	51	45.0	54	45.6	55	39.4	56	19.0	49	13.1	56	38.6	45	24.8
1927	49	39.9	57	36.2	64	29.9	51	52.0	53	56.1	56	43.2	56	24.3	50	14.2	57	50.8	43	26.4
1926	46	30.8	55	45.2	65	35.1	48	43.8	51	47.8	54	44.9	58	26.7	49	13.0	56	33.4	44	27.3
1925	48	31.4	56	32.7	66	33.4	51	44.4	53	41.7	56	32.4	57	23.1	49	12.6	57	23.2	45	20.9
1924	47	30.5	55	49.0	65	51.1	49	38.3	52	41.6	54	43.1	56	20.2	49	8.9	54	36.5	42	30.6
1923	47	34.9	57	36.7	66	46.6	50	44.6	53	40.7	56	39.2	56	11.0	50	14.2	56	41.7	45	20.2
1922	49	34.1	57	42.5	67	50.6	51	43.3	54	44.7	54	29.3	55	25.7	49	10.3	58	32.3	46	25.0
1921	51	29.7	58	37.7	67	45.6	52	41.8	55	37.8	55	35.4	56	19.7	50	17.8	60	41.1	45	24.8
1920	47	37.6	56	48.4	64	46.8	51	53.2	53	53.2	55	46.2	57	18.3	48	13.2	56	31.5	45	24.7
1919	49	29.8	55	37.5	67	36.7	49	52.6	52	50.8	54	49.1	56	19.0	48	20.8	57	40.8	44	30.4
1918	48	26.4	58	37.9	65	31.3	52	44.9	55	39.6	57	37.7	56	20.8	49	15.2	58	35.9	46	30.2
1917	46	32.1	55	36.0	64	33.6	50	39.3	53	36.7	54	39.4	55	9.0	48	5.0	54	41.8	40	24.9
1916	47	32.1	57	42.5	66	42.5	49	40.1	53	37.8	55	32.3	54	28.1	49	16.4	57	44.1	43	24.5
1915	49	28.5	56	46.4	65	46.4	51	45.5	53	43.1	55	44.8	56	28.3	48	17.9	55	49.3	45	20.9
1914	47	28.0	55	44.0	64	44.0	49	43.8	53	38.5	54	39.1	56	24.0	48	17.3	57	35.6	45	30.6
1913	50	28.4	58	36.1	66	41.5	52	46.6	55	56.1	57	47.4	56	19.0	47	15.0	58	38.7	46	20.2
1912	47	38.6	57	45.1	65	51.3	50	44.8	53	44.2	54	47.0	55	15.6	48	10.3	54	44.6	43	21.2
1911	49	32.5	56	48.6	67	31.7	50	46.9	53	46.5	55	51.4	55	26.0	48	17.1	57	36.1	45	40.4
1910	48	28.5	56	35.0	64	39.7	50	39.7	53	32.7	55	39.6	54	12.4	50	8.6	55	37.3	46	10.2
1909	49	28.0	56	34.7	65	38.7	50	43.7	53	39.9	55	37.4	54	31.4	47	12.3	56	47.5	44	31.8
1908	48	28.4	58	35.4	66	31.4	51	43.3	54	44.8	56	38.1	54	14.6	48	12.8	57	34.2	46	31.6
1907	47	38.6	54	49.1	66	31.7	48	46.3	52	43.8	53	48.7	55	22.5	49	15.2	55	41.4	42	23.1
1906	48	32.5	56	43.6	65	43.6	50	51.3	54	39.4	55	51.9	55	26.3	48	16.6	55	35.5	45	33.2
1905	47	27.0	54	46.6	65	34.8	49	43.3	53	35.5	54	41.6	55	16.2	47	17.2	55	38.5	44	30.8
1904	45	31.3	53	36.1	64	37.9	47	41.7	50	39.5	52	39.8	55	24.7	49	14.2	54	34.1	43	34.1
1903	48	34.1	55	46.3	64	42.9	49	41.2	52	55.5	54	41.5	54	18.3	48	9.8	56	33.8	44	37.9
1902	48	37.5	55	50.1	65	37.2	49	44.3	53	50.3	54	49.8	54	19.2	50	13.4	56	38.4	45	31.8
1901	48	40.5	54	43.0	64	32.7	49	52.6	52	47.0	54	45.5	54	19.8	50	17.4	57	24.8	46	25.8

[1] Values adjusted to city location from airport.
[2] Value corrected for typographical errors in *World Weather Record*.

Series J 246-265. Long-Record City Stations—Annual Mean Temperature and Annual Total Precipitation: 1780 to 1957—Con.

[Italicized figures are based on interpolated monthly values]

Year	Albany, N.Y. Annual mean temperature (°F.) 246	Albany, N.Y. Annual total precipitation (Inches) 247	Baltimore, Md. temp 248	Baltimore, Md. precip 249	Charleston, S.C. temp 250	Charleston, S.C. precip 251	New Haven, Conn. temp 252	New Haven, Conn. precip 253	New York, N.Y. temp 254	New York, N.Y. precip 255	Philadelphia, Pa. temp 256	Philadelphia, Pa. precip 257	San Francisco, Calif. temp 258	San Francisco, Calif. precip 259	Santa Fe, N. Mex. temp 260	Santa Fe, N. Mex. precip 261	St. Louis, Mo. temp 262	St. Louis, Mo. precip 263	St. Paul, Minn. temp 264	St. Paul, Minn. precip 265
1900	50	30.6	57	31.6	66	38.1	51	34.8	54	39.4	56	40.9	55	15.3	50	15.9	58	29.5	46	34.2
1899	49	28.9	55	40.6	66	44.3	49	35.3	53	36.8	54	40.0	54	23.2	49	10.0	56	34.6	44	27.5
1898	50	38.8	56	36.5	66	²46.4	50	33.7	54	46.2	56	49.2	54	9.3	48	13.0	57	49.2	45	25.3
1897	49	40.8	55	47.6	66	50.6	49	57.9	53	42.4	55	42.0	54	16.4	48	20.4	57	40.2	45	30.5
1896	48	27.9	56	38.6	66	47.8	49	38.4	53	40.1	54	32.2	55	28.2	50	14.3	58	37.6	44	34.7
1895	48	29.8	54	40.5	64	55.2	49	36.0	52	33.7	54	31.0	55	17.1	47	20.2	55	31.2	44	24.3
1894	49	35.1	56	38.3	64	56.8	50	37.7	52	39.3	55	40.3	54	24.8	49	13.8	57	27.4	46	25.8
1893	47	35.4	54	32.2	65	71.0	48	46.7	50	46.6	53	37.6	53	17.9	49	14.9	55	39.3	41	26.0
1892	48	34.8	54	45.0	66	53.3	49	37.8	52	34.1	54	34.8	55	22.1	48	11.6	55	41.6	43	32.6
1891	49	41.7	56	54.2	65	45.5	50	44.7	54	37.6	55	38.2	56	21.1	47	16.8	56	30.5	44	21.8
1890	48	44.9	57	47.0	67	47.8	49	49.0	52	43.7	55	34.0	55	25.4	50	12.9	56	37.7	44	23.4
1889	50	39.5	56	62.5	65	52.2	50	59.8	52	54.4	55	50.6	57	36.9	50	7.9	56	33.2	45	17.0
1888	46	44.7	54	43.6	65	49.5	47	60.3	49	51.0	53	44.1	56	23.0	50	12.0	54	41.2	41	25.9
1887	48	39.7	55	43.6	66	44.7	49	44.1	51	41.7	54	42.2	55	19.0	50	13.4	58	35.3	42	25.8
1886	46	34.0	54	52.1	64	35.9	48	42.3	51	38.3	54	37.2	56	20.0	48	15.9	53	44.3	43	22.9
1885	44	34.4	54	46.0	64	²67.9	47	38.3	51	38.5	52	33.4	56	24.9	48	14.9	55	45.6	42	25.3
1884	48	38.9	56	45.9	66	60.2	49	49.3	52	49.7	54	39.3	55	38.8		19.7	56	40.6	44	26.1
1883	48	39.4	55	40.5	66	²51.3	48	39.5	50	34.4	55	39.2	56	15.4		14.8	54	40.1	41	26.7
1882	50	33.8	56	42.1	67	57.0	49	47.9	52	43.0	55	45.6	54	18.7	49	11.4	58	43.2	46	23.1
1881	50	36.3	57	49.1	66	²43.2	50	51.3	52	35.0	54	30.2	55	23.7	49	²22.2	53	37.4	45	39.2
1880	49	32.5	56	41.9	67	46.7	52	46.5	53	34.7	55	33.6	54	30.1	46	9.9	55	34.7	44	29.8
1879	46	38.7	55	36.0	66	50.3	51	55.5	52	37.1	54	36.8	56	30.8	51	11.4	56	25.7	46	32.4
1878	49	49.4	57	50.1	66	77.4	53	58.1	53	46.0	54	34.5	56	33.9	48	19.6	58	40.8	48	22.8
1877	48	36.1	56	43.1	67	78.1	52	54.1	52	38.7	54	37.5	57	11.5	48	13.2	57	41.5	47	28.8
1876	47	38.2	54	46.7	66	78.4	51		52	40.6	53	47.4	56	23.5	48	15.1	56	48.5	42	23.7
1875	44	38.2	53	45.3	64	51.0	48	43.5	49	38.6	50	40.2	55	22.6	49	19.0	53	43.0	39	30.7
1874	47	37.4	55	33.6	64	62.5	48	55.5	51	44.2	53	46.2	55	18.6	49	19.9	57	37.9	44	35.5
1873	50	39.4	55	49.4	64	62.2	48	57.3	51	45.5	52	55.5	55	18.6	50	9.9	54	45.5	44	33.7
1872	50	39.1	55	34.8	64	57.1	48		51	40.3	52	48.4	56	22.4	50	²11.2	58	30.5	44	29.8
1871	50	56.8	56	32.7	66	²63.4	48		51	49.2	55	47.3		27.5	56		58	23.4	44	30.6
1870	50	55.8	58	22.4	66	48.3	49	45.4	53	37.8	57	44.1		16.2	53	13.9	56	27.1	46	30.5
1869	47	44.2	56	27.3	67	43.1	47	47.0	52	43.6	55	48.9		22.6	48	12.1	54	47.0	42	31.0
1868	46	41.9	55	32.6	66	61.1	47		50	57.4	55	51.4	54		49	8.9	54	45.6	40	31.0
1867	47	38.0	56	32.9	66	61.0	48		51	53.4	54	61.2		²30.6		7.8	55	37.8	40	33.3
1866	47	34.3	56	27.5	64	36.3	48		52	38.3	54	45.3	54	36.3	52	11.5	57	43.2	44	27.5
1865	48	36.4	58	33.2	67	57.2	49	41.9	54	45.0	56	56.3	54	14.1	49	23.2	56	46.9	44	38.0
1864	48	27.9	57	23.0	67	57.2	50		53	39.5	55	46.0	56	21.6	50	21.8	55	37.6	43	15.5
1863	46	43.2	54	43.0	66	33.1	50		52	43.4	55	49.2	54	15.1	51	7.8	56	40.4	43	15.5
1862	46	37.6	54	35.5	67	52.3	50		52	46.4	54	45.0	55	38.6		11.3	53	44.0	41	28.2
1861	50	36.0	55	43.6	66	44.5	50		53	37.2	55	46.3	56	25.5	52	15.8	57	38.0	42	30.1
1860	48	32.2	54	37.5	68	44.4	49		52	31.1	54	44.2	55	21.2	51	8.8	56	29.8	43	29.3
1859	51	32.0	54	55.6	66	50.2	48		52	59.7	54	58.1	56	23.5	48	9.5	54	61.4	41	29.4
1858		34.0	57	46.1	66	48.1	48		51	36.7	53	39.8	57	21.0	49	11.4	56	68.8	44	27.4
1857	47	41.9	55	38.4	67	38.1	49		50	38.7	53	48.3		22.3	50	8.5	53	39.0	42	32.1
1856	47	39.1	54	22.9	64	49.1	47		50	35.0	52	34.0			50	23.1	52	42.6	43	22.6
1855	50	42.5	57	29.3	66	34.8	49		51	43.2	54	44.1		26.4	51	24.2	54	50.4	44	24.8
1854	49	34.1	56	59.2	66	37.6	49		51	43.5	55	40.2	56	22.4	50	24.8	57	40.6	45	26.6
1853	49	45.8	54	36.0	67	43.7	50		52	46.4	54	40.7	55	21.2	50	21.8	55	30.9	42	20.5
1852	48	32.0	55	51.6	66	43.5	49		51	35.5	53	45.8		27.3		21.7	55	47.0	42	15.1
1851	47	34.6	57	38.1	66	33.1	49		52	38.8	54	35.5	56	15.6	50	13.2	55	46.8	47	23.4
1850	48	51.8	58	44.8	66	23.7	49		51	44.6	54	54.6			51		55	50.5	44	25.5
1849	48	36.7	56	30.6	66	30.7	48		50	30.1	53	42.1	56	17.4	52	9.1	54	46.7	42	49.7
1848	50	48.2	57	34.4	65	43.4	49		52	32.8	55	35.1	55		50		54	65.4	42	23.2
1847	49	41.4	56	33.0	65	43.8	49		52	44.5	55	45.1			50		54	52.7	42	21.8
1846	50	39.8	55	40.7	65	44.3	50		52	35.9	54	44.4					57	45.4	48	26.1

² Value corrected for typographical errors in *World Weather Record*.

Series J 246–265. Long-Record City Stations—Annual Mean Temperature and Annual Total Precipitation: 1780 to 1957—Con.

[Italicized figures are based on interpolated monthly values]

Year	Albany, N.Y. mean temp (246) °F.	Albany precip (247) In.	Baltimore, Md. mean temp (248) °F.	Baltimore precip (249) In.	Charleston, S.C. mean temp (250) °F.	Charleston precip (251) In.	New Haven, Conn. mean temp (252) °F.	New Haven precip (253) In.	New York, N.Y. mean temp (254) °F.	New York precip (255) In.	Philadelphia, Pa. mean temp (256) °F.	Philadelphia precip (257) In.	San Francisco mean temp (258) °F.	San Francisco precip (259) In.	Santa Fe mean temp (260) °F.	Santa Fe precip (261) In.	St. Louis, Mo. mean temp (262) °F.	St. Louis precip (263) In.	St. Paul, Minn. mean temp (264) °F.	St. Paul precip (265) In.
1845	50	39.4	55	28.4	64	46.4	50	---	53	33.7	54	40.2	---	---	---	---	56	38.0	46	25.3
1844	48	35.0	54	32.5	66	36.4	50	---	52	39.8	53	40.2	---	---	---	---	57	45.8	43	30.2
1843	47	48.4	54	48.8	64	54.7	47	---	51	35.7	52	46.9	---	---	---	---	54	34.8	40	23.8
1842	48	46.0	55	35.1	66	42.1	50	---	53	41.6	53	48.5	---	---	---	---	56	32.3	43	25.2
1841	48	38.0	53	43.9	66	53.9	50	---	51	44.6	52	55.5	---	---	---	---	56	42.7	44	21.7
1840	49	44.4	54	37.5	67	46.1	49	---	51	35.5	53	47.4	---	---	---	---	56	41.6	45	23.2
1839	48	38.1	56	51.7	67	53.0	49	---	51	33.4	52	43.7	---	---	---	---	55	47.4	47	21.2
1838	47	42.0	54	47.1	67	58.9	48	---	50	33.7	51	45.8	---	---	---	---	53	31.5	42	27.7
1837	46	41.2	54	46.0	67	²56.4	46	---	49	32.1	51	39.0	---	---	---	---	55	27.0	44	24.0
1836	45	44.6	52	54.6	66	40.9	45	---	47	36.6	50	42.7	---	---	---	---	53	---	43	---
1835	46	40.5	54	34.1	67	49.0	47	---	50	28.8	54	39.3	---	---	---	---	---	---	43	---
1834	48	32.4	57	29.5	68	68.6	49	---	51	33.6	55	34.2	---	---	---	---	---	---	47	---
1833	48	41.8	57	41.3	66	48.4	48	---	52	37.7	54	48.6	---	---	---	---	---	---	48	---
1832	48	44.4	57	34.3	67	45.0	48	---	52	39.2	54	39.5	---	---	---	---	---	---	46	---
1831	49	39.5	55	37.4	66	---	49	---	52	38.8	54	43.9	---	---	---	---	---	---	43	---
1830	51	41.8	58	39.0	70	---	51	---	55	43.3	55	45.1	---	---	---	---	---	---	48	---
1829	48	38.1	55	52.3	66	---	49	---	52	45.8	53	41.9	---	---	---	---	---	---	46	---
1828	51	37.7	58	33.0	71	---	52	---	54	48.9	56	38.0	---	---	---	---	---	---	46	---
1827	49	49.8	58	32.7	67	---	49	---	52	51.1	52	38.5	---	---	---	---	---	---	46	---
1826	51	33.1	58	30.7	66	---	50	51.4	52	55.7	54	35.2	---	---	---	---	---	---	45	---
1825	50	---	58	26.2	67	---	51	---	54	---	54	29.7	---	---	---	---	---	---	48	---
1824	48	---	57	42.3	67	---	50	---	52	---	---	49.9	---	---	---	---	---	---	43	---
1823	47	---	56	44.6	65	---	48	---	51	---	---	44.6	---	---	---	---	---	---	44	---
1822	49	---	59	29.2	---	---	50	---	54	---	---	40.6	---	---	---	---	---	---	44	---
1821	48	---	56	50.2	---	---	---	---	---	---	---	30.6	---	---	---	---	---	---	43	---
1820	49	---	55	42.5	---	---	48	44.6	---	---	---	36.2	---	---	---	---	---	---	43	---
1819	---	---	57	28.8	---	---	49	46.2	---	---	---	---	---	---	---	---	---	---	---	---
1818	---	---	55	32.6	---	---	47	33.9	---	---	---	---	---	---	---	---	---	---	---	---
1817	---	---	55	49.0	---	---	46	38.4	---	---	---	49.4	---	---	---	---	---	---	---	---
1816	---	---	55	---	---	---	47	38.0	---	---	---	---	---	---	---	---	---	---	---	---

Year	Albany, N.Y. mean temp (246) °F.	Charleston, S.C. precip (251) In.	New Haven, Conn. mean temp (252) °F.	New Haven, Conn. precip (253) In.
1815	---	---	47	50.6
1814	50	---	49	56.1
1813	48	---	49	53.4
1812	---	---	47	44.2
1811	---	49.3	50	47.7
1810	---	45.4	50	²39.4
1809	---	66.0	49	44.6
1808	---	40.8	50	49.4
1807	---	42.2	49	45.3
1806	---	---	50	38.6
1805	---	---	52	---
1804	---	---	50	40.8
1803	---	---	51	43.3
1802	---	---	51	---
1801	---	---	---	---
1800	---	---	50	---
1799	---	---	48	---
1798	---	---	49	---

Year	Albany, N.Y., annual mean temperature (246) °F.	New Haven, Conn., annual mean temperature (252) °F.
1797	---	48
1796	---	48
1795	---	---
1794	---	---
1793	---	50
1792	47	48
1791	50	50
1790	---	50
1789	---	50
1788	---	48
1787	---	48
1786	---	---
1785	---	48
1784	---	47
1783	---	49
1782	---	49
1781	---	50
1780	---	50

² Value corrected for typographical errors in *World Weather Record*.

chapter K

Agriculture

K 1–328. General note.

Basic statistics on agriculture are, for the most part, prepared by the Bureau of the Census which conducts the Census of Agriculture, and by the Agricultural Marketing Service and the Agricultural Research Service which prepare current estimates.

Annual agricultural statistics have been issued by the Department of Agriculture since May 1, 1863. Statistics compiled by the Agricultural Marketing Service on crops, livestock and livestock products, agricultural prices, farm employment, and related subjects are based mainly on data obtained by mail from nearly three-quarters of a million reporters, mostly farmers. They are located in every agricultural county in the United States and report on one or more items during a year.

Beginning with 1840, a Census of Agriculture has been taken every 10 years and, beginning in 1925, a middecade Census of Agriculture has also been taken. Census information is obtained by a personal canvass of individual farms. The first census was limited in scope. It included such items as an inventory of the principal classes of domestic animals, the production of wool, the value of poultry, the value of dairy products, and the production of principal crops. The number of farms and the acreage and value of farmland were first included in 1850 and in 1880 information on farm tenure was first secured. A detailed classification of farmland according to use was first obtained in 1925; in earlier censuses, farmland was classified only as improved land, woodland, and other unimproved land (see chapter J). For brief discussions of the comparability of various agricultural data, census to census, see Bureau of the Census, *U.S. Census of Agriculture: 1954*, vol. II.

For each decade from 1840 through 1900, the Census of Agriculture was taken as of June 1. The five decennial censuses since then have been taken as of April 15, 1910; January 1, 1920; April 1, 1930, 1940, and 1950. The 1925, 1935, and 1945 quinquennial Censuses of Agriculture were taken as of January 1; the 1954 Census was taken in October and November.

The definition of a farm has varied as follows from census to census:

For the 1954 Census of Agriculture, places of 3 or more acres were counted as farms if the annual value of agricultural products for sale or home use (exclusive of home-garden products) amounted to $150 or more. Places of less than 3 acres were counted as farms only if the annual value of sales of agricultural products amounted to $150 or more. Places for which the value of agricultural products for 1954 was less than these minima because of crop failure or other unusual conditions and places operated for the first time in 1954 were counted as farms if normally they could be expected to produce these minimum quantities of agricultural products.

If a place had croppers or other tenants, the land assigned each one was considered a separate farm, even though the landlord handled the entire holding as one operating unit in respect to supervision, equipment, rotation practice, purchase of supplies, or sale of products. Land retained by the landlord and worked by him with the help of his family and/or hired labor was likewise considered a farm.

For the 1950 Census of Agriculture, the definition of a farm was the same as for 1954. For the 1945 and earlier censuses, the definition of a farm was somewhat more inclusive. For 1925–1945, farms included (1) places of 3 or more acres on which there were agricultural operations and (2) places of less than 3 acres if the agricultural products for home use or for sale were valued at $250 or more. The only reports excluded from the 1925–1940 tabulations were those taken in error and those with very limited agricultural production, such as only a small home garden, a few fruit trees, a very small flock of chickens, etc. In 1945, reports for places of 3 acres or more with limited agricultural operations were retained only if (1) there were 3 or more acres of cropland and pasture or (2) the value of products in 1944 amounted to $150 or more.

The definition of a farm in the 1910 and 1920 Censuses was similar to that used from 1925 to 1940 but was even more inclusive. In those years, farms of less than 3 acres with products valued at less than $250 were to be included provided they required the continuous services of at least one person. In 1900, there were no acreage or production limits. Market, truck, and fruit gardens, orchards, nurseries, cranberry marshes, greenhouses, and city dairies were to be included provided the entire time of at least one person was devoted to their care. For 1870, 1880, and 1890, no tract of less than 3 acres was to be reported as a farm unless $500 worth of produce was sold from it during the year. For 1860, no definition was given the enumerators. For 1850, no acreage qualification was given, but there was a lower limit of $100 for value of products.

K 1. Number of farms, 1850–1957.

Source: 1850–1900, Bureau of the Census, *U.S. Census of Agriculture: 1954*, vol. II, p. 4; 1910-1956, Agricultural Marketing Service, *Number of Farms, by States, 1910-1956* (revised estimates), November 1957; 1957, "Number of Farms, by States, 1957" (mimeographed release), February 1958.

For 1910–1957, figures are adjusted estimates that are not exactly comparable with earlier data. Estimates for census years were adjusted for underenumeration and for changes in definition of a farm; estimates for intercensal years are based on trend and on indications of change in acreage and livestock surveys, in annual assessors' censuses in a number of States, in Agricultural Stabilization and Conservation records, and in other miscellaneous verifying data.

K 2. Land in farms, 1850–1954.

Source: Census years, Bureau of the Census, *Censuses of Agriculture*, various reports; intercensal years, Department of Agriculture, records (data obtained by straight-line interpolations).

Information on farmland values in scattered local areas is referred to by P. W. Bidwell and J. I. Falconer, *History of Agriculture in the Northern United States, 1620–1860*, pp. 70–71, 242, and 328. Similar information for Southern States is found in L. C. Gray, *History of Agriculture in the Southern*

United States to 1860, vol. I, pp. 403–406, and vol. II, pp. 640–645.

K 3. Total value of selected items of farm property, 1850–1957.

Source: Agricultural Research Service, *Balance Sheet of Agriculture*, annual issues.

Current market values of farm real estate, machinery and equipment, and livestock are combined in this series. Estimates of the value of farm real estate are based upon census reports and the annual index of farm real estate values, as described in series K 7. Inventory values for machinery and equipment and for livestock are based in part on census reports and supplemental estimates made by the Agricultural Marketing Service. A description of the estimates relating to machinery and equipment appears in *Major Statistical Series of the U.S. Department of Agriculture*, Agriculture Handbook No. 118, vol. 3.

K 4–5. Value of farmland and buildings, 1850–1957.

Source: Agricultural Research Service, *Current Developments in the Farm Real Estate Market*, various issues.

Data for years 1850-1910, 1920, 1925, 1930, 1940, 1950, and 1954 are from Census of Agriculture reports; figures for all other years are estimates derived by applying the change in the index of average value of land and buildings per acre to these census benchmarks, recognizing changes in acres of land in farms. All farm operators were asked to estimate the market value of their farms in each census from 1850 through 1945. In the 1950 and 1954 Censuses, data were obtained from all large farms and from a 20-percent sample of other farms.

Average value of land and buildings per acre is obtained by dividing the total value shown by the acres of land in farms, using unrounded data.

K 6. Total value of farm buildings, 1900–1957.

Source: See source for series K 4–5.

Data for 1900, 1910, 1920, 1925, 1930, and 1940 are from Censuses of Agriculture. Annual estimates since 1940 are extrapolations from this date based upon estimates of the market value of land with and without improvements obtained from the regular crop reporters of the Department of Agriculture. The average value per acre of unimproved land (without buildings) is expressed as a percentage of the value of improved land (with buildings) and converted to an index with 1940 as 100. This index is then applied to a comparable ratio obtained from the 1940 Census. Aggregate dollar values of buildings are obtained by applying the projected ratios for each State (buildings as a percentage of land and buildings) to the annual estimates of the total value of farm real estate mentioned in text for series K 3. The resulting dollar estimates reflect the amount added to the market value of farmland by buildings. They bear no direct relationship to the value of buildings that would be derived by applying the cost-less-depreciation principle to building valuation.

K 7. Index of average value of farm real estate per acre, 1912–1957.

Source: See source for series K 4–5.

See also *Major Statistical Series of the U.S. Department of Agriculture*, Agriculture Handbook No. 118, vol. 6, for a more complete description of methods used and limitations.

This index, which is available also by States, is designed to measure changes in the market value of farm real estate, including land, buildings, and such other permanent improvements as are customarily included when farms are sold. The index is constructed from estimates of average value of farm real estate per acre obtained from the regular crop reporters of the Department of Agriculture. It is not based upon the value of farm real estate obtained in the census. Between 15,000 and 20,000 reporters supply estimates of the market value of farms per acre in their localities as of March 1, July 1, and November 1. Although they undoubtedly base their estimates in part upon actual sales, no sales data are used directly in computing the index. Averages for crop-reporting districts are weighted by acres of land in farms as taken from the 1945 and 1950 Censuses to obtain weighted State averages which are, in turn, weighted by acres of land in farms to obtain regional and national averages. The weighted dollar values per acre are then expressed as index numbers.

K 8–52. Farms, by color and tenure of operator, and acreage and value, by tenure of operator, 1880–1954.

Source: Bureau of the Census, *U.S. Census of Agriculture: 1954*, vol. II, pp. 954–959.

Data on farm-operator status was not obtained until the Census of 1880. Studies of land tenure before 1860 are based, necessarily, upon fragments of information. See Bidwell and Falconer's *History of Agriculture . . .*, and Gray's *History of Agriculture . . .* (see text for series K 2).

The 1900 Census of Agriculture covered the ownership of rented farms, with particular reference to absentee ownership and the concentration of ownership. On a sample basis, the Department of Agriculture made a study of ownership of rented farms in 1920; the results were published as *Bulletins 1432 and 1433*. The Bureau of the Census and Department of Agriculture cooperated on sample surveys in 1945, 1950, and 1954 which were designed to show the portion of all farmland owned by each major class of owner. The results of these studies are published in Department of Agriculture, *Agricultural Economics Research*, vol. V, No. 4, 1953, and in Agricultural Research Service and Bureau of the Census, *Graphic Summary of Tenure, 1954*. A complete study of farmland ownership in the United States was made in 1945 and published as Department of Agriculture, *Miscellaneous Publication No. 699.*

In 1916, the Bureau of the Census published *Plantation Farming in the United States* from a 1910 Census study of plantations in 325 selected counties in 11 Southern States. In the selected plantation area, 39,073 plantations were reported as having 5 or more tenants. Another study of plantations was made in connection with the 1940 Census, but the results have not been published. In 1947, the Bureau of the Census published *Multiple Unit Operations* from a study made in connection with the 1945 Census of Agriculture. The Bureau has also published volumes on multiple unit operations from the 1950 and 1954 Censuses of Agriculture. In 1924, the Bureau of Agricultural Economics issued *Department Bulletin 1269*, the results of a study by C. O. Brannen, *Relation of Land Tenure to Plantation Organization*.

For the Censuses of 1880 and 1890 only the number of farms was classified by tenure. Classifications by the color of the farm operator and crossclassifications by color and tenure were first made in the Census of 1900.

A farm operator, according to the Census definition, is a person who operates a farm, either performing the labor himself or directly supervising it. The Census definition of a farm is based on operating units, rather than ownership tracts. A farm may consist of a number of separate tracts held under different tenures, some owned and some rented. Similarly, when a landowner has several tenants, renters, or croppers, the land operated by each is considered a separate farm. Therefore, the number of farm operators, for all practical purposes, is identical with the number of farms (series K 8) and these items are used interchangeably.

In the color classification of farm operators, Mexicans are reported as white. The nonwhite group includes Negroes, Indians, Chinese, Japanese, and other nonwhite races.

Each farm was classified according to the tenure under which the operator controlled the land. Land was considered owned if the operator or his wife held it under title, homestead law, purchase contract, or as one of the heirs or as trustee of an undivided estate. If both an owned and a rented tract were farmed by the same operator, these were to be considered as one farm even though the tracts were not contiguous and each was locally called a farm. Farm operators were classified as (a) full owners who own all the land they operate; (b) part owners who own a part and rent from others the rest of the land they operate; (c) managers who operate farms for others and receive wages or salaries for their services (persons acting merely as caretakers or hired laborers were not classed as managers, and farms operated for institutions or corporations were considered to be managed even where no person was specifically indicated as being employed as the farm manager); (d) tenants who operate hired or rented land only. Croppers are share tenants to whom landlords furnish all of the work animals or tractor power in lieu of work animals. Croppers were first classified separately in the 1920 Census.

In the 1920, 1925, and 1930 Censuses, croppers were defined as share tenants whose landlords furnished the work animals. The 1935 Census schedule carried no inquiry on the method of paying rent and, therefore, croppers for that year included all tenants whose landlords furnished the work animals. The furnishing of tractor power was not taken into account in classifying croppers until the 1940 Census.

The greatest difficulties in making a classification by tenure result from the sharecropper system. Briefly, the question involved is whether the sharecropper should be considered merely a type of laborer or a farm operator. In reality, croppers have some of the characteristics of both laborers and tenants.

K 53–60. Number, acreage, value, and amount of indebtedness of mortgaged farms, by tenure of operator, 1930–1956.

Source: Bureau of the Census and Agricultural Research Service, U.S. Census of Agriculture: 1954, vol. III, pt. 5.

Information on the number of mortgaged farms has been collected by both the Bureau of the Census and the Agricultural Research Service. Generally speaking, such data have been published with the data on amount of debt in census years, except in 1900 when no information on amount of debt was obtained. For a historical summary and an analysis of the data on number of mortgaged owner-operated farms for 1890–1935, see "Number and Percentage of Farms Under Mortgage," Agricultural Finance Review, vol. 1, No. 2, November 1938. The source cited above also includes State data on the number of mortgaged farms in each tenure class for 1940, 1945, 1950, and 1956.

Farm-mortgage debt includes the unpaid principal of mortgages, deeds of trust, sales contracts, vendors' liens, and all other debt for which farm real estate is pledged as security. Any farm which has a real estate mortgage is classified as a mortgaged farm even though only a portion of it is mortgaged.

These estimates are based on information obtained in the Census of Agriculture for owner-operated farms, mail surveys of samples of farm owners (including both operators and landlords), and reports from farm-mortgage lenders.

For each of the years shown, mortgage information was obtained from full-owner farm operators in the Census of Agriculture. Similar information was obtained by the Bureau of the Census for part owners for 1940, 1945, 1950, and 1956. This information was supplemented by data obtained in mail surveys for land operated by part owners, tenants, and managers. The 1930 mail survey was conducted by the Bureau of Agricultural Economics. Later surveys were cooperative undertakings of the Bureau of the Census and the Bureau of Agricultural Economics or the Agricultural Research Service.

For information by States and geographic divisions and descriptions of procedures, see the source cited, and U.S. Census of Agriculture: 1950, vol. V, pt. 8.

See also text for series K 8–52 for definition of tenure.

K 61–72. Farms and land in farms, by size of farm, 1880–1954.

Source: Bureau of the Census, U.S. Census of Agriculture: 1954, vol. II, pp. 352–354.

See general note for series K 1–364 for changes in definition of farm.

Since 1920, farms of 10 to 99 acres have shown a marked decrease, farms of 100 to 259 acres a slight decrease, and farms from 260 to 1,000 acres and over some increase. The greater number of very large farms does not mean that family farms are decreasing in relative importance. Rapid advances in technology have enabled a given family labor force to farm larger acreages.

With the development of better roads and more off-farm job opportunities, farms of less than 10 acres increased in number between 1940 and 1945, then decreased in 1950. This decrease may have been due to the change in the definition of a farm, which eliminated many small places previously counted as farms.

K 73–75. Farm employment, 1910–1957.

Source: Agricultural Marketing Service, Statistical Bulletin No. 236, September 1958.

For detailed descriptions of farm employment concepts, see Major Statistical Series of the U.S. Department of Agriculture, Agriculture Handbook No. 118, vol. 7, pp. 8–12. See source publication for geographic regional and State data.

These data are based on (1) data from the Census of Population used as benchmarks for 1910, 1920, and 1930, and data from the Census of Agriculture used for 1940, 1950, and 1954; (2) estimates of farm employment from nationwide enumerative sample surveys made at intervals during 1945–1948, together with historical data on the seasonal distributions of man-hour labor requirements in farm production, used to develop measures of seasonal variation; (3) returns from the monthly mailed questionnaire on employment on farms of crop reporters, available since 1925; and (4) annual estimates of the number of farms by States and regions used to expand "adjusted" average employment per farm to obtain regional and national estimates of total farm employment and of the family and hired worker components of the total.

The source also presents monthly estimates of total farm employment for 1950–1957 for the United States, for each of the 9 major geographic divisions, and State data for 35 selected States.

Family workers include working farm operators, plus members of their families who did unpaid farmwork or chores for 15 hours or more during the survey week. All persons working one hour or more during the survey week for pay at farmwork or chores are classified as hired farmworkers. Members of the operator's family receiving wages for work on their farms are counted as hired workers. Sharecroppers are considered family workers when working on their own crops but are classified as hired workers when doing farmwork for pay off their tracts. A person employed as both a family worker and a hired worker during the survey week on the same farm is counted as a hired worker. The survey week is the last complete calendar week in the month, but when that week includes the last day of the month the survey week is the next to the last full calendar week.

The average number of hired and family workers per farm is computed for the reporting farms for all States. The averages are then adjusted by factors based on comparisons with the last census level, labor requirements data, and the estimated seasonal pattern of employment based on the latest census and special studies in selected States. The adjusted averages are then multiplied by the estimated number of farms in each State to estimate the number of family and hired workers employed. Data from the census, State assessors' reports, Agricultural Stabilization and Conservation records, and indications of change from the larger acreage and livestock surveys are used in estimating the number of farms. Annual averages of employment are simple averages of last-of-month employment estimates. In addition to farm employment estimates, monthly indexes of farm employment are available.

Farm employment data were first collected through crop reporters in October 1923. In 1938, the National Research Project of the Works Progress Administration developed monthly farm employment estimates for 1925–1936 from the crop reporter data. See E. C. Shaw and J. A. Hopkins, *Trends in Employment in Agriculture, 1909–1936*, Works Progress Administration, Philadelphia, November 1938. Monthly estimates have been made by the Agricultural Marketing Service and the former Bureau of Agricultural Economics from crop reporter data for 1936–1957, using the methods developed in the Works Progress Administration project, plus certain recent refinements. Periodic revisions have been made as new benchmark data became available from national enumerative surveys or from Censuses of Agriculture. Following the 1950 Census of Agriculture, the entire historical series was re-examined and revised. Data for 1950–1957 reflect revisions following the 1954 Census of Agriculture.

K 76–80. Farm wage rates, 1866–1957.

Source: 1866–1909, Bureau of Agricultural Economics, *Farm Wage Rates, Farm Employment, and Related Data*, January 1943 (processed); 1910–1957, Agricultural Marketing Service, *Farm Labor*, January 1958.

Information on farm wages prior to 1866 is scattered; it consists of individual records or covers only certain States rather than the entire country. See Department of Agriculture, Bureau of Statistics, *Wages of Farm Labor in the United States*, Miscellaneous Series, Report No. 4, 1892; same agency's *Wages of Farm Labor*, by George K. Holmes, Bulletin 99, 1912; and T. M. Adams, *Prices Paid by Vermont Farmers for Goods and Services and Received by Them for Farm Products, 1790–1940*; see also Vermont Agricultural Experiment Station Bulletin 507, *Wages of Vermont Farm Labor, 1780–1940*, Burlington, February 1944.

The first investigation made by the Department of Agriculture of wage rates for hired farm workers was in 1866. In the next 44 years, 18 similar studies were made at irregular intervals. Then, for 1909–1923, inquiries were made annually and, since 1923, quarterly. In all these surveys, questionnaires were sent to the voluntary crop reporters.

For 1866–1909, crop reporters were requested to estimate the average wages in the locality for the year. Sometimes the inquiry was made in the spring and sometimes in the fall or winter. When it was made in the spring, the year to which the annual average refers is uncertain. For this reason, a dual date is designated for certain of these years as, for example, "1874 or 1875." In each of these 19 investigations, wage rates per day were obtained separately for harvest work and other work. The data published here for these years are the day rates for "other than harvest work."

The monthly wage rates (series K 77–78) shown for 1866–1909 are not strictly comparable throughout this period. For 1866–1890, monthly wage rates shown are for workers hired by the year. In addition, in the first three of the aforementioned inquiries, crop reporters were asked for monthly rates paid to workers hired for the season, which are published by Holmes (see above). For 1891–1909, the monthly rate requested was on a combined annual and seasonal basis. In 1909, the distinction was again made, but the two types of monthly rates were averaged. The weighted average (revised) is published here. For the original averages of the monthly rates for workers hired by the year and for those hired by the season, see Holmes, *Wages of Farm Labor*, referred to above. For 1866–1909, wage rates requested were those paid to men doing outdoor work. In 1902, 1906, and 1909, rates paid women for domestic work on farms were also requested.

Data from the 19 wage inquiries were published in 4 bulletins by the Bureau of Statistics of the Department of Agriculture—No. 4 (1892), 22 (1901), and 26 (1903) of the "Miscellaneous" series, and Bulletin 99 (1912) of the Bureau of Statistics series. In the first 3 bulletins, the rates were published without reducing currency to gold values, since the monetary system was not on a gold basis; but in Bulletin 99 and in subsequent reports the wage rates for the period of inflated currency values during and following the Civil War were reduced to gold values. In Bulletin 99 the weighting system, which was not uniform for all previous surveys, was revised and wage-rate data for all 19 surveys were recomputed. The number of male agricultural laborers in each State, as reported by the census of occupations, was used as the weight to obtain United States and major region averages from State average wage rates.

For 1909–1923, annual inquiries on farm wage rates in their localities were made of crop reporters. They were asked about monthly rates with and without board; and about daily rates with and without board "at harvest" and for "other than harvest labor." In 1923, to give an overlap for linking purposes, a quarterly inquiry was initiated. The new quarterly series eliminated the distinction between day rates for harvest work and for nonharvest work; it changed the time reference of day rates to "average wage rates being paid to hired labor at the present time in your locality," with an additional instruction to include in the estimates of day rates "average daily earnings of piece workers." The new rates obtained after 1923 are probably more nearly comparable with the old daily wage rates for "other than harvest work" than they are with either the old daily rates for harvest work or with a combination of the two types of daily rates.

For 1923–1948, the questions asked crop reporters on wage rates continued in almost exactly the same form. In 1948, the wage rate series was changed to include more different kinds of rates and to specify more clearly the perquisites received in addition to cash wages. Value of perquisites is not included in wage rates obtained—they are cash rates only. The types of rates currently obtained are as follows: Per month with board and room, per month with house (no meals), per week with board and room, per week without board or room, per day with board and room, per day with house (no meals), per day without board or room, per hour with house (no meals), and per hour without board or room.

Rates for 1949-1957 are not exactly comparable with rates for previous years. They only approximate the rates denoted in the series headings and represent averages for the following rates: Per month with board and room, per month with house, per day with board and room, and per day without board or room.

Average rates based on data reported by crop reporters are published quarterly and annually in Agricultural Marketing Service, *Farm Labor*, but annually only in the Department of Agriculture, *Agricultural Statistics*. Both quarterly and annual average rates are published for States, nine major geographic divisions, and the United States. The annual average rates are averages of the quarterly averages weighted by the number of hired farm workers employed each quarter.

Since employment data are for approximately the last week of the month and wage rates are usually reported a few days before the end of the month, they must be weighted to center on July 1 (the midpoint in the calendar year) in computing an annual average. The annual average is a 5-quarter average based on data for January of the current year and January of the following year. The use of only the January current year data would not properly weight the changes after October 1, especially when rates are rising or falling significantly.

K 81. Farmers' expenditures for hired labor, 1910-1957.

Source: Agricultural Marketing Service, *The Farm Income Situation*, July 1958 (No. 174).

Data for census years are from Bureau of the Census; intercensal year figures are Agricultural Marketing Service estimates. For a detailed description of concepts and methods, see *Major Statistical Series of the U.S. Department of Agriculture*, Agriculture Handbook No. 118, vol. 3.

Estimates of farmers' total expenditures for hired labor are available for 1929 and since 1949 for individual States. The total farm labor bill is divided between cash wages and the value of perquisites furnished. It is also divided between the wages paid to workers living on farms and those not living on farms.

K 82. Index man-hours of labor used for farmwork, 1910-1957.

Source: Department of Agriculture, *Changes in Farm Production and Efficiency*, Statistical Bulletin No. 233, August 1958.

Man-hours of labor used in farming are estimated by applying regional average man-hours per acre of crops and per head or unit of production of livestock to the official estimates of acreages and numbers made by the Agricultural Marketing Service.

Time for farm maintenance or general overhead work is calculated separately and added to the direct hours for crops and livestock to obtain the total number of man-hours. Annual man-hours per acre or per head are estimated by interpolating between or extrapolating from benchmarks.

Benchmarks are estimates of labor used per acre and per head in each State converted to a geographic-division basis. State estimates for 1939, 1944, and 1950 appear in two reports of the former Bureau of Agricultural Economics (*Labor Requirements for Crops and Livestock*, 1943, and *Labor Requirements in the United States*, 1939 and 1944) and in reports of the Agricultural Research Service (*Labor Used for Field Crops*, Statistical Bulletin No. 144, June 1954; and *Labor Used for Livestock*, Statistical Bulletin No. 161, 1955). Similar bench-

marks for 1910, 1919, and 1929 developed from data in the Works Progress Administration National Research Project reports were summarized in that agency's *Changing Technology and Employment in Agriculture*, 1941. These reports were based on extensive field surveys, while the first-mentioned studies were based on secondary data.

The interpolation of numbers of man-hours per acre or per animal between benchmarks and extrapolation beyond benchmarks are modified by several factors. For crops, these include such items as yields per acre, utilization of the crop, methods of harvest, and source of power as indicated by numbers of tractors and work stock on farms. For livestock, the modifiers include such factors as size of enterprise, production per animal, and extent of different methods and practices followed.

For more detailed explanation, for the aggregate man-hours upon which the indexes are based, and for other more detailed data, see *Major Statistical Series of the U.S. Department of Agriculture*, Agriculture Handbook No. 118, vol. 2.

K 83-97. Man-hours used to produce specified amounts of wheat, corn, and cotton, 1800-1950.

Source: 1800-1940, Department of Agriculture, *Progress of Farm Mechanization*, Miscellaneous Publication No. 630, October 1947; 1950, *Labor Used for Field Crops*, Statistical Bulletin No. 144, June 1954.

In Publication No. 630, the yield of cotton was reported in gross weight, including an allowance for the weight of bagging and ties on a standard bale. In series K 96, the yield was converted to pounds of cotton lint which corresponds to the current method of reporting yields of cotton.

The 1950 figures for yield per acre (series K 86, K 91, and K 96) are averages for 1948-1952. This agrees with the procedure for computing yields for the other years. Because of the higher 5-year average yield and because the time required to pick cotton is closely related to the yield, it was necessary to raise the number of man-hours used in harvesting cotton (series K 95) above those shown in Bulletin No. 144. The numbers of hours used in harvesting wheat and corn were not adjusted because the 5-year average yield did not differ significantly from the 1950 yield.

The numbers of man-hours per acre (series K 83-85, K 88-90, and K 93-95) are estimated from data on labor requirements published by State and Federal agencies. A list of such publications appears in Bureau of Agricultural Economics, *A Partial List of Publications on Farm Labor Requirements by Commodities*, 1943. For recent years, the estimates of man-hours per acre, like those in Bulletin No. 144, have been developed on a State basis. Related data used in preparing the estimates include sources of farm power as indicated by numbers of tractors, work stock and associated machines on farms, yield per acre, and methods of harvesting. These related materials are too numerous to list, but, as an example, see Department of Agriculture, *Harvesting Corn for Grain*, Statistical Bulletin No. 129, 1953.

The figures for yields (series K 86, K 91, and K 96) were developed from Agricultural Marketing Service acreage and production data (series K 265-266, K 269-270, and K 301-302).

K 98-103. Acreages of harvested crops, by use, and indexes of cropland used for crops and crop production per acre, 1910-1957.

Source: See source for series K 82.

These data measure changes in the total acreage of crops harvested and in acreages used for different broad purposes. Acreages for harvested crops do not include pasture. The total number of crop acres harvested consists of acreages of the 59 crops harvested (excluding duplication) plus acreages in tree fruits, small fruits, tree nuts, and farm gardens. Acreages of several minor crops, which are not included, have accounted for about 0.5 million acres in recent years. Basic data for the estimates are published in the releases of the Agricultural Marketing Service and in the Census of Agriculture reports from the Bureau of the Census.

Acreages used for production of each crop exported are determined by dividing the quantity exported by the average yield per acre. Two steps are necessary in computing the acreages of crops used to produce each of the livestock products exported. The first consists of estimating the quantities of each feed crop used to produce 100 pounds of pork, 100 pounds of milk, 100 dozen eggs, and so on. The second consists of determining the quantity of each feed crop used to produce the products exported, and then determining the acreages needed to produce each feed crop, at average yields per acre. Periodic 5-year average yields rather than yields for each year are used.

Yield data for the export estimates are from reports of the Crop Reporting Board. Data for volume of exports prior to 1940 are from *Agricultural Statistics*. For 1940–1957, export data are from reports and records of the Agricultural Marketing Service.

Estimates of feed consumed by horses and mules are based on the following average rations of corn, oats, and all hay: For 1910–1919, the calculations allow 800 pounds of oats, 1,600 pounds of shelled corn, and 1.8 tons of hay per head for farm horses and mules 3 years old and over and animal-unit equivalents for younger animals. For 1920–1940, it was assumed that as farm horses were worked less, they consumed less grain and more hay. Consequently, the rate of feeding corn was decreased 10 pounds per head per year and the rate of feeding hay was increased 20 pounds. Beginning with 1941, it was assumed that horses and mules would work less each year, and that on the average they would be fed less corn, oats, and hay and would consume more pasture.

For nonfarm horses and mules, it was assumed that, for 1910–1931, the quantities of grain and hay consumed per head per year were a third more than those consumed by farm work animals. Since 1932, the computations have rounded out to one million acres used in producing feed for nonfarm horses and mules.

Basic data on horses and mules are from publications of the Agricultural Marketing Service. The rations for horses and mules are based on data from many sources, especially from Bureau of Agricultural Economics, *Work Performed and Feed Utilized by Horses and Mules*, Farm Management 44, 1944, and on judgment of workers familiar with the subject.

The series on cropland used for crops (series K 102) is made up of three components—acres of harvested cropland (land from which one or more crops were harvested), crop failure, and summer fallow. The index is intended to measure changes in the land area in crops or being prepared for crops the following year; it excludes idle cropland and land in soil-improvement crops during the entire year and not harvested. These figures are based on estimates of principal crops harvested and crop losses of the former Bureau of Agricultural Economics and the Agricultural Marketing Service and on data from the 1925 to 1954 Censuses of Agriculture. Data from the 1950 and 1954 Censuses of Agriculture were adjusted

to cover some of the underenumeration indicated by post-enumeration surveys.

Acreages of crop failure were derived from the 1925 to 1945 Censuses of Agriculture, and interpolations for intervening years were based on BAE estimates of crop losses or differences between planted and harvested acreages of principal crops. Acreages of crop failure for recent years are based chiefly on crop losses as reported by AMS. Reported acreages of crop losses are adjusted for the replanting of part of the acreage on which winter wheat is abandoned. Hay land that produced nothing but pasture in some dry seasons is not included in crop failure in recent years.

Estimates of acreage of cultivated summer fallow were made only for the geographic divisions west of the Mississippi River. For 1945–1948, they were based chiefly on acreages seeded to wheat on summer fallow land, as estimated by BAE and according to data issued by the Great Plains Council. For 1949–1957, estimates of fallow were based partly on the 1950 and 1954 Censuses of Agriculture, estimates of wheat seeded on summer fallow made by AMS, and information obtained from the Great Plains Council. Estimates for years prior to 1945 were built up from fragmentary data available in BAE.

Indexes of total crop production were divided by indexes of cropland used for crops to derive indexes of crop production per acre (series K 103). Indexes of crop production were developed as one step in the calculation of farm output.

For a more detailed explanation of these series, see *Major Statistical Series of the U.S. Department of Agriculture*, Agriculture Handbook No. 118, vol. 2.

K 104–115. Index of supply and utilization of farm food commodities, 1924–1957.

Source: Agricultural Marketing Service, *National Food Situation*, quarterly issues.

This index involves the use of the basic disappearance data described in series G 552–584, converted to farm level, and of average 1947–49 farm prices to derive value aggregates in terms of constant dollars. Prices used are midmonth prices received by farmers in 1947–49 weighted by volume of monthly sales.

Each part of the index includes processed and unprocessed commodities. Where processing of farm commodities yields byproducts or joint products, the relative economic importance of the various products is retained by apportioning the farm value of the unprocessed commodity according to the ratio of the wholesale value of the several resulting end products. For processed commodities where no byproduct or joint product is involved direct conversion to the farm weight is made. See also Agriculture Handbook No. 91, *Measuring the Supply and Utilization of Farm Commodities*, 1955.

K 104, production. Includes harvested crops (including those used for feed and seed) and marketings of livestock products for consumption plus use on farms where produced.

K 105, imports and inshipments. Imports and inshipments from U.S. Territories include farm commodities similar to those produced in this country plus those not produced domestically but which are substitutes for United States products. Coffee, tea, cocoa, and bananas are included but rubber and silk are excluded. Dockside prices were used for commodities not produced in the United States. Imports include both processed and unprocessed commodities.

Reports on shipments to and from Alaska and Hawaii were discontinued in April 1948. For foods for which such trade is significant, estimates of inshipments have been made.

K 106, net change in available stocks. Changes in reported stocks other than those held for the USDA foreign supply programs are treated as a source of domestic supply. Such stocks include those accumulated under price support programs.

K 109, civilian food. Figures are derived as a residual by deducting feed, seed, and other nonfood uses, exports and shipments, Government purchases for the military and for export, and ending stocks from total supply of each food available for the year.

K 110, military food. No reliable information on military food procurement is available before 1941, but such takings were relatively small between 1919 and 1940. Data from reports of the Armed Services are supplemented by estimates to cover local procurement of some fresh commodities and items supplied daily. Civilian feeding in areas occupied by the Armed Forces is included.

K 111, domestic nonfood use. For data on nonfood use divided into feed, seed, and "other" (alcoholic beverages, soap, and industrial uses), see Supplement for 1956 to Agriculture Handbook No. 91, *Measuring the Supply and Utilization of Farm Commodities.*

K 112, commercial exports and shipments to U.S. Territories. Includes trade not handled by the Federal Government although Government financial aid may have been involved in the transaction in one way or another. Trade with Alaska and Hawaii has not been reported since April 1948 but shipments of some items are estimated.

K 113–115, USDA export program. Measures the annual takings of farm food commodities from commercial channels by the Department of Agriculture expressly for subsequent shipment abroad under foreign supply and special export programs. Quantities thus removed are designated as "net purchases" and are derived by adjusting the USDA deliveries of farm food commodities by the change in Department stocks.

K 116–118. Taxes levied on farm property, 1890–1957.

Source: Agricultural Research Service, *Agricultural Finance Review,* annual issues.

These data cover all ad valorem taxes levied upon farm property by State and local governments. They do not cover special assessments such as those levied by drainage, irrigation, or other special districts. Farm real estate comprises all land defined by the Bureau of the Census as land in farms, and structures thereon (see general note for series K 1–364). Farm personal property covers all livestock, machinery, automobiles, trucks, produce, and household and personal effects. Much personal property on farms is not taxed, either because of statutory exemptions or through faulty assessment.

Taxes include those levied on farm property whether owned by the operator or not. They do not necessarily represent taxes paid by farmers. "Levies" rather than "payments" are shown because the timing of actual payments is uncertain.

Real estate tax figures are developed from data for sample farms obtained from local tax officials and from data in the Censuses of Agriculture for 1930, 1940, and 1950. The acreages used in computing taxes per acre are census data for farmland in private ownership, with interpolations for intercensal years. The values used in computing taxes per $100 of value are based on census data of operator estimates of value, with interpolations for intercensal years based on the ARS index of farmland values. For a more detailed discussion, see Agricultural Research Service, *Taxes Levied on Farm Property in the United States and Methods of Estimating Them,* Statistical Bulletin No. 189, August 1956.

Personal property tax figures are developed from statistical data on assessed values and taxes published by State tax commissions, boards of equalization, or similar bodies; see "Taxation of Personal Property Owned by Farmers in the United States, 1940–49," *Agricultural Finance Review,* vol. 15, November 1952.

K 119. Automotive taxes paid by farmers, 1924–1957.

Source: See source for series K 116–118.

These data include payments of all registration and "tag" fees for automobiles and trucks on farms and for drivers' permits by farmers. Amounts paid for licenses and permits are based on estimates of vehicles on farms, and average charges per vehicle. The latter is the average charge for all vehicles registered, adjusted to the level of charges for vehicles on farms as determined from special surveys. State and Federal motor-fuel taxes are those arising out of the use of automobiles, trucks, tractors, and other machines by farmers. Motor-fuel figures represent net amount paid, after refunds, and are derived from estimates of fuel consumption of farm vehicles and the average tax rate on such fuel as developed from special surveys. For further discussion, see *Major Statistical Series of the U.S. Department of Agriculture,* Agriculture Handbook No. 118, vol. 6.

K 120–121. Farmers' mutual fire insurance, 1914–1957.

Source: Agricultural Research Service, *Agricultural Finance Review,* annual issues and records (compiled from published State reports and from data supplied by State insurance officials, company officials, and others).

Data include insurance against fire and lightning, and exclude, in most cases, insurance against windstorm, hail on growing crops, or other hazards. For 1914–1933, farmers' mutual fire insurance companies were defined as those which had more than 65 percent of their insurance on farm property. Since 1933, this has been reduced to 50 percent. During both periods, however, all business of such companies was considered farm business, although only about 85-88 percent of the total insurance was on farm property. The business of general-writing mutual and stock fire insurance companies, which also write insurance on farm property, is not included.

Figures for insurance in force (series K 120) include only companies for which reports were obtained and may not be entirely complete. For 1956 and 1957, the figures include an estimate for incompleteness. Figures for cost per $100 of insurance (series K 121) do not include any amounts collected from members which have been added directly to surplus or reserve funds. Such funds are, of course, available for payment of future losses and operating expenses. The average increase in these surplus funds during the 10-year period, 1947–1956, suggests that, on the average, annual assessments collected from members amounted to about 27.7 cents per $100 of insurance, compared with amounts actually paid out for losses and operating expenses of about 23.1 cents.

K 122–128. Cash receipts from farming and farm income, 1910–1957.

Source: Agricultural Marketing Service, *The Farm Income Situation,* July 1958 (No. 174).

These estimates refer to calendar-year income arising from commodities and services produced on all farms in the United States, as defined in the Census of Agriculture, to the expenses associated with such production, and to other income received by persons living on farms.

Estimates of farm income were started in 1924 on a crop-year basis. In 1936, a legislative formula for income parity for agriculture, based on a 1910-1914 comparison of farm and nonfarm per capita incomes, resulted in an extensive project of research designed to extend the estimates back to 1910, to put them on a full calendar-year basis comparable with estimates of nonagricultural income, and to improve and expand the data in other respects.

No adequate statistics are available on farm income and expenses before 1910. Willford I. King's early estimates of the total value produced in agriculture go back to 1850, but for census years only (published in *The Wealth and Income of the People of the United States*, Macmillan Co., 1915). They were based on inadequate information and are not comparable with any of the current series. Without data for intercensal years, King's decennial figures may be misleading even as an indication of the long-term trend. The decennial projections back to 1800 prepared by the National Industrial Conference Board, *National Income in the United States, 1799-1938*, 1939, are in much the same category, and must be regarded only as very rough approximations. Annual estimates of gross farm income extending back to 1869, and covering a substantial part of total farm production, are given in Department of Agriculture, *Gross Farm Income and Indices of Farm Production and Prices in the United States, 1869-1937*, Technical Bulletin No. 703, December 1940. Although not comparable with any of the current series, these estimates are probably fairly reliable as an indication of trends in the gross value of farm production.

In the absence of any direct reporting of farm income on an adequate scale, estimates have been developed by indirect methods using available data on production, disposition, prices, and costs. The procedure followed has been to treat agriculture as one tremendous enterprise, and to derive its net income by first computing "gross income," as defined below, and then deducting aggregate expenses of production.

Figures for series K 122-125 are estimates of realized gross farm income and its principal components. These estimates are "gross" in the sense that they represent the total value of commodities and services produced by farms without any deduction for costs incurred in their production, and without any consideration of who reaps the ultimate benefit from their sale or use, whether it be a farm operator, a landlord, a farm laborer, or a bank. Cash receipts from farm marketings, in the case of crops, include all sales of crops by farmers; purchases by other farmers for use as feed or seed are later deducted as production expenses. Similarly, in the case of livestock and products, the estimates include all sales by farmers, with purchases of livestock by other farmers included as a production expense in series K 126. Farm sales of firewood and other forest products are included in the crop totals.

For 1933-1957, total cash receipts from all farm marketings include Government payments to farmers. The latter include rental and benefit, conservation, price adjustment, parity, production, and Soil Bank payments—in short, all money paid directly to farmers by the Government in its farm programs. Indirect financial aid to farmers through commodity prices or loan values is covered in cash receipts from marketings. Government payments to landlords, as well as farm operators, are included but the former are also covered under farm production expense (series K 126) as rental payments to non-farm landlords.

Realized gross farm income (series K 125) represents total cash farm income, the value of farm-produced food and fuel consumed in farm households, and an imputed rental value for all farm dwellings. Farm-household consumption of farm products is valued at prices received for the sale of similar products. It includes food and fuel furnished to hired farm laborers, later deducted as a part of total labor costs to farm operators. The rental value of dwellings is on a gross basis; later deductions of rent, interest, taxes, insurance, maintenance, and depreciation are for farms as a whole with their buildings and equipment, and include shares allocable to farm dwellings.

The figures for gross farm income have been derived, commodity by commodity, from the periodic Crop Reporting Board estimates of production, disposition, price, and value. These estimates in turn are generally based on periodic census enumerations supplemented by regular reports from field statisticians, long lists of farmers, and special crop, livestock, and price correspondents, and by records and reports of public and private agencies concerned with the inspection, storage, marketing, transportation, or processing of farm products.

The figures for total farm-production expenses (series K 126) comprise the aggregate cost to farm operators, or all of that part of gross farm income not retained by farm operators. It includes (1) wages paid for hired labor, both in cash and in kind; (2) purchases of feed, livestock, fertilizer, and lime; (3) outlays for the operation of tractors, trucks, and automobiles (excluding the portion assigned to family use); (4) a large number of other current farm operating expenses; (5) charges for maintenance and depreciation of farm buildings, motor vehicles, machinery, and equipment; (6) taxes levied on farm property; (7) interest paid on farm-mortgage loans; and (8) net rents paid to landlords not living on farms, including that part of Government payments that goes to such landlords and not to farm operators. Other farm rents paid to landlords who are also farm operators are not included, as they constitute offsetting items of income and cost for farm operators as a group.

The estimates of production expenses are generally based on the Censuses of Agriculture, supplemented by special surveys. For years other than census or survey years, estimates for a specific item have for the most part been derived from relative changes in similar or related series. A combination of two series is frequently used, one indicating changes in quantity and the other, changes in price. For a few types of costs, however, the records of public or private agencies provide the basis for direct annual estimates.

The figures for realized net income of farm operators (series K 127) are obtained by subtracting total production expenses from realized gross farm income. The term "realized" is used because the estimates include the value only of farm products sold. In other words, they do not include changes in farm inventories of crops and livestock. These figures should not be confused with net income from agriculture or agriculture's contribution to the total national income. The latter includes farm wages, rent, and interest in addition to inventory changes and the realized net income of farm operators.

The figures for net income to persons on farms from farming (series K 128) include the realized net income of farm operators; the value, at annual average prices, of the net change during the year in crop and livestock inventories on farms; and wages, in cash or in kind, paid to farm laborers who live on farms. Inventory changes are included to achieve comparability with the net income of nonfarm businesses. Only about two-thirds of all hired farm workers live on farms; and only their wages are included. This series is the one previously used, together with corresponding estimates of the income of persons not on farms, in the now superseded legislative formula for computing income parity for agriculture.

The figures for series K 128 are generally comparable throughout the period shown and are believed to be fairly complete and reliable despite the indirect methods of estimation. For a more detailed discussion and for other series, see *Major Statistical Series of the U.S. Department of Agriculture*, Agriculture Handbook No. 118, vol. 3, December 1957.

K 129–131. Indexes of prices received by farmers, 1910–1957.

Source: 1910–1951, Agricultural Marketing Service, *Major Statistical Series of the U.S. Department of Agriculture*, Agriculture Handbook No. 118, vol. 1; 1952–1957, *Agricultural Prices*, January, February, and May 1959.

Data on prices received by farmers in their local markets are identified as "local market prices" in the source publication to distinguish them from "wholesale prices" of farm products at central markets.

The first comprehensive index-number series of prices of farm products was published in 1921 as Department of Agriculture Bulletin No. 999, *Prices of Farm Products in the United States*. Research in 1923 and 1924 resulted in the development of the aggregative type of index-number series first published in *Crops and Markets* in August 1924. Later revisions of the prices received index numbers were published in 1934, 1944, 1950, and 1959.

From the first indexes in 1921 to the 1950 revisions, the base period for index numbers of prices received by farmers was the 60-month period, August 1909–July 1914. This base was selected, because in these prewar years prices of farm products were relatively stable, and they were assumed to have a more nearly normal relationship with prices of other things than in any other period for which data were then available. In 1950, the base period was changed to January 1910–December 1914 pursuant to the provisions of the Agricultural Adjustment Act of 1938 as amended by the Agricultural Acts of 1948 and 1949.

The figures for prices received by farmers used to construct these indexes are based on reports from a group of voluntary respondents, most of whom are buyers of, or dealers in, farm products at country shipping points, and a few of whom are well-informed farmers. The number of these reporters has increased, and, as of 1958, reports were based upon returns from about 10,000 respondents. For most commodities, prices relate to a midmonth average, but for some, prices represent an average for the month.

These index numbers are based upon local market prices for 55 important agricultural commodities classified into 2 major groups, crops and livestock. There are 8 crop subdivisions (food grains, feed grains and hay, cotton, tobacco, oil-bearing crops, fruits, commercial vegetables, and potatoes, sweetpotatoes, and dry edible beans); and 4 livestock subdivisions (meat animals, dairy products, poultry and eggs, and wool). No single set of weights is representative of the long period covered by the index; but as a reasonably satisfactory compromise, weights for 1910–1935 are based on cash receipts in 1924–1929, and weights from 1935 to August 1952 are based on 1937–1941 receipts, and from September 1952 on, 1953–1957 receipts. For further details, see the first-listed source cited above.

K 132–137. Indexes of prices paid by farmers, interest and taxes payable per acre, and farm wage rates, 1910–1957.

Source: 1910–1951, see source for 1910–1951 for series K 129–131; 1952–1957, see source for same series for 1952–1957.

These indexes are based on monthly indexes which relate to prices as of the 15th of the month. For a detailed explanation, see the first-listed source above.

The indexes are a combination of the index of prices paid by farmers for commodities used for family living (6 groups—203 different commodity price series as of September 1958), the index of prices paid by farmers for commodities used in production (9 groups—232 different commodity price series as of September 1958), and of indexes of taxes on farm real estate, interest on loans secured by farm real estate mortgages, and farm wage rates. The index of prices paid for family living items (series K 132) represents prices of the following groups of commodities: Food and tobacco, 52 items; clothing, 39; household operation, 17; household furnishings, 40; building material for houses, 43; autos and auto supplies, 12. The index of prices paid for production items (series K 133) is based on the following groups of commodities: Feed, 26 items; livestock, 6; motor supplies, 15; motor vehicles, 12; farm machinery, 50; farm supplies, 37; fertilizer, 34; building and fencing material, 27; and seed, 25. Prices for individual commodities are collected monthly or periodically by mail, supplemented to some extent by interview, from independent stores and chain stores, hatcheries, etc., from a total of about 35,000 voluntary reporters. Prices by States for each commodity are weighted by estimated quantities purchased in each State to obtain the national average price.

National average prices for individual commodities are combined into group indexes by the weighted aggregative method. The commodity group indexes are weighted by estimated expenditures of farmers for commodities in the respective groups to obtain the family living and the production indexes.

There have been substantial changes in relative quantities of commodities bought by farmers during the period back to 1910. From 1910 to March 1935, the weights used in the index represent farmers' purchases during 1924–1929; from March 1935 to August 1952, the weights represent average purchases during 1937–1941, and from September 1952 on, the weights represent average purchases during 1955.

The index of interest payable per acre on farm mortgage indebtedness (series K 134) is constructed from estimates of interest charges on farm mortgages per acre. These interest charges are computed from the average of interest rates, as obtained from the various sources of farm credit, applied to the total mortgage indebtedness per acre of land in farms.

The index of taxes levied per acre on farm real estate (series K 135) is based on the Census of Agriculture and, for intercensal years, on data from local tax officials. Taxes levied during the year are, in most areas, payable in the following year. Figures for this series are available back to 1890.

The index of farm wage rates (series K 136) covers average wage rates paid hired farm workers. It is based on reports from crop reporters throughout the country and is seasonally adjusted before being combined with the other components of the parity index. The index is available on an annual basis back to 1866 for most years and quarterly since 1923.

The index of prices paid, including interest, taxes, and farm wage rates (series K 137), often referred to as the parity index, is used in computing parity prices of farm products under the formula prescribed by the Agricultural Adjustment Act of 1938 as amended by the Agricultural Acts of 1948 and 1949. It is the most comprehensive measure available of prices paid by farmers for the goods and services bought for both living and production purposes including interest, taxes, and hired farm labor. It is computed by weighting together the index of prices paid for living and production goods, the index of interest payable per acre of farm real estate, the index of taxes payable per acre of farm real estate, and the index of wage rates paid for hired farm labor.

K 138. Parity ratio, 1910–1957.

Source: See source for series K 129–131.

The parity ratio is the quotient (multiplied by 100) obtained by dividing the index of prices received by farmers (series K 129, by the index of prices paid by farmers, including taxes, interest, and wage rates (series K 137). If the ratio is 100 or over (i.e., if the prices received index is as high as, or higher than, the index of prices paid by farmers including interest, taxes, and wage rates), farmers' average purchasing power per unit of farm commodities is as high as, or higher than, it was in 1910–1914. If the ratio is lower than 100, this purchasing power is lower than it was in 1910–1914.

K 139–149. Value of farm gross output and product, in current and constant dollars, 1800–1900.

Source: M. W. Towne and W. E. Rasmussen, "Farm Gross Product and Gross Investment During the 19th Century," *Studies in Income and Wealth*, vol. 24, National Bureau of Economic Research (forthcoming).

These estimates are designed to measure the output of agriculture from 1800 to 1900 on a gross product, or "value-added" basis. The series for 1870–1900 are more reliable than for earlier years, and those for 1840–1860 are more reliable than for 1800–1830.

K 140–142, sales and home consumption of farm products, are totals of commodity values estimated separately from price and quantity estimates for individual commodities and groups of commodities. The data for 1870–1900 are based primarily on Department of Agriculture, *Gross Farm Income and Indices of Farm Production in the United States, 1869–1937*, Technical Bulletin No. 703, December 1940. Production estimates for 1840–1860 are based mostly on the Census of Agriculture. For 1800–1830, output is generally derived as the product of population and per capita production rates suggested by data for 1840–1860, although independent estimates were employed for the major cash crops, which amounted to about one-eighth of the total. Prices for current dollar valuation were obtained by extrapolating the 1870 farm price estimates of Technical Bulletin No. 703 to earlier years by changes in related wholesale prices and average prices received by farmers.

K 143, livestock inventory changes, is based on Department of Agriculture inventory and value-per-head data for 1870–1900. Inventory data from the Census of Agriculture were used for 1840–1860. For 1800–1830, the inventory estimates were projected backward from 1840 by population changes. Average values per head were projected to earlier years from 1870 by related wholesale price series.

K 144, gross rent from farm dwellings, represents imputed income from home ownership. Figures were obtained by multiplying the 1910–1914 average gross rent per farm (from the current farm income series) by the estimated number of farms in the decade years 1800–1900, and by inflating to current dollars by an index of construction costs. Estimates for number of farms were obtained from the Censuses of Agriculture for 1850–1900, and were extrapolated from 1850 to 1820 by the estimated number of persons engaged in agriculture, and from 1820 to 1800 by population figures.

K 146, intermediate products consumed, represents the cost of goods and services purchased for production purposes by farms from the nonfarm sector. It is deducted from gross output to derive the net contribution of the agricultural sector, or farm gross product (series K 145). The intermediate products and services originating off farms include fertilizer, cotton

ginning, horseshoeing, repairs, and rent paid to nonfarm landlords. For most items, estimates for 1800–1900 were constructed by extrapolating the 1910–14 average costs in the current series backward by changes in series closely related with respect to quantity or price. The estimates of intermediate products have as a whole less foundation in census or other contemporary benchmark sources and are less reliable than the gross output estimates.

K 148 and K 149, farm-produced improvements and home manufactures, although not included in current official measurements of gross farm output, are presented here because of their greater relative importance in the earlier years. The land improvement estimates were derived as the product of average annual number of acres improved and estimated per acre labor cost of improvement. The value of home manufactures series is based on survey and census estimates for 1810 and 1840–1870, with other decades estimated on the basis of trends in real output indicated by these benchmarks; a textiles price index was used for deflation.

Estimates of data in 1910–14 dollars, were derived in nearly all cases by multiplying estimated quantities of individual products by average prices for 1910–14.

K 150–157. Motor vehicles and specified machines on farms, 1910–1957.

Source: See source for series K 82.

Census counts were first made of tractors, automobiles, and motortrucks in the 1920 Census of Agriculture, of grain combines and farms with milking machines in the 1945 Census, of cornpickers and pickup balers in the 1950 Census, and of field forage harvesters in the 1954 Census. Estimates for intercensal years and before census data were available are as of January 1.

Before 1950, figures of machines shipped by manufacturers for farm use, with an allowance for disappearance, were used mainly as the basis for these estimates. Figures for automobiles and motortrucks were based on annual registrations for a limited number of agricultural States, and a few special sample surveys that were nationwide. Since 1950, estimates of motor vehicles and machines are based largely on information supplied by the voluntary crop reporters of the Agricultural Marketing Service adjusted to data from the 1954 Census of Agriculture.

K 158. Value of farm implements and machinery, 1850–1957.

Source: 1850–1900, Bureau of the Census, Thirteenth Census, 1910, *Agriculture*, vol. V, p. 51; 1910–1939, Agricultural Marketing Service, records; 1940–1957, Agricultural Research Service, *The Balance Sheet of Agriculture*, October 1957, p. 15.

Figures for 1910–1957 represent inventory value at the beginning of the year. They are closely tied to the values presented in the Censuses of Agriculture, the figures for intercensal years being estimated from information on manufacture and sales with due allowance for wear and tear and then adjusted for changes in price levels.

The data for 1850–1900 are not entirely comparable. They covered periods of vastly different price levels and attendant investment values, including the period of expansion into the West. According to the source, however, "the data are sufficiently comparable to indicate in a broad way the agricultural progress of the country . . . ."

K 159. Farmers' expenditures for fertilizer and lime, 1909–1957.

Source: See source for series K 122–128.

For a detailed discussion of concepts, coverage, and methods, see *Major Statistical Series of the U.S. Department of Agriculture*, Agriculture Handbook No. 118, vol. 3.

K 160. Commercial fertilizer consumed in U.S., 1850–1957.

Source: 1850–1956, Agricultural Research Service, *Statistics on Fertilizers and Liming Materials in the United States*, Statistical Bulletin No. 191, April 1957; 1957, *Preliminary Report on Consumption of Commercial Fertilizer and Primary Plant Nutrient in the United States*, December 1958.

Commercial fertilizer includes any substance containing nitrogen (N), phosphoric acid (P_2O_5), potash (K_2O), or any other recognized plant-food element or compound, such as lime (CaO), magnesia (MgO), boron (B), etc., which is consumed primarily for the purpose of supplying plant food to crops, excluding barnyard manures but including dried animal manures sold commercially. Ground phosphate rock, gypsum, sulfur, borax, copper sulfate, manganese sulfate, zinc sulfate, cottonseed meal, dried blood, animal tankage, etc., are included when sold to farmers for plant food, but are excluded when sold as fungicides, animal feeds, or for any other purpose than for plant food. Limestone, dolomite, magnesia, etc., are included when used as components of mixed fertilizers but excluded when sold as soil amendments (materials used to change the physical properties or the acidity of the soil rather than to supply plant food).

The data refer to all commercial plant food, including that distributed by the Production and Marketing Administration in its soil-building program and that used by the Tennessee Valley Authority in test demonstrations.

Beginning with 1920, the data related to consumption only in continental United States, but data for 1850–1919 include consumption in Alaska, Hawaii, and Puerto Rico. The total consumption in these outlying areas increased from about 3,000 tons in 1890 to 52,000 in 1900, 93,000 in 1910, 120,000 in 1920, 254,000 in 1930, 321,000 in 1940, and 444,000 in 1950. Most of this consumption occurred in Puerto Rico and Hawaii.

The earliest data on fertilizers were collected by State fertilizer control officials. The first volume of *American Fertilizer*, 1894, presents figures for Georgia for 1875–1892. In 1945, 36 States had a Fertilizer Control Office or similar agency which published tonnages of fertilizers consumed in the State. A bibliography of such reports is given in U.S. Department of Agriculture, Circular No. 756, 1946, which also gives considerable detail on fertilizer consumption.

Annual estimates of consumption made by the National Fertilizer Association (now a part of the National Plant Food Institute) were discontinued in 1955. *The Fertilizer Review*, vol. XXI, No. 2, pp. 11–14, presents figures for continental United States by decades from 1880 to 1910, and annually to 1945.

K 161. Lime consumed on farms, 1909–1957.

Source: See source for series K 82.

This series links two series not quite alike in coverage. For 1929–1945, the tonnage is in terms of ground limestone, materials in other forms being converted to that basis, except for some coarser materials used in Illinois. These figures were based on surveys made by State agricultural college agronomists and include county surveys of producers, and data from county extension agents and AAA offices, assembled by C. E. Carter of the Production and Marketing Administration. The data for 1910, 1920, and 1925–1928, however, were assembled by A. L. Mehring of the Bureau of Plant Industry, Soils,

and Agricultural Engineering. The intervening years were interpolated. Mehring's figures, with the interpolations, have been carried through 1939 in the Bureau of Agricultural Economics series, *Income Parity for Agriculture*, pt. II, sec. 2; hence, the figures given there for 1929–1939 differ from those presented here. Lime used by fertilizer manufacturers in their mixed goods is not included. Data for recent years are from National Agricultural Limestone Institute, Inc.

K 162–169. Farm-mortgage debt outstanding and loans closed, 1910–1957.

Source: Agricultural Research Service, Bureau of the Census, Farm Credit Administration, and Federal Deposit Insurance Corporation. For specific sources, see below. See also *Major Statistical Series of the U.S. Department of Agriculture*, Agriculture Handbook No. 118, vol. 6.

Farm-mortgage credit has been referred to as farm-real-estate credit, long-term credit, or capital credit. The data presented here, however, merely represent the amount of credit secured by farm real estate, whether it is extended for a short term or a long term, whether it is used for purchasing the farm, operating the farm, or financing nonagricultural activities, and whether the loan instrument is a mortgage, deed of trust, vendors' lien, or sales contract.

Estimates of the total amount of farm-mortgage debt outstanding at the beginning of each year (series K 162) are based upon census data and special surveys. Data on the amount of mortgage debt on farms operated by full owners appear in each census back to 1890, except that for 1900. In 1890, 1940, 1945, 1950, and 1956, similar information was collected on the owned part of part-owner farms.

Mortgage data may be found in the following reports of the Bureau of the Census: Eleventh Census, 1890, *Report on Real Estate Mortgages*; Thirteenth Census, 1910, *Agriculture*, vol. V, chap. 3; Fourteenth Census, 1920, *Agriculture*, vol. V, chap. 7; Census of Agriculture, 1925, *Summary Statistics by States*; Fifteenth Census, 1930, *Agriculture*, vol. IV, chap. 6; Sixteenth Census, 1940, *Agriculture*, vol. III, chap. 4. Data for 1935, 1945, 1950, and 1956 are in two cooperative publications—Bureau of the Census and Bureau of Agricultural Economics, *U.S. Census of Agriculture: 1950*, vol. V, pt. 8, and Bureau of the Census and Agricultural Research Service, *U.S. Census of Agriculture: 1954*, vol. III, pt. 5.

In 1920, 1928, and 1930 the Bureau of Agricultural Economics conducted surveys on which estimates of debt on farms operated by part owners, tenants, and managers were based. The Bureau of the Census and the Bureau of Agricultural Economics cooperated in the 1935, 1940, 1945, 1950, and 1956 surveys. The results of the 1928 survey, which included 1925 data, were published in Department of Agriculture, *Farm-Mortgage Credit*, Technical Bulletin No. 288, February 1932. Results of the later surveys appear in the two cooperative publications referred to above. Some earlier census-year estimates were revised on the basis of relationships established by the more recent surveys to make estimates for all census years more comparable.

Estimates for intercensal years are based on data on the amount of mortgages held by certain lending agencies, on estimates of the amount of farm mortgages recorded annually by major lender groups, and on the distribution by lenders of farm-mortgage debt in the last preceding census. Whenever a new census-year benchmark was established, the intercensal-year estimates were revised to reflect the new trend. For the years prior to 1935, the data on mortgages recorded were compiled from the records of selected counties through a nationwide Works Progress Administration project sponsored by the Bureau of Agricultural Economics. For 1935–1957, this information was collected by the Farm Credit Administration. Revisions of annual debt estimates for 1950–1957 appear in Agricultural Research Service, *Farm-Mortgage Debt Rises in 1957*, ARS 43–59, September 1957. A number of publications of the Bureau of Agricultural Economics contain annual estimates of farm-mortgage debt revised to the last census-year benchmark preceding the date of publication: *Agricultural Finance Review*, vol. 15, supplement I, May 1953, which has annual data by States for 1945–1953; *Farm-Mortgage Loans and Their Distribution by Lender Groups, 1940–1948*, USDA Circular No. 812, August 1949; *Revised Annual Estimates of Farm-Mortgage Debt by States*, 1930–1943, April 1944; *Distribution by Lender Groups of Farm-Mortgage and Real Estate Holdings, January 1, 1930–1945*, August 1945.

The Federal land banks were organized pursuant to the Federal Farm Loan Act of 1916 and became important lenders in the farm-mortgage field, particularly after 1933. The data on loans outstanding and loans closed (series K 163 and K 168) are from publications of the Farm Credit Administration or its predecessor, the Federal Farm Loan Board. Land Bank Commissioner loans, first made under the authority of the Emergency Farm-Mortgage Act of 1933, were taken over by the Federal Farm Mortgage Corporation upon its creation in 1934 and were continued until July 1, 1947, when authority to make new loans, except those incidental to liquidation, expired. In 1955, the remaining outstanding loans of the Corporation were sold to the Federal land banks. For a discussion of these agencies, see Department of Agriculture, *Farm-Mortgage Credit Facilities in the United States*, Miscellaneous Publication No. 478, 1942, and annual reports of the Farm Credit Administration.

Figures on farm-mortgage debt held by life insurance companies (series K 164) are estimates of the Bureau of Agricultural Economics and the Agricultural Research Service and refer to unpaid principal owed to the companies. The estimates are based on data from the annual statements of companies that hold a large part of all farm-mortgage debt held by life insurance companies, supplemented with other information obtained by mail from various companies. The data for 1910–1929 include the unpaid principal of regular mortgages only; for 1930–1957, they also include the unpaid principal of purchase-money mortgages and farm real estate sales contracts. Estimates of the Institute of Life Insurance have been used since 1945 for United States totals—and since 1950 for State totals—of the book value of this group's holdings of farm mortgages. See also the following Department of Agriculture publications: *Farm-Mortgage Loans Held by Life Insurance Companies*, ARS 43–58, October 1957; *Farm Investments of Life Insurance Companies, 1956*, ARS 43–57, October 1956; and *Farm-Mortgage Investments of Life Insurance Companies*, December 1943.

Figures on farm-mortgage debt held by commercial and savings banks (series K 165) for 1910–1947 do not cover all banks, but they do represent a very large proportion of all bank loans on farm real estate. For 1910–1934, the data include only open State and national banks, and are estimates prepared by the Bureau of Agricultural Economics from special surveys and reports of bank supervisory authorities. (See *Agricultural Loans of Commercial Banks*, USDA Technical Bulletin No. 521, July 1936, for a discussion of these special surveys.) For 1935–1947, the data include only farm-mortgage loans of insured commercial banks as summarized in reports of the Federal Deposit Insurance Corporation. For 1948–1957, the data include farm-mortgage debt held by all operating banks—commercial, savings, and private—as com-

piled by the Federal Deposit Insurance Corporation and published in annual reports of the Comptroller of the Currency. Sales contracts on farm real estate may or may not be included in the figures, because banks often classify such contracts with the real estate owned. The figures do not include loans of closed banks, of mutual savings banks before 1948, nor of noninsured commercial banks for 1935–1947.

The joint-stock land banks (series K 166 and K 169) also authorized under the Federal Farm Loan Act of 1916, were under Federal supervision and regulation, but differed from the Federal land banks in that they were privately owned. Their organization and growth are discussed in C. H. Schwartz, Jr., *Financial Study of the Joint-Stock Land Banks*, Washington College Press, Takoma Park, Md., 1938, as well as in the publications cited above for Federal land banks. Liquidation of the joint-stock banks was called for in the Emergency Farm Mortgage Act of 1933 and was completed in 1951. For several Federal and federally sponsored agencies, "loans closed" include only their regular loans as distinct from purchase-money mortgages and sales contracts, and they are not necessarily comparable with "loans recorded" by other lender groups.

Within the lender group identified as "individuals and others" (series K 167), individuals are by far the most important holders of farm mortgages. Because of its residual nature, this general lender group also includes many miscellaneous sources of farm-mortgage credit, including mortgage, real estate, finance, and investment companies; State and local governmental agencies; religious, educational, civic, and fraternal organizations; mercantile firms dealing largely in farm supplies; lending agencies operating chiefly in the urban mortgage field but sometimes lending on farmland; corporations and associations chiefly engaged in making production loans but sometimes requiring real estate as security; and the Farmers Home Administration (formerly Farm Security Administration). In addition to these are the loans of mutual savings banks, for 1910–1947, closed commercial banks, noninsured commercial banks for 1935–1947, insurance companies other than life insurance companies, and certain types of loans not specifically included in the figures for the major lending groups.

K 170–172. Interest payable on farm mortgages, 1910–1957.

Source: Agricultural Research Service and Farm Credit Administration, records.

These data represent average contract rates. They are averages of the rates charged by the various types of lenders weighted by the amount of mortgages recorded or held by each. Furthermore, they are averages of rates on all farm mortgages regardless of their priority. It should be pointed out that year-to-year changes in the average rates do not necessarily reflect changes in the level of interest rates charged by the different lenders but may represent changes in the distribution among the lender groups of loans recorded or held. The averages are based on the rates specified in the mortgage contract and payable by borrowers during the calendar year; they do not necessarily represent averages of the rates actually paid, except that for rates on outstanding mortgages, they do reflect the temporarily reduced rates of the Federal land banks for 1934–1944 and of the Federal Farm Mortgage Corporation for 1938–1945.

Some information either on interest rates or interest charges on outstanding mortgages was obtained in the Censuses of Agriculture for 1890, 1920, 1930, and 1940. Interest rates on mortgages recorded (series K 170) come from two sources. The averages for odd-numbered years from 1941 to 1953 are estimates of the Farm Credit Administration based on mortgages recorded during the month of March in approximately one-third of the counties in the United States. For 1955 and 1957, the average interest rates are based on mortgages recorded in the first quarter of the year. Rates for 1910–1935 were developed from data obtained in a nationwide Works Progress Administration project sponsored by the Bureau of Agricultural Economics (see that agency's *Average Rates of Interest Charged on Farm-Mortgage Recordings of Selected Lender Groups*, November 1940).

Average interest rates on outstanding mortgages (series K 171) for 1937–1957 are based on data obtained by the Bureau of Agricultural Economics, the Agricultural Research Service, and the Bureau of the Census in special surveys made in census years and from Farm Credit Administration surveys of farm-mortgage recordings made in selected months of intercensal years. For 1910–1936, the rates are based on the WPA data mentioned above. Rates on mortgages recorded as reported in the WPA project were converted to rates on outstanding mortgages by assuming that all mortgages recorded remained in effect for a period equal to the average of the terms of years specified in the mortgage contracts. This procedure was used for all lender groups except the Federal land banks and Federal Farm Mortgage Corporation for which averages were computed from information on the amount of loans outstanding at various interest rates. (See Bureau of Agricultural Economics, *Interest Charges Payable on Farm Indebtedness in the United States, 1910–40*, August 1942.) Some of the data for years after 1930 were later revised; see Bureau of Agricultural Economics, *Revised Annual Estimates of Interest Charges and Interest Rates on Farm-Mortgage Debt, 1930–43*, October 1944, and USDA Circular No. 821, *Farm-Mortgage Interest Charges and Interest Rates, 1940–48*, October 1949.

Figures for interest charges payable (series K 172) were developed from the estimates of farm-mortgage debt outstanding at the beginning of each year and the average interest rates charged thereon, except in the case of the Federal land banks and the Federal Farm Mortgage Corporation. Calendar-year estimates were computed by averaging the charges payable on debts outstanding at the beginning of each year and the beginning of the succeeding year. For the Federal land banks and the Federal Farm Mortgage Corporation, the actual amounts of interest charges payable on their outstanding loans during the calendar year were obtained from the Farm Credit Administration. These amounts, of course, excluded those charges no longer payable because of the interest reductions granted to borrowers. For more detailed discussion, see publications previously cited.

K 173–177. Non-real-estate agricultural loans to farmers, 1910–1957.

Source: Federal Farm Loan Board and Farm Credit Administration, records.

See also specific sources mentioned below.

Non-real-estate credit, variously called short-term credit, personal and collateral credit, or production credit, is obtained by farmers from many sources including banks, Federal and federally sponsored credit agencies, merchants, dealers, commission men, finance companies, landlords, and other individuals. Commercial banks have provided the bulk of this type of credit extended by credit institutions although, since the early 1930's, Federal and federally sponsored agencies and finance companies have become important in this lending field. The volume of non-real-estate credit extended by sources other than banks and Federal agencies is believed to have been about $3½ billion in recent years; however, data for precise estimates are lacking.

Since 1939, non-real-estate agricultural loan data of all operating banks have been available from the Comptroller of the Currency and the Federal Deposit Insurance Corporation. Since 1936, similar loans of insured commercial banks, whose loans comprise about 97 percent of the loans of all banks, have been regularly reported by the Federal Deposit Insurance Corporation. For earlier years, the only data of this type available are from Department of Agriculture surveys made in 1914, 1918, 1921, 1924, 1931, 1934, and 1936, all of which (except for 1936) are discussed in that Department's *Agricultural Loans of Commercial Banks*, Technical Bulletin No. 521, July 1936. Upon the basis of these survey data and of data on all loans of "country" national banks for intervening years, estimates have been made back to 1910. See the *Agricultural Finance Review*, "Short-Term Agricultural Loans of Commercial Banks, 1910–1945," vol. 8, November 1945; and *Major Statistical Series of the U.S. Department of Agriculture*, Agriculture Handbook No. 118, vol. 6.

The Federal Government first entered the non-real-estate agricultural credit field in 1918 when it made available $5 million for direct loans to farmers in the Northwest and Southwest where there had been two successive crop failures. During the 1920's, seed and feed loans were made available from time to time in certain "distressed" areas by special Acts of Congress. In the early 1930's, the basis for lending was broadened and the Emergency Crop and Feed Loan Office came to be a more-or-less permanent source of credit for farmers in distress. The Farmers Home Administration Act of 1946 transferred the activities of the Emergency Crop and Feed Loan Office from the Farm Credit Administration to the newly created Farmers Home Administration (successor to the Farm Security Administration) and provided for the liquidation of these loans. Thereafter, any loans of this character were made by the Farmers Home Administration under the provisions of the new law and are not included in this series. For a further discussion of the crop and feed loan program, see Department of Agriculture, *Federal Seed-Loan Financing and Its Relation to Agricultural Rehabilitation and Land Use*, Technical Bulletin No. 539, October 1936; and reports of the Farm Credit Administration.

The Agricultural Credits Act of 1923 created the Federal intermediate credit banks, the first permanent federally sponsored credit agencies making non-real-estate loans available to farmers. These banks make no loans directly to farmers, but they do make loans to and discount loans for private financing institutions (agricultural credit corporations and livestock loan companies). Loans discounted by the Federal intermediate credit banks for the production credit associations since their organization in 1933 are not included here. See Frieda Baird and Claude L. Benner, *Ten Years of Federal Intermediate Credits*, The Brookings Institution, Washington, D.C., 1933; and reports of the Farm Credit Administration.

The same 1923 Act also authorized the Federal intermediate credit banks to provide loans to and discounts for agricultural cooperatives; that is, direct loans to marketing cooperatives on the security of commodities. In 1933, special legislation authorized the creation of the "banks for cooperatives," which, by 1936, had largely taken over the function of the intermediate credit banks in making loans to cooperatives. A part of the loan funds of the "banks for cooperatives," however, is supplied by the Federal intermediate credit banks.

K 178–180. Indexes of deposits of country banks, 1923–1957.

Source: Department of Agriculture, records.

The indexes for demand, time, and total deposits are based upon deposits of member banks of the Federal Reserve System, located in places of less than 15,000 inhabitants in the 20 leading agricultural States. (See Department of Agriculture,

Demand Deposits of Country Banks, Technical Bulletin No. 575, August 1937; *Agricultural Finance Review Supplement,* vol. 15, May 1953; and *Major Statistical Series of the U.S. Department of Agriculture,* Agriculture Handbook No. 118, vol. 6.)

K 181–189. Number, memberships, and business of farmers, marketing and purchasing cooperatives, 1913–1956.

Source: 1913–1955, Farmer Cooperative Service, *Statistics of Farmer Cooperatives, 1954–1955;* 1956, *Statistics of Farmer Cooperatives, 1955–1956.*

These data were first compiled in 1913–1915 from questionnaires collected by mail from all cooperatives known to exist in the period 1912–1915. In 1919, data on the extent of cooperative marketing and farm supply purchasing were collected as a part of the Census of Agriculture. Other nationwide surveys were conducted in 1922 and for the fiscal years 1925–1926 and 1927–1928. Beginning with 1929–1930, annual nationwide surveys have been taken of farmer marketing, farm supply, and related services cooperatives. Data were collected by mail in each of these surveys except for 1936–1937 when information was collected in the field by Farm Credit Administration in cooperation with the banks for cooperatives and 33 State agricultural colleges.

A bona fide farmer cooperative is defined as one in which (1) farmers or agricultural producers hold the controlling interest; (2) no member is allowed more than one vote because of the amount of stock or membership capital he owns therein, or the cooperative does not pay dividends on stock or membership capital in excess of 8 percent a year; and (3) products of nonmembers are not handled in an amount greater in value than products of members. The annual survey includes all active bona fide farmer cooperatives responding to the initial questionnaire and showing their cooperative status, marketing of farm products, handling of farm supplies, or performing of services related to marketing or farm supply purchasing.

As cooperatives tended increasingly to diversify their operations, the annual survey figures became less satisfactory. Therefore, beginning with the survey covering fiscal 1951, revised questionnaires were used to develop information on a functional and commodity basis.

A very high percentage of response has been obtained in the annual survey. In the survey for fiscal 1955, 92 percent of the 9,887 associations in the survey furnished information. Estimates for nonreporting associations are based on every available source of information including periodicals and newspapers published by cooperatives.

K 190–194. Indexes of farm output and gross production of livestock, by groups, 1870–1957.

Source: 1870–1900, Department of Agriculture, *Gross Farm Income and Indices of Farm Production and Prices in the United States, 1869–1937,* Technical Bulletin No. 703, December 1940; 1910–1957, see source for series K 82. Census years, Bureau of the Census, *U.S. Census of Agriculture: 1954,* vol. II, p. 435.

The index of farm output (series K 190) includes all crops produced during the crop year except hayseeds, pasture seeds, cover crop seeds, and hay and concentrates fed to horses and mules on farms. The index also includes "net" livestock production (gross livestock production minus hay and concentrates fed) other than horses and mules on a calendar-year basis. This calculation is made to eliminate counting of feed crops in both livestock and crop production. The farm output index is also available for each of the nine census geographic divisions from 1919 to 1957. Although the indexes prior to 1910

are not strictly comparable with those for 1910–1957, they provide the best available measures for the early years.

The indexes on livestock production (as well as crop production) are measures of gross production, as they include items of production excluded in the index of farm output. They are subdivided into three livestock groups and nine crop groups.

Weighted average prices per unit of each commodity are used in constructing these indexes. Separate sets of weights are calculated for each of the nine census geographic divisions. Official reports of the Agricultural Marketing Service are the chief sources of data on both production and prices. The omission of production from farm forests and other minor items probably accounts for less than 5 percent of the total output in recent years. Commodities of little importance are omitted in some regions for earlier years.

Two weight periods are used: 1935–39 prices for 1939 and prior years, and 1947–49 prices for the period beginning in 1940. The index series for the two subperiods are "spliced" together in 1940 through the use of overlapped calculations for that year. Annual quantity-price aggregates for the United States are obtained by summing the regional data for 1919–1957.

For more detail, see *Major Statistical Series of the United States Department of Agriculture,* Agriculture Handbook No. 118, vol. 2.

K 195–204. Livestock on farms and value per head, 1867–1957.

Source: 1867–1919, Bureau of Agricultural Economics, *Livestock on Farms, January 1, 1867–1935,* January 1938; 1920–1939, *Livestock on Farms and Ranches on January 1,* Statistical Bulletin No. 88, 1950; 1940–1954, Agricultural Marketing Service, *Livestock and Poultry Inventory, January 1,* Statistical Bulletin No. 177, June 1956; 1955–1957, *Livestock and Poultry Inventory, January 1,* annual releases. Census years, see source for series K 190–194.

These estimates have been made by the Department of Agriculture since 1867. The early estimates were based on reports of the percentage change in numbers from the previous year by field agents and crop reporters. At 10-year intervals, the Census of Agriculture furnished the basic figures to which these percentage changes were applied. Since 1920, annual estimates are based primarily on survey returns from livestock producers who report on the number of livestock, by classes, on their own farms about December 1 each year. Records of livestock assessed for taxation in the various States have furnished indications of the annual percentage change in numbers, and records of marketings and slaughter have been used both by States and for the United States as check information.

Data from the Census of Agriculture have been used as periodic benchmarks for the January 1 estimates but there are few census years when the Department of Agriculture estimates and the census data are in close agreement. One of the main reasons for these differences is that there are only a few times when the census was taken as of January 1. In years when the census relates to a different date, adjustments are made to determine a January 1 equivalent number. The Department of Agriculture undertook in the midthirties a general revision of all estimates prior to 1920 to correct for irregularities in the early series and to utilize more fully the records of numbers assessed for taxation and other information not considered in preparing the original estimates; see first-cited source above.

Prior to 1920, crop reporters provided a single estimate of the value per head for a given species. Since 1920, the estimates are weighted averages based on values per head reported separately for the different age and sex classes of a given species—using as weights the estimated number in the respective class.

K 205, 208, 210. Live weight production of livestock, 1909–1957.

Source: 1909–1944, Bureau of Agricultural Economics, *Meat Animals, Farm Production, and Income, 1924–1944*, September 1947; 1945–1949, *Meat Animals, Farm Production, Disposition, and Income*, Statistical Bulletin No. 113, July 1952; 1950–1954, Agricultural Marketing Service, *Meat Animals, Farm Production, Disposition, and Income*, Statistical Bulletin No. 184; 1955–1957, annual releases of publication with same title.

Production in live weight relates to the total poundage produced on farms and ranches during a calendar year. The estimate of production is derived by determining for each State a balance sheet which shows as debit items the inventory at the beginning of the year, the births, and inshipments, and as credit items, the marketings, farm slaughter, death losses, and numbers on hand at end of year. Estimates of average live weight are based on reports from slaughterers, collected by the Department of Agriculture and in the Census of Manufacturers, and on records obtained from stockyards. In recent years, reports have been obtained from farmers on the average weight of livestock slaughtered on farms. The total live weight for beginning and end of year is obtained by multiplying estimates of the different age and sex classes for a species by an estimate of their respective average live weight. Live weight of marketings, farm slaughter, and inshipments is determined by multiplying the estimate for these items by the respective average live weight. To obtain production, the total weight of inshipments is subtracted from the combined weight of marketings and farm slaughter. Then the difference in the inventory weight between the beginning and end of year is added or subtracted as the case might be.

K 206, 207, 209, 211, 212. Annual average price received per hundred pounds of livestock by farmers, 1909–1957.

Source: 1909–1955, Agricultural Marketing Service, *Prices Received by Farmers, 1908–1955*, Statistical Bulletin No. 180, June 1956; 1956–1957, *Agricultural Prices, April 1958 and 1959*.

Price information is obtained from voluntary price reporters who furnish average local market prices each month. The estimates of monthly prices are weighted by monthly estimates of marketings to obtain the annual average. The monthly marketings are based on reports from stockyards and packers on monthly receipts of livestock by State of origin.

K 213. Workstock, 2 years old and over, on farms, 1920–1957.

Source: See source for series K 195–204.

K 214–225. Meat slaughtering, production, and price, 1899–1957.

Source: 1899–1945, Production and Marketing Administration, *Livestock Market News, Statistics and Related Data, 1946*, September 1947; 1946–1957, Agricultural Marketing Service, annual issues of publication with same title.

Figures for slaughter include federally inspected slaughter and estimates of all other slaughter (other commercial slaughter and farm slaughter). Before 1944, this information was obtained largely on an annual basis from various sources; but, beginning in 1944, information was collected by months, first under the slaughter control program of the War Food Administration, and later under the slaughter and meat control programs of Office of Price Administration. Current data on federally inspected slaughter, which includes animals condemned as unfit for human food, are compiled by the Agricultural Research Service in connection with its regulatory functions on meat inspection. The number of animals slaughtered

in other commercial channels is estimated by the Agricultural Marketing Service from monthly reports made by slaughterers who are not under Federal inspection. Estimates of farm slaughter are based on annual voluntary reports from livestock producers with periodic data from the Census of Agriculture as benchmarks. Production of the different kinds of meat are computed from estimated average live weights and dressing yields and, except for pork, is shown on a carcass weight basis. Pork production represents carcass weight excluding the raw fat rendered into lard.

The data on production under Federal inspection are based on records of production and yields reported monthly by slaughterers operating under Federal inspection. Monthly estimates of production under Federal inspection are not available prior to 1921. Reports of the biennial Census of Manufactures on slaughter were used as a basis for annual production estimates for years for which they are available. In other years, the estimates were based on information obtained from market records and other sources. Currently, information on weights and yields for other commercial slaughter is based on monthly reports from commercial slaughterers who are not under Federal inspection.

Prices of the different species of livestock at Chicago for the early years are from records published in the *Drovers Journal Yearbook*. Beginning in 1922, the price of beef steers at Chicago is based on records of all steers sold out of first hands for slaughter. The number of head, live weight, and total value of steers, by grades, are compiled by weeks. The annual prices represent the weighted average of all grades of steers sold during the year for slaughter. Since 1919, the average price for veal calves is based on the average of daily quotations. The average price of hogs at Chicago has been obtained from different sources; since 1920, it is the weighted average of packer and shipper purchases at the Chicago market. Since 1921, the price of lambs at Chicago represents an average computed from the bulk of sales price data.

K 226–233. General note.

Early development of the dairy industry in the United States is indicated by export statistics of 1790 which showed the New England States, New York, and Pennsylvania producing considerable amounts of butter and cheese in excess of their consumption requirements. The growth and spread of the industry between that time and 1849, when statistics on dairying were first available through the national census, are described in the *Agriculture Yearbook*, 1922, pp. 297–306. At the middle of the 19th century, milk cows were rather generally distributed over the eastern half of the United States as far west as southern Wisconsin, eastern Iowa, western Missouri and Arkansas, and the eastern third of Texas. By 1860, there were appreciable numbers of milk cows in the Pacific Coast States. In later years, they gradually spread over the intervening territory.

Dairy products sold by farmers in the early period were limited mainly to whole milk, farm-made butter, and farm-made cheese. Prior to 1850, these products were produced mainly on farms. The 1850 Census showed the bulk of cheese production for 1849 coming from farms in the area extending from northeastern Ohio eastward through New York and New England. Factory cheese production was in an experimental stage shortly before 1850, and made considerable progress during the next two decades. Although some butter was made in early cheese plants, the first commercial creamery was not established until 1861. Since that time, factories have largely supplanted farms in the production of both cheese and butter.

The first condensery was established in 1856, but little interest was given the product until the Civil War. Unsweetened condensed milk was first produced in 1885; the canned unsweetened product (evaporated milk) now makes up about nine-tenths of all evaporated and condensed whole milk. Ice cream was produced and sold by some retail stores in the first half of the 19th century, and wholesale plant distribution to dealers began about the middle of the century.

K 226–227. Cows and heifers kept for milk, 1850–1957.

Source: 1867–1929, Department of Agriculture, *Agricultural Statistics*, 1941; 1930–1939, *Agricultural Statistics*, 1946; 1940–1954, Agricultural Marketing Service, *Livestock and Poultry on Farms, January 1, Number, Value Per Head, and Total Value, Revised Estimates, 1940–1954*, June 1956; 1955–1957, *Livestock on Farms, January 1*, annual issues. (See also *Livestock on Farms, January 1, 1867–1935*, January 1938.) Census years, 1850–1920, Bureau of the Census, Sixteenth Census Reports, *Agriculture*, vol. III, pp. 606–607; 1925–1945, *Census of Agriculture, 1945*, vol. II, p. 381; 1950–1954, *U.S. Census of Agriculture: 1954*, vol. II, p. 440.

The estimates are based on interpretation of data from the Census of Agriculture, tax assessors, and other State agencies, together with the analysis of changes taking place in herds kept by a large sample of livestock reporters. With respect to the data on milk cow numbers obtained in the Censuses of Agriculture, the wording of the census questions has not necessarily been comparable with the definitions represented by the annual estimates and has varied somewhat from one census enumeration to another.

K 228. Milk production on farms, 1889–1957.

Source: 1889–1919, Bureau of the Census, various Censuses of Agriculture reports; 1924–1954, Agricultural Marketing Service, *Milk–Farm Production, Disposition, and Income*, Statistical Bulletin No. 175, April 1956; 1955–1957, same title, April 1959.

Beginning in 1924, the figures represent calendar-year estimates. The estimates are based on interpretations of census data, analysis of annual and monthly survey data on milk cows and milk production, and checks against information on milk utilization obtained from dairy plants and other sources. For 1919 and earlier years, the data are based on Censuses of Agriculture and converted from gallons to pounds by use of a conversion factor of 8.6 pounds per gallon. For 1889, the census totals are the reported figures. For 1899 they include estimates for incomplete reports, and for 1909 and 1919 they include estimates of production on farms that reported milk cows but failed to report milk produced. The 1889 and 1899 data were enumerated as of the following June, the 1909 data as of April 15, 1910, and the 1919 data as of January 1, 1920.

K 229–232. Production of dairy products, 1849–1957.

Source: 1849–1916, E. E. Vial, *Production and Consumption of Manufactured Dairy Products*, Department of Agriculture, Technical Bulletin No. 722, April 1940; 1917–1939, Agricultural Marketing Service, *Revisions in the Production of Creamery Butter, Cheese, and Ice Cream by States, 1916–1939*, and *Production and Utilization of Milk, United States, 1924–1952*; 1940–1957, same agency, *Production of Manufactured Dairy Products* (except for series K 232, 1940–1949, *Revisions of Ice Cream and Ice Milk Data, by States, 1940–1949*).

For 1940–1957, data are from the annual survey of output of dairy plants. For 1916–1939, data were based on the annual survey of dairy plants supplemented by estimates for incompleteness in some States based on data from the Census of

Manufactures or from State sources. For the years prior to 1916 or 1917, the level of the figures was based mainly on the Census Bureau's survey of the output of dairy plants with interpolations for intervening years for some products (see E. E. Vial, cited above).

Butter production data represent farm and factory production combined. Factory butter figures for 1917–1957 are for production of creamery butter and include some estimates for incompleteness. Figures for factory production for 1849, 1859, 1869, 1879, 1899, 1904, 1909, and 1914 are from the Census of Manufactures. The 1889 census data were revised upward to allow for incompleteness. Annual figures on factory butter production for the intercensal years were interpolated on the basis of receipts of butter at major central markets for 1879–1919 and on factory production for 1917–1957.

Cheese production figures include both farm and factory cheese production prior to 1927. Since 1926, farm cheese was negligible and is excluded. For 1909–1917, cheese figures exclude full-skim American. For 1918–1957, data are from plant reports of all types of cheese manufactured except cottage, pot, and bakers' cheese and full-skin American. For 1849, 1859, 1869, 1879, 1889, and 1909 the figures for total cheese production are from the decennial censuses. The census data for 1889 were revised upward to allow for incompleteness. Estimates for the intercensal years 1869–1899 were interpolated on the basis of market receipts. Data on factory production of cheese for 1904 and 1914 are from the Census of Manufactures; data for the intercensal years 1869–1919 were interpolated on the basis of market receipts. Production of farm cheese for the intercensal years 1899–1926 was roughly projected on the basis of average change between census years and added to the factory product to obtain total cheese figures.

Evaporated and condensed milk production includes evaporated whole milk, bulk unsweetened condensed whole milk, and case and bulk sweetened condensed whole milk. Production figures for 1879, 1899, 1904, 1909, and 1914 are census totals for all condensed and evaporated milk. For 1889, the census data were revised upward to allow for incompleteness. Data for 1869 are estimated; those for the noncensus years before 1919 represent an estimated trend of production based on intervening census data.

Ice cream production figures for 1916–1957 are based on the annual survey of dairy manufacturing plants supplemented by estimates for incompleteness in some States based on data from the Census of Manufactures or State sources. For 1914, data were estimated from the Census of Manufactures. For 1909 and earlier years, the data represent merely an estimated trend of production.

K 233. Milk equivalent of manufactured dairy products, 1849–1957.

Source: See source for series K 229–232.

For 1849–1923, the figures are based on national production of manufactured dairy products converted to milk equivalent on the basis of somewhat less refined conversion factors than those used for later years. As such they include no allowance for shifts in production between States or areas of high- or low-testing milk, and they assume standard butterfat content of the products for all years.

For 1930–1956, data were based on information of products made in each State and State conversion factors for each product. Duplication of milk usage involving the production of butter from whey fat recovered from cheese making and the use of butter and condensed milk in the production of ice cream were eliminated.

K 234-235. **Wholesale prices of cheese and butter, 1830-1957.**

Source: Agricultural Marketing Service, records.

The wholesale prices of cheese represent averages of weekly quotations on American twins on the Wisconsin cheese exchange at Plymouth. The wholesale price of butter is that for the New York City market. Since 1830, the data for butter differ somewhat in definition and source (see tabular footnote).

K 236-239. **Prices received by farmers for dairy products, 1909-1957.**

Source: 1909-1954, Agricultural Marketing Service, *Prices Received by Farmers*, Statistical Bulletin No. 180, June 1956; 1955, *Crops and Markets*, November 1957, p. 73; 1956, *Agricultural Prices*, April 1958; 1957, same title, April 1959.

Prices received by farmers for butter, butterfat, wholesale milk, and retail milk are estimates based on averages of survey data reported by dealers and farmers for their local market areas. Prices of butterfat (series K 237) represent the butterfat in farm-skimmed cream sold by farmers; before 1920, survey information was not collected, and estimates were extrapolated on the basis of trends in butter prices.

Wholesale milk prices (series K 238) are for milk sold by farmers to plants and dealers including such establishments as cheese factories, condenseries, creameries, or market milk plants. Prior to 1923, these prices were asked on a per-gallon basis and since that time on a per-100-pounds basis. Additional historic information on wholesale milk-price series was collected by direct plant contacts during the middle 1930's when the State estimates were revised. See also Bureau of Agricultural Economics, *Wholesale Prices Received by Farmers for Whole Milk, 1909-36*, February 1937 (mimeographed).

Retail milk prices (series K 239) represent the milk retailed by farmers directly to consumers. Before 1923, survey information was collected on a price per-gallon rather than per-quart basis. Some of the increase in price between 1909 and 1945 probably represents additional services rendered in process of distributing the milk. See also Bureau of Agricultural Economics, *United States Average Farm Prices of Dairy Products, 1910-34*, June 1934 (mimeographed).

K 240-241. **Shorn wool production and price, 1869-1957.**

Source: Series K 240, 1869-1908, *Agriculture Yearbook*, 1923; series K 241, 1869-1908, Department of Agriculture, *Gross Farm Income and Indices of Farm Production and Prices in the United States, 1869-1937*, Technical Bulletin No. 703, December 1940; series K 240-241, 1909-1956, *Livestock and Meat Statistics*, Statistical Bulletin No. 230, July 1958; 1957, Supplement to Statistical Bulletin No. 230.

The original source of data for 1869-1908 was the National Association of Wool Manufacturers. Estimates have been made by the Department of Agriculture since 1909. Wool production is estimated by ascertaining the number of sheep and lambs shorn and the average weight per fleece, and using data from the Censuses of Agriculture as periodic benchmarks. Extensive revisions of production estimates back through 1909 were made in 1936. The figures for 1869-1908 are not comparable to these revised estimates. To illustrate the lack of comparability, the unrevised production estimate of 287 million pounds for 1909, published in the *Agriculture Yearbook* for 1923, may be compared with the revised estimate of 310 million pounds.

K 242-253. **Poultry and eggs—number, production, and price, 1909-1957.**

Source: Series K 242-248, 1909-1944, Bureau of Agricultural Economics, *Farm Production, Disposition, and Income From Chickens and Eggs*, Statistical Bulletin No. 133, July 1953; 1945-1949, same title, June 1952; 1950-1953, Agricultural Marketing Service, same title, Statistical Bulletin No. 183; 1954, same title, April 1956 (mimeographed); 1955, same title, April 1957; 1956, same title, April 1958; 1957, same title, April 1959.

Series K 249-253, 1929-1944, Bureau of Agricultural Economics, *Farm Production, Disposition, and Income From Turkeys*, June 1953; 1945-1949, same title, May 1952; 1950-1954, Agricultural Marketing Service, same title, Statistical Bulletin No. 182; 1955, same title, March 1957 (mimeographed); 1956-1957, same title, March 1958.

Census data for chickens, 1910-1945, Bureau of the Census, *Census of Agriculture, 1945*, vol. II, pp. 406-407; 1950 and 1954, *U.S. Census of Agriculture: 1954*, vol. II, p. 531. Census data for chickens, 1910-1940, Sixteenth Census Reports, *Agriculture, Special Poultry Report*, p. 46; 1950 and 1954, *U.S. Census of Agriculture: 1954*, vol. II, p. 556.

The estimates are believed to indicate, within reasonable limits of accuracy, the actual number of farm chickens and turkeys; the production of chickens, turkeys, and eggs; and, with greater accuracy, the direction and extent of the changes from year to year.

Complete surveys of the hatchery industry are made every year in some States and every few years in all States. Monthly estimates of the production of baby chicks, based on returns from about 60 percent of total hatchery capacity, are also made. These figures of hatchery output together with a determination annually of the proportion of all farm chicks that came from hatcheries, give a dependable check on the actual level of chicken production.

Estimates of inventory numbers of chickens on farms January 1 (series K 242) are based primarily upon census enumerations. These enumerations for 1910-1955 were adjusted for changes between January 1 and the average date of enumeration in each State, and cover only farm flocks as defined by the Census Bureau. Estimates of change in numbers from year to year are based on rural carrier surveys made in December of each year, covering about 150,000 livestock farms, and on changes in flocks belonging to about 30,000 crop reporters, plus assessor and State farm census data where available.

Although census enumerations of chickens on farms were made in 1880, 1890, and 1900, the Department of Agriculture did not make annual estimates until 1909 because data showing annual changes were not available.

Estimates of inventory numbers of turkeys on farms January 1 (series K 249) are based primarily upon the census enumerations of turkeys on farms January 1, 1935, and April 1, 1940, adjusted for changes in numbers between January 1 and the date of enumeration. Turkeys on farms were not reported in the 1945 Census. The number on January 1, 1945, was estimated from the relationship between turkeys raised in 1944 and the number on hand January 1, 1945, as reported by crop and livestock reporters, using as a base the revised estimates of turkeys raised in 1944 based on the census enumeration. Annual changes in the estimates for intervening years are based mainly on the numbers on hand as reported on January 1 by crop and livestock reporters. Estimates of turkeys raised from 1954-1957 are based on poultry placement data secured from hatcheries. About an 88-percent sample is obtained. Although census enumerations of turkeys on farms were made in 1890, 1900, 1910, and 1920, the Department of Agriculture did not make annual estimates for years prior to 1929 because data showing annual changes were not available.

Chickens (series K 244) and turkeys (series K 251) produced on farms are computed from the number raised during

273

the year, minus the death loss of chickens and of turkeys that were on hand at the beginning of the year. Young chickens and young turkeys of the current year's hatchings that die are also excluded.

Egg production (series K 247) is estimated from returns from about 30,000 crop respondents and 5,000 commercial egg producers reporting on the first of each month for their own flocks the number of layers on hand and the eggs produced yesterday. Beginning with the estimated total number of layers on farms at the beginning of the year, the change in numbers from month to month is estimated from the changes shown by these survey farms. The monthly average number of layers and total egg production is revised at the end of the year if the change in number of layers shown by an annual survey with about 150,000 returns differs from the change estimated from monthly returns. Adjustment is also made for change in poultry farms on a monthly and annual basis.

K 254–328. General note.

For many crops, estimates of acreage, production, and prices begin in 1866, the year in which the Department of Agriculture began making regular reports. *Agricultural Statistics*, particularly the issues of 1941 and 1952, presents most of the available statistics, chiefly on a national basis, covering every phase, from acreage and production of individual commodities to utilization and consumption. *Crop Production* (Crop Reporting Board) presents monthly forecasts for the current season, beginning in March and carrying through the growing season.

The December issue provides a summary for the current season, revisions for the previous season, and comparisons with previous years. Forecasts and summary are on a State basis and for the United States. These data also appear in *Crops and Markets*. Other releases by the Crop Reporting Board present midmonth and season average prices received by farmers, value of sales and production, farm disposition, stocks in all positions, and other data. Periodic revisions connect current data with the longer historical series.

The censuses provide detailed data for counties. Census data are often not entirely comparable with the estimates shown, but furnish the benchmarks to establish the level of the estimates. For years before 1866, information from trade sources is available for some crops, such as cotton, tobacco, and rice.

Crop estimates are based chiefly upon reports from volunteer farmer-reporters who represent every part of every State. Check information is gathered from processors, from transportation and storage facilities, from buyers of farm products, from annual State farm enumerations, from various farm programs, and from other governmental agencies such as the Bureau of the Census, the Bureau of Internal Revenue, and the Bureau of Customs.

Season average prices are averages of the midmonth prices weighted by the quantity sold each month in the crop-marketing season, which is the 12-month period following the harvesting of the crop. This season may vary for different crops, and for any crop it may vary by States. The season average price of any crop is the average of all the State prices, weighted by the production of each State. Thus, it may be applied to production in any given year to obtain a measure of the value of that production. State season average prices may be weighted by quantities sold in each State to obtain an average for the United States which may be applied to total quantities sold in the United States to measure value of sales in the crop season. In neither case, however, should the computed value be confused with calendar-year income from the

crop. Monthly estimates of quantity sold are based upon reports of receipts by the chief purchasers of the commodity—in the case of grains, the interior mills and elevators.

Midmonth prices received by farmers are estimated by the Crop Reporting Board and are based upon reports from thousands of firms dealing directly with farmers (such as elevators, truckers, processors, produce dealers, etc.) and from farmers themselves. The estimates are issued monthly for the principal farm commodities in *Agricultural Prices*.

Season average prices for each State and the United States are summed up in the December issue of *Crop Values* and in *Field and Seed Crops Farm Production, Farm Disposition, and Value* issued each May. Data for season average prices begins for most commodities in 1908, but is supplemented for preceding years by the December 1 price series based on farmers' estimates on December 1 of average prices for the season's sales.

K 254–264. Indexes of gross production of crops, by groups, 1910–1957.

Source: See source for series K 82.

See text for series K 190–194 for description of the index and explanation of its construction.

K 265–268. Corn acreage, production, price, and stocks, 1839–1957.

Source: Series K 265–266, 1866–1943, Agricultural Marketing Service, *Acreage, Yield, and Production, 1866–1943*, June 1954 (processed); 1944–1948, *Crop Production*, Statistical Bulletin No. 108, March 1952 (processed); 1949–1954, *Field Crops, Acreage, Yield, and Production*, Statistical Bulletin No. 185, June 1956 (processed); 1955–1957, *Crop Production*, December annual summary, 1956, 1957, and 1958. For census years, Bureau of the Census, *U.S. Census of Agriculture, 1954*, vol. II, p. 568.

Series K 267, 1866–1938, Department of Agriculture, *Agricultural Statistics, 1952*; 1939–1954, *Agricultural Statistics, 1956*; 1955–1957, Agricultural Marketing Service, *Crop Values*, December 1956, 1957, and 1958.

Series K 268, 1926–1939, *Corn: Revised Estimates of Stocks on Farms, 1926–41*, April 1943 (processed); 1940–1943, *Revised Estimates of Stocks on Farms*, July 1947 (processed); 1944–1948, *Farms Stocks of Grains, Oilseeds, and Hay*, April 1952 (processed); 1949–1955, *Stocks of Grains, Oilseeds, and Hay*, Statistical Bulletin No. 203, January 1957 (processed); 1956, *Stocks of Grain in All Positions*, July 1957; 1957, *Stocks of Grain in All Positions*, October 1957.

See also general note for series K 254–328.

Corn figures include not only the production of corn on the acreage harvested for grain, but also an allowance for that harvested for silage and for forage, including some harvested by grazing farm animals (commonly called hogging off). Estimates of acreage harvested for grain, for silage, and for forage, including that hogged off, and production of corn for grain and silage are published by the Crop Reporting Board. Census figures for 1919 and previous years for both acreage and production represent corn harvested for grain only. For 1924–1939, census data for acreage represent corn harvested for all purposes, but those for production represent corn harvested for grain only.

The Crop Reporting Board has estimated farm stocks (series K 268), by States, quarterly since 1926 from reports of a large number of farmers. Farm stocks represent the farm carryover for crops of previous years, which become a part of the feed supply for the new season. In addition to farm stocks of corn, stocks in all off-farm positions have been estimated since 1943. Comparison with the farm-stocks data indicates that the bulk of carryover stocks of corn on October 1 of any year is still on farms.

K 269–273. Wheat acreage, production, price, and stocks, 1839–1957.

Source: Series K 269–270, 1866–1943, Agricultural Marketing Service, *Wheat Acreage, Yield, and Production, 1866–1943*, Statistical Bulletin No. 158, February 1955 (processed); for census data, 1944, *Census of Agriculture: 1950*, pp. 556–557, and other 1944–1957 data, see source cited for series K 265–266, above.

Series K 271, see source cited for series K 267, above.

Series K 272, 1926–1939, *Stocks of Wheat on Farms, Revised Estimates, 1926–41*, February 1943 (processed); 1940–1955, see source cited for series K 268, above; 1956–1957, *Stocks of Grain in All Positions*, July 1957 and 1958.

Series K 273, 1926–1929, Department of Agriculture, *Agricultural Statistics, 1941*; 1930–1933, *Agricultural Statistics, 1946*; 1934–1955, Agricultural Marketing Service, Statistical Bulletin No. 203, January 1957 (processed); 1956–1957, *Stocks of Grain in All Positions*, July 1957 and 1958.

Wheat figures are the combined estimates for winter, durum, and other spring wheat, harvested for grain. Separate series for each of these kinds, by market classes, are published by the Crop Reporting Board. The census data on acreage and production are regarded as comparable with the estimates in most cases. Wheat acreage harvested for hay is not included in these series.

Farm stocks of all wheat, by States, have been estimated quarterly since 1926 from reports of a large number of farmers. Farm stocks (series K 272) represent the farm carryover from previous crops at the beginning of a new crop year. The carryover added to the new crop is the supply for the new season. Stocks in interior mills, elevators, and warehouses (series K 273) have been estimated by the Crop Reporting Board since 1919, and data on stocks in other commercial storages have been gathered by other agencies for varying periods.

See also general note for series K 254–328.

K 274–276. Oats for grain acreage, production, and price, 1839–1957.

Source: Series K 274–275, 1866–1943, Agricultural Marketing Service, *Acreage, Yield, and Production, 1866–1943*, June 1954 (processed); 1944–1957 and for census years, see source for series K 265–266. Series K 276, see source for series K 267.

For 1866–1948, oats for grain figures include the acreage cut ripe and fed unthreshed; for 1949–1957, they include only the acreage and production combined or threshed. Estimates of harvested acreage exclude oats cut green for hay for all years and oats cut ripe and fed unthreshed, 1949–1957. Census data are comparable only with the estimates beginning in 1949. Data on farm stocks and stocks in off-farm positions are also available in publications of the Crop Reporting Board.

See also general note for series K 254–328.

K 277–279. Barley for grain acreage, production, and price, 1839–1957.

Source: Series K 277–278, 1866–1908, Department of Agriculture, *Agricultural Statistics, 1941*; 1909–1938, *Agricultural Statistics, 1952*; 1939–1943, Agricultural Marketing Service, *Field and Seed Crops, Acreage, Yield, and Production*, April

1947 (processed); 1944–1957 and for census years, see source for series K 265–266. Series K 279, 1866–1908, *Agricultural Statistics, 1941*; 1909–1938, *Agricultural Statistics, 1952*; 1939–1957, see source cited for series K 267.

The annual estimates of barley acreage and production and the census data are on a comparable basis. Barley cut for hay is excluded. Figures on farm stocks are available from 1933–1957, and stocks in off-farm positions have been estimated since 1943. These data are available in various publications of Agricultural Marketing Service.

See also general note for series K 254–328.

K 280–282. Flaxseed acreage, production, and price, 1849–1957.

Source: Series K 281, 1866–1888, Agricultural Marketing Service, *Revised Estimates of Flaxseed Production, 1866–1929*, July 1936 (processed). Series K 280–282, 1889–1957, see source for series K 277–279. Census years, Bureau of the Census, *U.S. Census of Agriculture, 1954*, vol. II, p. 570.

See also general note for series K 254–328.

Annual estimates and census data are on a comparable basis. Flax grown for fiber is not included in the acreage estimates; flaxseed deseeded from fiber flax is not included in the production estimates. Estimates of fiber flax are available in publications of the Crop Reporting Board. Farm-stocks data and stocks in off-farm positions, 1947–1957, are also available from the same source.

K 283–285. Soybeans for beans acreage, production, and price, 1924–1957.

Source: Series K 283–284, 1924–1953, Agricultural Marketing Service, Statistical Bulletin No. 211, June 1957 (processed); 1954, *Field Crops, Acreage, Yield, and Production*, Statistical Bulletin No. 185, June 1956 (processed); 1955–1957, *Crop Production*, December annual summary, 1956, 1957, and 1958. Series K 285, 1924–1953, Statistical Bulletin No. 211 (cited above); 1954–1957, *Crop Values*, December 1955, 1956, 1957, and 1958. Census years, Bureau of the Census, *U.S. Census of Agriculture: 1954*, vol. II, p. 571.

Price figures are season average prices prepared by weighting the midmonth prices received by farmers. Figures for acreage grown for all purposes, alone and interplanted, and acreage and production of soybeans for hay are also estimated by the Crop Reporting Board. Data on farm stocks and stocks in off-farm positions, 1942–1957, are also available in publications of the same agency.

See also general note for series K 254–328.

K 286–288. Rice acreage, production, and price, 1895–1957.

Source: Series K 286–287, 1895–1943, Agricultural Marketing Service, *Fluctuations in Crops and Weather*, Statistical Bulletin No. 101, June 1951 (processed); 1944–1957 and for census years, see source for series K 265–266. Series K 288, 1904–1928, Agricultural Marketing Service, records; 1929–1957, see source for series K 267.

See also general note for series K 254–328.

K 289–291. Rye for grain acreage, production, and price, 1866–1957.

Source: Series K 289–290, 1866–1908, Department of Agriculture, *Agricultural Statistics, 1941*; 1909–1943, *Agricultural Statistics, 1952*; 1944–1957 and for census years, see source for series K 265–266. Series K 291, 1866–1908, *Agricultural Statistics, 1941*; 1909–1957, see source for series K 267.

See also general note for series K 254–328.

Data on farm stocks are available from 1933–1957 and on stocks in off-farm positions from 1943.

K 292–294. Buckwheat acreage, production, and price, 1866–1957.

Source: 1866–1953, Agricultural Marketing Service, *Rice, Popcorn and Buckwheat Acreage, Yield, Production, Price and Value, 1866–1953*, Statistical Bulletin No. 238, October 1958; 1949–1957, see source for series K 269–271.

See also general note for series K 254–328.

K 295–297. Sugarcane acreage, production, and price, 1909–1957.

Source: 1909–1938, Department of Agriculture, *Agricultural Statistics, 1952*; 1939–1954, *Agricultural Statistics, 1956*; 1955–1957, Agricultural Marketing Service, *Crop Production*, June 1957 and 1958. Census years, Bureau of the Census, *U.S. Census of Agriculture: 1954*, vol. II, p. 576.

See general note for series K 254–328.

K 298–300. Hay acreage, production, and price, 1866–1957.

Source: **Series K 298–299**, 1866–1908, Department of Agriculture, *Agricultural Statistics, 1941*; 1909–1943, *Agricultural Statistics, 1952*; 1944–1957, see source for series K 265–266. **Series K 300**, 1866–1957, see source for series K 267. Census years, Bureau of the Census, *U.S. Census of Agriculture, 1954*, vol. II, p. 573.

See also general note for series K 254–328.

Census data are comparable to annual estimates in the series in which they are included. Farm stocks of hay, as of January 1 and May 1 of each year, are published in *Crop Production*.

K 301–306. Cotton and cottonseed acreage, production, price, and stocks, 1790–1957.

Source: **Series K 301**, 1866–1952, Agricultural Marketing Service, *Cotton and Cottonseed Acreage, Yield, Production, Disposition, Price, and Value, 1866–1952*, Statistical Bulletin No. 164, June 1955 (processed); 1953–1957, *Cotton and Cottonseed Production*, May 1955, 1956, 1957, and 1958. Census years, Bureau of the Census, *U.S. Census of Agriculture: 1954*, vol. II, p. 575.

Series K 302, 1790–1865, Department of Agriculture, Bureau of Statistics, Circular 32, August 1912; 1866–1957 and census years, see source for series K 301.

Series K 303, 1869–1875, Department of Agriculture, Bureau of Statistics, Circular 32, August 1912; 1876–1908, *Agricultural Statistics, 1941*; 1909–1952, Agricultural Marketing Service, Statistical Bulletin No. 164, June 1955 (processed); 1953–1955, Agricultural Marketing Service, *Cotton and Cottonseed Production*, May 1955, 1956, 1957, and 1958.

Series K 304, 1906–1928, Department of Agriculture, *Agricultural Statistics, 1941*; 1929–1945, *Agricultural Statistics, 1952*; 1946–1955, *Agricultural Statistics, 1956*; 1956–1957, Bureau of the Census, *Facts for Industry*, supplement to series M 22–P, August and September, 1957.

Series K 305, see source for series K 301.

Series K 306, see source for series K 303.

See also general note for series K 254–328.

Cotton production figures for census years are shown in running bales, and are not comparable with annual production estimates shown in 500-pound gross-weight bales. The net weight per running bale was 383 pounds in 1839, the first census period; 496.1 pounds in 1944; and 482.0 in 1954, the most recent census year.

Cotton production estimates are defined by statute as cotton actually ginned. For 1913–1924, annual ginnings as published by the Bureau of the Census included some cotton produced in lower California and Mexico and ginned in California; however, it is not included in U.S. production for, those years.

For those years, also, cotton ginned in the United States exceeds production by the quantity of the cross-border movement of seed cotton into this country. For all other years, beginning in 1899, production of cotton is the quantity of census ginnings by States adjusted for cross-State movement of seed cotton and rounded to thousands of bales. U.S. production is obtained by adding rounded State estimates and therefore differs slightly from the Census Bureau report on ginnings.

Before 1899, production figures were compiled from various current sources including exports and imports, rail and water shipments, mill receipts, etc., together with the decennial enumerations of the Bureau of the Census. These production estimates are the same as those in Department of Agriculture, Bureau of Statistics, Circular 32, cited above, except for minor adjustments caused by rounding State estimates.

Figures for stocks (series K 304) are in running bales, except that any small quantity of foreign cotton which is included is in equivalent 500-pound gross-weight bales. Before 1914, stocks are as of September 1. Data for 1906–1922 are from the New York Cotton Exchange Service; those for 1923–1957 were compiled by the Bureau of the Census.

Cottonseed production (series K 305) for 1866–1927 was computed from net lint production using a uniform ratio of 65 pounds of cottonseed for each 35 pounds of net lint. Beginning in 1928, ratios were estimated from data collected from cotton ginners.

The season average prices from 1908 to date for both cotton and cottonseed (series K 303 and K 306) are the weighted averages of midmonth prices. Before 1909, cottonseed prices are not available; before 1908, cotton prices were based on farmers' estimates on December 1 of average prices for the season.

The crop-marketing season for both cotton and cottonseed is August 1 to July 31 for all States except Texas where it begins about mid-July.

K 307–309. Tobacco acreage, production, and price, 1866–1957.

Source: **Series K 307–308**, 1866–1943, Agricultural Marketing Service, *Tobacco Acreage, Yield, Production, Price, and Value*, July 1948 (processed); 1944–1954, see source for series K 265–266, above; 1955–1957, *Crop Production*, July 1956–1958. **Series K 309**, 1866–1943, see source for series K 307–308; 1944–1954, Department of Agriculture, *Agricultural Statistics, 1956*; 1955–1957, Agricultural Marketing Service, *Crop Values*, December 1956, 1957, and 1958.

See also general note for series K 254–328.

Agricultural Marketing Service publications also present estimates of stocks of tobacco, 1929–1957, and of acreage and production of tobacco, by types, 1919–1957.

K 310–315. Irish potatoes and sweetpotatoes acreage, production, and price, 1849–1957.

Source: Census years, Bureau of the Census, *U.S. Census of Agriculture: 1954*, vol. II, p. 577.

Series K 310, 1866–1948, Agricultural Marketing Service, Statistical Bulletin No. 122, March 1953; 1949–1955, Statistical Bulletin No. 190, August 1956; 1956 and 1957, *Crop Production*, 1957 and 1958, annual summary.

Series K 311 and K 314, 1866–1918, Crop Reporting Board, records; 1919–1957, see source cited for series K 310.

Series K 312, 1866–1908, see source for series K 311; 1909–1955, Agricultural Marketing Service, *Agricultural Prices*, February 1957; 1956–1957, *Crop Values*, December 1957 and

1958. **Series K 313,** 1866–1918, Department of Agriculture, *Agricultural Statistics, 1941*; 1919–1957, see source for series K 310.

Series K 315, 1866–1908, see source for series K 311; 1909–1955, Agricultural Marketing Service, *Agricultural Prices,* January 1957; 1956–1957, see source for series K 312.

Estimates of potatoes and sweetpotatoes relate to the total crop harvested and include quantities used on farms where grown and losses from shrinkage, cullage, and dumping after harvest. The potato crop is divided into six seasonal groups: Winter, early spring, late spring, early summer, late summer, and fall. The seasonal estimates are based on the usual time of harvest. The schedule of estimates and the classification of States are shown in Agriculture Handbook No. 127, June 1957. Stocks on hand in the 26 fall States are published in separate reports, as of December 1, January 1, February 1, and March 1.

K 316–328. Fruit production and price, 1889–1957.

Source: Census years, Bureau of the Census, *U.S. Census of Agriculture: 1954*, vol. II, pp. 825–829 (for oranges and grapefruit for 1949 and 1954, see vol. I, parts 18, 24, 26, 30, and 33).

Series K 316–324, 1889–1943, Agricultural Marketing Service, *Fruits, Non-Citrus, Production, Farm Disposition, Value, and Utilization of Sales, 1889–1944,* May 1948; 1944–1948, Statistical Bulletin No. 114, October 1952; 1949–1954, Statistical Bulletin No. 192, September 1956; 1955, *Fruits, Non-Citrus Production, Use, and Value, 1955 and 1956,* July 1957; 1956–1957, *1957 and 1958 Annual Summary, Crop Production,* December 1957 and 1958, and *Crop Values,* December 1957 and 1958.

Series K 325–328, 1909–1944, Agricultural Marketing Service, *Citrus Fruits-Production, Farm Disposition, Value, and*

Utilization of Sales, Crop Season 1909–10 to 1943–44 (mimeographed), October 1945; 1944–1948, *Citrus Fruits, Production, Farm Disposition, Value, and Utilization of Sales, Crop Season 1944–45 to 1949–50* (mimeographed), October 1952; 1949–1954, Statistical Bulletin No. 201, January 1957; 1955, *Citrus Fruits, Production, Use, and Value,* October 1957 and 1958; 1957, *1958 Annual Summary, Crop Production,* December 1958, and *Crop Values,* December 1958.

See also general note for series K 254–328.

Estimates of fruit production include the harvested crop plus allowances for economic abandonment in years when appreciable quantities are not harvested because of low prices or other economic factors; they exclude losses from natural causes, such as windstorms, freezes, etc. For all crops except apples, production relates to the total crop within the State, including both commercial and home production. For apple production, estimates for 1935–1957 relate to the total crop within specified counties designated as "commercial" counties.

Since annual estimates of Agricultural Marketing Service were begun they have been checked and adjusted at the end of each marketing season on the basis of shipment and processing records from transportation agencies, processors, cooperative marketing associations, and other industry organizations. The estimates are again checked at 5-year intervals with the Census of Agriculture and revised. The Agricultural Marketing Service estimates for census years do not always agree with census data because of allowance for economic abandonment and of adjustments based on available shipment and processing records.

Citrus fruits are valued at equivalent per unit returns, excluding packing, grading, and container costs, rather than at average prices for all sales.

620722 O - 62 - 19

Series K 1–7.　Farms, Land in Farms, and Value of Farm Property and Real Estate: 1850 to 1957

[Census figures in italics]

Year	Number of farms [1] (1,000 farms)	Land in farms [2] (1,000 acres)	Selected items of farm property, total value [3] (Million dollars)	Farmland and buildings — Total value [4] (Million dollars)	Farmland and buildings — Average value per acre (Dollars)	Farm buildings, total value (Million dollars)	Index of average value of farm real estate per acre (1947–49 =100)
1957	4,857	(5)	137,977	109,469	94.52	24,594	147
1956	4,969	(5)	129,882	102,652	88.63	23,919	138
1955	5,087	(5)	125,930	98,780	85.29	24,534	133
1954	5,201	1,158,192	122,352	94,688	81.76	23,942	128
1953	5,308	1,158,285	126,802	96,688	83.43	25,454	132
1952	5,421	1,158,378	130,464	96,004	82.87	24,950	132
1951	5,535	1,158,471	116,722	86,798	74.92	22,768	119
1950	5,648	1,158,565	99,365	75,256	64.96	20,803	103
1949	5,722	1,155,174	100,368	76,623	66.33	20,778	105
1948	5,803	1,151,784	93,862	73,664	63.96	20,062	101
1947	5,871	1,148,394	85,462	68,463	59.62	18,521	94
1946	5,926	1,145,003	75,937	61,046	53.31	16,724	84
1945	5,967	1,141,614	69,186	53,884	47.20	14,906	74
1944	6,003	1,125,461	63,230	48,200	42.83	13,591	67
1943	6,089	1,109,308	56,153	41,604	37.50	11,923	58
1942	6,202	1,093,155	48,601	37,547	34.35	11,026	53
1941	6,293	1,077,002	42,979	34,400	31.94	10,386	49
1940	6,350	1,060,851	41,829	33,636	31.71	10,405	49
1939	6,441	1,059,582	42,213	34,085	32.17	---------	49
1938	6,527	1,058,315	43,202	35,170	33.33	---------	50
1937	6,636	1,057,047	42,926	35,213	33.31	---------	49
1936	6,739	1,055,780	41,803	34,260	32.45	---------	48
1935	6,814	1,054,512	38,959	33,264	31.54	10,245	45
1934	6,776	1,040,963	37,538	32,201	30.93	---------	44
1933	6,741	1,027,415	36,249	30,802	29.98	---------	42
1932	6,687	1,013,865	43,651	37,180	36.67	---------	51
1931	6,608	1,000,317	51,806	43,730	43.72	---------	61

Year	Number of farms [1] (1,000 farms)	Land in farms [2] (1,000 acres)	Selected items of farm property, total value [3] (Million dollars)	Farmland and buildings — Total value [4] (Million dollars)	Farmland and buildings — Average value per acre (Dollars)	Farm buildings, total value (Million dollars)	Index of average value of farm real estate per acre (1947–49 =100)
1930	6,546	986,768	57,689	47,873	48.52	12,949	68
1929	6,512	974,277	57,738	47,985	49.25	---------	69
1928	6,470	961,787	56,727	47,532	49.42	---------	70
1927	6,458	949,297	56,393	47,680	50.23	---------	71
1926	6,462	936,806	57,412	49,000	52.31	---------	74
1925	6,471	924,316	57,439	49,463	53.51	11,745	76
1924	6,480	930,628	58,519	50,487	54.25	---------	78
1923	6,492	936,941	60,902	52,629	56.17	---------	81
1922	6,500	943,253	61,982	54,050	57.30	---------	83
1921	6,511	949,566	71,401	61,523	64.79	---------	95
1920	6,518	955,878	78,386	66,310	69.37	11,485	103
1919	6,506	948,169	66,863	54,533	57.51	---------	84
1918	6,488	940,461	61,466	49,980	53.14	---------	78
1917	6,478	932,752	54,902	45,524	48.80	---------	70
1916	6,463	925,044	50,651	42,264	45.69	---------	65
1915	6,458	917,335	47,715	39,590	43.16	---------	61
1914	6,447	909,627	47,429	39,579	43.51	---------	61
1913	6,437	901,918	45,720	38,456	42.64	---------	60
1912	6,430	894,209	43,842	37,298	41.71	---------	58
1911	6,425	886,501	42,693	36,042	40.66	---------	---------
1910	6,406	878,792	40,959	34,793	39.59	6,324	---------
1900	5,737	838,592	20,365	16,603	19.81	3,555	---------
1890	4,565	623,207	16,439	13,273	21.31	---------	---------
1880	4,009	536,064	12,404	10,193	19.02	---------	---------
1870	2,660	407,723	9,412	7,441	18.26	---------	---------
1860	2,044	407,179	7,980	6,642	16.32	---------	---------
1850	1,449	293,534	3,967	3,270	11.14	---------	---------

[1] Except for data from Census of Agriculture, estimates have been adjusted for under-enumeration and changes in definition in the Census. Not strictly comparable with land in farms, value of farm property, or value of farm real estate.
[2] Intercensal estimates derived from straight-line interpolation. Excludes District of Columbia.
[3] Includes farmland and buildings, machinery and equipment, and all livestock.
[4] Census years as of date of enumeration. All other years as of March 1. District of Columbia excluded.
[5] Not available.

Series K 8–52.　Farms, by Color and Tenure of Operator, and Acreage and Value, by Tenure of Operator: 1880 to 1954

Series No.	Color and tenure of operator	1954 [1]	1950	1945	1940	1930	1920	1910	1900	1890	1880
	NUMBER OF FARMS										
8	U.S.	4,783,021	5,382,162	5,859,169	6,096,799	6,288,648	6,448,343	6,361,502	5,737,372	4,564,641	4,008,907
9	Full owner	2,744,708	3,089,583	3,301,361	3,084,138	2,911,644	3,366,510	3,354,897	3,201,947	3,269,728	2,984,306
10	Part owner	868,180	824,923	660,502	615,089	656,750	558,580	593,825	451,376		
11	Manager	20,894	23,527	38,885	36,351	55,889	68,449	58,104	59,085		
12	Tenant	1,149,239	1,444,129	1,858,421	2,361,271	2,664,365	2,454,804	2,354,676	2,024,964	1,294,913	1,024,601
13	White	4,301,420	4,801,243	5,169,954	5,377,728	5,372,578	5,498,454	5,440,619	4,969,608	---------	---------
14	Full owner	2,604,730	2,936,122	3,126,212	2,916,562	2,752,787	3,174,109	3,159,088	3,025,931	---------	---------
15	Part owner	814,112	769,573	629,734	581,517	612,887	517,759	548,413	420,875	---------	---------
16	Manager	20,236	23,056	38,263	35,634	52,767	66,223	56,560	57,261	---------	---------
17	Tenant	862,342	1,072,492	1,375,745	1,844,015	1,954,137	1,740,363	1,676,558	1,465,541	---------	---------
18	Nonwhite	481,601	580,919	689,215	719,071	916,070	949,889	920,883	767,764	---------	---------
19	Full owner	139,978	153,461	175,149	167,576	158,857	192,401	195,809	176,016	---------	---------
20	Part owner	54,068	55,350	30,768	33,522	43,863	40,821	45,412	30,501	---------	---------
21	Manager	658	471	622	717	3,122	2,226	1,544	1,824	---------	---------
22	Tenant	286,897	371,637	482,676	517,256	710,228	714,441	678,118	559,423	---------	---------
23	South	2,317,296	2,652,423	2,881,135	3,007,170	3,223,816	3,206,664	3,097,547	2,620,391	1,836,372	1,531,077
24	Full owner	1,275,226	1,411,123	1,509,056	1,327,690	1,190,683	1,405,762	1,329,390	1,237,114	1,130,029	977,229
25	Part owner	351,016	325,999	193,607	216,607	224,992	191,463	215,121	133,368		
26	Manager	9,571	9,979	13,193	13,580	17,358	18,318	16,284	18,765		
27	Tenant	681,483	905,322	1,165,279	1,449,293	1,790,783	1,591,121	1,536,752	1,231,144	706,343	553,848
28	Croppers	267,662	346,765	446,556	541,291	776,278	561,091				
29	White	1,853,820	2,093,333	2,215,722	2,326,904	2,342,129	2,283,750	2,207,406	1,879,721	---------	---------
30	Full owner	1,145,372	1,269,641	1,348,076	1,185,788	1,050,187	1,227,204	1,154,100	1,078,635	---------	---------
31	Part owner	300,280	274,135	165,355	185,246	183,469	152,432	171,944	105,171	---------	---------
32	Manager	9,190	9,740	12,751	13,215	16,529	16,548	15,084	17,172	---------	---------
33	Tenant	398,978	539,817	689,540	942,655	1,091,944	887,566	866,278	678,743	---------	---------
34	Croppers	107,416	148,708	176,260	242,173	383,381	227,378				
35	Nonwhite	463,476	559,090	665,413	680,266	881,687	922,914	890,141	740,670	---------	---------
36	Full owner	129,854	141,482	160,980	141,902	140,496	178,558	175,290	158,479	---------	---------
37	Part owner	50,736	51,864	28,252	31,361	41,523	39,031	43,177	28,197	---------	---------
38	Manager	381	239	442	365	829	1,770	1,200	1,593	---------	---------
39	Tenant	282,505	365,505	475,739	506,638	698,839	703,555	670,474	552,401	---------	---------
40	Croppers	160,246	198,057	270,296	299,118	392,897	333,713				

[1] Based on sample.

Series K 8-52. Farms, by Color and Tenure of Operator, and Acreage and Value, by Tenure of Operator: 1880 to 1954—Con.

Series No.	Color and tenure of operator	1954 [1]	1950	1945	1940	1930	1920	1910	1900
	LAND IN FARMS (1,000 acres)								
41	All farms	1,160,044	1,158,566	1,141,615	1,060,852	986,771	955,884	878,798	838,592
42	Full owner	397,214	418,970	412,358	382,098	372,450	461,250	464,923	431,261
43	Part owner	472,465	422,394	371,251	300,325	245,926	175,525	133,631	124,779
44	Manager	100,003	105,241	106,372	66,530	61,986	54,129	53,731	87,518
45	Tenant	190,362	211,960	251,634	311,899	306,409	264,980	226,513	195,034
46	Croppers (South)	9,413	14,166	18,922	23,313	31,605	22,531		
	AVERAGE VALUE PER FARM OF FARMLAND AND BUILDINGS (dollars)								
47	All farms	19,761	13,911	7,917	5,518	7,614	10,284	5,471	2,896
48	Full owner	14,511	10,716	6,393	4,960	7,255	9,122	5,160	2,851
49	Part owner	35,764	25,133	15,184	9,938	12,389	16,387	8,515	4,347
50	Manager	165,800	128,255	60,552	39,687	40,052	38,937	25,075	13,114
51	Tenant	19,464	12,943	6,941	4,569	6,148	9,690	4,662	2,345
52	Croppers (South)	3,972	3,333	1,981	1,433	1,802	2,633		

[1] Based on sample.

Series K 53-60. Number, Acreage, Value, and Amount of Indebtedness of Mortgaged Farms, by Tenure of Operator: 1930 to 1956

Year	Number of farms	Land in farms	Value of farm-land and buildings	Mortgage debt				Equity per mort-gaged farm
				Total	Ratio of mortgage debt to total value	Debt per acre	Debt per farm	
	53	54	55	56	57	58	59	60
	1,000 farms	1,000 acres	$1,000	$1,000	Percent	Dollars	Dollars	Dollars
ALL TENURES								
1956	(1)	348,687	36,282,284	9,066,153	25.0	26.00	(1)	(1)
1950	1,480	303,610	22,049,126	5,579,278	25.3	18.38	3,769	11,125
1945	1,714	373,123	16,375,954	4,940,915	30.2	13.24	2,883	6,672
1940	2,364	457,374	15,873,779	6,586,399	41.5	14.40	2,786	3,929
1935	2,350	(1)	(1)	7,584,459	(1)	(1)	3,227	(1)
1930	2,523	(1)	(1)	9,630,768	(1)	(1)	3,817	(1)
FULL OWNER								
1956	909	149,111	17,625,598	4,719,920	26.8	31.65	5,191	14,194
1950	894	135,343	11,273,372	3,116,297	27.6	23.03	3,485	9,123
1945	997	149,106	8,166,198	2,689,787	32.9	18.04	2,697	5,492
1940	1,278	180,452	7,887,163	3,353,376	42.5	18.58	2,623	3,547
1935	1,270	181,868	7,338,406	3,682,364	50.2	20.25	2,899	2,879
1930	1,232	182,081	10,955,133	4,337,225	39.6	23.82	3,521	5,373
PART OWNER [2]								
1956	368	117,087	9,086,969	2,311,978	25.4	19.75	6,278	18,397
1950	281	90,079	4,585,278	1,178,637	25.7	13.08	4,187	12,103
1945	274	89,898	2,862,721	875,086	30.6	9.73	3,194	7,256
1940	337	93,882	2,358,403	1,105,664	46.9	11.78	3,287	3,724
1935	349	(1)	(1)	(1)	(1)	(1)	(1)	(1)
1930	360	(1)	(1)	(1)	(1)	(1)	(1)	(1)
MANAGER AND TENANT [3]								
1956	(1)	82,489	9,569,717	2,034,255	21.3	24.66	(4)	(1)
1950	305	78,188	6,190,476	1,284,344	20.7	16.43	(4)	16,095
1945	443	134,119	5,347,035	1,376,092	25.7	10.26	(4)	8,969
1940	749	183,040	5,628,213	2,127,359	37.8	11.62	(4)	4,674
1935	731	(1)	(1)	(1)	(1)	(1)	(1)	(1)
1930	931	(1)	(1)	(1)	(1)	(1)	(1)	(1)

[1] Not available.
[2] Acres, value, and debt are for owned portion only.
[3] Acres, value, and debt include the rented portion of part-owner farms.
[4] Not shown because data for mortgage debt include rented portion of part-owner farms.

Series K 61-72. Farms and Land in Farms, by Size of Farm: 1880 to 1954

[In thousands]

Year	Total	Under 10 acres			10 to 29 acres	30 to 49 acres	50 to 99 acres	100 to 179 acres	180 to 259 acres	260 to 499 acres	500 to 999 acres	1,000 and over
		Total	Under 3 acres	3 to 9 acres								
	61	62	63	64	65	66	67	68	69	70	71	72
NUMBER OF FARMS												
1954	4,782	484	100	384	713	499	864	953	464	482	192	131
1950	5,382	485	77	408	854	624	1,048	1,103	487	478	182	121
1945	5,859	594	99	495	946	709	1,157	1,200	493	473	174	113
1940	6,097	506	36	470	1,013	767	1,291	1,310	486	459	164	101
1935	6,812	571	36	535	1,241	882	1,444	1,438	507	473	167	89
1930	6,289	358	43	315	2,000		1,375	1,864		451	160	81
1925	6,372	378	15	363	2,039		1,421	1,887		440	144	63
1920	6,448	289	20	269	2,011		1,475	1,980		476	150	67
1910	6,362	335	18	317	1,919		1,438	2,051		444	125	50
1900	5,737	267	41	226	1,664		1,366	1,912		378	103	47
1890	4,565	150	(1)	(1)	1,168		1,122	2,009			84	32
1880	4,009	139	4	135	1,036		1,033	1,696			76	29

[1] Not available.

Series K 61–72.   Farms and Land in Farms, by Size of Farm: 1880 to 1954—Con.

[In thousands]

Year	Total	Under 10 acres			10 to 29 acres	30 to 49 acres	50 to 99 acres	100 to 179 acres	180 to 259 acres	260 to 499 acres	500 to 999 acres	1,000 and over
		Total	Under 3 acres	3 to 9 acres								
	61	62	63	64	65	66	67	68	69	70	71	72
LAND IN FARMS (1,000 acres)												
1954	1,158,192	2,260	(1)	(1)	12,704	19,165	62,725	130,120	99,863	168,368	131,505	531,482
1950	1,159,789	2,429	(1)	(1)	15,391	23,945	75,628	149,942	105,388	166,584	125,981	494,501
1945	1,141,615	2,805	141	2,664	16,864	27,074	83,206	162,375	105,802	164,647	118,836	460,006
1940	1,060,852	2,668	51	2,617	18,111	29,388	93,317	177,508	104,288	159,568	111,935	364,069
1935	1,054,515	3,057	51	3,006	22,272	33,691	104,016	194,804	108,462	164,268	114,244	309,701
1930	986,771	1,908	61	1,847	54,041		98,685	290,478		156,522	108,924	276,213
1925	924,319	2,097	23	2,074	54,465		101,906	292,180		151,731	97,468	224,472
1920	955,884	1,600	33	1,567	55,553		105,631	307,244		164,244	100,976	220,636
1910	878,798			54,172			103,121	470,770			83,653	167,082
1900	838,592	1,478	79	1,399	47,240		98,592	295,962		129,672	67,864	197,784

¹Not available.

Series K 73–82.   Farm Employment, Wages, and Man-Hours Used for Farmwork: 1866 to 1957

Year	Employment [1]			Wage rates					Farmers' expenditures for hired labor [4]	Index man-hours of labor used for farmwork (1947–49 =100)
	Total farm	Family workers [2]	Hired workers	Index composite farm wage rates (1910–14 = 100)	Per month [3]		Per day [3]			
					With board	Without board	With board	Without board		
	73	74	75	76	77	78	79	80	81	82
	1,000	1,000	1,000		Dollars	Dollars	Dollars	Dollars	$1,000,000	
1957	7,577	5,682	1,895	560	133.00	168.00	5.80	5.80	2,867	79
1956	7,820	5,899	1,921	542	128.00	161.00	5.60	5.60	2,790	83
1955	8,364	6,347	2,017	519	123.00	154.00	5.40	5.30	2,736	85
1954	8,639	6,579	2,060	508	120.00	151.00	5.30	5.30	2,714	85
1953	8,864	6,775	2,089	517	122.00	151.00	5.40	5.30	2,792	88
1952	9,149	7,005	2,144	508	119.00	146.00	5.30	5.30	2,801	89
1951	9,546	7,310	2,236	481	113.00	137.00	5.00	5.00	2,931	91
1950	9,926	7,597	2,329	432	99.00	121.00	4.45	4.50	2,750	89
1949	9,964	7,712	2,252	430	99.00	121.00	4.45	4.45	2,865	97
1948	10,363	8,026	2,337	445	99.00	124.00	4.80	5.40	3,016	100
1947	10,382	8,115	2,267	424	92.00	117.00	4.50	5.10	2,808	103
1946	10,295	8,106	2,189	399	86.00	108.00	4.20	4.80	2,544	108
1945	10,000	7,881	2,119	366	79.00	101.00	3.85	4.35	2,299	112
1944	10,219	7,988	2,231	328	71.00	91.00	3.50	3.95	2,202	120
1943	10,446	8,010	2,436	274	59.00	77.00	2.90	3.30	2,027	121
1942	10,504	7,949	2,555	208	45.50	59.00	2.20	2.55	1,631	122
1941	10,669	8,017	2,652	160	34.50	44.50	1.65	1.95	1,249	117
1940	10,979	8,300	2,679	131	27.50	37.50	1.30	1.60	1,029	119
1939	11,338	8,611	2,727	129	27.00	36.00	1.25	1.55	988	121
1938	11,622	8,815	2,807	129	27.00	36.00	1.30	1.55	979	120
1937	11,978	9,054	2,924	133	27.50	36.50	1.35	1.65	988	129
1936	12,331	9,350	2,981	118	24.00	32.50	1.20	1.45	868	119
1935	12,733	9,855	2,878	110	22.00	30.50	1.10	1.35	775	123
1934	12,627	9,765	2,862	100	20.00	28.00	1.00	1.25	679	118
1933	12,739	9,874	2,865	89	18.00	25.50	.90	1.15	617	132
1932	12,816	9,922	2,894	100	20.50	29.00	.95	1.20	669	132
1931	12,745	9,642	3,103	133	28.50	38.00	1.30	1.65	914	137
1930	12,497	9,307	3,190	175	37.50	48.00	1.80	2.15	1,177	134
1929	12,763	9,360	3,403	187	40.00	51.00	2.00	2.30	1,300	135
1928	12,691	9,340	3,351	185	39.50	50.00	2.00	2.30	1,290	136
1927	12,642	9,278	3,364	185	39.50	50.00	2.00	2.35	1,302	134
1926	12,976	9,526	3,450	185	39.50	50.00	2.00	2.40	1,330	139
1925	13,036	9,715	3,321	183	38.50	49.00	2.00	2.35	1,267	139
1924	13,031	9,705	3,326	181	38.00	49.00	1.95	2.40	1,248	136
1923	13,162	9,798	3,364	177	37.50	47.50	1.95	2.35	1,251	135
1922	13,337	9,936	3,401	154	33.00	43.50	1.65	2.00	1,127	134
1921	13,398	10,001	3,397	156	33.50	44.50	1.65	2.05	1,170	129
1920	13,432	10,041	3,391	241	51.00	65.00	2.80	3.30	1,790	140
1919	13,243	9,968	3,275	206	43.00	56.00	2.40	2.90	1,515	138
1918	13,391	10,053	3,338	177	37.50	48.50	2.05	2.45	1,337	141
1917	13,568	10,121	3,447	141	31.00	40.50	1.55	1.90	1,127	139
1916	13,632	10,144	3,488	112	25.00	33.00	1.25	1.50	904	135
1915	13,592	10,140	3,452	102	22.50	30.00	1.10	1.40	815	136
1914	13,580	10,147	3,433	102	22.50	29.50	1.10	1.35	804	139
1913	13,572	10,158	3,414	104	22.50	30.00	1.15	1.40	804	134
1912	13,559	10,162	3,397	102	22.00	29.50	1.10	1.40	789	136
1911	13,539	10,169	3,370	98	21.50	28.00	1.05	1.35	758	134
1910	13,555	10,174	3,381	96	21.00	28.00	1.05	1.35	755	132

See footnotes at end of table.

Series K 73–82. Farm Employment, Wages, and Man-Hours Used for Farmwork: 1866 to 1957—Con.

Year	Index, composite farm wage rates (1910–14 =100)	Wage rates				Year	Index, composite farm wage rates (1910–14 =100)	Wage rates			
		Per month [3]		Per day [3]				Per month [3]		Per day [3]	
		With board	Without board	With board	Without board			With board	Without board	With board	Without board
	76	77	78	79	80		76	77	78	79	80
		Dollars	Dollars	Dollars	Dollars			Dollars	Dollars	Dollars	Dollars
1909	96	22.00	28.00	1.00	1.25	1887 or 1888	67	13.50	19.50	0.70	1.00
1906	91	18.50	26.00	1.05	1.30	1884 or 1885	64	13.00	19.00	.70	.95
1902	75	15.50	22.00	.85	1.10	1881 or 1882	64	13.00	19.00	.70	.95
1899	69	14.00	20.00	.75	1.00	1880 or 1881	62	12.50	18.50	.65	.90
1898	64	13.50	19.00	.70	.95	1879 or 1880	58	11.50	17.50	.65	.90
1895	60	12.50	18.50	.65	.85	1877 [5]	56	11.00	17.00	.60	.85
1894	60	12.50	18.50	.65	.85						
1893	67	14.00	20.00	.70	.90	1874 or 1875	58	11.00	17.00	.70	.95
1891 or 1892	67	13.50	20.00	.75	1.00	1869	54	10.00	15.50	.65	.85
1889 or 1890	67	13.50	19.50	.70	.95	1866 [6]	54	10.00	15.50	.65	.90

[1] These annual averages are simple averages of last-of-month employment estimates.
[2] Includes farm operators and members of their families doing farmwork without wages.
[3] Annual averages are weighted averages of wage rates as reported quarterly by crop reporters. Different wage rate categories used after 1948. See text.
[4] Cash wages and value of perquisites.
[5] 1877 or 1878, 1878 or 1879 (combined).
[6] Years 1866 to 1878 in gold.

Series K 83–97. Man-Hours Used to Produce Specified Amounts of Wheat, Corn, and Cotton: 1800 to 1950

Series No.	Crop and item	1950	1940	1920	1900	1880	1840	1800	Series No.	Crop and item	1950	1940	1920	1900	1880	1840	1800
	WHEAT									CORN—Con.							
83	Man-hours per acre	4.6	7.5	12.0	15	20	35	56	91	Yield per acre [1] __bu__	39.0	30.3	28.4	25.9	25.6	25	25
84	Before harvest	2.6	3.7	5.5	7	8	12	16	92	Man-hours per 100 bushels	39	83	113	147	180	276	344
85	Harvest	2.0	3.8	6.5	8	12	23	40		**COTTON**							
86	Yield per acre [1] __bu__	16.6	15.9	13.8	13.9	13.2	15	15	93	Man-hours per acre	74	98	90	112	119	135	185
87	Man-hours per 100 bushels	28	47	87	108	152	233	373	94	Before harvest	33	46	55	62	67	90	135
	CORN								95	Harvest	41	52	35	50	52	45	50
88	Man-hours per acre	15.2	25	32	38	46	69	86	96	Yield of lint per acre [1] __lb__	283	245	160	191	179	147	147
89	Before harvest	9.9	15	19	22	28	44	56	97	Man-hours per bale [2]	126	191	269	280	318	439	601
90	Harvest	5.3	10	13	16	18	25	30									

[1] Yields for 1800 and 1840 are estimates by the authors. Yields for the other years are 5-year averages of published data, centered on year shown.

[2] For statistical purposes, the bale of cotton is 500 pounds gross weight or 480 pounds net weight of lint. Prior to Aug. 1, 1946, the net weight was estimated at 478 pounds. Running bales reported prior to 1899 have been converted to bales of 478 pounds net weight. Actual bale weights vary considerably.

Series K 98–103. Acreages of Harvested Crops, by Use, and Indexes of Cropland Used for Crops and Crop Production Per Acre: 1910 to 1957

Year	Acreages of harvested crops, by use (1,000,000 acres)				Index (1947–49 =100)		Year	Acreages of harvested crops, by use (1,000,000 acres)				Index (1947–49 =100)	
	Total	Export products	Feed for horses and mules	Products for domestic use	Cropland used for crops	Crop production per acre		Total	Export products	Feed for horses and mules	Products for domestic use	Cropland used for crops	Crop production per acre
	98	99	100	101	102	103		98	99	100	101	102	103
1957 (prel.)	326	50	8	268	95	112	1933	340	28	59	253	100	71
1956 (prel.)	326	60	9	257	97	109	1932	371	35	60	276	101	79
1955	340	47	10	283	99	106	1931	365	36	62	267	101	83
1954	346	37	11	298	100	101	1930	369	39	65	265	101	75
1953	348	31	13	304	100	103	1929	365	44	67	254	100	79
1952	349	36	15	298	100	103	1928	361	49	70	242	99	83
1951	344	59	18	267	101	98	1927	358	49	73	236	98	81
1950	345	50	19	276	100	97	1926	359	54	76	229	98	82
1949	360	45	22	293	102	99	1925	360	44	78	238	98	80
1948	356	52	24	280	100	106	1924	355	53	81	221	96	79
1947	354	42	26	286	98	95	1923	354	47	84	223	96	79
1946	351	45	29	277	97	101	1922	355	50	86	219	96	79
1945	354	42	32	280	98	95	1921	359	66	87	206	97	73
1944	361	25	36	300	100	96	1920	360	60	90	210	97	86
1943	356	21	37	298	99	91	1919	364	56	91	217	99	77
1942	346	13	39	294	98	99	1918	362	62	92	208	98	77
1941	342	12	40	290	97	89	1917	349	44	92	213	94	80
1940	339	8	43	288	97	88	1916	340	53	92	195	92	76
1939	330	23	45	262	96	85	1915	340	49	93	198	92	85
1938	349	22	48	279	98	85	1914	334	57	92	185	90	83
1937	347	29	52	266	100	88	1913	333	43	92	198	90	76
1936	323	18	54	251	99	65	1912	329	42	91	196	89	87
1935	345	20	56	269	100	76	1911	330	40	90	200	89	75
1934	304	20	57	227	99	59	1910	325	37	88	200	87	79

Series K 104–115. Index of Supply and Utilization of Farm Food Commodities: 1924 to 1957

[Percent of total utilization in each year. Covers farm commodities normally used for food in the United States, including their nonfood use]

	Supply			Utilization									
					Domestic use					Commercial exports and shipments to U.S. Territories [4]	USDA export program		
Year	Production	Imports and inshipments	Net change in available stocks [1]	Total	Total	Food		Nonfood [3]			Stock change [5]	Deliveries [6]	Net purchases [7]
						Civilian	Military [2]						
	104	105	106	107	108	109	110	111			113	114	115
1957 (prel.)	94.9	6.5	−1.4	100.0	91.7	66.2	1.2	24.3		7.6	([8])	0.7	0.7
1956	94.7	6.4	−1.1	100.0	92.1	66.0	1.3	24.8		7.1	([8])	0.8	0.8
1955	95.7	6.5	−2.2	100.0	93.5	66.9	1.4	25.2		5.7	([8])	0.8	0.8
1954	96.3	6.4	−2.7	100.0	94.6	67.3	1.6	25.7		5.0	([8])	0.4	0.4
1953	95.5	7.3	−2.8	100.0	95.1	66.6	1.9	26.6		4.4	([8])	0.5	0.5
1952	94.8	7.0	−1.8	100.0	94.5	65.4	2.1	27.0		5.2	([8])	0.3	0.3
1951	90.0	6.9	3.1	100.0	93.7	62.8	2.7	28.2		4.6	([8])	1.7	1.7
1950	94.6	7.0	−1.6	100.0	95.4	65.2	1.4	28.8		3.2	−0.1	1.5	1.4
1949	94.9	6.8	−1.7	100.0	95.7	64.6	2.8	28.3		2.6	−0.2	1.9	1.7
1948	100.4	6.8	−7.2	100.0	96.0	65.7	2.9	27.4		2.4	−0.2	1.8	1.6
1947	91.6	6.0	2.4	100.0	94.1	64.1	2.4	27.6		3.3	0.4	2.2	2.6
1946	95.1	5.7	−0.8	100.0	95.0	63.7	2.2	29.1		1.9	−0.6	3.7	3.1
1945	92.8	5.8	1.4	100.0	95.9	57.6	8.5	29.8		1.1	−0.7	3.7	3.0
1944	93.0	6.9	0.1	100.0	95.0	55.7	9.0	30.3		0.8	−0.1	4.3	4.2
1943	90.4	5.7	3.9	100.0	94.3	54.5	6.1	33.7		0.6	0.4	4.7	5.1
1942	96.8	4.6	−1.4	100.0	95.1	59.3	4.1	31.7		0.8	1.1	3.0	4.1
1941	95.2	7.8	−3.0	100.0	97.1	64.9	1.3	30.9		1.3	0.3	1.3	1.6
1940	95.3	7.2	−2.5	100.0	98.3	67.5	----------	30.8		1.7	----------	----------	----------
1939	93.2	7.4	−0.6	100.0	97.5	66.6	----------	30.9		2.5	----------	----------	----------
1938	95.5	7.2	−2.7	100.0	96.7	66.1	----------	30.6		3.3	----------	----------	----------
1937	98.8	9.1	−7.9	100.0	98.3	69.4	----------	28.9		1.7	----------	----------	----------
1936	85.7	8.4	5.9	100.0	98.7	67.6	----------	31.1		1.3	----------	----------	----------
1935	96.2	9.0	−5.2	100.0	98.6	69.4	----------	29.2		1.4	----------	----------	----------
1934	87.5	6.6	5.9	100.0	98.3	68.9	----------	29.4		1.7	----------	----------	----------
1933	90.1	6.5	3.4	100.0	98.2	65.1	----------	33.1		1.8	----------	----------	----------
1932	96.1	6.0	−2.1	100.0	97.7	64.3	----------	33.4		2.1	----------	[9] 0.2	0.2
1931	96.0	6.8	−2.8	100.0	97.2	65.6	----------	31.6		2.6	----------	[9] 0.2	0.2
1930	92.3	7.3	0.4	100.0	96.9	65.4	----------	31.5		3.1	----------	----------	----------
1929	91.4	8.0	0.6	100.0	96.2	64.1	----------	32.1		3.8	----------	----------	----------
1928	94.3	7.2	−1.5	100.0	96.1	63.0	----------	33.1		3.9	----------	----------	----------
1927	92.8	7.2	([8])	100.0	95.4	63.0	----------	32.4		4.6	----------	----------	----------
1926	93.3	7.5	−0.8	100.0	96.0	64.3	----------	31.7		4.0	----------	----------	----------
1925	91.9	6.9	1.2	100.0	95.9	62.5	----------	33.4		4.1	----------	----------	----------
1924	93.4	6.6	([8])	100.0	94.5	63.5	----------	31.0		5.5	----------	----------	----------

[1] Includes farm and commercial stocks and holdings under price support and domestic supply programs. Minus sign means an addition to stocks.
[2] Includes civilian feeding in areas occupied by our Armed Forces.
[3] Includes seed, feed, industrial alcohol, alcoholic beverages, etc.
[4] Excludes deliveries by the Department of Agriculture.

[5] Stocks held for export. Minus sign means a withdrawal from stocks.
[6] Shipments out of this country.
[7] Represents net quantities withdrawn from domestic commercial channels.
[8] Less than 0.05 percent.
[9] Federal Farm Board exports.

Series K 116–121. Farm Taxes and Insurance: 1890 to 1957

	Taxes levied on farm property			Automotive taxes paid by farmers	Farmers' mutual fire insurance			Taxes levied on farm property			Automotive taxes paid by farmers	Farmers' mutual fire insurance	
	Real estate		Personal property		In force at end of year	Cost per $100 of insurance	Year	Real estate		Personal property		In force at end of year	Cost per $100 of insurance
Year	Total	Amount per acre						Total	Amount per acre				
	116	117	118	119	120	121		116	117	118	119	120	121
	Million dollars	Dollars	Million dollars	Million dollars	Million dollars	Cents		Million dollars	Dollars	Million dollars	Million dollars	Million dollars	Cents
1957	[1] 1,044	[1] 0.97	[1] 233	489	[1] 30,427	25.3	1935	392	0.37	42	142	11,083	23.2
1956	977	.91	226	455	29,297	23.5	1934	384	.37	40	132	10,572	26.9
							1933	398	.39	39	132	10,466	28.5
1955	928	.87	220	478	28,223	23.4	1932	461	.45	49	123	10,974	32.0
1954	870	.82	216	451	28,295	24.2	1931	526	.53	63	123	11,292	31.0
1953	840	.79	223	432	26,898	21.6							
1952	805	.76	233	409	27,716	22.0	1930	567	.57	81	127	11,382	31.6
1951	773	.72	214	369	25,494	22.1	1929	567	.58	84	119	11,119	28.4
							1928	556	.58	80	102	10,781	27.1
1950	741	.69	178	339	24,161	23.0	1927	545	.57	75	94	10,345	25.3
1949	706	.66	167	330	22,488	22.3	1926	526	.56	73	83	9,989	26.3
1948	656	.62	150	311	20,769	25.1							
1947	605	.57	128	287	19,264	24.3	1925	517	.56	72	72	9,477	27.8
1946	519	.49	99	261	16,941	24.6	1924	511	.55	72	55	9,487	26.9
							1923	516	.55	----------		9,058	26.4
1945	465	.44	92	248	15,170	23.6	1922	509	.54	----------		8,770	26.7
1944	419	.40	80	224	14,221	23.7	1921	510	.54	----------		8,410	27.2
1943	400	.38	77	219	13,778	23.9							
1942	400	.38	67	232	12,982	22.7	1920	483	.51	----------		7,866	25.8
1941	407	.39	56	200	12,519	24.6	1919	393	.41	----------		6,938	25.1
							1918	311	.33	----------		6,392	25.1
1940	401	.39	50	183	12,294	25.2	1917	292	.31	----------		5,877	24.6
1939	407	.39	49	170	12,144	26.6	1916	260	.28	----------		5,636	25.5
1938	400	.38	48	167	11,869	26.0							
1937	405	.39	47	163	11,569	24.1							
1936	394	.38	46	151	11,340	28.1							

[1] Preliminary.

Series K 116–121. Farm Taxes and Insurance: 1890 to 1957—Con.

Year	Taxes levied on farm real estate		Farmers' mutual fire insurance		Year	Taxes levied on farm real estate		Year	Taxes levied on farm real estate	
	Total	Amount per acre	In force at end of year	Cost per $100 of insurance		Total	Amount per acre		Total	Amount per acre
	116	117	120	121		116	117		116	117
	Million dollars	Dollars	Million dollars	Cents		Million dollars	Dollars		Million dollars	Dollars
1915	243	0.26	5,367	23.5	1905	130	0.15	1895	98	0.14
1914	222	.24	5,264	26.4	1904	125	.15	1894	93	.13
1913	218	.24			1903	123	.15	1893	92	.13
1912	191	.21			1902	113	.14	1892	87	.13
1911	183	.21			1901	111	.13	1891	84	.13
1910	166	.19			1900	106	.13	1890	82	.13
1909	163	.19			1899	105	.13			
1908	150	.17			1898	102	.13			
1907	141	.16			1897	101	.13			
1906	132	.16			1896	97	.13			

Series K 122–138. Farm Cash Receipts and Income, and Indexes of Prices Received and Paid by Farmers, and Parity Ratio: 1910 to 1957

Year	Cash receipts from farming ($1,000,000)			Farm income [1] ($1,000,000)				Indexes of prices received and paid by farmers, (1910–14 =100)								
	Total [1]	Crops	Live-stock	Realized gross farm income [2]	Total farm-production expenses	Realized net income of farm operators [3]	Net income to persons on farms from farming [4]	Prices received by farmers [5]			Prices paid by farmers		Payable per acre		Wage rates	Prices paid, including interest, taxes, and wage rates	Parity ratio [6]
								All farm products	Crops	Live-stock and products	Living	Pro-duc-tion	Inter-est pay-able	Taxes pay-able			
	122	123	124	125	126	127	128	129	130	131	132	133	134	135	136	137	138
1957	30,840	12,461	17,363	34,389	23,371	11,018	13,556	235	225	244	282	257	163	440	558	286	82
1956	31,117	14,252	16,312	34,626	22,594	12,032	13,358	230	235	226	274	250	150	421	536	278	83
1955	29,785	13,676	15,880	33,332	21,862	11,470	13,505	232	231	234	270	251	136	394	516	276	84
1954	30,210	13,669	16,284	33,865	21,664	12,201	14,447	246	242	249	270	255	126	381	510	277	89
1953	31,339	14,193	16,933	35,265	21,366	13,899	15,111	255	240	268	269	256	117	365	513	277	92
1952	32,906	14,380	18,252	37,016	22,600	14,416	17,262	288	267	306	271	274	108	350	503	287	100
1951	33,244	13,324	19,634	37,323	22,165	15,158	18,143	302	265	336	268	273	98	335	470	282	107
1950	28,795	12,410	16,102	32,482	19,297	13,185	15,696	258	233	280	246	246	89	320	425	256	101
1949	28,014	12,422	15,406	31,821	18,032	13,789	14,711	250	224	272	243	238	82	298	430	251	100
1948	30,484	13,098	17,129	34,914	18,857	16,057	19,810	287	255	315	251	250	78	276	442	260	110
1947	29,934	13,093	16,527	34,352	17,048	17,304	17,471	276	263	288	237	224	76	237	419	240	115
1946	25,574	11,016	13,786	29,706	14,483	15,223	17,050	236	228	242	202	191	74	213	387	208	113
1945	22,405	9,655	12,008	25,772	12,922	12,850	14,021	207	202	211	182	176	75	192	359	190	109
1944	21,312	9,185	11,351	24,412	12,195	12,217	13,352	197	199	196	175	173	79	185	318	182	108
1943	20,265	8,127	11,493	23,362	11,487	11,875	13,248	193	187	198	166	164	84	185	262	171	113
1942	16,215	6,526	9,039	18,767	9,942	8,825	11,074	159	145	171	149	148	94	189	197	152	105
1941	11,655	4,619	6,492	13,828	7,675	6,153	7,455	124	108	138	130	130	98	187	151	133	93
1940	9,105	3,469	4,913	11,038	6,749	4,289	5,299	100	90	109	121	123	102	189	129	124	81
1939	8,635	3,336	4,536	10,556	6,162	4,394	5,189	95	82	107	120	121	106	185	127	123	77
1938	8,169	3,200	4,523	10,101	5,828	4,273	5,101	97	80	112	122	122	110	187	130	124	78
1937	9,200	3,924	4,940	11,329	6,097	5,232	6,754	122	118	126	128	132	117	181	129	131	93
1936	8,669	3,649	4,742	10,712	5,574	5,138	4,954	114	108	119	124	122	125	180	114	124	92
1935	7,693	2,977	4,143	9,666	5,061	4,605	5,858	109	103	114	124	122	135	178	107	124	88
1934	6,803	3,021	3,336	8,541	4,670	3,871	3,428	90	98	81	122	114	147	188	99	120	75
1933	5,463	2,486	2,846	7,081	4,314	2,767	3,012	70	71	70	108	99	164	220	88	109	64
1932	4,748	1,996	2,752	6,371	4,443	1,928	2,510	65	57	72	106	99	185	254	104	112	58
1931	6,381	2,540	3,841	8,385	5,499	2,886	3,981	87	75	98	124	113	197	277	139	130	67
1930	9,055	3,868	5,187	11,432	6,909	4,523	5,060	125	115	134	144	135	206	281	177	151	83
1929	11,312	5,130	6,182	13,895	7,631	6,264	7,024	148	135	159	154	146	213	279	186	160	92
1928	10,991	4,956	6,035	13,553	7,727	5,826	6,844	148	142	155	156	148	219	277	184	162	91
1927	10,733	5,125	5,608	13,295	7,441	5,854	6,569	140	134	146	155	141	223	271	184	159	88
1926	10,558	4,875	5,683	13,256	7,356	5,900	6,810	145	139	151	158	141	228	270	183	160	91
1925	11,021	5,545	5,476	13,667	7,334	6,333	7,575	156	164	149	161	145	236	265	181	164	95
1924	10,225	5,413	4,812	12,736	7,436	5,300	5,681	143	159	128	156	140	250	266	182	160	89
1923	9,545	4,865	4,680	12,119	7,046	5,073	5,895	142	156	128	156	138	261	261	172	160	89
1922	8,575	4,300	4,275	11,009	6,608	4,401	5,081	131	136	126	153	127	260	259	154	151	87
1921	8,058	4,106	3,952	10,521	6,634	3,887	4,138	124	121	127	164	128	248	244	156	155	80
1920	12,600	6,644	5,956	15,907	8,837	7,070	9,009	211	235	190	228	195	216	200	241	214	99
1919	14,538	7,603	6,935	17,825	8,331	9,494	10,061	217	230	206	202	195	180	160	206	197	110
1918	13,467	6,974	6,493	16,447	7,507	8,940	9,736	206	220	194	170	180	159	151	177	173	119
1917	10,736	5,642	5,094	13,310	6,092	7,218	9,001	178	191	165	143	156	145	136	141	148	120
1916	7,746	4,035	3,711	9,643	4,836	4,807	5,103	119	120	117	115	115	132	128	112	116	103
1915	6,392	3,263	3,129	8,060	4,167	3,893	4,797	99	96	102	104	104	122	118	101	105	94
1914	6,036	2,899	3,137	7,718	4,029	3,689	4,677	101	96	107	102	102	116	117	101	103	98
1913	6,238	3,077	3,161	7,919	3,973	3,946	4,253	102	98	105	100	101	109	103	101	101	101
1912	6,008	3,095	2,913	7,663	3,833	3,830	4,975	99	100	98	100	102	101	99	104	101	98
1911	5,584	2,905	2,679	7,183	3,581	3,602	3,888	94	101	88	99	98	91	91	98	98	96
1910	5,780	2,929	2,851	7,477	3,531	3,946	4,703	104	105	102	99	97	83	90	96	97	107

[1] Includes Government payments from 1933 to 1957.
[2] Includes cash receipts from farm marketings, Government payments 1933 to date, value of home consumption, and rental value of farm dwellings.
[3] Realized gross farm income minus total farm-production expenses.
[4] Realized net income of farm operators plus value of inventory change plus wages paid to farm laborers living on farms.
[5] Base, 1910–1949: August 1909–July 1914=100; thereafter, January 1910–December 1914.
[6] Ratio of prices received by farmers (series K 129) to prices paid, including interest, taxes, and wage rates (series K 137).

Manufactures

P 1–10. Manufactures summary, 1849–1954.

Source: *U.S. Census of Manufactures: 1954*, vol. II, part 1, p. 3.

The basic source of comprehensive data on manufactures has been the *Census of Manufactures* conducted by the Bureau of the Census. The first *Census of Manufactures* covered 1809. A census was taken at 10-year intervals thereafter to 1899 (with the exception of 1829), at 5-year intervals for 1904–1919, and biennially for 1921–1939. The census was suspended during World War II, but was resumed for 1947. Legislation enacted in 1948 provided for a *Census of Manufactures* every 5 years, with annual sample surveys authorized for interim years. The 1954 Census was the first to be taken as a result of this legislation. Annual Surveys of Manufactures were taken for 1949–1953 and 1955–1957.

The reporting units in each census have been establishments (series P 1) rather than legal entities or companies. Conceptually, an establishment is a geographically isolated manufacturing unit maintaining independent bookkeeping records, regardless of its managerial or financial affiliations. An establishment may be a single plant, a group of closely located plants operated as a unit, or a group of closely located plants operated by a single company without separate records for each. The establishment is also the basic unit of industrial classification, being assigned to an industry on the basis of its reported product of chief value.

There have been changes in scope from one *Census of Manufactures* to another. For "factories and hand and neighborhood industries," data for 1849–1899 are for all establishments with products valued at $500 or more. For "factories, excluding hand and neighborhood industries," data for 1899–1919 are for establishments reporting value of shipments of $500 or more; for 1921–1939, for establishments reporting value of shipments of $5,000 or more; while data for 1947 and 1954 are for establishments employing one or more persons at any time during the census year. These changes in the minimum size limit have not appreciably affected the historical comparability of the census figures except for data on number of establishments.

There have also been a number of changes in the definition of manufacturing industries. Among the more important were changes in the treatment of "railroad repair shops" and "manufactured gas." These industries are included in the figures for 1899–1933, but excluded for 1935–1954. When the change results in the omission of an entire industry for which separate tabulations are available during each census, the adjustments are usually carried back through the previous censuses.

Employee figures (series P 3–4) for 1939–1954 exclude personnel reported by manufacturing establishments as in distribution and in construction work (the 1939 and subsequent censuses required separate reporting for such employees). Therefore, the employee figures for earlier years probably are not strictly comparable with those for 1939–1954. It is not known how many of the wage earners and the salaried employees reported in previous censuses were engaged in distribution and construction, and how many were engaged in manufacturing. The figures for "nonproduction employees" are derived by subtracting the figures for "production and

related workers" from those for "all employees." The category, "all employees," comprises all full-time and part-time employees on the payrolls of operating establishments who worked or received pay for any part of the pay period ended nearest the 15th of the month or months specified on the report form. Officers of corporations are included as employees; proprietors and partners of unincorporated firms are, however, excluded from the total. In recent censuses, employment at separate administrative offices and auxiliary units is excluded from this category.

There has not been a consistent treatment of employees in central administrative offices. The latter is defined as offices which operate one or more manufacturing plants located in a city or cities other than that in which the administrative office is located. For the Censuses of 1909–1923, data on employees in such offices were collected on a separate "administrative schedule" and were tabulated and included with those for salaried employees (and, therefore, with all employees) of the manufacturing plants. Thereafter, these data were collected and tabulated only for the Censuses of 1925, 1929, 1937, and 1954. For the 1947 Census, the data were collected but not tabulated. The figures for nonproduction employees (series P 3) for 1925 and 1929 include employees in central administrative offices. To make the 1937 figure for nonproduction employees more comparable to the figures for 1929 and earlier years (except 1927), 130,854 employees in central administrative offices should be added to the 1937 figure (*1937 Census of Manufactures*, p. 1652), and to make the 1954 figure more comparable to the figures for 1929 and earlier years (except 1927), 474,256 employees in administrative and auxiliary units should be added to the 1954 figure (*U.S. Census of Manufactures: 1954*, vol. II, part 1, p. 2).

Production and related workers (series P 4) are defined as workers (up through the working foreman level) engaged in fabricating, processing, assembling, inspection, receiving, storage, handling, packing, warehousing, shipping (but not delivering), maintenance, repair, janitorial, watchman services, product development, auxiliary production for plant's own use (e.g., power plant), recordkeeping, and other services closely associated with these production operations at the establishment covered by the report. Supervisory employees above the working foreman level are excluded from this category.

Decennial estimates of wage earners (production and related workers) excluding hand and neighborhood industries have been prepared for 1869–1899 by John W. Kendrick and Maude Pech for the National Bureau of Economic Research. The following is the estimated number of wage earners for each of these years: 1869, 1,803,000; 1879, 2,454,000; 1889, 3,562,000; 1899, 4,496,000. This estimate for 1899 differs from the official Census Bureau estimate (series P 4) by only one-tenth of one percent. For details of estimating procedure, see John W. Kendrick, *Productivity Trends in the United States*, National Bureau of Economic Research, New York, appendix D (forthcoming).

Figures for "value added by manufacture" (series P 8) are obtained by subtracting the cost of materials, supplies, containers, fuel, purchased electric energy, and contract work, from the value of shipments of manufacturing establishments. This procedure avoids the duplication in the "value of shipments" figures which result from the use of products of some establishments as materials by others. The "value added by manufacture" concept should not be confused with "national income originating in manufacturing," as presented in the national income estimates compiled by the Office of Business Economics. The latter is obtained by subtracting from the value of shipments not only the cost of materials, but also such other costs as depreciation charges, State and local taxes (other than corporate income taxes), allowance for bad debts, and purchases of services from nonmanufacturing enterprises such as services of engineering and management consultants, advertising, telephone and telegraph expense, insurance, royalties, patent fees, etc. It is, therefore, a more "net" concept of value added than that used in the *Census of Manufactures*. Value added by manufacture in 1954, for example, exceeded national income originating in manufacturing, as estimated by the Office of Business Economics, by 30 percent.

Robert E. Gallman has prepared estimates of value added for the census years 1839 to 1879 by adjusting manufacturing totals to exclude nonmanufacturing industries and by correcting for industries omitted from or poorly covered by the various censuses. These estimates are extrapolations based on data prepared by Richard A. Easterlin and published in "Estimates of Manufacturing Activity," *Population Redistribution and Economic Growth, United States, 1870–1950*, vol. I, by Everett S. Lee, Ann Ratner, Carol P. Brainerd, and Richard A. Easterlin, American Philosophical Society, Philadelphia, 1957, pp. 635–681. The following are Gallman's estimates:

Table I.　Value Added by Manufacturing

[In millions of dollars]

Year	Current prices	Prices of 1879
1899	5,044	6,252
1889	3,727	4,156
1879	1,962	1,962
1869	1,631	1,078
1859	815	859
1849	447	488
1839	240	190

Source: Robert E. Gallman, "Commodity Output in the United States, 1839–1899," *Studies in Income and Wealth*, National Bureau of Economic Research, New York, vol. 24, table A 13 (forthcoming).

P 11.　FRB index of manufacturing production, 1919–1957.

Source: Board of Governors of the Federal Reserve System, *Federal Reserve Bulletin*, April 1958, p. 476.

In the 1953 revision of this index, annual indexes of physical production based on about 1,400 separate product and industry series were constructed beginning with 1947. About 62 percent of the index is based on figures relating to quantities produced or shipped; figures on quantities of materials consumed by, delivered to, or produced mainly for certain industries account for about 12 percent. The remaining 26 percent is represented by estimates based on several types of data, including deflated value figures and man-hour figures with adjustments for estimated changes in output per man-hour. Man-hour figures account for only 4 percent. For weights and data used and description of method, see *Federal Reserve Bulletin*, December 1953, pp. 1239–1291. This series is extended back from 1947 to 1919 on the basis of the Federal Reserve Board series used prior to 1953 (1935–39= 100) after taking account of new levels established for 1947 relative to 1939 by the Census-Federal Reserve study of manufactures published in 1952 (see *Census of Manufactures: 1947, Indexes of Production*). These adjustments were relatively small, indicating that the 1947 levels of the old monthly and annual indexes for these aggregates were fairly accurate.

P 12.　NBER index of manufacturing production, 1899–1919.

Source: Bureau of the Census, records.

These data were prepared by extending and shifting the production indexes originally prepared from Census of Manufactures data by Solomon Fabricant, National Bureau of Economic Research. The original data were first presented in Solomon Fabricant, *The Output of Manufacturing Industries, 1899–1937*, National Bureau of Economic Research, New York, 1940. These indexes cover only those years for which a Census of Manufactures was taken. Because of the inadequacy of data for most groups, no attempt was made to interpolate between intercensal years. For details of method of construction, see Fabricant's book, chap. 2 and appendix A.

P 13.　Frickey index of manufacturing production, 1860–1914.

Source: Edwin Frickey, *Production in the United States, 1860–1914*, Harvard Economic Studies, Harvard University Press, 1947, p. 54.

In the derivation of these indexes, Frickey employed the weighted arithmetic mean of quantity relatives. With respect to weighting, he took the value-added principle as his standard and conformed to this standard as nearly as possible with existing data. For details on constituent series, see the source, appendixes A and B.

Making use of the figures for series P 11–13 and other data, John W. Kendrick has constructed an index of manufacturing, with 1929 as the base, for benchmark years 1869, 1879, and 1889, and annually thereafter through 1953. See appendix table D–II for figures and appendix D for description of this index in Kendrick's *Productivity Trends in the United States*, National Bureau of Economic Research, New York (forthcoming).

P 14–16.　Capital in manufacturing industries, in book value (NBER), 1879–1953.

Source: Daniel Creamer, Sergei Dobrovolsky, and Israel Borenstein, *Capital in Manufacturing and Mining: Its Formation and Financing*, Princeton University Press (forthcoming), appendix A, tables 8 and 9.

Estimates for 1879–1919 are based on data in various reports of the Census of Manufactures. For 1929–1953, the estimates are based on balance sheet data of corporations (raised to the level of all firms) published by the Internal Revenue Service (formerly Bureau of Internal Revenue) in *Statistics of Income*. Fixed capital includes land, buildings, and equipment (all net of depreciation). Working capital includes all other assets, other than investments in securities (chiefly cash, accounts and notes receivable, and inventories). Structures and equipment owned by the Federal Government but operated by private firms are excluded in all years. For a detailed description of data, adjustments and limitations, see appendix A, section A, of source.

P 17–19.　Capital in manufacturing industries, in 1929 dollars (NBER), 1879–1953.

Source: See source for series P 14–16.

Figures were derived by dividing the estimates of capital in book values (series P 15–17) by price indexes of book values expressed in 1929 prices. The latter are the implicit indexes derived by dividing the sum of the reported book values of the 15 major groups comprising all manufactures by the sum of the book values expressed in 1929 prices of the 15 major groups. For derivation of the deflators for each of the 15 major groups, see text for series P 30–133.

P 20–23. Real net value of assets in manufacturing, in 1947 dollars (Department of Commerce), 1928–1955.

Source: Office of Business Economics, *Survey of Current Business*, "Manufacturing Investment Since 1929," November 1956, p. 14.

Estimates are for privately owned structures and equipment assets in manufacturing establishments, and represent the undepreciated value remaining in past acquisitions. The latter were derived from the estimates of gross private domestic investment in newly constructed industrial buildings and producers' durable equipment that are included in the gross national product estimates of the Department of Commerce. The outlays on structures were adjusted to benchmarks, based mainly on expenditures for new plant construction by establishments included in the Census of Manufactures, and were supplemented by data on business purchases of Government surplus plant. The manufacturing purchases of equipment resulted from applying an allocation percentage to the total business purchases of each type of producers' durable equipment. The expenditures on equipment reported in the Bureau of the Census 1951 Annual Survey of Manufactures were used as a benchmark for these equipment purchases estimates. Purchases of structures and of equipment were converted to constant (1947) cost by the indexes used to deflate the corresponding components of the gross national product.

Depreciation at constant cost has been estimated by applying information on the length of useful lives to the constant dollar purchases of structures and equipment. Depreciation was allocated over the useful life by the straight-line method, which allots an equal amount of depreciation to each year. Net assets at constant cost were derived by adding up past purchases, and deducting the accumulated depreciation of these purchases. The useful life information was drawn largely from *Income Tax, Depreciation and Obsolescence, Estimated Useful Lives, and Depreciation Rates*, Bulletin F, Internal Revenue Service.

For additional information, see the source.

P 24–29. Capital expenditure for structures and equipment, 1915–1955.

Source: 1915–1929, see Lowell J. Chawner, "Capital Expenditures for Manufacturing Plant and Equipment—1915 to 1940," Office of Business Economics, *Survey of Current Business*, March 1941, pp. 10–11; 1929–1955, see source for series P 20–23, p. 9.

For 1929–1955, private purchases of structures and equipment for manufacturing establishments were derived from the estimates of gross private domestic investment in newly constructed industrial buildings and producers' durable equipment that are included in the gross national product estimates of the Department of Commerce. The outlays on structures were adjusted to benchmarks, based mainly on expenditures for new plant construction by establishments included in the Census of Manufactures, and were supplemented by data on business purchases of Government surplus plants. The manufacturing purchases of equipment resulted from applying an allocation percentage to the total business purchases of each type of producers' durable equipment. The expenditures on equipment reported in the Bureau of the Census 1951 Annual Survey of Manufactures were used as a benchmark for the equipment purchases estimates.

For 1915–1929, the plant expenditures (series P 25) refer to buildings (including heating, plumbing, and similar accessory equipment), and other fixed structures such as vats, blast furnaces, and docks. The estimates of factory building construction are based primarily on F. W. Dodge Corporation contract awards adjusted upward on the basis of information

from other sources to take care of underenumeration and regions not covered by the Dodge reports. Estimates of plant construction other than buildings were derived by allocating to manufacturing capital a portion of the value of the products included as reported by the Bureau of the Census. The absolute magnitude of this series depends in an important degree upon allowances for markup and for installation and transportation costs, and allowances for underreporting.

The equipment expenditures (series P 26) refer to movable equipment, and are based on Census of Manufactures data. For 1915–1922, allowance was made for underreporting. Those items not used entirely in manufacturing were allocated on the basis of data from trade associations and specialists in the various machinery industries. For 1923–1955, intercensal year interpolations were made on the basis of a Bureau of Labor Statistics index of payrolls of industrial machinery manufacturers. For the intercensal years between 1914 and 1919, estimates were made by using annual reports from five States. The series was then adjusted for imports and exports, inventory changes, for the differences between factory costs and cost to the industrial purchaser, and census under enumeration.

For 1929–1955, purchases of structures and of equipment were converted to constant (1947) cost by the indexes used to deflate the corresponding components of the gross national product. For 1915–1928, current year estimates were adjusted for price changes using appropriate indexes of actual costs of "shop machinery," "shops and engine houses," and similar items compiled by the Bureau of Valuation, Interstate Commerce Commission.

P 30–133. Total capital in major branches of manufactures, in book value and in 1929 dollars, 1879–1948.

Source: See source for series P 14–16, appendix A, table 8.

For the definition of total capital in book values, see text for series P 14–16.

The general procedure for deflating capital is to derive a composite index of prices underlying book values of buildings, machinery and equipment, and working capital for each of 15 major industrial groups. A construction cost index weighted by volume of construction depreciated over 50 years is used to represent the changes in the book value of land and buildings. This component of the composite index is identical for all 15 groups. For machinery and equipment, a price index of general machinery and equipment is used for all 15 groups, but in each group the index is weighted by volume of machinery and equipment produced, depreciated according to length of life typical for a given industry as reported by the Internal Revenue Service in *Income Tax, Depreciation and Obsolescence, Estimated Useful Lives, and Depreciation Rates*, Bulletin F (rev. January 1942). Because of these changing industry weights, a different deflator for machinery and equipment is obtained for each major group. The wholesale price index of the output of a given major industry is used to deflate working capital.

These 3 component indexes for each major group were combined into a composite price index for deflating *total capital* by computing the weighted harmonic mean of the 3 indexes. The weights used for 1879–1937, inclusive, were the average relative importance of the components in 1889, 1899, and 1904, as shown by Census Bureau data. Limited evidence indicates that there was little change in the relative importance of these 3 asset components from 1879 to 1937. By 1948, there were significant changes in their relative importance and new weights were used, based on balance-sheet data reported in Internal Revenue Service, *Statistics of Income*, 1948 and 1953 issues, part 2. The composite index for the major group was also applied to the total capital of minor industries within the group. For a full derivation of these price indexes, see source, appendix A, section B1.

P 134–137. Legal form of ownership of manufacturing establishments, 1899–1954.

Source: 1899, *Census of Manufactures: 1905*, part I, p. liv; 1904 and 1909, Thirteenth Census of the United States, 1910, *Manufactures: 1909*, vol. VIII, p. 135; 1914 and 1919, Fourteenth Census of the United States, 1920, *Manufactures: 1919*, vol. VIII, p. 108; 1929, Fifteenth Census of the United States, 1930, *Manufactures: 1929*, vol. I, p. 95; 1939, Sixteenth Census of the United States, 1940, *Manufactures: 1939*, vol. I, p. 229; 1947, *Census of Manufactures, 1947*, vol. I, p. 149; 1954, *U. S. Census of Manufactures: 1954*, vol. I, Bulletin MC–204–1, chapter IV (processed).

Percentages were computed from figures published in the various Bureau of the Census reports cited as sources.

P 138–146. Wage earners, by sex, 1869–1919.

Source: 1869–1899, Twelfth Census of the United States, 1900, Census Reports, vol. VII, *Manufactures*, part I, p. cxxvi; 1899–1904, Special Reports of the Census Office, *Manufactures, 1905*, part 1, p. lxxi; 1909–1919, Fourteenth Census of the United States, 1920, *Manufactures, 1919*, vol. VIII, p. 20.

P 147–168. Indexes of manufacturing production, by industry group, 1947–1957.

Source: Board of Governors of the Federal Reserve System, *Federal Reserve Bulletin*, December 1953 and later issues.

As the text for series P 11 indicates, this series is the successor series to the indexes based on 1935–39=100.

P 169–186. Indexes of manufacturing production, by industry group, 1899–1954.

Source: Bureau of the Census, records.

See text for series P 12.

For a listing of changes in industry classifications as of 1947, see *Census of Manufactures, 1947, Indexes of Production*, footnote to table 1, p. 1. For an annual index of durable and nondurable production (1899 = 100) for 1860–1914, see text for series P 13.

P 187. Wheat flour produced, 1860–1956.

Source: 1860–1914, see source for series P 13, pp. 8–9 and 135–139; 1915–1929, Arthur F. Burns, *Production Trends in the United States Since 1870*, National Bureau of Economic Research, New York, 1934, pp. 299 and 339; 1931 and 1933, Solomon Fabricant, *The Output of Manufacturing Industries, 1899–1937*, National Bureau of Economic Research, New York, 1940, p. 395 (data from Census of Manufactures); 1935–1956, Agricultural Marketing Service, Agriculture Handbook No. 62, *Supplement for 1956 to Consumption of Food in the United States, 1909–52*, p. 106.

Reported data in hundred weights converted to barrels containing 196 lbs. of flour. These estimates are based on commercial production of wheat flour reported by the Bureau of the Census. They include flour milled in bond from foreign wheat plus the estimated flour equivalent of farm wheat ground for flour or exchanged for flour for farm household use as reported by Agricultural Marketing Service.

P 188. Refined sugar produced, 1860–1955.

Source: 1860–1914, see source for series P 13, pp. 8–9 and 139–143; 1919–1933, see Solomon Fabricant, pp. 382 and 387, cited as source for series P 187; 1934–1945, Department of Agriculture, *Agricultural Statistics, 1952*, p. 111; 1946–1955, *Agricultural Statistics, 1956*, p. 83.

Figures represent production in cane-sugar refineries and in beet-sugar factories.

P 189. Coffee imported, 1860–1957.

Source: 1860–1914, see source for series P 13, pp. 8–9 and 143–144; 1915–1929, see Arthur F. Burns, pp. 292–293, cited as source for series P 187; 1930–1947, Bureau of the Census, *Foreign Commerce and Navigation of the United States;* 1948–1957, same agency, *Quarterly Summary of Foreign Commerce of the United States,* for those years.

The data for 1860–1933 are described as net imports (general imports) minus foreign trade; for 1934–1956, they are described as imports for consumption minus foreign exports. However, on duty-free commodities, like coffee, general imports equal imports for consumption.

P 190. Canned corn produced, 1885–1957.

Source: 1885–1929, see Arthur F. Burns, pp. 300–301 and 341, cited as source for series P 187; 1930–1951, Department of Agriculture, *Agricultural Statistics, 1952*, p. 322; 1952–1955, *Agricultural Statistics, 1956*, p. 251; 1956–1957, National Canners Association, *Canned Food Pack Statistics, 1957*, p. 16.

A case consists of 24 No. 2 cans. Figures for 1930–1955 are compiled mainly from reports of the National Canners Association.

P 191. Canned tomatoes produced, 1885–1957.

Source: 1885–1929, see Arthur F. Burns, pp. 300–301 and 341, cited as source for series P 187; 1930–1957, see source for series P 190.

A case consists of 24 No. 2 cans. The figures for 1885–1929 were published in the unit case of 24 No. 3 cans. They have been converted to a unit case of 24 No. 2 cans by multiplying by the factor of 1.707. The conversion factor is taken from National Canners Association, *Canned Food Pack Statistics: 1940, part 1—Vegetables*, Washington, D.C., March 1941, p. 19. Figures for 1930–1955 are compiled mainly from reports of the National Canners Association.

P 192. Fermented malt liquor produced, 1870–1957.

Source: 1870–1929, see Arthur F. Burns, pp. 292–293, cited as source for series P 187; 1930–1932, Internal Revenue Service (formerly Bureau of Internal Revenue), records; 1933–1938, Bureau of the Census, *Statistical Abstract of the United States, 1942*, p. 944; 1939–1945, *Statistical Abstract, 1946*, p. 859; 1946–1952, *Statistical Abstract, 1953*, p. 810; 1953–1956, *Statistical Abstract, 1957*, p. 805; 1957, *Statistical Abstract, 1958*, p. 796.

The unit "barrel" contains 31 wine gallons. Primary source of the data is the *Annual Report of the Commissioner of Internal Revenue*. For 1921–1933, only cereal beverages were permitted to be produced.

P 193. Distilled spirits produced, 1870–1955.

Source: 1870–1929, see Arthur F. Burns, pp. 292–293, cited as source for series P 187; 1930–1933, Department of Commerce, *Statistical Abstract of the United States, 1936*, p. 787; 1934–1941, *Statistical Abstract, 1942*, p. 944; 1942–1955, Internal Revenue Service (formerly Bureau of Internal Revenue), records.

The computation of taxable gallons excludes all fractional parts of a proof gallon less than one-tenth. Figures are for years ending June 30 and include data for Hawaii; beginning 1928, they also include data for Puerto Rico. Figures for all years include ethyl alcohol. Primary source of figures is the Internal Revenue Service (formerly Bureau of Internal Revenue).

P 194. Manufactured tobacco and snuff produced, 1870–1957.

Source: 1870–1879, see source for series P 13, pp. 14–15 and 192–193; 1880–1929, see Arthur F. Burns, pp. 296–297, cited as source for series P 187; 1930–1937, Bureau of the Census, *Statistical Abstract of the United States, 1938*, p. 802; 1938–1951, *Statistical Abstract, 1953*, p. 812; 1952–1956, *Statistical Abstract, 1958*, p. 798; 1957, *Statistical Abstract, 1959*, p. 804.

Primary source of the figures is the *Annual Report of the Commissioner of Internal Revenue.*

P 195.   Cigars produced, 1870–1957.

Source: 1870–1879, see source for series P 13, pp. 14–15 and 189–191; 1880–1929, see Arthur F. Burns, pp. 298–299, cited as source for series P 187; 1930–1937, Bureau of the Census, *Statistical Abstract of the United States, 1938*, p. 802; 1938–1951, *Statistical Abstract, 1953*, p. 812; 1952–1953, *Statistical Abstract, 1955*, p. 823; 1954–1956, *Statistical Abstract, 1958*, p. 798; 1957, *Statistical Abstract, 1959*, p. 804.

Primary source of the figures is the *Annual Report of the Commissioner of Internal Revenue.* For 1870–1953, figures exclude cigars weighing not more than 3 pounds per 1,000.

P 196.   Cigarettes produced, 1870–1957.

Source: 1870–1879, see source for series P 13, pp. 14–15 and 192; 1880–1929, see Arthur F. Burns, pp. 298–299, cited as source for series P 187; 1930–1957, see sources cited for these years for series P 195.

Figures represent large and small cigarettes and small cigars for 1870–1953, excluding those manufactured in bonded manufacturing warehouses. For 1953–1957, small cigars are excluded.

P 197.   Raw cotton consumed, 1860–1957.

Source: 1860–1909, Bureau of the Census, *Bulletin 160, Cotton Production and Distribution, 1926*, p. 49; 1910–1945, *Bulletin 183, Cotton Production and Distribution, 1946*, pp. 26–31; 1946–1949, *Statistical Abstract of the United States, 1953*, p. 814; 1950–1957, *Statistical Abstract, 1958*, p. 802.

Data are for years ending August 31 through 1910, July 31 thereafter. Figures are in running bales, except that figures for 1860–1870 are in equivalent 500-pound bales. Data include linters for 1909–1957; exclude linters for 1860–1908.

P 198.   Wool consumed, 1922–1957.

Source: 1922–1945, Bureau of the Census, *Statistical Abstract of the United States, 1946*, p. 655; 1946–1957, *Statistical Abstract, 1958*, p. 803.

Figures relate to scoured wool plus greasy wool reduced to a scoured basis, assuming average yields varying with class, origin, grade, and whether shorn or pulled. For 1946–1957, includes raw wool consumed in woolen and worsted systems only. Primary source of the figures is the Bureau of the Census.

For a series on apparent consumption of all wool, 1870–1929, see Arthur F. Burns, pp. 296–297, cited as source for series P 187.

P 199.   Unmanufactured silk imports for consumption, 1883–1957.

Source: 1883–1929, see Arthur F. Burns, pp. 294–295, cited as source for series P 187; 1930–1931, Bureau of Foreign and Domestic Commerce, *Foreign Commerce and Navigation of the U. S.*, vol. I, for respective years; 1932, Bureau of the Census, *Statistical Abstract of the United States, 1940*, p. 732; 1933–1949, *Statistical Abstract, 1950*, p. 638; 1950–1957, *Statistical Abstract, 1958*, p. 887.

Figures are derived by subtracting foreign exports from general imports of all types of unmanufactured silk. Spun silk is not included.

For a series on raw silk imports (excluding silk from cocoons and waste) for 1860–1914, see source for series P 13, pp. 8–9 and 153–155; and for 1870–1929, see Arthur F. Burns, cited above.

P 200.   Packaged rayon and acetate yarns produced, 1911–1957.

Source: 1911–1955, Textile Economics Bureau, Inc., *Textile Organon—Base Book of Textile Statistics*, vol. XXIX, No. 1, January 1958, p. 15; 1956 and 1957, Textile Economics Bureau, Inc., records.

Figures represent packaged or baled production ready for sale or fabrication and exclude staple, tow, waste, and other rayon and acetate products. Data for rayon relate to manmade fibers produced by the viscose, cuprammonium, and nitrocellulosic (discontinued after 1934) processes. Rayon horsehair and straw are included in the filament yarn figures for 1952–1957 (for 1940–51, production of these items averaged just under 1 million pounds per year). Acetate means manmade fibers composed of cellulose acetate.

For 1941–1957, figures for rayon and acetate are as actually reported by the entire industry; earlier data are estimated totals based on reports obtained from 86 percent or more of the industry, with adjustments for complete coverage in accordance with information from the Census of Manufactures.

P 201–202.   Men's and women's leather shoes produced, 1899–1954.

Source: 1899–1919, see Solomon Fabricant, cited as source for series P 187; 1921–1945, Department of Commerce, *Statistical Abstract of the United States*, various issues, 1929–1946; 1947–1954, Bureau of the Census, records.

Figures represent pairs of leather uppers for men's and women's shoes. They do not include youths' and boys', misses', children's, infants', athletic, part leather, or nonleather shoes. For 1930–1954, figures for men's shoes are not strictly comparable with earlier years because large quantities of heavy footwear included with men's shoes for later years were included with athletic shoes for earlier years.

P 203–207.   Steel ingots and castings produced, 1867–1957.

Source: Department of Commerce, *Statistical Abstract of the United States*, various issues, 1908–1958.

Primary source of figures is the *Annual Statistical Report* of the American Iron and Steel Institute. For 1934–1957, figures include only that part of steel castings made in foundries producing steel ingots.

P 208.   Rolled iron and steel produced, 1885–1957.

Source: 1885–1929, see Arthur F. Burns, p. 300, cited as source for series P 187; 1930–1957, Bureau of the Census, *Statistical Abstract of the United States*, various issues, 1947–1958.

Primary source of the figures is the *Annual Statistical Report* of the American Iron and Steel Institute. Figures include rails, plates and sheets, merchant bar and skelp production, wire rods, and structural shapes.

P 209.   Tinplate consumption, 1871–1957.

Source: 1871–1929, see Arthur F. Burns, p. 296, cited as source for series P 187; 1930–1957, American Iron and Steel Institute, *Annual Statistical Report*, various issues, 1932–1957.

Figures include both tinplate and terneplate. For 1871–1899, figures are for production plus imports; for 1900–1957, production plus imports minus exports.

P 210.   Rails produced, 1860–1957.

Source: 1860–1914, see source for series P 13, pp. 10–11 and 157–158; 1915–1929, see Arthur F. Burns, pp. 294–295, cited as source for series P 187; 1930–1957, American Iron and Steel Institute, *Annual Statistical Report*, various issues, 1930–1957.

Figures include both iron and steel rails, rerolled rails, and girder and high T rails. Rails are a component of "rolled iron and steel" (series P 208). For 1860–1867, figures include production of iron rails only.

P 211. Structural iron and steel shapes produced, 1879–1957.

Source: 1879–1914, see source for series P 13, pp. 10–11 and 158; 1915–1957, American Iron and Steel Institute, *Annual Statistical Report*, various issues, 1927–1957.

Structural shapes are a component of "rolled iron and steel" (series P 208).

P 212. Common and face brick produced, 1869–1957.

Source: 1869–1899 (decennially), 1904, 1909, 1914, 1919–1939 (biennially), 1947, and 1954, *Census of Manufactures*, reports for various years; 1894–1912, *Mineral Resources of the United States, 1900–1913*, various issues; 1913–1956, Bureau of the Census, *Statistical Abstract of the United States*, various issues, 1925–1958; 1957, Bureau of the Census, *Facts for Industry*, series M 32D.

The figures for 1869 and 1879 are for common brick only. For 1889, 1899, and 1904, the production of "fancy or ornamental brick" has been added to the production of "face brick," the reason being that "the best grade of 'face' or 'front' brick appears to have been classified as 'fancy or ornamental' brick" in these years. Beginning with 1943, common and face brick are classified as "unglazed" brick.

P 213. Locomotives produced, 1880–1945.

Source: 1880–1929, see Arthur F. Burns, pp. 300–301, cited as source for series P 187; 1930–1945, American Railway Car Institute, *Railway Age, Annual Statistical and Outlook Number*, January 6, 1945, p. 91, and *Annual Statistical and Outlook Number*, January 5, 1946, p. 88.

For 1905–1945, Canadian output is included although the U. S. output is shown separately beginning with 1929 (see, for example, *Railway Age, Annual Statistical Number*, January 4, 1947). For 1880–1911, locomotives built in railroad repair shops are excluded. For 1942–1944, figures exclude locomotives built for U. S. Government and for lend-lease program.

This series was discontinued when the new traction power was supplied almost exclusively by Diesel units. A locomotive may be composed of one or more Diesel units.

P 214. Railroad freight cars produced, 1871–1957.

Source: 1871–1914, see source for series P 13, pp. 14–15 and 193–196; 1915–1919, American Railway Car Institute, *Railway Age, Annual Statistical and Outlook Number*, January 7, 1939, p. 83; 1920–1957, *Railway Age, Annual Statistical and Outlook Number* (most recently entitled *Review and Outlook*), various issues, 1950–1958.

For 1920–1957, figures represent "freight cars delivered." For 1871–1919, figures represent domestic production of freight cars, exclusive of that in railroad repair shops; thereafter, figures include production in railroad repair shops.

P 215. Railroad passenger cars produced, 1871–1957.

Source: 1871–1914, see source for series P 13, pp. 14–15 and 196–197; 1915–1957, see source for series P 214.

For 1920–1957, figures represent "passenger train cars delivered." For 1871–1919, figures represent domestic production of passenger cars, exclusive of that in railroad repair shops; thereafter, figures include production in railroad repair shops.

P 216–217. Horse-drawn vehicles produced, 1899–1954.

Source: 1899–1937, see Solomon Fabricant, p. 585, cited as source for series P 187; 1939–1954, *Census of Manufactures*, reports for 1939, 1947, and 1954.

For 1899–1914, figures for farm wagons, trucks, and business vehicles include patrol wagons, ambulances, handcarts, and pushcarts; for 1919–1925, they exclude mail carrier wagons and public conveyances and relate to products made within the industry (as classified by the Bureau of the Census); for 1927–1954, figures relate to all products made regardless of the industry classification of the establishment.

For 1899–1925, figures for carriages, buggies, and sulkies exclude sulkies; for 1933, include two-wheeled carts.

P 218. Bicycles produced, 1899–1954.

Source: 1899–1937, see Solomon Fabricant, p. 590, cited as source for series P 187; 1939–1954, see source for series P 216–217.

For 1899–1921, figures relate to products made within the industry (as classified by the Bureau of the Census); for 1923–1954, figures relate to all products made regardless of the industry classification of the establishment.

P 219. Pneumatic tires and casings produced, 1914–1954.

Source: 1914–1937, see Solomon Fabricant, p. 480, cited as source for series P 187; 1939–1954, see source for series P 216–217.

Figures exclude tires for bicycles and motorcycles.

P 220. Light products of distillation, 1880–1956.

Source: 1880 and 1889, see *Twelfth Census of the United States*, vol. X, *Manufactures*, part IV, p. 685; 1899–1927, see Solomon Fabricant, p. 517, cited as source for series P 187; 1929–1956, Office of Business Economics, *Business Statistics, 1957, Biennial Edition*, a supplement to the *Survey of Current Business*, p. 173.

These figures relate essentially to the production of gasoline and naphtha. Figures for 1880–1927 and for 1929–1956 are not strictly comparable. The figure for 1929 on a basis comparable with preceding years is 18.4 billion gallons. For 1953–1956, figures for jet fuel are excluded.

The sum of the monthly average production of barrels of gasoline and naphtha from crude oil and natural gas liquids is multiplied by 12 to obtain the annual total. The latter is converted to gallons on the assumption of 42 gallons per barrel. The basic source of these data is the Bureau of Mines, *Minerals Yearbook*.

P 221. Illuminating oils (kerosene) produced, 1899–1956.

Source: 1899–1927, see Solomon Fabricant, p. 517, cited as source for series P 187; 1929–1956, see source for series P 220, p. 172.

Figures for 1899–1927 and for 1929–1956 are not strictly comparable. The figure for 1929 comparable with the preceding years is 2.34 billion gallons. For 1953–1956, figures exclude jet fuel.

The monthly average production of barrels of kerosene is multiplied by 12 to obtain the annual production. The latter is converted to gallons on the assumption of 42 gallons per barrel. The basic source of these data is the Bureau of Mines, *Minerals Yearbook*.

P 222. Fuel oils produced, 1899–1956.

Source: 1899–1927, see Solomon Fabricant, p. 517, cited as source for series P 187; 1929–1956, see source for series P 220, p. 171.

Figures for 1899–1927 and for 1929–1956 are not strictly comparable. The figure for 1929 comparable with the preceding years is 16.4 billion gallons. For 1953–1956, jet fuels are excluded.

The sum of the monthly average production of barrels of distillate and residual fuel oil is multiplied by 12 to obtain the annual total. The latter is converted to gallons on the assumption of 42 gallons per barrel. The basic source of these data is the Bureau of Mines, *Minerals Yearbook.*

P 223. Lubricating oils produced, 1899–1956.

Source: 1899–1927, see Solomon Fabricant, p. 518, cited as source for series P 187; 1929–1956, see source for series P 220, p. 173.

Figures for 1899–1927 and for 1929–1956 are not strictly comparable. The figure for 1929 comparable with preceding years is 1,554 million gallons.

The monthly average of barrels produced is multiplied by 12 to obtain the annual production. The latter is converted to gallons on the assumption of 42 gallons per barrel. The basic source of these data is the Bureau of Mines, *Minerals Yearbook.*

P 224. Paraffin wax produced, 1880–1956.

Source: 1880 and 1889, see *Twelfth Census of the United States*, vol. X, *Manufactures*, part IV, p. 685; 1899–1927, see Solomon Fabricant, p. 518, cited as source for series P 187; 1929–1956, see source for series P 220, p. 175.

For 1929–1956, figures are labelled petroleum wax. The monthly average of barrels produced is multiplied by 12 to obtain the annual production. The latter is converted to gallons on the assumption of 280 pounds per barrel and 7.5 pounds per gallon. The basic source of these data is the Bureau of Mines, *Minerals Yearbook.*

P 225. Super-phosphate produced, 1860–1957.

Source: 1860–1954, Department of Agriculture, *Statistics on Fertilizers and Liming Materials in the United States*, Statistical Bulletin No. 191, p. 43, April 1957; 1955–1957, Bureau of the Census, *Facts for Industries*, series M19D-06 and M19D-08.

P 226. Sulfuric acid produced, 1899–1956.

Source: 1899–1925, Bureau of the Census, records; 1929–1956, see source for series P 220, p. 119.

Figures are combined totals for sulfuric acid produced by the contact and chamber processes, including spent acid fortified in the contact plants with the simultaneous production of new acid. Production of Government-owned plants, which was large during the war period, is not included for that period; for the most part, this production was available only for military use. However, for 1954–1956, appreciable amounts of sulfuric acid produced in Government-owned privately operated plants are included. Figures for 1946–1950 include estimates based on annual totals of byproduct operations of a few smelters reporting to the Bureau of Mines; the estimated data included vary from 4 percent in 1946 to 2 percent in 1950. For 1899–1939, figures are based on reports of the Census of Manufactures; they are shown in those reports on a 50° Baume basis but are here converted to 100 percent H_2SO_4. Beginning January 1948, figures are not strictly comparable with earlier data because of the inclusion of additional plants; however, the addition of these plants increased the production of the specified chemical by less than 3.5 percent.

P 227. Soda ash produced, 1890–1954.

Source: 1890, *Twelfth Census of the United States*, vol. X, *Manufactures*, part IV, p. 539; 1899–1937, see Solomon Fabricant, p. 490, cited as source for series P 187; 1939–1954, see source for series P 216–217.

P 228. Mechanical refrigerators produced, 1921–1954.

Source: 1921–1937, American Gas Association (gas refrigerators), and Business News Publishing Co., *Air Conditioning and Refrigeration News*, and McGraw-Hill Publishing Co., *Electrical Merchandising* (electric refrigerators); 1939–1954, see source for series P 216–217.

Figures for 1921–1937 measure sales, not production, of household refrigerators.

P 229. Reed organs produced, 1899–1935.

Source: See Solomon Fabricant, p. 595, cited as source for series P 187.

P 230. Pianos produced, 1899–1954.

Source: 1899–1937, see Solomon Fabricant, pp. 597 and 598, cited as source for series P 187; 1939–1954, see source for series P 216–217.

P 231. Phonographs produced, 1899–1929.

Source: See Solomon Fabricant, p. 573, cited as source for series P 187.

P 232. Radios and radio-phonograph combinations produced, 1923–1954.

Source: 1923–1937, see Solomon Fabricant, pp. 573–574, cited as source for series P 187; 1939–1954, see source for series P 216–217.

Figures include home receiving sets, automobile sets, and radio-phonograph combinations.

P 233–249. General note.

Capacity is generally calculated on the basis of full-time operation of an industry (i.e., 365 days a year, 24 hours a day). Capacity as of January 1 is generally used as the basis of computation. Exceptions to these general rules are noted in the text for each series, where applicable.

P 233. Blast furnaces (pig iron), 1898–1957.

Source: 1898–1915, American Iron and Steel Institute, records; 1916–1957, same organization's *Annual Directory* and *Annual Statistical Report*, New York, various issues.

Figures include a 6.1 percent deduction from full-time operation to allow for rebuilding, relining, and repairing the equipment. Capacity is based on April 1 for 1898; November 1, 1901 and 1907; June 1, 1904; and the average of January 1 and July 1 for 1941–1944 and 1950.

P 234. Steel ingots and steel for castings, 1887–1957.

Source: See source for series P 233.

Figures include a 9.1 percent deduction from full-time operation to allow for rebuilding, relining, and repairing equipment, and for holiday shutdowns. Capacity is based on an average of January 1 and July 1 for 1941–1944.

P 235. Copper refining, 1907–1957.

Source: 1907–1930, Edwin G. Nourse, *America's Capacity to Produce*, The Brookings Institution, Washington, D. C., 1934, p. 557; 1931–1957, American Bureau of Metal Statistics, *Year Book*, New York, various issues.

P 236–237. Lead refining, 1921–1957.

Source: American Bureau of Metal Statistics, *Year Book*, New York, various issues.

P 238. Zinc refining, 1921–1957.

Source: See source for series P 236–237.

Figures are not comparable throughout because of changes in components. For 1921–1925, figures represent distillation zinc; 1926–1940, distillation and electrolytic zinc; 1941–1957, slab zinc. As an alternative source for data, see Bureau of Mines, *Minerals Yearbook*, various issues.

P 239. Aluminum ingots, 1889–1957.

Source: 1889–1895, J. D. Edwards, *et al.*, *The Aluminum Industry*, McGraw-Hill Publishing Co., New York, 1930; 1910–1919, Business and Defense Services Administration, *Materials Survey, Aluminum*, 1956; 1927–1938, Surplus Property Board, *Aluminum Plants and Facilities Report*, 1945; 1939–1957, American Bureau of Metal Statistics, *Year Book*, New York, various issues.

The general practice in this industry is to rate potline capacity on full-time operation. As an alternative source for data, see Bureau of Mines, *Minerals Yearbook*, various issues.

P 240. Portland cement, 1910–1957.

Source: 1910–1923, Geological Survey, *Mineral Resources of the United States*, annual volumes; 1924–1931, Bureau of Mines, *Mineral Resources of the United States*, annual volumes; 1932–1957, *Minerals Yearbook*, annual volumes.

A deduction from full-time operation is taken for estimated average number of days required for repair or other unavoidable shutdowns. Favorable labor, fuel, and transportation conditions are assumed.

P 241. Crude petroleum refining, 1918–1957.

Source: Bureau of Mines, *Petroleum Refineries, Including Cracking Plants in the United States, January 1, 1957*, Information Circular No. 7815, December 1957, Monthly Petroleum Statement No. 431 (also shown in *Minerals Yearbook*).

Capacity is defined as the maximum daily average throughput (converted to an annual basis) of the plant in complete operation, with allowance for necessary shutdown time for routine maintenance, repairs, etc. It approximates the maximum daily average crude runs to stills that can be maintained for an extended period. Capacity is based on November 1 for 1924 and May 1 for 1925.

P 242–243. Coke, 1909–1957.

Source: 1909–1920, see source for series P 235; 1921–1957, see source for series P 240.

P 244. Carbon black, 1929–1957.

Source: See source for series P 240.

P 245. Sulfuric acid, 1945–1957.

Source: American Chemical Society, *Chemical and Engineering News*, Washington, D. C., July 10, 1945; 1950–1957, Business and Defense Services Administration, *Chemical and Rubber Industry Report*, various issues.

Capacity is based on 350 days a year.

P 246. Phosphatic fertilizers, 1900–1957.

Source: 1900–1951, Agricultural Research Service, *Statistics on Fertilizers and Liming Materials in the United States*, Statistical Bulletin No. 191, April 1957; 1952–1957, National Plant Food Institute, *Plant Food Review*, vol. 4, Nos. 2 and 3, 1958.

These data are the total of normal superphosphate, concentrated superphosphate, and miscellaneous phosphatic materials. Capacity of normal superphosphate is based on 300 two-shift days a year. Capacity of concentrated superphosphate and other phosphatic materials is based on 350 days a year, continuous operations.

P 247. Synthetic nitrogen, 1924–1957.

Source: 1924–1950, see source for series P 246; 1951–1955, Business and Defense Services Administration, *Summary Information on Anhydrous Ammonia*, Bulletin No. 142, February 1956; 1956–1957, Business and Defense Services Administration, records.

Capacity is based on 350 days a year, continuous operations.

P 248. Rayon and acetate fibers, 1911–1957.

Source: 1911, *New York Times*, Special Chemistry Section, September 2, 1951; 1936–1957, Textile Economics Bureau, *Textile Organon* (prior to 1952, *Rayon Organon*), New York, various issues.

Capacity is as of November for all years except 1940 (July) and 1944 (April). Allowance was made for periodic shutdowns of machines for repair, overhaul, or cleaning on a set time schedule.

P 249. Paper and paperboard, 1900–1957.

Source: American Paper and Pulp Association, *The Statistics of Paper*, New York, December 1957.

Capacity for paper and building paper is based on 310 days a year, 24 hours a day; for paperboard, 313 days.

P 250–306. Value of output of finished commodities and construction materials destined for domestic consumption at current producers' prices, and implicit price indexes for major commodity groups (Shaw), 1869–1939.

Source: William H. Shaw, *Value of Commodity Output Since 1869*, National Bureau of Economic Research, New York, 1947, pp. 30, 66, and 290.

These estimates are derived from Census of Manufactures data, supplemented by less complete data for nonmanufactured finished commodities and construction materials and for intercensal year interpolations. The estimates before 1919 are based necessarily on less adequate information.

The estimates of finished commodities measure the value of commodities that have reached the form in which they are used by ultimate recipients—largely households in the case of consumers' goods, chiefly business and public enterprises in the case of producers' goods. The amount "destined for domestic consumption" is derived as the sum of domestic production, minus exports, plus imports. In most years and for most commodities, the differences between domestic production of finished commodities and finished commodities destined for domestic consumption were modest. Changes in the latter, therefore, can be used as an approximate measure of changes in domestic manufacturing output. For figures on domestic output of finished commodities at producers' prices for 1919–1933, see Kuznets, cited above, pp. 136–138 and 348.

The estimates presented here exclude transportation and distribution costs incurred after the production stage, and hence are not in terms of prices to final users. Nor do they measure domestic consumption for they make no allowance for inventory changes.

Perishable commodities include those usually lasting less than 6 months; semidurable, those usually lasting from 6 months to 3 years; and durable, those usually lasting more than 3 years. For a detailed discussion of sources and procedures, see the source, part II for estimates of the value of output, part III for exports and imports, and part IV for price indexes.

Series P 1–10. Manufactures Summary: 1849 to 1954

Year	Number of establishments	Persons engaged in manufacturing			Salaries and wages ($1,000)			Value added by manufacture [2] ($1,000)	Horsepower (1,000)	
		Proprietors and firm members	Nonproduction employees [1]	Production and related workers (average for year)	Total	Salaries	Wages		Prime movers	Motors run by purchased energy
	1	2	3	4	5	6	7	8	9	10
FACTORIES, EXCLUDING HAND AND NEIGHBORHOOD INDUSTRIES										
1954	286,817	197,850	[3] 3,278,264	12,373,030	62,993,321	18,397,864	44,595,457	116,912,526	35,579	72,783
1947	240,807	188,948	2,376,079	11,917,884	39,695,558	9,451,587	30,243,971	74,290,475		
1939 [4]	173,802	[5] 123,655	[6] 1,719,101	7,808,205	[6] 12,706,102	[6] 3,708,587	8,997,515	24,487,304	21,077	28,816
1937	166,794	99,268	1,217,171	8,569,231	12,829,749	2,716,866	10,112,883	25,173,539		
1935	167,916	81,521	1,058,501	7,203,794	9,564,754	2,253,425	7,311,329	18,552,553		
1933	139,325	72,267	[7] 770,314	5,787,611	[7] 6,237,800	[7] 1,297,654	4,940,146	14,007,540		
1931	171,450			6,163,144			6,688,541	18,600,532		
1929	206,663	132,686	1,290,037	8,369,705	14,284,282	3,399,363	10,884,919	30,591,435	19,328	21,794
1927	187,629	132,151	1,223,982	7,848,070	13,123,135	3,023,670	10,099,465	26,325,394		
1925	183,877	132,971	1,271,008	7,871,409	12,957,707	2,978,058	9,979,649	25,667,624	19,243	15,116
1923	192,096	147,958	1,280,488	7,871,409	12,996,460	2,847,836	9,979,649	24,569,487		
1921	192,059	172,291	1,081,890	6,475,474	9,870,199	2,418,900	7,451,299	17,252,775		
1919	270,231	249,865	1,371,885	8,464,916	12,426,902	2,762,893	9,664,009	23,841,624	19,432	8,965
1914	268,436	258,560	911,899	6,602,287	5,015,977	1,233,655	3,782,322	9,385,622	17,858	3,707
1909	264,810	272,421	750,330	6,261,736	4,105,470	900,257	3,205,213	8,160,075	16,393	1,669
1904	213,444	225,115	493,297	5,181,660	2,990,937	550,086	2,440,851	6,019,171	12,605	428
1899	204,754		348,100	4,501,919	2,258,654	366,080	1,892,574	4,646,981	9,633	178
FACTORIES AND HAND AND NEIGHBORHOOD INDUSTRIES										
1899	509,490		380,739	5,097,562	2,595,566	389,019	2,206,547	5,474,892	10,805	183
1889	353,864		457,139	4,129,355	2,209,058	388,204	1,820,854	4,102,301	5,939	
1879	253,852			2,732,595			947,954	1,972,756	3,411	
1869	252,148			2,053,996			620,467	1,395,119	2,346	
1859	140,433			1,311,246			378,879	854,257		
1849	123,025			957,059			236,755	463,983		

[1] 1954 figure is an average based on reported employment totals for payroll periods nearest the 15th of March, May, August, and November except in 1954 when a 12-month average was used. For 1947, figure represents the average of 12 monthly figures; for 1939 and earlier years, figures represent nonproduction workers reported for 1 payroll period (usually in October). For treatment of employees of central administrative offices, see text.

[2] For 1849-1933, cost of contract work was not subtracted from value of products in calculating value added by manufacture. For definition of value added, see text.

[3] Revised.

[4] Figures for 1939, but not for earlier years, represent figures which have been revised by retabulation of returns to exclude data for establishments classified as manufacturing in 1939 and prior years, but classified as nonmanufacturing beginning with

1947. Value added by manufacture for 1939, prior to revision and on a basis comparable with 1937 and previous years, was $24.7 billion.

[5] Not revised to exclude data for establishments classified as manufacturing in 1939 and prior years but classified as nonmanufacturing beginning with 1947.

[6] 1939 figures for "Nonproduction employees" revised on basis of estimates rather than by retabulation of 1939 reports. Estimates were made in the following manner: For nonproduction employees, by multiplying the retabulated figure for number of production and related workers by the ratio of all employees to production and related workers computed from unrevised 1939 statistics; for salaries and wages, by multiplying the retabulated wage figure by the ratio for salaries and wages also derived from the unrevised 1939 statistics.

[7] Excludes data for salaried officers of corporations and their salaries and, therefore, not strictly comparable with figures for other years.

Series P 11–13. Indexes of Manufacturing Production: 1860 to 1957

Year	FRB [1] (1947–49 =100)	Year	FRB [1] (1947–49 =100)	NBER [2] (1947 =100)	Frickey [3] (1899 =100)	Year	NBER [2] (1939 =100)	Frickey [3] (1899 =100)	Year	Frickey [3] (1899 =100)
	11		11	12	13		12	13		13
1957	145	1933	36			1905		140	1880	42
1956	144	1932	30			1904	19	121	1879	36
		1931	39			1903		126	1878	32
1955	140					1902		127	1877	30
1954	127	1930	48			1901		111	1876	28
1953	136	1929	58							
1952	125	1928	52			1900		100	1875	28
1951	121	1927	50			1899	15	100	1874	29
		1926	50			1898		91	1873	30
1950	113					1897		80	1872	31
1949	97	1925	48			1896		74	1871	26
1948	103	1924	43							
1947	100	1923	45			1895		81	1870	25
1946	90	1922	39			1894		68	1869	25
		1921	30			1893		70	1868	23
1945	110					1892		79	1867	22
1944	130	1920	39			1891		73	1866	21
1943	133	1919	38	34						
1942	110					1890		71	1865	17
1941	88	1914		29	192	1889		66	1864	18
		1913			203	1888		62	1863	17
1940	66	1912			194	1887		60	1862	15
1939	57	1911			162	1886		57	1861	16
1938	46									
1937	60	1910			172	1885		47	1860	16
1936	55	1909		24	166	1884		47		
		1908			127	1883		50		
1935	46	1907			156	1882		49		
1934	39	1906			152	1881		46		

[1] Federal Reserve Board index of manufactures.

[2] National Bureau of Economic Research, index of physical volume, all manufacturing industries.

[3] Edwin Frickey's indexes of production for manufacture.

Series P 14–23.   Capital in Manufacturing Industries: 1879 to 1955

[In millions of dollars]

Year	Capital in book value (NBER)			Capital in 1929 dollars (NBER)			Real net value in 1947 dollars (Dept. of Commerce)			
	Total	Fixed	Working	Total	Fixed	Working	Structures and equipment	Structures	Equipment	Inventories
	14	15	16	17	18	19	20	21	22	23
1955							64,300	33,200	31,100	37,200
1954							62,800	32,500	30,400	35,800
1953	[1] 164,853	[1] 69,323	[1] 95,530	[1] 97,245	[1] 43,463	[1] 53,782	61,700	32,200	29,500	37,800
1952							59,700	31,700	28,000	36,200
1951							57,700	31,300	26,400	34,300
1950							55,500	30,700	24,800	29,000
1949							54,200	30,800	23,400	27,100
1948	113,394	45,727	67,667	77,982	36,526	41,444	53,100	30,700	22,500	28,500
1947							50,500	30,000	20,400	27,600
1946							46,900	28,800	18,100	27,500
1945							42,900	26,600	16,300	24,100
1944							41,300	26,500	14,800	25,700
1943							41,500	27,400	14,100	26,600
1942							42,200	28,500	13,700	26,000
1941							42,400	29,000	13,400	24,000
1940							40,600	28,000	12,600	20,500
1939							39,900	27,900	12,000	18,700
1938							40,200	28,300	11,900	18,200
1937	50,166	23,282	26,884	55,319	25,851	29,468	40,800	28,800	12,000	19,300
1936							40,000	28,500	11,500	16,700
1935							40,100	28,800	11,300	15,200
1934							41,000	29,500	11,400	14,700
1933							42,100	30,100	11,900	14,100
1932							43,300	30,700	12,700	15,500
1931							45,200	31,700	13,500	17,800
1930							46,000	32,100	13,900	19,100
1929	59,072	27,410	31,662	63,022	30,853	32,169	45,500	31,600	13,900	18,400
1928							43,200	29,900	13,400	17,300
1919	40,289	[2]	[2]	46,094	[2]	[2]				
1914	20,784	[2]	[2]	36,737	[2]	[2]				
1909	16,937	[2]	[2]	31,563	[2]	[2]				
1904	11,588	5,596	5,992	23,295	12,316	10,979				
1899 [3]	8,168	[2]	[2]	17,452	[2]	[2]				
1899 [4]	8,663	4,223	4,440	18,626	9,651	8,975				
1889	5,697	2,646	3,051	11,157	5,553	6,336				
1879	2,718			4,821						

[1] Includes firms engaged in shipbuilding which were excluded in other years.
[2] Not available.
[3] Comparable with subsequent years; see text for series P 1–10.
[4] Comparable with preceding years; see text for series P 1–10.

Series P 24–29.   Capital Expenditure for Structures and Equipment: 1915 to 1955

[In billions of dollars]

Year	Current-year cost			Constant-year cost (1947 dollars) [1]			Year	Current-year cost			Constant-year cost (1947 dollars) [1]		
	Total	Structures	Equipment	Total	Structures	Equipment		Total	Structures	Equipment	Total	Structures	Equipment
	24	25	26	27	28	29		24	25	26	27	28	29
1955	8.6	3.0	5.6	6.4	2.4	4.0	1934	0.9	0.3	0.6	1.7	0.8	0.9
1954	8.0	2.4	5.6	6.0	1.9	4.1	1933	.7	.3	.4	1.5	.8	.7
1953	8.6	2.6	6.0	6.5	2.0	4.5	1932	.5	.1	.4	1.0	.3	.7
1952	8.4	2.6	5.9	6.5	2.0	4.5	1931	1.0	.3	.7	2.0	.9	1.1
1951	8.3	2.6	5.6	6.4	2.1	4.4	1930	1.8	.8	1.0	3.4	1.9	1.5
							1929	2.9	1.5	1.4	5.1	3.0	2.0
1950	6.3	1.6	4.6	5.5	1.5	4.0							
1949	5.7	1.8	3.9	5.1	1.7	3.4	1929	2.7	1.0	1.8	[1] 2.7	.9	[1] 1.8
1948	7.1	2.4	4.7	6.5	2.2	4.3	1928	2.3	.9	1.5	[1] 2.3	.7	[1] 1.5
1947	7.1	2.7	4.4	7.1	2.7	4.4	1927	2.1	.7	1.4	[1] 2.1	.6	[1] 1.5
1946	6.3	3.1	3.2	7.4	3.6	3.7	1926	2.4	.8	1.5	[1] 2.4	.7	[1] 1.6
1945	3.6	1.0	2.5	4.7	1.5	3.2	1925	2.0	.6	1.4	[1] 2.0	.5	[1] 1.5
1944	2.2	.3	1.9	2.9	.5	2.4	1924	1.7	.5	1.3	[1] 1.7	.4	[1] 1.3
1943	1.7	.2	1.5	2.3	.4	1.9	1923	2.1	.6	1.4	[1] 2.1	.5	[1] 1.5
1942	2.0	.6	1.5	2.8	.9	1.9	1922	1.5	.5	1.0	[1] 1.6	.5	[1] 1.1
1941	3.1	1.3	1.8	4.7	2.4	2.3	1921	1.4	.4	1.0	[1] 1.3	.3	[1] 1.0
1940	2.2	.7	1.5	3.5	1.5	2.0	1920	3.2	1.2	1.9	[1] 2.7	1.0	[1] 1.8
1939	1.5	.4	1.1	2.5	.9	1.5	1919	2.2	.8	1.4	[1] 2.1	.7	[1] 1.4
1938	1.3	.4	.9	2.1	.8	1.3	1918	2.5	.9	1.5	[1] 2.6	1.0	[1] 1.6
1937	2.1	.8	1.3	3.6	1.7	1.9	1917	1.7	.5	1.2	[1] 2.2	.6	[1] 1.6
1936	1.5	.4	1.0	2.6	1.0	1.6	1916	1.1	.3	.7	[1] 1.6	.5	[1] 1.1
1935	1.0	.3	.8	1.8	.6	1.2	1915	.6	.2	.4	[1] 1.0	.3	[1] .7

[1] Figures for 1915–1929 are in 1939 dollars.

Series P 30–133. Total Capital in Major Branches of Manufactures, in Book Value and in 1929 Dollars: 1879 to 1948

[In millions of dollars]

Series No.	Industry	1948 [1][2]	1937 [1]	1929 [1]	1919 [3]	1914 [3]	1909 [3]	1904 [3]	1899 [3]	1899 [4]	1889 [4]	1879 [4]
	BOOK VALUE											
30	Total manufacturing	113,394	50,166	59,072	40,289	20,784	16,937	11,588	8,168	8,663	5,697	2,718
31	Food and kindred products	16,071	8,069	8,881	6,272	3,668	2,935	2,230	1,576	1,647	925	498
32	Bakery and confectionery	1,757	1,131	1,568	911	426	295	173	114	123	72	28
33	Canned products	1,681	820	853	378	172	119	90	59	59	25	9
34	Mill products	1,060	496	471	802	380	349	265	189	219	208	177
35	Packinghouse products	1,975	1,114	1,385	1,185	537	378	238	189	189	117	49
36	Sugar	780	599	1,053	473	316	283	221	204	204	24	28
37	Liquor and beverages	3,158	1,371	692	782	1,016	873	660	516	534	310	135
38	Tobacco products	2,330	961	1,150	605	304	246	324	112	124	96	40
39	Other food products	3,302	1,577	1,709	1,136	517	392	259	193	195	73	32
40	Textiles and textile products	10,397	4,770	7,687	6,205	2,881	2,550	1,783	1,366	1,494	1,119	602
41	Cotton goods	3,693	866	1,603	2,145	1,039	936	702	528	528	392	246
42	Silk and rayon goods		441	869	533	210	152	110	81	81	51	19
43	Woolen and worsted goods		415	601	868	403	429	313	264	264	203	117
44	Carpets, floorcovering, tapestries, etc	483	199	262	179	112	97	69	53	53	43	25
45	Knit goods	929	433	709	516	216	164	107	82	82	51	16
46	Clothing	3,018	1,036	1,758	1,447	633	568	345	257	350	292	114
47	Textiles, n.e.c. [5]	2,253	1,380	1,887	517	268	204	137	101	136	87	65
48	Leather products	1,303	751	1,167	1,523	743	659	452	335	369	274	157
49	Boots and shoes	710	410	625	581	255	197	123	100	102	95	43
50	Other leather products	592	341	542	942	488	462	329	235	267	179	114
51	Rubber products	1,791	795	1,088	960	268	162	99	78	78	37	9
52	Tires and tubes	1,383	586	918	635	130						
53	Other rubber products	361	209	170	325	138						
54	Forest products	4,816	2,405	3,842	2,726	1,932	1,767	1,174	872	1,110	825	361
55	Sawmill and planing mill products	3,000	1,562	2,660	1,730	1,193	1,122	694	520	731	518	219
56	Other wood products	1,805	843	1,182	996	739	645	480	352	379	307	142
57	Paper, pulp, and products	3,692	1,942	2,060	1,195	689	523	354	218	219	115	58
58	Printing, publishing, and allied industries	3,984	2,320	2,622	1,189	745	611	450	342	342	234	80
59	Chemicals and allied substances	9,109	3,537	3,942	2,594	1,280	911	634	457	458	288	137
60	Fertilizers	334	198	335	312	217	122	69	61	61	41	18
61	Chemicals proper, acids, etc	2,580	1,125	973	941	390	273	194	144	145	96	49
62	Allied chemical substances, drugs, oils, etc	5,917	2,214	2,634	1,341	673	516	371	252	252	151	70
63	Petroleum refining	15,363	5,814	5,745	1,170	326	182	136	95	95	77	27
64	Stone, clay, and glass products	2,934	1,825	2,351	1,267	990	860	554	336	351	217	83
65	Iron and steel products	13,796	6,383	6,226	5,671	2,836	2,411	1,544	870	860	646	318
66	Iron and steel	9,521	4,394	4,155	4,456	2,147	1,845	1,185	657	657	469	258
67	Metal building materials and supplies	2,309	805	756	665	417	340	202	97	87	73	10
68	Hardware, tools, etc	1,177	1,184	1,315	549	273	225	156	116	117	104	49
69	Nonferrous metals and products	3,401	2,090	2,194	1,484	827	705	455	360	381	187	86
70	Precious metals, products and processes	515	247	352	315	196	181	126	97	97	70	29
71	Other metals, products and processes	2,663	1,843	1,842	1,169	631	524	329	263	284	117	57
72	Machinery, excluding transportation equipment	14,674	4,979	5,833	4,700	2,331	1,860	1,309	924	924	557	242
73	Electrical machinery and equipment; radios	4,874	1,120	1,514	963	390	282	183	87	86	19	2
74	Agricultural machinery	1,745	749	730	367	339	256	197	158	158	145	62
75	Office equipment, etc	815	413	430	167	95	72	41	24	24	8	6
76	Factory; household and miscellaneous machinery	6,962	2,697	3,159	3,203	1,507	1,250	888	655	656	385	172
77	Transportation equipment	8,382	3,294	3,264	2,326	685	390	169	173	167	73	9
78	Motor vehicles	6,006	2,504	2,575	1,816	426	184	29	36	30	2	
79	Locomotive and railroad equipment	927	610	578	491	259	206	139	137	137	71	9
80	Airplanes	1,114	180	111	18							
81	Miscellaneous manufacturing	3,681	1,192	2,168	1,007	583	411	245	166	168	123	51

[1] Covers factories having annual production of $5,000 or more.
[2] Some minor groups are not adjusted for investment in emergency facilities after "normal" depreciation or intangible assets. Therefore sum of detail does not equal totals.
[3] Covers factories having annual production of $500 or more.
[4] Includes custom and neighborhood shops.
[5] N.e.c. represents not elsewhere classified.

Series P 30–133.   Total Capital in Major Branches of Manufactures, in Book Value and in 1929 Dollars: 1879 to 1948—Con.

[In millions of dollars]

Series No.	Industry	1948[1][2]	1937[1]	1929[1]	1919[3]	1914[3]	1909[3]	1904[3]	1899[3]	1899[4]	1889[4]	1879[4]
	1929 DOLLARS											
82	**Total manufacturing**	77,982	55,319	63,292	46,094	36,737	31,563	23,295	17,452	18,626	11,157	4,821
83	**Food and kindred products**	10,488	9,180	9,591	7,593	6,515	5,517	4,656	3,598	3,760	1,839	897
84	Bakery and confectionery	1,146	1,287	1,693	1,103	757	555	361	256	281	143	50
85	Canned products	1,097	933	921	458	306	224	188	135	135	50	16
86	Mill products	691	564	509	971	675	656	553	432	500	414	319
87	Packinghouse products	1,288	1,267	1,496	1,435	954	711	497	432	432	233	88
88	Sugar	509	681	1,137	573	561	532	461	466	466	48	50
89	Liquor and beverages	2,061	1,560	747	947	1,805	1,641	1,378	1,178	1,219	616	243
90	Tobacco products	1,520	1,093	1,242	732	540	462	676	256	283	191	72
91	Other food products	2,154	1,794	1,846	1,375	918	737	541	441	445	145	58
92	**Textiles and textile products**	6,892	5,638	8,195	6,752	5,163	4,636	3,482	2,876	3,145	2,024	998
93	Cotton goods	2,447	1,024	1,709	2,334	1,862	1,702	1,371	1,112	1,112	709	408
94	Silk and rayon goods		521	926	580	376	276	215	171	171	92	32
95	Woolen and worsted goods		491	641	945	722	780	611	556	556	367	194
96	Carpets, floorcovering, tapestries, etc	320	235	279	195	201	176	135	112	112	78	41
97	Knit goods	616	512	756	561	387	298	209	173	173	92	27
98	Clothing	2,001	1,225	1,874	1,575	1,134	1,033	674	541	737	528	189
99	Textiles, n.e.c.[5]	1,493	1,631	2,012	563	480	371	268	213	286	157	108
100	**Leather products**	817	808	1,213	1,411	1,351	1,359	1,066	809	891	640	328
101	Boots and shoes	445	441	650	538	464	406	290	242	246	222	90
102	Other leather products	371	367	563	873	887	953	776	568	645	418	238
103	**Rubber products**	1,422	816	1,131	704	265	139	93	74	74	36	10
104	Tires and tubes	1,098	602	954	466	129						
105	Other rubber products	287	215	177	238	136						
106	**Forest products**	2,934	2,548	4,083	3,155	3,475	3,591	2,662	2,253	2,868	1,950	847
107	Sawmill and planing mill products	1,826	1,655	2,827	2,002	2,146	2,280	1,574	1,344	1,889	1,225	514
108	Other wood products	1,099	893	1,256	1,153	1,329	1,311	1,088	910	979	726	333
109	**Paper, pulp, and products**	2,476	2,062	2,239	1,524	1,246	1,002	670	453	455	200	90
110	**Printing, publishing, and allied industries**	2,571	2,505	2,737	1,556	1,444	1,265	939	801	801	466	144
111	**Chemicals and allied substances**	6,487	3,965	4,221	2,777	2,078	1,531	1,134	869	871	478	206
112	Fertilizers	237	222	359	334	352	205	123	116	116	68	27
113	Chemicals proper, acids, etc	1,830	1,261	1,042	1,007	633	459	347	274	276	159	74
114	Allied chemical substances, drugs, oils, etc	4,196	2,482	2,820	1,436	1,093	867	664	479	479	251	105
115	**Petroleum refining**	11,188	6,503	6,092	1,380	552	327	254	195	195	151	37
116	**Stone, clay, and glass products**	2,128	1,975	2,592	1,676	1,937	1,755	1,138	709	741	408	156
117	**Iron and steel and products**	9,645	6,719	6,666	6,735	5,166	4,305	2,886	1,599	1,581	1,143	472
118	Iron and steel	6,598	4,625	4,449	5,292	3,911	3,295	2,215	1,208	1,208	830	383
119	Metal building materials and supplies	1,600	847	809	790	760	607	378	178	160	129	15
120	Hardware, tools, etc	816	1,246	1,408	652	497	402	292	213	215	184	73
121	**Nonferrous metals and products**	2,520	2,338	2,364	1,808	1,365	1,203	804	610	646	276	116
122	Precious metals, products and processes	379	276	379	384	323	309	223	164	164	103	39
123	Other metals, products and processes	1,960	2,062	1,985	1,424	1,041	894	581	446	481	173	77
124	**Machinery, excluding transportation equipment**	10,352	5,286	6,166	5,595	4,293	3,654	2,710	1,917	1,917	1,160	414
125	Electrical machinery and equipment; radios	3,438	1,189	1,600	1,146	718	554	379	180	178	40	3
126	Agricultural machinery	1,226	795	772	437	624	503	408	328	328	302	106
127	Office equipment, etc	573	438	455	199	175	141	85	50	50	17	10
128	Factory; household and miscellaneous machinery	4,892	2,863	3,339	3,813	2,775	2,456	1,839	1,359	1,361	802	295
129	**Transportation equipment**	5,642	3,672	3,476	2,480	991	567	333	349	337	156	17
130	Motor vehicles	4,016	2,792	2,742	1,936	616	267	57	73	60	4	
131	Locomotive and railroad equipment	618	680	616	523	375	299	274	276	276	152	17
132	Airplanes	743	201	118	19							
133	**Miscellaneous manufacturing**	2,420	1,304	2,256	948	896	712	468	340	344	230	89

[1] Covers factories having annual production of $5,000 or more.
[2] Some minor groups are not adjusted for investment in emergency facilities after "normal" depreciation or intangible assets. Therefore sum of detail does not equal totals.
[3] Covers factories having annual production of $500 or more.
[4] Includes custom and neighborhood shops.
[5] N.e.c. represents not elsewhere classified.

Series P 134–137. Legal Form of Ownership of Manufacturing Establishments: 1899 to 1954

Year	Production workers, percent in establishments owned by—		Value added, percent in establishments owned by—		Year	Production workers, percent in establishments owned by—		Value added, percent in establishments owned by—	
	Corporations	Other [1]	Corporations	Other [1]		Corporations	Other [1]	Corporations	Other [1]
	134	135	136	137		134	135	136	137
1954	90.6	9.4	93.7	6.3	1914	80.3	19.7	83.2	16.8
1947	89.4	10.6	91.9	8.1	1909	75.6	24.4	77.2	22.8
1939	89.4	10.6	92.3	7.7	1904	70.6	29.4	71.9	28.1
1929	89.9	10.1	91.5	8.5	1899	(2)	(2)	[3] 65.0	[3] 35.0
1919	86.6	13.4	87.7	12.3					

[1] Includes sole proprietorships, firms (partnerships), and other forms of ownership, mostly cooperative societies.
[2] Not available.

[3] Based on value of product. Establishments covered include 66,143 establishments not covered by census of manufactures. These establishments produced value of products of $290 million in a total value of product of all manufactures of $11,701 million.

Series P 138–146. Wage Earners, by Sex: 1869 to 1919

[Annual average, except 1869, 1879, and 1889 based on months of operation only]

Year	All wage earners			Male			Female		
	Total	16 years and over	Under 16 years	Total	16 years and over	Under 16 years	Total	16 years and over [1]	Under 16 years
	138	139	140	141	142	143	144	145	146
1919	9,096,372	8,975,453	120,919	7,267,030	7,202,529	64,501	1,829,342	1,772,924	56,418
1914	7,036,247	6,914,474	121,773	5,590,907	5,525,108	65,799	1,445,340	1,389,366	55,974
1909	6,615,046	6,453,553	161,493	5,252,293	5,163,164	89,129	1,362,753	1,290,389	72,364
1904	5,470,321	5,310,422	159,899	(2)	4,244,538	(2)	(2)	1,065,884	(2)
1899 [3]	4,715,023	4,553,747	161,276	(2)	3,635,236	(2)	(2)	918,511	(2)
1899 [4]	5,308,406	5,139,823	168,583	(2)	4,110,527	(2)	(2)	1,029,296	(2)
1889	4,251,613	4,130,728	120,885	(2)	3,327,042	(2)	(2)	803,686	(2)
1879	2,732,595	2,550,674	181,921	(2)	2,019,035	(2)	(2)	531,639	(2)
1869	2,053,996	1,939,368	114,628	(2)	1,615,598	(2)	(2)	323,770	(2)

[1] Actually 15 years old and over in 1869, 1879, 1889.
[2] Not available.

[3] Comparable with later years; see text for series P 1–10.
[4] Comparable with preceding years; see text for series P 1–10.

Series P 147–168. Indexes of Manufacturing Production, by Industry Group: 1947 to 1957

[1947–49 = 100]

Year	Total manu- facturing	Durable manufactures									
		Total	Primary metals	Fabricated metal products	Machinery	Trans- portation equipment	Instruments and related products	Stone, clay, and glass products	Lumber and products	Furniture and fixtures	Miscel- laneous manufactures
	147	148	149	150	151	152	153	154	155	156	157
1957	145	160	131	139	168	213	172	155	114	120	140
1956	144	159	138	135	171	199	166	158	123	122	144
1955	140	155	140	134	155	203	149	149	127	119	141
1954	127	137	108	123	142	175	140	131	115	106	131
1953	136	153	132	136	160	189	155	133	118	117	140
1952	125	136	116	121	147	154	142	125	111	113	122
1951	121	128	126	122	130	135	128	131	113	111	120
1950	113	116	115	115	114	120	114	118	113	117	117
1949	97	95	90	93	93	102	95	97	93	96	95
1948	103	104	107	104	104	102	105	105	106	104	105
1947	100	101	103	103	103	96	100	98	101	100	100

Year	Nondurable manufactures										
	Total	Textile mill products	Apparel and allied products	Rubber products	Leather and products	Paper and allied products	Printing and publishing	Chemicals and allied products	Petroleum and coal products	Food and beverage manufactures	Tobacco manufactures
	158	159	160	161	162	163	164	165	166	167	168
1957	130	99	111	135	104	158	141	184	141	112	111
1956	129	104	112	133	104	159	136	177	141	113	107
1955	126	107	113	143	105	152	127	167	135	109	105
1954	116	95	105	115	95	134	120	148	125	106	103
1953	118	104	110	128	99	132	121	147	130	107	108
1952	114	103	108	116	99	120	116	137	123	105	110
1951	114	107	105	119	94	125	113	136	122	105	107
1950	111	111	108	119	101	118	111	121	110	103	101
1949	99	94	101	92	94	98	103	101	99	100	100
1948	102	105	102	102	100	102	103	103	104	99	101
1947	99	101	97	106	106	99	93	97	97	101	99

Series P 169–186.   Indexes of Manufacturing Production, by Industry Group: 1899 to 1954
[1947 = 100]

Year	All manufacturing industries	Durable manufactures							
		Primary metals	Fabricated metal products	Machinery, except electrical	Electrical machinery	Transportation equipment	Stone, clay, and glass products	Lumber and furniture	Instruments and miscellaneous [1]
	169	170	171	172	173	174	175	176	177
1954	128	103	114	116	165	189	124	116	178
1947	100	100	100	100	100	100	100	100	100
1939	57	52	50	38	35	49	87	72	52
1937	58	58	51	--------	--------	60	88	69	--------
1935	46	39	--------	--------	--------	48	61	54	--------
1933	35	27	--------	--------	--------	22	42	42	--------
1931	40	32	--------	--------	--------	30	60	57	--------
1929	56	65	--------	--------	--------	66	89	91	--------
1927	49	52	--------	--------	--------	45	88	90	--------
1925	46	53	--------	--------	--------	50	81	93	--------
1923	43	52	--------	--------	--------	50	--------	82	--------
1921	30	26	--------	--------	--------	25	--------	76	--------
1919	34	40	--------	--------	--------	40	--------	71	--------
1914	29	29	--------	--------	--------	13	--------	75	--------
1909	24	28	--------	--------	--------	7	--------	75	--------
1904	19	18	--------	--------	--------	5	--------	69	--------
1899	15	14	--------	--------	--------	5	--------	74	--------

Year	Nondurable manufactures								
	Textiles and apparel	Rubber products	Leather	Paper	Printing and publishing	Chemicals	Petroleum and coal products	Food	Tobacco
	178	179	180	181	182	183	184	185	186
1954	109	114	90	131	126	164	131	109	108
1947	100	100	100	100	100	100	100	100	100
1939	80	55	87	68	69	46	65	65	66
1937	72	51	86	63	73	43	61	61	65
1935	67	45	79	53	62	35	49	52	56
1933	57	39	68	44	52	29	42	37	48
1931	58	39	142	45	60	30	45	41	51
1929	67	57	79	52	72	35	54	46	55
1927	63	52	76	46	65	29	45	42	50
1925	58	48	67	40	59	24	40	40	45
1923	56	41	75	36	52	22	34	38	41
1921	43	24	60	26	37	15	30	31	36
1919	45	30	142	27	39	18	21	32	38
1914	48	--------	64	24	34	15	12	34	29
1909	41	--------	65	19	25	11	9	28	24
1904	32	--------	58	14	19	8	6	24	21
1899	26	--------	50	10	12	6	5	19	16

[1] Includes ordnance and accessories.

Series P 187–232.   Physical Output of Selected Manufactured Commodities: 1860 to 1957

Year	Foods					Beverages		Tobacco products			Textiles				Leather goods	
	Wheat flour produced [1]	Refined sugar produced	Coffee imported	Canned corn produced	Canned tomatoes produced	Fermented malt liquor produced [2]	Distilled spirits produced [2]	Manufactured tobacco and snuff produced	Cigars produced	Cigarettes produced	Raw cotton consumed	Wool consumed	Unmanufactured silk imports for consumption	Packaged rayon and acetate yarns produced	Men's leather shoes produced	Women's leather shoes produced
	187	188	189	190	191	192	193	194	195	196	197	198	199	200	201	202
	Mil. bbl.	Mil. lb.	Mil. lb.	1,000 cases	1,000 cases	1,000 bbl.	1,000 tax gallons	Mil. lb.	Millions	Millions	1,000 bales	Mil. lb.	Mil. lb.	Mil. lb.	1,000 pairs	1,000 pairs
1957	(3)	(3)	2,713	31,533	21,686	89,882	(3)	179	[4]5,952	[5]442,328	10,166	371.8	8.3	714.0	(3)	(3)
1956	117.6	(3)	2,776	35,668	29,883	90,698	(3)	185	[4]5,830	[5]424,247	10,930	440.7	12.7	750.0	(3)	(3)
1955	115.6	14,776	2,569	24,075	24,727	89,791	593,982	199	5,834	412,309	10,315	413.8	11.0	865.1	(3)	(3)
1954	113.5	14,410	2,234	30,619	21,827	92,561	563,496	204	[4]5,882	[5]401,849	9,900	380.8	8.5	706.8	91,125	202,025
1953	113.9	14,603	2,767	30,982	22,334	90,434	619,456	209	5,915	423,129	10,783	494.0	7.9	886.9	98,824	186,936
1952	117.0	13,811	2,665	32,329	27,981	89,601	689,256	220	5,825	435,616	10,426	466.4	12.6	828.8	100,742	183,933
1951	117.6	13,275	2,678	25,576	31,770	88,976	846,388	227	5,594	418,872	12,050	484.1	7.2	958.2	104,479	169,419
1950	115.4	14,665	2,429	18,241	21,108	88,807	521,770	235	5,399	392,025	10,467	634.8	10.5	953.9	102,526	195,186
1949	120.3	13,235	2,913	29,795	21,537	89,736	617,558	239	5,453	385,046	9,201	500.4	4.0	800.6	97,427	177,962
1948	143.2	12,202	2,752	31,483	24,393	91,291	576,409	245	5,645	386,916	10,510	693.1	7.4	856.1	104,401	176,545
1947	156.7	13,753	2,458	26,089	27,709	87,857	563,956	242	5,488	369,763	11,009	698.3	3.2	746.7	106,242	191,633
1946	143.2	10,224	2,664	30,951	23,857	84,978	634,454	253	5,618	350,132	10,218	737.5	15.6	677.5	106,044	181,351
1945	141.1	11,204	2,705	28,237	16,758	86,604	1,174,391	331	5,275	332,345	11,049	645.1	1.8	623.7	107,742	120,150
1944	125.4	12,160	2,604	25,089	26,099	81,726	1,011,763	307	5,199	323,734	11,308	622.8	--------	555.2	108,537	118,079
1943	122.8	10,635	2,194	28,755	29,269	71,018	772,267	327	5,363	296,305	12,401	636.2	--------	501.1	129,345	154,670
1942	114.6	9,637	1,712	32,118	41,252	63,717	675,482	330	5,841	257,657	12,658	603.6	0.2	479.3	142,975	181,685
1941	112.7	13,437	2,250	26,109	31,759	55,214	474,054	342	5,610	218,083	11,081	648.0	25.6	451.2	135,804	184,915
1940	110.9	12,098	2,044	15,524	29,533	54,892	387,183	344	5,235	189,508	8,845	407.9	47.6	390.1	102,383	151,944
1939	114.1	11,749	2,001	14,567	24,465	53,871	346,344	343	5,198	180,828	7,709	396.5	55.3	328.6	103,753	167,697
1938	111.8	11,908	1,981	20,470	23,131	56,340	351,190	345	5,015	171,842	6,463	284.5	57.1	257.6	96,660	147,755
1937	109.4	11,684	1,689	23,541	26,235	58,748	482,138	341	5,303	170,171	8,769	380.8	64.2	320.6	102,895	149,675
1936	111.0	11,181	1,732	14,621	24,414	51,812	449,994	348	5,172	159,076	7,085	406.1	67.5	277.6	103,784	161,858

See footnotes at end of table.

Series P 187–232. Physical Output of Selected Manufactured Commodities: 1860 to 1957—Con.

Year	Foods					Beverages		Tobacco products			Textiles				Leather goods	
	Wheat flour produced [1]	Refined sugar produced	Coffee imported	Canned corn produced	Canned tomatoes produced	Fermented malt liquor produced [2]	Distilled spirits produced [2]	Manufactured tobacco and snuff produced	Cigars produced	Cigarettes produced	Raw cotton consumed	Wool consumed	Unmanufactured silk imports for consumption	Packaged rayon and acetate yarns produced	Men's leather shoes produced	Women's leather shoes produced
	187	188	189	190	191	192	193	194	195	196	197	198	199	200	201	202
	Mil. bbl.	Mil. lb.	Mil. lb.	1,000 cases	1,000 cases	1,000 bbl.	1,000 tax gallons	Mil. lb.	Millions	Millions	1,000 bales	Mil. lb.	Mil. lb.	Mil. lb.	1,000 pairs	1,000 pairs
1935	106.4	10,891	1,745	21,471	26,985	45,229	349,772	343	4,685	140,147	6,080	417.5	72.4	257.5	99,525	145,231
1934		10,256	1,514	11,268	22,376	[6] 37,678	241,610	346	4,526	130,287	6,467	229.6	60.4	208.3	91,387	133,045
1933	97.2	11,132	1,574	10,193	20,461	[7] 9,798	123,405	342	4,300	115,087	6,898	317.1	73.0	213.5	88,821	130,742
1932			1,484	9,358	20,367	2,766	150,391	347	4,383	106,915	5,503	230.1	77.6	134.7	74,493	113,944
1931	115.0	11,172	1,730	19,415	16,341	3,137	170,394	371	5,348	117,402	5,977	311.0	87.6	150.8	77,420	112,603
1930	123.6		1,585	15,692	29,015	3,681	197,221	372	5,894	124,193	6,911	263.2	80.6	127.3	77,147	112,629
1929	123.6	12,376	1,475	17,487	24,146	3,900	203,300	381	6,519	122,822	7,970	368.1	85.9	121.4	94,770	131,303
1928	120.6		1,447	14,497	14,576	4,200	170,500	386	6,373	109,131	7,614	333.2	74.4	97.2	90,970	123,753
1927	122.0	12,046	1,419	10,347	22,425	4,400	185,500	396	6,519	100,260	7,996	354.1	72.7	75.5	95,328	116,259
1926	116.2		1,482	19,069	16,140	4,900	203,800	411	6,499	92,523	7,260	342.7	65.6	62.7	86,644	110,447
1925	117.5	12,972	1,269	24,320	33,747	5,100	167,500	414	6,463	82,712	6,852	349.9	63.1	51.0	86,546	104,782
1924	118.7		1,395	12,131	21,370	4,900	137,500	414	6,598	73,256	6,217	342.2	50.5	36.3	84,663	104,135
1923	114.7	10,358	1,388	14,106	25,045	5,300	124,600	413	6,950	67,239	7,312	422.4	49.1	34.9	100,283	109,676
1922	113.8		1,220	11,419	19,695	6,300	82,200	420	6,722	56,413	6,549	406.5	50.1	24.1	89,984	105,368
1921	97.2	9,586	1,304	8,843	6,857	9,200	87,900	387	6,726	52,770	5,409		44.9	15.0	69,458	101,474
1920	130.4		1,248	15,040	19,405	9,200	101,300	413	8,097	48,091	6,762		29.3	10.1		
1919	122.5	9,478	1,256	13,550	18,453	27,700	100,800	424	7,072	53,865	6,224		44.3	8.3	95,000	105,000
1918	115.4		1,014	11,722	27,111	50,300	178,800	497	7,054	47,528	7,685		32.3	5.8		
1917	115.8		1,218	10,803	25,735	60,800	286,100	483	7,560	36,323	7,658		36.0	6.5		
1916	118.7		1,132	9,130	22,433	58,600	253,300	466	7,042	26,203	7,279		32.0	5.8		
1915	119.2		1,137	10,124	14,457	59,800	140,700	442	6,599	18,945	6,009		30.8	3.9		
1914	115.0	8,617	975	9,789	25,984	66,200	181,900	441	7,174	17,944	5,885		25.5	2.4	98,000	80,900
1913	113.6	8,274	845	7,283	24,250	65,300	193,600	444	7,572	16,530	5,786		27.8	1.8		
1912	110.8	7,904	938	13,109	23,936	62,200	187,600	435	7,044	14,239	5,368		24.7	1.1		
1911	110.8	7,350	796	14,301	16,642	63,300	183,400	424	7,049	11,700	4,705		20.7	0.4		
1910	107.2	7,317	797	10,063	15,764	59,500	163,900	447	6,810	9,782	4,799		21.5			
1909	107.5	6,986	1,126	5,787	18,750	56,300	139,900	431	6,668	7,880	5,241		22.1		93,900	86,600
1908	109.8	6,479	926	6,779	19,595	58,800	133,900	408	6,489	6,833	4,493		18.6			
1907	111.5	6,451	930	6,654	22,051	58,600	174,700	388	7,302	6,345	4,974		15.6			
1906	109.5	6,433	844	9,137	14,733	54,700	150,100	391	7,148	5,502	4,877		16.7			
1905	105.4	5,699	859	13,019	9,517	49,500	153,300	368	6,748	4,477	4,523		15.4			
1904	104.7	5,963	1,074	11,163	14,539	48,300	139,500	354	6,640	4,170	3,981		16.4		83,400	69,500
1903	111.8	5,467	940	4,861	17,335	46,700	148,200	351	6,806	3,959	4,187		11.5			
1902	109.1	5,725	901	4,191	15,810	44,600	132,800	348	6,232	3,647	4,080		13.6			
1901	108.4	5,156	1,028	5,028	7,227	40,600	128,600	314	6,139	3,503	3,604		12.2			
1900	105.8	4,858	741	6,486	9,385	39,500	109,200	301	5,566	3,870	3,687		8.1			
1899	104.0	4,578	852	6,366	12,246	36,700	100,200	295	4,910	4,367	3,672		11.7		67,700	65,000
1898	100.3	4,107	781	4,315	9,651	37,500	83,700	275	4,459	4,843	3,472		8.4			
1897	95.7	4,241	787	2,787	6,767	34,500	64,300	297	4,136	4,927	2,841		10.0			
1896	96.5	3,957	621	2,539	5,845	35,900	90,000	261	4,048	4,967	2,500		4.9			
1895	93.6	3,961	634	2,992	6,888	33,600	81,900	274	4,099	4,238	2,984		9.1			
1894	93.7	4,281	601	3,278	10,971	33,400	92,200	269	4,164	3,621	2,300		7.8			
1893	92.5	4,050	535	4,184	7,337	34,600	131,000	251	4,341	3,661	2,416		4.4			
1892	92.1	3,896	601	3,417	5,502	31,900	118,400	274	4,675	3,282	2,847		7.8			
1891	86.3	4,069	574	2,837	5,660	30,500	117,800	271	4,422	3,137	2,604		7.1			
1890	83.3	3,233	481	1,523	5,280	27,600	111,100	253	4,229	2,505	2,518		4.6			
1889	80.8	3,170	534	1,726	5,022	25,100	91,100	246	3,787	2,413	2,309		5.8			
1888	79.5	3,048	507	3,437	5,580	24,700	71,700	209	3,668	2,212	2,205		5.4			
1887	79.5	3,014	423	2,276	4,720	23,100	79,400	226	3,662	1,865	2,050		4.8			
1886	75.7	2,949	521	1,675	3,921	20,700	81,800	210	3,462	1,607	2,095		4.8			
1885	74.0	2,912	534	1,062	2,362	19,200	76,400	207	3,294	1,080	1,687		3.9			
1884	72.5	2,732	494			19,000	76,500	172	3,373	920	1,814		3.4			
1883	70.8	2,466	488			17,800	75,300	194	3,232	844	2,038		3.3			
1882	67.8	2,368	484			17,000	107,300	159	3,118	599	1,849					
1881	65.6	1,940	426			14,300	119,500	172	2,806	595	1,866					
1880	64.3	1,988	396			13,300	91,400	146	2,510	533	1,501					
1879	61.9	1,709	438			11,100	72,900	136	2,217	371	1,457					
1878	59.8	1,778	325			10,200	57,300	125	1,923	210	1,459					
1877	56.5	1,698	349			9,800	61,400	123	1,816	157	1,314					
1876	56.1	1,583	267			9,900	58,600	124	1,776	113	1,256					
1875	54.4	1,642	360			9,500	62,700	124	1,828	59	1,098					
1874	53.6	1,638	283			9,600	69,600	124	1,835	35	1,213					
1873	51.3	1,526	292			9,600	71,200	118	1,755	28	1,116					
1872	49.2	1,454	289			8,700	69,400	112	1,578	24	1,147					
1871	49.0	1,413	308			7,700	57,000	107	1,353	20	1,027					
1870	47.9	1,196	272			6,600	72,600	102	1,183	16	797					
1869	46.8	1,254	235								860					
1868	44.9	1,149	235								844					
1867	44.3	841	220								715					
1866	42.8	886	175								615					
1865	42.5	733	126								344					
1864	42.4	565	105								220					
1863	42.5	607	101								287					
1862	42.4	590	94								369					
1861	41.6	978	146								842					
1860	39.8	788	180								845					

See footnotes at end of table.

Series P 187–232. Physical Output of Selected Manufactured Commodities: 1860 to 1957—Con.

Year	Primary and fabricated metals							Construction materials			Transportation equipment				
	Steel ingots and castings produced					Rolled iron and steel produced	Tinplate consumption	Rails produced	Structural iron and steel shapes produced	Common and face brick produced	Locomotives produced	Railroad freight cars produced	Railroad passenger cars produced	Horse-drawn vehicles produced	
	Total	Bessemer	Open hearth	Crucible	Electric and all other									Farm wagons, trucks, and business vehicles	Carriages, buggies, and sulkies
	203	204	205	206	207	208	209	210	211	212	213	214	215	216	217
	Long tons	Long tons	Long tons	Long tons	Long tons	1,000 long tons	1,000 long tons	1,000 long tons	1,000 long tons	Billions	Number	1,000	Number	1,000	1,000
1957	100,638,373	2,209,944	90,765,857		7,662,572	76,685	4,395	1,168	7,674	6.66		96.6	705		
1956	102,871,545	2,882,140	91,821,936		8,167,469	79,718	4,391	1,162	6,399	8.09		66.6	396		
1955	104,496,488	2,963,854	94,070,893		7,461,742	80,944	4,019	1,096	5,657	7.90		37.5	886		
1954	78,849,689	2,275,093	71,720,977		4,853,620	61,129	3,809	1,046	5,094	6.72		36.1	315	108	
1953	99,651,535	3,442,594	89,708,771		6,500,171	76,735	3,932	1,769	5,837	5.87		83.8	386		
1952	83,185,749	3,146,140	73,970,035		6,069,574	63,704	3,205	1,314	4,780	5.89		79.4	117		
1951	93,928,436	4,366,916	83,184,391		6,377,129	73,135	3,513	1,655	5,668	6.63		96.0	179		
1950	86,460,781	4,048,713	77,020,097		5,391,971	67,134	3,704	1,651	4,859	6.33		44.2	964		
1949	69,623,371	3,523,800	62,722,146		3,377,426	54,359	2,909	1,697	4,171	5.52		95.2	933		
1948	79,143,277	3,788,546	70,839,426		4,515,304	61,779	3,031	1,971	4,871	5.84		114.9	891	218	
1947	75,798,278	3,779,056	68,637,315		3,381,906	59,109	2,800	2,179	5,007	5.14		96.2	861		
1946	59,466,718	2,971,194	54,207,110		2,288,414	45,479	2,064	1,755	3,917	4.87		60.0	1,337		
1945	71,162,186	3,844,034	64,231,788	21	3,086,343	53,403	2,053	2,158	3,988	2.29	3,213	54.5	931		
1944	80,037,130	4,499,931	71,753,518	22	3,783,659	58,754	1,910	2,224	4,175	1.88	1,438	81.8	1,003		
1943	79,318,314	5,022,761	70,198,039	130	4,097,384	56,511	1,514	1,899	4,085	1.92	1,164	75.0	685		
1942	76,814,224	4,958,414	68,305,319	1,795	3,548,696	55,755	1,841	1,871	5,193	(³)	1,018	71.4	418		
1941	73,963,624	4,980,421	66,419,302	2,065	2,561,836	55,647	2,779	1,721	5,111	(³)	1,107	83.0	349		
1940	59,805,970	3,311,226	54,975,967	914	1,517,863	43,447	2,062	1,499	3,779	(³)	560	64.1	257		
1939	47,141,709	2,999,032	43,223,036	831	918,810	34,882	2,088	1,172	2,999	4.73	355	25.5	276	52.4	.592
1938	28,349,991	1,880,661	25,964,300	6	505,024	21,044	1,383	623	1,859	3.53	346	17.1	434		
1937	50,568,701	3,449,927	46,272,303	934	845,537	36,766	2,202	1,446	3,277	4.19	615	78.8	629	106.2	.900
1936	47,767,856	3,458,457	43,536,128	816	772,455	33,801	2,117	1,220	2,898	3.82	202	47.1	191		
1935	34,092,594	2,835,031	30,715,429	642	541,492	23,965	1,752	712	1,750	2.28	205	8.8	205	98.3	1.01
1934	26,055,289	2,162,357	23,531,105	531	361,296	18,970	1,419	1,010	1,425	1.40	110	25.3	195		
1933	23,232,347	2,428,791	20,381,672	681	421,203	16,735	1,674	416	1,109	1.29	63	2.2	7	52.8	1.07
1932	13,681,162	1,532,076	11,907,330	645	241,111	10,451	1,000	403	937	1.40	123	3.3	71		
1931	25,945,501	3,023,446	22,509,566	1,547	410,942	19,176	1,375	1,158	2,062	3.22	222	13.6	290	27.48	.711
1930	40,699,483	5,035,459	35,049,172	2,253	612,599	29,513	1,547	1,873	3,512	5.11	1,134	76.7	1,481		
1929	56,433,473	7,122,509	48,352,888	6,645	951,431	41,069	1,710	2,722	4,778	7.64	1,161	85.0	2,202	106.31	3.60
1928	51,544,180	6,620,195	44,113,956	7,769	802,260	37,663	1,590	2,647	4,096	8.83	747	47.5	1,462		
1927	44,935,185	6,191,727	38,068,335	9,036	666,087	32,879	1,436	2,806	3,742	9.47	1,176	63.8	1,975	112.3	7.63
1926	48,293,763	6,934,568	40,691,979	15,493	651,723	35,496	1,534	3,218	3,912	9.96	1,770	91.3	2,800		
1925	45,393,524	6,723,962	38,034,488	19,562	615,512	33,387	1,497	2,785	3,604	10.04	1,285	108.8	2,383	196.2	21.5
1924	37,931,939	5,899,590	31,577,350	22,473	432,526	28,086	1,259	2,433	3,284	9.19	2,036	115.3	2,491		
1923	44,943,696	8,484,088	35,899,657	44,079	515,872	33,277	1,392	2,905	3,405	9.21	3,785	177.7	1,963	192.8	39.8
1922	35,602,926	5,919,298	29,308,983	28,606	346,039	26,452	1,214	2,172	2,719	7.32	1,534	67.7	1,096		
1921	19,783,797	4,015,938	15,589,802	7,613	170,444	14,774	687	2,179	1,273	5.32	1,823	45.6	1,159	66.8	34.4
1920	42,132,934	8,883,087	32,671,895	72,265	505,687	32,348	1,220	2,604	3,307	5.64	3,672	75.6	903		
1919	34,671,232	7,271,562	26,948,694	63,572	387,404	25,102	947	2,204	2,614	5.54	3,272	156.8	391	342.4	216
1918	44,462,183	9,376,236	34,459,391	115,112	511,693	31,156	1,215	2,541	2,850	3.91	6,475	108.0	1,572		
1917	45,060,607	10,479,960	34,148,893	126,716	305,038	33,068	1,279	2,944	3,110	6.62	5,446	139.6	1,955		
1916	42,773,680	11,059,039	31,415,427	129,692	169,522	32,380	1,009	2,855	3,030	8.40	4,075	129.4	1,802		
1915	32,151,036	8,287,213	23,679,102	113,782	70,939	24,393	904	2,204	2,437	7.71	2,085	70.1	1,866		
1914	23,513,030	6,220,846	17,174,684	89,869	27,631	18,370	887	1,945	2,031	7.96	2,631	98.1	3,366	534	538
1913	31,300,874	9,545,706	21,599,931	121,226	34,011	24,791	787	3,503	3,005	8.92	5,332	185.7	2,779		
1912	31,251,303	10,327,901	20,780,723	121,517	21,162	24,657	883	3,328	2,846	9.37	4,915	126.4	2,818		
1911	23,676,106	7,947,854	15,598,650	97,653	31,949	19,039	737	2,823	1,912	9.20	3,530	62.2	3,466		
1910	26,094,919	9,412,772	16,504,509	122,303	55,335	21,621	777	3,636	2,267	9.92	4,755	170.8	4,288		
1909	23,955,021	9,330,783	14,493,936	107,355	22,947	19,645	665	3,024	2,276	10.61	2,887	86.8	2,749	588	828
1908	14,023,247	6,116,755	7,836,729	63,631	6,132	11,828	584	1,921	1,083	8.40	2,342	68.0	1,637		
1907	23,362,594	11,667,549	11,549,736	131,234	14,075	19,865	562	3,634	1,940	10.38	7,362	275.0	5,353		
1906	23,398,136	12,275,830	10,980,413	127,513	14,380	19,588	622	3,978	2,119	10.64	6,952	233.4	3,084		
1905	20,023,947	10,941,375	8,971,376	102,233	8,963	16,840	551	3,376	1,661	10.36	5,491	163.3	2,500	644	937
1904	13,859,887	7,859,140	5,908,166	83,391	9,190	12,013	524	2,285	949	9.10	3,441	60.8	2,144		
1903	14,534,978	8,592,829	5,829,911	102,434	9,804	13,208	527	2,992	1,096	8.90	5,152	152.8	2,007		
1902	14,947,250	9,138,363	5,687,729	112,772	8,386	13,944	419	2,948	1,300	8.93	4,070	162.6	1,948		
1901	13,473,595	8,713,302	4,656,309	98,513	5,471	12,349	476	2,875	1,013	8.45	3,384	137.0	2,055		
1900	10,188,329	6,684,770	3,398,135	100,562	4,862	9,487	440	2,386	815	7.49	3,153	115.6	1,636		
1899	10,639,857	7,586,354	2,947,316	101,213	4,974	10,294	420	2,273	850	8.13	2,475	119.9	1,305	570	905
1898	8,932,857	6,609,017	2,230,292	89,747	3,801	8,513	394	1,981	702	6.16	1,875	99.8	699		
1897	7,156,957	5,475,315	1,608,671	69,959	3,012	7,002	340	1,648	584	5.60	1,251	43.6	494		
1896	5,281,689	3,919,906	1,298,700	60,689	2,394	5,516	280	1,122	496	5.97	1,175	51.2	474		
1895	6,114,834	4,909,128	1,137,182	67,666	858	6,190	333	1,306	518	6.36	1,101	38.1	430		
1894	4,412,032	3,571,313	784,936	51,702	4,081	4,642	289	1,022	360		695	17.0	516		
1893	4,019,995	3,215,686	737,890	63,613	2,806	4,976	308	1,136	387		2,011	56.9	1,986		
1892	4,927,581	4,168,435	669,889	84,709	4,548	6,166	287	1,552	454		2,012	98.1	2,195		
1891	3,904,240	3,247,417	579,753	72,586	4,484	5,391	329	1,307			2,165	95.5	1,640		
1890	4,277,071	3,688,871	513,232	71,175	3,793	6,023	329	1,885			1,860	103.8	1,654		
1889	3,385,732	2,930,204	374,543	75,865	5,120	5,237	331	1,522	276	8.05	2,180	70.6	1,580		
1888	2,899,440	2,511,161	314,318	70,279	3,682	4,617	298	1,404			2,044	71.7	1,452		
1887	3,339,071	2,936,033	322,069	75,375	5,594	5,236	284	2,140			1,436	78.0	1,277		
1886	2,562,503	2,269,190	218,973	71,973	2,367	4,377	258	1,601				42.4	953		
1885	1,711,920	1,519,430	133,376	57,599	1,515	3,101	229	977			800	12.5	813		
1884	1,550,879	1,375,563	117,515	53,270	4,563		216	1,022			1,149	24.5	1,063		
1883	1,673,535	1,477,345	119,356	71,835	4,999		221	1,215			2,067	44.9	2,135		
1882	1,736,692	1,514,687	143,341	75,973	2,691		214	1,508			2,282	67.8	1,711		
1881	1,588,314	1,374,247	131,202	80,145	2,720		183	1,647			1,977	73.8	1,188		
1880	1,247,335	1,074,262	100,851	64,664	7,558		158	1,305			1,405	46.2	685		
1879	935,273	829,439	50,225	50,696	4,879		154	994	87	3.82		25.6	524		
1878	731,977	653,773	32,255	38,309	7,640		108	788				8.74	211		
1877	569,618	500,524	22,349	36,098	10,647		112	683				7.00	708		
1876	533,191	469,639	19,187	35,163	9,202		90	785				8.10	836		

See footnotes at end of table.

Series P 187–232. Physical Output of Selected Manufactured Commodities: 1860 to 1957—Con.

Year	Primary and fabricated metals — Steel ingots and castings produced					Tinplate consumption	Construction materials — Rails produced	Common and face brick produced	Transportation equipment — Railway freight cars produced	Railway passenger cars produced	Year	Construction materials, rails produced
	Total	Bessemer	Open hearth	Crucible	Electric and all other							
	203	204	205	206	207	209	210	212	214	215		210
	Long tons	Long tons	Long tons	Long tons	Long tons	1,000 long tons	1,000 long tons	Billions	1,000	Number		1,000 long tons
1875	389,799	335,283	8,080	35,180	11,256	91	708	----	9.13	185	1866	385
1874	215,727	171,369	6,250	32,436	5,672	80	651	----	4.63	256	1865	318
1873	198,796	152,368	3,125	31,059	12,244	97	795	----	5.69	280	1864	299
1872	142,954	107,239	2,679	26,125	6,911	86	893	----	8.69	387	1863	246
1871	73,214	40,179	1,785	31,250		83	693	----	1.78	185		
											1862	191
1870	68,750	37,500	1,339	29,911		----	554				1861	170
1869	31,250	10,714	893	19,643		----	530	2.80	----		1860	183
1868	26,786	7,589	----	19,197		----	452					
1867	19,643	2,679	----	16,964		----	413					

Year	Transportation equipment—Con. — Bicycles produced	Pneumatic tires and casings produced	Refined petroleum products — Light products of distillation	Illuminating oils (kerosene)	Fuel oils	Lubricating oils	Paraffin wax	Chemicals produced — Superphosphate produced (100% APA)	Sulfuric acid	Soda ash	Miscellaneous — Mechanical refrigerators produced	Reed organs produced	Pianos produced	Phonographs produced	Radios and radio-phonograph combinations produced
	218	219	220	221	222	223	224	225	226	227	228	229	230	231	232
	Millions	Millions	Bil. gal.	Bil. gal.	Bil. gal.	Mil. gal.	Mil. gal.	1,000 short tons	Million short tons	Million short tons	1,000	1,000	1,000	1,000	Millions
1957	(3)	(3)	(3)	(3)	(3)	(3)	(3)	2,455	16.0	(3)	(3)	(3)	(3)	(3)	(3)
1956	(3)	(3)	60.0	5.19	45.88	2,487	200.3	2,241	16.0	(3)	(3)	(3)	(3)	(3)	(3)
1955	(3)	(3)	57.7	4.92	42.96	2,345	197.6	2,272	16.0	(3)	(3)	(3)	(3)	(3)	(3)
1954	1.75	87.1	53.0	5.14	40.28	2,236	197.6	2,215	14.4	3.62	3,387	----	151.6	----	18.17
1953			53.2	5.17	41.08	2,207	185.9	2,147	14.0	----					
1952			50.1	5.56	40.92	2,335	161.7	2,165	13.3	----					
1951			47.9	5.70	39.70	2,582	179.6	2,044	13.4	----					
1950			43.0	4.98	34.61	2,173	166.7	1,993	13.0						
1949			40.4	4.29	32.16	1,906	119.6	1,892	11.4						
1948			38.7	5.12	35.57	2,160	131.3	1,900	11.5						
1947	2.88	102.7	35.3	4.64	31.92	2,174	135.3	1,857	10.6	3.14	3,975	----	148.3	----	21.06
1946			32.6	4.38	30.21	1,917	112.0	1,567	9.2						
1945			33.5	3.40	30.19	1,758	108.9	1,447	9.5						
1944			31.1	3.29	29.43	1,727	107.5	1,339	9.2						
1943			25.5	3.04	26.41	1,624	100.8	1,273	8.4						
1942			25.6	2.83	23.34	1,622	93.6	1,067	7.8						
1941			29.5	3.05	22.33	1,661	89.2	955	6.8						
1940			25.9	3.10	20.98	1,544	68.5	879							
1939	1.25	57.8	25.7	2.88	19.64	1,472	61.8	761	4.8	2.01	1,773		111.2		10.32
1938			23.9	2.71	18.76	1,295	58.2	685							
1937	1.13	53.4	24.0	2.74	19.27	1,483	69.4	805	4.9	2.32	2,824		103.1		7.78
1936			21.7	2.36	17.38	1,299	63.2	627							
1935	0.66	48.8	19.7	2.34	15.12	1,170	60.0	532	4.0	1.87	1,882	1.69	61.0		5.69
1934			17.8	2.26	14.08	1,108	62.7	509							
1933	0.32	45.4	17.1	2.06	13.29	998	62.7	463		1.65	1,160				3.68
1932			16.8	1.84	12.38	942	61.4	307							
1931	0.26	49.1	18.6	1.78	14.15	1,121	63.6	478	3.8	1.51	1,050	1.28	50.9		3.81
1930			18.7	2.07	15.65	1,436	73.0	794							
1929	0.31	69.8	18.6	2.35	17.99	1,443	84.2		5.3	1.81	890	2.70	121.1	755	4.98
1927	0.26	63.6	13.4	2.22	15.4	1,382	94.3		4.9	1.47	390	3.09	212.2	1,050	1.98
1925	0.30	58.8	11.3	2.37	14.6	1,361	89.8		4.4	1.37	75	4.36	302.5	642	2.35
1923	0.49	45.4	7.8	2.24	12.0	1,151	69.5		4.1	1.26	18	7.77	343.8	997	0.19
1921	0.22	27.3	5.4	1.94	9.75	949	58.4		2.7	0.78	5	7.88	218.3	596	--------
1920								863							
1919	0.47	32.8	4.1	2.31	7.77	822	68.0		3.5	1.03		26.4	337.9	2,230	
1914	0.30	8.0	1.5	1.94	3.73	518	57.5		2.5	0.94		40.5	323.0	514	
1909	0.17		0.5	1.67	1.70	537	47.3		1.7	0.65		64.1	364.2	345	
1904	0.23		0.3	1.36	0.36	315	39.7		1.2	0.52		113	261.2		
1899	1.11		0.3	1.26	0.31	170	38.7		1.0	0.39		107	171.5	151	
1890								84.1		0.47					
1889			0.165				12.1								
1880			0.075				10.5	35							
1870								12							
1860								1							

[1] Figures for 1915–1929 are for crop years ending June; all other figures are for calendar years. The 1914 crop-year figure is 114.2 million barrels. The 1929 calendar-year figure is 120.0 million barrels.
[2] Figures are for years ending June 30 and include data for Alaska and Hawaii.
[3] Not available.
[4] Includes small cigars.
[5] Excludes small cigars.
[6] Alcoholic content limited to 3.2 percent by weight from Apr. 7 to Dec. 5, 1933.
[7] Includes 1,588,788 barrels produced prior to Apr. 7 (effective date of the act of Mar. 22, 1933).

Series P 233–249. Total Production Capacity of Selected Manufacturing Industries: 1887 to 1957

[In thousands of short tons unless otherwise stated. Capacity is usually rated as of January 1. See text for exception]

Year	Blast furnaces (pig iron)	Steel ingots and steel for castings[1]	Copper refining[2]	Lead refining: Silver-lead refineries	Lead refining: Smelters and refiners of Missouri lead	Zinc refining[3]	Aluminum ingots	Portland cement	Crude petroleum refining (Millions 42-gal. bbls.)	Coke: By-product (slot type)	Coke: Beehive	Carbon black	Sulfuric acid	Phosphatic fertilizers[4]	Synthetic nitrogen	Rayon and acetate fibers	Paper and paperboard
	233	234	235	236	237	238	239	240	241	242	243	244	245	246	247	248	249
1957	86,818	133,459	2,064	560	258	1,161	1,776	64,699	3,330	79,965	5,766	1,016	19,500	4,550	3,711	768	32,579
1956	85,485	128,363	2,064	628	258	1,110	1,589	58,562	3,151	79,676	6,285	990	18,600	4,590	3,631	750	30,926
1955	83,971	125,828	1,862	628	258	1,081	1,388	55,324	3,074	78,596	8,078	966	17,440	4,329	3,194	785	30,025
1954	82,001	124,330	1,896	628	258	1,094	1,311	54,050	2,923	78,258	10,073	975	15,970	4,329	2,474	826	29,089
1953	79,380	117,547	1,647	628	242	1,014	1,142	52,624	2,788	76,428	12,005	1,030	14,560	3,720	2,002	805	27,854
1952	73,782	108,588	1,599	628	238	995	846	52,156	2,677	74,228	13,859	942	14,220	3,432	1,955	745	26,789
1951	72,472	104,230	1,599	628	238	966	750	49,712	2,542	72,488	11,572	744	13,410	3,349	1,593	708	26,059
1950	71,560	99,983	1,557	628	238	986	633	48,000	2,444	73,710	8,672	758	13,000	2,896	1,565	641	25,048
1949	70,542	96,121	1,547	628	238	974	679	47,326	2,350	74,500	9,076	736	----	----	1,389	587	23,389
1948	67,439	94,233	1,557	653	238	1,000	676	46,362	2,203	72,549	8,844	743	----	2,834	1,389	586	22,025
1947	65,709	91,241	1,585	653	238	1,000	762	45,086	2,033	71,113	8,427	668	----	2,604	1,394	511	20,420
1946	67,341	91,891	1,720	737	238	1,100	785	45,108	1,940	71,399	8,095	663	----	----	1,384	446	20,282
1945	67,314	95,505	1,720	767	246	1,084	704	44,915	1,935	72,330	10,438	472	10,500	2,291	1,327	----	19,260
1944	67,921	93,854	1,595	767	279	1,097	1,164	45,319	1,859	71,378	11,230	395	----	----	1,191	370	18,830
1943	64,188	90,589	1,563	767	(5)	1,069	771	46,669	1,789	64,555	10,409	330	----	----	797		18,772
1942	60,607	88,887	1,561	767	361	950	391	46,416	1,809	62,562	11,210	313	----	----	455		18,522
1941	57,775	85,158	1,549	845	313	787	245	47,707	1,722	62,220	(5)	317	----	----	390		16,891
1940	55,724	81,619	1,572	851	317	1,313	188	48,142	1,689	62,955	(5)	313	----	1,692	380	285	16,557
1939	56,326	81,829	1,642	851	317	1,346	131	48,071	1,646	61,272	(5)	317	----	----	375	243	16,191
1938	56,782	80,186	1,642	863	317	1,413	144	47,982	1,588	62,727	(5)	261	----	----	370	183	15,573
1937	55,557	78,148	1,642	809	317	1,368	133	48,035	1,568	62,076	(5)	261	----	----	359	180	14,458
1936	55,854	78,164	1,613	785	333	1,379	130	49,240	1,503	62,403	(5)	265	----	----	342	163	13,986
1935	57,098	78,452	1,624	799	333	1,489	130	49,389	1,481	62,757	(5)	240	----	----	341		13,888
1934	57,243	78,128	1,624	895	417	1,489	132	50,645	1,430	63,050	(5)	235	----	----	341		13,728
1933	56,511	76,767	1,612	823	417	1,458	134	51,006	1,420	62,645	(5)	227	----	----	347		13,728
1932	57,949	76,898	1,612	781	417	1,424	132	51,108	1,465	63,491	(5)	249	----	----	357		13,972
1931	58,979	75,328	1,630	775	417	1,447	125	50,768	1,439	61,468	(5)	270	----	----	261		13,643
1930	57,855	71,042	1,528	771	407	1,491	113	48,676	1,374	60,167	(5)	263	----	1,644	236		13,704
1929	57,382	69,584	1,520	711	407	1,575	100	45,816	1,281	60,357	(5)	228	----	----	212		12,933
1928	56,596	66,960	1,520	711	437	1,697	83	42,691	1,186	57,852	(5)	----	----	----	116		12,536
1927	58,701	65,344	1,490	----	437	1,692	82	40,476	1,117	52,666	(5)	----	----	----	66		12,000
1926	57,288	62,925	1,375	----	437	1,625		36,389	1,041	48,184	(5)	----	----	----	65		11,623
1925	59,847	65,962	1,335	----	427	1,478		32,919	1,042	46,809	(5)	----	----	----	55		10,500
1924	59,006	64,137	1,318	----	372	1,485		30,429	1,027	45,058	(5)	----	----	----	54		9,725
1923	59,009	63,383	1,348	----	372	1,409		27,486	----	43,763	(5)						8,970
1922	58,786	63,135	1,348	----	348	1,439		26,693	770	43,854	----						8,614
1921	57,950	61,928	1,348	----	342	1,439		27,523	689	42,821	----						8,540
1920	56,249	60,220	1,384	----	----	----		25,209	559	38,200	49,300			1,447			7,671
1919	55,182	59,174	1,408				63	25,869	473	33,700	51,000						7,500
1918	53,701	57,083	1,408					25,709	433	25,900	53,000						7,000
1917	51,368	53,914	1,244					25,132		21,600	55,000						
1916	50,438	49,266	946					24,402		18,400	55,000						6,440
1915	49,734	44,454	889				45	21,620		16,600	56,300						
1914	49,723	42,678	884					21,620		15,000	57,200						
1913	48,448	----	824					20,680		12,800	57,900						
1912	----	----	747					21,150		10,200	58,900					1	
1911	----		724					18,362		8,600	59,100						
1910	----		644				17	17,578		(5)	58,200			943			5,293
1909	----		587							(5)	57,100						
1908	----	36,545	581														
1907	34,074		568														
1906	----																
1905	----																3,858
1904	27,262	26,919															
1901	23,961	23,276												336			2,782
1900	----																
1898	18,124	15,639															
1896	----	13,236															
1895	----					(5)											
1894	----	10,780				(5)											
1892	----	8,332															
1891	----					(5)											
1889	----	7,195				(5)											
1887	----	5,852															

[1] From open hearth, Bessemer, crucible, and electric furnaces.
[2] 1944–1957 includes electrolytic refining capacity plus Lake Superior and fire-refined; 1907–1943, electrolytic capacity only.
[3] 1941–1957, slab zinc; 1926–1940, distillation and electrolytic zinc; 1921–1925, distillation zinc.
[4] Available phosphoric oxide (P₂O₅).
[5] Less than 500 tons.

Series **P 250–306.** Value of Output of Finished Commodities and Construction Materials Destined for Domestic Consumption at Current Producers' Prices, and Implicit Price Indexes for Major Commodity Groups (Shaw): 1869 to 1939

[In millions of dollars]

Year	Total, all finished commodities	Perishable								Semidurable				
		Total	Food and kindred products		Cigars, cigarettes, and tobacco	Drug, toilet, and household preparations	Magazines, newspapers, misc. paper supplies, etc.	Fuel and lighting products		Total	Dry-goods and notions	Clothing and personal furnishings	Shoes and other footwear	House-furnishings
			Manufactured	Non-manufactured				Manufactured	Non-manufactured					
	250	251	252	253	254	255	256	257	258	259	260	261	262	263
1939	31,277.7	16,073.5								5,490.6				
1938	28,156.7	15,721.6								4,852.7				
1937	33,667.8	17,295.3	9,402.3	3,683.0	1,274.1	818.4	601.9	1,335.0	180.6	5,591.3	712.9	3,258.6	828.3	340.1
1936	30,258.1	16,239.0								4,775.8				
1935	26,744.7	14,571.7	7,884.9	3,183.6	1,096.4	727.7	527.2	952.2	199.7	4,937.6	576.0	3,039.1	693.4	273.7
1934	23,166.7	12,987.2								4,501.6				
1933	18,454.1	10,872.9	5,509.5	2,451.1	910.7	626.0	470.1	707.2	198.3	3,772.8	390.4	2,274.6	597.3	218.2
1932	17,727.8	10,754.9	5,183.0	2,408.1	1,006.6	624.4	492.6	830.6	209.5	3,526.1	317.5	2,183.4	546.3	187.5
1931	24,243.3	13,431.7	6,730.2	3,133.4	1,154.9	809.0	573.5	740.2	290.5	4,931.4	1 459.4	3,087.9	705.1	256.6
1930	31,260.7	16,590.5	8,497.5	3,996.8	1,141.8	891.0	644.8	1,052.2	366.3	6,069.4	574.4	3,767.8	860.3	347.8
1929	37,782.6	18,384.0	9,463.9	4,358.3	1,243.6	984.2	683.9	1,237.8	412.3	7,458.3	791.0	4,516.4	1,081.9	416.5
1928	35,892.9	17,911.1	9,111.7	4,466.9	1,168.7	932.3	661.6	1,153.3	416.4	7,383.2	769.1	4,385.6	1,074.9	401.5
1927	34,410.2	17,263.6	8,827.3	4,360.2	1,164.5	851.9	648.4	958.9	452.5	7,390.7	798.6	4,360.2	1,077.6	396.9
1926	35,856.6	17,784.6	9,039.8	4,467.4	1,127.2	783.3	632.8	1,220.7	513.4	7,295.6	803.5	4,186.6	1,073.9	438.1
1925	34,046.3	16,870.5	8,684.0	4,335.8	1,094.4	767.0	615.7	990.1	383.5	7,134.0	816.0	4,149.2	1,044.8	404.8
1924	30,957.7	15,573.6	7,981.3	3,948.0	1,073.2	718.6	563.0	781.3	508.2	6,401.4	700.7	3,743.9	1,061.7	358.4
1923	32,168.5	15,176.0	7,554.6	4,012.9	1,050.3	698.5	550.7	746.4	562.7	7,230.3	861.9	4,347.4	1,128.2	377.3
1922	27,393.8	14,059.4	6,837.6	3,843.0	1,002.1	624.6	499.9	888.4	363.9	6,313.9	681.5	3,865.4	993.0	307.1
1921	25,864.0	14,022.9	6,548.7	4,182.4	1,053.0	562.2	474.5	714.9	487.3	5,631.7	607.4	3,345.3	953.5	277.9
1920	37,285.2	19,236.2	10,301.4	4,696.3	1,195.5	765.6	675.9	1,044.8	556.8	7,872.8	903.6	4,382.8	1,368.2	390.5
1919 ²	34,032.4	17,392.4	9,468.2	4,720.2	1,008.4	667.8	439.8	668.4	419.5	7,019.9	806.5	3,932.9	1,254.2	324.0
1919 ²	33,265.3	17,215.5	9,312.4	4,709.0	1,000.0	660.1	458.7	630.7	444.5	6,770.2	890.9	3,817.9	1,187.6	212.0
1918	29,979.8	15,807.2	8,583.6	4,280.8	864.0	636.1	445.5	580.7	416.5	6,076.1	854.8	3,361.1	1,043.2	199.9
1917	24,545.5	13,174.1	6,925.7	3,907.2	629.5	511.5	407.5	425.7	366.9	4,790.6	620.3	2,622.7	863.4	156.7
1916	18,389.4	9,893.2	5,380.1	2,693.6	522.4	420.7	352.2	262.5	261.7	3,573.7	461.6	2,025.3	705.5	112.2
1915	13,986.1	8,079.8	4,342.1	2,310.3	478.6	331.0	255.6	141.7	220.5	2,635.7	317.0	1,533.9	520.6	85.8
1914	14,054.0	8,296.5	4,484.8	2,380.1	500.9	289.0	254.4	160.4	226.9	2,709.5	337.8	1,598.1	523.8	90.0
1913	14,632.8	8,230.2	4,441.9	2,315.9	506.8	294.9	243.9	191.3	235.3	2,900.2	348.6	1,721.6	588.8	95.5
1912	14,028.0	8,100.8	4,342.3	2,410.5	468.9	289.4	233.6	142.0	214.0	2,754.4	363.2	1,656.7	531.4	85.5
1911	12,749.4	7,491.3	3,980.1	2,235.7	460.4	278.8	211.3	119.1	205.9	2,571.4	326.3	1,560.0	500.8	80.0
1910	³12,659.2	7,386.0	3,823.5	2,306.1	464.0	266.8	209.9	121.0	194.8	2,417.3	349.5	1,408.3	486.0	83.0
1909	11,825.3	6,922.1	3,617.7	2,112.5	430.5	250.3	210.6	124.7	175.8	2,447.0	368.0	1,459.7	467.9	75.0
1908	10,191.1	5,988.1	2,974.7	1,915.7	399.8	234.1	156.8	125.8	181.3	2,155.5	295.5	1,287.0	452.1	60.1
1907	11,524.3	6,452.7	3,389.7	1,886.9	405.2	249.3	196.7	128.5	196.5	2,310.1	375.5	1,335.4	454.4	68.2
1906	10,752.5	5,912.7	3,121.0	1,719.6	398.1	225.4	184.3	102.9	161.3	2,244.2	348.2	1,314.7	448.9	69.5
1905	9,451.0	5,403.6	2,856.7	1,540.0	357.2	215.8	172.5	94.4	167.0	1,925.3	318.3	1.099.7	395.9	55.7
1904	8,734.3	5,167.7	2,601.5	1,614.9	339.2	182.3	159.7	109.2	160.8	1,746.5	285.1	992.6	368.9	52.9
1903	8,702.1	5,012.7	2,516.7	1,518.9	346.0	183.1	154.2	111.5	182.3	1,734.7	302.1	981.8	352.5	53.9
1902	8,227.5	4,764.7	2,403.1	1,519.3	325.1	174.0	151.3	89.7	102.2	1,613.8	298.7	892.8	325.9	53.2
1901	7,782.2	4,620.5	2,365.0	1,420.8	327.9	155.2	134.9	84.7	132.0	1,528.5	271.1	837.9	327.4	49.4
1900	7,120.8	4,100.8	2,083.9	1,249.1	304.0	136.2	122.3	100.3	105.0	1,465.7	271.9	817.4	289.8	49.8
1899	6,586.2	3,820.9	1,955.0	1,160.9	267.4	134.6	113.0	87.7	101.8	1,374.4	255.8	743.7	292.9	42.5
1898	5,708.0	3,431.7	1,707.9	1,121.4	226.9	122.4	103.2	63.9	86.0	1,175.8	227.4	608.2	261.9	35.9
1897	5,376.1	3,222.6	1,633.7	1,032.1	197.3	115.6	92.6	62.4	89.0	1,154.0	232.3	596.8	246.3	35.7
1896	5,003.4	2,944.0	1,436.2	927.5	193.0	112.7	90.0	92.8	91.9	1,064.6	215.5	549.5	228.9	35.5
1895	5,227.2	3,119.1	1,443.7	1,079.0	202.4	111.3	94.1	95.8	92.9	1,114.7	265.7	542.2	236.0	36.4
1894	4,752.3	2,916.3	1,337.9	1,012.3	218.1	102.9	92.9	61.9	90.3	970.9	209.9	478.1	228.0	32.4
1893	5,500.4	3,314.4	1,555.3	1,182.7	218.5	104.9	98.3	54.0	100.7	1,124.2	259.4	566.9	233.6	35.9
1892	5,331.3	2,908.8	1,251.4	1,062.3	230.5	104.7	109.3	52.1	98.5	1,255.8	297.2	632.8	263.8	37.0
1891	5,284.3	2,964.9	1,308.5	1,079.2	226.6	97.9	101.2	62.7	88.9	1,196.9	289.3	603.3	244.2	35.3
1890	5,002.2	2,705.3	1,155.5	991.4	215.4	90.1	97.3	75.4	80.2	1,196.0	299.6	588.8	249.8	34.5
1889	5,080.4	2,905.7	1,434.3	956.6	202.5	81.6	93.9	59.5	77.2	1,132.9	281.7	560.8	236.1	32.1
1879	3,441.7	1,996.1	962.9	716.5	119.7	40.4	61.5	39.7	55.5	828.2	263.1	358.2	173.7	16.2
1869	2,813.3	1,594.2	673.1	699.1	74.7	37.7	30.6	29.4	49.7	665.4	224.5	229.8	185.3	12.8

¹ Does not agree with source, which is in error.
² Shaw's estimates for 1869–1919; Kuznets' estimates adjusted by Shaw for 1919–1939. See source, p. 104, for explanation.
³ Agrees with source; however, figures for components do not add to total shown.

Series P 250–306. Value of Output of Finished Commodities and Construction Materials Destined for Domestic Consumption at Current Producers' Prices, and Implicit Price Indexes for Major Commodity Groups (Shaw): 1869 to 1939—Con.

[In millions of dollars]

Year	Semidurable—Con.		Consumer durable											
	Toys, games, and sporting goods	Tires and tubes	Total	Household furniture	Heating and cooking apparatus, etc.	Electrical household appliances and supplies	Radios	Housefurnishings	China and household-utensils	Musical instruments	Jewelry, silverware, clocks, and watches	Printing and publishing books	Luggage	Passenger vehicles, motor
	264	265	266	267	268	269	270	271	272	273	274	275	276	277
1939			4,973.1											
1938			3,747.3											
1937	190.2	261.2	5,742.1	478.7	341.0	332.6	218.0	640.9	241.6	52.0	272.6	161.6	42.5	2,212.9
1936			5,158.0											
1935	140.3	215.1	4,256.8	323.7	237.5	217.8	167.4	468.3	204.8	31.5	189.5	131.1	31.0	1,688.3
1934			3,307.2											
1933	95.8	196.7	2,321.3	226.9	147.1	110.3	98.0	311.6	150.4	24.1	116.0	92.1	19.1	725.9
1932	96.9	194.5	2,047.4	205.4	123.0	82.2	94.2	252.0	138.9	35.0	108.5	102.9	18.4	603.2
1931	149.1	273.4	3,251.9	333.2	206.2	144.4	154.7	373.6	185.9	48.7	178.8	141.5	29.4	1,074.1
1930	182.2	336.9	4,272.6	441.4	254.2	160.0	230.6	402.7	196.4	103.4	263.8	174.3	44.5	1,538.0
1929	214.6	437.8	6,312.0	600.4	347.3	176.7	366.0	643.3	274.0	111.9	402.7	192.3	70.3	2,567.0
1928	200.9	551.0	5,936.1	629.3	314.2	152.7	298.7	627.5	275.7	148.6	396.3	179.7	67.9	2,294.9
1927	182.5	574.9	5,435.8	625.5	339.4	146.3	181.5	584.7	229.3	176.2	387.6	172.1	65.9	1,967.8
1926	177.2	616.3	6,109.0	638.2	364.3	137.5	206.7	591.6	271.6	189.3	398.9	155.4	66.4	2,504.3
1925	164.2	555.1	5,785.7	622.9	346.1	106.3	168.2	604.0	240.1	173.6	384.3	149.8	66.4	2,340.2
1924	154.6	382.0	5,034.3	614.0	322.2	83.4	139.3	547.1	181.5	178.5	363.9	145.0	57.8	1,922.5
1923	167.1	348.3	5,366.7	578.9	322.0	76.3	50.3	600.0	239.0	215.1	388.1	130.7	69.2	2,188.8
1922	131.1	335.8	4,056.5	501.1	239.2	58.6	26.9	470.0	167.7	187.7	327.0	124.9	52.6	1,546.1
1921	124.1	323.5	3,270.3	466.6	186.5	63.2	12.2	374.6	166.8	166.4	263.1	122.0	51.0	1,115.5
1920	148.8	678.9	4,899.3	620.5	345.6	82.8	17.0	574.8	265.7	264.2	383.2	140.0	78.2	1,628.3
1919 ²	155.8	546.6	4,075.6	509.0	242.5	65.1	14.3	430.2	201.7	242.0	427.8	128.2	70.4	1,292.6
1919 ²	146.4	515.4	3,921.2	494.7	263.5	84.5		375.2	230.1	248.3	409.7	127.4	64.2	1,286.9
1918	125.8	491.3	2,646.9	329.0	216.8	67.5		320.1	197.6	144.2	194.9	99.2	52.2	762.7
1917	198.5	329.1	2,799.0	300.6	194.2	58.8		288.6	221.7	134.7	219.2	89.8	36.7	996.7
1916	113.0	156.1	2,396.1	271.7	142.5	41.2		234.9	160.9	116.2	221.7	76.7	39.6	873.7
1915	73.5	104.9	1,700.2	212.3	119.4	23.7		181.4	126.1	90.2	144.1	73.3	25.9	537.8
1914	67.1	92.7	1,570.4	222.5	110.5	18.8		190.7	125.9	91.6	154.6	68.1	26.5	399.6
1913	64.0	86.6	1,675.1	236.7	124.9	22.2		209.3	130.2	104.4	196.0	77.8	34.0	372.8
1912	59.3	58.3	1,538.4	220.5	131.5	19.7		199.1	122.4	95.2	190.9	66.3	33.9	311.3
1911	58.7	45.5	1,339.2	204.1	104.1	15.7		187.5	116.7	81.3	186.1	59.1	36.1	209.2
1910	54.4	36.0	1,331.6	202.4	97.3	16.3		195.7	114.1	77.6	186.1	60.3	32.8	203.8
1909	52.9	23.4	1,212.8	192.0	93.8	11.8		184.2	102.9	76.8	175.9	62.9	28.5	154.3
1908	43.3	17.5	1,011.0	152.6	84.2	7.7		147.1	93.6	63.0	128.6	53.8	23.6	132.2
1907	60.9	15.6	1,178.1	185.1	101.2	10.2		182.8	120.7	87.8	180.9	56.8	27.7	89.6
1906	50.4	12.5	1,129.5	190.3	103.4	8.0		185.8	122.6	81.2	174.0	55.9	23.9	62.7
1905	46.3	9.3	954.8	160.8	85.8	4.7		156.7	108.7	71.1	144.1	56.7	20.1	35.6
1904	41.3	5.7	826.9	142.4	73.6	3.3		146.2	91.7	57.7	120.9	53.6	18.9	21.4
1903	40.1	4.3	825.7	139.2	78.8	3.8		152.5	90.8	65.1	120.5	51.5	15.8	11.3
1902	37.8	5.5	786.3	129.4	78.6	3.2		146.8	78.5	57.2	117.0	49.2	14.9	9.3
1901	36.5	6.2	718.9	118.7	70.7	2.6		128.8	73.5	48.8	103.6	47.4	13.1	7.8
1900	29.0	7.8	658.7	106.9	61.9	2.4		126.8	69.5	42.4	100.0	44.3	12.0	6.0
1899	27.0	12.7	634.3	104.1	59.2	1.9		115.6	60.9	34.2	97.1	45.0	12.6	4.2
1898	23.4	19.0	528.9	89.4	46.3			95.4	52.0	27.8	74.0	40.8	8.8	
1897	24.8	18.1	506.5	88.4	50.7			96.0	51.0	24.5	63.6	33.7	8.8	
1896	25.4	9.8	475.2	90.2	45.6			90.6	51.0	22.8	58.5	34.6	9.2	
1895	26.4	7.9	497.7	94.0	35.5			102.6	45.9	27.9	69.2	35.6	8.9	
1894	22.4		429.3	82.4	31.0			88.9	39.3	19.9	58.3	28.4	11.1	
1893	28.4		496.3	100.2	35.3			100.1	43.5	23.2	71.7	34.3	12.9	
1892	25.0		579.3	115.0	38.9			112.6	52.9	34.6	90.3	34.9	15.6	
1891	24.8		556.8	100.5	39.1			114.9	51.7	33.0	86.7	33.4	13.9	
1890	23.3		538.7	95.3	37.9			103.9	49.3	32.9	90.2	33.9	13.4	
1889	22.3		499.2	93.4	38.9			97.6	46.4	28.2	74.5	34.7	10.7	
1879	17.0		304.3	65.2	23.0			56.7	31.2	14.3	43.3	19.1	7.1	
1869	13.0		262.7	58.5	26.4			40.1	26.0	10.8	41.6	8.4	7.7	

² Shaw's estimates for 1869–1919; Kuznets' estimates adjusted by Shaw for 1919–1939.   See source, p. 104, for explanation.

Series **P 250–306.** Value of Output of Finished Commodities and Construction Materials Destined for Domestic Consumption at Current Producers' Prices, and Implicit Price Indexes for Major Commodity Groups (Shaw): 1869 to 1939—Con.

[In millions of dollars]

Year	Consumer durable—Con.						Producer durable							
	Motor vehicle accessories	Passenger vehicles (horse drawn) and accessories	Motorcycles and bicycles	Pleasure craft	Ophthalmic products and artificial limbs	Monuments and tombstones	Total	Industrial machinery and equipment	Tractors	Electrical equipment, industrial and commercial	Farm equipment	Office and store machinery and equipment	Office and store furniture and fixtures	Locomotive and railroad cars
	278	279	280	281	282	283	284	285	286	287	288	289	290	291
1939							4,740.5							
1938							3,835.1							
1937	594.6		30.8	25.4	70.9	26.0	5,039.1	1,883.7	223.7	673.8	668.5	204.9	176.8	119.1
1936							4,085.3							
1935	463.6		16.8	14.1	50.1	21.3	2,978.6	1,126.0	133.3	361.2	345.3	140.6	111.1	33.0
1934							2,370.7							
1933	228.2		7.5	4.8	39.1	20.8	1,487.1	577.1	12.6	200.9	78.8	78.8	70.3	13.6
1932	211.9		4.6	9.3	32.0	25.7	1,399.4	525.8	15.8	215.5	70.9	78.5	74.9	37.0
1931	273.1		7.7	16.8	40.3	43.6	2,628.3	938.2	19.6	499.5	163.4	116.5	151.7	78.0
1930	326.1		9.2	24.6	48.3	54.9	4,328.2	1,457.8	95.4	722.2	338.5	165.5	203.5	352.7
1929	407.6		10.6	26.2	52.1	63.6	5,628.4	2,017.2	121.8	1,000.1	386.5	217.8	288.7	347.6
1928	411.7		12.0	17.4	48.7	61.0	4,662.5	1,644.1	104.1	895.0	356.5	213.6	245.8	245.1
1927	419.8		10.1	17.8	49.7	61.9	4,320.2	1,476.0	91.3	741.2	340.4	201.2	249.0	318.5
1926	440.2		11.9	22.4	46.6	63.8	4,667.5	1,606.8	87.4	776.4	355.4	200.1	242.3	399.3
1925	444.3		11.3	15.0	46.6	66.8	4,256.0	1,486.4	70.3	666.2	306.5	196.4	236.1	353.1
1924	337.2		13.0	14.0	48.6	66.4	3,948.5	1,303.8	52.1	655.0	265.9	179.2	229.5	481.1
1923	355.8		16.3	12.1	58.5	65.6	4,395.5	1,510.9	63.5	598.1	315.5	182.0	201.3	635.5
1922	243.4		8.9	6.2	48.6	47.6	2,964.0	1,085.2	43.4	415.8	160.7	132.4	136.8	265.6
1921	169.5		10.2	9.4	46.6	46.9	2,939.1	922.8	49.6	406.6	248.1	114.0	115.5	313.6
1920	313.4		20.8	14.7	67.8	82.3	5,277.0	1,635.8	197.4	557.9	270.6	160.6	135.1	563.3
1919 [2]	282.6		24.0	13.9	58.2	73.4	5,544.5	1,434.3	171.6	460.8	394.6	156.4	100.3	560.7
1919 [2]	168.0	26.4	19.0	5.1	45.0	73.4	5,358.4	1,440.5	152.6	365.7	343.8	125.4	86.4	460.9
1918	85.8	35.3	18.9	1.5	71.1	50.0	5,449.7	1,575.8	136.6	339.9	301.8	157.8	65.7	734.0
1917	120.5	38.8	16.7	3.3	36.5	42.3	3,781.8	1,358.1	50.7	325.2	250.0	140.5	61.3	610.6
1916	104.0	31.0	16.3	4.0	23.9	37.9	2,526.3	906.0	25.8	253.9	237.1	98.8	51.6	363.4
1915	61.0	30.5	13.3	3.4	20.2	37.5	1,570.4	536.8	22.7	160.2	205.1	63.0	43.3	142.2
1914	49.9	35.6	16.2	3.6	15.5	41.0	1,477.6	460.2	16.7	147.0	187.8	50.9	50.8	203.2
1913	46.1	40.1	21.9	4.1	12.3	42.1	1,827.3	543.4	4.4	177.1	202.4	55.4	54.3	422.5
1912	39.3	41.6	12.0	3.9	10.6	40.3	1,634.5	517.1	8.1	162.1	187.3	50.2	54.3	303.4
1911	26.3	45.9	9.4	4.3	10.9	42.4	1,347.6	476.6		133.5	168.2	43.8	48.7	161.7
1910	26.9	53.3	7.3	4.4	10.7	42.6	[3]1,524.2	512.4		144.4	170.6	48.4	50.1	203.3
1909	21.1	49.8	5.6	4.3	10.5	38.4	1,243.4	446.9		111.2	166.5	40.1	48.6	127.0
1908	17.3	48.8	4.9	3.4	9.3	40.9	1,036.5	331.2		83.2	137.7	27.9	40.4	137.1
1907	11.3	63.8	6.5	6.1	9.4	38.3	1,583.5	510.9		127.5	161.6	42.7	49.1	351.2
1906	7.8	62.4	4.9	4.3	7.9	34.5	1,466.1	504.6		119.9	160.5	38.8	50.7	299.4
1905	4.3	61.2	5.4	3.8	7.1	28.7	1,167.3	404.7		84.9	130.2	28.0	4.31	214.3
1904	2.5	57.8	2.5	3.1	5.6	25.7	993.2	327.1		75.9	125.2	20.3	38.2	162.7

Year	Consumer durable—Con.					Producer durable—Con.						
	Passenger vehicles (horse drawn) and accessories	Motorcycles and bicycles	Pleasure craft	Ophthalmic products and artificial limbs	Monuments and tombstones	Total	Industrial machinery and equipment	Electrical equipment, industrial and commercial	Farm equipment	Office and store machinery and equipment	Office and store furniture and fixtures	Locomotive and railroad cars
	279	280	281	282	283	284	285	287	288	289	290	291
1903	56.7	4.2	3.6	5.8	25.9	1,129.0	405.9	91.9	120.2	23.9	37.8	194.6
1902	58.8	6.4	3.5	5.7	27.9	1,062.7	371.3	80.6	152.9	21.9	33.6	157.8
1901	64.1	7.7	3.7	5.2	23.2	914.3	330.3	68.5	110.4	18.9	30.2	127.4
1900	50.1	10.5	2.7	4.7	18.4	895.6	347.6	68.2	100.6	19.7	27.2	130.0
1899	53.5	18.9	2.1	4.8	20.3	756.6	267.5	56.1	99.4	14.3	24.2	114.1
1898	43.5	27.8	1.4	4.3	17.5	571.6	194.9	34.3	85.6	10.6	21.4	82.1
1897	40.9	27.0	1.2	4.0	16.6	492.9	182.3	24.4	58.4	9.7	21.8	67.7
1896	39.3	14.9	1.2	3.8	13.4	519.6	209.8	20.5	46.6	11.6	22.5	75.2
1895	45.2	14.1	1.3	3.7	13.8	495.7	193.1	20.0	59.3	10.7	23.7	53.7
1894	50.9		1.0	3.3	14.9	435.7	157.7	15.8	58.7	8.6	21.2	47.4
1893	58.5		1.4	3.3	11.9	565.5	184.9	16.6	71.2	9.5	26.1	104.1
1892	63.3		1.5	3.2	16.6	587.4	196.5	22.7	75.4	9.8	30.1	90.9
1891	62.4		1.6	2.9	16.7	565.7	185.5	23.7	75.3	9.0	26.8	87.6
1890	60.4		1.5	2.6	17.3	562.2	185.6	21.8	89.0	8.7	25.8	81.5
1889	54.0	1.9	1.5	2.3	15.2	542.6	184.5	13.1	83.9	8.2	25.6	87.3
1879	35.1		.9	.8	7.5	313.1	98.6	1.9	67.3	3.6	15.9	36.3
1869	35.7		.6	.4	6.6	291.0	110.4		50.0	3.1	13.6	40.8

[2] Shaw's estimates for 1869–1919; Kuznets' estimates adjusted by Shaw for 1919–1939. See source, p. 104, for explanation.
[3] Agrees with source; however, figures for components do not add to total shown.

Series P 250–306. Value of Output of Finished Commodities and Construction Materials Destined for Domestic Consumption at Current Producers' Prices, and Implicit Price Indexes for Major Commodity Groups (Shaw): 1869 to 1939—Con.

[In millions of dollars]

Year	Producer durable—Con.							Construction materials			Implicit price index (1913 =100)				
	Ships and boats	Business vehicles, motor	Business vehicles (horse drawn)	Aircraft	Professional and scientific equipment	Carpenters' and mechanics' tools	Misc. subsidiary durable equipment	Total	Manufactured	Non-manufactured	Perishable	Semidurable	Consumer durable	Producer durable	Construction materials
	292	293	294	295	296	297	298	299	300	301	302	303	304	305	306
1939								3,701.6			[4] 110.6	[4] 123.1	[4] 92.1	[5] 110.4	159.0
1938								3,159.0			[4] 114.6	[4] 122.7	[4] 92.8	[4] 112.8	159.0
1937	128.6	496.6		48.4	49.8	95.3	269.9	3,945.8			126.4	132.6	91.9	112.1	167.3
1936								3,331.5			[4] 122.6	[4] 120.6	[4] 90.8	[4] 102.0	152.2
1935	48.2	359.3		19.1	36.4	66.3	198.8	2,375.0			122.4	119.2	93.6	99.6	149.8
1934								1,909.9			[4] 107.8	[4] 120.6	[4] 98.5	[4] 107.6	151.4
1933	30.4	159.0		16.5	32.0	49.1	168.1	1,536.1			95.0	105.0	96.8	104.6	136.0
1932	49.7	125.5		14.1	31.7	31.0	129.0	1,362.7			96.7	93.6	98.0	112.9	126.8
1931	82.0	247.0		30.0	48.6	53.9	199.9	2,552.1			114.1	109.2	99.8	117.2	140.2
1930	94.9	373.0		28.8	91.6	99.8	304.7	3,779.8			135.1	122.0	104.3	125.6	158.4
1929	78.2	510.8		56.0	109.6	124.6	369.7	5,007.5			147.4	130.7	106.4	131.1	167.8
1928	60.4	318.3		51.1	92.1	131.6	304.9	4,793.8			150.0	131.7	105.4	136.5	165.6
1927	70.8	302.3		19.4	87.7	104.2	318.4	4,845.2			146.9	137.4	104.0	138.5	166.6
1926	86.5	377.2		17.6	86.5	110.2	321.9	5,111.5			154.3	150.4	98.8	138.4	175.6
1925	55.7	389.6		10.5	74.9	109.8	300.4	4,950.4			154.3	160.0	103.3	135.0	178.5
1924	67.4	323.4		10.9	66.0	106.4	208.0	4,465.3			143.5	164.9	108.5	134.8	179.5
1923	73.1	321.8		11.5	64.7	115.4	302.1	4,647.3			147.7	177.6	108.2	138.7	190.4
1922	93.6	237.2		8.8	51.7	87.8	245.1	3,568.9			141.2	163.2	113.4	135.2	170.7
1921	272.7	170.4		6.1	48.8	62.1	208.6	2,956.7			146.5	173.8	139.8	164.5	172.2
1920	808.1	332.9		8.7	74.8	128.7	403.0	4,777.1			213.4	265.6	157.8	181.0	262.0
1919 [2]	1,381.3	344.3		10.0	62.0	120.6	347.6	3,508.1			196.5	219.0	134.5	184.1	202.7
1919 [2]	1,389.5	344.0	42.5	8.4	74.5	174.8	349.3	3,703.2	3,224.5	478.7	199.9	212.4	136.4	185.0	202.7
1918	805.3	417.0	50.6	174.7	119.2	210.6	360.7	3,217.5	2,824.6	392.8	182.8	206.2	121.9	175.7	174.5
1917	243.8	189.1	51.1	21.3	57.0	131.7	291.6	3,058.6	2,702.9	355.7	161.1	161.0	100.8	145.5	154.9
1916	103.7	111.6	37.4	1.4	32.5	97.5	205.6	2,627.8	2,309.5	318.2	120.6	117.6	90.4	120.5	119.0
1915	66.8	68.6	34.0	.6	29.4	57.0	140.6	2,010.7	1,732.9	277.8	103.7	96.5	90.3	106.4	94.6
1914	43.5	36.2	36.9	.2	23.7	49.6	171.0	2,043.8	1,758.7	285.2	101.4	96.5	94.4	100.3	93.1
1913	47.6	47.1	39.9	.2	17.7	53.6	161.7	2,384.4	2,083.2	301.2	100.0	100.0	100.0	100.0	100.0
1912	44.4	49.9	41.9	.3	14.2	48.5	152.8	2,154.1	1,854.9	299.2	102.8	98.6	66.2	97.6	97.9
1911	42.7	25.9	44.2		13.4	41.9	147.1	1,942.8	1,655.4	287.4	96.2	97.4	95.8	99.1	97.0
1910	40.8	12.5	48.3		12.6	49.1	151.6	2,049.7	1,728.0	321.7	100.0	100.9	93.5	95.3	97.6
1909	38.2	7.3	43.0		12.4	47.7	154.6	1,992.5	1,686.7	305.8	96.9	99.3	90.4	94.3	94.8
1908	34.4	3.5	40.2		8.0	35.7	157.4	1,820.1	1,513.9	306.3	92.3	96.0	96.6	89.3	93.3
1907	66.3	2.3	49.5		11.8	52.7	157.9	2,111.5	1,770.1	341.4	89.7	102.6	97.7	93.6	101.0
1906	54.8	1.8	46.2		10.7	43.4	135.2	1,911.1	1,622.8	288.3	84.9	98.2	89.1	90.6	96.6
1905	55.6	1.5	43.1		8.2	37.9	115.6	1,578.1	1,334.0	244.1	86.9	90.5	85.3	89.7	87.0
1904	53.6	1.4	38.9		6.4	34.7	108.7	1,394.3	1,167.3	227.0	85.5	86.0	83.5	88.8	81.7
1903	61.3		37.6		7.8	37.7	110.4	1,447.4	1,218.9	228.4	83.3	86.0	82.7	86.2	84.5
1902	60.8		37.9		7.5	35.7	102.8	1,493.6	1,270.6	223.0	84.1	83.5	79.9	89.7	82.5
1901	64.7		40.2		5.0	29.2	89.5	1,306.3	1,119.2	187.1	79.6	81.9	77.5	88.9	80.7
1900	46.9		31.4		5.3	26.9	91.8	1,222.7	1,046.8	175.8	80.2	86.7	77.0	90.0	85.8
1899	36.1		32.5		4.0	24.5	83.9	1,006.3	855.7	150.6	75.4	81.0	70.0	88.1	80.7
1898	24.4		25.9		3.2	19.8	69.4	937.8	795.8	141.9	74.9	77.3	67.5	82.5	69.9
1897	20.7		24.2		2.7	16.8	64.2	963.4	821.0	142.4	72.0	75.5	63.0	75.9	67.1
1896	20.8		23.0		3.2	18.6	67.9	880.3	751.4	128.9	70.9	75.5	63.8	66.1	71.8
1895	22.7		25.7		3.0	19.1	64.8	1,033.2	881.2	152.0	75.0	77.1	67.4	72.2	70.7
1894	17.8		28.4		2.5	16.6	61.0	1,004.1	867.0	137.1	76.3	80.5	72.3	78.2	71.6
1893	23.9		32.1		3.0	22.5	71.7	1,074.3	933.1	141.3	84.7	90.5	74.8	78.4	75.4
1892	24.9		34.1		3.5	24.6	74.9	1,335.5	1,164.8	170.7	79.8	92.6	79.2	80.0	75.9
1891	26.9		33.5		3.2	24.7	69.5	1,076.0	940.0	136.0	84.8	92.6	82.1	81.1	80.2
1890	24.6		32.0		3.2	23.6	66.5	1,216.5	1,070.5	146.1	86.1	94.9	82.3	87.7	84.3
1889	24.7		28.4		2.9	20.8	63.3	838.9	712.2	126.7	88.3	95.6	81.9	88.2	85.0
1879	19.4		18.0		1.6	13.4	37.1	444.2	365.9	78.3	86.6	102.2	83.2	95.4	81.4
1869	11.5		18.1		1.6	10.5	31.4	377.4	324.8	52.6	141.2	158.5	119.4	163.8	107.4

[1] Does not agree with source, which is in error.
[2] Shaw's estimates for 1869–1919; Kuznets' estimates adjusted by Shaw for 1919–1939. See source, p. 104, for explanation.
[3] Agrees with source; however, figures for components do not add to total shown.
[4] Indexes derived by weighting the individual group indexes by the average current price estimates for 1933, 1935, and 1937. The composite indexes thus calculated were used to interpolate and extrapolate the implicit indexes for 1933, 1935, and 1937.
[5] Based on the movement of the NBER price index for processed capital equipment goods.

Transportation

RAIL TRANSPORTATION (Series Q 1–152)

Q 1–11. **Railroad and other domestic intercity freight traffic, by type of transportation, 1939–1957.**

Source: 1939–1954, Interstate Commerce Commission, *Intercity Ton-Miles, 1939–1954*, Statement No. 568 (mimeographed), 1956; 1955–1957, ICC, *Annual Report*, various issues.

For description of estimates, see Statement No. 568.

Q 12–14. **Indexes of transportation output, 1889–1953.**

Source: 1889–1946, Harold Barger, *The Transportation Industries, 1889 to 1946*, National Bureau of Economic Research, New York, 1951; 1947–1953, National Bureau of Economic Research, unpublished estimates by John W. Kendrick.

Sources of figures and methods of computation are described in Barger's book. The components of series Q 13, passenger traffic, are airlines, intercity buslines, waterways, and steam railroads. For series Q 14, freight traffic, the components are motor trucking, pipelines, waterways, and steam railroads.

Q 15–31. **Railroad mileage, equipment, and passenger and freight service, 1830–1890.**

Source: Interstate Commerce Commission, *Railway Statistics Before 1890*, Statement No. 32151 (mimeographed), 1932.

Before 1890, the principal source of continuous information on railroads is the annual *Poor's Manual of Railroads*. The figures in the *Manual* were revised in successive issues. The Interstate Commerce Commission consulted the issues from 1869 to 1900 and evidently took account of the revisions. Earnings and traffic figures are understatements of actual level; mileage covered is shown in the table below. Similar but not identical figures, with the degree of coverage similarly indicated in terms of mileage, appear in Bureau of the Census, *Report on Transportation Business in the United States at the Eleventh Census*, 1890, part I.

Table I.   Miles of Road Operated by Railroads

Year	Roads reporting earnings [1]	Roads reporting earnings and traffic statistics	Year	Roads reporting earnings [1]
1890	158,037	157,976	1879	79,009
1889	153,945	153,689	1878	78,960
1888	145,387	145,341	1877	74,112
1887	137,028	136,986	1876	73,508
1886	125,185	125,146		
			1875	71,759
1885	123,320	122,110	1874	69,273
1884	115,704	113,172	1873	66,237
1883	110,414	106,938	1872	57,323
1882	104,971	95,752	1871	44,614
1881	92,971			
1880	82,146		1851	8,836

[1] Includes elevated railways.

All figures except those for series Q 15 and Q 17 are based on reports of individual railroads for fiscal years ending in the calendar year indicated. The period of time covered is therefore not the same for all carriers included. Balance sheet and equipment data pertain to the ends of such fiscal years.

Data for 1890 shown in these series do not agree with 1890 data shown for series Q 44–72 because of different sources.

Q 32. **Freight service, ton-miles carried, 13 railroads, 1865–1885.**

Source: H. V. and H. W. Poor, *Manual of Railroads*, New York City, 1888, p. XXVIII.

The roads represented are 7 eastern roads (Pennsylvania; Pittsburgh, Fort Wayne, and Chicago; New York Central; Lake Shore; Michigan Central; Boston and Albany; New York, Lake Erie and Western) and 6 western roads (Illinois Central; Chicago and Alton; Chicago and Rock Island; Chicago; Burlington and Quincy; Chicago and Northwestern; Chicago, Milwaukee, and St. Paul).

Q 33–42. **Railroad property investment, capital, income, and expenses, 1850–1890.**

Source: See source for series Q 15–31.

See also text for same series.

Q 43. **Miles of railroad built, 1830–1925.**

Source: 1830–1879, Tenth Census Reports, vol. IV, *Report on the Agencies of Transportation in the United States*, p. 289; 1893–1925, *Railway Age*, vol. 104, No. 1, Simmons-Boardman Publishing Corp., New York, January 1, 1938, p. 66.

For a more detailed discussion of the problems of estimating miles of railroad built, see E. R. Wicker, "United States Railway Investment in the Pre-Civil War Period," and George R. Taylor, "Comments on E. R. Wicker's Paper," in *Studies in Income and Wealth*, Princeton University Press, vol. 24 (forthcoming).

The Tenth Census report (pp. 289–293, 300–375) contains materials on history of construction which includes figures on mileage built and existent, by groups of States, for individual companies, annually from 1830 to 1880. Somewhat similar data appear in Bureau of the Census, *Report on Transportation Business in the United States at the Eleventh Census: 1890*, part 1, pp. 3–5, 54–107.

According to the Bureau of the Census, information was received from every railroad known to exist in 1880. The letter of instructions from the Superintendent of the Census to the railroads said: "In cases . . . in which the records have been lost, the officers of such companies and roads are requested to obtain . . . this information in the best form possible. The recollection of officers and employees long in the service of a road may be used . . . if more reliable data be not accessible."

The *Railway Age* obtained its figures at annual intervals from individual railroads and from State railroad commissions.

It is not clear just when a mile of road would be reported as built. Construction of some lines extended over several years. Each annual segment may have been reported when finished, or nothing may have been reported until the whole line was completed. The year of physical completion may have differed from the year in which traffic was first carried. In such cases, the mileage may have been assigned to either year.

The Census Bureau figures pertain only to miles in operation in the census year. The figures for any year are, therefore, understatements to the extent that mileage constructed in that year may have been abandoned by June 1, 1880 (the date of the 1880 Census).

The change from year to year in miles operated (series Q 15) or miles owned (series Q 16) is sometimes used as a measure of miles constructed. The annual change in miles operated, however, is also affected by acquisitions of trackage rights, as a result of which the same line may be counted in the operation of two or more railroads. Both the change in miles operated and that in miles owned are affected by abandonments during the year (regardless of when constructed).

Q 44–152. General note.

The principal sources of these series are various issues of two annual publications of the Interstate Commerce Commission: For 1954–1957, *Transport Statistics of the United States*, part 1; and for all years prior to 1954, *Statistics of Railways in the United States*.

No attempt has been made to adjust the figures for the effect of changes in methods of accounting and reporting; hence, the data for the various years are often only approximately comparable.

Although railroads regulated by the ICC are still described legally as "steam railways," most train and switching operations are now performed by Diesel locomotives, and some divisions of the railways included are electrified. The Commission has also regulated a small and diminishing number of railways of the interurban electric type which are not included in the figures shown here.

Railway *operating* companies are those whose officers direct the actual transportation service and whose books contain operating as well as financial accounts. *Lessor* companies maintain a separate legal existence, but their properties are operated by the lessees. *Proprietary* companies are also nonoperating companies. Their outstanding capitalization is owned by other railway companies. The term "circular" refers to roads (operating or nonoperating) for which brief circulars showing date of incorporation, mileage, and a few of the facts were filed with the Interstate Commerce Commission. They include intrastate roads and roads under construction. The term "unofficial" is used to indicate roads for which official returns were not received by the ICC—the figures having been taken from the returns by roads in prior years, and items contained in railway and engineering periodicals and newspapers, corrected in accordance with the best information available.

Switching and terminal companies are those operating separately for joint account or for revenue. Services such as those of switching and terminal companies are mostly performed directly by the line-haul carriers as an ordinary part of their business. Line haul denotes train movements between terminals and stations on main and branch lines of the road, exclusive of switching.

Beginning in 1911, the ICC classified operating companies on the basis of operating revenues. Those of Class I had annual revenues above $1,000,000; Class II, above $100,000; Class III, below $100,000. Beginning in 1956, the minimum for Class I was raised to $3,000,000 and the other two classes were consolidated. If the revenues of a company fall below the limit, it is not reclassified until the decline appears to be permanent. The relative importance of Class I railroads has increased since 1911 because of the growth of traffic and the absorption of small roads in larger systems. The ratio of operating revenues of Class I line-haul companies to the total revenues of Classes I, II, and III was 96.48 percent in 1911, 97.45 percent in 1916, 98.07 percent in 1926, 98.76 percent in 1941, and 99.06 percent in 1945.

A collection of definitions of words or phrases frequently used in discussions of railway statistics has been issued by the ICC, entitled *Railway Statistical Terms*, Statement No. 4119, June 1941. For financial terms, see ICC, *Uniform System of Accounts for Steam Railroads.*

Statistics of mileage in existence and stocks of equipment, and balance sheet items, pertain to the end of the year indicated.

Q 44–72. Railroad mileage, equipment, and passenger traffic and revenue, 1890–1957.

Source: All series, except series Q 53–54, see general note for series Q 44–152. Series Q 53–54, American Railway Car Institute, *Railroad Car Facts*, New York, annual issues.

Q 45, mileage constructed. Miles on which operations were begun during the year. Figures exclude relocated road or road constructed to shorten distance without serving new territory.

Q 46, mileage abandoned. Miles on which operation was permanently abandoned during the year, the cost of which was written out of the investment accounts or was scheduled to be written out at the end of the year.

Q 49, track operated, first main track. Equivalent to miles of road operated. Figures exceed those for series Q 47, road owned, in some years because of two or more roads operating on same line under trackage agreements.

Q 60, average tractive effort. Figures represent the force in pounds exerted by locomotives, measured at the rim of the driving wheels.

Q 61–63, passenger-train cars. Includes coaches and parlor, sleeping, dining, club, lounge, observation, postal, baggage, express, and other cars, as well as cars serving a combination of purposes.

Q 64, freight-train cars. Includes cabooses as well as freight-carrying cars.

Q 71, passenger revenue. Excludes revenue from services such as handling of excess baggage or mail; sleeping and parlor or chair car reservations; dining and buffet service on trains; station, train, and boat privileges; parcel rooms; storage of baggage; or other miscellaneous services and facilities connected with the transportation of passengers. Passenger revenue depends upon the established tariffs (the published schedules of rates and fares) and includes extra fares on limited trains, additional railway fares for the exclusive use of space, mileage and scrip coupons honored, or revenue from the transportation of corpses.

Q 72, revenue per passenger mile. Represents figures for series Q 71 divided by those for series Q 67.

Q 73–86. Railroad freight traffic and revenue, 1890–1957.

Source: See general note for series Q 44–152.

Revenue-tons and ton-miles exclude the movement of a railroad company's materials and supplies on its own lines. A carload is a shipment of 10,000 pounds or more of one commodity from one shipper to one consignee.

Tons originated are tons identified as not having had previous line-haul transportation by other rail carriers; such shipments include import traffic and traffic from outlying possessions of the United States received from water carriers at the port of entry, and finished products from transit points. Tonmiles are computed by multiplying the weight of each shipment by the distance it moves and summing the products.

For definitions of Class I, II, and III roads, see general note for series Q 44–152.

Q 75, products of agriculture. Includes not only raw farm products but simple manufactures such as flour, corn meal, cottonseed meal, cake, and linters. On the other hand, such products as vegetable oils, sugar and molasses, canned fruits and vegetables, and manufactured tobacco are included in series Q 79, manufactures and miscellaneous.

Q 77, products of mines. Includes coke as well as coal and other raw minerals.

Q 78, products of forests. Includes not only raw forest products but lumber, shingles, lath; box, crate and cooperage materials; veneer and built-up wood.

Q 84, freight revenue. Includes revenue from the transportation of freight and from transit, stop, diversion, and reconsignment arrangements upon the basis of tariffs. Excludes revenue from such activities as switching of freight-train cars; water transfers of freight, vehicles, and livestock; movement of freight trains at a rate per train-mile or for a lump sum; storage of freight; demurrage; grain elevators; stockyards; or other miscellaneous services and facilities connected with the transportation of freight.

Q 87–88. Railroad passenger-miles per car-mile and per train-mile, 1890–1957.

Source: Interstate Commerce Commission, *Revenue Traffic Statistics*, December issues.

Figures for passenger-miles per car-mile for 1908–1919, and for passenger-miles per train-mile for 1890–1932, were computed by the National Bureau of Economic Research from figures for passenger-miles, car-miles, and train-miles presented in *Statistics of Railways in the United States*.

Q 89. Passenger train-miles per train-hour, 1936–1957.

Source: Interstate Commerce Commission, *Passenger Train Performance*, December issues.

The train-hour figures upon which these figures are based are reckoned from the time a train leaves its original terminal to the time it arrives at its final terminal. Time spent in stopping to take on and discharge traffic and other delays on the road is included.

Q 90–92. Railroad freight revenue ton-miles per loaded car-mile, train-mile, and mile of road, 1890–1957.

Source: See general note for series Q 44–152.

Q 93. Freight train-miles per train-hour, 1920–1957.

Source: Interstate Commerce Commission, *Freight Train Performance*, December issues.

For explanation of train-hour figures, see text for series Q 89.

Q 94. Freight car-miles per car-day, 1921–1957.

Source: See general note for series Q 44–152.

Days of unserviceable cars are included in the divisor.

Q 95–102. Railroad property investment and capital, 1890–1957.

Source: See general note for series Q 44–152.

Q 95, investment, book value. Figures represent recorded value, in the accounts of carriers, of land, fixed improvements such as roadbed and track, rolling stock, maintenance machinery, etc., owned by them. Figures include property held under contract for purchase.

Q 96, depreciation reserve. Figures represent the accumulated accounting allowance for loss in service value not restored by current maintenance. The loss in value is incurred in connection with the consumption or prospective retirement of physical property in the course of service from causes against which carriers are not protected by insurance, which are known to be in current operation, and the effect of which can be forecast with a reasonable approach to accuracy.

Q 100, funded debt unmatured. Funded debt is debt maturing more than one year from date of issue.

Q 101, net capitalization. Figures represent railway capital outstanding, series Q 97, minus stocks and debt of railroad companies held by other railroad companies.

Q 103–105. Railroad capital expenditures for additions and betterments, 1921–1957.

Source: Association of American Railroads, Bureau of Railway Economics, *Railroad Transportation*, annual issues.

Additions comprise: Additional facilities such as equipment (rolling stock), tracks, buildings and other structures; additions to such facilities, such as extensions to tracks, buildings and other structures; additional ties laid in existing tracks; and additional devices applied to facilities such as airbrakes applied to cars not previously thus equipped.

Betterments comprise improvements of existing facilities through the substitution of superior parts for inferior parts retired, such as the substitution of steel-tired wheels for cast wheels under equipment, the application of heavier rail in tracks, the strengthening of bridges by the substitution of heavier members, and the application of superior floors or roofs in buildings.

Q 106–116. Railroad income and expenses, and interest and dividends, 1890–1957.

Source: See general note for series Q 44–152.

Q 106, operating revenue. Includes revenue from freight, passenger, and other transportation and incidental services.

Q 107–109, operating expenses. Includes current depreciation.

Q 110, tax accruals. Taxes imposed by any form of government whether based on an assessed value of the property, on amounts of stocks and bonds, on earnings, income, dividends declared, payroll, number of passengers, quantity of freight, length of road, rolling stock, or other basis. Tax accruals do not include special assessments for street and other improvements, nor special benefit taxes such as water assessments.

Q 111, operating income. Figures represent net revenue from railway operations (series Q 106 minus series Q 107) less tax accruals (series Q 110).

Q 112, net operating income. Figures represent operating income (series Q 111) minus net payable balance of equipment and joint facility rents. The equipment rents deducted at this point are those for equipment leased for less than one year, or interchanged. They are usually on a per day or per mile basis.

Q 113, net income. Figures represent net operating income (series Q 112) plus other income, minus miscellaneous deductions and fixed and contingent charges. Fixed charges are mainly rent for leased roads and equipment (i.e., equipment leased for one year or more), and interest (except contingent interest).

Q 116, interest accrued on funded debt. Figures include interest not paid during year on debt in default of interest; exclude interest on debt owned by issuing company, or on debt incurred for new lines, extensions, additions or betterments, accrued before such property is completed or comes into service.

Q 117–123. Railroad tax accruals, 1921–1957.

Source: See general note for series Q 44–152.

Other taxes (series Q 123) are largely property taxes levied by State or local governments.

Q 124. Miles of railroad operated by receivers or trustees, 1894–1957.

Source: See general note for series Q 44–152.

Q 125–127. Railroad highway grade crossings, 1925–1957.

Source: See general note for series Q 44–152.

Specially protected highway grade crossings (series Q 126) include crossings with operated gates, watchmen, or both, during at least part of day, and those with audible signals, visible signals, or both; exclude those with fixed signs only.

Q 128–137. Fuel received, ties and rails laid, and purchases by railroads, 1917–1957.

Source: Series Q 128–134, see general note for series Q 44–152. Series Q 135–137, Association of American Railroads, *Railroad Transportation*, annual issues.

Q 128–130, fuel received. Figures include not only fuel for operation of trains but fuel for station, shop, or other use.

Q 131, new rails laid. Figures include both rails laid in replacement and rails laid in additional tracks, new lines, and extensions.

Q 132–133, cross-ties laid. Figures for 1917–1926 include only ties laid in replacement. In 1927, 78,340,000 ties were laid in replacement only. Treated ties are those which have been subjected to some preservative process, e.g., creosoting, before being placed in the track.

Q 138–140. Pullman Company operations, 1915–1957.

Source: Interstate Commerce Commission, *Statistics of Railways in the United States* and *Transport Statistics in the United States*, part 2, *The Pullman Company (Sleeping Car Companies)*, various annual issues; except **series Q 139**, 1915–1921, Office of Business Economics, *Survey of Current Business*, January 1939, p. 18.

Figures for series Q 139 exceed those in series Q 70, parlor and sleeping car passenger-miles, mainly because travel of

railroad employees, etc. (for which railroad companies receive no revenue) is not included in series Q 70; but if Pullman accommodations are paid for, the travel is included in series Q 139.

The number of Pullman employees (series Q 140) is the number on the payroll at the end of the year.

Q 141–142. Railroad employees and compensation, 1890–1957.

Source: See general note for series Q 44–152.

An employee is defined as a person in the service of a railroad, subject to its continuing authority to supervise and direct the manner of rendition of his service. Persons such as lawyers engaged to render only specifically defined service for specific cases and not under general or continuing retainer are not classed as employees. For 1890–1914, the number of employees is the number on the payroll at the end of the year. Thereafter, the nature of the figures included for the smaller (Class II and III) roads is not clear in the source. For Class I roads they appear to be averages of 4 quarterly counts, 1915–1920, and of 2 quarterly and 6 months counts, 1921; beginning 1922, they are averages of 12 monthly counts.

Q 143–152. Railroad accidents and fatalities, 1891–1957.

Source: Interstate Commerce Commission, *Accident Bulletin*, annual issues.

The Accident Reports Act approved May 1910 requires the filing of monthly reports of railway accidents and authorizes the Interstate Commerce Commission to investigate accidents. A reportable accident is one arising from the operation of a railway resulting . . . in the death of a person; or in the disability of an employee for more than 3 days during the 10 days following the accident; or in the disability of others for more than 1 day.

Series Q 1–11.   Railroad and Other Domestic Intercity Freight Traffic, by Type of Transportation: 1939 to 1957

[In millions of ton-miles.   A ton-mile is the movement of 1 ton (2,000 pounds) of freight traffic for the distance of 1 mile.   Comprises public and private traffic]

Year	Total traffic, volume	Railroads [1]		Motor vehicles		Inland waterways [2]		Oil pipelines		Airways [3]	
		Volume	Percent of total	Volume	Percent of total	Volume	Percent of total	Volume	Percent of total	Volume	Percent of total
	1	2	3	4	5	6	7	8	9	10	11
1957	1,352,131	626,222	46.31	260,856	19.29	231,792	17.14	232,660	17.21	601	0.044
1956	1,360,142	655,891	48.22	253,751	18.66	219,978	16.17	229,959	16.91	563	.041
1955	1,277,806	631,385	49.41	226,188	17.70	216,508	16.94	203,244	15.91	481	.037
1954	1,124,462	556,557	49.50	214,626	19.09	173,679	15.45	179,203	15.94	397	.035
1953	1,204,098	614,199	51.01	[4] 217,163	18.04	[5] 202,439	16.81	169,884	14.11	413	.034
1952	1,144,264	623,373	54.48	194,607	17.01	168,367	14.71	157,502	13.76	415	.036
1951	1,178,075	655,353	55.63	188,012	15.96	[5] 182,216	15.47	152,115	12.91	379	.032
1950	1,062,637	596,940	56.17	172,860	16.27	163,344	15.37	129,175	12.16	318	.030
1949	915,877	534,694	58.38	126,636	13.83	139,396	15.22	114,916	12.55	235	.026
1948	1,044,978	647,267	61.94	116,045	11.10	[5] 161,846	15.49	119,597	11.44	223	.021
1947	1,018,651	664,523	65.24	102,095	10.02	146,714	14.40	105,161	10.32	158	.016
1946	903,854	602,069	66.61	81,992	9.07	123,973	13.72	95,727	10.59	93	.010
1945	1,027,115	690,809	67.26	66,948	6.52	142,737	13.90	126,530	12.32	91	.009
1944	1,088,266	746,912	68.63	58,264	5.35	150,155	13.80	132,864	12.21	71	.007
1943	1,031,185	734,829	71.26	56,784	5.51	141,652	13.74	97,867	9.49	53	.005
1942	929,004	645,422	69.47	59,896	6.45	148,565	15.99	75,087	8.08	34	.004
1941	772,020	481,756	62.40	81,363	10.54	140,454	18.19	68,428	8.86	19	.002
1940	618,592	379,201	61.30	62,043	10.03	118,057	19.08	59,277	9.58	14	.002
1939	543,534	338,850	62.34	52,821	9.72	96,249	17.71	55,602	10.23	12	.002

[1] Revenue ton-miles.   Includes electric railroads, express, and mail.
[2] Includes Great Lakes.
[3] Domestic revenue service.   Includes express, mail, and excess baggage.

[4] Ton-miles revised upward on basis of new data; not applied to previous years.
[5] Part of these year-to-year changes resulted from coverage of waterways previously in use but not covered.

Series Q 12–14.   Indexes of Transportation Output: 1889 to 1953

[Weighted indexes, 1939=100]

Year	All traffic	Passenger	Freight	Year	All traffic	Passenger	Freight	Year	All traffic	Passenger	Freight
	12	13	14		12	13	14		12	13	14
1953	220	(1)	(1)	1942	183	(1)	(1)	1930	97	108	95
1952	219	(1)	(1)	1941	137	(1)	(1)	1929	110	118	108
1951	226	(1)	(1)					1928	106	117	103
				1940	110	108	114	1927	106	119	102
1950	206	(1)	(1)	1939	100	100	100	1926	108	121	104
1949	182	(1)	(1)	1938	89	97	87				
1948	205	(1)	(1)	1937	101	103	101	1925	102	120	97
1947	203	(1)	(1)	1936	93	99	92	1924	98	121	91
1946	192	248	176					1923	102	122	96
				1935	79	87	77	1922	88	116	81
1945	213	(1)	(1)	1934	76	84	74	1921	81	115	72
1944	222	(1)	(1)	1933	70	76	68	1920	103	127	96
1943	216	(1)	(1)	1932	66	79	62				
				1931	82	94	79	1889	18.5	25.5	16.5

[1] Not available.

Series Q 15–22.   Railroad Mileage and Equipment: 1830 to 1890

Year	Mileage			Equipment [2]					Year	Miles of road operated (Dec. 31)	Year	Miles of road operated (Dec. 31)
	Road operated (Dec. 31)	Road owned [1]	All track (Dec. 31)	Loco- motives	Revenue cars							
					Total	Passenger	Freight	Baggage, mail, express				
	15	16	17	18	19	20	21	22		15		15
1890	166,703	163,359	208,152	31,812	1,090,869	21,664	1,061,952	7,253	1870	52,922	1850	9,021
1889	161,276	159,934	202,088	30,566	1,080,665	21,471	1,051,141	7,053	1869	46,844	1849	7,365
1888	156,114	154,222	191,376	29,006	1,032,182	20,247	1,005,108	6,827	1868	42,229	1848	5,996
1887	149,214	147,953	184,935	27,275	[3] 976,772	19,339	950,889	6,554	1867	39,050	1847	5,598
1886	136,338	133,565	167,952	26,108	870,602	18,365	845,912	6,325	1866	36,801	1846	4,930
1885	128,320	127,689	160,506	25,662	828,058	16,497	805,517	6,044	1865	35,085	1845	4,633
1884	125,345	125,119	156,414	24,353	820,954	16,644	798,399	5,911	1864	33,908	1844	4,377
1883	121,422	120,519	149,101	23,405	800,741	16,230	778,663	5,848	1863	33,170	1843	4,185
1882	114,677	114,428	140,878	21,889	750,933	14,934	730,435	5,564	1862	32,120	1842	4,026
1881	103,108	103,530	130,455	19,911	667,218	13,947	648,295	4,976	1861	31,286	1841	3,535
1880	93,262	92,147	115,647	17,949	[3] 556,930	12,789	539,255	4,786	1860	30,626	1840	2,818
1879	86,556	84,393	104,756	17,084	496,718	12,009	480,190	4,519	1859	28,789	1839	2,302
1878	81,747	80,832	103,649	16,445	439,109	11,683	423,013	4,413	1858	26,968	1838	1,913
1877	79,082	79,208	97,308	15,911	408,082	12,053	392,175	3,854	1857	24,503	1837	1,497
1876	76,808	76,305	94,665	15,618	399,524	[4] 14,621	384,903	--------	1856	22,076	1836	1,273
1875	74,096	74,096	--------	--------	--------	--------	--------	--------	1855	18,374	1835	1,098
1874	72,385	72,623	--------	--------	--------	--------	--------	--------	1854	16,720	1834	633
1873	70,268	70,651	--------	--------	--------	--------	--------	--------	1853	15,360	1833	380
1872	66,171	57,323	--------	--------	--------	--------	--------	--------	1852	12,908	1832	229
1871	60,301	51,455	--------	--------	--------	--------	--------	--------	1851	10,982	1831	95
											1830	23

[1] Prior to 1882, includes elevated railways.
[2] Prior to 1881, includes elevated railways.

[3] Agrees with source; however, figures for components do not add to total shown.
[4] Includes baggage, mail, and express.

Series Q 23–32. Railroad Passenger and Freight Service: 1865 to 1890

Year	Passenger service				Freight service						Year	Passenger revenue service	Freight service		Year	Freight service	
	Passenger revenue	Passengers carried	Passenger miles	Revenue (passenger-mile)	Freight revenue	Total revenue tons carried [1]	Ton-miles carried, all roads	Revenue per ton-mile	Revenue ton-miles per train-mile	Ton-miles carried, 13 railroads			Freight revenue	Ton-miles carried, 13 railroads		Freight revenue	Ton-miles carried, 13 railroads
	23	24	25	26	27	28	29	30	31	32		23	27	32		27	32
	$1,000	1,000	Mil.	Cents	$1,000	1,000	Mil.	Cents		Bil.		$1,000	$1,000	Bil.		$1,000	Bil.
1890	272,321	520,439	12,522	2.174	734,822	691,344	79,193	0.927	163.99		1880	147,653	467,749	14.48	1870		4.92
1889	259,439	494,808	11,965	2.169	665,962	619,166	68,677	0.970	159.91		1879	142,336	386,676	13.07	1869	300,000	4.22
1888	251,356	451,354	11,191	2.246	639,201	590,857	65,423	0.977	159.36		1878	124,637	365,466	10.68	1868		3.44
1887	240,543	428,226	10,570	2.276	636,666	552,075	61,561	1.034	156.16		1877	125,205	347,705	8.75	1867		3.03
1886	211,930	382,285	9,660	2.194	550,359	482,245	52,802	1.042	150.99		1876	136,121	361,137	8.74	1866		2.62
															1865		2.16
1885	200,884	351,428	9,134	2.199	509,691	437,040	49,152	1.057	143.59	17.83	1875	139,105	363,960	7.84			
1884	206,791	334,571	8,779	2.356	502,870	399,075	44,725	1.124	133.58	16.81	1874	140,999	379,467	7.73			
1883	206,837	312,687	8,541	2.422	539,510	400,453	44,065	1.224	125.86	17.09	1873	137,384	389,036	7.48			
1882	188,137	289,031	7,688	2.447	485,778	360,490	39,302	1.236	128.81	16.23	1872	132,309	340,932	6.42			
1881	173,357				551,968					16.06	1871	108,899	294,430	5.57			

[1] Revenue tons carried for 1870 are 72,500,000 tons; for 1861, 55,073,000 tons.

Series Q 33–42. Railroad Property Investment, Capital, Income, and Expenses: 1850 to 1890
[In thousands of dollars]

Year	Property investment and capital					Income and expenses			Interest and dividends	
	Investment in railroad and equipment	Stock, mortgage bonds, equipment, obligations, etc.			Stock paying dividends	Total traffic earnings	Operating expenses	Net earnings	Dividends paid	Interest paid on funded debt
		Total	Capital stock	Bonded debt						
	33	34	35	36	37	38	39	40	41	42
EXCLUDING ELEVATED RAILWAYS										
1890		10,020,925	4,590,472	5,055,225		1,086,040		342,071	83,576	224,500
1889		9,576,940	4,447,104	4,784,173		991,935		317,867	79,532	216,878
1888		9,281,915	4,392,287	4,585,472		950,520		297,307	78,943	205,288
1887		8,595,041	4,146,958	4,155,628		931,373		331,174	90,013	202,009
1886		8,089,268	3,956,377	3,853,748		822,192	524,880	297,312	80,094	182,885
1885		7,775,858	3,778,610	3,740,255		765,311	498,822	266,489	77,672	179,681
1884		7,617,986	3,726,655	3,647,313		763,307		266,514	93,204	167,286
1883		7,423,040	3,675,793	3,479,412		807,113		291,588	101,579	[1]171,414
1882		6,960,649	3,478,914	3,214,084						
INCLUDING ELEVATED RAILWAYS										
1890	8,789,222	10,122,636	4,640,240	5,105,902	1,721,094	1,097,847		346,921	85,076	226,800
1889	8,598,081	9,680,942	4,495,099	4,828,366	1,790,842	1,002,926		322,123	81,263	218,974
1888	8,344,305	9,369,399	4,438,411	4,624,035	1,769,773	960,256		301,631	80,243	207,124
1887	7,799,472	8,673,187	4,191,562	4,186,943	1,805,488	940,151		334,989	91,573	203,790
1886	7,254,995	8,163,149	3,999,509	3,882,966	1,675,670	829,941		300,604	81,654	189,036
1885	7,037,627	7,842,533	3,817,698	3,765,727	1,304,802	772,569		269,494	77,672	187,426
1884	6,924,554	7,676,399	3,762,617	3,669,116	1,658,919	777,396		270,891	94,415	178,058
1883	6,684,756	7,477,866	3,708,061	3,500,880	1,713,702	823,773		298,367	102,053	173,140
1882	6,035,090	7,016,750	3,511,036	3,235,543	1,673,791	770,210		280,317	102,031	150,232
1881	5,577,997	6,278,565	3,177,375	2,878,424		701,781		272,407	93,344	128,587
1880	4,653,609	5,402,038	2,708,673	2,530,875		613,734		255,558	77,115	107,866
1879	4,416,511	4,872,018	2,395,647	2,319,489		525,621		216,544	61,681	112,238
1878	4,166,332	4,772,297	2,292,258	2,297,791		490,103	302,528	187,575	53,629	103,161
1877	4,180,192	4,806,202	2,313,279	2,255,319		472,909	301,933	170,977	58,556	98,821
1876	4,086,653	[2]4,468,592	2,248,359	2,165,141	937,025	497,258	310,805	186,453	68,040	93,560
1875		4,658,209	2,198,601	[3]2,459,607		503,066		185,506	74,294	
1874		4,221,764	1,990,997	[3]2,230,766		520,466	330,895	189,571	67,043	
1873		3,784,543	1,947,639	[3]1,836,904		526,420	342,609	183,811	67,121	
1872		3,159,423	1,647,844	[3]1,511,579		465,241		165,754	64,418	
1871		2,664,628	1,481,450			403,329		141,746	56,457	
1870		2,476,893								
1869		2,041,226								
1868		1,869,529								
1867		1,172,881	756,223	416,658		334,000	228,700	105,300	32,125	
1863						190,000				
1861						130,000				
1860		1,149,481								
1855		763,678	424,792	299,263		84,250	42,802			
1851						39,566				
1850		318,126								

[1] Includes other interest.   [2] Sum of capital stock, bonded debt, and $55,092,192 Pacific R.R., U.S. subsidiary bonds.   [3] Includes other debt.

Series Q 43. Miles of Railroad Built: 1830 to 1925

Year	Miles 43	Year	Miles 43	Year	Miles 43	Year	Miles 43	Year	Miles 43	Year	Miles 43	Year	Miles 43	Year	Miles 43
1925	644	1915	933	1905	4,388	1895	1,420	1871	6,660	1860	1,500	1850	1,261	1840	491
1924	579	1914	1,532	1904	3,832	1894	1,760	1869	4,103	1859	1,707	1849	1,048	1839	386
1923	427	1913	3,071	1903	5,652	1893	3,024	1868	2,468	1858	1,966	1848	1,056	1838	453
1922	324	1912	2,997	1902	6,026	1879	5,006	1867	2,541	1857	2,077	1847	263	1837	348
1921	475	1911	3,066	1901	5,368	1878	2,428	1866	1,404	1856	1,471	1846	333	1836	280
1920	314	1910	4,122	1900	4,894	1877	2,280	1865	819	1855	2,453	1845	277	1835	138
1919	686	1909	3,748	1899	4,569	1876	2,575	1864	947	1854	3,442	1844	180	1834	214
1918	721	1908	3,214	1898	3,265	1875	1,606	1863	574	1853	2,170	1843	288	1833	116
1917	979	1907	5,212	1897	2,109	1874	2,584	1862	720	1852	2,288	1842	505	1832	191
1916	1,098	1906	5,623	1896	1,692	1873	5,217	1861	1,016	1851	1,274	1841	606	1831	99
						1872	7,439							1830	40

Series Q 44–72. Railroad Mileage, Equipment, and Passenger Traffic and Revenue: 1890 to 1957

[Includes intercorporate duplications. Unless otherwise noted, covers Class I, II, and III railroads, except that prior to 1908 includes returns for switching and terminal companies where applicable]

Year ending—	Number of operating railroads [1]	Constructed	Abandoned	Road owned [2]	Track operated: Total [3]	First main track	Other main tracks	Yard tracks and sidings	Road operated, passenger service [4]	New cars delivered for domestic use: Freight train	New cars delivered for domestic use: Passenger train	Locomotives in service: Total [6]	Steam	Electric [7]	Diesel	Other	Average tractive effort [8] (Pounds)
	44	45	46	47	48	49	50	51	52	53	54	55	56	57	58	59	60
DEC. 31																	
1957	415	49	1,149	219,067	386,996	232,177	37,123	117,678	112,522	99,290	705	32,391	2,608	597	29,137	49	61,515
1956	422	74	613	220,221	389,668	233,509	37,908	118,251	115,749	67,080	396	32,593	3,918	616	28,001	58	68,745
1955	441	105	502	220,670	390,965	233,955	38,825	118,185	120,711	37,545	886	33,533	6,266	639	26,563	65	65,005
1954	443	49	694	221,098	392,580	234,342	39,520	118,718	124,572	35,696	349	35,033	9,041	669	25,256	67	63,152
1953	448	50	666	221,758	393,736	234,959	39,794	118,983	128,943	81,021	386	37,251	12,274	713	24,209	55	61,339
1952	454	76	965	222,508	394,631	235,545	39,977	119,109	132,903	77,833	117	39,697	16,737	790	22,118	52	59,966
1951	462	71	456	223,427	395,831	236,476	40,157	119,198	139,178	95,993	179	42,473	22,590	817	19,014	52	58,476
1950	471	33	755	223,779	396,380	236,857	40,456	119,067	147,511	43,991	964	42,951	26,680	827	15,396	48	57,075
1949	481	100	620	224,511	397,232	237,564	40,639	119,029	156,821	92,562	933	43,272	30,344	856	12,025	47	56,333
1948	485	71	529	225,149	397,203	237,756	40,845	118,602	160,140	112,640	891	44,474	34,581	867	8,981	45	55,170
1947	502	79	709	225,806	397,355	238,209	40,954	118,192	161,115	68,522	861	44,344	36,942	864	6,495	43	54,506
1946	513	20	381	226,438	398,037	239,069	41,015	117,953	161,407	41,955	1,337	45,511	39,592	867	5,008	44	53,735
1945	517	40	551	226,696	398,054	239,438	41,106	117,510	161,920	43,864	931	46,253	41,018	885	4,301	49	53,217
1944	524	46	705	227,335	398,437	240,215	41,178	117,044	162,290	43,003	1,003	46,305	41,921	902	3,432	50	52,822
1943	534	34	1,149	227,999	398,730	240,745	41,093	116,892	162,429	31,836	685	45,406	41,983	907	2,476	40	52,451
1942	543	38	2,886	229,174	399,627	241,737	41,137	116,753	163,658	62,873	418	44,671	41,755	892	1,978	46	51,811
1941	559	22	1,695	231,971	403,625	244,263	41,166	118,196	167,951	80,623	349	44,375	41,911	895	1,517	52	51,217
1940	574	19	1,284	233,670	405,975	245,740	41,373	118,862	170,175	62,341	257	44,333	42,410	900	967	56	50,905
1939	600	1	1,697	235,064	408,350	246,922	41,445	119,983	172,031	25,132	276	45,172	43,604	879	639	50	50,395
1938	611	35	1,621	236,842	411,324	248,474	41,589	121,261	173,616	16,470	434	46,544	45,210	882	403	49	49,803
1937	631	149	1,642	238,539	414,572	250,582	41,579	122,411	175,543	77,498	629	47,555	46,342	872	293	48	49,412
1936	641	38	1,577	240,104	416,381	251,542	41,731	123,108	178,403	46,612	191	48,009	46,923	858	175	53	48,972
1935	661	25	1,974	241,822	419,228	252,930	41,916	124,382	----	7,515	205	49,541	48,477	884	130	50	48,367
1934	678	33	1,784	243,857	422,401	254,882	42,109	125,410	----	25,176	275	51,423	50,465	805	104	49	47,712
1933	700	122	2,016	245,703	425,664	256,741	42,397	126,526	----	2,163	9	54,228	53,302	789	85	52	46,916
1932	709	321	1,370	247,595	428,402	258,869	42,556	126,977	----	3,252	77	56,732	55,831	764	80	57	46,299
1931	749	502	779	248,829	429,823	259,999	42,780	127,044	----	13,203	323	58,652	57,820	709	80	43	45,764
1930	775	460	954	249,052	429,883	260,440	42,742	126,701	----	74,920	1,534	60,189	59,406	663	77	43	45,225
1929	809	671	782	249,433	429,054	260,570	42,711	125,773	----	81,590	2,455	61,257	60,572	621	25	39	44,801
1928	849	946	710	249,309	427,750	260,546	42,432	124,772	----	46,000	1,571	63,311	62,642	617	(9)	9 52	43,838
1927	880	819	797	249,131	424,737	259,639	42,071	123,027	----	63,370	2,087	65,348	64,843	467	(9)	9 38	42,798
1926	929	881	892	249,138	421,341	258,815	41,686	120,840	----	88,862	2,814	66,847	66,381	435	11	20	41,886
1925	947	595	753	249,398	417,954	258,631	40,962	118,361	----	105,735	2,428	68,098	67,713	379	1	5	40,666
1924	995	635	617	250,156	415,028	258,238	39,916	116,874	----	113,711	2,517	69,486	69,114	372	----	----	39,891
1923	1,023	441	537	250,222	412,993	258,084	38,697	116,212	----	175,748	2,034	69,414	69,005	409	----	----	39,177
1922	1,041	318	1,188	250,413	409,359	257,425	37,888	114,046	----	66,289	977	68,518	68,121	397	----	----	39,177
1921	1,058	331	687	251,176	407,531	258,362	37,614	111,555	----	40,292	1,161	69,122	68,733	389	----	----	36,935
1920	1,085	----	----	252,845	406,580	259,941	36,894	109,744	----	60,955	831	68,942	68,554	388	----	----	36,365
1919	1,111	----	----	253,152	403,891	258,525	36,730	108,637	----	94,981	126	68,977	68,592	385	----	----	35,789
1918	1,131	----	----	253,529	402,343	258,507	36,228	107,608	----	67,063	750	67,936	67,563	373	----	----	34,995
1917	1,168	----	----	253,626	400,353	259,705	35,066	105,582	----	115,705	1,684	66,070	65,699	371	----	----	33,932
1916	1,216	----	----	254,037	397,014	259,705	34,325	102,984	----	111,516	1,344	65,595	65,253	342	----	----	32,840
JUNE 30																	
1916	1,243			254,251	----	259,211	33,864	101,869				65,314	65,021	293			32,380
1915	1,260			253,789	391,142	257,569	33,662	99,910		10 58,226	10 1,513	66,502	66,229	273			31,501
1914	1,297			252,105	387,208	256,547	32,376	98,285		10 97,626	10 3,589	67,012					31,006
1913	1,296			249,777	379,508	253,470	30,827	95,211		10 176,049	10 2,654	65,597					30,258
1912	1,298			246,777	371,238	249,852	29,367	92,019			10 2,509	63,463					29,049
1911	1,312			243,979	362,824	246,238	27,613	88,974			10 3,362	62,463					28,291
1910	1,306			240,293	351,767	240,831	25,354	85,582				60,019					27,282
1909	1,316			236,834	342,351	235,402	24,573	82,377				58,219					26,601
1908	1,323			233,468	333,646	230,494	23,699	79,453				57,698					26,356
1907	1,564			229,951	327,975	227,455	22,771	77,749				55,388					25,781
1906	1,491			224,363	317,083	222,340	20,982	73,761				51,672					24,741
1905	1,380			218,101	306,797	216,974	19,881	69,942				48,357					23,666
1904	1,314			213,904	297,073	212,243	18,338	66,492				46,743					22,804
1903	1,281			207,977	283,822	205,314	16,948	61,560				43,871					21,781
1902	1,219			202,472	274,106	200,155	15,820	58,221				41,225					
1901	1,213			197,237	265,352	195,562	14,876	54,915				39,584					
1900	1,224			193,346	258,784	192,556	14,075	52,153				37,663					
1899	1,206			189,295	250,143	187,535	13,384	49,224				36,703					
1898	1,192			186,396	245,334	184,648	13,096	47,589				36,234					
1897	1,158			184,428	242,013	183,284	12,795	45,934				35,986					
1896	1,111			182,777	239,140	181,983	12,440	44,718				35,950					
1895	1,104			180,657	233,276	177,746	12,348	43,181				35,699					
1894	1,043			178,709	229,796	175,691	12,163	41,941				35,492					
1893	1,034			176,461	221,864	169,780	11,633	40,451				34,788					
1892	1,002			171,564	211,051	162,397	10,846	37,808				33,136					
1891	991			168,403	207,446	161,275	10,428	35,742				32,139					
1890	1,013			163,597	199,876	156,404	9,760	33,711				30,140					

[1] Includes circular and unofficial.
[2] First track. Includes lessors, proprietary, circular and unofficial companies.
[3] For railroads reporting track by class. Excludes circular and unofficial, figures for which cover road, first track only.
[4] Class I line-haul railroads.
[5] Includes switching and terminal companies.
[6] For 1890–1927, number of locomotives; for 1928–1957, number of units, except for steam locomotives. (A unit is the least number of wheel bases together with superstructure capable of independent propulsion, but not necessarily equipped with an independent control.)
[7] For 1915–1922, identified as "other than steam," but all or almost all of the locomotives must be electric.
[8] For 1916–1956, represents steam locomotives and freight cars of Class I railroads excluding switching and terminal companies; for 1957, includes all Class I locomotives including switching and terminal companies.
[9] Diesel included with "Other."
[10] Calendar-year data.

Series Q 44–72. Railroad Mileage, Equipment, and Passenger Traffic and Revenue: 1890 to 1957—Con.

	Equipment [5]—Con.					Passenger traffic and revenue						
	Passenger-train cars in service			Freight-train cars in service [11]			Passenger-miles				Revenue	
Year ending—	Railroad only	Class I railroads and Pullman Co.		Number	Average capacity [8]	Passengers	Total	Commutation [4]	Coach [4]	Parlor and sleeping car [4]	Total	Per passenger-mile
		Total	Air conditioned									
	61	62	63	64	65	66	67	68	69	70	71	72
					Tons	1,000	Mil.	Mil.	Mil.	Mil.	$1,000	Cents
DECEMBER 31												
1957	29,564	32,231	14,323	1,777,557	54.5	412,625	25,914	4,828	15,875	5,185	736,408	2.842
1956	30,817		14,551	1,738,631	54.0	429,994	28,216	4,841	17,074	6,275	757,625	2.685
1955	32,118	35,455	14,784	1,723,747	53.7	433,308	28,548	4,776	17,314	6,441	743,688	2.605
1954	33,035	37,768	15,733	1,761,386	53.7	440,770	29,310	4,753	17,687	6,850	767,987	2.620
1953	34,106	39,532	16,231	1,801,874	53.5	458,252	31,679	4,757	18,955	7,950	842,663	2.660
1952	34,942	41,011	16,320	1,783,352	53.2	470,979	34,033	4,755	19,758	9,504	906,838	2.665
1951	36,326	42,406	16,502	1,777,878	52.9	485,468	34,640	4,866	19,524	10,226	901,019	2.601
1950	37,359	43,372	16,747	1,745,778	52.6	488,019	31,790	4,990	17,443	9,338	814,741	2.563
1949	38,006	43,578	16,008	1,778,811	52.4	556,741	35,133	5,478	20,273	9,349	862,139	2.454
1948	39,406	44,447	15,249	1,785,067	51.9	645,535	41,224	5,855	24,315	11,015	965,630	2.342
1947	39,057	44,841	14,628	1,759,758	51.5	706,551	45,972	6,011	27,660	12,261	965,005	2.099
1946	38,697	45,637	13,967	1,768,400	51.3	794,824	64,754	5,857	39,039	19,801	1,261,416	1.948
1945	38,633	46,863	12,685	1,787,073	51.1	897,384	91,826	5,418	59,415	26,912	1,719,316	1.872
1944	38,217	46,588	13,175	1,797,012	50.8	915,817	95,663	5,344	63,288	26,944	1,793,322	1.875
1943	38,331	45,764	13,165	1,784,472	50.7	887,674	87,925	5,261	57,909	24,675	1,655,814	1.883
1942	38,446			1,773,735	50.5	672,420	53,747	4,761	30,910	17,853	1,030,486	1.917
1941	38,334			1,732,673	50.3	488,668	29,406	4,088	16,106	9,166	515,851	1.754
1940	38,308			1,684,171	50.0	456,088	23,816	3,997	12,485	7,288	417,955	1.755
1939	38,977			1,680,519	49.7	454,032	22,713	4,012	11,118	7,527	417,716	1.839
1938	39,931			1,731,096	49.4	454,508	21,657	4,032	10,247	7,354	406,406	1.877
1937	40,949			1,776,428	49.2	499,688	24,695	4,116	12,417	8,126	443,532	1.796
1936	41,390			1,790,043	48.8	492,493	22,460	4,188			413,189	1.840
1935	42,426			1,867,381	48.3	448,059	18,509	4,118			358,423	1.936
1934	44,884			1,973,247	48.0	452,176	18,069	4,163			346,870	1.920
1933	47,677			2,072,632	47.5	434,848	16,368	4,308			329,816	2.015
1932	50,598			2,184,690	47.0	480,718	16,997	4,986			377,511	2.221
1931	52,096			2,245,904	47.0	599,227	21,933	6,018			551,726	2.515
1930	53,584			2,322,267	46.9	707,987	26,876	6,669			730,766	2.719
1929	53,838			2,323,683	46.3	786,432	31,165	6,898			875,929	2.811
1928	54,800			2,346,751	45.8	798,476	31,718	6,626			905,271	2.854
1927	55,729			2,378,800	45.5	840,030	33,798	6,650			980,528	2.901
1926	56,855			2,403,967	45.1	874,589	35,673	6,605			1,049,210	2.941
1925	56,814			2,414,083	44.8	901,963	36,167	6,592			1,064,806	2.944
1924	57,451			2,411,627	44.3	950,459	36,368	6,407			1,085,672	2.985
1923	57,159			2,379,131	43.8	1,008,538	38,294	6,401			1,158,925	3.026
1922	56,827			2,352,483	43.1	989,509	35,811	6,132			1,087,516	3.037
1921	56,950			2,378,510	42.5	1,061,131	37,706				1,166,252	3.093
1920	56,102			2,388,424	42.4	1,269,913	47,370				1,304,815	2.755
1919	56,290			2,426,889	41.9	1,211,022	46,888				1,193,431	2.548
1918	56,611			2,397,943	41.6	1,122,963	43,212				1,046,166	2.421
1917	55,939			2,379,472	41.5	1,109,943	40,100				840,910	2.097
1916	55,193			2,329,475	40.9	1,048,987	35,220				722,359	2.051
JUNE 30												
1916	54,774			2,313,378	40.5	1,015,338	34,309				689,627	2.010
1915	55,810			2,341,567	39.7	985,676	32,475				646,475	1.991
1914	54,492			2,349,734	39.1	1,063,249	35,357				703,484	1.990
1913	52,717			2,298,478	38.3	1,043,603	34,673				[12]695,988	[12]2.008
1912	51,583			2,229,163	37.4	1,004,081	33,132				660,373	1.987
1911	49,906			2,208,997	36.9	997,410	33,202				657,638	1.974
1910	47,179			2,148,478	35.9	971,683	32,338				628,992	1.938
1909	45,664			2,086,835	35.3	891,472	29,109				563,609	1.928
1908	45,292			2,100,784	34.9	890,010	29,083				566,833	1.937
1907	43,973			1,991,557	33.8	873,905	27,719				564,606	2.014
1906	42,262			1,837,914	32.2	797,946	25,167				510,033	2.003
1905	40,713			1,731,409	30.8	738,835	23,800				472,695	1.962
1904	39,752			1,692,194	30.1	715,420	21,923				444,327	2.006
1903	38,140			1,653,782	29.4	694,892	20,916				421,705	2.006
1902	36,987			1,546,101		649,879	19,690				392,963	1.986
1901	35,969			1,464,328		607,278	17,354				351,356	2.013
1900	34,713			1,365,531		576,831	16,038				323,716	2.003
1899	33,850			1,295,510		523,177	14,591				291,113	1.978
1898	33,595			1,248,826		501,067	13,380				266,970	1.973
1897	33,626			1,221,730		489,445	12,257				251,136	2.022
1896	33,003			1,221,887		511,773	13,049				266,563	2.019
1895	33,112			1,196,119		507,421	12,188				252,246	2.040
1894	33,018			1,205,169		540,688	14,289				285,350	1.986
1893	31,384			1,013,307		593,561	14,229				301,492	2.108
1892	28,876			966,998		560,958	13,363				286,806	2.126
1891	27,949			947,300		531,184	12,844				281,179	2.142
1890	26,820			918,491		492,431	11,848				260,786	2.167

[4] Class I line-haul railroads.
[5] Includes switching and terminal companies.
[8] For 1916–1956, represents steam locomotives and freight cars of Class I railroads excluding switching and terminal companies; for 1957, includes all Class I locomotives including switching and terminal companies.

[11] Excludes caboose cars.
[12] Class I and II railroads.

Series Q 73–86. Railroad Freight Traffic and Revenue: 1890 to 1957

[In tons of 2,000 pounds]

Year ending—	All tonnage	Revenue freight originated (Class I railroads)							Freight and revenue (Class I, II, and III railroads)					
		In carloads						Less than carload	Revenue-tons originated	Ton-miles	Haul per ton [2]	Revenue		
		Total	Products of agriculture	Animals and products	Products of mines	Products of forests	Manufactures and misc. [1]					Total	Per ton [2]	Per ton-mile
	73	74	75	76	77	78	79	80	81	82	83	84	85	86
	1,000	1,000	1,000	1,000	1,000	1,000	1,000	1,000	Mil.	Mil.	Miles	$1,000	Dol.	Cents
DECEMBER 31														
1957	1,380,327	1,374,884	137,618	11,074	769,675	77,497	379,020	5,443	1,449	621,907	429.20	9,063,749	6.26	1.457
1956	1,447,422	1,440,937	138,093	13,198	796,480	87,799	405,367	6,485	1,521	651,188	428.08	9,088,637	5.97	1.396
1955	1,396,339	1,389,346	133,789	13,161	761,993	82,584	397,819	6,993	1,459	626,893	430.67	8,665,379	5.95	1.382
1954	1,223,969	1,217,005	131,733	13,128	650,074	75,650	346,420	6,964	1,279	552,197	431.65	7,914,809	6.19	1.433
1953	1,384,301	1,376,046	131,137	13,768	754,292	82,107	394,742	8,255	1,448	608,954	420.66	9,077,996	6.27	1.491
1952	1,382,604	1,373,294	138,415	14,601	752,699	83,480	384,097	9,310	1,447	617,942	426.93	8,915,130	6.16	1.443
1951	1,477,402	1,467,023	140,811	14,362	819,373	86,522	405,955	10,379	1,547	649,831	419.99	8,757,874	5.66	1.348
1950	1,354,196	1,343,308	129,175	14,321	746,808	78,860	374,144	10,888	1,421	591,550	416.32	7,933,764	5.58	1.341
1949	1,226,503	1,213,911	140,383	15,284	653,759	69,257	335,228	12,592	1,284	529,111	412.02	7,151,237	5.57	1.352
1948	1,506,878	1,488,612	145,176	16,865	845,640	86,104	394,827	18,266	1,580	641,104	405.64	8,090,194	5.12	1.262
1947	1,537,546	1,514,985	158,168	19,716	847,807	87,027	402,267	22,561	1,613	657,878	407.82	7,140,881	4.43	1.085
1946	1,366,617	1,342,230	149,941	21,587	717,806	84,817	368,079	24,387	1,432	594,943	415.48	5,866,351	4.10	.986
1945	1,424,913	1,404,080	159,571	23,748	732,942	75,604	412,215	20,833	1,493	684,148	458.14	6,617,213	4.43	.967
1944	1,491,491	1,471,366	145,685	25,413	785,265	83,731	431,272	20,125	1,565	740,586	473.28	7,087,033	4.53	.957
1943	1,481,225	1,462,314	148,971	22,936	797,163	80,899	412,345	18,911	1,557	730,132	469.07	6,865,754	4.41	.940
1942	1,421,187	1,403,612	117,318	20,620	804,577	84,570	376,527	17,575	1,498	640,992	427.76	6,026,416	4.02	.940
1941	1,227,650	1,209,559	100,173	16,810	684,433	71,540	336,603	18,091	1,296	477,576	368.54	4,509,760	3.48	.944
1940	1,009,421	994,728	88,821	15,456	570,220	58,221	262,010	14,693	1,069	375,369	351.13	3,584,201	3.35	.955
1939	901,669	886,794	91,564	15,049	496,939	50,156	233,086	14,875	955	335,375	351.21	3,297,059	3.45	.983
1938	771,862	757,470	95,390	14,760	408,835	43,973	194,512	14,392	820	291,866	356.05	2,900,676	3.54	.994
1937	1,015,586	998,398	89,460	15,233	569,745	58,658	265,302	17,188	1,075	362,815	337.43	3,428,421	3.19	.945
1936	958,830	942,538	86,648	16,209	541,488	53,156	245,037	16,292	1,012	341,182	337.29	3,356,681	3.32	.984
1935	789,627	775,588	76,338	15,125	445,136	42,483	196,506	14,039	832	283,637	341.05	2,831,139	3.40	.998
1934	765,296	750,951	79,305	20,363	436,380	35,650	179,253	14,345	802	270,292	336.91	2,671,901	3.33	.989
1933	698,943	684,592	81,702	17,651	395,065	33,165	157,009	14,351	733	250,651	341.77	2,528,968	3.45	1.009
1932	646,223	630,989	80,917	18,055	362,226	26,109	143,682	15,234	679	235,309	346.63	2,485,475	3.66	1.056
1931	894,186	871,412	97,487	21,632	501,903	43,024	207,366	22,774	945	311,073	329.23	3,302,324	3.50	1.062
1930	1,153,197	1,123,530	110,728	23,129	642,537	69,371	277,765	29,667	1,220	385,815	316.21	4,145,015	3.40	1.074
1929	1,339,091	1,303,048	115,343	24,907	737,879	94,855	330,064	36,043	1,419	450,189	317.17	4,899,168	3.45	1.088
1928	1,285,943	1,248,989	118,022	25,634	696,583	96,737	312,013	36,954	1,371	436,087	318.00	4,771,562	3.48	1.094
1927	1,281,611	1,243,171	113,342	26,003	713,402	99,351	291,073	38,440	1,373	432,014	314.75	4,728,885	3.45	1.095
1926	1,336,142	1,296,651	111,787	26,244	757,703	104,851	296,066	39,491	1,440	447,444	310.81	4,905,981	3.41	1.096
1925	1,247,242	1,206,655	109,313	26,324	678,336	107,391	285,291	40,587	1,351	417,418	308.93	4,648,364	3.44	1.114
1924	1,187,296	1,146,747	116,587	27,747	637,582	108,094	256,737	40,549	1,287	391,945	304.44	4,437,380	3.45	1.132
1923	1,279,030	1,234,692	109,318	28,254	713,735	115,618	267,767	44,338	1,388	416,256	299.94	4,712,495	3.40	1.132
1922	1,023,745	980,516	111,787	26,230	532,998	89,059	220,442	43,229	1,112	342,188	307.77	4,085,742	3.67	1.194
1921	940,183	898,191	114,069	24,263	511,271	76,419	172,169	41,992	1,018	309,533	304.11	4,004,109	3.93	1.294
1920	[3]1,255,421	[3]1,202,219	110,840	26,595	712,155	100,765	251,864	53,202	1,363	413,699	303.52	4,420,833	3.24	1.069
1919	[3]1,096,449	[3]1,045,148	115,033	35,494	589,951	94,076	210,256	51,301	1,190	367,161	308.60	3,624,886	3.05	.987
1918	1,263,344	1,209,957	116,051	35,777	734,796	97,256	226,077	53,387	1,377	408,778	296.89	3,522,052	2.56	.862
1917	1,264,016	1,210,247	104,629	31,858	732,653	100,838	240,269	53,769	1,382	398,263	288.18	2,897,436	2.10	.728
1916	[3]1,203,367	[3]1,150,456	113,635	30,473	680,123	93,819	231,039	52,911	1,317	366,173	277.98	2,631,092	2.00	.719
JUNE 30														
1916									1,263	343,477	271.98	2,469,027	1.96	.719
1915	[3]925,697	[3]878,761	109,483	26,001	507,250	76,674	157,085	46,936	1,024	277,135	270.69	2,037,926	1.99	.735
1914	[3]1,023,131	[3]982,892	98,825	26,352	574,000	91,094	177,950	40,239	1,130	288,637	255.43	2,126,717	1.88	.737
1913	[3]1,067,978	[3]1,026,817	102,658	25,669	592,164	93,762	196,947	41,161	1,183	301,730	255.15	[4]2,198,931	[4]1.92	[4].729
1912	[3]926,990	[3]889,999	86,433	24,064	506,306	74,796	166,134	36,991	1,031	264,081	256.87	1,968,559	1.91	.744
1911	[3]901,573	[3]866,398	81,780	22,833	483,861	79,345	163,380	35,175	1,003	253,784	254.10	1,925,991	1.92	.757
1910	----	----	----	----	----	----	----	----	1,026	255,017	249.68	1,925,554	1.88	.753
1909	----	----	----	----	----	----	----	----	881	281,803	251.10	1,677,614	1.90	.763
1908	----	----	----	----	----	----	----	----	870	218,382	253.94	1,655,419	1.90	.754
1907	----	----	----	----	----	----	----	----	977	236,601	242.05	1,823,652	1.87	.759
1906	----	----	----	----	----	----	----	----	896	215,878	240.89	1,640,387	1.83	.748
1905	----	----	----	----	----	----	----	----	785	186,463	237.56	1,450,773	1.85	.766
1904	----	----	----	----	----	----	----	----	714	174,522	244.30	1,379,003	1.93	.780
1903	----	----	----	----	----	----	----	----	715	173,221	242.35	1,338,020	1.87	.763
1902	----	----	----	----	----	----	----	----	658	157,289	239.10	1,207,229	1.84	.757
1901	----	----	----	----	----	----	----	----	584	147,077	251.98	1,118,543	1.92	.750
1900	----	----	----	----	----	----	----	----	583	141,597	242.73	1,049,256	1.80	.729
1899	----	----	----	----	----	----	----	----	502	123,667	246.58	913,737	1.82	.724
1898	----	----	----	----	----	----	----	----		114,078	-------	876,728	-------	.753
1897	----	----	----	----	----	----	----	----		95,139	-------	772,849	-------	.798
1896	----	----	----	----	----	----	----	----		95,328	-------	786,616	-------	.806
1895	----	----	----	----	----	----	----	----		85,228	-------	729,993	-------	.839
1894	----	----	----	----	----	----	----	----		80,335	-------	699,491	-------	.860
1893	----	----	----	----	----	----	----	----		93,588	-------	829,054	-------	.878
1892	----	----	----	----	----	----	----	----		88,241	-------	799,316	-------	.898
1891	----	----	----	----	----	----	----	----		81,074	-------	736,794	-------	.895
1890	----	----	----	----	----	----	----	----		76,207	-------	714,464	-------	.941

[1] Includes forwarder traffic beginning 1939.
[2] United States as a system, i.e., ton-miles or revenue of connecting roads is included in the numerator, but only tonnage originated in the denominator.
[3] Includes the following amounts of unassigned carload tonnage (thousands): 1911, 35,199; 1912, 32,266; 1913, 15,617; 1914, 14,671; 1915, 2,268; 1916, 1,367; and 1919, 338.
[4] Class I and II railroads.

Series Q 87–94.   Railroad Passenger and Freight Operations: 1890 to 1957

[Tons are of 2,000 pounds.   Class I, II, and III railroads except as follows: Series Q 87, Class I beginning 1911; series Q 88, Class I beginning 1933; and series Q 89, Q 93, Q 94, Class I for all years]

Year ending—	Passenger service			Freight service					Year ending—	Passenger service, passenger-miles per—		Freight service, revenue ton-miles per—		
	Passenger-miles per—		Train-miles per train-hour	Revenue ton-miles per—			Train-miles per train-hour	Car-miles per car-day		Car-mile	Train-mile	Loaded car-mile [1]	Train-mile	Mile of road
	Car-mile	Train-mile		Loaded car-mile [1]	Train-mile	Mile of road								
	87	88	89	90	91	92	93	94		87	88	90	91	92
DECEMBER 31									**DECEMBER 31—**					
1957	18.1	93.9	40.2	32.42	1,369.56	2,676,573	18.8	43.7	**Con.**					
1956	18.1	96.9	40.0	31.98	1,347.21	2,789,340	18.6	45.0	1919	20.5	84.7	25.44	622.51	1,423,390
									1918	19.9	79.4	26.96	620.68	1,582,796
1955	17.8	95.2	39.8	30.99	1,296.86	2,679,482	18.6	45.7	1917	17.2	67.6	24.75	588.29	1,538,211
1954	17.4	92.0	39.5	30.27	1,216.54	2,356,646	18.7	41.2	1916	15.5	59.2	22.83	552.26	1,409,957
1953	17.7	94.8	39.1	30.66	1,219.03	2,592,188	18.2	44.3						
1952	18.1	98.4	38.3	31.02	1,210.90	2,622,463	17.6	44.0	**JUNE 30**					
1951	18.1	97.2	37.7	31.38	1,211.06	2,748,700	17.0	45.0						
									1916	15.3	58.2	22.39	536.67	1,325,089
1950	17.0	88.5	37.4	29.97	1,131.47	2,496,927	16.8	43.6	1915	15.0	56.0	21.14	476.13	1,075,962
1949	18.0	92.0	37.0	29.48	1,044.83	2,229,430	16.9	40.3	1914	15.4	58.4	21.09	446.96	1,125,084
1948	19.4	100.8	36.7	30.90	1,080.30	2,695,708	16.2	45.1	1913	15.4	58.5	[2]21.12	[2]445.43	1,190,397
1947	21.1	110.2	36.1	30.61	1,052.43	2,752,915	16.0	46.9	1912	15.1	56.5	20.18	406.76	1,078,580
1946	24.7	143.7	35.1	29.25	992.95	2,488,499	16.0	43.5	1911	15.6	57.9	19.74	383.10	1,053,566
1945	30.4	189.7	34.7	30.18	1,034.49	2,852,615	15.7	47.7	1910	15.7	58.9	19.84	380.38	1,071,086
1944	32.2	199.8	34.8	30.62	1,045.67	3,084,195	15.7	50.6	1909	15.4	57.5	19.26	362.57	953,986
1943	31.7	188.6	34.7	31.36	1,027.64	3,032,199	15.4	49.7	1908	15.5	57.5	19.62	351.80	974,654
1942	23.7	124.9	35.7	29.76	947.87	2,638,067	15.8	47.4	1907		54.5	19.68	357.35	1,052,119
1941	16.0	72.7	36.1	26.28	827.48	1,950,166	16.5	41.6	1906		52.5	18.92	344.39	982,401
1940	14.0	60.3	35.8	25.40	764.30	1,525,579	16.7	35.6	1905		51.7	18.14	322.26	861,396
1939	13.5	57.6	35.4	24.59	727.45	1,355,052	16.7	32.3	1904		49.8	17.72	307.76	829,476
1938	13.1	54.5	34.7	23.80	676.57	1,171,637	16.6	28.5	1903		49.2	17.60	310.54	855,442
1937	14.0	59.0	34.5	24.68	708.35	1,446,921	16.1	32.9	1902		48.5	16.92	296.47	793,351
1936	13.6	55.4	34.0	24.32	687.49	1,353,406	15.8	30.7	1901		45.1	16.55	281.26	760,414
1935	11.2	47.5	--	23.49	646.17	1,119,290	16.0	25.8	1900		44.2		270.86	735,352
1934	10.9	46.7	--	23.19	623.62	1,058,609	15.9	24.2	1899		41.2		243.52	659,565
1933	10.2	42.5	--	23.26	619.13	972,262	15.7	21.3	1898		39.1		226.45	617,810
1932	9.8	39.9	--	22.56	585.49	908,296	15.5	19.8	1897		36.6		204.62	519,079
1931	10.5	44.7	--	23.44	652.87	1,196,960	14.8	24.5	1896		39.2		198.81	523,832
1930	11.3	48.9	--	24.28	699.27	1,481,199	13.8	28.7	1895		38.3		189.69	479,490
1929	12.5	54.4	--	24.52	713.03	1,727,786	13.2	32.3	1894		43.7		179.80	457,252
1928	12.9	55.1	--	24.31	705.86	1,677,089	12.9	31.2	1893		42.4		183.97	551,232
1927	13.5	57.9	--	24.60	689.68	1,668,800	12.3	30.3	1892		42.0		181.89	543,365
1926	14.2	60.4	--	24.96	688.56	1,732,295	11.9	30.4	1891		41.7		181.67	502,705
									1890		41.4		175.12	487,245
1925	14.8	61.5	--	24.55	662.53	1,613,862	11.8	28.5						
1924	15.3	62.1	--	24.47	634.43	1,518,556	11.5	26.8						
1923	16.3	65.9	--	25.18	632.32	1,615,741	10.9	27.8						
1922	15.9	64.6	--	24.31	599.12	1,330,460	11.1	23.5						
1921	16.4	66.4	--	24.60	566.74	1,199,328	11.5	22.4						
1920	19.8	82.4	--	26.71	639.03	1,597,133	10.3	--						

[1] This average is obtained by dividing the revenue ton-miles by the total loaded car-miles, the latter item including some cars loaded with nonrevenue freight. This method is necessary to preserve comparability with figures for the earlier years, and the figures differ slightly from the average "net tons per loaded car" shown in the regular monthly statements of Freight and Passenger Service Operating Statistics based on revenue and nonrevenue ton-miles and car-miles.

[2] Class I and II railroads.

Series Q 95–105.   Railroad Property Investment, Capital, and Capital Expenditures: 1890 to 1957

Includes intercorporate duplications.   Figures subject to general exception that prior to 1908, the returns for switching and terminal companies were included where applicable   Capital expenditure represents total money outlay without deductions for property retired]

Year ending—	Property investment and capital (Class I, II, III railroads and their lessors)								Capital expenditures for additions and betterments (Class I railroads)		
	Road and equipment		Total	Railroad capital outstanding [4]			Net capitalization	Stock paying dividends	Total	Equipment	Roadway and structures
	Investment, book value [1][2]	Depreciation reserve [3]		Common stock	Preferred stock	Funded debt unmatured					
	95	96	97	98	99	100	101	102	103	104	105
DECEMBER 31	$1,000	$1,000	Mil. dol.	Mil. dol.	Mil. dol.	Mil. dol.	Mil. dol.	$1,000	$1,000	$1,000	$1,000
1957	[5]34,614,517	7,800,925	18,695	6,660	1,420	10,615	14,682	6,465,352	1,394,261	1,007,937	386,324
1956	[5]33,714,159	7,542,856	19,324	7,271	1,443	10,610	15,285	6,785,113	1,227,857	821,357	406,500
1955	[5]33,034,952	7,313,951	19,309	7,696	1,355	10,258	15,171	7,300,386	909,521	568,202	341,319
1954	[5]32,708,945	7,175,101	19,777	7,847	1,582	10,348	15,336	6,618,539	820,246	498,726	321,520
1953	[5]32,416,356	7,009,758	19,967	7,545	1,929	10,493	15,365	7,252,253	1,259,797	857,893	401,904
1952	[5]31,822,114	6,926,771	20,072	7,514	1,987	10,571	15,487	6,734,590	1,340,912	935,090	405,822
1951	[5]31,077,781	6,837,120	20,272	7,491	2,006	10,775	15,489	6,700,472	1,413,995	1,050,849	363,146
1950	[5]30,174,312	6,629,150	20,399	7,492	2,002	10,905	15,618	6,768,658	1,065,842	779,399	286,443
1949	[5]29,519,832	6,438,177	20,427	7,519	2,012	10,896	15,609	5,924,295	1,312,200	981,320	330,880
1948	[5]28,664,759	6,279,892	20,302	7,543	2,016	10,743	15,467	6,446,317	1,273,484	917,449	356,035
1947	[5]27,686,103	6,037,033	20,173	7,539	2,003	10,631	15,301	5,184,182	864,689	565,901	298,788
1946	[5]27,277,974	5,800,975	20,545	7,733	1,980	10,832	15,509	5,221,681	561,957	319,017	242,940
1945	[5]26,967,756	5,549,720	20,891	7,743	2,004	11,144	15,667	5,383,158	562,980	314,779	248,201
1944	[5]26,631,654	4,382,604	21,693	7,790	2,023	11,880	16,276	5,523,271	560,112	328,231	231,881
1943	[5]26,145,458	[*]3,939,562	22,149	7,842	1,936	12,371	16,755	5,466,566	454,282	255,981	198,301
1942	[5]25,838,351	3,561,570	22,742	7,882	1,959	12,901	17,315	5,355,928	534,897	349,374	185,523
1941	[5]25,668,984	3,240,145	22,952	7,832	1,980	13,140	17,568	3,861,658	543,021	367,568	175,453
1940	[5]25,646,014	3,095,237	23,371	8,005	2,064	13,302	17,630	3,741,132	429,147	271,906	157,241
1939	[5]25,538,157	3,102,779	23,609	8,025	2,050	13,534	17,698	3,190,115	262,029	133,388	128,641
1938	[5]25,595,739	3,044,972	23,855	8,040	2,049	13,766	17,988	3,139,486	226,937	115,408	111,529
1937	[5]25,636,082	2,950,848	24,123	8,064	2,050	14,009	18,319	3,890,177	509,793	322,877	186,916
1936	[5]25,432,388	2,809,063	24,003	7,993	2,036	13,974	18,336	3,594,789	298,991	159,104	139,887

See footnotes at end of table.

Series Q 95-105. Railroad Property Investment, Capital, and Capital Expenditures: 1890 to 1957—Con.

Year ending—	Property investment and capital (Class I, II, III railroads and their lessors)								Capital expenditures for additions and betterments (Class I railroads)		
	Road and equipment		Railroad capital outstanding [4]				Net capital-ization	Stock paying dividends	Total	Equipment	Roadway and structures
	Investment book value [1][2]	Depreciation reserve [3]	Total	Common stock	Preferred stock	Funded debt unmatured					
	95	96	97	98	99	100	101	102	103	104	105
DECEMBER 31— Con.	$1,000	$1,000	Mil. dol.	Mil. dol.	Mil. dol.	Mil. dol.	Mil. dol.	$1,000	$1,000	$1,000	$1,000
1935	[5]25,500,465	2,771,404	24,247	7,987	2,036	14,224	18,342	3,412,968	188,302	79,335	108,967
1934	[5]25,681,608	2,764,726	24,570	7,994	2,044	14,532	18,653	3,411,520	212,712	92,005	120,707
1933	[5]25,901,962	2,707,942	24,723	8,057	2,042	14,624	18,831	3,119,282	103,947	15,454	88,493
1932	[5]26,086,991	2,632,922	24,837	8,067	2,047	14,723	18,894	3,298,822	167,194	36,371	130,823
1931	[5]26,094,899	2,520,738	24,344	8,031	2,049	14,264	18,941	7,325,664	361,912	73,105	288,807
1930	[5]26,051,000	2,360,767	24,331	8,009	2,074	14,248	19,066	7,702,021	872,608	328,269	544,339
1929	[5]25,465,036	2,169,736	23,983	7,853	2,065	14,065	18,680	7,506,265	853,721	321,306	532,415
1928	[5]24,875,954	2,043,976	23,747	7,809	2,034	13,904	18,511	7,159,989	676,665	224,301	452,364
1927	[5]24,453,871	1,946,798	23,614	7,683	1,980	13,951	18,137	6,701,427	771,552	288,701	482,851
1926	[5]23,800,740	1,811,002	23,677	7,560	1,925	14,192	18,234	6,473,280	885,086	371,922	513,164
1925	[5]23,217,209	1,681,291	23,644	7,602	1,937	14,105	18,191	6,278,532	748,191	338,114	410,077
1924	[5]22,182,267	1,549,969	23,636	7,539	1,935	14,162	18,202	6,042,268	874,744	493,609	381,135
1923	[5]21,372,858	1,408,461	22,839	7,398	1,852	13,589	17,810	5,646,076	1,059,149	681,724	377,425
1922	[5]20,580,001	1,335,453	22,290	7,307	1,834	13,149	17,280	5,321,347	429,273	245,509	183,764
1921	[5]20,329,224	1,237,030	22,292	7,275	1,801	13,216	17,083	5,059,844	557,035	319,874	237,161
1920	19,849,320	1,081,342	21,891	7,215	1,898	12,778	16,994	5,075,040	----------	----------	----------
1919	19,300,121	1,009,322	20,950	7,193	1,898	11,859	16,550	5,298,321	----------	----------	----------
1918	18,984,756	936,979	20,785	7,249	1,806	11,730	16,454	5,138,851	----------	----------	----------
1917	18,574,298	796,395	21,249	7,454	1,848	11,947	16,402	5,610,774	----------	----------	----------
1916	17,842,777	628,934	21,049	7,594	1,455	12,000	16,333	5,430,123	----------	----------	----------
JUNE 30											
1916	17,689,425	571,360	21,092	7,603	1,456	12,033	16,336	5,279,428	----------	----------	----------
1915	17,441,420	511,452	21,128	7,600	1,395	12,133	16,308	5,219,847	----------	----------	----------
1914	17,153,786	435,835	[6]20,247	[6]7,304	[6]1,376	[6]11,567	[6]15,759	5,667,073	----------	----------	----------
1913	16,588,603	[7]327,847	[6]19,796	[6]7,232	[6]1,379	[6]11,185	[6]15,366	5,780,982	----------	----------	----------
1912	16,004,745	[7]259,661	19,753	7,249	1,374	11,130	15,126	5,581,289	----------	----------	----------
1911	15,612,379	[7]210,466	19,209	7,075	1,396	10,738	15,044	5,730,250	----------	----------	----------
1910	[8]14,557,816	----------	18,417	6,710	1,403	10,304	14,376	5,412,578	----------	----------	----------
1909	13,609,184	----------	17,488	6,218	1,468	9,802	13,914	4,920,174	----------	----------	----------
1908	13,213,767	----------	16,768	5,911	1,463	9,394	12,834	4,843,371	----------	----------	----------
1907	13,030,344	----------	16,082	5,933	1,424	8,725	----------	4,948,756	----------	----------	----------
1906	12,420,288	----------	14,570	5,403	1,401	7,766	11,672	4,526,959	----------	----------	----------
1905	11,951,849	----------	13,805	5,181	1,373	7,251	11,167	4,119,087	----------	----------	----------
1904	11,511,537	----------	13,213	5,051	1,289	6,873	10,712	3,643,427	----------	----------	----------
1903	10,973,505	----------	12,600	4,877	1,279	6,444	10,282	3,450,738	----------	----------	----------
1902	10,658,321	----------	12,134	4,722	1,302	6,110	9,926	3,337,645	----------	----------	----------
1901	10,405,095	----------	11,688	4,475	1,331	5,882	9,483	2,977,575	----------	----------	----------
1900	10,263,313	----------	11,491	4,522	1,323	5,646	9,548	2,668,970	----------	----------	----------
1899	9,961,841	----------	11,034	4,323	1,192	5,519	9,432	2,239,503	----------	----------	----------
1898	9,760,581	----------	10,819	4,269	1,119	5,431	9,297	1,818,113	----------	----------	----------
1897	9,709,329	----------	10,635	4,367	998	5,270	9,168	1,603,550	----------	----------	----------
1896	9,500,328	----------	10,567	4,257	970	5,340	9,066	1,559,024	----------	----------	----------
1895	9,203,491	----------	10,347	4,202	760	5,385	8,900	1,485,618	----------	----------	----------
1894	9,073,471	----------	10,191	4,104	730	5,357	8,647	1,767,926	----------	----------	----------
1893	8,937,546	----------	9,895	3,982	687	5,226	8,332	1,809,601	----------	----------	----------
1892	[9]8,690,083	----------	9,686	3,979	654	5,053	8,295	1,825,705	----------	----------	----------
1891	[9]8,444,856	----------	9,291	3,796	655	4,840	8,008	1,796,391	----------	----------	----------
1890	[9]8,133,665	----------	8,984	3,803	606	4,575	7,577	1,598,132	----------	----------	----------

[1] Includes proprietary.
[2] Increase in investment over a period of years cannot be obtained accurately by subtraction of 1 year's investment from that of another owing to reorganization, sale, or abandonment reclassification, etc.
[3] Includes depreciation on "Miscellaneous physical property," prior to 1920. Amortization of defense projects included subsequent to 1940, and, beginning in 1950, includes amortization applicable to proprietary companies.
[4] Figures subsequent to 1914 include actually outstanding, nominally issued, and nominally outstanding securities in order that they may be comparable with those of previous years in which these items were not segregated. Funded debt unmatured does not include equipment obligations subsequent to 1942, but they are included herein to preserve the comparability of the figures.
[5] For 1921-1924, includes investment of lessor companies; and for 1925-1957, investment of lessor and proprietary companies.
[6] Class I and II railroads and their lessor subsidiaries.
[7] Class I railroads.
[8] Includes $170,000,000, estimated reserve for accrued depreciation to put figure on a comparable basis with those of other years.
[9] Represents 1893 investments less increases each year on account of change in classification in 1893.

Series Q 106–116. Railroad Income and Expenses, and Interest and Dividends: 1890 to 1957

[In thousands of dollars. Includes intercorporate duplications. Unless otherwise noted, covers Class I, II, and III, railroads subject to general exception, that prior to 1908 the returns for switching and terminal companies were included where applicable]

Year ending—	Income and expenses									Interest and dividends [1]	
	Operating revenue	Operating expenses			Tax accruals	Operating income	Net operating income	Net income [1]	Ratio of operating expenses to operating revenues (percent)	Dividends declared	Interest accrued on funded debt
		Total	Maintenance of way and structures	Maintenance of equipment							
	106	107	108	109	110	111	112	113	114	115	116
DECEMBER 31											
1957	10,625,452	8,321,577	1,458,888	1,928,912	1,090,818	1,213,057	934,645	765,227	78.32	466,415	382,175
1956	10,686,492	8,199,792	1,433,037	1,907,606	1,144,446	1,342,254	1,083,708	908,416	76.73	476,083	373,207
1955	10,229,600	7,724,496	1,412,877	1,798,579	1,100,920	1,404,185	1,144,347	958,849	75.51	476,207	373,502
1954	9,484,015	7,460,507	1,376,478	1,704,985	877,304	1,146,203	887,817	712,252	78.66	405,403	376,020
1953	10,787,891	8,218,223	1,612,390	1,993,602	1,205,366	1,364,302	1,122,512	939,887	76.18	445,145	378,218
1952	10,702,877	8,134,811	1,546,613	1,965,327	1,282,144	1,285,922	1,091,657	900,472	76.01	394,042	376,907
1951	10,511,612	8,122,521	1,505,488	1,956,438	1,223,644	1,165,447	956,699	757,934	77.27	373,574	367,244
1950	9,587,000	7,135,055	1,311,775	1,718,660	1,212,084	1,239,861	1,055,309	854,951	74.42	348,811	367,218
1949	8,680,791	6,968,296	1,309,857	1,617,800	845,089	867,406	693,957	496,103	80.27	306,995	365,393
1948	9,784,332	7,552,630	1,374,058	1,713,967	1,043,036	1,188,666	1,014,815	767,949	77.19	335,313	361,879
1947	8,784,214	6,869,806	1,234,978	1,568,124	949,273	965,136	790,534	537,405	78.21	280,397	374,150
1946	7,709,171	6,422,494	1,169,887	1,478,302	506,480	780,197	624,868	334,966	83.31	283,171	406,147
1945	8,986,954	7,115,391	1,431,221	2,157,678	835,434	1,036,130	858,864	502,250	79.17	295,294	449,917
1944	9,524,628	6,345,035	1,283,208	1,597,155	1,861,652	1,317,941	1,113,153	733,461	66.62	292,248	488,877
1943	9,138,419	5,714,804	1,125,873	1,449,356	1,862,940	1,560,675	1,370,568	946,150	62.54	263,919	515,617
1942	7,547,826	4,653,705	811,206	1,219,460	1,211,775	1,682,347	1,499,364	992,843	61.66	254,088	564,174
1941	5,413,972	3,709,921	615,533	1,000,375	555,970	1,148,081	1,009,592	557,672	68.52	239,438	543,954
1940	4,354,712	3,131,598	508,328	826,242	402,953	820,161	690,554	243,148	71.91	216,522	547,333
1939	4,050,047	2,959,438	477,697	773,080	361,617	728,992	595,961	141,134	73.07	179,412	512,283
1938	3,616,072	2,762,681	431,021	683,529	346,236	507,155	376,865	−87,468	76.40	136,270	521,758
1937	4,226,325	3,165,154	508,319	834,820	331,013	730,158	597,841	146,351	74.89	227,596	532,237
1936	4,108,658	2,973,366	466,284	790,240	324,858	810,434	675,600	221,591	72.37	231,733	548,452
1935	3,499,126	2,630,177	404,105	688,678	240,760	626,973	505,415	52,177	75.17	202,568	559,187
1934	3,316,861	2,479,997	375,410	644,989	243,646	592,034	465,896	23,282	74.77	211,767	569,760
1933	3,138,186	2,285,218	331,653	605,409	253,522	598,222	477,326	26,543	72.82	158,790	590,230
1932	3,168,537	2,441,814	361,337	625,606	279,263	446,417	325,332	−121,630	77.06	150,774	591,340
1931	4,246,385	3,273,906	544,300	825,923	308,492	663,084	528,204	169,287	77.10	401,463	592,866
1930	5,356,484	3,993,621	723,525	1,030,482	353,881	1,007,907	874,154	577,923	74.56	603,150	588,742
1929	6,373,004	4,579,162	877,067	1,216,045	402,698	1,389,955	1,262,636	977,230	71.85	560,902	580,770
1928	6,212,464	4,508,606	861,846	1,181,251	395,631	1,306,620	1,182,467	855,018	72.57	510,018	578,831
1927	6,245,716	4,662,521	895,063	1,234,655	383,112	1,198,547	1,077,842	741,924	74.65	[2]567,281	583,452
1926	6,508,679	4,766,235	894,886	1,300,680	396,538	1,344,010	1,229,020	883,422	73.23	473,683	581,709
1925	6,246,884	4,633,497	844,186	1,278,227	365,790	1,245,622	1,136,728	771,053	74.17	409,645	583,875
1924	6,045,252	4,608,807	821,793	1,279,680	347,437	1,086,578	984,463	623,399	76.24	385,130	588,301
1923	6,419,210	4,999,383	843,224	1,485,555	339,577	1,078,226	974,918	632,118	77.88	411,882	551,705
1922	5,674,483	4,509,991	755,030	1,269,971	308,145	854,779	769,411	434,459	79.48	338,806	538,594
1921	5,632,665	4,668,998	787,537	1,271,921	283,163	678,551	601,139	350,540	82.89	456,482	529,398
1920	6,310,151	5,954,394	1,069,436	1,613,950	279,272	75,402	12,101	481,951	94.36	331,103	500,354
1919	5,250,420	4,498,817	800,912	1,245,264	239,136	511,546	454,132	496,609	85.68	335,242	476,075
1918	4,985,290	4,071,522	673,084	1,120,611	229,533	684,004	646,223	442,336	81.67	339,186	468,286
1917	4,115,413	2,906,283	460,447	700,073	218,632	988,776	950,557	658,225	70.62	381,852	474,123
1916	3,691,065	2,426,251	439,195	609,105	161,825	1,102,171	1,058,506	735,341	65.73	366,561	481,426
JUNE 30											
1916	3,472,642	2,277,202	421,501	570,326	150,015	1,044,603	1,002,935	671,398	65.58	342,109	474,535
1915	2,956,193	2,088,683	381,532	509,819	137,775	729,069	694,276	354,787	70.65	328,478	464,186
1914	3,127,730	2,280,416	[3]419,278	[3]532,139	140,470	706,844	674,190	395,492	72.91	451,653	442,595
1913	[3]3,193,118	[3]2,235,923	[3]421,232	[3]511,561	[3]122,005	[3]835,190	[3]805,266	[4]546,761	[3]70.02	369,078	[4]434,753
1912	2,906,416	2,035,058	367,448	450,373	113,819	757,540	727,458	453,125	70.02	400,315	429,027
1911	2,852,855	1,976,332	366,025	428,367	102,657	773,866	744,669	547,281	69.28	460,195	410,327
1910	2,812,142	1,881,879	368,507	413,110	98,035	832,228	805,097	583,191	66.92	405,771	399,582
1909	2,473,205	1,650,034	308,450	363,913	85,140	738,032	710,474	441,063	66.72	321,072	382,675
1908	2,440,639	1,710,402	329,373	368,354	78,674	651,562	634,794	443,987	70.08	390,695	368,296
1907	2,589,106	1,748,516	343,545	368,062	73,743	----------	766,846	488,014	67.53	308,089	344,243
1906	2,325,765	1,536,877	311,721	328,555	69,064	----------	719,824	434,229	66.08	272,796	322,556
1905	2,082,482	1,390,602	275,046	288,441	58,712	----------	633,168	364,811	66.78	237,964	310,632
1904	1,975,174	1,338,896	261,280	267,185	56,802	----------	579,476	317,308	67.79	221,941	297,675
1903	1,900,847	1,257,539	266,422	240,430	53,522	----------	590,056	338,324	66.16	196,728	283,953
1902	1,726,380	1,116,249	248,382	213,381	50,054	----------	560,077	314,989	64.66	185,392	274,422
1901	1,588,526	1,030,397	231,057	190,300	46,708	----------	511,421	273,450	64.86	156,736	262,095
1900	1,487,045	961,429	211,221	181,174	44,445	----------	481,171	252,760	64.65	139,598	252,950
1899	1,313,610	856,969	180,411	150,919	44,397	----------	412,244	177,225	65.24	111,010	251,158
1898	1,247,326	817,973	173,315	142,625	41,929	----------	387,424	147,167	65.58	96,153	246,127
1897	1,122,090	752,525	159,484	122,762	41,119	----------	328,446	85,802	67.06	87,111	247,880
1896	1,150,169	772,989	160,345	133,382	37,962	----------	339,219	94,794	67.20	87,603	249,624
1895	1,075,371	725,720	143,976	113,789	38,146	----------	311,505	60,133	67.48	85,288	252,513
1894	1,073,362	731,414	143,669	112,895	36,556	----------	305,391	60,174	68.14	95,515	252,780
1893	1,220,752	827,921	169,258	136,876	35,071	----------	357,760	114,015	67.82	100,930	250,177
1892	1,171,407	780,998	164,189	128,712	32,751	----------	357,658	120,091	66.67	97,615	240,075
1891	1,096,761	731,888	153,672	117,048	32,052	----------	332,822	114,965	66.73	91,118	219,521
1890	1,051,878	692,094	152,719	114,039	29,806	----------	329,978	106,270	65.80	87,072	221,500

[1] Includes lessors.
[2] Includes unusual items, amounting to $76,300,000, not representing cash.
[3] Class I and II railroads.
[4] Class I and II railroads and their lessor subsidiaries.

Series Q 117–123. Railroad Tax Accruals: 1921 to 1957

[In millions of dollars. Class I railroads]

Year	Total	U.S. Government taxes					Other taxes	Year	Total	U.S. Government taxes					Other taxes
		Total	Old-age retirement	Unemployment insurance	Income and excess profits	All other				Total	Old-age retirement	Unemployment insurance	Income and excess profits	All other	
	117	118	119	120	121	122	123		117	118	119	120	121	122	123
1957	1,068.4	664.2	258.7	82.9	320.3	2.4	404.2	1938	340.8	75.4	47.1	5.9	18.9	3.5	265.4
1956	1,121.3	728.5	269.3	64.9	392.0	2.3	392.8	1937	325.7	66.7	25.1	4.5	32.0	5.1	259.0
								1936	319.8	91.8	47.3	8.8	30.7	5.0	228.0
1955	1,080.4	700.9	262.5	21.3	414.3	2.7	379.5								
1954	861.3	499.6	250.6	20.0	226.4	2.6	361.7	1935	236.9	24.7	--------	--------	18.9	5.8	212.2
1953	1,185.0	822.4	266.8	21.2	533.1	1.3	362.6	1934	239.6	19.8	--------	--------	14.3	5.5	219.8
1952	1,261.8	906.4	269.8	21.6	612.6	2.4	355.4	1933	249.6	19.3	--------	--------	12.7	6.6	230.3
1951	1,203.3	855.8	264.1	22.0	567.1	2.6	347.5	1932	275.1	11.9	--------	--------	--------	--------	263.2
								1931	303.5	10.2	--------	--------	--------	--------	293.3
1950	1,194.6	866.5	242.1	20.2	601.2	3.0	328.1								
1949	832.5	517.8	233.8	19.4	261.6	3.0	314.7	1930	348.6	39.9	--------	--------	--------	--------	308.6
1948	1,028.5	721.2	243.9	21.1	448.4	7.9	307.3	1929	396.7	89.4	--------	--------	--------	--------	307.2
1947	936.4	654.0	232.2	121.2	297.6	3.0	282.4	1928	389.4	88.0	--------	--------	--------	--------	301.4
1946	498.1	242.1	136.9	117.4	-15.7	3.4	256.0	1927	376.1	84.6	--------	--------	--------	--------	291.5
								1926	388.9	108.3	--------	--------	--------	--------	280.6
1945	823.5	548.0	119.8	110.8	305.7	11.9	275.5								
1944	1,846.0	1,560.4	120.2	110.8	1,304.4	25.0	285.6	1925	358.5	86.5	--------	--------	--------	--------	272.0
1943	1,849.2	1,578.5	110.0	101.6	1,335.1	31.8	270.7	1924	340.3	73.4	--------	--------	--------	--------	266.9
1942	1,198.8	950.6	85.5	85.5	755.1	24.5	248.2	1923	331.9	77.1	--------	--------	--------	--------	254.8
1941	547.2	323.3	69.1	69.0	173.8	11.4	223.9	1922	301.0	51.9	--------	--------	--------	--------	249.1
								1921	275.9	37.3	--------	--------	--------	--------	238.6
1940	396.4	181.5	58.2	58.2	59.9	5.2	214.9								
1939	355.7	118.7	50.3	28.7	32.8	6.9	237.0								

Series Q 124. Miles of Railroad Operated by Receivers or Trustees: 1894 to 1957

[As of end of year. Class I, II, and III railroads]

Year ending—	Miles	Year ending—	Miles	Year ending—	Miles	Year ending—	Miles	Year ending—	Miles	Year ending—	Miles
	124		124		124		124		124		124
DEC. 31		DEC. 31—Con.		DEC. 31—Con.		DEC. 31—Con.		JUNE 30		JUNE 30 —Con.	
1957	1,022							1916	37,353		
1956	1,594	1945	39,714	1935	68,345	1925	18,687	1915	30,223	1905	796
		1944	50,497	1934	42,168	1924	8,105	1914	18,608	1904	1,323
1955	11,685	1943	64,758	1933	41,698	1923	12,623	1913	16,286	1903	1,185
1954	11,608	1942	66,904	1932	22,545	1922	15,259	1912	9,786	1902	1,475
1953	12,054	1941	69,859	1931	12,970	1921	13,512	1911	4,593	1901	2,497
1952	11,942										
1951	12,212	1940	75,270	1930	9,486	1920	16,290	1910	5,257	1900	4,178
		1939	77,013	1929	5,703	1919	16,590	1909	10,530	1899	9,853
1950	12,223	1938	76,938	1928	5,256	1918	19,208	1908	9,529	1898	12,745
1949	12,679	1937	70,884	1927	16,752	1917	17,376	1907	3,926	1897	18,862
1948	13,283	1936	69,712	1926	17,632	1916	34,804	1906	3,971	1896	30,475
1947	22,750									1895	37,856
1946	34,389									1894	40,819

Series Q 125–127. Railroad Highway Grade Crossings: 1925 to 1957

[Class I railroads. Includes switching and terminal companies]

Year	Total	Specially protected	Eliminated during year by separation of grades	Year	Total	Specially protected	Eliminated during year by separation of grades
	125	126	127		125	126	127
1957	223,381	39,884	113	1940	230,285	32,421	209
1956	224,519	39,324	72	1939	231,104	31,775	204
1955	226,318	39,060	84	1938	231,400	31,448	235
1954	226,522	38,528	80	1937	232,322	31,119	400
1953	227,110	37,990	53	1936	232,902	30,466	521
1952	227,291	37,242	95				
1951	227,415	36,682	50	1935	234,231	30,200	164
				1934	234,820	30,226	231
1950	227,364	35,968	61	1933	235,827	30,628	221
1949	226,791	35,243	53	1932	237,035	30,809	189
1948	226,844	34,507	26	1931	238,017	31,052	361
1947	226,501	33,789	24				
1946	226,143	33,320	23	1930	240,673	30,287	403
				1929	242,809	30,190	275
1945	226,153	33,321	7	1928	240,089	29,215	270
1944	226,357	33,211	14	1927	236,283	28,724	245
1943	226,938	33,124	37	1926	235,158	27,927	195
1942	227,496	33,075	149	1925	233,633	27,241	----------
1941	229,722	32,859	182				

Series Q 128–137. Fuel Received, Ties and Rails Laid, and Purchases by Railroads: 1917 to 1957

[Class I line-haul railroads]

Year	Fuel received			New rails laid	Cross-ties laid		Purchases			
	Bituminous coal	Fuel oil	Diesel oil		Total	Treated	Total, incl. miscellaneous	Fuel	Forest products	Iron and steel products
	128	129	130	131	132	133	134	135	136	137
	1,000 short tons	Mil. gal.	Mil. gal.	1,000 long tons	1,000	1,000	Mil. dol.	Mil. dol.	Mil. dol.	Mil. dol.
1957	8,160	279	3,633	698	25,123	24,497	1,816	460	128	609
1956	12,280	443	3,639	788	27,323	26,848	1,884	477	155	613
1955	15,188	613	3,453	860	27,173	26,490	1,637	454	119	510
1954	15,964	656	3,160	886	25,728	24,531	1,425	433	114	406
1953	28,005	1,153	3,067	1,163	33,462	32,144	1,920	510	176	613
1952	37,829	1,668	2,759	970	34,231	32,910	1,818	539	177	513
1951	54,226	2,335	2,323	1,145	32,457	30,804	2,176	621	188	704
1950	63,906	2,519	1,923	1,222	33,091	31,553	1,740	609	121	510
1949	64,671	2,638	1,486	1,293	32,926	31,198	1,641	564	142	454
1948	98,826	3,759	1,170	1,383	40,472	38,281	2,183	833	166	590
1947	109,884	4,052	785	1,464	40,206	37,920	1,909	692	172	504
1946	108,148	4,144	544	1,240	40,150	37,671	1,571	553	149	416
1945	123,007	4,706	441	1,628	46,624	43,657	1,572	555	137	418
1944	135,579	4,744	316	1,583	51,259	47,695	1,611	586	159	432
1943	129,738	4,802	219	1,293	49,344	44,822	1,394	527	150	340
1942	120,910	4,135	174	1,208	53,241	47,932	1,260	426	115	354
1941	104,100	3,368	114	1,210	50,077	43,872	1,161	350	104	380
1940	88,595	2,752	73	1,013	45,326	38,698	854	274	82	264
1939	81,813	2,573	44	886	46,410	39,654	769	257	70	236
1938	74,784	2,426	-----	606	42,508	34,589	583	244	57	127
1937	91,718	2,875	-----	1,038	49,738	39,674	966	294	105	311
1936	91,707	2,569	-----	931	49,117	38,206	803	272	77	239
1935	81,286	2,282	-----	587	45,260	33,939	593	233	57	135
1934	79,494	2,108	-----	639	44,131	32,367	600	217	64	151
1933	75,487	1,943	-----	408	38,007	26,818	466	181	42	104
1932	74,670	1,984	-----	407	40,137	30,107	445	178	52	95
1931	91,136	2,380	-----	1,030	54,449	41,851	695	245	76	189
1930	108,651	2,870	-----	1,592	69,325	54,529	1,039	307	135	305
1929	124,152	3,208	-----	2,037	81,964	64,724	1,330	364	158	407
1928	119,820	2,847	-----	2,147	84,585	64,331	1,271	385	161	375
1927	130,606	2,921	-----	2,212	86,243	62,963	1,396	439	176	407
1926	139,602	3,173	-----	2,210	[1]80,746	[1]55,558	1,559	473	186	507
1925	131,452	3,114	-----	1,950	82,717	50,090	1,392	459	170	419
1924	126,340	3,095	-----	1,791	83,073	44,490	1,343	472	181	366
1923	157,900	3,017	-----	1,730	84,435	41,656	1,739	618	233	465
1922	120,654	-----	-----	1,390	86,642	40,630	-----	-----	-----	-----
1921	127,630	-----	-----	1,464	86,522	36,072	-----	-----	-----	-----
1920	-----	-----	-----	1,412	86,829	37,792	-----	-----	-----	-----
1919	-----	-----	-----	2,335	80,903	-----	-----	-----	-----	-----
1918	-----	-----	-----	1,883	76,139	-----	-----	-----	-----	-----
1917	-----	-----	-----	2,047	79,070	-----	-----	-----	-----	-----

[1] Figures for this and earlier years less inclusive than for later years.

Series Q 138–140. Pullman Company Operations: 1915 to 1957

Year	Average miles of road over which operations conducted	Revenue passenger-miles [1] (millions)	Employees	Year	Average miles of road over which operations conducted	Revenue passenger-miles (millions)	Employees
	138	139	140		138	139	140
1957	85,068	5,388	14,890	1935	112,117	7,146	20,436
1956	87,472	6,630	16,793	1934	112,420	6,891	19,066
				1933	112,298	6,142	15,887
1955	89,124	6,882	18,061	1932	118,061	6,757	17,132
1954	91,920	7,271	19,866	1931	125,703	9,891	22,546
1953	94,518	8,200	21,529				
1952	96,390	9,336	22,588	1930	129,578	12,516	26,165
1951	99,592	9,893	23,862	1929	130,019	14,059	29,250
				1928	128,753	13,938	26,815
1950	102,722	10,558	22,820	1927	123,334	14,099	27,359
1949	104,287	10,544	22,286	1926	126,907	14,409	26,185
1948	104,940	12,172	23,724				
1947	105,950	13,516	29,046	1925	126,840	14,016	26,919
1946	100,653	20,672	36,982	1924	124,795	13,082	25,091
				1923	124,794	12,982	23,579
1945	95,765	27,276	41,601	1922	123,547	11,759	19,066
1944	103,766	28,267	39,703	1921	-----	11,295	-----
1943	104,128	25,891	33,182				
1942	106,408	19,072	26,591	1920	-----	14,334	-----
1941	108,034	10,070	22,704	1919	-----	13,720	-----
				1918	-----	10,679	-----
1940	109,595	8,214	20,877	1917	-----	11,072	-----
1939	109,886	8,485	21,335	1916	-----	9,285	-----
1938	110,728	8,270	20,750	1915	-----	8,925	-----
1937	111,507	9,170	23,406				
1936	111,522	8,355	21,711				

[1] 1939–1957 includes Pullman operations on Canadian and Mexican railroads; excludes that of chartered car passengers.

Series Q 141-152. Railroad Employment and Wages, and Accidents and Fatalities: 1890 to 1957

[Statistics on accidents and fatalities not strictly comparable because of changing definition of a reportable accident]

Year ending—	Employees [1]		Railroad accidents and fatalities (all steam railroads)									
	Number	Compensation	Total		Passengers [2][3]		Employees [4]		Other persons [3]		Trespassers [3][5]	
			Killed	Injured	Killed	Injured	Killed	Injured	Killed	Injured	Killed	Injured
	141	142	143	144	145	146	147	148	149	150	151	152
	1,000	$1,000										
DECEMBER 31												
1957	999	5,422,080	2,393	18,688	15	1,566	195	12,246	1,441	4,259	742	617
1956	1,058	5,387,631	2,578	28,676	57	2,756	288	19,608	2,233	6,312	818	724
1955	1,071	5,045,278	2,849	27,846	24	2,253	282	19,011	2,455	6,576	867	680
1954	1,078	4,906,584	2,575	25,547	30	2,247	235	17,219	2,310	6,081	870	727
1953	1,221	5,380,828	3,039	29,214	49	2,503	343	20,170	2,647	6,541	1,044	796
1952	1,242	5,382,489	3,011	30,001	24	2,049	386	21,339	2,601	6,613	1,043	807
1951	1,292	5,328,072	3,459	34,454	150	3,184	432	24,266	2,877	7,004	1,142	826
1950	1,237	4,644,890	3,486	33,267	180	3,419	392	22,586	2,914	7,262	1,215	942
1949	1,209	4,468,545	3,426	32,123	37	2,545	450	22,993	2,939	6,585	1,287	921
1948	1,345	4,820,747	3,883	43,107	59	3,607	622	31,961	3,202	7,539	1,445	964
1947	1,371	4,399,296	4,285	48,819	79	4,246	791	36,880	3,415	7,693	1,480	1,018
1946	1,378	4,213,530	4,508	52,026	128	4,714	738	39,472	3,642	7,840	1,635	987
1945	1,439	3,900,928	4,812	61,515	156	4,840	972	48,632	3,684	8,043	1,592	1,012
1944	1,434	3,897,755	4,908	61,251	267	4,854	1,087	48,613	3,554	7,784	1,550	964
1943	1,375	3,556,189	5,051	60,348	278	5,166	1,072	46,971	3,701	8,211	1,755	1,135
1942	1,291	2,966,062	5,337	48,123	122	3,501	1,005	36,032	4,210	8,590	2,013	1,353
1941	1,159	2,360,369	5,191	37,829	48	3,009	807	25,866	4,336	8,954	2,195	1,576
1940	1,046	1,990,631	4,740	29,606	83	2,597	583	18,350	4,074	8,659	2,095	1,773
1939	1,007	1,889,130	4,492	28,144	40	2,580	536	17,383	3,916	8,181	2,352	1,956
1938	958	1,771,083	4,649	27,275	81	2,345	513	16,569	4,055	8,361	2,360	2,108
1937	1,137	2,013,677	5,502	36,713	34	2,594	712	24,114	4,756	10,005	2,654	2,302
1936	1,086	1,873,819	5,550	34,723	41	2,548	720	22,409	4,789	9,766	2,801	2,418
1935	1,014	1,666,229	5,258	28,108	30	1,949	600	16,742	4,628	9,417	2,786	2,706
1934	1,027	1,541,313	5,020	28,641	38	1,945	556	17,338	4,426	9,358	2,697	2,785
1933	991	1,424,392	5,180	27,516	51	2,067	533	15,932	4,596	9,517	2,892	3,602
1932	1,052	1,535,066	4,905	29,232	27	1,912	579	17,742	4,299	9,578	2,577	3,364
1931	1,283	2,124,784	5,271	35,671	46	2,104	677	23,358	4,548	10,209	2,489	2,977
1930	1,517	2,588,598	5,665	49,443	61	2,666	977	35,872	4,627	10,905	2,409	2,675
1929	1,694	2,940,206	6,690	77,013	114	3,846	1,428	60,739	5,148	12,428	2,424	2,346
1928	1,692	2,874,429	6,680	86,205	91	3,468	1,329	70,873	5,260	11,864	2,487	2,367
1927	1,776	2,963,034	6,992	104,817	88	3,893	1,570	88,223	5,334	12,701	2,726	2,725
1926	1,822	3,001,804	7,090	130,235	152	4,461	1,672	111,903	5,266	13,871	2,561	2,545
1925	1,786	2,916,193	6,766	137,435	176	5,643	1,599	119,224	4,996	13,259	2,584	2,688
1924	1,795	2,882,658	6,617	143,739	153	6,023	1,543	125,319	4,925	13,066	2,556	2,853
1923	1,902	3,062,026	7,385	171,712	143	6,463	2,026	152,678	5,221	13,187	2,779	3,047
1922	1,670	2,693,292	6,325	134,871	203	6,712	1,657	117,197	4,468	11,521	2,430	2,844
1921	1,705	2,823,970	5,996	120,685	205	5,584	1,446	104,530	4,345	10,571	---------	---------
1920	2,076	3,754,281	6,958	168,309	229	7,591	2,578	149,414	4,151	11,304	---------	---------
1919	1,960	2,897,769	6,978	149,053	273	7,456	2,138	131,018	4,567	10,579	---------	---------
1918	1,892	2,665,013	9,286	174,575	471	7,316	3,419	156,013	5,396	11,246	---------	---------
1917	1,786	1,782,965	10,087	194,805	301	7,582	3,199	174,247	6,587	12,976	---------	---------
1916	1,701	1,506,961	10,001	196,722	246	7,152	2,941	176,923	6,814	12,647	---------	---------
JUNE 30												
1916	1,654	1,403,968	9,364	180,375	239	7,488	2,687	160,663	6,438	12,224	---------	---------
1915	1,548	1,277,663	8,621	162,040	199	10,914	2,152	138,092	6,270	13,034	---------	---------
1914	1,710	1,381,117	10,302	192,662	232	13,887	3,259	165,212	6,811	13,563	---------	---------
1913	[6]1,815	[6]1,373,831	10,964	200,308	350	15,130	3,715	171,417	6,899	13,761	---------	---------
1912	1,716	1,252,348	10,585	169,538	283	14,938	3,635	142,442	6,667	12,158	---------	---------
1911	1,670	1,208,466	10,396	150,159	299	12,042	3,602	126,039	6,495	12,078	---------	---------
1910	1,699	1,143,725	9,682	119,507	324	12,451	3,382	95,671	5,976	11,385	---------	---------
1909	1,503	988,324	8,722	95,626	253	10,311	2,610	75,006	5,859	10,309	---------	---------
1908	1,436	1,035,438	10,188	104,230	381	11,556	3,405	82,487	6,402	10,187	---------	---------
1907	1,672	1,072,386	11,839	111,016	610	13,041	4,534	87,644	6,695	10,331	---------	---------
1906	1,521	900,802	10,618	97,706	359	10,764	3,929	76,701	6,330	10,241	---------	---------
1905	1,382	839,945	9,703	86,008	537	10,457	3,361	66,833	5,805	8,718	---------	---------
1904	1,296	817,599	10,046	84,155	441	9,111	3,632	67,067	5,973	7,977	---------	---------
1903	1,313	757,321	9,840	76,553	355	8,231	3,606	60,481	5,879	7,841	---------	---------
1902	1,189	676,029	8,588	64,662	345	6,683	2,969	50,524	5,274	7,455	---------	---------
1901	1,071	610,714	8,455	53,339	282	4,988	2,675	41,142	5,498	7,209	---------	---------
1900	1,018	577,265	7,865	50,320	249	4,128	2,550	39,643	5,066	6,549	---------	---------
1899	929	522,968	7,123	44,620	239	3,442	2,210	34,923	4,674	6,255	---------	---------
1898	875	495,056	6,859	40,882	221	2,945	1,958	31,761	4,680	6,176	---------	---------
1897	823	465,602	6,437	36,731	222	2,795	1,693	27,667	4,522	6,269	---------	---------
1896	827	468,825	6,448	38,687	181	2,873	1,861	29,969	4,406	5,845	---------	---------
1895	785	445,508	6,136	33,748	170	2,375	1,811	25,696	4,155	5,677	---------	---------
1894	780	---------	6,447	31,889	324	3,034	1,823	23,422	4,300	5,433	---------	---------
1893	874	---------	7,346	40,393	299	3,229	2,727	31,729	4,320	5,435	---------	---------
1892	821	---------	7,147	36,652	376	3,227	2,554	28,267	4,217	5,158	---------	---------
1891	784	---------	7,029	33,881	293	2,972	2,660	26,140	4,076	4,769	---------	---------
1890	749	---------	---------	---------	---------	---------	---------	---------	---------	---------	---------	---------

[1] See headnote for series Q 106–116.
[2] Passengers on trains and travelers not on trains.
[3] Casualties sustained in nontrain accidents included with "Other persons." Nontrain accidents are those not caused directly by operation or movement of trains, locomotives, or cars, but attributable to shop machinery or use of tools and apparatus that result in reportable casualties.

[4] Prior to 1921 casualties sustained by employees not on duty in nontrain accidents included with "Other persons."
[5] Trespassers included with "Other persons" prior to 1922.
[6] Class I and II railroads.

chapter Q

WATER TRANSPORTATION (Series Q 153–245)

Q 153–245. General note.

Basic governmental sources of historical merchant-marine and water-traffic statistics include *American State Papers: Class IV, Commerce and Navigation*, vols. 1 and 2, for 1789–1823; the various annual issues of *Foreign Commerce and Navigation of the United States*, for 1821–1946, originally issued by the Register of the Treasury and then by the Treasury Department, later by the Department of Commerce and Labor, and finally by the Department of Commerce; the *Annual Report of the Commissioner of Navigation*, 1884–1923, the issuance of which followed a similar succession beginning with the Treasury Department; annual issues of *Merchant Marine Statistics*, 1924–1957, originally prepared by the Department of Commerce as successor to the statistical section of the *Annual Report of the Commissioner of Navigation*, and now issued annually by the Bureau of Customs; and the various annual issues of the *Annual Report of the Office of the Chief of Engineers*, Corps of Engineers. The *Statistical Abstract of the United States*, a secondary source, also contains historical merchant-marine and water-traffic statistics. The *Statistical Abstract* has been issued by the following agencies: 1878–1902, Bureau of Statistics (Treasury Department); 1903–1911, Bureau of Statistics (Department of Commerce and Labor); 1912, Bureau of Foreign and Domestic Commerce (Department of Commerce and Labor); 1913–1937, Bureau of Foreign and Domestic Commerce (Department of Commerce); 1938–1957, Bureau of the Census (Department of Commerce).

Congressional documents also contain historical series on the merchant marine, foreign commerce, and related fields. For 1789–1882, a particularly valuable collection of documents was found in the library of the Department of Commerce, bound together under the title *Decadence of American Shipping and Compulsory Pilotage*. The documents included are as follows: *Foreign Commerce and Decadence of American Shipping*, H. R. Ex. Doc. No. 111, 41st Congress, 2d session; *Causes of the Reduction of American Tonnage and the Decline of Navigation Interest . . .*, H. R. Report No. 28, 41st Congress, 2d session; *Foreign Commerce and the Practical Workings of Maritime Reciprocity*, H. R. Ex. Doc. No. 76, 41st Congress, 3d session; *Causes of the Decadence of Our Merchant Marine; Means for Its Restoration and the Extension of Our Foreign Commerce*, H. R. Report No. 342, 46th Congress, 3d session; *American Shipping*, H. R. Report No. 1827, 47th Congress, 2d session; *American Merchant Marine*, H. R. Report No. 363, 48th Congress, 1st session; *Ship-Building and Ship-Owning Interests*, H. R. Report No. 750, 48th Congress, 1st session; and reports of lesser interest, H. R. Misc. Doc. No. 37 and Report No. 1848, both of the 48th Congress, 1st session.

Since 1921, publications of the Maritime Commission and its predecessor agencies also should be consulted, particularly the reports entitled, *Ocean-Going Merchant Fleets of Principal Maritime Nations, Iron and Steel, Steam and Motor, Vessels of 2,000 Gross Tons and Over*, issued quarterly or semiannually, 1921–1941, and *Employment of American Flag Steam and Motor Merchant Vessels of 1,000 Gross Tons and Over*, issued quarterly, 1923–1941. Finally, the Bureau of the Census (and its predecessor Census Office) has published the results of five censuses of water tranportation, as follows: 1880, 1889, 1906, 1916, and 1926 (see general note for series Q 153–190, below).

Q 153–190. General note.

Statistics on documented merchant vessels and shipbuilding are from *Merchant Marine Statistics*, various annual issues, supplemented by records of the Bureau of Customs. Many are from the 1936 issue. Some of the estimates from the 1936 report have been modified, however, as explained below in table II. The text statements, and the correction of errors found in the published tables are based on reference to the primary sources, as follows: For 1789–1823, see *American State Papers: Class IV, Commerce and Navigation*, vols. 1 and 2 (published in 1834); for 1821–1892, see annual issues of *Commerce and Navigation of the United States*; for 1884–1923, see issues of *Annual Report of the Commissioner of Navigation*; for 1924–1945, see annual issues of *Merchant Marine Statistics*.

Of the Maritime Commission reports cited in the general note for series Q 153–245, above, the first, *Ocean-Going Merchant Fleets . . .*, provides data for each leading maritime nation on ocean-going merchant vessels of 2,000 gross tons and over, showing number and tonnage of such fleets classified by age, speed, size, boilers, engines, draft, etc., by major vessel type. The second, *Employment of American Flag Steam and Motor Merchant Vessels . . .*, shows for seagoing merchant vessels of 1,000 gross tons and over the number and tonnage of such vessels employed in U.S. foreign and domestic trade, arranged by major vessel type, ownership (government and private), and area of operation.

Census statistics on water transportation are not presented here. For reports of these censuses, see *Tenth Census Reports*, vol. IV, *Report on Agencies of Transportation*, 1880; *Eleventh Census Reports, Report on Transportation Business*, part 1, "Transportation by Water"; *Transportation by Water, 1906; Water Transportation, 1916;* and *Water Transportation, 1926*.

The first census, for 1880, was limited to steam vessels. The report of this census includes a detailed history of steam navigation in the United States with separate discussion and single-year construction statistics by geographic region, from the beginning to 1880. (See T. C. Purdy, "Report on Steam Navigation in the United States," *Tenth Census Reports*, 1880, vol. IV.) The report of the shipbuilding census, also taken the same year, includes a detailed technical history of shipbuilding in all aspects, with particular reference to sailing craft. Single-year figures are shown for New England shipbuilding, 1674–1714, classified by type of vessel and place where built. (See Henry Hall, "Report on the Ship-Building Industry of the United States," *Tenth Census Reports*, 1880, vol. VIII.)

The Censuses of 1889 and 1906 included all classes of vessels. However, the 1889 Census included fishing vessels for the Pacific Division only and the 1906 Census excluded fishing vessels. The Censuses of 1916 and 1926 provided data for all U.S., documented and undocumented, vessels and craft of 5 tons net register and over, whether propelled by machinery or sails, or unrigged, except that certain specified types of vessels were excluded. (See Bureau of the Census, *Water Transportation, 1926*, p. 5.) While the Census reports of 1850 and 1860 contain some statistics relating to water transportation, these statistics apparently were collected by other agencies.

Data shown here are for documented merchant vessels only, exclusive of yachts. The following definitions are those currently applicable:

Documented vessels include all vessels granted registers, enrollments and licenses, or licenses, as "vessels of the United States," and as such have certain benefits and privileges. Vessels of 5 net tons and over owned by citizens of the United States and otherwise complying with the requirements for documentation may be documented to engage in the foreign or coasting trades or the fisheries.

Registers are ordinarily issued to vessels engaged in the foreign trade or the whale fisheries. Historically, this group has included the major portion of the whaling fleet.

Enrollments and licenses are issued to vessels of 20 net tons and over engaged in the coasting trade or fisheries.

Licenses may be issued to vessels of less than 20 net tons engaged in the coasting trade or fisheries.

Undocumented craft are those not registered, enrolled, or licensed. Barges, scows, lighters, and canal boats, without any propelling power of their own, operated exclusively in a harbor, on the canals or other internal waters of a State, or on the rivers or lakes of the United States, not in any case carrying passengers, and vessels under 5 net tons are exempt from the requirements of the laws governing documentation.

Gross tonnage refers to *space* measurement, 100 cubic feet equalling 1 ton; it is not a measure of weight. Gross tonnage is the capacity of the entire space within the frames and the ceiling of the hull, together with those closed-in spaces above deck available for cargo, stores, passengers, or crew, with certain minor exemptions. Before 1865, 95 cubic feet equalled 1 ton, and the admeasurement method differed in other respects.

Changes in maritime law: Admeasurement method. "Admeasurement" refers to the method of calculating gross tonnage of ships or vessels. The first law of the United States on the subject appears to have been enacted September 1, 1789 (1 Stat. 55). The enactment then made was reenacted with certain minor amendments in the Acts of August 4, 1790 (1 Stat. 169), and of March 2, 1799 (1 Stat. 675), and as so enacted was in force until January 1, 1865.

A basic change in admeasurement method was provided in the act of May 6, 1864, effective January 1, 1865 (13 Stat. 70–72, R. S. 4153, 46 U. S. C. 77). The method described in the act of May 6, 1864, appears to have been substantially the same as that in force in 1945.

For the transition period, 1865–1868, the total tonnage figures for the fleet are "mixed." During those years, the total fleet tonnage was obtained by combining the "old admeasurement" tonnage of vessels not yet readmeasured and the "new admeasurement" tonnage of vessels which had been readmeasured or newly built. For a recapitulation of the "old" and "new" *components* of the fleet tonnage (not the same vessels) for each year, 1865–1868, see *Commerce and Navigation, 1870,* p. 798.

No table has been located comparing the tonnage of a substantial number of vessels under "new" and "old" admeasurement; hence, neither the magnitude nor the direction of the change can be stated here. Apparently it varied for different types of vessels. "Brigs, schooners, and sloops measure less under the 'new' admeasurement . . . while ships, barks, steamboats, and vessels having closed-in spaces above their hulls have their tonnage largely increased." Further, the difference between "old" and "new" was not believed to affect a comparison of New England shipbuilding for the years 1855 and 1868. (See *Treasury Annual Report,* 1868, p. 496.)

Another type of change in maritime law affecting the statistics is illustrated by the act of April 18, 1874 (18 Stat. 31), which exempted the greater amount of canalboat and other unrigged tonnage from documentation. (See U.S. Code, title 46, sec. 336.) For 1874–1876, the "balance sheets of tonnage," published annually in the source volumes, record the removal of 879,000 tons of vessels for this reason alone. However, *Merchant Marine Statistics, 1936,* lists 843,000 tons exempted in 1876, whereas the 1876 balance sheet of tonnage specified 601,000 tons exempted. The reason for this discrepancy is not clear. The tonnage exempted annually, 1874–1936, is shown on pp. 54–55 of *Merchant Marine Statistics, 1936.*

At irregular intervals, steps were taken to remove from the tonnage accounts those vessels lost, abandoned, captured, sold to aliens, etc., which had not been officially reported for removal purposes. From the outset, the failure to remove such vessels annually resulted in a cumulative error which inflated the statistics of tonnage. When general clearances of this cumulative error were made, the effect was concentrated in a single year or a small group of years.

For a basic statement on this subject, see *American State Papers,* cited above, vol. 1, p. 494, where Albert Gallatin, Secretary of the Treasury, outlines the problem and discusses the first attempt (1800) to deal with it. Recurrently, in the annual tonnage reports found in the source volumes, the problem is discussed, the announcement is made that the rolls have been finally cleared, and assurance is given that the problem has been solved for the future. However, as late as 1867, in spite of repeated clearances in earlier years, the "First Annual Report of the Director of the Bureau of Statistics" stated, "The tonnage returns were swelled with thousands of ghostly ships—ships that had gone to the bottom years ago." (See *Annual Report of the Secretary of Treasury, 1867,* p. 244.)

In 1869, the Register of the Treasury attributed the entire decline of tonnage reported for 1869 to this factor. (See *Treasury Report, 1869,* p. 300.) In the same year, Francis A. Walker, Deputy Special Commissioner of Revenue in Charge of the Bureau of Statistics, stated that the process of assigning a number to each vessel and the institution of an annual list of vessels, as required by the Act of July 28, 1866, "has succeeded in clearing from the lists of vessels . . . a vast amount of purely fictitious tonnage, which have been carried forward from year to year [although] thousands of vessels which this tonnage originally represented had been meanwhile lost at sea, broken up, or sold abroad." (See *Treasury Report, 1869,* p. 342.)

In the "balance sheets of tonnage" published annually in the source volumes, clearances of cumulative error are generally identified as "not heretofore credited" to distinguish them from listings of removals of the various types routinely reported as having occurred during the given year.

Some of the more important clearances of this cumulative error, and the tons of shipping thereby removed, were: 1800–1901, 197,000; 1811, amount not stated but the effect is evident in series Q 154; 1818, 182,000; 1829–1830, 604,000; 1837, 96,000; 1841–1842, 267,000; and 1855–1858, 945,000.

In later years, the terms "obsolete," "obsolete, not heretofore reported," and "correction of balance" found in annual balance sheets of tonnage, frequently reflect removal of cumulative errors. Examples are (in tons): 1864, 188,000; 1866, 1,063,000; 1867, 260,000; 1868, 128,000; 1869, 338,000; 1870, 58,000; 1871, 103,000; and 1881, 157,000.

Other factors which require that early merchant-vessel statistics should be used with some caution are the following: (1) In some instances, systematic differences in identically described statistical series appear in the source volumes (see text for series Q 178–182) which reflect conflicting series of figures, possibly originating from different primary sources of data (see table II below); (2) transcription and typographical errors have crept into historical tables in the source volumes in the process of repeated recopying and retypesetting; (3) statistically significant footnotes which appeared in early reports frequently were dropped in later years; and (4) caution is suggested in referring back to the earlier volumes in the search for explanations of discrepancies or major changes, since the earlier data may reflect the same or similar errors.

In this volume (see table II below), a number of the copying and typesetting errors have been corrected where the exact nature of the discrepancy could be determined beyond reasonable doubt; several broad differences in figures have been pointed out; and a few detailed tabular notes have been added based on information in various annual issues selected largely at random.

Table II. Merchant Marine Tonnage—Changes in Figures From Those Shown in Source

["Source" is *Merchant Marine Statistics, 1936*]

Series No.	Year	In source volume	In this volume
Q 153	1868	[1]28,118	[1]28,167
Q 154	1886	[2]4,131,116	[3]4,131,136
	1868	4,318,309	4,351,758
	1817	[4]1,339,912	[5]1,399,912
	1815	1,368,182	1,368,128
Q 155	1928	14,343,679	14,346,679
	1913	5,335,541	5,333,247
	1851	582,607	583,607
Q 161	1868	2,475,067	2,508,516
	1863	4,357,537	4,579,537
	1824	1,367,453	1,367,553
	1817	1,330,986	1,390,986
Q 162	1921	1,232,728	1,242,728
	1913	1,043,347	1,045,641
Q 163	1928	14,064,199	14,064,119
Q 165	1858	2,301,408	2,301,148
	1818	589,944	589,954
Q 166	1927	9,432,869	9,532,869
	1856	2,447,663	2,247,663
Q 167	1833	101,666	101,636
Q 168	1879	79,855	79,885
	1878	86,447	86,547
	1841	77,783	77,873
	1831	170,189	107,189
Q 169	1936	12,511,777	12,511,523
	1868	3,141,540	3,174,935
Q 170	1876	1,447,844	1,147,844
	1873	1,051,991	1,055,019
	1868	1,012,749	1,046,198
Q 171	1873	2,242,890	2,242,862
	1868	1,962,279	1,962,225
Q 173	1932	1,856,563	1,856,553
	1887	683,721	783,721
Q 174	1868	481,271	481,218
Q 180	1893	134,308	134,368
Q 181	1894	37,824	37,827
Q 182	1901	83,743	83,783
	1895	6,978	6,948
Q 183	1895	87,127	67,127
	1894	90,099	80,099
	1885	12,010	121,010
Q 184	1917	52,536	52,526
	1881	54,888	54,488
Q 185	1881	59,801	59,861
Q 187	1914	64,523	64,550
	1910	184,239	174,239
	1892	60,710	60,770

[1] Number of vessels. [2] As shown in table 10, p. 16, of source.
[3] As shown in table 16, p. 30, of source. [4] As shown in table 10, p. 14, of source.
[5] As shown in table 16, p. 28, of source.

Q 153–168. Documented merchant vessels, by major classes, material of which built, and trade, 1789–1957.

Source: Bureau of Marine Inspection and Navigation, *Merchant Marine Statistics, 1936*, and Bureau of Customs, records. (**Series Q 163–164**, 1884, Treasury Department, *Annual Report of Commission of Navigation, 1884*, p. 161.)

See also general notes for series Q 153–245 and Q 153–190.

For 1789–1793, tonnage figures are the "duty tonnage," i.e., the tonnage of vessels on which duties were collected during the year. (See *American State Papers*, cited above in general note for series Q 153–190, vol. 1, p. 895.) The "duty tonnage" appears to have been the tonnage on which duties were collected on registered vessels, including "the repeated voyages of the same vessel," plus tonnage of the enrolled and licensed vessels which paid tonnage duties once each year. (See *American State Papers*, cited above, vol. 1, pp. 494, 498, 528.) Beginning in 1794, "district tonnage returns" were used, derived from reports of District Collectors of Customs, which gave the tonnage of vessels in each district based on registers, enrollments, and licenses outstanding, as of December 31.

For 1794–1801, figures are district tonnage returns, with no attempt to correct for the cumulative error caused by failure to remove vessels lost, abandoned, sold to aliens, etc. (See *American State Papers*, vol. 1, pp. 494, 499.) The figures for 1800–1801 ignore the first clearing of tonnage accounts which took place during these years. (See *American State Papers*, vol. 1, pp. 494–499, 527–531.) The correction for the cumulative error for *registered vessels only* would reduce the 1800 total to 819,571 tons and the 1801 total to 903,235 tons. The sharp drop attributable to the clearing of tonnage accounts would thereby be shifted back to 1800 instead of appearing in 1802.

For 1802–1818, the figures in series Q 154 consist of the "corrected registered" tonnage plus the uncorrected enrolled or licensed tonnage (see 1813 tonnage report in *American State Papers*, cited above, vol. 1, p. 1017). The figures for 1811 and 1818 reflect two additional attempts to clear out the cumulative error of registered vessels improperly retained on the registers. (See *American State Papers*, vol. 1, pp. 876, 958, and vol. 2, p. 406.)

The figures shown below in table III are those which were derived by a method authorized by Secretary of the Treasury Gallatin. They were reported to Congress in the annual tonnage reports in *American State Papers* as being the "actual" or "more nearly correct" tonnage.

Table III. "Actual Tonnage" of Documented Vessels: 1800 to 1818

[In thousands of gross tons]

Year	Tons	Year	Tons
1818	1,150	1808	1,173
1817	1,341	1807	1,208
1816	1,264	1806	1,166
1815	1,262	1805	1,085
1814	1,029	1804	983
1813	1,032	1803	917
1812	1,127	1802	865
1811	1,131	1801	850
1810	1,329	1800	768
1809	1,266		

These were obtained by taking the "corrected registered tonnage" and adding to it the "duty tonnage" for enrolled and licensed vessels. Since duties were paid only once each year on enrolled and licensed vessels, and owners were not likely to pay duties on nonexistent vessels, it was reasoned that the lower "duty tonnage" figure more accurately reflected the true total for the enrolled or licensed craft than did the district returns of tonnage based on outstanding marine documents. This correction for enrolled and licensed craft was dropped after 1818, probably because, beginning 1819, the "duty tonnage" for this group exceeded the district tonnage returns for the group.

In *American State Papers*, vol. 1, p. 499, the tonnage described as "actual tonnage" in the comparative table for 1794–1799 is, in fact, the district returns of tonnage without correction of any kind. Elsewhere in the tonnage report for 1800 (pp. 494–499), and in tonnage reports for later years, the term "actual tonnage" normally means the district returns based on outstanding marine documents (registers, enrollments, and licenses) corrected for cumulative error. In table III, the term "actual tonnage" is used in the latter sense; the figures are from annual tonnage reports, 1800–1818, in *American State Papers*, vols. 1 and 2.

Q 163–164, vessels, by material of which built. The source publication also classifies tonnage of each material by type of propulsion (steam, motor, sail, canalboat, and barge).

Q 165–168, vessels, by trade in which engaged. The source publication also presents the number of vessels engaged in each type of trade as well as tonnage. The statutes do not recognize for documenting purposes any fisheries except the cod, mackerel, and whale. Vessels engaged in catching any other fish, such as salmon or menhaden, are documented for the mackerel fishery.

Figures in early reports identified as "registered," or as "registered in foreign trade," commonly include the registered vessels engaged in the whale fishery. Accordingly, figures on "whale fishery" found in early reports should be examined carefully to determine whether they represent the entire whaling fleet or only the "enrolled or licensed" portion. The term "fisheries" as used in early volumes refers to cod, and later, to cod and mackerel fisheries. It rarely includes the whale fishery.

In terms of documentation as "registered," "enrolled," "licensed," series Q 165–168 are composed broadly as follows:

Series Q 165 (foreign trade) represents the total "registered" minus "registered whale fishery." The "registered" whaling tonnage, is, however, included for 1794–1798.

Series Q 166 (coastwise and internal) represents the portion of the enrolled or licensed group engaged in this trade. The rest of the enrolled or licensed group is in series Q 168 (cod and mackerel fisheries).

Series Q 167 (whale fishery) is the "registered whale fishery" portion of the registered fleet plus the "whale fishery" portion of the enrolled or licensed fleet. For 1794–1798, however, the registered whaling tonnage is not included here, but in series Q 165.

Series Q 168 (cod and mackerel fishery) is the cod and mackerel fishery portion of the enrolled or licensed fleet. The rest of the enrolled or licensed group is in series Q 166 (coastwise and internal).

Q 169–174. Documented merchant vessels, by geographic region, 1816–1957.

Source: See source for series Q 153–168.

See also general notes for series Q 153–245 and Q 153–190.

Q 175–177. Documented merchant vessels, by type of service, 1934–1957.

Source: See source for series Q 153–168.

Series Q 177 includes cable, cod, dredging, elevator, ferry, fireboat, fishing, ice breaker, lightering, oil exploitation, oystering, passenger, pile driving, pilot boat, police boat, patrol boat, refrigerator, towing, waterboat, whaling, welding, wrecking,

and miscellaneous. The source presents details for each of these in recent years.

See also general notes for series Q 153–245 and Q 153–190.

Q 178–182. Merchant vessels built and documented, by type, 1797–1957.

Source: See source for series Q 153–168.

The source publication also presents statistics separately for steam, motor, and sailing vessels, canalboats, and barges. Statistics for motor vessels begin in 1893.

For 1938–1957, figures are not comparable with those for earlier years and are probably understated. They represent those vessels built during the 12-month period which were still existent and documented as part of the merchant fleet at the end of the period. Hence, they exclude vessels completed during the period which were lost, sold to U.S. Government, sold to aliens, or otherwise removed from merchant vessel documentation before the end of the period.

See also general notes for series Q 153–245 and Q 153–190.

Q 183–187. Merchant vessels built and documented, by region, 1817–1936.

Source: Bureau of Marine Inspection and Navigation, *Merchant Marine Statistics, 1936*, pp. 46–48, and table 2.

See general notes for series Q 153–245 and Q 153–190.

Q 188–190. Merchant vessels built and documented, by region, 1817–1850.

Source: Fold-in table on the history of shipbuilding (1817–1868) at back of the *Annual Report of the Secretary of the Treasury*, 1868.

Source also presents figures separately, for "The United States," "The Lakes," and "Western Rivers." For a discussion of these data see the *Annual Report*. The source table, with a more detailed discussion appears as Plate XXII in H. R., Ex. Doc. No. 111, 41st Congress, 2d Session, where the period covered is extended to 1869, and as Plate X (extended to 1870) in H.R. Ex. Doc. No. 76, 41st Congress, 3d Session. These three series do not add to series Q 179.

See also general notes for series Q 153–245 and Q 153–190.

Q 191. Persons entering the United States by ship, 1933–1957.

Source: Treasury Department, *Annual Report of the Secretary of the Treasury on the State of the Finances*, various issues.

Data include persons entering by documented vessels, excluding ferryboats.

Q 192–203. General note.

Net tonnage capacity, as used here, refers to net or registered tonnage of the vessel, not weight of cargo. The net tonnage is what remains after deducting from the gross tonnage (defined in general note for series Q 153–190) the spaces occupied by the propelling machinery, fuel, crew quarters, master's cabin, and navigation spaces. It represents, substantially, space available for cargo and passengers. It is the usual basis for tonnage taxes and port charges. The net tonnage capacity of a ship recorded as "entered with cargo" may bear little relation to actual weight of cargo. Gross tonnage and net tonnage are both measures of cubic capacity, not of weight, 100 cubic feet equalling 1 ton. These terms should not be confused with the cargo ton of 2,000 pounds. Tonnage figures shown in series Q 193 and Q 199 for U.S. vessels entered and cleared, respectively, in foreign trade are greater than the total tonnage of U.S. vessels documented for the foreign trade because the "entered" and "cleared" series include tonnage for each vessel as often as it "enters" or "clears" each year. The documented tonnage (series Q 154) includes the tonnage of each vessel once for each year.

These figures include the tonnage of all types of watercraft engaged in the foreign trade, whether entering or clearing with cargo or in ballast, which are required to make formal entrance and clearance under U.S. customs regulations. Vessels engaged in trade on the Great Lakes with Canada as well as in trade with Mexico are also included. Vessels touching at a U. S. port in distress or for other temporary causes without discharging cargo, and Army and Navy vessels carrying no commercial cargo, are not required by customs regulations to enter or clear and thus are not included in the figures.

Vessels are reported as entered at the first port in the United States at which entry is made, regardless of whether any cargo is unladen at that port; arrivals at subsequent ports are not counted. Vessels are reported as cleared from the last port in the United States where loading of outward cargo is completed or where the vessel cleared in ballast; departures from prior ports are not counted.

Q 192–194.   Vessels entered, all ports, 1789–1957.

Source: 1789–1820, Fred J. Guetter and Albert E. McKinley, *Statistical Tables Relating to the Economic Growth of the United States*, McKinley Publishing Co., Philadelphia, 1924, p. 39; 1821–1879, Bureau of Marine Inspection and Navigation, *Merchant Marine Statistics, 1936*, p. 93; 1880–1888, *Statistical Abstract of the United States, 1908*, p. 286; 1889–1916, *Statistical Abstract, 1916*, p. 338; 1917–1930, *Statistical Abstract, 1931*, p. 474; 1931–1944, *Statistical Abstract, 1947*, p. 558 (see general note for series Q 153–245 for the various agencies which have issued the *Statistical Abstract*); 1945–1946, *Foreign Commerce and Navigation of the United States, 1947*; 1947–1957, Bureau of the Census, *Vessel Entrances and Clearances*, Summary Report FT 975, various issues, and records.

Q 195.   Total vessels entered at seaports, 1840–1957.

Source: 1840, *Statistical Abstract of the United States, 1946*, p. 546; 1844–1855, *Statistical Abstract, 1878*, p. 134; 1856–1879, *Statistical Abstract, 1880*, p. 138; 1880–1957, see source for series Q 192–194.

Q 196–197.   U.S. and foreign vessels entered at seaports, 1856–1957.

Source: 1856–1879, see source for series Q 195; 1880–1957, see source for series Q 192–194.

Q 198–200.   Vessels cleared, all ports, 1821–1957.

Source: See sources cited for specific periods (except 1789–1820) for series Q 192–194; the following page numbers apply respectively to the sources cited: 93, 287, 475, 558, and 592.

Q 201.   Total vessels cleared at seaports, 1840–1957.

Source: 1840 and 1850, *Statistical Abstract of the United States, 1946*, p. 546; 1853–1879, *Statistical Abstract, 1881*, p. 138; 1880–1957, see source for series Q 192–194.

Q 202–203.   U.S. and foreign vessels cleared at seaports, 1857–1957.

Source: 1857–1879, *Statistical Abstract of the United States, 1881*, p. 136; 1880–1957, see source for series Q 192–194.

Q 204–209.   Value of waterborne imports and exports (including reexports) of merchandise, 1790–1946.

Source: 1790–1820, see source for series Q 192–194; 1821–1858, Bureau of Marine Inspection and Navigation, *Merchant Marine Statistics, 1936*, p. 91; 1859–1866, *Statistical Abstract of the United States, 1895*, pp. 399–400; 1867–1912, *Statistical Abstract, 1913*, pp. 318–319; 1913–1923, *Statistical Abstract,*

1924, p. 417; 1924–1935, *Statistical Abstract, 1946*, p. 552 (see general note for series Q 153–245 for the various agencies which have issued the *Statistical Abstract*); 1943–1946, Bureau of the Census, *Foreign Commerce and Navigation of the United States*, annual issues.

The primary source of figures for 1790–1820 is J. R. Soley, "The Maritime Industries of America," *The United States of America* (N. S. Shaler, Editor), vol. II, 1894, pp. 522–527, 534, 536, 538. The report gives the percent of imports and exports in U.S. vessels. Guetter and McKinley (cited above for series Q 192–194) have derived absolute figures by applying these percentages to total imports and exports of merchandise and specie. The primary source of figures for 1821–1935 is *Foreign Commerce and Navigation of the United States*, annual issues. Starting with 1943, import or export statistics by method of transportation showing shipping weight, as well as dollar value, have been compiled by the Bureau of the Census.

Q 210–215.   Waterborne imports and exports, by flag of carrier vessel, 1921–1957.

Source: 1921–1945, Bureau of the Census, *Foreign Commerce and Navigation of the United States*, annual issues; 1946–1957, Bureau of the Census, releases and records.

Excludes cargoes (small in the aggregate) carried by ships of less than 100 tons gross capacity prior to 1946. Beginning in 1946 excludes Army and Navy cargo, and includes Alaska, Hawaii, and Puerto Rico. Beginning in July 1950 excludes commodities classified for security reasons as "special category." From July 1953 to December 1955 and beginning July 1956, exports exclude shipments under $500 in value regardless of shipping weight; for January–June 1956, exports exclude shipments under $1,000. Beginning 1954, imports exclude shipments under 2,000 pounds shipping weight.

Q 216–229.   Waterborne cargo tonnage, foreign and domestic, 1924–1957.

Source: 1924–1953, Corps of Engineers, *Annual Report of the Chief of Engineers*, part 2; 1954–1957, *Annual Report of the Chief of Engineers, U. S. Army, on Civil Works Activities*, part 1.

In 1954, part 2 of the *Annual Report* was superseded by a separate publication entitled *Waterborne Commerce of the United States* (published in several regional parts). Part 5 of this report, *National Summaries*, presents separate figures for series Q 221–222 for "Canadian" and "overseas" for recent years.

Cargo tonnage refers to the weight of cargo and should not be confused with gross tonnage shown in series Q 153–190 or the net or registered tonnage capacity shown in series Q 192–203, which are measures of cubic capacity, not of weight. See also text for those series.

Q 230–234.   Waterborne bulk freight traffic on the Great Lakes, 1900–1956.

Source: Lake Carriers' Association, *Annual Report, 1956*, pp. 62–63.

Includes tonnage moving to or from Canadian or U.S. lake ports, in Canadian or U.S. bulk carriers.

Q 235–237.   Commercial ocean traffic on the Panama Canal, 1915–1957.

Source: 1915–1924, Governor of the Panama Canal, *Annual Report, 1948*, p. 10; 1925–1957, Panama Canal Company, *Annual Report*, various issues.

Does not include U.S. Government traffic.

Q 238–242. Freight traffic on the Sault Ste. Marie canals, 1855–1900.

Source: Corps of Engineers, *Statistical Report of Lake Commerce Passing Through Canals at Sault Ste. Marie, 1931.*

These series include traffic moving through the American and Canadian canals. Figures for later years may be obtained from various issues of Corps of Engineers, *Annual Report,* part 2, *Commercial Statistics.* They are not shown here because they pertain only to traffic between Lake Superior and the other lakes and series Q 230–234 therefore provide more comprehensive totals of Great Lakes traffic.

Q 243–244. Tonnage moved on New York State canals, 1837–1957.

Source: State of New York, Department of Public Works, *Annual Report of the Superintendent,* annual issues, and records.

Q 245. Federal expenditures for rivers and harbors, 1822–1957.

Source: 1822–1882, *Statement of Appropriations and Expenditures for Public Buildings, Rivers and Harbors, Forts, Arsenals, Armories, and Other Public Works from March 4, 1789 to June 30, 1882,* U. S. Senate Ex. Doc., vol. 7, No. 196, 47th Congress, 1st Session (Treasury Department Doc. No. 373), pp. 521–522; 1883–1919, Federal Works Agency, records (compiled from Treasury Department accounts); 1920–1957, Corps of Engineers, *Annual Report of the Chief of Engineers, U. S. Army,* part 1, vol. 1, annual issues (in 1954, changed to *Annual Report of the Chief of Engineers, U. S. Army, on Civil Works Activities,* part 1).

Figures include expenditures for rivers, harbors, and flood control prior to 1928. In 1928, expenditures for flood control amounted to less than $13,500,000. Figures for 1929–1957 exclude expenditures for flood control. The figures include amounts expended from emergency relief and Public Works Administration funds, 1933–1937, but exclude $5,500,000 for purchase of Cape Cod Canal, 1928, expended by and accounted for by Treasury Department.

Series Q 153–168. Documented Merchant Vessels, by Major Classes, Material of Which Built, and Trade: 1789 to 1957

[In thousands of tons except number of vessels. Gross tonnage of documented vessels of 5 tons or more. As of December 31, 1789–1834; September 30, 1835–1842; June 30, 1843–1940; January 1 thereafter]

Year	Total documented vessels		Major classes								Material of which built		Trade in which engaged			
			Total	Steam and motor					Sailing³	Canal-boats and barges	Metal⁴	Wood	Foreign trade	Coastwise and internal	Whale fisheries	Cod and mackerel fisheries⁵
				Steam			Motor									
	Number	Gross tons		Total¹	Coal burning¹	Oil burning¹	Total²	Diesel and semi-Diesel engines¹								
	153	154	155	156	157	158	159	160	161	162	163	164	165	166	167	168
1957	40,191	29,421	25,785	23,788	2,190	21,597	1,998	1,836	24	3,612	27,935	1,486	17,265	12,154	1	1
1956	39,499	29,610	26,251	24,210	2,204	22,005	2,041	1,886	34	3,326	28,073	1,537	17,765	11,843	1	1
1955	39,242	29,958	26,792	24,706	2,252	22,454	2,086	1,907	40	3,125	28,336	1,622	18,143	11,812	1	1
1954	39,008	30,764	27,631	25,489	2,321	23,168	2,142	1,960	46	3,087	28,982	1,782	18,974	11,787	1	2
1953	38,072	30,546	27,507	25,377	2,387	22,990	2,130	1,951	55	2,984	28,761	1,785	19,007	11,537	1	2
1952	37,389	30,416	27,459	25,356	2,405	22,951	2,103	1,923	66	2,891	28,559	1,857	19,280	11,134	1	2
1951	36,745	30,341	27,424	25,390	2,441	22,948	2,033	1,865	71	2,846	28,417	1,924	18,876	11,462	1	2
1950	36,083	31,215	28,327	26,273	2,507	23,765	2,055	1,885	82	2,806	29,263	1,952	19,154	12,048	[6]11	2
1949	35,264	32,182	29,323	27,225	2,543	24,682	2,099	1,932	87	2,771	30,212	1,969	20,654	11,525	1	3
1948	33,843	33,167	30,469	28,401	2,606	25,796	2,067	1,902	87	2,611	31,211	1,956	22,021	11,143	1	3
1947	32,760	37,832	35,149	32,941	2,699	30,242	2,208	2,058	95	2,588	35,897	1,936	26,535	11,294	1	3
1946	31,386	38,501	35,928	33,779	2,884	30,895	2,149	2,002	98	2,475	36,571	1,929	29,705	8,791	1	3
1945	29,797	32,813	30,247	28,669	2,931	25,737	1,578	1,433	115	2,452	30,898	1,915	26,043	6,766	1	3
1944	28,690	25,795	23,217	21,674	3,014	18,660	1,543	1,392	129	2,449	23,837	1,959	18,685	7,105	1	4
1943	27,612	16,762	14,052	12,547	3,048	9,499	1,505	1,361	142	2,568	14,647	2,115	9,285	7,471	2	5
1942	27,325	13,860	11,072	9,704	2,965	6,739	1,369	1,213	166	2,621	11,641	2,218	4,109	9,744	2	6
1941	27,075	13,722	11,047	9,814	3,058	6,756	1,233	1,075	182	2,493	11,393	2,329	3,047	10,654	14	7
1940	27,212	14,018	11,353	10,102	3,159	6,943	1,251	1,090	200	2,466	(⁷)	(⁷)	3,638	10,352	20	8
1939	27,470	14,632	11,952	10,760	3,250	7,510	1,192	1,028	221	2,459	12,159	2,473	3,312	11,288	21	11
1938	27,155	14,651	12,007	10,835	3,325	7,510	1,172	1,005	261	2,384	12,130	2,521	3,551	11,064	21	16
1937	26,588	14,676	12,170	11,055	3,322	7,559	1,115	878	312	2,194	12,233	2,443	3,833	10,798	20	25
1936	25,392	14,497	12,267	11,161	3,371	7,617	1,105	867	379	1,851	12,263	2,234	4,159	10,300	9	28
1935	24,919	14,654	12,535	11,433	3,496	7,748	1,102	841	441	1,677	12,469	2,185	4,560	10,049	9	35
1934	24,904	14,862	12,687	11,599	3,539	7,860	1,087	824	500	1,675	12,601	2,261	4,598	10,220	9	35
1933	24,868	15,060	12,862	11,788	3,615	7,971	1,075	812	563	1,635	12,736	2,324	4,701	10,313	9	37
1932	25,156	15,839	13,568	12,499	3,991	8,308	1,069	810	625	1,646	13,421	2,417	5,071	10,728	2	38
1931	25,471	15,908	13,528	12,475	4,103	8,202	1,053	792	673	1,707	13,344	2,565	5,576	10,286	7	40
1930	25,214	16,068	13,757	12,775	4,209	8,429	982	715	757	1,554	13,514	2,554	6,296	9,723	7	42
1929	25,326	16,477	14,162	13,301	4,462	8,751	861	609	825	1,490	13,910	2,567	6,906	9,526	7	39
1928	25,385	16,683	14,347	13,614	4,557	9,002	730	494	915	1,421	14,064	2,619	6,934	9,706	7	36
1927	25,778	16,888	14,507	13,874	4,919	8,907	633	397	1,092	1,392	14,160	2,728	7,309	9,533	8	38
1926	26,343	17,311	14,848	14,318	5,370	8,895	530	293	1,092	1,371	14,473	2,838	7,719	9,552	3	38
1925	26,367	17,406	14,976	14,495	5,512	8,931	481	254	1,125	1,304	14,499	2,907	8,151	9,216	4	35
1924	26,575	17,741	15,315	14,870	5,921	8,947	445	128	1,185	1,240	14,627	3,114	8,794	8,911	3	32
1923	27,017	18,285	15,821	15,426	6,556	8,870	397	17	1,254	1,209	14,775	3,510	9,069	9,177	4	35
1922	27,358	18,463	15,982	15,607	6,908	8,699	375	16	1,288	1,193	14,805	3,658	10,720	7,703	4	36
1921	28,012	18,282	15,745	15,376	7,069	8,302	374	15	1,294	1,243	14,426	3,856	11,077	7,163	4	37
1920	28,183	16,324	13,823	13,466	7,551	5,915	357	24	1,272	1,228	12,448	3,876	9,925	6,358	4	38
1919	27,513	12,907	10,416	--------	--------	--------	--------	--------	1,200	1,292	9,236	3,671	6,665	6,201	4	36
1918	26,711	9,925	7,471	--------	--------	--------	--------	--------	1,210	1,244	6,814	3,110	3,599	6,282	4	38
1917	26,397	8,871	6,433	--------	--------	--------	--------	--------	1,278	1,159	5,856	3,015	2,441	6,393	6	32
1916	26,444	8,470	6,070	--------	--------	--------	--------	--------	1,311	1,089	5,476	2,994	2,185	6,245	7	33
1915	26,701	8,389	5,944						1,384	1,061	5,305	3,085	1,863	6,486	9	32
1914	26,943	7,929	5,428						1,433	1,069	4,733	3,196	1,066	6,818	10	34
1913	27,070	7,887	5,333						1,508	1,046	4,608	3,278	1,019	6,817	9	42
1912	26,528	7,714	5,180						1,539	995	4,433	3,282	923	6,737	9	45
1911	25,991	7,639	5,074						1,598	967	4,299	3,340	863	6,720	9	46
1910	25,740	7,508	4,900						1,655	952	4,117	3,391	783	6,669	9	47
1909	25,868	7,389	4,749						1,711	928	3,925	3,464	879	6,451	9	50
1908	25,425	7,365	4,711						1,761	893	3,860	3,505	930	6,372	10	54
1907	24,911	6,939	4,279						1,814	845	3,438	3,501	861	6,011	10	57
1906	25,006	6,675	3,975						1,899	801	3,115	3,560	928	5,674	11	61
1905	24,681	6,457	3,741						1,962	753	2,850	3,607	944	5,442	11	60
1904	24,558	6,292	3,595						1,945	751	2,669	3,623	889	5,335	10	58
1903	24,425	6,087	3,408						1,966	713	2,440	3,647	879	5,141	10	58
1902	24,273	5,798	3,177						1,942	679	2,180	3,618	873	4,859	9	57
1901	24,057	5,524	2,921						1,933	670	1,901	3,623	880	4,583	10	52
1900	23,333	5,165	2,658						1,885	622	1,593	3,572	817	4,287	10	52
1899	22,728	4,864	2,476						1,825	563	1,376	3,489	837	3,965	11	51
1898	22,705	4,750	2,372						1,836	542	1,224	3,526	726	3,960	11	52
1897	22,633	4,769	2,359						1,904	506	1,207	3,562	793	3,897	13	67
1896	22,908	4,704	2,307						1,928	468	1,090	3,614	830	3,790	15	69
1895	23,240	4,636	2,213						1,965	458	970	3,666	822	3,729	16	69
1894	23,586	4,684	2,189						2,023	472	930	3,754	900	3,696	16	72
1893	24,512	4,825	2,183						2,118	524	896	3,930	883	3,855	17	71
1892	24,383	4,765	2,074						2,178	512	786	3,979	978	3,701	17	69
1891	23,899	4,685	2,016						2,172	497	742	3,943	989	3,610	17	69
1890	23,467	4,424	1,859						2,109	456	627	3,798	928	3,409	19	68
1889	23,623	4,307	1,766						2,099	443	554	3,753	1,000	3,211	22	74
1888	23,281	4,192	1,648						2,124	419	494	3,698	919	3,172	24	76
1887	23,063	4,106	1,543						2,170	393	475	3,631	989	3,011	26	80
1886	23,534	4,131	1,523						2,210	398	444	3,687	1,088	2,939	23	81

See footnotes at end of table.

Series Q 153–168. Documented Merchant Vessels, by Major Classes, Material of Which Built, and Trade: 1789 to 1957—Con.

[In thousands of tons except number of vessels

Year	Total documented vessels		Major classes			Material of which built		Trade in which engaged			
	Number	Gross tons	Steam and motor	Sailing [3]	Canal-boats and barges	Metal [4]	Wood	Foreign trade	Coastwise and internal	Whale fisheries	Cod and mackerel fisheries
	153	154	155	161	162	163	164	165	166	167	168
1885	23,963	4,266	1,495	2,374	397	430	3,836	1,263	2,895	25	83
1884	24,082	4,271	1,466	2,414	391	387	3,885	1,277	2,884	27	83
1883	24,217	4,235	1,413	2,387	436			1,270	2,838	32	95
1882	24,368	4,166	1,356	2,361	449			1,259	2,796	33	78
1881	24,065	4,058	1,265	2,350	442			1,297	2,646	39	76
1880	24,712	4,068	1,212	2,366	490			1,314	2,638	38	78
1879	25,211	4,170	1,176	2,423	571			1,452	2,598	40	80
1878	25,264	4,213	1,168	2,521	524			1,589	2,497	40	87
1877	25,386	4,243	1,171	2,580	491			1,571	2,540	41	91
1876	25,934	4,279	1,172	2,609	498			1,554	2,599	39	88
1875	32,285	4,854	1,169	2,585	1,100			1,516	3,220	38	80
1874	32,486	4,801	1,186	2,474	1,141			1,390	3,293	39	78
1873	32,672	4,696	1,156	2,383	1,156			1,379	3,163	45	110
1872	31,114	4,438	1,112	2,325	1,001			1,359	2,930	52	98
1871	29,651	4,283	1,088	2,286	909			1,364	2,765	61	93
1870	28,998	4,247	1,075	2,363	808			1,449	2,638	68	91
1869	27,487	4,145	1,104	2,400	641			1,496	2,516	70	63
1868	28,167	4,352	1,199	2,509	644			1,487	2,702	78	84
1867		4,304	1,192	3,113				1,516	2,660	52	76
1866		4,311	1,084	3,227				1,388	2,720	105	98

Year	Total documented vessels, gross tons	Major classes		Trade in which engaged			
		Steam and motor	Sailing	Foreign trade	Coastwise and internal	Whale fisheries	Cod and mackerel fisheries
	154	155	161	165	166	167	168
1865	5,097	1,067	4,030	1,518	3,382	84	113
1864	4,986	978	4,008	1,487	3,245	95	159
1863	5,155	576	4,580	1,927	2,961	99	168
1862	5,112	710	4,402	2,174	2,617	118	204
1861	5,540	877	4,663	2,497	2,705	146	193
1860	5,354	868	4,486	2,379	2,645	167	163
1859	5,145	769	4,376	2,322	2,481	186	157
1858	5,050	729	4,320	2,301	2,401	199	149
1857	4,941	706	4,235	2,268	2,337	196	140
1856	4,872	673	4,199	2,302	2,248	189	132
1855	5,212	770	4,442	2,348	2,543	187	134
1854	4,803	677	4,126	2,152	2,322	182	147
1853	4,407	605	3,802	1,910	2,134	193	169
1852	4,138	643	3,495	1,706	2,056	194	183
1851	3,772	584	3,189	1,545	1,900	182	146
1850	3,535	526	3,010	1,440	1,798	146	152
1849	3,334	462	2,872	1,259	1,770	180	125
1848	3,154	428	2,726	1,169	1,659	193	133
1847	2,839	405	2,434	1,047	1,489	194	109
1846	2,562	348	2,214	943	1,316	187	116
1845	2,417	326	2,091	904	1,223	191	98
1844	2,280	272	2,008	900	1,110	169	101
1843	2,159	237	1,922	857	1,076	153	73
1842	2,092	230	1,863	824	1,046	152	71
1841	2,131	175	1,956	788	1,107	157	78
1840	2,181	202	1,978	763	1,177	137	104
1839	2,096	195	1,901	702	1,154	132	108
1838	1,996	193	1,802	703	1,041	125	127
1837	1,897	155	1,742	683	957	129	127
1836	1,882	146	1,737	753	873	146	110
1835	1,825	123	1,702	788	797	98	142
1834	1,759	123	1,636	749	784	108	117
1833	1,606	102	1,504	649	744	102	111
1832	1,439	91	1,349	614	650	73	102
1831	1,268	69	1,198	538	540	83	107
1830	1,192	64	1,127	538	517	40	98
1829	1,261	54	1,207	593	509	57	102
1828	1,741	39	1,702	758	843	55	86
1827	1,621	40	1,580	702	789	46	84
1826	1,534	34	1,500	696	722	42	74

Year	Total documented vessels, gross tons	Major classes		Trade in which engaged			
		Steam and motor	Sailing	Foreign trade	Coastwise and internal	Whale fisheries	Cod and mackerel fisheries
	154	155	161	165	166	167	168
1825	1,423	23	1,400	665	641	35	81
1824	1,389	22	1,368	637	642	33	77
1823	1,337	25	1,312	600	618	41	78
1822	1,325	23	1,304	583	624	49	69
1821	1,299	23	1,276	594	615	28	62
1820	1,280	22	1,258	584	588	36	72
1819	1,261	17	1,243	581	571	32	76
1818	1,225	13	1,213	590	549	17	69
1817	1,400	9	1,391	805	525	5	65
1816	1,372	6	1,366	801	522	1	48
1815	1,368	3	1,365	854	476	1	37
1814	1,159	3	1,156	675	466	1	18
1813	1,167	3	1,164	673	471	3	20
1812	1,270	2	1,268	759	478	3	30
1811	1,233	1	1,231	764	420	5	43
1810	1,425	1	1,424	981	405	4	35
1809	1,350	1	1,350	907	405	4	34
1808	1,243	(8)	1,242	765	421	5	52
1807	1,269	(8)	1,268	840	349	9	70
1806	1,209	--------	1,209	799	341	11	59
1805	1,140	--------	1,140	744	333	6	57
1804	1,042	--------	1,042	661	318	12	52
1803	949	--------	949	586	299	12	52
1802	892	--------	892	558	290	3	42
1801	948	--------	948	631	275	3	39
1800	972	--------	972	667	272	3	29
1799	939	--------	939	657	247	6	30
1798	898	--------	898	603	251	1	43
1797	877	--------	877	598	237	1	41
1796	832	--------	832	577	218	2	35
1795	748	--------	748	529	184	3	31
1794	629	--------	629	439	163	4	23
1793	521	--------	521	368	122	--------	31
1792 [9]	564	--------	564	411	121	--------	32
1791 [9]	502	--------	502	363	106	--------	33
1790 [9]	478	--------	478	346	104	--------	28
1789 [9]	202	--------	202	124	69	--------	9

[1] For 1920–1937, tonnage for vessels with electric screw included in total (series Q 156 or Q 159) but excluded from series Q 157, Q 158, and Q 160. Maximum such tonnage included in series Q 156 is 201,246 in 1933 and maximum in series Q 159 is 91,470 in 1934.
[2] Includes gasoline engines, not shown separately.
[3] Includes canalboats and barges prior to 1868.
[4] Includes iron, steel, composite, concrete, bronze, and aluminum.
[5] Beginning 1937, excludes mackerel.
[6] Increase due to documentation of 1 large vessel on Atlantic Coast.
[7] Not available.
[8] Less than 500 tons.
[9] Figures for 1789 are for ships paying tonnage duties during the last 5 months of the year. Figures for 1790–1792 are for ships paying duties at some time during the year.

Series Q 169–174. Documented Merchant Vessels, by Geographic Region: 1816 to 1957

[In tons. Gross tonnage of documented vessels of 5 net tons or more. As of December 31, 1816–1834; September 30, 1835–1842; June 30, 1843–1940; January 1 thereafter

Year	Seaboard — Total seaboard	New England coast	Mid-Atlantic and Gulf coasts[1]	Pacific coast[2]	Northern lakes	Western rivers	Year	Seaboard — Total seaboard	New England coast	Mid-Atlantic and Gulf coasts[1]	Pacific coast[2]	Northern lakes	Western rivers
	169	170	171	172	173	174		169	170	171	172	173	174
1957	26,605,277	1,007,306	18,634,329	6,963,642	1,569,387	1,246,591	1886	3,033,673	1,054,551	1,631,437	347,685	762,560	334,902
1956	26,952,075	1,091,349	18,732,095	7,128,631	1,557,995	1,100,045	1885	3,169,930	1,089,760	1,719,562	360,608	749,948	346,055
1955	27,405,316	1,191,001	19,210,722	7,003,593	1,590,291	962,234	1884	3,181,803	1,142,319	1,704,815	334,669	733,069	356,356
1954	28,299,224	1,238,833	19,908,005	7,152,386	1,616,132	848,931	1883	3,150,529	1,121,039	1,701,925	327,565	723,911	361,047
1953	28,184,207	1,204,458	19,886,230	7,093,519	1,624,423	737,518	1882	3,061,655	1,095,189	1,664,032	302,434	711,269	393,009
1952	28,135,518	1,334,990	19,604,202	7,196,326	1,556,034	724,787	1881	3,000,302	1,044,884	1,669,033	286,385	663,383	394,049
1951	28,039,745	1,558,856	18,408,777	8,072,112	1,565,096	735,860	1880	2,989,140	1,072,580	1,644,199	272,361	605,102	473,792
1950	28,865,926	1,504,926	18,914,987	8,446,013	1,628,267	720,950	1879	3,070,415	1,094,760	1,705,307	270,348	597,376	501,809
1949	29,406,620	1,678,898	18,639,141	9,088,581	2,076,267	698,976	1878	3,150,351	1,140,013	1,757,404	252,934	604,656	457,757
1948	30,483,959	1,719,370	18,396,835	10,367,754	2,079,447	603,855	1877	3,196,422	1,146,359	1,798,507	251,556	610,160	436,017
1947	35,237,635	1,833,766	20,339,674	13,064,195	2,091,170	503,757	1876	3,265,735	1,147,844	1,864,496	253,395	613,211	400,512
1946	35,829,189	1,644,493	19,926,875	14,257,821	2,182,866	488,524	1875	3,596,876	1,142,995	2,224,624	229,257	837,892	418,964
1945	30,306,046	1,471,881	17,186,484	11,647,681	2,061,456	445,779	1874	3,520,597	1,076,818	2,232,162	211,617	842,381	437,674
1944	23,568,821	972,205	13,595,614	9,001,002	1,792,538	434,138	1873	3,489,199	1,055,019	2,242,862	191,318	788,412	418,415
1943	14,713,957	439,727	10,050,727	4,223,503	1,620,292	427,505	1872	3,265,251	1,053,420	2,031,483	180,348	724,493	448,001
1942	11,855,795	544,235	9,372,242	1,939,318	1,624,377	379,468	1871	3,163,862	1,049,723	1,946,704	167,435	712,027	406,718
1941	11,776,026	493,922	9,318,214	1,963,890	1,640,790	304,798	1870	3,163,597	1,056,563	1,916,636	190,398	684,704	398,206
1940	12,063,512	453,380	9,563,434	2,046,698	1,669,389	285,287	1869	3,090,372	1,066,337	1,839,461	184,574	661,366	392,902
1939	12,668,389	418,425	9,778,725	2,471,239	1,711,965	251,637	1868	3,174,935	1,046,198	1,962,225	166,512	695,604	481,218
1938	12,666,146	453,571	9,729,758	2,482,817	1,739,074	246,145	1867	3,340,095	1,008,015	2,170,795	161,285	612,645	351,747
1937	12,733,008	514,967	9,630,476	2,587,565	1,712,900	230,220	1866	3,515,248	1,126,382	2,208,841	180,025	571,637	223,893
1936	12,511,523	516,684	9,253,753	2,741,086	1,766,674	218,490	1865	4,179,920	1,269,247	2,756,323	154,350	671,004	245,858
1935	12,699,942	589,210	9,247,868	2,862,864	1,773,054	180,760	1864	4,099,610	1,340,566	2,654,147	104,897	697,798	188,992
1934	12,882,970	619,833	9,311,792	2,951,345	1,802,305	176,760	1863	4,381,901	1,645,743	2,617,958	118,200	631,456	141,699
1933	13,076,686	641,257	9,465,211	2,970,218	1,813,570	169,901	1862	4,424,612	1,805,210	2,515,720	103,682	561,003	126,549
1932	13,792,994	708,226	9,970,014	3,114,754	1,856,553	189,108	1861	4,888,140	1,839,158	2,959,041	89,941	478,788	172,885
1931	12,957,859	712,288	9,156,549	3,089,022	2,766,545	183,852	1860	4,723,006	1,827,671	2,810,224	85,111	463,123	167,739
1930	13,131,044	798,092	9,106,355	3,226,597	2,758,321	178,360	1859	4,674,799	1,832,513	2,754,385	87,901	328,735	141,504
1929	13,526,522	814,833	9,447,388	3,264,301	2,771,287	179,050	1858	4,648,029	1,738,984	2,824,201	84,844	260,698	141,081
1928	13,727,517	878,083	9,494,410	3,355,024	2,773,341	182,203	1857	4,562,408	1,776,993	2,700,630	84,785	237,955	140,480
1927	13,914,054	917,930	9,746,872	3,249,252	2,805,350	168,097	1856	4,525,309	1,862,725	2,578,894	83,690	222,475	123,869
1926	14,305,686	936,161	10,079,066	3,290,459	2,844,473	160,988	1855	4,876,720	2,004,364	2,778,901	93,455	205,894	129,387
1925	14,390,411	953,193	10,154,975	3,282,243	2,853,019	162,472	1854	4,531,280	1,806,242	2,622,588	102,450	161,020	110,602
1924	14,785,459	1,013,818	10,343,841	3,427,800	2,791,204	163,894	1853	3,871,716	1,678,509	2,087,935	105,272	253,712	281,582
1923	15,387,961	1,112,577	10,779,633	3,495,751	2,758,401	138,372	1852	3,566,215	1,557,216	1,906,282	102,717	217,087	355,138
1922	15,604,264	983,953	11,146,730	3,473,581	2,723,857	134,847	1851	3,258,723	1,414,290	1,784,934	59,499	195,766	317,950
1921	15,320,307	920,484	10,931,951	3,467,872	2,839,514	122,315	1850	3,051,390	1,368,049	1,664,686	18,655	181,235	302,829
1920	13,065,104	872,207	8,866,612	3,326,285	3,138,690	120,230	1849	2,874,015	1,289,260	1,584,033	722	173,525	286,476
1919	9,761,741	616,056	6,329,204	2,816,481	3,023,762	121,797	1848	2,728,516	1,258,314	1,470,202	----------	148,195	277,331
1918	7,003,673	599,988	4,756,988	1,646,697	2,797,503	123,342	1847	2,463,568	1,124,749	1,338,819	----------	134,030	241,448
1917	5,959,272	603,970	4,145,769	1,209,533	2,779,087	132,678	1846	2,256,786	1,070,842	1,185,944	----------	90,749	214,550
1916	5,574,082	616,192	3,826,832	1,131,058	2,760,815	134,752	1845	2,143,365	1,009,902	1,133,463	----------	85,897	187,740
1915	5,432,616	658,137	3,651,859	1,122,620	2,818,009	138,804	1844	2,033,237	962,572	1,070,665	----------	72,451	174,408
1914	4,904,330	767,421	3,035,933	1,100,976	2,882,922	141,436	1843	1,940,067	922,959	1,017,108	----------	66,207	152,329
1913	4,800,424	765,588	2,985,540	1,049,296	2,939,786	146,308	1842	1,888,134	915,237	972,897	----------	61,339	142,918
1912	4,618,279	765,476	2,867,990	984,813	2,949,924	145,980	1841	1,935,702	984,262	951,440	----------	57,782	137,260
1911	4,543,743	775,313	2,794,825	973,605	2,943,523	167,957	1840	2,014,214	1,012,343	1,001,871	----------	48,598	117,952
1910	4,459,264	799,811	2,722,862	936,591	2,895,102	153,716	1839	(³)	(³)	(³)	----------	(³)	(³)
1909	4,443,611	827,779	2,681,355	934,477	2,782,481	162,663	1838	1,836,564	901,058	935,506	----------	50,262	108,814
1908	4,468,865	821,849	2,684,702	962,314	2,729,169	167,411	1837	1,771,256	889,089	882,167	----------	34,644	90,786
1907	4,327,537	784,314	2,656,383	886,840	2,439,741	171,516	1836	1,773,125	877,371	895,754	----------	29,582	79,395
1906	4,272,580	781,118	2,651,427	840,035	2,234,432	167,957	1835	1,735,393	895,748	839,645	----------	16,851	72,697
1905	4,220,077	812,838	2,585,529	821,710	2,062,147	174,319	1834	(³)	(³)	(³)	----------	(³)	(³)
1904	4,058,943	794,866	2,457,500	806,577	2,019,208	213,384	1833	1,529,884	811,430	718,454	----------	16,678	59,589
1903	3,969,552	771,535	2,385,838	812,179	1,902,698	215,095	1832	1,367,411	700,433	666,978	----------	16,284	55,755
1902	3,759,267	758,288	2,226,768	774,211	1,816,511	222,124	1831	1,214,914	575,957	638,957	----------	9,080	43,852
1901	3,568,470	750,244	2,104,395	713,831	1,706,294	249,454	1830	1,145,929	581,173	564,756	----------	13,183	32,664
1900	3,340,796	770,578	1,957,314	612,904	1,565,587	258,456	1829	(³)	(³)	(³)	----------	(³)	(³)
1899	3,154,806	741,981	1,872,888	539,937	1,446,348	263,084	1828	1,691,744	786,971	904,773	----------	10,245	39,403
1898	3,050,506	774,965	1,778,774	496,767	1,437,500	261,732	1827	1,589,862	714,181	875,681	----------	8,803	21,942
1897	3,086,809	817,646	1,830,151	439,012	1,410,103	272,108	1826	1,500,910	706,167	794,743	----------	9,293	23,988
1896	3,105,287	857,219	1,810,097	437,971	1,324,067	274,526	1825	1,396,691	640,651	756,040	----------	7,027	19,393
1895	3,113,282	845,918	1,833,863	433,501	1,241,459	281,219	1824	1,361,776	613,340	748,436	----------	8,910	18,477
1894	3,169,303	879,261	1,833,684	456,358	1,227,400	287,325	1823	1,311,536	600,487	711,049	----------	7,311	17,719
1893	3,265,112	907,085	1,900,605	457,422	1,261,067	298,892	1822	1,298,385	600,977	697,408	----------	6,649	19,665
1892	3,270,537	931,756	1,874,162	464,619	1,183,582	310,802	1821	1,264,648	580,407	684,241	----------	7,150	27,160
1891	3,221,541	944,493	1,836,191	440,857	1,154,870	308,347	1820	1,245,416	564,816	680,600	----------	7,482	27,269
1890	3,066,988	947,366	1,691,231	428,391	1,063,063	294,446	1819	1,228,068	550,515	677,553	----------	7,492	25,192
1889	3,035,777	956,609	1,642,896	436,272	972,271	299,427	1818	1,194,372	527,768	666,604	----------	6,301	24,512
1888	3,012,731	1,009,426	1,603,416	399,889	874,102	305,082	1817	1,320,100	562,481	757,619	----------	6,866	12,946
1887	2,994,718	997,849	1,640,424	356,445	783,721	327,405	1816	1,357,072	569,093	787,979	----------	5,217	9,930

[1] Includes Puerto Rico and Virgin Islands.
[2] Includes Alaska and Hawaii.
[3] No returns reported.

Series Q 175–177. Documented Merchant Vessels, by Type of Service: 1934 to 1957

[In thousands of tons. Gross tonnage of documented vessels of 5 tons or more. As of June 30, 1934–1940; January 1 thereafter]

Year	Freight (dry cargo) 175	Tanker 176	All other 177	Year	Freight (dry cargo) 175	Tanker 176	All other 177	Year	Freight (dry cargo) 175	Tanker 176	All other 177
1957	22,024	4,934	2,464	1949	23,766	6,001	2,414	1941	8,115	3,053	2,553
1956	22,280	4,945	2,386	1948	24,047	4,171	4,949	1940	8,267	3,028	2,723
1955	22,298	5,279	2,381	1947	27,407	8,196	2,230	1939	8,615	3,089	2,929
1954	22,818	5,520	2,427	1946	28,087	8,336	2,077	1938	8,702	2,989	2,960
1953	22,605	5,478	2,463					1937	8,671	2,881	3,123
1952	22,556	5,451	2,409	1945	23,931	6,835	2,047				
1951	22,598	5,354	2,389	1944	18,878	4,802	2,115	1936	8,702	2,686	3,109
1950	23,209	5,554	2,452	1943	11,365	3,128	2,268	1935	8,748	2,668	3,238
				1942	8,226	3,261	2,373	1934	8,887	2,674	3,301

Series Q 178–182. Merchant Vessels Built and Documented, by Type: 1797 to 1957

[Gross tonnage of documented vessels of 5 tons or more. As of December 31, 1797–1834; September 30, 1835–1842; June 30, 1843–1940; January 1 thereafter]

Year	All vessels: Number of vessels 178	All vessels: Gross tons 179	Steam and motor 180	Sailing [1] 181	Canalboats and barges 182	Year	All vessels: Number of vessels 178	All vessels: Gross tons 179	Steam and motor 180	Sailing [1] 181	Canalboats and barges 182
1957	1,582	585,048	248,801	---	336,247	1916	937	325,413	250,125	14,765	60,523
1956	1,385	445,617	152,359	8	293,250	1915	1,157	225,122	154,990	8,021	62,111
1955	1,116	400,076	117,011	24	283,041	1914	1,151	316,250	224,225	13,749	78,276
1954	1,186	589,317	369,016	10	220,291	1913	1,475	346,155	243,408	28,610	74,137
1953	1,190	633,966	477,421	28	156,517	1912	1,505	232,669	153,493	21,221	57,955
1952	990	437,378	313,296	---	124,082	1911	1,422	291,162	227,231	10,092	53,839
1951	992	308,825	165,064	---	143,761						
1950	861	194,370	103,358	7	91,005	1910	1,361	342,068	257,993	19,358	64,717
1949	978	195,190	85,288		109,863	1909	1,247	238,090	148,208	28,950	60,932
1948	1,118	200,290	108,206	39	92,084	1908	1,457	614,216	481,624	31,981	100,611
1947	1,259	267,331	186,109	16	81,206	1907	1,157	471,332	365,405	24,907	81,020
1946	1,275	548,262	509,538	7	38,717	1906	1,221	418,745	315,707	35,209	67,829
1945	1,744	6,313,977	6,258,608	---	55,369	1905	1,012	330,316	197,702	79,418	53,196
1944	1,723	8,032,009	8,009,277	129	22,603	1904	1,184	378,542	255,744	64,908	57,890
1943	1,901	10,431,734	10,339,670	23	92,041	1903	1,311	436,152	271,781	89,979	74,392
1942	1,108	4,543,946	4,504,398	14	39,534	1902	1,491	468,831	308,178	97,698	62,955
1941	703	647,097	586,443	---	60,654	1901	1,580	483,489	273,591	126,165	83,733
1940 [2]	705	446,894	385,681	87	61,126	1900	1,447	393,790	202,528	116,460	74,802
1940 [3]	319	193,229	172,433	17	20,779	1899	1,273	300,038	151,058	98,073	50,907
1939	673	339,899	269,188	22	70,689	1898	952	180,458	105,838	34,416	40,204
1938	753	237,374	(4)	(4)	(4)	1897	891	232,233	106,154	64,308	61,771
1937	1,939	471,364	113,661	71	357,632	1896	723	227,097	138,029	65,236	23,832
1936	1,207	224,084	59,020	79	164,985	1895	694	111,602	69,754	34,900	6,948
1935	748	62,919	30,341	50	32,528	1894	838	131,195	83,720	37,827	9,648
1934	724	66,649	26,916	33	39,700	1893	956	211,639	134,368	49,348	27,923
1933	642	190,803	168,488	46	22,269	1892	1,395	199,633	92,531	83,217	23,885
1932	722	212,892	164,620	18	48,254	1891	1,384	369,302	185,037	144,290	39,975
1931	1,302	386,906	212,996	52	173,858	1890	1,051	294,123	159,046	102,873	32,204
1930	1,020	254,296	172,969	210	81,117	1889	1,077	231,134	159,318	50,570	21,246
1929	808	128,976	75,725	797	52,454	1888	1,014	218,087	142,007	48,590	27,490
1928	969	257,180	172,901	230	84,049	1887	844	150,450	100,074	34,633	15,743
1927	917	245,144	181,504	326	63,314	1886	715	95,453	44,468	41,238	9,747
1926	924	224,673	140,586	263	83,824	1885	920	159,056	84,333	65,362	9,361
1925	967	199,846	141,053	2,869	55,924	1884	1,190	225,514	91,328	120,621	13,565
1924	1,049	223,968	145,493	914	77,561	1883	1,268	265,430	107,229	137,046	21,155
1923	770	335,791	241,802	17,442	76,547	1882	1,371	282,270	121,843	118,798	41,629
1922	845	661,232	597,137	25,459	38,636	1881	1,108	280,459	118,070	81,209	81,180
1921	1,361	2,265,115	2,071,221	91,743	102,151	1880	902	157,410	78,854	59,057	19,499
1920	2,067	3,880,639	3,660,023	132,184	88,432	1879	1,132	193,031	86,361	66,867	39,803
1919	1,953	3,326,621	3,157,091	79,234	90,296	1878	1,258	235,504	81,860	106,066	47,578
1918	1,528	1,300,868	1,090,996	83,629	126,243	1877	1,029	176,592	47,514	106,331	22,747
1917	1,297	664,479	513,243	43,185	108,051	1876	1,112	203,586	69,251	118,672	15,663

[1] Includes canalboats and barges prior to 1868.
[2] Jan. 1–Dec. 31.
[3] July 1, 1939–June 30, 1940.
[4] Not available.

Series Q 178–182. Merchant Vessels Built and Documented, by Type: 1797 to 1957—Con.

Year	All vessels		Steam and motor	Sailing [1]	Canal-boats and barges	Year	All vessels		Steam and motor	Sailing [1]
	Number of vessels	Gross tons					Number of vessels	Gross tons		
	178	179	180	181	182		178	179	180	181
1875	1,301	297,639	62,460	206,884	28,295	1835 [5]	725	75,107	12,347	62,760
1874	2,147	432,725	101,930	216,316	114,479	1834	957	118,389	13,905	104,484
1873	2,261	359,246	88,011	144,629	126,606	1833	1,187	161,492	12,620	148,872
1872	1,643	209,052	62,210	76,291	70,551	1832	1,065	144,544	17,386	127,158
1871	1,755	273,227	87,842	97,179	88,206	1831	712	85,556	11,437	74,119
1870	1,618	276,953	70,621	146,340	59,992	1830	648	58,560	8,269	50,291
1869	1,726	275,230	65,066	149,029	61,135	1829	796	79,408	10,281	69,127
1868	1,802	285,304	63,940	142,742	78,622	1828	886	98,964	5,881	93,083
1867	1,518	305,594	72,010	233,584	----------	1827	951	106,456	11,010	95,446
1866	1,898	336,146	125,183	210,963	----------	1826	1,033	130,373	12,818	117,555
1865	1,789	394,523	146,433	248,090	----------	1825	1,000	116,464	9,171	107,293
1864	2,388	415,740	147,499	268,241	----------	1824	793	92,798	5,216	87,582
1863	1,816	311,045	94,233	216,812	----------	1823	630	75,857	3,766	72,091
1862	864	175,076	55,449	119,627	----------	1822	639	77,569	1,861	75,708
1861	1,146	233,194	60,986	172,208	----------	1821	519	57,275	3,017	54,258
1860	1,071	214,798	69,370	145,428	----------	1820	557	51,394	5,572	45,822
1859	875	156,602	35,305	121,297	----------	1819	876	86,670	5,824	80,846
1858	1,241	244,712	65,374	179,338	----------	1818	923	87,346	3,695	83,651
1857	1,443	378,804	74,459	304,345	----------	1817	1,087	87,626	2,543	85,083
1856	1,703	469,393	74,865	394,528	----------	1816	1,431	135,186	2,926	132,260
1855	2,024	588,450	78,127	505,323	----------	1815	1,329	155,579	546	155,033
1854	1,774	535,616	91,037	444,579	----------	1814	490	29,751	593	29,158
1853	1,710	425,572	109,402	316,170	----------	1813	371	32,583	1,140	31,443
1852	1,444	351,493	98,624	252,869	----------	1812	----------	85,148	118	85,030
1851	1,357	298,203	78,197	220,006	----------	1811	----------	146,691	1,145	145,546
1850	1,360	272,218	56,911	215,307	----------	1810	----------	127,575	----------	127,575
1849	1,547	256,577	61,241	195,336	----------	1809	----------	91,397	458	90,939
1848	1,851	318,075	66,652	251,423	----------	1808 [6]	----------	31,755	182	31,673
1847	1,598	243,732	53,979	189,753	----------	1807	----------	99,783	78	99,705
1846	1,420	188,203	51,778	136,425	----------	1806	----------	126,093	----------	126,093
1845	1,038	146,018	40,926	105,092	----------	1805	----------	128,507	----------	128,507
1844	766	103,537	30,976	72,561	----------	1804	----------	103,753	----------	103,753
1843 [5]	482	63,617	17,624	45,992	----------	1803	----------	88,448	----------	88,448
1842	1,021	129,083	29,158	99,925	----------	1802	(4)	(4)	(4)	(4)
1841	761	118,893	27,941	90,950	----------	1801	----------	124,755	----------	124,755
1840	871	118,309	19,811	98,498	----------	1800	995	106,261	----------	106,261
1839	899	125,260	34,219	91,041	----------	1799	767	77,921	----------	77,921
1838	913	115,905	23,607	92,298	----------	1798	635	49,435	----------	49,435
1837	972	125,913	33,811	92,102	----------	1797	----------	56,679	----------	56,679
1836	911	116,230	26,630	89,600	----------					

[1] Includes canalboats and barges prior to 1868.
[4] Not available.
[5] 9-month period.
[6] Figures by class of vessel do not add to the total for this year.

Series Q 183–190. Merchant Vessels Built and Documented, by Region: 1817 to 1936

[Gross tonnage of documented vessels of 5 tons or more. As of December 31, 1817–1834; September 30, 1835–1842; June 30 thereafter]

Year	Seaboard				Northern lakes and western rivers	Year	Seaboard				Northern lakes and western rivers
	Total	New England coast	Mid-Atlantic and Gulf coasts	Pacific coast			Total	New England coast	Mid-Atlantic and Gulf coasts	Pacific coast	
	183	184	185	186	187		183	184	185	186	187
1936	175,398	711	166,671	8,016	48,686	1910	167,829	23,442	127,517	16,870	174,239
						1909	131,748	27,237	81,752	22,759	106,342
1935	49,054	1,910	38,452	8,692	13,865	1908	266,937	70,903	138,984	57,050	347,279
1934	49,946	862	37,390	11,694	16,703	1907	219,753	44,428	140,134	35,191	251,579
1933	181,593	25,851	151,823	3,919	9,210	1906	146,883	32,311	94,311	20,261	271,862
1932	195,529	52,163	133,625	9,741	17,363						
1931	355,771	26,639	287,884	41,248	31,135	1905	230,716	119,377	91,224	20,115	99,600
						1904	208,288	51,417	135,263	21,608	170,254
1930	193,116	18,601	143,656	30,859	61,180	1903	288,196	66,973	177,887	43,336	147,956
1929	104,769	12,766	71,750	20,253	24,207	1902	290,122	75,852	161,211	53,059	178,709
1928	181,681	11,434	146,532	23,715	75,499	1901	291,516	82,971	153,977	54,568	191,973
1927	176,207	6,574	124,068	45,565	68,937						
1926	159,658	4,995	131,994	22,669	65,015	1900	249,006	72,179	135,473	41,354	144,784
						1899	196,120	68,761	85,825	41,534	103,918
1925	123,933	5,615	76,784	41,534	75,913	1898	112,879	23,944	39,146	49,789	67,579
1924	145,837	3,174	106,414	36,249	78,131	1897	103,504	21,942	74,067	7,495	128,729
1923	262,769	13,057	199,026	50,686	73,022	1896	102,544	39,582	52,143	10,819	124,553
1922	637,708	56,973	448,197	132,538	23,524						
1921	2,147,555	150,745	1,383,185	613,625	117,560	1895	67,127	26,783	33,200	7,144	44,475
						1894	80,099	28,665	46,042	5,392	51,096
1920	3,475,872	208,023	1,931,514	1,336,335	404,767	1893	102,830	37,091	52,018	13,721	108,809
1919	2,815,733	177,758	1,274,472	1,363,503	510,888	1892	138,863	60,624	57,469	20,770	60,770
1918	1,080,437	88,302	473,698	518,437	220,431	1891	237,462	105,491	112,901	19,070	131,840
1917	518,958	52,526	298,958	167,474	145,521						
1916	275,749	37,568	188,550	49,631	49,664	1890	169,091	78,577	78,179	12,335	125,032
						1889	111,852	39,983	53,930	17,939	119,282
1915	203,156	18,551	152,906	31,699	21,966	1888	105,125	33,813	49,356	21,956	112,962
1914	251,700	14,985	200,220	36,495	64,550	1887	83,061	24,035	49,886	9,140	67,389
1913	247,318	27,131	175,523	44,664	98,837	1886	64,458	30,624	27,920	5,914	30,995
1912	136,485	23,052	81,329	32,104	96,184						
1911	190,612	23,653	139,725	27,234	100,550						

Series Q 183–190.   Merchant Vessels Built and Documented, by Region: 1817 to 1936—Con.

Year	Seaboard				Northern lakes and western rivers	Year	Seaboard				Northern lakes and western rivers
	Total	New England coast	Mid-Atlantic and Gulf coasts	Pacific coast			Total	New England coast	Mid-Atlantic and Gulf coasts	Pacific coast	
	183	184	185	186	187		183	184	185	186	187
1885	121,010	48,128	61,844	11,038	38,046	1842	109,100	64,237	44,863		19,983
1884	178,419	84,046	83,753	10,620	47,095	1841	104,268	63,771	40,497		14,625
1883	210,349	110,226	83,385	16,738	55,081	1840	110,683	65,189	45,494		7,626
1882	188,084	93,965	78,342	15,777	94,186						
1881	125,766	54,488	59,861	11,417	154,693						

ALTERNATIVE SERIES

Year	Total	New England coast	Mid-Atlantic and Gulf coasts	Pacific coast	Northern lakes and western rivers	Year	The Coast [3]	Western lakes and rivers	New England States [3]
	183	184	185	186	187		188	189	190
1880	101,720	46,374	46,403	8,943	55,690				
1879	115,683	55,874	48,602	11,207	77,348				
1878	155,138	90,386	53,419	11,333	80,366				
1877	132,996	90,992	29,286	12,718	43,596	1850	247,847	24,372	142,367
1876	163,826	95,288	51,716	16,822	39,760	1849	217,264	39,313	120,234
						1848	262,581	55,495	146,111
1875	244,474	151,497	79,549	13,428	53,165	1847	185,493	58,240	104,682
1874	277,093	136,251	129,983	10,859	155,682	1846	149,332	38,872	82,347
1873	218,139	76,406	136,258	5,475	141,107				
1872	128,097	46,269	79,552	2,276	80,955	1845	116,156	29,862	63,835
1871	156,249	64,366	86,559	5,324	116,978	1844	71,732	31,805	36,268
						1843	90,017	26,293	46,251
1870	182,836	110,584	59,532	12,720	94,117	1842	108,302	20,782	56,234
1869	191,194	103,604	72,058	15,532	84,036	1841	103,576	15,318	63,770
1868	173,722	98,915	67,956	6,851	111,582				
1867 [1]	229,583	135,189	90,070	4,324	73,945	1840	109,706	8,603	65,189
1866	232,788	121,335	105,329	6,124	103,358	1839	107,232	13,757	59,204
						1838	100,074	13,061	53,054
1865 [1]	280,899	135,253	141,830	3,816	102,910	1837	98,997	23,990	51,981
1864	328,710	112,615	211,242	4,853	87,030	1836	98,130	15,497	58,330
1863 [1]	215,410	79,578	133,161	2,671	95,474				
1862	112,486	45,597	64,365	2,524	62,589	1835	101,906	14,072	60,054
1861	181,586	104,678	72,192	4,716	51,608	1834	105,683	12,647	61,779
						1833	153,455	8,171	95,143
1860	169,836	134,289	33,524	2,023	44,962	1832	130,064	14,475	100,585
1859 [1]	134,499	79,316	53,127	2,056	23,103	1831	80,541	5,222	49,793
1858 [1]	177,799	103,864	71,811	2,124	64,487				
1857	285,681	183,686	100,810	1,185	93,123	1830	52,686	5,398	24,169
1856	369,679	252,974	116,343	362	99,714	1829	71,055	6,044	38,117
						1828	95,349	3,027	54,282
1855	505,450	326,431	176,901	2,118	78,000	1827	99,343	5,000	57,156
1854	454,933	289,599	164,311	1,023	80,683	1826	121,908	4,530	72,668
1853	357,233	222,791	134,291	151	68,339				
1852	301,275	179,804	121,470		50,218	1825	112,616	2,381	65,616
1851	265,378	133,351	131,957	70	32,825	1824	89,166	1,773	52,445
						1823	73,942	1,066	42,725
1850	248,865	142,369	106,374	122	23,353	1822	75,242	105	44,206
1849	209,189	120,237	88,952		47,388	1821	55,607	249	36,651
1848	264,268	146,113	118,155		53,807				
1847	185,618	104,745	80,873		58,114	1820	47,696	88	29,353
1846	149,571	82,347	67,224		38,632	1819	79,551	267	50,614
						1818	82,232	189	48,823
1845	116,443	63,837	52,606		29,575	1817	85,144	1,250	46,605
1844	71,832	36,268	35,564		31,705				
1843 [2]	53,220	26,512	26,708		10,397				

[1] Figures for these years do not add to series Q 179.   [2] 9-month period.   [3] Figures for New England States included in series Q 188 "The Coast".

Series Q 191.   Persons Entering the United States by Ship: 1933 to 1957

[For years ending June 30]

Year	Persons entering	Year	Persons entering	Year	Persons entering	Year	Persons entering	Year	Persons entering
	191		191		191		191		191
1957	847,652	1952	899,639	1947	547,708	1942	305,190	1937	1,011,387
1956	841,656	1951	723,030	1946	1,660,107	1941	443,238	1936	898,267
1955	842,818	1950	762,353	1945	1,285,931	1940	733,338	1935	811,547
1954	845,424	1949	676,483	1944	676,312	1939	1,019,313	1934	754,190
1953	864,625	1948	641,262	1943	388,962	1938	1,071,896	1933	795,380

Series Q 192–203.   Net Tonnage Capacity of Vessels Entered and Cleared: 1789 to 1957

[In thousands of net tons.   For years ending September 20, 1789–1842; June 30, 1843–1918; December 31 thereafter.   Excludes domestic trade]

Year	Vessels entered						Vessels cleared					
	All ports			Seaports [1]			All ports			Seaports [1]		
	Total	U.S. vessels	Foreign vessels	Total	U.S. vessels	Foreign vessels	Total	U.S. vessels	Foreign vessels	Total	U.S. vessels	Foreign vessels
	192	193	194	195	196	197	198	199	200	201	202	203
1957	162,925	35,898	127,027	146,144	31,189	114,956	162,578	35,118	127,460	145,954	30,569	115,385
1956	147,844	36,247	111,598	130,767	31,254	99,514	148,269	36,317	111,952	131,391	31,510	99,881
1955	128,405	34,321	94,084	113,807	30,407	83,400	129,368	34,407	94,961	114,806	30,615	84,192
1954	109,524	33,860	75,664	97,198	30,133	67,065	109,899	33,579	76,321	97,674	29,969	67,706
1953	112,559	39,319	73,240	97,344	34,969	62,375	112,935	39,188	73,747	97,627	34,775	62,852
1952	116,375	45,223	71,152	101,263	40,732	60,532	114,797	43,726	71,071	99,703	39,273	60,429
1951	108,086	44,571	63,515	93,674	40,482	53,192	110,236	46,763	63,472	96,257	43,024	53,233
1950	86,629	35,376	51,251	73,451	31,757	41,693	87,829	36,043	51,778	74,785	32,510	42,269
1949	85,700	41,251	44,451	74,701	37,626	37,076	84,286	39,681	44,604	73,063	36,136	36,927
1948	90,927	47,726	43,199	76,910	43,270	33,640	89,449	45,775	43,667	75,714	41,348	34,358
1947	93,796	53,627	40,170	80,889	49,044	31,844	97,160	54,088	43,072	84,508	49,558	34,949
1946	80,258	53,045	27,213	69,520	49,143	20,378	77,225	49,124	28,101	66,376	45,113	21,263
1945	94,021	61,375	32,646	81,182	56,499	24,682	94,559	61,460	33,099	81,452	56,332	25,120
1944	81,860	48,071	33,789	66,305	42,196	24,109	87,385	53,050	34,335	71,717	46,919	24,798
1943	61,084	29,292	31,792	44,739	24,508	20,231	66,716	33,682	33,034	50,232	28,826	21,406
1942	43,942	13,611	30,331	28,258	10,326	17,932	47,706	16,354	31,352	31,976	13,149	18,827
1941	59,061	20,940	38,121	42,616	16,767	25,849	62,596	21,869	40,726	46,142	17,701	28,441
1940	58,544	19,220	39,324	45,393	15,740	29,652	62,171	20,248	41,923	48,996	16,766	32,230
1939	68,992	17,769	51,223	57,973	14,553	43,421	70,306	18,156	52,150	59,218	14,903	44,316
1938	70,516	19,020	51,496	59,223	15,899	43,324	71,286	18,829	52,456	60,064	15,742	44,322
1937	71,560	19,527	52,033	59,980	16,747	43,233	72,880	19,938	52,942	61,177	17,134	44,043
1936	65,972	20,682	45,290	55,038	17,510	37,528	66,066	20,069	45,997	55,381	16,967	38,414
1935	64,612	22,372	42,240	54,289	18,893	35,395	64,887	22,126	42,761	54,722	18,651	36,071
1934	63,787	23,192	40,594	53,132	19,186	33,946	63,702	22,799	40,903	53,162	18,901	34,261
1933	60,936	22,488	38,448	51,564	19,051	32,513	61,287	22,434	38,853	52,083	19,093	32,990
1932	64,837	24,278	40,559	55,229	20,643	34,587	64,446	23,865	40,582	54,900	20,204	34,695
1931	72,782	26,907	45,875	60,427	21,499	38,929	73,501	26,854	46,647	61,204	21,417	39,787
1930	81,253	31,866	49,387	66,499	24,620	41,879	81,307	31,560	49,747	66,500	24,154	42,346
1929	82,602	32,241	50,361	66,853	25,208	41,645	82,343	31,927	50,416	67,030	25,045	41,985
1928	80,211	31,285	48,926	62,809	22,991	39,818	80,667	31,734	48,933	63,331	23,180	40,151
1927	74,310	29,289	45,021	58,921	22,001	36,920	75,440	29,793	45,647	59,759	22,078	37,681
1926	76,933	26,890	50,043	63,759	21,091	42,668	79,041	28,532	50,509	65,583	22,234	43,349
1925	69,378	27,947	41,431	55,636	21,148	34,487	70,229	27,808	42,421	57,160	21,394	35,766
1924	68,292	29,628	38,664	54,726	22,462	32,264	68,910	30,092	38,818	55,294	22,896	32,397
1923	66,319	27,725	38,594	52,775	20,984	31,791	66,624	27,932	38,692	53,215	21,305	31,910
1922	65,191	31,738	33,453	51,701	23,633	28,068	64,839	31,759	33,080	51,799	23,755	28,044
1921	62,285	31,185	31,100	49,958	24,402	25,556	62,665	30,181	32,484	50,423	23,432	26,991
1920	64,104	32,119	31,985	51,531	26,225	25,306	67,817	34,053	33,764	54,980	27,875	27,106
1919	46,702	21,933	24,769	36,381	16,224	20,157	51,257	24,992	26,265	40,751	19,133	21,617
1918 [2]	45,456	19,284	26,173	31,101	11,256	19,845	46,014	19,206	26,808	31,869	11,280	20,589
1917	50,472	18,725	31,747	36,521	10,898	25,623	52,077	19,146	32,931	38,094	11,339	26,755
1916	51,550	17,928	33,622	37,744	9,446	28,298	52,423	17,902	34,521	38,946	9,763	29,182
1915	46,710	13,275	33,435	35,032	6,830	28,202	46,885	13,418	33,467	35,458	7,110	28,347
1914	53,389	13,730	39,659	40,052	5,436	34,616	53,183	13,740	39,443	39,743	5,185	34,558
1913	50,639	13,073	37,567	37,973	5,241	32,732	51,152	13,946	37,206	37,566	5,289	32,277
1912	46,158	11,257	34,901	34,659	4,572	30,087	46,417	11,703	34,713	34,706	4,794	29,912
1911	42,675	9,698	32,982	32,457	4,302	28,155	42,437	9,753	32,684	32,299	4,427	27,871
1910	40,236	8,888	31,347	30,917	4,214	26,703	39,706	8,809	30,897	30,510	4,196	26,314
1909	39,058	8,771	30,287	30,243	4,403	25,840	38,196	8,492	29,705	29,604	4,215	25,389
1908	38,539	8,473	30,066	30,444	4,314	26,130	38,282	8,435	29,846	30,198	4,288	25,910
1907	36,622	8,116	28,507	29,248	3,924	25,324	35,990	8,093	27,898	28,499	3,797	24,702
1906	34,155	7,613	26,543	27,401	4,023	23,379	33,784	7,581	26,204	26,970	3,923	23,047
1905	30,983	7,081	23,903	24,793	4,120	20,673	31,158	7,203	23,955	25,020	4,259	20,760
1904	29,952	6,679	23,273	24,111	3,806	20,305	30,016	6,641	23,374	24,192	3,836	20,356
1903	31,094	6,907	24,187	24,698	3,881	20,817	31,316	6,975	24,341	24,823	3,931	20,892
1902	30,654	6,961	23,693	24,361	4,020	20,342	30,444	6,822	23,623	24,242	3,956	20,287
1901	29,768	6,381	23,387	24,791	3,980	20,811	29,820	6,417	23,403	24,889	4,020	20,870
1900	28,163	6,136	22,027	23,534	3,974	19,559	28,281	6,209	22,072	23,618	4,006	19,612
1899	26,111	5,341	20,770	21,963	3,333	18,631	26,266	5,472	20,794	22,177	3,463	18,714
1898	25,579	5,240	20,339	21,700	3,362	18,338	25,748	5,111	20,637	21,892	3,231	18,661
1897	23,760	5,525	18,235	20,003	3,611	16,391	23,709	5,618	18,091	19,878	3,637	16,241
1896	20,989	5,196	15,793	17,453	3,673	13,779	21,415	5,330	16,085	17,819	3,741	14,078
1895	19,295	4,473	14,822	16,725	3,677	13,049	19,751	4,504	15,246	17,024	3,616	13,408
1894	19,990	4,655	15,335	17,025	3,649	13,376	20,272	4,740	15,532	17,306	3,747	13,560
1893	19,582	4,359	15,223	16,679	3,493	13,186	19,761	4,403	15,357	16,825	3,537	13,288
1892	21,013	4,470	16,543	18,180	3,747	14,434	21,161	4,536	16,625	18,258	3,751	14,507
1891	18,204	4,381	13,823	15,394	3,670	11,724	18,261	4,455	13,805	15,411	3,716	11,695
1890	18,107	4,083	14,024	15,366	3,405	11,961	18,149	4,067	14,082	15,429	3,390	12,039
1889	15,952	3,724	12,228	13,312	3,128	10,184	16,343	3,988	12,355	13,672	3,342	10,329
1888	15,393	3,367	12,026	12,956	2,914	10,042	15,669	3,415	12,254	13,252	2,944	10,308
1887	15,816	3,366	12,451	13,532	2,871	10,661	15,753	3,259	12,494	13,511	2,771	10,740
1886	15,136	3,232	11,904	12,230	2,762	9,468	15,328	3,303	12,024	12,413	2,806	9,607
1885	15,305	3,132	12,173	12,287	2,709	9,578	15,515	3,232	12,283	12,496	2,809	9,688
1884	15,069	3,202	11,867	12,085	2,821	9,264	15,205	3,237	11,968	12,206	2,845	9,361
1883	16,382	3,256	13,126	13,361	2,835	10,526	16,541	3,307	13,234	13,565	2,895	10,670
1882	17,601	3,341	14,260	14,656	2,968	11,688	17,757	3,318	14,439	14,846	2,936	11,911
1881	18,319	3,254	15,066	15,631	2,919	12,711	18,470	3,376	15,094	15,794	3,040	12,754

See footnotes at end of table.

Series Q 192–203. Net Tonnage Capacity of Vessels Entered and Cleared: 1789 to 1957—Con.

[In thousands of net tons]

Year	Vessels entered						Vessels cleared					
	All ports			Seaports [1]			All ports			Seaports [1]		
	Total	U.S. vessels	Foreign vessels	Total	U.S. vessels	Foreign vessels	Total	U.S. vessels	Foreign vessels	Total	U.S. vessels	Foreign vessels
	192	193	194	195	196	197	198	199	200	201	202	203
1880	18,011	3,437	14,574	15,251	3,140	12,111	18,043	3,397	14,646	15,296	3,078	12,218
1879	16,193	3,415	12,778	13,768	3,050	10,718	16,075	3,464	12,611	13,617	3,071	10,545
1878	14,464	3,642	10,821	11,531	3,009	8,521	14,808	3,872	10,935	11,844	3,196	8,647
1877	13,455	3,663	9,791	10,406	2,958	7,449	13,442	3,765	9,677	10,389	3,043	7,345
1876	12,511	3,611	8,899	9,716	2,928	6,788	12,655	3,732	8,923	9,839	3,037	6,802
1875	11,693	3,574	8,119	9,143	2,887	6,256	11,897	3,737	8,160	9,341	3,061	6,279
1874	13,092	3,894	9,198	10,010	2,915	7,095	13,189	3,982	9,207	10,058	2,961	7,097
1873	11,696	3,613	8,083	8,395	2,443	5,951	11,822	3,757	8,065	8,515	2,574	5,941
1872	10,806	3,712	7,095	7,770	2,585	5,185	10,734	3,682	7,051	7,739	2,598	5,141
1871	10,009	3,743	6,266	6,994	2,604	4,391	9,898	3,747	6,152	6,918	2,635	4,283
1870	9,156	3,486	5,670	6,270	2,452	3,818	9,169	3,507	5,662	6,362	2,530	3,832
1869	8,750	3,403	5,348	6,032	2,459	3,573	7,754	3,381	4,373	6,114	2,502	3,612
1868	8,046	3,551	4,495	5,572	2,466	3,106	8,279	3,718	4,561	5,811	2,625	3,186
1867	7,774	3,455	4,319	5,266	2,146	3,121	7,885	3,420	4,465	5,501	2,270	3,230
1866	7,782	3,372	4,410	5,008	1,891	3,117	7,822	3,383	4,438	5,161	2,030	3,131
1865	6,161	2,944	3,217	3,827	1,615	2,212	6,620	3,025	3,595	4,161	1,710	2,450
1864	6,538	3,066	3,471	4,167	1,655	2,512	6,832	3,091	3,741	4,279	1,662	2,617
1863	7,255	4,615	2,640	4,205	2,308	1,898	7,511	4,447	3,064	4,343	2,266	2,077
1862	7,363	5,118	2,245	4,191	2,629	1,562	7,339	4,962	2,377	4,205	2,568	1,637
1861	7,241	5,024	2,218	4,559	3,025	1,534	7,151	4,889	2,262	4,410	2,874	1,536
1860	8,275	5,921	2,354	5,000	3,302	1,698	8,790	6,166	2,624	5,257	3,501	1,756
1859	7,806	5,266	2,540	4,913	3,328	1,585	7,916	5,297	2,618	4,867	3,315	1,552
1858	6,605	4,396	2,209	4,338	3,051	1,287	7,803	4,490	3,313	4,436	3,128	1,309
1857	7,186	4,721	2,465	4,843	3,482	1,361	7,071	4,581	2,490	4,882	3,483	1,398
1856	6,872	4,385	2,487	4,464	3,194	1,270	7,000	4,538	2,462	4,695	----------	----------

Year	Vessels entered				Vessels cleared				Year	Vessels entered, all ports		
	All ports			Sea-ports [1]	All ports			Sea-ports [1]		Total	U.S. vessels	Foreign vessels
	Total	U.S. vessels	Foreign vessels		Total	U.S. vessels	Foreign vessels					
	192	193	194	195	198	199	200	201		192	193	194
1855	5,945	3,861	2,084	4,178	6,179	4,069	2,110	4,435	1820	880	801	79
1854	5,884	3,752	2,132	4,343	6,019	3,911	2,108	4,524	1819	869	784	86
1853	6,282	4,004	2,278	4,157	6,066	3,767	2,299	4,289	1818	917	755	161
1852	5,293	3,236	2,057	3,926	5,278	3,231	2,048	----------	1817	992	780	212
1851	4,993	3,054	1,939	3,466	5,130	3,201	1,930	----------	1816	1,136	877	259
1850	3,749	2,573	1,176	[3] 3,013	4,361	2,633	1,728	3,167	1815	918	701	217
1849	4,369	2,658	1,711	2,890	4,429	2,754	1,676	----------	1814	108	60	48
1848	3,799	2,393	1,405	2,503	3,865	2,461	1,404	----------	1813	351	238	114
1847	3,322	2,101	1,220	2,429	3,379	2,202	1,177	----------	1812	715	668	47
1846	3,111	2,151	960	2,022	3,189	2,221	968	----------	1811	981	948	33
1845	2,946	2,035	911	2,011	2,984	2,054	930	----------	1810	989	909	80
1844	2,894	1,977	917	1,897	2,918	2,011	907	----------	1809	705	605	99
1843	1,678	1,144	535	----------	1,792	1,268	524	----------	1808	586	539	48
1842	2,243	1,510	733	----------	2,277	1,536	740	----------	1807	1,203	1,116	87
1841	2,368	1,632	736	----------	2,371	1,634	737	----------	1806	1,135	1,044	91
1840	2,289	1,577	712	1,788	2,353	1,647	706	1,861	1805	1,010	922	88
1839	2,116	1,491	625	----------	2,090	1,478	612	----------	1804	944	822	122
1838	1,895	1,303	592	----------	2,013	1,409	604	----------	1803	951	787	164
1837	2,065	1,300	766	----------	2,023	1,267	756	----------	1802	944	799	146
1836	1,936	1,255	680	----------	1,990	1,316	674	----------	1801	1,007	849	157
1835	1,994	1,353	641	----------	2,031	1,401	631	----------	1800	804	683	121
1834	1,643	1,075	568	----------	1,712	1,134	578	----------	1799	732	625	108
1833	1,608	1,111	497	----------	1,639	1,142	497	----------	1798	610	522	88
1832	1,343	950	393	----------	1,362	975	388	----------	1797	681	608	73
1831	1,405	923	482	----------	1,244	973	272	----------	1796	722	675	47
1830	1,099	967	132	----------	1,105	972	133	----------	1795	637	580	57
1829	1,004	873	131	----------	1,078	945	133	----------	1794	609	526	83
1828	1,019	868	150	----------	1,048	897	151	----------	1793	611	448	164
1827	1,056	918	138	----------	1,112	981	131	----------	1792	659	415	244
1826	1,048	942	106	----------	1,052	953	99	----------	1791	604	364	241
1825	974	881	93	----------	1,055	960	95	----------	1790	606	355	251
1824	952	850	102	----------	1,022	919	103	----------	1789	234	127	107
1823	895	775	119	----------	931	811	120	----------				
1822	889	788	101	----------	911	814	97	----------				
1821	847	765	82	----------	888	805	83	----------				

[1] Comprises all ports except northern border ports.
[2] As of June 30; figures (in thousands of tons) for July-Dec. are as follows: Series Q 192, 25,029; series Q 193, 11,006; series Q 194, 14,023; series Q 195, 16,113; series Q 196, 5,747; series Q 197, 10,366; series Q 198, 25,472; series Q 199, 11,223; series Q 200, 14,249; series Q 201, 16,112; series Q 202, 5,614; and series Q 203, 10,498.
[3] Reported as 3,169 (thousands of net tons) in *Statistical Abstract, 1957*, p. 595, table 756.

Series Q 204–209. Value of Waterborne Imports and Exports (Including Reexports) of Merchandise: 1790 to 1946

[In millions of dollars. For years ending September 30, 1790–1842; June 30, 1843–1915; December 31 thereafter. Includes gold and silver coin and bullion to 1879, imports and exports by land prior to 1871; and all waterborne foreign commerce of ports on the Great Lakes]

Year	Imports Total 204	U.S. vessels 205	Foreign vessels 206	Exports Total 207	U.S. vessels 208	Foreign vessels 209
1946	3,691	2,239	1,452	7,705	4,692	3,013
1945	----	----	----	7,860	4,052	3,808
1944	----	----	----	11,382	5,582	5,800
1943	----	----	----	10,275	4,828	5,447
1935	1,813	649	1,164	1,973	705	1,268
1934	1,446	528	917	1,837	658	1,179
1933	1,287	461	826	1,471	515	956
1932	1,164	431	734	1,385	476	909
1931	1,829	619	1,210	2,043	732	1,311
1930	2,635	898	1,737	3,168	1,117	2,051
1929	3,807	1,205	2,602	4,322	1,487	2,835
1928	3,550	1,133	2,418	4,277	1,472	2,804
1927	3,662	1,215	2,447	4,097	1,434	2,663
1926	3,891	1,195	2,696	4,050	1,401	2,649
1925	3,716	1,151	2,565	4,224	1,473	2,751
1924	3,145	1,012	2,133	4,010	1,532	2,478
1923	3,312	1,040	2,272	3,539	1,358	2,181
1922	2,704	921	1,783	3,281	1,261	2,020
1921	2,187	765	1,422	3,888	1,402	2,486
1920	4,731	1,988	2,743	7,252	3,165	4,087
1919	3,414	1,228	2,186	7,090	2,596	4,494
1918	2,577	717	1,860	5,226	986	4,240
1917	2,590	733	1,857	5,403	946	4,457
1916	2,157	532	1,625	4,820	665	4,155
1915[1]	1,526	281	1,245	2,466	291	2,176
1914	1,738	199	1,539	2,048	170	1,878
1913	1,698	193	1,505	2,075	188	1,887
1912	1,551	171	1,380	1,880	152	1,729
1911	1,436	147	1,290	1,774	134	1,641
1910	1,467	147	1,319	1,516	114	1,403
1909	1,241	151	1,090	1,481	108	1,373
1908	1,123	152	971	1,670	121	1,550
1907	1,340	177	1,164	1,662	142	1,521
1906	1,140	168	971	1,550	154	1,396
1905	1,039	161	878	1,355	130	1,225
1904	923	132	791	1,308	97	1,211
1903	960	124	836	1,281	91	1,190
1902	847	102	745	1,258	84	1,174
1901	776	93	683	1,376	84	1,292
1900	806	104	701	1,284	91	1,193
1899	664	82	582	1,143	79	1,065
1898	586	94	492	1,158	68	1,090
1897	729	109	620	986	80	906
1896	744	117	627	821	70	751
1895	699	108	591	758	62	695
1894	625	122	504	843	74	769
1893	822	127	695	804	71	733
1892	788	139	649	997	81	916
1891	804	127	677	853	79	774
1890	749	125	624	825	78	747
1889	707	121	586	714	83	631
1888	692	124	568	674	67	606
1887	665	121	543	695	73	622
1886	611	119	492	660	78	582
1885	556	113	444	718	82	636
1884	648	135	513	714	99	615
1883	700	136	564	799	104	694
1882	702	130	572	738	97	641
1881	625	134	492	894	117	777
1880	653	149	503	830	109	721
1879	454	144	310	729	128	601
1878	454	146	307	736	167	570
1877	481	152	330	695	165	530
1876	465	143	321	660	168	492
1875	541	158	383	658	156	502
1874	581	176	405	708	174	534
1873	647	175	472	666	172	495
1872	623	177	445	562	168	394
1871	526	163	363	583	190	393
1870	462	153	309	530	200	330
1869	437	137	301	439	153	286
1868	372	123	249	477	175	302
1867	418	117	301	461	181	281
1866	446	112	333	565	214	352

Year	Imports Total 204	U.S. vessels 205	Foreign vessels 206	Exports Total 207	U.S. vessels 208	Foreign vessels 209
1865	249	74	174	356	93	263
1864	330	81	248	340	103	237
1863	253	110	143	332	132	200
1862	206	92	113	230	125	105
1861	336	202	134	249	180	69
1860	362	228	134	400	279	121
1859	339	216	123	357	250	107
1858	283	204	79	325	243	81
1857	361	259	102	363	251	112
1856	315	250	65	327	232	95
1855	261	202	59	275	203	72
1854	301	215	86	276	191	84
1853	268	192	76	231	155	76
1852	208	155	53	210	139	70
1851	216	164	53	218	152	66
1850	178	140	38	152	100	52
1849	148	120	27	146	101	45
1848	155	129	26	154	110	44
1847	147	113	33	154	100	54
1846	122	106	16	113	87	27
1845	117	102	15	115	87	28
1844	108	94	14	111	78	33
1843	65	50	15	84	65	19
1842	100	89	11	105	80	25
1841	128	113	15	122	95	27
1840	107	93	14	132	106	26
1839	162	144	18	121	95	26
1838	115	104	11	108	89	19
1837	141	122	19	117	91	26
1836	189	171	18	129	97	32
1835	150	135	15	122	94	28
1834	127	114	13	104	78	27
1833	108	98	10	90	68	22
1832	101	90	11	87	66	21
1831	103	94	9	81	66	16
1830	71	66	4	74	64	10
1829	74	69	5	72	62	10
1828	89	82	7	72	61	11
1827	79	75	5	82	72	10
1826	85	81	4	78	70	8
1825	96	92	4	100	89	11
1824	81	75	5	76	67	9
1823	78	72	6	75	65	9
1822	83	77	6	72	61	11
1821	63	58	5	65	55	10
1820	74	67	7	70	62	8
1819	87	67	20	70	58	13
1818	122	103	18	93	75	19
1817	99	78	21	88	65	23
1816	147	107	40	82	56	26
1815	113	87	26	53	37	15
1814	13	8	5	7	4	3
1813	22	16	6	28	18	10
1812	77	65	12	39	31	8
1811	53	48	5	61	53	9
1810	85	79	6	67	60	7
1809	59	52	7	52	44	8
1808	57	53	4	22	20	3
1807	139	130	8	108	98	11
1806	129	120	9	102	90	11
1805	121	112	8	96	85	11
1804	85	77	8	78	67	11
1803	65	56	9	56	46	9
1802	76	67	9	72	61	11
1801	111	101	10	93	81	12
1800	91	83	8	71	62	9
1799	79	71	8	79	68	10
1798	69	62	6	61	53	8
1797	75	69	6	51	45	6
1796	81	77	5	59	53	6
1795	70	64	6	48	42	6
1794	35	31	3	33	28	5
1793	31	26	6	26	20	6
1792	32	21	10	21	13	8
1791	29	17	12	19	10	9
1790	23	9	14	20	8	12

[1]Data are for years ending June 30. Figures (in millions of dollars) for July–Dec. are as follows: Series Q 204, 817; series Q 205, 179; series Q 206, 638; series Q 207, 1,625; series Q 208, 200; series Q 209, 1,425.

Series Q 210–215. Waterborne Imports and Exports, by Flag of Carrier Vessel: 1921 to 1957

[In thousands of short tons]

Year	Imports Total	U.S. vessels	Foreign vessels	Exports Total	U.S. vessels	Foreign vessels	Year	Imports Total	U.S. vessels	Foreign vessels	Exports Total	U.S. vessels	Foreign vessels
	210	211	212	213	214	215		210	211	212	213	214	215
1957	172,287	34,584	137,703	165,392	28,911	136,481	1938	36,756	13,527	23,230	62,286	11,602	50,684
1956	159,472	39,394	120,078	144,755	27,304	117,451	1937	47,110	14,967	32,143	61,105	12,189	48,916
1955	141,123	37,409	103,715	112,445	22,083	90,361	1936	43,003	14,780	28,223	44,480	9,650	34,830
1954	120,685	36,291	84,395	78,178	18,378	59,800	1935	38,042	15,820	22,221	42,723	9,789	32,935
1953	119,003	38,468	80,535	80,549	19,448	61,101	1934	33,392	14,299	19,092	42,360	10,567	31,792
1952	107,421	41,683	65,738	103,048	30,417	72,630	1933	29,755	12,340	17,415	36,272	9,357	26,914
1951	100,603	42,836	57,767	115,690	43,232	72,458	1932	32,156	14,923	17,232	35,666	9,125	26,541
							1931	40,168	19,168	21,000	44,855	12,396	32,459
1950	96,703	42,268	54,435	62,685	20,379	42,306							
1949	77,371	41,364	36,007	71,865	26,136	45,729	1930	53,270	27,801	25,469	55,699	16,703	38,995
1948	67,416	40,528	26,888	88,312	34,501	53,810	1929	57,103	28,260	28,844	64,372	20,071	44,301
1947	59,203	37,682	21,521	124,317	61,062	63,254	1928	53,083	27,089	25,993	65,889	21,602	44,287
1946	49,184	32,340	16,844	87,043	49,799	37,244	1927	47,245	24,033	23,212	63,768	20,939	42,829
							1926	50,049	23,638	26,411	76,316	19,177	57,140
1945[1]	39,426	31,415	8,011	61,603	37,729	23,874							
1944[1]	33,320	26,209	7,111	55,215	34,002	21,213	1925	48,311	23,760	24,551	55,626	17,603	38,024
1943[1]	30,988	24,740	6,248	47,765	25,302	22,463	1924	45,807	24,968	20,839	58,533	20,515	38,018
1942[1]	27,393	17,399	9,994	41,670	16,227	25,443	1923	48,491	25,518	22,973	54,970	18,131	36,838
							1922	50,044	31,286	18,758	47,602	18,871	28,731
1940	44,667	17,322	27,345	60,929	12,939	47,990	1921	37,167	26,269	10,898	54,477	20,784	33,692
1939	42,054	12,459	29,595	61,697	10,557	51,140							

[1] Excludes U. S. Army and Navy cargo, and Great Lakes.

Series Q 216–229. Waterborne Cargo Tonnage, Foreign and Domestic: 1924 to 1957

In thousands of short tons of 2,000 pounds. For definition of cargo tonnage, see text. Net totals are derived by deducting two types of duplications from unadjusted totals: (1) Traffic between seaports and river points, and (2) "Other duplications," comprising principally coastwise and lake traffic passing through canals and connecting channels other than the St. Marys Falls Canal and the Detroit River]

Year	Foreign and domestic commerce Net total	Unadjusted total	Foreign commerce Total	Through seaports Imports	Exports	Great Lakes ports Imports	Exports	Approximate net total [1]	Unadjusted total	Between ports Coastwise	Great Lakes	Local traffic of seaports and Great Lakes ports [2]	Between seaports and river ports	On rivers, canals, and connecting channels [3]
	216	217	218	219	220	221	222	223	224	225	226	227	228	229
1957	1,131,401	--------	358,540	176,236	146,890	10,116	25,298	772,862	--------	196,419	182,150	110,824	281,066	--------
1956	1,092,913	--------	326,690	163,349	126,448	10,865	26,027	766,223	--------	205,910	173,991	114,364	269,734	--------
1955	1,016,136	--------	271,103	144,276	95,404	8,681	22,742	745,033	--------	195,718	184,809	112,863	249,693	--------
1954	867,640	--------	213,844	123,503	65,244	5,921	19,176	653,796	--------	187,240	145,364	102,719	217,061	--------
1953	923,548	--------	217,396	120,595	63,780	7,387	25,635	706,151	--------	188,758	188,621	102,562	224,957	--------
1952	887,722	--------	227,326	108,674	85,072	7,287	26,293	660,396	--------	184,207	154,112	103,972	216,644	--------
1951	924,128	--------	232,056	101,813	97,603	6,935	25,705	692,073	--------	186,759	178,463	112,029	213,405	--------
1950	820,584	--------	169,225	96,299	43,640	5,683	23,603	651,359	--------	182,544	169,881	106,906	190,789	--------
1949	740,721	--------	165,358	77,153	45,740	4,839	17,626	575,363	--------	161,431	145,592	102,637	165,703	--------
1948	793,200	--------	162,971	68,078	65,404	4,219	25,270	630,229	--------	174,081	172,491	113,959	169,698	--------
1947	766,817	--------	188,256	57,366	101,996	4,796	24,098	578,561	--------	153,098	163,180	112,668	149,615	--------
1946	617,032	878,803	148,877	47,948	76,589	4,163	20,177	468,155	729,926	137,609	138,617	91,225	81,668	280,807
1945	618,906	870,282	172,094	44,526	100,333	6,511	20,724	446,812	698,188	90,705	157,900	97,822	87,073	264,688
1944	605,928	859,954	153,736	39,441	82,613	8,055	23,627	452,192	706,218	70,806	164,971	106,194	95,821	268,426
1943	580,581	804,104	127,284	33,077	63,086	7,120	24,001	453,297	676,820	60,009	159,458	106,278	93,689	257,386
1942	589,900	827,624	99,221	25,974	46,023	4,488	22,736	490,679	728,403	74,016	172,606	104,189	92,748	284,844
1941	653,600	920,634	120,652	54,616	40,605	4,628	20,802	532,948	799,982	155,927	163,161	98,728	85,368	296,798
1940	607,900	836,416	111,255	40,740	49,568	4,118	16,829	496,645	725,161	157,027	141,103	97,632	70,217	259,182
1939	569,400	769,689	112,667	37,854	57,711	4,941	12,161	456,733	657,022	150,983	113,309	87,710	62,014	243,006
1938	466,900	664,751	105,182	33,886	55,476	5,110	10,710	361,718	559,569	138,545	72,846	76,216	56,034	215,928
1937	583,100	745,032	114,413	43,764	52,910	4,102	13,637	468,687	630,619	149,740	135,075	91,059	55,295	199,450
1936	525,842	649,860	90,247	37,507	37,154	5,423	10,163	435,595	559,613	132,515	115,250	88,024	44,337	179,487
1935	453,331	543,270	81,639	33,942	33,922	4,716	9,059	371,692	461,631	115,561	83,628	76,583	35,720	150,139
1934	414,308	480,893	77,898	30,553	33,570	4,287	9,488	336,410	402,995	113,349	71,685	60,998	34,894	122,069
1933	394,104	447,244	69,466	27,670	31,197	3,034	7,565	324,638	377,778	110,675	68,911	55,207	26,030	116,955
1932	342,489	390,323	70,429	29,843	30,039	3,072	7,475	272,060	319,894	94,434	39,544	54,845	27,242	103,829
1931	445,648	493,442	89,525	37,375	38,841	4,016	9,293	356,123	403,917	113,949	71,788	67,530	37,327	113,323
1930	520,280	591,331	114,110	46,448	48,148	7,590	11,924	406,170	477,221	117,821	109,791	79,414	37,591	132,604
1929	588,800	655,045	127,510	51,591	55,761	6,385	13,773	456,290	527,534	124,999	135,838	89,528	41,995	135,174
1928	539,200	608,001	126,768	46,690	56,151	8,548	15,379	412,432	481,233	119,254	119,301	75,728	39,870	127,080
1927	532,500	594,755	120,523	43,388	56,550	8,098	12,487	411,977	474,232	121,036	112,805	78,020	40,559	121,812
1926	540,500	602,196	131,293	44,834	69,859	6,424	10,176	409,207	470,903	108,023	115,791	88,270	36,798	122,021
1925	483,400	548,200	108,548	42,793	49,251	7,317	9,187	374,852	439,352	105,090	110,626	59,981	49,787	114,168
1924	453,700	487,167	101,562	36,425	49,008	4,962	11,167	352,138	385,605	88,554	92,563	77,270	34,101	93,117

[1] Figures for 1924–1945 are approximations, excluding duplications in domestic traffic. There are, however, some minor duplications in figures for foreign traffic.
[2] Includes figures for harbor traffic of New York, Philadelphia, and San Francisco; local traffic of other seaports, and local traffic of lake ports.
[3] Excludes St. Marys Falls Canal traffic and additional Detroit River traffic, both of which are already counted in Great Lakes traffic; also excludes duplications relating to rivers and canals themselves.

Series Q 230–234. Waterborne Bulk Freight Traffic on the Great Lakes: 1900 to 1956

[In thousands of short tons]

Year	Total	Iron ore	Coal	Grain	Stone	Year	Total	Iron ore	Coal	Grain	Stone
	230	231	232	233	234		230	231	232	233	234
1956	192,267	89,819	57,375	14,320	30,753	1927	120,760	57,240	34,794	14,693	14,033
1955	193,759	99,871	53,378	10,788	29,722	1926	121,289	65,563	31,011	12,087	12,628
1954	151,298	68,090	46,367	11,866	24,975						
1953	199,697	107,346	51,035	14,317	26,999	1925	113,292	60,571	28,049	13,320	11,352
1952	168,677	83,900	46,284	15,215	23,278	1924	98,047	47,737	25,861	15,223	9,226
1951	189,750	99,783	50,946	13,150	25,871	1923	121,029	66,122	33,137	11,850	9,920
						1922	89,455	47,727	19,869	14,267	7,592
1950	177,953	87,591	57,640	9,327	23,395	1921	68,034	24,977	26,661	12,470	3,926
1949	151,697	77,902	40,930	12,543	20,322						
1948	185,612	92,890	60,564	9,877	22,282	1920	106,519	65,551	26,410	6,736	7,822
1947	177,606	87,246	58,060	11,409	20,891	1919	91,762	52,839	26,424	6,092	6,407
1946	147,955	66,478	53,727	10,198	17,552	1918	114,614	68,495	32,102	6,549	7,468
						1917	115,102	69,998	31,193	7,162	6,749
1945	175,083	84,801	55,246	18,718	16,318	1916	117,053	72,503	28,440	10,556	5,554
1944	184,159	90,911	60,163	16,229	16,856						
1943	175,653	94,534	51,969	11,810	17,340	1915	93,050	51,877	26,220	11,099	3,854
1942	182,731	103,125	52,534	8,502	18,570	1914	72,940	35,864	27,282	9,794	
1941	172,287	89,732	53,535	11,387	17,633	1913	100,018	54,959	33,362	11,697	
						1912	87,174	53,129	24,673	9,372	
1940	145,216	71,358	49,320	9,645	14,893	1911	68,646	35,987	25,700	6,959	
1939	114,230	50,482	40,368	11,172	12,208						
1938	75,118	21,575	34,623	10,679	8,241	1910	80,015	47,733	26,478	5,804	
1937	134,688	70,111	44,319	5,829	14,429	1909	71,954	46,686	18,617	6,651	
1936	114,415	50,201	44,699	7,434	12,081	1908	53,791	28,479	19,288	6,024	
						1907	74,743	46,245	21,487	7,011	
1935	82,887	31,766	35,289	6,750	9,082	1906	66,152	42,015	17,274	6,863	
1934	75,739	24,919	35,477	7,951	7,392						
1933	71,373	24,218	31,777	8,713	6,665	1905	58,008	37,494	14,401	6,113	
1932	41,673	3,997	24,857	8,890	3,929	1904	40,331	23,774	12,370	4,187	
1931	74,149	26,284	31,176	9,480	7,209	1903	45,571	26,488	13,351	5,732	
						1902	44,374	30,284	9,196	4,894	
1930	112,529	52,173	38,072	9,851	12,433	1901	37,064	22,576	9,820	4,668	
1929	138,574	73,028	39,255	10,021	16,270						
1928	127,331	60,458	34,823	16,372	15,678	1900	35,298	20,799	8,908	5,591	

Series Q 235–237. Commercial Ocean Traffic on the Panama Canal: 1915 to 1957

[For years ending June 30. Includes oceangoing tolls-paying vessels and foreign naval vessels of 300 net tons and over (Panama Canal measurement) for vessels rated on net tonnage, or 500 ton displacement and over for vessels rated on displacement tonnage]

Year	Number of transits	Tolls ($1,000)	Cargo (1,000 long tons)	Year	Number of transits	Tolls ($1,000)	Cargo (1,000 long tons)	Year	Number of transits	Tolls ($1,000)	Cargo (1,000 long tons)
	235	236	237		235	236	237		235	236	237
1957	8,579	38,444	49,702	1942	2,688	9,752	13,607	1928	6,253	26,922	29,616
1956	8,209	36,154	45,119	1941	4,727	18,158	24,951	1927	5,293	24,212	27,734
								1926	5,087	22,920	26,030
1955	7,997	33,849	40,646	1940	5,370	21,145	27,299				
1954	7,784	33,248	39,095	1939	5,903	23,661	27,867	1925	4,592	21,394	23,957
1953	7,410	31,918	36,095	1938	5,524	23,170	27,387	1924	5,158	24,285	26,993
1952	6,524	26,923	33,611	1937	5,387	23,102	28,108	1923	3,908	17,504	19,566
1951	5,593	23,906	30,073	1936	5,382	23,479	26,506	1922	2,665	11,192	10,883
								1921	2,791	11,269	11,596
1950	5,448	24,430	28,872	1935	5,180	23,307	25,310				
1949	4,793	20,541	25,305	1934	5,234	24,047	24,704	1920	2,393	8,508	9,372
1948	4,678	19,957	24,118	1933	4,162	19,602	18,161	1919	1,948	6,164	6,910
1947	4,260	17,597	21,671	1932	4,362	20,695	19,799	1918	1,989	6,429	7,526
1946	3,747	14,774	14,978	1931	5,370	24,625	25,065	1917	1,738	5,621	7,055
								1916 [1]	724	2,403	3,093
1945	1,939	7,244	8,604	1930	6,027	27,060	30,018				
1944	1,562	5,456	7,003	1929	6,289	27,111	30,648	1915 [2]	1,058	4,367	4,888
1943	1,822	7,357	10,600								

[1] Canal closed about 7 months by slides.   [2] Canal opened Aug. 15, 1914.

Series Q 238–242. Freight Traffic on the Sault Ste. Marie Canals: 1855 to 1900

[In thousands of short tons, except grain in thousands of bushels]

Year	Total traffic	Iron ore	Coal	Grain	Stone	Year	Total traffic	Iron ore	Coal	Grain	Stone
	238	239	240	241	242		238	239	240	241	242
1900	25,643	16,444	4,487	56,664	49	1887	5,495	2,498	1,353	23,872	13
1899	25,256	15,328	3,941	88,398	39	1886	4,528	2,088	1,010	19,707	9
1898	21,235	11,707	3,776	88,418	5						
1897	18,983	10,634	3,039	80,814	6	1885	3,257	1,235	895	15,697	8
1896	16,239	7,909	3,023	90,705	18	1884	2,875	1,136	706	12,503	6
						1883	2,267	792	714	6,677	2
1895	15,063	8,062	2,574	54,547	24	1882	2,030	987	430	4,202	5
1894	13,196	6,549	2,797	36,414	21	1881	1,568	748	296	3,825	1
1893	10,797	4,015	3,008	45,887	19						
1892	11,214	4,901	2,904	42,661	40	1880	1,322	677	171	4,659	2
1891	8,889	3,560	2,508	39,849	44	1879	1,051	540	111	3,578	2
						1878	937	556	92	2,138	3
1890	9,041	4,775	2,177	18,262	48	1877	913	568	92	1,728	3
1889	7,516	4,096	1,629	18,325	34	1876	1,074	610	125	2,396	2
1888	6,411	2,571	2,105	20,619	34						

Series Q 238-242. Freight Traffic on the Sault Ste. Marie Canals: 1855 to 1900—Con.

[In thousands of short tons, except grain in thousands of bushels]

Year	Total traffic 238	Iron ore 239	Coal 240	Grain 241	Stone 242
1875	833	493	101	1,486	3
1874	655	428	61	1,270	(1)
1873	888	504	97	2,430	2
1872	746	383	81	1,013	5
1871	586	327	47	1,686	6
1870	540	410	16	354	5
1869	368	239	28	324	
1868	299	192	26	285	
1867	325	223	23	249	
1866	239	152	20	230	
1865	182	147	----	----	
1864	284	214	11	144	
1863	237	182	8	78	
1862	162	113	11	59	
1861	88	45	12	77	
1860	154	120	----	133	
1859	122	66	9	72	
1858	57	31	4	21	
1857	52	26	5	41	
1856	34	12	4	82	
1855	15	1	1	----	

1 Less than 500 short tons.

Series Q 243-244. Tonnage Moved on New York State Canals: 1837 to 1957

[In short tons of 2,000 pounds]

Year	All canals 243	Erie division, freight originating 244
1957	4,468,539	2,675,853
1956	4,858,044	3,053,219
1955	4,616,399	2,779,491
1954	3,859,335	2,395,291
1953	4,497,231	3,211,932
1952	4,487,858	3,112,480
1951	5,211,472	3,673,104
1950	4,615,613	3,620,346
1949	3,949,739	2,685,635
1948	4,513,817	3,121,411
1947	3,790,050	2,514,643
1946	2,820,541	1,685,516
1945	2,968,682	1,665,447
1944	2,506,840	1,729,448
1943	2,824,160	2,166,393
1942	3,539,101	2,760,596
1941	4,505,059	3,512,829
1940	4,768,160	3,587,086
1939	4,689,037	3,643,782
1938	4,709,488	3,349,250
1937	5,010,464	4,173,700
1936	5,014,206	4,220,397
1935	4,489,172	3,898,506
1934	4,142,728	3,645,125
1933	4,074,002	3,574,951
1932	3,643,433	3,186,094
1931	3,722,012	3,277,936
1930	3,605,457	3,044,271
1929	2,876,160	2,422,204
1928	3,089,998	2,535,684
1927	2,581,892	2,047,774
1926	2,369,367	1,935,278
1925	2,344,013	1,945,466
1924	2,032,317	1,691,766
1923	2,006,284	1,626,062
1922	1,873,434	1,485,109
1921	1,270,407	993,639
1920	1,421,434	891,221
1919	1,238,844	842,164
1918	1,159,270	667,374
1917	1,297,225	675,083
1916	1,625,050	917,689
1915	1,858,114	1,155,235
1914	2,080,850	1,361,764
1913	2,602,035	1,788,453
1912	2,606,116	1,795,069
1911	3,097,068	2,031,735
1910	3,073,412	2,023,185
1909	3,116,536	2,031,307
1908	3,051,877	2,177,443
1907	3,407,914	2,415,548
1906	3,540,907	2,385,491
1905	3,226,896	1,999,824
1904	3,138,547	1,945,708
1903	3,615,385	2,414,018
1902	3,274,610	2,105,876
1901	3,420,613	2,257,035
1900	3,345,941	2,145,876
1899	3,686,051	2,419,084
1898	3,360,063	2,338,020
1897	3,617,804	2,584,906
1896	3,714,894	2,742,438
1895	3,500,314	2,356,084
1894	3,882,560	3,144,144
1893	4,331,963	3,235,726
1892	4,281,995	2,978,832
1891	4,563,472	3,097,853
1890	5,246,102	3,303,929
1889	5,370,369	3,673,554
1888	4,942,948	3,321,516
1887	5,553,805	3,840,513
1886	5,293,982	3,808,642
1885	4,731,784	3,208,207
1884	5,009,488	3,389,555
1883	5,664,056	3,587,102
1882	5,467,423	3,694,364
1881	5,179,192	3,598,721
1880	6,457,656	4,608,651
1879	5,362,372	3,820,027
1878	5,171,320	3,608,634
1877	4,955,963	3,254,367
1876	4,172,129	2,418,422
1875	4,859,958	2,787,226
1874	5,804,588	3,097,122
1873	6,364,782	3,602,535
1872	6,673,370	3,562,560
1871	6,467,888	3,580,922
1870	6,173,769	3,083,132
1869	5,859,080	2,845,072
1868	6,442,225	3,346,986
1867	5,688,325	2,920,578
1866	5,775,220	2,896,027
1865	4,729,654	2,523,490
1864	4,852,941	2,535,792
1863	5,557,692	2,955,302
1862	5,598,785	3,204,277
1861	4,507,635	2,500,782
1860	4,650,214	2,253,533
1859	3,781,684	1,753,954
1858	3,665,192	1,767,004
1857	3,344,061	1,566,624
1856	4,116,082	2,107,678
1855	4,022,617	2,202,463
1854	4,165,862	2,224,008
1853	4,247,853	2,196,308
1852	3,863,441	2,129,334
1851	3,582,733	1,955,265
1850	3,076,617	1,635,089
1849	2,894,732	1,622,444
1848	2,796,230	1,599,965
1847	2,869,810	1,661,575
1846	2,268,662	1,264,408
1845	1,977,565	1,038,700
1844	1,816,586	945,944
1843	1,513,439	819,216
1842	1,236,931	712,310
1841	1,521,661	906,442
1840	1,416,046	829,960
1839	1,435,713	845,007
1838	1,333,011	744,848
1837	1,171,296	667,151

Series Q 245. Federal Expenditures for Rivers and Harbors: 1822 to 1957

[In thousands of dollars. For years ending June 30]

Year	Total 245
1957	545,032
1956	489,118
1955	455,612
1954	475,418
1953	272,130
1952	214,957
1951	204,699
1950	190,456
1949	160,431
1948	115,728
1947	89,170
1946	79,542
1945	57,146
1944	64,366
1943	84,368
1942	88,664
1941	86,530
1940	107,082
1939	115,987
1938	135,921
1937	178,825
1936	106,239
1935	162,375
1934	104,873
1933	76,788
1932	84,260
1931	80,903
1930	73,970
1929	57,299
1928	70,197
1927	60,620
1926	63,464
1925	69,882
1924	62,025
1923	47,478
1922	43,393
1921	57,166
1920	47,188
1919	33,078
1918	29,594
1917	30,487
1916	32,450
1915	46,834
1914	50,762
1913	42,275
1912	35,861
1911	33,968
1910	29,273
1909	34,579
1908	30,361
1907	23,310
1906	25,955
1905	22,814
1904	22,546
1903	19,590
1902	14,948
1901	19,544
1900	18,736
1899	16,094
1898	20,792
1897	13,686
1896	18,119
1895	19,944
1894	19,888
1893	14,804
1892	13,024
1891	12,253
1890	11,740
1889	11,234
1888	7,007
1887	7,786
1886	4,197
1885	10,558
1884	8,237
1883	13,889
1882	11,624
1881	9,072
1880	8,080
1879	8,267
1878	3,791
1877	4,655
1876	5,736
1875	6,434
1874	5,704
1873	6,312
1872	4,962
1871	4,421
1870	3,528
1869	3,545
1868	3,457
1867	1,217
1866	295
1865	305
1864	102
1863	65
1862	37
1861	172
1860	228
1859	290
1858	427
1857	268
1856	161
1855	791
1854	937
1853	489
1852	40
1851	70
1850	42
1849	26
1848	24
1847	44
1846	219
1845	529
1844	313
1843	111
1842	82
1841	79
1840	145
1839	780
1838	1,054
1837	1,362
1836	869
1835	569
1834	598
1833	704
1832	538
1831	652
1830	574
1829	524
1828	188
1827	136
1826	87
1825	40
1824	26
1823	40
1822	1

chapter Q

HIGHWAY TRANSPORTATION (Series Q 246–344)

Q 246–264. General note.

In 1894, the Federal Government created an Office of Road Inquiry to initiate experiments and conduct inquiries concerning the best methods of road building. It was succeeded by the Office of Public Roads, which is now the Bureau of Public Roads (the latter was called the Public Roads Administration during 1939–1949). The Office of Public Roads made surveys of highway mileage, revenues, and expenditures in 1904, 1909, and 1914.

In 1916, Congress passed the first of the many Federal-aid highway acts, under which the Federal Government has contributed to the cost of constructing highways designated as parts of the Federal-aid system. The Bureau of Public Roads administers Federal legislation providing for the improvement, in cooperation with the States, of roads on the Federal-aid primary, secondary, and interstate highway systems. As the principal road-building agency of the Federal Government, it also cooperates with the Forest Service, the National Park Service, and other Federal agencies in the construction of roads in national forests, parks, and other areas.

Q 246–251. Mileage of rural roads and municipal streets, 1904–1957.

Source: 1904–1955, Bureau of Public Roads, *Highway Statistics, Summary to 1955*, 1957; 1956–1957, *Highway Statistics*, annual issues.

Rural roads, as used here, are defined roughly as those roads located outside of incorporated communities or delimited places generally having more than 1,000 inhabitants. Estimates for earlier years for total mileage of rural roads are (in thousands of miles): 1904, 2,151; 1909, 2,200; 1914, 2,446.

Municipal and other mileage figures for 1934 and 1935 represent only mileage on municipal extensions of State systems, which are State administered. Mileage not on State or county systems was initially included in 1936 (67,000 miles). Mileage on local city streets was first included in 1941 (274,000 miles for that year). Municipal extensions are continuations of State system roads through communities with more than 1,000 inhabitants. Although mileage in places having more than 2,500 inhabitants was not originally included in Federal-aid programs, those places have been eligible for such aid in more recent years.

Q 252–254. Existing surfaced mileage, 1904–1957.

Source: See source for series Q 246–251.

High-type surfaced roads include bituminous penetration, sheet asphalt, bituminous concrete, portland cement concrete, vitrified brick, and block pavements of asphalt, wood, and stone. For some years, they also include dual-type surfaces and a small amount of unclassified mileage. Low-type surfaced roads include sand, clay, selected soil, untreated gravel, bituminous surface-treated, mixed bituminous and treated gravel, chert, shale, waterbound macadam.

Q 255–259. Mileage built by State highway departments, 1923–1957.

Source: See source for series Q 246–251.

Mileage built is mileage on which construction work creates a newly located road or is regarded as significantly improving the condition of an existing road. It does not include work designed to maintain or restore the condition of an existing road without material betterment. Mileage resurfaced or rebuilt to higher standards is the bulk of mileage built. Construction of earth roads consists of aligning, grading, and draining. See also text for series Q 252–254.

Q 260–264. Mileage and cost of Federal-aid highway improvements, 1917–1957.

Source: See source for series Q 246–251.

In 1912, the Congress authorized $500,000 for an experimental program of rural post-road construction. However, it was not until the Federal-Aid Road Act of 1916 that the present cooperative Federal-State highway program was established on a continuing basis. In order to accelerate the improvement of the main traveled roads, Congress in 1921 authorized designation of a system of principal interstate and intercounty roads, limited to 7 percent of the total rural mileage then existing. The use of Federal aid was restricted to this system, and to rural mileage only.

Urban highway improvement first came in for its share of the Federal-State program when the Federal-Aid Highway Act of 1944 specifically authorized the use of funds for Federal-aid highways in urban areas. In addition, the Act provided for the designation of a Federal-aid secondary system and a National System of Interstate Highways. The Federal-Aid Highway Act of 1956 provided substantially increased sums for the Federal-aid primary and secondary systems for a 3-year period, and established a long-range plan for financing accelerated completion of the 41,000-mile interstate system.

Federal funds are available for expenditure only on the designated Federal-aid systems and, in general, must be matched by an equal amount of State funds. However, under the Federal-aid Act of 1954 the Federal share for the Interstate System was raised to 60 percent, and under the 1956 Act the proportion was increased to 90 percent. Federal aid may not be expended for maintenance. The cost of most Federal-aid projects is paid initially out of State highway funds, or in some cases by counties or other local governments. The Federal share is paid as reimbursement to the States as work progresses, with final payment made after completion.

Federal authorizations have usually been made on a biennial basis and apportioned among the States for use within a 3-year period. Figures for State funds shown here are based on legal matching ratios determined by applicable Federal-aid acts. In States having public lands in excess of 5 percent of their total area, the Federal share is proportionally increased.

Q 265–279. State highway finances, 1890–1957.

Source: See source for series Q 246–251.

A State highway-user tax is defined as a special tax or fee (except tolls) levied upon motor-vehicle users because of their use of the highways. Highway-user taxes include motor-fuel taxes, motor-vehicle registration and associated fees, and special taxes applicable only to motor carriers; these taxes are separable and apart from property, excise, business, or other taxes paid by the general public.

In many States, specific portions of the revenue from each type of highway-user tax are allocated to particular highway purposes. A number of States, however, place all highway-user revenue in a highway fund, and a few have a general State fund into which go all types of revenue. For the latter group of States, each particular appropriation or expenditure for highway purposes is considered to have been made from motor-fuel taxes, motor-vehicle registration fees and motor-carrier taxes in proportion to the relative amount of revenue received from each of these three sources.

The largest share of receipts from State highway-user taxes is expended on State highways, but a portion is also allocated for local roads and streets, and a small amount used for non-highway purposes.

Q 280–293. Funds contributed and disbursed for county and other local rural roads, 1921–1956.

Source: 1921–1955, the principal sources used were Bureau of Public Roads, *Highway Statistics, Summary to 1955; The Financing of Highways by Counties and Local Rural Governments, 1931–1941; The Financing of Highways by Counties and Local Rural Governments, 1942–51;* 1956, in great part from *Highway Finance, 1948–1957.* (Additional information obtained from Bureau of Public Roads, annual published local finance tables, 1921–1955, and records on file at the Bureau of Public Roads.)

Q 294–309. Funds contributed and disbursed for streets in incorporated and other urban places, 1921–1956.

Source: 1921–1955 (except for series Q 303, 1924–1939), Bureau of Public Roads, *Highway Statistics, Summary to 1955;* and annual published national summaries of urban finance data, UF series. **Series Q 303**, 1924–1939, "Municipal Bond Sales," published by *The Bond Buyer;* 1956, in great part from *Highway Finance, 1948–1957.* (Additional information is on file at the Bureau of Public Roads.)

Q 310–313. Motor-vehicle factory sales, 1900–1957.

Source: Automobile Manufacturers Association, *Automobile Facts and Figures,* 38th edition, 1958.

Production of passenger cars was discontinued in February 1942 to economize resources for war purposes, but some vehicles remaining in factory stocks were sold under rationing orders in subsequent war years.

Q 314–317. Motor-vehicle registrations, 1900–1957.

Source: 1900–1952, Bureau of Public Roads, *Highway Statistics, Summary to 1955;* 1953–1957, same agency, records (table MV-200, "Summary of Motor Vehicle Registrations by Years").

Figures are based on reports and records of State motor-vehicle registration departments. They include both privately and publicly owned vehicles.

Motor-vehicle data in the early years of the century are incomplete, largely because few States required their registration, and hence had no records of the number of vehicles using roads and streets. As production of vehicles increased, shortly before the first World War, so did the number of registration laws. By 1921, all States had adopted some form of motor-vehicle registration.

Accompanying the growth in motor-vehicle registrations has been a corresponding diversity in the registration practices among the States. In general, motor vehicles are classified as private passenger cars, passenger carriers for hire, trucks, trailers, motorcycles, and property carriers for hire. Several States, however, still register buses with either trucks or passenger cars. These differences have made it necessary for the Bureau of Public Roads to supplement the data submitted by the States with information obtained from special studies and from other sources.

Q 318–320. Motor-fuel usage, 1919–1957.

Source: 1919–1955, Bureau of Public Roads, *Highway Statistics, Summary to 1955,* p. 2; 1956–1957, same agency, records (table G 221, Analysis of Motor Fuel Consumption).

Fuel consumption figures for which reports from State authorities were not available have been estimated by Bureau of Public Roads. Motor fuel includes all gasoline used for any purpose (private and public), except military, plus any diesel or other fuels used solely for the propulsion of motor vehicles on public highways. Exports from the United States are excluded, and there is no duplication because of interstate shipment. Tractor fuels are not included. Nonhighway consumption includes all use off the highway, such as aviation, agriculture, marine, industrial, etc., and usually falls under the exemption or refund provisions of the motor-fuel tax law.

Q 321–327. Miles of travel by motor vehicles, 1921–1957.

Source: 1921–1935, Federal Works Agency, records, and Public Roads Administration, records (table VM-1 and table entitled "Estimates of Vehicle-Miles Traveled, 1921 to 1947"); 1936–1957, see source for series Q 246–251.

Q 328–329. State and Federal gasoline tax rates, 1930–1956.

Source: See source for series Q 246–251.

State average tax is weighted by net gallons taxed at the various rates in the several States. No data are shown before 1930 because it was the first year in which all States had motor fuel taxes in effect for the whole year.

The precise dates of the changes in the Federal tax are as follows: June 21, 1932, 1 cent; June 17, 1933, 1.5 cents; January 1, 1934, 1 cent; July 1, 1940, 1.5 cents; November 1, 1951, 2 cents; July 1, 1956, 3 cents.

Q 330–341. Public transit mileage, equipment, passengers, and passenger revenue, 1917–1957.

Source: American Transit Association, *Transit Fact Book,* various annual issues; *The Transit Industry in the United States, Basic Data and Trends,* 1943; mimeographed release on number of passengers, dated January 3, 1938.

Figures are estimates based on reports for about 85 percent of the industry, which includes local motorbuses, electric street railways, elevated and subway lines, interurban electric railways, and transit coach lines.

Mileage estimates for trolley coaches (series Q 331) are miles of negative overhead wire. Mileage estimates for motorbuses (series Q 332) are miles of route, round trip. Equipment owned, railway cars (series Q 333) includes surface, subway and elevated cars. The estimates for 1933 and 1934 for equipment owned, motorbuses (series Q 335) are probably understated. Revenue and nonrevenue passenger figures (series Q 336–339) exceed revenue passenger figures (series Q 340) chiefly because of free transfers.

Q 342–344. Oil pipelines operated and oil originated, 1921–1957.

Source: 1921–1953, Interstate Commerce Commission, *Statistics of Railways in the United States,* various annual issues; 1954–1957, *Transport Statistics in the United States,* part 6, *Oil Pipe Lines.*

Figures refer to pipelines operating in interstate commerce and regulated by ICC. Oil originated, crude, series Q 343, includes both gathering and trunk lines.

For a discussion of statistics of oil pipelines, see ICC, *A Review of Statistics of Oil Pipe Lines, 1921–1941,* Statement 4280, mimeographed, 1942. The figure for mileage in 1938, which appears to have been revised, is from this Statement.

Figures for barrels of oil carried are as follows, in millions: 1925, 831; 1926, 836; 1927, 989; 1928, 1,053; 1929, 1,156; 1930, 1,172; 1931, 987. In these figures, a barrel handled by two or more pipelines in succession is counted each time it is handled. In the figures for barrels originated, this duplication is avoided.

Series Q 246–259. Mileage of Rural Roads and Municipal Streets: 1904 to 1957

Year	Total existing mileage						Existing surfaced mileage			Mileage built by State highway departments					Year	Existing surfaced mileage, total
		Rural roads [1]				Muni-cipal and other mileage	Under State control [3]			Roads under State control						
	Total	Total	State administered		County roads under local control		Total [2]	High-type roads	Low-type roads	Total [4]	Total	Earth roads	High-type surface	Low-type surface		
			Prima-ry	Second-ary and county roads												
	246	247	248	249	250	251	252	253	254	255	256	257	258	259		252
	1,000 miles	*1,000 miles*	*1,000 miles*	*1,000 miles*	*1,000 miles*	*1,000 miles*	*1,000 miles*	*Miles*	*Miles*	*Miles*	*Miles*	*Miles*	*Miles*	*Miles*		*1,000 miles*
1957	3,453	2,966	391	232	2,343	487	2,371	287	338	52,971	39,675	374	19,476	19,825	1920	369
1956	3,430	2,957	389	226	2,342	473	2,323	281	335	57,454	44,016	486	20,726	22,804	1919	350
1955	3,418	2,954	387	222	2,345	464	2,273	270	340	53,559	41,120	694	17,672	22,754	1918	332
1954	3,395	2,941	379	218	2,344	454	2,228	262	333	55,488	42,053	866	19,730	21,457	1917	313
1953	3,366	2,925	377	214	2,334	441	2,160	252	332	52,886	41,744	1,264	17,807	22,673	1916	295
1952	3,343	2,925	371	219	2,335	418	2,070	245	328	57,847	46,354	1,238	17,811	27,305		
1951	3,326	2,925	367	217	2,341	401	1,998	236	323	51,471	41,864	1,603	15,122	25,139	1915	276
															1914	257
1950	3,313	2,922	363	210	2,349	391	1,939	227	316	55,487	44,265	1,784	13,379	29,102	1913	244
1949	3,322	2,934	358	206	2,370	388	1,865	174	350	45,176	35,241	1,517	7,487	26,237	1912	231
1948	3,323	2,929	350	206	2,373	394	1,815	172	338	41,968	35,085	1,403	7,753	25,929	1911	217
1947	3,326	2,933	337	212	2,384	393	1,785	170	330	32,870	29,579	1,013	6,224	22,342	1910	204
1946	3,316	2,934	342	205	2,387	382	1,730	170	317	21,713	20,858	417	4,900	15,541	1909	190
1945	3,319	2,939	339	202	2,398	380	1,721	168	312	15,278	14,827	250	3,971	10,606	1908	183
1944	3,311	2,932	335	200	2,397	379	1,655	167	309	15,080	13,924	289	3,925	9,710	1907	176
1943	3,311	2,930	333	200	2,397	381	1,646	166	306	15,971	14,692	458	4,446	9,788	1906	168
1942	3,309	2,925	334	199	2,392	384	1,630	165	302	19,673	18,081	1,038	4,170	12,873		
1941	3,309	2,926	332	196	2,398	383	1,607	162	296	32,634	30,554	1,343	6,304	22,907	1905	161
															1904	154
1940	3,017	2,920	329	195	2,396	97	1,367	153	296	32,594	29,695	1,423	5,223	23,049		
1939	3,007	2,913	328	194	2,391	94	1,318	151	286	32,996	30,671	1,720	5,021	23,930		
1938	2,992	2,898	327	194	2,377	94	1,276	149	277	36,328	34,604	1,187	5,757	27,660		
1937	2,982	2,894	327	189	2,378	88	1,232	144	265	35,627	28,945	1,828	6,532	20,585		
1936	3,006	2,920	340	177	2,403	86	1,175	131	262		32,274	3,361	4,706	24,207		
1935	3,050	3,032	332	173	2,527	18	1,080	128	246		26,814	3,284	3,806	19,724		
1934	3,050	3,034	325	170	2,539	16	992	124	237		41,730	5,917	6,386	29,427		
1933		3,029	346	135	2,548		914	116	195		33,471	6,258	7,412	19,801		
1932		3,040	358	84	2,598		879	110	156		35,971	6,394	10,009	19,568		
1931		3,036	329	45	2,662		830	96	146		44,634	10,095	12,513	22,026		
1930		3,009	324		2,685		694	84	142		35,277	7,813	10,787	16,677		
1929		3,024	314		2,710		662	75	133		32,522	7,451	8,847	16,224		
1928		3,016	306		2,710		626	68	125		29,252	8,675	8,748	11,829		
1927		3,013	293		2,720		589	60	117		26,723	7,151	6,733	12,839		
1926		3,000	288		2,712		550	54	109		26,552	7,060	6,132	13,360		
1925		3,006	275		2,731		521	48	97		23,152	5,316	6,686	11,150		
1924		3,004	261		2,743		472	41	90		23,164	5,957	6,697	10,510		
1923		2,996	252		2,744		439	34	78		20,311	5,814	5,628	8,869		
1922		2,960	227		2,733		412									
1921		2,925	203		2,722		387									

[1] Includes extensions of county, town, and township roads but excludes rural mileage not under State or local control.
[2] Includes all surfaced mileage whether under State or local control.
[3] Includes State highway extensions within cities.
[4] Beginning in 1937, includes special construction defined as mileage built by State Highway Departments on county and local roads not under State control; on city streets other than urban extensions of State highway system; on forest, park, and institutional roads; etc.

Series Q 260–264. Mileage and Cost of Federal-Aid Highway Improvements: 1917 to 1957

Year	Miles of highway		Cost ($1,000,000) [3]			Year or period	Miles of highway		Cost ($1,000,000) [3]		
	Total designated as part of Federal systems [1]	Completed during year [2]	Total	Federal funds	State funds		Total designated as part of Federal systems [1]	Completed during year [2]	Total	Federal funds	State funds
	260	261	262	263	264		260	261	262	263	264
1957	780,989	22,424	1,714	968	746	1938	229,905	11,766	309	183	125
1956	755,920	23,609	1,444	757	687	1937	226,829	21,330	521	348	173
						1936	224,450	12,258	238	225	13
1955	749,166	22,571	1,287	666	621						
1954	725,963	20,548	1,146	591	555	1935	219,869	12,811	242	218	24
1953	704,150	21,136	1,078	559	519	1934	212,496	21,203	358	311	47
1952	675,121	22,147	978	505	472	1933	207,194	18,219	264	223	41
1951	664,464	17,060	772	390	382	1932	205,025	10,855	205	95	110
						1931	198,967	15,902	325	228	97
1950	643,939	19,876	753	390	364						
1949	632,037	19,876	829	425	404	1930	193,652	10,339	237	100	137
1948	611,332	21,725	763	397	366	1929	189,853	8,581	197	80	117
1947	599,338	15,473	422	224	198	1928	188,017	9,756	196	83	113
1946	556,787	5,057	147	86	61	1927	187,035	10,220	189	84	105
						1926	184,162	10,723	215	93	122
1945	308,741	3,035	101	76	25						
1944	367,690	4,473	135	109	26	1925	179,501	11,001	221	100	121
1943	338,705	7,753	273	219	54	1924	174,507	10,946	205	93	112
1942	330,051	6,898	226	143	83	1923	169,007	7,494	130	57	73
1941	316,432	9,734	274	148	126	1922		11,188	186	80	106
						1917–1921		12,919	222	95	127
1940	235,482	11,549	269	150	119						
1939	232,834	11,776	306	176	130						

[1] Includes estimates on Federal-aid primary system throughout, Federal-aid on secondary systems beginning in 1942, and national system of interstate and defense highways beginning in 1951. Estimates as of end of calendar-year.
[2] Comprises new and rebuilt mileage.
[3] Represents actual expenditures of funds on calendar-year basis. Beginning 1935, includes money spent on public works and defense highways. Beginning 1940, includes secondary highways.

Series Q 265-279. State Highway Finances: 1890 to 1957

[In thousands of dollars]

Year	Total	Revenues — Receipts from current State imposts — Highway-user revenue — Total	Motor-fuel taxes	Motor vehicle and carrier taxes	Other [1]	Federal funds [2]	Receipts from issue of bonds, notes, etc. [3]	All other [4]	Disbursements — Total	For State-administered highways — Capital outlay for roads and bridges	Maintenance	Other [5]	For county and local roads and streets	All other [6]	State highway debt outstanding
	265	266	267	268	269	270	271	272	273	274	275	276	277	278	279
1957	7,067,566	4,544,558	2,894,719	1,649,839	357,391	1,256,005	727,157	182,455	7,702,319	4,139,322	812,426	903,523	1,347,618	499,430	7,945,208
1956	6,789,022	4,395,173	2,788,278	1,606,895	392,623	775,664	1,064,646	160,916	6,896,428	3,661,979	756,473	748,458	1,236,107	493,411	7,495,903
1955	5,794,659	4,014,449	2,533,126	1,481,323	295,103	670,259	658,168	156,680	6,033,880	3,102,994	675,629	686,738	1,130,444	438,075	6,618,507
1954	6,913,563	3,648,587	2,301,750	1,346,837	221,043	587,857	2,338,021	118,055	5,720,432	2,962,562	647,765	653,303	1,044,157	412,645	6,164,000
1953	5,401,670	3,420,590	2,167,956	1,252,634	213,299	540,883	1,101,546	125,352	4,884,672	2,271,434	620,405	566,375	994,005	432,453	4,015,481
1952	4,651,306	3,094,050	1,958,182	1,135,868	184,706	485,273	798,625	88,652	4,247,781	1,941,857	602,554	472,472	905,487	325,411	3,116,120
1951	4,051,205	2,863,225	1,809,310	1,053,915	158,192	415,628	536,926	77,234	3,980,534	1,739,579	562,272	484,092	808,823	385,768	2,475,803
1950	3,613,387	2,587,079	1,652,295	934,784	125,030	425,587	410,117	65,574	3,561,513	1,533,859	501,487	447,574	752,429	326,164	2,141,058
1949	3,278,984	2,337,089	1,473,366	863,723	153,001	429,198	303,177	56,519	3,201,008	1,361,950	488,037	355,816	735,340	259,865	1,928,330
1948	2,950,245	2,081,046	1,348,122	732,924	144,165	364,852	312,773	47,409	2,874,070	1,138,674	466,184	343,116	652,801	273,295	1,735,362
1947	2,345,032	1,888,741	1,196,480	642,261	91,585	288,336	89,349	37,021	2,383,150	882,351	375,097	343,497	537,349	244,856	1,536,939
1946	2,107,903	1,602,804	1,046,374	556,430	176,494	147,230	150,036	31,339	1,788,993	502,316	329,587	403,604	400,402	153,084	1,571,577
1945	1,449,147	1,235,780	773,817	461,963	87,234	59,964	47,617	18,552	1,302,073	210,467	289,368	342,633	309,883	149,722	1,637,904
1944	1,361,065	1,136,904	684,944	451,960	44,379	91,918	72,189	15,675	1,243,803	210,328	258,958	290,059	297,808	186,650	1,794,507
1943	1,425,077	1,117,377	663,646	453,731	56,425	152,189	83,873	15,213	1,309,358	268,695	224,884	303,117	315,520	197,142	1,869,559
1942	1,572,224	1,321,391	855,271	466,120	44,541	154,930	33,029	18,333	1,489,453	401,694	216,705	263,759	359,358	247,937	1,962,131
1941	1,899,100	1,452,011	948,038	503,973	45,742	168,862	204,857	27,628	1,888,851	525,233	234,833	505,848	359,000	263,937	2,069,639
1940	1,780,471	1,321,082	866,259	454,823	38,195	196,139	202,286	22,769	1,678,009	563,074	218,776	318,190	333,116	244,853	1,159,025
1939	1,611,091	1,226,916	816,629	410,287	34,109	203,830	120,230	26,006	1,606,672	500,113	211,927	337,022	333,575	224,035	2,177,883
1938	1,578,286	1,175,758	769,870	405,888	33,466	197,676	145,967	25,419	1,619,085	558,379	232,615	329,971	296,885	201,235	2,250,152
1937	1,634,818	1,195,651	767,467	428,184	30,298	264,087	111,559	33,223	1,601,760	589,242	228,793	270,695	312,820	205,210	2,243,648
1936	1,590,886	1,057,995	683,074	374,921	25,320	349,736	134,235	23,600	1,578,496	631,760	222,001	256,373	257,346	211,016	2,210,385
1935	1,330,589	940,436	615,581	324,855	24,886	219,381	117,150	28,736	1,257,838	438,306	187,122	219,893	233,238	179,279	2,169,299
1934	1,388,647	883,717	565,140	318,577	27,593	354,812	103,060	19,465	1,325,187	580,369	181,507	191,175	216,354	155,782	2,114,823
1933	1,182,027	815,688	514,014	301,674	43,747	223,586	79,848	19,158	1,219,624	527,012	181,565	189,043	195,392	126,612	2,108,839
1932	1,169,121	838,351	514,077	324,274	48,438	138,857	104,650	38,825	1,243,153	569,511	179,722	190,123	195,563	108,234	2,038,541
1931	1,389,970	881,763	537,443	344,320	47,634	218,383	174,781	67,409	1,393,590	796,902	162,943	167,264	217,067	49,414	1,879,797
1930	1,296,853	850,663	494,622	356,041	55,196	94,111	222,288	74,595	1,330,545	728,887	193,928	167,153	200,016	40,561	1,572,455
1929	1,209,487	778,950	431,354	347,596	75,819	77,952	191,229	85,537	1,089,411	575,475	173,601	136,909	170,423	33,003	1,438,994
1928	998,098	626,882	304,397	322,485	57,612	81,252	133,484	98,868	983,924	558,481	160,274	96,346	140,807	28,016	1,187,801
1927	879,243	559,690	258,771	300,919	52,001	80,160	90,979	96,413	847,863	418,820	139,130	129,367	136,206	24,280	1,085,867
1926	825,348	475,885	187,603	288,282	49,257	79,163	137,846	83,197	747,141	366,011	125,775	116,647	115,074	23,634	933,066
1925	783,159	405,699	145,492	260,207	56,175	93,343	141,402	86,540	761,914	403,843	119,304	115,972	101,197	21,598	789,347
1924	638,043	305,274	80,442	224,832	39,487	92,970	101,653	98,659	691,963	397,648	104,806	89,853	74,888	24,768	678,321
1923	532,574	227,983	38,566	189,417	62,482	73,308	88,187	80,614	493,317	279,993	75,329	74,436	57,459	6,100	565,450
1922	556,064	164,464	12,703	151,761	65,861	79,741	143,004	102,994	492,736	287,461	75,341	54,304	67,669	7,961	473,214
1921	430,210	127,828	5,382	122,446	69,721	77,741	114,804	40,116	444,413	300,609	64,833	41,897	29,546	7,528	372,945
1920	358,145	102,921	1,364	101,557	97,553	61,966	38,272	57,433	358,145	240,340	58,468	25,406	29,682	4,249	225,406
1919	221,260	65,719	1,023	64,696	27,787	11,730	34,322	81,702	221,260	124,981	53,093	19,259	19,016	4,911	191,441
1918	139,730	51,478	--------	51,478	30,235	2,109	7,083	48,825	139,730	71,913	34,975	13,581	14,718	4,543	159,502
1917	116,469	37,504	--------	37,504	6,379	--------	21,698	50,888	116,469	61,624	27,649	10,264	14,117	2,815	154,005
1916	87,217	25,866	--------	25,866	23,015	--------	4,809	33,527	87,217	49,884	18,453	6,722	10,203	1,955	134,490
1915	90,694	18,248	--------	18,248	20,104	--------	25,319	27,023	90,694	55,986	19,254	5,844	7,575	2,035	130,244
1914	75,423	12,385	--------	12,385	26,160	--------	11,684	25,194	75,423	53,880	14,527	5,200	1,816	--------	105,494

Year	State highway debt outstanding 279	Year	State highway debt outstanding 279	Year	State highway debt outstanding 279	Year	State highway debt outstanding 279
1913	94,213	1907	18,431	1901	13,109	1895	2,635
1912	65,697	1906	16,434			1894	1,385
1911	52,479			1900	12,797	1893	585
1905	15,431	1899	12,235	1892	48
1910	38,368	1904	15,014	1898	10,085	1891	40
1909	31,615	1903	14,567	1897	8,235		
1908	24,478	1902	14,000	1896	6,735	1890	11

[1] Includes road, bridge, and ferry tolls; property taxes; appropriations from general funds; and other State imposts.
[2] Includes funds of Bureau of Public Roads and other agencies paid as reimbursement to the States. Does not include direct Federal expenditures for highways.
[3] Includes refunding issues and toll revenue bonds.
[4] Includes funds transferred from local governments and miscellaneous receipts.

[5] Includes administration, engineering and equipment; State highway police; interest on obligations for State highways; and retirement of obligations for State highways.
[6] Includes expenditures and funds transferred for nonhighway purposes and expense of collecting and administering highway-user revenue.

Series Q 280–293. Funds Contributed and Disbursed for County and Other Local Rural Roads: 1921 to 1956

[In millions of dollars]

Year	Total [1]	Federal funds [2]	State sources				Local sources				Disbursements			
			Total	Highway-user imposts	Direct expenditures [3]	Other	Total	Property taxes, general funds, and other	Toll receipts	Borrowing [4]	Total	Capital outlay [2]	Maintenance and administration	Interest
	280	281	282	283	284	285	286	287	288	289	290	291	292	293
1956	1,767	89	933	680	225	28	[5] 744	[5] 606	[5] 16	122	1,482	[5] 646	[5] 806	[5] 30
1955	1,765	90	864	651	186	27	810	590	15	205	1,388	583	776	29
1954	1,573	77	818	628	163	27	677	569	14	94	1,313	540	744	29
1953	1,541	78	779	592	160	27	683	551	13	119	1,254	513	714	27
1952	1,431	67	728	554	148	26	634	521	13	100	1,160	456	678	26
1951	1,267	48	648	510	112	26	570	472	12	86	1,038	359	652	27
1950	1,199	45	603	470	108	25	550	448	12	90	966	331	608	27
1949	1,160	53	588	443	122	23	518	408	11	99	931	358	544	29
1948	1,055	41	539	403	97	39	474	381	10	83	870	325	515	30
1947	928	26	438	346	69	23	464	349	8	107	749	261	458	30
1946	729	12	355	287	32	36	361	305	7	49	601	164	404	33
1945	584	11	280	247	19	14	293	266	5	22	448	82	331	35
1944	542	16	273	234	32	7	253	242	5	6	435	80	318	37
1943	581	34	292	243	44	5	255	244	5	6	421	90	290	41
1942	683	95	307	266	37	4	281	257	5	19	510	190	276	44
1941	825	198	327	280	35	12	300	265	4	31	656	328	280	48
1940	937	309	318	272	35	11	309	277	3	29	765	447	267	51
1939	1,000	373	308	258	37	13	319	281	3	35	832	513	264	55
1938	1,022	401	289	246	30	13	332	280	3	49	868	547	261	60
1937	869	240	302	245	45	12	327	279	1	47	704	384	257	63
1936	894	341	235	224	--------	11	318	269	--------	49	771	464	244	63
1935	618	95	215	205	--------	10	308	265	--------	43	495	204	222	69
1934	654	154	223	218	--------	5	277	251	--------	26	540	252	212	76
1933	558	25	222	203	--------	19	311	296	--------	15	432	140	216	76
1932	649	(6)	208	204	--------	4	441	389	--------	52	518	177	259	82
1931	784	1	209	202	--------	7	574	493	--------	81	643	257	300	86
1930	819	--------	196	196	--------	--------	623	528	--------	95	701	297	321	83
1929	790	--------	154	154	--------	--------	636	525	--------	111	644	257	309	78
1928	835	--------	135	135	--------	--------	700	550	--------	150	659	282	297	80
1927	840	--------	125	125	--------	--------	715	534	--------	181	643	289	279	75
1926	776	--------	108	108	--------	--------	668	499	--------	169	588	266	255	67
1925	683	--------	102	102	--------	--------	581	437	--------	144	544	265	227	52
1924	603	--------	44	44	--------	--------	559	401	--------	158	534	256	223	55
1923	572	--------	40	40	--------	--------	532	403	--------	129	521	242	229	50
1922	580	--------	30	30	--------	--------	550	400	--------	150	590	330	225	35
1921	624	--------	22	22	--------	--------	602	400	--------	202	596	337	225	34

[1] For 1940–1956, includes contributions from urban places not shown elsewhere. ($1 million in 1956).
[2] The following amounts of Federal work-relief funds (mainly Works Progress Administration) are included for 1933–1942, respectively (in millions of dollars): 25, 150, 91, 339, 221, 389, 352, 295, 189, and 78.
[3] Work performed directly by State agencies on local projects; similar amounts included in disbursements.
[4] Refunding issues excluded after 1937.
[5] Estimated.
[6] Less than $500,000.

Series Q 294–309. Funds Contributed and Disbursed for Streets in Incorporated and Other Urban Places: 1921 to 1956

[In millions of dollars]

Year	Total [1]	Federal funds [2]	Funds contributed — State sources			Funds contributed — Local sources					Rural sources	Disbursements				
			Total	Highway-user imposts	Direct expenditure	Total	Highway-user imposts	Toll receipts	Property taxes, general revenues, miscellaneous	Borrowing [3]		Total	Capital outlay [2]	Maintenance and repair	Interest	Administration
	294	295	296	297	298	299	300	301	302	303	304	305	306	307	308	309
1956	1,445	4	282	⁴250	32	1,116	⁴58	⁴49	⁴767	242	⁴36	1,213	561	505	55	92
1955	1,473	3	274	238	36	1,161	56	46	736	323	30	1,154	531	484	52	87
1954	1,354	4	258	226	32	1,049	50	43	683	273	36	1,061	476	459	49	77
1953	1,195	2	223	197	26	932	48	42	646	196	31	1,007	443	446	45	73
1952	1,104	2	196	174	22	871	35	41	594	201	31	933	404	413	44	72
1951	976	1	177	156	21	767	25	37	523	182	25	839	356	382	42	59
1950	938	1	176	151	25	728	23	31	512	162	29	802	356	350	42	54
1949	947	3	165	143	22	747	23	26	511	187	30	796	350	350	43	53
1948	788	4	119	103	16	647	20	24	482	121	18	679	267	327	40	45
1947	677	2	109	95	14	554	17	21	394	122	12	562	221	267	39	45
1946	514	(⁵)	83	72	11	424	12	20	330	62	7	391	105	222	37	27
1945	408	(⁵)	52	46	6	347	11	14	302	20	9	310	58	194	39	19
1944	294	(⁵)	53	45	8	232	--------	--------	220	12	9	321	74	167	52	28
1943	282	1	58	48	10	217	--------	--------	205	12	6	321	68	171	54	28
1942	423	46	72	59	13	297	--------	--------	255	42	8	404	159	162	56	27
1941	544	105	61	54	7	368	--------	--------	295	73	10	480	241	155	58	26
1940	639	168	62	53	9	397	--------	--------	347	50	12	567	344	139	61	23
1939	708	233	62	52	10	401	--------	--------	382	19	12	665	434	150	56	25
1938	837	367	53	46	7	407	--------	--------	366	41	10	778	541	156	55	26
1937	615	203	56	48	8	350	--------	--------	335	15	6	584	375	133	54	22
1936	673	264	31	31	--------	367	--------	--------	348	19	11	643	401	156	60	26
1935	490	103	23	23	--------	352	--------	--------	335	17	12	461	223	146	68	24
1934	568	172	25	25	--------	366	--------	--------	337	29	5	534	286	148	75	25
1933	438	29	18	18	--------	386	--------	--------	373	13	5	420	167	147	82	24
1932	538	--------	17	17	--------	516	--------	--------	474	42	5	491	211	166	87	27
1931	741	--------	20	20	--------	716	--------	--------	643	73	5	663	350	193	88	32
1930	911	--------	12	12	--------	899	--------	--------	787	112	--------	799	478	197	91	33
1929	861	--------	14	14	--------	847	--------	--------	725	122	--------	739	429	196	82	32
1928	843	--------	10	10	--------	833	--------	--------	718	115	--------	728	444	180	74	30
1927	849	--------	4	4	--------	845	--------	--------	730	115	--------	734	453	182	69	30
1926	730	--------	6	6	--------	724	--------	--------	624	100	--------	630	373	167	62	28
1925	695	--------	4	4	--------	691	--------	--------	578	113	--------	582	357	147	54	24
1924	573	--------	--------	--------	--------	573	--------	--------	482	91	--------	482	285	130	45	22
1923	403	--------	--------	--------	--------	403	--------	--------	403	--------	--------	403	226	120	37	20
1922	376	--------	--------	--------	--------	376	--------	--------	376	--------	--------	376	213	115	29	19
1921	337	--------	--------	--------	--------	337	--------	--------	337	--------	--------	337	191	108	20	18

[1] Includes since 1949 other items not shown elsewhere.
[2] The following amounts of Federal work-relief funds (mainly Works Progress Administration) are included for 1933–1942 respectively (in millions of dollars): 29, 172, 103, 264, 203, 367, 233, 167, 104, and 44.
[3] Refunding issues excluded since 1940.
[4] Estimated.
[5] Less than $500,000.

Series Q 310–320.　Motor-Vehicle Factory Sales and Registrations, and Motor-Fuel Usage: 1900 to 1957

[Number sold includes sales of military vehicles.　Value of sales does not include Federal excise taxes.　Beginning 1937, standard equipment is included in the value estimate]

Year	Motor-vehicle factory sales				Motor-vehicle registrations				Motor-fuel usage		
	Passenger cars		Motor trucks and buses [1]		Total	Automobiles	Buses	Trucks	Total	Highway	Non-highway
	Number	Wholesale value	Number	Wholesale value							
	310	311	312	313	314	315	316	317	318	319	320
		$1,000		$1,000					1,000 gals.	1,000 gals.	1,000 gals.
1957	6,113,344	11,198,379	1,107,176	2,082,723	67,131,071	55,906,195	264,062	10,960,814	56,954,590	51,864,631	5,089,959
1956	5,816,109	9,754,971	1,104,481	2,077,432	65,153,810	54,200,784	258,764	10,694,262	55,149,647	50,214,299	4,935,348
1955	7,920,186	12,452,871	1,249,090	2,020,973	62,693,819	52,135,583	255,249	10,302,987	52,565,099	47,730,578	4,834,521
1954	5,558,897	8,218,094	1,042,174	1,660,019	58,510,253	48,461,219	248,346	9,800,688	49,118,918	44,365,465	4,753,453
1953	6,116,948	9,002,580	1,206,266	2,089,060	56,221,089	46,422,443	244,251	9,554,395	47,381,037	42,731,847	4,649,190
1952	4,320,794	6,455,114	1,218,165	2,319,789	53,265,406	43,817,580	240,485	9,207,341	45,037,336	40,584,530	4,452,806
1951	5,338,435	7,241,275	1,426,828	2,323,859	51,913,965	42,682,591	230,461	9,000,913	42,473,362	38,128,351	4,345,011
1950	6,665,863	8,468,137	1,337,193	1,707,748	49,161,691	40,333,591	223,652	8,604,448	39,830,606	35,652,940	4,177,666
1949	5,119,466	6,650,857	1,134,185	1,394,035	44,690,296	36,453,351	208,929	8,028,016	36,440,037	32,431,016	4,009,021
1948	3,909,270	4,870,423	1,376,274	1,880,475	41,085,531	33,350,894	196,726	7,537,911	34,329,147	30,460,641	3,868,506
1947	3,558,178	3,936,017	1,239,443	1,731,713	37,841,498	30,845,350	187,457	6,808,691	31,680,501	28,215,705	3,464,796
1946	2,148,699	1,979,781	940,866	1,043,247	34,373,002	28,213,336	173,585	5,986,081	28,876,546	25,648,998	3,227,548
1945	69,532	57,255	655,683	1,181,956	31,035,420	25,793,493	162,125	5,079,802	22,046,727	19,148,968	2,897,759
1944	610	447	737,524	1,700,929	30,479,306	25,566,464	152,592	4,760,250	19,292,047	16,429,668	2,862,379
1943	139	102	699,689	1,451,794	30,888,134	26,009,073	152,324	4,726,737	18,642,773	16,004,250	2,638,523
1942	222,862	163,814	818,662	1,427,457	33,003,656	27,972,837	135,957	4,894,862	22,438,925	19,939,887	2,499,038
1941	3,779,682	2,567,206	1,060,820	1,069,800	34,894,134	29,624,269	119,753	5,150,112	26,429,441	24,192,397	2,237,044
1940	3,717,385	2,370,654	754,901	567,820	32,453,233	27,465,826	101,145	4,886,262	24,038,525	22,001,356	2,037,169
1939	2,888,512	1,770,232	700,377	489,787	31,009,227	26,226,371	92,285	4,691,271	22,571,837	20,714,352	1,857,485
1938	2,019,566	1,241,032	488,841	329,918	29,813,718	25,250,477	87,664	4,475,577	21,311,675	19,611,643	1,700,032
1937	3,929,203	2,240,913	891,016	537,315	30,058,892	25,467,229	83,130	4,508,533	21,115,444	19,455,454	1,659,990
1936	3,679,242	2,014,747	782,220	463,719	28,506,891	24,182,662	62,618	4,261,611	19,561,677	18,099,138	1,462,539
1935	3,273,874	1,707,836	697,367	380,997	26,546,126	22,567,827	58,994	3,919,305	71,637,580	16,344,697	1,292,883
1934	2,160,865	1,140,478	576,205	326,782	25,261,710	21,544,727	51,530	3,665,453	16,557,921	15,414,896	1,143,025
1933	1,560,599	773,425	329,218	175,381	24,159,203	20,657,257	44,918	3,457,028	15,367,905	14,348,152	1,019,753
1932	1,103,557	616,860	228,303	137,624	24,391,000	20,901,401	43,476	3,446,123	15,427,340	14,339,151	1,088,189
1931	1,948,164	1,108,247	432,262	265,445	26,093,968	22,396,253	41,880	3,655,835	16,621,261	15,456,662	1,164,599
1930	2,787,456	1,644,083	575,364	390,752	26,749,853	23,034,753	40,507	3,674,593	15,777,707	14,753,911	1,023,796
1929	4,455,178	2,790,614	881,909	622,534	26,704,825	23,120,897	33,999	3,549,929	15,051,036	14,139,301	911,735
1928	3,775,417	2,572,599	583,342	460,109	24,688,631	21,362,240	31,982	3,294,409	13,090,282	12,361,460	728,822
1927	2,936,533	2,164,671	464,793	420,131	23,303,470	20,193,333	27,659	3,082,478	11,936,896	11,331,326	605,570
1926	3,692,317	2,607,365	608,617	484,823	22,200,150	19,267,967	24,320	2,907,863	10,552,161	10,063,951	488,210
1925	3,735,171	2,458,370	530,659	458,400	20,068,543	17,481,001	17,808	2,569,734	9,143,965	8,749,075	394,890
1924	3,185,881	1,970,097	416,659	318,581	17,612,940	15,436,102	----------	2,176,838	7,809,186	7,497,000	312,186
1923	3,624,717	2,196,257	409,295	308,538	15,102,105	13,253,019	----------	1,849,086	6,313,177	6,078,000	235,177
1922	2,274,185	1,494,514	269,991	226,050	12,273,599	10,704,076	----------	1,569,523	5,014,035	4,841,000	173,035
1921	1,468,067	1,038,191	148,052	166,071	10,493,666	9,212,158	----------	1,281,508	4,064,824	3,935,000	129,824
1920	1,905,560	1,809,171	321,789	423,249	9,239,161	8,131,522	----------	1,107,639	3,448,164	3,346,000	102,164
1919	1,651,625	1,365,395	224,731	371,423	7,576,888	6,679,133	----------	897,755	2,747,030	2,672,000	75,030
1918	943,436	801,938	227,250	434,169	6,160,448	5,554,952	----------	605,496	----------	----------	----------
1917	1,745,792	1,053,506	128,157	220,983	5,118,525	4,727,468	----------	391,057	----------	----------	----------
1916	1,525,578	921,378	92,130	161,000	3,617,937	3,367,889	----------	250,048	----------	----------	----------
1915	895,930	575,978	74,000	125,800	2,490,932	2,332,426	----------	158,506	----------	----------	----------
1914	548,139	420,838	24,900	44,219	1,763,018	1,664,003	----------	99,015	----------	----------	----------
1913	461,500	399,902	23,500	44,000	1,258,060	1,190,393	----------	67,667	----------	----------	----------
1912	356,000	335,000	22,000	43,000	944,000	901,596	----------	42,404	----------	----------	----------
1911	199,319	225,000	10,681	21,000	639,500	618,727	----------	20,773	----------	----------	----------
1910	181,000	215,340	6,000	9,660	468,500	458,377	----------	10,123	----------	----------	----------
1909	123,990	159,766	3,297	5,334	312,000	305,950	----------	6,050	----------	----------	----------
1908	63,500	135,250	1,500	2,550	198,400	194,400	----------	4,000	----------	----------	----------
1907	43,000	91,620	1,000	1,780	143,200	140,300	----------	2,900	----------	----------	----------
1906	33,200	61,460	800	1,440	108,100	105,900	----------	2,200	----------	----------	----------
1905	24,250	38,670	750	1,330	78,800	77,400	----------	1,400	----------	----------	----------
1904	22,130	23,358	700	1,273	55,290	54,590	----------	700	----------	----------	----------
1903	11,235	13,000	----------	----------	32,920	32,920	----------	----------	----------	----------	----------
1902	9,000	10,395	----------	----------	23,000	23,000	----------	----------	----------	----------	----------
1901	7,000	8,183	----------	----------	14,800	14,800	----------	----------	----------	----------	----------
1900	4,192	4,899	----------	----------	8,000	8,000	----------	----------	----------	----------	----------

[1] A substantial portion of the number of trucks and buses (series Q 312) consists of chassis only, without bodies; hence the value of bodies for these chassis (series Q 313) is not included.

Series Q 321–327.   Miles of Travel by Motor Vehicles: 1921 to 1957

[In million vehicle-miles]

Year	All motor vehicles			Passenger vehicles		Trucks and combinations	
	Total travel	Urban travel	Rural travel	Urban travel	Rural travel	Urban travel	Rural travel
	321	322	323	324	325	326	327
1957	647,004	296,699	350,305	256,563	277,235	40,136	73,070
1956	627,843	275,464	352,379	233,456	278,287	42,008	74,092
1955	603,434	267,281	336,153	226,380	265,667	40,901	70,486
1954	560,857	243,639	317,218	206,169	248,844	37,470	68,374
1953	544,433	236,058	308,375	199,754	240,046	36,304	68,329
1952	513,581	224,118	289,463	189,987	224,534	34,131	64,929
1951	491,093	222,671	268,422	188,670	207,579	34,001	60,843
1950	458,246	218,248	239,998	184,476	183,218	33,772	56,780
1949	424,461	205,364	219,097	175,686	171,044	29,678	48,053
1948	397,957	199,082	198,875	170,331	153,617	28,751	[1] 45,258
1947	370,894	184,088	186,806	158,770	145,921	25,318	[1] 40,885
1946	340,880	170,049	170,831	148,497	136,153	21,552	[1] 34,678
1945	250,173	130,161	120,012	111,401	92,831	18,760	[2] 27,181
1944	212,713	110,750	101,963	93,679	77,264	17,071	[2] 24,699
1943	208,192	108,990	99,202	91,942	74,592	17,048	[2] 24,610
1942	268,224	138,235	129,989	119,653	102,780	18,582	[2] 27,209
1941	333,612	163,591	170,021	143,101	135,558	20,490	[1] 34,463
1940	302,188	149,993	152,195	130,269	121,988	19,724	[1] 30,207
1939	285,402	142,253	143,149	122,805	115,378	19,448	27,771
1938	271,177	136,264	134,913	117,537	109,145	18,727	25,768
1937	270,110	138,072	132,038	118,216	107,743	19,856	24,295
1936	252,128	129,450	122,678	110,419	100,602	19,031	22,076

Year	All motor vehicles		
	Total travel	Urban travel	Rural travel
	322	323	324
1935	228,568	118,327	110,241
1934	215,563	112,513	103,050
1933	200,642	105,578	95,064
1932	200,517	106,366	94,151
1931	216,151	115,580	100,571
1930	206,320	111,202	95,118
1929	197,720	107,409	90,311
1928	172,856	--------	--------
1927	158,453	--------	--------
1926	140,735	--------	--------
1925	122,346		
1924	104,838		
1923	84,995		
1922	67,697		
1921	55,027		

[1] Includes travel on turnpikes not included in previously published figures.

[2] Includes travel on turnpikes as well as travel by military vehicles, not included in previously published figures.

Series Q 328–329.   State and Federal Gasoline Tax Rates: 1930 to 1957

[In cents per gallon. When 2 figures appear in a cell, the first is tax in effect at beginning of year, the last is tax at end of year]

Year	State average	Federal tax	Year	State average	Federal tax	Year	State average	Federal tax
	328	329		328	329		328	329
1957	5.58	3	1947	4.25	1.5	1938	3.96	1
1956	[1] 5.54	2–3	1946	4.16	1.5	1937	3.91	1
1955	5.35	2	1945	4.10	1.5	1936	3.85	1
1954	5.19	2	1944	4.06	1.5	1935	3.80	1
1953	5.10	2	1943	4.05	1.5	1934	3.66	1
1952	4.83	2	1942	3.99	1.5	1933	3.65	1–1.5
1951	4.74	1.5–2	1941	3.99	1.5	1932	3.60	0–1
1950	4.65	1.5	1940	3.96	1–1.5	1931	3.48	--------
1949	4.52	1.5	1939	3.96	1	1930	3.35	--------
1948	4.35	1.5						

[1] As of August 1.

Series Q 330-341. Public Transit Mileage, Equipment, Passengers, and Passenger Revenue: 1917 to 1957

Year	Mileage (Dec. 31)			Equipment owned (Dec. 31)			Revenue and nonrevenue passengers (millions)				Revenue passengers (mil.)	Passenger revenue (mil. dol.)
	Railway track	Trolley coach	Motor bus	Railway cars	Trolley coaches	Motor buses	Total	Railway	Trolley coach	Motor bus		
	330	331	332	333	334	335	336	337	338	339	340	341
1957	5,019	3,007	102,400	12,759	5,412	50,800	10,389	2,522	993	6,874	8,338	1,312.2
1956	5,746	3,292	100,700	13,225	5,748	51,400	10,941	2,756	1,142	7,043	8,756	1,346.4
1955	6,197	3,428	99,800	14,532	6,157	52,400	11,529	3,077	1,202	7,250	9,189	1,358.9
1954	6,765	3,630	99,000	15,600	6,598	54,000	12,392	3,401	1,367	7,624	9,858	1,410.0
1953	7,352	3,663	100,000	17,234	6,941	54,700	13,902	4,076	1,566	8,260	11,036	1,448.6
1952	8,532	3,736	99,600	19,176	7,180	55,980	15,119	4,601	1,640	8,878	12,022	1,438.1
1951	9,457	3,678	99,700	20,604	7,071	57,660	16,125	5,290	1,633	9,202	12,281	1,411.6
1950	10,813	3,513	98,000	22,986	6,504	56,820	17,246	6,168	1,658	9,420	13,845	1,386.8
1949	11,931	3,337	96,400	24,728	6,366	57,035	19,008	7,185	1,661	10,162	15,251	1,419.7
1948	12,964	2,905	96,500	26,280	5,687	58,540	21,368	9,112	1,528	10,728	17,312	1,416.8
1947	14,976	2,699	95,300	30,158	4,707	56,917	22,540	10,852	1,356	10,332	18,287	1,324.2
1946	16,716	2,354	91,100	33,479	3,916	52,450	23,372	11,862	1,311	10,199	19,119	1,331.5
1945	17,702	2,313	90,400	36,377	3,711	49,670	23,254	12,124	1,244	9,886	18,982	1,313.7
1944	18,082	2,245	87,700	37,199	3,561	48,400	23,017	12,137	1,234	9,646	18,735	1,296.9
1943	18,181	2,248	87,000	37,505	3,501	47,100	22,000	11,806	1,175	9,019	17,918	1,235.6
1942	18,171	2,273	85,500	37,508	3,385	46,000	18,000	9,856	899	7,245	14,501	979.1
1941	18,342	2,041	82,100	37,670	3,029	39,300	14,085	8,502	652	4,931	11,302	758.8
1940	19,602	1,925	78,000	37,662	2,802	35,000	13,098	8,325	534	4,239	10,504	701.5
1939	20,600	1,543	74,300	40,372	2,184	32,600	12,837	8,539	445	3,853	10,252	681.5
1938	21,800	1,398	70,400	42,605	2,032	28,500	12,645	8,781	389	3,475	9,985	662.9
1937	23,770	1,166	67,000	45,312	1,655	27,500	13,246	9,468	289	3,489	10,436	689.7
1936	25,300	859	62,200	48,103	1,136	23,900	13,146	9,824	143	3,179	10,512	685.5
1935	26,700	548	58,100	50,466	578	23,800	12,226	9,512	96	2,618	9,782	642.3
1934	28,500	423	54,700	54,118	441	18,700	12,038	9,600	68	2,370	--------	--------
1933	--------	--------	--------	58,124	310	17,200	11,327	9,207	45	2,075	--------	--------
1932	--------	--------	--------	--------	--------	--------	12,025	9,852	37	2,136	--------	--------
1931	--------	--------	--------	--------	--------	--------	13,924	11,583	28	2,313	--------	--------
1930	--------	--------	--------	--------	--------	--------	15,567	13,072	16	2,479	--------	--------
1929	--------	--------	--------	--------	--------	--------	16,985	14,358	5	2,622	--------	--------
1928	--------	--------	--------	--------	--------	--------	16,989	14,518	3	2,468	--------	--------
1927	--------	--------	--------	--------	--------	--------	17,201	14,901	--------	2,300	--------	--------
1926	--------	--------	--------	--------	--------	--------	17,234	15,225	--------	2,009	--------	--------
1925	--------	--------	--------	--------	--------	--------	16,651	15,167	--------	1,484	--------	--------
1924	--------	--------	--------	--------	--------	--------	16,301	15,312	--------	989	--------	--------
1923	--------	--------	--------	--------	--------	--------	16,311	15,650	--------	661	--------	--------
1922	--------	--------	--------	--------	--------	--------	15,735	15,331	--------	404	--------	--------
1921	--------	--------	--------	--------	--------	--------	--------	14,574	--------	--------	--------	--------
1920	--------	--------	--------	--------	--------	--------	--------	15,541	--------	--------	--------	--------
1919	--------	--------	--------	--------	--------	--------	--------	14,916	--------	--------	--------	--------
1918	--------	--------	--------	--------	--------	--------	--------	14,243	--------	--------	--------	--------
1917	--------	--------	--------	--------	--------	--------	--------	14,507	--------	--------	--------	--------

Series Q 342-344. Oil Pipelines Operated and Oil Originated: 1921 to 1957

Year	Miles of line operated	Oil originated Crude	Oil originated Refined
	342	343	344
		Mil. bbl.	Mil. bbl.
1957	145,236	2,183	668
1956	142,686	2,195	663
1955	140,374	2,038	586
1954	138,962	1,829	502
1953	133,900	1,861	435
1952	132,715	1,810	385
1951	131,152	1,774	345
1950	128,589	1,525	297
1949	124,984	1,415	241
1948	124,092	1,586	227
1947	119,298	1,431	187
1946	116,544	1,319	154
1945	113,351	1,292	150
1944	111,615	1,277	147
1943	108,783	1,123	144
1942	106,485	981	92
1941	105,435	971	82
1940	100,156	886	72
1939	98,681	803	70
1938	95,938	793	65
1937	96,612	885	63
1936	93,926	755	52
1935	92,037	723	44
1934	93,070	557	35
1933	93,724	538	29
1932	92,782	508	25
1931	93,090	489	16
1930	88,728	--------	--------
1929	85,796	--------	--------
1928	81,676	--------	--------
1927	76,070	--------	--------
1926	72,846	--------	--------
1925	70,009	--------	--------
1924	68,185	--------	--------
1923	64,760	--------	--------
1922	57,349	--------	--------
1921	55,260	--------	--------

Series R 1-9. Telephones and Average Daily Calls (Bell and Independent Companies): 1876 to 1956—Con.

[In thousands, except series R 2. Census figures in italics]

Year	Telephones				Average daily calls			
	Total		Bell	Independent companies not connecting with Bell	Bell		Independent companies	
	Number	Per 1,000 population			Local exchange	Toll	Local exchange	Toll
	1	2	3	5	6	7	8	9
1895	340	4.8	310	30	2,351	51	170	3
1894	285	4.1	270	15	2,088	38		
1893	266	3.9	266		1,872	34		
1892	261	3.9	261		1,868	41		
1891	239	3.7	239		1,585	34		
1890	*234*	*3.7*						
1890	228	3.6	228		1,438	10		
1889	212	3.4	212		1,240	8		
1888	195	3.2	195		1,052	7		
1887	181	3.0	181		1,012	7		
1886	167	2.9	167		856	7		
1885	156	2.7	156		747	7		
1884	148	2.6	148		698	8		
1883	124	2.3	124		590	5		
1882	98	1.8	98					
1881	71	1.4	71					
1880	*54*	*1.1*						
1880	48	0.9	48		237	2		
1879	31	0.6	31					
1878	26	0.5	26					
1877	9	0.2	9					
1876	3	0.1	3					

Series R 10-13. Telephone Toll Rates Between New York City and Selected Cities: 1902 to 1957

[Rate for station-to-station, daytime, 3-minute call]

Effective date	Between New York City and—				Effective date	Between New York City and—			
	Philadelphia	Chicago	Denver	San Francisco		Philadelphia	Chicago	Denver	San Francisco
	10	11	12	13		10	11	12	13
1957	$0.50	$1.50	$2.20	$2.50	1929, Feb.	$0.60	$3.00	$6.00	$9.00
1952, Mar.	.50	1.50	2.20	2.50	1927, Dec.	.60	3.25	6.00	9.00
1946, Feb.	.45	1.55	2.20	2.50	1926, Oct.	.60	3.40	7.25	11.30
1945, July	.45	1.75	2.35	2.50	1919, Jan.	.55	4.65	10.40	16.50
1941, July	.45	1.75	3.25	4.00	1917, June	[1] .75	[1] 5.00	11.25	18.50
1940, May	.45	1.90	3.25	4.00	1917, Mar.	(2)	(2)	11.25	19.80
1937, Jan.	.45	2.20	4.50	6.50	1915, Jan.	(2)	(2)	11.25	20.70
1936, Sept.	.50	2.50	5.25	7.50	1911	(2)	(2)	11.25	
1930, Jan.	.50	3.00	6.00	9.00	1902 [3]	.55	5.45		

[1] Rates in effect immediately prior to Jan. 21, 1919, according to an item in the New York Times for Jan. 23, 1919. [2] Not available. [3] Toll rates were $0.006 per mile for all mileages.

Series R 14-27. Bell Telephone Companies—Property, Revenues, Expenses, Interest, Net Income, Dividends, Employees, and Wages: 1880 to 1956

[In thousands, except series R 26. Census figures in italics]

Year	Telephone plant		Miles of wire	Operating revenues			Operating expenses [2]	Federal income taxes	Income from Western Electric Co. [3]	Interest expenses	Net income	Dividends declared [4]	Employees	
	Book value	Depreciation reserves		Total [1]	Local	Toll							Number	Wages and salaries
	14	15	16	17	18	19	20	21	22	23	24	25	26	27
1956	$17,555,590	$4,228,966	222,551	$5,964,876	$3,457,640	$2,220,488	$4,437,810	$714,260	$127,604	$147,778	$792,632	$546,924	652,974	$2,883,990
1955	15,773,373	4,007,118	203,474	5,424,246	3,168,480	1,999,553	4,039,159	644,404	90,084	133,910	696,857	483,619	629,769	2,631,154
1954	14,525,346	3,766,530	187,931	4,901,162	2,914,754	1,755,241	3,746,294	524,995	79,777	132,347	577,303	439,327	591,445	2,443,560
1953	13,419,650	3,555,901	175,390	4,523,707	2,713,501	1,603,608	3,500,599	472,994	69,359	117,668	501,805	389,057	600,618	2,327,884
1952	12,301,975	3,352,297	164,035	4,135,537	2,460,438	1,500,063	3,240,896	403,031	54,622	118,773	427,459	339,186	591,989	2,151,286
1951	11,250,819	3,125,706	153,924	3,727,632	2,205,117	1,369,682	2,929,122	350,134	54,244	118,857	383,763	296,541	563,540	1,927,900
1950	10,375,100	2,904,820	145,973	3,341,308	1,995,659	1,207,509	2,652,421	248,328	41,455	114,637	367,377	262,901	534,974	1,741,907
1949	9,688,160	2,724,745	137,013	2,965,852	1,746,771	1,092,395	2,530,899	125,878	52,224	113,469	247,830	227,929	528,276	1,704,105
1948	8,848,572	2,597,371	127,913	2,693,027	1,551,742	1,030,474	2,325,618	104,297	63,649	91,497	235,264	214,061	559,613	1,621,347
1947	7,552,159	2,447,046	116,169	2,282,446	1,311,401	880,227	2,013,725	77,024	40,613	63,420	168,890	198,469	536,737	1,395,042
1946	6,474,011	2,286,952	108,508	2,146,894	1,198,802	874,497	1,789,686	104,121	9,829	42,950	219,966	193,802	508,564	1,273,137
1945	5,865,065	2,108,385	102,816	1,978,418	1,072,731	845,008	1,454,133	259,274	[5] 30,198	47,177	187,656	187,972	396,198	910,929
1944	5,670,879	1,934,419	101,246	1,814,113	1,017,244	746,694	1,308,853	283,136	7,037	48,998	180,163	181,294	345,744	784,178
1943	5,543,992	1,763,868	100,381	1,690,720	981,094	666,238	1,212,515	243,608	5,989	52,525	188,061	177,877	350,998	731,276
1942	5,450,471	1,601,916	100,661	1,507,336	923,765	544,234	1,089,074	195,906	4,023	52,147	174,232	178,132	335,010	651,904
1941	5,196,319	1,482,590	98,115	1,333,064	872,089	424,521	986,412	110,375	17,118	49,886	203,509	179,341	321,422	586,207
1940	4,887,900	1,397,339	92,120	1,205,435	811,400	360,792	913,023	64,419	39,297	43,349	223,941	180,268	282,465	522,095
1939	4,727,050	1,339,563	88,219	1,136,412	766,956	338,391	870,762	41,387	23,222	43,597	203,888	180,360	266,806	497,276
1938	4,621,914	1,286,582	86,076	1,080,591	734,687	317,290	849,079	35,015	14,655	43,256	167,896	180,847	264,435	488,888
1937	*4,389,549*		*81,578*	*1,051,379*	*703,444*	*321,503*							*268,482*	*463,642*
1937	4,516,998	1,231,712	84,151	1,079,004	724,658	327,229	833,789	31,740	27,302	43,320	197,457	183,308	275,713	476,164
1936	*4,380,881*	*1,156,227*	*81,911*	*1,020,698*	*685,110*	*311,489*	*766,287*	*28,807*	*27,287*	*51,267*	*201,624*	*184,209*	*262,888*	*421,447*

See footnotes at end of table.

Series R 14–27. Bell Telephone Companies—Property, Revenues, Expenses, Interest, Net Income, Dividends, Employees, and Wages: 1880 to 1956—Con.

[In thousands, except series R 26. Census figures in italics]

| Year | Telephone plant | | Miles of wire | Operating revenues | | | Operating expenses [2] | Federal income taxes | Income from Western Electric Co. [3] | Interest expenses | Net income | Dividends declared [4] | Employees | |
| | Book value | Depreciation reserves | | Total [1] | Local | Toll | | | | | | | Number | Wages and salaries |
	14	15	16	17	18	19	20	21	22	23	24	25	26	27
1935	$4,196,671	$1,061,650	80,458	$934,371	$640,993	$273,483	$726,510	$20,843	$12,894	$52,373	$147,539	$183,145	244,599	$387,264
1934	4,177,950	968,214	80,118	884,582	607,676	258,691	685,951	19,586	3,918	57,561	125,352	183,181	248,996	371,727
1933	4,169,370	891,883	80,281	872,406	617,253	243,906	684,424	17,109	[5]1,942	54,351	114,580	183,240	248,563	356,287
1932	*4,269,268*		*80,586*	*956,355*	*670,737*	*263,148*							*281,350*	*414,342*
1932	4,188,749	820,195	80,491	943,540	670,737	263,148	747,713	19,073	17,717	55,135	139,336	185,032	266,288	414,342
1931	4,195,064	788,586	79,239	1,066,895	723,920	326,269	824,115	21,249	36,568	64,720	193,379	180,904	294,689	483,614
1930	4,043,422	740,006	76,248	1,094,883	728,709	348,541	852,703	21,931	47,626	66,229	201,646	156,625	324,343	534,468
1929	3,671,100	699,035	69,519	1,063,633	691,359	354,286	807,988	22,924	43,966	59,582	217,105	132,224	364,402	526,684
1928	3,275,687	650,621	62,193	969,237	644,209	309,334	728,544	25,591	27,621	51,635	191,088	119,349	333,794	466,362
1927	*3,085,613*		*56,819*	*894,699*	*604,266*	*271,174*							*308,865*	*429,877*
1927	3,013,985	600,664	56,823	888,987	604,266	271,174	670,397	23,908	21,888	50,511	166,059	112,401	309,005	429,877
1926	2,783,023	576,216	50,861	817,928	557,490	248,087	611,675	22,712	21,329	49,809	155,061	100,614	300,557	408,418
1925	2,524,906	530,071	45,474	736,648	506,026	219,913	557,295	16,829	19,920	45,941	136,503	93,243	293,095	381,857
1924	2,266,923	485,661	39,894	653,459	454,326	190,318	511,905	13,091	20,314	41,531	107,246	82,603	278,838	365,071
1923	1,978,948	443,130	34,524	598,153	412,009	178,427	470,556	11,748	21,526	37,751	99,624	72,429	271,979	333,786
1922	*1,783,079*		*30,614*	*546,820*	*374,719*	*163,098*	*438,592*		*15,186*	*36,790*	*86,623*	*60,305*	*242,710*	*299,350*
1922	1,729,220	395,297	30,617	543,747	374,719	163,098	426,302	10,162	17,209	37,869	86,623	60,305	243,045	297,301
1921	1,543,866	350,642	27,766	495,244	343,133	146,459	397,226	7,471	13,652	36,774	67,425	47,848	224,277	274,990
1920	1,363,826	309,556	25,377	448,233	301,283	141,883	376,171	4,246	11,693	31,724	47,785	40,000	231,316	263,729
1919	1,215,944	276,304	24,163	387,659				6,635		27,693	48,621	39,840	209,860	199,183
1918	1,142,498	235,395	23,349	326,524				5,893		23,111	46,383	39,735	187,458	156,451
1917	*1,140,640*	*206,863*	*23,134*	*303,864*	*214,119*	*86,814*	*237,002*		*5,539*	*21,266*	*51,135*	*37,021*	*198,700*	*144,915*
1917	1,064,893	201,090	22,610	293,666	207,472	84,560	224,766	4,342	7,976	21,820	50,714	36,863	192,364	137,861
1916	946,293	168,044	19,850	263,095	188,888	72,972	197,772	1,103	7,080	18,379	52,921	35,160	179,032	116,549
1915	880,069	142,307	18,506	232,721	169,156	62,930	171,888	674	6,023	18,096	48,086	32,897	156,294	99,454
1914	847,205	122,338	17,476	224,500	160,311	58,466	166,102	603	1,452	18,940	40,307	30,304	142,527	99,048
1913	797,159	105,720	16,111	214,126	151,260	57,009	156,883		1,447	16,653	42,037	30,302	156,928	95,209
1912	*780,018*		*15,133*	*206,131*			*163,024*				*43,107*	*29,710*	*141,903*	*76,901*
1912	742,288	92,458	14,611	197,798	139,630	53,037	142,285		1,374	14,205	42,681	29,460	141,340	
1911	666,661	73,832	12,933	178,267	126,238	47,413	127,892		1,211	13,611	37,975	25,967	129,724	
1910	611,000	54,051	11,642	164,245	114,896	45,004	114,618		1,368	11,557	39,438	25,161	121,310	
1909	557,417	38,980	10,480	148,951	103,502	40,095	101,547		964	10,222	38,146	23,911	104,956	
1908	528,717	17,819	9,831	137,363	93,964	35,800	93,377		781	10,874	33,894	20,719	98,533	
1907	*526,079*		*8,947*	*138,804*			*99,830*			*7,527*	*31,447*	*20,202*	*95,811*	*50,576*
1907	502,988	12,246	8,611	127,859	88,682	34,411	87,395		721		30,676	18,152	100,789	
1906	450,061		7,469	111,080	77,243	30,192	77,967		685		25,582	16,990	104,646	
1905	368,065		5,780	96,923	67,620	26,412	66,189		577	5,836	25,474	15,818	89,661	
1904	316,521		4,671	85,296	59,841	22,638	58,152		577		22,487	15,436	67,756	
1903	284,568		3,959	75,089	52,710	19,879	50,946		553		20,321	14,096	61,476	
1902			*3,388*							*1,745*		*13,714*	*56,405*	*28,875*
1902	250,013		3,282	64,176	44,845	16,906	44,338		457		16,129	10,608	55,403	
1901	211,780		2,445	54,177	37,971	14,329	35,824		373		15,464	9,884	45,990	
1900	180,700		1,962	46,086	32,414	12,098	30,632		300	2,390	13,364	7,894	37,067	
1899	145,511		1,519						198		12,095	6,647	29,818	
1898	118,124		1,159						168		10,577	6,294	22,955	
1897	104,488		951						144		9,735	6,127	19,603	
1896	95,242		806						144		8,833	5,481	16,558	
1895	87,859		675	24,059			15,488		138	656	8,053	5,067	14,699	
1894	77,731		577						117		7,708	4,662	12,553	
1893	73,136		508						105		8,630	4,967	11,862	
1892	67,636		441						84		8,114	4,631	11,602	
1891	62,190		382						83		6,741	4,398	9,713	
1890			*240*	*16,405*			*11,144*					*3,168*	*8,645*	
1890	58,512		332	16,153			9,068		59	279	6,866	4,101	8,740	
1889	51,572		280						60		6,202	3,802	7,550	
1888	44,436		244						75		5,747	3,658	7,445	
1887	40,799		203						42		5,506	3,444	6,683	
1886	38,325		172						32		5,160	3,246	6,162	
1885	38,619		156	10,002			5,124		32	28	4,882	3,107	5,766	
1884			137										5,769	
1883			115											
1882			83						8					
1881			52											
1880	*15,702*		*34*	*3,098*			*2,374*					*303*	*3,338*	
1880			30											

[1] Includes miscellaneous revenues not shown elsewhere.
[2] Excludes Federal income taxes.
[3] Beginning 1915, includes miscellaneous sources of income, less miscellaneous deductions.
[4] Excludes intercompany payments.
[5] Represents net loss.

Series R 28–42. Independent Telephone Companies—Property, Revenues, Expenses, Interest, Net Income, Dividends, Employees, and Wages: 1916 to 1956

[In thousands, except series R 28 and R 41.   Census figures in italics and represent "systems and lines" (see text)]

Year	Companies included	Telephone plant Book value	Telephone plant Depreciation reserves	Miles of wire	Operating revenues Total [1]	Local	Toll	Operating expenses [2]	Federal income taxes	Miscellaneous income items (net)	Interest expenses	Net income	Dividends declared	Employees Number	Employees Wages and salaries
	28	29	30	31	32	33	34	35	36	37	38	39	40	41	42
1956	437	$1,926,743	$364,616	17,478	$570,929	$370,587	$178,728	$402,318	$67,472	$2,035	$25,749	$76,686	$51,584	78,000	$261,218
1955	406	1,655,903	326,327	15,201	503,153	329,355	155,431	354,386	61,129	1,608	21,669	66,846	42,840	72,000	224,122
1954	392	1,444,320	293,008	13,587	449,464	295,965	137,820	327,318	48,841	1,767	19,271	55,136	37,209	70,000	214,073
1953	372	1,279,632	264,581	13,037	407,738	268,435	125,962	297,702	44,201	1,099	17,326	49,112	35,063	70,000	197,693
1952	372	1,124,094	239,885	11,337	347,307	226,436	109,943	265,597	31,140	984	15,038	36,368	24,598	68,000	163,349
1951	369	981,071	216,863	10,277	303,060	195,352	98,343	234,478	26,366	917	13,244	29,202	---	65,000	156,007
1950	379	878,167	203,265	9,176	270,347	170,536	91,512	211,493	18,762	1,217	11,974	28,765	---	63,000	147,317
1949	305	791,486	186,789	---	233,064	145,007	80,829	199,288	---	---	---	---	---	60,000	134,033
1948	291	667,762	174,735	7,128	203,578	124,219	72,898	161,499	12,843	874	8,015	21,621	4,877	54,000	112,565
1947	281	574,100	162,380	6,566	176,358	107,235	63,784	140,500	11,213	124	5,176	17,939	11,117	50,000	93,900
1946	265	498,567	151,959	6,609	154,757	93,857	56,754	117,195	12,522	1,188	5,067	18,781	11,108	44,000	73,211
1945	227	449,739	138,333	5,637	135,494	84,155	48,019	94,889	19,697	382	5,285	14,414	4,466	36,000	54,478
1944	229	438,962	126,970	5,521	126,081	80,752	42,519	86,482	18,704	327	5,289	14,329	4,538	31,409	46,177
1943	231	432,734	114,347	5,573	117,011	77,015	37,488	78,602	17,862	837	5,143	14,106	5,880	30,309	41,386
1942	210	412,440	98,980	5,829	97,071	68,786	25,801	66,459	11,875	283	5,323	12,725	6,695	32,196	40,473
1941	210	400,836	92,055	---	88,519	64,276	21,878	68,712	---	173	5,346	13,705	---	---	---
1940	210	383,315	85,453	---	80,846	59,993	18,676	61,478	---	181	5,541	11,768	---	---	---
1939	201	369,809	81,047	---	75,768	56,539	17,172	55,992	---	338	5,809	12,444	---	---	---
1938	201	357,472	76,290	---	71,508	53,678	15,923	53,366	---	338	5,823	10,573	---	---	---
1937	200	351,350	73,127	---	69,957	51,956	16,145	51,634	---	338	5,771	10,823	---	---	---
1937	*50,534*	*612,254*	---	*9,253*	*128,649*	---	---	*29,258*	---	---	---	---	---	*57,461*	*52,998*
1936	201	346,061	70,889	---	65,500	49,041	14,803	47,481	---	346	6,148	10,259	---	---	---
1935	202	341,949	67,001	---	61,170	46,273	13,029	43,974	---	396	6,347	8,830	---	---	---
1934	211	374,654	71,263	4,803	63,934	---	---	48,466	1,283	---	---	6,229	6,977	27,048	25,010
1933	261	429,087	74,832	5,027	68,533	---	---	51,940	1,073	---	---	6,727	8,179	28,836	23,861
1932	271	428,189	67,967	5,141	77,067	---	---	55,725	1,147	---	---	9,616	11,786	29,462	---
1932	*55,353*	*522,634*	---	*7,092*	*105,176*	*70,351*	*17,900*	---	---	---	---	---	---	*52,735*	*43,775*
1931	287	431,749	64,909	5,154	87,867	---	---	61,538	1,293	---	---	15,355	12,437	33,660	---
1930	314	418,456	59,758	4,880	90,884	---	---	63,860	1,454	---	---	16,628	12,940	35,715	---
1929	323	410,294	60,701	5,023	90,926	---	---	63,549	1,661	---	---	17,612	12,075	35,434	---
1928	316	376,955	56,284	4,756	83,866	---	---	59,446	1,740	---	---	14,966	10,834	35,310	---
1927	312	334,944	51,725	4,476	76,411	---	---	55,550	1,878	---	---	12,555	10,288	31,505	---
1927	*60,123*	*463,262*	---	*7,017*	*128,874*	*76,955*	*23,451*	---	---	---	---	---	---	*66,407*	*56,720*
1926	293	327,450	50,623	4,728	78,240	---	---	57,376	1,661	---	---	12,476	9,988	33,848	---
1925	268	289,157	49,051	4,045	73,122	---	---	54,339	---	---	---	11,714	8,809	---	---
1924	274	271,607	43,508	4,169	69,236	---	---	52,163	---	---	---	9,936	7,361	---	---
1923	268	270,076	48,686	3,770	67,486	---	---	51,078	---	---	---	9,231	6,816	---	---
1922	1,134	339,963	---	4,837	85,130	---	---	67,945	---	---	---	11,036	8,726	---	---
1922	*57,227*	*422,104*	*64,302*	*6,652*	*119,854*	*72,348*	*16,972*	*66,812*	---	---	---	*10,041*	*5,730*	*69,305*	*53,576*
1921	1,083	339,733	---	4,565	79,704	---	---	66,781	---	---	---	7,809	6,284	---	---
1920	1,034	349,795	---	4,735	80,561	---	---	67,548	---	---	---	7,559	8,204	---	---
1919	---	---	---	---	---	---	---	---	---	---	---	---	---	---	---
1918	---	---	---	---	---	---	---	---	---	---	---	---	---	---	---
1917	702	245,787	---	3,890	50,485	40,967	9,152	37,260	---	---	---	8,507	7,397	37,381	---
1917	*53,089*	*351,689*	*27,515*	*5,693*	*79,582*	*48,579*	*10,436*	*46,411*	---	*310*	*5,603*	*8,264*	*5,246*	*63,929*	*30,755*
1916	694	258,417	---	3,871	48,591	---	---	34,521	---	---	---	9,268	6,843	38,952	---

[1] Includes miscellaneous revenues not shown elsewhere.   [2] Excludes Federal income taxes.

Series R 43–52. Western Union Telegraph Company—Summary of Facilities, Traffic, and Finances: 1866 to 1915

[In thousands, except series R 43.   Census figures in italics.   Covers landline (domestic) and cable (international) operations]

As of, or for, year ending—	Telegraph offices	Miles of wire	Messages handled	Total book capitalization	Revenues	Expenses [1]	Miscellaneous income items (net)	Interest expenses	Net income	Dividends declared
	43	44	45	46	47	48	49	50	51	52
1915, Dec. 31	25,142	1,584	---	$167,338	$51,100	$40,797	$1,213	$1,348	$10,168	$4,986
1914, Dec. 31	25,784	1,582	---	162,678	45,880	40,138	972	1,343	5,371	3,989
1913, Dec. 31	25,060	1,561	---	158,855	45,784	42,327	1,116	1,338	3,235	2,992
1913, June 30	26,300	1,543	---	158,692	43,978	40,432	927	1,338	3,135	2,991
1912, Dec. 31	*30,864*	*1,814*	*109,378*	*226,387*	*62,822*	*55,610*	*1,941*	*2,769*	*6,384*	*6,180*
1912, June 30	25,392	1,517	---	159,394	39,438	34,846	1,107	1,697	4,002	2,991
1911, June 30	24,926	1,487	---	166,762	33,598	27,825	1,424	1,826	5,371	2,990
1910, June 30	24,825	1,429	75,135	164,382	30,741	24,544	1,133	1,951	5,379	2,987
1909, June 30	24,321	1,383	68,053	159,246	27,600	21,364	1,333	1,956	5,614	2,739
1908, June 30	23,853	1,359	62,371	156,371	25,890	23,553	1,063	1,731	1,670	1,715
1907, Dec. 31	*29,110*	*1,578*	*103,794*	*220,294*	*49,685*	*39,227*	*1,899*	*2,653*	*9,704*	*7,477*
1907, June 30	24,760	1,321	74,805	153,585	29,939	24,674	1,058	1,420	4,903	4,867
1906, June 30	24,323	1,256	71,487	146,349	27,828	21,838	1,093	1,335	5,749	4,867
1905, June 30	23,814	1,185	67,477	145,993	26,347	20,227	1,066	1,227	5,959	4,867
1904, June 30	23,458	1,155	67,904	141,271	26,571	19,783	1,116	1,175	6,729	4,867
1903, June 30	23,120	1,089	69,791	138,409	26,525	19,262	2,353	1,166	8,450	4,867
1902, Dec. 31	*27,377*	*1,318*	*91,655*	*162,947*	*39,486*	*28,999*	*1,444*	*1,950*	*9,982*	*6,257*
1902, June 30	23,567	1,030	69,375	133,150	25,602	18,941	670	1,008	6,323	4,867
1901, June 30	23,238	973	65,657	129,715	23,865	17,979	1,773	956	6,703	4,867
1900, June 30	22,900	933	63,168	128,856	22,811	16,934	405	991	5,292	4,867
1899, June 30	22,285	905	61,398	123,818	22,048	16,463	422	1,027	4,980	4,866
1898, June 30	22,210	874	62,174	123,718	21,683	16,231	671	992	5,130	4,866
1897, June 30	21,769	841	58,152	123,484	20,630	15,515	629	896	4,849	4,791
1896, June 30	21,725	827	58,760	121,436	20,820	15,406	474	909	4,980	4,766

[1] Including facility rentals and taxes.

Series R 43–52.　Western Union Telegraph Company—Summary of Facilities, Traffic, and Finances: 1866 to 1915—Con.

[In thousands, except series R 43.　Census figures in italics]

As of, or for, year ending—	Telegraph offices	Miles of wire	Messages handled	Total book capitalization	Revenues	Expenses [1]	Miscellaneous income items (net)	Interest expenses	Net income	Dividends declared
	43	44	45	46	47	48	49	50	51	52
1895, June 30	21,360	803	58,307	$121,278	$20,421	$14,756	$477	$898	$5,244	$4,766
1894, June 30	21,166	791	58,632	120,285	20,059	14,763	513	904	4,906	4,739
1893, June 30	21,078	769	66,592	120,364	22,983	16,057	575	899	6,602	4,632
1892, June 30	20,700	739	62,387	118,423	21,769	14,926	599	932	6,511	4,308
1891, June 30	20,098	716	59,148	116,255	21,135	15,012	499	903	5,719	4,308
1890, June 30	19,382	679	55,879	115,273	20,055	13,701	637	898	6,093	4,955
1889, June 30	18,470	648	54,108	108,430	19,075	13,328	725	820	5,651	4,308
1888, June 30	17,241	616	51,464	101,968	17,584	13,493	535	494	4,132	4,041
1887, June 30	15,658	525	47,395	96,481	15,683	12,021	504	608	3,557	812
1886, June 30	15,142	490	43,290	93,794	14,871	11,384	511	580	3,418	3,400
1885, June 30	14,184	462	42,097	92,616	15,298	11,029	509	505	4,274	5,198
1884, June 30	13,761	451	42,076	92,459	16,693	12,012	565	503	4,744	5,597
1883, June 30	12,917	433	41,181	90,961	16,596	10,490	459	433	6,132	4,999
1882, June 30	12,068	374	38,842	88,971	14,819	9,035	579	430	5,933	4,798
1881, June 30	10,737	327	32,500	87,123	11,552	7,630	2,228	437	5,713	3,733
1880, June 30	9,077	234	29,216	64,080	10,581	5,863	437	435	4,720	3,280
1880, June 1	*12,510*	*291*	*31,703*	*96,041*	*16,697*	*10,218*	----------	*564*	*5,970*	*4,137*
1879, June 30	8,534	212	25,070	62,699	9,118	5,239	395	438	3,836	2,295
1878, June 30	8,014	206	23,919	58,287	8,637	5,656	179	462	2,698	2,085
1877, June 30	7,500	194	21,159	56,318	9,039	6,096	194	443	2,694	1,521
1876, June 30	7,072	184	18,730	55,844	9,143	6,061	314	535	2,862	2,532
1875, June 30	6,565	179	17,154	54,673	[2] 4,330	[2] 2,832	[2] 33	[2] 228	[2] 1,304	1,351
1874, Dec. 31 [3]	6,188	176	16,329	54,773	8,872	5,935	148	333	2,752	151
1873, Dec. 31 [3]	5,740	154	14,457	53,331	8,612	6,506	155	266	1,995	269
1872, Dec. 31 [3]	5,237	137	12,444	----------	8,471	5,558	97	370	2,640	259
1871, Dec. 31 [3]	4,606	121	10,646	----------	7,384	4,916	74	318	2,224	222
1870, Dec. 31 [3]	3,972	112	9,158	----------	6,731	4,539	116	327	1,982	1,035
1869, Dec. 31 [3]	3,607	105	7,935	48,402	6,672	4,346	225	325	2,226	1,810
1868, Dec. 31 [3]	3,219	98	6,405	47,677	6,636	3,873	139	346	2,557	832
1867, Dec. 31 [3]	2,565	85	5,879	47,426	5,964	3,693	182	371	2,082	1,608
1866, Dec. 31 [3]	2,250	76	----------	24,205	4,619	2,686	185	162	1,956	1,051

[1] Including facility rentals and taxes.
[2] Income data are for 6 months ending June 30.
[3] Telegraph offices, miles of wire, messages handled, and total book capitalization are as of June 30.

Series R 53–67.　Domestic Telegraph Industry—Messages, Property, Revenues, Expenses, Net Income, Dividends, Employees, and Wages: 1916 to 1957

[In thousands, except series R 64 and R 66.　Census figures in italics]

Year	Messages handled	Private-line telegraph service revenues: Telegraph companies	Telephone companies	Telegraph plant: Book value	Depreciation reserves	Miles of wire	Operating revenues	Operating expenses [1]	Federal income taxes	Net income	Dividends declared	Employees: Number	Wages and salaries	Bell Teletypewriter Exchange (TWX) Service: Number of teletypewriters	Revenues
	53	54	55	56	57	58	59	60	61	62	63	64	65	66	67
1957	143,947	----------	----------	----------	$147,334	1,078	$245,549	$228,219	----------	----------	$7,165	36,467	$159,157	----------	----------
1956	151,600	$29,859	$66,074	$332,726	141,490	1,088	238,362	219,231	$6,665	$12,060	6,226	37,754	153,624	41,628	$44,872
1955	153,910	24,458	55,309	310,968	135,826	1,100	228,816	206,024	9,613	10,331	5,695	37,785	143,289	38,946	41,758
1954	152,582	20,163	48,732	300,126	130,183	1,129	209,635	194,657	6,208	4,480	3,730	37,009	137,521	36,672	38,349
1953	162,188	17,458	44,619	289,448	128,776	1,151	208,578	193,863	5,743	13,242	3,690	38,957	139,489	35,272	33,174
1952	151,712	15,031	40,828	286,372	126,580	1,194	184,336	183,395	199	[2] 724	3,689	39,853	126,974	33,338	26,503
1951	180,151	12,669	36,265	284,293	123,825	1,225	192,089	182,023	4,007	4,711	3,381	40,319	127,818	30,815	23,344
1950	178,904	9,139	31,747	294,451	128,227	1,298	177,994	167,280	2,050	7,353	2,459	40,482	116,937	28,393	20,445
1949	175,323	7,528	28,017	306,316	133,979	1,438	171,393	173,505	----------	[2] 3,468	----------	41,660	125,871	25,526	17,940
1948	191,013	5,696	25,225	310,295	136,267	1,632	183,429	185,362	----------	1,265	1,228	48,967	140,901	23,423	16,302
1947	213,780	4,320	21,829	314,275	142,664	1,743	199,654	185,314	2,176	906	----------	53,572	138,976	20,208	13,743
1946	212,072	3,681	20,732	361,618	161,826	2,044	175,536	183,366	----------	[2] 10,030	----------	57,644	137,293	14,838	12,946
1945	236,169	3,572	23,627	357,784	157,243	2,247	182,048	174,848	----------	[2] 7,834	2,433	63,446	126,662	13,031	16,798
1944	225,462	3,655	20,727	358,882	152,795	2,272	173,207	160,169	2,267	5,117	2,167	61,481	112,553	15,979	20,613
1943	231,692	3,688	17,590	366,347	153,730	2,303	166,963	159,020	3,236	[2] 746	2,090	61,037	111,872	16,013	23,456
1942	223,148	3,889	19,318	384,352	120,863	2,294	145,789	134,031	4,448	3,836	2,090	64,674	92,450	16,607	16,233
1941	210,928	3,079	14,830	380,501	114,174	2,281	130,519	121,841	1,450	4,016	2,090	65,363	84,267	16,130	10,169
1940	191,645	2,170	14,621	375,021	97,746	2,269	114,587	110,856	----------	372	1,045	59,670	74,736	14,855	8,436
1939	189,055	2,185	15,744	388,837	87,569	2,277	109,899	106,995	----------	[2] 3,152	----------	57,513	71,287	14,266	7,782
1938	185,639	2,056	16,834	387,897	83,827	2,279	106,813	105,996	----------	[2] 5,248	----------	57,190	70,124	----------	6,803
1937	200,711	1,981	19,098	387,749	80,678	2,275	117,228	111,614	----------	[2] 523	----------	64,084	77,745	12,499	6,775
1937	*206,987*	----------	----------	*418,231*		*[3] 2,302*	*117,032*	----------	----------	----------	*1,604*	*64,254*	*77,928*	----------	----------
1936	193,566	1,897	18,538	384,946	42,398	2,270	115,772	103,991	116	5,129	784	67,862	71,155	10,646	5,722
1935	176,250	1,782	17,007	383,216	42,254	2,245	106,262	96,076	----------	3,213	2,090	62,257	65,030	7,894	3,864
1934	155,215	1,749	19,131	383,165	42,940	2,247	102,557	96,069	----------	[2] 387	----------	62,839	65,810	5,776	2,300
1933	143,553	1,856	20,023	383,886	43,947	2,245	96,613	90,669	----------	330	----------	58,368	60,401	3,578	995
1932	143,075	1,830	21,284	383,960	44,191	2,239	97,902	96,339	----------	[2] 5,099	1,045	60,997	65,760	2,524	514
1932	*147,941*	----------	----------	*415,694*		*[3] 2,260*	*97,729*	----------	----------	----------		*60,933*	*66,988*	----------	----------
1931	183,373	1,787	25,245	382,737	46,222	2,250	126,697	120,166	----------	537	7,838	72,916	90,084	1,479	7

See footnotes at end of table.

Series R 53–67. Domestic Telegraph Industry—Messages, Property, Revenues, Expenses, Net Income, Dividends, Employees, and Wages: 1916 to 1957—Con.

[In thousands, except series R 64 and R 66. Census figures in italics]

Year	Messages handled	Private-line telegraph service revenues — Telegraph companies	Private-line telegraph service revenues — Telephone companies	Telegraph plant — Book value	Telegraph plant — Depreciation reserves	Miles of wire	Operating revenues	Operating expenses ¹	Federal income taxes	Net income	Dividends declared	Employees — Number	Employees — Wages and salaries
	53	54	55	56	57	58	59	60	61	62	63	64	65
1930	211,971	$1,881	$27,034	$379,869	$53,095	2,269	$148,223	$139,141	$486	$3,942	$8,188	84,962	$108,557
1929	234,050	1,947	25,197	357,343	53,710	2,251	163,358	146,867	1,307	12,796	8,188	87,435	113,928
1928	211,559	1,754	21,057	307,113	50,791	2,202	153,329	135,081	1,798	13,889	8,085	77,644	94,415
1927	203,365	1,853	18,016	292,817	46,991	2,095	147,845	128,940	2,126	14,105	7,981	76,183	91,493
1927	*215,595*			*338,143*		*³2,138*	*159,682*	*142,213*		*16,090*	*8,191*	*74,903*	*89,984*
1926	203,035	1,899	16,548	281,503	43,432	1,977	149,721	131,473	2,070	13,841	7,981	79,755	101,003
1925	185,187	1,601	15,153	266,571	40,675	1,944	141,680	122,613		15,153	7,232	73,262	90,911
1924	162,700	1,510	13,207	252,678	38,146	1,884	125,490	111,853	2,062	12,152	6,983	68,561	80,692
1923	158,468	1,502	13,106	238,923	35,326	1,836	124,172	109,197		13,094	6,983	69,045	79,341
1922	149,219	1,689	12,145	230,644	32,100	1,807	116,659	100,352		14,311	6,983	62,576	70,497
1922	*181,519*			*254,030*		*1,845*	*128,639*	*111,724*		*15,675*	*7,143*	*62,299*	*68,737*
1921	139,544	1,873	11,270	224,876	23,293	1,787	111,707	101,817		7,932	6,983	64,395	71,942
1920	155,884	1,489	10,541	214,986	19,289	1,711	124,379	113,253		9,199	6,983	74,448	86,037
1919	139,435	1,318	7,969	203,010	16,967	1,686	105,409	93,165		9,595	6,983	65,181	66,351
1918	134,031	1,121	5,811	190,712	12,965	1,620	90,369	80,511		8,103	6,983	69,528	58,376
1917	129,273	1,300	5,202	184,351	10,792	1,863	81,623	67,084		12,336	6,983	60,122	46,953
1917	*151,725*			*183,488*		*1,889*	*91,313*	*79,409*		*12,125*	*7,166*	*60,376*	*40,512*
1916		1,365	4,162			1,877	66,471	54,335		11,764	5,985		

¹ Excludes Federal income taxes.
² Figures represent net loss.
³ Excludes wire owned and operated wholly by Class I railroads and of landwire of ocean-cable companies.

Series R 68–71. Domestic Telegraph Message Rates and Teletypewriter Exchange Service (TWX) Rates Between New York City and Selected Cities: 1850 to 1956

Year	Between New York City and— Philadelphia	Chicago	Denver	San Francisco	Year	Between New York City and— Philadelphia	Chicago	Denver	San Francisco
	68	69	70	71		68	69	70	71
TELEGRAPH RATES ¹					**TELEGRAPH RATES ¹—Con.**				
Made effective:					In effect in—Con.				
1956, Aug. 26	$0.95	$1.30	$1.75	$1.75	1877	(²)	$0.50	$2.00	$2.00
1954, July 15	.85	1.25	1.70	1.70	1875	(²)	.25	(²)	(²)
1952, July 6	.65	1.10	1.55	1.70	1873	$0.30	1.00	2.50	2.50
1951, Sept. 1	.60	1.00	1.45	1.60	1870	.25	1.00	(²)	5.00
1950, Feb. 1	.40	.75	1.25	1.45	1869	.45	2.05	(²)	7.45
1946, Dec. 29	.36	.72	1.08	1.44	1866	.25	1.85	7.00	7.45
1946, June 12	.33	.66	.99	1.32	1850	.25	1.55		
1919, Apr. 1	.30	.60	.90	1.20	**TELETYPEWRITER EXCHANGE SERVICE RATES ³**				
In effect in—					Made effective:				
1908	.25	.50	.75	1.00	1953, July 1	.45	1.20	1.65	1.75
1890	.20	.40	.75	1.00	1946, Feb. 1	.35	1.05	1.55	1.75
1888	.25	.50	.75	1.00	1931, Nov. 21 ⁴	.35	1.10	1.80	2.40
1884	(²)	.50	(²)	1.00					
1883	.15	.50	1.25	1.50					
1877	(²)	.60	(²)	(²)					

¹ Beginning Sept. 1, 1951, minimum charge for 15 text words or less; prior to that, for 10 text words or less.
² Not available.
³ For 3 minutes or less, 2-way.
⁴ Beginning of service.

Series R 72–85. International Telegraph Industry—Messages, Property, Ocean-Cable Mileage, Countries Served by Radiotelegraph, Revenues, Expenses, Net Income, Employees, and Wages: 1907 to 1957

[In thousands, except series R 79 and R 84. Census figures in italics]

Year	Telegraph messages — Total	Telegraph messages — Cable	Telegraph messages — Radio	Overseas telephone calls	Telegraph plant — Book value	Telegraph plant — Depreciation reserves	Nautical miles of ocean-telegraph cable	Overseas countries served by direct radio-telegraph circuits	Operating revenues	Operating expenses ¹	Federal income taxes	Net income	Employees — Number	Employees — Wages and salaries
	72	73	74	75	76	77	78	79	80	81	82	83	84	85
1957	27,838	10,647	17,191		$149,439	$80,069	76		$76,845	$66,258			11,502	$41,994
1956	27,348	11,012	16,336	1,817	139,818	77,629	76	85	73,472	60,862	$5,783	$6,186	11,306	41,288
1955	25,642	10,671	14,971	1,553	135,178	76,432	76	85	68,050	58,366	6,328	5,020	11,844	40,548
1954	24,357	10,619	13,738	1,363	133,667	75,987	78	85	63,811	54,654	4,854	5,333	11,814	39,241
1953	23,725	10,085	13,640	1,279	131,168	75,348	78	85	59,727	53,217	4,308	3,390	11,686	37,507
1952	23,880	9,756	14,124	1,216	127,101	72,923	78	85	57,606	51,557	4,308	4,393	11,540	36,055
1951	24,043	10,059	13,984	1,130	127,310	73,929	78	85	56,949	49,087	2,434	4,526	11,081	33,120
1950	22,578	9,969	12,609	896	136,168	82,840	88	83	50,333	45,226	1,304	4,538	10,759	30,240
1949	20,891	10,390	10,501	764	134,332	82,897	88	83	46,595	45,959	525	619	11,150	31,269
1948	22,136	11,022	11,114	717	135,626	82,087	90	81	46,348	47,435	519	²778	11,644	31,717
1947	23,960	11,835	12,125	605	132,534	79,426	91	76	45,579	49,358	263	²2,715	12,404	33,678
1946	22,272	11,069	11,203	590	129,147	76,769	91	75	45,199	44,999	230	836	11,557	30,497

See footnotes at end of table.

Series R 72–85. International Telegraph Industry—Messages, Property, Ocean-Cable Mileage, Countries Served by Radiotelegraph, Revenues, Expenses, Net Income, Employees, and Wages: 1907 to 1957—Con.

[In thousands, except series R 79 and R 84.   Census figures in italics]

Year	Total (72)	Cable (73)	Radio (74)	Overseas telephone calls (75)	Book value (76)	Depreciation reserves (77)	Nautical miles of ocean-telegraph cable (78)	Overseas countries served by direct radio-telegraph circuits (79)	Operating revenues (80)	Operating expenses[1] (81)	Federal income taxes (82)	Net income (83)	Number (84)	Wages and salaries (85)
1945	21,047	10,531	10,516	326	$137,623	$86,197	91	72	$49,879	$37,905	$7,190	$7,907	9,579	$25,153
1944	17,266	10,386	6,880	166	136,329	84,550	91	69	46,981	34,340	6,983	7,454	7,898	20,002
1943	15,991	10,159	5,832	152	138,436	83,909	95	68	40,254	29,450	6,424	6,508	7,591	16,533
1942	13,020	8,012	5,008	134	139,360	83,807	95	65	35,812	28,423	4,600	4,525	7,232	14,553
1941	16,511	7,434	9,077	114	141,292	82,723	95	61	36,022	28,425	3,201	3,814	8,206	13,723
1940	16,619	7,667	8,952	72	142,015	81,240	95	60	32,087	27,035	1,359	3,598	8,083	12,809
1939	18,725	9,300	9,425	75	146,236	81,860	95	53	30,612	26,518	524	2,074	8,176	12,663
1938	18,306	9,612	8,694	74	147,747	81,263	95	53	26,895	25,577	219	[2]27	8,229	12,383
1937	*16,331*	*11,129*	*5,202*	----	*88,533*	----	*104*	----	*28,275*	----	----	----	*5,403*	*7,408*
1937	19,768	10,376	9,392	75	148,082	79,517	95	52	29,648	25,511	530	2,936	8,428	12,302
1936	17,641	9,819	7,822	48	147,723	78,082	95	52	27,173	24,042	306	2,004	8,182	11,538
1935	15,669	9,050	6,619	28	147,708	76,613	95	50	25,360	23,693	186	693	8,134	11,033
1934	14,464	9,287	5,177	26	147,662	75,473	97	49	25,449	23,177	259	1,395	7,851	10,754
1933	15,365	10,456	4,909	30	146,602	74,528	97	48	24,649	21,532	227	3,467	7,337	9,615
1932	*10,437*	*10,437*	----	----	*90,751*	----	*96*	----	*16,927*	----	----	----	*5,790*	*6,961*
1932	14,940	10,443	4,497	28	145,913	73,066	98	46	23,442	21,707	169	2,368	7,553	10,009
1931	17,414	12,551	4,863	33	148,847	62,050	98	43	28,584	23,919	201	5,610	8,114	11,178
1930	20,409	15,258	5,151	33	147,236	64,994	98	42	35,360	27,010	366	9,775	8,999	13,604
1929	21,565	16,473	5,092	30	135,797	72,671	97	34	39,656	27,559	798	13,705	8,579	13,129
1928	17,562	14,812	2,750	23	126,770	69,124	93	30	34,264	21,643	----	11,868	2,299	3,392
1927	*17,765*	*13,987*	*3,778*	----	*88,556*	----	*99*	----	*20,137*	*11,549*	----	*7,755*	*6,595*	*9,536*
1927	16,093	13,793	2,300	12	122,635	67,668	91	26	32,083	21,340	----	9,814	2,332	3,395
1926	15,493	13,298	2,195	9	116,179	60,904	88	20	32,672	22,293	----	11,159	2,309	3,469
1925	7,580	5,520	2,060	10	110,106	59,370	83	16	34,811	22,726	----	11,526	2,352	3,659
1924	7,088	5,198	1,890	12	107,357	54,834	83	14	33,636	21,360	----	10,962	2,340	3,463
1923	6,165	4,465	1,700	11	101,011	52,011	79	12	32,173	21,725	----	9,768	2,349	3,459
1922	*11,968*	*9,603*	*2,365*	----	*72,632*	----	*77*	----	*21,319*	*12,450*	----	*8,193*	*6,333*	*7,425*
1922	5,437	3,992	1,445	10	92,073	49,142	73	10	34,191	22,539	----	11,058	2,603	3,902
1921	4,947	3,987	960	6	90,139	46,467	76	9	35,976	22,570	----	10,399	3,111	4,283
1920	4,387	4,037	350	----	83,799	42,059	75	8	40,507	24,287	----	11,463	3,062	4,882
1919	----	581	----	----	74,090	37,145	69	4	22,584	12,267	----	5,357	2,688	3,938
1918	----	418	----	----	64,058	31,481	69	4	17,299	10,425	----	2,965	----	----
1917	*6,573*	*6,451*	*122*	----	*59,871*	----	*71*	----	*16,749*	*9,281*	----	*5,707*	*4,347*	*3,252*
1917	----	485	----	----	63,116	26,763	69	4	15,274	7,838	----	3,434	----	----
1916	----	378	----	----	63,256	21,349	68	4	10,878	4,706	----	3,318	----	----
1912	*6,121*	*5,841*	*280*	----	*58,136*	*7,600*	*68*	*1*	*8,469*	*4,008*	----	*2,953*	*[3]1,656*	*1,167*
1907	*6,024*	*5,869*	*155*	----	*57,438*	----	*46*	----	*7,672*	*2,205*	----	*4,029*	*1,207*	*915*

[1] Excludes Federal income taxes.
[2] Figures represent net loss.
[3] As of September 16.

Series R 86–89. International Cable and Radiotelegraph Rates and International Telephone Rates Between New York City and Selected Cities: 1866 to 1956

[Prior to 1924, rate changes are for messages by cable only (except as noted for radiotelegraph messages). Since 1924, rate changes are for both cable and radiotelegraph messages]

Effective date	London (86)	Cairo (87)	Tokyo (88)	Buenos Aires (89)
INTERNATIONAL CABLE AND RADIOTELEGRAPH RATES [1]				
1950, July 1, to 1956	$0.19	$0.30	$0.30	$0.27
1949, Feb. 2	.25	.40	.40	.35
1948, Apr. 28	.25	.30	.30	.28
1947, Aug. 5	.25	.30	.30	.22
1946, May 1	.20	.30	.20	.20
1945, May 1	.20	.42	.24	.20
1943, Aug. 16	.20	.42	.72	.26
1940	.20	.42	.72	.42
1937	.20	.42	.72	.42
1931	.20	.39	.80	.42
1928	.20	.39	.80	.42
1927	.20	.45	.80	.42
1925	.20	.42	.85	.42
1924	.20	(2)	1.09	.50
1924	.20	(2)	.85	.50
1923 [3]	.20	(2)	1.09	.50
1921 [3]	.18	(2)	.85	.50
1919	.25	(2)	1.09	.50
1917	.25	(2)	1.33	.50
1916 [3]	.17	(2)	.92	.65
1912	.25	(2)	1.33	.65
1910	.25	(2)	1.33	.85
1905	.25	.56	1.33	1.00
1903	.25	(2)	1.53	1.00
1903	.25	.61	1.76	1.00
1901	$0.25	(2)	$1.76	$1.00
1892, May 1	.25	(2)	2.21	1.50
1892, Jan. 26	.25	(2)	2.21	1.70
1890	.25	(2)	(2)	1.82
1888	.25	(2)	(2)	3.98
1886	.12	(2)	(2)	3.98
1884	.40	(2)	(2)	3.98
1882	.50	(2)	(2)	3.98
1882	.50	(2)	(2)	4.60
1880	.50	(2)	(2)	7.50
1868	1.575	(2)	(2)	(2)
1866	10.00	(2)	(2)	(2)
INTERNATIONAL TELEPHONE RATES [4]				
1946	12.00	$12.00	12.00	12.00
1945	12.00	30.00	19.50	12.00
1944	21.00	30.00	19.50	12.00
1940	21.00	30.00	19.50	15.00
1939	21.00	30.00	30.75	15.00
1937	21.00	30.00	30.75	21.00
1936	21.00	30.00	33.00	21.00
1934	30.00	36.00	39.00	30.00
1932	30.00	36.00	----	30.00
1930	30.00	----	----	30.00
1930	30.00	----	----	36.00
1928	45.00	----	----	----
1927	75.00	----	----	----

[1] Per plain language telegraph-word, including address and signature.
[2] Not available.
[3] Change in radiotelegraph messages.
[4] For 3-minute telephone conversations.

RADIO AND TELEVISION (Series R 90–138)

R 90–138. General note.

Federal regulation of radio communication has been continuous since 1912 when the Department of Commerce was given authority to license radio equipment and radio operators, and broadcast stations, which began operation in 1921. On February 23, 1927, Congress established the Federal Radio Commission with broad authority for the regulation of radio. In 1934, the powers of the Federal Radio Commission were transferred to the Federal Communications Commission.

Principal governmental sources of statistics in respect to broadcast and nonbroadcast radio services include the following:

1. Census reports: *Census of Business, 1935: Radio Broadcasting.* Fifteenth Census Reports, *Population*, vol. VI, *Families*, 1930. Sixteenth Census Reports, *Housing*, vol. II, part 1, 1940. *U.S. Census of Housing: 1950*, vol. I, part 1.

2. *Annual Report of the Secretary of Commerce*, 1913–1926.

3. *Annual Report of the Federal Radio Commission*, 1927–1933.

4. *Annual Report of the Federal Communications Commission*, 1938–1956.

5. Federal Radio Commission, *Commercial Radio Advertising*, 1931.

6. House Report No. 1273, 73d Cong., 2d sess., *Report on Communication Companies*, 1934.

7. Federal Communications Commission reports: *Report on Chain Broadcasting*, 1941; *The Public Service Responsibilities of Broadcast Stations*, 1946; "An Economic Study of Standard Broadcasting," October 1947 (processed); House Report No. 1297, 85th Cong., 2d sess., *Network Broadcasting*, 1958.

Since 1937, the FCC has obtained annual financial reports from networks and broadcast stations. Statistical tabulations of the data so reported have been made available by the FCC in its annual reports; in its annual *Statistics of the Communications Industry in the United States*, 1939-1949; and in annual processed reports. Unlike the telephone and telegraph industries, radio broadcasting is not classified as a common carrier and is not subject to rate or earnings regulation. The FCC, therefore, does not prescribe a uniform system of accounts for the radio industry. However, the Commission's Annual Report Form No. 324, and the accompanying instructions, ensures general uniformity in the reported data. The individual financial reports of networks and stations filed with the FCC are not available for public inspection. However, some individual network and station data have been published from time to time, as for example, in a Committee Print, 84th Cong., 2d sess. (Senator John W. Bricker), *The Network Monopoly: Report Prepared for Use of the Committee on Interstate and Foreign Commerce*, 1956; *Monopoly Problems in Regulated Industries; Hearings before the Antitrust Subcommittee of the Committee on the Judiciary*, 84th Cong., 2d sess., 4 vols., part 2, 1956.

R 90–94. General note.

Statistics of broadcast stations are commonly presented in terms of "authorized" and of "licensed" stations. A broadcast station is authorized when it receives a construction permit from the FCC (or predecessor licensing agencies). Normally, a station is expected to complete construction and begin regular operation within 8 months thereafter. However, not all authorized stations complete this process and become operating

stations. This has occurred mainly in the newer broadcast services, frequency modulation (FM) and television (TV).

Similarly, statistics of "licensed" stations can be misleading. A station permittee who has completed construction in accordance with the specifications of the construction permit or a modification thereof, usually receives a regular license, prior to start of regular on-the-air program service. However, for a variety of reasons, the FCC has permitted stations to undertake regular broadcast service under a Special Temporary Authorization. Many stations have operated under such authority for a number of years. Here, again, this statement applies particularly to FM and TV stations.

Figures for these series are for the most part presented in terms of operating stations. Stations are recorded in FCC records as operating when they have received permission to conduct program tests. In some instances, considerable time may elapse before such stations are in regular, daily operation. Adjustments for this factor have been made by the FCC on the basis of trade sources, and such adjustments are incorporated here. In sum, the data on operating stations are not precise, but are believed to be reasonably accurate.

R 90. Standard broadcast (AM) stations, operating, 1921–1956.

Source: 1921, FCC, records; 1922-1926, *Annual Report of the Secretary of Commerce*, various issues; 1927-1933, *Seventh Annual Report of the Federal Radio Commission for Fiscal Year 1933*, p. 18; 1934-1956, FCC, records.

Prior to 1948, data pertain to licensed stations which, in the AM service, generally approximated operating stations.

Figures are not available annually on the number of noncommercial AM stations because there is no separate noncommercial service. Usually, such stations are supported by educational or public bodies. In the early growth of radio prior to 1927, educational institutions were prominent in radio (see S. E. Frost, *Education's Own Stations; the History of Broadcast Licenses Issued to Educational Institutions*, University of Chicago Press, 1937). Since 1945, the number of noncommercial AM stations has remained fairly constant at about 35. In addition, a small number of educational institutions operate commercial stations.

The decline in the number of AM stations between 1927 and 1929 followed the transfer of the licensing function from the Secretary of Commerce to the Federal Radio Commission. The latter body tightened the licensing requirements, resulting in the withdrawal or deletion of a number of operating stations.

R 91–92. Frequency modulation (FM) stations operating, 1941–1956.

Source: FCC, records.

FM was authorized as a regular service in 1940, effective January 1, 1941, and the first commercial station was licensed in 1941. Noncommercial FM is a separate service with a specific spectrum allocation. The stations are licensed to nonprofit educational organizations.

R 93–94. Television (TV) stations operating, 1941–1956.

Source: FCC, records.

Television was authorized on a regular commercial basis, effective July 1, 1941, and 2 stations in New York began operating as of that date. Figures include very high frequency (VHF) stations, first authorized in 1941, and ultra high frequency stations (UHF), first authorized in 1952. Some stations (almost entirely UHF stations) began operation and subsequently ceased operation, but retained their FCC authorization. Such stations are not included in the years of nonoperation.

R 95–96. Sets produced, 1922–1956.

Source: Electronic Industries Association, *Electronics Industry Fact Book*, 1957, pp. 4, 5.

Figures are based on reports of members of the Electronic Industries Association (formerly Radio-Electronic-Television Manufacturers Association) adjusted for estimated production of nonmembers. Radio set figures include home sets for all years; auto sets, 1930-1956; portable sets, 1939-1956; and clock sets, 1951-1956. Auto sets have constituted over 30 percent of total radio set production for 1949-1956. The figures also include sets produced for export. As of July 1, 1957, it was estimated by Electronic Industries Association that there were 135 million radio sets in working order in the United States, including 90 million sets in homes, 35 million in automobiles, and 10 million in public places.

R 97. Families with radio sets, 1922–1956.

Source: Annual figures, National Broadcasting Company (NBC), records. Census data, as follows: 1930, Fifteenth Census Reports, *Population*, vol. VI, *Families*, table 39; 1940, Sixteenth Census Reports, *Housing*, vol. II, part 1, table 10; 1950, *U.S. Census of Housing: 1950*, vol. I, part 1, table 13.

NBC accredits data on radio ownership prior to 1950 to the National Association of Broadcasters (NAB), which is the national trade association of broadcasters, and to Broadcast Measurement Bureau, a private survey group, which conducted a detailed nationwide survey of radio listening. A survey conducted by the Columbia Broadcasting System (CBS), the results of which were published as "Lost and Found," purported to show 2,450,000 families with radios not enumerated in the 1930 Census of Population. Accordingly, the NAB adjusted the 1930 Census figure to 14,499,000. Similarly, 964,026 occupied dwelling units did not report concerning radio ownership in the 1940 Census of Population. The NAB estimated that 786,043 of these should be added to the 1940 Census figure of 28,048,219 occupied units with radio.

The figures include radio sets which may not be in working order. Sets temporarily out of order or being repaired at the time of enumeration were included in the census data. As of January 1, 1956, a joint network Radio Advertising Association estimate showed that there were 1,800,000 households with radio sets not in working order.

The figures exclude radio sets in places of business, institutions, and hotels.

R 98. Families with television sets, 1946–1956.

Source: National Broadcasting Company, records. Census data for 1950 from *U.S. Census of Housing: 1950*, vol. I, part 1, table 13.

An indication of the accuracy of the estimates is provided by several surveys of TV ownership in the Nation's households conducted by the Bureau of the Census for the Advertising Research Foundation. These studies have yielded the following estimates:

	June 1955	March 1956	August 1956
Total sets in TV homes	33,269,000	37,277,000	39,568,000
TV homes	32,106,000	35,495,000	37,410,000
Second sets in TV homes	1,163,000	1,782,000	2,158,000
TV homes as percent of total homes	67.2	72.8	76.1

All figures exclude sets in places of business, institutions, and hotels, but include households with television sets which may not be in current working order.

R 99–102 and R 110–113. Radio and television advertising expenditures, 1935–1957.

Source: 1935-1939, *Printers' Ink Advertisers' Guide to Marketing for 1956*, 1955, p. 68; 1940-1956, same publication, *1959*, 1958, pp. 154–155; 1957, *Printers' Ink*, Feb. 6, 1959, p. 9.

Historical-time series on advertising expenditures were first developed by L. D. H. Weld of the McCann-Erickson Advertising Agency, New York, in 1938. After Dr. Weld's death in 1946, McCann-Erickson continued to prepare the estimates.

Total advertising expenditures in radio and television are total time sales of networks and stations including commissions of advertising agencies and station representatives, as reported by the FCC, multiplied by the estimated "adjustment" factors. For a description of the method used in developing the annual adjustment factors, see the source. Total advertising expenditures are larger than total broadcast revenues as reported by the FCC in two respects: The inclusion of commissions paid to advertising agencies and station representatives; and the inclusion of sums paid by advertisers for talent, program, and production to organizations which do not operate networks or broadcast stations (included in the "adjustment" figures).

The elements in the FCC radio figures merit noting. First, the financial results of approximately 12 "key" stations owned by the networks in the major centers of New York, Chicago, and Los Angeles have been included with network time sales because of difficulties in allocations between national and station operations in these cities. This has had the effect of overstating network time sales and understating national spot and local time sales to some extent. In addition, the FCC data on time sales exclude stations with annual revenues of $25,000 or less. These stations have not been required to detail their time sales. Neither of these elements is present in the FCC series on television time sales.

The networks included in radio are the four national networks—American Broadcasting Company (ABC), Columbia Broadcasting System (CBS), National Broadcasting Company (NBC), and the Mutual Broadcasting System (MBS). The three large regional networks included for most years are the Don Lee Network, the Yankee Network, and the Texas State Network. The networks included in television are ABC, CBS, NBC (each of which operates a network in both radio and television) and until September 1955, the DuMont Network. At that time DuMont withdrew from the network field.

For a detailed discussion of the network system, see the FCC and other reports listed in the general note for series R 90-138; and 84th Cong., 2d sess., Robert F. Jones, *Investigation of Television Networks and the UHF-VHF Problems; Progress Report Prepared for the Committee on Interstate and Foreign Commerce*, 1955.

R 100 and R 111, network expenditures. Figures are total expenditures of network advertisers in radio or television for time (i.e., access to the individual stations broadcasting the program); for the program, including talent and production; and for the production of the commercial announcements. Such sums include commissions to advertising agencies but exclude discounts and allowances received by the advertiser. The figures are before disbursements by the networks to their affiliated and owned stations, and exclude the nonnetwork time sales of the stations owned by the networks.

The Publisher's Information Bureau (PIB) provides a monthly series on the billings of each nationwide television network, and through 1956 of each nationwide radio network. The PIB billings differ from either total advertiser expenditures or total broadcast revenues. They are limited to expenditures for time; and they are gross figures before trade or cash discounts or payment of commissions. The PIB figures are published by trade magazines such as *Broadcasting-Telecasting* and *Television Digest*.

R 101 and **R 112**, national spot expenditures. This type of advertising is commonly confused with commercial, or "spot," announcements. The term "spot" in this context refers to the purchase of time by national advertisers on individual stations "spotted" or selected in various communities. Predominantly, the advertiser expenditures are for commercial announcements adjacent to network or other programs carried by the individual stations. In addition, national spot advertisers sponsor programs or purchase "participations" in station-supplied programs. Thus, national spot advertiser expenditures include total time sales (after discounts but including commissions to advertising agencies and station representatives) multiplied by the estimated adjustment factor for program and production.

R 102 and **R 113**, local advertising expenditures. These include total time sales (after trade discounts but including commissions to advertising agencies) multiplied by the estimated adjustment factor for program and production. Local advertiser expenditures are made both in connection with the broadcast of commercial announcements and the supply of a program service. The main distinction between national spot and local advertising is, as follows: National spot advertisers are connected with firms or companies which produce or distribute goods or services on a national or regional basis, and which usually place their advertising message on a number of selected stations. Local advertisers are usually local retailers and other organizations whose goods or services are primarily for local distribution. As such, a local advertiser will place his advertising message only on the stations in his community or marketing area. However, in practice, the "national" and "local" categories are not completely differentiated.

R 103–109 and R 114–119. Networks and stations reporting broadcast revenues, expenses, income, gross investment, and employees, 1935–1957.

Source: 1935, *Census of Business, 1935, Radio Broadcasting*, pp. 15, 25; 1937–1957, Federal Communications Commission, *Annual Report*, various issues.

The basic sources of figures shown in the Annual Report are *Statistics of the Communications Industry in the United States*, annual issues, and processed releases of the FCC. Both sources are used prior to 1949; however, only the latter is used subsequently.

FCC began the regular annual collection of financial and operating data from networks and stations in 1937. The respondents each year usually include over 90 percent of commercial stations in operation, accounting for well over 95 percent of total industry revenues, expenses, and income. Statistics based on these reports, particularly prior to 1952, have included considerable detail. These statistics have been made available to the public in the *Annual Report* of the FCC, 1938–1956; *Statistics of the Communications Industry in the United States*, 1939-1949; and in processed releases.

R 103, R 104, and **R 114**, reporting networks and stations. Prior to 1949 the radio data are limited to commercial standard broadcasting (AM) stations and networks operating in the continental United States and its Territories and possessions, including Puerto Rico. Since 1949, the radio data also include reports of joint AM-FM stations, and reports of FM-only stations. The television data include stations operating in the continental United States and its Territories and possessions.

R 105 and **R 115**, broadcasting revenues. Figures include the amounts received by networks and stations from the sale of time (net of all trade and cash discounts and commissions to advertising agencies and station representatives) and from other broadcast activities as follows: Gross amount received

for services of talent under contract to and in the pay of networks or stations; net commissions, fees, and profits for services in obtaining, or for placing with others, talent not under contract to and in the pay of respondent; amounts received for furnishing manuscripts, transcriptions, productions, or other program materials or services; and amounts received for incidental broadcast activities such as charges for studio facilities and special charges in connection with remote broadcasts, fees or other charges for conducting studio tours, and fees or profits received for the right to operate concessions.

R 106 and **R 116**, broadcasting expenses. The broad expense categories reported include technical, program, selling, and general and administrative expenses. Among the expenses required to be included are the following: Salaries and wages; talent expenses; film and transcription expense; commissions to staff salesmen; insurance; depreciation and amortization of broadcast investments; rents paid for use of broadcast property; taxes (other than Federal taxes on income); and losses on notes, accounts, and other amounts receivable.

R 107 and **R 117**, broadcasting income. Figures represent net operating revenues (before Federal income tax), excluding income derived by the networks and stations from sources and operations other than broadcasting.

R 108 and **R 118**, gross investment. Figures represent investment in tangible broadcast property, before depreciation. The FCC report form requires that the costs be reported on an original-cost basis, and not on the basis of cost readjustments resulting from the sales or transfers of stations. Tangible broadcast property includes land and buildings, if owned, and transmitter and studio property; it excludes financial assets and good will. It is, therefore, not a measure of total investment in broadcasting.

R 109 and **R 119**, employees. Figures include all employees, staff and nonstaff, full and part time, not excluding general officers and other managerial officials, but excluding "uncompensated" employees. Figures for 1935 are employees reported as of 15th of each month, summed and divided by 12; 1938, week beginning Dec. 11; 1939–1943, middle week in October; 1944–1946, as of Dec. 31; 1946–1948, middle week in October; 1955–1956, as of Dec. 31.

R 120–126. Safety and special radio stations authorized, by class, 1913–1957.

Source: 1913–1926, *Annual Report of the Secretary of Commerce*, various issues; 1927–1934, Federal Radio Commission, *Annual Report*, various issues; 1935–1957, FCC, *Annual Report*, various issues.

Prior to 1948, the only data available to measure the use of radio in various nonbroadcast safety and special radio services were the number of authorized stations. The term "station," however, has not had a uniform significance among these services or within the same service over time. Primarily, the term reflects licensing procedures. A station is a single authorization issued by the FCC (or its predecessor licensing agencies) authorizing the use of one or more transmitters on assigned frequencies. A station may include one of the following: A single fixed transmitter, or a single mobile transmitter; a single frequency; a system including a land station and one or more mobile units; two or more fixed stations; a number of low-power mobile units in one authorization and a single higher-power mobile transmitter in another. Within most of the services, station authorizations have been changed from one to another form in an effort to simplify licensing procedures. As a result, year-to-year changes in the number of stations must be interpreted with caution, particularly if a decrease is shown.

In addition to the safety and special services, radio is assuming an ever larger role in the operations of the telephone and telegraph industries. By June 30, 1956, telephone companies operated 319 land mobile radio systems for 2-way communications.

R 127-138. Authorized land stations and mobile transmitters in the safety and special radio services, 1948-1956.

Source: See source for series R 120-126.

The distinctive characteristics of a land station are that it is located at a fixed site, has a fixed antenna and a panel control, and is used for communication in the mobile services (aviation, land transportation, etc.). In land transportation radio services, a land station is often referred to as a base station. Thus, in the taxicab radio service, the base station is used to send and receive communications to and from the associated mobile transmitter-receivers located in the taxicabs. In the marine radio services, coastal stations are examples of land stations, and in the aviation radio services, aeronautical stations are the land stations.

Fixed stations are similar to land stations but are employed in the nonmobile radio services to communicate, or transmit messages, to other land points.

Mobile transmitters, as the name implies, are installed in moving vehicles. They have relatively simple antenna and switching equipment, and are used for transmitting and/or receiving information. Such transmitters usually tie in with a land station, the latter serving as a central control point for communicating with the various mobile units.

One major shortcoming of the transmitter data, however, is that they measure authorized rather than operating transmitters. This divergence is not too great in the case of the land or fixed transmitters. It is estimated that over 90 percent of the authorized transmitters are in operation. However, an entirely different situation prevails with respect to mobile transmitters. As a rough approximation, only 50 percent of the authorized mobile transmitters were estimated as in operation in 1953. Licensees, in applying for authorizations, have wide latitude in estimating the number of mobile units they expect to have in operation within the license period.

See also text for series R 120-126.

Series R 90–98. Radio and Television Stations, Sets Produced, and Families With Sets: 1921 to 1956

[Census figures in italics]

Year	Operating broadcast stations — Standard broadcast (AM)[1] (90)	Frequency modulation (FM)[2] Commercial (91)	FM Non-commercial (92)	Television (TV)[3] Commercial (93)	TV Non-commercial (94)	Sets produced — Radio (95)	Television (96)	Families with — Radio sets (97)	Television sets (98)	Year	Operating standard broadcast stations (AM)[1] (90)	Radio sets produced (95)	Families with radio sets (97)
1956	2,824	540	123	442	16	13,982	7,387	46,800	34,900	1938	689	7,142	26,667
1955	2,669	553	122	411	10	14,529	7,757	45,900	30,700	1937	646	8,083	24,500
1954	2,521	560	112	349	2	10,400	7,347	45,100	26,000	1936	616	8,249	22,869
1953	2,391	616	98	125	----	13,369	7,216	44,800	20,400				
1952	2,331	637	85	108	----	10,935	6,096	42,800	15,300	1935	585	6,030	21,456
1951	2,232	676	73	107	----	12,627	5,385	41,900	10,320	1934	583	4,479	20,400
										1933	599	4,157	19,250
1950	2,086	733	48	97	----	14,590	7,464	40,700	3,875	1932	604	2,446	18,450
1950								*40,411*	*5,030*	1931	612	3,594	16,700
1949	1,912	700	30	50	----	11,400	3,000	39,300	940				
1948	1,621	374	22	[4]17	----	16,500	975	37,623	172	1930	618	3,789	13,750
1947	1,062	140	8	7	----	20,000	179	35,900	14	*1930*			*12,049*
1946	948	48	6	6	----	15,955	6	33,998	8	1929	606	4,428	10,250
										1928	677	3,250	8,000
1945	919	46	6	6	----	(5)	----	33,100	----	1927	681	1,350	6,750
1944	910	43	6	6	----	(5)	----	32,500	----	1926	528	1,750	4,500
1943	910	12	6	4	----	(5)	----	30,800	----				
1942[5]	887	2	5	4	----	4,307	----	30,600	----	1925	571	2,000	2,750
1941	831	1	4	2	----	13,642	----	29,300	----	1924	530	1,500	1,250
										1923	556	500	400
1940	765					11,831		28,500		1922	30	100	60
1940								*28,048*		1921	[6]1	----	----
1939	722					10,763		27,500					

[1] As of Sept. 15 for 1921; Jan. 1, 1922; Mar. 1, 1923; Oct. 1, 1924; June 30, 1925–1932; Jan. 1, 1933–1956.
[2] As of May 1 for 1941; June 30, 1942; Jan. 1, 1943–1956.
[3] As of July 1, 1941; June 30, 1942–1943; Jan. 1, 1944–1956.
[4] "Freeze" on new TV authorizations Sept. 1948–July 1952; only stations authorized before Sept. 30, 1948, permitted to operate in these years.
[5] Authorization of new radio stations and production of radio receivers for commercial use halted from April 1942 until Oct. 1945.
[6] First station to receive regular license as of Sept. 15; other stations in operation experimentally.

Series R 99–119. Radio and Television Advertising Expenditures, Revenues, Expenses, Income, Investment, and Employees: 1935 to 1957

Year	Radio — Advertising expenditures Total (99)	Network (100)	National spot (101)	Local (102)	Networks reporting (103)	Stations reporting (104)	Broadcasting revenues (105)	Broadcasting expenses (106)	Broadcasting income[1] (107)	Gross investment (108)	Employees (109)
	Mil. dol.	Mil. dol.	Mil. dol.	Mil. dol.	Number	Number	Mil. dol.	Mil. dol.	Mil. dol.	Mil. dol.	1,000
1957	618.9	64.7	187.1	367.1	7	3,164	517.9	463.3	54.6	328.2	48.9
1956	567.0	60.5	161.0	345.5	7	2,967	480.6	431.4	49.2	297.5	47.6
1955	544.9	84.4	134.1	326.4	7	2,742	453.4	407.4	46.0	284.7	45.3
1954	558.7	114.4	134.9	309.4	7	2,598	449.5	407.7	41.8	278.8	(2)
1953	611.2	141.2	145.6	324.4	7	2,479	475.3	420.3	55.0	276.2	(2)
1952	624.1	161.5	141.5	321.1	7	2,380	469.7	409.6	60.1	267.4	(2)
1951	606.3	179.5	138.3	288.5	7	2,266	450.4	392.9	57.5	254.7	(2)
1950	605.4	196.3	135.8	273.3	7	2,229	444.5	376.3	68.2	244.4	(2)
1949	571.4	203.0	123.4	245.0	7	2,125	415.2	362.5	52.7	230.6	52.0
1948	561.6	210.6	121.1	229.9	7	1,824	407.0	342.9	64.1	201.8	48.3
1947	506.4	201.2	106.4	198.8	7	1,464	363.7	291.9	71.8	150.0	(2)
1946	454.4	199.6	98.2	156.6	8	1,025	322.6	246.1	76.5	107.8	40.0
1945	423.9	197.9	91.8	134.2	10	901	299.3	215.7	83.6	88.1	37.8
1944	393.5	191.8	87.4	114.3	9	875	275.3	185.0	90.3	83.0	34.3
1943	313.6	156.5	70.9	86.2	9	841	215.3	148.8	66.5	81.1	31.8
1942	260.0	128.7	58.8	72.5	10	851	178.8	134.2	44.6	81.3	29.6
1941	247.2	125.4	52.3	69.5	8	817	168.8	124.0	44.8	78.0	27.6
1940	215.6	113.3	42.1	60.2	8	765	147.1	113.8	33.3	70.9	25.7
1939	183.8	98.6	35.0	50.2	3	705	123.9	100.1	23.8	64.4	23.9
1938	167.1	89.2	34.0	43.9	3	660	111.4	92.5	18.9	61.4	22.5
1937	164.6	88.5	28.0	48.1	3	629	114.2	91.6	22.6	55.1	--------
1936	122.3	75.6	22.7	24.0	--------	--------	--------	--------	--------	--------	--------
1935	112.6	62.6	14.9	35.1	8	[3]561	86.5	--------	--------	--------	14.6

[1] Before Federal income taxes.
[2] Not available.
[3] Includes 4 experimental stations.

Series R 99–119. Radio and Television Advertising Expenditures, Revenues, Expenses, Income, Investment, and Employees: 1935 to 1957—Con.

Year	Television Advertising expenditures Total	Net-work	National spot	Local	Stations reporting [4]	Broad-casting revenues	Broad-casting expenses	Broad-casting income [1]	Gross invest-ment	Employees	Year	Television Stations reporting [4]	Broad-casting revenues
	110	111	112	113	114	115	116	117	118	119		114	115
	Mil. dol.	Mil. dol.	Mil. dol.	Mil. dol.		Mil. dol.	Mil. dol.	Mil. dol.	Mil. dol.	1,000			Mil. dol.
1957	1,265.3	670.1	351.6	243.6	501	943.2	783.2	160.0	477.6	37.8	1947	15	1.9
1956	1,206.7	625.1	329.0	252.6	474	896.9	707.3	189.6	429.7	35.7	1946	7	.7
1955	1,025.3	540.2	260.4	224.7	437	744.7	594.5	150.2	364.7	32.3	1945	6	.3
1954	809.2	422.2	206.8	180.2	410	593.0	502.7	90.3	315.0	29.4	1944	6	.2
1953	606.1	319.9	145.5	140.7	334	432.7	364.7	68.0	233.1	18.2	1943	4	.1
1952	453.9	256.4	93.8	103.7	122	324.2	268.7	55.5	124.1	14.1			
1951	332.3	180.8	69.9	81.6	108	235.7	194.1	41.6	93.0	----------			
1950	170.8	85.0	30.8	55.0	107	105.9	115.1	[5] 9.2	70.3	----------			
1949	57.8	29.4	9.2	19.2	97	34.3	59.6	[5] 25.3	55.9	----------			
1948	----------	----------	----------	----------	50	8.7	23.6	[5] 14.9	----------	----------			

[1] Before Federal income taxes.   [4] Includes 4 networks (ABC, CBS, NBC, and DuMont) until Sept., 1955; at that time, DuMont withdrew.   [5] Represents net loss.

Series R 120–126. Safety and Special Radio Stations Authorized, by Class: 1913 to 1957

[As of June 30. Includes Alaska, Hawaii, Puerto Rico, and Virgin Islands]

Year	Amateur and disaster services	Aviation services	Industrial services	Land trans-portation services	Marine services	Public safety services	Other services	Year	Amateur and disaster services	Aviation services	Industrial services	Marine services	Public safety services	Other services
	120	121	122	123	124	125	126		120	121	122	124	125	126
1957	165,908	49,699	35,711	37,523	63,844	23,270	801	1935	45,561	678	146	2,157	298	975
1956	154,337	48,745	30,597	27,554	56,915	20,718	716	1934	46,390	671	129	2,195	220	681
								1933	41,555	646	121	2,192	152	255
1955	142,387	43,855	24,854	20,002	50,714	18,415	625	1932	30,374	579	134	2,225	123	168
1954	124,324	40,154	21,598	13,945	46,299	15,697	586	1931	22,739	463	130	2,392	91	160
1953	111,579	39,315	17,378	9,751	40,357	13,631	444							
1952	113,163	32,603	13,680	6,428	35,500	11,143	369	1930	18,994	281	----------	2,173	20	----------
1951	90,587	34,061	9,551	4,813	29,544	9,129	404	1929	16,829	131	----------	----------	12	----------
								1928	16,928	----------	----------	----------	----------	----------
1950	87,967	23,794	6,099	3,830	24,921	7,607	466	1927	16,926	----------	----------	----------	----------	----------
1949	81,675	27,227	4,266	3,588	20,004	5,700	501	1926	14,902	----------	----------	1,954	----------	----------
1948	78,434	20,858	2,855	3,122	15,024	4,903	652							
1947	75,000	15,943	1,787	1,692	11,955	4,620	532	1925	15,000	----------	----------	1,901	4	----------
1946	70,000	6,205	702	156	8,676	4,760	1,374	1924	15,540	----------	----------	2,741	3	----------
								1923	16,570	----------	----------	----------	3	----------
1945	60,000	3,793	576	----------	----------	4,446	487	1922	----------	----------	----------	----------	----------	----------
1944	60,000	3,445	468	----------	6,817	4,144	572	1921	----------	----------	----------	----------	----------	----------
1943	60,000	3,553	386	----------	6,609	3,772	453							
1942	60,000	4,713	356	----------	----------	3,455	497	1920	5,719	----------	----------	----------	1	----------
1941	60,000	3,000	306	----------	5,822	2,967	450	1919	----------	----------	----------	----------	----------	----------
								1918	----------	----------	----------	----------	----------	----------
1940	56,295	2,099	340	----------	4,945	2,334	295	1917	----------	----------	----------	----------	----------	----------
1939	53,558	1,824	307	----------	4,036	1,536	372	1916	----------	----------	----------	----------	1	----------
1938	49,911	1,460	232	----------	3,516	662	2,842	1915	----------	----------	----------	----------	----------	----------
1937	47,444	1,212	221	----------	2,422	535	1,971	1914	----------	----------	----------	----------	----------	----------
1936	46,850	852	195	----------	2,219	403	1,576	1913	1,312	----------	----------	701	----------	----------

Series R 127–138. Authorized Land Stations and Mobile Transmitters in the Safety and Special Radio Services: 1948 to 1956

[Includes Territories and possessions]

Year	Aviation Land or fixed stations	Aviation Portable or mobile units	Land transportation Land or fixed stations	Land transportation Portable or mobile units	Marine Land or fixed stations	Marine Portable or mobile units	Public safety Land or fixed stations	Public safety Portable or mobile units	Industrial Land or fixed stations	Industrial Portable or mobile units	Amateur and disaster Land or fixed stations	Amateur and disaster Portable or mobile units
	127	128	129	130	131	132	133	134	135	136	137	138
1956, Jan. 1	7,978	40,735	8,069	243,457	2,106	56,265	18,526	207,195	22,987	252,265	148,509	8,408
1955, Jan. 1	5,373	36,595	6,616	154,358	1,385	49,742	13,731	187,670	16,009	164,262	129,029	3,123
1954, Jan. 1	4,657	37,467	6,041	132,944	1,250	42,573	11,742	152,811	13,515	132,425	116,286	1,173
1953, March 1	6,145	37,951	5,277	110,514	1,174	37,629	10,306	131,549	12,074	115,024	116,902	252
1952, Jan. 1	2,716	39,307	4,302	92,000	1,102	34,187	7,732	104,559	8,676	81,418	113,159	335
1951, Jan. 1	3,181	32,575	3,721	74,966	1,273	28,085	6,579	80,433	6,458	64,172	90,601	61
1949, June 15	1,987	28,037	2,759	51,774	443	19,170	4,301	59,122	2,765	33,608	81,675	----------
1949, Jan. 1	----------	24,695	----------	[1] 49,650	----------	17,414	----------	53,783	----------	[2] 27,842	----------	----------
1948, Jan. 1	----------	20,517	----------	[3] 31,852	----------	13,180	----------	38,929	----------	10,924	----------	----------

[1] Includes Class 2 experimental stations as follows: 46,085 taxicab units and 668 trucks and buses.   [2] Includes 68 Class 2 experimental industrial units.   [3] Includes 30,000 Class 2 experimental taxicab units.

POSTAL SERVICE, NEWSPAPERS, AND BOOKS (Series R 139–186)

R 139. Post offices, 1789–1957.

Source: Post Office Department, *Annual Report of the Post-master General, 1958*, pp. 144-149.

The source also presents a classification of the number of post offices into first, second, third, and fourth class for 1946-1956.

R 140–141. Revenues and expenditures, 1789–1957.

Source: See source for series R 139.

For 1789–1953, revenues and expenses are stated on a cash basis and therefore include payments and receipts in one year applicable to the expenses and revenues of prior years. For 1954–1957, revenues and expenses are stated on an accrual basis, with expenses reported in the year which gave rise to the earnings, whether collected or accrued.

Comparability of figures from year-to-year are affected by various factors. For example, the Post Office discontinued payment of subsidies to airlines in 1954; the Department also began receiving reimbursement for penalty and franked mail in 1954, costs which the Post Office had previously absorbed.

Expenses include expenditures for plant and equipment of a capital nature and for inventories and supplies, but no provision for depreciation is made. Expenses also include certain public service costs paid by the Post Office Department, but which the Department considered to be unrelated to the determination of the proper operating costs of the Postal Service. These include in recent years unreimbursed services for other Government agencies; specific rate subsidies for mailings of second- and third-class mail by certain nonprofit organizations, free-in-county second-class mail, classroom publications, and mail for the blind; excess rates paid to foreign air carriers; and custodial services for other Government departments and agencies. These costs were estimated to have been approximately $43.2 million for 1956.

Expenses of the Post Office Department do not include costs applicable to postal operations which are paid by other Government departments and agencies for retirement pay accrual, workmen's compensation and unemployment compensation for postal employees, and certain custodial and maintenance expenses. These expenses amounted to $157.2 million in 1956.

R 142–143. Ordinary postage stamps and stamped envelopes and wrappers issued, 1848–1957.

Source: See source for series R 139.

R 144. Postal cards issued, 1873–1957.

Source: See source for series R 139.

The Government postal card was authorized in 1872. The post card, or private mailing card, was introduced in 1898. The rate for this service has been practically identical with that of the postal cards. Business reply cards and letters as a postal service was initiated in 1928. The rate for this service since October 1, 1928, has been 1 cent each plus regular postage collected on delivery.

R 145. Pieces of matter of all kinds handled by the Post Office, 1886–1957.

Source: See source for series R 139.

With the establishment of the Cost Ascertainment System in 1926, data on the volume of mail have been obtained from sample counts conducted quarterly for one week at representative post offices ranging in number from 255 to over 500. These sample data were then projected to include all originating mail at all post offices in the United States. The methods of estimating the number of pieces of matter handled prior to 1926 could not be ascertained. See also general note for series R 146-160.

R 146–160. General note.

The bulk of postal revenues and postal expenses cannot be allocated directly to the various classes of mail handled or to special services performed.

Postal revenues (except for about 10 percent which can be directly allocated or computed) are derived from postage acquired in the form of stamps and stamped paper and from payments under permits, which may be used by the purchaser generally on any class of mail. The result is a large common pool of revenues from numerous sources. Similarly, the several classes of mail and the special services are to a considerable extent handled by the same employees using the same buildings, equipment, operating facilities, house services, and supplies.

A regular, continuing Cost Ascertainment System was begun in 1926, pursuant to a Congressional Act of February 28, 1925 (39 U.S.C. 826). Selected post offices, grouped according to receipts, furnish basic data as to revenues and expenditures and the related weights and volumes of the several classes and subclasses of mail matter and special services. The data so obtained are used to develop ratios for segregating the audited revenues and the operating costs of each homogeneous group of offices in order to apportion the postal revenues and expenditures to the several classes of mail matter and to the special services.

Since 1926, various changes have been made in the number of offices used in the sample and the detailed revenue and expense apportionments and allocations. These are described in the annual *Cost Ascertainment Report* of the Post Office Department and in the *Report on Cost Ascertainment System of the Post Office Department*, December 29, 1944.

The statistics of expenses as published annually are subject to later readjustments as a result of increases in the charges of railroad or air or of other transportation services, or increases in the salaries of Post Office Department employees, if such increases are made retroactive to an earlier fiscal year.

R 146–148. First-class mail, 1926–1957.

Source: 1926–1946, Post Office Department, *Budget Digest, 1949*, chapter IV, tables 5-11; 1947-1957, Post Office Department, *Cost Ascertainment Report*, 1956 and 1958 issues, tables 250-252.

Figures include letters and packages (including local delivery letters), Government postal cards, and private mailing cards. For 1926–1929, domestic airmail could not be segregated and is included with first-class mail. Mail fees are included for 1950-1957. Box rent revenues, previously reported as unassignable are allocated to classes of mail, 1951–1955, and classified with special services for 1956–1957. For 1951–1956, the expense of free mail from members of the Armed Forces is included in first-class mail expenditures.

R 149-151. Second-class mail, 1926-1957.

Source: See source for series R 146-148.

This category includes newspapers, magazines, and pamphlets under the special low-rate "second-class privilege," the purposes of which are set forth in the Act of 1879. Revenues include postage payments (stamps or money order permit) and since 1932 payment of fees for use of the second-class privilege; transient second-class matter (mailings of second-class publications by other than the publisher or news agents); publishers' second-class matter forwarded or returned, 1950-1957; domestic mail fees, 1951-1957; and box rent revenue allocation, 1951-1955.

Expenses include cost of free-in-county service (delivery of newspapers free in the county of publication at offices not having city or village carrier service); publishers' second-class matter forwarded or returned, 1950-1957; and for 1953-1957, also includes the expense of sending notices to publishers regarding undelivered mail.

R 152-154. Third-class mail, 1926-1957.

Source: See source for series R 146-148.

Third-class mail embraces all matter not exceeding 8 ounces in weight and not qualifying as first or second class. A significant proportion of the matter mailed under third class is advertising material. In 1928, a special "bulk rate" was made applicable to separately addressed identical pieces of third-class matter mailed at one time in quantities of at least 20 pounds or 200 pieces. Revenues include postage revenues and permits; domestic mail fees, 1951-1957; and box rent revenue allocation, 1951-1955.

Prior to 1953, the revenues and expenses applicable to controlled circulation publications (publications consisting primarily of advertising and distributed free or mainly free) were included with third-class and fourth-class services. For 1953-1957, controlled circulation publications are shown separately.

R 155-157. Fourth-class mail, 1926-1957.

Source: See source for series R 146-148.

This class includes mailable matter exceeding 8 ounces in weight, not qualifying as first or second class. The major development in this class of mail was the establishment of the parcel post system effective January 1, 1913. Books, library books, catalogs, and matter for the blind included in fourth class carry special rates. Revenues include domestic mail fees for 1951-1957; box rent revenue allocations, 1951-1955; and special handling fees.

R 158-160. Domestic airmail, 1930-1957.

Source: See source for series R 146-148.

Since September 1948, domestic airmail includes a parcel post service and since January 1949 airmail postal and post card service. Paid airmail to and from the Armed Forces overseas and the outlying possessions of the United States, formerly in international airmail, is included with domestic airmail, 1947-1957. For 1951-1956, airmail expenses include the cost of free mail from members of the Armed Forces.

Airmail expenditures include subsequent payments, as of June 30, 1950, to airlines for retroactive rate increases where effective. The decline in airmail expenses between 1953 and 1954 resulted from the transfer of subsidy payments to airlines from the Post Office Department to the Civil Aeronautics Board effective October 1, 1953. The *Cost Ascertainment Report* for 1953 and prior years shows division of service costs and subsidy payments.

For 1954-1957, the Post Office Department experimented with the transporting of all mail by air between a number of major cities. Such mail, carrying first-class postage, is counted within first-class service.

R 161. Post Office employees, 1926-1957.

Source: 1926-1946, Post Office Department, *Budget Digest,* 1949, chapter II, table 1; 1947-1957, *Annual Report of the Postmaster General, 1957,* p. 107.

Includes regular or full-time employees and substitute, hourly rate, and part-time employees. Part-time employees are a substantial part of the Post Office labor force.

Prior to October 1933, the operating force for public buildings housing post offices and other Government agencies was on the rolls of the Treasury Department. On that date, the personnel were transferred to the Post Office Department. This increased the regular labor force of the Post Office Department by 8,000 employees.

R 162-163. Postal rates for first-class mail, letters and postal cards, 1792-1957.

Source: Post Office Department, *United States Domestic Postage Rates, 1789-1956,* table I.

The postage rates in effect in 1789 were those fixed by the Continental Congress in the Ordinance of 1782. These rates were continued until 1792. It was not until 1863 that mail was divided into "classes." In the early days of the postal service the recipient rather than the sender ordinarily paid the postage. In 1847 postage stamps were introduced, and in 1885 compulsory prepayment for all domestic letter mail was established.

The rates shown are for regular service. During the earlier years of the westward expansion, special local rates were often improvised. Thus, the first letter rate on the "pony express," which operated between Missouri and California from 1860 to 1861, was $5 for a half ounce, reduced in May 1861 to $2 for a half ounce, and in July 1861 to $1 for a half ounce because of a Government subsidy.

A considerable part of the domestic mail service between 1792 and 1863 was carried by ship, and was subject to ship-letter rates. These rates are detailed in the source, table II, p. 24. In 1863, a ship and steamboat rate, double the regular rate, was made applicable to domestic mail conveyed by ships not regularly employed in carrying mail. This classification is omitted after 1879 because of its diminishing importance but the double rate is still in effect although little or no matter is mailed under these rates.

In 1863, first-class mail was defined to include letters and matter wholly or partly in writing, except book manuscripts and corrected proof sheets. In 1872, first-class mail was described as including letters and all correspondence, wholly or partly in writing, except book manuscripts and corrected proof sheets passing between authors and publishers. In 1879, it was redefined to include letters, postal cards, and all matter wholly or partly in writing, except such writing as is authorized to be placed on mail of other classes. See Jane Kennedy, "Development of Postal Rates: 1845-1955," *Land Economics,* May 1957 issue, pp. 93-112, for additional materials on postal rates, particularly rates for second-, third-, and fourth-class mail.

R 164. Postal rates for domestic airmail, 1918-1957.

Source: See source for series R 162-163, table III, p. 25.

Until 1948, domestic airmail rates applied not only to letters but also to other mailable matter, including sealed parcels up to specified maxima (prescribed according to weight or according to length and girth). Effective September 1, 1948, an Air Parcel Post Service was established. Matter carried by air weighing 8 ounces or less was classified as "airmail" and over 8 ounces "air parcel post."

R 165–168. New books, new editions, and pamphlets published, 1880–1957.

Source: R. R. Bowker Co., New York, N.Y., *Publishers' Weekly* (usually the third or fourth weekly issue in January).

Figures represent the number of titles published, not the number of books which were printed. The data are compiled from information and actual books submitted to R. R. Bowker Company by the various book publishing firms. The source also contains the number of books by subject matter and the number of publications for some foreign nations.

R 169–172. Number and circulation of daily and Sunday newspapers, 1920–1957.

Source: Editor and Publisher, New York, N.Y., *International Year Book Number*, various issues.

The term "daily" refers to papers that are published either morning or evening. About 90 percent of the circulation figures are credited by the Audit Bureau of Circulations. The remaining 10 percent is based on publishers' statements to the Post Office Department. The compilation is checked annually with a questionnaire to every daily newspaper in the country. Source also presents data for individual States.

R 173–186. Number and circulation of newspapers and periodicals, 1850–1954.

Source: 1850-1899, Twelfth Census Reports, *Manufactures*, vol. IX, part III; 1904-1909, Thirteenth Census Reports, *Manufactures*, vol. X; 1914-1927, *Census of Manufactures* for each census year; 1929-1947, *Census of Manufactures: 1947, Product Supplement*, pp. 67 and 68; 1954, *U.S. Census of Manufactures: 1954*, vol. II, part I, p. 27A-16.

For data prior to 1850, which is not comparable to the data since that time, see Tenth Census Reports, S. N. D. North, *History and Present Conditions of the Newspaper and Periodical Press of the United States*, p. 47; and W. S. Rossiter, *A Century of Population Growth in the United States*, Government Printing Office, 1909, p. 32.

Series R 139–145. Postal Service—Post Offices, Revenues and Expenditures, Postage Stamps, Stamped Envelopes and Postal Cards Issued, and Pieces of Mail Handled: 1789 to 1957

[In thousands, except number of post offices. For years ending June 30]

Year	Post offices [1]	Revenues [2]	Expenditures [2]	Ordinary postage stamps issued [3]	Stamped envelopes and wrappers issued [4]	Postal cards issued [5]	Pieces of matter of all kinds handled
	139	140	141	142	143	144	145
1957	37,012	$2,496,614	$3,044,438	24,257,859	1,966,335	2,046,515	59,077,633
1956	37,515	2,419,353	2,883,305	23,722,489	2,571,416	2,911,276	56,441,216
1955	38,316	2,349,476	2,712,150	23,105,454	2,189,520	2,515,392	55,233,563
1954	39,405	2,268,516	2,667,664	22,219,068	2,265,309	2,360,534	52,213,170
1953	40,609	2,091,714	2,742,126	22,960,961	2,338,622	2,330,921	50,948,156
1952	40,919	1,947,316	2,666,860	22,067,082	2,274,659	2,984,123	49,905,874
1951	41,193	1,776,816	2,341,399	21,521,806	2,004,568	4,183,748	46,908,410
1950	41,464	1,677,487	2,222,949	20,647,164	2,052,155	3,872,300	45,063,736
1949	41,607	1,571,851	2,149,322	21,047,376	2,219,743	3,468,719	43,555,107
1948	41,695	1,410,971	1,687,805	20,432,059	2,117,572	3,656,590	40,280,374
1947	41,760	1,299,141	1,504,799	19,542,257	1,996,449	2,951,299	37,427,706
1946	41,751	1,224,572	1,353,654	19,180,426	1,815,915	2,477,853	36,318,158
1945	41,792	1,314,240	1,145,002	20,239,986	2,064,773	2,282,280	37,912,067
1944	42,161	1,112,877	1,068,986	19,106,171	1,902,312	1,912,990	34,930,685
1943	42,654	966,227	952,529	19,123,977	1,797,400	2,316,990	32,818,261
1942	43,358	859,817	873,950	19,492,121	1,676,573	2,370,061	30,117,633
1941	43,739	812,827	836,858	16,381,321	1,645,254	2,400,188	29,235,791
1940	44,024	766,948	807,629	16,381,427	1,649,548	2,256,519	27,749,467
1939	44,327	745,955	784,549	15,073,795	1,605,075	2,170,572	26,444,846
1938	44,586	728,634	772,307	14,912,092	1,643,815	2,186,720	26,041,979
1937	44,877	726,201	772,743	15,108,639	1,663,818	2,226,153	25,801,278
1936	45,230	665,343	753,616	13,835,399	1,647,891	1,917,793	23,571,315
1935	45,686	630,795	696,503	13,610,497	1,617,677	1,754,030	22,331,752
1934	46,506	586,733	630,732	12,525,716	1,580,819	1,590,257	20,625,826
1933	47,641	587,631	699,887	11,917,442	1,644,993	1,389,523	19,868,455
1932	48,159	588,171	793,684	14,650,970	2,384,792	1,334,753	24,306,743
1931	48,733	656,463	802,484	15,559,164	2,847,439	1,531,245	26,544,352
1930	49,063	705,484	803,667	16,268,856	3,164,127	1,643,212	27,887,823
1929	49,482	696,947	782,343	16,917,274	3,228,586	1,783,897	27,951,548
1928	49,944	693,633	725,699	16,676,492	3,201,458	1,872,040	26,837,005
1927	50,266	683,122	714,577	15,999,701	3,145,946	1,834,456	26,686,555
1926	50,601	659,819	679,704	16,333,410	3,001,858	1,668,240	25,483,528
1925	50,957	599,591	639,281	17,386,555	2,997,177	1,497,366	----------
1924	51,266	572,948	587,376	15,954,475	2,964,464	1,293,184	
1923	51,613	532,827	556,851	15,478,095	2,721,475	1,253,196	23,054,831
1922	51,950	484,853	545,644	14,261,948	2,364,372	1,111,124	----------
1921	52,168	463,491	620,993	13,869,934	2,738,934	1,081,206	----------
1920	52,641	437,150	454,322	13,212,790	2,350,073	986,156	----------
1919	53,084	[6] 436,239	362,497	15,020,470	1,844,884	456,924	
1918	54,347	[6] 388,976	324,833	13,065,784	1,819,307	707,111	
1917	55,414	329,726	319,838	12,451,522	2,161,108	1,112,337	
1916	55,935	312,057	306,204	11,671,842	1,853,791	1,047,894	
1915	56,380	287,248	298,546	11,226,386	1,793,764	975,542	----------
1914	56,810	287,934	283,543	11,112,254	1,864,713	962,072	
1913	58,020	266,619	262,067	10,812,507	1,724,730	946,861	18,567,445
1912	58,729	246,744	248,525	9,929,173	1,684,624	909,411	17,588,658
1911	59,237	237,879	237,648	10,046,068	1,690,775	975,138	16,900,552
1910	59,580	224,128	229,977	9,067,164	1,506,861	726,441	14,850,102
1909	60,144	203,562	221,004	8,731,875	1,509,626	926,478	14,004,577
1908	60,704	191,478	208,351	7,651,400	1,266,002	809,426	13,364,068
1907	62,658	183,585	190,238	7,061,036	1,418,840	805,568	12,255,666
1906	65,600	167,932	178,449	6,284,450	1,230,287	798,917	11,361,090
1905	68,131	152,826	167,399	5,751,017	1,074,918	728,285	10,187,505
1904	71,131	143,582	152,362	5,330,886	1,020,255	702,907	9,502,459
1903	74,169	134,224	138,784	5,270,549	948,654	770,658	8,887,467
1902	75,924	121,848	124,785	4,621,285	853,128	547,204	8,085,446
1901	76,945	111,631	115,554	4,239,273	772,839	659,614	7,424,390
1900	76,688	102,354	107,740	3,998,544	707,555	587,815	7,129,990
1899	75,000	95,021	101,632	3,692,775	628,456	573,634	6,576,310
1898	73,570	89,012	98,033	3,418,458	606,447	556,380	6,214,447
1897	71,022	82,665	94,077	3,063,633	585,032	523,608	5,781,002
1896	70,360	82,499	90,932	3,025,481	616,040	524,820	5,693,719
1895	70,064	76,983	87,179	2,795,424	598,848	492,305	5,134,281
1894	69,805	75,080	84,994	2,602,278	571,475	468,499	4,919,090
1893	68,403	75,897	81,581	2,750,293	636,279	530,505	5,021,841
1892	67,119	70,930	76,980	2,543,270	593,684	511,433	4,776,575
1891	64,329	65,931	73,059	2,397,503	556,226	424,216	4,369,900
1890	62,401	60,882	66,259	2,219,737	513,833	429,515	4,005,408
1889	58,999	56,175	62,317	1,961,980	451,864	386,808	3,860,200
1888	57,376	52,695	56,458	1,867,173	433,635	381,797	3,576,100
1887	55,157	48,837	53,006	1,746,985	381,611	356,939	3,495,100
1886	53,614	43,948	51,004	1,620,784	354,008	355,648	3,747,000
1885	51,252	42,560	50,046	1,465,122	322,751	339,416	----------
1884	48,434	43,326	47,224	1,459,768	322,232	362,876	----------
1883	46,820	45,508	43,282	1,202,743	259,266	379,516	----------
1882	46,231	41,876	40,482	1,114,560	256,565	351,498	----------
1881	44,512	36,785	39,592	954,128	227,067	308,536	----------

See footnotes at end of table.

Series R 139–145. Postal Service—Post Offices, Revenues and Expenditures, Postage Stamps, Stamped Envelopes and Postal Cards Issued, and Pieces of Mail Handled: 1789 to 1957—Con.

[In thousands, except number of post offices]

Year	Post offices [1]	Revenues [2]	Expenditures [2]	Ordinary postage stamps issued [3]	Stamped envelopes and wrappers issued [4]	Postal cards issued [5]	Year	Post offices [1]	Revenues [2]	Expenditures [2]	Ordinary postage stamps issued [3]	Stamped envelopes and wrappers issued [4]
	139	140	141	142	143	144		139	140	141	142	143
1880	42,989	$33,315	$36,542	875,682	207,137	272,550	1863	29,047	$11,163	$11,314	338,340	25,548
1879	40,588	30,042	33,449	774,358	177,562	221,797	1862	28,875	8,299	11,125	251,307	27,234
1878	38,253	29,277	34,165	742,461	183,560	200,630	1861	28,586	8,349	13,606	211,788	[8] 26,027
1877	37,345	27,531	33,486	689,580	170,651	170,015						
1876	36,383	28,644	33,263	698,799	165,520	150,815	1860	28,498	8,518	19,170	216,370	29,280
							1859	28,539	7,968	11,458	192,201	30,280
1875	35,547	26,791	33,611	682,342	149,766	107,616	1858	27,977	7,486	12,722	176,761	30,971
1874	34,294	26,471	32,126	632,733	136,418	91,079	1857	26,586	7,354	11,508	154,729	33,033
1873	33,244	22,996	29,084	601,931	131,172	31,094	1856	25,565	6,920	10,405	126,045	33,764
1872	31,863	21,915	26,658	541,445	113,925	---------						
1871	30,045	20,037	24,390	498,126	104,675		1855	24,410	6,642	9,968	72,977	23,451
							1854	23,548	6,255	8,577	56,330	21,384
1870	28,492	18,879	23,998	468,118	86,289	---------	1853	22,320	5,240	7,982	56,344	5,000
1869	27,106	17,314	23,698	421,047	81,675	---------	1852	20,901	5,184	7,108	54,136	---------
1868	26,481	16,292	22,730	383,470	73,364	---------	1851	19,796	6,410	6,278	1,246	---------
1867	25,163	15,237	19,235	371,599	63,086	---------						
1866	23,828	14,387	15,352	347,734	39,094	---------	1850	18,417	5,500	5,213	1,540	---------
							1849	16,749	4,705	4,479	955	---------
1865	20,550	14,556	13,694	387,419	[7] 26,206		1848	16,159	4,555	4,326	860	---------
1864	28,878	12,438	12,644	334,054	28,218	---------						

Year	Post offices [1]	Revenues [2]	Expenditures [2]	Year	Post offices [1]	Revenues [2]	Expenditures [2]	Year	Post offices [1]	Revenues [2]	Expenditures [2]
	139	140	141		139	140	141		139	140	141
1847	15,146	$3,880	$3,979	1827	7,300	$1,524	$1,470	1807	1,848	$478	$453
1846	14,601	3,487	4,076	1826	6,150	1,447	1,366	1806	1,710	446	417
1845	14,183	4,289	4,320	1825	5,677	1,306	1,229	1805	1,558	421	377
1844	14,103	4,237	4,298	1824	5,182	1,197	1,188	1804	1,405	389	337
1843	13,814	4,296	4,374	1823	4,043	1,130	1,157	1803	1,258	351	322
1842	13,733	4,546	5,672	1822	4,709	1,117	1,167	1802	1,114	327	281
1841	13,778	4,407	4,499	1821	4,650	1,059	1,165	1801	1,025	320	255
1840	13,468	4,543	4,718	1820	4,500	1,111	1,160	1800	903	280	214
1839	12,780	4,484	4,636	1819	4,000	1,204	1,117	1799	677	264	188
1838	12,519	4,238	4,430	1818	3,618	1,130	1,035	1798	639	233	179
1837	11,767	4,101	3,288	1817	3,459	1,003	916	1797	554	214	150
1836	11,091	3,408	2,841	1816	3,260	961	804	1796	468	195	131
1835	10,770	2,993	2,757	1815	3,000	1,043	748	1795	453	160	117
1834	10,693	2,823	2,910	1814	2,670	730	727	1794	450	128	90
1833	10,127	2,617	2,930	1813	2,708	703	631	1793	209	104	72
1832	9,205	2,258	2,266	1812	2,610	649	540	1792	195	67	54
1831	8,686	1,997	1,936	1811	2,403	587	499	1791	89	46	36
1830	8,450	1,850	1,932	1810	2,300	551	496	1790	75	37	32
1829	8,004	1,707	1,782	1809	2,012	506	498	1789	75	[9] 7	[9] 7
1828	7,530	1,659	1,689	1808	1,944	460	762				

[1] Excludes branches and stations.
[2] Accounting basis changed from cash to accrual basis in 1954.
[3] First issued under act of Mar. 3, 1847, and placed on sale at New York, July 1, 1847.
[4] Stamped envelopes first issued June 1853, under act of Aug. 31, 1852.
[5] First issued May 1, 1873, under Act of June 8, 1872.

[6] For 1918 and 1919, includes $44,500,000 and $71,392,000, respectively, war-tax revenue accruing from increased postage.
[7] Special-request envelopes first issued in this year.
[8] Newspaper wrappers first issued under act of Feb. 27, 1861; they were not made after Oct. 9, 1934.
[9] For 3 months only.

Series R 146–161. Postal Service—Revenues, Expenses, and Volume of Mail, by Classes of Mail, and Employees: 1926 to 1957

[In millions, except employees in thousands]

Year	First-class mail [1]			Second-class mail			Third-class mail			Fourth-class mail			Airmail, domestic [1][3]			Post Office employees
	Revenues [2]	Expenses	Pieces	Revenues [2]	Expenses	Pieces	Revenues [2]	Expenses	Pieces	Revenues [2]	Expenses	Pieces	Revenues [2]	Expenses	Pieces	
	146	147	148	149	150	151	152	153	154	155	156	157	158	159	160	161
1957	$1,066	$1,036	31,561	$66	$323	6,888	$281	$527	15,702	$586	$627	1,184	$139	$132	1,483	521
1956	1,013	978	30,078	65	318	6,915	266	471	14,676	592	607	1,173	137	127	1,487	508
1955	967	905	28,713	65	298	6,740	269	441	15,050	595	593	1,136	130	121	1,467	511
1954	908	844	27,085	61	293	6,483	252	399	13,866	587	608	1,195	127	127	1,470	507
1953	908	822	27,257	57	297	6,762	217	374	12,004	491	623	1,245	121	157	1,480	506
1952	842	786	26,502	51	287	6,956	170	360	11,630	484	619	1,257	120	148	1,391	523
1951	784	678	25,578	48	244	6,520	157	286	10,534	431	537	1,235	95	116	1,094	498
1950	741	665	24,500	45	242	6,265	153	291	10,343	403	506	1,179	74	109	853	500
1949	706	628	23,206	43	234	6,987	135	266	9,389	356	485	1,209	65	103	856	517
1948	668	518	21,948	41	209	6,344	112	200	8,188	271	368	1,143	53	82	796	503
1947	627	499	20,665	38	201	6,124	95	171	6,803	235	297	1,067	54	68	772	471
1946	597	454	20,059	33	181	5,832	83	135	6,055	208	251	994	68	49	716	487
1945	615	373	21,010	29	144	5,522	76	99	5,446	232	232	1,028	81	49	876	436
1944	540	369	20,760	29	137	4,635	62	87	4,409	202	216	961	79	49	1,092	389
1943	(4)	(4)	(4)	(4)	(4)	(4)	(4)	(4)	(4)	(4)	(4)	(4)	(4)	(4)	(4)	374
1942	459	293	16,972	26	112	4,571	74	98	5,435	150	168	779	33	37	463	369
1941	432	278	15,989	25	109	4,607	82	105	6,075	141	161	738	23	31	323	361
1940	413	267	15,224	24	110	4,577	75	101	5,556	133	155	712	19	28	259	353
1939	400	263	14,657	23	111	4,310	70	94	5,181	133	150	693	16	25	221	348
1938	389	259	14,226	24	114	4,377	71	94	5,272	129	146	670	15	22	210	345
1937	384	254	13,882	24	113	4,529	71	91	5,356	132	146	685	12	19	168	332
1936	355	246	12,731	22	112	4,353	63	86	4,674	121	139	618	9	16	134	323
1935	343	229	12,498	20	106	4,138	54	75	4,030	112	133	573	6	12	89	308
1934	325	205	11,557	21	98	3,956	50	67	3,612	101	121	531	5	15	57	314
1933	332	227	10,878	19	108	3,869	50	79	3,753	100	132	530	6	23	60	321
1932	310	276	14,598	23	125	4,552	50	79	3,641	113	146	617	6	23	89	332
1931	335	277	15,824	27	124	4,857	58	81	4,100	188	158	766	6	17	88	338
1930	359	278	16,832	30	120	4,968	61	83	4,325	151	167	837	5	15	69	339
1929	365	287	17,170	29	123	4,834	61	80	4,341	142	162	770	---	---	---	339
1928	355	268	16,706	34	119	4,678	66	72	3,838	143	150	752	---	---	---	336
1927	345	262	16,284	35	119	4,753	68	72	4,062	141	145	743	---	---	---	332
1926	321	247	15,266	34	117	4,658	69	71	3,962	144	147	770	---	---	---	329

[1] For 1926–1929, domestic airmail included with first-class mail.
[2] For 1951–1955, box rent revenue, previously classified as unassignable, allocated to classes of mail; thereafter, classified as "Special services."
[3] Beginning 1947, includes airmail to and from Armed Forces overseas, previously included with foreign mail. Beginning 1954, excludes reimbursement for airmail transportation.
[4] Not available.

Series R 162–163. Postal Rates for First-Class Mail, Letters and Postal Cards: 1792 to 1957

[First-class mail as a mail category not officially established until 1863. Ship and steamboat letters, 1792-1863, carried special rates]

Year of rate change	Letters, nonlocal	Postal cards (cents)
	162	163
1952 to 1957	3¢ per oz.	2
1940	(1)	(1)
1932	3¢ per oz.	1
1919	2¢ per oz.	1
1917	3¢ per oz.	2
1885	2¢ per oz.	1
1883	2¢ per ½ oz.	1
1872	3¢ per ½ oz.	[2]1
1863 [3]	3¢ per ½ oz.	---
1861 [4]	----[4] do	

Year of rate change	Single letters [5]	
	Distance (miles)	Rate (cents)
	162	163
1855	not over 3,000	3
	over 3,000 (all prepaid)	10
1851	not over 3,000 (prepaid)	3
	not over 3,000 (not prepaid)	5
	over 3,000 (prepaid)	6
	over 3,000 (not prepaid)	10
1847	(6)	(6)
1845	not over 300	5
	over 300	10
1816	not over 30	6
	31–80	10
	81–150	12½
	151–400	[7]18½
	over 400	25

Year of rate change	Single letters [5]	
	Distance (miles)	Rate (cents)
	162	163
1816	over 500	increase repealed
1815	----do----	50% increase
1799	not over 40	8
	41–90	10
	91–150	12½
	151–300	17
	301–500	20
	over 500	25
1794	----do----	[8]25
1792	not over 30	6
	31–60	8
	61–100	10
	101–150	12½
	151–200	15
	201–250	17
	251–350	20
	351–450	22
	over 450	25

[1] The 1940 rate change provided that the 3¢ letter rate was not to apply to first-class matter for local delivery or for delivery within a county with a population of over 1 million if county entirely within a corporate city.
[2] Government postal cards first authorized in 1872.
[3] A uniform rate regardless of distance, a free city delivery service, and a letter unit of ½ ounce instead of the former "single letter" were inaugurated.
[4] Rate between any point in the U.S. east of the Rocky Mountains and any State or Territory on the Pacific. For other rates, see those for 1855.
[5] A communication of 1 sheet. Proportionately higher rates charged for letters of 2, 3, and 4 or more sheets (packet).
[6] Various acts between 1847 and 1850 established special rates for the western and southwestern U.S.
[7] In 1825, rates for single letters, 151 to 400 miles, increased to 18¾ cents.
[8] Between 1794 and 1863, extra fees were charged for city delivery service. The proceeds went to the letter carrier.

Series R 164. Postal Rates for Domestic Airmail: 1918 to 1957

Effective date	Rate	Effective date	Rate		Effective date	Rate
1949, Jan. 1, to 1957	6¢ per oz., 4¢ each for airmail postal and post cards [1]	1926, Feb. 15	Contract air routes: Under 1,000 miles, 10¢ per oz. / 1,000–1,500 miles, 15¢ per oz. / Over 1,500 miles, 20¢ per oz.	plus 5¢ per oz. for each airmail zone	1925, July 1	10¢ per oz. for Government-operated overnight service New York to Chicago;
1948, Sept. 1	(2)				1924, July 1	8¢ per oz. daytime zone rate
1946, Oct. 1	5¢ per oz.				1919, July 18	8¢ per oz., per zone [3]
1944, Mar. 26	8¢ per oz.				1918, Dec. 15	2¢ per oz. [4]
1934, July 1	6¢ per oz.				1918, July 15	6¢ per oz.
1932, July 6	8¢ first oz.; 13¢ each additional oz.		Government routes: Daytime zone rate, 8¢ per oz. New York to Chicago (overnight), 10¢ per oz.		1918, July 15	16¢ per oz. and 6¢ each additional oz., of which 10¢ was for special delivery
1928, Aug. 1	5¢ first oz.; 10¢ each additional oz.				1918, May 15	24¢ per oz., of which 10¢ was for special delivery
1927, Feb. 1	10¢ per ½ oz., regardless of distance (both contract and Government-operated air routes)					

[1] Airmail postal and post card service started Jan. 1, 1949.
[2] Prior to 1948, weight and size limits for airmail were the same as for first-class mail; beginning Sept. 1, 1948, matter carried by air weighing 8 ozs. or less was classified as "airmail," and over 8 ozs. as "air-parcel post."
[3] Zones were (1) New York-Chicago, (2) Chicago-Cheyenne, (3) Cheyenne-San Francisco.
[4] Not strictly an "airmail rate." Between July 18, 1919, and July 1, 1924, there was no airmail rate and no offer of airmail service. Some mail, however, was carried by planes at the regular first-class rate of 2¢ per oz.

Series R 165–168. Books—New Books, New Editions, and Pamphlets Published: 1880 to 1957

Year	Total	New books	New editions
	165	166	167
1957	13,142	10,561	2,581
1956	12,538	10,007	2,531
1955	12,589	10,226	2,363
1954	11,901	9,690	2,211
1953	12,050	9,724	2,326
1952	11,840	9,399	2,441
1951	11,255	8,765	2,490
1950	11,022	8,634	2,388
1949	10,892	8,460	2,432
1948	9,897	7,807	2,090
1947	9,182	7,243	1,939
1946	7,735	6,170	1,565
1945	6,548	5,386	1,162
1944	6,970	5,807	1,163
1943	8,325	6,764	1,561
1942	9,525	7,786	1,739
1941	11,112	9,337	1,775
1940	11,328	9,515	1,813
1939	10,640	9,015	1,625
1938	11,067	9,464	1,603
1937	10,912	9,273	1,639
1936	10,436	8,584	1,852
1935	8,766	6,914	1,852
1934	8,198	6,788	1,410
1933	8,092	6,813	1,279
1932	9,035	7,556	1,479
1931	10,307	8,506	1,801

Year	Total	New books	New editions	Pamphlets [1]
	165	166	167	168
1930	10,027	8,134	1,893	
1929	10,187	8,342	1,845	
1928	10,354	7,614	1,562	1,178
1927	10,153	7,450	1,449	1,254
1926	9,925	6,832	1,527	1,566
1925	9,574	6,680	1,493	1,401
1924	9,012	6,380	1,158	1,474
1923	8,863	6,257	921	1,685
1922	8,638	5,998	865	1,775
1921	8,329	5,438	1,008	1,883
1920	8,422	5,101	1,086	2,235
1919	8,594	7,625	969	(2,853)
1918	9,237	8,085	1,152	(2,376)
1917	10,060	8,849	1,211	(2,051)
1916	10,445	9,160	1,285	(1,941)
1915	9,734	8,349	1,385	(1,532)
1914	12,010	10,175	1,835	(1,662)
1913	12,230	10,607	1,623	(1,920)
1912	10,903	10,135	768	
1911	[2]11,123	10,440	783	
1910	13,470	11,671	1,799	
1909	10,901	10,193	708	
1908	9,254	8,745	509	
1907	9,620	8,925	695	
1906	7,139	6,724	415	

Year	Total	New books	New editions
	165	166	167
1905	8,112	7,514	598
1904	8,291	6,971	1,320
1903	7,865	5,793	2,072
1902	7,833	5,485	2,348
1901	8,141	5,496	2,645
1900	6,356	4,490	1,866
1899	5,321	4,749	572
1898	4,886	4,332	554
1897	4,928	4,171	757
1896	5,703	5,189	514
1895	5,469	5,101	368
1894	4,484	3,837	647
1893	5,134	4,281	853
1892	4,862	4,074	788
1891	4,665		
1890	4,559		
1889	4,014		
1888	4,631		
1887	4,437		
1886	4,676		
1885	4,030		
1884	4,088		
1883	3,481		
1882	3,472		
1881	2,991		
1880	2,076		

[1] From 1880 to 1913, pamphlets were counted but were not separately identified. The number of pamphlets that are included with new books and new editions for 1913 to 1920 are shown in parentheses. After 1928, pamphlets were not counted.
[2] Agrees with source; however, figures for components do not add to total shown.

COMMUNICATIONS

Series R 169–172. Newspapers—Number and Circulation of Daily and Sunday Newspapers: 1920 to 1957

[Figures as of October 1 of each year]

Year	Daily Number 169	Daily Circulation 170	Sunday Number 171	Sunday Circulation 172	Year	Daily Number 169	Daily Circulation 170	Sunday Number 171	Sunday Circulation 172
1957	1,762	57,805,445	544	47,044,349	1938	1,936	39,571,839	523	30,480,922
1956	1,761	57,101,510	546	47,162,246	1937	1,993	41,418,730	539	30,956,916
1955	1,760	56,147,359	541	46,447,658	1936	1,989	40,292,266	520	29,962,120
1954	1,765	55,072,480	544	46,176,450	1935	1,950	38,155,540	518	28,147,343
1953	1,785	54,472,286	544	45,948,554	1934	1,929	36,709,010	505	26,544,516
1952	1,786	53,950,615	545	46,210,136	1933	1,911	35,175,238	506	24,040,630
1951	1,773	54,017,938	543	46,279,358	1932	1,913	36,407,689	518	24,859,888
1950	1,772	53,829,072	549	46,582,348	1931	1,923	38,761,187	513	25,701,798
1949	1,780	52,845,551	546	46,398,968	1930	1,942	39,589,172	521	26,413,047
1948	1,781	52,285,297	530	45,968,595	1929	1,944	39,425,615	528	26,879,536
1947	1,769	51,673,276	511	45,151,319	1928	1,939	37,972,488	522	25,771,588
1946	1,763	50,927,505	497	43,665,364	1927	1,949	37,966,656	526	25,469,037
1945	1,749	48,384,188	484	39,860,036	1926	2,001	36,001,803	545	24,435,192
1944	1,744	45,954,838	481	37,945,622	1925	2,008	33,739,369	548	23,354,622
1943	1,754	44,392,829	467	37,291,832	1924	2,014	32,999,437	539	22,219,646
1942	1,787	43,374,850	474	35,293,543	1923	2,036	31,453,683	547	21,463,289
1941	1,857	42,080,391	510	33,435,575	1922	2,033	29,780,328	546	19,712,874
1940	1,878	41,131,611	525	32,371,092	1921	2,028	28,423,740	545	19,041,413
1939	1,888	39,670,682	524	31,519,009	1920	2,042	27,790,656	522	17,083,604

Series R 173–186. Newspapers and Periodicals—Number and Circulation: 1850 to 1954

[Data for 1947 and 1954 are for establishments having 1 or more regularly paid employees for whom a social security account was maintained at the Bureau of Old-Age and Survivors Insurance. Data for 1921–1939 are for establishments reporting annual receipts of $5,000 or more. For prior years the corresponding limit was $500. Circulation figures are the totals of average circulation per issue]

	Newspapers										Periodicals			
	Total		Daily		Sunday		Weekly		Other		Total		Weekly	
Year	Number	Circu-lation (1,000)	Number	Circu-lation (1,000)	Number	Circu-lation (1,000)	Number	Circu-lation (1,000)	Number	Circu-lation (1,000)	Number	Circu-lation (1,000)	Number	Circu-lation (1,000)
	173	174	175	176	177	178	179	180	181	182	183	184	185	186
1954	9,022	136,353	1,820	56,410	510	46,350	6,249	30,336	443	3,257	3,427	449,285	487	82,066
1947	10,282	119,568	1,854	53,287	416	42,736	7,705	21,408	307	2,137	4,610	384,628	892	69,393
1939	9,173	96,476	2,040	42,966	542	33,007	6,212	18,295	379	2,209	4,985	239,693	1,109	55,825
1937	8,826	95,296	2,065	43,345	528	32,713	5,839	17,287	394	1,951	4,202	224,275	954	56,115
1935	8,266	87,096	2,037	40,871	523	29,196	5,337	15,185	369	1,844	4,019	178,621	966	42,648
1933	6,884	76,298	1,903	37,630	489	25,454	4,218	12,048	274	1,166	3,459	174,759	878	39,365
1931	9,299	86,457	2,044	41,294	555	27,453	6,313	16,173	387	1,537	4,887	183,527	1,066	30,782
1929	10,176	91,778	2,086	42,015	578	29,012	7,075	18,884	437	1,867	5,157	202,022	1,158	34,495
1927	9,693	87,617	2,091	41,368	511	27,696	6,661	16,879	430	1,674	4,659	191,000	1,099	39,107
1925	9,569	80,705	2,116	37,407	597	25,630	6,435	15,990	421	1,678	4,496	179,281	1,133	34,826
1923	9,248	[1]76,408	2,271	35,471	602	24,512	5,903	16,425	472	(2)	3,829	(2)	984	31,436
1921	9,419	[1]75,411	2,334	33,742	538	20,853	6,059	20,816	488	(2)	3,747	(2)	995	23,090
1919	15,697	[1]73,139	2,441	33,029	604	19,369	12,145	20,741	507	(2)	4,796	(2)	1,230	31,162
1914	[3]16,944	[1]67,108	2,580	28,777	571	16,480	13,793	21,851	(2)	(2)	--------	--------	1,379	28,486
1909	[3]17,023	[1]58,505	2,600	24,212	520	13,347	13,903	20,946	(2)	(2)	--------	--------	1,194	19,877
1904	[3]16,459	[1]50,464	2,452	19,633	494	12,022	13,513	18,809	(2)	(2)	--------	--------	1,493	17,418
1900	--------	--------	[4]2,226	[4]15,102	--------	--------	--------	--------	--------	--------	--------	--------	--------	--------
1890	--------	--------	[4]1,610	[4]8,387	--------	--------	--------	--------	--------	--------	--------	--------	--------	--------
1880	--------	--------	[4]971	[4]3,566	--------	--------	--------	--------	--------	--------	--------	--------	--------	--------
1870	--------	--------	[4]574	[4]2,602	--------	--------	--------	--------	--------	--------	--------	--------	--------	--------
1860	--------	--------	[4]387	[4]1,478	--------	--------	--------	--------	--------	--------	--------	--------	--------	--------
1850	--------	--------	[4]254	[4]758	--------	--------	--------	--------	--------	--------	--------	--------	--------	--------

[1] Does not include circulation of "other" newspapers (series R 182), not available prior to 1925.
[2] Not available.
[3] Does not include a number of "other" newspapers (series R 181), not available prior to 1919.
[4] Includes a small number of periodicals.

Power

S 1-93. General note.

Energy to meet the expanding power needs of our economy has been secured from various animate and inanimate sources. Among those of historical significance, whose use is generally within the control of mankind, are human and animal power, waterpower, windpower, wood and other vegetable matter used as fuel, coal, oil, and natural gas. Currently, efforts are being made to develop and control solar energy, atomic energy, internal heat of the earth, and, through chemical processing, certain additional natural resources such as shale and sea water. For those interested in developing a comprehensive understanding of power problems the following books are suggested: Eugene Ayers and Charles A. Scarlott, *Energy Sources —The Wealth of the World*, McGraw-Hill Publishing Company, Inc., 1952; Fred Cottrell, *Energy and Society*, McGraw-Hill Publishing Company, Inc., 1955; J. F. Dewhurst and Associates, *America's Needs and Resources, A New Survey*, The Twentieth Century Fund, 1955; P. C. Putnam, *Energy in the Future*, D. Van Nostrand Company, Inc., 1953.

Preparation of historical tables showing energy from various sources and total energy input on a per capita or other basis is complicated. The amounts shown will differ greatly depending on the basis and point of measurement used. End-use data, for example, will show far larger increases in total per capita over the last 100 years than will data presenting physical measures such as tons, gallons, cubic feet, or B.t.u.'s because of increased efficiency in conversion and utilization. During the 50-year period 1907–1957 reduction of the total energy required or lost in coal mining, in moving the coal from mine to point of utilization, in converting to electric energy, in delivering the electric energy to consumers, and in converting electric energy to end uses have increased by well over 10 times the energy needs supplied by a ton of coal as a natural resource.

Data on energy available from mineral fuels, waterpower for electric energy, and fuel wood are shown in series M 71–87. For total waterpower, net imports from waterpower sources in Canada and the energy equivalent of waterpower not converted to electric energy (direct drive from water wheels) must also be considered. Statistics available for power sources not included here are presented in the volumes by Ayers and Scarlott, Dewhurst, and Putnam, cited above. Government agencies such as the Bureau of Mines, Bureau of the Census, Rural Electrification Administration, Bureau of Labor Statistics, Federal Power Commission, Federal Reserve Board, Interstate Commerce Commission; the various trade associations such as the Edison Electric Institute, American Gas Association, Bituminous Coal Institute, American Petroleum Institute; and various technical journals, particularly in their statistical issues, compile or summarize and publish data on the development and use of energy for power and related purposes.

S 1-14. Total horsepower of all prime movers, 1849-1955.

Source: 1849–1952, J. F. Dewhurst and Associates, *America's Needs and Resources, A New Survey*, The Twentieth Century Fund, 1955, p. 1117; 1955, estimates prepared by John A. Waring for *Transactions of Canadian Sectional Meeting, World Power Conference, 1958* (in press).

Data for series S 4 (work animals), S 10 (sailing vessels), and S 12 (windmills), as shown on p. 1117 of *America's Needs and Resources*, are based on data presented in appendix 25-3 of that volume. All other data for 1849–1919 are from C. R. Daugherty, A. H. Horton, and R. W. Davenport, *Power Capacity and Production in the United States*, Water Supply Paper No. 579, Geological Survey, 1928. The original data from Daugherty, *et al.* were for 1849 and subsequent 10-year intervals through 1919. Estimates for 1850 and subsequent 10-year intervals through 1940 are based on straight-line interpolation of original data.

All data for 1929, 1939, 1950, and 1952 shown in Dewhurst were prepared by John A. Waring. According to Waring, estimates for 1952 as shown in Dewhurst are too low for mines and farms, and too high for railroad locomotives.

A technical and statistical bibliography of early data pertaining to the development of horsepower equipment in the United States appears on pp. 43 and 44 of Daugherty, *et al.* This source also contains a section on the sources and accuracy of the data. The following appraisal of the data appears on p. 21: "In general the accuracy of the statistics presented . . . increases with each successive decade. The data for the early years are almost wholly estimated, but it is believed that the estimates are supported by bases accurate enough to lend a degree of authenticity to them."

In addition to the classifications shown in series S 1–14, the installed mechanical horsepower in a number of special industries were also calculated for 1955 by Waring, as follows: Waterworks pumping stations, 1,700,000; communications standby reserve generators, 308,930; gas utility stations, 1,775,800; motorboats and yachts, 25,450,000; outboard-powered boats, 33,680,000; petroleum pipeline pumping stations, 3,603,750; natural gas pipeline pumping stations, 3,881,200; isolated nonindustrial power plants, 5,170,000; underground gas storage pools, 301,000; construction and contractors' building equipment, 53,403,750. These total 129,274,430 horsepower, which, when added to the 1955 total shown in series S 1, result in an aggregate total of 7,272,997,430 horsepower.

S 15-93. General note.

Some data on the production and use of electric energy are available since the beginning of commercial production in 1882. Data for 1882–1920, however, are difficult to evaluate because of changing bases of measurement and variations in coverage of the various censuses or other surveys made during the period. The Bureau of the Census published the results of censuses of the electric light and power industries made at 5-year intervals for 1902–1937, and the reports of the Census of Manufactures and of Mineral Industries contain important data on industrial use and production of electric energy. The Geological Survey, the *Electrical World* (McGraw-Hill Publishing Company, Inc., New York), and the National Electric Light Association also published considerable data applicable to the industry during this early period.

The chief gaps in the data for these years are in the production of electric energy by industrial establishments for their own use, and in the measurement of the sales by electric railroads and railways for public distribution. Early data on capacity must be converted from horsepower (hp.) to kilowatts (kw.) to be comparable; and capacity data in kilo-volt-amperes (kv.-a.) were often tabulated as kw. without adjustment for power factor. Data on generation were also often reported without allowance for the kilowatt-hours (kw.-hr.) used in production and, in many instances, where the prime mover was used both for direct drive and for electric generation, the kw.-hr. equivalent of power used directly was reported as generation. End uses were reported by appli-ances, as number of lamps, arc lights, or motors, rather than as kw.-hr. These variations in units of measurements, in classification, and in coverage often resulted in differences in estimated totals of as much as 20 to 25 percent. In present-ing historical data on electric energy since 1902, efforts have been made to resolve such differences and place the data on a comparable basis.

Referring to various historical sources it will be noted that data published in later years will frequently show material revisions to reflect changes in classification and coverage. In the utility series prior to 1945, for example, when a large generating plant was purchased from an industrial concern, the utility series would be adjusted to include the capacity and generation of this plant in prior years. Where such re-visions have been made, the revised data are shown.

Since 1920, comprehensive statistics on capacity and gener-ation of electric utilities for public use have been compiled and published by the Geological Survey for 1920-1936, and by the Federal Power Commission since 1936. Data on capacity and generation by nonutility establishments since 1939 have been compiled and published by the Federal Power Commission. The Commission also published financial, operating, sales, and rate statistics for the electric utility industry. Data on cus-tomers, revenues, sales, and related matters since 1926 are published by the Edison Electric Institute and the McGraw-Hill Publishing Co., Inc., *Electrical World*.

During the 20 years prior to 1957 there was a marked growth in the application of power from various fuels through electric energy produced not only in central stations but by generators in mobile equipment of many types. Among these are power plants in ships, railroad locomotives, trailers, barges, trucks, tractors, buses, and in machines used in mining and heavy construction which produce electric energy for driv-ing and operating the mobile unit and for other services re-lated thereto, or to supplement central stations for temporary periods. Also of interest are the electric generators for auxil-iary purposes operated directly or indirectly by the prime movers in automobiles, airplanes, and other mobile engines or by independent power units in refrigerator cars and trailers and many other installations to furnish electric energy directly or to maintain the electric charge in batteries for use as required. The importance of these small generators is indi-cated by the fact that the 65 million motor vehicles registered in the United States in 1956 alone have a total generator capacity in excess of that of all the Federally owned electric utilities. Except where large units in the general classifica-tion of mobile plants are connected to utility systems for power for extended periods neither capacity nor generation are in-cluded in the data indicating production and use of electric energy in the United States. In some cases, however, indus-tries will report the horsepower of such equipment as driving generators, but, in general, do not indicate power output in kw.-hr.

S 15-18. Net production of electric energy, by central stations, by type of prime mover, 1902-1957.

Source: Summation of series S 19-26.

S 19-22. Net production of electric energy, by electric utilities, by type of prime mover, 1902-1957.

Source: 1902-1917, Bureau of the Census, *Census of Elec-trical Industries: Central Electric Light and Power Stations;* 1920-1957, Federal Power Commission, *Production of Electric Energy and Capacity of Generating Plants,* monthly and annual reports.

Census data for 1902-1917 have been adjusted in some in-stances for classification and coverage by L. D. Jennings of the Federal Power Commission. The figures for electric energy produced by waterpower for 1912 and 1917, for exam-ple, differ from those published in *Central Electric Light and Power Stations: 1917,* table 26, because they have been ad-justed to exclude electricity produced by steam and internal combustion engines at plants which also produced energy by waterpower, and energy produced in plants subsequently in-cluded in series S 23-26.

For 1920-1957, data are based on monthly reports by elec-tric utilities to the Federal Power Commission. Coverage is substantially 100 percent. Included are plants of the privately owned electric utilities, the cooperatively owned systems, and the publicly owned electric utilities. The latter group is com-posed of the following classes: Municipal electric utilities, Federal projects, public utility power districts, and State power projects.

S 23-26. Net production of electric energy, by industrial es-tablishments, by type of prime mover, 1902-1957.

Source: 1902-1941, Federal Power Commission, records; 1942-1957, *Production of Electric Energy and Capacity of Generating Plants,* monthly and annual reports.

Data include the generation of electric energy by manufac-turing and extracting industries and by electric railroads and railways, but exclude electric energy generated by the follow-ing sources: Nonutility central station plants of less than 100 kw. capacity; plants operated by hotels, apartment houses, office buildings, or other commercial, transport, or service es-tablishments; plants in military installations; new industrial plants which are not added promptly as reporting establish-ments; and, in some instances, generation of newly installed utility plants during test periods. The total central station generation excluded is estimated as about 1½ percent of the annual total shown for both utility and industrial plants. This percentage has declined in recent years with the development of mobile type generators.

Data for steam and internal combustion prime movers are processed separately and are combined when annual reports are completed. For 1938-1942, data on capacity by type of prime mover, and on total generation, are available from data reported to the Commission. As most plants had only one type of prime mover, the area to be estimated was limited, and detailed data for subsequent years were available as a basis for preparing such distribution. For 1902-1940, data for a portion of these plants are available from FPC S-20, *Electric Power Statistics, 1920-1940,* and from the data pre-sented in the reports of the Census of Electrical Industries issued for each 5 years, 1902-1937. Data on capacity of prime movers driving generators also appear in various reports of the Census of Manufactures and the Census of Mineral Indus-tries, particularly those for 1929 and 1939; from papers pub-lished by the Geological Survey; from technical and trade publications; and from special studies made by various govern-mental agencies and others. For 1938-1950, there was con-siderable effort on the part of a number of Federal agencies (Department of Commerce, Department of the Interior, De-partment of Defense, War Production Board, Executive Offices of the President, Federal Power Commission, Atomic

Energy Commission, and others) to develop historical data relating to power by utilizing data on capacity and use to estimate generation for segments where reported data on generation were incomplete or not available. These studies resulted in the development of the data shown.

In interpreting the data, it should be noted that the coverage may have varied during the period. For 1955, for example, approximately 250,000 kw. capacity with related generation for plants operated by transport industries (pipelines and non-electrified railroads), and by certain miscellaneous establishments, were dropped because the plants were small, generally under 1,000 kw. capacity each, and the coverage for these industries was becoming increasingly incomplete. The cost of securing full coverage and processing these data was considered unreasonable for the relative amount of energy involved. At the same time, however, approximately an equivalent capacity and generation were added by the inclusion of plants in manufacturing industries previously excluded for security and other reasons. For 1956, however, additional information indicated that certain of the larger plants excluded with the pipeline group would now be classified in the extracting industry and they were again included. Further, in the usual methods for compiling such statistics there are delays in adding new plants while plants retired are excluded promptly. Changes in coverage of these types normally will not affect materially the relative annual amounts for nonutility central station electric generation excluded from this classification.

S 27–35. Net production of electric energy, by central stations, by class of ownership, 1902–1957.

Source: Series S 27–34, see source for series S 19–22; series S 35, see source for series S 23–26.

The FPC reports cited above show data for "noncentral stations" within the publicly owned group for 1920–1951. This category, which includes plants supplying electric power primarily for such functions as public street lighting, water pumping, and sewage disposal, have been included in municipal or other named classifications for 1952–1957. A similar adjustment using records available was made for 1920–1951.

Data for cooperatively owned utilities (series S 30) are shown in the source combined with power districts and State projects. The separate data for series S 30 were obtained from the detailed records of the Federal Power Commission. These amounts are slightly below those reported by the Rural Electrification Administration, *Annual Statistical Report— Rural Electrification Borrowers*, because a few plants financed by the REA are included in other classifications or are not, for various reasons, included in the Federal Power Commission totals.

S 36–43. Consumption of fuels by electric utilities, 1920–1957.

Source: Federal Power Commission, *Consumption of Fuel for Production of Electric Energy*, monthly and annual reports.

For series S 42–43, data for years prior to 1940 are from the records of the Federal Power Commission or may be computed from the data shown for fuel used and electric energy generated. For 1920–1938, the distribution of energy generated for plants using two or more kinds of fuel was estimated.

The data are based on individual generating plant reports submitted monthly by all electric utilities to the Federal Power Commission. Both the privately owned and publicly owned operations are included. The coal figures include anthracite, bituminous, and lignite coal—processed separately for the detailed report—and small amounts of coke; those for oil include crude oil, fuel oil, distillate pitch, sludge, and small

quantities of other liquid fuels. The consumption of gas includes both natural gas and byproduct manufactured gas. In general, the minor fuels are reported in units equivalent to those for the major class of fuel with which they are combined. The quantities of each fuel include the consumption of generating plants operating on a standby or other intermittent basis.

Data on fuels used in industrial electric generating plants are not solicited as many establishments do not keep such records separate from fuels used for other purposes.

Kilowatt-hour production represents the summation of net station output after deduction for energy used in the operation of auxiliary equipment and facilities within the generating plants. Where two or more kinds of fuel are used at a particular plant during the same month, allocation of the kilowatt-hour production to each fuel is reported. Where such allocations are not made by the reporting utility, they are estimated on the basis of the latest available annual average B.t.u. content of each fuel used at that plant and the average B.t.u. per kw.-hr. generated reported for each kind of fuel.

S 44–48. Number of electric utility generating plants, and production per kilowatt of installed generating capacity, 1902–1957.

Source: See source for series S 19–22.

Figures for series S 48 are based on beginning- and end-of-year average installed generating capacity, except for 1902–1920 when capacity of the end of the year was used.

In counting the number of generating plants, each prime mover type in combination plants was included separately. Generating capacity is based on the nameplate rating of generators.

S 49–52. Installed generating capacity in central stations, by type of prime mover, 1902–1957.

Source: Summation of series S 53–60.

See also text for series S 19–22 and S 23–26.

S 53–56. Installed generating capacity in electric utilities, by type of prime mover, 1902–1957.

Source: See source for series S 19–22.

See also text for series S 19–22.

S 57–60. Installed generating capacity in industrial establishments, by type of prime mover, 1902–1957.

Source: See source for series S 23–26.

See also text for series S 23–26.

S 61–69. Installed generating capacity, by class of ownership, 1902–1957.

Source: Series S 61–68, see source for series S 19–22; series S 69, see source for series S 23–26.

See also text for series S 27–35.

S 70. Annual use of electric energy per residential customer, 1912–1956.

Source: 1912, Bureau of the Census, *Census of Electrical Industries, 1912*; 1917–1925, National Electric Light Association, *Statistical Supplement to the Electric Light and Power Industry in the United States*, Publication 1106, New York, 1931, p. 27; 1926–1956, Edison Electric Institute, *Edison Electric Institute Statistical Bulletin*, New York, 1952 issue, table 32, and 1956 issue, table 40.

Averages are based on data for customers and on use reported by the electric utilities. Data for appliances used and related matters are published annually in the statistical issue of *Electrical Merchandising* (McGraw-Hill Publishing Company, Inc., New York).

S 71–73. Percentage of dwelling units with electric service, 1907–1956.

Source: For census years, Bureau of the Census, Census of Housing (decennial) and Census of Agriculture (quinquennial); for intercensal years, various annual issues of the following: National Electric Light Association, *Statistical Supplement to the Electric Light and Power Industry in the United States*, New York; McGraw-Hill Publishing Company, Inc., *Electrical World*, New York; and Edison Electric Institute, *Edison Electric Institute Statistical Bulletin*, New York.

Some adjustments for comparability and coverage have been made in the source data by L. D. Jennings of the Federal Power Commission.

In the annual *Statistical Bulletin* of the Edison Electric Institute and in the statistical reports of their predecessor organization, the National Electric Light Association (cited above), data on the electrification of farms (series S 72) are presented. The information shown in these publications includes Bureau of the Census data and data compiled by the Rural Electrification Administration as well as material collected by the Institute or the Association. In the annual statistical numbers of the *Electrical World* (cited above), data are presented showing the percent of the population living in wired homes (series S 71). These percentages are generally based on the relation between the number of residential electric customers and population in census years. Percentages presented by the different sources indicated may vary from one to the other for intercensal years, depending on the statistical procedures used to determine the number of farms and dwelling units and related concepts applied. Among the items causing variations in the percentages of farms electrified, for example, are the inclusion or exclusion of farms without permanent dwelling units, farms with their own electric power plants, farms without service where distribution lines are within ¼ mile of the dwelling unit, or interpolation for the number of farms in intervening years between the various Censuses of Agriculture. The percentages shown are those considered reasonable and comparable to those for census years.

S 74–76, and S 78. Average price of electricity by class of service, 1907–1956.

Source: 1907–1924, based on a study by W. G. Vincent, Pacific Gas and Electric Company, *Edison Electric Institute Bulletin*, June 1936, p. 224 (adjusted by L. D. Jennings for comparability with the Federal Power Commission series); 1925–1956, Federal Power Commission, annual report, *Typical Electric Bills: Cities of 50,000 Population and More* (except that average prices for 1925-1934 have been adjusted from as of October 1, as originally published, to as of January 1 for comparability with the series subsequent to 1934).

Data shown in source for series S 78 are labelled "Industrial" which, in general, includes customers in the "Large light and power" classification as used by the Edison Electric Institute for series S 79.

The average bills for specified consumption are based on typical bills for residential and industrial service in cities with 50,000 or more inhabitants. These cities include about one-third of the total U.S. population. Since populations in adjacent areas are frequently served under the rate schedules effective in these cities, the bills reported indicate rate levels applicable to more than 70 percent of the total population.

Specifications for the computation of typical net monthly bills are prepared by the Federal Power Commission. Special rates for refrigeration, cooking, or water heating, where generally applicable, are used in computing the bill. Sales taxes computed separately and added to the bill computed under the rate schedules are not included in the bills reported.

Average bills are determined by multiplying the bill as of January 1 for each city by its population and dividing the sum of these products by the sum of the populations. Where two or more utilities serve a community with different bills, the population for each bill is determined by the proportion of customers served by class of service. Except for possible disproportionate shifts in population to higher or lower rate areas, changes in these averages indicate changes in rate levels.

S 77, S 79, and S 80. Average price of electricity for all users, by class of user, 1902–1956.

Source: 1902–1925, Bureau of the Census, *Census of Electrical Industries*, 1917 and 1922 reports; 1926-1956, Edison Electric Institute, *Edison Electric Institute Statistical Bulletin*, New York, 1954 issue, table 37, and 1956 issue, table 41.

These averages indicate the average revenue from electric service and will vary with average use and rate levels.

S 81. Electric energy, total use, 1902–1956.

Source: Summation of series S 82–93.

Total amount is equal to (*a*) utility sales of electric energy by class of service, plus (*b*) industrial generation minus sales to utilities, plus (*c*) use by utilities except in connection with the operation of generating plants, plus (*d*) energy furnished others without charge, plus (*e*) reported losses and unaccounted for, plus (*f*) estimated production for nonutility central stations not included in industrial generation (series S 23) minus sales to utilities as shown by utility reports on purchased energy. This total by years was compared with total net generation of utility and industrial plants (series S 15), plus net imports (series S 93), plus estimates of energy produced by central stations not included in series S 15. Differences of significance were analyzed, sources checked, explanations of the differences considered and adjustments made as necessary to account for all production or use. For 1939-1956, an appreciable portion of the energy estimated for plants not included in series S 15 and related series are variously reported to the Federal Power Commission or available from related material. For prior years, the amount estimated is based on relationships in benchmark years for which census or comparable type data on capacity, production, or use were available.

S 82–83. Electric energy, residential and commercial use, 1912–1956.

Source: 1912–1925, based on McGraw-Hill Publishing Company, Inc., *Electrical World*, annual statistical numbers, New York, and Bureau of the Census, *Census of Electrical Industries*, 1902–1927, reports at 5-year intervals; 1926–1944, Edison Electric Institute, *Electric Light and Power Industry in the United States*, New York; 1945–1956, Federal Power Commission, *Sales of Electric Energy by Class of Service*, monthly reports.

For 1912–1945, some combinations and adjustments were necessary for comparability with data for later years. These adjustments were made by L. D. Jennings of the Federal Power Commission.

Series S 82 includes residential use on farms and in rural areas but does not include (*a*) residential service charged in the rent of dwelling units, (*b*) service where energy is submetered by large apartment houses or operators of housing projects, (*c*) residential service secured in connection with commercial or other enterprises purchasing energy usually under commercial service classifications, or (*d*) irrigation sometimes included in the sales classification "Rural (district rural rates)." The Federal Power Commission data include some residential service rendered by industrial and certain classes of publicly owned plants excluded from the Edison Electric Institute series.

Series S 83 includes purchases under commercial rate schedules for residential services by operators of apartment houses or housing projects where electric service is included in the rent of the facilities, and submetered service to small industrial establishments. Generally excluded are sales to very large commercial enterprises included in series S 91.

S 84. Electric energy, total industrial use, 1912–1956.

Source: Summation of series S 85 and S 90.

S 85. Use of electric energy for manufacturing industries, 1912–1956.

Source: 1912–1938, based on data in units of horsepower or kilowatt-hours presented in Bureau of the Census reports of the Census of Manufactures; 1939–1956, based on reports of the Census of Manufactures and Federal Power Commission report, *Industrial Electric Power, 1939-1946.*

Estimates or reported data were checked with information on industrial or large light and power sales of electric energy plus data available or developed for industrial generation with allowances for data applicable to series S 90, and, to a limited extent, series S 91. Adjustments that appeared reasonable in view of all information available, including that for later years, were made by L. D. Jennings of the Federal Power Commission for changes or variations in classification and coverage.

S 86. Use of electric energy for manufacture of nuclear fuels and related products, 1943–1956.

Source: 1943, Atomic Energy Commission, records; 1944–1956, Federal Power Commission, records.

Data for 1955–1956 were reported by suppliers of major installations of Atomic Energy Commission and by the Commission itself.

S 87. Use of electric energy for paper and chemical industries, 1912–1956.

Source: See source for series S 85.

The figures combine data for two major industry groups— paper and chemicals; they exclude major nuclear energy projects where included in the chemical industry group.

S 88. Use of electric energy for primary metals, 1912–1956.

Source: See source for series S 85.

Figures include ferrous and nonferrous metals.

S 89. Use of electric energy for other manufacturing industries, 1912–1956.

Source: See source for series S 85.

S 90. Use of electric energy for extracting industries, 1912–1956.

Source: 1912–1939, based on Bureau of the Census, *Census of Mineral Industries,* reports for 1919, 1929, and 1939; 1940–1946, Federal Power Commission, *Industrial Electric Power, 1939-1946;* 1947–1956, Federal Power Commission, records.

Data for 1947–1956 are based on generation reported by industrial plants in this classification. Data from trade associations and from technical publications on total output and on electric energy per unit computed for intercensal years for representative establishments were used to check data estimated for these years by other methods.

S 91. Use of electric energy for miscellaneous light and power, 1912–1956.

Source: See source for series S 82–83.

Depending on rate schedules applicable, figures include uses variously classified as other, industrial or large light and power (but not included in manufacturing or mineral industries), street and highway lighting, other sales to public authorities where service is not rendered under commercial or industrial rate schedules or purchased for resale by publicly owned systems, railroads and railways, interdepartmental or company use or furnished without charge by electric power systems, rural or other sales for irrigation, and generation in central stations and used by enterprises of various kinds not included in the use classifications shown separately. The figures include energy for certain classes of residential and commercial uses (series S 82–83), as noted for those series, and may also include some manufacturing and extracting plants for which data were not included in these series (S 85–90) for reasons indicated in text for series S 81.

S 92. Electric energy losses and use unaccounted for, 1912–1956.

Source: 1912–1936, Edison Electric Institute, *Edison Electric Institute Statistical Bulletin,* New York, monthly and annual issues, and *Electric Light and Power Industry in the United States* (annual); McGraw-Hill Publishing Company, Inc., *Electrical World* (annual), New York, and Bureau of the Census, *Census of Electrical Industries,* 1912–1932, reports at 5-year intervals; 1937–1956, Federal Power Commission, records.

Relation to total energy used varies from year to year with changes in the proportion of energy metered on the low or on the high side of transformers at the point of delivery or at the generating plant, as well as for changes in technological efficiency in the transmission and distribution of electric energy and its relation to the quantities handled.

S 93. Electric energy, net imports, 1912–1956.

Source: Federal Power Commission, records.

Data for 1940–1956 are based on annual survey for staff use. For prior years, data are based on FPC S-15, *Movement of Electric Energy Across State Lines and International Boundaries, 1940,* and on historical records and files to include exports and imports for industrial as well as utility purposes. Monthly and annual *Electric Power Statistics* published by the Dominion Bureau of Statistics, Ottawa, Canada, were also considered. Coverage in reports for the earlier years varied as did the treatment of energy delivered or received on long-term exchange agreements.

Series S 1–14.　Total Horsepower of All Prime Movers: 1849 to 1955

[In thousands]

Year	Total	Automotive [1]	Nonautomotive											
			Total	Work animals	Inanimate									
					Total	Factories [2]	Mines	Railroads	Merchant ships, powered	Sailing vessels	Farms [3]	Windmills	Electric central stations	Aircraft [4]
	1	2	3	4	5	6	7	8	9	10	11	12	13	14
1955	7,143,723	6,632,121	511,602	4,141	507,461	35,579	30,768	60,304	10,801	5	206,590	59	137,576	25,779
1952	5,726,886	5,361,386	365,500	5,980	359,520	35,045	9,523	101,690	13,207	9	73,590	62	103,453	22,941
1950	4,747,871	4,403,617	344,254	7,040	337,214	32,921	9,167	110,969	11,032	11	63,090	59	87,965	22,000
1940	2,759,018	2,511,312	247,706	12,510	235,196	21,768	7,332	92,361	10,094	26	42,488	130	53,542	7,455
1939		2,400,000				21,239	7,149	90,500	10,000		40,750		52,115	6,000
1930	1,663,944	1,426,568	237,376	17,660	219,716	19,519	5,620	109,743	9,115	100	28,610	200	43,427	3,382
1929		1,424,980				19,328	5,450	111,881	9,017		27,261		40,014	3,091
1920	453,450	280,900	172,550	22,430	150,120	19,422	5,146	80,182	6,508	169	21,443	200	17,050	
1919		230,432				19,432	5,112	76,660	6,229		20,796		15,250	
1910	138,810	24,686	114,124	21,460	92,664	16,697	4,473	51,308	3,098	220	10,460	180	6,228	
1909		7,714				16,393	4,401	48,491	2,750		9,311		5,225	
1900	65,045	100	64,945	18,730	46,215	10,309	2,919	24,501	1,663	251	4,009	120	2,443	
1899		32				9,633	2,754	21,835	1,542		3,420		2,134	
1890	44,086		44,086	15,970	28,116	6,308	1,445	16,980	1,124	280	1,452	80	447	
1889						5,939	1,300	16,440	1,078		1,233		260	
1880	26,314		26,314	11,580	14,734	3,664	715	8,592	741	314	668	40		
1879						3,411	650	7,720	703		605			
1870	16,931		16,931	8,660	8,271	2,453	380	4,462	632	314		30		
1869						2,346	350	4,100	624					
1860	13,763		13,763	8,630	5,133	1,675	170	2,156	515	597		20		
1859						1,600	150	1,940	503					
1850	8,495		8,495	5,960	2,535	1,150	60	586	325	400		14		
1849						1,100	50	435	305					

[1] Includes passenger cars, trucks, buses, and motorcycles.
[2] Excludes electric motors.
[3] Excludes horses and other work animals, which are included in series S 4.
[4] Includes private planes and commercial airliners.

Series S 15–26.　Net Production of Electric Energy, by Central Stations, by Type of Prime Mover: 1902 to 1957

[In millions of kilowatt-hours]

Year	Total utility and industrial				Electric utilities				Industrial establishments			
	Total	Hydro	Steam	Internal combustion	Total	Hydro	Steam	Internal combustion	Total	Hydro	Steam	Internal combustion
	15	16	17	18	19	20	21	22	23	24	25	26
1957	716,356	133,358	571,405	11,593	631,507	130,232	497,212	4,062	84,849	3,125	74,193	7,531
1956	684,804	125,237	548,306	11,261	600,668	122,029	474,552	4,087	84,136	3,208	73,754	7,174
1955	629,010	116,236	502,388	10,386	547,038	112,975	430,119	3,944	81,972	3,261	72,269	6,442
1954	544,645	111,640	423,151	9,854	471,686	107,069	360,834	3,783	72,959	4,571	62,317	6,071
1953	514,169	109,617	394,726	9,826	442,664	105,233	333,541	3,890	71,505	4,384	61,185	5,936
1952	463,055	109,708	344,695	8,652	399,224	105,102	290,385	3,737	63,831	4,606	54,310	4,915
1951	433,358	104,376	321,705	7,277	370,673	99,750	267,252	3,671	62,685	4,626	54,453	3,606
1950	388,674	100,884	281,000	6,790	329,141	95,938	229,543	3,660	59,533	4,946	51,457	3,130
1949	345,066	94,773	244,429	5,864	291,099	89,748	197,878	3,473	53,967	5,025	46,551	2,391
1948	336,808	86,992	243,730	6,086	282,698	82,470	196,928	3,300	54,110	4,522	46,802	2,786
1947	307,400	83,066	218,985	5,349	255,739	78,426	174,500	2,813	51,661	4,640	44,485	2,536
1946	269,609	83,150	181,825	4,634	223,178	78,406	142,412	2,360	46,431	4,744	39,413	2,274
1945	271,255	84,747	181,708	4,800	222,486	79,970	140,435	2,081	48,769	4,777	41,273	2,719
1944	279,525	78,905	195,664	4,956	228,189	73,945	152,328	1,916	51,336	4,960	43,336	3,040
1943	267,540	79,077	183,952	4,511	217,759	73,632	142,381	1,746	49,781	5,445	41,571	2,765
1942	233,146	69,133	159,725	4,288	185,979	63,871	120,479	1,629	47,167	5,262	39,246	2,659
1941	208,306	55,357	149,157	3,792	164,788	50,863	112,319	1,606	43,518	4,494	36,838	2,186
1940	179,907	51,659	124,941	3,307	141,837	47,321	93,002	1,514	38,070	4,338	31,939	1,793
1939	161,308	47,691	110,635	2,982	127,642	43,564	82,783	1,295	33,666	4,127	27,852	1,687
1938	141,955	48,394	93,561		113,812	44,279	68,423	1,110	28,143	4,115	24,028	
1937	146,476	48,272	98,204		118,913	44,013	73,891	1,009	27,563	4,259	23,304	
1936	136,006	42,750	93,256		109,316	39,058	69,359	899	26,690	3,692	22,998	
1935	118,935	42,253	76,682		95,287	38,372	56,144	771	23,648	3,881	19,767	
1934	110,404	35,922	74,482		87,258	32,684	53,939	635	23,146	3,238	19,908	
1933	102,655	36,730	65,925		81,740	33,457	47,709	574	20,915	3,273	17,642	
1932	99,359	35,998	63,361		79,393	32,878	45,922	593	19,966	3,120	16,846	
1931	109,373	32,106	77,267		87,350	29,028	57,685	637	22,023	3,078	18,945	
1930	114,637	34,874	79,763		91,112	31,190	59,293	629	23,525	3,684	19,841	
1929	116,747	37,038	79,709		92,180	32,648	58,965	567	24,567	4,390	20,177	
1928	108,069	37,297	70,772		82,794	32,874	49,370	550	25,275	4,423	20,852	
1927	101,390	32,924	68,466		75,418	28,474	46,615	329	25,972	4,450	21,522	
1926	94,222	30,355	63,867		69,353	25,603	43,422	328	24,869	4,752	20,117	
1925	84,666	26,112	58,554		61,451	21,798	39,367	286	23,215	4,314	18,901	
1924	75,892	24,138	51,754		54,662	19,489	34,955	218	21,230	4,649	16,581	
1923	71,399	23,421	47,978		51,229	18,940	32,093	196	20,170	4,481	15,689	
1922	61,204	21,262	39,942		43,632	16,875	26,579	178	17,572	4,387	13,185	
1921	53,125	18,732	34,393		37,180	14,703	22,311	166	15,945	4,029	11,916	
1920	56,559	20,311	36,248		39,405	15,760	23,489	156	17,154	4,551	12,603	
1917	43,429	13,948	29,481		25,438	10,100	15,338		17,991	3,848	14,143	
1912	24,752	7,387	17,365		11,569	4,500	7,069		13,183	2,887	10,296	
1907	14,121	4,003	10,118		5,862				8,259			
1902	5,969	2,166	3,803		2,507				3,462			

Series S 27–35. Net Production of Electric Energy, by Central Stations, by Class of Ownership: 1902 to 1957

[In millions of kilowatt-hours]

Year	Total utility and industrial	Electric utilities							Industrial establishments
		Total	Privately owned	Cooperatively owned [1]	Publicly owned				
					Total	Municipal	Federal	Other [1]	
	27	28	29	30	31	32	33	34	35
1957	716,356	631,507	480,943	3,020	147,544	27,850	109,176	10,518	84,849
1956	684,804	600,668	459,015	3,403	138,250	28,005	100,711	9,534	84,136
1955	629,010	547,038	420,869	3,034	123,135	25,852	89,064	8,219	81,972
1954	544,645	471,686	370,970	2,551	98,165	23,505	67,804	6,856	72,959
1953	514,169	442,664	354,271	1,972	86,421	21,625	58,064	6,732	71,505
1952	463,055	399,224	322,126	1,537	75,561	17,490	52,492	5,579	63,831
1951	433,358	370,673	301,845	1,324	67,504	17,617	44,120	5,767	62,685
1950	388,674	329,141	266,860	1,010	61,271	15,244	40,388	5,639	59,533
1949	345,066	291,099	233,112	847	57,140	13,410	38,102	5,628	53,967
1948	336,808	282,698	228,231	673	53,794	13,122	35,373	5,299	54,110
1947	307,400	255,739	208,105	406	47,228	12,415	29,877	4,936	51,661
1946	269,609	223,178	181,020	300	41,858	10,801	26,960	4,097	46,431
1945	271,255	222,486	180,926	242	41,318	9,624	28,000	3,694	48,769
1944	279,525	228,189	185,850	200	42,139	9,637	28,867	3,635	51,336
1943	267,540	217,759	180,247	187	37,325	9,223	24,485	3,617	49,781
1942	233,146	185,979	158,052	123	27,804	7,610	16,893	3,301	47,167
1941	208,306	164,788	144,290	78	20,420	7,023	10,793	2,604	43,518
1940	179,907	141,837	125,411	37	16,389	6,188	8,584	1,617	38,070
1939	161,308	127,642	115,078	----------	12,564	5,688	5,476	1,400	33,666
1938	141,955	113,812	104,090	----------	9,722	5,237	3,029	1,456	28,143
1937	146,476	118,913	110,464	----------	8,449	5,270	1,843	1,336	27,563
1936	136,006	109,316	102,293	----------	7,023	4,705	1,072	1,246	26,690
1935	118,935	95,287	89,330	----------	5,957	4,228	555	1,174	23,648
1934	110,404	87,258	82,079	----------	5,179	3,834	357	988	23,146
1933	102,655	81,740	76,668	----------	5,072	3,583	458	1,031	20.915
1932	99,359	79,393	74,488	----------	4,905	3,517	445	943	19,966
1931	109,373	87,350	82,597	----------	4,753	3,435	497	821	22,023
1930	114,637	91,112	86,109	----------	5,003	3,604	465	934	23,525
1929	116,747	92,180	87,514	----------	4,666	3,497	300	869	24,567
1928	108,069	82,794	78,207	----------	4,587	3,245	356	986	25,275
1927	101,390	75,418	70,920	----------	4,498	3,051	668	779	25,972
1926	94,222	69,353	65,480	----------	3,873	2,832	518	523	24,869
1925	84,666	61,451	58,685	----------	2,766	2,302	103	361	23,215
1924	75,892	54,662	52,315	----------	2,347	1,940	58	349	21,230
1923	71,399	51,229	49,044	----------	2,185	1,852	63	270	20,170
1922	61,204	43,632	41,660	----------	1,972	1,637	55	280	17,572
1921	53,125	37,180	35,456	----------	1,724	1,422	52	250	15,945
1920	56,559	39,405	37,716	----------	1,689	1,373	59	257	17,154
1917	43,429	25,438	24,399	----------	1,039	1,039	----------	----------	17,991
1912	24,752	11,569	11,032	----------	537	537	----------	----------	13,183
1907	14,121	5,862	5,573	----------	289	289	----------	----------	8,259
1902	5,969	2,507	2,311	----------	196	196	----------	----------	3,462

[1] Prior to 1940, cooperatively owned included in other publicly owned.

Series S 36–43. Consumption of Fuels by Electric Utilities: 1920 to 1957

Year	Net generation by fuel [1]	Fuel consumed						
		Total coal equivalent	Coal	Oil	Gas	Per kilowatt-hour		
						Coal	Oil	Gas
	36	37	38	39	40	41	42	43
	Mil. kw.-hr.	1,000 short tons	1,000 short tons	1,000 42-gal. bbl.	Mil. cu. ft.	Lb.	Gal.	Cu. ft.
1957	501,098	232,576	160,769	79,693	1,336,141	0.93	0.083	11.7
1956	478,487	223,733	158,279	72,711	1,239,311	0.94	0.085	11.9
1955	433,786	206,929	143,759	75,274	1,153,280	0.95	0.085	12.1
1954	364,354	180,367	118,385	66,745	1,165,498	0.99	0.089	12.4
1953	337,042	178,491	115,897	82,238	1,034,272	1.06	0.090	13.0
1952	293,640	160,872	107,071	67,218	910,117	1.10	0.095	13.3
1951	270,531	154,498	105,768	63,945	763,898	1.14	0.094	13.5
1950	232,813	138,421	91,871	75,420	628,919	1.19	0.094	14.1
1949	200,965	124,574	83,963	66,301	550,121	1.24	0.098	14.9
1948	199,796	130,122	99,586	42,645	478,097	1.30	0.107	15.9
1947	176,983	115,672	89,531	45,309	373,054	1.31	0.112	16.2
1946	144,555	93,471	72,197	36,316	306,942	1.29	0.108	16.3
1945	142,331	92,642	74,725	20,228	326,212	1.30	0.109	16.5
1944	153,868	99,251	80,084	20,862	358,784	1.29	0.109	16.6
1943	143,785	93,275	77,301	17,986	301,937	1.30	0.111	17.0
1942	121,585	79,075	66,257	15,236	235,208	1.30	0.115	16.7
1941	113,272	75,700	62,668	20,077	201,763	1.34	0.112	16.9
1940	93,963	62,942	51,474	16,325	180,096	1.34	0.112	16.5
1939	83,628	57,958	44,539	17,139	188,878	1.38	0.100	16.4
1938	69,255	48,560	38,394	12,942	165,504	1.40	0.113	17.1
1937	74,502	53,560	42,929	13,829	169,127	1.44	0.119	17.1
1936	69,823	50,144	40,085	14,079	154,084	1.44	0.118	17.1
1935	56,688	40,797	32,715	11,257	124,118	1.44	0.118	17.0
1934	54,418	39,367	34,414	10,258	127,071	1.45	0.120	17.2
1933	48,170	35,274	28,543	9,606	101,985	1.46	0.122	17.3
1932	46,422	34,489	28,056	7,583	107,103	1.49	0.122	17.6
1931	58,014	43,954	36,115	7,922	138,458	1.52	0.128	18.0

[1] Excludes generation by wood and waste fuels.

Series S 36-43. Consumption of Fuels by Electric Utilities: 1920 to 1957—Con.

Year	Net generation by fuel [1]	Fuel consumed						
		Total coal equivalent	Coal	Oil	Gas	Per kilowatt-hour		
						Coal	Oil	Gas
	36	37	38	39	40	41	42	43
	Mil. kw.-hr.	1,000 short tons	1,000 short tons	1,000 42-gal. bbl.	Mil. cu. ft.	Lb.	Gal.	Cu. ft.
1930	59,583	47,544	40,278	8,805	119,553	1.60	0.132	19.0
1929	59,154	49,039	41,827	9,783	112,353	1.66	0.137	19.7
1928	49,622	43,020	38,042	6,818	77,155	1.73	.143	20.9
1927	46,660	42,492	38,199	6,552	62,485	1.82	.153	21.5
1926	43,472	41,342	36,842	8,999	52,647	1.90	.157	22.9
1925	39,443	40,014	35,615	9,794	45,472	2.03	.165	23.9
1924	34,963	38,855	32,790	16,060	47,301	2.22	.182	26.3
1923	32,088	38,404	33,636	13,925	29,340	2.39	.195	29.3
1922	26,561	33,402	29,193	12,443	24,996	2.52	.209	31.2
1921	22,343	30,436	26,604	11,505	21,701	2.72	.220	31.0
1920	23,495	35,791	31,640	12,690	22,136	3.05	.254	36.9

[1] Excludes generation by wood and waste fuels.

Series S 44-48. Number of Electric Utility Generating Plants, and Production Per Kilowatt of Installed Generating Capacity: 1902 to 1957

Year	Number of plants				Production per kilowatt of capacity kw.-hr.	Year	Number of plants				Production per kilowatt of capacity kw.-hr.
	Total	Hydro	Steam	Internal combustion			Total	Hydro	Steam	Internal combustion	
	44	45	46	47	48		44	45	46	47	48
1957	3,517	1,360	1,043	1,114	5,056	1935	4,023	1,476	1,424	1,123	2,777
1956	3,534	1,365	1,037	1,132	5,108	1934	3,999	1,471	1,454	1,074	2,540
						1933	4,012	1,482	1,514	1,016	2,374
1955	3,587	1,381	1,045	1,161	5,037	1932	4,027	1,460	1,553	1,014	2,337
1954	3,627	1,387	1,045	1,195	4,862	1931	4,037	1,461	1,577	999	2,646
1953	3,686	1,406	1,041	1,239	5,098						
1952	3,698	1,412	1,030	1,256	5,051	1930	4,043	1,446	1,626	971	2,926
1951	3,806	1,428	1,048	1,330	5,124	1929	3,838	1,389	1,693	756	3,197
						1928	3,830	1,370	1,717	743	3,127
1950	3,867	1,458	1,051	1,358	4,984	1927	3,707	1,299	1,869	539	3,111
1949	3,888	1,465	1,054	1,369	4,862	1926	3,742	1,287	1,964	491	3,094
1948	3,879	1,467	1,045	1,367	5,191						
1947	3,865	1,479	1,045	1,341	4,984	1925	3,738	1,250	2,004	484	3,138
1946	3,854	1,488	1,046	1,320	4,441	1924	3,783	1,221	2,169	393	3,276
						1923	3,768	1,191	2,224	353	3,434
1945	3,886	1,505	1,057	1,324	4,487	1922	3,722	1,142	2,276	304	3,145
1944	3,933	1,510	1,082	1,341	4,699	1921	3,726	1,120	2,324	282	2,839
1943	3,959	1,507	1,101	1,351	4,687						
1942	3,899	1,489	1,100	1,310	4,257	1920	3,831	1,125	2,422	284	3,101
1941	3,882	1,473	1,116	1,293	4,003	1917	4,364	--------	--------	--------	2,828
						1912	3,520	--------	--------	--------	2,240
1940	3,918	1,474	1,153	1,291	3,601	1907	3,200	--------	--------	--------	2,164
1939	3,938	1,487	1,195	1,256	3,346	1902	2,250	--------	--------	--------	2,068
1938	3,903	1,479	1,252	1,172	3,110						
1937	3,918	1,473	1,283	1,162	3,364						
1936	3,896	1,471	1,337	1,088	3,145						

Series S 49–60. Installed Generating Capacity in Central Stations, by Type of Prime Mover: 1902 to 1957
[In thousands of kilowatts. As of December 31]

Year	Total utility and industrial				Electric utilities				Industrial establishments			
	Total	Hydro	Steam	Internal combustion	Total	Hydro	Steam	Internal combustion	Total	Hydro	Steam	Internal combustion
	49	50	51	52	53	54	55	56	57	58	59	60
1957	146,221	27,761	114,660	3,800	129,123	27,036	99,542	2,545	17,098	725	15,119	1,254
1956	137,342	26,386	107,251	3,705	120,697	25,654	92,591	2,452	16,645	732	14,660	1,253
1955	130,895	25,742	101,698	3,455	114,472	25,005	87,112	2,355	16,423	737	14,586	1,100
1954	118,878	24,238	91,250	3,390	102,592	23,211	77,102	2,279	16,286	1,027	14,148	1,111
1953	107,354	23,054	80,960	3,340	91,502	22,045	67,235	2,222	15,852	1,009	13,725	1,118
1952	97,312	21,416	72,620	3,276	82,227	20,419	59,679	2,129	15,085	997	12,941	1,147
1951	90,127	19,870	67,372	2,885	75,775	18,868	54,865	2,042	14,352	1,002	12,507	843
1950	82,850	18,674	61,495	2,681	68,919	17,675	49,333	1,911	13,931	999	12,162	770
1949	76,570	17,662	56,472	2,436	63,100	16,654	44,640	1,806	13,470	1,008	11,832	630
1948	69,615	16,635	50,751	2,229	56,560	15,652	39,304	1,604	13,055	983	11,447	625
1947	65,151	15,956	47,242	1,953	52,322	14,971	36,034	1,317	12,829	985	11,208	636
1946	63,066	15,828	45,442	1,796	50,317	14,848	34,313	1,156	12,749	980	11,129	640
1945	62,868	15,892	45,248	1,728	50,111	14,912	34,112	1,087	12,757	980	11,136	641
1944	62,066	15,696	44,637	1,733	49,189	14,586	33,541	1,062	12,877	1,110	11,096	671
1943	60,539	14,991	43,840	1,708	47,951	13,884	33,015	1,052	12,588	1,107	10,825	656
1942	57,237	13,947	41,593	1,697	45,053	12,842	31,169	1,042	12,184	1,105	10,424	655
1941	53,995	12,912	39,474	1,609	42,405	11,817	29,599	989	11,590	1,095	9,875	620
1940	50,962	12,304	37,138	1,520	39,927	11,224	27,775	928	11,035	1,080	9,363	592
1939	49,438	12,075	35,932	1,431	38,863	11,004	27,009	850	10,575	1,071	8,923	581
1938	46,873	11,682	35,191		37,492	10,657	26,066	769	9,381	1,025	8,356	
1937	44,370	11,186	33,184		35,620	10,176	24,763	681	8,750	1,010	7,740	
1936	43,582	11,037	32,545		35,082	10,037	24,441	604	8,500	1,000	7,500	
1935	42,828	10,399	32,429		34,436	9,399	24,471	566	8,392	1,000	7,392	
1934	42,545	10,345	32,200		34,119	9,345	24,253	521	8,426	1,000	7,426	
1933	43,037	10,330	32,707		34,587	9,334	24,759	494	8,450	996	7,454	
1932	42,849	10,258	32,591		34,387	9,258	24,646	483	8,462	1,000	7,462	
1931	42,287	10,190	32,097		33,698	9,090	24,162	446	8,589	1,100	7,489	
1930	41,153	9,650	31,503		32,384	8,585	23,385	414	8,769	1,065	7,704	
1929	38,708	8,925	29,783		29,839	7,813	21,704	322	8,869	1,112	7,757	
1928	36,782	8,800	27,982		27,805	7,702	19,790	313	8,977	1,098	7,879	
1927	34,574	7,927	26,647		25,079	6,802	18,078	199	9,495	1,125	8,370	
1926	32,936	7,650	25,286		23,386	6,405	16,792	189	9,550	1,245	8,305	
1925	30,087	7,150	22,937		21,472	5,922	15,368	182	8,615	1,228	7,387	
1924	25,923	6,224	19,699		17,681	5,024	12,535	122	8,242	1,200	7,042	
1923	23,235	5,682	17,553		15,643	4,507	11,026	110	7,592	1,175	6,417	
1922	21,317	5,229	16,088		14,192	4,129	9,965	98	7,125	1,100	6,025	
1921	20,605	5,002	15,603		13,519	3,902	9,527	90	7,086	1,100	5,986	
1920	19,439	4,804	14,635		12,714	3,704	8,920	90	6,725	1,100	5,625	
1917	15,494	3,886	11,608		8,994	2,786	6,128	80	6,500	1,100	5,400	
1912	10,980	2,794	8,186		5,165	1,694	3,395	76	5,815	1,100	4,715	
1907	6,809	1,906	4,903		2,709	906	1,765	38	4,100	1,000	3,100	
1902	2,987	1,140	1,847		1,212	290	914	8	1,775	850	925	

Series S 61–69. Installed Generating Capacity, by Class of Ownership: 1902 to 1957
[In thousands of kilowatts. As of December 31]

Year	Total utility and industrial	Electric utilities							Industrial establishments
		Total	Privately owned	Cooperatively owned [1]	Publicly owned				
					Total	Municipal	Federal	Other [1]	
	61	62	63	64	65	66	67	68	69
1957	146,221	129,123	97,376	922	30,824	8,640	19,649	2,535	17,098
1956	137,342	120,697	91,146	792	28,759	8,325	18,336	2,098	16,645
1955	130,895	114,472	86,887	776	26,809	7,795	16,962	2,052	16,423
1954	118,878	102,592	79,127	750	22,715	7,225	13,567	1,923	16,286
1953	107,354	91,502	71,201	619	19,682	6,570	11,358	1,754	15,852
1952	97,312	82,227	64,349	522	17,356	6,019	9,678	1,659	15,085
1951	90,127	75,775	60,192	482	15,101	5,293	8,099	1,709	14,352
1950	82,850	68,919	55,176	375	13,368	4,970	6,921	1,477	13,931
1949	76,570	63,100	50,484	283	12,333	4,727	6,210	1,396	13,470
1948	69,615	56,560	45,381	230	10,949	4,105	5,525	1,319	13,055
1947	65,151	52,322	41,986	168	10,168	3,825	5,027	1,316	12,829
1946	63,066	50,317	40,335	105	9,877	3,708	4,919	1,250	12,749
1945	62,868	50,111	40,307	87	9,717	3,586	5,081	1,050	12,757
1944	62,066	49,189	39,733	70	9,386	3,447	4,886	1,053	12,877
1943	60,539	47,951	39,128	66	8,757	3,419	4,322	1,016	12,588
1942	57,237	45,053	37,442	45	7,566	3,331	3,216	1,019	12,184
1941	53,995	42,405	36,041	30	6,334	3,158	2,371	805	11,590
1940	50,962	39,927	34,399	13	5,515	2,977	1,944	594	11,035
1939	49,438	38,863	33,908	----------	4,955	2,807	1,650	498	10,575
1938	46,873	37,492	33,246	----------	4,246	2,631	1,156	459	9,381
1937	44,370	35,620	31,958	----------	3,662	2,476	833	353	8,750
1936	43,582	35,082	31,787	----------	3,295	2,164	804	327	8,500
1935	42,828	34,436	31,820	----------	2,616	2,002	300	314	8,392
1934	42,545	34,119	31,547	----------	2,572	1,963	288	321	8,426
1933	43,037	34,587	32,163	----------	2,424	1,879	232	313	8,450
1932	42,849	34,387	32,033	----------	2,354	1,828	232	294	8,462
1931	42,287	33,698	31,498	----------	2,200	1,696	231	273	8,589

[1] Prior to 1940, cooperatively owned included in other publicly owned.

Series S 81–93. Use of Electric Energy: 1902 to 1956

[In millions of kilowatt-hours]

Year	Total	Residential	Commercial	Industrial						Extracting	Miscellaneous light and power	Losses and use unaccounted for	Net imports
				Total industrial	Manufacturing								
					Total	Nuclear energy	Paper and chemicals	Primary metals	Other				
	81	82	83	84	85	86	87	88	89	90	91	92	93
1956 (prel.)	693,625	143,476	86,840	341,123	325,100	60,655	72,265	78,500	113,680	16,023	54,873	62,765	4,548
1955	637,321	128,401	79,389	315,203	299,261	50,105	65,594	75,960	107,602	15,942	50,921	59,339	4,068
1954	553,727	116,228	72,141	263,527	247,666	26,559	58,146	66,781	96,180	15,861	45,687	53,804	2,340
1953	522,419	104,146	66,533	254,260	238,480	14,727	57,725	68,897	97,131	15,780	44,818	50,654	2,008
1952	472,071	93,545	63,935	224,487	209,507	8,473	51,049	54,493	95,492	14,980	39,949	47,886	2,269
1951	442,046	83,093	58,643	214,522	200,322	5,533	49,494	54,497	90,798	14,200	38,798	44,803	2,187
1950	396,346	72,200	52,091	194,835	181,335	3,794	45,123	50,111	82,307	13,500	34,166	41,268	1,786
1949	351,831	63,369	44,830	169,274	156,524	3,614	38,227	44,344	70,339	12,750	34,720	38,050	1,588
1948	343,410	57,421	41,698	172,658	159,358	3,477	38,970	45,206	71,705	13,300	33,096	36,992	1,545
1947	313,926	49,417	37,152	157,197	144,247	3,233	34,996	40,645	65,373	12,950	34,788	33,457	1,915
1946	276,044	42,919	32,060	137,308	125,598	3,548	32,104	34,895	55,051	11,710	32,584	28,782	2,391
1945	275,028	37,749	28,091	146,261	134,955	3,099	36,780	37,371	57,705	11,306	33,364	27,001	2,562
1944	283,718	34,636	29,837	156,365	145,015	1,164	40,285	43,158	60,408	11,350	31,965	28,400	2,515
1943	270,215	31,271	28,192	155,671	143,995	31	39,670	44,973	59,321	11,676	26,017	26,567	2,497
1942	235,477	29,187	27,233	133,899	122,762	----------	33,463	36,257	53,042	11,137	19,958	22,782	2,418
1941	210,389	26,574	24,628	113,931	104,037	----------	27,830	29,630	46,577	9,894	22,574	20,351	2,331
1940	181,706	24,068	22,373	92,390	83,276	----------	22,776	22,782	37,718	9,114	23,173	17,588	2,114
1939	162,921	21,433	20,722	78,603	70,518	----------	19,040	17,632	33,846	8,085	24,378	15,891	1,894
1938	143,375	19,371	19,137	65,850	58,452	----------	15,829	14,504	28,119	7,398	22,982	14,227	1,808
1937	147,941	17,691	18,075	73,300	64,757	----------	17,536	16,068	31,153	8,543	22,124	14,924	1,827
1936	137,366	15,659	15,612	70,500	62,949	----------	17,046	15,620	30,283	7,551	20,266	13,773	1,556
1935	120,124	13,978	13,588	63,265	56,706	----------	15,356	14,070	27,280	6,559	15,902	12,054	1,337
1934	111,508	12,658	12,278	56,695	50,593	----------	13,700	12,554	24,339	6,102	17,561	11,082	1,234
1933	103,682	11,747	11,589	52,358	46,561	----------	12,609	11,553	22,399	5,797	16,599	10,422	967
1932	100,353	11,875	12,106	48,614	43,504	----------	11,781	10,795	20,928	5,110	16,952	10,162	644
1931	110,467	11,738	13,544	56,512	50,410	----------	13,651	12,508	24,251	6,102	16,240	11,224	1,209
1930	115,783	11,018	13,944	61,023	53,930	----------	14,604	13,382	25,944	7,093	16,453	11,753	1,592
1929	117,914	9,773	13,106	63,279	55,122	----------	14,983	13,543	26,596	8,157	18,396	11,937	1,423
1928	109,150	8,619	11,692	59,750	52,699	----------	14,271	13,076	25,352	7,051	16,753	10,763	1,573
1927	102,404	7,676	10,766	57,383	51,012	----------	13,814	12,658	24,540	6,371	15,118	9,842	1,619
1926	95,164	6,827	9,485	52,750	46,350	----------	12,551	11,501	22,298	6,400	15,524	9,085	1,493
1925	85,513	6,020	9,345	45,500	39,725	----------	10,757	9,857	19,111	5,775	15,294	8,081	1,273
1924	76,651	5,080	8,634	40,300	34,967	----------	9,468	8,677	16,822	5,333	14,132	7,215	1,290
1923	72,113	4,580	8,027	38,250	32,585	----------	8,824	8,085	15,676	5,665	13,137	6,788	1,331
1922	61,816	3,916	7,180	32,200	27,364	----------	7,410	6,790	13,164	4,836	11,752	5,803	965
1921	53,656	3,532	6,125	28,000	23,993	----------	6,497	5,953	11,543	4,007	10,026	4,964	1,009
1920	57,125	3,190	6,150	31,500	26,913	----------	7,288	6,678	12,947	4,587	10,065	5,280	940
1917	43,863	1,731	5,213	23,750	20,750	----------	5,619	5,149	9,982	3,000	8,532	3,421	1,216
1912	25,000	910	4,076	11,250	9,250	----------	2,505	2,295	4,450	2,000	6,671	1,562	531
1907	14,262	----------	----------	----------	----------	----------	----------	----------	----------	----------	----------	----------	----------
1902	6,029	----------	----------	----------	----------	----------	----------	----------	----------	----------	----------	----------	----------

Distribution and Services

T 1–386. General note.

The data presented here, except for series T 346–351 (advertising), are based on distribution or service *establishments* rather than distribution or service *functions*, and therefore exclude the many distribution activities undertaken by other types of establishments, especially by manufacturers. The data for services are limited to types offered by retail-store-type establishments.

T 1–11. National income originating in distribution and selected service industries, 1869–1957.

Source: 1869–1929, Harold Barger, "Income Originating in Trade, 1869–1929," *Studies in Income and Wealth*, vol. 24 (forthcoming), Conference on Research in Income and Wealth, National Bureau of Economic Research, Princeton; 1929–1945, Office of Business Economics, *National Income: 1954 Edition, A Supplement to the Survey of Current Business*, pp. 176–177; 1946–1957, *U. S. Income and Output*, 1958, pp. 130–131.

Series T 5 combines the series shown in the source for "commercial and trade schools and employment agencies" with the series for "other business services."

T 12–22. Persons engaged in distribution and selected service industries, 1869–1957.

Source: 1869–1919, see source for series T 1–11; 1929–1945, see source for series T 1–11, pp. 202–203; 1946–1957, see source for series T 1–11, p. 214.

These figures show the man-years of full-time employment by persons working for wages or salaries and by active proprietors of unincorporated businesses devoting the major portion of their time to the business. Full-time equivalent employment measures man-years of full-time employment and its equivalent work performed by part-time workers. Full-time employment is defined simply in terms of the number of hours which is customary at a particular time and place. For a full explanation of the concept, see Office of Business Economics, *Survey of Current Business*, June 1945, pp. 7–18.

Unpaid family workers are excluded due. to unresolved difficulties in their definition and measurement.

Series T 16 combines the series shown in the source for "commercial and trade schools and employment agencies" with the series for "other business services."

T 23–48. Retail store sales, by kind of business, 1929–1957.

Source: 1929–1953, Office of Business Economics, records (except **series T 23, T 32, T 40, and T 43** for 1951–1956, Office of Business Economics, *Survey of Current Business*, June 1957, p. 28; and **series T 44–45** for 1929–1956, Bureau of the Census, *Statistical Abstract of the United States, 1953*, p. 851; *1954*, p. 862; and *1957*, p. 838); 1954–1956, *Statistical Abstract, 1957*, p. 838 (except **series T 23, T 32, T 40, and T 43** as noted above); 1957, Office of Business Economics, records.

Sales of multiunit stores, which are shown separately in series T 49–71, are also included in series T 23–48.

The definitions of retail stores and of kinds of business are in accordance with the 1948 Census of Business except as noted below. The classification of durable goods stores and nondurable goods stores is based on the durability of the commodities accounting for a major portion of the sales of each kind-of-business group. Census of retail trade data were used as benchmarks for 1929–1951. Estimates for intercensal years in this period were developed from sales tax collection data, special Internal Revenue Service compilations, business population trends, the Federal Reserve Board index of department store sales, and data from the Bureau of Public Roads and the American Petroleum Institute. Methods of compilation are described in Office of Business Economics, *Business Statistics, 1957, A Supplement to the Survey of Current Business*, p. 218.

Beginning in 1951, the figures are based on a new method of estimating retail sales and are not comparable to those shown for prior years. The new series for 1951–1957 is based on a sample consisting of about 30,000 organizations operating about 100,000 stores. The new series (as revised in 1957) also excludes milk dealers engaged in processing on the premises. Such establishments are treated as manufacturing plants in the 1954 Census. The sampling procedure for the new series is described in *Business Statistics, 1957*, cited above. Current monthly data are reported in the *Survey of Current Business*.

T 49–71. Retail sales of multiunit stores, by kind of business, 1929–1957.

Source: 1929–1953 and 1956–1957, Office of Business Economics, records; 1951 and 1954–1956, Bureau of the Census, *Statistical Abstract of the United States, 1957*, p. 849.

These series consist of 3 segments. The old series (designated as "Retail Sales of Chain Stores and Mail-Order Houses") represents sales of firms with 4 or more stores, and covers 1929–1951. Data from the Census of Business for 1929, 1933, 1935, 1939, and 1948 were used as benchmarks. The intercensal estimates were based on sample groups of organizations with 4 or more stores.

The new series, which covers 1951–1956, is based on a sample of firms which operated 11 or more units in 1948. The figures are not linked to the census of business. The new series, modified, covers 1956 and 1957, and is based on a new sample of firms which operated 11 or more units in 1954 and using 1954 classifications and definitions. As no adjustments are made for entries and exits from the "11 or more" category between censuses, the reported data cannot be subtracted from total retail sales to obtain sales by organizations operating 10 or fewer stores. Current monthly data for most of these series are reported in the *Survey of Current Business*.

T 72–182. Retail establishments, sales, and persons engaged, by kind of business, 1929–1954.

Source: 1929, 1939 (figures comparable with later years), 1948 (figures comparable with earlier years), *U. S. Census of Business: 1948*, Vol. I, *Retail Trade*, pp. 1.04–1.05; 1933; *Census of American Business: 1933*, Vol. I, *Retail Distribution*; 1935, 1939 (figures comparable with earlier years), *Census of Business: 1939*, Vol. I, *Retail Trade*, p. 57; 1948 (figures comparable with later years), 1954, *U. S. Census of Business: 1954*, Vol. I, *Retail Trade*, pp. 1-5 to 1-8. **Series T 84–86, T 93–95, T 177–179**, 1929, *Fifteenth Census of the United States: 1930*, Vol. I, *Distribution*.

Certain of these series have been combined for some years, and adjusted for others, by Professors Charles S. Goodman and Reavis Cox of the Wharton School of Finance and Commerce, University of Pennsylvania, in order to provide as comparable historical series as possible. Figures for 1933, in particular, have been adjusted for comparability. The reports of the census of business provide considerably more detail as to kinds of business.

Stores are classified according to their principal kind of business. Where a number of lines are carried, changes in relative importance may serve to shift a particular establishment from one category to another between censuses. The user of these figures is cautioned that sales figures shown are for kinds of establishments, not kinds of products.

Sales and excise taxes are included in sales figures for 1954 and excluded for 1948 and 1939. For earlier censuses, instructions called for the inclusion of sales taxes but these instructions were ignored in many instances.

Figures for persons engaged represent the total of the reported number of active proprietors and employees for the payroll period nearest November 15 for 1939 and later years, and of active proprietors plus the average number of employees for the year for 1939 and earlier years. Unpaid family workers are excluded from the definition of persons engaged. Such workers do represent an important additional labor force in some lines of retail trade. For retail trade as a whole, the 1948 Census enumerated 930,546 such workers, or 107 per thousand persons engaged (as defined above). For 1939, there were 923,878 unpaid family workers, or 144 per thousand persons engaged, of which 467,393 were full time and 456,485 were part time. Unpaid family workers were of greatest significance in grocery stores, without fresh meat, in which there were some 503 such workers per thousand persons engaged (as defined above) in 1948. Data for 1948 and 1939 are reported in the *Census of Business* for those years.

Establishments without paid employment and with less than $2,500 sales were excluded in 1954. The 1948 figures exclude stores which operated the entire year but had sales less than $500. The corresponding cutoff point for 1939 was $100.

There have been many changes in enumeration methods, in accuracy, and in classifications over the years. The principal ones are noted here; others are described in the various census volumes. The 1954 Census was conducted by a mail canvass of firms included in the active records of the Internal Revenue Service as subject to the payment of FICA taxes and which were in appropriate kind-of-business classifications. Such data cover only firms with paid employees. The nonemployer segment was derived from a 50-percent sample of 1954 tax returns. The 1948 and earlier censuses were conducted by field enumerations. The differences in enumeration affect particularly the coverage of establishments without easily recognized places of business (e.g., nonstore retailers) and those leaving business prior to the end of the year. The 1954 data are thus more complete in these areas. The 1933 and 1935 Censuses were not taken under mandatory reporting requirements and may be subject to some underenumeration.

Dairies which processed milk and cream were included as retailers in 1948 and earlier years if the major portion of their sales was by route delivery to the homes of consumers. They were excluded in 1954.

Nonstore retailers are treated as a separate kind of business for 1954. For earlier years, such retailers (to the extent enumerated) were classified in the appropriate product kind of business. For 1954, each leased department is treated as a separate establishment; for 1948 and earlier years, such

departments were consolidated with the establishments in which they were located.

Two sets of estimates are shown for 1948. The data for 1948 (comparable with later years) represent retabulations of 1948 data to make them comparable with 1954 as to treatment of dairies, nonstore retailers, and cutoff points for tabulation. Similarly, two sets of estimates are shown for the number of persons engaged in retail establishments in 1939. The data for 1939 (comparable with later years) represent the sum of active proprietors and paid employees for the payroll period nearest November 15 and are comparable with 1948 and 1954 data. The figures for 1939 (comparable with earlier years) represent the number of active proprietors and the average number of employees for the year, and are comparable with data for 1935 and earlier years.

T 183–187. Chains and chain stores, 1872–1928.

Source: Federal Trade Commission, *Chain Stores: Growth and Development of Chain Stores* (72d Congress, 1st session, Senate Document No. 100), p. 80.

Figures include chains of two or more stores reporting to the Federal Trade Commission or known to that agency. Grocery and meat chains have been combined with grocery chains. Ready-to-wear chains include men's ready-to-wear chains, women's ready-to-wear chains, and men's and women's ready-to-wear chains but not chains specializing in furnishings, accessories, millinery, and the like, nor dry goods chains whether carrying apparel or not. Data for each of the 26 lines of business shown in the total column are found in the source. The source publication also contains estimates of the number of chain outlets in different years but such data embody substantial estimating difficulties.

T 188–207. Retail trade margins, by kind of store, 1869–1947.

Source: Harold Barger, *Distribution's Place in the American Economy Since 1869*, National Bureau of Economic Research, Princeton University Press, 1955, pp. 57, 60, and 81.

The retail margin estimates are shown as a percent of retail value, and include both net profit and expenses of doing business. With regard to the reliability of the data, the source volume notes that "because of the extremely heterogeneous nature of the source material, it is not possible to offer any measures of dispersion within categories for the data." The source concludes, however, that we may "have some confidence that at least the larger differences reported . . . have a real existence."

T 208–210. Sales of wholesale establishments, 1939–1957.

Source: Office of Business Economics, records.

These series appear currently in the *Survey of Current Business*. The estimates exclude sales of corporate manufacturers, sales branches and offices, and the marketing stations of petroleum refiners which are included in the manufacturing series of the Office of Business Economics. Sales of agents and brokers are included here on the basis of actual receipts of the agents and brokers rather than on the total value of goods sold. Data for 1948–1957 are based on definitions and classifications in the 1954 Census of Business; for 1939–1947, on 1948 Census of Business definitions and classifications.

T 211–302. Wholesale establishments, sales, operating expenses, and persons engaged, by kind of business, 1929–1954.

Source: 1929, 1939, 1948 (figures comparable with earlier years), *U.S. Census of Business: 1948*, Vol. IV, *Wholesale Trade*, p. 105; 1933, *Census of American Business: 1933*, Vol. I, *Wholesale Distribution*, and *U.S. Summary of Wholesale Trade—Kinds of Business in Detail for 1933 and 1929*; 1935,

Census of Business: 1939, Vol. II, *Wholesale Trade*, pp. 1037–1044; 1948 (figures comparable with later years), 1954, *U. S. Census of Business: 1954*, Vol. III, *Wholesale Trade*, pp. 1-4 and 1-11. **Series T 213–214**, 1929, *Census of Business: 1939*, Vol. II, *Wholesale Trade*. **Series T 217, T 221, T 233, T 237, T 241, T 245, T 249, T 253, T 257, T 261, T 265, T 269, T 273, T 277, T 281, T 293, and T 297**, 1929, *Fifteenth Census of the United States: 1930*, Vol. II, *Distribution*.

Data shown are for wholesale establishments, other than chain store warehouses. Adjustments have been made in the published data for certain years by Professors Charles S. Goodman and Reavis Cox of the Wharton School of Finance and Commerce, University of Pennsylvania, in order to attain maximum comparability.

Persons engaged represents paid employment for the workweek ended nearest November 15 plus active proprietors of unincorporated firms.

There have been numerous changes over the years in the definitions of kinds of business, scope of the census (especially as regards size minima for enumeration), enumeration methods, and completeness of data. The statistics shown have been adjusted where possible to maintain maximum comparability over time. Significant changes are noted below. For treatment of lesser differences, see source publications.

The 1954 Census was conducted by mail canvass. Report forms were mailed to all firms included in the active records of the Internal Revenue Service as subject to the payment of FICA taxes and which were classified in appropriate kinds of business or were unclassified at the time the forms were mailed. The 1948 and earlier censuses were conducted by field canvasses. The 1933 and 1935 censuses were not taken under mandatory reporting requirements and may therefore be subject to some underenumeration.

Data for 1954 are for establishments with paid employees. The original 1948 tabulations include all establishments with sales of $5,000 or more irrespective of employment. For 1939, the corresponding cutoff point was $500. The figures for 1948 (comparable with later years) have been revised to reflect 1954 coverage and to incorporate certain changes in classification.

T 303–309. Wholesale trade margins of independent wholesalers, 1869–1947.

Source: See source for series T 188–207, p. 84.

See text for series T 188–207 for definition of "margin" and statement regarding reliability of the data.

T 310–345. Selected service establishments and receipts, 1914–1954.

Source: **Series T 320–323**, 1914–1935, *Biennial Census of Manufactures*, 1925, 1933, and 1935; **series T 342–343**, 1929–1935, *Census of Business: 1935, Hotels*. Except as noted above, 1933, *Census of American Business: 1933*, Vol. I, *Service Establishments*; 1935, *Census of Business: 1935*, Vol. I, *Service Establishments*; 1939 (figures comparable with earlier years), *Census of Business: 1939*, Vol. III, *Service Establishments*; 1939 (figures comparable with later years), 1948 (figures comparable with earlier years), *U.S. Census of Business: 1948*, Vol. VI, *Service Trade*; 1948 (figures comparable with later years), 1954, *U.S. Census of Business: 1954*, Vol. V, *Selected Services*.

Certain series have been combined for some years in order to provide as comparable historical series as possible. For some of the series, as noted below, data for some years were collected in other census programs. The series presented here cover that very limited segment of the services sector which bears greatest similarity to retail trade, specifically, personal, business, and automotive services, and hotels.

There have been numerous changes in enumeration methods, in accuracy, and in classifications over the years. The principal ones are noted here; others can be noted by reference to the various census volumes. The 1954 Census was conducted by a mail canvass of firms included in the active records of the Internal Revenue Service as subject to the payment of FICA taxes and which were in appropriate kind-of-business classifications. Such data cover only firms with paid employees. The nonemployer segment was derived from a 50-percent sample of 1954 tax returns. The 1948 and earlier censuses were conducted by field enumerations. The differences in enumeration methods affect particularly the coverage of establishments without easily recognizable places of business and those leaving business prior to the end of the year. The 1954 data are thus more complete in those areas. The 1933 and 1935 Censuses were not taken under mandatory reporting requirements and may therefore be subject to some underenumeration. There are important gaps in enumerators' reports for 1933 so that substantial underenumeration, particularly of the smaller establishments, exists for 1933. Underenumerations have more effect on the number of establishments than on receipts.

Establishments without paid employment and with less than $1,000 receipts were excluded in 1954 tabulations. The data for 1948 (comparable with later years) show 1948 figures adjusted to this cutoff point. The data for 1948 (comparable with earlier years) exclude establishments which operated the entire year but had receipts less than $500. For 1939 and earlier years establishments having receipts of $100 or more are included (except as noted). Where two estimates are shown for 1939, the figures for 1939 (comparable with later years) represent a revision to conform to 1948 kind-of-business definitions.

Receipts for 1954 include sales and excise taxes. These items are excluded for 1948 and 1939.

Establishments are classified according to their principal kinds of business. Changes in relative importance may thus serve to shift particular establishments among service categories or between service and retailing classifications from one census to another. Many service establishments derive some receipts from sales of merchandise; conversely, many establishments primarily engaged in the sale of goods, and hence included in retail trade, obtain some income from services. Receipts reported in each case represent *total receipts of establishments comprising the classification*, not receipts for the particular service indicated.

T 310–311, total personal services. Data for 1933 and 1935 represent groupings that correspond most closely to the 1939 scope. Power laundries and drycleaning plants with receipts under $5,000 have been excluded for 1933.

T 318–325, laundries and laundry service; cleaning and dyeing plants; and pressing, alteration, etc. Total laundries (series T 318–319) include self-service laundries for 1948 and subsequent years. Power laundries for 1919–1935 include only establishments with receipts of $5,000 or more. Cleaning and dyeing plants (series T 322–323) include plants primarily engaged in drycleaning and dyeing of apparel and household fabrics. Collecting and distributing units are included only if owned and operated by the plant. Establishments known as "cleaners" which do no drycleaning but have their cleaning done for them by cleaning and dyeing plants are included in series T 324–325. Rug cleaning plants are included as cleaning and dyeing plants for 1933 and later years; such establishments are treated as laundries for 1931 and earlier years.

T 326–327, photographic studios. Since the 1954 data were obtained by mail canvass, they are believed to be substantially more complete than data for earlier years for this industry in which nonrecognizable establishments are likely to result in substantial underenumeration in a field canvass.

T 330–331, automobile repair shops. Data for 1935 include specialized shops as enumerated in the census of service establishments, and general repair garages as enumerated in the *1935 Census of Business, Retail Distribution*, table 1A. Data for 1933 cover only general repair garages, as enumerated in the *1933 Census of American Business, Retail Distribution*, table 1A, and the following types of specialized shops as reported in *1933 Census of American Business, Service Industries*: Paint shops, radiator shops, top and body repair shops, tire repair shops, and brake repair shops.

T 338–341, miscellaneous repair services. Separate data are available for some or all of the indicated years for several of the repair services in this group including shops engaged in armature rewinding, bicycle repair, blacksmithing, harness and leather goods repair, musical instrument repair, saw and tool repair, typewriter repair, upholstering and furniture repair, watch, clock, and jewelry repair, etc. Since the 1954 data were obtained by mail canvass, they are believed to be substantially more complete than data for earlier years in these industries in which nonrecognizable establishments are likely to result in substantial underenumeration in a field canvass.

T 342–343, year-round hotels. Data for 1954 are for establishments with payrolls only.

T 346–351.   Volume of advertising, 1867–1957.

Source: 1867–1939, Printers' Ink Publications, New York, N. Y., *Printers' Ink Advertisers' Annual*, 1955 edition; 1940–1956, *Printers' Ink Advertisers' Guide to Marketing for 1958*, pp. 54–55; 1957, *Printers' Ink Advertisers' Guide to Marketing for 1959*, pp. 154–155.

The data are prepared by McCann-Erickson, Inc., from information furnished by the American Newspaper Publishers Association, A. C. Nielson Company, Publishers' Information Bureau, Farm Publication Reports, Inc., the Direct Mail Advertising Association, A. R. Venezian, Outdoor Advertising, Inc., and the Federal Communications Commission.

The data include the cost of preparation, and the cost of talent in the case of radio and television as well as the charges for space and time. Total advertising figures (series T 346) include, in addition to the figures for the media shown, advertising in regional farm publications and business papers, outdoor advertising, and miscellaneous advertising expenditures.

T 352–355.   Farm-to-retail price spreads of farm food products, 1913–1957.

Source: 1935–39 market basket: 1913–1950, Department of Agriculture, *Agricultural Statistics, 1952*, p. 669; 1951–1952, Agricultural Marketing Service, *The Marketing and Transportation Situation*, April 1953, p. 6. 1952 market basket: 1947–1956, Agricultural Marketing Service, *Farm-Retail Spreads for Food Products*, Misc. Pub. No. 741, 1957, p. 98; 1957, *The Marketing and Transportation Situation*, January 1958, p. 47.

The data are prepared by the Agricultural Marketing Service. The 1952 market basket contains quantities of food equal to the average annual purchases per wage-earner and clerical-worker family in 1952. The 1935–39 market basket contains quantities equivalent to the 1935–39 annual average purchases per family of 3 average consumers. Quantities do not change from year to year.

Retail costs are calculated from prices collected by the Bureau of Labor Statistics. Farm value represents payments to farmers, exclusive of government subsidies, for unprocessed products equivalent to the foods in the market basket. The marketing margin is the difference between farm value and retail cost. It comprises payments to agencies that assemble and process the food raw materials and perform other functions to get food products to consumers at the times and places desired.

T 356–358.   Retail cost, farm value, and marketing bill, for all farm food products purchased by domestic civilian consumers, 1913–1956.

Source: Agricultural Marketing Service, *Farm-Retail Spreads for Food Products*, Misc. Pub. No. 741, 1957, p. 49.

Unlike the market basket (series T 352–355) which measures a fixed quantity of food products, these series represent aggregates of all food products which originate on domestic farms and are bought by domestic civilian consumers. These estimates reflect not only price changes, but also changes in the total volume of products marketed, some variations in marketing services, and some of the effects of changes in the form in which goods are purchased by consumers, for instance the shift from flour to bread or the purchase of potato chips or frozen french fries instead of unprocessed potatoes.

In developing retail costs, different methods were used depending on the availability of data. Most commonly, such costs were estimated by dividing adjusted cash farm receipts by the farmers' share percentages for individual commodities as calculated for the market basket series. Thus they do not fully reflect changes in processing and other marketing services.

Food purchased in the form of meals is valued at what the food would have cost in retail stores, thus excluding services provided by such food preparers. For a similar series in which food purchased in eating establishments is valued at prices paid by consumers, see Department of Agriculture, *Agricultural Economics Research*, "The Farmer's Share: Three Measurements," April 1956, pp. 43–50.

The farm value represents only that part of farmers' cash receipts allocated to civilian domestic food use after making allowance for export and military use, interfarm transfers, the value of nonfood byproducts, and changes in stocks. These series do not include imported foods or nonfarm foods such as coffee, tea, and fish.

T 359–360.   Index of department store sales and stocks, 1919–1957.

Source: 1919–1946, Board of Governors of the Federal Reserve System, *Federal Reserve Bulletin*, December 1951, pp. 1490-1491; 1947–1956, *Federal Reserve Bulletin*, December 1957, p. 1340; 1957, *Federal Reserve Bulletin*, April 1958, p. 486.

The index for sales is based on the average per trading day. The stocks index is the annual average of monthly data of end-of-month stocks. Procedures used and the nature of periodic revisions are described in the December 1951 and December 1957 *Bulletins*. Current data appear monthly in the *Federal Reserve Bulletin*.

T 361–365.   Hotel operations, 1920–1957.

Source: Horwath and Horwath, New York, *Hotel Operations in 1957*, pp. 23 and 26–27.

Data are computed by Horwath and Horwath from about 400 hotels and are reported monthly in *The Horwath Hotel Accountant*. Data for 1926 and earlier years are based on relatively few hotels but do include two of the largest chains existing at that time. Sales and rate indexes based on 1951= 100 are also available, as are average room rates, in dollars, for the period since 1940.

T 366–386. Book value of inventories at end of year, 1929–1957.

Source: **Series T 366–374**, 1938–1952, Office of Business Economics, *Business Statistics, 1957*, pp. 49–50; 1953–1955, same agency, records; 1956, same agency, *Survey of Current Business*, February 1958, p. S-10; 1957, *Survey of Current Business*, May 1958, p. S-10. **Series T 375–377**, 1938–1947, Office of Business Economics, *Business Statistics, 1957*, p. 14; 1948–1950, same agency, records; 1951–1956, *Survey of Current Business*, August 1957, p. 32; 1957, *Survey of Current Business*, May 1958, p. S-3. **Series T 378–386**, 1929–1956 (except series T 380–382 and T 384–386 for 1953–1956), *Business Statistics, 1957*, pp. 17-20; **series T 380–382** and **T 384–386**, 1953–1956, *Survey of Current Business*, September 1957, p. 20; 1957, *Survey of Current Business*, May 1958, p. S-4.

In these series, trade inventories are valued at the cost of merchandise on hand while manufacturers' inventories are valued at cost or market price, whichever is lower. About 15 percent of manufacturers' inventories are valued on a last-in-first-out basis; this basis is much less prevalent in trade, although it is used extensively by department stores. Changes in book values reflect changes in unit costs as well as changes in physical quantities. Data for these series are published currently in the *Survey of Current Business*.

T 366–374, retail store inventories. Data for 1950–1957 represent the new series which are based on samples and are comparable in concept and coverage to the new series on retail sales. Data for 1938–1950 represent the old series which was linked to the 1954 Census of Business.

T 375–377, wholesale trade inventories. The scope includes all classes of wholesalers as defined by the 1954 Census of Business except that corporate manufacturers' sales branches and offices, and marketing stations of petroleum refiners have been excluded since they are included in the series on manufacturers' inventories. Data for 1947 and earlier are based on the definitions and classifications of the 1948 Census of Business instead of the 1954 Census. Inventories are valued at the cost of merchandise on hand; changes thus reflect changes in unit prices as well as changes in physical quantities.

T 378–386, manufacturers' inventories, by stage of fabrication. Seasonally adjusted series are not available prior to 1939. Data for 1929–1938 are without adjustment for seasonal variation. Unadjusted series are available since 1938 in the sources indicated.

Series T 1–11. National Income Originating in Distribution and Selected Service Industries: 1869 to 1957

[In millions of dollars. Net value added at factor costs]

Year	Whole-sale trade	Retail trade and automotive services	Hotels and other lodging places	Personal services	Business services [1]	Miscellaneous repair services and hand trades	Motion pictures	Amusement and recreation, except motion pictures	Legal services	Engineering and other professional services [1]	Nonprofit membership organizations [1]
	1	2	3	4	5	6	7	8	9	10	11
1957	20,929	38,693	1,814	4,019	4,841	1,488	867	1,335	2,095	1,952	2,653
1956	20,096	37,243	1,731	3,856	4,375	1,413	887	1,261	1,965	1,809	2,487
1955	18,729	36,271	1,657	3,652	3,795	1,310	926	1,187	1,900	1,474	2,311
1954	16,614	34,035	1,585	3,468	3,338	1,182	895	1,103	1,745	1,286	2,199
1953	16,551	33,202	1,566	3,395	3,133	1,176	815	1,032	1,595	1,245	2,060
1952	16,232	32,719	1,535	3,258	2,831	1,132	852	918	1,507	1,156	1,913
1951	15,905	31,282	1,461	3,149	2,533	1,046	853	865	1,449	948	1,758
1950	13,682	29,025	1,385	3,006	2,266	930	830	825	1,339	731	1,588
1949	12,401	28,166	1,354	2,898	2,018	877	879	815	1,253	680	1,471
1948	13,005	28,448	1,339	2,830	1,981	937	893	833	1,174	672	1,362
1947	11,651	25,690	1,287	2,634	1,748	938	1,054	794	1,033	560	1,242
1946	10,393	24,024	1,322	2,552	1,560	843	1,133	810	954	454	1,127
1945	8,242	19,755	1,085	2,121	1,251	703	930	613	930	335	983
1944	7,640	18,105	983	2,012	1,189	701	883	507	874	320	916
1943	6,911	16,920	877	1,893	1,074	610	830	436	814	344	819
1942	6,195	14,117	674	1,548	938	419	652	388	793	385	716
1941	5,228	12,026	584	1,286	836	350	513	368	763	264	640
1940	4,463	9,874	530	1,150	700	261	449	310	719	193	599
1939	3,830	8,623	481	1,049	672	261	434	288	692	181	556
1938	3,779	8,164	456	1,024	633	259	426	266	666	164	556
1937	3,926	8,286	471	1,110	646	247	437	305	680	156	547
1936	3,234	7,356	413	958	606	230	391	253	647	144	546
1935	2,919	6,281	371	857	502	218	329	211	624	121	528
1934	2,476	5,580	341	782	447	203	283	197	600	113	532
1933	1,781	3,704	271	695	350	191	210	154	561	98	527
1932	2,158	4,196	305	800	378	224	194	178	591	102	569
1931	3,181	6,562	442	1,030	476	273	361	269	701	152	626
1930	4,053	8,176	543	1,203	597	301	438	337	683	184	649
1929 [2]	4,222	9,136	599	1,279	601	312	440	381	689	206	640
1929 [3][4]	4,120	8,960	----	----	----	----	----	----	----	----	----
1919 [3]	3,130	5,920	----	----	----	----	----	----	----	----	----
1909 [3]	1,300	2,320	----	----	----	----	----	----	----	----	----
1899 [3]	810	1,340	----	----	----	----	----	----	----	----	----
1889 [3]	360	1,020	----	----	----	----	----	----	----	----	----
1879 [3]	220	560	----	----	----	----	----	----	----	----	----
1869 [3]	210	500	----	----	----	----	----	----	----	----	----

[1] Not elsewhere classified.   [2] Comparable with later years.   [3] Excludes inventory valuation adjustment.   [4] Comparable with earlier years.

Series T 12–22. Persons Engaged in Distribution and Selected Service Industries: 1869 to 1957

[In thousands of persons]

Year	Whole-sale trade	Retail trade and automotive services	Hotels and other lodging places	Personal services	Business services [1]	Miscellaneous repair services and hand trades	Motion pictures	Amusement and recreation, except motion pictures	Legal services	Engineering and other professional services [1]	Nonprofit membership organizations [1]
	12	13	14	15	16	17	18	19	20	21	22
1957	3,199	9,754	684	1,268	825	575	196	301	258	317	686
1956	3,158	9,664	669	1,267	760	549	206	301	256	303	675
1955	3,086	9,437	655	1,248	688	522	211	296	253	262	657
1954	2,969	9,220	643	1,241	635	486	214	288	251	238	647
1953	2,971	9,311	661	1,243	624	514	217	291	248	235	634
1952	2,922	9,225	643	1,246	590	522	225	288	244	220	619
1951	2,847	9,089	632	1,243	559	495	230	291	242	190	604
1950	2,711	8,728	609	1,225	542	451	234	294	234	157	581
1949	2,668	8,596	616	1,221	525	465	236	296	227	155	566
1948	2,712	8,597	640	1,241	525	504	234	299	217	160	554
1947	2,625	8,376	636	1,243	491	535	237	284	212	144	540
1946	2,419	7,973	632	1,210	448	504	236	275	210	131	514
1945	2,052	6,862	584	1,073	369	399	222	232	195	112	493
1944	1,936	6,598	584	1,053	361	394	221	232	200	104	479
1943	1,912	6,648	573	1,090	363	378	211	234	211	110	455
1942	2,041	6,916	561	1,115	357	328	200	255	228	129	448
1941	2,136	7,126	557	1,095	343	320	191	256	245	103	427
1940	2,015	6,768	538	1,050	315	293	181	240	244	91	390
1939	1,942	6,440	526	996	310	300	179	223	242	86	328
1938	1,857	6,218	522	1,008	297	314	178	212	236	82	331
1937	1,857	6,305	520	1,034	291	311	184	230	230	80	332
1936	1,690	5,949	494	994	285	311	171	212	225	78	342
1935	1,572	5,608	469	950	251	311	155	197	223	74	338
1934	1,530	5,431	453	910	246	309	141	193	216	72	339
1933	1,393	5,038	403	860	218	312	124	180	217	69	335
1932	1,395	5,058	417	886	213	315	128	200	214	69	341
1931	1,533	5,507	465	941	212	299	147	248	212	77	354
1930	1,685	5,839	504	996	229	281	153	277	202	85	358
1929	1,744	6,077	518	1,008	233	264	153	295	194	83	351
1919	1,233	3,977	----	----	----	----	----	----	----	----	----
1909	1,034	3,177	----	----	----	----	----	----	----	----	----
1899	783	2,218	----	----	----	----	----	----	----	----	----
1889	397	1,775	----	----	----	----	----	----	----	----	----
1879	250	1,087	----	----	----	----	----	----	----	----	----
1869	169	716	----	----	----	----	----	----	----	----	----

[1] Not elsewhere classified.

Series T 23–48. Retail Store Sales, by Kind of Business: 1929 to 1957

[In millions of dollars]

			Durable goods stores							Nondurable goods stores			
			Automotive group		Furniture and appliance group		Lumber, building, hardware group				Apparel group		
Year	All stores	Total sales [1]	Motor vehicle, other automotive dealers	Tire, battery, accessory dealers	Furniture, home-furnishings stores	Household appliance, radio stores	Lumber, building materials dealers	Hardware stores	Jewelry stores	Total sales [1]	Total	Men's and boys' wear stores	Women's apparel, accessory stores
	23	24	25	26	27	28	29	30	31	32	33	34	35
1957	200,010	68,460	36,298	2,293	6,601	3,984	7,950	2,737	(²)	131,550	12,277	2,487	4,914
1956	189,729	65,810	34,050	2,072	6,568	4,099	8,312	2,893	(²)	123,919	11,610	2,469	4,541
1955	183,851	66,978	36,267	1,959	6,116	3,939	8,242	2,788	(²)	116,873	10,791	2,294	4,207
1954	169,135	58,173	29,962	1,703	5,291	3,788	7,433	2,702	(²)	110,962	10,147	2,239	4,009
1953	169,094	60,371	31,498	1,822	5,136	3,989	7,715	2,706	(²)	108,723	10,256	2,249	4,089
1952	162,353	55,270	26,393	1,944	5,255	3,671	7,572	2,628	1,452	107,083	10,633	2,497	4,233
1951 ³	156,548	54,479	26,282	1,874	5,095	3,509	7,470	2,738	1,351	102,069	10,209	2,461	4,049
1951 ⁴	152,975	53,170	25,634	1,682	4,943	3,130	7,798	2,850	1,256	99,805	10,043	2,320	3,923
1950	143,689	52,935	26,702	1,587	4,847	3,402	7,458	2,634	1,174	90,754	9,333	2,175	3,606
1949	130,721	43,882	21,669	1,271	4,155	2,635	5,895	2,342	1,136	86,839	9,332	2,183	3,698
1948	130,521	41,876	18,744	1,360	4,371	2,543	6,272	2,494	1,225	88,645	9,803	2,309	3,961
1947	119,604	36,652	15,804	1,278	4,042	2,311	5,433	2,255	1,247	82,952	9,294	2,309	3,638
1946	102,488	27,570	10,647	1,275	3,264	1,575	4,106	1,911	1,260	74,918	8,880	2,195	3,591
1945	78,034	16,026	5,000	855	2,101	639	2,502	1,237	997	62,008	7,689	1,769	3,338
1944	70,208	13,942	4,420	739	1,848	462	2,102	1,030	909	56,266	6,704	1,524	2,964
1943	63,235	12,221	3,768	670	1,692	415	2,024	903	894	51,014	6,158	1,405	2,670
1942	57,212	12,320	3,404	623	1,776	594	2,332	973	710	44,892	5,089	1,268	2,042
1941	55,274	17,213	8,185	704	1,780	796	2,442	905	566	38,061	4,137	1,076	1,635
1940	46,375	13,576	6,429	560	1,386	625	2,023	712	422	32,799	3,451	886	1,388
1939	42,042	11,312	5,025	524	1,200	533	1,761	629	362	30,730	3,259	840	1,323
1938	38,053	9,475	3,909	457	1,014	476	1,530	563	299	28,578	2,998	765	1,211
1937	42,150	12,048	5,568	499	1,254	592	1,739	651	347	30,102	3,323	878	1,325
1936	38,339	10,751	5,102	457	1,082	533	1,463	576	297	27,588	3,102	855	1,205
1935	32,791	8,321	3,863	374	852	438	1,105	467	235	24,470	2,656	727	1,026
1933	24,517	5,384	2,142	226	646	313	854	311	175	19,133	1,930	542	754
1929	48,459	15,610	6,432	599	1,813	942	2,621	706	536	32,849	4,241	1,358	1,480

	Apparel group—Con.				Nondurable goods stores—Con.			General merchandise group					
					Food group		Gasoline service stations						Liquor stores
Year	Family and other apparel stores	Shoe stores	Drug and proprietary stores	Eating and drinking places	Total	Grocery stores		Total	Department stores, excl. mail order	Mail order (catalog sales)	Variety stores	Other general merchandise	
	36	37	38	39	40	41	42	43	44	45	46	47	48
1957	2,786	2,091	6,325	14,796	47,786	42,444	15,070	21,157	⁵16,157	1,477	3,523	(⁵)	4,212
1956	2,532	2,068	5,775	14,317	44,223	39,180	13,738	20,762	11,327	1,407	3,423	4,605	3,944
1955	2,281	2,009	5,232	13,662	42,010	36,919	12,411	20,100	10,882	1,331	3,295	4,592	3,546
1954	2,090	1,809	4,940	13,127	40,106	34,993	11,443	18,857	10,272	1,222	3,027	4,336	3,415
1953	2,182	1,736	4,790	13,003	39,130	33,623	10,536	19,006	10,370	1,327	3,095	4,214	3,325
1952	2,210	1,693	4,717	12,688	38,039	32,238	9,976	18,694	10,277	1,339	2,996	4,082	3,165
1951 ³	2,015	1,684	4,547	12,207	35,951	30,346	9,151	18,202	10,095	1,309	2,859	3,939	2,975
1951 ⁴	2,163	1,637	4,500	11,626	36,940	29,816	8,390	18,170	9,846	1,284	2,807	4,233	2,834
1950	2,041	1,511	4,166	10,626	32,768	26,412	7,553	17,235	9,403	1,235	2,587	4,010	2,550
1949	1,997	1,454	4,037	10,470	30,965	24,800	6,957	16,307	8,862	1,156	2,506	3,783	2,474
1948	2,066	1,467	4,013	10,683	30,966	24,770	6,483	17,135	9,344	1,301	2,507	3,983	2,580
1947	1,904	1,443	3,867	10,651	28,434	22,501	5,482	16,053	(²)	(²)	2,322	3,676	2,649
1946	1,717	1,377	3,723	10,619	24,155	18,646	4,511	14,724	(²)	(²)	2,158	3,383	2,688
1945	1,442	1,140	3,155	9,575	19,233	14,593	3,284	11,802	6,484	608	1,845	2,865	2,288
1944	1,215	1,001	2,924	8,305	17,918	13,665	2,812	11,076	(²)	(²)	1,774	2,814	1,926
1943	1,114	969	2,628	7,216	16,447	12,481	2,628	10,162	(²)	(²)	1,642	2,631	1,557
1942	865	914	2,213	5,699	14,788	11,368	3,089	9,204	(²)	(²)	1,536	2,279	1,212
1941	700	726	1,847	4,570	12,244	9,312	3,466	7,973	(²)	(²)	1,320	1,791	854
1940	545	632	1,636	3,787	10,732	8,169	2,970	6,859	(²)	(²)	1,153	1,578	681
1939	479	617	1,563	3,529	10,156	7,722	2,822	6,475	3,408	464	1,080	1,523	586
1938	431	591	1,474	3,188	9,505	7,187	2,696	6,145	(²)	(²)	1,015	1,536	539
1937	484	636	1,527	3,293	9,699	7,266	2,641	6,673	(²)	(²)	1,025	1,755	558
1936	456	586	1,409	2,748	9,008	6,850	2,318	6,366	(²)	(²)	967	1,731	475
1935	392	511	1,233	2,395	8,358	6,352	1,968	5,730	2,833	386	873	1,638	328
1933	209	425	1,066	1,434	6,772	5,004	1,532	4,982	(²)	(²)	756	1,766	17
1929	596	807	1,690	2,132	10,960	7,353	⁶1,787	9,015	3,903	447	904	3,761	--------

¹ Totals include subclasses not shown separately.
² Not available.
³ Comparable with later years.
⁴ Comparable with earlier years.
⁵ Other general merchandise stores combined with department stores.
⁶ Excludes garages primarily selling gasoline and oil.

Series T 49–71. Retail Sales of Multiunit Stores, by Kind of Business: 1929 to 1957
[In millions of dollars]

| | | Durable goods stores | | | | | | | Nondurable goods stores | | | | | | | |
| | | | Automotive group | | Furniture, appliance group | | Lumber, building, hardware group | | | Apparel group | | | | | | |
Year	All stores [1]	Total sales [1]	Motor vehicle, other automotive dealers	Tire, battery, accessory dealers	Furniture, home-furnishings stores	Household appliance, radio stores	Total	Lumber, building materials dealers	Total sales [1]	Total	Men's and boys' wear stores	Women's apparel, accessory stores	Family and other apparel stores	Shoe stores	Drug and proprietary stores	Eating and drinking places
	49	50	51	52	53	54	55	56	57	58	59	60	61	62	63	64
1957	41,782	2,914	(2)	815	444	480	1,053	723	38,868	2,696	232	1,141	523	800	1,032	868
1956 [3]	39,630	2,973	(2)	763	467	486	1,131	810	36,657	2,616	219	1,093	534	770	943	821
1956 [4]	36,291	2,836	(2)	732	349	361	1,316	818	33,455	2,249	175	861	433	781	834	755
1955	33,918	2,790	(2)	700	347	366	1,300	838	31,128	2,166	186	852	404	724	785	707
1954	31,690	2,582	(2)	609	346	378	1,178	750	29,108	2,041	187	794	385	675	760	662
1953	30,929	2,580	(2)	636	320	390	1,155	728	28,349	2,079	205	821	402	651	759	671
1952	30,120	2,605	(2)	611	317	383	1,224	785	27,515	2,068	214	834	378	642	737	622
1951 [3]	28,536	2,521	(2)	568	287	392	1,208	798	26,015	2,009	215	786	356	652	722	590
1951 [4]	34,000	3,825	389	575	569	572	1,582	1,147	30,175	2,763	342	1,137	539	745	905	779
1950	31,232	3,863	408	551	592	622	1,561	1,147	27,369	2,588	338	1,042	512	696	852	724
1949	29,041	3,240	331	448	519	482	1,336	957	25,801	2,588	342	1,049	517	680	847	721
1948	29,737	3,407	287	454	562	465	1,505	1,107	26,330	2,729	366	1,117	548	698	869	742
1947	26,958	3,100	262	437	533	417	1,315	962	23,858	2,566	385	1,012	483	686	864	714
1946	22,514	2,510	191	467	436	281	998	715	20,004	2,434	355	1,013	425	641	830	676
1945	17,280	1,627	96	295	277	112	739	565	15,653	2,090	272	968	329	521	704	593
1944	16,234	1,416	91	270	240	81	636	500	14,818	1,957	264	923	286	484	681	558
1943	14,926	1,316	82	254	224	71	589	478	13,610	1,791	241	843	232	475	654	518
1942	14,376	1,291	79	236	211	101	588	486	13,085	1,594	237	668	182	507	571	439
1941	12,635	1,465	200	293	226	134	552	480	11,170	1,280	229	504	135	412	479	374
1940	10,500	1,157	165	241	175	104	427	385	9,343	1,062	182	428	97	355	425	330
1939	9,570	1,024	136	236	151	88	375	350	8,546	992	173	394	80	345	400	304
1938	8,872	931	115	221	126	77	362	339	7,941	913	156	349	76	332	377	288
1937	9,426	1,065	182	225	150	93	381	357	8,361	989	177	371	90	351	378	290
1936	8,960	986	190	208	127	81	351	330	7,974	913	174	326	90	323	352	270
1935	8,040	813	168	187	97	65	274	256	7,227	758	141	260	78	279	317	248
1933	6,618	528	115	76	86	60	180	162	6,090	589	112	214	41	222	267	182
1929	10,412	1,683	624	122	235	157	509	488	8,729	1,197	271	413	144	369	312	299

| | Nondurable goods stores—Con. | | | | | | | | Nondurable goods stores—Con. | | | | | | |
| | Food group | | Gasoline service stations | General merchandise group | | | | | Food group | | Gasoline service stations | General merchandise group | | | |
Year	Total	Grocery stores		Total [1]	Department stores, excl. mail order	Mail order (catalog sales)	Variety stores	Year	Total	Grocery stores		Total [1]	Department stores, excl. mail order	Mail order (catalog sales)	Variety stores
	65	66	67	68	69	70	71		65	66	67	68	69	70	71
1957	18,223	17,379	818	13,092	(2)	(2)	2,667	1945	5,614	4,705	271	4,925	2,630	608	1,559
1956 [3]	16,636	15,894	732	12,805	7,630	1,362	2,619	1944	5,499	4,657	241	4,621	2,380	609	1,510
1956 [4]	16,545	15,454	625	10,342	4,918	1,306	2,611	1943	5,111	4,318	234	4,222	2,125	581	1,406
								1942	5,211	4,520	285	4,094	2,050	628	1,325
1955	15,247	14,222	561	9,726	4,575	1,233	2,508	1941	4,328	3,729	331	3,666	1,828	621	1,147
1954	14,344	13,357	538	8,862	4,092	1,130	2,357								
1953	13,390	12,404	498	8,962	4,058	1,233	2,350	1940	3,635	3,106	294	2,978	1,421	491	1,008
1952	12,554	11,606	474	8,916	4,002	1,254	2,322	1939	3,340	2,833	288	2,693	1,226	464	952
1951 [3]	11,705	10,718	478	8,575	3,820	1,220	2,233	1938	3,110	2,618	316	2,448	1,075	424	900
1951 [4]	12,921	11,569	609	9,950	6,149	1,284	2,326	1937	3,170	2,643	375	2,590	1,155	467	917
								1936	3,083	2,608	403	2,428	1,060	445	878
1950	11,344	10,140	548	9,300	5,743	1,235	2,143								
1949	10,636	9,468	505	8,560	5,159	1,156	2,077	1935	2,916	2,468	423	2,124	898	386	801
1948	10,493	9,319	470	8,930	5,373	1,301	2,077	1933	2,594	2,209	544	1,589	673	220	696
1947	9,418	8,284	416	7,916	4,636	1,171	1,987	1929	3,475	2,833	605	2,275	1,013	447	815
1946	7,259	6,192	357	6,713	3,788	959	1,812								

[1] Totals include subclasses not shown separately.   [2] Not available.   [3] Comparable with later years.   [4] Comparable with earlier years.

Series T 72–182. Retail Establishments, Sales, and Persons Engaged, by Kind of Business: 1929 to 1954
[Sales in millions of dollars]

| | Total [1] | | | Food group | | | | | | | | | | | | | | |
| | | | | Total [1] | | | Grocery stores, without fresh meat | | | Grocery stores, with fresh meat | | | Meat markets | | |
Year	Number	Sales	Persons engaged	Number	Sales	Persons engaged	Number	Sales	Persons engaged	Number	Sales	Persons engaged	Number	Sales	Persons engaged
	72	73	74	75	76	77	78	79	80	81	82	83	84	85	86
ALL ESTABLISHMENTS															
1954	1,721,650	169,967	8,890,083	384,616	39,762	1,439,397	--------	--------	--------	[2]279,440	[2]34,420	[2]1,109,440	22,896	1,944	71,836
1948 [3]	1,668,479	128,849	--------	460,913	29,207	--------	--------	--------	--------	[2]350,754	[2]24,729	--------	23,920	1,641	--------
1948 [4]	1,769,540	130,520	8,660,107	504,439	30,965	1,515,618	154,277	4,026	241,129	223,662	20,743	825,619	24,242	1,641	66,427
1939 [3]	1,770,355	42,041	6,435,479	560,549	10,165	1,331,722	200,303	2,225	309,725	187,034	5,496	595,290	35,630	700	85,485
1939 [4]	--------	--------	6,213,890	--------	--------	1,315,438	--------	--------	309,284	--------	--------	582,699	--------	--------	83,684
1935	1,587,718	32,791	5,338,366	532,010	8,362	1,235,069	188,738	2,202	326,446	166,233	4,149	508,037	32,555	565	77,236
1933	1,439,669	24,517	4,816,615	470,149	6,776	1,170,291	163,538	1,803	306,086	140,372	3,201	452,298	(5)	(5)	(5)
1929	1,476,365	48,329	5,721,220	481,891	10,837	1,174,665	191,876	3,449	365,094	115,549	3,903	354,671	43,788	1,253	113,407
ESTABLISHMENTS WITH PAYROLLS															
1954	1,124,040	157,932	--------	200,468	35,233	--------	--------	--------	--------	[2]142,968	[2]30,890	--------	14,984	1,697	--------
1948	1,118,692	118,352	--------	232,532	24,375	--------	--------	--------	--------	[2]168,131	[2]20,699	--------	--------	--------	--------

See footnotes at end of table.

Series T 72–182. Retail Establishments, Sales, and Persons Engaged, by Kind of Business: 1929 to 1954—Con.
[Sales in millions of dollars]

Year	Fruit stores, vegetable markets Number	Sales	Persons engaged	Candy, nut, confectionery stores Number	Sales	Persons engaged	Bakery products stores Number	Sales	Persons engaged	Eating places Number	Sales	Persons engaged	Drinking places Number	Sales	Persons engaged
	87	88	89	90	91	92	93	94	95	96	97	98	99	100	101
ALL ESTABLISHMENTS															
1954	13,136	484	27,691	20,507	568	46,892	19,034	862	104,929	195,128	8,731	1,280,398	123,887	4,360	438,559
1948 [3]	13,482	394	----	27,165	586	----	19,500	722	----	179,185	6,440	----	146,604	4,204	----
1948 [4]	15,763	399	32,273	32,876	649	75,021	20,152	725	103,415	194,123	6,468	1,175,331	152,433	4,215	533,899
1939 [3]	27,666	222	48,564	48,015	295	77,170	16,985	168	43,217	169,792	2,135	777,884	135,594	1,385	358,398
1939 [4]	----	----	48,357	----	----	76,353	----	----	41,225	----	----	764,650	----	----	348,452
1935	32,632	216	56,463	55,197	314	91,164	14,150	99	28,939	153,468	1,666	652,334	98,005	724	252,167
1933	21,897	170	43,419	54,243	271	91,237	19,380	188	63,563	170,434	1,324	606,600	29,901	105	54,798
1929	22,904	308	46,277	63,265	571	127,311	12,013	201	41,907	134,293	2,124	615,385	----	----	----
ESTABLISHMENTS WITH PAYROLLS															
1954	4,648	331	----	7,777	351	----	15,102	802	----	149,996	8,142	----	94,413	3,878	----
1948										141,163	5,982	----	104,316	3,626	----

Year	General stores Number	Sales	Persons engaged	Department, dry goods, general merch. Number	Sales	Persons engaged	Variety stores Number	Sales	Persons engaged	Apparel group Total [1] Number	Sales	Persons engaged	Shoe stores Number	Sales	Persons engaged
	102	103	104	105	106	107	108	109	110	111	112	113	114	115	116
ALL ESTABLISHMENTS															
1954	17,701	1,088	50,296	36,874	13,702	928,322	20,917	3,066	347,997	119,743	11,078	707,702	23,847	1,895	101,843
1948 [3]	20,588	1,157	----	31,302	12,134	----	18,917	2,504	----	110,944	9,716	----	19,201	1,460	----
1948 [4]	21,557	1,159	63,396	32,334	13,468	1,045,507	20,210	2,506	345,812	115,246	9,803	685,156	19,551	1,467	87,203
1939 [3]	39,688	810	101,069	33,321	4,688	762,905	16,946	976	239,341	106,959	3,258	499,725	20,487	617	78,262
1939 [4]	----	----	99,347	----	----	681,711	----	----	221,658	----	----	471,066	----	----	76,151
1935	66,701	1,110	149,624	32,910	3,838	584,134	11,741	780	177,221	95,968	2,656	401,043	18,967	511	68,799
1933	85,839	1,097	191,611	37,666	3,213	567,214	12,046	678	163,002	86,548	1,923	341,202	18,836	424	63,193
1929	104,089	2,570	254,231	42,526	5,540	695,700	12,110	904	167,058	114,296	4,240	494,524	24,259	806	83,355
ESTABLISHMENTS WITH PAYROLLS															
1954	9,901	884	----	23,014	13,428	----	17,639	3,014	----	97,829	10,701	----	19,723	1,817	----
1948										85,163	9,306	----	15,248	1,390	----

Year	Women's ready-to-wear stores Number	Sales	Persons engaged	Furniture group Total [1] Number	Sales	Persons engaged	Furniture stores Number	Sales	Persons engaged	Household appliance, radio, TV stores Number	Sales	Persons engaged
	117	118	119	120	121	122	123	124	125	126	127	128
ALL ESTABLISHMENTS												
1954	([5])	([5])	([5])	91,797	8,619	440,362	([5])	([5])	([5])	40,542	3,237	163,186
1948 [3]	29,788	3,277	----	80,423	6,592	----	28,465	3,413	----	35,331	2,410	----
1948 [4]	30,677	3,305	255,426	85,585	6,914	456,186	29,031	3,427	190,551	36,931	2,543	165,307
1939 [3]	25,820	1,009	164,696	52,827	1,733	263,441	[6]19,902	[6]973	[6]125,607	20,913	533	89,651
1939 [4]	----	----	154,297	----	----	256,126	----	----	[6]121,512	----	----	88,342
1935	21,975	795	124,537	45,215	1,289	209,795	[6]17,043	[6]694	[6]92,760	18,396	438	84,006
1933	17,759	568	99,702	42,976	958	197,663	[6]17,418	[6]553	[6]93,419	17,922	312	79,446
1929	18,253	1,087	131,116	58,941	2,754	319,212	25,854	1,578	159,624	25,366	950	129,877
ESTABLISHMENTS WITH PAYROLLS												
1954	26,893	3,577	----	65,773	8,151	----	25,475	4,170	----	27,774	3,003	----
1948				60,275	6,212	----	([5])	([5])	([5])			

Year	Automotive group Total [1] Number	Sales	Persons engaged	Passenger car dealers, franchised Number	Sales	Persons engaged	Passenger car dealers, nonfranchised Number	Sales	Persons engaged	Tire, battery, accessory dealers Number	Sales	Persons engaged	Gasoline service stations Number	Sales	Persons engaged
	129	130	131	132	133	134	135	136	137	138	139	140	141	142	143
ALL ESTABLISHMENTS															
1954	85,953	29,915	788,246	41,407	25,108	623,740	20,140	2,423	56,552	18,845	1,814	91,292	181,747	10,743	558,449
1948 [3]	85,285	20,100	----	43,960	15,951	----	16,634	2,440	----	20,224	1,358	----	179,647	6,470	----
1948 [4]	86,162	20,104	711,200	43,999	15,952	556,668	16,874	2,441	49,841	20,628	1,359	90,384	188,253	6,483	482,486
1939 [3]	60,132	5,548	451,404	33,609	4,810	353,757	6,980	193	20,552	18,525	523	74,224	241,858	2,822	478,075
1939 [4]	----	----	440,536	----	----	345,771	----	----	19,789	----	----	72,025	----	----	467,002
1935	50,459	4,236	356,374	30,294	3,725	282,638	4,751	122	14,603	14,343	373	56,135	197,568	1,967	383,623
1933	48,545	2,367	285,817	[7]30,646	[7]2,127	[7]237,185	([7])	([7])	([7])	16,027	226	44,510	170,404	1,531	328,263
1929	69,379	7,043	477,510	42,204	6,266	386,356	3,097	140	10,867	22,313	599	75,147	121,513	1,787	245,278
ESTABLISHMENTS WITH PAYROLLS															
1954	68,573	29,351	----	39,465	25,007	----	11,362	2,115	----	14,451	1,723	----	120,855	9,292	----
1948	72,655	19,565	----										112,372	5,310	----

See footnotes at end of table.

Series T 72–182. Retail Establishments, Sales, and Persons Engaged, by Kind of Business: 1929 to 1954—Con.

[Sales in millions of dollars]

Year	Lumber, building, hardware group											
	Total [1]			Lumber, building materials dealers			Hardware stores			Farm equipment dealers		
	Number	Sales	Persons engaged	Number	Sales	Persons engaged	Number	Sales	Persons engaged	Number	Sales	Persons engaged
	144	145	146	147	148	149	150	151	152	153	154	155
ALL ESTABLISHMENTS												
1954	100,519	13,123	540,326	30,177	6,502	232,329	34,858	2,694	143,323	18,689	2,804	99,825
1948 [3]	97,342	11,143	--------	25,978	5,126	227,722	34,009	2,491	--------	17,509	2,386	--------
1948 [4]	98,938	11,151	566,626	26,110	5,127	227,722	34,674	2,493	149,182	17,615	2,386	94,182
1939 [3]	79,313	2,734	323,396	25,067	1,478	152,959	29,147	629	86,707	10,499	344	35,831
1939 [4]	--------	--------	318,051	--------	--------	149,275	--------	--------	85,471	--------	--------	36,646
1935	73,186	1,864	253,829	21,149	866	101,677	26,996	467	72,130	9,637	291	31,879
1933	76,098	1,342	261,249	21,015	603	97,488	22,844	311	60,886	9,958	177	28,953
1929	90,386	3,845	405,836	26,377	1,981	164,571	25,330	706	81,277	12,242	518	43,443
ESTABLISHMENTS WITH PAYROLLS												
1954	78,507	12,642	--------	25,429	6,395	--------	25,266	2,478	--------	16,399	2,744	--------
1948	79,899	10,767	--------	--------	--------	--------	--------	--------	--------	15,944	2,332	--------

Year	Drug and proprietary stores			Liquor stores			Fuel, ice dealers			Hay, grain, feed stores		
	Number	Sales	Persons engaged	Number	Sales	Persons engaged	Number	Sales	Persons engaged	Number	Sales	Persons engaged
	156	157	158	159	160	161	162	163	164	165	166	167
ALL ESTABLISHMENTS												
1954	56,009	5,251	354,261	31,240	3,180	85,244	27,070	2,842	121,292	16,530	3,455	75,725
1948 [3]	55,282	4,011	--------	32,949	2,578	--------	21,473	2,425	--------	17,970	2,796	--------
1948 [4]	55,796	4,013	334,716	33,422	2,579	82,041	22,670	2,424	127,215	18,213	2,790	75,374
1939 [3]	57,903	1,562	241,969	19,136	586	40,735	41,172	1,013	149,094	16,772	624	50,321
1939 [4]	--------	--------	239,076	--------	--------	39,346	--------	--------	142,694	--------	--------	49,304
1935	56,697	1,232	207,493	12,105	328	25,234	35,293	859	123,199	11,132	346	28,376
1933	58,407	1,066	205,300	3,767	16	5,806	[8]23,875	[8]623	[8]104,858	([5])	([5])	([5])
1929	58,258	1,690	233,210	--------	--------	--------	[8]19,118	[8]1,013	[8]109,191	21,394	990	66,072
ESTABLISHMENTS WITH PAYROLLS												
1954	49,489	5,103	--------	21,926	2,853	--------	16,986	2,668	--------	13,196	3,345	--------
1948	47,628	3,832	--------	21,282	2,201	--------	17,855	2,350	--------	--------	--------	--------

Year	Jewelry stores			Cigar stores and stands			Florists			Gift, novelty, souvenir stores			Secondhand stores		
	Number	Sales	Persons engaged	Number	Sales	Persons engaged	Number	Sales	Persons engaged	Number	Sales	Persons engaged	Number	Sales	Persons engaged
	168	169	170	171	172	173	174	175	176	177	178	179	180	181	182
ALL ESTABLISHMENTS															
1954	24,266	1,407	90,908	6,068	233	14,255	16,279	495	50,111	12,149	283	27,538	14,364	424	41,041
1948 [3]	20,550	1,209	--------	12,791	385	--------	13,565	375	--------	10,266	185	--------	13,387	298	--------
1948 [4]	21,269	1,224	89,322	14,526	535	30,658	14,749	377	46,459	12,516	195	26,938	16,969	304	37,917
1939 [3]	14,559	361	50,686	18,504	207	31,197	16,055	148	38,635	7,429	53	13,665	23,962	138	48,146
1939 [4]	--------	--------	48,326	--------	--------	31,173	--------	--------	39,202	--------	--------	13,544	--------	--------	46,814
1935	12,447	234	36,805	15,350	183	28,828	11,242	98	28,296	5,512	31	9,655	22,550	113	43,543
1933	14,313	175	38,197	20,175	189	39,417	7,728	66	21,297	([5])	([5])	([5])	20,869	105	45,305
1929	19,998	536	62,853	33,248	410	67,377	9,328	176	37,889	5,186	61	13,771	15,065	148	33,516
ESTABLISHMENTS WITH PAYROLLS															
1954	15,548	1,287	--------	3,270	181	--------	10,247	421	--------	6,063	216	--------	7,956	359	--------
1948	14,583	1,128	--------	--------	--------	--------	--------	--------	--------	--------	--------	--------	--------	--------	--------

[1] Totals include subclasses not shown separately.
[2] Grocery stores without fresh meat combined with grocery stores with fresh meat.
[3] Comparable with later years.
[4] Comparable with earlier years.
[5] Not available.
[6] Excludes interior decorators.
[7] Nonfranchised dealers combined with franchised dealers.
[8] Excludes fuel oil dealers.

Series T 183–187. Chains and Chain Stores: 1872 to 1928

Year	26 lines of merchandise	Grocery	Drug	Shoes	Ready-to-wear	Year	26 lines of merchandise	Grocery	Drug	Shoes	Ready-to-wear	Year or period	26 lines of merchandise	Grocery	Drug
	183	184	185	186	187		183	184	185	186	187		183	184	185
1928	1,718	315	179	220	294	1911	292	69	39	17	39	1894	19	11	1
1927	1,689	335	175	206	281	1910	257	62	36	13	34	1893	17	10	1
1926	1,565	310	166	182	258	1909	231	59	30	12	31	1892	14	9	1
						1908	212	53	26	12	29	1891	12	7	1
1925	1,440	301	162	167	231	1907	193	49	25	10	28				
1924	1,267	270	150	146	201	1906	173	45	24	9	23	1890	10	6	1
1923	1,164	249	145	128	184							1889	9	5	1
1922	1,056	232	131	114	165	1905	154	44	19	9	21	1888	8	4	1
1921	905	198	117	95	137	1904	132	41	16	8	15	1887	6	3	1
						1903	107	36	13	7	10	1886	5	3	--
1920	808	180	107	79	125	1902	87	29	12	6	9				
1919	733	168	101	63	110	1901	66	23	9	4	7	1885	4	2	--
1918	645	148	89	46	104							1875–1884	3	1	--
1917	607	135	86	44	96	1900	58	21	7	3	5	1874	2	1	--
1916	557	125	80	40	87	1899	42	17	3	2	5	1873	2	1	--
						1898	38	15	3	1	5	1872	1	1	--
1915	505	112	81	38	73	1897	35	14	2	1	4				
1914	450	103	70	36	61	1896	25	11	1	1	3				
1913	376	85	52	27	52	1895	21	11	1	1	1				
1912	324	78	45	21	44										

Series T 188–207. Retail Trade Margins, by Kind of Store: 1869 to 1947

[Percent of retail value]

Year	Grocery Independent	Grocery Chain	Meat	Country general	Department	Mail order	Dry goods	Variety	Apparel
	188	189	190	191	192	193	194	195	196
1947	18.0	17.5	20.3	17.9	35.6	28.0	28.0	36.0	37.7
1939	19.0	18.2	23.6	17.9	36.4	27.4	28.0	34.6	36.0
1929	19.5	18.5	24.7	18.4	33.4	26.8	28.0	34.7	34.1
1919	19.5	18.0	25.8	19.0	32.8	26.2	29.0	34.7	31.8
1909	19.5	17.0	26.8	18.7	29.3	25.6	27.0	33.3	29.6
1899	19.5	----------	28.0	18.1	25.6	25.0	21.4	31.0	27.5
1889	19.0	----------	29.0	17.8	22.2	24.4	19.2	----------	25.4
1879	18.5	----------	----------	17.5	----------	----------	18.7	----------	23.2
1869	18.0	----------	----------	----------	----------	----------	----------	----------	21.1

Year	Shoes Independent	Shoes Chain	Furniture, independent	Automobile accessories	Filling stations	Coal and lumber	Hardware	Farm implements	Restaurants	Drugs	Weighted mean [1]
	197	198	199	200	201	202	203	204	205	206	207
1947	34.5	27.6	40.0	32.6	19.5	25.8	29.0	23.0	58.0	33.0	[2]29.7
1939	32.9	28.9	41.2	32.6	19.0	25.0	27.8	21.9	56.3	33.0	29.7
1929	31.2	30.5	41.2	29.1	16.5	24.0	26.4	20.6	54.3	34.6	28.6
1919	29.5	32.0	39.0	26.5	14.0	22.5	25.0	19.2	52.4	34.6	28.0
1909	28.0	33.5	31.2	26.5	22.0	20.5	23.6	18.0	52.0	33.6	27.6
1899	26.3	----------	31.2	----------	----------	19.5	22.2	18.0	----------	31.8	26.2
1889	24.7	----------	30.6	----------	----------	19.0	23.7	19.6	----------	30.2	25.1
1879	23.1	----------	30.0	----------	----------	18.5	25.2	21.4	----------	28.4	24.1
1869	21.4	----------	----------	----------	----------	18.0	----------	23.0	----------	----------	23.2

[1] Includes classes not shown.   [2] 1948 data.

Series T 208–210. Sales of Wholesale Establishments: 1939 to 1957

[In billions of dollars]

Year	Total	Durable goods establish-ments	Non-durable goods establish-ments	Year	Total	Durable goods establish-ments	Non-durable goods establish-ments	Year	Total	Durable goods establish-ments	Non-durable goods establish-ments	Year	Total	Durable goods establish-ments	Non-durable goods establish-ments
	208	209	210		208	209	210		208	209	210		208	209	210
1957	135.2	50.4	84.8	1952	114.8	39.3	75.4	1947	87.4	24.5	62.9	1942	41.2	9.6	31.6
1956	135.3	52.8	82.5	1951	112.4	39.6	72.8	1946	71.9	17.5	54.4	1941	36.4	10.2	26.2
1955	127.4	48.2	79.2	1950	101.0	35.4	65.6	1945	53.8	10.9	42.8	1940	28.9	7.6	21.4
1954	116.8	40.0	76.8	1949	86.6	27.2	59.3	1944	49.8	10.1	39.7	1939	26.3	6.2	20.0
1953	117.7	41.4	76.3	1948	90.6	29.2	61.4	1943	46.0	9.5	36.5				

Series T 211–302. Wholesale Establishments, Sales, Operating Expenses, and Persons Engaged, by Kind of Business: 1929 to 1954

[Sales in millions of dollars; operating expenses and commissions earned in percentage of sales]

Year	All wholesale establishments				Merchant wholesalers — Total [1]				Groceries, confectionery, meat				Farm products [2] (edible)			
	Number	Sales	Operating expenses	Persons engaged	Number	Sales	Operating expenses	Persons engaged	Number	Sales	Operating expenses	Persons engaged	Number	Sales	Operating expenses	Persons engaged
	211	212	213	214	215	216	217	218	219	220	221	222	223	224	225	226
1954 [3]	252,318	234,974.4	9.4	2,741,449	165,153	101,100.9	13.2	1,791,771	18,334	15,980.6	9.0	216,928	11,461	6,077.2	11.8	110,422
1948 [3][4]	216,099	180,576.7	8.3	2,436,281	129,117	76,533.3	11.5	1,526,089	15,707	11,213.1	8.8	195,072	10,966	5,858.6	9.0	106,809
1948 [5]	243,366	188,688.8	8.3	2,546,279	146,518	79,766.6	11.6	1,614,813	17,345	11,356.7	8.8	196,636	13,539	7,500.9	11.6	169,393
1939	199,726	54,888.5	10.0	[6]1,738,813	100,961	22,537.8	13.1	1,020,525	15,681	3,940.8	11.3	165,550	10,945	2,110.8	13.0	104,508
1935	176,756	42,802.9	9.7	1,399,480	88,931	17,661.7	12.6	843,016	15,989	3,636.7	10.5	164,486	11,188	1,941.1	11.0	89,043
1933	163,708	30,719.8	11.9	--------	82,865	12,997.3	15.0	--------	18,088	3,121.2	12.8	--------	10,386	1,589.9	14.8	--------
1929	168,262	66,739.6	9.0	[7]1,601,266	79,178	29,205.2	11.6	--------	15,224	5,386.9	10.2	--------	8,972	3,061.2	--------	--------

Merchant wholesalers—Con.

Year	Beer, wine, and distilled spirits				Tobacco distributors				Drugs, chemicals, and allied products				Dry goods, apparel [8]			
	Number	Sales	Operating expenses	Persons engaged	Number	Sales	Operating expenses	Persons engaged	Number	Sales	Operating expenses	Persons engaged	Number	Sales	Operating expenses	Persons engaged
	227	228	229	230	231	232	233	234	235	236	237	238	239	240	241	242
1954 [3]	7,309	5,686.9	12.0	78,340	2,858	3,208.9	5.9	30,848	5,837	3,369.9	15.9	71,366	9,389	5,689.7	13.3	83,811
1948 [3][4]	6,701	4,049.8	10.9	68,305	2,701	2,487.1	5.2	28,406	4,124	2,243.3	15.9	57,775	9,604	5,529.5	11.9	84,977
1948 [5]	7,195	4,069.7	10.9	69,059	3,019	2,529.6	5.2	28,886	4,671	2,282.2	15.8	58,679	11,733	5,727.7	11.8	88,745
1939	6,232	1,249.2	12.9	50,718	2,717	1,106.2	4.9	21,122	3,298	801.8	17.3	41,824	8,275	1,889.0	13.1	75,385
1935	5,496	698.5	13.1	37,266	2,253	783.4	5.5	16,862	2,989	722.9	15.6	35,926	7,567	1,634.3	12.8	69,624
1933	2,880	129.0	17.0	--------	1,738	523.7	6.4	--------	2,543	575.7	11.0	--------	6,392	1,262.2	14.5	--------
1929	--------	--------	--------	--------	1,721	858.3	7.4	--------	[9]2,376	[9]948.0	[9]15.9	--------	7,543	2,849.3	13.4	--------

Merchant wholesalers—Con.

Year	Furniture, homefurnishings [10]				Paper and allied products				Farm products (raw materials)				Automotive wholesalers			
	Number	Sales	Operating expenses	Persons engaged	Number	Sales	Operating expenses	Persons engaged	Number	Sales	Operating expenses	Persons engaged	Number	Sales	Operating expenses	Persons engaged
	243	244	245	246	247	248	249	250	251	252	253	254	255	256	257	258
1954 [3]	5,324	2,274.6	18.6	52,793	5,057	2,961.0	15.9	61,123	3,853	9,231.9	4.0	41,317	15,540	3,977.5	22.6	144,532
1948 [3][4]	3,189	1,249.2	17.3	34,402	3,630	1,880.0	15.5	50,553	2,059	6,771.0	3.6	24,326	13,563	3,917.6	18.1	145,023
1948 [5]	3,813	1,314.9	16.6	34,929	4,044	1,901.7	15.5	51,468	2,594	6,904.0	3.6	26,592	14,693	4,091.6	17.8	146,459
1939	2,214	373.5	17.2	20,265	2,898	575.0	17.2	33,605	2,086	1,628.7	6.9	29,281	7,818	1,055.4	17.5	72,616
1935	1,959	243.5	17.8	15,871	2,549	408.9	18.3	27,543	2,199	1,562.5	6.7	23,712	5,672	780.4	16.8	53,820
1933	1,788	175.0	22.5	--------	2,221	333.4	20.7	--------	2,433	1,224.7	6.9	--------	5,237	438.0	23.0	--------
1929	1,750	494.8	18.9	--------	2,297	704.4	16.4	--------	3,240	3,665.9	4.5	--------	3,451	1,383.1	15.0	--------

Merchant wholesalers—Con.

Year	Electrical, electronics appliance distributors				Hardware, plumbing and heating				Lumber, construction materials wholesalers				Machinery, equipment supplies distributors [11]			
	Number	Sales	Operating expenses	Persons engaged	Number	Sales	Operating expenses	Persons engaged	Number	Sales	Operating expenses	Persons engaged	Number	Sales	Operating expenses	Persons engaged
	259	260	261	262	263	264	265	266	267	268	269	270	271	272	273	274
1954 [3]	7,123	6,337.7	14.0	111,299	6,183	4,397.7	17.2	103,860	[12]10,314	[12]6,586.2	[12]16.1	[12]132,724	27,150	10,039.9	20.2	254,060
1948 [3][4]	5,041	4,309.3	12.8	91,772	5,189	3,680.2	15.2	100,721	5,576	3,890.0	14.1	89,427	19,573	6,723.1	18.2	203,642
1948 [5]	5,443	4,424.6	12.7	93,325	5,576	3,730.5	15.2	101,913	5,890	3,934.7	14.0	90,086	21,755	6,827.8	18.1	207,062
1939	3,072	788.0	16.6	40,147	3,568	972.0	18.4	64,358	3,303	804.4	15.2	38,918	11,270	1,440.4	20.0	96,311
1935	2,438	576.5	17.3	31,698	2,872	671.4	18.8	49,821	2,817	491.9	16.7	29,110	[13]7,583	[13]863.5	[13]21.1	[13]67,379
1933	2,125	275.8	22.3	--------	2,614	484.9	22.5	--------	2,636	278.7	22.7	--------	[13]6,226	[13]505.6	[13]25.4	--------
1929	2,182	846.7	16.9	--------	2,953	1,212.7	19.3	--------	3,774	1,283.9	15.8	--------	6,988	1,268.8	19.1	--------

See footnotes at end of table.

Series T 211–302. Wholesale Establishments, Sales, Operating Expenses, and Persons Engaged, by Kind of Business: 1929 to 1954—Con.

[Sales in millions of dollars; operating expenses and commissions earned in percentage of sales]

Year	Metals, metalwork (except scrap) distributors				Scrap, waste materials dealers				Manufacturers' sales branches (with stocks)				Manufacturers' sales offices [14] (without stocks)			
	Number	Sales	Operating expenses	Persons engaged	Number	Sales	Operating expenses	Persons engaged	Number	Sales	Operating expenses	Persons engaged	Number	Sales	Operating expenses	Persons engaged
	275	276	277	278	279	280	281	282	283	284	285	286	287	288	289	290
1954 [3]	[15]3,235	[15]3,362.6	[15]14.5	[15]53,641	8,189	2,405.6	17.8	75,499	[15]14,759	[15]36,811.2	[15]10.5	[15]404,098	7,831	32,722.5	4.5	111,888
1948 [3][4]	1,706	1,951.1	12.9	33,844	6,440	2,663.6	11.8	65,582	15,687	28,609.3	10.0	410,199	8,019	22,191.1	4.0	89,992
1948 [5]	1,803	2,056.7	12.1	34,395	7,717	2,699.3	11.9	67,227	15,716	29,229.7	10.9	412,252	8,052	23,508.9	4.3	90,144
1939	1,017	516.0	12.0	17,705	6,059	656.0	14.7	52,379	12,844	9,610.3	12.5	267,774	5,082	4,643.3	6.9	47,699
1935	810	282.0	13.2	11,343	4,793	399.7	14.5	34,830	11,541	7,403.6	11.8	[16]212,452	4,065	3,535.1	6.4	[16]39,607
1933	748	160.5	15.8	_____	3,360	272.2	10.8	_____	[17]12,444	[17]5,144.7	14.9	_____	4,429	2,412.7	7.4	_____
1929	856	672.6	8.1		3,919	474.5	12.3	_____	[18]16,863	[18]16,174.9	([19])	_____	([18])	([18])	([19])	_____

Year	Petroleum bulk stations, terminals				Agents and brokers				Assemblers (mainly farm products)			
	Number	Sales	Operating expenses	Persons engaged	Number	Sales	Commissions earned	Persons engaged	Number	Sales	Operating expenses	Persons engaged
	291	292	293	294	295	296	297	298	299	300	301	302
1954 [3]	29,189	16,038.4	10.0	154,760	22,131	39,250.5	3.1	148,595	[20]13,255	[20]9,050.8	[20]8.1	[20]130,337
1948 [3][4]	28,351	10,483.1	9.0	134,897	18,138	32,839.7	2.5	116,148	16,787	9,920.3	6.1	158,956
1948 [5]	29,451	10,615.7	9.0	136,418	24,361	34,610.1	2.6	123,470	19,268	10,957.9	6.1	169,182
1939	30,825	3,807.9	11.0	123,017	21,083	11,779.5	[21]2.8	111,125	28,931	2,509.6	9.3	168,673
1935	27,333	2,704.0	14.5	[16]105,118	18,147	8,908.1	[21]2.9	88,064	26,515	2,463.0	6.7	115,381
1933	[22]26,176	[22]1,884.6	[22]19.8	_____	13,818	6,502.4	[21]3.2	_____	23,962	1,774.1	9.8	_____
1929	19,587	2,101.1	16.0		18,467	14,517.2	[21]3.2		34,143	4,452.1	([17])	_____

[1] Totals include subclasses not shown separately.
[2] Fresh fruits and vegetable wholesalers and poultry and dairy products distributors. Milk bottling plants are included in the 1948 (unrevised) and earlier data.
[3] Based on 1954 scope of census for wholesale trade.
[4] Comparable with later years.
[5] Comparable with earlier years.
[6] Excludes commission bulk tank stations.
[7] Total of active proprietors plus the average number of employees (full time and part time) for the year.
[8] Includes dressed furs.
[9] Includes 42 distilled spirits wholesalers with sales of $12,785,473 and operating expenses of 24.7 percent.
[10] Includes musical instruments and sheet music wholesalers.
[11] Air conditioning and ventilating equipment distributors are included beginning 1948. Such distributors were classified in the plumbing and heating category in earlier years but were of negligible importance.
[12] Data for 1954 not strictly comparable with earlier years because of differences in treatment of sales to contractors and possible effects of differences in enumeration methods in the ready-mix concrete trade.

[13] Excludes wholesalers of shoe finding and cut stock. In 1929, 555 such establishments had sales of $55,810,553. Persons engaged in optical goods segment partially estimated.
[14] It is likely that there is a moderate amount of underenumeration in these series for 1954 as the mail canvass resulted in the activities of some branches and offices being reported as those of the manufacturing plant or as an auxiliary establishment.
[15] For 1954, 142 sales branches (with stocks) of steel works and rolling mill companies are included in metal distributors rather than as manufacturers' sales branches. These establishments had sales of $172,379,000.
[16] Partly estimated.
[17] Includes manufacturers' sales offices (without stocks).
[18] Combined with manufacturers' sales branches (with stocks).
[19] Not available.
[20] Data for assemblers for 1954 exclude fish and seafood assemblers which are included in the grocery, confectionery, meat group. In 1948 (adjusted) there were 544 such establishments with sales of $116,566,000, and operating expenses of 23.5 percent.
[21] Operating expenses.
[22] Includes district and general sales offices.

Series T 303–309. Wholesale Trade Margins of Independent Wholesalers: 1869 to 1947

[Percent of wholesale value]

Year	Dry goods	Furniture	Automobile accessories	Gasoline and oil	Lumber	Hardware	Drug (general line)	Year	Dry goods	Furniture	Lumber	Hardware	Drug (general line)
	303	304	305	306	307	308	309		303	304	307	308	309
1947	18	22.0	23.0	16.5	17.0	24.0	15.6	1899	17	14.0	10.0	19.0	13.6
1939	18	22.0	24.0	17.5	16.0	24.0	15.2	1889	16	14.0	10.0	19.0	12.2
1929	18	18.0	25.5	17.8	14.2	23.0	16.0	1879	15	14.0	10.0	19.0	11.0
1919	18	16.2	25.0	16.0	13.0	22.0	16.6	1869	14	14.0	10.0	19.0	10.0
1909	18	15.0	25.0	18.0	11.5	20.0	15.2						

Series T 310–345. Selected Service Establishments and Receipts: 1914 to 1954

[Receipts in millions of dollars]

Personal services

Year	Total¹ Number (310)	Total¹ Receipts (311)	Barber, beauty shops Number (312)	Receipts (313)	Funeral services, crematories Number (314)	Receipts (315)	Shoe repair shops, shoeshine parlors, hat cleaning shops Number (316)	Receipts (317)	Laundries, laundry service Total Number (318)	Receipts (319)	Power laundries Number (320)	Receipts (321)	Cleaning and dyeing plants Number (322)	Receipts (323)
1954	348,843	5,772.9	169,684	1,205.9	18,387	744.3	29,385	201.5	30,269	1,604.8	²9,612	²913.6	29,200	1,138.4
1948³	325,246	4,420.6	153,764	833.6	18,480	572.2	39,275	215.0	26,322	1,322.5	6,770	913.0	25,313	844.2
1948⁴	351,985	4,440.2	169,081	845.0	18,675	572.4	44,151	218.8	27,705	1,323.4	6,783	913.0	25,534	844.4
1939³	389,726	1,821.6	205,268	481.3	18,196	261.6	59,371	119.3	22,736	527.8	6,773	453.6	12,616	193.3
1939⁴	388,918	1,819.7	---	---	---	---	---	---	---	---	---	---	---	---
1935	369,081	1,517.0	186,810	401.6	17,144	230.0	61,046	109.7	23,915	429.7	6,470	369.5	6,910	141.4
1933	320,863	1,222.5	159,905	321.2	12,655	172.4	57,452	97.2	19,274	349.0	5,122	295.6	3,864	97.7
1931	---	---	---	---	---	---	---	---	---	---	6,400	466.0	4,568	147.5
1929	---	---	---	---	---	---	---	---	---	---	6,776	541.2	5,296	201.3
1927	---	---	---	---	---	---	---	---	---	---	6,013	454.0	3,175	142.8
1925	---	---	---	---	---	---	---	---	---	---	4,859	362.3	2,406	102.4
1919³	---	---	---	---	---	---	---	---	---	---	4,881	233.8	1,748	53.2
1919⁴	---	---	---	---	---	---	---	---	---	---	5,678	236.1	---	---
1914	---	---	---	---	---	---	---	---	---	---	6,097	142.5	---	---

Personal services—Con. / Automobile repair, garage, other services

Year	Pressing, alteration, garment repair, and fur storage Number (324)	Receipts (325)	Photographic studios (incl. commercial photography) Number (326)	Receipts (327)	Total Number (328)	Receipts (329)	Automobile repair shops Number (330)	Receipts (331)	Automobile, truck rentals (without drivers) Number (332)	Receipts (333)	Automobile storage, parking Number (334)	Receipts (335)	Automobile laundries Number (336)	Receipts (337)
1954	47,051	437.1	17,293	334.1	¹94,342	¹2,222.7	79,709	1,589.1	2,872	277.6	8,572	292.2	1,657	43.6
1948³	44,471	363.3	13,788	211.4	¹90,762	¹1,557.9	80,705	1,269.2	994	83.9	8,033	190.0	717	10.3
1948⁴	47,888	365.7	14,712	212.0	¹95,444	¹1,561.1	84,875	1,272.0	1,011	83.9	8,533	190.3	792	10.4
1939	54,696	153.3	10,957	64.2	78,881	440.9	66,178	315.6	648	20.3	11,095	102.1	960	2.9
1935	59,510	142.0	10,402	48.4	92,471	538.0	79,553	432.7	765	15.5	11,246	86.8	907	3.0
1933	56,769	140.7	8,330	31.9	100,149	584.5	⁵93,760	⁵550.0	381	5.4	5,275	27.0	733	2.1

Miscellaneous repair services / Hotels / Motels

Year	Miscellaneous repair services Total Number (338)	Receipts (339)	Electrical repair shops Number (340)	Receipts (341)	Hotels, year-round, 25 or more guest rooms Number (342)	Receipts (343)	Motels, tourist courts Number (344)	Receipts (345)
1954	113,429	1,795.8	32,195	501.5	²11,367	²2,075.2	29,432	457.1
1948³	71,338	941.3	17,076	213.3	(⁶)	(⁶)	23,316	193.5
1948⁴	80,023	947.4	19,440	214.8	14,547	1,854.8	25,919	195.5
1939³	75,262	224.2	15,644	47.8	14,084	759.0	13,521	36.7
1939⁴	72,130	195.0	---	---	---	---	---	---
1935	⁷71,426	⁷148.2	10,131	22.6	⁷11,373	⁷565.3	9,848	24.3
1933	53,010	91.0	⁸6,892	⁸17.3	⁸10,680	⁸398.7	---	---
1929	---	---	---	---	⁹11,873	⁹873.5	---	---

¹ Includes subclasses not shown separately.
² Establishments with payroll only.
³ Comparable with later years.
⁴ Comparable with earlier years.
⁵ Enumeration covers only general repair garages, paint shops, radiator shops, top and body repair shops, tire repair shops, and brake repair shops.
⁶ Not available.
⁷ Includes boat repair shops not included in other years.
⁸ Excludes refrigerator repair and washing machine repair establishments.
⁹ Excludes California which had 2,266 establishments in 1935.

Series T 346–351. Volume of Advertising: 1867 to 1957

[In millions of dollars]

Year	Total (346)	Newspapers (347)	Magazines (348)	Radio (349)	Television (350)	Direct mail (351)
1957	10,310.6	3,283.3	814.3	622.5	1,290.9	1,470.9
1956	9,904.7	3,235.6	794.7	567.0	1,206.7	1,419.2
1955	9,194.4	3,087.8	729.4	544.9	1,025.3	1,298.9
1954	8,164.1	2,695.3	667.9	558.7	809.2	1,202.4
1953	7,755.3	2,644.8	667.4	611.2	606.1	1,099.1
1952	7,156.2	2,472.8	615.8	624.1	453.9	1,024.3
1951	6,426.1	2,257.7	573.7	606.3	332.3	923.7
1950	5,710.0	2,075.6	514.9	605.4	170.8	803.2
1949	5,202.2	1,915.7	492.5	571.4	57.8	755.6
1948	4,863.6	1,749.6	512.7	561.6	---	689.1
1947	4,259.7	1,475.0	492.9	506.4	---	579.0
1946	3,864.2	1,158.3	426.5	454.4	---	334.4
1945	2,874.5	921.4	364.5	423.9	---	290.2
1944	2,723.6	888.0	323.6	393.5	---	326.2

Year	Total (346)	Newspapers (347)	Magazines (348)	Radio (349)	Direct mail (351)
1943	2,496.4	899.9	274.9	313.6	321.5
1942	2,156.1	797.5	198.7	260.0	329.1
1941	2,235.7	844.4	213.6	247.2	352.6
1940	2,087.6	815.4	197.7	215.6	333.7
1939	1,980.4	793.0	180.1	183.8	333.3
1938	1,904.0	782.4	168.7	167.1	323.7
1937	2,071.7	872.6	192.5	164.6	333.2
1936	1,902.4	843.5	162.0	122.3	319.0
1935	1,690.0	762.1	136.3	112.6	281.6
1934	1,627				
1933	1,302				
1932	1,627				

Year	Total (346)
1931	2,282.0
1930	2,607.0
1929	3,426.0
1928	3,262.0
1927	3,262.0
1926	3,262.0
1925	3,099.0
1924	2,935.0
1923	2,935.0
1922	2,607.0
1921	2,282.0
1920	2,935.0

Year	Total (346)
1919	2,282
1918	1,468
1917	1,627
1916	1,468
1915	1,302
1914	1,302
1909	1,142
1904	821
1900	542
1890	360
1880	200
1867	50

Series T 352–355. Farm-to-Retail Price Spreads of Farm Food Products: 1913 to 1957

Year	Market basket of farm food products			
	Retail cost	Farm value	Marketing margin	Farmer's share
	352	353	354	355
1952 MARKET BASKET	Dollars	Dollars	Dollars	Percent
1957	1,007	400	607	40
1956	972	390	582	40
1955	969	395	574	41
1954	986	421	565	43
1953	1,003	445	558	44
1952	1,034	482	552	47
1951	1,024	497	527	49
1950	920	432	488	47
1949	928	435	493	47
1948	982	497	485	51
1947	911	467	444	51
1935–39 MARKET BASKET				
1952	740	353	386	48
1951	722	360	362	50
1950	645	308	337	48
1949	646	308	338	48
1935–39 MARKET BASKET—Con.				
1948	690	350	340	51
1947	644	335	309	52
1946	528	279	249	53
1945	459	246	213	54
1944	451	233	218	52
1943	459	236	223	51
1942	409	195	214	48
1941	349	154	195	44
1940	319	127	192	40
1939	318	122	196	38
1938	329	127	202	39
1937	363	151	212	42
1936	350	141	209	40
1935	347	134	213	39
1934	312	106	206	34
1933	277	90	187	32
1932	285	90	195	32
1931	340	120	220	35
1935–39 MARKET BASKET—Con.				
1930	422	163	259	39
1929	436	183	253	42
1928	436	184	252	42
1927	434	177	257	41
1926	448	186	262	42
1925	442	186	256	42
1924	406	163	243	40
1923	413	164	249	40
1922	408	162	246	40
1921	427	170	257	40
1920	567	244	323	43
1919	511	247	264	48
1918	456	232	224	51
1917	441	207	234	47
1916	320	143	177	45
1915	267	118	149	44
1914	271	123	148	45
1913	263	122	141	46

Series T 356–358. Retail Cost, Farm Value, and Marketing Bill, for All Farm Food Products Purchased by Domestic Civilian Consumers: 1913 to 1956

[In billions of dollars]

Year	Retail cost	Farm value	Marketing bill
	356	357	358
1956	47.7	18.8	28.9
1955	46.2	18.3	27.9
1954	44.9	18.3	26.6
1953	44.6	19.0	25.6
1952	44.5	20.1	24.4
1951	43.0	20.2	22.8
1950	38.9	17.7	21.2
1949	37.9	17.1	20.8
1948	39.0	19.2	19.8
1947	36.5	18.7	17.8
1946	30.8	15.7	15.6
1945	24.4	12.6	12.5
1944	22.5	11.6	11.4
1943	22.3	11.4	11.1
1942	19.8	9.3	10.5
1941	16.3	7.1	9.2
1940	14.1	5.6	8.5
1939	13.37	5.17	8.19
1938	13.39	5.20	8.18
1937	14.18	5.98	8.20
1936	14.29	5.78	8.51
1935	12.94	5.02	7.58
1934	12.52	4.27	7.92
1933	10.93	3.56	7.30
1932	10.61	3.40	7.21
1931	13.06	4.66	8.40
1930	16.15	6.33	9.82
1929	17.08	7.22	9.86
1928	16.27	6.94	9.33
1927	16.23	6.72	9.51
1926	16.38	6.95	9.43
1925	15.73	6.77	8.96
1924	14.51	5.87	8.64
1923	14.00	5.62	8.38
1922	12.88	5.19	7.69
1921	12.57	5.05	7.52
1920	16.52	7.36	9.16
1919	15.22	7.55	7.67
1918	13.19	6.87	6.32
1917	12.40	6.05	6.35
1916	9.47	4.35	5.12
1915	7.99	3.63	4.36
1914	7.91	3.64	4.27
1913	7.41	3.53	3.88

Series T 359–360. Index of Department Store Sales and Stocks: 1919 to 1957

[1947–49 = 100]

Year	Sales index	Stocks index
	359	360
1957	136	152
1956	135	148
1955	128	136
1954	118	128
1953	118	131
1952	114	121
1951	112	131
1950	107	110
1949	99	100
1948	104	107
1947	98	94
1946	90	77
1945	70	59
1944	62	58
1943	56	55
1942	50	63
1941	44	46
1940	37	38
1939	35	35
1938	32	35
1937	35	39
1936	33	33
1935	29	31
1934	27	31
1933	24	29
1932	24	31
1931	32	39
1930	35	44
1929	38	48
1928	37	48
1927	37	48
1926	37	48
1925	36	48
1924	34	47
1923	34	46
1922	30	41
1921	30	41
1920	32	48
1919	27	37

Series T 361-365. Hotel Operations: 1920 to 1957

Year	Occupancy ratio (percent) 361	Total sales 362	Room sales 363	Restaurant sales 364	Room rate index (1929=100) 365	Year	Occupancy ratio (percent) 361	Total sales 362	Room sales 363	Restaurant sales 364	Room rate index (1929=100) 365	Year	Occupancy ratio (percent) 361	Total sales 362	Room sales 363	Restaurant sales 364	Room rate index (1929=100) 365
1957	70	238	214	274	204	1944	87	152	124	185	98	1932	51	55	58	52	79
1956	72	233	208	269	192	1943	84	137	114	164	94	1931	59	73	76	70	89
1955	72	224	200	261	185	1942	73	107	93	123	87	1930	65	90	91	88	97
1954	72	217	192	253	178	1941	67	93	82	105	84	1929	70	100	100	100	100
1953	74	219	192	256	173							1928	68	---	---	---	---
1952	76	215	188	251	165	1940	64	85	76	96	81	1927	69	---	---	---	---
1951	77	205	179	239	156	1939	62	82	74	90	82	1926	71	---	---	---	---
						1938	61	80	72	88	81						
1950	81	192	167	225	142	1937	66	85	78	95	80	1925	69	---	---	---	---
1949	82	188	162	221	137	1936	65	79	72	89	75	1924	70	---	---	---	---
1948	86	194	164	230	132							1923	75	---	---	---	---
1947	90	190	155	232	119	1935	60	71	64	80	72	1922	75	---	---	---	---
1946	93	181	141	230	105	1934	56	63	59	69	71	1921	79	---	---	---	---
1945	91	163	133	200	101	1933	51	51	52	49	71	1920	85	---	---	---	---

Series T 366-386. Book Value of Inventories at End of Year: 1929 to 1957

[In billions of dollars. All data except series T 378-386 for 1929-1939 adjusted for seasonal variations]

Year	Retail stores									Wholesale trade		
	Total inventories	Durable goods stores				Nondurable goods stores				Total inventories	Durable goods establishments	Nondurable goods establishments
		Total [1]	Automotive group	Furniture and appliance group	Lumber, building, hardware group	Total [1]	Apparel group	Food group	General merchandise group			
	366	367	368	369	370	371	372	373	374	375	376	377
1957	24.47	11.42	4.76	1.99	2.21	13.05	2.73	2.78	4.16	12.7	6.6	6.1
1956	23.86	10.70	4.02	2.02	2.22	13.16	2.85	2.70	4.18	13.0	6.6	6.4
1955	23.90	11.23	4.47	1.97	2.38	12.67	2.72	2.57	4.17	11.4	5.8	5.6
1954	22.09	10.06	3.43	1.90	2.41	12.03	2.57	2.31	3.92	10.4	5.1	5.3
1953	22.66	10.67	3.75	2.04	2.49	11.99	2.52	2.34	3.86	10.5	5.1	5.3
1952	21.59	9.91	3.17	1.98	2.52	11.69	2.49	2.30	3.68	10.0	4.9	5.1
1951	21.24	9.72	3.19	1.92	2.44	11.52	2.53	2.30	3.55	9.7	4.8	4.9
1950 [2]	19.94	8.82	2.79	1.88	2.27	11.12	2.47	2.21	3.51	---	---	4.8
1950 [3]	19.32	8.54	2.40	1.86	2.50	10.77	2.41	2.20	3.48	9.1	4.3	4.8
1949	15.31	6.44	1.84	1.25	1.82	8.87	2.05	1.75	2.85	7.6	3.5	4.1
1948	15.83	6.75	1.95	1.46	1.82	9.08	2.06	1.81	2.84	7.9	3.7	4.2
1947	14.06	5.49	1.49	1.22	1.52	8.57	1.84	1.71	2.80	7.6	3.2	4.4
1946	11.85	3.95	.98	.94	1.06	7.90	1.57	1.60	2.60	6.6	2.6	4.0
1945	7.95	2.43	.52	.48	.68	5.52	1.12	1.03	1.69	4.6	1.5	3.1
1944	7.64	2.24	.49	.42	.69	5.40	1.24	.97	1.60	3.9	1.1	2.8
1943	7.56	2.21	.56	.45	.59	5.35	1.21	1.08	1.68	3.7	1.1	2.6
1942	8.02	2.75	.81	.57	.68	5.27	1.15	1.12	1.66	3.8	1.1	2.7
1941	7.78	3.18	.95	.60	.88	4.60	.95	.96	1.59	4.0	1.4	2.7
1940	6.12	2.47	.77	.43	.71	3.65	.76	.69	1.34	3.2	1.1	2.1
1939	5.53	2.09	.58	.40	.64	3.45	.75	.66	1.27	3.1	1.0	2.0
1938	5.28	1.98	.54	.38	.62	3.30	.72	.61	1.20	2.9	.9	2.0

Year	Manufacturers'								
	Total inventories	Durable goods industries				Nondurable goods industries			
		Total	Purchased materials	Goods-in-process	Finished goods	Total	Purchased materials	Goods-in-process	Finished goods
	378	379	380	381	382	383	384	385	386
1957	53.520	31.148	8.3	12.7	10.1	22.372	8.8	3.1	10.5
1956	52.295	30.660	8.7	12.8	9.2	21.635	8.5	3.0	10.1
1955	46.364	26.664	7.4	11.1	8.2	19.700	8.1	2.8	8.8
1954	42.985	24.084	6.5	9.8	7.7	18.901	7.9	2.6	8.4
1953	45.431	26.244	7.4	10.7	8.1	19.187	8.1	2.7	8.4
1952	43.799	24.412	7.3	10.2	6.9	19.387	8.6	2.7	8.1
1951	42.815	22.806	7.4	8.6	6.8	20.009	9.1	2.7	8.2
1950	34.314	16.780	6.1	6.0	4.7	17.534	8.4	2.5	6.6
1949	28.860	13.974	4.6	4.7	4.7	14.886	6.5	2.1	6.3
1948	31.693	15.737	5.6	5.4	4.7	15.956	7.3	2.2	6.5
1947	28.874	14.298	5.1	5.2	4.0	14.576	7.2	2.2	5.2
1946	24.457	11.997	4.5	4.6	2.9	12.460	6.5	1.8	4.2
1945	18.390	8.767	3.2	3.5	2.1	9.623	4.9	1.5	3.2
1944	19.507	10.433	3.3	5.0	2.1	9.074	4.7	1.4	3.0
1943	20.098	11.175	3.9	5.2	2.1	8.923	4.5	1.4	3.0
1942	19.287	10.441	3.7	4.6	2.2	8.846	4.3	1.2	3.3
1941	16.960	8.601	3.1	3.2	2.3	8.359	4.0	1.2	3.2
1940	12.819	6.304	2.1	2.0	2.2	6.515	2.6	.9	3.0
1939	11.465	5.334	1.8	1.5	2.1	6.131	2.4	.8	2.9
1938 [2]	10.750	5.019	---	---	---	5.781	---	---	---
1938 [3]	10.803	5.017	1.6	1.3	2.1	5.786	2.2	.7	2.9
1937	12.071	5.693	---	---	---	6.378	---	---	---
1936	10.731	4.813	---	---	---	5.918	---	---	---
1935	9.145	4.052	---	---	---	5.098	---	---	---
1934	8.764	3.741	---	---	---	5.023	---	---	---
1933	8.189	3.533	---	---	---	4.656	---	---	---
1932	7.369	3.375	---	---	---	3.994	---	---	---
1931	9.151	4.241	---	---	---	4.910	---	---	---
1930	11.321	5.300	---	---	---	6.021	---	---	---
1929	12.889	5.919	---	---	---	6.920	---	---	---

[1] Includes kinds of business not shown separately.   [2] Comparable with later years.   [3] Comparable with earlier years.

Foreign Trade and Other International Transactions

FOREIGN TRADE (Series U 1-167)

U 1-167. General note.

Statistics on foreign trade of the United States are among the most useful, revealing, and, in spite of their deficiencies, reliable series relating to the growth of the American economy. This situation is especially true for the first 100 years of the Republic. The United States was more heavily dependent upon foreign markets and sources at that time than it has been in the 20th century. For a fuller discussion of the usefulness of such data, see G. G. Huebner's review of foreign trade of the United States in Emory Johnson, *History of Domestic and Foreign Commerce of the United States*, Carnegie Institution, Washington, D.C., 1915. This study has an excellent bibliography of material on foreign trade available at that time.

Since the first appearance of the *Statistical Abstract of the United States* in 1878, official time series on foreign trade have been presented in that publication and it is, therefore, cited here as a primary source for certain of the foreign trade data shown.

Foreign trade data are subject to a variety of special statistical problems relating to compilation, publication, coverage, valuation, and classification as to composition and direction. The record of gold movements, in particular, has been found to be subject to considerable error owing to its peculiar qualities which make it both a useful form of money and a likely candidate for smuggling (see R. G. D. Allen and J. Edward Ely, *International Trade Statistics*, John Wiley and Sons, New York, 1953; and Oskar Morgernstern, *Validity of International Gold Movement Statistics*, Special Paper in International Economics No. 2, International Finance Section, Princeton University Press, November 1955).

The first Congress of the United States provided for the compilation of statistics on foreign trade, and the Treasury Department, through its customhouses, began keeping a record of foreign trade beginning August 1, 1789. According to the Chief of the Bureau of Statistics, Treasury Department, Government records of the total values of our imports for 1790 to 1820 are fairly complete but do not show, except for a few years, the articles imported. They show, however, domestic exports by articles, but do not distinguish the values of merchandise from coin and bullion imported and exported, nor the value of the commerce with each country (see *Statistical Tables Exhibiting the Commerce of the United States With European Countries From 1790-1890*, Washington, D.C., 1893, p. vii).

Compared with currently compiled statistics, these earliest records left a great deal to be desired. J. Edward Ely, writing on the historical development of foreign trade statistics, observes that:

The United States may be said to have had an adequate set of import and export statistics only since about 1821. Prior to that time no information was compiled on the amount of imports of articles which were free of duty upon importation into the United States. No value figures were compiled on imports subject to specific rates of duty and the dollar value for imports subject to ad valorem rates of duty, although apparently accurate, was compiled only as a total with no information on how much of each commodity was imported. Existing figures on the total dollar value of imports during the years 1795 to 1801 were apparently estimated at the time by the Secretary of the Treasury, and the figures for 1790-1794 and from 1802-1820 were apparently estimated many years later. (Allen and Ely, cited above, p. 269.)

Douglass North observes that the 1789-1820 figures were "officially overhauled and published in the Report of the Secretary of the Treasury on Finances for 1835" (see North's "United States Balance of Payments, 1790-1860," *Studies in Income and Wealth*, vol. 24, National Bureau of Economic Research, forthcoming). In employing the early records, North found a number of deficiencies, and users of figures for 1790-1820 should note his revised figures and consider the criticisms in the appendix to his paper. The adequacy of the early records, of course, depends upon the use made of them. Some of the earliest records were not published officially and scholars have had to depend for information on the unofficial work of Tench Coxe, Samuel Blodget, Jr., Timothy Pitkin, and Adam Seybert (see Faith Williams, "The Origin and Development of Modern Trade Statistics," *Journal of the American Statistical Association*, vol. 17, 1920–21, footnote, p. 740). Such data as were published annually for 1790-1820 were brought together later in U.S. Congress, *American State Papers*, Class 4, "Commerce and Navigation," two volumes, Gales and Seaton, Washington, D.C., 1832 (vol. I) and 1834 (vol. II).

In 1820, Congress passed a law to provide for obtaining accurate statements of the foreign commerce of the United States and, at the same time, established the Division of Commerce and Navigation in the office of the Register of the Treasury. It required collectors of customs to compile and transmit annual reports to that office showing the detailed trade with foreign countries and the navigation employed therein. Beginning with 1821, these reports were consolidated and published annually in the *Commerce and Navigation of the United States*.

Foreign trade statistics published by the Federal Government after 1820 are regarded as superior to those for the earlier period but still subject to some deficiencies, notably with respect to valuation of imports. They also suffered in respect to coverage of overland exports (see North, cited above, app. II, and Allen and Ely, cited above, pp. 270-271).

The Civil War introduced two special difficulties. For the last three quarters of fiscal year ending June 30, 1861, certain ports of the Southern States failed to make reports, and it was necessary for the Treasury Department to introduce estimates of the exports of cotton by the Southern States during the war based on records of the main recipient countries in Europe (see Treasury Department *Statistics of the Foreign and Domestic Commerce of the United States*, Washington, D.C., 1864, p. 39).

The second difficulty was introduced in 1862 when the United States abandoned the specie backing for its money. The dollar fluctuated against foreign currencies and gold with each reverse or success of the northern forces. While imports and reexports continued to be valued in specie (dollars of a fixed parity to gold), since these goods were initially expressed in foreign currencies, domestic exports were recorded in "mixed values"—partly gold dollars and partly dollars of a fluctuating value—from 1862 until the resumption of specie payment in 1879. These deficiencies were recognized at the time both officially by the Director of the Bureau of Statistics (established in the Treasury Department in 1866) and by private observers (see, for example, Louis Blodgett's criticism and evaluation of United States foreign trade statistics in the early 1860's in *The Commercial and Financial Strength of the United States as Shown in the Balances of Foreign Trade and the Increased Production of Staple Articles*, King and Baird, Philadelphia, 1864). Treasury statisticians sought to adjust mixed currency values to specie values of total imports and exports and some other broad aggregates. The adjustments, however, were not carried through completely to country and commodity detail, and only a limited number of domestic export series are available for 1862-1879 in terms of "specie values" while the domestic export figures for countries and individual commodities are only available in mixed currency values.

When Congress established the Bureau of Statistics in 1866, it also specified that the kinds, quantities, and values of all articles exported and imported should be distinctly set forth in the statistical accounts, by countries of destination or of shipment, and that the exports of articles produced or manufactured in the United States should be shown separately from the reexports of foreign articles imported into the United States. Prior to 1866, only annual statistics of the foreign commerce of the United States were published; since then, monthly statistics have also been published.

The first report of the Director of the Bureau of Statistics in 1867 contains several pointed criticisms of the previous statistics, and the subsequent annual reports of the *Foreign Commerce and Navigation* emphasized the shortcomings of the figures presented, especially the difficulty which became important in the post-Civil War period of reporting on trade with Canada in the absence of any mandatory reporting requirement on the railroads (see, for example, the *Annual Report of the Chief of the Bureau of Statistics on the Commerce and Navigation of the United States for the Fiscal Year Ended June 30, 1877*, 1878, pp. xii-xiii, table showing " . . . the imports into Ontario, Quebec, and Manitoba, from the United States in excess of the domestic exports from the United States to Canada, as returned to the Bureau of Statistics by United States collectors of customs during the fiscal year ended June 30, 1877."). An act of March 3, 1893, provided for obtaining information on exports by rail and apparently eliminated this deficiency in the subsequent figures, but prior to that time trade totals and figures on trade with Canada suffer lack of coverage in varying degrees. Because of the deficiences in the earlier official United States trade statistics, an effort has been made to include here the account of trade with the United States as published by two of its leading partners throughout most of its history, Canada and the United Kingdom (see series U 152–155 and U 156–167).

For additional comments on foreign trade data for 1861-1900, see Matthew Simon, "Statistical Estimates of the Balance of International Payments and the International Capital Movements of the United States, 1861-1900," *Studies in Income and Wealth*, vol. 24, National Bureau of Economic Research (forthcoming).

In 1923, the function of compiling foreign trade statistics was transferred to the Department of Commerce; however, the release and publication of the annual figures had been done by that Department since 1903. In 1941, the function was transferred, within the Department of Commerce, from the Bureau of Foreign and Domestic Commerce to the Bureau of the Census.

A problem affecting comparability of value statistics arose between January 31, 1934, and March 10, 1953, when the foreign exchange value of the dollar was permitted to depreciate as a result of the restriction placed on gold shipments to foreign countries. For this period, unless otherwise noted, values stated are in United States dollars without reference to changes in the gold content of the dollar.

World War II and the special foreign aid programs following it introduced new complications into the handling of United States foreign trade statistics. Lend-lease during the war, surplus property disposal immediately after the war, War Department shipments to relieve disease and unrest, economic and military aid, and security shipments have all complicated the presentation as will be noted below.

Import data compiled by the Department of Commerce are from import entries (various Customs forms) which importers are required to file with Collectors of Customs for each shipment arriving. Import values are, in general, based on market or selling price and are f.o.b. the exporting country. Values do not include import duties. The country of origin is defined as the country in which the merchandise was grown, mined, or manufactured. If the importer cannot obtain the information as to the country of origin, it is credited (for statistical purposes) to the country of shipment.

Imports are classified either as general imports or imports for consumption. General imports represent total arrivals of imported goods (except for intransit shipments), that is, merchandise released from Customs custody immediately upon arrival plus merchandise entered into a bonded storage warehouse, bonded manufacturing warehouse, and bonded refining warehouse immediately upon arrival. Imports for consumption comprise merchandise entered into the U.S. consumption channels, that is, merchandise released from Customs custody immediately upon arrival, merchandise entered into a bonded manufacturing warehouse (other than smelting or refining warehouse), merchandise withdrawn from a bonded storage warehouse for release into domestic consumption channels, and imported ores and crude metals which have been processed in a bonded smelting warehouse and then withdrawn for consumption or for reexport.

Effective January 1954, imports valued at $250 or less, reported on formal consumption and informal entries (about 1 percent of total import value), are estimated from a 5-percent sample. The estimated import values are excluded from detailed commodity statistics but are included in the over-all totals and are distributed in the appropriate country, district, and economic class totals, and in the totals for groupings of commodity classifications (i.e., commodity group or subgroup). Some indication of the undercounting in the detailed commodity statistics for imports is presented in the appendixes to the annual issues of Bureau of the Census, Report FT 110, *United States Imports of Merchandise for Consumption*, beginning with the issue for 1954. Explanations of the sampling procedures are given in Report FT 110 for 1956 and in the same Bureau's *Quarterly Summary of Foreign Commerce of the United States*, January-December 1956.

Export data are from Shippers' Export Declarations which exporters are required to file with Collectors of Customs for each shipment leaving the United States. Export data include shipments made after World War II under the Department of the Army Civilian Supply Program only for 1948 and subsequent years. In addition, export data include United States exports under the Lend-Lease, United Nations Relief and Rehabilitation Administration, Economic Cooperation Administration, Mutual Defense Assistance, and other mutual security programs. Shipments to U.S. Armed Forces for their own use are not included in export statistics for any period.

Export value figures are based on the selling price (or on the cost, if not sold) of the commodity shipped and include inland freight, insurance, and other charges to the place of export. Transportation and other costs beyond the United States port of exportation are excluded. The country of destination is defined as the country of ultimate destination or country where the merchandise is to be consumed, further processed, or manufactured. In the event the exporter does not have definite information as to the country of ultimate destination for a shipment, it is credited (for statistical purposes) to the country to which it is consigned.

Certain export commodity classifications were grouped for security reasons into special categories beginning with May 1949, with periodic amendments to include additional commodities. With the adoption of new security regulations, effective July 1950, the publication of the country of destination and customs district detail for the special category commodities and groups was discontinued. Data for special category commodities are included, however, in all total export statistics (series U 1, U 10, U 11, U 21, U 22, U 61, and U 116); in the category of finished manufactures (series U 31, U 32, and U 66); and in the commodity categories of series U 73–93 (except automobiles and parts, series U 86, from which machinery and vehicles manufactured to military specifications have been excluded beginning in July 1949).

Shipments individually valued at less than $100 are not classified by commodity, but are reported in a single separate category. Effective with the statistics for July 1953 and continuing through December 1955, data for export shipments individually valued from $100 to $499 (about 4 to 6 percent of the total export value) were estimated on the basis of a 10-percent sample. From January through June 1956, the 10-percent sample was applied to shipments individually valued from $100 to $999 but, subsequently, the level was reduced to the previous level of $499. Details concerning sampling error and procedures are given in the Bureau of the Census, *Quarterly Summary of Foreign Commerce of the United States*, January-December 1956, and Report FT 410, *United States Exports of Domestic and Foreign Merchandise*, 1956.

The geographic area covered by these statistics, except as noted, is the United States Customs area, which includes Alaska, Hawaii, and Puerto Rico, and for 1935–1939, the Virgin Islands.

U 1–3. Total gold, silver, and merchandise exports and imports, 1821–1957.

Source: 1821-1880, except as noted, Bureau of Foreign and Domestic Commerce, *Foreign Commerce and Navigation of the United States*, 1912, pp. 43-44 (1821, **series U 1 and U 3**, revised estimates prepared by the Bureau of the Census); 1881-1903, Department of Commerce, *Statistical Abstract of the United States*, 1924, pp. 420-421; 1904-1941, *Statistical Abstract*, 1948, p. 903; 1942-1949 (except series U 1 for 1948 and 1949), *Statistical Abstract*, 1951, p. 828; **series U 1**, 1948 and 1949, *Statistical Abstract*, 1953, p. 899; 1950-1957, *Statistical Abstract*, 1958, p. 880.

U 4–9. Gold and silver exports and imports, 1821-1957.

Source: 1821-1864, Bureau of Foreign and Domestic Commerce, *Foreign Commerce and Navigation of the United States*, 1912, p. 43; 1865-1880, Treasury Department, *Statistical Abstract*, 1887, pp. 41, 42; 1881-1941, see source for series U 1–3

above; 1942-1957, Bureau of the Census, *Summary of Foreign Commerce of the United States*, various annual issues.

The data shown here for 1821-1864 for series U 6 and U 9 are not shown in the source but have been derived as the residual of the exports and imports data as shown in the source. Prior to 1895, figures for gold and silver relate to coin and bullion only; subsequently, they include ore also. Domestic exports of gold and silver cannot be separately stated prior to 1864, but it is probable that the greater portion of the exports was gold. In the series shown here, the data on exports of gold prior to 1864 include domestic exports of silver. The exports of silver for years prior to 1864, therefore, consist of only foreign exports or reexports.

U 10–14. Merchandise, exports and imports, 1790-1957.

Source: 1790, Bureau of Foreign and Domestic Commerce, *Foreign Commerce and Navigation of the United States*, 1912, p. 43; 1791-1880, except as noted, Treasury Department, Bureau of Statistics, *Monthly Summary of Imports and Exports of the United States for the Fiscal Year, 1896*, pp. 622-623 (1821, **series U 10, U 12, and U 14**, revised estimates prepared by the Bureau of the Census); 1881-1903, Department of Commerce, *Statistical Abstract of the United States*, 1924, pp. 420-421; 1904-1941, *Statistical Abstract*, 1948, pp. 902-903; 1942-1957, see source for series U 4-9.

Merchandise export statistics include data on all shipments of commodities and merchandise leaving the United States Customs area except: (*1*) Gold and silver and evidences of debt; (*2*) intransit merchandise; (*3*) bunker fuel, stores, supplies, and equipment for vessels and planes; (*4*) temporary exports; (*5*) merchandise having small value or no commercial value; (*6*) shipments of military and naval supplies and equipment to the U.S. Armed Forces; and (*7*) shipments to U.S. Government agencies or establishments.

Exports of United States merchandise (series U 11) consist of commodities grown, produced, or manufactured in the United States, and commodities of foreign origin which have been changed in the United States from the form in which they were imported, or which have been enhanced in value by further manufacture in the United States.

Reexports (series U 12) comprise withdrawals from customs-bonded storage warehouses for exportation and exports of foreign merchandise (principally duty-free articles) which have previously been formally entered through customs. Exports of foreign merchandise consist of commodities of foreign origin which have entered the United States as imports and which, at the time of exportation, are in the same condition as when imported.

Merchandise import statistics include data on all commodities and merchandise reaching the United States except: (*1*) Merchandise not entering the U.S. Customs area, such as articles excluded from the United States by law, bunker fuel, and ships' stores; (*2*) intransit merchandise; (*3*) certain domestic merchandise returned from foreign countries; (*4*) gold, silver, and evidences of debt; (*5*) merchandise having small value or no commercial value; and (*6*) commodities entered under special provisions, such as articles consigned to diplomatic officers. General imports (series U 13) consist of entries for immediate consumption and entries into warehouses, and therefore comprise the total arrivals of merchandise, whether they enter consumption channels immediately or are entered into warehouses under customs custody to be subsequently withdrawn for consumption or withdrawn for exportation.

U 15–20. Value of merchandise imports and duties, 1821-1957.

Source: 1821-1880, Bureau of Foreign and Domestic Commerce, *Foreign Commerce and Navigation of the United States*,

1912, p. 50; 1881-1915, *Foreign Commerce and Navigation of the United States*, 1924, p. lxvii; 1916-1941, Bureau of the Census, *Statistical Abstract of the United States*, 1948, p. 939; 1942-1949, *Statistical Abstract*, 1951, p. 854; 1950-1957, *Statistical Abstract*, 1958, p. 900.

Imports are "imports for consumption" consisting of entries for immediate consumption and withdrawals from warehouses for consumption. The term "entry for consumption" is the technical name of the import entry made at the customhouse, and implies that the goods have been delivered into the custody of the importer and that the duties have been paid on the dutiable portion. Some of them may be exported afterwards.

For 1821-1866, the figures for import values (series U 15–17) represent net general imports (total imports less reexports), the amount of duty collected (calculated) being the annual amounts collected on merchandise only. For 1867-1957, the figures of import values represent imports entered for consumption.

U 18, duties calculated. The series described here as "duties calculated" is the series identified in annual volumes of *Foreign Commerce and Navigation . . .* , through the 1925 issue, as "duties collected"; subsequent issues describe it as "duties calculated." In spite of its description, it was a computed figure at least back to 1876. The evidence indicates that the earlier years, at least in part, were on a "duties collected" basis. This series should not be confused with the modern series called "duties collected" (not shown here) which represents the total amount of duties actually collected (on individual shipments) as reported to the Treasury Department by Collectors of Customs, subject in certain cases to subsequent refund as well as drawback. In contrast, "duties calculated" is a statistical measure derived by applying the appropriate rates to totals for all imports of the given commodity received at all ports of entry; it does not reflect drawbacks or refunds and is subject to some time lag in reporting.

U 19–20, ratio of duties to total. The calculated ratio of duties to total is simply the relationship of series U 18 to series U 15 and series U 17, respectively, expressed in percentage form. Series U 19-20 are similar to, but not identical with, the series described as "ratios of duties to total" shown in annual issues of *Foreign Commerce and Navigation . . .* , 1925 to 1946, and as *"average ad valorem rates"* in earlier issues. These series have been computed as shown here because of conflicts in source volumes with respect to early years.

U 21–44. Indexes of quantity and unit value of exports and imports, 1879–1957.

Source: 1879-1921, unpublished estimates prepared by Robert E. Lipsey, National Bureau of Economic Research; 1921-1957, following editions of the Department of Commerce, *Statistical Abstract of the United States:*

Period	Edition	Page
1921–1929	1934	404
1930–1937	1941	532
1938–1940	1948	911
1941–1946	1950	846
1947–1949	1955	905
1950–1952	1957	900
1953–1957	1959	893

For 1879-1921, indexes were compiled by Robert E. Lipsey of the National Bureau of Economic Research using a method and materials similar to those employed by the Bureau of Foreign Commerce. However, the NBER series are Fisher "ideal" index numbers, constructed in four segments, 1913-1921, 1899-1913, 1889–1899, and 1879–1889, and then linked at the overlapping years. The last year of each segment was used as the base for weighting during that period. To secure the unit value index, the NBER used values, quantities, and indicated unit values for general imports and domestic exports of individual commodities from official reports supplemented by domestic and foreign price data and by customs data from foreign countries. These and other types of index numbers, quarterly as well as annual, in more commodity detail and with notes on sources and methods of computation will appear in a forthcoming NBER publication by Robert E. Lipsey. The figures presented here are preliminary and subject to revision in the final publication.

The basic source of the data for 1920-1957 is the Bureau of Foreign Commerce. The indexes for this period have been calculated using Fisher's "ideal formula," using both the weights of the given year and those of the preceding (or base) year. Commodities not directly entering the calculations, including special category exports, were taken into account in the weighting within the several economic classes of merchandise on the basis of certain assumptions regarding similarity of their price movements to price changes of selected commodities specifically covered.

U 45–50. Foreign trade related to various measures of production, 1869-1957.

Source: Series U 45–46, 1869-1939, computed as the ratios respectively of series U 10 and U 13 to gross national product (using series F 1 for all years except 1909-1918; for these years, the estimates of gross national product are from U.S. Senate, 79th Congress, 1st session, "Report to the Committee on Banking and Currency," *Basic Facts on Employment and Production*, Senate Committee Print No. 4) ; 1940–1957, Bureau of Foreign Commerce, *Exports in Relation to United States Production*, 1957, p. 2. Series U 47–48, 1919–1927, 1931, and 1935, Bureau of Foreign Commerce, *World Trade Information Service Statistical Reports*, part 3, No. 58-22; 1929, 1933, and 1937-1957, see source for series U 45–46, 1940–1957. Series U 49, 1910–1950, Foreign Agricultural Service, *United States Farm Products in Foreign Trade*, Statistical Bulletin No. 112, p. 10; 1951-1956, *The Problem of Maintaining High Level Agricultural Exports*, November 1957, p. 13; 1957, Department of Agriculture, records. Series U 50, Don D. Humphrey, *American Imports*, 20th Century Fund, New York, 1955, pp. 527-528.

For additional data on the relation of foreign trade to the domestic economy, see the following reports in World Trade Information Service: "Exports in Relation to U.S. Production," part 3, Nos. 55-27, 56-31, 57-36, and 58-22; "Contribution of Imports to United States Raw Material Supplies," part 3, Nos. 55-20, 55-40, 57-1, 57-46, and 58-30; "Contribution of Imports to U.S. Food Supplies," part 3, No. 58-38; and "Role of Foreign Trade in the U.S. Economy," part 3, No. 57-38.

U 51–60. Value of merchandise exports and imports, by groups of customs districts, 1860-1954.

Source: 1860-1880, Department of Commerce, *Statistical Abstract of the United States*, 1923, pp. 824-825; 1881-1903, *Statistical Abstract*, 1924, p. 441; 1904-1944, *Statistical Abstract*, 1947, p. 921; 1945-1954, Bureau of the Census, records.

The customs district in which merchandise is entered or withdrawn for consumption is the district shown in the "imports for consumption" statistics. The customs district shown in the "general imports" statistics is the district through which merchandise enters the United States either as an entry for immediate consumption or as an entry into a customs-bonded warehouse. Except for shipments by mail the customs district through which a shipment clears when it leaves the country is the district to which the export is credited statistically. Exports are not credited on the basis of the district in which the shipments originate. Exports and imports by mail are credited to the customs district at which the export or import entry is filed. For definition of terms, see text for series U 10–14 and U 15–20. Export figures for 1865 and 1870-1878 represent mixed gold and currency values and hence do not agree with the specie values given for total exports elsewhere.

U 61–72. Value of merchandise exports and imports, by economic classes, 1820–1957.

Source: The following editions of the Department of Commerce, *Statistical Abstract of the United States:*

Period	Edition	Page
1820–1881	1907	698–701
1882–1903	1926	448–449
1904–1939	1947	896–897
1940–1945	1950	845
1946–1949	1955	904
1950–1957	1958	888

For definition of terms, see text for series U 10–14 and U 15–20.

The economic classes shown here are broad categories based on groupings of more than 2,000 individual commodities listed in *Schedule B: Statistical Classification of Domestic and Foreign Commerce Exported From the United States and Regulations Governing Statistical Returns of Exports of Commodities,* "Part II, Numerical Classification and Articles Included (January 1, 1945, edition)," issued and kept current by the Bureau of the Census. Following are some of the important and typical commodities included in each of the economic classes:

Class	Exports	Imports
Crude materials	Crude petroleum	Crude rubber
	Coal	Raw silk
	Raw cotton	Hides and skins
Crude foodstuffs	Grains	Coffee
	Fruits	Tea
	Vegetables	Fruits
Manufactured foodstuffs	Meat	Sugar
	Lard	Meat
	Prepared fruits	Wheat flour
Semimanufactures	Iron and steel plates	Wood pulp
	Lumber	Copper in bars, etc.
	Refined copper	Tin in bars, etc.
Finished manufactures	Aircraft	Wool manufactures
	Cigarettes	Newsprint
	Radios and television sets	Automobiles and parts

In a report on *Exports of Manufactures from the United States and Their Distribution by Articles and Countries, 1800-1906* (1907), the Department of Commerce and Labor presented trade figures by economic classes annually back to 1850 and for selected years back to 1820. This study provided a different grouping of commodities than the Bureau of Statistics of the Treasury Department had previously employed for exports. In "Exports of Domestic Manufactures and Their Distribution" (*Monthly Summary of Commerce and Finance of the United States,* April 1903, p. 3239 ff.) the Treasury tabulated domestic exports for 1800–1850 by decade years and for 1851–1902 annually according to economic sector ("sources of production") as follows (p. 3249): Agriculture, manufactures, mining, forest, fisheries, and miscellaneous. But it tabulated imports "according to degree of manufacture and uses" for 1821, 1830, 1840, 1850, and 1851–1902 as follows (p. 3279–3280): Food and live animals, crude articles for domestic industries, articles manufactured wholly or partially for use as material in the mechanic arts, articles manufactured ready for consumption, and articles of voluntary use, luxuries, etc. This report noted that values for exports were in fluctuating currency for 1862-1879 and for those years gave specie values both for total exports and for exports of manufactures (p. 3315).

Trade in agricultural and forest products have been of special concern to the Department of Agriculture. Bulletin No. 51 of the Bureau of Statistics of the Department of Agriculture (1909) provides the "only compilation . . . ever to be completed (to that time)" of the "Foreign Trade of the United States in Forest Products, 1851-1908." Bulletins No. 74 and 75 in the same series, published in 1910, reviewed the "Imports of Farm Products into the United States, 1851-1908" and "Exports of Farm Products from the United States, 1851-1908," respectively.

U 73–115. General note.

The totals of the selected imports and exports (series U 73 and U 94) are shown to provide a means of judging the extent to which the selected items account for the total trade of this country. They include only the values of the items shown for each year and are, therefore, a total with a variable composition. Additional information on the composition of the foreign trade of the United States may be found in M. B. Hammond, *The Cotton Industry,* American Economic Association Series 2, No. 1, New York, 1897, and in reports by the Bureau of Statistics, Treasury Department, on the grain, provision, cotton, coal, iron and steel, and lumber trades of the United States which appeared in the *Monthly Summary of Commerce and Finance* (hereafter abbreviated as *MSCF*) for 1899-1900, 1900-1901, and 1902-3.

U 74–75. Cotton, unmanufactured, quantity and value, 1791-1957.

Source: 1791-1889, Treasury Department, Bureau of Statistics, *MSCF*, 1895-6, p. 290; 1890-1897, *MSCF*, March 1900, p. 2561; 1898-1940, following editions of the *Statistical Abstract of the United States:*

Period	Edition	Page
1898–1905	1907	417–477
1906–1915	1916	392–438
1916–1919	1920	435–511
1920–1922	1924	448–536
1923–1925	1928	480–552
1926–1929	1931	528–609
1930–1932	1934	440–521
1933–1935	1937	467–554
1936–1940	1942	575–669

1941-1957, Bureau of the Census, *Summary of Foreign Commerce,* various issues.

U 76–77. Leaf tobacco, unmanufactured, quantity and value, 1790–1957.

Source: 1790–1894, Treasury Department, Bureau of Statistics *MSCF*, June 1895, pp. 1418-1421; 1898-1957, see source for series U 74-75, 1898-1957.

U 78–79. Wheat, quantity and value, 1790-1957.

Source: 1790–1897, Treasury Department, Bureau of Statistics, *MSCF*, June 1895, pp. 1418-1421; 1898-1957, see source for series U 74-75, 1898-1957.

U 80–93. Value of exports of selected U.S. merchandise, 1810-1957.

Source: The following editions of the *Statistical Abstract of the United States* except as noted below for series U 86 and U 93:

Period	Edition	Page
1810–1881	1924	446–447
1882–1904 (1882–1907 for imports)	1926	470–473
1905–1945 (1908–1945 for imports)	1948	916–919
1946–1949	1954	910–911
1950–1957	1958	885–886

series U 86, 1860-1900, *Statistical Abstract,* 1924, p. 447; series U 93, 1903-1907, *Statistical Abstract,* 1947, p. 905.

U 95–96. Coffee imports, quantity and value, 1790–1957.

Source: 1790-1896, Treasury Department, Bureau of Statistics, *MSCF*, October 1896, pp. 670-672 and 679-681; 1898-1957, see source for series U 74–75, 1898-1957.

U 97–98. Tea imports, quantity and value, 1790-1957.

Source: 1790–1896, Treasury Department, Bureau of Statistics, *MSCF*, October 1896, pp. 684–685 and 688–689; 1898–1957, see source for series U 74–75, 1898–1957.

U 99–100. Sugar imports, quantity and value, 1790-1957.

Source: 1790-1897, Treasury Department, Bureau of Statistics, *MSCF*, November 1902, pp. 1366 and 1375; 1898-1957, see source for series U 74–75, 1898–1957.

U 101–104. Crude rubber and raw silk imports, quantity and value, 1855–1957.

Source: 1855–1897, Department of Commerce, *Statistical Abstract of the United States*, 1924, p. 445; 1898-1957, see source for series U 74–75, 1898-1957.

U 105–115. Value of imports of selected products, 1820-1957.

Source: See source for series U 80-93.

U 116–151. General note.

Imports are shown according to country of origin and exports according to ultimate destination. When the final destination is not known the shipment is credited statistically to the country to which it is consigned. Accurate information on country of origin is difficult to obtain. Consequently, the directional breakdown of foreign trade is at best approximate.

Trade with Canada and the United Kingdom, particularly, is difficult to measure. Considerable United States merchandise normally moves to foreign destination via Canada and some moves across Canada to destinations in the United States, notably from ports in Michigan to ports in New York. At times such movements have been counted as trade with Canada. Also considerable Canadian trade with other countries moves through the United States. A good deal of United States merchandise has been consigned to the United Kingdom and reexported to other markets by the United Kingdom, as can be observed by the difference between general imports and retained imports in the United Kingdom's record of trade with the United States.

Special studies of United States-Canadian trade have been made from time to time. In this connection, see the headnote to the table, p. 295 of *Commerce Yearbook*, vol. II, for 1931; and see *MSCF*, June and July 1898, pp. 2084–2089, where it is also noted (p. 2075) that "exports to Canada are incomplete prior to April 1, 1893, the date on which the law requiring exporters to clear their goods exported by railways went into effect." For an effort at adjusting the United States trade record for this deficiency and the similar lack of coverage in the report of trade with Mexico, see table II of Matthew Simon's "Statistical Estimates of the Balance of International Payments and the International Capital Movements of the U.S., 1861–1900" to be published by the National Bureau of Economic Research in *Studies in Income and Wealth*, vol. 24. For a discussion of shortcomings in the United States record of trade with the United Kingdom in the early years of the Civil War, see the Treasury's report in 1864 to Congress, *Statistics of the Foreign and Domestic Commerce of the United States*, p. 37 ff.

For certain periods, like the Civil War and the greenback era, partners' records of trade with the United States are more reliable than the United States record and in some ways more revealing of certain aspects of the trade. Accordingly, the records of two of the most important partners, Canada and the United Kingdom are shown in series U 152–161.

For 1862–1879, exports of domestic merchandise are mixed gold and currency values. Imports and reexports, however, are specie values. The extent of the adjustment can be observed by comparing figures from series U 116 with those in series U 10.

Prior to 1873, trade figures for Canada are actually trade figures for all of British North America, a somewhat larger area than the Dominion of Canada. Asia includes the Philippines in all years and Turkey in Europe for 1926-1951. Oceania includes Hawaii prior to 1901. Europe includes the Soviet Republic in Asia since 1923 and Iceland in all years (Iceland was included with northern North America in *Historical Statistics of the United States, 1789-1945*).

The source for these series for 1821-1881 is the Treasury Department, Bureau of Statistics, *Monthly Summary of Commerce and Finance*, hereafter abbreviated as *MSCF*.

U 116–133. Value of exports (including reexports) of U.S. merchandise, by country of destination, 1790-1957.

Source: 1790-1820, series U 116, see source for series U 10, 1790-1820; series U 117–133, Treasury Department, Bureau of Statistics, *Statistical Tables Exhibiting the Commerce of the U.S. With European Countries 1790–1890*, 1893, pp. xiii, xiv, xviii, and xix. 1821-1881, series U 116, *MSCF*, April 1898, p. 1632; series U 118, 1821-1872, *MSCF*, June 1898, p. 2091; 1873-1881, Department of Commerce and Labor, *Statistical Abstract of the United States*, 1907, p. 317; series U 119–121, *MSCF*, August 1901, pp. 618, 626-627, and 632-633; series U 123–127, *MSCF*, October 1896, pp. 718, 730-732, and 745-746; series U 128–131, *MSCF*, April 1898, pp. 1632, 1637, and 1638 (except for China, 1865-1881, *Statistical Abstract*, 1907, p. 350); series U 132–133, 1821-1864, *MSCF*, June 1896, pp. 1612, 1621-1622; 1865-1881, *Statistical Abstract*, 1907, pp. 366, 376 (data for total America and "other" series were obtained as residuals for 1821-1881); 1882-1957, the following editions of the *Statistical Abstract*:

Period	Edition	Page
1882–1889	1907	284, 288–369
1890–1906	1910	328–376
1907–1915	1916	347–381
1916–1920	1920	398–425
1921–1923	1926	452, 458–463
1924–1928	1930	482, 492–497
1929–1932	1934	418, 424–429
1933–1936	1938	456, 460–464
1937–1940	1943	530, 534–538
1941–1945	1948	922, 926–930
1946–1948	1952	856, 858–860
1949–1952	1957	901, 904–908
1953–1957	1958	892, 894–897

U 134–151. Value of general imports, by country of origin, 1790-1957.

Source: See source for series U 116–133.

See also general note for series U 116–151.

U 152–155. Trade with the United States as reported by Canada, 1850–1957.

Source: 1850–1867, Dominion of Canada, Department of Trade and Commerce, *Special Report of Trade Between Canada and the U.S. for the Use of the International Commission, Quebec, August 1898*, Dawson, Ottawa, 1898, pp. 258-259; 1868-1900, Dominion Bureau of Statistics, *Trade of Canada*, vol. I, 1956, p. 19; 1901–1918, series U 152 and U 155, *Review of Foreign Trade*, part II, p. 49; series U 153 and U 154, unpublished records of the Dominion Bureau of Statistics; 1919-1956, *Trade of Canada*, vol. I, 1956, pp. 24-25; 1957, *Review of Foreign Trade*, part II, pp. 50-51.

The Dominion Bureau of Statistics takes, as the value of goods exported, the actual amount received by the exporter in Canadian dollars, excluding such charges as freight, insurance, and handling. In effect, therefore, export values are taken f.o.b. point of shipment for export. The value of goods imported is the value as determined for customs duty purposes. In most cases, this corresponds to the value shown on the invoice accompanying the goods, converted to Canadian dollars at authorized exchange rates (usually the commercial rate prevailing on the date at which the goods were actually dispatched to Canada), and excluding such charges as freight, insurance, handling, and taxes. In effect, therefore, import values are taken f.o.b. point of shipment in the country of export.

U 156–167. Trade with the United States as reported by the United Kingdom, 1831-1957.

Source: 1831-1840, House of Lords, "Tables Shewing the Trade of the U.K. with Different Foreign Countries and British Possessions in each of 10 years," *Sessional Papers*, vol. xxxix, 1842, pp. 344-346, and 348; 1841-1848, Board of Trade, *Statistical Abstract of the United Kingdom, 1840–1854*, pp. 10, 13, 15; 1849-1923, the following editions of *Annual Statement of the Trade of the U.K. with Foreign Countries and British Possessions:*

Period	Edition	Page
1849–1859	1853	215
1854–1855	1855	255
1856–1857	1857	308
1858–1860	1860	323
1861–1865	1865	292
1866–1870	1870	270
1871–1875	1875	206
1876–1880	1880	208
1881–1885	1885	283
1886–1890	1890	308
1891–1895	1895	391
1896–1899	1900 (vol. II)	310
1900–1904	1904 (vol. II)	319
1905–1909	1909 (vol. II)	218
1910	1910	233
1911–1912	1915	309
1913, 1919–1922	1922 (vol. IV)	361
1914–1918	1918 (vol. II)	291
1923	1927 (vol. IV)	345

1924–1957, the following Department of Commerce publications: *Commerce Yearbook* (for years as noted); 1924–1926, vol. II, 1928 edition, p. 644; 1927-1929, vol. II, 1931 edition, p. 295; *Foreign Commerce Yearbook* (for years as noted); 1930-1932, 1933 edition, p. 145; 1931-1934, 1935 edition, p. 149; 1934-1936, 1937 edition, p. 168; 1937-1938 and 1946, 1948 edition, p. 209; 1947, 1950 edition, p. 508; 1948-1951, 1951 edition, p. 517; for 1952-1957, *World Trade Information Services*, part 3, Nos. 54-3, 56-37, and 58-16.

The basic source for all years is the official trade record of the United Kingdom and the sources quoted here for the data prior to 1923 are British publications. The figures from the British publications were converted at the following rates of exchange (dollars per pound sterling): 1923, $4.575; 1924, $4.417; 1925, $4.829; 1926, $4.858; and 1927-1933, $4.44. British imports are valued c.i.f. (cost, insurance, and freight); exports are valued f.o.b.

The sources used give wheat imports variously in quarters, hundredweight (cwt.), or bushels, and these have been converted to pounds at 8 bushels per quarter, 60 pounds per bushel, and 112 pounds per cwt. Cotton is given variously in pounds, centals (hundreds of pounds), or hundredweight (of 112 pounds).

Trade of the whole of Ireland is included with trade of Britain prior to April 1, 1923. Thereafter, trade of the Irish Free State is excluded.

The British system of reporting direction was changed in 1908 in accordance with recommendations of the departmental Committee on Trade Records [Cd 4345 (Command Paper by Parliament)] from country of shipment to country of consignment. Returns on both systems are reported in the *Annual Statement* (cited above) and its *Supplement* for 1904-1913. Figures given here were drawn from the *Annual Statement* for 1904 and 1909 (vol. II) giving the old basis through 1904 and the new beginning 1905. "The difference (between the two bases) arises mainly in the case of imports

from and exports to countries which do not possess a seaboard. . . ." Imports from the United States were affected somewhat by the adoption of the new system; exports to the United States of British produce, not at all. Imports of grain, especially, were affected; on the new basis of consignment United Kingdom grain imports from the United States were smaller than on the old country-of-shipment basis, indicating that more grain was consigned from Canada and shipped from United States ports than was consigned from the United States and shipped from Canadian ports (both movements are normal). See *Annual Statement* for 1910 *Supplement*, p. 317 ff.

The Department of Commerce and Labor in *MSCF*, April 1904, makes the following observation about the United Kingdom's trade record prior to the change in counting direction:

In the trade accounts of the United Kingdom imports are generally credited to the country whence they were shipped direct to the United Kingdom. Although efforts are made to trace the more important imports back to the actual countries of first shipment, yet in the absence of "certificates of origin" of imported goods this is not always possible. . . . The same practice is followed in the case of exports, which are charged to the country in which the port of first discharge is situated.

Similar inaccuracies appear in the United States trade account. As a rule the exports from the United States to countries having no direct steamship connections with American ports appear understated in the United States accounts, whereas the exports to countries containing the respective ports of discharge whence the goods are forwarded, either by land or water, to the ultimate country of destination as a rule are overstated. Thus the exports from the United States to Austria-Hungary, Russia, and Switzerland are understated, while those to United Kingdom and Germany appear overstated in the United States accounts. Generally a more correct idea of the trade relations between two countries can be obtained from a study of their respective import figures than their export figures. (p. 3727)

Prior to the issuance of the *Commerce Yearbooks* and their successor serials, various agencies of the U.S. Government from time to time published the official British record of trade with the United States converted into U.S. dollar equivalents. An early publication giving the dollar value of total United Kingdom imports and exports with the United States was the State Department's "Report on the Commercial Relations of the United States with all Foreign Nations" (S. Doc. 107, 34th Cong., 1st sess.). On p. 40 of vol. I of this work is a table giving a "View of trade between Great Britain and the part of the North American Colonies now included in the United States from 1697-1774 and between Great Britain and the United States from 1775-1820" compiled from British authorities. The sources of these figures are not more definitely specified, the problem of conversion is not discussed, nor is the basic record assessed critically, although much dissatisfaction developed late in the 18th century with the valuation of British trade statistics. From 1698, both imports and exports were valued according to official unit values which were altered from time to time but some of which remained fixed for over a century. The system of valuing exports of domestic products was changed to employ "real or declared" values beginning in 1805, and beginning in 1854 the system of valuing imports and exports of foreign and colonial merchandise was changed to give "computed real values" based on market quotations in the United Kingdom. An indication of the extent of the revision introduced by the change to market values can be obtained from the *Annual Statement* for 1854 (pp. iii-iv). Using market prices added 22¾ percent to the "official values" of all United Kingdom imports in 1854, 26 percent to imports from foreign countries, and 13⅓ percent to imports from British possessions. Curiously, the value of reexports was reduced by 38 percent. The new unit values were lower on raw cotton, coffee, and tea, but higher on cereals. In 1871, the "declared" value basis was introduced for imports and reexports. In spite of deficiencies, figures on trade in official values may serve as weighted indexes of quantities traded between the United States and United Kingdom, weights being the official unit values; and the State Department series may serve a useful purpose. The user would be well advised, however, to track down the original official returns in order to interpret the figures properly.

Another U.S. Government publication giving the dollar value of British trade with the United States is the 1864 report to Congress by the Treasury Department, *Statistics of the Foreign and Domestic Commerce of the United States*, which gives (p. 33 ff.) the values for United Kingdom trade with the United States from the official United Kingdom record, converted to U.S. dollar equivalents, for 1856-1862. A still later report is Department of State, Foreign Commerce Bureau, "Abstract of the Foreign Commerce of Europe, Australasia, Asia, and Africa 1873-1885," *Consular Report*, No. 85, vol. 24, 1887. It gives (p. 90 ff.) dollar values for the totals traded with the United States by the United Kingdom. However, this series appears to have required revision, for a subsequent compilation of the same nature in *Consular Report*, No. 91, vol. 25, 1888, p. 740, gives figures for the decade 1877–1886 showing an upward revision in both imports and exports for the years common to both tabulations. The 1888 tabulation is repeated, in part, in *Consular Report*, No. 141, vol. 39, 1892, p. 211, carrying similar figures for 1881-1890. The last year of this set of figures appears to have been revised. Somewhat different figures for 1890 are given by the Department of Commerce and Labor in *MSCF*, April 1904, p. 3848 ff., carrying the dollar values for United Kingdom trade with the United States 1890–1902. The series was extended to 1906 in Department of Commerce and Labor, Bureau of Statistics, *Statistical Abstract of Foreign Countries, parts I-III; Statistics of Foreign Commerce*, 1909, p. 120 ff.

From 1906 until the Department of Commerce began the serial publication of the dollar value of British trade with the United States in the *Commerce Yearbook* of 1926 and subsequent years, the publication of this series was spotty and irregular. The Bureau of Foreign and Domestic Commerce issued two compilations on the "Commercial Relations of the United States with Foreign Countries" for 1911 and 1912 giving the dollar value of total trade of the United Kingdom with the United States in 1910, 1911, and 1912. Figures for 1913 are given in the *Commerce Yearbook* for 1926 and subsequent years; and the Bureau of Foreign and Domestic Commerce, *Supplements to Commerce Reports* Nos. 19a, March 28, 1916, and 22b, April 12, 1920, give dollar values of United Kingdom trade with the United States in 1914 and 1917–1919. The last, however, are converted at par and there is some question as to whether this conversion is the best. The problem of conversion is discussed at some length in the *Supplement* for 1921, No. 1, p. 74. See also *Supplements* for 1922, No. 7, pp. 63 and 68, and 1923, No. 1, p. 21 ff.

Thus, for most of the last hundred years one agency or another of the U.S. Government has published dollar equivalent values for the official United Kingdom trade totals with the United States. However, until the publication of the *Commerce Yearbooks* the statistics were not always presented with descriptive notes giving exact sources and describing the method of conversion. Because of the frequency of revisions, one suspects, especially of consular reports, that the sources used for the most recent year given, and perhaps for other years, were preliminary figures which may or may not have been revised. Consequently, these series should be used with some caution. For additional information, see Albert Imlah, *Economic Elements in the Pax Britannica: Study in British Foreign Trade and Trade Policy in the 19th Century*, Harvard University Press, 1959.

Series U 1–14. Value of Exports and Imports: 1790 to 1957

[In millions of dollars. For years ending September 30, 1790–1842; June 30, 1843–1915; thereafter, calendar years]

Year	Total, gold, silver, and merchandise			Gold			Silver			Merchandise [2]				
										Exports and reexports			General imports	Excess of exports (+) or imports (−)
	Exports	Imports	Excess of exports (+) or imports (−)	Exports [1]	Imports	Excess of exports (+) or imports (−)	Exports [1]	Imports	Excess of exports (+) or imports (−)	Total	Exports of U.S. merchandise	Re-exports		
	1	2	3	4	5	6	7	8	9	10	11	12	13	14
1957	20,989	13,409	+7,580	168	273	−104	11	158	−147	20,810	20,630	179	12,978	+7,832
1956	19,124	12,877	+6,247	27	133	−106	7	129	−122	19,090	18,940	150	12,615	+6,475
1955	15,563	11,562	+4,001	7	105	−97	8	73	−65	15,547	15,419	128	11,384	+4,163
1954	15,136	10,333	+4,803	22	38	−16	5	80	−75	15,110	14,981	129	10,215	+4,894
1953	15,827	11,015	+4,812	45	47	−2	9	95	−86	15,774	15,652	122	10,873	+4,900
1952	15,262	11,525	+3,737	56	740	−684	5	67	−62	15,201	15,049	152	10,717	+4,483
1951	15,672	11,152	+4,520	631	81	+550	9	103	−94	15,032	14,879	153	10,967	+4,065
1950	10,816	9,125	+1,691	534	163	+372	7	110	−103	10,275	10,142	133	8,852	+1,423
1949	12,160	7,467	+4,693	85	771	−686	24	74	−50	12,051	11,936	115	6,622	+5,429
1948	12,967	9,176	+3,791	301	1,981	−1,680	13	71	−58	12,653	12,532	121	7,124	+5,529
1947	14,674	7,904	+6,770	213	2,080	−1,866	31	68	−37	[3]14,430	14,252	177	5,756	+8,673
1946	9,996	5,533	+4,464	221	533	−311	36	58	−21	[3]9,738	9,500	238	4,942	+4,796
1945	10,097	4,280	+5,816	200	94	+106	91	27	+64	[3]9,806	9,585	221	4,159	+5,646
1944	15,345	4,066	+11,279	959	114	+845	127	23	+104	[3]14,259	14,162	97	3,929	+10,330
1943	13,028	3,511	+9,517	33	102	−69	31	28	+3	12,965	12,842	123	3,381	+9,583
1942	8,081	3,113	+4,968	(4)	316	−316	2	41	−39	8,079	8,003	76	2,756	+5,323
1941	5,153	4,375	+778	(4)	982	−982	6	47	−41	5,147	5,020	127	3,345	+1,802
1940	4,030	7,433	−3,403	5	4,749	−4,744	4	58	−55	4,021	3,934	87	2,625	+1,396
1939	3,192	5,978	−2,786	1	3,575	−3,574	15	85	−71	3,177	3,123	54	2,318	+859
1938	3,107	4,170	−1,063	6	1,979	−1,974	7	231	−223	3,094	3,057	37	1,960	+1,134
1937	3,407	4,807	−1,400	46	1,632	−1,586	12	92	−80	3,349	3,299	50	3,084	+265
1936	2,495	3,750	−1,254	28	1,144	−1,117	12	183	−171	2,456	2,419	37	2,423	+33
1935	2,304	4,143	−1,839	2	1,741	−1,739	19	355	−336	2,283	2,243	40	2,047	+235
1934	2,202	2,944	−742	53	1,187	−1,134	17	103	−86	2,133	2,100	33	1,655	+478
1933	2,061	1,703	+358	367	193	+173	19	60	−41	1,675	1,647	28	1,450	+225
1932	2,434	1,706	+729	810	363	+446	14	20	−6	1,611	1,576	35	1,323	+288
1931	2,918	2,731	+186	467	612	−145	26	29	−2	2,424	2,378	46	2,091	+334
1930	4,013	3,500	+514	116	396	−280	54	43	+11	3,843	3,781	62	3,061	+782
1929	5,441	4,755	+686	117	292	−175	83	64	+19	5,241	5,157	84	4,399	+842
1928	5,776	4,328	+1,448	561	169	+392	87	68	+19	5,128	5,030	98	4,091	+1,037
1927	5,142	4,447	+695	201	208	−6	76	55	+21	4,865	4,759	107	4,185	+681
1926	5,017	4,714	+303	116	214	−98	92	70	+23	4,809	4,712	97	4,431	+378
1925	5,272	4,419	+852	263	128	+134	99	65	+35	4,910	4,819	91	4,227	+683
1924	4,763	4,004	+759	62	320	−258	110	74	+36	4,591	4,498	93	3,610	+981
1923	4,269	4,189	+79	29	323	−294	72	74	−2	4,167	4,091	77	3,792	+375
1922	3,931	3,459	+473	37	275	−238	63	71	−8	3,832	3,765	67	3,113	+719
1921	4,560	3,264	+1,297	24	691	−667	52	63	−12	4,485	4,379	106	2,509	+1,976
1920	8,664	5,784	+2,880	322	417	−95	114	88	+26	8,228	8,080	148	5,278	+2,950
1919	8,528	4,070	+4,457	368	77	+292	239	89	+150	7,920	7,750	171	3,904	+4,016
1918	6,443	3,165	+3,278	41	62	−21	253	71	+181	6,149	6,048	101	3,031	+3,118
1917	6,690	3,558	+3,131	372	552	−181	84	53	+31	6,234	6,170	64	2,952	+3,281
1916	5,709	3,110	+2,599	156	686	−530	71	32	+38	5,483	5,423	60	2,392	+3,091
1915 [5]	2,966	1,875	+1,091	146	172	−25	51	29	+22	2,769	2,716	52	1,674	+1,094
1914	2,532	1,991	+541	112	67	+46	55	30	+25	2,365	2,330	35	1,894	+471
1913	2,615	1,923	+692	78	69	+9	72	41	+30	2,466	2,429	37	1,813	+653
1912	2,327	1,749	+577	57	49	+8	65	47	+18	2,204	2,170	34	1,653	+551
1911	2,137	1,647	+490	23	74	−51	65	46	+19	2,049	2,014	36	1,527	+522
1910	1,919	1,646	+273	119	43	+75	55	45	+10	1,745	1,710	35	1,557	+188
1909	1,810	1,400	+410	92	44	+48	56	44	+12	1,663	1,638	25	1,312	+351
1908	1,991	1,387	+604	72	148	−76	58	45	+13	1,861	1,835	26	1,194	+666
1907	1,989	1,592	+397	51	115	−63	57	43	+14	1,881	1,854	27	1,434	+446
1906	1,848	1,367	+481	39	96	−58	66	44	+21	1,744	1,718	26	1,227	+517
1905	1,660	1,199	+461	93	54	+39	49	27	+21	1,519	1,492	27	1,118	+401
1904	1,592	1,118	+474	81	99	−18	49	28	+22	1,461	1,435	26	991	+470
1903	1,511	1,095	+417	47	45	+2	44	24	+20	1,420	1,392	28	1,026	+394
1902	1,480	984	+496	49	52	−3	50	28	+22	1,382	1,355	26	903	+478
1901	1,605	926	+680	53	66	−13	64	36	+28	1,488	1,460	27	823	+665
1900	1,499	930	+570	48	45	+4	57	35	+21	1,394	1,371	24	850	+545
1899	1,321	817	+504	38	89	−51	56	31	+26	1,227	1,204	23	697	+530
1898	1,302	767	+535	15	120	−105	55	31	+24	1,231	1,210	21	616	+615
1897	1,153	880	+273	40	85	−45	62	31	+31	1,051	1,032	19	765	+286
1896	1,056	842	+214	112	34	+79	61	29	+32	883	863	19	780	+103
1895	921	789	+133	66	36	+30	47	20	+27	808	793	14	732	+76
1894	1,020	741	+279	77	72	+5	50	13	+37	892	869	23	655	+237
1893	997	911	+86	109	21	+88	41	23	+18	848	831	17	866	−19
1892	1,113	897	+216	50	50	(4)	33	20	+13	1,030	1,016	15	827	+203
1891	993	881	+112	86	18	+68	23	18	+5	884	872	12	845	+40
1890	910	823	+87	17	13	+4	35	21	+14	858	845	13	789	+69
1889	839	774	+65	60	10	+50	37	19	+18	742	730	12	745	−3
1888	742	783	−41	18	44	−26	28	15	+13	696	684	12	724	−28
1887	752	752	(4)	10	43	−33	26	17	+9	716	703	13	692	+24
1886	752	674	+78	43	21	+22	30	18	+12	680	666	14	635	+44
1885	784	621	+164	8	27	−18	34	17	+17	742	727	16	578	+165
1884	808	705	+103	41	23	+18	26	15	+11	741	725	16	668	+73
1883	856	752	+104	12	18	−6	20	11	+9	824	804	20	723	+101
1882	800	767	+33	33	34	−2	17	8	+9	751	733	17	725	+26
1881	922	753	+169	3	100	−97	17	11	+6	902	884	18	643	+260

See footnotes at end of table.

Series U 1-14. Value of Exports and Imports: 1790 to 1957—Con.

[In millions of dollars]

Year	Total, gold, silver, and merchandise			Gold			Silver			Merchandise [2]				
										Exports and reexports			General imports	Excess of exports (+) or imports (−)
	Exports	Imports	Excess of exports (+) or imports (−)	Exports [1]	Imports	Excess of exports (+) or imports (−)	Exports [1]	Imports	Excess of exports (+) or imports (−)	Total	Exports of U. S. merchandise	Re-exports		
	1	2	3	4	5	6	7	8	9	10	11	12	13	14
1880	853	761	+92	4	81	−77	14	12	+1	836	824	12	668	+168
1879	735	466	+269	5	6	−1	20	15	+6	710	698	12	446	+265
1878	729	467	+262	9	13	−4	25	16	+8	695	681	14	437	+258
1877	659	492	+167	27	26	(4)	30	15	+15	602	590	13	451	+151
1876	597	477	+120	31	8	+23	25	8	+17	540	526	15	461	+80
1875	606	554	+52	67	14	+53	25	7	+18	513	499	14	533	−20
1874	653	596	+57	34	20	+15	33	9	+24	586	569	17	567	+19
1873	607	664	−57	45	9	+36	40	13	+27	522	505	17	642	−120
1872	524	640	−116	50	9	+41	30	5	+25	444	428	16	627	−182
1871	541	541	(4)	67	7	+60	32	14	+17	443	428	14	520	−77
1870	451	462	−11	34	12	+22	25	14	+10	393	377	16	436	−43
1869	343	437	−94	36	14	+22	21	6	+15	286	275	11	418	−131
1868	376	372	+4	72	9	+64	21	5	+16	282	269	13	357	−75
1867	355	418	−62	39	17	+22	22	5	+17	295	280	15	396	−101
1866	435	446	−11	71	8	+63	15	3	+12	349	338	11	435	−86
1865	234	249	−15	58	6	+52	9	3	+6	166	137	29	239	−73
1864	264	330	−65	101	11	+89	5	2	+3	159	144	15	316	−158
1863	268	253	+15	62	6	+57	2	4	−2	204	186	18	243	−39
1862	228	206	+22	35	14	+22	1	3	−1	191	180	11	189	+1
1861	249	336	−86	27	42	−15	2	4	−2	220	205	15	289	−70
1860	400	362	+38	58	3	+56	8	6	+2	334	316	17	354	−20
1859	357	339	+18	61	2	+59	3	5	−3	293	278	15	331	−38
1858	325	283	+42	50	12	+38	3	8	−5	272	251	21	263	+9
1857	363	361	+2	65	7	+59	4	6	−2	294	279	15	348	−55
1856	327	315	+12	45	1	+44	1	3	−2	281	266	15	310	−29
1855	275	261	+14	55	1	+54	1	3	−1	219	193	26	258	−39
1854	278	305	−26	40	3	+37	1	4	−3	237	215	22	298	−61
1853	231	268	−37	25	2	+23	2	2	(4)	203	190	14	264	−60
1852	210	213	−3	40	4	+36	3	2	+1	167	155	12	207	−40
1851	218	216	+2	23	4	+19	7	2	+5	189	179	10	211	−22
1850	152	178	−26	5	2	+3	3	3	(4)	144	135	9	174	−29
1849	146	148	−2	2	4	−2	3	3	+1	140	132	9	141	−1
1848	154	155	−1	11	3	+8	5	3	+2	138	130	8	149	−10
1847	159	147	+12	1	22	−21	1	3	−2	157	151	6	122	+34
1846	113	122	−8	2	1	+1	2	3	−1	110	102	8	118	−8
1845	115	117	−3	3	1	+2	6	3	+2	106	98	8	113	−7
1844	111	108	+3	1	2	(4)	4	4	(4)	106	100	6	103	+3
1843 [6]	84	65	+20	(4)	17	−17	1	5	−4	83	78	5	42	+40
1842	105	100	+5	2	1	+2	3	3	−1	100	92	8	96	+4
1841	122	128	−6	4	1	+2	6	4	+3	112	104	8	123	−11
1840	132	107	+25	4	3	+1	5	6	−1	124	112	12	98	+25
1839	121	162	−41	5	1	+4	4	4	(4)	112	102	11	156	−44
1838	108	114	−5	1	12	−10	2	6	−4	105	96	9	96	+9
1837	117	141	−24	3	2	+1	3	8	−5	111	94	17	130	−19
1836	129	190	−61	1	7	−7	4	6	−2	124	107	18	177	−52
1835	122	150	−28	1	2	−1	5	11	−6	115	100	15	137	−22
1834	104	127	−22	1	4	−3	1	14	−13	102	81	22	109	−6
1833	90	108	−18	1	1	(4)	2	6	−5	88	70	18	101	−14
1832	87	101	−14	2	1	+1	4	5	−2	82	62	20	95	−14
1831	81	103	−22	3	1	+2	6	6	(4)	72	59	13	96	−24
1830	74	71	+3	1	1	+1	1	7	−7	72	59	13	63	+9
1829	72	74	−2	2	1	+1	3	7	−3	67	55	12	67	(4)
1828	72	89	−16	2	1	+1	7	7	(4)	64	50	14	81	−17
1827	82	79	+3	2	1	+1	6	7	−1	74	58	16	71	+3
1826	78	85	−7	1	1	(4)	4	6	−3	73	52	20	78	−5
1825	100	96	+3	(4)	1	(4)	8	6	+3	91	67	24	90	+1
1824	76	81	−5	(7)	(7)	(7)	7 7	7 8	7 −1	69	51	18	72	−3
1823	75	78	−3	(7)	(7)	(7)	7 6	7 5	7 +1	68	47	21	72	−4
1822	72	83	−11	(7)	(7)	(7)	7 11	7 3	7 +7	61	50	11	80	−19
1821	65	63	+2	(7)	(7)	(7)	7 10	7 8	7 +2	55	44	11	55	(4)

Year	Merchandise [2]					Year	Merchandise [2]					Year	Merchandise [2]				
	Exports and reexports			General imports	Excess of exports (+) or imports (−)		Exports and reexports			General imports	Excess of exports (+) or imports (−)		Exports and reexports			General imports	Excess of exports (+) or imports (−)
	Total	Exports of U. S. merchandise	Re-exports				Total	Exports of U. S. merchandise	Re-exports				Total	Exports of U. S. merchandise	Re-exports		
	10	11	12	13	14		10	11	12	13	14		10	11	12	13	14
1820	70	52	18	74	−5	1810	67	42	24	85	−19	1800	71	32	39	91	−20
1819	70	51	19	87	−17	1809	52	31	21	59	−7	1799	79	33	46	79	(4)
1818	93	74	19	122	−28	1808	22	9	13	57	−35	1798	61	28	33	69	−7
1817	88	68	19	99	−12	1807	108	49	60	139	−30	1797	51	24	27	75	−24
1816	82	65	17	147	−65	1806	102	41	60	129	−28	1796	59	32	26	81	−23
1815	53	46	7	113	−60	1805	96	42	53	121	−25	1795	48	40	8	70	−22
1814	7	7	(4)	13	−6	1804	78	41	36	85	−7	1794	33	27	7	35	−2
1813	28	25	3	22	+6	1803	56	42	14	65	−9	1793	26	24	2	31	−5
1812	39	30	8	77	−39	1802	72	36	36	76	−4	1792	21	19	2	32	−11
1811	61	45	16	53	+8	1801	93	46	47	111	−18	1791	19	19	1	29	−10
												1790	20			23	−3

[1] Prior to 1864, domestic exports of silver included with gold.
[2] Figures include gold and silver prior to 1821.
[3] Figures which include estimates of civilian supplies shipped to occupied areas through U. S. Armed Forces and other relief agencies are as follows (in millions of dollars): 1944, 14,414; 1945, 10,530; 1946, 10,184; 1947, 15,338.
[4] Less than $500,000.

[5] Figures for 6-month period of July 1, 1915—Dec. 31, 1915, are as follows (in millions of dollars): Series U 1, 1,905; series U 2, 1,239; series U 3, +667; series U 4, 24; series U 5, 307; series U 6, −283; series U 7, 29; series U 8, 19; series U 9, +10; series U 10, 1,853; series U 11, 1,820; series U 12, 33; series U 13, 913; and series U 14, +940.
[6] Period beginning Oct. 1, 1842, and ending June 30, 1843.
[7] Data shown under silver are for gold and silver.

Series U 15-20. Value of Merchandise Imports and Duties: 1821 to 1957

[Merchandise imports entered for consumption. For years ending September 30, 1821-1842; June 30, 1843-1915; thereafter, calendar years]

Year	Value of imports			Duties calculated	Ratio of duties calculated to total imports	
	Total	Free	Dutiable		Free and dutiable	Dutiable
	15	16	17	18	19	20
	Mil. dol.	Mil. dol.	Mil. dol.	Mil. dol.	Percent	Percent
1957	12,921	6,012	6,909	746	5.77	10.80
1956	12,516	6,235	6,281	710	5.67	11.30
1955	11,337	6,037	5,300	633	5.59	11.95
1954	10,240	5,668	4,572	529	5.17	11.57
1953	10,779	5,920	4,859	584	5.42	12.02
1952	10,747	6,257	4,491	570	5.30	12.69
1951	10,817	5,993	4,824	591	5.47	12.26
1950	8,743	4,767	3,976	522	5.97	13.14
1949	6,592	3,883	2,708	365	5.53	13.46
1948	7,092	4,175	2,918	405	5.71	13.87
1947	5,666	3,455	2,212	428	7.55	19.34
1946	4,825	2,935	1,890	478	9.90	25.28
1945	4,098	2,749	1,349	381	9.29	28.24
1944	3,887	2,718	1,170	367	9.45	31.41
1943	3,390	2,193	1,197	393	11.57	32.79
1942	2,780	1,779	1,002	320	11.51	31.96
1941	3,222	2,031	1,191	438	13.59	36.75
1940	2,541	1,649	892	318	12.51	35.63
1939	2,276	1,397	879	328	14.41	37.33
1938	1,950	1,183	767	301	15.46	39.30
1937	3,010	1,765	1,245	471	15.63	37.80
1936	2,424	1,385	1,039	408	16.84	39.28
1935	2,039	1,206	833	357	17.52	42.88
1934	1,636	991	645	301	18.41	46.70
1933	1,433	904	529	284	19.80	53.58
1932	1,325	886	440	260	19.59	59.06
1931	2,088	1,392	697	371	17.75	53.21
1930	3,114	2,081	1,033	462	14.83	44.71
1929	4,339	2,880	1,458	585	13.48	40.10
1928	4,078	2,679	1,399	542	13.30	38.76
1927	4,163	2,680	1,483	575	13.81	38.76
1926	4,408	2,908	1,500	590	13.39	39.34
1925	4,176	2,709	1,467	552	13.21	37.61
1924	3,575	2,118	1,457	532	14.89	36.53
1923	3,732	2,165	1,567	567	15.18	36.17
1922	3,074	1,888	1,186	451	14.68	38.07
1921	2,557	1,564	993	292	11.44	29.46
1920	5,102	3,116	1,986	326	6.38	16.40
1919	3,828	2,711	1,116	237	6.20	21.27
1918	2,952	2,229	723	171	5.79	23.65
1917	2,919	2,141	778	205	7.01	26.28
1916	2,359	1,615	744	214	9.08	28.80
1915 [1]	1,648	1,033	616	206	12.49	33.46
1914	1,906	1,152	754	284	14.88	37.63
1913	1,767	987	780	313	17.69	40.08
1912	1,641	882	759	305	18.58	40.16
1911	1,528	777	751	310	20.29	41.27
1910	1,547	761	786	327	21.11	41.56
1909	[2]1,282	509	682	295	22.99	43.19
1908	1,183	526	657	283	23.88	42.98
1907	1,415	642	773	329	23.28	42.60
1906	1,213	549	665	294	24.22	44.22
1905	1,087	517	570	258	23.77	45.33
1904	982	454	528	258	26.29	48.92
1903	1,008	437	571	281	27.85	49.20
1902	900	397	503	251	27.95	49.97
1901 [3]	808	339	469	234	28.91	49.83
1900 [3]	831	367	464	229	27.62	49.46
1899	685	300	386	202	29.48	52.38
1898	587	292	296	145	24.77	49.20
1897	789	382	407	173	21.89	42.41
1896	760	369	391	157	20.67	40.18
1895	731	377	354	149	20.44	42.19
1894	630	372	258	130	20.56	50.29
1893	833	432	400	199	23.91	49.75
1892	804	449	356	174	21.65	48.98
1891	845	379	466	217	25.65	46.50
1890	766	258	508	227	29.59	44.63
1889	735	250	485	221	30.02	45.49
1888	707	239	468	216	30.55	46.15
1887	680	229	450	214	31.52	47.57
1886	624	210	414	189	30.35	45.78
1885	579	192	387	178	30.75	46.05
1884	668	211	457	190	28.50	41.67
1883	701	207	494	211	30.04	42.61
1882	717	211	506	216	30.16	42.71
1881	651	202	448	194	29.79	43.23
1880	628	208	420	183	29.12	43.54
1879	440	143	297	133	30.33	44.90
1878	439	141	297	127	29.00	42.77
1877	440	140	299	128	29.20	42.91
1876	465	140	324	145	31.25	44.76
1875	526	146	380	155	29.36	40.66
1874	568	151	416	161	28.29	38.58
1873	663	178	485	185	27.90	38.12
1872	560	47	513	213	37.99	41.46
1871	500	40	460	202	40.51	44.04
1870	426	20	406	192	44.89	47.13
1869	394	22	373	177	44.76	47.37
1868	345	15	330	161	46.56	48.70
1867	378	17	361	169	44.56	46.66
1866	423	57	366	177	41.81	48.33
1865	210	40	170	81	38.46	47.56
1864	301	38	263	96	32.04	36.69
1863	225	30	195	64	28.28	32.62
1862	178	50	128	47	26.08	36.20
1861	275	67	207	39	14.21	18.84
1860	336	68	268	53	15.67	19.67
1859	317	67	250	49	15.43	19.56
1858	243	55	187	42	17.33	22.44
1857	334	50	284	64	19.09	22.45
1856	296	50	246	64	21.68	26.05
1855	232	30	202	54	23.36	26.83
1854	276	23	254	65	23.52	25.61
1853	250	25	225	58	23.37	25.94
1852	195	22	174	48	24.35	27.38
1851	200	18	183	49	24.26	26.63
1850	164	16	148	40	24.50	27.14
1849	133	14	119	31	23.41	26.11
1848	141	15	126	33	23.49	26.28
1847	116	16	100	28	24.20	28.02
1846	110	19	91	30	27.70	33.35
1845	106	16	90	31	29.34	34.45
1844	96	17	80	29	30.50	36.88
1843 [4]	37	12	26	8	20.13	29.19
1842	88	23	65	17	18.96	25.81
1841	115	57	58	20	17.37	34.56
1840	86	42	44	15	17.60	34.39
1839	146	65	81	26	17.57	31.77
1838	87	38	48	20	23.11	41.33
1837	113	51	62	18	16.05	29.19
1836	159	70	89	31	19.51	34.94
1835	122	58	64	26	21.25	40.38
1834	87	40	47	19	21.83	40.19
1833	83	20	63	24	28.99	38.25
1832	75	7	68	29	38.97	42.96
1831	83	6	77	37	44.23	47.38
1830	50	4	46	28	57.32	61.69
1829	55	3	51	28	50.73	54.17
1828	67	4	63	30	44.74	47.59
1827	55	3	52	28	50.93	53.76
1826	58	5	53	26	45.28	49.26
1825	66	4	63	32	47.72	50.54
1824	54	3	51	26	47.39	50.26
1823	51	3	49	22	43.69	46.04
1822	68	4	65	24	35.23	37.16
1821	44	2	42	19	43.21	45.00

[1] Figures for 6-month period July 1, 1915—Dec. 31, 1915, are as follows (in millions of dollars): Series U 15, 935; series U 16, 631; series U 17, 303; series U 18, 96; series U 19, 10.26 percent; and series U 20, 31.61 percent.

[2] Agrees with source; however, figures for components do not add to total shown.

[3] During the period from May 1, 1900, to July 25, 1901, merchandise brought from Puerto Rico was dutiable at 15 percent of regular rates. The duties collected thereon were as follows: May 1, 1900, to June 30, 1900, $134,593.88; July 1, 1900, to July 25, 1901, $448,193.91.

[4] Period beginning Oct. 1, 1842, and ending June 30, 1843.

Series U 21–44.   Indexes of Quantity and Unit Value of Exports and Imports: 1879 to 1957

Year	Exports of U.S. merchandise											
	Total		Crude materials		Crude foodstuffs		Manufactured foodstuffs [1]		Semimanufactures		Finished manufactures	
	Quantity	Unit value	Quantity	Unit value	Quantity	Unit value	Quantity	Unit value	Quantity	Unit value	Quantity	Unit value
	21	22	23	24	25	26	27	28	29	30	31	32
1923–25=100												
1957	315	147	197	120	388	106	161	125	283	187	479	151
1956	299	142	160	119	385	107	182	120	237	191	476	142
1955	253	137	121	120	271	106	148	123	219	172	415	136
1954	248	135	120	120	209	110	107	135	184	162	441	134
1953	256	137	104	118	242	123	98	135	143	163	490	136
1952	244	138	120	125	323	131	98	131	158	167	423	135
1951	241	138	141	133	359	121	110	139	160	170	385	134
1950	188	121	127	112	217	109	99	111	133	138	291	121
1949	214	125	124	108	329	126	118	131	157	141	325	124
1948	208	134	99	114	274	143	139	164	150	149	334	130
1947	252	126	119	100	190	139	159	161	206	138	428	123
1946	201	106	125	86	167	121	201	130	137	107	293	105
1945	192	112	87	76	122	110	170	126	124	103	318	120
1944	283	112	55	75	41	101	219	128	171	105	545	121
1943	293	98	69	72	38	89	236	113	175	102	558	103
1942	201	89	48	65	30	71	150	106	152	98	374	93
1941	154	73	47	56	44	59	93	77	140	91	274	75
1940	129	68	70	49	46	50	44	65	179	83	196	73
1939	110	64	86	46	79	44	55	63	129	78	151	67
1938	105	65	95	47	148	52	47	68	106	78	137	68
1937	105	70	103	53	51	64	39	79	125	89	143	69
1936	82	66	93	54	30	59	33	74	88	73	107	66
1935	78	65	97	53	33	56	37	72	83	68	93	65
1934	74	63	94	52	34	54	47	62	81	69	84	64
1933	69	54	113	39	32	46	49	55	64	60	64	59
1932	69	51	115	34	59	47	50	52	55	58	61	62
1931	89	60	107	40	71	55	62	68	73	71	100	68
1930	109	78	106	59	69	80	71	88	97	87	137	85
1929	132	87	113	76	94	89	87	96	119	100	174	89
1928	128	88	124	78	98	93	84	96	124	94	154	90
1927	124	86	130	69	131	99	81	99	121	95	133	91
1926	115	92	134	70	105	99	81	107	106	101	119	101
1925	107	100	118	91	85	115	88	112	106	102	113	100
1924	102	99	99	101	122	100	105	94	103	97	98	99
1923	91	101	84	108	93	85	107	94	91	101	90	101
1922	89	94	87	85	167	85	110	92	77	93	75	105
1921	96	102	108	68	206	101	114	104	64	105	78	128
1913=100												
1921	113.4	157.5	81.3	156.4	252.8	155.7	153.9	136.2	72.2	143.5	125.6	163.9
1920	141.8	232.5	84.8	285.3	192.2	268.2	161.2	217.2	120.8	210.5	202.2	197.7
1919	146.6	215.7	86.7	241.3	156.3	241.7	257.6	237.4	126.4	199.5	179.9	174.4
1918	119.7	206.1	57.0	219.9	132.9	234.6	203.9	214.2	129.5	202.8	153.4	169.7
1917	142.2	177.0	64.4	166.8	134.5	214.9	147.0	170.5	168.5	198.4	225.0	150.4
1916	163.3	135.5	90.9	115.5	168.6	144.2	164.8	118.5	155.8	156.5	252.0	130.6
1915	135.7	105.1	103.1	86.0	200.6	133.8	160.5	106.5	111.7	113.2	163.6	100.9
1914	86.6	97.7	74.9	87.9	140.0	114.5	93.0	103.3	87.4	97.6	86.0	94.3
1913	100.0	100.0	100.0	100.0	100.0	100.0	100.0	100.0	100.0	100.0	100.0	100.0
1912	101.1	95.5	115.3	89.3	79.4	104.2	97.8	97.0	97.9	100.3	95.5	97.3
1911	90.0	93.5	96.2	90.9	68.5	97.9	103.2	93.3	89.7	93.2	84.0	95.5
1910	73.1	102.1	79.4	108.4	55.1	98.7	73.6	107.3	77.0	93.4	69.0	98.7
1909	73.7	94.3	83.5	91.4	65.1	104.2	94.3	93.7	69.8	91.0	60.7	97.4
1908	78.4	90.1	91.3	79.8	98.3	99.8	114.6	87.9	64.5	92.4	56.4	100.5
1907	81.3	95.2	89.3	87.4	118.2	95.0	121.8	86.5	62.6	109.9	62.5	102.2
1906	80.5	89.9	84.2	83.8	126.1	81.7	131.8	80.7	60.0	105.9	61.8	97.5
1905	78.0	83.7	84.7	75.6	108.8	82.5	129.8	75.7	58.4	93.6	58.5	94.5
1904	67.0	86.9	73.1	84.3	73.2	80.3	113.4	77.8	60.2	85.9	48.4	98.8
1903	68.8	86.6	77.2	81.0	123.1	81.4	123.1	81.8	46.0	87.3	43.2	98.9
1902	66.9	81.4	73.8	69.1	112.1	82.0	120.7	83.8	44.4	83.5	43.7	94.1
1901	74.0	79.4	77.0	67.9	182.7	77.4	143.4	76.0	40.0	86.0	42.9	94.2
1900	73.2	81.0	75.7	72.2	176.6	74.1	142.9	71.3	48.6	89.5	42.2	98.9
1899	70.8	72.3	66.8	55.1	186.5	74.2	148.2	66.9	41.8	84.9	41.4	90.3
1898	73.7	68.4	82.0	48.9	218.2	76.7	139.8	68.0	41.9	70.4	36.3	82.6
1897	63.8	69.1	67.2	54.3	197.7	71.3	121.8	64.8	39.6	69.6	30.6	88.1
1896	56.8	71.0	65.6	61.0	156.6	63.5	114.3	63.5	34.5	70.1	25.6	96.8
1895	46.0	71.8	59.0	56.7	92.0	69.4	100.5	69.5	25.5	71.7	22.2	91.4
1894	46.8	70.5	62.8	55.3	97.1	67.7	100.8	74.2	25.6	67.7	20.7	82.0
1893	43.5	80.2	54.7	66.4	107.8	77.7	89.6	85.6	23.1	71.8	19.7	87.0
1892	46.0	81.9	53.8	67.8	140.7	86.6	108.6	77.7	17.2	78.7	17.5	91.8
1891	44.5	87.9	60.1	74.1	119.1	100.1	94.5	76.7	18.3	81.7	17.1	100.3
1890	40.7	85.0	52.3	78.5	96.5	76.6	97.1	73.6	16.1	82.5	16.3	104.4
1889	38.7	86.0	55.4	77.5	85.9	75.4	82.9	76.7	15.8	81.9	15.6	106.7
1888	30.9	89.7	46.7	78.1	56.8	86.0	63.7	81.3	13.7	84.7	13.0	110.9
1887	33.6	85.5	46.6	74.5	85.3	81.6	72.4	76.3	12.8	82.2	13.1	106.1
1886	33.3	85.7	46.6	74.9	89.0	80.4	70.6	76.3	12.0	80.5	12.8	109.0
1885	30.2	91.0	39.0	80.2	70.9	85.4	73.8	80.9	12.1	83.7	12.1	115.5
1884	30.7	97.6	43.4	83.3	77.2	91.4	64.8	92.2	12.3	86.4	11.8	122.3
1883	31.3	101.4	43.7	82.1	82.7	104.0	64.1	99.7	12.1	90.8	12.6	121.8
1882	28.6	107.0	40.4	88.3	81.4	109.0	51.7	106.8	11.7	93.0	12.1	123.3
1881	32.0	103.8	39.8	86.8	117.7	102.6	67.3	97.6	10.4	92.1	11.6	124.8
1880	35.2	101.5	41.1	89.4	162.3	96.1	80.1	86.6	9.5	87.5	8.7	132.4
1879	33.3	92.5	37.0	80.1	148.5	93.4	74.4	76.7	10.1	79.3	9.7	119.3

[1] Includes beverages, and, beginning 1941, exports include private relief shipments of foodstuffs.

Series U 21–44. Indexes of Quantity and Unit Value of Exports and Imports: 1879 to 1957—Con.

Year	Imports [2]											
	Total		Crude materials		Crude foodstuffs		Manufactured foodstuffs [1]		Semimanufactures		Finished manufactures	
	Quantity	Unit value	Quantity	Unit value	Quantity	Unit value	Quantity	Unit value	Quantity	Unit value	Quantity	Unit value
	33	34	35	36	37	38	39	40	41	42	43	44
1923–25 = 100												
1957	208	163	174	125	159	298	231	117	225	184	279	166
1956	203	161	173	121	157	303	222	112	228	187	260	163
1955	188	158	163	118	149	314	213	111	224	176	214	160
1954	169	158	146	112	141	366	210	112	201	163	178	163
1953	182	155	153	115	167	306	206	114	227	167	177	163
1952	174	162	155	128	159	304	201	115	206	176	166	166
1951	165	171	147	155	161	302	190	114	200	174	149	168
1950	168	136	157	106	153	268	182	105	219	138	139	143
1949	138	125	130	97	160	195	150	104	143	141	112	146
1948	141	132	144	101	147	202	142	109	149	155	114	151
1947	124	119	133	90	130	183	130	107	130	136	93	139
1946	130	97	145	81	147	130	123	87	123	107	100	111
1945	122	87	100	80	157	103	129	76	137	96	113	96
1944	120	85	95	77	197	100	154	72	106	95	105	93
1943	112	79	97	73	151	90	127	71	104	92	104	84
1942	100	73	110	66	98	83	89	65	102	88	79	76
1941	134	63	161	58	141	62	140	49	128	80	81	69
1940	113	59	123	56	131	51	132	45	104	76	82	66
1939	108	55	99	51	128	53	144	46	100	69	98	59
1938	94	54	84	47	113	54	139	47	79	69	92	60
1937	131	60	119	56	145	67	172	54	118	76	130	56
1936	118	54	106	47	145	56	154	53	102	68	114	54
1935	106	50	100	40	140	54	137	49	87	67	97	55
1934	86	50	83	37	104	57	125	45	65	67	82	56
1933	86	43	91	31	100	50	102	40	73	57	79	53
1932	79	43	81	30	99	55	92	38	57	53	79	56
1931	98	55	102	43	109	65	97	46	79	67	103	69
1930	111	71	108	63	113	83	114	52	102	84	121	81
1929	131	87	133	80	112	113	137	63	127	98	141	91
1928	115	92	116	86	108	120	112	73	113	95	118	100
1927	113	95	116	94	107	111	111	82	105	100	120	95
1926	112	102	109	112	107	119	122	69	112	101	114	99
1925	104	105	105	113	97	120	118	74	105	101	99	104
1924	97	96	93	92	102	98	99	107	95	97	101	96
1923	99	99	101	95	103	82	90	119	100	101	100	99
1922	96	84	101	80	94	82	110	71	85	92	90	96
1921	74	88	81	72	95	74	74	101	51	101	75	107
1913 = 100												
1921	111.8	125.2	140.3	99.8	135.8	101.1	100.7	179.0	75.8	135.0	86.6	164.6
1920	134.4	219.1	159.9	179.1	155.7	166.4	133.3	472.4	112.7	204.2	89.9	223.5
1919	126.4	172.4	171.7	161.6	150.6	159.4	144.6	198.8	86.5	183.1	63.0	195.2
1918	104.9	161.3	137.2	147.3	132.4	110.5	92.9	216.5	92.3	180.4	63.4	180.1
1917	113.4	145.3	149.1	139.8	154.9	106.7	89.5	196.9	96.1	160.4	69.7	136.1
1916	111.0	120.2	144.9	113.1	117.0	98.7	98.1	172.3	96.8	128.1	75.2	112.2
1915	102.1	97.2	126.7	89.7	120.6	89.9	96.6	142.9	77.3	99.8	79.3	90.3
1914	106.5	93.7	106.0	92.9	117.5	91.1	117.1	110.7	87.1	93.3	110.2	90.7
1913	100.0	100.0	100.0	100.0	100.0	100.0	100.0	100.0	100.0	100.0	100.0	100.0
1912	100.4	101.0	104.6	100.4	103.2	104.0	87.8	119.0	97.0	96.9	103.0	95.4
1911	89.0	96.1	83.2	99.9	90.8	94.5	83.5	109.7	95.8	90.4	92.7	90.3
1910	92.2	94.6	85.1	104.8	85.7	80.9	86.0	113.8	102.4	85.7	99.7	86.5
1909	93.5	88.0	90.4	95.3	106.4	71.1	82.7	104.3	94.6	81.2	96.9	86.3
1908	70.7	88.1	65.6	89.7	87.0	72.8	74.8	105.8	64.2	83.9	74.5	90.4
1907	80.0	99.2	70.7	106.2	86.7	78.2	78.7	101.8	77.0	103.1	96.1	97.1
1906	77.8	94.7	71.1	100.7	79.6	75.9	75.0	97.1	78.8	97.4	90.2	93.2
1905	72.6	90.6	70.0	93.5	81.6	74.3	70.9	113.2	70.5	85.4	76.9	90.1
1904	67.3	85.8	62.4	89.2	89.9	73.0	73.6	93.7	60.3	83.4	68.3	87.7
1903	66.1	84.0	58.6	88.5	78.9	67.3	63.1	88.2	66.6	82.9	73.7	87.6
1902	67.0	80.8	61.8	83.0	79.0	67.9	67.6	80.5	66.2	80.0	71.5	86.9
1901	59.5	82.6	56.6	82.1	77.5	66.1	64.0	96.0	52.0	82.4	60.9	88.6
1900	53.4	86.7	47.7	87.7	64.2	72.9	61.7	106.1	48.8	82.7	58.8	87.4
1899	54.7	81.5	48.6	83.2	67.5	66.4	69.2	106.3	50.6	73.4	56.0	82.8
1898	46.8	75.7	40.7	76.2	59.3	68.4	55.6	99.3	43.7	60.8	50.9	79.4
1897	54.6	75.9	51.9	71.4	64.9	81.8	63.6	90.8	44.1	63.4	62.3	79.4
1896	47.1	80.7	35.7	71.0	53.2	99.5	63.8	101.1	40.7	64.9	60.4	81.2
1895	56.3	79.5	50.6	70.0	55.8	111.6	60.0	86.5	50.8	63.4	75.8	80.3
1894	44.9	83.5	37.6	68.5	52.5	114.8	65.6	109.0	40.9	65.2	48.2	80.5
1893	45.2	92.0	37.1	75.6	48.2	123.9	61.6	131.3	45.5	73.7	59.5	84.6
1892	50.9	88.5	42.9	74.9	52.1	113.7	61.4	120.8	50.3	72.4	64.0	84.8
1891	48.2	92.0	38.6	77.6	49.9	122.8	71.9	124.5	50.7	74.3	58.9	86.1
1890	47.4	93.2	36.4	82.2	49.0	123.7	56.0	121.5	49.7	75.3	71.6	86.4
1889	44.1	93.9	35.2	83.1	48.4	112.5	48.6	141.1	47.3	72.5	64.7	87.6
1888	43.9	88.8	32.2	81.3	49.4	108.4	51.6	118.1	47.6	69.5	64.8	85.1
1887	41.9	90.9	29.7	85.8	43.9	118.9	50.5	104.7	50.5	71.8	61.7	87.5
1886	40.7	87.5	29.7	84.5	48.2	87.3	51.6	115.1	43.7	73.1	57.9	87.4
1885	36.0	87.7	25.3	84.7	46.9	88.3	49.4	112.5	37.0	71.8	48.0	90.7
1884	35.4	95.4	23.4	91.9	46.1	95.5	47.8	125.0	36.0	80.1	51.5	96.1
1883	36.3	101.8	23.1	96.9	45.0	94.6	43.8	156.4	41.1	80.8	54.0	101.7
1882	37.4	108.3	23.0	104.5	46.1	105.2	42.5	171.2	43.8	84.9	59.1	103.6
1881	33.4	107.7	21.5	99.3	42.9	112.5	36.6	169.0	38.4	83.8	51.3	103.2
1880	33.1	113.1	22.9	104.2	36.8	123.3	35.6	170.2	41.5	91.1	52.8	105.4
1879	27.0	102.4	17.9	95.0	38.8	114.3	32.0	141.9	28.9	78.0	37.4	102.8

[1] Includes beverages, and, beginning 1941, exports include private relief shipments of foodstuffs.

[2] Based on "general imports" through 1933; on "imports for consumption" thereafter.

Series U 45–50. Foreign Trade Related to Various Measures of Production: 1869 to 1957

Year	Percent of gross national product — Exports (including reexports)	Percent of gross national product — General imports	Percent of production of movable goods — Exports (including reexports)	Percent of production of movable goods — General imports	Farm exports as percent of farm income	Index of finished goods imports as percent of output of finished goods (1919=100)	Year or period	Percent of gross national product — Exports (including reexports)	Percent of gross national product — General imports	Farm exports as percent of farm income	Index of finished goods imports as percent of output of finished goods (1919=100)
	45	46	47	48	49	50		45	46	49	50
1957	4.7	2.9	9.9	6.3	15.2	----	1915	6.6	4.0	25.1	111
1956	4.6	3.0	9.3	6.2	14.0	----	1914	6.1	4.9	16.5	115
							1913	6.2	4.5	18.3	111
1955	3.9	2.9	8.0	5.9	11.0	----	1912	5.7	4.3	18.8	117
1954	4.2	2.8	8.5	5.8	10.2	----	1911	5.6	4.1	17.8	109
1953	4.3	3.0	8.6	5.9	9.0	----					
1952	4.4	3.1	8.8	6.2	10.5	----	1910	4.8	4.2	15.9	113
1951	4.6	3.3	9.0	6.6	12.3	----	1909	4.9	3.9	----	114
							1908	----	----	----	99
1950	3.6	3.1	7.0	6.1	10.0	----	1907	----	----	----	112
1949	4.7	2.6	9.5	5.3	12.8	----	1906	----	----	----	111
1948	4.9	2.7	9.0	5.1	11.5	----					
1947	6.5	2.5	12.2	4.7	13.1	----	1905	----	----	----	113
1946	[1]4.8	2.3	9.8	4.9	12.9	----	1904	----	----	----	107
							1903	----	----	----	104
1945	[1]4.9	1.9	10.2	4.1	10.7	----	1902	----	----	----	106
1944	[1]6.8	1.9	13.6	3.7	10.5	----	1901	----	----	----	101
1943	6.7	1.8	12.9	3.4	10.8	----					
1942	5.1	1.7	9.0	3.1	7.7	----	1900	----	----	----	104
1941	4.1	2.7	7.8	5.2	6.0	----	1899	----	----	----	109
							1898	----	----	----	99
1940	4.0	2.6	8.3	5.5	6.2	----	1897	----	----	----	125
1939	3.5	2.5	7.5	5.6	8.4	66	1896	----	----	----	124
1938	3.6	2.3	----	----	10.7	----					
1937	3.7	3.4	7.4	6.9	9.0	84	1895	----	----	----	140
1936	3.0	2.9	----	----	8.5	----	1894	----	----	----	128
							1893	----	----	----	129
1935	3.1	2.8	6.6	6.0	10.6	70	1892	----	----	----	145
1934	3.3	2.5	----	----	11.6	----	1891	----	----	----	142
1933	3.0	2.6	6.5	5.7	13.1	70					
1932	2.8	2.3	----	----	14.0	67	1890	----	----	----	151
1931	3.2	2.7	7.2	6.4	12.9	77	1889	----	----	----	138
							1879	----	----	----	136
1930	4.2	3.4	----	----	13.3	87	1869	----	----	----	147
1929	5.0	4.2	9.6	8.2	15.0	103					
1928	5.2	4.2	----	----	17.0	100	1917–1921	8.7	4.7	----	----
1927	5.1	4.3	9.9	8.7	17.6	108	1912–1916	7.6	4.7	----	----
1926	4.9	4.5	----	----	17.2	110	1907–1911	5.8	4.4	----	----
							1902–1906	5.3	4.4	----	----
1925	5.4	4.6	10.0	8.7	19.4	110					
1924	5.2	4.1	----	----	20.7	103	1897–1901	7.4	4.3	----	----
1923	4.8	4.4	9.1	8.5	19.1	105	1892–1896	6.6	5.7	----	----
1922	5.2	4.2	----	----	21.9	99	1889–1893	6.5	6.0	----	----
1921	6.1	3.4	13.1	7.5	26.0	86					
							Kuznets concept: [2]				
1920	9.3	5.9	----	----	27.3	124	1889–1893	6.7	6.2	----	----
1919	10.0	4.9	16.4	8.3	28.1	100	1887–1891	6.3	6.2	----	----
1918	9.3	4.6	----	----	20.4	88	1882–1886	6.6	5.9	----	----
1917	10.5	5.0	----	----	18.4	105	1877–1881	8.2	5.8	----	----
1916	11.5	5.0	----	----	22.7	113	1872–1876	6.9	7.5	----	----
							1869–1873	6.2	7.9	----	----

[1] Includes an estimate for civilian supplies shipped to occupied areas through U. S. Armed Forces, which were not tabulated with the foreign trade statistics prior to 1947.

[2] For an explanation of this concept, see text for series F 1–5 and F 104–130.

Series U 51–60. Value of Merchandise Exports and Imports, by Groups of Customs Districts: 1860 to 1954

[In millions of dollars. Exports include reexports; general imports through 1933; thereafter, imports for consumption. For years ending June 30, 1860–1915; thereafter, calendar years]

Year	Atlantic coast — Exports	Atlantic coast — Imports	Gulf coast — Exports	Gulf coast — Imports	Mexican border — Exports	Mexican border — Imports	Pacific coast — Exports	Pacific coast — Imports	Northern border — Exports	Northern border — Imports
	51	52	53	54	55	56	57	58	59	60
1954	5,233	5,917	2,265	1,157	480	111	1,299	926	2,544	2,033
1953	[1]4,870	6,297	2,014	1,190	485	138	1,132	915	2,732	2,141
1952	[1]5,260	6,324	[1]2,588	1,217	[1]478	190	1,314	854	2,529	2,059
1951	[1]6,105	6,525	[1]2,799	1,219	[1]544	109	1,271	903	2,397	1,953
1950	(2)	5,310	(2)	882	[1]356	122	(2)	723	1,844	1,622
1949	(2)	3,826	(2)	765	360	113	(2)	549	1,779	1,279
1948	(2)	4,319	(2)	725	391	114	(2)	523	1,752	1,328
1947	7,874	3,570	2,235	570	483	102	1,071	426	1,918	953
1946	5,413	3,220	1,691	407	405	103	689	267	1,347	787
1945	5,733	2,268	1,150	453	256	117	1,302	233	[3]1,212	[3]942
1944	9,255	1,903	1,079	475	240	117	1,819	267	1,615	1,026
1943	7,744	1,692	1,068	395	185	120	2,377	250	1,538	889
1942	4,999	1,464	708	360	131	64	785	243	1,431	600
1941	3,246	2,161	364	227	91	31	376	308	1,032	459
1940	2,374	1,738	522	163	51	13	363	252	694	346
1939	1,640	1,601	576	157	86	13	390	179	470	301
1938	1,532	1,371	627	160	80	10	387	151	453	237
1937	1,680	2,116	662	214	102	11	404	232	483	404
1936	1,202	1,681	546	163	56	8	275	192	360	350

See footnotes at end of table.

Series U 51–60. Value of Merchandise Exports and Imports, by Groups of Customs Districts: 1860 to 1954—Con.

[In millions of dollars]

Year	Atlantic coast Exports 51	Atlantic coast Imports 52	Gulf coast Exports 53	Gulf coast Imports 54	Mexican border Exports 55	Mexican border Imports 56	Pacific coast Exports 57	Pacific coast Imports 58	Northern border Exports 59	Northern border Imports 60
1935	1,105	1,408	534	153	57	11	280	170	308	273
1934	1,018	1,158	510	113	48	6	259	123	298	217
1933	720	1,038	502	101	42	4	198	121	210	177
1932	665	914	467	94	33	8	203	130	234	168
1931	1,168	1,461	502	139	48	14	303	195	389	265
1930	1,801	2,041	822	198	102	26	449	343	648	427
1929	2,424	2,931	1,140	284	116	40	595	524	939	585
1928	2,290	2,677	1,228	285	95	30	561	505	925	564
1927	2,297	2,775	1,101	285	77	28	506	511	856	555
1926	2,309	2,953	1,121	326	73	26	519	546	759	543
1925	2,404	2,839	1,295	300	76	24	427	527	681	507
1924	2,246	2,358	1,164	282	73	20	447	477	639	442
1923	2,070	2,534	992	238	60	20	372	481	674	487
1922	1,938	2,024	914	188	57	11	312	430	610	440
1921	2,379	1,726	1,077	158	104	10	312	190	615	408
1920	4,905	3,802	1,683	340	84	38	511	391	1,044	666
1919	5,211	2,630	1,235	220	58	35	599	463	817	529
1918	3,759	1,830	776	156	48	52	539	569	1,027	403
1917	4,288	1,798	663	144	48	46	390	539	844	404
1916	3,826	1,654	624	114	24	43	338	295	670	269
1915 [4]	1,739	1,213	508	102	15	21	174	159	332	165
1914	1,304	1,375	566	120	17	33	136	138	341	205
1913	1,349	1,376	543	104	25	27	147	129	402	154
1912	1,263	1,268	464	92	27	23	128	111	322	138
1911	1,166	1,164	488	82	30	20	94	103	270	138
1910	1,018	1,227	399	69	29	23	73	89	225	129
1909	977	1,019	410	60	27	16	70	86	179	113
1908	1,156	907	397	59	33	11	94	82	181	15
1907	1,080	1,133	469	63	41	18	92	91	199	109
1906	1,062	975	369	54	35	17	102	66	177	98
1905	917	888	320	48	26	15	103	62	152	90
1904	897	779	335	44	29	12	66	57	134	84
1903	904	821	285	38	26	13	79	56	126	82
1902	895	724	263	31	24	14	88	54	111	68
1901	1,003	671	285	27	21	10	70	48	108	57
1900	964	693	234	24	22	5	70	59	104	60
1899	871	576	194	17	16	5	56	46	89	46
1898	862	502	202	13	12	5	74	50	81	39
1897	733	639	181	20	14	4	59	44	64	50
1896	636	645	131	18	11	4	44	49	60	56
1895	590	614	122	17	9	2	36	40	50	51
1894	670	538	127	21	7	8	35	41	53	42
1893	624	717	126	25	12	14	42	48	43	53
1892	753	689	175	22	7	13	56	50	40	46
1891	637	698	152	23	8	11	53	54	35	50
1890	629	654	141	18	6	9	45	51	37	50
1889	548	610	108	17	4	8	49	51	34	51
1888	523	596	105	14	3	6	36	49	29	51
1887	539	578	104	12	3	5	41	42	29	47
1886	505	534	105	10	2	4	40	39	27	44
1885	564	482	98	11	3	2	48	36	30	42
1884	543	583	110	13	5	2	46	37	37	32
1883	597	625	131	12	5	2	53	47	36	37
1882	557	620	94	16	5	2	65	42	30	43
1881	687	553	141	17	4	3	41	39	31	32
1880	651	590	118	13	4	2	39	36	24	28
1879	560	385	90	9	3	2	37	30	22	21
1878	540	374	110	14	3	2	29	27	27	21
1877	479	388	101	12	3	1	35	30	28	20
1876	437	391	118	15	3	2	28	29	24	25
1875	421	468	100	15	3	2	27	25	23	23
1874	463	493	126	17	2	1	28	27	30	29
1873	404	551	137	24	3	1	27	33	22	32
1872	344	544	119	22	2	1	11	28	16	31
1871	323	454	131	22	3	1	14	16	20	27
1870	293	371	146	17	2	1	15	16	15	32
1865	257	194	4	1	----------	----------	11	16	16	28
1860	160	305	154	22	1	1	5	7	14	19

[1] For security reasons, data for certain commodities and data on Department of Defense controlled cargo are excluded from export figures for individual customs districts, effective July 1950. Data on these shipments are included in total export statistics.

[2] Not available.

[3] Includes Omaha beginning April 1, 1945.

[4] Figures for 6-month period July 1, 1915–Dec. 31, 1915, are as follows (in millions of dollars): Series U 51, 1,304; U 52, 638; U 53, 224; U 54, 44; U 55, 10; U 56, 13; U 57, 97; U 58, 105; U 59, 218; and U 60, 105.

Series U 61–72. Value of Merchandise Exports and Imports, by Economic Classes: 1820 to 1957

[In millions of dollars.   General imports through 1933; thereafter, imports for consumption.   For years ending September 30, 1821–1840; June 30, 1850–1915; thereafter, calendar years]

Year	Exports of U. S. merchandise						Imports					
	Total	Crude materials	Crude food-stuffs	Manufactured foodstuffs [1]	Semi-manufactures	Finished manufactures	Total	Crude materials	Crude food-stuffs	Manufactured foodstuffs [1]	Semi-manufactures	Finished manufactures
	61	62	63	64	65	66	67	68	69	70	71	72
1957	20,630	3,109	1,330	1,168	[2]3,237	[2]11,786	12,921	3,186	2,019	1,268	2,920	3,527
1956	18,940	2,515	1,332	1,264	[2]2,775	[2]11,054	12,516	3,087	2,036	1,167	3,005	3,221
1955	15,419	1,907	930	1,012	[2]2,309	[2]9,260	11,337	2,845	1,998	1,118	2,777	2,599
1954	14,981	1,899	741	832	[2]1,819	[2]9,691	10,240	2,413	2,200	1,117	2,313	2,196
1953	15,652	1,626	962	759	[2]1,423	[2]10,881	10,779	2,613	2,185	1,108	2,678	2,194
1952	15,049	1,982	1,369	736	[2]1,619	[2]9,341	10,747	2,937	2,068	1,083	2,566	2,094
1951	14,879	2,471	1,401	881	[2]1,665	[2]8,462	10,817	3,365	2,077	1,022	2,459	1,896
1950	10,142	1,886	760	634	[2]1,121	[2]5,741	8,743	2,465	1,750	898	2,126	1,504
1949	11,936	1,780	1,342	908	1,356	6,551	6,592	1,854	1,333	741	1,418	1,246
1948	12,532	1,488	1,266	1,366	1,371	7,041	7,092	2,147	1,272	731	1,633	1,309
1947	14,252	1,579	849	1,483	1,734	8,607	5,666	1,766	1,017	656	1,245	983
1946	9,500	1,416	648	1,522	895	5,019	4,825	1,729	814	504	931	847
1945	9,585	871	432	1,246	780	6,257	4,098	1,183	693	462	928	832
1944	14,162	554	134	1,633	1,097	10,744	3,887	1,078	841	521	706	741
1943	12,842	662	109	1,551	1,089	9,431	3,390	1,037	584	421	678	670
1942	8,003	418	68	925	920	5,672	2,780	1,061	349	275	640	457
1941	5,020	362	84	418	771	3,385	3,222	1,376	376	322	724	423
1940	3,934	464	74	167	900	2,330	2,541	1,011	285	277	559	409
1939	3,123	545	111	202	599	1,667	2,276	745	291	313	487	440
1938	3,057	607	249	184	494	1,523	1,950	576	260	311	385	418
1937	3,299	731	105	178	669	1,617	3,010	971	413	440	634	551
1936	2,419	670	58	144	393	1,154	2,424	733	349	386	490	466
1935	2,243	683	59	157	350	994	2,039	582	322	319	410	406
1934	2,100	653	59	168	342	879	1,636	461	254	264	307	350
1933 [3]	1,647	591	48	155	237	617	1,450	418	216	201	292	322
1932	1,576	514	89	152	197	624	1,323	358	233	174	217	341
1931	2,378	567	127	247	318	1,120	2,091	642	305	222	372	549
1930	3,781	829	179	363	513	1,898	3,061	1,002	400	293	608	757
1929	5,157	1,142	270	484	729	2,532	4,399	1,559	539	424	885	994
1928	5,030	1,293	295	466	716	2,260	4,091	1,467	550	406	763	906
1927	4,759	1,193	421	463	700	1,982	4,185	1,601	505	451	750	879
1926	4,712	1,261	335	503	656	1,957	4,431	1,792	540	418	804	877
1925	4,819	1,422	318	574	662	1,843	4,227	1,748	495	433	755	796
1924	4,498	1,333	393	573	611	1,588	3,610	1,258	425	522	656	749
1923	4,091	1,208	257	583	564	1,478	3,792	1,407	363	530	721	771
1922	3,765	988	459	588	438	1,292	3,113	1,180	330	387	553	663
1921	4,379	984	673	685	410	1,627	2,509	859	300	368	362	620
1920	8,080	1,883	918	1,117	958	3,205	5,278	1,784	578	1,238	802	877
1919	7,750	1,623	678	1,963	922	2,564	3,904	1,701	545	556	609	493
1918	6,048	972	547	1,406	1,053	2,069	3,031	1,234	346	397	650	405
1917	6,170	833	509	807	1,315	2,706	2,952	1,286	386	352	537	392
1916	5,423	816	421	648	912	2,625	2,392	1,029	260	339	419	346
1915 [4]	2,716	591	507	455	356	807	1,674	591	224	286	237	336
1914	2,330	800	137	293	374	725	1,894	650	248	228	319	449
1913	2,429	740	182	321	409	776	1,813	649	212	194	349	408
1912	2,170	731	100	319	348	672	1,653	573	230	196	294	360
1911	2,014	721	103	282	309	598	1,527	525	181	172	288	361
1910	1,710	574	110	259	268	499	1,557	578	145	182	285	368
1909	1,638	529	136	303	231	440	1,312	461	164	166	222	299
1908	1,835	563	189	332	261	489	1,194	374	146	147	196	332
1907	1,854	601	167	346	259	481	1,434	488	150	159	274	364
1906	1,718	507	177	347	226	460	1,227	424	134	140	220	308
1905	1,492	479	118	283	210	402	1,118	396	146	145	178	252
1904	1,435	467	136	309	175	349	991	328	132	118	160	253
1903	1,392	416	185	323	141	327	1,026	336	119	117	196	258
1902	1,355	388	185	329	132	322	903	309	120	95	148	231
1901	1,460	411	246	337	148	318	823	254	110	126	128	206
1900	1,371	340	226	320	153	332	850	282	98	133	134	203
1899	1,204	286	233	305	118	263	697	213	99	123	92	170
1898	1,210	296	305	285	102	223	616	194	104	86	79	153
1897	1,032	304	181	235	98	213	765	201	128	129	88	218
1896	863	257	129	219	76	182	780	203	130	119	101	227
1895	793	269	99	219	62	144	732	188	141	107	96	200
1894	869	283	133	250	67	136	655	135	133	155	83	149
1893	831	252	153	247	49	130	866	217	132	154	136	229
1892	1,016	320	262	250	50	133	827	195	176	140	113	205
1891	872	351	106	226	48	140	845	193	151	148	136	218
1890	845	309	132	225	46	133	789	180	128	133	117	231
1889	730	291	99	175	43	123	745	172	123	122	115	212
1888	684	274	86	170	40	114	724	164	116	111	122	211
1887	703	253	125	176	37	112	692	151	106	112	120	203
1886	666	257	101	163	34	112	635	145	92	113	92	195

See footnotes at end of table.

Series U 61-72. Value of Merchandise Exports and Imports, by Economic Classes: 1820 to 1957—Con.

[In millions of dollars]

Year	Exports of U. S. merchandise						Imports					
	Total	Crude materials	Crude foodstuffs	Manufactured foodstuffs [1]	Semimanufactures	Finished manufactures	Total	Crude materials	Crude foodstuffs	Manufactured foodstuffs [1]	Semimanufactures	Finished manufactures
	61	62	63	64	65	66	67	68	69	70	71	72
1885	727	251	123	202	39	111	578	120	93	103	78	183
1884	725	244	130	195	38	118	668	131	103	131	95	208
1883	804	294	163	186	38	122	723	146	93	142	99	243
1882	733	238	155	178	37	125	725	143	105	139	99	243
1881	884	281	242	226	33	102	643	125	102	123	88	204
1880	824	243	266	193	29	93	668	142	100	118	111	197
1879	698	202	189	174	30	103	446	81	82	103	50	130
1878	681	216	155	170	29	110	437	79	84	102	47	125
1877	590	205	91	150	32	113	451	76	86	115	49	126
1876	526	204	94	122	31	74	461	78	94	92	51	146
1875	499	208	79	110	27	75	533	89	90	113	63	178
1874	569	229	119	114	26	81	567	89	94	120	72	192
1873	505	233	70	101	25	76	642	108	83	122	97	232
1872	428	198	59	84	21	76	627	103	77	122	88	238
1871	428	224	49	67	14	76	520	78	64	103	72	203
1870	377	214	42	51	14	56	436	57	54	96	56	174
1869	275	145	25	44	14	47	418	50	53	95	63	157
1868	269	133	35	42	17	43	357	41	52	78	53	133
1867	280	167	21	34	15	44	396	43	51	65	56	181
1866	338	228	17	41	12	39	435	48	61	72	56	198
1865	137	34	14	48	11	30	239	30	35	48	30	96
1864	144	29	25	55	10	25	316	40	44	52	52	128
1863	186	30	45	66	11	33	243	48	30	35	35	95
1862	180	18	56	70	8	27	189	33	32	35	24	66
1861	205	58	49	54	8	36	289	31	40	54	33	132
1860	316	217	12	39	13	36	354	40	46	60	35	172
1859	278	190	10	32	11	35	331	39	44	57	40	151
1858	251	155	18	39	10	30	263	34	36	46	31	116
1857	279	158	31	49	11	30	348	34	41	72	39	163
1856	266	145	29	53	8	31	310	27	39	46	41	157
1855	193	109	11	33	11	29	258	27	33	34	35	129
1854	⁵214	108	22	47	11	27	298	23	25	33	45	173
1853	190	124	8	27	6	24	264	18	26	33	42	144
1852	155	101	7	20	6	21	207	14	24	29	21	120
1851	179	125	5	20	6	23	211	17	20	29	27	118
1850	135	84	8	20	6	17	174	13	18	21	26	95
1840	112	76	5	16	5	11	98	12	15	15	11	44
1830	59	37	3	10	4	5	63	5	7	10	5	36
1821	----	----	----	----	----	----	55	3	6	11	4	31
1820	52	31	2	10	5	3	----	----	----	----	----	----

[1] Includes beverages.

[2] For security reasons, a small amount of semimanufactures included with finished manufactures.

[3] Imports for consumption are as follows (in millions of dollars): Series U 67, 1,433; series U 68, 420; series U 69, 215; series U 70, 191; series U 71, 290; and series U 72, 317.

[4] Figures for 6-month period July 1, 1915–Dec. 31, 1915, are as follows (in millions of dollars): Series U 61, 1,820; series U 62, 303; series U 63, 158; series U 64, 293; series U 65, 268; series U 66, 799; series U 67, 913; series U 68, 378; series U 69, 130; series U 70, 113; series U 71, 144; and series U 72, 147.

[5] Excludes exports from San Francisco valued at $1,343,064.

Series U 73–93.   Exports of Selected U. S. Merchandise: 1790 to 1957

[In millions of dollars and units.   For years ending September 30, 1790–1842; June 30, 1843–1915; thereafter, calendar years]

Year	Total selected commodities, value	Cotton, unmanufactured Quantity (lb.)	Cotton, unmanufactured Value	Leaf tobacco, unmanufactured[1] Quantity (lb.)	Leaf tobacco Value	Wheat Quantity (60-lb. bu.)	Wheat Value	Wheat and wheat flour, value	Cotton manufactures, value[2]	Animal fats and oils, value[3]	Fruits and nuts, value[4]	Meat products, value[5]	Naval stores, gums, and resins, value	Automobiles, incl. engines and parts, value[6]	Sawmill products, value[7]	Other wood manufactures, value[7]	Coal and related fuels, value[8]	Petroleum and products, value	Iron and steel mill products, value	Machinery, value	Copper and manufactures, value
	73	74	75	76	77	78	79	80	81	82	83	84	85	86	87	88	89	90	91	92	93
1957	12,241	3,648	1,059	492	358	415	732	846	314	198	213	113	42	1,306	89	45	845	992	[9]1,376	4,146	299
1956	10,880	2,511	729	506	333	409	694	798	293	207	230	99	39	1,357	88	42	745	766	[9]1,075	3,813	266
1955	8,667	1,415	477	535	355	222	386	483	293	190	161	70	39	1,238	89	38	495	646	[9]818	3,057	218
1954	7,982	2,231	788	450	303	192	350	427	317	181	171	61	38	1,036	70	30	312	658	[9]516	2,875	199
1953	7,845	1,497	521	513	339	236	506	590	329	130	129	60	27	963	65	29	346	692	[9]495	3,013	117
1952	8,825	2,141	874	391	245	369	841	942	370	147	125	52	25	987	77	33	510	793	[9]621	2,868	156
1951	9,415	2,618	1,146	518	325	423	887	997	478	214	108	60	48	1,191	96	37	605	783	611	2,615	101
1950	6,491	2,963	1,024	471	250	206	405	489	263	112	100	43	42	723	48	25	278	499	472	2,035	88
1949	7,750	2,708	874	493	252	340	835	1,002	366	135	140	51	32	753	60	31	308	562	732	2,355	97
1948	8,188	1,474	511	415	214	328	909	1,393	499	89	194	57	30	930	64	36	492	657	649	2,259	114
1947	8,789	1,380	423	493	270	167	429	868	852	111	199	129	48	1,149	121	68	632	641	824	2,352	102
1946	5,747	1,999	536	642	350	187	391	610	375	95	171	341	27	549	50	36	316	436	447	1,369	39
1945	4,949	1,282	279	470	239	129	240	330	236	103	128	290	13	588	34	55	198	753	457	1,191	55
1944	5,398	531	115	280	146	10	16	76	232	163	126	535	14	643	31	43	182	960	551	1,478	103
1943	4,407	842	184	393	170	12	16	56	192	144	80	617	14	279	26	38	172	517	615	1,194	109
1942	3,266	539	99	237	68	7	7	28	131	95	51	358	13	433	27	24	152	350	592	763	82
1941	2,608	625	83	263	65	13	11	35	135	41	52	99	15	339	30	21	119	285	501	740	48
1940	2,456	2,046	213	217	44	14	11	33	76	14	36	22	12	254	37	21	87	310	516	671	110
1939	2,198	2,562	243	327	77	63	37	61	68	23	83	32	15	254	41	14	67	385	236	502	97
1938	2,226	2,442	229	473	155	87	78	101	57	20	99	28	12	270	38	14	56	390	184	486	87
1937	2,513	3,223	369	418	134	35	39	64	60	18	82	25	22	347	56	18	67	378	300	479	94
1936	1,821	2,974	361	407	137	2	2	19	44	16	81	25	19	240	45	14	57	265	112	335	51
1935	1,719	3,234	391	381	134	----	----	15	39	15	93	28	17	227	42	13	52	251	88	265	49
1934	1,612	3,149	373	419	125	17	10	27	43	31	74	35	15	190	44	13	57	228	89	218	50
1933	1,268	4,523	398	420	82	8	5	19	39	40	70	26	15	91	33	11	40	201	46	132	25
1932	1,200	4,803	345	388	65	55	33	51	46	38	77	19	12	76	27	9	45	209	29	131	21
1931	1,782	3,667	326	504	110	80	50	84	60	60	109	36	15	148	47	17	65	271	63	316	55
1930	2,905	3,492	497	561	145	88	88	157	89	88	111	66	23	279	82	26	90	495	139	513	105
1929	4,363	3,982	771	555	146	90	112	192	135	124	137	79	31	541	115	37	106	962	200	604	183
1928	3,861	4,579	920	575	154	96	120	194	135	119	129	68	26	502	113	33	100	527	180	491	170
1927	3,641	4,897	826	506	139	168	240	325	133	116	122	71	34	389	111	34	110	487	161	433	150
1926	3,683	4,692	814	479	137	138	202	285	129	135	112	107	37	320	102	33	204	555	174	398	141
1925	3,707	4,384	1,060	468	153	87	149	234	146	148	102	127	32	318	103	32	107	474	144	366	161
1924	3,496	3,483	951	547	163	166	237	328	131	158	98	121	25	210	106	28	116	444	150	310	157
1923	3,124	2,743	807	475	152	99	116	205	136	158	69	154	25	171	107	30	166	367	167	281	129
1922	2,711	3,153	673	431	146	165	206	292	137	116	76	140	19	103	70	23	96	346	136	234	104
1921	3,263	3,339	534	515	205	280	433	551	116	140	70	157	11	84	55	26	171	401	236	408	98
1920	5,848	3,179	1,136	468	245	218	597	821	398	192	84	279	35	303	114	60	360	593	498	588	142
1919	5,229	3,368	1,137	766	260	148	357	650	270	326	126	698	31	156	80	49	126	377	450	362	131
1918	4,155	2,118	674	404	123	111	261	505	179	181	32	668	10	101	57	25	120	371	632	270	207
1917	3,534	2,476	575	251	46	106	246	384	157	100	35	274	14	124	42	25	119	275	645	356	363
1916	2,746	3,645	545	477	63	154	227	313	127	85	37	198	16	123	35	19	78	221	376	278	237
1915	1,804	4,404	376	348	44	260	334	428	70	79	35	132	11	70	31	15	58	148	85	120	102
1914	1,822	4,761	610	447	54	92	88	142	49	81	32	68	20	35	71	25	63	162	91	168	151
1913	1,831	4,562	547	414	49	92	89	142	52	89	37	68	26	33	78	30	68	150	124	195	143
1912	1,633	5,535	566	375	43	30	28	79	51	86	31	72	27	26	68	25	56	123	102	161	117
1911	1,528	4,034	585	352	39	24	22	71	41	86	24	66	25	16	64	23	48	105	79	151	105
1910	1,290	3,207	450	353	38	47	48	95	33	72	19	62	19	11	54	20	44	107	60	117	89
1909	1,255	4,448	417	283	31	67	68	119	32	87	17	82	15	6	45	19	40	112	47	99	87
1908	1,413	3,817	438	323	34	100	100	164	25	92	14	102	22	5	55	22	42	113	58	121	106
1907	1,404	4,518	481	332	33	77	60	122	32	94	18	108	22	6	59	20	38	94	55	125	97
1906	1,247	3,634	401	302	29	35	29	88	53	92	15	115	20	3	45	20	31	93	51	108	83
1905	1,102	4,305	380	328	30	4	4	44	50	70	16	99	16	2	37	17	31	88	45	89	88
1904	1,089	3,063	371	305	29	44	36	105	22	71	21	101	16	2	42	18	30	88	31	84	58
1903	1,044	3,543	316	357	35	114	88	162	32	72	18	104	13	1	34	19	23	77	21	76	41
1902	1,030	3,501	291	291	27	155	113	179	32	73	9	121	12	1	28	16	22	81	26	68	44
1901	1,058	3,331	314	307	27	132	97	166	20	68	11	121	11	1	32	15	24	78	40	73	45
1900	973	3,101	242	335	29	102	73	141	24	62	12	114	12	10	29	17	21	84	39	78	59
1899	875	3,773	210	272	25	139	104	177	24	61	8	109	10	10	24	14	14	63	29	61	36
1898	874	3,850	230	252	22	148	146	215	17	55	9	104	9	10	20	13	12	62	19	44	33
1897	725	3,104	231	(10)	(10)	80	60	116	21	43	8	88	9	10	22	14	12	68	11	38	34
1896	610	2,335	190	(10)	(10)	61	40	92	17	47	6	81	9	5	17	12	11	67	5	29	22
1895	586	3,517	205	(10)	(10)	76	44	95	14	48	5	81	7	2	15	10	11	50	3	24	16
1894	655	2,683	211	269	23	88	59	129	14	57	2	80	7	3	14	11	12	45	3	22	22
1893	651	2,212	189	248	22	117	94	169	12	51	4	79	7	3	15	9	10	47	3	22	9
1892	797	2,935	258	241	20	157	161	237	13	49	4	83	8	3	15	9	9	49	3	21	13
1891	703	2,907	291	237	21	55	51	106	13	51	2	81	8	3	15	9	8	56	3	21	13
1890	645	2,472	251	244	21	54	45	102	10	48	4	78	7	5	17	10	7	54	3	20	8
1889	576	2,385	238	212	19	46	42	87	10	36	5	59	6	3	16	10	7	52	2	16	10
1888	564	2,264	223	249	22	66	56	111	13	32	4	52	6	2	13	8	6	49	2	12	9
1887	575	2,169	206	294	26	102	91	143	15	32	3	53	5	2	11	8	5	49	1	11	4
1886	518	2,058	205	282	27	58	50	89	14	27	3	54	5	2	11	8	4	52	1	10	6
1885	565	1,892	202	219	22	85	73	125	12	32	4	63	5	2	11	8	5	52	1	16	10
1884	564	1,863	197	207	18	70	75	126	12	36	3	64	7	3	12	10	5	48	2	16	6
1883	659	2,288	247	236	19	106	120	175	13	35	3	61	7	4	13	11	4	46	1	17	2
1882	593	1,740	200	224	19	95	113	149	13	37	3	69	7	3	12	10	4	52	1	14	1
1881	654	2,191	248	227	19	151	168	213	14	(10)	(10)	134	5	2	18	(10)	(10)	(10)	(10)	(10)	1

See footnotes at end of table.

Series U 73-93. Exports of Selected U. S. Merchandise: 1790 to 1957—Con.

[In millions of dollars and units]

Year	Total selected commodities, value	Cotton, unmanufactured Quantity (lb.)	Value	Leaf tobacco, unmanufactured[1] Quantity (lb.)	Value	Wheat Quantity (60-lb.bu.)	Value	Year	Total selected commodities, value	Cotton, unmanufactured Quantity (lb.)	Value	Leaf tobacco, unmanufactured[1] Quantity (lb.)	Value	Wheat Quantity (60-lb.bu.)	Value
	73	74	75	76	77	78	79		73	74	75	76	77	78	79
1880	600	1,822	212	216	16	153	191	1835	73	387	65	94	8	(12)	(12)
1879	483	1,628	162	322	25	122	131	1834	56	385	49	88	7	(12)	(12)
1878	471	1,608	180	284	25	72	97	1833	42	325	36	83	6	(12)	(12)
1877	409	1,445	171	282	29	40	47	1832	38	322	32	107	6	(12)	(12)
1876	421	1,491	193	218	23	55	68	1831	31	277	25	87	5	(12)	1
1875	395	1,260	191	224	25	53	60	1830	45	298	30	84	6	(12)	(12)
1874	475	1,359	211	318	30	71	101	1829	32	265	27	77	5	(12)	(12)
1873	421	1,200	227	214	23	39	51	1828	27	211	22	96	5	(12)	(12)
1872	341	934	181	235	24	26	39	1827	36	294	29	100	7	(12)	(12)
1871	358	1,463	218	216	20	34	45	1826	30	205	25	64	5	(12)	(12)
1870	359	959	227	186	21	37	47	1825	43	176	37	76	6	(12)	(12)
1869	208	644	163	182	21	18	24	1824	27	142	22	78	5	(12)	(12)
1868	206	785	153	206	23	16	30	1823	26	174	20	99	6	(12)	(12)
1867	229	661	201	185	20	6	8	1822	30	145	24	83	6	(12)	(12)
1866	318	651	281	191	29	6	8	1821	26	125	20	67	6	(12)	(12)
1865	154	[11]9	[11]7	149	42	10	19	1820	39	128	22	84	8	(12)	(12)
1864	64	[11]12	[11]10	110	23	24	31	1819	29	88	21	69	8	(12)	(12)
1863	74	[11]11	[11]7	112	20	36	47	1818	41	94	31	84	10	(12)	(12)
1862	56	[11]5	[11]1	107	12	37	43	1817	32	86	23	62	9	(12)	(12)
1861	86	308	34	161	14	31	38	1816	37	82	24	69	13	(12)	--------
1860	270	1,768	192	167	16	4	4	1815	26	83	18	85	8	(12)	--------
1859	185	1,386	161	199	21	3	3	1814	3	18	3	3	(12)	--------	--------
1858	157	1,119	131	128	17	9	9	1813	2	19	2	5	(12)	(12)	--------
1857	174	1,048	132	157	20	15	22	1812	5	29	3	26	2	(12)	--------
1856	155	1,351	128	117	12	8	15	1811	12	62	10	36	2	(12)	--------
1855	151	1,008	88	150	15	1	1	1810	27	93	15	84	5	(12)	--------
1854	116	988	94	126	10	8	12	1809	13	51	9	54	4	(12)	--------
1853	124	1,112	109	160	11	4	4	1808	3	11	2	10	1	(12)	--------
1852	101	1,093	88	137	10	3	3	1807	19	64	14	62	5	1	--------
1851	122	927	112	96	9	1	1	1806	15	36	8	83	7	(12)	--------
1850	101	635	72	146	10	1	1	1805	15	38	9	71	6	(12)	--------
1849	74	1,027	66	102	6	2	2	1804	14	38	8	83	6	(12)	--------
1848	73	814	62	131	8	2	3	1803	14	41	8	86	6	1	--------
1847	66	527	53	136	7	4	6	1802	11	28	5	78	6	(12)	--------
1846	53	548	43	150	8	2	2	1801	--------	21	--------	104	--------	(12)	--------
1845	59	873	52	147	7	(12)	(12)	1800	--------	18	--------	79	--------	(12)	--------
1844	63	664	54	163	8	1	1	1799	--------	10	--------	96	--------	(12)	--------
1843[13]	54	792	49	94	5	(12)	(12)	1798	--------	9	--------	69	--------	(12)	--------
1842	59	585	48	159	10	1	1	1797	--------	4	--------	58	--------	(12)	--------
1841	68	530	54	148	13	1	1	1796	--------	6	--------	69	--------	(12)	--------
1840	94	744	64	119	10	2	2	1795	--------	6	--------	61	--------	(12)	--------
1839	71	414	61	79	10	(12)	(12)	1794	--------	2	--------	77	--------	1	--------
1838	69	596	62	111	7	(12)	(12)	1793	--------	(12)	--------	60	--------	1	--------
1837	69	444	63	100	6	(12)	(12)	1792	--------	(12)	--------	112	--------	1	--------
1836	81	424	71	109	10	(12)	(12)	1791	--------	(12)	--------	101	3	1	1
								1790	--------	--------	--------	118	4	1	1

Year	Wheat and wheat flour, value	Cotton manufactures, value	Meat products, value[5]	Naval stores, value	Automobiles, incl. engines and parts, value[6]	Other wood manufactures, value[7]	Copper and manufactures, value	Year	Wheat and wheat flour, value	Cotton manufactures, value	Meat products, value[5]	Naval stores, value	Automobiles, incl. engines and parts, value[6]	Other wood manufactures, value[7]	Copper and manufactures, value
	80	81	84	85	86	88	93		80	81	84	85	86	88	93
1880	226	10	114	5	1	15	1	1870	68	4	21	3	1	13	1
1879	160	11	102	4	1	15	3	1865	47	3	35	(12)	1	18	1
1878	122	11	107	5	2	17	2	1860	20	11	14	4	1	10	2
1877	69	10	101	5	1	20	3	1855	12	6	16	3	(12)	10	1
1876	93	8	79	4	1	17	3	1850	8	5	--------	1	(12)	5	(12)
1875	83	4	68	5	1	17	1	1840	12	4	--------	1	(12)	3	(12)
1874	131	3	71	6	2	21	(12)	1830	6	1	--------	(12)	(12)	2	(12)
1873	71	3	71	6	2	18	(12)	1820	5	--------	--------	--------	(12)	4	(12)
1872	57	2	55	6	1	15	(12)	1810	7	--------	--------	--------	--------	--------	(12)
1871	69	4	30	3	1	13	(12)								

[1] Prior to 1865, quantity in hogsheads. Includes some leaf tobacco which has been partly processed.
[2] Includes semimanufactures.
[3] Includes margarine of vegetable origin since 1948. Excludes inedible fish oils. Excludes lard compounds since 1921; now classified as vegetable cooking fats.
[4] Includes fruit and nut preparations since 1946.
[5] 1855-1881, "Meats and meat products"; 1882-1904, "Meats."
[6] "Cars, carriages, automobiles, etc.," prior to 1902. Excludes machinery and vehicles manufactured to military specifications beginning July 1949.
[7] Includes box, crate, and package shooks (except fruit and vegetables) beginning 1949; classified as "Sawmill products" in prior years. Prior to 1881, "Sawmill products" combined with "Other wood manufactures."
[8] "Coal and coke" prior to 1946.
[9] Includes a small amount of nonferrous metal articles.
[10] Not available.
[11] No record of cotton exports for southern ports.
[12] Less than one-half the unit indicated.
[13] or 9 months.

Series U 94–115. Imports of Selected Products: 1790 to 1957

[In millions of dollars and units. For years ending September 30, 1790–1842; June 30, 1843–1915; thereafter, calendar years. Last 6 months of 1915 omitted]

Year	Total selected commodities, value	Coffee Quantity (lb.)	Coffee Value	Tea Quantity (lb.)	Tea Value	Sugar Quantity (lb.)	Sugar Value	Rubber, crude Quantity (lb.)	Rubber, crude Value	Raw silk Quantity (lb.)	Raw silk Value	Wool and mohair, value	Wool manufactures (including rags, noils, waste), value	Iron and steel manufactures, value	Tin, including ore, value	Cotton manufactures, value [1]	Copper and manufactures, value [2]	Hides and skins, value	Furs and manufactures, value [3]	Fruits and nuts, value	Forest products, value [4]	Petroleum and products, value
	94	95	96	97	98	99	100	101	102	103	104	105	106	107	108	109	110	111	112	113	114	115
1957	6,431	2,761	1,376	102	51	8,273	458	1,243	350	6	25	211	191	(5)	131	143	384	49	86	194	1,234	1,548
1956	6,619	2,810	1,438	101	51	8,287	437	1,297	398	8	32	242	196	(5)	178	161	502	66	86	192	1,354	1,286
1955	6,142	2,599	1,357	105	65	7,806	414	1,423	440	8	34	260	168	(5)	179	132	455	57	88	201	1,266	1,026
1954	5,503	2,260	1,486	115	62	7,485	409	284	262	7	31	223	128	(5)	184	83	363	53	72	177	1,141	829
1953	5,747	2,786	1,468	108	48	7,613	426	1,450	331	5	26	296	140	(5)	271	80	433	74	73	188	1,131	762
1952	5,895	2,681	1,376	93	39	7,667	415	1,804	619	8	34	382	165	(5)	298	67	411	60	79	164	1,094	692
1951	6,143	2,693	1,361	87	41	7,278	387	1,642	807	5	19	714	152	(5)	159	81	280	133	114	169	1,125	601
1950	5,040	2,439	1,091	115	54	7,349	380	1,800	459	8	21	428	114	(5)	202	81	243	119	109	169	978	592
1949	3,796	2,924	796	95	46	7,457	372	1,480	240	3	7	222	72	(5)	212	50	224	73	109	147	748	478
1948	3,911	2,774	698	91	45	6,397	313	1,646	309	6	15	308	79	(5)	176	53	203	108	165	161	862	416
1947	3,233	2,501	600	68	28	8,330	411	1,587	317	2	16	209	40	(5)	86	31	176	86	126	136	721	250
1946	2,673	2,738	472	94	34	5,284	196	840	228	13	128	289	41	(5)	69	45	86	77	238	143	468	159
1945	2,005	2,717	346	84	29	6,574	202	312	99	(5)	1	241	25	(5)	42	38	195	50	144	110	331	152
1944	1,722	2,608	326	90	30	7,728	212	239	76	-----	-----	186	17	(5)	47	12	166	61	126	68	282	113
1943	1,577	2,200	273	89	29	6,684	184	117	33	(5)	(5)	296	16	(5)	38	12	157	66	91	41	256	85
1942	1,499	1,715	205	50	18	3,968	107	620	118	(5)	(5)	311	27	(5)	51	10	165	78	69	35	268	37
1941	1,974	2,255	177	107	29	5,807	117	2,294	418	23	62	205	28	(5)	177	23	142	83	109	62	260	82
1940	1,529	2,055	127	99	23	5,829	113	1,825	318	45	125	85	25	(5)	131	31	73	50	80	61	217	70
1939	1,243	2,014	140	98	21	5,807	125	1,114	178	52	121	50	26	(5)	71	40	44	47	55	58	223	44
1938	1,034	1,987	138	81	18	5,949	130	917	130	55	89	23	18	(5)	45	35	38	30	46	55	200	39
1937	1,560	1,697	151	95	21	6,395	166	1,339	248	58	107	96	32	(5)	104	57	53	71	86	67	256	45
1936	1,255	1,739	134	82	18	5,939	158	1,091	159	60	102	53	30	(5)	76	49	30	55	82	58	210	41
1935	1,063	1,756	137	86	17	5,910	133	1,045	119	68	96	30	20	(5)	70	41	35	46	53	55	175	38
1934	894	1,524	133	76	16	5,994	118	1,036	102	56	72	17	15	(5)	45	32	28	35	41	46	157	37
1933 [6]	820	1,586	124	97	14	5,669	105	988	46	67	103	21	16	(5)	51	32	18	46	38	37	143	26
1932	784	1,501	137	95	12	5,943	97	929	33	74	114	6	13	(5)	16	28	24	22	28	44	149	61
1931	1,207	1,742	175	87	19	6,353	113	1,124	74	84	191	22	23	(5)	37	41	49	50	56	60	204	93
1930	1,695	1,599	209	85	23	6,990	130	1,090	141	74	263	37	40	(5)	60	46	105	92	69	75	259	146
1929	2,477	1,482	302	89	26	9,777	209	1,263	241	87	427	87	79	(5)	92	69	154	137	126	87	296	145
1928	2,346	1,457	310	90	27	7,737	207	978	245	75	368	80	78	(5)	87	69	98	151	122	90	280	134
1927	2,430	1,433	264	89	28	8,431	258	955	340	74	390	83	79	(5)	101	66	85	113	138	85	285	115
1926	2,653	1,493	323	96	31	9,420	233	926	506	66	393	107	71	(5)	105	67	100	97	120	88	286	126
1925	2,534	1,284	286	101	31	8,920	246	888	430	64	396	142	74	(5)	95	79	84	97	117	89	259	109
1924	2,190	1,421	249	93	27	8,272	364	735	174	51	328	93	69	44	69	91	96	75	88	72	248	103
1923	2,302	1,410	190	105	30	7,709	380	692	185	49	392	130	69	54	63	100	96	119	89	70	255	80
1922	1,831	1,246	161	97	24	9,722	252	674	102	51	366	87	59	48	46	87	67	107	69	72	195	89
1921	1,429	1,341	143	76	14	5,967	235	415	74	45	259	60	51	29	22	75	46	68	41	74	159	79
1920	3,212	1,297	252	90	24	8,065	1,115	567	243	30	285	127	58	50	93	138	90	244	92	102	231	68
1919	2,309	1,334	261	81	20	7,020	393	536	216	45	329	217	19	27	63	53	86	307	76	79	130	33
1918	1,608	1,052	99	134	30	5,167	241	326	146	33	180	252	23	25	105	41	134	108	34	49	114	27
1917	1,692	1,287	123	127	26	4,941	222	406	233	37	184	172	23	28	68	56	138	210	29	45	113	22
1916	1,373	1,167	119	105	19	5,530	227	270	160	32	145	126	16	24	56	55	95	173	21	45	77	15
1915	908	1,119	107	97	18	5,093	166	172	83	26	81	68	30	23	31	46	32	104	10	41	57	11
1914	934	1,002	111	91	17	4,948	99	132	71	29	98	53	34	32	39	71	55	120	14	51	54	15
1913	913	863	119	95	17	4,533	99	113	90	26	82	36	16	34	53	66	60	117	24	41	48	11
1912	844	885	118	101	18	3,663	104	110	93	22	67	33	15	27	46	65	45	102	25	43	38	5
1911	749	876	91	103	18	3,703	90	72	76	22	73	23	19	36	38	67	40	71	24	40	40	3
1910	823	871	69	86	14	3,913	102	101	101	20	65	51	24	40	31	68	40	112	27	37	40	2
1909	711	1,050	79	115	19	4,184	96	88	62	23	79	45	18	22	26	63	38	78	21	30	34	1
1908	603	891	68	94	16	3,365	80	62	37	15	64	24	19	28	25	69	32	55	16	37	32	1
1907	755	985	78	86	14	4,384	93	77	59	17	70	42	22	41	38	75	48	83	22	36	34	------
1906	654	852	73	94	15	3,970	85	58	45	15	53	39	23	29	31	64	33	84	22	29	29	------
1905	626	1,048	85	103	16	3,658	97	67	50	18	60	46	18	24	23	50	25	65	18	26	23	------
1904	516	995	70	113	18	3,684	71	59	40	13	44	25	18	27	21	50	22	52	15	24	19	------
1903	535	915	59	109	16	4,163	71	55	30	14	49	22	20	52	24	53	21	58	15	24	21	------
1902	463	1,091	71	76	9	2,941	53	50	25	13	42	18	17	27	19	45	25	58	16	21	17	------
1901	438	855	63	90	11	3,865	88	55	28	9	29	13	15	18	20	40	21	48	11	20	13	------
1900	475	788	52	85	11	4,007	100	49	31	11	45	20	16	20	19	42	15	58	12	19	15	------
1899	387	832	55	74	9	3,917	93	51	32	10	32	9	14	12	12	32	7	42	11	18	9	------
1898	343	871	65	72	10	2,589	58	46	25	10	31	17	15	13	9	27	4	37	8	15	9	------
1897	355	(5)	(5)	-----	-----	4,720	94	(5)	17	(5)	18	53	49	16	7	35	2	28	6	17	13	------
1896	449	581	85	94	13	3,709	84	(5)	17	(5)	26	32	53	25	7	33	2	31	9	19	13	------
1895	416	646	95	97	13	3,516	75	(5)	18	(5)	22	26	39	23	7	33	1	26	10	17	11	------
1894	386	532	87	94	14	4,286	125	(5)	15	(5)	16	6	19	21	3	22	1	17	8	19	13	------
1893	475	541	77	89	14	3,733	115	(5)	18	(5)	29	21	38	35	12	34	1	28	11	24	18	------
1892	485	633	127	90	14	3,542	104	(5)	20	(5)	24	20	36	29	9	28	1	27	10	21	15	------
1891	483	520	96	83	14	3,479	106	(5)	18	(5)	18	18	41	54	8	30	1	28	10	26	15	------
1890	440	499	78	84	12	2,934	96	(5)	15	(5)	23	15	57	42	7	30	(7)	22	8	21	13	------
1889	418	578	75	80	13	2,762	89	(5)	12	(5)	19	18	53	42	7	27	(7)	25	7	19	12	------
1888	397	424	61	85	13	2,700	74	(5)	16	(5)	19	16	48	49	9	29	(7)	24	7	21	11	------
1887	392	526	56	90	17	3,136	78	(5)	14	(5)	19	16	45	49	7	29	(7)	24	7	21	10	------
1886	362	565	43	82	16	2,690	81	(5)	12	(5)	17	17	41	38	6	30	1	27	7	17	9	------
1885	317	573	47	72	14	2,718	73	(5)	9	(5)	12	9	36	34	4	27	(7)	21	5	17	9	------
1884	376	535	50	68	14	2,756	98	(5)	14	(5)	12	12	41	40	5	29	1	22	8	20	10	------
1883	403	516	42	73	17	2,138	92	(5)	16	(5)	14	11	44	58	6	37	(7)	28	8	20	10	------
1882	403	460	46	79	19	1,990	90	(5)	14	(5)	13	11	37	68	(5)	34	1	28	8	19	(5)	------
1881	320	455	57	82	21	1,947	87	(5)	11	(5)	11	10	31	61	(5)	31	(5)	(5)	(5)	(5)	(5)	------

See footnotes at end of table.

Series U 94–115. Imports of Selected Products: 1790 to 1957—Con.

[In millions of dollars and units]

Year	Total selected commodities, value	Coffee Quantity (lb.)	Coffee Value	Tea Quantity (lb.)	Tea Value	Sugar Quantity (lb.)	Sugar Value	Year	Total selected commodities, value	Coffee Quantity (lb.)	Coffee Value	Tea Quantity (lb.)	Tea Value	Sugar Quantity (lb.)	Sugar Value
	94	95	96	97	98	99	100		94	95	96	97	98	99	100
1880	341	447	60	72	20	1,830	80	1835	23	103	11	14	5	126	7
1879	217	378	47	60	15	1,834	72	1834	21	80	9	16	6	115	6
1878	222	310	52	65	16	1,538	73	1833	21	100	11	15	5	98	5
1877	239	332	54	58	16	1,654	85	1832	15	92	9	10	3	66	3
1876	231	340	57	63	20	1,494	58	1831	12	82	6	5	1	109	5
1875	272	318	51	65	23	1,797	73	1830	29	51	4	9	2	86	5
1874	298	285	55	56	21	1,701	82	1829	11	51	5	7	2	63	4
1873	344	293	44	65	24	1,568	83	1828	11	55	5	8	2	57	4
1872	334	299	38	64	23	1,509	81	1827	11	50	4	6	2	77	5
1871	260	318	31	51	17	1,276	65	1826	13	37	4	10	4	85	5
1870	205	235	24	47	14	1,197	57	1825	13	45	5	10	4	72	4
1869	99	254	25	44	14	1,247	60	1824	13	39	5	9	3	94	5
1868	85	249	25	38	11	1,121	49	1823	12	37	7	8	2	61	3
1867	69	187	21	40	12	849	36	1822	13	26	6	7	2	88	5
1866	73	181	21	43	11	998	41	1821	9	21	4	5	1	60	4
1865	101	106	11	20	5	651	27	1820	(5)	(5)	(5)	(5)	(5)	(5)	(5)
1864	57	132	16	37	11	632	30	1819	(5)	23	(5)	7	(5)	74	(5)
1863	37	80	10	30	8	517	19	1818	(5)	29	(5)	6	(5)	68	(5)
1862	41	123	14	25	7	557	20	1817	(5)	31	(5)	7	(5)	93	(5)
1861	59	184	21	26	7	809	31	1816	(5)	26	(5)	3	(5)	55	(5)
1860	170	202	22	32	9	694	31	1815	(5)	20	(5)	2	(5)	45	(5)
1859	63	264	25	29	7	656	31	1814	(5)	8	(5)	(7)	(5)	30	(5)
1858	48	189	18	33	7	519	23	1813	(5)	12	(5)	1	(5)	33	(5)
1857	71	241	22	20	6	776	43	1812	(5)	28	(5)	3	(5)	83	(5)
1856	53	236	22	23	7	544	24	1811	(5)	30	(5)	3	(5)	77	(5)
1855	118	191	17	25	7	474	15	1810	(5)	31	(5)	8	(5)	55	(5)
1854	36	162	15	24	7	455	14	1809	(5)	36	(5)	1	(5)	77	(5)
1853	39	199	16	23	8	464	15	1808	(5)	37	(5)	5	(5)	104	(5)
1852	36	194	14	29	7	457	15	1807	(5)	59	(5)	8	(5)	221	(5)
1851	31	153	13	17	5	368	13	1806	(5)	56	(5)	7	(5)	199	(5)
1850	87	145	11	30	5	218	8	1805	(5)	56	(5)	5	(5)	187	(5)
1849	21	165	9	16	4	259	8	1804	(5)	53	(5)	3	(5)	128	(5)
1848	23	151	8	24	6	255	9	1803	(5)	17	(5)	6	(5)	74	(5)
1847	23	157	9	17	4	236	10	1802	(5)	41	(5)	4	(5)	99	(5)
1846	18	133	8	20	5	128	5	1801	(5)	57	(5)	4	(5)	137	(5)
1845	17	108	6	20	6	114	5	1800	(5)	47	(5)	5	(5)	113	(5)
1844	21	161	10	16	4	185	7	1799	(5)	30	(5)	5	(5)	104	(5)
1843 [8]	12	93	6	14	4	71	2	1798	(5)	58	(5)	2	(5)	88	(5)
1842	20	113	9	16	5	172	6	1797	(5)	49	(5)	2	(5)	73	(5)
1841	22	115	10	12	3	184	9	1796	(5)	61	(5)	2	(5)	60	(5)
1840	47	95	9	20	5	121	6	1795	(5)	54	(5)	3	(5)	64	(5)
1839	22	107	10	9	2	195	10	1794	(5)	37	(5)	3	(5)	49	(5)
1838	19	88	8	14	3	154	8	1793	(5)	34	(5)	3	(5)	48	(5)
1837	22	88	9	17	6	136	7	1792	(5)	9	(5)	3	(5)	24	(5)
1836	28	94	10	16	5	191	13	1791	(5)	4	(5)	1	(5)	25	(5)
								1790	(5)	4	(5)	3	(5)	18	(5)

Year	Rubber, crude, value	Raw silk, value	Wool and mohair value	Wool manufactures, value	Iron and steel manufactures, value	Cotton manufactures, value [1]	Year	Rubber, crude, value	Raw silk, value	Wool and mohair value	Wool manufactures, value	Iron and steel manufactures, value	Cotton manufactures, value [1]
	102	104	105	106	107	109		102	104	105	106	107	109
1880	10	12	24	34	71	30	1870	3	3	7	34	40	23
1879	6	8	5	24	20	20	1865	1	1	8	22	17	9
1878	5	5	8	25	19	19	1860	1	----------	5	43	26	33
1877	6	7	7	26	19	19	1855	2	----------	2	28	29	18
1876	4	5	8	33	23	23	1850	----------	----------	2	20	20	21
1875	5	5	11	45	31	28	1840	----------	----------	1	11	8	7
1874	6	4	8	47	47	28	1830	----------	----------	----------	6	6	6
1873	7	6	20	51	74	35	1820	----------	----------	----------	6	----------	8
1872	5	6	26	52	68	35							
1871	4	6	10	44	53	30							

[1] Includes semimanufactures.
[2] "Copper including ore and manufactures" since 1946.
[3] Includes fur hats beginning 1921; formerly classified as miscellaneous textile products.
[4] Includes "Sawmill products," "Wood pulp," and "Paper and manufactures."
[5] Not available.

[6] Value in millions of dollars for "Imports for consumption" as follows: Series U 101, 19; series U 102, 16; series U 106, 51; series U 107, 31; series U 108, 15; series U 109, 45; series U 112, 37; series U 113, 37; series U 114, 144; series U 25, 26.
[7] Less than $500,000.
[8] For 9 months.

Series U 116–133.   Value of Exports (Including Reexports) of U. S. Merchandise, by Country of Destination: 1790 to 1957

[In millions of dollars.   Figures shown here are mixed values for 1862–1879.   For years ending September 30, 1790–1842; June 30, 1843–1915; thereafter, calendar years]

Year	Total value	America						Europe					Asia				Australia and Oceania	Africa
		Total	Canada [1]	Cuba	Mexico	Brazil	Other	Total	United Kingdom	France	Germany [2]	Other	Total	China [3]	Japan [4]	Other		
	116	117	118	119	120	121	122	123	124	125	126	127	128	129	130	131	132	133
1957	[5] 20,810	8,720	3,905	618	902	482	2,813	5,780	1,100	589	954	3,137	3,367	[6]	1,231	2,136	279	681
1956	[5] 19,090	8,009	4,016	519	851	309	2,314	5,190	910	562	785	2,933	2,781	[6]	902	1,879	245	676
1955	[5] 15,547	6,635	3,235	458	711	254	1,977	4,198	930	360	596	2,312	2,122	[6]	649	1,473	270	612
1954	[5] 15,110	6,213	2,778	435	642	475	1,883	3,409	696	335	494	1,884	1,970	[6]	682	1,288	248	590
1953	[5] 15,774	6,187	3,011	431	656	315	1,774	2,910	594	343	356	1,617	2,061	[6]	680	1,331	181	525
1952	[5] 15,201	6,331	2,796	516	666	565	1,788	3,349	677	365	445	1,862	2,113	[6]	622	1,491	227	569
1951	[5] 15,032	6,363	2,588	540	713	700	1,822	4,044	901	427	519	2,197	2,244	[6]	598	1,646	244	581
1950	[5] 10,275	4,762	1,995	456	512	343	1,456	2,893	511	334	439	1,609	1,505	[6]	416	1,089	133	349
1949	12,051	4,861	1,959	380	468	383	1,671	4,118	700	497	822	2,099	2,256	[6]	468	1,788	195	622
1948	12,653	5,307	1,944	441	522	497	1,903	4,279	644	591	863	2,181	2,130	[6]	325	1,805	153	785
1947	14,430	6,183	2,114	492	630	643	2,304	5,187	1,103	817	128	3,139	1,918	[6]	60	1,858	320	821
1946	9,738	3,684	1,442	272	505	356	1,109	4,122	855	709	83	2,475	1,327	[6]	102	1,225	117	489
1945	9,806	2,564	1,178	196	307	219	664	5,515	2,193	472	2	2,848	849	[6]	1	848	354	524
1944	14,259	2,627	1,441	167	264	218	537	9,364	5,243	18	[6]	4,103	996	[6]	------	996	410	861
1943	12,965	2,418	1,444	134	187	156	497	7,633	4,505	------	------	3,128	838	[6]	2	836	569	1,507
1942	8,079	2,205	1,334	133	148	105	485	4,009	2,529	1	------	1,479	688	[6]	------	688	361	816
1941	5,147	2,047	994	126	159	148	620	1,847	1,637	2	[6]	208	625	[6]	60	565	123	504
1940	4,021	1,501	713	85	97	111	495	1,645	1,011	252	[6]	382	619	[6]	227	392	94	161
1939	3,177	1,131	489	82	83	80	397	1,290	505	182	46	557	562	[6]	232	330	80	115
1938	3,094	1,040	468	76	62	62	372	1,326	521	134	107	564	517	[6]	240	277	94	118
1937	3,349	1,158	509	92	109	69	379	1,360	536	165	126	533	580	[6]	289	291	99	152
1936	2,456	821	384	67	76	49	245	1,043	440	129	102	372	399	[6]	204	195	79	114
1935	2,283	706	323	60	66	44	213	1,029	433	117	92	387	378	[6]	203	175	74	96
1934	2,133	648	302	45	55	40	206	950	383	116	109	342	401	[6]	210	191	57	77
1933	1,675	455	211	25	38	30	151	850	312	122	140	276	292	[6]	143	149	35	43
1932	1,611	462	241	29	32	29	131	784	288	112	134	250	292	[6]	135	157	37	36
1931	2,424	750	396	47	52	29	226	1,187	456	122	166	443	386	98	156	132	42	60
1930	3,843	1,357	659	94	116	54	434	1,838	678	224	278	658	448	90	165	193	108	92
1929	5,241	1,934	948	129	134	109	614	2,341	848	266	410	817	643	124	259	260	192	131
1928	5,128	1,802	915	128	116	100	543	2,375	847	241	467	820	655	138	288	229	180	117
1927	4,865	1,691	837	155	109	89	501	2,314	840	229	482	763	560	83	258	219	194	107
1926	4,809	1,620	789	160	135	95	491	2,310	973	264	364	709	565	110	261	194	213	101
1925	4,910	1,541	649	199	145	87	461	2,604	1,034	280	470	820	487	94	230	163	189	89
1924	4,591	1,404	624	200	135	65	380	2,445	983	282	440	740	515	109	253	153	157	70
1923	4,167	1,355	652	192	120	46	345	2,093	882	272	317	622	511	109	267	135	146	61
1922	3,832	1,142	577	128	110	43	284	2,083	856	267	316	644	449	100	222	127	102	56
1921	4,485	1,403	594	188	222	58	341	2,364	942	225	372	825	533	108	238	187	113	73
1920	8,228	2,553	972	515	208	157	701	4,466	1,825	676	311	1,654	872	146	378	348	172	166
1919	7,920	1,738	734	278	131	115	480	5,188	2,279	893	93	1,923	772	106	366	300	126	98
1918	6,149	1,628	887	227	98	57	359	3,859	2,061	931	------	867	498	53	274	171	105	59
1917	6,234	1,573	829	196	111	66	371	4,062	2,009	941	[6]	1,112	469	40	186	243	77	51
1916	5,483	1,145	605	165	54	48	273	3,813	1,887	861	2	1,063	388	32	109	247	83	54
1915	2,769	576	301	76	34	26	139	1,971	912	369	29	661	139	16	41	82	53	29
1914	2,365	654	345	69	39	30	171	1,486	594	160	345	387	141	25	51	65	56	28
1913	2,466	763	415	71	54	43	180	1,479	597	146	332	404	140	21	58	61	54	29
1912	2,204	648	329	62	53	35	169	1,342	564	135	307	336	141	24	53	64	48	24
1911	2,049	566	270	61	61	27	147	1,308	577	135	287	309	105	19	37	49	46	24
1910	1,745	479	216	53	58	23	129	1,136	506	118	250	262	78	16	22	40	34	19
1909	1,663	387	163	44	50	18	112	1,147	515	109	235	288	83	19	27	37	30	17
1908	1,861	409	167	47	56	19	120	1,284	581	116	277	310	113	22	41	50	35	20
1907	1,881	432	183	49	66	19	115	1,298	608	114	257	319	101	26	39	36	33	17
1906	1,744	383	157	48	58	15	105	1,200	583	98	235	284	111	44	38	29	30	20
1905	1,519	318	141	38	46	11	82	1,021	523	76	194	228	135	53	52	30	27	19
1904	1,461	286	131	27	46	11	71	1,058	537	84	215	222	65	13	25	27	28	24
1903	1,420	256	123	22	42	11	58	1,029	524	77	194	234	62	19	21	22	33	38
1902	1,382	242	110	27	40	10	55	1,008	549	72	173	214	69	25	21	23	29	33
1901	1,488	241	106	26	36	12	61	1,137	631	79	192	235	53	10	19	24	31	26
1900	1,394	227	95	26	35	12	59	1,040	534	83	187	236	68	15	29	24	41	19
1899	1,227	194	88	19	25	12	50	937	512	61	156	208	49	14	17	18	29	19
1898	1,231	174	84	10	21	13	46	974	541	95	155	183	45	10	20	15	22	18
1897	1,051	159	65	8	23	12	51	813	483	58	125	147	39	12	13	14	23	17
1896	883	153	60	8	19	14	52	673	406	47	98	122	26	7	8	11	17	14
1895	808	143	53	13	15	15	47	628	387	45	92	104	18	4	5	9	13	6
1894	892	153	57	20	13	14	49	701	431	55	92	123	22	6	4	12	12	5
1893	848	152	47	24	20	12	49	662	421	47	84	110	17	4	3	10	11	5
1892	1,030	139	43	18	14	14	50	851	499	99	106	147	20	7	3	10	16	5
1891	884	131	38	12	15	14	52	705	445	61	93	106	26	9	5	12	18	5
1890	858	133	40	13	13	12	55	684	448	50	86	100	20	3	5	12	16	5
1889	742	125	41	12	11	9	52	579	383	46	68	82	19	8	5	6	16	4
1888	696	110	36	10	10	7	47	549	362	39	56	92	20	5	4	11	15	3
1887	716	104	35	11	8	8	42	575	366	57	59	93	20	6	3	11	14	3
1886	680	98	33	10	8	7	40	541	348	42	62	89	23	8	3	12	15	3
1885	742	104	38	9	8	7	42	599	398	47	62	92	21	6	3	12	14	4
1884	741	123	44	11	13	9	46	584	386	51	61	86	17	5	3	9	13	3
1883	824	129	44	15	17	9	44	660	425	59	66	110	17	4	3	10	14	4
1882	751	113	37	12	15	9	40	600	408	50	54	88	19	6	3	10	13	6
1881	902	108	38	11	11	9	39	766	481	94	70	121	13	5	1	7	10	5
1880	836	93	29	11	8	9	36	719	454	100	57	108	12	1	3	8	7	5
1879	712	91	30	13	7	8	33	594	349	90	57	98	12	3	3	6	10	4
1878	710	100	37	12	7	9	35	584	387	55	55	87	12	4	2	6	9	4
1877	645	99	37	13	6	8	35	525	346	45	58	76	10	2	1	7	8	3
1876	610	96	33	13	6	7	37	497	336	40	51	70	8	1	1	6	5	4

See footnotes at end of table.

Series U 116–133. Value of Exports (Including Reexports) of U. S. Merchandise, by Country of Destination: 1790 to 1957—Con.

[In millions of dollars]

Year	Total value	America						Europe					Asia				Australia and Oceania	Africa
		Total	Canada[1]	Cuba	Mexico	Brazil	Other	Total	United Kingdom	France	Germany[2]	Other	Total	China[3]	Japan[4]	Other		
	116	117	118	119	120	121	122	123	124	125	126	127	128	129	130	131	132	133
1875	574	100	35	15	6	8	36	459	317	34	50	58	7	1	2	4	5	3
1874	651	110	42	17	6	8	37	528	345	43	63	77	5	1	1	3	5	3
1873	594	102	33	16	6	7	40	479	317	34	62	66	5	1	1	3	5	3
1872	492	89	29	14	6	6	34	393	265	31	41	56	4	3	1	—	4	2
1871	493	89	32	15	8	6	28	394	273	27	35	59	3	2	1	1	4	3
1870	471	79	25	14	6	6	28	381	248	46	42	45	4	3	1	—	5	2
1869	382	74	23	12	5	6	28	291	185	33	38	35	7	5	1	1	6	3
1868	383	81	24	15	6	6	30	287	198	26	31	32	6	4	1	1	6	3
1867	398	77	21	14	5	5	32	307	225	34	22	26	5	4	1	—	6	3
1866	479	80	24	15	5	6	30	386	288	51	22	25	5	3	1	2	7	2
1865	281	110	29	19	16	6	40	158	103	11	20	24	4	3	(6)	1	7	2
1864	235	92	27	13[7]	9	6	40	138	97	13	13	15	4	3	(6)	(6)		1
1863	268	83	28	14[7]	9	5	27	173	128	14	14	17	5	9	(6)	(6)	1	7
1862	193	57	21	9[7]	2	4	21	127	86	20	10	11	3	5	(6)	(6)		6
1861	220	61	23	10	2	5	21	147	108	15	11	13	6	7	(6)	(6)		6
1860	334	69	23	12	5	6	23	249	169	39	15	26	8	9	(6)	(6)		8
1859	293	70	28	12	3	6	21	210	133	30	15	32	6	7	(6)	(6)		7
1858	272	62	24	11	3	5	19	199	129	28	12	30	5	6	(6)	(6)		6
1857	294	64	24	9	4	5	22	218	135	32	15	36	4	4	(6)	(6)		8
1856	281	66	29	7	4	5	21	204	128	35	13	28	3	3	(6)	(6)		8
1855	219	62	28	8	3	4	19	148	92	29	9	18	3	*2*	(6)	—		6
1854	237	60	24	8	3	4	21	170	117	25	9	19	3	*2*	(6)	—		5
1853	203	43	12	6	4	4	17	151	103	22	7	19	4	*4*	—	—		5
1852	167	34	10	6	2	3	13	124	81	19	6	18	3	*3*	—	—		6
1851	189	39	12	5	2	3	17	146	101	21	6	18	3	*2*	—	—		2
1850	144	30	10	5	2	3	10	109	71	18	5	15	3	*2*	—	—		2
1849	140	29	8	5	2	3	11	107	78	13	3	13	3	*2*	—	—		1
1848	138	35	8	7	4	3	13	99	67	15	4	13	3	*2*	—	—		1
1847	157	31	7	6	1	3	14	123	87	19	5	12	2	*2*	—	—		1
1846	110	31	7	5	2	3	14	76	46	14	5	11	2	*1*	—	—		1
1845	106	29	6	6	1	3	13	73	45	12	6	10	2	*2*	—	—		1
1844	106	28	6	5	2	3	12	76	49	13	4	10	2	*2*	—	—		1
1843[8]	83	16	3	3	1	2	7	63	41	12	4	6	3	*3*	—	—		1
1842	100	27	6	5	2	3	11	72	40	17	5	10	2	*2*	—	—		
1841	112	30	6	6	2	3	13	80	47	18	5	10	2	*1*	—	—	—	
1840	124	30	6	6	3	2	13	92	55	20	4	13	1	*1*				1
1839	112	24	4	6	3	2	9	86	57	18	3	8	1	*2*				1
1838	105	23	2	6	2	2	11	80	52	15	3	10	1	*2*				1
1837	111	24	3	6	4	2	9	86	52	19	4	11	1	*1*				1
1836	124	26	3	6	6	2	9	96	58	21	4	13	2	*1*				
1835	115	30	3	5	9	2	11	83	52	19	4	8	2	*2*				1
1834	102	27	3	5	5	2	12	74	44	15	5	10	1	*1*				
1833	88	29	4	5	5	3	12	57	32	14	3	8	2	*1*				
1832	82	26	3	5	3	2	13	55	29	12	4	10	2	*1*				
1831	72	26	3	5	6	2	10	45	31	6	3	5	2	*1*				
1830	72	23	2	5	5	2	8	48	26	11	2	9	1	*1*				
1829	67	21	2	5	2	2	10	45	24	10	3	8	1	*1*				
1828	64	23	2	6	3	2	10	39	20	9	3	7	2	*1*				
1827	74	21	2	6	4	2	7	49	26	11	3	9	2	*4*				
1826	73	30	2	6	6	2	14	42	21	11	2	8	1	*3*				
1825	91	30	3	5	6	2	14	59	37	10	3	9	2	*6*				
1824	69	28	2	6	—	2	18	40	21	10	2	7	1	*5*				
1823	68	22	2	5	—	1	14	44	22	9	3	10	2	*5*				
1822	61	20	2	3	—	1	14	40	24	6	3	7	1	*6*				
1821	55	15	2	4	—	1	8	36	19	6	2	9		*4*				

Year	Total value	Europe Total	United Kingdom	France	Germany	Other
	116	123	124	125	126	127
1820	70	48	24	8	3	13
1819	70	47	24	9	4	10
1818	93	68	38	12	3	15
1817	88	58	33	9	3	13
1816	82	59	30	10	4	15
1815	53	38	18	7	2	11
1814	7	1	—	(6)	—	1
1813	28	22	—	4	(6)	18
1812	39	27	6	3	—	18
1811	61	40	14	2	(6)	24
1810	67	47	12	(6)	2	33
1809	52	34	6	—	2	26
1808	22	7	3	—	(6)	
1807	108	71	23	13	3	32
1806	102	65	16	11	6	32
1805	96	61	15	13	4	29
1804	78	51	13	9	6	23
1803	56	37	18	4	4	11
1802	72	44	16	8	6	14
1801	93	59	31	4	11	13
1800	71	41	19	(6)	8	14
1799	79	45	19	—	18	8
1798	61	39	12	1	15	11
1797	51	29	6	4	10	9
1796	59	39	17	3	10	9
1795	48	31	6	8	10	7
1794	33	21	6	1	5	9
1793	26	15	6	2	2	5
1792	21	12	5	2	1	4
1791	19	10	6	1	(6)	3
1790	20	13	7	1	(6)	5

[1] Prior to 1873, data are for trade with British North American Provinces which is a somewhat larger area than the Dominion of Canada. In the year ending June 30, 1873, the U. S. traded with British North American Provinces the following amounts: $34.6 million of exports and $37.6 million of imports. Beginning 1952, includes Newfoundland and Labrador.

[2] Prior to January 1952, East and West Germany; thereafter, only West Germany.

[3] Figures in italics include gold and silver.

[4] Beginning 1954, excludes Ryukyu Islands. No records available prior to 1855.

[5] Includes amounts not shown by continents for security reasons.

[6] Less than $500,000.

[7] Includes Puerto Rico.

[8] For 9 months.

Series U 134-151. Value of General Imports, by Country of Origin: 1790 to 1957

[In millions of dollars. Totals shown here in mixed values. For years ending September 30, 1790-1842; June 30, 1843-1915; thereafter, calendar years]

Year	Total value	America						Europe					Asia				Australia and Oceania	Africa
		Total	Canada [1]	Cuba	Mexico	Brazil	Other	Total	United Kingdom	France	Germany [2]	Other	Total	China [3]	Japan [4]	Other		
	134	135	136	137	138	139	140	141	142	143	144	145	146	147	148	149	150	151
1957	12,978	7,045	2,904	482	430	700	2,529	3,143	765	258	605	1,515	1,988	(5)	600	1,388	216	586
1956	12,615	6,856	2,894	457	401	745	2,359	2,963	726	236	494	1,507	1,996	(5)	558	1,438	203	597
1955	11,384	6,262	2,653	422	397	633	2,157	2,453	616	202	366	1,269	1,876	(5)	432	1,444	174	619
1954	10,215	5,896	2,377	401	328	682	2,108	2,083	501	157	278	1,147	1,467	(5)	279	1,188	165	605
1953	10,873	6,117	2,462	431	355	768	2,101	2,335	546	186	277	1,326	1,626	(5)	262	1,364	201	593
1952	10,717	6,025	2,386	440	410	808	1,981	2,029	485	167	212	1,165	1,813	(5)	229	1,584	243	607
1951	10,967	5,826	2,275	418	326	911	1,896	2,043	466	263	233	1,081	2,059	(5)	205	1,854	451	589
1950	8,852	5,063	1,960	406	315	715	1,667	1,387	335	132	104	816	1,699	(5)	182	1,517	208	494
1949	6,622	3,995	1,551	388	243	552	1,261	925	228	61	45	591	1,239	(5)	82	1,157	125	338
1948	7,124	4,099	1,554	375	246	514	1,410	1,121	290	73	32	726	1,346	(5)	63	1,283	164	394
1947	5,756	3,398	1,095	510	247	446	1,100	820	205	47	6	562	1,055	(5)	35	1,020	156	327
1946	4,942	2,762	883	324	232	408	915	804	158	63	3	580	887	(5)	81	806	183	306
1945	4,159	2,874	1,125	337	231	311	870	409	90	13	1	305	407	(5)	(5)	407	171	297
1944	3,929	2,965	1,260	387	204	293	821	289	84	(5)	(5)	205	322	(5)	(5)	322	130	222
1943	3,381	2,458	1,024	292	192	228	722	240	105	(5)	(5)	135	235	(5)	(5)	235	245	204
1942	2,756	1,762	717	161	124	165	595	220	134	1	(5)	85	340	(5)	(5)	340	231	204
1941	3,345	1,657	554	181	98	184	640	281	136	5	3	137	1,088	(5)	78	1,010	159	161
1940	2,625	1,089	424	105	76	105	379	390	155	37	5	193	981	(5)	158	823	35	131
1939	2,318	898	340	105	56	107	290	617	149	62	52	354	700	(5)	161	539	27	77
1938	1,960	753	260	106	49	98	240	567	118	54	65	330	570	(5)	127	443	16	55
1937	3,084	1,113	398	148	60	121	386	843	203	76	92	472	967	(5)	204	763	68	92
1936	2,423	910	376	127	49	102	256	718	200	65	80	373	708	(5)	172	536	36	51
1935	2,047	776	286	104	42	100	244	599	155	58	78	308	605	(5)	153	452	26	42
1934	1,655	628	232	79	36	91	190	490	115	61	69	245	489	(5)	119	370	15	33
1933	1,450	520	185	58	31	83	163	463	111	50	78	224	425	(5)	128	297	13	28
1932	1,323	539	174	58	37	82	188	390	75	45	74	196	362	(5)	134	228	8	24
1931	2,091	824	266	90	48	110	310	641	135	79	127	300	574	67	206	301	19	33
1930	3,061	1,195	402	122	80	131	460	911	210	114	177	410	854	101	279	474	33	68
1929	4,399	1,621	503	207	118	208	585	1,334	330	171	255	578	1,279	166	432	681	57	109
1928	4,091	1,530	489	203	125	221	492	1,249	349	159	222	519	1,169	140	384	645	53	90
1927	4,185	1,504	475	257	138	203	431	1,265	358	168	201	538	1,268	152	402	714	55	93
1926	4,431	1,580	476	251	169	235	449	1,278	383	152	198	545	1,409	143	401	865	68	96
1925	4,227	1,499	454	262	179	222	382	1,239	413	157	164	505	1,319	169	384	766	78	92
1924	3,610	1,461	399	362	167	179	354	1,096	366	148	139	443	931	118	340	473	49	73
1923	3,792	1,469	416	376	140	143	394	1,157	404	150	161	442	1,020	188	347	485	59	87
1922	3,113	1,181	364	268	132	120	297	991	357	143	117	374	827	135	354	338	49	65
1921	2,509	1,051	335	230	119	96	271	765	239	142	80	304	618	101	251	266	35	40
1920	5,278	2,424	612	722	179	228	683	1,228	514	166	89	459	1,397	193	415	789	80	150
1919	3,904	1,844	495	419	149	234	547	751	309	124	11	307	1,108	154	410	544	89	112
1918	3,031	1,585	452	279	159	98	597	318	149	60	(5)	109	939	111	302	526	103	86
1917	2,952	1,471	414	249	130	145	533	551	280	99	(5)	172	821	125	254	442	37	73
1916	2,392	1,086	237	244	105	132	368	633	305	109	6	213	551	80	182	289	60	62
1915	1,674	734	160	186	78	99	211	614	256	77	91	190	272	40	99	133	29	25
1914	1,894	650	161	131	93	101	164	896	294	141	190	271	305	39	107	159	24	19
1913	1,813	580	121	126	78	120	135	893	296	137	189	271	298	39	92	167	17	26
1912	1,653	549	109	120	66	124	130	820	273	125	171	251	249	30	81	138	13	23
1911	1,527	488	101	110	57	101	119	768	261	115	163	229	231	34	79	118	13	27
1910	1,557	503	95	123	59	108	118	806	271	132	169	234	210	30	66	114	20	17
1909	1,312	418	79	97	48	98	96	654	209	108	144	193	207	29	70	108	18	15
1908	1,194	364	75	83	47	75	84	608	190	102	143	173	191	26	68	97	15	16
1907	1,434	424	73	97	57	98	99	747	246	128	162	211	224	33	69	122	18	21
1906	1,227	375	68	85	51	80	91	633	210	108	135	180	192	29	53	110	12	13
1905	1,118	378	62	86	46	100	84	541	176	90	118	157	175	28	52	95	13	11
1904	991	319	52	77	44	76	70	499	166	81	109	143	156	29	47	80	8	9
1903	1,026	297	55	63	41	67	71	547	190	90	120	147	159	27	44	88	10	13
1902	903	271	48	35	40	79	69	475	166	83	102	124	136	21	38	77	8	13
1901	823	255	42	43	29	71	70	430	143	75	100	112	122	18	29	75	7	9
1900	850	224	39	31	29	58	67	441	160	73	97	111	146	27	33	86	29	11
1899	697	199	31	25	23	58	62	354	118	62	84	90	112	19	27	66	23	10
1898	616	183	32	15	19	62	55	306	109	53	70	74	96	20	25	51	23	7
1897	765	213	40	18	19	69	67	430	168	68	111	83	92	20	24	48	20	10
1896	780	236	41	40	17	71	67	419	170	66	94	89	95	22	26	47	20	11
1895	732	246	37	53	16	79	61	384	159	62	81	82	84	21	24	39	13	6
1894	655	267	31	76	29	79	52	295	107	48	69	71	75	17	19	39	14	3
1893	866	286	38	79	34	76	59	458	183	76	96	103	99	21	27	51	17	6
1892	827	325	35	78	28	119	65	392	156	69	83	84	89	20	24	45	17	5
1891	845	282	39	62	27	83	71	459	195	77	97	90	79	19	19	41	20	4
1890	789	238	39	54	23	59	63	450	186	78	99	87	81	16	21	44	17	3
1889	745	243	43	52	21	60	67	403	178	70	82	73	76	17	17	42	19	4
1888	724	224	43	49	17	54	61	407	178	71	78	80	73	17	19	37	16	3
1887	692	211	38	50	15	53	55	391	165	68	81	77	72	19	17	36	15	4
1886	635	191	37	51	11	42	50	358	154	63	69	72	69	19	15	35	14	3
1885	578	183	37	42	9	45	50	319	137	57	63	62	61	16	12	33	12	3
1884	668	212	38	57	9	50	58	371	163	71	65	72	68	16	11	41	13	4
1883	723	222	44	66	8	44	60	410	189	98	57	66	73	20	15	38	13	5
1882	725	238	51	70	8	49	60	398	196	89	56	57	73	20	14	39	12	5
1881	643	215	38	63	8	53	53	341	174	70	53	44	74	22	14	38	8	5

See footnotes at end of table.

Series U 134–151. Value of General Imports, by Country of Origin: 1790 to 1957—Con.

[In millions of dollars]

Year	Total value	America						Europe					Asia				Australia and Oceania	Africa
		Total	Canada[1]	Cuba	Mexico	Brazil	Other	Total	United Kingdom	France	Germany[2]	Other	Total	China[3]	Japan[4]	Other		
	134	135	136	137	138	139	140	141	142	143	144	145	146	147	148	149	150	151
1880	668	212	33	65	7	52	55	371	211	69	52	39	74	22	15	37	7	4
1879	446	172	26	64	5	39	38	216	109	51	36	20	52	16	10	26	4	2
1878	437	176	25	60	5	43	43	204	107	43	35	19	51	16	7	28	4	2
1877	451	182	24	66	5	43	44	214	114	48	33	19	49	11	14	24	4	2
1876	461	170	29	56	5	45	35	232	123	51	35	23	53	12	15	26	3	2
1875	533	191	28	65	5	42	51	281	155	60	40	26	52	13	8	31	5	3
1874	567	209	34	85	4	44	42	302	180	52	44	26	50	18	6	26	5	3
1873	642	204	37	77	4	39	47	361	237	34	61	29	66	26	8	33	5	5
1872	627	191	36	67	4	30	54	365	249	43	46	27	60	27	7	26	5	6
1871	520	170	33	58	3	31	45	297	221	28	25	23	48	20	5	23	1	4
1870	436	153	36	54	3	25	35	241	152	43	27	19	37	15	3	19	2	3
1869	418	147	29	57	2	25	34	235	159	30	25	21	31	13	3	15	2	3
1868	357	130	26	50	2	24	28	196	132	25	22	17	28	11	2	15	1	3
1867	396	111	25	38	1	19	28	245	172	29	27	17	30	12	3	15	7	2
1866	435 [5]	132	49	38	2	17	26	266	202	23	26	15	23	10	2	11	4	3
1865	239 [5]	100	33	30	6	10	21	109	85	7	10	7	13	*5*	(6)	8	1	3
1864	316	112	30	33	6	14	29	179	142	11	14	12	19	*10*	(6)	9		6
1863	243	71	17	21	3	11	19	148	113	11	13	11	20	*11*	(6)	9		4
1862	189	69	19	21	1	13	15	105	75	8	14	8	13	*7*	(6)	6		2
1861	289	94	23	31	1	18	21	166	105	32	15	14	26	*11*	(6)	15		8
1860	354	104	24	32	2	21	25	217	138	43	19	17	29	*14*	(6)	15		4
1859	331	102	19	33	1	22	27	201	126	41	18	16	25	*11*	(6)	14		3
1858	263	79	16	23	1	17	22	153	89	33	14	17	28	*11*	(6)	17		3
1857	348	116	22	45	1	21	27	205	127	46	15	17	25	*11*	(6)	17		2
1856	310	86	21	24	1	19	21	199	122	49	15	13	25	*10*	(6)	13		2
1855	258	70	15	18	1	15	21	165	106	32	13	14	21	*11*	(6)			2
1854	298	72	9	17	1	14	31	204	146	36	17	5	20	*11*	(6)	-------		2
1853	264	55	7	19	1	15	13	190	130	33	14	13	17	*11*	-------			2
1852	207	54	5	18	1	12	18	134	89	25	8	12	18	*11*	-------			1
1851	211	49	5	17	1	12	14	148	93	31	10	14	12	*7*	-------			2
1850	174	38	5	10	1	9	13	124	75	27	9	13	11	*7*	-------			1
1849	141	31	2	10	1	8	10	100	58	24	8	10	9	*6*	-------			1
1848	149	33	3	12	1	8	9	103	60	28	6	9	12	*8*	-------			1
1847	122	30	1	12	(6)	7	10	83	48	24	4	7	8	*6*	-------			1
1846	118	27	1	8	1	7	10	80	45	24	3	8	10	*7*	-------			1
1845	113	25	1	6	1	6	11	78	45	21	3	9	10	*7*	-------			(6)
1844	103	28	1	10	1	7	9	67	41	17	2	7	8	*5*	-------			(6)
1843 [7]	42	16	(6)	4	1	4	7	20	12	5	1	2	6	*4*	-------			1
1842	96	26	1	7	1	6	11	61	34	17	2	8	9	*4*	-------			(6)
1841	123	33	1	11	1	6	14	38	46	24	2	11	7	*5*	-------			(6)
1840	98	25		9	1	5	9	62	33	16	3	10	10	*7*	-------			1
1839	156	35	2	12	1	5	15	114	65	32	5	12	6	*4*	-------			1
1838	96	26	1	11	1	3	10	62	36	16	3	7	7	*5*	-------			1
1837	130	28	2	11	1	5	9	86	45	21	6	14	14	*9*	-------			2
1836	177	35	2	13	1	7	12	128	76	32	5	15	13	*7*	-------			1
1835	137	28	1	11	1	6	9	99	60	22	4	13	9	*6*	-------			1
1834	109	26	1	8	1	5	11	71	41	15	3	12	11	*8*	-------			1
1833	101	27	1	10	1	5	10	63	38	13	2	10	11	*8*	-------			(6)
1832	95	22	1	7	1	4	9	63	37	12	3	11	9	*5*	-------			1
1831	96	22	1	8	1	2	10	68	44	14	4	6	6	*3*	-------			1
1830	63	17	(6)	5	1	2	9	40	24	8	2	6	5	*4*	-------			1
1829	67	17	(6)	5	1	2	9	44	25	9	2	8	6	*5*	-------			(6)
1828	81	20	(6)	6	1	3	10	54	33	9	3	9	7	*5*	-------			(6)
1827	71	19	(6)	7	1	2	9	48	30	8	2	8	4	*5*	-------			(6)
1826	78	20	(6)	7	1	2	10	46	26	8	3	9	11	*7*	-------			1
1825	90	21	(6)	7	1	2	11	59	37	11	3	8	10	*8*	-------			(6)
1824	72	22	(6)	7	-------	2	13	44	28	7	2	7	6	*6*	-------			(6)
1823	72	18	(6)	7	-------	1	10	43	28	7	2	7	11	*7*	-------			(6)
1822	80	19	(6)	7	-------	1	11	51	35	6	2	8	9	*7*	-------			1
1821	55	15	(6)	5	-------	1	9	35	24	4	1	6	5	*3*	-------			(6)

Year	Total, value 134	Year	Total, value 134	Year	Total, value 134	Year	Total, value 134	Year	Total, value 134	Year	Total, value 134
1820	74	1815	113	1810	85	1805	121	1800	91	1795	70
1819	87	1814	13	1809	59	1804	85	1799	79	1794	35
1818	122	1813	22	1808	57	1803	65	1798	69	1793	31
1817	99	1812	77	1807	139	1802	76	1797	75	1792	32
1816	147	1811	53	1806	129	1801	111	1796	81	1791	29
										1790	23

[1] Prior to 1873, data are for trade with British North American Provinces which is a somewhat larger area than the Dominion of Canada. In the year ending June 30, 1873, the U.S. traded with British North American Provinces the following amounts: $34.6 million of exports and $37.6 million of imports. Beginning 1952, includes Newfoundland and Labrador.

[2] Prior to January 1952, East and West Germany; thereafter, only West Germany.

[3] Figures in italics include gold and silver.

[4] Beginning 1954, excludes Ryukyu Islands. No records available prior to 1855.

[5] Agrees with source; however, figures for components do not add to total shown.

[6] Less than $500,000.

[7] For 9 months.

FOREIGN TRADE AND OTHER INTERNATIONAL TRANSACTIONS

Series U 152–155. Trade With the United States as Reported by Canada: 1850 to 1957

[In millions of Canadian dollars. For calendar years 1850–1863 and 1901–1957; years ending June 30 for all other years]

Year	Recorded exports to the U.S.			Imports from U.S. for home consumption
	Total	Canadian products	Foreign products	
	152	153	154	155
1957	2,942	2,868	74	3,999
1956	2,879	2,819	60	4,162
1955	2,612	2,559	53	3,452
1954	2,367	2,317	50	2,961
1953	2,463	2,419	44	3,221
1952	2,349	2,307	42	2,977
1951	2,334	2,298	36	2,813
1950	2,050	2,021	29	2,130
1949	1,524	1,503	21	1,952
1948	1,522	1,501	21	1,806
1947	1,057	1,034	22	1,975
1946	909	888	21	1,405
1945	1,227	1,197	30	1,202
1944	1,335	1,301	33	1,447
1943	1,167	1,149	17	1,424
1942	897	886	11	1,305
1941	610	600	10	1,004
1940	452	443	9	744
1939	390	380	9	497
1938	279	270	8	425
1937	372	360	12	491
1936	345	334	11	369
1935	273	262	11	312
1934	224	219	5	294
1933	173	168	5	217
1932	165	159	6	264
1931	250	240	10	394
1930	390	373	16	654
1929	515	493	23	894
1928	503	482	21	826
1927	484	467	17	707
1926	471	458	13	669
1925	451	441	10	579
1924	395	385	10	524
1923	420	410	11	610
1922	348	336	11	510
1921	335	323	12	555
1920	581	555	26	921
1919	488	450	37	740
1918	441	423	19	741
1917	405	386	20	827
1916	252	243	9	595
1915	181	170	11	317
1914	169	158	11	309
1913	168	153	15	428
1912	129	118	11	410
1911	101	90	11	320
1910	108	101	8	262
1909	101	94	7	202
1908	80	75	5	166
1907	90	84	6	217
1906	80	75	5	188
1905	64	59	5	155
1904	55	51	5	149

Year	Recorded exports to the U.S.			Imports from U.S. for home consumption
	Total [1]	Canadian products [1]	Foreign products	
	152	153	154	155
1903	54	51	3	140
1902	52	49	3	117
1901	49	46	3	111
1900	60	58	2	102
1899	41	39	2	89
1898	41	39	2	75
1897	46	44	2	57
1896	40	38	2	54
1895	38	36	2	50
1894	34	33	1	51
1893	39	37	2	52
1892	38	35	3	52
1891	40	38	2	52
1890	38	36	2	51
1889	42	40	2	50
1888	42	40	2	46
1887	37	35	2	45
1886	36	34	2	43
1885	38	36	2	46
1884	36	34	2	50
1883	42	40	2	55
1882	48	46	2	47
1881	36	34		36
1880	32	30	2	28
1879	26	25	1	42
1878	25	24	1	48
1877	25	24	1	49
1876	31	30	1	44
1875	29	28	1	50
1874	34	33	1	52
1873	39	37	2	45
1872	33	33	---------	34
1871	29	29	---------	27
1870	30	30	---------	22
1869	27	27	---------	21
1868	25	25	---------	23
1867	[2]29	[2]29	---------	[2]17
1866	42	42	---------	23
1865	30	30	---------	23
1864	[3]12	[3]12	---------	[3]16
1863	25	25	---------	26
1862	20	20	---------	29
1861	19	19	---------	26
1860	25	25	---------	24
1859	19	19	---------	24
1858	16	16	---------	21
1857	17	17	---------	26
1856	23	23	---------	30
1855	23	23	---------	28
1854	13	13	---------	22
1853	13	13	---------	17
1852	9	9	---------	12
1851	6	6	---------	11
1850	7	7	---------	9

[1] Includes estimates of unrecorded exports for 1850–1900.
[2] Figures for Nova Scotia are for 9 months from September 1866, to June 30, 1867, and New Brunswick for 6 months only, to June 30, 1867.

[3] Figures for Ontario and Quebec are for 6 months only; fiscal year changed to end June 30.

Series U 156–167. Trade With the United States as Reported by the United Kingdom: 1831 to 1957

Value in millions of pounds sterling 1831–1923; of gold dollars 1923–1933; of gold dollars at former parity 1934; of U.S. dollars 1934 to present. Quantity in millions of pounds
For calendar years prior to 1923; thereafter, years ending March 31]

Year	U. K. exports to the U. S.			Imports from the U. S.								Other value
					Selected products							
	Total value	Exports	Re-exports	Total value	Total selected value	Cotton, raw		Wheat		Tobacco, unmanufactured		
						Quantity	Value	Quantity	Value	Quantity	Value	
	156	157	158	159	160	161	162	163	164	165	166	167
1957	728.6	687.7	[1]34.1	1,359.5	359.7	517	163.3	1,874	63.6	168	132.8	999.8
1956	727.6	683.1	[1]31.8	1,144.7	271.5	256	81.5	2,101	72.3	160	117.7	873.2
1955	558.8	514.9	44.0	1,180.3	237.0	237	74.0	1,062	34.2	179	128.8	943.3
1954	451.7	422.6	29.1	791.6	240.0	298	101.3	837	21.5	160	117.2	551.6
1953	481.8	444.6	37.2	710.6	235.4	192	71.3	998	38.6	174	125.5	475.2
1952	506.0	408.7	97.3	880.5	181.2	218	93.0	1,016	41.7	67	46.5	699.3
1951	428.9	381.7	47.2	1,064.6	343.8	220	94.7	2,380	104.9	212	144.2	720.8
1950	356.4	316.5	39.9	592.1	238.6	291	111.7	1,003	34.5	144	92.4	353.5
1949	224.0	205.3	18.7	822.3	269.0	412	151.6	621	30.4	154	87.0	553.3
1948	285.0	266.4	18.6	738.5	171.6	186	71.8	21	1.1	172	98.7	566.9
1947	247.1	193.3	53.8	1,197.4	227.8	194	65.5	776	37.8	201	124.5	969.6
1946	159.9	143.1	16.8	925.2	306.2	117	33.0	843	41.0	366	232.2	619.0
1938	140.6	100.2	40.4	576.9	165.4	444	46.2	1,770	33.0	257	86.2	411.5
1937	209.3	155.3	54.0	564.1	174.9	765	97.1	391	8.3	203	69.5	389.2
1936	183.1	137.3	45.8	463.8	155.5	617	83.5	5	.1	214	71.9	308.3
1935	147.6	112.2	35.4	429.1	145.7	572	76.0	66	.8	203	68.9	283.4
1934 [2]	117.0	88.5	28.5	413.0	129.4	458	61.6	15	.1	189	67.7	283.6
1934 [3]	69.8	52.8	17.0	246.6	77.2	458	36.7	15	.1	189	40.4	169.4
1933	86.8	63.4	23.4	251.2	87.9	786	60.5	1	[4]	160	27.4	163.3
1932	78.3	53.3	25.0	293.6	87.1	750	58.5	519	5.1	125	23.5	206.5
1931	119.7	83.3	36.4	471.1	97.0	449	45.5	1,259	13.7	157	37.8	374.2
1930	194.5	139.8	54.7	748.1	199.5	595	94.9	2,356	44.4	198	60.2	548.6
1929	301.8	221.7	80.1	953.7	314.9	846	185.0	2,494	57.1	205	72.8	638.8
1928	334.5	227.4	107.4	917.1	325.8	879	198.1	2,650	64.2	172	63.5	591.3
1927	325.4	221.1	104.3	974.2	340.0	947	164.2	3,989	106.8	177	69.0	634.2
1926	364.1	238.6	125.5	1,112.0	386.6	1,080	220.8	3,492	99.3	161	66.5	725.4
1925	401.8	251.5	150.3	1,184.4	502.9	1,236	347.3	2,969	90.7	163	64.9	681.5
1924	347.0	238.4	108.6	1,065.4	440.2	955	298.0	3,396	80.2	157	62.0	625.2
1923 [2]	391.8	273.1	118.7	964.0	359.5	670	220.2	3,524	77.1	155	62.2	604.5
1923 [3]	85.6	59.7	25.9	210.7	78.5	670	48.1	3,524	16.8	155	13.6	132.2
1922	77.3	55.5	21.7	221.8	90.4	915	52.0	4,173	22.5	167	15.9	131.4
1921	64.3	44.0	20.3	274.8	97.6	802	45.3	4,039	31.5	215	20.8	177.2
1920	131.1	77.1	53.9	563.3	264.2	1,395	166.8	5,087	69.8	178	27.6	299.1
1919	65.5	33.9	31.6	541.6	189.2	1,371	125.5	3,558	30.9	316	32.8	352.4
1918	26.8	23.3	3.5	515.4	132.2	976	94.8	2,773	22.7	163	14.7	383.2
1917	60.1	33.2	26.9	376.3	129.4	1,186	77.1	6,071	49.8	41	2.5	246.9
1916	64.5	32.7	31.9	291.8	112.5	1,647	60.6	7,229	46.0	153	5.9	179.3
1915	56.5	26.2	30.3	237.8	78.7	2,022	45.6	4,665	26.5	184	6.6	159.1
1914	64.0	34.0	30.0	138.6	55.4	1,284	35.0	3,833	14.9	139	5.5	83.2
1913	59.5	29.3	30.2	141.7	67.0	1,585	47.3	3,816	14.0	142	5.7	74.7
1912	64.6	30.1	34.6	134.6	67.8	2,165	55.2	2,237	8.3	122	4.3	66.8
1911	56.1	27.5	28.6	122.7	57.2	1,682	48.8	1,449	5.2	105	3.2	65.5
1910	62.2	31.4	30.7	117.6	56.4	1,470	48.8	1,226	4.8	99	2.8	61.2
1909	59.3	29.8	29.5	118.4	51.3	1,640	41.2	1,736	7.0	114	3.1	67.1
1908	42.5	21.3	21.2	123.9	53.5	1,589	39.3	2,886	10.9	107	3.3	70.4
1907	58.1	30.9	27.1	134.3	57.4	1,756	47.1	2,234	7.8	87	2.5	76.9
1906	53.2	27.8	25.5	131.1	49.3	1,488	38.7	2,526	8.1	104	2.5	81.8
1905	47.3	23.9	23.4	114.7	42.5	1,734	38.4	732	2.4	73	1.7	72.2
1904	39.3	20.2	19.1	119.2	45.0	1,491	40.2	790	2.5	95	2.4	74.2
1903	41.6	22.6	19.0	122.1	42.7	1,361	32.3	2,710	8.4	74	2.0	79.4
1902	43.1	23.8	19.3	127.0	47.2	1,364	29.3	4,851	14.5	116	3.4	79.8
1901	37.7	18.4	19.3	141.0	48.2	1,481	32.4	4,532	13.5	76	2.3	92.8
1900	37.3	19.8	17.6	138.8	43.9	1,365	30.2	3,650	11.2	89	2.5	94.9
1899	35.0	18.1	16.9	120.1	34.1	1,234	19.2	3,881	11.8	109	3.1	86.0
1898	28.5	14.7	13.8	126.1	44.8	1,805	27.5	4,240	15.3	70	2.0	81.3
1897	37.9	21.0	16.9	113.0	39.6	1,380	24.6	3,876	13.1	69	1.9	73.4
1896	32.0	20.4	11.6	106.3	39.7	1,394	28.0	3,438	9.7	74	2.0	66.6
1895	44.1	27.9	16.2	86.5	32.3	1,395	22.8	3,033	7.8	62	1.7	54.2
1894	30.8	18.8	12.0	89.6	33.7	1,393	24.7	2,762	6.9	76	2.1	55.9
1893	35.7	24.0	11.7	91.8	35.2	1,056	22.5	3,613	10.6	71	2.1	56.6
1892	41.4	26.5	14.9	108.2	44.2	1,406	29.2	3,795	13.3	52	1.7	64.0
1891	41.1	27.5	13.6	104.4	49.3	1,618	36.6	2,710	11.1	47	1.6	55.1
1890	46.3	32.1	14.2	97.3	39.9	1,317	31.4	1,927	6.9	53	1.6	57.4
1889	43.9	30.3	13.6	95.5	42.1	1,424	33.5	1,905	6.8	64	1.8	53.4
1888	41.2	28.9	12.3	79.8	37.9	1,349	31.1	1,640	5.7	37	1.1	41.9
1887	40.2	29.5	10.7	83.0	42.2	1,257	28.4	3,419	12.0	62	1.8	40.8
1886	37.6	26.8	10.8	81.6	40.1	1,293	28.6	2,761	9.5	70	2.0	41.5
1885	31.1	22.0	9.1	86.5	38.4	1,051	26.5	2,719	9.9	60	2.0	48.1
1884	32.7	24.4	8.3	86.3	41.9	1,212	30.8	2,536	9.9	37	1.2	44.4
1883	36.7	27.4	9.4	99.2	46.8	1,239	32.1	2,926	13.4	42	1.3	52.4
1882	38.7	31.0	7.7	88.4	50.2	1,155	30.4	3,935	19.2	22	0.6	38.2
1881	36.8	29.8	7.0	103.2	52.2	1,211	31.2	4,041	20.1	34	0.9	51.0
1880	38.0	30.9	7.1	107.1	53.3	1,224	31.8	4,053	20.2	47	1.3	53.8
1879	25.5	20.3	5.2	91.8	45.8	1,082	25.9	4,037	19.2	26	0.7	46.0
1878	17.5	14.6	3.0	89.1	43.8	1,026	25.4	3,255	16.5	73	1.9	45.3
1877	19.9	16.4	3.5	77.8	39.0	912	23.6	2,395	13.6	55	1.8	38.8
1876	20.2	16.8	3.4	75.9	37.5	933	25.1	2,164	10.3	62	2.1	38.4

[1] Excludes hides, skins, undressed fur skins, raw wool, and parcel post, which are included in total.
[2] Comparable with later years.
[3] Comparable with earlier years.
[4] Less than one-half the unit indicated.

Series U 156–167. Trade With the United States as Reported by the United Kingdom: 1831 to 1957—Con.

[Value in millions of pounds sterling 1831–1923; of gold dollars 1923–1933; of gold dollars at former parity 1934; of U.S. dollars 1934 to present. Quantity in millions of pounds]

Year	U.K. exports to the U.S. Total value	Exports	Re-exports	Imports from the U.S. Total value	Total selected value	Cotton, raw Quantity	Cotton, raw Value	Wheat Quantity	Wheat Value	Tobacco, unmanufactured Quantity	Tobacco Value	Other value
	156	157	158	159	160	161	162	163	164	165	166	167
1875	25.1	3.2	21.9	69.6	40.6	841	27.1	2,635	12.5	28	1.0	29.0
1874	32.2	4.0	28.2	73.9	45.3	875	29.3	2,586	14.2	54	1.8	28.6
1873	36.7	3.1	33.6	71.5	46.2	833	31.5	2,217	12.9	58	1.8	25.3
1872	45.9	5.2	40.7	54.7	32.3	626	25.9	977	5.7	24	.7	22.4
1871	38.7	4.5	34.2	61.1	42.8	1,089	33.1	1,499	8.1	55	1.6	18.3
1870	31.3	3.0	28.3	49.8	38.9	716	31.3	1,386	6.6	30	1.0	10.9
1869	26.8	2.2	24.6	42.6	31.8	457	23.7	1,476	6.9	37	1.2	10.8
1868	23.8	2.4	21.4	43.1	32.3	574	27.0	662	4.4	29	.9	10.8
1867	24.1	2.3	21.8	41.0	30.1	528	25.7	469	3.3	38	1.1	10.9
1866	31.8	3.3	28.5	46.9	36.4	520	35.0	71	.4	29	1.0	10.5
1865	25.2	4.0	21.2	21.6	14.4	136	12.0	132	.6	47	1.8	7.2
1864	20.2	3.5	16.7	17.9	7.0	14	1.7	884	3.7	40	1.6	10.9
1863	19.7	4.4	15.3	19.6	6.5	6	.6	975	4.4	32	1.5	13.1
1862	19.2	4.8	14.3	27.7	11.7	14	1.2	1,808	9.4	21	1.1	16.0
1861	11.0	2.0	9.1	49.4	34.9	820	26.6	1,217	7.0	34	1.3	14.5
1860	22.9	1.2	21.7	44.7	35.6	1,115	30.1	728	4.3	40	1.2	9.1
1859	24.4	1.9	22.6	34.3	29.6	962	28.3	18	.1	39	1.2	4.7
1858	15.8	1.3	14.5	34.3	27.8	833	24.9	285	1.4	43	1.5	6.5
1857	20.1	1.1	19.0	33.6	24.6	655	21.6	312	1.9	25	1.1	9.0
1856	22.6	.7	21.9	36.0	26.9	780	21.1	614	4.5	30	1.3	9.1
1855	18.0	.7	17.3	25.7	18.7	682	16.9	119	1.0	26	.8	7.0
1854	22.3	.9	21.4	29.8	19.5	722	17.3	200	1.5	24	.7	10.3
1853			23.7			658		342		34		
1852			16.6			766		232		27		
1851			14.4			597		97		24		
1850			14.9			493		48		30		
1849			12.0			635		52		38		
1848			9.6			600		38				
1847			11.0			365		206				
1846			6.8			402		83				
1845			7.1			627		11				
1844			7.9			517		1				
1843			5.0			575						
1842			3.5			414		8				
1841			7.1			358		5				
1840			5.3			488		36		35		
1839			8.8			312		2		34		
1838			7.6			431		(4)		29		
1837			4.7			321				26		
1836			12.4			290				51		
1835			10.6			284				25		
1834			6.8			269				38		
1833			7.6			238				21		
1832			5.5			220		3		20		
1831			9.1			219		21		33		

4 Less than one-half the unit indicated.

BALANCE OF INTERNATIONAL PAYMENTS AND INVESTMENT POSITION (Series U 168–213)

U 168–213. General note.

This section presents statistics on the balance of international payments and the international investment position of the United States. A separate table shows the value of United States direct investments in foreign countries by area and industry groups. The balance of international payments shows the economic transactions between residents of the United States and those of all other areas of the world during a stated time period. The international investment position indicates the value of United States investments abroad and of foreign investments in the United States at specified points of time. The change in the international investment position of the United States results partly from the movement of foreign and United States capital, as presented in the balance of international payments, and partly from other factors, such as changes in the valuation of assets or liabilities, including changes in the market value of securities, defaults, expropriations, writeoffs, and reinvested earnings of subsidiaries operating abroad and of foreign subsidiaries operating in the United States. Direct investments include all foreign enterprises whose voting stock is owned to the extent of at least 25 percent by United States organizations or individuals, or in the management of which Americans have an important voice. In addition, they include unincorporated foreign branches or other direct foreign operations of United States interests, including mining claims, oil concessions, and other property held for business purposes such as real estate.

In all the series of this section, international organizations, such as the International Monetary Fund, the International Bank for Reconstruction and Development, and the United Nations, though located within the United States, are considered extra-territorial. Consequently, transactions between the United States and these organizations are considered international transactions of the United States, while transactions between them and foreign countries do not enter the balance of payments of the United States. United States holdings of their obligations and United States liabilities to them are part of the United States investment position.

U 168–192. Balance of international payments, 1790–1957.

Source: 1790–1918 (except series U 191, 1874–1900), Office of Business Economics, records; series U 191, 1874–1900, Treasury Department, *Annual Report, Director of the Mint*, 1921, p. 130; 1919–1955, Office of Business Economics, *Balance of Payments Statistical Supplement*, 1958, pp. 10–13; 1956–1957, *Survey of Current Business*, June 1959, p. 20.

Basically the figures for 1790–1918 are from publications by private authors; therefore, they are unofficial figures. However, the figures, as shown by these authors, have been rearranged and adjusted, and in some cases supplemented, for this volume by the Office of Business Economics. The reclassified figures fit into the concepts and framework currently used in the official balance of payments statements prepared by OBE.

The original figures are from the following private publications: 1790–1860, Douglass C. North, "The United States Balance of Payments, 1790–1860," *Studies in Income and Wealth*, Princeton University Press, vol. 24 (forthcoming); 1861–1900, Matthew Simon, "The United States Balance of Payments,

1861–1900," *Studies in Income and Wealth*, Princeton University Press, vol. 24 (forthcoming); and 1901–1918 (with the exception of exports and imports of merchandise trade and silver), Paul D. Dickens, "The Transitional Period of American International Financing, 1897–1914," (unpublished doctoral dissertation, George Washington University, 1933) and C. J. Bullock, John H. Williams, and Rufus S. Tucker, "The Balance of Trade of the United States," *Review of Economic Statistics*, July 1919. Data on merchandise trade and silver for 1901–1918 were taken from Department of Commerce, *Monthly Summary of Foreign Commerce*, various issues.

The estimates for 1901–1918 were revised primarily to make them consistent with, and to link them to, data prepared for subsequent years. The revised estimates were published by Raymond W. Goldsmith, in *Study of Savings in the United States*, Princeton University Press, 1956, vol. 1, pp. 1078, 1080, 1081, 1084, and 1086.

The Department of Commerce began its series in 1922, later extending the data backward to cover 1919–1921. Data for annual and quarterly United States international transactions, total and with individual regions of the rest of the world, are available currently in the March, June, September, and December issues of the *Survey of Current Business*.

The balance of payments statement reflects all the exchanges of goods, services, gold, and capital claims between residents of the United States and residents of all other areas of the world. For 1919–1939, residents of the United States comprise residents of continental United States, Alaska, Hawaii, and Puerto Rico. Since 1940, residents of the Virgin Islands, the Panama Canal Zone, and American Samoa are also included. As noted above, international organizations are not regarded as residents of the United States.

Transactions entering into the balance of payments are divided into four categories—goods and services, unilateral transfers, capital movements, and changes in the monetary gold stock. The balance of payments statement is built on a double entry system, whereby, in principle, every transaction is recorded both as a debit and a credit. Debits represent increases in assets or decreases in liabilities, and credits represent decreases in assets or increases in liabilities. Thus, an export of merchandise in return for a check drawn on a foreign account in a bank in this country results in a credit for the export (a reduction in an asset) and a debit for the reduction in foreign-held bank deposits (a reduction in a liability). Unilateral transfers to foreign countries (payments) are debits (as are expense items in accounting), and unilateral transfers from foreign countries (receipts) are credits (as are income items in accounting). While all transactions have a debit and credit phase which are necessarily equal, both sides are not estimated simultaneously nor from the same sources; hence, the possibility of error. The resulting discrepancy, referred to as "errors and omissions," series U 192, is given a plus or minus sign, depending upon which is necessary to make the accounts balance.

The procedure generally followed by North and Simon in their studies was to estimate receipts and payments on account of merchandise trade, transportation, travel, interest, dividends, and remittances. The authors then assumed that the balance indicated net flows of United States and foreign capital. For 1790-1900, series U 185-190 represents this balance which, of course, includes any errors and omissions in the estimates.

Data on exports and imports of merchandise used in the study by North are reported to include gold and silver prior to 1821 (see *Statistical Abstract of the United States*, 1957, p. 890). A separate estimate, however, was made by North for net movements of gold, because he concluded on the basis of his research that specie movements were in fact not included in the merchandise trade figures prior to 1821. (See "The United States Balance of Payments, 1790-1860," pp. 24-25.) This estimate is included in series U 169 and U 176. Although the annual amounts are small, varying from net exports of $1 million to $2.5 million to net imports of $1 million to $4 million, the residual item, or net movement of capital, may be in error by the same amount.

North indicates that the reliability of the data on exports prior to 1820 is doubtful and that data on imports are incomplete. The paucity of information also made the estimates for other transactions for this period considerably less satisfactory than for subsequent years. Consequently, North suggests that 5-year averages may be more reliable than the annual data. Such averages are included in his study.

For the classification and contents of series U 168-192, 1900-1918, see Raymond W. Goldsmith, cited above. Three transactions have been entered which did not appear in this study. See text below for series U 184 and U 185.

For methods of estimating current data, see *Balance of Payments of the United States, 1949-1951, a supplement to the Survey of Current Business*, Office of Business Economics. Continued changes and improvements in the methods of collecting data have been made and the figures have become progressively more reliable over time.

U 169 and U 176, merchandise. The estimates for ship sales for 1790-1900 are included in exports, series U 169. For 1790-1819, the net export or import of specie is included in series U 169 or U 176, respectively. The gross movements of specie were not available. For 1820-1860, exports of specie are included in series U 169 and imports in series U 176. Exports and imports of gold for 1861-1873, of nonmonetary gold for 1874-1900, and of silver for 1861-1900 are included in series U 169 and U 176, respectively.

The data for 1901-1918 include merchandise trade proper, silver and nonmonetary gold. The basic data on merchandise trade for 1919-1957 are the official trade statistics published until 1946 in *Foreign Commerce and Navigation* and since then in the foreign trade compilations of the Bureau of the Census. For 1919-1957, adjustments in both exports and imports have been made to correct for known overvaluation or undervaluation, to exclude noncommercial items, to include an estimate for unrecorded trade, and to adjust for certain differences in territorial coverage, e.g., to exclude the trade with the Panama Canal Zone, beginning with 1940. For World War II and early postwar years, data on Government purchases were substituted for certain import data. For Government-financed transfers of merchandise, the figures based on fiscal records were used instead of the figures appearing in the recorded export statistics. For the years after World War I and World War II, sales and other transfers of surplus property located abroad were added to recorded export statistics. Series U 169 also includes the transfers with or without compensation to allied countries of military equipment, including that purchased abroad under the Mutual Defense Assistance Program. A small amount of services connected with these transfers is also included. Series U 169 and U 176 include nonmonetary

movements of gold. For the treatment of gold, see series U 191 below.

U 170 and U 177, transportation. For 1790-1819, series U 170 represents gross earnings on freight carried in United States ships. Some adjustment was made to eliminate earnings from carrying United States imports.

For 1820-1860, series U 170 includes earnings by United States ships from carrying United States exports and from carrying freight between foreign ports. It also includes American port charges paid by foreign ships. Transportation payments, series U 177, consist of freight payments to foreign ships for carrying United States imports, and expenditures of American ships in foreign ports. Port expenditures and receipts are estimated as a percentage of freight earnings by American and foreign ships, respectively. (Fare payments to American ships by immigrants are included in the estimate for immigrant funds. See discussion of series U 183, private unilateral transactions. For fare payments of tourists, see discussion of travel, series U 171 and U 178.) For 1861-1900, series U 170 includes ocean freight earnings from carrying United States exports and from carrying freight between foreign ports, and port expenditures in the United States of the foreign merchant marine and of passenger steamships. The estimates for the years 1871-1900 also include earnings from carrying overland freight. Payments for transportation, series U 177, includes ocean freight payments on United States imports, and expenditures in foreign ports by the United States merchant marine. Passenger fares are included in the travel account (series U 171 and U 178). The data for 1900-1918 include receipts and payments on account of ocean freight, and port charges. For 1916-1918, payments for charter hire were added.

For 1919-1957, the transportation category includes international freight, fares and shipboard expenses of travelers, revenues and expenditures resulting from the charter of vessels and the rental of freight cars, and the expenses of United States transportation companies abroad and foreign transportation companies in the United States. The data cover air and surface transportation.

U 171 and U 178, travel. For 1790-1819, no estimate was made for international travel expenditures. For 1820-1860, series U 171 includes tourist expenditures in the United States and their fare payments to American ships; series U 178 represents American tourist expenditures abroad. North assumed that American tourists going abroad and, for the most part, foreigners coming to the United States traveled on American ships during this period. The method employed in the source study for estimating tourism precludes the transfer of fare payments to the transportation account. For 1861-1900, series U 171 includes outlays of foreign travelers in the United States. It was assumed that alien travelers came to the United States on foreign lines, and therefore, no estimate was made for receipt of fares. Series U 178 includes payments abroad by American tourists for maintenance and for ocean fares. Simon assumed that the bulk of the travel during 1861-1900 was on foreign ships. The outlays for procurement of sundry items and luxury consumption goods were not included in his estimate for expenditures abroad by American tourists.

The data for 1900-1918 include fares paid to United States ships by foreign tourists and to foreign ships by United States tourists.

For 1919-1957, all expenditures made in the United States by foreign residents, except those of diplomats and other official personnel stationed here, are included in the travel receipts. Expenditures made in foreign countries by United States travelers for food, lodging, amusements, gifts, and other personal purchases constitute travel payments. Expenditures for transportation within or between foreign countries when purchased abroad are in general included as travel expenditures. However, passenger fares for overseas transportation to the ultimate destination (even if the ticket permits stopovers en-route) when paid to foreign carriers by United States residents, and when paid to United States carriers by foreign residents, are included in the transportation account.

U 172, U 173, and U 180, income on investments. For 1790-1900, series U 180 represents net payments of income on investments by the United States. The income was computed by applying an assumed yield rate to the net indebtedness of the United States.

For 1900-1918, separate estimates were made for receipts and payments. Series U 172 for 1915-1918 includes income on private and Government war loans. See Goldsmith, cited above, p. 1078.

For 1919-1957, income includes all interest, dividends, and branch profits effectively paid or credited during the period, after payment of all taxes in the country in which the payer of income resides.

Private income, series U 172, for 1919-1957 includes interest, dividends, and branch profits from direct investments, and interest and dividends received from holdings of foreign bonds by residents in the United States, from stocks issued by foreign corporations which are not United States direct investments, from loans by banks and other financial or commercial organizations, from miscellaneous assets such as commercial real estate, insurance policies, commercial claims of various kinds, trusts and estates, and mortgages. Reinvested earnings, or the parent company's equity in the undistributed earnings on common stock of foreign subsidiary companies, are not included except for 1919-1929. Reinvested earnings are, however, regularly tabulated and used for computing changes in the international investment position of the United States.

Government income, series U 173, for 1919-1957 includes interest received by the U.S. Government on long- and short-term loans and other investments.

Income payments, series U 180, for 1919-1957 include payments of interest, dividends, and branch profits by foreign direct investment companies in the United States, interest and dividend payments to foreign holders of other American bonds and stocks (including U.S. Government securities), and payments of income on various miscellaneous assets such as estates and trusts.

U 174 and U 181, other transactions. Marine insurance and brokers' commissions constitute series U 181 for 1790-1819. No estimate was made for these transactions between 1820 and 1860. For 1861-1900, series U 174 consists of receipts on marine insurance; series U 181 comprises payments for marine insurance and net payments for broker's commissions.

For 1900-1918, no estimates were made.

For 1919-1957, the coverage of miscellaneous service items has expanded and now includes receipts and payments from insurance transactions, communications, management services, motion picture and other royalties; receipts from fees of American engineering, construction and consulting firms from foreign contracts, from foreign governments in the United States, and expenditures of U.S. Government agencies abroad, except expenditures by the Department of Defense. The latter is included in series U 179, while receipts from abroad by the military agencies are included in series U 169.

U 179, military expenditures. This item includes direct outlays by the military agencies in dollars and in foreign currencies, as well as expenditures in the foreign economies by troops, civilian personnel of the military agencies, and post

exchanges. It does not include expenditures of deutsche marks received from the Federal Republic of Germany or of yen received from Japan for the support of Allied and United States Forces stationed in the respective countries. Offshore procurement under military assistance programs and the purchase of goods and services to be transferred to other foreign countries under aid programs are included in the expenditures by military agencies.

U 183-184, unilateral transfers, net. No estimate was made prior to 1820 for series U 183. For 1820-1860, series U 183 represents the excess of funds brought into the United States by immigrants and their fare payments to American shipping companies over the amounts remitted to abroad after their arrival in this country. For 1861-1916, series U 183 consists of the immigrant remittances and funds carried by immigrants into the country (+) and out (−). The estimate for immigrant remittances includes remittances through banks and an estimate for outlays by U.S. residents for prepayment of passage for friends and relatives planning to emigrate to the United States. For 1917 and subsequent years, remittances in cash and kind by religious, educational, and charitable institutions are also included. For series U 184, the entries of $0.6 million for 1794-1796 represent annual payments to the Barbary pirates. The payment of $11.2 million in 1803 was to France for the purchase of Louisiana Territory. The United States acquired sovereignty over this territory in 1803 and issued bonds for the amount of the purchase. These bonds carried an interest rate of 6 percent per year and were redeemed between 1812-1823. The interest during this period amounted to $8.2 million, $5.6 million of which was paid in the first 10 years. (See E. M. Douglas, *Boundaries, Areas, Geographic Centers and Altitudes of the United States and the Several States*, Washington, D.C., 1930.) Presumably the interest is included in the estimate for income payments, series U 180. The entries of $5.5 million for 1836-1838 represent receipts by the U.S. Government from France on behalf of American citizens in satisfaction of claims for indemnities arising from the Napoleonic wars. (See J. T. Adams, ed., *Dictionary of American History*, Scribner's, New York, 1940, Vol. II, p. 348.) Interest of $0.5 million ($0.3, $0.1, and $0.1 million for 1836-1838, respectively) is included. In 1848, at the end of the Mexican War, the United States and Mexico signed the treaty of Guadelupe-Hidalgo which gave to the United States the present States of Arizona, New Mexico, California, Nevada, Utah, and Colorado west of the Rockies. The payment by the United States of $15 million for this territory, plus interest of $1.4 million, is represented by the entries for 1849-1852. These entries were referred to in the study, "United States Balance of Payments, 1790-1860," as indemnity payments and entered in the capital account. The entries for 1854-1856, aggregating $10 million, represent the Gadsden purchase. Russia, in March 1867, agreed to sell Alaska to the United States for $7.2 million in gold. The United States took possession in fiscal year 1868, but payment was not made until fiscal year 1869. During the Civil War, Great Britain had sold to the Confederate States ships which were used as privateers to sink the Union ships. An international tribunal in 1873 held Great Britain liable to the extent of $15.5 million. Payment was made to the United States in 1873, as indemnity on behalf of its citizens. The treaty of peace with Spain in 1898, as a result of which the Philippines, Guam, and Puerto Rico were ceded to the United States, stipulated a payment to Spain of $20 million.

The figures for series U 184 include two transactions which are not included in Goldsmith's *Study of Saving . . .*, mentioned earlier for the 1900-1918 period. In 1904, the U.S.

Government paid $10 million to the Republic of Panama for lease of the Panama Canal, and in 1917, the United States bought the Virgin Islands from Denmark for $25 million. These transactions appear in series U 184.

For 1919–1957, series U 184 consists of Government transfers of goods, services, or cash, in both dollars and foreign currencies, for which payment by the foreign country has not been made, is not expected, or has not been specified, less reverse lend-lease, counterpart funds on certain foreign-aid programs, and other receipts. Series U 184 also includes Government payments of pensions, receipts or payments for idemnities, intangible rights, or other considerations.

U 185–190, United States capital, net, and foreign capital, net. For 1790–1900, the data for series U 185 and U 190 represent the net flow of United States and foreign capital, and were estimated as residuals, to balance the other items in the balance of payments. Consequently, they reflect errors and omissions in the estimates of the other items. For some of these years, particularly 1861–1900, the data shown here differ from those in the source studies because of adjustments in some of the other series. For 1900–1918, see Goldsmith, cited above, pp. 1080–1081.

In 1904, the figure for series U 185 includes the payment by the U.S. Government of $40 million for the original Panama Canal Company. This transaction was not included in Goldsmith's *Study of Saving*.

For 1919–1957, the data for series U 185–188 represent changes in assets or in investments of the United States abroad. The long-term transactions represent shifts in capital claims of indefinite maturity or of a stated original maturity of more than one year from the date of issuance. Short-term transactions represent changes in claims on foreigners with a maturity of one year or less. For 1919–1957, series U 185 (long-term) includes disbursements of foreign loans, net of repayments, by all U.S. Government agencies, whether made in dollars or in foreign currencies. Also included are movements of capital related to the operation by the U.S. Government of productive facilities abroad, and United States capital contributions to international organizations such as the International Monetary Fund, the International Bank for Reconstruction and Development, and the International Finance Corporation. Loan operations between these organizations and foreign countries are not included since such organizations are regarded as foreign entities in the United States balance of payments. Loans made by private banks and guaranteed by the Export-Import Bank are included in series U 187. Real property purchased by the Government for administrative purposes is included in series U 181, other transactions, while all expenditures of religious, educational, and charitable institutions are included in series U 183, unilateral transfers, even if they involve the purchase of fixed assets. For 1919–1957, series U 185 (short-term) includes changes in the U.S. Government short-term claims arising from holdings of foreign currencies (received as a counterpart to foreign grants or through sales of agricultural and other surplus products), deposits abroad, and various advances.

For 1919–1957, the shifts in capital claims in series U 186 and U 187 refer not only to securities (stocks, bonds, mortgages, etc.) but also to real property (farms, branch factories, and real estate). Series U 186 consists of net purchases of stocks in, and of changes in net claims by United States parent companies against foreign incorporated companies in the management of which United States companies have an important voice, and net changes in the equity in foreign branches of United States companies. Series U 187, other private long-term capital movements, consists of United States purchases of newly issued foreign securities, amortizations of foreign bonds, net transactions in outstanding foreign securities, and net changes in long-term claims reported by United States banks (including loans made by private banks and guaranteed by the Export-Import Bank) and other commercial enterprises.

Series U 188 includes changes in bank deposits, brokerage and commercial balances, and uncollected bills.

For 1919–1957, the data for series U 189–190 represent changes in liabilities of the United States to residents of foreign countries, or changes in assets held in the United States by residents of foreign countries. Series U 189 represents shifts in foreign claims on the United States with an original maturity of more than one year, including changes in the investments of foreign corporations in their branches and subsidiaries in the United States, and transactions by foreigners in the United States public debt obligations. Series U 190 represents shifts in the liabilities of the U.S. Government and of private individuals and institutions with an original maturity of one year or less. Foreign short-term claims on the U.S. Government include deposits with the Treasury and other Government agencies and changes in foreign holdings of U.S. Government short-term obligations. Foreign short-term claims on private Americans include foreign deposits in United States banks, changes in holdings of privately issued short-term securities, and other commercial liabilities. The data also include an estimate of movements of United States currency and coins.

U 191, gold. For 1874–1957, the gold entry is the net change in the monetary gold stock, including Stabilization Fund holdings. Thus, the gold stock is considered a special kind of international asset, all increases in which are debited and decreases credited in the balance of payments statement. Gold may enter the balance of payments account either in nonmonetary or in monetary form. If domestic consumption exceeds production, the excess is treated as an import or debit (−) in the merchandise account. It may be considered to be that part of the imported gold used as merchandise and not added to the monetary gold stock, or the part sold to the public from the monetary gold stock. Net domestic consumption of gold, which reduces the monetary gold stock of the United States, is treated as being comparable in its balance-of-payments effect to a merchandise import paid for by a net export of monetary gold to foreign countries. The sum of the merchandise entry and the monetary gold entry, it should be noted, still equals net international gold transactions.

U 192, errors and omissions. As indicated in the text for series U 168–192, this is the residual item which has been given the sign (+ or −) necessary to make the statement balance. It compensates for missing data, possible errors in the estimates, as well as for seasonal and other leads and lags in the reporting of the debit and credit phases of transactions which are compensating over a period of time.

U 193–206. International investment position of the United States, 1843–1957.

Source: 1843–1914, Cleona Lewis, *America's Stake in International Investments*, The Brookings Institution, Washington, D.C., 1938; 1919–1945, Office of Business Economics, various publications; 1946–1955, *Balance of Payments Statistical Supplement*, Washington, D.C.; 1956–1957, *Survey of Current Business*, September 1958.

The estimates for 1919–1945 are based on the following publications: (1) *The United States in the World Economy*, Economic Series No. 23, Washington, D.C., 1943, p. 123; (2) *The Balance of International Payments of the United States in 1931*,

Trade Information Bulletin No. 803, Washington, D.C., 1932, pp. 44, 48, and 62; (3) *Foreign Investments in the United States*, Washington, D.C., 1937, p. 5; (4) Cleona Lewis, *America's Stake in International Investments* (see source for 1843–1914); (5) *International Transactions of the United States During the War 1940-45* (as revised), Economic Series No. 65, 1948, p. 110.

In *America's Stake in International Investments*, direct investments are based on book value wherever possible; portfolio investments are calculated at par value for bonds and preferred stocks, and at market value for common stocks. Similar practices were followed in the estimates of the Department of Commerce for 1930, 1931, and 1935; miscellaneous portfolio investments for the same years were calculated at market values wherever possible. For 1940, 1945, and 1946–1957, the values of bonds and preferred stocks as well as of common stocks were calculated at market prices.

The estimates for these series prior to 1919 were prepared by compilers who used different valuation methods and whose data varied in completeness. While the estimates are therefore not homogeneous, they do present rough indications of the magnitudes involved.

U 207. International investment position of the United States (net liabilities), 1789–1900.

Source: 1789–1860, Douglass C. North, "The United States Balance of Payments, 1789–1860," cited in text for series U 168–192; and 1861–1900, Matthew Simon, "The United States Balance of Payments, 1861–1900," also cited in text for series U 168–192.

In the source studies, a net liability of $60 million was estimated for 1789. For the following years, the changes were computed by adding the annual net international flow of capital which is the balancing item, series 185–190, for exports and imports of goods, services, and unilateral transactions. For certain years, adjustments were made for defaults. Differences between the accumulating "net indebtedness" in the source studies and the data in series U 207 are due to adjustments incorporated in series U 168–192 as explained in the text for those series.

U 208–213. Value of direct investment in foreign countries, by area and industry groups, 1929–1957.

Source: See source for series U 193–206.

See also general note, U 168–213, and text for series U 186.

Series U 168–192. Balance of International Payments: 1790 to 1957

[In millions of dollars. For fiscal years, 1790–1900; thereafter, calendar years]

Year	Exports of goods and services							Imports of goods and services						
	Total	Merchandise, adjusted [1]	Transportation	Travel	Income on investments Private [2]	Income on investments Government	Other transactions [3]	Total	Merchandise	Transportation	Travel	Military expenditures	Income on investments [4]	Other transactions [3]
	168	169	170	171	172	173	174	175	176	177	178	179	180	181
1957	29,168	22,197	1,999	785	2,676	205	1,306	20,923	13,291	1,569	1,372	3,165	653	873
1956	26,284	20,116	1,642	705	2,417	194	1,210	19,829	12,804	1,408	1,275	2,955	580	807
1955	22,328	16,809	1,420	654	2,170	274	1,001	17,937	11,527	1,204	1,153	2,823	502	728
1954	21,110	16,139	1,171	595	1,955	272	978	16,088	10,354	1,026	1,009	2,603	419	677
1953	21,335	16,727	1,198	574	1,658	252	926	16,644	10,990	1,081	929	2,535	450	659
1952	20,708	15,922	1,488	550	1,624	204	920	15,760	10,838	1,115	840	1,957	390	620
1951	20,333	15,593	1,556	473	1,684	198	829	15,142	11,202	974	757	1,270	355	584
1950	14,427	10,643	1,033	419	1,484	109	739	12,098	9,108	818	754	576	345	497
1949	16,061	12,359	1,238	392	1,297	98	677	9,702	6,879	700	700	621	333	469
1948	17,089	13,493	1,317	334	1,238	102	605	10,349	7,563	646	631	799	280	430
1947	19,780	16,058	1,738	364	1,036	66	518	8,208	5,979	583	573	455	245	373
1946	14,804	11,776	1,383	271	751	21	602	6,991	5,073	459	462	493	212	292
1945	16,273	12,473	1,308	162	572	17	1,741	10,232	5,245	420	309	2,434	231	1,593
1944	21,438	16,969	1,306	117	556	17	2,473	8,986	5,043	399	225	1,982	161	1,176
1943	19,134	15,115	1,110	84	497	12	2,316	8,096	4,599	343	173	1,763	155	1,063
1942	11,769	9,187	689	82	496	18	1,297	5,356	3,499	263	155	953	158	328
1941	6,896	5,343	562	70	535	9	377	4,486	3,416	343	212	162	187	166
1940	5,355	4,124	402	95	561	3	170	3,636	2,698	334	190	61	210	143
1939	4,432	3,347	303	135	539	2	106	3,366	2,409	367	290	46	230	24
1938	4,336	3,243	267	130	583	2	111	3,045	2,173	303	303	41	200	25
1937	4,553	3,451	236	135	576	1	154	4,256	3,181	366	348	41	295	25
1936	3,539	2,590	158	117	567	2	105	3,424	2,546	247	297	38	270	26
1935	3,265	2,404	139	101	521	---------	100	3,137	2,462	206	245	41	155	28
1934	2,975	2,238	133	81	437	---------	86	2,374	1,763	196	218	34	135	28
1933	2,402	1,736	108	66	417	20	55	2,044	1,510	154	199	41	115	25
1932	2,474	1,667	171	65	460	67	44	2,067	1,343	255	259	47	135	28
1931	3,641	2,494	247	94	674	92	40	3,125	2,120	366	341	48	220	30
1930	5,448	3,929	325	129	876	164	25	4,416	3,104	477	463	49	295	28
1929	7,034	5,347	390	139	982	157	19	5,886	4,463	509	483	50	330	51
1928	6,842	5,249	372	121	922	158	20	5,465	4,159	460	448	44	275	79
1927	6,456	4,982	360	114	821	160	19	5,383	4,240	417	400	38	240	48
1926	6,381	4,922	370	110	793	160	26	5,555	4,500	415	372	43	200	25
1925	6,348	5,011	318	83	752	160	24	5,261	4,291	391	347	39	170	23
1924	5,911	4,741	315	77	602	160	16	4,560	3,684	361	303	36	140	36
1923	5,494	4,266	302	71	676	164	15	4,652	3,866	332	260	33	130	31
1922	4,954	3,929	286	61	544	126	8	3,957	3,184	341	243	42	105	42
1921	5,505	4,586	394	76	405	40	4	3,383	2,572	334	200	65	105	107
1920	10,264	8,481	1,119	67	588	8	1	6,741	5,384	848	190	123	120	76
1919	10,776	8,891	1,109	56	544	175	1	5,908	3,995	818	123	757	130	85
1918	7,272	6,432	346	44	450	---------	---------	4,814	3,103	510	83	1,018	100	---------
1917	7,072	6,398	290	34	350	---------	---------	3,597	3,006	391	100	---------	100	---------
1916	6,029	5,560	197	22	250	---------	---------	2,927	2,423	263	123	---------	118	---------
1915	3,948	3,686	38	24	200	---------	---------	2,200	1,813	91	160	---------	136	---------
1914	2,445	2,230	31	39	145	---------	---------	2,389	1,815	102	272	---------	200	---------
1913	2,816	2,600	29	50	137	---------	---------	2,442	1,829	92	311	---------	210	---------
1912	2,738	2,532	34	49	123	---------	---------	2,481	1,866	112	306	---------	197	---------
1911	2,405	2,228	22	41	114	---------	---------	2,131	1,576	76	289	---------	190	---------
1910	2,160	1,995	19	38	108	---------	---------	2,114	1,609	68	265	---------	172	---------
1909	2,013	1,857	15	41	100	---------	---------	1,987	1,522	50	251	---------	164	---------
1908	2,022	1,880	14	39	89	---------	---------	1,595	1,159	44	232	---------	160	---------
1907	2,192	2,051	19	35	87	---------	---------	1,896	1,469	60	214	---------	153	---------
1906	2,052	1,921	18	27	86	---------	---------	1,756	1,365	52	191	---------	148	---------
1905	1,859	1,751	14	18	76	---------	---------	1,561	1,215	41	160	---------	145	---------
1904	1,657	1,563	11	13	70	---------	---------	1,378	1,062	35	140	---------	141	---------
1903	1,663	1,575	12	9	67	---------	---------	1,323	1,019	38	127	---------	139	---------
1902	1,550	1,473	11	9	57	---------	---------	1,292	996	35	124	---------	137	---------
1901	1,651	1,585	11	8	47	---------	---------	1,213	912	36	130	---------	135	---------
1900 [5]	1,686	1,623	17	8	38		1	1,179	869	53	120		137	13
1900 [6]	1,578	1,534	23	19	---------	---------	1	1,149	894	30	98	---------	114	11
1899	1,400	1,363	19	17	---------	---------	1	973	735	26	77	---------	124	10
1898	1,340	1,304	19	16	---------	---------	1	896	653	25	76	---------	133	12
1897	1,173	1,136	21	15	---------	---------	1	1,041	803	30	69	---------	127	12
1896	1,082	1,048	18	15	---------	---------	1	1,048	816	26	71	---------	122	13
1895	888	855	18	14	---------	---------	1	1,015	774	28	75	---------	126	12
1894	981	943	17	20	---------	---------	1	883	692	22	45	---------	113	10
1893	1,021	974	20	26	---------	---------	1	1,140	898	26	62	---------	139	15
1892	1,122	1,084	23	14	---------	---------	1	1,142	888	28	69	---------	143	14
1891	1,035	997	24	13	---------	---------	1	1,124	875	31	69	---------	134	15
1890	960	921	23	15	---------	---------	1	1,109	866	36	68	---------	125	15
1889	880	841	23	14	---------	---------	1	1,046	817	35	62	---------	118	14
1888	786	750	22	14	---------	---------	1	1,013	791	34	67	---------	107	14
1887	810	774	21	14	---------	---------	1	967	759	31	65	---------	98	13
1886	817	781	20	15	---------	---------	1	894	698	30	60	---------	93	13
1885	830	792	20	17	---------	---------	2	818	635	28	58	---------	86	12
1884	862	822	23	15	---------	---------	2	921	730	31	56	---------	90	14
1883	915	875	25	13	---------	---------	2	927	748	31	45	---------	89	14
1882	859	824	26	7	---------	---------	2	915	747	30	39	---------	84	14
1881	971	936	26	6	---------	---------	2	834	672	27	34	---------	88	12

See footnotes at end of table.

Series U 168–192. Balance of International Payments: 1790 to 1957—Con.

[In millions of dollars]

Year	Exports of goods and services					Imports of goods and services					
	Total	Merchandise, adjusted	Transportation	Travel	Other transactions	Total	Merchandise	Transportation	Travel	Income on investments[4]	Other transactions
	168	169	170	171	174	175	176	177	178	180	181
1880	963	929	25	7	2	848	694	28	35	79	13
1879	813	784	22	5	2	612	469	20	36	78	8
1878	813	780	26	4	3	595	462	20	29	76	8
1877	716	687	24	3	3	614	475	21	23	86	9
1876	654	620	26	4	4	634	478	23	29	96	9
1875	623	590	26	3	3	722	556	26	30	99	11
1874	707	669	31	3	4	767	593	31	30	102	12
1873	675	631	39	2	4	856	683	36	25	99	13
1872	578	539	31	4	4	824	662	30	32	86	13
1871	603	564	29	6	4	704	557	24	28	84	11
1870	507	473	27	3	4	608	475	22	22	80	9
1869	395	365	24	2	3	567	450	23	17	69	9
1868	428	395	28	2	4	505	382	22	26	67	8
1867	401	369	27	1	4	550	430	29	25	58	9
1866	481	446	29	1	5	572	459	27	25	51	10
1865	279	261	16	---------	2	343	256	15	22	45	5
1864	304	288	14	---------	2	418	339	21	17	34	7
1863	313	287	19	1	7	328	260	13	15	31	5
1862	272	248	20	1	4	272	211	11	14	30	5
1861	303	261	36	1	5	406	344	17	15	24	6
1860	438	401	35	2	---------	438	376	17	20	25	---------
1859	384	358	25	1	---------	416	352	14	26	23	---------
1858	350	326	23	2	---------	334	293	8	17	15	---------
1857	385	366	18	2	---------	416	375	10	16	15	---------
1856	359	329	27	2	---------	378	327	9	19	23	---------
1855	303	279	22	2	---------	325	272	8	23	22	---------
1854	314	281	28	4	---------	377	316	15	25	20	---------
1853	258	231	23	4	---------	333	279	13	25	16	---------
1852	232	211	17	4	---------	265	221	9	20	15	---------
1851	251	219	28	4	---------	271	225	10	23	13	---------
1850	166	153	9	4	---------	210	185	5	8	12	---------
1849	166	146	16	3	---------	173	154	6	2	12	---------
1848	174	155	17	2	---------	188	161	6	2	12	7 8
1847	181	160	19	2	---------	178	151	7	4	9	7 8
1846	133	114	17	2	---------	143	126	5	3	9	---------
1845	135	115	19	1	---------	138	120	5	4	9	---------
1844	126	112	14	1	---------	126	111	4	5	7	---------
1843	101	85	15	1	---------	81	66	4	3	7	---------
1842	119	105	13	1	---------	119	102	4	5	8	---------
1841	136	122	13	1	---------	148	130	4	6	8	---------
1840	160	133	27	1	---------	134	109	7	6	12	---------
1839	135	121	12	1	---------	188	165	4	5	14	---------
1838	128	109	19	1	---------	135	116	5	5	10	---------
1837	133	118	13	2	---------	161	144	4	4	9	---------
1836	141	129	11	2	---------	209	194	4	4	9	---------
1835	132	122	9	1	---------	166	153	3	3	7	---------
1834	116	105	10	1	---------	140	129	3	2	6	---------
1833	101	90	9	1	---------	119	110	3	1	5	---------
1832	101	88	12	1	---------	112	103	4	1	5	---------
1831	97	82	14	1	---------	112	103	4	1	4	---------
1830	86	74	11	1		79	71	3	1	5	---------
1829	83	73	10			83	75	3	2	5	---------
1828	84	73	10	---------	1	97	89	3	2	4	---------
1827	98	83	14			90	80	3	2	5	---------
1826	91	78	13			95	85	3	2	5	---------
1825	112	100	12			106	96	3	2	5	---------
1824	90	77	14			90	81	3	1	5	---------
1823	89	75	14			87	78	3	1	5	---------
1822	83	73	10			92	83	3	1	5	---------
1821	76	66	11			72	63	3	1	5	---------
1820	84	70	14			84	75	3	2	5	---------

Year	Exports of goods and services			Imports of goods and services					Year	Exports of goods and services			Imports of goods and services				
	Total	Merchandise, adjusted	Transportation	Total	Merchandise	Transportation	Income on investments[4]	Other transactions		Total	Merchandise, adjusted	Transportation	Total	Merchandise	Transportation	Income on investments[4]	Other transactions
	168	169	170	175	176	177	180	181		168	169	170	175	176	177	180	181
1819	91	72	19	105	94	4	6	2	1804	114	81	34	102	87	7	5	4
1818	116	95	20	141	128	4	6	3	1803	88	59	30	80	67	6	4	3
1817	103	89	14	113	102	4	7	2	1802	98	75	23	91	78	5	5	3
1816	105	84	21	163	151	4	5	3	1801	134	95	39	132	114	8	5	5
1815	81	55	26	96	85	5	4	2	1800	107	74	33	108	93	7	5	4
1814	11	8	3	20	16	1	3	---------	1799	111	80	30	96	81	6	6	3
1813	45	32	13	30	22	3	4	3	1798	83	62	21	84	72	4	6	3
1812	75	39	36	96	83	7	3	2	1797	79	57	21	90	77	4	5	3
1811	114	63	51	78	61	10	5	---------	1796	94	67	27	97	84	5	5	3
1810	117	68	49	110	91	10	6	4	1795	72	48	24	85	73	5	4	3
1809	88	55	33	76	61	7	6	2	1794	55	36	19	46	36	4	5	1
1808	55	26	29	71	58	6	5	2	1793	43	28	15	42	33	3	5	1
1807	162	109	53	167	146	11	5	2	1792	32	23	9	40	33	2	4	1
1806	148	105	43	155	137	9	4	6	1791	29	21	8	37	31	2	4	1
1805	134	97	37	144	128	7	4	5	1790	29	21	7	30	24	2	4	1

See footnotes at end of table.

FOREIGN TRADE AND OTHER INTERNATIONAL TRANSACTIONS

Series U 168–192. Balance of International Payments: 1790 to 1957—Con.

[In millions of dollars]

Year	Balance on goods and services	Unilateral transfers, net [to foreign countries (-)]		U. S. capital, net [outflow of funds (-)]				Foreign capital, net [outflow of funds (-)]		Changes in monetary gold stock [increase(−)]	Errors and omissions [8]
		Private	Government [1]	Government, long- and short-term	Private			Long-term	Short-term		
					Direct [2]	Other long-term	Short-term				
	182	183	184	185	186	187	188	189	190	191	192
1957	8,245	−543	−4,210	−958	−2,058	−859	−258	309	382	−798	+748
1956	6,455	−530	−4,447	−629	−1,859	−603	−528	395	1,409	−306	+643
1955	4,391	−444	−4,367	−310	−779	−241	−191	875	579	41	+446
1954	5,022	−486	−4,937	93	−664	−320	−635	252	1,210	298	+167
1953	4,691	−476	−6,232	−218	−721	185	167	124	1,023	1,161	+296
1952	4,948	−417	−4,691	−420	−850	−214	−94	443	1,169	−379	+505
1951	5,191	−386	−4,576	−156	−528	−437	−103	−477	1,055	−53	+470
1950	2,329	−444	−4,089	−156	−621	−495	−149	994	918	1,743	−30
1949	6,359	−521	−5,316	−652	−660	−80	187	119	−47	−164	+775
1948	6,740	−683	−4,128	−1,024	−721	−69	−116	−172	524	−1,530	+1,179
1947	11,572	−669	−1,986	−6,969	−749	−49	−189	−98	363	−2,162	+936
1946	7,813	−650	−2,318	−3,024	−230	127	−310	−347	−633	−623	+195
1945	6,041	−473	−6,640	−1,019	−100	−354	−96	−104	2,189	548	+8
1944	12,452	−357	−13,785	−231	71	−62	−85	175	509	1,350	−37
1943	11,038	−249	−12,658	−109	98	−58	−12	−63	1,222	757	+34
1942	6,413	−123	−6,213	−221	19	−84	96	−84	182	23	−8
1941	2,410	−179	−957	−391	47	19	21	−327	−400	−719	+476
1940	1,719	−178	−32	−51	32	36	177	−90	1,353	−4,243	+1,277
1939	1,066	−151	−27	−14	9	104	226	−86	1,259	−3,174	+788
1938	1,291	−153	−29	−9	16	24	36	57	317	−1,799	+249
1937	297	−175	−60	2	35	241	43	245	311	−1,364	+425
1936	115	−176	−32	3	−12	189	52	600	376	−1,272	+157
1935	128	−162	−20	1	34	82	427	320	648	−1,822	+364
1934	601	−162	−10	−5	−17	202	104	[9]15	126	−1,266	+412
1933	358	−191	−17	−7	32	−80	42	[9]125	−454	131	+61
1932	407	−217	−21	26	−16	267	227	−26	−673	−53	+79
1931	516	−279	−40	14	−222	350	628	66	−1,265	133	+99
1930	1,032	−306	−36	77	−294	−70	−191	66	−288	−310	+320
1929	1,148	−343	−34	38	−602	−34	−200	358	196	−143	−384
1928	1,377	−346	−19	49	−558	−752	−231	463	−117	238	−104
1927	1,073	−355	−2	46	−351	−636	−349	−50	934	113	−423
1926	826	−361	−20	30	−351	−470	−36	95	455	−93	−75
1925	1,087	−373	−30	27	−268	−603	−46	[10]301	−60	100	−135
1924	1,351	−339	−25	28	−182	−703	−109	[10]185	228	−256	−178
1923	842	−328	−37	91	−148	−235	−82	[10]338	49	−315	−175
1922	997	−314	−38	31	−153	−669	----------	7	----------	−269	+408
1921	2,122	−450	−59	30	−111	−477	----------	−4	----------	−735	−316
1920	3,523	−634	−45	−175	−154	−400	----------	−278	----------	68	−1,905
1919	4,868	−832	−212	−2,328	−94	−75	----------	−215	----------	166	−1,278
1918	2,458	−268	----------	−4,028	----------	−396	----------	----------	422	−5	1,817
1917	3,475	−180	−25	−3,656	----------	−594	----------	−36	400	−312	+928
1916	3,102	−150	----------	----------	----------	−1,064	----------	−391	−900	−531	−66
1915	1,748	−150	----------	----------	----------	−790	----------	−789	450	−499	+30
1914	56	−170	----------	----------	−76	−14	----------	−432	450	100	+86
1913	374	−207	----------	----------	−138	−27	----------	252	----------	−25	−229
1912	257	−212	----------	----------	−139	−70	----------	232	----------	−81	+13
1911	274	−224	----------	----------	−95	−28	----------	171	----------	−90	−8
1910	46	−204	----------	----------	−124	34	----------	345	----------	−71	−26
1909	26	−187	----------	----------	−88	−24	----------	171	----------	18	+84
1908	427	−192	----------	----------	−48	−87	----------	89	----------	−44	−145
1907	296	−177	----------	----------	−89	24	----------	136	----------	−154	−36
1906	296	−147	----------	----------	−92	46	----------	114	----------	−171	−46
1905	298	−133	----------	----------	−46	−93	----------	56	----------	−71	−11
1904	279	−127	−10	−40	−80	11	----------	59	----------	−25	−67
1903	340	−115	----------	----------	−81	40	----------	20	----------	−71	−133
1902	258	−105	----------	----------	−65	−40	----------	−30	----------	−71	+53
1901	438	−104	----------	----------	−89	−123	----------	−33	----------	−61	−28
1900 [5]	507	−95	----------	----------	−56	−87	----------	−75	----------	−91	−103
1900 [6]	429	−54	----------			−296				−78	
1899	427	−48	−20			−229				−130	
1898	444	−44	----------			−279				−121	
1897	132	−41	----------			−23				−68	
1896	34	−49	----------			40				−25	
1895	−127	−55	----------			137				44	
1894	98	−54	----------			−66				22	
1893	−119	−44	----------			146				17	
1892	−20	−54	----------			41				33	
1891	−90	−50	----------			136				4	[11]
1890	−150	−45	----------			194				1	
1889	−166	−44	----------			202				8	
1888	−226	−30	----------			287				−30	
1887	−157	−28	----------			231				−46	
1886	−77	−28	----------			137				−32	
1885	12	−27	----------			34				−19	
1884	−59	−24	----------			105				−23	
1883	−12	−22	----------			51				−17	
1882	−55	−13	----------			110				−42	
1881	137	−5	----------			−41				−91	

See footnotes at end of table.

Series U 168–192. Balance of International Payments: 1790 to 1957—Con.

[In millions of dollars]

Year	Balance on goods and services (182)	Unilateral transfers, net [to foreign countries (−)] Private (183)	Government (184)	U.S. and foreign capital, net [outflow of funds (−)] (185–190)	Changes in monetary gold stock [increase (−)] (191)
1880	114	−4	--------	30	−140
1879	202	−8	--------	−160	−34
1878	218	−11	--------	−162	−44
1877	102	−13	--------	−57	−33
1876	20	−11	--------	2	−10
1875	−99	−14	--------	87	27
1874	−61	−11	--------	82	−11
1873	−181	−2	16	167	--------
1872	−246	4	--------	242	--------
1871	−101	--------	--------	101	--------
1870	−101	1	--------	100	--------
1869	−172	4	−7	176	--------
1868	−77	4	--------	73	--------
1867	−149	4	--------	145	--------
1866	−91	−4	--------	95	--------
1865	−64	5	--------	59	--------
1864	−114	3	--------	111	--------
1863	−15	3	--------	13	--------
1862	--------	--------	--------	--------	--------
1861	−103	−1	--------	103	--------
1860	−1	8	--------	−7	--------
1859	−32	6	--------	26	--------
1858	17	7	--------	−23	--------
1857	−30	14	--------	17	--------
1856	−20	9	−1	12	--------
1855	−22	10	−2	15	--------
1854	−63	28	−7	42	--------
1853	−75	19	--------	56	--------
1852	−33	20	−3	16	--------
1851	−20	18	−3	6	--------

Year	Balance on goods and services (182)	Unilateral transfers, net [to foreign countries (−)] Private (183)	Government[1] (184)	U.S. and foreign capital, net [outflow of funds (−)] (185–190)
1850	−44	20	−4	29
1849	−8	16	−6	−3
1848	−15	13	--------	2
1847	3	16	--------	−19
1846	−10	11	--------	−1
1845	−2	6	--------	−4
1844	--------	4	--------	−4
1843	20	2	--------	−22
1842	1	6	--------	−6
1841	−12	4	--------	8
1840	26	4	--------	−31
1839	−53	4	--------	49
1838	−7	2	1	3
1837	−28	6	1	22
1836	−68	6	4	59
1835	−33	3	--------	30
1834	−24	6	--------	19
1833	−19	5	--------	14
1832	−12	5	--------	7
1831	−15	1	--------	14
1830	6	2	--------	−8
1829	--------	2	--------	−2
1828	−14	2	--------	11
1827	8	2	--------	−10
1826	−4	1	--------	3
1825	6	1	--------	−7
1824	--------	1	--------	−1
1823	2	--------	--------	−2
1822	−9	--------	--------	8
1821	4	1	--------	−5
1820	1	1	--------	−1

Year	Balance on goods and services (182)	Unilateral transfers, net [to foreign countries (−)], government (184)	U.S. and foreign capital, net [outflow of funds (−)] (185–190)
1819	−15	--------	15
1818	−25	--------	25
1817	−11	--------	11
1816	−58	--------	58
1815	−15	--------	15
1814	−9	--------	9
1813	15	--------	−15
1812	−21	--------	21
1811	35	--------	−35
1810	7	--------	−7
1809	12	--------	−12
1808	−17	--------	17
1807	−5	--------	5
1806	−7	--------	7
1805	−10	--------	10
1804	12	--------	−12
1803	8	−11	3
1802	7	--------	−7
1801	2	--------	−2
1800	−2	--------	2
1799	15	--------	−15
1798	−2	--------	2
1797	−11	--------	11
1796	−3	−1	4
1795	−12	−1	13
1794	10	−1	−9
1793	2	--------	−2
1792	−8	--------	8
1791	−8	--------	8
1790	−1	--------	1

[1] Series U 169 and U 184 include transfer of military supplies and services under grants. For 1946–1957, these transfers amounted in millions of dollars to: $69 in 1946, $43 in 1947, $300 in 1948, $210 in 1949, $526 in 1950, $1,470 in 1951, $2,603 in 1952, $4,254 in 1953, $3,161 in 1954, $2,325 in 1955. $2,579 in 1956, $2,435 in 1957. Series U 169 also includes receipts from military cash and credit transactions, the major portion of which is merchandise.
[2] Includes reinvested earnings of subsidiaries for 1919–1929.
[3] Includes, for 1919–1939, certain adjustments to merchandise transactions.
[4] Net for 1790–1900.
[5] Comparable with later years.
[6] Comparable with earlier years.
[7] Military expenditures in Mexico.
[8] Included with series U 18.–19 prior to 1900.
[9] 1933 includes a net outflow of $40 million and 1934 a net inflow of $30 million of funds through arbitrage operation in securities which cannot be divided between domestic and foreign securities.
[10] Includes transactions in securities in 1923–1925 which cannot be separated between domestic and foreign securities.
[11] Included in figures for series U 185–190.

Series U 193–206. International Investment Position of the United States: 1843 to 1957

[In billions of dollars]

Year	U.S. investments abroad Total (193)	Private Total private (194)	Long-term Total long-term (195)	Direct (196)	Other (197)	Short-term (198)	U.S. Government (199)	Foreign investments in the U.S. Total (200)	Long-term Total long-term (201)	Direct (202)	Other (203)	Short-term Total short-term (204)	Private obligations (205)	U.S. Govt. obligations[1] (206)
1957 (prel.)	54.2	36.8	33.6	25.3	8.3	3.2	17.4	31.4	12.8	4.8	8.1	18.5	9.9	8.6
1956	49.5	33.0	30.1	22.2	7.9	2.9	16.5	31.6	13.4	4.5	8.8	18.3	9.5	8.8
1955	44.9	29.1	26.7	19.3	7.4	2.4	15.9	29.6	12.6	4.3	8.3	17.0	8.5	8.5
1954	42.2	26.6	24.4	17.6	6.7	2.2	15.6	26.8	10.9	4.0	7.0	15.9	8.5	7.3
1953	39.5	23.8	22.2	16.3	5.9	1.6	15.7	23.6	9.2	3.8	5.4	14.5	7.6	6.8
1952	37.3	22.8	21.1	14.8	6.3	1.7	14.4	22.5	8.9	3.5	5.4	13.6	7.3	6.3
1951	35.0	20.9	19.3	13.1	6.2	1.7	14.0	20.5	8.5	3.3	5.1	12.1	6.7	5.4
1950	32.8	19.0	17.5	11.8	5.7	1.5	13.8	19.5	7.7	3.1	4.6	11.7	6.5	5.2
1949	30.7	16.9	15.6	10.7	4.9	1.3	13.7	16.9	7.1	2.9	4.2	9.8	5.9	3.8
1948	29.4	16.3	14.7	9.6	5.1	1.6	13.1	16.5	6.8	2.8	4.0	9.8	5.8	4.0
1947	27.0	14.9	13.4	8.4	5.1	1.5	12.1	16.1	6.8	2.6	4.2	9.3	5.3	4.0
1946	18.7	13.5	12.3	7.2[2]	5.0	1.3	5.2	15.9	7.0	2.5	4.5	8.9	5.3	3.6
1945	16.8	14.7	13.7	8.4	5.3	1.0	2.1	17.6	8.0	2.5	5.5	9.6	5.3	4.3
1940	12.3	12.2	11.3	7.3	4.0	.9	.1	13.5	8.1	2.9	5.2	5.4	5.1	.3
1935	13.5	13.5	12.6	7.8	4.8	.9	(3)	6.4	5.1	1.6	3.5	1.2	1.2	(3)
1931	15.9	15.9	14.6	8.1	6.5	1.3	(3)	3.8	2.3	(3)	(3)	1.5	(3)	(3)
1930	17.2	17.2	15.2	8.0	7.2	2.0	(3)	8.4	5.7[4]	1.4[4]	4.3[4]	2.7	2.7	(3)
1927	13.8	13.8	12.5	6.6	5.9	1.3	(3)	6.6	3.7	(3)	(3)	2.9	(3)	(3)
1924	10.9	10.9	10.0	5.4	4.6	.8	(3)	3.9	2.9	1.0	1.9	1.0	1.0	(3)
1919	7.0	7.0	6.5	3.9	2.6	.5	(3)	3.3	2.5	.9	1.6	.8	.8	(3)
1914 (June 30)	3.5	3.5	3.5	2.7	.8	(3)	(3)	7.2	6.7	1.3	5.4	.5	.5	(3)
1908	2.5	2.5	2.5	1.6	.9	(3)	(3)	6.4	6.4	(3)	(3)	(3)	(3)	(3)
1897	.7	.7	.7	.6	.1	(3)	(3)	3.4	3.1	(3)	(3)	.3	(3)	(3)
1869	.1	.1	(3)	(3)	(3)	(3)	(3)	1.5	1.4	(3)	(3)	.2	(3)	(3)
1843	(5)	(5)	(3)	(3)	(3)	(3)	(3)	.2	(3)	(3)	(3)	(3)	(3)	(3)

[1] Includes long-term and short-term.
[2] New series for direct investments, based on *Investments of the United States*, Government Printing Office, 1953.
[3] Not available.
[4] 1929 data.
[5] Negligible.

Series U 207. International Investment Position of the United States (Net Liabilities): 1789 to 1900

[In millions of dollars]

Year	Amount 207	Year	Amount 207	Year	Amount 207	Year	Amount 207	Year	Amount 207	Year	Amount 207	Year	Amount 207	Year	Amount 207
1900	2,501	1886	1,980	1872	1,595	1858	358	1844	213	1830	75	1816	[5]118	1802	74
1899	2,797			1871	1,353	1857	381	1843	217	1829	83			1801	81
1898	3,026	1885	1,843			1856	364	1842	[5]239	1828	85	1815	80		
1897	3,305	1884	1,809	1870	1,252			1841	[5]257	1827	74	1814	65	1800	83
1896	3,328	1883	1,704	1869	1,152	1855	352			1826	84	1813	56	1799	81
		1882	1,653	1868	976	1854	337	1840	261			1812	71	1798	96
1895	3,288	1881	1,543	1867	903	1853	295	1839	292	1825	81	1811	50	1797	94
1894	3,151			1866	758	1852	239	1838	243	1824	88			1796	83
1893	3,217	1880	1,584			1851	223	1837	240	1823	89	1810	85		
1892	3,071	1879	1,554	1865	663			1836	218	1822	91	1809	92	1795	79
1891	3,030	1878	1,714	1864	604	1850	217			1821	83	1808	104	1794	66
		1877	1,876	1863	493	1849	188	1835	159			1807	87	1793	75
1890	2,894	1876	1,933	1862	480	1848	191	1834	129	1820	88	1806	82	1792	77
1889	2,700			1861	480	1847	189	1833	110	1819	[5]89			1791	69
1888	2,498	1875	1,931			1846	208	1832	96	1818	[5]104	1805	75		
1887	2,211	1874	1,844	1860	377			1831	89	1817	[5]109	1804	65	1790	61
		1873	1,762	1859	384	1845	209					1803	77	1789	60

[1] Includes defaults of $20 million in 1816 and 1817; $30 million in 1818 and 1819; and $12 million in 1841 and 1842.

Series U 208–213. Value of Direct Investment in Foreign Countries, by Area and Industry Groups: 1929 to 1957

[In millions of dollars. Figures for 1950 and subsequent years based on 1950 census of American direct investments abroad]

Year	Total, all areas 208	Canada 209	Latin American Republics[1] 210	Western Europe[2] 211	Western European dependencies 212	Other countries[3] 213	Year	Total, all areas 208	Canada 209	Latin American Republics[1] 210	Western Europe[2] 211	Western European dependencies 212	Other countries[3] 213
TOTAL							**MANUFACTURING**						
1957 (prel.)	25,252	8,332	8,805	3,993	906	3,216	1957 (prel.)	7,918	3,512	1,693	2,077	18	618
1956	22,177	7,460	7,459	3,520	805	2,933	1956	7,152	3,196	1,543	1,861	17	536
1955	19,313	6,494	6,608	3,004	637	2,570	1955	6,349	2,841	1,372	1,640	15	480
1954	17,626	5,871	6,244	2,639	599	2,273	1954	5,711	2,592	1,240	1,451	15	413
1953	16,286	5,242	6,034	2,369	601	2,040	1953	5,226	2,418	1,149	1,295	11	353
1952	14,819	4,593	5,758	2,146	468	1,854	1952	4,920	2,241	1,166	1,187	9	316
1951	13,089	3,972	5,176	1,979	446	1,516	1951	4,352	2,000	992	1,070	9	281
1950	11,788	3,579	4,735	1,720	435	1,318	1950	3,831	1,897	780	932	9	214
1940	7,000	2,103	2,771	1,420	(4)	706	1940	1,926	943	210	639	(4)	133
1936	6,691	1,952	2,847	1,245	(4)	[5]647	1936	1,710	799	192	611	(4)	108
1929	7,528	2,010	3,519	1,353	(4)	646	1929	1,813	820	231	629	(4)	134
AGRICULTURE							**TRANSPORTATION, COMMUNICATION, AND PUBLIC UTILITIES**						
1957 (prel.)	(6)	(6)	(6)	(6)	(6)	(6)	1957 (prel.)	1,702	340	1,210	47	18	87
1956	(6)	(6)	(6)	(6)	(6)	(6)	1956	1,817	351	1,291	54	21	100
1955	725	23	606	1	14	81	1955	1,614	326	1,143	42	25	79
1954	695	22	585	1	13	74	1954	1,547	302	1,120	30	20	75
1953	677	21	568	1	13	74	1953	1,508	300	1,093	28	18	68
1952	662	21	564	1	12	64	1952	1,469	287	1,076	28	18	61
1951	642	22	557	1	10	53	1951	1,431	285	1,044	27	18	56
1950	589	21	520	1	9	39	1950	1,425	284	1,042	27	18	54
1940	435	13	359		(4)	63	1940	1,514	407	962	74	(4)	71
1936	482	10	400		(4)	71	1936	1,640	520	937	91	(4)	92
1929	880	21	817		(4)	43	1929	1,610	542	887	145	(4)	36
MINING AND SMELTING							**TRADE**						
1957 (prel.)	2,634	996	1,238	50	132	218	1957 (prel.)	1,589	472	536	337	51	193
1956	2,399	940	1,096	45	122	197	1956	1,447	424	504	310	43	166
1955	2,209	862	1,024	40	111	173	1955	1,282	383	442	286	36	136
1954	2,078	792	1,002	35	103	147	1954	1,166	358	405	253	32	117
1953	1,981	677	999	30	133	92	1953	1,049	330	354	232	27	105
1952	1,642	550	871	26	118	76	1952	966	284	344	218	18	103
1951	1,317	400	736	23	98	61	1951	883	262	303	207	16	95
1950	1,129	334	628	21	88	57	1950	762	240	242	186	13	81
1940	782	187	512	53	(4)	30	1940	523	112	82	245	(4)	84
1936	1,032	239	708	43	(4)	42	1936	391	79	100	144	(4)	68
1929	1,185	400	732	(7)	(4)	53	1929	368	38	119	139	(4)	72
PETROLEUM							**OTHER**[8]						
1957 (prel.)	8,981	2,154	3,161	1,184	644	1,839	1957 (prel.)	2,197	793	875	264	37	228
1956	7,280	1,768	2,232	992	569	1,718	1956	2,312	847	886	291	40	247
1955	5,849	1,350	1,801	764	431	1,504	1955	1,285	709	220	232	6	118
1954	5,270	1,152	1,689	668	411	1,350	1954	1,160	653	204	201	5	97
1953	4,894	933	1,684	609	395	1,273	1953	1,001	562	187	173	3	74
1952	4,291	715	1,577	532	290	1,177	1952	869	494	162	152	1	59
1951	3,703	562	1,408	511	295	926	1951	762	440	136	138	1	45
1950	3,390	418	1,408	424	296	844	1950	661	385	116	129	1	30
1940	1,278	120	572	306	(4)	280	1940	544	320	74	104	(4)	46
1936	1,074	108	453	275	(4)	238	1936	362	197	57	80	(4)	28
1929	1,117	55	617	231	(4)	214	1929	555	136	116	209	(4)	94

[1] Western European dependencies in the Western Hemisphere included in Latin American Republics in 1929, 1936, and 1940.
[2] Includes Eastern Europe in 1929, 1936, and 1940, amounting to $89 million, $93 million, and $259 million, respectively. Excludes Turkey for 1936–1940.
[3] Includes Turkey for 1936 and 1940, and Western European dependencies for 1929, 1936, and 1940.
[4] Not shown separately.
[5] Includes $26 million reported as "International."
[6] Included in "other."
[7] Included in "Other countries."
[8] Excludes insurance in 1929; includes agriculture for 1956 and 1957.

Business Enterprise

BUSINESS POPULATION (Series V 1–64)

V 1–64. General note.

Statistics on the total number and the size distribution of business firms must be used with caution. No governmental process records all firms, and an entirely satisfactory definition of a firm seems impossible. The boundary between self-employment and conduct of a business firm is hazy at best. In addition, there are problems of inactive or partly (e.g., seasonally) inactive firms, joint ventures, partial interests, ownership of multiple firms by individuals and families, etc. Moreover, the characteristic which causes an enterprise to be counted as, for example, a corporation, an employer subject to social security, or an operator of an establishment requiring a sanitary or safety license, varies with the laws creating these categories and with the degree of thoroughness of administration of these laws.

These difficulties are compounded when an attempt is made to group firms into industrial categories, because industry boundaries must be arbitrary, and the assignment of a firm on one side of the boundary or another may be based on a 50-percent rule or on some convention lacking analytic justification. Or the activity may not fit well into any recognized category.

The statistical importance of these problems is great because of the unusual size distribution of the business population (see series V 20–29), which contains a large number of very small firms, and a minute proportion of larger firms accounting for a substantial or even predominant fraction of total activity. Many small firms are on the boundary line between recognition and nonrecognition (enumeration or nonenumeration), so that a slight difference in method or source, particularly one of which the statistician is unaware, may generate considerable but spurious change or absence of change in the total number of firms. If, however, the object of estimation is not number of firms but total activity, the radically unequal size distribution becomes a great advantage because it permits more efficient sample design at lower cost.

The number and percentage of business firms, therefore, must be used with a realization that the meaning of a business firm is not always certain and that the figures are subject to considerable error. The most meaningful statistics of the business population are those which are based on some consistent criterion or definition over a period of years. The business population studies of the Office of Business Economics may be said to have inaugurated the publication of such satisfactory statistics.

The statistics of business concentration in series V 57–64 do not share the defect of statistics of business population, since they require estimates only of total activity and the identification of some small number of the largest firms. However, the record of one particular year's activity is in effect a single observation out of the infinite number which might be generated by the structural condition which is the object of measurement. Strikes, accidents, and cyclical fluctuations, with highly unequal impact upon various branches of industry, cause a divergence of the actual year's activity from the theoretically true or representative (average) year. Furthermore, if the incidence of mergers (series V 30) is substantial, a given year may be the peak or trough of a short-run change in concentration. Moreover, concentration measures may be strongly affected by the arbitrary nature of industry subdivisions and changes in industry classification from census to census.

V 1–3. Concerns in business, failure rate, and average liability per failure, 1857–1957.

Source: 1857–1950, Dun & Bradstreet, Inc., *Dun & Bradstreet Reference Book and Failure Statistics* (a printed mail folder distributed by Dun & Bradstreet); 1951–1957, *Dun & Bradstreet Reference Book*, various issues.

Total concerns are the number of business enterprises listed in the *Reference Book*. The figures are for continental United States and represent listings in the books published nearest to July 1 of each year. The listings include types of business which are seekers of commercial credit in the accepted sense of the term; namely, manufacturers, wholesalers, retailers, contractors, and certain types of commercial service. Specific types of business not covered are finance, insurance, and real estate companies; railroads; terminals; amusements; and many types of small service and construction enterprises. Neither professions nor farmers are included.

Failure rate is obtained by dividing total failures by total number of enterprises. Failures are defined as concerns involved in court procedures or voluntary actions, probably ending in loss to creditors. These include, but are not limited to, discontinuances following assignment or attachment of goods, bankruptcy petitions, foreclosure, etc.; voluntary withdrawals with known loss to creditors; enterprises involved in court action such as receivership; businesses making voluntary arrangements with creditors out of court; and since June 1934 (enactment of the Bankruptcy Act), reorganization which may or may not lead to discontinuance.

Average liability per failure is obtained by dividing total liabilities by total concerns. Liabilities represent primarily current indebtedness, including accounts and notes payable on secured or unsecured obligations held by banks, officers, affiliates, suppliers, or government at all levels. For 1933–1957, certain types of enterprises characterized by heavy deferred obligations were eliminated from the data, thus conferring a slight downward bias in average liability figures as compared with earlier years.

V 4–12. Annual average number of firms in operation, by major industry group, 1929–1957.

Source: 1929–1950, Office of Business Economics, *Survey of Current Business*, January 1954, p. 12; 1951–1957, *Survey of Current Business*, May 1959, p. 18.

These estimates are based primarily on data from the Bureau of Old-Age and Survivors Insurance, and are revised from time to time by the Office of Business Economics. The last substantial revision was made in January 1954 and revealed errors in the earlier estimates for absolute number and rate of growth; these errors were due partly to the cumulative effect of imperfect estimates for discontinued businesses. OBE defines a firm as a business organization under one management, with either an established place of business or at least one paid employee. Concerns owned or controlled by the same interests are not combined. Agriculture and professional services are excluded. A firm conducting more than one kind of business is classified by industry according to the major activity of the firm as a whole. Revisions of the Standard Industrial Classification (see Bureau of the Budget, *Standard Industrial Classification Manual*, 1957) have, therefore, affected the industrial distribution of firms.

V 13–19. Annual average number of new, discontinued, and transferred businesses, by major industry group, 1940–1957.

Source: See source for series V 4–12.

Discontinued businesses include closures of all kinds without reference to the reason for going out of business. New businesses include only firms which have been newly established. A firm which is maintained as a business entity but which undergoes a change of ownership is counted as a transferred business, not as a discontinuance. Partnerships in which a member is added or dropped, corporations that are reorganized or reincorporated, and businesses sold or otherwise acquired by new owners or changed in legal form of organization (such as partnership to corporation) are considered transfers. Note should be taken of the large differences between the figures for failures in series V 2 and those for discontinued businesses in series V 13.

V 20–29. Number of firms in operation and paid employment, by size of firm, 1945–1951.

Source: Office of Business Economics, *Survey of Current Business*, May 1954, p. 18.

See general note for series V 1–64, as well as text for series V 4–12.

V 30–31. Recorded mergers in manufacturing and mining, 1895–1957.

Source: 1895–1920, Ralph L. Nelson, *Merger Movements in American Industry*, chap. III, app. B, Princeton University Press (forthcoming); 1919–1957, Federal Trade Commission, *Report on Corporate Mergers and Acquisitions*, 1955, pp. 17–36, and releases.

Methods of estimation of the Nelson figures are explained in chapters II and III of his book; the basic source of the figures is chiefly the *Commercial and Financial Chronicle*.

Figures for 1919–1957 include mergers reported by Moody's Investors Service and Standard and Poor's Corporation. For 1919–1939, the estimates were first made by Willard L. Thorp in various publications, and then continued by the Federal Trade Commission. For complete sources and related data, see the Federal Trade report cited above.

The annual totals of reported mergers are only a small fraction of all "transferred businesses," as shown in series V 13–19. Series V 30–31 are essentially a count of all mergers and acquisitions involving corporations with widely held or publicly traded securities outstanding. There are two offsetting biases of uncertain amount: Mergers may be announced but not actually accomplished; small acquisitions, particularly, may be accomplished without announcement.

The data for 1895–1920 and 1919–1957 use different sources, each of which changes in degree of coverage over time, and are not comparable. The estimates for 1919–1957 include a more complete recording of smaller mergers, so that average capitalization or assets per merger would on this account tend to decrease, and total assets to increase. As distinguished from the number of mergers per year, the relative rates of change are generally, though not precisely, comparable and the assets involved would not differ greatly in the aggregate in any one year, since the larger mergers are presumably counted in both sets of estimates.

V 32–44. Number of corporations, by major industry group, 1916–1956.

Source: 1916–1933, Bureau of Internal Revenue, *Statistics of Income*, various annual issues; 1934–1956, Internal Revenue Service, *Statistics of Income*, part II, *Corporation Income Tax Returns*, various annual issues.

After 1925, trade is divided into wholesale trade, retail trade, and trade not allocable. The latter figure appears at the end of the listing and varies widely owing to changes in inclusion. The joint figure of wholesale and retail trade for 1916 is not comparable with figures for subsequent years because the "merchandising companies" group was not as inclusive as the "wholesale trade" and "retail trade" groups. This is reflected in the very large figure for all other active corporations. The same is true of "finance, insurance, and real estate" for 1916, then labelled "banks and insurance companies."

V 45–56. Percent of total corporate net income reported by small and large corporations (with net income only), 1918–1939.

Source: Office of Business Economics, *Survey of Current Business*, March 1944, p. 11.

The data are based on a special tabulation of corporate income tax records by the then Bureau of Internal Revenue. See general note for series V 1–64.

V 57–64. Concentration in manufacturing, by industry group, 1901, 1947, and 1954.

Source: Series V 57, G. Warren Nutter, *The Extent of Enterprise Monopoly in the United States*, copyrighted 1951 by The University of Chicago, Press, 1951, tables 10 and 39. Series V 58, M. A. Adelman, "The Measurement of Industrial Concentration," *Review of Economics and Statistics*, vol. 33, November 1951, table 14 (based on *Hearings Before the Subcommittee on Study of Monopoly Power*, House of Representatives, 81st Congress, 1st session, Serial No. 14, part 2-B, pp. 1436–1456). Series V 59–60 are tabulations prepared by the Bureau of the Census from data reported in the *Census of Manufactures*. Series V 61–64, Irving Rottenberg, "New Statistics on Companies and on Concentration in Manufacturing From the 1954 Census," *Proceedings of the American Statistical Association*, 1957, table 5.

The basic source of most of the data in all columns is the *Census of Manufactures*. The concentration ratio is defined as the percent of total industry sales (or, occasionally, value added) made by the four largest sellers.

The entries for series V 57–58 represent the value added by manufacture in 4-digit (Standard Industrial Classification) industries with concentration ratios of 50 or higher, as a percentage of value added by all 4-digit industries included in each 2-digit industry group (e.g., "food and kindred products" is a 2-digit group containing "meat-packing plants" and 2 other 4-digit meat industries, "creamery butter" and 5 other 4-digit dairy industries, etc.).

The figures for series V 59–64 are average concentration ratios for each 2-digit industry group, i.e., the concentration ratio of each 4-digit industry is weighted in proportion to its employment or value added, as indicated, as a proportion of total employment or total value added by the whole 2-digit group.

Series V 59–60 include all industries for the given year—452 in 1947, and 434 in 1954. Because of changes in 4-digit industry definitions, concentration ratios are not fully comparable. Series V 61–64 are based on 375 comparable industries accounting for 85 percent of all value added by manufacture in 1947, and for 82 percent in 1954.

The first total line is a set of weighted averages based on value-added weights derived from the basic data for the respective years shown. Figures on the second total line (for series V 61–64) are averages of the concentration ratios shown for the 20 industry groups.

Where the change in concentration, 1947-1954, as shown in series V 59–60, is substantially different from that shown in series V 61–64, the difference is due to industry redefinition and to inclusion or exclusion of industries from the Census of Manufactures. A striking example is in group 39, "miscellaneous manufactures" from which major group 19, "ordnance and accessories," has been omitted for national security reasons.

Series V 1–3. Concerns in Business, Failure Rate, and Average Liability Per Failure (Dun & Bradstreet): 1857 to 1957

Year	Total concerns (1,000)	Failure rate per 10,000 concerns	Average liability per failure ($1,000)
	1	2	3
1957	2,652.2	52	44.8
1956	2,629.0	48	44.4
1955	2,633.1	42	41.0
1954	2,632.3	42	41.7
1953	2,666.7	33	44.5
1952	2,637.0	29	37.2
1951	2,608.0	31	32.2
1950	2,687.0	34	27.1
1949	2,679.0	34	33.3
1948	2,550.0	20	44.7
1947	2,405.0	14	58.9
1946	2,142.0	5	59.7
1945	1,909.0	4	37.4
1944	1,855.0	7	25.9
1943	2,023.0	16	14.1
1942	2,152.0	45	10.7
1941	2,171.0	55	11.5
1940	2,156.0	63	12.2
1939	2,116.0	70	12.4
1938	2,102.0	61	19.2
1937	2,057.0	46	19.3
1936	2,010.0	48	21.1
1935	1,983.0	62	25.4
1934	1,974.0	61	27.6
1933	1,961.0	100	23.0
1932	2,077.0	154	29.2
1931	2,125.0	133	26.0
1930	2,183.0	122	25.4
1929	2,213.0	104	21.1
1928	2,199.0	109	20.5
1927	2,172.0	106	22.5
1926	2,158.0	101	18.8
1925	2,113.0	100	20.9
1924	2,047.0	100	26.4

Year	Total concerns (1,000)	Failure rate per 10,000 concerns	Average liability per failure ($1,000)
	1	2	3
1923	1,996.0	93	28.8
1922	1,983.0	120	26.4
1921	1,927.0	102	31.9
1920	1,821.0	48	33.2
1919	1,711.0	37	17.6
1918	1,708.0	59	16.3
1917	1,733.0	80	13.2
1916	1,708.0	100	11.5
1915	1,675.0	133	13.6
1914	1,655.0	118	19.6
1913	1,617.0	98	17.0
1912	1,564.0	100	13.1
1911	1,525.0	88	14.2
1910	1,515.0	84	15.9
1909	1,486.0	87	11.9
1908	1,448.0	108	14.2
1907	1,418.0	83	16.8
1906	1,393.0	77	11.2
1905	1,357.0	85	8.9
1904	1,320.0	92	11.8
1903	1,281.0	94	12.9
1902	1,253.0	93	10.1
1901	1,219.0	90	10.3
1900	1,174.0	92	12.9
1899	1,147.6	82	9.7
1898	1,105.8	111	10.7
1897	1,058.5	125	11.6
1896	1,151.6	133	15.0
1895	1,209.3	112	13.1
1894	1,114.2	123	12.5
1893	1,193.1	130	22.8
1892	1,172.7	89	11.0
1891	1,143.0	107	15.5

Year	Total concerns (1,000)	Failure rate per 10,000 concerns	Average liability per failure ($1,000)
	1	2	3
1890	1,110.6	99	17.4
1889	1,051.1	103	13.7
1888	1,046.7	103	11.6
1887	994.3	97	17.4
1886	969.8	101	11.7
1885	920.0	116	12.6
1884	904.8	121	20.6
1883	864.0	106	18.8
1882	822.2	82	15.1
1881	781.7	71	14.5
1880	746.8	63	13.9
1879	702.2	95	14.7
1878	661.4	158	22.4
1877	636.6	139	21.5
1876	639.3	142	21.0
1875	602.8	128	26.0
1874	558.5	104	26.6
1873	493.5	105	44.1
1872	500.1	81	29.8
1871	456.9	64	29.2
1870	427.3	83	24.9
1869	(1)	(1)	26.8
1868	(1)	(1)	24.4
1867	(1)	(1)	34.8
1866	(1)	(1)	35.7
1865	(1)	(1)	33.3
1864	(1)	(1)	16.5
1863	(1)	(1)	16.0
1862	(1)	(1)	14.0
1861	(1)	(1)	29.6
1860	(1)	(1)	21.7
1859	229.7	170	16.5
1858	204.1	242	22.7
1857	(1)	(1)	59.2

[1] Not available.

Series V 4–12. Annual Average Number of Firms in Operation, by Major Industry Group: 1929 to 1957

[In thousands. Beginning 1951, figures as of January 1]

Year	All industries	Mining and quarrying	Contract construction	Manufacturing	Transportation, communication, and other public utilities	Wholesale trade	Retail trade	Finance, insurance, and real estate	Service industries
	4	5	6	7	8	9	10	11	12
1957	4,470.7	42.2	465.4	332.3	208.4	303.7	1,925.6	383.0	810.0
1956	4,381.2	40.9	451.7	327.3	200.1	296.9	1,903.2	371.5	789.6
1955	4,286.8	38.8	429.8	326.1	193.4	291.9	1,874.5	359.5	772.6
1954	4,239.8	37.8	416.7	331.3	192.9	288.2	1,861.4	351.6	760.0
1953	4,187.7	37.6	405.3	330.7	192.2	283.1	1,846.1	342.8	749.9
1952	4,118.2	37.4	387.2	328.2	184.6	275.8	1,830.8	334.6	739.6
1951	4,067.3	37.0	377.3	322.8	180.7	268.6	1,820.9	326.9	733.0
1950	4,050.7	37.0	370.5	320.7	179.5	266.2	1,815.8	325.5	735.6
1949	4,000.0	37.0	347.5	320.5	179.1	261.8	1,794.3	323.0	736.8
1948	3,948.4	37.2	329.0	320.0	178.8	257.9	1,763.8	323.4	738.3
1947	3,783.2	35.2	292.6	312.0	173.2	250.9	1,685.9	321.9	711.5
1946	3,487.2	33.8	243.8	285.9	162.2	229.2	1,555.4	320.3	656.5
1945	3,113.9	32.2	176.8	258.4	144.2	196.9	1,403.5	310.3	591.5
1944	2,916.5	31.4	153.3	250.2	132.2	177.9	1,322.6	297.0	551.8
1943	2,905.1	32.1	157.2	244.9	129.4	172.6	1,329.1	286.2	553.6
1942	3,185.8	35.4	176.9	241.5	144.3	193.5	1,491.3	298.4	604.6
1941	3,269.6	37.2	186.4	236.6	147.2	194.4	1,558.3	295.1	614.4
1940	3,290.8	35.6	198.8	226.0	149.6	186.4	1,567.4	300.6	626.3
1939	3,222.2	34.2	199.4	221.3	145.3	175.6	1,534.6	296.6	615.2
1938	3,073.7	33.9	193.5	202.2	135.7	167.1	1,451.6	285.0	604.8
1937	3,136.3	35.8	199.0	214.3	137.0	170.7	1,469.3	278.8	631.3
1936	3,069.8	35.8	191.7	210.8	132.3	164.7	1,430.1	275.8	628.6
1935	2,991.9	35.5	180.2	205.0	127.2	157.0	1,387.2	283.8	615.8
1934	2,884.0	35.5	179.7	187.9	116.6	152.0	1,337.3	282.5	592.5
1933	2,782.1	32.8	185.4	166.8	107.6	141.8	1,291.2	281.7	574.9
1932	2,828.1	32.0	202.2	164.4	107.7	141.6	1,301.8	288.4	588.0
1931	2,916.4	32.4	218.6	195.3	111.6	143.9	1,316.7	305.7	592.1
1930	2,993.7	33.4	230.2	228.1	116.0	146.6	1,325.5	315.2	598.7
1929	3,029.0	36.3	233.8	257.0	119.5	148.1	1,327.0	316.2	590.9

Series V 13–19. Annual Average Number of New, Discontinued, and Transferred Businesses, by Major Industry Group: 1940 to 1957

[In thousands]

Left panel

Year	All industries	Contract construction	Manufacturing	Wholesale trade	Retail trade	Service industries	All other[1]
	13	14	15	16	17	18	19
NEW BUSINESSES							
1957	405.1	56.1	25.1	23.4	173.1	71.8	55.4
1956	431.2	68.0	31.4	24.2	170.2	73.5	63.9
1955	408.2	68.7	29.4	22.3	161.4	67.4	59.0
1954	365.6	61.6	25.3	21.3	147.1	60.7	49.7
1953	351.6	59.8	28.2	21.1	139.7	55.8	46.9
1952	345.6	61.5	28.1	21.4	130.3	54.4	49.9
1951	327.1	53.7	28.0	20.7	122.9	53.3	48.3
1950	348.2	64.1	30.0	21.6	133.0	55.5	44.1
1949	331.1	54.2	25.8	21.1	135.5	57.5	36.8
1948	393.3	65.0	34.6	24.4	151.2	72.9	45.2
1947	460.8	73.8	39.7	29.8	179.5	90.3	47.7
1946	617.4	95.1	62.8	45.2	234.1	116.6	63.5
1945	422.7	55.8	37.2	30.2	161.4	84.5	53.6
1944	330.9	28.4	26.9	24.5	128.1	71.4	51.6
1943	146.0	8.8	25.2	7.8	49.9	28.3	25.9
1942	121.2	7.5	23.2	4.8	39.3	28.7	17.8
1941	290.0	19.9	30.9	22.6	117.4	61.7	37.4
1940	275.2	21.9	29.2	20.4	117.9	49.2	36.7
DISCONTINUED BUSINESSES							
1957	341.4	54.0	24.5	16.2	150.9	51.7	44.0
1956	341.7	54.3	26.4	17.3	147.8	53.1	42.8
1955	313.8	46.8	28.2	17.3	132.7	50.4	38.3
1954	318.7	48.4	30.5	17.6	134.0	48.0	40.2
1953	299.4	48.5	27.7	16.0	124.4	45.7	37.1
1952	276.1	43.3	25.5	14.2	115.1	44.2	34.0
1951	276.2	43.9	22.7	13.5	113.0	46.6	36.4
1950	289.6	39.2	24.7	16.3	115.0	57.8	36.5
1949	306.5	40.7	30.8	18.0	115.5	60.7	41.0

Right panel

Year	All industries	Contract construction	Manufacturing	Wholesale trade	Retail trade	Service industries	All other[1]
	13	14	15	16	17	18	19
DISCONTINUED BUSINESSES—Con.							
1948	282.0	36.3	27.4	19.1	98.5	62.3	38.4
1947	239.2	31.6	26.8	17.7	76.5	49.0	37.6
1946	208.7	26.0	24.3	11.4	65.5	43.9	37.6
1945	175.6	16.9	26.4	7.3	59.2	38.3	27.7
1944	174.6	15.2	20.2	8.3	63.3	39.7	27.7
1943	337.0	26.3	21.8	19.8	159.9	71.4	37.8
1942	386.5	30.0	21.0	23.7	199.4	69.6	42.9
1941	270.7	27.2	20.6	12.0	116.6	56.3	38.0
1940	318.1	30.0	21.7	13.9	137.6	73.7	41.1
TRANSFERRED BUSINESSES							
1957	376.2	13.2	15.0	12.4	251.7	56.2	27.6
1956	392.7	14.0	16.7	13.3	261.1	58.0	29.6
1955	384.3	13.4	16.6	12.6	258.7	55.0	28.1
1954	370.7	13.2	15.2	11.9	249.7	53.3	27.4
1953	377.6	13.5	17.3	12.7	252.5	55.4	26.3
1952	370.2	11.9	16.8	12.6	248.1	54.2	26.6
1951	358.2	11.3	16.1	11.3	241.3	52.7	25.4
1950	419.4	14.8	20.6	14.4	277.8	63.1	28.6
1949	434.7	15.7	21.9	16.0	286.1	66.0	29.0
1948	501.3	17.0	28.9	17.3	327.0	78.5	32.5
1947	571.9	18.1	31.3	20.4	374.8	93.6	33.7
1946	626.9	18.2	37.3	25.6	399.2	107.1	39.4
1945	473.2	9.9	21.3	15.7	307.6	82.9	35.8
1944	359.4	6.5	16.9	11.1	227.0	65.4	32.7
1943	249.5	4.3	17.4	7.2	121.6	60.3	38.8
1942	291.6	6.8	17.2	6.7	104.0	120.7	36.1
1941	320.2	9.8	22.5	8.7	73.7	157.8	47.7
1940	240.5	7.2	18.2	6.0	60.3	104.7	44.2

[1] Comprises mining and quarrying; transportation, communication, and other public utilities; finance, insurance, and real estate.

Series V 20–29. Number of Firms in Operation and Paid Employment, by Size of Firm: 1945 to 1951

[In thousands]

Year	All classes	Employee-size class								
		0 to 3	4 to 7	8 to 19	20 to 49	50 to 99	100 to 499	500 to 999	1,000 to 9,999	10,000 and over
	20	21	22	23	24	25	26	27	28	29
FIRMS IN OPERATION, JANUARY 1										
1951	4,067.3	3,040.0	513.2	311.8	124.7	40.7	30.3	3.4	2.9	0.2
1949	3,984.2	2,998.8	498.2	300.4	116.0	37.4	27.3	3.1	2.7	0.2
1948	3,872.9	2,876.6	497.2	307.8	118.0	38.3	28.7	3.3	2.8	0.2
1947	3,651.2	2,683.2	479.8	297.6	117.2	38.5	28.5	3.3	2.9	0.2
1946	3,242.5	2,347.5	438.8	274.9	111.2	36.9	27.4	3.1	2.6	0.2
1945	2,995.4	2,235.4	377.0	221.5	97.0	33.0	25.4	3.2	2.7	0.2
PAID EMPLOYMENT, MID-MARCH										
1951	38,390	2,416	2,702	3,769	3,786	2,812	6,038	2,316	7,340	7,211
1949	35,379	2,311	2,618	3,623	3,507	2,572	5,426	2,141	6,712	6,469
1948	36,475	2,211	2,597	3,677	3,604	2,663	5,713	2,291	7,101	6,618
1947	35,803	2,111	2,519	3,565	3,501	2,619	5,723	2,283	7,167	6,315
1946	33,631	1,938	2,384	3,360	3,387	2,553	5,537	2,172	6,934	5,366
1945	33,778	1,726	1,978	2,654	2,937	2,270	5,236	2,242	7,254	7,481

Series V 30–31. Recorded Mergers in Manufacturing and Mining: 1895 to 1957

Year	Recorded mergers [30]	Authorized capitalization or gross assets (Mil. dol.) [31]	Year	Recorded mergers [30]	Authorized capitalization or gross assets (Mil. dol.) [31]	Year	Recorded mergers [30]	Authorized capitalization or gross assets (Mil. dol.) [31]	Year	Recorded mergers [30]	Authorized capitalization or gross assets (Mil. dol.) [31]	Year	Recorded mergers [30]	Authorized capitalization or gross assets (Mil. dol.) [31]
1957 [1]	490	[2]	1945	333	[2,4]	1931	464	[2]	1920 [6]	206	1,089	1907	87	185
1956	537	[2]	1944	324	[2,4]				1919 [6]	171	982	1906	128	378
			1943	213	[2,4]	1930	799	[2]	1918	71	254			
1955	525	[2]	1942	118	[2,4]	1929	1,245	[2]	1917	195	679	1905	226	243
1954	387	[2,3]	1941	111	[2,4]	1928	1,058	[2]	1916	117	470	1904	79	110
1953	295					1927	870	[2]				1903	142	298
1952	288	[2,3]	1940	140	[2,4]	1926	856	[2]	1915	71	158	1902	379	911
1951	235	[2,3]	1939	87	[2]				1914	39	160	1901	423	2,053
			1938	110	[2]	1925	554	[2]	1913	85	176			
1950	219	[2]	1937	124	[2]	1924	368	[2]	1912	82	322	1900	340	442
1949	126	[2]	1936	126	[2]	1923	311	[2]	1911	103	210	1899	1,208	2,263
1948	223	[2]				1922	309	[2]				1898	303	651
1947	404	[2,4]	1935	130	[2]	1921	487	[2]	1910	142	257	1897	69	120
1946	419	[2,4]	1934	101	[2]				1909	49	89	1896	26	25
			1933	120	[2]	1920 [5]	760	[2]	1908	50	188	1895	43	41
			1932	203	[2]	1919 [5]	438	[2]						

[1] First 9 months.
[2] Not available.
[3] An estimate of assets involved in mergers in manufacturing and mining (plus wholesale and retail trade and miscellaneous) during the 42 months, 1951 through June 1954, inclusive, is $5.14 billion. See American Management Association, *Financial Management Series: No. 114*, 1957, p. 89.
[4] It is estimated that not over $5 billion was involved in all manufacturing and mining mergers during 1940–1947. See J. Keith Butters, John Lintner, and William L. Carey, *Effects of Taxation: Corporate Mergers*, Harvard Graduate School of Business Administration, Boston, 1951, chap. 10.
[5] Comparable with later years.
[6] Comparable with earlier years.

Series V 32–44. Number of Corporations, by Major Industry Group: 1916 to 1956

[In thousands]

Year	Total corporations [32]	Active corporations Total [33]	Agriculture [34]	Mining and quarrying [35]	Manufacturing [36]	Wholesale trade [37]	Retail trade [38]	Trade not allocable [39]	Services [40]	Finance, insurance, and real estate [41]	Public utilities [42]	Construction [43]	All other [44]
1956	925.0	885.7	11.0	11.7	132.8	95.0	168.3	23.0	81.6	265.0	36.2	48.3	12.8
1955	842.1	807.3	10.3	10.7	129.8	86.3	154.9	23.8	72.9	234.0	33.0	41.6	10.0
1954	754.0	722.8	8.8	9.6	120.9	77.1	140.0	21.5	64.8	205.3	29.1	36.1	9.6
1953	731.0	698.0	9.4	9.1	121.1	74.1	134.6	19.6	63.5	195.2	29.9	34.9	6.5
1952	705.5	672.1	8.9	9.1	119.4	72.1	131.5	17.7	61.6	185.9	28.5	31.8	5.6
1951	687.3	652.4	8.7	9.0	120.2	71.6	129.2	15.5	58.3	177.8	26.8	29.6	5.7
1950	666.0	629.3	8.3	9.1	115.9	68.9	125.5	15.0	55.2	171.8	26.3	27.7	5.6
1949	650.0	614.8	8.0	9.2	117.3	67.9	118.8	17.3	54.0	166.3	25.9	25.7	4.4
1948	630.7	594.2	7.7	9.1	116.7	64.8	110.8	21.1	50.5	160.6	25.2	23.5	4.2
1947	587.7	551.8	7.3	8.3	112.2	56.0	99.0	22.2	46.0	151.0	23.7	20.3	5.7
1946	526.4	491.2	6.7	7.7	98.1	47.7	84.8	19.1	39.6	144.4	21.8	15.8	5.5
1945	454.5	421.1	6.2	7.3	79.1	35.7	71.2	14.1	35.1	135.6	19.7	11.8	5.3
1944	446.8	412.5	6.4	7.6	76.6	33.6	69.1	14.6	34.7	133.9	19.2	11.5	5.0
1943	455.9	420.5	6.9	8.1	78.7	34.4	72.6	13.8	35.6	133.7	19.3	12.1	5.3
1942	479.7	442.7	7.3	8.9	82.2	36.3	78.3	14.4	38.4	136.9	20.2	13.7	6.1
1941	509.1	468.9	7.9	9.7	84.4	37.6	84.5	16.5	40.5	143.5	21.9	15.0	7.3
1940	516.8	473.0	8.4	10.4	85.6	37.5	85.8	16.5	41.4	142.6	22.1	15.7	7.0
1939	516.0	469.6	8.6	10.8	86.2	36.0	86.3	15.9	41.0	142.3	22.1	16.1	4.3
1938	520.5	471.0	9.0	10.9	88.1	37.0	86.7	15.5	41.0	140.4	22.0	16.3	4.1
1937	529.1	477.8	8.7	13.6	92.0	34.5	78.5	30.1	60.2	117.1	24.7	16.9	1.5
1936	530.8	478.9	8.9	13.8	92.0	35.2	83.0	27.3	59.7	115.7	24.9	16.6	1.8
1935	533.6	477.1	9.1	13.7	91.7	34.2	83.6	27.1	49.6	124.9	25.4	16.1	1.7
1934	528.9	469.8	9.3	13.5	91.3	33.2	79.7	27.9	45.9	126.1	25.4	15.9	1.6
1933	504.1	446.8	9.3	11.8	88.6	30.7	81.2	20.9	43.0	121.7	21.8	16.3	1.5
1932	508.6	451.9	9.8	12.0	87.9	29.9	77.9	24.6	43.3	125.1	21.7	17.3	2.4
1931	516.4	459.7	9.9	12.1	89.1	30.0	80.0	22.9	38.2	134.6	21.6	18.1	3.4
1930	518.7	463.0	9.9	12.2	91.5	30.2	79.2	22.1	38.2	136.6	21.6	18.5	2.9
1929	509.4	456.0	9.4	12.5	92.2	29.1	77.9	22.1	36.0	133.9	21.6	18.4	2.9
1928	495.9	443.6	9.2	12.9	91.6	28.5	73.0	24.9	33.5	129.1	21.3	17.3	2.3
1927	475.0	425.7	8.9	13.0	89.8	29.6	65.9	24.2	31.1	122.7	20.8	16.4	3.3
1926	455.3	[1]455.3	10.7	19.3	93.2	39.5	47.5	25.7	32.3	130.4	25.1	16.8	[1]14.8
1925	430.1	[1]430.1	9.9	19.1	88.7		109.6		29.0	115.9	23.6	15.3	[1]19.0
1924	417.4	[1]417.4	9.8	18.4	86.8		105.3		26.3	104.8	22.4	13.2	[1]30.4
1923	398.9	[1]398.9	9.4	18.5	85.2		100.6		25.1	96.8	21.1	12.6	[1]29.6
1922	382.9	[1]382.9	9.1	17.1	82.5		95.7		23.1	91.1	20.5	11.4	[1]32.4
1921	356.4	[1]356.4	8.7	17.7	79.7		88.2		19.1	82.8	19.1	10.4	[1]30.7
1920	345.6	[1]345.6	9.2	17.5	78.2		78.9		17.5	78.9	20.6	10.0	[1]34.8
1919	320.2	[1]320.2	8.3	18.5	67.8		70.2		15.7	72.8	20.5	8.2	[1]38.2
1918	317.6	[1]317.6	7.9	10.7	67.3		70.1		14.9	68.1	18.2	7.7	[1]52.7
1917	351.4	[1]351.4	9.6	12.9	79.6		91.1		18.6	68.4	26.4	10.7	[1]34.1
1916	341.3	[1]341.3	7.3	12.0	80.2		30.6		[2]	30.0	22.9	[2]	[1]158.3

[1] Includes inactive corporations.
[2] Included in "All other."

Series V 45–56. Percent of Total Corporate Net Income Reported by Small and Large Corporations (With Net Income Only): 1918 to 1939

[Size measured by net income]

Year	All industries				All industries except finance				Manufacturing			
	Total	Smallest 75%	Next 20%	Largest 5%	Total	Smallest 75%	Next 20%	Largest 5%	Total	Smallest 75%	Next 20%	Largest 5%
	45	46	47	48	49	50	51	52	53	54	55	56
1939	100.00	3.40	12.11	84.49	(1)	(1)	(1)	(1)	(1)	(1)	(1)	(1)
1938	100.00	3.52	12.05	84.43	(1)	(1)	(1)	(1)	(1)	(1)	(1)	(1)
1937	100.00	3.07	11.58	85.35	(1)	(1)	(1)	(1)	(1)	(1)	(1)	(1)
1936	100.00	3.32	12.85	83.83	(1)	(1)	(1)	(1)	(1)	(1)	(1)	(1)
1935	100.00	3.90	14.73	81.37	(1)	(1)	(1)	(1)	(1)	(1)	(1)	(1)
1934	100.00	3.70	14.77	81.53	(1)	(1)	(1)	(1)	(1)	(1)	(1)	(1)
1933	100.00	3.08	13.10	83.82	(1)	(1)	(1)	(1)	(1)	(1)	(1)	(1)
1932	100.00	2.71	10.70	86.59	(1)	(1)	(1)	(1)	(1)	(1)	(1)	(1)
1931	100.00	4.46	10.78	84.76	(1)	(1)	(1)	(1)	(1)	(1)	(1)	(1)
1930	100.00	4.09	10.63	85.28	100.00	3.50	9.84	86.66	100.00	3.42	11.82	84.76
1929	100.00	3.97	11.69	84.34	100.00	3.62	11.14	85.24	100.00	4.49	13.42	82.09
1928	100.00	4.43	13.03	82.54	100.00	4.03	12.45	83.52	100.00	4.94	14.69	80.37
1927	100.00	4.66	14.63	80.71	100.00	4.17	13.90	81.93	100.00	5.54	16.56	77.90
1926	100.00	4.52	14.35	81.13	100.00	3.94	13.29	82.77	100.00	5.28	15.12	79.60
1925	100.00	4.97	15.44	79.59	100.00	4.91	14.04	81.05	100.00	5.98	16.29	77.73
1924	100.00	5.52	16.06	78.42	100.00	4.96	15.23	79.81	100.00	6.16	16.92	76.92
1923	100.00	5.28	16.44	78.28	100.00	5.53	15.53	78.94	100.00	6.40	18.07	75.53
1922	100.00	5.62	16.71	77.67	100.00	5.51	16.21	78.28	100.00	6.72	19.19	74.09
1921	100.00	6.34	16.06	77.60	100.00	5.36	15.85	78.79	100.00	7.28	19.18	73.54
1920	100.00	5.77	15.31	78.92	100.00	5.77	16.16	78.07	100.00	6.42	17.92	75.66
1919	100.00	7.01	16.26	76.73	(1)	(1)	(1)	(1)	(1)	(1)	(1)	(1)
1918	100.00	6.03	14.37	79.60	100.00	6 56	14.51	78.93	100.00	6.33	17.58	76.09

[1] Not available.

Series V 57–64.   Concentration in Manufacturing, by Industry Group: 1901, 1947, and 1954

[Concentration ratio is defined as the percent of total "4-digit" SIC industry sales (or value added) made by 4 largest sellers (see text)]

SIC Code No.	Industry group (1947 and 1954 Census classification)	Value added by 4-digit industries with concentration ratio over 50 as percent of value added by all industries in a 2-digit industry group		Average concentration ratios						
				1947 value-added weights	1954 value-added weights	1947 employment weights		1954 employment weights	
		1901 [1]	1947 [2]	1947	1954 [3]	1947	1954	1947	1954
		57	58	59	60	61	62	63	64
	Total, all industries, value-added weights	32.9	24.0	35.3	36.9	36.3	37.0	37.7	39.0
	Total, all industries, employment weights					34.6	35.9	34.7	35.3
20	Food and kindred products	39.1	18.8	34.9	33.8	32.4	33.2	31.3	32.4
21	Tobacco manufactures	49.9	77.7	76.2	73.4	66.0	62.9	67.4	64.1
22	Textile mill products	20.3	9.0	24.3	26.5	27.6	28.8	26.5	27.8
23	Apparel and related products		2.2	12.6	13.0	14.0	14.7	13.6	14.3
24	Lumber and wood products	0.5	2.0	11.2	10.8	12.3	11.3	10.8	10.7
25	Furniture and fixtures		8.1	21.9	20.3	16.5	18.7	17.4	16.7
26	Pulp, paper, and products	71.0	1.6	21.2	24.8	24.2	24.3	24.5	24.4
27	Printing and publishing	1.0	0.0	19.7	17.7	18.8	17.2	18.6	16.9
28	Chemicals and products	24.3	33.7	51.0	48.6	25.8	29.7	29.7	32.5
29	Petroleum and coal products	46.8	13.6	39.5	36.6	39.5	37.0	39.4	36.7
30	Rubber products	100.0	59.9	58.6	54.1	57.0	56.0	52.1	51.0
31	Leather and leather products	26.3	0.0	26.2	26.4	26.1	26.6	25.9	26.6
32	Stone, clay, and glass products	13.3	43.9	43.4	46.4	80.6	78.8	79.0	77.7
33	Primary metal products	[4] 45.7	21.0	43.8	49.5	40.6	45.3	41.4	46.7
34	Fabricated metal products		8.4	25.3	26.1	26.7	26.0	26.6	25.4
35	Machinery, except electrical	[5] 41.4	18.5	38.0	33.2	38.2	38.9	37.6	37.8
36	Electrical machinery		53.2	54.1	48.2	53.4	50.5	50.8	47.9
37	Transportation equipment	57.3	84.2	54.4	58.7	54.0	63.3	53.7	56.6
38	Instruments and related products		45.0	45.3	47.4	52.8	52.5	54.0	53.5
39	Miscellaneous manufactures	2.7	21.2	34.9	16.1	31.5	30.1	29.0	28.6

[1] 319 (4-digit) industries. Various years 1895–1904; central date was approximately 1901 but weighting factors used were as of 1899.
[2] 452 (4-digit) industries.
[3] 434 (4-digit) industries.
[4] Excludes steel works and rolling mills for which the concentration ratio is 78.8.
[5] Includes electrical machinery.

chapter V

CORPORATE ASSETS, LIABILITIES, AND INCOME (Series V 65–237)

V 65–237. General note.

Aggregate balance sheet and income data for all U.S. corporations combined and for corporations classified by major industry have been published annually since 1926 by the Internal Revenue Service (and its predecessor, Bureau of Internal Revenue) in *Statistics of Income*, part 2. Data classified by asset-size class are also available since 1931. Series V 65–127 are based on the materials assembled in *Statistics of Income*. Other sources provide balance sheet and income data for public utilities, railroads, and commercial banks over considerably longer periods. Data for public utility corporations are presented, in condensed form, in series V 128–142. Data for railroads are presented in Chapter Q, Transportation, and for commercial banks in Chapter X, Banking and Finance.

Most of the series shown here include aggregates based on the values reported by corporations in their accounting statements. These book values are seldom, if ever, equal to current market values, nor do they correspond to theoretical values computed by economic analysts (e.g., values arrived at on the basis of the expected revenue streams). When the general price level remains stable, individual differences between the book value and the market value (or between the book value and the theoretical economic value) may largely cancel out in the process of aggregation. In times of a persistent inflation, however, book values show a general tendency to fall below current market valuations, while in times of persistent deflation the reverse is generally true. Some specific valuation problems, arising in connection with different types of business assets, are briefly discussed below.

Physical assets. Physical assets owned by business firms include inventories (of both finished goods and goods in process) and fixed assets (land, plant, and equipment).

Inventories are usually shown on the balance sheet at "cost or market, whichever is lower." Consequently, in periods of rising prices, book values tend to be below current market values. In periods of falling prices, however, conservative accounting practices require an adjustment in the book value so as to bring it down to the level of the current market value.

Until recently, book charges for inventories used up in production have been based almost universally on the "fifo" (first in, first out) method of valuation. But in recent years a substantial number of firms have switched to the "lifo" (last in, first out) method. These two valuation methods yield different results with respect to reported costs and profits and also with respect to the book value of the year-end inventory. Under "lifo" procedure, the most recent prices are used for the computation of costs. Consequently, reported profits (and, therefore, income tax liability) are reduced in periods of rising prices, but are increased in periods of falling prices, as compared with the amount that would be reported under "fifo."

On the other hand, the year-end inventories are valued at less recent prices on a "lifo" than on a "fifo" basis. Consequently, in periods of price instability the use of "lifo" tends to widen the gap between the book value and the current market value of the year-end inventories.

Except in special cases, a comparison of year-end inventory values does not provide an adequate indication of changes in the physical volume of inventories. When "lifo" is used, a change in the book value of inventory will correctly indicate the change in the physical volume valued at current prices, as long as the volume is increasing. If the physical volume is decreasing, however, a valuation adjustment is required in order to arrive at the current value of the physical decrement. When "fifo" is used, a valuation adjustment must be made whether the physical volume is increasing or decreasing.

Since the aggregate inventory values represent a combination of "fifo" and "lifo" inventories (the former being the predominant component), an inventory valuation adjustment is clearly required before any inferences regarding changes in the physical stock are to be drawn from these figures.

Fixed assets include durable capital goods, which are generally entered at cost and are written off gradually over a period of years by means of annual depreciation charges. A detailed balance sheet usually includes (*a*) the gross amount before depreciation, (*b*) the depreciation reserve accumulated to date, and (*c*) the net amount after depreciation, which is equal to (*a*) minus (*b*).

If the prices of capital goods remained constant, the gross amount of plant and equipment would equal their replacement cost (the cost of replacing the existing items, which vary in age from almost new to being close to the time of retirement, with brand new items of the same type). During periods of continual price increases, however, the gross amount falls considerably short of the replacement cost; while during periods of continual price declines, the opposite is true.

The net amount of plant and equipment would approach the current market value only if the annual depreciation allowances corresponded to the actual loss of value through wear and tear as well as obsolescence (and, furthermore, if the prices of new capital goods remained constant). This, however, hardly ever happens in actual practice. Most corporations have been using the "straight line" method of depreciation, under which durable equipment has been written off by equal amounts every year during its entire lifetime, irrespective of the actual degree of wear and tear or obsolescence. During and after World War II accelerated writeoffs were allowed in industries working for defense, whereby plant and equipment could be written off over an arbitrary 5-year period. This procedure, coupled with the fact that prices generally rose at a relatively fast rate during the war and the postwar period, has served to further widen the gap between the net book values and the actual market values of fixed assets.

Neither the gross nor the net amount of plant and equipment may be taken to reflect accurately changes in the physical stock of durable capital goods. If prices remained constant, changes in the gross amount would indicate changes in quantity, though not in quality, of capital goods. For example, if a firm owned 100 units of machinery and added 10 new units next year, the gross amount would show a 10-percent rise (assuming no retirements during the year); but the gross amount could not show the decline in quality of the original 100 units through the process of aging. The net amount does reflect the aging of durable equipment but, as stated above, the prevailing depreciation methods do not—and are not intended to—align the book values with changes in the actual market value over time.

Financial assets. Financial assets of corporations represent their claims on other business units, individuals, and government. Current (short-term) financial assets include cash, bank deposit accounts, notes receivable and marketable securities (mostly U.S. Government but frequently including marketable corporate stock as well). Noncurrent (long-term) financial assets consist of bonds, other long-term debt instruments, and nonmarketable securities which are largely permanent holdings of corporate stock. The problem of market valuation does not, of course, arise in connection with cash and bank deposits. If receivables are salable, their market value does not ordinarily deviate from the book amount by more than a moderate discount. But in the case of securities, especially common stocks, the current market value may differ widely from the original cost to the owner. Bonds tend to rise in price when the current interest rate declines relative to the coupon rate. Stocks tend to rise when the expected rate of profit and/or dividends earned by the issuer increases. Conservative accounting practice requires that securities be valued at "cost or market, whichever is lower." Thus, while the book values are not expected to exceed the market values for any considerable length of time the reverse relationship may continue indefinitely.

While the market value of stocks tends to rise with—though not necessarily in proportion to—the general level of prices, the market value of bonds is not directly affected by this factor. In fact, in times of inflation or deflation, the fixed amount debt instruments become especially variable in terms of real purchasing power represented by them.

A special problem arises in connection with financial assets when aggregate balance sheets are compiled. In a closed economic system all financial claims and liabilities would cancel out. A consolidated balance sheet for the entire system would show only physical property on the asset side and net claims to this property by individuals on the liability side.

Since the corporate sector of our economy is not a closed system, a consolidated balance sheet for all corporations combined would not eliminate all financial assets and liabilities, although it would eliminate a substantial part representing intercompany claims.

The aggregate balance sheets presented in this section are essentially unconsolidated data. Some large corporations submitted consolidated balance sheets comprising the parent company and its subsidiaries. (Consolidated returns were permitted prior to 1934 and then again after 1942. See text for series V 65–127.) But, in the main, the total amounts were obtained by mere aggregation rather than consolidation of individual companies' statements.

As a result, the total amounts of both receivables and payables include a certain (undetermined) amount owed by corporations to other corporations. The total amount of investments includes a certain (undetermined) amount of corporate securities owned by corporations. When claims of the creditor corporations on the debtor corporations are included in total assets of the sector as a whole, the total is inflated by the double-counting involved.

Liabilities. The valuation problems encountered in connection with corporate liabilities are generally similar to those discussed above in connection with financial assets. When the price level rises, the amount of debt shrinks in terms of real purchasing power. When the market value of assets increases, the dollar amount of debt remains unchanged, but its magnitude in relation to net worth (valued at market prices) declines. When unconsolidated data are aggregated, the total amount of debt is inflated because no adjustment is made for intercompany liabilities.

The item designated as "other liabilities" (series V 80) includes accrued income tax and other accrued liabilities. Tax accruals were a relatively minor item during the 1920's and 1930's, but assumed major proportions during and after World War II, when the income tax rates were sharply raised and the excess profits tax was imposed (during 1940–1945 and again during 1950–1953). Tax accruals rose substantially also in the years of World War I, but a sharp decline occurred after the war. These movements are reflected in the sample data for large manufacturing corporations, extending over the 1914–1943 period (see text for series V 217–237).

The amount of accrued taxes has not been reported as a separate balance sheet item in *Statistics of Income.* Until recently, the year-end amount of tax accruals usually was fairly close to the current year's total tax liability (series V 94, V 111, and V 126), but the acceleration program enacted in 1954 placed large corporate taxpayers on a partially pay-as-you-go basis, which tended to reduce their tax reserves.

The rise in the income tax accruals on the liability side of corporate balance sheets was accompanied by an increase in government security holding on the asset side. Thus, in a completely consolidated statement for the corporate sector, the debt owed by corporations to the government would be largely offset by the debt owed by the government to corporations, and the net balance of such claims would be relatively small.

Net worth. Net worth (or equity) is the stockholders' share in the total assets of a corporation. It is not measured by the capital stock account alone, but is equal to the sum of capital stock, capital reserves, paid-in surplus, and earned surplus; or, alternatively, it represents the difference between total assets on the one hand and the sum of all short-term and long-term liabilities on the other. Since the dollar amount of liabilities is fixed at any one time, a revaluation of assets results in a corresponding change in net worth.

In a newly established firm, net worth is equal to the amount of capital paid in by its first stockholders. This amount may be registered in the capital stock account alone, or partly (usually up to the par value per share) in the capital stock account and partly in the paid-in surplus (or capital surplus) account. A going concern, on the other hand, can increase its net worth from two sources—by selling additional shares of stock and by retaining profits. The latter method (known as internal financing) has generally been a very important source of funds for American corporations.

Net profit retained in a given year is reflected in the year-end balance sheet as an increase in the earned surplus account. However, the amount of earned surplus shown on the balance sheet may not generally be taken to represent the sum of all profit retentions over the company's entire lifetime. Many companies declare stock dividends from time to time, and this involves transfers from the earned surplus to the capital stock account. Other companies make occasional transfers from earned surplus to various reserve or special fund accounts. In some cases, earned surplus and paid-in surplus are combined into one account, which makes it impossible to separate paid-in equity from retained funds. Thus, generally speaking, while the balance sheet data for any one year indicate the total amount of net worth, they contain no accurate information as to what portion of net worth has been built up by stock sales and what portion has been accumulated through profit retentions.

Sales, income, and dividends. The sales, income, and dividend figures also represent unconsolidated aggregates, with no adjustment for intercompany transactions. Goods and services sold by corporations to other corporations are included in the total amount of sales two or more times. For example, the value of steel sold by steel producers to automobile manufacturers is included in the sales of the steel industry and also in the sales of the automobile industry (as part of the total value of the automobiles sold). In other words, total reported sales of all industries would exceed by a large margin the net value of corporate production (the sum of all net values added by individual companies) in any given period.

The net income and dividend totals also contain some duplication, since no adjustment has been made for intercompany dividends. When dividends are paid by one company to another, this is obviously a transfer payment which does not increase the actual total income of the corporate sector as a whole. Yet, since such payments are included in net income of the receiving companies without being deducted from net income of the paying companies, the aggregate amount of net income of all corporations is correspondingly inflated.

Problems of asset valuation and income computation have been extensively discussed in the accounting and economic literature. Useful basic discussions may be found in the following books: J. C. Bonbright, *The Valuation of Property*, McGraw-Hill, New York, 1937; N. S. Buchanan, *The Economics of Corporate Enterprise*, Henry Holt & Co., New York, 1940; B. Graham and D. L. Dodd, *Security Analysis*, McGraw-Hill, New York, 1951; J. P. Powelson, *Economic Accounting*, McGraw-Hill, New York, 1955.

The problems encountered in compiling the national income data from the balance sheets submitted by business firms are discussed in Office of Business Economics, *National Income: A Supplement to the Survey of Current Business*, 1954, and *U.S. Income and Output*, 1958.

V 65-127. General note.

Aggregate balance sheet data for all corporations submitting such data with their income tax returns have been published in *Statistics of Income* since 1926. Aggregate income data for all corporations submitting income tax returns have been available since 1916, but income data for corporations submitting balance sheets have been compiled only since 1931.

Companies which did not submit balance sheet data for 1926–1955 represented only a small fraction of the total corporate population in terms of total income and assets. Thus, companies not submitting balance sheets accounted for only 3 percent of the total compiled receipts in 1931 and 1 percent in 1953. The data presented here may, therefore, be taken as a fairly close approximation of the entire corporate population.

For 1926–1950, annual tabulations have been derived from all corporation returns filed. For 1951–1955, the aggregate data for small corporations were estimated on the basis of 10- and 20-percent samples, in order to reduce the cost and delay involved in tabulating all returns. In 1951, sampling procedures were confined to corporations with total assets under $250,000. The sample amounted to 10 percent of this population. In 1952, the companies with total assets under $250,000 were represented by a 10-percent sample. Furthermore, the companies with total assets between $250,000 and $500,000 were represented by a 20-percent sample. All returns with total assets of $500,000 and over together with all consolidated returns, life and mutual insurance companies, personal holding companies, and taxable returns with total income (total gross receipts less cost of sales or operations) of $200,000 and over, regardless of size of total assets, were tabulated.

For 1953–1955, the sampling rates no longer depended on total assets. A 10-percent sample was selected from the companies which had total gross receipts below $100,000. A 20-percent sample was selected from the companies with total gross receipts between $100,000 and $500,00. All companies with total gross receipts of $500,000 and over were tabulated.

Although small companies account for a very large share of the total corporate universe in terms of the number of returns, they represent a relatively small share of the total in terms of assets and receipts. Thus, in 1952 the total assets of small

companies accounted for only 7 percent of the aggregate figure for all corporations combined.

The data in each volume of *Statistics of Income* are from returns for the calendar year indicated, for fiscal years ending within the period July of the calendar year through June of the succeeding year, and for partial years with the greater number of months of the accounting period falling within the calendar year. The information is compiled from the returns as filed, prior to revisions that may be made as a result of audit by the Internal Revenue Service. Also, the data do not reflect loss carrybacks, renegotiation of war contracts, or recomputation of amortization of emergency facilities.

The returns included in each report are those filed for comparable periods of time. There are factors, however, which interfere with the precise comparability of the data over a period of years. While their influence has not been so strong as to obscure major historical trends, they must, of course, be borne in mind, especially when close comparisons are attempted. Some of the more important interfering factors are indicated below.

In general, the items for 1926–1933 are not precisely comparable with those for 1934–1941, because of the discontinuance, under the Revenue Act of 1934, of the privilege of filing consolidated income tax returns (except by railroad corporations and their related holding and leasing companies and, for 1940 and 1941, Pan-American trade corporations), and the consequent appearance, in the separate returns filed by corporations formerly included in an affiliated group, of items which, owing to "intercompany eliminations," did not appear on the consolidated return.

The discontinuance of consolidated returns also resulted in changes in industrial classification. A corporation is classified industrially according to the business reported on the return. When diversified activities are reported, the classification is determined by the industry which accounts for the largest percentage of receipts. Therefore, industrial groups may contain data for activities other than those on which the classification is based. Prior to 1934, a consolidated return was classified on the predominant activity of the group of affiliated concerns, whereas, for 1934 and subsequent years, the separate return filed by each concern which was formerly a part of an affiliated group is classified on its predominant industry. Beginning 1942, the consolidated return privilege was again extended, in general, to all corporations.

On the basis of the data contained in the 1934 issue of *Statistics of Income*, two sets of figures are given for 1934 in series V 98–112. In 1934 (comparable with later years), corporations which submitted consolidated returns in 1933 are classified according to the business reported on the deconsolidated returns for 1934. In 1934 (comparable with earlier years, insofar as industrial classification is concerned), corporations which submitted consolidated returns in 1933 are classified according to the business reported on consolidated returns in 1933. The latter data for 1934, however, are still not fully consistent with those for 1933 because they include items which are eliminated in consolidated returns but are present in deconsolidated statements.

There have been other changes in the content of various items, which have affected historical comparability. For example, notes payable with maturity of one year or more were included with bonds and mortgages for 1929–1936, but not for succeeding years. Surplus reserves were included with "surplus and undivided profits" for 1926–1937, whereas they have been shown as a separate item since 1938.

The changes in the Standard Industrial Classification from time to time do not substantially affect the comparability of these data. The figures have been revised historically to reflect these changes which are indicated in the annual volumes of *Statistics of Income.*

V 65–97. Corporate assets, liabilities, receipts, deductions, net profits, and dividends, for all industries combined, 1926–1955.

Source: Internal Revenue Service (and predecessor Bureau of Internal Revenue), *Statistics of Income*, part 2, *Corporation Income Tax Returns*, various annual issues.

V 65, number of returns. Excludes returns with fragmentary balance sheets and, except for 1926, returns of inactive corporations.

V 67, cash. Includes bank deposits.

V 70, investments, government obligations. Consists of obligations of all governmental units within the United States and its outlying areas. Where investments are not segregated as between "government" and "other," the entire amount is included in "other investments."

V 72, capital assets. Includes depreciable tangible assets such as buildings, fixed mechanical equipment, manufacturing and transportation facilities, furniture and fixtures; depletable tangible assets—natural resources; land; and, for 1939–1955, intangible assets such as patents, franchises, formulas, copyrights, leaseholds, goodwill, and trademarks. Prior to 1939, intangible assets were included in "other assets."

V 73, other assets. Consists of assets not elsewhere reported on tax return, such as sinking funds, other funds; deferred charges; organization expenses; prepaid and suspense items; interest, discount, coupons, and dividends receivable; and guarantee deposits. "Other assets" of life insurance companies include market value of real estate, bonds, and stocks in excess of book value; interest, rents, and premiums due; and agents' balances.

V 80, other liabilities. Consists of liabilities not elsewhere reported on tax return, such as deferred and suspense items; accrued expenses; dividends payable; funds held in trust; borrowed securities; outstanding coupons and certificates; and overdrafts. "Other liabilities" of life insurance companies include the net value of outstanding policies and annuities, and borrowed money. "Other liabilities" of banks include deposits (time, savings, demand, etc.) and bank notes in circulation.

V 83, surplus reserves. This item is included with surplus and undivided profits for 1926–1937.

V 84, surplus and undivided profits. Consists of paid-in or capital surplus and earned surplus and undivided profits.

V 85, deficit. Consists of negative amounts of earned surplus and undivided profits.

V 87, gross sales and receipts from operations. Gross sales consist of amounts received for goods, less returns and allowances, in transactions where inventories are an income-determining factor. Cost of goods sold is shown as a deduction. Gross receipts from operations consist of amounts received from transactions in which inventories are not an income-determining factor. Cost of operations is shown as a deduction. Gross receipts from operations and cost of operations are not available prior to 1932. The figure shown for 1931 represents gross profit from operations.

V 96, dividends paid in cash and assets other than own stock. Excludes liquidating dividends.

V 98–112. Selected corporate assets, liabilities, and income items, by industrial division, 1926–1955.

Source: See source for series V 65–97.

V 113–127. Selected corporate assets, liabilities, and income items, by size of total assets, 1931–1955.

Source: See source for series V 65–97.

V 128–142. Assets, liabilities, and selected income items for privately owned Class A and B electric companies, 1937–1956.

Source: All series except V 131–133, Federal Power Commission, *Statistics of Electrical Utilities in the United States*, various annual issues; series V 131–133, Federal Power Commission, records.

These data cover reports of all companies having annual electric revenues in excess of $250,000. In recent years, these concerns have represented approximately 98 percent of the total privately owned electric utility industry.

V 128, total assets or liabilities. For total assets, series V 128 is the sum of series V 129, V 130, V 133, and V 134. For total liabilities, series V 128 is the sum of series V 135–139.

V 129, current assets. Includes cash, special deposits, working funds, temporary cash investments, receivables (less reserve for uncollectible accounts), materials and supplies, prepayments, other current and accrued assets.

V 130, investments. Includes investments in associated companies (less reserve), other investments (less reserve), physical property other than utility plant (less reserve), sinking funds, miscellaneous special funds.

V 131–133, plant and equipment in service. Prior to 1932, firms in the electric utility industry included in their electric utility plant and equipment accounts an increasing amount of "phantom assets" which were created by "writing up" assets above their original cost. Changes in economic conditions and government regulation forced a "write-down" of these "assets" at intervals over subsequent years. Until such "write-downs" were made, however, the figures as published in the annual reports of the Federal Power Commission included decreasing amounts of "phantom assets." However, the figures shown here for series V 128–133 represent revised estimates of the Federal Power Commission and exclude "phantom assets."

V 134, other assets. Includes the "phantom assets" deducted from electric plant and equipment (see text for series V 131–133); electric plant not in service such as plant under construction, leased to others, or held for future use; net utility plant and equipment other than electric; deferred debits; capital stock discount and expenses; and reacquired securities. Although there was some decline in deferred debits, capital stock discount and expense, and reacquired securities, the major portion of the decline in this series between 1937 and 1945 is attributable to the writeoff of "phantom assets." The distribution of these assets for significant years was as follows (in millions):

Item	1937	1948	1956
Total other assets	$4,833.9	$3,657.3	$5,207.1
"Phantom assets"	2,100.0		
Electric plant not in service	450.0	1,472.1	1,945.0
Net utility plant other than electric	1,683.6	1,876.6	2,959.4
Other asset items	600.3	308.6	302.7

If the "phantom assets" were to be completely excluded from the asset side, a corresponding adjustment would have to be made in the companies' net worth. This has not been done, because it has been deemed advisable to present the capital and surplus figures as reported by the electric companies.

V 135, current liabilities. Includes notes and accounts payable, dividends declared, customers' deposits, accrued taxes and interest, miscellaneous current and accrued liabilities.

V 136, long-term debt. Includes bonds, receivers' certificates, advances from associated companies, miscellaneous long-term debt. Bonds held in treasury were deducted from the total amount of long-term debt outstanding.

V 137, other liabilities. Includes deferred credits, insurance, and other reserves.

V 138, capital stock. Includes common and preferred stock, stock liability for conversion, premiums and assessments on capital stock, capital stock subscribed, installments received on capital stock. Treasury stock was deducted from the total amount of stock outstanding.

V 139, net surplus. Includes capital and earned surplus.

V 140, total revenue. Includes operating revenues and other income, gross of operating expenses, and all other deductions.

V 141, net income. Equals total revenue less all operating and nonoperating income deductions (including depreciation, interest, and taxes).

V 142, dividends. Includes dividends on preferred and common shares. Excludes stock dividends.

V 143–157. Assets, liabilities, and selected income items for central electric light and power stations, commercial, 1902–1937.

Source: 1902–1912, Bureau of the Census, *Electrical Industries*, special reports and bulletins for 1902, 1907, and 1912; 1917–1937, *Census of Electrical Industries*, reports for 1917, 1922, 1927, 1932, and 1937.

See also text for series V 128–142.

Central electric stations are defined as plants owned or operated by individuals, companies, corporations, or municipalities, and furnishing current for public or commercial uses.

Although central electric stations, as defined by Bureau of the Census, do not represent a group completely identical with Class A and B electric companies, as defined by the Federal Power Commission, the coverage is nearly the same in terms of assets, liabilities, and revenues, as the figures for 1937 show. Consequently, the data in series V 128–142 and V 143–157 may be taken to indicate, with a high degree of approximation, financial trends in the electric utility industry over the entire 1902–1956 period.

Unfortunately, complete balance sheet data for series V 143–157 are available only for 1927, 1932, and 1937. The data for 1912, 1917, and 1922 do not include reserve for depreciation. Consequently, total assets for these years include the gross rather than net value of plant and equipment. The only balance sheet item available for 1902 and 1907 is the gross amount of plant and equipment. The gross revenue, net income, and dividend figures, however, are available for the entire 1902–1937 period.

The accounting nomenclature in series V 143–157 and also in series V 158–202 is similar to that described above for series V 128–142. However, financial statements were much less detailed in the early years and accounting procedures did not remain fully consistent over the entire 1902–1937 period.

V 158–172. Assets, liabilities, and selected income items for street and electric railways, 1902–1937.

Source: See source for series V 143–157.

See also text for series V 128–142.

These data relate to all electric railways in the United States irrespective of their length or location and all street railways irrespective of their motive power.

Data for 1902–1922 include companies which operated street and electric railways and were also engaged in other activities, while the data for 1922–1937 include only companies which were exclusively engaged in the operation of street and electric railways. The double set of figures given for 1922 should enable users to make an adjustment required for comparing the figures for 1927–1937 with those for 1902–1917. For 1917–1937, the amount of total assets includes net value of plant and equipment. For 1902–1912, on the other hand, gross value of plant and

equipment had to be included because of the lack of data on depreciation.

V 173–202. Assets, liabilities, and selected income items of telephone and telegraph companies, 1902–1937.

Source: See source for series V 143–157.

See also text for series V 128–142.

The data available for the telephone and telegraph companies for 1902–1937 are even more incomplete than those for the electric utilities. After 1922, the only data collected by the Bureau of the Census were value of plant and equipment, gross income, and dividends paid. During the entire 1902–1937 period, reserves for depreciation were included with other reserves on the liability side and could not, therefore, be used to obtain net value of plant and equipment. Treasury stocks and bonds were reported as a single item (Treasury securities) and could not, therefore, be subtracted from long-term debt and capital stock respectively, as was done for the other electrical industries.

Despite these serious deficiencies, however, the data throw some light on the rapid development of the telephone and telegraph industries in the early decades of the 20th century and should, therefore, be useful to those interested in financial trends of these two industries.

V 203–216. Net value of plant and equipment in regulated industries, 1870–1951.

Source: Melville J. Ulmer, *Capital in Transportation, Communications and Public Utilities*, National Bureau of Economic Research, Princeton University Press, 1959.

All values in these series are net of depreciation and relate to reproducible fixed assets: Road, plant and equipment. Investment in land and land rights has not been included. The coverage is confined to privately owned enterprises.

In general, the series have been obtained by cumulative addition (or subtraction) of the annual figures on net capital formation to a base value in some selected year. The series in 1929 dollars reflect changes in net physical stock of reproducible fixed assets. The series in current dollars indicate changes in the replacement value of such assets, less depreciation.

More specifically, the derivation of the series in 1929 dollars involved the following steps:

a. Finding a base-year figure. For steam railroads, the base-year value was derived from an ICC estimate for January 1, 1937. For electric light and power companies, the value of plant and equipment was assumed to be zero as of January 1, 1881. For telephones, the value for 1880 was derived from estimates of gross capital expenditures in 1878 and 1879. For street and electric railways, the value for 1870 was obtained from the reports submitted to State Railroad Commissions. For local bus lines, it was assumed that net value for 1910 was less than $100,000.

b. Converting the base-year figure into 1929 dollars.

c. Deriving the series on net capital expenditures in 1929 prices. This series was obtained by deducting the estimated annual amounts of "true" depreciation from the figures on gross capital expenditures for the corresponding years.

d. Applying the series on net capital expenditures to the base-year value.

The series in current dollars for each class of utilities was obtained by multiplying the values in 1929 dollars by the construction cost index applicable to that class.

V 217–237. Assets, liabilities, and selected income items for two samples of large manufacturing corporations, 1914–1943.

Source: National Bureau of Economic Research, records.

These series represent financial data for two samples of large corporations (companies with total assets over $10 million each). The data for 1914–1922 are based on a sample of 81 corporations, and the data for 1922–1943 are based on a sample of 84 corporations. These sample materials make it possible to examine financial developments in manufacturing during World War I and the early part of the interwar period, for which time no aggregate data are available.

For both samples, companies were selected from among the largest and most important concerns in 11 major manufacturing industries. A few of the very large corporations (e.g., Ford Motor Company) had to be omitted because of lack of published financial statements, but the number of such omissions was small. Consequently, both samples, though small in terms of the number of firms included, represent substantial portions of the entire manufacturing universe in terms of total assets and total volume of operations. For example, in 1933 the sample represented 29 percent of the total assets of all manufacturing corporations and as much as 45 percent of the total assets of all large manufacturing corporations (with total assets over $10 million). (See A. R. Koch, *The Financing of Large Corporations*, National Bureau of Economic Research, New York, 1943, p. 13.)

In the sample for 1914–1922, data were not available for 8 companies in 1914, 3 companies in 1915, 1 company in 1916, and 1 company in 1917. In the sample for 1922–1943, 3 companies had to be omitted in 1922, 1 in 1923, 1 in 1924, and 1 in 1925. Since the excluded firms were among the smallest in the samples, however, their omission had a relatively minor effect on the composite balance sheets and income statements.

The amounts of total assets, income, and dividends for the sample for 1922–1943 are considerably greater than those for the sample for earlier years. This is due to the fact that in a number of cases larger companies were substituted in the sample for 1922–1943 for smaller concerns included in the sample for 1914–1922. These differences should be borne in mind when trends over the entire period are examined.

For a more detailed description of these samples, see the unpublished manuscript, *Corporate Financial Data for Studies in Business Finance*, May 1945, available at the National Bureau of Economic Research.

The accounting terms used in these series are defined as follows:

Total assets: Sum of all asset items less depreciation and revaluation reserves.

Cash: Cash on hand and bank deposits.

Marketable securities: Government securities; call and time loans.

Receivables: Notes and accounts receivable less bad debt reserve.

Inventory: Raw materials; goods and work in process; finished goods; supplies—less reserves for inventory.

Investments and advances: Investment in, or advances, to subsidiaries or affiliates; other stocks and bonds.

Fixed assets (net): Land; plant; machinery; equipment; nonoperating property—less reserves for depreciation, depletion, and obsolescence.

Other assets: Prepaid expenses; deferred charges; intangibles; due from officers, directors, and stockholders; cash set aside for specific purposes or not available for immediate use.

Notes payable: All notes or bills to banks, trade, and others.

Accounts payable: Accounts payable to trade.

Other current liabilities: Accruals and current reserves.

Long-term debt: All funded debt or mortgages, whether current or not, less sinking fund when listed on asset side; purchase obligations.

Other liabilities: Minority interest; deferred liabilities; amounts appropriated from surplus for specific purposes; due to officers, employees, and affiliates.

Preferred stock: Preferred and debenture stock less treasury preferred stock when listed on asset side.

Common stock: Common stock (A and B) or capital stock less common treasury stock when listed on asset side.

Capital reserves: Special appropriations from income or surplus for contingencies.

Surplus: Capital and earned surplus less profit and undivided surplus when carried on asset side.

Net income: Net amount after all expenses, interest, and taxes.

Dividends: Cash dividends on preferred and common shares. Stock dividends are not included.

Series V 65–97. Corporate Assets, Liabilities, Receipts, Deductions, Net Profit, and Dividends, for All Industries Combined: 1926 to 1955

[Money figures in millions of dollars]

Series No.	Item	1955	1954	1953	1952	1951	1950	1949	1948	1947	1946
65	Number of returns with balance sheets	746,962	667,856	640,073	615,698	596,385	569,961	554,573	536,833	496,821	440,750
66	Total assets	888,621	805,300	761,877	721,864	647,524	598,369	543,562	525,136	494,615	454,705
67	Cash	87,375	81,723	80,171	79,597	76,853	71,018	63,864	65,737	64,369	58,502
68	Notes and accounts receivable less reserve	191,779	158,738	148,282	140,902	119,314	108,909	85,526	84,597	75,959	61,371
69	Inventories	70,920	62,914	65,519	64,520	63,776	54,496	44,726	48,293	44,009	36,965
70	Investments, government obligations	131,898	131,409	123,599	120,303	108,939	109,822	110,969	104,819	108,774	109,910
71	Other investments	179,558	160,553	147,188	132,512	104,883	96,760	91,152	84,202	78,363	77,089
72	Capital assets less reserves	206,388	191,437	180,612	169,546	159,325	144,691	135,617	125,650	112,194	100,329
73	Other assets	20,703	18,527	16,506	14,485	14,434	12,674	11,709	11,838	10,946	10,541
74	Total liabilities	888,621	805,300	761,877	721,864	647,524	598,369	543,562	525,136	494,615	454,705
77	Accounts payable	45,590	38,153	35,554	35,827	33,352	31,298	24,896	26,302	25,537	21,336
	Bonds, notes, and mortgages payable:										
78	Maturity less than 1 year [1]	30,458	23,239	21,394	20,996	19,240	15,845	11,801	12,225	11,289	9,504
79	Maturity 1 year or more [1]	98,399	90,797	86,607	80,628	72,835	65,719	61,851	57,326	50,108	44,968
80	Other liabilities	408,727	373,343	353,141	330,406	283,058	261,899	236,716	232,064	227,114	214,283
81	Capital stock, preferred	15,796	15,632	15,815	15,831	15,595	14,906	15,365	14,957	15,007	14,857
82	Capital stock, common	96,832	90,730	88,121	85,365	82,804	79,310	78,944	76,774	72,463	68,334
83	Surplus reserves	14,265	14,197	13,294	13,472	12,739	12,410	11,178	11,345	11,303	11,004
84	Surplus and undivided profits [2]	178,555	159,210	155,606	146,464	135,310	124,951	111,078	102,262	90,101	78,836
85	Less: Deficit [3]			7,655	7,125	7,411	7,968	8,269	8,118	8,307	8,416
86	Total compiled receipts	634,508	547,001	551,984	525,011	511,849	452,523	387,636	405,430	361,521	283,917
87	Gross sales and receipts from operations	605,408	521,478	528,638	503,365	492,373	434,666	372,005	390,382	347,946	270,984
88	Other receipts	29,100	25,523	23,344	21,647	19,476	17,856	15,629	15,049	13,575	12,933
89	Total compiled deductions	586,907	510,515	512,402	486,504	468,354	409,988	359,505	371,182	330,314	258,893
90	Cost of goods sold and of operations	443,172	384,226	388,214	371,597	363,046	317,373	275,585	290,405	258,146	199,552
91	Depreciation, depletion, and amortization	18,592	15,729	14,178	12,433	11,090	9,489	8,521	7,939	6,383	4,972
92	Other deductions	125,143	110,561	110,009	102,474	94,218	83,128	75,400	72,838	65,782	54,370
93	Compiled net profit or net loss	47,601	36,486	39,582	38,507	43,495	42,535	28,130	34,248	31,207	25,025
94	Income and excess profits taxes	21,536	16,682	19,693	19,002	21,902	17,168	9,688	11,771	10,787	8,710
95	Compiled net profit after taxes	26,065	19,804	19,889	19,504	21,593	25,368	18,442	22,477	20,420	16,314
	Dividends paid:										
96	Cash and assets other than own stock	13,468	11,832	11,533	11,196	11,219	11,471	9,464	9,305	8,285	7,378
97	Corporation's own stock	1,980	1,344	1,106	1,360	1,425	1,289	678	1,022	696	523

Series No.	Item	1945	1944	1943	1942	1941	1940	1939	1938	1937	1936
65	Number of returns with balance sheets	374,950	363,056	366,870	383,534	407,053	413,716	412,759	411,941	416,902	415,654
66	Total assets	441,461	418,324	389,524	360,018	340,452	320,478	306,801	300,022	303,357	303,180
67	Cash	57,717	52,783	50,271	46,464	41,629	41,423	34,054	27,973	24,346	26,102
68	Notes and accounts receivable less reserve	51,630	47,894	45,728	46,155	49,255	42,864	39,451	37,763	40,329	40,219
69	Inventories	26,067	26,476	27,187	26,832	25,058	19,463	17,718	16,582	18,515	16,584
70	Investments, government obligations	129,935	111,219	86,655	61,191	36,548	29,570	27,353	25,527	23,988	24,313
71	Other investments	74,026	74,392	72,064	70,899	80,354	80,429	81,155	82,701	85,065	86,208
72	Capital assets less reserves	92,057	95,128	97,728	99,772	100,698	100,214	100,226	99,299	100,320	97,873
73	Other assets	10,029	10,431	9,889	8,706	6,911	6,514	6,846	10,176	10,794	11,882
74	Total liabilities	441,461	418,324	389,524	360,018	340,452	320,478	306,801	300,022	303,357	303,180
75	Notes and accounts payable	--------	--------	--------	--------	--------	--------	--------	--------	--------	25,580
76	Bonded debt and mortgages	--------	--------	--------	--------	--------	--------	--------	--------	--------	47,023
77	Accounts payable	17,455	17,805	17,495	17,055	16,350	14,696	14,506	13,747	14,748	--------
	Bonds, notes, and mortgages payable:										
78	Maturity less than 1 year [1]	7,208	7,056	6,770	7,205	9,242	7,987	8,027	8,104	10,373	--------
79	Maturity 1 year or more [1]	40,987	42,454	43,735	45,040	49,542	49,199	49,388	50,278	49,326	--------
80	Other liabilities	221,286	200,550	175,859	151,088	122,728	110,210	98,016	90,455	87,276	97,109
81	Capital stock, preferred	14,764	15,112	15,067	15,473	16,214	17,138	17,213	18,108	18,364	18,591
82	Capital stock, common	64,747	64,785	64,481	65,828	71,577	72,292	73,482	74,792	77,339	78,072
83	Surplus reserves	11,057	12,200	12,409	10,581	10,065	8,358	7,889	7,301	} 58,524	48,043
84	Surplus and undivided profits [2]	72,528	67,557	63,427	58,201	56,593	53,275	51,302	50,367		
85	Less: Deficit [3]	8,571	9,195	9,720	10,454	11,858	12,676	13,022	13,131	12,594	11,237
86	Total compiled receipts	252,636	258,880	245,796	213,777	186,137	145,427	130,365	117,596	138,907	126,269
87	Gross sales and receipts from operations	241,456	249,129	236,610	204,981	176,717	136,535	121,601	109,210	130,004	117,375
88	Other receipts	11,180	9,750	9,186	8,795	9,420	8,891	8,763	8,384	8,903	8,895
89	Total compiled deductions	231,417	232,426	217,863	190,497	169,546	135,955	123,129	113,452	131,130	118,651
90	Cost of goods sold and of operations	178,187	183,179	171,698	146,596	125,737	97,240	86,828	78,271	94,149	84,447
91	Depreciation, depletion, and amortization	6,531	5,563	5,169	4,800	4,280	3,931	3,805	3,711	3,756	3,551
92	Other deductions	46,698	43,686	40,994	39,102	39,528	34,784	32,497	31,470	33,224	30,653
93	Compiled net profit or net loss	21,220	26,454	27,933	23,280	16,592	9,472	7,236	4,144	7,777	7,618
94	Income and excess profits taxes	10,702	14,769	15,752	12,138	7,064	2,525	1,217	844	1,246	1,145
95	Compiled net profit after taxes	10,518	11,685	12,181	11,141	9,528	6,947	6,019	3,300	6,531	6,473
	Dividends paid:										
96	Cash and assets other than own stock	6,009	5,957	5,628	5,512	6,556	6,019	5,639	4,834	7,281	7,163
97	Corporation's own stock	332	235	212	69	166	136	86	73	183	343

See footnotes at end of table.

Series V 65–97. Corporate Assets, Liabilities, Receipts, Deductions, Net Profit, and Dividends, for All Industries Combined: 1926 to 1955—Con.

[Money figures in millions of dollars]

Series No.	Item	1935	1934	1933	1932	1931	1930	1929	1928	1927	1926
65	Number of returns with balance sheets	415,205	410,626	388,564	392,021	381,088	403,173	398,815	384,548	379,156	359,449
66	Total assets	303,150	301,307	268,206	280,083	296,497	334,002	335,778	307,218	287,542	262,179
67	Cash	23,664	19,961	15,236	15,917	15,880	21,012	22,371	21,952	16,851	16,802
68	Notes and accounts receivable less reserve (except 1926)	38,690	40,529	35,835	39,564	48,667	59,675	66,810	62,804	50,959	23,552
69	Inventories	14,788	14,311	13,597	12,372	15,140	18,771	21,911	20,751	21,005	20,939
70	Investments, government obligations	21,863	19,084	13,571	11,917	10,667	10,228	10,338	10,116	9,781	8,694
71	Other investments	90,163	90,573	70,474	75,630	75,305	83,809	[3] 55,844	(4)	(4)	(4)
72	Capital assets less reserves	100,480	102,751	104,958	108,553	114,303	120,994	116,446	109,931	104,945	97,523
73	Other assets	13,501	14,097	14,535	16,129	16,534	19,511	[3] 42,057	[4] 81,663	[4] 84,001	[4] 94,669
74	Total liabilities	303,150	301,307	268,206	280,083	296,497	334,002	335,778	307,218	287,542	262,179
75	Notes and accounts payable	25,332	27,021	19,362	20,562	23,251	26,870	29,453	27,437	24,126	24,042
76	Bonded debt and mortgages	49,822	48,604	45,883	47,222	48,101	50,282	46,643	42,943	37,740	31,801
80	Other liabilities	89,066	84,096	75,384	78,730	81,782	95,568	99,314	93,950	93,274	87,076
81	Capital stock, preferred	19,533	19,976	18,394	19,076	19,217	19,117	19,738	18,475	17,800	17,146
82	Capital stock, common	82,733	84,970	74,088	78,413	79,794	87,067	85,520	77,256	74,081	67,517
83	Surplus reserves	} 48,828	48,986	44,792	45,664	51,976	61,832	60,699	52,069	45,415	39,154
84	Surplus and undivided profits [2]										
85	Less: Deficit [3]	12,163	12,347	9,696	9,584	7,624	6,734	5,588	4,913	4,893	4,557
86	Total compiled receipts	112,098	99,095	82,148	79,701	105,238					
87	Gross sales and receipts from operations	102,884	90,738	74,952	71,226	[5] 94,989					
88	Other receipts	9,214	8,357	7,196	8,475	10,249					
89	Total compiled deductions	106,599	96,058	82,787	83,211	105,725					
90	Cost of goods sold and of operations	73,926	64,656	51,969	50,261	[5] 57,374	(6)	(6)	(6)	(6)	(6)
91	Depreciation, depletion, and amortization	3,611	3,593	3,666	3,866	4,194					
92	Other deductions	29,061	27,808	27,151	29,084	44,158					
93	Compiled net profit or net loss	5,500	3,037	[7] 639	[7] 3,511	[7] 487					
94	Income and excess profits taxes	722	586	417	282	393					
95	Compiled net profit after taxes	4,778	2,451	[7] 1,056	[7] 3,792	[7] 880					
	Dividends paid:										
96	Cash and assets other than own stock	5,896	4,788	3,091	3,854	6,092					
97	Corporation's own stock	135	212	90	142	162					

[1] Prior to 1954, based on original maturity date; beginning 1954, based on date of balance sheet.

[2] Net amount beginning in 1954. For 1937–1953, this is the sum of all positive amounts reported; for 1926–1936, the sum of positive net surplus and undivided profits.

[3] For 1937–1953, this is the sum of all deficits reported; for 1926–1936, sum of net deficits.

[4] "Other investments" were included in "Other assets" for all corporations, 1926–1928, and for life insurance companies, 1929.

[5] For 1931, gross profit was reported in lieu of gross receipts and cost of operations.

[6] Not available separately for returns with balance sheets.

[7] Loss.

Series V 98–112. Selected Corporate Assets, Liabilities, and Income Items, by Industrial Division: 1926 to 1955

[Money figures in millions of dollars. Excludes returns not allocable to any industrial division]

Industrial division and tax year	Number of returns with balance sheets	Total assets or liabilities	Selected assets					Selected liabilities				Total compiled receipts	Compiled net profit or net loss before tax	Total tax	Dividends paid in cash and assets other than own stock
			Cash	Notes and accounts receivable less reserve	Inventories	Investments	Capital assets less reserves	Notes and accounts payable	Bonds and mortgages	Capital stock	Surplus and undivided profits				
	98	99	100	101	102	103	104	105	106	107	108	109	110	111	112
Mining and quarrying:															
1955	9,683	13,265	1,119	1,706	631	2,483	6,959	1,580	2,067	2,667	5,819	9,631	1,085	603	780
1954	8,704	11,891	1,059	1,496	640	2,221	6,111	1,245	1,713	2,563	5,407	8,181	736	425	736
1953	8,164	11,967	917	1,426	761	2,721	5,866	1,277	1,667	2,515	5,545	9,230	951	509	648
1952	7,998	12,034	970	1,423	803	2,349	6,208	1,321	1,833	2,577	5,354	9,475	973	504	613
1951	8,136	11,659	1,032	1,415	755	2,273	5,878	1,258	1,610	2,755	5,030	9,562	1,114	553	593
1950	8,045	10,844	1,031	1,312	643	2,187	5,395	1,139	1,629	2,682	4,584	8,493	1,086	443	549
1949	8,094	9,261	871	889	569	2,000	4,636	933	1,278	2,493	3,901	6,730	698	265	417
1948	8,025	9,042	971	991	551	2,023	4,271	916	1,176	2,526	3,653	7,782	1,143	408	463
1947	7,280	7,186	785	789	410	1,506	3,516	825	830	2,266	2,755	5,881	788	286	315
1946	6,759	5,949	641	601	341	1,152	3,050	639	719	2,055	2,162	4,240	332	131	207
1945	6,394	5,563	556	492	306	1,140	2,906	602	550	2,093	1,987	3,908	246	117	156
1944	6,581	5,480	527	480	273	1,106	2,919	569	561	2,135	1,831	3,969	318	156	187
1943	7,036	5,434	516	476	281	1,013	2,980	547	578	2,277	1,614	3,680	342	168	197
1942	7,619	6,221	527	485	343	1,039	3,625	618	619	2,778	1,753	3,945	392	195	264
1941	8,227	7,065	482	568	339	1,354	4,128	712	941	3,009	2,014	3,754	370	138	311
1940	8,885	7,362	488	556	309	1,355	4,432	753	1,056	3,285	1,937	3,219	212	67	280
1939	9,287	7,331	408	550	321	1,372	4,450	804	1,000	3,374	1,858	2,843	138	37	216
1938	9,468	7,545	314	502	342	1,406	4,688	838	999	3,547	1,846	2,489	52	28	200
1937	11,467	9,146	333	677	340	1,737	5,748	1,004	1,125	4,458	2,165	3,273	297	58	361
1936	11,531	9,199	315	678	278	1,671	5,850	1,041	1,046	4,590	1,853	2,756	168	36	274
1935	11,491	9,519	295	597	317	1,840	5,914	1,172	1,047	4,807	1,750	2,418	70	22	255
1934[1]	11,362	10,228	265	738	374	2,139	6,116	1,299	1,039	5,366	1,775	2,361	67	22	265
1934[2]	11,488	10,030	281	774	401	2,569	5,464	1,027	973	5,597	1,531	2,388	89	22	188
1933	9,950	9,007	255	504	411	1,213	6,053	730	928	5,046	1,460	1,936	[3]149	10	91
1932	10,020	9,485	236	515	392	1,366	6,415	768	957	5,460	1,528	1,653	[3]186	7	102
1931	9,576	10,050	242	603	474	1,455	6,683	849	996	5,564	1,776	2,191	[3]202	7	170
1930	10,025	11,395	331	730	444	1,734	7,259	1,028	941	5,785	2,166	(4)	(4)	(4)	(4)
1929	10,219	11,832	421	837	694	1,611	7,264	975	1,037	6,252	2,566	(4)	(4)	(4)	(4)
1928	10,366	10,799	413	745	516	264	6,647	854	976	5,793	2,004	(4)	(4)	(4)	(4)
1927	11,298	11,565	360	703	681	262	7,495	918	912	6,240	1,863	(4)	(4)	(4)	(4)
1926	11,641	12,172	409	763	636	299	7,967	902	1,008	6,714	1,638	(4)	(4)	(4)	(4)
Manufacturing:															
1955	124,199	201,360	15,999	32,380	44,422	34,095	69,892	25,853	22,426	42,986	88,007	303,211	25,816	12,891	6,770
1954	115,820	181,891	15,745	27,767	39,872	28,730	65,364	22,257	21,547	40,519	79,384	264,966	18,194	9,385	5,818
1953	115,254	176,805	14,847	26,368	42,992	27,267	61,657	22,258	19,372	39,265	74,549	278,495	21,290	12,054	5,848
1952	113,711	170,282	14,748	26,907	41,801	25,922	57,723	22,783	19,372	38,730	70,767	258,969	20,228	11,348	5,665
1951	114,142	160,876	14,542	24,011	40,774	26,014	52,643	20,823	15,797	37,676	67,049	252,956	24,697	14,060	5,715
1950	109,537	141,600	13,370	21,753	33,008	24,528	46,377	17,559	12,269	35,502	61,539	218,272	23,608	10,575	6,037
1949	110,269	123,755	12,610	16,067	27,780	20,789	44,118	13,286	12,262	34,780	54,105	185,285	14,158	5,446	4,838
1948	110,078	121,708	11,778	17,090	30,355	18,685	41,227	15,253	11,757	33,577	50,506	198,260	17,985	6,760	4,617
1947	105,390	111,356	11,884	16,138	27,634	17,774	35,380	14,750	9,906	32,577	44,097	178,173	16,477	6,241	4,143
1946	92,771	96,300	11,042	13,517	23,282	16,561	29,414	12,647	7,879	30,015	37,574	137,087	11,500	4,543	3,378
1945	75,215	91,030	11,270	13,569	17,256	21,076	25,145	11,056	6,385	28,445	35,705	140,155	10,179	6,064	2,801
1944	72,170	95,999	11,918	14,552	18,421	21,836	25,921	12,501	6,332	28,335	34,735	152,673	14,754	9,318	2,828
1943	73,149	94,768	11,752	15,010	19,155	18,501	27,037	12,540	6,573	27,378	33,310	144,560	16,428	10,430	2,596
1942	76,334	85,092	9,075	13,809	18,433	14,537	26,607	11,133	6,219	27,113	27,958	117,895	13,554	8,158	2,486
1941	78,645	70,071	6,149	10,858	16,178	10,781	24,727	9,151	5,702	25,476	22,922	91,606	10,310	4,881	2,800
1940	80,198	60,547	5,744	8,412	12,334	9,349	23,605	7,311	5,418	25,429	18,734	66,246	5,313	1,544	2,390
1939	80,860	56,739	4,570	7,427	10,993	9,507	23,060	6,996	5,255	25,640	16,798	57,603	3,571	629	2,170
1938	82,155	54,792	4,003	6,761	10,192	9,444	21,544	6,456	5,274	25,847	15,413	50,489	1,615	372	1,634
1937	85,474	55,723	3,283	7,004	11,454	9,525	21,537	7,271	4,904	25,951	15,288	61,560	3,686	641	2,899
1936	85,350	54,262	3,522	7,368	10,029	9,524	20,690	7,096	4,256	25,622	12,845	55,378	3,636	587	2,867
1935	85,817	52,682	3,389	7,376	8,705	9,688	20,231	6,745	4,387	25,882	11,729	47,473	2,494	355	2,184
1934[1]	85,499	52,531	3,006	7,483	8,319	9,663	20,451	6,768	4,025	26,930	11,201	40,581	1,387	263	1,578
1934[2]	88,371	66,626	3,371	10,178	8,612	17,130	22,889	9,653	5,122	33,347	13,981	44,754	1,959	289	2,071
1933	82,836	57,753	3,084	6,765	8,084	11,481	24,384	5,722	5,021	30,398	12,943	34,943	502	206	1,159
1932	82,083	59,023	3,343	6,541	7,310	11,651	25,622	5,507	5,226	31,186	12,790	31,850	[3]1,468	100	1,324
1931	80,106	63,801	3,458	7,819	9,003	11,120	27,286	6,017	5,581	32,329	15,310	43,534	[3]308	164	2,276
1930	85,520	69,245	3,960	8,730	11,157	11,062	28,987	6,852	5,879	33,855	18,267	(4)	(4)	(4)	(4)
1929	86,112	70,282	3,847	9,572	12,614	9,154	28,235	7,418	5,450	33,228	19,466	(4)	(4)	(4)	(4)
1928	84,925	67,060	3,895	9,502	12,011	2,183	27,025	7,449	5,446	32,491	17,526	(4)	(4)	(4)	(4)
1927	84,776	65,582	3,525	8,946	11,884	2,036	26,007	7,349	4,806	31,553	16,496	(4)	(4)	(4)	(4)
1926	84,251	64,727	3,528	8,567	12,284	1,822	26,619	7,216	4,340	31,412	14,862	(4)	(4)	(4)	(4)

[1] Comparable with later years.
[2] Comparable with earlier years. Adjusted for comparability with industry classification in 1933 when consolidated returns were permitted to be filed.
[3] Deficit or loss.
[4] Not available.

Series V 98–112.   Selected Corporate Assets, Liabilities, and Income Items, by Industrial Division: 1926 to 1955—Con.

[Money figures in millions of dollars]

Industrial division and tax year	Number of returns with balance sheets	Total assets or liabilities	Selected assets					Selected liabilities				Total compiled receipts	Compiled net profit or net loss before tax	Total tax	Dividends paid in cash and assets other than own stock
			Cash	Notes and accounts receivable less reserve	Inventories	Investments	Capital assets less reserves	Notes and accounts payable	Bonds and mortgages	Capital stock	Surplus and undivided profits				
	98	99	100	101	102	103	104	105	106	107	108	109	110	111	112
Public utilities:															
1955	29,704	106,378	3,634	3,904	2,623	9,436	83,444	5,164	38,727	30,183	24,157	47,983	5,763	2,895	2,380
1954	26,067	98,637	3,658	3,495	2,468	8,567	77,608	4,260	36,556	28,810	21,641	42,038	4,424	2,296	2,057
1953	26,314	95,220	3,281	3,732	2,381	10,429	72,862	4,213	35,053	28,517	20,303	40,570	5,018	2,537	2,012
1952	25,139	90,041	3,503	3,703	2,352	10,537	67,517	4,111	33,062	27,159	18,824	38,348	4,900	2,472	1,909
1951	23,641	84,707	3,170	3,553	2,360	10,258	62,955	3,902	31,275	26,084	16,747	36,007	4,676	2,299	1,782
1950	22,973	79,209	3,178	3,296	1,909	10,259	57,444	3,633	28,912	25,034	15,714	31,857	4,312	1,752	1,640
1949	22,496	71,620	2,853	2,621	1,756	8,295	53,986	3,411	25,534	24,349	13,624	28,410	2,835	1,041	1,303
1948	21,749	73,705	2,876	2,565	2,059	13,993	50,001	3,573	26,125	25,828	13,033	29,272	3,413	1,189	1,432
1947	20,376	68,087	2,921	2,476	1,811	12,512	46,092	3,349	23,425	24,182	11,947	25,957	2,662	979	1,292
1946	18,561	63,812	2,858	2,276	1,427	12,256	42,756	2,669	21,463	23,964	10,685	22,738	2,336	891	1,338
1945	16,656	63,217	2,754	2,203	1,115	12,962	41,955	2,287	20,902	23,619	10,701	22,485	2,928	1,538	1,238
1944	16,183	64,958	2,703	2,275	1,096	12,945	43,635	2,221	21,854	23,804	9,967	22,328	4,188	2,382	1,221
1943	16,227	64,910	3,130	2,391	991	12,171	44,117	2,233	22,863	23,593	9,149	21,186	4,500	2,402	1,171
1942	16,873	63,581	2,476	2,059	1,027	11,336	44,647	2,090	23,652	23,765	8,267	18,450	3,624	1,567	1,118
1941	18,405	58,472	2,024	1,628	1,013	6,179	45,966	2,059	23,709	21,926	6,183	15,739	1,918	695	1,068
1940	18,680	56,748	1,851	1,440	745	5,243	45,977	2,118	23,331	21,661	5,955	13,574	1,320	359	1,067
1939	18,744	60,230	1,582	1,394	715	8,031	46,694	2,801	23,994	23,602	6,250	12,945	1,179	215	1,196
1938	18,595	60,843	1,444	1,422	692	8,159	47,064	2,830	24,418	23,815	6,669	12,037	687	166	1,114
1937	20,775	64,648	1,181	1,592	818	8,825	49,629	2,925	25,803	25,420	7,172	13,235	1,084	192	1,334
1936	20,667	62,715	1,499	1,602	651	8,377	47,673	2,987	24,619	24,786	5,263	11,938	980	166	1,285
1935	21,149	66,478	1,233	1,869	617	10,050	49,581	3,189	26,391	26,119	6,243	11,353	638	126	1,281
1934 [1]	21,265	68,461	1,306	2,660	629	10,453	50,472	3,908	25,654	27,131	6,785	10,997	631	126	1,213
1934 [2]	21,329	83,990	1,510	4,027	729	23,505	50,501	5,178	29,726	34,352	8,291	11,556	669	118	1,299
1933	17,706	69,049	1,290	2,210	741	11,323	50,141	2,798	26,959	26,191	8,000	10,110	249	92	994
1932	17,547	72,149	1,299	2,539	713	12,956	50,058	3,382	27,006	27,793	8,036	10,735	341	97	1,300
1931	16,457	72,337	1,333	2,826	889	11,616	52,214	3,494	27,024	26,642	10,332	13,297	958	104	1,789
1930	17,248	80,479	1,693	3,670	973	14,505	55,060	4,146	28,739	28,345	12,431	(4)	(4)	(4)	(4)
1929	17,258	77,792	1,634	3,974	1,119	9,614	52,205	4,449	26,619	28,131	10,955	(4)	(4)	(4)	(4)
1928	16,770	71,380	1,571	3,628	1,000	475	48,887	3,585	25,696	25,741	9,837	(4)	(4)	(4)	(4)
1927	16,858	66,559	1,549	2,115	1,024	272	46,487	2,604	23,542	25,296	7,594	(4)	(4)	(4)	(4)
1926	18,297	57,245	1,358	1,528	942	285	40,699	2,337	19,932	20,466	6,045	(4)	(4)	(4)	(4)
Trade:															
1955	248,071	69,113	6,808	20,287	21,578	6,533	12,037	19,460	5,795	14,366	23,500	204,924	5,099	2,435	993
1954	222,801	59,132	6,317	16,594	18,138	5,651	10,695	15,402	4,973	12,856	21,066	170,589	3,629	1,867	909
1953	212,931	56,370	6,185	15,193	17,828	5,445	10,263	13,902	4,968	12,608	20,197	167,705	3,922	2,050	926
1952	205,848	55,792	6,023	15,365	17,802	5,169	10,145	14,043	4,572	12,468	20,058	166,063	4,388	2,226	989
1951	201,594	55,102	5,992	14,682	18,089	5,272	9,831	13,536	4,401	12,282	19,856	166,422	5,473	2,754	1,076
1950	193,496	51,759	5,547	14,068	17,394	4,558	9,028	13,115	3,951	11,518	18,585	152,895	6,273	2,593	1,135
1949	187,520	42,985	5,348	10,778	13,446	4,257	8,081	9,528	3,286	10,946	15,853	129,965	3,810	1,469	965
1948	181,353	42,270	5,322	10,354	14,016	4,120	7,417	9,770	3,088	10,505	15,025	135,092	5,681	2,094	1,063
1947	163,300	38,122	5,049	9,169	12,758	4,044	6,158	9,279	2,621	9,516	12,876	120,960	5,969	2,174	980
1946	139,816	31,958	4,300	7,130	10,746	4,213	4,732	7,803	2,017	8,434	10,469	94,936	5,487	1,992	915
1945	110,587	24,041	3,946	4,636	6,582	4,675	3,532	5,034	1,366	7,182	8,045	65,654	3,337	1,886	547
1944	106,193	22,674	3,505	4,678	5,941	4,289	3,543	4,673	1,305	6,999	7,320	60,660	3,228	1,895	543
1943	107,667	21,489	3,152	4,494	6,032	3,495	3,661	4,426	1,311	7,026	6,615	57,193	3,057	1,760	530
1942	114,165	21,063	2,687	5,021	6,313	2,564	3,870	4,977	1,467	7,063	5,795	54,642	2,548	1,385	487
1941	123,439	22,134	1,920	6,454	6,841	2,325	4,068	6,350	1,718	7,500	5,099	56,512	2,071	853	576
1940	125,474	19,514	1,684	5,626	5,522	2,203	4,003	5,366	1,537	7,494	4,172	46,060	1,089	292	504
1939	124,627	19,030	1,501	5,224	5,157	2,714	3,961	5,071	1,544	7,822	3,824	41,849	830	165	497
1938	124,765	18,346	1,452	4,990	4,808	2,660	3,655	4,781	1,461	7,900	3,456	37,974	435	113	432
1937	128,200	18,853	1,287	5,180	5,328	2,561	3,671	5,382	1,279	7,902	3,348	44,199	845	166	702
1936	130,073	18,224	1,314	5,224	5,054	2,160	3,615	5,381	998	7,648	2,788	40,532	915	167	736
1935	130,317	17,486	1,270	4,832	4,568	2,168	3,662	5,030	1,029	7,725	2,560	36,669	558	107	505
1934 [1]	127,457	17,434	1,251	4,787	4,374	2,267	3,698	4,951	892	8,054	2,445	32,170	415	93	392
1934 [2]	126,086	16,651	1,134	4,258	3,970	2,651	3,672	3,947	1,112	8,003	2,528	28,571	392	84	351
1933	120,064	15,654	990	3,944	3,809	2,032	3,810	3,625	1,126	7,732	2,155	23,653	36	62	213
1932	119,346	15,759	1,041	4,006	3,368	2,068	4,158	3,443	1,204	8,237	1,936	22,609	[3] 705	30	249
1931	113,886	17,900	1,033	4,688	3,986	2,120	4,729	4,074	1,315	8,520	2,925	29,540	[3] 453	45	430
1930	119,792	20,115	1,269	5,652	5,046	2,032	4,889	5,029	1,331	9,174	3,619	(4)	(4)	(4)	(4)
1929	117,583	21,842	1,283	6,305	5,862	1,764	4,967	5,730	1,252	9,317	4,204	(4)	(4)	(4)	(4)
1928	114,068	21,481	1,293	6,297	5,908	325	4,910	5,646	1,044	9,252	4,359	(4)	(4)	(4)	(4)
1927	110,280	20,083	1,198	5,614	5,631	403	4,309	5,046	846	8,858	3,832	(4)	(4)	(4)	(4)
1926	100,395	19,140	1,164	5,632	5,569	357	4,079	4,997	584	8,558	3,502	(4)	(4)	(4)	(4)

[1] Comparable with later years.
[2] Comparable with earlier years.   Adjusted for comparability with industry classification in 1933 when consolidated returns were permitted to be filed.
[3] Deficit or loss.
[4] Not available.

Series V 98–112. Selected Corporate Assets, Liabilities, and Income Items, by Industrial Division: 1926 to 1955—Con.

[Money figures in millions of dollars]

Industrial division and tax year	Number of returns with balance sheets	Total assets or liabilities	Selected assets					Selected liabilities				Total compiled receipts	Compiled net profit or net loss before tax	Total tax	Dividends paid in cash and assets other than own stock
			Cash	Notes and accounts receivable less reserve	Inventories	Investments	Capital assets less reserves	Notes and accounts payable	Bonds and mortgages	Capital stock	Surplus and undivided profits				
	98	99	100	101	102	103	104	105	106	107	108	109	110	111	112
Service:															
1955	66,011	11,264	1,296	1,808	630	1,666	5,334	2,244	2,413	2,169	3,283	14,103	699	361	173
1954	58,117	10,017	1,228	1,420	574	1,588	4,756	1,813	2,241	1,902	3,028	12,267	585	319	159
1953	56,473	9,471	1,110	1,309	551	1,469	4,652	1,543	2,133	1,962	2,897	11,815	607	318	157
1952	54,690	8,916	1,043	1,260	602	1,304	4,398	1,410	1,925	1,858	2,807	11,168	620	324	174
1951	51,357	8,667	973	1,144	633	1,328	4,284	1,321	1,903	1,855	2,711	10,432	637	325	179
1950	47,834	8,053	913	996	570	1,271	4,004	1,252	1,717	1,834	2,461	9,350	568	236	170
1949	46,588	7,063	854	810	467	911	3,726	1,059	1,531	1,750	2,059	8,850	534	212	154
1948	43,882	6,950	827	779	546	990	3,516	1,035	1,493	1,689	2,061	8,766	623	241	172
1947	39,896	6,517	814	724	618	919	3,135	1,003	1,389	1,595	1,867	8,285	720	260	184
1946	34,229	5,869	755	631	537	991	2,692	816	1,273	1,517	1,631	7,143	785	284	203
1945	30,043	5,017	660	502	419	994	2,240	640	1,193	1,354	1,283	5,801	596	312	130
1944	29,389	4,739	556	481	391	901	2,198	567	1,147	1,344	1,143	5,481	575	317	114
1943	29,799	4,584	530	427	351	756	2,331	573	1,122	1,370	1,000	4,964	537	303	104
1942	31,692	4,475	411	423	301	672	2,458	610	1,197	1,417	813	4,457	357	179	86
1941	33,296	4,366	313	420	264	611	2,605	656	1,307	1,465	614	4,029	189	74	97
1940	34,094	4,273	303	386	213	640	2,586	675	1,269	1,485	573	3,702	117	38	90
1939	34,177	4,255	261	388	218	626	2,610	686	1,289	1,579	422	3,512	85	26	85
1938	33,816	4,294	241	406	205	625	2,496	714	1,311	1,564	400	3,409	59	23	83
1937	49,751	10,835	356	558	175	970	8,271	1,384	5,128	3,101	529	4,605	36	33	148
1936	48,590	10,853	365	602	167	1,077	8,085	1,408	5,002	3,185	175	4,345	13	31	156
1935	40,093	8,427	285	526	157	826	6,033	1,231	3,560	2,734	[3]18	3,528	[3]97	18	71
1934 [1]	37,171	7,771	246	597	166	677	5,447	1,166	3,004	2,705	54	3,231	[3]144	15	63
1934 [2]	36,999	7,903	248	819	168	983	5,088	1,149	2,856	2,858	155	3,177	[3]151	14	58
1933	34,546	7,429	204	625	139	744	5,070	954	2,724	2,761	179	2,662	[3]255	9	42
1932	34,552	8,480	231	637	145	1,228	5,611	983	3,008	3,078	712	2,953	[3]371	9	71
1931	28,545	6,555	211	636	198	1,189	3,719	878	1,636	2,427	1,045	3,486	[3]67	11	115
1930	30,312	7,518	292	686	241	1,705	3,880	963	1,719	2,573	1,716	(4)	(4)	(4)	(4)
1929	28,710	7,820	440	833	191	1,876	3,814	954	1,563	2,519	1,982	(4)	(4)	(4)	(4)
1928	26,505	5,857	249	548	178	43	3,521	928	1,291	2,386	697	(4)	(4)	(4)	(4)
1927	25,388	5,618	240	459	177	37	3,340	869	1,163	2,189	736	(4)	(4)	(4)	(4)
1926	23,264	4,873	300	384	184	42	2,783	821	842	1,963	596	(4)	(4)	(4)	(4)
Finance, Insurance, real estate, and lessors of real property:															
1955	213,680	474,858	57,210	126,800	47	255,680	25,581	18,176	25,697	17,825	45,124	32,320	8,543	2,030	2,238
1954	187,172	432,477	52,413	103,697	48	243,959	24,129	13,502	22,724	17,484	39,979	29,406	8,308	2,068	2,027
1953	175,653	401,976	52,637	96,456	31	222,418	22,609	11,364	21,378	16,911	35,153	25,829	7,167	1,879	1,817
1952	166,749	374,891	52,174	88,544	27	206,476	20,970	10,818	18,779	16,424	32,351	23,343	6,662	1,745	1,712
1951	158,335	317,026	50,129	70,912	23	167,642	21,309	9,331	16,850	15,769	26,788	20,017	6,088	1,515	1,700
1950	151,540	298,624	46,104	64,529	20	162,872	20,111	8,406	16,508	15,750	24,318	18,233	5,849	1,228	1,748
1949	146,120	281,983	40,447	52,065	6	165,077	19,053	7,061	17,397	18,236	22,504	16,768	5,411	992	1,656
1948	140,872	265,124	43,254	50,699	11	148,524	17,380	6,628	13,143	15,928	19,550	15,132	4,612	792	1,428
1947	131,825	257,833	42,318	44,933	46	149,696	16,281	6,353	11,448	15,828	18,167	13,581	3,982	628	1,265
1946	124,564	246,364	38,404	35,984	69	151,177	16,363	5,294	11,232	15,822	17,878	12,097	4,146	713	1,261
1945	116,186	249,119	38,105	29,407	46	162,424	15,221	4,352	10,286	15,562	16,457	10,612	3,680	654	1,076
1944	113,221	221,043	33,152	24,624	35	143,870	15,836	3,675	10,937	16,000	14,818	9,614	3,123	544	1,004
1943	112,892	194,564	30,714	22,026	51	122,082	16,384	3,241	10,916	16,514	13,654	9,001	2,686	455	965
1942	114,866	175,483	30,837	23,185	68	101,264	17,255	3,937	11,507	17,631	13,079	8,749	2,385	387	1,004
1941	120,647	174,403	30,434	28,333	107	94,928	17,740	5,684	15,734	26,732	17,515	10,199	1,499	315	1,631
1940	120,725	168,414	31,103	25,616	61	90,565	18,131	5,609	16,159	28,264	17,394	9,455	1,369	192	1,622
1939	120,945	155,975	25,518	23,777	42	85,668	18,099	5,410	15,944	27,136	16,711	8,768	1,386	127	1,421
1938	118,631	150,926	20,314	23,040	53	85,377	18,489	5,504	16,451	28,582	16,688	8,548	1,273	127	1,326
1937	98,438	140,402	17,685	24,611	47	84,835	9,785	6,349	10,674	27,156	16,966	8,927	1,757	134	1,736
1936	96,869	144,109	18,872	24,028	65	87,108	10,238	6,814	10,707	29,046	13,606	8,692	1,834	136	1,738
1935	104,146	144,747	16,986	22,886	109	86,809	13,320	7,147	13,037	33,100	14,143	8,662	1,817	81	1,535
1934 [1]	105,535	140,840	13,702	23,640	134	83,626	14,689	8,031	13,611	32,739	14,074	8,022	721	59	1,226
1934 [2]	103,294	112,073	13,231	19,841	130	61,971	13,370	8,387	18,769	9,798	9,798	6,904	142	50	800
1933	100,989	105,475	9,252	21,235	141	56,518	13,712	4,825	8,652	18,482	9,965	7,422	[3]936	34	560
1932	104,141	110,753	9,581	24,647	151	57,397	14,634	5,625	9,395	19,635	10,619	8,155	[3]954	35	753
1931	107,892	121,043	9,385	31,202	249	57,611	17,638	6,962	11,000	21,583	12,167	10,565	[3]328	53	1,222
1930	114,275	140,035	13,207	39,158	462	62,136	18,792	7,640	11,079	24,356	16,177	(4)	(4)	(4)	(4)
1929	113,463	140,724	14,471	44,129	921	41,401	17,819	8,654	10,135	23,682	15,108	(4)	(4)	(4)	(4)
1928	108,123	125,692	14,278	41,029	675	6,690	16,969	7,724	8,103	18,056	11,995	(4)	(4)	(4)	(4)
1927	106,016	112,917	9,721	32,131	1,068	6,652	15,251	6,179	6,047	15,725	9,394	(4)	(4)	(4)	(4)
1926	98,417	99,452	9,778	5,790	923	5,823	13,429	6,682	4,740	13,733	7,436	(4)	(4)	(4)	(4)

[1] Comparable with later years.
[2] Comparable with earlier years. Adjusted for comparability with industry classification in 1933 when consolidated returns were permitted to be filed.
[3] Deficit or loss.
[4] Not available.

Series V 98–112. Selected Corporate Assets, Liabilities, and Income Items, by Industrial Division: 1926 to 1955—Con.

[Money figures in millions of dollars]

Industrial division and tax year	Number of returns with balance sheets	Total assets or liabilities	Cash	Notes and accounts receivable less reserve	Inventories	Investments	Capital assets less reserves	Notes and accounts payable	Bonds and mortgages	Capital stock	Surplus and undivided profits	Total compiled receipts	Compiled net profit or net loss before tax	Total tax	Dividends paid in cash and assets other than own stock
	98	99	100	101	102	103	104	105	106	107	108	109	110	111	112
Construction:															
1955	38,653	9,319	1,052	4,530	693	1,042	1,664	2,864	784	1,347	2,354	19,722	479	251	85
1954	33,700	8,254	1,074	3,694	886	789	1,438	2,302	631	1,216	2,189	17,215	483	252	75
1953	32,158	7,414	974	3,474	664	680	1,346	1,976	628	1,115	1,959	15,914	512	271	74
1952	29,433	7,307	918	3,372	793	673	1,336	1,904	713	1,035	1,946	15,047	596	304	75
1951	27,315	6,698	788	3,149	773	596	1,199	1,859	629	972	1,783	13,946	554	287	72
1950	25,344	5,661	661	2,670	614	502	1,025	1,496	434	911	1,568	11,262	545	238	81
1949	23,402	4,637	693	2,052	428	429	889	1,043	291	832	1,388	9,691	511	196	71
1948	21,293	4,203	523	1,881	475	364	810	1,020	297	749	1,168	9,198	569	207	67
1947	18,398	3,419	409	1,457	460	328	651	897	252	633	866	6,899	386	137	42
1946	14,406	2,497	319	993	332	287	459	645	181	517	636	4,234	231	83	38
1945	10,726	1,619	257	559	159	275	291	364	102	405	482	2,903	113	62	29
1944	10,326	1,629	263	555	147	308	274	345	101	401	492	3,106	138	89	25
1943	10,707	1,826	315	678	147	291	308	410	115	415	506	4,177	255	165	30
1942	11,729	2,082	315	934	177	262	309	568	107	430	500	4,661	337	204	32
1941	12,894	1,714	195	768	140	205	325	532	107	444	358	3,406	178	81	32
1940	13,795	1,445	157	608	117	182	321	434	93	458	260	2,439	70	23	30
1939	14,162	1,370	146	529	121	195	326	395	95	482	213	2,159	35	11	28
1938	14,308	1,364	134	460	116	188	385	341	98	515	225	1,882	28	10	23
1937	14,807	1,702	140	543	170	240	494	415	152	604	287	2,355	47	14	23
1936	14,574	1,689	126	544	159	244	493	436	135	608	188	1,927	38	11	49
1935	14,117	1,613	123	426	125	288	485	372	140	668	158	1,425	5	7	29
1934 [1]	14,082	1,700	110	418	125	325	546	392	131	707	198	1,220	[3]23	4	23
1934 [2]	14,059	1,624	106	403	113	365	469	366	162	690	199	1,147	[3]17	4	23
1933	14,398	1,833	100	390	125	479	555	376	235	734	263	1,035	[3]51	3	28
1932	15,382	2,141	132	479	138	517	674	448	274	791	332	1,384	[3]84	3	40
1931	15,350	2,475	155	643	180	545	704	580	297	809	450	2,131	[3]4	7	63
1930	16,496	3,012	215	800	248	554	896	773	350	932	524	(4)	(4)	(4)	(4)
1929	16,355	3,095	208	876	305	476	857	846	350	884	510	(4)	(4)	(4)	(4)
1928	15,289	2,690	197	816	263	84	756	818	220	808	442	(4)	(4)	(4)	(4)
1927	14,955	2,739	191	743	306	78	743	691	237	738	426	(4)	(4)	(4)	(4)
1926	13,981	2,358	213	668	273	48	654	645	233	639	317	(4)	(4)	(4)	(4)
Agriculture, forestry, and fisheries:															
1955	9,023	2,600	207	269	284	338	1,380	499	379	881	697	2,508	122	67	46
1954	7,790	2,620	191	452	278	376	1,251	508	334	870	696	2,226	122	65	49
1953	8,259	2,392	190	256	299	304	1,264	354	356	855	689	2,333	119	72	49
1952	7,738	2,355	191	257	332	318	1,186	384	332	827	683	2,500	139	77	58
1951	7,618	2,462	186	369	360	349	1,138	499	323	827	671	2,404	254	105	99
1950	7,094	2,260	177	211	322	321	1,174	435	246	799	640	2,052	287	99	106
1949	6,820	1,934	164	183	254	295	990	286	232	762	554	1,833	172	64	59
1948	6,539	1,855	160	176	266	256	934	278	205	754	510	1,812	217	78	62
1947	6,153	1,757	145	172	250	264	873	273	173	665	535	1,599	206	74	58
1946	5,554	1,583	139	149	207	270	764	232	152	648	437	1,239	181	66	33
1945	5,114	1,477	120	183	168	305	662	242	135	615	397	965	133	63	26
1944	5,224	1,436	117	174	160	262	684	215	141	631	357	896	119	62	31
1943	5,557	1,422	118	125	160	250	730	189	159	662	323	828	112	61	29
1942	5,893	1,409	85	109	152	232	793	195	159	675	284	771	81	39	25
1941	6,312	1,502	69	103	146	306	844	281	192	716	243	717	64	22	32
1940	6,816	1,516	62	107	141	259	900	233	224	762	216	617	19	9	25
1939	7,048	1,502	50	100	138	306	867	292	216	767	168	585	15	6	23
1938	7,304	1,523	57	107	145	290	872	299	212	828	122	575	[3]1	4	19
1937	7,046	1,987	77	141	179	346	1,174	362	254	1,055	214	746	26	8	48
1936	7,126	2,064	82	151	177	352	1,214	372	244	1,100	170	697	36	9	56
1935	7,143	2,107	76	151	187	340	1,229	392	217	1,135	186	566	18	6	35
1934 [1]	7,445	2,243	68	169	187	409	1,303	447	219	1,227	175	513	[3]11	4	26
1934 [2]	7,375	2,218	70	186	182	436	1,234	405	247	1,214	190	556	[3]36	4	26
1933	7,295	1,913	58	144	147	211	1,217	311	231	1,047	159	380	[3]34	2	5
1932	7,716	2,143	51	168	150	307	1,340	370	234	1,152	187	354	[3]77	1	14
1931	7,567	2,136	57	203	155	246	1,334	362	240	975	373	467	[3]70	1	25
1930	7,862	2,031	41	219	196	262	1,188	393	229	1,001	264	(4)	(4)	(4)	(4)
1929	7,443	2,140	60	218	198	230	1,231	376	222	1,051	341	(4)	(4)	(4)	(4)
1928	7,130	2,054	51	210	189	41	1,177	399	161	1,059	297	(4)	(4)	(4)	(4)
1927	7,195	2,177	57	197	217	32	1,230	387	178	1,082	202	(4)	(4)	(4)	(4)
1926	7,681	2,050	47	192	118	16	1,242	407	114	1,071	210	(4)	(4)	(4)	(4)

[1] Comparable with later years.
[2] Comparable with earlier years. Adjusted for comparability with industry classification in 1933 when consolidated returns were permitted to be filed.
[3] Deficit or loss.
[4] Not available.

Series V 113–127. Selected Corporate Assets, Liabilities, and Income Items, by Size of Total Assets: 1931 to 1955

[Money figures in millions of dollars]

Size of total assets and tax year	Number of returns with balance sheets	Total assets or liabilities	Cash	Notes and accounts receivable less reserve	Inventories	Investments	Capital assets less reserves	Notes and accounts payable	Bonds and mortgages	Capital stock	Surplus and undivided profits	Total compiled receipts	Compiled net profit or net loss before tax	Total tax	Dividends paid in cash and assets other than own stock
	113	114	115	116	117	118	119	120	121	122	123	124	125	126	127
Less than $50,000:															
1955	299,564	6,280	878	1,354	983	367	2,342	2,126	976	2,790	¹451	16,271	¹37	101	63
1954	273,045	5,750	802	1,229	962	322	2,108	1,825	933	2,597	¹292	14,623	¹87	86	66
1953	261,920	5,624	783	1,152	974	328	2,101	1,651	971	2,628	¹246	14,550	¹14	92	46
1952	253,029	5,429	752	1,089	971	333	2,055	1,560	936	2,462	¹139	13,905	46	97	57
1951	245,803	5,299	723	1,067	955	280	2,073	1,581	890	2,474	¹160	13,870	86	103	66
1950	236,854	5,081	658	1,016	939	262	1,987	1,519	835	2,453	¹274	12,381	59	78	74
1949	242,765	5,159	714	997	914	277	2,021	1,454	853	2,556	¹175	12,936	¹81	64	70
1948	234,590	5,007	719	946	920	261	1,913	1,347	797	2,463	¹114	13,215	54	84	80
1947	218,623	4,661	732	884	858	248	1,716	1,223	730	2,273	¹108	12,062	178	98	80
1946	199,076	4,196	749	778	740	243	1,496	1,064	652	2,095	¹97	10,902	363	119	86
1945	177,788	3,648	722	668	540	242	1,308	904	599	1,965	¹250	9,031	268	108	61
1944	176,212	3,528	624	652	558	229	1,313	967	614	2,034	¹441	9,004	257	106	66
1943	181,961	3,559	578	671	572	206	1,381	1,027	610	2,133	¹586	9,188	225	111	62
1942	196,642	3,753	477	753	663	175	1,521	1,198	668	2,328	¹799	9,461	132	82	50
1941	213,086	4,013	372	884	763	183	1,666	1,467	767	2,468	¹1,009	10,010	44	49	59
1940	225,000	4,136	354	958	738	206	1,740	1,610	731	2,722	¹1,260	9,617	¹96	24	56
1939	226,877	4,141	337	969	744	199	1,739	1,615	735	2,803	¹1,330	9,697	¹120	18	49
1938	227,491	4,140	324	977	748	193	1,604	1,563	673	2,875	¹1,313	9,347	¹204	15	53
1937	228,721	4,180	320	976	795	182	1,585	1,616	543	2,857	¹1,255	10,923	¹131	20	95
1936	227,343	4,151	339	998	778	168	1,528	1,602	459	2,875	¹1,244	10,325	¹101	22	90
1935	227,545	4,131	327	976	764	171	1,499	1,563	425	2,987	¹1,308	9,364	¹183	17	56
1934	223,073	4,038	302	961	730	173	1,495	1,498	419	3,023	¹1,315	8,588	¹250	15	62
1933	211,586	3,876	255	925	669	175	1,458	1,324	365	2,962	¹1,136	6,810	¹377	9	38
1932	206,477	3,870	237	934	636	177	1,503	1,323	340	2,994	¹1,136	6,340	¹609	5	40
1931	182,447	3,703	231	924	640	166	1,390	1,248	283	2,632	¹722	6,952	¹412	8	65
$50,000 to $99,999:															
1955	131,510	9,481	1,089	2,150	1,634	744	3,468	2,658	1,474	2,858	1,598	19,811	353	171	68
1954	117,001	8,430	981	1,858	1,494	585	3,153	2,160	1,334	2,631	1,491	17,606	260	144	61
1953	115,719	8,339	942	1,818	1,540	593	3,118	1,958	1,426	2,661	1,556	17,696	298	152	63
1952	109,780	7,939	941	1,689	1,518	599	2,952	1,846	1,347	2,541	1,555	16,711	390	166	68
1951	106,268	7,725	861	1,595	1,557	484	3,004	1,792	1,368	2,511	1,424	16,593	424	168	78
1950	101,645	7,317	785	1,527	1,475	422	2,865	1,727	1,243	2,452	1,331	15,257	438	138	89
1949	99,878	7,177	861	1,434	1,340	435	2,860	1,561	1,212	2,557	1,310	15,282	288	114	85
1848	96,747	6,948	844	1,352	1,366	414	2,710	1,512	1,137	2,462	1,245	15,444	471	152	92
1947	89,002	6,376	844	1,224	1,244	395	2,426	1,404	1,031	2,216	1,132	14,161	590	178	93
1946	76,821	5,491	801	1,034	985	387	2,075	1,133	904	1,972	953	11,904	649	185	92
1945	61,431	4,379	707	778	622	384	1,719	819	778	1,731	658	8,651	377	147	60
1944	56,831	4,050	584	704	589	364	1,661	750	746	1,683	524	7,929	351	148	64
1943	56,579	4,036	542	716	606	307	1,719	793	762	1,743	390	7,887	339	165	62
1942	58,338	4,164	442	797	685	249	1,843	935	809	1,844	245	7,772	270	123	51
1941	61,525	4,385	324	941	780	242	1,966	1,150	919	1,964	54	8,211	200	72	58
1940	61,053	4,342	297	942	693	269	2,015	1,152	886	2,083	¹58	7,358	57	30	65
1939	60,256	4,292	277	933	661	271	2,011	1,124	853	2,086	¹30	6,900	41	21	54
1938	59,582	4,238	261	912	642	266	1,878	1,095	784	2,151	¹86	6,412	¹21	16	48
1937	60,238	4,282	250	912	701	267	1,857	1,202	659	2,207	¹141	7,608	38	21	96
1936	59,528	4,233	263	936	664	259	1,790	1,171	609	2,205	¹150	7,156	56	23	103
1935	58,434	4,161	258	900	623	268	1,767	1,103	575	2,354	¹194	6,089	¹10	17	57
1934	57,840	4,120	243	893	582	278	1,777	1,062	547	2,326	¹197	5,402	¹47	14	44
1933	56,205	4,007	209	873	542	271	1,725	953	526	2,283	¹131	4,317	¹113	9	33
1932	58,320	4,153	204	924	534	286	1,827	1,067	543	2,415	¹149	4,101	¹312	5	38
1931	61,144	4,367	219	1,081	616	283	1,829	1,133	514	2,363	40	5,398	¹214	5	61
$100,000 to $249,999:															
1955	150,350	23,923	2,431	5,822	4,259	2,216	8,339	6,394	3,830	5,994	5,445	48,805	1,179	478	186
1954	134,299	21,379	2,263	5,025	3,772	1,847	7,681	5,247	3,488	5,635	5,121	42,249	834	391	160
1953	127,949	20,306	2,086	4,523	3,757	1,788	7,472	4,382	3,744	5,352	5,086	40,521	891	405	165
1952	122,123	19,362	2,070	4,375	3,698	1,714	6,984	4,175	3,534	5,213	4,796	39,489	1,101	451	175
1951	118,366	18,714	1,916	4,003	3,892	1,280	7,147	3,941	3,494	5,053	4,741	38,984	1,243	500	200
1950	111,503	17,687	1,760	3,844	3,605	1,246	6,713	3,817	3,195	4,924	4,342	35,585	1,371	448	224
1949	104,262	16,436	1,838	3,336	2,998	1,224	6,513	3,230	3,008	4,923	4,004	32,953	938	340	210
1948	100,341	15,832	1,767	3,119	3,086	1,152	6,161	3,166	2,829	4,731	3,689	33,606	1,388	480	236
1947	90,709	14,306	1,741	2,814	2,741	1,117	5,390	2,909	2,480	4,345	3,167	30,072	1,575	541	228
1946	76,592	12,094	1,563	2,267	2,152	1,123	4,557	2,361	2,181	3,820	2,509	23,988	1,495	509	217
1945	60,308	9,526	1,317	1,600	1,309	1,132	3,817	1,588	1,851	3,308	1,906	16,660	838	396	141
1944	56,782	8,964	1,150	1,487	1,220	1,085	3,694	1,461	1,774	3,256	1,632	15,587	848	433	145
1943	56,105	8,855	1,090	1,508	1,260	918	3,771	1,484	1,803	3,343	1,373	15,291	851	463	152
1942	57,865	9,067	935	1,686	1,420	735	3,992	1,731	1,864	3,493	1,150	14,808	729	367	130
1941	60,386	9,547	722	2,043	1,589	714	4,212	2,087	2,035	3,730	868	15,071	561	215	155
1940	59,059	9,316	653	2,015	1,331	781	4,279	1,986	1,981	3,924	633	12,742	275	83	154
1939	58,119	9,188	622	1,922	1,246	837	4,287	1,953	1,937	4,041	486	11,561	193	51	138
1938	57,733	9,112	577	1,853	1,195	841	4,096	1,902	1,789	4,112	391	10,535	50	37	120
1937	58,817	9,283	564	1,888	1,294	879	4,089	2,122	1,588	4,232	319	12,308	178	52	234
1936	58,442	9,229	600	1,930	1,212	872	3,980	2,097	1,511	4,337	160	11,394	225	53	258
1935	58,208	9,204	620	1,865	1,125	894	4,018	1,933	1,422	4,444	215	9,688	72	39	142
1934	58,186	9,231	566	1,835	1,065	963	4,080	1,898	1,399	4,616	138	8,466	¹28	32	113
1933	56,745	8,992	481	1,848	995	937	3,948	1,727	1,368	4,506	216	6,780	¹188	20	63
1932	59,500	9,414	457	1,994	945	1,000	4,249	1,779	1,427	4,751	247	6,561	¹484	11	83
1931	63,428	10,072	491	2,308	1,135	993	4,335	2,038	1,382	4,816	578	8,803	¹340	13	141
$250,000 to $499,999:															
1955	70,483	24,560	2,290	6,356	4,391	2,708	7,997	6,425	3,970	5,202	6,441	48,144	1,291	562	191
1954	60,356	21,046	2,143	5,193	3,686	2,235	7,044	5,088	3,416	4,622	5,835	39,745	966	447	176
1953	55,447	19,387	1,953	4,589	3,541	2,116	6,562	4,059	3,476	4,487	5,427	37,348	994	478	206
1952	52,976	18,571	1,884	4,343	3,488	2,072	6,303	3,927	3,292	4,239	5,197	36,678	1,143	545	202
1951	52,393	18,330	1,842	4,119	3,655	1,750	6,492	3,738	3,227	4,349	5,171	36,981	1,412	661	229
1950	49,735	17,365	1,721	3,954	3,503	1,576	6,112	3,618	2,934	4,250	4,859	33,737	1,605	621	259
1949	44,634	15,567	1,762	3,229	2,746	1,567	5,770	2,827	2,664	4,159	4,428	29,310	1,106	434	234
1948	43,366	15,145	1,681	3,039	2,924	1,521	5,489	2,872	2,510	4,042	4,121	30,510	1,577	603	262
1947	39,571	13,842	1,625	2,727	2,699	1,475	4,843	2,669	2,217	3,787	3,583	27,387	1,701	647	246
1946	34,264	11,997	1,464	2,254	2,228	1,493	4,135	2,217	1,945	3,469	2,951	22,270	1,584	603	253

¹ Deficit or loss.

Series V 113–127. Selected Corporate Assets, Liabilities, and Income Items, by Size of Total Assets: 1931 to 1955—Con.

[Money figures in millions of dollars]

Size of total assets and tax year	Number of returns with balance sheets	Total assets or liabilities	Selected assets					Selected liabilities				Total compiled receipts	Compiled net profit or net loss before tax	Total tax	Dividends paid in cash and assets other than own stock
			Cash	Notes and accounts receivable less reserve	Inventories	Investments	Capital assets less reserves	Notes and accounts payable	Bonds and mortgages	Capital stock	Surplus and undivided profits				
	113	114	115	116	117	118	119	120	121	122	123	124	125	126	127
$250,000 to $499,999—Con.:															
1945	27,583	9,667	1,256	1,567	1,398	1,561	3,523	1,527	1,663	3,063	2,255	15,829	914	511	154
1944	26,496	9,322	1,199	1,518	1,262	1,646	3,368	1,338	1,627	3,036	2,024	14,778	995	588	161
1943	26,757	9,418	1,236	1,585	1,294	1,474	3,538	1,348	1,655	3,096	1,858	14,646	1,015	606	171
1942	27,300	9,611	1,158	1,831	1,381	1,259	3,721	1,487	1,694	3,268	1,623	13,647	893	500	158
1941	28,751	10,122	975	2,270	1,493	1,152	3,986	1,830	1,860	3,455	1,407	13,053	691	289	189
1940	27,832	9,787	867	2,191	1,204	1,226	4,056	1,664	1,836	3,669	1,145	10,286	345	102	187
1939	27,447	9,649	812	2,064	1,130	1,302	4,092	1,590	1,819	3,796	1,013	9,335	248	59	175
1938	27,371	9,629	747	1,991	1,050	1,415	4,005	1,545	1,749	3,896	955	8,495	106	41	152
1937	27,992	9,868	720	2,007	1,159	1,523	4,052	1,745	1,706	3,990	915	9,794	242	59	256
1936	28,342	9,995	808	2,040	1,104	1,519	4,059	1,798	1,596	4,123	761	9,185	283	60	281
1935	28,605	10,076	775	1,933	1,016	1,483	4,160	1,687	1,486	4,363	633	7,888	132	41	162
1934	28,673	10,096	693	1,886	973	1,550	4,261	1,697	1,495	4,500	571	6,885	21	33	134
1933	26,773	9,421	535	1,823	891	1,420	3,976	1,419	1,419	4,222	733	5,505	[1]129	22	69
1932	28,422	9,988	491	2,023	846	1,533	4,322	1,486	1,500	4,521	790	5,297	[1]379	12	96
1931	31,052	10,930	555	2,436	1,036	1,557	4,544	1,747	1,547	4,685	1,071	7,210	[1]251	17	159
$500,000 to $999,999:															
1955	39,301	27,382	2,659	6,934	4,643	3,998	8,254	6,389	4,251	5,050	7,689	48,675	1,638	757	242
1954	33,617	23,491	2,475	5,728	3,788	3,357	7,409	4,976	3,617	4,628	6,982	38,904	1,214	594	232
1953	31,845	22,239	2,323	5,140	3,800	3,434	6,892	4,142	3,842	4,476	6,312	38,192	1,255	657	245
1952	31,290	21,847	2,375	5,162	3,847	3,230	6,697	4,077	3,418	4,562	6,474	37,896	1,462	762	258
1951	30,355	21,208	2,329	4,793	4,087	2,672	6,808	3,935	3,379	4,506	6,154	37,891	1,797	917	302
1950	29,093	20,338	2,181	4,610	3,824	2,779	6,402	3,805	3,055	4,437	5,929	34,453	1,991	830	352
1949	25,651	17,903	2,142	3,786	2,878	2,843	5,847	2,908	2,629	4,241	5,367	28,963	1,296	528	311
1948	24,803	17,362	2,048	3,593	3,119	2,718	5,497	2,898	2,410	4,133	5,040	30,900	1,861	721	346
1947	23,258	16,293	2,032	3,271	2,982	2,695	4,936	2,842	2,127	4,020	4,474	28,718	2,029	781	331
1946	20,803	14,585	1,878	2,692	2,544	2,739	4,324	2,435	1,909	3,772	3,744	23,611	1,840	718	305
1945	17,669	12,437	1,805	1,934	1,643	2,919	3,764	1,658	1,692	3,454	3,001	17,398	1,196	718	204
1944	17,625	12,391	1,804	1,959	1,508	2,974	3,746	1,513	1,627	3,463	2,782	16,545	1,304	817	215
1943	17,893	12,606	1,922	2,116	1,517	2,761	3,924	1,494	1,682	3,553	2,572	15,938	1,351	842	218
1942	18,109	12,715	1,906	2,475	1,601	2,295	4,119	1,615	1,717	3,699	2,301	14,785	1,185	702	208
1941	18,424	12,915	1,598	2,956	1,697	1,907	4,470	1,908	1,925	4,009	1,995	13,538	892	401	251
1940	17,505	12,227	1,338	2,687	1,322	1,987	4,607	1,714	1,977	4,174	1,683	10,419	427	135	220
1939	17,232	12,056	1,228	2,485	1,240	2,114	4,699	1,659	2,012	4,338	1,540	9,391	316	72	219
1938	17,079	11,966	1,087	2,370	1,144	2,275	4,597	1,627	1,953	4,415	1,481	8,406	162	51	190
1937	17,587	12,325	1,038	2,388	1,259	2,432	4,705	1,846	1,919	4,605	1,436	9,830	317	73	314
1936	17,941	12,560	1,142	2,394	1,192	2,467	4,807	1,909	1,836	4,766	1,243	9,214	364	77	333
1935	18,102	12,705	1,041	2,279	1,133	2,467	4,936	1,907	1,760	5,096	1,093	8,014	178	49	242
1934	18,339	12,856	923	2,248	1,076	2,571	5,175	1,923	1,764	5,310	1,062	7,115	55	39	209
1933	16,592	11,577	691	2,101	966	2,259	4,665	1,428	1,645	4,894	1,193	5,476	[1]101	27	98
1932	17,590	12,289	655	2,394	891	2,450	5,018	1,499	1,730	5,219	1,229	5,088	[1]395	15	125
1931	19,335	13,581	722	2,892	1,092	2,543	5,289	1,765	1,794	5,463	1,570	7,079	[1]252	19	198
$1,000,000 to $4,999,999:															
1955	40,853	87,950	10,225	22,331	10,799	23,468	19,038	13,421	9,857	11,996	22,255	97,583	4,820	2,338	881
1954	35,770	76,940	9,604	18,349	9,186	20,812	17,011	10,580	9,194	11,292	19,028	82,325	3,650	1,857	774
1953	33,805	72,960	9,284	17,089	9,255	19,759	15,960	8,984	8,467	10,373	18,980	81,805	3,996	2,115	880
1952	33,579	72,539	9,286	17,131	9,493	19,250	16,058	9,276	8,164	10,684	18,761	81,150	4,411	2,351	861
1951	32,041	68,596	9,437	15,645	9,872	16,287	16,069	8,790	7,644	10,665	18,100	81,724	5,297	2,804	970
1950	30,643	65,455	8,809	15,421	8,974	16,341	14,748	8,436	6,590	10,444	17,320	73,903	5,576	2,390	1,111
1949	27,793	59,298	8,453	12,846	6,900	16,400	13,670	6,154	5,728	10,281	15,398	61,613	3,663	1,401	973
1948	27,414	58,797	8,353	12,304	7,540	16,732	12,833	6,325	5,261	10,072	14,545	65,995	4,978	1,860	1,054
1947	26,447	57,167	8,458	10,937	7,272	17,774	11,696	6,307	4,747	10,009	13,282	61,785	5,336	1,995	1,014
1946	24,618	53,375	8,219	8,936	6,412	18,183	10,548	5,566	4,330	9,634	11,651	50,624	4,627	1,781	937
1945	22,057	47,907	8,199	6,572	4,477	18,114	9,486	4,241	3,906	9,359	9,676	42,251	3,450	2,047	680
1944	21,590	46,107	7,777	6,526	4,252	16,677	9,712	3,945	3,965	9,355	9,328	41,476	4,019	2,511	684
1943	20,737	43,611	7,291	6,664	4,245	14,255	10,096	3,804	3,930	9,488	8,817	39,471	4,139	2,567	681
1942	19,582	40,790	6,622	7,399	4,262	10,905	10,659	3,868	4,261	9,774	8,015	35,138	3,590	2,121	675
1941	18,832	39,214	5,313	8,155	4,324	8,694	11,927	4,399	5,032	10,898	7,149	31,307	2,655	1,214	838
1940	17,627	36,756	4,703	7,356	3,363	8,479	12,088	3,839	5,134	11,339	6,308	23,456	1,401	424	749
1939	17,337	36,150	4,144	6,770	3,140	8,887	12,404	3,782	5,232	11,553	6,311	21,091	1,104	211	740
1938	17,187	35,789	3,465	6,338	2,850	9,482	12,218	3,587	5,381	11,903	5,913	18,544	561	137	597
1937	17,897	37,278	3,266	6,541	3,246	10,115	12,701	4,262	5,338	12,455	6,024	21,930	1,108	220	974
1936	18,277	37,955	3,486	6,566	2,968	10,326	12,930	4,455	5,122	12,986	5,126	20,545	1,167	218	968
1935	18,407	38,298	3,067	6,273	2,691	10,533	13,542	4,699	5,288	13,986	4,785	18,446	674	132	817
1934	18,499	38,603	2,666	6,235	2,571	10,677	14,094	4,937	5,084	14,571	4,732	16,101	285	102	650
1933	15,840	32,723	1,928	5,549	2,220	8,829	11,835	3,095	4,299	12,781	4,424	11,448	[1]258	67	315
1932	16,705	34,432	1,927	6,321	1,972	9,359	12,658	3,138	4,512	13,573	4,730	10,744	[1]834	35	378
1931	18,345	37,955	2,067	7,666	2,438	9,843	13,440	3,710	4,649	14,118	5,625	14,595	[1]539	52	591
$5,000,000 to $9,999,999:															
1955	6,794	47,606	5,761	11,618	4,247	17,527	7,675	4,576	3,627	4,809	11,053	35,489	2,295	1,090	485
1954	6,324	44,205	5,713	9,718	3,916	16,765	7,323	3,707	3,433	4,493	10,536	32,269	1,870	926	470
1953	6,181	43,046	5,620	9,005	4,036	16,479	7,217	3,489	3,494	4,463	9,993	32,684	2,092	1,104	471
1952	6,139	42,817	5,635	9,280	4,195	15,757	7,298	3,619	3,257	4,698	9,955	32,718	2,205	1,188	501
1951	5,303	37,018	5,395	8,291	4,339	11,447	6,916	3,430	2,745	4,603	9,263	32,393	2,524	1,350	528
1950	4,987	34,767	4,882	7,778	3,857	11,266	6,430	3,046	2,406	4,574	8,833	28,430	2,631	1,117	598
1949	4,650	32,383	4,715	6,615	3,088	11,218	6,182	2,309	2,259	4,668	8,073	24,261	1,772	661	540
1948	4,733	33,061	4,869	6,524	3,641	11,339	6,154	2,635	2,222	4,728	8,026	28,292	2,545	927	604
1947	4,576	31,950	4,830	5,853	3,340	11,737	5,649	2,517	2,057	4,527	7,379	25,355	2,525	929	598
1946	4,241	29,627	4,409	4,669	2,922	11,860	5,179	2,063	1,901	4,565	6,591	20,234	2,133	809	548
1945	3,948	27,591	4,491	3,381	2,057	12,317	4,743	1,662	1,699	4,444	5,725	17,749	1,719	989	411
1944	3,646	25,285	4,055	3,170	2,066	10,357	5,015	1,687	1,891	4,504	5,346	18,684	2,073	1,292	388
1943	3,232	22,397	3,539	3,049	2,022	8,169	5,039	1,627	1,760	4,445	5,003	16,754	2,152	1,322	373
1942	2,905	20,258	3,151	3,168	2,014	6,141	5,301	1,617	1,895	4,566	4,479	14,552	1,766	1,072	356
1941	2,812	19,571	2,695	3,578	1,901	5,136	5,815	1,821	2,275	5,016	4,316	12,605	1,369	651	457
1940	2,603	18,142	2,404	3,105	1,434	4,912	5,894	1,550	2,376	5,221	3,863	9,186	687	212	390
1939	2,537	17,613	2,031	2,773	1,244	5,164	5,992	1,445	2,645	5,373	3,423	8,026	541	96	373

[1] Deficit or loss.

Series V 113-127.　Selected Corporate Assets, Liabilities, and Income Items, by Size of Total Assets: 1931 to 1955—Con.

[Money figures in millions of dollars]

Size of total assets and tax year	Number of returns with balance sheets	Total assets or liabilities	Selected assets					Selected liabilities				Total compiled receipts	Compiled net profit or net loss before tax	Total tax	Dividends paid in cash and assets other than own stock
			Cash	Notes and accounts receivable less reserve	Inventories	Investments	Capital assets less reserves	Notes and accounts payable	Bonds and mortgages	Capital stock	Surplus and undivided profits				
	113	114	115	116	117	118	119	120	121	122	123	124	125	126	127
$5,000,000 to $9,999,999—Con.:															
1938	2,542	17,584	1,745	2,639	1,158	5,428	5,961	1,470	2,718	5,631	3,198	7,192	302	63	312
1937	2,620	18,187	1,612	2,712	1,314	5,685	6,169	1,736	2,770	5,867	3,211	8,452	542	96	466
1936	2,719	18,967	1,711	2,806	1,265	5,920	6,459	1,861	2,776	6,180	2,998	8,352	605	101	498
1935	2,769	19,342	1,512	2,771	1,145	6,152	6,895	1,955	3,015	6,709	3,005	7,434	343	58	414
1934	2,844	19,789	1,323	2,931	1,108	6,337	7,151	2,215	2,994	7,000	2,903	6,589	172	50	332
1933	2,344	16,224	1,015	2,395	930	5,147	5,873	1,252	2,394	5,978	2,491	4,811	[1]110	33	191
1932	2,442	16,857	1,005	2,698	801	5,187	6,241	1,248	2,528	6,257	2,630	4,627	[1]335	21	228
1931	2,588	17,965	1,055	3,311	942	5,385	6,241	1,393	2,432	6,185	3,091	5,588	[1]138	28	345
$10,000,000 to $49,999,999:															
1955	6,246	126,472	13,607	27,557	10,153	52,241	20,622	8,796	9,665	11,257	29,799	77,254	6,530	3,039	1,723
1954	5,718	116,343	13,300	24,148	9,440	47,158	20,080	7,270	9,263	11,202	27,969	70,567	5,272	2,512	1,566
1953	5,550	112,990	13,163	22,922	9,928	44,569	20,407	7,116	9,344	11,928	26,537	73,302	5,966	3,130	1,631
1952	5,220	104,753	13,040	21,129	9,825	39,083	19,590	7,481	9,054	11,862	24,984	71,725	5,953	3,122	1,660
1951	4,481	90,506	12,394	18,330	10,143	29,064	18,637	7,326	8,063	11,647	23,378	71,510	7,195	3,803	1,805
1950	4,217	84,676	11,233	16,944	8,707	28,415	17,652	6,671	7,375	11,668	22,176	64,717	6,910	2,878	1,887
1949	3,761	75,812	10,051	13,006	7,015	27,606	16,505	4,603	6,862	11,334	19,448	53,772	4,486	1,589	1,529
1948	3,709	75,045	10,390	12,794	7,666	26,735	15,904	4,904	6,688	11,456	18,215	56,134	5,653	2,002	1,624
1947	3,565	71,789	10,063	11,646	7,208	26,977	14,325	5,040	5,708	11,613	16,511	51,621	5,188	1,878	1,487
1946	3,341	67,896	9,486	9,505	6,201	28,115	13,062	4,239	5,310	11,585	14,799	40,362	4,114	1,507	1,341
1945	3,197	65,335	9,724	7,523	4,591	30,143	11,852	3,798	4,817	11,134	13,513	39,917	3,900	2,163	1,072
1944	2,942	60,260	8,741	6,961	4,664	25,969	12,212	3,980	4,827	11,094	12,923	40,606	4,764	2,855	1,041
1943	2,719	55,215	7,966	6,757	4,670	21,737	12,487	3,763	5,003	11,063	12,047	37,959	5,093	3,120	1,016
1942	2,467	50,148	7,230	6,880	4,748	16,934	13,005	3,733	5,132	11,064	11,099	32,681	4,472	2,581	975
1941	2,411	49,186	6,615	7,685	4,249	14,964	14,576	3,646	6,288	12,671	10,877	29,132	3,071	1,440	1,252
1940	2,266	46,494	6,443	6,590	3,236	14,456	14,722	2,926	6,665	13,117	9,979	21,850	1,849	506	1,139
1939	2,217	45,767	5,485	6,186	3,009	15,156	14,887	2,838	6,972	13,651	9,465	19,199	1,565	246	1,154
1938	2,213	45,225	4,616	5,727	2,770	15,446	14,813	2,758	7,210	14,070	8,978	16,641	958	165	926
1937	2,281	46,642	4,263	6,086	3,040	16,063	15,228	3,495	7,100	14,536	9,325	19,522	1,640	252	1,372
1936	2,311	47,405	4,264	5,986	2,715	16,923	15,346	3,743	6,939	15,174	7,821	17,174	1,528	224	1,370
1935	2,393	49,080	3,926	6,122	2,428	17,935	16,313	4,244	8,050	16,268	8,099	16,386	1,202	152	1,308
1934	2,411	49,405	3,323	6,601	2,325	17,648	16,975	4,643	7,869	16,898	8,051	14,408	748	118	1,105
1933	1,885	38,592	2,365	4,932	2,029	13,314	13,657	2,391	6,194	13,442	6,270	10,430	[1]68	78	589
1932	1,947	39,839	2,494	5,628	1,752	13,369	14,122	2,485	6,271	14,319	6,054	9,905	[1]495	48	595
1931	2,117	43,167	2,482	7,051	2,141	13,859	14,857	2,980	6,282	14,890	7,154	13,365	[1]36	68	880
$50,000,000 to $99,999,999:															
1955	834	57,696	5,615	12,040	4,260	22,480	12,019	3,696	5,655	6,240	14,110	32,560	3,136	1,413	1,064
1954	794	55,544	5,801	10,288	4,234	21,808	12,026	3,204	5,431	6,297	13,580	31,400	2,667	1,223	972
1953	742	51,984	5,493	9,892	4,435	19,120	11,801	3,284	5,531	6,169	12,385	32,349	2,764	1,384	877
1952	708	49,986	5,551	8,995	4,224	18,463	11,542	3,230	5,442	6,012	11,748	30,361	2,755	1,382	926
1951	626	44,109	5,431	7,278	4,158	14,812	11,385	2,916	4,932	6,302	10,978	28,710	3,280	1,721	934
1950	596	41,555	4,989	7,113	3,659	14,191	10,555	2,594	5,145	6,335	9,798	27,249	3,205	1,297	959
1949	556	38,957	4,698	5,730	3,285	13,901	10,330	2,217	5,097	6,668	8,927	24,692	2,229	780	896
1948	529	37,169	4,760	5,358	3,443	13,415	9,146	2,142	4,442	6,263	7,909	23,985	2,507	866	849
1947	509	35,740	4,934	4,704	3,262	13,180	8,674	2,037	4,192	6,492	6,875	21,619	2,147	757	744
1946	463	32,457	4,125	3,660	2,645	12,918	8,235	1,712	3,808	6,463	6,125	15,675	1,587	559	651
1945	427	29,834	3,960	3,117	1,755	13,136	7,068	1,362	3,396	5,797	5,452	15,626	1,522	768	539
1944	415	28,953	3,927	2,950	2,112	11,740	7,274	1,555	3,623	5,820	5,023	17,351	1,986	1,169	506
1943	396	27,308	3,767	2,945	2,129	9,970	7,545	1,528	3,965	5,767	4,771	16,665	2,186	1,282	497
1942	371	25,623	3,545	2,975	2,072	8,546	7,567	1,422	3,895	5,833	4,141	13,665	1,760	952	477
1941	400	27,879	3,432	3,328	2,169	8,691	9,444	1,496	5,345	7,391	4,908	11,683	1,577	697	689
1940	368	25,565	3,200	2,822	1,624	7,861	9,383	1,152	5,209	7,265	4,523	8,488	939	245	643
1939	342	23,741	2,438	2,529	1,344	7,438	9,248	1,266	5,252	7,023	4,223	7,637	649	106	548
1938	349	24,220	2,134	2,613	1,260	7,927	9,334	1,400	5,348	7,357	4,383	7,210	474	84	527
1937	355	24,647	1,894	2,752	1,516	8,186	9,353	1,632	5,307	7,578	4,534	9,283	752	105	748
1936	355	24,295	2,000	2,646	1,223	8,610	8,848	1,614	4,977	7,703	3,667	7,201	775	92	729
1935 [2]	742	156,153	12,138	15,571	3,864	72,123	47,351	6,241	27,803	46,059	20,335	28,790	3,093	217	2,697
1934 [2]	761	153,168	9,922	16,309	3,882	69,461	47,743	7,149	27,033	46,701	20,695	25,542	2,080	183	2,140
1933 [2]	594	142,796	7,759	15,390	4,356	51,692	57,820	5,773	27,671	41,414	21,037	26,571	706	150	1,693
1932 [2]	618	149,241	8,448	16,648	3,993	54,185	58,614	6,538	28,371	43,440	21,684	27,037	332	132	2,270
1931 [2]	632	154,807	8,059	21,049	5,100	51,343	62,378	7,236	29,218	43,858	25,946	36,247	1,694	187	3,654
$100,000,000 or more: [2]															
1955	1,027	477,272	42,818	95,618	25,551	185,706	116,634	21,567	55,092	56,431	94,882	209,917	26,395	11,587	8,566
1954	932	432,171	38,641	77,202	22,435	177,072	107,541	17,334	50,689	52,965	83,157	177,314	19,840	8,502	7,355
1953	915	404,992	38,523	72,202	24,254	162,600	99,083	17,884	46,312	51,399	75,217	183,358	21,340	10,175	6,949
1952	854	378,622	38,062	67,708	23,261	152,314	90,066	17,632	42,183	48,925	69,478	164,378	19,040	8,938	6,490
1951	747	336,020	36,525	54,193	21,116	135,746	80,793	15,143	37,093	46,289	61,590	153,193	20,238	9,875	6,107
1950	688	304,127	33,999	46,701	15,954	130,085	71,224	11,908	32,941	42,678	55,080	126,812	18,751	7,370	5,916
1949	623	274,870	28,631	34,547	13,562	126,649	65,919	9,484	31,539	42,921	47,206	103,853	12,434	3,778	4,617
1948	601	260,770	30,306	35,569	14,590	114,736	59,843	10,726	29,029	41,379	42,811	107,250	13,214	4,077	4,159
1947	561	242,492	29,110	31,899	12,402	111,540	52,540	9,878	24,819	38,187	37,099	88,741	9,939	2,982	3,464
1946	531	222,988	25,806	25,575	10,136	109,938	46,716	8,051	22,029	35,816	32,199	64,349	6,632	1,920	2,947
1945	542	231,137	25,537	24,491	7,676	124,013	44,778	7,104	20,587	35,255	33,078	69,525	7,035	2,855	2,687
1944	517	219,462	22,922	22,966	8,244	114,571	47,135	7,665	21,759	35,654	31,419	76,920	9,858	4,852	2,687
1943	491	202,520	22,340	19,718	8,871	98,922	48,227	7,397	22,564	34,916	29,872	71,997	10,584	5,273	2,396
1942	455	183,889	20,997	18,191	7,986	84,851	48,042	6,654	23,105	35,433	26,074	57,268	8,482	3,621	2,431
1941	426	163,621	19,583	17,414	6,092	75,221	42,637	5,788	23,096	36,187	24,235	41,527	5,534	2,036	2,608
1940	403	153,712	21,165	14,199	4,519	69,823	41,431	5,091	22,404	35,917	22,139	32,026	3,587	764	2,417
1939	395	144,205	16,679	13,419	3,961	67,140	40,866	5,260	21,929	36,010	21,068	27,526	2,700	336	2,188
1938	394	138,119	13,016	12,343	3,764	64,956	40,792	4,906	22,673	36,490	20,637	24,815	1,755	236	1,911
1937	394	136,664	10,419	14,067	4,191	63,721	40,581	5,466	22,398	37,375	21,563	29,257	3,090	347	2,725
1936	396	134,389	11,489	13,918	3,463	63,457	38,126	5,331	21,198	36,315	16,423	25,723	2,716	274	2,533

[1] Deficit or loss.　　[2] For 1931–1935, data for returns with assets of $100,000,000 or more are included under the asset-size classification "$50,000,000 to $99,999,999."

Series V 128–202. Assets, Liabilities, and Selected Income Items for Electric Utility Industries: 1902 to 1956

[In millions of dollars]

Class A and B electric companies, privately owned

Year	Total assets or liabilities [1]	Current assets	Investments	Electric plant and equipment in service — Gross	Reserve for depreciation	Net	Other assets	Current liabilities	Long-term debt	Other liabilities	Capital stock	Net surplus	Total revenue	Net income	Dividends
	128	129	130	131	132	133	134	135	136	137	138	139	140	141	142
1956	33,341.2	2,617.6	937.2	30,817.4	6,238.1	24,579.3	5,207.1	2,627.4	15,231.2	562.4	11,877.5	3,042.7	9,114.4	1,332.2	1,021.8
1955	31,080.9	2,567.3	932.9	28,681.1	5,727.7	22,953.4	4,627.3	2,381.0	14,329.9	444.6	11,231.3	2,694.0	8,423.5	1,244.1	942.2
1954	29,053.9	2,436.9	1,009.1	26,011.4	5,269.4	20,742.0	4,865.9	2,254.3	13,322.2	380.9	10,635.2	2,461.2	7,654.8	1,134.1	868.0
1953	26,698.9	2,377.1	912.0	23,369.1	4,864.4	18,504.7	4,905.1	2,227.8	12,040.0	311.7	9,915.9	2,203.6	7,185.3	1,030.2	780.4
1952	24,580.6	2,442.6	1,255.2	20,996.3	4,525.0	16,471.3	4,411.5	2,090.4	10,809.4	284.7	9,228.3	2,167.9	6,619.4	947.1	724.8
1951	22,438.3	2,307.5	1,234.5	19,191.1	4,177.6	15,013.5	3,882.8	1,857.2	9,994.0	277.5	8,539.0	1,770.5	6,121.0	814.2	651.4
1950	20,589.7	2,058.1	1,234.9	17,340.6	3,851.6	13,489.0	3,807.7	1,527.2	9,188.6	260.5	7,943.9	1,669.5	5,595.7	821.9	619.1
1949	19,001.4	1,898.7	1,272.4	15,677.9	3,567.3	12,110.6	3,719.7	1,358.5	8,572.1	262.6	7,255.7	1,552.5	5,134.4	757.3	559.8
1948	17,346.9	1,985.2	1,154.6	13,918.9	3,369.1	10,549.8	3,657.3	1,359.7	7,718.7	267.6	6,590.0	1,410.9	4,895.9	656.8	493.1
1947	15,662.9	1,786.5	1,096.0	12,538.5	2,915.5	9,623.0	3,157.4	1,203.5	6,601.4	342.2	6,223.7	1,292.1	4,358.4	642.7	494.1
1946	14,733.3	1,726.7	1,066.8	11,827.5	2,715.8	9,111.7	2,828.1	1,003.4	6,140.7	378.6	5,939.2	1,262.4	3,877.2	637.6	458.1
1945	14,545.0	1,695.7	1,089.4	11,495.6	2,502.2	8,993.4	2,766.5	964.8	6,141.5	371.5	6,062.3	1,005.0	3,735.9	534.5	407.0
1944	15,275.5	1,679.0	1,297.4	11,279.2	2,272.3	9,006.9	3,292.2	959.8	6,397.3	434.0	6,380.1	1,104.3	3,670.7	506.8	397.6
1943	15,579.5	1,582.9	1,289.8	11,098.1	2,055.9	9,042.2	3,664.6	986.6	6,587.5	445.9	6,462.0	1,097.7	3,522.4	501.5	410.1
1942	15,703.8	1,364.7	1,320.0	10,825.6	1,860.4	8,965.2	4,053.9	908.0	6,753.6	384.5	6,596.9	1,060.7	3,275.0	489.9	407.5
1941	15,698.1	1,217.2	1,321.0	10,501.1	1,710.2	8,790.9	4,369.0	807.7	6,821.7	333.5	6,613.8	1,121.4	3,096.1	526.6	437.2
1940	15,579.2	1,122.9	1,380.4	10,165.0	1,593.8	8,571.2	4,504.7	692.0	6,895.5	303.6	6,570.9	1,117.3	2,864.8	547.7	447.4
1939	15,417.3	1,041.7	1,420.8	9,924.3	1,501.8	8,422.5	4,532.3	655.2	6,971.4	276.7	6,483.2	1,030.8	2,717.4	534.8	444.1
1938	15,591.4	1,083.7	1,468.4	9,710.3	1,413.9	8,296.4	4,742.9	750.4	7,060.3	270.4	6,485.9	1,024.4	2,615.5	487.2	417.6
1937	15,378.1	959.1	1,462.4	9,469.1	1,346.4	8,122.7	4,833.9	692.4	6,850.2	280.9	6,528.4	1,026.3	2,603.1	509.5	431.8

Central electric light and power stations, commercial

Year	Total assets or liabilities [1]	Current assets	Investments	Electric plant and equipment in service — Gross	Reserve for depreciation	Net	Other assets	Current liabilities	Long-term debt	Other liabilities	Capital stock	Net surplus	Total revenue	Net income	Dividends
	143	144	145	146	147	148	149	150	151	152	153	154	155	156	157
1937	15,553.6	972.5	1,308.1	14,048.7	1,346.4	12,702.3	570.6	707.5	6,837.6	467.1	6,540.5	1,000.9	2,603.3	514.2	434.0
1932	15,871.6	943.0	957.0	14,370.4	1,141.1	13,229.3	742.2	641.3	6,678.8	627.2	6,935.8	988.6	2,266.1	538.6	493.7
1927	12,239.6	982.2	622.4	10,586.8	700.2	9,886.6	748.3	671.6	5,309.9	450.7	5,095.1	712.3	1,841.2	505.8	338.2
1922	5,333.3	424.3	421.2	4,290.3	----	----	197.5	390.9	2,125.2	446.9	2,110.4	259.9	986.7	258.5	129.2
1917	3,555.1	178.9	238.9	2,964.2	----	----	173.1	348.6	1,262.7	234.6	1,543.5	165.8	486.6	91.5	64.6
1912	2,434.1	140.1	164.4	2,098.6	----	----	30.9	200.9	876.0	103.4	1,138.2	115.7	279.1	61.6	34.6
1907	----	----	----	1,054.0	----	----	----	----	----	----	----	----	161.6	37.8	19.3
1902	----	----	----	482.7	----	----	----	----	----	----	----	----	78.7	15.9	6.2

Street and electric railways

Year	Total assets or liabilities [1]	Current assets	Investments	Electric plant and equipment in service — Gross	Reserve for depreciation	Net	Other assets	Current liabilities	Long-term debt	Other liabilities	Capital stock	Net surplus	Total revenue	Net income	Dividends
	158	159	160	161	162	163	164	165	166	167	168	169	170	171	172
1937	6,454.6	289.1	397.4	5,867.2	666.5	5,200.7	567.4	556.2	3,022.3	854.3	2,073.1	−51.2	513.1	46.1	59.8
1932	3,967.6	137.0	693.6	3,314.0	308.4	3,005.6	131.4	363.6	1,914.1	446.3	1,294.8	−51.3	527.3	−20.2	19.0
1927	4,160.0	170.4	472.0	3,487.7	218.7	3,268.9	248.7	359.5	2,052.8	316.5	1,447.8	−16.6	813.3	40.7	32.8
1922 [2]	4,113.8	164.1	439.4	3,417.1	130.7	3,286.4	224.0	409.3	2,041.2	227.6	1,506.2	−70.4	784.9	35.7	22.7
1922 [3]	6,110.8	230.3	633.8	5,147.9	181.1	4,966.8	279.9	296.9	2,969.3	289.7	2,307.6	−26.7	1,049.8	74.2	53.7
1917	6,042.1	143.4	556.2	5,216.0	73.9	5,142.1	200.3	357.5	2,997.7	152.1	2,456.6	78.1	730.6	81.8	73.3
1912	5,317.4	178.9	399.9	4,596.6	----	----	142.1	441.1	2,273.1	159.5	2,348.5	95.3	586.4	81.4	71.0
1907	4,236.3	173.8	347.1	3,637.7	----	----	77.7	399.4	1,658.6	85.0	2,022.9	70.4	430.2	68.8	54.5
1902	2,533.8	61.1	152.5	2,167.6	----	----	152.6	118.7	974.1	133.4	1,266.9	40.7	250.5	47.4	33.0

Telephones

Year	Total assets or liabilities [1]	Current assets	Investments	Electric plant and equipment in service — Gross	Reserve for depreciation	Net	Other assets	Current liabilities	Long-term debt	Other liabilities	Capital stock	Net surplus	Total revenue	Net income	Dividends
	173	174	175	176	177	178	179	180	181	182	183	184	185	186	187
1937	----	----	----	4,941.3	----	----	----	----	----	----	----	----	1,167.4	----	----
1932	----	----	----	4,734.7	----	----	----	----	----	----	----	----	1,046.4	----	----
1927	----	----	----	3,475.2	----	----	----	----	----	----	----	----	996.9	----	----
1922	2,135.8	187.6	193.4	2,129.8	459.6	1,670.2	84.6	75.9	737.2	91.3	1,005.1	226.3	637.5	96.7	73.9
1917	1,424.5	108.5	75.2	1,435.8	234.4	1,201.5	39.3	46.4	497.3	60.9	670.9	149.0	363.8	59.4	45.3
1912	1,295.6	96.6	104.5	1,081.4	----	----	13.1	88.0	405.8	151.0	590.1	60.8	255.1	51.3	34.1
1907	940.3	83.0	60.7	794.1	----	----	2.6	85.0	302.5	45.2	459.4	48.2	176.7	41.2	23.4
1902	466.4	52.6	24.2	389.3	----	----	.3	44.5	[4]102.5	38.3	[4]269.7	21.3	86.8	21.7	15.0

Telegraphs

Year	Total assets or liabilities [1]	Current assets	Investments	Electric plant and equipment in service — Gross	Reserve for depreciation	Net	Other assets	Current liabilities	Long-term debt	Other liabilities	Capital stock	Net surplus	Total revenue	Net income	Dividends
	188	189	190	191	192	193	194	195	196	197	198	199	200	201	202
1937	----	----	----	506.8	----	----	----	----	----	----	----	----	135.8	----	3.1
1932	----	----	----	506.4	----	----	----	----	----	----	----	----	114.7	----	(5)
1927	----	----	----	426.7	----	----	----	----	----	----	----	----	177.6	----	14.2
1922	459.5	50.0	78.9	326.7	----	----	3.9	34.3	71.4	106.0	177.2	70.5	146.8	23.9	10.7
1917	363.1	59.4	56.0	243.4	----	----	4.3	31.9	61.8	67.3	167.3	34.8	107.0	17.8	9.8
1912	298.3	42.3	33.9	222.0	----	----	----	35.2	62.7	20.8	163.6	15.8	60.4	6.4	6.2
1907	261.8	15.3	36.5	210.0	----	----	----	12.9	65.2	8.3	155.1	20.3	45.3	9.7	7.5
1902	195.5	7.3	30.7	156.9	----	----	.6	6.6	45.9	7.9	117.1	18.1	35.3	10.0	6.3

[1] Includes net value of plant and equipment when a reserve for depreciation is shown; includes gross value when no reserve for depreciation is shown.
[2] Comparable with later years.
[3] Comparable with earlier years.
[4] Intercompany holdings of independent companies not deducted.
[5] Not available.

Series V 203-216. Net Value of Plant and Equipment in Regulated Industries: 1870 to 1951

[In millions of dollars. As of January 1]

Year	All regulated industries		Steam railroads		Electric light and power		Telephones		Street and electric railways		Local bus lines		All other	
	Current dollars	1929 dollars	Current dollars	1929 dollars	Current dollars	1929 dollars	Current dollars	1929 dollars	Current dollars	1929 dollars	Current dollars	1929 dollars	Current dollars	1929 dollars
	203	204	205	206	207	208	209	210	211	212	213	214	215	216
1951	87,254	48,394	39,213	22,601	19,145	9,335	8,377	5,056	1,299	749	628	351	18,592	10,303
1950	81,881	46,950	38,243	22,509	17,265	8,822	7,520	4,784	1,314	773	680	380	16,860	9,682
1949	77,416	45,299	37,695	22,265	15,069	8,145	6,650	4,341	1,375	812	696	405	15,932	9,331
1948	68,020	43,187	34,099	22,028	12,630	7,523	5,479	3,591	1,311	847	621	395	13,880	8,803
1947	58,495	41,752	30,769	22,009	10,326	7,136	3,978	3,007	1,356	970	449	333	11,617	8,295
1946	51,423	41,171	27,868	22,135	8,867	7,037	3,064	2,683	1,278	1,015	356	309	9,991	7,992
1945	49,842	41,260	26,905	22,217	8,726	7,089	3,001	2,668	1,301	1,074	349	308	9,559	7,904
1944	50,008	41,569	26,829	22,265	8,966	7,254	3,021	2,731	1,376	1,142	355	315	9,461	7,862
1943	48,430	42,150	25,369	22,391	9,052	7,383	3,057	2,810	1,376	1,215	380	340	9,195	8,011
1942	43,794	42,029	22,180	22,314	8,724	7,343	2,877	2,693	1,289	1,297	330	321	8,394	8,061
1941	40,475	41,555	20,533	22,270	8,171	7,174	2,478	2,487	1,251	1,357	264	274	7,777	7,993
1940	39,686	41,600	20,018	22,292	7,946	7,094	2,446	2,387	1,548	1,724	228	243	7,500	7,860
1939	39,855	41,909	20,220	22,517	7,899	7,110	2,398	2,355	1,590	1,771	212	223	7,535	7,933
1938	40,864	42,259	20,960	22,733	7,895	7,068	2,309	2,334	1,695	1,838	198	220	7,807	8,066
1937	38,021	42,012	19,491	22,638	7,166	6,985	2,308	2,284	1,640	1,904	169	201	7,247	8,000
1936	37,809	42,245	19,467	22,769	6,996	7,024	2,371	2,324	1,688	1,974	136	162	7,151	7,992
1935	37,898	42,920	19,453	23,076	7,010	7,161	2,446	2,418	1,740	2,064	115	133	7,133	8,068
1934	36,246	43,722	18,716	23,366	6,582	7,345	2,339	2,533	1,745	2,179	101	123	6,763	8,176
1933	37,560	44,714	19,434	23,729	6,629	7,533	2,466	2,656	1,900	2,320	103	120	7,029	8,357
1932	41,424	45,371	21,579	24,030	7,090	7,599	2,699	2,690	2,204	2,454	107	120	7,745	8,478
1931	43,584	45,212	23,273	24,142	7,090	7,424	2,568	2,576	2,466	2,558	109	115	8,078	8,397
1930	43,857	43,857	23,774	23,774	6,934	6,934	2,242	2,242	2,648	2,648	110	110	8,149	8,149
1929	41,728	42,407	23,120	23,401	6,215	6,535	1,968	1,899	2,711	2,744	98	100	7,616	7,728
1928	41,667	41,377	23,571	23,154	5,746	6,139	1,871	1,718	2,897	2,846	83	85	7,500	7,435
1927	40,516	40,234	23,132	22,858	5,427	5,683	1,773	1,596	2,990	2,955	75	74	7,119	7,069
1926	39,449	39,020	22,752	22,482	5,100	5,241	1,649	1,457	3,118	3,081	61	58	6,769	6,701
1925	39,503	37,947	23,270	22,204	4,606	4,729	1,526	1,332	3,355	3,201	47	44	6,699	6,437
1924	38,568	36,627	23,223	21,785	3,963	4,145	1,355	1,201	3,534	3,316	33	31	6,460	6,149
1923	33,937	35,388	20,367	21,260	3,317	3,633	1,246	1,112	3,254	3,397	14	12	5,739	5,974
1922	37,302	35,025	22,629	21,228	3,416	3,416	1,325	1,066	3,710	3,480	4	3	6,218	5,832
1921	46,384	35,060	28,841	21,191	3,591	3,343	1,291	1,064	4,920	3,615	4	3	7,737	5,845
1920	39,785	35,053	24,679	21,220	3,205	3,264	1,033	1,076	4,354	3,743	4	3	6,510	5,747
1919	36,123	35,276	22,309	21,410	3,085	3,310	992	1,112	3,980	3,819	3	2	5,755	5,623
1918	29,951	35,361	18,343	21,454	2,682	3,382	940	1,140	3,274	3,829	1	1	4,711	5,555
1917	23,992	34,822	14,776	21,322	2,110	3,216	762	1,109	2,656	3,833	1	1	3,687	5,341
1916	20,706	34,684	12,832	21,315	1,687	3,177	730	1,101	2,326	3,864	1	1	3,130	5,226
1915	20,318	34,614	12,687	21,358	1,595	3,133	738	1,143	2,286	3,849	1	1	3,011	5,131
1914	20,517	34,025	12,877	21,075	1,560	3,029	747	1,150	2,357	3,839	1	1	2,975	4,932
1913	19,464	32,989	12,184	20,443	1,535	2,925	709	1,145	2,288	3,825	(1)	(1)	2,748	4,652
1912	18,411	31,743	11,630	19,847	1,315	2,605	689	1,096	2,254	3,847	(1)	(1)	2,523	4,348
1911	17,638	30,463	11,265	19,190	1,109	2,311	650	1,079	2,255	3,816	(1)	(1)	2,359	4,068
1910	16,326	29,049	10,459	18,413	964	2,042	621	1,055	2,152	3,750	(1)	(1)	2,130	3,789
1909	15,219	27,925	9,790	17,735	792	1,795	590	1,067	2,086	3,745	--------	--------	1,961	3,583
1908	14,789	26,792	9,527	17,105	728	1,568	611	1,077	2,046	3,647	--------	--------	1,877	3,396
1907	13,584	25,533	8,848	16,477	629	1,413	545	1,000	1,855	3,422	--------	--------	1,707	3,221
1906	12,072	24,387	7,940	15,976	543	1,268	448	856	1,613	3,200	--------	--------	1,528	3,087
1905	11,197	23,524	7,483	15,688	474	1,130	385	752	1,444	2,970	--------	--------	1,411	2,984
1904	10,925	22,855	7,455	15,531	407	1,000	337	676	1,338	2,746	--------	--------	1,388	2,902
1903	10,356	22,271	7,179	15,439	361	875	292	585	1,205	2,542	--------	--------	1,319	2,830
1902	9,788	21,750	6,898	15,362	306	746	254	516	1,085	2,365	--------	--------	1,245	2,761
1901	9,681	21,276	6,944	15,295	267	638	226	456	1,012	2,190	--------	--------	1,232	2,697
1900	9,021	20,785	6,560	15,185	234	569	186	384	892	2,019	--------	--------	1,149	2,628
1899	8,091	20,328	6,000	15,113	185	490	144	321	749	1,889	--------	--------	1,013	2,566
1898	7,757	20,095	5,867	15,239	146	408	119	276	647	1,642	--------	--------	979	2,530
1897	7,869	19,973	6,100	15,444	108	347	90	235	580	1,440	--------	--------	991	2,508
1896	7,754	19,881	6,104	15,652	102	311	72	182	497	1,248	--------	--------	979	2,488
1895	7,736	19,735	6,194	15,801	96	264	59	137	430	1,072	--------	--------	957	2,461
1894	7,845	19,274	6,363	15,635	82	230	42	98	381	915	--------	--------	977	2,396
1893	7,462	18,200	6,098	14,873	69	193	40	92	328	783	--------	--------	927	2,259
1892	7,212	17,212	5,936	14,168	56	152	37	86	287	670	--------	--------	896	2,136
1891	7,184	16,747	5,955	13,882	48	123	38	84	252	576	--------	--------	891	2,083
1890	6,982	16,313	5,827	13,614	34	87	34	75	220	502	--------	--------	867	2,035
1889	6,872	15,907	5,766	13,348	23	60	29	64	195	441	--------	--------	859	1,995
1888	6,683	15,470	5,626	13,022	15	39	28	61	173	392	--------	--------	841	1,956
1887	6,509	14,964	5,494	12,631	9	23	27	60	150	337	--------	--------	829	1,913
1886	6,342	14,681	5,354	12,394	5	13	30	65	139	313	--------	--------	815	1,896
1885	6,378	14,529	5,390	12,278	3	8	26	56	133	294	--------	--------	827	1,893
1884	6,502	14,259	5,482	12,048	2	5	23	47	134	284	--------	--------	861	1,876
1883	6,412	13,789	5,401	11,641	1	2	20	38	131	272	--------	--------	859	1,836
1882	5,850	13,028	4,922	10,986	(1)	1	14	29	119	254	--------	--------	795	1,759
1881	5,357	12,121	4,494	10,191	(1)	(1)	9	18	116	248	--------	--------	788	1,664
1880	4,594	11,573	3,852	9,728	--------	--------	4	9	98	235	--------	--------	640	1,602
1879	4,576	11,384	3,853	9,584	--------	--------	--------	--------	93	219	--------	--------	680	1,580
1878	4,828	11,229	4,061	9,467	--------	--------	--------	--------	93	203	--------	--------	674	1,559
1877	5,199	11,086	4,380	9,360	--------	--------	--------	--------	94	188	--------	--------	725	1,538
1876	5,486	10,994	4,630	9,298	--------	--------	--------	--------	93	175	--------	--------	763	1,521
1875	5,729	10,912	4,844	9,244	--------	--------	--------	--------	91	162	--------	--------	794	1,506
1874	5,993	10,740	5,076	9,114	--------	--------	--------	--------	90	150	--------	--------	827	1,476
1873	5,656	10,340	4,799	8,789	--------	--------	--------	--------	81	138	--------	--------	776	1,413
1872	4,899	9,662	4,172	8,229	--------	--------	--------	--------	68	126	--------	--------	659	1,307
1871	4,484	8,810	3,829	7,523	--------	--------	--------	--------	61	112	--------	--------	594	1,175
1870	4,437	8,053	3,787	6,886	--------	--------	--------	--------	65	108	--------	--------	585	1,059

1 Less than $500,000.

Series V 217–237. Assets, Liabilities, and Selected Income Items for Two Samples of Large Manufacturing Corporations: 1914 to 1943

[In millions of dollars]

Year	Total assets or liabilities	Current assets Total [1]	Cash	Marketable securities	Receivables	Inventory	Investments and advances	Fixed assets (net)	Other assets
	217	218	219	220	221	222	223	224	225
1943	24,632.3	13,259.6	2,610.4	2,666.1	3,241.6	4,741.5	1,775.5	8,727.0	870.2
1942	23,074.1	11,664.6	2,120.6	1,751.2	3,168.2	4,624.6	1,833.5	8,853.4	722.6
1941	21,071.8	9,643.3	2,059.2	1,280.6	2,097.8	4,205.7	1,902.8	8,911.1	614.6
1940	19,048.2	7,858.0	2,184.0	602.5	1,511.0	3,560.5	1,985.9	8,715.6	488.7
1939	18,212.5	7,033.9	1,772.1	576.0	1,297.9	3,387.9	1,850.8	8,807.4	520.4
1938	17,769.2	6,641.1	1,593.9	451.9	1,223.8	3,371.5	1,650.2	8,937.8	540.1
1937	18,034.0	6,663.3	1,105.4	493.9	1,282.2	3,781.8	1,637.9	9,156.9	575.9
1936	16,985.4	6,280.8	1,270.1	522.6	1,266.7	3,221.4	1,594.0	8,592.7	517.9
1935	16,338.9	5,933.0	1,299.1	613.8	1,093.2	2,926.9	1,547.6	8,356.4	501.9
1934	16,257.0	5,553.1	1,109.1	705.8	947.8	2,790.4	1,604.7	8,600.2	499.0
1933	16,558.0	5,448.2	1,041.3	899.2	962.5	2,545.2	1,673.7	8,757.5	708.6
1932	16,799.4	5,360.4	1,219.5	782.2	987.3	2,371.4	1,466.2	9,391.6	581.2
1931	18,035.6	6,031.3	1,080.4	1,030.3	1,180.8	2,739.8	1,362.1	10,021.3	620.9
1930	18,689.2	6,855.1	1,219.1	910.0	1,453.9	3,272.1	1,434.7	9,735.3	664.1
1929	18,684.2	7,394.1	1,124.3	1,059.1	1,675.7	3,535.0	1,643.8	8,972.7	673.6
1928	17,292.3	6,999.5	1,187.2	1,079.6	1,529.9	3,202.8	1,221.7	8,459.8	611.3
1927	16,360.7	6,467.1	1,026.7	928.5	1,403.3	3,108.6	1,089.7	8,255.1	548.8
1926	16,048.3	6,651.5	937.1	877.9	1,658.2	3,178.3	1,035.9	7,847.6	513.3
1925	15,029.9	6,218.9	911.9	694.4	1,595.0	3,017.6	1,029.5	7,302.9	478.6
1924	14,030.7	5,728.9	818.6	665.0	1,472.8	2,772.5	1,025.7	6,752.3	523.8
1923	13,761.3	5,555.9	735.9	620.0	1,487.3	2,762.7	1,104.7	6,571.1	529.0
1922 [2]	12,701.1	5,102.3	650.7	583.9	1,379.6	2,488.1	1,032.6	6,005.8	560.4
1922 [3]	9,911.5	3,753.2	547.7	430.8	943.7	1,826.7	785.3	4,882.3	490.7
1921	9,915.1	3,786.5	526.6	432.2	985.4	1,837.1	775.4	4,874.8	478.4
1920	10,463.5	4,646.3	520.0	369.6	1,209.8	2,464.5	651.2	4,652.4	513.6
1919	9,693.5	4,500.6	573.8	534.7	1,065.5	2,242.2	563.2	4,136.1	493.6
1918	9,340.7	4,512.5	581.6	621.0	1,071.2	2,158.0	455.8	3,866.3	506.1
1917	8,197.0	3,662.7	552.9	461.2	863.0	1,717.6	407.8	3,667.6	458.9
1916	6,754.0	2,579.3	448.3	190.6	674.8	1,216.4	310.4	3,434.7	429.6
1915	5,919.1	1,920.5	316.4	99.8	581.8	886.4	306.1	3,277.1	415.4
1914	5,254.1	1,532.4	236.8	42.0	465.6	780.5	253.6	3,116.6	351.5

Year	Current liabilities Total [1]	Notes payable	Accounts payable	Other	Long-term debt	Other liabilities	Capital Preferred stock	Common stock	Capital reserves	Surplus	Net income	Dividends
	226	227	228	229	230	231	232	233	234	235	236	237
1943	5,870.8	202.7	1,466.3	4,201.8	1,984.3	495.7	1,831.1	6,843.0	1,408.8	6,198.6	1,247.7	770.7
1942	4,928.9	321.7	1,159.6	3,447.6	1,993.5	461.4	1,898.2	6,830.2	1,208.8	5,753.1	1,154.6	750.2
1941	3,547.7	263.9	925.1	2,358.7	2,014.3	444.5	1,907.4	6,821.4	960.5	5,376.0	1,501.6	949.8
1940	2,081.6	120.4	729.0	1,232.2	2,013.5	421.1	1,946.6	6,805.5	813.3	4,966.6	1,317.6	868.8
1939	1,440.4	88.2	626.2	726.0	2,089.9	423.2	1,963.1	6,856.5	639.2	4,800.2	1,048.4	750.7
1938	1,279.9	145.4	532.2	602.3	2,048.4	454.1	1,956.5	6,840.8	596.3	4,593.2	651.6	562.2
1937	1,597.1	289.2	557.0	750.9	1,717.0	469.5	1,956.0	7,110.4	634.0	4,550.0	1,427.4	1,019.2
1936	1,480.0	197.5	613.0	669.5	1,551.4	374.6	1,871.2	7,015.2	567.3	4,125.7	1,269.3	922.5
1935	1,201.0	193.6	504.0	503.4	1,592.0	440.8	1,882.4	6,805.0	519.3	3,897.8	791.7	514.6
1934	957.1	129.5	448.1	379.5	1,662.3	476.0	1,938.4	6,782.2	492.2	3,948.8	467.2	440.1
1933	787.2	65.0	465.7	256.5	1,768.9	413.0	1,945.2	7,243.3	461.2	3,969.2	314.3	384.0
1932	649.1	34.8	385.2	229.1	1,933.4	406.2	1,955.0	7,307.3	459.3	4,089.1	.5	497.1
1931	757.3	44.7	425.4	287.2	1,972.1	459.6	1,979.6	7,684.6	550.2	4,632.2	289.7	809.8
1930	1,059.6	72.4	588.9	398.3	2,001.2	299.4	1,995.1	7,521.9	544.9	5,267.1	964.1	971.7
1929	1,364.5	161.8	708.2	494.5	1,850.7	329.4	1,964.0	6,856.3	544.8	5,209.1	1,721.1	1,011.6
1928	1,344.7	171.7	685.5	487.5	2,162.2	279.9	1,918.9	6,582.8	456.4	4,547.4	1,485.3	905.3
1927	1,178.1	152.5	575.8	449.8	2,114.3	242.1	1,907.0	6,283.2	460.0	4,176.0	1,098.7	839.5
1926	1,385.0	166.6	760.2	458.2	1,887.0	67.4	2,041.1	5,974.0	429.1	4,264.7	1,311.0	764.8
1925	1,344.2	162.4	790.0	391.8	1,756.8	66.4	1,983.5	5,551.1	447.5	3,880.4	1,214.7	613.9
1924	1,225.9	232.7	689.5	303.7	1,745.2	55.4	1,935.2	5,384.8	423.8	3,260.4	889.7	527.2
1923	1,297.5	319.2	685.1	293.2	1,780.4	59.5	1,913.8	5,251.0	405.7	3,053.4	868.1	499.1
1922 [2]	1,111.0	273.0	604.1	233.9	1,648.6	59.7	1,877.2	4,864.2	435.4	2,705.0	645.2	410.5
1922 [3]	799.1	220.0	289.9	204.5	1,460.3	40.4	1,547.3	3,592.9	505.4	1,966.1	511.1	535.9
1921	948.2	436.9	230.9	198.8	1,470.6	60.0	1,450.1	3,028.0	552.5	2,405.7	139.2	297.2
1920	1,556.1	670.8	370.1	285.1	1,286.2	47.2	1,453.5	2,959.6	474.2	2,686.7	587.8	311.3
1919	1,459.9	511.3	385.0	323.7	1,204.0	88.4	1,404.1	2,610.7	440.7	2,485.7	610.7	297.1
1918	1,737.1	447.2	435.4	700.0	1,221.0	79.8	1,298.4	2,472.9	370.6	2,160.9	627.4	331.9
1917	1,331.3	345.4	332.8	471.1	1,114.2	82.4	1,236.4	2,337.9	237.7	1,857.1	875.1	357.4
1916	658.9	204.4	227.0	122.7	1,067.3	68.3	1,173.3	2,108.0	150.0	1,828.2	914.0	305.6
1915	527.8	177.4	220.0	67.5	1,030.0	122.5	1,149.6	1,955.9	126.8	1,006.5	381.5	172.1
1914	385.0	181.1	111.3	53.4	1,027.9	22.4	1,064.7	1,865.6	77.0	811.5	190.5	154.1

[1] For 1914–1922, exceeds sum of components by amount of unsegregable items.   [3] Comparable with earlier years.
[2] Comparable with later years.

Productivity and Technological Development

PRODUCTIVITY INDEXES (Series W 1-51)

W 1-51. General note.

Work in the field of productivity has been carried on by many individuals and organizations, especially the Bureau of Labor Statistics (BLS), the WPA National Research Project, and the National Bureau of Economic Research (NBER). Currently, extensive work is being done by BLS, which measures productivity for the economy and for selected major sectors and industries.

Productivity, which is a ratio of output to input, can have different meanings. For example, it may be computed as a ratio of output to capital, or to labor, or to a combination of the two. The latter measures, which have been developed by John W. Kendrick for NBER, are covered in series W 5-8. Their construction and meaning are described briefly in his *Productivity Trends: Capital and Labor*, Occasional Paper No. 53, NBER, 1956, and more fully in the forthcoming NBER volume, *Productivity Trends in the United States*. The indexes in series W 1-4 and W 9-51 were computed by dividing a product index by an index of man-hours or of employment.

Historically, the measure of productivity which is most commonly used has been output per unit of labor input—frequently called "labor productivity." Such a measure reflects not only labor's effort but also other factors, including state of technology, capital per worker, availability of materials, the efficiency of management, and rate of operations.

The output part of a labor productivity ratio may also be defined in several ways. The simplest one conceptually is what is called physical output, where the components are physical units such as pounds, bushels, number, etc. To arrive at total measures for an industry or an industry group, the units are weighted by man-hours or the closest equivalent (such as labor cost or value added). This type of measure is a weighted arithmetic average of the productivity change of its components. The BLS industry estimates are of this type.

Estimates for broad aggregates, such as manufacturing or the total private economy, are constructed in terms of another concept called net output or value added per man-hour. Purchased "intermediate" products consumed in the production process are excluded. This type of measure in relation to man-hours reflects not only the average of the individual productivity changes, but also reflects shifts in the relative importance of low- or high-productivity industries as well as savings in materials inputs.

The specific year chosen for the weight base may affect the trend of the productivity series. For example, net output valued in 1939 prices would undoubtedly show a different trend than net output valued in 1956 prices. In general, a current year-weighted productivity index gives a lower trend than a base year-weighted index, since items which increase most in volume of output tend to be those with price declines or lower price increases.

Productivity series suffer from statistical limitations which are common to most production estimates. They also have additional limitations arising out of the noncomparability of output and man-hour series. For example, quality change cannot be adequately accounted for in measuring changes in output, price indexes often do not cover a sufficiently broad industrial area, and man-hour weights for constructing physical output series are frequently not available. At the industry level, especially, the rigidities of the Bureau of the Budget Standard Industrial Classification system may result in man-hours and output being classified in different industries.

W 1-11. Indexes of national productivity, 1889-1957.

Source: **Series W 1-8**, John W. Kendrick, *Productivity Trends in the United States*, National Bureau of Economic Research, Princeton University Press (forthcoming); **series W 9-11**, Bureau of Labor Statistics, *Trends in Output Per Man-Hour in the Private Economy, 1909-1958*, Bulletin No. 1249, Dec. 1959, table 1.

These indexes are measures of aggregate productivity for the total private economy and the major segments thereof. The NBER series (W 1-8) show the change in real gross product per unit of factor input after adjustments to exclude general government and real net factor income from abroad. The BLS series (W 9-11) exclude only general government and retain real net factor income from abroad. Since the latter amount as a percent of total product is extremely small, the difference between the two series in this regard is relatively small. For both series, the numerator is derived from the Department of Commerce gross national product series (with some adjustments), carried back from 1929 in the case of the NBER series, chiefly by the national product estimates of Simon Kuznets, supplemented by estimates of government purchases by John W. Kendrick.

Although the numerator of the indexes is adjusted gross national product, the indexes are actually measures of the net productivity of the economy. This arises as the result of "netting" out all intermediate purchases of goods and services, thus eliminating duplication and measuring only the "end product" of the system. Indexes of net productivity may therefore move differently from gross productivity indexes according to changes in the efficiency of materials utilization which are not reflected in gross output indexes of productivity.

The indexes are "real" in the sense that price fluctuations have been eliminated by various means. In the NBER series, the net goods and services produced were combined in six segments or "comparison periods" by a Marshall-Edgeworth formula using as weights the average prices in the terminal years of each period. The final production index is thus a chain index with shifting weights between links, but fixed weights within links. Over the long period, therefore, the productivity index reflects the overall shifts in the industry composition of the aggregates. The comparison base is 1929.

The BLS index is derived from constant dollar aggregates of gross national product published by the Department of Commerce. These aggregates represent the deflation of current dollar values by weighted price indexes, wherever possible. The resultant indexes of net output approximate production indexes with 1954 representing the price base and 1947–49 the comparison base.

W 1–3, real gross private domestic product per man-hour. This series shows changes in over-all productive efficiency in terms of man-hours as the physical unit of labor input. In general, the estimates of man-hours were obtained by multiplying employment by average hours worked per year in the various industrial groupings. The industry hours were combined to the desired level of aggregation without explicit weights. The exception to the general rule for derivation of total hours occurred in the farm sector where the Agricultural Marketing Service estimates of *Farm Labor Requirements* in terms of "average adult man-hour equivalents" were used. The AMS estimates were adjusted upwards by 10 percent in all years to attain a level comparable to that of the other sectors. For an explanation of the man-hour equivalent concept, see text for series W 48–51.

For the private nonfarm sector, employment data are based upon establishment reports or represent extrapolations of establishment-type estimates. The estimates since 1929 are by the Office of Business Economics. Prior to 1929, they are extrapolations of various benchmark estimates and are largely those used in previous NBER studies of output and employment.

W 4, product per unit of labor input. This series measures net output per weighted man-hour. Man-hours for industry groups or segments were combined by average hourly earnings, using the Marshall-Edgeworth cross-weighting formula. The comparison periods conforming to those in the output index were used. Aside from making possible a comparative study of the movements of output per weighted and per unweighted man-hour, the construction of this index makes possible the combination of the capital and labor inputs and the derivation of indexes of net output per unit of total factor input.

W 5, product per unit of capital input. This series expresses the change in total productivity in terms of real capital assets. The capital input of the private domestic economy was defined to include land and replaceable assets, such as residential and nonresidential structures, equipment, and inventories. The estimates are based primarily on those by Raymond Goldsmith in *A Study of Saving in the United States*, vol. 3, Princeton University Press, 1956. Index numbers of real capital stocks for separate industry groups were combined by use of the Marshall-Edgeworth formula, using unit capital compensation as weights. The system parallels that used in the index of labor input.

W 6–8, product per unit of total factor input. These series are conceptually more inclusive measures than those shown in series W 1–5 since they relate the quantity of net output to the real quantity of total factor input required to produce it. The index of total factor input is the weighted average of the index of labor input and the index of capital input previously described. The weights are units of factor compensation and the combination was made by applying the Marshall-Edgeworth formula.

W 9–11, real gross private product. Aside from the previously discussed differences between the weighting systems used in the two output series, the BLS index also employs different concepts of man-hours in both sectors. Here, the concept is total hours paid for rather than hours worked. They include the time paid for in the form of paid holidays, sick leave, and vacation pay.

The hours of farmworkers are from the Bureau of the Census, *Current Population Survey*, and are derived as the product of average hours times the total number of workers, as distinct from the man-hour requirements estimates used in

series W 1–8. Hours of the nonfarm component are from the Bureau of Labor Statistics, *Employment and Earnings*. The index of man-hours is from a simple aggregation of the man-hours worked in the separate sectors.

W 12. Index of output per man-hour for total mining, 1890–1957.

Source: John W. Kendrick, *Productivity Trends in the United States*, National Bureau of Economic Research, Princeton University Press (forthcoming).

An earlier index appearing in Harold Barger and Sam H. Schurr, *The Mining Industries, 1899–1939: A Study of Output, Employment, and Productivity*, NBER, New York, 1944, provided the basis for this series. The earlier index has been extended back by Kendrick to cover years omitted by Barger and Schurr and to include the later period, 1939–1957. Since Kendrick's study of the mining industry was part of a study of national productivity, the need for consistency between the several sectors caused some modification of the Barger and Schurr index.

The mining industry covers all extraction of minerals including stone quarrying and the pumping of crude petroleum. The output index is a price-weighted aggregate of the Marshall-Edgeworth type and is of "modified chain" construction. Separate indexes were computed for each of several comparison periods using the mean of the commodity prices for the terminal years of each period. The indexes of the comparison periods were then linked to obtain an index covering the entire period.

The general weighting scheme of the original study was followed in the Kendrick revisions, except that he applied national income per unit of output as the weighting factor for combining the broad industry groups into the sector aggregate. These broad groups are metal mining, nonmetallic mining and quarrying, oil and gas wells, bituminous coal, and anthracite. For years prior to 1919, the 1919–1929 weights were used.

Basic sources of quantity and value data for the original production index were *Mineral Resources of the United States*, published annually for 1882–1931; and *Minerals Yearbook*, published annually since 1932–33. These volumes were prepared and issued by the Geological Survey from 1882 to 1923 and by the Bureau of Mines since 1924.

Labor input data for 1902 are from the Bureau of the Census, whereas later data are from accident statistics collected by the Bureau of Mines. The data are man-days used in actual mine operation; in most cases, the average number of employees times the number of days the mine operated during the year. BLS reports on employment and average hours have been used since 1939. The estimates of man-hours are the products of man-days times the "nominal" hours worked per day. Nominal hours are implicitly defined as the number of hours customarily worked on one shift in a regular workday by all persons "engaged in production."

W 13. Index of output per man-hour in all mining, 1880–1950.

Source: Bureau of Labor Statistics computations (1880–1935, based on WPA National Research Project, *Production, Employment, and Productivity in the Mineral Extractive Industries, 1880–1938*; 1935–1950, based on BLS, *Productivity Trends in Selected Industries, Indexes Through 1950*, Bulletin No. 1046).

For 1935–1945, the index for mining represents 6 individual mining industries, for 5 of which the BLS published separate series—bituminous coal, anthracite, iron, copper, and lead and zinc. The production index from which the combined index is derived is an average of the 5 separately published series plus a series for crude petroleum and natural gas weighted with current man-hours; the man-hours index is based on totals for the 6 industries. The productivity index for the years before 1935 is based on the WPA National Research Project study.

The individual mining series (W 14-21) are published annually in a BLS release, *Indexes of Output Per Man-Hour in Selected Industries*. The production data for these series are from the Bureau of Mines. Employment and average weekly hours series are those of BLS for 1939-1957. For 1935-1939, BLS series were used for the coal industry and Bureau of Mines data for metal mining. The employment definition adopted (average number of wage earners employed during the 12 months of each year, including months of no activity) is the concept used by the Bureau of the Census.

W 14-21. Indexes of output per man-hour in selected mining industries, 1935-1957.

Source: For selected years, Bureau of Labor Statistics, *Indexes of Output Per Man-Hour for Selected Industries: 1919-1958*, April 1959; all other years, BLS computations (based on BLS, *Trends in Output Per Man-Hour, 1935-1955, Selected Nonmanufacturing Industries*, Report No. 105, June 1956).

Production data on which the indexes are based come from the Bureau of Mines, *Minerals Yearbook*, and the Bureau of the Census, censuses of mineral industries. The man-hours components of the indexes are derived from the regularly published BLS series on employment and average weekly hours adjusted by data obtained from the censuses of mineral industries. Exceptions to this are the series of man-hours for copper mining and iron mining for 1935-1939, which were derived from accident analysis statistics of the Bureau of Mines; and the lead and zinc mining man-hours for 1935-1939, which were derived from special WPA National Research Project tabulations of Bureau of Mines data for 1935-1939. The man-hours cover only production and related workers, and exclude salaried officers, superintendents, other supervisory employees, and professional and technical employees. They include all hours worked or paid for.

W 22-23. Index of manufacturing, net output per man-hour, (1947-49=100), 1947-1957.

Source: Bureau of Labor Statistics, *Trends in Output Per Man-Hour in the Private Economy, 1909-1958*, Bulletin No. 1249, Dec. 1959.

The indexes of net output per man-hour in manufacturing measure changes in the real value added per production worker man-hour and per man-hour of all employees. The numerator of this index is real total output less the real costs of material, containers, fuel, and supplies. The residual value added is the same as adjusted value added in the 1954 Census of Manufactures, corrected for price changes.

Shipments, inventories, and materials consumed are deflated separately for each industry. Deflated shipments are adjusted by net changes in deflated inventories to estimate total production; deflated materials are deducted to arrive at net output. The index of net output is then divided by an index of total man-hours of production workers to obtain the index of net output per man-hour.

Data in current prices, by industry and commodity, are available from the census of manufactures and from the *Annual Survey of Manufactures* for intercensal years. For deflating output, the commodity indexes of BLS Wholesale Price Index are reweighted according to the commodity output of industries in the 1947 Census of Manufactures. Beginning and ending inventories are deflated separately by the price index at the beginning and ending of the year and the net change is computed in real terms.

Material cost deflators were derived by weighting the WPI commodity indexes according to the material consumption patterns of the separate industries as reflected in the 1947 BLS Interindustry Relations study.

Production worker man-hours represent the product of employment times the average weekly hours of production workers, as published by BLS, raised to annual levels. The hours of other workers are estimated by BLS.

W 24. Index of output per man-hour for all manufacturing industries, 1909-1953.

Source: 1909, 1914, and 1919-1939, Bureau of Labor Statistics computations (based on BLS, *Handbook of Labor Statistics*, 1947 edition); 1939, 1947, and 1949-1953, Bureau of Labor Statistics, *Trends in Output Per Man-Hour and Man-Hours Per Unit of Output-Manufacturing, 1939-53*, Report No. 100, 1955.

The production index used to derive the index of output per man-hour in manufacturing for 1909, 1914, and for the odd-numbered years 1919-1939, is from Solomon Fabricant, *Employment in Manufacturing, 1899-1939*, NBER, New York, 1942. The production index for even-numbered years to 1939 was computed by use of the Federal Reserve Index for Manufactures. The man-hours index was derived from an employment index based on Bureau of the Census and BLS data and BLS series for average weekly hours for 1909, 1919, and 1923-1939, supplemented with estimates of the WPA National Research Project for 1920-1922. For 1939, 1947, and 1949-1953, the production index was computed by BLS.

For the period before 1936, indexes of productivity are shown in *Production, Employment, and Productivity in 59 Manufacturing Industries, 1919-1936*, a 3-volume report prepared by WPA National Research Project on Reemployment Opportunities and Recent Changes in National Techniques. BLS made some revisions in these indexes and extended most of them to 1940. These measures, together with indexes of payrolls and unit labor cost, appear in the BLS report, *Productivity and Unit Labor Cost in Selected Manufacturing Industries, 1910-1940*, and were later revised. The revised output-per-man-hour series was published in the 1947 *Handbook of Labor Statistics*.

The production pattern changed radically when the United States began its World War II program. Statistics were inadequate for measuring overall changes in manufacturing efficiency during the period of transition from peace to war. Consequently, there is a gap in the measurements between 1939 and 1947.

The index of output per man-hour in manufacturing attempts to compare the labor time required in the current year to manufacture the current year's output of goods with the time required in the base year to produce the same quantity and mixture of goods. That is, it measures the change in output per man-hour, assuming that the proportion of goods produced by each industry and within each industry in each year under consideration were also produced in the base year. It is the ratio of a production index (consisting of an aggregate of quantities produced weighted by the labor time required to produce a single unit) to a man-hours index (based upon the time of production workers). The concept of physical output holds constant the relative importance of industries. Indexes developed under this concept reflect primarily the average change in productivity of plants and industries in manufacturing.

W 25-37. Indexes of output per man-hour for selected manufacturing industries, 1919-1957.

Source: For selected years, Bureau of Labor Statistics, *Indexes of Output Per Man-Hour for Selected Industries:*

1919–1958, April 1959; all other years, BLS computations (1919–1936, based on WPA National Research Project, *Production, Employment, and Productivity in 59 Manufacturing Industries*, May 1939; 1936–1939, based on BLS, *Productivity and Unit Labor Cost in Selected Manufacturing Industries, 1919–1940*, 1942; 1939–1950, based on BLS, *Productivity Trends in Selected Industries, Indexes Through 1950*, Bulletin No. 1046).

In 1939, the National Research Project on Reemployment Opportunities and Recent Changes in Industrial Techniques, a unit of the Works Progress Administration, published its indexes of production, employment, and productivity, based on data obtained from the Bureau of the Census, BLS, and other official and private agencies. BLS made some revisions in these series, and extended most of them through 1945. These extended and revised indexes were published, together with indexes of unit labor cost, in a series of BLS publications, *Productivity and Unit Labor Cost in Selected Manufacturing Industries, 1919–1940*, and several supplements to this report.

W 38. Indexes of output per man-year in the blast furnace industry, 1850–1925.

Source: Bureau of Labor Statistics, *Monthly Labor Review*, June 1928.

This series was constructed from data of the Bureau of the Census and the American Iron and Steel Association, and is one of the few well-defined industries for which definite figures for both production and employment were available over a long period of years.

W 39–43. Indexes of output per worker in transportation, 1869–1953.

Source: John W. Kendrick, *Productivity Trends in the United States*, National Bureau of Economic Research, Princeton University Press (forthcoming).

These series represent revisions and extensions of data by Harold Barger, *The Transportation Industries, 1889–1946: A Study of Output, Employment and Productivity*, NBER, New York, 1951. In addition to extending Barger's index, Kendrick also created an index for the trucking industry which was not separately presented in the earlier study.

W 39, output per worker in all transportation industries. This index measures the change in the movement of persons and property for hire per worker employed and includes the industry groupings of the national income accounts which follow closely the Bureau of the Budget, *Standard Industrial Classification Manual*.

The production index used as the numerator is based upon revenue passenger-miles and unweighted ton-miles wherever possible. Where these items were not available, less refined units were substituted, as indicated for individual industries below. Output figures were not available for industries which, in 1929, amounted to some 20 percent of the total. For these industries, output was derived from employment on the assumption that the productivity of the uncovered portion was the same as in the covered portion. The aggregate production index of the industry was derived by weighting together the group indexes using changing national income weights and applying a Marshall-Edgeworth formula. Sources of underlying data are indicated in the notes to the separate industries discussed below. These industries account for a significant part of total transportation output.

The employment index is based upon the Office of Business Economics employment series since 1929. For 1870–1930, the series was extrapolated by estimates of the distribution of gainfully employed workers in census years, adjusted to exclude the unemployed, and are largely from Daniel Carson, "Changes in the Industrial Composition of Manpower Since

the Civil War," *Studies in Income and Wealth*, vol. 11, NBER, 1949.

Although only output per worker is presented here, the Kendrick series afford measures of output per man-hour for total transportation and for most individual industries.

W 40, output per worker in steam railroads. The output of this industry includes the freight and passenger activities of Class I, II, and III line-haul roads, switching and terminal companies, the Pullman Company, and the Railway Express Agency and its predecessors.

The production index is a weighted average of simple ton-miles and revenue passenger-miles with different weights for the different classes of passenger service. The data are largely from the annual report of the Interstate Commerce Commission, *Statistics of Railways in the United States*. The combination of freight and passenger traffic was made by a Marshall-Edgeworth formula with average unit revenues in terminal years for the following periods: 1911–1922, 1922–1929, 1929–1939, and 1939–1947. Kendrick's extension to later years retained the 1939–1947 weights. The Barger index started with 1890. The index for 1889 is an extrapolation based on an index prepared by Melville J. Ulmer, *Trends and Cycles in Capital Formation by United States Railroads*, Occasional Paper 43, NBER. Since 1890, the index was multiplied by a "coverage" index to include evenly the output of segments for which quantities were not available, such as switching and terminal and express companies. Before 1890, the implicit assumption is that covered and uncovered components move together.

For 1929–1953, estimates of employment are from the Office of Business Economics. For earlier years, data were available from the Interstate Commerce Commission but the coverage was irregular. Adjustments were made for these deficiencies by Kendrick, and the extrapolation for 1889 was based on Daniel Carson (cited above).

W 41, output per worker for pipelines. This index covers companies primarily engaged in the pipeline transportation of crude petroleum and refined petroleum products. Transmission of natural gas is not included. It includes trunkline mileage in interstate as well as intrastate transmission. Gathering lines are excluded.

The physical unit of output is billions of ton-miles, available since 1936 from the ICC annual report, *Statistics of Oil Pipe-Line Companies*. For 1929, ton-miles were estimated from ICC data on oil received into the system, assuming that the 1936 ratio of barrels originated to barrels received was the same for earlier years. The figure for 1919 is an extrapolation of estimates of trunkline mileage by Walter Splawn, *Oil and Gas Journal*, Petroleum Publishing Co., Tulsa, and an extrapolation of the trend in the ratio of ton-miles transported to total line mileage, 1921–1952. Estimates for this industry for earlier years are not shown separately.

The employment index since 1929 is based upon data in *Statistics of Oil Pipe-Line Companies* and it covers primarily interstate companies. It is not exactly comparable to output since employment on gathering lines is also included. The ICC estimates were raised by 7 percent to correspond with the Office of Business Economics estimate of total employment for the sector. The employment estimate for 1919 is based on the report by Daniel Carson (cited above).

W 42, output per worker in waterways. The productivity estimates of waterways measure the output per person employed on U.S. flag vessels in coastwise, intercoastal, Great Lakes (domestic), inland, noncontiguous, and international water transportation. The exception is that Great Lakes passenger traffic is not included. The original index by Barger excluded coastwise and inland passenger traffic. Kendrick added these and made output and employment estimates for census years between 1899 and 1920, extrapolated intervening years by related series, and made extensions for the later years.

Separate indexes were prepared for freight and passenger traffic for the different types of service and weighted together by the relatives derived as 1939 unit revenues times 1929 units. The freight index is from weighted ton-miles derived from separate tonnage and average haul estimates. Data are from various reports of the Army Engineers, Maritime Commission, and Bureau of the Census. The net tons carried by U.S. flag vessels as shown in Census reports of water transportation were used to interpolate figures for 1906 and 1916. A weighted average of two tonnage series was used to interpolate figures for intercensal years. These were net tonnage capacity of U.S. flag vessels in foreign trade entered and cleared at all ports, adjusted where necessary to a calendar-year basis, and the gross tonnage of merchant vessels engaged in coastwise and internal trade of the United States. The index was extrapolated back to 1869 and 1879 by the 1889–1926 ratio to the index of combined vessel tonnage.

For 1928–1940, Barger's passenger index was based on Maritime Commission estimates of arrivals and departures, by type of service. Prior to 1928, it was based on arrivals and departures in U.S. ports of persons in foreign travel, adjusted by changes in the ratio of U.S. flag vessels to all entrances and clearances. (See August Maffry, *Overseas Travel and Travel Expenditures*, Bureau of Foreign and Domestic Commerce, Economic Series 4, 1939.) Kendrick used the Census transportation series for 1880, 1889, 1906, 1916, and 1926, interpolated by a series on gross tonnage of vessels engaged in coastwise and internal trade and linked with Army Engineers' data for 1926–1946 to derive passenger-miles for coastwise and inland waterways traffic, and thus to broaden the coverage of the original index.

For 1929–1953, the OBE estimates of full- and part-time employment in water transportation formed the basis of the employment index. Prior to 1929, employment estimates of the censuses of water transportation were used after several adjustments for coverage and comparability between censuses. Annual interpolations were made on the basis of gross tonnage estimates of documented merchant vessels. The OBE estimates for the later period were extrapolated back to 1926 and linked with the census-based series. The earlier estimates have most relevance for combination in the total index.

W 43, output per worker in airlines. The productivity estimates for this industry relate to scheduled airlines and unscheduled carriers and companies primarily engaged in operating fixed facilities or providing services to airlines.

The indexes are based on data collected by the Civil Aeronautics Administration (CAA) and predecessor agencies. For 1935–1953, the index of domestic traffic is based on a weighted aggregate of revenue passenger-miles and express (freight and mail) ton-miles. In earlier years, the index is based on total passenger-miles (or total passengers, 1928–1929). The U.S. flag international component represents passenger traffic throughout—revenue passenger-miles for 1937–1953, all passenger-miles for 1930–1937, and all passengers for 1928–1930. The sources of the data are CAA, *The Statistical Handbook of Civil Aviation, 1948* and *Statistical Handbook of Civil Aeronautics, 1954.*

For 1939 and earlier years, the weights are 1939 unit revenues; beginning 1940, average 1939 and 1947 unit revenues were used.

The employment index represents year-end averages of data compiled by CAA through 1941. For 1942 and subsequent years, OBE estimates based upon Social Security Administration data were used.

W 44. Index of output per man-hour in railroad transportation, 1916–1957.

Source: 1919, 1929, 1939, and 1947–1957, Bureau of Labor Statistics, *Indexes of Output Per Man-Hour for Selected Industries: 1919–1958,* April 1959; all other years, BLS computations (1916–1935, based on Witt Bowden, "Productivity, Hours, and Compensation of Railroad Labor, 1933–1936," *Monthly Labor Review,* July 1937; 1935–1947, based on BLS, *Trends in Output Per Man-Hour, 1935–1955, Selected Nonmanufacturing Industries,* Report No. 105, June 1956).

The index of output per man-hour for railroad transportation refers to Class I line-haul railroads. For 1935–1957, the production measure represents aggregate passenger-miles and freight ton-miles, each category being weighted by average unit revenues in the period 1947–1949. The man-hours index represents straight time worked and overtime paid for all hourly basis employees and also includes constructive allowance hours of train and engine employees. Constructive allowance time includes vacations, standby time, held-over time, court time, etc. All basic data are published by the Interstate Commerce Commission.

The indexes for the earlier period, 1916–1934, are based on a somewhat different index prepared by BLS. The components of the production index are combined with 1926 weights; and for the period from 1916 through July 1921, the man-hours represent time worked rather than paid for.

W 45. Output per man-hour for the electric light and power industry, 1935–1948.

Source: Bureau of Labor Statistics computations (based on BLS, *Productivity Trends in Selected Industries, Indexes Through 1950,* Bulletin No. 1046).

The index for the electric light and power industry refers to privately owned utilities generating and distributing electricity, and shows the trend of kilowatt-hours of electrical energy per man-hour. The production index is an aggregate of kilowatt-hours sold to ultimate consumers, and is derived from data of the quinquennial Census of Electrical Industries (suspended since 1937) and the Federal Power Commission. The employment index is based on the hours of all wage and salary employees, except executives and employees of appliance sales departments.

This series was discontinued after 1948 because of a growing lack of comparability between the production and the man-hour series.

W 46–47. Indexes of output per person and per man-hour in distribution, 1869–1953.

Source: John W. Kendrick, *Productivity Trends in the United States,* National Bureau of Economic Research, Princeton University Press (forthcoming).

These indexes represent revisions and extensions of an earlier index prepared by Harold Barger, *Distribution's Place in the American Economy Since 1869,* Princeton University Press, 1955. The original estimates by Barger represented real margin earned per man-hour on those goods reaching the public through retail stores only. The source of total commodity output was William H. Shaw, *Value of Commodity Output Since 1869,* NBER, New York, 1947. Distribution factors for amounts going through retail were from Simon Kuznets, *Commodity Flow and Capital Formation,* NBER, New York, 1938. The quantities sold through retail stores were weighted by average 1869 and 1929 distributive margins to derive the production aggregate. The index is thus a "net" concept, although it is more inclusive than the usual net productivity index since packaging and other supply materials customarily considered a part of margin are not eliminated.

The revisions in the numerator by Kendrick consisted of converting the weighting system in Shaw's commodity output from the original 1913 price base to a Marshall-Edgeworth formula with the average prices of key years as weights. For periods subsequent to 1929, Kendrick shifted to deflated values of final purchases of consumer goods and producer durable equipment by type and weighted by the corresponding distributive markups for 1929–1939 and 1939–1948, based on Department of Commerce estimates. Kendrick also added the margin on real outlays for construction materials to the series. The coverage of the new index was thus increased.

Since 1929, the Department of Commerce estimates of employment were used by Kendrick with interpolations between census years on the basis of BLS indexes. Extrapolation of the OBE series back to 1900 was based upon an employment series from an unpublished manuscript by Stanley Lebergott, *Estimates of Labor Force, Employment and Unemployment, 1900–1950.* Prior to 1900, the estimates used by Barger were retained. These were based upon the report by Daniel Carson (cited above).

W 48–51. General note.

Two types of gross productivity indexes for agriculture are currently available, both evolving directly from a WPA National Research Project series, *Output Per Worker in Agriculture,* May 1941. These indexes use a measure of gross output as distinct from the measure of net output which appears in series W 2.

W 48–50. Indexes of gross farm output per man-hour, 1910–1957.

Source: Department of Agriculture, *Changes in Farm Production and Efficiency,* Statistical Bulletin No. 233, August 1958.

The Agricultural Research Service (ARS) series are a continuation of the measures developed by Reuben Hecht and Glen Barton in their study, Department of Agriculture, *Gains in Productivity of Farm Labor,* Technical Bulletin No. 1020, December 1950. The indexes are also available for the United States, by major crops and by 9 geographic divisions.

The index includes only the man-hours utilized in the production of crops and livestock and products; does not include agricultural services, forestry, and fishing, which are included in the Bureau of the Budget Standard Industrial Classification definition of agriculture. The index measures only the volume of farm production for eventual human use; it excludes farm-produced power and other producer goods such as horses and mules and their feed, and certain hay, pasture, and cover crop seeds.

The production index which forms the numerator of the productivity index is of the fixed-base aggregative type with price weights. Weights for the period prior to 1939 are average 1935–1939 prices, whereas those for the period since 1939

are average 1947–1949 prices. The two subindexes were linked in 1940 by overlapping calculations in that year. Separate estimates are prepared for crops and livestock. The combination of the aggregates for crops and livestock is on a net basis—that is, the food consumed by livestock, while a part of the crop output index, is eliminated in deriving the sector index.

The labor input denominator of the index is not actual hours but "man-equivalent" hours, i.e., the total hours that would be required to produce the output by average adult males. The annual estimates are derived from benchmarks based upon farm management studies from numerous sources. The interpolations between, or extrapolations beyond, benchmark years are based upon changes in the number of crop acres and livestock units, modified to take into consideration changes in technology, yield, etc.

Although the index is shown here only for total farming and its major sectors (crops and livestock), additional detail is available annually for 12 smaller industry groups—meat animals, milk cows, poultry, feed grains, hay and forage, food grains, vegetables, fruits and nuts, sugar crops, cotton, tobacco, and oil crops—and in total by 9 geographic divisions.

W 51. Index of gross farm output per worker, 1909–1950.

Source: Bureau of Labor Statistics, *Productivity Trends in Agriculture,* March 1952.

The 1909–1935 estimates are derived by linking the original WPA series with the later index developed by BLS. Figures are available for the United States and 11 farming areas.

The production index of the BLS series is labor weighted. For most crops in the production aggregates, the unit man-hour requirements used as weights are for 1939, while the estimates for livestock products are for more recent years. The index is based on data of the Bureau of Agricultural Economics for the output of 73 farm products during the years 1935–1950. For the earlier period, 1909–1935, the series was derived from indexes prepared by the WPA National Research Project covering about 60 products.

The index includes "total farm production whatever its ultimate disposition." Horses and mules and their feed are thus included. Aside from this, the commodity coverage is the same as the ARS measure (see text for series W 48–50).

The labor input measure used in the index is total farm employment from *Farm Labor,* a monthly release by the Agricultural Marketing Service of the Department of Agriculture. Annual data appear in the January issue. Farm employment includes both hired and unpaid family workers above 10 years of age, as well as full- and part-time workers. Unpaid family workers are counted if they work 15 or more hours during the survey week. Farm operators and hired workers are counted if they work 1 or more hours during the period. Another measure of employment, different in coverage, is available from the Bureau of the Census for the period since 1939, and was used in series W 2.

Series W 1–11.   Indexes of National Productivity: 1889 to 1957

Year	Real gross private domestic product (NBER, 1929 =100)								Real gross private product per man-hour (BLS, 1947–49 =100)		
	Per man-hour			Per unit of labor input	Per unit of capital input	Per unit of total input					
	Total economy	Farm	Non-farm			Total economy	Farm	Non-farm	Total economy	Farm	Non-farm
	1	2	3	4	5	6	7	8	9	10	11
1957	211.7	265.6	192.3	192.6	142.4	179.4	198.0	175.0	132.8	166.7	124.9
1956	206.5	252.5	---------	188.0	145.1	177.1	194.1	---------	128.3	156.4	121.5
1955	204.8	240.3	---------	186.8	146.8	176.8	187.7	---------	128.0	153.5	121.9
1954	195.4	232.7	---------	178.4	138.9	168.4	181.1	---------	122.6	148.3	116.9
1953	190.9	217.7	176.3	173.1	145.3	166.4	171.2	163.8	120.4	138.6	115.1
1952	183.5	189.7	---------	167.7	145.6	162.5	152.8	---------	115.7	124.5	112.0
1951	179.4	180.3	---------	164.8	146.0	160.4	147.8	---------	113.2	114.5	110.6
1950	175.4	182.5	---------	162.8	145.5	158.7	153.0	---------	110.4	116.2	108.8
1949	162.7	165.9	---------	152.8	137.9	149.3	143.9	---------	103.1	102.2	103.3
1948	156.7	161.3	149.5	146.4	144.6	145.9	142.8	144.5	100.2	107.1	99.4
1947	151.5	146.1	---------	142.3	146.7	143.1	131.7	---------	96.7	90.5	97.5
1946	150.9	145.4	---------	143.1	150.3	144.5	133.0	---------	---------	---------	---------
1945	159.0	137.3	---------	150.9	160.7	152.9	127.2	---------	---------	---------	---------
1944	152.6	134.0	---------	144.5	161.4	147.9	126.6	---------	---------	---------	---------
1943	141.5	131.5	---------	134.1	150.4	137.3	124.6	---------	---------	---------	---------
1942	136.6	136.7	---------	131.3	140.2	133.1	130.4	---------	---------	---------	---------
1941	134.6	132.6	---------	131.3	131.7	131.3	126.2	---------	---------	---------	---------
1940	124.0	119.9	---------	124.4	114.9	122.0	115.7	---------	---------	---------	---------
1939	122.2	119.5	---------	123.6	110.4	120.2	116.5	---------	---------	---------	---------
1938	117.8	119.8	---------	120.3	100.8	115.2	116.8	---------	---------	---------	---------
1937	114.0	106.8	116.4	115.6	107.7	113.6	106.6	114.4	---------	---------	---------
1936	113.3	102.9	---------	114.4	102.2	111.2	99.9	---------	---------	---------	---------
1935	108.0	107.0	---------	111.9	90.6	105.9	104.8	---------	---------	---------	---------
1934	104.5	101.0	---------	108.6	82.0	100.8	97.2	---------	---------	---------	---------
1933	93.5	105.2	---------	99.3	72.5	91.3	104.5	---------	---------	---------	---------
1932	95.0	102.2	---------	100.8	71.9	91.9	100.9	---------	---------	---------	---------
1931	98.4	103.0	---------	102.1	82.3	96.4	103.4	---------	---------	---------	---------
1930	97.5	94.0	---------	98.8	89.0	96.3	93.9	---------	---------	---------	---------
1929	100.0	100.0	100.0	100.0	100.0	100.0	100.0	100.0	---------	---------	---------
1928	95.7	96.1	---------	95.9	96.1	96.0	96.7	---------	---------	---------	---------
1927	95.7	100.1	---------	95.6	97.5	96.1	100.3	---------	---------	---------	---------
1926	94.1	93.4	---------	94.4	99.2	95.7	95.3	---------	---------	---------	---------
1925	91.6	94.6	---------	92.5	96.4	93.6	96.6	---------	---------	---------	---------
1924	91.7	90.0	---------	92.9	95.3	93.6	91.2	---------	---------	---------	---------
1923	87.8	95.9	---------	88.2	95.9	90.2	96.5	---------	---------	---------	---------
1922	83.0	90.4	---------	84.9	85.7	85.1	90.2	---------	---------	---------	---------
1921	83.8	97.0	---------	86.8	81.1	85.1	85.7	---------	---------	---------	---------
1920	78.3	85.8	---------	79.6	85.4	81.2	86.4	---------	---------	---------	---------
1919	79.0	88.4	79.7	80.4	86.8	82.1	88.4	81.7	---------	---------	---------
1918	74.1	86.2	---------	75.0	86.1	78.0	87.3	---------	---------	---------	---------
1917	68.6	96.2	---------	69.5	82.6	73.0	97.3	---------	---------	---------	---------
1916	72.3	89.6	---------	73.7	87.5	77.4	89.9	---------	---------	---------	---------
1915	67.2	101.3	---------	70.2	77.0	72.0	102.1	---------	---------	---------	---------
1914	64.7	92.7	---------	67.9	76.6	70.3	95.3	---------	---------	---------	---------
1913	69.2	85.6	---------	71.8	86.0	75.6	87.2	---------	---------	---------	---------
1912	66.9	97.2	---------	69.7	85.1	73.7	99.8	---------	---------	---------	---------
1911	65.7	83.3	---------	69.0	83.0	72.7	85.4	---------	---------	---------	---------
1910	64.4	90.0	---------	67.7	82.4	71.6	92.5	---------	---------	---------	---------
1909	65.6	88.1	64.7	69.6	84.3	73.4	90.9	71.5	---------	---------	---------
1908	61.1	90.5	---------	65.6	76.2	68.2	93.7	---------	---------	---------	---------
1907	64.2	89.3	---------	68.0	86.2	72.7	92.5	---------	---------	---------	---------
1906	64.4	94.0	---------	68.5	88.1	73.5	93.1	---------	---------	---------	---------
1905	59.9	89.8	---------	64.2	81.7	68.8	93.5	---------	---------	---------	---------
1904	58.4	89.4	---------	63.5	78.0	67.2	93.3	---------	---------	---------	---------
1903	58.5	87.6	---------	62.9	81.7	67.7	91.6	---------	---------	---------	---------
1902	57.2	85.6	---------	61.9	80.7	66.7	90.0	---------	---------	---------	---------
1901	59.4	86.8	---------	65.2	83.2	69.8	93.1	---------	---------	---------	---------
1900	55.6	87.9	---------	61.7	77.0	65.7	92.8	---------	---------	---------	---------
1899	54.7	87.9	52.8	61.0	77.9	65.4	93.1	61.3	---------	---------	---------
1898	53.7	---------	---------	60.9	73.3	64.1	94.2	---------	---------	---------	---------
1897	52.9	---------	---------	60.0	74.3	63.7	91.5	---------	---------	---------	---------
1896	49.5	---------	---------	56.3	69.2	59.5	86.3	---------	---------	---------	---------
1895	50.7	---------	---------	57.7	73.5	61.7	81.3	---------	---------	---------	---------
1894	47.7	---------	---------	55.3	67.6	58.5	77.4	---------	---------	---------	---------
1893	47.4	---------	---------	54.1	71.9	58.7	75.5	---------	---------	---------	---------
1892	49.4	---------	---------	56.0	79.6	61.8	78.3	---------	---------	---------	---------
1891	46.6	---------	---------	53.2	77.1	59.1	83.6	---------	---------	---------	---------
1890	45.7	---------	---------	52.4	77.8	58.6	81.3	---------	---------	---------	---------
1889	43.6	77.0	41.1	50.0	74.8	56.0	83.9	51.6	---------	---------	---------

Series W 12–21. Productivity—Indexes of Output Per Man-Hour in Mining: 1880 to 1957

Year	Total mining (NBER, 1929=100)	Total and selected mining industries (BLS, 1947=100)									Year	Total mining (NBER, 1929=100)	Total mining (BLS, 1947=100)
		Total mining	Anthracite coal	Bituminous coal	Copper		Iron		Lead and zinc				
					Recoverable metal	Crude ore mined	Usable ore	Crude ore mined	Recoverable metal	Crude ore mined			
	12	13	14	15	16	17	18	19	20	21		12	13
1957	210.5	---------	148.0	166.9	125.7	145.7	107.9	133.7	123.0	104.3	1934	119.0	73.3
1956	206.1	---------	157.5	164.3	116.1	134.1	109.8	134.6	117.1	107.8	1933	116.0	70.9
											1932	112.9	69.8
1955	206.3	---------	132.9	159.9	120.4	131.3	117.1	132.7	116.6	111.1	1931	108.9	69.5
1954	197.0	---------	127.2	149.2	106.7	116.1	92.0	105.6	114.6	108.1			
1953	186.5	---------	104.4	129.0	106.8	112.9	107.3	116.3	116.0	102.8	1930	102.9	65.6
1952	176.8	---------	103.7	120.1	114.3	120.1	103.8	111.1	111.1	103.0	1929	100.0	62.9
1951	175.5	---------	104.0	113.8	114.5	115.1	110.7	118.0	116.4	104.4	1928	98.0	61.2
											1927	91.0	58.8
1950	164.0	105.7	95.4	114.5	114.3	115.7	102.5	107.4	127.0	103.2	1926	85.9	57.1
1949	151.9	97.7	102.2	104.4	98.8	97.7	95.9	96.8	114.7	94.1			
1948	149.9	99.8	101.9	100.0	97.4	95.6	99.4	101.4	108.3	88.8	1925	84.9	56.3
1947	144.2	100.0	100.0	100.0	100.0	100.0	100.0	100.0	100.0	100.0	1924	79.4	54.6
1946	141.0	96.5	103.4	97.8	89.7	89.0	98.8	96.1	92.0	120.1	1923	78.8	53.1
											1922	75.9	51.8
1945	144.1	95.5	98.6	94.2	102.8	99.8	104.1	102.3	103.4	129.5	1921	69.5	48.8
1944	136.2	94.2	101.8	91.4	102.1	93.1	93.8	90.4	102.8	124.5			
1943	135.3	91.4	96.7	88.1	93.4	81.3	91.4	88.3	98.5	109.1	1920	68.2	46.6
1942	133.2	93.6	113.9	91.6	91.7	75.4	101.4	99.3	119.0	117.7	1919	65.9	44.6
1941	138.3	93.5	111.0	93.0	89.8	71.0	110.3	104.5	129.1	124.0	1918	66.8	44.5
											1917	65.2	43.7
1940	145.6	91.9	109.1	92.6	93.1	71.0	110.4	101.5	127.6	114.4	1916	64.6	43.3
1939	144.9	90.0	110.6	89.1	90.2	66.3	94.2	84.9	132.3	114.7			
1938	138.8	81.1	108.4	85.9	83.8	55.0	66.2	60.0	129.4	107.0	1915	63.6	43.7
1937	130.9	79.2	96.8	81.6	84.8	59.7	99.7	90.8	120.2	110.6	1902	47.9	30.1
1936	138.6	77.9	95.3	79.7	91.7	55.7	93.0	85.1	123.5	109.0	1890	37.3	23.0
1935	127.6	76.4	87.8	76.1	88.2	43.3	82.6	77.8	131.0	101.9	1880	---------	17.8

Series W 22–23. Index of Manufacturing, Net Output Per Man-Hour (1947–49=100): 1947 to 1957

Year	Production workers	All persons	Year	Production workers	All persons	Year	Production workers	All persons
	22	23		22	23		22	23
1957	137.4	127.7	1953	121.7	118.3	1949	104.2	102.6
1956	134.3	127.1	1952	115.9	113.0	1948	99.7	100.1
1955	131.2	125.6	1951	112.4	111.2	1947	96.4	97.6
1954	123.6	117.4	1950	110.0	109.5			

Series W 24–38. Indexes for Manufacturing, Total and Selected Industries: 1850 to 1957

Year	Output per man-hour (1947=100)									Output per man-hour (1939=100)				
	Total manufacturing	Canning and preserving	Footwear	Hosiery	Paper and pulp	Steel	Tobacco products	Cigars	Cigarettes, etc.	Chemicals	Lumber and timber	Motor vehicles	Newspapers and periodicals	Blast furnaces
	24	25	26	27	28	29	30	31	32	33	34	35	36	37
1957	---------	159.9	---------	129.4	146.2	128.9	141.4	168.6	118.2	---------	---------	---------	---------	---------
1956	---------	154.9	---------	125.8	144.9	130.4	131.8	155.4	111.2	---------	---------	---------	---------	---------
1955	---------	145.3	---------	126.0	137.5	129.4	126.2	141.8	111.5	---------	---------	---------	---------	---------
1954	---------	140.0	---------	129.9	129.1	115.9	125.5	137.8	113.2	---------	---------	---------	---------	---------
1953	119.6	129.2	---------	126.6	123.8	118.8	127.4	134.1	120.3	---------	---------	---------	---------	---------
1952	116.3	128.2	---------	132.4	123.8	117.6	127.9	131.3	124.0	---------	---------	---------	---------	---------
1951	115.2	127.0	---------	122.9	125.3	113.0	124.0	126.6	120.9	---------	---------	---------	---------	---------
1950	114.3	118.3	---------	115.4	118.9	111.9	119.3	122.5	115.6	---------	---------	---------	---------	---------
1949	107.2	111.5	---------	110.3	106.7	102.8	113.2	114.3	111.8	---------	---------	---------	---------	---------
1948	---------	103.2	---------	---------	---------	---------	100.4	106.7	105.6	107.9	---------	---------	---------	---------
1947	100.0	100.0	100.0	100.0	100.0	100.0	100.0	100.0	100.0	---------	---------	---------	---------	---------
1946	---------	106.0	109.1	108.5	98.0	---------	98.1	102.4	93.5	---------	---------	---------	---------	---------
1945	---------	102.5	104.4	114.4	95.6	---------	96.5	106.9	86.3	---------	---------	---------	88.7	---------
1944	---------	100.5	99.5	109.7	95.0	---------	89.3	96.6	81.8	---------	96.0	---------	87.5	---------
1943	---------	92.3	101.6	106.1	98.1	---------	84.9	89.3	80.0	---------	95.1	---------	101.4	---------
1942	---------	93.2	100.4	99.6	109.1	---------	85.3	89.8	80.5	---------	98.1	---------	105.7	---------
1941	---------	97.8	101.8	95.6	115.9	87.2	84.1	89.3	78.7	---------	105.5	---------	106.2	---------
1940	---------	99.2	97.7	94.9	115.0	82.3	80.8	90.5	71.5	95.9	111.7	101.3	108.8	113.9
1939	93.2	90.0	93.8	87.0	109.2	79.3	80.0	91.3	69.6	100.0	100.0	100.0	100.0	100.0
1938	85.1	85.8	92.9	---------	103.2	67.2	76.1	84.5	67.8	89.6	87.6	99.7	92.8	68.2
1937	83.6	79.8	89.8	---------	101.1	65.9	73.1	79.5	66.6	91.3	82.4	100.4	93.0	98.7
1936	84.5	74.5	97.3	---------	99.9	64.7	75.0	78.4	71.3	88.5	84.9	102.1	93.7	101.2
1935	84.3	90.4	91.0	---------	95.5	62.9	69.4	75.8	62.8	84.1	90.8	99.5	92.1	86.4
1934	79.8	84.3	84.0	---------	90.0	58.6	60.3	63.6	56.7	76.0	89.5	85.2	85.4	68.7
1933	76.0	88.1	82.5	---------	94.9	59.5	61.3	57.1	67.1	86.7	86.1	83.8	75.3	67.8
1932	72.2	76.5	74.5	---------	92.7	55.4	56.1	52.9	60.7	85.7	79.6	69.4	74.4	51.2
1931	77.5	77.5	68.9	---------	93.1	53.0	58.5	58.1	59.0	81.3	90.6	79.6	75.4	83.3

Series W 24-38. Indexes for Manufacturing, Total and Selected Industries: 1850 to 1957—Con.

Year	Output per man-hour (1947=100)								Output per man-hour (1939=100)					Output per man-year (1850=100), blast furnaces
	Total manufacturing	Canning and preserving	Footwear	Paper and pulp	Steel	Tobacco products	Cigars	Cigarettes, etc.	Chemicals	Lumber and timber	Motor vehicles	Newspapers and periodicals	Blast furnaces	
	24	25	26	28	29	30	31	32	33	34	35	36	37	38
1930	74.3	68.9	71.0	81.3	54.7	52.7	49.6	56.9	72.6	78.5	89.1	74.3	98.8	----
1929	72.5	61.6	72.9	80.8	57.8	52.5	50.4	55.4	72.1	82.4	84.2	77.3	105.5	----
1928	69.7	65.2	72.8	80.2	57.5	45.2	46.2	44.1	65.9	78.2	70.6	78.6	92.5	----
1927	66.2	60.7	69.3	76.1	50.9	44.5	44.8	44.2	64.2	79.4	66.8	75.7	80.4	----
1926	64.5	64.1	64.2	71.8	50.3	45.8	45.9	45.6	61.1	76.4	66.1	77.5	82.0	----
1925	62.8	61.9	58.9	70.2	48.9	41.6	43.4	39.6	51.2	76.5	62.5	69.0	77.5	5,028
1924	58.9	65.0	60.0	66.5	43.1	39.3	43.3	35.3	45.9	72.7	59.6	65.0	62.0	----
1923	55.2	59.1	59.0	64.2	42.4	36.7	41.4	32.3	46.9	71.4	58.8	63.2	67.7	4,396
1922	56.2	----	63.0	60.5	43.8	33.0	40.8	26.7	43.5	67.5	51.5	59.4	64.7	----
1921	51.3	47.4	59.3	51.5	34.3	30.5	40.0	23.6	43.5	84.4	47.8	51.8	55.1	----
1920	44.6	----	62.5	51.3	37.7	27.2	45.8	18.2	49.6	75.6	39.1	51.9	59.7	----
1919	42.1	48.3	60.3	49.0	29.5	27.4	41.0	19.5	29.9	79.0	35.9	43.8	43.5	2,864
1914	42.2	----	----	----	----	----	----	----	----	----	----	----	----	3,180
1909	36.6	----	----	----	----	----	----	----	----	----	----	----	----	2,684
1904	----	----	----	----	----	----	----	----	----	----	----	----	----	1,880
1899														1,388
1890														1,060
1870														268
1860														220
1850														100

Series W 39-47. Indexes of Output Per Man-Hour and Output Per Worker in Transportation, Electric Light and Power, and Distribution: 1869 to 1957

Year	Transportation (NBER), output per worker					Railroad transportation (BLS), output per man-hour (1947=100)	Electric light and power (BLS), output per man-hour (1947=100)	Distribution (NBER)	
	Transportation (1929=100)	Steam railroads (1929=100)	Pipelines, etc. (1929=100)	Waterways (1929=100)	Airlines (1947=100)			Output per person (1929=100)	Output per man-hour (1929=100)
	39	40	41	42	43	44	45	46	47
1957	----	----	----	----	----	146.4	----	----	----
1956	----	----	----	----	----	143.5	----	----	----
1955	----	----	----	----	----	137.2	----	----	----
1954	----	----	----	----	----	124.0	----	----	----
1953	255.4	178.6	379.5	206.8	172.5	118.0	----	124.5	157.3
1952	253.3	179.3	345.0	206.7	160.7	117.3	----	----	----
1951	258.8	181.7	334.5	222.6	157.9	116.7	----	----	----
1950	247.1	172.8	290.7	207.0	142.9	110.5	----	----	----
1949	224.3	160.6	239.6	178.4	123.2	96.9	----	----	----
1948	231.6	174.0	233.5	170.7	108.4	98.5	102.4	117.1	144.2
1947	223.8	176.1	221.2	178.1	100.0	100.0	100.0	----	----
1946	207.3	169.0	211.5	----	----	88.2	95.8	96.2	----
1945	225.7	195.5	233.2	----	----	95.3	103.6	109.3	----
1944	242.2	211.2	241.6	----	----	75.3	110.1	114.4	----
1943	250.7	215.8	216.5	----	----	57.2	112.1	109.4	----
1942	231.3	191.0	186.4	----	----	60.2	103.7	87.3	----
1941	187.4	151.6	176.8	----	----	69.6	85.7	73.8	----
1940	163.7	132.0	159.6	115.7	66.4	78.2	65.0	----	----
1939	154.2	123.8	157.1	102.0	60.2	74.4	59.9	----	----
1938	141.0	114.6	148.2	97.5	53.3	70.4	53.3	----	----
1937	140.5	119.3	141.1	105.9	54.6	71.0	53.7	99.8	113.5
1936	132.2	116.7	----	99.2	57.3	70.0	52.6	----	----
1935	117.4	103.8	----	85.8	51.7	66.2	49.4	----	----
1934	111.5	98.2	----	84.6	36.4	63.2	----	----	----
1933	104.4	93.5	----	85.5	33.3	62.7	----	----	----
1932	94.5	83.7	----	77.2	26.5	55.7	----	----	----
1931	96.8	90.8	----	85.6	27.3	57.1	----	----	----
1930	97.7	95.3	----	93.9	37.1	56.7	----	----	----
1929	100.0	100.0	100.0	100.0	22.6	56.7	----	100.0	100.0
1928	96.1	98.4	----	----	----	55.7	----	----	----
1927	91.4	94.3	----	----	----	53.1	----	----	----
1926	90.6	95.6	----	----	----	53.2	----	----	----
1925	86.2	92.6	----	----	----	51.5	----	----	----
1924	81.1	87.6	----	----	----	48.8	----	----	----
1923	80.3	88.1	----	----	----	47.5	----	----	----
1922	76.0	84.2	----	----	----	46.0	----	----	----
1921	69.3	76.7	----	----	----	44.2	----	----	----
1920	76.2	83.9	----	----	----	43.5	----	----	----
1919	73.6	81.0	40.5	73.8	----	42.9	----	92.6	89.6
1918	80.2	88.8	----	----	----	40.4	----	----	----
1917	81.8	91.4	----	----	----	40.9	----	----	----
1916	78.2	87.3	----	69.7	----	39.0	----	----	----

Series W 39–47. Indexes of Output Per Man-Hour and Output Per Worker in Transportation, Electric Light and Power, and Distribution: 1869 to 1956—Con.

Year	Transportation (NBER), output per worker			Distribution (NBER)		Year	Transportation (NBER), output per worker			Distribution (NBER)	
	Transportation (1929=100)	Steam railroads (1929=100)	Waterways (1929=100)	Output per person (1929=100)	Output per man-hour (1929=100)		Transportation (1929=100)	Steam railroads (1929=100)	Waterways (1929=100)	Output per person (1929=100)	Output per man-hour (1929=100)
	39	40	42	46	47		39	40	42	46	47
1915	72.2	80.6				1905	59.1	64.1			
1914	65.3	71.2				1904	56.5	61.2			
1913	65.5	71.2				1903	56.0	60.5			
1912	64.3	70.2				1902	56.6	61.4			
1911	61.7	67.2				1901	56.4	61.7			
1910	62.5	68.2				1900	56.5	62.2			
1909	62.3	68.2		95.3	85.8	1899	55.8	61.5	46.7	90.5	73.7
1908	59.3	64.5				1889	42.3	47.5	30.8	82.1	66.0
1907	59.6	64.4				1879			18.9	93.0	75.0
1906	60.4	65.6	62.9			1869			18.1	59.4	47.8

Series W 48–51. Indexes of Gross Farm Output Per Man-Hour and Per Worker: 1909 to 1957

Year	Output per man-hour (ARS, 1947–49=100)			Output per worker (BLS, 1947=100)	Year	Output per man-hour (ARS, 1947–49=100)			Output per worker (BLS, 1947=100)
	Total farm	Livestock and products	Crops			Total farm	Livestock and products	Crops	
	48	49	50	51		48	49	50	51
1957	168	138	180		1932	56	75	55	80.6
1956	158	136	161		1931	56	75	54	85.4
1955	149	130	148		1930	53	76	50	77.5
1954	140	124	138		1929	54	76	51	79.0
1953	131	120	129		1928	54	76	53	79.2
1952	126	117	125		1927	53	77	52	76.2
1951	114	114	112		1926	51	76	50	78.8
1950	112	107	114	113.0	1925	49	73	49	76.4
1949	104	104	105	115.6	1924	49	74	49	72.3
1948	104	99	104	112.2	1923	50	76	50	70.7
1947	92	97	91	100.0	1922	50	75	51	68.8
1946	91	94	92	103.7	1921	47	72	49	63.6
1945	84	91	85	103.6	1920	49	71	51	74.6
1944	81	90	79	105.8	1919	47	72	48	70.1
1943	78	92	76	99.7	1918	46	72	46	70.1
1942	78	88	78	101.6	1917	46	73	47	67.5
1941	71	82	71	91.9	1916	45	72	45	63.3
1940	67	80	67	88.4	1915	49	74	50	66.4
1939	64	74	63	86.3	1914	46	72	46	68.5
1938	64	76	63	84.4	1913	43	72	43	62.6
1937	62	73	60	90.9	1912	47	71	48	66.8
1936	53	73	50	70.4	1911	43	71	42	63.2
1935	57	70	57	75.5	1910	45	70	45	60.5
1934	50	69	48	66.1	1909				57.3
1933	52	73	50	77.0					

chapter W

COPYRIGHTS, PATENTS, AND TRADEMARKS (Series W 52–78)

W 52–65. Copyright registrations, by type, 1870–1957.

Source: **Series W 52–62, W 64–65,** The Library of Congress, *Annual Report of the Librarian of Congress* and *Annual Report of the Register of Copyrights*, various issues. **Series W 63,** 1874–1896, Patent Office, *Annual Report of the Commissioner of Patents;* 1897–1940, records; 1941–1957, *Annual Report of the Register of Copyrights*, various issues.

Additional detail for some series is shown in the source volumes.

Figures are on a calendar-year basis for 1870–1896, and on a fiscal-year basis for subsequent years. Prior to 1870, copyright claims were entered at Federal District Courts. For additional information on this period, see Martin A. Roberts, *Records in the Copyright Office Deposited by the United States District Courts Covering the Period 1790-1870*, Washington, D. C., 1939.

The term "copyright" may be defined as the right to be protected from copying. It has come to mean that body of exclusive rights granted by Federal statute to authors for the protection of their writings. It includes the exclusive right to print, reprint, publish, copy, and vend the copyrighted work; to make other versions of the work; and, with certain limitations, to make recordings of the work and to perform the work in public. The Copyright Office does not examine material for originality; it is primarily an office of record, and registers claims if the provisions of the law and the regulations have been complied with. A certificate is issued to the applicant upon completion of each registration.

The first law, that of 1790, applied only to maps, charts, and books; subsequent amendments provided for prints (1802); musical compositions (1831); dramatic compositions with the right of public performance thereof (1856); photographs (1865); paintings, drawings, sculpture, and models or designs for works of the fine arts (1870); performance rights in music (1897); motion pictures and photoplays (1912); and performance rights in nondramatic literary works (1952). The original term of copyright was 14 years, with the privilege of renewal for 14 years. In 1831, the first term was increased to 28 years, and in 1909, the renewal term was also increased to 28 years. Before 1891, only citizens or residents of the United States could obtain copyrights. The Act of 1891 extended the privilege to citizens of countries with which the United States had reciprocal copyright agreements (in 1958, 38 countries). Claims in works by citizens of States adhering to international copyright conventions to which the United States is a party (Mexico City, 1902; Buenos Aires, 1910; and Universal Copyright Convention, 1952) may also be registered, as well as works first published in States adhering to the Universal Copyright Convention.

Detailed information on the various classes of works may be found in "Regulations of the Copyright Office," *Code of Federal Regulations*, Title 37, chap. II, 1956, or by writing to the Register of Copyrights, Library of Congress, Washington 25, D.C.

Copyright fees have always been nominal; they are now $4.00 except those for commercial prints and labels, which are $6.00, and renewals, which are $2.00.

W 52, total registrations. For 1870–1940, the figures shown in this series are equal to those given in the source plus those shown for series W 63, commercial prints and labels.

W 53–57, books, pamphlets, and periodicals. Serial publications issued at regular intervals of less than a year are considered periodicals; otherwise, they are considered books.

W 58, dramatic or dramatico-musical compositions. For 1909 and earlier years, this series pertains only to dramatic compositions.

W 63, commercial prints and labels. Registration of commercial prints and labels in the Patent Office was first authorized by the Act of June 18, 1874. Jurisdiction was transferred to the Register of Copyrights by Public Law 244, 53 Stat. 1142, effective June 30, 1940. In 1891, the registration of labels was questioned as the result of a Supreme Court decision, with a resulting temporary drop in registrations until 1896.

W 66–75. General note.

A patent is a grant by the Government to the inventor, his heirs or assigns, of the right to exclude others from making, using, or selling the invention patented. Patents can be obtained for any new and useful machine, manufacture, composition of matter or process, or any new and useful improvement thereof, subject to the requirements and conditions of the law, United States Code, Title 35, Patents. An invention is "useful" if it has lawful purpose and is operative. Since 1946, inventions useful solely in the utilization of fissionable material or atomic energy for military purposes have been unpatentable. If the subject matter patented can be used without infringement of the prior rights of others or violation of any applicable statute, the patent, in effect, gives its owner the exclusive right to make, use, or sell the subject of the patent. The subject matter covered by a patent must be sufficiently new as to be not obvious to one skilled in the art to which it relates.

Patents on inventions have been issued by the Federal Government since April 10, 1790. Both the fees charged and the term of patents have been changed occasionally by law. Except in the case of fees charged foreigners for a short period (see text for series W 76), these changes have generally been slight. Hence, the effect of the changes on patenting rates has tended to be small or negligible. A fee of $30, the same as now, was charged on application in 1793. However, whereas no charge was made in 1793 when a patent was granted, modern-day applicants pay an additional $30 at that time. Other smaller fees incidental to the processing of applications may also be charged by the Patent Office.

For 1790–1861, the term of a patent was 14 years. In addition, from 1836 until the patents granted in 1861 expired, patents were renewable for an additional 7 years upon application by the patentee and approval of a special board or the Commissioner. About 5 percent of the patents issued during the latter part of this period were renewed in this manner. Since 1861, the term of patents on inventions has been fixed at 17 years with renewals possible only by special act of Congress. The number of such renewals has been negligible.

From February 21, 1793, to July 4, 1836, patents were granted on demand of the applicant, upon compliance with the

603

formal requirements, without examination as to novelty and other requirements. Consequently, statistics of patents on inventions issued during this period are more comparable to subsequent statistics of applications for patents on inventions (series W 66) than to subsequent statistics of patents on invention. Different sources for patent statistics during this period show minor discrepancies.

Since July 4, 1836, the Patent Office has examined applications for novelty and for compliance with the requirements of the statute and not all applications which are filed become patents. See Department of Commerce, *The Story of the United States Patent Office, 1790–1956*, 1956, for a brief account of the development of the patent laws. See also, same agency, *General Information Concerning Patents*, 1957 (revised periodically), for an outline of the patent law.

Other kinds of patents issued are design patents, botanical plant patents, and reissued patents. Reissued patents are patents which are issued to replace another patent to correct some error, and hence have no significance in most uses of patent statistics. They are not shown in this compilation, although reissue applications are included in series W 66 for some years for which they could not be separated. Reissued patents were numbered separately from 1838 and the number of the first such patent issued in 1958 is 24,413.

Statistics on various phases of patents on invention are available in various sources. Analyses of aggregate patent statistics appear in S. C. Gilfillan, *The Sociology of Invention*, Chicago, 1935; Barkev S. Sanders, "The Course of Invention," *Journal of the Patent Office Society*, October 1936; Joseph Rossman and Barkev Sanders, "The Patent Utilization Study," *The Patent, Trademark, and Copyright Journal*, June 1957; Alfred B. Stafford, *Trends of Invention in Material Culture*, Ph.D. thesis, University of Chicago, 1950; Alfred B. Stafford, "Is the Rate of Invention Declining?" *American Journal of Sociology*, May 1952; Jacob Schmookler, *Technical Change and Patent Statistics*, a paper presented at the Social Science Research Council Conference on the Quantitative Description of Technological Change, Princeton University Press, 1951 (mimeographed); Jacob Schmookler, *Invention and Economic Development*, Ph.D. thesis, University of Pennsylvania, 1951; and Jacob Schmookler, "The Level of Inventive Activity," *Review of Economics and Statistics*, May 1954.

Statistics of patents issued by industry or by field of technology appear in Simon Kuznets, *Secular Movements in Production and Prices*, Boston, 1930; R. K. Merton, "Fluctuations in the Rate of Industrial Invention," *Quarterly Journal of Economics*, May 1935; *Trends of Invention in Material Culture*, cited above; and *Technical Change and Patent Statistics*, cited above. Statistics of patents issued by State and country of residence appear irregularly in the Patent Office, *Annual Report of the Commissioner of Patents*, and in the Bureau of the Census, *Statistical Abstract of the United States*. For an analysis of patents issued by States, see Jacob Schmookler, "Inventors Past and Present," *Review of Economics and Statistics*, August 1957.

W 66–68. Patent applications filed on inventions, designs, and botanical plants, 1836–1957.

Source: 1836–1839, Department of Commerce, *The Story of the United States Patent Office, 1790–1956;* 1840–1925, Patent Office, *Annual Report of the Commissioner of Patents;* 1926–1957, Patent Office, records.

Series W 66 involves a slight element of double counting prior to 1940. Before a change in the law on August 5, 1939, made it impossible, an applicant could permit his initial application to lapse and then file a new application covering the same invention. Possibly 2 to 4 percent of the applications filed before 1940 were of this character. For years prior to 1880, series W 66 includes design applications and for years prior to 1877, it also includes reissue applications.

W 69. Total patents issued on inventions, 1790–1957.

Source: 1790–1925, Patent Office, *Annual Report of the Commissioner of Patents;* 1926–1957, records.

Patents for inventions are numbered serially, the number of the first patent issued in 1958 being 2,818,567. This numbering system began with the first patent issued after the Patent Act of July 4, 1836. Most sources of patent statistics give, as the annual number of patents issued, the numbers derived by subtracting the serial numbers of the first patent in each year. However, some serial numbers were not used and are blank; that is, there may not be any patent corresponding to a particular number. This may arise when an application scheduled to be patented, with the patent number assigned, is withdrawn for some reason at a time when it is too late to assign that number to some other case. The blank numbers averaged 26 per year for 1939–1955. In the present series the number of blank numbers has been deducted in each year for which it could be ascertained. Therefore, the statistics of patents on inventions issued since 1836 may run a fraction of a percent below those appearing in some issues of the *Annual Report of the Commissioner of Patents* and in *Historical Statistics of the United States, 1789–1945*.

Patents granted in a given year cannot be compared with applications filed in the same year since there is a variable lag between the time of applying and the time of issuing a patent. During the last 10 years this lag varied between 3 years and 3 years and 8 months as the average time for issuing patents. Some variations in the number of patents issued in a given year may be due to administrative problems such as the loss or addition of examining personnel.

W 70–73. Patents on inventions issued to individuals, to U.S. and foreign corporations, and to the U.S. Government, 1901–1957.

Source: 1901–1935, Patent Office, records; 1936–1955, P. J. Federico, *Distribution of Patents Issued to Corporations, 1939–1955*, Washington, D.C., 1957, Study No. 3, table 6 (a report prepared for the Senate Subcommittee on Patents, Trademarks, and Copyrights); 1956–1957, Patent Office, records.

Statistics on patents issued to U.S. and foreign corporations are actual counts for 1931–1937 and 1955; for the other years they are estimates based on samples. Statistics of patents issued to the U.S. Government are based on actual count. This figure does not include patents issued to the Alien Property Custodian during and after World War II. Patents assigned after grant are not included. The patents issued to individuals are obtained by subtraction from the total.

W 74. Patents issued on designs, 1842–1957.

Source: Patent Office, *Annual Report of the Commissioner of Patents*.

Designs became patentable in 1842 and relate to the appearance, not to the structure or use, of articles of manufacture. The term for design patents was initially set at 7 years. Since 1861, the term has been 3½, 7, or 14 years, at the discretion of the applicant. Fees payable vary with the term. Design patents are numbered separately. The number of the first design patent issued in 1958 is 181,829.

W 75. Patents issued on botanical plants, 1931–1957.

Source: Patent Office, records.

Botanical plants became subject to patents for the first time in 1930. Patentable plants are those which are asexually reproduced—distinct and new varieties of plants other than tuber-propagated plants. The term and fees for plant patents are the same as for patents on inventions. Plant patents are numbered separately from the other patents. The number of the first plant patent issued in 1958 is 1,672.

W 76. Patents issued to residents of foreign countries, 1836–1957.

Source: Patent Office, *Annual Report of the Commissioner of Patents*, and records.

The volume of patents issued to citizens of foreign countries was influenced in the early years of the patent system by discriminatory legislation. For 1800–1836, only aliens who had resided in the United States for 2 years and who had declared their intention of becoming citizens could apply for U.S. patents. For 1836–1861, aliens paid higher fees than citizens on a theory of reciprocity. Discrimination based on nationality was eliminated in 1861.

This series is based on residence and not on citizenship. It includes patents on inventions, designs, and botanical plants. Separate statistics on components are not available except for a few recent years. For 7 recent years (1951–1957), design patents constituted 1.85 percent of patents issued to foreign residents, and plant patents were 0.23 percent. Looked at in another manner, foreign residents received 12.59 percent of invention patents, 3.28 percent of design patents, and 12.52 percent of the plant patents.

W 77–78. Trademarks registered and renewed, 1870–1957.

Source: Patent Office, *Annual Report of the Commissioner of Patents*, and records.

A trademark is a symbol—a picture, word, or phrase—applied by a manufacturer or merchant to distinguish his goods from those of others. Trademark rights are acquired by adoption of a mark and use of it on the goods in trade. The Federal law provides for the registration in the Patent Office of such marks which are used in interstate and foreign commerce. Applications for registration are examined and registration may be refused if the mark is of a character-prohibited registration (national emblems, deceptive marks, purely descriptive marks, etc.) or if it conflicts with a prior registered mark. Federal registration does not create ownership, but only gives additional advantages to the owner. See Department of Commerce, *General Information Concerning Trademarks*, 1958 (revised periodically), for an outline of the requirements for registering a trademark.

The first Federal trademark law, that of 1870, was based on the patent and copyright clause of the Constitution instead of the interstate and foreign commerce clause, and was held unconstitutional in 1879. The Trademark Act of 1881 was limited to marks used in foreign commerce. The Act of 1905 included marks used in interstate commerce as well. An Act of 1920 permitted registration of a secondary class of marks not previously registrable. A completely new Act, which came into effect in 1947, provided for a Principal Register on which marks of the type registrable under the Acts of 1881 and 1905 could be registered, and a Supplemental Register on which marks of the type registrable under the Act of 1920 could be registered. Registrations are for a term of 20 years, with renewal possible for successive 20-year terms, except for those trademarks registered on the Supplemental Register which generally are not renewable. Registrations under the Act of 1881 were for an initial term of 30 years but were made renewable for an additional term of 20 years.

Series W 52–65. Copyright Registrations, by Type: 1870 to 1957

| Year | Total registrations | Books and pamphlets | | | | Periodicals | Dramatic or dramatico-musical compositions | Musical compositions | Maps | Works of art, models, or designs | Motion pictures | Commercial prints and labels | Miscellaneous | Renewals, all classes |
| | | Total | Books proper (printed in U.S.) | Printed abroad in foreign language | Other | | | | | | | | | |
	52	53	54	55	56	57	58	59	60	61	62	63	64	65
1957	225,807	56,717	(1)	2,915	1 53,802	59,724	2,764	59,614	2,084	4,557	3,198	8,687	6,989	21,473
1956	224,908	57,432	(1)	3,115	1 54,317	58,576	3,329	58,330	2,242	4,168	3,012	9,491	7,402	20,926
1955	224,732	58,160	(1)	3,694	1 54,466	59,448	3,493	57,527	2,013	3,456	2,650	10,505	7,961	19,519
1954	222,665	55,057	(1)	3,697	1 51,360	60,667	3,527	58,213	2,390	3,170	2,556	10,784	7,793	18,508
1953	218,506	52,347	(1)	3,875	1 48,472	59,371	3,884	59,302	2,541	3,029	2,175	12,025	6,731	17,101
1952	203,705	49,403	11,623	3,382	34,398	56,509	3,766	51,538	2,422	3,305	2,079	11,770	6,223	16,690
1951	200,354	50,533	11,272	3,536	35,725	55,129	3,992	48,319	1,992	3,428	2,149	11,981	6,459	16,372
1950	210,564	54,894	11,323	3,710	39,861	55,436	4,427	52,309	1,638	4,013	1,895	13,320	8,101	14,531
1949	201,190	51,562	10,254	2,644	38,664	54,163	5,159	48,210	2,314	3,281	1,763	13,233	7,830	13,675
1948	238,121	54,774	9,786	2,545	42,443	59,699	6,128	72,339	1,456	3,938	1,631	10,619	11,721	15,816
1947	230,215	53,925	9,903	3,970	40,052	58,340	6,156	68,709	1,779	4,044	2,084	9,674	12,003	13,201
1946	202,144	47,860	7,679	3,513	36,668	48,289	5,356	63,367	1,304	3,094	2,024	7,975	10,359	12,516
1945	178,848	40,544	6,962	111	33,471	45,763	4,714	57,835	857	1,821	1,735	7,403	6,809	11,367
1944	169,269	40,682	7,585	82	33,015	44,364	4,875	52,087	494	1,743	1,872	5,953	6,952	10,247
1943	160,789	40,457	8,658	156	31,643	42,995	3,687	48,348	737	1,649	1,767	5,385	6,114	9,650
1942	182,232	50,276	10,377	651	39,248	45,145	4,803	50,023	1,217	2,110	2,219	7,162	7,789	11,488
1941	180,647	51,885	12,735	1,553	37,597	42,207	5,010	49,135	1,398	2,187	1,798	7,152	9,533	10,342
1940	179,467	64,051	11,976	2,504	49,571	40,173	6,450	37,975	1,622	3,081	1,611	2,470	11,827	10,207
1939	175,450	59,744	11,612	4,086	44,046	38,307	6,800	40,961	1,566	3,419	1,757	2,315	10,404	10,177
1938	168,663	57,351	11,625	3,646	42,080	39,249	7,369	35,334	1,200	3,330	1,889	2,415	10,586	9,940
1937	156,930	53,055	11,244	3,841	37,970	38,053	7,176	31,821	1,198	3,002	1,751	2,506	9,779	8,589
1936	159,268	54,749	11,748	3,853	39,148	38,418	6,569	33,250	1,444	2,977	1,708	2,306	9,667	8,180
1935	144,439	51,009	11,035	3,283	36,691	36,351	6,501	27,459	1,343	3,082	1,695	2,408	7,930	6,661
1934	2 141,217	48,398	9,660	3,593	35,145	35,819	5,945	27,001	1,250	5,447	1,513	2,170	6,989	6,989
1933	139,361	49,984	10,820	4,232	34,932	35,464	6,359	26,846	1,178	2,667	1,607	1,937	6,908	6,411
1932	154,710	57,065	13,460	4,784	38,821	39,177	6,296	29,264	1,774	2,590	1,539	2,975	8,142	5,888
1931	167,107	59,553	14,175	4,339	41,039	42,415	5,784	31,488	2,940	2,551	1,926	2,465	11,987	5,998
1930	175,125	61,835	15,221	4,664	41,950	43,939	5,734	32,129	2,554	2,734	2,195	2,333	15,735	5,937
1929	164,666	57,614	13,501	3,868	40,245	44,161	4,594	27,023	2,232	2,486	2,319	2,707	16,582	4,948
1928	196,715	77,081	13,401	4,405	59,275	47,364	4,473	26,897	2,862	3,152	2,304	2,801	24,334	5,447
1927	186,856	77,136	10,649	3,777	62,710	41,475	4,475	25,282	2,677	2,575	1,915	2,856	23,779	4,686
1926	180,179	73,455	---------	3,430	---------	41,169	4,130	25,484	2,647	3,173	1,623	2,544	21,925	4,029
1925	167,863	65,670	---------	3,266	---------	40,880	4,015	25,548	2,222	2,950	1,765	2,015	19,489	3,309
1924	164,710	61,982	---------	2,306	---------	39,806	3,409	26,734	2,265	2,873	1,473	2,016	20,719	3,433
1923	151,087	55,561	---------	2,886	---------	37,104	3,778	24,900	2,042	2,790	1,277	2,141	18,805	2,689
1922	140,734	46,307	---------	1,309	---------	35,471	3,418	27,381	1,930	2,954	1,487	2,101	16,959	2,726
1921	136,865	41,245	---------	1,134	---------	34,074	3,217	31,054	1,647	2,762	1,721	1,585	17,354	2,206
1920	127,342	39,090	---------	939	---------	28,935	2,906	29,151	1,498	2,115	1,714	780	19,041	2,112
1919	113,771	37,710	---------	855	---------	25,083	2,293	26,209	1,207	1,901	1,429	768	15,265	1,906
1918	107,436	33,617	---------	636	---------	25,822	2,711	21,849	1,269	1,858	1,838	708	15,907	1,857
1917	112,561	33,552	---------	914	---------	26,467	3,067	20,115	1,529	2,247	2,720	1,123	19,749	1,992
1916	117,202	32,897	---------	1,276	---------	26,553	3,223	20,644	1,612	2,220	3,240	1,235	23,950	1,628
1915	115,727	31,926	---------	1,843	---------	24,389	3,797	21,406	1,772	2,965	2,950	1,083	24,113	1,326
1914	124,213	31,891	---------	2,860	---------	24,134	3,957	28,493	1,950	3,021	2,148	1,059	26,329	1,231
1913	120,413	29,572	---------	2,369	---------	23,002	3,700	26,292	2,011	2,871	953	918	30,029	1,065
1912	121,824	29,286	---------	2,294	---------	22,580	3,767	26,777	2,158	3,224	---------	893	31,790	1,349
1911	115,955	26,970	---------	1,707	---------	23,393	3,415	25,525	2,318	3,355	---------	757	29,294	928
1910	109,309	24,740	---------	1,351	---------	21,608	3,911	24,345	2,622	4,383	---------	235	26,458	1,007
1909	121,141	32,533	---------	---------	---------	21,195	2,937	26,306	(3)	(3)	---------	1,010	3 37,160	---------
1908	120,657	30,191	---------	---------	---------	22,409	2,382	28,427	(3)	(3)	---------	915	3 36,338	---------
1907	124,814	30,879	---------	---------	---------	23,078	2,114	31,401	(3)	(3)	---------	985	3 36,357	---------
1906	118,799	29,261	---------	---------	---------	23,163	1,879	26,435	(3)	(3)	---------	1,095	3 36,966	---------
1905	114,747	29,860	---------	---------	---------	22,591	1,645	24,595	(3)	(3)	---------	1,373	3 34,683	---------
1904	104,431	27,824	---------	---------	---------	21,496	1,571	23,110	(3)	(3)	---------	1,301	3 29,129	---------
1903	99,122	26,466	---------	---------	---------	22,625	1,608	21,161	(3)	(3)	---------	1,143	3 26,119	---------
1902	93,891	24,272	---------	---------	---------	21,071	1,448	19,706	(3)	(3)	---------	913	3 26,481	---------
1901	93,299	---------	---------	---------	---------	(4)	(4)	(4)	---------	---------	---------	948	---------	---------

| Year | Total registrations | Periodicals | Dramatic or dramatico-musical compositions | Musical compositions | Maps | Commercial prints and labels |
	52	57	58	59	60	63
1900	95,573	(4)	(4)	(4)	(4)	775
1899	81,416	(4)	(4)	(4)	(4)	448
1898	75,634	(4)	(4)	(4)	(4)	89
1897	75,035	(4)	(4)	(4)	(4)	35
1896	73,372	12,892	907	20,951	1,198	33
1895	66,006	12,155	827	18,563	1,432	3
1894	62,790	12,149	465	18,460	1,922	4
1893	58,964	11,094	580	16,273	1,814	2
1892	56,006	10,327	813	14,649	(4)	6
1891	49,199	9,477	746	11,688	1,912	137
1890	43,093	8,164	715	9,132	---------	304
1889	41,297	7,646	620	8,958	---------	319
1888	38,910	7,086	589	8,066	---------	327
1887	35,472	6,708	536	7,744	---------	380
1886	31,638	6,089	672	7,514	---------	378

| Year | Total registrations | Periodicals | Dramatic or dramatico-musical compositions | Musical compositions | Commercial prints and labels |
	52	57	58	59	63
1885	28,746	6,060	625	6,808	391
1884	27,729	5,570	587	6,241	513
1883	25,912	5,489	498	6,280	906
1882	23,152	4,612	458	6,143	304
1881	21,266	4,339	415	5,578	202
1880	19,311	4,369	496	5,628	203
1879	18,528	3,608	414	4,688	355
1878	16,291	3,424	372	3,772	492
1877	16,082	---------	---------	---------	392
1876	15,393	---------	---------	---------	472
1875	14,464	---------	---------	---------	232
1874	16,206	---------	---------	---------	232
1873	15,648	---------	---------	---------	---------
1872	14,180	---------	---------	---------	---------
1871	12,831	---------	---------	---------	---------
1870 5	5,599	---------	---------	---------	---------

1 Books proper included with "Other."
2 Agrees with source; however, figures for components do not add to total shown.
3 Maps and works of art, models, or designs included with "Miscellaneous."
4 Not available.
5 July–December.

Series W 66-76. Patent Applications Filed and Patents Issued, by Type and by Patentee: 1790 to 1957

Year	Patent applications filed			Patents issued							
	Inventions	Designs	Botanical plants	Inventions					Designs	Botanical plants	To residents of foreign countries
				Total [1]	Individuals	Corporations		U.S. Government [2]			
						U.S.	Foreign				
	66	67	68	69	70	71	72	73	74	75	76
1957	74,197	4,714	101	42,744	15,154	23,255	3,372	963	2,362	129	6,282
1956	74,906	4,824	104	46,817	16,643	25,502	3,690	982	2,977	101	6,646
1955	77,188	5,764	118	30,432	11,914	16,084	1,744	689	2,713	103	4,065
1954	77,185	5,465	95	33,809	12,531	18,319	2,301	658	2,536	101	4,433
1953	72,284	5,450	99	40,468	16,284	21,230	2,294	658	2,713	78	4,331
1952	64,554	4,993	84	43,616	18,538	22,340	2,035	695	2,959	101	5,635
1951	60,438	4,279	71	44,326	19,192	22,305	2,163	659	4,163	58	4,888
1950	67,264	6,739	105	43,040	18,960	21,782	1,660	622	4,718	89	4,408
1949	67,592	6,998	70	35,131	14,957	18,536	1,127	485	4,450	93	3,105
1948	68,740	7,048	59	23,963	9,812	13,124	628	352	3,968	44	1,984
1947	75,443	7,644	92	20,139	7,784	11,448	669	155	2,102	52	1,617
1946	81,056	10,698	72	21,803	7,444	13,486	585	147	2,778	56	1,656
1945	67,846	8,066	52	25,695	8,981	15,665	580	87	3,524	17	2,112
1944	54,190	5,063	42	28,053	9,636	16,769	645	106	2,914	38	2,564
1943	45,493	2,986	41	31,054	11,654	18,022	524	48	2,228	47	2,625
1942	45,549	4,218	60	38,449	14,534	22,019	1,286	62	3,728	65	3,943
1941	52,339	7,203	67	41,109	16,322	22,632	2,112	43	6,486	62	5,311
1940	60,863	8,530	91	42,238	17,627	22,165	2,406	40	6,145	85	6,148
1939	64,093	7,137	76	43,073	18,583	21,800	2,640	50	5,592	45	6,338
1938	66,874	8,084	48	38,061	16,304	19,635	2,063	59	5,026	41	5,776
1937	65,324	7,207	45	37,688	15,995	19,881	1,824	33	5,136	55	5,688
1936	62,599	6,478	66	39,782	16,639	21,207	1,903	33	4,556	49	5,734
1935	58,117	5,728	72	40,618	17,757	20,821	2,018	22	3,864	45	5,980
1934	56,643	4,399	28	44,420	19,731	22,529	2,131	29	2,919	32	6,489
1933	56,558	3,600	27	48,774	22,713	23,667	2,343	51	2,411	33	7,170
1932	67,006	4,345	46	53,458	26,274	24,822	2,325	37	2,942	46	7,376
1931	79,740	4,190	37	51,756	26,618	23,149	1,961	28	2,935	5	6,897
1930	89,554	4,182	16	45,226	23,726	19,700	1,800	---------	2,710	---------	6,085
1929	89,752	4,520	---------	45,267	25,367	18,500	1,400	---------	2,905	---------	5,921
1928	87,603	4,761	---------	42,357	23,357	17,800	1,200	---------	3,182	---------	5,218
1927	87,219	4,473	---------	41,717	25,417	15,100	1,200	---------	2,387	---------	4,918
1926	81,365	4,343	---------	44,733	28,633	15,200	900	---------	2,597	---------	5,103
1925	80,208	4,082	---------	46,432	30,332	14,800	1,300	---------	2,819	---------	5,347
1924	76,987	3,635	---------	42,574	29,174	12,400	1,000	---------	2,670	---------	4,723
1923	76,783	3,550	---------	38,616	27,016	10,800	800	---------	1,927	---------	4,133
1922	83,962	4,763	---------	38,369	27,369	10,300	700	---------	1,609	---------	4,455
1921	87,467	5,596	---------	37,798	27,098	9,860	840	---------	3,265	---------	3,963
1920	81,915	4,660	---------	37,060				---------	2,481	---------	3,762
1919	76,710	3,627	---------	36,797				---------	1,521	---------	3,687
1918	57,347	2,234	---------	38,452				---------	1,206	---------	2,883
1917	67,590	2,545	---------	40,935				---------	1,505	---------	3,209
1916	68,075	2,684	---------	43,892	31,742	11,540	610	---------	1,745	---------	3,767
1915	67,138	2,734	---------	43,118				---------	1,538	---------	4,334
1914	67,774	2,454	---------	39,892				---------	1,711	---------	4,595
1913	68,117	2,060	---------	33,917				---------	1,677	---------	4,212
1912	68,968	1,850	---------	36,198				---------	1,341	---------	4,489
1911	67,370	1,534	---------	32,856	24,756	7,580	520	---------	1,004	---------	4,058
1910	63,293	1,155	---------	35,141				---------	636	---------	3,719
1909	64,408	1,234	---------	36,561				---------	679	---------	3,812
1908	60,142	1,131	---------	32,735				---------	755	---------	3,338
1907	57,679	896	---------	35,859				---------	589	---------	3,866
1906	55,471	806	---------	31,170	24,750	6,040	380	---------	620	---------	3,471
1905	54,034	781	---------	29,775				---------	486	---------	3,292
1904	51,168	818	---------	30,258				---------	553	---------	3,285
1903	49,289	770	---------	31,029				---------	536	---------	3,763
1902	48,320	1,170	---------	27,119				---------	639	---------	3,499
1901	43,973	2,361	---------	25,546	20,896	4,370	280	---------	1,729	---------	3,402
1900	39,673	2,225	---------	24,644				---------	1,754	---------	3,483
1899	38,937	2,400	---------	23,278				---------	2,137	---------	2,311
1898	33,915	1,843	---------	20,377				---------	1,799	---------	2,752
1897	45,661	2,150	---------	22,067				---------	1,620	---------	2,221
1896	42,077	1,828	---------	21,822				---------	1,441	---------	2,027
1895	39,145	1,463	---------	20,856				---------	1,108	---------	2,049
1894	36,987	1,357	---------	19,855				---------	927	---------	2,166
1893	37,293	1,060	---------	22,750				---------	899	---------	2,473
1892	29,514	1,130	---------	22,647				---------	816	---------	2,051
1891	39,418	1,025	---------	22,312				---------	835	---------	1,928
1890	39,884	1,046	---------	25,313				---------	886	---------	2,105
1889	39,607	857	---------	23,324				---------	723	---------	2,003
1888	34,713	971	---------	19,551				---------	832	---------	1,536
1887	34,420	1,041	---------	20,403				---------	948	---------	1,466
1886	35,161	645	---------	21,767				---------	594	---------	1,489
1885	34,697	862	---------	23,285				---------	769	---------	1,549
1884	34,192	1,230	---------	19,118				---------	1,150	---------	1,284
1883	33,073	1,238	---------	21,162				---------	1,017	---------	1,259
1882	30,270	948	---------	18,091				---------	858	---------	1,135
1881	24,878	678	---------	15,500				---------	565	---------	995
1880	21,761	634	---------	12,903				---------	514	---------	786

See footnotes at end of table.

Series W 66–76. Patent Applications Filed and Patents Issued, by Type and by Patentee: 1790 to 1957—Con.

Year	Inventions, patent applications filed [3]	Patents issued			Year	Inventions, patent applications filed [3]	Patents issued		
		Inventions	Designs	To residents of foreign countries			Inventions	Designs	To residents of foreign countries
	66	69	74	76		66	69	74	76
1879	20,059	12,125	591	648	1857	4,771	2,674	113	45
1878	20,260	12,345	590	581	1856	4,960	2,302	107	31
1877	20,308	12,920	699	590					
1876	21,425	14,169	802	787	1855	4,435	1,881	70	41
					1854	3,328	1,755	57	35
1875	21,638	13,291	915	563	1853	2,673	844	86	26
1874	21,602	12,230	886	547	1852	2,639	885	109	20
1873	20,414	11,616	747	493	1851	2,258	752	90	17
1872	18,246	12,180	884	581					
1871	19,472	11,659	903	522	1850	2,193	883	83	20
					1849	1,955	984	49	17
1870	19,171	12,137	737	644	1848	1,628	583	46	14
1869	19,271	12,931	506	377	1847	1,531	495	60	21
1868	20,420	12,526	445	337	1846	1,272	566	59	19
1867	21,276	12,277	325	275					
1866	15,269	8,863	294	244	1845	1,246	473	17	12
					1844	1,045	478	12	20
1865	10,664	6,088	221	181	1843	819	493	14	8
1864	6,932	4,630	139	181	1842	761	488	1	11
1863	6,014	3,773	176	125	1841	847	490	----------	21
1862	5,038	3,214	195	80					
1861	4,643	3,020	142	83	1840	765	458	----------	19
					1839	[4] 800	404	----------	10
1860	7,653	4,357	183	49	1838	[4] 900	514	----------	17
1859	6,225	4,160	107	47	1837	[4] 650	426	----------	7
1858	5,364	3,455	102	28	1836	[4][5] 400	[5] 103	----------	8

Year	Inventions, patents issued 69	Year	Inventions, patents issued 69	Year	Inventions, patents issued 69	Year	Inventions, patents issued 69	Year	Inventions, patents issued 69
1836	[6] 599	1825	304	1815	173	1805	57	1795	12
		1824	228	1814	210	1804	84	1794	22
1835	752	1823	173	1813	181	1803	97	1793	20
1834	630	1822	200	1812	238	1802	65	1792	11
1833	586	1821	168	1811	215	1801	44	1791	33
1832	474								
1831	573	1820	155	1810	223	1800	41	1790	3
		1819	156	1809	203	1799	44		
1830	544	1818	222	1808	158	1798	28		
1829	447	1817	174	1807	99	1797	51		
1828	368	1816	206	1806	63	1796	44		
1827	331								
1826	323								

[1] Since 1942, includes patents issued to Alien Property Custodian, not shown separately.
[2] Excludes patents issued to Alien Property Custodian.
[3] Applications for reissue included with inventions 1836–1876; design applications included with inventions 1836–1879.
[4] Estimate.
[5] From July 4 to end of year.
[6] To July 4.

Series W 77–78. Trademarks Registered and Renewed: 1870 to 1957

Year	Registered 77	Renewed 78	Year	Registered 77	Renewed 78	Year	Registered 77	Year	Registered 77
1957	17,483	3,488	1935	10,886	1,874	1913	5,065	1891	1,762
1956	20,753	3,756	1934	11,362	2,445	1912	5,020	1890	1,415
1955	18,207	4,268	1933	9,130	1,671	1911	4,205	1889	1,229
1954	15,946	3,491	1932	9,603	1,587	1910	4,239	1888	1,059
1953	15,610	3,103	1931	11,400	1,643	1909	4,184	1887	1,133
1952	16,172	3,419	1930	13,246	1,661	1908	5,191	1886	1,029
1951	17,376	3,350	1929	14,514	1,750	1907	7,878	1885	1,067
1950	16,817	3,564	1928	14,133	2,049	1906	10,568	1884	1,021
1949	15,968	3,788	1927	14,579	3,063	1905	4,490	1883	902
1948	11,472	5,056	1926	14,955	4,273	1904	2,158	1882	947
1947	8,976	6,139	1925	13,815	2,278	1903	2,186	1881	834
1946	8,106	5,725	1924	15,727	227	1902	2,006	1880	349
1945	7,490	4,210	1923	14,834	251	1901	1,928	1879	872
1944	6,025	4,052	1922	12,793	254	1900	1,721	1878	1,455
1943	5,595	3,835	1921	11,636	117	1899	1,649	1877	1,216
1942	6,795	2,894	1920	10,268	73	1898	1,238	1876	959
1941	8,530	2,765	1919	4,208	64	1897	1,671	1875	1,138
1940	9,974	2,547	1918	4,061	38	1896	1,813	1874	559
1939	10,521	1,398	1917	5,339	52	1895	1,829	1873	492
1938	10,204	1,051	1916	6,791	55	1894	1,806	1872	491
1937	11,242	1,524	1915	6,262	57	1893	1,677	1871	486
1936	10,722	1,888	1914	6,817	48	1892	1,737	1870	121

RESEARCH AND DEVELOPMENT (Series W 79–121)

W 79–121. General note.

Historical statistics on research and development expenditures and employment by various groups in the major sectors of the economy are of comparatively recent origin. Public interest in representing the input of research and development activity in terms of some widely used measure, such as funds expended or personnel employed, has been largely incidental to concern with major national issues. During the depression years of the 1930's this interest stemmed from the role that research played in the recovery of the economy. Groups such as the National Research Project of the Work Projects Administration (formerly the Works Progress Administration) and the National Resources Planning Board engaged in studies of the interrelationships among trends in research and development, technological change, unemployment, education, and other major economic and social factors. Their interest in measuring research and development was generally subsidiary to a larger preoccupation with such broad national issues as economic recovery, reemployment, and national planning. The research and development estimates which they published were intended to serve primarily as illustrative background materials.

The period of World War II and its aftermath dramatized the critical place of research and development in the Nation's military security program. Groups concerned with measuring research and development during this period included the Committee on Science and Public Welfare (Bowman Committee), the President's Scientific Research Board, and the Research and Development Board of the Department of Defense. Like the earlier groups, these organizations supplemented fragmentary data already on hand with special inquiries and analyses in order to develop background estimates on research and development trends.

More recent years have seen the recognition of scientific research and development both as a permanent component of a successful defense policy and as an essential element in peacetime economic growth and cultural achievement.

The National Science Foundation, a Federal agency established in 1950, undertook as one of its functions the development of such factual data and related analyses on research and development. As a first step, the Foundation initiated an annual survey of Federal funds for research and development, starting with data on funds for scientific research and development at nonprofit institutions for fiscal 1951 and 1952 and moving thereafter to annual surveys of the funds comprising the "Federal Research and Development Budget."

In 1954, the National Science Foundation undertook the first effort to measure the volume of research and development activity across the board, in terms of funds and personnel, through surveys of all major types of organizations in the several sectors of the economy which were known to be performing or financing this activity. Out of this effort grew a continuing Foundation program of surveys designed to facilitate preparation of annual estimates on funds and personnel employed in research and development by the major sectors of the economy.

Because the early inquiries concerning trends in research and development were sporadic and because many aspects of this subject are complex and abstract, there was no determined effort to develop a set of generally accepted concepts, definitions, and terms useful for statistical surveys. In particular, a clear distinction was slow to develop between expenditures for the financing or support of research and development and expenditures for the conduct or performance of research and development. Some exploration of concepts and definitions was undertaken by such groups as the National Resources Committee in 1938–1940 and the Subcommittee on War Mobilization of the Senate Committee on Military Affairs (Kilgore Committee) in 1945, but when the National Science Foundation undertook its first surveys, there was no general agreement on such fundamental matters as the definition of research and development; the distinction between the conduct of research and development and such related activities as academic instruction or industrial production; the distinction between basic and applied research and development; and the major characteristics distinguishing various types of research organizations. A broad review of the entire problem of defining research and development was therefore made a part of the Foundation's survey program.

National estimates for 1953–54—1957–58. National estimates of funds spent on the performance of research and development in the natural sciences by the four major sectors of the economy have thus far been made by the National Science Foundation for 1953–54 through 1957–58, with projected

Table I. Financing and Performance of Research and Development in the Natural Sciences, by Sectors: 1956–57

[In millions of dollars. Preliminary data. For accounting years coinciding with calendar 1956 or ending before mid–1957]

Source of research and development funds, by sector	Research and development performers				Total	
	Federal Government agencies	Industry	Colleges and universities	Other nonprofit institutions	Amount	Percent
Federal Government agencies	1,280	[1]3,230	[1]380	[1]70	[2]4,960	59
Industry		3,210	20	30	3,260	38
Colleges and universities [3]			170		170	2
Other nonprofit institutions [4]			30	40	70	1
Total	1,280	[1]6,440	[1]600	[1]140	8,460	100
Percent	15	76	7	2		100

[1] Includes funds from the Federal Government for the conduct of research and development at research centers administered by organizations in this sector under contract with Federal agencies.

[2] For an explanation of the difference between the total for Federal agencies as sources of funds as shown in this table and the total obligations for conduct of research and development by Federal agencies for fiscal year 1957 in series W 95, see the concluding paragraph in the text on series W 95–106.

[3] Includes all State and local funds, received by public institutions of higher education, which were used for research and development.

[4] Includes State and local funds, received by such nonprofit institutions as museums, zoological gardens, and academies of science, which were used for research and development.

estimates for 1958–59 and 1959–60. National estimates of funds received from various sources for the performance of research and development have been made for 1953–54, 1956–57, and 1957–58. These series appear in tables 1 and 2, respectively, of the National Science Foundation publication, "Funds for Research and Development in the United States, 1953–59," *Reviews of Data on Research and Development*, No. 16, 1959.

An analysis of intersectoral flows or transfers of funds for research and development for 1956–57 appears in table I, above. This table is based on information obtained in the National Science Foundation surveys of funds for research and development in 1956–57 and appears as table 4 in *Reviews of Data on Research and Development*, No. 16.

The estimates in table I must still be regarded as preliminary since some of the underlying data are subject to change. This fact, as well as the limitations described below, indicates that table I should be considered a general approximation rather than an exact statement of the extent to which the different sectors are participating in the financing and performance of research and development.

Research and development performed by industrial firms with funds from Federal production and procurement contracts has been represented in this tabulation insofar as industry reported the expenditure of such funds for research and development. (Federal reporting of funds flowing to "profit organizations" for research and development did not include a full accounting of expenditures for research and development made under production and procurement contracts for the year represented in the table.) Detailed information on the scope and limitations of the various surveys appears in the National Science Foundation publications listed below. Generally speaking, the National Science Foundation surveys seek full enumeration of the various segments. The outstanding exceptions are industrial firms and the smaller endowed philanthropic foundations, for which sampling procedures are employed.

The data in table I are derived basically from survey responses by *performers* of research and development as to how much they spent on this activity and where their funds originated. The estimates represent final through-transfers from source organizations financing research and development to performing organizations which ultimately used the funds. Every effort was made to net out intermediate transfers. Because of the many problems of survey response, including the fact that the accounting systems of most respondents did not easily lend themselves to reporting on funds for research and development, estimates were necessary where there were gaps or conflicts in the reported data.

The wide diversity in the understanding of "research and development" has led to the use of somewhat different definitions of this term in the National Science Foundation surveys. The central idea in all the definitions regards research (both basic and applied) as a "systematic and intensive study directed toward a fuller knowledge of the subject studied" and development as "the systematic use of scientific knowledge directed toward the production of useful materials, devices, systems, methods, or processes." For surveys covering the years 1953–54 through 1956–57, there was a significant conceptual difference between the surveys of the Federal agencies and those of the private industrial firms with respect to the point at which development was completed and production initiated. The Federal survey specifically excluded design and production engineering from development, whereas the industry survey included design and development of prototypes and processes. A somewhat wider range of activities was therefore implied by the data for industry than by the data for Federal agencies. Beginning with the Federal survey for fiscal year 1958, the Federal definition of development was revised and expanded to make it more comparable with that for the industry sector. In the case of colleges and universities and other nonprofit institutions, which employed the same definition as the Federal agencies, this difference was not significant, since these organizations supported and conducted little or no development.

The conduct of research and development refers only to current operating costs and excludes the acquisition of major capital items. Both direct and indirect costs are included and are defined in their usual sense, but it should be borne in mind that indirect cost is an item subject to wide differences in interpretation, not only from sector to sector, but also among respondents within a sector.

These estimates refer in general only to the natural sciences, defined as consisting of the physical sciences, that is, astronomy, chemistry, earth sciences, engineering, mathematics, and physics; and the life sciences, subdivided among the biological, medical, and agricultural. However, due to the difficulty of identifying them separately, some funds for research in social psychology and the social sciences are also included.

In the data for 1956–57, the government sector is represented only by agencies of the Federal Government, since data are not available on a national basis for State and local governments. However, on the basis of a special study of scientific activities in six States (see reference below), it is estimated that, aside from the State funds for research and development at the State universities and agricultural experiment stations, the total dollar amount of State funds for this purpose is not large. All State and local institutions of higher education, including agricultural experiment stations, are covered in the National Science Foundation surveys and are included with other institutions of higher education in the colleges and universities sector. The colleges and universities sector is treated as the source of those portions of university general funds which the educational institutions themselves allocated to research and development, including such general funds as were appropriated to educational institutions by State and local governments. Also attributed to the colleges and universities as a source are State and local government funds earmarked for research and development at educational institutions.

The National Science Foundation surveys include data on research and development by Federal contract research centers. These are laboratories or similar research undertakings supported wholly or predominantly by the Federal Government but operated under contract by an industrial, university, or independent organization. Data relating to the performance of research and development at these centers are included within the appropriate sector in the estimates for 1956–57.

Several groups of organizations comprise the industry sector as represented in table I. Private industrial firms account for about 95 percent of the total funds for performance of research and development in this sector. (Data for firms appear below in series W 107–121.) The remaining groups are Federal contract research centers operated by industrial concerns, independent commercial laboratories and engineering service firms trade associations, and certain other cooperative research organizations.

The colleges and universities sector consists of institutions of higher education with substantial research programs and of the Federal research centers operated under contract by educational institutions. Included in institutions of higher education are their affiliated research organizations, agricultural research centers, graduate and professional schools, and affiliated hospitals.

Other nonprofit institutions include privately endowed philanthropic foundations, nonprofit research institutes, voluntary health agencies, academies of science, professional societies, museums, zoological gardens, and arboretums, as well as several Federal research centers operated by independent organizations.

The data on transfers of funds were based on estimates from many institutions having somewhat different understandings of costs and expenditures. The estimates for Federal agencies, moreover, were based on obligations rather than expenditures, since information on transfers to the other sectors was available only for obligations.

Because of the diversity of accounting procedures the estimates for 1956–57 are based on a number of different time periods. For example, the entire Federal agency survey and the university estimates are based on the Federal fiscal year, July 1, 1956–June 30, 1957. In the industry sector the majority of private firms reported for fiscal years which either coincided with or began shortly after the opening of the calendar year 1953.

For detailed information on research and development funds and personnel at various types of organizations for 1953 and later years, see the following publications prepared for the National Science Foundation: Bureau of Labor Statistics, *Science and Engineering in American Industry, Final Report on a 1953–54 Survey*, 1956; Bureau of Labor Statistics, *Science and Engineering in American Industry, Report on a 1956 Survey*, 1960; Battelle Memorial Institute, *Research by Cooperative Organizations, A Survey of Scientific Research by Trade Associations, Professional and Technical Societies, and Other Cooperative Groups, 1953*, Washington, D.C., 1956; Maxwell Research Center, Syracuse University, *Research and Development by Nonprofit Research Institutes and Commercial Laboratories, 1953*, Washington, D.C., 1956; F. Emerson Andrews, *Scientific Research Expenditures by the Larger Private Foundations*, Washington, D.C., 1956.

Also see the following publications prepared by the National Science Foundation: *Federal Funds for Science*, Nos. VI and VII, 1957 and 1958; *Reviews of Data on Research and Development*, Nos. 1–3, 5–10, 12, and 14–16, 1957–1959; *Research Expenditures of Foundations and Other Nonprofit Institutions, 1953–54*, 1958; *Funds for Scientific Activities in the Federal Government, Fiscal Years 1953 and 1954*, 1958; *Scientific Research in Colleges and Universities—Expenditures and Manpower, 1953–54*, 1959; *Scientific Activities in Six State Governments, Summary Report on a Survey, Fiscal Year 1954*, 1958; and *Performance and Financing of Research and Development in American Industry, 1957*, 1960.

Early major efforts to estimate the volume of research and development. The methodology, scope, and limitations of the various series are often summarized in the publications cited below, and any use of these estimates in descriptive or analytical work should be preceded by a careful review of their limitations.

George Perazich and Philip M. Field, *Industrial Research and Changing Technology*, Work Projects Administration, National Research Project, Philadelphia, 1940, pp. 5–17 and 52–79. This report presents data on research personnel in industrial laboratories for 1920, 1921, 1927, 1931, 1933, and 1938. The data are based on the six directory listings of industrial research laboratories in the United States published by the National Research Council between 1920 and 1938.

National Resources Committee (later, National Resources Planning Board), *Research, A National Resource*, vol. 1, *Relation of the Federal Government to Research*, Report of the National Resources Planning Board Science Committee, 1938. Section 3, pp. 61–112, of this report presents estimates of Federal expenditures for research in 1937 and 1938. Table D, p. 91, summarizes from other sources a number of earlier estimates of Federal expenditures going back as far as 1901. Section 6, pp. 167–193, contains a discussion of research in American universities and colleges. It also provides a general estimate of the dollar volume of expenditures for research and development for 1935–1936.

National Resources Planning Board, *Research, A National Resource*, vol. II, *Industrial Research*, a report of the National Research Council to the National Resources Planning Board, 1941. Section IV, pp. 173–187 of this report, presents estimates of research personnel in industrial laboratories for 1940; and section II, part 7, pp. 120–123, shows research personnel and expenditures in 31 firms for 1937.

U.S. Senate, Committee on Military Affairs, Subcommittee on War Mobilization (Harley M. Kilgore, Chairman), *Report on the Government's Wartime Research and Development, 1940–44*, 1945. Part I of this report presents detail, and part II summarizes data on funds for research and development for each of 45 Federal agencies and bureaus, with detail on the fiscal sources of funds and the major categories of recipients for fiscal years 1940 through 1944.

Vannevar Bush, *Science, The Endless Frontier, A Report to the President*, July 1945, appendix 3, "Report of the Committee on Science and Public Welfare" (Isaiah Bowman, Chairman). The Bowman Committee's report to Dr. Bush presents the first known national estimates of trends in scientific research and development expenditures in table I, p. 80. It also contains series on scientific research expenditures (based largely on performance of research) for the following major groups: (a) Industry—annual expenditures estimates for 1920–1940; (b) nonprofit industrial research institutes—annual expenditures estimates for 1930–1942; (c) Government (Federal and State)—annual estimates for 1923–1932, 1934–1938, and 1940–1944; (d) colleges and universities—biennial estimates, 1930, 1932, 1934, 1936, 1938, 1940, and 1942; (e) research institutes (not connected with any industry nor an integral part of any university)—annual estimates for 1930–1940; and (f) total scientific research expenditures—total of the foregoing five series for 1930, 1932, 1934, 1936, 1938, and 1940.

The President's Scientific Research Board (John R. Steelman, Chairman), *Science and Public Policy, A Report to the President*, vols. I, II, and IV, 1947. Based on data in Vannevar Bush, *Science, The Endless Frontier* (cited above), vol. I, *A Program for the Nation*, presents for the even years of 1930–1940 estimated expenditures by the Federal Government, industry, universities, and others. Estimates are also made of the average annual expenditures by major groups for 1941–1945 and of expenditures for 1947. Vol. II, *The Federal Research Program*, presents estimates of Federal "expenditures for research and development in the physical and biological sciences" in fiscal year 1947 based on project reports from the individual agencies. Vol. IV, *Manpower for Research*, presents annual estimates and forecasts of scientists and engineers in industrial research laboratories for 1929–1956.

Helen Wood, Robert Cain, and Joseph H. Schuster, *Scientific Research and Development in American Industry, A Study of Manpower and Costs*, Bulletin No. 1148,

Bureau of Labor Statistics, prepared in cooperation with the Department of Defense, 1953. Data in this publication are based on the first survey specifically designed to obtain research and development performance costs and personnel for private firms. This survey was sponsored by the Research and Development Board, Department of Defense. The report presents estimates of expenditures for research and development performed in 1951 by firms reporting. Personnel data cover research and development scientists and engineers employed by these firms in January 1951 and 1952.

Office of the Secretary of Defense, *The Growth of Scientific Research and Development*, 1953. This publication presents annual estimates on sources of research and development funds and on performance of research and development for 1941–1952 for the Federal Government, industry, and nonprofit institutions including colleges and universities. Estimates of the number of scientists and engineers employed in research and development by these broad sectors are also shown for the same years. No methodological notes accompany the estimates. They are known to be based on materials in Wood, Cain, and Schuster (cited above); U.S. Senate, Committee on Military Affairs, Subcommittee on War Mobilization (cited above); and other published and unpublished sources. The series on sources and uses of funds have been continued to 1958 in the Bureau of the Census, *Statistical Abstract of the United States, 1959*, table 696.

Office of Education, *Statistics of Higher Education: Receipts, Expenditures and Property, 1953–54*, 1957. This report presents estimates, biennially, on expenditures for performance of "Organized research" by institutions of higher education, 1930–1954. See series H 355 in this volume. This is the oldest known current series on research expenditures.

More recently, beginning with Bureau of the Budget, *The Budget of the United States Government, 1955*, the Federal budget documents have carried a special analysis of "Federal Research and Development Programs" summarizing expenditures for scientific research and development on an agency basis and by budget function. In *The Budget*, 1959, this was Special Analysis H and covered fiscal years 1957, 1958, and 1959.

W 79–94. Federal Government expenditures for scientific research and development, by agency, 1940–1957.

Source: 1940–1944, U.S. Senate, Committee on Military Affairs, Subcommittee on War Mobilization (Harley M. Kilgore, Chairman), *Report on the Government's Wartime Research and Development, 1940–1944*, parts I and II, 1945; 1945–1951, Bureau of the Budget, records; 1952–1957, National Science Foundation, *Federal Funds for Science, The Federal Research and Development Budget*, various annual issues.

The data for 1940–1944 have been adjusted by the National Science Foundation for comparability with later estimates. Funds for increase of research and development plant for this period are included in these data but are not separately identifiable.

Expenditures are here defined as the amounts of checks issued and cash payments made during a given period regardless of when the funds were appropriated. The definitions of research and development followed in the three portions of the series differed somewhat, but these differences do not impair the usefulness of the series as a general indicator of trend. The definitions used and the periods to which they apply were, respectively: 1940–1944—research and development includes all the activities from pure research to the experimental testing

of new products, including all developmental work such as designing, engineering, the building and operation of pilot plants, etc.; 1945–1951—research and development consists of scientific research in the physical, mathematical, biological, medical, and engineering sciences; development of experimental models and prototypes; construction of research and development facilities and pilot plants; and experimental production; 1952–1957—scientific research is systematic and intensive study directed toward a fuller knowledge of the subject studied; and development is systematic use of that knowledge directed toward the production of useful materials, devices, systems, methods, or processes, exclusive of design and production engineering.

Routine testing activities, topographic and hydrographic surveys and mapping, collection of general purpose statistics, and routine production activities have been excluded from all portions of the series. Research in the social sciences was originally excluded from 1940–1951, but an estimate for research in those fields was added for these years by the National Science Foundation. The social sciences have been consistently included since 1952.

The major limitation of these data is that they are actually three rather than one series, each compiled at a different time and on a somewhat different basis. The first segment of the series (1940–1944) was based on a special retrospective study in which the data were examined and compiled after the period in question. Annual data for 1947–1951 were compiled by the Bureau of the Budget with interpolations for 1945 and 1946. In order to achieve as much chronological continuity as possible, the entire series has been reviewed by the National Science Foundation for consistency, and adjustments to improve comparability have been made wherever possible. The data represent estimates by informed persons, since Government accounting does not use research and development as a uniform expenditures bookkeeping category throughout all agencies and subdivisions.

A further limitation of the series is the exclusion of expenditures from Department of Defense production and procurement appropriations, which may be used by industrial firms for research and development purposes. The Department estimates that, in fiscal year 1958, $875 million was expended from these sources for engineering-type work in direct support of research and development, excluding quantity production of prototypes of weapons and equipment. It should be noted that the Department of Defense appropriation structure was revised in the Budget for 1960 to reflect a wider range of activities in the research and development appropriations. Subsequent data published later reflect this revision.

W 95–106. Federal Government obligations for scientific research and development, by agency, 1947–1957.

Source: 1947–1951, Bureau of the Budget, records; 1952–1957, see source for series W 79–94.

These series are based on budget data, and although they represent the best estimates of informed persons, some differences in the interpretation of terms and definitions have undoubtedly occurred. See also general note for series W 79–121 for other limitations.

Obligations are here defined as the amounts of orders placed, contracts awarded, services received, and similar transactions during a given period, regardless of when the funds were appropriated, and when future payment of money is required. Conduct of research and development includes the salaries and expenses of scientists engaged in these activities and all indirect, incidental, or related costs resulting from or necessary to the conduct of such research and development, regardless of whether the work was done by a Government agency, private individuals, or organizations under a contractual arrangement with the Government. It excludes routine testing, mapping, surveys, collections of general-purpose statistics, experimental production, and activities concerned primarily with dissemination of scientific information or the training of scientific manpower. Increase of research and development plant is a measure of funds made available for physical facilities, such as land, buildings, or equipment, where the primary intent is to enlarge the capital plant available for scientific research and development, regardless of whether the item is to be used by the Government or a private organization, and regardless of where title to the property may rest. Taken together, the conduct of research and development and increase of research and development plant are referred to as scientific research and development.

The difference in magnitude between the figure for the Federal conduct of research and development for fiscal year 1957 in this series and that presented for the Federal agencies as source in table I, p. 609, stems largely from the fact that data in table I were reported by organizations performing research and development for the Federal Government. Data in series W 95 were reported by the Federal agencies obligating the funds. In the case of the industry sector as a respondent in table I, a broader definition of research and development than the Federal definition resulted in the reporting of funds for research and development performed by industry under Federal production and procurement contracts which were not included in the Federal series W 95. This is the most significant cause of the difference.

W 107–121. Expenditures for research and development performed by private industrial firms, by major industry, 1953–1957.

Source: National Science Foundation, *Science and Engineering in American Industry, Final Report on a 1956 Survey*, 1959, and "Funds for Research and Development Performance in American Industry, 1957," *Reviews of Data on Research and Development*, No. 14, August 1959.

The report summarizing the results of the 1956 survey, conducted by the Bureau of Labor Statistics for the National Science Foundation, presents data on research and development expenditures by private firms during 1953–1956. The report for 1957, based on a survey conducted by the Bureau of the Census for the National Science Foundation, includes preliminary estimates of expenditures for 1956 and 1957. The Bureau of the Census survey reported total expenditures for research and development in 1956 approximately 4 percent lower than the comparable Bureau of Labor Statistics estimate for that year. Percentage differences for particular industries, however, were significantly larger than for the over-all total.

The differences between estimates of the Bureau of Labor Statistics and the Bureau of the Census for 1956 were due mainly to variation in methodology used by the two agencies in conducting these surveys and changes in reporting procedures by some respondents. The report on the 1956 survey, cited above, discusses in some detail the methodological differences between the two surveys.

Although Census data are not directly comparable to those of the Bureau of Labor Statistics, Census estimates for 1956 were included not only because of their comparability with 1957 estimates, but also because they mark the beginning of a series that will be continued through future annual surveys of expenditures for industrial research and development.

Research and development, as defined in these series, includes basic and applied research in the physical and life sciences (including medicine) and in engineering, and design and development of prototypes and processes. This definition excludes quality control, routine product testing, market exploration, research in the social sciences or psychology, or other nontechnological activities or technical services.

Expenditures, as defined in these series, include salaries of research and development scientists and engineers and their supporting personnel, other direct costs, service and supporting costs, plus attributable overhead expenses incurred in such items as administration, depreciation, and rent. Expenditures also include Federal funds for private industry performance of research and development ranging from about 40 percent of total expenditures in 1953 to about 50 percent in 1957. The totals exclude capital expenditures and patent expenses.

Series W 79–94. Federal Government Expenditures for Scientific Research and Development, by Agency: 1940 to 1957

[In millions of dollars. For years ending June 30. Includes expenditures for conduct of research and development and for increase of research and development plant]

Year	Total, excl. military pay and allowances	Total, incl. military pay and allowances	Department								Other offices, agencies, and establishments					
			Agriculture	Commerce	Defense [1]		Health, Education, and Welfare			Interior	Atomic Energy Commission	Manhattan Engineer District	National Advisory Committee for Aeronautics	Office of Scientific Research and Development	National Science Foundation	All other agencies
					Excl. military pay	Incl. military pay	Total	Public Health Service	Other							
	79	80	81	82	83	84	85	86	87	88	89	90	91	92	93	94
1957	2,835.9	3,031.3	97.0	19.8	1,889.7	2,085.3	143.5	138.8	4.7	42.3	512.2	--------	76.1	--------	30.6	24.7
1956	2,346.7	2,534.7	87.7	20.4	1,628.6	1,816.6	86.2	82.7	3.5	35.7	385.1	--------	71.1	--------	15.4	16.5
1955	2,133.4	2,290.6	72.0	9.9	1,550.9	1,708.1	70.2	67.9	2.3	31.9	289.8	--------	73.8	--------	8.5	26.4
1954	2,084.2	(2)	55.4	10.6	1,532.2	(2)	62.5	60.0	2.5	39.1	274.3	--------	89.5	--------	3.6	16.9
1953	2,099.0	(2)	54.9	13.6	1,569.2	(2)	65.2	61.7	3.5	35.2	261.8	--------	78.6	--------	2.1	18.5
1952	1,816.2	(2)	57.1	10.1	1,317.0	(2)	64.1	60.8	3.3	32.8	249.6	--------	67.4	--------	.5	17.6
1951	1,300.5	(2)	52.4	16.9	823.4	(2)	(2)	53.4	(2)	32.1	242.6	--------	61.6	--------	.1	18.2
1950	1,082.8	(2)	53.0	12.0	652.3	(2)	(2)	39.6	(2)	32.1	221.4	--------	54.5	--------	--------	17.7
1949	1,082.0	(2)	50.5	12.5	695.4	(2)	(2)	27.9	(2)	38.2	196.1	--------	48.7	--------	--------	12.8
1948	854.8	(2)	42.4	8.2	592.2	(2)	(2)	22.8	(2)	31.4	107.5	--------	37.5	.9	--------	11.8
1947	899.9	(2)	39.2	4.8	550.8	(2)	(2)	10.1	(2)	20.3	37.7	186.0	35.2	5.6	--------	10.2
1946	917.8	(2)	36.8	5.0	418.0	(2)	(2)	3.5	(2)	17.0	--------	366.0	23.7	36.8	--------	11.0
1945	1,590.7	(2)	33.7	5.0	513.0	(2)	(2)	3.4	(2)	18.0	859.0	--------	24.1	114.5	--------	20.0
1944	1,377.2	(2)	32.1	5.2	448.1	(2)	(2)	3.3	(2)	20.7	730.0	--------	18.4	86.8	--------	32.6
1943	602.4	(2)	30.7	5.2	395.1	(2)	(2)	3.2	(2)	17.0	77.0	--------	9.8	52.2	--------	12.2
1942	280.3	(2)	29.9	3.2	211.1	(2)	(2)	3.2	(2)	13.5	--------	--------	5.0	11.0	--------	3.4
1941	197.9	(2)	28.3	3.1	143.7	(2)	(2)	3.0	(2)	9.5	--------	--------	2.6	5.3	--------	2.4
1940	74.1	(2)	29.1	3.3	26.4	(2)	(2)	2.8	(2)	7.9	--------	--------	2.2	--------	--------	2.4

[1] Total Department of Defense includes expenditures of the Departments of the Army, Navy, and Air Force, as well as departmentwide funds. Excluded is the research and development financed from production and procurement funds.
(2) Not available.

Series W 95–106. Federal Government Obligations for Scientific Research and Development, by Agency: 1947 to 1957

[In millions of dollars. For years ending June 30]

Year	Total, excl. military pay and allowances	Total, incl. military pay and allowances	Department		Defense[1]		Health, Education, and Welfare	Interior	Other offices, agencies, and establishments			
			Agriculture	Commerce	Excl. military pay	Incl. military pay			Atomic Energy Commission	National Advisory Committee for Aeronautics	National Science Foundation	All other agencies
	95	96	97	98	99	100	101	102	103	104	105	106
TOTAL OBLIGATIONS												
1957	2,980.4	3,176.0	102.8	19.3	1,953.7	2,149.3	177.9	47.5	530.5	83.4	37.1	28.2
1956	2,504.8	2,692.8	83.6	18.4	1,747.0	1,935.0	89.0	38.5	424.6	65.7	17.4	20.5
1955	2,094.7	2,251.9	73.3	15.9	1,510.6	1,667.8	70.8	34.6	294.4	64.5	10.4	20.3
1954	1,900.2	(2)	67.2	8.3	1,379.3	(2)	62.0	38.7	266.3	57.0	4.6	16.7
1953	2,148.0	(2)	56.6	11.3	1,632.4	(2)	58.7	34.4	250.3	78.6	2.3	23.4
1952	2,194.5	(2)	55.7	14.2	1,706.6	(2)	52.0	36.0	228.8	81.7	.9	18.5
1951	1,811.9	(2)	55.2	12.3	1,278.0	(2)	53.0	32.2	278.5	84.4	.1	18.2
1950	1,175.9	(2)	57.7	22.7	636.2	(2)	65.3	31.4	284.2	62.7	____	15.7
1949	1,105.5	(2)	53.9	11.9	652.0	(2)	39.9	35.6	246.9	50.4	____	14.6
1948	867.7	(2)	46.4	9.8	485.8	(2)	27.1	28.0	212.5	44.4	____	13.5
1947	690.8	(2)	40.2	6.4	503.3	(2)	18.8	16.9	64.6	29.9	____	10.8
CONDUCT OF RESEARCH AND DEVELOPMENT												
1957	2,528.8	2,724.0	99.8	17.7	1,689.3	1,884.9	144.2	47.4	419.5	55.3	30.0	25.6
1956	2,231.3	2,419.3	83.0	18.2	1,585.0	1,773.0	86.0	38.0	335.5	49.5	16.0	20.0
1955	1,887.4	2,044.6	72.2	15.0	1,371.5	1,528.7	68.0	34.5	253.4	43.0	9.7	20.2
1954	1,744.0	(2)	59.3	7.8	1,282.9	(2)	58.2	37.7	229.6	47.4	4.6	16.4
1953	1,900.1	(2)	56.0	11.0	1,476.8	(2)	49.9	32.1	204.4	48.4	2.3	19.1
1952	1,887.3	(2)	55.3	10.4	1,508.5	(2)	43.6	30.7	168.8	50.5	.9	18.5
1951	1,481.9	(2)	55.1	11.0	1,125.9	(2)	37.9	30.4	157.9	45.4	.1	18.1
1950	973.2	(2)	56.9	22.4	600.3	(2)	34.2	28.7	172.2	42.8	____	15.6
1949	938.1	(2)	53.2	10.9	626.2	(2)	25.2	30.2	140.0	38.3	____	13.9
1948	776.6	(2)	45.7	8.9	485.8	(2)	24.3	20.3	145.4	33.0	____	13.0
1947	619.4	(2)	40.0	5.7	469.3	(2)	10.6	16.9	39.9	26.7	____	10.3
INCREASE OF RESEARCH AND DEVELOPMENT PLANT												
1957		451.6	3.0	1.6	264.4		33.7	.1	111.0	28.1	7.1	2.6
1956		273.5	.6	.2	162.0		3.0	.5	89.1	16.2	1.4	.5
1955		207.3	1.1	.9	139.1		2.8	.1	41.0	21.5	.7	.1
1954		156.2	7.9	.5	96.4		3.8	1.0	36.7	9.6	(3)	.3
1953		247.9	.6	.3	155.6		8.8	2.3	45.9	30.2	____	4.3
1952		307.2	.4	3.8	198.1		8.4	5.3	60.0	31.2	(2)	
1951		330.0	.1	1.3	152.1		15.1	1.8	120.6	39.0	____	.1
1950		202.7	.8	.3	35.9		31.1	2.7	112.0	19.9	____	.1
1949		167.4	.7	1.0	25.8		14.7	5.4	106.9	12.1	____	.7
1948		91.1	.7	.9	____		2.8	7.7	67.1	11.4	____	.5
1947		71.4	.2	.7	34.0		8.2	____	24.7	3.2	____	.5

[1] Total Department of Defense includes obligations for the Departments of the Army, Navy, and Air Force, as well as departmentwide funds. Excluded is the research and development financed from production and procurement funds.
[2] Not available.
[3] Less than $50,000.

Series W 107–121. Expenditures for Research and Development Performed by Private Industrial Firms, by Major Industry: 1953 to 1957

[In millions of dollars]

Series No.	Industry	1957 (prel.)	1956[1] (prel.)	1956[1]	1955	1954	1953	Series No.	Industry	1957 (prel.)	1956[1] (prel.)	1956[1]	1955	1954	1953
107	**All industries**	7,155	6,018	6,231	4,449	3,950	3,538	114	Fabricated metal products and ordnance	143	122	176	124	109	104
108	Food and kindred products	68	58	76	65	58	54	115	Machinery	688	562	611	434	347	322
109	Paper and allied products	50	44	40	33	31	27	116	Electrical equipment	1,170	941	1,038	800	755	682
110	Chemicals and allied products	596	521	512	429	395	365	117	Aircraft and parts	2,544	2,109	2,079	1,170	916	758
111	Petroleum products and extraction[2]	230	187	201	163	162	146	118	Professional and scientific instruments	240	200	221	169	191	172
112	Stone, clay, and glass products	61	51	66	45	42	38	119	Other manufacturing industries[3]	921	844	846	715	641	586
113	Primary metal industries	113	93	88	71	66	60	120	Telecommunications and broadcasting	206	177	171	148	127	113
								121	Other nonmanufacturing industries	[4]126	[4]107	107	86	112	110

[1] See text for series W 107–121.
[2] Includes a few companies with relatively small research programs engaged primarily in manufacturing coal products.
[3] Includes rubber products, tobacco manufactures, lumber and wood products, furniture and fixtures, printing and publishing, leather, motor vehicles and other transportation equipment except aircraft and parts, and miscellaneous manufacturing industries.
[4] Estimated.

Banking and Finance

BANKING (Series X 1–265)

X 1–265. General note.

For general statistical purposes it may be said that a bank is a financial institution which accepts money from the general public for deposit in a common fund, subject to withdrawal or transfer by check on demand or on short notice, and makes loans to the general public. The historical series on assets and liabilities of banks reflect these activities and are the basic series on banking. Series X 1–128 on principal assets and liabilities of banks and on number and total assets by class of bank cover all banks and all commercial banks. Series X 129–265 provide information on selected aspects of banking: Insured banks, branch banking, suspension of banks, earnings and expenses, bank debits and clearings, savings deposits, and Federal Reserve Banks.

Collection and publication of banking and monetary statistics in the United States have been conditioned by the development of the banking and monetary system. Banks in this country have been in part under the jurisdiction of State governments and in part under the Federal Government. At the same time some banks operated before 1933 outside the jurisdiction of both governments, while other banks operated within the jurisdiction of both.

Supervision and regulation of banks have been a primary responsibility of the chartering authority. National banks, organized under Federal law enacted in 1863, are supervised by the Comptroller of the Currency, and State banks, by officials of the respective States.

Two other Federal entities with additional supervisory authority have been superimposed upon the existing banking structure: The Federal Reserve System, established in 1914 to exercise central banking functions, and the Federal Deposit Insurance Corporation, created in 1933 to insure bank deposits. The Federal Reserve System includes all national banks and such State banks as voluntarily join the System. Insurance of bank deposits was made obligatory for banks belonging to the Federal Reserve System and optional for others.

All the supervisory agencies have published some statistics for the banks under their jurisdiction, but there was no centralized collection of statistics for all classes of banks on a uniform basis until 1947. Prior to the National Banking Act of 1863, the only official collection of banking figures for the entire country was made by the Treasury Department under authority of a resolution of the House of Representatives passed in 1832. For 1833–1863, reporting by banks to the Secretary of the Treasury was voluntary. With the exception of some years, the Secretary of the Treasury included in his reports to Congress information regarding the number of State banks which reported to him. For 1863–1873, statistics of national banks only were published in the *Annual Report of the Comptroller of the Currency*.

The need for complete reporting was recognized in the act of 1873, which authorized the Comptroller to obtain balance-sheet data for nonnational banks from State banking authorities, Territorial authorities, or individual incorporated banks. Although coverage was improved, the data obtained were neither uniform nor complete because the various State and Territorial authorities did not request the same information from banks and some States had no department to collect the information. Moreover, in some States many so-called private or unincorporated banks operated outside the jurisdiction of State authority. The Comptroller annually requested that these banks report directly to him, but this procedure met with only limited success.

In spite of the difficulties of collecting statistics for all banks, the coverage and uniformity of the data became progressively better. This improvement came about principally because of greater uniformity in classification of balance-sheet information requested of banks, and because of the creation of banking departments in States that formerly had none, as well as more adequate collection and tabulation of data.

Efforts to promote uniformity in bank statistics culminated in 1938 when representatives of all Federal supervisory agencies worked out a standardized balance-sheet report form. This form was approved by the National Association of State Bank Supervisors and was adopted by the three Federal banking agencies and by many of the State banking departments. Nearly all States now use a form that is substantially consistent with the standard one.

In 1947, the Comptroller of the Currency, the Board of Governors of the Federal Reserve System, and the Federal Deposit Insurance Corporation, which compiled somewhat different balance-sheet data for all banks, worked out an arrangement for the Federal Deposit Insurance Corporation to compile semiannually a uniform series of statistics for all banking institutions.

To provide more adequate historical banking statistics comparable to those available beginning in 1947, the Board of Governors of the Federal Reserve System—with the cooperation of the Comptroller of the Currency, the Federal Deposit Insurance Corporation, and the State bank supervisory authorities—recently compiled a revised series for all banks in continental United States as of June 30 of each year, 1896–1955. These data were published in 1959 in Board of Governors of the Federal Reserve System, *All-Bank Statistics, United States, 1896–1955*. The series cover number of banks and principal assets and liabilities for major classes of banks. The publication also includes similar data for individual States, and for the Territories and possessions, which are not included in U.S. totals. Revisions in the earlier data affect primarily the nonnational components, and are largest for figures before 1920.

Compilation of the revised series for national banks presented no major problems. Since 1864, the Comptroller of the Currency has collected condition reports from 3 to 6 times annually from national banks, and has tabulated and published summaries of these reports showing principal assets and liabilities. National bank balance-sheet data are published in detail in *Abstract of Reports of Condition of National Banks* (usually 3 or 4 times a year) and in summary form in the *Annual Report*.

Compilation of revised statistics for nonnational banks beginning in 1896 required extensive research into all types of available banking statistics. The main sources of information, other than the records of several large private banks, were the annual reports and statistical publications and records of the Comptroller of the Currency, the Bureau of Internal Revenue, the Board of Governors of the Federal Reserve System, the Federal Deposit Insurance Corporation, and State banking departments, as well as compilations published in bankers' directories. Unofficial compilations of figures for banks in several States were also used.

Under the arrangements made for all-bank data beginning with 1947, the 1947–1955 data in Board of Governors of the Federal Reserve System, *All-Bank Statistics, United States, 1896–1955,* are based on compilations of the Federal Deposit Insurance Corporation, except that data for "other areas," that is, the Territories and possessions, have not been included in U.S. totals.

A financial institution is considered a bank in the revised all-bank series if it accepts deposits from the general public or if it conducts principally a fiduciary business. This is the definition used by the Comptroller of the Currency, the Federal Deposit Insurance Corporation, and the Board of Governors of the Federal Reserve System in the all-bank statistics published beginning with 1947. For complete description of the types of institutions included and of those excluded, see Federal Deposit Insurance Corporation, *Annual Report, 1956,* pp. 88–89.

X 1–96. General note.

Assets and liabilities are defined here in their usual accounting meaning. Assets are the resources of banks, such as loans, investments, reserves, cash, and balances with other banks; liabilities are the obligations of banks, such as demand and time deposits and capital accounts.

X 1–5. State banks—number of banks and assets and liabilities, 1811–1830.

Source: *Writings of Albert Gallatin,* edited by Henry Adams, J. B. Lippincott and Company, Philadelphia, 1879, vol. III, pp. 286, 291, and 296.

These are believed to be the most consistent series for the period before 1834. The figures are reprinted in Comptroller of the Currency, *Annual Report, 1876,* p. xl, which also contains estimates derived from an unofficial source of the number of banks, specie holdings, banknote circulation, and capital of banks in the United States for selected years 1774–1804, and some discussion of early banking statistics. Figures in the Comptroller's report for 1876, together with some additional banking data for the period prior to 1834, are included in Comptroller of the Currency, *Annual Report, 1920,* vol. 2, p. 846.

X 6–19. Second Bank of the United States—assets, liabilities, and profits, 1817–1840.

Source: Series X 6–17, Comptroller of the Currency, *Annual Report, 1876,* app. p. lxxxiii (except series X 17 for 1818–1837, *Annual Report, 1916,* p. 912); series X 18–19, Ralph C. H. Catterall, *The Second Bank of the United States,* University of Chicago Press, Chicago, 1903, p. 504.

The Second Bank was chartered by Congress in 1816 for 20 years. Renewal of the charter was denied and reorganization of the bank was effected by the Legislature of the State of Pennsylvania. The bank failed in 1841 and was finally liquidated in 1856. See headnote, table 94, p. 912, Comptroller of the Currency, *Annual Report, 1916,* vol. II; that page also shows assets and liabilities of the First Bank of the United

States in 1809 and 1811, the only two years for which data appear to be available.

X 20–41. All banks—number of banks and principal assets and liabilities, 1834–1957.

Source: 1834–1896, Comptroller of the Currency, *Annual Report, 1931,* pp. 1018–1025; 1896–1955, Board of Governors of the Federal Reserve System, *All-Bank Statistics, United States, 1896–1955,* pt. I, pp. 30–33; 1956–1957, Federal Deposit Insurance Corporation, records.

These series represent a combination of data on two different bases: For 1896–1957, on the revised all-bank series basis and for 1834–1896, on the basis published in annual reports of the Comptroller of the Currency, which is known to provide incomplete coverage, especially of nonnational banks.

The historical tables in the 1931 *Annual Report of the Comptroller of the Currency* provide summary statistics by single years beginning in 1834 for (*a*) all reporting banks, (*b*) national banks (beginning in 1863), and (*c*) all reporting State and private banks (that is, nonnational banks). For nonnational bank data prior to 1873 the sources are as follows: For 1834–1840, Executive Document No. 111, 26th Congress, 2d Session; for 1841–1850, Executive Document No. 68, 31st Congress, 1st session. For 1851–1863 (except 1852–1853), figures are from the report on the condition of banks for 1863. Those for 1853 are from Executive Document No. 66, 32d Congress, 2d session, and are incomplete. For 1852, the figures are estimates based on number of banks in 5 years, 1847–1851, and on assets and liabilities in 10 years, 1854–1863. For 1864–1872, all figures except number of banks and capital accounts are estimates based on data for the previous 10 years, 1854–1863.

Prior to 1896, figures shown here include all national banks and all State banks that voluntarily reported to State banking departments in the United States including mutual and stock savings banks, loan and trust companies, and private banks. A few banks in U.S. possessions are included. Data for nonnational banks for the earlier years are reported for dates other than June 30 and are known to be incomplete; many of the items have been estimated, as noted above. Where more reliable estimates prior to 1896 are available, they are included in alternate series X 86–90.

Beginning in 1896, more comprehensive data for nonnational banks than those included in the Comptroller's annual reports are available in *All-Bank Statistics, 1896–1955,* cited above. More detailed data than are shown here, by States and by class of banks, are available in this source, together with a description of the composition of the balance-sheet items, the methods by which the figures were compiled, and the classification of banks used.

The figures beginning in 1896 include national banks and chartered or incorporated State banks, loan and trust companies, stock savings banks, and mutual savings banks. In conformity with the definition of a bank adopted in 1947, they also include unincorporated financial institutions which meet the definition of "bank"; cooperative exchanges in Arkansas which receive deposits; cash depositories in South Carolina; and Morris Plan and industrial banks (unless engaged merely in making loans and investments). In 1933 and 1934 only licensed banks, that is, those operating on an unrestricted basis, are included.

X 25–28, investments. For the national bank component, 1863–1865, total investments exclude securities other than those of the U.S. Government, which are included in "other assets" in the source. U.S. Government obligations (series X 26) include all direct obligations and, since 1933, those fully guaranteed as to interest and principal by the U.S. Government. Obligations of States and political subdivisions (series X 27) include securities issued by States, counties, and municipalities; by school, irrigation, drainage, and reclamation districts; and by local housing authorities. Other securities (series X 28) include primarily obligations of domestic corporations, those of Government agencies not guaranteed by the United States, and foreign securities.

X 34–38, deposits. Total deposits for national banks for 1863–1865 include State banknotes in circulation and for 1866–1868, bills payable and rediscounts. Beginning 1942, deposit figures exclude reciprocal balances.

X 39, banknotes. Prior to 1864, figures represent State banknotes only and beginning 1896, national banknotes only. In 1865, a prohibitive tax was imposed on State banknotes and as a result only a few such notes were in circulation thereafter. Data for 1870–1910 exclude comparatively small amounts of State banknotes outstanding for which national banks, converted from State banks or merged with State banks, assumed liability.

X 40, capital accounts. Capital accounts include capital, surplus, net undivided profits, reserves for contingencies, and certain other reserve accounts. Capital is here used to designate primarily the original contribution of bank owners to the bank and is ordinarily evidenced by bank stock certificates. Surplus is ordinarily the amount of bank earnings specifically set aside as capital funds. Net undivided profits are earnings not yet set aside for dividends or allocated to surplus. In addition to reserves for contingencies, capital accounts include reserves for undeclared dividends and for accrued interest on capital notes and debentures as well as reserves for retirement of preferred stock or capital notes and debentures. Valuation reserves set up in connection with prospective but undetermined losses on loans, securities, and other assets *are not included* but are deducted from these assets. Prior to 1873, figures for nonnational banks include capital only, and beginning 1933, the figures include preferred stock and capital notes and debentures.

X 42–63. National banks—number of banks and principal assets and liabilities, 1863–1957.

Source: See source for series X 20–41.

See also general note for series X 1–265.

National banks are those chartered by the Federal Government and are under the general supervision of the Comptroller of the Currency.

X 64–85. Nonnational banks—number of banks and principal assets and liabilities, 1863–1957.

Source: See source for series X 20–41.

Nonnational banks comprised all banks prior to 1863 (see general note for series X 1–265). These banks include State commercial banks, mutual and stock savings banks, private banks, loan and trust companies, and other institutions enumerated in the text for series X 20–41. For comment on incompleteness of nonnational bank data prior to 1896, see text for series X 20–41.

X 86–90. Nonnational banks—number of banks and selected assets and liabilities, alternate series, 1865–1896.

Source: **Series X 86–88,** 1875–1882, Comptroller of the Currency, *Annual Report, 1885,* pp. clxix–clxxiii (discussion of figures, p. lxviii). **Series X 88,** 1865–1866, Federal Deposit Insurance Corporation, *Annual Report, 1934,* pp. 103, 112–113; 1867–1876, James K. Kindahl, *Estimates of Nonnational Bank Deposits for the United States, 1867–1875,* unpublished doctoral dissertation on file at University of Chicago, 1954, and

Federal Deposit Insurance Corporation, *Annual Report, 1934,* pp. 112–113. **Series X 89–90,** David I. Fand, *Banks in the Post-Civil War Period in the United States, 1875–1896,* unpublished doctoral dissertation on file at University of Chicago.

Data for all nonnational banks were compiled from tax returns submitted by banks during this period. Figures for capital accounts and total deposits (series X 87–88) are based on information included on semiannual tax returns and are monthly averages for 6 months ending May 31, 1876–1882, and for 6 months ending November 30, 1875.

The figures shown for total deposits (series X 88) for 1865–1876 are the sum of separate estimates for deposits of nonnational commercial banks and mutual savings banks. The methods of estimation are described in the sources cited above. The original source figures for commercial banks were adjusted for nonreporting banks but not for underreporting by banks.

X 89–90, adjusted deposits and vault cash. Adjusted deposits as used here are total deposits (with original source figures adjusted for nonreporting banks and for underreporting by banks) less cash items in process of collection. Data are as of August, 1875–1881, and June, 1882–1896. In the source volume, figures for nonnational commercial banks are shown separately from mutual savings banks.

X 91–96. Nonnational banks—number of banks and total assets, by class, 1875–1957.

Source: 1875–1896, Comptroller of the Currency, *Annual Report,* various issues; 1896–1955, see source for series X 20–41, pts. I and II; 1956–1957, see source for series X 20–41.

These series are a breakdown of number and total assets of nonnational banks shown in series X 64–65.

See also sources and text for series X 20–41.

State commercial banks are all banks other than national and mutual savings banks. The classification of banks as "commercial" is based on function or type of deposit business. Commercial banks are those banks the business of which includes the holding of checking accounts and other deposits subject to withdrawal on demand, and the making of short-term self-liquidating loans to commerce, agriculture, and industry. Mutual savings banks, on the other hand, carry only savings and other time deposits (with some unimportant exceptions) and they invest their funds mostly in mortgage loans and securities. While the distinction between mutual savings and commercial banks is not strictly functional, since the great majority of commercial banks also carry varying proportions of savings and time deposits, it serves to segregate from banks holding demand deposits the group of banks that hold a large amount of deposits which represent principally savings. See series X 97–118 for balance-sheet data for all commercial banks, that is, national and State commercial banks combined.

Private banks are unincorporated institutions that operate ordinarily without a charter from either State or Federal Government. The number and relative importance of these banks has declined over the past half century.

The differences for 1896 in the data compiled by the Federal Reserve Board and by the Comptroller of the Currency indicate the incompleteness of early compilations of banking data, particularly in the case of private banks. Balance-sheet data are available in the Comptroller's annual reports for those banks submitting information to that agency. For separate figures for number and deposits of mutual savings banks, 1865–1896, see Federal Deposit Insurance Corporation, *Annual Report, 1934,* pp. 112–113.

In the source volume for 1896–1955, principal assets and liabilities are available separately for State commercial and mutual savings banks, by States, and for private banks in 18

States; in the remaining States, private banks were not segregated from other banks.

X 97–128. General note.

The following quotation concerning the role of commercial banks in the economy is taken from Board of Governors of the Federal Reserve System, *Banking Studies*, 1941, p. 169:

> Commercial banks are part of the economic organization of the nation. They operate as business concerns and earn a living by rendering services to the public. By lending and investing money, they assist productive processes; by providing checking account services they facilitate and expedite the settlement of financial obligations. There are numerous other banking services, but most of them are related to the primary banking functions of making loans and investments and handling deposits. All these services and operations have to do with money, which may be viewed as the stock in trade of banks.

For further comment on commercial banks and the reason for their separate classification, see text for series X 91–96. See also text for series X 20–41 and general note for series X 1–265. The data presented in series X 97–128 are for continental United States.

X 97–118. All commercial banks—number of banks and principal assets and liabilities, 1896–1957.

Source: 1896–1955, see source for series X 20–41, pt. I, pp. 34–37; 1956–1957, see source for series X 20–41.

X 119–128. All commercial banks—number of banks and total assets, by Federal Reserve membership and class, 1896–1957.

Source: **Series X 119–120** and **series X 125–126**, see source for series X 20–41; **series X 121–122**, Board of Governors of the Federal Reserve System, *Member Bank Call Report*, various issues (with adjustments to bring these data into conformity with the revised all-bank series); **series X 123–124**, derived by deducting from the totals for all commercial banks (series X 97–98) the figures for all member banks (series X 119–122); **series X 127–128**, are all commercial banks (series X 97–98) less national banks (series X 42–43).

State member commercial banks are those banks chartered by the various States which have voluntarily requested membership in the Federal Reserve System and met the necessary requirements. Nonmember commercial banks are all other State-chartered banks (other than mutual savings banks). See general note for series X 1–265 and text for series X 20–41 and series X 91–96.

X 129–154. General note.

The Federal Deposit Insurance Corporation was created in June 1933 to pay depositors of failed banks the amount of their insured deposits. All national banks and all other member banks of the Federal Reserve System are required by law to be members of the Federal Deposit Insurance Corporation. Banks that are not members of the Federal Reserve System may be admitted to Federal deposit insurance upon meeting certain prescribed conditions.

X 129–142. All banks—number of banks and total assets, by deposit insurance status and class, 1934–1957.

Source: 1934–1955, Board of Governors of the Federal Reserve System, records (data compiled in connection with *All-Bank Statistics, United States, 1896–1955*); 1956–1957, Federal Deposit Insurance Corporation, records.

See general note for series X 1–265 and text for series X 20–41.

Detailed statistics on assets and liabilities and earnings, expenses, and dividends of insured banks by class are available in Federal Deposit Insurance Corporation, *Annual Report*.

X 143–151. Number of banking offices, by deposit insurance status, 1900–1957.

Source: 1900–1941, Board of Governors of the Federal Reserve System, *Monetary Policy and the Management of the Public Debt*, Joint Committee on the Economic Report, 82d Congress, 2d session, pt. I, p. 553; 1942–1957, Federal Deposit Insurance Corporation, *Annual Report*. various issues.

Additional statistics on the number of banking offices are included in Board of Governors of the Federal Reserve System, *Federal Reserve Bulletin* and *Annual Report*, and in Federal Deposit Insurance Corporation, *Annual Report*.

The figures for 1900–1932 comprise national and all State-chartered banks except (*a*) mutual savings banks (data for which are not available until 1933) and (*b*) unincorporated or private banks not reporting to State banking authorities, other than certain large private banks which began to report to State banking authorities in 1934 and for which data are extended back to 1928. Separate data for State member banks are not available until 1933 (see text for series X 155–164). Beginning in 1942, the figures include banking facilities at military and other Government establishments. See series X 164. See also text for series X 20–41 and X 155–164.

X 152–154. Proportion of total bank deposits insured by the Federal Deposit Insurance Corporation, 1934–1957.

Source: 1934–1955, **series X 152**, the sum of figures in series X 34 and deposits of banks in U.S. Territories and possessions, shown in Federal Deposit Insurance Corporation, *Assets, Liabilities, and Capital Accounts, Commercial and Mutual Savings Banks*, various issues; **series X 153**, Federal Deposit Insurance Corporation, *Annual Report, 1955*, p. 16; 1956–1957, **series X 152** and **X 153**, FDIC, *Annual Report*, 1956 and 1957, and records; **series X 154**, FDIC computations (ratio of insured deposits to total deposits).

The Federal Deposit Insurance Corporation insured deposits in each account up to a maximum of $5,000 from 1934 to September 1950, and thereafter to a maximum of $10,000. Series X 153 shows the estimated portion of total deposits in all banks which was insured by the Corporation in each year.

X 155–164. Branch banking, 1900–1957.

Source: Number of banks and loans and investments or deposits, 1900–1941, Board of Governors of the Federal Reserve System, *Banking and Monetary Statistics*, pp. 297, 311 (for data on private and mutual savings banks, see also annual tables in the *Federal Reserve Bulletin*); number of branches, 1900–1951, see first source cited for series X 143–151, pt. I, p. 555; all series for all other years, *Federal Reserve Bulletin*, April, May, June, or July issues.

The figures for number of branches represent some revisions of data previously published in *Banking and Monetary Statistics*. Detailed statistics on branch banking by States, by class of bank, and by location of branches relative to the head office, for selected years since 1900, are available in the sources indicated.

Branch banking is defined as a type of multiple-office banking under which a bank as a single legal entity operates more than one banking office. If a bank operates a single branch office, irrespective of size or functions, other than a "facility" as defined below, it is included here.

The statistics on branches include all branches or additional offices in continental U.S. within the meaning of section 5155, United States Revised Statutes, which defines a branch as "any branch bank, branch office, branch agency, additional office, or any branch place of business . . . at which deposits are received, or checks paid, or money lent." Branch figures, however, do not include banking facilities at military and other Government establishments, which began in 1942 through arrangements made by the Treasury Department with banks designated as depositaries and financial agents of the Government. The number of such facilities is shown separately in series X 164.

Branch banking is not to be confused with group and chain banking. Group and chain banking refers to types of multiple-office banking which differ from branch banking principally in legal form and type of control. For data on group and chain banking, see sources cited above.

For mutual savings banks, data are not available for banks operating branches and number of branches until 1933; deposits are available only for the years indicated. Branches of unincorporated (private) banks not reporting to State banking authorities are not included prior to 1934. Separate data for State member and nonmember banks of the Federal Reserve System are available only for the years shown.

Wherever available, figures on loans and investments or deposits of banks operating branches are shown. These figures include the combined deposits or loans and investments of banks and their branches. For 1900–1936, the figures present loans and investments; for 1937–1941 and 1949, they are deposits, except as noted.

X 165–179. Bank suspensions—number and deposits of suspended banks, 1864–1933.

Source: Series X 165 and X 172, summation of series X 166–169 and X 173–176. Series X 166–178 (except X 169 and X 176 for 1864–1920) 1864–1891, see first source cited for series X 20–41, p. 1040; 1892–1933, see first source cited for series X 155–164, pp. 283 and 292. Series X 169 and X 176, 1864–1920, Federal Deposit Insurance Corporation, *Annual Report, 1934*, pp. 112–113. Series X 179, FDIC, *Annual Report, 1940*, p. 66.

More detailed statistics for 1921–1941 are available in *Banking and Monetary Statistics*, including the number and deposits of suspended banks, by States and by class of bank, and in the *Federal Reserve Bulletin* for September 1937, pp. 866–910, and December 1937, pp. 1204–1224. The annual reports of the Comptroller of the Currency contain considerable material relating to national banks placed in receivership and losses sustained by depositors and stockholders of national banks.

Comprehensive and dependable statistics on bank suspensions are available only for comparatively recent years, that is, beginning with 1921. Prior to 1921, the figures are useful principally in showing the periods of abnormal banking mortality. Statistics for State banks prior to 1892 are fragmentary and incomplete. While figures for 1892–1920 are believed to be somewhat more reliable than for earlier years, they are not strictly comparable with the figures shown for 1921–1933.

Beginning with 1921, detailed data on the number and deposits of suspended banks were compiled from original reports on bank suspensions. The term "bank suspension" has been defined to comprise all banks closed to the public, either temporarily or permanently, by supervisory authorities or by the banks' boards of directors on account of financial difficulties, whether on a so-called moratorium basis or otherwise, unless the closing was under a special banking holiday declared by civil authorities. In the latter case, if the bank remained closed only during such holiday, it was not counted as a suspension. Banks which, without actually closing, merged with other banks or obtained agreements with depositors to waive or to defer withdrawal of a portion of their deposits likewise were not counted as suspended.

The figures for number of suspended banks for 1933 are not wholly comparable with those for other years. It was difficult in that year to determine the status of some banks because of the changes brought about by the State and national banking

holidays and the subsequent reorganization of the banking system. The 1933 figures comprise banks suspended before the banking holiday, licensed banks suspended or placed on a restricted basis following the banking holiday, unlicensed banks placed in liquidation or receivership, and all other unlicensed banks which were not granted licenses to reopen by June 30, 1933. This date was selected because by that time supervisory authorities had completed their examination of practically all the banks not granted licenses immediately following the banking holiday, and had authorized the reopening of banks that could qualify for licenses. Since 1933, suspensions of insured banks have been handled by the Federal Deposit Insurance Corporation.

Deposits for suspended banks are as of the date of suspension for member banks of the Federal Reserve System and for nonmember banks, as of the date of suspension or latest available call date prior thereto, with the exception of unlicensed banks included for 1933. Deposits of unlicensed banks included in suspensions for 1933 are (*a*) for national banks, as of the date of conservatorship; (*b*) for State member banks, as of June 30, 1933, or the nearest call date prior to liquidation or receivership; and (*c*) for nonmember banks, the latest figures available at the time the banks were reported as having been placed in liquidation or receivership, or (for those which later reopened) as of the date license was granted to reopen.

Methods used in deriving the figures for losses borne by depositors (series X 179) for the periods 1865–1880, 1881–1900, and 1901–1920, are described in Federal Deposit Insurance Corporation, *Annual Report, 1940*, pp. 61–73.

X 180–191. Banks closed because of financial difficulties, 1934–1957.

Source: Federal Deposit Insurance Corporation, *Annual Report, 1957*, pp. 146, 150, and records.

The Federal Deposit Insurance Corporation has used two procedures in fulfilling its responsibility to protect bank depositors from loss. It has paid depositors of insured banks placed in receivership up to the maximum limit prescribed by law and it has made loans to, or purchased assets of, financially distressed banks, thereby facilitating assumption of their deposits by another insured bank. The assumption of deposits by another bank enables business to continue with little or no deviation from normal routine, whereas a receivership may disrupt the economic life of the community.

Deposit figures at date of closing are adjusted to reflect subsequent corrections. In the case of banks placed in receivership, deposits at date of closing may be changed to include deposits discovered or reclassified after that date.

Data for losses to depositors in noninsured banks are not available.

X 192–215. General note.

The earliest available bank earnings data on a nationwide basis are those for national banks beginning in 1869. National banks were required to make earnings reports for the years 1869–1871 whenever dividends were declared; for 1872–1916, at least semiannually whether dividends were declared or not declared; and beginning with 1917, for the periods ending in June and December. At first the report form included only cash dividends declared, net profits, and a few related items, but it became progressively more detailed and more comprehensive. Beginning with 1917 a breakdown as to the sources and disposition of earnings has been required.

X 192–199. National banks—earnings and expenses, 1869–1957.

Source: 1869–1941, see first source cited for series X 155–164, pp. 260–261; 1942–1957, Comptroller of the Currency, *Annual Report, 1943*, pp. 30–31; *1946*, pp. 98–99; *1949*, pp. 100–102; *1952*, pp. 124–126; *1955*, pp. 150–152; *1958*, pp. 147–149.

More detailed data are available for 1919–1941 for all Federal Reserve member banks (national and State member banks combined) in *Banking and Monetary Statistics*, pp. 262–265, and thereafter in various issues of the *Federal Reserve Bulletin*. For example, earnings and expenses are available by type; recoveries and profits, losses and charge-offs, and transfers to and from valuation reserves (beginning in 1948) are shown by character of asset. Data are also available for banks grouped by Federal Reserve District, State, class of bank, and size of bank. Various earnings ratios are available for part of the period.

The figures for gross and net current earnings before 1927 include profits on securities sold; such profits during the second half of 1926, when first reported separately, were $17,388,000. The figures for gross and net earnings up to and including the fiscal year ending June 1919 also include recoveries on charged-off assets; such recoveries in the fiscal year ending June 30, 1919, were $21,066,000. Beginning in 1927 and 1919, respectively, these items are included in series X 196, which is the excess of total losses, charge-offs (including depreciation), and transfers to reserve accounts over total recoveries, profits, and transfers from reserve accounts, or vice versa.

X 200–215. Insured commercial banks—earnings and expenses, 1934–1957.

Source: 1934–1941, Federal Deposit Insurance Corporation, *Annual Report, 1941*, pp. 158–159 (except ratio of net profits to capital accounts which are from FDIC records); 1942–1957, *Annual Report, 1950*, pp. 250–251; *1955*, pp. 134–135; *1957*, pp. 118–120.

For a definition of commercial banks, see general note for series X 1–265 and especially text for series X 91–96 and X 97–118.

More detailed data than are shown here are available in the source. See description of additional data available for national and other Federal Reserve member banks in the text for series X 192–199.

Reports of earnings, expenses, and dividends are submitted to the Federal supervisory agencies on either a cash or an accrual basis. For national banks and for State banks in the District of Columbia, not members of the Federal Reserve System, the data are collected by the Comptroller of the Currency; for State bank members of the Federal Reserve System, by the Board of Governors of the Federal Reserve System; for other insured banks, by the Federal Deposit Insurance Corporation.

Earnings data are included for all insured banks operating at the end of the respective years, unless indicated otherwise. Appropriate adjustments have been made for banks in operation during part of the year but not at the end of the year.

Series X 211 is the excess of total losses, charge-offs, and transfers to reserve accounts over total recoveries, profits, and transfers from reserve accounts, or vice versa.

X 216–255. General note.

Deposits in commercial banks are the major portion of the current means of payment. The extent to which such deposits are used is measured by statistics of bank debits. In conjunction with deposit figures, debits figures are a means of determining the rate of turnover of deposits in commercial banks. While these two measurements throw light upon current economic developments, the data must be used with care to measure changes in business conditions. Since factors not related to business activity may affect debits and deposits,

these data reflect changes in general business conditions only in a broad way.

X 216–219. Bank debits to deposit accounts, except interbank accounts, at reporting centers, 1919–1952.

Source: 1919–1941, see first source cited for series X 155–164, pp. 234–237; 1942–1952, *Federal Reserve Bulletin*, June 1946, p. 630; June 1951, p. 665; and June 1953, p. 612.

Data for individual reporting centers, by months, for 1919–1941, are available in *Banking and Monetary Statistics*; for 1942–1952, they are available upon request from the Board of Governors of the Federal Reserve System.

Figures represent debits or charges on books of reporting member and nonmember commercial banks to deposit accounts of individuals, partnerships, and corporations, the U.S. Government, and State, county, and municipal governments, including debits to time and savings accounts, payments from trust funds on deposit in the banking department, and payments of certificates of deposit. Debits to accounts of other banks or in settlement of clearinghouse balances, payment of certified and officers' checks, charges to expense and miscellaneous accounts, corrections, and similar charges are not included. For a more detailed description of the data, see *Banking and Monetary Statistics*, pp. 230–233, and George Garvy, *Development of Bank Debits and Clearings and Their Use in Economic Analysis*, published in 1952 by the Board of Governors of the Federal Reserve System, especially chap. III, pp. 27–48.

Satisfactory figures are available for New York City and 140 other reporting centers, but the number of other reporting centers, and consequently the total number of all reporting centers, increased substantially for 1919–1952. (For details, see *Banking and Monetary Statistics*, p. 231, and *Federal Reserve Bulletin*, May 1952, p. 514.)

Beginning with March 1953, the Board of Governors of the Federal Reserve System has published a revised monthly bank debits series comprising only debits to demand deposit accounts of individuals, partnerships, and corporations, and of States and political subdivisions. This series, which classifies reporting centers into 3 groups—New York City, 6 other centers, and 338 centers—is a better measure of the activity of checking accounts than the discontinued series presented here. Monthly data on debits and annual turnover for the period beginning in 1943 are available in the *Federal Reserve Bulletin*, including a seasonally adjusted series for turnover.

X 220–225. Bank debits and deposit turnover, at all commercial banks, 1919–1941.

Source: See first source cited for series X 155–164, p. 254.

For a definition of debits, see text for series X 216–219. The annual rate of turnover of deposits is obtained by dividing the total volume of debits for a year by the average amount of deposits during the same period. Figures shown here are in part estimated; for a description of these series, see source, p. 232.

X 226–229. Bank clearings at principal cities, 1854–1956.

Source: 1854–1881, Comptroller of the Currency, *Annual Report, 1920*, vol. 2, p. 849; 1882–1955 (except as noted below for series X 229), Department of Commerce, *Statistical Abstract of the United States, 1937*, p. 268; *1947*, p. 444; *1951*, p. 384; *1954*, p. 447; *1956*, p. 429. **Series X 229**, 1920–1936, *Statistical Abstract, 1938*, p. 275; 1956, *Commercial and Financial Chronicle*, New York, January 14, 1957.

The Comptroller of the Currency, *Annual Report, 1920*, vol. 2, p. 849, gives for New York the number of banks, capital, clearings, balances, average daily clearings, and average daily balances, for years ending September 30, 1854–1920.

For 1882–1919, figures are for all cities reporting to New York Clearing House Association and cover years ending September 30. Beginning 1920, all figures are for calendar years. For 1920–1935, series X 228 is for 146 identical cities. The comparability of figures over the years is affected by (a) changes in the number of cities reporting and (b) the tendency toward consolidation of banks, eliminating former clearings between two or more banks. The source volume suggests that bank debits, series X 216–219, are a better measure of volume of payment.

X 230–237. Number of depositors and savings deposits, by class of bank, 1910–1942.

Source: Bureau of the Census, *Statistical Abstract of the United States, 1946*, p. 404.

These data were originally furnished by the American Bankers Association, which discontinued this series after 1942. Savings and other time deposits include deposits evidenced by savings passbooks, time certificates of deposit payable in 30 days or over, time deposits (open account), postal savings redeposited in banks, and for some States, Christmas savings and similar accounts.

Series X 232 and 236 include commercial, stock savings, and private banks and trust companies. Data shown for some of the years for these banks are incomplete for some States or have been estimated for others. Figures exclude 6 States in 1926 and 1927, 4 in 1928–1930, 3 in 1931, 2 in 1932 and 1933, and 1 in 1934–1937. For 1929–1942, depositors at national banks are represented by the number of savings passbook accounts.

The amounts of savings and other time deposits shown in series X 234–237 differ from and are less reliable than similar figures shown in series X 36, X 58, and X 80. The series on time and savings deposits by class of bank, presented earlier, generally provide a more complete coverage of banks and probably are more consistent with respect to deposits included than the series shown here.

X 238–239. Number of depositors and savings deposits in savings banks, 1820–1910.

Source: 1820–1896, Comptroller of the Currency, *Annual Report, 1896*, vol. I, p. 720; 1897–1910, *Annual Report, 1920*, vol. 1, p. 241.

Data include both mutual and stock savings banks. Figures for savings deposits in series X 239 differ from those in series X 234–237; the latter are based on savings and other time deposits in national and State banks, whereas series X 239 covers mutual and stock savings banks only. Also series X 234–237 are based on reports voluntarily submitted by banks to the American Bankers Association. This may result in different coverage of banks and of deposit figures.

X 240–244. Postal Savings System, 1911–1957.

Source: Post Office Department, *Annual Report of the Postmaster General, 1957*, p. 142, and records.

Data are for fiscal years since the inception of the Postal Savings System.

X 245–265. General note.

For purposes of administering the Federal Reserve System, the country is divided into 12 districts. There is a Federal Reserve bank in each district and most have one or more branches. Federal Reserve banks are organized as Federal corporations with capital stock subscribed by member banks in the respective districts. Member banks include all national banks and those State banks which have voluntarily requested membership and have met the requirements for joining the System. The number and total assets of national and State

member banks are shown separately in series X 119–122 and for the two groups combined in series X 133–134.

The Federal Reserve banks are the principal medium through which the credit policies and general supervisory powers of the Federal Reserve authorities are carried out; they hold the legal reserves of member banks and perform for member banks many services related to those that commercial banks perform for the public, such as furnishing currency for circulation, facilitating the collection and clearance of checks, and providing discount facilities. The Reserve banks also act as fiscal agents, depositaries, and custodians for the U.S. Treasury and other Government units and perform numerous other important functions. The Federal Reserve banks are coordinated and supervised by the Board of Governors of the Federal Reserve System.

X 245–254. Federal Reserve banks—principal assets and liabilities, 1914–1957.

Source: 1914–1941, Board of Governors of the Federal Reserve System, *Banking and Monetary Statistics*, pp. 330–332; 1942–1957, *Annual Report*, various issues.

Complete and detailed balance sheets for all Federal Reserve banks combined and for each bank are included in the source.

Since 1934, the reserves of the Federal Reserve banks have consisted principally of the gold certificate account, which is backed dollar for dollar by gold in the Treasury. The supply of these reserves is dependent primarily upon the size of the monetary gold stock, or more precisely upon that part of the gold stock against which the Treasury has issued gold certificates or gold certificate credits. For a discussion of changes in the items affecting the reserves of Federal Reserve banks, 1914–1934, see *Banking and Monetary Statistics*, p. 325.

Deposits of Federal Reserve banks consist mainly of reserves of member banks, shown in series X 252. They also include the checking account of the U.S. Treasurer, deposits of foreign banks and governments, and other accounts, such as accounts of certain nonmember banks maintained for use in clearing and collecting checks and checking accounts of Government agencies. For further description of the items included in this table, see *Banking and Monetary Statistics*, pp. 324–329, and *Federal Reserve System—Purposes and Functions*, chap. XIII, pp. 173–190.

For statistical series presenting Federal Reserve balance-sheet i'ems and monetary data related to member bank reserves, see *Banking and Monetary Statistics*, pp. 360–401; *Federal Reserve System—Purposes and Functions*, chap. VIII, pp. 107–119; and the opening pages of the tabular section of *Federal Reserve Bulletin*, for example, February 1958, pp. 147–149.

X 255–261. Federal Reserve banks—earnings and expenses, 1914–1957.

Source: Board of Governors of the Federal Reserve System, *Annual Report, 1957*, pp. 94–95.

Federal Reserve banks are not operated for profit but they are self-supporting. The nature and the amount of Reserve bank earnings depend largely upon the demand for Reserve bank credit on the part of the member banks and upon Federal Reserve policy as to open-market operations. Most of the expenses of the Reserve banks are incurred in collecting checks, supplying currency, and performing other services from which no earnings are derived.

Until 1933, the law required that the net earnings of the Federal Reserve banks, after deduction of the annual 6 percent cumulative dividend on paid-in capital stock, be allocated to surplus and to a franchise tax paid to the U.S. Government. In 1933, Congress abolished the franchise tax at a time when

Reserve bank earnings were small and after Congress had directed the Reserve banks to contribute half of their surplus to the capital of the Federal Deposit Insurance Corporation. In 1947, when Reserve bank earnings were once more large, the Federal Reserve adopted the procedure by which it pays to the Treasury nine-tenths of its earnings above expenses and dividends as interest on Federal Reserve notes. The remaining one-tenth is added to the surplus of the banks.

X 262–265. Federal Reserve banks—member bank reserve requirements, 1917–1957.

Source: Board of Governors of the Federal Reserve System, *Federal Reserve Bulletin*, January 1958, p. 34.

These data represent minimum reserve requirements as specified by law (amendment to the Federal Reserve Act effective June 21, 1917). Since 1935, the Board of Governors of the Federal Reserve System has been authorized to increase, at its discretion, the minimum statutory requirements up to double the percentages as authorized in the 1917 amendment to the Federal Reserve Act.

The Federal Reserve Act as approved December 23, 1913, provided for temporary reserve requirements for member banks to be effective for a period of approximately 3 years. These requirements authorized member banks to hold a part of their reserves as cash in their own vaults and a part on deposit with other banks. For a fuller discussion of these requirements and the 1917 amendment of the Federal Reserve Act, see *Federal Reserve Bulletin*, November 1938, pp. 957–959. Since June 21, 1917, only balances with Reserve banks have counted as legal reserves.

Net demand deposits are demand deposits subject to reserve requirements. In general, prior to April 24, 1917, net demand deposits were made up of (*a*) the gross amount of all demand deposits except those due to other banks, and (*b*) the net excess (if any) of demand deposits due to other banks over demand balances due from other banks and cash items in process of collection. From April 24, 1917, to August 23, 1935, the definition was substantially the same, except that U.S. Government deposits were exempt by law from all reserve requirements and were therefore excluded from net demand deposits. Beginning August 23, 1935, net demand deposits have been total demand deposits minus cash items in process of collection and demand balances due from domestic banks (also minus war loan and series E bond accounts during the period April 13, 1943–June 30, 1947).

A list of the cities classified as "central reserve" and "reserve" for 1914–1941, is shown in *Banking and Monetary Statistics*, p. 401, and thereafter in the *Member Bank Call Report*.

Series X 1-5.   State Banks—Number of Banks and Assets and Liabilities: 1811 to 1830

[Money figures in millions of dollars.   As of January 1]

Year	Number of banks	Capital	Circulation	Deposits	Specie
	1	2	3	4	5
1830	329	110.2	48.3	40.8	14.9
1820	307	102.1	40.6	31.2	16.7
1816	246	89.8	68.0	--------	19.0
1815	208	82.3	45.5	--------	17.0
1811	88	42.6	22.7	--------	9.6

Series X 6-19.   Second Bank of the United States—Resources, Liabilities, and Profits: 1817 to 1840

[In thousands of dollars, except series X 17, where figures in parenthesis are in millions.   Resources and liabilities as of January 1]

| | Resources | | | | | | | Liabilities | | | | | Profits | | | |
| | | | | | | | | | | | | | Six months ending January | | Six months ending July | |
Year	Loans and discounts	Stocks	Real estate	Banking houses	Due from State and foreign banks	Notes of State banks	Specie	Capital	Circulation	Deposits	Due to State and foreign banks, etc. [1]	Other liabilities [1]	Amount	Dividend rate (percent)	Amount	Dividend rate (percent)
	6	7	8	9	10	11	12	13	14	15	16	17	18	19	18	19
1840	36,840	16,316	1,229	611	7,469	1,384	1,470	35,000	6,696	3,339	9,127	8,119	------	------	------	------
1839	41,619	17,957	1,055	424	5,833	1,792	4,154	35,000	5,983	6,779	15,832	9,260	------	------	------	------
1838	45,257	14,862	1,062	443	3,657	867	3,771	35,000	6,768	2,617	17,449	7,987	------	------	------	------
1837	57,394	--------	817	420	2,285	1,207	2,638	35,000	11,448	2,332	9,211	(6.8)	------	------	------	------
1836	59,232	--------	1,487	967	4,161	1,736	8,418	35,000	23,075	5,061	2,661	(10.1)	------	------	------	------
1835	51,809	--------	1,761	1,219	6,532	1,506	15,708	35,000	17,340	11,757	3,119	(11.3)	------	------	------	------
1834	54,911	--------	1,741	1,189	4,861	1,983	10,039	35,000	19,208	10,839	1,522	(8.2)	1,430	3.50	1,498	3.50
1833	61,696	--------	1,855	1,181	6,795	2,293	8,952	35,000	17,518	20,348	2,092	(8.0)	1,594	3.50	1,602	3.50
1832	66,294	2	2,137	1,160	4,037	2,172	7,038	35,000	21,356	22,761	1,951	(1.6)	1,716	3.50	1,861	3.50
1831	44,032	8,675	2,629	1,345	2,383	1,495	10,808	35,000	16,251	17,297	735	(2.0)	1,345	3.50	1,590	3.50
1830	40,664	11,610	2,886	1,445	2,730	1,465	7,608	35,000	12,924	16,046	--------	(4.5)	1,392	3.50	1,414	3.50
1829	39,220	16,099	2,346	1,557	2,206	1,294	6,098	35,000	11,902	17,062	1,448	(3.4)	1,325	3.50	1,381	3.50
1828	33,683	17,625	2,295	1,634	357	1,447	6,170	35,000	9,856	14,497	3,165	(.6)	1,203	3.00	1,349	3.50
1827	30,938	17,764	2,089	1,678	2,144	1,068	6,457	35,000	8,549	14,320	280	(4.1)	1,148	3.00	1,274	3.00
1826	33,425	18,304	1,848	1,793	1,169	1,115	3,960	35,000	9,475	11,215	251	(5.5)	1,162	2.75	1,218	3.00
1825	31,813	18,422	1,495	1,853	2,154	1,056	6,747	35,000	6,068	12,033	2,407	(8.0)	1,031	2.50	1,155	2.75
1824	33,432	10,874	1,303	1,872	2,722	705	5,814	35,000	4,647	13,702	1,020	(2.4)	929	2.50	977	2.50
1823	30,736	11,019	627	1,957	1,432	766	4,425	35,000	4,361	7,622	1,293	(2.6)	884	2.50	932	2.50
1822	28,061	13,319	563	1,856	2,825	918	4,761	35,000	5,579	8,075	2,040	(1.7)	719	2.00	1,010	2.25
1821	30,905	9,156	--------	1,887	1,262	677	7,643	35,000	4,567	8,075	2,053	(2.0)	734	(2)	750	1.50
1820	31,401	7,193	--------	1,297	2,989	1,443	3,393	35,000	3,589	6,569	2,054	(.5)	785	(2)	719	(2)
1819	35,786	7,392	--------	434	3,246	1,878	2,667	35,000	6,564	5,793	1,434	(2.6)	899	2.50	983	(2)
1818	41,182	9,476	--------	175	2,238	1,837	2,516	35,000	8,339	12,279	1,358	(.4)	1,382	4.00	1,266	3.50
1817	[3]13,485	4,829	--------	--------	8,848	587	1,724	35,000	1,911	11,233	--------	--------	--------	--------	1,022	2.60

[1] Comptroller of the Currency, *Annual Report, 1916*, pp. 912–913, shows somewhat different figures as follows (in millions of dollars): Series X 16—1840, 17.3; 1839, 25.1; 1838, 25.5.   Series X 17—1840, 3.0; 1839, no entry; 1838, 0.2.
[2] Carried to contingent fund.

[3] Comptroller of the Currency, *Annual Report, 1916*, p. 912, shows $32.2 million; *American State Papers, Finance*, vol. 3, p. 353, shows $32.4 million as of "last of October."

Series X 20-41.   All Banks—Number of Banks and Principal Assets and Liabilities: 1834 to 1957

[Money figures in millions of dollars.   As of June 30 or nearest available date]

| | | | Assets | | | | | | | | | |
| | | | Loans [1] | | | Investments | | | | Cash | |
Year	Number of banks	Total assets or liabilities	Total	Real estate	Other	Total	U.S. Government obligations	Obligations of States and political subdivisions	Other	Total	Cash items in process of collection
	20	21	22	23	24	25	26	27	28	29	30
1957	14,142	242,629	111,509	42,909	70,462	85,942	64,540	13,993	7,409	40,831	8,953
1956	14,205	238,128	105,523	40,395	66,697	85,547	64,915	13,596	7,035	43,360	11,106
1955	14,308	229,626	91,353	35,951	56,731	92,897	71,946	13,440	7,511	42,013	9,799
1954	14,464	218,896	81,225	31,108	51,293	92,115	72,524	12,463	7,128	42,555	8,911
1953	14,533	207,760	77,117	28,343	49,890	85,965	68,109	10,911	6,945	42,024	8,854
1952	14,598	201,795	69,742	25,573	45,201	87,786	70,784	10,078	6,924	41,668	8,655
1951	14,636	188,338	63,841	23,281	41,521	83,901	68,726	8,595	6,580	38,236	7,439
1950	14,676	179,165	52,001	19,740	33,098	90,962	77,322	7,477	6,163	34,101	6,843
1949	14,681	170,810	47,078	17,197	30,565	86,794	74,879	6,005	5,910	34,967	6,121
1948	14,721	170,052	45,100	15,590	30,062	87,982	76,774	5,668	5,540	35,000	6,054
1947	14,715	166,336	38,365	12,911	25,454	92,729	82,673	5,029	5,027	33,544	5,848
1946	14,685	171,529	31,506	10,126	21,380	105,163	95,969	4,173	5,021	33,163	5,268
1945	14,660	162,169	27,996	8,740	19,256	101,724	93,708	3,880	4,136	30,740	3,412
1944	14,674	138,842	25,435	8,797	16,638	83,329	75,775	3,628	3,926	28,195	4,136
1943	14,734	116,729	22,248	9,155	13,093	65,674	57,774	3,751	4,149	26,696	3,560
1942	14,891	91,930	25,063	9,617	15,446	38,954	30,320	3,952	4,682	25,595	2,701
1941	14,975	87,324	25,273	9,599	15,674	32,667	23,559	4,206	4,902	26,785	2,527

See footnotes at end of table.

Series X 20–41. All Banks—Number of Banks and Principal Assets and Liabilities: 1834 to 1957—Con.

[Money figures in millions of dollars]

Year	Number of banks	Total assets or liabilities	Loans[1] Total	Real estate	Other	Investments Total	U.S. Government obligations	Obligations of States and political subdivisions	Other	Cash Total	Cash items in process of collection
	20	21	22	23	24	25	26	27	28	29	30
1940	15,076	79,729	22,311	9,227	13,084	29,040	19,705	4,161	5,174	25,603	1,607
1939	15,210	73,193	21,300	8,911	12,389	28,339	18,779	3,932	5,628	20,550	2,256
1938	15,419	67,730	21,033	8,689	12,344	26,267	16,761	3,483	6,023	17,374	1,958
1937	15,646	68,402	22,435	8,610	13,825	27,212	16,983	3,592	6,687	15,520	2,262
1936	15,884	66,854	20,640	8,487	12,153	27,857	17,392	3,646	6,819	15,038	2,208
1935	16,047	59,951	20,240	8,691	11,549	24,176	14,316	3,555	6,305	12,318	1,230
1934	15,913	55,915	21,309	9,141	12,168	21,262	11,308	3,256	6,698	10,158	1,102
1933	14,771	51,359	22,337	9,954	12,383	18,125	8,229	3,178	6,718	7,793	1,510
1932	19,317	57,295	28,071	10,857	17,214	18,406	6,937	3,256	8,213	7,407	1,376
1931	22,242	70,070	35,416	11,626	23,790	19,973	6,601	3,472	9,900	10,405	2,531
1930	24,273	74,290	40,990	11,780	29,210	18,090	5,373	3,031	9,686	11,201	3,663
1929	25,568	72,315	41,944	11,796	30,148	17,305	5,477	2,860	8,968	9,222	2,397
1928	26,401	71,121	39,946	11,364	28,582	18,146	5,671	2,898	9,577	9,454	2,413
1927	27,255	67,893	37,949	10,752	27,197	16,649	5,345	2,740	8,564	10,156	2,894
1926	28,350	65,079	36,658	10,105	26,553	15,562	5,384	2,481	7,697	9,806	2,687
1925	29,052	62,232	34,378	9,196	25,182	15,056	5,529	2,235	7,292	9,903	2,758
1924	29,601	57,420	32,030	8,239	23,791	13,843	5,381	2,060	6,402	9,034	2,508
1923	30,444	54,144	30,734	7,329	23,405	13,474	5,715	1,852	5,907	7,595	1,680
1922	30,736	50,368	28,000	6,386	21,614	12,328	4,818	1,843	5,667	7,830	1,991
1921	31,076	49,633	29,236	5,857	23,379	11,169	4,201	1,723	5,245	6,980	1,669
1920	30,909	53,094	31,189	5,516	25,673	11,043	4,420	1,594	5,029	8,489	2,010
1919	29,767	47,603	25,132	4,709	20,423	12,024	5,425	1,695	4,904	8,286	1,740
1918	29,480	41,097	22,863	4,578	18,285	9,609	3,243	1,708	4,658	6,837	872
1917	28,919	37,540	20,902	4,504	16,398	7,925	1,349	1,727	4,849	7,250	771
1916	28,362	32,697	18,263	4,108	14,155	6,833	753	1,638	4,442	6,385	778
1915	28,017	28,363	15,976	3,875	12,101	5,982	778	1,477	3,727	5,300	435
1914	27,864	27,349	15,502	3,678	11,824	5,701	793	1,407	3,501	5,125	590
1913	27,285	26,103	14,821	3,590	11,231	5,500	783	1,340	3,377	4,853	491
1912	26,472	25,372	14,124	3,354	10,770	5,440	787	1,280	3,373	4,925	496
1911	25,815	24,026	13,228	3,084	10,144	5,136	755	1,224	3,157	4,842	520
1910	25,151	22,922	12,766	2,892	9,874	4,839	750	1,173	2,916	4,543	758
1909	23,734	21,489	11,548	2,548	9,000	4,746	747	1,131	2,868	4,499	566
1908	23,161	19,946	10,763	2,430	8,333	4,456	722	1,017	2,717	4,043	432
1907	21,986	20,114	11,319	2,393	8,926	4,284	636	1,001	2,647	3,848	488
1906	20,407	18,740	10,442	2,228	8,214	4,080	620	973	2,487	3,635	520
1905	18,767	17,511	9,540	1,991	7,549	3,974	600	959	2,415	3,455	446
1904	17,659	15,848	8,545	1,805	6,740	3,595	600	916	2,079	3,202	292
1903	16,433	14,901	8,257	1,697	6,560	3,341	588	875	1,878	2,828	347
1902	15,112	14,026	7,664	1,564	6,100	3,098	579	823	1,696	2,855	378
1901	14,054	13,037	6,914	1,445	5,469	2,891	603	785	1,503	2,866	522
1900	13,053	11,388	6,093	1,342	4,751	2,544	611	736	1,197	2,395	277
1899	12,459	10,679	5,689	1,261	4,428	2,254	574	718	962	2,382	340
1898	12,163	9,218	4,976	1,197	3,779	1,970	533	673	764	1,914	152
1897	12,079	8,432	4,596	1,169	3,427	1,802	514	621	667	1,703	154
1896[2]	12,112	8,048	4,615	1,164	3,451	1,689	506	584	599	1,421	136

Year	Number of banks[3]	Total assets or liabilities	Total loans[1]	Total investments	Total cash[3]
	20	21	22	25	29
1896[4]	9,469	7,554	4,251	1,675	1,266
1895	9,818	7,610	4,269	1,565	1,442
1894	9,508	7,291	4,085	1,445	1,473
1893	9,492	7,192	4,369	1,366	1,190
1892	9,336	7,245	4,337	1,284	1,378
1891	8,641	6,562	4,031	1,179	1,125
1890	8,201	6,358	3,854	1,173	1,123
1889	7,244	5,945	3,478	1,129	1,144
1888	6,647	5,471	3,161	1,131	989
1887	6,170	5,193	2,943	1,011	999
1886	4,338	4,542	2,434	1,052	773
1885	4,350	4,427	2,272	1,042	876
1884	4,113	4,221	2,261	1,041	678
1883	3,835	4,208	2,234	1,028	712
1882	3,572	4,031	2,051	1,055	755
1881	3,427	3,869	1,902	985	782
1880	3,355	3,399	1,662	904	655
1879	3,335	3,313	1,507	1,139	505
1878	3,229	3,081	1,561	875	493
1877	3,384	3,204	1,721	852	483
1876	3,448	3,183	1,727	818	503
1875	3,336	3,205	1,748	802	527
1874	[5]3,552	2,891	1,564	732	510
1873	[5]3,298	2,731	1,440	721	487
1872[6]	2,419	2,145	1,123	480	490
1871[6]	2,175	2,003	990	479	485
1870[6]	1,937	1,781	864	470	406
1869[6]	1,878	1,736	801	480	418
1868[6]	1,887	1,736	766	520	418
1867[6]	1,908	1,674	709	536	398
1866[6]	1,931	1,673	682	483	480

Year	Number of banks[3]	Total assets or liabilities	Total loans[1]	Total investments	Total cash[3]
	20	21	22	25	29
1865[6]	1,643	1,357	518	412	392
1864[6]	1,556	973	555	150	236
1863	1,532	1,209	654	186	307
1862	1,492	1,012	647	99	221
1861	1,601	1,016	697	74	198
1860	1,562	1,000	692	70	196
1859	1,476	983	657	64	229
1858	1,422	849	583	60	170
1857	1,416	953	684	59	177
1856	1,398	880	634	49	167
1855	1,307	817	576	53	155
1854	1,208	795	557	44	163
1853[7]	750	577	409	22	127
1852[8]	913	620	430	23	137
1851	879	597	414	22	132
1850	824	532	364	21	115
1849	782	479	332	24	97
1848	751	512	345	27	112
1847	715	458	310	20	94
1846	707	456	312	22	95
1845	707	434	289	20	93
1844	696	427	265	23	104
1843	691	393	255	28	74
1842	692	472	324	25	82
1841	784	608	387	65	112
1840	901	658	463	42	99
1839	840	702	492	36	129
1838	829	682	486	34	119
1837	788	707	525	12	140
1836	713	622	458	12	129
1835	704	498	365	9	108
1834	506	419	324	6	76

See footnotes at end of table.

Series X 20–41. All Banks—Number of Banks and Principal Assets and Liabilities: 1834 to 1957—Con.

[Money figures in millions of dollars]

Year	Assets—Con. Cash—Con. Currency and coin	Assets—Con. Cash—Con. Bankers' balances (including reserves)	Assets—Con. Cash—Con. Other	Liabilities Deposits Total	Liabilities Deposits Interbank	Liabilities Deposits U.S. Government	Liabilities Deposits Other demand	Liabilities Deposits Other time	Liabilities Bank-notes [9]	Liabilities Capital accounts	Liabilities Other
	31	32	33	34	35	36	37	38	39	40	41
1957	2,843	29,036	4,347	216,970	14,423	3,625	114,653	84,270	----------	19,878	5,782
1956	2,382	29,871	3,698	215,504	15,242	5,536	115,848	78,878	----------	18,811	3,812
1955	2,800	29,414	3,363	208,845	15,245	5,417	113,032	75,151	----------	17,663	3,118
1954	2,777	30,867	3,001	199,505	15,500	5,895	107,042	71,068	----------	16,664	2,727
1953	2,699	30,471	2,654	189,176	13,601	3,942	105,769	65,864	----------	15,791	2,793
1952	2,497	30,516	2,599	184,147	13,513	6,121	103,426	61,087	----------	15,038	2,610
1951	1,972	28,825	2,360	171,879	11,947	6,332	96,417	57,183	----------	14,235	2,224
1950	1,919	25,339	2,101	163,789	11,436	3,801	91,900	56,652	----------	13,577	1,799
1949	2,169	26,677	1,971	156,488	10,938	2,304	88,015	55,231	----------	12,846	1,476
1948	2,195	26,751	1,970	156,373	11,436	2,180	88,769	53,988	----------	12,239	1,440
1947	1,934	25,762	1,698	153,375	11,682	1,367	88,044	52,282	----------	11,719	1,242
1946	1,594	26,301	1,697	159,293	12,309	13,415	84,838	48,731	----------	11,104	1,132
1945	1,586	25,742	1,709	151,128	12,587	24,385	72,535	41,621	----------	10,126	915
1944	1,576	22,483	1,883	128,684	11,201	19,512	64,262	33,709	----------	9,333	825
1943	1,563	21,573	2,111	107,297	10,888	8,027	59,667	28,715	----------	8,765	667
1942	1,413	21,481	2,318	82,765	10,278	1,837	44,614	26,036	----------	8,500	665
1941	1,366	22,892	2,599	78,212	10,929	748	39,919	26,616	----------	8,441	671
1940	1,111	22,885	2,775	70,854	10,168	824	33,649	26,213	----------	8,252	623
1939	1,014	17,280	3,004	64,303	8,220	788	29,694	25,601	----------	8,236	654
1938	993	14,423	3,056	59,000	6,838	596	26,398	25,168	----------	8,107	623
1937	924	12,334	3,235	59,485	6,337	669	27,582	24,897	----------	8,123	794
1936	994	11,836	3,319	58,068	6,903	1,144	26,100	23,921	----------	8,016	770
1935	772	10,316	3,217	51,270	5,644	820	21,733	23,073	222	7,815	644
1934	691	8,365	3,186	46,480	4,582	1,735	17,798	22,365	695	7,865	875
1933	641	5,642	3,104	41,684	3,467	858	16,022	21,337	727	7,388	1,560
1932	767	5,264	3,411	45,569	3,323	433	17,114	24,699	649	8,525	2,552
1931	851	7,023	4,276	57,187	5,150	447	22,573	29,017	636	9,872	2,375
1930	831	6,707	4,009	60,365	5,129	298	25,658	29,280	649	10,372	2,904
1929	770	6,055	3,844	58,269	3,975	375	25,169	28,750	649	9,750	3,647
1928	797	6,244	3,575	58,138	4,283	274	24,864	28,717	649	8,954	3,380
1927	921	6,341	3,139	56,700	4,528	232	25,265	26,675	650	8,301	2,242
1926	937	6,182	3,053	54,416	4,289	235	25,010	24,882	651	7,841	2,171
1925	920	6,225	2,895	52,301	4,330	182	24,332	23,457	648	7,384	1,899
1924	882	5,644	2,513	47,961	4,246	185	22,076	21,454	729	7,073	1,657
1923	770	5,145	2,341	44,376	3,417	305	20,835	19,819	720	6,818	2,230
1922	807	5,032	2,210	41,227	3,353	158	20,112	17,604	725	6,599	1,817
1921	879	4,432	2,248	38,934	2,904	405	18,934	16,691	704	6,385	3,610
1920	1,038	5,441	2,373	41,838	3,728	261	21,579	16,270	688	6,019	4,549
1919	965	5,581	2,161	37,982	3,949	914	19,285	13,834	677	5,409	3,535
1918	888	5,077	1,788	33,061	3,718	1,542	15,751	12,050	681	5,113	2,242
1917	1,489	4,990	1,463	30,855	4,014	146	15,088	11,607	660	4,988	1,037
1916	1,486	4,121	1,216	26,738	3,511	39	12,921	10,267	676	4,718	565
1915	1,477	3,388	1,105	22,504	2,811	48	10,706	8,939	722	4,643	494
1914	1,636	2,899	1,021	21,665	2,720	66	10,309	8,570	722	4,503	459
1913	1,564	2,798	929	20,523	2,585	49	9,252	8,637	722	4,443	415
1912	1,575	2,854	883	20,013	2,636	58	9,220	8,099	708	4,269	382
1911	1,574	2,748	820	18,860	2,633	48	8,629	7,550	681	4,133	352
1910	1,441	2,344	774	17,950	2,304	54	8,567	7,025	675	3,984	313
1909	1,472	2,461	696	16,883	2,492	70	8,119	6,202	636	3,750	220
1908	1,373	2,238	684	15,440	2,213	130	7,382	5,715	613	3,627	266
1907	1,141	2,219	663	15,759	2,094	180	7,710	5,775	548	3,492	315
1906	1,052	2,063	583	14,703	1,908	90	7,404	5,301	510	3,285	242
1905	1,018	1,991	542	13,772	1,909	75	6,899	4,889	445	3,066	228
1904	1,031	1,879	506	12,341	1,756	110	6,058	4,417	399	2,935	173
1903	881	1,600	475	11,612	1,479	147	5,772	4,214	359	2,760	170
1902	878	1,599	409	11,103	1,498	124	5,541	3,940	309	2,473	141
1901	848	1,496	366	10,374	1,437	99	5,279	3,559	319	2,200	144
1900	774	1,344	356	8,922	1,261	99	4,346	3,216	265	2,075	126
1899	749	1,293	354	8,472	1,126	76	4,295	2,975	199	1,907	101
1898	717	1,045	358	7,044	872	53	3,431	2,688	190	1,878	106
1897	655	894	331	6,270	726	16	2,999	2,529	197	1,877	88
1896 [2]	568	717	323	5,859	571	15	2,844	2,429	199	1,893	97

Year	Total deposits [3] (34)	Bank-notes [9] (39)	Capital accounts [3] (40)
1896 [4]	5,486	199	1,746
1895	5,539	179	1,780
1894	5,268	172	1,753
1893	5,065	155	1,781
1892	5,298	141	1,721
1891	4,683	124	1,649
1890	4,576	126	1,558
1889	4,311	129	1,428
1888	3,891	156	1,348
1887	3,719	167	1,259
1886	3,186	245	1,076
1885	3,078	269	1,040
1884	2,849	295	1,036
1883	2,884	312	973
1882	2,777	309	901
1881	2,649	313	864

Year	Total deposits [3] (34)	Bank-notes [9] (39)	Capital accounts [3] (40)
1880	2,222	318	826
1879	2,149	308	827
1878	1,921	300	826
1877	2,006	290	875
1876	1,993	295	864
1875	2,009	318	847
1874	1,740	339	789
1873	1,625	339	749
1872	927	405	748
1871	888	370	706
1870	775	336	648
1869	772	329	616
1868	798	329	596
1867	744	329	578
1866	759	309	560
1865	689	180	452

Year	Total deposits [3] (34)	Bank-notes [9] (39)	Capital accounts [3] (40)
1864	380	176	391
1863	504	239	412
1862	357	184	418
1861	319	202	430
1860	310	207	422
1859	328	193	402
1858	237	155	395
1857	288	215	371
1856	265	196	344
1855	236	187	332
1854	239	205	301
1853	195	146	208
1852	182	161	237
1851	175	155	228
1850	146	131	217
1849	121	115	207

Year	Total deposits [3] (34)	Bank-notes [9] (39)	Capital accounts [3] (40)
1848	143	129	205
1847	120	106	203
1846	125	106	197
1845	114	90	206
1844	117	75	211
1843	78	59	229
1842	88	84	260
1841	108	107	314
1840	120	107	358
1839	143	135	327
1838	146	116	318
1837	190	149	291
1836	166	140	252
1835	122	104	231
1834	102	95	200

[1] Beginning 1948, figures for loan items are shown gross (i.e., before deduction of valuation reserves); they do not add to the total and are not entirely comparable with prior figures. Total loans continue to be shown as net.

[2] Comparable with later data.

[3] See series X 86–90 for supplementary figures for nonnational banks: Number of banks, 1875–1882; capital accounts, 1875–1882; vault cash, 1875–1896; deposits, 1865–1896.

[4] Comparable with earlier data.

[5] Number of nonnational banks estimated.

[6] For nonnational banks, all figures except number of banks and capital accounts are estimated; see footnote 5, series X 64–85.

[7] Incomplete.

[8] Estimates based on previous 5 years for number of banks and on 10 years 1854–1863 for assets and liabilities.

[9] Includes circulating notes of both State and national banks. For State banknotes in circulation chiefly for 1834–1872, see series X 83, and for more complete figures for this series, 1860–1878, see series X 290, and the source (see p. 645) for that series for figures from 1800–1859. For national banknotes in circulation, 1864–1935, see series X 61.

Series X 42–63.　National Banks—Number of Banks and Principal Assets and Liabilities: 1863 to 1957

[Money figures in millions of dollars.　As of June 30 or nearest available date]

Year	Number of banks	Total assets or liabilities	Loans [1] Total	Loans [1] Real estate	Loans [1] Other	Investments Total [2]	Investments U.S. Government obligations	Investments Obligations of States and political subdivisions	Investments Other	Cash Total	Cash items in process of collection
	42	43	44	45	46	47	48	49	50	51	52
1957	4,645	112,443	48,408	12,019	37,273	39,487	30,337	7,243	1,907	22,522	5,187
1956	4,666	110,697	45,858	11,551	35,035	39,593	30,553	7,079	1,961	23,544	6,175
1955	4,743	107,736	39,422	10,366	29,646	43,890	34,671	7,011	2,208	22,890	5,405
1954	4,834	108,607	37,671	9,109	29,136	44,808	35,757	6,941	2,110	24,635	5,489
1953	4,874	103,418	36,420	8,443	28,517	41,429	32,958	6,209	2,262	24,279	5,547
1952	4,925	101,253	33,054	7,785	25,763	42,982	34,604	5,800	2,578	23,927	5,271
1951	4,946	94,394	30,479	7,224	23,664	40,535	32,965	4,959	2,611	22,198	4,616
1950	4,971	89,691	24,591	6,335	18,593	44,132	37,548	4,288	2,296	19,914	4,334
1949	4,987	84,853	22,505	5,677	17,089	41,012	35,487	3,406	2,119	20,324	3,692
1948	4,998	85,081	22,243	5,250	17,192	41,395	36,092	3,204	2,099	20,415	3,829
1947	5,012	83,149	18,764	4,215	14,549	44,218	39,271	2,898	2,049	19,341	3,558
1946	5,012	85,698	14,469	2,740	11,729	51,809	47,271	2,451	2,087	18,607	3,004
1945	5,015	81,491	12,369	2,077	10,292	50,808	47,051	2,196	1,561	17,544	2,184
1944	5,036	70,143	11,213	2,032	9,181	42,130	38,640	2,029	1,461	15,998	2,509
1943	5,060	58,783	9,173	2,129	7,044	33,632	30,102	2,022	1,508	15,154	2,258
1942	5,101	44,584	10,880	2,237	8,643	18,584	14,878	1,956	1,750	14,274	1,671
1941	5,130	41,228	10,897	2,172	8,725	14,922	11,111	2,016	1,795	14,496	1,512
1940	5,164	36,816	9,156	1,993	7,163	12,882	9,094	1,926	1,862	13,857	980
1939	5,203	33,119	8,553	1,821	6,732	12,528	8,753	1,691	2,084	11,061	1,257
1938	5,242	30,317	8,316	1,621	6,695	11,618	7,973	1,424	2,221	9,438	1,107
1937	5,293	30,272	8,797	1,503	7,294	12,097	8,206	1,462	2,429	8,365	1,284
1936	5,368	29,643	7,749	1,367	6,382	12,459	8,435	1,535	2,489	8,368	1,236
1935	5,425	26,009	7,353	1,293	6,060	10,698	7,164	1,396	2,138	6,857	689
1934	5,417	23,854	7,681	1,326	6,355	9,331	5,847	1,225	2,259	5,688	633
1933	4,897	20,813	8,102	1,322	6,780	7,358	4,026	1,158	2,174	4,110	764
1932	6,145	22,318	10,265	1,612	8,653	7,183	3,347	1,114	2,722	3,480	692
1931	6,800	27,430	13,162	1,580	11,582	7,662	3,251	1,107	3,304	4,988	1,262
1930	7,247	28,828	14,874	1,468	13,406	6,875	2,748	893	3,234	5,408	1,808
1929	7,530	27,260	14,805	1,412	13,393	6,651	2,801	838	3,012	4,279	1,228
1928	7,685	28,265	14,921	1,285	13,636	7,141	2,888	839	3,414	4,738	1,412
1927	7,790	26,455	13,849	1,062	12,787	6,388	2,593	743	3,052	4,978	1,635
1926	7,972	25,202	13,322	725	12,597	5,837	2,466	647	2,724	4,788	1,568
1925	8,066	24,252	12,592	636	11,956	5,701	2,512	594	2,595	4,789	1,605
1924	8,080	22,525	11,955	535	11,420	5,103	2,446	505	2,152	4,455	1,468
1923	8,236	21,454	11,778	463	11,315	5,027	2,655	401	1,971	3,660	1,023
1922	8,244	20,633	11,191	371	10,820	4,514	2,240	414	1,860	3,969	1,251
1921	8,150	20,475	11,976	280	11,696	3,919	1,917	393	1,609	3,535	1,106
1920	8,024	23,267	13,499	230	13,269	4,048	2,137	338	1,573	4,493	1,406
1919	7,779	21,105	10,903	184	10,719	4,809	2,941	322	1,546	4,395	1,183
1918	7,699	18,262	10,077	185	9,892	3,836	2,025	320	1,491	3,570	598
1917	7,599	16,231	8,936	185	8,751	2,961	1,043	315	1,603	3,739	530
1916	7,571	13,920	7,767	161	7,606	2,319	703	278	1,338	3,352	522
1915	7,597	11,790	6,663	151	6,512	2,025	749	245	1,031	2,695	250
1914	7,518	11,477	6,443	114	6,329	1,870	764	176	930	2,770	358
1913	7,467	11,032	6,160	77	6,083	1,845	752	175	918	2,659	295
1912	7,366	10,857	5,972	75	5,897	1,822	745	179	898	2,714	295
1911	7,270	10,378	5,632	65	5,567	1,724	717	164	843	2,691	317
1910	7,138	9,892	5,454	65	5,389	1,575	712	149	714	2,549	483
1909	6,886	9,365	4,986	57	4,929	1,594	705	157	732	2,496	338
1908	6,817	8,710	4,639	52	4,587	1,518	679	105	734	2,264	271
1907	6,422	8,472	4,662	52	4,610	1,361	587	93	681	2,157	306
1906	6,047	7,781	4,236	47	4,189	1,240	562	78	600	2,071	345
1905	5,664	7,325	3,928	41	3,887	1,204	527	76	601	1,982	296
1904	5,330	6,653	3,625	38	3,587	1,091	514	67	510	1,740	172
1903	4,935	6,285	3,441	37	3,404	1,025	486	63	476	1,633	250
1902	4,532	6,007	3,246	35	3,211	945	460	57	428	1,685	269
1901	4,163	5,674	2,980	31	2,949	885	450	51	384	1,681	326
1900	3,731	4,944	2,644	26	2,618	775	418	41	316	1,400	180
1899	3,582	4,709	2,508	24	2,484	652	346	36	270	1,428	229
1898	3,581	3,978	2,164	20	2,144	555	304	29	222	1,129	112
1897	3,610	3,563	1,978	18	1,960	484	279	24	181	982	101
1896 [3]	3,689	3,354	1,972	18	1,954	464	274	22	168	801	89

Year	Number of banks	Total assets or liabilities	Assets Total loans [1]	Assets Total investments [2]	Assets Total cash	Year	Number of banks	Total assets or liabilities	Assets Total loans [1]	Assets Total investments [2]	Assets Total cash	Year	Number of banks	Total assets or liabilities	Assets Total loans [1]	Assets Total investments [2]	Assets Total cash
	42	43	44	47	51		42	43	44	47	51		42	43	44	47	51
1896 [4]	3,689	3,536	1,972	464	801	1885	2,689	2,422	1,258	432	663	1874	1,983	1,852	926	451	430
1895	3,715	3,471	2,017	447	894	1884	2,625	2,283	1,270	449	488	1873	1,968	1,851	926	445	439
1894	3,770	3,422	1,944	435	935	1883	2,417	2,365	1,286	465	541	1872	1,853	1,771	872	450	412
1893	3,807	3,213	2,021	357	733	1882	2,239	2,344	1,209	471	598	1871	1,723	1,703	789	456	422
1892	3,759	3,494	2,128	347	919	1881	2,115	2,326	1,145	484	627	1870	1,612	1,566	719	453	361
1891	3,652	3,113	1,964	309	747	1880	2,076	2,036	995	452	518	1869	1,619	1,564	686	466	382
1890	3,484	3,062	1,934	311	730	1879	2,048	2,020	836	715	398	1868	1,640	1,572	656	507	384
1889	3,239	2,938	1,779	323	757	1878	2,056	1,751	835	460	388	1867	1,636	1,494	589	522	361
1888	3,120	2,731	1,628	356	671	1877	2,078	1,774	902	431	371	1866	1,634	1,476	550	468	439
1887	3,014	2,637	1,560	329	677	1876	2,091	1,826	934	427	400	1865	1,294	1,127	362	[5] 394	344
1886	2,809	2,475	1,399	407	593	1875	2,076	1,913	973	443	432	1864	467	252	71	[5] 93	86
												1863	66	17	6	[5] 6	5

See footnotes at end of table.

Series X 42–63. National Banks—Number of Banks and Principal Assets and Liabilities: 1863 to 1957—Con.

[Money figures in millions of dollars]

Year	Assets—Con. Cash—Con. Currency and coin	Assets—Con. Cash—Con. Bankers' balances (including reserves)	Assets—Con. Cash—Con. Other	Liabilities Deposits Total	Liabilities Deposits Interbank	Liabilities Deposits U.S. Government	Liabilities Deposits Other demand	Liabilities Deposits Other time	Liabilities National bank-notes	Liabilities Capital accounts	Liabilities Other
	53	54	55	56	57	58	59	60	61	62	63
1957	1,387	15,948	2,025	100,972	7,963	2,013	61,731	29,265	----------	8,721	2,750
1956	1,162	16,206	1,703	100,820	8,404	3,166	62,120	27,130	----------	8,232	1,645
1955	1,364	16,121	1,534	98,631	8,314	3,099	60,917	26,301	----------	7,714	1,391
1954	1,369	17,777	1,493	99,358	9,750	3,576	60,826	25,206	----------	7,686	1,563
1953	1,336	17,396	1,290	94,475	8,594	2,434	60,186	23,261	----------	7,220	1,723
1952	1,239	17,417	1,290	92,719	8,584	3,629	58,862	21,644	----------	6,879	1,655
1951	968	16,614	1,182	86,589	7,625	3,870	55,014	20,080	----------	6,504	1,301
1950	946	14,634	1,054	82,430	7,362	2,363	52,748	19,957	----------	6,180	1,081
1949	1,077	15,555	1,012	78,219	6,945	1,417	50,130	19,727	----------	5,815	819
1948	1,105	15,481	1,028	78,753	7,305	1,327	50,680	19,441	----------	5,533	795
1947	966	14,817	826	77,146	7,482	843	49,932	18,939	----------	5,296	707
1946	788	14,815	813	80,212	7,816	7,648	47,356	17,392	----------	4,862	624
1945	801	14,559	770	76,534	8,251	13,138	40,638	14,507	----------	4,461	496
1944	803	12,686	802	65,585	7,402	10,746	36,214	11,223	----------	4,101	457
1943	793	12,103	824	54,590	7,156	4,542	33,715	9,177	----------	3,816	377
1942	715	11,888	846	40,533	6,497	1,146	24,737	8,153	----------	3,671	380
1941	703	12,281	913	37,273	6,589	516	21,812	8,356	----------	3,590	365
1940	575	12,302	921	33,014	6,083	537	18,189	8,205	----------	3,468	334
1939	527	9,277	977	29,416	4,881	500	15,999	8,036	----------	3,382	321
1938	525	7,806	945	26,763	4,210	392	14,210	7,951	----------	3,266	288
1937	441	6,640	1,013	26,716	3,790	377	14,785	7,764	----------	3,205	351
1936	528	6,604	1,067	26,153	4,167	690	13,786	7,510	----------	3,160	330
1935	402	5,766	1,101	22,477	3,410	435	11,517	7,115	222	3,080	230
1934	350	4,705	1,154	19,896	2,767	887	9,469	6,773	695	2,995	268
1933	286	3,060	1,243	16,742	2,000	448	8,141	6,153	727	2,850	494
1932	336	2,452	1,390	17,428	1,814	212	8,196	7,206	649	3,274	967
1931	367	3,359	1,618	22,164	2,862	234	10,653	8,415	636	3,749	881
1930	340	3,260	1,671	23,235	2,850	170	11,682	8,533	649	3,969	975
1929	297	2,754	1,525	21,586	2,219	226	10,908	8,233	649	3,672	1,353
1928	314	3,012	1,465	22,645	2,701	184	11,466	8,294	649	3,569	1,402
1927	363	2,980	1,240	21,778	2,820	138	11,507	7,313	650	3,237	790
1926	359	2,861	1,255	20,644	2,864	143	11,325	6,312	651	3,088	819
1925	359	2,825	1,170	19,912	2,855	106	11,028	5,923	648	2,969	723
1924	345	2,642	1,012	18,349	2,794	121	10,175	5,259	729	2,915	532
1923	290	2,347	989	16,899	2,384	191	9,570	4,754	719	2,874	962
1922	325	2,393	959	16,323	2,482	102	9,628	4,111	725	2,847	738
1921	373	2,056	1,045	15,142	2,132	247	9,068	3,695	704	2,795	1,834
1920	449	2,638	1,227	17,159	2,824	174	10,676	3,485	688	2,621	2,799
1919	424	2,788	998	15,935	2,974	565	9,612	2,784	677	2,362	2,131
1918	382	2,590	779	14,015	2,796	1,036	7,840	2,343	681	2,249	1,317
1917	752	2,457	595	12,767	3,025	133	7,430	2,179	660	2,197	607
1916	818	2,012	482	10,872	2,713	39	6,391	1,729	675	2,102	271
1915	857	1,588	407	8,817	2,208	48	5,235	1,326	722	2,105	146
1914	1,022	1,390	394	8,560	2,186	66	5,107	1,201	722	2,049	146
1913	968	1,396	368	8,140	2,120	49	4,603	1,368	722	2,045	125
1912	996	1,423	349	8,061	2,178	58	4,611	1,214	708	1,983	105
1911	998	1,376	331	7,673	2,147	48	4,394	1,084	681	1,932	92
1910	865	1,201	314	7,254	1,900	54	4,286	1,014	675	1,850	113
1909	926	1,232	289	6,932	2,037	70	4,082	743	636	1,728	69
1908	889	1,104	289	6,328	1,823	130	3,850	525	613	1,667	102
1907	721	1,130	292	6,188	1,686	180	3,890	432	547	1,603	134
1906	681	1,045	234	5,691	1,545	90	3,766	290	511	1,490	89
1905	679	1,007	211	5,406	1,547	75	3,538	246	445	1,406	68
1904	689	879	197	4,834	1,412	110	3,113	199	399	1,349	71
1903	581	802	186	4,561	1,212	147	3,026	176	359	1,285	80
1902	597	819	131	4,467	1,243	124	2,945	155	309	1,184	47
1901	567	788	128	4,249	1,207	99	2,811	132	319	1,062	44
1900	529	691	125	3,621	1,063	99	2,361	98	265	1,014	44
1899	512	687	121	3,539	933	76	2,443	87	199	947	24
1898	493	524	130	2,799	720	53	1,943	83	190	955	34
1897	435	446	119	2,386	597	16	1,700	73	196	962	19
1896 [3]	363	349	117	2,141	454	16	1,603	68	199	983	31

Year	Liabilities Total deposits	Liabilities National bank-notes	Liabilities Capital accounts	Year	Liabilities Total deposits	Liabilities National bank-notes	Liabilities Capital accounts	Year	Liabilities Total deposits	Liabilities National bank-notes	Liabilities Capital accounts
	56	61	62		56	61	62		56	61	62
1896 [4]	2,141	199	983	1885	1,420	269	725	1873	836	339	662
				1884	1,233	295	739	1872	805	327	626
1895	2,279	179	987	1883	1,337	312	707	1871	791	308	594
1894	2,228	172	1,001	1882	1,365	309	660				
1893	1,939	155	1,029	1881	1,364	312	642	1870	706	291	562
1892	2,327	141	1,011					1869	716	293	549
1891	1,974	124	988	1880	1,085	318	625	1868	745	295	530
				1879	1,090	307	615	1867	685	292	512
1890	1,979	126	935	1878	814	300	629	1866	695	268	494
1889	1,920	129	875	1877	818	290	656				
1888	1,716	155	842	1876	842	294	679	1865	614	[6] 132	380
1887	1,650	167	806	1875	897	318	687	1864	147	[6] 26	79
1886	1,459	245	760	1874	828	339	676	1863	10	----------	7

[1] Beginning 1948, figures for loan items are shown gross (i.e., before deduction of valuation reserves); they do not add to the total and are not entirely comparable with prior figures. Total loans continue to be shown net.
[2] Before 1903, includes securities borrowed.
[3] Comparable with later data.
[4] Comparable with earlier data.
[5] U. S. Government securities only.
[6] Includes State banknotes outstanding.

Series X 64–85. Nonnational Banks—Number of Banks and Principal Assets and Liabilities: 1863 to 1957

[Money figures in millions of dollars. As of June 30 or nearest available date]

Year	Number of banks	Total assets or liabilities	Loans [1] Total	Loans Real estate	Loans Other	Investments Total	Investments U.S. Government obligations	Investments Obligations of States and political subdivisions	Investments Other	Cash Total	Cash items in process of collection
	64	65	66	67	68	69	70	71	72	73	74
1957	9,497	130,187	63,101	30,890	33,188	46,455	34,203	6,751	5,502	18,309	3,766
1956	9,539	127,431	59,665	28,844	31,662	45,954	34,362	6,517	5,075	19,816	4,931
1955	9,565	121,890	51,931	25,585	27,085	49,007	37,275	6,429	5,303	19,123	4,394
1954	9,630	110,289	43,554	21,999	22,157	47,307	36,767	5,522	5,018	17,920	3,422
1953	9,659	104,342	40,697	19,900	21,373	44,536	35,151	4,702	4,683	17,745	3,307
1952	9,673	100,542	36,688	17,788	19,438	44,804	36,180	4,278	4,346	17,741	3,384
1951	9,690	93,944	33,362	16,057	17,857	43,366	35,761	3,636	3,969	16,038	2,823
1950	9,705	89,474	27,410	13,405	14,505	46,830	39,774	3,189	3,867	14,187	2,509
1949	9,694	85,957	24,573	11,520	13,476	45,782	39,392	2,599	3,791	14,643	2,429
1948	9,723	84,971	22,857	10,340	12,870	46,587	40,682	2,464	3,441	14,585	2,225
1947	9,703	83,187	19,601	8,696	10,905	48,511	43,402	2,131	2,978	14,203	2,290
1946	9,673	85,831	17,037	7,386	9,651	53,354	48,698	1,722	2,934	14,556	2,264
1945	9,645	80,678	15,627	6,663	8,964	50,916	46,657	1,684	2,575	13,196	1,228
1944	9,638	68,699	14,222	6,765	7,457	41,199	37,135	1,599	2,465	12,197	1,627
1943	9,674	57,946	13,075	7,026	6,049	32,042	27,672	1,729	2,641	11,542	1,302
1942	9,790	47,346	14,183	7,380	6,803	20,370	15,442	1,996	2,932	11,321	1,030
1941	9,845	46,096	14,376	7,427	6,949	17,745	12,448	2,190	3,107	12,289	1,015
1940	9,912	42,913	13,155	7,234	5,921	16,158	10,611	2,235	3,312	11,746	627
1939	10,007	40,074	12,747	7,090	5,657	15,811	10,026	2,241	3,544	9,489	999
1938	10,177	37,413	12,717	7,068	5,649	14,649	8,788	2,059	3,802	7,936	851
1937	10,353	38,130	13,638	7,107	6,531	15,115	8,727	2,130	4,258	7,155	978
1936	10,516	37,211	12,891	7,120	5,771	15,398	8,957	2,111	4,330	6,670	972
1935	10,622	33,942	12,887	7,398	5,489	13,478	7,152	2,159	4,167	5,461	541
1934	10,496	32,061	13,628	7,815	5,813	11,931	5,461	2,031	4,439	4,470	469
1933	9,874	30,546	14,235	8,632	5,603	10,767	4,203	2,020	4,544	3,683	746
1932	13,172	34,977	17,806	9,245	8,561	11,223	3,590	2,142	5,491	3,927	684
1931	15,442	42,640	22,254	10,046	12,208	12,311	3,350	2,365	6,596	5,417	1,269
1930	17,026	45,462	26,116	10,312	15,804	11,215	2,625	2,138	6,452	5,793	1,855
1929	18,038	45,055	27,139	10,384	16,755	10,654	2,676	2,022	5,956	4,943	1,169
1928	18,716	42,856	25,025	10,079	14,946	11,005	2,783	2,059	6,163	4,716	1,001
1927	19,465	41,438	24,100	9,690	14,410	10,261	2,752	1,997	5,512	5,178	1,259
1926	20,378	39,877	23,336	9,380	13,956	9,725	2,918	1,834	4,973	5,018	1,119
1925	20,986	37,980	21,786	8,560	13,226	9,355	3,017	1,641	4,697	5,114	1,153
1924	21,521	34,895	20,075	7,704	12,371	8,740	2,935	1,555	4,250	4,579	1,040
1923	22,208	32,690	18,956	6,866	12,090	8,447	3,060	1,451	3,936	3,935	657
1922	22,492	29,735	16,809	6,015	10,794	7,814	2,578	1,429	3,807	3,861	740
1921	22,926	29,158	17,260	5,577	11,683	7,250	2,284	1,330	3,636	3,445	563
1920	22,885	29,827	17,690	5,286	12,404	6,995	2,283	1,256	3,456	3,996	604
1919	21,988	26,498	14,229	4,525	9,704	7,215	2,484	1,373	3,358	3,891	557
1918	21,781	22,835	12,786	4,393	8,393	5,773	1,218	1,388	3,167	3,267	274
1917	21,320	21,309	11,966	4,319	7,647	4,964	306	1,412	3,246	3,511	241
1916	20,791	18,777	10,496	3,947	6,549	4,514	50	1,360	3,104	3,033	256
1915	20,420	16,573	9,313	3,724	5,589	3,957	29	1,232	2,696	2,605	185
1914	20,346	15,872	9,059	3,564	5,495	3,831	29	1,231	2,571	2,355	232
1913	19,818	15,071	8,661	3,513	5,148	3,655	31	1,165	2,459	2,194	196
1912	19,106	14,515	8,152	3,279	4,873	3,618	42	1,101	2,475	2,211	201
1911	18,545	13,648	7,596	3,019	4,577	3,412	38	1,060	2,314	2,151	203
1910	18,013	13,030	7,312	2,827	4,485	3,264	38	1,024	2,202	1,994	275
1909	16,848	12,124	6,562	2,491	4,071	3,152	42	974	2,136	2,003	228
1908	16,344	11,236	6,124	2,378	3,746	2,938	43	912	1,983	1,779	161
1907	15,564	11,642	6,657	2,341	4,316	2,923	49	908	1,966	1,691	182
1906	14,360	10,959	6,206	2,181	4,025	2,840	58	895	1,887	1,564	175
1905	13,103	10,186	5,612	1,950	3,662	2,770	73	883	1,814	1,473	150
1904	12,329	9,195	4,920	1,767	3,153	2,504	86	849	1,569	1,462	120
1903	11,498	8,616	4,816	1,660	3,156	2,316	102	812	1,402	1,195	97
1902	10,580	8,019	4,418	1,529	2,889	2,153	119	766	1,268	1,170	109
1901	9,891	7,363	3,934	1,414	2,520	2,006	153	734	1,119	1,185	196
1900	9,322	6,444	3,449	1,316	2,133	1,769	193	695	881	995	97
1899	8,877	5,970	3,181	1,237	1,944	1,602	228	682	692	954	111
1898	8,582	5,240	2,812	1,177	1,635	1,415	229	644	542	785	40
1897	8,469	4,869	2,618	1,151	1,467	1,318	235	597	486	721	53
1896 [2]	8,423	4,694	2,643	1,146	1,497	1,225	232	562	431	620	47

Year	Number of banks [3]	Total assets or liabilities	Assets Total loans [1]	Assets Total investments	Assets Total cash [3]	Year	Number of banks [3]	Total assets or liabilities	Assets Total loans [1]	Assets Total investments	Assets Total cash [3]	Year	Number of banks [3]	Total assets or liabilities	Assets Total loans [1]	Assets Total investments	Assets Total cash [3]
	64	65	66	69	73		64	65	66	69	73		64	65	66	69	73
1896 [4]	5,780	4,200	2,280	1,211	465	1885	1,661	2,005	1,015	610	213	1874	[6] 1,569	1,039	638	281	80
1895	6,103	4,139	2,252	1,118	549	1884	1,488	1,939	991	592	190	1873	[6] 1,330	880	514	276	48
1894	5,738	3,869	2,141	1,010	538	1883	1,418	1,843	948	563	171	1872 [7]	566	375	252	30	78
1893	5,685	3,979	2,348	1,010	456	1882	1,333	1,687	842	584	157	1871 [7]	452	299	201	24	62
1892	5,577	3,752	2,209	936	459	1881	1,312	1,543	757	501	154	1870 [7]	325	215	144	17	45
1891	4,989	3,449	2,067	870	378	1880	1,279	1,364	668	453	138	1869 [7]	259	171	115	14	36
1890 [5]	4,717	3,296	1,920	863	393	1879	1,287	1,293	671	424	107	1868 [7]	247	164	110	13	34
1889 [5]	4,005	3,007	1,699	806	387	1878	1,173	1,330	726	414	105	1867 [7]	272	180	121	14	38
1888	3,527	2,739	1,533	775	318	1877	1,306	1,430	819	421	112	1866 [7]	297	197	132	16	41
1887	3,156	2,556	1,383	682	322	1876	1,357	1,357	793	391	103	1865 [7]	349	231	155	18	48
1886	1,529	2,068	1,035	644	180	1875	1,260	1,291	775	359	95	1864 [7]	1,089	721	484	57	150
												1863	1,466	1,192	649	181	303

See footnotes at end of table.

Series X 64–85. Nonnational Banks—Number of Banks and Principal Assets and Liabilities: 1863 to 1957—Con.

[Money figures in millions of dollars]

Year	Assets—Con. Cash—Con. Currency and coin	Bankers' balances (including reserves)	Other	Liabilities Deposits Total	Interbank	U.S. Government	Other demand	Other time	State bank-notes	Capital accounts	Other
	75	76	77	78	79	80	81	82	83	84	85
1957	1,456	13,087	2,322	115,997	6,460	1,611	52,922	55,004	----------	11,157	3,032
1956	1,220	13,665	1,996	114,684	6,838	2,370	53,727	51,748	----------	10,579	2,168
1955	1,436	13,293	1,829	110,214	6,931	2,318	52,115	48,850	----------	9,949	1,727
1954	1,408	13,090	1,508	100,147	5,750	2,319	46,216	45,862	----------	8,978	1,164
1953	1,363	13,075	1,364	94,701	5,007	1,508	45,583	42,603	----------	8,571	1,070
1952	1,258	13,099	1,309	91,428	4,929	2,492	44,564	39,443	----------	8,159	955
1951	1,004	12,211	1,178	85,290	4,322	2,462	41,403	37,103	----------	7,731	923
1950	973	10,705	1,047	81,359	4,074	1,438	39,152	36,695	----------	7,397	718
1949	1,092	11,122	959	78,269	3,993	887	37,885	35,504	----------	7,031	657
1948	1,090	11,270	942	77,620	4,131	853	38,089	34,547	----------	6,706	645
1947	968	10,945	872	76,229	4,250	524	38,112	33,343	----------	6,423	535
1946	806	11,486	884	79,081	4,493	5,767	37,482	31,339	----------	6,242	508
1945	785	11,183	939	74,594	4,336	11,247	31,897	27,114	----------	5,665	419
1944	773	9,797	1,081	63,099	3,799	8,766	28,048	22,486	----------	5,232	368
1943	770	9,470	1,287	52,707	3,732	3,485	25,952	19,538	----------	4,949	290
1942	698	9,593	1,472	42,232	3,781	691	19,877	17,883	----------	4,829	285
1941	663	10,611	1,686	40,939	4,340	232	18,107	18,260	----------	4,851	306
1940	536	10,583	1,854	37,840	4,085	287	15,460	18,008	----------	4,784	289
1939	487	8,003	2,027	34,887	3,339	288	13,695	17,565	----------	4,854	333
1938	468	6,617	2,111	32,237	2,628	204	12,188	17,217	----------	4,841	335
1937	483	5,694	2,222	32,769	2,547	292	12,797	17,133	----------	4,918	443
1936	466	5,232	2,252	31,915	2,736	454	12,314	16,411	----------	4,856	440
1935	370	4,550	2,116	28,793	2,234	385	10,216	15,958	----------	4,735	414
1934	341	3,660	2,032	26,584	1,815	848	8,329	15,592	----------	4,870	607
1933	355	2,582	1,861	24,942	1,467	410	7,881	15,184	----------	4,538	1,066
1932	431	2,812	2,021	28,141	1,509	221	8,918	17,493	----------	5,251	1,585
1931	484	3,664	2,658	35,023	2,288	213	11,920	20,602	----------	6,123	1,494
1930	491	3,447	2,338	37,130	2,279	128	13,976	20,747	----------	6,403	1,929
1929	473	3,301	2,319	36,683	1,756	149	14,261	20,517	----------	6,078	2,294
1928	483	3,232	2,110	35,493	1,582	90	13,398	20,423	----------	5,385	1,978
1927	558	3,361	1,899	34,922	1,708	94	13,758	19,362	----------	5,064	1,452
1926	578	3,321	1,798	33,772	1,425	92	13,685	18,570	----------	4,753	1,352
1925	561	3,400	1,725	32,389	1,475	76	13,304	17,534	----------	4,415	1,176
1924	537	3,002	1,501	29,612	1,452	64	11,901	16,195	----------	4,158	1,125
1923	480	2,798	1,352	27,477	1,033	114	11,265	15,065	1	3,944	1,268
1922	482	2,639	1,251	24,904	871	56	10,484	13,493	----------	3,752	1,079
1921	506	2,376	1,203	23,792	772	158	9,866	12,996	----------	3,590	1,776
1920	589	2,803	1,146	24,679	904	87	10,903	12,785	----------	3,398	1,750
1919	541	2,793	1,163	22,047	975	349	9,673	11,050	----------	3,047	1,404
1918	506	2,487	1,009	19,046	922	506	7,911	9,707	----------	2,864	925
1917	737	2,533	868	18,088	989	13	7,658	9,428	----------	2,791	430
1916	668	2,109	734	15,866	798	----------	6,530	8,538	1	2,616	294
1915	620	1,800	698	13,687	603	----------	5,471	7,613	----------	2,538	348
1914	614	1,509	627	13,105	534	----------	5,202	7,369	----------	2,454	313
1913	596	1,402	561	12,383	465	----------	4,649	7,269	----------	2,398	290
1912	579	1,431	534	11,952	458	----------	4,609	6,885	----------	2,286	277
1911	576	1,372	489	11,187	486	----------	4,235	6,466	----------	2,201	260
1910	576	1,143	460	10,696	404	----------	4,281	6,011	----------	2,134	200
1909	546	1,229	407	9,951	455	----------	4,037	5,459	----------	2,022	151
1908	484	1,134	395	9,112	390	----------	3,532	5,190	----------	1,960	164
1907	420	1,089	371	9,571	408	----------	3,820	5,343	1	1,889	181
1906	371	1,018	349	9,012	363	----------	3,638	5,011	1	1,795	153
1905	339	984	331	8,366	362	----------	3,361	4,643	----------	1,660	160
1904	342	1,000	309	7,507	344	----------	2,945	4,218	----------	1,586	102
1903	300	798	289	7,051	267	----------	2,746	4,038	----------	1,475	90
1902	281	780	278	6,636	255	----------	2,596	3,785	----------	1,289	94
1901	281	708	238	6,125	230	----------	2,468	3,427	----------	1,138	100
1900	245	653	231	5,301	198	----------	1,985	3,118	----------	1,061	82
1899	237	606	233	4,933	193	----------	1,852	2,888	----------	960	77
1898	224	521	228	4,245	152	----------	1,488	2,605	----------	923	72
1897	220	448	212	3,884	129	----------	1,299	2,456	1	915	69
1896 [2]	205	368	206	3,718	117	1	1,241	2,361	----------	910	66

Year	Liabilities Total deposits [3]	State bank-notes [8]	Capital accounts [3]	Year	Liabilities Total deposits [3]	State bank-notes [8]	Capital accounts [3]	Year	Liabilities Total deposits [3]	State bank-notes [8]	Capital accounts [3]
	78	83	84		78	83	84		78	83	84
1896 [4]	3,345	----------	763	1885	1,659	(9)	315	1874	912	(9)	114
1895	3,260		793	1884	1,616	(9)	297	1873	789	(9)	86
1894	3,039	(9)	751	1883	1,547	(9)	266	1872	121	78	122
1893	3,126	(9)	752	1882	1,412	(9)	240	1871	97	62	111
1892	2,970	(9)	710	1881	1,285	(9)	223	1870	70	45	87
1891	2,709	(9)	661	1880	1,137	(9)	201	1869	56	36	67
1890	2,598	(9)	624	1879	1,059	(9)	211	1868	53	34	66
1889	2,391	(9)	552	1878	1,107	(9)	196	1867	58	38	65
1888	2,175	(9)	506	1877	1,188	(9)	219	1866	64	41	67
1887	2,069	(9)	453	1876	1,151	(9)	185	1865	75	48	71
1886	1,727	(9)	316	1875	1,111	(9)	160	1864	233	150	312
								1863	494	239	405

[1] Beginning 1948, figures for loan items are shown gross (i. e., before deduction of valuation reserves); they do not add to the total and are not entirely comparable with prior figures. Total loans continue to be shown net.
[2] Comparable with later data.
[3] See series X 86–90 for supplementary figures: Number of banks, 1875–1882; capital accounts, 1875–1882; vault cash, 1875–1896; deposits, 1865–1896.
[4] Comparable with earlier data.

[5] Revised from source publication.
[6] Estimated.
[7] All figures except number of banks and capital accounts are estimated, using as a basis the previous 10 years, 1854–1863, inclusive.
[8] For more complete estimates of State banknotes in circulation, 1860–1878, see series X 290, and the source (see p. 645) for that series for figures from 1800–1859.
[9] Less than $500,000.

Series X 86–90. Nonnational Banks—Number of Banks and Selected Assets and Liabilities, Alternate Series: 1865 to 1896

[Money figures in millions of dollars]

Year	Adjusted deposits	Vault cash	Year	Number of banks	Capital accounts	Total deposits	Adjusted deposits	Vault cash	Year	Total deposits
	89	90		86	87	88	89	90		88
1896	3,545	207							1876	1,408
			1885				2,141	161	1875	1,399
1895	3,604	229	1884				2,057	131	1874	1,307
1894	3,311	226	1883				2,016	106	1873	1,276
1893	3,312	221	1882	5,063	235	1,719	1,844	109	1872	1,255
1892	3,409	218	1881	4,681	211	1,527	1,823	109	1871	1,045
1891	3,082	187								
			1880	4,456	194	1,319	1,495	112	1870	868
1890	2,971	181	1879	4,312	201	1,180	1,272	84	1869	751
1889	2,694	186	1878	4,400	205	1,243	1,275	86	1868	665
1888	2,569	191	1877	4,501	224	1,352	1,383	84	1867	597
1887	2,528	186	1876	4,520	219	1,362	1,453	85	1866	443
1886	2,395	177	1875	4,488	214	1,372	1,450	90	1865	635

Series X 91–96. Nonnational Banks—Number of Banks and Total Assets, by Class: 1875 to 1957

[Money figures in millions of dollars. As of June 30 or nearest available date. Figures prior to 1896 are known to be incomplete; for explanation, see text for series X 20–41]

Year	State commercial banks (including private) Number	Total assets	Private banks[1] Number	Total assets	Mutual savings banks[2] Number	Total assets	Year	State commercial banks (including private) Number	Total assets	Private banks[1] Number	Total assets	Mutual savings banks[2] Number	Total assets
	91	92	93	94	95	96		91	92	93	94	95	96
1957	8,972	95,932	89	344	525	34,254	1915	19,793	12,316	2,101	857	627	4,257
1956	9,012	95,010	92	355	527	32,421	1914	19,718	11,679	2,201	610	628	4,194
							1913	19,197	11,024	2,305	583	621	4,047
1955	9,037	91,508	92	355	528	30,382	1912	18,478	10,638	2,319	595	628	3,877
1954	9,102	81,974	92	374	528	28,315	1911	17,913	9,941	2,374	576	632	3,706
1953	9,131	78,009	95	357	528	26,333							
1952	9,144	76,164	105	362	529	24,378	1910	17,376	9,432	2,442	590	637	3,598
1951	9,161	71,109	115	382	529	22,835	1909	16,212	8,780	2,467	625	636	3,344
							1908	15,714	7,954	2,525	557	630	3,281
1950	9,175	67,223	118	372	530	22,252	1907	14,939	8,390	2,784	565	625	3,252
1949	9,164	64,852	122	378	530	21,105	1906	13,739	7,820	2,726	575	621	3,139
1948	9,191	64,718	131	374	532	20,252							
1947	9,170	63,825	134	394	533	19,362	1905	12,488	7,217	2,777	572	615	2,969
1946	9,140	67,810	136	362	533	18,021	1904	11,707	6,382	2,914	604	622	2,814
							1903	10,879	5,905	3,017	584	619	2,711
1945	9,111	64,754	137	317	534	15,924	1902	9,956	5,420	2,896	633	624	2,599
1944	9,102	54,889	149	276	536	13,810	1901	9,261	4,897	2,855	610	630	2,466
1943	9,137	45,539	152	261	537	12,407							
1942	9,252	35,691	160	237	538	11,655	1900	8,696	4,115	2,825	507	626	2,328
1941	9,304	34,128	167	228	541	11,969	1899	8,253	3,780	2,761	461	624	2,190
							1898	7,949	3,193	2,698	453	633	2,048
1940	9,370	30,988	174	223	542	11,925	1897	7,828	2,912	2,637	441	641	1,957
1939	9,464	28,303	183	812	543	11,771	1896[3]	7,785	2,813	2,597	457	638	1,881
1938	9,625	25,868	191	665	552	11,545							
1937	9,801	26,635	202	837	552	11,496	1896[4]	4,792	2,057	824	94	988	2,143
1936	9,961	25,929	213	761	555	11,283	1895	5,086	2,085	1,070	131	1,017	2,054
							1894	4,714	1,888	904	105	1,025	1,981
1935	10,063	22,896	223	623	559	11,046	1893	4,655	1,965	848	108	1,030	2,014
1934	9,931	21,124	235	508	565	10,938	1892	4,520	1,788	1,161	147	1,059	1,964
1933	9,310	19,698	294	486	564	10,848	1891	3,978	1,595	1,235	152	1,011	1,855
1932	12,589	23,985	391	512	583	10,991	1890[5]	3,594	1,539	1,344	164	921	1,743
1931	14,854	31,587	481	760	588	11,052	1889[5]	3,115	1,380	1,324	143	849	1,623
1930	16,432	35,297	591	963	594	10,164	1888	2,726	1,219	1,203	164	801	1,520
1929	17,440	35,181	654	874	598	9,873	1887	2,472	1,179	1,001	175	684	1,378
1928	18,113	33,298	696	901	603	9,557	1886	891	807			638	1,261
1927	18,860	32,518	766	915	605	8,920	1885	1,015	802			646	1,203
1926	19,770	31,579	823	809	608	8,298	1884	852	761			636	1,178
1925	20,376	30,150	879	736	610	7,831	1883	788	724			630	1,119
1924	20,908	27,612	944	820	613	7,284	1882	704	634			629	1,053
1923	21,593	25,878	1,024	647	615	6,812	1881	683	576			629	968
1922	21,876	23,473	1,108	546	616	6,262	1880	650	482			629	882
1921	22,306	23,194	1,160	588	620	5,964	1879	648	428			639	865
1920	22,267	24,242	1,691	741	618	5,586	1878	510	389			663	941
1919	21,368	21,351	1,808	804	620	5,141							
1918	21,157	18,090	1,926	953	624	4,745	1877	631	507			675	923
1917	20,699	16,571	1,974	863	621	4,739	1876[6]	671	406			686	951
1916	20,168	14,297	2,057	766	623	4,480	1875[6]	586	395			674	896

[1] Figures for 1896–1946 are for private banks in 18 States only; private banks were not segregated from other banks in the remaining States in this period.

[2] Includes mutual and stock savings banks, 1875–1896; thereafter mutual savings banks only.

[3] Comparable with later years.

[4] Comparable with earlier years.

[5] The total of series X 91 and X 95 and the total of series X 92 and X 96 differ from series X 64 and X 65, respectively. The latter are revised data published in the *Annual Report of the Comptroller of the Currency, 1931,* without breakdown by class of bank.

[6] Revised data for number of mutual savings banks, 781 in 1876 and 771 in 1875, are included in *Annual Report of the Comptroller of the Currency, 1920,* vol. 1, p. 241, but total assets for these banks are not available.

Series X 97–118. All Commercial Banks—Number of Banks and Principal Assets and Liabilities: 1896 to 1957

[Money figures in millions of dollars.   As of June 30 or nearest available date]

Year	Number of banks	Total assets or liabilities	Loans [1] Total	Real estate	Other	Investments Total	U.S. Government obligations	Obligations of States and political subdivisions	Other	Cash Total	Cash items in process of collection
	97	98	99	100	101	102	103	104	105	106	107
1957	13,617	208,375	91,022	22,527	70,134	73,479	56,634	13,314	3,531	39,992	8,920
1956	13,678	205,707	86,884	21,786	66,447	73,120	56,618	12,929	3,573	42,442	11,063
1955	13,780	199,244	75,181	19,779	56,527	80,080	63,270	12,785	4,025	41,024	9,762
1954	13,936	190,581	67,335	17,226	51,099	79,046	63,508	11,930	3,608	41,568	8,880
1953	14,005	181,427	65,025	16,230	49,734	72,932	58,645	10,533	3,754	41,157	8,826
1952	14,069	177,417	59,233	15,019	45,067	75,204	61,178	9,844	4,182	40,703	8,619
1951	14,107	165,503	54,821	14,144	41,392	71,224	58,521	8,514	4,189	37,385	7,409
1950	14,146	156,914	44,798	12,411	32,978	76,973	65,753	7,392	3,828	33,270	6,813
1949	14,151	149,705	41,028	11,023	30,459	72,750	63,221	5,929	3,600	34,167	6,102
1948	14,189	149,799	39,866	10,233	29,963	73,990	64,798	5,588	3,604	34,168	6,038
1947	14,182	146,974	33,679	8,310	25,369	79,076	70,533	4,965	3,578	32,705	5,831
1946	14,152	153,507	27,159	5,845	21,314	92,417	84,549	4,082	3,786	32,418	5,253
1945	14,126	146,245	23,697	4,501	19,196	90,917	84,136	3,778	3,003	30,157	3,402
1944	14,138	125,031	21,029	4,447	16,582	74,784	68,480	3,472	2,832	27,662	4,126
1943	14,197	104,322	17,673	4,633	13,040	59,020	52,495	3,517	3,008	25,976	3,550
1942	14,353	80,276	20,249	4,875	15,374	33,431	26,439	3,564	3,428	24,844	2,691
1941	14,434	75,356	20,324	4,742	15,582	27,319	20,139	3,670	3,510	25,819	2,517
1940	14,534	67,804	17,393	4,392	13,001	23,793	16,597	3,610	3,586	24,626	1,598
1939	14,667	61,422	16,411	4,099	12,312	23,004	15,740	3,286	3,978	19,852	2,249
1938	14,867	56,185	16,128	3,863	12,265	21,109	14,081	2,779	4,249	16,798	1,953
1937	15,094	56,907	17,471	3,727	13,744	22,138	14,583	2,799	4,756	14,993	2,257
1936	15,329	55,572	15,600	3,530	12,070	23,077	15,344	2,873	4,860	14,497	2,204
1935	15,488	48,905	14,950	3,494	11,456	19,735	12,778	2,689	4,268	11,799	1,226
1934	15,348	44,978	15,719	3,661	12,058	17,072	10,324	2,360	4,388	9,648	1,097
1933	14,207	40,511	16,457	4,202	12,255	14,078	7,496	2,267	4,315	7,368	1,506
1932	18,734	46,304	22,001	4,955	17,046	14,277	6,250	2,299	5,728	6,970	1,372
1931	21,654	59,017	29,307	5,757	23,550	15,686	6,011	2,434	7,241	10,017	2,526
1930	23,679	64,125	35,043	6,146	28,897	14,392	4,874	2,111	7,407	10,910	3,659
1929	24,970	62,442	36,114	6,313	29,801	13,683	4,872	1,955	6,856	9,004	2,394
1928	25,798	61,563	34,488	6,193	28,295	14,466	4,933	1,999	7,534	9,215	2,409
1927	26,650	58,973	32,932	5,992	26,940	13,165	4,494	1,912	6,759	9,901	2,890
1926	27,742	56,781	32,084	5,781	26,303	12,224	4,414	1,723	6,087	9,568	2,683
1925	28,442	54,401	30,222	5,273	24,949	11,755	4,454	1,527	5,774	9,663	2,755
1924	28,988	50,136	28,278	4,710	23,568	10,679	4,260	1,382	5,037	8,787	2,504
1923	29,829	47,332	27,397	4,243	23,154	10,325	4,604	1,182	4,539	7,377	1,677
1922	30,120	44,106	25,040	3,671	21,369	9,359	3,846	1,146	4,367	7,602	1,988
1921	30,456	43,669	26,386	3,354	23,032	8,360	3,262	1,043	4,055	6,771	1,665
1920	30,291	47,509	28,562	3,225	25,337	8,398	3,638	944	3,816	8,264	2,007
1919	29,147	42,462	22,814	2,609	20,205	9,521	4,864	947	3,710	8,061	1,737
1918	28,856	36,352	20,571	2,484	18,087	7,478	3,043	924	3,511	6,613	869
1917	28,298	32,802	18,581	2,395	16,186	5,837	1,300	863	3,674	7,010	768
1916	27,739	28,217	16,067	2,122	13,945	4,870	740	786	3,344	6,148	775
1915	27,390	24,106	13,834	1,960	11,874	4,156	767	663	2,726	5,092	434
1914	27,236	23,155	13,416	1,812	11,604	3,861	782	565	2,514	4,930	587
1913	26,664	22,056	12,820	1,809	11,011	3,697	770	536	2,391	4,681	490
1912	25,844	21,495	12,239	1,677	10,562	3,676	774	530	2,372	4,758	495
1911	25,183	20,320	11,455	1,513	9,942	3,431	742	466	2,223	4,672	519
1910	24,514	19,324	11,072	1,392	9,680	3,156	737	408	2,011	4,387	757
1909	23,098	18,145	10,015	1,199	8,816	3,153	733	412	2,008	4,340	565
1908	22,531	16,664	9,243	1,104	8,139	2,912	706	335	1,871	3,885	431
1907	21,361	16,862	9,810	1,111	8,699	2,744	616	316	1,812	3,706	487
1906	19,786	15,601	9,013	1,026	7,987	2,563	598	279	1,686	3,502	519
1905	18,152	14,542	8,220	870	7,350	2,523	571	286	1,666	3,321	445
1904	17,037	13,035	7,299	756	6,543	2,226	562	259	1,405	3,066	291
1903	15,814	12,190	7,052	698	6,354	2,016	542	223	1,251	2,706	345
1902	14,488	11,427	6,521	617	5,904	1,821	517	199	1,105	2,731	377
1901	13,424	10,572	5,835	545	5,290	1,676	525	190	961	2,740	521
1900	12,427	9,059	5,065	484	4,581	1,410	506	169	735	2,274	276
1899	11,835	8,489	4,718	446	4,272	1,207	435	157	615	2,264	339
1898	11,530	7,170	4,060	420	3,640	1,002	386	128	488	1,800	151
1897	11,438	6,475	3,701	417	3,284	886	358	113	415	1,604	153
1896	11,474	6,167	3,741	436	3,305	818	348	102	368	1,330	136

[1] Beginning 1948, figures for loan items are shown gross (i.e., before deduction of valuation reserves); they do not add to the total and are not entirely comparable with prior figures. Total loans continue to be shown net.

Series X 97–118. All Commercial Banks—Number of Banks and Principal Assets and Liabilities: 1896 to 1957—Con.

[Money figures in millions of dollars]

| Year | Assets—Con. Cash—Con. | | | Liabilities | | | | | | | |
| | Currency and coin | Bankers' balances (including reserves) | Other | Deposits Total | Inter-bank | U.S. Government | Other demand | Other time | National bank-notes | Capital accounts | Other |
	108	109	110	111	112	113	114	115	116	117	118
1957	2,737	28,336	3,882	186,292	14,421	3,622	114,626	53,623	----------	16,836	5,248
1956	2,273	29,106	3,260	186,320	15,239	5,533	115,822	49,726	----------	15,926	3,460
1955	2,681	28,581	2,959	181,512	15,242	5,414	112,981	47,875	----------	14,906	2,826
1954	2,659	30,029	2,632	174,065	15,497	5,892	106,995	45,681	----------	14,038	2,478
1953	2,590	29,741	2,313	165,548	13,598	3,940	105,735	42,275	----------	13,276	2,603
1952	2,396	29,688	2,277	162,365	13,512	6,118	103,402	39,333	----------	12,599	2,453
1951	1,873	28,103	2,073	151,475	11,946	6,329	96,399	36,801	----------	11,950	2,078
1950	1,829	24,628	1,873	143,845	11,435	3,799	91,882	36,729	----------	11,389	1,680
1949	2,072	25,993	1,760	137,538	10,938	2,302	87,999	36,299	----------	10,781	1,386
1948	2,103	26,027	1,775	138,162	11,435	2,178	88,754	35,795	----------	10,284	1,353
1947	1,851	25,023	1,514	135,933	11,681	1,365	88,030	34,857	----------	9,877	1,164
1946	1,510	25,655	1,513	143,042	12,309	13,413	84,824	32,496	----------	9,392	1,073
1945	1,509	25,246	1,474	136,727	12,586	24,384	72,526	27,231	----------	8,652	866
1944	1,503	22,033	1,556	116,235	11,201	19,511	64,254	21,269	----------	8,011	785
1943	1,485	20,941	1,653	96,175	10,888	8,026	59,661	17,600	----------	7,521	626
1942	1,334	20,819	1,752	72,394	10,278	1,837	44,611	15,668	----------	7,254	628
1941	1,290	22,012	1,894	67,588	10,929	748	39,915	15,996	----------	7,131	637
1940	1,037	21,991	1,992	60,246	10,168	824	33,646	15,608	----------	6,960	598
1939	950	16,653	2,155	53,894	8,220	788	29,691	15,195	----------	6,896	632
1938	936	13,909	2,150	48,814	6,838	596	26,387	14,993	----------	6,770	601
1937	875	11,861	2,305	49,345	6,336	669	27,578	14,762	----------	6,786	776
1936	945	11,348	2,398	48,118	6,903	1,144	26,096	13,975	----------	6,703	751
1935	729	9,844	2,421	41,462	5,644	820	21,731	13,267	222	6,601	620
1934	642	7,909	2,539	36,810	4,581	1,735	17,796	12,698	695	6,625	848
1933	582	5,280	2,608	32,078	3,467	858	16,019	11,734	727	6,190	1,516
1932	715	4,883	3,056	35,658	3,323	433	17,111	14,791	649	7,484	2,513
1931	816	6,675	4,007	47,277	5,150	447	22,569	19,111	636	8,746	2,358
1930	799	6,452	3,780	51,267	5,129	298	25,648	20,192	649	9,318	2,891
1929	740	5,870	3,641	49,385	3,975	375	25,160	19,875	649	8,780	3,628
1928	768	6,038	3,394	49,582	4,282	274	24,857	20,169	649	7,968	3,364
1927	893	6,118	2,975	48,704	4,527	232	25,257	18,688	650	7,392	2,227
1926	911	5,974	2,905	46,952	4,289	235	24,993	17,435	651	7,021	2,157
1925	892	6,016	2,761	45,230	4,330	182	24,325	16,393	648	6,636	1,887
1924	855	5,428	2,392	41,343	4,247	185	22,069	14,842	729	6,420	1,644
1923	743	4,957	2,233	38,175	3,417	305	20,829	13,624	719	6,220	2,218
1922	776	4,838	2,105	35,532	3,353	158	20,106	11,915	725	6,044	1,805
1921	856	4,250	2,152	33,432	2,904	405	18,926	11,197	703	5,936	3,598
1920	1,012	5,245	2,285	36,682	3,729	261	21,571	11,121	688	5,599	4,540
1919	941	5,383	2,066	33,254	3,948	914	19,282	9,110	677	5,014	3,517
1918	865	4,879	1,690	28,708	3,718	1,541	15,747	7,702	681	4,742	2,221
1917	1,464	4,778	1,374	26,501	4,015	146	15,085	7,255	660	4,612	1,029
1916	1,463	3,910	1,132	22,613	3,510	39	12,917	6,147	676	4,367	561
1915	1,452	3,206	1,024	18,612	2,811	48	10,703	5,050	722	4,286	486
1914	1,615	2,728	948	17,806	2,720	66	10,306	4,714	722	4,169	458
1913	1,548	2,643	858	16,808	2,585	49	9,249	4,925	722	4,116	410
1912	1,559	2,704	822	16,455	2,636	58	9,217	4,544	709	3,955	376
1911	1,559	2,594	762	15,452	2,633	48	8,625	4,146	681	3,843	344
1910	1,421	2,209	709	14,644	2,304	54	8,566	3,720	675	3,694	311
1909	1,453	2,322	637	13,789	2,492	70	8,115	3,112	636	3,501	219
1908	1,351	2,103	624	12,425	2,213	130	7,381	2,701	613	3,364	262
1907	1,120	2,099	602	12,727	2,094	180	7,708	2,745	547	3,274	314
1906	1,036	1,947	523	11,791	1,908	89	7,403	2,391	511	3,060	239
1905	1,001	1,875	478	11,028	1,909	75	6,898	2,146	445	2,844	225
1904	1,014	1,761	444	9,739	1,756	110	6,057	1,816	399	2,727	170
1903	865	1,496	416	9,107	1,479	147	5,771	1,710	359	2,555	169
1902	862	1,492	354	8,713	1,498	124	5,541	1,550	309	2,266	139
1901	831	1,388	321	8,114	1,437	99	5,279	1,299	319	1,996	143
1900	756	1,242	310	6,792	1,261	99	4,345	1,087	265	1,878	124
1899	732	1,193	300	6,472	1,126	76	4,295	975	199	1,720	98
1898	701	948	308	5,175	872	53	3,431	819	190	1,701	104
1897	638	813	284	4,486	726	16	2,999	745	197	1,705	87
1896	550	644	278	4,142	571	15	2,844	712	199	1,730	96

Series X 119–128. All Commercial Banks—Number of Banks and Total Assets, by Federal Reserve Membership and Class: 1896 to 1957

[Money figures in millions of dollars. As of June 30 or nearest available date]

Year	National banks Number (119)	National banks Total assets (120)	State member banks [1] Number (121)	State member banks [1] Total assets (122)	Nonmember banks Number (123)	Nonmember banks Total assets (124)
1957	4,645	112,443	1,795	64,019	7,177	31,913
1956	4,666	110,697	1,829	64,090	7,183	30,920
1955	4,743	107,736	1,864	61,919	7,173	29,589
1954	4,834	108,607	1,883	53,568	7,219	28,406
1953	4,874	103,418	1,888	50,817	7,243	27,192
1952	4,925	101,253	1,887	50,266	7,257	25,898
1951	4,946	94,394	1,910	47,199	7,251	23,910
1950	4,971	89,691	1,911	44,033	7,264	23,190
1949	4,987	84,853	1,913	42,388	7,251	22,464
1948	4,998	85,081	1,924	42,199	7,267	22,519
1947	5,012	83,149	1,913	41,630	7,257	22,195
1946	5,012	85,698	1,872	45,686	7,268	22,123
1945	5,015	81,491	1,822	44,930	7,289	19,824
1944	5,036	70,143	1,734	38,528	7,368	16,360
1943	5,060	58,783	1,640	32,028	7,497	13,511
1942	5,101	44,584	1,543	25,353	7,709	10,340
1941	5,130	41,228	1,423	23,620	7,881	10,508
1940	5,164	36,816	1,234	21,030	8,136	9,958
1939	5,203	33,119	1,127	18,789	8,337	9,514
1938	5,242	30,317	1,096	16,826	8,529	9,042
1937	5,293	30,272	1,064	17,181	8,737	9,454
1936	5,368	29,643	1,032	16,881	8,929	9,048
1935	5,425	26,009	985	14,710	9,078	8,186
1934	5,417	23,854	958	13,529	8,973	7,595
1933	4,897	20,813	709	12,226	8,601	7,472
1932	6,145	22,318	835	13,538	11,754	10,448
1931	6,800	27,430	982	17,406	13,872	14,181
1930	7,247	28,828	1,068	18,521	15,364	16,776
1929	7,530	27,260	1,177	18,194	16,263	16,988
1928	7,685	28,265	1,244	16,390	16,869	16,908
1927	7,790	26,455	1,309	16,144	17,551	16,374
1926	7,972	25,202	1,403	15,436	18,367	16,143
1925	8,066	24,252	1,472	14,694	18,904	15,455
1924	8,080	22,525	1,570	13,192	19,338	14,419
1923	8,236	21,454	1,620	12,212	19,973	13,666
1922	8,244	20,633	1,648	10,960	20,228	12,513
1921	8,150	20,475	1,595	10,375	20,711	12,820
1920	8,024	23,267	1,374	10,351	20,893	13,891
1919	7,779	21,105	1,042	8,629	20,326	12,727
1918	7,699	18,262	513	6,104	20,644	11,987
1917	7,599	16,231	53	756	20,646	15,815
1916	7,571	13,920	34	307	20,134	13,990
1915	7,597	11,790	17	97	19,776	12,219

Year	National banks Number (125)	National banks Total assets (126)	State banks Number (127)	State banks Total assets (128)
1914	7,518	11,477	19,718	11,679
1913	7,467	11,032	19,197	11,024
1912	7,366	10,857	18,478	10,638
1911	7,270	10,378	17,913	9,941
1910	7,138	9,892	17,376	9,432
1909	6,886	9,365	16,212	8,780
1908	6,817	8,710	15,714	7,954
1907	6,422	8,472	14,939	8,390
1906	6,047	7,781	13,739	7,820
1905	5,664	7,325	12,488	7,217
1904	5,330	6,653	11,707	6,382
1903	4,935	6,285	10,879	5,905
1902	4,532	6,007	9,956	5,420
1901	4,163	5,674	9,261	4,897
1900	3,731	4,944	8,696	4,115
1899	3,582	4,709	8,253	3,780
1898	3,581	3,978	7,949	3,193
1897	3,610	3,563	7,828	2,912
1896	3,689	3,354	7,785	2,813

[1] Beginning in 1941, excludes 3 mutual savings banks which are members of the Federal Reserve System; and in 1955–1957, includes 1 nondeposit trust company which is not insured by the Federal Deposit Insurance Corporation.

Series X 129–142. All Banks—Number of Banks and Total Assets, by Deposit Insurance Status and Class: 1934 to 1957

[Money figures in millions of dollars. As of June 30 or nearest available date. Includes data for U.S. Territories and possessions]

Year	All banks Insured Number (129)	All banks Insured Total assets (130)	All banks Noninsured Number (131)	All banks Noninsured Total assets (132)	Commercial Insured Member banks [1] Number (133)	Commercial Insured Member banks [1] Total assets (134)	Commercial Insured Nonmember banks Number (135)	Commercial Insured Nonmember banks Total assets (136)	Commercial Noninsured nonmember Number (137)	Commercial Noninsured nonmember Total assets (138)	Mutual savings Insured Number (139)	Mutual savings Insured Total assets (140)	Mutual savings Noninsured Number (141)	Mutual savings Noninsured Total assets (142)
1957	13,445	233,423	739	10,432	[2]6,441	[2]176,479	6,770	30,703	[2]447	[2]2,419	234	26,241	292	8,013
1956	13,449	228,524	798	10,743	[2]6,495	[2]174,793	6,734	29,460	[2]490	[2]2,593	220	24,271	308	8,150
1955	13,505	220,327	845	10,359	[2]6,607	[2]169,660	6,680	27,906	[2]534	[2]2,738	218	22,761	311	7,621
1954	13,619	209,880	888	10,038	6,718	162,179	6,682	26,464	578	2,960	219	21,237	310	7,078
1953	13,648	199,176	926	9,579	6,762	154,235	6,673	25,351	610	2,836	213	19,590	316	6,743
1952	13,655	193,222	983	9,547	6,812	151,519	6,638	23,820	658	3,052	205	17,883	325	6,495
1951	13,652	179,946	1,026	9,309	6,856	141,592	6,595	21,759	697	3,069	201	16,595	329	6,240
1950	13,641	170,364	1,077	9,679	6,882	133,724	6,567	20,977	738	3,090	192	15,663	339	6,589
1949	13,614	161,888	1,109	9,788	6,900	127,241	6,523	19,975	769	3,355	191	14,672	340	6,433
1948	13,613	161,177	1,154	9,805	6,922	127,280	6,498	19,964	814	3,485	193	13,933	340	6,320
1947	13,582	157,542	1,179	9,747	6,925	124,779	6,466	19,594	836	3,554	191	13,169	343	6,193
1946	13,526	162,881	1,203	9,646	6,884	131,384	6,451	19,359	860	3,763	191	12,138	343	5,883
1945	13,474	154,115	1,228	9,010	6,837	126,421	6,445	17,036	885	3,744	192	10,658	343	5,266
1944	13,461	131,766	1,254	7,894	6,770	108,671	6,499	13,976	909	3,203	192	9,119	345	4,691
1943	13,363	105,414	1,411	11,927	6,700	90,811	6,602	11,594	934	2,529	61	3,009	477	9,398
1942	13,456	80,765	1,474	11,582	6,644	69,937	6,759	8,772	988	1,983	53	2,056	486	9,599
1941	13,479	74,976	1,540	12,679	6,553	64,848	6,873	8,149	1,051	2,689	53	1,979	489	9,990
1940	13,534	67,187	1,585	12,825	6,398	57,846	7,085	7,756	1,093	2,485	51	1,585	492	10,340
1939	13,621	60,832	1,630	12,604	6,330	51,968	7,242	7,531	1,135	2,226	49	1,393	495	10,378
1938	13,783	55,520	1,676	12,449	6,338	47,144	7,389	7,239	1,179	2,041	56	1,137	497	10,408
1937	13,943	56,047	1,744	12,585	6,357	47,452	7,530	7,456	1,247	2,228	56	1,139	497	10,357
1936	14,121	54,718	1,807	12,343	6,400	46,524	7,665	7,072	1,307	2,182	56	1,122	500	10,161
1935	14,242	48,468	1,849	11,672	6,410	40,719	7,769	6,554	1,352	1,821	63	1,195	497	9,851
1934	14,150	50,946	1,807	5,149	6,375	37,383	7,540	6,066	1,476	1,708	235	7,497	331	3,441

[1] Beginning in 1941, the figures for member commercial banks exclude and the figures for mutual savings banks include 3 mutual savings banks which are members of the Federal Reserve System.

[2] Figures for member commercial banks exclude and figures for noninsured nonmember commercial banks include 1 member nondeposit trust company which is not insured by the Federal Deposit Insurance Corporation.

Series X 143–151. Number of Banking Offices, by Deposit Insurance Status: 1900 to 1957

Year [1]	All banking offices	Commercial bank offices					Mutual savings bank offices			Year [1]	Commercial bank offices		
		Total	Member banks [2]		Nonmember banks		Total	Insured [3]	Non-insured		Total	National banks	State banks [5]
			National	State [3]	Insured	Non-insured							
	143	144	145	146	147	148	149	150	151		144	145	146–148
1957	22,699	21,772	8,795	3,969	8,545	463	927	535	392	1932	20,997	7,231	13,766
1956	22,123	21,230	8,459	3,884	8,405	482	893	480	413	1931	22,842	7,478	15,364
1955	21,494	20,638	8,055	3,785	8,263	535	856	454	402	1930	25,694	8,075	17,619
1954	20,982	20,147	7,844	3,598	8,132	573	835	439	396	1929	27,379	8,398	18,981
1953	20,608	19,810	7,602	3,536	8,062	610	798	411	387	1928	28,106	8,563	19,543
1952	20,288	19,513	7,465	3,436	7,947	665	775	383	392	1927	28,714	8,482	20,232
1951	20,003	19,244	7,309	3,365	7,879	691	759	367	392	1926	29,454	8,327	21,127
1950	19,708	18,966	7,188	3,271	7,766	741	742	346	396	1925	30,163	8,366	21,797
1949	19,465	18,735	7,060	3,216	7,679	780	730	333	397	1924	30,482	8,299	22,183
1948	19,234	18,520	6,956	3,156	7,582	826	714	325	389	1923	30,931	8,383	22,548
1947 [4]	19,046	18,342	6,875	3,096	7,521	850	704	318	386	1922	31,259	8,384	22,875
1946	18,863	18,165	6,794	3,022	7,464	885	698	306	392	1921	31,243	8,222	23,021
1945	18,781	18,096	6,831	2,963	7,397	905	685	293	392	1920	30,368	8,088	22,280
1944	18,741	18,058	6,840	2,866	7,430	922	683	291	392	1915	26,660	7,624	19,036
1943	18,646	17,965	6,782	2,744	7,487	952	681	279	402	1910	22,034	7,150	14,884
1942	18,562	17,878	6,675	2,619	7,602	982	683	91	592	1905	15,032	5,669	9,363
1941	18,524	17,841	6,682	2,514	7,742	903	683	84	599	1900	8,857	3,736	5,121
1940	18,561	17,875	6,683	2,344	7,892	956	686	84	602				
1939	18,663	17,980	6,705	2,177	8,099	999	683	75	608				
1938	18,774	18,084	6,723	2,106	8,226	1,029	690	64	626				
1937	18,927	18,236	6,745	2,075	8,342	1,074	691	67	624				
1936	19,066	18,373	6,723	2,032	8,440	1,178	693	67	626				
1935	19,153	18,455	6,715	1,953	8,562	1,225	698	67	631				
1934	19,196	18,491	6,705	1,961	[5] 9,825		705	(5)	(5)				
1933	17,940	17,236	6,275	1,817	[5] 9,144		704	(5)	(5)				

[1] For 1925, 1926, and 1932–1957, figures are as of December; for earlier years they are as of different dates for banks and branches: For banks, 1927–1931 and 1923–1924, as of December; for 1915–1922, as of June; for branches, 1924 and 1927–1931, as of June; prior to 1924, not for any uniform month. Figures in this table prior to 1947 have not yet been revised to bring them into conformity with the revised all-bank data referred to in the text for series X 1–265.
[2] Federal deposit insurance is compulsory for member banks of the Federal Reserve System.
[3] Beginning in 1941, the member bank figures exclude and the insured mutual savings bank figures include 3 mutual savings banks which became members of the Federal Reserve System during 1941.
[4] In 1947, the series was revised. See footnote 6 to series X 155–164.
[5] Federal insurance of bank deposits did not become effective until Jan. 1, 1934, and the number of nonmember banking offices by insurance status is not available prior to 1935.

Series X 152–154. Proportion of Total Bank Deposits Insured by the Federal Deposit Insurance Corporation: 1934 to 1957

[Money figures in millions of dollars. As of June 30 or nearest available date. Includes data for U.S. Territories and possessions]

Year	Total deposits at all banks	Estimated insured deposits [1]	Insured deposits as percentage of all deposits	Year	Total deposits at all banks	Estimated insured deposits [1]	Insured deposits as percentage of all deposits	Year	Total deposits at all banks	Estimated insured deposits [1]	Insured deposits as percentage of all deposits
	152	153	154		152	153	154		152	153	154
1957	218,026	118,931	54.5	1949	157,258	74,212	47.2	1941	78,501	27,398	34.9
1956	216,483	114,601	52.9	1948	157,197	73,705	46.9	1940	71,091	24,708	34.8
1955	209,771	110,437	52.6	1947	154,262	74,097	48.0	1939	64,505	24,237	37.6
1954	200,401	105,031	52.4	1946	160,219	70,486	44.0	1938	59,191	22,540	38.1
1953	190,057	100,743	53.0	1945	152,023	60,373	39.7	1937	59,679	22,544	37.8
1952	185,010	96,215	52.0	1944	129,459	50,542	39.0	1936	58,239	21,139	36.3
1951	172,698	89,753	52.0	1943	107,870	38,437	35.6	1935	51,417	18,954	36.9
1950	164,574	76,891	46.7	1942	83,140	28,873	34.7	1934	46,613	16,831	36.1

[1] Estimated by applying to the deposits in the various types of accounts, at the regular call dates, the percentages insured as determined from special reports secured from insured banks.

Series X 155–164. Branch Banking: 1900 to 1957

Year [1]	Total	Commercial banks					Mutual savings banks			Number of banking facilities [4]
		Total	Member banks [2]		Nonmember banks [3]		Total	Insured	Non-insured	
			National	State [3]	Insured	Noninsured				
	155	156	157	158	159	160	161	162	163	164
NUMBER OF BANKS OPERATING BRANCHES										
1957	2,066	1,893	677	340	856	20	173	106	67	---
1956	1,962	1,790	627	327	815	21	172	100	72	---
1955	1,814	1,659	543	304	790	22	155	94	61	
1954	1,720	1,571	502	276	769	24	149	92	57	
1953	1,609	1,474	444	258	745	27	135	85	50	
1952	1,483	1,359	385	237	708	29	124	78	46	
1951	1,422	1,299	352	226	692	29	123	75	48	
1950	1,354	1,241	324	218	669	30	113	67	46	
1949	1,268	1,162	287	206	636	33	106	(5)	(5)	
1948	1,242	1,140	276	202	626	36	102	62	40	
1947 [6]	1,188	1,089	253	194	604	38	99	60	39	
1946	1,143	1,053	235	193	591	34	90	56	34	
1945	1,101	1,016	222	190	570	34	85	52	33	
1944	1,082	999	216	188	563	32	83	51	32	
1943	1,069	989	214	181	563	31	80	49	31	
1942	1,065	985	212	177	565	31	80	---	---	
1941	1,054	973	205	174	563	31	81	---	---	
1940	1,040	959	200	170	560	29	81	---	---	
1939	1,019	939	195	165	549	30	80	---	---	
1938	1,001	921	194	161	566		80	---	---	
1937	987	909	194		715		78	---	---	
1936	938	859	188		671		79	---	---	
1935	901	822	181		641		79			
1934	807	729	176		553		78			
1933	660	584	146		438		76			
1932	---	681	157		524		---			
1931	---	723	164		559		---			
1930	---	751	166		585		---			
1929	---	764	167		597		---			
1928	---	775	171		604		---			
1927	---	740	153		587		---			
1926	---	744	148		596		---			
1925	---	720	130		590		---			
1924	---	706	112		594		---			
1923	---	671	91		580		---			
1922	---	610	55		555		---			
1921	---	547	23		524		---			
1920	---	530	21		509		---			
1915	---	397	12		385		---			
1910	---	292	9		283		---			
1905	---	196	5		191		---			
1900	---	87	5		82		---			
NUMBER OF BRANCHES										
1957	8,373	7,968	3,993	2,173	1,765	37	405	296	109	236
1956	7,728	7,362	3,629	2,053	1,643	37	366	257	109	227
1955	7,040	6,710	3,196	1,916	1,563	35	330	234	96	213
1954	6,416	6,108	2,900	1,710	1,462	36	308	221	87	198
1953	5,897	5,627	2,590	1,631	1,365	41	270	192	78	199
1952	5,520	5,274	2,403	1,530	1,300	41	246	177	69	191
1951	5,225	4,994	2,244	1,449	1,260	41	231	165	65	159
1950	4,934	4,721	2,136	1,343	1,190	52	213	152	61	122
1949	4,578	4,386	1,969	1,247	1,104	66	192	141	51	88
1948	4,461	4,279	1,913	1,219	1,079	68	182	132	50	70
1947	4,261	4,090	1,817	1,168	1,038	67	171	124	47	71
1946	4,059	3,902	1,721	1,118	1,001	62	157	115	42	79
1945	3,866	3,723	1,641	1,061	964	57	143	101	42	224
1944	3,772	3,632	1,589	1,035	954	54	140	99	41	292
1943	3,716	3,580	1,573	1,020	935	52	136	95	41	217
1942	3,712	3,575	1,571	1,020	932	52	137	35	102	27
1941	3,699	3,564	1,565	1,015	932	52	135	32	103	---
1940	3,666	3,531	1,539	1,002	940	50	135	31	104	---
1939	3,629	3,497	1,518	1,002	927	50	132	24	108	---
1938	3,580	3,445	1,499	992	908	46	135	16	119	---
1937	3,540	3,412	1,485	994	891	42	128	11	117	---
1936	3,399	3,271	1,398	981	848	44	128	11	117	---
1935	3,284	3,156	1,329	952	828	47	128	11	117	---
1934	3,133	3,007	1,243	981	783		126	---	---	
1933	2,911	2,786	1,121	960	705		125	---	---	
1932	---	3,195	1,220		1,975		---			
1931	---	3,467	1,110		2,357		---			
1930	---	3,522	1,042		2,480		---			
1929	---	3,353	995		2,358		---			
1928	---	3,138	934		2,204		---			
1927	---	2,914	723		2,191		---			
1926	---	2,703	421		2,282		---			
1925	---	2,525	318		2,207		---			
1924	---	2,297	256		2,041		---			
1923	---	2,054	204		1,850		---			
1922	---	1,801	140		1,661		---			
1921	---	1,455	72		1,383		---			
1920	---	1,281	63		1,218		---			
1915	---	785	26		759		---			
1910	---	548	12		536		---			
1905	---	350	5		345		---			
1900	---	119	5		114		---			

See footnotes at end of table.

Series X 155–164. Branch Banking: 1900 to 1957—Con.

LOANS AND INVESTMENTS OR DEPOSITS [7] ($1,000,000)

Year [1]	Total	Commercial bank branches Total	Member banks [2] National	Member banks [2] State [3]	Non-member banks [3] Insured	Non-member banks [3] Non-insured	Mutual savings bank branches, total
	155	156	157	158	159	160	161
1949	83,260	71,833	39,339	26,703	5,103	688	11,427
1941	43,449	38,496	19,094		19,402		4,953
1939	35,733	30,813	14,924		15,889		4,920
1938		26,587	12,828		13,759		
1937		24,989	12,054		12,935		
1936		20,706	9,713		10,993		
1935		18,744	8,602		10,142		4,457
1933		15,528	6,963		8,565		
1932		17,279	7,339		9,940		
1931		20,680	8,529		12,151		
1930		22,491	9,169		13,322		
1929		21,420	8,016		13,404		
1928		20,068	7,840		12,228		

LOANS AND INVESTMENTS OR DEPOSITS [7]—Con. ($1,000,000)

Year [1]	Commercial bank branches Total	Member banks [2] National	Member banks [2] State [3]
	156	157	158–160
1927	17,591	6,294	11,297
1926	16,511	5,243	11,268
1925	14,763	4,447	10,316
1924	12,480	3,606	8,874
1923	10,922	2,841	8,081
1922	9,110	2,330	6,780
1921	8,354	1,581	6,773
1920	6,897	689	6,208
1915	2,187	98	2,089
1910	1,272	44	1,228
1905	637	6	631
1900	119	5	114

[1] For years prior to 1924, figures are not for any uniform month. For 1925, 1926, 1932–1948, and 1950–1957, figures are as of December; for 1924, 1927–1931, and 1949, as of June.

[2] Federal deposit insurance is compulsory for member banks of the Federal Reserve System.

[3] Figures for 1900–1932 comprise State-chartered commercial banks operating branches and their branches and those unincorporated (private) banks operating branches and their branches reporting to State banking authorities. Beginning in 1934, the proportion of private banks reporting was larger than in prior years.

[4] Banking facilities are provided at military and other Government establishments through arrangements made by the Treasury Department with banks. Some of these facilities are operated by banks that have no other type of branch or additional office.

[5] Not available.

[6] In 1947, the series was revised to conform (except that it excludes Territories and possessions) to the number of banks in the uniform all-bank series inaugurated in 1947 by the Federal bank supervisory authorities. The revision resulted in a net addition of 115 banks and 9 branches.

[7] Loans and investments 1900–1936, and deposits 1937–1941 and 1949, of banks operating branches, except for mutual savings banks for 1935 which are deposits. For other years data are not available. Prior to 1949, commercial bank figures exclude a small amount of deposits of private banks, data for which are available for selected years only as follows: 1935, $46 million; 1939, $102 million; 1941, $138 million.

Series X 165–179. Bank Suspensions—Number and Deposits of Suspended Banks: 1864 to 1933

Year [1]	Total	National	State commercial Incorporated	State commercial Private (unincorporated)	Mutual savings	Federal Reserve System Member	Federal Reserve System Non-member
	165	166	167	168	169	170	171
1933 [2]	4,004	1,101	2,790	109	3	1,275	2,729
1932	1,456	276	1,140	37	1	331	1,125
1931	2,294	409	1,804	80	2	516	1,778
1930	1,352	161	1,131	58	--	188	1,164
1929	659	64	564	31	1	81	578
1928	499	57	422	19		73	426
1927	669	91	545	33	----	122	547
1926	976	123	801	52		158	818
1925	618	118	461	39	----	146	472
1924	775	122	616	37	----	160	615
1923	646	90	533	23	----	122	524
1922	367	49	294	23	1	62	305
1921	505	52	409	44	----	71	434
1920	168	7	136	24	1	----	----
1919	63	2	59	1	1	----	----
1918	47	2	35	10		----	----
1917	49	5	29	15		----	----
1916	52	8	32	12		----	----
1915	152	20	93	39		----	----
1914	151	15	107	27	2	----	----
1913	105	13	75	15	2	----	----
1912	80	6	51	21	2	----	----
1911	87	5	58	22	2	----	----
1910	63	6	40	12	5		
1909	79	8	37	33	1		
1908	155	19	83	51	2		
1907	91	12	58	20	1		
1906	53	6	34	13	----		
1905	80	20	25	35	----		
1904	128	22	53	50	3		
1903	52	13	22	17			
1902	54	4	30	20			
1901	69	9	15	41	4		
1900	36	5	14	16	1		
1899	36	10	8	14	4		
1898	67	11	19	33	4		
1897	145	28	64	47	6		
1896	155	34	66	41	14		
1895	124	34	51	25	14		
1894	89	23	39	21	6		
1893	496	69	228	194	5		
1892	83	12	32	36	3		
1891	62	16	44	------	2		
1890	37	6	30		1		
1889	18	3	15				
1888	33	12	17		4		

Year [1]	Total	National	State commercial [3]	Mutual savings
	165	166	167–168	169
1887	25	5	19	1
1886	20	6	13	1
1885	46	9	32	5
1884	63	6	54	3
1883	33	1	27	5
1882	22	3	19	--
1881	11	----	9	2
1880	18	5	10	3
1879	37	7	20	10
1878	140	10	70	60
1877	99	8	63	28
1876	59	8	37	14
1875	28	3	14	11
1874	57	10	40	7
1873	41	4	33	4
1872	19	6	10	3
1871	10	----	7	3
1870	3	1	1	1
1869	7	1	6	----
1868	14	6	7	1
1867	8	4	3	1
1866	7	2	5	
1865	6	1	5	----
1864	2		2	----

See footnotes at end of table.

Series X 165–179.   Bank Suspensions—Number and Deposits of Suspended Banks: 1864 to 1933—Con.

Year [1]	Total	National	State commercial Incorporated	Private (unincorporated)	Mutual savings	Federal Reserve System Member	Non-member	Losses borne by depositors [4]	Year [1]	Total	National	State commercial Incorporated	Private (unincorporated)	Mutual savings	Federal Reserve System Member	Non-member	Losses borne by depositors [4]
	172	173	174	175	176	177	178	179		172	173	174	175	176	177	178	179
1933 [2]	3,599	1,611	1,975	13	[5]2	2,394	1,205	540	1926	260	44	207	9	--------	67	193	83
1932	716	214	494	8	9	269	446	168									
1931	1,691	439	1,230	21	([6])	733	958	391	1925	168	56	104	8	--------	65	102	61
									1924	210	65	138	8	--------	79	132	79
1930	853	170	668	15	16	373	481	237	1923	150	34	114	2	--------	47	103	62
1929	231	42	181	8	--------	58	173	77	1922	93	20	69	2	2	27	66	38
1928	143	36	103	3	([5])	47	96	44	1921	172	21	143	9	--------	38	134	60
1927	199	46	149	4		63	136	61									

[1] For 1864–1891, all series except mutual savings banks are for year ending June 30; for mutual savings banks the date is not specified in the source. For 1892–1920, for all banks other than private, figures are for calendar year; for private banks, figures vary in ending date of reporting year as follows: 1892, June 30; 1893 (14 months), Aug. 31; 1894–1899, Aug. 31; 1900–1919, June 30; and 1920 (18 months), Dec. 31. For 1921–1933, all series are for calendar year. Series X 165 is composite as to reporting period since it comprises the summation of series X 166–169.
[2] Figures not wholly comparable with earlier years; see text.

[3] Prior to 1892, the figures shown include all State commercial banks; separate figures for private bank suspensions are not available.
[4] In commercial banks only. Estimated losses to depositors in mutual savings banks were as follows: 1922, $213,000; 1928, $31,000; 1930, $6,530,000; 1931, $157,000; 1932, $4,738,000; 1933, $7,085,000. (See *Annual Report* of the Federal Deposit Insurance Corporation, *1934*, p. 113.)
[5] Figures not comparable with losses to depositors shown in footnote 4 because source data differ for these series.
[6] Less than $500,000.

Series X 180–191.   Banks Closed Because of Financial Difficulties: 1934 to 1957

[Money figures in thousands of dollars]

Year	Number of banks Total	Insured by Federal Deposit Insurance Corporation Total insured [1]	With disbursements by FDIC Deposit payoff cases [2]	Deposit assumption cases [3]	Not insured by FDIC [4]	Deposits Total	In banks insured by Federal Deposit Insurance Corporation Total insured [1]	With disbursements by FDIC Deposit payoff cases [2]	Deposit assumption cases [3]	In banks not insured by FDIC [4]	Losses in banks insured by Federal Deposit Insurance Corporation By FDIC [5]	By depositors [6]
	180	181	182	183	184	185	186	187	188	189	190	191
1957	3	2	1	---------	1	12,502	11,247	1,163	---------	1,255	57	3
1956	3	2	1	1	1	11,644	11,283	4,703	6,581	360	341	71
1955	5	5	4	1	--------	11,968	11,968	6,503	5,465	---------	277	8
1954	4	2	--------	2	2	2,947	997	---------	997	1,950	266	--------
1953	5	4	--------	2	1	45,101	44,711	---------	18,262	390	--------	--------
1952	4	3	--------	3	1	3,313	3,170	---------	3,170	143	790	--------
1951	5	2	--------	2	3	6,097	3,408	---------	3,408	2,689	5	--------
1950	5	4	--------	4	1	5,543	5,501	---------	5,501	42	1,375	--------
1949	9	5	--------	4	4	9,108	6,665	---------	5,475	2,443	369	--------
1948	3	3	--------	3	--------	10,674	10,674	---------	10,674	---------	641	--------
1947	6	5	--------	5	1	7,207	7,040	---------	7,040	167	74	--------
1946	2	1	--------	1	1	494	347	---------	347	147	--------	--------
1945	1	1	--------	1	--------	5,695	5,695	---------	5,695	---------	40	3
1944	2	2	1	1	--------	1,915	1,915	456	1,459	---------	40	3
1943	5	5	4	1	--------	12,525	12,525	6,637	5,888	---------	123	12
1942	23	20	6	14	3	19,516	19,186	1,816	17,369	331	688	5
1941	16	14	7	7	2	18,805	18,726	3,739	14,987	79	591	33
1940	48	43	19	24	5	142,788	142,429	5,657	136,773	358	3,853	31
1939	72	60	32	28	12	160,211	157,772	32,738	125,034	2,439	7,157	936
1938	80	73	49	24	7	60,445	59,406	10,018	49,388	1,039	2,425	40
1937	83	76	49	25	7	34,141	33,613	14,896	18,389	528	3,550	110
1936	72	69	42	27	3	28,100	27,508	11,241	16,267	592	2,459	171
1935	32	26	24	1	6	13,988	13,404	9,091	4,229	583	2,716	416
1934	62	9	9	---------	53	37,332	1,968	1,968	---------	35,364	207	20

[1] Includes the following banks not shown separately which reopened or had their deposits assumed by another insured bank without financial aid of the Federal Deposit Insurance Corporations: 1935, 1 bank with deposits of $85 thousand; 1937, 2 banks with deposits of $328 thousand; 1949, 1 bank with deposits of $1,190 thousand; 1953, 2 banks with deposits of $26,449 thousand; and 1957, 1 bank with deposits of $10,084 thousand. (See following *Annual Reports* of Federal Deposit Insurance Corporation, *1941*, pp. 99 and 101; *1949*, p. 191; *1953*, p. 80; *1957*, p. 8.)
[2] Banks placed in receivership with deposits paid, to insurance maximum, by Federal Deposit Insurance Corporation, adjusted to exclude: 1937, 1 bank in voluntary liquidation; 1938, 1 noninsured bank with insured deposits at date of suspension (insured status having been terminated prior to suspension); 1941, 1 foreign-owned bank closed by order of the Federal Government.

[3] Banks in financial difficulties with deposits assumed by other insured banks, with financial aid of Federal Deposit Insurance Corporation.
[4] Previously published data adjusted to add 4 cases in 1934; 1 in 1937; 1 in 1938; 2 in 1939; 1 in 1940; 1 in 1941; and to exclude 1 case in 1935; and 1 case in 1938. Deposits not available for 1 bank in 1938; 2 in 1939; 1 in 1940; 1 in 1941; and 1 in 1954.
[5] Includes loss in the 1938 case mentioned in footnote 2 and estimated loss in cases not yet closed.
[6] Tabulated by Federal Deposit Insurance Corporation from receivership records. Includes loss in the 1938 case mentioned in footnote 2 and estimated loss in cases not yet closed.

Series X 192–199. National Banks—Earnings and Expenses: 1869 to 1957

[Money figures in millions of dollars. Includes data for U.S. Territories and possessions]

Year [1]	Number of banks	Gross earnings	Expenses [2]	Net current earnings [2]	Net losses including depreciation (−) or net recoveries (+)	Net profits	Cash dividends declared	Net profits as percent of total capital accounts	Year [1]	Number of banks	Gross earnings	Expenses [2]	Net current earnings [2]	Net losses including depreciation (−) or net recoveries (+)	Net profits	Cash dividends declared	Net profits as percent of total capital accounts
	192	193	194	195	196	197	198	199		192	193	194	195	196	197	198	199
1957	4,627	4,284	3,252	1,031	−301	730	364	8.3	1922	8,225	1,043	717	326	−115	211	161	7.4
1956	4,659	3,833	2,768	1,065	−418	647	330	7.9	1921	8,169	1,121	775	347	−166	181	153	6.5
1955	4,700	3,437	2,551	885	−242	643	310	8.1	1920	8,130	1,211	817	393	−132	261	162	9.9
1954	4,796	3,226	2,528	699	+42	741	300	9.6	1919	7,890	993	671	322	−73	249	135	10.2
1953	4,864	3,068	2,310	758	−185	573	275	7.9	1918	7,705	814	510	304	−91	212	130	9.4
1952	4,916	2,751	2,067	684	−122	561	259	8.2	1917	7,604	667	411	257	−62	194	126	8.8
1951	4,946	2,454	1,812	642	−135	507	248	7.8	1916	7,579	591	371	220	−62	157	115	7.5
1950	4,965	2,193	1,593	600	−63	538	230	8.7	1915	7,605	528	322	206	−78	127	114	6.0
1949	4,981	2,005	1,442	563	−88	475	205	8.2	1914	7,525	516	301	214	−65	149	121	7.3
1948	4,997	1,900	1,361	540	−116	424	194	7.6	1913	7,473	499	285	215	−54	161	120	7.9
1947	5,011	1,725	1,263	461	−8	453	184	8.6	1912	7,372	450	259	191	−42	149	120	7.5
1946	5,013	1,574	1,138	436	+59	495	170	10.1	1911	7,277	429	232	197	−40	157	115	8.1
1945	5,023	1,349	987	362	+128	490	156	11.0	1910	7,145	403	210	193	−39	154	106	8.3
1944	5,031	1,206	846	360	+52	412	144	10.0	1909	6,926	349	177	172	−40	131	93	7.5
1943	5,046	1,062	746	315	+35	350	132	9.1	1908	6,824	332	151	182	−51	131	97	7.9
1942	5,087	963	695	268	−24	243	128	6.6	1907 [4]	6,429	315	132	183	−31	152	100	[5] 11.4
1941	5,123	926	642	284	−15	269	133	7.5	1906	6,053	279	120	159	−31	128	89	8.6
1940	5,150	865	599	265	−24	241	133	7.0	1905	5,668	249	112	136	−30	106	73	7.5
1939	5,193	848	581	267	−16	252	131	7.4	1904	5,331	249	103	146	−33	113	76	8.4
1938	5,230	838	577	261	−62	199	123	6.1	1903	4,939	235	93	141	−32	110	64	8.6
1937	5,266	859	586	273	−45	228	122	7.1	1902	4,535	221	85	136	−29	107	68	9.0
1936	5,331	825	565	260	+54	314	120	10.0	1901	4,165	188	78	111	−29	82	52	7.7
1935	5,392	794	549	245	−87	158	113	5.1	1900	3,732	194	73	121	−34	87	48	8.6
1934 [3]	5,467	809	558	251	−405	−153	91	−5.2	1899	3,583	157	68	88	−34	54	47	5.7
1933 [3]	5,159	802	565	236	−523	−286	72	−9.6	1898	3,582	143	62	81	−31	50	44	5.2
1932	6,016	1,000	750	250	−415	−165	135	−5.0	1897	3,610	138	61	77	−32	44	42	4.6
1931	6,373	1,153	850	303	−358	−55	193	−1.5	1896	3,689	142	61	81	−32	50	46	5.1
1930	7,038	1,325	990	336	−177	158	211	4.0	1895	3,715	135	60	75	−29	47	46	4.8
1929	7,408	1,407	988	418	−126	292	227	7.8	1894	3,770	140	60	80	−38	42	45	4.2
1928	7,635	1,351	988	363	−72	291	195	8.2	1893	3,807	152	61	91	−22	69	50	6.7
1927	7,765	1,227	919	308	−50	258	184	7.9	1892	3,759	149	59	90	−23	67	50	6.6
1926	7,912	1,212	857	354	−109	245	169	8.0	1891	3,652	151	55	96	−21	76	51	7.7
1925	8,054	1,160	823	338	−93	244	163	8.2	1890	3,484	145	51	93	−21	72	51	7.7
1924	8,049	1,094	776	318	−104	214	155	7.4	1889	3,239	135	50	86	−16	70	47	8.0
1923	8,184	1,065	758	307	−112	195	152	6.7	1888	3,120	129	45	84	−18	65	47	7.8

Year [1]	Number of banks	Net profits	Cash dividend declared	Net profits as percent of total capital accounts	Year [1]	Number of banks	Net profits	Cash dividend declared	Net profits as percent of total capital accounts	Year [1]	Number of banks	Net profits	Cash dividend declared	Net profits as percent of total capital accounts
	192	197	198	199		192	197	198	199		192	197	198	199
1887	3,014	65	44	8.0	1880	2,076	45	36	7.2	1874	1,983	60	48	8.8
1886	2,809	55	42	7.3	1879	2,048	32	35	5.1	1873	1,968	65	50	9.8
1885	2,689	44	41	6.0	1878	2,056	31	37	4.9	1872	1,853	58	47	9.3
1884	2,625	52	41	7.1	1877	2,078	35	44	5.3	1871	1,723	55	44	9.2
1883	2,417	54	41	7.6	1876	2,091	44	47	6.4	1870	1,612	56	43	9.9
1882	2,239	53	41	8.1	1875	2,076	58	49	8.4	1869 [6]	1,619	29	22	10.7
1881	2,115	54	38	8.4										

[1] All data except number of banks are for calendar year, 1919–1957; year ending June 30, 1907–1918; and year ending Aug. 31, 1869–1906. Number of banks are as of end of period.

[2] Income taxes have been treated as an expense throughout. Beginning in 1943, these figures differ from those shown in the source volume, because income taxes in the source volume are shown separately from other expenses and as a deduction from net current earnings.

[3] Licensed banks, i.e., those operating on an unrestricted basis.

[4] 10 months only.

[5] Annual basis.

[6] 6 months only.

Series X 200–215. Insured Commercial Banks—Earnings and Expenses: 1934 to 1957

[Money figures in millions of dollars. Includes data for U.S. Territories and possessions]

Year	Number of banks	Earnings					Expenses				Net current earnings [2]	Net losses (−) or net recoveries (+)	Taxes on net income [1]	Net profits (after income taxes)	Cash dividends	Net profits as percent of capital accounts
		Total	On loans	On securities	Service charges on deposit accounts	Other	Total	Salaries and wages	Interest on time deposits	Other [1]						
	200	201	202	203	204	205	206	207	208	209	210	211	212	213	214	215
1957	13,165	8,050	4,880	1,855	441	875	5,119	2,313	1,142	1,665	2,931	−559	998	1,374	678	8.30
1956	13,218	7,232	4,340	1,713	386	793	4,457	2,136	806	1,516	2,775	−743	815	1,217	617	7.82
1955	13,237	6,378	3,626	1,685	340	727	3,960	1,935	678	1,346	2,418	−468	794	1,156	566	7.90
1954	13,323	5,774	3,206	1,598	312	659	3,638	1,799	618	1,221	2,136	+79	908	1,307	517	9.50
1953	13,432	5,484	3,108	1,505	271	600	3,376	1,687	534	1,154	2,108	−296	786	1,026	474	7.93
1952	13,439	4,932	2,742	1,376	245	569	3,029	1,526	458	1,044	1,903	−218	695	990	442	8.07
1951	13,455	4,395	2,390	1,233	231	542	2,701	1,378	385	938	1,694	−226	559	908	419	7.82
1950	13,446	3,931	1,976	1,241	212	501	2,445	1,226	343	875	1,486	−121	428	937	391	8.51
1949	13,436	3,607	1,734	1,215	194	464	2,284	1,133	328	822	1,323	−167	325	831	354	7.98
1948	13,419	3,404	1,578	1,198	174	454	2,164	1,065	317	782	1,240	−219	275	745	332	7.49
1947	13,403	3,098	1,264	1,259	148	427	1,982	966	298	717	1,116	−32	302	781	315	8.20
1946	13,359	2,863	937	1,395	125	406	1,763	848	269	646	1,100	+125	323	902	299	10.01
1945	13,302	2,482	708	1,300	110	365	1,523	706	233	584	960	+245	299	906	274	10.87
1944	13,268	2,215	681	1,090	107	337	1,357	640	187	530	858	+96	203	751	253	9.73
1943	13,274	1,959	692	861	95	310	1,256	594	164	498	703	+62	128	638	233	8.82
1942	13,347	1,791	805	610	84	291	1,222	564	175	483	569	−48	80	441	228	6.34
1941	13,427	1,730	848	509	373		1,266	527	190	549	464	−10	-------	455	253	6.72
1940	13,438	1,631	769	500	363		1,193	498	201	495	438	−37	-------	401	237	6.01
1939	13,534	1,606	727	522	357		1,160	484	215	461	446	−57	-------	389	232	5.96
1938	13,657	1,584	705	532	347		1,159	474	230	455	425	−125	-------	300	222	4.67
1937	13,795	1,634	710	572	352		1,167	463	235	468	467	−86	-------	381	226	5.94
1936	13,969	1,567	663	574	330		1,126	437	237	451	441	+83	-------	524	223	8.28
1935	14,123	1,486	643	548	295		1,083	411	262	410	403	−196	-------	207	208	3.34
1934	14,137	1,518	691	550	35	243	1,117	402	303	413	401	−741	-------	−340	188	−5.49

[1] Prior to 1942, taxes on net income have been included with other expenses. Taxes on net income for insured nonmember commercial banks for 1936–1941 are available separately in *Annual Reports* of the Federal Deposit Insurance Corporation.

[2] Prior to 1942, represents net current earnings after deduction of income taxes; thereafter, net current earnings before deduction of income taxes. See footnote 1.

Series X 216–225. Bank Debits and Deposit Turnover: 1919 to 1952

[In millions of dollars except rates]

Year	Bank debits to deposit accounts, except interbank accounts, at reporting banks [1]				Bank debits and deposit turnover, all commercial banks [3]					
					Total demand and time deposits			Demand deposits		
	All reporting centers [2]	New York City	140 other centers	Other reporting centers [2]	Debits	Deposits	Annual turnover rate	Debits	Deposits	Annual turnover rate
	216	217	218	219	220	221	222	223	224	225
1952	1,692,136	615,670	895,906	180,560	-------	-------	-------	-------	-------	-------
1951	1,577,857	551,889	854,050	171,917	-------	-------	-------	-------	-------	-------
1950	1,403,752	513,970	742,458	147,324	-------	-------	-------	-------	-------	-------
1949	1,231,053	452,897	648,976	129,179	-------	-------	-------	-------	-------	-------
1948	1,249,630	449,002	667,934	132,695	-------	-------	-------	-------	-------	-------
1947	1,125,074	405,929	599,639	119,506	-------	-------	-------	-------	-------	-------
1946	1,050,021	417,475	527,336	105,210	-------	-------	-------	-------	-------	-------
1945	974,102	404,543	479,760	89,799	-------	-------	-------	-------	-------	-------
1944	891,910	345,585	462,354	83,970	-------	-------	-------	-------	-------	-------
1943	792,935	296,368	419,413	77,153	-------	-------	-------	-------	-------	-------
1942	[4] 641,778	[4] 226,865	[4] 347,837	[4] 67,074	-------	-------	-------	-------	-------	-------
1941	537,343	197,724	293,925	45,694	756,000	54,110	14.0	740,000	38,220	19.4
1940	445,863	171,582	236,952	37,329	627,000	48,610	12.9	611,000	33,040	18.5
1939	423,933	171,382	218,295	34,256	592,000	43,670	13.6	577,000	28,550	20.2
1938	405,930	168,778	204,744	32,408	566,000	40,410	14.0	551,000	25,520	21.6
1937	469,462	197,836	235,207	36,419	650,000	40,290	16.1	635,000	25,710	24.7
1936	461,889	208,936	219,669	33,284	628,000	38,660	16.2	614,000	24,810	24.7
1935	402,718	184,006	190,167	28,545	547,000	34,610	15.8	534,000	21,480	24.9
1934	356,613	165,948	165,555	25,110	491,000	30,640	16.0	479,000	18,220	26.3
1933	303,216	[5] 148,449	[5] 134,259	[5] 20,508	437,000	28,500	15.3	424,000	15,850	26.8
1932	347,264	167,964	154,401	24,899	471,000	31,720	14.8	456,000	16,720	27.3
1931	515,294	263,834	217,523	33,937	685,000	37,830	18.1	658,000	19,810	33.2
1930	702,959	384,639	277,317	41,003	931,000	41,550	22.4	892,000	22,090	40.4
1929	982,531	603,088	331,942	47,501	1,276,000	42,720	29.9	1,237,000	23,080	53.6
1928	850,521	500,211	306,194	44,116	1,114,000	42,570	26.2	1,075,000	22,950	46.8
1927	714,328	391,558	282,303	40,467	952,000	40,670	23.4	915,000	22,340	41.0
1926	646,587	339,055	268,902	38,630	872,000	39,340	22.2	838,000	22,210	37.7
1925	605,843	313,373	256,689	35,781	820,000	37,720	21.7	788,000	21,720	36.3
1924	522,627	263,530	228,161	30,936	716,000	34,590	20.7	687,000	19,990	34.4
1923	494,412	238,396	225,331	30,685	685,000	32,920	20.8	658,000	19,280	34.1
1922	451,513	239,855	199,510	12,148	643,000	29,750	21.6	620,000	18,150	34.2
1921	409,338	207,096	191,942	10,300	591,000	28,400	20.8	569,000	17,470	32.6
1920	490,468	241,431	241,595	7,442	721,000	30,350	23.8	700,000	19,800	35.4
1919	460,249	244,119	211,175	4,955	681,000	27,060	24.5	646,000	18,480	35.0

[1] Beginning in May 1942, 60 new reporting centers (affecting series X 216 and X 219) and a number of banks in previously included reporting centers (affecting all series) were added to those centers and banks included for the years prior to 1942. The figures for the period 1942–1952 are therefore not strictly comparable with those for the earlier years. The extent of the change in coverage is reflected for 1942 by comparing the figures shown above with those derived on the old basis, as follows: Series X 216, 607,071; series X 217, 210,961; series X 218, 342,430; series X 219, 53,679. (See *Federal Reserve Bulletin*, Aug. 1943, p. 717.)
[2] The number of centers in this group varied considerably; see text.
[3] Excludes interbank deposits and collection items.
[4] Partly estimated for first 4 months.
[5] 11 months only; data for Mar. 1933 not available because of bank holiday.

639

Series X 226–229. Bank Clearings at Principal Cities: 1854 to 1956
[In millions of dollars]

Year	New York City (227)	36 cities outside New York City [1] (229)	Year	Total, United States (226)	New York City (227)	Outside New York City (228)	36 cities outside New York City [1] (229)	Year	Total, United States (226)	New York City (227)	Outside New York City (228)
1956	559,157	569,803	1935	300,913	181,551	119,362	103,948	1915	163,189	90,843	72,347
1955	530,883	547,803	1934	264,268	161,507	102,761	89,940	1914	163,850	89,760	74,089
1954	532,029	500,884	1933	243,891	157,414	86,477	75,301	1913	173,193	98,122	75,071
1953	470,289	492,594	1932	258,523	160,138	98,385	85,625	1912	168,686	96,672	72,014
1952	461,724	470,403	1931	411,754	263,270	148,484	129,855	1911	159,540	92,420	67,119
1951	431,775	455,621									
1950	399,309	403,905	1930	544,542	347,110	197,433	173,045	1910	168,987	102,554	66,433
1949	358,845	356,111	1929	715,692	477,242	238,450	208,914	1909	158,877	99,258	59,620
1948	371,554	374,727	1928	623,366	391,727	231,638	201,727	1908	126,239	73,631	52,608
1947	361,238	338,537	1927	544,414	321,234	223,180	195,124	1907	154,477	95,315	59,161
1946	366,065	298,129	1926	512,567	290,355	222,212	194,271	1906	157,681	103,754	53,927
1945	334,433	260,331	1925	500,354	283,619	216,734	190,358	1905	140,502	91,879	48,623
1944	286,349	249,685	1924	445,747	249,868	195,878	171,736	1904	102,356	59,673	42,684
1943	248,560	234,757	1923	404,512	213,996	190,515	166,092	1903	113,963	70,834	43,130
1942	192,939	201,060	1922	384,977	217,900	167,076	145,730	1902	115,892	74,753	41,139
1941	183,263	172,272	1921	349,757	194,331	155,426	135,699	1901	114,820	77,021	37,799
1940	160,878	135,789	1920	439,792	243,135	196,657	177,044	1900	84,582	51,965	32,618
1939	165,914	124,286	1919	387,854	214,703	173,151	----------	1899	88,829	57,368	31,461
1938	165,156	114,054	1918	320,989	174,524	146,464	----------	1898	65,925	39,853	26,072
1937	186,740	130,340	1917	305,062	181,534	123,528	----------	1897	54,180	31,338	22,842
1936	193,549	120,054	1916	242,236	147,181	95,055	----------	1896	51,936	29,351	22,585

Year	Total, United States (226)	New York City (227)	Outside New York City (228)	Year	New York City (227)	Year	New York City (227)
1895	50,975	28,264	22,711	1880	37,182	1865	26,032
1894	45,028	24,230	20,798	1879	25,179	1864	24,097
1893	58,881	34,421	24,460	1878	22,508	1863	14,868
1892	60,884	36,280	24,604	1877	23,289	1862	6,871
1891	57,181	34,054	23,127	1876	21,597	1861	5,916
1890	59,882	37,661	22,221	1875	25,061	1860	7,231
1889	53,501	34,796	18,705	1874	22,856	1859	6,448
1888	48,751	30,864	17,887	1873	35,461	1858	4,757
1887	52,127	34,873	17,254	1872	33,844	1857	8,333
1886	48,212	33,375	14,837	1871	29,301	1856	6,906
1885	37,770	25,251	12,519	1870	27,805	1855	5,363
1884	47,387	34,092	13,295	1869	37,407	1854	5,750
1883	53,536	40,293	13,243	1868	28,484		
1882	61,054	46,553	14,501	1867	28,675		
1881	----------	48,566	----------	1866	28,717		

[1] Excludes Los Angeles.

Series X 230–237. Savings—Number of Depositors and Savings Deposits, by Class of Bank: 1910 to 1942
[As of June 30 or nearest available date]

Year	Number of depositors (1,000)				Amount of savings and other time deposits [1] ($1,000,000)			
	Total (230)	Mutual savings banks (231)	State, etc., banks (232)	National banks (233)	Total (234)	Mutual savings banks (235)	State, etc., banks (236)	National banks (237)
1942	45,417	14,441	14,923	16,053	25,487	10,351	7,294	7,842
1941	46,151	14,621	15,046	16,484	26,149	10,601	7,494	8,053
1940	45,791	14,524	15,129	16,138	25,750	10,584	7,272	7,894
1939	45,104	14,193	14,988	15,924	25,081	10,385	7,003	7,693
1938	44,549	14,132	14,549	15,868	24,626	10,151	6,876	7,599
1937	44,226	13,526	14,977	15,723	24,492	10,164	6,794	7,534
1936	42,397	13,374	13,988	15,035	23,464	10,010	6,265	7,188
1935	41,315	13,415	13,631	14,269	22,614	9,872	5,873	6,869
1934	39,562	13,342	12,734	13,486	21,753	9,803	5,452	6,498
1933	39,262	12,995	14,289	11,978	21,126	9,760	5,453	5,912
1932	44,352	12,735	17,520	14,097	24,281	10,040	7,283	6,958
1931	51,399	12,544	23,662	15,193	28,220	10,034	10,141	8,045
1930	52,729	12,077	25,115	15,537	28,479	9,206	11,176	8,097
1929	52,764	11,875	25,467	15,422	28,218	8,904	11,426	7,889
1928	53,188	11,643	25,364	16,181	28,413	8,668	11,695	8,050
1927	48,355	11,190	22,828	14,337	26,091	8,040	10,963	7,088
1926	46,762	10,950	23,242	12,570	24,696	7,525	10,993	6,178
1925	----------	10,639	----------	11,865	23,134	7,152	10,172	5,810
1924	----------	10,384	----------	11,068	21,189	6,693	9,337	5,158
1923	----------	10,045	----------	9,899	19,727	6,273	8,767	4,686
1922	----------	9,687	----------	8,873	17,579	5,818	7,687	4,074
1921	----------	9,662	----------	8,109	16,501	5,568	7,255	3,677
1920	----------	9,079	----------	7,980	15,189	5,058	6,668	3,463
1919	----------	9,040	----------	6,763	13,040	4,732	5,532	2,776
1918	----------	8,326	----------	(2)	11,535	4,382	4,817	2,336
1917	----------	8,651	----------	(2)	10,876	4,339	4,364	2,173
1916	----------	7,917	----------	(2)	9,459	4,102	3,641	1,716
1915	----------	7,643	----------	(2)	8,807	3,945	3,541	1,321
1914	----------	7,901	----------	(2)	8,712	3,910	3,348	1,454
1913	----------	8,034	----------	2,965	8,548	3,812	3,368	1,369
1912	----------	7,880	----------	2,675	8,404	3,609	3,260	1,536
1911	----------	7,691	----------	2,341	7,963	3,459	3,024	1,480
1910	----------	----------	----------	2,087	6,835	(3)	(3)	1,014

[1] Figures differ from similar data included in series X 38, X 60, and X 82; for explanation, see text.

[2] Not available.

[3] Combined data for cities other than national banks included in total.

Series X 238–239. Number of Depositors and Savings Deposits in Savings Banks: 1820 to 1910

[As of June 30 for later years; earlier years as of various dates]

Year	Number of depositors	Amount of deposits [1] ($1,000,000)	Year	Number of depositors	Amount of deposits [1] ($1,000,000)	Year	Number of depositors	Amount of deposits [1] ($1,000,000)	Year	Number of depositors	Amount of deposits [1] ($1,000,000)
	238	239		238	239		238	239		238	239
1910	9,142,908	4,070.5	1892	4,781,605	1,712.8	1875	2,359,864	924.0	1857	490,428	98.5
1909	8,831,863	3,713.4	1891	4,533,217	1,623.1	1874	2,293,401	864.6	1856	487,986	95.6
1908	8,705,848	3,660.6				1873	2,185,832	802.4			
1907	8,588,811	3,690.1	1890	4,258,893	1,524.8	1872	1,992,925	735.0	1855	431,602	84.3
1906	8,027,192	3,482.1	1889	4,021,523	1,425.2	1871	1,902,047	650.7	1854	396,173	77.8
			1888	3,838,291	1,364.2				1853	365,538	72.3
1905	7,696,229	3,261.2	1887	3,418,013	1,235.2	1870	1,630,846	549.9	1852	308,863	59.5
1904	7,305,443	3,060.2	1886	3,158,950	1,141.5	1869	1,466,684	457.7	1851	277,148	50.5
1903	7,035,228	2,935.2				1868	1,310,144	392.8			
1902	6,666,672	2,750.2	1885	3,071,495	1,095.2	1867	1,188,202	337.0	1850	251,354	43.4
1901	6,358,723	2,597.1	1884	3,015,151	1,073.3	1866	1,067,061	282.5	1849	217,318	36.1
			1883	2,876,438	1,024.9				1848	199,764	33.1
1900	6,107,083	2,449.5	1882	2,710,354	966.8	1865	980,844	242.6	1847	187,739	31.6
1899	5,687,818	2,230.4	1881	2,528,749	892.0	1864	976,025	236.3	1846	158,709	27.4
1898	5,385,746	2,065.6				1863	887,096	206.2			
1897	5,201,132	1,939.4	1880	2,335,582	819.1	1862	787,943	169.4	1845	145,206	24.5
1896	5,065,494	1,907.2	1879	2,268,707	802.5	1861	694,487	146.7	1840	78,701	14.1
			1878	2,400,785	879.9				1835	60,058	10.6
1895	4,875,519	1,810.6	1877	2,395,314	866.2	1860	693,870	149.3	1830	38,085	7.0
1894	4,777,687	1,748.0	1876	2,368,630	941.4	1859	622,556	128.7	1825	16,931	2.5
1893	4,830,599	1,785.2				1858	538,840	108.4	1820	8,635	1.1

[1] Coverage of these figures differs from series X 234–237; see text.

Series X 240–244. Postal Savings System: 1911 to 1957

[As of June 30]

Year	Offices in operation	Number of depositors [1]	Deposits ($1,000)	Withdrawals ($1,000)	Balance to credit of depositors [2] ($1,000)	Year	Offices in operation	Number of depositors [1]	Deposits ($1,000)	Withdrawals ($1,000)	Balance to credit of depositors [2] ($1,000)
	240	241	242	243	244		240	241	242	243	244
1957	6,483	2,200,508	353,628	656,830	1,462,268	1933	7,071	2,342,133	1,166,327	763,961	1,187,186
1956	6,623	2,482,026	606,100	848,627	1,765,470	1932	6,743	1,545,190	860,196	422,792	784,821
						1931	6,665	770,859	366,901	194,756	347,417
1955	6,708	2,711,110	1,140,503	1,383,926	2,007,996						
1954	6,816	2,934,795	1,197,325	1,403,454	2,251,419	1930	5,998	466,401	159,959	138,332	175,272
1953	7,181	3,162,176	1,342,675	1,502,691	2,457,548	1929	5,976	416,584	112,446	110,945	153,645
1952	7,200	3,339,378	1,460,415	1,631,050	2,617,564	1928	5,897	412,250	96,386	91,602	152,143
1951	7,208	3,529,527	1,603,327	1,912,444	2,788,199	1927	5,896	411,394	103,607	90,426	147,359
						1926	5,853	399,305	90,751	88,746	134,179
1950	7,215	3,779,784	1,827,913	2,007,999	3,097,316						
1949	7,213	3,964,509	1,947,238	2,048,965	3,277,402	1925	5,896	402,325	89,708	90,349	132,173
1948	7,234	4,111,373	2,055,651	2,069,295	3,379,130	1924	5,995	412,584	94,933	93,790	132,814
1947	7,225	4,196,517	2,163,619	1,890,502	3,392,773	1923	6,047	417,902	88,000	94,073	131,671
1946	7,187	4,135,565	2,127,038	1,666,956	3,119,656	1922	6,020	420,242	96,508	111,161	137,736
						1921	5,554	466,109	133,575	138,461	152,390
1945	7,162	3,921,937	1,739,341	1,113,902	2,659,575						
1944	7,183	3,493,079	1,363,028	906,417	2,034,137	1920	5,583	508,508	139,209	149,256	157,276
1943	7,199	3,064,054	1,033,550	771,548	1,577,526	1919	5,715	565,509	136,690	117,838	167,323
1942	7,211	2,812,806	895,080	883,710	1,315,523	1918	5,926	612,188	116,893	100,376	148,471
1941	7,203	2,882,886	923,660	912,916	1,304,153	1917	6,423	674,728	132,112	86,177	131,955
						1916	7,701	602,937	76,776	56,441	86,020
1940	7,172	2,816,408	923,266	892,149	1,293,409						
1939	7,162	2,767,417	897,339	886,846	1,262,292	1915	8,832	525,414	70,315	48,074	65,685
1938	7,245	2,741,569	929,480	945,355	1,251,799	1914	9,639	388,511	47,815	38,190	43,444
1937	7,266	2,791,371	972,743	936,743	1,267,674	1913	12,158	331,006	41,701	28,120	33,819
1936	7,299	2,705,152	933,071	906,261	1,231,673	1912	9,907	243,801	30,732	11,172	20,237
						1911	400	11,918	778	101	677
1935	7,301	2,598,391	944,960	938,017	1,204,863						
1934	7,247	2,562,082	966,651	955,917	1,197,920						

[1] Includes depositors whose accounts are reflected on balance sheet as unclaimed.   [2] Includes items shown on balance sheet as unclaimed.

Series X 245–254. Federal Reserve Banks—Principal Assets and Liabilities: 1914 to 1957

[In millions of dollars.   As of December 31]

Year	Reserves, total	Reserve bank credit outstanding				Total assets or liabilities and capital accounts	Deposits		Federal Reserve notes in actual circulation [2]	Capital accounts
		Total loans and securities [1]	Discounts and advances	Bills bought	U.S. Government securities		Total	Member bank reserve account		
	245	246	247	248	249	250	251	252	253	254
1957	22,085	24,360	55	66	24,237	53,028	20,117	19,034	27,535	1,291
1956	21,269	25,034	50	69	24,915	52,910	20,249	19,059	27,476	1,209
1955	21,009	24,921	108	28	24,785	52,340	20,355	19,005	26,921	1,132
1954	21,033	25,076	143	--------	24,932	50,872	20,371	18,876	26,253	1,084
1953	21,354	25,945	28	--------	25,916	52,315	21,422	20,160	26,558	1,025
1952	21,986	24,857	156	--------	24,697	51,852	21,344	19,950	26,250	972
1951	21,468	23,825	19	--------	23,801	49,900	21,192	20,056	25,064	909
1950	21,458	20,848	67	--------	20,778	47,172	19,810	17,681	23,587	869
1949	23,176	18,965	78	--------	18,885	45,643	18,906	16,568	23,483	832
1948	22,966	23,556	223	--------	23,333	50,043	22,791	20,479	24,161	761
1947	21,497	22,646	85	--------	22,559	47,712	19,731	17,899	24,820	696
1946	18,381	23,513	163	--------	23,350	45,006	17,353	16,139	24,945	678

See footnotes at end of table.

Series X 245–254. Federal Reserve Banks—Principal Assets and Liabilities: 1914 to 1957—Con.

[In millions of dollars]

Year	Reserves, total	Reserve bank credit outstanding				Total assets or liabilities and capital accounts	Deposits		Federal Reserve notes in actual circulation [2]	Capital accounts
		Total loans and securities [1]	Discounts and advances	Bills bought	U.S. Government securities		Total	Member bank reserve account		
	245	246	247	248	249	250	251	252	253	254
1945	17,863	24,513	249		[3]24,262	45,063	18,200	15,915	24,649	587
1944	18,687	18,930	80		[3]18,846	40,269	16,411	14,373	21,731	486
1943	20,096	11,558	5		[3]11,543	33,955	15,181	12,886	16,906	429
1942	20,908	6,208	6		[3]6,189	29,019	15,194	13,117	12,193	381
1941	20,764	2,267	3		[3]2,254	24,353	14,678	12,450	8,192	373
1940	20,036	2,195	3		[3]2,184	23,262	16,127	14,026	5,931	369
1939	15,524	2,502	7		[3]2,484	19,027	12,941	11,653	4,959	349
1938	12,166	2,584	4	1	2,564	15,581	10,088	8,724	4,452	344
1937	9,481	2,592	10	1	2,564	12,880	7,577	7,027	4,284	341
1936	9,121	2,461	3	3	2,430	12,525	7,109	6,606	4,284	341
1935	7,835	2,473	5	5	2,431	11,026	6,386	5,587	3,709	335
1934	5,401	2,457	7	6	2,430	8,442	4,405	4,096	3,221	331
1933	3,794	2,670	98	133	2,437	7,041	2,865	2,729	3,080	445
1932	3,331	2,128	235	33	1,855	6,115	2,561	2,509	2,739	430
1931	3,158	1,825	638	339	817	5,672	2,125	1,961	2,624	420
1930	3,082	1,352	251	364	729	5,201	2,517	2,471	1,664	444
1929	3,011	1,548	632	392	511	5,458	2,414	2,355	1,910	448
1928	2,709	1,783	1,056	489	228	5,352	2,440	2,389	1,838	401
1927	2,867	1,591	582	392	617	5,346	2,531	2,487	1,790	366
1926	2,948	1,335	637	381	315	5,150	2,276	2,194	1,851	354
1925	2,824	1,395	643	374	375	5,109	2,257	2,212	1,838	338
1924	3,047	1,249	320	387	540	5,096	2,311	2,220	1,862	330
1923	3,169	1,211	723	355	134	5,066	1,960	1,898	2,247	331
1922	3,166	1,326	618	272	436	5,252	1,974	1,934	2,396	326
1921	3,010	1,524	1,144	145	234	5,151	1,876	1,753	2,409	319
1920	2,250	3,235	2,687	260	287	6,254	1,861	1,781	3,336	302
1919	1,990	3,090	2,215	574	300	6,324	2,022	1,890	3,009	208
1918	2,146	2,291	1,766	287	239	5,250	1,808	1,636	2,659	104
1917	1,672	1,060	660	273	122	3,164	1,583	1,447	1,247	71
1916	757	222	29	129	55	1,211	[4]879	[4]722	275	56
1915	555	84	32	24	16	697	[4]452	[4]401	189	55
1914	268	11	10			330	[4]301	[4]265	11	18

[1] Includes industrial advances not shown separately.
[2] Includes Federal Reserve notes held by the U.S. Treasury or by a Federal Reserve bank other than the issuing bank.
[3] Includes guaranteed obligations which were not issued until late in 1933. Reserve banks were first authorized to purchase them in 1934. The only holdings of such securities prior to 1939 were $181,000 at the end of 1935, which were included in "other securities."
[4] Figures not comparable with later years in part because prior to June 21, 1917, member banks were not required to keep all of their legal reserves with the Reserve banks; also, for 1914–1916, deferred availability accounts, subsequently shown separately in the source, are included in total deposits.

Series X 255–261. Federal Reserve Banks—Earnings and Expenses: 1914 to 1957

[In thousands of dollars]

Year	Current earnings	Current expenses	Net earnings before payments to U.S. Treasury [1]	Disposition of net earnings				Year	Current earnings	Current expenses	Net earnings before payments to U.S. Treasury [1]	Disposition of net earnings		
				Dividends paid	Franchise tax paid to U.S. Treasury [2]	Paid to U.S. Treasury [3]	Transferred to surplus					Dividends paid	Franchise tax paid to U.S. Treasury [2]	Transferred to surplus
	255	256	257	258	259	260	261		255	256	257	258	259	261
1957	763,348	131,814	624,393	20,081	542,708		61,603	1935	42,752	31,577	9,438	8,505		635
1956	595,649	121,182	474,443	18,905	401,556		53,983	1934	48,903	29,241	15,231	8,782		6,450
								1933	49,487	29,223	7,957	8,874		−917
1955	412,488	110,060	302,162	17,712	251,741		32,710	1932	50,019	26,291	22,314	9,282	2,011	11,021
1954	438,486	109,733	328,619	16,442	276,289		35,888	1931	29,701	27,041	2,972	10,030		−7,058
1953	513,037	113,515	398,463	15,558	342,568		40,337							
1952	456,060	104,694	352,950	14,682	291,935		46,334	1930	36,424	28,343	7,988	10,269	17	−2,298
1951	394,656	95,469	297,059	13,865	254,874		28,321	1929	70,955	29,691	36,403	9,584	4,283	22,536
								1928	64,053	26,905	32,122	8,458	2,585	21,079
1950	275,839	80,572	231,561	13,083	196,629		21,849	1927	43,024	27,518	13,048	7,755	250	5,044
1949	316,537	77,478	226,937	12,329	193,146		21,462	1926	47,600	27,350	16,612	7,329	818	8,464
1948	304,161	72,710	197,133	11,920	166,690		18,523							
1947	158,656	65,393	95,236	11,523	75,224	36	8,453	1925	41,801	27,528	9,449	6,916	59	2,474
1946	150,385	57,235	92,524	10,962		67	81,495	1924	38,340	28,431	3,718	6,682	114	−3,078
								1923	50,709	29,764	12,711	6,553	3,613	2,546
1945	142,210	48,717	92,662	10,183		248	82,232	1922	50,499	29,559	16,498	6,307	10,851	−660
1944	104,392	49,176	58,438	9,500		327	48,611	1921	122,866	34,464	82,087	6,120	59,974	15,993
1943	69,306	43,546	49,528	8,911		245	40,372							
1942	52,663	38,624	12,470	8,669		198	3,604	1920	181,297	28,258	149,295	5,654	60,725	82,916
1941	41,380	32,963	9,138	8,430		141	566	1919	102,381	19,340	78,368	5,012	2,704	70,652
								1918	67,584	10,960	52,716	5,541		48,334
1940	43,538	29,165	25,860	8,215		82	17,563	1917	16,128	5,160	9,582	6,804	1,134	1,134
1939	38,501	28,647	12,243	8,110		25	4,108	1916	5,218	2,274	2,751	1,743		
1938	36,261	28,912	9,582	8,019		120	1,443							
1937	41,233	28,801	10,801	7,941		177	2,684	1915 [4]	2,173	2,321	−141	217		
1936	37,901	29,874	8,512	7,830		227	455							

[1] Current earnings less current expenses plus other additions and less other deductions.
[2] The Banking Act of 1933 eliminated the provision in the Federal Reserve Act requiring payments of a franchise tax. Beginning in 1947, payments represent interest on Federal Reserve notes; see text.
[3] Payments made pursuant to section 13b of the Federal Reserve Act, relating to loans and discounts for industrial purposes provided for by act of June 19, 1934.
[4] Figures for 1914 and 1915.

Series X 262-265. Federal Reserve Banks—Member Bank Reserve Requirements: 1917 to 1957

[Percent of deposits]

Effective date of change	Net demand deposits [1]			Time deposits (all member banks)	Effective date of change	Net demand deposits [1]			Time deposits (all member banks)
	Central reserve city banks	Reserve city banks	Country banks			Central reserve city banks	Reserve city banks	Country banks	
	262	263	264	265		262	263	264	265
1957—Dec. 31	20	18	12	5	1948—Sept. 16, 24 [2]	26	22	16	7½
1954—July 29, Aug. 1 [2]	20	18	12	5	June 11	24	20	14	6
June 16, 24 [2]	21	19	13	5	Feb. 27	22	20	14	6
1953—July 1, 9 [2]	22	19	13	6	1942—Oct. 3	20	20	14	6
1951—Jan. 25, Feb. 1 [2]	24	20	14	6	Sept. 14	22	20	14	6
Jan. 11, 16 [2]	23	19	13	6	Aug. 20	24	20	14	6
1949—Sept. 1	22	18	12	[3] 5	1941—Nov. 1	26	20	14	6
Aug. 25	22½	18½	12	[3] 5	1938—Apr. 16	22¾	17½	12	5
Aug. 16, 18 [2]	23	19	12	[3] 5	1937—May 1	26	20	14	6
Aug. 1, 11 [2]	23½	19½	13	[3] 5	Mar. 1	22¾	17½	12½	5½
June 30, July 1 [2]	24	20	14	6	1936—Aug. 16	19½	15	10½	4½
May 1, 5 [2]	24	21	15	7	1917—June 21	13	10	7	3

[1] For definition of net demand deposits over the period 1917–1957, see text.

[2] First-of-month or midmonth dates are changes at country banks, and other dates (usually Thursdays) are at central reserve or reserve city banks.

[3] Requirement became effective at central reserve and reserve city banks on Aug. 11, and at country banks on Aug. 16.

chapter X

MONEY SUPPLY AND GOLD (Series X 266–304)

X 266–304. General note.

The supply of money, in the sense of a means of payment, is defined broadly to include bank deposits and currency. A more restricted definition of the active money supply includes demand deposits and currency held by the public. Time deposits, including funds deposited in the Postal Savings System, have occasionally been included in the definition of the money supply. Prior to 1934, gold was also a part of the means of payment but in January of that year it was withdrawn from circulation, and since then gold has served as a means of settlement of international accounts only and is purely reserve money domestically.

As used here, the term "currency" includes coin and paper money issued by the Government and by banks. All currency is now issued by the Federal Reserve banks and the U.S. Treasury. In the series in this section three types of currency figures are shown: (*a*) Total currency stock (series X 281); (*b*) currency in circulation (series X 284–298), defined as coin and paper money outside the Treasury and Federal Reserve banks; and (*c*) currency outside banks, that is, currency in circulation less cash in the vaults of banks (series X 269 and X 277).

Figures on currency in circulation have been compiled by the Treasury Department since 1800. They exclude currency held in the Treasury and Federal Reserve banks, gold and silver coin known to have been exported and, beginning with January 31, 1934, all gold coin. They include currency held by the public within the United States, cash in the vaults of banks, currency lost or destroyed, and currency carried abroad and not appearing in the official gold and silver export figures.

At one time gold was the basic form into which all other types of currency could generally be converted. At present, however, the gold stock in most countries is held largely or entirely by central banks and Government treasuries as legal reserves against note and deposit liabilities or for stabilizing exchange rates. All gold belonging to the United States is held by the Treasury Department. Private gold holdings are forbidden except in limited amounts for licensed purposes. Gold may be held by Federal Reserve banks for account of foreign central banks or governments. Such earmarked gold, however, is not a part of the monetary gold stock of this country.

Prior to 1934, when gold coin and gold certificates were a part of the means of payment, they are included in series X 282, "currency held in Treasury"; series X 283, "currency in Federal Reserve banks"; and series X 284, "currency in circulation"; as well as in series X 285 and X 286, "gold coin" and "gold certificates" in circulation.

X 266–274. Deposits adjusted and currency outside banks, 1892–1957.

Source: 1892–1941 (except series X 274, 1916–1947), Board of Governors of the Federal Reserve System, *Banking and Monetary Statistics*, pp. 34–35; 1942–1947, *Federal Reserve Bulletin*, January 1949, p. 41; 1948–1957, September issues of *Bulletin*. Series X 274, 1916–1947, Board of Governors, records.

These figures provide an indication of the total volume of money, or the means of payment, outstanding in the country. They have been adjusted to show as nearly as possible the deposits and currency owned by the public. Currency held as vault cash has been deducted from the total amount of currency outside the Treasury and Federal Reserve banks. Deposit figures have been adjusted to exclude interbank deposits, which do not represent money available to the public, and items in process of collection, inclusion of which would represent a double counting of deposits. Deposits of the U.S. Government, which are not included in deposits adjusted, are shown separately. Deposit figures, which are partly estimated, include all deposits in banks in the United States and in the Postal Savings System. For a detailed description of the individual items comprising adjusted deposits and currency outside banks, see *Banking and Monetary Statistics*, pp. 11–12.

X 275–280. Deposits adjusted and currency outside banks, 1867–1896.

Source: National Bureau of Economic Research, records.

These figures are unpublished estimates by Milton Friedman and Anna Jacobson Schwartz. They supplement series X 266–274, but they differ in several important respects. Series X 275–280 are seasonally adjusted figures; figures without seasonal adjustment, such as shown in X 266–274, are not available for the earlier period. Series X 275 and X 276 are total deposits adjusted, i.e., total deposits less U.S. Government deposits, interbank deposits, and cash items in process of collection. A distribution showing demand and time deposits is not available for this period. Figures for vault cash (series X 278) are deducted from currency in circulation to arrive at currency outside banks.

Series X 275 is the sum of national bank figures, *Annual Report of the Comptroller of the Currency, 1918*, vol. 2, pp. 248–269, and nonnational commercial bank estimates: For 1867–1874, by James K. Kindahl (series X 88); for 1875–1896, by David Fand (series X 89). Figures for series X 276, 1867–1874, were derived from E. W. Keyes, *A History of Savings Banks in the United States* (New York, 1878), vol. 2, table facing p. 532; figures for 1875–1896 were estimated by Fand (series X 89). Series X 277 is the residual remaining after deducting series X 278 from published figures of currency in circulation corrected for a presumed error in the gold component, the omission of fractional currency, and national banknotes in vaults of issuing banks. Series X 278 is the sum of national bank figures, *Annual Report of the Comptroller of the Currency, 1918*, vol. 2, pp. 248–269, and nonnational bank estimates: For 1867–1874, for commercial banks, by James K. Kindahl; for mutual savings banks, derived from cash in New York mutual savings banks, *Annual Report of the Superintendent of the Banking Department Relative to Savings Banks and Trust Companies*, 1867–1875, and in Massachusetts savings banks, *Annual Report of the Massachusetts Savings Bank Commissioners*, 1867–1875; for 1875–1896, by David Fand. Series X 279 is derived from *Annual Report of the Secretary of the Treasury on the State of the Finances, 1928*, p. 550. Series X 280 is derived from *Annual Report of the Comptroller of the Currency, 1918*, vol. 2, pp. 248–269. For more detail, see the forthcoming volume by Friedman and Schwartz, *The Stock of Money in the United States, 1867–1957.*

X 281–284.   Currency stock and currency in circulation, 1800–1957.

Source: 1800–1859, Comptroller of the Currency, *Annual Report, 1896,* vol. I, p. 544; 1860–1957, Treasury Department, *Annual Report of the Secretary of the Treasury, 1928,* pp. 550–551; *1945,* p. 675; *1949,* p. 545; *1957,* p. 550.

See general note for series X 266–304.

Currency stock (series X 281) and the total of its components (series X 282–284) involve a duplication to the extent that U.S. notes, Federal Reserve notes, Federal Reserve banknotes, and national banknotes, all included in full, are in part secured by gold, also included in full. The duplication of gold certificates, silver certificates, and Treasury notes of 1890 resulting from the equal amounts of gold or silver held as security therefor has been eliminated. For a statement on this point, see footnotes to series X 281 and X 282. A description of security and reserves by type of currency is included in the text for series X 285–298, below. The text for series X 285–298 also describes more refined estimates of gold coin in circulation, 1873–1907 and 1913–1933, which, if incorporated into series X 281–284, would require similar adjustments in "total currency in the United States" and "currency in circulation."

The *Annual Report of the Secretary of the Treasury* for 1922 and subsequent years includes the following information concerning changes in the compilation of series X 281–284. The figures for 1860–1889 have been revised from the best data available in annual reports of the Secretary of the Treasury. The records are not complete and the figures for gold and silver in those years are only estimates. Beginning with 1890, the compilation is based on revised figures for June 30 of each year and therefore differs slightly from the monthly circulation statements issued by the Treasury. The compilation reflects revisions to take account of other changes in the circulation statement, chiefly in 1922 and 1927. These revisions are explained in the *Annual Report of the Secretary of the Treasury* as follows: *1922,* p. 433; *1928,* pp. 70–71 and 551.

X 285–298.   Currency in circulation, by kind, 1860–1957.

Source: Treasury Department, *Annual Report of the Secretary of the Treasury, 1928,* pp. 554–555; *1949,* p. 547; *1958,* p. 584.

See general note for series X 266–304 and text for series X 281–284.

More detailed annual data on currency stock and circulation, by kind, are shown in the annual reports of the Secretary of the Treasury and the Comptroller of the Currency. For a continuation of series X 290 (State banknotes, 1860–1878), annually back to 1830, decennially to 1800, see *Annual Report of the Comptroller of the Currency, 1916,* vol. II, p. 45.

The security and reserve provisions for the different types of currency are described in the *Annual Report of the Secretary of the Treasury, 1957,* p. 551, as follows:

A part of the gold and silver included in the stock of currency is held by the Treasury as a reserve against other kinds of currency as follows: (1) As a reserve for United States notes and Treasury notes of 1890—gold bullion (gold coin and bullion prior to gold conservation actions of 1933 and 1934), varying in amount from $150,000,000 to $156,039,431 during the years 1913–1957; (2) also as security for Treasury notes of 1890—an equal dollar amount in standard silver dollars (these notes are being cancelled and retired on receipt); (3) as security for outstanding silver certificates—silver in bullion and standard dollars of monetary value equal to the face amount of such silver certificates; and (4) as security for gold certificates— gold bullion (gold coin and bullion before gold actions of

1933 and 1934) of a value at legal standard equal to the face amount of such gold certificates. Federal Reserve notes are obligations of the United States and a first lien on all the assets of the issuing Federal Reserve Bank. Federal Reserve notes are secured by deposit with Federal Reserve agents of a like amount of gold certificates (gold prior to actions of 1933 and 1934) or of gold certificates and such discounted or purchased paper as are eligible under the terms of the Federal Reserve Act as amended, or (from February 27, 1932) of direct obligations of the United States. Federal Reserve Banks must maintain a reserve in gold certificates (gold for 1933 and prior years) of at least 25 percent (40 percent prior to passage of Act of June 12, 1945) including a redemption fund, which must be deposited with the Treasurer of the United States, against Federal Reserve notes in actual circulation. "Gold certificates," as herein used for 1934 and subsequent years include credits with the Treasurer of the United States payable in gold certificates. Federal Reserve Bank notes at time of issuance were secured by direct obligations of United States or commercial paper; however, lawful money has been deposited with the Treasurer for their redemption and they are in process of retirement. National bank notes at issuance were secured by direct obligations of the United States; lawful money has been deposited with the Treasurer for their redemption and they are being retired.

The monetary value of gold was changed from $20.67 per fine ounce to $35.00 per fine ounce on January 31, 1934. The weight of the gold dollar was reduced from 25.8 to 15-5/21 grains of gold, 0.9 fine.

More refined estimates of the amount of gold coin in circulation, 1873–1907, are contained in Bureau of the Mint, *Annual Report of the Director of the Mint, 1907,* p. 87; a discussion of the errors for which adjustments were made is given on pp. 66–95. For 1914–1933, the Board of Governors of the Federal Reserve System has published revised estimates of gold coin in circulation (see *Banking and Monetary Statistics,* p. 409), which exclude $287 million of gold coin reported in January 1934 as still in circulation because this amount is believed to have been largely lost or melted down, or otherwise to have disappeared from circulation over the years. The Federal Reserve series has been adjusted in this way for 1914–1933; no similar adjustment has been made in the data included in this volume for gold coin in circulation, total currency in circulation, or total currency stock.

X 299–304.   Changes in gold stock, 1914–1957.

Source: 1914–1941, Board of Governors of the Federal Reserve System, *Banking and Monetary Statistics,* p. 536; 1942–1957 (except series X 304), *Federal Reserve Bulletin,* June 1949, p. 745, and April 1958, p. 503. Series X 304, 1942–1957, *Federal Reserve Bulletin,* January issues.

For a discussion of the items shown here, see *Banking and Monetary Statistics,* pp. 522–523. See also general note for series X 266–304.

Also available in *Banking and Monetary Statistics* are annual data on gold inflow into the United States and contributing factors, net gold imports to the United States by country, and gold production by country.

The data for domestic gold production (series X 301) are those reported by the Director of the Mint, adjusted through 1945 to exclude Philippine Islands production received in the United States. The data for net gold imports or exports (series X 302) are those compiled by the Department of Commerce. The figures for gold under earmark (series X 303–304) represent gold held by the Federal Reserve banks for foreign and international accounts; in the calculation of the changes in gold under earmark, however, consideration has also been given to gold held under earmark abroad for the account of the Federal Reserve banks in 1917–1933.

Series X 266–274.   Deposits Adjusted and Currency Outside Banks: 1892 to 1957

[In millions of dollars. As of June 30 or nearest available date]

Year	Total deposits adjusted and currency	Demand deposits adjusted and currency			Time deposits				U.S. Government deposits [6]
		Total	Demand deposits adjusted [1]	Currency outside banks	Total	Commercial banks [2][3]	Mutual savings banks [3][4]	Postal Savings System [5]	
	266	267	268	269	270	271	272	273	274
1957	219,439	133,724	105,706	28,018	85,715	53,605	30,647	1,463	4,098
1956	213,643	133,028	104,744	28,284	80,615	49,698	29,152	1,765	6,059
1955	207,738	130,609	103,234	27,375	77,129	47,846	27,277	2,007	5,798
1954	198,517	125,225	98,132	27,093	73,292	45,653	25,388	2,251	6,770
1953	192,560	124,267	96,898	27,369	68,293	42,245	23,589	2,459	4,074
1952	184,904	121,228	94,754	26,474	63,676	39,302	21,755	2,619	6,454
1951	174,684	114,736	88,960	25,776	59,948	36,781	20,382	2,785	6,649
1950	169,964	110,225	85,040	25,185	59,739	36,719	19,923	3,097	4,751
1949	165,626	107,143	81,877	25,266	58,483	36,292	18,932	3,259	2,742
1948	165,695	108,335	82,697	25,638	57,360	35,788	18,194	3,378	4,108
1947	164,140	108,485	82,186	26,299	55,655	34,835	17,428	3,392	2,123
1946	157,821	105,992	79,476	26,516	51,829	32,429	16,281	3,119	14,249
1945	138,403	94,150	69,053	25,097	44,253	27,170	14,426	2,657	24,980
1944	116,666	80,946	60,065	20,881	35,720	21,217	12,471	2,032	20,156
1943	102,113	71,853	56,039	15,814	30,260	17,543	11,141	1,576	8,503
1942	80,126	52,806	41,870	10,936	27,320	15,610	10,395	1,315	2,127
1941	73,400	45,521	37,317	8,204	27,879	15,928	10,648	1,303	1,733
1940	66,124	38,661	31,962	6,699	27,463	15,540	10,631	1,292	1,062
1939	60,151	33,360	27,355	6,005	26,791	15,097	10,433	1,261	1,736
1938	55,966	29,730	24,313	5,417	26,236	14,776	10,209	1,251	1,459
1937	56,592	30,687	25,198	5,489	25,905	14,513	10,125	1,267	759
1936	53,910	29,002	23,780	5,222	24,908	13,706	9,971	1,231	1,832
1935	49,070	25,216	20,433	4,783	23,854	12,820	9,830	1,204	913
1934	44,228	21,353	16,694	4,659	22,875	11,988	9,691	1,196	1,797
1933	40,828	19,172	14,411	4,761	21,656	10,849	9,621	1,186	887
1932	44,997	20,241	15,625	4,616	24,756	14,049	9,927	780	422
1931	52,444	23,483	19,832	3,651	28,961	18,691	9,928	342	486
1930	54,067	25,075	21,706	3,369	28,992	19,705	9,117	170	341
1929	54,790	26,179	22,540	3,639	28,611	19,557	8,905	149	417
1928	54,407	25,881	22,259	3,622	28,526	19,802	8,576	148	295
1927	52,004	25,539	21,983	3,556	26,465	18,306	8,016	143	256
1926	50,342	25,601	22,000	3,601	24,741	17,125	7,483	133	239
1925	48,143	24,949	21,376	3,573	23,194	15,974	7,089	131	205
1924	44,321	23,062	19,412	3,650	21,259	14,492	6,635	132	232
1923	42,419	22,697	18,958	3,739	19,722	13,374	6,217	131	361
1922	38,828	21,391	18,045	3,346	17,437	11,592	5,709	136	203
1921	37,373	20,790	17,113	3,677	16,583	10,917	5,518	148	461
1920	39,555	23,721	19,616	4,105	15,834	10,509	5,168	157	329
1919	34,640	21,217	17,624	3,593	13,423	8,522	4,734	167	1,016
1918	29,858	18,141	14,843	3,298	11,717	7,207	4,362	148	1,631
1917	27,320	15,777	13,501	2,276	11,543	7,038	4,373	132	1,102
1916	24,162	13,849	11,973	1,876	10,313	6,088	4,140	85	140
1915	20,634	11,403	9,828	1,575	9,231	5,264	3,901	66	48
1914	19,965	11,615	10,082	1,533	8,350	4,441	3,866	43	66
1913	19,354	10,998	9,140	1,858	8,356	4,606	3,716	34	49
1912	18,807	10,918	9,156	1,762	7,889	4,313	3,556	20	58
1911	17,714	10,377	8,668	1,709	7,337	3,928	3,408	1	48
1910	16,923	9,979	8,254	1,725	6,944	3,636	3,308	----------	54
1909	15,724	9,459	7,768	1,691	6,265	3,170	3,095	----------	70
1908	14,588	9,095	7,384	1,711	5,493	2,427	3,066	----------	130
1907	14,922	9,572	7,872	1,700	5,350	2,295	3,055	----------	180
1906	14,032	9,263	7,504	1,759	4,769	1,860	2,909	----------	89
1905	13,162	8,698	7,069	1,629	4,464	1,727	2,737	----------	75
1904	11,863	7,818	6,256	1,562	4,045	1,443	2,602	----------	110
1903	11,305	7,505	5,962	1,543	3,800	1,288	2,512	----------	147
1902	10,715	7,150	5,719	1,431	3,565	1,185	2,380	----------	124
1901	9,914	6,599	5,204	1,395	3,315	1,055	2,260	----------	99
1900	8,766	5,751	4,420	1,331	3,015	881	2,134	----------	99
1899	7,960	5,343	4,162	1,181	2,617	656	1,961	----------	76
1898	6,979	4,582	3,432	1,150	2,397	572	1,825	----------	53
1897	6,189	3,884	2,871	1,013	2,305	568	1,737	----------	16
1896	6,033	3,813	2,839	974	2,220	532	1,688	----------	15
1895	6,019	3,931	2,960	971	2,088	491	1,597	----------	13
1894	5,773	3,779	2,807	972	1,994	456	1,538	----------	14
1893	5,854	3,847	2,766	1,081	2,007	456	1,551	----------	14
1892	5,824	3,895	2,880	1,015	1,929	470	1,459	----------	14

[1] For definition of deposits adjusted, see text.
[2] Excludes U.S. Treasurer's time deposits, open account, beginning with 1939, and postal savings redeposited in banks.
[3] Beginning with 1941, the commercial bank figures exclude and the mutual savings bank figures include 3 member mutual savings banks.
[4] Prior to 1947, includes a relatively small amount of demand deposits.

[5] Includes both amounts redeposited in banks and amounts not so redeposited; excludes amounts at banks in U.S. possessions.
[6] Includes Government deposits at commercial and savings banks and at Federal Reserve banks. Beginning with 1939, includes U.S. Treasurer's time deposits, open account.

Series X 275–280. Deposits Adjusted and Currency Outside Banks: 1867 to 1896

[In millions of dollars. Seasonally adjusted figures. As of January 1867–1872; February 1873–1874; August 1875–1881; and June 1882–1896]

Year	Deposits adjusted - Commercial banks	Deposits adjusted - Mutual savings banks	Currency outside banks	Commercial and savings banks' vault cash	U.S. Government balances - Treasury cash	U.S. Government balances - Commercial and savings banks	Year	Deposits adjusted - Commercial banks	Deposits adjusted - Mutual savings banks	Currency outside banks	Commercial and savings banks' vault cash	U.S. Government balances - Treasury cash	U.S. Government balances - Commercial and savings banks
	275	276	277	278	279	280		275	276	277	278	279	280
1896	3,434	1,693	832	567	288	17	1881	1,702	957	797	316	235	12
1895	3,596	1,650	881	621	215	15	1880	1,380	829	662	310	209	11
1894	3,341	1,571	883	686	142	14	1879	1,201	744	574	241	212	43
1893	3,203	1,546	985	529	138	14	1878	1,026	772	529	238	176	40
1892	3,541	1,517	929	600	147	14	1877	1,092	818	525	234	113	10
1891	3,098	1,427	921	512	173	26	1876	1,152	847	506	245	99	11
1890	3,020	1,373	888	478	245	31	1875	1,185	837	510	257	93	11
1889	2,724	1,300	819	499	268	47	1874	1,066	745	526	275	79	12
1888	2,541	1,237	821	488	308	58	1873	1,070	684	550	231	67	13
1887	2,486	1,183	793	464	305	23	1872	1,041	612	521	240	83	15
1886	2,330	1,125	753	442	306	17	1871	844	521	504	230	111	11
1885	2,057	1,067	780	453	240	14	1870	779	436	466	248	128	10
1884	1,922	1,034	842	347	240	14	1869	735	374	477	232	126	16
1883	1,955	1,004	856	328	236	14	1868	713	324	523	244	135	28
1882	1,787	951	807	317	231	13	1867	729	276	585	267	148	30

Series X 281–284. Currency Stock and Currency in Circulation: 1800 to 1957

[In thousands of dollars. As of June 30]

Year	Total currency in U.S.[1]	Currency held in Treasury[2]	Currency outside Treasury - In Federal Reserve banks	Currency outside Treasury - In circulation	Year	Total currency in U.S.[1]	Currency held in Treasury[2]	Currency outside Treasury in circulation	Year[4]	Total currency in U.S.[1]	Currency held in Treasury[2]	Currency outside Treasury in circulation
	281	282	283	284		281	282	284		281	282	284
1957	55,363,063	19,887,518	4,393,632	31,081,913	1913	3,777,021	358,329	3,418,692	1870	899,876	124,909	774,966
1956	54,008,743	19,060,827	4,232,727	30,715,189	1912	3,701,965	366,744	3,335,220	1869	873,759	133,118	740,641
					1911	3,606,989	343,935	3,263,053	1868	888,413	116,529	771,884
1955	53,308,618	18,989,892	4,089,403	30,229,323					1867	1,020,927	161,567	859,360
1954	53,429,405	19,234,197	4,273,259	29,921,949	1910	3,466,856	318,172	3,148,684	1866	1,068,066	128,388	939,678
1953	54,015,346	19,729,629	4,160,765	30,124,952	1909	3,451,521	302,695	3,148,826				
1952	53,853,745	20,610,303	4,217,518	29,025,925	1908	3,423,068	343,913	3,079,155	1865	1,180,197	96,657	1,083,541
1951	50,985,939	18,979,646	4,197,063	27,809,230	1907	3,158,111	344,248	2,813,863	1864	1,062,841	55,226	1,007,615
					1906	3,109,380	334,690	2,774,690	1863	1,010,747	79,473	[5] 931,274
1950	52,440,353	21,464,308	3,819,755	27,156,290					1862	629,452	23,754	[5] 605,698
1949	53,103,980	21,736,254	3,874,816	27,492,910	1905	2,919,494	296,154	2,623,340	1861	488,006	3,600	[5] 484,406
1948	52,601,129	20,769,375	3,928,896	27,902,859	1904	2,838,023	285,117	2,552,906				
1947	50,599,352	18,538,131	3,763,994	28,297,227	1903	2,717,646	317,914	2,399,732	1860	442,102	6,695	[5] 435,407
1946	49,648,011	17,539,072	3,863,941	28,244,997	1902	2,593,910	314,796	2,279,114	1859	443,307	4,339	438,968
					1901	2,511,472	308,275	2,203,198	1858	415,208	6,398	408,810
1945	48,009,400	17,517,449	3,745,512	26,746,438					1857	474,779	17,710	457,069
1944	44,805,301	18,489,163	3,811,797	22,504,342	1900	2,366,220	284,989	2,081,231	1856	445,748	19,901	425,847
1943	40,868,266	19,676,674	3,770,331	17,421,260	1899	2,190,094	286,022	1,904,072				
1942	35,840,908	19,937,577	3,520,465	12,382,866	1898	2,073,574	235,714	1,837,860	1855	436,952	18,932	418,020
1941	32,774,611	19,781,266	3,380,914	9,612,432	1897	1,906,770	265,787	1,640,983	1854	445,689	20,138	425,551
					1896	1,799,975	293,540	1,506,435	1853	424,181	21,943	402,238
1940	28,457,960	17,124,764	3,485,695	7,847,501					1852	375,673	14,632	361,041
1939	23,754,736	13,271,527	3,436,467	7,046,743	1895	1,819,360	217,392	1,601,968	1851	341,165	10,912	330,254
1938	20,096,865	10,132,397	3,503,576	6,460,891	1894	1,805,079	144,270	1,660,809				
1937	19,376,690	9,475,429	3,454,205	6,447,056	1893	1,738,808	142,107	1,596,701	1850	285,367	6,605	278,762
1936	17,402,493	7,800,438	3,360,854	6,241,200	1892	1,752,219	150,872	1,601,347	1849	234,743	2,185	232,558
					1891	1,677,794	180,353	1,497,441	1848	240,506	8,101	232,405
1935	15,113,035	8,398,521	1,147,422	5,567,093					1847	225,520	1,701	223,819
1934	[3] 13,634,381	6,953,734	1,305,985	5,373,470	1890	1,685,123	255,872	1,429,251	1846	202,552	9,126	193,426
1933	10,078,417	2,085,971	2,271,682	5,720,764	1889	1,658,672	278,311	1,380,362				
1932	9,004,505	1,513,985	1,795,349	5,695,171	1888	1,691,441	319,270	1,372,171	1845	185,609	7,658	177,950
1931	9,079,624	2,031,632	2,226,059	4,821,933	1887	1,633,413	315,874	1,317,539	1844	175,168	7,857	167,310
					1886	1,561,408	308,707	1,252,701	1843	148,564	1,449	147,114
1930	8,306,564	2,043,489	1,741,087	4,521,988					1842	163,734	230	163,504
1929	8,538,796	1,935,513	1,856,986	4,746,297	1885	1,537,434	244,865	1,292,569	1841	187,290	987	186,303
1928	8,118,091	1,738,889	1,582,576	4,796,626	1884	1,487,250	243,324	1,243,926				
1927	8,667,282	2,062,851	1,753,110	4,851,321	1883	1,472,494	242,189	1,230,306	1840	189,969	3,663	186,305
1926	8,428,971	2,070,588	1,473,118	4,885,266	1882	1,409,398	235,108	1,174,290	1839	222,171	2,467	219,704
					1881	1,349,592	235,355	1,114,238	1838	203,639	[5] 5,000	198,639
1925	8,299,382	2,116,582	1,367,591	4,815,208					1837	222,186	[5] 5,000	217,186
1924	8,846,542	2,620,299	1,376,935	4,849,307	1880	1,185,550	212,169	973,382	1836	205,301	[5] 5,000	200,301
1923	8,702,788	2,671,678	1,207,836	4,823,275	1879	1,033,641	215,009	818,632				
1922	8,276,070	2,515,005	1,297,893	4,463,172	1878	984,225	164,221	820,004	1835	154,692	8,893	145,800
1921	8,174,528	2,001,446	1,262,089	4,910,992	1877	916,548	102,458	814,090	1834	135,840	11,703	124,137
					1876	905,238	98,114	807,124	1833	122,150	2,012	120,138
1920	8,158,496	1,675,026	1,015,881	5,467,589					1832	121,900	4,503	117,397
1919	7,688,413	2,001,139	810,636	4,876,638	1875	925,702	91,912	833,789	1831	[3] 109,100	6,015	93,085
1918	6,906,237	1,568,557	855,984	4,481,697	1874	950,116	86,510	863,606				
1917	5,678,774	796,005	816,365	4,066,404	1873	903,316	65,065	838,252	1830	93,100	5,756	87,344
1916	4,541,730	299,127	593,345	3,649,258	1872	900,571	71,361	829,209	1820	69,100	[5] 2,000	67,100
					1871	894,376	100,220	794,156	1810	58,000	[6] 3,000	55,000
1915	4,050,783	348,236	382,965	3,319,582					1800	28,000	[6] 1,500	26,500
1914	3,797,825	338,391		3,459,434								

[1] Excludes gold certificates, silver certificates, and Treasury notes of 1890, since the gold and silver held as security against them are included.

[2] Prior to 1860 consists of specie only; thereafter includes coin, bullion, and paper money. Includes the following categories of currency held in Treasury as published in the circulation statement: Reserves held against U.S. notes and Treasury notes of 1890, held for Federal Reserve banks and agents, and all other money. Excludes amount held as security against gold and silver certificates and Treasury notes of 1890 since the certificates and notes are included elsewhere; for 1860–1933 they are included as currency outside the Treasury, and beginning 1934 they are included either as cur-

rency outside the Treasury or as amounts held in the Treasury for Federal Reserve banks and agents, payable in gold certificates.

[3] Agrees with source; however, figures for components do not add to total shown.

[4] Prior to 1860 the exact date of the figures is not known.

[5] Includes total stock of silver dollars and subsidiary silver, 1860–1863; and of gold coin and bullion, 1862–1863. It is not practical to present the amounts in circulation separately for the years mentioned.

[6] Estimated.

Series X 285–298.   Currency in Circulation, by Kind: 1860 to 1957

[In thousands of dollars.   As of June 30]

Year	Gold coin [1]	Gold certificates [2]	Silver dollars	Silver certificates [2]	Treasury notes of 1890 [2]	Subsidiary silver	Minor coin	Federal Reserve notes [2]	Federal Reserve banknotes [2]	U.S. notes [2]	National banknotes [2]
	285	286	287	288	289	291	292	293	295	297	298
1957		32,541	252,607	2,161,589	1,142	1,315,325	473,904	26,329,345	132,566	321,148	61,745
1956		33,483	236,837	2,148,369	1,142	1,258,555	453,044	26,055,247	146,629	317,643	64,239
1955		34,466	223,047	2,169,726	1,142	1,202,209	432,512	25,617,775	162,573	319,064	66,810
1954		35,481	211,533	2,135,016	1,142	1,164,912	418,754	25,384,606	180,277	320,224	70,005
1953		36,596	202,424	2,121,511	1,143	1,150,499	412,952	25,608,669	200,054	317,702	73,403
1952		37,855	191,306	2,087,811	1,145	1,092,891	393,482	24,605,158	220,584	318,330	77,364
1951		39,070	180,013	2,092,174	1,145	1,019,824	378,350	23,456,018	243,261	318,173	81,202
1950		40,772	170,185	2,177,251	1,145	964,709	360,886	22,760,285	273,788	320,781	86,488
1949		42,665	163,894	2,060,852	1,145	939,568	355,316	23,209,437	308,821	318,688	92,524
1948		45,158	156,340	2,060,869	1,146	918,691	346,112	23,600,323	353,499	321,485	99,235
1947		47,794	148,452	2,060,728	1,147	875,971	331,039	23,999,004	406,260	320,403	106,429
1946		50,223	140,319	2,025,178	1,149	843,122	316,994	23,973,006	464,315	316,743	113,948
1945		52,084	125,178	1,650,689	1,150	788,283	291,996	22,867,459	527,001	322,587	120,012
1944		53,964	103,325	1,587,691	1,154	700,022	262,775	18,750,201	597,030	322,293	125,887
1943		56,909	83,701	1,648,571	1,155	610,005	235,672	13,746,612	584,162	322,343	132,130
1942		59,399	66,093	1,754,255	1,158	503,947	213,144	9,310,135	18,717	316,886	139,131
1941		62,872	52,992	1,713,508	1,161	433,485	193,963	6,684,209	20,268	299,514	150,460
1940		66,793	46,020	1,581,662	1,163	384,187	168,977	5,163,284	22,373	247,887	165,155
1939		71,930	42,407	1,453,573	1,166	361,209	154,869	4,483,552	25,593	265,962	186,480
1938		78,500	39,446	1,230,156	1,169	341,942	145,625	4,114,338	30,118	262,155	217,441
1937		88,116	38,046	1,078,071	1,172	340,827	144,107	4,168,780	37,616	281,459	268,862
1936		100,771	35,029	954,592	1,177	316,476	134,691	4,002,216	51,954	278,190	366,105
1935		117,167	32,308	701,474	1,182	295,773	125,125	3,222,913	81,470	285,417	704,263
1934		149,740	30,013	401,456	1,189	280,400	119,142	3,068,404	141,645	279,608	901,872
1933	320,989	265,487	27,995	360,699	1,186	256,865	112,532	3,060,793	125,845	268,809	919,614
1932	452,763	715,683	30,115	352,605	1,222	256,220	113,619	2,780,229	2,746	289,076	700,894
1931	363,020	996,510	34,326	377,149	1,240	273,147	117,393	1,708,429	2,929	299,427	648,363
1930	357,236	994,841	38,629	386,915	1,260	281,231	117,436	1,402,066	3,206	288,389	650,779
1929	368,488	934,994	43,684	387,073	1,283	284,226	115,210	1,692,721	3,616	262,188	652,812
1928	377,028	1,019,149	46,222	384,577	1,304	278,175	111,061	1,626,433	4,029	298,438	650,212
1927	384,957	1,007,075	48,717	375,798	1,327	275,605	108,132	1,702,843	4,606	292,205	650,057
1926	391,703	1,057,371	51,577	377,741	1,356	270,072	104,194	1,679,407	5,453	294,916	651,477
1925	402,297	1,004,823	54,289	382,780	1,387	262,009	100,307	1,636,108	6,921	282,578	681,709
1924	393,330	801,381	54,015	364,414	1,423	252,995	96,952	1,843,106	10,066	297,790	733,835
1923	404,181	386,456	57,262	364,258	1,460	247,307	93,897	2,234,660	19,969	302,749	711,076
1922	415,937	173,342	57,973	265,335	1,510	229,310	89,157	2,138,715	71,868	292,343	727,681
1921	447,272	200,582	65,883	158,843	1,576	235,295	91,409	2,599,598	129,942	259,170	721,421
1920	474,822	259,007	76,749	97,606	1,656	248,863	90,958	3,064,742	185,431	278,144	689,608
1919	474,875	327,552	79,041	163,445	1,745	229,316	81,780	2,450,278	155,014	274,119	639,472
1918	537,230	511,190	77,201	370,349	1,851	216,492	74,958	1,698,190	10,970	291,859	691,407
1917	666,545	1,082,926	71,754	468,365	1,970	193,745	68,411	506,756	3,702	311,595	690,635
1916	624,989	1,050,266	66,234	476,279	2,098	171,178	62,998	149,152	1,683	328,227	716,204
1915	587,537	821,869	64,499	463,147	2,245	159,043	58,516	70,810		309,796	782,120
1914	611,545	1,026,149	70,300	478,602	2,428	159,966	57,419			337,846	715,180
1913	608,401	1,003,998	72,127	469,129	2,657	154,458	54,954			337,215	715,754
1912	610,724	943,436	70,340	469,224	2,916	145,034	50,707			337,697	705,142
1911	589,296	930,368	72,446	453,544	3,237	138,422	49,049			338,989	687,701
1910	590,878	802,754	72,433	478,597	3,663	135,584	46,328			334,788	683,660
1909	599,338	815,005	71,988	477,717	4,203	132,332	42,585			340,118	665,539
1908	613,245	782,977	76,329	465,279	4,964	124,178	41,139			339,396	631,649
1907	561,697	600,072	81,710	470,211	5,976	121,777	40,907			342,270	589,242
1906	668,655	516,562	77,001	471,520	7,337	111,630	38,043			335,940	548,001
1905	651,064	485,211	73,584	454,865	9,272	101,438	35,458			332,421	480,029
1904	645,818	465,655	71,314	461,139	12,902	95,528	33,763			333,759	433,028
1903	617,261	377,259	72,391	454,733	19,077	92,727	32,040			334,249	399,997
1902	632,394	306,399	68,747	446,558	29,803	85,721	29,724			334,292	345,477
1901	629,791	247,036	66,921	429,644	47,525	79,235	27,890			330,045	345,111
1900	610,806	200,733	65,889	408,466	75,304	76,161	26,080			317,677	300,115
1899	679,738	32,656	61,481	402,137	92,562	69,066				328,627	237,805
1898	657,950	35,812	58,483	390,127	98,306	64,057				310,134	222,991
1897	517,590	37,285	51,940	357,849	83,470	59,616				306,915	226,318
1896	454,905	42,198	52,117	330,657	95,045	60,204				256,140	215,168
1895	479,638	48,381	51,986	319,623	115,943	60,350				319,094	206,953
1894	495,977	66,340	52,565	326,991	134,681	58,511				325,525	200,220
1893	408,536	92,642	56,930	326,824	140,856	65,470				330,774	174,670
1892	408,569	141,094	56,817	326,693	98,259	63,294				339,400	167,222
1891	407,319	120,063	58,826	307,236	40,349	58,219				343,207	162,221
1890	374,259	130,831	56,279	297,556		54,033				334,689	181,605
1889	376,482	117,130	[3]54,457	257,156		51,477				316,439	207,221
1888	391,114	121,095	[3]55,527	200,760		50,362				308,000	245,313
1887	376,541	91,225	55,549	142,118		48,584				326,667	276,855
1886	358,220	76,044	[3]52,669	88,116		46,174				323,813	307,665
1885	341,668	126,730	39,087	101,531		43,703				331,219	308,631
1884	340,624	71,147	40,690	96,427		45,661				318,687	330,690
1883	344,653	59,807	35,651	72,621		46,474				323,242	347,856
1882	358,251	5,029	32,404	54,506		46,380				325,255	352,465
1881	315,313	5,760	29,342	39,111		46,839				328,127	349,746

See footnotes at end of table.

Series X 285–298. Currency in Circulation, by Kind: 1860 to 1957—Con.

[In thousands of dollars]

Year	Gold coin [1]	Gold certificates [2]	Silver dollars	Silver certificates [2]	State banknotes	Subsidiary silver	Fractional currency	Other U.S. currency	U.S. notes [2]	National banknotes [2]
	285	286	287	288	290	291	294	296	297	298
1880	225,696	7,964	20,111	5,790	----------	48,512	----------	----------	327,895	337,415
1879	110,505	15,280	8,036	414	----------	61,347	----------	----------	301,644	321,405
1878	84,740	24,898	1,209	7	806	58,918	16,368	428	320,906	311,724
1877	78,111	32,298	----------	----------	909	42,885	20,242	456	337,899	301,289
1876	74,839	24,175	----------	----------	1,047	26,055	32,939	500	331,447	316,121
1875	64,446	17,549	----------	----------	964	22,141	37,905	551	349,686	340,547
1874	78,948	18,015	----------	----------	1,162	14,940	38,234	620	371,421	340,266
1873	62,718	34,251	----------	----------	1,399	13,679	38,076	701	348,464	338,962
1872	76,575	26,412	----------	----------	1,701	12,064	36,403	849	346,169	329,037
1871	72,391	17,790	----------	----------	1,968	12,022	34,446	1,064	343,069	311,406
1870	81,183	32,085	----------	----------	2,223	8,978	34,379	2,507	324,963	288,648
1869	62,129	29,956	----------	----------	2,559	5,695	30,442	3,343	314,767	291,750
1868	63,758	17,643	----------	----------	3,164	6,520	28,999	28,859	328,572	294,369
1867	72,882	18,678	----------	----------	4,484	7,082	26,306	123,727	319,438	286,764
1866	109,705	10,505	----------	----------	19,996	8,241	24,687	162,739	327,792	276,013
1865	148,557	----------	----------	----------	142,920	8,713	21,729	236,567	378,917	146,138
1864	184,346	----------	----------	----------	179,158	9,375	19,133	169,252	415,116	31,235
1863	[4]260,000	----------	----------	----------	238,677	[4]11,000	15,884	93,230	312,481	----------
1862	[4]283,000	----------	----------	----------	183,792	[4]13,000	----------	53,040	72,866	----------
1861	266,400	----------	----------	----------	202,006	[4]16,000	----------	----------	----------	----------
1860	207,305	----------	----------	----------	[5]207,102	[4]21,000	----------	----------	----------	----------

[1] More refined estimates are available for gold coin in circulation, 1873–1907 and 1914–1933; see text.
[2] For description of reserves held against various kinds of money, see text.
[3] Figures corrected for apparent errors. Components now add to total series X 284.
[4] Total stock; circulation figures not available.
[5] Data for this series are available in source back to 1800; see text.

Series X 299–304. Changes in Gold Stock: 1914 to 1957

[In millions of dollars; gold valued at $20.67 per fine ounce through January 1934; at $35 thereafter]

Year	Gold stock (end of period) [1]	Increase in gold stock	Domestic gold production [2]	Net gold import (+) or export (−)	Earmarked gold, decrease (+) or increase (−)	Gold under earmark (end of period)	Year	Gold stock (end of period) [1]	Increase in gold stock	Domestic gold production [2]	Net gold import (+) or export (−)	Earmarked gold, decrease (+) or increase (−)	Gold under earmark (end of period)
	299	300	301	302	303	304		299	300	301	302	303	304
1957	22,857	798.8	63.6	+104.3	+600.1	6,022.7	1935	10,125	1,887.2	110.7	+1,739.0	+0.2	8.8
1956	22,058	305.9	65.3	+106.1	+318.5	6,622.8	1934	8,238	4,202.5	92.9	+1,133.9	+82.6	9.0
							1933	4,036	−190.4	47.1	−173.5	[5]−58.0	59.1
1955	21,753	−40.9	65.7	+97.6	−132.4	6,941.3	1932	4,226	52.9	45.9	−446.2	[5]+457.5	73.7
1954	21,793	−297.2	65.1	+16.6	−325.2	6,808.9	1931	4,173	−133.4	45.8	+145.3	−320.8	458.5
1953	22,091	−1,161.9	69.0	+2.0	−1,170.8	6,483.8							
1952	23,252	379.8	67.4	+684.3	−304.8	5,313.0	1930	4,306	309.6	43.4	+280.1	−2.4	137.7
1951	22,873	52.7	66.3	−549.0	+617.6	5,008.2	1929	3,997	142.5	42.5	+175.1	−55.4	135.3
							1928	3,854	−237.9	44.3	−391.9	+119.5	79.9
1950	22,820	−1,743.3	80.1	−371.3	−1,352.4	5,625.7	1927	4,092	−112.8	43.8	+6.1	−160.2	199.4
1949	24,563	164.6	67.3	+686.5	−495.7	4,273.3	1926	4,205	92.6	46.3	+97.8	−26.3	39.3
1948	24,399	1,530.4	70.9	+1,680.4	−159.2	3,777.7							
1947	22,868	[3]2,162.1	75.8	+1,866.3	+210.0	3,618.4	1925	4,112	−100.1	48.0	−134.4	+32.2	13.0
1946	20,706	623.1	51.2	+311.5	+465.4	3,828.4	1924	4,212	255.6	50.6	+258.1	−42.2	45.2
							1923	3,957	315.1	50.2	+294.1	+0.7	3.0
1945	20,083	−547.8	32.0	−106.3	−356.7	4,293.8	1922	3,642	268.5	47.3	+238.3	−3.7	3.7
1944	20,631	−1,349.8	35.8	−845.4	−459.8	3,937.2	1921	3,373	734.6	48.8	+667.4	[5]+18.7	----------
1943	21,981	−757.9	48.3	+68.9	−803.6	3,477.4							
1942	22,739	−23.0	125.4	+315.7	−458.4	2,673.8	1920	2,639	−68.4	49.9	+95.0	[5]−145.0	22.0
1941	22,737	741.8	169.1	+982.4	−407.7	2,215.4	1919	2,707	−165.8	59.5	−291.7	[5]+127.4	5.0
							1918	2,873	4.9	67.4	+21.0	−46.7	6.9
1940	21,995	4,351.2	170.2	+4,744.5	−644.7	1,807.7	1917	2,868	312.2	82.3	+180.6	[5]+51.7	6.9
1939	17,644	3,132.0	161.7	+3,574.2	−534.4	1,163.0	1916	2,556	530.7	91.1	+530.2	−6.1	6.1
1938	14,512	1,751.5	148.6	+1,973.6	−333.5	628.6							
1937	[4]12,760	1,502.5	143.9	+1,585.5	−200.4	295.1	1915	2,025	499.1	99.7	+420.5	----------	----------
1936	[4]11,258	1,132.5	131.6	+1,116.6	−85.9	94.7	1914	1,526	−100.2	93.4	−165.2	----------	----------

[1] Beginning 1942, gold stock includes Treasury gold stock plus gold in Exchange Stabilization Fund; prior to that time represents Treasury gold stock only.
[2] Estimates of the U.S. mint.
[3] Net after payment of $687.5 million in gold as United States gold subscription to the International Monetary Fund.
[4] Includes gold in the inactive account amounting to $27,000,000 on Dec. 31, 1936, and $1,228,000,000 on Dec. 31, 1937.
[5] Adjusted for changes in gold held under earmark abroad by the Federal Reserve banks.

chapter X

MONEY RATES AND SECURITY MARKETS (Series X 305–388)

X 305–388. General note.

Available statistics on interest rates and security prices indicate the cost of credit to borrowers—mainly business concerns and the Federal Government; and the income received by those who lend and invest—primarily individuals, trusts, endowments, banks, and other financial institutions. This section presents a variety of money rate and security market statistics, including principal short-term open-market rates in New York City, the discount rate of the Federal Reserve Bank of New York, commercial paper and bankers' acceptances outstanding, bank rates on short-term loans to business, bond and stock yields and prices, security issues, margin requirements, stock market credit, and the volume of stock exchange trading.

X 305–313. Short-term interest rates—open market rates in New York City and Federal Reserve Bank discount rate, 1890–1957.

Source: 1890–1941, Board of Governors of the Federal Reserve System, *Banking and Monetary Statistics*, pp. 439–442, 448, 460; 1942–1957, March issues of *Federal Reserve Bulletin*, 1945–1958, and Federal Reserve Board, records.

The rates shown here cover the most important short-term open market instruments in New York City, which is the chief money market of the country. The New York money market is composed of a number of specialized markets for certain types of borrowing and there are usually differences in rates corresponding to differences in the supply of funds relative to the demand for particular types of short-term funds in which the market deals. These markets are called "open" markets since transactions in them are usually made on an impersonal basis with the borrower and lender dealing through agents, as distinct from a "customer" market where the borrower and lender deal directly with each other and where transactions are often made on a personal basis. As a result, lenders may sell paper held, call loans, or refrain from renewing credits upon maturity more freely in the case of open-market paper than in the case of customer loans. Monthly and weekly figures for most of the series shown here are given in the source.

Rates on stock exchange loans are no longer published by the Board of Governors of the Federal Reserve System but data for these series for 1942–1957 were supplied by that agency. For stock exchange call loans (series X 307–308), a single rate only is available beginning in 1957.

Government securities maturing within one year are represented prior to 1930 by the average yield on 3- to 6-month Treasury notes and certificates (series X 310); this series was discontinued after 1933. The figures for series X 310 are averages of daily yields published by the Treasury Department on all outstanding issues of these securities with periods to maturity from 3 to 6 months.

Beginning 1929, a new measure of short-term rates became available with the issuance by the Treasury of a new type of security—the Treasury bill, which differs from other types of Treasury marketable securities in that it is sold on a discount basis instead of being offered in the market with a fixed coupon rate. Maturities of Treasury bills have varied up to 9 months, but usually have been 3 months. A continuous series (X 311) is available beginning with 1931.

The Federal Reserve Bank of New York discount rates shown (series X 312–313) are the lowest and highest rates during the year on discounts for and advances to member banks under sections 13 and 13b of the Federal Reserve Act. Rates also apply to advances secured by obligations of Federal intermediate credit banks maturing in 6 months. For 1942–1946, the low rate shown is the preferential rate for advances secured by Government securities maturing or callable in one year or less. In this period the rate of 1 percent was continued for discounts of and advances secured by eligible paper. The discount rates at all Federal Reserve banks and a description of the series through 1941 is contained in *Banking and Monetary Statistics*, pp. 422–424, 439–442, and thereafter in the *Federal Reserve Bulletin*.

X 314–321. Commercial paper and bankers' acceptances outstanding, 1918–1957.

Source: 1918–1941, Board of Governors of the Federal Reserve System, *Banking and Monetary Statistics*, pp. 465–467; 1942–1957, *Federal Reserve Bulletin*, February 1944, p. 170; January 1946, p. 59; February 1953, p. 146; May 1958, p. 572.

Figures for commercial paper represent the amount of paper outstanding as reported by the principal commercial paper dealers in the country. Some finance company paper sold in the open market is included. Figures for bankers' acceptances are amounts outstanding as reported by makers of bankers' acceptances, including banks and bankers in the United States and agencies of foreign banks in this country.

X 322–329. Bank rates on short-term business loans, 1919–1957.

Source: 1919–1938, Board of Governors of the Federal Reserve System, *Banking and Monetary Statistics*, pp. 463–464; 1939–1948, *Federal Reserve Bulletin*, March 1949, p. 233; 1949–1957, March issue of *Bulletin* in each year.

Data by months through 1938 and by quarters thereafter are available in the source volume. These data are compiled by the Board of Governors from reports submitted by member banks in leading cities throughout the country.

The reporting cities are representative financial centers having large loan markets. Interest rates charged by banks in these cities are more responsive to changes in general monetary conditions than are rates in other places. Because of the financial importance of the cities, their influence would predominate in any compilation designed to show movements of interest rates in large cities.

Figures for series X 326–329 represent averages of prevailing rates reported monthly by banks in a varying number of leading cities on commercial loans and time and demand security loans. These figures are not strictly comparable with those in series X 322–325 but they are believed to represent bank rates on business loans. For series X 322–325, the figures for 1928–1938 are averages of prevailing rates reported monthly by banks in 19 principal cities on business loans only; beginning in 1939, the figures are averages of interest rates charged by banks in the 19 cities on short-term business loans made during the first half of March, June, September, and December. For a description of the figures prior to 1939, see *Banking and Monetary Statistics*, pp. 426–427, and beginning 1939, see *Federal Reserve Bulletin* for March 1949, pp. 228–237. Beginning 1939, the source publication includes data on average interest rates by size of loan.

X 330. Yields on U.S. Government bonds, 1919–1957.

Source: 1919–1941, Board of Governors of the Federal Reserve System, *Federal Reserve Bulletin*, May 1945, p. 483; 1942–1957, *Federal Reserve Bulletin*, October 1947, p. 1251; January 1950, p. 72; January 1951, p. 66; January 1954, p. 58; January 1958, p. 84.

Figures are unweighted averages of yields. For 1919–1925, yields cover all outstanding partially tax-exempt Government bonds due or callable after 8 years; for 1926–1934, all such bonds due or callable after 12 years; for 1935–1941, all such bonds due or callable after 15 years. For further description of series, see *Banking and Monetary Statistics*, p. 429, and *Federal Reserve Bulletin*, May 1945, pp. 483 and 490. Beginning 1942, the series is for fully taxable bonds. Yields cover 1942–March 31, 1952, the bonds due or callable after 15 years; April 1, 1952–March 31, 1953, due or callable after 12 years; April 1, 1953–1957, due or callable in 10 years or more.

X 331. Municipal high-grade bond yields, 1900–1957.

Source: 1900–1956, Standard and Poor's Corporation, Trade and Securities Statistics, *Security Price Index Record*, New York, 1957 edition, p. 172; 1957, same source, January 1959 Supplement, p. 22.

Prior to 1929, this series is an arithmetic average of the yield to maturity of 15 high-grade municipal bonds, based on the mean of monthly high-low prices. Beginning 1929, the series is an average of the 4 or 5 weekly indexes for the month. Annual figures are averages of monthly data. Monthly and weekly data are available in the source.

X 332. Unadjusted index number of yields of American railroad bonds, 1857–1936.

Source: Frederick R. Macauley, *Some Theoretical Problems Suggested by the Movements of Interest Rates, Bond Yields and Stock Prices in the United States Since 1856*, National Bureau of Economic Research, 1938, pp. A 142–161.

The railroad industry was selected as the basis for a long-time study of bond yields because no other industry had securities of comparable importance as early as 1857, and for many years no other industry had as high a credit rating. The series is available before and after adjustment to eliminate economic drift due to secular changes in the quality of the bonds included. The unadjusted series is more comparable with currently available series. The series is a chain index number based on the arithmetic average of yields on long-term high-grade railroad bonds. Yields for individual bonds are based on arithmetic averages of monthly high and low sale prices. With a few exceptions the index includes no bonds with maturities under 10 years, and since 1909 the minimum has been 14 years. The number of bonds on which the index is based was 13 in 1857 and increased gradually to 37 in 1900; it varied between 36 and 45 until 1930 and declined to about 28 in 1935. Annual figures are averages of monthly data.

X 333. Corporate Aaa bond yields, 1919–1957.

Source: Moody's Investors Service, *Moody's Industrial Manual*, New York, 1958 edition, p. a19.

This series is an unweighted arithmetic average of the yields for individual bonds, based on closing prices. Prior to 1928, yields are based on the average of the month's high and low sale price for each bond; for 1928 and 1929, on bi-weekly closing quotations; for 1930 through October 1931,

on weekly quotations; beginning November 1931, on daily closing quotations. Annual figures are averages of monthly data.

X 334. Yields on preferred stocks, 1910–1957.

Source: See source for series X 331, 1957 edition, p. 97, and January 1959 Supplement, p. 19.

For January 1910–January 1928, this index is computed from the average of the monthly high and low prices of 20 high-grade issues. All prices are converted to a price equivalent to $100 par and a $7 annual dividend before averaging. The yield index is computed from the average price. Beginning February 1928, the index is based on an average of the weekly yields, which are based on Wednesday's closing quotations for 15 (currently 14) high-grade noncallable issues. The yield is determined for each issue and the average of the 9 (currently 8) median yields represents the group yield. Annual figures are averages of monthly data.

X 335–338. Yields on common stocks (Cowles Commission), 1871–1937.

Source: Alfred Cowles and Associates, *Common Stock Indexes, 1871–1937*, Principia Press Inc., Bloomington, Ind., 1939, pp. 372–373.

Yields are total actual dividends paid in each calendar year divided by total stock values as represented by an average of the monthly values for the year. The data employed in the construction of this index include, for 1871–1917, all industrial and public utility common stocks, and about 93 percent in market value of the railroad stocks traded on the New York Stock Exchange. The stocks and the periods of their inclusion are given in appendix II of the source volume. Subsequent to 1917 (in some cases 1926 or later) the stocks included in the Standard Statistics weekly indexes are used, which represent 90 percent of all common shares listed on the New York Stock Exchange. For further description of index, see source volume, pp. 1–50.

X 339–342. Yields on common stocks (Moody's), 1929–1957.

Source: Moody's Investors Service, *Moody's Industrial Manual*, New York, 1958 edition, p. a25.

Annual figures are averages of monthly data which are dividends at annual rates based on latest company declarations divided by end-of-month prices.

X 343–347. Basic yields of corporate bonds, by term to maturity, 1900–1957.

Source: 1900–1942, David Durand, *Basic Yields of Corporate Bonds, 1900–1942*, New York, 1942; 1943–1957, National Bureau of Economic Research, records.

Greater detail than is shown here as to yield by years to maturity appears in Durand's volume.

The basic yield series represents the yield estimated as prevailing in the first quarter of each year on the highest grade corporate issues, classified by term to maturity. This series is based on monthly high and low quotations of practically all the actively traded high-grade corporate issues outstanding since 1900.

X 348. U.S. Government bond prices, 1919–1957.

Source: 1919–1944, Board of Governors of the Federal Reserve System, *Federal Reserve Bulletin*, May 1945, p. 483; 1945–1957, *Federal Reserve Bulletin*, October 1947, p. 1251; January 1950, p. 73; January 1951, p. 67; January 1954, p. 58; May 1958, p. 612.

Prior to 1942, the prices are derived from average yields of partially tax-exempt bonds shown in series X 330 on basis of a 4 percent 16-year bond through December 1930 and on the basis of a 2-3/4 percent 16-year bond 1931–1941. For further description of series, see *Banking and Monetary Statistics*, p. 429.

For 1942–March 31, 1952, figures for fully taxable issues are average prices of bonds due or first callable after 15 years; for April 1, 1952–March 31, 1953, average prices of fully taxable marketable 2-1/2 percent bonds first callable after 12 years; beginning April 1, 1953, prices are derived from average yields on basis of an assumed 3 percent 20-year bond. The yield averages used are those on bonds maturing or callable in 10 years or more.

X 349–350. Municipal and corporate high-grade bond prices, 1900–1957.

Source: See source for series X 331, 1957 edition, pp. 150 and 173, and January 1959 Supplement, p. 18.

The prices are a conversion of the yield indexes, assuming a 4-percent coupon with 20 years to maturity. For a description of the yield series for high-grade municipal bonds, see text for series X 331. The high-grade corporate bond series is based upon the following: For 1900–1928, the monthly high-low price of 45 high-grade corporate bonds; for 1929–March 1937, a varying group of A1+ bonds, one price monthly (first of month); beginning April 1937, the average of the weekly A1+ indexes. Annual data are averages of weekly figures.

X 351–354. Index of common stock prices, 1871–1957.

Source: See source for series X 331, 1957 edition, pp. 94–95, and January 1959 Supplement, pp. 18–22.

These indexes, which are based on the aggregate market value of the common stocks of all the companies in the sample, currently 500 stocks, express the observed market value as a percentage of the average market value during the base period. From January 1908 to date, these indexes are based on monthly averages of the Standard and Poor's stock price indexes. The indexes for earlier years have been converted to the 1941–43 base from the Cowles Commission stock price indexes, which are an extension of the Standard and Poor's indexes. The same method of construction was used for both, and, as far as possible, the same companies. The formula used for this index is generally defined as a "base-weighted aggregative" expressed in relatives with the average value for the base period (1941–43) equal to 10 and with adjustments for arbitrary price changes caused by the issuance of rights, stock dividends, splitups, etc.

X 355–365. Security issues and net change in outstanding corporate securities, 1934–1957.

Source: **Series X 355–362**, Securities and Exchange Commission, *Annual Report, 1952*, pp. 210–221, and *1958*, pp. 208–216; and *Statistical Bulletin*, May 1958, pp. 9–11. **Series X 363–365**, same agency, records.

The data for series X 355–362 cover substantially all new issues of securities offered for cash sale in the United States in amounts over $100,000 and with terms to maturity of more than one year. Figures include issues privately placed and publicly offered, whether unregistered or registered with the Securities and Exchange Commission.

The figures for privately placed issues include securities actually issued but exclude securities which institutions had contracted to purchase but had not actually taken during the period covered by the statistics. Also excluded are intercorporate transactions; U.S. Government "Special Series" issues, and other sales directly to Federal agencies and trust accounts; notes issued exclusively to commercial banks; and corporate issues sold through continuous offering, such as issues of open-end investment companies. Issues sold by competitive bidding directly to ultimate investors are classified as publicly offered issues. The figures for new capital include all issues other than those whose proceeds are intended to be used for retirement of securities already outstanding.

The figures for series X 363–365 on net change in outstanding corporate securities are derived by deducting from estimated gross proceeds received by corporations through the sale of securities the amount of estimated gross payments by corporations to investors for securities retired. Included in the latter figures are payments for issues retired with internal funds as well as with proceeds from new issues sold for refunding purposes. These series are based primarily on cash transactions but include conversions and exchanges of one type of security for another, e.g., bonds for stocks.

X 366–371. Corporate security issues, 1910–1934.

Source: 1910–1918, Bureau of Foreign and Domestic Commerce, *Statistical Abstract of the United States, 1932*, p. 292; 1919–1934, Board of Governors of the Federal Reserve System, *Banking and Monetary Statistics*, p. 487.

The *Commercial and Financial Chronicle* data used for these series, for 1919–1934, include all security issues publicly offered for sale by companies incorporated in the United States. Securities sold privately are included when the compilers are aware of the sale. Issues of foreign companies sold in the United States are excluded. Data are based on the offering price for preferred stock of no par value and for common stock, and on par amounts for bonds, notes, and preferred stock with stated par value. The data prior to 1919 include offerings of foreign corporations.

These series differ from those compiled by the Securities and Exchange Commission (series X 355–362) in a number of respects. The latter include issues on the basis of gross and/or net proceeds, whereas the *Chronicle* series include issues on the basis noted above. The *Chronicle* series include issues for exchange purposes, while the SEC figures include only that portion of such an offering that is sold for cash. The SEC series also include foreign corporate security issues sold in the United States, while the *Chronicle* series exclude them except for the period noted. The basis for inclusion of privately sold securities also differs.

X 372. New State and municipal security issues, 1919–1957.

Source: 1919–1933, Board of Governors of the Federal Reserve System, *Banking and Monetary Statistics*, p. 487; 1934–1951, Securities and Exchange Commission, *Annual Report, 1952*, part 3, p. 211; 1952–1957, Board of Governors of the Federal Reserve System, *Federal Reserve Bulletin*, February 1959, p. 182.

Data represent principal amounts of securities offered publicly for sale in the United States by all political subdivisions either for new money or for refunding, retiring, or otherwise acquiring existing securities. For 1919–1933, figures are as compiled and published by the *Commercial and Financial Chronicle*, and for 1934–1957, they are from totals published by the *Chronicle* and the *Bond Buyer*.

X 373–377. Volume of sales on New York Stock Exchange, 1900–1957.

Source: 1900–1909, Board of Governors of the Federal Reserve System, *Banking and Monetary Statistics*, p. 485; 1910–1957, Department of Commerce, *Statistical Abstract of the United States, 1936*, p. 289; *1947*, p. 452; *1958*, p. 467.

These data are published currently in the *Commercial and Financial Chronicle*.

Data on stocks (series X 373) show the volume of share trading in round lots on the New York Stock Exchange, as reported by the Exchange ticker; this series excludes odd lots, stopped sales, private sales, split openings, crossed transactions, and errors of omission. Data on bonds are exclusive of stopped sales, and beginning in July 1947, include bonds of the International Bank for Reconstruction and Development.

Beginning 1935, the Securities and Exchange Commission has compiled statistics on the total volume sold and the money value of stock and bond sales on all registered exchanges. These are available in the source volumes.

X 378–380. Margin requirements, 1934–1957.

Source: 1934–1941, Board of Governors of the Federal Reserve System, *Banking and Monetary Statistics*, p. 504; 1942–1957, Federal Reserve Board, *Annual Report, 1948*, p. 77, and *1957*, p. 102.

Regulations T and U administered by the Federal Reserve Board, limit the amount of credit that may be extended on a security by prescribing a maximum loan value, which is a specified percentage of its market value at the time of extension; the "margin requirements" shown are the differences between the market value (100 percent) and the maximum loan value.

X 381–384. Stock market credit, 1931–1957.

Source: **Series X 381–383**, 1931–1941, Board of Governors of the Federal Reserve System, *Banking and Monetary Statistics*, p. 501; 1942–1952, Federal Reserve Board, records; 1953–1957, *Federal Reserve Bulletin*, January 1958, p. 50. **Series X 384**, 1938–1952, FRB, records; 1953–1957, *Federal Reserve Bulletin*, February 1958, p. 166.

Series X 381–383 relate to credit extended by stock brokers on the basis of reports made by a group of firms estimated to account for at least 90 percent of total credit extended by security brokers and dealers in the United States. Data for 1931–1934 are estimates based on data collected by the New York Stock Exchange, and for 1935–1957 are based on reports collected by the Federal Reserve Board. Customers' debit balances represent credit extended by brokers to their customers, and money borrowed represents most of the credit obtained by these brokers, including money borrowed against customer collateral as well as that for their own activities. Customers' free credit balances represent customers' funds held by brokers pending investment or pending remittances to customers.

Customer credit in the stock market (series X 384) is defined as the sum of customers' net debit balances of the reporting firms, exclusive of those secured by U.S. Government obligations, and bank loans to others than brokers and dealers for purchasing and carrying securities exclusive of U.S. Government securities. As a result of changes in reporting, this series is not continuous. Prior to 1955, customers' net debit balances include balances secured by U.S. Government obligations. Bank loans to others for purchasing and carrying securities are figures of weekly reporting member banks for the last Wednesday of the year, a series beginning in 1938. At the end of 1957 these banks accounted for about seven-tenths of all loans for this purpose. Loans for purchasing and carrying U.S. Government securities are excluded for all reporting banks for 1944–1952, and for reporting banks in New York City and Chicago for 1953–1957. For further details concerning the series, see *Banking and Monetary Statistics*, pp. 435 and 437–438, and *Federal Reserve Bulletin*, January 1958, p. 50.

X 385–388. Brokers' loans, by groups of lenders, 1918–1938.

Source: Board of Governors of the Federal Reserve System, *Banking and Monetary Statistics*, p. 494.

These data were assembled from various sources and where gaps occurred estimates were made. The figures represent loans to brokers by principal groups of lenders—New York City banks, outside banks, and others. Other lenders comprise foreign banking agencies, corporations, other brokers, and individuals. The figures cover primarily loans to brokers and dealers in New York City, most of whom are members of the New York Stock Exchange, but they include also loans to certain investment banking houses that do not have Stock Exchange seats and to brokers and dealers belonging to other stock exchanges. Comparable data are not available after 1938. For a more detailed description of the series, see *Banking and Monetary Statistics*, pp. 434–435.

Series X 305–313. Short-Term Interest Rates—Open Market Rates in New York City and Federal Reserve Bank Discount Rate: 1890 to 1957

[Percent per annum]

Year	Stock exchange time loans, 90 days [1]	Prime commercial paper, 4 to 6 months [1]	Stock exchange call loans [2] New	Stock exchange call loans [2] Renewals	Prime bankers' acceptances, 90 days [1]	U.S. Treasury notes and certificates [2]	U.S. Treasury bills [3]	Federal Reserve Bank of New York discount rate [4] Low	Federal Reserve Bank of New York discount rate [4] High
	305	306	307	308	309	310	311	312	313
1957	4.35	3.81	4.50		3.45	----------	3.23	3.00	3.50
1956	3.89	3.31	4.08	4.03	2.64	----------	2.62	2.50	3.00
1955	3.01	2.18	3.20	3.20	1.71	----------	1.73	1.50	2.50
1954	2.80	1.58	3.05	3.05	1.35	----------	0.94	1.50	2.00
1953	2.85	2.52	3.06	3.06	1.87	----------	1.90	1.75	2.00
1952	2.42	2.33	2.48	2.48	1.75	----------	1.72	1.75	1.75
1951	2.15	2.16	2.17	2.17	1.60	----------	1.49	1.75	1.75
1950	1.59	1.45	1.63	1.63	1.15	----------	1.20	1.50	1.75
1949	1.50	1.49	1.63	1.63	1.13	----------	1.11	1.50	1.50
1948	1.50	1.44	1.55	1.55	1.11	----------	1.05	1.50	1.50
1947	1.50	1.03	1.38	1.38	0.87	----------	0.61	1.00	1.00
1946	1.35	0.81	1.16	1.16	0.61	----------	0.38	[5]0.50	1.00
1945	1.25	0.75	1.00	1.00	0.44	----------	0.38	[5]0.50	1.00
1944	1.25	0.73	1.00	1.00	0.44	----------	0.38	[5]0.50	1.00
1943	1.25	0.69	1.00	1.00	0.44	----------	0.38	[5]0.50	1.00
1942	1.25	0.66	1.00	1.00	0.44	----------	0.34	[5]0.50	1.00
1941	1.25	0.53	1.00	1.00	0.44	----------	0.13	1.00	1.00
1940	1.25	0.56	1.00	1.00	0.44	----------	0.01	1.00	1.00
1939	1.25	0.59	1.00	1.00	0.44	----------	0.02	1.00	1.00
1938	1.25	0.81	1.00	1.00	0.44	----------	0.05	1.00	1.00
1937	1.25	0.94	1.00	1.00	0.43	----------	0.45	1.00	1.50
1936	1.16	0.75	0.91	0.91	0.15	----------	0.14	1.50	1.50
1935	0.55	0.75	0.56	0.55	0.13	----------	0.14	1.50	1.50
1934	0.90	1.02	1.00	1.00	0.25	----------	0.26	1.50	2.00
1933	1.11	1.73	1.14	1.16	0.63	0.26	0.52	2.00	3.50
1932	1.87	2.73	2.05	2.05	1.28	0.78	0.88	2.50	3.50
1931	2.15	2.64	1.74	1.74	1.57	1.15	1.40	1.50	3.50
1930	3.26	3.59	2.87	2.94	2.48	2.23	----------	2.00	4.50
1929	7.75	5.85	7.74	7.61	5.03	4.42	----------	4.50	6.00
1928	5.86	4.85	6.10	6.04	4.09	3.97	----------	3.50	5.00
1927	4.35	4.11	4.05	4.06	3.45	3.10	----------	3.50	4.00
1926	4.60	4.34	4.52	4.50	3.59	3.23	----------	3.50	4.00
1925	4.23	4.02	4.20	4.18	3.29	3.03	----------	3.00	3.50
1924	3.64	3.98	3.10	3.08	2.98	2.77	----------	3.00	4.50
1923	5.14	5.07	4.87	4.86	4.09	3.93	----------	4.00	4.50
1922	4.53	4.52	4.36	4.29	3.51	3.47	----------	4.00	4.50
1921	6.15	6.62	5.97	5.97	5.28	4.83	----------	4.50	7.00
1920	8.06	7.50	8.07	7.74	6.06	5.42	----------	6.00	7.00
1919	5.83	5.37	6.70	6.32	4.37	----------	----------	4.00	4.75
1918	5.90	6.02	----------	5.28	4.19	----------	----------	3.50	3.50
1917	4.62	5.07	----------	3.43	----------	----------	----------	3.00	3.50
1916	3.25	3.84	----------	2.62	----------	----------	----------	3.00	4.00
1915	2.85	4.01	----------	1.92	----------	----------	----------	4.00	4.00
1914	4.37	5.47	----------	3.43	----------	----------	----------	5.00	6.00

Year	Stock exchange time loans, 90 days [1] 305	Prime commercial paper, 4 to 6 months [1] 306	Stock exchange call loans, renewals [2] 308	Year	Stock exchange time loans, 90 days [1] 305	Prime commercial paper, 4 to 6 months [1] 306	Stock exchange call loans, renewals [2] 308	Year	Stock exchange time loans, 90 days [1] 305	Prime commercial paper, 4 to 6 months [1] 306	Stock exchange call loans, renewals [2] 308
1913	4.64	6.20	3.22	1905	3.82	5.18	4.44	1897	2.68	4.72	1.75
1912	4.16	5.41	3.52	1904	3.10	5.14	1.78	1896	4.83	7.02	4.28
1911	3.22	4.75	2.57	1903	4.84	6.16	3.71	1895	2.82	5.80	1.88
1910	4.03	5.72	2.98	1902	5.05	5.81	5.15	1894	2.30	5.22	1.07
1909	3.26	[6]4.67	2.71	1901	4.24	5.40	4.00	1893	5.08	7.64	4.57
1908	3.24	[6]5.00	1.92	1900	3.94	5.71	2.94	1892	3.80	5.40	3.08
1907	6.49	[6]6.66	7.01	1899	4.19	5.50	5.08	1891	4.83	6.48	3.42
1906	5.71	6.25	6.54	1898	3.31	5.34	2.18	1890	5.31	6.91	5.84

[1] Averages of weekly prevailing rates through 1934; averages of daily prevailing rates thereafter.
[2] Averages of daily quotations.
[3] 1931–1940 figures are average rates on new issues offered within period; thereafter they are market yields. Beginning 1941, figures are average of closing bid quotations, except Jan. 1950–Mar. 1953 when the mean of bid and ask quotation is shown. For Aug. 1942–June 1947 the yield was pegged at 0.375 percent.
[4] See text.
[5] Preferential rate on advances secured by Government securities; see text.
[6] Includes 1 or more interpolated items.

Series X 314–321. Commercial Paper and Bankers' Acceptances Outstanding: 1918 to 1957

[In millions of dollars. As of end of year]

Year	Commercial paper [1]	Dollar acceptances Total	Held by— Accepting banks	Held by— Federal Reserve banks	Held by— Others	Based on— Imports into U.S.	Based on— Exports from U.S.	Based on— Other
	314	315	316	317	318	319	320	321
1957	551	1,307	287	142	878	278	456	574
1956	506	967	227	119	621	261	329	377
1955	510	642	175	61	405	252	210	180
1954	733	873	289	19	565	285	182	406
1953	564	574	172	24	378	274	154	147
1952	552	492	183	20	289	232	125	135
1951	449	490	197	21	272	235	133	122
1950	333	394	192	--------	202	245	87	62
1949	257	272	128	--------	144	184	49	39
1948	269	259	146	--------	112	164	57	38
1947	287	261	197	--------	64	159	63	39
1946	228	227	169	--------	58	162	29	36
1945	159	154	112	--------	42	103	18	33
1944	166	129	93	--------	35	86	14	28
1943	202	117	90	--------	27	66	11	39
1942	230	118	93	--------	25	57	9	52
1941	375	194	146	--------	49	116	15	63
1940	218	209	167	--------	42	109	18	81
1939	210	233	175	--------	57	103	39	92
1938	187	270	212	--------	58	95	60	116
1937	279	343	278	2	63	117	87	139
1936	215	373	315		57	126	86	161
1935	171	397	368	--------	29	107	94	196
1934	166	543	497	1	46	89	140	314
1933	109	764	442	131	190	94	207	463
1932	81	710	604	44	62	79	164	468
1931	120	974	262	556	156	159	222	594
1930	358	1,556	371	767	417	221	415	919
1929	334	1,732	191	939	602	383	524	825
1928	383	1,284	76	813	395	316	497	472
1927	555	1,081	105	619	357	313	391	377
1926	526	755	77	437	242	284	261	211
1925	621	774	93	442	239	311	297	165
1924	798	821	(2)	430	(2)	292	305	223
1923	763	----	----	----	----	----	----	----
1922	722	----	----	----	----	----	----	----
1921	663	----	----	----	----	----	----	----
1920	948	----	----	----	----	----	----	----
1919	1,186	----	----	----	----	----	----	----
1918	881	----	----	----	----	----	----	----

[1] Beginning 1954, data are not strictly comparable with earlier years because of a change in the number of dealers reporting.　　[2] Not available.

Series X 322–329. Bank Rates on Short-Term Business Loans: 1919 to 1957

[Percent per annum]

Business loan rates

Year	Total, 19 cities	New York City	7 northern and eastern cities	11 southern and western cities
	322	323	324	325
1957	4.6	4.5	4.6	4.8
1956	4.2	4.0	4.2	4.4
1955	3.7	3.5	3.7	4.0
1954	3.6	3.4	3.6	4.0
1953	3.7	3.5	3.7	4.0
1952	3.5	3.3	3.5	3.8
1951	3.1	2.8	3.1	3.5
1950	2.7	2.4	2.7	3.2
1949	2.7	2.4	2.7	3.1
1948	2.5	2.2	2.6	2.9
1947	2.1	1.8	2.2	2.6
1946	2.1	1.8	2.1	2.5
1945	2.2	2.0	2.5	2.5
1944	2.4	2.1	2.7	2.8
1943	2.6	2.2	2.9	2.8
1942	2.2	2.0	2.3	2.6
1941	2.0	1.8	1.9	2.5
1940	2.1	1.8	2.0	2.5
1939	2.1	1.8	2.0	2.5
1938	2.5	1.7	2.8	3.3
1937	2.6	1.7	2.9	3.3
1936	2.7	1.7	3.0	3.4
1935	2.9	1.8	3.4	3.8
1934	3.5	2.5	3.7	4.3
1933	4.3	3.4	4.5	5.0
1932	4.7	4.2	4.8	5.2
1931	4.3	3.8	4.3	4.9
1930	4.9	4.4	4.8	5.4
1929	5.8	5.8	5.8	5.9
1928	5.2	5.0	5.2	5.4

Customer loan rates

Year	Total, leading cities	New York City	Northern and eastern cities	Southern and western cities
	326	327	328	329
1929	6.0	5.9	6.0	6.1
1928	5.4	5.2	5.3	5.7
1927	5.0	4.5	4.9	5.6
1926	5.1	4.7	5.1	5.6
1925	5.0	4.5	5.0	5.6
1924	5.1	4.6	5.1	5.7
1923	5.5	5.2	5.5	5.9
1922	5.5	5.1	5.5	6.1
1921	6.7	6.3	6.8	7.0
1920	6.6	6.3	6.7	6.8
1919	5.7	5.5	5.7	6.0

Series X 330–342. Bond and Stock Yields: 1857 to 1957

[Percent per annum]

Year	Bonds				Preferred stocks	Common stocks							
			Corporate			Cowles Commission				Moody's			
	U.S. Government	Municipal high grade	Unadjusted index number of yields of American railroad bonds	Corporate Aaa (Moody's)		Total	Industrial	Railroad	Utilities	Total	Industrial	Railroad	Utilities
	330	331	332	333	334	335	336	337	338	339	340	341	342
1957	3.47	3.60	--------	3.89	4.63	--------	--------	--------	--------	4.33	4.11	6.77	4.92
1956	3.08	2.93	--------	3.36	4.25	--------	--------	--------	--------	4.07	3.89	5.51	4.68
1955	2.84	2.53	--------	3.06	4.01	--------	--------	--------	--------	4.06	3.93	4.88	4.50
1954	2.55	2.37	--------	2.90	4.02	--------	--------	--------	--------	4.78	4.70	6.20	4.81
1953	2.94	2.72	--------	3.20	4.27	--------	--------	--------	--------	5.49	5.51	6.48	5.33
1952	2.68	2.19	--------	2.96	4.13	--------	--------	--------	--------	5.50	5.55	5.88	5.39
1951	2.57	2.00	--------	2.86	4.11	--------	--------	--------	--------	6.12	6.29	6.31	5.77
1950	2.32	1.98	--------	2.62	3.85	--------	--------	--------	--------	6.27	6.51	6.50	5.66
1949	2.31	2.21	--------	2.66	3.97	--------	--------	--------	--------	6.63	6.82	3.47	5.86
1948	2.44	2.40	--------	2.82	4.15	--------	--------	--------	--------	5.78	5.87	6.04	5.85
1947	2.25	2.01	--------	2.61	3.79	--------	--------	--------	--------	5.13	5.06	6.16	5.32
1946	2.19	1.64	--------	2.53	3.53	--------	--------	--------	--------	3.97	3.75	5.33	4.22
1945	2.37	1.67	--------	2.62	3.70	--------	--------	--------	--------	4.19	4.00	5.51	4.99
1944	2.48	1.86	--------	2.72	3.99	--------	--------	--------	--------	4.81	4.56	6.75	6.28
1943	2.47	2.06	--------	2.73	4.06	--------	--------	--------	--------	4.89	4.54	6.93	6.84
1942	2.46	2.36	--------	2.83	4.31	--------	--------	--------	--------	6.67	6.44	7.73	9.75
1941	2.05	2.10	--------	2.77	4.08	--------	--------	--------	--------	6.25	6.33	6.47	8.02
1940	2.26	2.50	--------	2.84	4.14	--------	--------	--------	--------	5.31	5.30	5.41	5.99
1939	2.41	2.76	--------	3.01	4.19	--------	--------	--------	--------	4.15	3.85	3.75	5.31
1938	2.61	2.91	--------	3.19	4.34	--------	--------	--------	--------	4.38	3.86	5.29	6.27
1937	2.74	3.10	--------	3.26	4.45	4.87	4.91	3.76	5.12	4.77	4.79	4.29	5.40
1936	2.69	3.07	3.88	3.24	4.33	4.35	4.27	5.32	4.31	3.50	3.36	2.74	3.66
1935	2.79	3.40	4.24	3.60	4.63	3.88	3.51	2.94	5.97	4.06	3.52	3.97	5.11
1934	3.12	4.03	4.53	4.00	5.29	3.92	3.45	3.09	6.56	4.11	3.43	3.01	5.86
1933	3.31	4.71	5.35	4.49	5.75	4.05	3.56	2.50	6.27	4.42	3.71	2.63	5.81
1932	3.68	4.65	5.73	5.01	6.13	6.69	6.58	5.30	7.36	7.36	7.28	6.15	7.53
1931	3.34	4.01	4.66	4.58	5.04	5.58	5.82	6.89	4.43	6.17	6.37	7.83	5.20
1930	3.29	4.07	4.41	4.55	4.95	4.26	4.45	5.27	3.19	4.54	4.93	5.55	3.45
1929	3.60	4.27	4.60	4.73	5.12	3.48	3.65	4.29	2.29	3.41	3.84	4.36	2.10
1928	3.33	4.05	4.35	4.55	5.12	3.98	3.82	4.76	4.09	--------	--------	--------	--------
1927	3.34	3.98	4.34	4.57	5.51	4.77	4.72	4.89	4.96	--------	--------	--------	--------
1926	3.68	4.08	4.47	4.73	5.78	5.32	5.24	5.52	5.57	--------	--------	--------	--------
1925	3.86	4.09	4.73	4.88	5.90	5.19	4.75	5.66	6.13	--------	--------	--------	--------
1924	4.06	4.20	4.84	5.00	6.08	5.87	5.25	6.44	7.35	--------	--------	--------	--------
1923	4.36	4.25	4.98	5.12	6.12	5.94	5.40	6.29	7.59	--------	--------	--------	--------
1922	4.30	4.23	4.85	5.10	6.14	5.80	5.37	5.95	7.62	--------	--------	--------	--------
1921	5.09	5.09	5.57	5.97	6.80	6.49	5.84	7.08	8.29	--------	--------	--------	--------
1920	5.32	4.98	5.81	6.12	6.79	6.13	5.54	6.81	8.06	--------	--------	--------	--------
1919	4.73	4.46	5.29	5.49	6.31	5.75	5.18	6.26	7.37	--------	--------	--------	--------

Year	Bonds		Preferred stocks	Common stocks, Cowles Commission			
	Municipal high grade	Corporate, unadjusted index number of yields of American railroad bonds		Total	Industrial	Railroad	Utilities
	331	332	334	335	336	337	338
1918	4.50	5.23	6.70	7.24	7.71	6.32	7.57
1917	4.20	4.79	6.42	7.82	9.79	6.12	6.75
1916	3.94	4.49	6.19	5.62	6.16	5.13	5.72
1915	4.16	4.62	6.48	4.98	4.19	5.21	6.01
1914	4.12	4.44	6.49	5.01	5.32	4.64	6.06
1913	4.22	4.44	6.57	5.87	5.71	5.16	5.66
1912	4.02	4.23	6.27	4.85	4.98	4.73	5.11
1911	3.98	4.19	6.28	4.92	5.36	4.68	5.28
1910	3.97	4.18	6.30	4.84	5.33	4.63	5.04
1909	3.78	4.07	--------	4.31	3.64	4.47	4.57
1908	3.93	4.22	--------	4.93	4.81	4.97	4.93
1907	3.86	4.27	--------	5.38	6.16	5.21	4.78
1906	3.57	4.00	--------	3.96	4.17	3.58	4.67
1905	3.40	3.89	--------	3.53	3.76	3.20	4.77
1904	3.45	3.98	--------	4.18	4.83	3.85	4.64
1903	3.38	4.03	--------	4.65	6.77	3.90	4.60
1902	3.20	3.84	--------	3.71	4.83	3.21	4.03
1901	3.13	3.83	--------	3.85	5.25	3.25	3.84
1900	3.12	3.89	--------	4.50	5.74	3.93	5.30
1899	--------	3.85	--------	3.21	3.62	3.03	3.47
1898	--------	4.03	--------	3.72	5.04	3.38	3.91
1897	--------	4.11	--------	3.90	5.32	3.47	4.73
1896	--------	4.34	--------	4.15	5.56	3.77	4.76
1895	--------	4.27	--------	3.97	5.46	3.50	4.99

Year	Corporate, unadjusted index number of yields of American railroad bonds	Common stocks, Cowles Commission			
		Total	Industrial	Railroad	Utilities
	332	335	336	337	338
1894	4.41	4.62	6.03	4.17	5.94
1893	4.65	5.03	8.12	4.35	5.45
1892	4.53	4.16	5.51	3.77	5.05
1891	4.71	4.28	5.96	3.83	5.44
1890	4.55	4.01	5.07	3.54	6.03
1889	4.43	3.88	4.41	3.35	6.26
1888	4.59	4.18	4.29	3.84	6.11
1887	4.65	4.24	5.13	4.09	4.88
1886	4.55	3.85	5.46	3.75	3.75
1885	4.89	5.09	6.02	4.71	8.14
1884	5.15	6.31	6.25	6.13	8.03
1883	5.23	5.69	6.26	5.47	7.34
1882	5.24	5.18	5.23	5.07	6.18
1881	5.19	4.84	5.06	4.84	4.64
1880	5.60	4.78	6.85	4.64	4.08
1879	5.98	4.70	4.76	4.64	5.25
1878	6.45	5.12	5.34	5.15	4.61
1877	6.62	5.78	5.11	5.94	5.01
1876	6.68	7.02	6.99	7.02	6.98
1875	7.06	6.51	6.06	6.41	7.90
1874	7.53	6.89	6.72	6.80	7.92
1873	7.76	6.54	6.49	6.98	2.81
1872	7.60	5.70	5.10	6.18	2.12
1871	7.78	5.26	4.80	5.48	2.98

Year	Corporate, unadjusted index number of yields of American railroad bonds
	332
1870	7.92
1869	8.13
1868	7.80
1867	7.87
1866	7.95
1865	7.62
1864	6.27
1863	6.34
1862	7.56
1861	8.88
1860	8.59
1859	8.91
1858	9.34
1857	10.25

Series X 343–347. Basic Yields of Corporate Bonds, by Term to Maturity: 1900 to 1957

[Percent per annum]

Year	1 year (343)	5 years (344)	10 years (345)	20 years (346)	50 years (347)
1957	3.50 [1]	3.50 [1]	3.50	3.50 [1]	3.78
1956	2.70	2.78	2.86	2.99	3.17
1955	(2)	2.70 [1]	2.80	2.95	3.10
1954	2.40	2.52	2.66	2.88	3.05
1953	2.62 [1]	2.75 [1]	2.88	3.05	3.22
1952	2.73 [1]	2.73 [1]	2.73	2.88	3.09
1951	2.05 [1]	2.22 [1]	2.39	2.59	2.72
1950	1.42 [1]	1.90 [1]	2.30	2.48	2.63 [1]
1949	1.60	1.92	2.32	2.62	2.80
1948	1.60	2.03	2.53	2.73	2.85
1947	1.05 [1]	1.65	2.08 [1]	2.40	2.55
1946	.86 [1]	1.32	1.88 [1]	2.35	2.45
1945	1.02	1.53	2.14	2.55	2.55 [3]
1944	1.08 [1]	1.58	2.20	2.60	2.60 [3]
1943	1.17	1.71	2.16	2.61	2.65 [3]
1942	0.81	1.50	2.16	2.61	2.65 [1]
1941	0.41	1.21	1.88	2.50	2.65 [1]
1940	0.41	1.28	1.95	2.55	2.70 [1]
1939	0.57	1.55	2.18	2.65	2.75 [1]
1938	0.85	1.97	2.60	2.91	3.00 [1]
1937	0.69	1.68	2.38	2.90	3.22 [1]
1936	0.61	1.86	2.64	3.04	3.29
1935	1.05	2.37	3.00	3.37	3.50
1934	2.62 [1]	3.48	3.70	3.91	4.00
1933	2.60 [1]	3.68	4.00	4.11	4.15
1932	3.99 [3]	4.58 [4]	4.70	4.70	4.70
1931	3.05	3.90	4.03	4.10	4.10
1930	4.40	4.40	4.40	4.40	4.40
1929	5.27	4.72	4.57	4.45	4.40
1928	4.05	4.05	4.05	4.05	4.05
1927	4.30	4.30	4.30	4.30	4.30
1926	4.40	4.40	4.40	4.40	4.40
1925	3.85	4.46	4.50	4.50	4.50
1924	5.02	4.90	4.80	4.69	4.65
1923	5.01	4.90	4.80	4.68	4.60
1922	5.31	5.19	5.06	4.85	4.61
1921	6.94 [1]	6.21	5.73	5.31	5.15
1920	6.11	5.72	5.43	5.17	5.10
1919	5.58	5.16	4.97	4.81	4.75
1918	5.48	5.25	5.05	4.82	4.75
1917	4.05	4.05	4.05	4.05	4.05
1916	3.48	4.03	4.05	4.05	4.05
1915	4.47	4.39	4.31	4.20	4.15
1914	4.64	4.45	4.32	4.16	4.10
1913	4.74	4.31	4.12	4.02	4.00
1912	4.04	4.00	3.96	3.91	3.90
1911	4.09	4.05	4.01	3.94	3.90
1910	4.25	4.10	3.99	3.87	3.80
1909	4.03	3.97	3.91	3.82	3.75
1908	5.10 [4]	4.30 [4]	4.02 [4]	3.95	3.95
1907	4.87 [4]	3.87 [4]	3.80	3.80	3.80
1906	4.75 [4]	3.67 [4]	3.55	3.55	3.55
1905	3.50	3.50	3.50	3.50	3.50
1904	3.60	3.60	3.60	3.60	3.60
1903	3.45	3.45	3.45	3.45	3.45
1902	3.30	3.30	3.30	3.30	3.30
1901	3.25	3.25	3.25	3.25	3.25
1900	3.97 [4]	3.36 [4]	3.30	3.30	3.30

[1] More than usually liable to error.
[2] Not available.
[3] Represents bonds 40 years to maturity. More than usually liable to error.
[4] One alternative value; the other is equal to the longest term yield shown.

Series X 348–354. Bond and Stock Prices: 1871 to 1957

Year	Bonds (price per $100 bond) U.S. Government (348)	Municipal high grade (349)	Corporate high grade (350)	Index of common stocks (1941–43=10) Total (351)	Industrial (352)	Railroad (353)	Utilities (354)
1957	$ 93.2	$105.8	$101.3	44.38	47.63	28.11	32.19
1956	98.9	116.3	109.1	42.62	49.80	33.65	32.25
1955	102.4	123.1	114.4	40.49	42.40	32.94	31.37
1954	107.0	125.8	117.2	29.69	30.25	23.96	27.57
1953	99.1	119.7	112.1	24.73	24.84	22.60	24.03
1952	97.3	129.3	115.8	24.50	24.78	22.49	22.86
1951	98.9	133.0	117.7	22.34	22.68	19.91	20.59
1950	102.5	133.4	121.9	18.40	18.33	15.53	19.96
1949	102.7	128.9	121.0	15.23	15.00	12.83	17.87
1948	100.8	125.3	118.2	15.53	15.34	15.27	16.77
1947	103.8	132.8	122.1	15.17	14.85	14.02	18.01
1946	104.8	140.1	123.4	17.08	16.48	19.09	20.76
1945	102.0	139.6	121.6	15.16	14.72	18.21	16.84
1944	100.3	135.7	118.7	12.47	12.34	13.47	12.81
1943	100.5	131.8	118.3	11.50	11.49	11.81	11.34
1942	100.7	126.2	117.4	8.67	8.78	8.81	7.74
1941	109.5	130.9	117.7	9.82	9.72	9.39	10.93
1940	106.6	123.6	116.3	11.02	10.69	9.41	15.05
1939	104.5	119.0	114.7	12.06	11.77	9.82	16.34
1938	101.8	116.6	111.7	11.49	11.39	9.15	14.17
1937	100.1	113.3	110.2	15.41	14.97	16.86	19.07
1936	100.8	113.8	109.6	15.47	14.69	17.71	22.47
1935	99.5	108.6	105.5	10.60	10.13	11.78	15.15
1934	95.4	99.7	98.2	9.84	9.00	11.45	15.79
1933	93.1	91.0	91.2	8.96	7.61	12.75	19.72
1932	88.9	91.7	84.4	6.93	5.37	8.75	20.65
1931	92.8	100.0	92.8	13.66	10.51	23.72	37.18
1930	108.8	99.0	90.9	21.03	16.42	39.82	53.24
1929	104.8	96.5	89.1	26.02	21.35	46.15	59.33
1928	108.3	99.3	91.8	19.95	16.92	40.40	36.86
1927	108.1	100.3	91.6	15.34	12.53	38.17	27.63
1926	103.8	99.0	90.1	12.59	10.04	32.72	24.11
1925	101.7	98.8	88.3	11.15	8.69	29.21	23.28
1924	99.3	97.4	86.6	9.05	6.83	25.02	19.34
1923	95.9	96.7	85.0	8.57	6.54	23.45	18.11
1922	96.6	96.9	85.5	8.41	6.35	23.71	17.39
1921	88.2	86.5	76.6	6.86	5.07	20.15	14.18
1920	85.9	87.7	75.2	7.98	6.50	20.86	13.36
1919	91.9	93.9	81.9	8.78	7.13	22.94	14.79
1918		93.5	82.3	7.54	5.57	22.40	14.70
1917		97.3	87.6	8.50	6.15	24.89	18.24
1916		100.9	90.7	9.47	6.62	28.35	20.26
1915		97.8	89.5	8.31	5.22	26.38	18.65
1914		98.4	90.4	8.08	4.50	27.39	18.14
1913		97.0	90.0	8.51	4.56	29.48	18.92
1912		99.7	92.2	9.53	5.18	32.83	20.92
1911		100.2	92.5	9.24	4.82	32.43	20.00
1910		100.4	92.3	9.35	5.02	32.90	19.08
1909		103.1	93.3	9.71	4.99	34.79	19.39
1908		100.9	90.3	7.78	3.74	28.18	16.11
1907		102.0	90.8	7.84	3.84	28.09	17.36
1906		106.2	95.0	9.64	4.82	34.06	23.25
1905		108.7	96.2	8.99	4.11	31.85	25.59
1904		108.0	93.6	7.05	2.92	24.61	24.19
1903		108.9	93.2	7.21	3.20	24.71	24.48
1902		111.8	95.5	8.42	3.92	28.37	28.25
1901		112.8	94.9	7.84	4.00	25.01	27.82
1900		113.1	93.6	6.15	3.38	18.62	24.22

Index of common stocks (1941–43=10)

Year	Total (351)	Industrial (352)	Railroad (353)	Utilities (354)
1899	6.29	3.67	18.21	27.76
1898	5.05	2.74	14.71	23.44
1897	4.45	2.32	13.06	20.55
1896	4.23	2.22	12.48	18.84
1895	4.53	2.50	13.29	19.25
1894	4.39	2.41	12.95	18.09
1893	4.78	2.66	14.15	18.47
1892	5.55	3.19	16.58	19.10
1891	5.03	2.88	15.22	16.16
1890	5.27	2.99	15.80	18.14
1889	5.32	3.24	15.70	18.59
1888	5.20	2.70	15.78	16.96
1887	5.53	2.60	17.11	16.93
1886	5.36	2.48	16.57	16.80
1885	4.60	2.19	14.14	14.81
1884	4.74	2.06	14.68	15.16
1883	5.63	2.25	17.44	19.14
1882	5.90	2.41	18.18	20.31
1881	6.25	2.45	19.38	21.09
1880	5.21	2.10	16.08	17.36
1879	4.12	1.90	12.44	14.83
1878	3.38	1.78	10.00	12.54
1877	3.14	1.80	9.22	10.94
1876	4.06	2.27	12.00	13.92
1875	4.45	2.27	13.16	16.43
1874	4.57	2.40	13.53	16.44
1873	4.80	2.37	14.34	17.06
1872	5.03	2.38	15.02	18.79
1871	4.69	2.00	14.26	15.91

Series X 355–365.　Security Issues and Net Change in Outstanding Corporate Securities: 1934 to 1957

[In millions of dollars]

| Year | Non-corporate | Total security issues — Corporate [1] | | | Classes of corporate securities [2] — Bonds and notes | | Stocks | | Net change in outstanding corporate securities | | |
| | | Total | New capital | Retirement of securities | Publicly offered | Privately placed | Preferred | Common | Total | Bonds and notes | Stocks |
	355	356	357	358	359	360	361	362	363	364	365
1957	17,687	12,661	12,447	214	6,118	3,839	411	2,516	11,129	7,455	3,675
1956	11,467	10,749	10,384	364	4,225	3,777	636	2,301	8,065	4,752	3,313
1955	16,532	10,049	8,821	1,227	4,119	3,301	635	2,185	6,875	4,188	2,687
1954	20,249	9,365	7,490	1,875	4,003	3,484	816	1,213	6,065	3,799	2,265
1953	19,926	8,755	8,495	260	3,856	3,228	489	1,326	7,121	4,755	2,366
1952	17,675	9,380	8,716	664	3,645	3,957	564	1,369	7,927	4,940	2,987
1951	13,523	7,607	7,120	486	2,364	3,326	838	1,212	6,277	3,577	2,700
1950	13,532	6,261	4,990	1,271	2,360	2,560	631	811	3,724	2,004	1,720
1949	15,059	5,959	5,558	401	2,437	2,453	425	736	4,856	3,284	1,572
1948	13,172	6,959	6,652	307	2,965	3,008	492	614	5,887	4,655	1,232
1947	13,364	6,466	5,114	1,352	2,889	2,147	762	779	4,359	3,004	1,355
1946	11,786	6,757	3,889	2,868	3,019	1,863	1,127	891	2,382	1,096	1,286
1945	48,701	5,902	1,347	4,555	3,851	1,004	758	397	−449	−1,072	623
1944	53,108	3,142	753	2,389	1,892	778	369	163	−475	−698	223
1943	48,348	1,147	408	739	621	369	124	56	−796	−804	8
1942	34,376	1,043	646	396	506	411	112	34	−313	−398	85
1941	12,490	2,623	1,041	1,583	1,578	811	167	110	−24	−125	101
1940	3,887	2,615	761	1,854	1,628	758	183	108	−273	−337	64
1939	3,523	2,115	420	1,695	1,276	703	98	87	−539	−611	72
1938	3,771	2,110	904	1,206	1,353	691	86	25	569	588	−19
1937	3,018	2,239	1,138	1,100	1,291	327	406	285	72	−429	501
1936	5,411	4,431	1,062	3,368	3,660	369	271	272	759	598	159
1935	4,352	2,266	401	1,865	1,840	385	86	22	−242	−187	−55
1934	4,512	384	152	231	280	92	6	19	−168	−244	76

[1] Estimated net proceeds which represent the amount received by the issuers after payment of compensation to distributors and other costs of flotation.　　[2] Estimated gross proceeds, which represent the amount paid for the securities by investors.

Series X 366–371.　Corporate Security Issues: 1910 to 1934

[In millions of dollars]

| Year | Corporate securities — Total | New capital | Retirement of securities | Bonds and notes | Stocks — Preferred | Common | Year | Corporate securities — Total | New capital | Retirement of securities | Bonds and notes | Stocks — Preferred | Common |
	366	367	368	369	370	371		366	367	368	369	370	371
1934	490	178	312	456	3	31	1921	2,270	1,702	568	1,994	75	200
1933	380	161	219	227	15	137	1920	2,788	2,563	225	1,750	483	555
1932	644	325	319	620	10	13	1919	2,668	2,246	422	1,122	793	753
1931	2,372	1,551	821	2,028	148	195	1918				1,047	298	
1930	4,957	4,483	474	3,431	421	1,105	1917				1,076	455	
1929	9,376	8,002	1,374	2,620	1,695	5,062	1916				1,405	782	
1928	6,930	5,346	1,584	3,439	1,397	2,094							
1927	6,507	4,657	1,850	4,769	1,054	684	1915				1,111	325	
1926	4,574	3,754	820	3,354	543	677	1914				1,175	262	
							1913				1,194	452	
1925	4,223	3,605	618	2,975	637	610	1912				1,350	904	
1924	3,521	3,029	492	2,655	346	519	1911				1,387	352	
1923	3,165	2,635	530	2,430	407	329							
1922	2,949	2,215	734	2,329	333	288	1910				1,113	405	

Series X 372.　New State and Municipal Security Issues: 1919 to 1957

[In millions of dollars]

Year	Amount 372	Year	Amount 372	Year	Amount 372	Year	Amount 372	Year	Amount 372	Year	Amount 372	Year	Amount 372	Year	Amount 372
1957	6,958	1950	3,532	1945	795	1940	1,238	1935	1,232	1930	1,487	1925	1,400
1956	5,446	1949	2,907	1944	661	1939	1,126	1934	939	1929	1,431	1924	1,399
		1948	2,690	1943	435	1938	1,108	1933	520	1928	1,415	1923	1,063
1955	5,977	1947	2,324	1942	524	1937	908	1932	849	1927	1,510	1922	1,101
1954	6,969	1946	1,157	1941	956	1936	1,121	1931	1,256	1926	1,366	1921	1,207
1953	5,558											1920	683
1952	4,121											1919	691
1951	3,189												

Series X 373–377.   Volume of Sales on New York Stock Exchange: 1900 to 1957

[Money figures in millions of dollars]

Year	Stocks (1,000,000 shares)	Bonds, par value				Year	Stocks (1,000,000 shares)	Bonds, par value			
		Total	Corporate	U.S. Government	State, municipal, foreign			Total	Corporate	U.S. Government	State, municipal, foreign
	373	374	375	376	377		373	374	375	376	377
1957	560	1,082	1,031	(1)	50	1928	920	2,903	1,967	188	749
1956	556	1,069	1,013	(1)	56	1927	577	3,269	2,142	290	837
1955	650	1,046	962	(1)	84	1926	451	2,987	2,004	262	721
1954	573	980	856	(1)	124	1925	454	3,384	2,332	391	661
1953	355	776	683	(1)	93	1924	282	3,804	2,345	877	582
1952	338	773	693	(1)	80	1923	236	2,790	1,568	796	425
1951	444	824	730	2	92	1922	259	4,370	1,905	1,873	592
						1921	173	3,324	1,043	1,957	324
1950	525	1,112	1,008	2	103						
1949	271	818	725	(1)	93	1920	227	3,977	827	2,861	289
1948	295	1,014	925	1	87	1919	317	3,809	622	2,901	286
1947	254	1,076	970	3	102	1918	144	2,063	356	1,436	271
1946	364	1,364	1,265	19	81	1917	186	1,057	471	286	300
						1916	233	1,150	845	1	304
1945	378	2,262	2,148	8	106						
1944	263	2,695	2,585	6	104	1915	173	961	907	3	51
1943	279	3,255	3,130	4	120	1914	48	462	427	1	34
1942	126	2,311	2,181	7	124	1913	83	502	471	2	29
1941	171	2,112	1,929	20	163	1912	131	675	648	1	26
						1911	127	890	795	3	92
1940	208	1,669	1,414	39	216						
1939	262	2,046	1,480	311	255	1910	164	635	592	(1)	43
1938	297	1,860	1,484	127	249	1909	212	------	------	------	------
1937	409	2,793	2,097	349	347	1908	195	------	------	------	------
1936	496	3,576	2,899	319	359	1907	195	------	------	------	------
						1906	282	------	------	------	------
1935	382	3,339	2,287	674	378						
1934	324	3,726	2,239	885	602	1905	261	------	------	------	------
1933	655	3,369	2,099	501	769	1904	187	------	------	------	------
1932	425	2,967	1,642	570	755	1903	159	------	------	------	------
1931	577	3,051	1,846	296	908	1902	187	------	------	------	------
						1901	265	------	------	------	------
1930	810	2,764	1,927	116	721						
1929	1,125	2,982	2,182	142	658	1900	139	------	------	------	------

[1] Less than $500,000.

Series X 378–380.   Margin Requirements: 1934 to 1957

[**Percent of market value.**   Prescribed by Board of Governors of Federal Reserve System in accordance with Securities Exchange Act of 1934]

Period	Regulation T		Regulation U, for loans by banks on stocks	Period	Regulation T		Regulation U, for loans by banks on stocks
	For extensions of credit by brokers and dealers on listed securities	For short sales			For extensions of credit by brokers and dealers on listed securities	For short sales	
	378	379	380		378	379	380
1957, Dec. 31–1955, Apr. 23 [1]	70	70	70	1946, Jan. 20–1945, July 5	75	75	75
1955, Apr. 22–1955, Jan. 4 [1]	60	60	60	1945, July 4–1945, Feb. 5	50	50	50
1955, Jan. 4–1953, Feb. 20	50	50	50	1945, Feb. 4–1937, Nov. 1	40	50	40
1953, Feb. 20–1951, Jan. 17	75	75	75	1937, Oct. 31–1936, Apr. 1	[2] 55	(3)	55
1951, Jan. 16–1949, Mar. 30	50	50	50	1936, Mar. 31–1936, Feb. 1	[4] 25–55	(3)	----------
1949, Mar. 29–1947, Feb. 1	75	75	75	1936, Jan. 31–1934, Oct. 1	[4] 25–45	(3)	----------
1947, Jan. 31–1946, Jan. 20	100	100	100				

[1] Effective after close of business.
[2] Effective May 1, 1936.
[3] Requirement prior to Nov. 1, 1937, was margin "customarily required" by broker.

[4] Exact requirement on each security determined by relation of its current price to its lowest price since July 1, 1933.

Series X 381–384. Stock Market Credit: 1931 to 1957

[In millions of dollars. As of end of year]

Year	Customers' net debit balances [1]	Money borrowed [2]	Customers' net free credit balances	Customer credit in stock market [3]	Year	Customers' net debit balances [1]	Money borrowed [2]	Customers' net free credit balances	Customer credit in stock market [3]	Year	Customers' net debit balances [1]	Money borrowed [2]	Customers' net free credit balances	Customer credit in stock market [3]
	381	382	383	384		381	382	383	384		381	382	383	384
1957	2,550	1,831	896	3,576	1948	550	257	586	968	1939	906	637	266	1,412
1956	2,856	2,178	880	3,984	1947	578	240	612	1,032	1938	991	754	247	1,551
					1946	540	218	694	976	1937	985	688	278	--------
1955	2,825	2,297	894	4,030						1936	1,395	1,048	342	--------
1954	2,429	1,598	1,019	3,436	1945	1,138	795	654	1,374					
1953	1,696	1,162	713	2,445	1944	1,041	726	472	1,394	1935	1,258	930	286	--------
1952	1,365	907	727	1,980	1943	789	557	354	1,367	1934	1,170	--------	170	--------
1951	1,292	695	816	1,826	1942	543	378	270	925	1933	1,270	--------	220	--------
					1941	600	368	289	1,022	1932	800	--------	230	--------
1950	1,356	745	890	1,798						1931	1,300	--------	260	--------
1949	881	523	633	1,249	1940	677	427	281	1,142					

[1] Excludes balances with reporting firms of other member firms of major security exchanges and balances of the reporting firms and of general partners of the reporting firm. Figures for November 1931 to August 1935, inclusive, are estimates based on data made available through the courtesy of New York Stock Exchange; such estimates are available only for "Customers' debit balances" and for "Customers' free credit balances."

[2] Includes money borrowed from banks and trust companies in New York City and elsewhere in U.S. and also money borrowed from other lenders (not including members of national securities exchanges). Prior to September 1935, figures reported on a different basis.

[3] For an explanation of this series, see text.

Series X 385–388. Brokers' Loans, by Groups of Lenders: 1918 to 1938

[In millions of dollars. As of end of year]

Year	Total	New York City banks	Outside banks	Others	Year	Total	New York City banks	Outside banks	Others	Year	Total	New York City banks	Outside banks	Others
	385	386	387	388		385	386	387	388		385	386	387	388
1938	770	715	15	40	1931	715	540	35	140	1924	2,230	1,150	530	550
1937	770	705	35	30	1930	2,105	1,280	215	610	1923	1,580	720	410	450
1936	1,185	1,095	50	40	1929	4,110	1,200	460	2,450	1922	1,860	945	410	505
					1928	6,440	1,640	915	3,885	1921	1,190	545	265	380
1935	1,080	1,020	30	30	1927	4,430	1,550	1,050	1,830					
1934	905	660	180	65	1926	3,290	1,160	830	1,300	1920	1,080	390	285	405
1933	915	705	135	75						1919	1,610	715	420	475
1932	430	335	20	75	1925	3,550	1,450	1,050	1,050	1918	1,000	575	145	280

chapter X

CREDIT AND OTHER FINANCE (Series X 389–434)

X 389–434. General note.

Financing institutions other than commercial banks provide credit by making loans and purchasing securities. Such agencies include—in addition to mutual savings banks—savings and loan associations, personal loan and other small-loan companies, credit unions, sales finance and commercial finance companies, mortgage companies, insurance companies, and credit agencies owned or sponsored by the Federal Government.

While the available data for most of these institutions are much less comprehensive than those for commercial banks, when used in conjunction with the data for commercial banks, they provide a broader view of finance in the United States. Historical series for institutions not included in other chapters are incorporated in this section.

Among the private noncommercial bank financing institutions included elsewhere in this volume are life insurance companies (series X 435–468), mutual savings banks (series X 95–96), and savings and loan associations (series N 156 and N 169). Included in this section (series X 389–434) are Federal agencies (both those owned and those sponsored by the Federal Government) that provide direct loans and underwrite, by insurance or guarantee, credit extended by privately owned agencies; and credit unions which make primarily short-term loans to consumers.

Other broad measures of finance relate to oustanding credit (or debt) which represents financing by all lenders and investors. This volume includes series on farm credit (series K 162–180), home mortgage debt (series N 150–178 and N 190–195), and in this section, short- and intermediate-term consumer credit and aggregate public and private debt.

X 389–402. Outstanding loans and loan insurance or guarantees of Federal and Federally sponsored agencies, by economic sector served, 1917–1953.

Source: R. J. Saulnier, Harold G. Halcrow, and Neil H. Jacoby, *Federal Lending and Loan Insurance*, Princeton University Press, 1958, appendix A, pp. 365–380.

These series are combinations of data shown separately in the source volume for Federal and Federally sponsored agencies; the source volume shows amount extended during the year as well as amount outstanding at year end. The economic sectors shown here are the major sectors shown in the source volume—agriculture, business, financial institutions, and housing—and an "other group" which combines minor governmental units and miscellaneous sectors. The coverage and classification are described in the source chapter I, pp. 3–27, the footnote on pp. 28–29, and in footnotes of tables A1 to A8. The following paragraphs are adapted from that text.

Federally sponsored agencies include all those having a special financial or administrative connection with the Federal Government, whether or not Federal funds are presently invested in them. Thus, they include agencies that are in some respects private or cooperative in ownership and organization but that operate in part with Federal funds; and agencies that, although no longer using Treasury funds, are specially connected with some Federal agency through the latter's power to appoint policymaking officers and in some cases to review policy decisions.

The Federal agencies represented under the various categories of loans, insurance or guarantees, and stock purchases are summarized in the source in footnotes to the economic sector tables (pp. 365–380) and are shown in greater detail in the source tables covering individual agencies (pp. 381–418). For example, among agencies making direct loans to the business sector are the Export-Import Bank of Washington, the Departments of Army and Navy, and the Public Works Administration, as well as the War Finance Corporation, the Reconstruction Finance Corporation, and the Smaller War Plants Corporation. Federal Reserve bank loans and participations in loans of private financing institutions to business under section 13b of the Federal Reserve Act are also included. Guarantees of loans to the business sector include guarantees by the Veterans Administration and by Federal agencies under Regulation V of the Board of Governors of the Federal Reserve System, as well as deferred participation commitments of the Reconstruction Finance Corporation. (For further details, see source, p. 374.)

Credit programs not covered by the tabulation shown here include loans to foreign governments, except the Export-Import Bank as noted here, direct and guaranteed loans by the Commodity Credit Corporation, and loans to State governments. Loans of the Export-Import Bank of Washington which could not be fully separated from lending to foreign concerns and to domestic concerns engaged in foreign trade are included in the business sector.

Outstanding amounts relate to three basic categories of Federal credit activities.

X 389–394, direct loans. These include (*a*) the full amounts of loans extended by specified Federal and Federally sponsored agencies; (*b*) the amounts disbursed to private lenders by Federal agencies in purchasing outstanding loans made under Federal insurance or guarantee; and (*c*) the amounts disbursed on loans made in participation with private lenders.

Loans exclude credit extended (usually on an accounts-receivable basis) incident to some other activity, as when the U.S. Commercial Company gave open book credit during World War II in connection with its sales of commodities. Grant-in-aid programs are also excluded. Loans made indirectly—as when the Federal intermediate credit banks discount paper for production credit associations, enabling the latter to make loans to farmers—are included, as well as loans going directly to the ultimate borrower; but there is no double counting that would result from interagency loans, such as purchase by the Treasury of debentures of the Reconstruction Finance Corporation.

X 395–399, loan insurance or guarantees. Loan insurance covers the full amounts of loans extended by private lenders and insured by Federal agencies. Loan guarantees cover (*a*) the amounts Federally guaranteed, ranging from 100 percent to seldom lower than 50 percent of a privately made loan; and (*b*) the amounts of the Federal shares authorized under deferred participations, where the Government stands ready to take up an agreed percentage of a privately made loan. Thus, credit actually extended under participation agreements with private lenders is included under direct loans; but during the time when there is merely a commitment outstanding to

620722 O - 62 - 43

661

take up all or some part of a loan at the option of the private lender, the amount of the obligation is included as a loan guarantee.

X 400–402, stock purchases. Such purchases are included if identifiable as primarily credit aid, and they cover the amount of Federal funds invested. Stock purchases represent purchases of, and loans on, preferred stocks of banks and insurance companies, and purchases of capital notes and debentures of banks, by the Reconstruction Finance Corporation; purchases of shares of savings and loan associations by the Home Owners' Loan Corporation and the Treasury Department; purchases of stock of agricultural cooperative associations by the Tennessee Valley Associated Cooperatives, Inc.; and purchases of Class A stock of production credit associations by the production credit corporations.

X 403–414. State and Federally chartered credit unions—number, share capital, loans, and total assets, 1931–1957.

Source: Bureau of Federal Credit Unions, *Report of Operations of Federal Credit Unions, 1957*, p. 1; *State-Chartered Credit Unions in 1957*, pp. 1 and 3; and records.

Annual data on operations of credit unions are also published in Bureau of Labor Statistics, *Monthly Labor Review*, 1936–1953 (usually in the latter part of the year), and in BLS Bulletin Nos. 797 and 850.

Data for Federal credit unions, which were authorized by legislation enacted in 1934, represent all operating unions. Data on State-chartered credit unions have been furnished annually by State officials charged with the supervision of such credit unions, to the Bureau of Federal Credit Unions since 1951, and to the Bureau of Labor Statistics prior to 1951. Figures for State credit unions represent reporting unions, which in recent years have included 97 percent or more of all active unions; prior to 1939, the proportion reporting was about 80 percent.

Loans of credit unions (series X 409–411) are principally short-term consumer loans, but they include some real estate mortgage loans and a small amount of business loans.

X 415–422. Short- and intermediate-term consumer credit, by major types, 1929–1957.

Source: Board of Governors of the Federal Reserve System, *Federal Reserve Bulletin*, April 1953, pp. 346–347, 354; June 1955, p. 638; October 1956, pp. 1035–1036; and February 1960, p. 198.

Short- and intermediate-term consumer credit includes credit used to finance the purchase of commodities and services for personal consumption or to refinance debt originally incurred for such purposes. It also includes credit extended to individuals for the purchase of consumer goods that may be used in part for business. The installment component includes credit

scheduled to be repaid in a number of installments. Noninstallment debt includes single-payment loans, charge accounts, and service credit.

Among types of installment credit, automobile and other consumer-goods paper includes credit extended for the purpose of purchasing such goods, in most cases secured by the item purchased. This credit may be extended to the consumer by a retail dealer, arranged by a retail dealer through a financing institution, or extended directly to the consumer by a financial institution. All other installment credit (series X 418) includes other consumer-goods paper, repair and modernization loans, and personal loans.

Estimates are described in the *Bulletin* for April 1953, pp. 336–345. They are based for the most part on sample reports submitted monthly and are adjusted periodically to more comprehensive data. Figures prior to 1940 are based largely on estimates of the Department of Commerce.

X 423–434. Net public and private debt, by major sectors, 1916–1957.

Source: Office of Business Economics, *Survey of Current Business*, September 1953, p. 14; May 1957, p. 17; and May 1959, pp. 12 and 14.

The source publications include details for the sectors shown here as well as data on gross debt.

Net debt for the public sectors of the economy represents total outstanding indebtedness minus intrasector holdings of such debt, e.g., total Federal debt minus such portions of that debt as are held by the Treasury and by Federal agencies. State and local debt includes State loans to local units. Net corporate debt represents total corporate debt minus intercompany debts of affiliated companies. Figures for the noncorporate private debt are gross, with no adjustment for intrasector holdings.

All sectors of both gross and net debt exclude (a) deposit liability of banks and banknotes in circulation, (b) value of outstanding policies and annuities of life insurance carriers, (c) short-term debt of individuals and unincorporated nonfinancial business concerns held by other individuals and unincorporated businesses, and (d) nominal corporate debt, such as bonds authorized but not issued, and issued but reacquired.

Series X 425 includes debt of Federal agencies. Figures for State and local debt (series X 426) beginning 1950 differ slightly from earlier years, because of changes in Bureau of Census classifications. Series X 433 represents agricultural loans to farmers and farmers' cooperatives by institutional lenders. Series X 434 comprises debt incurred for commercial (nonfarm), financial, and consumer purposes, and includes debt owed by farmers for financial and consumer purposes.

Series X 389–402. Outstanding Loans and Loan Insurance or Guarantees of Federal and Federally Sponsored Agencies, by Economic Sector Served: 1917 to 1953

[In millions of dollars. As of end of year]

Year	Direct loans						Loan insurance or guarantees [4]					Stock purchases [6]		
	Total	Agriculture [1]	Business [2]	Financial institutions	Housing	Other [3]	Total	Agriculture [1]	Business	Housing	Other [5]	Total	Agriculture	Financial institutions
	389	390	391	392	393	394	395	396	397	398	399	400	401	402
1953	13,615	4,939	3,757	952	3,003	965	29,327	124	765	26,504	1,933	46	5	42
1952	13,026	4,748	3,481	864	2,638	1,294	25,737	123	929	23,618	1,067	54	8	47
1951	11,648	4,405	3,329	806	2,161	948	22,876	119	733	21,219	806	96	11	84
1950	10,217	3,972	3,201	816	1,543	684	18,601	109	191	17,886	414	119	16	103
1949	9,108	3,576	3,244	433	1,244	604	14,318	92	246	13,760	221	139	22	116
1948	8,306	3,241	3,112	515	746	691	11,166	81	290	10,576	219	164	29	135
1947	7,264	2,944	2,583	436	651	650	8,239	65	381	7,567	226	195	35	160
1946	6,170	2,736	1,796	315	694	629	6,097	31	395	5,438	234	253	46	207
1945	5,464	2,749	918	220	932	645	5,518	(7)	537	4,751	229	363	56	308
1944	6,308	3,087	1,147	160	1,279	685	6,333	----	1,564	4,542	226	438	64	374
1943	7,088	3,445	1,170	190	1,549	733	6,335	----	1,715	4,394	225	536	76	460
1942	7,842	3,717	1,096	240	1,917	872	5,082	----	727	4,096	259	674	82	592
1941	8,063	3,825	912	337	2,090	899	3,744	----	38	3,503	203	727	82	645
1940	7,882	3,718	852	374	2,227	712	3,079	----	35	2,796	248	788	61	726
1939	7,750	3,702	768	353	2,254	673	2,234	----	47	2,136	51	848	75	773
1938	7,761	3,670	727	407	2,314	642	1,545	----	34	1,511		909	76	833
1937	8,159	3,650	638	450	2,474	946	1,023	----	4	1,020	(7)	924	76	848
1936	8,453	3,642	642	468	2,807	895	705	----	4	701	(7)	943	75	868
1935	8,645	3,537	771	622	2,903	812	310	----	3	308	----	1,063	77	986
1934	7,815	3,126	703	928	2,366	691	32	----	1	30	----	984	90	893
1933	4,303	2,015	533	1,121	142	493	----					271	2	269
1932	3,324	1,835	450	832	--------	207								
1931	2,031	1,800	140	--------	--------	90								

Year	Direct loans					Year	Direct loans					Year	Direct loans				
	Total	Agriculture [1]	Business [2]	Financial institutions	Other [3]		Total	Agriculture [1]	Business [2]	Financial institutions	Other [3]		Total	Agriculture [1]	Business [2]	Financial institutions	Other [3]
	389	390	391	392	394		389	390	391	392	394		389	390	391	392	394
1930	1,779	1,582	125	--------	72	1925	1,476	1,106	353	--------	16	1920	1,034	355	680	--------	(8)
1929	1,486	1,313	120	--------	53	1924	1,487	1,034	442	--------	11	1919	395	299	94	2	--------
1928	1,438	1,288	113	--------	37	1923	1,431	915	508	--------	8	1918	190	159	30	2	--------
1927	1,474	1,241	204	--------	29	1922	1,303	791	506	--------	5	1917	39	39	--------	--------	--------
1926	1,527	1,184	321	--------	22	1921	1,260	519	740	--------	1						

[1] Classification by real-estate and non-real-estate loans available in source tables. Excludes loans and loan guarantees of Commodity Credit Corporation; see text.
[2] Includes loans of Export-Import Bank; see text.
[3] Includes minor governmental units and miscellaneous purposes.
[4] Federal agencies only.
[5] Minor governmental units.
[6] For details on types of stock purchased, see text.
[7] Not available.
[8] Less than $500,000.

Series X 403–414. State and Federally Chartered Credit Unions—Number, Share Capital, Loans, and Total Assets: 1931 to 1957

[Money figures in millions of dollars. As of end of year]

Year	Operating credit unions			Paid-in share capital			Outstanding loans			Total assets		
	Total	Federal	State [1]	Total	Federal [2]	State	Total	Federal [2]	State	Total	Federal [2]	State
	403	404	405	406	407	408	409	410	411	412	413	414
1957	18,070	8,735	9,335	3,298	1,589	[3]1,709	2,788	1,257	1,531	3,810	1,789	2,021
1956	17,113	8,350	8,763	2,837	1,366	[3]1,471	2,326	1,049	1,277	3,271	1,529	1,742
1955	16,064	7,806	8,258	2,378	1,135	[3]1,243	1,934	863	1,071	2,743	1,267	1,476
1954	14,940	7,227	7,713	1,977	931	[3]1,046	1,552	682	870	2,270	1,033	1,237
1953	13,564	6,578	6,986	1,638	768	[3]870	1,308	574	734	1,895	854	1,041
1952	12,249	5,925	6,324	1,309	597	[3]712	985	415	570	1,516	662	854
1951	11,284	5,398	5,886	1,040	457	583	748	300	448	1,199	505	694
1950	10,569	4,984	5,585	851	362	489	680	264	416	1,005	406	599
1949	9,897	4,495	5,402	701	285	416	515	186	329	827	316	511
1948	9,329	4,058	5,271	603	235	368	399	138	261	701	258	443
1947	8,942	3,845	5,097	509	192	317	280	91	189	591	210	381
1946	8,715	3,761	4,954	431	160	271	188	57	131	495	173	322
1945	8,615	3,757	4,858	367	141	226	126	35	91	435	153	282
1944	8,722	3,815	4,907	339	134	205	121	34	87	398	144	254
1943	9,062	3,938	5,124	308	117	191	122	35	87	355	127	228
1942	9,545	4,145	5,400	289	110	179	149	43	106	341	120	221
1941	9,734	4,228	5,506	274	97	177	220	69	151	323	106	217
1940	8,931	3,756	5,175	212	66	146	191	56	135	254	73	181
1939	7,859	3,182	4,677	160	43	117	149	38	111	194	48	146
1938	6,737	2,760	3,977	114	27	87	108	24	84	148	30	118
1937	5,441	2,313	3,128	83	18	65	78	16	62	116	19	97
1936	4,485	1,751	2,734	(4)	9	(4)	(4)	7	(4)	83	9	74
1935	2,894	772	2,122	35	2	33	36	2	34	50	2	48
1934	2,028	----------	2,028	26	----------	26	28	----------	28	40	----------	40
1933	1,772	----------	1,772	22	----------	22	26	----------	26	40	----------	40
1932	1,472	----------	1,472	22	----------	22	26	----------	26	35	----------	35
1931	1,244	----------	1,244	(4)	----------	(4)	25	----------	25	34	----------	34

[1] Reports not received from all operating credit unions; see text.
[2] Data for 1935–1944 partly estimated.
[3] Excludes small amounts of members' deposits.
[4] Not available.

Series X 415–422. Short- and Intermediate-Term Consumer Credit, by Major Types: 1929 to 1957

[In millions of dollars. Estimated credit outstanding as of end of year]

Year	Total	Installment			Noninstallment credit			
		Total	Automobile paper	All other	Total	Single-payment loans	Charge accounts	Service credit
	415	416	417	418	419	420	421	422
1957	45,286	34,183	15,409	18,774	11,103	3,364	5,146	2,593
1956	42,511	31,897	14,459	17,438	10,614	3,253	4,995	2,366
1955	38,882	28,958	13,472	15,486	9,924	3,002	4,795	2,127
1954	32,464	23,568	9,809	13,759	8,896	2,408	4,485	2,003
1953	31,393	23,005	9,835	13,170	8,388	2,187	4,274	1,927
1952	27,401	19,403	7,733	11,670	7,998	2,120	4,011	1,867
1951	22,617	15,294	5,972	9,322	7,323	1,934	3,605	1,784
1950	21,395	14,703	6,074	8,629	6,692	1,821	3,291	1,580
1949	17,305	11,590	4,555	7,035	5,715	1,532	2,795	1,388
1948	14,398	8,996	3,018	5,978	5,402	1,445	2,673	1,284
1947	11,570	6,695	1,924	4,771	4,875	1,356	2,353	1,166
1946	8,384	4,172	981	3,191	4,212	1,122	2,076	1,014
1945	5,665	2,462	455	2,007	3,203	746	1,612	845
1944	5,111	2,176	397	1,779	2,935	624	1,517	794
1943	4,901	2,136	355	1,781	2,765	613	1,440	712
1942	5,983	3,166	742	2,424	2,817	713	1,444	660
1941	9,172	6,085	2,458	3,627	3,087	845	1,645	597
1940	8,338	5,514	2,071	3,443	2,824	800	1,471	553
1939	7,222	4,503	1,497	3,006	2,719	787	1,414	518
1938	6,338	3,691	1,099	2,592	2,647	777	1,362	508
1937	6,689	4,015	1,494	2,521	2,674	797	1,336	541
1936	6,135	3,623	1,372	2,251	2,512	707	1,300	505
1935	4,911	2,694	992	1,702	2,217	575	1,183	459
1934	3,904	1,871	614	1,257	2,033	493	1,102	438
1933	3,482	1,588	493	1,095	1,894	450	990	454
1932	3,567	1,521	356	1,165	2,046	549	1,020	477
1931	4,760	2,207	684	1,523	2,553	772	1,265	516
1930	5,767	2,687	986	1,701	3,080	1,037	1,476	567
1929	6,444	3,151	1,384	1,767	3,293	1,112	1,602	579

Series X 423–434. Net Public and Private Debt, by Major Sectors: 1916 to 1957

[In billions of dollars. As of end of year, except as noted]

Year	Total	Public			Private							
		Total public	Federal	State and local [1]	Total private	Corporate			Individual and noncorporate			
						Total	Long-term [2]	Short-term [2]	Mortgage		Nonmortgage	
									Farm	Nonfarm	Farm	Nonfarm
	423	424	425	426	427	428	429	430	431	432	433	434
1957	736.0	271.1	224.4	46.7	464.9	243.9	111.5	132.3	10.5	131.6	9.8	69.2
1956	707.2	268.1	225.4	42.7	439.1	231.7	100.1	131.7	9.9	121.2	9.6	66.5
1955	672.2	269.9	231.5	38.4	402.3	212.1	90.0	122.2	9.1	108.8	9.7	62.6
1954	611.8	263.6	230.2	33.4	348.2	182.8	82.9	100.0	8.3	94.7	9.3	53.1
1953	586.4	256.7	228.1	28.6	329.7	179.5	78.3	101.2	7.8	83.8	9.2	49.6
1952	555.2	248.7	222.9	25.8	306.5	171.0	73.3	97.7	7.2	75.2	8.0	45.2
1951	524.0	241.8	218.5	23.3	282.2	162.5	66.6	95.9	6.6	67.4	7.0	38.8
1950	490.3	239.4	218.7	20.7	250.9	142.0	60.1	81.9	6.1	59.4	6.2	37.2
1949	448.4	236.7	218.6	18.1	211.7	118.0	56.5	61.5	5.6	50.6	6.4	31.2
1948	433.6	232.7	216.5	16.2	200.9	117.8	52.5	65.3	5.3	45.1	5.5	27.3
1947	417.4	237.7	223.3	14.4	179.7	108.9	46.1	62.8	5.1	38.7	3.5	23.5
1946	397.4	243.3	229.7	13.6	154.1	93.5	41.3	52.2	4.9	32.5	2.7	20.5
1945	406.3	266.4	252.7	13.7	139.9	85.3	38.3	47.0	4.8	27.0	2.5	20.4
1944	370.8	226.0	211.9	14.1	144.8	94.1	39.8	54.3	4.9	26.1	2.8	16.9
1943	313.6	169.3	154.4	14.9	144.3	95.5	41.0	54.5	5.4	26.2	2.8	14.4
1942	259.0	117.5	101.7	15.8	141.5	91.6	42.7	49.0	6.0	26.8	3.0	14.1
1941	211.6	72.6	56.3	16.3	139.0	83.4	43.6	39.8	6.4	27.2	2.9	19.2
1940	189.9	61.3	44.8	16.5	128.6	75.6	43.7	31.9	6.5	26.0	2.6	17.9
1939	183.2	58.9	42.6	16.3	124.3	73.5	44.4	29.2	6.6	25.0	2.2	17.0
1938	179.6	56.5	40.5	16.0	123.1	73.3	44.8	28.4	6.8	24.5	2.2	16.4
1937	182.0	55.3	39.2	16.1	126.7	75.8	43.5	32.3	7.0	24.3	1.6	18.0
1936	180.3	53.9	37.7	16.2	126.4	76.1	42.5	33.5	7.2	24.4	1.4	17.3
1935	174.7	50.5	34.4	16.0	124.2	74.8	43.6	31.2	7.4	24.7	1.5	15.7
1934	171.4	46.3	30.4	15.9	125.1	75.5	44.6	30.9	7.6	25.5	1.3	15.1
1933	168.5	41.0	24.3	16.7	127.5	76.9	47.9	29.1	7.7	26.3	1.4	15.2
1932	174.6	37.9	21.3	16.6	136.7	80.0	49.2	30.8	8.5	29.0	1.6	17.6
1931	181.9	34.0	18.5	15.5	147.9	83.5	50.3	33.2	9.1	30.9	2.0	22.4
1930	191.0	30.6	16.5	14.1	160.4	89.3	51.1	38.2	9.4	32.0	2.4	27.3
1929	190.9	29.7	16.5	13.2	161.2	88.9	47.3	41.6	9.6	31.2	2.6	28.9
1928	185.9	29.8	17.5	12.3	156.1	86.1	46.1	40.0	9.8	29.6	2.7	27.9
1927	177.3	29.7	18.2	11.5	147.6	81.2	44.4	36.8	9.8	26.9	2.6	27.1
1926	168.8	29.9	19.2	10.7	138.9	76.2	41.7	34.5	9.7	24.0	2.6	26.4
1925	162.6	30.3	20.3	10.0	132.3	72.7	39.7	33.0	9.7	21.3	2.8	25.8
1924	153.0	30.0	21.0	9.0	123.0	67.2	38.5	28.7	9.9	18.6	2.7	24.6
1923	146.3	30.0	21.8	8.2	116.3	62.6	36.2	26.4	10.7	16.3	3.0	23.7
1922	140.0	30.5	22.8	7.7	109.5	58.6	34.4	24.2	10.8	14.1	3.1	22.9
1921	135.8	29.6	23.1	6.5	106.2	57.0	33.8	23.2	10.7	12.8	3.3	22.4
1920	135.4	29.6	23.7	5.9	105.8	57.7	32.6	25.1	10.2	11.7	3.9	22.3
1919	128.0	30.8	25.6	5.2	97.2	53.3	31.0	22.3	8.4	10.1	3.5	21.9
1918	117.4	25.9	20.9	5.0	91.5	47.0	30.2	16.8	7.1	9.6	2.7	25.1
1917	94.4	12.0	7.3	4.7	82.4	43.7	29.7	14.0	6.5	9.3	2.5	20.4
1916	82.1	5.6	1.2	4.4	76.5	43.4	29.1	11.1	5.8	8.4	2.0	20.1

[1] Data for State and local governments are for June 30.
[2] Long-term debt is defined as having an original maturity of 1 year or more; short-term, as less than 1 year.

PRIVATE INSURANCE (Series X 435–500)

X 435–468.   General note.

There are three general sources of primary data about life insurance as a whole: The various State insurance departments through their reports of the life insurance companies operating within their jurisdictions; commercial publishers of life insurance company data; and the trade and other associations of the life insurance companies.

Probably the most widely used of the State insurance department reports are those published annually by the New York Insurance Department.   For the approximate period 1860–1880 these reports, which give data on the companies domiciled in the State and the companies of other States authorized to transact business in the State, are most frequently made use of to exhibit the progress of life insurance.   The data presented in these reports for this period represent a very high percentage of the total life insurance business.   Other State reports often consulted by researchers are those of Massachusetts and Connecticut.

Of the commercial publications, the most frequently used to study the progress of life insurance as a whole is the *Spectator Insurance Year Book*, published annually since 1873 by the Spectator Company, Philadelphia.   (For 1873–1937, the publication was known as *The Insurance Year Book*.   There has been a separate "Life" volume since 1923.)

A number of the trade and other associations in the life insurance business prepare industrywide statistics on different aspects of life insurance.   The Institute of Life Insurance, New York, a public relations organization formed by the life insurance companies, compiles a number of such statistics and publishes these, as well as data from other associations and from commercial publishers, annually in the *Life Insurance Fact Book*.   Two major sources of insurance statistics included in the Institute compilations are the Life Insurance Association of America and the Life Insurance Agency Management Association.

To obtain a series of figures over a long period it is not necessary to consult each annual edition of the publications mentioned above.   Many of the *New York Insurance Reports* (known also as the *Annual Report of the Superintendent of Insurance*) contain a chronology which gives some of the salient statistics over a long period (sometimes only for selected years).   The annual *Spectator Insurance Year Book* often gives the aggregates for all available companies for the preceding 10 years and, for the early years of this publication, a summary of data was presented for the companies operating in New York State.

The most recent *Life Insurance Fact Book* will generally give most of the preceding statistics compiled, as well as historical statistics from other sources, as far back as 1890 for some series.

In addition to the *Life Insurance Fact Book*, there are two compilations of historical statistics which are often consulted: J. Owen Stalson, *Marketing Life Insurance, Its History in America*, Harvard University Press, Cambridge, 1942 (the appendixes give data on the number of companies, life insurance sales, life insurance in force, and income as well as many other items from earliest available figures to 1937); and Frederick L. Hoffman, "Fifty Years of American Life Insurance Progress," *Quarterly Publications of the American Statistical Association*,

New Series, No. 95, vol. XII, Boston, 1911 (tables of salient statistics, 1860–1910).   The statistics presented in these publications do not always agree with the figures given here because in some cases different sources have been used, and in some cases adjustments and corrections of the source material have been made by the Institute of Life Insurance.

Because it represents the exception rather than the rule, it may be of interest to note two instances in which data on life insurance were collected in the decennial census of the United States.   *Statistics of the United States in 1860*, 1866, pp. 293–294, contains some statistics on the number of life insurance companies, the amount of life insurance, the number of persons insured, and the annual premium income for 1860.   Data on the life insurance business are also shown in the *Report on Insurance Business in the United States at the Eleventh Census: 1890, Part 2, Life Insurance*, 1895.   This report contains statistics on life insurance for the decade 1880–1890 for the companies in operation as of December 31, 1889.   It does not, however, reflect the business in this decade of companies which ceased to do business before December 31, 1889.

The basic reporting form utilized by all three types of primary sources in preparing their statistics is the annual statement convention blank.   This is the prescribed accounting statement which each company must submit to the insurance department of each State in which it is licensed to transact business, setting forth the company's balance sheet, income and disbursement accounts, policy exhibit, and many supporting schedules.   The collecting agencies supplement the data from the annual statement form from time to time through mail questionnaires, mostly among the life insurance companies.

An understanding of the historical statistics of life insurance requires some knowledge of the annual statement convention blank—the accounting methods used in preparing the form and changes in the form and methods over the years—and some knowledge of the history of life insurance.

Uniformity in the annual statement convention blank required by the States has been achieved through the efforts of the National Association of Insurance Commissioners.   This association is a national organization composed of the officials of the various States who have supervision of insurance affairs within their respective States.   It was formed in 1871 (under the name of the National Convention of Insurance Commissioners) and adopted its first convention blank in 1874.   This organization has also achieved a degree of uniformity in insurance legislation and departmental rulings among the different States.

The convention blank has undergone revisions from time to time.   The most recent significant revision in the annual statement convention blank took place in the form used for reporting the operations for 1951.   Where these changes have affected the statistics shown, they are discussed below in the text for the specific series.   For a complete discussion of the annual statement form now in use, and a comparison with the superseded form, see E. C. Wightman, *Life Insurance Statements and Accounts*, Life Office Management Association, New York, 1952.   For a detailed discussion of two of the earlier forms, see *Life Insurance Accounts*, 1935 and 1941, by the same author and publisher.

There are many nonstatistical histories of life insurance. A few that may be consulted are: Charles K. Knight, *The History of Life Insurance in the United States to 1870*, unpublished thesis, University of Pennsylvania, 1920; *Marketing Life Insurance, Its History in America* (cited above); and *The Bible of Life Insurance*, George W. Wadsworth, 1932.

The data presented here cover only life insurance as it relates to the insurance companies which are usually referred to as the legal reserve life insurance companies. These are life insurance companies operating under insurance laws specifying the minimum basis for the reserves a company must maintain on its policies. Other types of life insurance include fraternal life insurance which is provided by societies, lodges, and similar fellowship organizations; life insurance with assessment associations, mutual aid groups, and burial societies; life insurance available through savings banks in three States; and veterans life insurance (consisting of U.S. Government Life Insurance and National Service Life Insurance) issued by the Federal Government to members of the Armed Forces and veterans of World Wars I and II.

Though in very recent years the greatest part of all life insurance in force in the United States has been provided by the legal reserve life insurance companies, veterans insurance at its peaks during or immediately after the World Wars exceeded or nearly equaled the totals achieved by the life insurance companies. Fraternal and assessment life insurance combined for the period 1879–1928 was a significant proportion of the life insurance company total (actually exceeding it for a year or two in the 1890's and never amounting to less than 10 percent of the life insurance company total for the period stated).

For historical statistics of veterans, fraternal, and assessment life insurance, see Stalson, *Marketing Life Insurance*, cited above, pp. 806–808 and 816–819.

The data for legal reserve life insurance companies which are presented here are subject to three types of limitations: (a) Changes in the annual statement convention blank on which the companies report their operations; (b) incompleteness of the data in terms of the number of companies for which information is available; and (c) lack of uniformity among the companies in the allocation of certain items to the categories of the convention blank, changes in allocation, and changes made by the publishers of life insurance data in their reporting methods.

Changes in the annual statement blank over the years have been discussed previously. With regard to the completeness of the statistics available, it is extremely difficult to obtain data for any given period on the operations of *all* the life insurance companies operating in the United States. Theoretically, one should be able to compile complete statistics by consulting the insurance reports of each State and the District of Columbia, but in practice this is not feasible. State insurance reports began in the 1850's but it was not until 1919 that all States (and the District of Columbia) were issuing reports. (A list of the first reports on insurance companies by State departments of insurance is given in Stalson, *Marketing Life Insurance*, cited above, pp. 775–776.) Therefore, until 1919, there is no way of obtaining data from State reports for companies which operated in only those States for which reports were not available. Subsequent to 1919, the difficulties in compiling complete statistics arise from the lack of uniformity in the various reports with regard to the selection of items to be presented and the basis of reporting, and from the failure of some States to issue reports on a regular annual basis.

The life insurance companies omitted from the sources utilized are very small in size relative to those for which data are available. Therefore, even when a fairly large number of these very small companies are omitted, they account for a very small percentage of the total business. For example, in 1956, according to the Institute of Life Insurance, the 789 companies for which life insurance in force data were available accounted for 99.7 percent of the total which would have been obtained from the 1,189 companies in existence at the end of 1956. This percentage is doubtlessly lower for the earlier years and for some of the other categories, but it is highly probable that even the oldest figures presented here represent 90 percent or more of the total for all companies. This is true both with regard to the figures taken from sources, such as the *Spectator Insurance Year Book*, which collect data from all available companies, and for the figures for about 1860–1880 which are taken from the reports of the New York Insurance Department. (For a discussion of the percentage of total business accounted for by the New York Insurance Department reports, see Hoffman, "Fifty Years of American Life Insurance Progress," cited above, pp. 11–13.)

The third limitation with regard to the data of legal reserve life insurance companies pertains to the lack of uniformity in allocation of certain items to the categories of the convention blank and changes in allocation. There are many instances where neither the categories of the annual statement convention blank nor the instructions for filing the blank are detailed enough to specify clearly how a certain transaction is to be allocated, so that the treatment becomes a matter of the company's judgment. Thus, for example, of two companies writing monthly debit insurance (a form of life insurance with some of the features of both ordinary and industrial insurance), one may classify it as ordinary and one as industrial. Moreover, a company may decide to change the classification of an item; for the example just cited, a company may transfer at some point its monthly debit business from the industrial to the ordinary classification. Such problems can arise in all the series presented. Even when an accounting procedure tends to become widespread, it is often adopted by different companies at different times.

A further problem arises from the fact that the sources which compile industrywide statistics must often combine the many categories of the annual statement convention blank into broader classifications. From time to time, the manner of combining the categories may be altered or the manner of treating special categories, which are sometimes found in a few companies' convention blank, may be changed.

Related to the problems of changes in the annual statement convention blank and variations in the allocation of items is the problem of changes in method of valuation of policy reserves and assets. The amount of policy reserves reported in a company's convention blank is determined by the types of policies issued, the length of time they have been in force, and the age at issue. The policy reserves are also affected by the mortality table used, the interest assumption, and the reserve basis specified by the various States as the minimum basis for valuation. The assets of a company, and hence its surplus, are also affected by the method of valuation of assets. The problems of changes in valuation of assets and reserves do not appear to be factors of major significance, however, with regard to long-term historical trends of these series.

The general procedure used in preparing these statistics was to examine the various sources and compare the series available as to bases of reporting, completeness of coverage, etc. In those cases where alternative series were available, the selection was determined by completeness of coverage in terms of the number of companies for which data were obtainable, and the basis of reporting most consistent with current practice, on two conditions: (a) That the series be available for a sufficiently long period to preserve the trend, and (b) that component items could be obtained on the same basis or level of coverage as the totals. An illustration might make this clear. For 1879–1887, total assets can be obtained for all the companies operating in New York State. For the same period, totals for a larger group of companies can be obtained from the 1888 *Spectator Insurance Year Book*. The distribution of assets, by type, however, is available only for the companies operating in New York State. Rather than estimate a distribution for the larger asset totals or report a distribution which would not add to the total shown, the New York State figures were used for the total and for the distribution by type. For the period under discussion, the assets of companies operating in New York State represented from 92 to 97 percent of the assets given by the *Spectator Insurance Year Book* for all available companies.

In most cases, the various sources were identical with regard to bases of reporting and completeness of coverage. In these cases, the procedure was to compare the various sources presenting the same data for the same period. Thus for the early period, comparisons were made among the individual *New York Insurance Reports* and the summaries of these reports given in various issues of the *Spectator Insurance Year Book*, *Marketing Life Insurance*, and "Fifty Years of American Life Insurance Progress." For later years, comparisons were made among the various issues of the *Spectator Insurance Year Book* which covered the same period (mainly the 10-year aggregates as compared with the aggregates given in each *Year Book*), *Marketing Life Insurance*, and the *Life Insurance Fact Book* (which utilizes a great deal of material from the *Spectator Insurance Year Book*).

Where the figures in the various sources were in agreement, the data presented were accepted unless some limitations were uncovered while making the comparisons. Where the sources were not in agreement, the reasons for the differences were investigated and the figures considered to be most accurate and complete were accepted.

Some of the figures presented here are original in the sense that they represent adjustments by the Institute of Life Insurance of existing figures for errors in addition or for omissions. Wherever possible, published material has been utilized.

X 435. Number of life insurance companies, 1759–1957.

Source: 1759–1936, J. Owen Stalson, *Marketing Life Insurance, Its History in America*, Harvard University Press, Cambridge, 1942, pp. 748–753; 1937–1939, Institute of Life Insurance estimates; 1940–1949, same agency, records; 1950–1957, same agency, *The Tally of Life Insurance Statistics*, September 1957, p. 2 and August 1958, p. 1 (data shown here are slightly revised figures of data given in these references).

The figures comprise the total number of companies in operation at the end of the year and domiciled in the United States. This number is larger than the number of companies for which life insurance in force data are available (see general note for series X 435–468). For 1941–1949, figures do not include companies which started and then ceased operations within this period. For data on the number of companies formed, discontinued, and in operation, classified by stock and mutual for 1759–1937, see Stalson, cited above, pp. 748–753.

X 436–440. General note.

For 1854–1894, the series were derived by deducting from the insurance in force figures of U.S. life insurance companies the amount of their Canadian and other foreign business, and adding thereto the U.S. business of Canadian and other foreign companies. Data for 1895–1948 were derived from the totals of individual State estimates given in the "Life Insurance in Force by States" section of each *Spectator Insurance Year Book*.

For ordinary life insurance, the figures for 1815–1850 are for all available companies; for 1854–1877, the figures are for life insurance companies reporting to the New York Insurance Department. Beginning with 1878, the data are for all available companies. All the data for group, industrial, and credit life insurance are for all available companies.

Life insurance in force is the sum total of the face amounts (plus additions purchased with dividends) of the life insurance outstanding at a given time. The additional amount of life insurance payable under accidental death provisions (providing for payment of an additional death benefit in case of death as a result of accidental means, often called double indemnity) is not included.

Life insurance in force figures have been adjusted to represent insurance in force on the lives of residents of the United States whether issued by U.S. or foreign companies. For statistics of life insurance in force with U.S. life insurance companies, whether the policyholders are residents of the United States or of some other country, and for the number of policies outstanding, for 1900–1957, see *Life Insurance Fact Book, 1958*, pp. 15, 25, 27, 31, 33. Estimates by States are available from the "Life Insurance in Force by States" section of the annual *Spectator Insurance Year Book* and the *Life Insurance Fact Book*. For information of life insurance in force by plan of insurance, 1950, 1954, and 1957, see *The Tally of Life Insurance Statistics*, January 1959, pp. 1 and 2.

For an alternative series of life insurance in force in the United States, for selected years, 1815–1937, see *Marketing Life Insurance*, cited above, pp. 816–817. The alternative series includes fraternal, assessment, and other types of life insurance, and is derived from aggregate figures of U.S., Canadian, and foreign companies, rather than as totals of State figures.

X 436. Total life insurance in force in the United States, 1815–1957.

Source: 1815–1850, see Stalson, cited above for series X 435, p. 787 (1850 estimate corrected for addition error); 1854–1899, a summation of series X 437 and X 439; 1900–1957, Institute of Life Insurance, *Life Insurance Fact Book, 1957*, p. 8, and *1958*, p. 10.

X 437. Ordinary life insurance in force in the United States, 1815–1957.

Source: 1815–1850, see Stalson, cited above for series X 435, p. 787; 1854–1894, Institute of Life Insurance, records; 1895–1957, same agency, *Life Insurance Fact Book, 1958*, p. 25.

The 1854–1894 figures were compiled from the following sources, using the method described in the general note for series X 436–440: Ordinary insurance in force of U.S. companies: 1854–1858, Spectator Company, *Spectator Insurance Year Book*, 1878, p. 71; 1859–1877, Stalson, cited above for series X 435, p. 820; 1878–1894, *Spectator Insurance Year Book*, various issues (for certain years, adjustments were made). Ordinary business of U.S. companies in Canada: 1869–1894, Stalson, cited above for series X 435, pp. 833–834 (1873 figure adjusted; 1885–1894, industrial business in Canada of U.S. companies subtracted to get ordinary business in Canada). Ordinary business of U.S. companies in foreign countries other than Canada: 1868–1885, Stalson, cited above for series X 435, p. 824; 1886–1888, Hoffman, "Fifty Years of American Life Insurance Progress," cited above in general note for series X 435–468, p. 86; 1889–1894, *Spectator Insurance Year Book*, 1899, p. 466. Ordinary business of Canadian companies in the U.S.: 1889–1894, Stalson, cited above for series X 435, p. 839. Ordinary business of other foreign companies in the U.S.: 1854–1870, series for U.S. branches of British companies estimated by the Institute of Life Insurance; 1871–1881, 1885–1886, State of New York Insurance Department, *New York Insurance Report*, various issues; 1882–1884, data not available, but probably insignificant.

Ordinary life insurance refers to life insurance usually issued in amounts of $1,000 or more, with premiums payable on an annual, semiannual, quarterly, or monthly basis.

X 438. Group life insurance in force in the United States, 1911–1957.

Source: Institute of Life Insurance, *Life Insurance Fact Book, 1958*, p. 27, and records.

Group life insurance is life insurance issued, usually without medical examination, on a group of persons under a master policy. It is usually issued to an employer for the benefit of employees. The individual members of the group hold certificates as evidence of their insurance.

X 439. Industrial life insurance in force in the United States, 1876–1957.

Source: 1876–1894, Institute of Life Insurance, records; 1895–1957, see source for series X 438, p. 31.

The 1876–1894 figures were compiled from the following sources, using the method described in the general note for series X 436–440: Industrial insurance in force of U.S. companies: 1876–1894, Spectator Company, *Spectator Insurance Year Book*, various issues (for certain years, adjustments were made). Industrial business of U.S. companies in Canada: 1885–1894, *Spectator Insurance Year Book*, various issues. Canadian and other foreign companies have never written industrial life insurance in the U.S., according to available information.

Industrial life insurance is life insurance issued in small amounts, usually not over $500. Premiums are payable on a weekly or monthly basis and are generally collected at the home by an agent of the company.

X 440. Credit life insurance in force in the United States, 1917–1957.

Source: See source for series X 438, p. 33.

Credit life insurance is term life insurance sold through a lender or lending agency to cover payment of a loan, installment purchase, or other obligation, in case of death. Lending agencies are defined to include agencies that sell merchandise on time and mortgage departments of life insurance companies, as well as banks, finance companies, and other institutions or agencies to or through which financial obligations are incurred.

X 441–444. General note.

Figures represent U.S. life insurance companies' sales (including reinsurance acquired) in the United States and in other countries. Credit life insurance is excluded.

Life insurance sales represent the sum total of the face amount of life insurance sold in a given period (in this case, one year). The additional amount of life insurance payable under accidental death provisions is not included. For definitions of ordinary, group, and industrial, see text for series X 437–439.

X 441. Total sales of life insurance by U.S. life insurance companies, 1854–1957.

Source: 1854–1920, a summation of series X 442–444; 1921–1957, see source for series X 438, p. 23.

Total life insurance sales in the United States, representing all sales to residents of the United States, whether issued by U.S. or foreign companies, are available, beginning with 1940, from the source, p. 20. These series give number of policies and amount of insurance, by type.

X 442. Sales of ordinary life insurance by U.S. life insurance companies, 1854–1957.

Source: 1854–1910, Spectator Company, *Spectator Insurance Year Book*, various issues (for certain years, adjustments were made by the Institute of Life Insurance); 1911–1920, Institute of Life Insurance, records (based on data from summary table of Spectator Company, *Spectator Compendium of Official Life Insurance Reports* for each year); 1921–1957, see source for series X 438, p. 23.

The estimates for 1854–1877 are for life insurance companies reporting to the New York Insurance Department. Thereafter, the data are for all available companies. Beginning 1888, the data are on a paid-for basis; beginning 1893, they exclude revivals, increases, and dividend additions.

Monthly sales and annual sales by States since 1923 are available in Life Insurance Agency Management Association, *Monthly Sales Survey*, various issues. See also *Life Insurance Fact Book*, 1947–1958 editions. For regional data, see Department of Commerce, *Business Statistics, 1957 Biennial Edition*.

X 443. Sales of group life insurance by U.S. life insurance companies, 1911–1957.

Source: 1911–1920, Institute of Life Insurance, records (1911–1918, estimated from a survey of companies writing group life insurance at that time; 1919–1920, compiled from Group Life Exhibit in Spectator Company, *Spectator Compendium of Official Life Insurance Reports*, various issues); 1921–1957, see source for series X 438, p. 23.

The group life insurance figures are on a paid-for basis. Figures for 1912–1918 may reflect increases in existing contracts to some extent. Beginning 1919, figures exclude revivals, increases, and dividend additions.

X 444. Sales of industrial life insurance by U.S. life insurance companies, 1873–1957.

Source: 1873–1910, Spectator Company, *Spectator Insurance Year Book*, various issues; 1911–1920, *Spectator Compendium of Official Life Insurance Reports*, various issues; 1921–1957, see source for series X 438, p. 23.

Beginning 1893, figures exclude revivals, increases, and dividend additions.

X 445–458. General note.

The data for 1854–1887 are for life insurance companies reporting to the New York Insurance Department. Thereafter, the data are for all available companies.

In general, before 1951, income and disbursement items were reported on a cash basis (in the accounting use of the term). Beginning 1951, income and disbursement items are reported on an accrual basis (reflecting earned income and incurred claims and expenses).

Before 1951, gross investment income (without deduction of investment expenses) was reported as income, and investment expenses were reported as disbursements (included with "Commissions, expenses, taxes, and other disbursements"). Beginning 1951, investment expenses are deducted from gross investment income and the resulting net figure is reported as income.

X 445–448. Income of life insurance companies, 1854–1957.

Source: 1854–1910, see first source for series X 444; 1911–1957, see source for series X 438, p. 53.

X 446, life insurance premiums. For 1911–1957, this series was obtained by subtracting from premium income as reported in the source, the annuity premium series (series X 447) described below. Since 1947, accident and health premiums have also been subtracted from premium income.

This series includes premiums for ordinary, group, industrial, and credit life insurance, including disability and accidental death provisions. A premium is defined as the payment, or one of the regular periodical payments, a policyholder is required to make for an insurance policy.

X 447, annuity premiums. For 1911–1931, data were obtained by subtracting from the "consideration for annuities" figures given in the aggregates of the *Spectator Compendium* each year, the amount of supplementary contracts involving life contingencies. The series on supplementary contracts involving life contingencies was compiled by the Institute of Life Insurance from data in the *New York Insurance Reports* and the annual editions of Alfred M. Best Co., *Best's Life Insurance Reports*, New York. For 1932–1951, data were obtained directly by summing annuity income items from *Spectator Compendium* aggregates each year. For 1952–1955, data were obtained by summing group and individual annuity data given in Institute of Life Insurance, *The Tally of Life Insurance Statistics*, August 1956, p. 1. For 1956, Institute of Life Insurance, records; for 1957, same agency, *Life Insurance Fact Book, 1958*, p. 54.

This category includes considerations for group and individual annuities. Before 1911, figures include considerations for supplementary contracts with life contingencies. An annuity is defined as a contract that provides an income for a specified period of time, such as a number of years or for life. A supplementary contract is an agreement by the company to retain the lump sum payable under an insurance policy and to make payments in accordance with the settlement option chosen.

X 448, investment and other income. For 1911–1957, figures include considerations for supplementary contracts both with and without life contingencies. Before 1911, figures include considerations for supplementary contracts without life contingencies.

X 449–458. Disbursements of U.S. life insurance companies, 1854–1957.

Source: 1854–1918, Spectator Company, *Spectator Insurance Year Book*, various issues (for certain years, adjustments were made by the Institute of Life Insurance); 1919–1951, *Spectator Compendium of Official Life Insurance Reports* for each year; 1952–1957, Institute of Life Insurance, records.

Annual additions to policy reserves are not included. These constitute the greatest portion of the difference between income and disbursements. For data on policy reserves, see series X 467.

Figures for life insurance benefit payments paid to residents of the United States, either by U.S. or foreign companies, may be obtained, for 1940–1957, from the *Life Insurance Fact Book, 1958*, p. 39. Death benefit payments in the United States by type of insurance, number of policies, and by State may also be obtained from the annual editions of the *Life Insurance Fact Book*. Monthly benefit figures and quarterly death benefits by States may be obtained from the *Tally of Life Insurance Statistics*. A summary of monthly data for several years may be obtained from Department of Commerce, *Business Statistics, 1957 Biennial Edition*, pp. 90, 243.

X 452, matured endowment payments. This series is defined as the proceeds paid under a policy which provides that a definite sum of money be paid to the policyholder after a specified number of years if he is then living. If the policyholder dies during the endowment period, payment is made to a beneficiary (such proceeds are included as death benefits).

X 454, policy dividends. A policy dividend is defined as a refund of part of the premium on a participating life insurance policy. It is a share of the surplus earnings apportioned for distribution and reflects the difference between the premium charged and actual experience.

X 455, surrender values. A surrender value payment is the amount paid to policyholders upon surrender, for cash, of a policy before it becomes payable by death or maturity.

X 456, disability and accidental death benefits. Disability benefits are payments under a feature added to a life insurance policy, providing for waiver of premium and sometimes payment of monthly income if the insured becomes totally and permanently disabled. For definition of accidental death benefits, see text for series X 436–440.

Disability provisions became general around 1910 and benefits under these were usually included with annuity payments until 1920. Accidental death benefit provisions became general around 1917 and benefits under these were usually included with death benefits until 1920.

X 457, commissions, expenses, taxes, and other disbursements. This series includes payments on supplementary contracts, with and without life contingencies, and payments of dividends which have been left on deposit.

X 458, dividends to stockholders. Dividends to stockholders were shown as a disbursement in the annual statement convention blank before 1951. For 1951–1957, dividends to stockholders have been shown as a deduction from surplus in the surplus account.

X 459–464. Assets of U.S. life insurance companies, 1854–1957.

Source: 1854–1889, see first source for series X 444; 1890–1957, see source for series X 438, pp. 64–91.

The data for 1854–1887 are for life insurance companies reporting to the New York Insurance Department. Thereafter, the data are for all available companies.

Assets are on an admitted asset value basis, which is the aggregate value of all the assets used for determination of a company's balance sheet in accord with principles adopted by the insurance departments of the various States. Until about 1909, stocks and bonds were reported at market value. Until 1906, this value was determined by each individual company and, since 1907, by the insurance commissioners. In 1909, New York State required amortization of amply secured bonds, and this soon became the general practice. Stocks and nonamortizable bonds are generally reported at market value. Assets include the assets, distributed by type, of the accident and health departments of life insurance companies.

Shares of Federal savings and loan associations are included with series X 461. Series X 463 includes real estate sold on contract but does not include real estate owned subject to redemption. Foreclosed liens subject to redemption are included in "mortgages" and not transferred to "real estate" until the redemption period is past.

X 465. Net rate of interest earned on assets, 1872–1957.

Source: 1872–1909, see first source for series X 444; 1910–1914, Institute of Life Insurance, records; 1915–1957, see source for series X 438, p. 59.

The net rate of interest earned is the ratio of the investment income for the year to the mean assets decreased by one-half the investment income. For 1872–1909, the investment income is gross investment income—i.e., there was no deduction of investment expenses. For 1910–1940, the investment income is net of investment expenses (including direct investment taxes) and the Federal income taxes treated as investment expenses. Beginning 1941, the investment income is net of investment expenses (including direct investment taxes) and all Federal income taxes. For 1872–1950, the assets used in the formula are ledger assets; beginning 1951, the assets are invested assets (including cash) and interest due and accrued.

For a discussion of the level of interest earnings before 1872, see Lester W. Zartman, *The Investments of Life Insurance Companies*, Henry Holt Company, 1906.

X 466. Total liabilities, 1859–1957.

Source: 1859–1917, see first source for series X 444; 1918–1951, see second source for series X 444; 1952–1957, Institute of Life Insurance, *Life Insurance Fact Book*, 1953–1958 editions.

Data include operations of accident and health departments of life insurance companies. The 1918–1931 figures were compiled by subtracting from total liabilities as given, the amount shown as "amounts set apart." The 1932–1942 figures were compiled by subtracting from total liabilities as given, the amounts shown as "special, voluntary, contingency, etc., reserves." The 1943–1951 figures are those shown as total liabilities. The 1952–1957 figures were compiled by adding all the reserve and obligation items shown, excluding only special surplus funds, unassigned surplus, and capital.

X 467. Policy reserves, 1860–1957.

Source: 1860–1864, State of New York Insurance Department, *New York Insurance Report*, 1865, pp. clxxv–clxxix; 1865–1889, see first source for series X 444 (for certain years, adjustments were made by Institute of Life Insurance); 1890–1957, see source for series X 438, p. 61.

This series includes life, annuity, supplementary contract, disability, and accidental death reserves and, beginning 1947, business of accident and health departments of life insurance companies.

Policy reserves are defined as the funds that an insurance company holds specifically for the fulfillment of its policy obligations. Reserves are so calculated that, together with future premiums and interest earnings, they will enable the company to pay all future claims.

X 468. Capital and surplus, 1859–1957.

Source: 1859–1917 (except 1868, 1869, 1870, 1879, and 1881 which are from various *New York Insurance Reports*), see first source for series X 444; 1918–1951, see second source for series X 444; 1952–1957, Institute of Life Insurance, *Life Insurance Fact Book*, 1953–1958 editions.

The 1919–1931 figures were compiled by adding to the "unassigned funds and capital" as given, the amounts shown as "amounts set apart." The 1932–1950 figures were compiled by adding to the "unassigned funds and capital" as given, the amounts shown as "special, voluntary, contingency, etc., reserves" (for 1932–1942, "special, voluntary, contingency, etc., reserves" are shown as "liabilities"; for 1943–1950, this item is shown separately). The 1951–1957 figures were compiled by adding the items "special surplus funds," "unassigned surplus," and "capital."

This series includes operations of accident and health departments of life insurance companies.

X 469–482. Estimated enrollment in medical care insurance and rate per 1,000, by type of insurance, 1939–1957.

Source: Social Security Administration, records; and Health Insurance Institute, *Source Book of Health Insurance Data*, New York, 1959.

The data for insurance companies (series X 470, X 471, X 475, X 476, X 480, and X 481) are from the *Source Book* and were developed from surveys of the Life Insurance Association of America, the Health Insurance Association, the U.S. Chamber of Commerce, and other trade organizations.

The data relating to Blue Cross hospitalization plans (series X 472) were furnished directly by the Blue Cross Commission. Similarly, data for the Blue Shield plans on surgical insurance (series X 477) were furnished by the Blue Shield Commission.

Data for "All other plans" under each type of insurance (series X 473, X 478, and X 482) were compiled by the Social Security Administration for 1947–1957. Data for earlier years were estimated from reports relating to some of those years.

There are many voluntary health insurance companies or plans in the United States. The benefits of one plan for the same expense may differ markedly from the benefits under another plan, so that there may be wide variation in the adequacy of the protection afforded for the same benefit. Such differences may be reflected in the premium rates but other factors also influence premiums, so that there is not necessarily any close correlation between size of premium and type of benefits.

Both life and property insurance companies write accident and health insurance. Some are mutual companies and others are stock companies. Any company may sell both group and individual policies.

Because one plan may provide only one type of benefit and because the benefits may be limited, families frequently carry several forms of health insurance simultaneously. For this reason, the enrollment under the different categories of insurers is not additive. It is not unusual for a family to have Blue Cross hospitalization insurance, Blue Shield surgical insurance, in-hospital medical expense insurance, and an insurance policy applicable to all three types of expenses.

In general, medical insurance relates to policies that pay benefits for physicians' visits in the hospital and a limited amount of outpatient diagnostic services such as X-rays. However, some of the independent plans provide services regardless of the location of the patient, whether in the hospital, in the doctor's office, or in the patient's home.

X 483–500. Private pension and deferred profit-sharing plans—estimated coverage, contributions, reserves, beneficiaries, and benefit payments, 1930–1957.

Source: Social Security Administration, *Social Security Bulletin*, March 1960, p. 3.

These series were compiled by the Social Security Administration from releases of the Institute of Life Insurance, Securities and Exchange Commission, Department of Labor, and Internal Revenue Service, supplemented by various other reports, such as those of nonprofit organizations and the annual statements of the leading life insurance companies writing group annuities. Information was also received from various industrial concerns. In addition, for the earlier years, M. W. Latimer's studies were utilized (see M. W. Latimer, *Industrial Pension Systems in the United States and Canada*, Industrial Relations Counselors, Inc., New York, 1932).

These series present estimates with respect to formal private pension and deferred profit-sharing plans. Included are plans covering employees of industrial and nonprofit organizations. Most of them are funded although some of the self-insured plans are on a pay-as-you-go basis. The majority are single-employer plans with (in recent years) an increasing number of multiemployer plans, industry- or area-wide.

Under insured plans, insurance carriers are the medium through which benefits are provided; sponsors of the plans pay premiums to these carriers. Under self-insured plans, the sponsors themselves perform the functions of insurance carriers.

Series X 483–485 exclude pensioners and potential members who have not yet met the entrance requirements (age and/or service). The latter applies particularly to plans underwritten by life insurance companies. For insured plans, the estimated number of beneficiaries was subtracted from total coverage as reported by the Institute of Life Insurance. The larger groups under insured plans are covered by group annuity contracts, whereas individual-policy pension trusts, often providing both life insurance and annuities, cover smaller groups.

Contributions to insured plans (series X 487 and X 490) are on a net basis with dividends and refunds deducted. Those of self-insured plans (series X 488 and X 491) are for the most part on a gross basis, refunds appearing as benefit payments.

For pay-as-you-go plans, contributions have been assumed to equal benefit payments.

Reserves for insured plans (series X 493) were furnished by the Institute of Life Insurance. Reserves for self-insured plans (series X 494) include those of corporate pension plans, obtained from releases of the Securities and Exchange Commission; to these were added estimated reserves of self-insured nonprofit organization and multiemployer plans.

The number of beneficiaries (series X 495–497) relate to those in receipt of periodic payments at the end of the year, thus excluding those receiving lump sums during the year. Payments under insured plans (series X 499) are net amounts. Estimates of such payments and of the number of beneficiaries (series X 496) are based on data from the annual statements of the leading life insurance companies writing group annuities (filed with State insurance departments), with estimated additions for the other types of insured coverage, largely individual pension trusts. Payments for the self-insured plans (series X 500) were obtained by adding to the Securities and Exchange Commission data the estimated payments under formal pay-as-you-go plans and under noninsured multiemployer and nonprofit organization plans. The data from SEC include lump sums and refunds from corporate pension funds (types not segregated). Therefore, dividing the payments of the year by the mean number of beneficiaries results in an overstatement of the average annual periodic payment.

Series X 435–440. Life Insurance Companies and Life Insurance in Force in the United States, by Type: 1759 to 1957

[In millions of dollars, except number of companies. As of December 31]

Year	Number of companies (435)	Total (436)	Ordinary (437)	Group [1] (438)	Industrial (439)	Credit [2] (440)
1957	1,271	458,359	264,678	133,794	40,139	19,748
1956	1,189	412,630	238,099	117,324	40,109	17,098
1955	1,107	372,332	216,600	101,300	39,682	14,750
1954	917	333,719	198,419	86,395	38,664	10,241
1953	833	304,259	184,859	72,913	37,781	8,706
1952	731	276,591	170,795	62,913	36,448	6,435
1951	680	253,140	159,054	54,398	34,870	4,818
1950	650	234,168	149,071	47,793	33,415	3,889
1949	612	213,672	138,847	40,207	32,087	2,531
1948	584	201,208	131,158	37,068	31,253	1,729
1947	539	186,035	122,393	32,026	30,406	1,210
1946	514	170,066	112,818	27,206	29,313	729
1945	473	151,762	101,550	22,172	27,675	365
1944	451	145,771	95,085	23,922	26,474	290
1943	437	137,158	89,596	22,413	24,874	275
1942	435	127,721	85,139	19,316	22,911	355
1941	438	122,178	82,525	17,359	21,825	469
1940	444	115,530	79,346	14,938	20,866	380
1939	446	111,569	77,121	13,641	20,500	307
1938	435	108,927	75,772	12,503	20,396	256
1937	436	107,794	74,836	12,638	20,104	216
1936	372	102,653	72,361	11,291	18,863	138
1935	373	98,464	70,684	10,208	17,471	101
1934	371	96,677	70,094	9,472	17,036	75
1933	375	96,246	70,872	8,681	16,630	63
1932	392	101,559	75,898	8,923	16,669	69
1931	413	106,970	79,514	9,736	17,635	85
1930	438	106,413	78,576	9,801	17,963	73
1929	438	102,086	75,686	8,994	17,349	57
1928	433	92,590	68,430	7,889	16,231	40
1927	407	84,775	63,334	6,333	15,078	30
1926	396	77,642	58,453	5,362	13,803	24
1925	379	69,475	52,892	4,247	12,318	18
1924	369	61,327	47,283	3,127	10,905	12
1923	358	55,097	43,077	2,393	9,618	9
1922	347	48,342	38,053	1,795	8,486	8
1921	339	43,944	34,777	1,527	7,633	7
1920	335	40,540	32,018	1,570	6,948	4
1919	314	32,971	25,783	1,092	6,092	4
1918	295	27,924	21,818	630	5,474	2
1917	295	25,243	19,868	349	5,026	(3)

Year	Number of companies (435)	Total (436)	Ordinary (437)	Group (438)	Industrial [4] (439)
1916	293	22,853	18,081	155	4,617
1915	295	21,029	16,650	100	4,279
1914	307	19,737	15,661	65	4,011
1913	302	18,683	14,827	31	3,825
1912	305	17,301	13,709	13	3,579
1911	304	16,125	12,772	(3)	3,353
1910	284	14,908	11,783	----	3,125
1909	254	13,878	10,960	----	2,918
1908	211	13,085	10,450	----	2,635
1907	190	12,639	10,103	----	2,536
1906	163	12,285	9,871	----	2,414
1905	126	11,863	9,585	----	2,278
1904	106	11,165	9,059	----	2,106
1903	101	10,217	8,264	----	1,953
1902	95	9,369	7,594	----	1,775
1901	86	8,369	6,766	----	1,603
1900	84	7,573	6,124	----	1,449
1899	82	6,822	5,547	----	1,275
1898	73	6,053	4,952	----	1,101
1897	69	5,555	4,563	----	992
1896	67	5,207	4,323	----	884
1895	67	4,988	4,170	----	818
1894	66	4,846.6	4,047.7	----	798.9
1893	66	4,609.4	3,948.4	----	661.0
1892	66	4,267.4	3,685.1	----	582.3
1891	63	3,868.1	3,387.5	----	480.6
1890	60	3,522.2	3,094.7	----	427.5
1889	60	3,122.6	2,758.1	----	364.5
1888	60	2,742.0	2,437.8	----	304.2
1887	60	2,456.3	2,201.8	----	254.5
1886	59	2,096.9	1,899.1	----	197.8
1885	56	2,007.1	1,861.3	----	145.8
1884	56	1,995.9	1,884.8	----	111.1
1883	56	1,872.1	1,784.9	----	87.2
1882	55	1,720.8	1,664.6	----	56.2
1881	58	1,606.5	1,573.0	----	33.5
1880	59	1,522.7	1,502.2	----	20.5
1879	61	1,474.9	1,469.5	----	5.4
1878	65	1,519.7	1,517.7	----	2.0
1877	69	1,512.1	1,511.1	----	1.0
1876	76	1,690.6	1,690.2	----	.4

Year	Number of companies (435)	Total (436)	Ordinary (437)
1875	86	1,873.9	1,873.9
1874	96	1,947.6	1,947.6
1873	96	2,040.8	2,040.8
1872	108	2,079.2	2,079.2
1871	123	2,083.0	2,083.0
1870	129	2,006.1	2,006.1
1869	127	1,824.8	1,824.8
1868	113	1,534.6	1,534.6
1867	100	1,168.0	1,168.0
1866	79	874.2	874.2
1865	61	589.9	589.9
1864	53	404.3	404.3
1863	50	276.1	276.1
1862	48	191.8	191.8
1861	44	173.3	173.3
1860	43	173.3	173.3
1859	38	151.7	151.7
1858	36	130.5	130.5
1857	37	120.6	120.6
1856	38	106.5	106.5
1855	42	106.0	106.0
1854	43	94.0	94.0
1853	41	----	----
1852	45	----	----
1851	50	----	----
1850	48	97.1	97.1
1849	38		
1848	30		
1847	25		
1846	20		

Year	Number of companies (435)	Total (436)	Ordinary (437)
1845	18	14.5	14.5
1844	16		
1843	15		
1842	15		
1841	14		
1840	15	4.7	4.7
1839	17		
1838	18		
1837	18		
1836	17		
1835	15	2.8	2.8
1834	13		
1833	12		
1832	10		
1831	9		
1830	9	.6	.6
1829	7		
1828	7		
1827	7		
1826	7		
1825	7	.2	.2
1824	7		
1823	7		
1822	7		
1821	6		
1820	6	.1	.1
1819	5		
1818	5		
1817	4		

Year	Number of companies (435)	Total (436)	Ordinary (437)
1816	4		
1815	4	(5)	(5)
1814	4		
1813	3		
1812	4		
1811	2		
1810	2		
1809	2		
1808	2		
1807	2		
1806	2		
1805	2		
1804	2		
1803	2		
1802	2		
1801	4		
1800	4		
1799	4		
1798	4		
1797	4		
1796	4		
1795	4		
1794	4		
1793	2		
1792	2		
1791	2		
1790	3		
1789	3		
1788	3		

Year	Number of companies (435)
1787	3
1786	2
1785	2
1784	2
1783	2
1782	2
1781	2
1780	2
1779	2
1778	2
1777	2
1776	2
1775	2
1774	2
1773	2
1772	2
1771	2
1770	2
1769	2
1768	1
1767	1
1766	1
1765	1
1764	1
1763	1
1762	1
1761	1
1760	1
1759	1

[1] Initial year 1911.
[2] Initial year, 1917.
[3] Less than $500,000.
[4] First weekly premium policy issued 1873; industrial agency system introduced 1875.
[5] Less than $50,000.

Series X 441-444. Sales of Life Insurance, by U.S. Life Insurance Companies, by Type: 1854 to 1957

[In millions of dollars]

Year	Total 441	Ordinary 442	Group 443	Industrial [1] 444	Year	Total 441	Ordinary 442	Group 443	Industrial [1] 444	Year	Total 441	Ordinary 442	Industrial [1] 444
1957	71,748	48,937	16,016	6,795	1922	8,885	6,720	298	1,867	1887	696.5	537.7	158.8
1956	60,037	38,941	14,518	6,578	1921	7,957	6,248	128	1,581	1886	609.2	476.5	132.7
1955	[2]50,243	32,207	[2]11,637	6,399	1920	9,415	7,634	441	1,340	1885	432.2	338.5	93.7
1954	[2]47,453	26,824	[2]13,669	6,960	1919	7,882	6,369	433	1,080	1884	418.1	328.9	89.2
1953	38,134	24,908	6,609	6,617	1918	4,731	3,520	268	943	1883	394.3	317.3	77.0
1952	32,954	21,579	5,285	6,090	1917	4,553	3,500	184	869	1882	320.7	268.6	52.1
1951	28,857	19,000	4,261	5,596	1916	3,893	2,986	90	817	1881	267.6	230.5	37.1
1950	29,989	18,260	6,237	5,492	1915	3,285	2,437	48	800	1880	228.2	193.4	34.8
1949	24,215	15,848	2,911	5,456	1914	3,098	2,305	41	752	1879	178.4	173.4	5.0
1948	23,380	15,787	2,998	4,595	1913	3,175	2,414	22	739	1878	167.6	165.8	1.8
1947	23,637	16,131	2,768	4,738	1912	2,886	2,125	13	748	1877	179.3	178.3	1.0
1946	22,805	16,244	2,152	4,409	1911	2,688	2,008	[3]	680	1876	233.4	232.7	.7
1945	15,391	10,577	1,302	3,512	1910	2,371	1,742	----------	629	1875	299.3	299.3	[1]
1944	14,124	9,184	1,621	3,319	1909	2,232	1,574	----------	658	1874	351.8	351.8	[1]
1943	13,281	8,022	1,924	3,335	1908	1,884	1,379	----------	505	1873	465.6	465.6	[1]
1942	11,888	7,041	1,657	3,190	1907	1,782	1,272	----------	510	1872	489.9	489.9	--------
1941	12,564	7,935	1,197	3,432	1906	1,963	1,377	----------	586	1871	488.7	488.7	--------
1940	11,087	7,022	747	3,318	1905	2,283	1,666	----------	617	1870	587.9	587.9	--------
1939	10,935	6,886	844	3,205	1904	2,316	1,729	----------	587	1869	614.8	614.8	--------
1938	11,045	6,745	507	3,793	1903	2,217	1,660	----------	557	1868	579.7	579.7	--------
1937	12,572	7,593	800	4,179	1902	2,064	1,488	----------	576	1867	471.6	471.6	--------
1936	12,165	7,314	626	4,225	1901	1,895	1,326	----------	569	1866	404.5	404.5	--------
1935	12,298	7,550	715	4,033	1900	1,755	1,221	----------	534	1865	245.4	245.4	--------
1934	11,928	7,363	534	4,031	1899	1,609	1,118	----------	491	1864	155.8	155.8	--------
1933	10,846	6,786	427	3,633	1898	1,286	883	----------	403	1863	89.8	89.8	--------
1932	12,305	7,896	720	3,689	1897	1,196	803	----------	393	1862	43.5	43.5	--------
1931	15,066	10,161	927	3,978	1896	1,034	687	----------	347	1861	25.0	25.0	--------
1930	17,265	11,905	1,381	3,979	1895	1,113	744	----------	369	1860	35.6	35.6	--------
1929	17,755	12,305	1,379	4,071	1894	1,274.0	712.1	----------	561.9	1859	30.1	30.1	--------
1928	16,942	11,654	1,508	3,780	1893	1,131.4	797.3	----------	334.1	1858	23.1	23.1	--------
1927	15,582	10,777	1,008	3,797	1892	1,095.7	818.8	----------	276.9	1857	20.5	20.5	--------
1926	15,217	10,508	1,174	3,535	1891	1,006.4	779.2	----------	227.2	1856	20.2	20.2	--------
1925	14,278	10,060	1,075	3,143	1890	984.3	742.1	----------	242.2	1855	16.6	16.6	--------
1924	12,039	8,764	649	2,626	1889	871.0	669.0	----------	202.0	1854	15.3	15.3	--------
1923	11,061	8,273	549	2,239	1888	722.8	544.5	----------	178.3				

[1] First weekly premium policy issued in 1873; industrial agency system introduced 1875. Yearly sales, 1873-1875, probably less than $500,000.   [2] Includes Federal employees group life insurance of $6,756 million in 1954 and $1,928 million in 1955.   [3] Less than $500,000.

Series X 445-458. Income and Disbursements of U.S. Life Insurance Companies: 1854 to 1957

[In millions of dollars]

	Income				Disbursements									
						Payments to policyholders								
Year	Total income [1]	Life insurance premiums	Annuity premiums	Investment and other income	Total disbursements	Total [1]	Death benefits	Matured endowments	Annuity payments	Policy dividends [2]	Surrender values	Disability and accidental death benefits	Commissions, expenses, taxes, and other disbursements	Dividends to stockholders
	445	446	447	448	449	450	451	452	453	454	455	456	457	458
1957	19,333	10,241	1,408	4,558	14,197.3	9,222.7	[3]2,785.7	733.4	529.4	1,473.7	1,290.5	[3]127.9	4,837.3	137.3
1956	17,865	9,592	1,293	4,281	12,492.4	8,055.6	[3]2,495.3	655.5	502.7	1,358.2	1,024.4	[3]117.8	4,302.1	134.7
1955	16,544	8,903	1,288	3,998	11,273.9	7,267.5	[3]2,289.6	615.0	453.2	1,270.9	922.5	[3]118.2	3,891.5	114.9
1954	15,280	8,239	1,209	3,717	10,246.8	6,570.1	[3]2,111.6	543.1	417.3	1,117.6	868.6	[3]118.9	3,585.6	91.1
1953	14,271	7,778	1,190	3,424	9,416.4	5,976.5	[3]2,023.7	475.5	411.7	985.2	714.3	[3]118.2	3,347.6	92.3
1952	13,076	7,228	1,094	3,193	8,467.4	5,371.4	[3]1,881.4	440.7	369.0	868.4	644.0	[3]112.8	3,037.0	59.0
1951	12,012	6,785	961	2,972	7,838.6	4,983.4	[3]1,749.2	504.0	345.7	796.9	618.6	[3]101.7	2,803.2	52.0
1950	11,337	6,249	939	3,148	7,189.7	4,402.7	1,593.3	493.8	257.2	679.3	666.3	132.7	2,696.6	90.4
1949	10,376	5,926	768	2,865	6,475.6	3,997.4	1,483.7	469.7	239.7	634.5	588.7	128.5	2,416.1	62.1
1948	9,751	5,679	799	2,594	5,955.5	3,670.7	1,443.3	436.2	229.9	600.5	472.9	124.9	2,240.2	44.6
1947	9,114	5,370	718	2,461	5,469.4	3,338.3	1,335.7	415.6	214.4	567.0	389.9	122.0	2,092.6	38.5
1946	8,068	4,982	644	2,442	4,611.1	2,848.3	1,274.5	404.6	199.0	507.2	327.3	135.7	1,728.9	33.9
1945	7,674	4,589	570	2,515	4,218.6	2,718.8	1,282.2	413.7	184.8	472.4	240.7	125.0	1,469.3	30.5
1944	7,011	4,265	528	2,218	3,972.1	2,527.9	1,203.1	360.6	173.7	437.7	235.4	117.4	1,420.1	24.1
1943	6,442	3,942	415	2,085	3,781.2	2,407.5	1,092.5	324.6	165.2	410.1	295.0	120.1	1,335.5	38.2
1942	6,029	3,753	368	1,908	3,739.6	2,443.2	993.0	268.1	159.3	434.5	453.8	134.5	1,282.2	14.2
1941	5,855	3,607	413	1,835	3,827.4	2,550.2	989.7	264.3	152.0	429.7	573.1	141.4	1,258.7	18.5
1940	5,658	3,501	386	1,771	3,914.0	2,680.7	976.9	275.1	142.3	456.1	688.5	141.8	1,215.2	18.1
1939	5,453	3,431	345	1,677	3,826.9	2,641.6	943.2	241.6	133.6	456.5	731.6	135.0	1,165.9	19.5
1938	5,357	3,368	393	1,596	3,744.4	2,578.1	934.0	175.9	123.2	446.9	771.2	126.9	1,152.7	13.6
1937	5,257	3,354	376	1,527	3,610.3	2,437.0	937.3	154.7	109.9	435.4	669.3	130.4	1,155.1	18.2
1936	5,180	3,216	440	1,524	3,518.0	2,429.2	919.2	154.2	94.8	418.3	712.7	130.0	1,076.1	12.7
1935	5,072	3,182	491	1,399	3,593.0	2,535.1	877.4	145.0	76.1	424.2	882.5	129.9	1,047.5	10.4
1934	4,786	3,107	400	1,279	3,661.7	2,704.9	875.4	129.4	58.2	437.7	1,077.8	126.4	945.2	11.6
1933	4,622	3,057	254	1,311	3,917.4	3,016.4	877.1	121.0	42.2	499.4	1,356.6	120.1	891.9	9.1
1932	4,653	3,314	181	1,158	3,997.7	3,087.0	905.3	122.6	36.5	562.7	1,346.1	113.8	896.7	14.0
1931	4,850	3,477	176	1,197	3,537.8	2,606.6	915.2	117.0	29.0	584.6	861.0	99.8	914.2	17.0
1930	4,594	3,416	101	1,077	3,198.5	2,246.8	855.8	112.0	23.3	553.7	614.2	87.8	929.8	21.9
1929	4,337	3,251	92	994	2,882.3	1,961.5	807.8	108.8	21.2	513.2	448.0	62.5	898.5	22.3
1928	4,088	3,037	98	953	2,547.9	1,698.7	705.9	89.9	16.8	465.8	369.2	51.1	828.1	21.1
1927	3,673	2,814	52	807	2,295.2	1,499.9	613.5	89.2	13.0	417.9	324.5	41.8	777.0	18.3
1926	3,330	2,577	39	714	2,123.8	1,373.2	569.1	98.7	11.3	376.9	282.9	34.3	737.4	13.2

See footnotes at end of table.

Series X 445–458.　Income and Disbursements of U.S. Life Insurance Companies: 1854 to 1957—Con.

[In millions of dollars]

Year	Total income	Life insurance premiums	Annuity premiums	Investment and other income	Total disbursements	Total	Death benefits	Matured endowments	Annuity payments	Policy dividends	Surrender values	Disability and accidental death benefits	Commissions, expenses, taxes, and other disbursements	Dividends to stockholders
	445	446	447	448	449	450	451	452	453	454	455	456	457	458
1925	3,018	2,340	38	640	1,936.5	1,246.2	493.4	114.5	10.0	351.1	248.6	28.6	675.8	14.5
1924	2,703	2,096	20	587	1,813.2	1,205.1	449.7	138.6	10.1	351.1	235.7	19.9	596.4	11.7
1923	2,427	1,881	13	533	1,680.4	1,089.1	420.8	142.9	10.0	274.7	225.3	15.4	579.0	12.3
1922	2,149	1,671	11	467	1,493.9	1,005.7	370.1	138.3	9.5	259.8	218.4	9.6	477.5	10.7
1921	1,951	1,523	11	417	1,289.0	840.0	338.9	121.9	10.7	192.0	167.2	9.3	443.0	6.0
1920	1,764	1,374	7	383	1,198.3	744.6	350.0	101.2	9.4	157.5	119.0	7.5	448.4	5.3
1919	1,560	1,187	17	356	1,105.7	739.9	354.1	103.7	10.9	159.5	111.7	----------	361.6	4.2
1918	1,325	980	11	334	998.9	710.2	372.9	80.0	11.1	145.2	101.0	----------	283.6	5.0
1917	1,249	916	10	323	845.8	590.2	264.6	74.6	10.0	136.7	104.3	----------	251.8	3.8
1916	1,118	835	10	273	792.4	566.4	256.4	63.5	9.1	125.3	112.0	----------	220.9	5.2
1915	1,043.1	776.4	5.7	261.0	768.5	544.7	237.4	63.4	8.9	111.3	123.8	----------	220.5	3.3
1914	985.0	738.8	5.4	240.8	704.7	509.5	222.1	60.7	8.1	107.9	110.6	----------	192.0	3.3
1913	945.6	708.5	4.6	232.5	660.6	469.6	209.6	56.0	8.4	101.2	94.4	----------	186.9	4.1
1912	893.4	666.3	4.9	222.2	629.2	448.8	205.2	55.7	7.8	92.8	87.4	----------	178.2	2.1
1911	836.1	625.9	4.2	206.0	579.9	414.3	194.1	48.5	7.4	83.1	81.2	----------	163.6	2.0
1910	781.0	587.7	5.7	187.6	540.3	387.3	180.7	46.4	7.4	75.4	77.5	----------	150.9	2.1
1909	748.0	560.2	5.0	182.8	505.4	360.7	172.3	41.2	7.4	63.0	76.8	----------	143.2	1.4
1908	703.9	542.0	3.9	158.0	467.7	335.8	164.7	34.9	7.2	54.5	74.5	----------	130.2	1.7
1907	678.7	528.4	4.7	145.6	438.8	309.7	164.2	33.0	7.3	46.3	58.9	----------	128.0	1.1
1906	667.2	521.5	5.1	140.6	426.9	287.3	153.0	29.3	7.1	40.3	57.7	----------	138.6	1.0
1905	642.1	507.7	8.3	126.1	411.9	265.0	149.7	28.0	6.8	36.1	44.4	----------	145.9	1.0
1904	599.1	477.2	11.1	110.8	391.8	247.1	144.5	25.3	6.3	33.6	37.4	----------	143.9	.9
1903	553.6	438.7	8.8	106.1	360.5	225.8	131.7	24.6	5.6	31.4	32.6	----------	133.8	.9
1902	504.5	396.5	10.4	97.6	322.0	199.9	118.4	22.4	4.9	26.9	27.3	----------	121.2	.9
1901	458.0	357.6	8.7	91.7	302.8	192.4	117.9	21.3	4.4	24.3	24.6	----------	109.6	.8
1900	400.6	318.4	6.3	75.9	267.6	168.7	100.7	18.3	4.1	22.9	22.7	----------	97.9	1.0
1899	365.4	285.6	6.2	73.6	250.3	160.0	96.2	15.4	3.7	21.4	23.4	----------	89.5	.9
1898	325.5	252.6	5.1	67.8	222.5	146.8	82.7	14.0	3.4	20.0	26.8	----------	74.9	.9
1897	304.9	237.3	6.0	61.6	209.0	139.4	78.6	12.4	3.0	18.5	27.0	----------	68.8	.8
1896	283.7	222.9	5.0	55.8	202.6	136.2	77.3	12.3	2.6	17.2	26.7	----------	65.5	.9
1895	271.9	216.1	3.6	52.2	189.8	125.1	73.1	10.9	2.4	15.4	23.4	----------	63.8	.8
1894	262.0	207.1	2.6	52.3	182.3	118.4	69.3	8.3	2.3	14.8	23.6	----------	63.1	.8
1893	241.7	195.0	2.0	44.7	170.4	112.7	66.6	8.5	2.3	15.1	20.2	----------	56.9	.8
1892	227.6	181.9	2.6	43.1	156.4	104.5	63.9	8.0	2.1	14.7	15.9	----------	51.2	.7
1891	213.4	170.0	2.9	40.5	144.6	97.0	55.8	8.5	2.0	14.2	16.5	----------	46.9	.6
1890	195.6	153.6	3.2	38.8	134.2	90.0	50.9	8.9	1.8	14.5	14.0	----------	43.7	.5
1889	176.2	137.2	2.9	36.1	120.8	82.1	44.9	9.1	1.5	14.1	12.4	----------	38.3	.5
1888	153.9	117.9	2.4	33.6	108.7	76.5	41.1	8.1	1.4	14.5	11.5	----------	31.7	.5
1887	133.7	101.6	1.9	30.2	96.0	68.9	35.9	6.5	1.2	14.9	10.4	----------	26.6	.4
1886	119.1	89.1	1.7	28.3	84.1	61.5	30.8	6.9	1.1	13.2	9.4	----------	22.3	.3
1885	107.0	78.8	1.2	27.0	82.8	61.6	30.3	7.6	1.1	13.0	9.6	----------	20.8	.4
1884	98.1	71.8	1.3	25.0	78.6	59.5	27.1	8.8	1.0	13.0	9.5	----------	18.8	.4
1883	93.4	66.0	2.2	25.2	72.5	56.4	25.4	7.9	.8	13.4	8.8	----------	15.8	.3
1882	85.7	59.4	1.7	24.6	66.7	52.8	23.0	6.4	.6	13.6	9.3	----------	13.6	.3
1881	80.2	54.9	1.9	23.4	66.3	52.7	22.8	7.9	.5	12.6	8.9	----------	13.3	.3
1880	77.7	53.0	1.2	23.5	67.5	53.2	21.9	7.9	.3	13.2	9.9	----------	13.9	.3
1879	77.8	53.1	.7	24.0	69.0	57.4	22.6	8.8	.3	13.5	12.2	----------	11.3	.3
1878	80.5	56.8	.5	23.2	72.1	60.9	19.7	9.2	.3	14.6	17.1	----------	11.0	.2
1877	86.2	62.7	.3	23.2	74.3	60.7	21.0	4.9	.2	15.4	19.2	----------	13.3	.4
1876	96.4	71.8	.3	24.3	76.6	63.1	22.3	3.0	.2	16.2	21.4	----------	13.2	.3
1875	108.6	83.4	.4	24.8	80.0	65.5	25.0	2.0	.2	17.9	20.4	----------	14.1	.4
1874	115.7	89.2	.2	26.3	81.2	64.9	[4]25.7	[4]	.1	16.6	22.5	----------	16.0	.4
1873	118.4	95.8	.2	22.4	84.5	66.8	[4]27.1	[4]	.1	22.9	16.7	----------	17.2	.5
1872	117.3	96.5	.1	20.7	78.2	59.7	[4]25.6	[4]	.1	20.1	13.9	----------	18.0	.5
1871	113.5	96.6	.1	16.8	77.5	56.7	[4]28.7	[4]	.1	14.6	13.3	----------	20.2	.4
1870	105.0	90.2	.1	14.7	63.9	44.9	[4]19.5	[4]	.1	15.8	9.6	----------	18.3	.6
1869	98.5	86.0	.1	12.4	54.5	36.6	[4]15.6	[4]	.1	15.7	5.1	----------	17.3	.6
1868	77.4	67.8	.1	9.5	41.0	26.5	10.1	.9	.1	11.7	3.8	----------	13.8	.6
1867	56.5	50.4	[5]	6.1	26.3	16.5	7.6	.6	[5]	6.2	2.1	----------	9.5	.4
1866	40.4	35.8	[5]	4.6	17.2	10.2	6.1	.3	[5]	2.5	1.2	----------	6.8	.2
1865	24.9	[6]21.6	[6]	3.3	10.6	6.3	[7]4.1	[7]	[7]	1.5	.7	----------	4.0	.3
1864	16.1	[6]13.1	[6]	3.0	7.0	4.6	[7]3.1	[7]	[7]	1.0	.4	----------	2.3	.1
1863	10.6	[6]8.5	[6]	2.1	5.8	3.7	[7]2.3	[7]	[7]	1.0	.4	----------	1.9	.1
1862	7.4	[6]5.7	[6]	1.7	3.8	2.8	[7]1.7	[7]	[7]	.6	.5	----------	.9	.1
1861	6.3	[6]4.9	[6]	1.4	3.6	2.8	[7]1.5	[7]	[7]	.6	.7	----------	.8	.1
1860	6.0	[6]4.8	[6]	1.2	2.9	2.1	[7]1.4	[7]	[7]	.5	.2	----------	.7	.1
1859	5.2	[6]4.0	[6]	1.2	2.6	1.9	[7]1.3	[7]	[7]	.4	.1	----------	.8	[5]
1858	4.5	[6]3.6	[6]	.9	2.4		1.2	----------	----------	----------	----------	----------	----------	----------
1857	4.0	[6]3.2	[6]	.8	2.1		1.2	----------	----------	----------	----------	----------	----------	----------
1856	3.8	[6]3.0		.8	2.0		1.0	----------	----------	----------	----------	----------	----------	----------
1855	3.5	[6]3.0	[6]	.5	2.0		1.2	----------	----------	----------	----------	----------	----------	----------
1854	3.2	[6]2.6	[6]	.6	2.0		1.0	----------	----------	----------	----------	----------	----------	----------

[1] Beginning 1947, includes data on operations of accident and health departments of U.S. life insurance companies, not shown separately, therefore components will not add to totals.

[2] Beginning 1947, includes policy dividends paid by accident and health departments of U.S. life insurance companies.

[3] Beginning 1951, accidental death benefits included with death benefits; figures for series X 456 are for disability benefits only. Accidental death benefits approximately $30 million in 1951.

[4] Matured endowments included with death benefits.

[5] Less than $50,000.

[6] Annuity premiums included with life insurance premiums.

[7] Matured endowments and annuity payments included with death benefits.

Series X 459–468. Assets, Earning Rate, Liabilities, and Capital and Surplus of U.S. Life Insurance Companies: 1854 to 1957

[In millions of dollars, except net rate of interest earned on assets. As of December 31]

Year	Assets						Net rate of interest earned on assets	Liabilities		Capital and surplus
	Total	Bonds	Stocks	Mortgages	Real estate	Other [1]		Total	Policy reserves	
	459	460	461	462	463	464	465	466	467	468
1957	101,309	51,356	3,391	35,236	3,119	8,207	3.44	93,085	84,075	8,224
1956	96,011	49,107	3,503	32,989	2,817	7,595	3.33	88,321	79,738	7,690
1955	90,432	47,741	3,633	29,445	2,581	7,032	3.23	83,424	75,359	7,008
1954	84,486	46,294	3,268	25,976	2,298	6,650	3.24	78,103	70,903	6,383
1953	78,533	44,402	2,573	23,322	2,020	6,216	3.15	72,819	66,683	5,714
1952	73,375	41,974	2,446	21,251	1,903	5,801	3.07	68,119	62,579	5,256
1951	68,278	39,650	2,221	19,314	1,631	5,462	2.98	63,428	58,547	4,850
1950	64,020	39,366	2,103	16,102	1,445	5,004	3.00	59,381	54,946	4,639
1949	59,630	39,274	1,718	12,906	1,247	4,485	2.98	55,472	51,498	4,158
1948	55,512	37,979	1,428	10,833	1,055	4,217	2.96	51,803	48,158	3,709
1947	51,743	36,757	1,390	8,675	860	4,061	2.88	48,307	44,882	3,436
1946	48,191	35,350	1,249	7,155	735	3,702	2.89	44,885	41,702	3,306
1945	44,797	32,605	999	6,636	857	3,700	3.05	41,556	38,667	3,241
1944	41,054	28,711	756	6,686	1,063	3,838	3.14	38,318	35,577	2,736
1943	37,766	24,836	652	6,714	1,352	4,212	3.23	35,343	33,049	2,423
1942	34,931	21,558	608	6,726	1,663	4,376	3.36	32,775	30,797	2,156
1941	32,731	19,051	601	6,442	1,878	4,759	3.42	30,769	28,945	1,962
1940	30,802	17,092	605	5,972	2,065	5,068	3.45	28,964	27,238	1,838
1939	29,243	15,734	587	5,683	2,139	5,100	3.54	27,512	25,827	1,731
1938	27,755	14,473	586	5,445	2,179	5,072	3.59	26,122	24,495	1,633
1937	26,249	13,272	558	5,230	2,192	4,997	3.69	24,706	23,202	1,543
1936	24,874	11,869	615	5,128	2,149	5,113	3.71	23,274	21,800	1,600
1935	23,216	10,041	583	5,357	1,990	5,245	3.70	21,826	20,404	1,390
1934	21,844	8,533	482	5,875	1,693	5,261	3.92	20,417	19,030	1,427
1933	20,896	7,189	487	6,701	1,267	5,252	4.25	19,475	18,077	1,421
1932	20,754	6,843	574	7,336	935	5,066	4.65	19,308	17,839	1,446
1931	20,160	6,806	567	7,673	684	4,430	4.93	18,750	17,384	1,410
1930	18,880	6,431	519	7,598	548	3,784	5.05	17,524	16,231	1,356
1929	17,482	6,001	416	7,316	464	3,285	5.05	16,159	14,948	1,323
1928	15,961	5,655	285	6,778	403	2,840	5.05	14,711	13,596	1,250
1927	14,392	5,146	145	6,200	351	2,550	5.05	13,238	12,279	1,154
1926	12,940	4,653	125	5,580	303	2,279	5.09	11,919	11,061	1,021
1925	11,538	4,333	81	4,808	266	2,050	5.11	10,623	9,927	915
1924	10,394	4,034	64	4,175	239	1,882	5.17	9,551	8,939	843
1923	9,455	3,783	57	3,662	243	1,710	5.18	8,657	8,130	798
1922	8,652	3,656	56	3,122	197	1,621	5.12	7,943	7,449	709
1921	7,936	3,390	69	2,792	186	1,499	5.02	7,332	6,903	604
1920	7,320	3,298	75	2,442	172	1,333	4.83	6,752	6,338	568
1919	6,791	3,241	76	2,094	168	1,212	4.66	6,209	5,830	582
1918	6,475	3,012	82	2,075	179	1,127	4.72	5,903	5,407	572
1917	5,941	2,537	83	2,021	179	1,121	4.81	5,336	5,033	605
1916	5,537	2,309	83	1,893	174	1,078	4.80	4,967	4,696	570
1915	5,190	2,095	81	1,779	173	1,062	4.77	4,648	4,399	542
1914	4,935	1,982	83	1,706	171	993	4.69	4,364	4,166	571
1913	4,659	1,909	86	1,618	166	880	4.67	4,137	3,934	522
1912	4,409	1,859	96	1,485	176	793	4.59	3,880	3,695	529
1911	4,164	1,787	100	1,358	171	748	4.59	3,646	3,473	518
1910	3,876	1,660	130	1,227	173	686	4.55	3,386	3,226	490
1909	3,644	1,616	146	1,084	167	631	4.79	3,171	3,029	473
1908	3,380	1,473	147	987	167	606	4.77	2,939	2,829	441
1907	3,053	1,281	133	921	170	548	4.80	2,736	2,651	317
1906	2,924	1,299	160	826	170	469	4.68	2,557	2,473	367
1905	2,706	1,211	173	724	171	427	4.68	2,372	2,295	334
1904	2,499	1,066	173	672	181	407	4.63	2,168	2,101	331
1903	2,265	897	165	624	178	401	4.61	1,979	1,916	286
1902	2,092	872	132	573	170	345	4.58	1,798	1,738	294
1901	1,911	792	103	532	166	318	4.61	1,640	1,584	271
1900	1,742	707	95	501	158	281	4.67	1,493	1,443	249
1899	1,595	654	83	468	154	236	4.81	1,366	1,322	229
1898	1,463	581	72	455	145	210	4.87	1,246	1,203	217
1897	1,345	503	56	452	138	196	4.86	1,141	1,119	204
1896	1,244	445	54	442	135	168	4.91	1,067	1,048	177
1895	1,160	423	53	412	125	147	5.00	998	980	162
1894	1,073	369	50	394	117	143	4.93	931	915	142
1893	988	323	47	374	105	139	4.95	869	853	119
1892	919	306	39	351	97	126	5.08	802	789	117
1891	841	270	31	334	86	120	5.36	740	727	101
1890	771	241	30	310	81	109	5.10	679	670	92
1889	714.5	251.7	(2)	283.3	75.7	103.8	5.27	624.3	616.3	90.2
1888	657.1	231.6	(2)	262.5	68.6	94.4	5.43	574.6	566.8	82.5
1887	597.6	207.8	(2)	244.9	63.4	81.5	5.47	524.7	518.4	72.9
1886	561.6	197.7	(2)	227.5	59.9	76.5	5.39	459.8	452.8	101.8
1885	524.7	182.6	(2)	212.9	58.0	71.2	5.42	431.5	425.0	93.2
1884	492.2	152.1	(2)	205.7	54.6	79.8	5.48	410.1	403.3	82.1
1883	472.4	137.6	(2)	187.6	51.7	95.5	5.54	391.9	385.2	80.5
1882	450.0	124.0	(2)	172.7	51.4	101.9	5.55	373.1	366.4	76.9
1881	429.6	129.2	(2)	160.2	51.1	89.1	5.51	357.1	349.9	72.5

See footnotes at end of table.

Series X 459–468.   Assets, Earning Rate, Liabilities, and Capital and Surplus of U.S. Life Insurance Companies: 1854 to 1957—Con.

[In millions of dollars, except net rate of interest earned on assets]

Year	Assets						Net rate of interest earned on assets	Liabilities		Capital and surplus
	Total	Bonds	Stocks	Mortgages	Real estate	Other [1]		Total	Policy reserves	
	459	460	461	462	463	464	465	466	467	468
1880	418.1	124.8	(2)	164.8	51.6	76.9	5.48	346.5	338.8	71.6
1879	401.7	116.2	(2)	173.8	49.2	62.5	5.83	336.3	328.3	65.4
1878	404.1	112.8	(2)	189.1	42.8	59.4	5.94	339.6	329.5	64.5
1877	396.4	100.8	(2)	201.1	31.6	62.9	6.37	334.8	326.3	61.6
1876	407.4	85.7	(2)	217.9	29.2	74.6	6.55	346.3	337.5	61.1
1875	403.1	73.9	(2)	219.7	22.6	86.9	6.79	342.3	334.1	60.8
1874	387.3	65.3	(2)	210.1	18.3	93.6	6.89	328.4	320.3	58.9
1873	360.1	56.6	(2)	189.8	15.0	98.7	6.93	311.5	300.2	48.6
1872	335.2	54.7	(2)	164.3	12.5	103.7	6.90	288.3	277.4	46.9
1871	302.6	52.4	(2)	134.9	10.8	104.5	----------	254.6	243.3	48.0
1870	269.5	48.1	(2)	108.0	9.0	104.4	----------	221.0	209.3	48.5
1869	229.1	45.1	(2)	83.6	7.0	93.4	----------	180.3	170.9	48.8
1868	176.8	40.9	(2)	58.0	4.8	73.1	----------	135.8	126.0	41.0
1867	125.6	33.2	(2)	37.0	3.6	51.8	----------	88.6	81.2	37.0
1866	91.6	28.3	(2)	23.7	2.3	37.3	----------	65.6	59.8	26.0
1865	64.2	22.4	(2)	16.5	1.7	23.6	----------	49.3	42.8	14.9
1864	49.0							34.7	31.0	14.3
1863	37.8							28.6	24.0	9.2
1862	30.1							23.8	17.5	6.3
1861	26.7							18.3	15.3	8.4
1860	24.1							17.1	14.4	7.0
1859	20.5							15.4	----------	5.1
1858	15.9									
1857	14.0									
1856	15.0									
1855	12.7									
1854	11.4									

[1] Includes cash, policy loans, collateral loans, due and deferred premiums, and all other assets.   [2] Included with bonds.

Series X 469–482. Estimated Enrollment in Medical Care Insurance and Rate Per 1,000, by Type of Insurance: 1939 to 1957

Year	Hospitalization insurance — Total[1] (469)	Insurance companies — Group policies (470)	Insurance companies — Individual policies (471)	Blue Cross plans (472)	All other plans[2] (473)	Surgical insurance — Total[1] (474)	Insurance companies — Group policies (475)	Insurance companies — Individual policies (476)	Blue Shield plans[3] (477)	All other plans[4] (478)	Medical insurance[5] — Total[1] (479)	Insurance companies — Group policies (480)	Insurance companies — Individual policies (481)	All other plans[6] (482)
ENROLLMENT (1,000)														
1957	121,432	48,439	28,673	51,857	8,013	108,931	48,955	24,928	39,343	11,637	71,813	28,317	7,371	42,945
1956	115,949	45,211	27,629	50,108	7,709	101,325	45,906	23,074	36,896	10,585	64,891	25,177	6,789	39,183
1955	107,662	39,029	26,706	47,719	7,525	91,927	39,725	22,445	34,071	9,410	55,506	20,678	6,264	34,090
1954	101,493	35,090	25,338	44,243	8,468	85,890	35,723	21,442	30,067	9,700	47,248	15,778	6,513	29,576
1953	97,303	33,575	23,475	42,857	8,112	80,982	34,039	20,212	26,822	9,879	42,684	13,787	5,824	27,010
1952	91,667	29,455	21,412	40,495	7,145	73,161	29,621	18,354	23,522	8,949	35,797	10,157	4,965	23,471
1951	85,991	26,663	20,802	38,424	6,043	65,535	26,376	15,623	20,193	6,585	27,723	7,946	4,230	17,138
1950	76,961	22,305	17,296	37,435	5,006	54,477	21,219	13,718	16,054	6,512	21,589	5,587	2,714	14,301
1949	66,044	17,697	14,729	33,381	4,694	47,141	15,590	9,315	11,894	6,554	16,862	2,736	2,350	12,343
1948	60,995	16,741	11,286	30,448	4,563	34,060	14,199	6,944	8,399	5,831	12,895	1,927	1,810	9,551
1947	52,584	14,190	7,584	27,489	3,775	26,247	11,103	4,875	5,732	3,829	8,898	1,098	1,111	6,829
1946	42,065	11,315	3,000	24,250	3,500	18,697	8,661	2,000	4,436	3,600	6,400	567	300	-------
1945	32,685	7,804	2,700	18,881	3,300	13,172	5,537	1,800	2,535	3,300	4,700	335	200	-------
1944	29,648	8,400	2,400	15,748	3,100	12,093	5,625	1,600	1,768	3,100	3,800	100	100	-------
1943	23,900	6,800	2,100	12,600	2,400	9,735	4,700	1,400	1,235	2,400	3,400	-------	-------	-------
1942	19,395	5,080	1,800	10,215	2,300	7,740	3,275	1,200	965	2,400	3,400	-------	-------	-------
1941	16,049	3,850	1,500	8,399	2,300	6,375	2,300	1,000	775	2,300	3,200	-------	-------	-------
1940	12,012	2,500	1,200	6,012	2,300	4,950	1,430	850	370	2,300	3,000	-------	-------	-------
1939	7,976	1,260	(7)	4,410	2,300	3,103	630	(7)	167	2,300	3,000	-------	-------	-------
RATE PER 1,000 POPULATION[8]														
1957	721	288	170	308	48	647	291	148	234	69	426	168	44	255
1956	701	273	167	303	47	613	278	140	223	64	392	152	41	237
1955	663	240	165	294	46	566	245	138	210	58	342	127	39	210
1954	638	221	159	278	53	540	225	135	189	61	297	99	41	186
1953	624	215	150	275	52	519	218	130	172	63	274	88	37	173
1952	598	192	140	264	47	477	193	120	153	58	233	66	32	153
1951	569	176	138	254	40	434	175	103	134	44	184	53	28	113
1950	512	148	115	249	33	363	141	91	107	43	144	37	18	95
1949	448	120	100	226	32	279	106	63	81	44	114	19	16	84
1948	420	115	78	210	31	235	98	48	58	40	89	13	12	66
1947	369	100	53	193	26	184	78	34	40	27	62	8	8	48
1946	304	82	22	175	25	135	63	14	32	26	46	4	2	-------
1945	256	61	21	148	26	103	43	14	20	26	37	3	2	-------
1944	234	66	19	124	24	95	44	13	14	24	30	1	1	-------
1943	188	53	16	99	19	76	37	11	10	19	27	-------	-------	-------
1942	148	39	14	78	18	59	25	9	7	18	24	-------	-------	-------
1941	122	29	11	64	17	48	17	8	6	17	24	-------	-------	-------
1940	91	19	9	46	17	38	11	6	3	17	23	-------	-------	-------
1939	61	10	-------	34	18	24	5	-------	1	18	23	-------	-------	-------

[1] Unduplicated total. Since 5 to 15 percent of the population with each type of insurance benefit had protection under more than 1 of the kinds of policies or plans appearing under the benefits, the number of persons insured and the rates per 1,000 are lower than the sum of the numbers appearing under the different categories of insurance underwriters. Data for 1939–1946 have not been adjusted for duplication since the extent of overlapping was not known; it was less important in the earlier years.

[2] Includes members of those Blue Shield plans that provide hospitalization benefits, and members of the independent plans (i.e., fraternal, community, consumer, employer-employee, union and physician-controlled plans) that provide hospitalization benefits.

[3] Excludes medical-society-sponsored plans that are not affiliated with the Blue Shield Commission.

[4] Includes members of those Blue Cross plans that provide surgical benefits and members of medical-society-sponsored plans not affiliated with the Blue Shield Commission and of the independent plans that provide surgical benefits.

[5] Includes insurance against the costs of (a) in-hospital, medical (nonsurgical), physicians' visits, (b) visits to the doctor's office, and (c) physician visits to the patient's home. Since about 1948 most of the increase in enrollment shown has been for insurance limited to (a) in-hospital medical care. Total estimated for 1939–1946; detail not available.

[6] For 1947–1957, includes members of Blue Shield plans, those Blue Cross plans that provide in-hospital medical benefits, and the medical-society-sponsored and all other independent plans.

[7] Not available.

[8] For 1939, based on total population; all other years based on civilian population as of July 1.

BANKING AND FINANCE

Series X 483–500. Private Pension and Deferred Profit-Sharing Plans—Estimated Coverage, Contributions, Reserves, Beneficiaries, and Benefit Payments: 1930 to 1957

[Includes pay-as-you-go plans, nonprofit organization plans, and deferred profit-sharing plans. Excludes railroad plans other than those supplementing Federal Railroad Retirement Act.   In 1930 and 1935, respectively, private railroad plans covered an average of 1.3 and 1.1 million employees; had about 50,000 and 60,000 beneficiaries; and paid about $30 million and $40 million in benefits]

Year	Coverage [1] [2] (1,000)			Employer contributions ($1,000,000)			Employee contributions ($1,000,000)		
	Total	Insured plans	Self-insured plans	Total	Insured plans	Self-insured plans	Total	Insured plans	Self-insured plans
	483	484	485	486	487	488	489	490	491
1957	18,200	4,400	13,800	3,900	1,230	2,670	680	300	380
1956	16,800	4,000	12,800	3,490	1,110	2,380	610	290	320
1955	15,400	3,800	11,600	3,190	1,100	2,090	550	280	270
1954	14,200	3,600	10,600	2,930	1,030	1,900	510	270	240
1953	13,200	3,400	9,800	2,930	1,010	1,920	480	260	220
1952	11,700	3,200	8,500	2,510	910	1,600	430	240	190
1951	11,005	2,900	8,100	2,260	820	1,440	380	210	170
1950	9,800	2,600	7,200	1,750	720	1,030	330	200	130
1945	6,400			830			160		
1940	4,100			180			130		
1935	2,700			140			90		
1930	2,700			130			70		

Year	Reserves [2] ($1,000,000,000)			Number of monthly beneficiaries [2] (1,000)			Amount of benefit payments [3] ($1,000,000)		
	Total	Insured plans	Self-insured plans	Total	Insured plans	Self-insured plans	Total	Insured plans	Self-insured plans
	492	493	494	495	496	497	498	499	500
1957	34.8	14.0	20.8	1,250	380	870	1,150	260	890
1956	30.3	12.4	17.9	1,110	340	770	1,010	230	780
1955	26.5	11.2	15.3	990	300	690	860	200	660
1954	23.1	10.0	13.1	880	270	610	720	170	550
1953	19.8	8.8	11.0	750	230	520	620	150	470
1952	16.9	7.7	9.2	650	200	450	540	130	410
1951	14.2	6.6	7.6	540	170	370	460	110	350
1950	11.7	5.6	6.1	450	150	300	380	90	290
1945	5.4			310			220		
1940	2.4			160			140		
1935	1.3			110			100		
1930	.8			100			90		

[1] Excluding pensioners.
[2] As of end of the year.

[3] Includes refunds to employees and lump-sum payments under deferred profit-sharing plans.

Government

ELECTIONS AND POLITICS (Series Y 1–204)

Y 1–26. Methods of electing presidential electors, 1788–1836.

Source: Charles O. Paullin, *Atlas of the Historical Geography of the United States*, Carnegie Institution of Washington and American Geographical Society of New York, 1932, p. 89.

The presidential electors of each State, now chosen by popular vote in all States, are selected, according to the Constitution, "in such manner as the legislature thereof may direct." The development of political party direction of the electoral college was not anticipated in the Constitution, and during the early years of the Republic electors were chosen in the several States by a number of different devices. The principal methods were election by the State legislature itself, by State electors popularly chosen to elect presidential electors, and by direct popular vote for the electors. With few exceptions, presidential electors have been elected by popular vote since 1828. The Legislature of South Carolina, however, continued to elect presidential electors until 1860. Since the Civil War, legislatures have chosen electors only twice—in Florida in 1868 and in Colorado in 1876.

Y 27–128. General note.

The election of the President of the United States is provided for in the Constitution, article II, section 1, through the establishment of an electoral college in each State, for each presidential election. The method of casting the electoral vote was modified in 1804 by the adoption of the 12th amendment to the Constitution. The number of electors, and therefore of electoral votes, is "equal to the whole number of Senators and Representatives to which the State may be entitled in Congress." Because of the varied practices in choosing electors in earlier years, the record of popular votes is inadequate to explain the elections until after 1824.

In four elections the entire electoral vote of certain States remained uncast: (a) 1789—no electoral vote was cast in New York because the legislature failed to agree on electors; (b) 1864—no vote in Confederate States (Alabama, Arkansas, Florida, Georgia, Louisiana, Mississippi, North and South Carolina, Tennessee, Texas, and Virginia); (c) 1868—no vote in Mississippi, Texas, and Virginia because these States had not yet been "readmitted" to the Union; (d) 1872—the vote of Arkansas was rejected, the count of the popular vote in Louisiana was disputed, and the votes of both sets of electors were rejected by Congress.

In addition to the sources cited below, the following references were employed in compiling the data for series Y 27–128: U.S. Congress, Clerk of the House of Representatives, *Platforms of the Two Great Political Parties, 1932 to 1944*, pp. 437–447, and *Statistics of the Presidential and Congressional Elections*, various issues; Julius F. Prufer and Stanley J. Folmesbee, *American Political Parties and Presidential Elections*, McKinley Publishing Company, Philadelphia, 1928; Charles O. Paullin, cited above for series Y 1–26, pp. 88–104; Bureau of the Census, *Vote Cast in Presidential and Congressional Elections, 1928–1944*.

Y 27–31. Electoral and popular vote cast for President, by political party, 1789–1956.

Source: 1789–1832, Edward Stanwood, *A History of the Presidency*, two volumes, Houghton Mifflin Company, Boston, 1928, various pages; 1836–1892, W. Dean Burnham, *Presidential Ballots, 1836–1892*, Johns Hopkins Press, Baltimore, 1955, pp. 246–257 and 887–889; 1896–1932, Edgar Eugene Robinson, *The Presidential Vote*, Stanford University Press, Stanford, 1934, pp. 46 and 402; 1936–1944, Edgar Eugene Robinson, *They Voted for Roosevelt*, Stanford University Press, Stanford, 1947, p. 183; 1948–1956, Governmental Affairs Institute, *America Votes*, Macmillan Company, New York, 1958, pp. 1–6.

Y 32–79. Electoral vote cast for President, by political party, for States, 1804–1956.

Source: For complete citation of the following, see sources cited for series Y 27–31: 1804–1832, Edward Stanwood, various pages; 1836–1892, W. Dean Burnham, pp. 887–889; 1896–1932, Robinson, *The Presidential Vote*, p. 402; 1936–1944, Robinson, *They Voted for Roosevelt*, pp. 56–57; 1948–1956, *America Votes*, pp. 1–6.

Y 80–128. Popular vote cast for President, by political party, by States, 1836–1956.

Source: For complete citation of the following, see sources cited for series Y 27–31: 1836–1892, W. Dean Burnham, pp. 246–257; 1896–1932, Robinson, *The Presidential Vote*, pp. 46–53; 1936–1944, Robinson, *They Voted for Roosevelt*, pp. 59–182; 1948–1956, *America Votes*, pp. 1–6.

Variations in figures reported for some States account for small differences between the sum of State data and the total shown for the United States.

Y 129–138. Congressional bills, acts, and resolutions, 1789–1958.

Source: U.S. Congress, *Calendars of the U.S. House of Representatives and History of Legislation*; Library of Congress, Legislative Reference Service, unpublished (typewritten) tabulations; U.S. Congress, *Congressional Record*, various issues.

Some measure of the activities of the U.S. Congress can be gained from the number of bills and resolutions which have been introduced in Congress and from the number of public and private laws which have been passed. The abrupt reduction in the number of private bills enacted into law beginning with the 60th Congress was the result of combining many private bills, particularly pension bills, into omnibus enactments.

Y 139–145. Political party affiliations in Congress and the Presidency, 1789–1958.

Source: 1st to 74th Congresses, Library of Congress, Legislative Reference Service, "Political Trends—Both Houses of Congress—1789–1944" (typewritten tabulation based on *Encyclopedia Americana*, 1936 edition, vol. 7, pp. 516–518, 1st to 69th Congresses; and on Harold R. Bruce, *American Parties and Politics*, 3d edition, Henry Holt and Co., New York, 1936, pp. 174–179, 70th to 74th Congresses); 75th to 85th Congresses, U.S. Congress, *Congressional Directory*, annual volumes.

It is generally recognized today that popular government operates only through the agency of organized political parties. During the early development of the United States, party alignments and the function of political parties were neither fully appreciated nor provided for. Party alignments developed during the formative period, but designations for the different groups were not firmly fixed.

In the classification by party, the titles of parties during early years have been so designated as to be recognizable in the records of the periods concerned, and also to show the thread of continuity which tends to run from early alignments into the present 2-party system. Inasmuch as the party of Thomas Jefferson (generally known at the time as the Republican party) has with a considerable measure of continuity survived to the present time as the Democratic party, the name later accepted by the Jeffersonian Republicans of "Democratic-Republican" is used in the tables to avoid any confusion of the early Jeffersonian Republican with the present-day Republican party. Opposed to the early Republican party was the Federalist party which was dominant in the first national administration and which, with interruptions, can be traced tenuously by elements of popular support through the National Republican, the Whig, and the Free Soil parties to the Republican party of today.

Y 146–149. Vote cast for Representatives, by political party, 1896–1956.

Source: Governmental Affairs Institute, Washington, D. C., records. (Figures adapted by Richard M. Scammon from Cortez A. M. Ewing, *Congressional Elections, 1896–1944*, University of Oklahoma Press, Norman, 1947, and from unpublished work sheets used in its preparation; the first and second editions of Governmental Affairs Institute, *America Votes*, Macmillan Company, New York, 1956 and 1958; and the biennial reports of the Clerk of the House of Representatives giving statistics of Congressional voting.)

Y 150–154. Apportionment of Representatives among the States, 1790–1950.

Source: Bureau of the Census, *U. S. Census of Population: 1950*, vol. I, p. xix, and records.

The number of members in the House of Representatives was fixed by the Congress at the time of each apportionment; since 1912 it has remained constant. The 14th amendment to the Constitution, in effect since 1868, provides that "Representatives shall be apportioned among the several States according to their respective numbers, counting the whole number of persons in each State, excluding Indians not taxed." At the time of the 1940 apportionment, it was determined that there were no longer any Indians who should be classed as "not taxed" under apportionment law.

Prior to the passage of the 14th amendment, Representatives were apportioned among the States "according to their respective numbers, which shall be determined by adding to the whole number of free persons, including those bound to service for a term of years, and excluding Indians not taxed, three-fifths of all other persons." (Art. I, sec. 2.) The original assignment of Representatives for each State, to be in effect until after the first enumeration of the population, and the requirement that each State have at least one Representative, are also included in the Constitution.

Y 155–204. Apportionment of membership in House of Representatives, by States, from adoption of Constitution to 1950.

Source: Bureau of the Census, *Statistical Abstract of the United States, 1958*, p. 350.

Membership is shown as at the date of the fixing of the new House apportionment plus members added for new States admitted during the subsequent decade. No reapportionment was made following the 1920 Census, and no change in total House membership has been made since 1912. Major boundary changes affecting State representation in the House occurred in 1820, when Maine was separated from Massachusetts, and during the Civil War with the separation of West Virginia from Virginia.

Series Y 1–26.   Methods of Electing Presidential Electors: 1788 to 1836

[L—by legislature; G T—by people, on general ticket; D—by people, in districts; A—by people, in the State at large; E—by electors.   The number in parentheses following the symbol "D" is the number of districts into which the State was divided.   As a rule, each district elected 1 elector.   The number in parentheses following the symbol "A" is the number of electors elected at large]

Series No.	State	1836	1832	1828	1824	1820	1816	1812	1808	1804	1800	1796	1792	1788–1789
1	New Hampshire	G T	G T	G T	G T	G T	G T	G T	G T	G T	L	G T and L [1]	G T [2]	G T and L [1]
2	Massachusetts	G T	G T	G T	G T	D (13) and A (2)	L	D (6) [3]	L	D (17) and A (2)	L	D (14) and L [4]	D (4) and L [5]	D (8) and L [6]
3	Rhode Island	G T	G T	G T	G T	G T	G T	G T	G T	G T	G T	L	L	--------
4	Connecticut	G T	G T	G T	G T	G T	L	L	L	L	L	L	L	L
5	New York	G T	G T	D (30) and E [7]	L	L	L	L	L	L	L	L	L	--------
6	New Jersey	G T	G T	G T	G T	G T	G T	L	G T	G T	L	L	L	L
7	Pennsylvania	G T	G T	G T	G T	G T	G T	G T	G T	G T	L	G T	G T	G T
8	Delaware	G T	G T	L	L	L	L	L	L	L	L	L	L	D (3) [8]
9	Maryland	G T	D (4) [9]	D (9) [10]	D (9) [10]	D (9) [10]	D (9) [10]	D (9) [10]	D (9) [10]	D (9) [10]	D (10)	D (10)	G T	G T
10	Virginia	G T	G T	G T	G T	G T	G T	G T	G T	G T	G T	D (21)	D (21)	D (12)
11	North Carolina	G T	G T	G T	G T	G T	G T	L	D (14)	D (14)	D (12)	D (12)	L [11]	--------
12	South Carolina	L	L	L	L	L	L	L	L	L	L	L	L	L
13	Georgia	G T	G T	G T	L	L	L	L	L	L	L	G T	L	L
14	Vermont	G T	G T	G T	L	L	L	L	L	L	L	L	L	--------
15	Kentucky	G T	G T	G T	D (3) [12]	D (3) [13]	D (3) [13]	D (3) [13]	D (2) [13]	D (2) [13]	D (4)	D (4)	D (4)	--------
16	Tennessee	G T	G T	D (11)	D (11)	D (8)	D (8)	D (8)	D (5)	D (5)	E [14]	E [14]	--------	--------
17	Ohio	G T	G T	G T	G T	G T	G T	G T	G T	G T	--------			
18	Louisiana	G T	G T	G T	L	L	L	L	--------					
19	Indiana	G T	G T	G T	G T	L	L	--------						
20	Mississippi	G T	G T	G T	G T	G T	--------							
21	Illinois	G T	G T	G T	D (3)	D (3)	--------							
22	Alabama	G T	G T	G T	G T	L	--------							
23	Maine	G T	G T	D (7) and A (2)	D (7) and A (2)	D (7) and A (2)	--------							
24	Missouri	G T	G T	G T	D (3)	L	--------							
25	Arkansas	G T	--------											
26	Michigan	G T	--------											

[1] A majority of the popular vote was necessary for a choice.   In case of a failure to elect, the legislature supplied the deficiency.

[2] A majority of votes was necessary for a choice.   In case of a failure to elect 1 or more electors a second election was held by the people, at which choice was made from the candidates in the first election who had the most votes.   The number of candidates in the second election was limited to twice the number of electors wanted.

[3] 1 district chose 6 electors; 1, 5 electors; 1, 4 electors; 2, 3 electors each; and 1, 1 elector.

[4] A majority of votes was necessary for a popular choice.   Deficiencies were filled by the General Court, as in 1792.   It also chose 2 electors at large.   In 1796 it chose 9 electors, and the people, 7.

[5] 2 of the districts voted for 5 members each, and 2 for 3 members each.   A majority of votes was necessary for a choice.   In case of a failure to elect by popular vote the General Court supplied the deficiency.   In the election of 1792, the people chose 5 electors and the General Court, 11.

[6] Each of the 8 districts chose 2 electors, from which the General Court (i.e., the legislature) selected 1.   It also elected 2 electors at large.

[7] 1 district elected 3 electors; 2, 2 electors each; and 27, 1 elector each.   The 34 electors thus elected chose 2 presidential electors.

[8] Each qualified voter voted for 1 elector.   The 3 electors who received most votes in the State were elected.

[9] 1 district chose 4 electors; 1, 3 electors; 1, 2 electors; 1, 1 elector.

[10] During the years 1804–1828, Maryland chose 11 electors in 9 districts, 2 of the districts elected 2 members each.

[11] The State was divided into 4 districts, and the members of the legislature residing in each district chose 3 electors.

[12] 2 districts chose 5 electors each, and 1 chose 4 electors.

[13] Each district elected 4 electors.

[14] In 1796 and 1800, Tennessee chose 3 presidential electors—1 each for the districts of Washington, Hamilton, and Mero. 3 "electors" for each county in the State were appointed by the legislature, and the "electors" residing in each of the 3 districts chose 1 of the 3 presidential electors.

Series Y 27–31. Electoral and Popular Vote Cast for President, by Political Party: 1789 to 1956

[Excludes unpledged tickets and minor candidates polling under 10,000 votes; various party labels may have been used by a candidate in different States; the more important of these are listed below]

Year	Number of States	Presidential candidate	Political party	Electoral	Popular
	27	28	29	30	31
1956	48	Dwight D. Eisenhower	Republican	457	35,590,472
		Adlai E. Stevenson	Democratic	¹73	26,022,752
		T. Coleman Andrews	States' Rights		107,929
		Eric Hass	Socialist Labor		44,300
		Enoch A. Holtwick	Prohibition		41,937
1952	48	Dwight D. Eisenhower	Republican	442	33,936,234
		Adlai E. Stevenson	Democratic	89	27,314,992
		Vincent Hallinan	Progressive		140,023
		Stuart Hamblen	Prohibition		72,949
		Eric Hass	Socialist Labor		30,267
		Darlington Hoopes	Socialist		20,203
		Douglas A. MacArthur	Constitution		17,205
		Farrell Dobbs	Socialist Workers		10,312
1948	48	Harry S. Truman	Democratic	303	24,105,812
		Thomas E. Dewey	Republican	189	21,970,065
		Strom Thurmond	States' Rights	39	1,169,063
		Henry Wallace	Progressive		1,157,172
		Norman Thomas	Socialist		139,414
		Claude A. Watson	Prohibition		103,224
		Edward A. Teichert	Socialist Labor		29,244
		Farrell Dobbs	Socialist Workers		13,613
1944	48	Franklin D. Roosevelt	Democratic	432	25,606,585
		Thomas E. Dewey	Republican	99	22,014,745
		Norman Thomas	Socialist		80,518
		Claude A. Watson	Prohibition		74,758
		Edward A. Teichert	Socialist Labor		45,336
1940	48	Franklin D. Roosevelt	Democratic	449	27,307,819
		Wendell L. Willkie	Republican	82	22,321,018
		Norman Thomas	Socialist		99,557
		Roger Q. Babson	Prohibition		57,812
		Earl Browder	Communist		46,251
		John W. Aiken	Socialist Labor		14,892
1936	48	Franklin D. Roosevelt	Democratic	523	27,752,869
		Alfred M. Landon	Republican	8	16,674,665
		William Lemke	Union		882,479
		Norman Thomas	Socialist		187,720
		Earl Browder	Communist		80,159
		D. Leigh Colvin	Prohibition		37,847
		John W. Aiken	Socialist Labor		12,777
1932	48	Franklin D. Roosevelt	Democratic	472	22,809,638
		Herbert C. Hoover	Republican	59	15,758,901
		Norman Thomas	Socialist		881,951
		William Z. Foster	Communist		102,785
		William D. Upshaw	Prohibition		81,869
		Verne L. Reynolds	Socialist Labor		33,276
		William H. Harvey	Liberty		53,425
1928	48	Herbert C. Hoover	Republican	444	21,391,993
		Alfred E. Smith	Democratic	87	15,016,169
		Norman Thomas	Socialist		267,835
		Verne L. Reynolds	Socialist Labor		21,603
		William Z. Foster	Workers		21,181
		William F. Varney	Prohibition		20,106
1924	48	Calvin Coolidge	Republican	382	15,718,211
		John W. Davis	Democratic	136	8,385,283
		Robert M. LaFollette	Progressive	13	4,831,289
		Herman P. Faris	Prohibition		57,520
		Frank T. Johns	Socialist Labor		36,428
		William Z. Foster	Workers		36,386
		Gilbert O. Nations	American		23,967
1920	48	Warren G. Harding	Republican	404	16,143,407
		James M. Cox	Democratic	127	9,130,328
		Eugene V. Debs	Socialist		919,799
		P. P. Christensen	Farmer-Labor		265,411
		Aaron S. Watkins	Prohibition		189,408
		James E. Ferguson	American		48,000
		W. W. Cox	Socialist Labor		31,715
1916	48	Woodrow Wilson	Democratic	277	9,127,695
		Charles E. Hughes	Republican	254	8,533,507
		A. L. Benson	Socialist		585,113
		J. Frank Hanly	Prohibition		220,506
		Arthur E. Reimer	Socialist Labor		13,403
1912	48	Woodrow Wilson	Democratic	435	6,296,547
		Theodore Roosevelt	Progressive	88	4,118,571
		William H. Taft	Republican	8	3,486,720
		Eugene V. Debs	Socialist		900,672
		Eugene W. Chafin	Prohibition		206,275
		Arthur E. Reimer	Socialist Labor		28,750
1908	46	William H. Taft	Republican	321	7,675,320
		William J. Bryan	Democratic	162	6,412,294
		Eugene V. Debs	Socialist		420,793
		Eugene W. Chafin	Prohibition		253,840
		Thomas L. Hisgen	Independence		82,872
		Thomas E. Watson	People's		29,100
		August Gillhaus	Socialist Labor		14,021
1904	45	Theodore Roosevelt	Republican	336	7,628,461
		Alton B. Parker	Democratic	140	5,084,223
		Eugene V. Debs	Socialist		402,283
		Silas C. Swallow	Prohibition		258,536
		Thomas E. Watson	People's		117,183
		Charles H. Corregan	Socialist Labor		31,249
1900	45	William McKinley	Republican	292	7,218,491
		William J. Bryan	Democratic ²	155	6,356,734
		John C. Wooley	Prohibition		208,914
		Eugene V. Debs	Socialist		87,814
		Wharton Barker	People's		50,373
		Jos. F. Malloney	Socialist Labor		39,739
1896	45	William McKinley	Republican	271	7,102,246
		William J. Bryan	Democratic ²	176	6,492,559
		John M. Palmer	National Democratic		133,148
		Joshua Levering	Prohibition		132,007
		Charles H. Matchett	Socialist Labor		36,274
		Charles E. Bentley	Nationalist		13,969
1892	44	Grover Cleveland	Democratic	277	5,555,426
		Benjamin Harrison	Republican	145	5,182,690
		James B. Weaver	People's	22	1,029,846
		John Bidwell	Prohibition		264,133
		Simon Wing	Socialist Labor		21,164
1888	38	Benjamin Harrison	Republican	233	5,447,129
		Grover Cleveland	Democratic	168	5,537,857
		Clinton B. Fisk	Prohibition		249,506
		Anson J. Streeter	Union Labor		146,935
1884	38	Grover Cleveland	Democratic	219	4,879,507
		James G. Blaine	Republican	182	4,850,293
		Benjamin F. Butler	Greenback-Labor		175,370
		John P. St. John	Prohibition		150,369
1880	38	James A. Garfield	Republican	214	4,453,295
		Winfield S. Hancock	Democratic	155	4,414,082
		James B. Weaver	Greenback-Labor		308,578
		Neal Dow	Prohibition		10,305
1876	38	Rutherford B. Hayes	Republican	185	4,036,572
		Samuel J. Tilden	Democratic	184	4,284,020
		Peter Cooper	Greenback		81,737
1872	37	Ulysses S. Grant	Republican	286	3,596,745
		Horace Greeley	Democratic	(²)	2,843,446
		Charles O'Connor	Straight Democratic		29,489
		Thomas A. Hendricks	Independent-Democratic	42	
		B. Gratz Brown	Democratic	18	
		Charles J. Jenkins	Democratic	2	
		David Davis	Democratic	1	
		(Not voted)		17	
1868	37	Ulysses S. Grant	Republican	214	3,013,421
		Horatio Seymour	Democratic	80	2,706,829
		(Not voted)		23	
1864	36	Abraham Lincoln	Republican	212	2,206,938
		George B. McClellan	Democratic	21	1,803,787
		(Not voted)		81	
1860	33	Abraham Lincoln	Republican	180	1,865,593
		J. C. Breckinridge	Democratic (S)	72	848,356
		Stephen A. Douglas	Democratic	12	1,382,713
		John Bell	Constitutional Union	39	592,906
1856	31	James Buchanan	Democratic	174	1,832,955
		John C. Fremont	Republican	114	1,339,932
		Millard Fillmore	American	8	871,731
1852	31	Franklin Pierce	Democratic	254	1,601,117
		Winfield Scott	Whig	42	1,385,453
		John P. Hale	Free Soil		155,825

See footnotes at end of table.

Series Y 27–31. Electoral and Popular Vote Cast for President, by Political Party: 1789 to 1956—Con.

Year	Number of States	Presidential candidate	Political party	Vote cast Electoral	Vote cast Popular	Year	Number of States	Presidential candidate	Political party	Vote cast, electoral
	27	28	29	30	31		27	28	29	30
1848	30	Zachary Taylor	Whig	163	1,360,967	1804	17	Thomas Jefferson	Democratic-Republican	162
		Lewis Cass	Democratic	127	1,222,342					
		Martin Van Buren	Free Soil	----------	291,263			C. C. Pinckney	Federalist	14
1844	26	James K. Polk	Democratic	170	1,338,464	1800 [6]	16	Thomas Jefferson	Democratic-Republican	73
		Henry Clay	Whig	105	1,300,097			Aaron Burr	Democratic-Republican	73
		James G. Birney	Liberty	----------	62,300			John Adams	Federalist	65
1840	26	William H. Harrison	Whig	234	1,274,624			C. C. Pinckney	Federalist	64
		Martin Van Buren	Democratic	60	1,127,781			John Jay	Federalist	1
1836	26	Martin Van Buren	Democratic	170	765,483					
		William H. Harrison	Whig	73	}	1796 [6]	16	John Adams	Federalist	71
		Hugh L. White	Whig	26	[4] 739,795			Thomas Jefferson	Democratic-Republican	68
		Daniel Webster	Whig	14				Thomas Pinckney	Federalist	59
		W. P. Mangum	Anti-Jackson	11	----------			Aaron Burr	Anti-Federalist	30
1832	24	Andrew Jackson	Democratic	219	687,502			Samuel Adams	Democratic-Republican	15
		Henry Clay	National Republican	49	530,189			Oliver Ellsworth	Federalist	11
		William Wirt	Anti-Masonic	7	----------			George Clinton	Democratic-Republican	7
		John Floyd	Nullifiers	11	----------			John Jay	Independent-Federalist	5
		(Not voted)		2	----------			James Iredell	Federalist	3
1828	24	Andrew Jackson	Democratic	178	647,286			George Washington	Federalist	2
		John Q. Adams	National Republican	83	508,064			John Henry	Independent	2
								S. Johnston	Independent-Federalist	2
1824	24	John Q. Adams	No distinct party designations	[5] 84	108,740			C. C. Pickney	Independent-Federalist	1
		Andrew Jackson		[5] 99	153,544					
		Henry Clay		37	47,136	1792 [6]	15	George Washington	Federalist	132
		W. H. Crawford		41	46,618			John Adams	Federalist	77
1820	24	James Monroe	Republican	231	----------			George Clinton	Democratic-Republican	50
		John Q. Adams	Independent-Republican	1	----------			Thomas Jefferson		4
		(Not voted)		3	----------			Aaron Burr		1
1816	19	James Monroe	Republican	183	----------					
		Rufus King	Federalist	34	----------	1789 [6]	11	George Washington		69
		(Not voted)		4	----------			John Adams		34
1812	18	James Madison	Democratic-Republican	128	----------			John Jay		9
		De Witt Clinton	Fusion	89	----------			R. H. Harrison		6
		(Not voted)		1	----------			John Rutledge		6
								John Hancock		4
1808	17	James Madison	Democratic-Republican	122	----------			George Clinton		3
								Samuel Huntington		2
		C. C. Pinckney	Federalist	47	----------			John Milton		2
		George Clinton	Independent-Republican	6	----------			James Armstrong		1
								Benjamin Lincoln		1
		(Not voted)		1	----------			Edward Telfair		1
								(Not voted)		12

[1] 1 Democratic elector voted for Walter Jones.
[2] Includes a variety of joint tickets with People's Party electors committed to Bryan.
[3] Greeley died shortly after the election and presidential electors supporting him cast their votes as indicated, including 3 for Greeley, which were not counted.
[4] Whig tickets were pledged to various candidates in various States.
[5] No candidate having a majority in the electoral college, the election was decided in the House of Representatives.

[6] Prior to the election of 1804, each elector voted for 2 candidates for President; the one receiving the highest number of votes, if a majority, was declared elected President, the next highest, Vice President. This provision was modified by adoption of the 12th amendment which was proposed by the 8th Congress, Dec. 12, 1803, and declared ratified by the legislatures of three-fourths of the States in a proclamation of the Secretary of State, Sept. 25, 1804.

Series Y 32–79. Electoral Vote Cast for President, by Political Party, for States: 1804 to 1956

[Electoral votes are given for the period following the revision of the method of election in 1804, using these letter symbols for the various political parties: A—American; AJ—Anti-Jackson; AM—Anti-Masonic; C—Coalition; CU—Constitutional Union; D—Democratic; DR—Democratic-Republican; F—Federalist; N—Nullification; NR—National Republican; PP—People's Party; PR—Progressive; R—Republican; SD—Southern Democratic; SR—States' Rights; W—Whig. In the 1824 election, party lines were so indistinct that names of the individual candidates have been used]

Series No.	State	1956	1952	1948	1944	1940	1936	1932	1928	1924	1920	1916	1912	1908
32	Alabama	[1]10D	11D	11SR	11D	11D	11D	11D	12D	12D	12D	12D	12D	11D
33	Arizona	4R	4R	4D	4D	3D	3D	3D	3R	3R	3R	3D	3D	------
34	Arkansas	8D	8D	9D	9D	9D	9D	9D	9D	9D	9D	9D	9D	9D
35	California	32R	32R	25D	25D	22D	22D	22D	13R	13R	13R	13D	2D, 11PR	10R
36	Colorado	6R	6R	6D	6R	6R	6D	6D	6R	6R	6R	6D	6D	5D
37	Connecticut	8R	8R	8R	8D	8D	8D	8R	7R	7R	7R	7R	7D	7R
38	Delaware	3R	3R	3R	3D	3D	3D	3R	3R	3R	3R	3R	3D	3R
39	Florida	10R	10R	8D	8D	7D	7D	7D	6R	6D	6D	6D	6D	5D
40	Georgia	12D	12D	12D	12D	12D	12D	12D	14D	14D	14D	14D	14D	13D
41	Idaho	4R	4R	4D	4D	4D	4D	4D	4R	4R	4R	4D	4D	3R
42	Illinois	27R	27R	28D	28D	29D	29D	29D	29R	29R	29R	29R	29D	27R
43	Indiana	13R	13R	13R	13R	14R	14D	14D	15R	15R	15R	15R	15D	15R
44	Iowa	10R	10R	10D	10R	11R	11D	11D	13R	13R	13R	13D	13D	13R
45	Kansas	8R	8R	8R	8R	9R	9D	9D	10R	10R	10R	10D	10D	10R
46	Kentucky	10R	10R	11D	11D	11D	11D	11D	13R	13R	13D	13D	13D	13D
47	Louisiana	10R	10D	10SR	10D	10D	10D	10D	10D	10D	10D	10D	10D	9D
48	Maine	5R	5R	5R	5R	5R	5R	5R	6R	6R	6R	6R	6D	6R
49	Maryland	9R	9R	8R	8D	8D	8D	8D	8R	8R	8R	8D	8D	2R, 6D
50	Massachusetts	16R	16R	16D	16D	17D	17D	17D	18D	18R	18R	18R	18R	16R
51	Michigan	20R	20R	19R	19D	19R	19D	19D	15R	15R	15R	15R	15PR	14R
52	Minnesota	11R	11R	11D	11D	11D	11D	11D	12R	12R	12R	12R	12PR	11R
53	Mississippi	8D	8D	9SR	9D	9D	9D	9D	10D	10D	10D	10D	10D	10D
54	Missouri	13D	13R	15D	15D	15D	15D	15D	18R	18R	18R	18D	18D	18R
55	Montana	4R	4R	4D	4D	4D	4D	4D	4R	4R	4R	4D	4D	3R
56	Nebraska	6R	6R	6R	6R	7R	7D	7D	8R	8R	8R	8D	8D	8D
57	Nevada	3R	3R	3D	3D	3D	3D	3D	3R	3R	3R	3D	3D	3D
58	New Hampshire	4R	4R	4R	4R	4D	4D	4R	4R	4R	4R	4D	4D	4R
59	New Jersey	16R	16R	16R	16D	16D	16D	16D	14R	14R	14R	14R	14D	12R
60	New Mexico	4R	4R	4D	4D	3D	3D	3D	3R	3R	3R	3D	3D	------
61	New York	45R	45R	47R	47D	47D	47D	47D	45R	45R	45R	45R	45D	39R
62	North Carolina	14D	14D	14D	14D	13D	13D	13D	12R	12D	12D	12D	12D	12D
63	North Dakota	4R	4R	4R	4R	4R	4D	4D	5R	5R	5R	5D	5D	4R
64	Ohio	25R	25R	25D	25R	26D	26D	26D	24R	24R	24R	24D	24D	23R
65	Oklahoma	8R	8R	10D	10D	11D	11D	11D	10R	10D	10D	10D	10D	7D
66	Oregon	6R	6R	6R	6R	5D	5D	5D	5R	5R	5R	5R	5R	4R
67	Pennsylvania	32R	32R	35D	35D	36D	36D	36R	38R	38R	38R	38R	38PR	34R
68	Rhode Island	4R	4R	4D	4D	4D	4D	4D	5D	5R	5R	5R	5D	4R
69	South Carolina	8D	8D	8SR	8D	8D	8D	8D	9D	9D	9D	9D	9D	9D
70	South Dakota	4R	4R	4R	4R	4R	4D	4D	5R	5R	5R	5R	5PR	4R
71	Tennessee	11R	11R	11D, 1SR	12D	11D	11D	11D	12R	12D	12D	12D	12D	12D
72	Texas	24R	24R	23D	23D	23D	23D	23D	20R	20D	20D	20D	20D	18D
73	Utah	4R	4R	4D	4D	4D	4D	4D	4R	4R	4R	4D	4R	3R
74	Vermont	3R	3R	3R	3R	3R	3R	3R	4R	4R	4R	4R	4R	4R
75	Virginia	12R	12R	11D	11D	11D	11D	11D	12R	12D	12D	12D	12D	12D
76	Washington	9R	9R	8D	8D	8D	8D	8D	7R	7R	7R	7D	7PR	5R
77	West Virginia	8R	8D	8D	8D	8D	8D	8D	8R	8R	8R	7R, 1D	8D	7R
78	Wisconsin	12R	12R	12D	12R	12D	12D	12D	13R	13PR	13R	13R	13D	13R
79	Wyoming	3R	3R	3D	3R	3D	3D	3D	3R	3R	3R	3R	3D	3R

Series No.	State	1904	1900	1896 [2]	1892	1888	1884	1880	1876	1872 [3]	1868 [4]	1864 [5]	1860	1856
32	Alabama	11D	11D	11D	11D	10D	10D	10D	10D	10R	8R	--------	9SD	9D
34	Arkansas	9D	8D	8D	8D	7D	7D	6D	6D	--------	5R	--------	4SD	4D
35	California	10R	9R	8R, 1D	1R, 8D	8R	8R	1R, 5D	6R	6R	5R	5R	4R	4D
36	Colorado	5R	4D	4D	4PP	3R	3R	3R	3R	--------	--------	--------	--------	--------
37	Connecticut	7R	6R	6R	6D	6D	6D	6R	6D	6R	6R	6R	6R	6R
38	Delaware	3R	3R	3R	3D	3D	3D	3D	3D	3R	3D	3D	3SD	3D
39	Florida	5D	4D	4D	4D	4D	4D	4D	4R	4R	3R	--------	3SD	3D
40	Georgia	13D	13D	13D	13D	12D	12D	11D	11D	[6]8D	9D	--------	10SD	10D
41	Idaho	3R	3D	3D	3PP	--------	--------	--------	--------	--------	--------	--------	--------	--------
42	Illinois	27R	24R	24R	24D	22R	22R	21R	21R	21R	16R	16R	11R	11D
43	Indiana	15R	15R	15R	15D	15R	15D	15R	15D	15R	13R	13R	13R	13D
44	Iowa	13R	13R	13R	13R	13R	13R	11R	11R	11R	8R	8R	4R	4R
45	Kansas	10R	10R	10D	10PP	9R	9R	5R	5R	5R	3R	3R	--------	--------
46	Kentucky	13D	13D	12R, 1D	13D	13D	13D	12D	12D	12D	11D	11D	12CU	12D
47	Louisiana	9D	8D	8D	8D	8D	8D	8D	8R	--------	7D	--------	6SD	6D
48	Maine	6R	6R	6R	6R	6R	6R	7R	7R	7R	7R	7R	8R	8R
49	Maryland	1R, 7D	8R	8R	8D	8D	8D	8D	8D	8D	7D	7R	8SD	8A
50	Massachusetts	16R	15R	15R	15R	14R	14R	13R	13R	13R	12R	12R	13R	14R
51	Michigan	14R	14R	14R	9R, 5D	13R	13R	11R	11R	11R	8R	8R	6R	6R
52	Minnesota	11R	9R	9R	9R	7R	7R	5R	5R	5R	4R	4R	4R	--------
53	Mississippi	10D	9D	9D	9D	9D	9D	8D	8D	8R	--------	--------	7SD	7D
54	Missouri	18R	17R	17D	17D	16D	16D	15D	15D	15D	11R	11R	9D	9D
55	Montana	3R	3D	3D	3R	--------	--------	--------	--------	--------	--------	--------	--------	--------
56	Nebraska	8R	8R	8D	8R	5R	5R	3R	3R	3R	3R	--------	--------	--------
57	Nevada	3R	3D	3D	3PP	3R	3R	3D	3R	3R	3R	2R	--------	--------
58	New Hampshire	4R	4R	4R	4R	4R	4R	5R	5R	5R	5R	5R	5R	5R
59	New Jersey	12R	10R	10R	10D	9D	9D	9D	9D	9R	7D	7D	4R, 3D	7D
61	New York	39R	36R	36R	36D	36R	36D	35R	35D	35R	33D	33R	35R	35R

See footnotes at end of table.

Series Y 32–79. Electoral Vote Cast for President, by Political Party, for States: 1804 to 1956—Con.

[Electoral votes are given for the period following the revision of the method of election in 1804, using these letter symbols for the various political parties: A—American; AJ—Anti-Jackson; AM—Anti-Masonic; C—Coalition; CU—Constitutional Union; D—Democratic; DR—Democratic-Republican; F—Federalist; N—Nullification; NR—National Republican; PP—People's Party; PR—Progressive; R—Republican; SD—Southern Democratic; SR—States' Rights; W—Whig. In the 1824 election, party lines were so indistinct that names of the individual candidates have been used]

Series No.	State	1904	1900	1896 [2]	1892	1888	1884	1880	1876	1872 [3]	1868 [4]	1864 [5]	1860	1856
62	North Carolina	12D	11D	11D	11D	11D	11D	10D	10D	10R	9R	----	10SD	10D
63	North Dakota	4R	3R	3R	(7)									
64	Ohio	23R	23R	23R	22R, 1D	23R	23R	22R	22R	22R	21R	21R	23R	23R
66	Oregon	4R	4R	4R	3R, 1PP	3R	3R	3R	3R	3R	3D	3R	3R	
67	Pennsylvania	34R	32R	32R	32R	30R	30R	29R	29R	29R	26R	26R	27R	27D
68	Rhode Island	4R	4R	4R	4R	4R	4R	4R	4R	4R	4R	4R	4R	4R
69	South Carolina	9D	9D	9D	9D	9D	9D	7D	7D	7R	6R	----	8SD	8D
70	South Dakota	4R	4R	4D	4R									
71	Tennessee	12D	12D	12D	12D	12D	12D	12D	12D	12D	10R	----	12CU	12D
72	Texas	18D	15D	15D	15D	13D	13D	8D	8D	8D			4SD	4D
73	Utah	3R	3R	3D										
74	Vermont	4R	4R	4R	4R	4R	4R	5R	5R	5R	5R	5R	5R	5R
75	Virginia	12D	12D	12D	12D	12D	12D	11D	11D	11R			15CU	15D
76	Washington	5R	4R	4D	4R									
77	West Virginia	7R	6R	6R	6D	6D	6D	5D	5D	5R	5R	5R		
78	Wisconsin	13R	12R	12R	12D	11R	11R	10R	10R	10R	8R	8R	5R	
79	Wyoming	3R	3R	3D	3R									

Series No.	State	1852	1848	1844	1840	1836 [8]	1832	1828	1824	1820	1816	1812	1808	1804
32	Alabama	9D	9D	9D	7D	7D	7D	5D	5 Jackson	3DR				
34	Arkansas	4D	3D	3D	3D	3D								
35	California	4D												
37	Connecticut	6D	6W	6W	8W	8D	8NR	8NR	8 Adams	9DR	9F	9C	9F	9F
38	Delaware	3D	3W	3W	3W	3W	3NR	3NR	(9)	4DR	[10]3F	4C	3F	3F
39	Florida	3D	3W											
40	Georgia	10D	10W	10D	11W	11W	11D	9D	9 Crawford	8DR	8DR	8DR	6DR	6DR
42	Illinois	11D	9D	9D	5D	5D	5D	3D	(11)	3DR				
43	Indiana	13D	12D	12D	9W	9W	9D	5D	5 Jackson	3DR	3DR			
44	Iowa	4D	4D											
46	Kentucky	12W	12W	12W	15W	15W	15NR	14D	14 Clay	12DR	12DR	12DR	[10]7DR	8DR
47	Louisiana	6D	6W	6D	5W	5D	5D	5D	(12)	3DR	3DR	3DR		
48	Maine	8D	9D	9D	10W	10D	10D	8NR, 1D	9 Adams	9DR				
49	Maryland	8D	8W	8W	10W	10W	[13]5NR, 3D	6NR, 5D	(14)	11DR	[15]8DR	5C, 6DR	2F, 9DR	2F, 9DR
50	Massachusetts	13W	12W	12W	14W	14W	14NR	15NR	15 Adams	15DR	22F	22C	19F	19DR
51	Michigan	6D	5D	5D	3W	3D								
53	Mississippi	7D	6D	6D	4W	4D	4D	3D	3 Jackson	[10]2DR				
54	Missouri	9D	7D	7D	4D	4D	4D	3D	3 Clay	3DR				
58	New Hampshire	5D	6D	6D	7D	7D	7D	8NR	8 Adams	[16]7DR	8DR	8C	7F	7DR
59	New Jersey	7D	7W	7W	8W	8W	8D	8NR	8 Jackson	8DR	8DR	8C	8DR	8DR
61	New York	35D	36W	36D	42W	42D	42D	16NR, 20D	(17)	29DR	29DR	29C	[18]13DR	19DR
62	North Carolina	10D	11W	11W	15W	15D	15D	15D	15 Jackson	15DR	15DR	15DR	3F, 11DR	14DR
64	Ohio	23D	23D	23W	21W	21W	21D	16D	16 Clay	8DR	8DR	[10]7DR	3DR	3DR
67	Pennsylvania	27D	26W	26D	30W	30D	30D	28D	28 Jackson	[10]24DR	25DR	25DR	20DR	20DR
68	Rhode Island	4D	4W	4W	4W	4D	4NR	4NR	4 Adams	4DR	4DR	4C	4F	4DR
69	South Carolina	8D	9D	9D	11D	11AJ	11N	11D	11 Jackson	11DR	11DR	11DR	10DR	10DR
71	Tennessee	12W	13W	13W	15W	15W	15D	11D	11 Jackson	[10]7DR	8DR	8DR	5DR	5DR
72	Texas	4D	4D											
74	Vermont	5W	6W	6W	7W	7W	7AM	7NR	7 Adams	8DR	8DR	8DR	6DR	6DR
75	Virginia	15D	17D	17D	23D	23D	23D	24D	24 Crawford	25DR	25DR	25DR	24DR	24DR
78	Wisconsin	5D	4D											

[1] 1 elector voted for Walter Jones.
[2] Electors classed here as Democratic were elected in many States on joint Democratic and People's Party fusion tickets.
[3] Electoral votes from Arkansas and Louisiana were not counted. Due to the death of Greeley, Democratic electors divided their votes among Hendricks (42), Brown (18), Jenkins (2), and Davis (1).
[4] Mississippi, Texas, and Virginia did not participate in the election.
[5] Confederate States did not participate in the election.
[6] Excludes 3 votes for Greeley, which were not counted.
[7] 1 each for Republican, Democratic, and People's Party.
[8] Whig electors divided their votes among Harrison (73), White (26), and Webster (14).

[9] Vote was as follows: 2 for Crawford, 1 for Adams.
[10] 1 elector did not vote.
[11] Vote was as follows: 2 for Jackson, 1 for Adams.
[12] Vote was as follows: 3 for Jackson, 2 for Adams.
[13] 2 electors did not vote.
[14] Vote was as follows: 7 for Jackson, 3 for Adams, 1 for Crawford.
[15] 3 electors did not vote.
[16] 1 elector voted for John Quincy Adams.
[17] Vote was as follows: 26 for Adams, 5 for Crawford, 4 for Clay, 1 for Jackson.
[18] 6 electors voted for George Clinton.

Series Y 80–128.   Popular Vote Cast for President, by Political Party, by States: 1836 to 1956

[In thousands. Rep.—Republican; Dem.—Democratic. Vote listed is normally that of the highest candidate for presidential elector for each party. Democratic vote in 1896 and 1900 includes a variety of joint elector tickets with the People's Party, and party totals generally include votes cast for the presidential candidate under other designations than that of the party itself]

Series No.	State	1956 Total	Rep.	Dem.	1952 Total	Rep.	Dem.	1948 Total	Rep.	Dem.	States' Rights	1944 Total	Rep.	Dem.	1940 Total	Rep.	Dem.
80	**United States**	62,034	35,590	26,023	61,551	33,936	27,315	48,691	21,970	24,106	1,169	47,969	22,015	25,607	49,891	22,321	27,308
81	Alabama	497	196	281	426	149	275	215	41	----	171	245	45	199	294	42	251
82	Arizona	290	177	113	261	152	109	177	78	95		138	56	81	150	54	95
83	Arkansas	407	186	213	405	177	226	242	51	150	40	213	64	149	200	42	157
84	California	5,466	3,028	2,420	5,142	2,897	2,198	4,022	1,895	1,913	1	3,521	1,513	1,989	3,269	1,351	1,878
85	Colorado	664	394	258	630	380	246	515	240	267		505	269	234	549	280	266
86	Connecticut	1,117	712	405	1,097	611	482	884	438	423		832	391	435	782	361	418
87	Delaware	178	98	79	174	90	83	139	70	68		125	57	68	136	61	75
88	Florida	1,126	644	480	989	544	445	578	194	282	90	483	143	339	485	126	359
89	Georgia	670	223	445	656	199	457	419	77	255	85	328	57	268	313	24	265
90	Idaho	273	167	106	276	181	95	215	102	107		208	100	107	235	107	128
91	Illinois	4,407	2,623	1,776	4,481	2,457	2,014	3,984	1,961	1,995		4,036	1,939	2,079	4,218	2,047	2,150
92	Indiana	1,975	1,183	784	1,955	1,136	802	1,656	821	808		1,672	876	781	1,783	899	874
93	Iowa	1,235	729	502	1,269	809	452	1,038	494	522		1,053	547	500	1,215	632	579
94	Kansas	866	567	296	896	616	273	789	423	352		734	442	287	860	489	365
95	Kentucky	1,054	572	476	993	495	496	823	341	467	10	868	392	473	968	410	557
96	Louisiana	618	329	244	652	307	345	416	73	136	204	349	68	282	372	52	320
97	Maine	352	249	102	352	232	119	265	150	112		296	155	141	321	164	156
98	Maryland	933	560	373	902	499	395	597	295	287	2	608	293	315	660	270	385
99	Massachusetts	2,349	1,393	948	2,383	1,292	1,084	2,107	909	1,152		1,961	921	1,035	2,027	940	1,077
100	Michigan	3,080	1,714	1,360	2,799	1,552	1,231	2,110	1,039	1,003		2,205	1,084	1,107	2,086	1,040	1,033
101	Minnesota	1,340	719	618	1,379	763	608	1,212	484	693		1,126	527	590	1,251	596	644
102	Mississippi	248	61	144	286	113	173	192	5	19	168	180	12	169	176	7	168
103	Missouri	1,833	914	918	1,892	959	930	1,579	655	917		1,572	761	807	1,834	871	958
104	Montana	271	155	116	265	157	106	224	97	119		207	93	113	248	100	146
105	Nebraska	577	378	199	610	422	188	489	265	224		563	330	233	616	352	264
106	Nevada	97	56	41	82	51	32	62	29	31		54	25	30	53	21	32
107	New Hampshire	267	177	90	273	166	107	231	121	108		230	110	120	235	110	125
108	New Jersey	2,484	1,607	850	2,419	1,374	1,016	1,950	981	895		1,964	961	988	1,974	945	1,016
109	New Mexico	254	147	106	239	132	106	187	80	105		152	71	81	183	79	104
110	New York	7,096	4,346	2,748	7,128	3,953	3,105	6,177	2,841	2,780		6,317	2,988	3,304	6,302	3,027	3,252
111	North Carolina	1,166	575	591	1,211	558	653	791	259	459	70	791	263	527	823	214	609
112	North Dakota	254	157	97	270	192	77	221	115	96		220	119	100	281	155	124
113	Ohio	3,702	2,263	1,440	3,701	2,100	1,600	2,936	1,446	1,453		3,153	1,582	1,571	3,320	1,587	1,733
114	Oklahoma	859	474	386	949	518	431	722	269	453		722	319	401	826	349	474
115	Oregon	736	406	329	695	421	271	524	261	243		480	225	249	481	220	258
116	Pennsylvania	4,577	2,585	1,982	4,581	2,416	2,146	3,735	1,902	1,752		3,795	1,835	1,940	4,078	1,890	2,171
117	Rhode Island	388	226	162	414	211	203	328	136	189		299	123	175	321	139	182
118	South Carolina	301	76	136	341	168	173	143	5	34	103	103	5	91	100	2	95
119	South Dakota	294	172	122	294	204	90	250	130	118		232	135	97	308	177	131
120	Tennessee	939	462	457	893	446	444	550	203	270	74	511	200	309	523	169	352
121	Texas	1,955	1,081	860	2,076	1,103	969	1,147	282	751	107	1,144	192	816	1,117	212	905
122	Utah	334	216	118	330	194	135	276	124	149		248	98	150	248	93	154
123	Vermont	153	110	43	154	110	43	123	76	46		125	72	54	143	78	64
124	Virginia	698	386	268	620	349	269	419	172	201	43	388	145	242	347	109	236
125	Washington	1,151	620	523	1,103	599	493	905	386	476		856	362	487	794	322	462
126	West Virginia	831	449	382	874	420	454	749	316	429		716	323	393	868	372	496
127	Wisconsin	1,551	955	587	1,607	980	622	1,277	591	647		1,339	675	650	1,406	679	705
128	Wyoming	124	75	50	129	81	48	101	48	52		101	52	49	112	53	59

Series No.	State	1936 Total	Rep.	Dem.	1932 Total	Rep.	Dem.	1928 Total	Rep.	Dem.	1924 Total	Rep.	Dem.	Progressive	1920 Total	Rep.	Dem.
80	**United States**	45,643	16,675	27,753	39,732	15,759	22,810	36,812	21,392	15,016	29,086	15,718	8,385	4,831	26,748	16,143	9,130
81	Alabama	276	35	238	242	35	205	249	121	128	165	43	113	8	234	75	156
82	Arizona	124	33	87	118	36	79	91	53	39	74	31	26	17	67	37	30
83	Arkansas	179	32	147	219	27	190	202	78	123	139	41	85	13	183	72	106
84	California	2,638	836	1,767	2,266	848	1,324	1,797	1,162	614	1,282	733	106	425	943	625	229
85	Colorado	489	181	295	457	190	251	392	254	133	342	195	75	70	292	173	105
86	Connecticut	691	279	382	594	288	282	553	297	252	400	246	110	42	366	229	121
87	Delaware	128	54	70	113	57	54	105	69	35	90	52	33	5	95	53	40
88	Florida	327	78	249	275	69	206	254	144	102	109	31	62	9	145	45	91
89	Georgia	293	37	255	256	20	234	231	65	130	166	30	123	13	149	43	106
90	Idaho	200	66	126	187	71	109	154	100	53	148	70	24	54	136	89	47
91	Illinois	3,957	1,570	2,283	3,408	1,433	1,882	3,107	1,769	1,313	2,470	1,453	577	432	2,095	1,420	534
92	Indiana	1,651	692	935	1,575	677	862	1,421	848	563	1,272	703	492	72	1,263	696	511
93	Iowa	1,143	488	622	1,037	414	598	1,010	624	379	972	537	160	274	895	635	228
94	Kansas	859	394	462	790	348	423	713	514	193	662	408	156	98	570	369	185
95	Kentucky	923	370	539	983	395	581	941	558	381	814	397	376	38	919	452	456
96	Louisiana	330	37	293	269	19	249	216	51	165	122	25	93	4	126	39	88
97	Maine	304	169	126	298	167	129	262	180	81	192	138	42	11	198	136	59
98	Maryland	625	231	390	511	184	314	528	301	224	359	162	148	47	428	236	181
99	Massachusetts	1,840	769	943	1,580	737	800	1,578	776	793	1,130	703	281	141	994	681	277
100	Michigan	1,805	700	1,017	1,665	740	872	1,372	965	397	1,160	875	152	122	1,038	756	231
101	Minnesota	1,130	350	699	1,003	364	601	971	561	396	822	421	56	339	736	519	143
102	Mississippi	162	4	157	146	5	140	152	26	125	112	8	100	3	82	12	69
103	Missouri	1,829	698	1,111	1,610	565	1,025	1,501	834	663	1,310	648	575	84	1,332	727	575

Series Y 80-128. Popular Vote Cast for President, by Political Party, by States: 1836 to 1956—Con.

[In thousands. Rep.—Republican; Dem.—Democratic]

Series No.	State	1936 Total	1936 Rep.	1936 Dem.	1932 Total	1932 Rep.	1932 Dem.	1928 Total	1928 Rep.	1928 Dem.	1924 Total	1924 Rep.	1924 Dem.	1924 Progressive	1920 Total	1920 Rep.	1920 Dem.
104	Montana	231	64	160	216	78	127	194	113	79	174	74	34	66	179	109	57
105	Nebraska	608	248	347	570	201	359	547	346	198	464	219	137	106	383	248	120
106	Nevada	44	12	32	41	13	29	32	18	14	27	11	6	10	27	15	10
107	New Hampshire	218	105	108	206	104	101	197	115	81	165	99	57	9	159	95	63
108	New Jersey	1,819	719	1,084	1,630	775	806	1,548	925	616	1,086	675	298	109	904	611	257
109	New Mexico	169	62	106	151	54	95	118	70	48	114	55	49	10	106	58	47
110	New York	5,596	2,181	3,293	4,689	1,938	2,535	4,406	2,193	2,090	3,264	1,820	951	475	2,899	1,871	781
111	North Carolina	839	223	616	712	208	498	635	349	286	482	191	284	7	538	233	305
112	North Dakota	274	73	163	256	72	178	240	131	107	199	95	14	90	204	160	37
113	Ohio	3,012	1,128	1,747	2,610	1,228	1,302	2,508	1,628	864	2,016	1,176	478	358	2,021	1,182	780
114	Oklahoma	750	245	501	705	188	516	618	394	219	528	226	256	41	489	248	218
115	Oregon	414	123	267	369	136	214	320	205	109	279	143	68	68	239	144	80
116	Pennsylvania	4,138	1,690	2,354	2,859	1,454	1,296	3,160	2,055	1,077	2,145	1,401	409	308	1,853	1,218	504
117	Rhode Island	310	125	164	266	115	147	237	118	119	210	125	77	8	168	107	55
118	South Carolina	115	2	114	104	2	102	69	3	63	51	1	49	1	67	2	64
119	South Dakota	296	126	160	288	99	184	262	158	103	204	101	27	75	182	111	36
120	Tennessee	477	147	328	390	127	259	353	195	157	301	131	159	11	428	219	207
121	Texas	850	103	742	856	98	753	708	367	340	656	130	483	43	486	115	288
122	Utah	217	65	150	207	85	117	177	95	81	157	77	47	33	146	82	57
123	Vermont	144	81	62	137	79	56	135	90	44	103	80	16	6	90	68	21
124	Virginia	335	98	235	298	90	204	305	165	140	224	73	140	10	231	87	142
125	Washington	692	207	460	615	209	353	501	336	157	422	220	43	151	399	223	84
126	West Virginia	830	325	503	744	331	405	643	376	264	584	289	257	37	510	282	221
127	Wisconsin	1,259	381	803	1,115	348	707	1,017	544	450	841	312	68	454	701	499	113
128	Wyoming	103	39	63	97	40	54	83	53	29	80	42	13	25	55	35	17

Series No.	State	1916 Total	1916 Rep.	1916 Dem.	1912 Total	1912 Rep.	1912 Dem.	1912 Progressive	1908 Total	1908 Rep.	1908 Dem.	1904 Total	1904 Rep.	1904 Dem.	1900 Total	1900 Rep.	1900 Dem.
80	**United States**	**18,531**	**8,534**	**9,128**	**15,037**	**3,487**	**6,297**	**4,119**	**14,884**	**7,675**	**6,412**	**13,521**	**7,628**	**5,084**	**13,968**	**7,218**	**6,357**
81	Alabama	131	29	99	118	10	82	23	105	26	74	109	22	80	160	56	97
82	Arizona	58	21	33	23	3	10	7	-----								
83	Arkansas	168	47	112	124	24	69	22	152	57	88	117	48	64	128	45	81
84	California	1,000	463	466	678	4	283	284	387	214	127	332	205	89	303	165	125
85	Colorado	294	102	179	266	58	114	72	264	124	127	244	135	100	221	93	123
86	Connecticut	214	107	100	190	68	75	34	190	113	68	191	111	73	180	103	74
87	Delaware	52	26	25	49	16	23	9	48	25	22	44	24	19	42	23	19
88	Florida	81	15	56	52	4	36	5	49	11	31	39	8	27	40	7	28
89	Georgia	160	11	128	121	6	94	21	132	41	72	130	24	84	121	34	81
90	Idaho	135	55	70	106	33	34	26	98	53	36	73	48	18	58	27	29
91	Illinois	2,193	1,153	950	1,146	254	405	386	1,155	630	451	1,076	633	328	1,132	598	503
92	Indiana	719	341	334	654	151	282	162	721	349	338	682	369	274	663	335	310
93	Iowa	515	279	221	492	120	185	162	495	275	201	486	308	149	530	308	209
94	Kansas	628	276	314	365	75	144	120	376	197	161	329	213	86	352	186	161
95	Kentucky	520	242	270	453	116	219	102	490	235	244	436	205	217	468	227	235
96	Louisiana	93	6	80	79	4	60	9	76	9	64	54	5	48	68	14	54
97	Maine	136	70	64	130	27	51	48	106	67	35	97	65	28	108	66	38
98	Maryland	262	117	138	232	55	113	58	239	117	116	224	109	109	264	136	122
99	Massachusetts	532	269	248	489	156	174	142	457	266	156	445	258	166	415	239	157
100	Michigan	647	338	284	548	151	150	213	538	333	175	520	362	134	544	316	211
101	Minnesota	387	180	179	334	64	106	126	330	196	109	293	217	55	316	190	113
102	Mississippi	86	4	80	64	2	57	4	67	4	60	59	3	53	58	6	51
103	Missouri	787	369	398	699	208	331	124	716	347	347	644	321	296	684	314	352
104	Montana	178	67	101	80	19	28	22	69	32	29	64	35	22	64	25	37
105	Nebraska	287	118	159	249	54	109	73	267	127	131	226	139	53	241	122	114
106	Nevada	33	12	18	20	3	8	6	25	11	11	12	7	4	10	4	6
107	New Hampshire	89	44	44	88	33	35	18	90	53	34	90	54	34	92	55	35
108	New Jersey	494	269	211	434	89	179	146	467	265	183	432	245	165	401	222	165
109	New Mexico	67	31	34	49	18	20	8									
110	New York	1,706	869	759	1,588	455	656	390	1,688	870	667	1,618	860	684	1,548	822	678
111	North Carolina	290	121	168	244	29	144	69	252	115	137	208	82	124	292	133	158
112	North Dakota	115	53	55	86	23	30	26	95	58	33	70	53	14	58	36	21
113	Ohio	1,164	514	604	1,037	278	425	230	1,122	572	503	1,004	600	345	1,040	544	475
114	Oklahoma	292	97	148	253	91	119	-----	256	107	127						
115	Oregon	262	127	120	137	35	47	38	111	63	38	90	60	17	84	47	33
116	Pennsylvania	1,297	704	522	1,218	273	396	445	1,265	746	447	1,237	841	338	1,173	713	424
117	Rhode Island	88	45	40	78	28	30	17	72	44	25	69	42	25	57	34	20
118	South Carolina	64	2	62	50	1	48	1	66	4	62	56	3	53	51	4	47
119	South Dakota	129	64	59	117	-----	59		115	68	40	101	72	22	96	55	40
120	Tennessee	273	117	153	253	60	133	55	257	118	136	243	105	132	274	123	145
121	Texas	373	65	287	302	29	220	27	298	69	218	233	51	167	422	131	268
122	Utah	143	54	84	112	42	37	24	109	61	43	102	62	33	93	47	45
123	Vermont	64	40	23	63	23	15	22	53	40	11	52	40	10	56	43	13
124	Virginia	154	49	103	137	23	90	22	137	53	83	131	48	81	264	116	146
125	Washington	381	167	183	322	70	87	114	184	106	58	145	102	28	108	57	45
126	West Virginia	290	143	140	264	57	113	79	258	138	111	240	133	101	221	120	99
127	Wisconsin	447	221	192	400	131	164	62	454	248	167	443	280	124	442	266	159
128	Wyoming	52	22	28	42	15	15	9	36	21	15	31	20	9	25	14	10

Series Y 80–128. Popular Vote Cast for President, by Political Party, by States: 1836 to 1956—Con.

[In thousands. Rep.—Republican; Dem.—Democratic]

Series No.	State	1896 Total	1896 Rep.	1896 Dem.	1892 Total	1892 Rep.	1892 Dem.	1892 People's	1888 Total	1888 Rep.	1888 Dem.	1884 Total	1884 Rep.	1884 Dem.	1880 Total	1880 Rep.	1880 Dem.
80	United States	13,907	7,102	6,493	12,061	5,183	5,555	1,030	11,383	5,447	5,538	10,053	4,850	4,880	9,217	4,453	4,414
81	Alabama	195	56	130	233	9	138	85	175	57	117	154	59	93	152	56	91
83	Arkansas	140	38	101	148	47	88	12	157	60	86	126	51	73	109	42	61
84	California	299	147	123	270	118	118	25	250	125	118	197	102	89	164	80	80
85	Colorado	187	26	159	96	39	---	54	91	50	37	64	36	28	54	28	25
86	Connecticut	174	110	57	165	77	82	4	154	75	75	137	66	67	133	67	64
87	Delaware	32	17	13	37	18	19	---	30	13	16	30	13	17	29	14	15
88	Florida	46	11	31	35	---	30	5	67	27	40	60	28	32	52	24	28
89	Georgia	156	59	93	221	48	129	42	142	40	100	143	48	94	157	54	103
90	Idaho	30	6	23	19	9	---	11									
91	Illinois	1,088	607	465	874	399	426	22	748	370	348	673	337	312	622	318	277
92	Indiana	637	324	306	552	254	263	22	537	263	261	495	239	245	471	232	226
93	Iowa	521	289	224	443	220	196	21	404	212	180	377	197	178	323	184	106
94	Kansas	336	159	172	325	157	---	163	331	183	103	266	154	90	201	122	60
95	Kentucky	446	218	218	341	136	175	24	344	155	184	276	118	153	267	106	149
96	Louisiana	101	22	77	114	26	88	---	116	31	85	109	46	63	103	38	65
97	Maine	118	80	35	116	63	48	2	128	74	50	130	72	52	144	74	65
98	Maryland	251	137	105	213	93	114	1	211	100	106	186	86	97	173	79	94
99	Massachusetts	402	279	106	391	203	177	3	345	184	152	303	147	122	283	165	112
100	Michigan	546	293	237	467	223	202	20	475	236	213	403	193	150	353	185	132
101	Minnesota	342	194	140	268	123	101	30	262	143	104	190	112	70	151	94	53
102	Mississippi	70	5	63	53	1	41	10	115	29	85	121	44	78	116	34	76
103	Missouri	674	305	364	542	228	268	41	521	236	262	441	203	236	397	154	209
104	Montana	53	10	42	44	19	18	7									
105	Nebraska	223	103	115	200	87	24	83	203	108	80	134	77	54	87	55	29
106	Nevada	10	2	8	11	3	1	7	12	7	5	13	7	6	18	9	10
107	New Hampshire	84	57	21	89	46	42	---	91	46	43	84	43	39	86	45	41
108	New Jersey	371	221	134	336	156	171	1	304	144	152	261	123	128	246	121	123
110	New York	1,424	820	551	1,337	609	655	16	1,320	650	636	1,167	562	563	1,104	556	535
111	North Carolina	330	154	175	278	101	133	45	286	135	148	268	125	143	241	116	125
112	North Dakota	47	26	21	36	18	---	18									
113	Ohio	1,014	526	477	851	405	405	15	839	416	395	785	400	368	725	375	341
115	Oregon	97	49	45	78	35	14	27	62	33	27	53	27	25	41	21	20
116	Pennsylvania	1,194	728	427	1,003	516	452	9	998	526	447	900	473	395	875	445	407
117	Rhode Island	55	37	14	53	27	24	---	41	22	18	33	19	12	29	18	11
118	South Carolina	66	7	59	71	13	55	2	80	14	66	93	22	70	171	58	112
119	South Dakota	83	41	41	71	35	9	27									
120	Tennessee	315	149	164	266	101	136	24	304	139	159	259	124	134	243	108	130
121	Texas	539	163	369	423	75	240	101	364	94	236	326	93	226	241	57	156
122	Utah	78	13	65													
123	Vermont	64	51	10	56	38	16	---	63	45	17	59	40	17	65	46	18
124	Virginia	295	135	155	292	113	164	12	304	150	152	285	139	145	212	84	97
125	Washington	94	39	52	88	37	30	19									
126	West Virginia	202	105	94	171	80	84	4	159	78	79	132	63	67	113	46	57
127	Wisconsin	447	268	166	371	171	177	10	355	177	155	320	161	146	266	144	114
128	Wyoming	21	10	10	17	8	---	8									

Series No.	State	1876 Total	1876 Rep.	1876 Dem.	1872 Total	1872 Rep.	1872 Dem.	1868 Total	1868 Rep.	1868 Dem.	1864 Total	1864 Rep.	1864 Dem.	1860 Total	1860 Rep.	1860 Dem.	1860 Southern Dem.	1860 Constitutional Union
80	United States	8,422	4,037	4,284	6,460	3,597	2,843	5,720	3,013	2,707	4,011	2,207	1,804	4,690	1,866	1,383	848	593
81	Alabama	172	69	103	170	90	79	149	76	72				90	---	14	49	28
83	Arkansas	97	39	58	79	41	38	41	22	19				54	---	5	29	20
84	California	156	79	76	96	54	41	109	55	54	106	62	44	120	39	38	34	9
86	Connecticut	122	59	62	96	50	46	99	51	48	87	45	42	80	43	17	16	3
87	Delaware	24	11	13	22	11	10	19	8	11	17	8	9	16	4	1	7	4
88	Florida	48	24	24	33	18	15							13	---	---	8	5
89	Georgia	181	51	130	143	63	76	160	57	103				107	---	12	52	43
91	Illinois	553	277	259	430	242	185	448	250	198	348	190	159	337	171	158	2	5
92	Indiana	430	207	214	350	186	164	344	177	167	280	150	130	272	139	116	12	5
93	Iowa	295	174	112	205	132	71	194	120	74	135	86	48	128	70	55	1	2
94	Kansas	124	78	38	100	67	33	44	30	14	21	17	4					
95	Kentucky	260	97	160	189	89	100	155	39	116	90	27	63	146	1	26	53	66
96	Louisiana	146	75	71	129	72	57	114	33	80				51	---	8	23	20
97	Maine	116	66	50	91	61	29	113	70	42	109	64	45	101	63	30	6	2
98	Maryland	164	72	92	135	67	68	93	30	62	70	37	32	93	2	6	42	42
99	Massachusetts	259	150	109	199	133	65	196	136	59	175	127	49	169	107	34	6	22
100	Michigan	317	167	141	222	139	79	226	129	97	160	89	72	155	88	65	1	---
101	Minnesota	124	73	49	91	56	35	72	44	28	42	25	17	35	22	12	1	---
102	Mississippi	165	53	112	129	82	47							69	---	4	40	25
103	Missouri	351	145	202	271	119	151	152	87	66	104	73	31	165	17	59	31	58
105	Nebraska	53	32	17	25	17	8	15	10	6								
106	Nevada	20	10	9	15	8	6	12	6	5	16	10	7					
107	New Hampshire	80	42	39	69	37	31	68	38	31	69	36	33	66	38	26	2	---
108	New Jersey	220	104	116	168	92	77	163	80	83	129	61	68	121	58	63		
110	New York	1,016	490	522	830	441	387	850	420	430	731	369	362	677	363	314		
111	North Carolina	234	108	125	165	95	70	181	97	85				96	---	3	49	45
113	Ohio	659	331	323	529	282	244	519	280	239	471	266	206	443	232	187	11	12
115	Oregon	30	15	14	20	12	8	22	11	11	18	10	8	14	5	3	5	---
116	Pennsylvania	755	385	362	562	349	213	656	342	314	574	296	277	476	268	17	179	13
117	Rhode Island	26	16	11	19	14	5	20	13	6	23	14	9	20	12	8		
118	South Carolina	183	92	91	95	72	23	108	62	45								
120	Tennessee	223	90	133	181	86	95	82	57	25				144	---	11	64	69
121	Texas	151	45	106	116	48	68							63	---	---	48	15
123	Vermont	65	44	20	52	41	11	56	44	12	56	42	13	45	34	9	---	2
124	Virginia	237	96	141	185	93	92							167	2	16	74	74
126	West Virginia	100	42	57	62	32	30	49	29	20	34	23	10					
127	Wisconsin	257	130	124	192	105	86	194	109	85	145	80	63	152	86	65	1	---

Series Y 80–128. Popular Vote Cast for President, by Political Party, by States: 1836 to 1956—Con.

[In thousands. Rep.—Republican; Dem.—Democratic]

Series No.	State	1856				1852			1848			1844			1840		
		Total	Rep.	Dem.	American	Total	Whig	Dem.	Total	Whig	Dem.	Total	Whig	Dem.	Total	Whig	Dem.
80	**United States**	4,045	1,340	1,833	872	3,162	1,385	1,601	2,879	1,361	1,222	2,701	1,300	1,338	2,412	1,275	1,128
81	Alabama	75	----	47	29	44	15	27	62	30	31	63	26	37	63	29	34
83	Arkansas	33	----	22	11	20	7	12	17	8	9	15	6	10	12	5	7
84	California	110	21	53	36	77	36	41	----	----	----	----	----	----	----	----	----
86	Connecticut	81	43	35	3	67	30	33	62	30	27	65	33	30	57	32	25
87	Delaware	14	----	8	6	13	6	6	12	6	6	12	6	6	11	6	5
88	Florida	11	----	6	5	7	3	4	7	4	3	----	----	----	----	----	----
89	Georgia	99	----	57	42	62	17	35	92	48	45	86	42	44	72	40	32
91	Illinois	239	96	106	38	155	65	80	125	53	56	108	46	59	93	46	47
92	Indiana	235	94	119	22	184	81	95	153	70	75	140	68	70	117	65	52
93	Iowa	90	44	36	9	35	16	18	22	10	11	----	----	----	----	----	----
95	Kentucky	133	----	70	63	111	57	54	115	67	49	113	61	52	91	59	33
96	Louisiana	43	----	22	21	36	17	19	34	18	15	27	13	14	19	11	8
97	Maine	110	67	39	3	82	33	42	87	35	40	85	34	46	93	47	46
98	Maryland	87	----	39	47	75	35	40	72	38	34	69	36	33	62	34	29
99	Massachusetts	167	108	39	20	125	53	45	134	61	35	130	68	52	126	73	52
100	Michigan	126	72	52	2	83	34	42	65	24	31	56	24	28	44	23	21
102	Mississippi	59	----	34	24	45	18	27	52	26	27	46	20	26	37	20	17
103	Missouri	106	----	58	49	69	30	39	73	33	40	73	31	41	53	23	30
107	New Hampshire	70	37	32	----	51	15	29	50	15	28	49	18	27	59	26	33
108	New Jersey	100	28	47	24	84	39	44	78	40	37	76	38	37	64	33	31
110	New York	597	276	196	125	525	235	263	456	219	114	486	232	238	442	226	213
111	North Carolina	85	----	48	37	79	39	40	80	44	36	82	43	39	79	46	34
113	Ohio	386	187	171	28	353	153	169	329	139	155	312	155	149	273	148	124
116	Pennsylvania	460	148	231	82	386	179	199	369	185	173	331	160	167	288	144	144
117	Rhode Island	20	11	7	2	17	8	9	11	7	4	12	7	5	9	5	3
120	Tennessee	140	----	74	66	115	59	57	122	64	58	120	60	60	108	60	48
121	Texas	48	----	32	16	20	5	15	17	5	12	----	----	----	----	----	----
123	Vermont	51	40	11	1	44	22	13	48	23	11	49	27	18	51	32	18
124	Virginia	150	----	90	60	133	59	74	92	45	47	96	45	51	86	43	44
127	Wisconsin	120	66	53	1	62	21	32	39	14	15	----	----	----	----	----	----

Series No.	State	1836			Series No.	State	1836—Con.			Series No.	State	1836—Con.		
		Total	Whig	Dem.			Total	Whig	Dem.			Total	Whig	Dem.
80	**United States**	1,505	740	765	95	Kentucky	69	37	33	108	New Jersey	52	26	26
					96	Louisiana	7	4	4	110	New York	306	139	167
81	Alabama	37	17	21	97	Maine	38	15	23	111	North Carolina	50	24	27
83	Arkansas	4	1	2	98	Maryland	48	26	22	113	Ohio	203	106	97
86	Connecticut	38	19	19	99	Massachusetts	78	42	35	116	Pennsylvania	179	87	91
87	Delaware	9	5	4	100	Michigan	12	6	7	117	Rhode Island	6	3	3
89	Georgia	47	24	23	102	Mississippi	20	10	10	120	Tennessee	62	36	26
91	Illinois	33	15	18	103	Missouri	18	7	11	123	Vermont	35	21	14
92	Indiana	74	41	32	107	New Hampshire	25	6	19	124	Virginia	54	23	30

Series Y 129–138. Congressional Bills, Acts, and Resolutions: 1789 to 1958

[Excludes simple and concurrent resolutions]

Period of session	Congress	Measures introduced			Measures passed						
		Total	Bills	Joint resolutions	Total	Public			Private		
						Total public	Acts	Resolutions	Total private	Acts	Resolutions
		129	130	131	132	133	134	135	136	137	138
Jan. 1957–Aug. 1958	85th	19,112	18,205	907	1,720	936	936	(1)	784	784	(1)
Jan. 1955–July 1956	84th	17,687	16,782	905	1,921	1,028	1,028	(1)	893	893	(1)
Jan. 1953–Dec. 1954	83d	14,952	14,181	771	1,783	781	781	(1)	1,002	1,002	(1)
Jan. 1951–July 1952	82d	12,730	12,062	668	1,617	594	594	(1)	1,023	1,023	(1)
Jan. 1949–Jan. 1951	81st	14,988	14,219	769	2,024	921	921	(1)	1,103	1,103	(1)
Jan. 1947–Dec. 1948	80th	10,797	10,108	689	1,363	906	906	(1)	457	457	(1)
Jan. 1945–Aug. 1946	79th	10,330	9,748	582	1,625	733	733	(1)	892	892	(1)
Jan. 1943–Dec. 1944	78th	8,334	7,845	489	1,157	568	568	(1)	589	589	(1)
Jan. 1941–Dec. 1942	77th	11,334	10,793	541	1,485	850	850	(1)	635	635	(1)
Jan. 1939–Jan. 1941	76th	16,105	15,174	931	1,662	1,005	894	111	657	651	6
Jan. 1937–June 1938	75th	16,156	15,120	1,036	1,759	919	788	131	840	835	5

[1] Public and private resolutions are carried only as public and private laws beginning with the 77th Congress.

Series Y 129–138. Congressional Bills, Acts, and Resolutions: 1789 to 1958—Con.

Period of session	Congress	Measures introduced			Measures passed						
		Total	Bills	Joint resolutions	Total	Public			Private		
						Total public	Acts	Resolutions	Total private	Acts	Resolutions
		129	130	131	132	133	134	135	136	137	138
Jan. 1935–June 1936	74th	18,754	17,819	935	1,724	987	851	136	737	730	7
Mar. 1933–June 1934	73d	14,370	13,774	596	975	539	486	53	436	434	2
Dec. 1931–Mar. 1933	72d	21,382	20,501	881	843	516	442	74	327	326	1
Apr. 1929–Mar. 1931	71st	24,453	23,652	801	1,522	1,009	869	140	513	512	1
Dec. 1927–Mar. 1929	70th	23,897	23,238	659	1,722	1,145	1,037	108	577	568	9
Dec. 1925–Mar. 1927	69th	23,799	23,250	549	1,423	879	808	71	544	537	7
Dec. 1923–Mar. 1925	68th	17,462	16,884	578	996	707	632	75	289	286	3
Apr. 1921–Mar. 1923	67th	19,889	19,133	756	930	654	549	105	276	275	1
May 1919–Mar. 1921	66th	21,967	21,222	745	594	470	401	69	124	120	4
May 1917–Dec. 1919	65th	22,594	21,919	675	453	405	349	56	48	48	--------
Dec. 1915–Mar. 1917	64th	30,052	29,438	614	684	458	400	58	226	221	5
Mar. 1913–Mar. 1915	63d	30,053	29,367	686	700	417	342	75	283	271	12
Apr. 1911–Mar. 1913	62d	38,032	37,459	573	716	530	457	73	186	180	6
Mar. 1909–Mar. 1911	61st	44,363	43,921	442	884	595	526	69	289	286	3
Dec. 1907–Mar. 1909	60th	38,388	37,981	407	646	411	350	61	235	234	1
Mar. 1905–Mar. 1907	59th	34,879	34,524	355	7,024	775	692	83	6,249	6,248	1
Mar. 1903–Mar. 1905	58th	26,851	26,504	347	4,041	575	502	73	3,466	3,465	1
Mar. 1901–Mar. 1903	57th	25,460	25,007	453	2,790	480	423	57	2,310	2,309	1
Dec. 1899–Mar. 1901	56th	20,893	20,409	484	1,942	443	383	60	1,499	1,498	1
Mar. 1897–Mar. 1899	55th	18,463	17,817	646	1,437	552	449	103	885	880	5
Dec. 1895–Mar. 1897	54th	14,585	14,114	471	948	434	356	78	514	504	10
Dec. 1893–Mar. 1895	53d	12,226	11,796	430	711	463	374	89	248	235	13
Dec. 1891–Mar. 1893	52d	14,893	14,518	375	722	398	347	51	324	318	6
Mar. 1889–Mar. 1891	51st	19,630	19,163	467	2,251	611	531	80	1,640	1,633	7
Dec. 1887–Mar. 1889	50th	17,078	16,664	414	1,824	570	508	62	1,254	1,246	8
Mar. 1885–Mar. 1887	49th	15,002	14,618	384	1,452	424	367	57	1,028	1,025	3
Dec. 1883–Mar. 1885	48th	11,443	10,961	482	969	284	219	65	685	678	7
Dec. 1881–Mar. 1883	47th	10,704	10,194	510	761	419	330	89	342	317	25
Mar. 1879–Mar. 1881	46th	10,067	9,481	586	650	372	288	84	278	250	28
Mar. 1877–Mar. 1879	45th	8,735	8,413	322	746	303	255	48	443	430	13
Mar. 1875–Mar. 1877	44th	6,230	6,001	229	580	278	251	27	302	292	10
Mar. 1873–Mar. 1875	43d	6,434	6,252	182	859	415	392	23	444	441	3
Mar. 1871–Mar. 1873	42d	5,943	5,725	218	1,012	531	515	16	481	479	2
Mar. 1869–Mar. 1871	41st	5,314	4,466	848	769	470	313	157	299	235	64
Apr. 1867–Mar. 1869	40th	3,723	3,003	720	765	354	226	128	411	380	31
Mar. 1865–Mar. 1867	39th	2,348	1,864	484	714	427	306	121	287	228	59
Mar. 1863–Mar. 1865	38th	1,708	1,402	306	515	411	318	93	104	79	25
Mar. 1861–Mar. 1863	37th	1,661	1,370	291	521	428	335	93	93	66	27
Mar. 1859–Mar. 1861	36th	1,746	1,595	151	370	157	131	26	213	192	21
Mar. 1857–Mar. 1859	35th	1,686	1,544	142	312	129	100	29	183	174	9
Dec. 1855–Mar. 1857	34th	1,608	1,515	93	433	157	127	30	276	265	11
Mar. 1853–Mar. 1855	33d	1,660	1,552	108	540	188	161	27	352	329	23
Mar. 1851–Mar. 1853	32d	1,167	1,011	156	306	137	113	24	169	156	13
Mar. 1849–Mar. 1851	31st	1,080	978	102	167	109	88	21	58	51	7
Dec. 1847–Mar. 1849	30th	1,433	1,305	128	446	176	142	34	270	254	16
Mar. 1845–Mar. 1847	29th	1,051	956	95	303	142	117	25	161	146	15
Dec. 1843–Mar. 1845	28th	1,085	979	106	279	142	115	27	137	131	6
Mar. 1841–Mar. 1843	27th	1,210	1,146	64	524	201	178	23	323	317	6
Dec. 1839–Mar. 1841	26th	1,122	1,081	41	147	55	50	5	92	90	2
Mar. 1837–Mar. 1839	25th	1,631	1,566	65	532	150	138	12	382	376	6
Dec. 1835–Mar. 1837	24th	1,107	1,055	52	459	144	130	14	315	314	1
Dec. 1833–Mar. 1835	23d	993	946	47	390	128	121	7	262	262	--------
Dec. 1831–Mar. 1833	22d	1,000	976	24	462	191	175	16	271	270	1
Mar. 1829–Mar. 1831	21st	856	842	14	369	152	143	9	217	217	--------
Dec. 1827–Mar. 1829	20th	632	612	20	235	134	126	8	101	100	1
Mar. 1825–Mar. 1827	19th	622	609	13	266	153	147	6	113	113	--------
Dec. 1823–Mar. 1825	18th	498	481	17	335	141	137	4	194	194	--------
Dec. 1821–Mar. 1823	17th	492	492	--------	238	136	130	6	102	102	--------
Dec. 1819–Mar. 1821	16th	480	480	--------	208	117	109	8	91	91	--------
Mar. 1817–Mar. 1819	15th	507	507	--------	257	156	136	20	101	101	--------
Dec. 1815–Mar. 1817	14th	465	465	--------	298	173	163	10	125	124	1
Mar. 1813–Mar. 1815	13th	400	400	--------	273	185	167	18	88	88	--------
Mar. 1811–Mar. 1813	12th	406	406	--------	209	170	163	7	39	39	--------
Mar. 1809–Mar. 1811	11th	348	348	--------	119	94	91	3	25	25	--------
Oct. 1807–Mar. 1809	10th	266	266	--------	105	88	87	1	17	17	--------
Mar. 1805–Mar. 1807	9th	219	219	--------	106	90	88	2	16	16	--------
Oct. 1803–Mar. 1805	8th	217	217	--------	111	93	90	3	18	18	--------
Mar. 1801–Mar. 1803	7th	161	161	--------	95	80	78	2	15	15	--------
Dec. 1799–Mar. 1801	6th	157	157	--------	112	100	94	6	12	12	--------
Mar. 1797–Mar. 1799	5th	234	234	--------	155	137	135	2	18	18	--------
June 1795–Mar. 1797	4th	132	132	--------	85	75	72	3	10	10	--------
Mar. 1793–Mar. 1795	3d	122	122	--------	127	103	94	9	24	24	--------
Mar. 1791–Mar. 1793	2d	105	105	--------	77	65	64	1	12	12	--------
Mar. 1789–Mar. 1791	1st	144	144	--------	118	108	94	14	10	8	2

Series Y 139–145. Political Party Affiliations in Congress and the Presidency: 1789 to 1958

[Letter symbols for political parties: Ad—Administration; AM—Anti-Masonic; C—Coalition; D—Democratic; DR—Democratic-Republican; F—Federalist; J—Jacksonian; NR—National Republican; Op—Opposition; R—Republican; U—Unionist; W—Whig. Figures are for the beginning of the first session of each Congress

Year	Congress	House			Senate			President
		Majority party	Principal minority party	Other (except vacancies)	Majority party	Principal minority party	Other (except vacancies)	
		139	140	141	142	143	144	145
1957–1958	85th	D–233	R–200	--------	D–49	R–47	--------	R (Eisenhower)
1955–1956	84th	D–232	R–203	--------	D–48	R–47	1	R (Eisenhower)
1953–1954	83d	R–221	D–211	1	R–48	D–47	1	R (Eisenhower)
1951–1952	82d	D–234	R–199	1	D–49	R–47	--------	D (Truman)
1949–1950	81st	D–263	R–171	1	D–54	R–42	--------	D (Truman)
1947–1948	80th	R–245	D–188	1	R–51	D–45	--------	D (Truman)
1945–1946	79th	D–242	R–190	2	D–56	R–38	1	D (Truman)
1943–1944	78th	D–218	R–208	4	D–58	R–37	1	D (F. Roosevelt)
1941–1942	77th	D–268	R–162	5	D–66	R–28	2	D (F. Roosevelt)
1939–1941	76th	D–261	R–164	4	D–69	R–23	4	D (F. Roosevelt)
1937–1938	75th	D–331	R–89	13	D–76	R–16	4	D (F. Roosevelt)
1935–1936	74th	D–319	R–103	10	D–69	R–25	2	D (F. Roosevelt)
1933–1934	73d	D–310	R–117	5	D–60	R–35	1	D (F. Roosevelt)
1931–1933	72d	D–220	R–214	1	R–48	D–47	1	R (Hoover)
1929–1931	71st	R–267	D–167	1	R–56	D–39	1	R (Hoover)
1927–1929	70th	R–237	D–195	3	R–49	D–46	1	R (Coolidge)
1925–1927	69th	R–247	D–183	4	R–56	D–39	1	R (Coolidge)
1923–1925	68th	R–225	D–205	5	R–51	D–43	2	R (Coolidge)
1921–1923	67th	R–301	D–131	1	R–59	D–37	--------	R (Harding)
1919–1921	66th	R–240	D–190	3	R–49	D–47	--------	D (Wilson)
1917–1919	65th	D–216	R–210	6	D–53	R–42	--------	D (Wilson)
1915–1917	64th	D–230	R–196	9	D–56	R–40	--------	D (Wilson)
1913–1915	63d	D–291	R–127	17	D–51	R–44	1	D (Wilson)
1911–1913	62d	D–228	R–161	1	R–51	D–41	--------	R (Taft)
1909–1911	61st	R–219	D–172	--------	R–61	D–32	--------	R (Taft)
1907–1909	60th	R–222	D–164	--------	R–61	D–31	--------	R (T. Roosevelt)
1905–1907	59th	R–250	D–136	--------	R–57	D–33	--------	R (T. Roosevelt)
1903–1905	58th	R–208	D–178	--------	R–57	D–33	--------	R (T. Roosevelt)
1901–1903	57th	R–197	D–151	9	R–55	D–31	4	R (McKinley) R (T. Roosevelt)
1899–1901	56th	R–185	D–163	9	R–53	D–26	8	R (McKinley)
1897–1899	55th	R–204	D–113	40	R–47	D–34	7	R (McKinley)
1895–1897	54th	R–244	D–105	7	R–43	D–39	6	D (Cleveland)
1893–1895	53d	D–218	R–127	11	D–44	R–38	3	D (Cleveland)
1891–1893	52d	D–235	R–88	9	R–47	D–39	2	R (B. Harrison)
1889–1891	51st	R–166	D–159	--------	R–39	D–37	--------	R (B. Harrison)
1887–1889	50th	D–169	R–152	4	R–39	D–37	--------	D (Cleveland)
1885–1887	49th	D–183	R–140	2	R–43	D–34	--------	D (Cleveland)
1883–1885	48th	D–197	R–118	10	R–38	D–36	2	R (Arthur)
1881–1883	47th	R–147	D–135	11	R–37	D–37	1	R (Arthur) R (Garfield)
1879–1881	46th	D–149	R–130	14	D–42	R–33	1	R (Hayes)
1877–1879	45th	D–153	R–140	--------	R–39	D–36	1	R (Hayes)
1875–1877	44th	D–169	R–109	14	R–45	D–29	2	R (Grant)
1873–1875	43d	R–194	D–92	14	R–49	D–19	5	R (Grant)
1871–1873	42d	R–134	D–104	5	R–52	D–17	5	R (Grant)
1869–1871	41st	R–149	D–63	--------	R–56	D–11	--------	R (Grant)
1867–1869	40th	R–143	D–49	--------	R–42	D–11	--------	R (Johnson)
1865–1867	39th	U–149	D–42	--------	U–42	D–10	--------	R (Johnson) R (Lincoln)
1863–1865	38th	R–102	D–75	9	R–36	D–9	5	R (Lincoln)
1861–1863	37th	R–105	D–43	30	R–31	D–10	8	R (Lincoln)
1859–1861	36th	R–114	D–92	31	D–36	R–26	4	D (Buchanan)
1857–1859	35th	D–118	R–92	26	D–36	R–20	8	D (Buchanan)
1855–1857	34th	R–108	D–83	43	D–40	R–15	5	D (Pierce)
1853–1855	33d	D–159	W–71	4	D–38	W–22	2	D (Pierce)
1851–1853	32d	D–140	W–88	5	D–35	W–24	3	W (Fillmore)
1849–1851	31st	D–112	W–109	9	D–35	W–25	2	W (Fillmore) W (Taylor)
1847–1849	30th	W–115	D–108	4	D–36	W–21	1	D (Polk)
1845–1847	29th	D–143	W–77	6	D–31	W–25	--------	D (Polk)
1843–1845	28th	D–142	W–79	1	W–28	D–25	1	W (Tyler)
1841–1843	27th	W–133	D–102	6	W–28	D–22	2	W (Tyler) W (W. Harrison)
1839–1841	26th	D–124	W–118	--------	D–28	W–22	--------	D (Van Buren)
1837–1839	25th	D–108	W–107	24	D–30	W–18	4	D (Van Buren)
1835–1837	24th	D–145	W–98	--------	D–27	W–25	--------	D (Jackson)
1833–1835	23d	D–147	AM–53	60	D–20	NR–20	8	D (Jackson)
1831–1833	22d	D–141	NR–58	14	D–25	NR–21	2	D (Jackson)
1829–1831	21st	D–139	NR–74	--------	D–26	NR–22	--------	D (Jackson)
1827–1829	20th	J–119	Ad–94	--------	J–28	Ad–20	--------	C (John Q. Adams)
1825–1827	19th	Ad–105	J–97	--------	Ad–26	J–20	--------	C (John Q. Adams)
1823–1825	18th	DR–187	F–26	--------	DR–44	F–4	--------	DR (Monroe)
1821–1823	17th	DR–158	F–25	--------	DR–44	F–4	--------	DR (Monroe)
1819–1821	16th	DR–156	F–27	--------	DR–35	F–7	--------	DR (Monroe)
1817–1819	15th	DR–141	F–42	--------	DR–34	F–10	--------	DR (Monroe)
1815–1817	14th	DR–117	F–65	--------	DR–25	F–11	--------	DR (Madison)
1813–1815	13th	DR–112	F–68	--------	DR–27	F–9	--------	DR (Madison)
1811–1813	12th	DR–108	F–36	--------	DR–30	F–6	--------	DR (Madison)
1809–1811	11th	DR–94	F–48	--------	DR–28	F–6	--------	DR (Madison)

Series **Y 139–145.** Political Party Affiliations in Congress and the Presidency: 1789 to 1958—Con.

[Letter symbols for political parties: Ad—Administration; AM—Anti-Masonic; C—Coalition; D—Democratic; DR—Democratic-Republican; F—Federalist; J—Jacksonian; NR—National Republican; Op—Opposition; R—Republican; U—Unionist; W—Whig]

Year	Congress	House		Senate		President
		Major party	Principal minority party	Major party	Principal minority party	
		139	140	142	143	145
1807–1809	10th	DR–118	F–24	DR–28	F–6	DR (Jefferson)
1805–1807	9th	DR–116	F–25	DR–27	F–7	DR (Jefferson)
1803–1805	8th	DR–102	F–39	DR–25	F–9	DR (Jefferson)
1801–1803	7th	DR–69	F–36	DR–18	F–13	DR (Jefferson)
1799–1801	6th	F–64	DR–42	F–19	DR–13	F (John Adams)
1797–1799	5th	F–58	DR–48	F–20	DR–12	F (John Adams)
1795–1797	4th	F–54	DR–52	F–19	DR–13	F (Washington)
1793–1795	3d	DR–57	F–48	F–17	DR–13	F (Washington)
1791–1793	2d	F–37	DR–33	F–16	DR–13	F (Washington)
1789–1791	1st	Ad–38	Op–26	Ad–17	Op–9	F (Washington)

Series **Y 146–149.** Vote Cast for Representatives, by Political Party: 1896 to 1956

[In thousands]

Year	Total	Republican	Democratic	Other	Year	Total	Republican	Democratic	Other
	146	147	148	149		146	147	148	149
1956	58,886	28,697	29,832	357	1926	20,435	11,643	8,284	508
1954	42,580	20,034	22,175	371	1924	26,884	14,932	10,854	1,098
1952	57,571	28,399	28,336	836	1922	20,409	10,548	9,131	730
1950	40,342	19,750	19,785	807	1920	25,214	14,773	9,038	1,403
1948	45,933	20,920	23,820	1,193	1918	12,579	6,600	5,421	558
1946	34,398	18,400	15,221	777	1916	16,140	7,810	7,468	862
1944	45,103	21,303	22,808	992	1914	13,275	5,650	5,727	1,898
1942	28,074	14,203	12,934	937	1912	13,517	4,602	6,128	2,787
1940	46,951	21,393	24,092	1,466	1910	11,669	5,427	5,536	706
1938	36,236	17,047	17,612	1,577	1908	14,021	6,975	6,466	580
1936	42,886	17,003	23,944	1,939	1906	10,552	5,350	4,659	543
1934	32,256	13,558	17,385	1,313	1904	12,697	6,837	5,298	562
1932	37,657	15,575	20,540	1,542	1902	10,654	5,250	4,980	424
1930	24,777	13,032	11,044	701	1900	13,626	6,973	6,086	567
1928	33,906	19,163	14,361	382	1898	11,513	5,258	5,373	882
					1896	14,652	6,845	6,339	1,468

Series **Y 150–154.** Apportionment of Representatives Among the States: 1790 to 1950

Year	Congress	Population base [1] (1,000)	Apportionment act			Apportionment population per Representative	Year	Congress	Population base [1] (1,000)	Apportionment act			Apportionment population per Representative
			Number of States	Number of Representatives [2]	Date of act					Number of States	Number of Representatives [2]	Date of act	
		150	151	152	153	154			150	151	152	153	154
1950	83d	149,895	48	435	Nov. 15, 1941	344,587	1850	33d–37th	21,767	31	234	May 23, 1850 [6]	93,020
1940	78th–82d	131,006	48	435	Nov. 15, 1941	301,164	1840	28th–32d	15,908	26	223	June 25, 1842	71,338
1930	73d–77th	122,093	48	435	June 18, 1929	280,675	1830	23d–27th	11,931	24	240	May 22, 1832	49,712
1920	(3)	(3)	(3)	435		(3)	1820	18th–22d	8,972	24	213	Mar. 7, 1822	42,124
1910	63d–72d	91,604	48	435	Aug. 8, 1911	210,583	1810	13th–17th	6,584	17	181	Dec. 21, 1811	36,377
1900	58th–62d	74,563	45	386	Jan. 16, 1901	193,167	1800	8th–12th	4,880	16	141	Jan. 14, 1802	34,609
1890	53d–57th	61,909	44	356	Feb. 7, 1891	173,901	1790	{3d–7th	3,616	15	105	Apr. 14, 1792	34,436
1880	48th–52d	49,371	38	325	Feb. 25, 1882	151,912		{1st–2d		13	65	Constitution 1789	[7] 30,000
1870	43d–47th	38,116	37	292	Feb. 2, 1872 [4]	130,533							
1860	38th–42d	29,550	34	241	May 23, 1850 [5]	122,614							

[1] Excludes the population of the District of Columbia, the population of the Territories, the number of Indians not taxed, and (prior to 1870) two-fifths of the slave population.
[2] Actual number apportioned at the beginning of the decade.
[3] No apportionment was made after the Census of 1920.

[4] Amended by the act of May 30, 1872.
[5] Amended by the act of March 4, 1862.
[6] Amended by the act of July 30, 1852.
[7] The minimum ratio of population to Representatives stated in the Constitution (art. I, sec. 2).

Series Y 155–204. Apportionment of Membership in House of Representatives, by States, From Adoption of Constitution to 1950

[Population figures used for apportionment purposes are those determined for States by each decennial census. Until 1940, population for apportionment purposes excluded Indians not taxed and until 1870, excluded two-fifths of slaves. Until 1850, apportionment ratios were chosen arbitrarily; 1850 to 1900, ratios were apportionment population of U.S. divided by predetermined number of Representatives; from 1910 on, apportionment ratios shown were computed by dividing fixed number (435) of Representatives into apportionment population but were not used in the original calculations, which were based on priority lists. No reapportionment based on 1920 Population Census. For discussion of apportionment methods, see S. Doc. No. 304, 76th Cong. 3d sess., *A Survey of Methods of Apportionment in Congress*, by Edward V. Huntington]

Series No.	Item	1950	1940	1930	1910	1900	1890	1880	1870	1860	1850	1840	1830	1820	1810	1800	1790	Constitution
155	Apportionment ratio _____1,000	[1]345	[1]301	[1]281	[1]211	194	174	152	131	127	93	71	48	40	35	33	33	[2]30
	STATE																	
156	Total number of representatives	435	435	435	435	391	357	332	[3]293	[4]243	[5]237	232	242	213	186	142	106	65
157	Alabama	9	9	9	10	9	9	8	8	6	7	7	5	3	[6]1			
158	Arizona	2	2	1	[7]1													
159	Arkansas	6	7	7	7	7	6	5	4	3	2	1	[6]1					
160	California	30	23	20	11	8	7	6	4	3	2	[6]2						
161	Colorado	4	4	4	4	3	2	1	[6]1									
162	Connecticut	6	6	6	5	5	4	4	4	4	4	4	6	6	7	7	7	5
163	Delaware	1	1	1	1	1	1	1	1	1	1	1	1	1	2	1	1	1
164	Florida	8	6	5	4	3	2	2	2	2	1	1	[6]1					
165	Georgia	10	10	10	12	11	11	10	9	7	8	8	9	7	6	4	2	3
166	Idaho	2	2	2	2	1	1	[6]1										
167	Illinois	25	26	27	27	25	22	20	19	14	9	7	3	1	[6]1			
168	Indiana	11	11	12	13	13	13	13	13	11	11	10	7	3	[6]1			
169	Iowa	8	8	9	11	11	11	11	9	6	2	[6]2						
170	Kansas	6	6	7	8	8	8	7	3	1								
171	Kentucky	8	9	9	11	11	11	11	10	9	10	10	13	12	10	6	2	
172	Louisiana	8	8	8	8	7	6	6	6	5	4	4	3	3	[6]1			
173	Maine	3	3	3	4	4	4	4	5	5	6	7	8	7	[8]7			
174	Maryland	7	6	6	6	6	6	6	6	5	6	6	8	9	9	9	8	6
175	Massachusetts	14	14	15	16	14	13	12	11	10	11	10	12	13	13	17	14	8
176	Michigan	18	17	17	13	12	12	11	9	6	4	3	[6]1					
177	Minnesota	9	9	9	10	9	7	5	3	2	[6]2							
178	Mississippi	6	7	7	8	8	7	7	6	5	5	4	2	1	[6]1			
179	Missouri	11	13	13	16	16	15	14	13	9	7	5	2	1				
180	Montana	2	2	2	2	1	1	[6]1										
181	Nebraska	4	4	5	6	6	6	3	1	[6]1								
182	Nevada	1	1	1	1	1	1	1	1	[6]1								
183	New Hampshire	2	2	2	2	2	2	2	3	3	3	4	5	6	6	5	4	3
184	New Jersey	14	14	14	12	10	8	7	7	5	5	5	6	6	6	6	5	4
185	New Mexico	2	2	1	[7]1													
186	New York	43	45	45	43	37	34	34	33	31	33	34	40	34	27	17	10	6
187	North Carolina	12	12	11	10	10	9	9	8	7	8	9	13	13	13	12	10	5
188	North Dakota	2	2	2	3	2	1	[6]1										
189	Ohio	23	23	24	22	21	21	21	20	19	21	21	19	14	6	[6]1		
190	Oklahoma	6	8	9	8	[6]5												
191	Oregon	4	4	3	3	2	2	1	1	1	[6]1							
192	Pennsylvania	30	33	34	36	32	30	28	27	24	25	24	28	26	23	18	13	8
193	Rhode Island	2	2	2	3	2	2	2	2	2	2	2	2	2	2	2	2	1
194	South Carolina	6	6	6	7	7	7	7	5	4	6	7	9	9	9	8	6	5
195	South Dakota	2	2	2	3	2	2	[6]2										
196	Tennessee	9	10	9	10	10	10	10	10	8	10	11	13	9	6	3	[6]1	
197	Texas	22	21	21	18	16	13	11	6	4	2	[6]2						
198	Utah	2	2	2	2	1	[6]1											
199	Vermont	1	1	1	2	2	2	2	3	3	3	4	5	5	6	4	2	
200	Virginia	10	9	9	10	10	10	10	9	11	13	15	21	22	23	22	19	10
201	Washington	7	6	6	5	3	2	[6]1										
202	West Virginia	6	6	6	6	5	4	4	3									
203	Wisconsin	10	10	10	11	11	10	9	8	6	3	[6]2						
204	Wyoming	1	1	1	1	1	1	[6]1										

[1] See headnote.
[2] Number of Representatives not to exceed 1 for each 30,000 inhabitants.
[3] Membership originally fixed at 283 but increased to 292 by act of May 30, 1872 (17 Stat. L. 192). One Member assigned to Colorado after apportionment.
[4] Membership increased from 233 to 241 by act of Mar. 4, 1862 (12 Stat. L. 353). See footnote 6.
[5] Membership increased from 233 to 234 by act of July 30, 1852 (10 Stat. L. 25). See footnote 6.
[6] Assigned after apportionment.
[7] Included in apportionment act in anticipation of statehood.
[8] Included in the 20 Members originally assigned to Massachusetts but credited to Maine after its admission as a State, Mar. 15, 1820 (3 Stat. L. 555).

GOVERNMENT EMPLOYMENT AND FINANCES (Series Y 205–714)

Y 205–714. General note.

Governmental services in the United States are provided through a complex organizational structure made up of numerous public bodies and agencies. In addition to the widely recognized pattern of Federal, State, county, municipal, and township governments, there exist many offshoots in the form of single-function and multiple-function districts, authorities, commissions, boards, and other entities that have varying degrees of autonomy. The basic pattern differs widely from State to State. Within a particular State, the various classes of local units may also differ in their characteristics.

Identification and enumeration of governmental units is, of course, a prerequisite to comprehensive reports on their activities. Thus, the report *U.S. Census of Governments: 1957*, vol. I, No. 1, *Governments in the United States*, provides information on numbers of governmental units by type, size, and location.

The summary historical table from the 1957 Census of Governments, reproduced below, presents the numbers of different types of governmental units, for 1942, 1952, and 1957.

Table I. Governmental Units, by Type: 1942, 1952, and 1957

Type of government	Number of units			Change in number	
	1957	1952	1942	1952 to 1957	1942 to 1957
Total	102,328	116,743	155,116	−14,415	−52,788
U. S. Government	1	1	1		
States	48	48	48		
Counties	3,047	3,049	3,050	−2	−3
Municipalities	17,183	16,778	16,220	+405	+963
Townships and towns	17,198	17,202	18,919	−4	−1,721
School districts	50,446	[1]67,346	108,579	−16,900	−58,133
Special districts	14,405	12,319	8,299	+2,086	+6,106

[1] Corrected figure.

Comparable data for the number of governments are not available for earlier years, principally because definition of the concept of "a governmental unit" and enumeration of the units in existence are beset with many difficulties. Professor William Anderson of the University of Minnesota has done extensive work in this field, and the enumerations by the Bureau of the Census in 1942 and later reflect his contributions.

Anderson's classic monograph, *The Units of Government in the United States: An Enumeration and Analysis*, first published in 1934 and revised in 1936, was extensively revised in 1942 and finally republished in 1945 with an appendix comparing the author's enumeration of governments with that of the 1942 Census of Governments. (Public Administration Service, Chicago, 1945.) Anderson reported 175,418 governments in the United States in 1930–33 and 165,049 in 1941. The 1942 Census of Governments adopted a more selective definition, eliminating 9,729 school districts and 204 other units from enumeration as separate entities. Anderson reported that he had "good reason to believe that the Bureau's figures represent a more accurate enumeration." (Source cited above, p. 48.)

The comparative totals reported by Anderson, on the basis of his definitions and procedures, are summarized below.

Table II. Governmental Units, by Type: 1930–33 and 1941

Type of government	1941	1930–33	Change in number
Total	165,049	175,418	−10,369
U.S. Government	1	1	
States	48	48	
Counties	3,050	3,053	−3
Incorporated places (cities, villages, etc., and D.C.)	16,262	16,366	−104
Towns (as in New England) and organized townships (in a total of 23 States)	18,998	20,262	−1,264
School districts	118,308	127,108	−8,800
Other units	8,382	8,580	−198

The definition of a governmental unit employed in the 1957 Census of Governments (*Governments in the United States*, cited above, p. 9) is as follows:

A government is an organized entity which, in addition to having governmental character, has sufficient discretion in the management of its own affairs to distinguish it as separate from the administration structure of any other governmental unit. To be defined as a government, any entity must possess all three of the attributes reflected in the foregoing definition: Existence as an organized entity, governmental character, and substantial autonomy.

Characteristics taken as evidence of the "essential attributes" of a separately existing governmental unit include organization, active operation, and the possession of specific corporate powers; the popular election or appointment of officers; the power to levy taxes or to issue debt that bears interest exempt from Federal taxation; responsibility for performing a function commonly regarded as governmental; public accountability; and considerable administrative and fiscal independence.

Despite the variety and apparent simplicity of these criteria, the proper classification of some local governmental entities remains doubtful, and in such cases, account has been taken of (*a*) local attitudes as to whether the type of unit involved is independent, and (*b*) the effect of the classification upon the collection and presentation of statistics of governmental finances and employment.

Two broad categories of governmental units may be distinguished—special-purpose organizations, such as school, park, and sanitary districts; and general-purpose governments, each with a broad spectrum of powers and duties, ranging in size from small village and town governments to the large metropolitan city, State, and Federal governments.

These diverse units can be represented by at least two kinds of measures that are universally applicable: (*a*) the number of persons serving in each governmental unit and their compensation, and (*b*) the broad financial aspects of the operations, as represented by revenues, expenditures, and indebtedness. The collection and reporting of such data are complicated by the large numbers and frequent changes of the governmental units to be covered, by changes (often unrecorded) in their internal structures and external relationships, and by the great diversity that exists in organizational forms, employment relationships, financial procedures, the adequacy and availability of records, and the categories and terminologies used in those records and in public reporting. For the most part, data for the Federal Government are derived from regular personnel and fiscal reports, published annually or oftener. Those for the States and large cities are compiled from annual public reports or other official records of each unit and its component organizational subdivisions; and those of other local governments are derived from surveys based on similar reports and records of carefully selected samples of each type of government.

Complete censuses of governments, covering governmental structure, personnel, expenditures, revenues, debt, and other selected aspects of all governments in the United States, were conducted for 1932, 1942, and 1957. Earlier periodic censuses (for decennial years for 1850–1890 and for 1902, 1912, and 1922) were narrower in scope, particularly with reference to expenditures and personnel.

The various censuses of governments and also the annual reports on personnel and finances, differ not only in completeness, but also in some of the basic concepts and classifications. Consequently, the preparation of historically comparable data covering all governmental units is extremely difficult. As is evident in the historical series for the Federal Government, events and changing concepts greatly affect the comparability, over long periods, of data for a single government. The problem of continuity in concepts and classifications is greatly multiplied in summaries for all governmental entities.

For such reasons, the consolidated historical series now available are for selected years beginning with 1902. The data available for earlier years are either inadequate for classifications now used or require more extensive reworking than could be achieved with available resources.

State and local government data in this chapter relate to continental United States. They omit Alaska, Hawaii, and possessions outside the continental limits. The District of Columbia is classified as a local government.

For references to publications containing the original data and statistics for individual State and local governments, see text below for series Y 517–714.

For still another approach to the role of Government operations in the economy, see series F 81–86, reporting Government purchases of goods and services, in which the Federal Government totals for 1938–1957 are subdivided between national security and other purposes. For national income originating in "Government" as an industry, see series F 32; and for estimates of "Government product" in the national income accounts, see series F 48.

Y 205-253. General note.

Statistics on government employment and payrolls in the United States appear in the appendix to a comprehensive study by Solomon Fabricant, assisted by Robert E. Lipsey, *The Trend of Government Activity in the United States since 1900*, National Bureau of Economic Research, New York, 1952, pp. 161–203. Fabricant and Lipsey relate their figures to the government employment data for 1929–1949 and earlier periods published by the Office of Business Economics and predecessor agencies. The latter figures differ from the former chiefly in omitting, for national income accounts, all Federal Government employees abroad. Also differentiated are earlier estimates prepared for the National Bureau of Economic Research by Simon Kuznets in *National Income and Its Composition, 1919–1938*, New York, 1941, vol. II, pp. 811–826. This study did not have data from the Work Projects Administration-Bureau of Labor Statistics compilations noted below. For reference to other studies for earlier years, see text for series Y 251–253.

The WPA-BLS figures, mentioned above, cover 1929–1939. They were obtained as part of a larger survey of State and local governments conducted in 1938–1943 by the Bureau of Labor Statistics and financed and staffed by the Work Projects Administration. Annual estimates of employment and payrolls of State and local governments and the underlying detailed estimates of States, by classes of governments and major fields of employment, were published by the Bureau of Labor Statistics in *Employment and Pay Rolls of State and Local Governments*, January 1946 (processed).

Sample surveys by the Bureau of the Census began in 1940 on a quarterly basis, giving reports of January, April, July, and October data. After January 1955, the surveys were made annually for the month of October, except for 1957, the year of the detailed census of governments.

School data prior to 1946 were from the Office of Education and reported only in terms of State and local aggregates, so that detail by level and type of government relates only to the nonschool data.

Beginning with 1955, the Bureau of Labor Statistics assumed responsibility for providing monthly statistics on government employment and payrolls. Census publication of monthly data on a quarterly reporting basis ceased at that time. Comparability between the payroll series compiled by the two agencies was maintained, so that the payroll statistics are continuous. Monthly estimates of employment compiled by the Bureau of the Census include nominal employees of local governments and exclude, during the summer months, regular members of school faculties who were not paid for those months. The Bureau of Labor Statistics series excludes the nominal employees and includes school employees throughout the year. To this extent, it differs from the earlier Census Bureau series.

The BLS employment and payroll data for 1955–1957 were issued in a processed monthly release, *State and Local Government Employment and Payrolls*, with occasional issues carrying cumulative tabulations and explanatory notes. The employment estimates (but not the payroll series) were included also in the BLS monthly publication, *Employment and Earnings*, table A-5.

Both series Y 207–209 and Y 251–253 cover all types of special-purpose districts as well as general-purpose local governments and all branches of the State governments; and both include the employees of government utilities as well as of general government services and agencies. School employment includes noninstructional staff and the educational employees of State as well as local governments. Both tabulations omit military personnel and persons on work relief.

Federal Government employment and payrolls, series Y 206 and Y 224, respectively, are originally from the Civil Service Commission for 1952–1957. Prior to 1952 these data are basically the Bureau of Labor Statistics figures and, therefore, differ in coverage and date from the Civil Service Commission's historical tabulations for the Federal Government alone (series Y 241–250).

Differences from labor force data.—Data collected from the governmental employers, such as the Bureau of the Census and Bureau of Labor Statistics compilations on public employment referred to above, necessarily differ from government employment statistics derived from broad surveys of the labor force.

Data on the labor force, and therefore on government workers, are collected by the Bureau of the Census in monthly surveys and published in its *Current Population Reports*. These surveys involve direct personal interviews with selected samples of households throughout the Nation. Governments are listed as an industry group, and members of the labor force who report that they are government workers are so classified. However, these compilations do not yield information on the employment and payroll totals of individual governments, types of governments, governments in specified geographic areas, or the functions of public employees. These aspects of public administration require the collection of information from employing governments.

Moreover, statistics resulting from the labor force surveys are affected by the shifts of individuals between jobs; by movements of individuals from government to nongovernment employment, or to unemployment or retirement from the labor force; and by multiple jobholding and other factors. The Fabricant-Lipsey study, cited above, compares the differing approaches to analyses of statistics of governmental employment and payrolls.

Y 205–240. Public employees and government monthly payrolls, by type of government, 1940–1957.

Source: 1940–1956, Bureau of the Census, *State Distribution of Public Employment in 1956*, 1957, p. 7; 1957, *U.S. Census of Governments: 1957*, vol. II, No. 1, *Summary of Public Employment*, p. 13.

Data on Federal employment and payrolls were obtained from the Bureau of Labor Statistics prior to 1952 and the Civil Service Commission since that time. BLS figures were based on Civil Service data. Substantially all basic data for State and local governments were collected by mail surveys of the Bureau of the Census. However, prior to 1946, data on school employment were obtained from Office of Education, *Biennial Survey of Education in the United States.*

Public employees, as defined for the purpose of the Bureau of the Census survey of government employment, include all paid officials and civilian employees of Federal, State, and local governmental units. Employees of contractors, other persons serving governments on a contract basis, and persons on work relief are not considered public employees. The term, however, does include fee officials, paid volunteer firemen, student help, and other persons serving on a part-time basis even though they may receive only nominal compensation for their services. Military personnel and their pay are omitted.

Full-time employees are those persons employed during the pay period for the number of hours per week prescribed for full-time work in the jurisdiction concerned. The term includes temporary and emergency employees working on a full-time basis during the pay period.

Payrolls, series Y 223–240, include salaries, wages, fees, and other compensation earned in the calendar month by officials and other employees. (Amounts reported for semimonthly, biweekly, weekly, or other nonmonthly periods are adjusted to monthly equivalents.) Amounts reported are gross pay before deductions for withholding taxes, retirement contributions, social security, and other purposes. Full-time payrolls, series Y 225–240, are amounts paid to full-time employees as defined above.

Figures for State governments include, in addition to data for the regular departments and agencies, data for boards, commissions, authorities, institutions of higher education, and other semiautonomous agencies of State government. State employees include all persons paid by the State government. Thus, employees of the public school system, usually a local government function, are classified in North Carolina as State government employees because their salaries are paid directly by the State government. Some public school system employees in Delaware and Maine and a scattering of such employees in a few other States are similarly treated.

Employees on paid vacations are included in the data for State and local employment. Those on extended unpaid absence are excluded.

Figures for cities (series Y 216–217, Y 234–235) are for city, borough, village, and—except in New England, New York, and Wisconsin—town governments. They include boards, commissions, and semiautonomous districts and authorities controlled by such governments, as well as the regular municipal departments and agencies. In a number of States, some or all of the public schools serving city areas are operated by city governments, and city figures include their employees.

Figures for counties (series Y 218–219, Y 236–237) include data for semiautonomous county agencies and for public schools or school facilities operated by county governments in a few of the States.

Data on school districts are restricted to independent districts operating public schools. They do not include data for school systems operated by State, city, county, or town governments. Between 76 and 81 percent of all local government education employees in October of each year, 1946–1956, were employees of independent school districts.

In addition to townships of the Midwestern States, which have limited governmental functions and play a minor role, township data include figures for New England, New York, and Wisconsin towns, and Pennsylvania and New Jersey townships, where town and township governments are important in the local government structure. The New England town figures include school information in five States (all except New Hampshire) in which town governments administer public schools. Data on special districts are for special-purpose units of local government set up to perform a specific service or services in a local area, but which are administratively and fiscally independent of the broader types of local government having jurisdiction in the area. These units range in size from drainage districts and other agricultural-resources districts having only intermittent activity or employment up to such entities as the Chicago Transit Authority, the Port of New York Authority, and other large-scale governmental employers.

Y 241–250. Paid civilian employment of the Federal Government, 1816–1957.

Source: Civil Service Commission, records.

The data for 1816–1891 were compiled by the Civil Service Commission from *Official Register of the United States;* for 1901–1911, from the *Annual Report* of the Civil Service Commission and *Official Register;* for 1908–1957, from the Civil Service Commission, *Annual Report* and *Monthly Report of Federal Employment,* and supplemented throughout by Civil Service Commission records.

Prior to 1938, the data are for employees on the rolls, with or without pay; for 1938–1942, the number on the payroll with pay; and for 1943–1957, the number in active duty status.

Employees and officials of the legislative, judicial, and executive branches are included throughout. Employees of the District of Columbia are not included; they are considered employees of a local government.

The figures exclude military personnel but include civilian employees of the military departments. However, mechanics and other workmen at army arsenals and navy yards are not included prior to 1881.

The data for the Post Office, series Y 247, exclude contractors but include substitutes, partly estimated.

Series Y 244 represents personnel employed under the act of January 16, 1883, establishing the Civil Service Commission and the competitive (classified) service. This service includes all civilian positions in the executive branch of the Federal Government that are not specifically exempted by or pursuant to statute, or by the Civil Service Commission. It also includes all positions in the legislative and judicial branches which are specifically made subject to the civil service laws by statute. Figures represent positions prior to 1947; for 1948–1957, they represent employees serving under competitive appointment.

Y 251–253. State and local government employment, 1929–1957.

Source: Bureau of Labor Statistics, records.

Data for 1929–1939 are derived from a WPA-BLS survey (see general note for series Y 205–253). Figures for 1940–1954 are from Bureau of the Census reports on public employment (incorporating data for 1940–1945 from the *Biennial Survey of Education* of the Office of Education), and for 1955–1957, from the Bureau of Labor Statistics compilations.

These data differ from series Y 207–209 for 1940–1957 because they measure average monthly employment in each calendar year, whereas series Y 207–209 are for October 31 of each year (except for 1957, when the date is April 30). In the annual averages for 1929–1957, regular teachers are included for the summer vacation period, whether or not they were specifically paid in those months; and nominal employees are omitted.

For a discussion of studies conducted by Federal agencies, see general note for series Y 205–253. Estimates of employment and payrolls for the years 1909–1927 appear in Wilford I. King, *The National Income and Its Purchasing Power*, National Bureau of Economic Research, 1930, pp. 360–365; and for 1926, a study by William E. Mosher and Sophie Polah based on approximately 500 reports from State and local governments, published in "Public Employment in the United States," supplement to *National Municipal Review*, vol. XXI, No. 1, January 1932.

Relying heavily on the Mosher-Polah article and public employment data issued by the Bureau of Foreign and Domestic Commerce in connection with certain of its national income studies, Simon Kuznets, in *National Income and Its Composition, 1919–1938*, National Bureau of Economic Research, 1941, vol. II, pp. 811–826, published revised estimates of government employees and payrolls for 1919–1938.

Y 254–257. Summary of Federal Government finances, 1789–1957.

Source: Treasury Department, *Annual Report of the Secretary of the Treasury, 1958*, pp. 392–397 and 469–470.

Receipts and expenditures for 1789–1915 are based on warrants issued; for 1916–1952, on daily Treasury statements; for 1953–1957, on the Treasury's *Monthly Statement of Receipts and Expenditures of the United States Government*. Total gross debt is on the basis of public debt accounts for 1791–1915, and on the basis of daily Treasury statements for 1916–1957. For description of the *Daily* and *Monthly Statements of the Treasury*, explanation of "warrants issued," "public debt accounts," and other pertinent items, see the source, pp. 385–388.

The receipts and expenditures data exclude amounts received in trust and expended from trust accounts. They also exclude amounts borrowed through the sale of Government securities and amounts paid to retire public debt. Receipts include the proceeds of sales of some types of Government-owned assets, including land. For recent years, however,

proceeds from the disposition of some categories of Government property (including sales of commodities and securities purchased and repayments received on account of loans made by the Government) are reported as deductions from expenditures, rather than as receipts. Postal receipts and expenditures are included net for each year throughout the series; that is, a postal surplus is included in receipts and a postal deficit in expenditures.

Subject to the foregoing qualifications, figures for Federal Government receipts (series Y 254) represent "total receipts" through 1930 and "net receipts" thereafter. In determining net receipts, the following items are deducted from total receipts:

Refunds of receipts, principally for the overpayment of taxes, 1931–1957. (For earlier years, such refunds are included in expenditures.)

Transfers of tax receipts to the Federal old-age and survivors insurance trust fund, 1937–1957; to the railroad retirement account, 1938–1957; to the Federal disability insurance trust fund and the highway trust fund, 1957.

Capital transfers, consisting of payments to the Treasury principally by wholly owned Government corporations for retirement of capital stock and for disposition of earnings. (Although the exclusion applies to all fiscal years for 1931–1957, the only transfer of this kind identified for 1931–1939 was an item of $250 thousand in 1937.)

Figures for expenditures for 1931–1957 likewise are net of refunds paid and of capital transfers, but include any such payments in earlier years. For 1951–1957, investments of wholly owned Government corporations in public debt securities are excluded.

The surplus or deficit (series Y 256) is the difference between receipts and expenditures in any fiscal year. The change in public debt during any year is usually determined in large part by the surplus or deficit; it is, however, affected also by the increase or decrease in the Treasury cash balance and by various other financial operations. Consequently, there is only an approximate relationship between series Y 256 and the year-to-year differences in the debt reported in series Y 257.

For comments on the total gross debt (series Y 257) and other aspects of the public debt, see text for series Y 368–379. For the differences between series Y 254–257 and the data on receipts from and payments to the public, see text for series Y 380–383.

In a statement on "Some Historical Aspects of Federal Fiscal Policy, 1790–1956" (in *Federal Expenditure Policy for Economic Growth and Stability*, papers submitted by panelists appearing before the Subcommittee on Fiscal Policy, Joint Economic Committee, 85th Congress, 1st sess., Nov. 5, 1957, Joint Committee Print, pp. 60–83), the official historical series on Federal receipts and expenditures—such as series Y 254 and Y 255—were characterized by Professor Paul B. Trescott as subject to "certain deficiencies for the economist" stemming in part from "capricious patterns of inclusion and exclusion." Important before 1870, according to Trescott, was lack of conformity between the accounts of the Treasury, which the official data summarize, and the accounts of the collecting and disbursing officers who actually dealt with the public. He reported that the payment of $28 million of surplus revenue to the States in 1837 was omitted from Treasury accounts; that more than $100 million reported in Treasury figures of expenditures in the Civil War years was accumulated in disbursing officers' balances; and that various other adjustments were desirable. In compiling alternative totals of receipts and expenditures on the basis of various official records additional to Treasury accounts, Trescott has adopted special concepts, so that the resulting totals are designed primarily to measure money-flows. To some extent, his work incorporates a revised expenditure series compiled by M. Slade Kendrick in *A Century and a Half of Federal Expenditures*, National Bureau of Economic Research, New York, Occasional Paper 48, revised, 1955. Kendrick's data are as nearly as possible on a cash-payment basis for 1917–1952 (see Appendix B, especially p. 67).

Y 258–263. Federal Government receipts, 1789–1957.

Source: All series except Y 263, Treasury Department, *Annual Report of the Secretary of the Treasury, 1958*, pp. 392–396; series Y 263, 1796–1945, *Annual Report of the Secretary of the Treasury, 1946*, pp. 422–423, and 1946–1948, *Monthly Statement of Receipts and Expenditures of the United States Government*.

These data exclude receipts from borrowing. For the distinction between "total receipts" (series Y 259) and "net receipts" (series Y 258), see text for series Y 254–257. In recent years, these totals have been designated in the President's annual budget and in Treasury reports as "Gross budget receipts" and "Net budget receipts"; and the Bureau of the Budget, *Budget of the United States Government*, has included annually a special analysis giving detailed explanations and comparisons for the last-completed fiscal year, the current year, and the budget year.

In both the "total" and the "net" receipts, postal receipts are included net for each year when they exceeded postal expenditures, and they are included only to the extent of any such excess. For historical series relating to postal receipts and expenditures for 1789–1957, see the *Annual Report of the Secretary of the Treasury, 1946*, pp. 419–421, and *1958*, p. 461. (See also series Y 416, Y 460, and Y 496, below.)

Y 264–279. Internal revenue collections, 1863–1957.

Source: Treasury Department, *Annual Report of the Secretary of the Treasury, 1929*, pp. 419–424; *1946*, pp. 406–409; and *1958*, pp. 454–458.

The three *Annual Reports* overlap as to years covered. To the extent that they differ in the grouping of items in any given year, the tabulation shown here generally follows the later compilation; however, some exceptions are indicated below.

In *Historical Statistics of the United States, 1789–1945*, series P 109–119, the corresponding figures exclude trust fund receipts for 1935–1945. The data shown here for series Y 264–279 follow later Treasury practice by including, among internal revenue collections, all taxes collected by the Internal Revenue Service, whether assigned to general revenue or to trust funds.

These data are from Internal Revenue Service reports of collections. They differ from figures shown in other series, particularly series Y 261 (although the deviations in some years are small and the two series agree for 1904, 1909, 1955, and 1957). The variations reflect differences in the time or stage of operations when the receipts are recorded. Taxes are included in budget receipts when reported in the account of the Treasurer of the United States. Internal Revenue Service reports of collections through 1954 included taxes for which returns (and payments) had been received in internal revenue offices. Under arrangements begun in 1950 for withheld individual income tax and old-age and survivors insurance taxes, and later extended to railroad retirement taxes and many excises, these taxes are paid directly into Treasury depositaries. The depositary receipts, issued as evidence of such payment, are attached to quarterly returns submitted to

the Internal Revenue Service by employers and taxpayers. Under this procedure, the amounts are included in budget receipts in the month and year when the depositary receipts are issued.

Effective July 1, 1954, this accounting practice was extended to Internal Revenue Service reports of collections, so that the reported collections after fiscal 1954 likewise include depositary receipts in the month when the depositary receipts are issued.

Excise taxes paid into depositaries cannot be fully classified in terms of specific taxes until the supporting returns are received. Consequently, the collections shown for designated excise taxes in fiscal years after 1954 are subject to an undistributed adjustment. (For the amounts involved, see *Annual Report of the Secretary of the Treasury, 1958*, p. 458.)

The principal taxes included in totals but not shown separately are as follows:

1863–1915. Income and profits, largely 1863–1874 and 1914–1915 (see comments below for series Y 265); corporation excise, 1910–1914; occupational (special) taxes, 1863–1871, 1898–1902, and 1915.

1916–1957. Occupational (special) taxes, 1916–1928; insurance, 1918–1922; soft drinks, 1918–1924; and agricultural adjustment taxes, 1934–1936.

Y 264, total collections. For items included in this series but not shown separately in series Y 264–279, see source publications.

Y 265, individual income taxes. Although not shown separately for 1863–1915, this was an important tax source under revenue legislation enacted during the Civil War. The first collections in 1863 and for other years are shown below as tabulated in the *Annual Report of the Secretary of the Treasury, 1929*, p. 419.

Table III. Individual Income Tax Collections: 1863 to 1895
[In thousands of dollars. For years ending June 30]

Year	Amount	Year	Amount	Year	Amount	Year	Amount
1895	77	1874	139	1870	37,776	1866	72,982
1884	56	1873	5,062	1869	34,792	1865	60,979
1881	3	1872	14,437	1868	41,456	1864	20,295
1876	1	1871	19,163	1867	66,014	1863	2,742

The income tax legislation of the Civil War period expired in 1871 (see text for series Y 292–311). The collections in 1895 were under an act of 1894 that was declared unconstitutional. This type of tax was not imposed in other years during 1872–1913. The amounts shown in table III for 1873, 1874, 1876, 1881, and 1884 were late collections.

Separate figures for the individual income tax collections are not available for 1914, 1915, and 1918–1924.

Since 1951, withheld income taxes and old-age and survivors insurance taxes on employees and employers, and since 1957, disability insurance taxes on employees and employers have been paid into the Treasury in combined amounts without separation as to type of tax. Similarly, for the same periods, the old-age and survivors insurance and the disability insurance taxes on self-employment incomes have been paid in combination with income tax other than that withheld. The distribution of these collections by type of tax is based on estimates made in accordance with section 201(a) of the Social Security Act (42 U.S.C. 401(a)). Included in income taxes withheld by employers for 1951–1956 are amounts subsequently transferred to the Government of Guam under an act approved August 1, 1950 (48 U.S.C. 1421h). For 1957, these amounts are excluded.

The relative importance of withholding by employers as a method of income tax collection is shown in table IV for the period since withholding was instituted.

Table IV. Individual Income Tax Collections, by Method of Collection: 1943 to 1957

[In millions of dollars. For years ending June 30]

Year	Total	Withheld by employers	Other collections	Year	Total	Withheld by employers	Other collections
1957	39,030	26,728	12,302	1949	18,052	10,056	7,996
1956	35,338	24,016	11,322	1948	20,998	11,534	9,464
1955	31,650	21,254	10,396	1947	19,343	9,842	9,501
1954	32,814	22,077	10,737	1946	18,705	9,858	8,847
1953	32,536	21,132	11,404	1945	19,034	10,264	8,770
1952	29,274	17,929	11,345	1944	18,261	7,823	10,438
1951	22,997	13,090	9,908	1943	6,630	686	5,944
1950	17,153	9,889	7,264				

Y 266, corporation income taxes. Includes excess profits tax, 1917 and 1934–1946; unjust enrichment tax, 1937–1946; and undistributed profits tax, 1937–1939.

The corporation income tax law, effective March 1, 1913, was preceded by a corporate excise tax enacted in 1909, under which collections were as shown in table V (see Treasury Department, *Annual Report of the Secretary of the Treasury, 1929*, p. 420).

Table V. Collections Under the Corporate Excise Tax Act of 1909: 1910 to 1914

[In thousands of dollars. For years ending June 30]

Year	Amount	Year	Amount
1914	10,671	1911	33,512
1913	35,006	1910	20,960
1912	28,583		

For 1914, 1915, and 1918–1924, the Treasury reports do not separate corporate income tax from individual income tax collections.

Collections shown for 1952–1957 include taxes on business income of exempt corporations. Also included is the income tax on the Alaska Railroad, which was repealed for taxable years after June 30, 1952.

Y 267, employment taxes. Comprises the employer, employee, and self-employed taxes for the Federal old-age, survivors, and disability insurance system; the Federal unemployment insurance tax on employers; and the railroad retirement tax on employers and employees. Collections are received in combination with individual income taxes and the distribution by type of tax is based on estimates, as noted above in text for series Y 265.

Omitted from this series are railroad unemployment insurance contributions, collected by the Railroad Retirement Board under the Railroad Unemployment Insurance Act of 1938, as amended (45 U.S.C. 360). Although based on payrolls, this levy is not considered an internal revenue tax.

State unemployment insurance taxes also are not internal revenue collections, although the proceeds are deposited in the unemployment trust fund in the Federal Treasury.

Y 268, estate and gift taxes. Comprises, for 1863–1871 and 1899–1907, taxes on legacies, successions, and inheritances. The estate and gift taxes are shown separately for 1917 and later in the Treasury reports cited above. The figures for 1917–1924 and 1927–1932, inclusive, are for estate tax only. As indicated below for series Y 333–342, estate tax rate increases under the Revenue Act of June 2, 1924, were repealed retroactively February 26, 1926. Gift tax rates levied in 1924 were also reduced retroactively by the act of 1926. Estate and gift tax collections reported for 1925 and 1926 may include amounts collected at the higher rates and subsequently

refunded; the refunds were reported as expenditures rather than as deductions from revenue. (See Bureau of Internal Revenue, *Statistics of Income, 1946*, part 1 pp. 430–431; *Annual Report of the Secretary of the Treasury, 1926*, pp. 291 and 350; *1927*, pp. 965–966.)

Y 269–277 and Y 279, excise taxes. Series Y 269, excise taxes total, and series Y 272, manufacturers' excise tax subtotal, are shown for years in which these totals appear in the Treasury annual reports cited above. Taxes of these types were collected also in other years.

For the years for which they are shown, these totals include various taxes not specified in the table. The "manufacturers' excise taxes" include special taxes relating to manufacture and sale. For 1863–1868, the manufacturers' excise subtotal includes a tax on raw cotton. For 1916–1957, the series includes taxes on sales under the act of October 22, 1914; manufacturers', consumers', and dealers' excise taxes under war revenue and subsequent acts; and for 1932 and later, manufacturers' excises under the act of 1932, as amended. Excise taxes on soft drinks are in the total for series Y 269 but not in series Y 272.

Y 270, alcohol. Comprises taxes on distilled spirits, beer, wines, and other products and includes occupational taxes. Includes amounts collected by the customs service on imports of distilled spirits and beer. For 1954–1957, the reported amounts include taxes collected in Puerto Rico on alcohol products of Puerto Rican manufacture coming into the United States; for prior years, this is excluded.

Y 271, tobacco. Comprises taxes on cigarettes, cigars, and other tobacco products. Amounts reported for 1954–1957 include tax collected in Puerto Rico on Puerto Rican tobacco products coming into the United States; excluded prior to 1954.

Y 273, automobiles and accessories. Combines the Treasury series for "passenger automobiles and motorcycles," "automobile trucks and busses," and "parts and accessories for automobiles."

Y 276, admissions. Comprises "general admissions" and "cabarets," as shown separately in the *Annual Report of the Secretary of the Treasury, 1958*, p. 457, for 1929–1957.

Y 277, telephone, telegraph, radio, and cable facilities. Includes in all years the taxes on "telephone, telegraph, radio, and cable facilities," and also, for 1942 and later, the tax on "local telephone services."

Y 278, capital stock tax. This tax was not levied for years ending in the period July 1, 1926, through June 30, 1932, and for years ending after June 30, 1945. Collections after the fiscal year 1950 are included in excises, series Y 269.

Y 280–291. Corporation income tax returns, 1909–1956.

Source: 1909–1915, Bureau of Internal Revenue, *Annual Report of the Commissioner of Internal Revenue*, various issues; 1916–1956, Internal Revenue Service (and predecessor, Bureau of Internal Revenue), *Statistics of Income*, corporation income tax returns, annual issues.

Income tax returns are required annually of all corporations except those specifically exempt, such as fraternal, civic, and charitable organizations not operating for profit.

Data for 1916–1956 are for returns with accounting periods that ended between July 1 of the year specified and June 30 of the following year (for example, figures for 1916 are for accounting periods ending July 1, 1916, to June 30, 1917). A large proportion of the corporations' accounting periods coincide with the calendar year, and the calendar year is therefore used to identify the "income year." For the "income year" 1956, for example, 50.7 percent of the returns were for accounting periods that ended in December 1956; 17.6 percent for periods that ended during July–November 1956; 26.4 percent for periods that ended in the first half of 1957; and 5.2 percent, part-year returns.

Data for 1909–1915 are from returns received during the fiscal year beginning July 1 of the year specified. The data for 1915 include information from approximately 32,000 returns received during the preceding fiscal year.

Data are based on returns as filed, prior to audit adjustments, carrybacks, renegotiation of war contracts, or other changes made after the returns were filed. For 1951–1956, data are based on a probability sample described in the annual *Statistics of Income*. Only the most important changes in law affecting historical comparability of the data can be noted here; others are specified in the annual *Statistics of Income*— for example, the varying provisions regarding life insurance company taxation.

Because of consolidated returns for affiliated corporations, the number of returns (series Y 280, Y 281, Y 285, and Y 291) is not the same as the number of corporations.

Total compiled receipts of the corporations (series Y 282 and Y 286) include gross sales and receipts from operations, interest less amortizable bond premium, rents, royalties, net gain from capital assets (as defined by law) and other property, dividends, and other taxable income—all before "compiled deductions." These series also include nontaxable dividends from domestic corporations for 1918–1935 and nontaxable interest, but exclude all other nontaxable income. The data for 1916–1922 represent gross income. This was smaller than the total compiled receipts by the amounts of wholly tax-exempt interest received on certain government obligations and, for 1918–1921, of nontaxable dividends.

Compiled deductions include the cost of goods sold and (beginning in 1932) the cost of operations, as well as other negative amounts reported under sources of income.

Net income (less deficit) (series Y 283 and Y 287) is gross taxable income less allowable current-year deductions, except statutory deductions for dividends and Western Hemisphere trade corporations. This category excludes tax-exempt interest on government obligations and, for 1918–1935, dividends from domestic corporations; these are included in total compiled receipts. Beginning in 1936, contributions or gifts were deductible in determining net income. A deduction for amortization of emergency facilities was first allowable in 1940; the deduction was later extended to grain facilities and other items.

Income tax (series Y 288), as shown for 1909–1915, represents tax collections. For 1909–1912, these amounts correspond to the corporate excise tax collections noted for the fiscal years 1910–1913 in the text for series Y 266, above. For the income year 1913, the amount represents income tax and excise tax. Beginning with 1916, "income tax" is the tax liability on the returns, but before deduction of credit for taxes paid to foreign countries or U.S. possessions. For 1936–1938, the amounts include surtax on undistributed profits, as well as normal tax. For 1940 and 1941, the series includes the income defense tax; for 1941–1956, normal tax and surtax; and for 1942–1956, alternative tax.

Excess profits tax (series Y 289) for 1917–1922 comprises war profits tax and excess profits tax, and for 1933–1945, a declared-value excess profits tax effective for tax years that ended before July 1, 1946. Data for 1940 include the declared-value excess profits defense tax, and for 1940–1946, the excess profits tax under the Second Revenue Act of 1940. Amounts for 1942–1944 are for tax liability on the excess profits tax returns less a credit for debt retirement and the net postwar refund. Deferments under section 710(a)(5) of the 1939 Internal Revenue Code (relating to abnormalities under section 722) are reflected in the data for 1942 but not for 1943–1946. Amounts for 1943–1946 are after adjustments under various other relief provisions. The data for 1950–1954 are for the excess profits tax effective with respect to tax years from July 1, 1950, to December 31, 1953. For all years, the tax shown is before credit for foreign taxes paid.

Dividends paid (series Y 284 and Y 290) exclude liquidating dividends. They include all other dividends. In including dividends paid in the corporation's own stock, this series differs from similar series published elsewhere (e.g., Bureau of the Census, *Statistical Abstract of the United States, 1958*, p. 381, and Internal Revenue Service, *Statistics of Income, 1956–57, Corporation Income Tax Returns*, p. 120). For selected years, the amounts paid in stock, as included in the historical table, are as shown in table VI.

Table VI. Stock Dividends Paid: 1935 to 1956
[In thousands of dollars]

Income year	Included in series Y 284	Included in series Y 290	Income year	Included in series Y 284	Included in series Y 290
1956	2,725,210	2,676,783	1950	1,292,460	1,278,908
1955	1,996,477	1,965,391	1940	139,989	130,578
1954	1,350,041	1,316,460	1935	135,851	112,162
1953	1,110,260	1,089,355			

Inactive corporation returns (series Y291) are those which show no items of income or deductions.

Y 292–311. Individual income tax returns, 1913–1957.

Source: Internal Revenue Service, *Statistics of Income*, individual income tax returns, annual issues.

The data represent returns of residents and citizens, including those with addresses outside Alaska, Hawaii, and continental United States. Detailed tabulations for each year, 1948–1957, with data by levels of gross income and by States, appear in *Statistics of Income, 1957, Individual Income Tax Returns*, 1959, pp. 60–67.

As noted above in the text for internal revenue collections (series Y 265), the individual income tax has been a continuing element of the revenue system since 1913, but was included in Federal revenue legislation in two earlier periods.

During the Civil War decade, this tax was included in the first revenue act of the war, in 1861, at a flat rate of 3 percent on incomes above $800. Before the initial rate took effect, it was superseded in 1862 by rates of 3 percent on up to $10,000, 5 percent above that amount of net income, and an individual exemption of $600. Rates were raised further in 1864. The highest rates, levied for a single year, were 10 percent on net income of $600 to $5,000, 12.5 percent on $5,000 to $10,000, and 15 percent above $15,000. In 1867, the rate became a flat 5 percent on income of more than $1,000; for 1870 and 1871, the rate was 2.5 percent and the exemption $2,000. The law expired at the end of 1871.

An individual income tax law adopted in 1894 was patterned generally after the law of 1867. It provided a 2 percent tax rate on individual and corporate net income, with a $4,000 exemption for individuals. Personal property received by gift or inheritance was to be included in net income. The act was declared unconstitutional in 1895 in a Supreme Court decision (Pollock v. Farmers' Loan and Trust Co., 157 U.S. 429, 158 U.S. 601). The personal income tax was not again levied until after adoption in 1913 of the Sixteenth Amendment to the Constitution.

The data for 1913–1957 relate to returns filed under the income tax laws of 1913 and subsequent years. A return is required of every citizen or resident with gross or net income above a specified minimum. The requirements for filing have changed from time to time and are summarized below.

Table VII. Requirements for Filing Individual Income Tax Returns: 1913 to 1957

| Year | Return required if net or gross income equalled or exceeded amount specified | |
	Single, or married and not living with spouse	Married couple, joint return [1]
1954–1957	Gross, $600 [2]	Gross, $600 each spouse [2]
1948–1953	Gross, $600	Gross, $600 each spouse
1944–1947	Gross, $500	Gross, $500 each spouse
1942–1943	Gross, $500 [3]	Gross, $1,200 [4]
1941	Gross, $750	Gross, $1,500
1940	Gross, $800	Gross, $2,000
1932–1939	Net, $1,000 or gross, $5,000	Net, $2,500 or gross, $5,000
1925–1931	Net, $1,500 or gross, $5,000	Net, $3,500 or gross, $5,000
1924	Net, $1,000 or gross, $5,000	Net, $2,500 or gross, $5,000
1921–1923	Net, $1,000 or gross, $5,000	Net, $2,000 or gross, $5,000
1917–1920	Net, $1,000	Net, $2,000
1913–1916	Net, $3,000	Net, $3,000

[1] Through 1943, amount shown is combined net or combined gross income.
[2] Gross income of $1,200 for each person aged 65 or older.
[3] Also, for 1943, required to file if liable for 1942 tax, regardless of 1943 gross income.
[4] Also, for 1943, required to file if gross income of either spouse exceeded $624 or f either was liable for 1942 tax, regardless of 1943 gross income.

A joint return could be filed by husband and wife if income of both was included or if one spouse had no income.

For 1951–1957, a return was required of any individual whose net earnings for self-employment tax were $400 or more, regardless of the gross income requirement for filing.

In addition, under the current tax payment system instituted in 1943, returns were filed to claim refunds of taxes overpaid, even though the individual was not otherwise required to file.

Fiduciary income of an estate or trust for 1913–1936 was reported on an individual return form when there remained in the hands of the fiduciary net income which was taxable to him and not distributed to beneficiaries. Such a return for net income taxable to the fiduciary was required under the same conditions as those stated above for single persons during this period.

Data for 1913–1915 were derived from annual reports of the Commissioner of Internal Revenue, net income being determined on the basis of number of returns filed and the average net income in each class. Subsequent data were taken from returns, unaudited except to insure proper execution. Data for 1916 were tabulated from each return, but for later years were compiled by sampling techniques to represent the universe of returns, Form 1040 and 1040A (replaced by W–2 for 1944–1947). Tabulated data cover individual and fiduciary returns with net income of $3,000 or more, 1913–1916; returns with net income of $1,000 or more, 1917–1920; all returns with net income, 1921–1927; all individual and fiduciary returns with net income, but only individual returns with no net income, 1928–1936; all individual returns with net income or no net income, 1937–1943; and all individual returns with adjusted gross income or no adjusted gross income, 1944–1957, except that returns with no information were excluded for 1953–1956.

In the great majority of cases, the returns are for the calendar year, although some returns are for accounting periods ended during the calendar year. Also, some returns cover income attributable to several tax years. Prior to 1957, the tabulations of adjusted gross income (series Y 297) included only income attributed to the current tax year. For 1957, adjusted gross income includes the whole amount received by the taxpayer within his tax year even if it was reported as income earned over a period of time that included prior tax years.

Adjusted gross income for 1944–1957 is total income reported for tax purposes less deductions for certain expenses generally related to the acquisition of income. These deductions include business and rental expenses, certain travel and transportation expenses of employees, depreciation allowed life tenants of property held in trust, allowable loss from the sale of capital assets and other property, adjustments for long-term capital gain, net operating loss deductions, and for 1954–1957, excludable sick pay, the limited exclusion of dividends, and expenses of salesmen.

Under the Internal Revenue Code of 1954, taxable income (series Y 298) for 1954–1957 is the base on which the tax is computed. It consists of adjusted gross income less nonbusiness deductions. These deductions are for taxes, contributions, interest, and other specified purposes, and also include all personal exemptions. The figures for taxable income embrace all returns, including those showing the so-called "optional tax," i.e., a tax determined by reference to a simplified tax table involving standardized deductions rather than itemized nonbusiness deductions.

During 1948–1957, personal exemptions were $600 a year for each person—the taxpayer, his spouse, and dependents. A taxpayer aged 65 or older was allowed an additional $600 exemption for himself and, if a joint return was filed, for his wife if she was 65 or older. Likewise, an additional $600 exemption was allowed a blind taxpayer or a blind spouse.

Total income (series Y 305 and Y 309) for 1913–1943 is the gross income reported for income tax purposes under the act in effect for the income year. It is the total income after deduction of business and rental expenses and allowable loss on sales of capital assets and other property. Capital gain is included to the extent provided under successive acts.

Net income (series Y 306) for 1913–1943 is total income less authorized deductions. However, in the *Statistics of Income* for 1922–1931 the allowable prior-year loss was not deducted, and for 1924–1933 a capital loss that gave rise to a tax credit was not deducted. In the case of fiduciary net income, distribution to the beneficiary was an authorized deduction for 1913–1936. Net income in all years is measured before deduction of personal exemptions; it is not the tax base. The series is not available after 1943.

The small amounts of tax reported for 1938–1941 for returns with no net income (series Y 311) are an alternative tax on a small number of returns which showed a long-term capital loss and, for 1940 and 1941, a defense tax. For 1943, a victory tax was due on 17,438 returns with no net income.

Y 312–318. Fiduciary income tax returns, 1937–1956.

Source: Internal Revenue Service, *Statistics of Income*, fiduciary income tax returns, annual issues.

For more detailed information for 1947–1956, and for data by levels of income, see 1959 issue of source, pp. 24–25.

These series were tabulated from returns (Form 1041) before official audit. All returns were used for 1937–1939, but only taxable returns were used for 1940–1951. Taxable and nontaxable data for 1952, 1954, and 1956 were compiled by sampling techniques to represent all returns filed. Data were not tabulated for 1953, 1955, and 1957.

Fiduciary returns show annual income from estates in process of settlement or any other trust for which the fiduciary acts as administrator. Only certain small trusts are excused from filing. For the period covered, returns were required if income equalled or exceeded the amounts specified for the following years:

Income of an estate—for 1937–1939, gross income of $5,000 or net income taxable to the fiduciary of $1,000; 1940, gross income of $800; 1941, gross income of $750; 1942–1947, gross income of $500; 1948–1956, gross income of $600.

Income of a trust—for 1937, gross income of $5,000 or net income taxable to the fiduciary of $1,000; 1938 and 1939, gross income of $5,000 or net income of $100; 1940, gross income of $800 or net income of $100; 1941, gross income of $750 or net income of $100; 1942–1947, gross income of $500 or net income of $100; 1948–1953, gross income of $600 or net income of $100; 1954–1956, gross income of $600 or any taxable income of the fiduciary.

For any tax year, a return was required if any beneficiary of the estate or trust was a nonresident alien.

Total income (series Y 313) is gross income reported in accordance with the law for each tax year. For 1937–1952, this is after business and rental expenses and allowable loss from sales of capital assets and other property, and it includes capital gains as required under the various acts. For 1954 and 1956, it includes gross profit from business, gross rents, and the entire capital gain without adjustment.

Net income or taxable income (series Y 314) as shown for 1954 and 1956 is less inclusive than the amounts shown for earlier years. For 1937–1952, this series represents total income less allowable nonbusiness deductions and the amount distributable to beneficiaries. For these years, it is not the amount taxed, since the exemption allowed to trusts and estates has not been deducted from the net income taxable to the fiduciary. For 1954 and 1956, the series shows income taxable to the fiduciary. This is total income after deduction of the exemption as well as all business and rental expenses, the authorized nonbusiness deductions, distributions to beneficiaries, and the fiduciary's share of dividend exclusions and of long-term capital gain.

Y 319–332. Individual income tax liability and effective rates, for selected income groups, 1913–1957.

Source: Treasury Department, records.

Maximum earned net income is assumed where it affects the amount of tax liability. In the case of the married couple (four exemptions), the computations assume prior to 1948 that only one spouse had income. Beginning with the income year 1948, all married couples have been permitted to combine their incomes in a joint return and to split the taxable income equally for purposes of the tax computation; a joint return on the split-income basis is therefore assumed for the married couple for the income years 1948–1957.

For the same years, persons of age 65 or older and blind persons were allowed additional exemptions; consequently, the illustrative data for 1948–1957 apply equally to any married couple claiming 4 exemptions, whether the additional exemptions were for dependents, age, or blindness.

The effective tax rate is the tax liability as a percentage of the amount of net income. The liability is the amount for income tax only, including the defense and victory taxes of 1940 and 1943; it does not include the self-employment tax for social security, applicable for 1951–1957.

Net income, as used here, is gross income (after 1943, adjusted gross income) minus nonbusiness deductions for contributions, interest, taxes, medical and dental expenses, and other allowable expenses, but before deduction of personal exemptions. Also excluded from net income (and from adjusted gross income) is tax-exempt interest on government obligations, excludable sick pay under the Revenue Act of 1954, certain expenses related to the acquisition of income, and other nontaxable income.

Statutory changes have been made from time to time in the allowable nonbusiness deductions. For example, the deduction for medical expenses was amended several times during 1944–1957. Another type of nonbusiness deduction, the amount allowed for contributions, was limited to 20 percent of adjusted gross income prior to 1954; for 1954–1957, taxpayers were allowed to deduct more than 20 percent to the extent that the excess (limited to 10 percent of adjusted gross income) was for contributions to hospitals, churches, or educational institutions.

In consequence of these and other changes, a given amount of net income could be associated with somewhat different amounts of gross income in different years. Even in any one year, a given amount of net income could be associated with different amounts of gross income for different taxpayers in accordance with their varying allowable deductions.

Beginning with the income year 1941, taxpayers with gross income of not more than $3,000 from specified sources were allowed to use a simplified return Form 1040A, with the tax determined by a table that allowed a standard percentage of earned income credit and deductions from income. Taxpayers who did not use the short form were required to itemize deductions. In either case, the 1943 victory tax had to be computed separately. Legislation simplifying the filing of tax returns made available (beginning in 1944) the option of a standard deduction of 10 percent of adjusted gross income, limited to $500 for 1944–1947. For 1948–1957, the limit was raised to $1,000 for single persons and for married persons filing joint returns. In general, this implies that, for 1944–1947, net incomes of $4,500 or less and, for 1948–1957, net incomes of $9,000 or less, as shown in the table, would represent adjusted gross incomes at least ten-ninths as large. (That is, $800 net represents at least $889 of adjusted gross income; $1,000 net, at least $1,111 gross; $4,500 net, at least $5,000 gross; etc.)

For some types of analysis, effective rates based on gross rather than net income might be more pertinent. Such rates can be computed by making uniform assumptions about the deductions associated with the several specified levels of net income. For example, if it is assumed that the standard deductions made up the whole difference between adjusted gross and net income in cases in which the standard deduction was available, the effective percentage rate of tax on adjusted gross income in these cases would be nine-tenths of the effective rates shown in series Y 319–332. For another type of computation of effective tax rates, see Internal Revenue Service, *Statistics of Income, 1957, Individual Income Tax Returns*, p. 38.

The history since 1913 of the personal exemptions (including credits for dependents) and of the range of tax rates applicable to taxable individual incomes is summarized below in table VIII, from the following publications: 1913–1950, Treasury Department, *Annual Report of the Secretary of the Treasury, 1940*, pp. 466–467, and *1950*, p. 251; and 1951–1957, Joint Economic Committee, *The Federal Revenue System: Facts and Problems, 1959*, 86th Congress, 1st session, p. 189.

Table VIII. Federal Individual Income Tax Exemptions, and First and Top Bracket Rates: 1913 to 1959

Income year	Personal exemptions					Tax rates			
	Single	Married				First bracket		Top bracket	
		Dependents				Rate	Amt. of income	Rate	Income over
		None	1	2	3				
1954–1959[1]	$600	$1,200	$1,800	$2,400	$3,000	20	$2,000	[2]91	$200,000
1952–1953[1]	600	1,200	1,800	2,400	3,000	22.2	2,000	[2]92	200,000
1951[1]	600	1,200	1,800	2,400	3,000	20.4	2,000	[2]91	200,000
1950[1]	600	1,200	1,800	2,400	3,000	17.4	2,000	[2]84.36	200,000
1948–1949[1]	600	1,200	1,800	2,400	3,000	16.6	2,000	[2]82.13	200,000
1946–1947	500	1,000	1,500	2,000	2,500	19	2,000	[2]86.45	200,000
1944–1945	500	1,000	1,500	2,000	2,500	23	2,000	[2]94	200,000
1942–1943[3]	500	1,200	1,550	1,900	2,250	[4]19	2,000	88	200,000
1941	750	1,500	1,900	2,300	2,700	[4]10	2,000	81	5,000,000
1940	800	2,000	2,400	2,800	3,200	[4]4.4	4,000	81.1	5,000,000
1936–1939	1,000	2,500	2,900	3,300	3,700	[4]4	4,000	79	5,000,000
1934–1935	1,000	2,500	2,900	3,300	3,700	[4]4	4,000	63	1,000,000
1932–1933	1,000	2,500	2,900	3,300	3,700	4	4,000	63	1,000,000
1930–1931	1,500	3,500	3,900	4,300	4,700	[5]1⅛	4,000	25	100,000
1929	1,500	3,500	3,900	4,300	4,700	[5]⅜	4,000	24	100,000
1925–1928	1,500	3,500	3,900	4,300	4,700	[5]1⅛	4,000	25	100,000
1924	1,000	2,500	2,900	3,300	3,700	[5]1½	4,000	46	500,000
1923	1,000	[6]2,500	2,900	3,300	3,700	3	4,000	56	200,000
1922	1,000	[6]2,500	2,900	3,300	3,700	4	4,000	56	200,000
1921	1,000	[6]2,500	2,900	3,300	3,700	4	4,000	73	1,000,000
1919–1920	1,000	2,000	2,200	2,400	2,600	4	4,000	73	1,000,000
1918	1,000	2,000	2,200	2,400	2,600	6	4,000	77	1,000,000
1917	1,000	2,000	2,200	2,400	2,600	2	2,000	67	2,000,000
1916	3,000	4,000	4,000	4,000	4,000	2	20,000	15	2,000,000
1913–1915	3,000	4,000	4,000	4,000	4,000	1	20,000	7	500,000

[1] Additional exemptions of $600 are allowed to taxpayers and their spouses on account of blindness and/or age 65 or older.

[2] Subject to maximum effective rate limitation: 90 percent for 1944–45, 85.5 percent for 1946–47, 77 percent for 1948–49, 80 percent for 1950, 87.2 percent for 1951, 88 percent for 1952–53, and 87 percent for 1954–59.

[3] Exclusive of victory tax.

[4] Before earned income credit allowed as a deduction equal to 10 percent of earned net income.

[5] After earned income credit equal to 25 percent of tax on earned income.

[6] If net income exceeds $5,000, married person's exemption is $2,000.

Y 333–342. Federal estate tax returns, 1916–1957.

Source: Internal Revenue Service, *Statistics of Income*, estate tax returns, annual issues.

The Federal estate tax is a levy upon the transfer of property by a decedent. It differs from inheritance taxes, in which, generally, the tax is on the privilege of receiving property by inheritance and is levied upon the heirs.

The base of the tax is the value of the gross estate transferred, adjusted for exclusions, deductions, and exemptions. The tax is imposed at graduated rates, and certain credits are allowed against the tax so computed.

The estate tax in its present form became a permanent part of the Federal tax system in 1916, but four times earlier death taxes had been imposed by the Federal Government. During 1797–1802, a stamp tax applied to succession to personal property by inheritance. The Civil War Revenue Act of 1862 included an inheritance tax which was substantially increased in 1864; this tax was repealed in 1870. The income tax act of 1894 included an inheritance tax that was abandoned when the income tax was declared unconstitutional. The Revenue Act of 1898, for financing the Spanish-American War, included a short-lived tax applicable to all estates of over $10,000, except those inherited by spouses.

Table IX summarizes the history of Federal estate tax rates and exemptions for 1916–1957. An estate tax return was required if the value of the gross estate at the date of death exceeded the allowable specific exemption as shown in the table and footnote 1.

The estate of an individual who died in the period June 6, 1932, through August 16, 1954, was subject to two estate taxes—basic and additional. Basic tax was at the rates provided in the 1926 act; additional tax was the excess of a tentative tax at rates provided by the act in force at date of death, over the basic tax. Under the 1954 Code, these two taxes were combined and a single tax rate applied to the net taxable estate.

Table IX. Estate Tax Rates, Specific Exemption, and Insurance Exclusion: 1916 to 1957

Date of death	Tax rates range (percent)	Minimum rate applies to first—	Maximum rate applies above—	Specific exemption[1]	Insurance exclusion
Oct. 22, 1942–1957	3.0–77	$5,000	$10,000,000	$60,000	————
Sept. 21, 1941–Oct. 21, 1942	3.0–77	5,000	10,000,000	40,000	$40,000
Aug. 31, 1935–Sept. 20, 1941	[2]2.0–70	10,000	50,000,000	40,000	40,000
May 11, 1934–Aug. 30, 1935	1.0–60	10,000	10,000,000	40,000	40,000
June 6, 1932–May 10, 1934	1.0–45	10,000	10,000,000	50,000	40,000
Feb. 26, 1926–June 6, 1932	1.0–20	50,000	10,000,000	100,000	40,000
Feb. 24, 1919–Feb. 26, 1926	[3]1.0–25	50,000	10,000,000	50,000	40,000
Oct. 4, 1917–Feb. 24, 1919	2.0–25	50,000	10,000,000	50,000	————
Mar. 3–Oct. 3, 1917	1.5–15	50,000	5,0000,00	50,000	————
Sept. 9, 1916–Mar. 2, 1917	1.0–10	50,000	5,000,000	50,000	————

[1] For estate of resident citizen or alien. The same specific exemption was granted for estates of nonresident citizens dying after May 10, 1934. Exemptions were not granted to estates of nonresident aliens until Oct. 22, 1942, when a $2,000 exemption became available.

[2] For deaths from June 26, 1940, to Sept. 20, 1941, a defense tax was added equal to 10 percent of the net estate tax (computed at the rates of 2 to 70 percent) after deduction of credits for gift taxes and State death taxes.

[3] Higher rates, ranging from 1 percent to a top-bracket rate of 40 percent on the excess over $10,000,000, were provided in the Revenue Act of June 2, 1924, but the rates of the 1921 act were restored retroactively Feb. 26, 1926. Refunds were authorized for overpayments made at the higher rates. The net tax (series Y 338 and Y 342) was computed at the lower rates (*Statistics of Income, 1925*, pp. 70–71, 82).

Source: Adapted from Internal Revenue Service, *Statistics of Income*, various issues; Treasury Department, *Annual Report of the Secretary of the Treasury, 1940*, pp. 478–479, and *1950*, p. 258.

A marital deduction for bequests to the surviving spouse applied to the estates of persons who died after 1947. The deduction is limited to the smaller of either one-half the value of the adjusted gross estate or the value of the qualifying property interests which pass to the surviving spouse. The impact of this provision is reflected in the statistics.

Gross estate (series Y 335 and Y 340) includes all property possessed to the extent of the decedent's interest therein at death, including certain transfers made during life without full consideration, joint estates, tenancies by the entirety, dower and curtesy of surviving spouse, and life insurance on the life of the decedent if the estate was administered under the 1942 or subsequent acts. The value of the gross estate may be either the value at date of death or as of the date one year after death, whichever the executor elected in case death occurred on or after August 31, 1935.

Net taxable estate (series Y 336 and Y 341) is gross estate less the deductions and specific exemptions allowed under the act in effect at date of death. These have varied somewhat among the different acts.

Y 343–349. Federal gift tax returns, 1924–1956.

Source: Internal Revenue Service, *Statistics of Income*, gift tax returns, annual issues.

These data are from returns filed, before audit. Data for 1952, 1954, 1955, and 1957 were not tabulated.

The Federal gift tax, like the estate tax, is a levy upon transfers of property by gift. The tax is a liability of the person making the gift and is based upon the value of the transferred property.

The gift tax was first levied for 1924 and 1925. For these years, a return was required for gifts of property located in the United States, made by individuals, corporations, associations, partnerships, trusts, or estates, if total gifts exceeded the sum of authorized deductions for exemption, charitable gifts, and previously taxed property, and if the aggregate exceeded $500 to any one donee.

The present gift tax was introduced in 1932 in connection with substantial revisions in the estate tax. The rates were three-fourths of those in the estate tax, and this relationship was maintained through subsequent revisions (subject, however, to differences in the effective dates of rate and exemption changes). A return was required during 1932–1956 if aggregate gifts in the year to any donee exceeded the allowable annual exclusion per donee and for gifts of future interests regardless of value. Tax rates, specific exemptions, and annual exclusions are summarized in table X.

Table X. Gift Tax Rates, Exemptions, and Exclusions: 1924 to 1956

Calendar year of gift	Tax rates, range (percent)	Minimum rate applies to first—	Maximum rate applies above—	Specific exemption [1]	Annual exclusion per donee
1943–1956	2.25–57.75	$ 5,000	$10,000,000	$30,000	$3,000
1942	2.25–57.75	5,000	10,000,000	40,000	4,000
1939–1941	[2] 1.5–52.5	10,000	50,000,000	40,000	4,000
1936–1938	1.5–52.5	10,000	50,000,000	40,000	5,000
1935	.75–45	10,000	10,000,000	50,000	5,000
1932 [3]–1934	.75–33.5	10,000	10,000,000	50,000	5,000
1924 [4]–1925	1–25	50,000	10,000,000	50,000	500

[1] During 1924–1925, allowed in each calendar year; in later years, allowed only once.
[2] From June 26, 1940, through 1941, subject to additional defense tax equal to 10 percent of basic tax liability.
[3] In effect for gifts June 7, 1932, and later.
[4] In effect June 24, 1924.
Source: Adapted from Internal Revenue Service, *Statistics of Income*, various issues; Treasury Department, *Annual Report of the Secretary of the Treasury, 1940*, pp. 478–479, and *1950*, p. 258.

Since 1932 the tax has applied to individuals only (citizens, residents, or nonresident aliens) for transfer of property situated in the United States.

Gift tax rates are progressive in application; that is, current graduated rates are applied to (*a*) the aggregate net taxable gifts made after June 6, 1932, and to (*b*) the aggregate net gifts exclusive of those made in the current year—the excess of tax in (*a*) over (*b*) being the current tax liability.

As indicated in table X, the donor is allowed to exclude gifts of less than a specified amount to each recipient in each year. This annual exclusion was $3,000 for each donee for the years 1943–1956. In addition, a specific exemption ($30,000 during 1943–1956) is allowed each citizen or resident and may be taken, at his option, entirely in a single year or spread over a number of years. After April 2, 1948, a marital deduction of one-half of the value of gifts made between a husband and wife was allowed citizens and residents.

Total gifts (series Y 345 and Y 349) is the value of property (real property or tangible or intangible personal property) transferred without full consideration in money or money's worth, whether transferred in trust or otherwise, whether direct or indirect, or of future interests. Generally, gifts of less than the allowable annual exclusion for each donee are not reported, except that gifts of future interests must be included regardless of value (and, for 1939–1942, gifts in trust).

Net taxable gift (series Y 346) is the tax base. It is the value of total gifts minus the exclusion for each donee, deductions, and specific exemptions.

Y 350–356. Expenditures of the Federal Government, 1789–1957.

Source: Series Y 350–355, Treasury Department, *Annual Report of the Secretary of the Treasury, 1958*, pp. 393–397. Series Y 356, 1789–1946, Treasury Department, *Annual Report, 1946*, pp. 422–423, 1947–1957, Bureau of the Budget, *Budget of the United States Government*, annual issues, 1949–1959.

These series exclude amounts paid to retire public debt and expenditures from trust accounts. They include the transactions of all other Federal funds. In the case of public enterprise funds (including the postal service) and various intra-governmental funds, expenditures included in the total are on a *net* basis—that is, their collections are deducted from gross expenditures and the results are the net expenditures included in Federal Government expenditure accounts. In the case of the postal service, the net postal expenditure is included in the total and "other" (series Y 350 and Y 355) expenditures in the years in which there was a postal deficit. For a historical series showing gross postal expenditures in relation to postal receipts, see references in text for series Y 258–263.

Expenditures for 1789–1915 are based on warrants issued; for 1916–1952, on the *Daily Statement of the United States Treasury;* for 1953–1957, on the Treasury's *Monthly Statement of Receipts and Expenditures of the United States Government.*

In the *Monthly Statement*, expenditures are reported on the basis of checks issued by disbursing officers, except for interest on the public debt and payments made in cash. Where payment is made by the issuance of bonds or by an increase in their redemption value, instead of by the issuance of checks, such an issuance or increase is an expenditure. Interest on the public debt is reported on an accrual basis. For years prior to those reported in the *Monthly Statement*, interest on the public debt is reported on the same basis as other expenditures.

The figures for 1916–1952 were compiled from daily reports received by the Treasurer of the United States from Government depositaries and Treasury offices holding Government funds. On this basis, the expenditures include payments on checks outstanding at the beginning of the fiscal year and do not include checks unpaid at the end of the year. Beginning with the fiscal year 1947, expenditures of several departments and establishments were reported on the basis of checks issued, so that the detail in the daily statement was partly based on checks issued, partly on checks paid. The change to the monthly statement basis eliminated the necessity for showing an item of "adjustment to daily Treasury statement basis" in tabulations presenting components of the expenditure total.

Y 357–367. Budget expenditures of the Federal Government, by major function, 1900–1957.

Source: Bureau of the Budget, records.

Basic data are from the following:

1900–1914. Adapted from Bureau of the Budget compilation for 1900–1948 in U.S. Congress, *Congressional Record*, 80th Congress, 2d session, vol. 94, pt. 2, March 11, 1948, pp. 2576–2577. Series Y 360, veterans services and benefits supplied from the Treasury compilation in series Y 356 (see below). Tax refunds of $10 million a year deducted from 1913 and 1914 to conform to the *1959 Federal Budget Midyear Review* (September 1958), p. 42, where budget receipt and expenditure totals are shown for each year, 1900–1959, with refunds excluded starting in 1913.

1915–1920. *Congressional Record*, cited above, but with tax refunds deducted.

1921–1938. Unpublished Bureau of the Budget table for 1920–1959, September 17, 1958; but with series Y 359, International affairs and finance, supplied from *Congressional Record*, cited above.

1939–1950. Unpublished Bureau of the Budget table for 1939–1950, February 1959.

1951–1957. Bureau of the Budget, *Federal Budget in Brief*, fiscal year 1960 (1959), p. 55, summarizing the *Budget* for 1960, special analysis L, pp. 1013–1014.

As Federal Government operations expanded in volume and variety, the limited classification of expenditures exemplified in series Y 350–356 (even when supplemented with additional items and subdivided to give more specific categories) was inadequate to delineate the scope of Government programs and to focus attention on significant shifts in the purpose of expenditures.

A systematic classification of expenditures by major functional categories and more specific subfunctions was introduced in the *Budget* for the fiscal year 1948. Although each succeeding annual *Budget* modified some of the categories or shifted particular items from one classification to another, continuity of the series was maintained by explanatory statements and a revised historical special analysis included at the end of each year's *Budget* volume. See, for example, special analysis L, in the *Budget* for 1960, pp. 1013–1014, showing expenditures for each major function and subfunction for the fiscal years 1951–1957, using the classification system as revised for the 1960 *Budget*. The content of each functional category may be determined from the subfunctions listed in the special analysis, from the explanatory comments in the President's Budget Message, and by examination of the detailed *Budget*.

Series Y 360, veterans services and benefits, may be slightly understated for 1900–1914, as it comprises only the payments for veterans compensation and pensions, the same as series Y 356. Any such understatement in series Y 360 apparently would not exceed $12 million a year and is balanced by an equal overstatement in the residual series, Y 361–365, for "All other."

Refunds are excluded from series Y 357–367 since 1912. Consequently, total expenditures, series Y 357, for 1913–1930 deviate from those shown in series Y 255 and Y 350 by the amount of refunds.

As to series Y 367, adjustment to daily Treasury statement, see text for series Y 350–356.

Y 368–379. Public debt of the Federal Government, 1791–1957.

Source: **Series Y 368–372,** Treasury Department, *Annual Report of the Secretary of the Treasury, 1891,* p. xcii, *1946,* pp. 455–456, and *1958,* p. 470. **Series Y 373–374,** 1855 and 1892–1915, Bureau of Foreign and Domestic Commerce, *Statistical Abstract of the United States, 1921,* p. 829; 1856–1891 and 1916–1957, Treasury Department, *Annual Report, 1891,* p. XCIV, *1946,* p. 546, and *1958,* p. 563. **Series Y 375–379,** 1880–1915, Treasury Department, records; 1916–1957, *Annual Report, 1946,* p. 459, and *1958,* pp. 472–473.

The total gross debt (series Y 368) as reported at the end of each fiscal period is essentially the formal funded debt of the Federal Government, both long-term and short-term. It includes savings bonds at current redemption value. The total gross debt is also designated as "the public debt." Outside that total, but included in "total debt outstanding," are guaranteed obligations held outside the Treasury—comprising obligations issued by certain Government corporations and credit agencies, which are guaranteed by the United States as to both principal and interest. These were first authorized in 1932 but none were outstanding at the end of the fiscal years 1932 and 1933. (See the *Annual Report of the Secretary of the Treasury, 1958,* pp. 391, 471.)

Studies by Paul B. Trescott and others have suggested that the debt totals (series Y 368) as compiled by the Treasury Department for the early years of the Republic—1791 into the early 1800's—may omit obligations incurred otherwise than by the issuance of Treasury obligations and may include some contingent liabilities that would be excluded by the definitions adopted in later years. (Trescott, unpublished memoranda; see also Paul Studenski and Herman E. Krooss, *Financial History of the United States,* McGraw-Hill, New York, 1952, p. 3, footnote 1.) See also text for series Y 254–257.

Although nearly all the public debt is interest-bearing, the total includes some obligations that bear no interest and matured debt on which interest has ceased. In recent years, a substantial part of the public debt has been held in the trust funds and other Treasury investment accounts. (For the ownership of Federal public debt obligations at several dates for 1941–1958, see the *Annual Report of the Secretary of the Treasury, 1958,* pp. 34, 576.) Certain unfunded obligations of the Government are not counted in the public debt, for example, a potential obligation of the Government for unpaid employer contributions to the civil service retirement and disability fund.

The formal concept of "the public debt," as used in Federal fiscal reports, appears to have emerged following initial enactment of a statutory ceiling on the debt of the Federal Government. Such a ceiling was first provided in the Second Liberty Bond Act of 1917; prior to May 26, 1938, the limitation applied to particular segments of the debt, not to the total. The debt ceiling has been modified from time to time in subsequent legislation. For a tabular summary of the debt limit legislation, 1917–1958, see Marshall A. Robinson, *The National Debt Ceiling, An Experiment in Fiscal Policy,* The Brookings Institution, Washington, D.C., 1959, p. 3.

Despite the close relationship of "the public debt" or total gross debt (series Y 368) to the debt limitation, series Y 368 includes a relatively small amount of obligations not subject to statutory limitations. Robinson, cited above, points out (p. 8) that "the Federal debt is part of a larger structure of Federal Government obligations. . . . The legally defined gross Federal debt . . . is the debt that falls under the debt limitation, and it is what general usage calls the national debt." For a rough estimate of some additional obligations not included in "total gross debt," see a compilation by the Comptroller General of the United States, in *Investigation of the Financial Condition of the United States: Hearings before the Senate Committee on Finance,* 85th Congress, 1st session, vol. 1, June 26, 1957, pp. 81–82, 269.

Various writers, including Robinson, have contended that the most meaningful measure of the national debt in economic terms is "debt owed to the public." (See series Y 383, which shows yearly changes in terms of "net cash borrowing from the public or repayment.") It should be noted, however, that any such series is a subdivision of the total gross public debt and does not incorporate Federal Government obligations that are not counted in the formal public debt.

The computed annual interest charge (series Y 373) represents the amount of interest that would be paid if each interest-bearing issue outstanding at the end of the year should remain outstanding for a year at the applicable annual rate of interest. The charge is computed for each issue by applying the appropriate annual interest rate to the amount outstanding on that date. The aggregate charge is the total of the computed amounts for all interest-bearing issues. The average annual rate is computed by dividing the computed annual interest charge for the total of outstanding issues by the corresponding principal amount.

Y 380–383. Cash receipts from and payments to the public by the Federal Government, 1929–1957.

Source: **Series Y 380–382,** all fiscal years, and calendar years 1929–1956, U.S. Congress, Joint Economic Committee, 85th Congress, 1st session, *1957 Historical and Descriptive Supplement to Economic Indicators,* p. 73; calendar 1957, Council of Economic Advisers, *Economic Indicators,* June 1959. (Basic data from Bureau of the Budget and Treasury Department.) **Series Y 383,** 1930–1940, Bureau of the Budget, records; 1941–1949, Treasury Department, *Treasury Monthly*

Bulletin, August 1948 and 1950; 1950–1957, *Annual Report of the Secretary of the Treasury, 1958,* p. 462.

The series summarize the flow of money between the public and the Federal Government as a whole. This type of compilation is often referred to as a consolidated-cash statement. The totals represent in effect a summation of all Federal transactions with the public—other than borrowing and debt repayment.

The public is defined to include individuals, banks, other private corporations and associations, unincorporated businesses, the Federal Reserve System, the Postal Savings System, State and local governments, foreign governments, and international organizations.

For the statistical procedures by which the data are derived, see *1957 Historical and Descriptive Supplement . . . ,* pp. 72 and 74. For presentation and derivation of the annual data and reconciliations with the administrative budget totals and with Treasury accounts, see the annual *Budget of the United States Government* for 1949 and later fiscal years, special analysis A.

Federal Government transactions comprised within these totals include not only those receipts and expenditures counted in the administrative budget but also the transactions of trust and deposit funds held by the Government and certain transactions of Government-sponsored enterprises that are outside the conventional budget—mainly the Federal Deposit Insurance Corporation, Federal land banks, Federal home loan banks, and banks for cooperatives. Major intragovernmental and noncash transactions are eliminated in the consolidated summation of transactions with the public. A few items of expenditure that are made in the form of additions to the public debt (such as interest accruing on savings bonds) are counted as cash payments only when the actual disbursement is subsequently made, in contrast with the administrative budget totals in which such items are reported as a budget expenditure at the time when the increase in the public debt occurs.

The excess of Federal cash receipts from the public or payments to the public is often referred to as the "cash surplus or deficit." As the tabulated series indicate, the excess of receipts from or payments to the public is not necessarily the same as the Government's net cash borrowing from the public or repayment of debt owed to the public. The difference is accounted for mainly by increases or decreases in cash balances (both in the Treasury and outside it) and to a minor extent by receipts from the exercise of monetary authority. Net cash borrowing or repayment of borrowings from the public excludes Treasury borrowing from Federal trust accounts and Government-sponsored enterprises and also excludes certain types of public-debt transactions such as the issuance and redemption of Armed Forces leave bonds.

Because the cash accounts include receipts and payments of trust funds, exclude various intragovernmental and noncash transactions, and are affected by other types of adjustments, the amounts reported as receipts from several major sources and the expenditures reported for several major functions differ significantly from the amounts reported for the same sources or functions in Treasury and budget accounts that tie to the administrative budget totals.

In the case of tax receipts, the principal differences during 1948–1957 were in employment taxes, which were predominantly trust fund revenues; and, in 1957, certain excise taxes on motor fuel, tires, and vehicles that were earmarked, beginning in that year, for the highway trust fund. Also, the cash receipts accounts include other types of trust fund receipts (such as unemployment insurance deposits by States,

and veterans life insurance premiums) that are not included in budget receipts. For Federal Government receipts from the public, by major sources, in the fiscal years 1948–1957, see the *Budget of the United States Government* for fiscal year 1960, p. 929.

The figures in the 1960 *Budget* are not the same, however, as those shown under similar headings in series Y 264–279, not only because there are conceptual differences between budget receipts and receipts from the public, but also because series Y 264–279 are in terms of internal revenue collections, so that the amounts are reported at a point in the flow of receipts different from the point at which they are reported in the annual budget total.

On the expenditure side, the functional categories most substantially affected for 1948–1957 by the differences between Federal payments to the public and budget expenditures were those for labor and welfare and for veterans services and benefits, both of which involve extensive payments from trust funds. In 1957, the commerce and housing category—which includes Federal expenditures for highway construction grants—also showed a substantial difference between budget expenditures and payments to the public.

The 1960 *Budget* (p. 929) reports Federal payments to the public for each major function for the fiscal years 1948–1957. The amounts shown there may be compared with budget expenditures for the same categories as reported in series Y 357–367.

Because the totals of receipts from and payments to the public are more comprehensive than the budget totals, they are widely used in assessing the impact of Government transactions on the economy. However, the magnitude of Government operations is understated somewhat, even in these totals, because they include only the net receipts or net expenditures of wholly owned and Government-sponsored enterprises. This procedure affects the totals of cash receipts and payments equally and therefore does not affect the excess of receipts from or payments to the public.

Similar data for State and local governments (and for the Federal Government for calendar years) are shown for 1946–1957 in the Council of Economic Advisers, *Economic Report of the President,* annual issues.

Y 384–714. General note.

The concepts and terms used in these series were originally developed for Census Bureau reporting on finances of State and local governments. These concepts have also been applied to Federal Government data to provide comparable comprehensive aggregates covering all levels of government.

For a full discussion of basic concepts and terminology and of the classifications of revenue and expenditure, see the source for series Y 384–445, pp. 1–9. A few of the more important items are discussed here.

General revenue and general expenditure, as used in these series, refer to all sources or purposes other than certain specifically defined utility, liquor store, and insurance trust operations.

Intergovernmental revenue and intergovernmental expenditure refer to transactions between the Federal, State, and local governments. To avoid double counting, such transactions are netted out of aggregates comprising the groups of governments concerned. Transactions with governments of other countries are not defined as intergovernmental. The value of intergovernmental aid "in kind" (for example, commodities or other property given by the Federal Government to State or local government agencies) is **not** included in **either** intergovernmental or other revenue of the receiving government; the expenditures involved in granting such aid are included in direct expenditure of the granting government.

Besides intergovernmental aid "in kind," the following types of transactions between governments have not been isolated for special treatment as intergovernmental revenue or expenditure:

a. Contributions by local governments to State-administered retirement systems that cover their employees. These are included without distinction as part of the "current operation" expenditure of the local governments, and the receipts are included with State insurance trust revenue.

b. Interest paid or received on obligations of one government held by another government.

c. Transactions in which governments deal as ordinary suppliers and customers—e.g., in purchasing property, utility services, or supplies from one another.

Direct expenditure comprises all expenditure other than intergovernmental expenditure.

Since the data utilized for each individual government represent a consolidation of amounts from its various funds, payments between funds are eliminated for Census reporting. Thus, a government employer contribution to a retirement fund it administers is not counted as expenditure, nor is the receipt of this contribution by the retirement fund considered revenue; only the payment out of the fund for retirement benefits is classified in the Census tabulations as a governmental expenditure (in this particular illustration, an insurance trust expenditure).

The substantial amount of interest paid by the U.S. Treasury to the Federal insurance trust funds, which have all their reserves invested in Federal securities, is excluded from Federal interest expenditure and insurance trust revenue to avoid double counting in Federal financial aggregates. However, the principle of eliminating interfund transactions is not followed in the case of interest paid by a State or local government on any of its own securities held as an investment by insurance funds it administers—mainly because of the difficulty of identifying such transactions.

Y 384–445. Federal, State, and local government finances, 1902–1957.

Source: Bureau of the Census, *U.S. Census of Governments: 1957*, vol. IV, No. 3, *Historical Summary of Governmental Finances in the United States*, 1959.

These data are a consolidation of data for the Federal Government in series Y 446–516 and for State and local governments in series Y 517–574. The amounts in these series are net of intergovernmental transactions between the Federal, State, and local governments.

Y 446–516. Federal Government finances, 1902–1957.

Source: See source for series Y 384–445.

The 1957 Census of Governments classification of Federal fiscal data was applied in an annual *Summary of Governmental Finances* for the fiscal years 1952 through 1957. Derivation of the Federal Government data for earlier years is described on pp. 8–9 of the *Historical Summary*, cited above.

For the *Historical Summary* and the annual *Summary of Governmental Finances*, Federal budget data are recast into the Census framework which is used for reporting State and local government finances. Accordingly, Census figures on Federal revenue and expenditure differ from "budget receipts" and "budget expenditures" (series Y 254–367) as reported in the *Budget of the United States* and annual reports of the

Secretary of the Treasury. The major differences are discussed in the following paragraphs.

In the 1957 Census of Governments report, the introductory text includes detail for 1942–1957 for the Census category, "National defense and international relations," showing how related items in Federal budget reports are regrouped in the census of governments classifications; and for 1902–1957, showing the Census treatment of items grouped in Federal budget reports under "Veterans services and benefits." Other functional categories also differ from those shown for the Federal Government in series Y 357–367.

Loans made by the Government are included in "budget expenditures" and receipts from the repayment of loans are included in "budget receipts." These transactions are excluded from revenue and expenditure as defined by the Bureau of the Census.

Financial transactions of government enterprises are included in Federal budget figures only to the extent of their net effect (plus or minus) upon "budget expenditures"; Census figures include gross revenue and expenditure of government enterprises (other than loan and investment transactions). Illustrative of this difference is the treatment of transactions of the Post Office Department in Census and Budget sources.

In series Y 416 and Y 496, postal service, expenditure for the Post Office Department is reported gross, without deduction for postal revenue. Gross postal receipts are included in series Y 392 and Y 460 as a category of general revenue. This treatment differs from the tabulations based on Treasury and budget accounts (series Y 254–367) which include only the difference between postal receipts and payments.

Federal "budget receipts" and "budget expenditures" omit the financial transactions of trust funds. These are included in Census reporting of Federal revenue and expenditure, except for trust funds handled on an agency basis for State and local governments (e.g., the State accounts in the unemployment compensation fund, and District of Columbia funds).

Certain kinds of reimbursements from non-Federal sources and receipts from charges for quarters and subsistence furnished to employees are treated in the Federal Budget as "appropriation credits" and result in the reduction of budget expenditures by the amount of such credits. For Census purposes, these amounts are counted as revenue and added to expenditure.

Federal budget receipts and expenditures include amounts transferred between general and special accounts, on the one hand, and enterprise and trust funds, on the other. Census figures exclude such interfund transfers.

Federal budget expenditures include interest on an accrual basis. Census data on interest expenditure are on a disbursement basis. Furthermore, interest paid to Federal insurance trust funds is included in Federal budget expenditures, while Census data exclude such interfund transfers.

Data on "cash receipts from and payments to the public" (series Y 380–383) also differ from the Census figures on Federal revenue and expenditure. Thus, that series treats the financial transactions of government enterprises on a net basis (as does the series on budget receipts and expenditures); it includes lending transactions to the extent that they are included in budget receipts and expenditures; and it handles "appropriation credits" the same way they are handled in budget receipts and expenditures. On the other hand, the data on "cash receipts from and payments to the public" differ from the budget series and more closely resemble the Census data in their treatment of trust funds, interfund transfers, and interest amounts.

Federal Government indebtedness and the change in debt outstanding (series Y 480–483) correspond with "public debt" as reported by the U.S. Treasury. Consequently, series Y 480 is the same as series Y 257.

Y 517–714. State and local government finances, 1902–1957.

Source: See source cited for series Y 384–445.

Periodic surveys of State and local government finance began in 1850; for that year and 1860 the data were published in conjunction with reports of the population census. For 1870–1922, the State and local government data were reported at approximately decennial intervals under the title, *Wealth, Debt, and Taxation;* for 1932, as *Financial Statistics of State and Local Governments;* and for 1942 and 1957, as the *Census of Governments.*

In all these reports and the specialized annual series mentioned below, concepts, classifications, and coverage have undergone frequent revisions significantly affecting historical continuity and comparability. For a historical resume of 10 decennial censuses of governments, 1850–1942, see Bureau of the Census, *Governmental Finances in the United States: 1942,* pp. 130–135. The *Historical Summary* for 1902–1957, the source for the series presented here, represents a reworking of summaries for all State governments and all local governments (and the Federal Government) on a comparable basis. Except for the Federal Government, it does not report individual units of government.

For financial statistics of the individual State and local governments in 1957, see the detailed reports of the *U.S. Census of Governments: 1957,* especially vol. VI, presenting a separate bulletin for each State area.

For financial statistics in detail for the individual State governments, see the annual compilation by the Bureau of the Census issued for 1942–1957, as *Compendium of State Government Finances;* and for 1915–1941, as *Financial Statistics of States.* There were no volumes for 1920 and for 1932–1936; partial data were published for 1921; and data for 1932 were collected for 41 States but were not compiled fully or published.

Reports for earlier years used systems different than those applied since 1951. Figures for individual States on the later reporting basis are available in Bureau of the Census, *Revised Summary of State Government Finances, 1942–1950* (State and Local Government Special Studies No. 32, 1953).

For detail for individual large city governments, and in many years for every city with population above 25,000 or 30,000, see the annual compilations published by the Department of Labor for 1898–1901 and by the Bureau of the Census for 1902–1941 (with gaps for the years 1914 and 1920), as *Financial Statistics of Cities* (with early variations in title), and for 1942–1957, as *Compendium of City Government Finances.* Prior to 1932, the city statistics covered cities of 30,000 inhabitants or more in the preceding decennial census. For 1932–1941, coverage was limited to cities of 100,000 or more, and beginning 1942, the compilation relates to cities of 25,000 inhabitants or more. Through 1940, the city series included data for overlying local governments as well as the city government itself (except that the county governments were included only for cities of 300,000 inhabitants or more). For 1941, basic data related only to city governments, but supplementary tables provided figures for overlying local governments other than counties. For 1941–1957, the compilation was limited to the city government, omitting the overlying county government, school and other special districts, or other local governments.

A series on county governments also was published for 1943–1946, following the inclusion of all county governments in the Census of Governments for 1942. The county series yielded nationwide aggregates of county transactions and individual statistics for large counties.

Series Y 205–222.   Public Employees, by Type of Government: 1940 to 1957

[In thousands.   As of October 31 except as noted]

Year	All governments	Federal[1] (civilian)	State and local			State			Local										
			Total	School	Non-school	Total	School	Non-school	All local			City		County		School district	Township and special district		
									Total	School	Non-school	Total	Non-school only	Total	Non-school only		Total	Non-school only
	205	206	207	208	209	210	211	212	213	214	215	216	217	218	219	220	221	222
ALL EMPLOYEES																		
1957[2]	8,047	[3]2,439	5,608	2,461	3,147	1,358	433	925	4,249	2,028	2,221	1,539	1,319	668	562	1,649	394	341
1956	7,685	2,410	5,275	2,283	2,992	1,322	407	915	3,953	1,876	2,077	1,485	1,277	620	530	1,531	318	270
1955	7,432	2,378	5,054	2,169	2,886	1,250	384	866	3,804	1,784	2,020	1,436	1,239	597	512	1,455	315	269
1954	7,232	2,373	4,859	2,050	2,809	1,198	359	839	3,661	1,691	1,970	1,420	1,220	579	497	1,365	297	254
1953	7,048	2,385	4,663	1,949	2,714	1,129	341	788	3,533	1,607	1,926	1,382	1,187	550	473	1,293	308	267
1952	7,105	2,583	4,522	1,873	2,649	1,103	336	768	3,418	1,537	1,881	1,342	1,154	530	454	1,234	312	273
1951	6,802	2,515	4,287	1,759	2,528	1,070	316	754	3,218	1,443	1,774	1,297	1,102	505	435	1,136	280	238
1950	6,402	2,117	4,285	1,723	2,562	1,057	312	745	3,228	1,411	1,817	1,311	1,106	500	429	1,102	317	282
1949	6,203	2,047	4,156	1,658	2,497	1,037	306	731	3,119	1,352	1,767	1,281	1,082	476	410	1,056	307	275
1948	6,042	2,076	3,966	1,581	2,385	963	286	677	3,002	1,295	1,707	1,249	1,039	469	406	986	298	263
1947	5,791	2,002	3,789	1,529	2,260	909	271	638	2,880	1,258	1,622	1,202	996	434	375	962	282	251
1946	6,001	2,434	3,567	1,457	2,110	804	233	572	2,762	1,224	1,539	1,155	955	417	361	934	257	223
1945	6,556	3,375	3,181	1,267	1,914	(4)	(4)	473	(4)	(4)	1,441	(4)	879	(4)	316	(4)	(4)	246
1944	6,537	3,365	3,172	1,311	1,861	(4)	(4)	456	(4)	(4)	1,405	(4)	855	(4)	329	(4)	(4)	221
1943	6,358	3,166	3,192	1,320	1,872	(4)	(4)	464	(4)	(4)	1,408	(4)	858	(4)	322	(4)	(4)	228
1942	5,915	2,664	3,251	1,320	1,931	(4)	(4)	503	(4)	(4)	1,428	(4)	872	(4)	333	(4)	(4)	223
1941	4,970	1,598	3,372	1,320	2,052	(4)	(4)	547	(4)	(4)	1,505	(4)	901	(4)	335	(4)	(4)	268
1940	4,474	1,128	3,346	1,320	2,026	(4)	(4)	551	(4)	(4)	1,475	(4)	887	(4)	345	(4)	(4)	242
FULL-TIME EMPLOYEES ONLY																		
1957[2]	6,897	2,304	4,593	1,986	2,607	1,154	277	877	3,439	1,710	1,729	1,263	1,081	568	475	1,391	216	172
1956	6,814	2,282	4,532	1,961	2,571	1,143	276	867	3,389	1,685	1,704	1,256	1,071	564	481	1,375	194	152
1955	6,592	2,255	4,337	1,868	2,469	1,085	268	817	3,252	1,600	1,652	1,218	1,041	541	462	1,303	189	149
1954	6,349	2,203	4,146	1,754	2,391	1,015	239	776	3,132	1,516	1,615	1,201	1,026	524	447	1,228	179	142
1953	6,167	2,199	3,968	1,669	2,299	954	229	726	3,014	1,441	1,570	1,167	998	501	428	1,162	183	144
1952	6,216	2,372	3,844	1,609	2,235	936	227	708	2,909	1,381	1,527	1,141	977	479	408	1,113	176	142
1951	(4)	(4)	3,643	1,512	2,132	903	214	690	2,740	1,298	1,442	1,112	942	442	375	1,024	161	125

[1] Includes Federal civilian employees outside continental United States. Prior to 1953, figures are as of Sept. 30.
[2] As of Apr. 30.
[3] Includes 30,000 employees of the National Guard not previously included.
[4] Not available.

Series Y 223–240.   Government Monthly Payrolls, by Type of Government: 1940 to 1957

[In millions of dollars.   For October except as noted]

Year	All governments	Federal[1] (civilian)	State and local			State			Local										
			Total	School	Non-school	Total	School	Non-school	All local			City		County		School district	Township and special district		
									Total	School	Non-school	Total	Non-school only	Total	Non-school only		Total	Non-school only
	223	224	225	226	227	228	229	230	231	232	233	234	235	236	237	238	239	240
ALL EMPLOYEES																		
1957[2]	2,533.1	[3]918.6	1,614.5	757.8	856.7	388.4	111.1	277.3	1,226.1	646.6	579.5	461.0	375.9	169.1	142.4	519.4	76.6	61.2
1956	2,509.4	943.7	1,565.7	734.3	831.4	381.6	108.2	273.4	1,184.1	626.1	558.0	450.0	365.4	161.8	138.4	503.2	69.0	54.2
1955	2,264.5	845.7	1,418.8	661.7	757.1	340.4	97.5	242.9	1,078.4	564.2	514.2	413.8	337.0	147.8	126.2	452.8	64.0	51.0
1954	2,103.1	784.8	1,318.3	600.0	718.2	314.6	87.3	227.3	1,003.6	512.8	490.8	396.2	324.4	138.2	118.9	409.5	59.7	47.6
1953	2,013.6	793.1	1,220.5	552.0	668.5	291.8	81.8	210.0	928.7	470.2	458.6	367.6	301.1	127.8	110.5	375.6	57.8	46.9
1952	1,979.6	855.9	1,123.7	502.9	620.8	270.8	75.6	195.3	852.9	427.3	425.6	345.0	282.7	113.7	97.0	338.6	55.7	45.8
1951	1,865.4	857.4	1,008.0	452.5	555.5	245.8	68.1	177.7	762.3	384.5	377.8	314.9	253.9	101.3	86.1	298.6	47.5	37.8
1950	1,527.9	613.4	914.6	409.4	505.2	218.4	61.0	157.4	696.2	348.4	347.8	290.0	230.2	92.5	78.7	267.1	46.7	39.0
1949	1,406.1	539.2	866.7	384.8	481.9	209.8	58.5	151.3	656.9	326.3	330.6	277.2	219.7	86.4	74.8	249.2	44.3	37.3
1948	1,329.0	533.9	795.1	353.0	442.0	184.9	50.9	134.0	610.1	302.1	308.0	266.0	206.2	78.1	66.6	223.4	42.6	35.2
1947	1,183.7	481.4	702.3	318.5	383.7	160.8	44.8	116.0	541.5	273.7	267.7	236.3	181.2	68.4	58.1	202.0	34.8	28.4
1946	1,155.5	571.5	584.0	260.1	323.9	128.0	34.6	93.5	456.0	225.6	230.4	205.8	160.0	58.4	50.7	166.4	25.4	19.8
1945	1,109.9	642.3	467.6	200.0	267.6	(4)	(4)	72.9	(4)	(4)	194.7	(4)	133.2	(4)	42.6	(4)	(4)	19.0
1944	1,103.0	684.8	418.2	172.2	246.0	(4)	(4)	64.2	(4)	(4)	181.8	(4)	125.0	(4)	39.4	(4)	(4)	17.4
1943	1,084.4	672.7	411.7	175.7	236.0	(4)	(4)	64.0	(4)	(4)	172.0	(4)	119.3	(4)	36.9	(4)	(4)	15.7
1942	880.2	486.1	394.1	175.4	218.7	(4)	(4)	59.5	(4)	(4)	159.2	(4)	109.7	(4)	34.5	(4)	(4)	14.9
1941	649.4	254.1	395.3	175.4	219.9	(4)	(4)	62.1	(4)	(4)	157.8	(4)	108.4	(4)	34.5	(4)	(4)	14.8
1940	565.8	177.0	388.8	175.3	213.5	(4)	(4)	58.8	(4)	(4)	154.7	(4)	104.9	(4)	34.3	(4)	(4)	15.5
FULL-TIME EMPLOYEES ONLY																		
1957[2]	(4)	(4)	1,543.8	717.3	826.5	369.9	98.4	271.5	1,173.9	619.0	554.9	445.2	365.0	160.8	134.9	498.2	69.7	54.9
1956	(4)	(4)	1,514.0	707.8	806.2	366.1	99.0	267.2	1,147.9	608.9	539.0	437.8	355.8	157.1	134.1	489.5	63.5	49.1
1955	(4)	(4)	1,371.5	638.0	733.5	326.4	89.6	236.9	1,045.0	548.5	496.6	402.7	328.0	143.7	122.6	439.9	58.6	46.0
1954	(4)	(4)	1,268.0	575.6	692.4	296.1	77.7	218.5	971.8	497.9	473.9	385.8	316.3	134.0	114.9	397.7	54.3	42.7
1953	(4)	(4)	1,172.6	529.3	643.2	274.2	73.3	200.9	898.3	456.0	442.3	357.0	293.1	123.8	106.8	364.5	52.9	42.4
1952	(4)	(4)	1,078.5	482.2	596.3	254.0	67.5	186.4	824.5	414.6	409.9	335.5	275.4	109.4	93.1	328.8	50.8	41.4
1951	(4)	(4)	962.7	433.8	528.9	228.1	60.8	167.4	734.6	373.1	361.5	305.9	245.4	97.7	82.6	288.4	42.7	33.5

[1] Federal payroll figures represent pay for the number of working days in month specified. Thus, changes in amount of payroll reflect in part differences in number of working days covered. Prior to 1953, data are for the month of September.
[2] Data are for the month of April.
[3] Includes $10.9 million for employees of the National Guard not previously included.
[4] Not available.

Series Y 241–250. Paid Civilian Employment of the Federal Government: 1816 to 1957

[As of June 30 except as noted]

Year	Employees			Competitive civil service employees (classified)	Executive branch				Legislative branch	Judicial branch [3]
	Total	Washington, D.C. [1]	All other areas		Total	Defense [2]	Post Office	Other		
	241	242	243	244	245	246	247	248	249	250
1957	2,417,565	236,330	2,181,235	2,067,285	2,390,561	1,160,915	521,198	708,448	22,340	4,664
1956	2,398,736	232,707	2,166,029	2,042,007	2,372,266	1,179,836	508,587	683,843	22,115	4,355
1955	2,397,309	231,873	2,165,436	2,004,853	2,371,462	1,186,580	511,613	673,269	21,711	4,136
1954	2,407,676	228,501	2,179,175	1,992,057	2,381,659	1,208,892	507,135	665,632	21,972	4,045
1953	2,558,416	242,678	2,315,738	2,138,899	2,532,150	1,332,068	506,555	693,527	22,312	3,954
1952	2,600,612	261,569	2,339,043	2,247,692	2,574,132	1,337,095	507,779	729,258	22,517	3,963
1951	2,482,666	265,980	2,216,686	2,144,882	2,455,901	1,235,498	482,281	738,122	22,835	3,930
1950	1,960,708	223,312	1,737,396	1,656,803	1,934,040	753,149	484,679	696,212	22,896	3,772
1949	2,102,109	225,901	1,876,208	1,771,927	2,075,148	879,875	501,743	693,530	23,382	3,579
1948	2,071,009	214,544	1,856,465	1,707,220	2,043,981	870,962	474,911	698,108	23,551	3,477
1947	2,111,001	213,515	1,897,486	1,692,065	2,082,258	859,142	445,683	777,433	25,669	3,074
1946	2,696,529	242,263	2,454,266	----	2,665,520	1,416,225	453,953	795,342	27,946	3,063
1945	3,816,310	264,770	3,551,540	----	3,786,645	2,634,575	416,314	735,756	26,959	2,706
1944	3,332,356	276,758	3,055,598	----	3,304,379	2,246,454	374,758	683,167	25,314	2,663
1943	3,299,414	284,665	3,014,749	----	3,273,887	2,200,064	339,005	734,818	22,903	2,624
1942	2,296,384	276,352	2,020,032	----	2,272,082	1,291,093	338,090	642,899	21,657	2,645
1941	1,437,682	190,588	1,247,094	990,233	1,416,444	556,073	335,008	525,363	18,712	2,526
1940	1,042,420	139,770	902,650	726,895	1,022,853	256,025	323,481	443,347	17,099	2,468
1939	953,891	129,314	824,577	662,832	935,797	195,997	314,478	425,322	15,802	2,292
1938	882,226	120,744	761,482	562,909	864,534	163,457	311,440	389,637	15,609	2,083
1937	895,993	117,020	778,973	532,073	878,214	160,737	304,852	412,625	15,609	2,170
1936	867,432	122,937	744,495	498,725	850,395	148,369	281,314	420,712	14,976	2,061
1935	780,582	108,673	671,909	455,229	765,712	147,188	275,483	343,041	12,970	1,900
1934	698,649	94,244	604,405	450,592	685,108	133,092	281,770	270,246	11,667	1,874
1933	603,587	70,261	533,326	456,096	590,984	101,228	286,935	202,821	10,847	1,756
1932	605,496	73,455	532,041	467,161	592,560	100,420	296,136	196,004	11,159	1,777
1931	609,746	76,303	533,443	468,050	596,745	107,980	297,159	191,606	11,192	1,809
1930	601,319	73,032	528,287	462,083	588,951	103,462	297,895	187,594	10,620	1,748
1929	579,559	68,266	511,293	445,957	567,721	103,098	295,695	168,928	10,240	1,598
1928	560,772	65,506	495,266	431,763	549,238	94,005	293,023	162,210	9,894	1,640
1927	547,127	63,814	483,313	422,998	535,599	85,717	291,249	158,633	9,848	1,680
1926	548,713	64,722	483,991	422,300	537,251	92,208	288,573	156,470	9,742	1,720
1925	553,045	67,563	485,482	423,538	541,792	94,772	284,550	162,470	9,493	1,760
1924	543,484	68,000	475,484	415,593	532,048	92,331	279,679	160,038	9,636	1,800
1923	536,900	70,062	466,838	411,398	525,746	94,001	268,951	162,794	9,314	1,840
1922	543,507	73,645	469,862	420,688	532,210	107,126	260,100	164,984	9,417	1,880
1921 [4]	561,142	82,416	478,726	448,112	550,020	138,293	251,800	160,427	9,202	1,920
1920 [4]	655,265	94,110	561,155	497,603	645,408	237,212	242,400	165,796	7,897	1,960
1919 [5]	794,271	106,073	688,198	592,961	784,180	(6)	(6)	(6)	8,091	2,000
1918	854,500	120,835	733,665	642,432	844,480	(6)	(6)	(6)	7,980	2,040
1917	438,500	48,313	390,187	326,899	429,727	91,982	215,883	121,862	6,693	2,080
1916	399,381	41,804	357,577	296,926	391,133	63,395	212,215	115,523	6,128	2,120
1915	395,429	41,281	354,148	292,291	387,294	58,286	212,012	116,996	5,975	2,160
1914	401,887	40,016	361,871	292,460	393,555	57,989	212,973	122,593	6,132	2,200
1913	396,494	38,975	357,519	282,597	388,217	55,476	213,103	119,638	6,037	2,240
1912	400,150	38,555	361,595	217,392	391,918	60,015	214,770	117,133	5,942	2,290
1911	395,905	39,782	356,123	227,657	387,673	60,283	211,546	115,844	5,902	2,330
1910	388,708	38,911	349,797	222,278	380,428	58,320	209,005	113,108	5,910	2,370
1909	372,379	35,936	336,443	234,940	364,078	54,425	205,360	104,293	5,891	2,410
1908	356,754	34,647	322,107	206,637	348,479	50,665	199,904	97,910	5,825	2,450
1907	----	----	----	194,323	----					
1906				184,178						
1905				171,807						
1904				154,093						
1903				135,453						
1902				107,990						
1901	239,476	28,044	211,432	106,205	231,056	44,524	136,192	50,340	5,690	2,730
1900				94,893						
1899				93,144						
1898				89,306						
1897				85,886						
1896				87,044						
1895				54,222						
1894				45,821						
1893				43,915						
1892				37,523						
1891	157,442	20,834	136,608	33,873	150,844	20,561	95,449	34,834	3,867	2,731
1890				30,626						
1889				29,650						
1888				22,577						
1887 [7]				19,345						
1886 [8]				17,273						
1885 [9]				15,590						
1884 [10]				13,780						
1881	100,020	13,124	86,896	----	94,679	16,297	56,421	21,961	2,579	2,762
1871	51,020	6,222	44,798	----	50,155	1,183	36,696	12,276	618	247
1861	36,672	2,199	34,473	----	36,106	946	30,269	4,891	393	173
1851	26,274	1,533	24,741	----	25,713	403	21,391	3,919	384	177
1841	18,038	1,014	17,024	----	17,550	598	14,290	2,662	332	156
1831	11,491	666	10,825	----	11,067	377	8,764	1,926	289	135
1821	6,914	603	6,311	----	6,526	161	4,766	1,599	252	136
1816	4,837	535	4,302	----	4,479	190	3,341	948	243	115

[1] Beginning 1950, includes D.C.; Arlington and Fairfax Counties, Falls Church and Alexandria cities, Va.; and Montgomery and Prince Georges Counties, Md. In 1941–1949, only parts of Fairfax, Montgomery, and Prince Georges Counties were included; prior to 1941, D.C. only.
[2] Prior to 1947, War and Navy Departments; beginning 1881, includes mechanics and other workmen at army arsenals and navy yards.
[3] Estimated for 1908–1928.   [4] As of July 31.   [5] As of Nov. 11.
[6] Not available.   [7] Jan. 16, 1886–June 30, 1887.   [8] Jan. 16, 1885–Jan. 15, 1886.
[9] Jan. 16, 1884–Jan. 15, 1885.   [10] July 16, 1883–Jan. 15, 1884.

Series Y 251–253. State and Local Government Employment: 1929 to 1957

[In thousands. Excludes nominal employees. Estimated monthly average]

Year	Total 251	School 252	Other functions 253	Year	Total 251	School 252	Other functions 253	Year	Total 251	School 252	Other functions 253
1957	5,409	2,402	3,007	1947	3,582	1,468	2,114	1937	2,923	1,206	1,717
1956	5,068	2,220	2,849	1946	3,341	1,386	1,955	1936	2,842	1,174	1,668
1955	4,727	2,061	2,666	1945	3,137	1,353	1,784	1935	2,728	1,152	1,577
1954	4,563	1,966	2,597	1944	3,116	1,352	1,764	1934	2,647	1,122	1,525
1953	4,340	1,856	2,484	1943	3,174	1,361	1,813	1933	2,601	1,122	1,479
1952	4,188	1,750	2,438	1942	3,270	1,383	1,887	1932	2,667	1,148	1,518
1951	4,087	1,677	2,410	1941	3,320	1,363	1,957	1931	2,704	1,160	1,544
1950	4,098	1,644	2,454	1940	3,206	1,299	1,907	1930	2,622	1,150	1,472
1949	3,948	1,585	2,363	1939	3,090	1,267	1,823	1929	2,532	1,121	1,411
1948	3,787	1,516	2,271	1938	3,054	1,239	1,815				

Series Y 254–257. Summary of Federal Government Finances: 1789 to 1957

[In thousands of dollars. For 1789–1842, years ending December 31; 1844–1957, June 30; 1843 figures are for January 1–June 30]

Year	Receipts[1] 254	Expenditures[2] 255	Surplus or deficit[3] (−) 256	Total gross debt[4] 257	Year	Receipts[1] 254	Expenditures[2] 255	Surplus or deficit[3] (−) 256	Total gross debt[4] 257	Year or period	Receipts[1] 254	Expenditures[2] 255	Surplus or deficit[3] (−) 256	Total gross debt[4] 257
1957	71,028,650	69,433,078	1,595,572	270,527,172	1900	567,241	520,861	46,380	1,263,417	1845	29,970	22,937	7,033	15,925
1956	68,165,330	66,539,776	1,625,553	272,750,814	1899	515,961	605,072	−89,112	1,436,701	1844	29,321	22,338	6,984	23,462
					1898	405,321	443,369	−38,047	1,232,743	1843	8,303	11,858	−3,555	32,743
1955	60,389,744	64,569,973	−4,180,229	274,374,223	1897	347,722	365,774	−18,052	1,226,794	1842	19,976	25,206	−5,230	20,201
1954	64,655,387	67,772,353	−3,116,966	271,259,599	1896	338,142	352,179	−14,037	1,222,729	1841	16,860	26,566	−9,706	13,594
1953	64,825,044	74,274,257	−9,449,213	266,071,062						1840	19,480	24,318	−4,837	5,251
1952	61,390,945	65,407,585	−4,016,640	259,105,179	1895	324,729	356,195	−31,466	1,096,913	1839	31,483	26,899	4,584	3,573
1951	47,567,613	44,057,831	3,509,788	255,221,977	1894	306,355	367,525	−61,170	1,016,898	1838	26,303	33,865	−7,562	10,434
					1893	385,820	383,478	2,342	961,432	1837	24,954	37,243	−12,289	3,308
1950	36,494,901	39,617,003	−3,122,102	257,357,352	1892	354,938	345,023	9,914	968,219	1836	50,827	30,868	19,959	337
1949	37,695,549	39,506,989	−1,811,440	252,770,360	1891	392,612	365,774	26,839	1,005,807					
1948	41,488,179	33,068,709	8,419,470	252,292,247						1835	35,430	17,573	17,857	38
1947	39,786,181	39,032,393	753,788	258,286,383	1890	403,081	318,041	85,040	1,122,397	1834	21,792	18,628	3,164	38
1946	39,771,404	60,447,574	−20,676,171	269,422,099	1889	387,050	299,289	87,761	1,249,471	1833	33,948	23,018	10,931	4,760
					1888	379,266	267,925	111,341	1,384,632	1832	31,866	17,289	14,577	7,012
1945	44,475,304	98,416,220	−53,940,916	258,682,187	1887	371,403	267,932	103,471	1,465,485	1831	28,527	15,248	13,279	24,322
1944	43,635,315	95,058,708	−51,423,393	201,003,387	1886	336,440	242,483	93,957	1,555,660	1830	24,844	15,143	9,701	39,123
1943	21,986,701	79,407,131	−57,420,430	136,696,090	1885	323,691	260,227	63,464	1,578,551	1829	24,828	15,203	9,624	48,565
1942	12,555,436	34,045,679	−21,490,243	72,422,445	1884	348,520	244,126	104,394	1,625,307	1828	24,764	16,395	8,369	58,421
1941	7,102,931	13,262,204	−6,159,272	48,961,444	1883	398,288	265,408	132,879	1,721,959	1827	22,966	16,139	6,827	67,475
1940	5,144,013	9,062,032	−3,918,019	42,967,531	1882	403,525	257,981	145,544	1,856,916	1826	25,260	17,036	8,225	73,987
1939	4,996,300	8,858,458	−3,862,158	40,439,532	1881	360,782	260,713	100,069	2,019,286	1825	21,841	15,857	5,984	81,054
1938	5,615,221	6,791,838	−1,176,617	37,164,740						1824	19,381	20,327	−945	83,788
1937	4,978,601	7,756,021	−2,777,421	36,424,614	1880	333,527	267,643	65,884	2,090,909	1823	20,541	14,707	5,834	90,270
1936	4,068,937	8,493,486	−4,424,549	33,778,543	1879	273,827	266,948	6,879	2,298,913	1822	20,232	15,000	5,232	90,876
					1878	257,764	236,964	20,800	2,159,418	1821	14,573	15,811	−1,237	93,547
1935	3,729,914	6,520,966	−2,791,052	28,700,893	1877	281,406	241,334	40,072	2,107,760	1820	17,881	18,261	−380	89,987
1934	3,064,268	6,693,900	−3,629,632	27,053,141	1876	294,096	265,101	28,995	2,130,846	1819	24,603	21,464	3,140	91,016
1933	2,021,213	4,622,865	−2,601,652	22,538,673	1875	288,000	274,623	13,377	2,156,277	1818	21,585	19,825	1,760	95,530
1932	1,923,913	4,659,203	−2,735,290	19,487,002	1874	304,979	302,634	2,345	2,159,933	1817	33,099	21,844	11,255	103,467
1931	3,115,557	3,577,434	−461,877	16,801,281	1873	333,738	290,345	43,393	2,151,210	1816	47,678	30,587	17,091	123,492
1930	4,177,942	3,440,269	737,673	16,185,310	1872	374,107	277,518	96,589	2,209,991	1815	15,729	32,708	−16,979	127,335
1929	4,033,250	3,298,859	734,391	16,931,088	1871	383,324	292,177	91,147	2,322,052	1814	11,182	34,721	−23,539	99,834
1928	4,042,348	3,103,265	939,083	17,604,293						1813	14,340	31,682	−17,341	81,488
1927	4,129,394	2,974,030	1,155,365	18,511,907	1870	411,255	309,654	101,602	2,436,453	1812	9,801	20,281	−10,480	55,963
1926	3,962,756	3,097,612	865,144	19,643,216	1869	370,944	322,865	48,078	2,545,111	1811	14,424	8,058	6,365	45,210
					1868	405,638	377,340	28,298	2,583,446	1810	9,384	8,157	1,228	48,006
1925	3,780,149	3,063,105	717,043	20,516,194	1867	490,634	357,543	133,091	2,650,168	1809	7,773	10,281	−2,507	53,173
1924	4,012,045	3,048,678	963,367	21,250,813	1866	558,033	520,809	37,223	2,755,764	1808	17,061	9,932	7,128	57,023
1923	4,007,135	3,294,628	712,508	22,349,707	1865	333,715	1,297,555	−963,841	2,677,929	1807	16,398	8,354	8,044	65,196
1922	4,109,104	3,372,608	736,496	22,963,382	1864	264,627	865,323	−600,696	1,815,831	1806	15,560	9,804	5,756	69,218
1921	5,624,933	5,115,928	509,005	23,977,451	1863	112,697	714,741	−602,043	1,119,774	1805	13,561	10,506	3,054	75,723
1920	6,694,565	6,403,344	291,222	24,299,321	1862	51,987	474,762	−422,774	524,178	1804	11,826	8,719	3,107	82,312
1919	5,152,257	18,514,880	−13,362,623	25,484,506	1861	41,510	66,547	−25,037	90,582	1803	11,064	7,852	3,212	86,427
1918	3,664,583	12,696,702	−9,032,120	12,455,225	1860	56,065	63,131	−7,066	64,844	1802	14,996	7,862	7,134	77,055
1917	1,124,325	1,977,682	−853,357	2,975,619	1859	53,486	69,071	−15,585	58,498	1801	12,935	9,395	3,541	80,713
1916	782,535	734,056	48,478	1,225,146	1858	46,655	74,185	−27,530	44,913	1800	10,849	10,786	63	83,038
1915	697,911	760,587	−62,676	1,191,264	1857	68,965	67,796	1,170	28,701	1799	7,547	9,666	−2,120	82,976
1914	734,673	735,081	−408	1,188,235	1856	74,057	69,571	4,486	31,974	1798	7,900	7,677	224	78,409
1913	724,111	724,512	−401	1,193,048	1855	65,351	59,743	5,608	35,588	1797	8,689	6,134	2,555	79,229
1912	692,609	689,881	2,728	1,193,839	1854	73,800	58,045	15,755	42,244	1796	8,378	5,727	2,651	82,064
1911	701,833	691,202	10,631	1,153,985	1853	61,587	48,184	13,403	59,805	1795	6,115	7,540	−1,425	83,762
1910	675,512	693,617	−18,105	1,146,940	1852	49,847	44,195	5,652	66,199	1794	5,432	6,991	−1,559	80,748
1909	604,320	693,744	−89,423	1,148,315	1851	52,559	47,709	4,850	68,305	1793	4,653	4,482	171	78,427
1908	601,862	659,196	−57,334	1,177,690	1850	43,603	39,543	4,060	63,453	1792	3,670	5,080	−1,410	80,359
1907	665,860	579,129	86,732	1,147,178	1849	31,208	45,052	−13,844	63,062	1789–				
1906	594,984	570,202	24,782	1,142,523	1848	35,736	45,377	−9,641	47,045	1791	4,419	4,269	150	77,228
1905	544,275	567,279	−23,004	1,132,357	1847	26,496	57,281	−30,786	38,827					
1904	541,087	583,660	−42,573	1,136,259	1846	29,700	27,767	1,933	15,550					
1903	561,881	517,006	44,875	1,159,406										
1902	562,478	485,234	77,244	1,178,081										
1901	587,685	524,617	63,068	1,221,572										

[1] Excludes receipts from borrowing. Prior to 1931, total receipts; thereafter, net receipts (see text).
[2] Excludes debt repayment. Prior to 1931, total expenditures; thereafter, net expenditures (see text).
[3] Receipts compared with expenditures.
[4] As of end of period.

Series Y 258–263. Federal Government Receipts: 1789 to 1957

[In thousands of dollars. For 1789–1842, years ending December 31; 1844–1957, June 30; 1843 figures are for January 1–June 30]

Year	Net (258)	Total (259)	Customs (260)	Internal revenue (261)	Other receipts Total (262)	Sales of public lands (263)
1957	71,028,650	83,675,305	754,461	80,171,971	2,748,872	(1)
1956	68,165,330	78,820,426	704,898	75,109,083	3,006,445	(1)
1955	60,389,744	69,454,196	606,397	66,288,692	2,559,107	(1)
1954	64,655,387	73,172,936	562,021	70,299,652	2,311,264	(1)
1953	64,825,044	72,649,135	613,420	70,170,974	1,864,741	(1)
1952	61,390,945	67,999,370	550,696	65,634,894	1,813,779	(1)
1951	47,567,613	53,368,672	624,008	51,106,095	1,638,569	(1)
1950	36,494,901	41,310,628	422,650	39,448,607	1,439,370	(1)
1949	37,695,549	42,773,506	384,485	40,307,285	2,081,736	(1)
1948	41,488,179	46,098,807	421,723	41,853,485	3,823,599	214
1947	39,786,181	44,508,189	494,078	39,379,409	4,634,702	143
1946	39,771,404	44,238,135	435,475	40,310,333	3,492,327	127
1945	44,475,304	47,750,306	354,776	43,902,002	3,493,529	184
1944	43,635,315	45,441,049	431,252	41,684,987	3,324,810	99
1943	21,986,701	23,402,322	324,291	22,143,969	934,063	129
1942	12,555,436	13,676,680	388,948	12,993,118	294,614	90
1941	7,102,931	7,995,612	391,870	7,361,675	242,067	178
1940	5,144,013	5,893,368	348,591	5,303,134	241,643	117
1939	4,996,300	5,667,824	318,887	5,161,221	187,765	248
1938	5,615,221	6,241,661	359,187	5,674,318	208,156	96
1937	4,978,601	5,293,590	486,357	4,597,140	210,094	71
1936	4,068,937	4,115,957	386,812	3,512,852	216,293	74
1935	3,729,914	3,800,467	343,353	3,277,690	179,424	87
1934	3,064,268	3,115,554	313,434	2,640,604	161,516	99
1933	2,021,213	2,079,697	250,750	1,604,424	224,523	103
1932	1,923,913	2,005,725	327,755	1,561,006	116,964	170
1931	3,115,557	3,189,639	378,354	2,429,781	381,504	230
1930	----	4,177,942	587,001	3,039,295	551,646	396
1929	----	4,033,250	602,263	2,938,019	492,968	315
1928	----	4,042,348	568,986	2,794,971	678,391	385
1927	----	4,129,394	605,500	2,869,414	654,480	621
1926	----	3,962,756	579,430	2,837,639	545,686	754
1925	----	3,780,149	547,561	2,589,176	643,412	624
1924	----	4,012,045	545,638	2,795,157	671,250	522
1923	----	4,007,135	561,929	2,624,473	820,734	657
1922	----	4,109,104	356,443	3,213,253	539,408	895
1921	----	5,624,933	308,564	4,596,426	719,943	1,530
1920	----	6,694,565	322,903	5,405,032	966,631	1,910
1919	----	5,152,257	184,458	4,315,285	652,514	1,405
1918	----	3,664,583	179,998	3,186,034	298,550	1,969
1917	----	1,124,325	225,962	809,366	88,996	1,893
1916	----	782,535	213,186	512,702	56,647	1,888
1915	----	697,911	209,787	415,670	72,455	2,167
1914	----	734,673	292,320	380,041	62,312	2,572
1913	----	724,111	318,891	344,417	60,803	2,910
1912	----	692,609	311,322	321,612	59,675	5,393
1911	----	701,833	314,497	322,529	64,807	5,732
1910	----	675,512	333,683	289,934	51,895	6,356
1909	----	604,320	300,712	246,213	57,396	7,701
1908	----	601,862	286,113	251,711	64,088	9,732
1907	----	665,860	332,233	269,667	63,960	7,879
1906	----	594,984	300,252	249,150	45,582	4,880
1905	----	544,275	261,799	234,096	48,380	4,859
1904	----	541,087	261,275	232,904	46,908	7,453
1903	----	561,881	284,480	230,810	46,591	8,926
1902	----	562,478	254,445	271,880	36,153	4,144
1901	----	587,685	238,585	307,181	41,919	2,965
1900	----	567,241	233,165	295,328	38,748	2,837
1899	----	515,961	206,128	273,437	36,395	1,678
1898	----	405,321	149,575	170,901	84,846	1,243
1897	----	347,722	176,554	146,689	24,479	865
1896	----	338,142	160,022	146,763	31,358	1,006
1895	----	324,729	152,159	143,422	29,149	1,103
1894	----	306,355	131,819	147,111	27,426	1,674
1893	----	385,820	203,355	161,028	21,437	3,182
1892	----	354,938	177,453	153,971	23,514	3,262
1891	----	392,612	219,522	145,686	27,404	4,030
1890	----	403,081	229,669	142,607	30,806	6,358
1889	----	387,050	223,833	130,882	32,336	8,039
1888	----	379,266	219,091	124,297	35,878	11,202
1887	----	371,403	217,287	118,823	35,293	9,254
1886	----	336,440	192,905	116,806	26,729	5,631
1885	----	323,691	181,472	112,499	29,720	5,706
1884	----	348,520	195,067	121,586	31,866	9,811
1883	----	398,288	214,706	144,720	38,861	7,956
1882	----	403,525	220,411	146,498	36,617	4,753
1881	----	360,782	198,160	135,264	27,358	2,202
1880	----	333,527	186,522	124,009	22,995	1,017
1879	----	273,827	137,250	113,562	23,016	925
1878	----	257,764	130,171	110,582	17,012	1,080
1877	----	281,406	130,956	118,630	31,820	976
1876	----	294,096	148,072	116,701	29,323	1,129
1875	----	288,000	157,168	110,007	20,825	1,414

Year or period	Total (259)	Customs (260)	Internal revenue (261)	Other receipts Total (262)	Sales of public lands (263)
1874	304,979	163,104	102,410	39,465	1,852
1873	333,738	188,090	113,729	31,919	2,882
1872	374,107	216,370	130,642	27,094	2,576
1871	383,324	206,270	143,098	33,955	2,389
1870	411,255	194,538	184,900	31,817	3,350
1869	370,944	180,048	158,356	32,539	4,020
1868	405,638	164,465	191,088	50,086	1,349
1867	490,634	176,418	266,028	48,189	1,164
1866	558,033	179,047	309,227	69,759	665
1865	333,715	84,928	209,464	39,322	997
1864	264,627	102,316	109,741	52,569	588
1863	112,697	69,060	37,641	5,997	168
1862	51,987	49,056	----	2,931	152
1861	41,510	39,582	----	1,928	871
1860	56,065	53,188	----	2,877	1,779
1859	53,486	49,566	----	3,921	1,757
1858	46,655	41,790	----	4,866	3,514
1857	68,965	63,876	----	5,089	3,829
1856	74,057	64,023	----	10,034	8,918
1855	65,351	53,026	----	12,325	11,497
1854	73,800	64,224	----	9,576	8,471
1853	61,587	58,932	----	2,655	1,667
1852	49,847	47,339	----	2,507	2,043
1851	52,559	49,018	----	3,542	2,352
1850	43,603	39,669	----	3,935	1,860
1849	31,208	28,347	----	2,861	1,689
1848	35,736	31,757	(2)	3,978	3,329
1847	26,496	23,748	(2)	2,748	2,498
1846	29,700	26,713	3	2,984	2,694
1845	29,970	27,528	4	2,438	2,077
1844	29,321	26,184	2	3,136	2,060
1843	8,303	7,047	(2)	1,256	898
1842	19,976	18,188	(2)	1,788	1,336
1841	16,860	14,487	3	2,370	1,366
1840	19,480	13,500	2	5,979	3,293
1839	31,483	23,138	3	8,342	7,076
1838	26,303	16,159	2	10,141	3,082
1837	24,954	11,169	5	13,779	6,776
1836	50,827	23,410	(2)	27,416	24,877
1835	35,430	19,391	10	16,028	14,758
1834	21,792	16,215	4	5,573	4,858
1833	33,948	29,033	3	4,913	3,968
1832	31,866	28,465	12	3,389	2,623
1831	28,527	24,224	7	4,295	3,211
1830	24,844	21,922	12	2,910	2,329
1829	24,828	22,682	15	2,131	1,517
1828	24,764	23,206	17	1,541	1,018
1827	22,966	19,712	20	3,234	1,496
1826	25,260	23,341	22	1,898	1,394
1825	21,841	20,099	26	1,716	1,216
1824	19,381	17,878	35	1,468	984
1823	20,541	19,088	34	1,418	917
1822	20,232	17,590	68	2,575	1,804
1821	14,573	13,004	69	1,500	1,213
1820	17,881	15,006	106	2,769	1,636
1819	24,603	20,284	230	4,090	3,274
1818	21,585	17,176	955	3,454	2,607
1817	33,099	26,283	2,678	4,138	1,991
1816	47,678	36,307	5,125	6,246	1,718
1815	15,729	7,283	4,678	3,768	1,288
1814	11,182	5,999	1,663	3,520	1,136
1813	14,340	13,225	5	1,111	836
1812	9,801	8,959	5	837	710
1811	14,424	13,313	2	1,108	1,040
1810	9,384	8,583	7	793	697
1809	7,773	7,296	4	473	442
1808	17,061	16,364	8	689	648
1807	16,398	15,846	13	539	466
1806	15,560	14,668	20	872	765
1805	13,561	12,936	22	602	540
1804	11,826	11,099	51	677	488
1803	11,064	10,479	215	370	166
1802	14,996	12,438	622	1,936	189
1801	12,935	10,751	1,048	1,137	168
1800	10,849	9,081	809	958	(2)
1799	7,547	6,610	779	157	----
1798	7,900	7,106	644	150	12
1797	8,689	7,550	575	564	84
1796	8,378	6,568	475	1,334	5
1795	6,115	5,588	338	188	----
1794	5,432	4,801	274	357	----
1793	4,653	4,255	338	60	----
1792	3,670	3,443	209	18	----
1789–1791	4,419	4,399	----	19	----

¹ Not available.   ² Less than $500.

Series Y 264–279. Internal Revenue Collections: 1863 to 1957

[In thousands of dollars. For years ending June 30. Total columns include components not shown separately]

Columns under "Excise taxes" (269–277); "Manufacturers'" spans 272–275.

Year	Total collections	Individual income taxes	Corporation income taxes	Employment taxes	Estate and gift taxes [1]	Total [2]	Alcohol	Tobacco	Manufacturers' Total [3]	Automobiles and accessories	Tires, tubes, and tread rubber	Gasoline, lubricating oils	Admissions	Telephone, telegraph, radio, and cable facilities [4]	Capital stock tax [2]
	264	265	266	267	268	269	270	271	272	273	274	275	276	277	278
1957	80,171,971	39,029,772	21,530,653	7,580,522	1,377,999	10,637,544	2,973,195	1,674,050	3,761,925	1,500,822	251,454	1,531,818	119,088	613,210	--------
1956	75,112,649	35,337,642	21,298,522	7,295,784	1,171,237	10,004,195	2,920,574	1,613,497	3,456,013	1,711,603	177,872	1,104,981	146,273	557,233	--------
1955	66,288,692	31,650,106	18,264,720	6,219,665	936,267	9,210,582	2,742,840	1,571,213	2,885,016	1,319,327	164,316	1,024,496	145,357	520,449	
1954	69,934,980	32,813,691	21,546,322	5,107,623	935,122	9,532,222	2,797,718	1,580,512	2,689,133	1,152,155	152,567	904,922	310,264	771,981	
1953	69,686,535	32,536,217	21,594,515	4,718,403	891,284	9,946,116	2,780,925	1,654,911	2,862,788	1,173,672	180,047	964,000	359,522	775,873	
1952	65,009,586	29,274,107	21,466,910	4,464,264	833,147	8,971,158	2,549,120	1,565,162	2,348,943	889,729	161,328	808,461	376,305	705,771	
1951	50,445,686	22,997,308	14,387,569	3,627,480	729,730	8,703,599	2,546,808	1,380,396	2,383,677	894,123	198,383	666,286	389,138	644,980	
1950	38,957,132	17,153,308	10,854,351	2,644,575	706,226	7,598,405	2,219,202	1,328,464	1,836,053	664,429	151,795	604,342	412,697	559,620	266
1949	40,463,125	18,051,822	11,553,669	2,476,113	796,538	7,578,846	2,210,607	1,321,875	1,771,533	589,747	150,899	585,407	434,701	535,911	6,138
1948	41,864,542	20,997,781	10,174,410	2,381,342	899,345	7,409,941	2,255,327	1,300,280	1,649,234	485,872	159,284	559,525	438,628	468,776	1,723
1947	39,108,386	19,343,297	9,676,459	2,024,365	779,291	7,283,378	2,474,762	1,237,768	1,425,395	366,711	174,927	515,691	456,223	417,690	1,597
1946	40,672,097	18,704,536	12,553,602	1,700,828	676,833	6,684,178	2,526,165	1,165,519	922,671	131,908	118,092	480,297	415,268	380,082	352,121
1945	43,800,388	19,034,313	16,027,213	1,779,177	643,055	5,944,630	2,309,866	932,145	782,511	72,845	75,257	498,428	357,466	341,587	371,999
1944	40,121,760	18,261,005	14,766,796	1,738,372	511,211	4,463,674	1,618,775	988,483	503,462	36,020	40,334	323,690	205,289	231,474	380,702
1943	22,371,386	6,629,932	9,668,956	1,498,705	447,496	3,797,503	1,423,646	923,857	504,746	26,132	18,345	332,104	154,451	158,161	328,795
1942	13,047,869	3,262,800	4,744,083	1,185,362	432,542	3,141,183	1,048,517	780,982	771,898	123,621	64,811	416,019	115,033	75,022	281,900
1941	7,370,108	1,417,655	2,053,469	925,856	407,058	2,399,417	820,056	698,077	617,373	105,234	51,054	381,242	70,963	27,331	166,653
1940	5,340,452	982,017	1,147,592	833,521	360,071	1,884,512	624,253	608,518	447,152	77,847	41,555	257,420	21,888	26,368	132,739
1939	5,181,574	1,028,834	1,156,281	740,429	360,716	1,768,113	587,800	580,159	396,975	56,666	34,819	237,516	19,471	24,094	127,203
1938	5,658,765	1,286,312	1,342,718	742,660	416,874	1,730,853	567,979	568,182	417,152	58,051	31,567	235,213	20,801	23,977	139,349
1937	4,653,195	1,091,741	1,088,101	265,745	305,548	1,764,561	594,245	552,254	450,581	84,382	40,819	227,996	19,740	24,570	137,499
1936	3,520,208	674,416	753,032	48	378,840	1,547,293	505,464	501,166	382,716	62,311	32,208	204,443	17,112	21,098	94,943
1935	3,299,436	527,113	578,678	--------	212,112	1,363,802	411,022	459,179	342,145	50,617	26,638	189,332	15,380	19,741	91,508
1934	2,672,239	419,509	400,146	--------	113,138	1,287,854	258,911	425,169	385,291	43,271	27,630	227,830	14,614	19,251	80,168
1933	1,619,839	352,574	394,218	--------	34,310	838,738	43,174	402,739	243,600	17,825	14,980	141,162	15,521	14,565	--------
1932	1,557,729	427,191	629,566	--------	47,422	453,550	8,704	398,579	87				1,859		
1931	2,428,229	833,648	1,026,393	--------	48,078	520,110	10,432	444,277	138				2,779		
1930	3,040,146	1,146,845	1,263,414	--------	64,770		11,695	450,339	2,665				4,231		47
1929	2,939,054	1,095,541	1,235,733	--------	61,897	565,070	12,777	434,445	5,712				6,083		5,956
1928	2,790,536	882,727	1,291,846	--------	60,087	539,927	15,308	396,450	51,952				17,725		8,689
1927	2,865,683	911,940	1,308,013	--------	100,340		21,196	376,170	66,850				17,941		8,970
1926	2,836,000	879,124	1,094,980	--------	119,216		26,452	370,666	150,220				23,981		97,386
1925	2,584,140	845,426	916,233	--------	108,940		25,905	345,247	140,877				30,908		90,003
1924	2,796,179	---------	---------	--------	102,967		27,586	325,639	200,922						
1923	2,621,745	---------	---------	--------	126,705		30,358	309,015	185,117				77,713	34,662	87,472
1922	3,197,451	---------	---------	--------	139,419		45,609	270,759	174,361				70,175	30,381	81,568
1921	4,595,357	---------	---------	--------	154,043		82,623	255,219	229,398				73,385	29,272	80,612
1920	5,407,580	---------	---------	--------	103,636		139,871	295,809	267,969				89,731	28,442	81,526
1919	3,850,150	---------	---------	--------	82,030		483,051	206,003	79,400				76,721	27,677	93,020
1918	3,698,956	---------	---------	--------	47,453		443,841	156,189	36,637				50,920	17,902	28,776
1917	809,394	180,108	207,274	--------	6,077		284,009	103,202	775				26,357	6,299	24,996
1916	512,723	67,944	56,994	--------	--------		247,454	88,064	4,219				--------	--------	10,472

Year	Total collections	Estate and gift taxes [1]	Alcohol	Tobacco	Total manufacturers' [3]	Stamp taxes (including playing cards)
	264	268	270	271	272	279
1915	415,681	---------	223,949	79,957	---------	24,130
1914	380,009	---------	226,180	79,987	---------	714
1913	344,424	---------	230,146	76,789	---------	655
1912	321,616	---------	219,660	70,590	---------	616
1911	322,526	---------	219,648	67,006	---------	582
1910	289,957	---------	208,602	58,118	---------	566
1909	246,213	---------	192,324	51,887	---------	502
1908	251,666	---------	199,966	49,863	---------	460
1907	269,664	50	215,905	51,811	---------	573
1906	249,103	142	199,036	48,423	---------	489
1905	234,188	774	186,319	45,660	---------	427
1904	232,904	2,072	184,893	44,656	---------	376
1903	230,741	5,357	179,501	43,515	---------	423
1902	271,868	4,843	193,127	51,938	---------	13,807
1901	306,872	5,212	191,698	62,482	1	39,558
1900	295,316	2,884	183,420	59,355	3	41,295
1899	273,485	1,235	167,928	52,493	5	44,109
1898	170,867	---------	132,062	36,231	1	1,055
1897	146,620	---------	114,481	30,710	9	251
1896	146,831	---------	114,454	30,712	1	260
1895	143,246	---------	111,503	29,705	(5)	382
1894	147,168	---------	116,674	28,618	2	---------
1893	161,005	---------	127,269	31,890	7	---------
1892	153,858	---------	121,347	31,000	2	1
1891	146,035	---------	111,901	32,796	4	(5)
1890	142,559	---------	107,696	33,959	9	8
1889	130,894	---------	98,136	31,867	6	(5)
1888	124,326	---------	92,630	30,662	10	(5)
1887	118,837	---------	87,752	30,108	22	8
1886	116,903	---------	88,769	27,907	24	8
1885	112,421	---------	85,742	26,407	23	2
1884	121,590	---------	94,990	26,062	24	166
1883	144,553	---------	91,269	42,104	72	7,053
1882	146,523	---------	86,027	47,392	82	7,569
1881	135,230	---------	80,854	42,855	149	7,375
1880	123,982	---------	74,015	38,870	228	7,134
1879	113,450	---------	63,300	40,135	299	6,238
1878	110,654	---------	60,358	40,092	430	5,937
1877	118,549	---------	66,950	41,107	238	6,004
1876	116,768	---------	65,998	39,795	509	6,049
1875	110,072	---------	61,226	37,303	864	6,084
1874	102,191	---------	58,749	33,243	625	5,683
1873	113,504	---------	61,424	34,386	1,267	7,131
1872	130,890	---------	57,734	33,736	4,616	15,296
1871	143,198	2,505	53,671	33,759	3,632	14,530
1870	184,303	3,092	61,925	31,351	3,017	15,611
1869	159,124	2,435	51,171	23,431	3,345	15,505
1868	190,375	2,823	24,612	18,730	61,650	14,047
1867	265,065	1,865	39,600	19,765	91,531	15,239
1866	310,120	1,171	38,489	16,531	127,231	14,258
1865	210,856	547	22,466	11,401	73,318	10,889
1864	116,966	311	32,619	8,592	36,223	5,715
1863	41,003	57	6,805	3,098	16,525	4,140

[1] Prior to 1916, series entitled "legacies, successions, inheritances" taxes.
[2] Beginning 1951, capital stock taxes included in excise taxes.
[3] Prior to 1916, series entitled "manufactures and products" taxes.
[4] Beginning 1942, includes excise taxes on local telephone service.
[5] Less than $500.

Series Y 280–291.   Corporation Income Tax Returns: 1909 to 1956

[Money figures in thousands of dollars.   Includes data for Alaska and Hawaii]

Income year	Number of corporation returns	Active corporation returns										Number of inactive corporation returns [4]
		All returns				Returns with net income						
		Number of returns	Total compiled receipts [1]	Net income (less deficit)	Dividends paid [2]	Number of returns	Total compiled receipts [1]	Net income	Income tax [3]	Excess profits tax	Dividends paid [2]	
	280	281	282	283	284	285	286	287	288	289	290	291
1956	924,961	885,747	679,868,168	46,884,912	17,223,610	559,710	614,857,002	50,184,217	21,364,290	----------	16,870,178	39,214
1955	842,125	807,303	642,248,036	47,478,271	15,588,909	513,270	584,975,387	50,328,887	21,740,890	----------	15,366,051	34,822
1954	754,019	722,805	554,822,450	36,328,435	13,263,471	441,177	484,727,486	39,572,830	16,823,241	37,711	12,907,270	31,214
1953	730,974	697,975	558,242,262	39,484,687	12,711,017	441,767	506,450,081	41,819,445	18,255,625	1,613,424	12,511,979	32,999
1952	705,497	672,071	531,307,298	38,456,179	12,626,377	442,577	486,441,344	40,431,697	17,596,969	1,550,725	12,475,019	33,426
1951	687,310	652,376	517,039,188	43,545,590	12,728,622	439,047	479,243,451	45,333,173	19,623,441	2,458,676	12,576,500	34,934
1950	665,992	629,314	458,130,069	42,613,304	12,845,423	426,283	430,687,780	44,140,741	15,929,488	1,387,444	12,733,663	36,678
1949	649,957	614,842	393,449,692	28,194,837	10,253,335	384,772	350,168,722	30,576,517	9,817,308	----------	10,068,108	35,115
1948	630,670	594,243	410,965,648	34,425,024	10,411,182	395,860	379,309,471	36,273,250	11,920,260	----------	10,287,867	36,427
1947	587,683	551,807	367,745,578	31,422,728	9,065,813	382,531	343,273,851	33,381,291	10,981,482	----------	8,914,555	35,876
1946	526,363	491,152	288,954,237	25,192,886	8,024,178	359,310	265,597,448	27,184,592	8,606,695	268,145	7,762,034	35,211
1945	454,460	421,125	255,447,753	21,138,957	6,415,201	303,019	239,045,611	22,165,206	4,182,705	6,612,045	6,246,856	33,335
1944	446,796	412,467	262,200,531	26,304,481	6,304,239	288,904	252,962,944	27,123,741	4,353,620	10,530,430	6,210,584	34,329
1943	455,894	420,521	249,682,493	27,819,245	5,952,524	283,735	240,766,898	28,717,966	4,479,166	11,446,417	5,851,265	35,373
1942	479,677	442,665	217,680,512	23,051,611	5,679,802	269,942	206,160,215	24,052,358	4,337,728	7,918,668	5,559,812	37,012
1941	509,066	468,906	190,432,017	16,332,542	6,879,727	264,628	175,181,820	18,111,095	3,744,568	3,423,334	6,676,037	40,160
1940	516,783	473,042	148,236,787	8,919,429	6,228,770	220,977	125,180,472	11,203,224	2,144,292	404,254	6,018,903	43,741
1939	515,960	469,617	132,878,224	6,734,565	5,836,617	199,479	105,658,338	8,826,713	1,216,450	15,806	5,649,475	46,343
1938	520,501	471,032	120,453,946	3,672,882	5,098,013	169,884	80,267,477	6,525,979	853,578	5,988	4,856,345	49,469
1937	529,097	477,838	142,443,379	7,353,991	7,702,687	192,028	109,202,739	9,634,837	1,232,837	43,335	7,479,719	51,259
1936	530,779	478,857	132,722,602	7,326,218	7,724,305	203,161	105,011,693	9,478,241	1,169,765	21,613	7,514,539	51,922
1935	533,631	477,113	114,649,717	1,695,950	6,076,471	164,231	77,638,952	5,164,723	710,156	[5] 24,969	4,763,164	56,518
1934	528,898	469,804	101,489,954	94,170	5,074,142	145,101	63,118,536	4,275,197	588,375	[5] 7,673	3,996,018	59,094
1933	504,080	446,842	84,234,006	[6] 2,547,367	3,229,502	109,786	46,906,664	2,985,972	416,093	6,976	2,466,339	57,238
1932	508,636	451,884	81,637,988	[6] 5,643,574	4,028,677	82,646	31,855,481	2,153,113	285,576	----------	2,410,341	56,752
1931	516,404	459,704	108,056,952	[6] 3,287,545	6,314,613	175,898	52,267,013	3,683,368	398,994	----------	3,949,767	56,700
1930	518,736	463,036	136,588,320	1,551,218	8,598,422	221,420	89,910,937	6,428,813	711,704	----------	7,073,549	55,700
1929	509,436	456,021	151,186,206	8,739,758	9,808,454	269,430	130,064,831	11,653,886	1,193,436	----------	9,199,848	53,415
1928	495,892	443,611	153,304,973	8,226,617	7,632,852	268,783	127,787,507	10,617,741	1,184,142	----------	7,104,022	52,281
1927	475,031	425,675	144,899,177	6,510,145	7,125,677	259,849	113,732,970	8,981,884	1,130,674	----------	6,427,654	49,356
1926	455,320	455,320	142,629,445	7,504,693	6,702,942	258,134	118,420,378	9,673,403	1,229,797	----------	6,246,430	----------
1925	430,072	430,072	134,779,997	7,621,056	5,733,906	252,334	114,086,725	9,583,684	1,170,331	----------	5,319,791	----------
1924	417,421	417,421	119,746,703	5,362,726	4,849,349	236,389	97,560,316	7,586,652	881,550	----------	4,461,811	----------
1923	398,933	398,933	119,019,865	6,307,974	5,060,403	233,339	97,793,737	8,321,529	937,106	----------	4,607,787	----------
1922	382,883	382,883	[7] 100,920,515	4,770,035	6,784,765	212,535	[7] 80,331,680	6,963,811	775,310	8,466	6,349,786	----------
1921	356,397	356,397	[7] 91,249,274	457,829	(8)	171,239	[7] 60,051,123	4,336,048	366,444	335,132	(8)	----------
1920	345,595	345,595	[7] 118,205,562	5,873,231	(8)	203,233	[7] 93,824,225	7,902,655	636,508	988,726	(8)	----------
1919	320,198	320,198	[7] 99,918,749	8,415,872	(8)	209,634	[7] 88,261,006	9,411,418	743,536	1,431,806	(8)	----------
1918	317,579	317,579	[7] 86,464,281	7,671,739	(8)	202,061	[7] 79,706,659	8,361,511	653,198	2,505,566	(8)	----------
1917	351,426	351,426	[7] 84,693,239	10,100,753	(8)	232,079	[7] 79,540,005	10,730,360	503,698	1,638,748	(8)	----------
1916	341,253	341,253	[7] 35,327,631	8,109,005	(8)	206,984	[7] 32,531,097	8,765,909	171,805	----------	(8)	----------
1915	366,443	366,443	(8)	(9)	(8)	190,911	(8)	5,310,000	56,994	----------	(8)	----------
1914	299,445	299,445	(8)	(9)	(8)	174,205	(8)	3,940,000	39,145	----------	(8)	----------
1913	316,909	316,909	(8)	(9)	(8)	188,866	(8)	4,714,000	43,128	----------	(8)	----------
1912	305,336	305,336	(8)	(9)	(8)	61,116	(8)	4,151,000	35,006	----------	(8)	----------
1911	288,352	288,352	(8)	(9)	(8)	55,129	(8)	3,503,000	28,583	----------	(8)	----------
1910	270,202	270,202	(8)	(9)	(8)	54,040	(8)	3,761,000	33,512	----------	(8)	----------
1909	262,490	262,490	(8)	(9)	(8)	52,498	(8)	3,590,000	20,960	----------	(8)	----------

In 1918–1924, railroads and other public utility corporations frequently reported only net income, resulting in understatements estimated at $5 billion in 1918 and 1919 and nearly twice that amount in 1920 and 1921; not estimated for 1922–1924. [2] Excludes liquidating dividends. [3] For 1941–1943, includes a small amount of surtax from returns with no net income but with partially tax-exempt interest from Government obligations. For 1941–1956, includes a small amount of tax from returns with no net income because of special provisions for insurance companies.

[4] Prior to 1927, included among those reporting no net income. [5] The declared-value excess profits tax includes a small amount of tax from returns with no net income because the excess profits tax applied to interest on Government obligations exempt from income tax. [6] Deficit. [7] Gross income. "Total compiled receipts" is not available separately for returns with net income and returns with no net income. [8] Not tabulated. [9] Amount of deficit for returns with no net income is not available.

Series Y 292–301.   Individual Income Tax Returns: 1944 to 1957

[Money figures in thousands of dollars]

Income year	Number of returns			Returns with adjusted gross income					Returns with no adjusted gross income	
	Total	Taxable	Non-taxable [1]	Number		Adjusted gross income	Taxable income	Income tax (after credits)	Number [1]	Adjusted gross deficit
				Total	Taxable					
	292	293	294	295	296	297	298	299	300	301
1957	59,825,121	46,865,315	12,959,806	59,407,673	46,865,315	281,308,431	149,363,077	34,393,639	417,448	987,865
1956	59,197,004	46,258,646	12,938,358	58,798,843	46,258,646	268,583,814	141,532,061	32,732,132	398,161	859,546
1955	58,250,188	44,689,065	13,561,123	57,818,164	44,689,065	249,429,182	128,020,111	29,613,722	432,024	898,865
1954	56,747,008	42,633,060	14,113,948	56,306,704	42,633,060	230,235,855	115,331,301	26,665,753	440,304	1,014,480
1953	57,838,184	45,223,151	12,615,033	57,415,885	44,159,622	229,863,409	----------	29,430,659	422,299	1,155,153
1952	56,528,817	43,876,273	12,652,544	56,107,089	42,833,675	216,087,449	----------	27,802,831	421,728	797,541
1951	55,447,009	42,648,610	12,798,399	55,042,597	41,594,222	203,097,033	----------	24,227,780	404,412	760,548
1950	53,060,098	38,186,682	14,873,416	52,655,564	38,186,682	179,874,478	----------	18,374,922	404,534	726,202
1949	51,814,124	35,628,295	16,185,829	51,301,910	35,628,295	161,373,205	----------	14,538,141	512,214	799,280
1948	52,072,006	36,411,248	15,660,758	51,745,697	36,411,248	164,173,861	----------	15,441,529	326,309	657,847
1947	55,099,008	41,578,524	13,520,484	54,799,986	41,578,524	150,295,275	----------	18,076,281	299,072	559,198
1946	52,816,547	37,915,696	14,900,851	52,600,470	37,915,696	134,830,006	----------	16,075,913	216,077	247,206
1945	49,932,783	42,650,502	7,282,281	49,750,991	42,650,502	120,301,131	----------	17,050,878	181,792	292,472
1944	47,111,495	42,354,468	4,757,027	46,919,590	42,354,468	116,714,736	----------	16,216,401	191,905	249,771

[1] Includes returns with no information, 1944–1952 and 1957.

Series Y 302–311. Individual Income Tax Returns: 1913 to 1943

[Money figures in thousands of dollars]

Income year	Returns with net income [1]						Returns with no net income			
	Number of returns			Total income	Net income [2]	Income tax [3]	Number of returns	Total income	Net deficit	Tax
	Total	Taxable	Non-taxable							
	302	303	304	305	306	307	308	309	310	311
1943	43,506,553	40,222,699	3,283,854	106,614,214	99,209,862	14,449,441	215,485	170,866	225,683	643
1942	36,456,110	27,637,051	8,819,059	85,876,118	78,589,729	8,823,041	163,136	181,486	198,598	----
1941	25,770,089	17,502,587	8,267,502	63,841,047	58,527,217	3,815,415	99,828	264,032	292,023	2,326
1940	14,598,074	7,437,261	7,160,813	40,277,645	36,309,719	1,440,967	112,697	239,583	311,385	473
1939	7,570,320	3,896,418	3,673,902	25,816,147	22,938,918	890,934	82,461	228,690	284,327	300
1938	6,150,776	2,995,664	3,155,112	21,549,277	18,660,929	726,120	100,233	318,769	354,156	615
1937	6,301,833	3,326,912	2,974,921	23,891,481	20,941,302	1,093,163	83,904	250,394	308,518	----
1936	5,413,499	2,861,108	2,552,391	21,888,373	19,240,110	1,214,017	73,272	248,530	286,632	----
1935	4,575,012	2,110,890	2,464,122	17,316,505	14,909,812	657,439	94,609	288,653	381,353	----
1934	4,094,420	1,795,920	2,298,500	15,092,960	12,796,802	511,400	104,170	344,055	412,859	----
1933	3,723,558	1,747,740	1,975,818	13,393,825	11,008,638	374,120	168,449	725,817	1,141,331	----
1932	3,877,430	1,936,095	1,941,335	14,392,080	11,655,909	329,962	206,293	831,592	1,480,922	----
1931	3,225,924	1,525,546	1,700,378	17,268,451	13,604,996	246,127	184,583	1,299,750	1,936,878	----
1930	3,707,509	2,037,645	1,669,864	22,319,446	18,118,635	476,715	144,867	1,204,383	1,539,452	----
1929	4,044,327	2,458,049	1,586,278	29,844,758	24,800,736	1,001,938	92,545	902,251	1,025,130	----
1928	4,070,851	2,523,063	1,547,788	28,987,634	25,226,327	1,164,254	72,829	420,649	499,213	----
1927	4,101,547	2,440,941	1,660,606	26,208,561	22,545,091	830,639	(4)	(4)	(4)	----
1926	4,138,092	2,470,990	1,667,102	25,447,436	21,958,506	732,471	(4)	(4)	(4)	----
1925	4,171,051	2,501,166	1,669,885	25,272,035	21,894,576	734,555	(4)	(4)	(4)	----
1924	7,369,788	4,489,698	2,880,090	29,578,997	25,656,153	704,265	(4)	(4)	(4)	----
1923	7,698,321	4,270,121	3,428,200	29,247,593	24,777,466	661,666	(4)	(4)	(4)	----
1922	6,787,481	3,681,249	3,106,232	24,871,908	21,336,213	861,057	(4)	(4)	(4)	----
1921	6,662,176	3,589,985	3,072,191	23,328,782	19,577,213	719,387	(4)	(4)	(4)	----
1920	7,259,944	5,518,310	1,741,634	26,690,270	23,735,629	1,075,054	(4)	(4)	(4)	----
1919	5,332,760	4,231,181	1,101,579	22,437,686	19,859,491	1,269,630	(4)	(4)	(4)	----
1918	4,425,114	3,392,863	1,032,251	17,745,761	15,924,639	1,127,722	(4)	(4)	(4)	----
1917	3,472,890	2,707,234	765,656	[5] 14,538,146	13,407,303	691,493	(4)	(4)	(4)	----
1916	437,036	362,970	74,066	8,349,902	6,298,578	173,387	(4)	(4)	(4)	----
1915	336,652	(4)	(4)	(4)	4,600,000	67,944	(4)	(4)	(4)	----
1914	357,515	(4)	(4)	(4)	4,000,000	41,046	(4)	(4)	(4)	----
1913 [6]	357,598	(4)	(4)	(4)	3,900,000	28,254	(4)	(4)	(4)	----

[1] Includes fiduciary returns with net income filed on Form 1040, 1913–1936.
[2] For 1941–1943, total income on Form 1040A was also used as net income.
[3] Tax for 1924–1931, after earned income credit and capital loss credit; 1932–1933, after capital loss credit only; 1943, after foreign tax credit and tax paid at source. Tax for 1940–1941 includes defense tax and for 1943, victory tax.
[4] Not available.
[5] Somewhat understated because net income was used also as total income on returns with income of $1,000 to $2,000.
[6] Data pertain to last 10 months of year.

Series Y 312–318. Fiduciary Income Tax Returns: 1937 to 1956

[Money figures in thousands of dollars]

Income year	Taxable returns				Nontaxable returns		
	Number of returns	Total income	Net income or taxable income [1]	Income tax (after credits) [2]	Number of returns [3]	Total income [4]	Deficit (reduced by net income)
	312	313	314	315	316	317	318
1956	172,185	2,543,617	901,626	326,945	318,511	2,340,802	192,716
1954	127,779	1,868,922	696,999	263,893	297,136	1,993,002	149,568
1952	132,927	1,307,721	626,760	234,933	289,736	1,480,439	56,808
1951	116,210	1,202,376	590,847	210,765	(5)	(5)	(5)
1950	115,252	1,233,957	615,614	208,756	(5)	(5)	(5)
1949	99,577	926,824	462,775	144,030	(5)	(5)	(5)
1948	101,283	986,806	530,360	176,309	(5)	(5)	(5)
1947	109,997	973,583	509,244	173,071	(5)	(5)	(5)
1946	121,725	1,065,765	594,924	205,457	(5)	(5)	(5)
1945	113,560	856,594	478,495	175,605	(5)	(5)	(5)
1944	92,369	655,623	357,017	131,078	(5)	(5)	(5)
1943	97,156	695,395	375,766	189,933	(5)	(5)	(5)
1942	81,483	572,753	299,633	103,670	(5)	(5)	(5)
1941	84,884	700,790	340,808	90,210	(5)	(5)	(5)
1940	67,388	583,926	278,827	54,963	(5)	(5)	(5)
1939	62,879	574,502	252,953	37,460	150,461	817,334	58,763
1938	52,881	506,172	236,444	39,098	147,945	785,816	60,816
1937	44,531	556,811	294,990	48,406	138,442	976,511	26,862

[1] Prior to 1954, net income taxable to fiduciary before exemptions; thereafter, taxable income after exemptions.
[2] For 1937–1942 and 1944, income tax before credits. Tax for 1940–1941 includes defense tax, and for 1943, victory tax.
[3] For 1954–1956, excludes returns with no information.
[4] For 1952–1956, represents total income less deficit in total income.
[5] Not available.

Series Y 319–332. Individual Income Tax Liability and Effective Rates, for Selected Income Groups: 1913 to 1957

Group and revenue act	Income year or period	$600 (319)	$1,000 (320)	$2,000 (321)	$3,000 (322)	$5,000 (323)	$6,000 (324)	$8,000 (325)	$10,000 (326)	$15,000 (327)	$20,000 (328)	$25,000 (329)	$50,000 (330)	$100,000 (331)	$1,000,000 (332)
1 EXEMPTION															
Liability [1] (dol.):															
1954 [2]	1954–1957 [3]		80	280	488	944	1,204	1,780	2,436	4,448	6,942	9,796	26,388	66,798	[4]870,000
1951	1952–1953 [3]		89	311	542	1,052	1,342	1,992	2,728	4,968	7,762	10,940	28,466	69,688	[4]880,000
	1951 [3]		82	286	498	964	1,234	1,816	2,486	4,528	7,072	9,976	26,758	67,274	[4]872,000
1950	1950		70	244	428	843	1,080	1,604	2,201	4,032	6,301	8,898	23,997	60,770	[4]800,000
1948	1948–1949		66	232	409	811	1,040	1,546	2,124	3,894	6,098	8,600	23,201	58,762	[4]770,000
1945	1946–1947	19	95	285	485	922	1,169	1,720	2,347	4,270	6,645	9,362	25,137	63,541	[4]840,147
1944 [5]	1944–1945	23	115	345	585	1,105	1,395	2,035	2,755	4,930	7,580	10,590	27,945	69,870	[4]900,000
1942	1943 [6][7]	17	107	333	574	1,105	1,401	2,052	2,783	4,968	7,626	10,644	28,058	69,665	[4]899,500
	1942 [6]	15	89	273	472	920	1,174	1,742	2,390	4,366	6,816	9,626	25,811	64,641	854,616
1941	1941		21	117	221	483	649	1,031	1,493	2,994	4,929	7,224	20,882	53,214	733,139
1940	1940 [8]		4	44	84	172	255	449	686	1,476	2,666	4,253	14,709	44,268	718,404
1936, 1938 [9]	1936–1939			32	68	140	216	378	560	1,104	1,834	2,804	9,334	33,354	680,184
1934	1934–1935			32	68	140	216	378	560	1,104	1,834	2,804	9,334	31,404	572,324
1932	1932–1933			40	80	160	240	420	600	1,140	1,800	2,640	8,720	30,220	571,220
1928	1929 [10]			2	6	13	22	52	90	285	555	922	4,250	14,930	230,930
	1928, 1930–1931			6	17	40	56	101	154	386	694	1,099	4,664	15,844	240,844
1926	1925–1927 [11]			6	17	40	56	101	154	386	694	1,234	4,954	16,134	241,134
1924	1924			15	30	60	90	150	225	585	1,045	1,635	6,165	22,645	429,645
1921	1923			30	60	120	180	315	450	855	1,350	1,980	6,540	22,665	413,040
	1922			40	80	160	240	420	600	1,140	1,800	2,640	8,720	30,220	550,720
	1921			40	80	160	250	450	670	1,310	2,070	2,960	9,270	31,270	663,270
1918	1919–1920			40	80	160	250	450	670	1,310	2,070	2,960	9,270	31,270	663,270
	1918			60	120	240	370	650	950	1,790	2,750	3,840	11,150	35,150	703,150
1917	1917			20	40	120	170	275	395	770	1,220	1,820	5,220	16,220	475,220
1916	1916					40	60	100	140	240	340	490	1,340	3,940	102,940
1913	1913–1915 [12]					20	30	50	70	120	170	270	770	2,520	60,020
Effective rate [13] (percent):															
1954 [2]	1954–1957 [3]		8.0	14.0	16.3	18.9	20.1	22.3	24.4	29.7	34.7	39.2	52.8	66.8	[4]87.0
1951	1952–1953 [3]		8.9	15.5	18.1	21.0	22.4	24.9	27.2	33.1	38.8	43.8	56.9	69.7	[4]88.0
	1951 [3]		8.2	14.3	16.6	19.3	20.6	22.7	24.9	30.2	35.4	39.9	53.5	67.3	[4]87.2
1950	1950		7.0	12.2	14.3	16.9	18.0	20.0	22.0	26.9	31.5	35.6	48.0	60.8	[4]80.0
1948	1948–1949		6.6	11.6	13.6	16.2	17.3	19.3	21.2	26.0	30.4	34.4	46.4	58.8	[4]77.0
1945	1946–1947	3.2	9.5	14.3	16.2	18.4	19.5	21.5	23.5	28.5	33.2	37.5	50.3	63.5	[4]84.0
1944 [5]	1944–1945	3.8	11.5	17.3	19.5	22.1	23.3	25.4	27.6	32.9	37.9	42.4	55.9	69.9	[4]90.0
1942	1943 [6][7]	2.8	10.7	16.7	19.1	22.1	23.4	25.7	27.8	33.1	38.1	42.6	56.1	69.7	[4]90.0
	1942 [6]	2.5	8.9	13.7	15.7	18.4	19.6	21.8	23.9	29.1	34.1	38.5	51.6	64.6	85.5
1941	1941		2.1	5.9	7.4	9.7	10.8	12.9	14.9	20.0	24.6	28.9	41.8	53.2	73.3
1940	1940 [8]		0.4	2.2	2.8	3.4	4.3	5.6	6.9	9.8	13.3	17.0	29.4	44.3	71.8
1936, 1938 [9]	1936–1939			1.6	2.3	2.8	3.6	4.7	5.6	7.4	9.2	11.2	18.7	33.4	68.0
1934	1934–1935			1.6	2.3	2.8	3.6	4.7	5.6	7.4	9.2	11.2	18.7	31.4	57.2
1932	1932–1933			2.0	2.7	3.2	4.0	5.3	6.0	7.6	9.0	10.6	17.4	30.2	57.1
1928	1929 [10]			0.1	0.2	0.3	0.4	0.7	0.9	1.9	2.8	3.7	8.5	14.9	23.1
	1928, 1930–1931			0.3	0.6	0.8	0.9	1.3	1.5	2.6	3.5	4.4	9.3	15.8	24.1
1926	1925–1927 [11]			0.3	0.6	0.8	0.9	1.3	1.5	2.6	3.5	4.9	9.9	16.1	24.1
1924	1924			0.8	1.0	1.2	1.5	1.9	2.3	3.9	5.2	6.5	12.3	22.7	43.0
1921	1923			1.5	2.0	2.4	3.0	3.9	4.5	5.7	6.8	7.9	13.1	22.7	41.3
	1922			2.0	2.7	3.2	4.0	5.3	6.0	7.6	9.0	10.6	17.4	30.2	55.1
	1921			2.0	2.7	3.2	4.2	5.6	6.7	8.7	10.4	11.8	18.5	31.3	66.3
1918	1919–1920			2.0	2.7	3.2	4.2	5.6	6.7	8.7	10.4	11.8	18.5	31.3	66.3
	1918			3.0	4.0	4.8	6.2	8.1	9.5	11.9	13.8	15.4	22.3	35.2	70.3
1917	1917			1.0	1.3	2.4	2.8	3.4	4.0	5.1	6.1	7.3	10.4	16.2	47.5
1916	1916					0.8	1.0	1.3	1.4	1.6	1.7	2.0	2.7	3.9	10.0
1913	1913–1915 [12]					0.4	0.5	0.6	0.7	0.8	0.9	1.1	1.5	2.5	6.0
4 EXEMPTIONS															
Liability [1] (dol.):															
1954 [2]	1954–1957 [3][14]				120	520	720	1,152	1,592	2,900	4,464	6,268	18,884	51,912	[4]857,456
1951	1952–1953 [3][14]				133	577	799	1,282	1,774	3,236	5,005	7,004	21,088	56,032	[4]871,224
	1951 [3][14]				122	530	734	1,174	1,622	2,972	4,552	6,406	19,232	52,640	[4]858,408
1950	1950 [14]				104	452	626	1,016	1,417	2,607	4,030	5,672	17,152	47,208	[4]791,430
1948	1948–1949 [14]				100	432	598	974	1,361	2,512	3,888	5,476	16,578	45,643	[4]769,314
1945	1946–1947				190	589	798	1,292	1,862	3,639	5,890	8,522	24,111	62,301	[4]838,850
1944 [5]	1944–1945	3	15	45	275	755	1,005	1,585	2,245	4,265	6,785	9,705	26,865	68,565	[4]900,000
1942	1943 [6][7]	1	14	58	267	730	979	1,553	2,208	4,207	6,693	9,574	26,392	67,803	[4]898,800
	1942 [6]			13	191	592	810	1,322	1,914	3,758	6,088	8,814	24,845	63,479	853,384
1941	1941			58	271	397	717	1,117	2,475	4,287	6,480	19,967	52,160	731,980	
1940	1940 [8]					75	114	246	440	1,118	2,143	3,571	13,741	42,948	717,036
1936, 1938 [9]	1936–1939					48	84	184	343	831	1,469	2,327	8,621	31,997	678,436
1934	1934–1935					48	84	184	343	831	1,469	2,327	8,621	30,162	570,898
1932	1932–1933					68	108	236	416	956	1,616	2,456	8,536	30,036	571,036
1928	1929 [10]					3	6	14	40	201	471	838	4,166	14,846	230,846
	1928, 1930–1931					8	19	42	83	281	589	994	4,559	15,739	240,739
1926	1925–1927 [11]					8	19	42	83	281	589	1,129	4,849	16,029	241,029
1924	1924					26	41	81	141	475	935	1,525	6,055	22,535	429,535
1921	1923					51	96	207	342	747	1,242	1,872	6,432	22,557	412,932
	1922					68	128	276	456	996	1,656	2,496	8,576	30,076	550,576
	1921					68	138	306	526	1,166	1,886	2,816	9,126	31,126	663,126
1918	1919–1920				24	104	154	338	558	1,198	1,958	2,848	9,158	31,158	663,158
	1918				36	156	226	482	782	1,622	2,582	3,672	10,982	34,982	702,982
1917	1917				12	64	114	219	339	714	1,164	1,764	5,164	16,164	475,164
1916	1916					20	40	80	120	220	320	470	1,320	3,920	102,920
1913	1913–1915 [12]					10	20	40	60	110	160	260	760	2,510	60,010

See footnotes at end of table.

Series Y 319–332. Individual Income Tax Liability and Effective Rates, for Selected Income Groups: 1913 to 1957—Con.

Group and revenue act	Income year or period	Income groups													
		$600	$1,000	$2,000	$3,000	$5,000	$6,000	$8,000	$10,000	$15,000	$20,000	$25,000	$50,000	$100,000	$1,000,000
		319	320	321	322	323	324	325	326	327	328	329	330	331	332
4 EXEMP-TIONS—Con.															
Effective rate [13] (percent):															
1954 [2]	1954–1957 [3][14]				4.0	10.4	12.0	14.4	15.9	19.3	22.3	25.1	37.8	51.9	85.7
	1952–1953 [3][14]				4.4	11.5	13.3	16.0	17.7	21.6	25.0	28.0	42.2	56.0	87.1
1951	1951 [3][14]				4.1	10.6	12.2	14.7	16.2	19.8	22.8	25.6	38.5	52.6	85.8
1950	1950 [14]				3.5	9.0	10.4	12.7	14.2	17.4	20.2	22.7	34.3	47.2	79.1
1948	1948–1949 [14]				3.3	8.6	10.0	12.2	13.6	16.7	19.4	21.9	33.2	45.6	76.9
1945	1946–1947				6.3	11.8	13.3	16.2	18.6	24.3	29.5	34.1	48.2	62.3	83.9
1944 [5]	1944–1945	0.5	1.5	2.3	9.2	15.1	16.8	19.8	22.5	28.4	33.9	38.8	53.7	68.6	[6] 90.0
1942	1943 [6][7]	0.2	1.4	2.9	8.9	14.6	16.3	19.4	22.1	28.0	33.5	38.3	52.8	67.8	[6] 89.9
	1942 [6]			0.7	6.4	11.8	13.5	16.5	19.1	25.1	30.4	35.3	49.7	63.5	85.3
1941	1941				1.9	5.4	6.6	9.0	11.2	16.5	21.4	25.9	39.9	52.2	73.2
1940	1940 [8]					1.5	1.9	3.1	4.4	7.5	10.7	14.3	27.5	42.9	71.7
1936, 1938 [9]	1936–1939					1.0	1.4	2.3	3.4	5.5	7.3	9.3	17.2	32.0	67.8
1934	1934–1935					1.0	1.4	2.3	3.4	5.5	7.3	9.3	17.2	30.2	57.1
1932	1932–1933					1.4	1.8	3.0	4.2	6.4	8.1	9.8	17.1	30.0	57.1
1928	1929 [10]					0.1	0.1	0.2	0.4	1.3	2.4	3.4	8.3	14.8	23.1
	1928, 1930–1931					0.2	0.3	0.5	0.8	1.9	2.9	4.0	9.1	15.7	24.1
1926	1925–1927 [11]					0.2	0.3	0.5	0.8	1.9	2.9	4.5	9.7	16.0	24.1
1924	1924					0.5	0.7	1.0	1.4	3.2	4.7	6.1	12.1	22.5	43.0
1921	1923					1.0	1.6	2.6	3.4	5.0	6.2	7.5	12.9	22.6	41.3
	1922					1.4	2.1	3.5	4.6	6.6	8.3	10.0	17.2	30.1	55.1
	1921					1.4	2.3	3.8	5.3	7.8	9.6	11.3	18.3	31.1	66.3
1918	1919–1920				0.8	2.1	2.6	4.2	5.6	8.0	9.8	11.4	18.3	31.2	66.3
	1918				1.2	3.1	3.8	6.0	7.8	10.8	12.9	14.7	22.0	35.0	70.3
1917	1917				0.4	1.3	1.9	2.7	3.4	4.8	5.8	7.1	10.3	16.2	47.5
1916	1916					0.4	0.7	1.0	1.2	1.5	1.6	1.9	2.6	3.9	10.3
1913	1913–1915 [12]					0.2	0.3	0.5	0.6	0.7	0.8	1.0	1.5	2.5	6.0

[1] Actual tax liability on selected net incomes and necessary assumptions.
[2] Internal Revenue Code of 1954. [3] Excludes self-employment tax.
[4] Taking into account the following maximum effective rate limitations: For 1944–1945, 90 percent; 1946–1947, 85.5 percent; 1948–1949, 77 percent; 1950, 80 percent; 1951, 87.2 percent; 1952–1953, 88 percent; 1954–1957, 87 percent.
[5] Individual Income Tax Act of 1944.
[6] Tax liabilities unadjusted for transition to current payment basis.
[7] Includes net victory tax. Computed by assuming that deductions are 10 percent of victory tax net income; i.e., that victory tax net income is ten-ninths of selected net income.

[8] Includes defense tax.
[9] Rates and exemptions for 1936 and 1938 acts were identical and resulted in the same tax liabilities.
[10] Normal tax rates of 1928 act were reduced for 1929 only by Joint Resolution of Congress.
[11] Provisions of 1926 act were retroactive to 1925.
[12] Mar. 1, 1913–Dec. 31, 1915.
[13] Tax liability divided by stated net income. [14] Split income basis.

Series Y 333–342. Federal Estate Tax Returns: 1916 to 1957

[Money figures in thousands of dollars]

Filing year	Total number of returns	Citizens and resident aliens [1]					Nonresident aliens [4]			
		Number of returns (taxable and nontaxable)	Gross estate	Net taxable estate [2]	Credit for State inheritance taxes paid	Net estate tax [3] (after credits)	Number of returns (taxable and nontaxable)	Gross estate	Net taxable estate [2]	Net estate tax [3] (after credits)
	333	334	335	336	337	338	339	340	341	342
1957	47,381	46,473	10,293,669	4,342,072	146,769	1,176,710	908	28,884	20,987	4,589
1955	37,565	36,595	7,467,443	2,990,810	86,249	778,342	970	22,803	15,948	2,913
1954	37,672	36,699	7,411,754	2,969,174	85,842	778,504	973	23,383	16,206	3,096
1951	29,002	27,958	5,504,961	2,188,878	64,535	577,401	1,044	20,666	16,052	3,081
1950	27,144	25,858	4,918,094	1,916,645	48,940	483,520	1,286	24,157	18,192	3,229
1949	25,904	24,552	4,933,215	2,106,827	65,881	567,421	1,352	24,511	19,356	3,407
1948	24,381	23,356	4,774,783	2,584,595	82,725	714,707	1,025	16,266	12,602	1,825
1947	22,007	20,899	4,224,210	2,319,310	69,850	621,966	1,108	27,198	21,872	4,389
1945	16,550	15,898	3,436,901	1,900,159	64,517	531,052	652	13,524	10,997	1,876
1944	14,857	14,303	2,907,620	1,508,953	46,285	404,635	554	8,712	7,272	1,146
1943	16,033	15,187	2,627,367	1,396,697	35,966	362,164	846	10,471	8,703	1,212
1942	17,396	16,215	2,724,513	1,524,881	45,626	308,342	1,181	12,620	11,455	1,349
1941	17,122	15,977	2,777,657	1,561,215	53,636	291,758	1,145	15,783	14,553	1,641
1940	16,876	15,435	2,632,659	1,479,268	45,337	250,360	1,441	15,540	13,916	1,196
1939	16,926	15,221	2,746,143	1,537,975	53,111	276,707	1,705	21,745	20,347	2,231
1938	17,642	15,932	3,046,977	1,724,589	59,842	314,620	1,710	22,648	20,670	2,182
1937	17,032	15,037	2,767,739	1,622,618	58,252	305,784	1,995	26,019	23,995	2,665
1936	13,321	11,605	2,296,257	1,245,395	44,218	195,301	1,716	16,163	14,627	1,069
1935	12,724	11,110	2,435,282	1,316,838	43,864	153,763	1,614	24,609	22,888	1,703
1934	11,853	10,353	2,244,107	1,150,533	33,922	95,228	1,500	23,178	20,033	988
1933	10,275	8,727	2,026,931	970,868	28,295	59,429	1,548	34,025	30,056	1,986
1932	8,507	7,113	2,795,818	1,391,569	61,642	22,364	1,394	34,570	31,868	1,310
1931	9,889	8,333	4,042,381	2,327,319	137,663	44,540	1,556	33,195	29,013	660
1930	10,382	8,798	4,108,517	2,376,973	113,388	250,360	1,584	57,106	50,481	2,614
1929	10,343	8,582	3,843,514	2,268,323	122,110	43,303	1,761	49,732	45,653	1,085
1928	10,236	8,079	3,503,239	1,943,429	94,452	40,561	2,157	51,032	49,075	1,398
1927	10,700	9,353	3,146,290	1,735,840	59,600	40,931	1,347	26,945	25,777	755
1926	14,567	13,142	3,386,267	1,951,969	36,732	101,324	1,425	21,656	20,567	481
1925	16,019	14,013	2,958,364	1,621,008	10,707	86,223	2,006	42,725	37,861	1,099
1924	14,513	13,011	2,540,922	1,372,421	----------	71,451	1,502	25,600	23,395	488
1923	15,119	13,963	2,774,741	1,504,621	----------	88,384	1,156	29,587	27,440	726
1922 (Jan. 15–Dec. 31)	13,876	12,563	2,955,959	1,652,832	----------	117,624	1,313	58,113	52,142	2,938
1916–1922 [5]	45,126	42,230	8,785,642	5,407,674	----------	351,138	2,896	107,597	101,849	5,378

[1] Includes returns for nonresident citizens who died on or after May 11, 1934.
[2] Net taxable estate includes net estate for returns filed under 1926 and prior acts, net estate for additional tax for returns filed under 1932 through 1953 acts, and net taxable estate for returns filed under 1954 Code.

[3] Net estate tax is the combined basic tax and additional tax whenever applicable, and includes defense tax for returns filed under 1940 act.
[4] Includes returns for nonresident citizens who died prior to May 11, 1934.
[5] Sept. 9, 1916–Jan. 15, 1922.

Series Y 343–349.   Federal Gift Tax Returns: 1924 to 1956

[Money figures in thousands of dollars]

Year of gift	Total number of returns	Taxable returns				Nontaxable returns		Year of gift	Total number of returns	Taxable returns				Nontaxable returns	
		Number of returns	Total gifts	Net taxable gift	Gift tax	Number of returns	Total gifts			Number of returns	Total gifts	Net taxable gift	Gift tax	Number of returns	Total gifts
	343	344	345	346	347	348	349		343	344	345	346	347	348	349
1956	(1)	14,736	923,470	517,583	113,005	(1)	(1)	1940	15,623	4,930	346,679	225,972	34,445	10,693	223,363
1953	44,695	8,464	474,767	258,478	55,528	36,231	537,287	1939	12,226	3,929	219,594	131,577	18,701	8,297	152,010
1951	41,703	8,360	501,377	304,131	67,426	33,343	498,141	1938	11,042	3,515	230,763	138,801	17,839	7,527	169,010
								1937	13,695	4,128	317,787	180,939	22,758	9,567	250,322
1950	39,056	8,366	578,431	337,719	77,605	30,690	485,769	1936	13,420	3,770	258,000	134,979	15,664	9,650	224,783
1949	31,547	6,114	325,682	178,035	36,087	25,433	382,699								
1948	26,200	6,559	377,889	209,148	45,338	19,641	363,034	1935	22,563	8,718	1,710,061	1,196,001	162,798	13,845	420,453
1947	24,857	6,822	438,681	256,534	64,402	18,035	338,932	1934	9,270	2,528	692,428	537,083	68,383	6,742	196,325
1946	24,826	6,808	425,640	265,246	62,336	18,018	329,964	1933	3,683	878	155,859	101,793	8,943	2,805	85,149
								1932 (June 7–Dec. 31)	1,747	245	36,025	17,879	1,111	1,502	45,363
1945	20,095	5,540	288,739	169,625	36,633	14,555	246,820								
1944	18,397	4,979	276,121	148,420	37,781	13,418	222,891								
1943	16,987	4,656	208,738	123,936	29,637	12,331	203,916	1925	848	768	[2] 187,275	91,289	2,715	80	15,789
1942	16,906	4,380	222,296	120,653	24,665	12,526	257,927	1924	1,528	1,411	328,803	170,182	7,242	117	18,289
1941	25,788	8,940	714,400	484,319	69,819	16,848	367,082								

[1] Not available.   [2] Exclusive of total gifts on 4 returns of nonresident donors.

Series Y 350–356.   Expenditures of the Federal Government: 1789 to 1957

[In thousands of dollars.   For 1789–1842, years ending December 31; 1844–1957, June 30; 1843 figures are for January 1–June 30]

Year	Total [1]	Department of the Army (formerly War Department)	Department of the Navy	Department of the Air Force	Interest on the public debt	Other [1]		Year	Total [1]	Department of the Army (formerly War Department)	Department of the Navy	Interest on the public debt	Other [1]	
						Total	Veterans compensation and pensions [2]						Total	Veterans compensation and pensions [2]
	350	351	352	353	354	355	356		350	351	352	354	355	356
1957	69,433,078	9,704,788	10,397,224	18,360,926	7,244,193	23,725,947	2,869,989	1905	567,279	126,094	117,550	24,591	299,044	141,774
1956	66,539,776	9,274,301	9,743,715	16,749,648	6,786,599	23,985,513	2,797,509	1904	583,660	165,200	102,956	24,646	290,857	142,559
								1903	517,006	118,630	82,618	28,556	287,202	138,426
1955	64,569,973	9,450,383	9,731,611	16,405,038	6,370,362	22,612,579	2,680,834	1902	485,234	112,272	67,803	29,108	276,051	138,489
1954	67,772,353	13,515,388	11,292,804	15,668,473	6,382,486	20,913,202	2,481,514	1901	524,617	144,616	60,507	32,343	287,151	139,324
1953	74,274,257	17,054,333	11,874,830	15,085,228	6,503,580	23,756,286	2,420,140							
1952	65,407,585	17,452,710	10,231,265	12,851,619	5,859,263	19,012,727	2,177,893	1900	520,861	134,775	55,953	40,160	289,973	140,877
1951	44,057,831	8,635,939	5,862,549	6,358,604	5,612,655	17,588,085	2,171,475	1899	605,072	229,841	63,942	39,897	271,392	139,395
								1898	443,369	91,992	58,824	37,585	254,968	147,452
1950	39,617,003	5,789,468	4,129,546	3,520,633	5,749,913	20,427,444	2,222,926	1897	365,774	48,950	34,562	37,791	244,471	141,053
1949	39,506,989	7,862,397	4,434,706	1,690,461	5,339,396	20,180,029	2,153,828	1896	352,179	50,831	27,148	35,385	238,816	139,434
1948	33,068,709	7,698,556	4,284,619	----------	5,211,102	15,874,432	2,080,130							
1947	39,032,393	9,172,139	5,597,203	----------	4,957,922	19,305,129	1,929,226	1895	356,195	51,805	28,798	30,978	244,615	141,395
1946	60,447,574	27,986,769	15,164,412	----------	4,721,958	12,574,435	1,261,415	1894	367,525	54,568	31,701	27,841	253,415	141,177
								1893	383,478	49,642	30,136	27,264	276,436	159,358
1945	98,416,220	50,490,102	30,047,152	----------	3,616,686	14,262,280	772,190	1892	345,023	46,895	29,174	23,378	245,576	134,583
1944	95,058,708	49,438,330	26,537,634	----------	2,608,980	16,473,764	494,959	1891	365,774	48,720	26,114	37,547	253,393	124,416
1943	79,407,131	42,525,563	20,888,349	----------	1,808,160	14,185,059	442,394							
1942	34,045,679	14,325,508	8,579,589	----------	1,260,085	9,880,496	431,294	1890	318,041	44,583	22,006	36,099	215,352	106,937
1941	13,262,204	3,938,943	2,313,058	----------	1,110,693	5,899,510	433,148	1889	299,289	44,435	21,379	41,001	192,473	87,625
								1888	267,925	38,522	16,926	44,715	167,761	80,289
1940	9,062,032	907,160	891,485	----------	1,040,936	6,222,452	429,178	1887	267,932	38,561	15,141	47,742	166,488	75,029
1939	8,858,458	695,256	672,722	----------	940,540	6,549,939	416,721	1886	242,483	34,324	13,908	50,580	143,671	63,405
1938	6,791,838	644,264	596,130	----------	926,281	4,625,163	402,779							
1937	7,756,021	628,104	556,674	----------	866,384	5,704,859	396,047	1885	260,227	42,671	16,021	51,386	150,149	56,102
1936	8,493,486	618,587	528,882	----------	749,397	6,596,620	399,066	1884	244,126	39,430	17,293	54,578	132,826	55,429
								1883	265,408	48,911	15,288	59,160	142,053	66,013
1935	6,520,966	487,995	436,266	----------	820,926	4,775,779	373,805	1882	257,981	43,570	15,032	71,077	128,302	61,345
1934	6,693,900	408,587	296,927	----------	756,617	5,231,768	319,322	1881	260,713	40,466	15,687	82,509	122,051	50,059
1933	4,622,865	434,621	349,373	----------	689,365	3,149,506	234,990							
1932	4,659,203	476,305	357,518	----------	599,277	3,226,103	232,521	1880	267,643	38,117	13,537	95,758	120,231	56,777
1931	3,577,434	486,142	353,768	----------	611,560	2,125,964	224,402	1879	266,948	40,426	15,125	105,328	106,069	35,121
								1878	236,964	32,154	17,365	102,501	84,944	27,137
1930	3,440,269	464,854	374,166	----------	659,348	1,941,902	220,609	1877	241,334	37,083	14,960	97,125	92,167	27,964
1929	3,298,859	425,947	364,562	----------	678,330	1,830,020	229,781	1876	265,101	38,071	18,963	100,243	107,824	28,257
1928	3,103,265	400,990	331,335	----------	731,764	1,689,175	229,401							
1927	2,974,030	369,114	318,909	----------	787,020	1,498,987	230,556	1875	274,623	41,121	21,498	103,094	108,912	29,456
1926	3,097,612	364,090	312,748	----------	831,938	1,588,841	207,190	1874	302,634	42,314	30,933	107,120	122,268	29,038
								1873	290,345	46,323	23,526	104,751	115,745	29,359
1925	3,063,105	370,981	346,142	----------	881,807	1,464,176	218,321	1872	277,518	35,372	21,250	117,358	103,538	28,533
1924	3,048,678	357,017	332,249	----------	940,603	1,418,809	228,262	1871	292,177	35,800	19,431	125,577	111,370	34,444
1923	3,294,628	397,051	333,201	----------	1,055,924	1,508,452	264,148							
1922	3,372,608	457,756	476,775	----------	991,001	1,447,076	252,577	1870	309,654	57,656	21,780	129,235	100,982	28,340
1921	5,115,928	1,118,076	650,374	----------	999,145	2,348,333	260,611	1869	322,865	78,502	20,001	130,694	93,668	28,477
								1868	377,340	123,247	25,776	140,424	87,894	23,782
1920	6,403,344	1,621,953	736,021	----------	1,020,252	3,025,118	213,344	1867	357,543	95,224	31,034	143,782	87,503	20,937
1919	18,514,880	9,009,076	2,002,311	----------	619,216	6,884,278	221,615	1866	520,809	284,450	43,324	133,068	59,968	15,605
1918	12,696,702	4,869,955	1,278,840	----------	189,743	6,358,163	181,138							
1917	1,977,682	377,941	239,633	----------	24,743	1,335,365	160,318	1865	1,297,555	1,031,323	122,613	77,398	66,221	16,339
1916	734,056	183,176	153,854	----------	22,901	374,125	159,302	1864	865,323	690,792	85,726	53,685	35,119	4,984
								1863	714,741	599,299	63,222	24,730	27,490	1,079
1915	760,587	202,160	141,836	----------	22,903	393,688	164,388	1862	474,762	394,368	42,668	13,190	24,535	853
1914	735,081	208,350	139,682	----------	22,864	364,186	173,440	1861	66,547	22,981	12,421	4,000	27,144	1,036
1913	724,512	202,129	133,263	----------	22,899	366,221	175,085							
1912	689,881	184,123	135,592	----------	22,616	347,550	153,591	1860	63,131	16,410	11,515	3,177	32,029	1,103
1911	691,202	197,199	119,938	----------	21,311	352,753	157,981	1859	69,071	23,244	14,643	2,638	28,546	1,220
								1858	74,185	25,485	13,985	1,567	33,148	1,217
1910	693,617	189,823	123,174	----------	21,343	359,277	160,696	1857	67,796	19,262	12,748	1,678	34,108	1,312
1909	693,744	192,487	115,546	----------	21,804	363,907	161,710	1856	69,571	16,948	14,092	1,954	36,577	1,298
1908	659,196	175,840	118,037	----------	21,426	343,893	153,892							
1907	579,129	149,775	97,128	----------	24,481	307,744	139,310	1855	59,743	14,774	13,312	2,314	29,342	1,450
1906	570,202	137,326	110,474	----------	24,309	298,093	141,035	1854	58,045	11,734	10,799	3,071	32,442	1,238

See footnotes at end of table.

Series Y 350–356. Expenditures of the Federal Government: 1789 to 1957—Con.

[In thousands of dollars]

Year	Total [1] (350)	Department of the Army (formerly War Department) (351)	Department of the Navy (352)	Interest on the public debt (354)	Other [1] — Total (355)	Other [1] — Veterans compensation and pensions [2] (356)
1853	48,184	9,947	10,919	3,666	23,652	1,778
1852	44,195	8,225	8,953	4,000	23,017	2,404
1851	47,709	11,812	9,006	3,697	23,195	2,290
1850	39,543	9,400	7,905	3,782	18,456	1,870
1849	45,052	14,853	9,787	3,566	16,846	1,330
1848	45,377	25,502	9,408	2,391	8,076	1,211
1847	57,281	38,306	7,901	1,119	9,956	1,748
1846	27,767	10,793	6,455	843	9,676	1,810
1845	22,937	5,753	6,297	1,040	9,847	2,397
1844	22,338	5,179	6,498	1,834	8,826	2,031
1843	11,858	2,957	3,728	524	4,649	843
1842	25,206	6,612	8,397	774	9,423	1,379
1841	26,566	8,806	6,001	285	11,474	2,388
1840	24,318	7,097	6,114	175	10,932	2,604
1839	26,899	8,917	6,182	400	11,400	3,143
1838	33,865	12,897	6,132	15	14,821	2,156
1837	37,243	13,683	6,647	----------	16,914	2,672
1836	30,868	12,169	5,808	----------	12,891	2,883
1835	17,573	5,759	3,865	58	7,891	1,955
1834	18,628	5,696	3,956	202	8,773	3,364
1833	23,018	6,704	3,901	304	12,108	4,589
1832	17,289	5,446	3,956	773	7,114	1,184
1831	15,248	4,842	3,856	1,384	5,166	1,171
1830	15,143	4,767	3,239	1,914	5,223	1,363
1829	15,203	4,724	3,309	2,543	4,627	950
1828	16,395	4,146	3,919	3,099	5,232	851
1827	16,139	3,939	4,264	3,486	4,450	976
1826	17,036	3,943	4,219	3,973	4,900	1,557
1825	15,857	3,660	3,049	4,367	4,781	1,309
1824	20,327	3,341	2,905	4,997	9,085	1,499
1823	14,707	3,097	2,504	4,923	4,183	1,781
1822	15,000	3,112	2,224	5,173	4,491	1,948
1821	15,811	4,461	3,319	5,087	2,943	243
1820	18,261	2,630	4,388	5,126	6,116	3,208
1819	21,464	6,506	3,848	5,164	5,946	2,416
1818	19,825	5,623	2,954	6,016	5,232	891
1817	21,844	8,004	3,315	6,389	4,136	297
1816	30,587	16,012	3,908	7,213	3,453	189
1815	32,708	14,794	8,660	5,755	3,499	70
1814	34,721	20,351	7,311	4,593	2,466	90
1813	31,682	19,652	6,447	3,599	1,984	87
1812	20,281	11,818	3,959	2,451	2,052	91
1811	8,058	2,033	1,966	2,466	1,594	75
1810	8,157	2,294	1,654	2,845	1,363	84
1809	10,281	3,346	2,428	2,866	1,641	88
1808	9,932	2,901	1,884	3,428	1,719	83
1807	8,354	1,289	1,722	3,370	1,974	71
1806	9,804	1,224	1,650	3,723	3,206	82
1805	10,506	713	1,598	4,149	4,047	82
1804	8,719	875	1,190	4,267	2,388	80
1803	7,852	822	1,215	3,849	1,966	63
1802	7,862	1,179	916	4,125	1,642	85
1801	9,395	1,673	2,111	4,413	1,197	74
1800	10,786	2,561	3,449	3,375	1,402	64
1799	9,666	2,467	2,858	3,186	1,155	95
1798	7,677	2,010	1,381	3,053	1,232	105
1797	6,134	1,039	383	3,300	1,412	92
1796	5,727	1,260	275	3,195	997	101
1795	7,540	2,481	411	3,189	1,459	69
1794	6,991	2,639	61	3,490	800	81
1793	4,482	1,130	----------	2,772	580	80
1792	5,080	1,101	(3)	3,202	777	109
1789–1791	4,269	633	1	2,349	1,286	176

[1] Prior to 1930, includes tax refunds paid and capital transfers for wholly owned Government corporations; thereafter, excludes them.

[2] Includes compensation for service-connected injuries and deaths as well as pension for nonservice-connected disabilities and deaths.

[3] Less than $500.

Series Y 357–367. Budget Expenditures of the Federal Government, by Major Function: 1900 to 1957

[In millions of dollars. For years ending June 30]

Year	Total (357)	Major national security (358)	International affairs and finance (359)	Veterans services and benefits (360)	Labor and welfare (361)	Agriculture and agricultural resources (362)	National resources (363)	Commerce and housing (364)	General Government (365)	Interest (366)	Adjustment to daily Treasury statement (367)
1957	69,433	43,270	1,976	4,793	3,022	4,526	1,296	1,455	1,787	7,308	----------
1956	66,540	40,641	1,846	4,756	2,821	4,868	1,104	2,030	1,627	6,846	----------
1955	64,570	40,626	2,181	4,457	2,575	4,389	1,202	1,504	1,199	6,438	----------
1954	67,772	46,904	1,732	4,256	2,485	2,557	1,315	817	1,235	6,470	----------
1953	74,274	50,363	2,216	4,298	2,426	2,936	1,476	2,504	1,472	6,583	----------
1952	65,408	43,976	2,826	4,863	2,168	1,045	1,366	2,624	1,463	5,934	−857
1951	44,058	22,444	3,736	5,342	2,065	650	1,267	2,217	1,327	5,714	−705
1950	39,617	13,009	4,674	6,646	1,963	2,783	1,206	1,991	1,186	5,817	+341
1949	39,507	12,908	6,052	6,725	1,563	2,512	1,049	1,904	1,076	5,445	+272
1948	33,069	11,771	4,566	6,653	1,322	742		1,302	1,277	5,248	−388
1947	39,032	14,368	6,536	7,381	1,277	1,243	548	1,003	1,358	5,012	+305
1946	60,448	43,176	3,107	4,415	1,030	747	337	687	1,054	4,816	+1,077
1945	98,416	81,216	3,312	2,095	1,109	1,607	317	3,964	884	3,662	+252
1944	95,059	76,696	3,642	745	1,057	1,215	402	8,062	978	2,623	−360
1943	79,407	63,159	3,299	606	1,257	610	501	7,560	788	1,825	−197
1942	34,046	23,987	1,839	558	2,034	1,482	533	2,802	512	1,272	−924
1941	13,262	6,086	145	566	2,637	1,314	452	676	407	1,123	−94
1940	9,062	1,498	51	552	3,079	1,538	471	456	370	1,056	−7
1939	8,858	1,075	20	560	3,925	1,199	349	501	343	950	−63
1938	6,792	1,030	19	581			4,229			933	----------
1937	7,756	937	18	1,137			4,792			872	----------
1936	8,494	914	18	2,350			4,456			756	----------
1935	6,521	711	19	607			4,358			826	----------
1934	6,694	540	12	557			4,815			770	----------
1933	4,623	648	16	863			2,395			701	----------
1932	4,659	703	19	985			2,333			619	----------
1931	3,578	733	16	1,040			1,161			628	----------
1930	3,320	734	14	821			1,054			697	----------
1929	3,127	696	14	812			886			719	----------
1928	2,933	656	12	806			728			731	----------
1927	2,837	578	17	786			669			787	----------
1926	2,888	586	17	772			681			832	----------

Series Y 357–367. Budget Expenditures of the Federal Government, by Major Function: 1900 to 1957—Con.

[In millions of dollars]

Year	Total	Major national security	International affairs and finance	Veterans services and benefits	Interest	All other	Year	Total	Major national security	International affairs and finance	Veterans services and benefits	Interest	All other
	357	358	359	360	366	361–365		357	358	359	360	366	361–365
1925	2,881	591	15	741	882	652	1912	690	284	5	154	23	224
1924	2,890	647	15	676	941	611	1911	691	283	(1)	158	21	[1] 229
1923	3,137	680	14	747	1,056	640							
1922	3,285	929	10	686	991	669	1910	694	284	(1)	161	21	[1] 228
1921	5,058	2,581	83	646	999	749	1909	694	308	(1)	162	22	[1] 202
							1908	659	294	(1)	154	21	[1] 190
1920	6,357	3,997	435	332	1,024	569	1907	579	247	(1)	139	24	[1] 169
1919	18,448	13,548	3,500	324	616	460	1906	570	247	(1)	141	24	[1] 158
1918	12,662	7,110	4,748	235	198	371							
1917	1,954	602	891	171	25	265	1905	567	244	(1)	142	25	[1] 156
1916	713	305	6	171	23	208	1904	584	268	(1)	143	25	[1] 148
							1903	517	202	(1)	138	29	[1] 148
1915	746	297	5	176	23	245	1902	485	180	(1)	138	29	[1] 138
1914	725	298	5	173	23	226	1901	525	206	(1)	139	32	[1] 148
1913	715	293	5	175	23	219	1900	521	191	(1)	141	40	[1] 149

[1] Prior to 1912, figures for "International affairs and finance" included with "All other."

Series Y 368–379. Public Debt of the Federal Government: 1791 to 1957

[For 1791–1842, as of January 1; thereafter, as of June 30]

Year	Principal of public debt outstanding					Computed annual interest charge	Computed rate of interest	Composition of interest-bearing debt				
	Total gross debt		Matured	Non-interest-bearing [2]	Interest-bearing [3]			Bonds		Treasury bills, etc. [4]	Notes [5]	Special issues [6]
	Amount [1]	Per capita						U.S. savings bonds	Other bonds			
	368	369	370	371	372	373	374	375	376	377	378	379
	1,000 dollars	Dollars	1,000 dollars	1,000 dollars	1,000 dollars	1,000 dollars	Percent	Million dollars	Million dollars	Million dollars	Million dollars	Million dollars
1957	270,527,172	1,579.91	529,242	1,512,368	268,485,563	7,325,147	2.730	54,622	92,170	43,893	30,973	46,827
1956	272,750,814	1,621.84	666,052	2,201,694	269,883,068	6,949,700	2.576	57,497	94,210	37,111	35,952	45,114
1955	274,374,223	1,660.16	588,601	2,044,354	271,741,268	6,387,226	2.351	58,365	94,133	33,350	42,642	43,250
1954	271,259,599	1,670.14	437,185	1,912,648	268,909,767	6,298,069	2.342	58,061	93,660	37,920	37,039	42,229
1953	266,071,062	1,666.74	298,421	1,826,623	263,946,018	6,430,991	2.438	57,886	95,084	35,561	34,878	40,538
1952	259,105,179	1,650.06	418,692	1,823,625	256,862,861	5,981,357	2.329	57,685	90,221	45,642	25,575	37,739
1951	255,221,977	1,653.42	512,047	1,858,165	252,851,765	5,739,616	2.270	57,572	93,881	23,123	43,624	34,653
1950	257,357,352	1,696.68	264,771	1,883,228	255,209,353	5,612,677	2.200	57,536	104,490	31,951	28,876	32,356
1949	252,770,360	1,694.75	244,757	1,763,966	250,761,637	5,605,930	2.236	56,260	112,306	40,964	8,456	32,776
1948	252,292,247	1,720.71	279,752	1,949,146	250,063,348	5,455,476	2.182	53,274	114,464	36,345	15,769	30,211
1947	258,286,383	1,792.05	230,914	2,942,058	255,113,412	5,374,409	2.107	51,367	121,607	41,071	13,702	27,366
1946	269,422,099	1,905.42	376,407	934,820	268,110,872	5,350,772	1.996	49,035	119,929	51,843	24,972	22,332
1945	258,682,187	1,848.60	268,667	2,056,904	256,356,616	4,963,730	1.936	45,586	107,149	51,177	33,633	18,812
1944	201,003,387	1,452.44	200,851	1,259,181	199,543,355	3,849,255	1.929	34,606	80,132	43,557	26,962	14,287
1943	136,696,090	999.83	140,500	1,175,284	135,380,306	2,678,779	1.979	21,256	58,164	28,425	16,663	10,871
1942	72,422,445	537.13	98,300	355,727	71,968,418	1,644,476	2.285	10,188	38,588	5,604	9,703	7,885
1941	48,961,444	367.09	205,000	369,044	48,387,400	1,218,239	2.518	4,314	30,652	1,603	5,698	6,120
1940	42,967,531	325.23	204,591	386,444	42,376,496	1,094,620	2.583	2,905	27,012	1,302	6,383	4,775
1939	40,439,532	308.98	142,283	411,280	39,885,970	1,036,937	2.600	1,868	25,698	1,308	7,243	3,770
1938	37,164,740	286.27	141,362	447,452	36,575,926	947,084	2.589	1,238	22,361	1,154	9,147	2,676
1937	36,424,614	282.75	118,530	505,974	35,800,109	924,347	2.582	800	20,522	2,303	10,617	1,558
1936	33,778,543	263.79	169,363	620,390	32,988,790	838,002	2.559	316	18,312	2,354	11,381	626
1935	28,700,893	225.55	230,662	824,989	27,645,241	750,678	2.716	62	14,874	2,053	10,023	633
1934	27,053,141	214,07	54,267	518,387	26,480,488	842,301	3.181		16,510	2,921	6,653	396
1933	22,538,673	179.48	65,911	315,118	22,157,643	742,176	3.350		14,223	3,063	4,548	323
1932	19,487,002	156.10	60,079	265,650	19,161,274	671,605	3.505		14,250	3,341	1,261	309
1931	16,801,281	135.45	51,819	229,874	16,519,589	588,987	3.566		13,531	2,246	452	291
1930	16,185,310	131.51	31,717	231,701	15,921,892	606,032	3.807		12,111	1,420	1,626	764
1929	16,931,088	139.04	50,749	241,398	16,638,941	656,654	3.946		12,125	1,640	2,267	607
1928	17,604,293	146.09	45,335	241,264	17,317,694	671,353	3.877		13,021	1,252	2,582	462
1927	18,511,907	155.51	14,719	244,524	18,252,665	722,676	3.960		15,222	686	1,986	359
1926	19,643,216	167.32	13,360	246,086	19,383,771	793,424	4.093		16,928	453	1,799	204
1925	20,516,194	177.12	30,259	275,028	20,210,907	829,680	4.105		16,842	533	2,740	95
1924	21,250,813	186.23	30,278	239,293	20,981,242	876,961	4.180		16,025	808	4,148	
1923	22,349,707	199.64	98,739	243,925	22,007,044	927,331	4.214		16,535	1,031	4,441	
1922	22,963,382	208.65	25,251	227,793	22,710,338	962,897	4.240		15,965	1,829	4,916	
1921	23,977,451	220.91	10,688	227,862	23,738,900	1,029,918	4.339		16,119	2,700	4,920	
1920	24,299,321	228.23	6,745	230,076	24,062,500	1,016,592	4.225		16,218	2,769	5,075	
1919	25,484,506	242.56	11,176	236,383	25,236,947	1,054,205	4.178		17,188	3,625	4,422	
1918	12,455,225	119.13	20,243	237,475	12,197,508	468,619	3.910		9,911	1,706	369	
1917	2,975,619	28.77	14,232	248,837	2,712,549	83,625	3.120		2,412	273	27	
1916	1,225,146	12.02	1,473	252,110	971,563	23,085	2.376		967		4	

See footnotes at end of table.

Series Y 368–379.   Public Debt of the Federal Government: 1791 to 1957—Con.

Year	Total gross debt		Matured	Non-interest-bearing [2]	Interest-bearing [3]	Computed annual interest charge	Other bonds	Treasury bills, etc. [4]
	Amount [1]	Per capita						
	368	369	370	371	372	373	376	377
	1,000 dollars	Dollars	1,000 dollars	1,000 dollars	1,000 dollars	1,000 dollars	Million dollars	Million dollars
1915	1,191,264	11.85	1,507	219,998	969,759	22,937	970	---
1914	1,188,235	11.99	1,553	218,730	967,953	22,891	968	---
1913	1,193,048	12.27	1,660	225,682	965,707	22,835	966	---
1912	1,193,839	12.52	1,760	228,301	963,777	22,787	964	---
1911	1,153,985	12.29	1,880	236,752	915,353	21,337	915	---
1910	1,146,940	12.41	2,125	231,498	913,317	21,276	913	---
1909	1,148,315	12.69	2,884	232,114	913,317	21,276	913	---
1908	1,177,690	13.28	4,130	276,056	897,504	21,101	883	14
1907	1,147,178	13.19	1,087	251,257	894,834	21,629	895	(7)
1906	1,142,523	13.37	1,128	246,236	895,159	23,248	895	(7)
1905	1,132,357	13.51	1,370	235,829	895,158	24,177	895	(7)
1904	1,136,259	13.83	1,971	239,131	895,157	24,177	895	(7)
1903	1,159,406	14.38	1,205	243,659	914,541	25,542	915	(7)
1902	1,178,031	14.88	1,281	245,680	931,070	27,543	913	(7)
1901	1,221,572	15.74	1,416	233,016	987,141	29,789	987	(7)
1900	1,263,417	16.60	1,176	238,762	1,023,479	33,541	1,023	(7)
1899	1,436,701	19.21	1,218	389,434	1,046,049	40,848	1,046	(7)
1898	1,232,743	16.77	1,263	384,113	847,367	34,387	847	(7)
1897	1,226,794	16.99	1,347	378,082	847,365	34,387	847	(7)
1896	1,222,729	17.25	1,637	373,729	847,364	34,387	847	(7)
1895	1,096,913	15.76	1,722	378,980	716,202	29,141	716	(7)
1894	1,016,898	14.89	1,851	380,005	635,042	25,394	635	(7)
1893	961,432	14.36	2,094	374,301	585,037	22,894	585	(7)
1892	968,219	14.74	2,786	380,404	585,029	22,894	585	(7)
1891	1,005,807	15.63	1,615	393,663	610,529	23,616	610	(7)
1890	1,122,397	17.80	1,816	409,268	711,313	29,418	711	(7)
1889	1,249,471	20.23	1,911	431,705	815,854	33,752	816	(7)
1888	1,384,632	22.89	2,496	445,613	936,523	38,992	936	(7)
1887	1,465,485	24.75	6,115	451,678	1,007,692	41,781	1,008	(7)
1886	1,555,660	26.85	9,704	413,941	1,132,014	45,510	1,132	(7)
1885	1,578,551	27.86	4,101	392,299	1,182,151	47,014	1,182	(7)
1884	1,625,307	29.35	19,656	393,088	1,212,564	47,926	1,212	(7)
1883	1,721,959	31.83	7,831	389,899	1,324,229	51,437	1,324	(7)
1882	1,856,916	35.16	16,261	390,845	1,449,810	57,365	1,449	(7)
1881	2,019,286	39.18	6,724	386,994	1,625,568	75,019	1,625	1
1880	2,090,909	41.60	7,621	373,295	1,709,993	79,634	1,709	1
1879	2,298,913	46.72	37,015	374,181	1,887,716	83,774	---	---
1878	2,159,418	44.82	5,594	373,089	1,780,736	94,654	---	---
1877	2,107,760	44.71	16,649	393,223	1,697,889	93,161	---	---
1876	2,130,846	46.22	3,902	430,258	1,696,685	96,104	---	---
1875	2,156,277	47.84	11,426	436,175	1,708,676	96,856	---	---
1874	2,159,933	49.05	3,216	431,786	1,724,931	98,796	---	---
1873	2,151,210	50.02	51,929	402,797	1,696,484	98,050	---	---
1872	2,209,991	52.65	7,927	401,270	1,800,794	103,988	---	---
1871	2,322,052	56.72	1,949	399,406	1,920,697	111,949	---	---
1870	2,436,453	61.06	3,570	397,003	2,035,881	118,785	---	---
1869	2,545,111	65.17	5,112	388,503	2,151,495	125,524	---	---
1868	2,583,446	67.61	1,246	390,874	2,191,326	128,460	---	---
1867	2,650,168	70.91	1,739	409,474	2,238,955	138,892	---	---
1866	2,755,764	75.42	4,436	429,212	2,322,116	146,068	---	---
1865	2,677,929	75.01	2,129	458,090	2,217,709	137,743	---	---
1864	1,815,831	52.08	367	455,437	1,360,027	78,853	---	---
1863	1,119,774	32.91	172	411,767	707,834	41,854	---	---
1862	524,178	15.79	231	158,591	365,356	22,049	---	---
1861	90,582	2.80	159	---	90,423	5,093	---	---
1860	64,844	2.06	161	---	64,683	3,444	---	---
1859	58,498	1.91	165	---	58,333	3,126	---	---
1858	44,913	1.50	170	---	44,743	2,447	---	---
1857	28,701	0.99	198	---	28,503	1,673	---	---
1856	31,974	1.13	169	---	31,805	1,869	---	---
1855	35,588	1.30	170	---	35,418	2,314	---	---
1854	42,244	1.59	199	---	42,045	---	---	---
1853	59,805	2.32	162	---	59,642	---	---	---
1852	66,199	2.67	---	---	---	---	---	---
1851	68,305	2.85	---	---	---	---	---	---

Year	Gross debt [1] (368) — 1,000 dollars
1850	63,453
1849	63,062
1848	47,045
1847	38,827
1846	15,550
1845	15,925
1844	23,462
1843	32,743
1842	13,594
1841	5,251
1840	3,573
1839	10,434
1838	3,308
1837	337
1836	38
1835	38
1834	4,760
1833	7,012
1832	24,322
1831	39,123
1830	48,565
1829	58,421
1828	67,475
1827	73,987
1826	81,054
1825	83,788
1824	90,270
1823	90,876
1822	93,547
1821	89,987
1820	91,016
1819	95,530
1818	103,467
1817	123,492
1816	127,335
1815	99,834
1814	81,488
1813	55,963
1812	45,210
1811	48,006
1810	53,173
1809	57,023
1808	65,196
1807	69,218
1806	75,723
1805	82,312
1804	86,427
1803	77,055
1802	80,713
1801	83,038
1800	82,976
1799	78,409
1798	79,229
1797	82,064
1796	83,762
1795	80,748
1794	78,427
1793	80,359
1792	77,228
1791	75,463

[1] Figures for 1791 through 1852 are not entirely comparable with later figures.

[2] Includes old demand notes; U.S. notes (gold reserve deducted since 1900); postal currency and fractional currency less the amounts officially estimated to have been destroyed; and also the deposits held by the Treasury for the retirement of Federal Reserve banknotes, and for national banknotes of national banks failed, in liquidation, and reducing circulation, which prior to 1890 were not included in the published debt statements. Does not include gold, silver, or currency certificates, or Treasury notes of 1890 for redemption of which an exact equivalent of the respective kinds of money or bullion was held in the Treasury.

[3] Exclusive of the bonds issued to the Pacific Railways (provision having been made by law to secure the Treasury against both principal and interest) and the Navy pension fund (which was in no sense a debt, the principal being the property of the United States). The Statement of the Public Debt included the railroad bonds from issuance and the Navy fund from Sept. 1, 1896, until the Statement of June 30, 1890.

[4] Includes certificates of indebtedness. Also includes refunding certificates of deposit, 1880–1907, inclusive.

[5] Includes old Treasury (War) savings securities from 1918 through 1929.

[6] Comprises special issues to Government agencies and trust funds.

[7] Less than $500,000.

Series Y 380–383. Cash Receipts From and Payments to the Public by the Federal Government: 1929 to 1957

Fiscal year	Cash receipts from the public	Cash payments to the public	Excess of receipts (+) or payments (−)	Net cash borrowing from the public (+) or payments (−)	Fiscal year	Cash receipts from the public	Cash payments to the public	Excess of receipts (+) or payments (−)	Net cash borrowing from the public (+) or payments (−)	Calendar year	Cash receipts from the public	Cash payments to the public	Excess of receipts (+) or payments (−)
	380	381	382	383		380	381	382	383		380	381	382
	Bil. dol.	Bil. dol.	Bil. dol.	Bil. dol.		Bil. dol.	Bil. dol.	Bil. dol.	Bil. dol.		Mil. dol.	Mil. dol.	Mil. dol.
1957	82.1	80.0	+2.1	−3.1	1942	15.1	34.5	−19.4	+19.7	1957	84,520	83,326	+1,194
1956	77.1	72.6	+4.5	−4.4	1941	9.2	14.0	−4.8	+5.4	1956	80,330	74,807	+5,524
1955	67.8	70.5	−2.7	+1.8	1940	6.9	9.6	−2.7	+1.7	1955	71,448	72,188	−740
1954	71.6	71.9	−.2	+2.5	1939	6.6	9.4	−2.9	(²)	1954	68,589	69,661	−1,072
1953	71.5	76.8	−5.3	+2.9	1938	7.0	7.2	−.1	(²)	1953	70,141	76,289	−6,148
1952	68.0	68.0	(¹)	−.5	1937	5.6	8.4	−2.8	(²)	1952	71,436	73,082	−1,646
1951	53.4	45.8	+7.6	−5.8	1936	4.2	7.6	−3.5	(²)	1951	59,268	58,034	+1,234
1950	40.9	43.1	−2.2	+4.2	1935	3.8	6.3	−2.4	+1.5	1950	42,411	41,962	+450
1949	41.6	40.6	+1.0	−2.5	1934	3.1	6.5	−3.3	(²)	1949	41,339	42,635	−1,295
1948	45.4	36.5	+8.9	−7.3	1933	2.1	4.7	−2.6	(²)	1948	44,914	36,892	+8,023
1947	43.5	36.9	+6.6	−19.4	1932	2.0	4.8	−2.7	(²)	1947	44,282	38,616	+5,666
1946	43.5	61.7	−18.2	+7.4	1931	3.2	4.1	−1.0	(²)	1946	41,441	41,399	+42
1945	50.2	95.2	−45.0	+49.5						1945	49,423	86,142	−36,719
1944	47.8	94.0	−46.1	+56.8	1930	3.8	2.9	+.9	(²)	1944	48,131	94,810	−46,679
1943	25.1	78.9	−53.8	+60.2	1929	4.0	3.1	+.9	−.9	1943	37,863	88,987	−51,124

¹ Less than $50 million.   ² Not available.

Series Y 384–400. Federal, State, and Local Government Revenue, by Source: 1902 to 1957

[In millions of dollars]

Year	Total revenue ¹	General revenue Total	Taxes Total taxes	Individual income	Corporation income	Sales, gross receipts, and customs	Property	Other taxes, including licenses	Charges and miscellaneous	Utility and liquor stores revenue	Insurance trust revenue Total	Employee retirement	Unemployment insurance Total	Contributions	Interest (credited by U.S. Government)	Old-age and survivors insurance	Other
	384	385	386	387	388	389	390	391	392	393	394	395	396	397	398	399	400
1957	129,151	112,723	98,632	37,374	22,151	20,594	12,864	5,650	14,091	4,127	12,301	2,130	1,799	1,588	211	6,857	1,515
1956	119,651	104,494	91,593	33,725	21,770	19,160	11,749	5,190	12,900	3,854	11,303	1,872	1,536	1,349	187	6,442	1,453
1955	106,404	93,264	81,072	29,984	18,604	17,221	10,735	4,527	12,192	3,688	9,452	1,622	1,345	1,157	188	5,087	1,398
1954	108,255	95,844	84,476	30,669	21,879	17,643	9,967	4,317	11,369	3,496	8,914	1,502	1,488	1,284	204	4,554	1,370
1953	104,781	93,124	83,704	30,881	22,055	17,279	9,375	4,112	9,420	3,324	8,333	1,332	1,571	1,389	182	4,060	1,369
1952	100,245	89,230	79,066	28,919	22,072	15,689	8,652	3,735	10,163	3,108	7,907	1,253	1,612	1,452	160	3,547	1,495
1950	66,680	58,486	51,100	16,533	11,081	12,997	7,349	3,140	7,386	2,712	5,482	965	1,190	1,042	148	2,107	1,219
1948	67,005	59,666	51,218	19,848	10,270	12,092	6,126	2,881	8,448	2,511	4,828	672	1,337	1,193	144	1,616	1,203
1946	61,532	55,130	46,380	16,579	12,280	9,950	4,986	2,586	8,750	2,033	4,369	571	1,282	1,154	128	1,201	1,316
1944	64,778	58,617	49,095	20,043	15,188	7,012	4,604	2,249	9,522	1,633	4,528	498	1,518	1,432	86	1,260	1,251
1942	28,352	24,347	20,793	3,481	4,999	5,776	4,537	2,000	3,554	1,277	2,728	285	1,218	1,159	59	869	356
1940	17,804	14,858	12,688	1,183	1,279	4,109	4,430	1,687	2,170	998	1,948	214	931	896	35	538	265
1938	17,484	15,023	12,949	1,495	1,498	3,815	4,440	1,701	2,074	877	1,584	182	731	706	25	387	284
1936	13,588	12,533	10,583	819	858	3,389	4,093	1,424	1,950	747	308	158	23	23			127
1934	11,300	10,463	8,854	485	435	2,885	4,076	973	1,609	590	247	136					111
1932	10,289	9,578	7,977	479	677	1,485	4,487	849	1,601	463	248	126					122
1927	12,191	11,551	9,451	949	1,351	1,558	4,780	862	2,100	403	237	92					145
1922	9,322	8,894	7,387	2,040		1,306	3,321	721	1,507	−266	162	59					103
1913	2,980	2,862	2,271	--------	35	670	1,332	234	591	116	2	2					
1902	1,694	1,632	1,373	--------		515	706	152	259	62							

¹ To avoid duplication, transactions between governments have been excluded; see text.

Series Y 401–411. Federal, State, and Local Government Expenditure, by Character and Object, and Governmental Debt: 1902 to 1957

[In millions of dollars]

Year	Total expenditure ¹	Capital outlay Total	Construction	Other	Current operation	Assistance and subsidies	Interest on debt ²	Insurance benefits and repayments	Expenditure for personal services	Debt outstanding at end of fiscal year	Increase or decrease (−) in debt during year
	401	402	403	404	405	406	407	408	409	410	411
1957	125,463	28,866	13,782	15,084	68,966	9,488	6,873	11,269	39,486	323,566	1,947
1956	115,796	26,363	12,771	13,592	64,110	9,215	6,531	9,576	37,573	321,619	2,978
1955	110,717	28,736	12,612	16,125	58,133	8,942	5,904	9,002	34,916	318,641	8,450
1954	111,332	27,369	11,739	15,631	62,494	8,271	5,713	7,484	33,538	310,190	10,338
1953	110,054	26,403	10,498	15,904	63,051	8,933	5,660	6,006	33,070	299,852	10,648
1952	99,847	24,873	9,723	15,151	56,112	8,387	4,986	5,489	29,766	289,205	5,867
1950	70,334	(³)	6,840		51,584		5,017	6,894	20,530	281,472	7,703
1948	55,081	(³)	4,376		43,226		4,866	2,614	17,345	270,948	−4,153
1946	79,707	(³)	2,536		70,356		4,422	2,392	28,413	285,339	9,986
1944	109,947	(³)	5,117		101,201		2,786	842	26,760	218,482	63,013
1942	45,576	(³)	8,232		34,625		1,732	986	10,966	92,128	22,891
1940	20,417	(³)	3,139		14,624		1,686	968	7,649	63,251	2,748
1938	17,675	(³)	2,662		12,835		1,624	554	7,047	56,601	714
1936	16,758	(³)	2,427		12,551		1,558	222	6,353	53,253	5,305
1934	12,807	(³)	2,155		8,888		1,571	193	5,338	45,982	3,855
1932	12,437	(³)	1,876		8,968		1,422	171	4,729	38,692	2,918
1927	11,220	(³)	2,095		7,560		1,426	139	4,255	33,393	−57
1922	9,297	(³)	1,397		6,398		1,418	84	3,303	33,072	432
1913	3,215	(³)	561		2,451		196	7	1,427	5,607	(²)
1902	1,660	(³)	202		1,350		108	----------	700	3,285	(²)

¹ See footnote 1, series Y 384.   ² Includes interest on debt of utilities operated by local governments.   ³ Not available.

Series Y 412–445. Federal, State, and Local Government Expenditure, by Function: 1902 to 1957

[In millions of dollars]

Year	Total expenditure [1]	General expenditure Total	National defense and international relations Total	Military services only	Postal service	Education Total	State institutions of higher education	Local schools	Other education	Highways	Public welfare Total	Categorical public assistance	Other public assistance	Other public welfare	Hospitals	Health	Police
	412	413	414	415	416	417	418	419	420	421	422	423	424	425	426	427	428
1957	125,463	109,765	45,803	39,073	3,034	15,098	1,958	11,871	1,269	7,931	3,453	2,538	229	686	3,445	787	1,623
1956	115,796	102,156	42,680	35,553	2,899	14,161	1,678	11,250	1,233	7,035	3,185	2,319	258	607	3,067	672	1,487
1955	110,717	97,828	43,472	35,782	2,726	12,710	1,468	10,186	1,056	6,520	3,210	2,278	382	550	2,721	707	1,358
1954	111,332	100,365	49,265	40,519	2,669	11,196	1,324	8,990	882	5,586	3,103	2,234	349	520	2,676	692	1,254
1953	110,054	100,733	53,583	43,847	2,686	10,117	1,277	7,857	983	5,053	2,956	2,167	300	488	2,548	698	1,160
1952	99,847	91,291	48,187	38,962	2,612	9,598	1,180	6,903	1,515	4,714	2,830	2,033	327	469	2,460	739	1,080
1950	70,334	60,701	18,355	12,118	2,270	9,647	1,107	5,879	2,661	3,872	2,964	2,010	538	416	2,050	661	864
1948	55,081	50,088	16,075	10,642	1,715	7,721	895	4,347	2,479	3,071	2,144	1,473	357	314	1,398	536	724
1946	79,707	75,582	50,461	42,677	1,381	3,711	397	2,872	442	1,680	1,435	1,014	216	205	762	380	549
1944	109,947	107,823	85,503	74,670	1,085	2,805	380	2,331	94	1,215	1,150	842	166	142	568	289	497
1942	45,576	43,483	26,555	22,633	878	2,696	296	2,213	187	1,765	1,285	761	345	179	517	197	444
1940	20,417	18,125	1,590	1,567	808	2,827	290	2,281	256	2,177	1,314	611	438	265	537	195	386
1938	17,675	16,273	1,041	1,021	776	2,653	268	2,161	224	2,150	1,233	483	485	265	496	182	378
1936	16,758	15,835	932	916	751	2,365	231	1,894	240	1,945	997	731		266	461	131	331
1934	12,807	12,086	553	541	651	2,005	177	1,616	212	1,829	979	796		183	416	119	306
1932	12,437	11,748	721	702	794	2,325	234	2,042	49	1,766	445	366		79	462	121	349
1927	11,220	10,590	616	599	711	2,243	196	2,017	30	1,819	161	79		82	347	84	290
1922	9,297	8,854	875	864	553	1,713	143	1,541	29	1,296	128	57		71	287	65	204
1913	3,215	3,022	250	245	270	582	49	522	11	419	57	17		40	80	33	92
1902	1,660	1,578	165	162	126	258	13	238	7	175	41	11		30	45	18	50

Year	Local fire protection	Local sanitation	Natural resources Total	Stabilization of farm prices and income	Local parks and recreation	Housing and community redevelopment	Veterans services, not elsewhere classified	General control	Interest on general debt	Nonhighway transportation [2]	Other and unallocable [2]	Utility and liquor stores expenditure	Insurance trust expenditure Total	Employee retirement	Unemployment compensation	Old-age and survivors insurance	Other
	429	430	431	432	433	434	435	436	437	438	439	440	441	442	443	444	445
1957	810	1,443	7,699	4,980	608	624	3,224	2,405	6,603	1,478	3,696	4,429	11,269	1,534	1,633	6,515	1,589
1956	737	1,326	7,338	4,926	541	562	3,185	2,235	6,297	1,413	3,335	4,065	9,576	1,332	1,383	5,361	1,500
1955	694	1,142	6,338	3,892	509	611	3,058	2,060	5,684	1,223	3,085	3,886	9,002	1,152	1,990	4,333	1,527
1954	653	1,058	6,377	3,863	424	742	2,913	1,997	5,515	1,193	3,050	3,482	7,484	1,090	1,648	3,276	1,471
1953	598	908	4,816	2,271	374	768	2,823	1,866	5,477	1,361	2,943	3,316	6,006	948	1,008	2,728	1,321
1952	586	992	3,252	638	324	875	2,570	1,801	4,814	1,118	2,735	3,067	5,489	831	1,022	1,983	1,653
1950	488	834	5,005	2,712	304	573	3,258	1,555	4,862	661	2,478	2,739	6,894	629	1,980	726	3,559
1948	406	670	2,223	592	243	245	3,926	1,325	4,722	571	2,373	2,379	6,614	541	821	512	740
1946	294	370	3,111	2,012	179	221	2,588	1,163	4,286	1,201	1,810	1,733	2,392	503	985	321	584
1944	251	245	2,731	1,532	123	574	530	1,087	2,650	4,753	1,767	1,281	842	298	70	185	289
1942	236	229	2,468	929	128	622	481	828	1,591	894	1,668	1,106	986	247	386	110	243
1940	235	207	2,730	694	162	267	501	789	1,552	377	1,521	1,324	968	209	509	16	234
1938	231	226	2,089	326	130	109	590	725	1,513	269	1,482	848	554	193	202	5	154
1936	205	204	2,158	602	104	71	1,699	662	1,455	271	1,093	701	222	157	--------	--------	65
1934	189	177	1,241	382	126	3	508	533	1,473	215	763	528	193	135	--------	--------	58
1932	210	223	326	--------	147	--------	928	601	1,323	200	807	518	171	103	--------	--------	68
1927	203	312	206	--------	153	1	579	526	1,348	257	734	491	139	64	--------	--------	75
1922	158	189	140	--------	85	1	505	439	1,370	306	540	359	84	36	--------	--------	48
1913	76	97	44	--------	57	--------	177	256	170	90	272	186	7	7	--------	--------	--------
1902	40	51	17	--------	29	--------	141	175	97	22	128	82	--------	--------	--------	--------	--------

[1] To avoid duplication, transactions between governments have been excluded; see text.
[2] For 1902–1950, Federal only; State and local expenditure for "Nonhighway transportation" included with "other and unallocable."

Series Y 446–468. Federal Government Revenue, by Source: 1902 to 1957

[In millions of dollars]

Year	Total revenue	General revenue Total	Total taxes	Individual income	Corporation income	Sales, gross receipts, and customs Total	Customs duties	Motor fuel	Alcoholic beverages	Tobacco products	Other	Death and gift	Other taxes
	446	447	448	449	450	451	452	453	454	455	456	457	458
1957	87,066	78,403	69,815	35,620	21,167	11,127	735	1,498	2,893	1,669	4,333	1,365	537
1956	81,294	73,162	65,226	32,188	20,880	10,469	682	1,055	2,846	1,607	4,279	1,161	528
1955	71,915	65,822	57,589	28,747	17,861	9,578	585	972	2,694	1,571	3,757	924	478
1954	75,835	69,798	62,409	29,542	21,101	10,367	542	845	2,716	1,580	4,684	934	465
1953	74,239	68,687	62,796	29,816	21,238	10,352	596	906	2,781	1,655	4,414	881	508
1952	71,798	66,615	59,744	27,921	21,226	9,332	532	720	2,549	1,565	3,966	818	446
1951	56,731	52,125	46,032	21,643	14,106	9,143	609	589	2,494	1,378	4,073	708	432
1950	43,527	40,061	35,186	15,745	10,488	7,843	407	534	2,165	1,325	3,412	698	412
1948	47,254	44,277	37,876	19,305	9,678	7,650	403	479	2,208	1,297	3,268	890	353
1946	46,405	43,629	36,286	16,157	11,833	6,964	424	406	2,479	1,156	2,499	669	[1] 663
1944	51,899	48,663	40,321	19,701	14,737	4,723	417	271	1,592	986	1,457	507	[1] 653
1942	16,062	14,788	12,265	3,205	4,727	3,425	369	370	1,087	779	870	421	[1] 487

See footnotes at end of table.

Series Y 446–468. Federal Government Revenue, by Source: 1902 to 1957—Con.

[In millions of dollars]

Year	Total revenue	General revenue				Taxes								Death and gift	Other taxes
		Total	Total taxes	Individual income	Corporation income	Sales, gross receipts, and customs									
						Total	Customs duties	Motor fuel	Alcoholic beverages	Tobacco products	Other				
	446	447	448	449	450	451	452	453	454	455	456			457	458
1940	7,000	6,194	4,878	959	1,123	2,127	331	226	613	607	350			357	[1]312
1938	7,226	6,595	5,344	1,277	1,333	2,021	343	204	556	567	351			413	[1]300
1936	5,176	5,086	3,882	666	745	1,905	372	177	493	499	[2]364			377	[1]189
1934	3,886	3,801	2,942	405	386	1,877	299	203	248	424	[2]703			110	[1]164
1932	2,634	2,542	1,813	405	598	733	311	----------	8	398	16			41	36
1927	4,469	4,396	3,364	879	1,259	1,088	585	----------	20	376	107			90	47
1922	4,261	4,221	3,371	1,939		1,152	318	----------	44	270	520			139	[1]142
1913	962	962	662	----------	35	612	310	----------	223	77	2			----------	15
1902	653	653	513	----------		487	243	----------	187	49	8			5	21

Year	General revenue—Con.				Insurance trust revenue					
	Charges and miscellaneous general revenue									
	Total	Postal receipts	Sales of agricultural products [3]	Other	Total	Employee retirement	Unemployment compensation	Old-age and survivors insurance	Veterans life insurance	Railroad retirement
	459	460	461	462	463	464	465	466	467	468
1957	8,588	2,512	2,092	3,984	8,663	644	74	6,857	472	616
1956	7,936	2,435	1,324	4,177	8,132	577	31	6,442	441	641
1955	7,733	2,363	1,187	4,183	6,594	442	16	5,087	450	599
1954	7,390	2,269	1,134	3,987	6,037	432	18	4,554	430	603
1953	5,891	2,093	544	3,254	5,552	423	15	4,060	428	625
1952	6,871	1,967	800	4,104	5,183	418	10	3,547	473	735
1951	6,093	1,777	1,772	2,544	4,606	377	15	3,119	520	575
1950	4,875	1,677	933	2,265	3,466	359	10	2,107	440	550
1948	6,401	1,411	414	4,576	2,977	239	131	1,616	434	557
1946	7,343	1,221	700	5,422	2,776	282	117	1,201	893	283
1944	8,342	1,113	343	6,886	2,736	270	109	1,260	834	263
1942	2,523	860	385	1,278	1,274	90	76	869	98	141
1940	1,316	767	----------	549	806	45	46	538	56	121
1938	1,251	729	----------	522	631	39	----------	387	59	146
1936	1,204	665	----------	539	90	33	----------		57	----------
1934	859	587	----------	272	85	29	----------		56	----------
1932	730	588	----------	142	91	33	----------		58	----------
1927	1,032	683	----------	349	73	25	----------		48	----------
1922	850	485	----------	365	40	14	----------		26	----------
1913	300	267	----------	33	----------	----------	----------		----------	----------
1902	140	122	----------	18	----------	----------	----------		----------	----------

[1] Includes capital stock tax.
[2] Includes agricultural adjustment taxes.
[3] In connection with price support program; excludes sales to Federal Government agencies.

Series Y 469–483. Federal Government Expenditure, by Character and Object, and Federal Government Debt: 1902 to 1957

[In millions of dollars]

Year	Expenditure											Debt			
	Total	Intergovernmental expenditure to State and local governments	Direct expenditure									Outstanding at end of fiscal year			Increase or decrease (−) during year
			Total	Capital outlay			Current operation	Assistance and subsidies	Interest on debt	Insurance benefits and repayments	Expenditure for personal services	Total	Held by Federal Government	Other	
				Total	Construction	Other									
	469	470	471	472	473	474	475	476	477	478	479	480	481	482	483
1957	81,783	3,873	77,910	16,250	3,396	12,854	40,983	6,660	5,497	8,520	20,779	270,527	55,501	215,026	−2,224
1956	75,991	3,347	72,644	14,956	3,416	11,540	38,582	6,595	5,311	7,200	20,454	272,751	53,470	219,281	−1,623
1955	73,441	3,099	70,342	18,030	3,564	14,467	34,947	6,238	4,845	6,238	19,377	274,374	50,536	223,838	3,114
1954	77,692	2,967	74,725	18,244	4,001	14,244	40,986	5,637	4,796	5,061	19,195	271,260	49,340	221,920	5,189
1953	79,990	2,873	77,117	18,498	3,735	14,763	43,086	6,376	4,863	4,294	19,970	266,071	47,560	218,511	6,966
1952	71,568	2,585	68,984	17,437	3,337	14,100	37,579	5,916	4,262	3,790	17,721	259,105	44,335	214,770	3,883
1951	48,935	2,383	46,552	[1]	2,218		37,312		4,221	2,801	13,564	255,222	40,958	214,264	−2,135
1950	44,800	2,371	42,429	[1]	1,671		31,839		4,404	4,515	10,487	257,357	37,830	219,527	4,587
1948	35,592	1,771	33,821	[1]	1,291		26,790		4,323	1,417	8,915	252,292	35,761	216,531	−5,994
1946	66,534	894	65,640	[1]	1,566		59,123		3,865	1,086	22,468	269,422	29,121	240,301	10,740
1944	100,520	1,072	99,448	[1]	4,555		92,254		2,151	488	21,772	201,003	18,920	182,083	64,307
1942	35,549	887	34,662	[1]	6,991		26,276		1,026	369	6,451	72,422	10,340	62,082	23,461
1940	10,061	884	9,177	[1]	1,311		6,686		899	281	3,347	42,968	6,803	36,165	2,528
1938	8,449	762	7,687	[1]	1,124		5,552		840	171	3,023	37,165	4,466	32,699	740
1936	9,165	908	8,257	[1]	1,162		6,312		717	66	2,797	33,779	1,959	31,820	5,008
1934	5,941	976	4,965	[1]	985		3,186		734	60	2,144	27,053	1,332	25,721	4,514
1932	4,266	232	4,034	[1]	318		3,083		582	51	1,188	19,487	607	18,880	2,686
1927	3,533	123	3,410	[1]	174		2,442		764	30	1,110	18,512	759	17,753	−1,131
1922	3,763	118	3,645	[1]	161		2,487		988	9	919	22,963	432	22,531	−1,014
1913	970	12	958	[1]	119		816		23	----------	401	1,193	[2]	1,193	−1
1902	572	7	565	[1]	38		498		29	----------	160	1,178	[1]	1,178	−44

[1] Not available. [2] Less than $500,000.

Series Y 484–516. Federal Government Expenditure, by Function: 1902 to 1957

[In millions of dollars]

Year	Total expenditure	Total general expenditure (direct and intergovernmental)	Intergovernmental expenditure						Direct expenditure							
			Total	Education	Highways	Public welfare	Employment security administration	Other and unallocable	Total direct	General expenditure						
										Total general	National defense and international relations		Postal service	Education	Highways	Public welfare
											Total	Military services only				
	484	485	486	487	488	489	490	491	492	493	494	495	496	497	498	499
1957	81,783	73,263	3,873	604	944	1,557	245	523	77,910	69,390	45,803	39,073	3,034	964	115	49
1956	75,991	68,792	3,347	535	732	1,458	224	397	72,645	65,445	42,680	35,553	2,899	940	82	45
1955	73,441	67,203	3,099	521	589	1,429	187	373	70,342	64,104	43,472	35,782	2,726	802	68	42
1954	77,692	72,631	2,967	475	530	1,489	198	325	74,725	69,664	49,265	40,519	2,669	639	60	43
1953	79,990	75,696	2,873	508	510	1,332	196	327	77,117	72,823	53,583	43,847	2,686	727	66	42
1952	71,568	67,778	2,585	436	415	1,181	182	369	68,984	65,193	48,187	38,962	2,612	1,280	64	42
1951	48,935	46,134	2,383	311	400	1,194	176	302	46,552	43,751	25,953	19,136	2,403	1,885	56	25
1950	44,800	40,285	2,371	369	429	1,131	215	227	42,429	37,914	18,355	12,118	2,270	2,470	69	24
1948	35,592	34,175	1,771	418	318	724	158	153	33,821	32,404	16,075	10,642	1,715	2,342	35	45
1946	66,534	65,448	894	149	79	424	75	167	65,640	64,554	50,461	42,677	1,381	355	8	26
1944	100,520	100,032	1,072	193	147	420	36	276	99,448	98,960	85,503	74,670	1,085	12	15	17
1942	35,549	35,180	887	76	164	383	72	192	34,662	34,293	26,555	22,633	878	110	275	60
1940	10,061	9,780	884	154	195	278	62	195	9,177	8,896	1,590	1,567	808	189	604	158
1938	8,449	8,278	762	112	264	218	46	122	7,687	7,516	1,041	1,021	776	162	500	164
1936	9,165	9,099	908	147	285	290	3	183	8,257	8,191	932	916	751	188	520	170
1934	5,941	5,881	976	61	279	495	1	140	4,965	4,905	553	541	651	174	320	90
1932	4,266	4,215	232	12	191	1	----	28	4,034	3,983	721	702	794	14	25	1
1927	3,533	3,503	123	10	83	1	----	29	3,410	3,380	616	599	711	8	10	10
1922	3,763	3,754	118	7	92	1	----	18	3,645	3,636	875	864	553	8	2	9
1913	970	970	12	3	----	2	----	7	958	958	250	245	270	5	----	5
1902	572	572	7	1	----	1	----	5	565	565	165	162	126	3	----	4

Direct expenditure—Con.

Year	General expenditure—Con.										Insurance trust expenditure					
	Hospitals	Health	Police	Natural resources		Housing and community redevelopment	Veterans services, not elsewhere classified	General control	Interest on general debt	Non-highway transportation	Other and allocable	Total	Employee retirement	Unemployment compensation	Old-age and survivors insurance	Veterans life insurance	Railroad retirement
				Total	Stabilization of farm prices and income												
	500	501	502	503	504	505	506	507	508	509	510	511	512	513	514	515	516
1957	797	235	155	6,668	4,980	119	3,186	680	5,497	970	1,118	8,520	591	133	6,515	612	670
1956	752	215	156	6,432	4,926	125	3,097	675	5,311	872	1,162	7,200	507	106	5,361	628	599
1955	667	238	129	5,545	3,892	112	2,997	607	4,845	818	1,035	6,238	430	206	4,333	698	570
1954	714	245	124	5,615	3,863	131	2,811	622	4,796	856	1,073	5,061	411	140	3,276	749	485
1953	685	271	122	4,111	2,271	138	2,710	602	4,863	1,084	1,134	4,294	363	98	2,728	645	460
1952	715	299	141	2,476	638	106	2,428	608	4,262	886	1,085	3,790	300	49	1,983	1,073	384
1951	668	299	104	3,027	1,360	124	2,601	547	4,221	697	1,141	2,801	270	51	1,498	665	317
1950	666	297	88	4,335	2,712	121	2,796	514	4,404	661	844	4,515	268	131	726	3,088	302
1948	461	244	80	1,727	592	69	3,293	445	4,323	571	979	1,417	244	62	512	377	222
1946	195	129	70	2,809	2,012	107	2,534	460	3,865	1,201	953	1,086	266	17	321	330	152
1944	100	101	83	2,499	1,532	528	529	488	2,151	4,753	1,097	488	103	1	185	65	134
1942	85	38	50	2,254	929	386	480	250	1,026	894	951	369	78	9	110	46	126
1940	87	36	21	2,512	694	37	501	178	899	377	899	281	69	15	16	68	113
1938	96	31	19	1,867	326	106	590	183	840	269	872	171	64	----	5	22	80
1936	110	15	17	1,965	602	71	1,699	162	717	271	603	66	44	----	----	22	----
1934	107	10	15	1,082	382	3	508	101	734	215	342	60	39	----	----	21	----
1932	113	14	31	161	----	----	928	131	582	200	268	51	28	----	----	23	----
1927	68	8	20	112	----	1	579	114	764	257	102	30	14	----	----	16	----
1922	87	7	14	79	----	1	425	126	988	306	156	9	6	----	----	3	----
1913	1	4	3	30	----	----	177	45	23	90	55	----	----	----	----	----	----
1902	2	1	----	8	----	----	141	34	29	22	30	----	----	----	----	----	----

Series Y 517–535. State and Local Government Revenue, by Source: 1902 to 1957

[In millions of dollars]

Year	Revenue from all sources		Intergovern-mental revenue (from Federal Government)	Revenue from State and local sources									Charges and miscellaneous general revenue
				Total [1]	General revenue								
	Total	General revenue (direct and intergovernmental)			Total general revenue	Taxes							
						Total	Individual income	Corporation income	Sales and gross receipts	Property	Other taxes		
	517	518	519	520	521	522	523	524	525	526	527		528
1957	45,929	38,164	3,843	42,085	34,320	28,817	1,754	984	9,467	12,864	3,748		5,503
1956	41,692	34,667	3,335	38,357	31,332	26,368	1,538	890	8,691	11,749	3,501		4,964
1955	37,619	31,073	3,131	34,489	27,942	23,483	1,237	744	7,643	10,735	3,125		4,459
1954	35,386	29,012	2,966	32,420	26,046	22,067	1,127	778	7,276	9,967	2,918		3,979
1953	33,411	27,307	2,870	30,541	24,437	20,908	1,065	817	6,927	9,375	2,723		3,529
1952	31,013	25,181	2,566	28,447	22,615	19,323	998	846	6,357	8,652	2,471		3,292
1950	25,639	20,911	2,486	23,153	18,425	15,914	788	593	5,154	7,349	2,030		2,511
1948	21,613	17,250	1,861	19,752	15,389	13,342	543	592	4,442	6,126	1,638		2,047
1946	15,983	12,356	855	15,128	11,501	10,094	422	447	2,986	4,986	1,254		1,407
1944	14,333	10,908	954	13,379	9,954	8,774	342	451	2,289	4,604	1,089		1,180
1942	13,148	10,418	858	12,290	9,560	8,528	276	272	2,351	4,537	1,092		1,031
1940	11,749	9,609	945	10,804	8,664	7,810	224	156	1,982	4,430	1,018		854
1938	11,058	9,228	800	10,258	8,428	7,605	218	165	1,794	4,440	988		823
1936	9,360	8,395	948	8,412	7,447	6,701	153	113	1,484	4,093	858		746
1934	8,430	7,678	1,016	7,414	6,662	5,912	80	49	1,008	4,076	699		750
1932	7,887	7,267	232	7,655	7,035	6,164	74	79	752	4,487	772		871
1927	7,838	7,271	116	7,722	7,155	6,087	70	92	470	4,730	725		1,068
1922	5,169	4,781	108	5,061	4,673	4,016	43	58	154	3,321	440		657
1913	2,030	1,912	12	2,018	1,900	1,609	--------	--------	58	1,332	219		291
1902	1,048	986	7	1,041	979	860	--------	--------	28	706	126		119

Year	Revenue from State and local sources—Con.						
	Utility and liquor stores revenue	Insurance trust revenue					
		Total	Employee retirement	Unemployment compensation			Other
				Total	Contributions	Interest (credited by U.S. Govt.)	
	529	530	531	532	533	534	535
1957	4,127	3,638	1,486	1,725	1,514	211	427
1956	3,854	3,171	1,295	1,505	1,318	187	371
1955	3,688	2,858	1,180	1,329	1,141	188	349
1954	3,496	2,877	1,070	1,470	1,266	204	337
1953	3,324	2,781	909	1,556	1,374	182	316
1952	3,108	2,724	835	1,602	1,442	160	287
1950	2,712	2,016	606	1,180	1,032	148	229
1948	2,511	1,851	433	1,206	1,062	144	212
1946	2,033	1,593	289	1,165	1,037	128	140
1944	1,633	1,792	228	1,409	1,323	86	154
1942	1,277	1,454	195	1,142	1,083	59	117
1940	998	1,142	169	885	850	35	88
1938	877	953	143	731	706	25	79
1936	747	218	125	23	23	----------	70
1934	590	162	107	--------	--------	----------	55
1932	463	157	93	--------	--------	----------	64
1927	403	164	67	--------	--------	----------	97
1922	266	122	45	--------	--------	----------	77
1913	116	2	2	--------	--------	----------	
1902	62	--------	--------	--------	--------	----------	

[1] To avoid duplication, transactions between State and local governments have been excluded; see text.

Series Y 536–546. State and Local Government Expenditure, by Character and Object, and State and Local Government Debt: 1902 to 1957

[In millions of dollars]

Year	Expenditure									Debt	
	Total [1]	Current operation	Capital outlay			Assistance and subsidies	Interest on debt [2]	Insurance benefits and repayments	Expenditure for personal services	Outstanding at end of fiscal year	Increase or decrease (−) during year
			Total	Construction	Other						
	536	537	538	539	540	541	542	543	544	545	546
1957	47,553	27,983	12,616	10,386	2,230	2,828	1,376	2,749	18,707	53,039	4,171
1956	43,152	25,528	11,407	9,355	2,052	2,620	1,220	2,376	17,118	48,868	4,601
1955	40,375	23,186	10,706	9,048	1,658	2,660	1,059	2,764	15,539	44,267	5,336
1954	36,607	21,508	9,125	7,738	1,387	2,634	916	2,423	14,343	38,931	5,149
1953	32,937	19,965	7,905	6,763	1,142	2,558	797	1,711	13,100	33,782	3,682
1952	30,863	18,533	7,436	6,386	1,051	2,472	724	1,698	12,045	30,100	1,984
1950	27,905	15,948	6,047	5,169	879	2,918	613	2,379	10,043	24,115	3,116
1948	21,260	13,415	3,725	3,085	640	2,381	543	1,197	8,430	18,656	1,841
1946	14,067	9,690	1,305	970	334	1,209	557	1,306	5,945	15,917	−754
1944	10,499	7,848	709	562	147	952	635	354	4,988	17,479	−1,294
1942	10,914	7,057	1,477	1,241	236	1,056	706	617	4,515	19,706	−570
1940	11,240	6,176	2,515	1,828	687	1,075	787	687	4,302	20,283	220
1938	9,988	5,969	1,858	1,538	320	994	784	383	4,024	19,436	−26
1936	8,501	5,228	1,524	1,265	259	752	841	156	3,556	19,474	297
1934	7,842	4,650	1,407	1,170	237	815	837	133	3,194	18,929	−659
1932	8,403	5,179	1,876	1,558	318	388	840	120	3,541	19,205	232
1927	7,810	4,590	2,356	1,921	435	93	662	109	3,145	14,881	1,074
1922	5,652	3,477	1,518	1,236	282	152	430	75	2,384	10,109	1,446
1913	2,257	1,505	548	442	106	24	173	7	1,026	4,414	(³)
1902	1,095	796	205	164	41	15	79	----------	540	2,107	(³)

[1] See footnote 1, series Y 520. — [2] Includes interest on debt of utilities operated by local governments. [3] Not available.

Series Y 547–574. State and Local Government Expenditure, by Function: 1902 to 1957

[In millions of dollars]

Year	Total	Total general	Education Total	State institutions of higher education	Local schools	Other education	Highways	Public welfare Total	Categorical public assistance	Other public assistance	Other public welfare	Hospitals	Health	Police
	547	548	549	550	551	552	553	554	555	556	557	558	559	560
1957	47,553	40,375	14,134	1,958	11,871	305	7,816	3,404	2,525	201	678	2,648	552	1,468
1956	43,152	36,711	13,220	1,678	11,250	292	6,953	3,139	2,310	258	571	2,316	456	1,330
1955	40,375	33,724	11,907	1,468	10,186	254	6,452	3,168	2,269	382	517	2,053	456	1,330
1954	36,607	30,701	10,557	1,324	8,990	243	5,527	3,060	2,224	349	486	1,962	471	1,229
1953	32,937	27,910	9,390	1,277	7,857	256	4,987	2,914	2,159	300	454	1,863	447	1,130
1952	30,863	26,098	8,318	1,180	6,903	235	4,650	2,788	2,023	327	437	1,745	440	939
1950	27,905	22,787	7,177	1,107	5,879	191	3,803	2,940	2,010	538	392	1,384	364	776
1948	21,260	17,684	5,379	895	4,347	137	3,036	2,099	1,473	357	269	937	292	644
1946	14,067	11,028	3,356	397	2,872	87	1,672	1,409	1,014	216	179	567	251	479
1944	10,499	8,863	2,793	380	2,331	82	1,200	1,133	842	166	125	468	188	414
1942	10,914	9,190	2,586	296	2,213	77	1,490	1,225	761	345	119	432	159	394
1940	11,240	9,229	2,638	290	2,281	67	1,573	1,156	611	438	107	450	159	365
1938	9,988	8,757	2,491	268	2,161	62	1,650	1,069	483	485	101	400	151	359
1936	8,501	7,644	2,177	231	1,894	52	1,425	827	731		96	351	116	314
1934	7,842	7,181	1,881	177	1,616	38	1,509	889	796		93	309	109	291
1932	8,403	7,765	2,311	234	2,042	35	1,741	444	366		78	349	107	318
1927	7,810	7,210	2,235	196	2,017	22	1,809	151	79		72	279	76	270
1922	5,652	5,218	1,705	143	1,541	21	1,294	119	57		62	200	58	190
1913	2,257	2,064	577	49	522	6	419	52	17		35	79	29	89
1902	1,095	1,013	255	13	238	4	175	37	11		26	43	17	50

General expenditure—Con.

Year	Local fire protection	Local sanitation	Natural resources	Local parks and recreation	Housing and community redevelopment	General control	Interest on general debt	Non-highway transportation	Other and unallocable	Utility and liquor stores expenditure	Insurance trust expenditure Total	Employee retirement	Unemployment compensation	Other
	561	562	563	564	565	566	567	568	569	570	571	572	573	574
1957	810	1,443	1,031	608	505	1,725	1,106	508	2,616	4,429	2,749	943	1,500	307
1956	737	1,326	906	541	437	1,560	986	541	2,263	4,065	2,376	825	1,277	274
1955	694	1,142	793	509	499	1,452	838	405	2,112	3,886	2,764	722	1,784	258
1954	653	1,058	762	424	611	1,375	718	337	2,080	3,482	2,423	679	1,507	237
1953	598	908	705	374	631	1,263	614	277	1,921	3,316	1,711	585	910	216
1952	586	992	776	324	769	1,193	552	232	1,792	3,067	1,698	530	973	195
1950	488	834	670	304	452	1,041	458		2,096	2,739	2,379	361	1,849	169
1948	406	670	496	243	176	880	399		2,027	2,379	1,197	297	759	141
1946	294	370	302	179	114	708	421		911	1,733	1,306	237	968	102
1944	251	245	232	123	46	599	499		672	1,281	354	195	69	90
1942	236	229	214	128	236	578	565		718	1,106	617	169	377	71
1940	235	207	218	162	230	561	653		622	1,324	687	140	494	53
1938	231	226	222	130	3	542	673		610	848	383	129	202	52
1936	205	204	193	104	―――	500	738		490	701	156	113	―――	43
1934	189	177	159	126	―――	432	739		421	528	133	96	―――	37
1932	210	223	165	147	―――	470	741		539	518	120	75	―――	45
1927	203	312	94	153	―――	412	584		632	491	109	50	―――	59
1922	158	189	61	85	―――	313	382		464	359	75	30	―――	45
1913	76	97	14	57	―――	211	147		217	186	7	7	―――	
1902	40	51	9	29	―――	141	68		98	82			―――	

¹ To avoid duplication, transactions between State and local governments have been excluded; see text.

Series Y 575–600. State Government Revenue, by Source: 1902 to 1957

[In millions of dollars]

Year	Revenue from all sources Total	General revenue (direct and intergovernmental)	Intergovernmental revenue From Federal Government	From local governments	Revenue from State sources Total	General revenue Total general	Taxes Total	Individual income	Corporation income	Sales and gross receipts Total	General	Motor fuel	Alcoholic beverages	Tobacco products	Other
	575	576	577	578	579	580	581	582	583	584	585	586	587	588	589
1957	24,656	20,382	3,500	427	20,728	16,454	14,531	1,563	984	8,436	3,373	2,828	569	556	1,109
1956	22,199	18,389	3,027	269	18,903	15,093	13,375	1,374	890	7,801	3,036	2,687	546	515	1,017
1955	19,667	16,194	2,762	226	16,678	13,205	11,597	1,094	737	6,864	2,637	2,353	471	459	944
1954	18,834	15,299	2,668	215	15,951	12,417	11,089	1,004	772	6,573	2,540	2,218	463	464	889
1953	17,979	14,511	2,570	191	15,218	11,750	10,552	969	810	6,209	2,433	2,019	465	469	823
1952	16,815	13,429	2,829	156	14,330	10,944	9,857	913	838	5,730	2,229	1,870	442	449	740
1950	13,903	11,262	2,275	148	11,480	8,839	7,930	724	586	4,670	1,670	1,544	420	414	621
1948	11,826	9,257	1,643	97	10,086	7,517	6,743	499	585	4,042	1,478	1,259	425	337	542
1946	8,576	6,284	802	63	7,712	5,419	4,987	89	442	2,803	899	886	402	198	419
1944	7,695	5,465	926	55	6,714	4,484	4,071	16	446	2,153	720	684	267	159	323
1942	6,870	5,132	802	56	6,012	4,274	3,903	19	269	2,218	632	940	257	130	258
1940	5,737	4,382	667	58	5,012	3,657	3,313	206	155	1,852	499	839	193	97	224
1938	5,298	4,141	633	48	4,612	3,460	3,132	218	165	1,674	447	777	176	55	219
1936	4,023	3,672	719	39	3,265	2,914	2,618	153	113	1,394	364	687	126	44	173
1934	3,421	3,212	933	36	2,452	2,243	1,979	80	49	978	173	565	62	25	153
1932	2,541	2,428	222	45	2,274	2,156	1,890	74	79	726	7	527	―――	19	173
1927	2,152	2,015	107	51	1,994	1,857	1,608	70	92	445	―――	259	―――		186
1922	1,860	1,254	99	27	1,234	1,128	947	43	58	134	―――	13	―――		121
1913	376	376	6	10	360	360	301	―――	―――	55	―――		2	―――	53
1902	192	190	3	6	188	181	156	―――	―――	28	―――			―――	28

Series Y 575–600. State Government Revenue, by Source: 1902 to 1957—Con.
[In millions of dollars]

Year	General revenue—Con. Taxes—Con. Property (590)	Motor vehicle and operators' licenses (591)	Other (592)	Charges and miscellaneous general revenue (593)	Liquor stores revenue (594)	Insurance trust revenue Total (595)	Employee retirement (596)	Unemployment compensation Total (597)	Contributions (598)	Interest (credited by U. S. Govt.) (599)	Other (600)
1957	479	1,368	1,701	1,923	1,065	3,209	1,063	1,719	1,510	209	427
1956	467	1,295	1,548	1,718	1,019	2,791	919	1,500	1,315	185	371
1955	412	1,184	1,306	1,608	962	2,511	837	1,325	1,138	187	350
1954	391	1,098	1,251	1,328	974	2,560	757	1,466	1,263	203	337
1953	365	949	1,250	1,198	967	2,501	634	1,551	1,370	181	316
1952	370	924	1,082	1,087	924	2,462	579	1,597	1,438	159	287
1950	307	755	888	909	810	1,831	425	1,176	1,028	148	229
1948	276	593	747	774	857	1,711	296	1,203	1,059	144	212
1946	249	439	616	482	798	1,494	193	1,162	1,034	128	140
1944	243	394	520	413	528	1,702	142	1,405	1,319	86	154
1942	264	431	472	370	373	1,366	115	1,134	1,076	58	117
1940	260	387	453	344	281	1,074	108	878	844	34	88
1938	244	359	472	328	262	890	85	726	702	24	79
1936	228	360	370	296	183	168	75	23	23	------	70
1934	273	305	294	264	90	119	64	------	------	------	55
1932	328	335	348	266	------	118	54	------	------	------	64
1927	370	301	330	249	------	137	40	------	------	------	97
1922	348	152	212	181	------	106	29	------	------	------	77
1913	140	5	101	59	------	------	------	------	------	------	------
1902	82	------	46	25	2	------	------	------	------	------	------

Series Y 601–647. State Government Expenditure, by Character and Object, by Function, and State Government Debt: 1902 to 1957
[In millions of dollars]

Expenditure by character and object

Year	Total (601)	Intergovernmental expenditure (602)	Direct expenditure Total (603)	Current operation (604)	Capital outlay Total (605)	Construction (606)	Other (607)	Assistance and subsidies (608)	Interest on debt (609)	Insurance benefits and repayments (610)	Expenditure for personal services (611)	Debt Outstanding at end of year (612)	Increase or decrease (−) during year (613)
1957	24,235	7,315	16,921	7,455	5,163	4,318	845	1,639	351	2,313	4,590	13,738	848
1956	21,686	6,538	15,148	6,758	4,564	3,872	692	1,531	311	1,984	4,132	12,890	1,692
1955	20,357	5,986	14,371	6,234	3,992	3,404	589	1,482	251	2,412	3,795	11,198	1,598
1954	18,686	5,679	13,008	5,886	3,347	2,831	515	1,486	193	2,096	3,491	9,600	1,776
1953	16,850	5,384	11,466	5,540	2,847	2,472	375	1,501	162	1,416	2,956	7,824	950
1952	15,834	5,044	10,790	5,173	2,658	2,323	336	1,402	144	1,413	2,450	6,874	652
1950	15,082	4,217	10,864	4,450	2,237	1,966	272	1,891	109	2,177	1,960	5,285	1,137
1948	11,181	3,283	7,897	3,837	1,456	1,268	188	1,499	86	1,020	1,240	3,676	708
1946	7,066	2,092	4,974	2,701	368	292	75	663	84	1,158	1,061	2,353	−154
1944	5,161	1,842	3,319	2,134	330	288	42	527	101	226	961	2,776	−214
1942	5,343	1,780	3,563	1,827	642	560	82	466	122	505	505	3,257	−233
1940	5,209	1,654	3,555	1,570	737	643	94	517	130	601	902	3,590	58
1938	4,598	1,516	3,082	1,503	701	612	89	448	128	302	848	3,343	−32
1936	3,862	1,417	2,445	1,192	634	553	81	416	124	79	685	3,413	−9
1934	3,461	1,318	2,143	985	619	540	79	356	119	64	576	3,248	167
1932	2,829	801	2,028	982	786	686	100	83	114	63	616	2,832	223
1927	2,047	596	1,451	762	492	430	62	43	83	71	465	1,971	145
1922	1,397	312	1,085	562	302	263	39	122	45	54	343	1,131	230
1913	388	91	297	218	48	42	6	17	14	------	125	379	47
1902	188	52	136	114	2	2	------	10	10	------	65	230	11

Intergovernmental expenditure by function / Direct expenditure by function

Year	Total expenditure (direct and intergovernmental) (614)	Total general expenditure (direct and intergovernmental) (615)	Intergovernmental expenditure by function Total (616)	Education (617)	Highways (618)	Public welfare (619)	Other specified purposes (620)	Purposes unspecified (621)	Direct expenditure by function — General expenditure Total (622)	Total general (623)	Education Total (624)	State institutions of higher education (625)	Local schools (626)	Other education (627)	Highways (628)	Public welfare Total (629)	Categorical public assistance (630)
1957	24,235	21,087	7,315	4,087	1,082	1,025	453	668	16,921	13,772	2,466	1,958	237	272	4,875	1,745	1,481
1956	21,686	18,857	6,538	3,541	984	1,069	313	631	15,148	12,319	2,138	1,678	219	241	4,367	1,603	1,364
1955	20,357	17,176	5,986	3,150	911	1,046	288	591	14,371	11,190	1,905	1,468	227	210	3,899	1,600	1,321
1954	18,686	15,788	5,679	2,930	871	1,004	274	600	13,008	10,109	1,715	1,324	199	192	3,254	1,548	1,298
1953	16,850	14,678	5,384	2,737	803	981	271	592	11,466	9,294	1,634	1,277	150	207	2,781	1,534	1,307
1952	15,834	13,697	5,044	2,523	728	976	268	549	10,790	8,653	1,494	1,180	125	189	2,556	1,410	1,192
1950	15,082	12,250	4,217	2,054	610	792	279	482	10,864	8,033	1,358	1,107	87	164	2,058	1,566	1,337
1948	11,181	9,469	3,283	1,554	507	648	146	428	7,897	6,186	1,081	895	65	121	1,510	962	820
1946	7,066	5,245	2,092	953	339	376	67	357	4,974	3,153	518	397	48	73	613	680	589
1944	5,161	4,508	1,842	861	298	368	41	274	3,319	2,666	489	380	40	69	540	577	506
1942	5,343	4,549	1,780	790	344	390	32	224	3,563	2,769	391	296	30	65	790	523	414
1940	5,209	4,384	1,654	700	332	420	21	181	3,555	2,730	375	290	29	56	798	527	321
1938	4,598	4,092	1,516	656	317	346	17	180	3,082	2,576	347	268	28	51	815	453	257
1936	3,862	3,640	1,417	573	285	245	151	163	2,445	2,223	297	231	24	42	754	422	395
1934	3,461	3,327	1,318	434	247	211	281	145	2,143	2,009	228	177	20	31	738	363	337
1932	2,829	2,766	801	398	229	28	6	140	2,028	1,965	278	234	------	44	843	74	61
1927	2,047	1,976	596	292	197	6	3	98	1,451	1,380	218	196	------	22	514	40	29
1922	1,397	1,343	312	202	70	4	1	35	1,085	1,031	164	143	------	21	303	16	10
1913	388	388	91	82	4	------	------	5	297	297	55	49	------	6	6	16	10
1902	188	186	52	45	2	------	------	5	136	134	17	13	------	4	4	10	6

Series Y 601–647. State Government Expenditure, by Character and Object, by Function, and State Government Debt: 1902 to 1957—Con.

[In millions of dollars]

	Direct expenditure by function—Con.																
	General expenditure—Con.													Insurance trust expenditure			
Year	Public welfare—Con.		Hospitals	Health	Police	Natural resources	Veterans services, not elsewhere classified	General control	Interest on general debt	Employment security administration	Correction	Other and unallocable	Liquor stores expenditure	Total	Employee retirement	Unemployment compensation	Other
	Other public assistance	Other public welfare															
	631	632	633	634	635	636	637	638	639	640	641	642	643	614	645	646	647
1957	55	209	1,402	250	179	787	38	531	351	234	328	586	836	2,313	511	1,495	307
1956	51	189	1,268	202	159	670	88	477	311	215	295	526	845	1,984	437	1,273	2⁹4
1955	97	181	1,145	193	139	597	61	447	251	207	268	478	770	2,411	373	1,780	258
1954	73	177	1,089	187	130	563	102	419	193	190	250	469	803	2,096	355	1,504	237
1953	65	162	1,014	170	119	531	113	399	162	187	238	411	757	1,416	292	908	216
1952	61	158	968	164	106	539	142	361	144	177	223	369	723	1,413	247	971	195
1950	92	137	788	159	85	468	462	317	109	172	198	293	654	2,177	163	1,845	169
1948	58	84	533	130	65	344	633	266	86	150	153	273	691	1,020	123	756	141
1946	35	56	308	116	45	207	54	192	84	60	97	179	663	1,158	92	965	102
1944	32	39	253	78	41	164	1	162	101	35	83	142	426	226	71	65	90
1942	72	37	235	64	40	159	1	164	122	59	80	141	288	505	65	369	71
1940	170	36	236	64	34	144	--------	151	130	64	86	126	224	601	56	492	53
1938	165	31	209	59	30	128	--------	146	128	48	85	128	204	302	48	202	52
1936	(¹)	27	180	41	19	93	--------	130	124	3	73	87	143	79	36	--------	43
1934	(¹)	26	167	36	15	85	--------	108	119	1	70	79	70	64	27	--------	37
1932	(¹)	13	181	34	15	119	--------	114	114	--------	87	106	--------	63	18	--------	45
1927	(¹)	11	146	24	7	94	--------	96	83	--------	64	94	--------	71	12	--------	59
1922	(¹)	11	105	20	4	61	80	69	45	--------	64	78	--------	54	9	--------	45
1913	(¹)	6	47	6	1	14	--------	38	14	--------	28	52	--------	--------	--------	--------	--------
1902	(¹)	4	28	4	--------	9	--------	23	10	--------	14	15	2	--------	--------	--------	--------

¹ Not available; included with categorical public assistance, series Y 630.

Series Y 648–669. Local Government Revenue, by Source: 1902 to 1957

[In millions of dollars]

	Revenue from all sources		Intergovernmental revenue		Revenue from local sources									
						General revenue								
Year	Total	General revenue (direct and inter-governmental)	From Federal Government	From State governments	Total	Total general	Taxes							Charges and misc. general revenue
							Total	Individual income	Corporation income	Sales and gross receipts	Property	Other taxes ¹	
	648	649	650	651	652	653	654	655	656	657	658	659	660
1957	28,896	25,406	343	7,196	21,358	17,866	14,286	191	----------	1,081	12,385	679	3,579
1956	26,352	23,137	309	6,590	19,453	16,238	12,992	164	----------	889	11,282	657	3,246
1955	24,166	21,092	368	5,987	17,811	14,737	11,886	143	7	779	10,323	634	2,851
1954	22,402	19,562	298	5,635	16,468	13,629	10,978	122	7	703	9,577	569	2,651
1953	21,007	18,371	300	5,384	15,323	12,687	10,356	96	7	718	9,010	523	2,331
1952	19,398	16,952	237	5,044	14,117	11,671	9,466	85	8	627	8,282	465	2,205
1950	16,101	14,014	211	4,217	11,673	9,586	7,984	64	7	484	7,042	387	1,602
1948	13,167	11,373	218	3,283	9,666	7,872	6,599	44	7	400	5,850	298	1,273
1946	9,561	8,227	53	2,092	7,416	6,082	5,157	33	5	183	4,737	199	925
1944	8,535	7,340	28	1,842	6,665	5,470	4,703	26	5	136	4,361	175	767
1942	8,114	7,122	56	1,780	6,278	5,286	4,625	27	3	133	4,273	189	661
1940	7,724	6,939	278	1,654	5,792	5,007	4,497	18	1	130	4,170	178	510
1938	7,329	6,651	167	1,516	5,646	4,968	4,473	--------	--------	120	4,196	157	495
1936	6,793	6,179	229	1,417	5,147	4,533	4,083	--------	--------	90	3,865	128	450
1934	6,363	5,820	83	1,318	4,962	4,419	3,933	--------	--------	30	3,803	100	486
1932	6,192	5,690	10	801	5,381	4,879	4,274	--------	--------	26	4,159	89	605
1927	6,333	5,903	9	596	5,728	5,298	4,479	--------	--------	25	4,360	94	819
1922	4,148	3,866	9	312	3,827	3,545	3,069	--------	--------	20	2,973	76	476
1913	1,755	1,637	6	91	1,658	1,540	1,308	--------	--------	3	1,192	113	232
1902	914	854	4	52	858	798	704	--------	--------	--------	624	80	94

	Revenue from local sources—Con.								
	Utilities revenue					Liquor stores revenue	Insurance trust revenue		
Year	Total	Water supply system	Electric power system	Transit system	Gas supply system		Total	Employee retirement	Unemployment compensation ²
	661	662	663	664	665	666	667	668	669
1957	2,944	1,235	1,011	541	157	118	429	423	6
1956	2,718	1,162	887	542	127	117	380	376	5
1955	2,609	1,092	870	544	104	117	347	343	4
1954	2,403	971	787	554	90	119	317	313	4
1953	2,237	939	713	500	85	120	280	275	5
1952	2,071	839	683	479	70	113	262	256	5
1950	1,808	705	574	468	61	94	185	181	4
1948	1,565	640	474	399	52	89	140	137	3
1946	1,169	556	348	227	38	66	99	96	3
1944	1,066	521	305	208	32	39	90	86	4
1942	887	439	251	170	27	17	88	80	8
1940	704	401	220	58	25	13	68	61	7
1938	605	371	169	47	18	10	63	58	5
1936	558	369	131	41	17	6	50	50	--------
1934	499	342	115	32	10	1	43	43	--------
1932	463	317	111	25	10	--------	39	39	--------
1927	403	247	111	35	10	--------	27	27	--------
1922	266	175	72	13	6	--------	16	16	--------
1913	116	99	16	--------	1	--------	2	2	--------
1902	60	56	3	--------	1	--------	--------	--------	--------

¹ Including licenses.   ²Washington, D.C., only.

Series Y 670–682. Local Government Expenditure, by Character and Object, and Local Government Debt: 1902 to 1957

[In millions of dollars]

			Expenditure									Debt	
			Direct expenditure										
		Inter-govern-mental expend-iture (to States)			Capital outlay			Assist-ance and subsidies	Interest on debt [1]	Insurance benefits and repayments	Expend-iture for personal services	Out-standing at end of fiscal year	Increase or decrease (−) during year
Year	Total		Total	Current operation	Total	Construc-tion	Other						
	670	671	672	673	674	675	676	677	678	679	680	681	682
1957	30,932	300	30,632	20,528	7,453	6,068	1,385	1,189	1,025	436	14,117	39,301	3,323
1956	28,273	269	28,004	18,771	6,843	5,482	1,361	1,089	910	392	12,986	35,978	2,909
1955	26,230	226	26,004	16,951	6,713	5,644	1,069	1,179	807	353	11,744	33,069	3,738
1954	23,814	215	23,599	15,622	5,778	4,907	871	1,148	723	327	10,851	29,331	3,374
1953	21,662	191	21,471	14,425	5,058	4,291	767	1,057	635	296	9,868	25,957	2,731
1952	20,229	156	20,073	13,360	4,778	4,063	715	1,070	580	285	9,089	23,226	1,332
1950	17,041	(2)	[1]17,041	11,498	3,810	3,203	607	1,027	504	202	7,593	18,830	1,979
1948	13,363	(2)	[1]13,363	9,578	2,269	1,817	452	882	457	177	6,470	14,980	1,133
1946	9,093	(2)	[1]9,093	6,989	937	678	259	546	473	148	4,705	13,564	−600
1944	7,180	(2)	[1]7,180	5,714	379	274	105	425	534	128	3,927	14,703	−1,080
1942	7,351	(2)	[1]7,351	5,230	835	681	154	590	584	112	3,554	16,449	−337
1940	7,685	(2)	[1]7,685	4,606	1,778	1,185	593	558	657	86	3,400	16,693	162
1938	6,906	(2)	[1]6,906	4,466	1,157	926	231	546	656	81	3,176	16,093	6
1936	6,056	(2)	[1]6,056	4,036	890	712	178	336	717	77	2,871	16,061	306
1934	5,699	(2)	[1]5,699	3,665	788	630	158	459	718	69	2,618	15,681	−826
1932	6,375	(2)	[1]6,375	4,197	1,090	872	218	305	726	57	2,925	16,373	9
1927	6,359	(2)	[1]6,359	3,828	1,864	1,491	373	50	579	38	2,680	12,910	929
1922	4,567	(2)	[1]4,567	2,915	1,216	973	243	30	385	21	2,041	8,978	1,216
1913	1,960	(2)	[1]1,960	1,287	500	400	100	7	159	7	901	4,035	(3)
1902	959	(2)	[1]959	682	203	162	41	5	69	--------	745	1,877	(3)

[1] Includes interest on debt of utilities operated by local governments.
[2] Minor amounts of intergovernmental expenditure to States not segregable from "Direct expenditure."
[3] Not available.

Series Y 683–714. Local Government Expenditure, by Function: 1902 to 1957

[In millions of dollars]

			Direct expenditure													
			General expenditure													
		Inter-govern-mental expend-iture (to States)			Education			High-ways	Public welfare				Hos-pitals	Health	Police	Fire pro-tection
Year	Total		Total	Total general	Total	Local schools	Other educa-tion		Total	Cate-gorical public as-sistance	Other public assist-ance	Other public welfare				
	683	684	685	686	687	688	689	690	691	692	693	694	695	696	697	698
1957	30,932	300	30,632	26,603	11,668	11,635	33	2,941	1,659	1,043	146	470	1,246	303	1,290	810
1956	28,273	269	28,004	24,392	11,082	11,031	51	2,586	1,536	946	207	382	1,048	254	1,172	737
1955	26,230	226	26,004	22,534	10,003	9,959	45	2,553	1,568	947	285	336	908	277	1,091	694
1954	23,814	215	23,599	20,593	8,842	8,791	51	2,272	1,512	927	276	309	873	260	1,000	653
1953	21,662	191	21,471	18,616	7,756	7,706	50	2,207	1,380	853	236	292	849	258	919	598
1952	20,229	156	20,073	17,444	6,824	6,778	46	2,094	1,378	831	266	280	777	276	833	586
1950	17,041	(1)	[1]17,041	14,754	5,819	5,792	27	1,745	1,374	673	446	255	596	205	691	488
1948	13,363	(1)	[1]13,363	11,498	4,298	4,282	16	1,526	1,137	653	299	185	404	162	579	406
1946	9,093	(1)	[1]9,093	7,875	2,838	2,824	14	1,059	729	425	181	123	259	135	434	294
1944	7,180	(1)	[1]7,180	6,197	2,304	2,291	13	660	556	336	134	86	215	110	373	251
1942	7,351	(1)	[1]7,351	6,421	2,195	2,183	12	700	702	347	273	82	197	95	354	236
1940	7,685	(1)	[1]7,685	6,499	2,263	2,252	11	780	629	290	268	71	214	95	331	235
1938	6,906	(1)	[1]6,906	6,181	2,144	2,133	11	835	616	226	320	70	191	92	329	231
1936	6,056	(1)	[1]6,056	5,421	1,880	1,870	10	671	405		336	69	171	75	295	205
1934	5,699	(1)	[1]5,699	5,172	1,603	1,596	7	771	526		459	67	142	73	276	189
1932	6,375	(1)	[1]6,375	5,800	2,033	2,025	8	898	370		305	65	133	52	263	203
1927	6,359	(1)	[1]6,359	5,830	2,017		2,017	1,295	111		50	61	95	38	186	158
1922	4,567	(1)	[1]4,567	4,187	1,541		1,541	991	81		30	51	32	23	88	76
1913	1,960	(1)	[1]1,960	1,767	522		522	393	36		7	29	15	13	50	40
1902	959	(1)	[1]959	879	238		238	171	27		5	22				

Direct expenditure—Con.

	General expenditure—Con.							Utilities expenditure					Liquor stores expend-iture	Insurance trust expenditure		
Year	Sanita-tion	Natural re-sources	Parks and recrea-tion	Housing and com-munity redevel-opment	General control	Interest on general debt	Other and unallo-cable	Total	Water supply system	Electric power system	Transit system	Gas supply system		Total	Em-ployee retire-ment	Unem-ployment compen-sation [2]
	699	700	701	702	703	704	705	706	707	708	709	710	711	712	713	714
1957	1,443	244	608	503	1,195	755	1,939	3,494	1,584	1,103	652	156	98	436	432	4
1956	1,326	236	541	435	1,083	675	1,681	3,119	1,461	895	636	128	101	392	388	4
1955	1,142	196	509	497	1,005	587	1,504	3,023	1,479	819	600	125	93	353	348	5
1954	1,058	199	424	609	956	525	1,410	2,577	1,150	751	586	90	102	327	323	4
1953	908	173	374	628	864	452	1,250	2,457	1,084	723	582	68	102	296	294	2
1952	992	237	324	766	832	408	1,117	2,246	973	631	581	61	98	285	283	2
1950	834	202	304	452	724	349	971	2,005	849	534	570	52	80	202	198	4
1948	670	152	243	176	614	313	818	1,612	628	438	499	47	76	177	174	3
1946	370	95	179	114	511	337	521	1,014	426	305	247	36	56	148	145	3
1944	245	68	123	46	437	398	411	822	355	227	215	25	33	128	124	4
1942	229	55	128	236	414	443	437	804	368	216	201	19	14	112	104	8
1940	207	74	162	230	410	523	346	1,090	404	257	411	18	10	86	84	2
1938	226	94	130	3	396	545	349	636	385	156	82	13	8	81	81	--------
1936	204	100	104	--------	370	614	327	553	344	117	81	11	5	77	77	--------
1934	177	74	126	--------	324	620	271	457	292	102	57	6	1	69	69	--------
1932	223	46	147	--------	356	627	346	518	320	92	99	7	--------	57	57	--------
1927	312	--------	153	--------	316	501	474	491	349	94	38	10	--------	38	38	--------
1922	189	--------	85	--------	244	337	242	359	255	75	25	4	--------	21	21	--------
1913	97	--------	57	--------	173	133	137	186	159	25	1	1	--------	7	7	--------
1902	51	--------	29	--------	118	58	69	80	71	8	1	1	--------	--------	--------	--------

[1] Minor amounts of intergovernmental expenditure to States not segregable from "Direct expenditure."   [2] Washington, D.C., only.

chapter Y

ARMED FORCES AND VETERANS (Series Y 715–854)

Y 715–762. Selected characteristics of the Armed Forces, by war.

Source: The President's Commission on Veterans Pensions, *Veterans' Benefits in the United States*, vol. I; Staff Report No. IV, "Veterans in our Society," House Committee Print 261, 84th Cong., 2d session; and revised estimates prepared by the Department of Defense.

The time coverage for a particular war may vary from series to series. See source for exact coverage.

The number of personnel serving in the Revolutionary War is not known, but estimates range from 184,000 to 250,000. In the War of 1812, it is estimated that 286,730 served and in the Mexican War, 78,718. In the Civil War, estimates for Confederate forces range from 600,000 to 1,500,000.

Y 763–775. Military personnel on active duty, 1789–1957.

Source: Department of Defense, reports and records.

Primary sources of Army data are as follows: 1789, 1794, and 1795, *American State Papers, Military Affairs*, vol. 1 (except for officers, 1789, Thomas H. S. Hamersly, *Complete Regular Army Register of the United States for One Hundred Years (1779–1879)*, Washington, D.C., 1880); 1801–1821, *American State Papers, Military Affairs*, vol. 2; 1822–1939, *War Department Annual Reports* (except as follows: Regular Army, 1847 and 1866, Francis B. Heitman, *Historical Register and Dictionary of the United States Army*, vol. 2, Washington, D.C., 1903; Army Nurse Corps, 1920, Army field clerks, 1917, and Quartermaster Corps field clerks, 1917 and 1918, *Special Report 196*, Revised, Statistics Branch, War Department, General Staff, 1927; 1919 and 1920, Quartermaster Corps field clerks, *Regular Report 189*, Statistics Branch, War Department, General Staff, 1922; 1940–1957, Office of The Adjutant General, *Strength of the Army*, monthly reports. For data on U.S. Military Academy cadets, 1802–1821, *American State Papers, Military Affairs*, vol. 2; 1822–1920, *Official Register of the Officers and Cadets at the United States Military Academy* (except as follows: 1871, 1910, 1913, 1915, 1917, and 1918, *War Department Annual Reports*); 1921–1941, *War Department Annual Reports*; 1942–1957, *Strength of the Army*, monthly reports.

Some of the figures for the Navy and Marine Corps appear in the following sources: Gordon R. Young (ed.), *Army Almanac*, Stackpole Company, Harrisburg, Pennsylvania, 1959; Bureau of Navy Personnel, *Navy and Marine Corps, Military Personnel Statistics*, June and December 1956; Navy Department, Bureau of Personnel, *Progress Report*, March 1948.

Officers include warrant officers, flight officers, nurses, medical specialists, and field clerks. Enlisted personnel includes U.S. Military Academy cadets, U.S. Naval Academy midshipmen, U.S. Air Force Academy cadets, and other officer candidates.

Army data (series Y 764–766) begin with 1789, the year in which the Department of War (now Department of the Army) was established. Although a "regular" Army has existed continuously from that time, the total strengths cannot be documented from available records, nor can reliable estimates be made for 1790–1793 and 1796–1800. Beginning 1861, the data include all military personnel on extended active duty with the Army (Regulars, volunteers, militia, inductees, Reserves, National Guardsmen, and reactivated retired Regular personnel) and U.S. Military Academy cadets. Data prior to 1861 are for Regular Army and cadets only, except for 1836–1840 (Seminole Indian War) and 1846–1848 (Mexican War). Source documents for other years do not contain adequate strength statistics on nonregular personnel called out during the War of 1812 or for short periods of service during the numerous Indian disturbances. For most years prior to 1878, data were compiled from the latest returns received; some of the reports used, especially those from the frontier garrisons, were weeks or months in transit.

The Army figures include the Army Nurse Corps beginning 1898; Army field clerks and field clerks in the Quartermaster Corps for 1917–1925; warrant officers beginning 1919; flight officers for 1943–1947; and the Women's Army Corps (formerly the Women's Army Auxiliary Corps) and the Women's Medical Specialist Corps (later redesignated the Army Medical Specialist Corps), beginning 1943. All data for these categories are as of June 30, except the 1898 figure for the Army Nurse Corps which is as of September 15.

The Army Nurse Corps became a part of the permanent Army military establishment in 1901. It traces its origin, however, to 1898, when authority was received to employ by contract as many nurses as needed during the war with Spain. For this reason, data on nurses have been included for 1898–1900.

The positions of Army field clerks and field clerks in the Quartermaster Corps were created by Act of Congress, August 29, 1916. Field clerks of both classes were subject to the rules and articles of war, and had the status of officers, although not commissioned officers. By Act of Congress, April 27, 1926, the Secretary of War was authorized and directed to appoint as warrant officers all field clerks then in active service.

The Army figures for 1908–1947 include strength of the Army Air Force and predecessor agencies. Those beginning with 1948 consist of military personnel under the command of the Army only, resulting from the establishment of the Department of the Air Force as an executive department by the National Security Act of 1947. Data for 1948 and 1949 include a small number of Department of the Air Force military personnel assigned for duty with Army commands, and data for 1948–1955 exclude a larger number of Department of the Army military personnel assigned for duty with Air Force commands.

Navy data for 1794, 1795, and 1798 are an approximation of the "on board" personnel authorized by Congress in conjunction with the construction of six frigates to reconstitute a Navy which had existed for 1775–1785 under the Continental Congress. A separate Navy Department was authorized and organized in 1798. Since the crews usually were obligated, during the early years of the Navy, for only a specific sailing or mission, rather than a continuous tour of duty, the strengths shown are more in the nature of averages and are therefore noted as estimated. Data exclude an unknown number of Naval militia, supplied by the States, who served during the War of 1812, the Mexican War, and the Spanish-American

War. Since 1916, Naval Reservist and retired personnel on extended active duty have been included.

The Marine Corps was founded in 1775 by the Continental Congress and served during the Revolutionary War, but ceased to exist in 1783. It was reactivated in 1794 when Congress authorized the building of the six frigates and a small number of Marines were used as guards. The data in series Y 773–775 begin with 1798, since reliable estimates are not available for prior years. Since 1917, Reservist and retired personnel on active duty have been included.

Y 776–786. Estimated number of veterans in civil life, by war, 1865–1955.

Source: Veterans Administration, estimates based primarily on Armed Forces records.

The estimates for the War of 1812 were derived by a backward chain computation involving the application of appropriate survival rates to the age distribution of the 165 living veterans of this war on the pension rolls in 1892. It was assumed that all living veterans of the War of 1812 were on the pension rolls after 1873.

Estimates for the Mexican War were computed by applying appropriate survival rates to the age distribution of the 2,195 living Mexican War veterans on the pension rolls in 1907. For 1890 and later years, the estimates were based on the assumption that 90 percent of the living Mexican War veterans were on the pension rolls. Estimates for years prior to 1890 were based on a backward chain computation.

The Civil War estimate for 1865 was based on Armed Forces data. Estimates for years after 1865 were computed from actuarial projections, based on the American Experience Mortality Table, 1868, applied to the age distribution of one million Civil War participants included in Surgeon General, *The Medical Department of the U.S. Army in the World War,* Vol. XV, *Statistics,* part I, 1921. The totals so obtained were modified by the assumptions that 75 percent of the living Civil War veterans were on the pension rolls in 1900–1915 and that practically all living Civil War veterans were on the rolls in 1920 and later years. The estimates pertain to Union forces only.

For the Spanish-American War, estimates for 1905 and later years were computed by application of appropriate survival rates to the 1902 age distribution of Spanish-American War participants (not shown here). For 1900, estimate is based on total participants, inservice deaths, and discharges to civil life.

Estimates for World War I were computed by applying appropriate survival rates to the 1918 distribution of World War I participants by year of age based on records of 3.7 million War Risk Insurance applications (*The Medical Department of the U.S. Army . . . ,* cited above).

For World War II and the Korean conflict, the estimates were derived from Armed Forces data on the number of persons returned to civil life less Veterans Administration estimates of deaths and less the number who reenlisted from civil life.

Estimates for the Indian wars include only veterans on pension rolls of the Veterans Administration or predecessor agencies. Data on the Regular Establishment include only former members of the peacetime forces receiving disability compensation or pension from the Veterans Administration or predecessor agencies.

The following periods are covered by the above-mentioned wars for determining veterans status:

War of 1812—June 18, 1812, through February 17, 1815
Mexican War—April 25, 1846, through May 30, 1848
Indian wars—1860 through 1898 (approximately)
Civil War—April 15, 1861, through August 20, 1866
Spanish-American War—April 21, 1898, through July 4, 1902 (includes the war with Spain, Boxer Rebellion, and Philippine Insurrection. For persons serving in the Moro Province, hostilities ended July 15, 1903)
World War I—April 6, 1917, through November 11, 1918 (for persons serving in Russia, the war ended April 1, 1920)
World War II—September 16, 1940, through July 25, 1947
Korean conflict—June 27, 1950, through January 31, 1955

Y 787–800. Estimated number of veterans in civil life, by age, 1865–1955.

Source: Veterans Administration, estimates.

Age distribution for veterans of World War I, Spanish-American War, Civil War, Mexican War, and War of 1812 were obtained by procedures used in estimating the numbers of living veterans in civil life, as described in the text for series Y 776–786. The ages for veterans of Indian wars and Regular Establishment (peacetime service) were obtained from records of the Veterans Administration and predecessor agencies.

The ages of World War II veterans included in the total for 1945 were based on the ages of those veterans on the Veterans Administration disability compensation rolls on June 30, 1945. The estimated number of veterans by age, for 1950 and 1955, were derived by the application of appropriate survival rates to the male and female components of the potential World War II veteran population as of July 25, 1947. In this particular case, the potential World War II veteran population is defined as: (*a*) The estimated number of men and women who had served in World War II and who had returned to civil life prior to July 25, 1947, and (*b*) those still in the service as of July 25, 1947. The age distribution of this population was derived from the Veterans Administration's scientific sample of approximately 1 percent of the records of the men and women separated from the Armed Forces between September 16, 1940, and July 25, 1947, and from estimates provided by the Armed Forces for World War II participants who were still in service on the latter date.

The ages of Korean conflict veterans included for 1955 were derived from the Veterans Administration's sample of approximately 1 percent of Department of Defense records for persons returning to civil life between June 27, 1950, and June 30, 1955.

Y 801–811. Expenditures of Veterans Administration and predecessor agencies from appropriated funds, by war, 1790–1957.

Source: Veterans Administration, records.

Original data are taken from annual reports of the Administrator of Veterans Affairs, Veterans Bureau, Bureau of Pensions, National Home for Disabled Volunteer Soldiers, and records of the Veterans Administration.

The data pertain to expenditures from appropriated funds (see text for series Y 812–825) for veterans and their dependents through June 30, 1957. Thus, they include expenditures for pensions since 1790 and for care in the National Homes (now Veterans Administration domiciliaries) since 1867. Grants-in-aid for the care of veterans in State homes were first made in 1889 and are included thereafter.

Expenditures on behalf of World War I veterans, made originally as allowances for the dependents of enlisted men in the Armed Forces, compensation for death and disability, medical care and treatment, vocational rehabilitation and training, and insurance against death or permanent disability, are included since October 1917. Subsequent adjustments of benefits for World War I veterans and for veterans of the earlier wars (e.g., extension of hospital benefits) are reflected in the ensuing years. Expenditures for World War II veterans began in 1941, and for veterans of the Korean conflict in 1951.

Trust and working fund expenditures (e.g., the U.S. Government Life and National Service Life Insurance Trust Funds, the Adjusted Service Certificate Trust Fund, and the General Post Fund) are excluded; transfers from appropriations to the insurance trust funds, however, are included. Also excluded are expenditures made by other Federal and State agencies (e.g., unemployment compensation paid to Korean conflict veterans by the Department of Labor, expenditures for retirement pay by the Department of Defense, and bonus payments made by State governments).

Of the $88.8 billion in total expenditures through 1957, $74.4 billion (84 percent) was directly allocated by war. The distribution of the remaining expenditures was estimated. Therefore, the figures are subject to a varying and unknown degree of error. For example, variations in average hospital costs between wars, or unusual administrative workloads are not reflected in the distribution factors used.

Y 812–825. Expenditures for veterans benefits and services by Veterans Administration and predecessor agencies, 1790–1957.

Source: Veterans Administration, records.

Data are based on checks paid through December 31, 1947, and on vouchers approved for payment thereafter. The data are gross, since they include expenditures made from amounts earned (in the form of reimbursements) by the various accounts. Expenditures from revolving funds are also gross, i.e., receipts have not been netted out of these funds except in minor instances noted elsewhere. Accordingly, these data do not agree with those reported in the statements of the Treasury Department and the Bureau of the Budget.

Y 812, total expenditures. This series measures the gross cost of benefits and services (including capital expenditures and administrative costs) provided veterans and their beneficiaries, irrespective of the source of funds. Included are expenditures from general and special funds appropriated by the Congress, revolving and management funds authorized to finance a continuing cycle of operations using receipts derived from these operations, trust funds held by the Government for the benefit of veterans and their beneficiaries, and veterans funds held on deposit by the Government. Transfers from appropriations to insurance trust funds, from which the actual expenditures are made, are not included in the total, in order to avoid duplication. Expenditures from the Veterans Administration Revolving Supply Fund, established July 1, 1954, also are excluded from the total, since these amounts generally duplicate expenditures made by Veterans Administration administrative appropriations for supplies, equipment, and certain services procured through the fund.

Y 813, compensation and pensions. Data represent total expenditures less refund of overpayments.

Y 814, insurance and servicemen's indemnities. Data include direct payments to beneficiaries from insurance appropriations, servicemen's indemnities, and benefits and dividends paid from insurance trust funds. Some noncash transactions (e.g., interest credited to dividends left on deposit) also are included as expenditures from the trust funds. Transfers from appropriations to the insurance trust funds, from which the benefit payments are made, are not included in these amounts. Beginning fiscal year 1949, the reporting of expenditures from the U.S. Government Life Insurance and National Service Life Insurance trust funds was changed from a net to a gross basis. This resulted in an understatement in varying amounts for prior years. The cumulative differences for the prior years between the net figures and what the figures would have been on a gross basis have been added in a lump sum to the 1948 figures. This adjustment amounted to $295,651,000.

Y 815, education and training. This series includes subsistence allowances, tuition, supplies, and equipment of veterans training under Public Law 346, education and training allowances of veterans training under Public Law 550, and war orphans educational assistance under Public Law 634.

Y 816, vocational rehabilitation. Data include subsistence allowances, tuition, supplies, and equipment of veterans training under Public Laws 16 and 894, and vocational rehabilitation allowances for World War I veterans.

Y 817, unemployment and self-employment allowances. Includes weekly and monthly allowances to World War II veterans to assist in their readjustment to civilian employment. Credit figures reflect the excess of overpayments refunded over expenditures during the various years. Similar allowances paid to Korean conflict veterans by the Department of Labor are excluded.

Y 818, loan guaranty. Includes 4 percent gratuity payments to veteran borrowers, payments on defaulted loans, and the cost of property and securities acquired. The amounts are gross and do not reflect the cost of the loan guaranty program to the Government. Refunds and recoveries on claims paid and returned to the general fund have amounted to $84 million through June 30, 1957. Other losses of the program are subject to further recovery from the liquidation of securities and repayments by borrowers.

Y 819, direct loans. Includes direct mortgage loans and advances to veterans, interest expenses on capital borrowed from the U.S. Treasury, and other expenses (excluding Veterans Administration administrative expenses) of the direct loan program. Expenditures are gross and do not reflect the cost of this program to the Government. Through June 30, 1957, receipts paid into the direct loan fund amounted to $225 million, bringing net expenditures to $492 million. This will be further reduced, as the program matures, by payments of interest and principal by borrowers.

Y 820, miscellaneous benefit payments. Includes statutory burial allowances; expenditures not classified as to purpose from the Compensation and Pensions appropriation; automobiles and other conveyances for disabled veterans; specially adapted homes for paraplegic veterans; payments to participants in the yellow fever experiments; military and naval family allowances of World War I veterans; marine and seamen's insurance in World War I; adjusted service compensation (World War I bonus); General Post Fund expenditures; withdrawals of the personal funds of patients held by the Veterans Administration as banker and funds due incompetent beneficiaries; soldiers' and sailors' civil relief; and the vocational rehabilitation revolving fund. These expenditures are gross with the exceptions of soldiers' and sailors' civil relief and the vocational rehabilitation revolving fund, which are on a net basis.

Y 821, medical, hospital, and domiciliary services. Figures include expenditures for hospital and domiciliary care, outpatient medical and dental treatment, medical research, and related costs; appropriations to the Canteen Service Revolving Fund; and grants to the Republic of the Philippines for medical care and treatment of veterans. Beginning 1921, the data are estimated. Prior to July 1, 1879, the fiscal year of the National Home for Disabled Volunteer Soldiers ended on various dates. For this period, the data have been proportionately adjusted by the Veterans Administration to reflect expenditures for years ending June 30.

Y 822, hospital and domiciliary facilities. These data include expenditures for the construction and equipping of hospitals and domiciliary facilities, and major alterations, improvements, and repairs thereof; grants to the Republic of the Philippines for the construction and equipping of a hospital; expenditures from funds allotted under the National Recovery Act of 1933 and Public Works Administration Act of 1938; and $436,623,692 transferred to the Department of the Army, Corps of Engineers, for the construction of hospitals.

Y 823, administration and other benefits. Includes expenses for vocational counseling of veterans, beneficiary travel for certain programs, reporting allowances paid schools for certifying the attendance of veteran trainees, private laws for relief, and all administrative salaries and expenses.

Y 824-825, expenditures from general and special fund appropriations. Series Y 824 represents expenditures from appropriations made by the Congress to finance the general and ordinary operations of the Veterans Administration and predecessor agencies. The figures differ from amounts shown under total expenditures (series Y 812) after 1917 in that they do not include expenditures from trust funds, working funds, and deposit funds. Transfers from appropriations to insurance trust funds (series Y 825) are included in the figures for series Y 824.

Y 826-837. **Veterans pensions and compensation—number of veterans and expenditure, by type, 1866-1957.**

Source: Veterans Administration, records. Data were compiled from various annual reports of the Administrator of Veterans Affairs, and of the Commissioner of Pensions.

The basic distinction between pension and compensation is that pension is a benefit payable for total and permanent disability or death which is not attributable to the veteran's military service. Compensation is payable for disability or death resulting from injury or disease incurred in, or aggravated by, military service. In the series relating to death benefits, the number of veterans refers to the number of deceased veterans whose dependents are receiving benefits, rather than to the number of dependents in receipt of such benefits; the data on expenditures refer to the amount received by these dependents. In the disability cases, the data refer to the number of veterans, and the amount of money paid to these veterans in the form of retirement pay administered by the Veterans Administration or its predecessor agencies.

For 1866-1890, separate data are not available for the death and disability series. Likewise, information is not available which would permit a separation of the data on the pensions and compensation earned for military service prior to 1904. As a result, all data on veterans of the Spanish-American and earlier wars have been arbitrarily included in the pension series.

The compensation data refer to (with the qualifications as noted above for the series on deaths) the number of, or expenditures paid to, veterans of the Regular Establishment, World War I, World War II, and the Korean conflict. Data on these veterans were first included in 1904, 1918, 1942, and 1951, respectively.

Y 838-850. **Patients receiving hospital or domiciliary care authorized by Veterans Administration, 1921-1957.**

Source: Veterans Administration, records.

These data do not in all cases agree with information previously published in some of the earlier annual reports of the Veterans Administration. Revisions were made to adjust some of the data for earlier years for comparability with current data.

The data for all veterans receiving hospital care (series Y 839) and veterans with service-connected disabilities (series Y 844) are identical prior to 1925. The act which made Veterans Administration hospital care available to veterans with nonservice-connected disability was passed in 1924, and it was not until 1925 that such patients were admitted to Veterans Administration hospitals.

Data for veterans receiving hospital care for service-connected disabilities (series Y 844-847) exclude those veterans with service-connected disabilities who are being treated for nonservice-connected ailments.

Series Y 843 shows the number of nonveteran patients in Veterans Administration hospitals. This group of patients is made up for the most part of persons still in the military service who have not yet attained veteran status, and cases admitted to Veterans Administration hospitals for humanitarian reasons.

Domiciliary care was provided by the National Homes for Disabled Volunteer Soldiers through July 30, 1930; later, it was provided by other agencies. However, the data for years prior to 1933 are not comparable with the 1933-1957 data. The number of veterans in State homes receiving domiciliary care (series Y 850) is shown because the Veterans Administration contributes to the support of veterans cared for in approved State homes, who would be eligible for admission to Veterans Administration domiciliaries.

Y 851-854. **Government life insurance administered by Veterans Adminstration—number of policies, income received, and benefits paid, 1921-1957.**

Source: Veterans Adminstration, records.

The U.S. Government, through the Veterans Administration, operates two life insurance programs for veterans and servicemen. The insurance program which had its origin in World War I is known as U.S. Government Life Insurance (USGLI); and the program which had its inception in 1940 is called National Service Life Insurance (NSLI). The administrative expenses of these programs are borne by the U.S. Government. All USGLI is participating (that is, entitled to dividends from any earnings). This program was closed to new issues effective April 25, 1951. All NSLI issued prior to April 25, 1951, with some minor exceptions, is participating and entitled to dividends. This type of insurance also was closed to new issues in 1951. Veterans separated from military service without a service-connected disability on or after April 25, 1951, and before January 1, 1957, could apply for nonparticipating NSLI on the 5-year nonconvertible term plan only. This insurance is known as veterans special term insurance. Those separated with a service-connected disability on or after April 25, 1951, are eligible to apply, within one year after service-connection is established, for permanent plan or term policies. This insurance is known as service-disabled veterans insurance. The maximum amount of all Government insurance for veterans is $10,000 on one life. Excluded from these series are data on the Servicemen's Indemnity program, which was in effect from June 27, 1950, to January 1, 1957. This program provided free life insurance in the amount of $10,000 (less any USGLI or NSLI in force) while in military service and for 120 days thereafter.

Income received (series Y 853) includes: (a) Premiums received from policy holders for insurance and disability income benefits, including premiums waived because of disability, (b) advances from Congressional appropriations to the service-disabled veterans insurance fund, (c) interest on investments in U.S. Treasury Certificates of Indebtedness and in U.S. Treasury notes, (d) interest on policy loans and on premiums paid in arrears, (e) dividends credited to insureds or deposited to accumulate at interest, and (f) reimbursements from the U.S. Government as the Government's contribution for death and disability claims due to the extra hazards of military or naval service, for gratuitous insurance, and for other obligations.

Benefits paid (series Y 854) include: (a) The actual cash payments to beneficiaries of deceased insureds, (b) cash payments to insureds under the total and permanent disability provisions of USGLI policies, (c) monthly income payments under total disability income provisions of USGLI and NSLI policies issued before April 25, 1951, (d) premiums waived for total disability, (e) cash surrender values paid on contracts surrendered, (f) payments on matured endowment policies, (g) dividends paid and dividends previously credited or left on deposit and later withdrawn, (h) interest added on dividend credits and deposits, and (i) adjustments in policy liens, receivables, and overpayments waived.

Series Y 715–762. Selected Characteristics of the Armed Forces, by War

Series No.	Characteristic	Civil War (Union forces only)	Spanish-American War	World War I	World War II	Korean conflict
715	Military personnel___1,000__	2,213	307	4,744	16,354	5,764
716	Army___do___	2,129	281	4,057	11,260	2,834
717	Air Force___do___					1,285
718	Navy___do___	84	23	599	4,183	1,177
719	Marines___do___		3	79	669	424
720	Coast Guard___do___			9	241	44
	Draftees:					
721	Classified___do___	777		24,234	36,677	9,123
722	Examined___do___	522		3,764	17,955	3,685
723	Rejected___do___	160		803	6,420	1,189
724	Inducted___do___	46		2,820	10,022	1,560
725	Average duration of service___months__	20	8	12	33	19
726	Officers___do___	[1]	8	14	39	24
727	Enlisted___do___	[1]	8	12	33	18
	Overseas service:					
728	Percent of total who served overseas___	[1]	29	53	73	56
729	Average months served overseas [2]___	[1]	1.5	5.5	16.2	13.4
730	Occupation of enlisted personnel___percent__	[3]100.0	[3]100.0	[3]100.0	100.0	100.0
731	Technical and scientific___do___	0.2	0.5	3.7	10.4	12.7
732	Administrative and clerical___do___	0.7	3.1	8.0	12.6	18.1
733	Mechanics and repairmen___do___	0.1	1.0	8.5	16.6	15.3
734	Craftsmen___do___	0.5	.1	13.0	5.9	4.7
735	Service workers___do___	2.4	6.5	12.5	9.6	12.4
736	Operators and laborers___do___	2.9	2.2	20.2	6.1	6.5
737	Military-type occupations, not elsewhere classified___do___	93.2	86.6	34.1	38.8	30.3
	Casualties, number:					
738	Total deaths___	364,511	2,446	116,516	405,399	54,246
739	Battle deaths___	140,414	385	53,402	291,557	33,629
740	Other deaths___	224,097	2,061	63,114	113,842	20,617
741	Wounds not mortal___	281,881	1,662	204,002	670,846	103,284

Series No.	Characteristic	Civil War (Union forces only)	Spanish-American War	World War I	World War II	Korean conflict
	Annual rate per 1,000 average strength:					
742	Total deaths___	104.4	36.6	35.5	11.6	5.5
743	Battle deaths___	40.1	[1]	17.1	8.6	3.4
744	Other deaths___	64.3	[1]	18.4	3.0	2.1
	Medical care: Army: Admissions for care, all causes:					
745	Number___1,000___	6,455	317	4,039	17,919	2,717
746	Annual rate per 1,000 average strength___	2,477.9	2,146.2	978.2	704.4	511.3
	Noneffectiveness, total:					
747	Man-days lost_1,000__	[1]	4,355	86,947	413,393	49,810
748	Daily rate per 1,000 average strength___	[1]	80.7	57.7	44.5	25.7
749	Wounded who died subsequently___percent__	13.3	6.3	8.1	4.5	2.6
750	Annual nonbattle death rate per 1,000 average strength___	68.7	25.9	15.4	3.0	2.0
	Navy and Marine Corps: Admissions for care, all causes:					
751	Number___1,000___	[1]	25	1,073	5,514	1,200
752	Annual rate per 1,000 average strength___	[1]	1,037.5	1,024.1	553.3	337.3
	Noneffectiveness, total:					
753	Man-days lost_1,000__	[1]	248	12,705	115,700	23,998
754	Daily rate per 1,000 average strength___	[1]	28.3	33.2	31.8	18.5
755	Wounded who died subsequently___percent__	[1]	5.9	9.0	3.2	2.2
756	Annual nonbattle death rate per 1,000 average strength___	[1]	17.6	11.6	2.8	1.9
	Military pay (current dol.): Basic pay (annual rate):					
757	All personnel__dollars___	231	282	510	1,017	1,776
758	Officers___do___	717	2,101	2,141	2,442	4,453
759	Enlisted___do___	202	205	417	856	1,473
	Pay and allowances (annual rate):					
760	All personnel dollars___	510	528	968	1,811	2,940
761	Officers___do___	1,912	2,489	2,698	3,777	6,234
762	Enlisted___do___	427	444	870	1,587	2,584

[1] Not available.   [2] During hostilities only.   [3] Army personnel only.

Series Y 763–775.　Military Personnel on Active Duty: 1789 to 1957

[As of June 30 beginning 1878 for Army, 1900 for Navy, and 1798 for Marine Corps.　For prior years, the month for which most complete records were available was used. Excludes Coast Guard]

Year	Grand total	Army			Air Force [1]			Navy			Marine Corps		
		Total	Officers	Enlisted	Total	Officers	Enlisted	Total	Officers	Enlisted	Total	Officers	Enlisted
	763	764	765	766	767	768	769	770	771	772	773	774	775
1957	2,795,798	997,994	111,187	886,807	919,835	140,563	779,272	677,108	73,703	603,405	200,861	17,434	183,427
1956	2,806,441	1,025,778	118,364	907,414	909,958	142,093	767,865	669,925	71,770	598,155	200,780	17,809	182,971
1955	2,935,107	1,109,296	121,947	987,349	959,946	137,149	822,797	660,695	74,527	586,168	205,170	18,417	186,753
1954	3,302,104	1,404,598	128,208	1,276,390	947,918	129,752	818,166	725,720	77,280	648,440	223,868	18,593	205,275
1953	3,555,067	1,533,815	145,633	1,388,182	977,593	130,769	846,824	794,440	81,731	712,709	249,219	18,731	230,488
1952	3,635,912	1,596,419	148,427	1,447,992	983,261	128,742	854,519	824,265	82,247	742,018	231,967	16,413	215,554
1951	3,249,455	1,531,774	[2] 130,540	1,401,234	788,381	107,099	681,282	736,680	70,513	666,167	192,620	15,150	177,470
1950	1,460,261	593,167	72,566	520,601	411,277	57,006	354,271	381,538	44,641	336,897	74,279	7,254	67,025
1949	1,615,360	660,473	77,272	583,201	419,347	57,851	361,496	449,575	47,975	401,600	85,965	7,250	78,715
1948	1,445,910	554,030	68,178	485,852	387,730	48,957	338,773	419,162	45,416	373,746	84,988	6,907	78,081
1947	1,582,999	991,285	132,504	858,781	----------	----------	----------	498,661	52,434	446,227	93,053	7,506	85,547
1946	3,030,088	1,891,011	267,144	1,623,867	----------	----------	----------	983,398	141,161	842,237	155,679	14,208	141,471

Year	Grand total	Army			Navy			Marine Corps		
		Total	Officers	Enlisted	Total	Officers	Enlisted	Total	Officers	Enlisted
	763	764	765	766	770	771	772	773	774	775
1945	12,123,455	8,267,958	891,663	7,376,295	3,380,817	331,379	3,049,438	474,680	37,067	437,613
1944	11,451,719	7,994,750	776,980	7,217,770	2,981,365	276,153	2,705,212	475,604	32,788	442,816
1943	9,044,745	6,994,472	579,576	6,414,896	1,741,750	179,676	1,562,074	308,523	21,384	287,139
1942	3,858,791	3,075,608	206,422	2,869,186	640,570	69,564	571,006	142,613	7,138	135,475
1941	1,801,101	1,462,315	99,536	1,362,779	284,427	29,092	255,335	54,359	3,339	51,020
1940	458,365	269,023	18,326	250,697	160,997	13,604	147,393	28,345	1,800	26,545
1939	334,473	189,839	14,486	175,353	125,202	12,023	113,179	19,432	1,380	18,052
1938	322,932	185,488	13,975	171,513	119,088	10,739	108,349	18,356	1,359	16,997
1937	311,808	179,968	13,740	166,228	113,617	10,367	103,250	18,223	1,312	16,911
1936	291,356	167,816	13,512	154,304	106,292	10,247	96,045	17,248	1,208	16,040
1935	251,799	139,486	13,471	126,015	95,053	10,115	84,938	17,260	1,163	16,097
1934	247,137	138,464	13,761	124,703	92,312	9,972	82,340	16,361	1,187	15,174
1933	243,845	136,547	13,896	122,651	91,230	9,947	81,283	16,068	1,192	14,876
1932	244,902	134,957	14,111	120,846	93,384	9,967	83,417	16,561	1,196	15,365
1931	252,605	140,516	14,159	126,357	93,307	9,849	83,458	18,782	1,196	17,586
1930	255,648	139,378	14,151	125,227	96,890	9,540	87,350	19,380	1,208	18,172
1929	255,031	139,118	14,047	125,071	97,117	9,434	87,683	18,796	1,181	17,615
1928	250,907	136,084	14,019	122,065	95,803	9,401	86,402	19,020	1,198	17,822
1927	248,943	134,829	14,020	120,809	94,916	9,440	85,476	19,198	1,198	18,000
1926	247,396	134,938	14,143	120,795	93,304	9,091	84,213	19,154	1,178	17,976
1925	251,756	137,048	14,594	122,454	95,230	8,918	86,312	19,478	1,168	18,310
1924	261,189	142,673	13,784	128,889	98,184	8,651	89,533	20,332	1,157	19,175
1923	247,011	133,243	14,021	119,222	94,094	8,410	85,684	19,674	1,141	18,533
1922	270,207	148,763	15,667	133,096	100,211	8,334	91,877	21,233	1,135	20,098
1921	386,542	230,725	16,501	214,224	132,827	9,979	122,848	22,990	1,087	21,903
1920	343,302	204,292	18,999	185,293	121,845	10,642	111,203	17,165	1,104	16,061
1919	1,172,602	851,624	91,975	759,649	272,144	19,357	252,787	48,834	2,270	46,564
1918	2,897,167	2,395,742	130,485	2,265,257	448,606	23,631	424,975	52,819	1,503	51,316
1917	643,833	421,467	34,224	387,243	194,617	8,383	186,234	27,749	776	26,973
1916	179,376	108,399	5,175	103,224	60,376	4,022	56,354	10,601	348	10,253
1915	174,112	106,754	4,948	101,806	57,072	3,593	53,479	10,286	338	9,948
1914	165,919	98,544	5,033	93,511	56,989	3,406	53,583	10,386	336	10,050
1913	154,914	92,756	4,970	87,786	52,202	3,273	48,929	9,956	331	9,625
1912	153,174	92,121	4,775	87,346	51,357	3,074	48,283	9,696	337	9,359
1911	144,846	84,006	4,585	79,421	51,230	2,886	48,344	9,610	328	9,282
1910	139,344	81,251	4,585	76,716	48,533	2,699	45,834	9,560	328	9,232
1909	142,200	84,971	4,299	80,672	47,533	2,630	44,903	9,696	328	9,368
1908	128,500	76,942	4,047	72,895	42,322	2,463	39,859	9,236	283	8,953
1907	108,375	64,170	3,896	60,274	36,119	2,238	33,881	8,086	279	7,807
1906	112,216	68,945	3,989	64,956	35,053	2,133	32,920	8,218	278	7,940
1905	108,301	67,526	4,034	63,492	33,764	2,079	31,685	7,011	270	6,741
1904	110,129	70,387	3,971	66,416	32,158	2,014	30,144	7,584	255	7,329
1903	106,043	69,595	3,927	65,668	29,790	1,893	27,897	6,658	213	6,445
1902	111,145	81,275	4,049	77,226	23,648	1,822	21,826	6,222	191	6,031
1901	112,322	85,557	3,468	82,089	20,900	1,742	19,158	5,865	171	5,694
1900	125,923	101,713	4,227	97,486	18,796	1,683	17,113	5,414	174	5,240
1899	100,166	80,670	3,581	77,089	16,354	1,588	14,766	3,142	76	3,066
1898	235,785	209,714	10,516	199,198	22,492	1,432	21,060	3,579	98	3,481
1897	43,656	27,865	2,179	25,686	11,985	1,399	10,586	3,806	71	3,735
1896	41,680	27,375	2,169	25,206	12,088	1,425	10,663	2,217	72	2,145
1895	42,226	27,495	2,154	25,341	11,846	1,412	10,434	2,885	71	2,814
1894	42,101	28,265	2,146	26,119	11,460	1,405	10,055	2,376	67	2,309
1893	39,492	27,830	2,158	25,672	9,529	1,486	8,043	2,133	63	2,070
1892	38,677	27,190	2,140	25,050	9,448	1,468	7,980	2,039	66	1,973
1891	37,868	26,463	2,052	24,411	9,247	1,510	7,737	2,158	66	2,092
1890	38,666	27,373	2,168	25,205	9,246	1,489	7,757	2,047	61	1,986
1889	39,452	27,759	2,177	25,582	9,921	1,530	8,391	1,772	54	1,718
1888	39,035	27,019	2,189	24,830	10,115	1,528	8,587	1,901	72	1,829
1887	38,763	26,719	2,200	24,519	10,113	1,542	8,571	1,931	61	1,870
1886	38,636	26,727	2,102	24,625	9,909	1,549	8,360	2,000	66	1,934
1885	39,098	27,157	2,154	25,003	10,057	1,611	8,446	1,884	65	1,819
1884	39,400	26,666	2,147	24,519	10,846	1,660	9,186	1,888	66	1,822
1883	37,278	25,652	2,143	23,509	9,842	1,819	8,023	1,784	60	1,724
1882	37,850	25,811	2,162	23,649	10,170	1,911	8,259	1,869	63	1,806
1881	37,845	25,842	2,181	23,661	10,101	1,866	8,235	1,902	70	1,832
1880	37,894	26,594	2,152	24,442	9,361	1,713	7,648	1,939	69	1,870
1879	38,022	26,601	2,127	24,474	9,453	1,695	7,758	1,968	62	1,906

See footnotes at end of table.

Series Y 763–775. Military Personnel on Active Duty: 1789 to 1957—Con.

Year	Grand total	Army			Navy			Marine Corps		
		Total	Officers	Enlisted	Total	Officers	Enlisted	Total	Officers	Enlisted
	763	764	765	766	770	771	772	773	774	775
1878	36,444	26,023	2,153	23,870	8,087	1,582	6,505	2,334	77	2,257
1877	34,094	24,140	2,177	21,963	8,057	1,591	6,466	1,897	73	1,824
1876	40,591	28,565	2,151	26,414	10,046	1,646	8,400	1,980	76	1,904
1875	38,105	25,513	2,068	23,445	10,479	1,571	8,908	2,113	76	2,037
1874	43,609	28,640	2,081	26,559	12,700	1,595	11,105	2,269	85	2,184
1873	43,228	28,812	2,076	26,736	11,654	1,655	9,999	2,762	87	2,675
1872	42,205	28,322	2,104	26,218	11,680	1,699	9,981	2,203	77	2,126
1871	42,238	29,115	2,105	27,010	10,610	1,702	8,908	2,513	74	2,439
1870	50,348	37,240	2,541	34,699	10,562	1,551	9,011	2,546	77	2,469
1869	51,632	36,953	2,700	34,253	12,295	1,649	10,646	2,384	70	2,314
1868	66,412	51,066	2,835	48,231	[3]12,268	1,976	10,292	3,078	81	2,997
1867	74,786	57,194	3,056	54,138	14,081	1,801	12,280	3,511	73	3,438
1866	76,749	57,072	[4]	[4]	16,340	2,297	14,043	3,337	79	3,258
1865	1,062,848	1,000,692	[4]	[4]	58,296	6,759	51,537	3,860	87	3,773
1864	1,031,724	970,905	[4]	[4]	57,680	5,679	52,001	3,139	64	3,075
1863	960,061	918,354	[4]	[4]	38,707	4,209	34,498	3,000	69	2,931
1862	673,124	637,264	[4]	[4]	[3]33,454	3,224	30,230	2,406	51	2,355
1861	217,112	186,845	[4]	[4]	27,881	1,114	26,767	2,386	48	2,338
1860	27,958	16,215	1,080	15,135	9,942	1,150	8,792	1,801	46	1,755
1859	28,978	17,243	1,070	16,173	9,884	1,117	8,767	1,851	47	1,804
1858	29,014	17,678	1,099	16,579	9,729	1,068	8,661	1,607	52	1,555
1857	27,345	15,918	1,097	14,821	9,676	1,031	8,645	1,751	57	1,694
1856	25,867	15,715	1,072	14,643	8,681	1,027	7,654	1,471	57	1,414
1855	26,402	15,911	1,042	14,869	8,887	1,236	7,651	1,604	52	1,552
1854	21,134	10,894	956	9,938	8,879	1,254	7,625	1,361	49	1,312
1853	20,667	10,572	961	9,611	8,841	1,250	7,591	1,254	49	1,205
1852	21,349	11,376	957	10,419	8,805	1,232	7,573	1,168	47	1,121
1851	20,699	10,714	944	9,770	8,792	1,246	7,546	1,193	43	1,150
1850	20,824	10,929	948	9,981	8,794	1,273	7,521	1,101	46	1,055
1849	23,165	10,744	945	9,799	11,345	1,282	10,063	1,076	46	1,030
1848	60,308	47,319	2,865	44,454	11,238	1,141	10,097	1,751	42	1,709
1847	57,761	44,736	[3]2,863	[3]41,873	11,193	1,126	10,067	1,832	75	1,757
1846	39,165	27,867	[3]2,003	[3]25,864	10,131	1,053	9,078	1,167	41	1,126
1845	20,726	8,509	826	7,683	11,189	1,095	10,094	1,028	42	986
1844	20,919	8,730	813	7,917	11,103	1,063	10,040	1,086	40	1,046
1843	20,741	9,102	805	8,297	[3]10,555	1,055	9,500	1,084	43	1,041
1842	22,851	10,780	781	9,999	10,782	998	9,784	1,289	46	1,243
1841	20,793	11,319	754	10,565	8,274	940	7,334	1,200	44	1,156
1840	21,616	12,330	789	11,541	8,017	932	7,085	1,269	46	1,223
1839	19,317	10,691	749	9,942	7,676	922	6,754	950	34	916
1838	17,948	9,197	717	8,480	7,656	847	6,809	1,095	28	1,067
1837	22,462	12,449	873	11,576	8,452	801	7,651	1,561	37	1,524
1836	16,874	9,945	[3]857	[3]9,088	5,588	787	4,801	1,341	43	1,298
1835	14,311	7,337	680	6,657	5,557	756	4,801	1,417	68	1,349
1834	13,396	7,030	669	6,361	5,451	695	4,756	915	46	869
1833	12,895	6,579	666	5,913	5,420	664	4,756	896	43	853
1832	12,478	6,268	659	5,609	5,312	642	4,670	898	38	860
1831	11,173	6,055	613	5,442	4,303	612	3,691	815	35	780
1830	11,942	6,122	627	5,495	4,929	615	4,314	891	37	854
1829	12,096	6,332	608	5,724	4,869	555	4,314	895	43	852
1828	11,431	5,702	540	5,162	4,797	506	4,291	932	40	892
1827	11,627	5,885	546	5,339	4,796	505	4,291	946	43	903
1826	11,586	5,989	540	5,449	4,762	471	4,291	835	39	796
1825	11,089	5,903	562	5,341	4,405	505	3,900	781	35	746
1824	11,008	5,973	532	5,441	4,095	531	3,564	940	50	890
1823	10,871	6,117	525	5,592	[3]4,053	553	3,500	701	20	681
1822	9,863	5,358	512	4,846	3,774	534	3,240	731	23	708
1821	10,587	5,773	547	5,226	3,935	484	3,451	879	35	844
1820	15,113	10,554	696	9,858	3,988	537	3,451	571	19	552
1819	13,259	8,506	705	7,801	[3]4,068	568	3,500	685	21	664
1818	14,260	8,155	697	7,458	[3]5,545	545	5,000	560	24	536
1817	14,606	8,446	647	7,799	[3]5,494	494	5,000	666	14	652
1816	16,743	10,231	735	9,496	[3]6,040	500	5,540	472	21	451
1815	40,885	33,424	2,272	31,152	6,773	531	6,242	688	8	680
1814	46,858	38,186	2,271	35,915	[3]8,024	524	7,500	648	11	637
1813	25,152	19,036	1,476	17,560	[3]5,525	525	5,000	591	12	579
1812	12,631	6,686	299	6,387	5,452	442	5,010	493	10	483
1811	11,528	5,608	396	5,212	5,364	454	4,910	556	14	542
1810	11,554	5,956	441	5,515	[3]5,149	450	4,699	449	9	440
1809	12,375	6,977	533	6,444	[3]4,875	450	4,425	523	10	513
1808	8,200	5,712	327	5,385	1,616	191	1,425	872	11	861
1807	5,523	2,775	146	2,629	2,145	191	1,954	403	11	392
1806	4,076	2,653	142	2,511	1,105	191	914	318	11	307
1805	6,498	2,729	159	2,570	[3]3,191	191	3,000	578	22	556
1804	5,323	2,734	216	2,518	[3]2,200	200	2,000	389	25	364
1803	4,528	2,486	174	2,312	[3]1,700	200	1,500	342	25	317
1802	5,432	2,873	175	2,698	[3]2,200	200	2,000	359	29	330
1801	7,108	4,051	248	3,803	[3]2,700	200	2,500	357	38	319
1800	[4]	[4]	[4]	[4]	[3]5,400	400	5,000	525	38	487
1799	[4]	[4]	[4]	[4]	[3]2,200	200	2,000	368	25	343
1798	[4]	[4]	[4]	[4]	[3]1,856	150	1,706	83	25	58
1795	5,296	3,440	212	3,228	[3]1,856	150	1,706	---	---	---
1794	5,669	3,813	[3]235	3,578	[3]1,856	150	1,706	---	---	---
1789	718	718	46	672	---	---	---	---	---	---

[1] Included with Army prior to 1948. Includes Army personnel assigned to Air Force Command. See text.
[2] Includes 178 Navy medical officers on duty with the Army.
[3] Estimated.
[4] Not available.

Series Y 776–786. Estimated Number of Veterans in Civil Life, by War: 1865 to 1955

[In thousands. As of June 30]

Year	Total, all wars	War of 1812	Mexican War	Indian wars [1]	Civil War	Spanish-American War	World War I	World War II [2]	Korean conflict — Total	Korean conflict — Without World War II service	Regular Establishment [3]
	776	777	778	779	780	781	782	783	784	785	786
1955	21,861			[4]	[4]	72	3,150	15,405	3,999	3,171	63
1950	19,076			[4]	[4]	118	3,518	15,386			54
1945	6,498			1	[4]	164	3,821	2,469			43
1940	4,286			2	2	206	4,040				36
1935	4,494			4	13	244	4,201				32
1930	4,680			5	49	274	4,336				16
1925	4,894		[4]	4	127	298	4,453				12
1920	5,146		[4]	4	244	317	4,566				15
1915	773		1	1	424	332					15
1910	977		2	2	624	349					
1905	1,192		5	2	821	364					
1900	1,224		9	1	1,000	214					
1895	1,187		14	3	1,170						
1890	1,341	[4]	19		1,322						
1885	1,475	3	23		1,449						
1880	1,593	10	26		1,557						
1875	1,698	16	28		1,654						
1870	1,802	28	30		1,744						
1865	1,908	46	32		1,830						

[1] Includes only veterans on the benefit rolls of the Veterans Administration or predecessor agencies.
[2] Includes veterans who served both in World War II and the Korean conflict.
[3] Includes only former members of Regular Establishment (peacetime) receiving disability compensation from the Veterans Administration or predecessor agencies.
[4] Less than 500.

Series Y 787–800. Estimated Number of Veterans in Civil Life, by Age: 1865 to 1955

In thousands. As of June 30. Includes all veterans of the Korean conflict, World War II, World War I, Spanish-American War, Civil War, Mexican War, and War of 1812, as well as those veterans of the Indian wars and former members of the Regular Establishment (peacetime) who were on the benefit rolls of Veterans Administration or predecessor agencies. Veterans who served in 2 or more wars prior to the Korean conflict are included 2 or more times; veterans who served in both World War II and the Korean conflict are included only once]

Year	Total, all ages	Under 20 years	20 to 24 years	25 to 29 years	30 to 34 years	35 to 39 years	40 to 44 years	45 to 49 years	50 to 54 years	55 to 59 years	60 to 64 years	65 to 69 years	70 years and over	Unknown
	787	788	789	790	791	792	793	794	795	796	797	798	799	800
1955	21,861	22	1,397	3,870	5,144	4,094	2,155	1,265	445	1,288	1,483	555	143	
1950	19,076	1	2,194	5,024	4,064	2,153	1,279	458	1,390	1,655	652	70	136	
1945	6,498	28	637	740	497	380	130	1,295	1,764	718	77	111	77	44
1940	4,286					16	1,287	1,848	773	86	131	72	35	38
1935	4,494				16	1,323	1,917	815	93	149	86	31	28	36
1930	4,680			17	1,356	1,974	849	98	162	97	37	13	56	21
1925	4,894		17	1,386	2,026	877	103	172	105	41	15	6	130	16
1920	5,146	17	1,416	2,075	903	107	180	112	44	18	7	3	245	19
1915	773			[1]	19	145	100	40	16	8	8	3	417	17
1910	977		[1]	20	150	105	42	17	8	4	11	380	238	2
1905	1,192	[1]	21	156	109	44	18	9	4	13	458	208	150	2
1900	1,224	12	91	64	26	11	5	3	14	521	251	121	104	1
1895	1,187							13	578	289	148	85	71	3
1890	1,341						14	628	321	171	105	67	35	
1885	1,475					15	670	347	189	121	82	44	7	
1880	1,593				16	710	370	203	133	93	53	5		10
1875	1,698			17	748	390	216	142	103	59	7	[1]		16
1870	1,802		17	784	411	228	152	109	65	8	[1]	[1]		28
1865	1,908	18	820	430	239	159	116	70	9	1	[1]		9	37

[1] Less than 500.

Series Y 801–811. Expenditures of Veterans Administration and Predecessor Agencies From Appropriated Funds, by War: 1790 to 1957

[In thousands of dollars. For years ending June 30]

Year	Total, all wars 801	War of 1812 802	Mexican War 803	Indian wars 804	Civil War 805	Spanish-American War 806	World War I 807	World War II 808	Korean conflict 809	Regular Establishment 810	Undistributed and other 811
Total	88,820,062 [1]	48,747 [2]	64,272 [3]	118,072	8,544,456 [4]	4,254,226	21,638,567	48,811,950	4,109,250	1,143,688	16,789 [5]
1957	4,884,506	---	3	863	2,839	137,279	1,349,830	2,059,223	1,231,723	102,742	4
1956	4,801,885	---	4	983	3,257	145,738	1,284,202	2,135,904	1,140,840	90,955	2
1955	4,483,137	---	5	1,101	3,697	152,663	1,188,768	2,137,246	914,123	85,532	2
1954	4,282,592	---	5	1,192	4,112	164,889	1,067,701	2,416,000	548,801	79,891	1
1953	4,354,220	---	8	1,326	4,739	163,000	1,019,190	2,869,785	216,054	80,116	2
1952	4,944,187	---	11	1,348	5,168	160,434	903,432	3,747,014	53,706	73,070	4
1951	5,356,639	---	13	1,532	6,974	164,525	851,288	4,255,015	4,003	73,284	5
1950	6,627,657	---	14	1,719	6,864	168,449	793,337	5,593,899	---	63,369	6
1949	6,660,350	---	17	1,920	7,938	174,787	717,947	5,705,569	---	52,166	6
1948	6,497,681	---	23	1,971	9,081	175,716	647,393	5,624,766	---	38,725	6
1947	7,470,600	---	26	2,008	9,104	153,191	573,034	6,696,915	---	36,316	6
1946	4,425,001	(6)	27	2,169	10,513	145,783	444,965	3,794,869	---	26,667	8
1945	2,084,668	(6)	31	2,348	12,007	148,109	400,440	1,494,977	---	26,747	9
1944	743,596	(6)	39	2,324	14,070	132,116	355,691	213,346	---	25,999	11
1943	605,693	(6)	50	2,517	16,776	130,189	375,435	54,327	---	26,385	14
1942	556,198	(6)	55	2,782	19,791	132,593	370,162	7,851	---	22,949	15
1941	553,013	(6)	66	3,025	23,504	133,744	366,260	5,244	---	21,155	15
1940	557,690	(6)	85	3,313	28,255	134,166	372,522	---	---	19,334	15
1939	555,175	(6)	103	3,554	33,615	131,774	371,627	---	---	14,487	15
1938	581,923	1	117	3,671	39,791	125,160	398,895	---	---	14,273	15
1937	579,352	1	133	3,664	47,292	121,591	392,619	---	---	14,036	16
1936	580,249	1	155	3,911	56,340	116,189	391,916	---	---	11,720	17
1935	556,857	3	181	4,013	64,400	83,413	393,314	---	---	11,515	18
1934	496,215	3	199	3,887	70,797	61,415	350,201	---	---	9,695	18
1933	780,758	4	286	5,039	99,204	131,328	537,434	---	---	7,437	26
1932	789,251	4	327	4,865	109,315	122,829	544,910	---	---	6,977	24
1931	714,022	5	347	4,797	123,400	110,375	468,926	---	---	6,172	---
1930	639,213	6	397	4,786	127,458	91,700	409,307	---	---	5,559	---
1929	631,248	7	475	4,646	145,301	84,230	391,305	---	---	5,284	---
1928	625,144	9	547	4,123	151,718	77,476	386,452	---	---	4,819	---
1927	618,791	10	572	2,141	169,124	63,338	379,084	---	---	4,522	---
1926	628,271	7	438	1,951	174,645	35,806	411,088	---	---	4,336	---

Year	Total, all wars [7] 801	War of 1812 802	Mexican War 803	Indian wars 804	Civil War 805	Spanish-American War 806	World War I 807	Regular Establishment 810	Undistributed and other 811
1925	607,246	9	511	2,011	190,003	29,929	380,780	4,003	---
1924	647,283	13	585	1,970	207,148	25,197	408,400	3,970	---
1923	737,000	18	724	1,964	243,965	21,071	465,051	4,207	---
1922	736,731	20	781	1,844	241,662	18,933	474,415	4,076	---
1921	652,157	24	894	1,614	252,792	8,046	384,582	4,205	---
1920	494,183	21	683	1,784	207,948	5,748	273,806	4,193	---
1919	499,311	18	765	1,594	217,640	4,813	270,236	4,245	---
1918	260,898	21	892	971	176,653	5,379	72,622	4,360	---
1917	169,264	19	852	428	159,237	4,948	---	3,780	---
1916	167,393	19	815	488	157,447	4,887	---	3,737	---
1915	173,729	23	939	526	163,778	4,821	---	3,642	---
1914	180,866	28	1,077	575	170,928	4,663	---	3,586	9
1913	183,138	33	1,207	545	173,038	4,735	---	3,569	11
1912	162,125	38	1,191	538	152,355	4,585	---	3,418	---
1911	166,448	45	1,348	592	156,651	4,508	---	3,302	2
1910	169,492	52	1,492	640	159,861	4,343	---	3,102	---
1909	171,458	64	1,647	659	161,747	4,279	---	2,972	---
1908	162,398	70	1,512	553	153,267	4,009	---	2,853	---
1907	147,482	86	1,381	587	138,808	3,770	---	2,727	---
1906	148,421	103	1,423	650	139,767	3,726	---	2,614	---
1905	150,851	117	1,572	686	142,191	3,667	---	2,512	---
1904	150,716	144	1,739	778	142,248	3,318	---	2,376	---
1903	147,079	165	1,687	447	142,295	2,369	---	3	---
1902	146,575	188	1,729	435	142,253	1,865	---	2	---
1901	147,275	216	1,788	488	143,409	1,247	---	(6)	---
1900	146,887	255	1,893	545	143,726	344	---	---	---
1899	146,822	301	2,014	601	143,775	31	---	---	---
1898	152,814	357	2,150	644	149,559	---	---	---	---
1897	147,903	400	2,190	707	144,455	---	---	---	---
1896	145,789	471	2,277	777	142,093	---	---	---	---

Year or period	Total, all wars [7] 801	War of 1812 802	Mexican War 803	Indian wars 804	Civil War 805
1895	147,606	561	2,340	820	143,821
1894	147,408	668	2,291	871	143,366
1893	165,315	758	2,257	251	161,783
1892	147,784	876	2,254	---	144,295
1891	125,351	1,115	2,499	---	121,284
1890	112,647	1,359	2,598	---	---
1889	95,066	1,521	2,672	---	---
1888	84,512	1,755	2,624	---	---
1887	79,451	1,984	142	---	---
1886	68,931	1,727	---	---	---
1885	70,196	1,911	---	---	---
1884	62,184	2,157	---	---	---
1883	64,361	2,448	---	---	---
1882	56,882	2,656	---	---	---
1881	52,771	3,135	---	---	---
1880	58,585	3,573	---	---	---
1879	35,526	3,317	---	---	---
1878	28,764	1,128	---	---	---
1877	30,145	1,373	---	---	---
1876	29,887	1,622	---	---	---
1875	31,106	1,981	---	---	---
1874	31,908	2,305	---	---	---
1873	28,681	2,875	---	---	---
1872	31,454	2,411	---	---	---
1871	30,081	---	---	---	---
1870	30,543	---	---	---	---
1869	29,658	---	---	---	---
1868	24,164	---	---	---	---
1867	21,276	---	---	---	---
1866	15,858	---	---	---	---
1790–1865	96,445	---	---	---	---

[1] Includes $70,045,000 for the Revolutionary War spent prior to 1911.
[2] Includes $132,000 spent prior to 1872, not shown by year.
[3] Includes $78,000 spent prior to 1887, not shown by year.
[4] Includes $1,168,119,000 spent prior to 1891, not shown by year.
[5] Includes $16,487,000 spent prior to 1911, not shown by year.
[6] Less than $500.
[7] Amounts in footnotes 1 to 5, which affect years prior to 1911, are not shown annually by war but are distributed by years in this column.

Series Y 812–825. Expenditures for Veterans Benefits and Services by Veterans Administration and Predecessor Agencies: 1790 to 1957

[In thousands of dollars. For years ending June 30]

Year	Total expenditures	Compensation and pensions	Insurance and servicemen's indemnities [1]	Readjustment benefits — Education and training	Readjustment benefits — Vocational rehabilitation	Readjustment benefits — Unemployment and self-employment allowances	Loan guaranty	Direct loans	Miscellaneous benefit payments	Medical, hospital, and domiciliary services	Hospital and domiciliary facilities	Administration and other benefits	Expenditures from general and special fund appropriations — Total	Transfers to insurance trust funds
	812	813	814	815	816	817	818	819	820	821	822	823	824	825
Total	[2]99,354,257	42,515,015	13,241,159	16,964,187	2,344,257	3,804,872	651,749	717,140	5,135,504	9,026,212	1,095,177	3,860,772	88,820,062	4,832,104
1957	[2]5,553,871	2,828,516	696,646	776,277	30,598	5	60,125	130,219	58,915	768,076	36,342	168,799	4,884,506	19,993
1956	[2]5,402,035	2,748,989	686,013	766,900	38,134	[3]2	40,062	103,118	55,726	760,409	26,882	176,944	4,801,885	79,041
1955	5,170,768	2,634,293	724,069	664,514	40,770	[3]200	28,881	125,126	51,000	696,750	32,510	173,105	4,483,137	31,160
1954	5,075,185	2,450,518	869,579	544,119	41,294	[3]245	44,640	117,709	51,537	712,828	51,043	192,163	4,282,592	73,477
1953	5,013,733	2,376,307	737,575	667,802	57,768	[3]516	65,843	92,760	63,809	662,858	88,183	201,344	4,354,220	84,725
1952	5,869,841	2,105,973	1,110,193	1,325,403	97,902	76	78,355	87,276	53,267	662,683	113,011	235,702	4,944,187	204,644
1951	5,953,879	2,035,988	607,104	1,943,341	176,875	8,378	90,108	60,932	62,530	594,084	103,878	270,661	5,356,639	44,555
1950	9,278,335	2,009,462	3,108,957	2,595,728	272,292	138,191	58,671	....	41,222	592,082	151,532	310,198	6,627,657	474,648
1949	6,987,596	1,891,283	401,454	2,703,862	335,200	509,592	40,038	....	40,700	574,178	124,025	367,264	6,660,350	89,154
1948	7,040,503	1,820,685	[4]676,932	2,497,986	333,313	677,256	64,354	....	39,780	519,722	16,980	393,495	6,497,681	144,458
1947	6,972,077	1,731,973	328,211	2,118,735	221,147	1,447,916	75,493	....	44,409	415,813	153,880	434,500	7,470,600	833,278
1946	3,382,777	1,215,688	340,594	350,019	45,087	1,000,909	5,229	....	18,007	213,816	34,313	159,115	4,425,001	1,389,296
1945	1,140,829	732,535	175,935	9,501	8,348	23,512	....	....	21,744	101,611	15,801	51,842	2,084,668	1,130,490
1944	723,445	494,364	86,392	....	659	[3]3	....	....	10,077	98,041	4,851	29,061	743,596	104,947
1943	619,764	442,360	55,508	....	[3]3		....	....	8,063	86,623	2,720	24,493	605,693	36,492
1942	642,917	431,284	56,516	....	[3]4		....	....	49,974	81,973	4,046	19,128	556,198	4,813
1941	612,721	433,114	69,588	....	[3]4		....	....	9,626	78,458	4,541	17,398	553,013	1,636
1940	637,611	429,138	87,899	....	[3]3		....	....	15,690	74,497	13,468	16,752	557,690	1,516
1939	597,461	416,704	70,965	....	[3]2		....	....	14,045	69,651	10,958	15,140	555,175	2,760
1938	627,399	402,769	111,727	....	[3]1		....	....	20,757	66,626	9,347	16,174	581,923	2,431
1937	891,426	396,030	114,880	....	[3]9		....	....	289,957	64,154	8,964	17,450	579,352	2,568
1936	3,835,661	398,992	118,862	....	[3]6		....	....	3,234,247	62,481	2,938	18,147	580,249	3,459
1935	605,686	374,407	123,297	....	[3]9		....	....	29,802	57,047	2,903	18,239	556,857	4,230
1934	540,991	321,377	124,494	....	[3]7		....	....	28,065	45,962	3,170	17,930	496,215	4,847
1933	827,825	550,559	145,426	....	[3]16		....	....	27,034	65,435	13,517	25,870	780,758	5,674
1932	835,357	545,777	146,397	....	[3]17		....	....	25,958	75,020	12,876	29,346	789,251	6,080
1931	752,816	488,389	137,325	....	[3]22		....	....	21,862	68,591	9,040	27,631	714,022	6,551
1930	675,788	418,433	139,212	....	[3]20		....	....	23,263	60,426	8,241	26,233	639,213	8,235
1929	665,342	418,821	135,704	....	[3]3		....	....	26,191	54,682	4,044	25,903	631,248	7,946
1928	652,712	410,765	131,277	....	234		....	....	27,189	53,121	5,222	24,904	625,144	7,158
1927	640,549	403,630	128,415	....	2,206		....	....	24,180	53,235	4,599	24,284	618,791	4,413
1926	649,143	372,281	142,507	....	25,840		....	....	20,927	53,113	4,511	29,964	628,271	4,350
1925	617,486	346,748	109,762	....	60,486		....	....	7,657	55,024	3,895	33,914	607,246	3,336
1924	652,101	345,490	106,036	....	106,962		....	....	17	48,422	9,215	35,959	647,283	2,685
1923	740,783	388,607	103,334	....	149,433		....	....	[3]264	59,262	2,644	37,767	737,000	2,785
1922	740,624	377,158	104,801	....	166,051		....	....	5,231	77,062	917	9,404	736,731	4,273
1921	664,538	380,026	96,961	....	99,065		....	....	23,831	53,128	....	11,527	652,157	....
1920	514,980	316,418	85,974	....	34,652		....	....	54,084	5,829	....	18,023	494,183	....
1919	701,131	233,461	43,798	....	67		....	....	400,589	5,512	....	17,704	499,311	....
1918	327,100	180,177	840	....			....	....	134,806	6,920	....	4,357	260,898	....

Year	Expenditures from general and special fund appropriations and trust, deposit, and working funds — Total expenditure	Compensation and pensions	Medical, hospital, and domiciliary services	Administration and other benefits	Expenditures from general and special fund appropriations	Year or period	Total expenditure	Compensation and pensions	Medical, hospital, and domiciliary services	Administration and other benefits	Expenditures from general and special fund appropriations
	812	813	821	823	824		812	813	821	823	824
1917	169,264	160,895	6,806	1,563	169,264	1890	112,647	106,094	3,027	3,526	112,647
1916	167,393	159,155	6,581	1,657	167,393	1889	95,066	88,843	2,756	3,467	95,066
1915	173,729	165,518	6,431	1,780	173,729	1888	84,512	78,951	2,046	3,515	84,512
1914	180,866	172,418	6,382	2,066	180,866	1887	79,451	73,753	1,945	3,753	79,451
1913	183,138	174,172	6,423	2,543	183,138	1886	68,931	64,091	1,595	3,245	68,931
1912	162,125	152,986	6,690	2,449	162,125						
1911	166,448	157,325	6,606	2,517	166,448	1885	70,196	65,172	1,631	3,393	70,196
						1884	62,184	57,912	1,437	2,835	62,184
1910	169,492	159,974	6,860	2,658	169,492	1883	64,361	60,428	1,341	2,592	64,361
1909	171,458	161,974	6,632	2,852	171,458	1882	56,882	54,313	1,103	1,466	56,882
1908	162,398	153,093	6,504	2,801	162,398	1881	52,771	50,583	1,116	1,072	52,771
1907	147,482	138,155	6,018	3,309	147,482						
1906	148,421	139,000	5,897	3,524	148,421	1880	58,585	56,689	961	935	58,585
						1879	35,526	33,664	1,024	838	35,526
1905	150,851	141,143	5,986	3,722	150,851	1878	28,764	26,786	945	1,033	28,764
1904	150,716	141,094	5,773	3,849	150,716	1877	30,145	28,183	928	1,034	30,145
1903	147,079	137,760	5,326	3,993	147,079	1876	29,887	27,936	936	1,015	29,887
1902	146,575	137,504	5,240	3,831	146,575						
1901	147,275	138,531	4,875	3,869	147,275	1875	31,106	29,270	853	983	31,106
						1874	31,908	30,207	734	967	31,908
1900	146,887	138,462	4,583	3,842	146,887	1873	28,681	26,982	695	1,004	28,681
1899	146,822	138,355	4,320	4,147	146,822	1872	31,454	29,753	750	951	31,454
1898	152,814	144,652	4,048	4,114	152,814	1871	30,081	28,519	699	863	30,081
1897	147,903	139,950	3,965	3,988	147,903						
1896	145,789	138,221	3,577	3,991	145,789	1870	30,543	29,351	591	601	30,543
						1869	29,658	28,513	580	565	29,658
1895	147,606	139,812	3,456	4,338	147,606	1868	24,164	23,102	509	553	24,164
1894	147,408	139,987	3,457	3,964	147,408	1867	21,276	20,785	....	491	21,276
1893	165,315	156,907	3,540	4,868	165,315	1866	15,858	15,451	....	407	15,858
1892	147,784	139,394	3,491	4,899	147,784						
1891	125,351	117,313	3,338	4,700	125,351	1790–1865	96,445	96,445	....	....	96,445

[1] Largely includes payments from trust accounts.
[2] Detail does not add to total because of adjustments for overpayments collected and items written off as uncollectible under the readjustment benefits program. These amounted to $1,140,000 in 1956 and $647,000 in 1957.　　[3] Credit.　　[4] Includes adjustments for prior years; see text.

Series Y 826–837. Veterans Pensions and Compensation—Number of Veterans and Expenditure, by Type: 1866 to 1957

[For years ending June 30]

Year	Number of veterans [1] (1,000)						Expenditure ($1,000,000)					
	Total		Pensions		Compensation		Total		Pensions		Compensation	
	Death	Disability	Death	Disability	Death	Disability	Death	Disability	Death	Disability	Death	Disability
	826	827	828	829	830	831	832	833	834	835	836	837
1957	863	2,797	478	720	385	2,076	729	2,100	295	657	434	1,443
1956	837	2,739	454	654	383	2,085	694	2,055	281	604	413	1,451
1955	808	2,669	426	832	382	1,837	664	1,970	265	538	400	1,432
1954	778	2,590	403	533	375	2,057	612	1,838	243	475	369	1,364
1953	748	2,506	379	485	369	2,021	608	1,768	231	431	377	1,337
1952	707	2,418	353	437	353	1,981	538	1,568	195	364	343	1,204
1951	683	2,374	339	394	343	1,980	501	1,535	190	330	311	1,205
1950	658	2,368	322	345	336	2,023	485	1,524	181	295	304	1,229
1949	636	2,314	302	290	334	2,024	457	1,434	171	253	286	1,181
1948	603	2,315	279	249	324	2,066	385	1,436	152	234	233	1,201
1947	566	2,354	253	233	314	2,121	367	1,365	138	194	229	1,171
1946	502	2,130	227	219	275	1,911	305	910	108	167	198	744
1945	369	1,144	177	220	193	924	185	547	69	166	116	381
1944	253	813	124	221	129	593	126	368	50	80	76	288
1943	239	622	127	227	112	395	113	330	52	139	61	190
1942	236	624	129	231	107	392	111	320	53	132	58	188
1941	238	619	130	229	108	390	113	320	54	132	59	188
1940	239	610	130	224	110	386	115	314	55	130	60	184
1939	240	603	130	225	109	378	109	308	55	129	54	179
1938	236	601	132	225	104	375	101	301	56	126	45	176
1937	243	599	136	227	107	371	96	300	60	121	37	179
1936	251	601	144	230	107	371	100	299	63	119	37	180
1935	253	586	146	215	107	371	96	278	61	96	35	182
1934	258	581	153	218	105	363	94	228	59	80	34	148
1933	273	998	169	636	103	362	122	428	85	228	37	200
1932	284	994	182	641	102	354	124	421	87	215	38	206
1931	289	791	192	468	97	323	124	365	91	168	32	197
1930	298	543	203	241	95	301	128	290	94	120	34	170
1929	306	526	215	245	91	281	132	287	100	126	32	162
1928	318	517	229	245	89	271	124	287	92	132	32	154
1927	327	490	240	233	86	257	126	278	96	131	30	147
1926	334	473	252	233	83	240	125	247	93	111	32	136
1925	334	457	264	232	70	224	124	223	97	117	26	107
1924	335	427	274	236	62	191	122	223	102	125	20	99
1923	341	437	282	241	59	196	133	256	113	146	20	110
1922	341	431	286	244	55	187	124	253	106	144	17	109
1921	346	423	294	254	52	169	127	253	108	147	19	106
1920	350	420	302	271	48	149	115	201	93	117	22	85
1919	336	338	307	299	29	40	101	133	95	124	6	9
1918	308	342	302	325	6	16	81	99	80	97	1	3
1917	303	370	298	354	5	16	55	106	54	103	1	3
1916	306	403	302	388	5	16	46	113	45	110	1	3
1915	310	438	306	422	4	15	47	119	46	116	1	3
1914	315	471	310	456	4	15	47	125	46	123	1	3
1913	317	504	312	489	4	15	47	127	46	124	1	3
1912	322	538	318	524	4	14	48	105	47	103	1	2
1911	322	570	317	557	4	14	48	109	47	107	1	2
1910	318	603	314	589	4	13	48	112	47	110	1	2
1909	314	633	310	620	4	12	47	115	46	113	1	2
1908	293	659	289	647	4	12	35	118	34	116	1	2
1907	287	680	283	669	4	11	35	104	34	102	1	2
1906	284	701	281	691	4	11	35	104	34	103	1	2
1905	281	718	277	708	3	10	35	106	34	104	1	2
1904	274	721	271	711	3	10	35	106	34	104	1	2

Year	Number of veterans [1] (1,000)		Expenditure ($1,000,000)	
	Death	Disability	Death	Disability
	826	827	832	833
1903	267	729	34	104
1902	260	739	33	104
1901	249	749	32	106
1900	241	753	31	107
1899	237	754	32	107
1898	235	759	35	110
1897	229	747	34	106
1896	222	749	32	106
1895	219	751	32	108
1894	215	754	33	107
1893	206	760	37	120
1892	173	703	31	109
1891	139	537	31	86

Year	Number of veterans [1] (1,000)	Expenditure ($1,000,000)
	826–827	832–833
1890	538	106
1889	490	89
1888	453	79
1887	406	74
1886	366	64
1885	345	65
1884	323	58
1883	304	60
1882	286	54
1881	269	51
1880	251	57
1879	243	34
1878	224	27

Year	Number of veterans [1] (1,000)	Expenditure ($1,000,000)
	826–827	832–833
1877	232	28
1876	232	28
1875	235	29
1874	236	30
1873	238	27
1872	232	30
1871	207	29
1870	199	29
1869	188	29
1868	170	23
1867	155	21
1866	127	15

[1] Series Y 826, 828, and 830 represent the number of deceased veterans whose dependents were receiving pension or compensation. Series Y 827, 829, and 831 represent the number of living veterans who were receiving pension, compensation, disability allowance, or retirement pay.

Series Y 838–850.　Patients Receiving Hospital or Domiciliary Care Authorized by Veterans Administration: 1921 to 1957

[1921-1954, as of June 30; thereafter, as of May 31.　Includes beneficiaries cared for in Army, Navy, and other Federal, and State and civil (contract) hospitals]

Year	Patients receiving hospital care						Veterans with service-connected disabilities receiving hospital care				Veterans receiving domiciliary care		
	Total	Veterans				Non-veterans	Total	Tuber-culosis	Neuro-psychi-atric	General	Total	Veterans Adminis-tration	State [1]
		Total	Tuber-culosis	Neuro-psychi-atric	General								
	838	839	840	841	842	843	844	845	846	847	848	849	850
1957	110,715	110,247	12,224	61,550	36,473	468	39,063	3,138	32,083	3,842	25,329	[2]16,391	8,938
1956	112,660	112,131	13,595	61,703	36,833	529	40,195	3,769	32,536	3,890	25,162	[2]16,423	8,739
1955	110,257	109,649	14,836	59,349	35,464	608	41,078	4,576	32,312	4,190	25,660	[2]16,858	8,802
1954	108,357	107,509	[3]15,636	[3]54,916	[3]36,957	848	40,711	[3]5,150	[3]30,106	[3]5,455	25,226	16,880	8,346
1953	102,323	101,470	[3]15,292	[3]52,559	[3]33,619	853	39,092	[3]5,638	[3]28,502	[3]4,952	24,745	16,629	8,116
1952	103,774	102,974	15,362	53,570	34,042	800	36,182	5,917	26,564	3,701	24,635	16,710	7,925
1951	100,517	99,800	14,825	52,987	31,988	717	35,597	6,253	25,397	3,947	24,108	16,279	7,829
1950	102,303	101,862	14,361	54,419	33,082	441	34,596	5,323	25,347	3,926	24,131	16,694	7,437
1949	107,073	106,685	14,810	55,150	36,725	388	35,919	6,242	24,755	4,922	22,967	16,267	6,700
1948	103,576	103,263	13,045	54,790	35,428	313	34,872	6,158	23,478	5,236	20,425	14,275	6,150
1947	104,443	104,176	12,436	53,913	37,827	267	35,525	6,408	22,854	6,263	19,058	13,458	5,600
1946	87,257	86,998	8,475	48,687	29,836	259	28,806	3,921	20,282	4,603	15,963	11,320	4,643
1945	70,246	69,965	6,864	44,078	19,023	281	23,375	3,219	18,072	2,084	13,029	8,870	4,159
1944	63,890	63,581	6,314	40,076	17,191	309	18,476	2,398	14,608	1,470	13,052	8,647	4,405
1943	56,850	56,597	5,149	36,345	15,103	253	14,580	1,491	12,312	777	13,967	9,069	4,898
1942	56,103	55,847	5,090	34,596	16,161	256	13,324	1,185	11,393	746	17,236	11,506	5,730
1941	58,241	57,988	4,758	34,257	18,973	253	12,825	849	11,098	878	19,892	13,926	5,966
1940	56,450	56,216	4,848	32,882	18,486	234	12,670	873	10,826	971	22,456	16,238	6,218
1939	53,745	53,472	5,041	31,080	17,351	273	12,534	1,013	10,383	1,138	21,175	15,197	5,978
1938	50,640	50,385	5,062	29,299	16,024	255	12,394	1,045	10,209	1,140	19,728	14,106	5,622
1937	46,235	45,935	4,987	26,246	14,702	300	12,182	1,133	9,956	1,093	15,962	11,030	4,932
1936	41,251	40,899	4,553	24,025	12,321	352	11,906	1,123	9,818	965	12,337	7,604	4,733
1935	41,728	41,316	5,283	22,781	13,252	412	12,168	1,340	9,669	1,159	14,694	10,534	4,160
1934	38,733	38,026	5,283	21,475	11,268	707	11,451	1,145	9,241	1,065	13,761	9,404	4,357
1933	33,844	33,518	5,804	19,791	7,923	326	13,925	1,574	11,056	1,295	17,205	11,187	6,018
1932	43,469	43,334	6,985	19,528	16,821	135	15,199	1,991	11,414	1,794	(4)	--------	--------
1931	35,145	35,055	6,560	16,936	11,559	90	15,773	2,616	11,342	1,815	(4)	--------	--------
1930	30,556	30,447	6,733	15,035	8,679	109	16,418	3,278	11,170	1,970	(4)	--------	--------
1929	27,897	27,784	6,547	13,781	7,456	113	16,024	3,399	10,777	1,848	(4)	--------	--------
1928	26,257	26,139	6,542	13,057	6,540	118	16,597	3,802	10,809	1,986	(4)	--------	--------
1927	25,440	25,318	6,956	12,748	5,614	122	18,087	4,818	10,988	2,281	(4)	--------	--------
1926	25,965	25,858	7,863	12,902	5,093	107	20,811	6,576	11,438	2,797	(4)	--------	--------
1925	27,218	27,071	9,792	12,224	5,055	147	23,266	8,848	11,038	3,380	(4)	--------	--------
1924	22,978	22,726	8,831	9,875	4,020	252	22,726	8,831	9,875	4,020	(4)	--------	--------
1923	23,805	23,604	9,886	9,403	4,315	201	23,604	9,886	9,403	4,315	(4)	--------	--------
1922	27,240	26,869	10,849	9,231	6,789	371	26,869	10,849	9,231	6,789	(4)	--------	--------
1921	26,237	26,237	10,337	7,499	8,401	--------	26,237	10,337	7,499	8,401	(4)	--------	--------

[1] Average daily number.
[2] Data are for June 30.
[3] Estimated.
[4] Not available.

Series Y 851–854.　Government Life Insurance Administered by Veterans Administration—Number of Policies, Income Received, and Benefits Paid: 1921 to 1957

[As of June 30]

Year	Policies in force		Income received	Benefits paid	Year	Policies in force		Income received	Benefits paid
	Number	Face value				Number	Face value		
	851	852	853	854		851	852	853	854
		1,000 dol.	*1,000 dol.*	*1,000 dol.*			*1,000 dol.*	*1,000 dol.*	*1,000 dol.*
1957	6,565,985	44,202,158	(1)	(1)	1939	606,071	2,562,354	130,808	97,397
1956	6,442,956	42,890,932	758,047	649,903	1938	602,963	2,569,893	159,772	99,481
					1937	596,982	2,578,339	185,251	120,396
1955	6,449,437	42,623,425	810,683	662,750	1936	593,213	2,590,922	193,146	123,785
1954	6,530,816	42,802,077	784,615	755,058					
1953	7,003,942	46,706,290	797,789	804,819	1935	590,865	2,605,400	193,617	130,670
1952	7,538,729	50,837,910	838,360	822,818	1934	598,266	2,666,733	196,844	141,810
1951	7,625,694	51,559,594	896,129	1,026,661	1933	616,069	2,782,709	208,826	149,112
					1932	641,247	2,977,330	216,342	158,712
1950	6,113,308	37,972,928	814,455	3,144,507	1931	646,055	3,024,445	210,865	148,982
1949	6,038,865	37,952,323	1,128,508	450,525					
1948	6,291,263	38,065,025	783,577	376,281	1930	648,248	3,042,743	208,080	142,870
1947	6,380,103	37,535,634	1,347,322	383,374	1929	650,066	3,059,919	206,157	141,523
1946	9,814,873	67,514,994	2,280,700	369,715	1928	660,374	3,113,649	204,143	136,978
					1927	587,980	2,893,045	196,352	130,536
1945	16,512,099	126,034,439	2,412,815	287,219	1926	553,660	2,781,587	185,682	136,784
1944	15,068,150	110,707,707	1,263,124	124,864					
1943	9,394,598	63,304,655	693,624	76,414	1925	552,340	2,865,029	167,735	127,005
1942	3,217,499	16,986,809	263,188	66,176	1924	562,000	2,984,573	142,936	109,103
1941	972,860	3,847,972	121,498	71,816	1923	560,065	3,070,210	137,521	105,218
					1922	581,778	3,348,400	131,865	104,363
1940	609,094	2,565,327	116,159	91,989	1921	651,054	3,849,376	115,109	101,410

[1] Not available.

Colonial Statistics

Z 1–405. General note.

It would have been possible to distribute these series for the colonial period among the chapters covering each of the appropriate subject fields. It was felt, however, that a separate chapter especially organized to cover this period would be more valuable in itself and would also provide a more suitable, less-exacting context for the statistics, many of which are relatively roughhewn.

In the past, statistics for the colonial period were largely dependent on compilations made during the 17th and 18th centuries by historians such as Whitworth and Macpherson. Present-day scholars, however, no longer solely rely upon such compilations. They are ferreting out statistical information from original records hitherto left unused in archives and reconstructing statistical series of their own from other sources.

Only five of the tables presented here might be said to be old standbys. Twenty-two are the work of modern scholars, half reprinted as originally published, and half supplemented by reference to other data.

Of those which never before have appeared in print, Stella H. Sutherland compiled series Z 1–19; Jacob M. Price, series Z 223–237 and part of series Z 238–240; J. R. House, series Z 267–273; Austin White, series Z 388–405; and Lawrence A. Harper (assisted by graduate students), the remainder.

The Public Records Office in London (sometimes hereafter abbreviated PRO) contains many collections of records which throw light on commerce between England and the colonies and to some extent on the development of agriculture and manufacturing in the colonies, particularly when considered with reference to the mercantilist laws passed by the mother country, as has been done here. The laws in question are cited at various points in the text below by reference to their regnal year and chapter numbers—for example, 5 Geo. II c 22 (the fifth year of the reign of King George II, chapter 22).

The collections in the Public Records Office in London, which are the original sources for much of the data presented here, are identified there by title and call numbers. For example, one collection is titled "American Inspector General's Ledgers" and is further identified as "PRO Customs 16/1." The most important of these collections or ledgers of imports and exports are the following: The English Inspector General's Ledgers (PRO Customs 3); the Scottish Inspector General's Ledgers (PRO Customs 14); the American Inspector General's Ledgers (PRO Customs 16/1); and the colonial naval office lists (usually found in C. O. 5).

The English, Scottish, and American Inspector Generals' Ledgers are conveniently arranged for statistical purposes, but are so voluminous that it is far more convenient to utilize contemporary tabulations drawn from them when such secondary sources are available. The lists kept by the naval officers of that period (for the purpose of helping to enforce the navigation laws) merely provide chronological data concerning the ships which entered and cleared port, together with their cargoes and destinations.

The task of using the naval office lists has in some instances been lightened by colonial newspapers, such as the *South Carolina Gazette*, which published data taken from customhouse records. Also of general assistance in the preparation of many series presented in this chapter are the compilations from naval office lists prepared by a Works Progress Administration project conducted at the University of California, entitled "Trade and Commerce of the English Colonies in America," and referred to below as WPA compilations.

Z 1–19. Estimated population of American Colonies, 1610–1780.

Source: Compiled by Stella H. Sutherland, Oakland City College, Oakland City, Indiana, chiefly from the following sources: B. J. Brawley, *A Short History of the American Negro*, MacMillan, 1913; Elizabeth Donnan (editor), *Documents Illustrative of the History of the Slave Trade to America*, 4 vols., Carnegie Institution of Washington, D.C., 1930–35; Evarts B. Greene and Virginia D. Harrington, *American Population Before the Federal Census of 1790*, Columbia University Press, New York, 1932; Stella H. Sutherland, *Population Distribution in Colonial America*, Columbia University Press, New York, 1936; E. R. Turner, "The Negro in Pennsylvania," *Prize Essays of the American Historical Association*, Washington, D.C., 1911; Bureau of the Census, *A Century of Population Growth*, 1909; Thomas J. Wertenbaker, *The Planters of Colonial Virginia*, Princeton, 1922; and George W. Williams, *The History of the Negro Race in America From 1619 to 1880*, 2 vols., New York, 1883. (Also, a wide variety of source material was consulted for general information.)

The original data were obtained from the reports of the colonial officials to the Lords Commissioners of Trade and Plantations. Not infrequently a census supplied sworn evidence of the number of inhabitants; for other reports, the militia or the tax lists or both were used, commonly accompanied by an estimate of the whole population as indicated by the rolls or lists. Estimates made by colonial officials and by other informed contemporaries who did not disclose the figures upon which their conclusions were based have occasionally been included in these series. However, such estimates were selected in accordance with the general pattern of population growth.

The ratio of the militia to the whole population was generally 1 to 5⅓, but there were many exceptions. In Massachusetts, it was 1 to 6 in 1751 and 1 to 4 in 1763; in Connecticut, 1 to 6 in 1722 and 1756 and 1 to 7 in 1749, 1761, and 1774; it was 1 to 6 in Virginia and 1 to 7 in South Carolina at various times. No generalization can safely be made as to the ratio borne by the northern polls and ratables and by the southern taxables and tithables to the whole population of the Colonies. In every Province the figure was different. In the North, it ranged from 1 to 4 to 1 to 5½; in Pennsylvania, it was 1 to 7 in the 1750's, but 1 to 5.8 was the more common figure; in Maryland and Virginia, where both male and female slaves appeared on the tax lists, the ratio was 1 to 3 or 3.5 in the 17th century and 1 to 2.4 or 2.6 in the 18th century. The North Carolina white taxables were multiplied by 4 and the Negro taxables by 2.

The figures for Negroes for the 17th century, which are doubtlessly too low, are largely estimates based upon references to purchase and sale, to laws governing slavery, and occasionally to reports of more or less exact numbers.

Z 20. Percent distribution of the white population, by nationality, 1790.

Source: American Council of Learned Societies, "Report of Committee on Linguistic and National Stocks in the Population of the United States" (based on studies by Howard F. Barker and Marcus L. Hansen), *Annual Report of the American Historical Association, 1931*, vol. I, Washington, D.C., 1932, p. 124.

Distribution was made primarily on the basis of family names. For explanation of methods used, see source.

Z 21–34. Value of exports to and imports from England, by American Colonies, 1697–1776.

Source: 1697–1773, Charles Whitworth, *State of the Trade of Great Britain in Its Imports and Exports Progressively from the Year 1697*, G. Robinson, London, 1776; 1774–1776, David Macpherson, *Annals of Commerce, Manufactures, Fisheries and Navigation*, vol. III, Mundell & Son, Edinburgh, 1805, pp. 564, 585, and 599.

The English Inspector General's Ledgers (Public Records Office, London, Customs 2 and 3) provide the original source for these figures. Unfortunately, Whitworth's erroneous title has caused many to believe the figures relate to Britain rather than to England but otherwise his volume has much value. The source tables cover all countries and appear in two formats: One gives England's trade with any one country, annually; the other shows all the countries with which England traded each year. Those interested in studying broader trends will find value in the decennial averages in John Lord Sheffield, *Observations on the Commerce of the American States*, 6th edition, London, 1784. G. N. Clark's *Guide to English Commercial Statistics, 1696–1782* (Royal Historical Society Guides and Handbooks, No. 1, London, 1938) provides a valuable history and analysis of the basic statistics and a useful appendix which has a chronological list of statistical material for 1663–1783 and specifies where the data may be found.

Users of this material should note the basis on which the values rest. Smuggling (which so often attracts greater attention but which must always be considered commodity by commodity, country by country) does not constitute a material factor during the years under consideration. However, other difficulties arise with respect to the question of the volume of exports and the value of all the trade. The repeal of the export duties on woolen manufactures in 1701 (11 W. III c 20) and of the remaining export duties in 1721 (Geo. II c 15) removed the penalty for false entries on exports, and some merchants overstated their quantity for reasons of real or fancied prestige—a practice which may have injected an element of error of about 4 percent (Clark, cited above, pp. 16, 27, and 35).

Another problem arose in determining the value of the merchandise imported as well as exported. The authorities of the early 18th century were greatly interested in the balance of trade and at first tried to ascertain the real commercial value of merchandise. However, the difficulties of doing so, and the increasing recognition that there were intangible elements which the records could not disclose, led to the abandonment of attempts to keep the values current by the end of the second decade of the 18th century.

The so-called "official values" became stereotyped between 1705 and 1721 (Clark, cited above, pp. 17–23), a fact which diminished their value for use in striking a balance of trade but increased their usefulness as a rough-and-ready index of the relative increase or decrease of the volume of trade.

See also general note for series Z 1–405.

Z 35–42. Value of exports to and imports from England by New York, 1751–1775.

Source: Virginia D. Harrington, *The New York Merchant on the Eve of the Revolution*, Columbia University Press, New York, 1935, p. 354.

Foreign manufactures "In time" are those which could receive a drawback (refund) of duties; "Out of time" are those which could not. Outports are all ports in England other than London.

Z 43–55. Tonnage capacity of ships and value of exports and imports of American Colonies, by destination and origin, 1769 and 1770.

Source: David Macpherson, cited above in source for series Z 21–34, vol. III, pp. 571–572.

The tonnage figures shown are those used commercially— not those computed when the Royal Navy was purchasing vessels (see text for series Z 56–75). The statistics given by Macpherson are substantially the same as those given in Public Records Office, London, Customs 16/1, except that Macpherson put the 1769 inward-bound tonnage data for Southern Europe in the West Indies column (and vice versa)—an error which has been corrected here.

The value figures for 1769 provide only a rough-and-ready index of the relationship among the different trades. Totals include figures for the Islands of Newfoundland, Bahama, and Bermuda (a factor which statistically makes only a minor difference). These data are based on the official valuations used in the customhouse which, according to Macpherson, considerably understate the true amount. This defect, however serious for some purposes, does not destroy the value of the figures for comparative purposes. Also, it must be remembered that the value figures exclude the intercolonial coastwise trade which the tonnage figures show to have been as large as any other.

See also series Z 21–34, which provide a broader and more representative base for studying the relative relationship of the Thirteen Colonies' trade with England.

It should be noted that the use of these figures on volume of the traffic for the various trades for estimating the amount of shipping given full-time employment must allow for repeated voyages of the same vessel.

Z 56–75. Number and tonnage capacity of ships outward and inward bound, by destination and origin, 1714–1772.

Source: Compiled by Lawrence A. Harper, University of California, from photographic copies of the naval office lists in the British Public Records Office (C. O. 5), except for: 1714–1717, Boston, and 1715–18, New York City, E. B. O'Callaghen, ed., *Documents Relative to the Colonial History of the State of New York*, vol. V, Weed, Parsons, and Company, Albany, 1855, p. 618; 1733 and 1734, Philadelphia, *Pennsylvania Gazette* for those years; 1752, Port Hampton, Francis C. Huntley, "The Seaborne Trade of Virginia in Mid-Eighteenth Century: Port Hampton," *Virginia Magazine of History and Biography*, vol. LIX, No. 3, July 1951, pp. 302–303; 1763 and 1764, New York, and 1765 and 1766, New York, Boston, and Philadelphia, see source for series Z 35–42, pp. 356–358; and 1768–1772, all ports, American Inspector General's Ledgers, Public Records Office, London, Customs 16/1.

Where the classification in *Documents Relative to the Colonial History . . .* did not correspond to that used here, the necessary adjustments were made by reference to the Colonial Naval Office lists (PRO C.O.5).

The colonial naval officers appointed to enforce the English navigation laws as well as the collectors appointed by the English Commissioners of Customs under the act of 1673 (25 Car. II c 7) were charged with reporting the entry and clearance of ships as well as their cargoes. Many of the copies of the naval office lists have survived from the 18th century. When they have not, records of the names and destinations of the ships (but not their tonnages) may be obtained from the shipping news in the colonial newspapers. Such data of entries and clearances provide the best rough-and-ready index of the course of trade and its relative volume.

Although the figures concerning the entry of goods such as molasses might be distorted by illicit trade, the severity of the penalty (forfeiture) for failure to enter one's ship and the difficulty of concealing the offense help to warrant the accuracy of ship entry figures. Tonnage figures, however, present a special problem. Ralph Davis in "Organization and Finance of the English Shipping Industry in the Late Seventeenth Century" (doctoral thesis, University of London, 1955) states (pp. 476–479) that *the tonnage* as calculated when the English Navy was contracting *for the purchase* of a vessel was 25 to 33 percent greater than the *conventional "tons burden"* recorded in the customhouse books. Since the "tons burden" figures for the same ship remain constant in the passbooks and customs entries during the span of time here involved (although not necessarily for all periods), the difference between this purchase tonnage and the conventional tonnage will ordinarily not affect use of the data shown here.

See also general note for series Z 1–405.

Z 76. Value and quantity of articles exported from British Continental Colonies, by destination, 1770.

Source: David Macpherson, cited above in source for series Z 21–34, vol. III, pp. 572–573, supplemented by American Inspector General's Ledgers, Public Records Office, London, Customs 16/1.

Data do not include coastwise shipments as do the figures in the American Inspector General's Ledgers (PRO Customs 16/1). Macpherson (see source for series Z 21–34) states that he omitted fractional parts of the quantities but their value is retained in the value column. Because of this and an error which Macpherson saw but had no means of correcting, the value column may not be entirely comparable with the quantity columns. The value figures are not the market values (which Macpherson believes to have been higher) but are the official customhouse values at the ports of exportation. Customs 16/1 presents the quantities in all cases for a longer time span, 1768–1772, but the data there are not so conveniently totaled as in Macpherson.

See also general note for series Z 1–405.

Z 77–86. Coal exported from James River ports in Virginia, by destination, 1758–1765.

Source: Howard N. Eavenson, *The First Century and a Quarter of American Coal Industry*, Waverly Press, Inc., Baltimore, 1942, pp. 32–34, and WPA compilations (see general note for series Z 1–405) of naval office lists at the University of California.

These figures were compiled from the colonial naval office lists by Eavenson. They represent only the years for which records are complete in the case of both the Upper and Lower James. Comparison with the colonial exports for 1768–1772 (compiled by Eavenson, p. 36, from PRO Customs 16/1) shows that the James River shipments constituted the great bulk of the exports from the Thirteen Colonies. Out of a total of 2,798 net tons recorded, 1,220 net tons were shipped from the Upper James, 180 from the Lower James, 1,100 from Nova Scotia, 117 from New Hampshire, and only minor quantities from other ports (which may have been used as ballast and originally may have come from Great Britain).

Chaldrons were not converted into tons at the Newcastle rate of 5,936 pounds equal to 2.97 net tons but on the measure used after the Revolutionary War, a chaldron equaling 36 bushels or 1.44 net tons.

Z 87–107. Coal imported, by American ports, 1768–1772.

Source: American Inspector General's Ledgers, Public Records Office, London, Customs 16/1.

Chaldrons and bushels were converted to net tons as described in text for series Z 77–86.

The WPA compilations (see general note for series Z 1–405) from the naval office lists show earlier entries of coal in the several ports, from time to time. The great bulk came from Britain, the remainder (except in the case of exports from James River ports) apparently were transshipments, but it is not until 1768 that records give a good cross section of the traffic.

Z 108–121. Value of furs exported to England, by British Continental Colonies, 1700–1775.

Source: Murray G. Lawson, "Fur—A study in English Mercantilism, 1700–1775," *University of Toronto Studies*, History and Economics Series, vol. IX, University of Toronto Press, Toronto, 1943, pp. 108–109.

As pointed out in the source, the fur trade is inextricably interwoven with the manufacture of beaver hats. Thus, the Hat Act of 1732 (5 Geo. II c 22) forbidding the exportation of hats by any colony, combined with the enumeration of beaver skins and furs in 1722 (8 Geo. I c 15), sought to protect the English hat manufacturers. These series show the importance to the English of their colonial supply of fur. Comparison of these figures with those shown in series Z 21–34 will demonstrate the relative unimportance of fur in the colonial balance of trade.

The source also specifies the different kinds and quantity of fur England imported from the colonies and elsewhere, as well as the quantity and value of the different markets of the world—data given in even greater detail in the original tables which Lawson has left with the WPA compilations at the University of California in Berkeley.

See also general note for series Z 1–405.

Z 122–125. Indigo and silk exported from South Carolina and Georgia, 1747–1775.

Source: Series Z 122–124, Lewis C. Gray, *History of Agriculture in the Southern United States to 1860*, vol. II, Carnegie Institution of Washington, D.C., 1933, p. 1024 (except 1766, WPA compilations of colonial naval office lists, Public Records Office, London, C. O. 5; and 1768–1772, photographic copies of the American Inspector General's Ledgers, Public Records Office, London, Customs 16/1). Series Z 125, Lewis C. Gray, cited above, vol. I, p. 187.

See also general note for series Z 1–405.

The data on indigo are reasonably complete. Although South Carolina contemplated the production of indigo as early as 1672 little came of it, presumably because of the competition from the British West Indies. When the British Islands began to emphasize sugar rather than indigo, England had to depend upon the French West Indies for her supplies of indigo until South Carolina (thanks to the enterprise of Eliza Lucas) again entered the field. The first successful crop in 1744 was largely devoted to seed but South Carolina was soon exporting in quantity. In due course, Georgia became a competitor but British Florida did not enter the picture until late. Even during the last 5 years of the colonial period British Florida's production ranged only between 20,000 and 60,000 pounds (Gray, cited above, vol. I, pp. 54 and 291–295).

The great bulk of indigo went to Britain (which wanted it as a source of blue dye), not only because of its enumeration in the act of 1660 (12 Charles II c 18), but also because of the bounty England paid of 6 pence per pound (21 Charles II c 30). However, Customs 16/1 and the WPA compilations (see general note for series Z 1–405) show that minor quantities went to other Continental Colonies. Gray's Carolina figures, which were taken by him from an English source, apparently do not include coastwise shipments. This omission is relatively unimportant since the coastwise figures for 1768–1773 (as shown in Customs 16/1) represented only 1.6 percent of the total exports. The figures for Georgia (compiled by an American customs official) include shipments coastwise as well as to England—a matter of statistical significance as they constituted 5.1 percent of Georgia's total for 1768–1773.

Comparison of Gray's figures for 1747–1765 with those for 1768–1773 in Customs 16/1 suggests that Gray's figures are not for Charleston and Savannah alone, as shown by his headings, but for South Carolina and Georgia. In the case of South Carolina, the two series agree exactly in 1768, the one year when we have figures from both sources. Since Gray's source (British Museum, Kings Manuscripts, 206, f. 29) is the same for the earlier years, 1747–1765, it seems probable that the figures for these years also refer to South Carolina as a whole.

Customs 16/1 does not conclusively answer the problem in the case of Savannah. It shows for 1768–1772 that Savannah was the only Georgia port exporting indigo except in 1772. For this year, Gray's figures differ slightly from those shown in Customs 16/1 for Savannah alone and also those for Georgia as a whole. The decision to change the heading from Savannah to Georgia rests upon the fact that Bernard Romans (*A Concise Natural History of East and West Florida*, vol. I, New York, 1775, p. 104) specifies Georgia rather than Savannah.

Whether or not the figures are for Savannah or Georgia seems statistically insignificant. In South Carolina, however, ports other than Charleston provided 7.8 percent of that colony's exports to England for 1768–1773. Whatever may be true of Gray's figures, those given for 1768–1773 from Customs 16/1 do include all South Carolina ports and all of Georgia, but the only figure available for South Carolina for 1766 (from the WPA compilations) is for Charleston alone.

The figures on silk are from records compiled by the Georgia Comptroller of Customs (Gray, cited above, vol. I, p. 187). See also text for series Z 126–130.

Z 126–130. Silk exported and imported by North and South Carolina, 1731–1755.

Source: Chapman J. Milling, ed., *Colonial South Carolina*, University of South Carolina Press, Columbia, 1951, p. 104.

Despite vigorous efforts to encourage colonial silk production by both British and colonial governments, more silk moved west than east across the Atlantic. Early figures gathered by Gray (cited above for series Z 122–125, vol. I, pp. 184–187) show that in 1654 Virginia reported the production of only 8 pounds; in 1656, 10 pounds (wound silk); in 1668, 300 pounds (sent to Charles II, type unspecified); in 1730, 300 pounds (raw), and that the Carolinas sent "several bales" to London in 1710 and again in 1716. Georgia's first efforts succeeded

in sending only 20 pounds of silk to England in 1739. In 1741, she produced 600 pounds of cocoons (of which 16 pounds made 1 pound of silk) as against 37 pounds of wound silk in all the previous years of the colony. In 1749, the Salzburgers (a religious colony of industrious peasants and artisans) alone produced 762 pounds of cocoons and 50 pounds, 13 ounces, of spun silk. In 1764, the Colonies' total product amounted to 15,212 pounds of cocoons. See also text for series Z 122–125.

The figures for the Carolinas (1731–1755) were taken from British records and appear in Governor James Glen's *Description of South Carolina* (Milling, cited above, p. 104).

Z 131–222. General note.

Iron was listed in colonial commerce as "pig iron" which derived its name from the shape assumed by the molten iron when poured from the furnace, after being separated from the ore, and "bar iron" which consisted of malleable iron produced in bloomeries or at the forge. Iron manufactures not specifically described by name, such as anchors, axes, pots, nails, scythes, etc., were listed as "cast iron" if poured into forms and "wrought iron" if forged from malleable iron except in the English Inspector General's records (PRO Customs 3) where the term "wrought iron" seems to have included both cast and malleable iron products.

The statistical picture of iron in the colonies can be reconstructed in part from data concerning iron works in the colonies and in part from the records of colonial trade. The beginning of this industry came early in the various American colonies—in Virginia in 1622, Massachusetts in 1645, Connecticut in 1657, New Jersey in 1680, Maryland in 1715, Pennsylvania in 1716, and New York shortly before 1750. By 1775, the colonies had at least 82 charcoal furnaces which produced about 300 tons each, or a total of 24,600 tons, of pig iron and more than 175 iron forges, some being bloomeries which made bar iron directly from the ore. Most of them, however, were refinery forges which used pig iron. Each of the 175 forges produced an average of 150 tons of bar iron a year, or 26,250 tons in all. In addition, there were slitting mills and other iron works.

Arthur C. Bining, in *British Regulation of the Colonial Iron Industry*, cited below for series Z 131–135, p. 134, provides a table comparing American production with the world total (see text table I). These estimates include pig iron, cast iron wares made at blast furnaces, and bar iron produced at bloomeries directly from the ore.

Table I. Iron Production of American Colonies and the World
[In tons]

Year	American Colonies	World
1800	45,000	400,000
1790	38,000	325,000
1775	30,000	210,000
1750	10,000	150,000
1700	1,500	100,000

The figures shown in series Z 131–222 for the movement of the various types of iron in commerce throw light on England's efforts to encourage Americans to produce pig and bar iron by freeing those products from import duties in England, and to limit further manufacture by prohibiting the erection of any new slitting or rolling mills, tilt hammer forges, or steel furnaces (23 Geo. II c 29; 30 Geo. II c 16). Iron was not added to the list of enumerated products which could only be shipped to Britain (or another colony) until 1764 (4 Geo. III c 15), and even then the law only forbade shipments to Europe.

Comparisons of colonial production with export figures will help provide estimates of the home market, which can be reduced to an approximate *per capita* base by reference to series Z 1–19.

See also general note for series Z 1–405.

Z 131–135. Pig iron exported to England, by colony, 1723–1776.

Source: 1723–1755, and, **series Z 131** only, 1761–1776, Arthur Cecil Bining, *British Regulation of the Colonial Iron Industry*, University of Pennsylvania Press, Philadelphia, 1933, pp. 126–133; 1756–1760, and **series Z 132–135**, 1761–1776, English Inspector General's Ledgers, Public Records Office, London, Customs 3.

Basically, all the figures come from the Inspector General's accounts although Bining obtained his from House of Lords MSS., No. 185, and Harry Scrivenor, *Comprehensive History of the Iron Trade*, Longman, Brown, Green, and Longmans, London, 1841.

J. L. Bishop, *A History of American Manufactures . . .*, cited below for series Z 153–158, p. 625, gives an earlier figure when he states that the first iron sent to England from America was from Nevis and St. Christopher, followed in 1718 by 3⅓ tons from Virginia and Maryland. Series Z 131 is that of Bining and, where possible, footnotes explain the reasons for differences between his totals and those of the extended figures. The customs records were stated in terms of tons, hundredweights, quarters, and pounds, but they have here been rounded to tons.

Z 136–142. Pig iron exported from American Colonies, by destination and colony, 1768–1772.

Source: American Inspector General's Ledgers, Public Records Office, London, Customs 16/1.

The difference in total exports given in series Z 136 for Great Britain and that in series Z 131 for England should reflect trade with Scotland except for the variation in terminal dates and the lapse of time required to cross the Atlantic. The trade, however, seems to have been minor. J. L. Bishop, *A History of American Manufactures . . .*, cited below for series Z 153–158, p. 628, gives figures showing that the pig iron exported to Scotland totaled only 264 tons in the 10 years from 1739 to 1749 and 229 tons in the 6 years from 1750 to 1756.

No figures are available for pig iron imported from England by the colonies. Such imports were probably negligible.

Z 143–152. Pig iron imported by American Colonies from other Continental Colonies, 1768–1772.

Source: See source for series Z 136–142.

In addition to the colonies shown, these series also cover New Hampshire, New Jersey, Georgia, and Florida. However, these colonies imported no pig iron for 1768–1772.

Z 153–158. Bar iron imported from England, by American Colonies, 1710–1750.

Source: 1710–1735, J. L. Bishop, *A History of American Manufactures From 1608 to 1860*, vol. I, Edward Young & Co., Philadelphia, 1861, p. 629; 1750, English Inspector General's Ledgers, Public Records Office, London, Customs 3.

Shipments of bar iron from England to the Colonies declined sharply in the last quarter century before the Revolution. Figures are not available for 1736–1749 to determine when the decline first became evident.

Imports were relatively few after 1750. The English and American Inspector Generals' Ledgers show that New England

imported 6 tons in 1764, and again in 1769, and 1,053 bars in 1773. South Carolina imported 19 bars in 1770 and 3 hundredweight in 1773.

Z 159–164. Bar iron exported to England, by colony, 1718–1776.

Source: 1718–1755, and **series Z 159**, 1761–1776, Bining, cited above for series Z 131–135, pp. 128–133; 1756–1760, and **series Z 160–164**, 1761–1776, English Inspector General's Ledgers, Public Records Office, London, Customs 3.

The original sources show data in tons, hundredweights, quarters, and pounds, but they have here been rounded by Lawrence A. Harper (University of California) to the nearest ton.

The source indicates that no bar iron was exported during 1710–1717 and for years which have been omitted in these series.

Z 165–178. Bar iron imported by American Colonies from other Continental Colonies, 1768–1772.

Source: See source for series Z 136–142.

Z 179–188. Bar iron exported by American Colonies, by destination and colony, 1768–1772.

Source: See source for series Z 136–142.

The difference in total exports given in series Z 179 for Great Britain and those in series Z 159 for England should reflect exports to Scotland, except for the variation in terminal dates and the lapse of time required to cross the Atlantic. According to J. L. Bishop, these exports were minor—only 11 tons from 1739 to 1749 (see text for series Z 136–142).

Z 189–202. Cast iron imported and exported by American Colonies, by origin and destination, 1768–1772.

Source: See source for series Z 136–142.

Additional information may be obtained concerning imports from England in the English Inspector General's Ledgers (PRO Customs 3) and in the WPA compilations (see general note for series Z 1–405) of the colonial naval office lists. English exports to the Colonies list, in addition to the generic heading "cast iron," such items as ordnance, iron pots, melting pots, and Flemish iron pots. The WPA compilations show an active coastal trade in pots as well as a surprisingly large quantity of sugar pots and sugar molds going to Kingston, Jamaica, especially from Philadelphia.

The figures for 1769–1771 may include some shipments from Scotland but the amounts probably are negligible.

Source also indicates additional minor quantities of cast iron exported to Southern Europe, Wine Islands, and West Indies.

Z 203–210. Wrought iron imported from England by American Colonies, 1710–1773.

Source: 1710–1735, Bishop, cited above for series Z 153–158, p. 629; 1750–1764, and 1773, English Inspector General's Ledgers, Public Records Office, London, Customs 3; 1769–1771, see source for series Z 136–142.

The figures for 1769–1771 may include some shipments from Scotland but the amounts probably are negligible.

The American Inspector General's figures for 1768–1772 (PRO Customs 16/1) disclose no exports of wrought iron from the Colonies to England, but the figures do show some shipments to the West Indies.

Z 211–222. Selected iron products imported and exported by American Colonies, 1768–1772.

Source: See source for series Z 136–142.

Figures are probably underestimated since the items included may have been listed under more general designations. The colonists were not necessarily dependent upon importation but may have manufactured their own nails and other articles from bar iron which was either home-produced or imported.

Since colonial imports of axes and scythes came so predominantly from the other colonies, and steel and nails from Great Britain, no note has been taken of the negligible importations of these items from other sources.

Z 223–253. General note.

Colonial statistics concerning production and consumption of tobacco have not been developed yet, and perhaps they can never advance beyond the rough estimate stage. For the present, only general deductions from export statistics and other evidence can be made.

Figures for trans-Atlantic shipments of tobacco in the 17th century leave much to be desired (see text for series Z 238–240) but those for the 18th century are reasonably satisfactory. The 18th century statistics of English imports rest upon contemporary compilations from customhouse entries. The figures for Scotland are less exact and in the early years they do not rise above mere estimates. However, Scotland's tobacco imports were relatively minor in those years. Fortunately, as their relative importance grew, the Scottish statistics became more reliable.

British imports represented virtually all the colonial exports. The figures given in series Z 223–229 and Z 230–237 give the landed weight in Britain. Due to the tobacco's loss of moisture while crossing the Atlantic, the landed weight in Britain is about 5 percent less than the shipping weight in America (Arthur P. Middleton, *Tobacco Coast*, the Mariners' Museum, Newport News, Va., 1953, p. 104; Rupert C. Jarvis, *Customs Letter-Books of the Port of Liverpool, 1711-1813*, the Chetham Society, Manchester, 1954).

Unfortunately, the English Inspector General's Ledgers of Imports and Exports (PRO Customs 3) do not differentiate between shipments from Virginia and Maryland as do the Scottish (PRO Customs 14) and the American (PRO Customs 16/1).

The validity of British statistics as a reflection of the American tobacco trade depends, of course, upon colonial obedience to the regulations requiring shipment (with minor exceptions) of colonial tobacco to England (Britain after 1707)—at first by royal order and after 1660 by the Navigation Act of 12 Car. II, c 18.

Until the English drove the Dutch from New Netherland (first in 1664 and finally in 1674) great opportunities existed for illicit trade in America. The rules also appear not to have been consistently enforced in Europe (see text for series Z 238–240). In the 1680's there was a flareup of illegal shipments to Ireland but it reflected a sudden change in the law. The offending vessels were apprehended and the great bulk of the Irish trade thereafter seems to have followed legal channels. There were lurid accounts of smuggling to Scotland at the turn of the century but the quantity of tobacco involved should be viewed in proportion to the trade as a whole. One cannot reasonably expect the illegal shipments at that time to exceed the shipments made a decade later with full sanction of the law. In fact, the illegal shipments presumably were much less because Scotland as a whole at the end of the 17th century had only one-fourth of the shipping it had within 5 years after direct trade was permitted. The Clyde ports, which were most concerned with the American trade, had only one-tenth of their later shipping (L. A. Harper, *The English Navigation Laws*, Columbia University Press, New York, 1939, pp. 260–261). In view of this difference in the shipping available, the volume of illegal trade

would seem not to have been more than 250,000 pounds, and a comparison with series Z 223–229 shows that it represented at most 1 percent of the tobacco crossing the Atlantic lawfully.

During the 18th century there was undoubtedly some smuggling of tobacco but it does not seem likely to impair the validity of the colonial import statistics. The illicit trader's greatest profit did not lie in evading the provisions of the Navigation Act but in escaping the high taxes laid on tobacco in England. The most effective technique consisted in importing the tobacco and reexporting it legally to a nearby port (such as the Isle of Man) whence small craft could "run" it ashore again duty-free (for details, see Jacob M. Price, *The Tobacco Trade and the Treasury, 1685–1733: British Mercantilism in its Fiscal Aspects*, unpublished doctoral dissertation, Harvard University, 1954).

American historians have pointed to the small amount of the "plantation duties" collected on intercolonial trade as evidence of the breakdown of the laws. If the American colonists consumed the 5 pounds per capita of the Bermudians in the early 18th century, the 2 pounds of the English at the beginning of the 18th century, or even their 1 pound per capita at the end of the 18th century (Alfred Rive, "The Consumption of Tobacco Since 1600," *Economic Journal Supplement, Economic History Series*, vol. I, Jan. 1926, p. 63; H. C. Wilkinson, *Bermuda in the Old Empire*), Oxford University Press, London, 1950, p. 14), the colonies would have provided a sizable market of 2,000,000 to 10,000,000 pounds at the time of the Revolution. But that is a figure which can and must be greatly discounted. In the first place, it should be cut in half because the southern colonies had about half the population and provided their own source of supply. Similarly, allowance must be made for tobacco produced in the northern colonies. Pennsylvania, Delaware, New York, Rhode Island, Connecticut, and Massachusetts all at one time or another grew tobacco (George L. Beer, *The Origins of the British Colonial System, 1578–1660*, Macmillan, New York, 1908, p. 88; J. B. Killebrew, *Report on the Culture and Curing of Tobacco in the United States*, Department of the Interior, Census Office, Washington, D.C., 1884, pp. 147 and 237; Vertrees J. Wyckoff, *Tobacco Regulation in Colonial Maryland*, Johns Hopkins University Studies in Historical and Political Science, Extra Volumes, New Series, No. 22, Baltimore, 1936, pp. 37, 38, and 65). Philadelphia, Lewes, and New Castle appear in the WPA compilations (see general note for series Z 1–405) as suppliers to other ports like New York and Boston. New York itself exported tobacco (and even more snuff) coastwise as well as to England, and the exports from New England continued large even into the 1750's. In the 1760's, Rhode Island tobacco crops provided surpluses sufficient to warrant shipping 200,000 pounds to Surinam, a colony in South America (James B. Hedges, *The Browns of Providence Plantations*, Harvard University Press, Cambridge, 1952, pp. 30–40).

It need not be assumed that the colonists were averse to violating the law. It may be that violations on a significant scale were not good business. The fact that the 200,000 pounds of Rhode Island tobacco sent to Surinam went there illegally means little. It was a type of tobacco not in general demand and constituted less than one-third of one percent of the annual legal trade.

Z 223–229. Tobacco imported by England, by origin, 1697–1775.

Source: Compiled by Jacob M. Price, the University of Michigan.

The basic sources used by Price are the same as those used by him for his doctoral dissertation (see below).

The English Inspector General's Ledgers (PRO Customs 3), which are the original source of the data, distinguish between entries in London and in the rest of the Kingdom (the outports) but Price has combined them in the interest of saving space.

Z 230–237. American tobacco imported and reexported by Great Britain, 1697–1775.

Source: Jacob M. Price, *The Tobacco Trade and the Treasury, 1685–1733: British Mercantilism in its Fiscal Aspects*, unpublished doctoral dissertation, Harvard University, 1954.

The basic sources of the data for England in Price's doctoral dissertation were the Inspector General's Ledgers of Imports and Exports (PRO Customs 2 and 3) except as follows (see general note for series Z 1–405 for an explanation of the call numbers which follow): 1703–1722, from PRO CO 390/5/47; 1717–1722, confirmed in PRO T. 1/281/18, BM Add. MS. 33,038 fol. 159; 1722 (London import only), from PRO T 64/276B/327; 1763–1769 (import only), from PRO T. 64/276B/328; 1770–1773 (import only), from PRO T. 64/276B/332; 1770–1771 (export), from PRO T. 64/276/330; 1772, 1774–1775 (import and export), from PRO T. 17/1,3,4; 1773–1775 (export), from Adam Anderson, *An Historical and Chronological Deduction of the Origin of Commerce*, vol. IV, J. Walter, London, 1707–1709, p. 447.

For Scotland, Price's data came from the Scottish Ledgers of Imports and Exports (PRO Customs 14), except as follows: 1707–1711 (import and export), from PRO T. 1/39/29; 1715–1717 (import and export), from PRO CO 390/5/13; 1721–1724 (import and export), from PRO T. 1/282/23; 1725–1731, 1752–1754, 1763, 1769 (import and export), from PRO T. 36/13; 1738–1747 (import and export), from PRO T. 1/329 fol. 125.

Total imports and reexports for 1708–1731 and 1752–1754 were obtained by adding figures not strictly comparable with each other. Scottish imports and reexports for 1708–1717 are averages of estimates for several years.

Z 238–240. American tobacco imported by England, 1616–1693.

Source: 1616–1621, Vertrees J. Wyckoff, *Tobacco Regulation in Colonial Maryland*, Johns Hopkins University Studies in Historical and Political Science, Extra Volumes, New Series, No. 22, Baltimore, 1936, pp. 20–36; 1622–1631, Neville Williams, "England's Tobacco Trade in the Reign of Charles I," *The Virginia Magazine of History and Biography*, October 1957, pp. 403–449; 1637–1640, Stanley Gray and V. J. Wyckoff, "The International Tobacco Trade in the Seventeenth Century," *Southern Economic Journal*, VII, July 1940, pp. 18–25; 1663–1693, compiled by J. M. Price from PRO CO 388/2 ff.7,13 (1663, 1669), B. M. Sloane MS.1815 ff.34–7 (1683–1689), PRO T.1/36/9 fo.50 (1689–1693), and Gray and Wyckoff, cited above (1672–1682).

The figures here are not as satisfactory as those given in series Z 223–229 and Z 230–237. The total imports for 1686 and 1688 were obtained by adding figures not strictly comparable with each other. Imports of the outports (English ports other than London) for 1682–1688 are averages of estimates for several years. In a few instances the figures from Gray and Wyckoff include minor quantities of Spanish and Brazilian tobacco.

As indicated in the general note for series Z 223–253, the figures shown prior to the time when the Dutch were driven from New Netherland should not be relied upon too greatly. Rive (cited in source above, pp. 57–75) suggests that the doubling of the London import figures between 1637 and 1638 may have been due to better patrolling of the Channel. There is much evidence to show that the laws restricting tobacco importations to London and excluding Spanish tobacco were disregarded at least in part (Beer, cited above in general note for series Z 223–253, pp. 197 ff; Williams, cited in source above, pp. 419–420; Wyckoff, cited in source above, pp. 32–34).

An alternate approach to studying the import figures is to consider the estimates of tobacco which might be produced or purchased. English proposals for limitations on tobacco importation included the following: 55,000 pounds in 1620; 200,000 pounds in 1625 and 1626; 250,000 pounds in 1627; 600,000 pounds in 1635; and 1,600,000 pounds in 1638 (Beer, cited above in general note for series Z 223–253, pp. 120, 138, 154, and 158). Virginia meantime wanted the King in 1628 to take at least 500,000 pounds annually and by 1639 sought to reduce the tobacco crop to 1,500,000 that year and 1,300,000 pounds for each of the next two years (Killebrew, cited above in general note for series Z 223–253, pp. 215–216).

Another weakness of the figures for these series lies in their failure to show which colonies supplied the tobacco; however, other data provide some opportunities to estimate the quantity which the various colonies contributed. Virginia and Bermuda ran neck and neck in 1620 at 50,000 to 55,000 pounds each. In 1628, Virginia's shipments were twice those of Bermuda, and thereafter Virginia drew far ahead (Beer, cited above in general note for series Z 223–253, p. 120; and Williams, cited in source above, pp. 421–449). Her production had risen from 20,000 pounds in 1619 and went on to 18,150,000 in 1688 and 18,295,000 pounds in 1704 (R. A. Brock, "A Succinct Account of Tobacco in Virginia, 1607–1790," in J. B. Killebrew, cited above in general note for series Z 223–253, p. 224). Bermuda's production increased to 500,000 pounds at the most in the 1680's (George L. Beer, *The Old Colonial System, 1660–1754*, vol. II, Macmillan, New York, 1912, p. 91). At the end of the century, Bermuda's exports to England became negligible, and by the first quarter of the 18th century Bermuda was importing from Virginia some of the 20,000 pounds consumed by her population, which was estimated at 3,600 whites and 5,000 slaves in the 1680's (H. C. Wilkinson, *Bermuda in the Old Empire*, Oxford University Press, London, 1950, p. 14).

The West Indies were said to have begun growing tobacco as early as 1625; by 1628, reports show the shipment of about 100,000 pounds, but by the middle of the century sugar began to take over as the predominant crop (Beer, *The Origins . . .*, cited above in general note for series Z 223–253, pp. 89–90).

Meanwhile Maryland, which probably had produced no more than 100,000 pounds annually by 1639 (Wyckoff, cited in source above, p. 49), so increased her output that she contributed about 36 percent of the combined Virginia-Maryland total in 1688—a percentage she approximated at the turn of the 17th century (Margaret Shove Morriss, *Colonial Trade of Maryland, 1689–1715*, Johns Hopkins University Studies in Historical and Political Science, Series XXXII, No. 3, Baltimore, 1914, pp. 31–36) and during the period 1768 to 1773 (see series Z 248–249).

In the Colonies further south, North Carolina was said to be growing about 2,000 hogsheads, or 1,000,000 pounds, of tobacco in the 1670's—an estimate which seems more generous than the subsequent pattern of exports justifies (Beer, *The Old Colonial System, 1660–1754*, cited above, vol. II, p. 195).

Z 241–253. American tobacco exported and imported, by origin and destination, 1768–1772.

Source: Compiled by Lawrence A. Harper, University of California, from American Inspector General's Ledger of Imports and Exports, Public Records Office, London, Customs 16/1.

Although they cover only a few years, these series provide the only known comprehensive data which permit a complete analysis of the pre-Revolutionary colonial tobacco trade.

In the source, some export figures for 1768 and 1770 for Virginia, North Carolina, and South Carolina were shown in hogsheads or barrels. When the weights of these units were not indicated, they were converted to pounds by Harper, by using the average weights of these units as reflected in the shipments to Great Britain from the respective colonies for 1768–1772.

Also, the source shows the South Carolina export to Great Britain for 1771 as 433 hogsheads totaling 40,333 pounds. This obviously is an erroneous ratio. Since the hogshead figure is more comparable to other data shown here than the pounds figure, the former is assumed to be correct. It has been converted to pounds in the same manner as the 1770 export figures mentioned above.

Z 254–261. Tea imported from England by American Colonies, 1761–1775.

Source: Compiled by Lawrence A. Harper, University of California, from the English Inspector General's Ledgers, Public Records Office, London, Customs 3.

Figures for tea imports shown in the American Inspector General's Ledgers (PRO Customs 16/1) for 1768–1772 closely approximate those shown here for the corresponding years (O. M. Dickerson, *The Navigation Acts and the American Revolution*, University of Pennsylvania Press, Philadelphia, 1951, pp. 99–100).

Z 262–280. General note.

Information on rice in the colonial period is limited primarily to the material on the clean rice which entered commercial trading. Presumably, the weight of this rice bore approximately the same ratio to the rough rice of the plantation at that time as it does now, that is, 100/162. There are no known satisfactory statistics on rice production and only scattered data concerning domestic consumption. Lord Carteret told the Board of Trade in 1715 that South Carolina "spent in the country" one-third of the 3,000 tons of rice she was producing at that time. By the pre-Revolutionary period, comparison of total exports with net imports for 1769–1772 indicates that only 3 percent of total exports was consumed in the nonrice-producing colonies.

The basic sources of statistics on clean rice in commerce are the records of importations in the British Public Records Office kept by the English Inspector General of Imports and Exports (Customs 2 and 3, since 1696), by the Scottish Inspector General (Customs 14, since 1755), by the American Inspector General (Customs 16/1, 1768–1772), and the records kept by the colonial naval officers (supplemented by those kept by the deputies of the London Commissioners of Customs for the comparatively few instances when these records have survived).

Data from these basic sources appear in: Gray, *History of Agriculture* . . ., cited above for series Z 122–125, pp. 1020–1023; Francis Yonge, *A View of the Trade of South Carolina*, London, 1722; C. J. Gayle, "The Nature and Volume of Exports From Charleston, 1724–1774," *The Proceedings of the South Carolina Historical Association*, Columbia, 1937, pp. 30–31; G. K. Holmes, *Rice Crop of the United States, 1712–1911* (Circular 34, Department of Agriculture, Bureau of Statistics, 1912); Francis Yonge, *Narratives of the Proceedings of the People of South Carolina*, in B. R. Carroll, *Historical Collections of South Carolina*, vol. II, Harper & Bros., New York, 1836, p. 156; *The Case of the Province of South Carolina* (Carroll, vol. II, p. 265); Gov. James Glen, *Description of South Carolina* (Carroll, vol. II, p. 26); "An Account of Sundry Goods Imported and . . . Exported . . . From the First of November 1738 to the First of November 1739" (printed as a broadside by P. Timothy, Charleston, 1739), Bernard Romans, *Natural History of East and West Florida*, New York, 1775; and WPA compilations from the Charleston Naval Office lists (see general note for series Z 1–405).

Fortunately, the British records measure the quantities imported in hundredweights, but the American statistics usually give only the number of barrels and other containers exported. Where half-barrels were reported, the number was divided by two and the result included in the barrel totals.

Miscellaneous units in the American figures have been converted to barrels. The term "cask" has been considered synonymous with "barrel," following the usage of the American Inspector General's Accounts for 1768, but the remaining figures are rough approximations suggested by the weights of other commodities as given in M. Postlethwayt, *The Universal Dictionary of Trade and Commerce*, W. Strahan, London, 1774; J. H. Alexander, *Universal Dictionary of Weights and Measures*, D. Van Nostrand, New York, 1867, and the *Oxford English Dictionary*. A tierce has been considered to equal 1⅓ barrels; a hogshead, 2 barrels; a puncheon, 2⅔ barrels; a butt, 4 barrels; small barrels and small casks, ½ of a barrel; seroons, boxes, and bags, ⅖ of a barrel; kegs, ⅛; and bushels, ⅛. Colonial containers varied so greatly that these estimates seldom, if ever, represented the exact relationship. When discussing weights and measures for other uses, additional information should be obtained and corrections, as may be necessary, should be made in the formulas employed here. For present purposes, these maverick units constitute such a negligible part of the whole that errors in estimating their weight seem unlikely to exceed those involved in rounding.

The significant problem lies in determining the weight of the barrel, the principal unit. Holmes (cited above, p. 4) stated that it weighed 350 pounds in 1717; 400 pounds, 1718–1729; and 500 pounds, 1730–1788, but as Gray (cited above, vol. II, p. 1020) points out, these figures conflict with those given by others. Although Governor Johnson of South Carolina stated in 1719 that the average barrel contained about 350 pounds, Francis Yonge, the collector at Charleston, gave the figure of 400 pounds for 1719–1721; a Savannah Rice Association study declared it to be 325 pounds for 1720–1729; a contemporary report in 1731 and Governor Glen of South Carolina in 1749 said the barrel contained 500 pounds, but other documents say that it was 500–600 pounds in 1763; "something over 600 pounds in 1768–1769"; 550 pounds for 1764–1772; and 540 pounds net in 1772. O. M. Dickerson, *The Navigation Acts and the American Revolution* (cited above in text for series Z 254–261, p. 59) states that the formula used by the customs service for converting barrels to hundredweight had each barrel containing 4½ hundredweight, or 504 pounds (but the records do not disclose when the formula was calculated nor how often it was revised).

Fortunately, an examination of the surviving official statistics enables one to obtain averages calculated on broad bases. The decennial totals for 1720–1729 and 1730–1739 (Gov. James Glen, cited above) give both the number of barrels and the total weight shipped, showing the average barrel to weigh 373 pounds during the first decade and 448 pounds during the second. Similarly, the naval office lists for 1756–1767, which record both the number of barrels and pound weights shipped to Southern Europe and the West Indies, give a weighted average of about 525 pounds each for some 20,000 barrels.

Comparisons of the number of barrels shipped to Britain from America with the weight recorded for the rice arriving there provide another means of estimating the average weight of the rice barrel. For present purposes, it can be assumed to have been 350 pounds until 1720, and then to have risen 10 pounds a year until 1730, when it remained at a plateau of 450 pounds until after 1740; then it began to ascend at the rate of 5 pounds a year until it reached its pre-Revolutionary peak of 525 pounds in 1755. It must be remembered, however, that the weight of the barrels might vary radically. New York's Naval Office list for 1764 shows one shipment averaging 183½ pounds a barrel and another 698 pounds.

Z 262–266. Rice exported from producing areas, 1698–1774.

Source: Compiled by Lawrence A. Harper, University of California, from references discussed below.

These series attempt to provide a comprehensive statistical summary comparable to those available for the postcolonial period. Barrels have been converted to pounds on the bases described in the general note for series Z 262–280.

There was the problem of totaling the exports from the three South Carolina ports (Charleston, Beaufort-Port Royal, and Georgetown-Wynyaw) and those of Georgia. Shipments from other colonies can be considered as having originated in South Carolina and Georgia, except possibly those of North Carolina, and even in this case most of the exports probably went through South Carolina. In any event, North Carolina's exports are grouped with South Carolina's shipments in the English import figures, under the generic heading, "Carolinas." Shipments to Scotland seem to have been infrequent and insignificant until the French and Indian War (1754–1763).

The Charleston figures, with the exceptions noted below, are those compiled by Gayle (cited above in general note for series Z 262–280) from the *South Carolina Gazette*, although his figures for less than 12 months have been extended to full year bases for 1750, 1756, 1757, 1763, and 1767. For 1698–1724, the figures have been calculated on the assumption that all American rice imports recorded in the English Inspector General's Ledgers were equal to ⅞ of Charleston's total exports, as suggested in 1719 by Francis Yonge, the customs collector at Charleston, a conclusion corroborated by a comparison of the WPA compilations of Charleston exports with the English imports for 1717, 1718, 1719, and 1724, and by Edward Randolph's remark in 1700 that ⅒ of Charleston's exports went to the West Indies alone (Carroll, cited above in general note for series Z 262–280). For 1731, the figures come from the WPA compilations of the Charleston Naval Office list (see general note for series Z 1–405), and for 1734 and 1758, directly from the *South Carolina Gazette;* for 1765, from the *Charleston Year Book* (1880) as copied by Holmes (cited above in general note for series Z 262–280); for 1766, from photographic copies of the Charleston Naval Office list (PRO C. O. 5); for 1768–1772, from the American Inspector General's Ledgers (PRO Customs 16/1); for 1773 and 1774, from Gray (cited above for series Z 122–125, p. 1022), although his partial figure for 1773 has been extended to complete the year. The years terminate October 31 except 1698 (September 28); 1699–1724, 1731 (December 24); and 1768–1773 (January 4 of the following year).

Neither Beaufort-Port Royal nor Georgetown-Wynyaw (South Carolina) seem to have had much importance until 1732. Although the former had its first collector in 1729, there was a lapse of 2½ years before his successor took over (PRO AO 1/804/1038, AO 1/805/1039); and the latter appears to have had its first collector in June 1732 (*South Carolina Gazette*, June 24, 1732). Scattered naval office records show Georgetown exporting 385 barrels for the year 1734 and 509 for the first quarter in 1735; and Beaufort, 342 during the first half of 1736. In 1739, Georgetown exported 2,202 barrels and Beaufort, 2,165 barrels (broadside, cited above, general note for series Z 262–280), an approximate equality which also existed in the period 1768–1772 (PRO Customs 16/1). For lack of a better basis, their exports will be considered for present purposes to have been equal from 1733 to 1768, when exact figures are available and were used. In 1739, the exports of the two together equalled 6½ percent of South Carolina's exports—a percentage which dropped by 1769–1772 to 4.4 percent. Thus, from 1739 to 1768, the Beaufort and Georgetown contributions have been assumed to be 5 percent of the total South Carolina exports. A different formula was used for the years prior to 1739, when their percentage was growing from the 2½ percent which they enjoyed in 1734 (calculated by doubling the Georgetown figures which have survived for that year). On the necessarily arbitrary assumption that the rate of increase was uniform, the two ports each year from 1734 to 1739 added 0.7 percent to their share of South Carolina's exports. Extending the same formula backwards, their share of the Carolina total was 1.8 percent in 1733 and 1.1 percent in 1732.

Romans, cited above, general note for series Z 262–280, provides figures for Georgia for 1756–1767. A comparison of his figures for Georgia's total exports with those of receipts from Georgia in England (see series Z 274–280) for the decade 1756–1765 shows a ratio of one barrel exported for every 2.07 hundredweight received; and for 1740, 1742, 1750, and 1753–1755, the barrels shipped from Georgia have been computed in accordance with that formula, on the basis of English receipts (series Z 274–280). Figures for 1768–1772 come from PRO Customs 16/1. In 1773 and 1774, Georgia is assumed to have contributed 13.9 percent of the total exports, as it did from 1768 to 1772. Years end January 4 of the year following, except for the years for which figures are calculated, as noted above. For those years, no exact date can be assigned and the data are therefore not strictly comparable.

The figures for 1768–1772 provide the best basis for the later period, but for present purposes the 1768 list was not included in the basic calculations described above because it lacks data for coastwise exports; however, it provides the best base for estimating the imports for that year. All that need be assumed is that the ratio of the coastwise exports to the other exports was the same in 1768 as the average of the other four years.

The coastwise entries for 1769–1773 show both inward and outward entries. Thus, to avoid duplications in the Carolina and Georgia entries, only the net exports coastwise have been included. This adjustment cannot be made prior to 1769, but samples from the WPA compilations (see general note for series Z 1–405) indicate that it is very minor.

The data for the various colonies are shown here, not because the individual details are necessarily accurate, but in order that scholars possessing more complete information may adjust the figures wherever possible.

The object of presenting these series is to provide the best possible pattern of the over-all development. The errors in detail are as likely as not to offset one another. Except for

1713–1731, when the estimates of the size of the barrels varied radically, the totals shown here should be within 5 percent of the true figure.

Z 267–273. Rice exported from Charleston, S.C., by destination, 1717–1766.

Source: Compiled by J. R. House from the WPA compilations of naval office lists at the University of California, Berkeley (see general note for series Z 1–405).

The differences in totals here and in series Z 262–266 may result in part from the differences in year-ending dates, as shown in the tabular headnotes.

Z 274–280. Rice exported to England, by origin, 1698–1776.

Source: Compiled by Lawrence A. Harper, University of California, from English Inspector General's Ledgers of Imports and Exports, Public Records Office, London, Customs 3 (except 1727, from PRO T.64/276B/323).

A large proportion of the exported rice was reexported by England, not only to Northern but also to Southern Europe.

Z 281–303. General note.

The two basic sources for the study of the colonial Negro are population statistics (see series Z 1–19) and commercial statistics concerning slave importations. Although direct knowledge of the colonial Negro's natural increase is scarce, available evidence indicates that this increase must have been considerable. It is reported in 1708 that about half of Boston's 400 Negro servants were born there, and Governor James Glen of South Carolina stated in 1749 that the number of Negroes in his colony increased rather than diminished during the nine years when prohibitive taxes and war "prevented any from being imported" (Elizabeth Donnan, ed., *Documents Illustrative of the History of the Slave Trade to America*, Carnegie Institution of Washington, D.C., 1935, vols. III and IV, pp. 24 and 303, respectively). Otherwise, discrepancies between import and population figures (especially in later years) would call for the existence of an illegal trade in Negroes of an extent to which other evidence gives little support.

Donnan's *Documents . . .*, cited above, provides the greatest single source on the subject of the slave trade. She supplies references to many of the varied sources which provide such knowledge as we have of the 17th century, most helpful of which are the statistical reports prepared to help settle disputes between the Royal African Company and the separate traders.

After the first quarter of the 18th century, data on the slave trade usually rest upon the colonial naval office lists (PRO C. O. 5). Colonial newspapers sometimes reported the tallies which had been made in the customhouse; Donnan, *Documents . . .*, cited above, reproduces the individual entries for most of the lists which have survived, and the WPA compilations (see general note for series Z 1–405) give annual totals. In preparing the series on slaves, photographic copies of the naval office lists (PRO C. O. 5) were used when the Donnan entries and the WPA compilations did not agree. It is important to note, however, that the naval office lists report importations by sea rather than overland movements of slaves. Also, it is not always known how many of the Negroes survived after their entry was recorded. The Virginia statistics for 1710–1718 (Donnan, cited above, vol. IV, pp. 175–181) show that of 4,415 Negro slaves entered, 231 died within the time allowed to recover the duty and 103 were drawn back for exportation—7.5 percent of the total importations.

In the case of the southern colonies, the statistics for Virginia and South Carolina are reasonably complete; those for Maryland and Georgia are spotty; and those for North Carolina are virtually nonexistent.

In New England the Negro population appears to have been due to natural increase rather than extensive importations. Governor Dudley of Massachusetts reported in 1708 that about one-half of Boston's Negro servants were born there (Donnan, cited above, vol. III, p. 24), and a comparison of the 1768–1773 trade figures (series Z 281–293) with the population figures (series Z 1–19) suggests that natural increase had become even more important than importations by the revolutionary era.

In the middle colonies the first Negroes were probably brought to New York from Spanish or Dutch prizes in 1625 or 1626. Dutch records are meager but show a consignment of 5 in 1660 and another of 300 in 1664. After the English conquest, New York for a time had an indeterminate trade in slaves with the pirates of Madagascar (Donnan, cited above, vol. III, pp. 405–406, 420, and 423). In Pennsylvania, the number of slaves was always small and their entry often discouraged by high taxes. Donnan (cited above, vol. III, pp. 408–409) believes that data about the slave trade there must be sought in merchant's account books, newspaper advertisements, and items of ship news, some of which appear in Edward R. Turner, "The Negro in Pennsylvania," *Prize Essays of American Historical Association*, Washington, D.C., 1911. In New Jersey, the slave trade centered in the eastern part of the colony, but here too the number of slaves imported was relatively small.

Z 281–293. Slave trade, by origin and destination, 1768–1772.

Source: Compiled by Lawrence A. Harper, University of California, from the American Inspector General's Ledgers of Imports and Exports, Public Records Office, London, Customs 16/1.

Z 294–297. Slave trade in Virginia, 1619–1767.

Source: 1619–1699, Elizabeth Donnan, ed., *Documents Illustrative of the History of the Slave Trade to America*, Carnegie Institution of Washington, D.C., 1935, vol. IV, pp. 4–6, 49–65, and Philip A. Bruce, *Economic History of Virginia in the Seventeenth Century*, vol. II, Macmillan, New York, 1895, pp. 66–85; 1700–1726, Donnan, *Documents Illustrative . . .*, vol. IV, pp. 173–187; 1727–1767, Donnan, vol. IV, pp. 187–234, and WPA compilations of colonial naval office lists (see general note for series Z 1–405).

The title of these series refers to "slaves" because that was the status of most Negroes listed, but it should be remembered that until the middle of the 17th century Negroes came as servants, not as slaves. Unless otherwise noted, these figures show the total trade at all Virginia ports. When one or more quarters of a port's naval office lists are missing, the total for the full year has been estimated, the calculations resting upon a chronological or geographic extension—whichever involved the least element of conjecture. The totals depend upon such estimates in all years after 1726 except 1737–1740, 1743–1745, 1750, 1758, 1761–1762, and 1764, when full records exist for all the ports except Accomack, which can be disregarded because of its lack of direct participation in the slave trade. No figure is given in which the total includes more than 20 percent estimate.

In the case of slaves exported, the highly variable nature of this trade did not warrant estimative totals. Of the slaves exported, 1,055 went to Maryland, 12 to North Carolina, 9 to Rhode Island, 8 and a shipment (number unspecified) to Barbados, 3 to Madeira, 2 to Great Britain, 2 to Georgia, and 1 to Boston.

Z 298–302. Slave trade in New York, 1701–1764.

Source: 1701–1718, E. B. O'Callaghan, ed., *Documents Relative to the Colonial History of the State of New York*, vol. V, Weed, Parsons & Co., Albany, 1855, p. 814; 1719–1764, Donnan, cited above for series Z 294–297, vol. III, pp. 462–509, and WPA compilations of colonial naval office lists (see general note for series Z 1–405).

Figures for New York for 1731 were partially estimated, for missing quarters, by Lawrence A. Harper, University of California. The estimates were derived by obtaining the ratio of the number of slaves imported for each quarter to the number annually imported. This ratio was based on figures covering a period of eight years in which quarterly data were available.

Z 303. Slaves imported into Charleston, S.C., 1706–1773.

Source: 1706–1726, 1749–1751, Donnan, cited above for series Z 294–297, vol. IV, pp. 255, 267, and 301–302; 1727–1739, WPA compilations of the colonial naval office lists (see general note for series Z 1–405); 1752, *South Carolina Gazette*, Charleston, S.C., October 30, 1752; 1753–1772, O. M. Dickerson, *The Navigation Acts and the American Revolution*, University of Pennsylvania Press, Philadelphia, 1951, p. 62; 1773, Leila Sellers, *Charleston Business on the Eve of the American Revolution*, University of North Carolina Press, Chapel Hill, 1934, p. 132.

Z 304–307. Pitch, tar, and turpentine exported from Charleston, S.C., 1725–1774.

Source: 1725–1755, 1760–1764, 1767–1771, Charles J. Gayle, "The Nature and Volume of Exports from Charleston, 1724–1774," *The Proceedings of the South Carolina Historical Association*, Columbia, 1937, p. 31; 1756–1759, 1765, 1772–1774, *South Carolina Gazette*, Charleston, S.C., various issues.

The basic source for these series has been the *South Carolina Gazette*, which obtained the figures from the customhouse books and ran them as cumulative totals from November 1st of most years. The editorial policy of the *Gazette* was not consistent, however; it did not always list the same commodities each year, and sometimes it discontinued the cumulative totals before October 31st.

The WPA compilations (see general note for series Z 1–405) from the English copies of these same records (PRO C. O. 5) provide an alternate source for some years. They also distinguish in detail the destination of the various shipments.

Z 308–313. Timber and timber products exported from Charleston (S.C.) and Savannah, 1754–1774.

Source: Series Z 308–310, 1754–1755, 1760–1764, 1767–1771, Gayle, cited above for series Z 304–307, p. 31; 1756–1759, 1765, 1772–1774, *South Carolina Gazette*, Charleston, S.C., various issues. Series Z 311–313, Oliver M. Dickerson, cited above for series Z 303, pp. 26–27.

The original figures for Savannah were compiled by the Comptroller at that port. For discussion of Charleston figures, see text for series Z 304–307.

Z 314–317. Number of vessels engaged in whaling, and quantity and value of oil acquired, Nantucket, Mass., 1715–1789.

Source: 1715–1785, Obed Macy, *The History of Nantucket*, Hilliard, Gray & Co., Boston, 1835, pp. 54–55 and 232–233; 1787–1789, U.S. Congress, *American State Papers*, Class 4, "Commerce and Navigation" (two volumes), vol. I, Gales and Seaton, Washington, D.C., 1832, p. 16.

The figures shown on pp. 232–233 of the source are stated to be from the Massachusetts Historical Society's Collections. Those on pp. 54–55 cite no authority; however, the Macy

family descended from the first settlers and Obed Macy's data, which are generally consistent with information from other sources, provide the best figures now available.

The development of whaling in Nantucket followed the process typical of all the colonies [Walter S. Tower, *A History of the American Whale Fishery* (publications of the University of Pennsylvania, series in Political Economy and Public Law, No. 20), Philadelphia, 1907]. The early settlers first processed drift whales, then they engaged in the offshore fisheries which probably reached their height at Nantucket in 1726 when 86 whales were taken (Alexander Starbuck, *The History of Nantucket*, C. E. Goodspeed & Co., Boston, 1924, p. 356). The first deep-sea venture occurred about 1712 when a strong wind blew an offshore vessel to sea where it caught a spermaceti whale (Macy, cited above, p. 36). By 1746, Nantucket whalers were making their way to Davis Straits and by 1774 they were sailing as far away as the coast of Brazil (Macy, cited above, p. 54).

The figures for Nantucket may be viewed in better perspective by noting that in 1730 the New England whaling fleet totaled 1,300 tons, and in 1763 that of Massachusetts consisted of 180 sailing vessels. (Raymond McFarland, *A History of the New England Fisheries*, D. Appleton and Company, New York, 1911, p. 86.) At the time of the Revolution, New England had 304 whalers totaling 27,840 tons out of an estimated American fleet of 360 vessels (Tower, cited above, p. 45; Starbuck, cited above, p. 176).

Z 318–329. Daily wages of selected types of workmen, by area, 1621–1781.

Source: 1621–1670 and 1776–1781, Richard B. Morris, *Government and Labor in Early America*, Columbia University Press, New York, 1946; 1710, Richard Walsh, *The Charleston Sons of Liberty*, University of South Carolina Press, Columbia, 1959.

The figures do not represent actual payments, which may have been higher, but they represent what the lawmakers believed was the proper maximum wage rate. Figures are payments to master craftsmen; journeymen received less (for example, 20 pence instead of 2 shillings in 1641).

For New Haven there were two wage rates—one for the summer, which is shown in these series, and one for the winter. For each occupation the winter rate was 6 shillings less in 1640 and 4 shillings less in 1641. Apparently the lower rate for the winter was paid because of the shorter workday.

The legislative rates also throw light on other labor facts. When New Haven set the rate for mowers in 1640, correlation of the daily wage (2 s. 6 d.) with the rate for mowing an acre of fresh marsh shows that they considered it a day's work, although they believed that mowing a salt marsh would take longer and be worth 3 shillings. The next year they confessed the ratio was inadequate when they lowered the daily wages without board to 20 d. and raised the rate for mowing to 3 s. per acre for fresh marsh and 3 s. 6 d. for salt marsh (Morris, cited above, pp. 79–80).

For discussion of the working day, see text for series Z 330–335.

Z 330–335. Daily and monthly wages of agricultural laborers in Maryland, 1638–1676.

Source: Manfred Jonas, "Wages in Early Colonial Maryland," *Maryland Historical Magazine*, vol. LI, March 1956, pp. 27–38.

The source also gives additional information on the cost of living. Its basic data come from scattered items in the *Archives of Maryland* (a series of annual volumes published by the Maryland Historical Society, Baltimore).

In Maryland, during the first half of the 17th century, the working month seems to have extended from 23 to 25 days and the working day from 10 to 12 hours. The 3 winter months were generally not included within the terms of labor contracts. Persons hired by the day worked the same hours and did not get lodging, but received at least 2 meals at the job (Jonas, cited above, pp. 30 and 34–35). In the other colonies the working day was probably much the same. New Haven, for example, specified in 1640 that a day's work was from 10 to 12 hours in summer and 8 hours in winter (Morris, *Government and Labor* . . ., cited above for series Z 318–329, pp. 59, 79, and 84).

Z 336. Index of wholesale prices estimated for the United States, 1720–1789.

Source: U.S. Congress, *Hearings Before the Joint Economic Committee*, 86th Congress, 1st session, Part II, *Historical and Comparative Rates of Production, Productivity, and Prices* (statement presented by Ethel D. Hoover, Bureau of Labor Statistics).

This index (which extends to 1958 in the source) was obtained by combining and splicing index numbers constructed by various investigators for different markets, to approximate a continuous series. The annual indexes were calculated by working forward and backward from the selected base period, 1850–59. No adjustments were made to the original series for differences in coverage or in methods of calculation. However, when wholesale prices in two or more markets were combined, the necessary conversions to a common base period were made, and occasional estimates, as noted in other parts of the source, were used.

For this series, weighted combinations were made of the available index series for three major markets (Philadelphia, New York, and Charleston), except for the years prior to 1732 and the Revolutionary War years. For these years, the estimates were based on Philadelphia prices only. The weights used to combine markets were rough approximations, based chiefly on estimates of the population and trade for each area and on the representative character and adequacy of the available indexes.

Z 337–356. Average annual wholesale prices of selected commodities in Philadelphia, 1720–1775.

Source: Anne Bezanson, Robert D. Gray, and Miriam Hussey, *Prices in Colonial Pennsylvania*, University of Pennsylvania Press, Philadelphia, 1935, pp. 422–424.

The primary source of the original data was the list of "prices current" which first appeared in 1719 in the *American Mercury* and which was continued in that and other newspapers. Gaps were usually filled by reference to merchants' account books and letterbooks (as discussed and listed in the source cited, pp. 3–5, 351–354, and 434–438). The annual averages were computed "by taking the arithmetic mean of the 12 average monthly prices in each year. When any monthly price was missing the available data were averaged quarterly and the annual figure derived from the quarterly averages. . . . In some cases it was necessary to estimate a quarterly price by averaging the last monthly quotation in the previous quarter with the first monthly quotation in the following quarter. No annual price was estimated completely. . . ."

The source volume was sponsored by the International Scientific Committee in Price History, as were a number of other studies of colonial prices drawn together in A. H. Cole, *Wholesale Commodity Prices in the United States: 1700–1861*, Harvard University Press, Cambridge, 1938. In addition to discussion and analyses of prices, this publication offers a statistical supplement of monthly prices for the principal commercial

centers. The tables in it, however, rest primarily upon the Philadelphia prices until the 1750's. Prior to 1750, Boston has only two series, wheat and molasses, which begin in 1720. Although there are gaps in the data, Charleston has series for bread, corn, rice, rum, wine, molasses, and staves beginning 1732; sugar beginning 1744; beef, pork, and indigo in 1747; and coffee, leather, and lumber in 1749. New York has series for flour, bread, rice, sugar, salt, rum, and molasses beginning 1748; and for wheat, beef, and pork beginning 1749.

Price series for the following Philadelphia commodities are shown in the source (not included here because of space limitations): Brown bread, white bread, London loaf sugar, Pennsylvania loaf sugar, indigo, bar iron, pig iron, hogshead staves, pipe staves, turpentine, and gunpowder. In addition to the annual averages, the source contains average monthly prices and monthly and annual indexes (both arithmetic and geometric) of 20 commodities in Philadelphia.

The unit of measure of Madeira wine (pipe) consists of 110 gallons and hundredweights equal 112 pounds, except for tobacco where it equals 100 pounds. Barrels, in the case of beef and pork, consist of 31.5 gallons.

Z 357. Annual rate of exchange on London for Pennsylvania currency, 1720–1775.

Source: See source for series Z 337–356, p. 432.

This series is derived from data in papers of Pennsylvania merchants and the Minutes of the Provincial Council (1739), supplemented in some years by Victor S. Clark, *History of Manufactures in the United States, 1893–1928*, vol. III, Carnegie Institution of Washington, D.C., 1916–1949, pp. 361–362. Bezanson et al., in *Prices* . . ., cited above, p. 431, also give monthly rates of exchanges during the same period.

Z 358. Annual price of an ounce of silver at Boston, 1700–1749.

Source: A. H. Cole, *Wholesale Commodity Prices in the United States: 1700–1861*, Harvard University Press, Cambridge, 1938, p. 119.

The original shilling prices were taken from the Suffolk files by A. M. Davis, *Currency and Banking in the Province of Massachusetts Bay*, vol. I, Macmillan, New York, 1901, pp. 368 and 370. Where more than one price was given for a year, the high and low figures were averaged to determine the price for that year.

Z 359–370. Partial list of bills of credit and Treasury notes issued by American Colonies, 1703–1775.

Source: B. U. Ratchford, *American State Debts*, Duke University Press, Durham, 1941, pp. 26–27.

These series attempt to show the issues of bills of credit and treasury notes emitted by the Colonies between 1703 and 1775. The £82,000 in bills issued by Massachusetts between 1690 and 1702 are not included, nor are the issues of Georgia, which never had a large debt. Under the trustees, the principal circulating medium in Georgia was the "sola" bills, issued only in the original by the trustees. A total of £135,000 of these bills of exchange were issued but only £1,149 remained unredeemed in 1752. Thereafter, Georgia emitted at least two issues of bills: One of £3,000 in 1756 and one of £7,410 in 1761 (Ratchford, cited above, p. 19).

Ratchford concedes that the list may be incomplete and that many of the issues listed were not made at the time nor in the exact amount stated. Sometimes the law authorizing the issue constitutes the only evidence, and nothing indicates "how, when, or to what extent the issue was actually made."

The original source for 1737–1748 for Massachusetts is A. M. Davis, cited above in text for series Z 358. Davis expressed all issues in the terms of old tenor (the form of bills which existed in February 1737). Ratchford did not follow this procedure because he did not feel sufficiently acquainted with the circumstances in each case to make the conversion with assurance. For all other years, the data rest upon a variety of sources cited in the footnotes of Ratchford's first chapter, which provide a helpful bibliography for further reference.

The footnotes to these series indicate the principal purposes for which the larger issues were made. For years when several issues appeared for different purposes, the footnotes indicate the purpose for issuing the majority of the bills.

Z 371–382. Paper money outstanding in American Colonies, 1705–1775.

Source: See source for series Z 359–370, p. 28.

The original sources of the data are various monographs cited in Ratchford's first chapter. Unfortunately, the authors of these monographs did not always attempt to find or to make estimates themselves. Some of the estimates are those of legislative committees or public officials and, less frequently, of contemporary writers. Many of the estimates for 1739 and 1748 come from William Douglass whose work is discussed in Charles Bullock, Introduction, *Economic Studies of the American Economic Association*, vol. II, No. 1. Georgia did not warrant a separate series, the only estimate being one for £5,500 for 1761.

For approximately a fifth of the figures, the actual year of issuance differs from that indicated in this table by one or two years; for exact year of issuance, see source.

Z 383–387. Tax collections in America under the different revenue laws, 1765–1774.

Source: O. M. Dickerson, cited above for series Z 303, p. 201.

Tax records have long been an untapped source of economic data. Dickerson has gathered figures from the English Treasury Papers for both the revenues collected under the Navigation Act of 1673 (25 Car. II c 7) and the new revenue measures which followed the French and Indian War (1763). He estimates (p. 202) that seizures (often highly technical) under the new revenue program cost the Americans not less than £60,956 "exclusive of fees, direct plunder, and costs of defending suits in the admiralty courts."

Z 388–405. Basic weekly diets in Britain and America, 1622–1790.

Source: Compiled by Austin White (graduate student, University of California) based on the following: **Series Z 388,**

M. S. Rose, *A Laboratory Handbook for Dietetics*, Macmillan, New York, 1937. **Series Z 389–405,** 1622, see source for series Z 43–55, vol. II, p. 318; 1632, E. M. Leonard, *The Early History of English Poor Relief*, Cambridge University Press, Cambridge, 1900, pp. 198–199; 1638, John Josselyn, "An Account of Two Voyages to New England Made During the Years 1638–1663," *Massachusetts Historical Society Collections*, Third Series, III, 1833, pp. 220–221; 1676, Philip A. Bruce, *Institutional History of Virginia in the Seventeenth Century . . .*, vol. II, Putnam, New York, 1910, p. 87; first half of 18th century, William Douglass, *A Summary, Historical and Political, of the First Planting, Progressive Improvement, and Present State of the British Settlements in North America*, vol. I, R & J Dodsley, London, 1760, p. 536; 1735, Abbot Smith, *Colonists in Bondage*, University of North Carolina Press, Chapel Hill, 1947, p. 212; 1744–1746, Howard Chapin, *The Tartar, the Armed Sloop of the Colony of Rhode Island in King George's War*, Providence, 1922, p. 17; 1747, Isabel M. Calder, *Colonial Captivities, Marches, and Journeys*, Macmillan, New York, 1935, p. 40; 1755, Basil Sollers, "The Acadians (French Neutrals) Transported to Maryland," *Maryland Historical Magazine*, vol. III, March 1908, pp. 8–10; 1757, John Fitzpatrick, ed., *The Writings of George Washington*, vol. II, U.S. Government Printing Office, Washington, D.C., 1931, p. 72; 1761, "Brigade Order Books, Montreal, September 29, 1761," *Journals of the Hon. William Hervey, from 1755 to 1814*, Paul and Mathew, Bury St. Edmunds, England, 1906, p. 154; about 1770, Walter Besant, *London in the Eighteenth Century*, A & C Black, London, 1903, p. 556; 1775, Fitzpatrick, cited above, vol. III, p. 409; 1776, "Journal of the Committees of Observation of the Middle District of Frederick County, Maryland," *Maryland Historical Magazine*, vol. XI, December 1916, p. 310; 1780 (Continental Army), John W. Wright, "Some Notes on the Continental Army," *William and Mary Quarterly*, vol. XI, 1931, p. 105; 1780 (French prisoners), Rupert C. Jarvis, ed., *Customs Letter-Book of the Port of Liverpool*, Manchester, 1954, p. 106; about 1790, Fitzpatrick, cited above, vol. XXXI, pp. 186–187; before 1861 (majority of slaves), Kenneth Stampp, *The Peculiar Institution*, Alfred A. Knopf, New York, 1956, p. 282.

The caloric contents of the weekly diet have been divided by 7 for greater ease in comparing them with modern charts which are usually stated in daily terms.

The data from *The Writings of George Washington* have been calculated on the basis of the ratio for an adult male. Women slaves referred to in Washington's diary were assumed to require ⅚ of that of a man; children, ⅙. A barrel of corn was calculated as weighing 196 pounds; a barrel of fish, 290 pounds.

COLONIAL STATISTICS

Series Z 1-19. Estimated Population of American Colonies: 1610 to 1780

Series No.	Colony	1780	1770	1760	1750	1740	1730	1720	1710	1700	1690	1680	1670	1660	1650	1640	1630
	WHITE AND NEGRO																
1	Total	2,780,369	2,148,076	1,593,625	1,170,760	905,563	629,445	466,185	331,711	250,888	210,372	151,507	111,935	75,058	50,368	26,634	4,646
2	Maine (counties)[1]	49,133	31,257												1,000	900	400
3	New Hampshire	87,802	62,396	39,093	27,505	23,256	10,755	9,375	5,681	4,958	4,164	2,047	1,805	1,555	1,305	1,055	500
4	Vermont	47,620	10,000														
5	Plymouth[2]										7,424	6,400	5,333	1,980	1,566	1,020	390
6	Massachusetts[1][2]	268,627	235,308	222,600	188,000	151,613	114,116	91,008	62,390	55,941	49,504	39,752	30,000	20,082	14,037	8,932	506
7	Rhode Island	52,946	58,196	45,471	33,226	25,255	16,950	11,680	7,573	5,894	4,224	3,017	2,155	1,539	785	300	----
8	Connecticut	206,701	183,881	142,470	111,280	89,580	75,530	58,830	39,450	25,970	21,645	17,246	12,603	7,980	4,139	1,472	
9	New York	210,541	162,920	117,138	76,696	63,665	48,594	36,919	21,625	19,107	13,909	9,830	5,754	4,936	4,116		350
10	New Jersey	139,627	117,431	93,813	71,393	51,373	37,510	29,818	19,872	14,010	8,000	3,400	1,000				
11	Pennsylvania	327,305	240,057	183,703	119,666	85,637	51,707	30,962	24,450	17,950	11,450	680					
12	Delaware	45,385	35,496	33,250	28,704	19,870	9,170	5,385	3,645	2,470	1,482	1,005	700	540	185		
13	Maryland	245,474	202,599	162,267	141,073	116,093	91,113	66,133	42,741	29,604	24,024	17,904	13,226	8,426	4,504	583	
14	Virginia	538,004	447,016	339,726	231,033	180,440	114,000	87,757	78,281	58,560	53,046	43,596	35,309	27,020	18,731	10,442	2,500
15	North Carolina	270,133	197,200	110,442	72,984	51,760	30,000	21,270	15,120	10,720	7,600	5,430	3,850	1,000			
16	South Carolina	180,000	124,244	94,074	64,000	45,000	30,000	17,048	10,883	5,704	3,900	1,200	200				
17	Georgia	56,071	23,375	9,578	5,200	2,021											
18	Kentucky	45,000	15,700														
19	Tennessee	10,000	1,000														
	NEGRO																
1	Total	575,420	459,822	325,806	236,420	150,024	91,021	68,839	44,866	27,817	16,729	6,971	4,535	2,920	1,600	597	60
2	Maine (counties)[1]	458	475														
3	New Hampshire	541	654	600	550	500	200	170	150	130	100	75	65	50	40	30	
4	Vermont	50	25														
6	Massachusetts[1]	4,822	4,754	4,866	4,075	3,035	2,780	2,150	1,310	800	400	170	160	422	295	150	
7	Rhode Island	[3]2,671	3,761	3,468	3,347	2,408	1,648	543	375	300	250	175	115	65	25		
8	Connecticut	[3]5,885	5,698	3,783	3,010	2,598	1,490	1,093	750	450	200	50	35	25	20	15	
9	New York	21,054	19,112	16,340	11,014	8,996	6,956	5,740	2,811	2,256	1,670	1,200	690	600	500	232	10
10	New Jersey	10,460	8,220	6,567	5,354	4,366	3,008	2,385	1,332	840	450	200	60				
11	Pennsylvania	7,855	5,761	4,409	2,872	2,055	1,241	2,000	1,575	430	270	25					
12	Delaware	2,996	1,836	1,733	1,496	1,035	478	700	500	135	82	55	40	30	15		
13	Maryland	80,515	63,818	49,004	43,450	24,031	17,220	12,499	7,945	3,227	2,162	1,611	1,190	758	300	20	
14	Virginia	220,582	187,605	140,570	101,452	60,000	30,000	26,559	23,118	16,390	9,345	3,000	2,000	950	405	150	50
15	North Carolina	91,000	69,600	33,554	19,800	11,000	6,000	3,000	900	415	300	210	150	20			
16	South Carolina	97,000	75,178	57,334	39,000	30,000	20,000	12,000	4,100	2,444	1,500	200	30				
17	Georgia	20,831	10,625	3,578	1,000												
18	Kentucky	7,200	2,500														
19	Tennessee	1,500	200														

Series No.	Colony	1620	1610
	WHITE AND NEGRO		
5	Plymouth		102
14	Virginia	[4]2,200	350

[1] For 1660-1760, Maine Counties included with Massachusetts.
[2] Plymouth became a part of the Province of Massachusetts in 1691.
[3] Includes some Indians.
[4] Includes 20 Negroes.

Series Z 20. Percent Distribution of the White Population, by Nationality: 1790

Area	Total	English	Scotch	Irish Ulster	Irish Free State	German	Dutch	French	Swedish	Spanish	Unassigned
Total colonies	100.0	60.9	8.3	6.0	3.7	8.7	3.4	1.7	0.7	---------	6.6
Maine	100.0	60.0	4.5	8.0	3.7	1.3	0.1	1.3			21.1
New Hampshire	100.0	61.0	6.2	4.6	2.9	0.4	0.1	0.7			24.1
Vermont	100.0	76.0	5.1	3.2	1.9	0.2	0.6	0.4			12.6
Massachusetts	100.0	82.0	4.4	2.6	1.3	0.3	0.2	0.8			8.4
Rhode Island	100.0	71.0	5.8	2.0	0.8	0.5	0.4	0.8		0.1	18.6
Connecticut	100.0	67.0	2.2	1.8	1.1	0.3	0.3	0.9			26.4
New York	100.0	52.0	7.0	5.1	3.0	8.2	17.5	3.8	0.5		2.9
New Jersey	100.0	47.0	7.7	6.3	3.2	9.2	16.6	2.4	3.9		3.7
Pennsylvania	100.0	35.3	8.6	11.0	3.5	33.3	1.8	1.8	0.8		3.9
Delaware	100.0	60.0	8.0	6.3	5.4	1.1	4.3	1.6	8.9		[1]4.4
Maryland and District of Columbia	100.0	64.5	7.6	5.8	6.5	11.7	0.5	1.2	0.5		1.7
Virginia and West Virginia	100.0	68.5	10.2	6.2	5.5	6.3	0.3	1.5	0.6		.9
North Carolina	100.0	66.0	14.8	5.7	5.4	4.7	0.3	1.7	0.2		1.2
South Carolina	100.0	60.2	15.1	9.4	4.4	5.0	0.4	3.9	0.2		1.4
Georgia	100.0	57.4	15.5	11.5	3.8	7.6	0.2	2.3	0.6		1.1
Kentucky and Tennessee	100.0	57.9	10.0	7.0	5.2	14.0	1.3	2.2	0.5		1.9
OTHER AREAS											
Northwest Territory	100.0	29.8	4.1	2.9	1.8	4.3		57.1			
Spanish, United States	100.0	2.5	0.3	0.2	0.1	0.4				96.5	
French, United States	100.0	11.2	1.6	1.1	0.7	8.7		64.2		12.5	

[1] Corrected figure; does not agree with source.

Series Z 21–34. Value of Exports To and Imports From England, by American Colonies: 1697 to 1776

[**In pounds sterling.** For years ending December 24, except as noted]

Year	Total Exports	Total Imports	New England Exports	New England Imports	New York Exports	New York Imports	Pennsylvania Exports	Pennsylvania Imports	Virginia and Maryland Exports	Virginia and Maryland Imports	Carolina Exports	Carolina Imports	Georgia Exports	Georgia Imports
	21	22	23	24	25	26	27	28	29	30	31	32	33	34
1776	103,964	55,415	762	55,050	2,318		1,421	365	73,226		13,668		12,569	
1775	1,920,950	196,162	116,588	71,625	187,018	1,228	175,962	1,366	758,356	1,921	579,549	6,245	103,477	113,777
1774	1,373,846	2,590,437	112,248	562,476	80,008	437,937	69,611	625,652	612,030	528,738	432,302	378,116	67,647	57,518
1773	1,369,229	1,979,412	124,624	527,055	76,246	289,214	36,652	426,448	589,803	328,904	456,513	344,859	85,391	62,932
1772	1,258,515	3,012,635	126,265	824,830	82,707	343,970	29,133	507,909	528,404	793,910	425,923	449,610	66,083	92,406
1771	1,339,840	4,202,472	150,381	1,420,119	95,875	653,621	31,615	728,744	577,848	920,326	420,311	409,169	63,810	70,493
1770	1,015,535	1,925,571	148,011	394,451	69,882	475,991	28,109	134,881	435,094	717,782	278,907	146,273	55,532	56,193
1769	1,060,206	1,336,122	129,353	207,993	73,466	74,918	26,111	199,909	361,892	488,362	387,114	306,600	82,270	58,340
1768	1,251,454	2,157,218	148,375	419,797	87,115	482,930	59,406	432,107	406,048	475,954	508,108	289,868	42,402	56,562
1767	1,096,079	1,900,923	128,207	406,081	61,422	417,957	37,641	371,830	437,926	437,628	395,027	244,093	35,856	23,334
1766	1,043,958	1,804,333	141,733	409,642	67,020	330,829	26,851	327,314	461,693	372,548	293,587	296,732	53,074	67,268
1765	1,151,698	1,944,114	145,819	451,299	54,959	382,349	25,148	363,368	505,671	383,224	385,918	334,709	34,183	29,165
1764	1,110,572	2,249,710	88,157	459,765	53,697	515,416	36,258	435,191	559,408	515,192	341,727	305,808	31,325	18,338
1763	1,106,131	1,631,997	74,815	258,854	53,998	238,560	38,228	284,152	642,294	555,391	282,366	250,132	14,469	44,908
1762	742,632	1,377,160	41,733	247,385	58,882	288,046	38,091	206,199	415,709	417,599	181,695	194,170	6,522	23,761
1761	847,892	1,652,078	46,225	334,225	48,648	289,570	39,170	204,067	455,083	545,350	253,002	254,587	5,764	24,279
1760	761,099	2,611,764	37,802	599,647	21,125	480,106	22,754	707,998	504,451	605,882	162,769	218,131	12,198	
1759	639,909	2,345,453	25,985	527,067	21,684	630,785	22,404	498,161	357,228	459,007	206,534	215,255	6,074	15,178
1758	670,720	1,712,887	30,204	465,694	14,260	356,555	21,383	260,953	454,362	438,471	150,511	181,002		10,212
1757	610,684	1,628,348	27,556	363,404	19,168	353,311	14,190	268,426	418,881	426,687	130,889	213,949		2,571
1756	659,356	1,352,178	47,359	384,371	24,073	250,425	20,095	200,169	337,759	334,897	222,915	181,780	7,155	536
1755	939,553	1,112,997	59,533	341,796	28,054	151,071	32,336	144,456	489,668	285,157	325,525	187,887	4,437	2,630
1754	1,007,759	1,176,279	66,538	329,433	26,663	127,497	30,649	244,647	573,435	323,513	307,238	149,215	3,236	1,974
1753	972,740	1,452,944	83,395	345,523	50,553	277,864	38,527	245,644	632,574	356,776	164,634	213,009	3,057	14,128
1752	1,004,182	1,148,127	74,313	273,340	40,648	194,030	29,978	201,666	569,453	325,151	288,264	150,777	1,526	3,163
1751	835,651	1,233,168	63,287	305,974	42,363	248,941	23,870	190,917	460,085	347,027	245,491	138,244	555	2,065
1750	814,768	1,313,083	48,455	343,659	35,634	267,130	28,191	217,713	508,939	349,419	191,607	133,037	1,942	2,125
1749	663,524	1,230,386	39,999	238,286	23,413	265,773	14,944	238,637	434,618	323,600	150,499	164,085	51	5
1748	716,626	830,433	29,748	197,682	12,358	143,311	12,363	75,330	494,852	252,624	167,305	160,172		1,314
1747	660,715	726,669	41,771	210,640	14,992	137,984	3,832	82,404	492,619	200,088	107,500	95,529		24
1746	559,500	755,926	38,612	209,177	8,841	86,712	15,779	73,699	419,371	282,545	76,897	102,809		984
1745	554,431	535,253	38,948	140,463	14,083	54,957	10,130	54,280	399,423	197,799	91,847	86,815		939
1744	667,524	640,881	50,248	143,982	14,527	119,920	7,446	62,214	402,709	234,855	192,594	79,141		769
1743	880,807	829,273	63,185	172,461	15,067	135,487	9,596	79,340	557,821	328,195	235,136	111,499	2	2,291
1742	659,227	800,052	53,166	148,899	13,536	167,591	8,527	75,295	427,769	264,186	154,607	127,063	1,622	17,018
1741	912,291	885,492	60,052	198,147	21,142	140,430	17,158	91,010	577,109	248,582	236,830	204,770		2,553
1740	718,416	813,382	72,389	171,081	21,498	118,777	15,048	56,751	341,997	281,428	266,560	181,821	924	3,524
1739	754,276	695,869	46,604	220,378	18,459	106,070	8,134	54,452	444,654	217,200	236,192	94,445	233	3,324
1738	620,212	751,270	59,116	203,233	16,228	133,438	11,918	61,450	391,814	258,860	141,119	87,793	17	6,496
1737	775,382	682,434	63,347	223,923	16,833	125,833	15,198	56,690	492,246	211,301	187,758	58,986		5,701
1736	699,764	677,624	66,788	222,158	17,944	86,000	20,786	61,513	380,163	204,794	214,083	101,147		2,012
1735	652,326	668,664	72,899	189,125	14,155	80,405	21,919	48,804	394,995	220,381	145,348	117,837	3,010	12,112
1734	611,350	556,275	82,252	146,460	15,307	81,758	20,217	54,392	373,090	172,086	120,466	99,658	18	1,921
1733	669,633	548,890	61,983	184,570	11,626	65,417	14,776	40,565	403,198	186,177	177,845	70,466	203	1,695
1732	519,036	531,253	64,095	216,600	9,411	65,540	8,524	41,698	310,799	148,289	126,207	58,298		828
1731	650,863	536,266	49,048	183,467	20,756	66,116	12,786	44,260	408,502	171,278	159,771	71,145		
1730	572,585	536,860	54,701	208,196	8,740	64,356	10,582	48,592	346,823	150,931	151,739	64,785		
1729	575,282	422,958	52,512	161,102	15,833	64,760	7,434	29,799	386,174	108,931	113,329	58,366		
1728	605,324	517,861	64,689	194,590	21,141	81,634	15,230	37,478	413,089	171,092	91,175	33,067		
1727	637,135	502,927	75,052	187,277	31,617	67,452	12,823	31,979	421,588	192,965	96,055	23,254		
1726	526,303	553,297	63,816	200,882	38,307	84,866	5,960	37,634	324,767	185,981	93,453	43,934		
1725	415,650	549,693	72,021	201,768	24,976	70,650	11,981	42,209	214,730	195,884	91,942	39,182		
1724	462,681	461,584	69,585	168,507	21,191	63,020	4,057	30,324	277,344	161,894	90,504	37,839		
1723	461,761	411,590	59,337	176,486	27,992	53,013	8,332	15,992	287,997	123,853	78,103	42,246		
1722	437,696	424,725	47,955	133,722	20,118	57,478	6,882	26,397	283,091	172,754	79,650	34,374		
1721	493,871	331,905	50,483	114,524	15,681	50,754	8,037	21,548	357,812	127,376	61,858	17,703		
1720	468,188	319,702	49,206	128,767	16,836	37,397	7,928	24,531	331,482	110,717	62,736	18,290		
1719	463,054	393,000	54,452	125,317	19,596	56,355	6,564	27,068	332,069	164,630	50,373	19,630		
1718	¹457,471	¹425,333	61,591	131,885	27,331	62,966	5,588	22,716	316,576	191,925	46,385	15,841		
1717	¹426,090	¹439,666	58,898	132,001	24,534	44,140	4,499	22,505	296,884	215,962	41,275	25,058		
1716	¹424,389	¹402,042	69,595	121,156	21,971	52,173	5,193	21,842	281,343	179,599	46,287	27,272		
1715	¹297,246	¹452,366	66,555	164,650	21,316	54,629	5,461	17,182	174,756	199,274	29,158	16,631		
1714	¹395,774	¹333,443	51,541	121,288	29,810	44,643	2,663	14,927	280,470	128,873	31,290	23,712		
1713	¹303,222	¹284,556	49,904	120,778	14,428	46,470	178	17,037	206,263	76,304	32,449	23,967		
1712	¹365,971	¹309,691	24,699	128,105	12,466	18,524	1,471	8,464	297,941	134,583	29,394	20,015		
1711	¹324,698	¹297,626	26,415	137,421	12,193	28,856	38	19,408	273,181	91,535	12,871	20,406		
1710	¹249,814	¹293,659	31,112	106,338	8,203	31,475	1,277	8,594	188,429	127,639	20,793	19,613		
1709	¹324,534	¹269,596	29,559	120,349	12,259	34,577	617	5,881	261,668	80,268	20,431	28,521		
1708	286,435	240,183	49,635	115,505	10,847	26,899	2,120	6,722	213,493	79,061	10,340	11,996		
1707	284,798	413,244	38,793	120,631	14,283	29,855	786	14,365	207,625	237,901	23,311	10,492		
1706	187,073	161,691	22,210	57,050	2,849	31,588	4,210	11,037	149,152	58,015	8,652	4,001		
1705	150,961	291,722	22,793	62,504	7,393	27,902	1,309	7,206	116,768	174,322	2,698	19,788		
1704	321,972	176,088	30,823	74,896	10,540	22,294	2,430	11,819	264,112	60,458	14,067	6,621		
1703	204,295	296,210	33,539	59,608	7,471	17,562	5,160	9,899	144,928	196,713	13,197	12,428		
1702	335,788	186,809	37,026	64,625	7,965	29,991	4,145	9,342	274,782	72,391	11,870	10,460		
1701	309,134	343,826	32,656	86,322	18,547	31,910	5,220	12,003	235,738	199,683	16,973	13,908		
1700	395,021	344,341	41,486	91,918	17,567	49,410	4,608	18,529	317,302	173,481	14,058	11,003		
1699	255,397	403,614	26,660	127,279	16,818	42,792	1,477	17,064	198,115	205,078	12,327	11,401		
1698²	226,055	458,097	31,254	93,517	8,763	25,279	2,720	10,704	174,053	310,135	9,265	18,462		
1697²	279,852	140,129	26,282	68,468	10,093	4,579	3,347	2,997	227,756	58,796	12,374	5,289		

¹ Corrected figures. Figures shown in source for 1709–1718 incorrectly presented as totals of components.
² For years ending Sept. 28.

Series Z 35–42.　Value of Exports To and Imports From England by New York: 1751 to 1775

[In pounds sterling.　For years ending December 24.　Foreign manufactures "In time" are those which could receive a drawback (refund) of duties; "Out of time" are those which could not. Outports are all ports in England other than London]

	Between New York and London				Between New York and outports			
	Exports to London	Imports from London			Exports to outports	Imports from outports		
Year		English manufactures	Manufactures of other nations			English manufactures	Manufactures of other nations	
			In time	Out of time			In time	Out of time
	35	36	37	38	39	40	41	42
1775	95,106	1,140	55	---------	91,912	---------	33	---------
1774	49,381	250,728	61,908	10,612	30,627	108,271	5,673	746
1773	54,476	127,433	69,942	4,205	21,771	71,470	16,166	---------
1772	58,743	183,663	30,809	10,246	23,964	111,175	7,688	390
1771	72,895	393,345	66,842	23,031	22,981	158,764	11,588	52
1770	55,192	284,973	45,494	15,248	14,691	119,451	10,555	272
1769	38,585	48,991	3,900	2,325	34,881	16,327	3,230	146
1768	50,510	299,481	96,381	8,111	36,606	72,484	6,180	293
1767	35,502	258,012	57,586	17,705	25,921	75,249	9,067	339
1766	45,688	184,866	18,940	47,374	21,338	58,024	18,285	3,341
1765	38,233	217,488	20,288	81,312	16,727	42,285	19,909	1,068
1764	28,922	336,352	37,486	99,032	24,776	34,250	7,837	459
1763	29,978	133,444	30,094	34,140	24,011	38,024	2,828	30
1762	17,730	216,165	23,357	28,091	41,152	19,962	472	---------
1761	16,721	89,631	25,851	7,103	31,927	18,449	3,927	232
1760	6,328	387,839	42,124	18,065	14,797	28,628	2,995	455
1759	10,012	483,952	59,804	58,826	11,673	23,903	4,300	---------
1758	3,442	263,290	30,136	43,946	10,819	16,154	2,772	256
1757	9,828	228,378	43,149	37,522	9,340	34,780	8,864	620
1756	13,136	169,234	31,753	9,478	10,937	31,311	8,253	396
1755	17,987	114,451	17,097	4,191	10,067	14,756	525	51
1754	21,289	87,499	13,501	7,845	5,374	13,600	5,052	---------
1753	45,866	199,578	25,769	24,951	4,687	16,825	10,418	325
1752	38,485	124,329	21,846	28,916	2,164	13,113	5,213	613
1751	36,997	124,190	25,530	48,177	5,367	33,191	17,072	780

Series Z 43–55.　Tonnage Capacity of Ships and Value of Exports and Imports of American Colonies, by Destination and Origin: 1769 and 1770

[Value of exports and imports in pounds sterling.　For years ending January 4 of following year]

| Year and destination or origin | Total | New Hampshire | Massachusetts | Rhode Island | Connecticut | New York | New Jersey | Pennsylvania | Maryland | Virginia | North Carolina | South Carolina | Georgia |
	43	44	45	46	47	48	49	50	51	52	53	54	55
1770 TONNAGE													
Outward bound	351,664	20,192	70,282	20,661	20,263	26,653	1,181	49,654	33,474	45,179	21,490	32,031	10,604
Great Britain and Ireland	[1]98,825	1,910	13,778	955	426	7,357	---------	7,999	17,967	25,123	7,393	12,457	3,460
Southern Europe and Africa	37,237	185	5,419	755	180	3,018	---------	11,395	5,337	3,682	655	6,291	320
British and foreign West Indies	[1]108,050	12,419	20,957	6,779	9,923	7,005	648	14,839	5,118	10,096	6,893	8,194	5,179
America, Bermuda, and Bahamas	107,552	5,678	30,128	12,172	9,734	9,273	533	15,421	5,052	6,278	6,549	5,089	1,645
Inward bound	331,942	15,362	65,271	18,667	19,223	25,539	1,018	50,901	30,477	44,803	20,963	29,804	9,914
Great Britain and Ireland	82,934	1,200	13,916	400	210	5,722	---------	7,917	13,693	21,236	6,202	10,163	2,275
Southern Europe and Africa	37,717	---------	6,213	101	---------	3,354	140	15,010	5,005	4,403	440	2,256	795
British and foreign West Indies	106,713	10,300	19,917	7,121	8,656	8,695	365	15,883	5,093	9,547	5,930	10,588	4,618
America, Bermuda, and Bahamas	104,578	3,862	25,225	11,045	10,357	7,768	513	12,091	6,686	9,617	8,391	6,797	2,226
1769 TONNAGE													
Outward bound	339,302	19,744	63,666	17,775	17,966	26,859	1,093	42,986	30,996	52,008	23,113	33,855	9,241
Great Britain and Ireland	99,121	2,822	14,044	540	580	6,470	---------	7,219	16,116	24,594	7,805	15,902	3,029
Southern Europe and Africa	42,601	170	5,102	863	200	3,483	---------	12,070	6,224	7,486	1,030	5,773	200
British and foreign West Indies	96,382	12,878	17,532	6,060	9,201	5,466	555	11,959	3,358	11,397	6,945	6,377	4,654
America, Bermuda, and Bahamas	101,198	3,874	26,988	10,312	7,985	11,440	538	11,738	5,298	8,531	7,333	5,803	1,358
Inward bound	332,146	16,446	66,451	16,836	18,016	26,632	936	45,028	30,688	47,237	23,076	31,107	9,693
Great Britain and Ireland	90,710	915	14,340	415	150	5,224	---------	9,309	15,486	20,652	6,415	15,281	2,523
Southern Europe and Africa	34,151	480	6,595	226	105	2,730	25	10,745	4,095	4,600	700	3,325	525
British and foreign West Indies	94,916	9,500	17,898	5,958	7,790	6,964	257	12,521	4,533	11,612	6,702	6,893	4,288
America, Bermuda, and Bahamas	112,369	5,551	27,618	10,237	9,971	11,714	654	12,453	6,574	10,373	9,259	5,608	2,357
1769 VALUE													
Exports	2,852,441		550,090			231,906	2,532	410,757	991,402		569,585		96,170
Great Britain	1,531,516		142,776			113,382	---------	28,112	759,961		405,015		82,270
Southern Europe and Africa	573,015	561	86,503	9,255	2,567	52,199	---------	204,313	66,556	73,635	3,310	73,501	614
West Indies	747,910	40,431	123,394	65,207	79,395	66,325	2,532	178,331	22,303	68,946	27,944	59,815	13,286
Imports	2,623,412		564,034			188,976	1,991	399,821	851,140		535,714		81,736
Great Britain	1,604,976		223,696			75,931	---------	204,980	714,944		327,084		58,341
Southern Europe and Africa	228,682	652	21,908	2,761	267	15,625	327	14,249	10,083	16,462	2,013	130,347	13,987
West Indies	789,754	48,529	155,387	56,840	53,994	97,420	1,664	180,592	32,198	77,454	10,604	65,666	9,408

[1] Figures disagree with source used here (Macpherson); corrected to agree with sum of components and with original source (PRO Customs 16/1).

Series Z 56–75. Number and Tonnage Capacity of Ships Outward and Inward Bound, by Destination and Origin: 1714 to 1772

[Prior to 1768, for years ending December 24, except as noted; 1768–1772, January 4 of following year. In some years, detail will not add to total since ships were sometimes counted twice; see text]

Series No.	Destination or origin	1772 Number	1772 Tonnage	1771 Number	1771 Tonnage	1770 Number	1770 Tonnage	1769 Number	1769 Tonnage	1768 Number	1768 Tonnage	1765–66, tonnage[1]	1755 Number	1755 Tonnage	1754 Number	1754 Tonnage	1714–17[2] Number	1714–17[2] Tonnage
	BOSTON																	
56	Outward bound	845	42,506	794	38,995	800	36,965	828	37,045	612	33,695	30,444	406	21,295	447	26,669	416	20,927
57	Great Britain	57	6,178	55	5,750	56	5,819	66	6,707	67	6,428	5,286	35	2,975	26	2,510	48	3,985
58	Ireland	1	170					1	60	2	170	436	2	100	3	165		
59	Europe	11	555	22	1,113	15	813	20	1,081	22	1,333	1,075	29	1,853	31	2,465	19	1,185
60	Africa	5	420	4	267	6	415	4	495			275			1	75		
61	Bahama Islands	8	215	12	320	5	100	6	175			50	1	50	5	260	4	124
62	Bermuda Islands	1	70	1	40			1	20						3	80	5	124
63	Caribbean	178	10,703	136	9,171	131	8,248	143	8,995	147	10,095	7,806	133	7,945	149	10,521	191	10,897
64	Thirteen Colonies	443	17,528	439	16,764	464	16,638	457	16,132	281	11,451	11,926	122	4,854	156	7,052	117	3,583
65	Other American Colonies	141	6,667	125	5,570	123	4,932	130	3,380	93	4,218	3,590	81	3,438	76	3,621	28	891
66	Inward bound	852	43,633	821	39,420	819	38,360	879	40,483	549	31,983	33,786	287	14,585	303	17,575	[3]	[3]
67	Great Britain	93	9,325	72	7,502	74	6,830	75	7,333	69	6,946	7,163	32	3,040	43	4,448		
68	Ireland							1	100	3	220	80	2	85	2	110		
69	Europe	20	1,343	17	1,055	23	1,640	31	2,129	22	1,871	2,018	27	1,963	37	2,763		
70	Africa																	
71	Bahama Islands	11	340	9	215	4	110	5	160			163			7	345		
72	Bermuda Islands	1	70	2	85	1	45	1	20			80	2	60				
73	Caribbean	204	12,469	196	12,155	188	11,088	172	10,495	160	10,811	6,295	48	2,391	71	4,482		
74	Thirteen Colonies	427	14,713	382	12,827	422	14,118	430	14,200	204	8,266	14,375	149	5,651	139	5,347		
75	Other American Colonies	96	5,373	143	5,581	107	4,529	164	6,046	91	3,869	3,612	28	1,475	11	445		

Series No.	Destination or origin	1772 Number	1772 Tonnage	1771 Number	1771 Tonnage	1770 Number	1770 Tonnage	1769 Number	1769 Tonnage	1768 Number	1768 Tonnage	1765–66, tonnage[1]	1764, tonnage[4]	1763, tonnage[4]
	NEW YORK													
56	Outward bound	700	28,574	524	25,433	612	26,653	787	26,859	480	23,566	19,862	16,982	15,741
57	Great Britain	39	4,280	45	4,830	46	4,665	47	3,955	56	5,130	2,872	2,952	2,079
58	Ireland	19	1,610	27	2,476	29	2,692	30	2,515	30	2,522	2,035	1,882	1,460
59	Europe	48	2,449	40	2,029	58	2,920	78	3,278	45	2,360	3,190	1,087	1,000
60	Africa	9	260	4	115	2	98	5	205	2	35	290	140	70
61	Bahama Islands	5	88	7	135	8	144	2	35	4	67	50	93	35
62	Bermuda Islands	3	85	6	153	4	95	8	127	7	172	190	230	115
63	Caribbean	199	8,076	194	7,708	189	7,005	125	5,466	156	6,981	8,385	7,898	7,507
64	Thirteen Colonies	324	8,859	134	4,968	188	5,655	430	9,068	125	3,754	1,129	1,495	2,450
65	Other American Colonies	54	2,867	67	3,019	88	3,379	62	2,210	55	2,545	1,721	1,205	1,025
66	Inward bound	710	28,861	557	25,042	600	25,539	725	26,650	462	21,847	18,214	16,750	11,129
67	Great Britain	61	6,117	63	6,850	39	4,055	41	3,785	79	7,158	4,842	4,040	3,980
68	Ireland	11	915	13	1,411	19	1,667	18	1,435	15	1,387	880	1,647	550
69	Europe	38	2,480	27	1,344	44	3,124	39	2,700	31	1,500	710	2,385	1,390
70	Africa					4	230	1	30	2	130	295		65
71	Bahama Islands	11	268	9	210	11	284	4	42	9	204	75	103	205
72	Bermuda Islands	5	215	4	105	1	30	2	90	3	115	45	370	200
73	Caribbean	208	8,170	220	8,191	226	8,695	179	6,964	158	6,301	8,265	7,430	4,124
74	Thirteen Colonies	352	9,247	184	5,416	217	5,941	394	9,884	139	3,952	2,450	645	615
75	Other American Colonies	24	1,449	37	1,515	39	1,513	47	1,720	26	1,100	652	130	

Series No.	Destination or origin	1754[4] Number	1754[4] Tonnage	1739 Number	1739 Tonnage	1735 Number	1735 Tonnage	1734 Number	1734 Tonnage	1733 Number	1733 Tonnage	1727 Number	1727 Tonnage	1726 Number	1726 Tonnage	1715–18[2] Number	1715–18[2] Tonnage
	NEW YORK—Con.																	
56	Outward bound	322	13,322	269	10,012	207	7,358	184	6,374	223	7,704	214	8,052	211	7,855	215	7,464
57	Great Britain	31	2,085	9	795	12	838	8	645	9	690	11	1,030	12	988	21	1,461
58	Ireland	23	1,615	16	820	3	200	2	160	5	160						
59	Europe	19	725	21	1,040	17	904	9	475	6	275	6	465	8	515	10	630
60	Africa	4	130					1	60							1	40
61	Bahama Islands	3	60	1	20	3	60	1	20	4	145					3	75
62	Bermuda Islands	3	75	3	78	1	45	4	90	6	168	5	160	3	90	5	107
63	Caribbean	180	6,351	113	4,333	95	2,836	87	2,771	103	3,624	104	4,149	95	3,878	104	3,608
64	Thirteen Colonies	51	2,076	97	2,451	73	2,321	70	1,959	85	2,349	86	2,138	90	2,761	68	1,406
65	Other American Colonies	12	440	10	505	5	250	5	278	6	305	2	110	5	155	3	137
66	Inward bound	266	10,921	261	9,738	196	6,759	213	7,442	217	7,433	215	7,672	202	7,716	[3]	[3]
67	Great Britain	28	2,475	27	2,224	26	1,648	18	1,350	24	1,823	17	1,473	31	2,470		
68	Ireland	10	650	4	360	3	240	4	215	3	100			1	80		
69	Europe	25	1,055	22	1,320	25	1,436	24	1,571	12	640	7	420	10	615		
70	Africa	5	205							1	120			1	25		
71	Bahama Islands	6	120	1	20	2	40	6	145	3	65	2	40				
72	Bermuda Islands	3	80	14	426	13	365	19	525	15	426	11	305	9	275		
73	Caribbean	177	6,020	105	3,643	83	2,509	78	2,707	97	3,271	95	3,775	85	3,072		
74	Thirteen Colonies	23	931	93	2,069	47	882	71	1,366	78	1,629	87	1,753	69	1,452		
75	Other American Colonies	7	280	11	321	5	124	5	241	6		3	204	5	135		149

[1] Ending date of year unknown. For Boston, figures given in source for trade with the remainder of Massachusetts do not follow pattern of other entries and are, therefore, not a component of total. Totals were not taken from source but represent sum of detail as shown in source.

[2] Annual averages for years ending June 23. For Boston, the sum of the detail does not equal the total shown since the total includes entries for unknown ports.

[3] Not available.

[4] For year ending January 4 of following year.

Series Z 56–75. Number and Tonnage Capacity of Ships Outward and Inward Bound, by Destination and Origin: 1714 to 1772—Con.

Series No.	Destination or origin	1772 Number	1772 Tonnage	1771 Number	1771 Tonnage	1770 Number	1770 Tonnage	1769 Number	1769 Tonnage	1768 Number	1768 Tonnage	1765–66, tonnage [1]	1734, number	1733, number
	PHILADELPHIA													
56	**Outward bound**	759	44,822	741	43,029	769	47,292	678	40,871	641	36,944	39,262	191	185
57	Great Britain	23	3,123	27	3,222	25	3,208	37	4,049	40	4,134	1,830	21	12
58	Ireland	24	2,491	25	3,470	49	4,791	32	3,170	38	3,482	4,830	16	17
59	Europe	88	8,415	79	7,110	125	10,940	136	12,040	88	7,255	4,455	22	20
60	Africa	1	20	3	90					1	30	300		
61	Bahama Islands	11	282	13	253	10	126					317		
62	Bermuda Islands	4	125	3	55	2	75			3	100	242	6	2
63	Caribbean	268	15,674	230	13,449	243	13,842	202	11,114	206	12,019	13,494	74	87
64	Thirteen Colonies	307	12,872	332	13,655	283	12,370	246	9,085	229	8,116	10,834	50	45
65	Other American Colonies	33	1,820	29	1,725	32	1,940	24	1,383	37	1,838	2,960	2	2
66	**Inward bound**	730	42,300	719	41,740	750	47,489	698	42,333	528	34,970	36,872	210	190
67	Great Britain	63	7,757	71	8,157	42	4,705	46	5,504	60	6,924	4,455	24	26
68	Ireland	12	1,125	16	1,545	26	2,267	32	2,995	15	1,470	4,100	11	8
69	Europe	88	8,120	69	6,345	154	13,620	108	9,685	63	5,001	4,230	17	16
70	Africa											40		
71	Bahama Islands	10	247	12	208	11	156					405		
72	Bermuda Islands	2	70	6	155	1	10			3	110	425	12	10
73	Caribbean	247	12,947	232	13,397	221	14,946	214	11,726	139	11,677	11,724	79	77
74	Thirteen Colonies	287	11,024	294	11,058	274	10,670	243	9,160	218	7,978	9,688	68	58
75	Other American Colonies	21	1,010	19	875	21	1,115	55	3,263	30	1,810	1,805		

Series No.	Destination or origin	1772 Number	1772 Tonnage	1771 Number	1771 Tonnage	1770 Number	1770 Tonnage	1769 Number	1769 Tonnage	1768 Number	1768 Tonnage	1752 Number	1752 Tonnage	1739 Number	1739 Tonnage	1733 Number	1733 Tonnage	1731 Number	1731 Tonnage	1727 Number	1727 Tonnage
	HAMPTON																					
56	**Outward bound**	356	22,293	301	18,593	244	13,851	266	17,046	246	15,776	156	8,008	98	3,966	82	3,769	101	4,501	104	4,577
57	Great Britain	36	5,454	34	4,530	27	3,184	29	4,110	33	5,252	20	2,285	6	745	11	1,110	16	1,633	22	2,046
58	Ireland			3	360	2	270	1	100	1	200										
59	Europe	14	1,155	20	1,790	15	1,405	20	2,096	14	1,209	14	1,195	7	410	6	440	5	300	2	60
60	Africa											1	25								
61	Bahama Islands	3	60	3	55	1	30	6	65	5	115	1	15								
62	Bermuda Islands	10	235	5	123	12	306	3	68	7	205	8	220	8	240	5	140	13	332	19	483
63	Caribbean	205	11,930	180	9,450	141	7,410	146	8,136	148	7,376	81	3,462	44	1,607	50	1,664	53	1,795	41	1,366
64	Thirteen Colonies	88	3,459	56	2,285	42	1,156	59	2,396	37	1,369	31	806	33	964	10	415	14	441	20	622
65	Other American Colonies					2	90	2	75	1	50										
66	**Inward bound**	332	23,966	317	21,857	282	18,915	281	19,843	254	19,673	169	10,557	102	5,746	87	4,816	88	5,009	94	4,023
67	Great Britain	62	9,623	62	8,216	56	8,320	59	8,532	55	8,411	37	4,912	21	2,535	19	2,285	21	2,525	18	1,785
68	Ireland	1	170	1	130	2	195	1	105												
69	Europe	10	1,050	10	878	13	1,080	15	1,595	9	1,065	10	1,015	5	330	4	440	1	40	2	130
70	Africa	1	150			1	103					2	140			1	25				
71	Bahama Islands	3	80	5	105	5	55	7	80	3	35	1	15			2	60			1	120
72	Bermuda Islands	7	185	6	150	8	198	9	236	3	75	4	120	9	330	5	131	5	127	16	421
73	Caribbean	158	8,598	156	8,532	132	6,298	134	7,575	134	8,152	78	3,580	40	1,579	50	1,769	46	1,760	37	1,273
74	Thirteen Colonies	88	4,025	77	3,846	64	2,656	50	1,425	50	1,935	37	775	29	1,122	10	351	15	557	20	294
75	Other American Colonies					1	10	6	295												

Series No.	Destination or origin	1772 Number	1772 Tonnage	1771 Number	1771 Tonnage	1770 Number	1770 Tonnage	1769 Number	1769 Tonnage	1768 Number	1768 Tonnage	1735 Number	1735 Tonnage	1734 Number	1734 Tonnage	1732 Number	1732 Tonnage	1731 Number	1731 Tonnage
	CHARLESTON (S.C.)																			
56	**Outward bound**	485	31,548	487	31,031	451	29,976	433	31,147	429	31,551	247	14,530	219	12,841	183	10,322	198	12,366
57	Great Britain	115	15,610	119	15,792	81	11,727	109	14,681	121	15,873	88	7,919	81	7,330	73	6,234	94	8,424
58	Ireland																		
59	Europe	16	1,774	26	2,882	53	6,291	56	5,773	48	5,515	30	2,685	22	1,830	20	1,665	15	1,185
60	Africa	2	290	1	30														
61	Bahama Islands	25	452	25	497	21	690	16	333	22	345	41	582	28	385	22	249	23	404
62	Bermuda Islands	11	323	12	398	11	343	8	205	9	293			1	40	1	20		
63	Caribbean	129	5,749	163	6,131	163	7,374	113	5,807	113	5,808	22	670	28	1,359	33	1,134	34	1,280
64	Thirteen Colonies	166	6,724	124	4,875	98	3,012	106	3,698	83	2,852	65	2,644	59	1,897	33	1,000	31	1,059
65	Other American Colonies	21	626	17	426	24	539	25	650	33	865	1	30					1	14
66	**Inward bound**	452	29,933	489	31,592	455	27,554	433	29,096	448	34,449	232	13,220	226	13,278	174	9,504	191	12,101
67	Great Britain	79	10,932	79	11,878	61	9,153	115	14,551	139	18,125	57	4,896	53	5,122	43	3,650	55	5,375
68	Ireland	11	1,110	3	310	5	440			11	1,010	4	320	7	700	3	204	1	74
69	Europe	24	2,565	21	2,361	20	2,256	13	1,310	18	2,023	38	3,130	17	1,500	12	980	10	870
70	Africa	25	2,171	11	993			21	2,215	21	2,215	9	885	7	645	5	495	9	755
71	Bahama Islands	22	585	29	517	22	466	20	245	21	355	27	453	30	445	21	293	18	264
72	Bermuda Islands	14	386	20	606	15	395	10	395	9	273	1	70	4	115	7	230	9	198
73	Caribbean	120	6,121	163	8,208	184	9,563	114	6,123	129	8,238	42	2,039	60	3,665	46	2,225	55	3,501
74	Thirteen Colonies	188	5,538	132	5,788	115	4,223	104	3,071	88	3,410	57	2,743	64	2,825	42	1,843	42	2,030
75	Other American Colonies	19	525	31	931	33	1,058	36	1,186	33	1,015	15	254	4	56	2	74	3	74

[1] Ending date of year unknown.

Series Z 76.   Value and Quantity of Articles Exported From British Continental Colonies, by Destination: 1770

[Value in pounds sterling, quantities in units as indicated.   For year ending January 4 of following year.   Includes Newfoundland, Bahamas, and Bermuda]

Article	Value, total	Total [1]	Great Britain	Ireland	Southern Europe	West Indies	Africa	Article	Value, total	Total [1]	Great Britain	Ireland	Southern Europe	West Indies	Africa
				Value							Quantity shipped [3]				
Total_____	3,437,715	(2)	1,752,515	118,777	691,912	848,934	21,678	Butter____lb_	3,492	167,613	_____	_____	_____	167,313	300
								Cheese____do_	933	55,997	_____	_____	_____	55,997	_____
Foreign merchandise (mostly from West Indies)_____	81,555	(2)	65,860	4,698	5,992	4,755	297	New England rum_____gal_	21,836	4 349,381	600	7,931	45,310	2,574	292,966
								Rice_____bbl_	340,693	4 151,418	74,073	_____	36,296	4 40,932	117
								Rough rice _bu_	615	8,200	_____	_____	_____	8,200	_____
Articles shipped as American produce____	3,356,160	(2)	1,686,654	114,079	685,920	844,179	21,382	American loaf sugar_____lb_	333	10,648	_____	_____	600	8,548	1,500
								Raw silk___do_	542	541	541	_____	_____	_____	_____
			Quantity shipped [3]					Soap_____do_	2,165	86,585	_____	_____	550	85,035	1,000
								Shoes____pairs_	394	3,149	_____	_____	_____	3,140	_____
								Ship stuff__bbl_	9,959	7,964	_____	_____	7,327	640	_____
Potash___tons_	35,192	1,173	1,173	_____	_____	_____	_____	Onions__value_	6,495	(2)	_____	_____	117	6,379	_____
Pearlash___do_	29,469	737	737	_____	_____	_____	_____	Pitch_____bbl_	3,200	9,144	8,265	_____	_____	822	57
Spermaceti candles___lb_	23,688	379,012	4,865	450	14,167	351,625	7,905	Tar, common_do_	24,427	81,422	78,115	_____	_____	3,173	134
Tallow candles___do_	1,238	59,420	_____	_____	1,630	57,550	240	Tar, green_do_	261	653	653	_____	_____	_____	_____
Coal____chaldrons_	25	20	_____	_____	_____	20	_____	Turpentine_do_	6,806	17,014	15,125	_____	_____	1,807	82
Castorium__lb_	1,680	7,465	7,465	_____	_____	_____	_____	Rosin_____do_	279	223	195	_____	_____	28	_____
Fish, dried quintals_	375,394	660,003	22,086	450	431,386	206,081	_____	Oil of turpentine_do_	103	41	11	_____	_____	30	_____
Fish, pickled__bbl_	22,551	30,068	123	25	307	29,582	31	Masts, yards, etc____tons_	16,630	3,045	3,043	_____	_____	2	_____
Flaxseed___bu_	35,169	312,612	6,780	305,083	749	_____	_____	Walnut wood__value_	115	(2)	106	9	_____	_____	_____
Indian corn_do_	43,376	578,349	_____	150	175,221	402,958	20	Pine, oak, cedar boards____ft_	58,618	42,756,306	6,013,519	329,741	486,078	35,922,168	4,800
Oats_____do_	1,243	24,859	_____	_____	3,421	21,438	_____	Pine timber _tons_	4,405	11,011	10,582	50	64	315	_____
Wheat_____do_	131,467	4 751,240	11,739	149,985	588,561	955	_____	Oak timber___do_	3,487	3,874	3,710	10	10	144	_____
Peas and beans___do_	10,077	50,383	_____	_____	1,046	49,337	_____	Houses framed number_	3,260	163	_____	_____	_____	163	_____
Ginseng_____lb_	1,243	74,604	74,604	_____	_____	_____	_____	Staves and heading_do_	61,619	20,546,326	4,921,020	2,828,762	1,680,403	11,116,141	_____
Hemp_____cwt_	130	86	86	_____	_____	_____	_____	Hoops_____do_	8,668	3,852,383	18,912	_____	7,072	3,817,899	8,500
Iron, pig__tons_	30,089	6,017	5,747	267	_____	_____	_____	Shook hogsheads_do_	7,835	62,678	_____	_____	549	62,099	30
Iron, bar__do_	36,961	4 2,470	2,102	85	4 10	4 273	_____	Cattle_____do_	14,328	3,184	_____	_____	_____	3,184	_____
Iron, cast _do_	33	2	_____	_____	_____	2	_____	Horses_____do_	60,228	6,692	_____	_____	_____	6,692	_____
Iron, wrought _____tons_	167	8	_____	_____	_____	8	_____	Sheep and hogs_____do_	4,479	12,797	_____	_____	_____	12,797	_____
Indigo_____lb_	131,552	584,672	584,593	_____	_____	83	_____	Poultry___doz_	1,177	2,615	_____	_____	_____	2,615	_____
Whale oil_tons_	85,013	5,667	5,202	22	175	268	_____	Furs____value_	91,486	(2)	91,486	_____	_____	_____	_____
Whale fins_lb_	19,121	112,971	112,971	_____	_____	_____	_____	Deer skins__lb_	57,750	799,807	799,622	185	_____	_____	_____
Linseed oil _____tons_	488	168	161	_____	_____	7	_____	Tobacco_value_	906,638	(2)	904,982	_____	_____	1,569	87
Copper ore_____do_	854	41	41	_____	_____	_____	_____	Tallow and lard _____lb_	3,857	185,143	800	_____	_____	183,893	450
Lead ore_do_	83	6	6	_____	_____	_____	_____	Beeswax____do_	6,426	128,523	62,794	10,980	50,529	1,820	2,400
Bread and flour___do_	504,553	45,868	263	3,583	18,501	23,449	72								
Meal_____bu_	443	4,430	_____	_____	_____	4,430	_____								
Potatoes___do_	127	3,382	_____	_____	_____	3,382	_____								
Beef and pork___bbl_	66,035	(2)	_____	_____	244	5 2,870	439								

[1] Fractional quantities have been dropped; therefore, total may not equal sum of components.   [2] Information needed to provide totals is not available.   [3] Except for a few items where value is shown.

[4] Figures disagree with source used here (Macpherson); corrected to agree with sum of components and with original source (PRO Customs 16/1).   [5] Quantity in tons of beef and pork.

Series Z 77–86.   Coal Exported From James River Ports in Virginia, by Destination: 1758 to 1765

[In net tons of 2,000 pounds.   For years ending January 4 of following year]

Series No.	Destination	1765	1763	1762	1761	1760	1758	Series No.	Destination	1765	1763	1762	1761	1760	1758
77	Salem_____	161	112	____	____	____	____	82	Piscataway_____	214	168	____	____	____	____
78	Boston_____	60	232	288	____	____	____	83	Philadelphia_____	21	102	47	60	____	____
79	Nantucket_____	____	34	____	____	____	____	84	New Castle_____	____	24	____	____	____	____
80	Rhode Island_____	256	136	156	____	____	____	85	Lower James_____	____	____	____	____	____	8
81	New York_____	____	247	40	136	182	24	86	West Indies and Bermuda_____	____	21	____	15	12	____

Series Z 87–107.   Coal Imported, by American Ports: 1768 to 1772

[In net tons of 2,000 pounds.   For years ending January 4 of following year]

Series No.	Port	Imports from Continental Colonies				Imports from Great Britain			Series No.	Port	Imports from Continental Colonies, 1771	Imports from Great Britain		
		1772	1771	1770	1768	1771	1770	1769				1771	1770	1769
87	New Hampshire_____	____	50	____	130	89	158	293						
88	Falmouth_____	____	____	____	____	____	3	12						
89	Salem and Marblehead_	83	183	23	101	162	30	____						
90	Boston_____	204	174	____	153	527	989	1,894	98	Rappahannock_____	____	96	____	150
91	Rhode Island_____	____	13	76	206	208	159	____	99	James River—lower_	____	384	432	815
92	New Haven_____	____	____	____	____	69	37	____	100	James River—upper_	____	____	____	56
93	New London_____	____	37	____	____	____	____	____	101	York River_____	____	181	____	____
94	New York_____	226	____	____	2,248	337	1,537	____	102	Roanoke_____	____	19	____	____
95	Philadelphia_____	122	____	69	86	1,119	1,507	____	103	Brunswick_____	____	46	____	3
96	Patuxent_____	____	40	____	____	239	65	107	104	Charleston_____	244	774	901	1,819
97	North Potomac_____	____	____	____	316	____	____	65	105	Savannah_____	4	93	69	74
									106	Sunbury_____	____	15	____	____
									107	St. Augustine_____	3	23	____	____

Series Z 108–121.   Value of Furs Exported to England, by British Continental Colonies: 1700 to 1775

[In pounds sterling.   For years ending December 24]

Series No.	Colony	1775	1770	1765	1760	1750	1739 [1]	1730	1725	1720	1710	1700
108	Total	53,709	47,758	49,293	19,985	22,817	25,196	22,348	23,541	19,377	7,840	16,284
109	Continental Colonies	51,058	44,394	45,925	14,637	17,491	22,536	19,804	21,903	19,128	5,165	13,712
110	Canada	34,486	28,433	24,512	1,930							
111	Carolina	128	26	491	20	12	9	57	46	4	27	576
112	Florida	108	68									
113	Georgia	63	9	53	3							
114	Hudson's Bay	5,640	9,213	9,770	8,321	8,143	13,452	12,335	11,180	9,839		2,360
115	New England	1,642	2,453	2,811	946	1,015	2,481	2,010	1,862	2,119	1,595	2,435
116	Newfoundland	1,913	403	648	470	420	551	500	452	457	553	223
117	New York	3,939	2,340	5,565	1,023	5,710	5,073	2,611	6,952	5,393	2,148	4,962
118	Nova Scotia	210	132	78	24			156				
119	Pennsylvania	2,866	1,148	1,927	1,879	1,909	329	1,642	923	849	88	723
120	Virginia and Maryland	63	169	70	21	282	641	493	488	467	754	2,433
121	All other colonies	2,651	3,364	3,368	5,348	5,326	2,660	2,544	1,638	249	2,675	2,572

[1] Since the English customs records for 1740 are not complete, the records for 1739 were used.

Series Z 122–125.   Indigo and Silk Exported From South Carolina and Georgia: 1747 to 1775

[For years ending January 4 of following year, except as noted]

Year	Indigo (1,000 pounds) Total	South Carolina	Georgia	Silk [1] (pounds)	Year	Indigo (1,000 pounds) Total	South Carolina	Georgia	Silk [1] (pounds)	Year	Indigo, South Carolina (1,000 pounds)
	122	123	124	125		122	123	124	125		123
1775 [2]	(3)	1,122.2	(3)	(3)	1764	543.2	529.1	14.2	898	1754	129.6
1774 [4]	(3)	747.2	(3)	(3)	1763	447.7	438.9	8.7	953	1753	28.5
1773 [5]	(3)	720.6	(3)	(3)	1762	264.4	255.3	9.1	380	1752 [11]	3.8
1772	[6] 759.8	[6] 746.7	13.1	485	1761	385.6	384.1	1.6	332	1751 [12]	19.9
1771	454.1	434.2	19.9	438							
					1760	519.3	507.6	11.7	558	1750 [12]	63.1
1770	573.1	550.8	22.3	290	1759	696.2	695.7	0.6	734	1749 [12]	138.3
1769	416.6	402.7	13.9	332	1758	572.6	563.0	9.6	358	1748 [12]	62.2
1768	[7][8] 517.7	[7] 498.0	[8] 19.7	541	1757	894.5	876.4	18.2	358	1747 [12]	138.3
1767	(3)	(9)	12.9	671	1756	232.1	222.8	9.3	268		
1766	[10] 506.2	491.8	14.4	1,084	1755	308.0	303.5	4.5	438		
1765	351.9	335.8	16.0	711							

[1] Savannah, Ga., only.   [2] For 6½ months ending Feb. 24.
[3] Not available.   [4] For 11 months ending Oct. 6.
[5] For year ending Nov. 11.   [6] Plus 302 casks and 5 boxes.
[7] Plus 196 casks.   [8] Plus 357 casks.
[9] From Oct. 31, 1767, to Sept. 8, 1768, Charleston exported 530,092 pounds of indigo.
[10] Figures given are for Charleston's exports, the only South Carolina port for which data are available; other South Carolina ports averaged 7.8 percent of the colony's total for 1768-1773.
[11] For 9½ months ending Jan. 5 of following year.
[12] For year ending Mar. 24 of following year.

Series Z 126–130.   Silk Exported and Imported by North and South Carolina: 1731 to 1755

[In pounds.   For years ending December 24]

Year	Exports of raw silk	Imports of British silk manufactures Silk, wrought	Silk with worsted	Silk with inkle	Silk with grosgrain	Year	Exports of raw silk	Imports of British silk manufactures Silk, wrought	Silk with worsted	Silk with inkle	Silk with grosgrain	Year	Imports of British silk manufactures Silk, wrought	Silk with worsted
	126	127	128	129	130		126	127	128	129	130		127	128
1755	5.5	3,416	2,634	337		1746		929	590	330	3	1738	1,111	1,177
1754		2,682	2,300	374	150	1745		544	615	184	40	1737	691	790
1753	11	3,027	2,236	190		1744		1,035	1,296	181		1736	1,223	516
1752		3,365	2,860	218	7	1743		1,427	1,262	122				
1751		2,404	1,933	291		1742	18.5	1,576	1,350	144		1735	1,487	864
						1741		2,798	2,452	440	7	1734	943	937
1750	118	1,519	1,258	223	50							1733	1,015	1,341
1749	46	1,772	1,065	74		1740		1,454	1,492			1732	774	892
1748	52	1,772	1,658	155	34	1739		1,273	877			1731	970	537
1747		1,313	2,050	386										

Series Z 131–135.   Pig Iron Exported to England, by Colony: 1723 to 1776

[In tons of 2,240 pounds.   For years ending December 24]

Year	Total	Virginia and Maryland	New York	Pennsylvania	Other [1]	Year	Total	Virginia and Maryland	New York	Pennsylvania	Other [1]	Year	Total	Virginia and Maryland	Pennsylvania	Other [1]
	131	132	133	134	135		131	132	133	134	135		131	132	134	135
1776	[2] 316	208	43		60	1758	[3] 3,717	3,448	49	195	25	1740	2,275	2,020	159	96
1775	2,996	1,467	1,015	385	130	1757	[3] 2,699	2,462	157	80		1739	2,418	2,242	170	6
1774	[2] 3,452	1,458	1,533	323	131	1756	[3] 3,011	2,468	201	234	[3] 108	1738	2,359	2,113	228	18
1773	2,938	1,581	984	209	163	1755	3,441	2,133	457	836	15	1737	2,316	2,120	169	27
1772	[2] 3,725	1,879	756	706	364	1754	3,245	2,591	116	513	25	1736	2,729	2,458	271	
1771	[2] 5,303	2,624	778	1,553	379	1753	2,738	2,347	97	243	51					
						1752	2,979	2,762	41	156	20	1735	2,561	2,362	196	3
1770	4,233	1,572	1,031	1,381	248	1751	3,210	2,950	33	200	27	1734	2,196	2,042	147	7
1769	3,402	1,616	864	634	288							1733	2,405	2,310	95	
1768	2,953	1,718	520	665	50	1750	2,924	2,509	76	318	21	1731	2,333	2,226	107	
1767	3,313	2,070	357	785	101	1749	1,759	1,575	17	167		1731	2,250	2,081	169	
1766	[2] 2,887	1,741	548	299		1748	2,156	2,018	22	115	1					
						1747	2,157	2,119	13	25		1730	1,717	1,527	189	1
1765	[2] 3,264	2,071	564	301	29	1746	1,861	1,729	29	103		1729	1,132	853	274	5
1764	2,554	1,837	371	307	40							1728	886	643	243	
1763	2,566	2,325	108	132		1745	2,274	2,131	19	97	27	1727	484	407	77	
1762	[2] 1,767	1,733	19	7	23	1744	1,862	1,748	6	88	20	1726	296	263	33	
1761	2,766	2,512	76	149	29	1743	3,005	2,816	81	63	45	1725	137	137		
1760	[3] 3,265	3,123	51	61	30	1742	2,075	1,926		144	5	1724	202	202		
1759	[2][3] 1,596	1,429	103	128	12	1741	3,457	3,261		153	43	1723	15	15		

[1] Includes pig iron exported from New England, Carolina, Barbados, Canada, Newfoundland, and Jamaica.
[2] Reason for discrepancy in total and sum of components is unknown.
[3] 13 American Colonies only.

Series Z 136–142. Pig Iron Exported From American Colonies, by Destination and Colony: 1768 to 1772

[In hundredweights. For years ending January 4 of following year]

Year and destination	Total	Massachusetts	Rhode Island	New York	Pennsylvania	Maryland	Virginia
	136	137	138	139	140	141	142
1772							
Total	98,098	1,521	6,325	26,755	9,408	33,405	20,684
Great Britain	74,320	1,301	1,075	15,585	8,840	27,215	20,304
Ireland	610				160	150	300
Continental Colonies	22,688	220	5,250	11,170	8	6,040	
West Indies	480				400		80
1771							
Total	128,306 [1]	810	7,820	15,770	30,886	45,245	27,455
Great Britain	101,316	810	2,760	10,300	29,986	30,005	27,455
Ireland	1,280			700		580	
Continental Colonies	25,680 [1]		5,060	4,740	900	14,660	
West Indies	30			30			
1770							
Total	133,079	1,020	6,957	26,490	31,947	35,150	31,515
Great Britain	114,944	1,020	3,697	21,515	31,387	25,810	31,515
Ireland	5,350			1,250	560	3,540	
Continental Colonies	12,725		3,260	3,725		5,740	
West Indies	60					60	
1769							
Total	112,186	2,365	5,980	23,795	21,896	24,830	33,320
Great Britain	93,866	1,360	2,310	14,960	21,676	20,240	33,320
Ireland	930	370		40	220	300	
Continental Colonies	17,390	635	3,670	8,795		4,290	
1768							
Total	71,194 [2]	1,077	2,220	31,119	12,102	6,422	17,494
Great Britain	62,356 [2]	1,077	1,820	29,819	10,006	1,780	17,094
Continental Colonies	8,838		400	1,300	2,096	4,642	400

[1] Includes 320 hundredweights exported by Connecticut.

[2] Includes 760 hundredweights exported by New Jersey.

Series Z 143–152. Pig Iron Imported by American Colonies From Other Continental Colonies: 1768 to 1772

[In hundredweights. For years ending January 4 of following year]

Year	Total	Massachusetts	Rhode Island	Connecticut	New York	Pennsylvania	Maryland	Virginia	North Carolina	South Carolina
	143	144	145	146	147	148	149	150	151	152
1772	25,768	5,680	9,620	620	4,770	160		4,918		
1771	27,625	3,640	3,875	1,420	1,980	5,590	1,060	10,040	20	
1770	14,127	2,710	3,405	1,640	740	2,872		2,700		60
1769	15,535	4,555	3,020	1,340	3,280	20		3,320		
1768	12,447	1,654		360	1,920	4,523	430	3,560		

Series Z 153–158. Bar Iron Imported From England, by American Colonies: 1710 to 1750

[In tons of 2,240 pounds. For years ending December 24]

Year	Total	New England	New York	Pennsylvania	Virginia and Maryland	Carolina
	153	154	155	156	157	158
1750	5	1			3	1
1735	218	101	108		3	6
1734	363	263	90		2	8
1733	465	371	55	2	12	25
1732	488	413	58	3	5	9
1731	365	243	102	5	4	11
1730	250	150	92		2	6
1729	405	338	58	4	1	4
1718	190	154	3	4	27	2
1717	207	141	43	9	10	4
1716	539	373	147	10	9	
1715	511	373	111	8	17	2
1714	419	279	98	25	8	9
1713	302	211	49	7	8	27
1712	326	282	32	2	5	5
1710	226	201	10	13	2	

Series Z 159–164. Bar Iron Exported to England, by Colony: 1718 to 1776

[In tons of 2,240 pounds. For years ending December 24]

Year	Total	New England	New York	Pennsylvania	Virginia and Maryland	Other [1]
	159	160	161	162	163	164
1776	28				28	
1775	916	5	361	88	462	
1774	639 [2]		284	114	244	
1773	838 [2]	5	498	137	289	
1772	966 [2]		561		382	18
1771	2,222	1	1,493	18	709	
1770	1,716	9	984	93	598	32
1769	1,780	46	861	208	659	5
1768	1,990	7	909	357	712	3
1767	1,326	13	401	342	569	
1766	1,258	9	400	88	744	15
1765	1,079		194	85	639	160
1764	1,059 [2]		241	272	247	1
1763	310 [2]		39	21	234	3
1762	110 [2]			3	107	3
1761	39			3	36	
1760	127			29	98	
1759	273			199	74	
1758	355			10	341	4 [3]
1757	73		19	19	35	
1756	181		2	31	148	
1755	390		12	79	299	
1754	271		7	110	154	
1753	248	2		148	98	
1752	82			65	17	
1751	5			2	3	
1750	6				6	
1748	4				4	
1747	83				83	
1746	196			3	193	
1745	4				4	

Year	Total	Virginia and Maryland	Other [1]
	159	163	164
1744	57	57	
1741	5	5	
1740	5	5	
1736	5		5 [4]
1735	55	44	11 [4]
1733	1		1 [5]
1730	9		9
1727	3	3	
1726	1		1 [6]
1724	7	7	
1721	15	15	
1720	4	4	
1719	1	1	
1718	3	3	

[1] Includes bar iron exported from Antigua, Canada, Jamaica, Barbados, and others as noted.

[2] Reason for discrepancy between total and sum of components is unknown.

[3] From Carolina.

[4] From Pennsylvania.

[5] From New York.

[6] From New England.

Series Z 165–178.   Bar Iron Imported by American Colonies From Other Continental Colonies: 1768 to 1772

[In hundredweights. For years ending January 4 of following year]

Year	Total	New Hampshire	Massachusetts	Rhode Island	Connecticut	New York	New Jersey	Pennsylvania	Maryland	Virginia	North Carolina	South Carolina	Georgia	Florida
	165	166	167	168	169	170	171	172	173	174	175	176	177	178
1772	33,156	4,169	14,367	2,304	1,588	220	6	940	16	4,540	1,749	2,778	352	127
1771	28,064	3,079	10,869	2,240	2,351	880	--------	494	47	2,420	2,604	2,590	419	91
1770	28,338	3,717	[1]13,052	1,240	2,295	120	--------	166	--------	2,105	1,186	3,961	324	172
1769	21,860	2,390	8,648	1,175	1,734	710	--------	530	97	1,546	1,352	3,127	525	28
1768	16,905	1,500	7,977	2,322	271	236	145	684	45	71	1,401	1,775	317	161

[1] Plus 154 bars.

Series Z 179–188.   Bar Iron Exported by American Colonies, by Destination and Colony: 1768 to 1772

[In hundredweights. For years ending January 4 of following year]

Year and destination	Total	Massachusetts	Rhode Island	Connecticut	New York	New Jersey	Pennsylvania	Maryland	Virginia	Other[1]
	179	180	181	182	183	184	185	186	187	188
1772										
Total	60,916	1,110	354	538	17,245	140	22,008	17,272	2,091	158
Great Britain	19,708				9,930		900	7,797	1,081	
Continental Colonies	35,848	1,110	314	504	4,805	100	19,253	8,875	729	158
West Indies	4,620		40	34	2,370	40	[2]1,595	260	281	
Other	740				140		260	340		
1771										
Total	76,513	985	500	85	28,892	94	21,942	20,080	3,713	222
Great Britain	42,300	2	20		23,650		200	15,531	2,897	
Continental Colonies	29,310	983	320	65	3,607	14	19,413	4,207	489	212
West Indies	3,980		120	20	935	80	2,196	302	327	
Other	923		40		700		133	40		10
1770										
Total	78,168	1,029	686	180	33,569	108	22,967	14,823	4,453	353
Great Britain	42,047	100	40		25,985		1,577	10,530	3,815	
Continental Colonies	28,949	929	[3]606		4,674	108	18,776	3,200	484	172
West Indies	5,457		40	180	1,635		[4]2,594	673	154	181
Other	1,775				1,335		20	420		
1769										
Total	75,869	1,009	641	556	24,358	230	21,805	17,965	9,184	121
Great Britain	43,105	124	98		17,090		4,415	12,925	8,453	
Continental Colonies	26,378	885	543	446	5,223	230	14,628	3,789	514	120
West Indies	4,826			110	1,385		2,652	461	217	1
Other	1,560				660		110	790		
1768										
Total	77,857	1,127	3,199	223	4,422	140	20,969	35,114	12,307	356
Great Britain	50,271	(5)	739	38			[6]6,189	[7]31,265	[8]11,704	336
Continental Colonies	24,403	1,107	2,400	171	3,874	140	12,621	3,714	356	20
West Indies	3,123	20		14	548		[9]2,159	135	247	
Other	60		60				(10)			

[1] Includes N.H., N.C., S.C., Ga., and Fla.
[2] Includes 40 cwt. exported through New Castle, Del.
[3] Plus 150 bars.
[4] Includes 134 cwt. exported through New Castle, Del.
[5] Plus 42 bars.
[6] Plus 10,627 bars exported to Great Britain and 166 bars to Ireland.
[7] Plus 730 bars.
[8] Plus 11,664 bars.
[9] Includes 45 cwt. exported through New Castle, Del. In addition to the 2,159 cwt., there were 2,125 bars exported.
[10] Source states that 735 bars were exported to Southern Europe.

Series Z 189–202.   Cast Iron Imported and Exported by American Colonies, by Origin and Destination: 1768 to 1772

[In hundredweights. For years ending January 4 of following year]

Series No.	Origin or destination	Imports								Exports							
		From other Continental Colonies					From Great Britain			To other Continental Colonies					To West Indies		
		1772	1771	1770	1769	1768	1771	1770	1769	1772	1771	1770	1769	1768	1771	1770	1769
189	Total	4,936	4,884	4,039	3,824	4,733	968	969	2,621	5,231	5,503	6,309	3,926	2,025	97	42	165
190	New Hampshire	217	402	[1]72	40			(1)		5	11	18	29	18			
191	Massachusetts	128	138	[1]121	44	43	8	(1)		2,070	1,714	[2]2,029	1,972	860		25	10
192	Rhode Island	72	97	194	7					2,538	2,795	[2]1,206	1,422	711	21		65
193	Connecticut	964	2,364	[1]1,150	1,581	256				77	315	[2]37	129	41		7	
194	New York	1,773	422	[1]150	318	785			(1)	180	206	[2]61	142	20	20	6	
195	New Jersey			10	24	116					2						
196	Pennsylvania[3]	58	45	[1]1,357	155	359		106	[1]231	311	290	356	137	188	3		70
197	Maryland	280	266	236	285	1,496	(1)	[1]30	[1]1,426	4	39	2,513	95	51	53		
198	Virginia	138	290	347	391	65	733	626	528	8	82			99			
199	North Carolina	1,131	532	297	633	1,066	[1]178	78	6	8	12			2			20
200	South Carolina	142	313	192	67	363		60	359	30	37	89		35			
201	Georgia	3	5	3		270	[1]49	69	[1]71							4	
202	Florida	30		90		23	(1)		(1)								

[1] In addition, the following number of pots were imported: From other Continental Colonies, 1770, N. H.–4, Mass.–20, Conn.–103, N. Y.–52, Pa.–130; from Great Britain, 1771, Md.–2,432, N. C.–169, Ga.–150, Fla.–4; 1770, N. H.–187, Mass.–12 pots and 250 pounds, Md.–107; 1769, N. Y.–100, Pa.–231, Md.–34, Ga.–71, Fla.–2.
[2] In addition, the following number of pots were exported: Mass.–510, R.I.–116, Con.–20, N.Y.–104, and 35 potash kettles from Mass.
[3] Includes figures for New Castle, Del., as follows: Imports from other Continental Colonies, 1770, 1 cwt.; 1771, 40 cwt. Exports to other Continental Colonies, 1771, 3 cwt.

Series Z 203–210. Wrought Iron Imported From England by American Colonies: 1710 to 1773

[In hundredweights. For years ending December 24 except 1769–1771, January 4 of following year]

Year	Total	New England	New York	Pennsylvania	Virginia and Maryland	Carolina	Georgia	Florida	Year or period	Total	New England	New York	Pennsylvania	Virginia and Maryland	Carolina
	203	204	205	206	207	208	209	210		203	204	205	206	207	208
1773	56,988	2,634	5,972	19,652	12,554	12,155	1,855	2,166	1731	26,753	9,727	2,628	2,946	9,682	1,770
1771	59,186	4,209	11,497	--------	38,546	[1]3,212	1,068	[2]654	1730	20,604	7,330	2,775	2,629	6,390	1,480
1770	19,756	2,250	3,860	176	7,664	4,393	1,402	11	1729	16,357	7,394	1,904	851	4,866	1,342
1769	33,685	[3]2,907	620	[4]1,565	21,734	[5]5,773	[6]878	[7]208	1718	13,097	3,110	1,396	887	6,735	969
1764	29,720	6,290	4,883	5,303	4,866	7,993	385	--------	1717	15,705	3,819	1,145	1,147	8,728	866
1758	35,549	3,455	6,280	8,687	10,128	6,849	150	--------	1716	15,571	5,398	1,094	963	7,446	670
1750	29,508	7,884	4,384	4,765	8,684	3,733	58	--------	1715	17,802	5,796	1,380	988	8,947	691
1735	23,845	6,544	2,137	2,102	9,709	3,353	--------	--------	1714	14,343	4,633	1,137	924	6,598	1,051
1734	23,155	6,192	2,291	3,150	8,641	2,881	--------	--------	1713	11,176	4,883	986	1,040	2,860	1,407
1733	22,643	7,105	1,610	2,420	8,815	2,693	--------	--------	1712	13,729	5,345	639	540	5,654	1,551
1732	22,800	8,598	2,380	2,208	7,446	2,168	--------	--------	1710–1711	10,309	4,597	567	988	3,014	1,143

[1] Plus 5 casks and 4 cases.   [2] Plus 15 casks and 1 case.   [3] Plus 41 casks and 13 packs.   [4] Plus 1 cask.   [5] Plus 49 packs.   [6] Plus 11 packs.   [7] Plus 7 packs.

Series Z 211–222. Selected Iron Products Imported and Exported by American Colonies: 1768 to 1772

[For years ending January 4 of the following year. Data are for imports from or exports to other colonies unless otherwise noted]

Year	Imports						Exports					
							Wrought iron		Anchors	Scythes	Axes	
	Wrought iron	Anchors	Scythes	Nails [1]	Steel [1]	Axes	Other colonies	West Indies			Other colonies	West Indies
	211	212	213	214	215	216	217	218	219	220	221	222
	Cwt.	Number	Dozens	Cwt.	Cwt.	Number	Cwt.	Cwt.	Number	Dozens	Number	Number
1772	351	494	(²)	(²)	(²)	5,603	301	47	[3]80	454	6,800	2,673
1771	513	[4]109	[5]340	5,668	1,599	7,144	391	153	70	[6]540	7,574	2,385
1770	[7]256	[7]126	297	[8]22,283	[9]1,578	6,063	[10]103	167	[11]156	377	7,483	1,961
1769	[11]1,289	[1]12	[5]102	[8]3,161	[9]2,126	6,665	[12]1,101	--------	[13]	400	5,606	4,059
1768	(²)	(²)	(²)	(²)	(²)	5,568	[12]162	279	[14]	(²)	2,688	(²)

[1] Imported from Great Britain.   [2] No listing.
[3] Plus 36 to West Indies.   [4] Plus, from Great Britain, 15 in 1771.
[5] Plus, from Great Britain, 129 bundles in 1771 and 46 bundles and 1 dozen in 1769.   [6] 30 dozen to West Indies.
[7] Wrought iron entry coastwise in source includes 43 cwt. of anchors which may not have been included in number of anchors. Also, 27 anchors were imported from Great Britain.
[8] Plus 1,993 casks in 1770 and 84 casks in 1769 from Great Britain and 102 barrels in 1770 from other colonies.

[9] Plus 4,030 bars, 12.5 faggots, and 36 long steel in 1770, and 1 bundle and 41 faggots in 1769.
[10] Includes 110 cwt of anchors which have also been included in the number of anchors.
[11] Wrought iron entry coastwise included 363 cwt. of anchors which may not have been included in the number of anchors.
[12] Anchors only.
[13] 15 anchors to Africa. All the wrought iron entries this year consisted of anchors.
[14] In addition to coastwise exports listed under wrought iron, 1 anchor went to the West Indies.

Series Z 223–229. Tobacco Imported by England, by Origin: 1697 to 1775

[In thousands of pounds. For years ending December 24, except as noted]

Year	Total	Virginia and Maryland	Carolina	Georgia	Pennsylvania	New England	Other [1]	Year	Total	Virginia and Maryland	Carolina	Pennsylvania	New England	New York	Other [1]
	223	224	225	226	227	228	229		223	224	225	226	227	228	229
1775	55,968	54,458	834	109	--------	--------	57	1735	40,069	39,818	--------	250	--------	--------	1
1774	56,057	54,785	1,191	71	--------	--------	510	1734	35,563	35,216	--------	338	1	--------	8
1773	55,929	54,915	964	50	--------	--------	10	1733	40,085	39,854	--------	169	--------	--------	62
1772	51,501	50,667	684	135	--------	--------	(²)	1732	30,891	30,847	--------	21	14	--------	9
1771	58,093	56,888	1,136	35	--------	--------	15	1731	41,595	41,194	2	90	--------	--------	
1770	39,188	38,986	190	8	--------	--------	34	1730	35,080	34,860	16	73	--------	--------	131
1769	33,797	33,552	203	1	--------	--------	4	1729	39,951	39,785	--------	161	(²)	--------	5
1768	35,555	35,457	88	--------	--------	--------	41	1728	42,588	42,328	--------	155	1	--------	103
1767	39,145	39,096	44	--------	--------	--------	9	1727	43,275	43,026	1	225	--------	--------	24
1766	43,318	43,193	114	--------	--------	--------	4	1726	32,311	32,159	--------	142	1	--------	9
1765	48,320	47,600	704	--------	--------	3	13	1725	21,046	20,968	--------	66	--------	2	12
1764	54,433	53,662	765	--------	4	--------	2	1724	26,634	26,612	(²)	13	--------	1	9
1763	65,179	64,500	647	--------	6	--------	27	1723	29,297	29,259	6	23	(²)	2	7
1762	44,111	41,862	2,226	--------	10	--------	13	1722	28,543	28,383	8	140	--------	1	10
1761	47,075	45,818	796	--------	450	--------	11	1721	37,292	36,949	47	254	41	--------	1
1760	52,347	51,283	989	--------	10	7	59	1720	34,526	34,138	8	365	4	1	10
1759	34,782	34,652	120	--------	4	--------	6	1719	33,684	33,503	1	177	2	(²)	1
1758	43,969	43,623	273	--------	--------	--------	73	1718	31,840	31,740	4	94	1	--------	(²)
1757	42,232	41,542	369	--------	--------	--------	321	1717	29,600	29,450	(²)	102	47	(²)	1
1756	33,291	32,943	289	--------	1	(²)	58	1716	28,316	28,305	(²)	3	(²)	--------	8
1755	49,084	48,610	241	--------	14	2	217	1715	17,810	17,783	--------	18	(²)	--------	9
1754	58,867	57,977	836	--------	46	--------	8	1714	29,264	29,248	--------	1	--------	9	6
1753	62,686	61,913	451	--------	35	285	2	1713	21,598	21,573	(²)	--------	12	2	11
1752	57,250	56,591	83	--------	68	505	3	1712	30,523	30,502	--------	7	4	4	6
1751	45,979	45,745	162	--------	67	4	(²)	1711	28,122	28,100	--------	--------	1	6	15
1750	51,339	50,785	12	--------	34	447	61	1710	23,498	23,351	2	117	2	(²)	26
1749	44,648	44,190	321	--------	122	15	15	1709	34,547	34,467	1	65	--------	2	12
1748	50,695	49,646	393	--------	66	319	271	1708	28,975	28,716	7	184	57	1	10
1747	51,289	50,765	287	--------	107	124	6	1707	28,088	27,684	6	83	192	46	77
1746	39,990	39,567	81	--------	228	--------	114	1706	19,780	19,379	5	94	17	5	280
1745	41,073	40,897	--------	--------	166	--------	10	1705	15,661	15,573	--------	47	9	--------	32
1744	41,434	41,119	35	--------	159	3	118	1704	34,864	34,665	7	86	9	2	95
1743	56,767	55,666	515	--------	18	--------	568	1703	20,075	19,451	2	313	113	3	193
1742	43,467	42,838	558	--------	30	(²)	41	1702	37,209	36,749	3	304	67	--------	86
1741	59,449	59,007	70	--------	221	7	144	1701	32,189	31,754	--------	270	44	1	120
1740	36,002	35,372	49	--------	427	48	106	1700	37,840	37,166	2	398	23	12	233
1739	46,724	45,866	552	--------	305	--------	1	1699	31,253	30,641	8	65	16	32	496
1738	40,120	39,868	--------	--------	226	--------	26	1698 [3]	8,478	8,359	(²)	67	(²)	9	43
1737	50,208	49,946	86	--------	154	--------	22	1698 [4]	23,052	22,738	(²)	22	2	7	283
1736	37,904	37,682	108	--------	100	--------	14	1697 [4]	35,632	35,329	1	118	1	27	156

[1] Includes Portugal and Madeira Islands, rest of Europe, Turkey, Africa, East Indies, Antigua, Barbados, Bermuda, Jamaica, St. Kitts, and others and prize.   [2] Less than 500 lbs.   [3] For Sept. 29–Dec. 24.   [4] For years ending Sept. 28.

Series Z 230–237. American Tobacco Imported and Reexported by Great Britain: 1697 to 1775

[In millions of pounds. For years ending December 24 unless otherwise noted. Leaders denote no satisfactory data available. Outports are English ports other than London]

Year	Imports Total (230)	Imports England Total (231)	Imports England London (232)	Imports England Outports (233)	Imports Scotland [1] (234)	Reexports Total (235)	Reexports England (236)	Reexports Scotland [1] (237)
1775	102	56	----	----	46	74	44	30
1774	97	56	----	----	41	79	45	34
1773	100	56	38	18	45	97	50	46
1772	97	51	36	15	45	94	50	44
1771	105	58	43	15	47	87	41	46
1770	78	39	27	12	39	73	33	40
1769	70	34	24	9	36	59	24	35
1768	69	36	23	12	33	67	31	36
1767	68	39	26	14	29	63	36	26
1766	73	43	27	16	29	63	33	30
1765	81	48	29	20	33	68	39	29
1764	81	54	37	17	26	85	54	31
1763	98	65	47	18	33	65	41	24
1762	71	44	22	22	27	62	36	25
1761	73	47	27	20	26	66	37	29
1760	85	52	28	24	32	64	40	25
1759	50	35	18	16	15	50	32	19
1758	70	44	24	20	26	43	26	17
1757	60	42	22	20	18	46	28	18
1756	46	33	19	14	12	38	26	12
1755	64	49	27	22	15	45	34	10
1754	79	59	33	26	20	73	53	20
1753	87	63	37	25	24	74	50	23
1752	78	57	33	24	21	69	49	20
1751	----	46	26	20	----	----	39	----
1750	----	51	26	26	----	----	33	----
1749	----	45	21	23	----	----	44	----
1748	----	51	28	23	----	----	43	----
1747	64	51	29	23	13	52	39	13
1746	52	40	19	21	12	49	32	16
1745	55	41	22	19	14	43	33	10
1744	52	41	24	17	11	51	42	10
1743	67	57	33	24	11	58	47	11
1742	53	43	24	19	10	52	44	8
1741	68	59	41	19	9	54	46	8
1740	41	36	19	17	5	42	35	7
1739	53	47	31	16	7	43	38	5
1738	45	40	25	15	5	37	33	4
1737	----	50	32	19	----	----	41	----
1736	----	38	25	13	----	----	32	----
1735	----	40	26	14	----	----	33	----
1734	----	36	24	12	----	----	27	----
1733	----	40	27	13	----	----	26	----
1732	----	31	20	11	----	----	31	----
1731	46	42	29	13	4	34	29	5
1730	41	35	24	11	6	33	27	5
1729	47	40	27	13	7	38	31	7
1728	50	43	29	14	7	35	29	6
1727	50	43	28	16	7	32	26	5
1726	36	32	20	12	4	31	28	3
1725	25	21	14	7	4	16	13	3
1724	32	27	18	8	6	28	18	11
1723	34	29	21	9	5	24	22	1
1722	35	29	19	9	7	25	21	4
1721	41	37	----	----	4	30	26	4
1720	----	35	----	----	----	----	23	----
1719	----	34	----	----	----	----	20	----
1718	----	32	----	----	----	----	19	----
1717	32	30	----	----	2	21	19	2
1716	31	28	----	----	2	19	17	2
1715	20	18	----	----	2	15	13	2
1714	----	29	----	----	----	----	20	----
1713	----	22	----	----	----	----	17	----
1712	----	31	----	----	1	16	15	1
1711	30	28	----	----	1	16	15	1
1710	25	23	----	----	1	16	15	1
1709	36	35	----	----	1	22	21	1
1708	30	29	----	----	1	18	17	1
1707	----	28	15	13	----	----	21	----
1706	20	20	12	8	----	----	11	----
1705	----	16	----	----	----	----	11	----
1704	----	35	25	10	----	----	20	----
1703	----	20	----	11	----	----	17	----
1702	----	37	25	12	----	----	14	----
1701	----	32	21	11	----	----	21	----
1700	----	38	25	12	----	----	25	----
1699	----	31	18	13	----	----	22	----
1698 [2]	----	23	10	13	----	----	18	----
1697 [2]	----	36	26	10	----	----	18	----

[1] For 1721–1731 and 1752–1754, for years ending Sept. 28; 1755–1775, years ending Jan. 4 of following year.
[2] For years ending Sept. 28.

Series Z 238–240. American Tobacco Imported by England: 1616 to 1693

[In thousands of pounds. For years ending September 28 except 1637–1640, unknown; 1672–1682, December 24; 1690–1693, November. Leaders denote no satisfactory data available. Outports are English ports other than London]

Year	Total (238)	London (239)	Outports (240)
1693	----	19,866.0	----
1692	----	13,423.5	----
1691	----	14,830.5	----
1690	----	12,638.0	----
1689	----	14,392.6	----
1688	28,385.5	14,890.5	13,495.0
1687	27,567.0	14,072.0	13,495.0
1686	28,036.5	14,541.5	13,495.0
1684	----	----	13,495.0
1683	----	----	13,495.0
1682	21,399.0	12,592.0	8,807.0
1681	----	14,472.0	----
1680	----	11,943.0	----
1679	----	12,983.0	----
1678	----	14,455.0	----
1677	----	11,735.0	----
1676	----	11,127.0	----
1672	17,559.0	10,539.0	7,020.0
1669	----	9,037.3	----
1663	----	7,371.1	----
1640	----	1,257.0	----
1639	----	1,345.0	----
1638	----	3,134.0	----
1637	272.3	209.7	62.5
1631	----	1,537.0	----
1630	458.2	360.6	97.5
1629	178.7	89.0	89.7
1628	552.9	420.1	132.8
1627	376.9	335.3	41.6
1626	333.1	213.3	119.8
1625	131.8	111.1	20.7
1624	203.0	187.3	15.6
1623	134.6	119.4	15.2
1622	61.6	59.4	2.2
1621	73.8	73.8	----
1620	119.0	118.0	1.0
1619	45.8	45.8	----
1618	49.7	49.5	0.2
1617	18.8	18.8	----
1616	2.5	2.3	0.2

Series Z 241–253. American Tobacco Exported and Imported, by Origin and Destination: 1768 to 1772

[In thousands of pounds. For years ending January 4 of following year]

Year and destination	Total	New Hampshire	Massachusetts	Rhode Island	Connecticut	New York	Pennsylvania	Maryland	Virginia	North Carolina	South Carolina	Georgia	Florida
	241	242	243	244	245	246	247	248	249	250	251	252	253
1772													
Exports	106,979.4	2.0	23.7	14.0	1.7	58.6	26.4	33,909.2	70,632.3	1,604.8	527.6	179.1	
Great Britain	106,574.0							33,902.0	70,449.4	1,573.4	479.0	170.2	
West Indies	178.0		0.5	1.8	0.3	6.7		2.5	147.0	11.8	7.4		
Coastwise	194.4	2.0	23.2	4.1	1.4	36.6	¹22.3	4.7	35.9	19.6	35.7	8.9	
Southern Europe and Africa	33.0				8.1	15.3	4.1				5.5		
Imports, coastwise	²87.4		13.7	16.6	0.6	25.1	30.8			0.1	(³)		0.5
1771													
Exports	112,921.2	4.4	58.0	11.4	5.0	48.2	4.4	38,963.0	71,468.7	1,886.6	436.6	34.9	
Great Britain	112,508.6							38,931.4	71,268.7	1,872.2	401.4	34.9	
West Indies	181.7				2.9		1.0	15.3	160.5	2.0			
Coastwise	197.5	4.4	55.6	9.9	2.1	29.1	1.1	16.3	39.5	12.4	27.1		
Southern Europe and Africa	33.4		2.4	1.5		19.1	2.3				8.1		
Imports, coastwise	141.5	12.2	39.3	7.2	1.0	66.7	14.8	0.1				0.2	
1770													
Exports	89,744.3	3.7	20.9	0.4	13.5	34.6	6.5	27,272.0	61,048.5	1,097.3	233.2	13.4	0.3
Great Britain	89,321.4							27,266.8	60,811.1	1,084.7	145.5	13.3	
West Indies	165.4				10.8	3.4		3.1	145.6	2.4		0.1	
Coastwise	248.2	3.7	20.9	0.4	2.7	21.9	6.5	2.1	91.8	10.2	87.7		0.3
Southern Europe and Africa	9.3					9.3							
Imports, coastwise	158.7	5.9	39.0	5.4		72.6	32.4					0.5	2.9
1769													
Exports	84,207.3		46.7	11.2	29.3	12.6	1.2	25,790.8	57,445.2	554.7	310.4	5.2	
Great Britain	83,945.2							25,781.8	57,337.8	549.6	275.4	0.6	
West Indies	102.3		0.3	2.3	13.9	1.3		1.2	78.2	3.4	0.1	1.6	
Coastwise	155.2		45.5	6.6	15.4	10.6	1.2	7.8	29.2	1.0	34.9	3.0	
Southern Europe and Africa	4.6		0.9	2.3		0.7				0.7			
Imports, coastwise	95.2	10.6	38.1		1.2	34.4	¹4.7			1.0	0.2		5.0
1768													
Exports	69,683.1		11.8	3.1	23.2	5.0		24,382.3	44,876.9	380.8			
Great Britain	69,519.1							24,382.3	44,769.7	367.1			
West Indies	139.2			1.4	23.2	1.0			107.2	6.4			
Coastwise	20.5		11.8	1.4						7.3			
Southern Europe and Africa	4.3			0.3		4.0							
Imports, coastwise	22.1		3.7			10.0	5.5				0.8	0.7	1.4

¹ Coastwise exports for 1772 include 14,589 lbs. exported by Delaware; coastwise imports for 1769 include 224 lbs. imported by the Jerseys.   ² Plus 5 pigtails.   ³ 5 pigtails.

Series Z 254–261. Tea Imported From England by American Colonies: 1761 to 1775

[In pounds. For years ending December 24]

Year	Total	New England	New York	Pennsylvania	Virginia and Maryland	Carolina	Georgia	Florida
	254	255	256	257	258	259	260	261
1775	22,198	8,005			8,825	4,332		5,368
1774	73,274	30,161	1,304		31,273	4,076	3,661	2,543
1773	739,221	206,312	208,385	208,191	26,491	83,959	5,070	813
1772	264,882	151,184	530	128	78,117	22,916	10,265	1,742
1771	362,257	282,857	1,035	495	32,961	36,385	5,420	3,104
1770	110,386	85,935	269		18,270	1,175	2,980	1,757
1769	229,439	86,004	4,282	81,729	37,355	12,982	4,426	2,661
1768	873,744	291,899	320,214	174,883	41,944	34,639	5,212	4,953
1767	480,376	152,435	177,111	87,741	36,088	24,261	2,325	415
1766	361,001	118,982	124,464		29,177	20,112	6,798	672
1765	518,424	175,389	226,232	54,538	23,280	36,067	2,918	
1764	489,252	143,234	265,385	41,949	18,249	18,374	1,989	72
1763	188,785	37,525	83,870	18,281	23,481	22,860	2,768	
1762	161,588	51,618	70,460	7,884	12,773	17,850	1,003	
1761	56,110	6,992	3,837	144	22,244	22,893		

Series Z 262–266. Rice Exported From Producing Areas: 1698 to 1774

[In barrels, except as indicated. Data are for various terminal dates, primarily December 24, January 4 (of the succeeding year), and October 31; see text]

Year	Total: Pounds	Total: Barrels¹	Charleston, S.C.	Beaufort and Georgetown, S.C.	Georgia
	262	263	264	265	266
1774	76,265,700	145,268	118,482	6,594	20,192
1773	81,476,325	155,193	126,940	6,681	21,572
1772	69,218,625	131,845	104,821	4,076	22,948
1771	81,755,100	155,724	125,151	5,209	25,364
1770	83,708,625	159,445	131,805	5,568	22,072
1769	73,078,950	139,198	115,582	6,900	16,716
1768	77,284,200	147,208	125,588	7,045	14,625
1767	63,465,150	120,886	104,125	5,480	11,281
1766	48,396,600	92,184	74,031	3,896	14,257
1765	65,710,575	125,163	107,292	5,647	12,224
1764	55,907,250	106,490	91,960	4,840	9,690
1763	61,959,450	118,018	104,800	5,516	7,702
1762	47,435,325	90,353	79,652	4,192	6,509
1761	58,480,275	111,391	101,389	5,336	4,666
1760	35,327,250	67,290	60,807	3,200	3,283
1759	30,472,575	58,043	51,718	2,722	3,603
1758	38,527,650	73,386	67,464	3,551	2,871
1757	33,976,950	64,718	58,634	3,086	2,998
1756	45,344,250	86,370	79,203	4,170	2,997
1755	59,057,775	112,491	104,682	5,510	2,299
1754	49,179,520	94,576	88,570	4,662	1,344
1753	19,747,675	38,345	35,523	1,870	952
1752	42,245,850	82,835	78,208	4,116	511
1751	32,751,270	64,854	61,611	3,243	
1750	27,372,500	54,745	51,190	2,694	861
1749	21,381,030	43,194	41,034	2,160	
1748	28,368,550	57,895	55,000	2,895	
1747	27,643,060	56,996	54,146	2,850	
1746	27,335,040	56,948	54,101	2,847	
1745	29,813,375	62,765	59,627	3,138	
1744	39,963,630	85,029	80,778	4,251	
1743	35,985,200	77,280	73,416	3,864	
1742	22,706,060	49,361	46,196	2,431	734
1741	38,720,955	85,101	80,846	4,255	
1740	43,326,000	96,280	91,110	4,785	385

¹ Number of pounds per barrel varied from year to year; see text.

Series Z 262–266. Rice Exported From Producing Areas: 1698 to 1772—Con.

[In barrels, except as indicated]

Year	Total Pounds	Total Barrels[1]	Charleston, S.C.	Beaufort and Georgetown, S.C.
	262	263	264	265
1739	32,167,800	71,484	67,117	4,367
1738	16,327,350	36,283	34,324	1,959
1737	20,201,400	44,892	42,827	2,065
1736	24,804,000	55,120	52,971	2,149
1735	21,259,800	47,244	45,732	1,512
1734	13,991,850	31,093	30,323	770
1733	23,245,200	51,656	50,726	930
1732	16,866,000	37,480	37,068	412
1731	21,753,450	48,341	48,341	----------
1730	18,774,900	41,722	41,722	----------
1729	14,248,960	32,384	32,384	----------
1728	12,884,950	29,965	29,965	----------
1727	11,291,280	26,884	26,884	----------
1726	9,442,710	23,031	23,031	----------
1725	7,093,600	17,734	17,734	----------

Year	Total, pounds (262)	Year	Total, pounds (262)
1724	8,654,447	1710	1,600,983
1723	8,797,304	1709	1,510,679
1722	9,732,377	1708	675,327
1721	7,963,615	1707	561,185
		1706	267,309
1720	6,485,662	1704	759,536
1719	4,001,210	1703	694,493
1718	2,956,727	1702	612,646
1717	2,881,335	1701	194,618
1716	4,584,927	1700	394,130
1715	2,367,605	1699	131,207
1714	3,139,361	1698[2]	10,407
1713	3,850,533		
1711	1,181,430		

[1] Number of pounds per barrel varied from year to year; see text.　[2] Year ending Sept. 28; exports from Sept. 29 to Dec. 24, 1698, were 1,597 pounds.

Series Z 267–273. Rice Exported From Charleston, S.C., by Destination: 1717 to 1766

[In barrels. For 1717–1738, for years ending December 24; for 1758–1766, ending January 4 of following year]

Year	Total	England	Scotland	Continental Colonies	British West Indies	Foreign West Indies	Countries south of Cape Finisterre
	267	268	269	270	271	272	273
1766	85,862	39,468	2,862	3,297	11,730	3,369	25,136
1763	103,451	51,335	3,703	16,117	16,466	1,490	14,340
1762	82,159	33,217	4,573	10,921	20,239	1,970	11,239
1759	51,037	18,517	9,359	4,546	5,962	490	12,163
1758	61,501	30,687	7,214	4,611	6,432	--------	12,557
1738	32,372	27,331	--------	596	643	--------	3,802
1737	37,896	32,322	--------	511	594	--------	4,469
1736	53,376	38,158	--------	798	1,164	--------	13,256

Year	Total	England	Scotland	Continental Colonies	British West Indies	Countries south of Cape Finisterre
	267	268	269	270	271	273
1735	44,418	28,345	--------	667	713	14,693
1734	37,303	24,849	--------	605	1,061	10,788
1732	38,942	26,766	--------	1,417	1,504	9,255
1731	48,337	38,331	--------	1,737	1,872	6,397
1724	19,908	16,452	--------	2,199	1,257	--------
1719	13,357	8,423	31	3,210	1,693	--------
1718	8,421	6,187	--------	1,005	1,229	--------
1717	10,380	7,257	--------	1,980	1,143	--------

Series Z 274–280. Rice Exported to England, by Origin: 1698 to 1776

[In hundredweights. For years ending December 24, except as noted]

Year	Total	Carolina	Georgia	New England	New York	Pennsylvania	Virginia and Maryland
	274	275	276	277	278	279	280
1776	6,342	3,507	2,835	--------	--------	--------	--------
1775	576,916	452,822	110,020	4,232	7,312	2,530	--------
1774	425,988	339,911	69,387	870	5,696	9,980	144
1773	457,073	378,291	72,469	--------	2,455	3,858	--------
1772	[1]479,226	405,121	64,078	--------	360	6,321	2,146
1771	[1]452,664	375,727	59,417	349	7,666	9,399	52
1770	280,847	222,556	48,846	8,183	66	1,196	--------
1769	434,444	362,063	71,484	92	305	500	--------
1768	431,891	380,720	41,398	6,457	565	2,719	32
1767	288,537	257,936	27,530	193	1,650	1,072	156
1766	[1]238,680	193,915	44,387	88	24	175	--------
1765	357,099	319,164	28,495	554	6,916	1,501	469
1764	320,734	291,546	20,377	1,631	4,574	2,277	329
1763	271,505	251,476	9,494	1,537	5,354	3,644	--------
1762	148,754	138,777	7,786	750	408	1,033	--------
1761	238,750	224,964	7,220	164	4,562	1,840	--------
1760	108,673	95,773	11,628	--------	309	958	5
1759	109,596	102,001	6,358	481	523	233	--------
1758	102,794	95,741	(2)	305	4,819	1,929	--------
1757	74,741	72,785	(2)	1,375	67	514	--------
1756	167,261	156,279	5,931	1,359	3,621	71	--------
1755	312,845	306,720	3,945	342	1,837	1	--------
1754	276,935	273,862	2,782	62	204	25	--------
1753	123,682	120,221	1,970	--------	225	--------	1,266
1752	267,210	261,387	1,047	1,815	1,387	174	1,400
1751	202,943	196,863	--------	4,363	923	794	--------
1750	166,672	164,378	1,783	505	--------	6	--------
1749	122,401	121,614	--------	748	--------	39	--------
1748	144,068	143,515	(2)	--------	209	344	--------
1747	86,018	85,939	(2)	79	--------	--------	--------
1746	51,736	50,202	(2)	1,094	431	--------	9
1745	75,153	73,792	(2)	38	317	1,006	--------
1744	196,968	195,249	(2)	1,323	156	240	--------
1743	243,091	241,820	--------	244	60	888	79
1742	136,117	134,368	1,518	52	--------	179	--------
1741	263,093	261,110	(2)	360	1,006	613	4
1740	313,571	308,178	798	1,597	1,374	1,624	--------
1739	254,879	253,380	--------	1,350	105	--------	44
1738	128,337	128,187	--------	149	--------	--------	1

Year	Total	Carolina	Georgia	New England	New York	Pennsylvania	Virginia and Maryland
	274	275	276	277	278	279	280
1737	154,318	154,010	(2)	128	--------	180	--------
1736	151,234	150,797	(2)	--------	--------	437	--------
1735	118,295	116,441	1,444	--------	309	97	4
1734	80,263	79,448	--------	286	222	300	7
1733	147,272	147,021	--------	124	--------	83	44
1732	101,838	101,387	--------	401	--------	50	--------
1731	164,515	161,246	--------	1,784	37	1,448	--------
1730	139,384	136,578	--------	1,365	507	922	12
1729	119,202	117,550	--------	1,120	232	300	--------
1728	100,466	95,973	--------	1,986	1,918	589	--------
1727	89,942	89,942	--------	(2)	(2)	(2)	[4](2)
1726	69,092	67,041	--------	499	1,465	87	--------
1725	53,670	52,268	--------	754	585	63	--------
1724	63,383	59,385	--------	3,115	556	327	--------
1723	67,613	60,952	--------	5,746	488	425	2
1722	76,034	72,238	--------	2,457	366	940	33
1721	62,215	54,873	--------	5,574	620	1,058	90
1720	50,669	44,915	--------	5,444	175	118	17
1719	31,259	26,233	--------	4,035	147	813	31
1718	23,097	19,530	--------	2,303	1,130	129	5
1717	22,509	17,484	--------	3,822	641	439	123
1716	35,820	27,555	--------	5,709	871	1,424	261
1715	18,497	14,405	--------	2,013	1,272	807	--------
1714	24,527	22,264	--------	1,620	210	433	--------
1713	30,083	28,517	--------	1,393	165	--------	8
1711	9,231	8,678	--------	174	379	--------	--------
1710	12,508	12,265	--------	128	105	--------	10
1709	11,802	11,274	--------	289	232	--------	7
1708	5,276	5,220	--------	49	--------	--------	7
1707	4,385	4,120	--------	173	83	--------	9
1706	2,089	2,058	--------	--------	3	21	7
1704	5,933	5,550	--------	217	79	28	59
1703	5,426	5,320	--------	17	62	--------	27
1702	4,786	4,568	--------	--------	218	--------	--------
1701	1,521	1,457	--------	--------	64	--------	--------
1700	3,079	3,037	--------	26	4	--------	12
1699	1,025	1,018	--------	--------	--------	7	--------
1698[3]	81	81	--------	--------	--------	--------	--------

[1] Includes exports from Florida in 1766, 91 cwt.; 1771, 54 cwt.; 1772, 1,200 cwt.
[2] Not available.
[3] Year ending Sept. 28. Data for Sept. 29 to Dec. 24, 1698, were 11 cwt. for Carolina and 2 cwt. for Virginia and Maryland.

Series Z 281–293. Slave Trade, by Origin and Destination: 1768 to 1772

[For years ending January 4 of following year]

Year and origin or destination	Total 281	New Hampshire 282	Massachusetts 283	Rhode Island 284	Connecticut 285	New York 286	Pennsylvania 287	Maryland 288	Virginia 289	North Carolina 290	South Carolina 291	Georgia 292	Florida 293
1772													
Imports	10,165	4	4	2		23		175	2,104	155	7,201	328	169
Africa	6,638					19		86	1,271		5,145	117	
West Indies	3,146	4		2		4		82	794	145	2,027	69	19
Continental Colonies	381		4					7	39	10	29	142	150
Exports	495	4				2	20			5	463	1	
West Indies	3					2						1	
Continental Colonies	492	4					20			5	463		
1771													
Imports	4,970			12		9		227	762	82	3,100	758	20
Africa	2,754							194	13	7	2,051	489	
West Indies	2,020			7		8		27	744	68	998	148	20
Continental Colonies	196			5		1		6	5	7	51	121	
Exports	341		1	6	1		1	2			297	5	28
West Indies	3							2			1		
Continental Colonies	338		1	6	1		1				296	5	28
1770													
Imports	3,069					69		532	905	115	123	1,144	181
Africa	2,266					67		517	631			875	176
West Indies	600					2		14	274	103	81	126	
Continental Colonies	203							1		12	42	143	5
Exports	144		1	13				1		19	88	22	
West Indies	27							1		14	5	7	
Continental Colonies	117		1	13						5	83	15	
1769													
Imports	6,736	4		6		10		203	493	169	4,888	687	276
Africa	5,161			6				180	234	36	4,138	448	119
West Indies	1,222	4				10		23	258	79	675	91	82
Continental Colonies	353								1	54	75	148	75
Exports	336			4				1		5	298	28	
West Indies	9							1		5	3		
Continental Colonies	327			4							295	28	
1768													
Imports	2,496	12		70	14	19		301	354	198	249	1,001	278
West Indies [1]	2,204	12		59	14	19		288	354	170	187	971	130
Continental Colonies	292			11				13		28	62	30	148
Exports	282	1		34				14		14	39	61	119
West Indies	107			8				1		1		5	92
Continental Colonies	175	1		26				13		13	39	56	27

[1] Includes Africa.

Series Z 294–297. Slave Trade in Virginia: 1619 to 1767

[For years ending December 24, except 1619–1699, unknown. Italic figures do not purport to be complete. For 1619 and 1727–1767, leaders denote zero except as noted; 1621–1726, indicate no data available]

Year	Total 294	Africa 295	Elsewhere 296	Exported 297
1767	61	([1])	61	([1])
1766	112	108	4	4
1765	66	([1])	66	([1])
1764	967	922	45	10
1763	1,195	1,080	115	3
1762	1,810	1,787	23	92
1761	1,581	1,470	111	28
1760 [2]	1,158	1,152	6	52
1758	43		43	
1757	4	([1])	4	([1])
1756	1	([1])	1	2
1755 [2]	565	456	109	2
1754 [2]	399	249	150	([1])
1753	21	([1])	21	9
1752	[1]3,515	[2]3,515	([1])	11
1751 [2]	1,194	982	212	([1])
1750	1,010	849	161	
1749 [2]	2,338	1,826	512	([1])
1747	28	([1])	28	([1])
1746	1,647	1,299	348	10
1745	654	512	142	
1744	672	486	186	
1743	1,428	1,320	108	
1742	1,529	1,095	434	63
1741	947	687	260	36
1740	1,646	934	712	6
1739	1,710	1,623	87	7
1738	1,101	839	262	

Year	Total 294	Africa 295	Elsewhere 296	Exported 297
1737	2,174	2,044	130	263
1736 [2]	3,222	3,166	56	52
1735	2,104	1,798	306	([1])
1734	1,587	1,231	356	47
1733 [2]	1,720	1,245	475	21
1732	1,291	1,223	68	149
1731	184	130	54	([1])
1730	[1]276	[2]276	([1])	([1])
1729	4	([1])	4	([1])
1728	26	24	2	4
1727	735		735	24
1726		2,149		55
1725	781			142
1724	464			
1723	694			
1722	239			
1721	1,960			
1720	1,368			
1719	1,842			
1710–1718 [3]	552	233	319	
1709	326			
1708	593			
1707	713			
1706	1,013			
1705	1,639			
1704	987			
1703	156			
1702	481			

Year	Total 294	Africa 295	Elsewhere 296
1701		796	
1700		229	
1699 [4]	349		
1687		120	
1685	191	[5]190	1
1684		34	
1679		245	
1678		120	
1677		[5]150	
1674		[5]650	
1665 [4]	59		
1662 [4]	80		
1656 [4]	30		
1652 [4]	7		
1649 [4]	17		
1643 [4]	18		
1642 [4]	7		
1639 [4]	46		
1638 [4]	30		
1637 [4]	28		
1636 [4]	7		
1635 [4]	26		
1628		100	
1623		1	
1622		1	
1621		1	
1619	21		21

[1] Information lacking or too incomplete to calculate.
[2] Figures have been extended on basis of partial data.
[3] Annual average. Source also shows 72 Indian slaves imported; 231 slaves died and 103 drawn back for exportation during the 9 years.
[4] Number of headrights granted.
[5] Number of Negroes shipped, not those actually arrived.

Series Z 298–302. Slave Trade in New York: 1701 to 1764

[For years ending December 24, except 1701–1718, unknown; 1754–1764, January 4 of following year]

Year	Imported Total (298)	Africa (299)	Continental Colonies (300)	Elsewhere (301)	Exported (302)	Year	Imported Total (298)	Africa (299)	Continental Colonies (300)	Elsewhere (301)	Exported (302)
1764	35	----	----	35	1	1726	176	----	32	144	6
1763	205	196	----	----	9	1725	211	59	6	146	6
1754	65	65	----	----	41	1724	64	----	8	56	5
1748	¹10	----	----	10	¹0	1723	101	----	1	100	3
						1722	96	----	----	96	----
1743	7	----	----	7	¹0	1721	205	117	2	86	4
1742	14	----	2	12	----						
1741	55	----	7	48	----	1720	77	----	11	66	4
						1719	104	----	----	104	¹8
1740	56	----	4	52	5	1718	517	70	----	447	(³)
1739	100	----	11	89	----	1717	334	266	----	68	(³)
1738	118	3	51	64	----	1716	62	43	----	19	(³)
1737	99	----	3	96	¹0						
1736	¹13	----	----	13	¹0	1715	55	38	----	17	(³)
						1714	53	----	----	53	(³)
1735	121	----	2	119	----	1712	77	77	----	----	(³)
1734	52	----	1	51	----	1711	55	55	----	----	(³)
1733	257	100	1	156	7						
1732	¹139	¹0	1	138	5	1710	53	53	----	----	(³)
1731	²309	²130	²2	²177	¹0						
						1705	24	24	----	----	(³)
1730	165	----	7	158	¹4	1704	8	----	----	8	(³)
1729	211	----	11	200	8	1703	16	----	----	16	(³)
1728	130	----	4	126	14	1702	165	----	----	165	(³)
1727	221	----	3	218	1	1701	36	----	----	36	(³)

¹ Partial year.
² Figures have been extended on basis of partial data.
³ Not available.

Series Z 303. Slaves Imported Into Charleston, S.C.: 1706 to 1773

[For years ending: 1706–1724, unknown; 1725–1726, September 28; 1727–1751, December 24; 1752–1772, October 31; 1773, September 27.   Italics indicate figures do not purport to be complete]

Year	Number	Year	Number	Year	Number	Year	Number	Year	Number	Year	Number
1773	8,050	1764	3,057	1755	1,436	1737	1,781	1725	433	1715	81
1772	4,865	1763	1,145	1754	2,532	1736	3,176	1724	604	1714	419
1771	3,079	1762	602	1753	1,398			1723	436	1713	159
		1761	1,395	1752	1,572	1735	2,516	1722	323	1712	76
1770	149	1760	3,449	1751	831	1734	1,719	1721	165	1711	170
1769	4,612					1733	190				
1768	¹178	1759	1,879	1750	442	1732	1,003	1720	601	1710	131
1767	¹12	1758	3,177	1749	72	1731	1,775	1719	541	1709	107
1766	¹101	1757	1,438	1739	996			1718	529	1708	53
		1756	1,952	1738	2,654	1727	658	1717	573	1707	22
1765	7,184					1726	1,751	1716	67	1706	24

¹ Prohibitive taxes limited importation.

Series Z 304–307. Pitch, Tar, and Turpentine Exported From Charleston, S.C.: 1725 to 1774

[In barrels. For years ending October 31. Leaders denote no data available]

Year	Pitch (304)	Tar (305)	Turpentine (306)	Tar (green) (307)	Year	Pitch (304)	Tar (305)	Turpentine (306)	Tar (green) (307)	Year	Pitch (304)	Tar (305)	Turpentine (306)
1774 ¹	870	1,176	1,394	----	1757 ³	4,962	2,103	337	397	1740	11,377	2,436	577
1773 ²	821	1,236	1,043	396	1756 ⁵	3,058	2,711	1,195	1,070	1739	7,890	2,722	33
1772 ³	4,125	2,728	864	2,995	1755	5,869	2,596	2,171	547	1738	16,088	5,417	845
1771	7,429	2,259	1,353	1,142	1754	11,025	2,295	5,375	369	1737	11,987	8,501	4,411
					1753	15,220	6,008	6,496	----	1736	11,736	1,491	5,193
1770	4,133	827	1,335	2,111	1752	20,483	2,651	6,271	----				
1769	5,256	1,278	3,201	3,849	1751	11,441	5,070	1,401	----	1735	24,036	5,636	8,061
1768 ³	6,948	1,454	5,761	822						1734	28,874	7,336	4,552
1767 ³	12,339	2,232	3,787	----	1750 ⁴	11,157	3,858	812	----	1733	18,165	6,604	2,212
					1749	7,796	3,765	1,582	----	1732	32,593	4,575	2,466
1765 ²	8,751	2,183	653	392	1748	5,521	3,075	2,397	----	1731	9,385	1,725	1,560
1764	7,459	3,093	1,643	65	1747	13,737	4,422	5,162	----				
1763 ⁴	6,087	1,265	3,042	411	1746	18,016	1,519	4,262	----	1730	10,825	2,014	1,073
1762	6,315	1,244	1,438	289						1729	8,377	3,441	1,913
1761 ⁴	6,626	1,438	4,874	----	1745	8,823	1,286	988	----	1728	3,186	2,269	1,232
					1744	7,678	17,552	1,245	----	1727	13,654	10,950	1,252
1760	5,754	886	2,420	97	1743	9,755	2,206	2,012	----	1726	29,776	8,322	715
1759	7,813	2,236	1,333	405	1742	15,808	3,115	1,986	----	1725	57,422	2,333	133
1758	2,521	1,720	937	328	1741	11,831	1,811	1,691	----				

¹ Data for only 4 months.
² Data for only 7 months.
³ Data for only 10 months.
⁴ Data for only 11 months.
⁵ Data for only 9 months.

Series Z 308–313. Timber and Timber Products Exported From Charleston (S.C.) and Savannah: 1754 to 1774

[Charleston, for years ending October 31; Savannah, unknown. Leaders indicate no data available]

Year	Charleston (S.C.) Lumber (feet)	Charleston (S.C.) Shingles	Charleston (S.C.) Staves	Savannah Timber (feet)	Savannah Shingles	Savannah Staves	Year	Charleston (S.C.) Lumber (feet)	Charleston (S.C.) Shingles	Charleston (S.C.) Staves	Savannah Timber (feet)	Savannah Shingles	Savannah Staves
	308	309	310	311	312	313		308	309	310	311	312	313
1774 [1]	119,923	858,100	27,400	--------	--------	--------	1764	948,121	1,553,365	228,015	1,043,535	2,061,151	423,251
1773 [2]	528,637	1,313,500	79,875	--------	--------	--------	1763 [4]	647,112	1,225,160	362,065	917,384	1,470,120	594,356
1772 [2]	647,047	1,392,075	207,280	2,163,582	3,525,930	988,471	1762	414,754	896,500	163,990	417,449	685,265	325,477
1771	675,000	709,000	101,228	2,159,072	2,224,598	403,253	1761	610,952	1,354,500	236,327	307,690	606,650	50,969
1770	697,393	1,305,625	117,860	1,805,992	2,896,991	466,276	1760	545,333	1,354,500	135,992	--------	--------	--------
1769	592,026	2,072,947	282,180	1,634,331	3,474,588	747,903	1759	1,018,490	1,204,890	146,172	--------	--------	--------
1768 [3]	760,125	2,131,000	182,940	1,787,258	3,669,477	806,609	1758	639,012	724,000	145,529	--------	--------	--------
1767 [3]	450,118	1,717,800	240,813	1,767,199	2,570,725	748,166	1757 [3]	234,303	664,100	83,617	--------	--------	--------
1766	--------	--------	--------	1,101,466	2,036,947	737,898	1756 [5]	202,316	522,420	109,890	--------	--------	--------
							1755	780,776	952,880	168,121	--------	--------	--------
1765 [2]	697,648	--------	186,375	1,879,454	3,722,050	661,416	1754	764,607	822,120	102,290	--------	--------	--------

[1] Charleston data only for 4 months.
[2] Charleston data only for 7 months.
[3] Charleston data only for 10 months.
[4] Charleston data only for 11 months.
[5] Charleston data only for 9 months.

Series Z 314–317. Number of Vessels Engaged in Whaling, and Quantity and Value of Oil Acquired, Nantucket, Mass.: 1715 to 1789

[Year ending date unknown. Leaders indicate no data available]

Year or period	Number of vessels	Tons burden, each vessel	Oil Barrels	Oil Value [1] (£)	Year	Number of vessels	Tons burden, each vessel	Oil Barrels	Oil Value [1] (£)	Year	Number of vessels	Tons burden, each vessel	Oil Barrels	Oil Value [1] (£)
	314	315	316	317		314	315	316	317		314	315	316	317
1787–1789	36	113	--------	12,060	1770	[3] 125	75–110	[3] 14,331		1763	60		9,238	--------
1785	15	--------	([2])	([2])	1769	119		19,140		1762	78	--------	9,440	--------
1784	28	--------	5,400	14,500	1768	[3] 125	75	[3] 15,439		1756	80	75	12,000	27,600
1783	19	--------	2,260	16,280	1767	108		16,561		1748	60	50–75	11,250	19,648
1772–1775	150	90–180	30,000	167,000	1766	118		11,969		1730	25	38–50	3,700	3,200
1772	98	--------	7,825	--------	1765	101		11,512		1715	6	38	600	[4] 1,100
1771	115	--------	12,754	--------	1764	72		11,983						

[1] £, pound sterling. See source for value per ton.
[2] Ships still at sea at time of reporting.
[3] Different figures are quoted by the source (p. 233) from the Massachusetts Historical Society Collection.
[4] Includes the value of 11,000 pounds of whale bone.

Series Z 318–329. Daily Wages of Selected Types of Workmen, by Area: 1621 to 1781

[£, pound sterling; s., shilling; d., pence. Pay in local currency; not comparable from colony to colony. Leaders indicate no data available]

Year and area	With board furnished Carpenters	With board furnished Masons and bricklayers	With board furnished Joiners and riggers	With board furnished Coopers	With board furnished Tailors	With board furnished Laborers	Without board furnished Carpenters	Without board furnished Masons and bricklayers	Without board furnished Joiners and riggers	Without board furnished Coopers	Without board furnished Tailors	Without board furnished Laborers
	318	319	320	321	322	323	324	325	326	327	328	329
	£ s. d.	£ s. d.	£ s. d.	£ s. d.	£ s. d.	£ s. d.	£ s. d.	£ s. d.	£ s. d.	£ s. d.	£ s. d.	£ s. d.
Virginia, 1781	--------	--------	--------	--------	--------	--------	5–0	5–0	--------	5–0	5–0	2–0
Providence, 1779	--------	--------	--------	--------	--------	--------	72–0	73–0	72–0	--------	[1] 17–0–0	48–0
Rhode Island, 1776	--------	--------	--------	--------	[1] 3–0	--------	5–0	6–6	5–0	5–0	--------	3–0
South Carolina, 1710	--------	--------	--------	--------	--------	--------	3 to 5–0	6–0	3 to 5–0	4–0	5–0	([3])
Massachusetts, 1670	--------	--------	--------	--------	--------	2–0	2–0	2–0	--------	[2] 2–8	1–8	1–3
New Haven, 1641	--------	--------	--------	--------	--------	--------	2–0	2–0	2–0	2–0	--------	18
New Haven, 1640	--------	--------	--------	--------	--------	--------	2–6	2–6	2–6	2–6	--------	2–0
Massachusetts, 1633	14	14	14	--------	12	8	2–0	2–0	2–0	--------	--------	18
Virginia, 1621	3–0	3–0	4–0	3–0	2–0	2–0	4–0	4–0	5–0	4–0	3–0	3–0

[1] Per suit.
[2] For 32-gal. barrel.
[3] 1s. 3d. to 2s.

Series Z 330–335. Daily and Monthly Wages of Agricultural Laborers in Maryland: 1638 to 1676

[s., shilling; d., pence. Leaders indicate no data available]

Year	Daily wages In tobacco Pounds of tobacco	Daily wages In tobacco Price per pound	Daily wages Sterling	Monthly wages In tobacco Pounds of tobacco	Monthly wages In tobacco Price per pound	Monthly wages Sterling	Year	Daily wages In tobacco Pounds of tobacco	Daily wages In tobacco Price per pound	Daily wages Sterling	Monthly wages In tobacco Pounds of tobacco	Monthly wages In tobacco Price per pound	Monthly wages Sterling
	330	331	332	333	334	335		330	331	332	333	334	335
		s.	s. d.		s.	s. d.			s.	s. d.		s.	s. d.
1676	--------	--------	--------	300	[1] 1.0	25–0	1654	--------	--------	--------	600	[1] 2.0	100–0
1670	--------	--------	--------	175	[1] 1.5	21–10	1652	--------	--------	--------	600	[1] 2.0	100–0
1669 [2]	20	1.5	2–6	320	1.5	40–0	1649	10	3.0	2–6	--------	--------	--------
1669 [2]	--------	--------	--------	125	1.5	15–8	1648	15	[1] 2.0	2–6	250	[1] 2.0	41–8
1669 [2]	--------	--------	--------	150	1.5	18–9	1647	20	1.5	2–6	170	1.5	21–3
1667	--------	--------	--------	600	0.5	25–0							
							1645	--------	--------	--------	170	1.5	21–3
1662	--------	--------	--------	266	1.2	26–8	1644 [2]	10	[1] 1.5	1–3	187	[1] 1.2	23–4
1660 [2]	--------	--------	--------	200	1.0	16–8	1644 [2]	--------	--------	--------	167	[1] 1.2	20–10
1660 [2]	--------	--------	--------	250	1.0	20–10	1644 [2]	--------	--------	--------	133	[1] 1.2	16–8
1656 [2]	15	[1] 2.0	2–6	--------	--------	--------	1642	15	0.6	9	100	0.6	5–0
1655 [2]	25	2.0	4–2	--------	--------	--------	1641	20	[1] 1.2	2–0	--------	--------	--------
1655 [2]	20	2.0	3–4	--------	--------	--------	1638	--------	--------	--------	--------	--------	8–4

[1] Estimate.
[2] Source does not explain why 2 (or 3) sets of figures are given.

Series Z 336.   Index of Wholesale Prices Estimated for the United States: 1720 to 1789

[1850–59 = 100]

Year	Index	Year	Index	Year	Index	Year	Index	Year	Index	Year	Index	Year	Index
1789	94.0	1779	2,969.1	1769	81.2	1759	85.8	1749	76.1	1739	59.6	1729	62.9
1788	97.4	1778	598.1	1768	80.7	1758	73.9	1748	74.3	1738	69.4	1728	63.1
1787	103.9	1777	329.6	1767	81.7	1757	69.6	1747	65.6	1737	69.3	1727	66.3
1786	105.1	1776	108.0	1766	81.7	1756	69.5	1746	55.0	1736	62.6	1726	68.7
1785	105.0	1775	78.0	1765	76.7	1755	71.2	1745	53.7	1735	66.3	1725	65.7
1784	112.7	1774	84.3	1764	77.2	1754	71.4	1744	57.1	1734	67.0	1724	60.4
1783	119.1	1773	90.9	1763	83.5	1753	78.2	1743	59.7	1733	59.7	1723	57.3
1782	139.6	1772	98.2	1762	83.4	1752	75.6	1742	69.7	1732	58.0	1722	55.5
1781	5,085.8	1771	84.9	1761	77.5	1751	72.0	1741	73.6	1731	59.2	1721	53.4
1780	10,544.1	1770	80.0	1760	81.5	1750	73.9	1740	59.6	1730	66.6	1720	58.6

Series Z 337–356.   Average Annual Wholesale Prices of Selected Commodities in Philadelphia: 1720 to 1775

[In Pennsylvania currency; in shillings per unit of quantity indicated, except series Z 352, in pounds.   Leaders indicate no data available]

Year	Corn	Wheat	Tobacco	Rice	Bread Middling	Bread Ship	Flour	Beef	Pork	Salt Coarse	Salt Fine	Molasses	Sugar, muscovado	Rum New England	Rum West Indies	Madeira wine	Barrel staves	Pitch	Tar	Cotton
	337	338	339	340	341	342	343	344	345	346	347	348	349	350	351	352	353	354	355	356
	Bu.	Bu.	Cwt.[1]	Cwt.	Cwt.	Cwt.	Cwt.	Bbl.	Bbl.	Bu.	Bu.	Gal.	Cwt.	Gal.	Gal.	Pipe	Mil.	Bbl.	Bbl.	Lb.
1775	2.90	5.68	......	17.38	15.36	......	......	57.00	64.88	2.13	3.71	1.75	52.96	......	3.05	64.06	......	......	......	......
1774	2.83	6.93	......	16.92	31.08	14.57	18.12	54.31	69.50	1.38	2.05	1.79	55.56	2.17	3.03	55.17	72.54	15.13	13.81	1.48
1773	3.14	7.42	......	18.34	30.93	17.30	18.92	54.58	83.97	1.69	2.22	1.74	50.02	2.20	3.25	56.75	63.49	14.70	13.79	1.44
1772	3.69	7.74	32.29	23.39	31.23	19.95	20.26	57.05	93.46	1.85	1.85	1.75	49.18	2.19	3.44	54.03	71.85	14.54	14.32	1.27
1771	3.50	6.78	32.50	16.86	28.93	15.68	17.50	51.48	80.31	1.65	1.55	1.77	50.86	2.18	3.35	50.00	75.15	12.19	12.41	1.24
1770	3.60	5.92	28.73	16.29	28.53	14.11	15.71	51.39	77.04	1.63	1.89	1.86	51.80	2.19	3.01	49.58	68.68	11.54	11.33	1.32
1769	2.80	5.48	25.12	17.71	25.45	13.65	15.04	55.21	80.29	1.43	1.81	1.78	52.74	2.16	3.29	48.02	61.32	11.93	10.17	1.37
1768	2.57	6.31	21.83	17.74	26.38	15.91	16.89	52.41	73.43	1.61	1.53	1.81	46.42	2.23	3.34	47.73	65.47	14.34	11.01	1.71
1767	2.93	6.25	21.89	17.54	27.47	16.80	17.16	55.35	71.76	1.64	1.76	1.74	49.43	2.08	3.00	50.97	79.60	16.16	11.69	1.93
1766	3.29	5.73	20.42	16.69	24.54	15.44	14.81	55.21	76.88	1.70	......	1.92	55.74	2.23	3.02	48.92	67.71	17.25	11.90	......
1765	3.01	4.70	18.13	14.34	24.92	13.88	13.50	58.75	74.36	1.70	......	1.76	52.94	2.04	3.02	47.29	70.63	17.33	12.40	......
1764	2.74	4.60	17.71	14.52	23.84	12.95	12.81	60.00	98.26	1.92	......	1.63	48.73	2.05	3.26	50.56	64.90	15.28	12.36	......
1763	3.75	6.06	19.48	15.50	30.18	17.82	16.94	60.29	86.95	2.21	......	1.99	49.79	2.59	3.72	49.34	66.04	14.93	12.30	1.87
1762	3.48	5.66	21.42	13.90	28.88	17.49	16.82	58.04	85.63	2.86	......	2.29	52.15	2.79	3.94	50.79	90.85	13.47	10.04	2.04
1761	2.42	5.03	21.52	16.58	25.18	12.67	14.82	54.91	73.92	1.98	2.86	2.42	49.14	3.04	3.93	48.83	86.91	14.06	11.25	1.45
1760	2.96	5.11	20.43	19.00	24.36	13.40	14.96	53.72	69.30	2.14	2.97	2.70	47.85	3.54	4.73	50.31	68.82	14.47	10.82	1.32
1759	2.99	4.96	20.42	......	22.14	14.33	14.59	48.66	69.19	2.13	2.40	2.87	45.18	3.94	4.99	45.26	60.69	16.07	10.68	1.51
1758	1.94	3.89	18.33	......	21.84	13.98	12.27	48.18	59.49	2.36	2.41	2.51	47.70	3.12	3.72	41.77	60.73	15.11	9.75	1.40
1757	1.72	3.79	17.74	14.84	21.24	14.16	11.31	46.43	60.94	2.83	2.56	2.45	47.99	2.74	3.17	39.46	50.82	15.19	9.85	1.52
1756	2.50	4.34	15.88	14.50	21.21	13.65	12.76	48.96	61.42	2.15	2.39	2.04	48.83	2.35	2.73	32.78	41.63	13.93	11.42	1.49
1755	2.16	4.49	15.08	16.50	21.42	14.50	13.76	47.85	65.94	1.49	1.54	1.89	48.39	2.27	2.84	29.56	51.54	14.92	11.54	1.40
1754	2.34	4.46	17.77	17.06	21.64	15.89	14.11	45.13	61.19	1.47	1.63	2.00	50.85	2.44	3.22	28.96	55.94	15.71	10.67	1.58
1753	2.91	4.48	19.47	20.97	21.52	13.87	12.80	45.70	63.20	1.43	1.85	2.03	51.70	2.47	3.08	30.70	56.87	16.05	9.76	1.65
1752	2.56	4.38	19.90	16.32	21.94	13.17	13.13	51.01	72.35	1.26	1.53	1.94	48.00	2.39	3.22	30.10	53.28	20.06	10.08	1.90
1751	2.79	4.28	20.19	17.29	22.37	14.20	12.34	48.44	69.97	1.16	1.30	1.86	47.04	2.51	3.49	30.07	51.50	21.56	11.07	2.18
1750	2.56	4.51	19.98	20.63	23.82	15.23	13.10	38.17	63.99	1.41	1.69	1.69	51.98	2.53	3.46	29.74	68.36	18.91	12.89	1.89
1749	2.63	5.66	17.10	18.98	26.30	17.60	16.59	37.31	60.16	2.18	2.51	2.08	46.83	2.72	3.77	28.77	68.79	15.41	10.49	1.65
1748	2.28	5.04	18.00	15.83	19.67	13.89	15.41	44.29	61.04	3.17	3.07	2.82	51.63	3.60	4.63	25.60	61.06	14.76	11.06	1.77
1747	1.92	3.29	16.38	11.40	16.48	11.53	10.01	40.55	57.66	3.58	3.84	2.63	55.01	3.62	4.46	24.42	56.03	13.19	10.30	1.94
1746	1.82	2.87	13.93	6.99	14.95	10.15	9.07	41.13	53.79	3.76	3.75	2.50	47.15	2.69	3.03	22.90	40.63	11.42	9.11	1.83
1745	1.69	2.60	13.05	10.00	13.06	8.81	8.01	36.88	53.02	2.63	2.56	2.34	43.02	2.65	3.25	27.50	39.79	13.50	10.38	1.33
1744	1.53	2.49	12.65	11.03	13.32	8.47	7.68	41.94	60.49	2.05	2.23	1.80	49.97	2.52	3.20	27.85	40.00	13.90	10.92	1.19
1743	2.14	2.84	16.25	11.96	14.31	9.06	8.69	44.75	68.52	1.94	2.20	1.87	38.94	2.36	3.16	27.38	40.85	14.25	10.40	.99
1742	2.69	3.58	17.65	16.17	15.96	11.77	10.98	36.63	54.17	2.90	2.67	2.28	40.94	2.84	3.64	24.35	47.81	16.21	12.75	1.01
1741	2.74	4.47	14.83	16.58	19.58	15.83	13.66	40.63	49.83	2.47	2.19	1.82	36.40	2.46	2.96	21.83	49.17	17.54	14.08	1.16
1740	1.50	3.25	13.92	12.75	13.56	10.31	8.72	35.63	46.04	1.67	2.20	1.65	37.88	1.81	2.53	20.17	39.42	14.29	10.88	1.29
1739	1.41	2.82	15.63	18.08	13.01	9.60	8.03	35.75	54.88	1.24	2.16	1.59	38.08	......	2.33	21.58	44.58	11.42	9.42	1.33
1738	2.10	3.48	17.00	20.67	16.75	12.58	11.16	36.67	59.58	1.35	2.19	1.60	38.98	......	2.29	22.00	47.56	11.33	8.63	1.22
1737	2.08	3.88	17.41	17.44	15.21	11.78	11.71	36.06	54.41	1.22	2.24	1.58	35.64	......	2.65	20.88	45.36	10.85	8.56	1.17
1736	1.89	3.24	15.08	17.15	12.77	10.94	9.61	33.50	41.72	1.36	1.92	1.68	32.81	......	2.24	21.58	35.21	12.25	8.98	1.09
1735	1.58	3.85	15.65	18.50	14.58	12.33	11.47	30.61	37.59	1.56	2.08	1.65	35.64	......	2.36	21.47	36.37	12.83	9.63	1.07
1734	2.02	3.55	......	......	13.75	10.90	10.51	30.56	43.58	......	2.04	1.50	29.20	......	2.63	......	......	12.92	10.14	1.01
1733	2.10	3.06	......	......	12.85	10.39	8.84	......	47.54	......	2.36	1.39	28.94	......	2.30	......	......	17.17	12.25	1.08
1732	1.81	2.70	15.53	......	11.91	......	8.17	......	49.41	1.95	2.40	1.37	33.35	......	2.50	......	......	13.75	10.10	.97
1731	1.65	2.47	13.45	15.04	11.72	......	8.02	36.31	55.97	1.88	3.14	1.36	33.21	......	2.64	......	......	14.31	11.10	1.13
1730	1.93	3.68	......	......	14.88	......	11.56	......	59.24	......	3.09	1.54	32.13	......	2.51	......	......	15.00	11.04	......
1729	2.15	3.70	15.08	18.74	14.00	......	10.65	......	51.65	......	2.15	1.53	35.00	......	2.60	......	......	12.08	11.00	......
1728	2.26	3.39	16.06	......	13.72	......	10.02	36.72	59.17	......	1.85	1.51	35.17	......	2.61	......	......	13.11	11.92	......
1727	2.02	3.27	17.87	......	13.46	......	11.46	......	47.79	......	2.07	1.43	32.63	......	2.87	......	......	18.40	......	......
1726	2.13	3.82	17.22	......	14.08	......	12.51	......	48.58	......	1.85	1.45	36.35	......	3.19	......	......	19.19	......	......
1725	2.13	3.87	33.46	19.98	12.79	......	12.12	30.17	39.29	2.51	2.83	1.46	33.44	......	2.85	......	......	18.42	......	......
1724	2.12	3.36	......	14.56	11.92	......	10.95	30.65	50.65	2.23	3.14	1.49	29.42	......	2.35	......	......	15.50	10.67	......
1723	1.86	2.73	......	14.13	11.67	......	8.80	30.58	40.48	2.05	2.81	1.30	36.88	......	2.57	......	22.50	12.63	11.38	......
1722	1.73	2.97	10.25	13.92	12.54	......	8.93	30.67	45.00	1.19	1.65	1.24	31.88	......	2.94	20.50	22.50	12.63	13.50	......
1721	1.76	3.05	10.04	15.44	13.00	......	8.83	30.00	45.00	1.46	1.85	1.16	33.13	......	2.31	19.08	22.50	12.00	8.33	......
1720	1.73	3.08	13.79	16.92	13.31	......	9.26	30.00	46.46	2.31	2.31	1.34	35.52	......	2.68	17.99	22.50	14.17	9.83	......

[1] Cwt. of tobacco was an exception to the rule that cwt. equaled 112 lbs.; it equaled only 100 lbs.

Series Z 357. Annual Rate of Exchange on London for Pennsylvania Currency: 1720 to 1775
[Pennsylvania currency for 100 £ sterling]

Year	Rate	Year	Rate	Year	Rate
1775	166.04	1758	159.21	1741	145.18
1774	169.74	1757	165.95	1740	164.06
1773	165.80	1756	172.52	1739	170.00
1772	161.21	1755	168.88	1738	167.50
1771	165.57	1754	168.15	1737	167.50
		1753	167.96	1736	165.13
1770	153.99	1752	166.66		
1769	158.31	1751	170.63	1735	162.50
1768	166.36			1733	165.00
1767	166.20	1750	171.10	1732	161.10
1766	165.35	1749	172.36	1731	153.13
		1748	174.33		
1765	171.58	1747	184.56	1729	151.69
1764	172.38	1746	179.25	1728	150.00
1763	173.13				150.00
1762	175.84	1745	175.70	1727	150.00
1761	174.12	1744	167.35	1722	133.33
1760	160.30	1743	160.31	1720	133.33
1759	154.71	1742	159.69	1720	133.33

Series Z 358. Annual Price of an Ounce of Silver at Boston: 1700 to 1749
[In paper shillings. Base 1700]

Year	Price	Year	Price	Year	Price
1749	60.00	1730	20.00	1715	9.00
1747	55.00	1729	20.50	1714	9.00
1746	38.50	1728	17.25	1713	8.50
		1727	16.00	1712	8.50
1745	36.00	1726	16.00	1711	8.33
1744	30.00				
1741	28.00	1725	15.50	1710	8.00
		1724	16.25	1709	8.00
1739	28.50	1723	15.00	1708	8.00
1738	27.00	1722	14.25	1707	8.00
1737	26.75	1721	13.00	1706	8.00
1736	26.75				
1735	27.50	1720	12.33	1705	8.00
1734	25.50	1719	12.00	1704	7.00
1733	22.00	1718	11.00	1703	7.00
1732	20.00	1717	10.00	1702	7.00
1731	18.75	1716	10.00	1701	7.00
				1700	7.00

Series Z 359–370. Partial List of Bills of Credit and Treasury Notes Issued by American Colonies: 1703 to 1775
[In thousands of colonial pounds except for Maryland in 1769 and 1773, which are in thousands of dollars. Leaders indicate no data available]

Year	Massachusetts 359	Connecticut 360	New Hampshire 361	Rhode Island 362	New York 363	Pennsylvania 364	New Jersey 365	Maryland 366	Delaware 367	Virginia 368	North Carolina 369	South Carolina 370
1775				60		6						
1773						162		[1]480		[2]36		
1772						25						
1771			2		[1]120	15				30	[3]66	
1770												70
1769						30		[1]318		10		[2]107
1768											20	
1767				2		20						
1766				1				65				
1764		[3]7				55	[3]25					
1763		[3]10					[3]10					
1762	[3]60	[3]65	20	[3]13			[3]30		1	20		
1761	[3]70	[3]45	[3]20				[3]25				[3]20	
1760		[3]70	[3]15	[3]27	[3]60	[3]100	[3]45		[3]4	52	[3]12	[3]392
1759		[3]70	[3 4]13	[3]20	[3]100	[3]100	[3]50		[3]27	62		
1758		[3]30	[3]21	21	[3]100	[3]100	[3]60		[3]12	89	[3]11	
1757			[3]20			[3]100	[3]40			180	[3]15	[3]229
1756			[3]36	[3 4]14	[3]62	[3]85	[3]18	[3]40	[3]2	35	[3]4	
1755		[4]62	[3]40	[3]240	[3]63	[2]15	[3]40			[3]60		33
1754	10							[2]4			[3]40	
1753									[2]3			
1752												[2]20
1751				[1 4]25								
1748	[3]400			30							[2 4]21	[2]107
1747	[3]348			[3]15	[3]28							
1746	[3]662	[3]23	[3]60	[3]11	[3]53	5	[3]16	[2]6	20			[1]210
1745	[3]1,040	[3]40	[1]27	[3]9								
1744	[3]344	[3]19		[1 4]50		[2]10		[2]1				
1743	85		1							[1]6		
1742	117		[4]30									
1741	120			16				[2]1				
1740	80	[3 4]49	[3]2	[1 4]30				[2]8				
1739						[2]10	[2]80			[2]6		
1738	26			[1]110								
1737	81		10	30	[1]48							
1736	48							[2]1				[1]210
1735	39										[2]53	
1734	30			2	12					[1]12		
1733	79	[1]30		[1]104			[1]40	90				
1731	24			[1]60								[2]107
1730	13		1		[2]3		[1]20					
1729	20	6	[2]2			[1]30				[1]12	[1]40	
1728	36	4		[1]48								
1727	88	4	2		[2]3		[2]25					[2]20
1726	25		3	[2]50								
1725	70		[3]2		7							
1724	55	4	[3]2									63
1723	40			2	2	[1]45	[1]40			[1]11		
1722	45	4	[2]10								[2]12	
1721	17			[1]100								
1720	[1]65											34
1719	15	4										
1718	11											
1717	9		[1]15		17							
1716	[1]111		2				5					[3]15
1715	44		1	[1]40							[2]24	[3]35
1714	[1]50		1		28							
1713	14	[2]22									[3]8	
1712	25		[2]2								[3]4	[1]52
1711	[1]95	10	4	6	[3]10						[3]5	[3]7
1710	44	5	3	[3]7								
1709	46	[3]19	[3]3		13						[3]3	[3]6

Year	Massachusetts 359	South Carolina 370
1708	32	8
1707	32	8
1706	44	
1705	18	
1704	32	
1703	32	

[1] Loans.
[2] Reissues or exchanges.
[3] War costs.
[4] Indicates years in which there were issues of different tenor on a different basis from previous issues.

Series Z 371–382. Paper Money Outstanding in American Colonies: 1705 to 1775

[In thousands of colonial pounds. Leaders indicate no data available]

Year	Massachusetts	Connecticut	New Hampshire	Rhode Island	New York	Pennsylvania	New Jersey	Delaware	Maryland	Virginia	North Carolina	South Carolina
	371	372	373	374	375	376	377	378	379	380	381	382
1775	------	27	------	------	120	422	------	------	295	------	80	------
1770	------	------	------	------	------	344	190	------	------	88	79	498
1765	------	------	------	------	260	432	248	------	------	303	75	------
1760	------	------	212	------	------	486	155	------	------	------	50	------
1752	------	340	114	------	------	84	------	------	60	------	------	------
1748	2,135	281	114	550	------	85	38	------	60	------	21	133
1744	305	------	30	------	------	85	------	14	90	------	------	------
1739	243	60	23	340	80	80	60	17	90	------	53	250
1735	309	------	22	------	------	69	23	20	90	------	53	------
1730	311	------	27	320	------	69	18	------	------	------	40	107
1725	351	------	27	------	------	39	37	11	------	------	------	116
1720	230	------	22	------	------	------	------	------	------	------	12	------
1715	170	27	8	51	36	------	5	------	------	------	24	74
1710	89	20	------	7	7	------	------	------	------	------	------	------
1705	28	------	------	------	------	------	------	------	------	------	------	------

Series Z 383–387. Tax Collections in America Under the Different Revenue Laws: 1765 to 1774

[In pounds sterling]

Year	New revenue measures: Total	Sugar act (1764, 1766)	Stamp act (1765)	Townshend revenue act (1767)	Navigation act (1673)
	383	384	385	386	387
1774	27,995	27,074		921	672
1773	42,103	39,531		2,572	2,517
1772	45,870	42,570		3,300	1,490
1771	31,761	27,086		4,675	1,446
1770	33,637	30,910		2,727	1,828
1769	45,499	39,938	------	5,561	1,294
1768	37,861	24,659	------	13,202	1,160
1767	34,041	33,844	------	197	3,905
1766	26,696	26,696	------	------	7,373
1765	17,383	14,091	3,292	------	2,954

Series Z 388–405. Basic Weekly Diets in Britain and America: 1622 to 1790

[In pounds or gallons unless otherwise specified]

Year	Calories per day	Biscuits	Bread	Flour	Oatmeal	Peas	Rice	Cornmeal	Fish	Beef	Pork	Bacon	Cheese	Butter	Beer	Molasses	Rum	Other
	388	389	390	391	392	393	394	395	396	397	398	399	400	401	402	403	404	405
Before 1861, majority of slaves in U.S.	4,187–5,287	------	------	------	------	------	------	1 peck	------	------	3½ or 3½		------	------	------	------	------	------
About 1790, slaves on Washington's plantation	3,752	------	------	------	------	------	------	14.4	3.6	------	------	------	------	------	------	------	------	[1] 0.55
1780, French prisoners returned to France and English repatriates	3,284	------	7	------	------	------	------	------	------	7	------	------	------	------	3½	------	------	------
1780, Continental Army ration	2,478–3,741	------	7	7	------	------	------	1¾ pts	------	7 or 6⅛		------	------	------	------	------	------	------
1776, Tory prisoners in Maryland	3,226–3,917	------	7 or 7		------	3 pts	------	1 qt	------	7 or 5¼		------	------	------	------	7 gills	------	[2] 7 gills
1775, Continental Army ration	3,032–4,058	------	7 or 7		------	[3] 3 pts	------	[4] 1 pt		7 or 7 or 5¼		------	------	------	1¾ or 9/25		------	[5] ⅞
About 1770, convicts sent to Va., Md., and Carolinas from England	2,061	------	4⅔	------	1⅔	1	------	------	------	⅔	½	------	⅔	------	------	1¼ lb	------	[6] ⅓ gill
1761, British Army in Canada	2,552–2,921	------	------	7	------	3 pts	½	------	------	7 or 4		------	------	⅜	------	------	------	------
1757, Va. militia in the field	2,600	------	------	7	------	------	------	------	------	------	------	------	------	------	------	------	------	[1] 7
1755, Acadians sent to Md.	1,934	------	2	5	------	------	------	------	------	1	------	------	------	------	------	------	------	------
1747, English prisoners of French, at Quebec	1,934–2,278	------	7	------	------	[7] 1¾ pts	------	------		1⅙ or 3½ or 1¾		------	------	------	1⅘	9/25		(8)
1744–1746, R. I. Armed Sloop	3,951	------	7	------	------	[3] 2 qts	------	------	------	4	2	------	------	1	------	------	7/16	------
1735, Ga. trustees, diet for passengers	3,392	------	6⅛	2	------	1 pt	------	------	½	3⅕	2	------	------	1/10	21 pts	------	------	[9] ⅖
First half of 18th century, Mass. Militia:																		
Post allowance	2,480	------	7	------	------	3½ pts	------	------	------	------	4⅔	------	------	------	------	⅙	------	------
Marching allowance	2,688	------	7	------	------	------	------	------	------	------	7	------	------	------	------	------	7 gills	------
First half of 18th century, Mass. privateers	4,748	------	7	------	------	1 qt	1 pt	------	------	3	4	------	------	------	7	------	------	------
1676, Va. Militia	4,156	7	------	------	------	------	------	------	------	3½	------	3½	3½	------	------	------	------	------
1638, Josslyn voyage to New England, immigrants	4,527	------	7	------	7/50 gal	1½ pts	------	------	1½	4⅞	------	------	¾	¼	7	------	------	(10)
1632, children's hospital at Norwich, England	2,754	------	6 9/16	------	------	------	------	------	------	1⅛	------	------	1⅜	14½ oz	2 3/16	------	------	[11] 3 pts
1622, British naval vessels [12]	4,737–5,459	7	------	------	------	------	------	------	1½	8	------	------	¾	⅜	7	------	------	------
		7	------	------	------	2	------	------	1½	4	2	------	¾	⅜	7	------	------	------
		7	------	------	------	2	------	------	1½	4	------	2	¾	⅜	7	------	------	------

[1] Meat.
[2] Vinegar.
[3] Peas or beans.
[4] ½ pint of rice or 1 pint of cornmeal.
[5] Milk.
[6] Gin.
[7] With pork ration only.
[8] 10½ spoonfuls of oil, and 21 spoonfuls of vinegar, with fish only.
[9] Suet or plums.
[10] Vinegar and mustard; quantity unknown.
[11] Pottage.
[12] Sailors received 1 of the 3 different diets.

Index